Curtis P. Nettels

Cornell University

The Roots of
American Civilization

A HISTORY OF AMERICAN COLONIAL LIFE

SECOND EDITION

D0002121

 New York

APPLETON - CENTURY - CROFTS

Division of Meredith Corporation

To

ELSIE PATTERSON NETTELS

 # Editor's Foreword

"THE basic institutions of American government and the prevailing philosophy of today were shaped in large measure during the colonial period." With this striking summary statement Professor Nettels begins his chapter on government and religion, but its application will be recognized in every part and phase of his book; wherefore it is properly entitled *The Roots of American Civilization.*

If it could be assumed that the number of people involved in a transaction, either in the cause or in the immediate effect, should be taken as an index of its comparative historical importance, then of course colonial history would sink into insignificance. But the few men who start an enterprise may be more significant than the vast number who carry it on long afterwards. The pioneer is immensely important; his ideals and his purposes may prove to be as fundamental influences in conditioning the lives of a people many generations later as the geographical facts of rivers and soils and mountains or those strong new economic forces which have come with changes in the form and character of work. As the twig is bent, runs the old adage, so grows the tree. Of course, the changing winds may alter its shape somewhat in later years, but the original bent continues to account for much of its peculiarity. America is what it is, partly, at least, because men like John Winthrop, William Penn, John Wise, John Peter Zenger, Thomas Jefferson, and George Washington were what they were. Conjecturing the viewpoint of historians two or three centuries hence is a hazardous business, but it seems safe to say that any one of these men was more important because he lived in the colonial period than he would have been if he had lived in the twentieth century.

It would certainly be a mistake to assume, too, that colonial history is a "dead" subject, that productive research in that field, largely speaking, has been finished. Put an able, industrious mind to work on the first half of our life as Americans, judged by years, and you will get as fresh and novel a history as you will get from the same kind of mind set to the second half. Professor Nettels' book is a proof of it, if there were nothing more at hand. Scholars have discovered as much about the America of the seventeenth and eighteenth centuries in the past forty years as they knew before that time. The astonishing number of books published in this field during the nineteen-thirties, which the author here cites, illustrates how the fruitful work proceeds. The identification and analysis of economic forces, of group rivalries, of stirring ideas, of the fundamental reasons why wars were fought and won or lost in that period, has gone on and is going on with constantly increasing result. The discovery that there was a British colonial policy maturing through many vicissitudes from the days of Elizabeth to those of George III, and of some of the factors that made its execution difficult, indeed impossible, is the work of men who for the most part are still alive.

But in no other single volume, I believe, has so much of this modern scholarship been laid under contribution, or its results so clearly analyzed and fused into so coherent an account, informed throughout by the author's own original investigations, as in the book before us. Its main thesis is the emergence and definition of social classes in colonial America, with their respective economic foundations and their social and political conflicts. There were aristocratic tendencies flowing from a persistent tradition and from personal and family ambition; there were democratic tendencies encouraged by American environment; and the two could not work together in peace. Neither could imperial and local interests. These conflicts insisted upon expression not only in politics, but also in religion, military administration, education, and, indeed, in every phase of popular culture.

This, however, is not to say that every event, every policy, every life is interpreted in terms of this conflict. It is well to have a thesis, if it is come by after long, industrious, and honest study of the data, but it is not well to attempt to jam everything into its pattern and to reject as unimportant all that does not contribute to its argument. The process of colonization is considered as a challenge to intelligence and courage, those of statesmen and promoters on the one hand and those of colonist families on the other. All took a risk, and in large part their hopes were joined. "Plantations," remarked Lord Bacon, "are amongst ancient, primitive and heroic works." No reader of these pages can escape vicarious thrills as he follows the first strike into the wilderness on a strange continent. The life of a people, however, holds abundant interest even when it is not thrilling. Curtis Nettels, I believe, has given us a fuller, clearer picture of the common day of American colonials than is to be found in other one-volume histories, and has done so in a rational order of treatment so often missed by writers on the social scene.

Reference has been made to the colonial people. There are obvious inherent difficulties in treating thirteen colonies as one people, though we may realize that they were much alike and undergoing similar experiences. Despite these difficulties the author has made a notable contribution in attempting to view them as a whole rather than in a series, and reflective readers will remark with satisfaction how well he has succeeded. Certain social or political phenomena appeared in one colony before they did in another; in consequence chronology is less regarded here than logical arrangement.

The author has designed a scheme of references to make additional reading as attractive and convenient as possible. Instead of the usual consolidated bibliography at the back of the book, so dismaying to the average reader, he has introduced occasional citations and counsel after appropriate paragraphs of the text, where they may satisfy awakened curiosity, and, at the chapter's end, a more extended note, listing books in designated parts which deal with the subject at hand, a few atlas maps of special application, and with cautious restraint some source materials that the ordinary reader might actually desire to read; here and there, for the benefit of more hearty appetites he discusses specialized, "technical" works, which are not recommended for the many. Much care has been given to these devices to lure the reader into further inquiry; from them he will be aware of at least some of the material that lies behind the present volume, and occasionally he will be tempted, beyond the resistance of our common natural indolence, to explore a few parts of it for himself.

Dixon Ryan Fox

Preface

HISTORY is man's guide to action in the present and future. And such action is certain to be most constructive when it is informed by an understanding of the problems and conditions which, having emerged slowly from the past, mold and limit the activities of today and tomorrow. Those who know the circumstances of their country's development and who understand the elements of its civilization will be the ones best qualified to meet present issues with decision, intelligence, and economy of effort.

Such is the conception of the uses of history that underlies this book. My effort has been to understand and to describe the essentials of American society as they have appeared in the course of its development. One who studies the colonial period is continually pulled in two directions: toward the time that has passed since then, that one may relate colonial origins to contemporary trends; and toward the remote past, that one may understand the sources of those enduring influences which have outlived the colonial period. For this reason I have emphasized the European background of American history—not for itself, but in order to explain the forces that have made the United States what it is today.

It is impossible to acknowledge all intellectual debts incurred in preparing this book. Among those who have read parts of the manuscript and have saved me from errors are Dean G. C. Sellery and Professor Robert L. Reynolds of the University of Wisconsin, Professor Marcus W. Jernegan of the University of Chicago, Mr. Louis M. Hacker of Columbia University, Dr. Dixon Ryan Fox, President of Union College, and Dr. Carl Bridenbaugh of the Massachusetts Institute of Technology.

To the University of Wisconsin I am indebted for the aid of research assistants and the opportunity for four months of uninterrupted study, both of which were made possible by grants from research funds. I have also profited from studies of several graduate students in American history at Wisconsin, particularly those of John M. Weidman, Bertha M. Hamilton, George T. Hunt, Merrill M. Jenson, Milton Longhorn, Alexander C. Kern, Leo Wearing, Katherine Ragen, Emil F. Heintz, Clarence M. Weiner, Raymond Plath, Marion Hoffman Gottfried, William Marsh, and Ruth Dunham.

The eight original population maps printed in the text were prepared by Mr. H. R. Friis, to whom I am deeply obliged for his generous permission to include them in this book.

Many notable studies bearing on the subject of this volume have appeared since it was first published. In making a revision I have improved several statements but have left the original structure intact. In the bibliographical notes at the ends of chapters I have cited works which seem to me to merit the attention of readers. The citations in the footnotes are guides to reading rather than authorities for statements in the text. I am indebted to three historians, Evarts B. Greene, Marcus W. Jernegan, and Oliver P. Chitwood, whose books I once used as texts in courses in colonial history.

CURTIS P. NETTELS

Contents

Maps and Illustrations

I

Factors in the Expansion of Europe

THE United States which we know today is the product of two principal forces. One—the immigration of many European peoples—introduced a variety of European ideals, customs, and racial characteristics.[1] Yet European cultural traits have not remained distinctly European in their American setting; they have been greatly modified by the second factor, the environment of the new country—natural resources, the climate, the lie of the land. The history of the United States is a story of the impact of a rich and undeveloped continent upon transplanted European ideas and ways of life. The outcome is a social order in many ways similar to European societies, yet possessing an unmistakably American character.

THE NORSE REVIVAL IN EUROPE

After the barbarian invasions in Europe had prostrated the Roman empire, a state of lethargy and economic stagnation settled upon the peoples of Western Europe. Among the forces which finally aroused them from this slumber was an infusion of vital energy from the northern kingdoms of Denmark, Norway, and Sweden. The consolidation of the Norse people into these three kingdoms, accomplished between 900 and 1050, was accompanied and followed by tidal waves of expansion and conquest, motivated at first by lust for plunder, and later by hunger for more fertile lands. To the east the Northmen established a kingdom in Russia, and reached Constantinople, where they became a symbol of military power. To the south, they conquered Normandy in France and twice overran large parts of England. Their descendants, the Normans, aided in the reconquest of Spain from the Moors, made settlements in southern Italy and Sicily, and seized outposts in northern Africa. Westward, the Northmen subdued Ireland and discovered and colonized Iceland and Greenland. Then, between

[1] The best survey of the early European background for the general student is Edward P. Cheyney's *The Dawn of a New Era* (New York, 1936)—a book that combines learning, breadth of view, insight, and literary charm.

986 and 1003, two Norwegians, Biarni Heriulfson and Leif Ericsson, on separate voyages, reached the shores of America somewhere between Labrador and Cape Cod. Several later voyages failed to accomplish an intended colonization of "Vinland," the wooded, vine-covered shore which Leif Ericsson first explored.[2]

In retrospect, the Northmen are less important for their discovery of America than for the mighty impetus they gave to the renewal of European life. It is likely that the knowledge of their discovery was lost to most of Europe, and that it did not contribute to the final opening of the New World. But as pioneers in seafaring, shipbuilding, and colonization, they entered the main stream of European expansion. They were the first to build vessels which could safely ride the turbulent waters of the Atlantic. Their conquests, affording a thousand contacts of kinship within the known world, led to an expansion of trade which helped to dissolve the isolation in which the villagers of Western Europe had previously lived. Prodigious was the energy of the Northmen, while their capacity for political leadership and their genius for organization and assimilation were unexcelled. Their zeal for Christianity was blended with an ardor for military renown and a primitive reverence for sacred sites and objects. They felt that their church should be a militant warrior chastising its enemies in glorious physical combat and redeeming the holy places of the faith. In consequence, the descendants of Northmen who settled in Europe became the foremost leaders of the Crusades.[3]

EUROPE AND THE ORIENT

These pilgrimages of the twelfth and thirteenth centuries—inspired by curiosity, by religious fervor, and by love of glory, plunder, and adventure—supplied another powerful force to break the shell of isolation which had encased the people of early medieval Europe. The armies of crusaders voyaging to Palestine gave a tremendous stimulus to the building of ships. New transports had to be constructed, and when crusading activity subsided, such vessels were used in ordinary trade. Merchants of Italian cities like Genoa and Venice grew rich upon the profits of transporting and provisioning the warrior pilgrims; capital for commerce thus accumulated in the northern

[2] A scholarly study is Geoffrey M. Gathorne-Hardy's *The Norse Discoverers of America* (Oxford, 1921). An older work of merit is Joseph Fischer's *The Discoveries of the Norsemen in America* (London, 1903). An especially good treatment is William Hovgaard, *The Voyages of the Norsemen* . . . (New York, 1914).

[3] Charles H. Haskins, *The Normans in European History* (Boston, 1915), is a model of historical writing.

Mediterranean towns. In Syria and Egypt the crusaders beheld rare and costly articles of the Orient—spices, fine cloth, and precious stones —and new visions of wealth and splendor opened before the West. Likewise, European merchants came into contact with the terminal cities on the routes of oriental trade. There they later established trading posts in order to obtain the precious commodities of the East.[4]

The products which came from Arabia, India, Ceylon, China, and the Spice Islands wrought a transformation of European life. Before 1100, living conditions had been extremely mean and hard. The arts of cooking and preserving food were little known. Even at the tables of the nobles the fare was monotonous and coarse. It is not strange, then, that the Europeans relished the spices of the Orient—pepper, nutmeg, cinnamon, ginger, cloves, and mace. Such seasoning made stale food more palatable in the days before refrigeration. The nobles likewise welcomed the elegant fabrics of the East which satisfied the craving for display to set apart the noble from the lowly serf. Oriental rugs and carpets—then as now the best in the world—beautiful chinaware, fine glass, tapestries, diamonds and pearls from India and rubies from Ceylon—all these brought a glow of warmth and color into a previously drab existence. Perfumes provided a crude but welcome substitute for baths. And there were soothing drugs—camphor, medicinal rhubarb, and musk, and opium, the only drug then known which deadened pain.[5]

These oriental goods could be carried great distances because they were abundant and cheap in the East and scarce and expensive in the West. All were of slight weight and bulk; this made long-range transportation possible. They were brought to Europe over three principal routes of trade. One led from Japan and China by way of the China Sea, or from the Spice Islands—athwart the equator—and past the rich East Indies, to the port of Malacca, a great center where Chinese merchants met Arab and Indian traders from the West. Thence the goods were conveyed by sea to Calicut in India; then across the Arabian Sea and by way of the Red Sea to Alexandria. The second or central route touched at points along the western coast of India and led to Ormuz in the Persian Gulf. Next the goods went by Bozra and the Tigris River to Bagdad, whence some were taken by caravan to Jaffa or Antioch. To Trebizond on the Black Sea other wares were

---

[4] *The Crusades*, by Richard A. Newhall (New York, c. 1927), is the best brief discussion for the general reader.

[5] Clive Day's *History of Commerce* (New York, 1936) discusses medieval trade admirably in chapters 9–14.

carried north from Bagdad. The third route began near Peking, and crossed the inland provinces of China and Turkestan to the Caspian Sea. Thence it proceeded through Tabriz to the Black Sea and across to Constantinople.

At Alexandria, Antioch, and other terminals of these three routes the trading towns of France and Spain and particularly of Italy established business headquarters called *fondachi*. These consisted of warehouses, market places, offices, churches, dwellings, and baths. The traders bought from native princes the privileges of self-government and protected trade. Their business was to obtain the incoming oriental wares and to reship them to their home cities, such as Pisa, Genoa, or Venice.[6]

These cities in the late Middle Ages came to resemble trading corporations, in which the merchants controlled the government for their own advantage. All Venetian traders were required to send to Venice the wares they purchased in the East. These were to be stored in warehouses and exported only on government license. After 1300, fleets of vessels with galley convoys were fitted out and dispatched for trade with Western Europe. The "Flanders fleet" usually made a yearly voyage to Spain, Portugal, France, Britain, and Flanders. The expense was borne and the profit made by the Venetian merchants. Oriental goods were also carried to northern Europe by German traders who traveled by the Danube and the Rhine, or through towns brought into new importance, like Augsburg and Nuremberg, and over the Alpine passes to Venice. The great distributing agency in northwestern Europe was the Hanseatic League—an association of German towns which included Lübeck, Hamburg, and Bremen. These towns had banded together to secure outside commercial privileges for their traders. The Hanseatic merchants bought their oriental wares in Italy, Antwerp and other towns, and at fairs in Western Europe. Then they supplied the markets of England, Russia, Poland, Scandinavia, and Germany. They also set up trading agencies abroad, with special privileges and protection. In London, the Hanse merchants were called Easterlings, and their walled settlement on the Thames was known as the Steelyard. The word *sterling* survives as a tribute to the quality of the silver money current among the Easterlings.

Most of the commodities exported from Western Europe to the Orient were raw materials such as quicksilver, tin, copper, lead, amber,

---

[6] The best one-volume text on its subject is Herbert Heaton's *Economic History of Europe* (New York, 1936). For the Middle Ages see chapters 5-11.

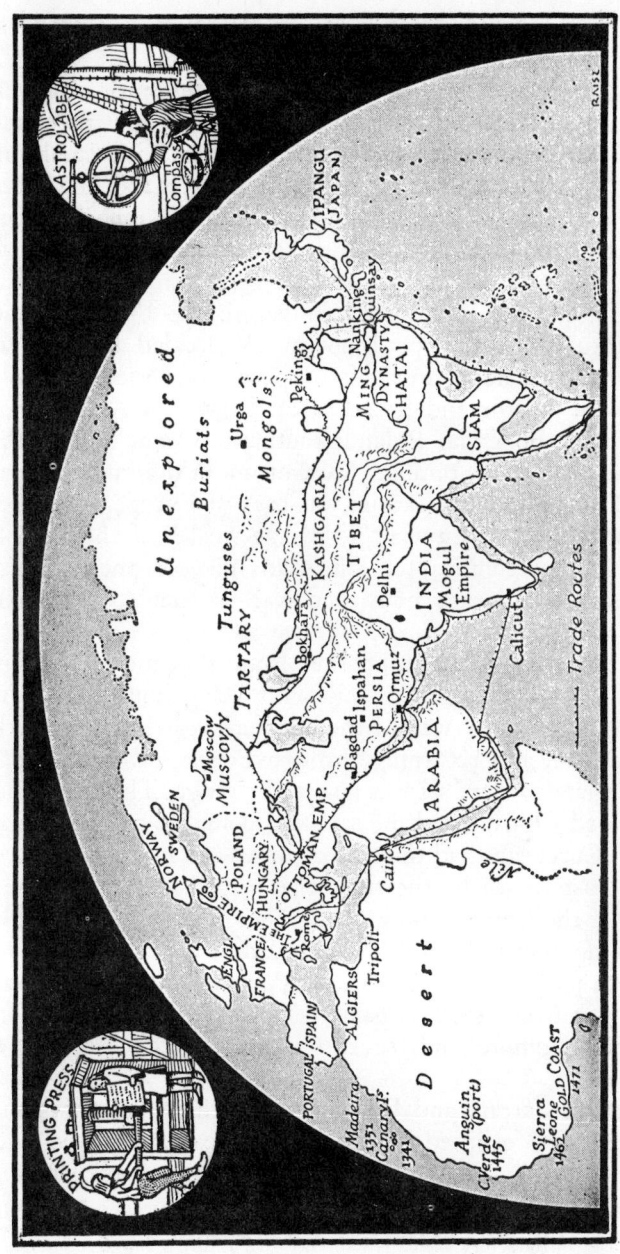

From Wertenbaker and Smith's *"The United States of America."* © *Charles Scribner's Sons.*

MEDIEVAL TRADE ROUTES TO THE ORIENT

and tar, and manufactured goods like woolen cloth. Gold and silver money also flowed from west to east.[7]

The regeneration of commerce stirred anew the spirit of adventure and the quest for knowledge, and eased the path for travelers who sought a fuller understanding of the mysterious East. In the meantime great events were stirring there. Between 1206 and 1227 occurred the conquests of the Mongols under their renowned leader, Genghis Khan. Soon afterward the Tartars invaded Armenia and southern Russia, and in 1241 one of their generals captured Budapest. Christian Europe was terror-stricken before the threat of another barbarian invasion, and Pope Innocent IV decided to send ambassadors to the great khan. For this purpose he selected one John of Plano Carpini, disciple and friend of St. Francis of Assisi, who proceeded through Bohemia, Poland, southern Russia, and Turkestan and met the khan at his camp at Karakorum, in the midst of oriental splendor. Two years later Carpini was back in Europe. His carefully written accounts of his travels told of the wealth of the Orient and pictured the opportunities for Christian missions there. This was the first recorded journey of a medieval traveler to the unknown East.

A few years later, in 1253, another Franciscan monk, William de Rubruquis, was sent on a similar mission by King Louis IX of France. Going to Karakorum by way of the northern coasts of the Black Sea and the Caspian, and returning through Persia and Syria, he spent two years in lands where all was new and strange. The description he wrote included China, which he said was bounded by an eastern sea. Previously, Europeans had thought of Asia as an indefinite land mass. Could this eastern sea be the same that stretched away to the west of Spain? Of the Chinese, he wrote: "These Cathayans are little fellows, speaking much through the nose, and, as in general with all those eastern people, their eyes are very narrow. . . . They do their writing with a pencil such as painters paint with, and a single character of theirs comprehends several letters, so as to form a whole word." [8]

The fame of Carpini and Rubruquis and the wonders which they related were soon eclipsed by the adventures experienced and the marvels described by the greatest of medieval travelers, Marco Polo. In 1260, the father and uncle of young Marco had set out from

[7] A good brief introductory sketch is Laurence B. Packard's *The Commercial Revolution* (New York, c. 1927).

[8] For a collection of excellent recent studies of the medieval background of discovery see Arthur P. Newton (ed.), *Travel and Travellers of the Middle Ages* (New York, 1926).

Constantinople on a trading voyage which finally carried them to the court of Kubla Khan. Here they were well received and allowed to return to Venice with a commission to ask the pope to send a hundred wise men to instruct the Mongolians in Western arts and the Christian faith. When the Polo brothers went forth again to China in 1271 they took the enterprising Marco with them. Three and a half years elapsed before they reached the court of Kubla Khan. Marco speedily won the confidence of the great ruler, who made him governor of a great Chinese city and sent him on diplomatic missions to eastern Tibet, Cochin China, and India. Having accumulated a fortune, Marco returned to Venice in 1295. Captured soon afterward in a war between Venice and Genoa, he was clapped into prison by the Genoese. There he dictated the famous narrative of his travels, *The Book of Ser Marco Polo concerning the Kingdoms and Marvels of the East.*[9]

What a panorama of wonders this remarkable book unfolded! It was the first account "to reveal China in all its wealth and vastness, its mighty rivers, its huge cities, its rich manufactures, its swarming population, the inconceivably vast fleets that quickened its seas and inland waters." Into the city of Peking entered every day a thousand cartloads of silk; there stood the palace of the Great Khan, with its walls and ceilings of gold and its banquet hall large enough to accommodate six thousand guests. Japan, or Cipangu, appeared as a very large island, rich in "rose-tinted pearls" and precious stones. There were the pearls and diamonds, the spices, the cotton, the indigo, and the dyestuffs of India, the golden pagodas of Burma and the rubies of Ceylon. In the eastern sea lay hundreds of small islands, every one of which produced "valuable and odorous woods, and gold and gems, and all manner of spices—pepper as white as snow, and also the black kind, in great quantity." And from the south came rumors of strange lands—of Abyssinia and Zanzibar and Madagascar —with tales of Negroes and ivory and gold, while from the north came reports of the vast expanse of Siberia, where ranged the dog sledge, the reindeer, and the white bear.

Marco Polo was the first European traveler to traverse the whole length of Asia. The wonders he had seen and the still greater marvels of which he had heard intensified the interest of traders, scholars, and missionaries in the East, and inspired other travelers to journey thither during the next century. His book cast an enduring spell over

[9] C. R. Beazley, "Marco Polo and the European Expansion of the Middle Ages," *Atlantic Monthly*, CIV (Oct. 1909). The latest study, authoritative and readable, is Sir Percy Sykes, *The Quest for Cathay* (London, 1937).

European minds. Printed in 1477, it was read by Columbus and probably inflamed his imagination with a desire to visit wondrous lands. Next to the voyages of Columbus himself, the travels of Marco Polo form the most important chapter in the history of geographical discovery.[10]

THE RENAISSANCE AND THE AGE OF DISCOVERY

The extending contacts of commerce and travel helped to prepare the way for another great movement—the Renaissance. This surge of intellectual and artistic energy may be traced in part to the renewed intercourse between Italy and the East which revealed a fuller knowledge of the civilizations of the ancient world. The growth of commerce and industry in towns provided the wealth, the leisure and security necessary for the work of artist and scholar. Italian merchants became promoters of learning, partly in order that they might apply the fruits of knowledge to the advancement of their trade.

Two aspects of the life of the spirit had been prominent before the Renaissance. One was religious faith. The earlier scholars were churchmen who accepted the Scriptures as the revealed word of God. Man attained the truth only when he accepted divine revelation as the premise of his reasoned thought. It is true that after the tenth century, the Greek philosopher, Aristotle, had been widely studied in Latin translations. But Aristotle had expounded the deductive method of logic—reasoning from accepted principles. The medieval schoolmen were thus able to apply the method of Aristotle to the Bible, taking its teachings as accepted truths to be demonstrated by deductive logic. One would not dare to oppose the Bible with contrary conclusions drawn from personal observations of the natural world.

A second feature of religious life was the ascetic ideal of the monasteries. Man was regarded as a weak and erring creature; his life on earth was a prison of woes; his works of pride and vanity were an abomination in the sight of God. His sinful flesh must be purified by prayerful contemplation of the divine spirit. Through the agency of the Church he might renounce the corruption of the world and enter into the incorruptible and eternal life to come.[11]

One stream of the Renaissance, Humanism, flowed from an ap-

[10] An older coöperative work, the massive *Narrative and Critical History of America* (ed. Justin Winsor, 8 vols., Boston, 1884–89), is still valuable on discovery and exploration. See Vol. I, chapters 1–2.

[11] See an illuminating essay, "The Christian Life," by F. M. Powicke, in *The Legacy of the Middle Ages* (ed. C. G. Crump, Oxford, 1926).

preciative study of the classics of Greece and Rome. These cultural treasures gave an enlarged view of the dignity of man. He had fashioned exquisite works of art, probed the mysteries of nature, and produced inspiring literature recording heroic deeds and elevated thought. To students of such achievements man did not appear as an unworthy tenant of a corrupting earth. He might at least roughhew the ends of his own destiny, find joy in the cultivation of the arts, and expand the comprehending powers of his mind. By intelligence and effort he might subdue the earth and make it minister to his emotional and intellectual needs. Life should become a blessing to be enjoyed, not a curse to be endured.

In several fields of inquiry the thinkers of ancient Greece had gone beyond the scholars of early medieval Europe. Many of the studies which the Greeks had cultivated—mathematics, astronomy, and geography—were to play important parts in the advancement of science and navigation which led to the age of discovery. For many years the scholars of Europe accepted the classical writers as sources of truth second only to the Bible. But the ancient authorities did not always agree with one another. This led eventually to classifications and comparisons, and to critical appraisals and verifying investigations. Where the Greeks had contented themselves with bold speculative inquiry, the scholars of the late Middle Ages were moved to check with actual measurements. Such advances pointed toward the great era of geographical discovery, whose guiding philosophy was to take nothing for granted but to learn by observation and experience. Moreover, the spirit of Greek philosophers had been distinctly critical. Accordingly, they helped to instruct their later European disciples in the art of examining into the nature of the visible world.[12]

The development of science in Europe took a more practical turn than it had in ancient Greece. The Greek philosophers, living in a society supported by slaves, had been free from the petty cares of daily toil. Breathing a somewhat rarefied intellectual atmosphere, they had dwelt upon the ideal and the abstract. But the European bourgeoisie, not having slaves, became interested in making science do a part of the world's work. Astronomy helped the navigator, geometry was a boon to architects, and arithmetic and algebra (newly derived from Arabian mathematicians), facilitated business and trade. A similar trend was disclosed in scores of inventions introduced in Europe after the twelfth century. Such were magnifying glasses, gun-

[12] Lord Acton's *Lectures on Modern History* (London, 1918) gives a broad view of important themes, emphasizing the influence of ideas. See chapters 1, 3.

powder, compasses, printing presses, bellows, blast furnaces, thermometers, water-power machines, and clocks.[13]

Ancient writers exerted a particularly strong influence upon the study of geography in medieval times. Prior to 1400 the size of the world known to Europeans was smaller than the area still unknown. The continent of Africa, excepting its Mediterranean shore and the valley of the Nile, was as yet a closed book. Europe, north of the Baltic and the Caspian Sea, was another *terra incognita*. Europeans could only estimate roughly the size and relationships of oriental countries. Beyond the Atlantic, shrouded in darkness, lay the two Americas, the Pacific Ocean, and the lands of Australasia.

Lacking first-hand knowledge of much of the world's surface, European scholars could only speculate about its full nature and extent. From the ancient Greeks they derived the idea that the earth is round. This view was commonly accepted by learned men after the time of the Crusades. The Byzantine emperors carried a ball as a symbol of their world dominion; Dante in the *Divine Comedy* pictured the world as a globe; and Columbus later testified that he had always read that ancient geographers had proved the sphericity of the earth.[14]

One of these geographers was Claudius Ptolemy, who lived at Alexandria about 127–151 A. D. His works exerted a stronger influence on medieval scholars than those of any other writer. He conceived the earth as the center of the universe; around it, every twenty-four hours, with incredible speed, revolved the sun and stars, all fixed in a succession of hollow and transparent spheres. He estimated that most of the unknown world consisted of land; hence his "continental theory." In consequence, he exaggerated the size of Asia, and described Africa as extending far to the south and east, joining Asia in a continuous land mass and making the Indian Ocean an inland sea. If these views were correct, the Orient could not be reached from Western Europe by sailing south around Africa. But perhaps one might proceed directly west across the Atlantic.

A greater scientist than Ptolemy, but one less honored in the Middle Ages, was the Greek astronomer, Eratosthenes (276–196 B. C.). His studies convinced him that the unknown parts of the world consisted mainly of water. According to his "oceanic theory," both Eu-

---

[13] Book I of Henry S. Lucas's *The Renaissance and the Reformation* (New York, c. 1934) is a good recent discussion of the Renaissance.

[14] John Fiske's *The Discovery of America* (2 vols., Boston, 1892) begins his history of the colonial period. Not an outstanding historical scholar, Fiske wrote for the general public. His writings are still of interest for their vigorous expression and literary excellence. See Vol. I, chapters 2, 3.

rope at the north and Africa at the south were bounded by immense seas.

Three questions had an important bearing upon geographical discovery. (1) How large was the earth? (2) What was the relation in size of the known world to the unknown? (3) Was there a continuous water passage from west to east? [15]

Although Eratosthenes calculated the earth's circumference at very nearly its true figure, Ptolemy computed it as considerably less than it actually is. Aristotle regarded the earth as a small sphere. Eratosthenes believed that the unknown world covered two-thirds of the earth's surface; the immense extent of the Atlantic made the crossing of it well-nigh impossible. Aristotle, on the other hand, said that the unknown world was so small that a mariner might easily sail from Spain to China. Ptolemy estimated the known world as at least half of the whole. The Roman moralist, Seneca, shared the view of Aristotle. In his play, *Medea*, Seneca said: "And the time shall come when the raging ocean itself, instead of being a limit and an obstacle, shall become a means of communication. The world will thus be thrown open; the pilots of the ocean will discover new worlds, and there shall no longer be a 'remotest Thule' on the map." As the Orient became better known through the medieval travelers, its great extension eastward seemingly reduced in size the ocean supposed to roll between China and the West.

Even though many ancient writers, including Aristotle, Strabo, and Cicero, hinted at the possibilities of the existence of unknown continents beyond the Atlantic, this idea did not strike root in Europe. Africa, Asia, and Europe seemed to be the only habitable parts of the world; the rest was water. If the earth was relatively small, and the unknown world but a fraction of the whole, then there could not be room for other great continents beyond the western sea.[16]

The ideas of Aristotle, Seneca, and Ptolemy appear in the works of two of the foremost European students of geography. One was Roger Bacon, the great Oxford scholar of the thirteenth century. The other was Cardinal Pierre d'Ailly, a fifteenth-century popularizer of other men's ideas and author of the *Imago Mundi*, a series of short treatises devoted partly to cosmography. Both of these writers believed that the known world exceeded half of the earth's surface, and that the Atlantic was but a narrow strip of ocean connecting the

[15] On geographical studies and early discoveries, the outstanding work is C. R. Beazley's *The Dawn of Modern Geography* (3 vols., London and Oxford, 1897–1906).
[16] Medieval conceptions of geography are described in John K. Wright's *The Geographical Lore of the Time of the Crusades* (New York, 1925).

Orient and Spain. Cardinal d'Ailly's *Imago Mundi* may have had a direct influence upon Columbus. He appears to have possessed a copy of the book, which he covered with marginal notes.

Since several of the geographical ideas of the Middle Ages were conducive to exploration in the West, the question arises: Why was the discovery of America so long delayed? Many strange fears held mariners back. Some believed that, if the world was round, Europe must be on top; hence if a vessel went too far "downhill," it might not be able to get back up. At the bottom of the globe, rain would fall away from the land, trees would grow downward, and people and animals would all go tumbling off into space. Even scholars believed that intense heat beat upon the earth at the equator, making it impossible for man to cross the tropics to the southern temperate zone. And there were legends of early voyagers into the unknown who had been forced to turn back because great distances, fruitlessly traversed, had exhausted their ships' supplies.[17]

The progress of the art of navigation eventually helped to dissipate such fears. In the twelfth century, crusaders learned from Arabs the secret of the compass. An iron needle, rubbed with loadstone, was found to point invariably to the north. By 1320, the magnet had been set in a box to indicate directions marked on a card. For a long time, however, the compass was regarded as an instrument of evil spirits, and superstitious mariners would not venture upon vessels where they knew that it was used.

Two devices where employed to determine position at sea—the cross-staff and the astrolabe. Both measured the elevation of stars and indicated the degrees of latitude on metal strips. Ascertaining longitude was a more difficult matter, because the time element entered into the calculation. However, by the fifteenth century clocks had come into use, and tables of data called ephemerides were prepared. If a mariner knew the time of day, and the height of certain stars, by referring these facts to the prepared tables he could readily ascertain degrees of longitude. With the aid of compass, astrolabe, and ephemerides, it became safer for vessels to venture into unknown seas.[18]

Improvements in map making also had an important place in the progress of navigation. Before 1300, maps had been imaginary and crude. They were based on myths and poetical lore and did not even

[17] Joseph Jacobs, *The Story of Geographical Discovery* (London, 1901), is a brief, readable, popular account. For a more extended survey see John N. L. Baker's *A History of Geographical Discovery* . . . (London, 1931).

[18] For a short introductory sketch see James E. Gillespie, *A History of Geographical Discovery* (New York, c. 1933).

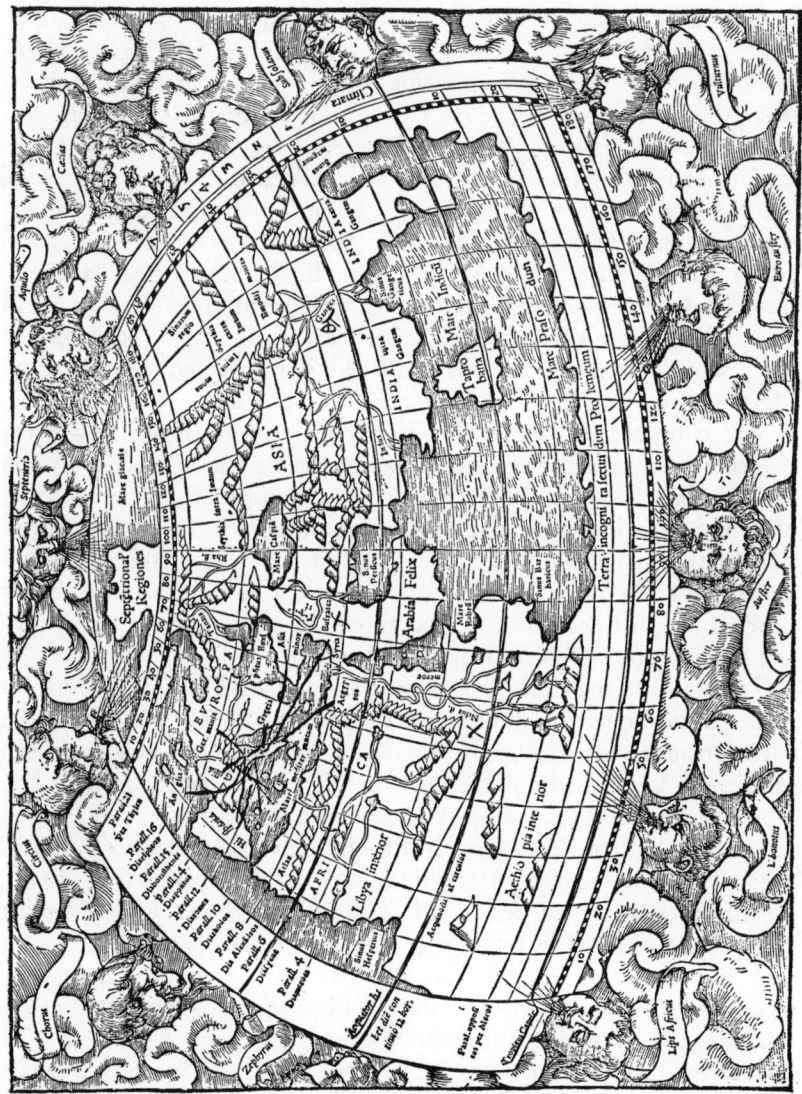

This map, entitled *Typus Orbis a Ptol. Descriptus*—the world according to Ptolemy—from an edition of Ptolemy published at Basel in 1540, represents the type of map inherited from Greek geography as re-drawn in the sixteenth century. It is especially interesting on account of the insertion of lines—apparently by the hand of its sixteenth-century owner—of the trade routes.

register all the known facts of the time. Little effort was made to
achieve exact measurements, and latitudinal and longitudinal lines
were missing. The advance came during the fourteenth century
through the gradual refinement of mariners' maps, known as *por-
tolani*. Such maps were probably developed by seamen of the towns
of northern Italy. They described only the features of the shore line,
but this was done in the minutest and most accurate detail. Exact
measurements were attempted on a stated distance scale. The *por-
tolani* still lacked longitudinal and latitudinal lines; instead, they included loxodromes, or lines indicating the prevailing winds. By 1450
the coasts of the known world had been mapped with the utmost
care. Such achievement preserved all additions to geographical knowledge for the convenience of explorers of a later day.

The culmination of the map maker's art came in 1492, when a
Nuremberg cosmographer, Behaim, constructed the first globe. Made
of papier-mâché, with a covering of plaster and outside strips of vel-
lum, and with lettering in colors and gold, it gave the fullest expression to the geographical knowledge of its day. It pictured the unknown ocean between Europe and the Orient as a little more than a
third of the earth's surface. It was about this time, also, that maps began to show lines of latitude and longitude.[19]

The way for the explorer was further prepared by improved techniques in the construction of ships. In early medieval times, when the
Mediterranean was the main channel of commerce, vessels had been
small and light, built in the fashion of an oar-driven galley. The
Northmen had then developed a sturdier, larger, more rounded vessel, with a higher mast, suitable for the more tempestuous Atlantic.
After 1400 the most popular ship among explorers was the caravel,
especially favored and developed in Portugal. The caravel was swift
before the wind, quick in turning, well adapted to shallow water, and
distinguished by high castles fore and aft. But in spite of the advances
in shipbuilding, for many years after 1500 small coasting vessels often had to be employed for ocean voyages.

Perhaps the greatest spur to enterprise along all fronts was given
by the invention, about 1450, of movable metal type for the printing
press. The writings of geographers and travelers could now be broadcast far and wide at a fraction of the cost of the old laborious method
of copying by hand. The tidings of every discovery could be carried
quickly and with accuracy into every land. The barriers which had

[19] Edward J. Payne's *History of the New World Called America* (2 vols., New
York, 1892) devotes Book I to the age of discovery. See pp. 12–112.

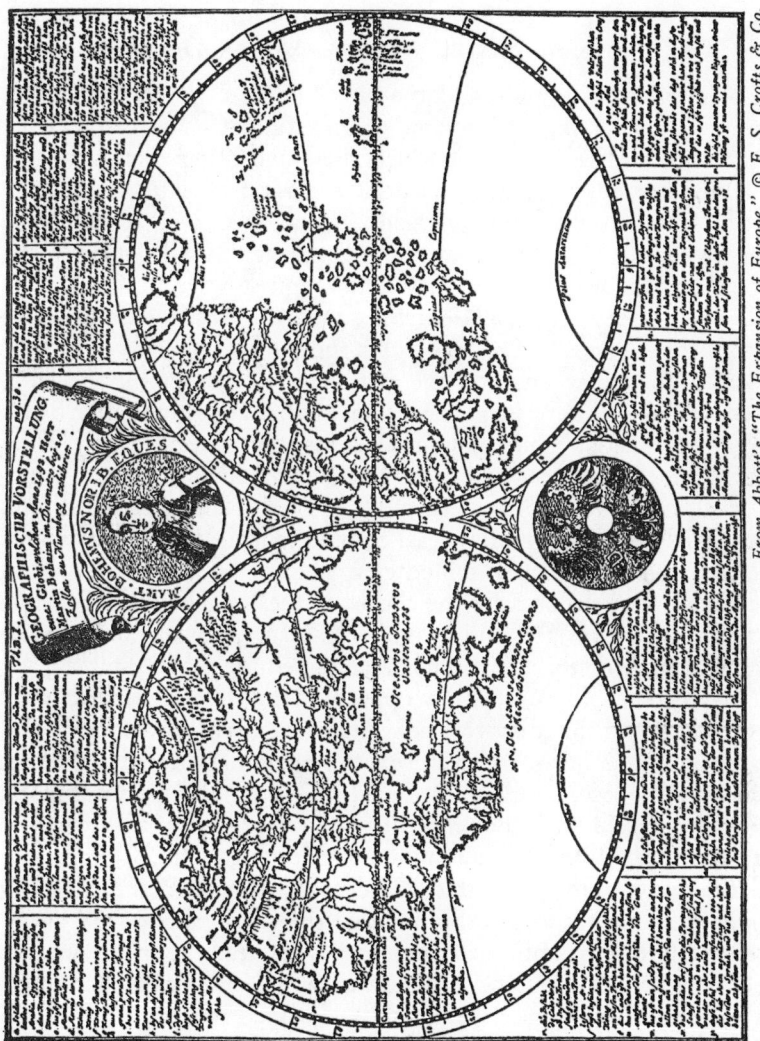

From Abbott's "The Expansion of Europe." © F. S. Crofts & Co.

MARTIN BEHAIM'S GLOBE OF 1492

isolated scientists were removed, and the accelerated spread of knowledge lessened superstition, ignorance, and fear.[20]

THE NATIONAL STATES AND THE AGE OF DISCOVERY

The intellectual impulses of the late Middle Ages in themselves do not account for the opening and colonization of new worlds. Some agency was necessary through which these and other impulses—zest for adventure, religious zeal, scientific curiosity, invention, and commercial profit—could find expression. Such an agency appeared in the fifteenth century in the form of the national state. Under its auspices, the stupendous feats of discovery and conquest were performed. It alone had the resources sufficient for supporting costly enterprises in which success and gain were doubtful in the extreme.

Before the emergence of the nation-state, Europe had been a curious blend of interests, general and local. Each community dwelt largely in isolation, ruled by local lords. But covering all like a blanket was the Universal Church. The Holy Roman Empire, including what are now Germany, Austria, the Netherlands, and Belgium, kept alive the memory of the all-embracing rule of ancient Rome. The common use of Latin united clergy, scholars, and officials. And spreading over Europe were the classes of the feudal order, from the lord who held the land and lived for pleasure, power, and war, to the impoverished serf whose labor maintained the lord's estate.[21]

This feudal society stood in opposition to the forces that were moving toward the discovery of America. Such forces emanated largely from the towns, which were bitter enemies of the feudal lords. Occupying the second rank in medieval society (the Church was first), the nobles looked with contempt upon the bourgeoisie, who were, in fact, often descended from humble itinerant peddlers or serfs who had run away from some estate. The nobles despoiled the traveling merchants of their goods and plundered the inhabitants of the towns. Incessant fighting diminished the security of trade. Surplus wealth, which might have become productive capital, was expended upon castles, armor, tournaments, and bands of armed retainers.

In some respects the medieval Church did not contribute to the forces leading to the economic expansion of Europe. In general, the

[20] A recent coöperative work, *The Pageant of America* (ed. Ralph H. Gabriel, 15 vols., New Haven, 1925–29), is compact, readable, and well-illustrated. The first volume, *Adventurers in the Wilderness* (1925), by Clark Wissler, Constance L. Skinner, and William Wood, devotes chapters 1 and 2 to medieval backgrounds.

[21] Wilbur C. Abbott's urbane and lucid *The Expansion of Europe*, reprinted in one volume (New York, 1929), stresses ideas and politics. See Vol. I, chapters 1–2, 4.

BOOKMAKING

From the woodcuts of Jost Amman, 1562, illustrating type founding, paper-making, printing, and binding.

writers of the Church approved of feudalism and looked askance upon commerce and finance. Peasants and artisans were the main producers of wealth; trade was a sort of necessary evil. Merchants should be allowed to make only such profit as would reward them for their work. Fair prices ought to govern sales—not the rule of buying low and selling high. Profiteering and monopoly were the offspring of avarice, a deadly sin. Man accumulated riches only at the expense of his fellow man. Money itself was not productive; a lender should not charge interest or "usury" as it was called, especially to the poor. All these ideas were contrary to the spirit of merchant capitalism which animated the growth of medieval trade. The economic activity which was to open and exploit new worlds was based upon credit, interest-taking, monopoly, and a desire for larger gain.[22]

The national states of Europe rose in conjunction with the growth of towns and trade, and at the expense of feudalism and the sway of the Universal Church. Between 1200 and 1600 the modern states of Portugal, Spain, France, England, and Holland were taking form. They developed through the consolidation of a compact territory under a central government. The distinguishing feature of the nation-state was the spirit of patriotism which united people of similar traditions, language, memories, and race.

The enlargement of the royal authority was another tendency at work within the national states. In struggles for supremacy with their feudal lords, the medieval kings were prone to seek alliances with the towns. The burgesses were granted charters of freedom which allowed them to own and dispose of property, to have their own courts and local government, to build walls for their defense, and to be exempt from dues to near-by nobles. In return the townsmen paid the king a regular revenue, granted him extraordinary taxes for emergencies, and put the town militia at his command against the feudal lords.

Secure under such shelter, the towns forged ahead in industry and trade. Freedom, association, and competition all served as spurs to productive work. Permitted to retain most of the property they obtained, the townsmen were impelled to industry and improved techniques. The more ambitious serfs ran away from the manors and became free artisans in towns. Thus the progressive forces of economic life tended to center there. Even after industry in towns had been

---

[22] The intellectual and political background of the age of discovery is sketched in chapters 1–9 and 11 of Edward M. Hulme's *The Renaissance and the Protestant Revolution* . . . (New York, 1920).

improved by a multitude of inventions, the methods of farming used were still those of ancient times.[23]

Receiving a steady revenue from taxes on commerce and the towns, the kings became less needful of the military aids once given by the nobles. Royal armies of hired troops took form. These could be used, if need arose, against the nobles themselves. The introduction of gunpowder finally unhorsed the feudal knights, while movable cannon battered down their once impregnable walls and castles. With town allies, with enlarged revenues, and with hired troops, the king was able to break the military power of the nobles, and so to unify the state.

An illustration of the alliance of king and merchant appears in the impetus given after 1200 to the study of the Roman law. In the early Middle Ages the canon law had been the principal legal code common to Europe. However, because the Church mistrusted trade, this body of law did not give adequate security to the merchant class. The merchants accordingly promoted the extension of the Roman law, with its well-developed commercial code. This movement received the benediction of the kings, for the Romans had defined the ruler as the source of law. One of the principal cornerstones of the developed nation-state was thus a body of national law formulated by the king and his advisers, which applied to all communities alike.

Equally potent as a nationalizing force was the evolution of vernacular literature and speech. The English language, a mixture of Latin, French, Anglo-Saxon, and Celtic, had achieved mature expression by the time of Chaucer (1340?–1400). Dante (1265–1321) wrote his greatest work in the Italian vernacular. In Spain the language of the people was derived from Castile. This had assumed literary form by 1250, largely through the influence of a poem, *Poema del Cid.* Two principal dialects prevailed in early France, the *langue d'oïl* and the *langue d'oc*, the former becoming the language of the nation as a whole. The emergence of vernacular literature and speech made Europeans conscious of separate identities. Often the awareness of people concerning the differences between themselves and foreigners is a more cohesive force than dimly realized similarities in one another.[24]

Geography also played some part in national unification. The

---

[23] Henri Pirenne's *Economic and Social History of Medieval Europe* (London, 1936) and *Medieval Cities* (Princeton, 1925) are works of one of the greatest of modern scholars.

[24] Carlton J. H. Hayes, *A Political and Cultural History of Modern Europe* (revised ed., 2 vols., New York, 1936), is an exceptionally good text. See Vol. I, chapter 1 on political backgrounds; chapter 3 on early culture.

English were set apart from the Continent, the Spaniards were isolated by the Pyrenees, and the French were somewhat isolated by
the Atlantic, the Pyrenees, and the Alps. In addition, patriotic sentiments were engendered and inflamed by wars to rid native lands of
alien foes. The efforts to expel the Moors from Europe aroused and
united both Portugal and Spain; French patriotism received its baptism in the long crusade to expel the English invader; and later the
Dutch Republic was born in the throes of war with Spain.

All the rising nation-states bordered the ocean highway that disappeared in the unknown west. Remote from the source of oriental
goods, they were obliged to buy such products from the Italian cities
—and on terms unfavorable to themselves. The prices they paid were
high; what they received for their own products seemed too small.
They realized that they were paying heavy charges to many middlemen. East of the Mediterranean, where the Arabs had a monopoly
of the oriental trade, numerous taxes were levied by rulers on the
shipments passing through their lands. Between India and Alexandria, goods moving westward had to pay, at five different ports, a
set of duties which quadrupled prices. All the while, the Italian
cities prospered through the profits of their merchants and the earnings of their ships which served the West.[25]

The general result of all this was that the western states were confronted with an adverse balance of trade. Their coined money was
drained away to Italy and the East. The accumulation of treasure in
the Italian towns gave rise to the first medieval banking houses, such
as the Bardi, Alberti, and Frescobaldi—firms which received deposits,
issued notes, dealt in bills of exchange, and extended credit throughout Europe, thereby adding interest to their earnings in the West.
Loans to kings were given in exchange for concessions within the
state, or secured by royal taxes due to be collected. Thus, in England,
Florentine bankers supplied the money for equipping the early expeditions of the Hundred Years' War.

As the wealth of Europe increased and the products of the East
became more widely used, the commercial groups in the nation-states
desired to secure a better place in the oriental trade. Unable to dominate the established routes of commerce, they sought to find new
routes of their own. This motive guided exploration for nearly two
hundred years. Three principal objects inspired the long pursuit. One
was the desire of the merchants (who were also manufacturing employers) to retain at home an adequate supply of coin—the very life-

[25] Ferdinand Schevill's *A History of Europe* (New York, 1925) is an excellent
summary. See pp. 8–90.

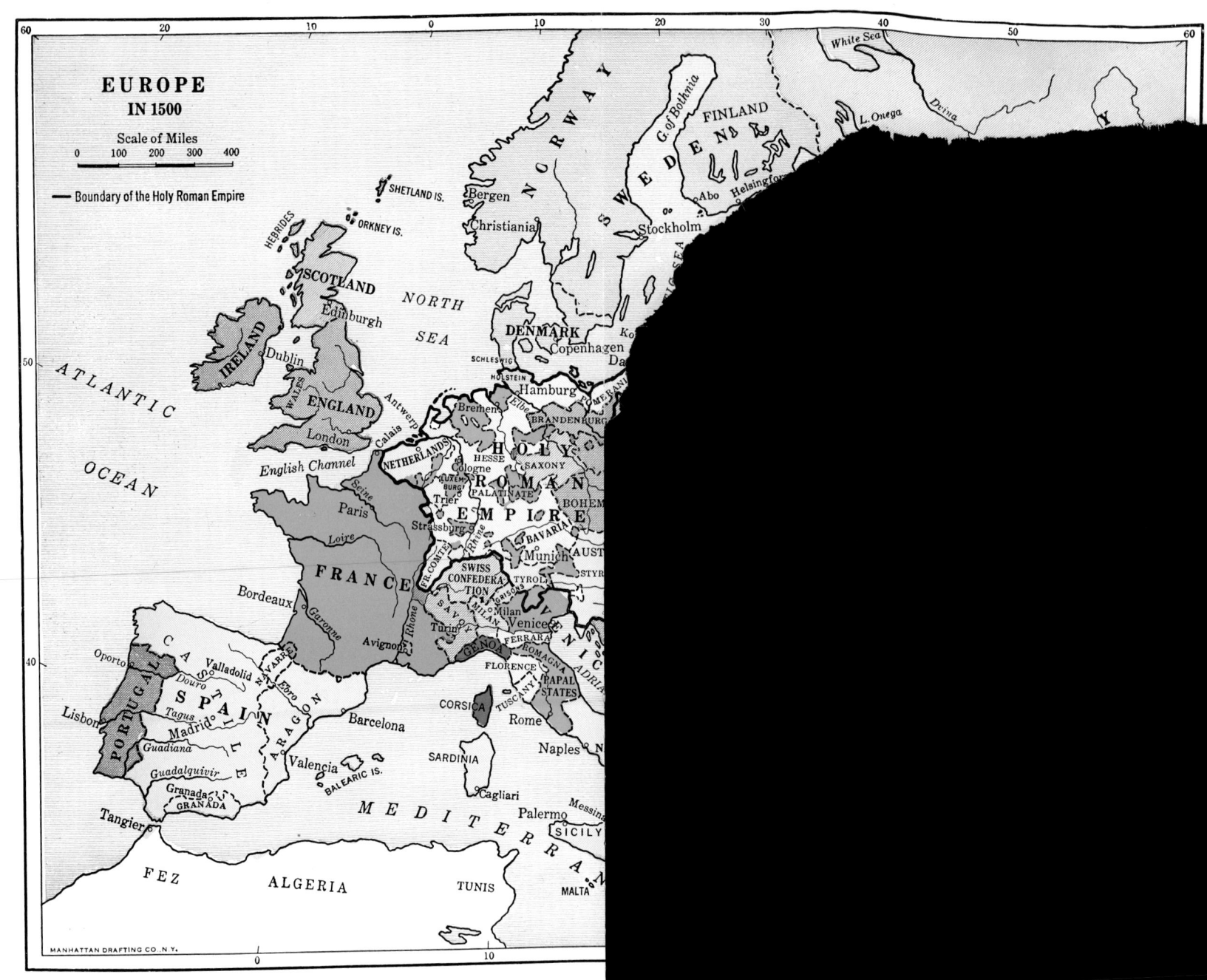

EUROPE
IN 1500

Scale of Miles

0   100   200   300   400

— Boundary of the Holy Roman Empire

60   20   10   0   10   20   30   40   50   60

White Sea

L. Onega   *Dvina*

NORWAY   SWEDEN   FINLAND

G. of Bothnia

SHETLAND IS.   Bergen

Christiania   Stockholm   Åbo   Helsingfor

ORKNEY IS.

HEBRIDES

SCOTLAND

NORTH   DENMARK   Ko

Edinburgh   *SEA*   Copenhagen   Da

IRELAND   SCHLESWIG

Dublin   HOLSTEIN

WALES   Hamburg

ENGLAND   Bremen   BRANDENBURG

Antwerp   Elbe

ATLANTIC   London   NETHERLANDS   HOLY

Calais   Cologne   HESSE   SAXONY

English Channel   LUXEM-   ROMAN

OCEAN   BURG   PALATINATE   BOHEM

Trier   EMPIRE

Paris   Strassburg   *Rhine*

Seine   BAVARIA

Loire   Munich   AUST

FRANCE   SWISS   STYR

CONFEDERA-   TYROL

Bordeaux   TION

Garonne   *Rhone*   Milan   VENICE

FR COMTE   SAV   Turin   Venice

Avignon   GENO   FERRARA   ADRIA

CA   Valladolid   ROMAGNA

Oporto   NAVAR   FLORENCE   TUSCANY

PORTUGAL   *Douro*   *Ebro*   CORSICA   PAPAL

SPAIN   ARAGON   Barcelona   STATES   Rome

Lisbon   Madrid   Valencia

Tagus   *Guadiana*   BALEARIC IS.   SARDINIA   Naples   N

Guadalquivir   Granada

GRANADA   Cagliari

Tangier   *MEDITERRA*   Palermo   Messin

SICILY

FEZ   ALGERIA   TUNIS   MALTA

MANHATTAN DRAFTING CO. N.Y.

0   10

blood of industry and trade, far more important in the town economy of that day than in these times of checking accounts and paper money. If a nation could find a new route to the Orient, it would no longer have to pay out profits, freights, and interest to Italian and Arab merchants. Such earnings would go to native merchants, whose stock of capital would remain at home.[26]

Secondly, if a nation-state discovered a shorter and more economical route to the Orient, its merchants would reap the benefits long enjoyed by the Italian cities. The westerners would supply all neighboring lands with oriental wares. Foreigners would thus pay every year a stream of profits, freights, and interest to the fortunate possessor of the better route. The wealth that had made the Italian cities great would fertilize the West. And when a state became the emporium of the oriental trade, its king could play the old game of the eastern princes—that of taxing goods which passed through his domain to other lands.

Outside the five nation-states of France, Spain, Portugal, England, and Holland, social conditions were unfavorable to participation in the enterprise of discovery. The Scandinavian kingdoms were too far removed from the Mediterranean to feel the full impact of the Renaissance. Germany was divided into a multitude of small states, each of which lacked the resources needed for financing visionary schemes. The commercial cities of Germany had not developed under the protection of a powerful king; instead they had been able, through coöperation among themselves, to achieve a virtual independence, and so to delay the final union of the German people. Very much the same thing happened in Italy. Besides, the Italian city-states were exhausted during the fifteenth century by wars against the Turks. And, as beneficiaries of the older routes of trade, the Italians did not feel the urge to find another passage to the Orient which animated the nations in the West.[27]

The discovery of America was a result of the progressive forces at work in medieval times. The rise of commerce stimulated travel and the hope of private gain. Under its invigorating influence, wealth increased, the resources for new enterprise accumulated, and the desire for easier access to oriental products grew apace. The progress of learning tended to dispel the ignorant fear of unknown scenes, and new inventions afforded technical aids for great achievements on the

---

[26] *The Cambridge Medieval History* (ed. H. M. Gwatkin and J. P. Whitney, 8 vols., Cambridge, 1911–36) contains excellent essays on medieval economy by H. Pirenne and J. H. Clapham (Vol. VI, chapters 14, 15).

[27] Carl Stephenson's *Mediaeval History* (New York, 1935) is comprehensive, well-written, and compact. See chapters 9, 15, 26–28.

ocean. Through the consolidation of the nation-states, local anarchy gave place to internal order, and an effective agency arose to provide support for daring undertakings overseas. One force of earlier days, crusading zeal, survived the transition from medieval to modern times and continued to inspire devout men to conquer distant lands.[28]

[28] Of exceptional value to the general student is E. P. Cheyney's interesting *European Background of American History* (New York, 1904). See chapters 1-3, 6. This book is the first volume of *The American Nation: A History* (ed. A. B. Hart, 27 vols., New York, 1904-08)—a coöperative work that stresses the political aspects of American history.

BIBLIOGRAPHICAL NOTE

BIBLIOGRAPHIES: Oscar Handlin and others, *Harvard Guide to American History* (Cambridge, 1954), is pre-eminent. The literature of the frontier before 1800 is surveyed in R. W. G. Vail, *The Voice of the Old Frontier* (Philadelphia, 1949). *The Cambridge History of the British Empire* (ed. J. H. Rose and others) contains in Volume I (*The Old Empire*, New York, 1929) the best bibliography on imperial aspects of colonial history. Books on social and economic themes are evaluated in *A History of American Life* (ed. A. M. Schlesinger and D. R. Fox, 13 vols., 1927–1948). Clarence S. Brigham, *History and Bibliography of American Newspapers* (2 vols., Worcester, 1947), is the standard guide.

The most useful collections of maps are: *Harper's Atlas of American History* (ed. D. R. Fox, New York, 1920); *Atlas of the Historical Geography of the United States* by Charles O. Paullin (ed. J. K. Wright, Washington, 1932)—very important; and James T. Adams and R. V. Coleman (eds.), *Atlas of American History* (New York, 1943)—useful for early settlements. W. P. Cumming, *The Southeast in Early Maps* (Princeton, 1958), reveals the growth of knowledge concerning the Old South.

An indispensable work is Allen Johnson, Dumas Malone, and others (eds.), *Dictionary of American Biography* (22 vols., New York, 1928–58).

The best collection of statistical data pertaining to the colonies is that compiled by Lawrence A. Harper in U. S. Bureau of the Census, *Historical Statistics of the United States, Colonial Times to 1957* (Washington, 1960), pp. 743–774.

An outstanding collection of sources is Merrill Jensen (ed.), *American Colonial Documents to 1776* (New York, 1955).

The foremost studies of the intellectual, cultural, and social life of the colonies are: *The Cambridge History of American Literature* (ed. W. P. Trent and others, 3 vols., New York, 1917); *The Literature of the American People* (ed. A. H. Quinn, New York, 1951)—see essay by K. B. Murdock; Daniel J. Boorstin, *The Americans: The Colonial Experience* (New York, 1958); Merle Curti, *The Growth of American Thought* (New York, 1943); Vernon L. Parrington, *The Colonial Mind* (New York, 1927); Clinton Rossiter, *Seedtime of the Republic* (New York, 1953); Max Savelle, *Seeds of Liberty* (New York, 1948); R. E. Spiller and others, *Literary History of the United States* (3 vols., New York, 1948); Moses C. Tyler, *A History of American Literature* (2 vols., New York, 1878); Harvey Wish, *Society and Thought in Early America* (New York, 1950); Louis B. Wright, *The Cultural Life of the American Colonies* (New York, 1957), and L. B. Wright, *The Atlantic Frontier* (New York, 1947).

SECONDARY WORKS FOR CHAPTER I: J. R. Strayer, *Western Europe in the*

Middle Ages (New York, 1955), is a compact, well-written summary. A comprehensive survey of life in the later Middle Ages is G. G. Coulton, *Medieval Panorama* (New York, 1938). Among the most useful studies of Norse discoveries are H. R. Holand, *Explorations in America before Columbus* (New York, 1956); and Einar Haugen, *Voyages to Vinland* (New York, 1942). Steven Runciman, *A History of the Crusades* (3 vols., Cambridge, 1951–52) is a distinguished work. A brief, popular sketch is Harold Lamb, *The Crusades* (New York, 1930). Richard Ehrenberg, *Capital and Finance in the Age of the Renaissance* (London, 1928) is a standard authority. Important works on medieval trade are F. C. Lane, *Venetian Ships and Shipbuilders of the Renaissance* (Baltimore, 1934); A. A. Ruddock, *Italian Merchants and Shipping in Southampton, 1270–1600* (Southampton, 1951); and Raymond de Roover, *Money, Banking and Credit in Mediaeval Bruges* (Cambridge, 1948). For medieval maps see E. G. Ravenstein, *Martin Behaim* (London, 1908); and E. L. Stevenson, *Atlas of Portolan Charts* (New York, 1911). Henry H. Hart, *Venetian Adventurer* (Stanford University, 1942), is a good introduction to the career of Marco Polo. Attractive surveys of European life and thought are Sidney Painter, *Mediaeval Society* (Ithaca, 1951); Carl Stephenson, *Mediaeval Feudalism* (Ithaca, 1942); Wallace K. Ferguson, *The Renaissance* (New York, 1940); and G. C. Sellery, *The Renaissance* (Madison, 1950). An outstanding study of humanism is J. Huizinga, *Erasmus of Rotterdam* (New York, 1924; London, 1952).

SOURCES FOR CHAPTER I: The first two volumes of A. B. Hart (ed.), *American History Told by Contemporaries* (5 vols., New York, 1897–1926), relate to the colonial era. J. Franklin Jameson served as general editor of an important series of source materials, *Original Narratives of Early American History* (19 vols., New York, 1906–17). The first volume, *The Northmen, Columbus and Cabot* (ed. J. E. Olson and E. G. Bourne, New York, 1906), contains documents relative to the Norse. Arnold W. Lawrence and Jean Young have presented in attractive form the *Narratives of the Discovery of America* (New York, 1931). The standard edition of *The Book of Ser Marco Polo the Venetian* is that of Sir Henry Yule (revised Henri Cordier, 2 vols., London, 1903). The Everyman's Library edition by John Masefield of *The Travels of Marco Polo* is the most accessible. C. R. Beazley has edited the *Texts and Versions of John de Plano Carpini and William de Rubruquis* for the Hakluyt Society (London, 1903). E. L. Stevenson (ed.), *Geography of Claudius Ptolemy* (New York, 1932), is the first full translation in English. The edition of Pierre d'Ailly's *Imago Mundi* by Edmond Buron (3 vols., Paris, 1930–31), contains the marginal notes of Columbus.

II

 European Pioneers

PORTUGUESE DISCOVERIES

FIRST among the nation-states to embark upon a career of discovery was the little kingdom of Portugal. Founded in 1095, its territorial growth completed by 1263, this state in 1383 entered an era of national greatness at the beginning of the reign of John I, a patriot king. The Portuguese were unified and aroused to aggressive action by wars against their Moorish foes. Imbued with a fierce spirit of independence, they maintained their borders against onslaughts of the ambitious rulers of Castile, but the barrier of that powerful neighbor stopped expansion toward the east. The whole length of their land fronted the sea; the rugged coast furnished many splendid harbors and the earliest national center was a port. Hemmed in on land, the Portuguese turned outward upon the Atlantic.[1]

Their genius for seamanship was fostered by the maritime policies of the state. Foreign traders were encouraged to visit Lisbon; treaties of alliance were formed with England in 1294 and 1386; and Genoese seamen were employed to man the Portuguese navy. During the fourteenth century, Portuguese vessels visited the Canary Islands and probably reached the Madeiras and the Azores. Maritime crusades against Moorish pirates stimulated the building of ships. Moreover, the Kings of Portugal coöperated with the native merchant class. Shipbuilders received timber gratis from the royal forests; shipowners were granted a partial exemption from military service; and a coöperative scheme of marine insurance was devised. Lisbon became a bustling town, its harbor fringed with foreign ships and its streets thronged with foreign mariners and traders.

The foremost patron of seafaring in Portugal, Prince Henry the Navigator, became a national figure in 1415. Son of King John I, grandson of Edward III of England, a devout champion of the Church, an ardent student of science, and a practical business man of

---

[1] *The Portuguese Pioneers* (London, 1933), by Edgar Prestage, is an attractive account by a leading authority.

large affairs, Prince Henry devoted his life to one great cause—the exploration of the western coasts of Africa. The guiding impulse of his early work was his ardor for the war against the Moors. From Morocco, Tunis, and Algeria, the Mohammedans had been wont to launch attacks upon their Christian foes. In Portugal, crusades against the infidel were the noblest causes in which a Christian could engage. Prince Henry in 1415 participated in the successful siege of a Moorish stronghold, Ceuta, and later served as governor of the garrison established there. As a result, he heard reports of the interior of Africa— of the river Senegal, supposed to traverse the land of Guinea, whose people were as yet uncontaminated by the Moors. Other rumors hinted of a Christian country far up the valley of the Nile, the fabled kingdom of Prester John, who waged a gallant fight against encircling Arabs. And there were tales of a caravan trade into the heart of Africa by which the Moors enriched themselves with ivory, slaves, and gold.[2]

Upon these rumors Prince Henry built an imperial design. He would explore the western shore of Africa and learn how far the power of the Moors extended toward the south. Then he would find the land of Guinea, Christianize its people, and unite them in the war against the Moors. If he gained the realm of Prester John, he would obtain a new ally; then after forming a Christian power in the heart of Africa, he might strike the Moors from the south and drive them from their strongholds on the northern coast. In consequence the inland trade which the Saracens had carried on with the Sudan would be diverted by an ocean route to Lisbon.

The lure of science also animated Prince Henry's work. Eager for knowledge for its own sake, he sought to learn by observation the truth about the unknown world. Probably he hoped his explorations would open a new passage to the East. In Africa Portugal might achieve a career of imperial greatness such as she could never realize in Europe.

Appointed governor for life of the southern province of Portugal, Prince Henry built a small town, Villa do Infante, on the tip of Cape St. Vincent—an ideal point for vessels sailing to the south. Here he also erected an observatory where he immersed himself in studies of mathematics and cosmography. He used his personal fortune to equip expeditions in a systematic course of exploration and to provide his mariners with the best of instruction, maps, and instruments of navigation. His work was blessed at Rome, when the papacy twice called

[2] C. R. Beazley's *Prince Henry the Navigator* (New York, 1895), a history of Portuguese maritime enterprise, is especially recommended.

upon Christian Europe to join him in a new crusade against the Moors.[3]

Between 1420 and 1431 Prince Henry's mariners rediscovered the Madeira Islands and the Azores. Then, in 1434, the Portuguese sailed beyond Cape Bojador—a feat which carried them for the first time into unknown waters. The following year they made their first landing upon the African coast. Already they had passed the land of the Moors. In 1441, after capturing several natives, they inaugurated the European trade in Negro slaves. A burst of enthusiasm now greeted Prince Henry's schemes, previously considered as devoid of private gain. So lucrative did slave-hunting become that later navigators sent out to discover Guinea preferred to stop and capture natives who might be ransomed by their tribes with ivory and gold or sold elsewhere as slaves. Although Prince Henry condoned slavery as a means of Christianizing the Negroes, he remained interested primarily in discovery. The last achievements of his lifetime were the sighting of Cape Verde in 1446 and the discovery of the Cape Verde Islands in 1455.

After Prince Henry's death in 1460, his work was carried forward by his nephew, King Alfonso V. An expedition in 1471 crossed the equator, and another in 1484 reached the Congo River. Then, in 1486, Bartholomew Diaz rounded the Cape of Good Hope. Motivated by scientific rather than commercial interest, Diaz was seeking the kingdom of Prester John. After reaching the eastern shore of Africa, he was forced to turn back by the fears and weariness of his crew. Only on the return voyage did he realize what he had accomplished; the Orient now seemed within the reach of Portugal. In 1497–98 occurred the memorable voyage of Vasco da Gama to Calicut in India. His return to Lisbon in 1499 with valuable spices and precious stones (which more than paid the expenses of the expedition) announced that Portugal had gained admittance to the oriental trade by a cheap and expeditious route.[4]

The Portuguese now prepared for commercial war with the Arabs who dominated the routes of trade in the Indian Ocean and the Red Sea, and the second Portuguese fleet, under Cabral in 1500, seized and burned several Moorish ships. During the next decade two great admirals, Almeida and Albuquerque, captured the Moorish stations

[3] See two excellent articles on Prince Henry by C. R. Beazley in the *American Historical Review*, XVI (Oct. 1910) and XVII (Jan. 1912).
[4] E. G. Bourne's *Essays in Historical Criticism* (New York, 1901) contains an admirable discussion of Prince Henry.

on the eastern coast of Africa and secured a trading center at Goa on the western coast of India. Then the Portuguese, having gained control of distant Malacca, established themselves, too, in Ormuz at the entrance to the Persian Gulf, thus enabling them to levy duties on the products moving westward over one of the older routes.

These victories ushered in the commercial revolution of the sixteenth century, which transferred the seat of commercial power from the Mediterranean to the West. As Portugal diverted the oriental trade to Lisbon, the Italian cities declined. Eager for a monopoly of this commerce, the Portuguese admitted only their own vessels and merchants to the eastern ports which they controlled. However, by reason of limited commercial resources, the Portuguese could not distribute the oriental wares throughout Europe, and consequently other European traders were permitted to come to Lisbon and purchase goods for exportation. In the north, Antwerp rose to take the place of the free towns of Germany as chief distributor of eastern wares in Western Europe.

In the meantime, Portugal had erected a colonial empire in the eastern Atlantic. During the fifteenth century, the papacy conferred upon Prince Henry the title to all lands lying south of Cape Bojador, and excluded all Christians from settling there unless with his consent. From the Portuguese government he received permission to colonize the Azores, the exclusive privilege of navigating the waters of the western coast of Africa, and the right to receive in full the profits of his ventures. Colonies were founded under his auspices in the Azores, the Madeiras, and the Cape Verde Islands. These supplied Portugal with wine, sugar, cattle, sheep, and lumber. In founding settlements the Portuguese government granted land to leaders who were required to develop its resources, to promote exploration, and to share their profits with the king. To protect themselves, the Portuguese endeavored to suppress the news of their discoveries, and in 1480 King Alfonso V ordered that mariners found on foreign ships in Portugal's new sphere of influence should be thrown into the sea.[5]

Although the most spectacular achievements of Portugal came after the death of Prince Henry, he nevertheless deserves the credit for their success. He presents one illustration of individual influence in history—of a leader who devoted his talent and fortune to one undertaking that proved immensely significant in later times. He in-

---

[5] Albert G. Keller's *Colonization* (Boston, c. 1908) in chapters 3–8 presents a good summary of Portuguese and Spanish enterprise.

spired his nation with a patriotic enthusiasm for discovery. Likewise, he altered the method of exploration, substituting systematic experimentation in place of the earlier reliance upon the views of ancient writers. Every technical improvement in the art of navigation received his encouraging support. It is probable that his success inspired Columbus with his vision of a western voyage. During the lifetime of Prince Henry the hardest part of the circumnavigation of Africa was achieved. When he died, the Dark Continent had been revealed as a populous, fertile land, rich in opportunities for Christian missions and economic gain.

The activities of Portugal throw light upon the motives which dominated the age of discovery. Formerly it was supposed that the conquests of the Ottoman Turks, their plundering of Mediterranean towns, and their capture of Constantinople in 1453 dammed the older routes of trade, deprived Europe of her usual supply of oriental goods, and so impelled the western states to seek a new approach to the East. This view, however, no longer holds. One of the most important routes—the southern, with its terminus at Alexandria—did not fall under the control of the Turks until their conquest of Egypt in 1517—nineteen years after Vasco da Gama arrived in India. Moreover, Portuguese pioneering began in 1417, long before the Turks were supposed to have choked the older channels of trade. Originally the Portuguese were motivated by religious and scientific interests; the search for a new route was in all probability an afterthought. During the fifteenth century, the prices of oriental spices in Europe actually declined. Had the Turks seriously interfered with the eastern trade, such prices must have risen very sharply in response to added charges or reduced supplies.[6]

It must be concluded that the national states finally undertook the search for a new route, not because the older channels were closed, but because they desired to avoid paying the heavy charges to foreign middlemen. Each state sought independent access to the East. After Portugal opened her route, Spain, France, England, and Holland endeavored for many years to acquire separate routes of their own. It was not a matter of single route—or of the general supply of oriental commodities in the West. Each nation-state desired to have its own approach to the East in order that its payments to foreign middlemen might cease and that its own merchants might reap the profits earned by distributors of oriental wares.

[6] A very significant article is A. H. Lybyer's "Influence of the Rise of the Ottoman Turks upon the Routes of Oriental Trade," *Report*, American Historical Association, 1914, Vol. I.

THE UNIFICATION OF SPAIN

Many of the impulses which urged Portugal to colonizing activity were likewise powerful in Spain. The way for Spanish enterprise was prepared by the consolidation of many separate kingdoms into a unified state. Prior to 1450, national unity in Spain had not been won. Five distinct kingdoms existed on the Iberian peninsula—Aragon, including Barcelona and Valencia; Castile, which had annexed Leon; the Moorish kingdom of Granada; the independent state of Portugal; the northern kingdom of Navarre. Racially, there were the Spanish descendants of the original inhabitants and of early German invaders, along with a large element of Moors, whose forefathers had overrun the peninsula early in the eighth century. Jews, who had always been encouraged by the Moors, formed another important group. The Spanish Christians were bitterly hostile to both the Jewish faith and the Mohammedanism of the Moors. "Judaizing Christians" were Jews who outwardly conformed to Christian beliefs but in secret continued to practice Jewish rites.

The early monarchies of Aragon and Castile were weakened by the military power of the feudal knights, whose services were so essential in the contest with the Moors. A law unto themselves, the nobles readily defied the king's authority and seized estates from his domain. Centuries of warfare and crusading had given rise to three powerful military orders in Castile—the Knights of Santiago, of Calatrava, and of Alcantara. Possessed of towns and extensive lands, many gained by bequests of the pious, the masters of these orders commanded so many tenants, soldiers, revenues, and honors as to make them rivals of the king.[7]

The royal houses of Aragon and Castile finally welded the Spanish territories into a unified state. In 1469 occurred the marriage of Ferdinand of Aragon and Isabella of Castile. The latter became queen of Castile in 1474; the former, king of Aragon in 1479. Although each kingdom remained legally independent, the two sovereigns effected a common rule. The final territorial consolidation of Spain was accomplished through the conquest of Granada in 1492 and the annexation of southern Navarre in 1512. After the death of Isabella, Ferdinand ruled as regent of Castile. Then, in 1516, the united possessions of the two sovereigns passed into the hands of their grandson, King Charles I of Spain.

Little by little the power of the feudal lords gave way before the

---

[7] Edward D. Salmon's *Imperial Spain* (New York, c. 1931) is especially valuable for the general reader.

encroachments of the state. After 1480 the two sovereigns destroyed the fortifications of the castles of the nobles and compelled them to disband their knights. Duels and private warfare were proscribed. A middle-class league was used to stamp out lawlessness and crime. This society, the *hermandad,* through coöperation among its widely scattered members, captured criminals and punished with a heavy hand. Ferdinand and Isabella placed their ministers in the offices of

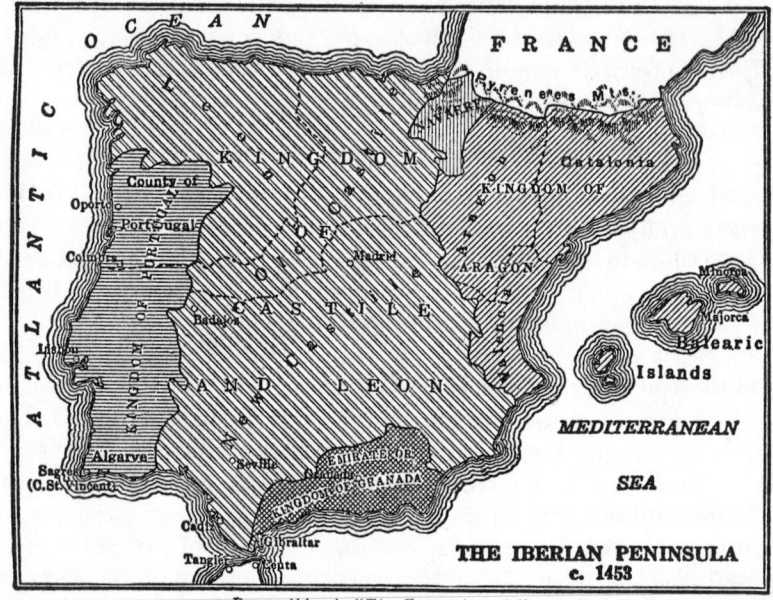

From Abbott's "The Expansion of Europe." © F. S. Crofts & Co.

this league and used it to subdue the nobles. Royal agents investigated claims to land and confiscated estates once wrested from the Crown. After the nobles were shorn of military power, they were encouraged, by means of titles, honors, and exemption from taxation, to ally themselves with the Spanish court.

Meanwhile the three great military orders were subordinated to the state. Taking for himself the offices of Grand Master in these societies, King Ferdinand practically appropriated their offices and funds. He also sent agents to the towns to assert the royal supremacy over local rights. Gradually a centralized government took form. Its mainspring was a royal council composed principally of lawyers whose training in the Roman law inclined them to assert the absolute power of the state. Out of this body developed several other powerful councils which held the reins of power for the king.

Absolutism assumed its harshest features in religious persecution.

In 1480, the Spanish Inquisition was devised, with papal sanction, to stamp out heresy. The Jews were expelled in 1492—an act that drove from Spain a hundred thousand of their race and persuaded fifty thousand others to embrace the Catholic Church. Then followed a similar expulsion of the Moors. As an agency of the state, the Inquisition labored ceaselessly to uproot heresy and to force all people to accept the king's religion as the national faith.

All these measures made the royal will supreme. The wars against the Moors had unified the Spanish people and subordinated them to the military leadership of the crowns of Aragon and Castile. Final success enhanced the prestige of the two sovereigns and gave them command of the armies and the treasure of their states. Spain soon became the most progressive military power in Europe—the first to organize its army on modern lines. The suppression of the feudal nobles rallied the middle classes to the royal cause. The sovereign power reduced the Spanish parliament, or Cortes, to the impotence of an advisory body which merely ratified the king's commands. By 1500, Spain was ready for expansion overseas. The powerful monarchy could assert its authority over Spanish conquerors and thus extend its arbitrary rule to foreign lands.[8]

COLUMBUS

Some time between 1446 and 1451 there was born in Genoa, of humble parents, a boy who was destined, some forty-odd years later, to lead Spain upon the path of colonial empire. Having taken to the sea at an early age, the youthful Christopher Columbus was educated in the school of hardship. What he learned of Latin, navigation, and geography was self-taught. About the year 1473, he appeared in Portugal, whence he made a voyage down the African coast to Guinea. Later, in 1477, he visited Iceland. But it has not been proved that while there he ever heard of Leif Ericsson's discovery of Vinland; the sagas which recited the Norse discoveries in the Western World, it happened, were not then current.[9]

By 1484, Columbus had conceived his idea of a western voyage. There are two interpretations of his original aim. One is that he had derived from his study of Aristotle, Ptolemy, and Cardinal d'Ailly

---

[8] Edward Channing in his *History of the United States* (6 vols., New York, 1905–25) exhibits a mastery of narration, description, and characterization, although his work does not emphasize social forces. See Vol. I, pp. 14–114, on Spain and France.

[9] Clements R. Markham's *Life of Columbus* (London, 1892) presents the most widely held view of Columbus's career. A more formal but equally scholarly biography is Justin Winsor's *Christopher Columbus* (Boston, 1891).

the theory that the western ocean was so small that one might readily sail from Spain to China. Accordingly, he wrote to a Florentine astronomer, Toscanelli, for additional information. Toscanelli sent him a copy of a letter and a map. These described in glowing terms the wealth of the Indies, and indicated that the distance thither across the Atlantic was only about four thousand miles. Fed with these ideas and fired by hope, Columbus sought deliberately to reach the Orient by a western route.

The other view is less flattering to Columbus. While he was sojourning in Portugal, he is supposed to have sheltered a Portuguese mariner who had accidentally discovered a strange land in the Atlantic. This narrative harmonized with contemporary legends of islands in the western sea. To one of these (Antilia), the last Gothic king of Spain had fled before the avalanche of the Moors. Another land, Brazil, was supposed to lie to the west of the British Isles. A third, St. Brandan's, had presumably been peopled in the sixth century by three thousand monks. Columbus must have been familiar with these legends. Was he seeking some such fabled land? If so, the length of his voyage convinced him that he had gone far beyond his intended destination and had accidentally reached the Indies. Either he or his friends then wished to show that he had made his discovery, not by accident, but through design. Thus it is inferred that someone forged the Toscanelli letter to prove that Columbus had acted with a scientific aim.[10]

Whatever his original object, it seems certain that in 1483 or 1484 Columbus asked the King of Portugal to provide the vessels for a voyage, but to no avail. The king was irritated by the boastful manner of Columbus and by his inordinate demands. Moreover, the Portuguese were occupied with their explorations of the African coast. Thereupon Columbus turned to Isabella of Castile. He enlisted the aid of a leader of the Spanish nobles, the Count of Medina-Celi, who later said that he had brought the novel plan before the queen. It was then referred to a committee whose presiding officer believed that the views of Columbus were contrary to the teachings of the Bible. For several years Columbus made fruitless pleas for aid. Even though the queen was favorably disposed, the energies of her court were devoted to a war against the Moors. In a final effort Columbus persuaded a former confessor of the queen to make a fresh appeal. This

[10] Examples of brilliant scholarship are Henri Vignaud's *The Columbian Tradition* (Oxford, 1920) and *Toscanelli and Columbus* (London, 1902)—very important. See also G. E. Nunn's "The *Imago Mundi* and Columbus," *American Historical Review*, XL (Oct. 1934) and his *The Geographical Conceptions of Columbus* (New York, 1924)—important.

coincided with the conquest of Granada early in 1492, and at last the queen was free to act. Accordingly, a commission was issued to Columbus at Santa Fé in April 1492.

Columbus was to be recognized as admiral and governor of the islands and mainlands which he might discover. He was privileged to contribute one-eighth of the money for the voyage and to receive a like share of the profits. Otherwise, after expenses were deducted, a tenth of the proceeds should go to him, and the remainder to the queen. Isabella advanced more than a fourth of the funds, Columbus or his friends contributed an eighth, and the rest was probably lent to Castile by the treasurer of Aragon. During the early summer three vessels were fitted out—the *Santa Maria,* of about one hundred and twenty tons burden, the *Pinta* of fifty tons, and the *Nina* of forty tons. The crew of ninety common sailors was a cosmopolitan lot.[11]

Sailing from Palos on August 3, Columbus proceeded first to the Canary Islands and then took the path of the trade winds to one of the Bahama Islands, which was sighted in the early morning of October 12. But for the fears and opposition of his men, which Columbus tried to quiet with false reports of the distance traveled, the voyage was easily performed. After the initial landing, probably at Watling Island, Columbus pushed on to Cuba, and then discovered Haiti. The former, he thought at first, was Asia; the latter, Japan. At Cuba he sent envoys in search of the court of the great khan of China. Meanwhile, he hunted for some valuable products which might provide a profit for the voyage, or at least give cause for another expedition. Taking along several natives—whom he had named Indians—he returned to Europe, arriving in Portugal in March 1493.

The news of the discovery spread like wildfire. The exaggerated accounts which Columbus related of the wealth of the Indies made him a hero overnight. "From all the neighboring places the people gathered along the highway to see him and the Indians and the other things so novel that he brought . . ." Spanish gentlemen of means and position were eager to share the anticipated spoils of conquest. A fleet of seven vessels was now equipped at Cadiz, whence Columbus with fifteen hundred followers embarked in the autumn of 1493 upon his second voyage. Proceeding by way of the Leeward Islands and Puerto Rico, he planted at Haiti the first Spanish colony in the New World. Next he discovered Jamaica, only to return to

[11] Cecil Jane has edited for the Hakluyt Society a handsome collection of *Select Documents Illustrating the Four Voyages of Columbus* (London, 1930, 1933). Volume I contains a splendid essay on the objective of Columbus.

Haiti to find his settlers in revolt. He was then obliged to go back to Spain to answer charges against him which his enemies had carried to the queen.

On his third voyage, in 1498, Columbus reached the mouth of the Orinoco River on the mainland of South America. Such a mighty fresh-water stream, he was persuaded, did not issue from an island. Yet this new land was apparently too far south for Asia; it must be a separate continent, an *otro mundo*. On his last voyage in 1502 he endeavored to sail around the northwestern end of the new continent in order to reach the wealthy parts of Asia. He coasted along Central America between Honduras and Panama, always seeking

> . . . the wealth of Ormuz and of Ind,
> Or where the gorgeous East with richest hand
> Showers on her kings barbaric pearl and gold.

Until his death in 1506 Columbus remained convinced that he had visited the outlying lands of Asia.[12]

The mistakes of Columbus and the defects of his character should not obscure the greatness of his achievement. Vain, boastful, arrogant, and deceitful he certainly was, and in his last years highly visionary; yet his tenacity, courage, hardihood, and independence indicate a man of heroic stature. Although many men had thought that a western voyage was possible, he was the first to venture into perilous seas on the strength of that belief. His success affected profoundly every important phase of later European history.

PORTUGAL AND SPAIN

When Columbus arrived in Portugal in 1493 and described his first discovery, the Portuguese insisted that he had not reached the Indies but had merely visited lands belonging to them. In 1480, Castile and Portugal had agreed to a treaty which consigned the Canary Islands to Castile, and northern Africa, Guinea, and other western islands in the southern ocean to Portugal. This treaty confirmed earlier grants from the papacy to the two states. It had been the custom in the Middle Ages for the pope to confer title to lands conquered from the infidel. Accordingly, Spain in 1493 felt it necessary to obtain papal sanction to her claims arising from the voyage of Columbus.

[12] *The Discovery of North America*, by Henry Harrisse (London, 1892), is the chief reference work in English of a great French-American scholar.

At this time Spain exerted a strong influence over Pope Alexander VI. It is probable that Spanish officials prepared three decrees which were issued in May and September 1493 by the pope. These decrees provided that a line of demarcation should be drawn through a point a hundred leagues west and south of the Azores and the Cape Verde Islands. As far to the west of this line as the Indies, Spain was to have title to, and a monopoly of the commerce with, the lands she had discovered or might discover, provided they did not already belong to a Christian prince. Portuguese subjects should not pass beyond the line without consent of Spain.

These decrees did not satisfy Portugal because the line was placed too far to the east. An appeal to Spain resulted in the Treaty of Tordesillas (June 7, 1494), which declared that the line should run north and south through a point three hundred and seventy leagues west of the Cape Verde Islands. Not until 1506 did this shift of the line receive papal confirmation. The so-called papal line was in reality a line agreed upon by Portugal and Spain. It did not divide all new territories between the two states; it merely mapped out areas in which discovery would confer title to land. Each state agreed to keep out of the other's sphere of activity.[13]

The wariness of Portugal in demanding a more western location of the line of demarcation was soon rewarded. In 1500, a Portuguese fleet under Cabral, carried out of its course around Africa to India, arrived at the coast of Brazil. The "papal" line so fell in South America as to include Brazil in the Portuguese sphere of influence, thus enabling Portugal to establish a colony there. In 1501, the Portuguese sent out an expedition which sailed hundreds of miles along the coast to South America. One member of this party was a Florentine merchant, Americus Vespucius, who later claimed that he had made four western voyages between 1497 and 1503. He wrote a letter in 1503 describing the land which he had seen and insisting that it was a new world. A German scholar, Martin Waldseemüller, included a second letter by Vespucius in a popular geography (1507), and suggested that the new land be called Amerige, or Americ's land, in honor of Americus. The name caught the fancy of Europe and stuck. Vespucius was not a navigator, and in all probability had not seen the mainland of America before Columbus. Chance, literary

[13] Henry Harrisse, *The Diplomatic History of America* (London, 1897), should be supplemented by H. Vander Linden's "Alexander VI and the Demarcation of the . . . Domains of Spain and Portugal, 1493–1494," *American Historical Review*, XXII (Oct. 1916).

talent, and self-assertiveness brought an honor to his name which he did not deserve.[14]

In 1518 the Spaniards contended that the line of 1494 extended around the globe. How it divided the eastern hemisphere was not known. Were the valuable Spice Islands within the Portuguese or the Spanish sphere? Meanwhile, the exploration of America had demonstrated that the wealthy parts of Asia had not yet been reached by the western route. A Portuguese navigator, Ferdinand Magellan, convinced Charles I that a strait could be found through America that would lead to Asia, thus giving Spain a direct route to the oriental lands which might lie within the Spanish zone. Having secured a royal patent, Magellan sailed from Spain in September 1519 intent upon discovering a western passage to the Indies.

Proceeding by way of the coast of Brazil, Magellan finally entered the strait that now bears his name. For thirty-eight days his vessels threaded their way through this tortuous passage, often in the face of terrific winds. When at last he saw the western ocean, it seemed so calm that he named it the Pacific. Then followed the long, harassing voyage across its vast, dreary expanse. After intense suffering from hunger, when rats were sold on shipboard as food, Magellan's men and three of his vessels reached the Philippines. The resolute commander, who had withstood all manner of hardship and opposition, was killed by natives at the island of Matan. One of his vessels, however, visited Borneo and Moluccas, and returned to Spain by way of India and the Cape of Good Hope. It brought back a cargo of spices, which paid in full the cost of the expedition.[15]

The dispute between Spain and Portugal over the partition of the Indies now broke out afresh. In 1524 an attempt of the two states to locate the line of demarcation in the Orient failed. Finally, however, Charles I sold the Spanish claims to the Spice Islands to Portugal. Later, the Portuguese recognized Spain's claim to the Philippine Islands. The outcome of negotiations concerning the islands was to leave Portugal in the strongest position in the commerce of the East Indies, while Spain carried on a slight trade with the Philippines by way of the western coast of America.

[14] E. G. Bourne, "The Naming of America," *American Historical Review*, X (Oct. 1904).

[15] Edward F. Benson's *Ferdinand Magellan* (New York, 1930) presents its subject in an interesting manner. The best older study is F. H. H. Guillemard, *The Life of Ferdinand Magellan* (London, 1890).

Spanish Exploration and Conquest

The first half of the sixteenth century witnessed a series of Spanish exploits unmatched in the annals of exploration. The fortune hunters who accompanied Columbus on his second voyage were outraged by the meager resources of the new Indies. His false accounts inspired hopes of gain which disillusionment speedily transformed into hatred of himself. His enemies returned to Spain and obtained from the queen special licenses for independent explorations in the region over which he had been made admiral and governor. His monopoly rights vanished into thin air. By 1502 his rivals had sailed along three thousand miles of the coast of South America. They searched for pearls, made raids to capture Indian slaves, and endeavored to find the desired strait to Asia, which was then thought to lie close beyond America. When such a strait was not found, the Spaniards turned their attention to the mainland. Lust for gold inspired imperial conquests. The natives who resisted were pursued with fire and sword, and the dread of Spanish arms spread far and wide. By 1550 the Spaniards had explored the eastern coast of America from Panama to Labrador and the western coast from Oregon to the Strait of Magellan.[16]

The conquests of the Spaniards were performed, not by the state through royal expeditions, but by small bands of adventurers whose leaders provided the necessary funds. First, however, such a leader had to secure a license from the king, without which an explorer was not permitted to sail in American seas. In order to obtain a royal license, the leader was obliged to show that he had financial backing sufficient to assure success; he then received the right to recruit soldiers and settlers and to fit out ships. He and his men (who were bound to him as if to the king) were entitled to the profits of the expedition. Royal agents went along to keep record of the treasure taken, one-fifth of which belonged to the leader and another fifth to the king. If the intended conquest promised to be especially important, it might receive financial assistance from the Crown. The leader was commonly required to take along a certain number of missionaries to convert the natives who submitted to Spanish rule.

When once a conquest had been made, the title to the land was vested in the king. The leader, however, received the right to hold a personal estate, the privilege of making land grants to his followers, and the power of putting the natives to forced labor on private lands.

[16] John Bartlet Brebner's *The Explorers of North America* (New York, 1933) is a superior introductory study. See chapters 1–9.

As an agent of the king, the conqueror might erect forts, serve as governor or captain-general of the colony, and appoint the local officers to govern it during its first year. The methods of Spanish conquest intensified individual leadership in America and established there the supreme power of the parent state.

During the early years of conquest the Spaniards used their settlements in the West Indies as bases for launching expeditions to the mainland. From Haiti in 1511 an adventurous planter, Vasco de Balboa, fled from his creditors to the Isthmus of Darien, where warfare with the natives brought him in touch with a leader who told of a region "flowing with gold where you may satisfy your ravening appetites," and reported that beyond the western mountains lay another sea. In the summer of 1513 Balboa, with a selected band of Spaniards and Indians, fought his way across the Isthmus of Panama, through forests and over cliffs, until on September 25 he reached a mountain summit, where—first among Europeans—he beheld the waters of the Pacific, "the great South Sea." His discovery was soon followed by Spanish exploration of the coasts of the new ocean.[17]

A few months before Balboa's exploit, another gold hunter, Ponce de Leon, had sailed from Puerto Rico and discovered Florida. A trader and first governor of Puerto Rico, he had heard from slave raiders of a strange land called Bimini, which in Indian legend was rich in gold and blessed with a fountain whose waters made men perpetually young. After his return from Florida to Puerto Rico in 1513, eight years elapsed before Ponce de Leon set out again to the desired land. This time he took settlers and livestock for a colony. Little is known of his attempted settlement in 1521 except that it was dispersed by hostile Indians. Severely wounded in the attack, Ponce de Leon returned to Havana to die.

An official at Santo Domingo, Lucas Vasquez de Ayllon, who was also interested in the North American coast, dispatched a vessel thither in 1521 under the command of one Francisco Gordillo. After falling in with some slave hunters, Gordilla sailed to the coast at 33° 30′ north latitude. The Indian slaves whom he captured contrary to Ayllon's instructions were freed in Santo Domingo. Ayllon next secured a royal patent for colonization and exploration, and in 1526 headed an expedition which planted a settlement somewhere

---

[17] An outstanding figure in American historical writing is George Bancroft, whose *History of the United States* (6 vols., New York, 1885) was the most influential work of its time. Bancroft is noted for his democratic and patriotic bias. See Vol. I, chapters 1–2 on France and Spain.

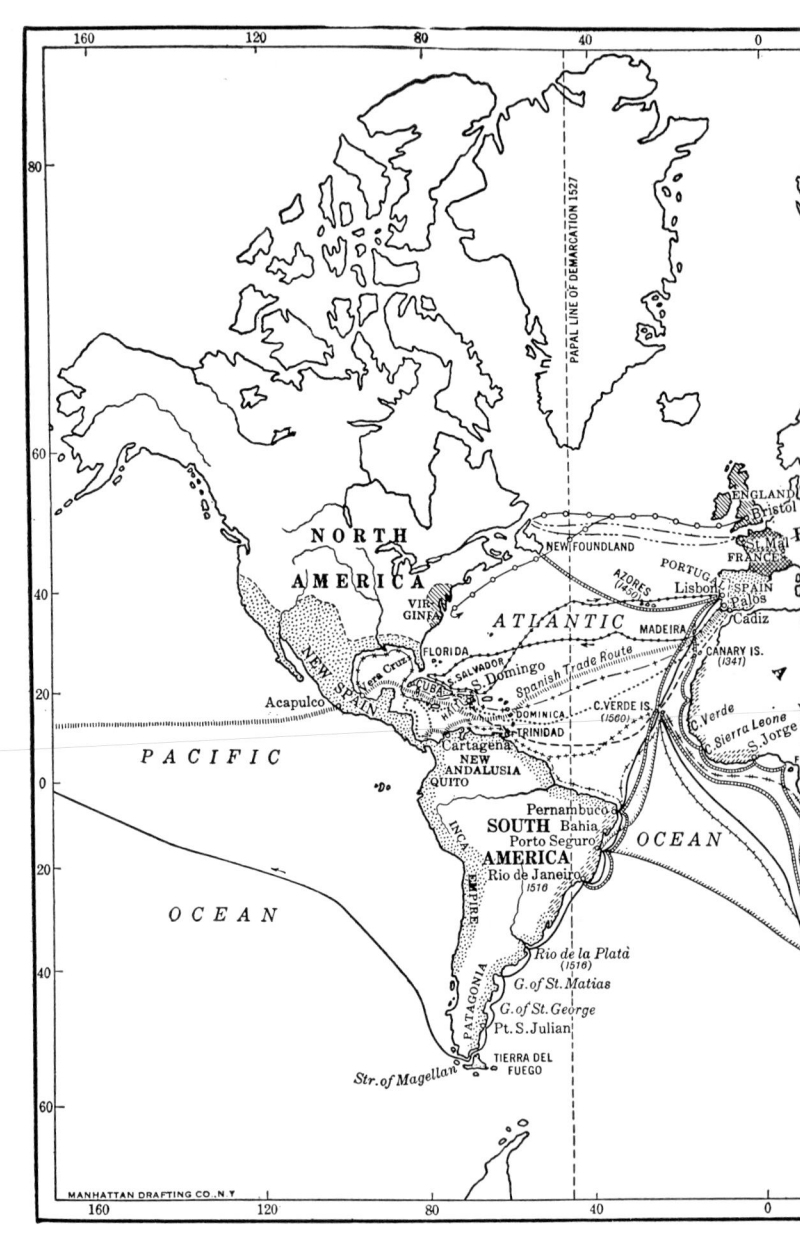

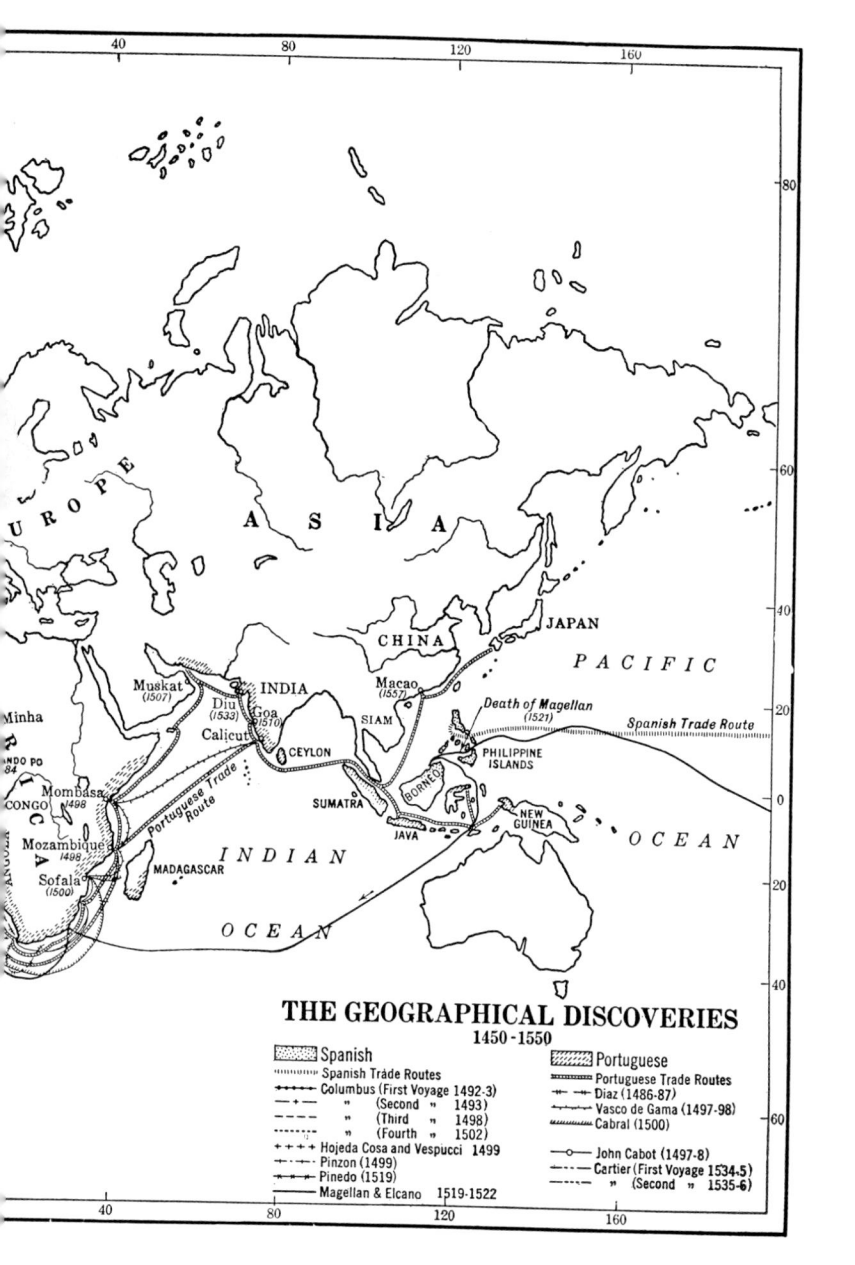

THE GEOGRAPHICAL DISCOVERIES
1450 - 1550

between the Cape Fear River and the James. Engulfed by a sea of troubles and losing their leader, a victim of fever, the colonists abandoned the project in despair. Fewer than a fourth of their number finally returned to Santo Domingo.[18]

Shortly before Ayllon's failure, a Portuguese mariner, Estevan Gomez, sailing under Spanish auspices, had skirted the North American coast between Newfoundland and the fortieth parallel. Nowhere did he find evidence of gold or precious stones, while the trees, fruits, and fish which he beheld did not seem valuable. His unattractive picture of the coast, in conjunction with the failure of Ayllon's colony, led the Spaniards to concentrate upon Central and South America, thereby leaving the northern shore open to later occupation by the English, French, Dutch, and Swedes.

A turning point in Spanish enterprise occurred in 1519–22 when Hernando Cortés conquered the Aztecs of Mexico. While commanding an expedition under the governor of Cuba, Cortés violated his orders and became a conqueror in his own right. Posing as a deliverer of the oppressed Aztecs, he played one faction among them against another, and captured their emperor, Montezuma, and their capital, Mexico City. He then successfully defied the governor of Cuba and in 1522 gained recognition from the King of Spain as independent ruler of Mexico. His conquests brought to the Spaniards for the first time a large store of gold and silver and put them in command of an agricultural people who might be profitably exploited. Visions of inland wealth now dimmed the old lure of the East, and other Spanish conquerors strove to imitate Cortés—to subdue similar empires rich in silver and gold. Since the mines of America were widely distributed, the Spaniards undertook a series of extended explorations which finally carried them over the vast territory stretching between present-day Kansas and Peru.[19]

In 1520 the governor of Cuba sent an army to Mexico to arrest Cortés. Its leader was Panfilo Narvaez. Defeated and imprisoned for a time by Cortés, Narvaez conceived the design of conquering another empire on the northern shore of the Gulf of Mexico. Having returned to Spain, he obtained in 1526 a patent to Florida and the next year he set out with five vessels and six hundred followers. After two disasters in the West Indies, his expedition arrived at the coast of Florida in 1528. Lured inland by reports of an Indian city,

---

[18] Woodbury Lowery's *The Spanish Settlements* . . . (2 vols., New York, 1911) treats Spanish enterprise "within the present limits of the United States."

[19] F. A. Kirkpatrick's *The Spanish Conquistadores* (New York, 1934) is unsurpassed as a one-volume history (to 1550).

Apalache, supposed to abound with gold and pearls, he found only a miserable village. He pursued his explorations a few weeks until sickness and Indian hostilities obliged him to construct new boats and to embark for Mexico. A storm in the Gulf cast his shipwrecked followers upon the coast of Texas.

Four survivors finally reached Mexico in 1536. One of these was the treasurer of the expedition, Cabeza de Vaca, who had wandered far and wide between the Mississippi and the Gulf of California— "from the land of the cactus on the south to the ranges of the buffalo on the north." His fascinating account of his travels and the rumors he reported gave confirmation to Indian legends of populous and wealthy cities somewhere toward the north.[20]

In 1537, Cabeza de Vaca returned to Spain, where his narrative reached the ears of another adventurer, Hernando de Soto—lately returned from participation in the conquest of Peru. De Soto had brought back a share of the plunder of the Incas, and was already seeking new realms to conquer. After obtaining a royal license to colonize Florida, he set forth with a band of six hundred noblemen, officials, and servants, and arrived at Tampa Bay in 1539. Intent upon capturing Indian slaves, he brought along iron neck collars attached to chains and by cruelties inflicted upon the natives spread hatred and terror as the expedition advanced. Its route led to the Savannah River, across the piedmont of North Carolina, southward toward Mobile Bay, and thence to the Mississippi near the present site of Memphis.

The discovery of the "Father of Waters" did not delight de Soto; he regarded the river only as an obstacle in his search for wealth. After crossing the stream, he proceeded into the lands of present-day Arkansas and Oklahoma, and then floated down the Arkansas River to its mouth, where he died and was secretly buried in the Mississippi. Later, his followers constructed boats which carried them down the river, along the Texan coast, and finally to Panuco in Mexico (1543). For a half century afterward the Spaniards believed that the Mississippi had its source in a chain of mountains supposed to extend east and west between the highlands of Carolina and the Ozarks.[21]

---

[20] *The Chronicles of America* (ed. Allen Johnson, 50 vols., New Haven, 1918–21) is a series of short, entertaining volumes which combine readability and scholarship. Early Spanish enterprise is treated in this series in Herbert E. Bolton's *The Spanish Borderlands* (1921), chapters 1–4, and in Irving B. Richman's *The Spanish Conquerors* (1919).

[21] Theodore Maynard, *De Soto and the Conquistadores* (New York, 1930), is a delightfully written narrative.

At about the same time another romantic adventure was inspired in part by Cabeza de Vaca. In 1536 his narrative reached the viceroy of New Spain at Mexico City—Don Antonio de Mendoza. Indian legends then current told that north of Mexico lay great towns suggesting to the Spanish fancy the fabled land of Cibola, famed for its seven wealthy cities whose golden towers glistened in the sun. Such legends were seemingly confirmed by the tales of Cabeza de Vaca. Earlier Spanish expeditions to find the cities had failed for want of systematic preparations, but now, determined to extend the power of Spain over this mythical kingdom, Mendoza sent an advance party of Franciscan monks to chart the way. One of their number—Friar Marcos—penetrated far enough northward to see, at a distance, a promising Indian village. His description of its storied houses, built of stone, seemed to his uncritical hearers assurance that Cibola, in all the gorgeous splendor with which European tales time out of mind had invested it, was here at hand to be rediscovered.

Mendoza accordingly organized an ambitious expedition and chose as its commander the governor of the northwestern province of Mexico, Francisco de Coronado. So firm was the conviction of success and gain that Coronado had difficulty, not to enlist followers, but to persuade enough Spaniards to remain behind to protect their settlements. With three hundred and seventy soldiers, a large band of Indians, and a long train of cattle, horses, mules, and sheep, Coronado in 1540 ventured forth in search of the seven cities.

After traversing a mountainous wilderness and gaining the plains of southern Arizona, the Spaniards came upon the Indian village which Friar Marcos had descried in the distance. This they conquered, only to find an ordinary pueblo instead of a magnificent city rich in gold. Visits to other villages soon dispelled the illusion of the towered cities of Cibola, but the Indians told that farther north or east lay a land, Quivera, which was indeed a golden realm. Taking a band of twenty picked men, Coronado now pressed on to the plains of Texas where, first of Europeans, he beheld herds of buffalo, and then, turning sharply, he crossed wide, grassy wastes to central Kansas, where he again found only miserable tented villages destitute of gold. Bitterly disappointed, he returned to Mexico—an abject failure. Although he had penetrated to the heart of the northern continent, the Spaniards did not then care to conquer the disappointing lands which he had seen. But whatever their immediate value to statesmanship and commerce, the two explorations of de Soto and Coronado, reaching points but nine days' distance from each other, had made a striking contribution to the geographical knowledge of the New World.[22]

The Spanish Empire in the Sixteenth Century

Long before England established successful colonies, the Spaniards had designed an elaborate system of colonial policy and administration. In 1600 the imperial area was twenty times larger than Spain. Theoretically, the colonies belonged to the king, who ruled them without interference from the Spanish parliament. They formed two distinct kingdoms, each of which in organization was somewhat similar to the kingdom of Spain, and united to it only through the king. In all its features the government of the colonies was monarchical in form.

The agency through which the Spanish king governed the colonies was the Council of the Indies. Formally organized in 1524, this body consisted of powerful officials appointed by and responsible to him alone. It selected colonial officials for his approval, superintended the imperial administration, shaped important policies, and also served as a supreme court to which the more serious cases arising in the colonies might be appealed. Its routine business was transacted in committees, but when it enacted laws (it was the source of colonial legislative power) at least three-fourths of its members had to attend.

Another governing body was the Casa de Contratacion—a sort of board of trade. Its officials gathered information about the commerce of the colonies, supervised all voyages to the New World, considered ways and means of promoting imperial trade, and operated at Seville a great trading house, or *casa*, used as a depot for all goods going to or coming from America. The primary object of this board was to strengthen the monopoly of colonial trade which Spain reserved to herself.

The two colonial kingdoms which existed in 1600 were known as New Spain and Peru. The former included the mainland north of the Isthmus of Panama, the West Indian islands, and the region that is now Venezuela. The kingdom of Peru comprised all territory south of New Spain except Brazil. Over each kingdom ruled a viceroy—a personal agent of the king, by whom he was appointed and removed —serving a three-year term, after which he was subject to a royal investigation or *residencia*. Such inquiries enabled the king's subjects to present complaints but did not offer any means of day-to-day con-

[22] A standard work is George P. Winship's *The Coronado Expedition, 1540–1542* (Washington, 1896).

trol of the viceroy's actions. Ordinarily the viceroy was reappointed at the end of his three-year term.

Even Spaniards in the colonies did not enjoy the privilege of self-government, for representative assemblies were never granted by the king. Only the towns (of which there were two hundred in 1575) had the right to elect councils, but such councils could act only with reference to matters such as sanitation and police regulations—not with respect to fundamental issues of taxation and economic policy. In the early days, the towns had sent delegates to general congresses, but this trend toward representative government was checked when Charles I ordered in 1530 that the townsmen should not assemble without his consent. All important officers, from viceroy to district magistrate, received their places from the king, and after 1557 offices were sold to the highest bidders. Officials were thus regarded as contractors with the king rather than as agents of the people.[23]

More important as an obstacle to self-government was the imperial policy respecting taxation. Generally speaking, popular control over taxes and appropriations is the final measure of self-government. The Spanish colonists, as has been observed, did not exercise such control; the king's revenues were collected without their consent. Every male native of working age had to pay a poll tax, excise duties were levied on goods sold within the colonies, and customs duties were collected on American exports and imports. The king regularly sold monopoly rights for the marketing of common products such as gunpowder, tobacco, and salt. Each vessel paid a convoy tax of 2 per cent of the value of its cargo, while contractors who purchased the monopoly of the slave trade paid a fee on every Negro slave imported into the colonies. The sale of offices also added to the income of the king. Finally, he received a fifth of the gold and silver from the American mines. All this revenue made it unnecessary for him to ask his subjects for money, and because they were not able to coerce him by withholding needed supplies they could not compel him to concede other political rights.

Agriculture supported the mass of the Spanish colonists. To favored leaders and the Church the king granted economic allotments known as *encomiendas*, grants which allowed the receiver to utilize the forced labor of the resident natives. Although such workers received wages, it was easy to keep them permanently in debt, and thus cause them to forfeit such liberties as they had theoretically retained, reducing

---

[23] Of major importance is Roger B. Merriman's *The Rise of the Spanish Empire in the Old World and the New* (4 vols., New York, 1918–34). See particularly Vols. II, III.

their status to one which was little better than that of serfs. The native population in 1575 numbered approximately five million souls, and about four thousand *encomiendas* existed then. American products raised in the colonies included cacao, vanilla, and Indian corn. The Spaniards introduced a great variety of European and other animals and plants: cattle, horses, sheep, mules, and hogs; wheat, barley, rye, and rice; sugar cane, alfalfa, beans, and peas; apples, quinces, pears, bananas, apricots, lemons, oranges, and cherries. On the other hand, the colonists were not allowed to raise certain products culti-vated.extensively in Spain, such as olives, grapes, flaxseed, and hemp. Wheat, Indian corn, and cattle supplied the common articles of food. The native workers merely eked out a bare existence, and even the overlords or *encomenderos* enjoyed only a life of rude plenty.[24]

Among the colonial industries, mining ranked second in impor-tance. The silver mines of Mexico and Peru yielded the treasure which paid the administrative costs of the agricultural areas, and made it possible and profitable for Spain to retain her vast imperial possessions. The output of the mines increased nearly ninetyfold be-tween 1500 and 1750. The extension of colonial mining was not entrusted to ordinary prospectors; instead, well-to-do promoters went forth with caravans of workers, mules, and supplies to locate new veins of ore. When the search was successful, buildings were erected around a courtyard into which the ore was brought for treatment. Mules were then used to tramp in quicksilver and salt which released the silver. After the quicksilver was removed by smelting, the silver was cast into bars and carried once a year by pack train to the colonial mints. The most common coins issued in the colonies were Mexican and Peruvian pieces of eight, ancestors of the American dollar.[25]

Not all the Spanish settlers in America, of whom there were 152,500 in 1574, were *encomenderos* or large-scale miners. Small farmers, attorneys, officials, traders, soldiers, and clergymen all played important parts in colonial life. Commercial manufacturing in the colonies, however, was successfully discouraged, and the use of manu-factured goods—judged by European standards—was very slight.

Restrictions upon European emigration to Spanish America un-doubtedly retarded its industrial progress. After 1555 only native Spaniards of Catholic faith were allowed to enter the colonies, a policy which aimed to exclude undesirable adventurers who might

[24] E. G. Bourne's comprehensive *Spain in America* (New York, 1904) is one of the best volumes of the *American Nation* series. A convenient survey is Charles E. Chapman, *Colonial Hispanic America* (New York, 1933).

[25] One of the most significant studies of recent times is Earl J. Hamilton's *American Treasure and the Price Revolution in Spain, 1501–1650* (Cambridge, 1934).

exploit the natives, to prevent the diffusion throughout Europe of knowledge of the wealth of the Spanish Indies, and to check the spread of heresy to the New World. In consequence, European culture and institutions transplanted to the colonies were exclusively Spanish, while the small number of Spanish settlers necessitated their intermarriage with the native Indians. The exclusion of non-Catholics from Spanish America accounts in part for their later migrations to the English colonies and for the latter's predominantly Protestant character.

One alien element admitted by the Spaniards was the Negro slave, first brought into the islands about 1503 and to the mainland in 1510. Slavery spread rapidly in Cuba, Haiti, and Puerto Rico, where the hard work on plantations rapidly decimated the Indians who were subjected to forced labor. Another region where slavery became prominent was the northern coast of South America. In Mexico the natives performed most of the work, while in the southern part of South America the altitude was unfavorable to the Negro.[26]

After 1510 Spain provided for the systematic importation of slaves. Not possessing slave trading stations in Africa, the Spaniards did not conduct this traffic as a government enterprise. Instead the king granted contracts which conferred monopoly rights upon private traders, such a contract being known as the assiento, and the contractors as assientists. Only a fixed number of slaves, usually between three and four thousand, could be imported legally into the colonies each year. The contractors paid a large bonus for the monopoly, which was commonly granted for a term varying from seven to ten years. Only Spanish vessels could be used for transporting the slaves, although Flemings, Genoese, Portuguese, Dutch, French, and English trading interests obtained the assiento at various times. Its effect was to limit the supply of slaves, to keep prices high, and thus to invite smuggling by interlopers. Prior to 1750 Spanish importations of Negroes averaged about three thousand a year.

Government control and monopoly extended to all branches of colonial commerce. Spanish exports to America consisted of wines, figs, olives, oil, quicksilver, iron, dry goods and other manufactures for which the colonists made payment with sugar, cacao, vanilla, cochineal, drugs, and gold and silver coin and bullion. Only Spanish vessels and merchants could engage in the trade. Even more striking was the commercial monopoly of the port of Seville. Between 1503

[26] Herbert I. Priestley, *The Coming of the White Man* (New York, 1929), an excellent study, begins the notable Schlesinger-Fox series, *A History of American Life*. See chapters 1–7.

and 1718 this city alone was allowed to sell to the colonies and to receive their products. Under the auspices of the government, two fleets were fitted out each year at Seville and provided with a naval convoy. The combined fleets sailed first to the island of Dominica, where they separated, one going to the mainland and the other to the islands. Only a few licensed ports in America—such as Porto Bello, Havana, Cartagena, and Vera Cruz—had the right to trade with the outside world. When the fleet arrived in harbor, a great fair was held for the exchange of products. The American traders would sell the native commodities which they had collected and buy European merchandise from agents of Spanish merchants who traveled with the fleet. The local traders then distributed their purchases throughout the settlements, while the two fleets proceeded to Havana and returned together to Seville under their naval escort.[27]

This scheme of commercial regulation imposed severe hardships upon the colonists. Let us consider how it affected a settler living on the banks of the Plata River in the Argentine. He was not allowed to ship his products to Buenos Aires to be conveyed directly to markets in Europe or in the eastern settlements of America, nor could he import directly from Europe. If he bought goods made in Holland, they had to be shipped first to Seville, whence they went to the Plata by way of Porto Bello, the Isthmus of Panama, and Peru. Over this roundabout route the settler also had to send his exports. In consequence, he paid exorbitant charges for European goods, while the lack of markets for his own products kept their prices at extremely low levels. Even after 1700, an ox could be bought at Buenos Aires for a dollar, a sheep for three or four cents, and a mare for ten cents. Only favored places along the established channels of trade—such as Mexico City and Lima—could afford to buy many European manufactured goods. Thus the mass of the people had to depend upon native handicrafts.

In spite of the protests of the colonial settlers, the monopoly of Seville remained intact until 1718, when Cadiz became the entrepôt of the American trade. This method of commercial control survived partly because it enabled the government to collect its import and export duties at a single place, while the fleet system justified itself also as a means of protection against European pirates who habitually plundered vessels carrying gold and silver to Spain. Moreover, the merchants of Seville formed one of the principal bulwarks of the monarchy. They exerted a lobbying influence at court somewhat com-

---

[27] Clarence H. Haring's *Trade and Navigation between Spain and the Indies* . . . (Cambridge, 1918) is the work of a leading authority on Spanish America.

parable to that of manufacturers upon tariff legislation in the United States since the Civil War.[28]

During the eighteenth century the Spanish government gradually relaxed its commercial restrictions. By 1778 the fleet system had been discontinued, and any port in the colonies was allowed to trade with any port either in Spain or in the other Spanish dominions. Before this time, however, the commercial policy of Spain had been much more rigid than that which England applied to her colonies. The Spanish system led eventually to a widespread contraband trade from which the English and the Dutch made the principal gains. Meanwhile, the colonies did not promote the industrial growth of Spain; they experienced too much difficulty in buying goods which were legally imported from Seville. In the end the stifling effects of regulation contributed a major cause of the successful revolt of the colonies during the Napoleonic wars.

Even so, the Spanish empire endured for a period nearly a hundred and fifty years longer than England's rule of her colonies in North America. In the Spanish empire religion bound the settlers closely to the king; in the English colonies it was mainly a dividing force. The King of Spain was virtually the head of the Catholic Church in the colonies, where it enjoyed an uncontested supremacy. From the papacy he had received the right to establish colonial churches and monasteries and to collect the tithes which all the people had to pay. He also possessed the exclusive right of appointment to ecclesiastical offices. The organization of the colonial Church resembled its European model. In 1600 there were four hundred monasteries directly under the king's supervision and four hundred local districts served by the secular clergy. The latter were grouped into bishoprics, which in turn formed the two archbishoprics of Mexico and Peru. The bishops, archbishops, and their cathedral chapters received half of the tithes collected; consequently, they possessed great wealth, prestige, and influence. Eventually the Church acquired about half of the property in the colonies.[29]

The king's privilege of collecting tithes carried with it the obligation to use the money in the service of the Church, a duty faithfully performed. Through the Church the government exerted a continuing influence against oppression, idolatry, and heresy. Royal funds were employed to send missionaries to the colonies, to erect monas-

---

[28] *The Establishment of Spanish Rule in America*, by Bernard Moses (New York, 1898), is brief, scholarly, and readable.

[29] For detailed studies see Bernard Moses, *The Spanish Dependencies in South America* (2 vols., New York, 1914)—particularly Vol. I, chapter 14; Vol. II, chapters 12–13, 20.

teries on the king's estates, and to assist also in establishing convents on private holdings. Priests and monks were not allowed to act as attorneys, to engage in business, or to work in the mines, lest such activity bring discredit upon the Church. The ecclesiastical courts could not impose fines upon the natives, condemn them to forced labor, or defraud them of their wages. Irresponsible soldiers and sailors who had committed offenses could not use the churches as sanctuaries. A law of 1619 called upon the clergy to learn the language of the natives, and another act (1634) required that the Indians should be taught Spanish—measures designed to bring instruction in the doctrines of Christianity to the people. In every town or district a time was set apart for religious worship when masters had to allow their Indian workers and Negro slaves to attend the services of the Church.

Religion thus relieved the harsher features of economic exploitation and at the same time buttressed the king's authority over the colonies. The bond of union between the colonial prelates and the Spanish court was especially intimate and strong. The clergy taught submission to the king's government, and through the Inquisition rooted out doctrines subversive to the blended authority of Church and state.[30]

FRANCE IN THE NEW WORLD

The expansion of Portugal and Spain inspired France to follow their example. During the reign of Francis I (1515–47), the French government promoted four expeditions to America. Although the French monarchy was fairly well centralized in 1520, France had not yet become a first-rate power in Europe. Not until 1453 had she expelled the armies of England and overthrown the English claim to a large part of her territory; not until 1516 did the king obtain control over the Catholic Church in France when he received from the papacy the right to nominate bishops and abbots. In the days of Francis I, the French were surrounded by the lands of a powerful enemy—the Hapsburg emperor, Charles V, whose imperial dominions included Austria, Germany, northern Italy, the Netherlands, Spain, and the Spanish colonies. Moreover, Charles V aspired to annex the province of Burgundy which had been taken from his grandmother by an earlier French king. Encircled by the Hapsburg territories,

[30] H. C. Lea's *The Inquisition in the Spanish Dependencies* (New York, 1911) paints a dark picture.

France was in danger of being crushed and absorbed into the empire of her stronger rival.[31]

In a series of wars between 1521 and 1559 the French fought for their national existence. Other issues at stake were the mastery of Naples, Milan, the Netherlands, and Burgundy. Finally concluded by the Treaty of Cateau-Cambrésis (1559), these wars decided that France was to remain an independent state. Although she relinquished her claims to Italy, her acquisition of the three border bishoprics of Metz, Toul, and Verdun during the reign of Henry II (1547–59) began her historic advance toward the Rhine. Despite the fact that these wars absorbed the energies of the monarchy they nevertheless inspired the earliest French efforts to gain a foothold in America.

The cod fishery of Newfoundland first brought France into contact with the New World. It is probable that French fishermen were visiting Newfoundland as early as 1497, and after 1510 the markets of Normandy were supplied regularly with cod by fishing fleets from the Grand Banks. Shortly after Magellan's party returned to Spain in 1522, the chronicler of the expedition, Antonio Pigafetti, visited the French court, where he presented to the queen mother of Francis I a copy of the journal of the voyage. Soon afterward the king, who was one of the foremost patrons of the Renaissance in Europe, became interested in opening a French route to China. Doubtless he hoped to use the profits of the oriental trade to finance his wars with Charles V. Accordingly he engaged the services of a Florentine mariner, Giovanni Verrazano, a resident of Dieppe—then the base of French operations in the Newfoundland fishery.[32]

Summoned to court by Francis I, Verrazano displayed a matured interest in discovering a new route to Asia and revealed himself as a scholar and capable man of affairs. With a royal commission and four vessels provided by the king, he embarked in the early summer of 1523 and proceeded to the Madeira Islands, whence one of his vessels crossed the Atlantic and reached the coast of North America at about the thirty-fourth parallel. Later, he skirted the shore northward as far as Newfoundland and returned to France in July 1524. His success established the original claim of France to North America.

The exigencies of war did not allow Francis I to continue Ver-

[31] Due to its literary excellence, painstaking scholarship, and comparative freedom from personal bias, Francis Parkman's history of the French and English in America ranks as a masterpiece. On French explorations see his *Pioneers of France in the New World* (Boston, 1871), pp. 168–207.

[32] William B. Munro, *Crusaders of New France* (*Chronicles of America*, New Haven, 1918), chapters 1–2.

razano's work until after the Peace of Cambrai in 1529. Three voyages were then made to the Gulf of St. Lawrence by Jacques Cartier, a Breton pilot of the port of St. Malo. The first two voyages (in 1534 and 1535–36) were financed by Francis I, who continued to display a deep interest in exploration. The initial motive—to find a passage to the Orient—was supplemented after 1535 by the desire to obtain gold and silver, to plant a settlement on the St. Lawrence River, and to Christianize the Indians. The third expedition (in 1541–42) was promoted and commanded by a nobleman of Picardy, Jean François Roberval, to whom Francis I gave the title to the lands which Cartier discovered in 1535.

On his first voyage (1534) Cartier explored the Gulf of St. Lawrence and took possession of the region in the name of Francis I. He returned to France with two Indians whose tale of a great inland stream gave promise of the desired passage to Asia. The second voyage (1535–36) carried Cartier up the St. Lawrence River past the site of Quebec to an Indian village, Hochelaga, which lay at the foot of a mountain which the French named Mount Royal or Montreal. From its heights Cartier saw the Ottawa and St. Lawrence branches of the imperial stream. The Indians related that westward lay two or three great lakes beyond which stretched a fresh-water sea whose end was unknown, while the interior lands were thought to abound with silver and gold. After passing a difficult winter near Quebec, Cartier returned to France in July 1536.[33]

Employed as pilot for the third expedition, Cartier preceded Roberval in 1541 and planted a settlement twelve miles above Quebec, but his efforts to explore the St. Lawrence were halted by the rapids of the river and by fear of the Indians. The sufferings of another severe winter apparently bred despair; at any rate Cartier decided to return to France. He met Roberval in a Newfoundland harbor but managed to slip away, homeward bound. Roberval proceeded westward, and occupied the colony which Cartier had abandoned. He held on until the autumn of 1543, when he followed Cartier to France. Except that the colony disappeared, its fate is unknown.

These three expeditions designated the line of advance which France later followed in North America. For the time, however, the pressure of war in Europe made it impossible for the government to continue the work of Cartier, and France did not resume her activi-

[33] George M. Wrong and H. H. Langton have edited a series of short, popular volumes, *The Chronicles of Canada* (32 vols., Toronto, 1914–16). See the second volume, *The Mariner of St. Malo* (1914), by Stephen Leacock.

ties in the St. Lawrence region until after 1600. Efforts made between 1550 and 1565 by French Protestants to found colonies in Brazil and Florida also failed. Thus when the sixteenth century closed, Spain and Portugal alone among European pioneers had established colonial empires in the New World.[34]

The treasure which Spain received from her American empire enabled her to play a decisive role in European politics during the sixteenth century. As the outstanding champion of Catholicism in Europe, she drew upon her imperial wealth to oppose the progress of Protestantism, particularly in France, the Netherlands, and England. In the ensuing conflicts, the enemies of Spain quickly perceived the advantage which she derived from her colonies. In consequence, the English and the Dutch carried the war against Spain to the New World. First they endeavored to plunder Spanish settlements and ships. Such warfare gave birth to an ambition to acquire colonial sources of wealth comparable to Spain's, and to establish outposts in America which might be used as bases for attacks upon the Spanish empire. The conflict between Protestantism and Catholicism thus ushered in the second phase of European colonization in America.[35]

[34] The best recent general work on the French in North America is G. M. Wrong, *The Rise and Fall of New France* (2 vols., New York, 1928). See Vol. I, chapter 4.

[35] Philip A. Means, *The Spanish Main, Focus of Envy* (New York, 1935), is a vivid, interesting summary of research on international conflicts in Spanish America, 1492–1700.

BIBLIOGRAPHICAL NOTE

SECONDARY WORKS: A. P. Newton (ed.), *The Great Age of Discovery* (London, 1932), contains nine essays by leading authorities on the principal voyages and their backgrounds. Harold Lamb, *New Found World* (Garden City, 1955), records the growth of geographical knowledge as revealed by the great discoveries. Boies Penrose, *Travel and Discovery in the Renaissance, 1420–1620* (Cambridge, 1952), is a good introductory survey. Myron P. Gilmore, *The World of Humanism, 1453–1517* (New York, 1952), emphasizes the discoveries and the new trade routes.

Samuel E. Morison, *Portuguese Voyages to America in the Fifteenth Century* (Cambridge, 1940), rejects claims that the Portuguese discovered America before Columbus. Henry H. Hart, *Sea Road to the Indies* (New York, 1950), presents a lively account of Portuguese voyages, with a sharply critical estimate of Vasco da Gama.

S. E. Morison, who retraced several parts of the voyages of Columbus, using the means of navigation of his time, gives in *Admiral of the Ocean Sea* (Boston, 1942), an oceanic interpretation, presenting him as a skilled mariner whose discoveries revitalized European society. Frederick J. Pohl, *Amerigo Vespucci* (New York, 1944), is the leading commentary on problems concerning the voyages of the Florentine traveler. Germán Arciniegas, *Amerigo and the New World* (New York, 1955), is a readable, popular biography which reasserts the dubious claim that Vespucius first reached the mainland. Stefan Zweig, *Conqueror of the Seas: The Story of Magellan* (New York, 1938), is an interesting, well-written narrative.

The best introduction to Spanish activity in America is C. H. Haring, *The Spanish Empire in the New World* (New York, 1947). The expeditions of Ponce de Leon and de Ayllon are described in *Barcia's Chronological History of the Continent of Florida* [1723] (translated by Anthony Kerrigan, Gainesville, Fla., 1951). Herbert E. Bolton, *Coronado* (New York, 1949), re-creates the Coronado adventure in a graphic manner. Leslie B. Simpson, *The Encomienda in New Spain* (rev. ed., Berkeley, 1950), is the standard authority.

The works of one of the foremost American historians, William H. Prescott, are well worth reading. They include *History of the Reign of Ferdinand and Isabella* (3 vols., Boston, 1857); *History of the Conquest of Mexico* (3 vols., Boston, 1856–58); and *History of the Conquest of Peru* (2 vols., Boston, 1857). Prescott also wrote the concluding section of a work of extraordinary vitality, William Robertson, *The History of the Reign of the Emperor Charles the Fifth* (3 vols., Boston, 1857). No works excel Prescott's in the art of bringing the past to life.

SOURCES: Volume I of F. G. Davenport (ed.), *European Treaties bearing on the History of the United States* . . . (3 vols., Washington, 1917), contains Spanish-French-Portuguese treaties to 1600. *The Life of the Admiral Christopher Columbus by His Son Ferdinand* (ed. Benjamin Keen, New Brunswick, 1959), is a new edition of a work that was long one of the most widely used accounts of Columbus. *Narratives of the Career of Hernando de Soto* (ed. E. G. Bourne, 2 vols., New York, 1904), is a convenient collection. For de Vaca, de Soto, and Coronado see *Spanish Explorers in the United States, 1528–1543* (ed. F. W. Hodge and T. H. Lewis, New York, 1907). *The Journey of Coronado* (ed. G. P. Winship, New York, 1904), is a standard edition. For Cartier documents see *The Precursors of Jacques Cartier, 1497–1534* (ed. H. P. Biggar, Ottawa, 1911); H. P. Biggar's *The Voyages of Jacques Cartier* (Ottawa, 1924); James P. Baxter, *A Memoir of Jacques Cartier* (New York, 1906); and H. S. Burrage (ed.), *Early English and French Voyages* (New York, 1906).

III

The Reformation
and the New World

The Protestant Reformation, inaugurated by Martin Luther in 1519, affected profoundly the colonization of America and the later history of the United States. The strife between Protestant and Catholic and internal conflicts among Protestants provided one of the mainsprings of European migration to America. Under the influence of religious beliefs the domestic institutions of the English colonies took shape, while the repeated colonial wars between England and France revolved in part around religious issues. The dominantly Protestant character of the United States, and the cultural traits which Protestantism has fostered—such as intellectual freedom, individualism, self-government, and independence—have determined largely the mold and spirit of American life.

LUTHERANISM

The two leading movements of the Reformation were Lutheranism and Calvinism. In the history of colonial America, however, Calvinism far overshadowed Lutheranism. The early Lutherans did not migrate to the New World. At the outset the Lutheran movement appealed to a large number of German princes, who openly embraced the new faith. In 1530 they formed the League of Schmalkald to resist the efforts of the emperor of the Germanies, Charles V, to restore Catholicism. A religious war broke out in 1546 and continued intermittently until the Peace of Augsburg in 1555. This settlement established in Germany the principle that the prince might determine the religion of his subjects. It applied, however, only to Lutheran and Catholic princes. Thereafter, Lutherans living under a Lutheran prince enjoyed protection; those living under Catholic princes could move to near-by Lutheran states. A similar trend occurred in the Scandinavian countries. Lutheranism became the official state religion of Denmark and Norway in 1537 and of Sweden in 1593. Protected wherever they were numerous in Europe, the Lutherans did not need

---

[1] For the general student no book on its subject surpasses Preserved Smith's *The Age of the Reformation* (New York, 1920). See chapters 1–9, 14.

to migrate to the New World in order to enjoy religious freedom.[2]

At the same time the Lutherans alienated a large class of people whose unsatisfactory social status was conducive to emigration. An economic upheaval occurred in Germany in 1524—the Peasants' Revolt against serfdom and the privileges of nobles and clergy. Luther's favorable disposition toward the peasants soon changed into animosity when in 1525 they attacked Lutheran nobles as well as Catholics. He urged the suppression of the revolt, which was effected in 1525 with terrible cruelty. Fifty thousand peasants were killed, serfdom remained, and Lutheranism lost its hold upon the lower classes in central and southern Germany. The peasants turned either to Catholicism or to radical Protestantism.

In the wake of the Peasants' Revolt arose a party of Anabaptists, whose central doctrine denied the efficacy of infant baptism. The Lutherans met this idea by defining rebaptism as a capital crime. From the nucleus of Anabaptists emerged a variety of radical sects— Mennonites, Amish, Familists, Dunkers, and Schwenkfelders. Believing in the literal application of the teachings of Christ to daily life, these groups objected to war, tithes, oaths, a paid ministry, and forms of social inequality. During the sixteenth century the Anabaptists were severely persecuted in Bohemia, Austria, Switzerland, Bavaria, the Palatinate, and the cities of Augsburg, Nuremberg, and Strassburg. Only their industry, steadfastness and moral courage enabled these humble people to survive. They were always on the defensive, always unprotected and exposed to persecution. After 1680 thousands of German peasants of these Protestant sects migrated to Pennsylvania. Thus the Lutherans and Catholics in Germany contributed toward the early peopling of English America—not by coming themselves, but by expelling the radical Protestants.[3]

CALVINISM

Few men have exerted so pervasive an influence upon early American development as the French reformer, John Calvin. Born at Noyon in Picardy in 1509, Calvin received a dual education in theology and law. His precise, legalistic mind was suffused with an overpowering sense of the divine spirit. Retiring from France to

---

[2] For a good brief survey of the background of the Reformation see Summerfield Baldwin's *The Organization of Medieval Christianity* (New York, 1929).

[3] Jacob S. Schapiro's *Social Reform and the Reformation* (New York, 1909) discusses some economic factors in the Lutheran movement.

II

European Pioneers

FIRST among the nation-states to embark upon a career of discovery was the little kingdom of Portugal. Founded in 1095, its territorial growth completed by 1263, this state in 1383 entered an era of national greatness at the beginning of the reign of John I, a patriot king. The Portuguese were unified and aroused to aggressive action by wars against their Moorish foes. Imbued with a fierce spirit of independence, they maintained their borders against onslaughts of the ambitious rulers of Castile, but the barrier of that powerful neighbor stopped expansion toward the east. The whole length of their land fronted the sea; the rugged coast furnished many splendid harbors and the earliest national center was a port. Hemmed in on land, the Portuguese turned outward upon the Atlantic.[1]

Their genius for seamanship was fostered by the maritime policies of the state. Foreign traders were encouraged to visit Lisbon; treaties of alliance were formed with England in 1294 and 1386; and Genoese seamen were employed to man the Portuguese navy. During the fourteenth century, Portuguese vessels visited the Canary Islands and probably reached the Madeiras and the Azores. Maritime crusades against Moorish pirates stimulated the building of ships. Moreover, the Kings of Portugal coöperated with the native merchant class. Shipbuilders received timber gratis from the royal forests; shipowners were granted a partial exemption from military service; and a coöperative scheme of marine insurance was devised. Lisbon became a bustling town, its harbor fringed with foreign ships and its streets thronged with foreign mariners and traders.

The foremost patron of seafaring in Portugal, Prince Henry the Navigator, became a national figure in 1415. Son of King John I, grandson of Edward III of England, a devout champion of the Church, an ardent student of science, and a practical business man of

---

[1] *The Portuguese Pioneers* (London, 1933), by Edgar Prestage, is an attractive account by a leading authority.

Middle Ages (New York, 1955), is a compact, well-written summary. A comprehensive survey of life in the later Middle Ages is G. G. Coulton, *Medieval Panorama* (New York, 1938). Among the most useful studies of Norse discoveries are H. R. Holand, *Explorations in America before Columbus* (New York, 1956); and Einar Haugen, *Voyages to Vinland* (New York, 1942). Steven Runciman, *A History of the Crusades* (3 vols., Cambridge, 1951–52) is a distinguished work. A brief, popular sketch is Harold Lamb, *The Crusades* (New York, 1930). Richard Ehrenberg, *Capital and Finance in the Age of the Renaissance* (London, 1928) is a standard authority. Important works on medieval trade are F. C. Lane, *Venetian Ships and Shipbuilders of the Renaissance* (Baltimore, 1934); A. A. Ruddock, *Italian Merchants and Shipping in Southampton, 1270–1600* (Southampton, 1951); and Raymond de Roover, *Money, Banking and Credit in Mediaeval Bruges* (Cambridge, 1948). For medieval maps see E. G. Ravenstein, *Martin Behaim* (London, 1908); and E. L. Stevenson, *Atlas of Portolan Charts* (New York, 1911). Henry H. Hart, *Venetian Adventurer* (Stanford University, 1942), is a good introduction to the career of Marco Polo. Attractive surveys of European life and thought are Sidney Painter, *Mediaeval Society* (Ithaca, 1951); Carl Stephenson, *Mediaeval Feudalism* (Ithaca, 1942); Wallace K. Ferguson, *The Renaissance* (New York, 1940); and G. C. Sellery, *The Renaissance* (Madison, 1950). An outstanding study of humanism is J. Huizinga, *Erasmus of Rotterdam* (New York, 1924; London, 1952).

Sources For Chapter I: The first two volumes of A. B. Hart (ed.), *American History Told by Contemporaries* (5 vols., New York, 1897–1926), relate to the colonial era. J. Franklin Jameson served as general editor of an important series of source materials, *Original Narratives of Early American History* (19 vols., New York, 1906–17). The first volume, *The Northmen, Columbus and Cabot* (ed. J. E. Olson and E. G. Bourne, New York, 1906), contains documents relative to the Norse. Arnold W. Lawrence and Jean Young have presented in attractive form the *Narratives of the Discovery of America* (New York, 1931). The standard edition of *The Book of Ser Marco Polo the Venetian* is that of Sir Henry Yule (revised Henri Cordier, 2 vols., London, 1903). The Everyman's Library edition by John Masefield of *The Travels of Marco Polo* is the most accessible. C. R. Beazley has edited the *Texts and Versions of John de Plano Carpini and William de Rubruquis* for the Hakluyt Society (London, 1903). E. L. Stevenson (ed.), *Geography of Claudius Ptolemy* (New York, 1932), is the first full translation in English. The edition of Pierre d'Ailly's *Imago Mundi* by Edmond Buron (3 vols., Paris, 1930–31), contains the marginal notes of Columbus.

THE RELIGIONS OF EUROPE
IN 1580

Scale of Miles
0   100   200   300   400

escape persecution, he lived at Basel, Switzerland, where he wrote his famous *Institutes of the Christian Religion*, aptly described as "the finest work of Reformation literature." By 1630, seventy-four editions, nine translations, and fourteen abridgments of this remarkable book had appeared in Europe. After 1536 Calvin lived at Geneva, where he fashioned and controlled the government of the city-republic. His untiring writing, preaching, correspondence, conferences, and educational activity made him so clearly the focus of Reformation thought that he became widely known as the Protestant pope.

Calvin's influence permeated four countries of Europe and affected vitally their internal history between 1560 and 1650. In France his followers were the Huguenots; in Holland, the members of the Dutch Reformed Church; in Scotland, the Presbyterians; in England, the Puritans. These four groups contributed the largest body of emigrants to English America. Calvinism thus became the strongest single religious force in the thirteen colonies. In consequence the ideas of Calvin and of his immediate successors have left enduring marks upon American thought.[4]

The theology of the Calvinists conditioned all their other beliefs. Man, in their sight, was an unworthy sinner; the world was a habitation of evil and temptation; life was a journey of sorrow and suffering leading the footsore pilgrim to his eternal home. Not earthly pleasure but the welfare of his immortal soul was man's imperative concern. His mission on earth was to glorify God, the omnipotent ruler of the universe, who decreed the destiny of His creatures and by means of His special providences warned, punished, and rewarded His saints on earth.

Calvin accepted the Bible as the inspired word of God, giving to man a divine rule of conduct and an approved form of worship. Every feature of the church should have the expressed authorization of the Scriptures; all traditions and ceremonies not thus sanctioned should be eliminated. In Calvinistic churches the laity exercised more influence than in the Catholic Church. The laity not only selected the pastors and the elders but also admitted new members and managed the finances of the congregation. Although the clergy were regarded as the authorized interpreters of the Bible, the final control over the church was vested in the whole body of true believers. Thus Calvin-

---

[4] *Calvin: a Modern Biography*, by Jean Moura and Paul Louvet (Garden City, N. Y., 1932), is a vigorous, readable account. See also James MacKinnon, *Calvin and the Reformation* (London, 1937).

ism was an expression of the religious thought of the individual members of the congregation rather than a creed imposed and interpreted by outside ecclesiastical authorities.

Fundamental in Calvinist theology was the doctrine of predestination. The sin of Adam had rent man from his Creator and implanted in the sons of man a corrupt love of self and material gain which caused them to struggle one against another. However, the Son of God, Christ, in His infinite compassion for man's suffering, had entered into a covenant with God for the salvation of a chosen few among the descendants of Adam. The vicarious sacrifice of Christ on earth had thus conferred the boon of eternal salvation upon the elect. The remainder of mankind were condemned to an afterlife of everlasting suffering. Wholly unworthy and insignificant in comparison with God, man could do nothing to achieve his own salvation. If he chanced to be among the elect his good fortune was due solely to the grace of God and the love of Christ. As a recipient of such a transcendent blessing, the sincere believer was naturally filled with an overpowering sense of gratitude and devotion to his divine benefactor.[5]

The theology of the Calvinists did not provide for compromise or a middle ground; it was compounded of two irreconcilable extremes. On the one hand were God, heaven, morality, and the elect; on the other, Satan, hell, evil, and the damned. Between these two forces there could be only warfare to the end. Thus the Calvinists rejected the idea of purgatory, and defined all actions as either godly or ungodly, condemning idle pastimes, merrymaking, card playing, dancing, and frivolity as sinful waste of God-given time and talent. In such a creed, toleration could have no sanction. Those who opposed the Calvinists were certainly not among the elect; and if God had condemned them to eternal suffering, it did not become His saints to countenance their false doctrines and evil ways. Toleration was thus regarded as defiance of God's will. Even those whom God had condemned were required to obey His laws in order that they might glorify Him on earth, for such was the duty of every man.

It might seem that this doctrine of predestination would fill men with a sense of futility and cover life with a shroud of gloom. But the true believers in Calvin's creed regarded themselves as the elect. Upon them God had set the seal of his special approval and thereby had exalted them—humble folk, as many of them were—above man-made nobles, priests, and even kings. In consequence the ardent Cal-

[5] An excellent introduction to European thought is Preserved Smith's *The History of Modern Culture* (2 vols., New York, 1930–34). See Vol. I.

vinists were confident and aggressive. Instead of becoming a prey to
pessimism and despair, they plunged eagerly into the work of the
world, determined to assert their divinely ordained right to rule.
Trivial amusements seemed unnecessary to a people who attempted
to reform church and society, took up arms against kings, waged
righteous wars, and founded new commonwealths beyond the sea.[6]

The aggressive spirit of Calvinism and its idea of divinely appointed saints bred intense opposition among people of more moderate views. Particularly harsh appeared the Calvinists' view of predestination, because it condemned not only the mature man of evil
ways but also the good heathen, the majority of children, and moral
people of other creeds. This doctrine seemed to picture its author as
heartless in the extreme—

> The monster dread who from the poison chalice
> Pours out the drug of hell in unctuous malice
> And makes the gracious God a very fiend.

The political philosophy of the Calvinists took form under the pressure of persecution which they endured at the hands of their Catholic
enemies, particularly in France. Fundamentally, the Calvinists believed that the duty of government—both of ruler and subject—was
to glorify God. Government had originated by means of a contract
between the prince and his people by which the two parties were to
labor together to realize the kingdom of God on earth. This contract
implied a fundamental written law which was binding upon the ruler
and his subjects alike. Such a law consisted of the moral code of the
Scriptures—especially of the Mosaic law of the Old Testament—and
of certain great charters and agreements entered into by the king and
the people. The fundamental law therefore guaranteed to the subjects
certain inherent rights—particularly the right of worshipping God
in the manner approved by the Scriptures. If the sovereign usurped
these rights, if he deserted the true faith, if he led the people away
from God to false idols, then he violated the contract and forfeited
his crown. Through their chosen representatives, the true believers
might rise against such a prince and depose him. The Calvinists, however, did not approve of mob resistance; if the elected magistrates
refused to oppose an unorthodox ruler, the only alternative open to
the people was to select a new magistracy.[7]

These ideas implied a partnership of religion and government in

---

[6] James T. Adams's vigorous and well-written *The Founding of New England*
(Boston, 1921) is hostile toward Calvinism. See chapter 4.

[7] H. D. Foster, "The Political Theories of the Calvinists," *American Historical Review*, XXI (Oct. 1915).

which the state served as a protecting arm of the church. To the church was entrusted the duty of education, while the state was obliged to maintain the purity of religious doctrine and to impose a moral and godly way of life upon the people. The state could never tolerate non-Calvinist doctrines. As Calvin's successor, Beza, said: "But obstinate heretics are worse than parricides and deserve death, even if they repent." "It is the duty of the state to punish them, for the whole ecclesiastical order is upheld by the political."

If the Calvinistic ideas are shorn of their religious aspects there remain the doctrines of contract, fundamental law, representative government, and the right of resistance. And if to these remaining ideas is grafted the principle of democracy, the result is the political philosophy which has prevailed in the United States.[8]

In their economic views the Calvinists stood midway between medieval and modern times. First of all they sanctified every form of productive labor. Calvin rejected the monastic ideal of withdrawal from the world; man at work was more Godlike than man in idle contemplation of the divine spirit. By the sweat of his brow should man earn his bread. *Navigation Spiritualized, Husbandry Spiritualized,* and *The Religious Weaver* were Calvinistic books which expressed the ideal that the production and enjoyment of wealth were wholly consistent with a godly life.[9]

It followed, therefore, that private property enjoyed a divine sanction; in fact, the Creator rewarded the pious man with material wealth; while an evil commonwealth could not prosper. "If God," wrote Richard Baxter, "show you a way in which you may lawfully get more than in another way . . ., if you refuse this, and choose the less gainful way, you cross one of the ways of your calling, and refuse to be God's steward." Social inequalities were a part of the divine order, because God had decreed that some men should be rich and some poor, "some high and eminent in power and dignity; others mean and in subjection." In general the Calvinists approved heartily of business, trade, and profit-making; even the taking of interest was legitimate in many circumstances.

But all these economic sanctions were subject to religious restraints. Continuous work insured against temptation. The man of large property was merely a steward of the Lord, a custodian who should use his surplus to advance the kingdom of God on earth. In times of

[8] H. L. Osgood, "The Political Ideas of the Puritans," *Political Science Quarterly,* VI (March, June 1891).

[9] R. H. Tawney's *Religion and the Rise of Capitalism* (New York, 1926), a profound, scholarly analysis, is especially recommended.

calamity the rich should share generously with the poor. Private wealth should not be used in any way detrimental to the public welfare. Merchants were entitled only to a fair profit; they should charge only just prices, and shun profiteering and monopoly as devices of Satan. The community should regulate prices and wages in the common good. Interest rates should not be extortionate; the charge to a poor man should be less than to the rich. Workmen ought not to ask for leisure and high wages, lest they spend their time and money upon tobacco, liquor, and idle amusements.

Thus the economic order was divinely arranged. The custodians of wealth had social duties to perform—to advance religion and education, to rule justly, and to enforce morality. If the servant must obey his master, so also the master should not exploit the servant, because "no man is made more honorable or more wealthy . . . out of any particular and singular respect to himself, but for the glory of his Creator, and the common good of the creature, man." [10]

This philosophy extolled the economic virtues of industry, thrift, frugality, prudence, temperance, and honesty—which all together imposed a godly discipline upon sinful man. In the English colonies Calvinism found a fertile soil. The trend of American development, however, weakened the religious restraints which the early Calvinists placed upon economic practices. But the other features of Calvinism remained and waxed strong. The sanctification of work, of private property, of the acquisitive spirit, of social inequality, of profit-making and interest-taking—these traits so characteristic of American life eventually came to be known as "rugged individualism." [11]

THE FRENCH HUGUENOTS

The first Calvinists to attempt colonization in America were the French Huguenots. These Protestants, who probably represented 5 per cent of the population of France in 1550, belonged mainly to the upper middle class. On the whole they were industrious, earnest, thrifty, and prosperous—a group which exerted an influence greater than their numbers alone would have warranted. In 1559 the Huguenots formed a national church and adopted Calvin's confession of

[10] E. A. J. Johnson, "Economic Ideas of John Winthrop," *New England Quarterly*, III (April 1930). See also A. W. Griswold, "Three Puritans on Prosperity," *New England Quarterly*, VII (Sept. 1934).

[11] Max Weber's *The Protestant Ethic and the Spirit of Capitalism* (New York, 1930), a creative book, finds in Calvinism the germs of the capitalistic spirit. For a criticism of this view see H. M. Robertson, *Aspects of the Rise of Economic Individualism* (Cambridge, 1933).

faith as their creed. They were not content merely to be tolerated; they desired also to shape the religious policy of the state. Their compact organization added greatly to their strength.

Throughout the sixteenth century the Huguenots were subject to recurring persecutions. Francis I (1515–47) not only banished Calvin from France but consented to attacks upon his followers as the price of Catholic support of the monarchy. The successor of Francis I, Henry II (1547–59), was an intolerant foe of Protestantism. Having been educated in Spain, he desired to introduce the Inquisition into France; hence he created a special criminal court, *Chambre Ardente* (court of fire), which employed persecution to suppress heresy. Between 1562 and 1593 a series of religious wars threatened the Calvinists with destruction. Their political doctrines did not harmonize with the ideal of an absolute monarchy, since their desire for self-government in religion incited them to political agitation against enforced uniformity and subordination to the king's power and faith.[12] Courageous and self-righteous, they became involved in plots against the Catholic monarchy and by "image-breaking, assaults on processions, and general violence they made the part of tolerant Catholics difficult to play."

After 1550 Calvin's principal lieutenant in France was an influential nobleman, Gaspar de Coligny, who eventually became the Admiral of France, and a power in the government of Charles IX (1560–74). Earlier, Coligny had engaged in privateering enterprises directed against Spanish commerce. This business gave him an interest in establishing a base in America from which the Huguenot privateers might operate. He found an agent for this task in the person of Nicolas Durand de Villegagnon—a versatile but rather unstable adventurer. Converted to Calvinism, Villegagnon conceived the plan of establishing a Huguenot colony in Brazil. Both Calvin and Coligny approved, hoping to provide a refuge for persecuted Calvinists. Catholic leaders likewise consented, seeking to rid the land of obnoxious heretics. In July 1555, therefore, Villegagnon sailed from France with a band of Huguenot colonists and a sprinkling of seamen and bankrupt nobles and arrived at the harbor of Rio de Janeiro in November.

In 1557 a second party arrived. Unhappily, however, it included five disputatious Calvinist ministers. Villegagnon, who had a natural taste for theological argument, soon engaged in a sharp controversy with the ministers which resulted in his reconversion to Catholicism.

---

[12] Franklin C. Palm's *Calvinism and the Religious Wars* (New York, c. 1932) is an excellent brief introduction.

After sending three of the ministers back to France, he deserted the settlers and returned home. In 1558 Portuguese soldiers fell upon the weakened colony and destroyed it.

Undismayed by this failure, Coligny made new plans. While governor of the fortress of Le Havre in 1561, he summoned his followers and announced his intention of sending an expedition preparatory to the colonization of Florida. Again he aimed to provide a shelter for the Huguenots. In accordance with this plan, a Huguenot captain, Jean Ribaut, sailed in 1562 and explored the northern coast of Florida—"a country full of havens, rivers, and islands, of such fruitfulness as cannot with tongue be expressed." Proceeding northward, Ribaut planted a settlement (which he called Charlesfort), near the present site of Beaufort, South Carolina; then, leaving a band of thirty men to hold the garrison, he returned to France for reinforcements.[13]

After enduring innumerable sufferings, the settlers built a rude craft and embarked for France. Motionless calm was succeeded by violent winds; hungry and athirst on their water-soaked vessel the desperate survivors resorted to killing and eating one of their fellows. Finally they were rescued and taken as prisoners to England.

The promoters of the Huguenot colony, however, were not idle. In 1564 they sent forth another expedition under René de Laudonnière, which established a settlement, Fort Caroline, on the St. John's River in Florida. Nearly every ill which could beset an infant colony visited these pioneers: sickness, hunger, Indian hostilities, insubordination, and mutiny. Bent upon finding gold, the colonists neglected to till the soil. Laudonnière was on the verge of abandoning the project when Ribaut arrived in August 1565 with fresh supplies and a large party of soldiers, artisans, and fortune-hunting noblemen.

But the damage already done proved fatal. Several malcontents at Fort Caroline had seized two vessels from the colony and had taken to buccaneering in the West Indies at the expense of the Spaniards. Captured by their intended victims, they were carried to Havana, where they divulged the news of the Huguenot colony in Florida. The Spaniards believed that the French were colonizing with the intention of preying upon Spanish commerce from an American base. As Protestants the French were all the more odious, for they might corrupt the Indians of New Spain. A champion of militant Catholicism now stepped forward in Spain—Pedro Menéndez de Avilés. Fired with the ambition of extending the empire of Spain over Florida, Menéndez in 1565 secured a royal patent authorizing him to

[13] See again Francis Parkman, *Pioneers of France in the New World.*

explore, conquer, and colonize the region. Success was to confer upon him the powers of governor of Florida. Since he intended to attack the French he received assistance from the Spanish court—three vessels and six hundred troops. With this small army he sailed from Cadiz in June and founded St. Augustine in Florida, September 6, 1565.

Menéndez lost little time in marching overland and destroying Fort Caroline. More than two hundred of the French were put to the sword, and only a hundred were spared. Informed of Menéndez's conduct, Philip II remarked: "Say to him as to those he has killed he has done well: and as to those he has spared they shall be sent to the galleys." The death of Ribaut pleased Menéndez particularly, since "he was the most expert sailor and corsair known, and very skillful in the navigation of the Indies and the coast of Florida."

The story of Huguenot colonization was thus a tale of dismal failure. The Protestants did not have the ardent backing of the French government—a necessary requisite for new projects at the time. Moreover, France was distracted by factional warfare at home. Above all, these early ventures were falsely conceived. "The foundation was forgotten. There were no tillers of the soil. Such, indeed, were rare among the Huguenots; for the dull peasants . . . clung with blind tenacity to the ancient faith. Adventurous gentlemen, reckless soldiers, discontented tradesmen, all keen for novelty and heated with dreams of wealth—these were they who would build for their country and their religion an empire beyond the sea" (Parkman).

The Huguenot failures meant that later French Protestants did not enjoy a French retreat in America. In consequence many of their number, when afflicted with later persecutions, migrated to the English colonies in America.[14]

THE CHURCH OF ENGLAND

While the French Huguenots were attempting to found colonies, England was in the throes of religious change. The Anglican Church, which took form during the reign of Queen Elizabeth (1558–1603), exerted a threefold influence upon English settlements in America. The policies of the Anglican leaders provided one of the potent causes of Puritan migration to New England. In the southern colonies, the

[14] *The Cambridge Modern History* (ed. A. W. Ward, G. W. Prothero, and S. Leathes, 13 vols., New York, 1907–11), a scholarly English work for advanced students, emphasizes ideas and politics. The second volume deals with the Reformation. See also Vol. I, chapter 19; Vol. III, chapters 1, 10, 17; and Vol. IV, chapters 8–12.

From the De Bry engraving made about 1595. Courtesy of the New York Public Library.

THE COAST OF FLORIDA

Anglican Church, although considerably modified, was established in law and served as the center of the social and religious life of the well-to-do planters. Finally, the fear that England might appoint American bishops—and tax the colonists for their support—contributed an active cause of the Revolutionary War.

The roots of the Reformation in England extend backward to the reign of Henry VIII (1509–47) and far beyond. His desire to secure a "divorce" from Catherine of Aragon—his Spanish queen—led him to induce Parliament to repudiate the authority of the papacy over the English Church (1534–35). Similarly the king effected the dissolution of the monasteries and the confiscation of their lands. But Henry VIII was not a Protestant. He sought to exercise supreme authority over the English Church; but aside from this he favored the ecclesiastical doctrines, ceremonies, and organization of pre-Reformation times.

During the reign of Edward VI (1547–53) England became radically Protestant. But his successor, Queen Mary (1553–58), was a devout Roman Catholic who obliterated nearly all official traces of English Protestantism. However, her reign was a period of hard times and national humiliation in foreign affairs, and the harsh persecution of Protestants which the queen instituted stirred up a wave of popular feeling against extreme Catholicism. At the time of her death her religious policy had been generally discredited.[15]

The problem which confronted Queen Elizabeth in 1558 was exceptionally delicate. She was the daughter of Henry VIII and Anne Boleyn, whose marriage had never been sanctioned by the papacy, and accordingly Pope Paul IV asserted that Elizabeth could not become queen without his consent, since her illegitimate birth nullified her natural claim. But Elizabeth resolutely refused to admit that her right to rule depended upon the will of an outside power. Hence she had to defy the papacy at the outset, and to look to the Protestants for support. She was not at heart a Protestant; all her preferences inclined her toward Roman Catholic beliefs and practices. Yet, since she depended upon the Protestants, she had to make concessions to them. At the same time she believed that it was the proper function of her government to determine the religious beliefs of her subjects. She did not have a deep interest in theology; her concern was with politics, and her aim was to promote the material welfare of the nation. Internal peace was necessary to this end, and religious uniform-

---

[15] Conyers Read's *The Tudors* (New York, 1936) consists of five stimulating essays on personalities and policies.

ity afforded the best assurance of peace. Elsewhere she saw that religious diversity led to destructive civil war. To avoid such a calamity in England she was determined to impose a common religion upon the country—one that would assert and uphold the supremacy of her own power.[16]

Two features of the religious settlement of her reign formed part of the background of English colonization. The first was the national character of the Anglican Church. The Reformation in England was "the last and greatest conquest of the State, the assertion of its authority over the Church, and of its absolute, undisputed supremacy within the national frontiers." The Act of Supremacy (1559) defined the sovereign as the Supreme Governor of the Church and required that all clergy take an oath affirming the royal authority. An Act of Uniformity (1559) prescribed that an English Book of Common Prayer should be used in the services of all the churches. Ministers who did not comply were to be punished, and any person who refused to attend the authorized ceremonies was obliged to pay a fine. The Bible was Anglicized by translation and an English litany and an English order of communion were introduced. Church and state formed a partnership in which the state was the dominating member. The sovereign became the custodian of the national faith, armed with far-reaching powers to compel submission among the people. Resolute opponents of the Established Church were therefore plunged into open conflict with the royal power.[17]

The second feature of the Elizabethan settlement was its compromise nature. The Anglican Church was neither Roman Catholic nor radically Protestant. The sovereign's title, "Supreme Governor," replaced the earlier title, "Supreme Head," in order to appease both Catholics and Calvinists. The former regarded the pope as Christ's vicar, and the latter considered Christ only and immediately, as the supreme head of the Church. While rejecting the authority of the papacy, the English Church retained the Catholic hierarchy of archbishops and bishops, and although the services of the prayer book were expressed in the English language, they were drawn largely from the old Church. But the Anglican creed (formulated in the Thirty-nine Articles in 1563) was dominantly Protestant. The Roman Catholic doctrine of transubstantiation was rejected, as well as the institution of an unmarried priesthood. Whereas the Roman Catholic

---

[16] C. Read, "Good Queen Bess," *American Historical Review*, XXXI (July 1926).

[17] A. F. Pollard, *Factors in Modern History* (New York, 1926) gives the penetrating conclusions of a leading English scholar. See chapters 4, 7–8.

faith embraced seven sacraments, the Anglican creed recognized only two—baptism and communion. Nor did Queen Elizabeth restore the monasteries.[18]

The English Reformation was not the work of a great reformer like Calvin or Luther; it was rather the product of political leaders. It has been likened to "the policy of a cabinet, full of compromise, not entirely satisfactory to any one, but tolerable to many" (Pollard). It had enough features of Roman Catholicism to satisfy the moderate Catholics, and enough of Protestantism to satisfy the moderate Protestants. It was accordingly accepted by the majority of the English people. However, neither extreme Protestants nor Roman Catholics were appeased. Their hostility produced a century of political agitation which had profound effects upon English colonization in America.

Soon after the Elizabethan settlement was effected, England became involved in a quasi-war with Spain. Under Philip II, the Spaniards, assuming the leadership of the Catholics in Europe, determined to suppress Protestantism and therefore assisted the English Catholics who desired to restore the authority of the papacy in England. In 1568 the Catholic queen of Scotland, Mary Stuart, fled to England from her Protestant foes. Her claim to the English crown and her religious faith made her the focus of anti-Protestant plots in England. In a general way these conspiracies anticipated a Spanish invasion of England and an uprising of English and Irish Catholics that would depose Elizabeth, restore the Roman Catholic Church, and place the exiled Scottish queen upon the English throne. Such plots, together with the commercial rivalry between England and Spain, brought the two countries to open war in 1587. One issue of the struggle was the right of England to maintain a national church free from foreign dictation. Accordingly, the extreme English Catholics found themselves in alliance with the alien enemies of the queen. Parliament in consequence enacted a series of anti-Catholic laws in order to strengthen the Established Church.[19]

One group of the English Catholics—the papists—sought to restore the papal supremacy; a second—the recusants—while not denying the queen's authority over the Church, desired to adhere to the Roman Catholic ritual and doctrines. The earliest laws against the

[18] Charles Sydney Carter's *The English Church and the Reformation* (London, 1925), a brief manual, emphasizes the period to 1565.

[19] Henry O. Wakeman's *An Introduction to the Church of England* (London, 1919) is the best short history from the point of view of conservative Anglicanism. See chapters 10–17.

Roman Catholics barred them from offices in Church and state, and required them to attend the services of the Established Church under pain of a fine of a shilling a week for non-compliance. After the pope had excommunicated Queen Elizabeth (1570) Parliament imposed the death penalty upon the partisans of Mary Stuart, as well as upon anyone who brought a papal decree into England. Two acts of 1581 made reconciliation with Rome a capital crime and raised the fine for non-attendance at the Anglican services to £20 a month. In 1585 all Catholic priests who had been trained in foreign colleges were expelled, and all English subjects studying in Jesuit schools abroad were ordered home. Two years later another law provided that the goods and two-thirds of the lands of recusants who did not pay the fines for non-attendance at Anglican services should be confiscated by the Crown. Finally, in 1593, Catholics who were too poor to pay fines were banished from the realm.

Most of these acts were intended not only to uphold the queen's authority in religion but also to augment the revenues of the state at the expense of the Roman Catholics. The laws against them became progressively more severe as the strife between England and Spain grew more acute. It was not intended, however, to expel the body of the Roman Catholics; the government preferred that they remain in England, subject to royal scrutiny, lest their migration to Europe should strengthen England's enemies there.[20]

In spite of these oppressive laws, the Elizabethan Catholics did not endeavor to establish colonies in the New World. First of all, the acts were not uniformly enforced. Queen Elizabeth preferred to ignore them, except in time of political crisis. Moreover, the Roman Catholics believed that better times would come. From the Spanish war, and later from James I and Charles I, they hoped for a Catholic restoration or at least for toleration. On the whole they were conservative, even reactionary, in their views: they yearned for the old ways—not for a new social order; consequently they did not wish to pull up their roots in England for the sake of establishing an experimental society in America. Belonging mainly to the landed class, they likewise did not respond to the lure of commercial profit with which the New World beckoned to merchants and capitalists. In addition, the Roman Catholic prelates discouraged emigration, lest the old Church should be completely uprooted in England. Proposals to establish Catholic colonies were therefore treated as Protestant plots. Eng-

[20] R. B. Merriman, "Some Notes on the Treatment of the English Catholics in the Reign of Elizabeth," *American Historical Review*, XIII (April 1908).

land was too important a country to be abandoned to Protestantism through the emigration of ardent Catholics, who—staying at home—would labor to restore the old faith.

For these reasons the English Catholics, harsh as the penal laws against them were, did not play an important part in the colonization of America. That was left to the other critics of the Anglican Church —the more extreme and uncompromising Protestants.[21]

THE ENGLISH PURITANS

When Henry VIII confiscated the lands of the monasteries he distributed them among his followers, thereby creating a new order of aristocrats who supported the Anglican Church with heart and soul, since a reversion to Catholicism would have stripped them of their titles and estates. This feudal basis of the Anglican Church found expression in its decorous ritual, which was in keeping with the ceremonials of aristocratic life, and which denied to the people an active part in divine service, thus carrying into religion the ideal of the supremacy of the aristocratic class. However, there were other groups in the community who were not long content with a passive role. Such were many of the clergy and the lesser landowners, as well as the rising artisans and merchants of the towns. Their growing sense of importance dictated that they should participate in the affairs of state and shape the policy of the church in response to their social and spiritual needs.[22]

Thus during the reign of Elizabeth there arose a body of radicals known as Puritans. Prior to about 1630 they desired merely to reform the Established Church from within. After 1630, however, the term Puritan came to have a broader meaning. In the intellectual sphere, the Puritans insisted upon the right of individual judgment as against the formulation of belief by nobles, priests, or kings. To achieve this end the Puritans fostered education in order that the individual might know the sources of religious truth. Other traits of the Puritans were a highly ingrained sense of the divine presence and an awareness of the sinful nature of man which must be repressed by rigid discipline and an austere moral life. Above all, a highly developed conscience was the mark of sincere Puritans. In practical affairs they were generally aggressive and self-reliant, somewhat in-

[21] Walter H. Frere, *The English Church in the Reigns of Elizabeth and James I* (London, 1904), is useful on the rise of Puritanism.

[22] A suggestive study is Oscar H. Marti's *Economic Causes of the Reformation in England* (New York, 1929).

tolerant of human weaknesses, hostile to compromise, inclined to impose their views on others, and actuated by a craving for self-expression and an eager desire to shape the course of human development toward spiritual ends.

Calvinism appeared in England around 1540, and rose to prominence during the Protestant reign of Edward VI. Expelled during the reign of Mary Tudor, many of the English Calvinists sought refuge at Geneva where their association with Calvin enhanced their ardor for the new faith. They returned to England after 1558, determined to realize their ideas at home. The first notice of a Puritan society in England refers to a London group which in 1566 was styled as "Puritans or unspotted lambs of the Lord." [23]

Several factors explain the growth of Puritanism after 1560. First was the feeling among many Protestants that the Elizabethan religious settlement was an insincere compromise, not truly Protestant or Christian. Many abuses disfigured the Established Church—pluralism in office-holding, ignorant and corrupt clergymen, and a yawning chasm between highly paid prelates and pauperized parish priests. Milton later spoke of the Anglican clergy as shepherds whose

> Hungry sheep look up and are not fed
> But swoln with wind and the rank mist they draw
> Rot inwardly and foul contagion spread.

Moreover, to the Puritans the society of their day seemed coarse, vicious, brutal, and corrupt, with crime rampant and idleness uncontrolled. Believing that the Church was the guardian of public morals, they held the clergy responsible for the evils of the time. In addition, many influential men who had the disposal of offices in the Anglican Church embraced the Puritan faith, with the result that some of the clergy assumed a Puritan pose in order to obtain appointments. Finally, the Puritans entered into an alliance with other opponents of the monarchy—those who resisted the sovereign's claims to absolute power. This alliance made each party much more powerful than if it had acted alone, and eventually (1642–49) enabled both to triumph over the Stuart monarchy and the Anglican Church.

The earliest manifestation of Puritanism was an attack upon the ceremonies of the Established Church, which exemplified the medieval view of the correct mode of worshipping God. The older theory was that man (whose mind was not attuned by nature to God) must apprehend Him through the senses—by means of beautiful services,

---

[23] Henry W. Clark's *History of English Nonconformity* (2 vols., London, 1911, 1913) is one of the best books on religion in England.

images, symbols, and music. The Puritans, on the other hand, believed that the elect who received Divine grace might know God directly through a spiritual medium; consequently ritual and elaborate ceremonies were unnecessary, and a sacrament was only a sign. As Milton said, faith needed not "the weak and fallible office of the senses to be . . . interpreters of heavenly mysteries." Catholics made "God earthy and fleshy because they could not make themselves heavenly and spiritual." [24]

In accordance with such views the Puritans objected to many features of the Anglican ceremony. Some targets of their criticism were the making of the sign of the cross on a child's head at baptism, the practice of kneeling in the communion service, the use of organ music, the observance of saints' days, and the wearing of the cap and surplice and the changing of robes by the clergy. Failing to obtain reforms from the body of Anglican divines assembled in convocation (1563), the Puritan leaders began to hold private services, or conventicles, in which they replaced the Book of Common Prayer with their own observances. After Parliament in 1567 prohibited the holding of conventicles, the Puritans organized themselves into bodies of Protestant dissenters.

After 1570 the Puritan clergy became interested in modifying the government of the Established Church. A craving for self-expression led their leaders to hold meetings called prophesyings at which they exchanged ideas and practiced extemporaneous preaching. Queen Elizabeth objected to individual sermons, lest they destroy the uniformity of belief. She preferred that the clergy should merely read homilies prepared by the proper officials. The task of suppressing individual preaching was assigned to the bishops. In enforcing such policies the bishops naturally incurred the bitter enmity of the Puritan divines, and as a result the bishop's office became another target of Puritan discontent. In two "Admonitions to Parliament" (1572) the Puritans argued that the authority of a bishop over his diocese was no more justifiable than the authority of the pope over the Christian church. The court of the Archbishop of Canterbury was described as "the filthy quagmire and poisoned splash of all abominations that do infect the whole realm." Since the names of archbishops, archdeacons, lord bishops, and chancellors were "drawn out of the pope's shop, together with their offices, so the government which they use . . . is anti-Christian and devilish and contrary to the Scriptures."

In the 1570's most of the Puritans favored the Presbyterian scheme

---

[24] Edward Eggleston's *The Beginners of a Nation* (New York, 1897), a work both interesting and scholarly, emphasizes religious ideas. See Book II.

of Calvinistic church government which had been evolved in Scotland under the leadership of John Knox. The chief advocate of this system in England was Thomas Cartwright, a professor at Cambridge University, intellectual center of Puritan teaching.[25] The Presbyterian plan provided that each church should be governed by presbyters—its minister and lay elders—and that each church should be included in a district, the controlling agency of which was a presbytery or assembly of the local ministers and elders. Above the presbytery stood a larger regional conference—the synod—to which the presbyteries sent delegates. Crowning the structure there was to be a general assembly for the whole nation. In this arrangement the power of church government—shared jointly by the ministers and the lay elders—was concentrated chiefly in the presbytery and the local congregation. Authority ascended from the individual church to the larger conferences; under the Anglican rule, authority descended from the king and the archbishops through the bishops to the parish churches. The first presbytery was organized in England in 1572, and by 1590 there were probably five hundred ministers sustaining a Presbyterian organization within the Established Church.

Along with the Puritans arose a party of ultra-radical Protestants known as Separatists, who believed that each individual had the right to form his own religious creed. Such extreme individualism meant that, since different people would not reach identical conclusions, a single faith could not be imposed upon all. The only solution was to allow like-minded persons to form separate congregations and to worship free from all restraint. This attitude pointed directly toward religious toleration. Since the Established Church denied individual freedom of worship, the radicals felt that they must separate themselves from its errors.

The creed of the English Separatists was formulated by an Anglican clergyman, Robert Browne, who argued in the 1580's that the only church organization sanctioned by the Bible was that of a self-governing congregation. Hence the English Separatists became known as Brownists or Congregationalists. Because they rejected the authority of the state over religion they soon ran afoul of the national government. Two of their leaders, Barrow and Greenwood, were hanged at Tyburn in 1587; elsewhere their meetings were broken up, their property seized, and their leaders imprisoned. In 1597 a group of those imprisoned asked permission to migrate to America. This

<hr>

[25] A. F. Scott Pearson, *Thomas Cartwright and Elizabethan Puritanism* (Cambridge, 1925), a careful, dignified study, treats religion without reference to other social forces.

was wholly natural, since the position of the Separatists in England was extremely weak. Their number in 1593 probably did not exceed six hundred; their primary ideas worked against an effective organization among themselves; their practices were contrary to the ingrained habits of the English people; and their defiance of the government required too much courage to be widely popular.[26]

The last years of the reign of Elizabeth brought a policy of increasingly severe anti-Puritanism. After the defeat of the Spanish Armada in 1588, the Spanish menace diminished and the persecution of English Catholics tapered off. The Puritans now emerged as the principal enemies of the monarchy, inasmuch as their ideas threatened to divide the people into hostile camps, and by destroying the unity of the queen's Church to undermine the royal authority within the state. Elizabeth accordingly appointed strict Anglicans to the highest ecclesiastical offices and proceeded to punish heretics and to dismiss a large number of Puritan clergy from their posts. For this purpose she utilized a special tribunal—the Court of High Commission—reorganized in 1583 with the object of imposing religious uniformity upon the land. This court was merely a mouthpiece of the sovereign, not an ordinary court of justice; it did not allow trial by jury or exempt the accused from testifying against himself. At this time, also, the queen's partisans advanced the theory that the office of bishop was divinely ordained.

A similar course was pursued by the successor of Elizabeth, James I, who ruled from 1603 to 1625. At the outset of his reign he refused to reform the Anglican Church along Presbyterian lines and warned the Puritans that he would make them conform or harry them out of the realm. A similar break with the Roman Catholics compelled the new sovereign to depend upon the Established Church —a natural alliance, since the Anglican principle of royal authority in religion harmonized with his view of the divine right of kings. But in spite of the animosity of the court, Puritanism continued to gain strength. Their ousted clergy gave unofficial lectures attended by their former parishioners, while the un-English foreign policies and the personal unpopularity of the king won allies and new recruits. Puritanism ceased to be a minor pest plaguing a popular queen who dominated a subservient Parliament; it became the central opposition to an unpopular king contending with a hostile Parliament. The movement reached its zenith during the reign of Charles I (1625–49), when some of England's greatest men—Sir John Eliot,

---

[26] Winnifred Cockshott's *The Pilgrim Fathers* (New York, 1909) opens with two chapters on the Separatists.

John Pym, John Selden, John Milton, and Oliver Cromwell—were Puritans.[27]

As the strife between king and Parliament grew apace, Charles I gathered about him a party of high-church Anglican prelates extremely odious to the Puritans. This party became indoctrinated with the ideas of a Dutch theologian, Jacob Arminius, who criticized the theory of predestination because it seemed to make God the author of sin. The Arminian creed asserted that all who believed in Christ might be saved; divine grace was given freely to all who would seek it; salvation depended in part upon good works; and infants and virtuous heathens would not be eternally damned. Such beliefs were gall and wormwood to the Puritans—not only because they were an affront to Calvin, but also because they seemed to point backward to the creed of the Catholic Church. The first great victory of the Puritans occurred in 1628, when their leaders drafted and imposed upon Charles I the famous Petition of Right, which asserted the Calvinistic theory of fundamental law superior even to kings, and revealed that the Puritans had found powerful allies who resisted, on constitutional grounds, the claim of Charles I to tax his subjects without Parliament's consent.

The following year the Puritans struck at the religious policy of the king, when in March 1629 they attacked the Anglican clergy for discarding Calvinistic doctrines in favor of Arminianism. Resentful of what he considered impudent meddling, Charles I ordered parliament to adjourn. When the speaker of the Commons was about to read the royal order for adjournment, he was held down in his chair by two members, while Sir John Eliot read three resolutions to the House. One of these declared a public enemy any person who should "bring in innovation in religion, or by favor of countenance seem to introduce popery or Arminianism." The House became a scene of confusion as the doors were locked and the resolutions put to vote and carried. The speaker was then released, the doors were thrown open, and the members thronged out. Charles I immediately dissolved Parliament and thereby inaugurated a personal rule which was to have momentous consequences in both the Old World and the New.[28]

Unhampered by parliamentary restraints, the king now plunged

[27] A good brief account of the years 1628–60 by an outstanding authority is Samuel R. Gardiner's introduction to his edition of *The Constitutional Documents of the Puritan Revolution* (Oxford, 1880).

[28] George M. Trevelyan's *England under the Stuarts* (New York, 1930) contains a brilliant survey of the religious struggles, 1603–89. Another excellent treatment is Godfrey Davies, *The Early Stuarts, 1603–1660* (Oxford, 1937).

heedlessly along his own course. In 1633 he appointed William Laud Archbishop of Canterbury—a sincere and diligent but rigid and headstrong Anglican who had asserted the divine right of bishops and was suspected of Arminian sympathies. Laud tried to sweep away the evils of immorality, ignorance, sloth, and hypocrisy among the clergy, and to accomplish this he attempted to impose a hard-and-fast uniformity upon all the churches. He believed that the existence of a separate church outside the Anglican fold would create a state within the state. However, the reforms upon which he insisted were hateful to the Puritans, since they emphasized the externals of worship and showed a partiality to the Roman Catholic aspects of Anglican ritual. When the Puritans resisted what the archbishop regarded as his righteous aims, he attributed their opposition to irreligion, and classed them with wicked and dissolute persons—an intolerable insult to their spiritual pride. As head of the Court of High Commission Laud used it to enforce his decrees. The expelled Puritan clergy were hounded, their unofficial lectures were broken up, and their followers were arrested. A rigorous censorship of the press was enforced upon several vocal Puritans—Alexander Leighton, John Lilburne, and William Prynne—who were fined, whipped, shorn of their ears, imprisoned, or branded. The mass of the Puritans were not brutally persecuted, but they were threatened, harassed, and above all denied any influence in the affairs of Church and state—an unhappy circumstance for a party overstocked with strong leaders whose ardent spirits craved the right of translating their beliefs into official acts.[29]

Soon after Charles I began his personal rule one of the Puritan leaders—John Winthrop—wrote to his wife: "I am verily persuaded God will bring some heavy affliction upon this land, and that speedily; but if the Lord seeth it will be good for us, He will provide a shelter and a hiding place for us and others." God "is turning the cup toward us also, and because we are the last, our portion must be drunk to the very dregs which remain."

Gloomy indeed was the outlook for the Puritans in the 1630's. A wave of triumphant Catholicism seemed to be rolling over Europe. The Thirty Years' War was favoring the Catholic cause; the French Huguenots suffered a sorrowful defeat in 1628; the English queen, Henrietta Maria of France, was a devoted Catholic; the impecunious government of Charles I refused to aid the Protestants on the Continent; and the policies of Archbishop Laud seemed to the Puritans

[29] William H. Hutton's *The English Church* (London, 1903) is a standard work on the period 1625–1714.

to proclaim a forthcoming reunion between England and Rome. In 1633 the king issued the Declaration of Sports, which, in the old Catholic manner, allowed the people to play games on Sunday. Abhorrent as this was in itself to the Puritan believers in a joyless Sabbath, it was doubly obnoxious because it had to be read by the clergy from their pulpits on pain of losing their positions. Meanwhile, the parliamentary leaders of the Puritans had been cast into prison, where the purest soul among them—Sir John Eliot—contracted tuberculosis and died.

Such then was the religious background of the great Puritan migration to America. Ministers no longer allowed to preach in England gathered their flocks about them and departed for New England. The severity of Laud's rule over the church stimulated the movement westward until the collapse of the personal government of the king and the forward thrust of the Puritans in England in 1640 halted the exodus. By this time, however, a Puritan stamp had been placed upon a half dozen English colonies in the New World.[30]

THE QUAKERS

The Civil War and the Puritan regime in England (1642–59) temporarily overthrew the Anglican Church and unloosed new forces of social unrest, but with the restoration of the Stuart dynasty in 1660 and the reëstablishment of the old religious order, a vigorous reaction set in. As a result there ensued another bitter conflict in which the government and the aristocracy were pitted against dissatisfied groups of the lower and middle classes that had become indoctrinated with radical ideas of freedom and individual right.

Foremost among such groups stood the English Quakers. The founder of this sect, George Fox, had displayed as a youth a precocious desire for religious truth which accepted creeds were unable to satisfy. "Not of high degree or elegant speech or learned after the way of this world," but by virtue of much solitude and long reflection this youthful seeker fashioned an individual faith consonant with his personal humility, gravity, and earnestness. Feeling himself divinely called to a public ministry, he preached and traveled with unwearied diligence, and drew about him a group of ardent evangelists who carried the tidings of the new salvation throughout England and to Germany and the Netherlands.

To George Fox and his followers the true religion had been prac-

[30] N. M. Crouse, "Causes of the Great Migration, 1630–1640," *New England Quarterly*, V (Jan. 1932).

ticed by the primitive Christians, but this had later been perverted by kings and emperors to worldly uses. The Reformation had sought to restore the pristine purity of the Church, but the triumph of reforming sects had corrupted them with a sense of power that induced persecution—a negation of the Christian spirit. The object of the Quakers was to restore religion to its primitive simplicity, charity, and spirituality.[31]

The core of Quaker belief was the idea of the inner light or of man's kinship with God. In every person there dwelt a spark of divinity that might be enlarged by man's conscious effort until he became wholly Godlike. The divine attributes of meekness, truthfulness, faith, love, charity, purity, and mercy should be cultivated as opposed to the evil attributes of vanity, pride, envy, sloth, falsehood, and anger. Divine grace and salvation were freely available to all on condition that the sinner acknowledge his sins, repent, and mend his ways. The ideal that salvation was to be achieved by man's works or effort appealed with particular force to those classes in English society which were engaged in useful labor.

As members of the middle and non-privileged class in England the Quakers readily embraced a faith which rejected ceremony, authority, and inequality. Inasmuch as man might commune directly with God, the office of priest was eliminated. Ministers need not be trained in dogma or ritual, because they could speak truly only as the divine spirit moved them. Church services became informal by virtue of the right of each member to rise at will and utter words divinely inspired. Marriages were performed without the services of a minister, since God sealed the union, not man. Taxes for the support of churches were proscribed: "freely ye have received, freely give." The Scriptures condemned oaths, even when legally administered, since man was commanded to "swear not at all." Persecution was regarded as spiritual murder, out of harmony with the merciful spirit of Christ. Since war and fighting issued from the sinful nature of man, they were sternly outlawed. Such forms of social respect as the tipping of hats and bowing to superiors were likewise rejected. The words "thee" and "thou," then customarily addressed to servants and children, were applied by the Quakers to the highborn and the lowly alike.[32]

At the outset of the Quaker movement its popular appeal attracted

[31] Rufus M. Jones, *The Story of George Fox* (New York, 1919), is good reading—the work of a leading American historian of Quakerism.

[32] On radical tendencies see George P. Gooch's able, concise *The History of English Democratic Ideas in the Seventeenth Century* (Cambridge, 1898).

many of the more ignorant and superstitious poor, who marred the meetings with unseemly emotional demonstrations. Others asserted that the divine spirit directed their actions—evil ones included—and that they were thus above ordinary moral restraints. The Quaker leaders accordingly were obliged to develop a church organization and an effective discipline to check such excesses. The local congregation was made the central authority, acting through its monthly meeting. This body selected the minister, supervised the morals of members, investigated proposed marriages, kept records, and excommunicated the wayward who refused to reform. In addition to the monthly meetings there were quarterly meetings attended by representatives of the churches in a given county, and over all was the yearly meeting held at London. The quarterly and yearly meetings, composed of the most eminent and zealous Friends, afforded mutual counsel and aid—particularly in supporting missions and in defending Quakers persecuted in any part of the world.

In one respect the Quakers did not insist upon the ideals of primitive Christianity; they did not believe in poverty. In fact, they showed a marked capacity for acquiring and retaining wealth. They were generally intelligent and industrious people, conscious and resentful of social inequalities and privileges based upon force. Although they did not share the benefits of the ruling class, they were not of the servile or ignorant poor, but, rather, enterprising farmers, artisans, and merchants who felt the need of a larger place in the sun. Accordingly they disliked the aristocratic Anglican Church which denied to rising members of the community an active part in the conduct of divine service. Their doctrines which asserted the equality of man and the right of the individual to an active part in worship thus coincided with their growing economic importance and independence.[33]

In England the Quakers were regarded as upstarts who refused to pay homage to their privileged superiors. Their principles of equality were odious to a society based upon inflexible class distinctions. Their refusal to take oaths, to pay tithes, or to bear arms laid them open to the charge of refusing to support the state, and such refusal strongly suggested to the authorities a hidden impulse toward revolution.

One of the acts of Parliament known as the Clarendon Code (1661–65), which reëstablished the Church of England, provided that the Quakers, as dissenters, could not attend private religious meetings or conventicles. A fourth violation of this law was punisha-

[33] David Ogg's *England in the Reign of Charles II* (2 vols., Oxford, 1934), an important study, devotes most of Vol. II to religion and politics.

ble by a seven-year sentence to penal servitude in the West Indies. By another act the Quakers were fined £20 a month or two-thirds of their property if they refused to attend the Anglican services. Accordingly, they were sorely persecuted: their meetings were broken up; they were arrested, fined, imprisoned, and in extreme cases transported to the colonies; they suffered "mockings, contradictions, beatings, prisons, and many other jeopardies," so that "they seemed indeed to be as poor sheep appointed to the slaughter, and as a people killed all the day long." Like the Puritans before them, the Quakers looked to America as a land where they might live in peace and realize their peculiar aspirations, and accordingly they were active in colonizing schemes from 1675 until 1689—the year in which England finally adopted the general policy of religious toleration.[34]

Conclusion

The religious contests after 1500 arose largely from the prevailing conception that church and state should be united. The sovereigns of Europe, and the privileged groups identified with them, felt that a single religion was necessary to unify the country and to maintain the authority and dignity of the ruling classes. In France, Spain, Germany, Holland, and England the Reformation established the principle that the secular power should preside over the national church. The adherents of state churches, protected at home, were not driven to seek shelter in other lands. Such protected groups were the Catholics in France and Spain, the Anglicans in England, the Calvinists in Holland, and the Lutherans in Germany and the Scandinavian kingdoms. Hence emigration inspired by religious motives was relatively slight among such protected groups. The opponents of state churches, however, were exposed to persecution, and consequently responded more readily to the lure of emigration. All these groups were prone to resist the absolute power of government. The mass of their members were drawn from the classes engaged in farming, industry, or trade. They could not settle in the colonies of France or Spain, which were closed to all but Roman Catholics. As a result they sought refuge in the American colonies of England and thus laid the foundations of a Protestant society prone to assert individual rights in defiance of external authority and to proclaim the freedom of farmers, artisans, and traders from the dominance of nobles,

---

[34] W. C. Dudley, "Nonconformity under the Clarendon Code," *American Historical Review*, XVIII (Oct. 1912). See also W. C. Abbott, "English Conspiracy and Dissent, 1660–1674," *American Historical Review*, XIV (April, July 1909).

priests, and kings. A further result was that English America soon made a strong appeal to the common folk of Europe and Britain who were not actuated by religious motives, but who desired to be free from the social and economic shackles which bound them in the Old World.

BIBLIOGRAPHICAL NOTE

Secondary Works: Marshall W. Baldwin, *The Mediaeval Church* (Ithaca, 1953), describes the features of the Church and traces its history to about 1250. G. G. Coulton, *Inquisition and Liberty* (London, 1938), is a vigorous, interesting account. E. Harris Harbison, *The Age of the Reformation* (Ithaca, 1955), is an excellent résumé. E. G. Schwiebert, *Luther and His Times* (St. Louis, 1950), is the most extensive biography, from a Protestant point of view. W. Gordon Zeeveld, *Foundations of Tudor Policy* (Cambridge, 1948), is an original study of the interaction of humanism and the Reformation. H. Maynard Smith, *Henry VIII and the Reformation* (London, 1948), regards the interests of the king as the matrix of religious strife.

John T. McNeil, *The History and Character of Calvinism* (New York, 1954), is a readable, well-informed survey. Charles D. Cremeans, *The Reception of Calvinist Thought in England* (Urbana, 1949), combines a statement of Calvin's political beliefs with an account of the diffusion of Calvinist theology in England. J. H. M. Salmon, *The French Religious Wars in English Political Thought* (Oxford, 1959), traces the influence of French Calvinism in England. William Haller, *The Rise of Puritanism* (New York, 1938), an erudite work, gives a full account of the activities of the Puritans within the Church of England. M. M. Knappen, *Tudor Puritanism* (Chicago, 1939), interprets Puritanism as an idealistic impulse and explains its strength and limitations. Alan Simpson, *Puritanism in Old and New England* (Chicago, 1955) consists of six attractive essays which describe the essentials of Puritanism as a trans-Atlantic force. William C. Braithwaite, *The Beginnings of Quakerism* (2d ed., Cambridge, Eng., 1955), is a standard work. Arthur Raistrick, *Quakers in Science* (New York, 1950), records and explains Quaker contributions of a practical cast. Arnold Lloyd, *Quaker Social History, 1669–1738* (New York, 1950), an outstanding work, attributes the survival and mellowing of Quakerism to discipline and organization.

Sources: Henry Gee and W. J. Hardy (eds.), *Documents Illustrative of English Church History* (London, 1896), devotes nos. 46–124 to the Reformation. John Calvin, *Institutes of the Christian Religion* (2 vols., Philadelphia, 1921), is of primary importance. John L. Nickalls (ed.), *The Journal of George Fox* (New York, 1952), is the best version.

IV

The Economic Background
of English Colonization

ENGLISH colonization was in the main an outgrowth of an economic revolution which marked the passing of the Middle Ages. Prior to about 1350, England occupied a minor place in the economy of Europe. But a series of profound changes occurred during the two centuries afterward—changes in agriculture, industry, and foreign trade that effected the transition in England from economic localism to importance in world commerce.

MEDIEVAL ENGLISH ECONOMY

During the Middle Ages, agriculture supported the mass of the English people. The methods and organization of farming, however, were not conducive to economic progress. Spread over the country were a host of large estates in which the peasants carried on a semi-communal form of production. What gave their essential character to such estates or manors was the relation between the tillers of the soil and their lords, who held the land directly or indirectly from the king. The labor of the serfs provided the good things of life for the manorial lord, and consequently the serfs were bound to the soil— were not allowed to leave the manor even temporarily without the lord's consent. Since they had to work two or three days a week upon the land reserved to the lord (the demesne), it was imperative that they always be within his reach. During the remaining time they worked for themselves on little plots of ground, but they could eke out only a bare existence after the demands of the lord had been met.[2]

As long as this system remained, England could not become im-

---

[1] The best survey of the English background appears in E. Lipson's *The Economic History of England* (3 vols., London, 1920, 1931). Volume I is devoted to the medieval period and to early modern times; Vols. II and III to the age of mercantilism. A very valuable work.

[2] N. S. B. Gras, *An Introduction to Economic History* (New York, 1922) should be read by all students. It is original, scholarly and excellently written. See chapters 1–5. For more detailed studies by Professor Gras see *A History of Agriculture* (New York, 1925) and *Industrial Evolution* (Cambridge, 1930).

portant on the world stage of economic affairs. The country was too small to be a great producer of the commodities raised on the manor —grains and livestock—and obviously a people bound to the soil could not engage in seafaring, business, foreign trade, and colonization. Serfdom closed the avenues of economic progress; only when each person could go as he liked where opportunity beckoned could the maximum productive power of the nation be utilized. The manor itself cast a pall upon personal initiative—partly because so much of the fruits of the serf's toil went to the lord, and partly because the work of the serfs was regulated by custom and performed in common, so that the man of enterprise was held down to the speed of his more sluggish fellows. The methods of farming did not improve; the manor produced little surplus except for the overlord; the serfs, therefore, could not buy much of anything from the outside world. In the absence of money they paid their dues to the lord in labor and produce.

Such manufacturing as England carried on in the Middle Ages was performed chiefly in rising but struggling towns. Here the central feature was the craft gild. Since England did not as yet export manufactured products in quantity or conduct an extensive trade within the country, each town could exploit only a small market in its immediate vicinity, and consequently the gilds enforced a policy of restricting production within narrow limits. Each gild applied rigid rules to guarantee that every member should have his share of the available work. Only gild members were tolerated, and admission depended upon a long-term apprenticeship, while the number of apprentices was kept down in order to prevent overcrowding in any trade. Even the masters were closely regulated by the gild as to the quality and quantity of their work. Membership was a boon not to be surrendered lightly; hence the craftsmen were not disposed to leave their towns in search of better opportunities. Although such restrictions assured that apprentices would be properly chosen and well trained and that a high quality of work would be upheld, the gild ideal of monopoly and restricted production tended to keep industry within a narrow groove. Industrial expansion had to wait until wider markets appeared.[3]

The backwardness of England in agriculture and industry was reflected in foreign trade. In this sphere England depended largely upon foreign merchants. The area of external trade included only the Mediterranean, the Black Sea, the North Sea, the Baltic, and the

---

[3] L. F. Salzman's *English Industries of the Middle Ages* (Oxford, 1923) describes particular industries. Many illustrations. See chapters 9, 11, 13.

eastern border of the Atlantic Ocean. Moreover, the national state had not yet taken complete control over commerce; instead, merchants operated under the protection of their towns. Commercial treaties were negotiated and tariff duties imposed by the towns, to the infinite multiplication of restrictions upon trade. The exports of England consisted principally of raw materials—tin, copper, and raw wool. These were carried to distant markets by foreign merchants— by Italians who brought in the luxuries of the Orient, by German traders who imported forest products from the Baltic countries, and by Flemings who came with cloth from the Netherlands.

Such domination of foreign trade by alien merchants expressed the economic backwardness of medieval England, although in the long run it prepared the way for economic independence. In the days when the English monarchy was struggling for supremacy within the nation it was not opposed by a group of all-powerful commercial cities which frustrated political unification and the nationalization of commercial activity. England thus eventually became a compactly organized economic unit. But in the Middle Ages, the foreign merchants did not aggressively promote England's external trade. They were generally unpopular and consequently obliged to buy concessions and protection from the king, and were often exploited in a right royal manner. Frequently they were mobbed and despoiled of their property by an angry populace, as at the time of the Peasants' Revolt, when the German traders were a special target of the English mob. In the best of times trade could be carried on with only a few countries, and this the foreigners were prone to monopolize at the expense of their English customers. Moreover, the alien merchant regarded England as on the periphery, not as in a central area, of world trade. He did not seek to create a world market for English products, but only to export as many of them as could be sold through a single outlet—his own particular town and the commercial channels which it controlled. And since he did not engage in either industrial or agricultural production in England, he did not feel the powerful urge of a producer to widen the markets for his wares. All in all, then, the restrictions upon foreign trade harmonized with the restraints upon agriculture and industry which kept England in the background of European commercial progress during the early Middle Ages.[4]

[4] L. F. Salzman, *English Trade in the Middle Ages* (Oxford, 1931), is a satisfactory introduction, topically arranged.

The Economic Revolution, 1350–1600

Such handicaps, however, were only relative, because a train of economic change was gradually undermining the old order. The basic revolution occurred in the breakdown of the medieval manor, an event which speedily transformed both industry and foreign trade. The essential change in agriculture was the alteration in the status of the worker from that of soil-bound serf to that of independent yeoman, rent-paying tenant, or hired laborer.

As industry and trade expanded in Europe—particularly in the towns of the Netherlands, Germany, northern France, and Italy—the standard of bourgeois well-being rose to new heights, accompanied by an increasing demand for good clothing. In those days woolen cloth was in well-nigh universal use, neither silk nor cotton having yet become widely practicable. England happened to be peculiarly suited to the raising of wool, and her farmers were soon supplying the looms of Europe with the finest grades available. The progress of sheep raising in turn revolutionized English agriculture. Small patches of land formerly cultivated by serfs were taken from them and enclosed as large sheep pastures. The evicted tenants could not all find new employment, since sheep tending required less labor per acre than the grain farming of manorial days. A large class of unemployed workers began to roam about as idlers and vagabonds. At the same time the population of England grew steadily—from about three million souls in 1485 to four million in 1603. The diversion of land from food growing to sheep raising meant that food supply did not keep pace with population growth, with the result that the growing army of unemployed struggled with a rising cost of living. Between 1461 and 1603 half the manors of England were enclosed. The rapidity of the revolution confronted the government with the specter of food shortage and the danger of internal strife due to high rents and prices and unemployment. Threats of class war induced the government to pass laws forbidding enclosures; nine such measures were enacted between 1485 and 1624. But because of the resistance of the landowners profiting by higher rents and of the merchants who reaped the profits of the wool trade, the enclosure movement could not be seriously checked.[5]

The exports of English wool to the Continent paid for the returning imports, part of which were gold and silver money. This came first into the towns, thereby enabling the bourgeoisie to buy more

[5] The best treatment of agricultural change is R. H. Tawney's *The Agrarian Problem in the Sixteenth Century* (New York, 1912).

farm products from neighboring manors. The unevicted peasants might sell a little surplus food to the towns for ready cash. The accelerating circulation of money not only raised the price of food but also gave the peasants a means whereby they could relieve themselves of payments to their lords in labor and produce. Instead of working two or three days a week upon the lord's demesne land, the peasants preferred to pay money rents which allowed them to work on their own plots of ground all the time. Having lost the customary workers for his demesne by this process of commutation, the lord could either put the land to sheep pasture or hire laborers to cultivate it for a money wage. The lord now ceased to care whether the peasants were bound to the soil or not, since he no longer expected them to be on hand for work upon his land. They in turn devoted themselves wholly to their own little farms, gained the freedom to come and go as they pleased, and discharged their former obligations of work and produce payments in a money rent.[6]

Hard upon the heels of the enclosure movement and the emancipation of the serfs followed a revolution within industry. Its essence was the progress of manufacturing, the decline of the gilds, and above all the emergence of woolen cloth working as England's foremost enterprise. In 1613 an English writer, John May, described the manufacture of woolen cloth as "the glory of our traffic and maintenance of our poor, many hundred thousands depending wholly on the same, chief pillar to our prince's revenue, the life of our merchant, the living of our clothier."

The plentiful supply of raw wool afforded by the enclosure movement gave the initial impetus to this all-important English industry. The universal demand for woolens furnished a large market, close at hand. Labor was plentiful, as the evicted peasants and runaway serfs sought the freedom of the manufacturing towns, and skilled artisans from abroad were welcomed into England to teach the secrets of cloth manufacture. About 1335, Flemings fled from the ravages of the Hundred Years' War, and Dutch craftsmen, whose finely made cloth was called in England the "new drapery," came in during the reign of Elizabeth, as did also a company of Huguenot weavers who sought relief from religious persecution in France. The protection and encouragement extended to such foreigners were but a part of a general policy of the English government to foster the woolen industry. Acts of Parliament, passed intermittently after 1337, aimed to restrain the exportation of raw wool and unfinished cloth and the im-

---

[6] E. P. Cheyney's *An Introduction to the Industrial and Social History of England* (New York, 1920) is compact, lucid, and well organized. See chapters 1–7.

portation of finished articles, in order that English producers might have prior access to raw materials and markets, foreign and domestic alike.[7]

One other factor necessary to manufacturing was present in England after 1400—ready capital. At that time capital was thought to consist of trading goods and money rather than of plants, machinery, and transportation facilities. The capitalist was one who circulated his trading stock rapidly with a profit to himself, not, as at present, one who deals primarily in long-term securities. Coined money was especially prized as capital, since it so readily effected the exchange of the country's stock of trading goods.

England's exportation of raw wool to the Continent accounted in part for her increasing supply of gold and silver, as did also the plundering of French towns and estates during the Hundred Years' War. During the reign of Henry VIII Parliament cut off money payments to the papacy, and thus put an end to one principal drain on the country's supply of coin. The working of silver mines in Bohemia and Germany between 1448 and 1492 augmented the European stock of money just before the Spanish colonies in America began to pour their treasure into Spain, whence it quickly seeped out, especially to the Netherlands, France, and England. The decline of feudalism and the dissolution of the monasteries released capital for industry and trade. As early as the close of the fifteenth century a Venetian observer wrote of London: "In a single street named the Strand leading to St. Paul's there are fifty-two goldsmiths' shops, so rich and full of silver vessels, great and small, that in all the shops in Milan, Rome, Venice and Florence put together I do not think there would be found so many of magnificence." [8]

The growing utilization of money as capital effected a change of attitude toward interest and moneylenders. Previously loans at interest had been made to kings and nobles, mainly for high living or war, and consequently were not regarded as productive of wealth. The Church condemned any person who lent at interest to humble folk, since money itself was unproductive. But as the rising capitalist class began to use money as a medium of exchange, thereby facilitating trade and extending production, the medieval attitude toward usury broke down. In England Parliament in 1545 legalized interest charges up to 10 per cent. This act acknowledged that a class of

---

[7] E. Lipson's *History of the Woollen and Worsted Industries* (London, 1921) is unexcelled.

[8] N. S. B. Gras exhibits a mastery of generalization in "The Economic Activity of the Towns," in *The Legacy of the Middle Ages* (ed. C. G. Crump, Oxford, 1926).

merchant-capitalists had arisen who were becoming increasingly important to the state.[9]

In the woolen industry the capitalist was both employer and merchant. He bought the raw wool, hired artisans to manufacture it into cloth, and sold the finished product. As the market for English cloth widened, the merchant-capitalists objected to the restrictions imposed upon production by the craft gilds and accordingly employed artisans in villages that were not under the rule of the gilds. There followed then a lively war between the older industrial towns and the new—a war which ended in the decay of the gilds and the established supremacy of the capitalist-employers within the woolen industry. Under the new domestic system the workers did not own the raw materials which they fabricated nor did they have any part in the marketing of the finished products. The wage system, subdivision of labor among carders, spinners, weavers, fullers, and dyers, improved tools and machines, the ideal of maximum production at minimum cost, and control of marketing by the employers—all these announced the coming of modern capitalistic economy.

In response to the advance of manufacturing, England's foreign trade assumed a new character as woven cloth replaced raw wool as the nation's primary export. About 1350 such exports consisted of thirty thousand sacks of raw wool and about five thousand pieces of cloth; in 1500 only five thousand sacks of wool were sold abroad as against sixty thousand pieces of cloth exported by one society of merchants alone. During these years another momentous change occurred. Foreign traders were gradually squeezed out of England's commerce and English merchants ventured throughout Europe in search of markets for their wares. In 1350 there were only 169 English merchants of consequence engaged in foreign trade; in 1500 there were at least three thousand.[10]

The change in exports from raw wool to manufactures was the principal factor making possible the commercial expansion of England. As long as the country exported only raw products, its available market was restricted, for they could be sent only to a relatively few Continental manufacturing towns. When, however, England had cloth to sell, her immediate markets widened immensely, for woolens could be carried directly to the consumer in every quarter of the

[9] R. D. Richards, *The Early History of Banking* (London, 1929), is an outstanding study.

[10] *Studies in Economic History: The Collected Papers of George Unwin* (London, 1927) consists of penetrating accounts of medieval and early modern themes.

known world. Likewise, England became interested in colonies largely because she had manufactures to sell. Had she had only raw wool, hides, tin, and the like for export, she could have traded with advanced industrial regions, but hardly with the backward peoples of Africa and America.

From the merchant-employers came the driving impulse for commercial expansion. Here was a class of energetic, ambitious producers who pushed the sale of their goods throughout Europe with boldness and dispatch. With a potential market of unlimited extent and with seemingly boundless possibilities of production in England, the merchant-employers refused to depend upon foreign traders whose interest in selling English goods was not uppermost in their concerns. And so the English merchants went abroad, forcing their way into new markets, selling their goods with the ardor of an army bent upon conquering the world.[11]

AN ENGLISH MERCHANT OF THE SIXTEENTH CENTURY

Before the rise of the English woolen industry the principal traders of England—called the Merchants of the Staple—exported only raw products, which had to be shipped to a few designated ports. Sometimes these staple towns were located in England, sometimes on the Continent. The staplers declined as cloth replaced raw wool in England's export trade, being superseded by a new Company of Merchant Adventurers, whose main business was the exportation of cloth. Each merchant traded as an individual, owning the vessels he used and keeping private accounts. But the adventurers were banded together into a company which imposed common regulations upon all. Each merchant had to pass through a long apprenticeship, to pay a membership fee, and to abide by the decisions of the company's court in disputes with his fellows. A charter from the king (1407) had al-

[11] George Unwin's *Industrial Organization in the Sixteenth and Seventeenth Centuries* (Oxford, 1914) is an excellent, highly important survey of England's economy at the beginning of the colonizing era.

!owed the English traders abroad to act together through officers chosen by themselves, and eventually they established their own governing centers—one in London and one in the Netherlands, where most of their cloth was then sold. As a semi-political agency the company secured privileges for its members abroad and provided for their defense. During the fifteenth and sixteenth centuries the Merchant Adventurers controlled the bulk of England's foreign trade. Their very name indicates the aggressive and daring spirit that was then animating England's commercial expansion.

The gradual opening of new trading areas resulted in a need for commercial specialization; consequently, after 1550, the Merchant Adventurers were supplemented by new chartered companies, each with a monopoly of the commerce of a particular region. First came the Russia or Muscovy Company (1553 and 1555), then the Levant or Turkey Company (1581), next the Barbary or Morocco Company (1585), then the Guinea Company (1588), and finally the great East India Company, chartered in 1600. These companies, like the Merchant Adventurers, exported English manufactures, principally cloth, and they evinced the same all-powerful desire for extended markets.[12]

Two types of corporate organization were employed. The regulated company resembled the Merchant Adventurers—a society of private merchants conducting their trade on an individual basis, but submitting to a governor and court established by themselves, obeying common regulations, and by joint action securing privileges and providing for their own defense. Only merchants were admitted into these companies, and only after they had paid high membership fees. Such companies stood midway between the medieval gild merchant and the modern joint-stock corporation, which became increasingly popular after 1550. In the joint-stock company, membership was thrown open to investors in all walks of life who purchased shares. Each shareholder then had the right to attend the general court or stockholders' meeting, and to vote for the governor, treasurer, and board of assistants (or company directors) who managed the company's affairs. All assets were pooled and the business was carried on in a corporate capacity, profits being divided periodically among the shareholders. The first joint-stock companies were organized for single ventures, and endured only a few years, but by 1600 they were being established on a permanent basis. Widely utilized between 1560 and 1590 as a means of financing privateering and exploring

[12] Abbott P. Usher's *An Introduction to the Industrial History of England* (Boston, c. 1920) gives essential facts in well-organized form. See chapters 4–9.

ventures, the joint-stock companies earned enticing profits of 20 per cent or better, and thus exerted a tremendous popular appeal.[13]

Particularly suited to the promotion of foreign trade, the joint-stock company enabled England to seize the major commercial advantages of modern times. England's opportunity lay not in the mastery of the trade of Europe, which was already partitioned among a score of zealous and jealous states, but rather in the exploitation of areas which the age of discovery was revealing with bewildering rapidity—unappropriated areas that beckoned to a nation seeking fresh fields of endeavor. In the conduct of such trade, however, combined action was desirable. The great distances of the new areas from England and the necessity of winning the favor of native rulers as a condition to trade called for large capital outlays, while the hazard of uncharted enterprise clouded the prospect of success. In those days of small individual fortunes if one merchant were to venture his all upon the unknown his failure might spell his ruin. The joint-stock company, however, enabled a large number of investors to share the risk, each with but a fraction of his fortune, and thus to provide a large capital with little danger of ruining anyone.

As a condition to their hazardous ventures the promoters of new companies demanded and secured from the English government royal charters conferring monopolies of the trade with the areas which they proposed to open. Large initial expenditures might be necessary and profits slow; hence the exclusion of outsiders who might reap in the future where the promoters had sown. The conflicting claims of rival states made trading in new areas a thinly disguised maritime war, and if naval protection were provided by the original promoters, even their countrymen who did not bear the expense should not enjoy its benefits. Moreover, a single company was necessary in the trade with native peoples in order to exclude unscrupulous Englishmen who might, by plunder and fraud, give the whole English nation a bad name and turn the undiscriminating natives against English traders of more honorable intent.[14]

As exporters using their own vessels the English merchants were obliged to import return cargoes; hence their opposition to foreign merchants who had previously held the lion's share of the nation's import trade. After a century of conflict with their alien rivals the

[13] W. R. Scott's *The Constitution and Finance of English, Scottish and Irish Joint Stock Companies to 1720* (3 vols., Cambridge, 1910, 1912) is a monumental work.

[14] Alfred C. Wood, *A History of the Levant Company* (Oxford, 1935), explains trading organization and methods of this period. See chapters 1–5.

English merchants succeeded in dislodging them during the reign of Elizabeth. The Hansards at the Steelyard first lost their ancient privilege of paying duties lower than those exacted from English merchants and were excluded from the English cloth trade with the Netherlands (1560). Between 1588 and 1598 they were driven from the Steelyard, which was handed over to the City of London. The leader of this attack was Sir Thomas Gresham, prince of English merchants, founder of the Royal Exchange and friend and adviser of the queen. By 1532 the Flanders fleet had ceased to visit Southampton from Venice, and England's alliance with Portugal enabled her merchants to import oriental wares from Lisbon on advantageous terms.[15]

MERCANTILISM

The transition from medieval to modern economy introduced a new economic philosophy which the eighteenth century designated as mercantilism—not a systematic program but a collection of regulations exhibiting a major trend. Politically mercantilism was an expression of the militant nationalism which arose upon the ruins of feudalism. Its objects were threefold: to achieve an economic self-sufficiency for the nation, to provide maximum profits to influential landowners, manufacturers, and merchants, and to yield an ample revenue to the Crown.

In the opinion of mercantilists the external trade of a country was similar to the business of a private merchant. Imports were analogous to the merchant's purchases, and exports to his sales; the nation's gain consisted in an excess of exports over imports, or in a favorable balance of trade, likened to the merchant's profit. Such excess value should, in part, assume the form of gold or silver money imported into the country.[16]

How was the desired excess of exports over imports to be achieved? Chiefly by fostering the exportation of manufactured goods. In English mercantilism the role of agriculture was to supply raw materials and foodstuffs for the country rather than for exportation; to this end the landowners received favors from the government through high duties on imports of foreign grain (the corn laws) and through acts which restricted the importation of foreign wool. Manufactured goods were preferred as exports because they bore higher prices than

---

[15] A standard work of great value is Sir William Ashley's *An Introduction to English Economic History and Theory* (2 vols., London, 1925). See Vol. II.

[16] A highly valuable recent work, *Mercantilism*, by Eli F. Heckscher (London, 2 vols., 1935), considers Europe as a whole, with special emphasis on England. Very important.

raw materials and hence tended to create a more favorable balance of trade. Consequently, parliament fostered home industries by enacting laws which placed high import duties on foreign manufactured articles (the protective tariff), which prohibited the exportation of needed raw products and semi-finished goods, and which encouraged the importation of raw materials not produced in England. The exportation of manufactured goods was more or less a necessity in the capitalistic scheme of production. Under the wage system and farm tenancy the workers did not receive enough buying power to enable them to purchase all the products of domestic agriculture and industry—for the simple reason that the total prices of all goods included profits to landowners and merchant-employers as well as the wages paid to the workers: the sum of wages did not equal the sum of prices. The profits of employers and landlords therefore represented a part of the product of industry that could not be sold to domestic workers; hence the need of foreign markets for such surplus goods. Similarly, it was undesirable to receive foreign goods of a value equal to that of manufactured goods exported; such imports would have curtailed the English market for English goods, a market that was inadequate to begin with. Hence the government assisted the merchant-employers to enlarge their outside markets by chartering companies which enabled the merchants to act in unison abroad.[17]

For similar reasons England fostered the development of an English-owned merchant marine. If goods were imported in vessels owned by foreigners, England had to pay the freight charges. But if English merchants carried their wares abroad in their own vessels, the foreigner had to purchase English labor and the use of English capital. Foreign-owned shipping was thus regarded as an import, English-owned shipping as an export. Moreover, if merchandise were carried away from England by foreigners in their own ships they would make the profits of selling abroad, but if English vessels were employed they would generally go out laden with goods belonging to English merchants, who would thus reap the profit of selling directly to foreigners. One leading mercantilist wrote: "If the Italian merchants should come hither in their own vessels to fetch our corn, . . . in this case the kingdom should have but ordinarily 25s. for a quarter of wheat . . . , whereas if we carry these wares ourselves into Italy . . . , it is likely we shall obtain 50 shillings . . . , which is a great difference in the . . . vent of the kingdom's stock." As early as 1485 Parliament passed a navigation act requiring that certain articles in

---

[17] A leading French economic historian, Henri Sée, presents mature conclusions in his *Modern Capitalism* (New York, 1928). See chapters 2–5.

English trade should be carried only in English ships. The acquisition of a strong merchant marine also contributed toward the ideal of national independence in that age of small navies when commerce was the nursery of seamen—when England in time of war had to enlarge her fighting forces by pressing merchantmen into the naval service.[18]

A favorable balance of trade and the resulting influx of money were supposed to serve the nation well. As the sinews of war—*nervi bellorum*—money gave assurance of national security, particularly after the armed knights of feudal days had given way to the hired armies of modern times. Money was regarded as the motive power of industry and trade. Since paper currency and bank checks had not yet come into vogue, gold and silver coin had to serve as the common medium of exchange. It was the only convenient form of wealth that could be hoarded without deterioration. To the early capitalists it was peculiarly desirable because they periodically acquired surplus profits which they desired to convert into a form of non-perishable wealth that would be inexpensive to keep. Coined money was also in universal demand; hence the possessor of it could dispose of it at any time, either through loans at interest or through commercial purchases in any quarter of the world where an unusual opportunity for profits occurred. Neither of these benefits could be obtained if the capitalist had to keep his surplus wealth in perishable commodities for which there was not a continuous and general demand. Most important of all, money was indispensable to the new capitalistic mode of production. The hired artisans of the domestic system did not own the products upon which they worked. As specialists in industry they could not conveniently receive their wages in the finished product because they had neither the time nor the facilities for exchanging it for other things they needed. Hence the necessity of some measure of value that would express their share in the finished product; and coined money—or credit instruments based upon it—performed this function better than any other medium of exchange.[19]

Despite England's commercial advantages, there were, prior to 1600, many weak spots in her economy. First of all she did not possess either gold or silver mines, and thus was forced to rely upon trade as her source of specie. But certain branches of her commerce did not conform to the mercantilist creed. From the Baltic coun-

[18] Thomas Mun, *England's Treasure by Forraign Trade* (1664, reprinted Oxford, 1928), is a classic statement of mercantilism.

[19] Jacob Viner, *Studies in the Theory of International Trade* (New York, 1937), an erudite work by a leading authority, discusses the trade theories of mercantilism in chapters 1 and 2.

tries—Sweden, Russia, Poland, and Germany—she obtained naval stores and potash for her cloth industry; from southern Europe she purchased wine, silk, salt, sugar, and dried fruits; from Holland she imported fish; and oriental goods came through Portugal. Each of these trades had certain drawbacks. Each might be cut off unexpectedly by piracy or war, thus depriving the nation of essentials like naval stores, potash, and fish. Again, the commodities were subject to foreign duties and regulations manipulated in the interest of foreign princes or alien merchants at the expense of their English customers. It was also commonly believed that in these particular trades the balance of payments was against England, thereby inducing an outward flow of specie badly needed at home.[20]

In other words England's commerce did not provide sufficient markets in which the products of her own industry could profitably be exchanged for desired imports. Between 1530 and 1635 there was acute unemployment; the nascent industries of the country could not absorb all the workers who had been thrown off the land by the enclosure movement. The oversupply of labor was indicated by a heated contest between the older towns dominated by the gilds and the newly emerging towns patronized by the merchant-employers—a contest for manufacturing supremacy or control of markets not large enough to support all workers. In a futile effort to check the new trend in industry Parliament in 1557 prohibited the manufacture of cloth except in the older, gild-ridden towns. Severe social unrest had flared up in three major revolts between 1536 and 1552 and had threatened the existence of the monarchy itself. Most informed men thought England to be seriously overpopulated; in places a third of the people lived on poor relief. Vagabonds roved throughout the countryside—bands of "idle persons, which having no means of labor to relieve their misery, do likewise swarm in lewd and naughty practices, . . . pestering the land with pestilence and penury, and infecting one another with vice and villainy worse than the plague itself."[21]

Economic Motives of Colonization

Such vagabonds and dissolute persons were regarded as the scum of English society. Above them in the social scale were servants, wage-earners, artisans, tenants, and farm hands. The latter suffered par-

---

[20] Gustav Schmoller, *The Mercantile System* (New York, 1931), an older brief introduction (1884), stresses the role of the state in mercantilism.

[21] E. Lipson, "England in the Age of Mercantilism," *Journal of Economic and Business History,* IV (Aug. 1932).

ticularly as a result of new economic trends, since the government had
passed laws forbidding the farm worker to leave his parish in search
of work and making it impossible for his sons to train themselves for
the skilled trades. The new class of merchant-employers was separated from the wage-earners as by a gulf. Socially superior to the
capitalists were the larger landowners—the gentry or squires; below
them stood the yeomen who owned small farms. The landowners had
stood to gain by the increased prices of agricultural produce but this
boon was offset by the heavy burden of poor relief carried by each
locality through taxes on the land. So crushing was this burden that
the gentry found themselves sinking in the social scale, menaced by
the rising capitalists who sought prestige by buying estates and living
in a style of grandeur which the gentry could not afford. Despising
the *nouveaux riches* as upstarts, many of the gentry thought that
England was "going to the dogs." [22]

The crest of English society was graced by the aristocracy and
nobility—owners of vast estates who were profiting by the enclosure
movement—particularly the new magnates to whom Henry VIII
gave the lands he confiscated from the monasteries. Politically the
landed aristocracy was the most powerful group within the state.
Comprising as it did the House of Lords, it was the bulwark of the
Established Church and the Protestant monarchy—all three having
profited by the seizure of the lands of the Roman Catholic Church.

To each of these classes colonies in the New World made an appeal.
The paupers, vagabonds, and criminals, it was assumed, might find
freedom, escape disgrace, and get a new start in life. Unemployed
artisans and farm hands might secure work with a prospect of independence in the near future. The small landowners who sold out in
England could secure larger estates in America and at the same time
cast off the crushing burden of English taxes. Traders of small capital who were hard pressed in competition with the merchant princes
and monopolistic corporations might earn larger profits in trades not
yet preëmpted. The merchants as a class desired wider markets for
their goods, and the gentry, as well-to-do emigrants, might keep from
being overshadowed in society by their onetime inferiors. Many of
the aristocracy in turn saw in colonies a chance of investing surplus
funds at handsome profits. [23]

[22] A classic of major importance is William Cunningham's *Growth of English Industry and Commerce* (3 vols., Cambridge, 1921–27). Volume II, Part I, on mercantilism is especially recommended.

[23] A work of exceptional excellence is G. N. Clark's *The Seventeenth Century* (Oxford, 1929). See chapters 1–4, 10, 12.

One important group in England occupied a peculiar position. Contrary to the practice of European nobility, by which each son received a title and lands, English law provided that titles and estates should pass only to the eldest sons. This rule of primogeniture thus created a class of landless younger sons, bred with all advantages of social position and culture, men who shared the tastes of the aristocracy, yet educated with the idea that they must shift for themselves. If they desired to live as aristocrats—and they generally did—they had to achieve success in some field of endeavor. Thus while the eldest son remained upon the ancestral estate to raise a large family, the younger sons went afield—into the law or the Church, the army or navy, into business, colonization, and even piracy. The English aristocracy did not remain aloof from the work of the world; it not only preserved the principle of aristocracy in the eldest son but also created a class of ambitious, energetic leaders who carried the traditions of the English gentleman into other walks of life and into all corners of the world.[24]

These various motives for migration and colonization were intensified by a severe economic depression which swept over England between 1620 and 1635. Having its origin in the closing of England's markets on the Continent during the Thirty Years' War, it reached its height in 1629, paralyzing particularly the southeastern and central parts of England, chief seats of the cloth industry. "Overflowing multitudes" could not find work; even the best artisans could not earn more than a bare living; hard-pressed traders resorted to trickery and fraud, exposing the more honorable to unfair competition; and riots moved an observer to write that "it is not certain where this disturbance will end, but things certainly can not go on thus." Bad crops between 1629 and 1633 added to the distress. Food prices soared, causing merchants to refuse to export grain in fear of the people's wrath and forcing the government to prohibit the exportation of beer. Coinciding with the troubles of the Puritans, this protracted depression reinforced their purpose of emigration to America.

All the striving states of Europe embraced the ideas of mercantilism; consequently England could not find relief from her difficulties by compelling foreigners to trade with her on her own terms. Colonies, however, offered a better prospect of adjustment. The second promoter of English colonies, Sir Walter Raleigh, was preëminently a gold hunter who hoped that England might imitate Spain's success

---

[24] Volume I of *The Cambridge History of the British Empire* is the work of leading English and American scholars. It is excellent for imperial themes, but does not stress American conditions. See Vol. I, pp. 22–70, 93–135.

in exploiting American mines. The search for gold largely inspired the settlement of Virginia: an early English play referred to the colony as a place "where gold and silver is more plentiful than copper is with us." Colonies, moreover, would assist England in finding and holding a new route to the Orient—first as exploring bases, later as ports of call. As American resources became better known after 1600 these early interests abated, and colonies thereafter promised to supply England with products she had formerly bought from foreigners—fish, naval stores, tobacco, iron, potash, lumber, furs, wines, dyes, sugar, fruits, and silk.[25]

Such commodities would be produced by England's unemployed turned colonists and paid for with English manufactures. "Now if her Majesty take these western discoveries in hand, and plant there," wrote Richard Hakluyt in 1584, "it is likely that in short time we shall vent as great a mass of cloth in those parts as ever we did in the Netherlands, and in time much more." The colonial demand for English wares would in turn employ the poor at home "who live here idly to the annoy of the whole state," and taxes for poor relief would be correspondingly reduced. England would no longer have to buy her imports from foreigners who refused to take her own exports in payment. As dependencies of the king, colonies, moreover, might be regulated to England's advantage. Their trade would not be burdened by duties imposed by a hostile government or cut off at the edict of a foreign prince in time of war, thereby endangering the supply of needed commodities like naval stores. The long voyages to America would employ a fine fleet of English vessels, and the freights, insurance premiums, and profits would flow into the pockets of the English merchant-shipowners. Every increase of trade would swell the custom duties collected for the king. If the colonies produced commodities in excess of England's needs, the surplus could be reëxported to Europe—another source of profit to the English merchants. In other words, the trade of colonies might be regulated so that the balance of payments would favor England. Reduced purchases from foreigners would check the outflow of specie, while the exports to the colonies would induce a returning stream of money and commodities which would make England the financial center of the world.[26]

[25] William Cunningham's *An Essay on Western Civilization in Its Economic Aspects* (2 vols., Cambridge, 1923) presents the broad views of a great scholar. See chapter 2. A briefer essay, equally stimulating, is Cunningham's *The Rise of Capitalism in England* (Cambridge, 1925).

[26] Sir Charles P. Lucas gives an excellent brief summary of commercial evolution in his *Beginnings of English Overseas Enterprise* (Oxford, 1917).

ENGLAND AND THE ORIENTAL TRADE

Commerce between Europe and the newly opened areas of Asia, Africa, and America harmonized perfectly with the principle of mercantilism which stressed the profits of the merchant class. The products of those continents brought high prices in Europe, and because the native peoples did not have the same economic values as the Europeans they were willing to give liberally of their spices, precious stones, gold, ivory, furs, etc., in exchange for low-priced European wares. Hence the European trader could buy such foreign articles cheap and sell them dear, thereby operating on a wide margin of profit. For this reason the exploitation of new areas was woven into the central pattern of mercantilism.[27]

The first outpost in England of western seafaring was the port of Bristol, whence a trade with the Madeiras and the Azores had been developed late in the fifteenth century. Residing there in 1496 was John Cabot, a naturalized Venetian, Genoese by birth, who believed that Columbus had not discovered the wealthy parts of Asia, which presumably extended far enough toward the east to be reached by crossing the Atlantic. A patent was issued in March to Cabot by Henry VII, authorizing him to search in the east, west, or north for lands as yet unknown to Europeans. Cabot was to enjoy a monopoly of newly opened trade and the king was to receive a fifth of the profits of the voyage. Sailing in March 1497, the explorer gained the coast of America at Nova Scotia, Newfoundland, or Labrador, and returned to Bristol in August, convinced that he had visited Asia. During the following winter merchants of London and Bristol were busy fitting out a fleet of four or five vessels for a second voyage, with the object of erecting a trading post in the Orient. Should England divert the Far Eastern trade to her shores, Bristol would become a great commercial center. What happened to Cabot's second expedition is unknown, save that it failed. England at the time was too poor a state to spend freely upon exploration: Henry VII gave Cabot only £10 for the discovery which initiated England's claim to North America.[28] Yet Englishmen did not relinquish the hope of finding a trade route for themselves. The councillors of Henry VIII urged in 1511:

[27] On the English background, 1485–1558, no work excels James A. Williamson's *Maritime Enterprise* (Oxford, 1913). By the same author: *A Short History of British Expansion* (London, 1930).

[28] For the general reader the best introduction is C. R. Beazley's *John and Sebastian Cabot* (London, 1908). Henry Harrisse's *John and Sebastian Cabot* (London, 1896) is detailed and technical. A careful, precise study is J. A. Williamson, *Voyages of the Cabots . . .* (London, 1929).

". . . when we would enlarge ourselves, let it be that way we can, and to which . . . the eternal Providence has destined us, which is by the sea. The Indies are discovered and vast treasures brought from thence every day. Let us therefore bend our endeavors thitherward; and if the Spaniards and Portuguese suffer us not to join them, there will be yet region enough for all to enjoy."

Not until 1553, however, did England resume the search for a new route in earnest, when a joint-stock company with a capital of £6,000 was organized to open a passage around northern Europe. Three vessels then sailed forth under the command of Sir Hugh Willoughby and Richard Chancellor. Willoughby perished during the following winter, but Chancellor entered the White Sea and proceeded to Moscow, where he met the Russian czar, Ivan the Terrible, whose lands were then closed to European traders except the members of the Hanseatic League. When Chancellor returned to England he brought an agreement with the czar which opened Russia to English trade, via the White Sea, and thus furnished the impetus for the organization of the Russia or Muscovy Company on a permanent basis (1555). Although an active trade resulted, the voyage of Chancellor and Willoughby—together with the expedition of Anthony Jenkinson from Moscow down the Volga and across the Caspian Sea into the heart of Asia (1558–60)—convinced the English that a passage through the icebound Northeast was a frigid illusion.[29]

England's adventures into the frozen North had occurred during the reign of Queen Mary, a most pious Catholic and ally of Spain, who respected the claims of Portugal and Spain (derived in part from the papacy) to the routes which they had opened. After Elizabeth's quarrel with the pope, however, such inhibitions were speedily dispelled, and England no longer hesitated to encroach upon the preserves of her Catholic rivals. In the meantime English fishermen had kept the scene of John Cabot's discovery in view, as they visited the Banks of Newfoundland and returned with codfish to western England. The fishermen of France, Portugal, and Spain were similarly engaged, and many a lively contest among them and the English accompanied the quarrels of their respective states.

When the animosity between England and Spain was deepening, a faithful courtier and friend of the Virgin Queen, Sir Humphrey Gilbert, published in 1576 his *Discourse of a Discovery of a New Passage to Cataia.* Sir Humphrey argued that America was an island,

---

[29] This theme is treated attractively in Sir William Foster's *England's Quest of Eastern Trade* (London, 1933).

around whose northern coasts a water passage might be found which would lead to the Pacific Ocean and the populous parts of Asia.[30] First to act upon this idea was one of England's most intrepid seamen, Martin Frobisher. On his first voyage in 1576 he explored Frobisher's Bay, discovered Baffin's Land, encountered the Esquimaux, and brought home some ore which assayers pronounced rich in gold. This news, along with Frobisher's belief that he had found an open course to India, gave good cause for the second expedition of 1577, in which the queen invested £500. Great was the expectation of gold, now the principle lure. "Considering the greedy desire our country hath to a present savor and return of gain," Frobisher "bent his whole endeavor only to find a mine, to freight his ships, and to leave the rest (by God's help) hereafter to be well accomplished." Not until his third expedition of 1578 had brought back eight hundred tons of ore which proved to be worthless did the golden bubble burst and the original interest in the Northwest passage resume its sway.[31]

The first project of an English colony in America had its origin in the determination of Sir Humphrey Gilbert to realize his dream of a Northwest passage. A settlement at Newfoundland would not only strengthen the English fishery there and provide Sir Humphrey with a vast personal estate; it would also afford a station on the anticipated route to India. Accordingly, he obtained in 1578 a patent from Queen Elizabeth and made two preparatory voyages to America in 1578 and 1583, but without advancing the discovery of the desired route. And yet the belief in the Northwest passage would not die. Between 1585 and 1587 John Davis led three expeditions in the path of Frobisher, penetrating to Davis Straits and Baffin's Bay in the fruitless endeavor to find a track through the intricate network of seas, inlets, and bays. So also the pioneers of the Virginia Colony (1607–10) continued the search, hoping that the rivers emptying into Chesapeake Bay would disclose a continuous passage to the great South Sea.

The recession of English interest in a new route after 1610 followed a memorable event—the launching of the East India Company during the Anglo-Spanish war. Spain had annexed Portugal in 1581, thereby taking charge of the Portuguese monopoly of the oriental

[30] Nellis M. Crouse, *In Quest of the Western Ocean* (New York, 1928), scholarly and well written, discusses the search for a North American passage to the Orient. See chapters 1–4. See also George B. Manhart, *The Search for a Northwest Passage in the Time of Queen Elizabeth* (Philadelphia, 1924).

[31] William McFee's *The Life of Sir Martin Frobisher* (New York, 1928) is the work of a skilled writer who knows the sea.

trade. No longer were the English constrained to respect the claims of Portugal, and the India Company hustled to usurp as much of the established traffic as England's power would allow.

THE ANGLO-SPANISH CONFLICT IN AMERICA

England and Spain adopted conflicting theories of the title to unappropriated lands in the New World. The Spaniards affirmed that prior discovery established the full right of possession, while the English insisted that occupation or utilization was the final test of ownership. Having taken little part in the feats of discovery, England did not propose to be excluded forever from idle lands merely because a Spanish explorer had happened first to sail along their coasts. Similarly the English, after their break with Rome, denied that the pope had authority to grant lands on the basis of discovery alone. The Spaniards, on the other hand, desiring to monopolize the commerce of their colonies, not only excluded English merchants from them on pain of death, but also withheld from England the right to make near-by settlements which might serve as bases for illegal trade.[32]

As the military power of Spain threatened to deprive Elizabeth of her throne, to overthrow the newly established national church, and to impose upon England the rule of pope and Spaniard, the loyal subjects of the queen readily struck at the principal source of that power, the wealth which Spain derived from her colonies. Hatred of Spain thus became a ruling passion among English seamen—that "nation of ravenous strangers which more greedily thirst after the English blood than after the lives of any other people of Europe." The Spaniards in turn perceived that England's strength lay in her foreign trade, and, when war came, did all in their power to ruin it. "The Spaniard," wrote an Englishman in 1588, "knowing the welfare of our country to depend upon the vent of our native commodities, not only forbade the use and bringing [of them] into any part of his dominions, but also then practised with the emperor and his Hanse towns and no less with the Easterly countries to the like effect," seeking to force the English merchant "to surcease his trade" and thereby to reduce a "great number of . . . unemployed to hard extremities." [33]

Through their trade with the Canaries and the Madeiras the sea-

---

[32] William Wood, *Elizabethan Sea-Dogs* (*Chronicles of America*, New Haven, 1918).

[33] An attractive, readable survey is Arthur P. Innes, *The Maritime and Colonial Expansion of England* (London, 1931).

men of western England became familiar with the traffic of the Atlantic which linked Spain and Portugal with Africa and America. Thus in the 1530's William Hawkins visited and traded with Brazil by way of Guinea. Shortly afterward, the English began to prey upon Spanish vessels engaged in American commerce, since Spain did not then protect them with naval convoys, and international law did not restrain the subjects of two nations at peace from acts of violence in distant waters. Such piracy became more pronounced after 1560 and provided the setting for the exploits of the first notorious English sea dog, Sir John Hawkins (son of William Hawkins), who as a boy had voyaged along the African coast in slave-trading vessels. The Spanish assiento then in force limited the number of slaves imported into the Spanish colonies and by raising the prices charged to the settlers offered ideal conditions for smuggling. The younger Hawkins rationalized slavery as a means of Christianizing the natives and justified smuggling as a means of enriching England and impoverishing Spain; his Protestant piety was equaled only by his intense hatred of the Spaniard. Accordingly, in 1562 he went to Sierra Leone in Africa whence he took three hundred Negroes to Haiti and returned to England with ginger, sugar, and pearls, which netted a profit of 60 per cent. He repeated the feat in 1564–65 but on his third voyage of 1567–68 he fell in with a Spanish fleet sent out by Philip II to stop his depredations. Hawkins allowed the Spaniards to enter the port of Vera Cruz, which he then commanded, but their pledges of friendship served merely as a cloak for a surprise attack which cost the lives of scores of Englishmen and sent Hawkins and two of his vessels scurrying away in a narrow escape.[34]

One fellow adventurer with Hawkins was his kinsman, Francis Drake. After the "treachery" of the Spaniards at Vera Cruz, Drake was animated by a consuming hatred of his "perfidious" foes. He now devised a scheme more profitable than smuggling slaves; he would plunder Spanish towns and treasure ships in the Caribbean. To this end he spent over a year (1572–73) in the vicinity of the West Indies and Panama, but found the Spaniards there too well protected to be an easy prey. His imagination then conceived one of the boldest adventures in history. He knew that the Pacific Ocean was a Spanish lake to which no foreigner had penetrated since Magellan's heroic voyage, and that the Spanish settlements and treasure vessels there were quite defenseless. Intent upon reaping "some of the Spaniards' harvest which they got out of the earth and sent to Spain to trouble all the earth," Drake in December 1577 sailed from England with the

[34] J. A. Williamson's *Sir John Hawkins* (Oxford, 1927) is especially recommended.

connivance of the queen and a faction among her statesmen who favored war with Spain, and with the backing of a joint-stock company in which she was a secret investor.

The consummate seamanship of Drake effected a safe passage of the Strait of Magellan in August 1578. As he proceeded northward along the western coast of America he looted unprotected ports and treasure vessels, almost at will, until his ship was ballasted with silver. Fearing to return as he had come lest the Spaniards waylay him, he sailed along the western coast of North America in search of a Northwest passage that would carry him eastward to the Atlantic, but, discouraged by the arctic conditions he encountered, he crossed the Pacific and took the route of the Spice Islands and the Cape of Good Hope to England, arriving in September 1580. The treasure he brought home amounted to £600,000, which netted £263,000 to the queen and profits of 4,600 per cent to his other sponsors.[35]

The Spanish ambassador forthwith demanded that Elizabeth censure Drake and return the plunder to Spain. The wily queen, however, intimated that the Spaniards had brought their troubles on themselves by attempting to exclude her subjects from America, and went aboard Drake's vessel, the *Golden Hind,* at Deptford and knighted him—"the most important knighthood ever conferred by an English sovereign, for it was a direct challenge to Spain and an appeal to the people of England to look to the sea for their strength." [36]

In view of Spain's priority of colonial power and her pretensions to dominion over America, England could realize her dreams of empire only through her prowess on the sea. The Spaniards, who were enchanted with the vision of ruling Europe, regarded their colonies as tributary to that end. They conceived themselves primarily as a military people, destined for glory and conquest through the deeds of their soldiers, whom they exalted above ordinary men. As the most progressive military leaders of the time, they applied their ideas of land combat to warfare at sea. A naval encounter should be a contest of armies on floating battlefields. Thus they filled transports with soldiers drawn up in proud array and sought to destroy the enemy by ramming his vessels, boarding them, and dispatching his soldiers in hand-to-hand fighting. To the Spaniards a sailor was but a menial servant of the soldier. For convoys to their transports they depended

[35] A careful, intensive study is Henry R. Wagner, *Sir Francis Drake's Voyage Around the World* (San Francisco, 1926).

[36] Edward F. Benson, *Sir Francis Drake* (New York, 1927), is a briefer, more popular account, as also is John D. Upcott, *Sir Francis Drake and the Beginnings of English Sea Power* (London, 1927).

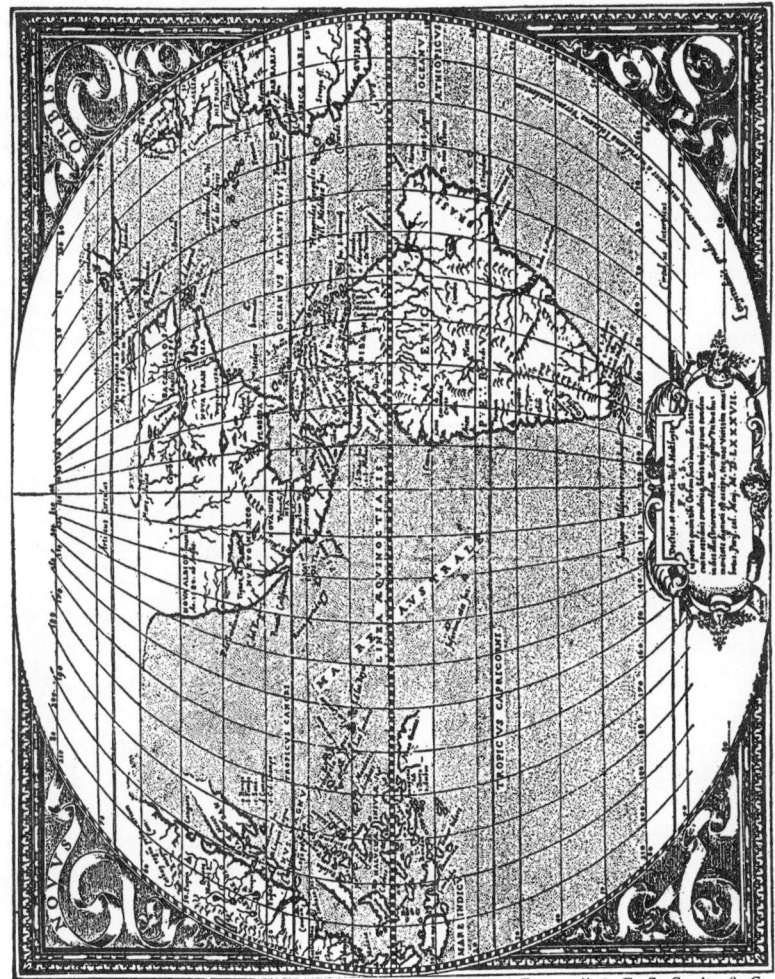

THE NEW WORLD IN 1587

This map, dedicated to Richard Hakluyt, represents the English knowledge of the American continents and of the Atlantic and Pacific oceans after Drake's voyage. It will be noted that there is no hint of the existence of Australia.

upon oar-driven galleys manned mostly by slaves. Such warships were not suited for the long voyages to America because of the strain placed upon the oarsmen and because the reliance upon man power for navigation necessitated the carrying of larger supplies than could be conveniently managed. Above all, a galley could fire only straight ahead—not broadside—and thus could not fight in line formation and attack the enemy from the side or rear.[37]

The art of warfare developed in another direction in England. After she relinquished her ambitions of military conquests in Europe, England had little need of a strong army, since her shores could be invaded only by sea, and consequently the soldier was less esteemed than the sailor. As an old song put it—

> We care not for your martial men
> That do the state disdain.
> But we care for your sailor lads
> That do the state maintain.

During the reign of Henry VIII the basis of English sea power was laid when the sailing vessel was adapted to open fighting. The English "wasps" learned how to fire broadside and were thus able to dart in and out around their enemies, inflicting telling blows and keeping out of the range of floating armies that sought to board them. Moreover, the sailing warship could make the long voyages to the New World with comparative ease, since wind and sails, unlike the galley oarsmen, did not have to be fed en route. The official English navy contained only a score of vessels, but overnight it could be augmented by hundreds of private vessels manned by the hardiest, boldest, most accomplished seamen of the age. The day had dawned when England honored such men:

> As full of peril and adventurous spirit,
> As to o'erwalk a torrent roaring loud,
> On the unsteadfast footing of a spear,

—when Drake decreed that gentlemen at sea should "hale and draw with the mariner" and when Raleigh proclaimed that he "who rules the sea, rules the commerce of the world and to him that rules the commerce of the world belongs the treasure of the world and indeed the world itself."

In 1588 the destruction of Spain's "Invincible Armada," bound to the Netherlands preparatory to an invasion of England, attested the

---

[37] Julian S. Corbett, *Drake and the Tudor Navy* (2 vols., London, 1898)—a vigorous, interesting narrative (important).

superiority of the new naval tactics adopted by the island state. From that day England's mastery of the seas was never long in doubt. With it came her golden opportunity in the West: across the Atlantic the rich prize of colonies beckoned to her, and Spain was no longer able to delay her advance.[38]

[38] Sir John R. Seeley's *The Expansion of England* (London, 1883) was a pioneer work in stimulating the study of English imperialism.

BIBLIOGRAPHICAL NOTE

SECONDARY WORKS: Good brief summaries of economic change in England are J. L. Hammond and Barbara Hammond, *The Rise of Modern Industry* (New York, 1926); and E. A. J. Johnson, *Some Origins of the Modern Economic World* (New York, 1936).

Valuable studies of the economic background of English colonization include Eileen Power, *The Wool Trade in English Medieval History* (New York, 1941); Sylvia L. Thrupp, *The Merchant Class of Medieval London* (Chicago, 1948); E. M. Carus-Wilson, *Medieval Merchant Venturers* (London, 1954); Dorothy Burwash, *English Merchant Shipping, 1460–1540* (Toronto, 1947); T. S. Willan, *The Early History of the Russia Company, 1553–1603* (Manchester, 1956); and John U. Nef, *Industry and Government in France and England, 1540–1640* (Philadelphia, 1940).

James A. Williamson, *The Tudor Age* (New York, 1953), gives a comprehensive review of the background of early English expansion. J. B. Black, *The Reign of Elizabeth* (New York, 1936), is an outstanding survey.

James A. Williamson, *The Age of Drake* (New York, 1938), is the best summary for the general reader. Rayner Unwin, *The Defeat of John Hawkins* (New York, 1960), is a vivid narrative of the beginnings of the Anglo-Spanish conflict.

SOURCES: On English economy the best collection is R. H. Tawney and Eileen Power (eds.), *Tudor Economic Documents* (3 vols., London, 1924). A smaller collection, A. E. Bland, P. A. Brown, and R. H. Tawney (eds.), *English Economic History, Select Documents* (London, 1914), devotes Parts I–II to the period before 1650. The Everyman's Library edition of Hakluyt's *The Principal Navigations, Voyages, Traffiques and Discoveries of the English Nation* (8 vols., London,) is readily accessible. A more convenient selection from Hakluyt is E. J. Payne and C. R. Beazley (eds.), *Voyages of Elizabethan Seamen* (Oxford, 1907). Vilhjalmur Stefansson, *The Three Voyages of Martin Frobisher . . .* (2 vols., London, 1938), brings together seven contemporary records, related data, an outstanding essay on exploration in Northern America before 1580, and a biography of Frobisher.

V

The English Promoters of Colonies

As IN the other states of Europe, so in England the course of internal political development determined the nature of colonization. The English government did not itself perform the task of planting colonies abroad but rather left it to private initiative. Prior to the reign of Henry VII (1485–1509) the monarchy had been weakened by the destructive War of the Roses, so that the work of restoring the royal authority and of pacifying the country occupied the first Tudor sovereign. Then followed the English Reformation and the protracted religious strife, absorbing the energies of Henry VIII (1509–47), Edward VI (1547–53), Mary Tudor (1553–58), and Elizabeth. More important, perhaps, as a deterrent to the participation of the government in colonization was the financial status of the monarchy. The English sovereigns did not attain absolute power of taxation but were obliged to act with the consent of Parliament, and the funds voted by it barely met the most pressing needs of domestic pacification and defense. Henry VII, who favored English expansion overseas, spent less than £300 on exploration during his whole reign.

When England's economic progress, sea power, and domestic tranquillity warranted expansion, the government fell under the control of the Scottish kings, James I and Charles I. Their reigns proved to be a time of rising prices when they could barely make the royal ends meet, and consequently they were forever seeking new sources of revenue. The intense struggle over taxes between king and Parliament after 1603 indicates that the English king was not free to spend money upon every project which caught his fancy. The checks which Parliament placed upon the royal income therefore necessitated that private persons supply the funds if exploration and colonization were to be carried forward in the New World.[1]

Such individuals, however, would not embark upon an untried

[1] Every student should become familiar with the extremely important work of Charles M. Andrews, *The Colonial Period of American History* (4 vols., New Haven, 1934–38), which affords the best account of promotional activities of English colonizers. See particularly Vol. I, chapters 1–4, 13, 15–18, Vol. II, chapters 6, 8, and Vol. III, chapters 4–5, 7.

venture without the backing of the government. The theory of English exploration was that the title to newly discovered land and political jurisdiction over it were vested in the sovereign. Thus the promoters of colonies had to seek a royal grant of land and the right of governing it in a manner conducive to their own profit. They also needed commercial privileges in or monopolies of the trade of the region upon which they spent their money. Moreover, they desired exemption from certain laws—those, for instance, which forbade an Englishman to leave the country or prohibited the exportation of various commodities required in a new colony. Such rights and privileges were conferred by the sovereign in a royal patent or charter. The preferred method was to obtain letters of patent under the Great Seal, in which case the Secretary of State directed the Attorney-General to prepare the document in coöperation with the agent of the promoters, whereupon it was engrossed upon the patent roll. Inasmuch as this was a costly business, involving much red tape and fees or bribes to officials and clerks, the men who obtained charters had to possess wealth, social position, and influence at court. By means of such grants a marriage was effected between private enterprise and government patronage.

PIONEERS OF ENGLISH COLONIZATION

The Englishmen of the age of Elizabeth lived in spacious days when the national spirit of daring and adventure attained its greatest heights. Intense patriotism, self-confidence, and faith in their destiny inspired their leaders to unprecedented achievements. The vitality and originality of Elizabethan England found their fullest expression in Shakespeare, whose uniquely imaginative mind encompassed the world of his own day and ranged the epic heights of past times. From the vantage of

> This sceptered isle
> This earth of majesty, this seat of Mars,
> This other Eden, demi-paradise,

he and his contemporaries viewed the panorama of life. They perceived, as if suddenly revealed, the splendors of the earth—its strange peoples, remote kingdoms, and infinitely varied resources—and strove to conquer for honor, wealth, and fame.[2]

The peculiar English trait of blended insularity and cosmopolitan-

---

[2] Walter Raleigh's *The English Voyages of the Sixteenth Century* (Glasgow, 1906) is a brief discussion from the literary point of view.

ism characterized the work of a humble clergyman, Richard Hakluyt of Oxford. Like so many other Elizabethans, Hakluyt would make the whole world tributary to England. When nearly every breeze brought home a vessel with tales of new lands and wonders beyond sea, Hakluyt conceived the idea of systematically publishing this record, and in 1582 printed his first work, *Divers Voyages Touching the Discovery of America.* As the English "press-agent of adventure," he continued to issue the narratives of "the principal voyages of the English nation," which disclosed the tremendous sweep of English enterprise and familiarized his countrymen with every quarter of the globe. The poet Drummond celebrates his labors in verse:

> Thy voyages attend
> Industrious Hakluyt,
>   Whose reading shall inflame
>   Men to seek fame,
> And much commend
> To aftertimes thy wit.

Hakluyt also wrote a discourse in favor of planting colonies in North America, stressing their value as markets, as producers of commodities needed by England, as a boon to English navigation, and as sources of private profit. Above all, they might serve as bases for plundering the Spaniards in America, on the theory that as the "Spanish empire falls to the ground," the Spanish king "shall be left as bare as Aesop's proud crow," for "if you touch him in the Indies, you touch the apple of his eye." [3]

Closely associated with Hakluyt was a group of Devonshire men, whose leader, Sir Humphrey Gilbert, is rightly called the father of English colonization. In 1578 Queen Elizabeth issued a patent to Gilbert, conferring upon him the exclusive right "to inhabit and possess at his choice all remote and heathen lands not in the actual possession of any Christian prince." Thus equipped Sir Humphrey sailed in September 1578, for America, but was carried out of his course by a gale to the West Indies, where an unhappy encounter with the Spaniards forced him to return. Again, in June 1583, he ventured forth, to Newfoundland, with five vessels and two hundred and fifty men. After taking possession of the island in the name of the queen, he left a small band of servants on its bleak shore and set forth to discover a better site. The dismal setting dismayed the colonists, who

[3] George B. Parks, *Richard Hakluyt and the English Voyages* (New York, 1928) is excellent. E. G. R. Taylor has a splendid introductory sketch in her edition of *The Writings and Correspondence of the Two Richard Hakluyts* (printed for the Hakluyt Society, 2 vols., London, 1935).

soon dispersed to parts unknown.[4] Gilbert himself was lost at sea, in September 1583.

> He sat upon the deck,
> The Book was in his hand;
> "Do not fear! Heaven is as near,"
> He said, "by water as by land."

After the death of Gilbert his rights to America passed to his half-brother, Sir Walter Raleigh, politician, courtier, adventurer, and favorite of the queen. In 1584 Raleigh received a royal patent almost identical with that granted to Gilbert in 1578. Hakluyt's narratives had already awakened in Sir Walter an ardent interest in the New World, and he consequently commissioned the Oxford compiler to prepare his discourse of 1584 on "western planting." Raleigh's love of the sea, which had been kindled when he was a boy by tales of the mariners of southwestern England, was reinforced by his hatred of Spain, his devotion to the queen, and his passion for gold. The Newfoundland misadventure of Gilbert turned Raleigh's gaze toward more hospitable shores—toward the warmer climate and verdant slopes to which the Spaniards had naturally gravitated. Convinced that England was the best of all possible worlds, he believed that an English colony should be a miniature England, duplicating the class distinctions and aristocratic tone of society which, as a landed gentleman, he dearly cherished.[5]

Raleigh sponsored three expeditions to the island of Roanoke, off the coast of present-day North Carolina. The first party, in 1584, explored the country and returned with such favorable reports that Sir Walter rose to new heights in the favor of Queen Elizabeth, who honored Raleigh, herself, and the new land by naming it Virginia. The second venture of 1585–86, under the command of Sir Richard Grenville and Ralph Lane, and which had aspired to plant a colony, taught Raleigh that a settlement composed of gold hunters, sword polishers, and seekers for a Northwest passage, all dependent upon England for supplies, could not survive. His interest in permanent colonization, however, was already attested by the presence in the expedition of a chronicler, Thomas Hariot, and a painter, John White, who prepared sketches of the Indians, animals, and plants of the new

---

[4] A standard, scholarly biography is William G. Gosling's *The Life of Sir Humphrey Gilbert* (London, 1911). David B. Quinn, *The Voyages and Colonizing Enterprises of Sir Humphrey Gilbert* (2 vols., London, 1940), a definitive work, presents a factual essay and the principal documentary evidence.

[5] Of the older biographies, William Stebbing, *Sir Walter Raleigh* (Oxford, 1891), is the best.

country. The failure of his first colony convinced Raleigh that a better site should be selected northward in the Chesapeake Bay, inasmuch as Roanoke Island was exposed to severe storms, although Lane had described it "as the goodliest and most pleasing territory of the world," whose natives were "most courteous and very desirous to have clothes." In his modified plans—indicative of the capacity of the English to adapt themselves readily to new situations which was to assure their later success as colonizers and to transform emigrants from Englishmen into Americans—Raleigh prepared to make the colony self-sustaining, a normal community of families engaged in diversified economic pursuits. Accordingly the third expedition of 1587 brought the first English women and children to America. The colony was to be ruled on the aristocratic principle by a governor and a council of twelve gentlemen and to be held together by the cement of military discipline.[6]

With John White in command, the third expedition arrived at Roanoke in July 1587, where the colonists remained, contrary to Raleigh's wise instructions. White lacked the force of will necessary for the government of a band of people suddenly released from traditional restraints, and made the mistake of returning to England for supplies after only a month's stay in the colony. He found England astir with preparations for warding off the Spanish invasion; Raleigh, the court, and all the great English seamen were preoccupied with that paramount task and the colony could not be reinforced. White did set out with two vessels in 1588 but Spanish pirates at Madeira drove them back to England. It was not until 1591 that he again set foot on Roanoke Island, where he had left as pledges of his return his daughter and his granddaughter, Virginia Dare, the first English child born in America. But the colonists had vanished and no authentic trace of them has ever been found.[7]

THE FOUNDERS OF VIRGINIA

The early experiences of Raleigh taught him that the expense of planting a colony was too great to be borne by one man. Hence in 1589 he enlisted the aid of a group of London merchants and investors, selling to them the privileges of trading with his projected colony. However, this group was not active until Raleigh in 1603 was

[6] The best modern biography is Willard M. Wallace, *Sir Walter Raleigh* (Princeton, 1959).

[7] David B. Quinn (ed.), *The Roanoke Voyages, 1584–1590* (2 vols., London, 1955), combines a narrative of Raleigh's Virginia with a collection of sources and critical comments on technical problems.

convicted of treason and stripped of his colonizing rights. Then in
1604 England made peace with Spain, but failed to secure from the
Spaniards a recognition of England's right to take part in the exploitation of the New World. Many of the ardent anti-Spanish Protestants
in England now sought a peaceful means of penetration into the Spanish sphere of influence in America. Accordingly the men to whom
Raleigh had granted concessions organized a new colonizing venture
and in 1606 obtained a charter from James I.

This charter authorized two groups of English promoters to plant
settlements in America. One group was domiciled chiefly in Plymouth,
the other in London. Each obtained a grant of 10,000 square miles of
land. The Plymouth group received the exclusive right to colonize
between the forty-fifth and forty-first parallels; the London group
alone could operate between the thirty-eighth and thirty-fourth parallels. The intervening space, between the forty-first and thirty-eighth
parallels, was open to occupancy by either group, provided however
that the two colonies should be at least a hundred miles apart.[8]

In 1607 the London promoters established at Jamestown what became the first permanent English settlement in the area of the United
States. Before 1609, however, this colony accomplished but meager
results, due to a variety of causes later to be explained. The promoters in London felt that the colony needed additional resources, and accordingly they obtained a new royal charter in 1609. This enlarged
vastly the territory of the colony. Its eastern boundary was to extend
two hundred miles north and two hundred miles south of Old Point
Comfort. Rather vaguely the grant said that the colony was to extend
"west and northwest" to the Pacific Ocean. Moreover, the patent of
1609 incorporated the promoters into a joint-stock company. Fifty-
six London companies and 659 persons were listed as charter members. The Virginia Company of London immediately took over the
Jamestown colony and developed it until the company's dissolution
in 1624.

Men of wealth and power dominated the Virginia Company and
colony during this formative stage. There was, for instance, Sir
Thomas Smith, perhaps the greatest merchant prince of the day, chief
of English expansionists, a veritable embodiment of the commercial
motives of colonization. Sir Thomas began his career with a large
capital inherited from his grandfather, a founder of the Muscovy
Company, and from his father, who had amassed a fortune while serving as collector of the queen's revenue. The younger Smith in turn

[8] E. P. Cheyney, "Some English Conditions surrounding the Settlement of Virginia,"
American Historical Review, XII (Nov. 1907).

was an organizer of the Levant Company in 1581, a principal figure
and onetime governor of the Muscovy Company, a founder and first
governor of the East India Company, and treasurer and a moving
spirit in the Virginia Company. His career thus indicated the growing
solidarity of merchant capitalism, anticipating the modern age of interlocking directorates. Politically he belonged to the anti-Spanish party
led by the Earl of Essex, and when Essex was executed in 1601 Sir
Thomas was sent to the Tower where he remained a prisoner until
the accession of the ally of Essex, James I. The interests of Smith in
the Levant and East India Companies focused his attention upon the
search for an American passage to the Orient: as a merchant he strove
to enlarge the whole domain of English commerce. Thus the motives
of personal profit and hatred of Spain found expression in the work of
this prominent builder of the Virginia colony.[9]

A much greater figure, socially, than Smith was Robert Rich, second Earl of Warwick, nephew of the Earl of Essex and head of a
powerful clan of relatives and Puritan merchants of London. Forsak-
ing the pleasures of the court, Warwick embraced the strenuous life,
"for his spirit aimed at the more public adventures, planting colonies
in the western world." His early interests centered in privateering depredations upon the Spaniards, and perhaps he was mainly interested
in Virginia as a base for such attacks. His fleet of vessels resembled
a private navy, ever ready to strike at Spain. His speculative ventures
also included the Council for New England, the Bermuda Company,
the East India Company, and the Guinea Company of 1618. His ship
the *Treasurer* carried the first cargo of Negro servants sold in Virginia. The details of Warwick's vast interests were in the hands of his
kinsman, Sir Nathaniel Rich, the business agent of the family. After
1619 Warwick and Rich, with Sir Thomas Smith, headed a faction
in the Virginia Company which regarded colonization as a form of
profitable exploitation. As insiders at court these leaders had benefited
by and therefore favored the commercial monopolies granted by the
sovereign to various trading companies and their capitalistic promoters.

Of somewhat different stamp was a fourth leader of the Virginia
Company, Sir Edwin Sandys—"a religious gentleman," son of a Puritan Archbishop of Canterbury, high in the social order, educated at
Oxford where he had studied under Richard Hooker, author of the
famous *Ecclesiastical Polity*. As a young man Sandys had observed at

[9] Edward Keble Chatterton's *Seed of Liberty* (Indianapolis, 1929), published also
as *English Seamen and the Colonization of America* (London, 1930), is a splendid
study of early relations between England and America.

Geneva the Calvinistic institutions of government (somewhat republican in form) and considered them as almost divinely ordained. He became an ardent foe of James I, opposing divine right of kings with the Puritan doctrines of covenant between prince and people and of a fundamental law limiting the powers of government. The vigorous opposition of Sandys to private commercial monopolies was also in keeping with his Puritan faith. From the time he drafted the Virginia charter of 1609 until the end of the Virginia Company, Sandys played a prominent role in its affairs, leading a faction which came to blows with the Smith-Warwick party—a strife which eventually destroyed the company itself.[10]

Sir Edwin Sandys found an ally in a nobleman of vast wealth, the Earl of Southampton, a Catholic born but converted to Protestantism, probably by Sandys. Southampton, as a friend and ally of Essex, had been imprisoned in the Tower. Following his release by James I he had failed to realize his ambition for great political influence, due to his impetuosity and rashness; hence he busied himself with colonizing schemes and with patronizing the drama, particularly the work of Shakespeare. Bitterly hostile to Spain, he regarded the Virginia colony as a weapon of warfare against the ancient enemy. As treasurer of the Virginia Company, 1620–24, he fought the battle with Sandys against Smith and Warwick.

THE COUNCIL FOR NEW ENGLAND

Through the fisheries of Newfoundland, certain adventurers and merchants in western England—at Bristol and Plymouth especially— kept in touch with the region of Sir Humphrey Gilbert's ill-fated colony. Three notable voyages were made after 1600 to what is now New England. Expeditions commanded by Bartholomew Gosnold in 1602, by Martin Pring in 1603, and by George Weymouth in 1604 were financed by Bristol merchants or the Earl of Southampton. They disclosed good prospects in New England of a lucrative fishery, a trade in furs with friendly natives, and fine resources of virgin timber. Such favorable accounts appealed particularly to two West country leaders of means and influence.

Sir John Popham, a Somerset lawyer and chief justice of England, believed that England's paupers might profitably be sent to build settlements in northern America. The other leader, Sir Ferdinando Gorges, governor of the port of Plymouth and onetime friend

[10] A. P. Newton, *The Colonising Activities of the English Puritans* (New Haven, 1914), emphasizes the interest of Puritans in regions other than New England.

of the Earl of Essex, had heard of Weymouth's voyage to the coast of Maine, which news, he said, "must be acknowledged the means under God of putting on foot and giving life to all our plantations." Gorges and Popham acted as a link connecting the government and interested promoters in western England. Largely through the influence of Popham the charter of 1606 was issued. This authorized a group of Plymouth patentees to colonize in the northern part of "Virginia." In 1607 they sent out an expedition commanded by George Popham, brother of Sir John, and by Raleigh Gilbert, son of Sir Humphrey, who made a settlement at the mouth of the Kennebec River. However, the sufferings of a terrible winter, 1607–08, coinciding with the death of Chief Justice Popham, caused the abandonment of this first attempt to colonize New England.[11]

During the next thirteen years Gorges sent trading and fishing vessels to the coast of Maine, advertised the region, and persuaded other West countrymen to join in the work of exploitation. Captain John Smith, of earlier Virginia fame, voyaged along the northern coast in 1614 and named the country New England. Then he entered the service of the Plymouth promoters, made a trading voyage for them, and in 1616 published his *Description of New England*—a glowing tribute to the region and its fishery. Soon afterward came news that a plague had nearly wiped out the Indians residing along the New England coast between the Penobscot River and Narragansett Bay. This calamity promised to open the northern area to peaceable settlement by the English.

In 1620 the Plymouth promoters reorganized and secured a royal charter which established the Council for New England—a limited body of forty members, representing the nobility rather than the merchants and more in the nature of a land company than a trading corporation. Chief among its leaders were Warwick, Southampton, Rich, and Gorges. The Council received title to all land between the fortieth and the forty-eighth parallels, from sea to sea, together with a monopoly of the trade and fishery of the territory and seas adjacent, as well as the right of selling licenses to traders and fishermen operating in this imperial domain.[12]

So dominant in the Council for New England was Sir Ferdinando Gorges that the Council has been called a "gorgeous affair." Its signifi-

[11] An excellent, scholarly history of these events is H. S. Burrage, *The Beginnings of Colonial Maine* (Portland, 1914). See chapters 1–8.

[12] On enterprise before 1628 see Charles K. Bolton, *The Real Founders of New England* (Boston, 1929).

cance lies in the fact that it possessed the title to all New England and that directly or indirectly it created the initial land grants of five colonies—Plymouth, Massachusetts, New Hampshire, Maine, and Connecticut. The original policy of Gorges, to sell licenses to English fishermen who fished in the waters of the company's grant and to use the money for promoting settlement, provoked a bitter contest between the Council and the West country fishermen, who not only objected to the monopoly, but also feared that rival fishing settlements in New England would destroy the industry as carried on from English ports.

Foremost among the associates of Gorges was John Mason, Anglican, ardent royalist, naval officer, adventurer, colonizer, businessman, and friend of the Duke of Buckingham, that shining favorite of Charles I who was eventually assassinated at Mason's house in Portsmouth. Between 1611 and 1621 Mason had been active in exploring and colonizing Newfoundland, where he served as governor after 1615. Upon Mason and Gorges the Council for New England in August 1622 conferred an extensive domain extending sixty miles inland between the Merrimack and the Kennebec Rivers. After making, in 1623, a futile effort to develop and govern its territory, the Council lapsed into inactivity. It was unable to obtain sufficient capital or settlers; between 1624 and 1629 the energies of Gorges were absorbed by wars involving England with France and Spain; and the Council thereafter could not enforce its rights or control the fishermen and settlers who were then pouring into New England. During the early 1630's occurred a heated rivalry between Gorges and the Puritan settlers of Massachusetts over land and fishing rights. Since the Council for New England was unable to cope with the Puritans, Gorges enlisted the aid of Charles I, seeking to substitute his potent authority for that of the moribund Council. In order to facilitate action by the king against the Puritans, the Council in 1635 surrendered its charter and ceased to function.[13]

In 1629 the Mason-Gorges grant of August 1622 was divided. Mason received the land between the Merrimack and the Piscataqua Rivers, which he now called New Hampshire, and Sir Ferdinando retained the area between the Piscataqua and the Kennebec, thereafter called Maine. Mason, who became a member of the Council for New England in 1632, received from it a final confirmation of his title in

[13] James P. Baxter's *Sir Ferdinando Gorges and His Province of Maine* (3 vols., Boston, 1890) is the standard authority. Volume I is a biography; Volumes II and III are documents.

1635, and Gorges obtained in 1639 a royal patent which made him the proprietor and governor of Maine.[14]

THE PILGRIM FATHERS

While the great men of London, Plymouth, and Bristol were busy with projects of promotion, a little band of humble country folk were meeting at the village of Scrooby in Nottinghamshire to worship in defiance of the Established Church. Their leader, William Brewster, village postmaster and bailiff of Scrooby Manor—an estate belonging to the archbishopric of York—had been educated at Cambridge University, and afterward pursued a lively interest in theology, history, and religious poetry. He was described as "of a very cheerful spirit, very sociable and pleasant among his friends." The pastor of the Scrooby Separatists, John Robinson, was a mild, spiritual man who exemplified the Christian virtues of modesty, charity, and love of truth. A young farmer, William Bradford, devout reader of the Bible and later a student of many languages, shared the tolerant spirit of the group. "It is too great arrogance," he said, "for any man or church to think that he or they have . . . sounded the word of God to the bottom." Bradford later told the trials of the Pilgrims in his *History of Plymouth Plantation*, written in a straightforward, dignified manner that reveals the honesty and sincerity of his nature and his familiarity with the Geneva version of the Bible.[15]

Not long had the Scrooby group been active before they were molested by their neighbors, who regarded them as "freaks." Jeered at and insulted at home, and investigated by the church authorities of the province of York, the Pilgrims felt so exposed to attack that they decided to move to Holland, "where they had heard was freedom for all men." During the years 1607–09 they left in small bands, by stealth, for the law of England forbade a subject to leave the country without the king's consent. Arriving at Amsterdam they found so much religious strife among the Dutch that they moved to Leyden. Here they lived peaceably, working as laborers and "enjoying much sweet and delightful society and spiritual comfort together in the ways of God." But despite such felicity the exiles were not satisfied. They preferred to live under their "natural prince" and

---

[14] Charles W. Tuttle, *Life of Captain John Mason* (Boston, 1887) includes important documents.

[15] Of the many accounts of the Pilgrims see Ronald G. Usher, *The Pilgrims and Their History* (New York, 1918), Daniel Plooij, *The Pilgrim Fathers from a Dutch Point of View* (New York, 1932), and Arthur Lord, *Plymouth and the Pilgrims* (Boston, 1920).

feared that their children would be assimilated by the Dutch. So hard was their lot that their children had to work at a tender age and "their bodies bowed under the weight of the same, and became decrepit in their early youth." Others of their children were corrupted by the Dutch, "getting the reins from their neck, and departing from their parents. Some became soldiers, others took upon them far voyages by sea, and others some worse courses, tending to dissoluteness and the destruction of their souls." [16]

And thus a part of the Leyden congregation decided to migrate to Virginia. Through the influence of Sir Edwin Sandys they obtained permission to settle on the Virginia Company's lands and to enjoy the status of an independent community. James I promised that they would not be molested if they lived peaceably, although he did not guarantee protection or toleration. But his decision nevertheless opened the way to the settlement of English America by dissenters and is therefore one of the great landmarks in American history. By means of an agreement with London promoters the Pilgrims obtained capital for the emigration, and in 1620 they made the historic voyage from Delft Haven via Southampton and Plymouth, England, to the New England coast, where they began their settlement of Plymouth at Christmas time. Only a minority of the Leyden group voted to leave Holland. Since it had been agreed that the pastor, John Robinson, should serve the majority, he had to remain behind, while Brewster and Bradford led the Pilgrims who came to America in the *Mayflower*.

Landing, apparently by accident of weather, within the territory of the Council for New England rather than within that of the Virginia Company, the Pilgrims were obliged to obtain a land grant from the Council. This was done by the London promoters in 1621, when a patent was issued to John Pierce acting in their behalf. The leaders in Plymouth purchased this title in 1629–30, but never received a royal charter from the king. The little colony retained its separate identity until it was merged with its powerful neighbor, Massachusetts, in 1691. Life at Plymouth flowed along smoothly and uneventfully in the short and simple annals of a rural community. The Pilgrims' sojourn in Holland had left few marks upon their ways of life; only their custom of marriage by a civil magistrate can be traced to the Dutch.[17]

[16] Raymond P. Stearns, "The New England Way in Holland," *New England Quarterly*, VI (Dec. 1933).
[17] C. M. Andrews, *The Fathers of New England* (*Chronicles of America*, New Haven, 1919), chapters 1–3.

The Genesis of Massachusetts

About the year 1622 a group of businessmen in Dorchester, England, decided to transform the English fishery as carried on in American waters. Previously annual fishing fleets had gone out from England in the late winter, returning at the close of autumn. The Dorchester men proposed to erect a fishing settlement in New England where the fishermen would reside throughout the year, selling their catches to trading vessels from England. This plan was designed to cut the labor cost by eliminating the idleness of the fishermen on the outward and inward voyages. Accordingly the Dorchester men formed a company, secured, perhaps, a land grant from the Council for New England, and in 1623 established a fishing settlement at the present site of Gloucester, Massachusetts. But profits were not forthcoming and in 1626 the Dorchester promoters withdrew. The settlers, under the leadership of one Roger Conant, removed from Gloucester and founded the town of Salem, "the peaceful."

High in the confidence of the businessmen of Dorchester was their pastor, Master John White, a moderate Puritan, philanthropist, organizer of poor relief—a true patriarch who presided over his parish as a father over his family. In close touch with the Dorchester Company, the good pastor believed that its settlement might become a retreat for the worthy poor and a base of missionary work among the Indians.[18] Hence when the company expired he appealed to many influential Puritan gentry and merchants of London, and in 1628 a group of them formed the New England Company to take over the defunct Dorchester concern. The new company obtained through the Earl of Warwick a huge land grant from the Council for New England. This was made while Sir Ferdinando Gorges was away at war, and he soon denounced the grant as improperly obtained and as conflicting with previous grants to his son Robert and to John Mason. The Puritan leaders of the New England Company needed a stronger sanction for their claim, and so they appealed to Charles I, who granted them a royal charter in March 1629, incorporating them into the Massachusetts Bay Company. Their land grant, reaching from three miles north of the Merrimack River to three miles south of the Charles River, and extending from the Atlantic to the Pacific, cut the heart out of the territory of the Council for New England. By what means this unusual encroachment upon the Council's land was effected is unknown.

The Massachusetts Bay Company, like its two immediate predeces-

[18] *John White*, by Frances Rose-Troup (New York, 1930), is a definitive biography.

sors, concerned itself at first with maintaining the Salem settlement as a commercially profitable venture. However, during the year 1629 two parties developed within the company. One, composed of moderate Puritans content to stay in England, preferred to operate the company for profit. The other party, headed by John Winthrop and consisting of dissatisfied Puritans who wished to escape the repression of Charles I, conceived that the company might be used as a Puritan shelter and as an instrument for building a godly kingdom or "a garden of the Lord" in the New England wilderness.[19]

John Winthrop, father of Massachusetts, leading Puritan of early America, well-educated country squire of the Manor of Groton, Suffolk County, was an exceptional leader of rare stability, judgment, power of decision, and force of character. Early in life he had made a covenant with the Lord whereby he pledged himself to shun the sins of vanity, sloth, pride, and worldliness. Sorely distressed by events in England in 1629, and dismayed by the harsh conditions which decreed that "children, servants, and neighbors, especially if they be poor, are counted the greatest burdens, which if things were right, would be the chiefest earthly blessing," he conceived that a Puritan colony might contribute to "the comfort and increase of the body of Christ, whereof we are all members." Aristocratic in temper and scornful of the *nouveaux riches* who were overreaching their social superiors, he felt in his commanding soul that if he remained in England "that talent which God hath bestowed upon him for public service is like to be buried." If life should be hard in New England, man must "learn with Paul to want as well as to abound"; the Lord had once "carried the Israelites into the wilderness and made them forget the flesh-pots of Egypt." [20]

A second leader of the Winthrop party was Thomas Dudley, steward of the Earl of Lincoln, a great Puritan noble. Although Dudley's English career had been undistinguished, he had demonstrated good business ability and had acquired a modest fortune. Austere, domineering, cold, intolerant, and imperious, he was the strictest of the strict, a strong believer in the right of government to coerce men in religion, and withal something of a scholar and poet. His last poem urged:

> Let men of God in courts and churches watch
> O'er such as do a toleration hatch.

---

[19] S. E. Morison's excellently written *Builders of the Bay Colony* (Boston, 1930) re-creates the Puritans as human beings. See chapters 1–3.

[20] The best formal biography is Robert C. Winthrop, *Life and Letters of John Winthrop* (2 vols., Boston, 1864, 1867). Volume I to 1630.

In August 1629 twelve members of the Winthrop party signed the Cambridge agreement, in which they pledged to migrate to New England provided that the government and charter of the Massachusetts Bay Company might be transferred with them to the colony. Immediately afterward the company at London voted that this should be done. The charter did not prescribe that the governing body of the company should be domiciled in England—an omission so unusual for the time as to create suspicion that the framers of the charter intended originally to transfer the government of the company to New England. The insistence of the Winthrop group that the transfer be made is more easily explained. The Puritans who agreed to migrate hoped to create a new religious commonwealth, and hence they demanded independence and self-rule. The Massachusetts Bay Company was an open corporation; any person could join simply by purchasing a share of stock. This meant that the company in England might easily fall into the hands of non-Puritans. Thus if the power over the Massachusetts colony remained with the company in England, the enemies of the Puritans might gain control and destroy the godly commonwealth which Winthrop envisaged in the New World. But such a calamity could not befall if the charter and governing body were in possession of Winthrop and his friends.[21]

With the charter transfer authorized, Winthrop was elected governor of the company and Dudley deputy-governor. In 1630 they led the first large migration to Massachusetts and founded Boston and several adjacent towns. The good tidings of success soon induced many ministers and devout Puritans to follow. Foremost among these was Master John Cotton, sometime fellow of Emmanuel College in Cambridge University and vicar of St. Botolph's church in Boston, Lincolnshire—which latter post he is said to have obtained when the mayor of Boston broke a deadlock in town council by unwittingly voting twice. The fame of Cotton as a persuasive preacher and his Puritan proclivities set the ecclesiastical authorities after him and in 1633 he fled from old Boston to new Boston. At once he achieved a commanding position and it was soon observed that whatever he preached in the pulpit became the law of the colony.[22]

High-minded, devout, and sincere as these Puritans certainly were, they can hardly be considered pioneers in the narrow sense. They

[21] Augustine Jones, *The Life and Work of Thomas Dudley* (Boston, 1900), is sympathetic toward its subject.

[22] Cotton Mather's *Magnalia Christi Americana* (2 vols., Hartford, 1820) contains many laudatory sketches of early New England worthies. For John Cotton, see Book III, chapter 1.

did not act until the technique of colonization was well developed. They studied their task in the light of much accumulated knowledge and they brought to bear upon it ample means and remarkable caution, foresight, and mastery of practical detail. None of the leaders had held important offices in England or had exercised much influence there. If it was heroic to face the wilderness so also it required courage for Puritans to remain in England and fight the battle against Charles I and Laud. James Truslow Adams suggestively points out that the migration of the Puritans is in keeping with the later American tendency to escape the complex problems of an old society by resorting to a simple and primitive frontier environment. But such a resort to the primitive is evidence of man's faith in his ability to create from new materials a better world.

PROMOTERS OF THE 1630's

High in the councils of the English Puritans was an impecunious nobleman of great personal ambition—Lord Saye and Sele. In the 1620's he had been the parliamentary strategist or "oracle" of the Puritans in opposition to the Stuart kings. Finding this theater of achievement closed by the personal rule of Charles I, Lord Saye turned to colonization, primarily to enhance his waning fortune. His chief ally, Lord Brooke, was a less active Puritan but nevertheless highly valued for his immense wealth. These two noble lords, with other prominent Puritans including Warwick, established in 1630 the Providence Company, intending to colonize three islands in the Caribbean, thus reflecting the anti-Spanish bias that had long found vent in privateering exploits against Spain. The Massachusetts Puritans were urged to settle under the Providence Company, but they decided that the get-rich-quick environment of the West Indies would be destructive to moral character. Both Saye and Brooke in turn offered to settle in Massachusetts, provided a titled ruling aristocracy could be created there with themselves at the head. This proposal was rejected, "with thanks."

In 1632 Saye and Brooke, with nine other leading Puritans, obtained from Warwick or the Council for New England a large tract of land about the mouth of the Connecticut River. Here in 1635 they established a small settlement called Saybrook which was intended as a retreat for the settlers of the Providence Company, should that venture fail, and as a means of preëmpting more New England soil for the Puritan cause. Under the command of John Winthrop, Jr.,

Saybrook survived as an independent settlement until it was purchased by the colony of Connecticut in 1644.[23]

The success of Massachusetts inspired two other Puritan worthies
to found in 1638 the little colony of New Haven, which became in
1664 the western part of Connecticut. Theophilus Eaton, London
merchant, and John Davenport, London divine, had been boyhood
friends at grammar school in Coventry, England. Both were of well-
to-do and established families. In early life their paths diverged,
Eaton going to London as a merchant's apprentice to become an independent trader to the Baltic, member of the Eastland Company,
and perhaps onetime agent of Charles I at the Danish court. Like
other good Puritans Eaton did not believe in drinking toasts, and, as
tradition relates, was once rescued from this offense by divine interference when, just as he was called upon to drink to the Danish king,
the latter had a fit. Davenport had gone to Oxford and then to London, where he affiliated with Puritans and fell in again with Eaton,
now the wealthiest parishioner in Davenport's church, St. Stephen's.

Davenport came to grips with Laud, took part in organizing the
Massachusetts Bay Company, then left his church and went to Holland, where he became so deeply embroiled in theological disputes
that he was not allowed to preach. Returning to England in 1637 he
found Eaton ready to establish a colony in New England which
would enable him to share the profits of American trade. To Davenport the plan opened an outlet for his suppressed energies. Outspoken, hearty, commanding, vigorous, and aggressive, he felt the
need of the free air of America and the opportunity of creating a new
commonwealth over whose destinies he could preside.

These two strong leaders gathered about them a band of colonists
and embarked for Boston in 1637. Spending the winter there in spiritual concert with the Bay Puritans, but spurning entreaties that they
remain in Massachusetts, they sailed in the following spring and
formed their independent settlement, New Haven.[24]

Illustrative of the diversity of factors making for English expansion is the genesis of Maryland. Its chief founder, Sir George Calvert,
owed his rise in life largely to a warm friendship with James I, by
whom he was knighted and made Secretary of State. A cultivated
gentleman, holder of two Oxford degrees, and an accomplished
courtier, Calvert shared the prevailing enthusiasm for colonial ex-

[23] C. M. Andrews, *Our Earliest Colonial Settlements* (New York, 1933), contains
six admirable essays. See chapters 1–3, 6.

[24] Isabel M. Calder's *The New Haven Colony* (New Haven, 1934) is the best
account of its subject. See chapters 1–3.

ploitation. Between 1620 and 1627 he endeavored to develop a colony at Newfoundland, which he named Avalon, but when he visited it in 1627 he was disheartened by the illness of his settlers and by the long winter "from October to May." Meanwhile, he had become an ardent and avowed Roman Catholic and as a result had to vacate his office of Secretary of State—a loss for which James I compensated him by raising him to the Irish peerage as Baron Baltimore. When secretary he had appeared "as an honorable, well-intentioned man, courteous to strangers, full of respect toward ambassadors, zealously intent upon the welfare of England, but by reason of these good qualities, entirely without consideration or influence." [25]

Seeking a better site than Newfoundland for a province, Baltimore visited Virginia in 1629. The unoccupied land of the colony then belonged to the king, but Charles I had promised the Virginians that they should retain their territory as defined in the charter of 1609. The authorities at Jamestown, aware that Baltimore had designs upon their land, asked him to take the oath renouncing the pope's authority over the English Church. As a conscientious Catholic he refused and had to leave, which was precisely what the Virginians had intended. But this stratagem accomplished little, because in 1632 a royal charter to Baltimore carved out of the lands of Virginia a new colony named Maryland in honor of Queen Henrietta Maria. Its bounds were: at the north, the fortieth parallel; at the west, the meridian running through the western fountain of the Potomac; at the south, the southern bank of the Potomac; and at the east, the Atlantic Ocean.

Before the charter of 1632 was issued, Baltimore died, and the province was granted to his son Cecilius Calvert, second Baron Baltimore. Thus to the father belongs the credit of conceiving and initiating the enterprise, while to the son fell the task of actual colonization. Both had in mind the creation of a refuge for English Catholics and the extension of their faith in America. They also anticipated that a vast new estate would enhance materially the fortunes, dignity, and prestige of the house of Calvert.[26]

PROMOTERS OF THE AGE OF CHARLES II

The Civil War and the rule of Cromwell put a halt to the founding of new colonies in North America, but with the restoration of

[25] William H. Browne's *George Calvert and Cecilius Calvert* (New York, 1890) is brief, informed, sympathetic toward the Calverts.

[26] Clayton C. Hall in *The Lords Baltimore and the Maryland Palatinate* (Baltimore, 1904) gives a good brief résumé in chapter 1.

the Stuarts occurred another wave of colonizing activity. In 1660 Charles II returned to the throne of his fathers, and immediately drew about him a host of devoted royalists, aristocrats, and believers in hereditary right—most of them outraged by the Puritan upheaval and now hastening as to a feast after long years of privation.

During the ensuing twenty-five years were laid the English foundations of six of the thirteen colonies—the two Carolinas, New Jersey, New York, Pennsylvania, and Delaware. It was an age of robust growth of English industry, shipping, and trade. Charles II himself did all in his power to extend the territorial and commercial dominion of his subjects. A divine-right Catholic at heart who might play fast and loose with his subjects' wishes in religion, court politics, and morals, he never betrayed the material interests of the country. His marriage to Catherine of Braganza, sister of the King of Portugal, added Bombay in India and Tangier in Africa to the English empire. He chartered two new commercial companies of primary importance— the Royal African Company and the Hudson's Bay Company, and in these he took a deep personal interest. His brother, James, Duke of York, a Roman Catholic of autocratic temperament, was equally active in these practical affairs. The two royal brothers appreciated fully the value to England of her rising colonies, and labored diligently to make them profitable to the Crown.

Surrounding the king was a small ring of favorites and statesmen who imposed upon England an aristocratic rule. They served as members of the Privy Council and on royal committees for colonies and trade, belonged to and shared the profits of the great monopolistic companies, presided over their own large estates, and received gladly the numerous titles and honors conferred upon them by the king. Under their guidance the House of Lords was restored; the Church of England, with bishops, prayer book, and ritual, was reëstablished; the Puritans were fully suppressed; other dissenters were persecuted; a subservient Parliament was retained by dispensing with elections; the Acts of Trade and Navigation were passed with the purpose of giving English merchants a monopoly of the commerce of the empire; and huge territories in the New World were bestowed by the king as an earnest of his gratitude to men who had served him during the dark years of exile.

The first new colony created by Charles II was the province of Carolina. Among the devoted followers of the king in England in 1660 was Sir John Colleton, recently a planter in the English sugar island, Barbados. That colony had originally been settled by small farmers but the introduction and spread of sugar culture had led, about 1650, to the growth of large plantations manned by Negro slaves. The small farmers, finding themselves relentlessly squeezed by the large producers, were acutely discontented. Colleton knew that on the American mainland between Virginia and Spanish Florida lay an immense country occupied only by Indians, where there was room for every hard-pressed planter of Barbados. Even though the region was claimed by Spain and though it had failed to attract English settlers by reason of its inaccessibility and reputed unwholesomeness, Sir John believed that it could be used for both the relief of Barbados and the profit of enterprising promoters. Moreover, by 1660 independent emigrants from Virginia had gone south to what is now Albemarle Sound and were making a success of an infant settlement there.[27]

One of Colleton's associates was Anthony Ashley Cooper, a landed gentleman, once an owner of a plantation in Barbados and now in 1660 an expert on colonies and trade. In 1671 he became Lord Ashley; later, as the Earl of Shaftesbury (after 1672), he achieved fame as the founder of the Whig party in England. Another man associated with Colleton in 1660 was Sir William Berkeley, governor of Virginia, who contributed much information about the Carolina country and his confidence in the success of a colony there. Since none of these men had large influence at court and since Cooper was actually mistrusted by the royalists (he had sided with the Puritans in the Civil War), they were obliged to secure the aid of more powerful men. In this they succeeded admirably. The most powerful ally they obtained was Edward Hyde, Earl of Clarendon, Lord High Chancellor, father-in-law of James, Duke of York, and grandfather of the later queens, Mary and Anne. Clarendon had opposed Cromwell, had gone into exile, and returning with Charles II had become a titan of the new regime, chief author of the Clarendon Code, and an ardent patron of colonization. Equally prominent was General George Monck, Duke of Albemarle, who more than any one man effected the return of Charles II. Something of a popular idol, Albemarle was also a closefisted businessman who was not averse to profiting by his influence at court. A lesser figure, the Earl of Craven, companion of the aunt of the king, had plenty of money to invest in new projects which caught his fancy. John, Lord Berkeley, brother of Sir William, had served the Duke of York as governor of his exiled

---

[27] See again C. M. Andrews, *The Colonial Period of American History*, Vol. III, chapter 5. For sketches of English leaders who did not migrate see the *Dictionary of National Biography* (ed. Leslie Stephen and Sidney Lee, 63 vols. and index. London, 1885–   ).

household, raising funds in the hour of Stuart adversity. So also, Sir George Carteret, "the richest man in England," as governor of the Island of Jersey, had sheltered Charles II in 1649 and had defended the island against the Puritans in 1653. Both Lord Berkeley and Carteret were rewarded with offices, lands, titles, and charter membership in the Royal African Company, organized in 1660 with the Duke of York as its head.

To these eight men—Albemarle, Carteret, Ashley, Colleton, Craven, Clarendon, and the two Berkeleys—Charles II granted on March 24, 1663, the regal domain of Carolina, extending from sea to sea between the thirty-sixth and the thirty-first parallels. A second charter, of June 30, 1665, moved the southern boundary to the twenty-ninth parallel and the northern boundary to the now famous line, 36° 30'—a change which brought the existing settlement at Albemarle Sound within the limits of Carolina. As in the case of Maryland, the Carolina charter sliced a large strip of land from the territory given to Virginia in 1609.

Uppermost in the minds of the Carolina proprietors was the purpose of making money from their huge province; their interest was that of landlord or real-estate promoter rather than that of merchant. Like Lord Baltimore they intended to sell part of their lands, to keep and develop large estates for themselves, and to collect quit-rents from all purchasers or receivers of individual tracts. In developing the province they endeavored to produce commodities not yet raised in England or her dominions—products such as silk, wine, olives, raisins, currants, almonds, and naval stores, for which there was a ready demand and for which England had to resort to foreigners, paying for them presumably with specie in violation of the current principles of a favorable balance of trade. Socially, the proprietors hoped to duplicate the English order of nobles, yeoman farmers, tenants, and dependents, instituting in the American wilderness the class distinctions and feudal allegiance to superiors so strongly entrenched at home. The chosen model was the large English estate owned by a titled magnate who governed his dependents in a patriarchal fashion. All tendencies toward the growth of a "numerous democracy" such as the proprietors identified with Puritan New England and the turmoils of the Puritan Revolution in England were to be vigorously suppressed.[28]

For these various reasons the proprietors concentrated upon the southern part of their province, where they founded in 1670 a settle-

[28] A scholarly, thorough, detailed biography is Louise F. Brown, *The First Earl of Shaftesbury* (New York, c. 1933).

ment at old Charles Town, relocated at Charleston in 1680, nucleus of the colony of South Carolina. The northern settlement at Albemarle Sound, though taken under the proprietors' control, was allowed to develop much in its own way. Prior to 1668 all the proprietors took an active part in Carolina affairs, with Colleton perhaps the most influential, but afterward Lord Ashley was the dominating member of the group, and he impressed his ideal of a landed aristocracy strongly upon the early history of Carolina. With the imagination of an empire builder he visualized a chain of supplementary settlements—at Charles Town, at Albemarle Sound, on the Edisto River, and in the Bahama Islands. Fearful that the latter might be used by the Spaniards as a base for attacking Charles Town, he obtained from Charles II on November 1, 1670, a grant of the Bahamas to himself and to the five remaining Carolina proprietors. Upon these islands also he endeavored to impose a landed aristocracy of the English pattern.

Of equal importance with the creation of Carolina was the grant on March 12, 1664, to the Duke of York of the region between the Connecticut and Delaware Rivers, occupied at the time by weak, scattered Dutch settlements which were conquered by the English in the following August. This grant severed at the Connecticut River the territory of Massachusetts, supposed by the charter of 1629 to extend to the Pacific Ocean. From his newly created domain the Duke of York on June 24, 1664, separated the land lying between the Delaware and the Hudson Rivers and between the fortieth parallel at the north and Cape May at the south, and conferred it upon his faithful friends and servants, Sir George Carteret and John, Lord Berkeley, naming it New Jersey in honor of Carteret's loyal services as governor of the Island of Jersey. Berkeley and Carteret valued this province for its potential profits, which they expected to realize through a large-scale real-estate business. The Duke of York retained the remainder of his grant of March 12 as his personal principality or estate, and accordingly its name was changed from New Netherland to New York. The duke's territory also included Long Island, but he did not make good his claim to the Connecticut River as the eastern boundary of his province.

Berkeley retained his share of New Jersey only ten years—until 1674, when he sold it for £1,000 to John Fenwick, acting for a fellow Quaker, Edward Byllinge. This sale marks the entrance of the Quakers upon the stage of colonial promotion. In 1673 George Fox had returned from a tour of America full of zeal for building there a Quaker commonwealth. It is possible that Byllinge was acting for the

Quakers as a whole, now intent upon realizing Fox's ideal. At any rate, in 1676 Carteret consented to the division of New Jersey into East New Jersey, which he retained, and West New Jersey, which he recognized as the property of the Byllinge Quaker interest. Then in 1692 Byllinge's rights (having been acquired in 1687 by Dr. Daniel Coxe) were purchased by a body of proprietors called the West New Jersey Society. East New Jersey, on the other hand, was purchased in 1680 from Carteret's estate, and soon passed into the hands of a numerous group of proprietors and business partners, a number of whom were Friends. Although after 1682 the Quaker interest in both parts of New Jersey was strong, they were not reunited into a single province until 1702.

The intent and spirit of the Quakers as colonizers found fullest expression in the work of William Penn, liberal, mystic, philosopher, and man of practical affairs.[29] Educated at Oxford, at a Huguenot academy in France, and in the law at Lincoln's Inn, London, he was exposed to the main intellectual currents of his time. His precocity and yearning for an independent spiritual life resulted in his expulsion from Oxford for worshipping with a group of nonconforming seekers for new truth. Through his father, Sir William Penn, admiral of the royal navy and friend of the Duke of York, the younger Penn occupied a high station in society. Fearful that his son's youthful radicalism would block his advancement in the world, the father had sent him to France to acquire the manners and tastes of a gentleman who would adorn the court. Then the young William went to Ireland to manage his father's estates but while there came in touch with a Quaker preacher, Thomas Loe, and was converted to the faith of the Friends. Numerous quarrels between father and son ensued, but the breach was always closed, due largely to their mutual respect and honorable conduct. After 1667 the younger Penn, in close touch with George Fox, sought by direct political action in England and by missionary tours in Holland and Germany to extend and to realize his Quaker ideals of peace, toleration, and liberty. As a result of his outspoken condemnation of injustice and oppression he was several times arrested and imprisoned in England. On the whole he remained steadfast in his faith, demonstrating in his voluminous writings and personal conduct a commendable purpose of integrating thought and conviction with the practical concerns of life.

Penn inherited in 1670 his father's estates and a claim to £16,000

[29] The best of the earlier accounts is Sydney G. Fisher, *The True William Penn* (Philadelphia, c. 1899).

owed to the admiral by the king. His wealth thereupon enhanced his influence among the Quakers and he was soon able to grapple with the material difficulties of colonization. In 1675 he entered the West New Jersey enterprise and became one of its proprietors and probably prepared the plans for the principal Quaker settlement at Burlington in 1677. On March 4, 1681, he received from Charles II the province of Pennsylvania, named at the insistence of the king to honor Penn's father, and granted in consideration of the debt which the Crown had never paid to the Penns. Bounded on the east by the Delaware River, on the north by the forty-third parallel, on the west by a line five degrees west of the Delaware, and on the south by the fortieth parallel, Penn's imperial domain was the largest, most valuable estate in America ever granted to an individual by the Crown.

After the founding of Pennsylvania by settlers sent out in 1681 under Penn's deputy, William Markham, Philadelphia soon became one of the four principal towns in English America. Penn visited his colony in 1682, at which time he also received from his friend, the Duke of York, the territory of present-day Delaware. This he immediately united with Pennsylvania proper, and so it remained for twenty years until it was created into a separate colony in 1704. Penn, however, retained his rights as proprietor and governor of the little province.[30]

Like the Carolina proprietors and the Duke of York, Penn hoped to obtain a revenue from land sales, rents, and his personal estates in his colony. But perhaps he was more interested in his "Holy Experiment"—his design for a commonwealth in which men should live in peace, brotherly love, toleration, sobriety, and charity, under an orderly, mild, and equitable government that would confer the twin blessings of liberty and property. "Colonies," he wrote, "are the seeds of nations, begun and nourished by the care of wise and populous countries; as conceiving them best for the increase of human stock, and beneficial for commerce." His ideas, particularly those on religious freedom, entered the main stream of American thought. "No man, nor number of men upon earth," he wrote, "hath power or authority to rule over men's consciences in religious matters." He may not have been a brilliant or original thinker, but his sincerity, benevolent nature, and courage cannot be questioned. "He was a man of

---

[30] There are three excellent recent biographies: Bonamy Dobrée, *William Penn, Quaker and Pioneer* (Boston, 1932); Arthur Pound, *The Penns of Pennsylvania and England* (New York, 1932); and Mabel R. Brailsford, *The Making of William Penn* (London, 1930). The last is devoted to Penn's struggles before 1680.

great abilities, of an excellent sweetness of disposition, quick of thought, and ready utterance. . . . He may without straining his character be ranked among the learned good and great."

With the exception of the Pilgrim fathers, all the promoters who launched colonies from an English base were men of means, position, and political influence—aristocrats, landed gentry, or well-to-do merchants who shared the English philosophy of aristocracy and class distinctions. Their expectations of private profit from colonies induced them to extend to America the social and economic inequalities which they took for granted in England. By virtue of commercial monopolies and personal estates they intended to utilize the services of dependent classes to augment their own wealth. One result was the planting of the seeds of aristocracy in the American wilderness. Another was the extension from England to the colonies of the conflict between privileged and non-privileged groups. The genesis of class distinctions and group conflicts in America will become apparent as we survey the methods employed in founding colonies.

BIBLIOGRAPHICAL NOTE

Secondary Works: Louis B. Wright, *Religion and Empire* (Chapel Hill, 1943), interprets English expansion in terms of a national spirit animated by religious zeal. Henry F. Howe, *Prologue to New England* (New York, 1943), describes early voyages along the New England coast. Richard A. Preston, *Gorges of Plymouth Fort* (Toronto, 1953), is a careful, scholarly biography. C. K. Shipton, *Roger Conant* (Cambridge, 1944), sketches the career of a Massachusetts pioneer. John E. Pomfret, *The Province of West New Jersey* (Princeton, 1956), and John E. Pomfret, *The Province of East New Jersey* (Princeton, 1962), are the best studies of the origin of New Jersey. Catherine O. Peare, *William Penn* (Philadelphia, 1957), is a good introductory study. E. W. Kirby, *George Keith* (New York, 1942), relates the story of the Quakers before 1700.

Useful studies of English backgrounds are: A. L. Rowse, *The Expansion of Elizabethan England* (New York, 1955); Harold Hume, *The Life of Sir John Eliot, 1592 to 1632* (New York, 1957); Catherine D. Bowen, *The Lion and the Throne* (Boston, 1957)—a life of Sir Edward Coke; and Allen French, *Charles I and the Puritan Upheaval* (Boston, 1955).

Sources: G. P. Winship has edited *Sailors' Narratives of Voyages along the New England Coast, 1524–1624* (Boston, 1905). William Bradford, *Of Plymouth Plantation* (ed. S. E. Morison, New York, 1952), is a good version. An attractive collection is Stewart Mitchell (ed.), *The Founding of Massachusetts* (Boston, 1930). Some of Penn's writings appear in an Everyman's Library edition as *The Peace of Europe.*

VI

The Founding of Colonies

THE English colonies did not just happen; they were products of careful business planning and management and of considerable expenditures of money. Settlers had to be transported three thousand miles across the sea and equipped with utensils, clothing, seed, tools, building materials, livestock, arms, and ammunition. Moreover, food had to be provided until a settlement could become self-sustaining. The cost of transporting and establishing a colonial family certainly amounted to several hundred dollars, as calculated today.

From the point of view of colonization three classes of people in England may be distinguished. First, there were moderately well-to-do members of the middle class who were willing to migrate to America and able to pay their own expenses. Secondly, there was a group of nobles and prosperous merchants and lesser people who had surplus funds to invest in colonies, but did not choose to leave England. The third group consisted of the mass of the workers, tenants, paupers, and unemployed who might be compelled to emigrate or be persuaded that they could improve their lot in America, but who lacked the means of paying their passage thither. The ordinary English laborer did not earn in a year enough to meet the cost of emigration; in fact his earnings barely sufficed for a mere subsistence, so that savings for this class were impossible. Since the members of the group first mentioned were not sufficiently numerous to people a colony, one problem of settlement reduced itself to this: how might the poor who were willing but unable to go, be financed by the well-to-do who were willing to invest but unwilling to go? [1]

This problem was solved in various ways. Two English colonies, Virginia and Massachusetts, were founded by chartered companies whose funds were provided by investors and used in the first instance to equip, transport, and maintain the colonists. By a second method, employed in the settlement of New Haven and of Massachusetts after 1629, well-to-do emigrants brought over their families and their

[1] Attention is again called to C. M. Andrews, *The Colonial Period of American History*, Vol. I, chapters 3–4, 13, 15–18; Vol. II, chapters 6, 8; and Vol. III, chapters 5, 7.

property and in addition paid for the transportation of personal servants. The method of founding Plymouth resembled that used for Virginia, with this exception—that the investors in England who paid the costs of the migration were not incorporated by a royal charter. The other colonies—New Hampshire, Maine, Maryland, the Carolinas, New Jersey, and Pennsylvania—belonged to proprietors who as landlords advanced or endeavored to advance out of their own resources the funds for settling tenants and servants upon their feudal estates. This method was also employed earlier by Gilbert and Raleigh.[2]

Inasmuch as the promoters of colonies depended upon the exploitation of the land as a principal source of profit, their relations with their servants and tenant colonists were shaped by the tenure upon which land was held from the king. Theoretically all land in England and her dominions belonged to the king, who granted individual estates to his subjects, exacting feudal dues and services from the recipients, who were called his tenants-in-chief or vassals. Prior to the year 1290 the tenant-in-chief had the right to "subinfeudate," that is, to grant his estate to a third person, exacting from him services and payments similar to those which were owed to the king by the tenant-in-chief. However, the statute *quia emptores* (1290) prohibited further subinfeudation by providing that if a tenant-in-chief granted his land to a third person he lost all his rights and the new holder paid his services and dues directly to the king. But in spite of the fact that prior to 1600 subinfeudation had long been illegal in England, it was revived and extended to the colonies by the charters issued after 1630.

Technically both the proprietors and the chartered companies with colonial grants were tenants-in-chief of the king. However, they paid next to nothing for their lands. The charters did reserve to the king a tenth or a fifth of all gold and silver discovered in the colonies, but none being found, none was paid. Otherwise the payments were trifling. Lord Baltimore, for instance, had to give the king each year two Indian arrowheads and William Penn had to contribute yearly two beaver skins. Regular payments of value were not required of the proprietors because the land was practically worthless when given to them by the king and because the prospects of profit from the colonies

---

[2] *The South in the Building of the Nation* (12 vols., Richmond, c. 1909–13) comprises a series of articles, some by leading Southern historians. Volume I, *History of the Southern States*, contains a good article on Virginia's beginnings by J. A. C. Chandler; on Maryland by B. C. Steiner; on North Carolina by R. D. W. Connor.

were so uncertain that the promoters would not have acted if they had been obliged to make large yearly contributions to the crown.[3]

The early charters created two types of land tenure. The Virginia Company, the Massachusetts Bay Company, and the Council for New England did not receive the right to subinfeudate or to establish manors. These three companies might grant to individuals the lands they had received from the king, but when that was done the company was not overlord of the landholder and could not exact feudal services and dues. The grantee thus became a tenant, not of the company, but of the king. On the other hand the charters of Maryland, Maine, Carolina, and Pennsylvania conferred upon the proprietors the right to subinfeudate and to create manors and new forms of land tenure. In the proprietary colonies, therefore, the proprietor (as tenant-in-chief of the king) might grant lands, exacting from the recipients various feudal services and payments and also conferring upon them the power to govern the tenants on their estates. Hence a principle of feudal land law which had been abandoned in England since 1290 was applied to five of the American colonies.

THE PROCURING OF CAPITAL

Inasmuch as prospective settlers could not emigrate without money, the prerequisite of colonization was the procuring of capital. Both Gilbert and Raleigh met the problem by using their own funds and by soliciting aid from friends to whom they promised American estates and from merchants to whom they offered commercial concessions. Raleigh, who derived a large income from monopolies, licenses, and offices bestowed upon him by Queen Elizabeth, claimed that he spent £40,000 on Virginia without earning a penny on the investment. The conflict with Spain then diverted much capital to war and privateering, but with the advent of peace in 1604, surplus funds rapidly sought more normal sources of profit. Moreover, the East India Company had turned out to be a financial success. Not only did its example stimulate new colonial-commercial enterprises, but the profit-makers of the company acquired excess funds which needed additional channels of investment.

The Virginia patentees of 1606 intended to duplicate the activities of the East India Company, and therefore conceived of their James-

---

[3] Viola F. Barnes, "Land Tenure in English Colonial Charters of the Seventeenth Century," in *Essays in Colonial History Presented to Charles M. Andrews . . .* (New Haven, 1921).

town settlement more as a trading post than as an agricultural colony. They advanced the capital for the support of their gold-hunting, Indian-trading settlers, expecting to derive profits, not from land sales, but from trade. The early failure at Jamestown arose in part from the fact that the backers in England, a small number of patentees, did not have enough capital. Accordingly the charter of 1609, by creating a joint-stock company, invited all English investors to participate in the enterprise. Every purchaser of a share of stock (the par value of which was £12 10s., or the cost of equipping and transporting one settler) became an adventurer in the company, entitled to dividends and to a land grant in Virginia. The company used its capital to send over settlers to labor as its employees for seven years. Any surplus they produced went to the company, which also carried on all trade with the colony. At the end of the seven years, the improved lands were to be divided among the company members, each receiving a hundred acres for every share of stock which he owned.[4]

The Virginia Company of 1609 was launched amidst an active campaign in which letters, pamphlets, and handbills were widely distributed, and the result of which was a large number of initial members. But afterward the company, due to its inability to make profits, met a stubborn sales resistance from the investors it solicited. Accordingly, a third charter issued by James I in 1612 authorized the company to raise money by lotteries, which were spoken of thereafter "as the real and substantial food" by which Virginia was nourished.

In 1618 the Virginia Company sank to its lowest ebb, financially. The peculations of Samuel Argall, its governor in the colony, had dissipated most of its property there. Lacking funds in its treasury in England, the company adopted a new policy. The initial seven-year period having expired, the members of the company were entitled to their hundred-acre tracts. Some of the leading members had invested sums ranging from £200 to £500, and hence were entitled to estates varying from fifteen hundred to four thousand acres. Moreover, each member was promised a second tract equal to the first, provided he settled colonists upon the first within a given time. This situation induced the company to authorize its members to form sub-companies or associations to which it granted large plantations, and these associations of wealthy "insiders" thereupon assumed the burden of financing new settlements. Between 1619 and 1624, seventy-eight patents were granted to such associations. The largest estate thus

---

[4] For a detailed chronicle of the founding of Virginia see Alexander Brown's *The First Republic of America* (Boston, 1898).

created, called Smyth's Hundred, contained 200,000 acres. Its proprietors sent out 310 settlers in May 1620. To a similar estate, Martin's Hundred, came 250 colonists in 1619. However, such plantations were only well begun when in 1622 a destructive Indian massacre wiped out most of their servants and tenants and spread havoc and ruin. The associations in England later sold their plantations to individuals, who thereafter supplied the capital for further development.[5]

The Virginia Company attracted capital to the colony by another method—that of granting lands to well-to-do families and individuals who would colonize at their own expense. The famous "head-right" system, introduced in 1618, gave fifty acres to any person who transported to the colony a settler who remained three years. Such head-rights became the chief means of acquiring land in Virginia during the seventeenth century. The system was later extended so that each family head received fifty acres for every member of his family who emigrated and for every servant he brought into the colony. As a result, merchants and shipmasters who imported settlers, as well as families who came at their own expense, were compensated with land for their capital outlays toward peopling the colony.

The Pilgrims, in founding Plymouth, resorted to methods of financing similar to those employed by the Virginia Company. They formed an agreement with seventy English "adventurers" who contributed £7,000 toward the cost of the migration. An unincorporated joint-stock company was formed with shares of a par value of £10. The Pilgrims and other settlers who were sent over agreed to work for the company as its servants or employees, although the emigrants were also members of the company. After seven years of such corporate labor, the goods and lands of the company were to be divided among the members according to the shares of stock held by each. Plymouth, like Virginia, failed to produce money profits for the English investors, and accordingly in 1624 they refused to contribute further and soon afterward withdrew from the enterprise.[6]

The first precursors of the Massachusetts Bay Company consisted of 120 investors of the Dorchester Company who advanced a total capital of £3,000, which was used to found the fishing settlement at

[5] Herbert L. Osgood's *The American Colonies in the Seventeenth Century* (3 vols., New York, 1904, 1907) is one of the great works of American history—the best older study of the origins of political institutions. See Vol. I, pp. 3–135; Vol. II, chapters 1–8, 10.

[6] Lyon G. Tyler's *England in America, 1580–1652* (New York, 1904—*American Nation* series) is a useful compilation, though not outstanding. See chapters 1–4, 7, 9–12.

Cape Ann. When the Dorchester group failed to make a profit and was replaced by the New England Company in 1628, some of the Dorchester men received stock in the new company and were designated as the "Old Planters." The New England Company operated the settlement, now at Salem, selling new stock and sending out colonists who as servants or employees were supposed to produce profits for the investors. Then in 1629 the New England Company became the Massachusetts Bay Company. The decision of the latter in August 1629 to transfer its charter and governing body to Massachusetts created an unusual situation. The great majority of the members of the company did not intend to migrate. Those who did intend to go did not care to be employees of the company and work to produce profits for the stockholders in England. Winthrop therefore suggested that the company contribute most of its existing assets to the emigrants and exempt them from future payments to the members who proposed to remain in England. But the latter felt that they were entitled to some return on their investments. Finally a compromise was arranged. The stockholders agreed to write off two-thirds of the value of their shares and receive four hundred acres of land in Massachusetts for each £50 of their adjusted claims. Moreover, the investors received four concessions: (1) a monopoly of the business of transporting settlers to the colony, (2) one-half of the beaver trade, (3) a monopoly of the manufacture of salt, and (4) the privilege of trading with the colony through a "magazine." However, these concessions were to endure but seven years and were so hedged about that they could not be used to exploit the colonists. By virtue of this arrangement the members of the company who remained in England relinquished their claims to money dividends from the colonists, and consequently the company, when moved to Massachusetts in 1630, did not function there as a profit-making body.[7]

After the decision to transfer the charter was made in 1629, investors in England did not contribute additional capital except for the purchase of new "common stock," the proceeds of which were to be put to public uses, such as building churches in the colony, providing for its defense, and transporting poor families thither. The subscribers to this stock were promised a two hundred-acre tract of land in Massachusetts for each £50 contributed. Such contributions were made in part for philanthropic reasons and in part by London merchants who hoped to trade with the colony.

From these arrangements it appears that the Massachusetts Bay

---

[7] A good study of the business angle of colonization is Frances Rose-Troup, *The Massachusetts-Bay Company and Its Predecessors* (New York, 1930).

Company after 1629 did not have any funds to spend except the proceeds from the common stock; consequently it could not promote much additional settlement. The great migration of the 1630's was therefore financed by individual Puritans who bore the expense of transporting their own families. They sold their English estates and transferred the proceeds to New England. Thus the sale of Winthrop's estate netted £4,200. Another leader, John Haynes, brought some £7,000 into the colony. A later estimate revealed that the early emigrants invested £400,000, besides initial expenditures of £192,000 for the transportation of settlers, for the purchase and shipment of livestock, and for supplies of food, glass, iron goods, and arms and ammunition. These financial arrangements, which freed the Massachusetts settlers from debts to English promoters, indicate that the colony was developed after 1630 by men of considerable wealth.

The founders of New Haven Colony did not organize a chartered company, nor did they contract debts or other financial obligations as a means of procuring capital for the migration. Instead, the well-to-do parishioners of John Davenport utilized their own fortunes and thus established their colony on an independent economic basis. Theophilus Eaton, who was worth £4,000 in England, is said to have transferred £3,000 to the colony. Although the New Haven settlers were not numerous, they were relatively the wealthiest group which went to America during the seventeenth century.[8]

The methods of financing adopted by the proprietors of New Hampshire, Maryland, Carolina, and Pennsylvania bear a striking resemblance. In the first place, the proprietors made personal investments with the object of providing a nucleus of settlement that would attract future colonists and thus increase the value of the lands which the proprietors offered for general sale. All lands given away or sold were subject to a quit-rent or yearly payment which would provide the proprietors with a permanent income. The proprietors also retained for themselves American estates to be worked for their profit by servants or tenants whom they transported to their colonies. Lord Baltimore spent about £30,000 on the development of Maryland. The Calvert wealth is indicated by the family's possession of valuable Irish estates and by the fact that Sir George Calvert received £6,000 when he sold his claim to the office of Secretary of State. Similarly Captain John Mason spent large sums upon his New Hampshire colony on the Piscataqua, but never received any profit from it.

In 1663 the eight wealthy proprietors of Carolina reserved for themselves estates of twenty thousand acres each, and a new arrange-

[8] See again J. T. Adams, *The Founding of New England*, chapters 1–3, 5–6.

ment in 1669 set aside a fifth of all the lands of the province for their benefit. They financed in part the expedition which settled Old Charles Town in 1670; a decade later they wrote: "We have been at great expense, some 17 or £18,000 sterling, and have brought the colony to so prosperous a condition that men of estates have for years gone there on their own accounts." Each proprietor agreed in 1674 to spend £100 a year on the colony for five years—indicating not only the need for more capital but also their reluctance to become more deeply involved. Lord Shaftesbury at this time endeavored to establish a personal manor of twelve thousand acres to which he sent a shipload of servants and supplies. In 1679 the proprietors were unwilling to make further outlays, asserting that their previous investments had put the colony on its feet.

Like Lord Baltimore, William Penn derived an income from family estates in Ireland. His initial plans for Pennsylvania reserved to himself a tenth of all surveyed lands of his province, upon which he intended to establish personal estates. He said about 1698 that he had invested £30,000 in Pennsylvania, and complained that he had not received a sixpence profit during the preceding twelve years. His expenditures strained his credit, with the result that he was later thrown into a debtors' prison and eventually forced to mortgage the province and assign to his creditors the revenues he derived from quit-rents, land sales, and other Pennsylvania sources.[9]

As in earlier days, the proprietors active after 1630 found the cost of colonization too great to be borne singlehanded, and therefore enlisted the aid of wealthy men who may be called "proprietary associates." Thus Captain Mason joined with six London merchants in 1631 for the financing of New Hampshire settlement but two years without profit sufficed for the merchants and they retired. Lord Baltimore originally obtained associates by giving them a thousand acres of land for every five men they transported to Maryland. The size of such grants was increased to two thousand acres in 1636 and reduced to five hundred acres in 1649. These associates spent about £20,000 toward peopling their estates. Three of them—Thomas Cornwallis and two Jesuit fathers, White and Copley—transported 130 settlers to the colony.

The Carolina proprietors in particular relied upon wealthy associates. In the South Carolina expedition of 1669 were many adventurers, each transporting at his own expense a small group of servants.

[9] C. M. Andrews, *Colonial Self-Government, 1652–1689* (New York, 1904—*American Nation* series), gives essential facts, emphasizing legal foundations. See chapters 7–9, 11.

Proposals made for the colony in 1669 anticipated that a fifth of all its land should be assigned to such associates, who were also to form an order of nobles—landgraves and caciques. Lord Ashley said in 1671 that nothing would so foster "the growth and prosperity of the plantation as that men of estate should come to settle amongst you." Accordingly, during the 1670's generous grants were made to individuals and partners who transported groups of between ten and twenty servants. Each servant imported secured for the associate a tract of 100 or 150 acres of land. Thus Seth Sothell in 1675 received a manor of twelve thousand acres on condition that within five years he build thirty houses and "seat" 120 colonists. Between 1675 and 1684, nine grants bestowed estates ranging from one thousand to three thousand acres, while Sir Peter Colleton, then one of the proprietors, obtained title to 35,800 acres.

William Penn once said that the success of his province was due partly to the fact that it was "begun by men of estates." He enlisted many wealthy Quaker associates, each of whom bought for £100 a tract of five thousand acres which included a lot of one hundred acres in Philadelphia. Nearly half of the land sold by Penn in 1681–82 was purchased by about forty of these wealthy associates who probably intended to people their colonial estates with tenants.[10]

Besides investing their own funds and enlisting wealthy associates, the proprietors encouraged moderately well-to-do families to settle in their colonies. They did this by giving away land or by selling it at bargain prices. Lord Baltimore in 1636 offered land gratis to self-paying families: one hundred acres for each adult, including servants, and fifty acres for each child under sixteen. In 1658 the allotments were reduced to fifty acres for each person; in 1683 they were discontinued. The Carolina proprietors, prior to 1670, gave 150 acres for each man servant and one hundred acres for each woman servant and for each male servant under sixteen. In 1672 such grants were reduced to seventy acres and sixty acres respectively. The majority of farms established in South Carolina before 1685 did not contain more than three hundred acres. William Penn sold land at the rate of about 1s. an acre or one hundred acres for £5. To a company of German emigrants headed by Daniel Francis Pastorius he disposed of fifteen thousand acres for £300. The list of original purchasers who bought land from Penn before 1683 shows that 307 procured tracts ranging from 250 to one thousand acres—representing about three-fourths of the purchasers and half of all the land then sold. Penn at

<hr>

[10] John Fiske's *The Dutch and Quaker Colonies* (2 vols., Boston, 1899) is a readable narrative. On Pennsylvania see Vol. II, chapter 12.

this time advised the self-paying settler to bring over two-thirds of his property in goods and the other third in money.

THE PROCURING OF SETTLERS

The resources of English America required a large supply of labor for their exploitation—a demand far in excess of the supply afforded by the settlers who paid their own way. The promoters therefore had to recruit workers among the dependent classes in England. Accordingly, the colonies were pictured attractively to the poor as "places where food shall drop into their mouths." In 1630 Thomas Dudley, then in New England, observed that "honest men out of a desire to draw over others to them, wrote somewhat hyperbolically of many things here." America seemingly spread a table heaped up with fruits, berries, vegetables, and nuts; the rivers teemed with fish; and the forests abounded with game which had no keepers.

The most common method of procuring workers—adopted alike by companies, proprietors, and independent families—was the labor contract. Such a contract or indenture stipulated that the contractor should transport and maintain a servant for a given term during which the latter was bound to labor for his master. This system had its roots deep in the soil of England's aristocratic past. Earlier statutes had provided that laborers must work at fixed wages and that minors between the ages of twelve and twenty-one might be apprenticed by their parents or guardians and thus be obliged to work for a master until they became adults. Another act allowed magistrates to bind vagabonds to property owners who would put them to work and maintain them.[11]

However, the procuring of indentured servants for colonization raised new problems. If a worker were to remain forever a servant or tenant it was better for him to stay in England rather than to add the hardships and dangers of a wilderness frontier life to his dependent lot. As early as 1612 it was reported that escaped servants had returned from Virginia to England where they "endeavored by most vile and slanderous reports . . . of the country of Virginia . . . to bring the said voyage and plantation into disgrace and contempt." Such reports, added to the native repugnance of less enterprising groups in England for novelty and change, had to be counteracted by the promoters. Accordingly, many servants were obtained by force.

[11] Volume II of E. P. Cheyney's *A History of England from the Defeat of the Armada to the Death of Elizabeth* (2 vols., New York, 1914, 1926) gives a vivid picture of social conditions.

Kidnaping was resorted to by "spirits" who carried off drunkards from the taverns, seized poor people by "strong-arm" methods, and enticed others on board ships where they were held as prisoners. Moreover, judges sentenced criminals to servitude in the colonies where their services were sold to promoters or prosperous settlers. As early as 1612 we hear of servants in Virginia "sent thither as misdoers and offenders." [12]

The right sort of servants, however, could not be obtained by such methods, and accordingly the promoters (except in New England) were obliged to make attractive concessions which would induce the more industrious and responsible members of the dependent classes to enter into voluntary service. First, the promoters promised the servant his freedom after a term generally between four and seven years; secondly, the servant when free should receive a small tract of land, usually fifty acres in the back country; then thus emancipated he would be entitled to vote, and, if a Protestant, to enjoy religious toleration. By such concessions the promoters met the criticism of Lord Bacon that "it is a shameful and unblessed thing to take the scum of people and wicked, condemned men to be the people with whom you plant."

Under the Virginia charter of 1606 the promoters sent over three hundred settlers—a miscellaneous group of adventurers, gentlemen of decayed fortunes, and some of the "scum" of whom Bacon complained. Their utter incompetence as colonists induced the Virginia Company, after 1609, to seek hard-working farmers and artisans. The company's efforts to people Virginia were supplemented after 1618 by the associations formed within the company and by private planters who purchased servants for personal use. In each case the importers of poor immigrants offered land as the principal inducement. Under the charter of 1609 a servant over ten years of age who went to Virginia became a member of the company, entitled to one hundred acres at the end of seven years in its service. Similarly the associations formed within the company after 1617 offered their servants twenty-five acres each after a labor term of from three to eight years. It also became the custom for private planters to give to their servants the fifty-acre head-rights which the planters received as a bonus for importing the servants in the first instance. Thus most of the servants eventually emerged as landowning farmers. As such, if Protestants, they enjoyed religious toleration, because the promoters of Virginia did not impose any religious restraints except the oath of supremacy.

[12] A. E. Smith, "The Transportation of Convicts to the American Colonies in the Seventeenth Century," *American Historical Review*, XXXIX (Jan. 1934).

The charter of 1606, moreover, guaranteed to the colonists and their descendants all the "liberties, franchises, and immunities . . . to all intents and purposes as if they had been abiding and born within this our realm of England. . . ." This extension to the colonies of the liberties enjoyed by citizens of England laid the foundations of colonial self-government. Such liberties which were of most consequence, however, were enjoyed by English property owners, and thus the colonial servants had to become landholders before they attained the substantial benefits promised in the charter of 1606.[13]

The Pilgrims came to Plymouth Colony as both servants and members of the joint-stock company which they had formed with their English backers. Each emigrant received one share in the company, and for every £10 of property which he brought to the colony he received an additional share. Besides the Pilgrims, the English promoters dispatched a company of other settlers in the *Mayflower:* only thirty-five of its 102 passengers were Pilgrims. Until 1624 the company reinforced the colony with additional colonists from England. Among the non-Pilgrim group were several of the now historic figures of Plymouth—John Alden, Miles Standish, and Richard Warren.

Indentured servants occupied a minor place in the great Puritan migration of the 1630's. After 1629 the Massachusetts Bay Company did not transport settlers except certain poor families for whom a special fund was created. Some of the well-to-do ministers charitably financed the removal of deserving but needy families. Otherwise emigrants unable to pay their way were brought as servants of the wealthier Puritans. However, the leaders of both Massachusetts and New Haven did not seek servants merely as a labor force. They sought, rather, fit "instruments" for a religious commonwealth, feeling that the troubles of other colonies arose from the character of the settlers —"a multitude of rude and misgoverned persons, the very scum of the land." Hence the Puritans did not offer tempting concessions which would appeal to people whose "main end was carnal and not religious"—not even such concessions as freedom of worship and political rights. Individual Puritans and towns may have given land to worthy and devout servants at the end of their terms, but neither the Massachusetts Bay Company nor the New Haven leaders promised land wholesale to every servant who might arrive. By virtue of such

[13] The best one-volume political history of Virginia in the seventeenth century is Thomas J. Wertenbaker's *Virginia under the Stuarts* (Princeton, 1914). See chapter 1 and pp. 45–54.

precautions the Puritans could feel with complacency that all England had been sifted for the choicest grain for their New England planting.[14]

In early Maryland the indentured servants were entitled to land grants—at first from the individuals who transported them. There developed a traffic whereby shipmasters imported servants and secured the head-rights, which were sold to planters along with the servants. Until 1646 the servant could claim fifty acres from his employer or master; between 1646 and 1683, the proprietor gave the land. Lord Baltimore also recruited settlers by assuring religious freedom to Christians.

After 1665 the theory that England was overpopulated gave way before a contrary view that the nation was in danger of losing its man power. The effects of the emigration of thousands of able-bodied workers prior to 1640 were now severely felt. The Civil War had taken a heavy toll, while a destructive plague, originating in London in 1665, swept throughout the country—the greatest calamity of its kind since the Black Death of the fourteenth century. Wagons went through the London streets at night to the doleful cry of the drivers: "Bring out your dead." In spite of these population losses England was forging ahead rapidly as an industrial and commercial power, but this very growth augmented the demand for workers. Whereas the colonies had formerly been prized as an outlet for the unemployed, they now became a source of alarm. "Ireland and our plantations," said a publicist of the time, "rob us of all the growing youth and industry of the nation, whereby it becomes weak and feeble, and the strength, as well as trade, becomes decayed and diminished."

This new theory of population affected the policies of both the English government and the promoters of colonies. The establishment of the Royal African Company in the 1660's proclaimed the intention of supplying colonial employers with Negro slaves rather than with English servants. Between 1664 and 1684 measures were adopted to prevent kidnaping, which business supposedly was then draining the country of ten thousand workers annually. At the same time English judges with increasing frequency ordered criminals transported to the colonies, so that in 1670 Virginia, in view of "the great numbers of felons and other desperate villains sent hither from

---

[14] Charles Edward Banks has made valuable studies of the process of colonization in Massachusetts. His writings include *The Winthrop Fleet of 1630* (Boston, 1930) and *The Planters of the Commonwealth* (Boston, 1930). Banks stresses economic forces in emigration.

the several prisons of England," passed an act prohibiting such importations. The English convict policy obviously aimed to supply the colonies with workers whom England did not want.

With the shrinkage of English emigration the promoters of colonies began to solicit settlers in Europe. The Carolina proprietors and the English government coöperated in 1679 in locating French Huguenots near Charles Town. A short time later Penn began to seek settlers, not only in Ireland and Wales, but also in Germany and the Netherlands. He prepared two tracts, *A Brief Account of the Province of Pennsylvania* and *Some Account*, while in 1686 appeared a third, *A Further Account*. In the Netherlands his friend, agent, and fellow Quaker, Benjamin Furly, translated *Some Account* into Dutch, while one Jan Claus prepared a translation for circulation in Germany. In these pamphlets Penn gave a pleasant picture of his province, described his liberal purposes, and advised prospective settlers as to the practical details of pioneering. The sort of people he desired were "industrious husbandmen, carpenters, masons, weavers, shoemakers, and other mechanics, industrious spirits that are oppressed about a livelihood, younger brothers, and men of universal spirits who understand the promotion of a just government among a plain and well intending people." By means of such writings Pennsylvania became, perhaps, the best advertised and certainly the most cosmopolitan of the English colonies, notable for the presence of Dutch, Germans, Swedes, Irish, Finns, Welsh, and English in its early population.[15]

The proprietors of Carolina, New Jersey, and Pennsylvania also bid for settlers who were dissatisfied in the older colonies, particularly in Barbados, Virginia, and New England. Unable to attract enough wealthy associates the proprietors again had to fall back upon self-paying families. The competition for settlers tended to liberalize the concessions offered. The Carolina charters granted freedom of worship to law-abiding Christians, and the proprietors issued a list of concessions in 1665 and 1667 which promised a representative legislature with power to assent to laws and taxes. Prior to 1670 a servant in Carolina received one hundred acres of land at the end of service; after 1670 his "freedom dues" included a grant of seventy acres. From pamphlets advertising Carolina in 1682 we learn that servants there enjoyed a Saturday afternoon vacation, that work was not done

[15] This theme is treated at length in William I. Hull, *William Penn and the Dutch Quaker Migration* (Swarthmore, 1935). See also Sydney G. Fisher, *The Quaker Colonies* (*Chronicles of America*, New Haven, 1919).

on the Sabbath, that "juries were chosen by lot," and that "lawyers could not charge fees."

When Carteret and Berkeley were proprietors of New Jersey in 1665 they offered concessions identical with those granted to Carolina settlers—land grants, religious freedom, a representative assembly, and free elections. The Quakers who took possession of West New Jersey issued in 1677 a more generous charter of popular liberties than any drawn up before that time. It guaranteed the rights of jury trial and religious freedom, protected the settlers from arbitrary imprisonment for debt, and did not provide for capital punishment. The colony was promised a legislature, to be elected yearly by the settlers, which should enjoy free speech, hold meetings open to the public, and legislate freely without a governor's veto.

William Penn, who probably drafted the West New Jersey concessions, extended similar privileges to Pennsylvania. In addition Penn bestowed upon indentured servants (whose term in Pennsylvania was commonly four years) farms of fifty acres. Such privileges as those granted by Penn were more than a competitive bid for labor; they embodied the Quaker ideals of human freedom.

About 1830 an English observer noted the democratic spirit in the United States, which he explained by the character of the early settlers. "We sent them forth," he wrote, "poor and struggling only for the means of subsistence. . . . We severed the humble from the nobles of our land and formed the embryo of a plebeian nation. Is it we that should find fault with their extravagant abhorrence of rank, or their want of high breeding and gentle blood which we so sparingly bestowed upon them?"

The American Scene

Let us take passage with a shipload of emigrants bound from England to the colonies. The vessels engaged were small craft, mostly of not more than two hundred tons. The voyage commonly lasted between six and twelve weeks, during which time the passengers subsisted on bread, salted meats, and fish, beer and stronger drinks—and these in meager rations too. Vessels were unmercifully overcrowded, and the horses and cattle on board did not improve sanitary conditions. Storms and diseases, particularly scurvy, carried away perhaps a fourth of the emigrants, while infants rarely survived. On the *Arbella*—flagship of the Winthrop fleet—when the seasick "lay groaning in the cabins" a line was stretched on deck and they were brought out and made "to sway it up and down till they were warm, and by this means they soon grew well and merry." Ever on the lookout for pirates and enemy privateers, the passengers kept their swords sharp for the threatening encounter. No wonder that the Puritans punctuated the voyage with morning and evening prayers, relished two sermons on the Sabbath, and changed watches to the singing of psalms and prayers that were "*not* read out of a book." A tempest might blow the vessel out of its course or a total calm might seem to threaten the fate of the Ancient Mariner. And what relief when the American shore was sighted! And even before! "The air at twelve leagues distance smelt as sweet as a new-blown garden."

Coming in view of the new land the immigrant received his first glimpse of the dense forest that spread backward from the water's edge and extended from Maine to Carolina. The effect of the American scene upon the European newcomer was to invite him to remain and to enable him to obtain a foothold.[16] The climate generally appealed. "Heaven and earth," wrote John Smith in praise of Virginia, "never agreed better to frame a place for man's habitation," while Penn said of his colony: "The air is sweet and clear, the heavens serene, like the south parts of France, rarely overcast." And from a New Englander, Mr. Higginson, came this tribute: "Experience doth manifest itself that there is hardly a more healthful place to be found in the world that agreeth better with our English bodies. Many that have been weak and sickly in old England, by coming hither have been thoroughly healed and grown healthful strong. For here is a most extraordinary clear and dry air that is of a most healing nature to all such as are of a cold, melancholy, phlegmatic, or rheumatic temper of body." A later observer noted the keenness and brilliance of the air. "The fog of an English town is wanting; you are in a new world, and a world which knows the sun." Such a climate contributed to make the early settlers, when adapted to it, energetic, industrious, and optimistic.

The "forest primeval," with its profusion of white pines (from Maine to Massachusetts), its maples, poplars, beeches, hickories, oaks, and walnut trees offered the settler an abundance of cheap fuel and lumber for his houses, barns, furniture, and tools.

> And the ambitious vine
> Crowns with its purple mass
> The cedar reaching high
> To kiss the sky

[16] Ellen C. Semple, *American History and Its Geographic Conditions* (Boston, 1903; new ed., 1933) is the best short treatment.

The cypress, pine
And useful sassafras.

To England the virgin forest seemed a veritable treasure-house, for wood occupied a place in her economy comparable to that of coal and iron today. It was the raw material for ships, potash, and dyes, the source of the pitch, tar, and resin which made vessels seaworthy and watertight, and the fuel for iron, glass, and copper manufactures. Thus the virgin forest promised to the early settlers a prosperous export trade with the Old World.[17]

Equally inviting were the native food products of America. Of fish and seafood there were oysters, crabs, sturgeon, bass, cod, lobsters, eels, herring, shad, catfish, trout, and salmon. Turkeys, "fat and incredible of weight," ducks ("when they flew up there was a rushing and vibration of the air like a great storm coming through the trees"), rabbits, squirrels, partridges, quail, pheasants, elk, geese, and deer "bigger than ours" in England and "in places so many that venison is accounted a tiresom meat"—all these created a hunter's paradise. The woods displayed a wealth of raspberries, blackberries, strawberries, gooseberries, cranberries, grapes red and black, whortleberries, plums, crab apples, hickory nuts, black walnuts, chestnuts, butternuts, hazelnuts, and pecans. For a more substantial fare the settlers, like the Indians, could easily cultivate peas, beans, Indian corn, pumpkins, squashes, cucumbers, and melons, as well as sweet potatoes, tomatoes, and onions.

The land and climate were also suited to the common English grains—wheat, oats, barley, and rye. Imported swine fattened cheaply, if not copiously, upon acorns and ground nuts in the woods. When protected from wolves, sheep and goats did well, and cattle grew "to a far greater bulk of body" than in England. Transplanted fruit trees—apple, cherry, apricot, pear, quince, and peach—soon found their way into colonial orchards and afforded the settlers a varied bill of fare.[18]

Despite the richness of American resources, the settlers had to keep in touch with Europe in order to import a multitude of articles they could not produce. In this connection the coast-line served them well, providing as it did innumerable inlets and harbors which became the cradles of colonies. Only North Carolina and southern New Jersey

---

[17] T. J. Wertenbaker, *The First Americans* (New York, 1929). Chapter 1 discusses American resources in relation to English interests.

[18] Philip A. Bruce's *Economic History of Virginia in the Seventeenth Century* (2 vols., New York, 1896) presents a mass of detailed information, conveniently classified. See Vol. I, chapters 2–3 on aboriginal Virginia.

lacked harbors for ocean vessels, but even their shores could be readily visited by smaller boats from adjacent settlements. Majestic rivers such as the Kennebec, the Piscataqua, the Connecticut, the Delaware, the Susquehanna, the Potomac, the James, the York, the Rappahannock, the Santee, and the Savannah linked the coastal plain with the seaports and through them with Europe. Since the seaboard area was not tributary to one river system alone, many independent colonies could develop, each with its own outlets to the sea. The shore line and the rivers, therefore, at first spread population north and south along a narrow band of the coast so traversed by arteries of travel, especially at Chesapeake Bay, as to resemble a "sylvan Venice." [19]

On the other hand, the American environment prevented a rapid extension into the interior. The forests retarded a westward march— not only as an obstacle to travel and trade but also by virtue of the hard task of clearing the heavily wooded lands for farming. Of the rivers of North America, only two gave easy access to the interior— the St. Lawrence, held by the French, and the Hudson, dominated by the Dutch. The Appalachian Mountains, from which the rivers of the English colonies flowed to the sea, long arrested westward traffic for all save trappers and traders with pack trains carrying light and precious furs. The coastal plain, which below Delaware Bay reaches inland between a hundred and two hundred miles and widens as it extends to the south, meets the piedmont region at the fall line, where the falls impose a serious obstacle to navigation. The piedmont rises between a thousand and two thousand feet above sea level, until it merges into the mountains proper, whose lofty ridges and peaks include the White Mountains in New Hampshire and the Green Mountains in Vermont, separated by the Connecticut River, the Adirondacks and the Catskills, divided by the Hudson, and the Blue Ridge, rearing its massive wall before the Shenandoah valley. Within the Appalachian system as it extends to the southwest from Pennsylvania lies that great valley which is in reality a broad plateau at points two hundred miles wide and which, with its numerous hills and ridges running parallel to bordering mountains on the east, imposed a formidable barrier to westward travel and for a hundred years forced the English colonists to build compact settlements on the coastal plain and in the piedmont region.

In the long run, geography and resources shaped the industries of English America. Abundant rainfall and good soil fostered agriculture. New England, a glaciated area, was strewn with boulders, but

[19] Livingston Farrand's *Basis of American History* (New York, 1904—*American Nation* series) deals with the Indians and physiographic features of North America.

Based on Charles O. Paullin's "Atlas of the Historical Geography of the United States."
© Carnegie Institution of Washington. Reprinted by courtesy of the American Geographical
Society of New York.

INDIANS OF THE EASTERN UNITED STATES

once cleared the land did not quickly lose its fertility. However, the small area of level land and the short summers and long winters of New England made it an inferior farming country. The soil of eastern Pennsylvania and eastern New Jersey was good, but less fertile than the alluvial lands about the rivers of the coastal plain to the south where, in Maryland, Virginia, and North Carolina, a soil ideally suited to tobacco raising was found. However, as the coastal plain was originally a part of the ocean bed, the southern lands between the alluvial deposits in the river valleys were sandy and unproductive.

The slender farming resources of New England soon forced its people to develop a thriving lumber industry in the northeastern woods and to transform oak and pine into sturdy vessels. The cod fishery rapidly became the basis of prosperity in Massachusetts. And to all the infant colonies the forest beckoned with alluring profits from the trade in the furs and skins of beaver, deer, raccoon, panther, wolf, squirrel, fox, mink, muskrat, opossum, bear, elk, bison, and otter.[20]

> Instead of foxes, wolves and hungry bear
> That oft the Massachusetts herd do tear,
> Pequot has beaver, otter and the wary hare.

It was inevitable that the Indians of North America should come in conflict with the white intruders from England. Considering the vast extent of the continent, the Indians did not form a large population; they averaged scarcely more than two inhabitants to a square mile. Yet they probably felt the pressure of overcrowding, because their way of life required much land to support a few people. Although they did a little farming they relied chiefly on hunting and fishing. They lived in permanent villages to which the adjacent territory was attached; the idea of land ownership was well developed amongst them, and the various tribes had appropriated most of the lands suited to Indian economy. If a tribe moved from its traditional locality it was certain to encroach upon the lands of neighbors and enemies, thus precipitating war. The advance of the English therefore threatened a more intense pressure upon the Indians' means of subsistence.

This situation arose from the means of production employed by the red men. Before the arrival of the whites, the Indians utilized stone and wooden tools of a very primitive nature. They knew nothing of plows, wheels, axles, gunpowder, and firearms; they were ignorant

---

[20] Ralph H. Brown, *Historical Geography of the United States* (New York, 1948), shows effectively the influences of the physical environment.

of horses, cattle, swine, and sheep. "Their houses," wrote Penn, "are mats or barks of trees set on poles . . . , but out of the power of the winds, for they are hardly higher than a man; they lie on reeds or grass. In travel they lodge in the woods about a great fire, with the mantle of duffels they wear by day wrapt about them, and a few boughs stuck round them." For clothing they depended chiefly upon skins. Their spoken language seemed abrupt, being confined to the use of major words without the shading supplied by tenses, moods, adverbs, and participles; and they were familiar with neither calendar nor writing. Their customs denoted a hunters' society quite at odds with the farmers' civilization brought to America by the early European settlers.[21]

From the English the Indians might readily have acquired advanced industrial methods which would have enabled them to support a larger population on a smaller area. Yet this did not happen, largely because the Indian differed so materially in outlook from the white. To the red man physical labor was repulsive and degrading, and consequently the bearing of burdens and work in the fields were assigned to women, who were primarily servants of the men. Hunting, fishing, war, and feats of prowess were the honorable pursuits which occupied the "braves." The adoption of European civilization required either that the warriors degrade themselves with labor in the fields or that the women perform all such work, with the one-time warrior-hunters degenerating in idleness. The Indians preferred to fight. The resulting wars, both with the English and among themselves, adjusted the native population to its contracting means of support. Moreover, the Indian's ignorance of medicine and his susceptibility to distempers spread by the whites—such as alcoholism, smallpox, tuberculosis, measles, and social diseases—kept the population within bounds and thus enabled the natives to adhere to their hunting, roving, predatory ways of life.

Temperamentally the practical, acquisitive, businesslike English settler was the antithesis of the easygoing, easily contented Indian. "The most merry creatures that live" who "feast and dance perpetually," the Indians were respectful of private property and yet exceedingly generous toward friends. "They are not disquieted with bills of lading and exchange, nor perplexed with chancery suits or exchequer reckonings. We sweat and toil to live"; said Penn, "their pleasure

---

[21] William C. MacLeod, *The American Indian Frontier* (New York, 1928), factual but controversial, states the case of the Indians against the settlers. A modern, readable study is Paul Radin, *The Story of the American Indian* (New York, 1934). The best survey is Clark Wissler, *The American Indian* (New York, 1922).

feeds them: I mean their hunting, fishing and fowling." "Give them a fine gun, coat, or other thing, it may pass twenty hands before it sticks. . . . Wealth circulateth like the blood, all parts partake, and . . . none shall want what another hath." [22]

The superiority of European weapons, together with the relative sparseness of the native population, enabled the English settlers to secure a foothold and to benefit by early contacts with the tribes. To the white strangers the Indians sold food in times of distress, taught the secret of cultivating important crops like tobacco and maize, revealed the trails of wilderness travel, and furnished fields already cleared. The fruits of immemorial experience with forest life became available to the settlers, almost overnight.

Contact with the Indian kept the colonists in close touch with his government—the channel through which all agreements between the two were made. The unit of Indian society was the tribe, and the tribes have been grouped, according to their language forms, into fifty-nine families. The Algonquin family—the most numerous of the eastern Indians—occupied both the seaboard area above North Carolina and vast stretches of the interior adjacent to the Great Lakes. Among its tribes were the Abenaki and Penobscot in Maine, the Pennacook in New Hampshire, the Massachuset and Wampanoag in Massachusetts, the Narraganset in Rhode Island, the Pequot and the Mohegan in Connecticut, the Delaware in eastern Pennsylvania and New Jersey, the Nanticoke in Maryland and Delaware, the Powhatan in eastern Virginia, and the Pamlico in North Carolina. Superior to the Algonquins in energy, prowess, and organization were the Iroquois, whose leading tribes, the Seneca, the Onondaga, the Cayuga, the Mohawk, and the Oneida (known as the Five Nations), occupied the Mohawk valley between the Hudson River and Lake Erie. The Tuscarora in North Carolina also belonged to the Iroquoian family. The third principal family of the East, the Muskhogean, held sway in the lower South and included the Creek, Chickasaw, Choctaw, and Seminole. The various tribes were grouped into confederacies, some of which, such as the Five Nations, were alliances of equals; others, like the kingdom of Powhatan, resembled an empire of conquered provinces.[23]

Within the tribe or village each person belonged to a clan—the

---

[22] Ellsworth Huntington, *The Red Man's Continent* (*Chronicles of America*, New Haven, 1919).

[23] A modern coöperative work consisting of scholarly essays is the *History of the State of New York* (ed. A. C. Flick, 10 vols., New York, 1933–37). Chapters 1–4 of the first volume, *Wigwam and Bouwerie*, discuss the land and the Indians.

PLAN OF A COLONIAL TOWN

This view, made at the end of the seventeenth century, shows fort, pinks, ocean ships and smaller craft, Indians, carts, settlers, well, guns, and houses.

unit which regulated daily life, protected its members, educated the young in the ancient customs, entertained visiting kinsmen, and exacted revenge for injuries on the principle of "an eye for an eye." Children belonged to the clan of their mothers; and inheritance was so devised that the property of a man would not pass to his own children but to his brothers or to his sister's children. Each clan had its symbol or "totem," such as the "bear," "beaver," or "wolf," and each elected its sachem or wise man who presided over his people as a supreme judge and custodian of morals and also represented them in the village council of the whole tribe. Smaller groups within the clan elected chiefs who led the warriors to battle. Such bands often made plundering forays against enemies, acting independently of the rest of the clan.

The ruling body of the tribal village consisted of a council attended by the chiefs and sachems. Here were decided issues of war, peace, and disposal of land which affected the whole tribe. In general the Indian government suggests an oligarchy in which old, experienced, forceful leaders—elected from hereditary ruling families, and mighty as the guardians of customs which did not change—held the reins of power. Among such leaders one might become a king, ruling his subordinate chiefs and sachems with cunning, energy, and tact, and bringing to conferences with the whites no little shrewdness, caution, and address.[24]

THE PROCESS OF SETTLEMENT

The initial task of first settlers was to choose a site for their colony. Immediately afterward arose a fourfold problem of defense, shelter, food supply, and health. The pioneers of Virginia in May 1607 selected as the site of Jamestown a peninsula extending into the James River. There they could readily observe the approach of Spanish enemies by water and defend themselves against the attacks of natives by guarding a small strip of land. Located near the entrance to Chesapeake Bay and close to the great rivers of Virginia, Jamestown was also well placed for trade. But due to a near-by malaria-breeding swamp, the site proved to be fatally unhealthful.

Immediately the Virginians set to work constructing a fort, log huts, a storehouse, and a church. Then they planted wheat, pump-

[24] Francis Parkman's *History of the Conspiracy of Pontiac* (2 vols., Boston, 1885) opens with a brilliant chapter on the Indians.

kins, potatoes, and melons, but their agriculture did not sustain them for a long time to come. They were not farmers and they dissipated their energies in hunting gold, seeking a Northwest passage, and endeavoring to manufacture pitch, tar, soap ashes, and glass. Nor could they depend upon food sent from England. Such supplies were often damaged, destroyed, lost, or consumed en route, and other colonists who arrived before 1610 did not bring enough food for their own support, thus increasing rather than relieving the strain upon the slender rations of the colony. Only trade with the Indians enabled the settlers to survive.[25]

On the banks of the York River lay the capital of the emperor Powhatan, who ruled in lordly fashion some thirty-four tribes of his confederacy, which extended from the Roanoke River to the head of Chesapeake Bay. "He had such a grave, majestical countenance," said Captain John Smith, "as drove me into admiration to see such a state in a naked savage." Although frequently receiving the English with a show of friendship, and giving them Indian corn, turkeys, venison, bread, and vegetables in exchange for beads, knives, kettles, copper, and fishhooks, Powhatan suspected them from the start and planned to destroy them. "You have come here," he said, "not to trade but to invade my people and possess my country."

But among the English there arose a leader more than a match for the aged Powhatan. Captain John Smith was an adventurer whose exploits and hairbreadth escapes in the Netherlands, Austria, France, Transylvania, Russia, and Morocco read like tales from the Arabian Nights, and may have somewhat the same authenticity. An emblem of three Turks' heads on his coat of arms celebrated a hand-to-hand encounter in which he had dispatched three Turkish warriors. In command of expeditions which explored the Virginia rivers, Smith visited various Indian villages, where he proved to be a master trader, exciting the natives with dramatically displayed beads and other trifles or striking fear into their hearts by attacking them before they could attack him—always warily retaining his weapons when in the presence of Powhatan and his chiefs. The dauntless, resolute spirit of Smith is embodied in his phrase: "It is less perilous to go forward than to go backward." In 1608 he visited Powhatan with instructions to crown him as a king under English protection. Gifts of regal splendor were tendered and the emperor was asked to kneel to receive his copper crown. Fearing foul play, he refused, but the English "by leaning

[25] John Fiske, *Old Virginia and Her Neighbors* (2 vols., Boston, 1897). See Vol. I, chapters 8–9; Vol. II, chapter 15.

hard on his shoulders" forced him to stoop a bit, while a salvo from their boats proclaimed the coronation and startled him, with "a horrible fear." "Then remembering himself, to congratulate their kindness, he gave his old shoes and mantle to Captain Newport." [26]

Prior to 1610 the colonists were generally on the verge of starvation. They had settled on wooded land which could be cleared only with great effort, and they feared the Indians too much to risk a seizure of their open fields. In the resulting crisis John Smith assumed the powers of dictator, imposed military discipline, and forced all to work. But after his departure in 1609 a terrible winter—"the starving time"—ensued, and when relief came in the spring of 1610 only sixty of the five hundred left by Smith had survived, "subsisting on roots, herbs, acorns, walnuts, wild fruits, and snakes, with occasionally a little fish." [27]

The Virginia Company in London now breathed new life into the colony. Three expeditions arrived in 1610 and 1611 bearing fresh supplies and colonists who had been instructed to concentrate on farming. The Virginians obtained cleared lands from the Indians and thereafter kept large tracts under cultivation. They continued to secure food from the natives, developed a fishery, and imported livestock which increased rapidly. In 1612 occurred the memorable marriage of John Rolfe and the Princess Pocahontas, favorite daughter of Powhatan and, by tradition, savior of John Smith. Rolfe, who was interested in raising tobacco, saw the value of a peaceful alliance with the Indians which would provide the security and assistance needed for the new industry. Pocahontas, long a friend and protégée of the English, later visited the court of James I as the Lady Rebecca Rolfe and there enjoyed the attentions paid to her as a princess and social lioness of the season. [28]

During the decade after 1610 conditions steadily improved until 1619, when a new period of hard times set in with the arrival of a host of unseasoned settlers. An epidemic swept over the colony, taking a toll of nearly four thousand lives between 1619 and 1624. This pestilential fever seems to have been brought into the colony by the newly arrived immigrants. And while the plague was in progress occurred a terrible Indian massacre in 1622. Powhatan had been succeeded by his brother, Opechancanough, who witnessed with dismay

---

[26] John Gould Fletcher's *John Smith—also Pocahontas* (New York, c. 1928) is a brilliantly written personal narrative.

[27] Edward Keble Chatterton's *Captain John Smith* (New York, 1927) is the most interesting brief biography.

[28] P. A. Bruce's *The Virginia Plutarch* (2 vols., Chapel Hill, 1929) contains readable essays on early leaders. See Vol. I, chapters 1–5.

the encroachments of the English plantations upon his peoples' lands. The Indians had thus far proved ineffectual in battle with the soldier because their arrows could not penetrate his coat of mail, while their war paint did not stop his bullets. Only by a surprise attack could the Indians defeat the English. Feigning good will and friendship, Opechancanough and his men caught the settlers off guard and massacred 357 of them. Unable to engage the Indians in open fighting, the Virginians burned their cornfields. For a dozen years a guerilla warfare raged about the outskirts of the settlement with the result that the Indians were gradually pushed back. By 1630 the Virginians had demonstrated that an American colony could survive.[29]

The Pilgrims of the *Mayflower* selected, in December 1620, as the site of their colony a small clearing in the woods which fronted a good harbor—a scene somewhat suggestive of Plymouth in England. A recent plague had all but destroyed the Indians of the vicinity. The Pilgrims at first began to erect houses for communal dwellings, but soon decided "that every man should build his own house, thinking by that course men would make more haste." Disease immediately visited the little company; by March 1621 nearly half of the settlers were dead from scurvy and exposure. But the spring restored health and spirits, and none of the survivors deserted the colony.

The Pilgrims' fears of the natives were largely dissipated by visits late in March from two friendly Indians, Samoset and Squanto, who told of the recent plague among the near-by tribes. Squanto, who had previously been in England and had learned to speak English, remained at Plymouth, where he proved invaluable to the Pilgrims as guide, interpreter, and instructor in the arts of wilderness life. The chief of the nearest tribe, Massasoit of the Wampanoags, also paid his respects in person, and entered into a treaty of peace with Plymouth which was faithfully kept by both sides until his death in 1662. From a more remote tribe, the Narragansets, came the famous challenge of arrows in a snakeskin which the Pilgrims met by returning the skin filled with powder and shot. The Narragansets were apparently overawed by this display of courage or magic and did not attack. Beyond such threats and the petty thievery of an occasional prowler, the Pilgrims were not molested.

Meanwhile they were busily engaged in farming, fishing, trading, and receiving settlers sent by their London partners. The health of the colony steadily improved, although minor pests moved Bradford to write that "they are too delicate and unfit to begin new plantations

[29] Mary N. Stanard's *The Story of Virginia's First Century* (Philadelphia, 1928) is a trustworthy narrative of the familiar events.

that cannot endure the biting of a mosquito." By the end of 1624 the problem of food supply had been permanently solved.[30]

Nearly a thousand settlers came to Massachusetts in the Winthrop migration of 1630. The leaders selected Boston Bay instead of Salem as the center of the colony, and moved the capital first to Charlestown, where a lack of fresh water forced a removal to Boston. Winthrop had hoped to build one compact settlement protected by a fort at Newtown, now Cambridge, but the many agreeable sites about Boston intrigued his companions and they divided and founded the towns of Roxbury, Dorchester, Watertown, Medford, and Lynn.[31]

Arriving too late for planting crops, the Puritans had to eke out a bare existence during the winter of 1630–31, living on salt pork, hard-tack, shellfish, and a few supplies obtained from Indians. Against the blasts of winter the bark wigwams and sail-cloth tents of the settlers offered only a precarious shelter. Scurvy and some dread disease (probably typhus from the water at Charlestown) caused two hundred deaths and much illness, "so that in every family, lamentation, mourning and woe was heard, and no fresh food to be had to cherish them." The colony had reached its lowest depths in February 1631, when at last a vessel sent by Winthrop to Bristol returned with grain, peas, beef, and lemon juice, a cure for scurvy. Other supply ships soon arrived from Virginia or Ireland, boats were built for fishing, and farming was soon under way. In less than a year the crisis at Boston had been passed.[32]

Since the strength of the Indians depended largely upon their agriculture, the tribes in contact with the rocky New England soil were neither numerous nor powerful. Accordingly they did not menace the Puritan pioneers about Boston. In April 1631 the sachem of the neighboring tribe came to the English as a supplicant for aid in intertribal wars, and the Puritans gladly established relations of friendship.

The band of colonists who founded Maryland in 1634 settled upon the St. Mary's River, a small tributary of the lower Potomac. Finding the resident Indians on the point of leaving to escape an enemy tribe, the newcomers secured the use of the Indians' houses and purchased their cleared lands. The site of the settlement (named St. Mary's) proved to be more healthful than that of Jamestown and the

---

[30] Although an older book, William B. Weeden's *Economic and Social History of New England* (2 vols., Boston, 1890) is still useful for its mass of well selected but poorly classified information. See Vol. I, chapters 1–3.

[31] Charles F. Adams discusses the settlement of Boston Bay in Volume I of his incisive essays, *Three Episodes of Massachusetts History* (2 vols., Boston, 1892).

[32] John Fiske, *The Beginnings of New England* (Boston, 1889), chapters 2–3.

winter climate was not so rigorous as in New England. The settlers—the great majority of whom were farmers and artisans braced for hard work—arrived in March 1634 and were able to raise a good crop of maize during the year. In Virginia the Marylanders had an adequate base of provisions; in fact the first expedition had reached the Potomac after a sojourn in Virginia where fresh supplies were procured. Because of these initial supplies, Maryland was able to export Indian corn after the first harvest. All in all, the colonists at St. Mary's accomplished the first tasks of settlement with a minimum of privation.[33]

After their failure in 1666–67 to establish a colony on the Cape Fear River to the south of Virginia the proprietors of Carolina dispatched a second expedition in 1669 which proceeded by way of Barbados and Bermuda to the Kiawha River, where in 1670 a settlement was begun at Albemarle Point. The country appeared "so delicious, pleasant and fruitful that were it cultivated it would prove a second paradise." A comparison of the early experiences of Virginia and New England had convinced the Carolina proprietors of the superiority of compact over scattered settlement, and accordingly they directed their colonists to settle in towns. The nucleus of the colony at Albemarle Point was called Charles Town and the Kiahwa River was renamed the Ashley.

At the outset the Charles Town settlers had to pay particular attention to defense. Not only did they fear hostile Indians, but they also realized that the Spaniards, who claimed the South Carolina country as part of Florida, had a strong garrison at St. Augustine from which they could readily smite their ancient English foes. The settlers, therefore, turned to the construction of a fort and of a palisade across Albemarle Point but the time consumed in this prevented them from clearing land and raising sufficient food during the first year, although they did plant corn and potatoes. By August 1670, provisions were exhausted, but a supply ship from Virginia saved the day. Meanwhile, the Indians had not offered resistance; in fact, a near-by tribe, the Kiawhas, welcomed the English as allies against their ferocious enemies, the Westoes. Among the colonists was Dr. Henry Woodward, versed in the Indian language, who won the friendship of the neighboring tribes and thus procured food from them in times of extremity. The climate at Charles Town was good; sickness was not acute; and only a few of the pioneers died.

By 1671 some of the Indians had become hostile and had turned to the Spaniards as allies in a war for the extermination of Charles

<hr>

[33] Bernard C. Steiner's *Beginnings of Maryland, 1631–1639* (Baltimore, 1903) is a carefully written narrative.

Town. The scarcity of food persisted; so that in 1672 all but carpenters and smiths were ordered to farm and idlers were placed at
forced labor. The proprietors sent provisions and cattle from Virginia, Bermuda, and New York, but in 1673 Sir Peter Colleton wrote:
"our friends in Carolina sing the same song they did in the beginning
—great want of vituals, clothes and tools." However, conditions
gradually improved, and by 1675 the colonists had gained a secure
foothold.[34]

The technique of pioneering learned by the English since 1607
enabled William Penn to establish his colony with a minimum of
hardship and suffering. He instructed his colonists who sailed in
1681 to select on the western side of the Delaware River a spot "most
navigable, high, dry and healthy, . . . where most ships may best
ride, of deepest draught of water, if possible to load and unload at
the bank . . . without boating." His plan for compact settlement in
a "great town"—where the houses should be set in lawns "that it may
be a green country town"—aimed to assure the benefits of society in
"help, trade, education and government, also roads, travel, entertainment, etc." Arriving in 1682 Penn helped to lay out the city of
Philadelphia on a neck of land two miles wide between the Delaware
and Schuylkill Rivers. Ships could "ride in good anchorage in both
rivers in six or eight fathoms of water," and the land was "level,
dry and wholesome"—"a situation scarcely to be paralleled." The
town plan of wide, straight streets and regular squares introduced
the design of the later typical American city.

Penn's colony prospered from the beginning, by reason of the
wealth of many of the Quaker settlers, the abundance of provisions in
near-by colonies, the presence of Swedish and Dutch farmers in the
lower Delaware valley, the friendly attitude of the Pennsylvania
Indians, and the pains Penn had taken in planning the initial settlement. In 1684 there were nearly four hundred houses in Philadelphia,
"divers of them large and well built with good cellars, three stories,
and some with balconies." [35]

Believing that the Indians were the rightful owners of the soil,
Penn joined them at the council fire and purchased from them the
southeastern part of his province. His benevolent, peaceful spirit, his
refusal to debauch them with rum or other "fire-water," his steadfastness in keeping agreements, and his avoidance of fraud, treachery,

---

[34] Mary Johnston, *Pioneers of the Old South* (*Chronicles of America*, New Haven,
1918), chapters 1–7, 9, 14.

[35] *Political Leaders of Provincial Pennsylvania*, by Isaac Sharpless (New York,
1919), contains interesting sketches of well-to-do emigrants.

and violence endeared him to his red brethren, who affectionately called him Onas (a pen) and revered him as a paragon of virtue among the English leaders. The peace and friendship thus established were major factors in the rapid growth of Pennsylvania.

BIBLIOGRAPHICAL NOTE

SECONDARY WORKS: Mildred Campbell, *The English Yeoman under Elizabeth and the Early Stuarts* (New Haven, 1942), is an intensive study of English antecedents of the most important group in the colonies. See also Mildred Campbell, "Social Origins of Some Early Americans," in *Seventeenth-Century America* (ed. James Morton Smith, Chapel Hill, 1959). David Mathew, *The Social Structure in Caroline England* (Oxford, 1948), emphasizes the upper crust of English society.

Marshall Harris, *Origin of the Land Tenure System in the United States* (Ames, 1953), gives special attention to the colonial era.

Roy H. Pearce, *The Savages of America* (Baltimore, 1953), explains the fate of the Indians by the hostility of the whites.

John Bakeless, *The Eyes of Discovery* (New York, 1950), reveals the primitive state of North America as it appeared to the first white explorers. *William Byrd's Natural History of Virginia* (ed. R. C. Beatty and W. J. Mulloy, Richmond, 1940), describes the resources of the colony.

Valuable accounts of colonial beginnings appear in W. F. Craven, *The Southern Colonies in the Seventeenth Century* (Louisiana State University Press, 1949); Richard L. Morton, *Colonial Virginia* (2 vols., Chapel Hill, 1960); Robert Beverley, *The History and Present State of Virginia* [London, 1725] (ed. L. B. Wright, Chapel Hill, 1947); and Nathaniel C. Hale, *Virginia Venturer* (Richmond, 1951), which relates the exploits of William Claiborne.

Sophie H. Drinker, *Hannah Penn and the Proprietorship of Pennsylvania* (Philadelphia, 1958), discloses the financial straits of the Penns, 1713–1726.

Jarvis M. Morse, *American Beginnings* (Washington, 1952), throws light on early colonization by surveying contemporary writings and their authors.

SOURCES: A widely used collection is William MacDonald's *Documentary Source Book of American History* (3d ed., New York, 1926). For colonial charters see nos. 1–3, 6, 8, 11, 16–18, 21, 23. The Jameson *Original Narratives* series contains four useful collections: Clayton C. Hall (ed.), *Narratives of Early Maryland, 1633–1684* (1910); Lyon G. Tyler (ed.), *Narratives of Early Virginia, 1606–1625* (1907); Alexander S. Salley (ed.), *Narratives of Early Carolina, 1650–1708* (1911); and Albert C. Myers (ed.), *Narratives of Early Pennsylvania, West New Jersey and Delaware, 1630–1707* (1912). See also John Smith, *The Generall Historie of Virginia* in *The Travels of Captaine John Smith* (2 vols., Glasgow, 1907). On the southern Indians [James] *Adair's History of the American Indians* (ed. S. C. Williams, Johnson City, Tenn., 1930) is a classic eighteenth-century account.

VII

Government and Religion

THE basic institutions of American government and the prevailing political philosophies of today were shaped in large measure during the colonial period. The office of governor, an elected, representative assembly, a two-house legislature, written constitutions, the order of local government with counties and townships, sheriffs and justices of the peace, the common law and the system of inferior and superior courts—all these have their roots in the colonial past. The English origin of the colonies has placed an indelible stamp upon the political habits of the United States.[1]

And yet American political development has not slavishly duplicated that of England. New forces emerged from the American environment which gave to transplanted English institutions an American twist. When the colonies were founded, England adhered to the principle of a close union between religion and government as expressed in the Established Church, which survives today. That principle was planted in the colonies, but the American climate proved unsuited to it; instead, the American trend was toward separation of church and state—a goal attained soon after 1776 as the result of colonial experience. In England after 1600 the central government became increasingly important; in the colonies and the United States the vast extent of the country and a resulting social diversity strengthened local government at the expense of a central sovereign authority. Whoever would understand the United States must think of it not as a centralized nation but as a confederation of communities in which the habit of local government remains a powerful force.

Four pervasive factors affected the political growth of the colonies. First, the leaders—as men of large property—favored a government that would lodge power in the hands of the few. The American frontier, however, created economic opportunities for the lesser folk, enabled them to achieve a measure of independence, and caused them to champion the democratic principle of the rule of the many. Both groups received the English heritage of political liberty—the rights of jury

[1] Attention is again called to H. L. Osgood, *The American Colonies in the Seventeenth Century*, Vol. I (Virginia, New England); Vol. II (proprietary provinces).

trial, representative government, and protection of one's home, family, person, and property from arbitrary action on the part of governing bodies. Finally, the colonial charters conferred definite powers upon political agencies and implied that the king's government must respect certain rights reserved to freemen or property owners. The charters therefore accustomed the colonists to the idea of a written, fundamental law, superior to the officers of government.[2]

American history exhibits a profound, continuing conflict between two opposing tendencies. One is the trend toward the concentration of wealth and power in the hands of the few; the other, a movement for the dispersion of wealth and power among the mass of the people. In colonial days the first or aristocratic tendency was introduced by promoters of colonies who sought to establish a rule by landlords, capitalists, and clergy. However, in order to obtain settlers, the promoters were obliged to grant land to the rank and file of the immigrants. There arose accordingly a mass of small landowners, who by virtue of property owning became entitled to the guarantees of English liberty. In England the class of property owners who enjoyed political rights was small, so that English political liberty was then quite consistent with aristocracy. When large numbers of American settlers acquired property, the result was a democratizing of English liberty. Thousands of transplanted Englishmen became entitled in America to political rights which they had not enjoyed in England—the right, for instance, to vote and to hold office. They escaped the dependent status of servant or tenant and became independent farmers or artisans. The American frontier conferred economic freedom and property, and these entitled the settler to the benefits of English liberty. However, the large property owners, endeavoring to protect their interests by controlling government, came into conflict with the lesser folk who were impelled by a similar motive. The ensuing strife has been a central theme of American history. Both the aristocratic and democratic groups endeavored to interpret or use the charters to their special advantage. Inasmuch as the New England charters diffused political power rather widely among the settlers, they tended to advance the democratic principle. The charters of Maryland and Carolina, on the other hand, concentrated power in a few hands, thus fostering the aristocratic principle and sharpening the conflict between the many and the few.[3]

[2] Vernon L. Parrington's *The Colonial Mind* (New York, 1927) is a brilliant analysis of colonial thought. Very important. See Book I, Part I.

[3] Thomas F. Moran, *The Rise and Development of the Bicameral System in America* (Baltimore, 1895), is a formal study for the specialist.

THE GENESIS OF REPRESENTATIVE GOVERNMENT

The royal charters affirmed the sovereignty of the king over the colonies, conferred upon promoters the powers of government, and invested the settlers, if freemen, with the liberties of English subjects. The Virginia charter of 1606 created a royal council of thirteen members appointed by the king, who were to reside in England and exercise the king's sovereign power over the colony. A second council of thirteen members, appointed by the royal council and empowered to elect its president and fill vacancies in its membership, was given the task of applying in Virginia the regulations of the royal council. This scheme of dual control proved ineffectual. The councillors in Virginia were of equal rank; their president was their own creature; authority was not sufficiently centralized. The first president, Edward M. Wingfield, a mild, unaggressive man, failed to rule with a firm hand and was deposed by his fellow councillors, as was also the second president. When John Smith became president and dictator in 1608 he demonstrated the value of a strong, centralized authority as against "the equality of governors" and "some outrages and follies committed by them," which had "shaken so tender a body."

The charters of 1609 and 1612 shifted the control over the colony into the hands of the Virginia Company. Its general court of stockholders received the right to elect the officers of the company, including its treasurer, to make laws for the colony, and to dispose of its lands. The company ruled Virginia through its governor and council residing there. Between 1610 and 1618 the governors enforced an iron discipline, imposed harsh laws, and meted out severe punishments. The councillors assumed military titles, the settlers were essentially soldiers, and the colony resembled a military outpost of the company.[4]

But such government by dictatorship did not make the colony pay, and the company in 1618 adopted a new policy. Previously all the land had belonged to the company and all the settlers labored as its servants. When, however, the company decided to grant land to individuals, it created a class of property owners, who—in English practice—became entitled to a voice in government. Moreover, the members of the company resident in Virginia were entitled equally with the English members to a part in the management of the colony. Accordingly, in 1618, the company appointed Sir George Yeardley governor and sent him to Virginia with instructions to set up a representative

---

[4] P. A. Bruce, *The Institutional History of Virginia* . . . (2 vols., New York, 1910), is a thorough, technical study of religion and government in the seventeenth century. See Vol. I, Parts I, III; Vol. II, Parts IV–V.

assembly. In 1619, Yeardley arranged for a division of the company's lands, assigning a hundred acres to each settler who had come to the colony before 1616 and fifty acres to those who had arrived afterward. A call was also issued for an election of representatives to a House of Burgesses, which first met at Jamestown, August 9, 1619. Sitting with the governor and council it passed laws on a variety of subjects. The elected body was by no means independent because its acts could be vetoed by the governor or set aside by the company in England, and the latter could impose its decrees upon the colony. But nevertheless the germ of self-government had been introduced into the political order of English America.

With the dissolution of the Virginia Company in 1624 its rights and powers reverted to the king. The political framework of the colony, however, remained unchanged. The king now appointed the governor and his council, but the House of Burgesses continued as before. The royal governor, who was always an Englishman and generally a man of high rank, was supposed to guard England's stake in the colony. He received from Westminster royal instructions which he was required to put into effect. He enforced the laws of the colony, commanded the militia, and issued land patents in the name of the king. His office combined the duties of head of the Anglican Church in Virginia and of foreign secretary in charge of the colony's external affairs. He had a vote in the council, of which he was a member; he summoned the legislature into session; he could veto its acts, adjourn its meetings, or dissolve it and order a new election. He appointed the local officials such as the justices of the peace, who dispensed justice in the localities, and the sheriffs, who collected taxes and enforced the law. This power of appointment enabled him to build up a party of followers and thus at times to control the House of Burgesses. An act of 1680 made him independent of the legislature by granting his salary from a permanent tax of 2s. on each hogshead of tobacco exported, so that he did not have to curry the favor of the burgesses in order to obtain his yearly means of support.[5]

Like the governor, the council after 1624 was appointed by the king, and its members held office at his pleasure, although ordinarily they served for life. They composed a small group of the wealthiest and most influential Virginians. Their familiarity with local affairs gave them an advantage over the governor, who as a stranger and an outsider had frequently to depend upon them for information and advice. Moreover, the governor could not act without their consent. Should

[5] L. G. Tyler, "Virginia as a Royal Province," in *The South in Making of the Nation*, Vol. I, chapter 2.

he seek personal profit from his office, he could distribute favors to the wealthiest men of the colony, who generally approached him through the council. As the upper house of the legislature the council could propose bills and vote down measures offered by the elected assembly; as the highest court of the colony it could dominate the local courts and magistrates. The strategic position of the council made it the political center of gravity in Virginia during most of the seventeenth century—an oligarchy that could frustrate the elected house, thwart a hostile governor, dominate one who was weak, and bargain with one who was disposed to sell favors at a price.

Because of the checks which the governor and councillors could impose upon House of Burgesses, it occupied before 1689 a position of secondary importance. However, since its consent was necessary to the enactment of laws and the levying of taxes, it could restrain the governor and council, although it could not control them. It appears that before 1670 all freemen of Virginia (i. e., all men not slaves or indentured servants) had the right to vote in the election of burgesses, but acts of 1670 and 1684 limited the suffrage franchise to freeholders or landowners. In early times most of the freemen, except tenants, had been landowners; and as voting was by voice, the tenants had to declare their votes publicly and were therefore somewhat constrained to vote as their landlords dictated. But by 1670 a class of freemen who had neither property nor masters had arisen and were making "tumults" at elections and choosing "improper" persons as burgesses. From this class the suffrage was taken by the acts of 1670 and 1684, which thus strengthened the hold of the oligarchy of wealth upon the government of the colony.[6]

The aristocratic temper of the Virginia leaders found expression in the establishment of the Anglican faith as the official religion of Virginia. The first assembly of 1619 met in the Anglican church at Jamestown, the session was opened with Anglican prayers, and the members took the oath of supremacy. As the only colony in which the majority of the people were Anglicans, Virginia established the parish as the unit of local government, imported its ministers from England, and required all property owners to pay taxes for the support of their parish clergymen.

As the wealthy Virginians shaped the colonial government and generally controlled the governor, so also they dominated the Anglican

[6] J. A. C. Chandler, *Representation in Virginia* (Baltimore, 1896), and *History of Suffrage in Virginia* (Baltimore, 1901). These are detailed monographs for the special student.

Church and modified it to suit American needs. Due to the dispersion of settlements in Virginia, the parishes combined a large territory with a small population. One result was inadequate financial support for the churches; another was extremely irregular attendance at divine worship; a third was a marked deviation from English forms of service; and a fourth was the domination of the Church by the Virginians themselves rather than by English officials. Although Virginia formed a part of the diocese of the Bishop of London, his control over the planters was only nominal. The wealthy men of each parish, serving as vestrymen, selected the ministers and managed the finances of the church. The meager salaries and perquisites offered to the clergy did not attract men of the best caliber. The difficulties of travel made heavy inroads upon church attendance, so that the more conscientious ministers complained of a general neglect of religion, became discouraged, and departed. Those who remained enjoyed little influence in public affairs, were continually reminded of their dependence upon the planters, and bitterly complained of their want of income.[7]

Although one function of the Anglican Church in Virginia was to express, through its decorous services, the aristocratic aspirations of the planters, even in this sphere it departed from its English model. Unable to maintain an adequate ministry, the Virginians had to admit lay readers to the pulpit and allow laymen to read funeral services. Burial in a distant churchyard gave way to burial on the planters' private grounds. Marriages were commonly performed in private houses, the sacraments were administered without the proper ornaments and vessels, the holy days of the church were not observed, and communion was partaken by people who had not been confirmed. Thus even the Anglican Church—solace of kings and nobles—became somewhat popularized under the impact of the American wilderness.[8]

The decision of the Pilgrims in November 1620 to settle outside the territory of the Virginia Company nullified the privilege of self-government which had been given them. Since they had never received a royal charter, and because some of their companions talked of mutiny and anarchy, the leaders signed the Mayflower Compact, in which they agreed to erect a civil society and to enact laws to which they pledged obedience—the first American example of government of the people and by the people. Afterward the settlers met together

---

[7] See again T. J. Wertenbaker, *The First Americans*, chapters 4–5.

[8] A detailed and scholarly work, H. J. Eckenrode's *Separation of Church and State in Virginia* (Richmond, 1910), devotes chapter 1 to the Anglican Church.

in an assembly or General Court, where they framed laws and elected a governor and a council of assistants. When the Plymouth colony gained independence from its English backers in 1627, the settlers divided all property among themselves and formed a quasi-corporation known as the "old comers," who thereafter composed the General Court of the colony. As freemen they possessed the right to vote and to hold office. Newcomers were given political rights when the General Court voted to include them as freemen. For eighteen years the General Court was a primary assembly of all freemen who could attend the yearly meetings, but in 1638 and afterward each of the towns (of which there were ten in 1643) elected deputies to a representative assembly, which now became the General Court.

The right to vote for deputies was liberally bestowed, in that non-freemen, called inhabitants, were so privileged, although only the freemen could serve as deputies and participate in electing the governor and assistants. The legislature of Plymouth always consisted of a single house. Since the governor and his council were elected by the freemen and were not allowed to veto measures passed by the deputies, Plymouth approximated a democracy. Its foundations were Congregationalism in religion and a fairly even distribution of wealth among the people.

True to their Separatist principles, the Pilgrim Fathers did not at first create a state church, impose religious qualifications for voting, or require that churches be supported by taxes. Each congregation was a self-governing unit, unrestrained by superior church authorities. And yet the Pilgrim conception of liberty did not mean license. All freemen had to take an oath of allegiance to the king and an oath of fidelity to the colony, to possess "competent estates" (£20 value in 1669), and to qualify as men of good character and conversation. By an act of 1659, Quakers were denied the ballot; so also were opponents of "the true worship of God," as well as "liars, drunkards, swearers." After 1640 probably only a third of the adult males of Plymouth were freemen.[9]

Intent upon transforming Massachusetts into a "Bible commonwealth," John Winthrop, Thomas Dudley, and their Puritan associates felt that they must retain to themselves the powers of governing the Bay Colony; otherwise their opponents might seize control and overthrow the Puritan state. The rule of the many therefore must give way to the rule of the enlightened few. Neither Winthrop nor Cotton believed in democracy; both considered it the meanest, most contempti-

---

[9] A standard work is Albert E. McKinley, *The Suffrage Franchise in the Thirteen English Colonies* . . . (Philadelphia, 1905).

ble form of government. For his chosen people, the Israelites, God had ordained monarchy and aristocracy as the proper trustees of political power.[10]

The situation in Massachusetts in 1630 seemed propitious for the realization of Winthrop's ideals. The charter of Massachusetts lodged all power over the colony in the general court of the company, which in turn was composed of its shareholders, called freemen. Now only a very few freemen came to Massachusetts with Winthrop, less than one per cent of the inhabitants, and yet they possessed all the political power. However perfectly this situation suited Winthrop, it did not suit the men who were denied a part in government. Accordingly a group of 108 settlers demanded in 1630 that they be admitted as freemen of the Massachusetts Bay Company. Winthrop found himself in a quandary: if all who demanded admittance were accepted, the control of the General Court would pass to the multitude; if the petitioners were denied, they would probably leave with a large following, thus weakening the colony at its very inception. In deciding the issue, the leaders admitted the 108 petitioners but about the same time devised a means of withholding political rights from men who were not of their mind.

An act of 1631 ordered that only members of an approved Puritan church might be made freemen of the company. A second act in 1636 provided that new churches could be created only with the consent of the Puritan authorities. These laws laid the foundation of the Puritan state as it endured until 1664—a state dominated by upper-class leaders acting as magistrates (also called assistants). The clergy, as advisers of the magistrates on all sorts of subjects, exerted a great political influence which was enhanced by their right to exclude new applicants from church membership. Only freemen could vote and hold office; only church members could become freemen; only men approved by the clergy could become church members. Admission to a church entailed a threefold scrutiny of the applicant's religious experience: first by the pastor (who might reject the applicant), then by the church officers, and finally by the congregation. From this ordeal timid persons shrank, but that was held to be their fault. In the seventeenth century only a minority of the people were church members, and all church members were not necessarily freemen; only by a special vote of the General Court could·one be made a freeman.[11]

Although the body of freemen was enlarged in 1630, Winthrop

[10] Stanley Gray, "The Political Thought of John Winthrop," *New England Quarterly*, III (Oct. 1930).

[11] See again C. M. Andrews, *Colonial Period of American History*, Vol. I, chapter 20.

and the magistrates were not willing to allow them to exercise the rights conferred upon them by the charter, which stated explicitly that the freemen assembled in General Court should pass laws, grant lands, elect officers, and levy assessments. The leaders kept the charter out of sight and—between 1630 and 1634—limited the power of the freemen to the election of the governor and the council of assistants. Once a year the freemen assembled, usually at Boston, and cast their votes in the General Court. Then the governor and assistants exercised the real powers of government. However, the spirit that had moved the 108 petitioners to demand that they be admitted as freemen also moved them, when admitted, to insist that they have a larger part in managing the colony's affairs.

The first complaint came in 1632 from the people of Watertown, who objected to paying taxes that had been imposed by the governor and assistants, declaring that "it was not safe to pay moneys after that sort, for fear of bringing themselves and posterity into bondage." Winthrop rebuked the Watertown remonstrants and they apologized. But the Watertown spirit seems to have spread throughout the colony. It appears that in 1634 each of the towns selected two representatives who met at Boston and demanded to see the charter. There in black and white they read that the powers of enacting laws and of levying assessments were vested in the General Court of the freemen. Winthrop explained that the governor and the assistants had usurped these powers because the body of freemen had been so enlarged that the General Court could not function efficiently as a legislature. This explanation did not appease the representatives, however, and they declared emphatically that only the General Court had the power to raise taxes, dispose of lands, make laws, and admit freemen—in short that it was "the chief civil power of this commonwealth." [12]

To meet Winthrop's criticism about the size of the General Court and to obviate the expense and trouble incident to a yearly meeting of all the freemen, the General Court in October 1634 adopted a representative plan. The freemen of each town thereafter selected two or three deputies to represent them in the General Court, which now became a chamber composed of the deputies and assistants. The two arms of the court, however, did not always move in harmony. The assistants expressed the ideals of the few wealthy aristocratic leaders; the deputies reflected the more democratic spirit of the laboring settlers. The division widened until in 1644 it split the General Court into two

[12] George H. Haynes, *Representation and Suffrage in Massachusetts, 1620–1691* (Baltimore, 1894), is concise and clear. See again S. E. Morison, *Builders of the Bay Colony*, chapter 3 and pp. 339–346.

houses—the court of deputies and the court of assistants. A poor widow, Mrs. Sherman, had become embroiled in a lawsuit with a rich merchant, Captain Keayne. Early in the case, the issue of which was the ownership of a stray pig, the decision had favored merchant Keayne. Then when the widow accused him of theft, he sued her for defaming his character and obtained a verdict of £20 damages. Knowing that he was widely unpopular as an oppressor of the poor, the embattled widow appealed to the General Court. The majority of the assistants favored Keayne, but the widow had a majority of the votes of the deputies and assistants combined. The case exposed the danger that the assistants might be subordinated to the more numerous deputies, and thus led the next year to the division of the court into two houses, with each chamber receiving a power of veto over the other—a distinct triumph for the assistants.[13]

Through these developments the Massachusetts Bay Company, originally a trading corporation, was transformed into the governing body of a commonwealth. Membership in a Puritan church replaced the purchasing of stock as the means of becoming a freeman. The General Court ceased to be a primary assembly of the freemen, due to the adoption of representation, and the division into the two houses conformed to English parliamentary tradition rather than to the practice of English trading companies. The charter of 1629 remained unchanged, but by a course of "broad construction" it had been adapted to practical needs.[14]

THE FOUNDING OF CONNECTICUT AND RHODE ISLAND

The unrest in Massachusetts which led to the uprising of the freemen in 1634 also embroiled the colony in serious internal strife and eventually induced an exodus of malcontents who founded the new commonwealths of Connecticut and Rhode Island.

The conservative spirit of the Winthrop party which dictated the withholding of political rights from the settlers also cropped out in the granting of lands. The early settlements at Dorchester, Roxbury, Newtown, and Watertown had been planted close together, so that by 1634 many of their inhabitants felt that their lands were inadequate. What they heard of the rich soil of the Connecticut River valley made their dissatisfaction with the rule of the Massachusetts oligarchy in-

[13] E. E. Brennan, "The Massachusetts Council of the Magistrates," *New England Quarterly*, IV (Jan. 1931).

[14] A concise, well-written, modern treatment is John F. Sly, *Town Government in Massachusetts* (Cambridge, 1930), which summarizes various theories of the origins of New England towns.

creasingly acute. The Winthrop regime did not afford sufficient scope for the political talents of all the Puritans, and the stony land of Massachusetts offered but a feeble compensation.

In 1633 the Reverend Thomas Hooker arrived at Boston and forthwith took up residence as pastor at Newtown. Before long Hooker found many things of which to complain. He had been a very eminent divine in England, but he soon felt himself somewhat overshadowed by John Cotton, now the spiritual father of the Bay Colony. Apparently Hooker disliked the Massachusetts policy of admitting only a minority of the people as members of the approved churches, and he certainly disapproved of the oligarchy which Cotton sponsored. Cotton urged that the assistants should have a vested interest in their offices—that they should be reëlected annually and not be ousted except for grave cause—just as they could not "turn a private man out of his freehold, etc., without a public trial." Practice adhered to this theory because the same leaders were repeatedly elected assistants. To Hooker such a ruling caste savored of tyranny. He preferred a government in which power was more widely dispersed among the proper people, to whom the assistants should be, not superior, but subordinate.[15]

On one other point Hooker criticized the Massachusetts oligarchy. The assistants performed the functions of judges or magistrates in hearing and deciding cases at law. Cotton believed that in framing sentences the assistants should consult with the clergy who would advise what laws and punishments to apply. The colony did not yet have a codified body of law, so that the assistants were free to enforce the Mosaic law of the Scriptures, the law of England, or other legal principles. To Hooker such a procedure seemed to be a government not of laws but of men. In his opinion all offenses and penalties should be clearly and specifically defined: "Let the judge do according to the sentence of the law."

In 1634 some of Hooker's parishioners in Newtown petitioned the General Court for permission to migrate to the Connecticut valley. The deputies were willing to comply but Cotton and the assistants opposed, so that a decision was postponed, while the Newtowners were offered additional land in Massachusetts. But having already expressed "the strong bent of their spirits to remove thither," they persisted and gained, in May 1635, permission for themselves and for residents of Watertown, Roxbury, and Dorchester to move where they would, provided that they remain under the government of Massachusetts.

[15] George L. Walker's *Thomas Hooker* (New York, c. 1891) is the best biography available.

In 1635 the exodus began and continued during the following year. Driving their cattle and hacking their laborious way through the New England forest, little bands of pioneers journeyed to the promised land where they settled in the three river towns of Hartford, Windsor, and Wethersfield. Hooker arrived with his Newtown congregation in 1636, locating at Hartford, which became the capital of the newborn colony.

Although Massachusetts had created, in March 1636, a special commission to govern the Connecticut towns, the emigrés held steadfastly to their ideal of independence. When threatened by an Indian war early in 1637 the three settlements each elected three deputies who met at Hartford as a General Court and assumed the powers of a sovereign government. Success in the Pequot war entitled the Connecticut people to a permanent government of their own. Accordingly on May 31, 1638, Hooker expounded in his famous election day sermon the political creed of the colony. "The foundation of authority," he said, "is laid . . . in the free consent of the people, to whom belongs the choice of public magistrates, by God's own allowance." "They who have the power to appoint officers and magistrates, it is in their power also to set the bounds and limitations of the power and place unto which they call them." On these lofty principles the residents of Hartford, Windsor, and Wethersfield erected their frame of government when they adopted in January 1639 the "Fundamental Orders of Connecticut." [16]

This charter of the "people" declared their purpose of forming a confederation to preserve the purity of the Gospel and the discipline of the churches, and to provide laws for a civil government. Once a year all the freemen were to assemble in a court of election and there to choose a governor and court of assistants. Hartford, Windsor, and Wethersfield were each to select four deputies who were to meet with the governor and the assistants, thus forming a General Court. Its powers included the granting of lands, the levying of taxes, the framing of laws, and the admitting of freemen, who alone were entitled to hold office and to vote for governor, assistants, and deputies. The General Court outranked the governor in importance: it could be adjourned and dissolved only by a vote of the majority of its members; it could be called into session without his approval. The governor lacked the power to veto its measures and he could vote only in case of a tie. He could not serve two consecutive years or become eligible for the office until he had been an assistant. Similarly the assistants were

[16] H. L. Osgood, "Connecticut as a Corporate Colony," *Political Science Quarterly*, XIV (June 1899).

restricted to one-year terms. The assistants and the deputies sat together as a single house until 1698, although the assistants in 1645 received the right to reject measures passed by the deputies.[17]

The "Fundamental Orders" were not a constitution in the modern sense, inasmuch as they could be discarded or modified by a majority vote of the General Court. Although they did not create a democracy, they registered the gains that the freemen of Massachusetts had wrung from the Puritan leaders prior to 1635. Particularly significant were the safeguards imposed to prevent the assistants from becoming a permanent, self-perpetuating ruling caste. And yet the aristocratic spirit asserted itself in the action of 1645 giving the assistants a negative voice in the General Court.

Otherwise the social order in Connecticut resembled that in Massachusetts. True, there was no religious qualification for voting as in the Bay Colony, but the suffrage was restricted to freemen; and the General Court in admitting freemen accepted only men of orthodox belief. Only a member of an approved congregation could serve as governor. All the Connecticut leaders scornfully rejected the ideal of toleration; they believed with Winthrop and Cotton that the state should labor with the church to maintain uniformity of religious creed. The colony's laws of 1642 provided that if "any man after legal conviction shall have or worship any other God but the Lord God, he shall be put to death." Two years later the General Court enacted that residents who refused to contribute voluntarily to the Puritan church should be taxed for its support. Other acts fined both the negligent who failed to attend divine service and troublemakers who spoke contemptuously of the doctrines preached by the clergy. Neither Massachusetts nor Connecticut welcomed the dissenter. The chief difference between the leaders of the two colonies was that Hooker would base the government on the consent of the orthodox church members whereas Winthrop and Cotton preferred an oligarchy of ministers and assistants.[18]

Connecticut expanded both by planting new settlements about the three river towns and by absorbing the colonies of Saybrook and New Haven. In 1635 John Winthrop, Jr., arrived in Massachusetts commissioned to govern the territory near the Connecticut River to which Lord Saye and Sele, Lord Brooke, and others laid claim by virtue of a patent issued to them in 1632 by the Earl of Warwick. The younger

[17] Perry G. Miller, "Hooker and Connecticut Democracy," *New England Quarterly*, IV (Oct. 1931).

[18] M. Louise Greene's *The Development of Religious Liberty in Connecticut* (Boston, 1905) is admirable. See chapters 1–3.

Winthrop in November 1635 founded the town of Saybrook at the mouth of the river. By a doubtful purchase Connecticut annexed it in 1644.[19]

The Puritanism of John Davenport and Theophilus Eaton, founders of New Haven, was the purest of the pure. They and their associates, called free planters, met at New Haven in June 1639 and declared that the Scriptures offered perfect guidance for a commonwealth, and expressed their willingness to submit to a government which would enforce the laws of God. Then they selected twelve men who in turn chose seven of their number "to begin the church." Only the settlers admitted as church members by the committee of seven could become free burgesses or voters privileged to choose the governor and a court of magistrates and "to have the power of transacting all the public civil affairs of this plantation, of making and repealing laws, dividing inheritances, deciding differences that may arise, and doing all things . . . of like nature."

Rapidly a cluster of towns sprang up around New Haven—Fairfield, Medford, Guilford, Stamford, Greenwich, and Branford—and in 1643 they united to form the colony of New Haven. Their representatives provided for a general government of the now familiar New England type. The fundamental law of the colony, like the earlier law of New Haven town, limited the privileges of voting and office-holding to members of an approved Puritan church. The freemen or free burgesses, either personally or by proxies, elected the governor and a court of magistrates who met with deputies (elected by the free burgesses of each town) to form a one-house General Court which levied taxes, enacted laws, scrutinized and restrained the magistrates, and served as a supreme court to which all cases might be appealed. So strongly entrenched was the power of the inner ruling group that Theophilus Eaton occupied the governor's chair during the first seventeen years of the colony's existence. Otherwise the similarity of the political order in New Haven to that in Connecticut facilitated the unification of the two colonies in 1664-65.[20]

The stern, inflexible Puritanism of Massachusetts drove into exile four courageous leaders of independent spirit who founded the colony of Rhode Island. Roger Williams, the foremost liberal of seventeenth-

<hr />

[19] The Tercentenary Commission of Connecticut has published sixty brief essays on Connecticut history (New Haven, 1933–36). Of particular value are: Dorothy Deming, *The Settlement of the Connecticut Towns*, no. 6 (1933), Warren S. Archibald, *Thomas Hooker*, no. 4 (1933), and Charles M. Andrews, *The Beginnings of Connecticut*, no. 32 (1934).

[20] C. M. Andrews, *The Rise and Fall of the New Haven Colony* (New Haven, 1936 —Connecticut Tercentenary Commission, no. 48).

century America, came to New England in 1631 where he preached both
at Plymouth and at Salem. He was essentially a humanitarian—a man
who could see the good in all sorts of people and who was prone to
resist oppression of the weak and lowly by the powerful. Combining
the traits of martyr and prophet, he judged issues by the test of justice
and equity rather than by expediency or legality, and threw petty
considerations of personal advantage and comfort to the winds. Insight and intuition moved him to eloquent, passionate utterance of
truth as he felt it, irrespective of logic and authority. Although a man
of fine presence, charming personality, and deep moral earnestness,
he was not of the dictatorial, commanding type of leader before whom
followers prostrate themselves in blind obedience.

In championing the cause of religious toleration Roger Williams
declared war upon the most powerful forces of his time. Persecution
was an instrument which all the entrenched churches employed to uphold their supremacy. In Massachusetts the Puritan leaders conceived
of themselves as agents of God to whom He had entrusted a monopoly
of divine truth. Toleration of contrary views would propagate errors
which would corrupt the commonwealth and so anger the Lord that
He would punish or destroy it. The persecution of His enemies was
therefore necessary to propitiate a jealous God.

Roger Williams questioned all these assumptions. First, he denied
that any church had a full understanding of the divine mysteries.
"The experiences of our fathers' errors," he wrote, "our own mistakes,
. . . and the great profession of light to come . . . may abate the
edge, yea sheath up the sword of persecution." He also denied that
only a Puritan state could enjoy divine favor; many great cities had
prospered without adhering to the Puritan creed. Persecution tended
to defeat its own ends because it inspired and strengthened the persecuted and gained sympathy and converts for their cause. Above all,
the state should not persecute, because political power was often held
by irreligious leaders who would use it to oppress the truly devout.[21]

Roger Williams also differed with the Massachusetts leaders over
the treatment of the Indians, whom he visited, studied, and befriended.
He reminded the Bay Puritans that the conversion of the Indian had
been presented to the English public as the main purpose of the Massachusetts colony, and chided them for failing to carry on the good
work with the funds contributed. And to whom did the land of
America belong? Williams insisted that the Indians were the real

[21] James E. Ernst, *Roger Williams* (New York, 1932), is the most complete modern
biography—a study in ideas rather than in personality.

owners. The Massachusetts authorities were willing to recognize and purchase the right of the natives to land they occupied and cultivated. But even though the Indians' hunting lands were as necessary to them as were their cleared fields, the Puritans insisted that all land not actually occupied belonged to the colony by virtue of its charter. The contrary views of Williams on this point were particularly obnoxious in Boston because they questioned the validity of the charter—the sacred shield of the colony's independence.

While preaching at Salem, Williams charged that the Massachusetts churches were not Christian because they upheld the right of the state to coerce and punish dissenters. He also complained that the Puritans had never formally separated from the Church of England. The Massachusetts leaders insisted that they had separated only from the *errors* of the mother church. In fact, however, they adopted the congregational system which had been first introduced by the Pilgrims at Plymouth and later accepted by John Endicott when governor at Salem before the arrival of Winthrop. Thus there were neither bishops, hierarchy, nor Anglican ritual in the New England towns. In this case the substance did not satisfy Roger Williams and he called upon his fellow Puritans to complete the separation from the Anglican Church by an open declaration.[22]

At another point Williams took issue with the Boston authorities. They believed it proper for the magistrates on occasion to administer to all inhabitants an oath required by law, whereas he insisted that the administering of an oath was an act of worship which should be performed only by truly religious people. If an oath were administered indiscriminately it would be taken by irreligious persons, and the magistrate would be guilty of having communion with wicked men in the worship of God, and thus of taking the name of the Lord in vain.

Once admonished by the Boston leaders, Williams continued to assert his unorthodox views and in 1635 was summoned to trial before the General Court. In the crisis the majority of his congregation at Salem failed to support him. His opinions respecting land titles, oaths, and the relation of the Massachusetts churches to the Church of England, together with his view that the power of magistrates extended only to the "bodies, goods and outward estate of men"—not to their consciences—provided the charges against him. The court found him guilty of unsound belief and banished him from the colony. Although

---

[22] Emily Easton, *Roger Williams* (Boston, 1930), is a straightforward narrative, with many excerpts from Williams's writings. Edmund J. Carpenter's *Roger Williams* (New York, c. 1909) is a brief, sympathetic study.

permitted to remain until spring because of illness, he returned to Salem and resumed his "offensive" preaching. Warned by Winthrop of the intention to arrest him, he fled in January 1636 to Plymouth and then in the spring repaired with a few friends to Narragansett Bay where he founded Providence, the nucleus of Rhode Island colony.[23]

Perhaps the most painful thorn to the Massachusetts Puritans was Mrs. Anne Hutchinson, disciple of John Cotton, who landed in Boston in 1634. Winthrop described her as "of a haughty and fierce carriage, of nimble wit and active spirit and a very voluble tongue"—"more bold than a man, though in understanding . . . inferior to many women." Consumed with a passion for theology and self-expression, she began to hold Thursday meetings in her commodious house where she repeated the gist of the Sunday sermons for the benefit of hard-working wives unable to attend church. Before long she was expounding her own views and passing judgment upon the ministers.

The chief pastor of the Boston church, the Reverend John Wilson, was a rather dour, uninspired gentleman for whom Mrs. Hutchinson conceived a violent dislike. On the other hand, she considered that the second pastor (or "teacher"), John Cotton, was blessed with rare spiritual gifts and that her brother-in-law, John Wheelwright, another minister, also enjoyed the divine favor in uncommon measure. In her discourses on religion, Mrs. Hutchinson intimated that Wilson lacked spiritual insight, or that he was under "a covenant of works"—meaning, presumably, that he was deficient in divine grace and could only repeat at second-hand the revelations to earlier men of God as recorded in the Scriptures. But it was not thus with Cotton and Wheelwright. They were under "a covenant of grace"; in them dwelt the Holy Spirit; they received fresh inspiration from on high and thus were able to interpret correctly the divine mysteries.[24]

Out of these vague concepts arose a veritable tempest. Mrs. Hutchinson and her followers, who controlled the Boston church, were called Antinomians and accused of an heretical belief that a truly spiritual person was above the written moral law. To the defense of Wilson rallied Winthrop, Dudley, and most of the ministers. In their

[23] H. B. Parkes, "Cotton and Williams Debate Religious Toleration," *New England Quarterly*, IV (Oct. 1931). G. A. Stead, "Roger Williams and the Massachusetts-Bay," *New England Quarterly*, VII (June 1934).

[24] Mrs. Hutchinson receives friendly treatment in three popular biographies, none definitive: Helen Augur, *An American Jezebel* (New York, c. 1930), Winnifred K. Rugg, *Unafraid* (Boston, 1930), and Edith Curtis, *Anne Hutchinson* (Cambridge, 1930).

sight Mrs. Hutchinson's conduct was unbecoming to women, whose place was in the home. She had bred a faction in the Boston church, humiliated its pastor, Wilson, and had therefore besmirched the prestige and authority of the clergy upon whom the integrity of the colony rested.

In January 1637 Wheelwright preached a fast-day sermon to the Boston church in which he urged his partisans to wage spiritual warfare against their enemies. When nearly all the clergy testified that their beliefs classified them as Wheelwright's enemies, the General Court found him guilty of sedition and contempt of the constituted authorities. Then in the summer of 1637 the clergy held a synod with the object of winning Cotton away from the Antinomians. In the end he said that he saw the light as the other clergy saw it, and Mrs. Hutchinson was thus isolated. In November the General Court (the colonial government now strongly opposing the Antinomians) banished Wheelwright, found Mrs. Hutchinson guilty of "slandering the ministers," and ordered her to depart. In the proceedings against her she was not allowed counsel or a jury trial and was not even informed of the reasons for her expulsion. Wheelwright went north at the beginning of winter in 1637 and founded Exeter, New Hampshire, while Mrs. Hutchinson's Boston friends established the town of Portsmouth in Rhode Island in 1638.[25]

The defeat of the Antinomian party tightened the control of the clergy in Massachusetts. The issue at stake had been: were the clergy as interpreters of the Scriptures the final source of religious truth, or did religious persons, including laymen (and laywomen), receive revelations and inspiration directly from God? The decision in 1637 favored the clergy and thereafter their influence prevailed.

While the Antinomian controversy was raging in Boston there arrived one Samuel Gorton, a London clothier and self-appointed "professor of the mysteries of Christ." Perceiving that his unorthodox views and his extreme distaste for authority would never appeal to the Bay Puritans, he departed for Plymouth, where he soon was at swords' points with the minister at whose house he lived, and was ordered out of the colony. Thence he proceeded to Portsmouth, the new stronghold of the Antinomians, ruled in patriarchal fashion by William Coddington, formerly champion of Anne Hutchinson in Boston. Gorton was soon leading a faction against Coddington, whereupon the latter again sought the wilderness and in 1639 founded the town of Newport

[25] Brooks Adams traces the growth of religious liberty in *The Emancipation of Massachusetts* (Boston, 1886). See chapters 1–2, 4.

on Rhode Island. But Coddington continued to claim the land at Portsmouth, and eventually his followers and Gorton's engaged in a hand-to-hand fight in which Gorton was beaten and expelled.[26]

Gorton now journeyed to Providence, where new troubles over land titles caused his enemies to seek aid from Massachusetts. Threats from the Bay Colony forced him to move once more, and this time he founded in 1643 his own settlement, Shawomet, twelve miles from Providence. But at the behest of Indians who claimed the land at Shawomet, Massachusetts sent an armed band thither which brought Gorton to Boston. After a stay in prison he and his followers were ordered to leave the colony. In 1645 he went to England, where a parliamentary commission (headed by the Earl of Warwick) granted him the right to live at Shawomet. After his return in 1648 he renamed his town Warwick, and thereafter he was not molested by the Massachusetts authorities.

In 1643 the settlements about Rhode Island found themselves in a precarious position. None of them had obtained a royal charter from the king or an official title to its lands. Massachusetts asserted a hostile attitude (fearful lest neighbors so unorthodox might spread their heretical opinions) and repeatedly attempted to bring them under her own authority. But the people whom she had expelled had no intention of submitting again to her yoke, and accordingly they united to ward off her encroachments. In 1640 Portsmouth and Newport combined under a common government. Then in 1643 Roger Williams went to England, where in March 1644 he procured from a parliamentary commission on colonial affairs a charter which organized the people of Providence, Newport, and Portsmouth into the corporation of Providence Plantations in Narragansett Bay. The inhabitants received permission to form a government of their own choice (by majority vote), to enact and enforce laws, and to appoint and dismiss judicial officers. The charter also defined rather vaguely an area thus to be governed.[27]

Inasmuch as in securing the parliamentary charter of 1644 the Rhode Islanders had ignored the king's authority, they waited until he had been decisively defeated in the Civil War (1647) before they united the four towns of Providence, Newport, Portsmouth, and Shawomet under a common government. The landowners of each town after 1650 elected deputies who met with a governor and a council of assistants (also elected by the freeholders) to form a general

[26] K. W. Porter, "Samuel Gorton," *New England Quarterly*, VII (March 1934).
[27] J. E. Ernst, *The Political Thought of Roger Williams* (Seattle, 1929), stresses Williams's opposition to the power of the state.

assembly. The spirit of localism found expression in the rules that the voters of the towns might either propose measures to the general assembly, or refuse to accept for their localities any of its enacted laws—rules that continued in force until 1663. The Rhode Islanders insisted upon complete separation of church and state; religious liberty meant to them the right to worship without coercion from the civil authorities, although it did not exempt one from paying taxes or sanction revolution or even resistance to established government. The institutions which developed under the charter of 1644 were approved and continued when Charles II issued a royal patent to the colony in 1663 (July 8).

Although not a democracy in the strict sense, Rhode Island made a notable advance in the direction of popular or local government. The voluntary union of the four towns exemplified the idea of federalism which later created the United States. And the little colony was the first to proclaim what has become the traditional American policy of religious freedom. Of the felicities of its settlers Roger Williams wrote in 1654: "We have long drunk of the cup of as great liberties as any people we can hear of under the whole heaven. We have not only been long free . . . from the iron yoke of wolfish bishops, and their popish ceremonies. . . . We have not felt the new chains of Presbyterian tyrants, nor in this colony have we been consumed with the over-zealous fire of the (so-called) godly Christian magistrates. Sir, we have not known what an excise means; we have almost forgotten what tithes are, yea, or taxes either, to church or commonwealth." [28]

GOVERNMENT IN THE PROPRIETARY COLONIES

The governments of the proprietary provinces exhibit a fundamental similarity, whether the province belonged to an individual (Maryland, Maine, Pennsylvania) or to a group of men (as in the case of Carolina). The charters of all these colonies (except Pennsylvania) conferred upon the proprietors the powers of the Bishop of Durham in England —an office which had arisen in the days of incessant warfare between England and Scotland when a powerful ruler was needed to defend the northern border against the Scots. The Bishop of Durham was virtually a king over his domain, subject to the English kings chiefly in that decisions might be appealed from his courts to Westminster.

---

[28] The best full-length work is I. B. Richman's philosophical history, *Rhode Island, Its Making and Its Meaning* (2 vols., New York, 1902). The same author's *Rhode Island, A Study in Separatism* (Boston, 1905) gives a compressed account in chapters 1–2.

The proprietors who received the powers of the Bishop of Durham therefore became virtually sovereign in their territory, and the governments they established were monarchical in form.

The proprietors of Maryland, Maine, and Carolina were the owners and grantors of all lands within their provinces. As the source of honor they might confer titles of nobility and appoint all provincial officers, and such appointments did not need to be confirmed by the king. As the fountain of justice, the proprietors could erect courts, hear appeals, and punish or pardon offenders; their powers included the right to create, equip, and command armies and to defend their colonies; they could establish churches and make ecclesiastical appointments. Not only did they receive all revenues arising in their provinces; the king promised not to subject them to royal taxes. They could make laws, issue ordinances, enforce decrees, administer oaths, and establish towns, ports, markets, and fairs. Their laws, however, must conform to the laws of England, and judgments might be appealed from their courts to the king.

The charter of Pennsylvania did not confer upon Penn the right to create titles of nobility or grant to him the powers of the Bishop of Durham. Laws passed in the colony had to be submitted within five years to the king, who might nullify them within six months after they were received. Penn was also required to keep an agent in England to answer charges brought against him there. The king and Parliament together might tax the colony. Otherwise, the rights of Penn duplicated those bestowed upon Baltimore, Gorges, and the Carolina magnates.[29]

All the proprietary charters for those colonies begun by Englishmen contained one clause of momentous importance: laws should be enacted and taxes levied with the advice and consent of the freemen of the respective colonies. This guaranteed some sort of a legislature through which influential colonists might resist the proprietary interest. However much the proprietors might resemble the king in theory, actually they were but a shadow of royalty. They commonly lived in England, not in their provinces, and thus had to rule through deputies. In their persons they reflected none of the splendor of the divinity that doth hedge a king. Nor did they possess financial resources equal to their rights and pretensions. The colonists therefore were not inhibited from encroaching upon their privileges. As the House of Commons in England strove to limit even the king's power, so also the colonists en-

[29] H. L. Osgood, "The Proprietary Province as a Form of Colonial Government," *American Historical Review*, II (July 1897) and III (Oct. 1897, Jan. 1898). See also Osgood's "The Corporation as a Form of Colonial Government," *Political Science Quarterly*, XI (June, Sept., Dec. 1896).

deavored to frustrate the proprietors. The ensuing conflict endured until the Revolutionary War finally overthrew the monarchical principle as embedded in the then remaining proprietary governments of Maryland and Pennsylvania.

In all the proprietary colonies the proprietors appointed the governors, removed them at will, invested them with their powers, and advised them what acts to perform. The governor was both the political agent of the proprietor and the overseer of his landed estates. "Wherever the governor was, there also was the proprietor." The vast powers conferred upon the proprietors by the charters—executive, legislative, judicial, appointive, ecclesiastical, and military—were exercised in their behalf by the governors, whose primary business was to protect the proprietary interest.

With respect to other features of the proprietary governments—the governor's council, the legislature, and religious policy—variations occurred in the early development of Maryland, South Carolina, and Pennsylvania which gave each colony an individual character.

In Maryland the members of the governor's council were appointed by Lord Baltimore (usually upon recommendation of the governor) and served at the pleasure of the proprietor. As his personal representatives they were supposed to supervise the governors and to compel them to act as he directed. The council during the seventeenth century was a small body varying from three to ten members, who, once appointed, generally held office for life.

Since the Maryland charter did not specify the nature of the legislature to be created, and since it came into being after the governor and council were appointed, its development depended largely upon concessions made to the freemen or landowners by the proprietor. Before 1650 the governor consulted with the freemen in the enactment of law. Sometimes they were all summoned to a general assembly; at other times they elected representatives—the method employed being determined by the governor, who called the legislature into session. The plan of a direct primary assembly of all the landowners obliged those unable to attend to assign their proxies to others present at the meeting. This practice tended to concentrate too many votes or proxies in a few hands; hence in 1650 the freemen petitioned that the scheme of elected delegates be adopted permanently. With this request Lord Baltimore complied, and thereafter the Maryland legislature adhered to the representative plan.[30]

[30] Newton D. Mereness, *Maryland as a Proprietary Province* (New York, 1901), is one of the best monographs on colonial government but is too detailed for the general reader.

In the early days the freemen or their delegates had met in joint session with the governor and the council. However, the freemen felt somewhat overawed and constrained by the power and dignity of these officials, and accordingly requested that they might meet together in a separate chamber where they would enjoy greater freedom of action—a proposal that was granted, also in 1650. The resulting division of the legislature into two houses gave the council a veto over the delegates and *vice versa*. Although the impetus for the change came from the freemen, in the long run this division strengthened the council by giving it power to thwart the delegates. Otherwise, had a single chamber existed, the delegates would have gained control as their number and independence increased.

Lord Baltimore attempted to limit the right of the freemen in the legislature to the mere privilege of ratifying measures proposed by himself. But the freemen insisted that they too should propose or initiate bills. A heated contest broke out over this issue and a deadlock ensued when the freemen refused to assent to the proprietor's measures and he refused to recognize their demands. Finally, in 1650 he gave way and conceded to the delegates the right of proposing measures on their own initiative.

Another major dispute arose between the freemen and the proprietor over his exercise of the veto power. They pointed out that his governor could veto acts of the legislature and contended that one such veto was enough. Lord Baltimore, however, insisted upon his right to veto laws that had been signed by the governor. A survey made in 1674 showed that, of all the acts of the previous forty years, only thirty had been approved by the proprietor. His right to veto at will all the others created a sense of insecurity as to the legal foundations of the colony. On this issue, however, the Calverts would not surrender; all the delegates could obtain was the promise that if the laws were not vetoed by the proprietor within eighteen months after their passage, they were to stand as approved.[31]

Despite the gains made by the freemen, the government of Maryland in the seventeenth century was essentially a Calvert oligarchy. The governor could adjourn or dissolve the legislature and veto its acts. By virtue of his exercise of the appointing power, he built up a family party which controlled the public administration. The council, which could thwart the House of Delegates, consisted generally of picked men: in 1669 it included three Calverts, a Calvert brother-in-law, and two intimate friends of the family. Only landowners could

[31] See again C. C. Hall, *The Lords Baltimore*, chapters 2–4.

vote for the delegates, and they in turn might be overridden by the council, by the governor, and by the proprietary veto. The people had no control over appointments, land grants, or executive action. However, some steps toward popular government had been taken. The House of Delegates had established the representative principle, won the right to initiate bills, and wrung from the proprietor his promise to exercise his veto power within eighteen months. Above all, taxes could not be imposed or laws enacted without the consent of the elected house. The freemen therefore could resist, even if they could not dominate, the proprietor.

The interest of Lord Baltimore largely determined the religious policy of Maryland. As a Roman Catholic he desired to provide a shelter for his co-religionists, but he could not establish a state church contrary to the laws of England; consequently he could neither make Catholicism an official religion nor in any way discriminate against Anglicans. Neither Catholics nor Anglicans came to Maryland in large numbers, so that in order to obtain settlers he had to offer religious toleration to other Protestants. Catholics, Protestants, and Anglicans therefore all found a welcome.

Realizing the dangers of religious strife, Baltimore warned the Catholic leaders in charge of the colony not to persecute or give offense to Protestants, who composed a majority of the laboring settlers. Eventually he had to suppress a small but ardent group of Jesuit priests who attempted to shape the destinies of the colony. They arrived with the first expedition in 1634 and procured large tracts of land from the proprietor. Then through their Indian missions they acquired other great grants from the natives. Soon they were asserting their virtual independence of the proprietor, implying for instance that they were exempt from taxes and the jurisdiction of his courts. Determined to be master in his own household, and fearing that the Jesuits would turn the English government against his colony, Lord Baltimore asserted the supremacy of his laws over the priests, and in 1641 he extended to Maryland the English statute of mortmain, which provided that religious orders could not acquire additional lands. Meanwhile, the papacy had decreed that the Jesuits should surrender the lands obtained from Indians and refrain from sending other priests to the colony. The existing Jesuit missions remained, but in strict subordination to the proprietor.[32]

In the 1640's the relative importance of the Catholics in Maryland

[32] The special student may consult George Petrie, *Church and State in Maryland* (Baltimore, 1892).

declined as the Protestants—especially Puritans from Virginia—increased in numbers. The triumph of the Puritans in the English Civil War further exposed the proprietor to attack. Accordingly in 1648 Lord Baltimore appointed a Protestant governor and sent over to the colony a bill which became the famous Toleration Act of 1649. It guaranteed freedom of conscience to all Christians who respected the rights of the proprietor. Any person who disturbed a Christian in his chosen worship should pay treble damages and a fine of twenty shillings. Should any troublemaker call a fellow colonist an offensive name—such as heretic, schismatic, idolator, popish priest, or roundhead—he was to be punished by fine or whipping and imprisonment. The act asserted openly its underlying principle of political expediency: "the enforcing of conscience in matters of religion hath frequently fallen out to be of dangerous consequences in those commonwealths where it hath been practised."

Except for a brief period, 1654–58, the Toleration Act of 1649 guided the religious policy of the proprietors, and as a result the radical Protestants multiplied until they accounted for three-fourths of the population, as against a sixth who were Anglicans and a twelfth who were Roman Catholics. Later, when the king had taken charge of the government of Maryland, the Anglican Church was officially established in 1692, but it did not attain the supremacy which it enjoyed in Virginia.

The proprietors of Carolina never achieved an effective control over their two colonies. The division of the proprietary rights among eight men, most of whom were preoccupied with other affairs in England, deprived their councils of a strong, guiding hand. By the time Old Charles Town was founded in 1670, two of the proprietors (Colleton and Albemarle) had died, Clarendon was in exile, and John, Lord Berkeley had lost interest. Within twenty years after 1663 the entire personnel of the proprietary board had changed, and the new proprietors were generally incompetent or indifferent. Although two or three men usually dominated the proprietary board, the necessity of considering the rights of the others restricted their power to act. That there were two colonies to be managed instead of one also complicated matters. By and large the proprietors devoted their efforts to the Charles Town settlement, and left the northern colony about Albemarle Sound to shift for itself. They provided a separate government for each colony until 1691, when North Carolina was placed under a deputy of the governor at Charles Town. In effect, however, each colony retained a separate government, and in 1712 an independent governor was appointed for North Carolina. About 1700 the names North Carolina and South Carolina came into vogue.[33]

When Lord Ashley was the moving force in Carolina affairs in 1669 he had prepared a scheme of government known as the Fundamental Constitutions of Carolina. Despite the failure of the proprietors to impose it upon the colonies, it had an important effect on their political development. It designated the most important proprietor as the "palatine," and anticipated that each proprietor should exert an individual influence in provincial affairs. Instead of the single authority of the proprietary board there was to be a division of powers among the individual proprietors, with provision for their coöperation in matters of joint interest. This division of power contributed materially toward the weakness of the proprietary rule.

The peculiar feature of government in the Carolinas was the position of the governor and the council. The chief proprietor, or palatine, appointed the governor for each colony, while each of the other proprietors appointed a deputy councillor. The deputy councillors formed the proprietary council in each province, with the result that the governor, as deputy of one proprietor, was only a leader among equals. Powers exercised by the governor alone in Maryland were exercised in each of the Carolinas by the governor and deputy councillors jointly—powers such as the calling, proroguing, and dissolving of the legislature, the appointing of officials, the spending of proprietary funds, and the ratifying or vetoing of colonial legislation. The governor and the deputy councillors also sat with elected delegates as a part of the legislature or local parliament.

The proprietors allowed the landowners in each colony to elect another set of councillors, who often met with the deputy councillors to form a sort of grand council. The elected councillors served for indefinite terms, save that they might be removed at the pleasure of the proprietors. Acting together, the two sets of councillors prepared bills for the legislature to consider, expended money appropriated by it, raised military forces, declared war and negotiated treaties. The elected councillors did not share the other functions of the deputy councillors, nor were they members of the legislature. The joint council survived until 1691; afterward, all the councillors were appointed by the proprietors.

The legislature in each of the two colonies consisted of the governor, the deputy councillors, and delegates elected by the resident

[33] John S. Bassett, *The Constitutional Beginnings of North Carolina, 1663–1729* (Baltimore, 1894), is a good brief statement.

freeholders. Since measures of the delegates could be vetoed by the deputy councillors, or set aside by the proprietors, and because the delegates could consider only bills presented to them by the grand council, their legal position was secondary. However, in 1693 the proprietors conceded to the delegates the right to prepare and submit bills of their own. Originally, the legislature of each colony had been unicameral, but in each case the representatives separated from the governor and the council to form a two-house parliament (about 1700).[34]

During the formative period, 1670–90, conditions in South Carolina were favorable to the growth of a small ruling class of the wealthiest colonists. Only freeholders could vote for delegates to the legislature, and the powers of the delegates were narrowly circumscribed; consequently the most influential men were the councillors, whom the remote and indifferent proprietors could not keep in check. On the most vital issues—such as the enforcement of the Fundamental Constitutions—the deputy councillors defied the proprietors and united with the elected councillors to defeat them. The refusal of the proprietors to continue the elected councillors after 1691 is evidence that a colonial oligarchy was developing which acted in defiance of the proprietary interests.

With reference to religious policy, the Carolina proprietors intended that the colonial legislatures should provide for the erection and maintenance of Anglican churches. Other law-abiding sects which professed a belief in God should enjoy freedom of worship, although their ministers should not be supported by public taxes. By 1700 the Anglicans, who then composed half of the population of South Carolina, had erected two churches there. Baptists and Quakers had each an organized congregation, and there were three French Huguenot societies, as well as a church supported jointly by Presbyterians and Congregationalists. A South Carolina act of 1697 granted religious toleration to all Christians except papists. Not until 1672 did North Carolina receive the benefit of public worship, when Quaker preachers came into the colony, and not until 1702 was a meeting-house erected. Quakerism was the dominant faith among the North Carolinians during those early years.[35]

The government of Pennsylvania evolved in experimental fashion. Penn was not a doctrinaire; he believed that governments "like clocks go from the motion men give them, and as governments are made

[34] Edson L. Whitney, *Government of the Colony of South Carolina* (Baltimore, 1895)—a technical study, for the advanced student.
[35] Stephen B. Weeks, *The Religious Development of North Carolina* (Baltimore, 1892), is a monograph of the detailed type.

and moved by men, so by them they are ruined, too . . . Let men be good and the government cannot be bad; if it be ill, they will cure it." Once he urged the Pennsylvanians "not to give away anything of liberty and property that they do at present enjoy," and again he wrote: "Any government is free to the people under it . . . where the laws rule and the people are a party to those laws. . . ."

In April 1682 Penn issued his "first frame of government" as a constitution for the colony. It provided for a council of seventy-two members who were to be elected by the resident landowners. As a part of the legislature, the council alone could propose measures; as an executive body it was to function through four committees. The first frame also created an assembly of two hundred members, likewise selected by the landowners, which had the privilege of accepting or rejecting the bills submitted by the council. The governor, appointed by Penn, had a triple vote in the council, but was not authorized to veto the acts approved by the council and assembly. Both of these bodies proved to be too large for the infant colony; consequently in 1683 Penn issued a "second frame," which reduced the number of assemblymen and councillors to thirty-six and eighteen respectively. It also gave to the assembly the right to amend the bills proposed by the council and conferred the suffrage franchise upon owners of fifty acres of land or of other property worth £50.[36]

Penn's governor, William Markham, issued in 1696 a "third frame," which provided that the council should consist of twelve members and the assembly of twenty-four. The assembly now gained the right to propose legislation. By the "fourth frame" in 1701 Penn vested all legislative power in the assembly, thus creating a one-house legislature and confining the council to executive and judicial functions. Thereafter Penn appointed the councillors and endowed the governor with the veto power. He issued the fourth frame because the elected council and the elected assembly had quarreled incessantly, each claiming to represent the voting property owners. The change to a one-house legislature was urged by the most wealthy men of the colony, and since they generally controlled it afterward, the innovation did not spell a triumph for democracy.

In accordance with their religious convictions, Penn and his fellow Quakers did not give legal preference or support to any church in the colony. All believers in God enjoyed the blessing of free worship,

---

[36] Two attractive, readable sketches are Isaac Sharpless, *Two Centuries of Pennsylvania History* (Philadelphia, 1900) and *A History of the Quaker Government in Pennsylvania* (2 vols., Philadelphia, 1898, 1899). See again C. M. Andrews, *The Colonial Period of American History*, Vol. III, chapter 7.

while all Christians were eligible for the right to vote and to hold office. Pennsylvania thus became a secure retreat for Protestants of every persuasion.

The seventeenth century witnessed the rapid emergence of a colonial ruling class. In the major colonies the council became the most powerful political force. Its members, who represented the families of superior wealth, held office year after year and thus mastered the technique of politics and the details of local administration. As the social elite in each colony, they were the natural associates of governors or officials sent from England by proprietors or the king. In constant touch with such officials, they had every opportunity to influence their views and conduct and thus to frustrate in large measure the efforts to shape American development from England. Similarly the councillors had an advantage over the lesser colonists represented in the elected house—not only by means of their negative voice in the legislature but also by virtue of their long tenure, intimate association together, and compact organization. Even the elected house was not a democratic body, inasmuch as the suffrage was generally limited to property holders, thus excluding indentured servants, tenants, and wage-earners from participation in politics.

On the other hand the establishment of the elected house and its success in winning the right to initiate legislation, together with its right to share the powers of legislation and taxation, afforded an agency through which the smaller property owners could resist the aristocratic council. As the body of small landowners increased they found ready at hand in the elected house an instrument for democratic action. The aristocracy of large landowners and the democracy of small or expectant landowners readily came into conflict, because— among many other interests—both strove to possess available lands which at any given time were limited in extent.

BIBLIOGRAPHICAL NOTE

SECONDARY WORKS: William W. Sweet, *Religion in Colonial America* (New York, 1942), a comprehensive survey, finds in sectarianism a principal clue to the growth of religious liberty. W. H. Seiler, "The Anglican Parish in Virginia," in *Seventeenth-Century America* (ed. James M. Smith), describes clearly the workings of the Anglican Church. Perry Miller, *The New England Mind: The Seventeenth Century* (New York, 1939), is a learned disquisition, best suited to readers who are well grounded in the philosophy of religion. Contradictions within Puritanism as they afflicted John Winthrop are dealt with in Edmund S. Morgan's *The Puritan Dilemma* (Boston, 1958). Richard S. Dunn, *Puritans and Yankees* (Princeton, 1962), traces leading trends in early New England, to 1717.

George L. Haskins, *Law and Authority in Early Massachusetts* (New York, 1960), is an important study of the legal foundations and practices of the colony and of the emergence of a distinctive body of law. A similar work, more technical in treatment, is Elwin L. Page, *Judicial Beginnings in New Hampshire, 1640–1700* (Concord, 1959). Samuel H. Brockunier, *The Irrepressible Democrat: Roger Williams* (New York, 1940), is outstanding. Raymond P. Stearns, *The Strenuous Hugh Peter* (Urbana, 1954), is an authoritative treatment of Puritanism in England and New England, 1630–1660. Thomas O. Hanley, *Their Rights and Liberties* (Westminster, Md., 1959), traces the origin of religious freedom in pioneer Maryland.

Standard studies of early colonial governments, considered from an institutional point of view, are: P. S. Flippin, *The Royal Government in Virginia, 1624–1775* (New York, 1919); C. J. Hilkey, *Legal Development in Colonial Massachusetts, 1630–1686* (New York, 1910); Elmer I. Miller, *The Legislature of the Province of Virginia* (1907); William R. Sheperd, *History of Proprietary Government in Pennsylvania* (New York, 1896); E. P. Tanner, *The Province of New Jersey, 1664–1738* (New York, 1908); N. P. Mead, *Connecticut as a Corporate Colony* (Lancaster, 1906); and C. H. Karraker, *The Seventeenth-Century Sheriff* (Philadelphia, 1930).

SOURCES: Collections which contain the colonial charters are: Francis N. Thorpe, *The Federal and State Constitutions, Colonial Charters and Other Organic Laws* (7 vols., Washington, 1909), and Benjamin P. Poore, *The Federal and State Constitutions, Colonial Charters, and Other Organic Laws of the United States* (2 vols., Washington, 1877). The *Original Narratives* series includes J. F. Jameson (ed.), *Johnson's Wonder-Working Providence* (New York, 1910), and James K. Hosmer (ed.), *Winthrop's Journal,* "History of New England, 1630–1649" (2 vols., New York, 1908). An attractive collection is the *Documentary History of Rhode Island* (ed. Howard M. Chapin, 2 vols., Providence, 1916). H. Shelton Smith and others, *American Christianity,* Volume I, *1607–1820* (New York, 1960), is a useful collection of important sources. Perry Miller and Thomas H. Johnson, *The Puritans* (New York, 1938), an outstanding collection, is prefaced by an essay on Puritan ideas and traits. Perry Miller, *Roger Williams* (Indianapolis, 1953), provides a good introduction to the thought of Williams, with selections from his writings. An important source is Richard D. Pierce (ed.), *The Records of the First Church in Boston, 1630–1868* (3 vols., Boston, 1961).

VIII

 Colonial Neighbors

DURING the seventeenth century three European powers besides Spain challenged England's growing ascendancy in North America. The most immediate threat came from the Dutch Republic, which in 1624 planted on the Hudson River a colony which later menaced the unity of England's colonial possessions. Rivalry and warfare between these two aspiring powers continued for fifty years until the Dutch were defeated and forced to surrender their North American territories. By what means and for what reasons were the Dutch able to get a foothold in the Hudson and Delaware valleys, and why did they ultimately fail as colonizers there?

DUTCH AND SWEDISH COLONIZATION

The birth of the Dutch Republic unfolds some striking parallels to the formation of the United States. Seven provinces of the northern Netherlands—Holland, Utrecht, Friesland, Gröningen, Overyssel, Gelderland, and Zealand—united in 1579 to form a loose confederation. Inhabited by people of Teutonic stock, these provinces—once a part of the Holy Roman Empire—had passed under the control of the Duke of Burgundy, from whose grandson they were inherited by Charles I, King of Spain. The Dutch nobles and burghers had long enjoyed extensive rights. Each province had its own assembly which made voluntary grants of money to the reigning duke or king. About 1550 Protestantism, especially Calvinism, spread rapidly among the Dutch, indoctrinating the landed nobles and the townsmen alike.[1] Holland, with its busy industrial and commercial towns—Amsterdam, Rotterdam, Haarlem, and Leyden—towered above its sister provinces. Economically, the Dutch occupied at the mouth of the Rhine a tremendously valuable region which united the rich hinterland of Germany with the outside world. Due to the small extent of their land and their strategic location for trade the Dutch had concentrated upon industrial and maritime pursuits. Their manufactures of woolen and linen cloth, especially after 1550, were

[1] Petrus J. Blok, *A History of the People of the Netherlands* (5 vols., New York, 1908–12) is the outstanding modern authority. See Vol. III.

unexcelled. Amsterdam, it has been said, was founded upon the herring fishery. The supremacy of the Dutch in commerce arose from a variety of factors: "Their cheap freights due to building ships which cost less, sailed with fewer hands, and were adapted to particular trades . . .; the light customs which made their ports the center of the world's traffic; their low rates of interest which facilitated the conduct of business on the most advantageous terms; their banking system which served 'to make a small sum equivalent in trade to a greater' . . .; their education of children, daughters as well as sons; their practice of equal inheritance; their thrift; their toleration in religion; their encouragement of immigration and inventions; their swift determination of suits in which mercantile interests were involved; and, lastly, the presence of experienced merchants in their councils of state." [2]

Under the Emperor Charles V (King Charles I of Spain), who ruled the Netherlands from 1519 till 1555, the Dutch were on the whole well satisfied. The emperor, himself born and bred in the Netherlands, elicited warm personal support from his Dutch subjects. However, his successor, Philip II, was spiritually an alien who hated the spirit of independence abroad in the Netherlands and used the Inquisition in a merciless campaign to eradicate Protestantism. When the Dutch resisted his invasion of their traditional rights, he imposed upon them a ruthless military despotism which provoked one of the most savage wars in history. Seemingly impotent in the face of the mighty King of Spain, the Dutch found a leader of inflexible purpose and courage in Prince William of Orange, a large landowner in Holland, and a convert from Catholicism to Calvinism, whose refusal to compromise led his followers to call him William the Silent. In 1579 the seven provinces formed the Union of Utrecht and in 1581 declared their independence of Philip II, thereby creating the United Netherlands. They erected a loose federal government ruled by a weak Council of State and an Estates-General composed of delegates from the provincial assemblies, which, by retaining to themselves the power of taxation, asserted their individual sovereignty. The weakness of the central government greatly militated against unified resistance, but William the Silent and his son, Maurice of Nassau, by personal leadership provided the necessary cement of union.

In 1609 Spain agreed to a twelve-year truce which contained a veiled recognition of the independence of the Dutch. One great asset in their favor had been their superior prowess on the sea which had

---

[2] Quoted from E. Lipson, *Economic History of England*, by permission of the publishers, A. & C. Black, London.

enabled them to plunder Spanish trading and treasure ships. England in 1585 entered a military alliance with the Dutch which eventually led to the defeat of the great Spanish Armada in 1588. Spain then became involved in war with the French Protestants; in 1592 her greatest agent in the Netherlands, Alexander Farnese, Duke of Parma, died; and Philip II passed away in 1598. These events sealed the doom of the power of Spain in the northern Netherlands. Although she resumed the war in 1621, the futility of her efforts forced her in 1648 to recognize at Westphalia the unconditional independence of the Dutch Republic.

As the pressure from Spain abated, the Dutch people divided into two bitterly hostile parties. Maurice of Nassau commanded one faction, the Orange party, which stood for a strong central government (even a monarchy) and for a vigorous continuation of the war with Spain. In opposition were the Republicans, led by John of Oldenbarneveldt, advocate of peace and champion of the sovereignty and independence of the provinces. Religion finally brought the two factions into open conflict. The Republicans favored toleration and inclined toward the Arminian creed which questioned the Calvinist doctrine of predestination in its harshest form. Like other strict Calvinists, the leaders of the Orange party believed in persecution and the regulation of religion, morals, and popular amusements by law. Nor would they modify their conviction that God had irrevocably predetermined the salvation or damnation of all individual souls.

The war with Spain inevitably drew the Netherlands into the race for colonial empire. After Spain had annexed the Portuguese colonies in the Far East in 1581 it was only natural for the Dutch to encroach upon her new preserves. In 1602 John of Oldenbarneveldt organized the Dutch merchants who had become concerned in the oriental trade into the Dutch East India Company—a move to forestall a similar action by the Orange party. However, the peaceful inclinations of the Republican leaders who controlled the company dictated a Spanish policy of appeasement and hence they avoided giving unnecessary offense to Spain. It is probable that, at the approach of peace, they sought a non-Spanish, non-Portuguese route to the Orient, and thus commissioned an English navigator, Henry Hudson, to discover an all-Dutch passage around northern Europe. Hudson sailed from Amsterdam in April 1609, but soon despaired of penetrating the frozen North, abandoned his original plan, and crossed the Atlantic to North America in search of the elusive Northwest passage.[3]

---

[3] Henry C. Murphy, *Henry Hudson in Holland* (The Hague, 1909), is the best study of the object of Hudson's voyage.

From the coast of Maine Hudson sailed to Chesapeake Bay, then discovered Delaware Bay and finally reached the mouth of the great river which now bears his name. His little vessel, the *Half-Moon*, proceeded up the river, perhaps to the present site of Albany, where he entertained a band of Mohawk Indians and made them merry with brandy. His return to England ended his service with the Dutch, but the sailors of the *Half-Moon* brought to Holland the story of the discovery, the lure of a rich trade in furs, and the promise of a country "pleasant with grass and flowers and as goodly trees as ever they had seen." [4]

During the first years of the truce the influence of the Republicans prevented a grand offensive against the Spanish power in America. However, individual merchants of Holland and Friesland obtained from their provincial governments the privilege of exploring the country visited by Hudson and of trafficking with the Indians for beaver, mink, and otter skins. A few trading houses were erected on Manhattan Island and Dutch voyagers in 1614 explored the Delaware region and pushed eastward through Long Island Sound, ascended the Connecticut River, visited Narragansett Bay, rounded Cape Cod, and sailed northward to Massachusetts Bay. Shortly afterward a group of Amsterdam merchants who had promoted this exploration formed the New Netherland Company and procured from the Estates-General a three-year monopoly of trade with the country between Cape Cod and Delaware Bay.

This monopoly expired just before a political revolution occurred in the Netherlands. In 1618–19 Maurice of Nassau and the Orange party overthrew the Republicans, executed John of Oldenbarneveldt, seized control of the Dutch governments, imposed their stern Calvinism upon the country by promulgating the Dordrecht Creed, and expelled two hundred of the Republican preachers from their pulpits. Closely allied with the Orange leaders was an exiled Fleming, William Usselinx, a restless promoter who had fled to Amsterdam from Antwerp to escape the Spaniards. Usselinx since 1606 had been urging upon the Dutch a grand project for colonization in America—partly as a means of crushing Spain, partly to obtain gold and silver, partly to increase the sale of Dutch manufactures, and above all to gain a rich trade in American products which could be procured cheap and sold dear. Since Usselinx had proposed to colonize in Spanish America he had been an ardent advocate of the war. The triumph of the war

---

[4] The best biography, Llewelyn Powys, *Henry Hudson* (New York, 1928), presents new material with literary skill. A slight biography is Thomas A. Janvier's *Henry Hudson* (New York, 1909).

party in 1618 and the end of the truce in 1621 finally gave the signal for a determined attack upon Spain in the New World.[5]

On June 3, 1621, the Estates-General incorporated the Dutch West India Company and bestowed upon it a twenty-four-year monopoly of the trade of western Africa, of the eastern coasts of North and South America, and of all the islands in between. Conceived very largely as a weapon against Spain, the company was empowered to build forts, maintain troops, make alliances with natives, and wage war; and toward these ends it received from the Estates-General a promise of a million florins and the use of "sixteen well-appointed ships and four yachts." Although the inside promoters of the company regarded it primarily as a means of plundering the Portuguese in Brazil and the Spaniards in the Caribbean, its charter authorized it to "advance the peopling of fruitful and unsettled parts." A governor and a board of nineteen directors managed the company's affairs and appointed and discharged its subordinate officers. The union of public and private interests was further effected by allowing the civil officers of the provinces to choose the company's directors from among the largest stockholders.

The first settlers sent to North America by the Dutch West India Company arrived at Manhattan Island in 1624—about thirty families of French-speaking Walloons—Protestant exiles from the southern Netherlands, which had remained Spanish and Catholic. Since these settlers were under strict orders from the company as to where they should go and what they should do, and because the company's interest in North America centered in the fur trade, they divided into small bands and located in four or five scattered trading posts. The largest group proceeded up the Hudson and founded Fort Orange at the present site of Albany. The next largest group went to the Delaware River and founded Fort Nassau, opposite the site of present-day Philadelphia. A few men proceeded to the mouth of the Connecticut River, while another band remained at Manhattan to hold the island and to build Fort Amsterdam—the seat of government for these widely dispersed forts. The company then sent over an engineer instructed to lay out ten farms on Manhattan Island along the waterfront. Behind these was to be erected a pentagonal fort, surrounded by a wide moat, with gates on two sides connecting a main street traversing the fort and leading to a central market place. Within the fort were located the residences and offices of the officials, a school, hospital, church, warehouse, magazine, and quarters for the com-

[5] The outstanding study is J. Franklin Jameson, *Willem Usselinx* (New York, 1887).

+ Fort nieuw Amsterdam op de Manhatans

From Abbott's "The Expansion of Europe." © F. S. Crofts & Co.

NEW AMSTERDAM ABOUT 1630

From Hartgers's *Beschrijvingh van Virginia*. Interesting not only in itself, but also as an example of the many descriptions of the world produced in Holland during the seventeenth century.

pany's employees. By 1626 the fort had been constructed and farmers had arrived with tools and livestock; New Netherland was well under way.[6]

Although Usselinx had taken a leading part in launching the Dutch West India Company, it did not assume the form which he intended. It was so organized as to aggrandize a few great capitalists, whereas he had advocated a large measure of state control. When in 1623 he was refused adequate compensation for his services to the company, he left Holland and later visited Sweden. Under the leadership of their brilliant king, Gustavus Adolphus, the Swedes were then rapidly forging ahead in all lines of endeavor. Sweden (which in 1624 controlled Norway and a part of Denmark) was commercially backward and deficient in capital, but Gustavus Adolphus, an advocate of mercantilism, was striving by state action to force a rapid growth of national industry and commerce. Usselinx in 1624 laid before the great king a plan for a vast Swedish trading company designed to operate throughout the world. Much as the king approved of the scheme, he was prevented from carrying it out by his participation in the Thirty Years' War. His death occurred in 1632, just after he had attained the leadership of the forces which were fighting to save Protestantism in Germany and northern Europe against the onslaughts of the ardent Catholic emperors of the Holy Roman Empire.

After the death of Gustavus Adolphus, the project of a Swedish trading company was revived by the regent and chancellor, Oxenstiern. The South Company, as chartered in 1637, received a rather indefinite land grant on the shores of Delaware Bay—a region which the Dutch had not yet fully occupied. The company might establish a colony and appoint its governor, while its trade with Europe was confined to Swedish ports. An expedition sent by the company established Fort Christina in 1638, located at the present site of Wilmington, Delaware, and some twenty-seven miles below the then Dutch post, Fort Nassau. In 1643 the Swedes erected a second settlement, New Gottenberg, about fifteen miles above Fort Christina. A few farmers took up land in the vicinity, but the settlements under the Swedish company, called New Sweden, did not ever include more than four hundred souls or extend more than thirty-five miles along the Delaware. The company focused its main interest upon the fur trade, so that farming was encouraged mainly as a means of support

[6] Thomas A. Janvier, *The Dutch Founding of New York* (New York, 1903), a collection of readable magazine articles, is concerned chiefly with the Dutch West India Company.

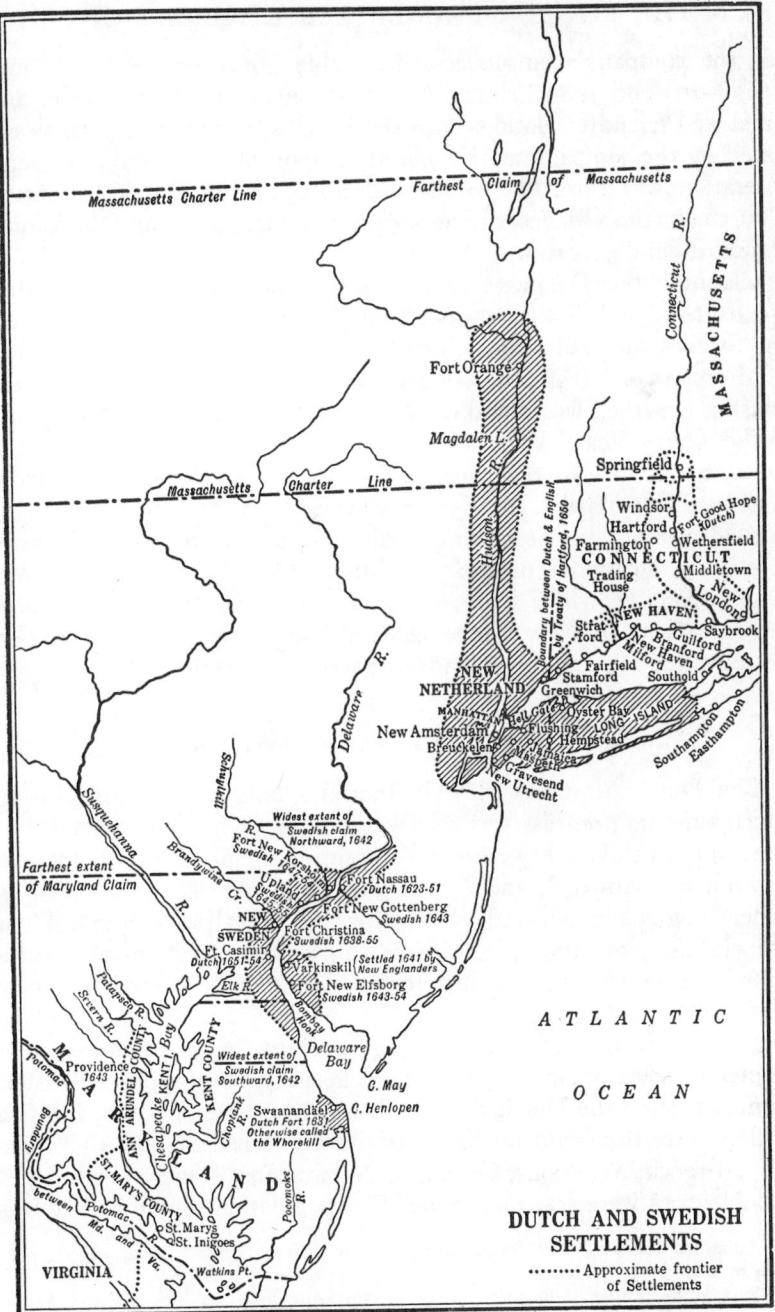

Massachusetts Charter Line

Farthest   Claim   of   Massachusetts

Connecticut R.

MASSACHUSETTS

Fort Orange

Magdalen I.

Massachusetts   Charter   Line

Springfield

Windsor
Hartford   Ft Good Hope
                        (Dutch)
Farmington   Wethersfield
CONNECTICUT
Trading   Middletown
House   New
                        London
NEW HAVEN
Strat-   Saybrook
ford   Branford
                Guilford
Fairfield   New Haven
                Milford
NEW
NETHERLAND   Stamford   Southold
                Greenwich
MANHAT.   Bell Gate   Oyster Bay
New Amsterdam   Flushing   LONG   ISLAND
Breuckelen   Hempstead
                Jamaica
Gravesend   Southampton
New Utrecht   Easthampton

Hudson R.

Boundary between Dutch & English
by Treaty of Hartford, 1650

Delaware R.

Widest extent of
Swedish claim
Northward, 1642
Fort New
Swedish

Farthest extent
of Maryland Claim

Schuylkill

Brandywine Cr.

Susquehanna

Fort Nassau
Dutch 1623-51
Upland
Fort New Gottenberg
Swedish 1643
NEW
SWEDEN   Fort Christina
Ft Casimir   Swedish 1638-55
Dutch 1651-54
Tarkinskil   Settled 1641 by
Elk R.   New Englanders
Fort New Elfsborg
Swedish 1643-54

ATLANTIC

OCEAN

Delaware
Bay
C. May
C. Henlopen

Severn R.

Patapsco R.

Patuxent R.

Potomac

MARYLAND

Providence
1643

ANN ARUNDEL COUNTY

KENT COUNTY

Chesapeake   Bay

Choptank R.

Widest extent of
Swedish claim
Southward, 1642

Swaanandael
Dutch Fort 1631
Otherwise called
the Whorekill

ST. MARY'S COUNTY

Boundary between
Md. and
Potomac R.
Va.

St. Marys
St. Inigoes

VIRGINIA

Watkins Pt.

Peomoke R.

DUTCH AND SWEDISH
SETTLEMENTS
········· Approximate frontier
of Settlements

Based on "Atlas of American History." © Harper & Brothers.

for the company's employees. Two able governors, Peter Minuit (1638–40) and John Printz [7] (1643–53) maintained good order and preserved friendly relations with the Indians. Lutheranism was designated by the company as the official religion of the colony, although toleration was extended to the Calvinists of the Dutch Reformed Church. In the villages, divine service was marked by an Old World regularity and decorum.

Claiming the Delaware region as they did, the Dutch protested against the Swedish occupation, although they did not seriously molest the Swedes for many years. The Swedish forts on the Delaware cut off Fort Nassau from the sea and made it worthless to the Dutch. Inasmuch as the Swedes and the Dutch were fighting on the same side in the Thirty Years' War, the latter tolerated the little colony on the Delaware as long as they needed Swedish aid in their war for independence from Spain. In 1655, however, when the Dutch no longer needed such aid, they sent an expedition of seven vessels which easily forced the surrender of Fort Christina, since the Dutch army was larger than the whole body of Swedish settlers. New Sweden now became a part of New Netherland, although the Swedes were permitted either to retain their lands or to return to Sweden.[8]

WHY THE DUTCH FAILED IN NORTH AMERICA

The Dutch possessed New Netherland only forty years, during which time its progress was relatively slight. Why was this so? For one reason, the Dutch were not a migrating people. Their homeland was not overcrowded, and New Netherland offered no advantages, either religious or political, which they did not already enjoy. Their fishery, carrying trade, commerce, agriculture, and manufactures afforded economic opportunities for all classes. Only a few Dutch people became permanent settlers in New Netherland; consequently the colony had to depend upon alien groups. In 1644 it was said that eighteen different languages were spoken at and near Fort Amsterdam. Although the Dutch composed the largest racial group, English settlers were dominant on Long Island and Swedes along the Delaware. French, Walloons, Germans, Norwegians, Danes, Irish, Scots, and Negroes were less numerous. The population of the colony was

[7] Amandus Johnson, *The Instruction for John Printz* (Philadelphia, 1930), contains the best biographical sketch.

[8] The authoritative, definitive history is Amandus Johnson, *The Swedish Settlements on the Delaware, 1638–1664* (2 vols., New York, 1911). Johnson's material is presented in more attractive form in Christopher Ward, *The Dutch and Swedes on the Delaware, 1609–64* (Philadelphia, 1930).

declining in 1638, and in 1650 the governor, Peter Stuyvesant, welcomed refugees from New Haven Colony, whether "noble or ignoble, freeman or slave, debtor or creditor, yea, to the lowest prisoner included." As late as 1667 the inhabitants numbered only about eight thousand souls.[9]

The colony, moreover, made but a feeble appeal to farmers. Local leaders complained in 1649 of "petty traders who swarm hither with great industry, reap immense profits and exhaust the country without adding anything to its population or security," while "agriculture and many necessary matters remain neglected." The diversity of racial stocks magnified the problem of government and the dispersion of the settlers among widely scattered posts multiplied contacts with hostile neighbors and imposed a heavy burden of defense. The conquest of New Sweden, financed by a loan from the city of Amsterdam, saddled the colony with a huge debt, the repayment of which dictated a policy of commercial exploitation of the settlers.

A further weakness is traceable to the attitude of the Dutch West India Company. Its magnates saw little profit in New Netherland comparable to the gains from plundering Spaniards in the Caribbean. The capture of the Spanish silver fleet in 1627 netted the company a tremendous sum, but instead of devoting it to the development of New Amsterdam, the magnates declared a dividend for themselves. So profitable was the war at this time that the Dutch rejected a peace overture from Spain in 1629. Moreover, the company had a monopoly of Dutch trade with Africa, whose gold, ivory, pepper, and Negro slaves made even the furs of New Netherland seem insignificant. The capital subscriptions of the company were not large to begin with, and no stock was issued after 1623. Due to ill-advised expenditures in Brazil, the company became bankrupt about 1645, and was thereafter forced to neglect New Netherland—even its most necessary defenses. The profit-makers of the company did not cherish an unprofitable colony.[10]

In the 1620's, however, a faction within the company favored the development of an agricultural colony near Manhattan Island, but, since the company as a whole refused to act, the promotion of farming was entrusted to private enterprise. A charter of privileges issued in 1629 provided that a member of the company might secure a large

[9] S. G. Fisher, *Men, Women and Manners in Colonial Times* (2 vols., Philadelphia, 1898), a group of discursive essays, has a readable account of the Dutch in Vol. II, chapter 8. See again C. M. Andrews, *The Colonial Period of American History*, Vol. III, chapter 3.

[10] J. H. Innes, *New Amsterdam and Its People* (New York, 1902), is a scholarly essay in local history, too specialized for the general reader.

estate in the colony on condition that he people it with fifty adults within four years. The landlord, or patroon, should supply his tenants with cattle, tools, buildings, and mills; they in turn paid him rent, had their grain ground in his mill, gave him the first opportunity to buy their surplus produce, and submitted to the jurisdiction of his manorial court. The tenant was free to leave the estate after his lease expired, but livestock could not be removed from the colony. The company promised the patroons an eight-year exemption from duties on trade and gave their settlers a ten-year exemption from taxes.

Only five men took up patroonships, and only one succeeded—a certain Kiliaen Van Rensselaer, Amsterdam diamond merchant, who obtained the land of present-day Albany County, to which he sent settlers in 1630. By 1635 the other patroonships had reverted to the company. A primary cause of failure was the difficulty of securing settlers who would accept the dependent status of long-term tenancy. The patroonships thus indicate another weakness of New Netherland —the refusal of the company to offer attractive conditions to settlers. Tenancy was no lure to colonial farmers who could own land outright in Virginia or New England. The company liberalized the patroon system somewhat in 1638 and 1640, but this gesture was soon canceled by the effects of a devastating Indian war.[11]

The interests of the Dutch and the Iroquois tribes of the Mohawk valley proved to be supplementary. The Iroquois held one of the keys to the fur trade of the Great Lakes region and were thus able to supply the Dutch traders at Fort Orange with pelts on very profitable terms. The Dutch in turn furnished the Iroquois with firearms, which not only increased their efficiency as hunters but also gave them a tremendous advantage in war over enemy tribes. Among the enemies of the Iroquois were the Algonquin tribes which occupied the territory about the mouth of the Hudson—tribes which had already been conquered and rendered tributary to the Iroquois. The Dutch, however, refused to sell firearms to the Indians in the vicinity of Fort Amsterdam, and thus made them more than ever a prey to the Iroquois. Moreover, as farms began to extend on Manhattan Island, Staten Island, Long Island, and the mainland, the Algonquins began to fear for their own fields and hunting grounds. Occasionally disputes and fights occurred over such prosaic things as stray cattle or stolen pigs. Apparently the Indians were becoming restive when the company's agent, William Kieft, levied a tax upon the river Indians for repairs at Fort Amsterdam. Hostilities broke out in 1641 which inspired

[11] Attention is again called to A. C. Flick (ed.), *History of the State of New York*, Vol. I, chapters 6–9, and Vol. II, chapters 2–4 (important).

Kieft with hatred of the tribes and a desire to crush them. In February 1643 a band of Algonquins fled down the river and sought protection near Fort Amsterdam from a war party of Mohawks, armed with rifles. Kieft seized the occasion to launch a treacherous attack upon two camps of the unsuspecting Algonquins—a massacre that cost 120 Indian lives. Eleven Algonquin tribes immediately took up the tomahawk against the Dutch and attacked the farms and settlers between the Raritan River and the New Haven Colony. The colonists who escaped deserted their homes and crowded about Fort Amsterdam, while the Indians plundered and burned with a free hand. The tide turned early in 1644 when the Dutch sent a force of 130 men against an Indian rendezvous in the eastern part of present-day Westchester County. The soldiers advanced in stealth upon the village. "It was a full moon, . . . and the white snow made it like day, when at midnight they rushed upon the stronghold. . . . Before daybreak all was over. The village was in ashes, eight Indians had escaped and seven hundred corpses lay reddening the snow." Fifteen soldiers were wounded, but none killed.[12]

By the time peace was restored in August 1645, New Netherland was exhausted. Perhaps two thousand settlers had been slain during the war. "Our fields lie fallow, our dwellings and other buildings are burnt . . . the crops which God permitted to come forth during the past summer remain in the fields standing and rotting"—such was the colony's lament in October 1644. Kieft's Indian war dealt New Netherland a blow from which the Dutch never fully recovered.

Perhaps the most fatal weakness of New Netherland was its government. The Dutch West India Company appointed the local officials and allowed the settlers no semblance of home rule. Its chief representative at New Amsterdam, the director, received his orders from the company and held office at its pleasure. He was assisted by a council, also selected by the company, which issued local regulations and served as a court in both civil and criminal cases. The company imposed laws upon the colony from Amsterdam and sent over subordinate officials such as the schout fiscal (or sheriff and prosecuting officer), the koopman (or bookkeeper of wages), the clergymen, and the schoolmasters. Local government was exceedingly undemocratic. The town officials of New Amsterdam, appointed originally by the director, formed a close corporation which filled vacancies in its membership. There were neither town meetings in the localities nor elected assemblies for the whole colony.

[12] Maud W. Goodwin, *Dutch and English on the Hudson* (*Chronicles of America*, New Haven, 1919).

In view of the great influence of the director, it was unfortunate that the company thrice appointed men who were not properly qualified. Director Wouter Van Twiller (1633–38) embroiled the colony in heated quarrels in which he was accused of profligacy and drunkenness, while his indecisiveness earned him the sobriquet, "Wouter the doubter." The treachery, blundering, and cowardice of his successor, William Kieft (1638–46), prompted the settlers to demand his removal. Then came Peter Stuyvesant (1647–64), a harsh, irascible, overbearing soldier to whom the company once remonstrated: "You have now learned by experience how too much vehemence may draw upon you the hatred of the people." He announced that he intended to rule as a father over children, proclaimed contemptuously that popular elections would place thieves, rogues, and drunkards in office, and with dire threats commanded the settlers not to appeal to the Estates-General in Holland. He packed the council with his own henchmen, appropriated the company's property to his own use, and ruled more autocratically than any other governor of the colony.[13]

The directors of New Netherland made a gesture toward representative government when they selected leading citizens to act as an unofficial advisory council. Thus there were the "twelve men" and the "eight men" under Kieft and the "nine men" of Stuyvesant. The latter allowed the property owners to nominate eighteen men, from whom he chose nine—three merchants, three burghers (artisans and tradesmen), and three landowners. Although these special bodies had only advisory powers, they often opposed the director. For such resistance Kieft dismissed his "eight men" in 1645 and Stuyvesant successfully defied his "nine," so that this institution was significant chiefly as a mouthpiece of discontent.

Stuyvesant's difficulties arose because the company expected that he make the colony profitable but did not provide him with the necessary resources. His rule therefore assumed the character of exploitation of the settlers, and on many occasions they protested. In 1649 the "nine men" petitioned that the Estates-General take over the government of the colony from the company and presented a long remonstrance which attributed their ills to "1. Unsuitable government; 2. Scanty privileges and exemptions; 3. Onerous imposts, duties, exactions and such like." This remonstrance breathes an American spirit; it expressed the view of men who regarded New Netherland as their home and who desired a government that would promote education, religion, and peace and guarantee property rights. Complaining of the power of the director to confiscate private property, the remonstrance

[13] Bayard Tuckerman, *Peter Stuyvesant* (New York, 1893), is a brief sketch.

observed that "a covetous chief makes poor subjects." Although the Estates-General recommended concessions, the company stood pat and replied by confirming the autocratic powers of the director.

Again, in 1653, the leading men of the colony, assembled in a "landtag," demanded that they be given a part in the enactment of ordinances and the selection of officials. This action, however, was immediately declared illegal and the assembly was ordered to disperse. The English settlers in New Netherland who were familiar with New England's representative scheme may have intensified the popular discontent, particularly after 1650. At any rate, the widespread dissatisfaction with the rule of the Dutch West India Company caused New Netherland to become an easy prey to English conquest in 1664. In the meantime arbitrary government had given the colony a bad name and had deterred people "from going thither to settle." After 1664 the English discarded the institutions of New Netherland, so that the Dutch made but a slight impression upon the thirteen colonies, their chief contribution being that of a good racial stock.[14]

NEW FRANCE AND NEW ENGLAND

While the Dutch were fighting for their independence from Spain, France was emerging as a great power in Europe. In 1589 the strife between French Catholics and Protestants placed upon the throne the Protestant leader, Henry of Navarre. His religion was offensive to the mass of his subjects, yet his claim to the crown was incontestable, and the only alternative to his rule was the subjection of France to the power of Spain—a condition as humiliating to French patriotism as a heretic king was offensive to French Catholicism. From this dilemma Henry IV rescued the nation in 1593 when he embraced the Catholic faith. By 1598 he had freed France from Spanish domination and had granted a large measure of toleration to the Huguenots. He proved to be an immensely popular king whose guiding purpose was the material progress of the country. His "new deal" for France included domestic pacification, the fostering of agriculture, a public works program of roads and bridges, and the introduction of new industries, particularly silk manufacturing. His vision of national wealth and grandeur also encompassed projects of empire in America.[15]

From Verrazano and Cartier France had acquired a title to North

---

[14] A. E. McKinley, "The English and Dutch Towns of New Netherland," *American Historical Review*, VI (Oct. 1900).

[15] Justin Winsor, *Cartier to Frontenac* (Boston, 1894), is an excellent general account. See chapters 4–8.

America and knowledge of the St. Lawrence region. Moreover, fishermen of Normandy and Brittany for a century had visited the area
between Nova Scotia and the St. Lawrence and had engaged in the
fur trade with the resident natives, from whom they heard rumors
of inland seas (the Great Lakes) which supposedly connected the Atlantic and Asia. The early English efforts to colonize Newfoundland
having failed, the great northern region lay open to French enterprise in fur trading, fishing, seeking a new route to the Orient, and
missionary work among the Indians.

Such enterprise had to be entrusted at first to individuals, due to
the poverty of the government; and in order to attract investors
Henry IV granted monopolies of the northern fur trade, the only
ready source of profit. The colonizing efforts of two such monopolists
failed before a successful promoter, the Sieur de Monts, acquired the
rights in 1603. Having visited the St. Lawrence, de Monts favored a
more southern site for a settlement; and accordingly he obtained a
grant to the region between the fortieth and forty-sixth parallels—a
land supposed to be so pleasant that it was called Arcadia or Acadia.
In 1605 de Monts established a colony at Port Royal harbor. Although the "Acadians" who settled there were dispersed in 1613 by
an expedition from Virginia, they returned to hold Acadia or Nova
Scotia as a province of France.[16]

The colonization of Canada was largely the work of a French
navigator, map maker, and friend of Henry IV—Samuel de Champlain. After taking part in expeditions under de Monts to Acadia in
1604–07, when he explored and mapped the region as far south as
New England, Champlain became convinced that this area was unsuited to the fur trade and persuaded de Monts to concentrate upon
the St. Lawrence. Thus it came to pass that Champlain led the expedition which founded Quebec, July 3, 1608. Despite a first winter
of hardship and sickness the little colony survived—partly because
the resident Indians (the Montagnais) were too weak and degraded
to resist.[17]

Fascinated by the American scene and eager to promote the fur
trade, to find a passage to the Orient, and to Christianize the natives,
whose savagery appalled him, Champlain was immediately drawn
into the vortex of Indian warfare and politics. To gain his ends he
supported the tribes near Quebec against their dreaded enemies, the

---

[16] H. P. Biggar's *The Early Trading Companies of New France* (Toronto, 1901)
is a valuable, standard work. See chapters 1–9.

[17] Charles W. Colby, *The Founder of New France* (*Chronicles of Canada* series,
Toronto, 1915).

Iroquois, who were bent upon mastering the country between the St. Lawrence and the Mississippi. In 1609 Champlain proceeded along the Richelieu River to Lake Champlain, where he encountered a party of Iroquois. The firearms of the French threw the latter into a panic-stricken flight. Thus began a century of warfare between the two.

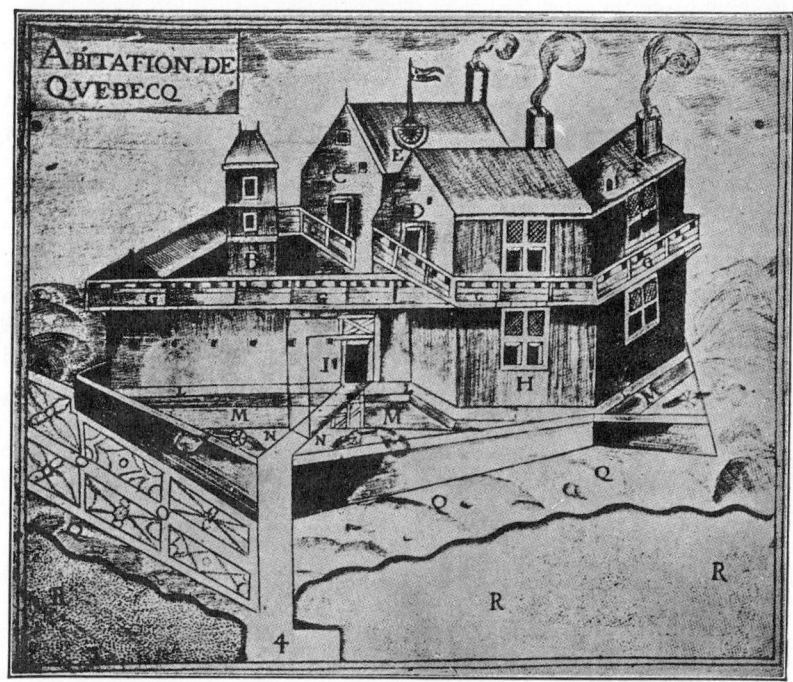

From Champlain's "Voyages," published in 1613. Courtesy of the New York Public Library.

CHAMPLAIN'S "HABITATION" AT QUEBEC

The enemies of the Iroquois, particularly the Hurons, adhered to the arms of France and brought their furs to Quebec, where they obtained the kettles, axes, knives, and firearms which were soon indispensable to the red man, while the Iroquois turned to the Dutch at Fort Orange as their source of supply.[18]

Later Champlain pursued westward exploration. He lived among the Hurons and learned their customs; then in 1615 he traveled by the Ottawa River to Lake Huron and thence to Lake Ontario. One of his lieutenants, Jean Nicolet, in 1634 pushed on to the Straits of Mackinac, Lake Michigan, Green Bay, and the Fox River in present-

---

[18] Louise P. Kellogg's *The French Regime in Wisconsin and the Northwest* (Madison, Wis., 1925) is a book of great merit. See chapters 1–8.

day Wisconsin. Sent by Champlain to make an alliance with western Indians in order to open the interior to trade and exploration, Nicolet visited the Winnebago tribe, from whose chiefs he heard of a great river (the Mississippi) leading to a "great water," presumably the Pacific. Thus Champlain's work not only revealed the Great Lakes but also kept alive the dream of a Northwest passage through Canada.[19]

Beyond such achievements New France made but slight progress, largely because of inadequate backing in France. The death of Henry IV in 1610 resulted in canceling the monopoly of de Monts, although Champlain remained in command at Quebec. The control over New France was now given to great nobles interested only in a personal income from the colony. This they obtained by selling trading monopolies to French merchants who opposed settlement as injurious to the fur trade, which netted profits as high as 40 per cent. However, by 1624 France had fallen under the sway of Cardinal Richelieu, apostle of absolutism, defender of Catholicism, and champion of colonization. He revoked all previous concessions in Canada, and in 1628 formed the Company of New France, composed of a hundred associates who contributed a total capital of £13,000. The company received a perpetual monopoly of the fur trade and absolute title to the lands of New France. Richelieu insisted upon colonization; hence the company was required to transport four thousand settlers within fifteen years, to support each settler for three years after arrival, and to maintain three priests in each settlement.[20]

The plans of Richelieu for a populous, agricultural colony were not realized and the fur trade remained the economic basis of New France. The profits of the trade were not sufficient to enable the company to establish the required quota of settlers. Moreover, a war between England and France weakened the company by virtue of English seizures of several of the company's ships and a conquest of Quebec in 1629, although France recovered Canada by the treaty of St. Germain in 1632. Only Frenchmen who were Roman Catholics were admitted as settlers, and the French were not a migrating people, believing that "next to heaven, France is the most beautiful of all lands." As late as 1637 only two agricultural settlers had arrived. The population consisted of traders, officials, soldiers, employees, and priests.[21]

---

[19] Reuben G. Thwaites, *France in America* (New York, c. 1905), a brief survey by a great editor, is available in the *American Nation* series.

[20] *Canada and Its Provinces* (ed. Adam Shortt and Arthur G. Doughty, 23 vols., Toronto, 1914–17) is a coöperative work consisting of reliable articles by qualified writers. See Vols. I and II entitled *New France* (1914).

[21] A group of attractive biographical essays is C. W. Colby, *Canadian Types of the Old Regime* (New York, 1908). See chapters 1–4.

New France was without benefit of clergy until 1615, when four fathers of the Recollect order arrived—followers of St. Francis of Assisi who served the poor in a spirit of love and self-sacrifice. However, the Recollects, who were pledged to poverty, lacked funds for missions, and because the fur traders did not choose to bear the expense, the work was entrusted after 1625 to the Society of Jesus—a rich, powerful order, whose members displayed an almost superhuman courage in facing danger and privation for the salvation of souls and the glorification of the Roman Catholic Church. Since the Jesuits labored chiefly with the Indians their efforts contributed to the success of France in extending her sway in the northern fur trade. The willingness of the French to treat the Indians as human beings, to associate with them on friendly terms, to adapt themselves to the natives' way of life, and to aid them in war also explains the secret of France's early ascendancy in Canada.[22]

The country south of Acadia, now Maine and New Hampshire, was destined to become a theater of strife between New England and France. Massachusetts coveted this territory, partly that she might so control it as to protect her Puritan churches from undesirable neighbors, partly that she might share the wealth of its rich timber resources, its fur trade, and its fishery, and partly that she might defend herself against the French. Since 1622 this region had been subject to the claims of Captain John Mason, whose title applied to the land between the Piscataqua and the Merrimack Rivers, and of Sir Ferdinando Gorges, who held the area between the Piscataqua and the Kennebec.

The principal towns of New Hampshire were founded between 1623 and 1640: Dover and Portsmouth by Anglicans; Exeter by the unorthodox Puritan followers of Wheelwright; and Hampton by orthodox Puritans acting under the authority of Massachusetts. All were annexed by Massachusetts, 1641–43, an act explained in part by the death of Mason in 1635 and by the Puritan uprising in England against his party, the royalists. In justification, Massachusetts interpreted her charter in such a way as to include New Hampshire within her territory. Although the charter of 1629 indicated that the northern boundary of Massachusetts was to be located three miles north of the *mouth* of the Merrimack, the Bay leaders insisted that the boundary should extend three miles north of the source of the Merrimack. Moreover, Massachusetts had received from Lords Saye and

[22] Francis Parkman, *The Jesuits in America* (Boston, 1870), is a masterpiece. See also Thomas G. Marquis, *The Jesuit Missions* (*Chronicles of Canada* series, Toronto, 1916).

Brooke and other English Puritans a title to Portsmouth and Dover which they had previously purchased.

Due to the religious diversity of the New Hampshire towns and to their former privileges of self-government, Massachusetts granted them a liberal measure of home rule. They managed their local affairs in their town meetings, elected deputies to the General Court at Boston, and were exempted from the church membership requirement for voting then in force in Massachusetts. They remained a part of Massachusetts until 1677, when English judges decided that New Hampshire was not a part of the Bay Colony. In 1679 England converted New Hampshire into a royal province whose governor and council thereafter were appointed by the king, while the elected representatives formed a separate assembly.

The hold of Massachusetts on Maine proved to be more enduring. Four groups took part in founding settlements there. Sir Ferdinando Gorges was responsible for establishing the towns of York, Kittery, Wells, and Saco—all on the southern coast of Maine; the Pilgrims of Plymouth erected a fur trading post on the Kennebec at the modern site of Augusta; English merchants set up similar posts at Pemaquid and on Monhegan Island; and rivals of Gorges developed settlements at Casco Bay, where Portland and Scarborough now stand. Between 1652 and 1658 Massachusetts annexed the four Gorges settlements and those at Casco Bay. After the death of Gorges in 1647 had left his colonists without a guiding hand, the towns of York, Kittery, and Wells endeavored to form an independent union akin to that of Rhode Island. In this they were frustrated by Massachusetts, whose leaders justified the annexation by their interpretation of the northern boundary, which gave Massachusetts a claim to more than half of Maine. Massachusetts had also purchased the claims of one of Gorges' rivals. Moreover, the annexation occurred after the Puritans in England had lessened the influence of the Gorges family, adherents of the royalist cause.[23]

After the restoration of Charles II, Ferdinando Gorges, grandson of Sir Ferdinando, carried on a long struggle with Massachusetts for the possession of southern Maine. In 1677 the Privy Council decided against the Bay Colony, and the latter then secretly purchased the Gorges rights for £1,250. Previously Massachusetts had regarded Maine as an integral part of her territory and had granted the northern towns privileges similar to those enjoyed by New Hampshire when a part of Massachusetts. Between 1677 and 1684 Massachusetts

[23] See again H. S. Burrage, *Beginnings of Colonial Maine*, chapters 10–23, and J. P. Baxter, *Sir Ferdinando Gorges*, Vol. I.

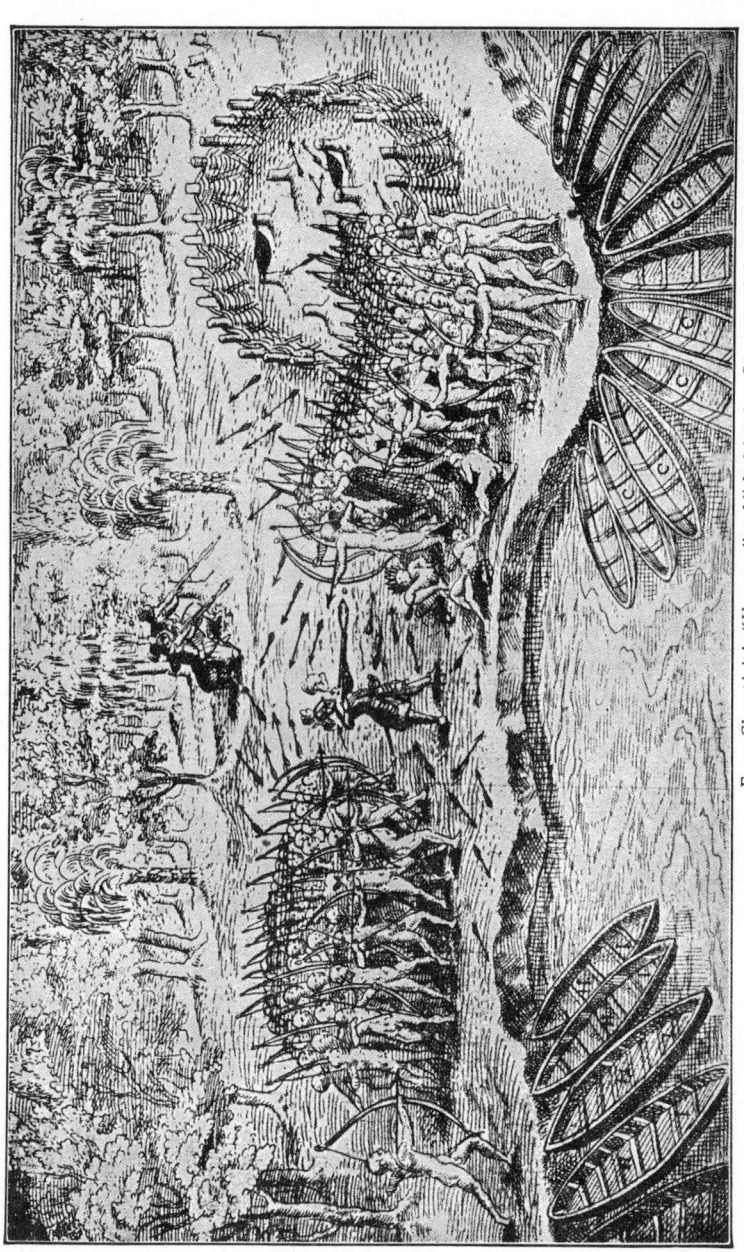

From Champlain's "Voyages," published in 1613. Courtesy of the New York Public Library.

CHAMPLAIN'S FIRST FIGHT WITH THE IROQUOIS

held Maine as proprietor in place of Gorges and endeavored to collect quit-rents from the northern settlers.

The Confederation of New England

The presence of the Dutch, French, and Indians, coupled with a
series of boundary disputes among the New England colonies, induced them in 1643 to form the first voluntary American union. The
original impetus for this came from hostilities with the Pequot Indians on the Connecticut frontier. The extension of Puritan settlement into the Connecticut valley brought into bold relief the irreconcilable conflict between two economic orders. The Indian's dependence
upon hunting and trapping necessitated a large area to support a small
population, whereas the New Englanders required additional lands to
support a rapidly growing farming population. Accordingly, the Puritans refused to recognize the title of the Indians to lands they did not
occupy and cultivate, advancing the theory that cultivation conferred
the right of ownership and thus denying to the red man his hunting
lands which were as indispensable to him as was farming land to the
English settler.

The penetration of the Puritans into the Connecticut valley gave
rise to numerous quarrels with the resident Pequots which resulted
in the murder of several settlers at Saybrook and Wethersfield in
1635–36. Prior to this, Massachusetts, in order to avenge the death of
an English trader, John Oldham, had sent into the Pequot country
an expedition which plundered the Indians and infuriated them. A
leader at Saybrook remarked to John Endicott, in charge of the expedition, "You come hither to raise these wasps about my ears, and
then you will take wings and flee away." And so it happened. When
the resulting Indian outrages had become general, Massachusetts appealed to Plymouth for aid and succeeded, through the influence of
Roger Williams, in detaching the Narragansets from an alliance with
the Pequots. But the settlers on the Connecticut could not wait for
aid from Boston, and in May 1637 they raised a force of ninety men
which was placed under the command of John Mason and John
Underhill, two accomplished Indian fighters. The Pequot stronghold was on the Pequot River, between Saybrook and Narragansett
Bay. At the suggestion of Mason, the Connecticut force sailed from
Saybrook to Narragansett Bay, thus suggesting to the Pequots that
the force was returning to Massachusetts and throwing them off their
guard. Then the settlers landed and made an all-day march to the
Pequot fort, to which they set fire at night. Five hundred Pequots

were burned alive or killed as they tried to escape over the palisade, while the New Englanders lost but two men. Reinforcements now arrived from Massachusetts, and the surviving Pequots were ruthlessly tracked down, captured, and turned over to other tribes, enslaved by the Puritans, or sold to the West Indies. The Pequots were virtually exterminated, while the prowess and diplomacy of the Connecticut Puritans enabled them to make a treaty with the Narragansets, and peace prevailed on the New England frontier for nearly forty years after the Pequot War.[24]

The New Englanders also came into conflict with the Dutch, who claimed that New Netherland extended to the Connecticut River, and who in 1633 built a trading post, the House of Good Hope, at the site of Hartford. Plymouth established a similar outpost at Windsor about the same time. The Dutch in 1634 and 1635 sent expeditions against the Pilgrims' fort and Saybrook, but the New Englanders refused to move and appeared to be too strong to be dislodged by force. By 1640 the founding of New Haven and the westward expansion of Connecticut brought the English within forty miles of Manhattan Island. The two parties also struggled for possession of Long Island as the New Englanders occupied its eastern end and expanded westward toward the Dutch settlements there. Neither Connecticut nor New Haven had a legal claim to the territory in dispute but they enjoyed the backing of the English government, which persistently refused to recognize the Dutch claim to the land between the Connecticut and the Delaware. The English position was expressed by an English representative at The Hague, who advised his countrymen to "crowd on, crowding the Dutch out of those places they have, but without hostility or any act of violence." The English had the better title by virtue of discovery; the Dutch defended their right by prior occupation; while in the disputed area east of the Hudson the English outnumbered the Dutch at least three to one.[25]

The relations among the New England colonies furnished another source of trouble. Massachusetts, the most populous and powerful colony, felt a mission to dominate her weaker neighbors and to control the whole of New England. Since the smaller colonies did not possess land patents issued by the king, and because of conflicting grants and the uncertainty of geographical locations, Massachusetts was in a position to extend her claims in all directions. Thus, when

[24] Howard Bradstreet, *The Story of the War with the Pequots, Re-Told*, (New Haven, 1933—Connecticut Tercentenary Commission, no. 5).

[25] John G. Palfrey's *A Compendious History of New England* (4 vols., Boston, 1884), a learned, well-written political narrative, devotes much space to intercolonial relations.

Plymouth established a trading post on the Connecticut in 1633, Massachusetts refused to coöperate and then in 1635 laid claim to the Pilgrims' land when it was desired by emigrants from Massachusetts. The dispute was finally settled by allowing the Massachusetts settlers to occupy fifteen-sixteenths of the land, although the Bay Colony had no legal title. Governor Bradford spoke of the incident as an "unkindness not so soon forgotten."

Again, Massachusetts interfered in a dispute that had arisen in 1634 at the trading post established by the Pilgrims on the Kennebec. In this case also Massachusetts had no title to the land in question, yet she took upon herself the settlement of the quarrel, arrested one of the Plymouth magistrates, and obliged other Plymouth leaders to go to Boston to adjust the matter. After the establishment of Connecticut, that colony contended with Massachusetts over their common boundary, while the Bay leaders refused to consent to a scientific survey. Likewise, Massachusetts laid claim to a large part of the territory of Plymouth. Such frontier disputes revealed the need of some scheme of united action by which the smaller colonies might protect themselves from the aggrandizement of Massachusetts.[26]

At the same time, however, the Puritan colonies had many things in common. New England was a geographical and economic unit, with Boston its commercial center; a few settlements excepted, there was a fundamental unity in government, religion, and ideals; the people were exclusively of English stock: all these factors favored coöperation. Moreover, after 1642, the New Englanders could not refer their disputes to a common umpire in England or look thither for protection—torn as England was by civil war. Nor could England coerce or punish the colonies for usurping sovereign rights when they united to form a miniature league of nations with the object of exercising powers which properly belonged to England.

In 1637 Massachusetts proposed a union of the colonies with the suggestion that she be given some preëminence in its deliberations. Connecticut declined the offer, fearful that she would thus fall under the domination of her more powerful neighbor. But when Connecticut was having Indian troubles in 1642, she advanced a similar proposal, with the result that in May 1643 representatives of four colonies met in Boston and adopted articles creating "The Confederation of the United Colonies of New England." Its members were Massachusetts, Connecticut, Plymouth, and New Haven. The towns of Rhode Island, Maine, and New Hampshire were not admitted, partly

[26] See again J. T. Adams, *Founding of New England*, pp. 175–188, chapters 9–10, 14.

because their people did not see eye to eye with the orthodox Puritans of the four member colonies, and partly because Massachusetts desired to annex those towns—and therefore could not recognize them as independent colonies by admitting them to a confederation of equals. When Rhode Island applied for membership in 1648 the condition was imposed that she become incorporated into Massachusetts—and to this she would not consent.[27]

The articles declared the purpose of the united colonies to be "a firm and perpetual league of friendship, for offense and defense, mutual advice and succor upon all just occasions, both for preserving and propagating the truths of the Gospel and for their mutual safety and welfare." Each colony received a guarantee of its independence and territory. New members could not be admitted or a member colony merged with another member except by vote of the Confederation. The general court of each colony elected two commissioners to meet regularly once a year and on special occasions with similar commissioners from the other three colonies. The eight commissioners had the power to declare war, make peace, and apportion military expenses among the colonies in proportion to their adult male population, although the general court of each colony actually levied the taxes. Six of the eight commissioners had to vote for such measures before they became effective. The commissioners were also authorized to settle boundary disputes, to provide for the capture and return of fugitives from justice, and to make recommendations to the respective colonies. The only executive provided was the president of the commissioners (chosen yearly), who was merely a moderator presiding over equals.

The Confederation was fairly active until 1665; afterward its influence was negligible. Its functioning exposed two fundamental weaknesses. First, its work necessarily involved foreign powers—the Dutch and the French—yet in this sphere England refused to recognize, and thus negatived, its actions. For instance: in 1650 the commissioners negotiated with Peter Stuyvesant the Treaty of Hartford, which aimed to dispose of pending conflicts between New England and New Netherland and to locate a definite boundary between the two. Although this treaty was ratified by Holland, England refused to acknowledge it, insisting that the Dutch had no rights in North America.[28]

The second weakness arose from the fact that Massachusetts would

---

[27] Richard Hildreth's *The History of the United States* (6 vols., New York, 1854–55) is a vigorous, realistic work. Writing from the Federalist point of view, Hildreth, a New England journalist, stressed the historical background of the American Union.
[28] John Fiske, *New France and New England* (Boston, 1902), chapters 2–4.

not treat the smaller colonies as equals and that the latter would not recognize her as superior. Massachusetts therefore felt free to ignore the Confederation and to act alone when her interests so dictated. A bitter conflict broke out over the town of Springfield, located within Massachusetts in the Connecticut valley. In 1644 Connecticut purchased Saybrook and proceeded to collect the purchase price by levying duties on goods shipped down the river. Springfield, claiming that she was outside of Connecticut's jurisdiction, refused to pay the duties; Connecticut insisted that she should, since the fort at Saybrook protected her commerce. When the matter was referred to the Confederation, Plymouth and New Haven supported Connecticut, while Massachusetts supported Springfield. Unable to obtain exemption for Springfield from the duties, Massachusetts in 1649 retaliated by taxing the products of Plymouth, New Haven, and Connecticut which entered Boston—the port from which most of such exports were shipped to Europe. Massachusetts would not yield, and this led the commissioners to ask whether her opposition agreed "with the law of love and with the tenure and import of the articles of confederation," adding that they desired "to be spared in all farther agitations concerning Springfield."

A second defiance on the part of Massachusetts occurred during the first war between England and Holland (1652–54). Connecticut and New Haven, asserting that the Dutch at New Netherland were plotting to attack western New England with Indian allies, induced seven of the eight commissioners to vote for a war against the Dutch. However, Massachusetts, having little interest in the issue at stake, refused to participate, affirming that the commissioners could declare only a defensive, not an offensive, war, although the articles clearly sanctioned warfare of both kinds. A European peace ended the war without a New England campaign against the Dutch, and hence Massachusetts was credited with another victory over the Confederation.

The leaders of Massachusetts also ignored the Confederation in their dealings with the French. Soon after France recovered Acadia from England in 1632 that region became the object of rivalry between two French magnates, each of whom aspired to dominate it as governor. Charles d'Aulnay, who held the land to the north and east of the Bay of Fundy and was an uncompromising Catholic and enemy of the English, insisted that France possessed all North America to Florida. His rival, Claude de La Tour, who claimed the territory on the western side of the Bay of Fundy, was a lax Catholic with leanings toward Protestantism and friendship with New England, whose merchants he allowed to trade with Nova Scotia. After a series of conflicts, La Tour appealed to Boston for aid against Aulnay. It was decided by Governor Winthrop and an inner group of leaders that Massachusetts could not act officially, but they permitted La Tour to raise volunteers who went forth and plundered Aulnay's settlement. In the end, however, Aulnay secured the backing of the French court, crushed La Tour's plantation, and became governor of Acadia. Massachusetts then had to recognize Aulnay and recompense him for its part in La Tour's attack. The Winthrop group had acted without submitting the matter to the General Court, because, as Winthrop explained, "We knew they would not have given him [La Tour] aid without consent of the commissioners of the other colonies, and for a bare permission, we might do it without the court." The commissioners, on the other hand, resolved against any future acts of war such as the Massachusetts leaders had permitted. The episode showed that the men in control of the strongest colony were not willing to be bound by the Confederation when coöperative action entailed a sacrifice of their particular interests.[29]

Some of the most effective work of the Confederation was performed in the shaping of a general New England policy. The commissioners made numerous recommendations, many of which were adopted by the several colonies, thus contributing to their social solidarity. For instance, the Confederation suggested that well-to-do Puritans should make gifts to its president for the support of the Puritan center of learning, Harvard College. Each colony was advised to tax its inhabitants who did not contribute voluntarily toward the maintenance of the Puritan ministers and to banish all Quakers under pain of death for returning. Each church was called upon to keep a careful watch over its membership, so that only those persons might be admitted who had "had an effectual calling and had entered by an express covenant," while all errors contrary to the Scriptures, to Sabbath observance, and to the authority of the clergy were to be rigorously suppressed. Thus in the religious sphere the spirit of the Confederation was one of intolerant orthodoxy. Moreover, the Confederation served as an agency for missionary work among the Indians. It coöperated with an English Society for Propagating the Gospel in New England, from which the commissioners received funds for disbursement. One branch of this work was a program for educating young Indians at Harvard College.

Several factors finally put an end to the Confederation. The conquest of New Netherland by England in 1664 removed one of the

---

[29] Richard Frothingham, *The Rise of the Republic* . . . (Boston, 1873), presents a political interpretation of American history. See chapter 2.

hostile neighbors who had made the union necessary, while in 1665 Connecticut, contrary to the terms of the articles, absorbed New Haven, thus leaving only three member colonies. Moreover, after the reëstablishment of the English monarchy in 1660, the home government resumed its authority over America in matters of diplomacy and defense, and since the New Englanders had never had a legal warrant for their union, they could no longer act together as semi-independent states without incurring the displeasure of the king. Finally, the charter of Massachusetts was annulled in 1684 and England then imposed upon the New England colonies an imperial union which deprived them of their powers of independent action. The Confederation, however, had enabled the New Englanders to coöperate during the time when England was paralyzed by civil upheaval, and thus it fostered among them a spirit of self-reliance and independence which could not be eradicated afterward.

The weakness of the Confederation became apparent again in 1675–78, when New England faced a grave domestic crisis, King Philip's War, which was essentially a struggle for land.[30] During the thirty-five years after 1640, the settlements of New England had been expanding until they extended fifty miles or more along the eastern and southern coasts and reached up the Connecticut valley to the northern boundary of Massachusetts, while the white population had increased from 22,500 in 1640 to 52,000 in 1675. This steady advance threatened eventual disaster to the Indians as they felt a growing pressure upon their scanty means of subsistence and saw that the land hunger of the whites could not be appeased. Two weeks after the outbreak of the war a letter from Boston said that Indian lands worth £10,000 had already been gained from the struggle, and the land factor was further indicated by an act of Massachusetts promising land bounties to soldiers who expelled the natives from the Narraganset country.[31]

Meanwhile, the attitude of the settlers toward the red man had become increasingly hostile and contemptuous. Although many Puritans had sincerely desired and labored to Christianize the Indians, their efforts could not prevent the inevitable conflict between two antagonistic ways of life. The New Englanders did not establish isolated forest missions, but rather endeavored to bring the Indians at the fringe of settlement into the English villages for the services at the

[30] The best earlier narrative is George W. Ellis and John E. Morris, *King Philip's War* (New York, c. 1906).

[31] J. A. Doyle's *English Colonies in America* (5 vols., New York, 1882–1907), a formal and conventional English treatment, emphasizes political institutions and events. Valuable as a reference work.

community churches. In consequence, the natives who were Christianized lived close to the whites—at Nantucket, Martha's Vineyard, and along the Massachusetts frontier, while their remoter brethren retained their savage customs and beliefs. Foremost among the New England missionaries was the Reverend John Eliot, a saintly Christian and man of humane spirit who translated the Bible into the Indian language and who protested against Indian slavery, saying that "to sell souls for money seemeth to me a dangerous merchandise." Nearly four thousand Indians who had been Christianized remained loyal to the English. Had they too taken up arms the war might have been far more costly to New England.

As the Puritans gained knowledge of the Indians and became the more powerful they adopted an overbearing attitude. Cotton Mather once referred to the natives as those "pernicious creatures," while another Puritan leader called their foremost warrior a "great naked dirty beast." The colonial governments forced the red man to acknowledge the English as overlords, to pay tribute, to submit his disputes to English arbiters, to secure the consent of the colonial authorities to his land sales, and to surrender his firearms upon demand. English laws and customs were forced upon him, and his misdemeanors were punished by fines, whipping, or confiscation of lands.

Many of these indignities were inflicted by Plymouth Colony upon Philip, son of the Wampanoag chieftain, Massasoit. A humiliating treaty imposed upon him in 1671 spurred him to opposition which in 1675 set the frontiers ablaze. Philip's forces were not organized, but his sporadic raids on isolated settlements caught them off guard before a general alarm could be sounded. Other tribes, the Narragansets and the Nipmucks, joined King Philip and the Wampanoags and gained repeated victories during 1675. The turning point came in December, when the New Englanders surrounded an Indian stronghold and killed between four hundred and a thousand of the foe, after the manner of the earlier Pequot massacre. In 1676 peace was made with the southern New England tribes, but meantime the war had spread to New Hampshire and Maine, where it continued in unorganized fashion until 1678.

The New Englanders demonstrated that they were good fighters, although unused to military discipline and disinclined to coöperate with forces from other colonies. Every male inhabitant between the ages of sixteen and sixty was liable to military service; hence the war reached into every quarter, regardless of personal disinclinations to military service. Massachusetts provided the death penalty for those who refused to serve, while Connecticut forbade the emigration of able-bodied men. The colonies at the start had no system of war supply, so that some expeditions had to be abandoned because provisions failed to arrive in time. On the other hand, the Indians were outnumbered four to one and they received no assistance from the French, except on the Maine frontier, where they were supplied with ammunition and arms. The principal weakness of the tribes was due to their hand-to-mouth way of living. They had no food reserves, and were unable to fight and support themselves at the same time; hence in 1676 they stood face to face with starvation, the primary cause of their failure.[32]

The war cast a pall of gloom over New England; the Puritans felt that Providence was punishing them for their sins—because they had been lenient toward Quakers and because men had been wearing periwigs and women were guilty of "cutting, curling and immodest laying out of their hair." Twenty towns in Rhode Island and Massachusetts were destroyed or abandoned, while the war took a toll of a sixteenth of the male population of New England and cost Plymouth, Massachusetts, and Connecticut upward of £90,000. Hatreds deepened on both sides as the colonists exacted vengeance by executing the native leaders and forced captives into servitude or sold them as slaves to the West Indies. The participating tribes were not utterly prostrated as the Pequots had been, and thereafter they turned to the French for assistance against their New England foes.

[32] Elroy M. Avery, *A History of the United States* (7 vols., Cleveland, 1904–10), is an accurate, profusely illustrated narrative, written for the general reader but now useful as a reference work.

BIBLIOGRAPHICAL NOTE

SECONDARY WORKS: C. V. Wedgwood, *William the Silent* (New Haven, 1944), is an admirable biography of the great Dutch leader. Thomas J. Wertenbaker, *The Founding of American Civilization: The Middle Colonies* (New York, 1938), devotes chapters 2 and 3 to New Netherland. Ellis S. Raesly, *Portrait of New Netherland* (New York, 1945), consists of attractive, sympathetic sketches of the people, politics, and social life of the Dutch colony. Henry H. Kessler and Eugene Rachlis, *Peter Stuyvesant and His New York* (New York, 1959), relates in a readable manner the conflicts between Stuyvesant and the settlers. Allen W. Trelease, *Indian Affairs in Colonial New York: The Seventeenth Century* (Ithaca, 1960), is the foremost authority on its subject. George T. Hunt, *The Wars of the Iroquois* (Madison, 1940), states the thesis that the Iroquois gained formidable power among eastern Indians after 1625.

Douglas E. Leach, *Flintlock and Tomahawk* (New York, 1958), is a thorough, well-written study—the best history of King Philip's War.

Morris Bishop, *Champlain, the Life of Fortitude* (New York, 1948), an interesting, readable narrative, is the best biography of the French explorer.

SOURCES: The Jameson *Original Narratives* series contain a volume on the

Dutch, *Narratives of New Netherland, 1609–1664* (ed. J. F. Jameson, New York, 1909). W. L. Grant has edited the *Voyages of Samuel de Champlain, 1604–1618* (New York, 1907—Jameson *Original Narratives* series). For another selection see E. G. Bourne (ed.), *The Voyages and Explorations of Samuel de Champlain* (2 vols., Toronto, 1911); R. G. Thwaites (ed.), *The Jesuit Relations* (73 vols., Cleveland, c. 1895–1901), gives original French texts and English translations of reports of Jesuit missionaries. *The Indians in North America* (ed. Edna Kenton, 2 vols., New York, c. 1927) contains excerpts from *The Jesuit Relations* pertaining to the Indians of New France. See Vol. I. On French colonial economy see H. A. Innis (ed.), *Select Documents in Canadian Economic History, 1478–1783* (Toronto, 1929). For King Philip's War see Charles H. Lincoln (ed.), *Narratives of the Indian Wars* (New York, 1913—Jameson *Original Narratives* series).

IX

 Economic Foundations

The Genesis of Individual Enterprise

The mainspring of American economic development has been private enterprise—the ownership and conduct of businesses by individuals, rather than by the community. The founders of the colonies did not seek to create an economic order different from the one with which they were familiar in Europe; instead they hoped to make money in accustomed ways. The New World did inspire one famous plan for an ideal society—that set forth in Sir Thomas More's *Utopia* (1516). To Sir Thomas the ills of mankind—crime, poverty, and war—issued from the lust and strife for the possession of land. In the New World he saw an extent of land so vast that all inhabitants might share it in common, and accordingly he conceived of Utopia as a place where the land would be owned jointly by the people and would be rotated among them, free from rents to overlords. Even houses were to be exchanged every ten years by lot. Under a planned community life each person would have to work only six hours a day, dividing his time equally between city and rural pursuits. "Shun the precious metals," urged Sir Thomas, "till the land, let all share alike and so build up a new community founded on peace, good will and equity." However, colonial promoters did not follow this idealistic advice. Instead they searched diligently for the precious metals and introduced private ownership of land, economic inequality, and the profit motive.[1]

In the first colonies, Virginia and Plymouth, individual enterprise did not take root until after experiments with corporate production and trade had failed. The promoters of each colony devised a scheme whereby the settlers labored as servants of the company, which was domiciled in England. The produce of their labor went into a company storehouse, from which they were fed and clothed. Any surplus they produced belonged to the company, to be sold in England to provide profits for the company's investors. If the settlers' produce

[1] An attractive and able study is E. A. J. Johnson, *American Economic Thought in the Seventeenth Century* (London, 1932).

proved inadequate for their maintenance, they were supported by supplies sent by the company from England. This scheme meant that all land in each colony temporarily belonged to the company, and that the company had to carry on all trade, since all the produce raised in the colony belonged to it. However, both the Virginia and Plymouth promoters had provided that after a seven-year term all the improved lands and other property were to be divided among the company investors in proportion to the shares of stock owned by each.

This plan did not yield good results. In Virginia the settlers "loafed on the job," since they got a living, irrespective of their personal efforts. They could receive but little, if any, benefit from the colony's surplus; hence a surplus was not produced. The Plymouth colonists became acutely dissatisfied for a number of reasons. The labor of unmarried men benefited other men's families; married men did not like to have their wives work for other settlers; the older men objected to being placed on a par with the younger; and the industrious workers thought it unjust that they received no more than the idlers. Since the plan provided only a niggardly subsistence for the settlers and because it failed to provide profits for the English investors, it was soon abandoned: in Virginia in 1614–18, in Plymouth in 1623–24.[2]

The first step toward a new economy was the transfer of land from the companies to individual settlers in order that they might enjoy in full the fruits of their labor and thus feel a stronger incentive to work. The Virginia Company accomplished this change in four ways: by renting small plots to farmers; by giving hundred-acre tracts to settlers who had labored for the company seven years; by issuing patents for large tracts to societies composed of wealthy English investors with the understanding that they would develop extensive plantations; and by offering head-rights to emigrants who would establish themselves in the colony at their own expense. By 1624 the improved lands of Virginia had passed into private hands, and thereafter the English government, as the owner of ungranted lands, continued the policy of selling or giving farms to individual settlers.

Similarly, the Pilgrims at Plymouth became owners of their lands after 1627. In 1623 a food shortage in the colony caused a temporary abandonment of the corporate method of farming, and in 1624 the English investors wrote that they did not intend to spend any more money on the colony and offered to sell their claims to the Pilgrims

---

[2] Harry J. Carman's *Social and Economic History of the United States* (Boston, 1930) contains a store of well selected information, presented in an interesting manner. See Vol. I, pp. 62–83.

if the latter would pay certain debts due in England. After negotiations, 1627–30, the Pilgrim leaders acquired title to the land of Plymouth Colony and agreed to pay (in nine annual £200 installments) debts due in England amounting to £1,800. The leaders then divided the lands and other property of the colony among the settlers, who thereby became known as the "purchasers" or "old comers" and who made themselves responsible for paying the £1,800 debt. The "purchasers" also acquired a monopoly of the fur trade and fishery of the colony, which they assigned to a group of "undertakers," who managed it for the benefit of the settlers and thereby procured the money to discharge the English debt. Some of the "undertakers" operated in the colony and some in England. Due to misappropriation of funds by the latter, the debt was not fully paid until 1648.

The introduction of private landowning is a major landmark in American history because it determined the course of later economic development. Essentially it came about because the English people had a deep-seated desire for title to land, which had become the basis of social position to which they were accustomed. When the early settlers saw such great stretches of idle land about them they were not satisfied to work as employees or tenants of English companies. Only with individual ownership did the colonist feel the spur to industry necessary in subduing a hostile wilderness.[3]

As soon as settlers of Virginia and Plymouth became owners of their farms, they also owned the produce they raised and therefore demanded the right to sell it to the highest bidder. No longer could a company in England insist upon a monopoly of trade, as it had done when it owned all lands and produce. Obviously a monopolistic company might set prices on both the farmer's produce and the wares sold to him, and thus appropriate his surplus and destroy the advantages of ownership. Hence the introduction of private ownership was soon followed by the abandonment of corporate trading monopolies. After 1624 the trade of Virginia and Plymouth was carried on by private traders, either as individuals or in partnerships, who usually operated with a small capital and at first competed among themselves for the business both of supplying the farmer with the wares he needed and of marketing his crops.

The unhappy experience of Virginia and Plymouth with the corporate scheme of ownership, production, and trade demonstrated its weakness to later colonial promoters. All the English colonies founded

---

[3] A work of great value is the *Encyclopaedia of the Social Sciences* (ed. E. R. A. Seligman and Alvin Johnson, 15 vols., New York, 1930–35). Excellent articles on economic topics are arranged alphabetically.

after 1629—Massachusetts, Maryland, Connecticut, Rhode Island, New Hampshire, New Haven, New Jersey, the Carolinas, and Pennsylvania—immediately introduced private landowning and with it a competitive trade in farm produce, carried on by individual merchants.

Another business enterprise in the colonies, the fur trade, also resisted monopolization or corporate control. This traffic, by virtue of the large profits it afforded, appeared to promoters and traders as a certain road to riches.[4] The wealthy nobles and bourgeoisie of Europe were willing to pay high prices for luxurious furs which proclaimed the superior affluence and social status of their possessors. Such furs could be obtained at low cost in America in exchange for cheap articles like hoes, axes, knives, beads, trinkets, bright colored cloth, guns, ammunition, and strong drink, particularly rum. Transportation charges were not excessive; all the goods could be carried overland by pack horse or along the rivers in small boats or canoes. When the natives became better acquainted with the value of their furs, unscrupulous traders resorted to various frauds such as using false weights and measures or supplying the Indians with rum, then driving hard bargains while they were intoxicated. William Penn reported that profits in the fur trade ran as high as 100 per cent. "For a sixpence worth of rum," he wrote, "one may buy the fur from them [the Indians] that five shillings in any other commodity shall not purchase."

Five regions in English America yielded furs during the seventeenth century. In New England, Plymouth Colony established trading posts on the Connecticut, Kennebec, and Penobscot Rivers, while Connecticut and Massachusetts, prior to 1650, operated in the Connecticut valley, where Springfield was a trafficking center. New Netherland had its posts at Fort Orange, Fort Nassau, and the House of Good Hope. Pennsylvania soon developed a trade with the Susquehanna region, and traders from Virginia and South Carolina ranged throughout the back country of those colonies. The principal furs of the middle and New England colonies were beaver, otter, mink, bear, raccoon, and fox; south of Maryland, the importance of deerskins made the traffic primarily a leather trade, although raccoon, fox, beaver, and mink furs were also obtained. By 1650 the fur trade of western New England had practically disappeared, but that carried on by New Netherland with the Iroquois was still the mainstay of that colony. In 1656 Fort Orange exported about 35,000 beaver and

---

[4] Clarence A. Vandiveer, *The Fur-Trade and Early Western Exploration* (Cleveland, 1929), is a clear, concise, brief introduction. See chapters 1–7.

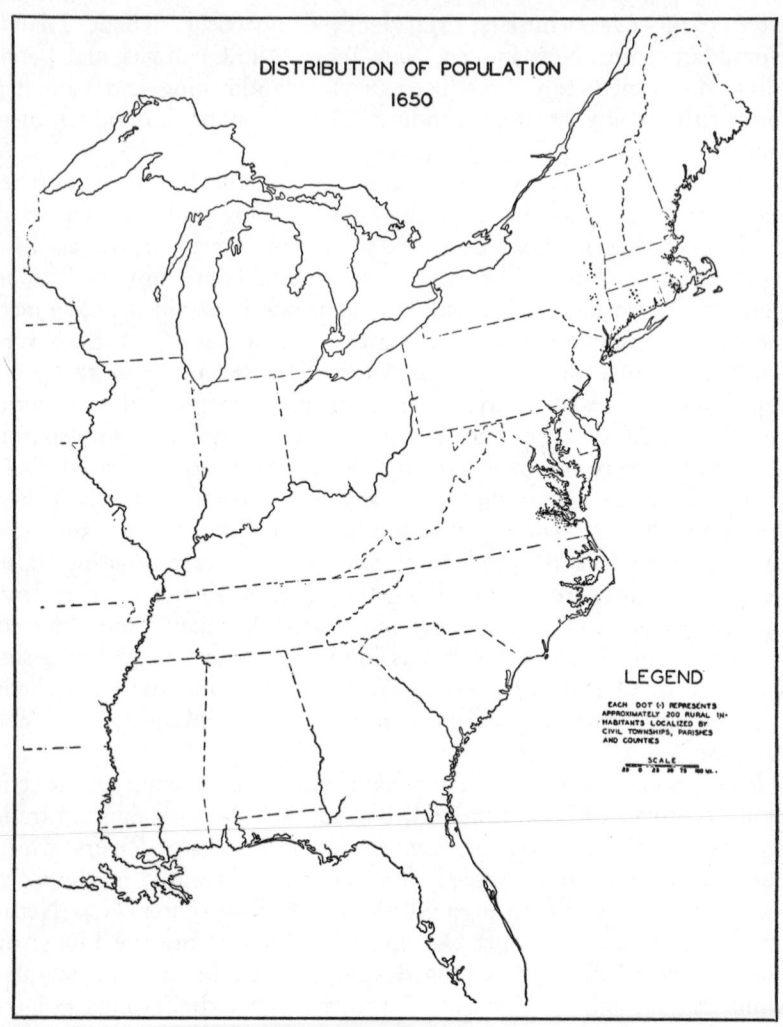

DISTRIBUTION OF POPULATION
1650

LEGEND

EACH DOT (·) REPRESENTS
APPROXIMATELY 200 RURAL IN-
HABITANTS LOCALIZED BY
CIVIL TOWNSHIPS, PARISHES
AND COUNTIES

SCALE

otter furs. Exports from South Carolina in 1687 did not exceed £2,000, but by 1705 the fur trade was the chief branch of the colony's commerce.[5]

North of Maryland the English and Dutch fur traders conducted their business through posts, "trucking houses," or "mansion houses" to which the Indians brought their furs, whereas the traders of Virginia and South Carolina traveled long distances to bargain with the

[5] Francis X. Maloney's *The Fur Trade in New England, 1620–1676* (Cambridge, 1931) shows what an undergraduate can do with a bachelor's thesis.

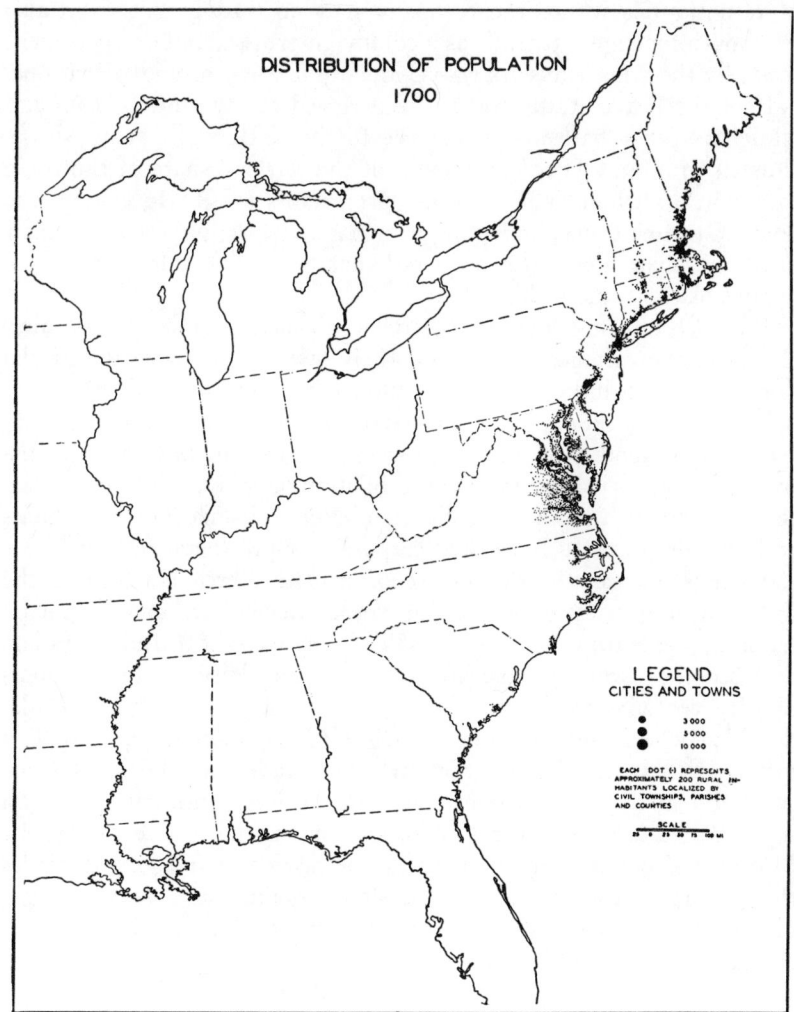

DISTRIBUTION OF POPULATION
1700

LEGEND
CITIES AND TOWNS

natives in their villages. The French also sought out the Indians in their forest haunts, even accompanying them on the hunt. The advantage to the French of their intimate contacts was offset by the high price of their trading goods. The English at Albany often charged less than half of French prices at Montreal. Low production costs in English industry accounted in part for this difference.

The profits of the fur trade led colonial promoters to attempt to monopolize it. Thus the Dutch West India Company reserved the New Netherland traffic to itself, even excluding the patroons, except in communities where the company had no trading posts. So also Plymouth managed its trade as a colony enterprise, and an agreement made by the Massachusetts Bay Company in 1629 provided that one-half of the beaver trade was to be reserved to investors in England, while the other half was to be free to the settlers. In 1632 Massachusetts granted a year's monopoly of the settlers' share of the trade to a Mr. Pynchon. The Carolina proprietors sought to control the South Carolina traffic, by having it managed by the governor for their profit. William Penn also proposed that he receive a long-term monopoly of the trade in his colony.[6]

But such efforts generally failed largely because officials and merchants in the colonies "traded on their own"; and by virtue of the difficulty of excluding such "interlopers" from the vast American wilderness, the monopolists could not enforce their claims. Thus in New Netherland both the employees of the company and the patroons traded privately in defiance of its monopoly, while in Massachusetts, Virginia, South Carolina, and Pennsylvania local merchants and officials successfully resisted corporate or proprietary control.

In consequence, the dominance of private merchants became the distinguishing feature of the fur trade. Such merchants imported trucking goods from Europe and sold them on credit to Indian traders or hired the latter to make inland trading expeditions. The business rapidly centered in a few places—Albany, Charleston, and Philadelphia—where the furs were brought to the merchants, who then exported them to Europe. Similarly the trade soon fell under the sway of a small group of rich merchants, largely because it required a considerable capital. A year's shipment of trucking goods might cost £1,000, and because the goods had to be carried inland long distances the returns to the merchant were slow. Again, there were strategic points like the Mohawk valley which might be controlled by merchants who had established friendly contacts with the resident tribes. For these reasons only a few men could engage in the trade on a profitable basis—a fact which tended to reduce competition among the merchants, since they could agree among themselves upon prices at which their goods were bartered. However, competition was not eliminated, as indicated by the rivalry after 1680 between New York merchants and Pennsylvania merchants for the trade of the Susquehanna region, and by the struggle between South Carolina and Virginia for control of the southwestern trade (1695–1710). In the lat-

---

[6] Sydney Greenbie, *Frontiers and the Fur Trade* (New York, 1929), is a popular, discursive account.

ter contest the Charleston merchants emerged victorious and tightened their grip upon the great southern traffic in deerskins.[7]

The westward advance of the fur trade further entrenched the wealthy merchants, by virtue of the larger capital outlays required for distant operations. The extension of the trade proceeded more rapidly than the growth of settlement. The demand created by the white trader led the Indians to destroy furbearing animals to an extent greatly in excess of the red man's primitive needs, and thus compelled trappers and traders to go farther and farther inland. By 1700 the New England fur trade centered in Maine; New York traders were then visiting Lakes Erie and Ontario; Pennsylvanians had penetrated, via the Susquehanna, Allegheny, and Ohio Rivers, to the mouth of the Wabash; Virginians had explored the upper waters and southern tributaries of the Ohio; and South Carolinians had journeyed a thousand miles inland from Charleston.[8]

COLONIAL AGRICULTURE

During the seventeenth century between 90 and 95 per cent of the settlers were engaged in agriculture, although the colonial farmer was also generally a hunter, builder, artisan, and in places a lumberman and a fisherman. The New England and middle colonies developed a diversified, nearly self-sufficient economy centering in grains, livestock and household manufactures. The surplus and therefore the exports of the middle colonies consisted chiefly of wheat, flour, beef, and pork, while New England—less adapted to farming—produced little or no surplus of foodstuffs and depended more upon household manufacturing and specialized trades such as lumbering, shipbuilding, shipping, and fisheries. Thus New England's exports which matched the grains, cattle, and meat of the middle colonies were fish, lumber, ships, shipping services, earthenware, woodenware, leather goods, woolen cloth, and even ironware. Virginia and Maryland produced more pork, Indian corn, vegetables, and fruits than did New England but less than the middle colonies. Tobacco, the great staple of Virginia and Maryland, taking the place occupied by manufactures and the fishery in New England and by wheat in the middle colonies,

[7] For the best description of the southern fur trade see Verner W. Crane, *The Southern Frontier* (Durham, 1929), chapter 5.

[8] A. H. Buffinton, "New England and the Western Fur-Trade, 1629–1675," in *Publications,* Colonial Society of Massachusetts, XVIII (Boston, 1917); H. Broshar, "The First Push Westward of the Albany Traders," *Mississippi Valley Historical Review,* VII (Dec. 1920).

enabled the Southerners to purchase such provisions and merchandise as they needed. By 1700 New England did not produce all its own foodstuffs, and hence exported its manufactures, shipping services, and fish to pay for the balance it imported. The middle colonies produced a surplus of foodstuffs which they sold abroad in order to buy manufactures, since their industries were less developed than New England's. Virginia and Maryland supplied themselves with most of their food but, lacking manufactures, they were obliged to exchange their tobacco for finished articles and some provisions. North Carolina resembled Virginia and Maryland save that tobacco was less important and food production and household manufactures relatively more important. The agriculture of South Carolina was of the diversified type until the growth of rice production in the 1690's.[9]

The colonial farmer labored in the shadow of the American forest. His first great task, and an arduous one too, was to clear a planting field. From the Indians he learned how to "girdle" trees—to cut a ring around them and thus to kill them by preventing the sap from rising. Then, after clearing away the underbrush, he could plant his crop in the spaces between the tree stumps. Energetic pioneers cut down the trees and rooted out the stumps. One method used was to cut part way through the trunks of several trees and then to fell a "monarch" at the head of the line thus bringing them all crashing to earth like ninepins. Fallen branches and tree trunks were burned and the ashes left as fertilizer. So laborious was this work that a family could clear only an acre a month. In New England the removal of stones doubled the pioneer's burden. The early clearings looked ragged, gaunt, and rather dismal.[10]

In cultivating these irregular patches the pioneer could use only spades, hoes, and rakes, a limitation which prevented his raising wheat at first, since it could be grown only after wilderness land had been thoroughly plowed. Indian corn proved to be the ideal initial crop. Not only could it be cultivated in hills by hand labor but its seed yielded a seventyfold increase, and it provided a variety of dishes for the settler and feed for his livestock. Beans planted in the hills entwined themselves about the cornstalks, while pumpkins could be grown in between. Indian corn gave American agriculture its start, from Carolina to Maine.

[9] Albert H. Sanford's *The Story of Agriculture in the United States* (Boston, c. 1916) is a satisfactory elementary sketch. See chapters 1–8.
[10] Joseph Schafer, *The Social History of American Agriculture* (New York, 1936), contains two able lectures on the colonial period. See chapters 1 and 2.

The absorbing interest of the Virginia Company in profit led to early efforts to develop products for sale in Europe rather than to create a self-sustaining economy for the settlers. However, experiments with the production of wine, hemp, flax, naval stores, iron, silk, potash, and glassware came to little, save that they emphasized the desirability of commodities which might be exported at a profit. Such a commodity was soon found in tobacco, first successfully raised by John Rolfe in 1612. Thereafter tobacco growing spread with phenomenal rapidity. Here was a product which satisfied the demands of mercantilism. Whereas in 1615 England was exporting £200,000 in specie to buy foreign tobacco, principally from Spain, Virginian tobacco could now be paid for with English goods and handled by English traders, thus preserving England's stock of specie, enlarging the markets for her wares, and affording profits to her merchants. The rich alluvial lands of Virginia were perfectly suited to tobacco production, and because of high prices prevailing in England the settlers could make five or six times more from tobacco than from any other crop. By 1627 Virginia's exports amounted to 500,000 pounds and tobacco was so basic in her economy that one writer said the colony was in danger of being founded upon smoke. In the 1630's Maryland became a producer and North Carolina followed in the 1660's, so that "king tobacco" thereafter guided the social, political, and economic destinies of his subjects in three of the English colonies.[11]

Tobacco paved the way for large units of production and for the employment of servile or slave labor. The demand in Europe seemed unlimited since by 1620 smoking had become something of a social craze; accordingly it was possible for the planters to concentrate upon tobacco, exchanging it for other things they desired. Such specialization in turn meant that large farms could be operated profitably, provided that enough laborers could be found, but at this point the tobacco grower encountered his greatest problem. The abundance of open land in America constantly drew workers from employers to the frontier with its promise of land ownership and independence. A relatively large number of landowners, all bidding against each other for a limited supply of laborers, sent wages to levels much higher than in Europe and thus created among employers a prejudice against the free, independent wage-earner. They found a way out by obtaining indentured servants and Negro slaves. The indentured servant labored for four years or more without pay in return for his transportation to

[11] Meyer Jacobstein, *The Tobacco Industry in the United States* (New York, 1907), is a standard work. See chapter 1.

America, his maintenance, and possibly a tract of land at the end of his term. The Negro slave, of course, was condemned to a lifetime of labor, without pay other than a bare subsistence.[12]

In Virginia and Maryland indentured servants formed the bulk of the non-free laboring population until about 1680. Although Negroes had been imported into Virginia as early as 1619, they did not become of primary importance until more than sixty years later. Negro slavery spread after 1680 partly because of a rapid development at that time of the English and Dutch slave traffic, partly because the increasing competition among tobacco planters necessitated lower production costs and therefore cheaper labor, and partly because the opening of Pennsylvania in 1681 diverted thither thousands of indentured servants from Europe when the supply of English servants was diminishing. In addition the system of indentured servants had inherent defects. The worker received his freedom just as he became most valuable to his employer, who thereupon had to train new hands, while the freed servant might set up as a planter, thereby competing with his former master.[13]

Since neither the indentured servant nor the Negro slave received direct payment, his labor was generally given reluctantly and therefore tended to be unskillful and inefficient. Furthermore the Negroes of the seventeenth century, recently arrived from Africa, were ignorant of the white man's ways. Both servants and slaves therefore could be used to most advantage in an employment which called for little skill and enabled the employer to supervise their activities within a restricted area. Tobacco cultivation met this requirement perfectly, consisting as it did of a series of simple operations that extended throughout the year. First the seed was sown in winter in a forest soil. The tobacco plant had to be cultivated separately and the seeds were so small (about ten thousand to a teaspoonful) that this could not be done without transplanting. Hence when the seedbeds had been prepared the growing field was made ready by ridging it into hills about three feet apart. When the spring rains had moistened the hills the shoots were transplanted. Later care consisted of hoeing, removing hornworms, and cutting off the top and lower leaves of the plant so that it would produce a suitable number of large, heavy leaves. At the close of summer the plants were cut as they turned yellow and the stalks were fastened to laths and hung to dry on the rafters of

[12] An outstanding work is Lewis C. Gray's *History of Agriculture in the Southern United States* (2 vols., Washington, 1933)—one of the foremost products of American scholarship. See Vol. I, chapters 1–3, 5–10, 14–15, 17. Very important.

[13] Ulrich B. Phillips, *American Negro Slavery* (New York, 1918), is the best one-volume work in its subject. See chapters 1–4, 6.

barns. In the following spring the dried leaves were stripped from the stalk, then sorted and packed into hogsheads, which were rolled to the planter's wharf where vessels took them for exportation. All these operations were simple and easily learned; hence they could be performed by ignorant slaves, while large-scale production made possible the working of several hands under the direction of an overseer.[14]

Although practically all the planters of Virginia and Maryland were tobacco growers, they also produced food for their families, servants, and slaves. They raised Indian corn, a little wheat, beans, peas, hogs, cattle, poultry, and fruits, while the woods afforded venison, partridges, turkeys, and other game. Virginia's stock of cows, oxen, bulls, and calves increased fivefold in sixteen years—from 20,-000 in 1649 to 100,000 in 1665. Sheep raising, however, was impracticable, due to the scarcity of pasture land. Without tobacco, the native products of the southern colonies would have afforded only a rude living, but tobacco exports enabled the planters to supply themselves with hardware and tools, as well as wine, sugar, household goods, clothing, and other amenities of life.[15]

Small farms usually varying in size from ten to two hundred acres dotted the landscape in New York, Long Island, western New Jersey, and Pennsylvania. The people did not live together in villages but more or less isolated on their individual holdings. Economic pursuits were highly diversified, most of the labor being performed by the farmer, his family, and his indentured servants. The variety of tasks involved and the impossibility of working several hands in one series of large-scale operations precluded the widespread use of ignorant and indifferent slaves who labored most efficiently under close supervision. The worker on the farms of the middle colonies had to be a "Jack-of-all-trades"—farmer, woodsman, and artisan.[16]

Once the pioneering stage had passed wheat became a principal crop. After the land was prepared by three plowings, the seed was sown broadcast by hand, most commonly in September, and harvested with sickles in July. Then the sheaves were stored in barns, where the threshing took place in fall or winter when the weather prevented outdoor work. The colonial "threshing machine" was a wooden hand flail consisting of a handle about four feet in length to which a "striker" about two feet long was attached by a leather thong. After

[14] U. B. Phillips, *Life and Labor in the Old South* (Boston, 1929), gives mature conclusions in an entertaining manner. See chapters 1–3.

[15] P. A. Bruce, "Economic and Social Life of Virginia in the Seventeenth Century," in *The South in the Making of the Nation*, Vol. I, chapter 3.

[16] Lyman Carrier's *The Beginnings of American Agriculture* (New York, 1923) affords the best introduction to farming techniques.

the kernels had been separated the grain was thrown against the wind to remove the chaff. In raising Indian corn, the farmer plowed his fields in March and planted the seed by hoe and hand in April or May. When, after much "backbreaking" hoeing, the plants were full grown in September, the blades were stripped from the stalks and fed to the cattle as fodder. The ripened ears were harvested and stored in October and then the farm children did the shelling during their spare time, scraping the ears over shovel edges or the handles of frying pans.

Flax also became an important crop in the middle colonies. Late in March the seed was sown broadcast on newly plowed ground. Then when the plants were three or four inches high, barefoot women and children weeded the fields. The plants, having ripened by July, were pulled up by the roots, tied in bundles, and dried in the sun. Next the heads of the stalks were pulled through a comb, thus removing the seed "bob," and the bundles were then stacked in a pool of water and left to rot. When the pith between fibers had rotted, the stalks were dried in a flax kiln—an E-shaped stone wall within which a fire was built while the stalks were placed on poles laid across the top. Thus were the fibers made ready for linen manufacture.[17]

Other crops grown in the middle colonies included barley, oats, rye, buckwheat, and tobacco—the latter for family consumption. Gardens yielded beets, parsnips, onions, parsley, radishes, beans, peas, red peppers, lettuce, and sage. Cabbage was often planted two or three times a year, the heads being cut down for sauerkraut or stored in the cellar to be used as greens. Orchards, fence-enclosed, consisted mainly of apple, cherry, and peach trees. Surplus peaches (the clingstone was a colonial favorite) were fed to hogs, and apples to the cows and horses.[18]

The middle colony farm raised its own poultry and livestock. The best cows (generally small, tough, and weather-beaten) yielded about four quarts of milk daily in times of good pasturage but little or none during the winter months. The colonial horse, small and rarely shod, resembled a pony more than a modern work horse. From the meadow came the supply of hay, which was cut in May and August, dried, and placed in cone-shaped stacks raised on poles a few feet from the ground. Although the farmer's sheep were of the English variety, they produced a staple only a third as long as that of their English

[17] Percy W. Bidwell and John I. Falconer, *History of Agriculture in the Northern United States, 1620–1860* (Washington, 1925), is the standard work on its subject. Important.

[18] An ably written, comprehensive text is Edward C. Kirkland, *A History of American Economic Life* (New York, 1932). See chapter 2.

rivals. The colonial hog—a fierce, tough, fleet, long-legged fellow of the "racer" or "razorback" sort—had to hold his own among the wild animals of the woods, where he picked up his scanty livelihood from plants and acorns.[19]

Seventeenth-century New England wore an aspect altogether different from that of the southern and middle colonies. The New Englanders lived in villages which resembled medieval English farming communities. On the outskirts of the village lay a community grazing field for horses and cattle; near the center were located the "home lots"—tracts varying from three to five acres where the farmers had their houses, barns, orchards, gardens, and cattle yards. Behind the home lots lay the arable fields devoted to grain. In most villages there was uncleared and ungranted land held in common by the town proprietors where they could obtain timber, firewood, and stone. Low, marshy land served as the meadows which produced an inferior sort of hay.[20]

The early New England farmer did not own one large arable field; instead he possessed small tracts scattered throughout the township—a fact explained by the slow process of clearing land. The founders or proprietors of a new village would first allot only a part of its arable land, each receiving a small parcel; later clearings would be similarly divided, so that in the end the farmer's fields would be scattered throughout the village, and these he reached by paths or roads. In many cases, however, the tracts were enclosed by a single fence forming a large "common field" and the farmers in their town meeting would decide what crop should be grown there, although each cultivated his own tract. After harvest, the common fields became pasture as the cattle were turned in to graze on the stubble, each landowner having the right to pasture a certain number of animals, depending upon the amount of land he owned. Such a right might entitle the landowner to pasture one ox, horse, or cow for every four acres he held in the common field.[21]

In New England Indian corn took the place occupied by wheat in the middle colonies. About 1660 the black-stem rust attacked the northern wheat and although the Connecticut valley remained a good wheat-growing country, Sir Edmund Andros, referring to Massachusetts in 1690, spoke of "no wheat having grown but blasted there

[19] Louis B. Schmidt and Earle D. Ross (eds.), *Readings in the Economic History of American Agriculture* (New York, 1925), is a valuable collection.

[20] Anne B. MacLear's *Early New England Towns* (New York, 1908) is a competent monograph.

[21] Melville Eggleston, *The Land System of the New England Colonies* (Baltimore, 1886), is a good short essay.

for about thirty years past, nor have they cattle or other grain beyond their own consumption." Sheep raising depended upon protection from wolves; hence it first took root on islands where they could be exterminated—on Martha's Vineyard, Nantucket, and the islands in Narragansett Bay. Only when the frontier had been pushed well inland could sheep growing thrive on the mainland. New England raised rye and barley in small quantities, as well as all sorts of garden produce and fruits, particularly apples, which in the form of cider, pies, dumplings, and apple butter figured largely in New England's diet.[22]

The village system of scattered tracts and common field cultivation did not result in efficient production. The farmer spent too much time going to and coming from his small holdings. When the village cattle mingled promiscuously on the common pasture selective stock breeding was impossible. Moreover, regulated cultivation in the common fields prevented crop experimentation and confined the more enterprising farmers within a routine geared to suit the slower workers.

All in all, it was a hard, primitive, meager life which the ordinary farmer endured. His tools would have been familiar in ancient Babylonia. His plow, awkward and cumbersome, operated something like a shovel pulled through the earth, was so prone to pull out of the soil that it took two men to hold it down and two or three horses or four or five oxen to draw it along. Since the farmer could raise only as large a crop as he could harvest, his dependence upon the sickle set the limits of his productivity, and one man could harvest only five acres a season. The cheapness and abundance of land bred a type of farming which quickly "mined" the fertility of the soil. The seventeenth-century farmer used neither fertilizer nor crop rotation, preferring to let exhausted land stand idle and become overgrown with weeds, a practice which failed to restore its productivity.[23] Pasturage was generally very poor. Speaking of New England cattle in 1723 a writer said: "Our flesh [are] like carrion for want of feeding, there being no provender or pasture but rancid sour stuff, never renewed since the days of Adam, nor any hay but what spontaneously arrives, etc., no straw to litter our cattle, so that most of them die for hunger and cold." An exaggerated picture, perhaps, and yet colonial cattle generally had "a lean and hungry look." Horses and pigs, always tempted by the growing grain fields, orchards, and gardens, were prone to

[22] Albert L. Olson, *Agricultural Economy and the Population in . . . Connecticut* (New Haven, 1935, Connecticut Tercentenary Commission, no. 40).

[23] R. R. Walcott, "Husbandry in Colonial New England," *New England Quarterly*, IX (July 1936).

jump over the crude wooden fences in order to partake of a self-invited feast. Such encroachments were the source of many a rural argument, in spite of the practice of fastening wooden yokes about the necks of the stock to restrain their leaping propensities. Fruit trees grew without benefit of pruning and grafting, attacked by a variety of parasites which the farmer did not understand. Clouds of mosquitoes and flies harassed both man and beast; chickens fell a prey to raccoons, weasels, and minks; rabbits helped themselves to turnips and cabbage; and squirrels and crows made merry in the cornfields. Is it surprising that a pious traveler found the colonial farmer a profane man? [24]

HOUSEHOLD MANUFACTURING

The colonial settler was determined not only to retain his European way of life but also to improve his economic condition as much as possible. Because a rising standard of living entailed an increasing utilization of manufactured products, the procuring of such goods was a paramount interest. These the settler purchased partly in England, but due to his limited buying power he had to produce many commodities with his own labor. Two types of industrial production developed during the seventeenth century. The more prominent was household manufacturing—the making of articles by members of the family, primarily for their own use. The second—commercialized industry which produced goods to be sold at a profit in a general market—made but slow progress before 1700. The open frontier drew laborers away from the older settlements, thereby creating a labor shortage that kept wages two or three times as high as in Europe and hence retarded industries dependent upon hired workers. Moreover, the colonists lacked capital, not only machines and large workshops, but also a surplus of specie or cash which employers need in order to support their operations while advancing goods to their customers on credit. Above all, the market of the colonies was too small to nourish large-scale enterprises. As late as 1700 the population of the mainland settlements did not exceed 300,000 souls; hence the American demand for manufactured goods was not great enough to support large plants that could cut production costs by utilizing machinery and a subdivision of labor. England, on the other hand, manufactured for a world market and accordingly benefited by increasing production economies due to the division of labor, specialized skills, and improved tools.

[24] Percy W. Bidwell, *Rural Economy in New England at the Beginning of the Nineteenth Century.* (New Haven, 1916) gives an intimate view of rural New England.

The colonial industries which developed before 1700 had two things in common. First, they took advantage of the resources which America afforded so abundantly and so cheaply, and secondly, the manufacturing processes employed were so simple as to require but little capital. By and large, colonial industries merely converted raw materials into crude products.

First of all the colonial household supplied itself with articles of food now prepared in bakeries, creameries, cheese factories, packing houses, canning factories, sugar refineries, and breweries. The busy housewife, using the wheat, rye, or Indian corn that had been raised on the farm and ground at the neighborhood mill, baked the family's supply of bread, as well as hardtack biscuits which were made in copious quantities and served with bowls of milk. The women and children labored at the hand churn to produce a potent, salty kind of butter. After the farmer had slaughtered his hogs the hams and shoulders were kept for six or eight weeks in brine and then smoked in the smokehouse. A large part of the family meat supply went into head cheeses and sausage. Since the housewife did not have sealed jars, preserves had to be made so rich that they would keep uncovered. Apples, melons, and gourds were cut into pieces and strung up to dry in the kitchen, while peaches were cut in quarters, dried in the oven, and packed away in bags. Applesauce boiled in cider made apple butter. Unable to obtain much white sugar, the household used honey, molasses, and maple sugar for sweetening. In the early spring the sugar maple trees were tapped; when the sap began to run in the trunks it was drained into wooden troughs and then boiled in kettles over a woodland fire. The light work involved and a holiday spirit made maple sugar time a sort of picnic when the family camped out in the forest.[25]

The colonial farmer was not a prohibitionist. He manufactured his own beer, using not hops but malt from barley, rye, or wheat. His "table beer" was made from persimmons, his "small beer" from molasses. Honey and water thoroughly boiled gave him mead, an ancient and very potent drink; brandy he made from peaches, persimmons, and apples; while cherry, blackberry, wild grape, raspberry, or currant wine might grace his table. Not content with these beverages he concocted many others: "grog," a mixture of rum, water, and sweetening; "cider royal," made of cider and brandy; "milk punch," consisting of rum, milk, and sweetening; and "cherry bounce," a combination of cherry wine and rum.

[25] Rollo M. Tryon's *Household Manufactures in the United States, 1640–1860* (Chicago, 1917), the standard authority, is a careful analysis. See chapters 1–3.

The farmer in the middle colonies and New England acquired no little skill with axe, saw, and hammer. He felled the timber for his house and barn, shaped planks, rafters, shingles, clapboards, and flooring, and did much of the actual construction, although his neighbors helped him to put the heavy framework into place. He also quarried and dressed stone but he generally employed a stonemason to build the chimneys and foundation of his house. Using twisted tree limbs or branches he fashioned sled runners, scythe handles, ox yokes, harness hames, and hay forks. In place of a wagon he depended upon a cart, the wheels of which he made from ends of large tree trunks cut crosswise, while the feed troughs for his stock were probably hollowed-out logs. Spade and shovel handles, flails, plows, harrows, axe-helves, rakes with wooden teeth, brooms made from hickory saplings or hemlock branches, baskets fashioned from birch bark—all these testified to his skill as a woodworker. His house contained homemade chairs, benches, tables, bedsteads, stools, cradles, chests, spoons, and plates or trenchers (blocks of wood hollowed out on top). As a cooper he manufactured boxes, casks, and barrels. In the tobacco colonies indentured servants who were coopers or carpenters specialized in their trades, thus leaving the planter free to farm or manage his estate.[26]

The rural household north of Maryland habitually manufactured its own supply of linen and woolen cloth. By 1710 it had been said that in New Hampshire from the governor's family "to the meanest peasant" homespun was worn, that the Long Islanders made serge "that any man may wear," and that the people of New York produced two-thirds of their linens and woolens. The tobacco colonies, on the other hand, turned to the manufacture of cloth only in times of trade depression when tobacco exports would not pay for imported goods— and then the planters found themselves unskilled in the textile crafts.

The manufacture of woolens occupied the farmer's whole family. After the sheep had been shorn, the wool was mixed with hog's lard to make it soft and pliable. Next came the carding process which straightened the fibers of the fleece. Then the farmer combed the fibers, using T-shaped combs with iron teeth, the wool being placed upon one comb and carefully stroked with the other so as to make the long hairs smooth for spinning. The farm women operated the spinning wheel, the wool being fastened to the spindle, and as the wheel spun around the yarn was drawn and twisted into an even thread. If

[26] L. H. Bailey (ed.), *Cyclopedia of American Agriculture* (4 vols., New York, 1907–09) contains in Volume IV "Aboriginal Agriculture—The American Indian," by G. K. Holmes, and "Historical Sketch of American Agriculture," by Thomas N. Carver: both significant articles.

a strong thread were desired, the yarn was spun twice, such thread making a stiff, wiry cloth, while a single spinning sufficed to produce knitting yarn for softer garments. Weaving, a laborious task, was performed by the men at a hand loom operated by a hand shuttle. A single weaver could make a piece of cloth only as wide as the reach of his arm. After the grease had been washed from the cloth the material was scraped several times to even the threads. Finally, homemade dyes were applied, the colors being obtained from bark, leaves, flowers, and berries, or from imported products such as indigo, logwood, or cochineal. The colonial housewife used a large part of the yarn for knitting bags, stockings, shawls, and mittens.[27]

The manufacture of linen was also a complicated process. When the flax had been rotted, washed, and dried in the flax kiln, the stalks were opened, thus exposing the fibers. The latter were combed in order to remove the pith, then pulled through finer combs to separate the tow, and finally sorted as to fineness. Coarse tow was used to make bags, the finer tow for trousers, shirts, and bed ticking, the finest tow for suiting, towels, and fine linen goods. After the fibers had been spun into thread the skeins were washed and bleached in a solution of ashes and hot water. Since the cloth—which was woven on a semi-homemade frame—had a light brown color, it was washed and bleached in the sun. Pure white fabrics could be obtained by soaking bleached linen in buttermilk.

So great was the labor of making cloth and clothing that textiles had to be carefully conserved. Servants had to wear the cast-off garments of master and mistress, and children ordinarily "inherited" the clothes of their older brothers and sisters. When cloth was finally discarded it was completely worn out.

As leather workers the northern farmers made their coonskin caps and deerskin leggings and breeches and lined their overcoats with fur. Calfskins from the farm were generally taken to a near-by tanner, who kept part of the leather as his pay. The men of the household might work the leather into shoes, but because the farmer was ordinarily not a skilled leather worker he commonly hired a traveling shoemaker. This work was so crudely done that a shoe fitted either foot equally well (or poorly). The northern farm also produced its own harness, utilizing raw leather, wood, and hemp, while collars for horses were made of straw. A series of acts passed in Maryland, Connecticut, Massachusetts, New Jersey, Pennsylvania, and New York between 1662 and 1717 prohibited the exportation of raw hides

[27] One of the most outstanding studies of an industry is Arthur H. Cole's *The American Wool Manufacture* (2 vols., Cambridge, 1926). See Vol. I, chapters 1–3.

and tanned calfskins, thus denoting the growing importance of the colonial leather industry. Homemade shoes were mentioned at this time as a principal manufacture in Maryland, although they were "not to be had but at far dearer rates than from Great Britain." In Virginia, however, a writer noted in 1705 that hides were either wasted or used only "for covering dry goods in a leaky house." [28]

The commercial industries which nowadays provide fuel and light for the home were carried on by the seventeenth-century household. The settler's axe and brawn supplied him with firewood from the forest, used alike for heating and cooking. At night his house was lighted by the glow of the open fire and by homemade candles, the manufacture of which was a special art. During the autumn months the farmer boiled tallow, deer suet, moose fat, or bear's grease in great iron kettles. Then the melted tallow was twice skimmed and poured into another kettle containing boiling water. If candles were made by "dipping" the farmer used candle rods—short sticks to which were attached six or eight strings or candle wicks. The wicks were dipped into the molten tallow and the candle rod then hung in a cool room in order that the tallow might harden. With each dipping the wicks acquired more tallow until the candle attained the desired size. A good candlemaker worked slowly, taking particular pains to allow the tallow to cool and harden thoroughly before the wicks were again dipped; otherwise the candles became brittle and broke easily. Two hundred candles were a good day's output for an accomplished worker. The colonial household also made candles by a molding process. Candle molds consisted of several metal cylinders in each of which a wick was fastened before the melted tallow was carefully poured in. The largest molds had as many as twenty-four cylinders. Since candlemaking with molds required some little skill and special equipment it was often done by traveling chandlers who brought their own molds, though the farm supplied the tallow.

The colonial household was also a soap factory and a laundry. Refuse fats from cooking and slaughtering were preserved during the winter and then boiled with lye to produce a soft "jelly" soap. The farmer obtained lye by filtering water through a barrel containing wood ashes from the fireplace. A better grade of soap, hard and sweet-scented, was made of oil pressed from bayberries. About once a month the women of the household did the family laundry at the washhouse, located on a near-by stream. Here the clothes were boiled in a large iron kettle which contained a generous quantity of jelly soap. A crude

[28] Frederick J. Allen's *The Shoe Industry* (New York, 1922) is *the* book on its subject.

washing machine consisting of a wooden barrel and a wooden pounder sufficed for the coarser clothes while the finer fabrics were rubbed, rinsed, and wrung by hand. The housewife had neither washtub, washboard, nor wringer to lessen the drudgery of her work. The rural folk also had to do their own dry cleaning. When powdered soapstone spread over spots on clothes had absorbed some of the grease the powder was rubbed off, thus cleaning the garment. Crude as such methods were, laundering did not impose an intolerable hardship for the simple reason that the ordinary colonial household possessed only a small quantity of fabrics and clothing, and most textiles were dyed in dark blues, grays, and browns.

COMMERCIAL INDUSTRIES

Commercialized industry differed from the household crafts in that it produced goods to be sold at a profit, not for the immediate use of the manufacturer. It required a fairly substantial capital in the form of tools, ships, or mills owned by a capitalist and operated for his profit by workers to whom he paid wages. The principal commercial industries which developed during the seventeenth century were the fishery, lumbering, shipbuilding, flour milling, and the manufacture of iron.

Throughout colonial times Massachusetts dominated the fishing industry. The reports of mariners who explored New England between 1600 and 1615 had called attention to the fishery as the most likely source of wealth, Captain John Smith, for instance, having taken forty thousand fish in 1614 from the waters off the Maine coast. He observed that "the main staple from hence to be extracted for the present, to produce the rest, is fish; which however it may seem a base commodity, yet who will but truly take the pains and consider the sequel, I think will allow it well worth the labor." By this time merchants in western England were turning from dreams of fabulous golden riches to more solid prospects of profit from timber, tobacco, and codfish and had already developed a lucrative fishery at Newfoundland, which they carried on by means of vessels sent out yearly from their home ports. New England promised an even better opportunity. Not only did its waters teem with a variety of fish—hake, haddock, halibut, mackerel, and pollock—but, more important, the chief profit-maker, the codfish, was larger, more numerous and earlier in its arrival in the fishing season than at Newfoundland. The New England fishery could be operated from the shore throughout the year; in consequence New England fish sold at higher prices in Europe than Newfoundland fish "because 'tis taken all winter and in cold weather is better cured."

Massachusetts did not achieve her mastery of the fishing industry without a struggle. When the Council for New England obtained its patent in 1620 it received the right to sell licenses giving to fishermen the privilege of operating from the shore. By charging 3s. 4d. a ton for every vessel entering New England harbors, the Council aroused the wrath of the fishermen of western England and the leaders of the Virginia Company—both of whom cast covetous eyes upon the New England fishery. Under the leadership of Sir Edwin Sandys the opponents of the Council sought through Parliament to cancel the monopoly but in this they were defeated by the king. Several vessels fishing without licenses were seized in 1623 when the royal navy undertook to enforce the monopoly. Legitimate promoters, therefore, had to operate with the consent of the Council, and this was done, prior to 1630, by the colonists at Plymouth, by the Dorchester Company, and by its two successors, the New England Company and the Massachusetts Bay Company.[29]

The capital for the initial development of the New England fishery was contributed by English merchants, some of whom operated by sending vessels from England and others by financing fishing settlements on the American coast. The number of vessels engaged rose from eight in 1616 to thirty-five in 1622 and fifty in 1624. However, after the arrival of the Massachusetts Puritans in 1630 the financial control of the fishery rapidly passed into the hands of the resident settlers. They fished at the start simply to supply themselves with food, but when they produced a surplus they soon felt that the profits earned by English capitalists might as well enrich themselves. In the 1620's English merchants furnished the settlements with fishing supplies (salt, hooks, lines, knives, and boats) at a 40 per cent price increase and reaped 30 per cent profit on the sale of the fish they purchased. As early as 1633 the New Englanders were building their own fishing shallops—and more cheaply than they could be made in England. Meanwhile the efforts of the Council for New England to enforce its monopoly had forced most of the English fishermen to withdraw from New England and to concentrate upon Newfoundland. Then when the Council ceased to function in 1635 the path was cleared for New England enterprise, while the disruption of England's trade and fishing during the Civil War gave relief from English competition for nearly a decade. Massachusetts fostered the fishery

[29] Raymond McFarland, *A History of the New England Fisheries* (New York, 1911), covers this subject most completely. See chapters 1–4.

by excusing seamen from military service during the fishing seasons and by granting a seven-year tax exemption to owners of property used in taking, curing, and transporting fish. In 1642 the Bay Colony sent 300,000 dried fish to market; by 1660 she had established her supremacy in the New England waters.

Gloucester, Marblehead, and Salem became the principal bases of operations, which were conducted by small capitalists who owned the boats, fishing supplies, and stages. They obtained the utmost labor from their workers by giving them between a sixth and a tenth of the season's catch. By 1720 complaints were made that the fishery had fallen under the sway of a few wealthy capitalists. The fish were sold to Boston or Salem merchants (some of whom were also operators in the industry) and exported to distant markets. The better grades, called merchantable, went to Spain, Portugal, France, the Madeiras, the Canaries, and Ireland, while the inferior fish, called refuse, were sent to the West Indies for the use of Negro slaves. Wholesale prices for the refuse were only about half as high as those for the merchantable grades.

As in the fisheries so in lumbering the abundance of raw material, the utilization of concentrated capital, and an extensive foreign market provided conditions suited to capitalistic enterprise. The forest products prepared for commercial sale included ship timber, for which pine, cedar, spruce, and oak were utilized as masts, spars, yards, bowsprits, and planks. Shingles, clapboards, and building frames, preferably of cedar, were in great demand, while red and white oak served admirably in the manufacture of staves for pipes, barrels, and casks in which meat, fish, flour, sugar, molasses, and rum were carried to market. The lumber-timber industry first took root on the New England coast between Boston and the Kennebec River, and this region remained the chief producing center during the seventeenth century. Lumbering also developed to a considerable extent in the Hudson valley and after 1680 in Pennsylvania and North Carolina. England and the shipbuilding towns of New England bought the northern masts and ship timbers, while the West Indies and the mainland settlements along the coast purchased most of the building lumber and cooperage stock.[30]

A fair degree of specialization marked the progress of lumbering in New Hampshire and Maine. The farmer-lumbermen lived in forest villages; many of the northern settlements were primarily logging

[30] Victor S. Clark, *History of Manufactures in the United States, 1607–1860* (Washington, 1916), the most comprehensive and authoritative work on American industry, gives a pragmatic view. See chapters 1–9. Very important.

camps. The woodsman felled the trees with his axe, whereupon they were hauled overland to a near-by sawmill or harbor, forty oxen being needed to drag the largest mast trees; in winter the logs could be pulled over the snow or loaded onto sleds. The small, crude sawmills which dotted the northern region stood at the falls of the rivers, which fortunately in northern New England were but a few miles from the sea. The water wheel of the mill operated a saw in crosswise motion, the rotary saw not having yet been invented. The first mill erected in Maine was probably built near York in 1623 and the first in New Hampshire in 1635.

Whatever the deficiency of the early sawmills they offered a vast improvement over the strenuous work of sawing logs by hand, since the labor of one mill operator was about twenty times more effective than that of a hand sawyer. This fact gave to the mill owner a strategic position in the industry. The first mills carried only one saw and could be operated by the owner assisted by his son or a hired worker. A mill that cost between $500 and $1,000 would produce a thousand feet of lumber a day and net its owner a daily return of between five and ten dollars. Such profits were commonly invested in additional mill equipment. In the development of the industry it became cheaper for owners of the established mills to add additional saws rather than to erect new plants; consequently the control of the industry tended to center in a few hands. By 1700, when the New Hampshire mills were generally operating four saws or more, it was reported that the lumber-timber trade was dominated by a dozen men; and although there were then forty mills in New York, the erection of a new mill operating twelve saws indicated the trend toward the concentration of capital. The enlargement of the mills in turn increased the number of wage-earners employed by the owners. The sawmills of New England had done their work so well by 1720 that a stretch of the coast six miles wide between Boston and the Kennebec had been denuded of trees, and there was keen rivalry among the northern lumbermen to obtain title to the remaining timber lands.

The initial impetus to shipbuilding in New England arose from the fishery; as early as 1614 Captain John Smith constructed seven small fishing boats on the coast of Maine and after 1630 the growth of colonial commerce added to the demand. From the northern forests came the best of white oak planks for the construction of the lower parts of ships and the best of white pine timbers for the decks and superstructures; needed materials which the colonies did not produce, such as anchors, sailcloth, and cordage, could readily be imported from England, while skilled shipwrights migrated to the colonies at an early date. One arrived at Plymouth in 1624; others came with Winthrop in 1630; and artisans emigrating to Pennsylvania had orders for vessels before the town of Philadelphia was laid out.[31]

Economic conditions in England favored the growth of colonial shipbuilding and gave the industry its larger significance. The opening of new world trades—with India, Africa, America, and the West Indies—created an almost insatiable demand for new vessels as shipping became one of the most fruitful sources of profit to seventeenth-century capitalists. On the other hand, due to the scarcity of ship timber in England, the expense of constructing vessels there was excessively high in comparison with the costs paid by the Dutch, England's chief rival on the sea. Early in the seventeenth century England had permitted the Dutch to carry much of her commerce, but after 1651 she excluded their vessels from most of her foreign and all her colonial trade—a policy adopted at a time when she did not have enough ships to meet her rapidly growing needs. By virtue of the abundance of timber in New England shipbuilding costs there were from 20 to 50 per cent lower than in England. So great was the competition in shipping that English merchants sought the cheapest vessels afloat; hence they fostered American production by purchasing ships in New England, and the government permitted skilled shipwrights to migrate thither. England found it more profitable to build in the colonies the vessels needed in her world-wide trade than to import the timbers for home construction. By loading the colonial built vessels with cargoes bound for England, the timber of which the vessels were made not only paid its own way across the Atlantic but also earned the freights on the cargoes carried.[32]

The launching at Boston in 1631 of a thirty-ton vessel, the *Blessing of the Bay*, built for Governor Winthrop, may be regarded as the inauguration of the colonial industry. A New England built vessel of fifty tons put to sea in 1641 and a three hundred ton ship in 1650. By 1670 Massachusetts had turned out 730 vessels and between 1696 and 1713 the colony's production amounted to at least 1,118 vessels of 69,500 tons—over half of which were built at Boston. All the New England shipwrights in 1721 produced about 160 vessels of which 40 per cent were sold to England and the West Indies and the other 60 per cent to colonial investors, principally the merchants of Boston. The average burden of these vessels was sixty-two tons.

[31] John L. Bishop, *History of American Manufactures, 1608–1860* (3 vols., Philadelphia, 1866–68) is a useful compilation for the advanced student. See Vol. I.
[32] Malcolm Keir, *The Epic of Industry* (*Pageant of America*, V, New Haven, 1926), chapters 1–2.

During the seventeenth century Boston and Charlestown built more than half of the vessels made in New England. Salem ranked second and Scituate third. A number of other Massachusetts towns engaged in the industry to a lesser extent, as did also Maine, Connecticut, and Rhode Island. Much of the capital employed was contributed by English merchants who placed orders for vessels in advance of construction and forwarded the necessary ship iron, canvas, and cordage. Thirty vessels were thus ordered in 1670 and more than fifty in 1709. Despite the dispersion of the industry it was affected by the trend toward concentrated operations. A master shipwright performed the work on contract with merchants, such contracts being very carefully drawn as to the size and cost of the vessel. He owned his own tools and shipyard, purchased the necessary timber, and employed apprentices and skilled artisans to whom he paid wages. As early as 1641 Massachusetts provided for the careful inspection of the shipwrights and the work they performed, so that the trade was restricted to artisans of proper training. As the industry expanded the best shipwrights received more orders than they could execute by themselves; consequently they devoted themselves to supervising the work of their artisans and to the business side of the industry. That the average burden of the vessels constructed was about sixty-two tons is explained, not by the inability of the shipwrights to build larger ships, but by the hazards of seventeenth-century trade. The toll of shipping taken by storms, wrecks, pirates, privateers, and accidents was so high that shipowners preferred to invest in a number of small vessels rather than in a few large ones. Fishing boats and vessels built for the New England coasting trade ranged from ten to thirty tons; the ketches used in the West Indian trade averaged about sixty-eight tons; and the ships sold to English merchants averaged about 102 tons.[33]

From American resources early colonial promoters had hoped to develop an iron industry beneficial to England. Before 1700, when iron ore was smelted with charcoal, England's position as an iron producer was precarious due to the depletion of her forests by virtue of the clearing of land for sheep and wheat raising. Since the colonies possessed bog iron deposits in swamps and ponds and a superabundance of wood, they might furnish England with smelted iron at low cost, thus preserving England's timber resources and taking off England's manufactured goods in payment. Experiments made in Virginia resulted in sending several tons of iron ore to England in 1608 and in the erection of a colonial ironworks in 1620, which, however, was de-

[33] R. H. Gabriel, *Toilers of Land and Sea* (*Pageant of America*, III, New Haven, 1926), chapters 1–4.

stroyed in 1622. The industry was not resumed during the next hundred years; tobacco crowded out iron production in the Old Dominion.

New England made a little progress during the seventeenth century—not, however, in producing iron for exportation but in supplying some of its own needs. Two types of crude iron were prepared: pig or cast iron, hard and brittle, used for making pots, kettles, pans, etc., and wrought iron, tough and malleable, manufactured into edged tools. In its simplest form the equipment of an ironworks consisted of a bloomery which produced "blooms" or pig iron, and an anvil where the carbon impurities in pig iron were removed by hammering, thus yielding wrought iron. More advanced equipment included a furnace in which iron ore, charcoal, and limestone were melted and the ore refined (the furnace draft being furnished by bellows operated by water power). Then the pig iron was hammered into wrought iron at a forge where the hammers were also operated by water power.

The first successful ironworks in New England were established at Lynn and Braintree, Massachusetts, about 1644. Despite many efforts to develop the industry in Connecticut, Rhode Island, Plymouth, and Massachusetts only five plants existed in 1673. The sponsors of the industry secured capital by organizing partnerships or companies of "undertakers," securing subscriptions both in England and the colonies. Then they engaged skilled managers for their works and employed hired helpers. One drawback to progress was the hostility of the Indians, since the works were often located on the frontier where timber was plentiful. The Indians destroyed the Virginia ironworks in 1622 and a plant at Pawtucket in 1675, when they also crippled the well-established Raynham works on the Plymouth frontier. The foremost promoter of the New England industry was John Winthrop, Jr., who visited England in 1641 to secure capital for the enterprise and succeeded in 1643 in organizing a "company of undertakers for the iron works." Massachusetts granted the company a twenty-one-year monopoly with the right to obtain three square miles of land in six different places and exempted its property from taxation and its workers from military service. Although the company erected plants at Lynn and Braintree it became involved in so many quarrels "that instead of drawing out bars for the country's use, there was hammered out nothing but contention and lawsuits, which was but a bad return for the undertakers." [34]

In all the colonies flour milling overshadowed the iron manufacture.

---

[34] John R. Commons and Associates, *History of Labor in the United States* (2 vols., New York, 1918) discusses in Vol. I the relation of the laborer to industrial organization.

Gristmills commonly made their appearance as soon as a community was settled. Operated in the main by water power and located on small streams (due to the cost of damming the larger rivers), the ordinary gristmills ground the farmers' grain into meal preparatory to the bolting process of sifting the refuse from the meal so as to produce a high-grade flour. Most seventeenth-century gristmills were small local affairs which produced only ten or twenty barrels of flour or meal a week.

The owner of a gristmill operated it himself with the aid of his family or an assistant or two. Since the work was of a seasonal nature it did not provide employment throughout the year; hence the mill owner had to find supplementary work. In slack times the mill was used to grind malt for beer or rags for paper manufacture or its water wheel was attached to saws and converted into a sawmill. Frequently the owner engaged in farming on the side and more commonly in trade. The farmers who brought in grain paid the miller by giving him a share of their meal or flour. In New England he received a twelfth of the Indian corn and a sixteenth of the other grains; in Virginia and Maryland, where mills were less numerous, the charge was commonly a sixth. Gristmills were regarded as vested with a public interest and their charges were accordingly regulated by law. Since the miller received payment in grain he had to find a buyer for it; thus he became a trader. He could also act as an agent or buyer in the marketing of the surplus grain which the farmers had to sell. His trading contacts led him to import foreign merchandise as a stock for a general store and then to advance goods to the farmers on credit in anticipation of their future grain deliveries. In the middle colonies the milling establishments gradually increased in size and capital equipment as the owner supplemented his gristmill with a bolting mill, erected a cooper's shop and a flour packing house, and even operated a bakery where hardtack biscuits were prepared for the export trade. The milling business thus offered the mill owner an opportunity to acquire considerable wealth and local influence.[35]

Between the commercialized industries and the household crafts there was an intermediate form of industrial organization represented by skilled artisans. In a new, sparsely settled community such specially trained craftsmen traveled from farm to farm where they labored in the household on materials furnished by the farmer, receiving their pay in board, lodging, and produce or money. Chief among such traveling artisans were shoemakers, chandlers, carpenters, weavers,

[35] Charles B. Kuhlmann, *The Development of the Flour-Milling Industry in the United States* (Boston, 1929), devotes chapter 1 to the colonial period.

blacksmiths, and masons. As a community became more compactly settled the traveling artisan established a permanent workshop. In the
earliest stage of this development, the settled artisan received orders
from his neighbors who furnished the raw materials and paid him
with produce or money. He then devoted his spare time to producing
goods for general sale—goods which he might display at his shop, sell
to near-by storekeepers, or dispose of to peddlers or town merchants.
Should his business expand he would take apprentices and hired journeymen into his home and shop. He commonly owned a plot of ground
sufficient to supply him with fruits, vegetables, meat, and dairy products. The crafts represented by the settled artisan in New England
and the middle colonies during the seventeenth century included
brick-making, leather tanning, weaving, fulling and dyeing, shoemaking, candlemaking, blacksmithing, and the manufacture of pot-
tery, paper, and hats. Some of these trades could not be carried on by
traveling artisans and consequently did not appear until communities
were developed sufficiently to support a settled craftsman.[36]

[36] N. S. B. Gras, "Stages in Economic History," *Journal of Economic and Business
History*, II (May 1930).

BIBLIOGRAPHICAL NOTE

SECONDARY WORKS: Ernest L. Bogart, *Economic History of the American
People* (2d ed., New York, 1939), is a convenient summary of essential data,
Joseph Dorfman, *The Economic Mind in American Civilization, 1606–1867*
(2 vols., New York, 1946), is a technical, analytical work, useful as a guide to
specialists.

Paul C. Phillips, *The Fur Trade* (2 vols., Norman, 1961), a monumental
survey, is the basic study of its subject. Nathaniel C. Hale, *Pelts and Palisades*
(Richmond, 1959), is a good introduction to the fur trade in North America
before 1650. Stevenson W. Fletcher, *Pennsylvania Agriculture and Country Life*
(Harrisburg, 1950), is an attractive, readable survey. Wheaton J. Lane, *From
Indian Trail to Iron Horse* (Princeton, 1939), is a careful, comprehensive study
of transportation in New Jersey, 1620–1860, describing conditions that existed
in the colonies as a whole. Lura W. Watkins, *Early New England Potters and
Their Wares* (Cambridge, 1950), says the last word on its subject.

SOURCES: A good collection is E. L. Bogart and C. M. Thompson, *Readings in
the Economic History of the United States* (New York, 1929).

X

Commerce, Business, and Finance

DESPITE the diversity and extent of their manufactures the colonies were unable to produce all the articles they needed in order to uphold a European standard of living and to sustain a growing system of production. Necessity dictated that they buy from the older industrial communities of Europe a wide range of capital goods (commodities used to produce or acquire wealth). Such imports included mill machinery, ship iron, canvas, cordage, Indian trading goods, hardware, bricks, nails, bellows, paint, and instruments of navigation. The colonial farmers and artisans generally worked with tools of European manufacture—spades, shovels, axes, saws, knives, chisels, grindstones, planes, hammers, cant hooks, trowels, and the iron parts of plows and other implements. Throughout the seventeenth century colonial soldiers waged war with imported cannon, powder, shot, and firearms. To the colonial housewife came a variety of kitchen utensils—kettles, measuring cans, milk trays, bowls, ladles, sieves, pans, graters, funnels, pepperboxes, flour boxes, punch strainers, and woodenware, while her table might display imported spoons, platters, porridge dishes, saucers, salts, tankards, and other pewter ware. As a seamstress she probably used English buttons, thread, needles, thimbles, pins, tape, ribbons, and filleting. Miscellaneous household aids from abroad included mousetraps, beer taps, lanterns, tinderboxes, calendars, combs, basins, and inkhorns. Wealthier families imported textiles—woolens, crepe, damask, flannel, lace, calico, gauze, cambric, gingham, cottons, and linsey-woolsey. Such families also purchased various foreign luxuries like wine, brandy, spices, sugar, books, and paper as well as some of their furniture—looking glasses, candlesticks and snuffers, curtain rings, chests, chairs, and cradles. From the beginnings of settlement the importation of such commodities increased in volume and variety until by 1700 most of them were coming into the colonies in three or four sizes, grades, or colors. To determine the wealth of a colonial family one needed only to observe how large a proportion of its possessions were of European manufacture. No family was so poor as to be without at least a few imported articles. After the coming of the

251

white man to America even the Indians could not get along without the goods which he brought from the Old World.[1]

This import trade was the fundamental fact around which revolved the economic development of the colonies. From it sprang in large measure their value to England. The central feature of colonial trade was the exchange of American products for European wares; the central economic problem facing the colonies was that of finding the means of paying for their imported supplies.

THE TOBACCO TRADE

The foreign commerce of Virginia, Maryland, and Carolina during the seventeenth century consisted of a direct exchange of tobacco and furs for European goods. For the most part this trade was carried on with England, although the Dutch managed to obtain a large share of it in the years 1630–60. So great was its importance to Virginia and Maryland that their economic position depended almost exclusively upon it. What was that position? Was the balance of trade so adjusted as to place them in a situation of independence and affluence or in a plight of dependence and uncertainty? Did the planters or European merchants reap the chief advantages of the trade, how did it affect the prosperity of England, and what part did it play in shaping the relations between colonies and mother country? The answers to these questions are keys to major issues of colonial history.

The essential features of the tobacco trade remained constant throughout the seventeenth and eighteenth centuries, although we do not have adequate statistics of its volume until after the year 1696.[2] The English customs records show that in eighteen years after 1698 Virginia, Maryland, and South Carolina bought goods from England which had an average value of £154,200 a year. In return the three colonies shipped to England commodities of a yearly average value of £245,900. Thus it appears at first glance that these colonies had an annual balance of trade in their favor amounting to £91,700. However, these figures give a false impression of the real balance of payments. The estimates of colonial imports represent the value of the goods before they were shipped from England and the estimates of colonial exports represent the value of the products before they were shipped from the colonies. Consequently the customs records do not

---

[1] C. M. Andrews, "Colonial Commerce," *American Historical Review*, XX (Oct. 1914).

[2] George L. Beer's *The Origins of the British Colonial System* (New York, 1908), one of the foremost studies of the colonial period, discusses commerce in relation to British policy. See chapter 9.

reveal several invisible charges which the southern planters had to pay. Chief among such invisible charges were freight payments to English shipowners, the profits and commissions earned by English merchants, the outlays made by the planters to purchase indentured servants and slaves, the insurance premiums on cargoes carried, and the interest charges assessed against the planters on loans extended to them by English capitalists.

All these invisible earnings were made by the merchant capitalists of England who conducted a highly diversified business. They bought and sold colonial produce, purchased English and foreign wares for resale to the planters, owned ships and thus provided shipping, carried on the servant and slave trade, supplied the capital for the insurance business, and from their surplus earnings lent money to the planters at interest. In their employ was a host of attorneys who protected their interests in the courts and constantly sought and obtained support from the English government. The stake of the merchant class in the southern colonies was all-important—so paramount in fact that the regulations imposed on colonial trade by England were dictated by the necessity of preserving the profit opportunities and investments of this dominant class.[3]

Not, however, that the merchants formed a harmoniously unified group; rather they were divided into two competing factions. The merchants of London composed one bloc which struggled incessantly against the merchants of the "outports"—Bristol, Liverpool, South-ampton, Plymouth, and many lesser seacoast towns. Each party fought for the lion's share of the colonial trade but year by year the London merchants strengthened their position of dominance until by 1700 London was the great entrepôt of English commerce. The two groups used different methods in the conduct of colonial trade, the analysis of which will reveal the manner in which each derived profit from the colonies and explain why the planters were confronted with an adverse balance of payments.

The merchants of the outports commonly purchased in England the various commodities needed in America, carried them abroad in their own vessels, sold them to the planters or colonial traders, and used the proceeds to purchase colonial tobacco and furs. In this process the outport merchants supplied the capital and assumed the risks of trade. Obviously they added to the English price of their wares the cost of bringing them from England to the southern colonies. Such costs included the freights and insurance on the voyage across and the

---

[3] For the advanced student: Violet Barbour, "Marine Risks and Insurance in the Seventeenth Century," *Journal of Economic and Business History*, I (Aug. 1929).

profits earned by the merchants as exporters. Moreover the outport merchants sold goods to colonial planters and merchants on credit, thus adding interest charges to their earnings. We know but little about the total gains made by the outport traders save that they carried on only a minor part of the southern trade. We do know, however, that the prices of English goods in the colonies were two or three times as high as English prices, so that the English customs records which value colonial imports at their English prices do not indicate the bill which the planters had to pay to the outport merchants in the form of freights, insurance, profit, and interest.[4]

Far more important were the earnings of the London merchants. Ordinarily they did not engage in the trade independently, nor did they invest their capital in trading goods or assume the risks involved. Instead they acted as commission agents for the planters. To Virginia and Maryland they dispatched each year their vessels which sailed along the coast from plantation to plantation where they loaded the planters' tobacco for shipment to England. The London merchants did not buy the tobacco outright; instead the planter consigned the shipment to the merchant with instructions to sell it on the London market. At the same time the planter would place with the merchant an order for various European goods to be purchased with the proceeds from the sale of the tobacco, with the understanding that such goods would be delivered to the planter in the ships that came the following year. The payments which the planters made to the London merchants included commissions for buying the merchandise sent to the colonies—a charge of 2½ per cent of the English price of the goods. Next the merchant was entitled to the freight and insurance on shipments to America. The London merchants must have earned, in the period 1690–1718, at least £18,000 a year from such freights, insurance, and commissions. Above all, the planters purchased their servants and slaves from English merchants and paid for them, year by year throughout the seventeenth century, considerably in excess of £30,000.

When the tobacco of the planters was sold in London not all the proceeds belonged to the planter. From the English wholesale price several charges had to be deducted. First, the merchant was entitled to the freight charges on the voyage to England, since he owned the ships employed. Freight charges (including insurance) on tobacco and furs to London varied between £6 and £9 a ton in time of peace, rising to £12, £14, or £16 a ton in time of war. In the years 1703–18

---

[4] Attention is again called to L. C. Gray's *History of Agriculture in the Southern United States*, Vol. I, chapters 11–12, 18.

the average freight earnings from tobacco carried to England amounted to at least £82,000 a year. Secondly, the planters were obliged to pay various charges connected with the handling of tobacco in London—for unloading, trucking, inspection, and storage; and moreover the planters had to stand any loss due to shrinkage or damage. Thirdly, the English import duties had to be deducted from the wholesale price. During the seventeenth century such duties were steadily increased until by 1703 they amounted to $6\frac{1}{3}d.$ a pound although the price of tobacco in the colonies was then only $1d.$ a pound. When tobacco was reëxported from England to the Continent (and about two-thirds of the colonial tobacco was so reëxported) the government remitted all the import duty except $\frac{1}{2}d.$ a pound, but considering the low price of tobacco in the colonies this was still a high charge, and meanwhile the planters had to provide bond for the payment of the full import duties on tobacco in storage in England before it was reëxported. Finally, the merchant deducted from the wholesale price a commission to pay him for the trouble of handling it and of finding a buyer. The most common commission charge was $2\frac{1}{2}$ per cent. This was based, not upon the colonial price of the product, but upon English wholesale prices, which included freight and customs. Such charges increased the English price, which for this reason was five or six times above the colonial price. An estimate of the commissions earned in London in 1720 gives a figure between £12,500 and £15,000.[5]

Theoretically all these charges deducted from the planter's proceeds should have represented items in excess of his cost of production and his profit. In actual practice, however, this did not always occur. On several occasions, especially in time of war when the European market for colonial tobacco was curtailed, English wholesale prices fell to such a low level that they barely covered, or failed to cover, customs, freights, insurance, commissions, and handling charges. In such situations neither the government nor the London merchants abated their claims against the tobacco and accordingly the planters found that all the proceeds went to pay the English charges. A leading planter of Virginia, William Byrd I, complained that "When there's any hopes of profit, then we may have a little after the owners [of vessels], masters and sailors are served"; a colonial governor wrote in 1713 that "though the merchant takes care to secure his freight and commission, the owners [planters] are often brought in debt over and above the loss of their principal venture"; and London merchants admitted in

[5] M. S. Morriss, *Colonial Trade of Maryland, 1685–1715* (Baltimore, 1914), is a superior study.

1714, "that of late years plantation tobacco hath been often sold for less than custom, freight and charges, [and] that the exports of our woolen and all other manufactures to Virginia and Maryland are diminished at least one-half."

When tobacco prices fell so low that they would provide only for customs, freight, and commissions the planters obviously had no proceeds with which to pay for English goods. But the merchants were willing to provide them with supplies on credit; otherwise the whole trade would soon have been ruined. The planters generally seem to have been hopeful of getting high prices for their tobacco and were accordingly prone to place large advance orders for goods. Frequently when the proceeds from tobacco were not sufficient to pay for the English goods ordered, the merchant would supply the planter on credit, for thereby the merchant was assured that he would handle the next year's crop through which the planter would have to pay the debt. Moreover, the planters borrowed funds outright from the merchants, pledging future tobacco deliveries as security. As a result of these business methods the planters became increasingly indebted to the merchants as short-term loans secured by crop liens were gradually converted into long-term loans secured by mortgages on the planters' lands and slaves. Indebtedness in turn created an additional invisible item in the balance of payments against the planters in that they were obliged to pay an interest charge of 6 per cent or more to their merchant creditors.[6]

That the balance of payments favored England as against the southern colonies is attested by several facts. The southern planters repeatedly complained of a scarcity of European goods in their colonies and lamented that such wares were commonly sold at two or three times above their English prices. Moreover, the coined money which came into the tobacco colonies was quickly exported as a partial means of redressing the unfavorable trade balance. An acute shortage of specie resulted which forced the planters to utilize tobacco as their common medium of exchange. Finally, the planters became seriously involved in debt. In 1706 Governor Seymour of Maryland observed "how much the country is indebted" to London merchants, "very many plantations being mortgaged to them, of which there seems little probability of redemption, considering the growing interest." Similarly the London merchants in 1709 described how loans were advanced to the planters on their future crops—"the very foundation

[6] J. S. Bassett, "The Relation between the Virginia Planter and the London Merchant," *Report*, American Historical Association, 1901, I, pp. 551–575.

on which the credit was solely given, and by which those plantations have been supported and peopled, and the trade itself sustained and without which it had been altogether unable to have been carried on." Again in 1714 a Maryland act recited how the planters "are become vastly indebted, and no prospect as yet appearing of any means whereby they may extricate themselves out of their miserable and deplorable circumstances."

From the standpoint of mercantilism the colonial tobacco trade suited England perfectly. It brought a huge yearly revenue to the government in import duties and relieved the country from dependence on foreign tobacco supplies which presumably had been purchased with English specie. The southern colonies afforded a market for English merchandise, thus providing profit to manufacturers and employment to artisans which in turn reduced the English tax burden for the support of unemployed workers on poor relief. To the merchant class the tobacco trade offered handsome incomes from profit, commissions, freights, and insurance, and provided a field for the investment of surplus funds. One vital feature of the rising capitalistic system of England was the accumulation of capital surpluses which the merchants desired to invest in profitable channels. Investments made in the tobacco colonies by extending loans to the planters were not only productive of interest and protected by mortgages which were safeguarded by the English government but also had the effect of strengthening the merchant's control of the trade by forcing the planter to market his future crops through his creditor in order to pay his past debts. These benefits to England explain why her merchants and her government were united in a firm alliance to control the colonial trade in tobacco.

On the other hand the conditions of the trade were less satisfactory to the planters. The employment of seagoing vessels to carry European goods in small lots directly to their private wharves and to collect their individual crops was certainly not an economical practice. Moreover, the planter was at a disadvantage in that he could not supervise the sale of his produce or the purchase of his supplies in England. His merchant could have at best only a vicarious interest in his welfare; the freedom of the merchant from the planter's scrutiny must have been conducive to carelessness or fraud—perhaps both. At any rate the correspondence of the planters bristles with charges that the merchants sold tobacco at excessively low prices and sent over inferior English goods at excessive prices—the very refuse of the shops of London. Indebted planters often felt themselves "in the clutches" of their creditors. Thus William Byrd II once sold lands and slaves to clear his debt to his merchant, asserting that "I had rather incommode myself a little than continue in the grip of that usurer." [7]

Why did the organization of the tobacco trade persist in face of its obvious disadvantage to the planters? Had they supplied their own shipping and marketing facilities they might have retained more of the profit of the trade for themselves, but this, they were unable to do. When the tobacco industry first took root in the colonies it was the most profitable means of employing capital and labor; hence the planters invested their surplus in additional lands, servants, and slaves. In an expanding economy the rise in land values increased the planter's credit, while an enlarged output seemed to justify borrowing for the purchase of new workers and productive equipment. Since the planters' capital thus went into agriculture and since their produce had to be sold in Europe there was no alternative to the employment of European capital in the marketing of their crops. Then when the productive system of the tobacco colonies declined after 1700 the planters found themselves with heavy fixed investments in land, labor, and equipment that could not readily be transferred to other pursuits. Moreover, they could borrow new capital only from England—and to obtain this they were obliged to continue the tobacco industry in order to provide the means of paying their debts. Finally, the English government excluded foreign merchants and vessels from the tobacco trade, thus increasing the dependence of the planters on England for ships, marketing services, credit facilities, and manufactured products.

The Trade of New England and the Middle Colonies

The mechanism of the trade of Virginia and Maryland differed materially from that of the commerce of the middle colonies and New England—a fact explained by the lack of staples in the northern settlements which could be exchanged directly for English goods. In order to protect English agriculture Parliament after 1660 prohibited the importation into England of colonial fish, flour, wheat, and meat. Since such commodities were the staples of the northern colonies, the sale of their native products to England was limited to small quantities of ship timber, furs, whale oil, and whalebone. On the other hand the desire for European goods was as insistent in the North as in the South. In eighteen years, 1698–1717, New England and New York purchased each year from England goods of an average value of

[7] G. L. Beer's *The Old Colonial System* (2 vols., New York, 1912), a work of major importance, gives in Vol. II much information on trade.

£103,500 and sent in return products having a yearly average value of only £37,400, thus incurring an unfavorable balance of trade of £66,100 a year. And not all the exports of those colonies consisted of their native products; the latter paid for about only one-sixth of the goods imported. The central problem which faced the northerners was that of converting their fish, lumber, wheat, flour, livestock, and meat products into some means of paying for European wares.[8]

In solving this problem the northern colonies attained a much stronger commercial position than did their southern neighbors. For one reason invisible items did not figure largely in the balance of payments between England and the northern mainland. Boston, Philadelphia, and New York each contained merchants who traded in their own vessels. The freights, profits, and commissions earned by English merchants as exporters to the northern colonies were nearly balanced by similar earnings of the northern merchants in carrying their products to England and selling them in the English market. Moreover, the northern towns did not consume all the European goods they imported; their function was that of distributor to surrounding communities. Besides, the Northerners engaged in a variety of outside trades which enabled them to get remittances to England on terms highly favorable to themselves. Such trading activities are explained largely by three things: shipbuilding, shipowning, and the methods of marketing goods—all intimately related.[9]

Boston, Philadelphia, and New York each served as an entrepôt to which foreign goods were brought in ocean-going ships and then carried in small vessels to the surrounding mainland settlements. Similarly, to the three northern towns were transported the products of the colonial fishery, farms, and forests preparatory to exportation abroad. Thus the three commercial towns acted as exchange centers, receiving all sorts of commodities from all parts of America, the West Indies, and Europe and making up cargoes suitable to every market of the time. Although Boston, Philadelphia, and New York all traded with every region on the mainland, each town had a special trading area which it dominated. Thus Boston was supreme in New England and eastern Long Island; New York (New Amsterdam before 1664) served western Long Island, eastern New Jersey, and the province of New York; and Philadelphia after 1682 dominated western New Jersey, Delaware, northern Maryland, and Pennsylvania. During the

---

[8] Roland M. Hooker, *The Colonial Trade of Connecticut* (New Haven, 1936—Connecticut Tercentenary Commission, no. 50).
[9] N. S B. Gras, "The Rise of Big Business," *Journal of Economic and Business History*, IV (May 1932).

seventeenth century Boston ranked first in importance, New York second, and Philadelphia third. Boston's supremacy arose from the fact that she had the most populous hinterland, that she was well situated with reference to all centers of colonial commerce (particularly the fishing and lumbering regions), and that her merchants had arrived early on the scene and had always pushed aggressively into every available trade. Prior to 1700 New York and Philadelphia were commercial satellites of Boston, and Philadelphia was a lesser satellite of New York.

The relations of these three towns with the mainland communities resembled in miniature the relations between London and the tobacco colonies. Each town supplied the American settlements with European goods, rum and molasses from the West Indies, and needed products from the other colonies. Moreover, the northern merchants owned most of the vessels engaged in the trade and therefore earned the freights on shipments to the adjacent settlements. Similarly the merchants provided the marketing services and thereby reaped profits on their sales. Such freights and profits, added to the first cost of the goods, meant that the settlers had to pay high prices. On the other hand they received only the first cost of the articles they produced. Moreover, the need of foreign goods among the settlers was so great that they were prone to buy more than their own produce would pay for; in consequence the balance of trade between country and town generally favored the latter. One result of this was that the hard money which came into the rural settlements quickly flowed away to the towns. Boston drew money from all parts of America—even from New York and Philadelphia—and thus became the financial center of the colonies.[10]

The rural communities, particularly Virginia and Maryland, also made additional payments to the towns by sending bills of exchange drawn on England. Bills of exchange, which always played a vital part in colonial commerce, were somewhat similar to modern bank checks. When a colonial merchant or planter shipped a cargo of produce from America to England with instructions to an English merchant that it be sold on arrival, the colonist was due to have funds at his disposal there. Accordingly he could write an order (or draw a bill of exchange) upon his English correspondent directing that a certain sum be paid to the receiver of the bill. Such a bill could then be used like a modern check; endorsed from person to person it would circulate until sent to England and paid from the proceeds of the sale

[10] Bernard Bailyn, *The New England Merchants in the Seventeenth Century* (Cambridge, 1955), shows the relation of business to the world in which it operated.

of the produce which the drawer of the bill had previously shipped. Since the tobacco planters were constantly anticipating credits from the sale of their tobacco in England they could buy foreign merchandise from the northern towns by giving bills drawn on English merchants.[11]

Remittances from the rural settlements to the towns by money and bills did not generally redress the unfavorable balance of trade; hence the town merchants were obliged to extend credit to their country customers. In their trade with the southern colonies the northern merchants consigned their goods to agents who sold to the planters on credit and as attorneys protected the merchants' interests. In the northern colonies the merchants advanced goods to local traders or storekeepers and the latter sold to the settlers on credit. The settlers would pay their existing debts by delivering their surplus produce to the country traders and they in turn would consign it to the town merchant in payment of their debts. This arrangement placed the settlers in a somewhat exposed position due to the fact that the charges imposed by the merchant—freights, profit, and interest—tended to remain fixed whereas the price of what the farmer produced might fall abruptly, and thus in time of depression all his surplus might be needed to pay existing debts.

As previously noted the produce shipped from the colonial towns to England did not begin to pay for their importations. In order to secure additional remittances the northern merchants carried on external trades with Newfoundland, southern Europe, the Wine Islands, and the West Indies whereby they obtained coin, bills of exchange, and commodities which could be marketed in England. Prior to 1700 Boston practically monopolized the trade with the fishing settlements of Newfoundland. The Bostonians exported provisions, lumber, and rum which were exchanged for the settlers' fish and this in turn was sold for coin, bills of exchange, or European goods to vessels that came to Newfoundland from Britain or Europe. It was said that the Bostonians never loaded fish when they could get money or bills, that their vessels returned to Boston in ballast and in departing left not a shilling of coin behind. One English official observed that the Newfoundland trade enabled New England to make remittances to England which equaled in value the native products which she shipped directly to the mother country.[12]

[11] Emory R. Johnson *et al*, *History of Domestic and Foreign Commerce of the United States* (2 vols., Washington, 1915, 1922), is a useful compilation for the special student. See Vol. I, chapters 1–2, 4–5, 10–11.

[12] Ralph G. Lounsbury's *The British Fishery at Newfoundland* (New Haven, 1934) is a careful monograph, very detailed. See chapter 6. For a good résumé see R. G.

Boston also carried on an extensive trade with Portugal, Spain, and France, sending thither the best grades of fish, which were sold for coin, bills of exchange, or southern European produce. Such proceeds were then carried to England and there used to pay for part of New England's imports of English goods. After 1690 ship timber was also exported from New England to southern Europe and in similar fashion converted into buying power in the English market. A large part of New England's fish was taken to southern Europe by English vessels which procured the fish at Boston in exchange for English goods imported. After 1700 Salem rapidly superseded Boston as the exporting center in the southern European trade.

To the Spanish and Portuguese Wine Islands (the Canaries, Madeira, and Fayal) the northern colonies sent fish, lumber, and provisions—all used to purchase wine. Part of the wine procured was carried back to the colonies and part of it was shipped to England, where its sale enabled the northern merchants to obtain additional purchasing power for English goods.

Far overshadowing all these trades was that carried on between the northern towns and the Caribbean.[13] The northern exports consisted of fish, horses, lumber, wheat, flour, biscuit, beef, pork, bacon, peas, and Indian corn. The Northerners sold such products to the sugar planters of the British islands of Jamaica, Barbados, Antigua, Montserrat, Nevis, and St. Christopher's or St. Kitt's, to the Danish sugar island St. Thomas, and to the Dutch sugar colony Surinam (Guiana). Similar northern commodities reached the Spanish colonies in America by way of Jamaica and the Dutch island Curaçao; other shipments went to Yucatan or Campeche Bay. This diversified trade enabled the Northerners to procure various commodities for exportation to England. First of all they obtained Spanish money—chiefly pieces of eight —which flowed into Jamaica, Curaçao, and Barbados in payment for European goods, Negroes, and northern colonial products sold by English and Dutch traders to the Spaniards at Havana, Vera Cruz, Porto Bello, and Cartagena. From the sugar colonies the northern towns also secured sugar, molasses, rum, indigo, fustic, dyewoods, cotton-wool, and minor commodities including lime juice, lignum vitae, and ginger. The sugar islands also paid for northern products with bills of exchange drawn on English merchants. At Campeche

Lounsbury, "Yankee Trade at Newfoundland," *New England Quarterly*, III (Oct. 1930).

[13] A splendid introductory study is A. P. Newton, *The European Nations in the West Indies, 1493–1688* (London, 1933).

Bay the Northerners procured logwood, highly valued as a dyestuff for the woolen industry. Most of the commodities thus obtained by the northern traders—coin, bills of exchange, sugar, logwood, ginger, fustic, cotton-wool, and indigo—were shipped to England and there exchanged for English goods or taken to the mainland towns and later reëxported to England. Rum and molasses (the raw material of rum) were carried to the mainland colonies where they were used in the fur trade, the New England fishery, and the Newfoundland trade—in each instance enabling the Northerners to obtain additional remittances to England. Another important commodity returned to the mainland was salt, procured chiefly at the island of Tortuda. Indispensable to the fishery and to cattle raising, it contributed its part to all the trades in which colonial fish and cattle were important items. The northern merchants further increased their buying power in England by earning the freight charges and profits on the cargoes they carried in their vessels directly to England from the Wine Islands, the West Indies, and southern Europe.[14]

In all these external trades the balance of payments favored the northern towns. Their merchants owned most of the shipping employed and thus earned the freight charges on voyages to and from the various markets. Similarly, the Northerners sold their cargoes through their agents or stores abroad, thereby obtaining the profits of both importer and exporter. Their gains are indicated by the fact that prices of northern products in the West Indies were fully 50 per cent higher than in the northern towns. By selling their exports on credit the Northerners added interest charges to their earnings and attained a position of dominance over their customers (particularly at Newfoundland) comparable to the position of London in the tobacco trade. These varied external contacts not only made it possible for the northern towns to complete their payments for English imports; they also provided handsome profits which accumulated in the hands of the merchants and thus fostered a rising capitalistic class.[15]

New England possessed one other form of remittance to England— the ships that were built in her seacoast towns on order of English merchants. During the latter part of the seventeenth century such vessels must have netted New England between £20,000 and £40,000

---

[14] Three excellent books on the West Indies are Vincent T. Harlow, *A History of Barbados* (Oxford, 1926); J. A. Williamson, *The Caribbee Islands under the Proprietary Patents* (Oxford, 1926); and Charles S. S. Higham, *The Development of the Leeward Islands under the Restoration, 1660–1688* (Cambridge, 1921).

[15] Malcolm Keir, *The March of Commerce* (*Pageant of America*, IV, New Haven, 1927), chapter 1.

a year. Certainly their value exceeded that of all the other New England commodities—fur, ship timber, and whale products—which were exported from Boston to England.

While the external trades of the northern colonies remained open and adequate they supplied the resident merchants with attractive opportunities for profit making. England also benefited in that the northern settlements provided an expanding market for her own wares, while external trade afforded the colonists the necessary means of payment. Moreover England prized her sugar colonies in the West Indies as extremely lucrative sources of revenue to the Crown and of profit to her merchants. Hence the northern colonies had an added value in that they furnished the sugar planters with indispensable work animals, foodstuffs for their slaves, and lumber for hogsheads, sugar works, and houses. In other respects, however, the activities of the northern merchants seemed injurious to English merchants and in consequence there occurred an intense conflict between the two—a conflict which will be discussed in the succeeding chapter.[16]

CURRENCY AND FINANCE

The course of American commerce determined the currency problems with which the colonists had to contend. Their principal monetary troubles issued from an acute and persistent shortage of specie or coin. The very process of founding colonies created a scarcity of money by virtue of the necessity which impelled the first emigrants to take with them things that were essential for life in their new homes. What money they may have had at the start they were obliged to exchange in England for goods with which they could stock the detached farms on which they were to settle. However, a few years after a settlement had been planted coined money began to filter in—brought by newly arriving settlers wherewith to purchase provisions, or returned in the course of external trade. But such money never remained long in the colonies; it speedily accumulated in the commercial towns whence it was remitted to England to redress the unfavorable balance of trade. In other words the colonists found it more profitable to use coined money for purchases abroad than to retain it as a domestic medium of exchange.[17]

Meanwhile the English government did not desire to supply the colonies with a large stock of coined money. English officials insisted

---

[16] J. W. McElroy, "Seafaring in Seventeenth-Century New England," *New England Quarterly*, VIII (Sept. 1935).

[17] Curtis P. Nettels, *The Money Supply of the American Colonies before 1720* (Madison, Wis., 1934), chapters 2–5 (commerce), 6–7, 9 (finance).

that the colonies should provide England with specie—not England the colonies. The ideal colony exchanged its produce in England for manufactured goods, and the transactions involving money should preferably be performed in England rather than America. The creed of mercantilism placed great emphasis upon a country's supply of coin. As the most permanent and flexible form of wealth, specie enabled the merchant class to convert their surplus profits into a stable type of property that could be utilized in any additional profit-making enterprise, due to the universal demand for silver and gold. Coined money was also highly esteemed as the lifeblood of manufacturing industries, providing as it did a ready means of purchasing raw materials and a wage fund for specialized artisans who could not be paid conveniently in the products of their labor. England objected to the growth in the colonies of industries that would compete with her own; consequently she did not desire them to obtain a large stock of specie which would provide a currency in which the wages of specialized artisans might be paid. Furthermore, English officials believed that England's own stock of precious metals was inadequate to her threefold needs of currency, trade, and war. Particularly important in this connection was England's commerce with the Orient. During the seventeenth century silver was regarded as the metal best suited to currency purposes, but it so happened that silver had a higher intrinsic value in India than it had when minted into English coins. The great demand for silver in the India trade led to the melting and clipping of English coins, since the metal could be more profitably employed in the Orient than in England. The English silver coinage became seriously deranged; incessant complaints bewailed the scarcity of money at home; and the East India Company was roundly berated as a thief of the nation's treasure. So great were the profits of the India trade, however, that in 1663 Parliament legalized the exportation of foreign coins and bullion, although it refused to lift the ban against the exportation of English coin. In the face of these conditions it seemed out of the question for England to supply her American colonies with hard money. Prior to 1663 she did not permit the exportation of any coin or bullion to the colonies and after 1663 did not allow the exportation of English coin. She did not erect special mints in America to provide an American coinage and when the New Englanders independently erected their own mint she speedily dismantled it. Nor would she allow the colonies to prohibit the exportation of coin and bullion from America to England.[18]

[18] See again W. B. Weeden, *Economic and Social History of New England*, Vol. I, chapters 5, 7; pp. 314–336, 379–387.

Although the colonists possessed practically no English coins they continued to make their financial reckonings in English monetary terms (or to use pounds, shillings, and pence as their money of account). Out of the scarcity of English coin issued a series of currency makeshifts which never adequately solved the financial problems of the colonies. During the seventeenth century all the colonies resorted to the use of commodity money. The colonial legislatures enacted that certain important local products should be designated as money— lumber in New Hampshire; wheat, pork, beef, cattle, peas, Indian corn, barley, and rye in New England, the middle colonies, and North Carolina; and tobacco in Virginia and Maryland. Before 1660 beaver and wampum (shells or beads much sought after by the Indians) figured largely in the currency system of New England and New Netherland. The laws of the colonies uniformly provided that commodity money should be legal tender in all public payments and legal tender in private payments unless contracts called for another kind of currency. Ordinarily the receiver of commodities used as money did not want them for personal use; sooner or later they had to be sold in commercial markets and thus converted into some more durable form.[19]

One of the persistent defects of commodity money was the difficulty of determining its real value. The legislatures generally decreed that the money commodities should pass at fixed legal prices in public payments. Thus Connecticut at one time valued wheat at 4s. a bushel. In private transactions, however, the legal prices did not apply; the parties concerned agreed between themselves as to the value of the commodity tendered; failing in this they referred the issue to impartial judges who decided it for them. Due to the wide variations in the quality of different units of a given commodity the task of determining value was a most baffling one. The products used as currency in a locality were its staples; nearly every farmer raised them and hence operated a mint. Great was the temptation to debase the currency by using inferior products for local payments. In the respectable town of New Haven the deacons of the church once complained "that the wampum that is put into the church treasury is generally so bad, that the elders to whom they pay it cannot pay it away but it is returned to them again." The tendering of such inferior products evoked much protective legislation. Connecticut ordered that no wampum should pass unless it was "in some measure strung suitably, not small . . . and disorderly mingled as formerly," and the New England and

[19] William Z. Ripley, *The Financial History of Virginia, 1609–1776* (New York, 1893), is a precise, discriminating study.

middle colonies appointed inspectors of products to guarantee that corn "be sweet and clean and every way well conditioned" and that prepared meats be properly packed. Despite such precautions the settlers commonly paid their taxes in their inferior products and even private creditors were often at the mercy of local judges who favored debtors by overvaluing the commodities tendered in payment of debts that were recorded in pounds, shillings, and pence.[20]

The transportation of commodity money proved to be another serious disadvantage. Frequently the colonial prices of products were so low that commodity currency worth 5s. weighed fifty or sixty pounds. The costs of carrying tax money from the localities to the seat of government usually consumed between 5 and 10 per cent of the produce. In Massachusetts, when cattle were driven to Boston as a means of remitting tax money, the General Court provided that "if they be weary, or hungry, or fall sick or lame, it shall be lawful to rest and refresh them for a competent time in any open place that is not corn, meadow, or inclosed for some particular use." Once commodity money had been delivered there arose the added problem of storing it. Ordinary barns had to serve as banks where produce deposits were exposed to fire, theft, shrinkage, or deterioration. Instead of earning interest on his deposits the owner had to pay a high storage fee. In one case the cost of storing Indian corn eleven months amounted to 18 per cent of the quantity stored.

Merchants and creditors had other objections to commodity money. In times of high prices their debtors endeavored to pay their worst products; in times of low prices the commodities received became a drug on the market and could not be sold abroad. North of Maryland there was another difficulty—the money commodities could not be sent to England and exchanged for European goods. "The ordinary estates which we have in plantations," wrote John Winthrop, Jr., "cannot be converted into such as may suit correspondence with Europe, or carrying on such works as require the labor and help of such artificers who expect pay in the commodities of England, or such as will presently procure them." Only when the northern staples had been sent to the West Indies or other intermediate markets could they be exchanged for English goods. The costs of such roundabout shipments added to the colonial price of English goods imported and correspondingly depressed the price of the northern staples. The northern legislatures then placed a legal value on their products higher than their prices when sold for exportation—hoping thus to correct the price

<hr>

[20] On wampum see W. B. Weeden, *Indian Money as a Factor in New England Civilization* (Baltimore, 1884).

disparity between European imports and their own produce. This resulted only in creating two price levels: commodity money or "country pay" prices which governed strictly local transactions, and foreign exchange or sterling prices which governed foreign trade. The merchants commonly reckoned in the lower foreign exchange price scale and hence it was also called the "merchant's price." These different price levels contained the seeds of protracted conflicts in which colonial debtors strove to pay their debts in commodities valued at the higher colonial level rather than at the lower figure of sterling or foreign exchange prices.[21]

Another remedy for the low price of northern staples when exchanged for European goods was widely advocated during the seventeenth century—that of producing commodities in the north which might be exchanged directly for English goods. John Winthrop, Jr., and William Penn were the leading advocates of this solution. They secured laws in their colonies encouraging the production of hemp, tobacco, and cotton, the opening of mines, and the building of ships. Such products might be exported to England at low cost, thereby purchasing English goods for the northern colonies on more favorable terms or at lower prices.

Despite the drawbacks of commodity money it served the colonists reasonably well during the seventeenth century. Its use was most common in the rural districts where the need for money was not so acute as in the towns. The colonial family produced so many of its own foodstuffs and manufactures that exchange was reduced to a minimum. Moreover, a large part of local trade was carried on by simple barter; each settler became an expert in bargaining his surplus products for other articles possessed by his neighbors. This rural trait, vividly described in Mark Twain's *Tom Sawyer*, had its origins in the remote colonial past. Credit likewise loomed large in colonial economy. The settlers ordinarily purchased goods from the local stores on credit, paying with later deliveries of farm produce. The stores also bartered products; a housewife, for instance, might buy a dozen eggs' worth of butter or cloth. Credit instruments provided another substitute for money. A man of means and reputation would give his promissory notes payable after several months and these would pass from hand to hand on endorsement until they became due and were paid. Bills of exchange circulated in the same manner. So also the colonial treasurers issued notes in advance of tax collections—notes which served as a crude form of paper money until the taxes were collected and the

[21] See again P. A. Bruce, *Economic History of Virginia in the Seventeenth Century*, Vol. II, chapters 17–20.

notes redeemed. Similarly coined money played a very small part in the colonial labor system, since apprentices, indentured servants, and slaves received payment, not in money, but in food, lodging, clothing, medical care, and vocational instruction. Such currency substitutes, common to all the colonies, helped to fill the void occasioned by the scarcity of coin.[22]

The New England colonies eliminated money payments in many other ways. The general courts and the towns granted lands without cash payments and did not exact quit-rents from the freeholders. They also paid salaries or wages to soldiers, officers, ministers, and public officials with land bounties; and compensation was given to public servants and encouragement to new undertakings like an ironworks by exempting the individuals concerned from paying taxes. Every able-bodied man between the ages of sixteen and sixty had to serve in the militia and the town police; thus these vital services were secured without money payments. Similarly the settlers were required to work without wages on certain public works such as highways, dams, harbors, bridges, and meeting-houses. Voluntary coöperation among the people further enabled them to carry on without using money, as at house-raisings, huskings, quilting parties, and funerals, or when misfortune disabled a farmer from caring for his fields.

The defects of commodity money prompted the colonists at an early date to seek a metallic currency. The establishment of colonial mints seemingly offered a way out of the difficulty. Massachusetts erected a mint in 1652 and at one time or another most of the other colonies desired to follow her example. The coining of money, however, was a prerogative of the king; his subjects could not operate mints without his permission and the charters issued to the colonies generally did not confer this privilege. Only when the king was in exile did Massachusetts venture to erect the Boston mint and although it continued to function until 1684, the coins it issued were all stamped with the date 1652.[23]

In the opinion of the colonists local mints were required by two major conditions. The foreign coins of Spain, France, Holland, and Portugal which came into the colonies after 1640 varied so widely in weight and alloy that the ordinary settler knew little of their real value in terms of English money. Due to the clipping, shaving, or "sweating" of coins even those of the same denomination differed considerably in metallic content. This made the use of coin so confusing

[22] See again E. L. Bogart and C. M. Thompson (eds.), *Readings in the Economic History of the United States,* chapters 2–3.

[23] See again S. E. Morison, *Builders of the Bay Colony,* chapters 5, 9.

that frauds could readily be practiced on the unwary. The colonists therefore assumed that if local mints were erected the confusing foreign coins could be melted down and the bullion converted into uniform pieces. Furthermore, English and European coins had the habit of speedily departing from the colonies. Seeing their specie leave, the colonists concluded that they needed a special kind of money—a coin so designed that it would always remain in America and provide all the advantages of a metallic currency.

The various proponents of colonial mints suggested that if coins issued in the colonies contained less silver than corresponding English coins they would have a higher value in the colonies than in England and would thus remain at home. Massachusetts acted upon this assumption in operating her mint. The famous pinetree shilling minted at Boston contained only seventy-two grains of silver as against ninety-three grains in the standard English shilling; consequently the province debased its coin, in comparison with sterling, to the extent of 22½ per cent. If seventy-two grains of silver were worth a shilling in Boston (so the argument ran) and worth only three-fourths of a shilling in England, then the pinetree coins would always remain in the colony. But this assumption proved to be false. The importers of goods raised the price of their wares so that they would get for a given article a certain amount of silver regardless of how it was coined. Prices of imported goods were therefore higher in pinetree shillings than in English shillings. On the other hand the prices of Massachusetts produce in pinetree shillings did not rise so rapidly as the pinetree prices of imported goods. This outcome, declared the deputies of the General Court, brought "an undervalue upon all commodities raised among ourselves" and so utterly frustrated "the end and use of money amongst us." So rapidly were the pinetree shillings exported as bullion that in 1654 the General Court prohibited such exportations under heavy penalties. The experiment of Massachusetts exposed two monetary theories common to the colonies: first, that a specially designed colonial currency would remain in America, and second, that by declaring a given amount of silver to be worth more shillings in the colonies than it was worth in England in English shillings, the colonial supply of money would be increased, the prices of colonial produce would rise, and the colonists would therefore be able to buy more foreign goods. What actually happened was that the price of foreign goods (as measured in pinetree shillings) rose more rapidly than the price of colonial produce (also measured in pinetree shillings), that importers obtained as much silver for their wares as formerly, and that in consequence the pinetree shillings were exported as bullion in order to pay for European goods.[24]

The Boston mint brought upon Massachusetts the accusation that she had usurped the king's prerogative—one of the charges which led to the annulment of her royal charter in 1684. Immediately afterward the authorities of the province petitioned that the mint be allowed to continue, asserting that an ample supply of coined money was necessary in order to uphold the value of colonial produce and property. English officials, however, rejected the plea on the ground that separate colonial mints would create a dozen or more coinage or price systems in America, to the infinite annoyance of merchants. English officialdom preferred that all the colonies use a common standard of value, that of sterling coin issued at the royal mint in the Tower of London. An earlier opinion delivered by English treasury officials in 1662 was now reasserted: "the preserving one certain standard of weight and fineness of . . . gold and silver coins in all your Majesty's kingdoms and dominions is very much for the security and advantage of your Majesty, and the altering or debasing of the . . . standard . . . cannot be practised or allowed in any one of your Majesty's dominions without eminent prejudice to all the rest." Inasmuch as the chief purpose behind projected colonial mints was that of issuing a debased coinage, this opinion sealed the fate of the Boston mint and it was not allowed to resume operations.

Underneath the English ban on colonial mints lay the fear that they would draw to the colonial towns a fund of specie which would provide them with a money economy and thereby stimulate colonial commerce and manufacturing industries in competition with English enterprises and investments in America. In the philosophy of mercantilism the power over the currency was an attribute of sovereignty and independence; consequently the English government refused to allow its colonial dependencies to influence debts, prices, and the movement of commodities in trade by managing coinage systems of their own.[25]

Another element in the money supply of the colonies consisted of the foreign coins previously mentioned. Since the colonists kept accounts in pounds, shillings, and pence, the various foreign coins which they used had to be evaluated in terms of sterling. The colonial legis-

[24] For the economic background see M. H. Gottfried, "The First Depression in Massachusetts," New England Quarterly, IX (Dec. 1936).

[25] E. A. J. Johnson, "Some Evidence of Mercantilism in Massachusetts-Bay," New England Quarterly, I (July 1928).

latures accordingly enacted laws declaring that various foreign coins should pass in the colony concerned as worth a certain number of shillings. In this case also the colonies declared that the silver in a foreign coin should be worth more shillings in America than it would have been worth if minted into English shillings. A Spanish piece of eight, for instance, which had a bullion content equal to 4s. 6d. in English coin was declared to be worth 5s. or more in the colonies. After 1680 occurred a currency war among the colonies in which the various legislatures progressively raised the legal value of foreign coin until the piece of eight in places was rated as high as seven or eight shillings. A similar policy at the present time would provide that a dollar of today should pass at a dollar and a half tomorrow.[26]

Two underlying reasons dictated this practice of raising the shilling value of foreign coins. In Massachusetts, Pennsylvania, and New York it was assumed that higher rates there would draw in money from the outside. If a foreign coin was declared to be worth 5s. in the West Indies and 6s. in Pennsylvania, then presumably the owners of money would send it to Philadelphia in order to make purchases there, thus giving a great stimulus to local trade. For a short time high money rates did draw in coin because the price of colonial produce did not rise so rapidly as the change in currency values was effected, and accordingly the possessors of money would have more shillings and thus be able to buy more produce at former price levels. Before long, however, local prices would rise high enough to reduce the purchasing power of the overvalued coins to their old figure. When such a point was reached the inflow of money would decline and merchants were then tempted to repeat the process by placing a still higher value on foreign coins. An act of one colony tended to draw money from its neighbors, so that in self-defense each felt it necessary to boost its own money rates. With a dozen colonies involved it seemed that the contest might never end.[27]

This competitive bidding for foreign coin coincided with a wave of piracy and privateering which washed a considerable amount of treasure upon the colonial shores. Rumor surmised that the pirate crews brought in £50,000 of treasure or more at a time, although records of seizures by officials indicate more modest sums—between £1,300 and £12,000 to a vessel. At any rate the supply of coin in the

[26] W. G. Sumner, "The Spanish Dollar and the Colonial Shilling," *American Historical Review*, III (July 1898).

[27] An outstanding though brief study is Charles J. Bullock, *Essays on the Monetary History of the United States* (New York, 1900). See Part I, chapters 1–3.

colonies was particularly abundant in the 1680's and 1690's when piracy was at its height. It also happened that the colonies which saw the most of the outlaws—South Carolina, New York, Pennsylvania, and Massachusetts—placed the highest shilling value on the foreign coins which were taken from vessels in the Caribbean and the Red Sea.[28]

A second reason which motivated the raising of the shilling value of foreign coins applied to Virginia and Maryland and the sugar islands, Barbados and Jamaica. In those colonies a large proportion of the planters staggered under the debts they owed to English merchants and the Royal African Company—debts which might be reduced by a revaluation of the currency. When a piece of eight was valued at 5s. the payment of a debt of 60s. would require twelve pieces of eight; if the piece of eight were then revalued at 6s., the debtor might pay with only ten pieces. But inasmuch as England's trade and investments centered in these four colonies the home government kept a sharp watch over their currency measures in order to protect English merchants and creditors. Moreover, these colonies paid substantial revenues to the Crown or (in the case of Maryland) to a proprietor resident in England—payments which also might be reduced by currency revaluation. For these reasons England forbade the sugar and tobacco colonies to raise the legal value of foreign coins. On the other hand, because the Crown did not derive any revenues from New England, Pennsylvania, and South Carolina and because the English merchants had only slight investments in those colonies, their currency measures were not called into question until they had all succeeded in establishing much higher foreign coin rates than those prevailing in the tobacco and sugar colonies. The latter then complained that their coin was rapidly drawn away to the commercial towns. English merchants had no particular desire to provide the southern planters with a large stock of money, but they did object to the drainage of coin from the sugar and tobacco colonies to Boston, Philadelphia, and New York. Such a trend in the movement of money meant that the southern planters bought their supplies from colonial merchants instead of from English merchants. The profits and specie thus accumulated by the northern merchants increased their capital and strengthened their position as competitors of their English rivals. But should all money pass at a single rate in America, the advantage of the mainland towns would be taken from them and the

[28] Shirley C. Hughson, *The Carolina Pirates and Colonial Commerce* (Baltimore, 1894), a pioneer study, is of interest to the specialist.

coin of the southern colonies might go directly to England, to the profit of English merchants and shipowners.[29]

In order to effect the desired uniformity of coin values the English government in 1704 issued a royal proclamation which prescribed that a piece of eight of 17½ pennyweight should not pass in any colony at more than 6s. All other foreign coins were rated proportionately, depending upon their bullion content. In this manner England created the fiction of "proclamation money." Since the piece of eight rated at 6s. was intrinsically worth 4s. 6d., the proclamation meant that coin worth £100 sterling might pass in the colonies at £133⅓ proclamation money. This measure aimed to lower the rates of foreign coin money in South Carolina, Pennsylvania, New England, and New York—the colonies which had previously valued foreign money at a higher level—while Virginia and Maryland were permitted, although not required, to raise their lower values to the new maximum level. But the proclamation contained no provision for its own enforcement, and accordingly the northern colonies and South Carolina ignored it completely and with perfect immunity. At the same time the governors of Virginia and Maryland prevented its violation there. Foreign coin rates in the tobacco colonies remained disproportionately low with resulting complaints that specie continued to flow away to neighbors who retained the higher rates.[30]

With the object of giving legal force to the proclamation, Parliament in 1708 enacted it into law and provided that any person who paid or received foreign coin when valued in excess of the proclamation rate should be imprisoned six months or pay a fine of £10. Even Parliament, however, could not bring the colonists to terms. The assemblies resorted to a new device; they now valued silver as worth a certain number of shillings an ounce instead of defining the value in shillings of each foreign coin. When England protested that excessive evaluation of bullion violated the proclamation Massachusetts and New York refused to make appropriations for the support of government unless the money appropriated bore the former (and higher) values. After a long contest with the Assembly of New York Governor Hunter surrendered. " 'Tis not in the power of men or angels," he wrote, "to beat the people of this continent out of a silly notion of their being gainers by the augmentation of the value of plate [bullion]." Only Maryland adopted the official standard; Virginia put

---

[29] Clarence P. Gould, *Money and Transportation in Maryland* (Baltimore, 1915), is one of the best discussions of colonial currency.

[30] Viola F. Barnes, *The Dominion of New England* (New Haven, 1923), a standard work, has a good technical chapter (7) on currency and trade.

into effect a new rate slightly below the proclamation level, while New York, Pennsylvania, South Carolina, and the New England colonies all retained values at a higher figure. Whereas by the proclamation foreign coins were not to be valued in excess of 33⅓ per cent above English values, most of the colonies rated silver bullion at 8*s.* an ounce, which amounted to 55 per cent more than its value in English shillings. The Northerners objected to the lowering of their foreign money values, fearful that such a measure would make it difficult if not impossible for them to draw in foreign money from the outside. Meanwhile, England prevented the violation of the proclamation in Maryland, Virginia, Barbados, and Jamaica, so that uniform money rates throughout the colonies were not established. After 1710 the interest of the colonists in altering the value of foreign coins declined as paper money became the center of the currency question.[31]

The legislation of the colonies pertaining to currency exhibits one common tendency and two resulting causes of strife between them and England. When they evaluated either the silver which was minted into coin or the commodities they used as money the colonies set the monetary values at higher figures than the commercial price of such commodities and silver. Two reasons for this policy are evident. First, the indebted farmers and planters desired to increase the supply of shillings, to raise the price of their produce, and thus more readily to obtain the money with which to pay their debts. Secondly, the merchant class desired high rates on coin in order to attract it from the outside, thereby enabling them to pay cash in Europe for the imports around which all colonial trade revolved. Coined money also afforded a durable form of wealth in which surplus profits could be safely conserved pending future investments, and provided a reliable and convenient medium of exchange highly essential to the merchant class. For contrary reasons England did not favor the currency policies of the colonies. Money rates which benefited colonial debtors injured English creditors, while measures to attract coin to the colonial towns strengthened their merchants in competition with English merchants for the profits of American trade. Moreover, a money economy in the colonies might stimulate the growth of colonial manufactures, cut down American imports from abroad, and in the end make the colonies economically independent of their parent state.[32]

[31] A brief outline of colonial problems appears in chapter 1 of Davis R. Dewey, *Financial History of the United States* (New York, 1922).

[32] For the advanced student: A. H. Cole, "Evolution of the Foreign Exchange Market in the United States," *Journal of Economic and Business History*, I (May 1929).

XI

 England and the Colonies

UPPERMOST in the political history of the United States has been the federal problem—the relationship between the states and the federal government. The origins of this problem are to be found in the contacts between England and the thirteen colonies; British imperialism was the parent of American federalism. The distinct individuality and interests of the colonies, together with the vast extent of the territory occupied by the settlers, made it impossible for England to impose upon them a centralized and unified government. Each colony instead was treated as a separate unit and permitted to exercise particular privileges which fostered a feeling of independence, localism, or "state rights."

And yet, since all the colonies fell within the circle of England's rule, they were subject to common regulations framed by Parliament and the king. The problems of English imperial government, like those of American federalism, embraced first of all a series of economic contacts among the various communities of the empire. Commerce, navigation, manufacturing, currency, and property rights cut across colonial boundaries and necessitated some common regulations for the protection of England's interests in America. Relations with foreign states required a uniform system of diplomacy and a single navy. Such common agencies and regulations in turn called for a central or imperial government which could exercise both legislative and administrative powers. But since each colony had its separate legislature there arose at once a delicate problem of dividing powers between the imperial government and the colonial governments. Economic policy, diplomacy, and war gave birth to an imperial government and with it to the problem of dividing powers between the Crown and Parliament of England and the colonial legislatures in America.[1]

[1] A. C. McLaughlin, "The Background of American Federalism," *American Political Science Review*, XII (May 1918).

The Conflict between England and the Dutch

Of the various influences which shaped England's colonial policy prior to 1675 the most profound was her prolonged struggle with the Dutch for the mastery of the world's commerce—and of this the colonial trade formed no inconsiderable part. After 1616 England's interest in American commerce revolved primarily around the tobacco exports of Virginia and Maryland. Here were sources of wealth which might readily enrich the English merchant class. In the direct trade with Virginia the English merchants desired first of all to supply the colony with English goods and to reap the profits on the sales. Secondly, the merchants desired to market the tobacco in England, thereby earning commissions or profits on such transactions. The transportation of the tobacco would employ the vessels owned by the merchants and bring them an income from freight and insurance charges. Any tobacco exported from Virginia to Europe should similarly be handled by the English merchants, involving as it did added freight earnings and commissions, while such sales would augment England's favorable trade balance and bring home an increased stock of the precious metals, so vital to the merchant class. Before 1615 England had purchased most of her tobacco from Spain—a trade to which the merchants objected because it did not afford employment for their vessels or payments for their marketing services. They said in 1620 that England's importation of Spanish tobacco drained the kingdom yearly of £120,000 of specie and was the chief cause of a scarcity of hard money in England. Could England obtain tobacco only from her own colonies, her merchants might pay for it with English manufactures instead of money, earn the freights, profits, and insurance premiums involved, and export to Europe the surplus tobacco which England did not need, thereby gaining additional profits and procuring in payment an increased fund of specie.[2]

In their efforts to realize this aim the English merchants encountered sharp competition from Dutch merchants, whose trading activities and whose shipping surpassed England's at this time. The Dutch used Fort Amsterdam on the Hudson as a base from which their vessels carried European goods to Virginia and obtained tobacco for the European markets, thus threatening to crowd the English merchants out of the trade. The latter took their case to the English government and secured a series of protecting regulations—a natural outcome, because both King James I and Charles I desired to obtain

---

[2] See again *The Cambridge History of the British Empire*, Vol. I, chapters 6–7, 9 (important).

a large revenue from the importation into England of Virginia tobacco, and that in turn depended upon driving Dutch merchants out
of the English colonies.

In furthering these interests the English government required that
tobacco exported from Virginia should be shipped directly to England.
This policy was adopted in 1620–23, when James I endeavored to limit
the amount of tobacco which the Virginia Company could legally ship to
England and the company in retaliation threatened to send its entire supply to the Netherlands. A compromise in 1622 provided that
the company could import into England unlimited quantities on condition that none of the tobacco be carried from the colony directly to
a foreign port. Later orders and proclamations of the king in 1623,
1624, and 1631 continued this policy of requiring that all Virginia tobacco be first exported to England, in order that English merchants
might reap the full profit of marketing it.[3]

A second regulation in 1624 prescribed that all Virginia tobacco
should be exported from the colony in English ships—a rule which
guaranteed that English merchants would earn the freights involved
and that the tobacco would be carried directly to England, as previously ordered. In 1633–34 the king further directed that all foreign
traders be excluded from Virginia, thus tightening the monopoly of
the English merchants. Inasmuch as the levying of English import
duties on Virginia tobacco hampered the reëxportation of that part of
the crop not consumed in England, the crown in 1628 granted a
"drawback" or remission of half the import duty for all such reëx-
ports. The position of the merchants was further strengthened by
royal orders (1620–36) which forbade the growing of tobacco in England, authorized constables to destroy home-grown plants, and imposed fines upon violators of the orders. Finally, the Crown favored
the English merchants by prohibiting the importation of all foreign
tobacco except a small yearly quantity of the Spanish variety, and
upon this the import duty was greatly in excess of that levied on tobacco from the English colonies. By giving the colonial planters a
virtual monopoly of the English tobacco market these regulations appeared to benefit them as well as the English merchants.

Soon after these regulations for the protection of the English merchants had been proclaimed the Civil War broke out in England,
affording the Dutch an opportunity to usurp a large share of England's colonial trade as English merchants found themselves at a

---

[3] G. L. Beer's *The Commercial Policy of England toward the American Colonies*
(New York, 1893) is a general, preliminary survey.

competitive disadvantage.[4] In the first place the Civil War greatly disrupted English industry, due to the military service of a large part of the working people and a widespread destruction of property. The costs of production in England soared, thus forcing upward the price of English manufactures and enabling Dutch merchants to undersell their English rivals in outside markets. Secondly, the war drastically curtailed English shipping. The country was roughly divided into two military sections, the king and his forces controlling the northwestern part and the Puritan-Parliamentary party controlling the southeast. Each faction pressed as many commercial vessels as possible into service as privateers to prey upon the commerce of the ports in the hands of its enemies. Vessels bound for Puritan ports were seized by the king's privateers, while Puritan privateers captured vessels trading with the king's ports, so that England waged a destructive warfare on her own commerce. Due to the high prices of English goods and the danger that cargoes bound for England might be seized by privateers, Dutch vessels met a welcome reception in the English colonies. They brought cheap products—"all sorts of domestic manufactures," particularly dry goods, beer, liquors, and hardware. At least fifty Dutch merchants were trading to Virginia and England's West Indian colonies in 1651. They procured and marketed the two colonial staples, sugar and tobacco, carrying them directly to European ports and thus depriving England of the profits of her former colonial trade. So extensive was the commerce of the Dutch with New England that Dutch money became there a common medium of exchange. Virginia in 1643 and Maryland in 1649 formally opened their ports to Dutch traders and vessels in defiance of orders from England. In the English sugar colonies, Barbados and the Leeward Islands, Dutch capitalists supplied goods to the planters on credit, equipped them with machinery for their sugar works, and sold them Negro slaves from African trading posts which the Dutch had seized from the Portuguese. As a result it was reported in 1652 that the Dutch had engrossed the whole commerce of Barbados. The French statesman, Colbert, indicated the power of the Dutch at this time when he estimated that they owned sixteen thousand of the twenty thousand vessels engaged in Europe's trade.[5]

The execution of Charles I in 1649 and the establishment of the

---

[4] The best introduction to its subject is George Edmundson's *Anglo-Dutch Rivalry during the First Half of the Seventeenth Century* (Oxford, 1931).

[5] Violet Barbour, "Dutch and English Merchant Shipping in the Seventeenth Century," *Economic History Review*, II (Jan. 1930).

Puritan regime under Oliver Cromwell inaugurated a new era in colonial policy. The Puritan merchants of London had formed the backbone of the opposition to the king, and London carried on three-quarters of England's external commerce. When installed in power the Puritans were determined to recapture the trade of the English colonies and to deprive the Dutch of the gains they had made during the Civil War. Accordingly, in 1650 the Puritan Parliament, now a mouthpiece of the London merchants, passed a Navigation Act which prohibited the vessels of any foreign nation from trading with England's American colonies—an act which anticipated that all colonial commerce would be carried on with England, to the enrichment of the merchants of London.

On issues of colonial and foreign policy the Puritan leaders divided into two parties. One group, headed by Cromwell, looking backward to Elizabethan times, stressed religious issues, regarded Spain as England's great rival in the New World, and desired to conquer Spain's colonies, thereby diverting their wealth to the Protestant cause in Europe. A second party believed that the Spanish power had passed its zenith and that the energetic and aggressive Dutch held out the greatest threat to England's commerce and prosperity. The programs of these two parties, however, were antagonistic. If England went to war against Spain she needed Protestant allies, and since the Dutch were the strongest Protestant power in Europe, England should join them in a Protestant league against Spain. Cromwell approved of a plan whereby England and the Dutch should divide and monopolize all colonial trade—the Dutch to enjoy the commerce of India, the English to possess all America except Brazil, and the two to divide the slave trading stations of Africa. Behind this scheme was Cromwell's theory that the Caribbean islands and the Spanish lands in lower America offered the most lucrative sources of colonial profit. An advocate of "tropical colonization," he hoped to acquire the Spanish colonies and to transfer English settlers from North America to the Caribbean region.[6]

In order to establish a Protestant league against Spain Cromwell carried on negotiations with the Dutch in 1650–51, but to no avail. The Dutch demanded as their price the privilege of a free trade with England's American and West Indian colonies—a concession to which the Puritan merchants of London would not consent. After the failure of the negotiations in 1651 the anti-Spanish plans of Cromwell were shelved, the commercial rivalry with the Dutch flared up anew, and

[6] For this period an excellent brief account is Charles H. Firth, *Oliver Cromwell and the Rule of the Puritans* . . . (New York, 1900). See chapters 18–19.

in October 1651 parliament passed a sweeping Navigation Act which precipitated the First Anglo-Dutch War of 1652–54.

This act aimed to eliminate the Dutch not only from the commerce of the English colonies (which exclusion had already been decreed by the act of 1650) but also from the carrying trade between England and other countries. Goods from America, Asia, and Africa could enter England, Ireland, and the English colonies only if carried in English, Irish, or colonial ships; and goods from Europe could enter England, Ireland, and the colonies only if brought in English ships or foreign ships of the country "of which the said goods are the growth, production or manufacture." Fish, oil, and whalebone could be imported into and exported from England only in English ships, and the coasting trade between English ports was confined to English vessels. Under the terms of the acts of 1650 and 1651 the only important shipping business with England open to the Dutch was that of importing Dutch goods into England directly from Holland and of exporting English goods (except fish) to Europe. And since Amsterdam was an entrepôt to which the Dutch brought products from all parts of the world, the act of 1651 forbade even English vessels to bring from the Netherlands any articles except those produced by the Dutch.[7]

This measure to exclude the Dutch from most of England's trade, together with numerous commercial disputes between the two powers and the fact that the Dutch were sheltering the exiled heir to the English throne, culminated in the First Dutch War—a naval conflict in which England made the larger gains. The Dutch had neglected their navy, and having far more vessels afloat than England, suffered disproportionate losses as English privateers captured fifteen hundred prizes. The peace concluded in 1654 provided for a defensive alliance between the two powers, for the exclusion of the Stuarts from the Netherlands, for the continuation of England's Navigation Acts, and for the settlement of other English grievances. Cromwell was now free to push his earlier designs against Spain.

The Spaniards still adhered to their policy of excluding English subjects from the trade of Spanish America and even denied to England the right to hold her possessions in the Caribbean. In 1635 they had seized from the English the island of Tortuga and in 1641 they conquered the Puritan colony of Providence in the Caribbean. Cromwell, having pacified England, Scotland, and Ireland, decided in 1654 to retaliate against the Spaniards by seizing one of their important

[7] G. L. Beer, "Cromwell's Policy in Its Economic Aspects," *Political Science Quarterly*, XVI (Dec. 1901) and XVII (March 1902).

colonies which might serve as a base for the eventual conquest of Spanish America. He therefore dispatched a fleet under Robert Venables and William Penn, the elder, with instructions to occupy Puerto Rico, Hispaniola, or Cartagena on the mainland. "The design in general," he wrote, "is to gain an interest in that part of the West Indies in possession of the Spaniard, for the effecting whereof we shall not tie you up to a method by any particular instructions." The force sent out from England, about twenty-five hundred civilians of poor fighting quality, failed to conquer Hispaniola, but did succeed in taking Jamaica in 1655—an island of slight value then but destined to loom large in the British empire as a profitable sugar colony and a center of English trade with Spanish America.[8]

The return of Charles II to England represented a compromise between contending parties. The restoration of the Stuart monarchy and the reëstablishment of both the Church of England and the House of Lords appeased the royalist and aristocratic forces, while Charles II consented to a commercial policy which gratified the London merchants. This policy was embodied in the famous Acts of Trade and Navigation, the foundation stones of England's colonial system until after the American Revolution. Of the first importance was the Navigation Act of 1660, reënacted in 1661, sometimes called the English Magna Carta of the sea. With respect to the colonies it contained three momentous provisions. All trade of the colonies had to be carried in English ships—vessels that were English built and owned, commanded by an English captain, and manned by a crew three-fourths of whom were English sailors. The word "English" was defined in 1662 as meaning "only his Majesty's subjects of England, Ireland, and the plantations." Second, the act of 1661 excluded all foreign merchants from the commerce of the English colonies, and, third, it required that certain enumerated articles produced in the colonies be exported only to England, Ireland, Wales, Berwick-on-Tweed, or to other English colonies. Sugar, tobacco, cotton-wool, indigo, ginger, and such dyewoods as fustic, logwood, and braziletto composed the original list of commodities thus enumerated.

The second act of major importance, the Staple Act of 1663, provided that goods produced in Europe and destined for the colonies should first be sent to England, Wales, or Berwick-on-Tweed before going to America. Direct exportation to the colonies of European commodities was permitted in only a few cases: servants, horses, and

[8] F. Strong, "The Causes of Cromwell's West Indian Expedition," *American Historical Review*, IV (Jan. 1899).

provisions from Scotland or Ireland, wine from Madeira or the Azores, and salt for the North American fisheries.[9]

These acts intended to give England a monopoly of the trade of her colonies—not a monopoly to particular persons, but a national monopoly in which all English merchants should share. The Staple Act meant not only that English merchants would get the business of selling to the colonies but also that English manufacturers might dispose of their wares at an advantage in that the foreign goods which had to pass through England en route to the colonies might be taxed, thereby raising their prices and enabling English goods to undersell them. Similarly, the enumerated article principle assured that most of the colonial staples important to England would be exported by English merchants, who were also guaranteed employment for their vessels through the exclusion of foreign vessels from the English colonies. Since the colonists had to do most of their buying and selling in England, the London merchants could safely sell their wares on credit, thus adding interest charges to the freights, profits, and commissions which they reaped from their American trade.

The acts of 1660–63 threatened to exclude the Dutch completely from the English colonies and consequently new fuel was added to the old rivalry. In 1664 occurred the Second Anglo-Dutch War, notable for England's conquest of New Netherland—a move for the stricter enforcement of English colonial policy. Since the Dutch had long used New Amsterdam as a center from which they conducted their trade with Virginia, Maryland, and New England, the English desired to hold Manhattan as a means of enforcing their Navigation Acts by depriving the Dutch of their American trading base. The English also desired New Netherland in order to complete the chain of English territory along the coast, to acquire the Hudson River fur trade, and to obtain land for additional settlement. The treaty of 1667 which closed the Second Dutch War ceded New Netherland to England while England withdrew from the Spice Islands, limiting her oriental trade to the mainland of India. England also obtained the Dutch slave trading stations in Africa, and her Navigation Acts remained in force.[10]

Despite these material gains England again went to war against the Dutch in 1672—largely through personal intrigues of King Charles

---

[9] For a British view see Hugh E. Egerton, *A Short History of British Colonial Policy* (London, 1897), Book I, and Book II, chapters 1–3.

[10] Gerald B. Hertz, *The Old Colonial System* (Manchester, 1905), an English study, contains a chapter (3) on colonial policy.

II, in secret alliance with France. Although a Dutch fleet recaptured New Amsterdam in August 1673 the treaty of peace in 1674 once more restored it to England—an act which marked the passing of the Dutch menace to England's North American trade. Never a successful colonizing nation, the Dutch afterward confined themselves to the commerce of Europe, Africa, the Far East, and the Caribbean.[11]

The Conflict between the Merchants

England versus New England

The Navigation Acts and the exclusion of the Dutch from the English colonies presented to the merchants of Puritan New England a commercial opportunity of which they quickly took advantage. Ever since 1645 the trade of Massachusetts had been growing by leaps and bounds. The initial impulse to its development was a severe economic depression which struck New England in 1640 by virtue of the cessation of Puritan emigration from England. In the 1630's New England's economy had been in a fair state of balance. The two basic needs of the settlements—an adequate supply of foreign goods and a market for the surplus products of the New England farms—had been met by the arrival of thousands of immigrants who brought their property to the colonies chiefly in the form of English goods, which they exchanged there for livestock, seed, foodstuffs, other New England products, and land. When the immigration ceased in 1640 the settlers lost this steady market for their surplus produce and were unable to obtain sufficient supplies of foreign goods. Prices of New England commodities dropped drastically as the farmers could not find buyers and prices of foreign goods soared in face of an extreme and sudden shortage.

From this impasse New England extricated herself through the development of external trade. The merchants of Boston collected the surplus farm products, lumber, and fish of the surrounding settlements and carried them to the West Indies, southern Europe, the tobacco colonies, and Newfoundland, where they exchanged them for European goods or the means of buying such imports. The disruption of England's external trade in the 1640's aided the New Englanders much in the same manner as it had aided the Dutch. By 1660 the merchants of Boston and Salem, closely identified with the fishery,

---

[11] John Beresford, *The Godfather of Downing Street* (London, 1925), is primarily a study of Anglo-Dutch relations. See chapters 9–11.

shipbuilding, and New Hampshire lumbering, formed the dominant economic interest in the New England colonies.[12]

The Navigation Acts further strengthened the position of New England, in that they decreed the exclusion from the colonies of Dutch merchants and vessels—then the chief competitors of the Boston merchants. Moreover, England excluded foreign vessels before she had enough vessels to carry on all her colonial trade, and New England merchants and shipbuilders (to whom the Navigation Acts gave the same privileges which were conferred upon English shippers) rushed forward to fill the gap. During the Civil War and the Puritan regime England had been too busy at home and in Europe to supervise the colonies closely; hence the New England traders had been free to trade wherever they could make a profit, and they came to feel that they were independent of English restrictions such as were imposed upon them by the acts of 1660 and 1663. Accordingly, they proceeded to ship the enumerated articles directly from the colonies to European ports and to import European wares on the return voyage without bringing them first to England as the Staple Act required. Such illegal trade caused the utmost concern among the English merchants because the New England trader could undersell them in America, exempt as he was from paying the customs duties on goods that passed through England. Moreover, direct shipments between Europe and the colonies were less expensive than the roundabout trade which the English merchants carried on through English ports.

In other words, the Boston merchants were rapidly succeeding the Dutch as the competitors of English merchants in the contest for the American trade. By supplying the colonies with European instead of English manufactures, the Bostonians threatened to deprive the English manufacturer of the colonial market. Their marketing of colonial produce in Europe similarly robbed the English merchants of the profits of such business, as well as the profit of supplying the colonies with needed imports, while the employment of New England vessels in colonial trade reduced the freight earnings of English merchant-shipowners. Above all, New England's direct trade with Europe diminished the king's revenues, since the products involved did not pass through English ports and accordingly did not yield custom duties to the Crown. Once more the allied interests of the king and the English merchants were threatened and once more they prepared vigorous measures to protect their stake in the colonies.

[12] The third volume of H. L. Osgood's *American Colonies in the 17th Century* deals with imperial relations (important).

Massachusetts in the meantime had taken the stand that she was not subject to acts of Parliament, arguing that "our allegiance binds us not to the laws of England any longer than we live in England." Not only did the Massachusetts Puritans fear that Parliament might overthrow their religious system but the Boston merchants were loath to admit that parliamentary statutes could regulate American trade so as to restrict colonial profits. For these reasons Massachusetts between 1630 and 1680 stubbornly resisted every effort toward imperial control. Her government refused to recognize Charles II as king in 1660 and consistently supported the Boston merchants in their defiance of the Acts of Trade and Navigation.[13]

The headstrong attitude of Massachusetts brought a royal commission to Boston in 1664 to investigate charges that the colony had rejected England's authority. The four commissioners met only obstruction and hostility from the Boston government and accomplished nothing—an outcome which encouraged the Bay merchants in their violation of both the Staple Act and the clause in the Navigation Act of 1661 pertaining to the enumerated articles. A common method of evading the latter act was that of shipping sugar and tobacco from the southern colonies to Boston and then reëxporting the products to foreign ports. By an oversight this act permitted the exportation of the enumerated articles from one English colony to another without requiring the payment of any duties. Boston merchants could obtain such articles tax free, whereas English merchants had to pay English import duties, a difference which enabled the Bostonians to undersell their competitors in foreign markets. To relieve this situation, Parliament in 1673 passed another trade act which placed a "plantation duty" on enumerated articles exported from one English colony to another—a tax equivalent to the duty on such articles when imported into England, so that the colonial merchant lost his former advantage of tax exemption. Furthermore, English officials construed the act of 1660 so as to prohibit the reëxportation of enumerated articles from intermediate colonial ports to foreign countries.[14]

The act of 1673 necessitated a staff of officials in the colonies to collect the export duties on the enumerated articles shipped to the other English colonies. Foremost among such custom officials was one Edward Randolph, who was sent to New England in 1676 to investigate colonial trade. Two years later he was appointed collector of

---

[13] A. H. Buffinton, "The Isolationist Policy of New England," *New England Quarterly*, I (Jan. 1928).

[14] Lemuel A. Welles, *The History of the Regicides in New England* (New York, 1927), gives the American careers of three of the judges who condemned Charles I.

The London Customs House

During the great days of Elizabeth, especially after the fall of Spanish sea power, English commerce spread apace. East, south, and west, farther and farther from the Thames, went the adventurous traders of England. The old customs house in London received the cargoes of a swiftly growing merchant fleet. England was taking a new place in the world.

the king's revenue in Massachusetts. A staunch Anglican and royalist, Randolph despised nearly everything cherished by the Massachusetts Puritans. As a "watchdog" of the English merchants it was his duty to expose and stamp out all illegal trade in New England and in so doing to safeguard the king's revenue. Related to the Mason family in England which claimed New Hampshire, he vigorously combated the pretensions of Massachusetts to that region, and was largely instrumental in having it separated from Massachusetts and set apart as a royal province in 1679. When he returned from a visit to New Hampshire in 1679 he was greeted with this welcoming verse:

> Welcome, Sir, welcome from the eastern shore
> With a commission stronger than before
>   To play the horse-leech, rob us of our fleeces,
>   To rend our land, and tear it all to pieces
> Welcome now back again.

Determined, tactless, and overbearing, Randolph persistently harassed the Massachusetts Puritans over a half-dozen years, relentlessly prying into all their affairs with the sole object of making out as strong a case against them as possible. In 1680 he drew up twenty-nine charges against the colony, twenty-three of which related to violations of the Navigation Acts. He accused the Puritans of operating their mint at Boston—a manifest usurpation of the king's prerogative—and of fitting out pirates who preyed upon the commerce of the Caribbean. The authorities of Massachusetts, he said, worked hand in glove with the lawbreaking merchants and put every sort of obstacle in his path. Such was an act in 1681 creating a colonial naval station whereby the colony was to receive all fines arising from judgments against violators of the Navigation Acts, whereas the king's instructions directed that such fines should go half to the king and half to the informer— and Randolph was the principal informer. Local juries, he charged, refused to convict merchants accused of illegal trade. He concluded as early as 1679 that the king's revenues and the English merchants could be protected only if the charter of Massachusetts were revoked and the locally elected officers of the colony were replaced by agents appointed by the king. In season and out he urged this policy upon the English government.[15]

During the years 1660–80 many other charges were leveled against Massachusetts. Her religious policies, which discriminated against Anglicans by denying them the right to vote and by forcing them to

[15] H. L. Osgood, "England and the Colonies in the Seventeenth Century," *Political Science Quarterly*, XVII (June 1902).

pay taxes for the support of the Puritan churches, manifestly violated the colony's charter, requiring as it did that colonial laws should be consistent with the laws of England. In her boundary quarrels with Connecticut, Rhode Island, and New Hampshire, Massachusetts brought upon herself the accusation of unfair and illegal treatment of her smaller neighbors. In the 1650's the Boston Puritans assumed the attributes of sovereignty when, for purely religious causes, they executed four Quakers—an act clearly outside the province of a corporation such as the Massachusetts Bay Company. Above all, the Puritan leaders claimed virtual independence when they refused to take the oath of allegiance to the king or to recognize the authority of Parliament, insisted that judgments of the local courts could not be appealed to the Privy Council, asserted that the king possessed no powers over the colony except those mentioned in the charter, and claimed the sole right to judge whether the colony's laws were consistent with the laws of England. Orders and requests from the king were consistently ignored or evaded. And when this spirit of independence expressed itself in violations of the Navigation Acts and threatened to deprive England of the economic value of her colonies, an intolerable situation called for drastic action. After long negotiations in which the Puritan authorities refused to yield an inch, the Privy Council brought suit in the court of chancery against the Massachusetts Bay Company. Finding its charter privileges had been abused, the court on October 23, 1684, declared the charter forfeited.

Imperial Administration

After the revocation of the Massachusetts charter the English government imposed upon New England a highly centralized administration—a scheme of control toward which English officials had been striving (rather fitfully, to be sure) since 1620. In order to induce promoters and investors to establish colonies it had been necessary to grant them liberal powers of governing their territories, but as the economic value of the colonies increased, such powers were often used to deprive English merchants and the Crown of the profits from colonial resources and trade. It therefore seemed desirable to curtail colonial privileges and so to regulate the colonies that they might be of maximum value to English interests. The Dominion of New England, 1686–89, exhibited this tendency at its height, but behind it lay a long trend toward imperial control.[16]

[16] An excellent discussion of English backgrounds appears in George N. Clark's *The Later Stuarts, 1660–1714* (Oxford, 1934), chapters 1–5, 12.

The initial step was taken by the Crown in 1624 when it assumed the power of governing Virginia. Under the charters of 1609 and 1612 the Virginia Company had acquired and exercised that power— not, however, with very satisfactory results. Between 1620 and 1624 the company was split into two bitterly hostile factions, headed respectively by Sir Edwin Sandys, leader of the party in control, and Sir Thomas Smith, spearhead of the opposition. In 1622–23 the Smith faction leveled a series of charges against the administration by the Sandys group. It was asserted that Sandys and his friends had only slight investments in the company, that they kept control by manipulating votes, that they suppressed free discussion and criticism, and that they spent the company's money recklessly and unprofitably. Settlers had been sent to Virginia faster than the colony could absorb them; adequate provision was not made for their support, health, or protection; the company's agents in the colony had embezzled the company's funds there; and even the Indian massacre of 1622 was attributed to the mismanagement of Sandys. So appallingly high was the death rate in the colony that it was likened to a slaughterhouse. Moreover, with reference to plans for granting the company a monopoly of importing tobacco into England, it was charged in 1623 that the Sandys group was preparing to give its partisans some needless "soft jobs" at excessively high pay.[17]

The strife within the company and distress in the colony moved the king's Privy Council to appoint in April 1623 an investigating commission which soon brought in a report that strongly condemned the policies of Sandys. When he had taken charge in 1618 there were one thousand settlers in Virginia; four thousand emigrants had been sent afterward, and yet in 1623 there were only twelve hundred alive. The tactics of Sandys had disgusted many important members of the company, causing them to lose interest, while the intense factional strife was imperiling the colony. The Privy Council accordingly recommended that the company surrender its charter and place the government of Virginia in the king's hands. When the company refused to do this the Privy Council brought against it a suit of *quo warranto* which terminated in 1624 in a decision annulling the charter. Although the powers of governing the colony were now transferred to the king, the company was allowed to operate as a trading body. Its failure, however, to earn profits ended its commercial activities in

[17] Alexander C. Brown's *English Politics in Early Virginia History* (Boston, 1901) contains much information but has been superseded by Wesley F. Craven's *Dissolution of the Virginia Company* (New York, 1932)—a first-rate monograph. See also W. F. Craven, "The Dissolution of the London Company for Virginia," *American Historical Review*, XXXVII (Oct. 1931).

1632, when bankruptcy revealed that it had lost more than £200,000 in the Virginia enterprise.

Having taken over the government of Virginia the king now was confronted by the task of evolving a colonial administration. Should the province be managed by Parliament or the king? Both James I and Charles I insisted that colonial administration fell solely within the prerogative of the sovereign, who had originally asserted his power by issuing the charters which conferred land titles and the right to govern the colonies. During the contest between the Sandys and Smith factions James I had directed Parliament not to interfere on the ground that his Privy Council had charge of the matter, and immediately after 1624 the king continued to supervise the colonies, Parliament not even being in session between 1629 and 1640. The royal authority was made effective during these years through the agency of the Privy Council, but since it was too large a body to consider details, small temporary committees of its members—usually experts on trade—performed the task of drafting and enforcing regulations for the colonies. After 1624 the general administration of Virginia was assigned to such a special commission. Due, however, to the preoccupation of Charles I and his court with issues foreign and domestic, this commission was inactive and the real government was entrusted to the king's governor and his council in Virginia.[18]

The economic relations between the tobacco planters and the English merchants illustrate the part played by the king's government in colonial administration. It was customary after 1620 for the merchants to sell goods to the planters on credit and to receive payment in tobacco. The initial profits of tobacco growing forced a rapid increase in production so that Virginia's exports multiplied seventy-fivefold between 1617 and 1640. In consequence, the price of tobacco, which was as high as five shillings a pound in 1617, had dropped below the cost of production by 1630, and between 1627 and 1638 its average was only about twopence a pound. The drastically reduced incomes of the planters were not sufficient both for the payment of debts incurred when tobacco prices were high and for the purchase of new supplies of English goods, whose prices did not fall at a corresponding rate. As a remedy the planters, through their local legislature, experimented with statutory price-fixing. An act of 1619 required that the better grades of tobacco should be sold in the colony at 3s. a pound, and the inferior grades at 1s. 6d. a pound. A second act

[18] C. M. Andrews, *British Committees, Commissions, and Councils of Trade and Plantations, 1622–1675* (Baltimore, 1908), the standard work, is detailed and technical.

(1631–32) imposed heavy penalties on planters who sold their tobacco at less than 6d. a pound, while a similar measure of 1640 provided for the inspection of all tobacco and the destruction of all the
bad and half of the good, the remainder being valued for payments
of debts at the rate of forty pounds of the selected product for one
hundred pounds of ordinary tobacco.

Such acts did not appeal to the English merchants, who argued
that the actual price of tobacco was determined by general European
market conditions and that if they paid a higher legal price to the
planters they would be ruined. In self-protection the merchants priced
the goods they sold to the planters so as to correspond with the inflated tobacco prices. The planters then complained to the king that
the merchants were guilty of profiteering. In this contest the king
and his advisers sought to protect the merchants by ordering the governors of Virginia in 1626 and 1634 not to enforce any colonial
statutes which arbitrarily fixed the price of tobacco. In the meantime
the Crown had framed its regulations granting in substance a monopoly of the colonial tobacco trade to English merchants. Thus the
planters could neither trade with foreign merchants nor dictate prices
to the English monopolists.[19]

New England also engaged the attention of the king's advisers during the reign of Charles I. Several non-Puritans whom Massachusetts
had expelled charged in a petition to the Privy Council in 1632 that
the New Englanders had withdrawn from the Anglican Church and
were striving for complete independence from England. After 1633,
Archbishop Laud extended his ecclesiastical investigations to the Puritan migration, and Charles I, convinced that the exodus to New England was weakening England and strengthening the stiff-necked Puritan colony, created in 1634 a special commission known as the
Lords Commissioners for Plantations in General. Composed of England's leading churchmen and statesmen, though actually functioning
through a sub-commission of lesser men who made recommendations
to guide the decisions of the great men, this commission had a general
jurisdiction over the colonies, with special instructions to regulate
emigration and to examine the colonial charters in order to ascertain
whether any "privileges hurtful to us or our Crown . . . have been
prejudicially suffered or granted."

The commission immediately brought suit against Massachusetts

---

[19] G. L. Beer's *Origins of the British Colonial System* is very important here. Beer
emphasizes England's concern with the colonies as sources of supply. For a criticism,
see C. P. Nettels, "The Place of Markets in the Old Colonial System," *New England
Quarterly*, VI (Sept. 1933).

and called upon the company to produce its charter and to answer the charges that the local authorities had violated its terms. But the Bay Puritans refused to send the charter to England, and since the governing body of the company was in New England, the legal proceedings could not be completed and the charter was not officially annulled. Charles I nevertheless assumed control of the colonies and appointed as governor-general of New England the most bitter and active foe of the Bay Puritans—Sir Ferdinando Gorges—then quarreling with Massachusetts about land titles and the control of the New England fishery. It was at this time that the Council for New England surrendered its patent in order to expedite the proceedings against the Massachusetts charter. The year 1635–36 witnessed preparations on the part of Gorges to raise a force to subdue Massachusetts, impose his authority on the colony, and compel the surrender of the charter. Determined to resist by force of arms such an "invasion," the Bay Puritans were equally busy with preparations for defense. However, Charles I failed to back Gorges with financial aid and his plans had not been carried out when the rumblings of civil war in England forced the king to ignore the remote colony. Massachusetts escaped unscathed—its first successful resistance to English authority. The colonial leaders had not desired nominal independence but they did crave the right to manage their affairs in their own way.[20]

When Parliament functioned without the king during the Civil War it asserted that it possessed supreme authority over the colonies and thereupon created a special commission upon which it conferred almost unlimited powers to govern them. The high-priest of Puritan colonial promoters, the Earl of Warwick, headed this commission with the title of Governor-in-Chief and Lord High Admiral of all the English colonies. Having escaped from the regulations which Charles I was seeking to impose upon them, the colonies had no intention of submitting to the potentially stronger authority of Parliament. Particularly was this the case in Virginia, where the planters realized that the London merchants who desired to monopolize the tobacco trade at the expense of the planters formed the backbone of the parliamentary party. The Virginians therefore proclaimed their loyalty to Charles I but this amounted to little more than a declaration that they opposed the regulation of their trade by the London merchants. Massachusetts also rejected the authority of Parliament, even refusing to accept legislation friendly to the colony "lest in after times . . . hostile forces might be in control, and meantime a prece-

[20] Attention is again called to G. L. Beer's *The Old Colonial System*, Vols. I and II (important).

dent would have been established." So occupied was Parliament with the war that it could not interfere with the colonies and they hastened to shake off all imperial authority and to carry on a free trade with foreign countries.

After the parliamentary forces had disposed of the king and established their uncontested supremacy in England they proceeded to bring the refractory colonies to terms. New England had not openly defied the English Puritans but Virginia, along with the island colonies, had proclaimed their loyalty to Charles II when their legislatures declared anyone guilty of treason who denied his right to the throne. In 1652 Cromwell sent to the colonies an expedition which forced the islands, Virginia, and Maryland to recognize the newly won authority of Parliament. Terms of surrender in 1652 provided that Virginia and Maryland should not be taxed except through their own legislatures and that they should enjoy a free trade with "friendly" nations. The latter concession occasioned a dispute as English officials interpreted it as subject to the Navigation Acts of 1650 and 1651 which excluded foreign vessels and merchants from colonial trade, while the planters construed it to mean free trade in a literal sense. Some effort was made to enforce those acts, naval vessels being employed to seize foreign ships trading with the colonies. On the whole, however, Cromwell and his fellow Puritans were too much preoccupied with European affairs to impose a firm rule upon the colonies. The Virginia House of Burgesses was allowed to elect its own governor and to function as a miniature republic, while the New England colonies managed their own affairs and operated their independent league of nations, the Confederation of New England.

The compromise between the London merchants and the English aristocracy which placed Charles II upon the throne in 1660 meant a continuance of the commercial policies of the Puritan regime. As far as the new king had a consistent policy it was that of promoting England's industrial, commercial, and imperial growth—a policy which was bound to lead to a strict control of colonial trade. He conceded to Parliament a share in the regulation of the colonies by assenting to the Acts of Trade and Navigation; he favored the merchants by appointing select councils of trade and plantations whose primary duty was to make the colonies profitable to the merchants and the Crown.[21] These councils had a checkered career until 1675 when they were superseded by a committee of the Privy Council known as the Lords of Trade—a body of men of high station, influence, and wealth.

[21] R. Bieber, "British Plantation Councils of 1670–1672," *English Historical Review*, XL (Jan. 1925).

Both the Lords of Trade and the earlier councils acted upon royal instructions which embodied the views of the London merchants. Such instructions directed the councils to supervise the colonies with an eye to making them valuable to England as markets, as sources of raw materials, merchants' profits, freights, and Crown revenues, and as fields for the investment of English capital. To this end the councils were ordered to obtain all possible information about the colonies, to prepare instructions for the colonial governors, to scrutinize colonial acts and court proceedings, and to investigate and expose all violations of English orders and statutes. The councils did not possess actual authority; they merely gave advice to the king and his Privy Councillors, who in turn appointed colonial officials, framed regulations, and ordered their enforcement in the colonies.

During the first decade of his reign Charles II pursued a fairly conciliatory policy toward the colonies. With the memory of the Civil War only too fresh in mind he refrained from oppressive measures that would antagonize his subjects before he was securely established on the throne.[22] Responding to the declarations of loyalty issued by the leaders of Connecticut and Rhode Island he granted those colonies their liberal charters of 1662 and 1663 which recognized them legally as virtual republics, empowered through their assemblies to pass laws and elect their own governors. He appointed Sir William Berkeley governor of Virginia after he had been chosen by the House of Burgesses. When Massachusetts refused to submit to the royal commissioners in 1664 the king did not press the charges against the colony, allowing it to go its own way unmolested. Liberal powers of government were conferred upon the proprietors of New York and Carolina, while after the conquest of New Netherland the Dutch settlers were granted religious freedom and permitted to retain their property and customs. However, this policy of leniency toward the colonies proved to be merely a prelude to measures which aimed to reduce them to a state of abject subordination to England's authority.[23]

THE DOMINION OF NEW ENGLAND

The close of the Third Dutch War in 1674 definitely removed the Dutch menace to England's colonial trade. Charles II, now fourteen years upon the throne, had acquired a sense of security that dis-

[22] Percy L. Kaye, *English Colonial Administration under Lord Clarendon* (Baltimore, 1905), treats adequately the years 1660–67.

[23] Ralph P. Bieber, *The Lords of Trade and Plantations, 1675–1696* (Allentown, Pa., 1919), is a formal study of administration. See also W. T. Root, "The Lords of Trade and Plantations, 1675–1696," *American Historical Review*, XXIII (Oct. 1917).

posed him to assert, however secretly, his father's theory of absolute rule. Year by year the colonies were becoming more valuable to England, although the evasion of the Navigation Acts by New England merchants remained a disturbing challenge to England's supremacy. After Dutch competition in North America had been crushed, the king was at last in a position to discipline New England. In this policy he could count upon the aid of the English merchants, who were firmly resolved to make their New England competitors respect the Navigation Acts.

The trend toward a closer control of the colonies by England appeared in the Revenue Act of 1673. Two years later Charles II created the Lords of Trade, thus dignifying colonial administration by entrusting it to the most powerful men in the kingdom. Another step was taken in 1679 when the right of the Mason family to govern New Hampshire was restored to the king and a royal governor was placed over the province. The charter of Pennsylvania of 1681 made the colony subject to taxes levied by Parliament and required the proprietor to enforce the Navigation Acts, to submit the laws of the province for the king's approval or disapproval, and to maintain an agent in England to answer charges brought against the province. Refusing to approve of a proposal to erect a new proprietary province in Florida the Lords of Trade in 1682 declared it inexpedient "to constitute any new proprieties in America or to grant any further powers that may render the plantations less dependent on the Crown." Then followed the annulment of the Massachusetts charter in 1684. The trend was reinforced in 1685 when Charles II was succeeded by his brother, James II. Determined to rule as an absolute monarch over England, the new king naturally did not intend to allow the dependent colonies to defy his royal will.[24]

Two obstacles to a firmer control over the colonies had come to light prior to 1675. First, the charters had conferred extensive rights behind which the colonists had been able to resist England's authority. Hence it seemed urgent that the charters, particularly those of the New England colonies, be revoked and their privileges returned to the king. Secondly, the existence of many separate colonial governments greatly complicated the task of imperial administration. If, on the other hand, all New England, New York, and New Jersey could be brought into direct dependence upon England, the king could appoint one set of officials who would act as a unit in enforcing the

---

[24] An admirable study of colonial administration is Louise P. Kellogg's *The American Colonial Charter*, *Report*, American Historical Association, 1903, Vol. I, chapter 1.

Acts of Trade and Navigation. A single government, moreover, would be far less expensive to England than the maintenance of six or eight separate colonies. Should the whole northern and middle area be converted into one large royal province its economic resources might be so developed, and its commercial activities so directed, as to yield maximum returns to English interests. Although the northern area was already immensely valuable to England, it presented an acute problem in that its people were not producing staples that could be marketed directly in England. The lack of such staples had forced the Northerners to engage in external trade (in which they had rapidly become effective competitors of English merchants) and to develop home manufactures that threatened to deprive England of the northern colonial market for textiles, leather goods, earthenware, woodenware, and ironware. But if England established a uniform, all-powerful government over the whole northern area, its resources might be developed so as to divert the people from manufacturing and foreign trade. They might develop lead and copper mines and produce hemp and naval stores, thus obtaining staple raw materials that could be exchanged directly for English manufactures. Such a direct trade would halt the growth of colonial manufactures and at the same time lessen the dependence of the northern area on outside trades, which, while they provided it with purchasing power for English goods, also fostered a class of merchants who competed with English merchants for the profits of the commerce of the New World.[25]

A new factor in British policy came into play after 1675. As the Anglo-Spanish rivalry had been succeeded by the Anglo-Dutch rivalry, so also the Dutch menace was followed by a menace from France. At Newfoundland and Nova Scotia and on the New England and New York frontiers the expansion of the English and French was drawing the two people into a new contest for colonial supremacy. It therefore happened that the French menace focused attention upon the northern area just when it was so notorious for its violation of the Navigation Acts. And in the impending contest France was likely to derive an advantage from her scheme of imperial government. All Canada was included in one dominion, administered by a single body of officials who were appointed by the king and unrestrained by colonial legislatures. Since both Charles II and James II felt a spiritual partiality for French absolutism it is quite understandable that they used the Dominion of Canada as their model for the Dominion of New England.

[25] See again Viola F. Barnes's important *The Dominion of New England.*

This experiment in colonial absolutism endured but three years. In May 1686 James II appointed Sir Edmund Andros as governor of New England with autocratic powers over all the northern colonies except Connecticut and Rhode Island. The colonial legislatures were abolished and their powers transferred to Andros and a local council whose members were appointed by the king. Andros and his council were authorized to levy taxes, enact laws, erect courts, and grant lands in the name of the king. All such acts might be set aside by the king, while judgments of the colonial courts involving £300 or more might be appealed to the Privy Council. Land grants made in the future were subject to a quit-rent of 2s. 6d. a hundred acres. So drastic were these provisions that they constituted a complete overthrow of the Puritan social and political order, and it is not surprising that the Puritans afterwards referred to the years 1686–89 as the period of usurpation.

Andros did not arrive in Massachusetts until December 1686; in the meantime a temporary government had been erected, consisting of a council of which the secretary was Edward Randolph and the president was Joseph Dudley, son of Thomas Dudley the founder.[26] On the whole the people of Massachusetts submitted tamely to the new regime. The strict Puritans accepted it as a divine judgment upon the people for their sins; the non-Puritans even welcomed it as an escape from the harsh, discriminating features of the old order. Dudley, however, soon found himself between two fires. He was regarded by the Puritans as a traitor to the colony—as an agent of tyranny—while Randolph felt that, because the institutions of the colony were left intact, Dudley was indifferent toward England's interests. After the arrival of Andros both Connecticut and Rhode Island were brought into the Dominion and organized into counties, although Andros admitted important men from both colonies into his council and neither had its charter legally annulled. A new commission issued to Andros in 1688 by James II made him governor of all New England, New Jersey, and New York. Accordingly, he formally annexed those middle colonies to the Dominion—an act, however, of little significance, for a few months later the whole new system toppled to the ground.

The Dominion expired in 1689, primarily because it had engendered intense opposition among the New Englanders. It introduced the Anglican Church into Massachusetts, imposed an Anglican governor upon the Puritans, brought an Anglican rector to Boston,

[26] Everett Kimball's *The Public Life of Joseph Dudley* (New York, 1911) devotes chapters 1–3 to the imperial problem in Massachusetts.

and destroyed the legal foundations of the Puritan church. These grievances were aggravated when the Puritans were forced to allow Anglicans to worship in their own South Meeting House in Boston. All the religious ideals for which they had struggled seemed doomed.

As Andros strove to enforce the Navigation Acts he was accused of stifling New England's trade, while his powers over land grants resembled a sword suspended over property rights. Acting with his council he might investigate, confirm, or annul all existing land titles. And it so happened that most of such titles were of doubtful legality, derived from sub-corporations of town proprietors which had been created by the general courts. The New England charters, however, did not authorize the general courts to incorporate towns, and hence the town grants and the individual titles derived from them might be declared illegal. Most of the land had been granted in this manner; consequently the whole body of landowners felt that their most cherished property might be taken from them. Furthermore, in order to obtain money for the support of the Dominion government, Andros was authorized to require that all lands to be newly granted should be subject to a quit-rent. Thus existing titles might be set aside and the landowner forced to pay a permanent quit-rent as the price of a new title. The money thus paid would support a "tyrannical" government and also, perhaps, an odious church.

Andros, however, did not seriously disturb existing land titles; nor was he able to obtain sufficient revenue from quit-rents to support his government and to provide for colonial defense. His council therefore was forced to impose taxes upon the property owners in defiance of the New England tradition that taxes should be levied only by the General Court. Protests soon filled the air, particularly in the towns of Topsfield and Ipswich—chief hotbeds of resistance—where one of the foremost colonial liberals, the Reverend John Wise, vehemently denounced Andros's levies as illegal and proclaimed that only the elected representatives of the property owners could levy taxes. That the Andros regime was no shadowy threat to Puritan liberties soon became evident when thirty "rebels" were arrested, of whom six were clapped into jail and fined.[27]

In the face of these issues the most bitter enmity was bound to separate the New England Puritans and Andros. Although he was an able and honest man, his foes accused him of the harshest tyranny and ill will. His failure to conciliate the Puritans did not arise from his personality; his task was inherently too odious. Nearly all the important groups were outraged by the policies which he was instructed

[27] See again J. T. Adams, *The Founding of New England*, chapters 12–17.

to carry out. The devout Puritans could not stomach the preference shown to the Anglican Church, the merchants feared a stricter enforcement of the Acts of Trade, the landowners were outraged by the unsettling of land titles and the menace of quit-rents, and the voters in all the colonies deplored the loss of their local liberties and elected assemblies. No governor who was ordered to tear up a country's institutions by the roots could be popular, whatever his personality. Perhaps the best work of Andros was done in improving the defenses of New England, yet such was the animosity toward him that his absence from Boston on defense and Indian affairs gave birth to the baseless rumor that he was in league with the French, plotting an Indian war against the Puritans which was to deliver New England to France and the pope. As long as Andros endeavored to obey his instructions from England (and this he conscientiously tried to do) there was not the remotest likelihood of a friendly adjustment—unless the New England Puritans submissively abandoned everything which they had previously cherished. They regarded him as a usurper and awaited an opportunity to renounce him and all his works.

On the 18th of December 1688, King James II, the sponsor of Andros, fled from England to France. In less than three years of his reign he had so antagonized the most influential groups in England that they united to invite William of Orange, Stadtholder of Holland, to invade England in order to preserve her ancient liberties. Bishops, archbishops, and landed aristocrats had been outraged by the apparent determination of the king to foster his own religious faith, Catholicism, even to the point of undermining the Anglican Church. Landowners and townsmen bitterly resented his claim that he was privileged to suspend the enforcement of acts of Parliament. In foreign affairs he had defied the English merchants by courting France, now their chief rival in colonization and overseas trade. The opposition crystallized in June 1688 when the birth of a royal son threatened to perpetuate indefinitely a Catholic monarchy in a Protestant country. On February 13, 1689, William of Orange was proclaimed King of England.[28]

When the news of the "Glorious Revolution" reached Massachusetts in March 1689 it fanned the embers of Puritan discontent into the flame of revolution. In April a mob in Boston, probably instigated by the Puritan leaders, seized and jailed Randolph and other Dominion officials. Andros later surrendered and was imprisoned at

[28] The political struggle in England, 1603–89, is ably presented in George B. Adams, *Constitutional History of England* (New York, c. 1921), chapters 11–14.

Castle William on an island in Boston harbor, where the "usurpers" remained until they were sent to England the following February. The dominion immediately fell apart as Connecticut, Rhode Island, and Plymouth resumed their separate identities and reinstated their elected governors and assemblies. A council of safety ruled Massachusetts during the revolutionary interim; then, hoping that the colony might return to the good old days of the charter, the Puritans placed in office the officials who had been serving when the charter was annulled.

But such good fortune was not in store for Massachusetts. The attack upon her liberties represented more than the whims of two tyrannical kings; it represented the fixed purpose of the English merchants and the Crown to force the New England merchants to conform to the English colonial system. To William III and his advisers, therefore, a return to the old course of independence was inadmissible. As early as 1688 "the foremost American Puritan," Increase Mather, had gone to England to seek a modification of the Dominion government, and after its complete overthrow he strove to restore to Massachusetts her charter of 1629. When the Lords of Trade rejected this plan, Mather—a practical man not averse to compromise—agreed to a new charter, issued in 1691, which restored many of the essential features of the earlier government.[29] New Hampshire remained a separate province but Plymouth and Maine were joined to Massachusetts. Several important changes were intended to subordinate the colony to England's authority. No longer was the governor to be elected by the Puritan freemen; now he was to be appointed and removed by the king and to act as the king directed. No longer was the legislature to be a law unto itself; its acts might now be vetoed by the royal governor and, even when signed by him, reviewed and disallowed by the Privy Council. Nor did the freemen continue to elect the governor's council. The first councillors to serve under the new charter were appointed by the king; afterward vacancies were filled by vote of the house of representatives and the council in joint session, while the governor might reject the nominees thus designated. The charter forbade religious tests for voting, requiring property ownership instead. Judgments of the colonial courts which involved £300 or more might be appealed to the Privy Council. On the other hand, the property owners retained many of their former privileges by virtue of the continuation of the town meet-

[29] Kenneth B. Murdock discusses this subject in his definitive biography, *Increase Mather* (Cambridge, 1925).

ings and the restoration of the elected house of the legislature. Thus was effected a compromise between imperial authority and home rule by property owners in the colony.[30]

The Revolution of 1688 in England enabled New England to defend its liberties very much in the manner that the Puritan uprising after 1640 had warded off the encroachments of Charles I. The English revolutions emphasized the political and economic rights of English property owners, and to such rights the propertied groups in the colonies also laid claim (and successfully, thanks largely to English examples). But there was a difference between 1640 and 1689. When the Puritan Revolution broke out the colonies were of minor importance to English merchants and moreover the merchants were not strong enough to overthrow a hostile king until after nearly a decade of warfare. In 1689 the colonial empire was of major value to the merchants and they were strong enough to dispose of a hostile king without bloodshed, thus preventing another decade of neglect of the colonies such as had occurred after 1640. Instead, the Massachusetts charter of 1691 proclaimed that they were to be kept in close dependence upon England. Both revolutions had augmented the powers of Parliament, the agency through which the rising merchant class now strove to monopolize colonial trade. As the interests of the English merchants and the colonists diverged, so also the colonists and Parliament were to draw farther apart. Thus the revolutions of the 1640's and of 1688 sowed the seeds of a third and—to America—more significant revolt.[31]

[30] For additional material on colonial administration see Gertrude A. Jacobsen's scholarly, technical *William Blathwayt* (New Haven, 1932).

[31] H. L. Osgood, "England and the Colonies," *Political Science Quarterly*, II (Sept. 1887).

BIBLIOGRAPHICAL NOTE

SECONDARY WORKS: Readable and scholarly accounts of European backgrounds in the seventeenth century are David Ogg, *Europe in the Seventeenth Century* (7th ed., London, 1959), and Carl J. Friedrich, *The Age of the Baroque* (New York, 1952), a history of Europe, 1610–1660, which gives much attention to England. David Ogg, *England in the Reigns of James II and William III* (New York, 1955), portrays the English setting of the Dominion of New England. F. C. Turner, *James II* (New York, 1948), presents a realistic appraisal of the last Stuart monarch.

Lawrence A. Harper, *The English Navigation Laws* (New York, 1939), is the leading authority on a subject of primary importance.

Violet Barbour, *Capitalism in Amsterdam in the Seventeenth Century* (Baltimore, 1950), is pre-eminent as a portrayal of the economy of Holland, as it figured in the Anglo-Dutch wars.

Books which deal with conditions and actions in New England that affected its relations with England, and studies of English colonial policy and administration include the following works: Perry Miller, *The New England Mind: From Colony to Province* (Cambridge, 1953), although primarily a study of religous thought, reflects the influence of the English connections of the Puritans during the second half of the seventeenth century. This is a somewhat abstruse treatise, suitable for the specialist in Protestant theology. Thomas J. Wertenbaker, *The Puritan Oligarchy* (New York, 1947), is a lively, readable criticism of the orthodox Puritans which relates the decline of the original Puritan state. Michael G. Hall, *Edward Randolph and the American Colonies, 1676–1703* (Chapel Hill, 1960), a scholarly, detailed study of colonial administration, gives the best account of its subject. George Allan Cook, *John Wise, Early American Democrat* (New York, 1952), is the most satisfactory biography of a leading opponent of the Dominion of New England.

SOURCES: Two important seventeenth-century essays on trade and policy are Sir Dudley North, *Discourses upon Trade* [1691] (ed. J. H. Hollander, Baltimore, 1907), and Sir Josiah Child, *A New Discourse of Trade* (London, 1804). On the revolution in New England (1689) see C. M. Andrews (ed.), *Narratives of the Insurrections* (New York, 1915—Jameson *Original Narratives* series), pp. 167–297.

XII

 The Social Structure

THE transition from medieval to modern society effected a change in the social structure of Europe. The three estates of the Middle Ages —the clergy, the nobles, and the peasants—were replaced by the new groupings of the upper class, the middle class, and the propertyless working class. This change was brought about by the growth of industry and commerce which produced a society more complex than that which prevailed in early medieval times, when agriculture was supreme. Inasmuch as the colonists were steeped in the social traditions of Europe and because the economic forces active there also operated in America, the settlers tended to duplicate the social structure of the Old World, with certain important exceptions to be noted later.

During the seventeenth century a colonial upper class took form, although this incipient aristocracy was numerically weak. Its members consisted of the largest landowners, the most wealthy merchants, and the royal and proprietary governors. The latter may be regarded rather as representatives of English upper-class groups than as aristocrats in their own right. Economically, the basis of the colonial aristocracy was the ownership of wealth so extensive that the owner could support an ostentatious way of living without engaging in manual labor. The upper class, therefore, occupied itself with leisure interests, military affairs, government, business management, and intellectual pursuits. Its activities were self-directed and its members never served in a dependent capacity. All their social arrangements and usages— such as dress, manners, and etiquette—proclaimed their exemption from toil and their possession of leisure and means sufficient to enable them to acquire the decorative graces of a refined way of living. Judged by English standards the social techniques of the colonial aristocracy may have been somewhat crude, but nevertheless they were sufficiently advanced to differentiate its members sharply from the laboring farmers and artisans.[1]

Due to the widespread ownership of land in the colonies the middle

[1] An original, penetrating study which all students should know is Thorstein Veblen, *The Theory of the Leisure Class* (The Modern Library, New York).

class occupied a particularly important place. Its members included professional men (principally clergymen and teachers), lesser merchants who conducted their own small businesses, landowning farmers, artisans who employed servants or hired workers, officials of the proprietors and the king, shopkeepers, clerks of the great merchants, overseers of plantations, and ship captains. Such people were set apart from the upper class either because they did not possess enough wealth to exempt them from laborious work or because they depended upon employment by the upper class or upon the custom of their fellow settlers, as in the case of shopkeepers, who, however, preferred the patronage of the well-to-do. Socially, the middle class copied the manners and dress of the aristocracy. But having neither the wealth nor leisure to warrant an intensive cultivation of refined manners they failed to attain the aristocratic standards. As a whole they aspired to enter the upper class, strove to acquire property, felt themselves superior to the propertyless laboring groups, and endeavored to eliminate all evidence of degrading toil from the appearance they presented to the world.

THE UPPER CLASS

The aristocracy or planter class which emerged in Virginia, Maryland, and South Carolina during the seventeenth century had its basis in extensive private landowning and in a labor system which exempted the wealthy planter from physical toil. Prior to 1680 the labor force consisted chiefly of indentured servants, afterward increasingly of Negro slaves. How deep was the social gulf between owner and worker appeared in the layout of the plantation, where the owner's house stood apart amidst shrubs, while the workers occupied cabins at a distance, not far from the pens and barns which housed the livestock. By 1700 there were fifty planters in Virginia whose wealth amounted to $50,000 as calculated in values of today. The estates of two men, Robert Beverley and William Byrd I, were probably worth a quarter of a million dollars each. Beverley owned at least 37,000 acres of land and Byrd over 15,000 acres. Other large estates were those of John Carter (18,570 acres), Richard Lee (12,000 acres), and Samuel Mathews (9,000 acres), although the average large holding included only about 5,000 acres.[2] As early as 1624–25 there were fifteen planters who owned ten or more servants and one who owned forty. An observer writing in 1649 told of a planter who "hath a fine house and all things answerable to it; he sows yearly [a] store of

[2] J. T. Adams's *Provincial Society, 1690–1763* (New York, 1928) contains a mass of well-classified facts. See chapters 3 and 4.

hemp and flax, and causes it to be spun; he keeps weavers, and hath a tan-house, causes leather to be dressed, hath eight shoemakers employed in their trade, hath forty Negro servants, brings them up to trades in his house. He yearly sows abundance of wheat, barley, etc. The wheat he selleth at four shillings the bushel, kills store of beeves, and sells them to victual the ships when they come hither; hath abundance of kine, a brave dairy, swine great store and poultry."

In founding Maryland Lord Baltimore endeavored to introduce manors on the European model and to people them with tenants subject to the political and judicial authority of the owner. However, workers could not be obtained who would place themselves permanently in the dependent status of tenants, and the early manors were forced to rely upon indentured servants and Negro slaves; in consequence the manor was converted into a plantation of the Virginia type, although the name survived.[3] Similarly, the proprietors of Carolina failed in their efforts to graft a landed nobility and a manorial regime of tenants or serfs on the Charles Town colony. However, the plantation readily developed in South Carolina. Between 1675 and 1684 nine planters received land grants varying from 1,000 to 3,000 acres, one received 12,000 acres, and another 35,800 acres. In 1670 the ownership of one Negro slave and three indentured servants justified the employment of an overseer; in 1677 the estate of Sir John Yeamans possessed fourteen slaves; in 1694 the largest plantations were rated as worth about £5,000. After the development of rice culture in South Carolina in the 1690's, the plantation multiplied rapidly; as early as 1700 Negro slaves outnumbered the white residents of the colony.

Since many of the planters were descended from well-to-do members of the English middle class they were able to establish themselves in the colonies by virtue of inheritance and family assistance. William Fitzhugh, for instance, a son of an English barrister, migrated to Virginia about 1670, purchased an estate on the Potomac, and settled at once into the leisurely life of a planter. As estates grew in size the owners entrusted the supervision of the daily work to overseers and devoted themselves to sports (hunting and horse racing were prime favorites), business management, land speculation, politics, social affairs, and military pursuits. They drank heartily, gambled freely, relished vigorous physical exertion out of doors, cultivated the refined manners of drawing-room society, and attended, none too punctually, the religious observances of the Anglican Church. The need of defending their property and of upholding the social struc-

[3] John Johnson, *Old Maryland Manors* (Baltimore, 1883), is a brief sketch.

ture, coupled with the desire to maintain individual physical prowess, induced them to an active military life, serving as they almost invariably did as captains and colonels in the county militia. They readily developed a political philosophy of isolation, self-rule, or "estate rights," whereby each man should order his economic affairs without external restraint. Through their influence on the governor's council they could defeat proposed laws hostile to their interests; as local magistrates they dispensed justice among their lesser neighbors; as plantation owners they governed their servants and slaves. Living in isolation with numerous dependents they deemed it imperative to maintain their authority and prestige at a high pitch; consequently they could not tolerate insubordination from inferiors. In personal intercourse among their equals they were governed by a code of honor, the chief purpose of which was to preserve their dignity and good repute.[4]

During the seventeenth century a progressive improvement in the planter's way of living was evident, although it still remained somewhat rough and crude, judged by modern standards. His dwelling, its furnishings, and his personal apparel all proclaimed his affluence and his superior social status. He lived in the "great house" or "manor house," usually a simple, plain building, square or rectangular, with chimneys at each end, lacking architectural graces and not as yet set off by beautiful lawns and flower gardens, although bushes and shrubs softened its harsher aspects. As his wealth increased the planter added rooms to the main structure; by 1700 the largest mansions, as that of William Fitzhugh, contained a dozen rooms—a great hall or dining room, a parlor, bedchambers, kitchens, a dairy, an overseer's room, and closets. The great hall, where the planter dispensed a generous hospitality, was furnished with a long center table flanked with benches. Side tables and cupboards resplendent with pewter plates, knives and spoons and various silver dishes gave an impression of wealth while perhaps a few original portraits adorned the paneled walls of cedar or walnut. Lighted by narrow windows or at night by candles and the glow of the open hearth, the room presented a rather somber aspect; in winter it was cold and draughty. Linen, even damask, napkins and tablecloths graced the dining table on special occasions. Colored and decorative fabrics gave a warmer tone to the bedchambers—curtains, woven rugs, tapestry on the walls, and figured coverlets and quilts. The large bed, not yet canopied, stood high above the floor, so that a child's trundle bed could be rolled underneath

---

[4] See again P. A. Bruce, *Economic History of Virginia in the Seventeenth Century*, Vol. I, chapter 9; Vol. II, chapters 10–14.

during the day, where it was screened by valances. Canvas mattresses, feather-stuffed, sheets, pillows, and blankets all bore evidence of gentility. In a chest or trunk, usually of leather, highly ornamented, were stored the most highly prized possessions of the household, while a chest of drawers, with mirror above, served for everyday articles of apparel. Chairs with leather, rush, or embroidered seats, screens, escritoires, and brass andirons also suggested means and refinement. All such furnishings, imported from England, resembled those in vogue among the upper classes there.[5]

The class feeling of the planters expressed itself likewise in dress. In their wardrobes were to be found such articles as linen shirts with pewter or silver buttons, silk and woolen stockings, leather shoes with brass, steel, or silver buckles, periwigs, felt and beaver hats, linen neckcloths, broadcloth, camlet, or serge coats with decorative buttons and cuffs or ruffles on the sleeves, waistcoats of many colors, plush or broadcloth breeches, and scarfs edged with lace. The attire of the women of the planter's family included silk and flowered gowns, laced shoes, decorated fans, colored scarfs, white, scarlet, and black hose, calico hoods, palmetto hats, lace-trimmed bonnets, and black tippets. And when adorned with pearl necklace, gold pendant, silver earrings, and gold rings a lady was not to be mistaken for a woman who worked at menial tasks, nor could her husband or father be ranked as other than a member of the upper class.

Somewhat similar to the southern plantations were the large estates which took form in New York during the seventeenth century, vast holdings of certain wealthy Dutch, Scottish, or English families—the Van Rensselaers, Schuylers, Beekmans, Morrises, Livingstons, Van Cortlandts, Heathcotes, Philipses, and Lloyds. The founders of the colonial branches of these families had come to New Netherland, for the most part, during the years between 1634 and 1664, bringing with them considerable wealth which was invested in land and the Indian trade. Located chiefly in the Hudson valley their estates were gradually enlarged by various devices until in the eighteenth century they covered immense areas. Rensselaerswyck, which extended on both sides of the Hudson, with its geographical center at Albany, included 700,-000 acres, while the Van Cortlandt, Livingston, and Beekman estates consisted of 140,000, 160,000, and 240,000 acres respectively. The early grants made by the Dutch West India Company were confirmed by the Duke of York as a means of winning the support of the most influential men in the province, and after 1664 new patents were is-

---

[5] P. A. Bruce, "Economic and Social Life of Virginia in the Seventeenth Century," in *The South in the Making of the Nation*, Vol. I, chapter 3.

sued in order to build up a party loyal to the proprietor.[6] Boundaries were but vaguely described and surveys long delayed; the resulting uncertainty enabled the magnates to enlarge their holdings, often by sheer force. Politics, favoritism, and bribery, rather than *bona fide* purchase, seem to have been the legal means of obtaining the estates. Governor Benjamin Fletcher particularly offended by receiving bribes for excessive grants during the 1690's.

Such vast holdings, of course, included much waste land, with only a small part under cultivation. The requirement that the landlord pay the proprietor or the king a yearly quit-rent of a bushel of wheat per hundred acres was more honored in the breach than in the observance. Due to the difficulty of obtaining tenants the magnates could not develop their estates rapidly; consequently they did not appear so affluent as the southern planters, although their social ideals, pastimes, manor houses, and living standards were of the same pattern. The cleared land was cultivated by tenants who were generally supplied by the owner with tools and farm animals and were therefore forced to give him a share of the increase of the livestock, as well as to pay regular rents in grain, most commonly wheat. Not until the late seventeenth century were these estates legally converted into manors. Politically the magnates dominated local government through the sheriffs, their allies; they dispensed justice among their tenants, and in the provincial legislature they acted after 1693 chiefly through the elected house—entitled in some instances to representatives for their estates, and always dominating elections in their districts. Religious fellowship in the Anglican and Dutch Reformed churches, together with multiple ties of marriage and blood relationship, sealed the bonds of union among these wealthy, aristocratic families.[7]

In the northern towns the growth of merchant capitalism had produced, by 1700, the nucleus of an upper class. Here also wealth distinguished the leading merchants from their lesser competitors. When a merchant acquired extensive property and devoted his time to its general supervision rather than to routine business, and when his income was derived primarily from his investments, he had attained a distinctly upper-class standing. The secret of his economic progress was his accumulation of profits beyond his needs for current expenditure and the investment of his surplus in income-producing enterprises.

[6] Clarence W. Rife, "Land Tenure in New Netherland," in *Essays in Colonial History Presented to Charles M. Andrews.*

[7] Ernest Wilder Spaulding's *New York in the Critical Period, 1783–1789* (New York, 1932) has an excellent chapter (3) on the landed aristocracy. S. G. Nissenson, *The Patroon's Domain* (New York, 1937), is thorough and legalistic.

At the close of the seventeenth century such wealthy merchants were to be found in the northern towns. At Boston the most prominent were Samuel Lillie, Andrew Faneuil, Andrew Belcher, John Foster, Samuel Phillips, William Clarke, and Benjamin Gallop; at Philadelphia, Samuel Carpenter, Robert Turner, James Claypoole, Isaac Norris, and Edward Shippen; at New York, Stephen De Lancey, John, Abraham, and Cornelius Van Horn, Caleb Heathcote, Andrew Fresneau, Benjamin Faneuil, Abraham De Peyster, and Rip Van Dam. A very large majority of these merchants came to the colonies with trading capital they had inherited or acquired as merchants in Europe, and to which many of them added by marriage into wealthy families. As early as 1670 there were thirty merchants in Massachusetts with estates ranging between £10,000 and £30,000. The rate of profit in the seventeenth century was exceptionally high: an observer said of Pennsylvania in 1686 that "merchants find themselves encouraged by the profit, which is seldom less than 50 per cent, the which is a great advance." [8]

Such profits went into many channels of investment. The wealthy merchant owned his own private wharves and his warehouses, where his counting-room or business office was located and where he often operated a retail shop. Equally important was his investment in ships. Most commonly he preferred to purchase shares in several vessels rather than to own a few outright; thus he spread the risk of loss at sea. In 1700 seventeen Boston merchants owned shares in ten or more vessels, and in 1715 eight New York merchants owned shares in five or more. The advance of goods on credit to fur traders or the erection of trading posts afforded another source of profit to the merchants. They also dealt in real estate. Thus the first outstanding merchant of Boston, Robert Keayne, as a large investor in the Massachusetts Bay Company, received four hundred acres of land in the colony in 1639. The leading merchants of Philadelphia bought five or ten thousand acres apiece in the province in 1681–82—a good investment, since lands that sold for £2 a hundred acres in 1682 brought between £8 and £25 in 1701. A New England merchant, Philip English, owned fourteen houses at Salem in 1692. John Hull of Boston, goldsmith, merchant, and mintmaster, similarly owned several farms in Massachusetts and an estate on Block Island, the products of which he carried to market in his own vessels. Likewise Hull and his fellow mer-

[8] Carl L. Becker, *The History of Political Parties in the Province of New York* (Madison, Wis., 1909), a work of major importance, discusses New York society in chapter 1.

chants invested in sawmills or gristmills; at Philadelphia Samuel Carpenter anticipated that such investments would yield 8 per cent.

An especially fruitful source of income to the merchants was the loan business. An interest charge always accompanied the advance of goods on credit to farmers or country traders—a charge compounded semi-annually. As the bankers of the time the merchants also made long-term loans on real estate or short-term loans on personal security. In most cases they insisted upon ample security, the merchants of Philadelphia once refusing to lend to William Penn because he could not provide sufficient guarantees. So also they insisted upon prompt payment and the precise fulfillment of contracts; John Hull, though lenient, even threatened to sue a Puritan minister for a debt long over-due. Interest charges in the northern colonies during most of the seventeenth century were nominally 8 per cent. Massachusetts in 1693 reduced the charge to 6 per cent, excepting maritime contracts, and New York followed in 1717. Such phrases in colonial laws as "the great and excessive usury now commonly taken in this province" indicate that moneylending was a very profitable business.[9]

With mounting incomes derived from commercial profits, land sales, rents, freights, warehouse charges, and interest the merchants were able to extend their investments and at the same time to support an increasingly opulent manner of living. Their houses, furniture, dress, and social standards all resembled those of the southern planters, copied as they were after a common model, that of the landed aristocracy of England, to whose social eminence the English bourgeoisie had always aspired. As a colonial merchant prospered he moved his residence from the business quarter of the town to the "suburbs," where he could enjoy a semi-country estate surrounded by lawns and gardens and travel to and fro in his own carriage. The northern merchants also matched the southern planter class in political influence. They generally controlled the governor's council and the local governments of their towns. A host of colonial acts reveal their influence— New York acts which, until 1695, gave the town of New York a monopoly of flour making; a Pennsylvania act of 1711 providing that in the settlement of estates, debts due to residents of the province be paid before debts due to outsiders; and a Massachusetts act of 1682 which prohibited sales to seamen on credit lest the imprisonment of seafaring debtors delay the departure of vessels. Whenever the in-

[9] On social classes see chapters 8 and 10 in *Under Duke and King* (1933), the second volume of A. C. Flick (ed.), *History of the State of New York*. On the aristocracy see chapter 5 of the third volume, *Whig and Tory* (1933).

terests of the merchants were concerned they acted in unison, chiefly by presenting petitions to the local authorities. It is not misleading to regard the governor's councils of New York, Massachusetts, and Pennsylvania as committees acting in behalf of this powerful class.

In many respects the psychology of the northern merchants distinguished them from the southern planters. In religion they inclined toward the Calvinistic churches—the Congregational, Presbyterian, French Huguenot, and Dutch Reformed—while the Quakers were well represented in Philadelphia. As their wealth increased they exerted a conservative influence within the churches, favoring refined, decorous, formal, and conventional services. Samuel Sewall, a Salem merchant, indicated this social trend in his spiritual reflections: "I had a sweet and very affectionate meditation concerning the Lord Jesus, nothing was to be objected against his person, parentage, relations, estate, house, home." Living as they did in towns—not isolated amidst a host of dependents—employing workers rather than owning slaves, obliged to maintain a multitude of contacts with business associates of all degrees, the merchants were not prone to vigorous physical sports, preferred calculation to gambling, eschewed dueling and the ideals of a code of honor in favor of amicable settlement of disputes, avoided military pursuits and did not covet the title of captain or colonel. Instead of depending upon personal force and mastery they relied upon the sanctity of contracts, the give-and-take of bargaining, and the letter of the law, over which they kept a watchful eye.[10]

The demands of business required that the merchant possess a diversified knowledge and a cosmopolitan point of view. As an employer and creditor he had to be a good judge of human character; as a buyer he must know the humble details of farming and industry in order to determine accurately the quality of all sorts of products; as a shipper he had to be familiar with the art of navigation and the geography of remote places; as a trader he needed to keep posted on prices, market conditions, rates of exchange, currencies, tariffs and treaties pertaining to all parts of the world, and to be advised about politics, foreign and domestic, and wars and rumors of wars. Fresh news of this sort he sought with avidity. Such practical concerns also directed his intellectual interests to mathematics, accounting, modern languages, law, politics, and the economics of business, while travel enlarged his outlook by giving him contact with the cultural life of other countries.

[10] D. R. Fox's *Caleb Heathcote* (New York, 1926) is a spirited portrait of a New York merchant.

Farmers and Workers

The mass of the colonial population was composed of working farmers and artisans, who were roughly divisible into three groups. A minority of the farmers were moderately well-to-do, owners of land up to a thousand acres and regular employers of farm hands or indentured servants. Similarly, certain master artisans—shipwrights, millers, shoemakers, hat makers, fullers, blacksmiths, and weavers—owned their shops and tools and employed journeymen or apprentices. Economically, such artisans were less independent than the substantial farmers, depending as they did upon the custom of their neighbors, although employed by the community as a whole rather than by a single person. Both groups generally enjoyed the right to vote and their social station depended upon the amount of their property and the number of their employees. Most of them doubtless came to the colonies with a small amount of capital and established themselves as independent settlers, although many indentured servants, when free, rose into this class.[11]

Such farmers and artisans exhibited several common characteristics. Ambitious, energetic, highly skilled and efficient in their occupations, with a well-developed instinct of workmanship and a deep respect for work, they possessed more than a usual fund of initiative and managerial ability which qualified them as employers and directors of labor. Actuated by a competitive and emulative spirit, they steadily strove to improve their standing in society, and the social standards to which they aspired were those of the upper class. Their ownership of property, an upper-class attribute, and their desire to increase their wealth through the employment of dependent workers, also indicate their spiritual kinship with the privileged groups. However, their investments were not large enough to exempt them from work or to afford them leisure to cultivate the refined graces of aristocratic society; consequently they blended the traits and attitudes of the laboring workers and of the leisured upper class. They generally lived well and comfortably but did not consume their substance in ostentatiously extravagant living, preferring rather to save their surplus and invest it in additional land or equipment—a process by which they could gain the respect of their neighbors more effectually than by lavish personal expenditures. As the settlements expanded the farmers and artisans of this class were increasingly concentrated in the older, thickly settled

[11] Edward Eggleston's *The Transit of Civilization* (New York, 1933) is good reading. On classes see chapter 6.

parts of the colonies, which afforded the best opportunities for extended operations wherein several workers could profitably be employed.

Numerically the largest group in the colonies consisted of the less affluent farmers—men who owned a hundred and fifty or fewer acres, who worked their own land with the assistance of their families and the occasional aid of a hired hand, who possessed a little capital in the form of tools and livestock, and who commonly were entitled to vote. This class was sprung largely from immigrants who came to the colonies as employees or indentured servants.[12] Lack of initial capital compelled such farmers to borrow money in order to purchase land, or to equip their farms, and since their debts often became a permanent possession they developed a pronounced debtor psychology. Equally conspicuous was a spirit of independence—a dislike of being "bossed"—which induced them to prefer a free life in the wilderness to a dependent status in older settlements. Although they toiled at heavy, laborious work, they were generally easygoing, easily contented, not unusually gifted with foresight, inclined to live from day to day; many of them were actually shiftless. Living very largely in isolation they relished the companionship of strangers and neighbors, displayed a sociable, familiar, and inquisitive manner, had few if any intellectual interests beyond the Bible and the church, felt only a slight urge to neatness and orderliness, and concerned themselves with immediate, practical tasks which limited their conversation to crops, the weather, neighborhood news, and family happenings. Since they worked "from sun to sun" their dress and appearance openly proclaimed their occupation and place in society, even on holidays. Among them the emulative spirit was not strongly developed; instead of striving for social advancement they preferred an out-of-door life under the spell of nature and the privilege of working on their own terms. Simple-hearted, neighborly, coöperative, narrow in outlook, and firm in their convictions, they lived their uneventful and useful lives, obeying the scriptural command to replenish the earth, for they brought more children into the world than they could provide with a generous patrimony and many of their descendants were forced to move on and build new settlements in the West.

Even though these less wealthy farmers and their families were essentially working people, they too shared an attribute of the upper class—the ownership of land. They too coveted more acres, more ad-

---

[12] On the small farmer in the South the most important works are those of T. J. Wertenbaker: *Patrician and Plebeian in. Virginia* (Charlottesville, 1910) and *The Planters of Colonial Virginia* (Princeton, 1922). See also his *The First Americans*, pp. 27–48, 283–301.

vantages, more of the good things of life. Their economic independence bred a sense of self-importance and self-respect. When a farmer's son went forth "to make his way in the world," his father might advise him: "Remember that you are as good as any man—and also that you are no better." Despite their property ownership, the farmers remained primarily workers, drawing their income from their labor rather than from investments, treating the occasional servant as one of the family, showing without concern the evidences of toil so odious to the upper class, and retaining their deep-seated respect for useful work and the man who could perform it well. Thus the American environment acted upon the European social heritage so as to produce a property-conscious democracy of farmers and workers who sought a share in social advantages previously confined to the upper classes in the Old World.[13]

Below the settled yeoman there existed a class of nomad farmers who made a business of pioneering. They went into the virgin forest, erected cabins and cattle pens, cleared a few acres of timberland, planted a little Indian corn, corralled some livestock—and later sold their improved property to permanent settlers who came after them. This class usually possessed few worldly goods beyond a cart, a pack horse, a gun, axe, hoe, the coarsest of clothing, and the crudest of household utensils; they merely "squatted" on the land, and sold, not the title to their clearings, but the improvements they had made. They lived partly by hunting and fishing, performed heavy, unskilled labor, presented an extremely unkempt and uncouth appearance; true denizens of the forest, they seemed to outsiders as half-civilized wretches, hardly distinguishable from the Indians among whom they consorted and with whom they fought.

Other groups inferior to the yeomen included tenant farmers, traveling artisans, and wage-earners such as dock hands, journeyman artisans, and farm hands. Possessing little or no property and not privileged to vote, such workers were doomed to a life of dependence unless they managed to save enough of their earnings to buy land or displayed force and ambition sufficient to gain them a place among the employing artisans. In the southern colonies skilled workers commonly gave up their trades and became farmers, due partly to the loss of time involved in traveling between remote plantations and partly to the absence of money, which compelled them to accept payment in heavy, bulky raw products which they could not conveniently transport, store, and exchange for consumer's articles. Another dependent group consisted of fur traders, sailors, and fishermen—all wage-earners without capital

[13] See again L. C. Gray, *History of Agriculture in the Southern United States*, Vol. I, chapters 16, 21–22.

who labored at dangerous and strenuous work which did not appeal to men of that cautious, prudential temperament which delights in saving, accumulation, and investment. The letdown after intense physical exertion in isolated and hazardous circumstances was often followed by periods of protracted idleness when such workers freely distributed their accumulated wages at taverns, over the gambling table, and in other dubious ways.[14]

The mode of living attained by the mass of the colonial farmers and workers gives a striking illustration of their place in society. In the first stage of settlement the colonists had to live in huts, caves, or tents. Soon they erected log houses or cabins—probably first constructed by the Swedes on the Delaware and afterward particularly characteristic of new settlements in the middle region and the South. Selecting a site near a stream or a fresh-water spring, the settler usually built upon high land a cabin which faced south. With the aid of his neighbors he erected a rectangular, one-story hut consisting of a kitchen and sleeping room, with a small attic above—a rude structure held together by joints and wooden pegs. A stone fireplace and chimney built within the cabin was the center of the household's activities; openings sawed in the log walls served as windows; a single door was swung on leather hinges; the ground sufficed at first as the cabin floor; and the roofing consisted of clapboards which resembled barrel staves. In the kitchen a ladder led to the attic, used as a storehouse, while an opening in the interior wall gave into the sleeping room, which, having neither windows nor fireplace, was ventilated by cracks in the wall. Two tiny windows in the kitchen were covered with paper made weatherproof with lard.

If a settler remained at his first clearing he worked several years at odd hours preparing materials for a permanent house—cutting, hewing, and squaring timbers, quarrying and dressing stone, splitting clapboards from logs, and making shingles by slicing chips from cedar blocks. Then in the spring, when the frost had left the ground, he dug the cellar, employed a local mason to lay the foundation, and put together the frames for the sides of the house. With all in readiness a call was sent to his neighbors and on an appointed day they gathered with their own tools, and, working under the direction of the mason, they lifted the frames into place on the foundation, made them fast with crossbeams, braces, floor joists, and rafters, and laid the flooring of oak plank. This completed the house-raising, which closed with a christening ceremony and a general celebration. Afterward the farmer laid the roof boards, pegged down the shingles, built the fireplace and nailed on

[14] Samuel McKee's *Labor in Colonial New York* (New York, 1935) contains the best short account of free labor.

the laths (dried split saplings) which he covered with plaster made of straw, clay, and lime. Whitewash applied to the plaster gave the only decorative effect; wainscoting, paint, varnish, and wallpaper were beyond the ordinary farmer's means.

The architectural designs of the houses varied, but like the interiors they were uniformly simple and plain. In the northern and middle colonies the most common type was a house two stories in front with a single pitched roof that sloped to one story in the rear. Downstairs a central hall separated five low-ceilinged rooms; the upstairs was divided lengthwise into two rooms. The principal room on the ground floor, the kitchen, was located on the the south side of the front; behind was a storeroom or workroom, while across the hall were three bedrooms. The room upstairs over the kitchen and workroom served as a bedchamber, the other room as an attic. A ladder in the kitchen gave access to the upper floor. Each room had at least one window (the kitchen usually had three); sliding shutters served as blinds.[15]

By far the most important as well as the largest room was the kitchen —parlor, living room, workshop, and dining room, scene of constant bustle and activity where the family toiled, ate, relaxed, and enjoyed life. Its furniture, chiefly homemade, was designed with two primary objects in mind—to be useful and to conserve space. Thus the table, consisting of boards laid on movable legs, could be lengthened into a dining table and then taken down when not in use, while a bed drawn up against the wall during the day could be lowered into the room at night. On one side of the table-boards plates were formed by hollowed spaces so that dishwashing consisted of scrubbing the table top and the "dishes" could be put away by turning over the boards. Since the houses contained no closets clothes had to be stored in chests or hung on pegs in the rooms, and for chairs the family had to use blocks of wood, stools, benches, or remodeled barrels. A narrow cupboard housed such articles as wooden spoons and trenchers, iron forks, and leather, wood, or gourd cups, bowls, bottles, and dippers. About the fireplace stood the warming pan, flatirons, skillets, teapots, gridirons, and kettles. Some of the cooking utensils were fastened to legs so that they could be set into the fire; others were placed upon movable trivets. Above the fireplace was hung the trusty fowling piece, while the mantelpiece was graced with tinderbox, clock or hourglass, tobacco box, pipe tongs (to extract coals from the fire), and candlebox. Other objects within the kitchen included a flour bin, water barrel, candle molds, spinning wheel, mortars for

---

[15] The books of Alice M. Earle are popular, readable accounts. Among them see *Home Life in Colonial Days* (New York, 1913), and *Two Centuries of Costume in America* (2 vols., New York, 1903).

pounding mustard or corn, hanks of yarn or thread, and a Bible or Bible-box.

The bedrooms were exceptionally plain. Bedsteads (high enough that children's trundle beds could be rolled underneath and often made of cedar as a deterrent to pests) supported brown linen cases stuffed with straw and placed on a network of cords instead of springs. Furnished only with a chair or chest, generally devoid of curtains, rugs, dressers, mirrors, and wall ornaments, poorly lighted, unheated in winter, such bedrooms were dreary and cheerless in the extreme. On winter nights a warming pan was used to take the chill from the beds, but even so, the intense cold discouraged the retiring farmer from taking off more than his shoes and heavy outer garments.[16]

Three storerooms in the rural houses held the miscellaneous possessions of the family. In the downstairs workroom or tool shed the farmer kept his carpenter's tools, anvil, and loom, together with such articles as wool, seed, cordwood, feed, charcoal, and empty boxes and barrels. The attic contained the smokehouse and housed certain objects not in regular or current use—quilting frames, discarded furniture, old clothing and bedding. Entering the cellar by an outside sloping door, one found a single room with dirt floor, lighted only by narrow openings which were kept closed in the winter with dirt or manure, and pervaded by a dark, dank atmosphere. Here the farmer stored his reserve food supply. On shelves, away from rats and mice, were placed preserves, smoked hams, bacon, cheese, sausages, butter, and eggs, while the floor space was devoted to jars of pickles, boxes of apples, barrels of sauerkraut, heaps of potatoes, parsnips, and turnips, kegs or barrels of vinegar, cider, and ale, and jars of rum.

Few indeed were the conveniences of the rural household. Water had to be carried in from the outside unless the farmer was fortunate enough to live near a spring from which it could be conveyed by a trough to the kitchen water barrel, whence the overflow was taken off by a lower trough. The brackish water of creek and river was generally unfit to drink; hence the popularity of wine, cider, beer, rum, mead, and ale. "Early to bed" was sensible advice when houses were fitfully lighted by the glare of the fireplace, tallow candles, and ill-smelling, dismal lamps—shallow containers filled with tallow, lard, or grease into which a cotton rag wick was inserted through a projecting spout. In winter the kitchen was the only heated room and even there on cold days water froze a few yards from the fireplace. Since matches were unknown, great care was taken to preserve the fire, generally kindled by sparks

---

[16] P. A. Bruce, *Social Life of Virginia in the Seventeenth Century* (Richmónd, 1907), is a good brief survey of classes.

from stone on steel which ignited scorched linen used as tinder. Within the fireplace, about five feet from the floor, was placed a lug-pole from which hung kettles, spits, and other cooking utensils. A backlog of hickory (so huge that two men were needed to put it in place) and a smaller front log made a firebox that was filled with corn cobs or chips. At the side of the fireplace was placed the oven, in which, after a fire had been built and the coals removed, the accumulated heat did its baking work.

The sanitary arrangements of these rural homes left much to be desired. Floors were swept and then sanded. No screens protected the windows, so that the household was at the mercy of gnats, mosquitoes, and flies, while other pests disturbed the night's slumber. Lice in children's hair were treated with a solution of itch-weed and boiled water. Winter bathing was confined to the hands and face; in the summer the boys and men went swimming. Shaving was a luxury in which the men indulged only upon occasion. All in all, it was not an easy or effete way of life.[17]

In summer the clothing of the men consisted of long pantaloons, linen shirts, and cloth caps, sans shoes and stockings, while winter attire included home-knitted woolen stockings and mittens, coonskin caps, buckskin breeches and leggings, fur-lined overcoats, shirts of homespun tow cloth, and heavy work shoes. The women of the household had to be content with such garments as homespun dresses and petticoats of linen and wool, dyed in sober colors. Exposure to the weather and the kitchen fire gave a leathery, reddish complexion against which face powder would have been utterly ineffectual.

SERVANTS AND SLAVES

Indentured servants composed the largest dependent class during the seventeenth century. These were workers who served under a labor contract in return for their transportation to America. Some of these servants entered into agreements in England so that they knew in advance who their masters would be. Others—called redemptioners or free-willers—made bargains with ship captains or merchants which entitled the servant to find a master in the colonies who would pay the transportation costs; if the immigrant failed to do this, his services could be sold by the importer to the highest bidder. Ordinary indentured servants—the most numerous group—were auctioned to farmers or traders when the vessel arrived at a colonial port. Although thousands of immigrants came as voluntary servants, a considerable minority

[17] See again S. G. Fisher, *Men, Women, and Manners in Colonial Times.*

arrived through accident or force—convicts from prison who were sentenced to labor service in the colonies, vagrants or vagabonds who were seized by ship captains, and innocent people without social influence who were kidnaped by "spirits." After a stated term of employment the servant became a freedman privileged to go where he pleased. The common term of service in Maryland, Virginia, Pennsylvania, New Jersey, and Carolina was four years; in New England, about seven years. The prices paid by masters for such servants ranged between £10 and £20 sterling, depending upon the length of service. Of this about £5 represented the cost of transportation and the remainder went to the importer as profit. In case of voluntary agreements made in England either the servant, his family, or his creditors received the excess above the transportation charge.[18]

Employed chiefly as farm hands and domestic servants these workers composed the principal dependent labor force in English America prior to 1690. Between 1635 and 1705 the tobacco colonies imported between fifteen hundred and two thousand servants each year; in Virginia they composed 40 per cent of the population in 1625, while in 1683, when they numbered about twelve thousand, they represented 16 per cent of the whole. Of the people arriving in Maryland in the 1630's about 16 per cent came as indentured servants, whereas this class accounted for 36 per cent of the emigrants to Pennsylvania in the 1680's. Although the wealthier landowners of New England imported many servants, the niggardly soil of New England and the poverty of the mass of the farmers compelled them to depend upon the labor of their families and the assistance of their neighbors. "Our want of servants and help . . . in our harvest," wrote John Winthrop, Jr., of Connecticut in 1666, "is great, so that all hands are fully improved," while such an important man as Cotton Mather later made it "an article of special supplications before the Lord, that He would send a good servant." [19]

Each colony at a very early date devised a legal code to govern the indentured servants. Such acts required that masters should feed and clothe their servants and provide them with medical care, shelter, and certain "freedom dues" prescribed in their contracts. William Penn ordered in 1683 that "servants be not kept longer than their time, and [that] such as are careful be both justly and kindly used in their service, and put in fitting equipage at the expiration, according to custom." The

[18] Marcus W. Jernegan, *Laboring and Dependent Classes in Colonial America* (Chicago, n.d.), is a group of important, definitive essays. See pp. 45-56.

[19] A good brief discussion appears in chapter 3 of Lucy M. Salmon's *Domestic Service* (New York, 1901).

legal privileges of the servant included the right to sue his master for breach of contract, in which case a local magistrate might free the servant, reduce the time of servitude, or order that compensation be given to him by his master at the end of his term. Thus a Maryland act of 1715 imposed such penalties upon any master who failed to supply "sufficient meat, drink, lodging and clothing, or shall unreasonably burden servants beyond their strength, or debar them of their necessary rest or sleep, or excessively beat or abuse them, or shall give them more than ten lashes for any one offense." In Pennsylvania and the southern colonies the freedom dues included fifty acres of land granted either by the master or by the colony; in New England they consisted of tools, clothing, and livestock, or, in lieu of these, money payments varying from £2 to £5.[20]

In return for such benefits the servants were required to labor diligently and obediently at the behest of their masters and were forced to accept a legal status midway between that of minors and slaves. They could not buy liquor or frequent taverns, nor could they leave their master's premises without his consent, stay out late at night, or engage in buying and selling, lest they surreptitiously dispose of his property. Neither could they marry without his permission, and they might be transferred by sale or bequest from one master to another. New Haven Colony in 1656 imposed fines upon any persons who "shall harbor or entertain any such servants in the night, . . . or shall suffer them disorderly . . . or to play at shovel-board or other . . . games, to drink, spend money or provisions, or shall . . . suffer any sinful carriage, conference, counsel or songs." Since the servants did not possess property they could not be required to pay fines, and they could not be imprisoned without injuring the master. Accordingly they were punished in two ways: by whipping and by requiring that they serve additional time beyond the terms of their indentures. When a court fine was assessed against a servant it was paid by the master who compensated himself by exacting additional service.[21]

What treatment the servants received depended upon the disposition of their masters, although it is safe to assume that most of them endured a pretty hard lot. Not only was the work performed inherently strenuous and virtually without end; the master who could command the labor of the servant only a few years had no material interest in him save that of obtaining the maximum service within a short time. In this

[20] M. W. Jernegan, "Forgotten Slavery of Colonial Days," *Harper's Magazine*, CXXVII (Oct. 1913).
[21] James C. Ballagh, *White Servitude in the Colony of Virginia* (Baltimore, 1895), is a pioneer work, not superseded.

respect, servitude wore a harsher aspect than chattel slavery: the owner of a slave would at least conserve his personal property. The legal right of the master to whip the servant often placed excessive power in irresponsible hands; in extreme cases masters were accused of whipping servants to death. One observer said of Maryland servants that "they groan beneath a worse than Egyptian bondage," while a versifier attributed these sentiments to a servant in 1708:

> In better times, e'er to this land
> I was unhappily trapanned
> Perchance as well I did appear
> As any lord or lady here. . . .
> But things are changed, now at the hoe,
> I daily work and barefoot go,
> In weeding corn or feeding swine,
> I spend my melancholy time.
> Kidnaped and fooled, I thither fled . . .
> And to my cost already find
> Worse plagues than those I left behind.

Such dissatisfaction explains the ease with which the servants succumb to the temptation to run away—a practice so common that the legislatures provided stringent penalties. An apprehended fugitive was required to serve several additional days without pay for every day that he was absent without leave. Moreover, the colonies had their fugitive servant laws which enjoined the local officers to pursue the escaped servants and authorized them, at public expense, to requisition boats for the pursuit. Similarly, rewards were granted to captors and heavy fines assessed against persons who knowingly assisted a fugitive in any way.[22]

Undoubtedly the blame in the servant question was not always wholly attributable to the masters. The servant class included many convicts, idlers, and ne'er-do-wells whose aversion to work was prodigious, as well as many who were "stubborn, refractory and discontented" and those who "withdrew themselves from their master's service to improve their time to their own advantage." A particularly grave problem arose from the relations between white servants and the Negro slaves; nearly all the colonial legislatures had to prohibit the marriage of such workers. In this connection, however, some masters were culpable. A Maryland act of 1664 provided that, if a servant woman married a slave, the children should belong to the master, but this act had to be repealed because unscrupulous masters encouraged

---

[22] An able, compact study is Karl F. Geiser, *Redemptioners and Indentured Servants in . . . Pennsylvania* (New Haven, c. 1901).

such marriages. Expenditures which the parishes in Virginia made for the care of illegitimate mulatto children give further light on the character of one element in the servant class.[23]

In spite of such undesirables a large majority of the servants were industrious and reliable workers who, when free, became independent artisans and farmers. During the seventeenth century a hundred thousand persons passed through the servant class of the tobacco colonies into the ranks of freemen. An observer in New England, about 1650, noted that "there are many hundreds of laboring men who had not enough to bring them over, yet are now worth scores, and some hundreds of pounds." Of Maryland servants a writer said in 1666 that they are no sooner free "but they are ready to set up for themselves, and when once entered live surprisingly well." Probably a majority of the small farmers of the middle and southern colonies rose from the servant class. Entitled to vote and to hold office, such emancipated yeomen formed the main current of the democratic movement in the colonies. In 1663, the Virginia House of Burgesses included thirteen members (43 per cent of the total) who had come to the colony as indentured servants.[24]

An important group in the servant class consisted of boys and girls who were bound to work for a master until they became of age. A large number of such minors were sent under contract from England and sold for sums varying from £5 to £10. Likewise many poor children or orphans in the colonies were assigned to masters—only, however, with the consent of parents, guardians, or magistrates. When a master took charge of a poor child he ordinarily did not make a payment; he merely promised to provide a home for the child in return for such labor as the child could perform. In one case, however, a New Haven master offered to give a cow to a poor widow in exchange for her son. Legally indentured children occupied the same position as an adult servant; their masters might transfer them to other employers and they were subject to strict discipline. A refractory servant boy was told by the New Haven town magistrates in 1661 that since he "stood bound to do faithful service" he was "not upon every dislike to run away" and was reminded "how he had carried stubbornly, stoutly and rebelliously,"—"which were carriages not to be borne." "After which he was committed to prison." On the other hand, fines were imposed upon masters who failed to give proper care to their servants of tender

[23] E. I. McCormac, *White Servitude in Maryland* (Baltimore, 1904), is an outstanding study of colonial labor.

[24] Cheesman A. Herrick, *White Servitude in Pennsylvania* (Philadelphia, 1926), is thorough, comprehensive, reliable. See also J. S. Bassett, *Slavery and Servitude in North Carolina* (Baltimore, 1896).

years. At the age of twenty-one the servant gained his freedom and received two suits of clothing and often a small sum of money. If he had inherited any estate he received that also from his guardian-master.[25]

Distinct from the children serving as indentured servants (who worked at all sorts of tasks about the household and the farm) were apprentices bound to an artisan on condition that he support them and give instruction in reading, writing, accounting, and the secrets of his trade. As a rule such indentures required that the parents of the boy pay to the master an advance sum of between £2 and £6; hence the apprentices were socially a step higher than ordinary servants—children of artisans or farmers of some means. Quite commonly an artisan trained one of his sons in his own trade and apprenticed the others to workers in other lines. The terms of service varied usually from six to eight years in New England and the middle colonies, where apprenticeship was more common than in the South. If the master died or failed to give the intended instruction the apprentice would be transferred to another artisan in the same trade. Freedom dues consisted of apparel and money. In one case a master was to pay £4 if he had taught the apprentice a trade and £10 if he had not. Coopers, carpenters, merchants, ship captains, tailors, blacksmiths, and shipwrights were the chief employers of apprentices. When free the latter customarily served at first as traveling artisans or journeyman employees of settled craftsmen.

By accustoming employers to the complete though temporary control of their workers, bonded servitude prepared the way for the introduction and spread of actual slavery.[26] Perhaps the first Negroes brought to Virginia in 1619 were sold as servants; at any rate, slavery took root soon afterward. The institution, however, was not an invention of the colonists; from time out of mind natives in Africa had been held as slaves—captives taken in war or evildoers punished for their crimes. It was not unnatural, therefore, that when European traders appeared in Africa the native chiefs should have exchanged their slaves and other property for European goods. With the growth of the traffic the Portuguese and later the Dutch and English established trading posts or garrisons along the slave coast to which traders periodically brought hordes of slaves who were bound together by leather thongs and marched overland, single-file, to be exchanged for cloth, ironware, rum, and trinkets. At the garrisons the European traders refused to buy

[25] Alice M. Earle's *Child Life in Colonial Days* (New York, 1909) is brief and interesting.
[26] See again U. B. Phillips, *American Negro Slavery*, chapters 1–4, 6.

any Negroes who were old or sick; such were left on the coast to die as the vessel departed with its strange cargo. After the slaves had been branded and placed in chains they were packed in a space between the decks so low that they were unable to stand. Overcrowding on shipboard and exposure to tropical heat and disease took a heavy toll of these unwilling passengers, for it was cheaper to let many of them die than to provide decent accommodations for all.[27]

During the seventeenth century the slaves were first landed at the West Indies and there seasoned before they were sold to mainland colonies. This required about three years, during which the novices were placed in the company of experienced hands and cared for by an old slave skilled in the art of nursing. So severe was the change from native to European ways that about half of the Negroes died within three or four years after their removal from Africa. On the other hand, the psychological adjustment to plantation life was not difficult: the Negroes had been accustomed to a tribal system in which the authority of the chief resembled that of the plantation owner. Generally, they were healthier on the North American continent than in the islands, due largely to better food and fewer disease-breeding insects. Adjustment was further facilitated by the selection of young Negroes who evinced a pliant disposition. Since they came from different tribes and spoke different dialects they were obliged to learn English in order to converse among themselves. By and large they proved to be highly cheerful and adaptable people who readily adjusted themselves to a new life. One writer remarked that "their juvenile minds entertain no regrets for the loss of their connections. They acquire the English language with great ease, and improve daily in size, understanding and capacity for labor."

In 1700, when the Negroes in the mainland settlements numbered between twenty and twenty-five thousand, they accounted for less than a tenth of the inhabitants, although they were to be found in nearly all the colonies. They were brought into New Netherland by the Dutch West India Company—one of the leading slave trafficking agencies of its time. Virginia's slave population rose from 2,000 in 1671 to 4,000 in 1690, while South Carolina's in 1708 was 4,100. Although the New England Puritans had few moral scruples against slavery they found it unsuited to their region. Their small diversified farms called for a servant who could perform a variety of operations and who would work effectively without close supervision, whereas the Negroes were profitable only in regions where they could labor in gangs at a common

[27] See the introduction to Vol. I of the monumental *Documents Illustrative of the History of the Slave Trade* (ed. Elizabeth Donnan, 4 vols., Washington, 1930–35).

task, and in climates that did not require expensive winter clothing and housing. Nor did the industries of New England suit the Negro. Navigation and shipbuilding were trades too specialized for his skills, while fishing exposed him to rigors of winter too severe for his constitution. In 1680 there were only about two hundred slaves in New England, of whom twenty were owned in Connecticut and 120 in Massachusetts—most of them being employed in domestic service.[28]

Even among the slaves in the plantation area a tendency toward social differentiation soon appeared. Those who worked about the household partook somewhat of the honor and dignity of the master, to whom they had especially commended themselves and with whom they were in close contact. Attendance upon the planter's family required that such domestics should conform to its standards of decorum and appear in decent attire. On the larger plantations some of the most intelligent slaves were trained as artisans, and their special skills made them more highly esteemed than the ordinary field hands, the group at the very bottom of the social scale. The crude huts in which the field hands lived, their diet of corn and salt pork, and their cheap clothing —linsey-woolsey pantaloons and shirts—all proclaimed the inferior status of their class.[29]

As a species of private property the slaves of course enjoyed no legal or political rights. In New England they were not allowed to buy liquor or to sell any property; if they struck a white person or stayed out-of-doors at night they were severely whipped. Their unhappy position is well indicated by an act passed by the humanitarian Quakers of Pennsylvania in 1693 which authorized any persons "to take up Negroes, male or female, whom they shall find gadding abroad on the first days of the week without a ticket from their master or mistress . . . [and] to take them to jail, there to remain that night, and that without meat or drink, and to cause them to be publicly whipped next morning with 39 lashes, well laid on their bare backs, at which their said master or mistress shall pay 15*d.* to the whipper." [30]

In three notable respects the social order of the colonies differed from that of Europe—a divergence explained largely by the influence of the American environment. First, the colonies did not produce a class of serfs bound to the soil or a titled, hereditary nobility dependent

---

[28] Carter G. Woodson's *The Negro in Our History* (Washington, c. 1922) is a reliable factual survey. See chapters 1–2.

[29] Jeffrey D. Brackett, *The Negro in Maryland* (Baltimore, 1889)—for advanced students.

[30] Edward Raymond Turner, *The Negro in Pennsylvania* (Washington, 1911), is an exceptionally good study. See chapters 1–4.

upon such a class. Secondly, Negro slavery, especially in the plantation area, became a peculiarly American institution. And finally, while social classes existed in the colonies, each individual was not permanently placed at one level. It was relatively easy for a servant to become a small landowner or independent artisan, although very difficult for the latter to enter the ranks of the upper class. Excepting the fixed status of slaves, the flexibility of colonial society was its distinguishing feature.[31] And yet the notion of class distinctions was firmly imbedded in the colonial mind. An act of Massachusetts in 1650 states: "We declare our utter detestation and dislike that men and women of mean condition should take upon themselves the garb of gentlemen, by wearing gold or silver lace or buttons, or points at their knees, or to walk in boots, or women of the same rank to wear silk or tiffany . . . scarfs, which though allowable to persons of greater estates, or more liberal education, yet we cannot but judge it intolerable in persons in such like condition."

This act epitomizes social trends in the colonies. It reveals the class consciousness of the leaders in control and manifests their desire to keep their inferiors in their places. Class lines in New England were also indicated by the forms of address in vogue. Some of the titles denoting good repute were: "esquire" or "gentleman" for wealthy landowners and merchants who had belonged to the English upper middle class; "master" for clergymen who possessed the degree of master of arts; "mister" for professional people and substantial landowners and merchants (about one man in fourteen was addressed as Mr.); and "goodman" for ordinary yeoman farmers. Such military titles as captain and ensign also signified an honorable station. Indentured servants, tenants, and wage-earners were unceremoniously called by their family or given names. Church pews were assigned on the basis of social status, while the names on the student register at Harvard College were listed, not alphabetically, but according to family rank.

The Massachusetts act of 1650 further reveals that the standards of social decorum of the colonial upper class stemmed from the aristocracy of England. It also exposes the social aspirations of many of the lesser folk—their desire to emulate the upper class—and it indicates that the American environment was enabling them to improve their external condition and appearance. That the act of 1650 was powerless to check the determination of the people to attain a higher standard of living appears in a comment on Boston in 1720: "The tradesmen or

[31] Two specialized studies for the advanced student are Edward McCrady, "Slavery in . . . South Carolina, 1670–1770," *Report*, American Historical Association, 1895; and Henry S. Cooley, *A Study of Slavery in New Jersey* (Baltimore, 1896).

mechanical part, they are very ambitious of appearing above themselves, and will not be seen in anything beneath the merchant or more substantial, which is the produce of Europe." The tendency of the times was not to abolish class distinctions but for the individual to strive to rise in the social scale.

BIBLIOGRAPHICAL NOTE

SECONDARY WORKS: Thomas J. Wertenbaker, *The Old South* (New York, 1942), is notable for its descriptions of the planter aristocracy, with lesser attention to pioneers, small farmers, and artisans. Louis B. Wright, *The First Gentlemen of Virginia* (San Marino, 1940), delineates the planter class. Susie M. Ames, *Studies of the Virginia Eastern Shore in the Seventeenth Century* (Richmond, 1940), emphasizes the importance of large landholdings and tenancy in an isolated quarter of Virginia. Bernard Bailyn, "Politics and Social Structure in Virginia," in *Seventeenth-Century America* (ed. James M. Smith), traces the emergence and renewal of the planter group.

Three scholarly contributions which amplify the history of indentured servitude are Abbot Emerson Smith, *Colonists in Bondage* (Chapel Hill, 1947), with emphasis on emigrants from Britain; Richard B. Morris, *Government and Labor in Early America* (New York, 1946), an excellent general discussion; and Warren B. Smith, *White Servitude in Colonial South Carolina* (Columbia, 1961), a specialized monograph.

Thomas T. Waterman, *The Dwellings of Colonial America* (Chapel Hill, 1950), describes the evolution of houses, in all the colonies. Anthony N. B. Garvan, *Architecture and Town Planning in Colonial Connecticut* (New Haven, 1951), emphasizes the importance of English origins. William Haller, Jr., *The Puritan Frontier* (New York, 1951), provides a good, readable introduction to the New England towns of the era before 1660. Harold R. Shurtleff, *The Log Cabin Myth* (Cambridge, 1939), attributes the origin of the log cabin to Swedish settlers. Thomas T. Waterman, *The Mansions of Virginia* (Chapel Hill, 1946), is an attractive account of English-colonial architecture, profusely illustrated.

John Hope Franklin, *From Slavery to Freedom* (2d ed., New York, 1956), treats the history of slavery in the Americas before 1775, with a preliminary survey of African backgrounds. Lorenzo J. Greene, *The Negro in Colonial New England* (New York, 1942), a definitive work, shows that slaves in New England fared better than in the South.

SOURCES: Bartlett B. James and J. F. Jameson (eds.), *Journal of Jasper Danckaerts* (Jameson *Original Narratives* series, New York, 1913), is replete with observations on social life in 1679–80.

XIII

 Social Conflicts

DESPITE the diversity and fluidity of early colonial society two dominant classes emerged during the seventeenth century—the aristocracy
of wealthy landowners and merchants and the democracy of the small
yeoman farmers. And in spite of the ideals of individual improvement
entertained by members of the latter class they were not averse to
united action in their struggle for social betterment. At many points,
however, the democracy found the way to advancement blocked by the
influence of the upper class. In consequence there ensued a series of
social conflicts between the hostile forces—conflicts common to all the
colonies because the underlying causes were present throughout the
whole settled area. Assuming various forms of expression and flaring
up intermittently in different localities, these conflicts exhibited one
major issue: who should control the land and the products it yielded
to the labor of the settlers?

With the growth of settlement along most of the seacoast there appeared a uniform tendency for a small group of wealthy men to acquire
large landholdings worked by servants, tenants, or slaves. The temporary efficiency of larger producing units gradually forced the smaller
farmers in the oldest areas to fall behind in the competitive struggle.
If they sold their farms to the landed magnates or lost them through
foreclosure proceedings, the trend toward larger holdings was accelerated. In the interior, however, lay vast stretches of virgin land to which
the dispossessed farmers or the propertyless freedmen might repair
for a new start. But even here they did not escape the influence of the
magnates. The property and enterprise of men of wealth in the seaboard areas yielded increasing profits which demanded fresh fields of
investment—and one such outlet was found in the financing of settlers
in new areas.

Due to the cheapness of land it was usually easy for the poor freedman to acquire fifty acres of back country, but he generally lacked tools,
seed, and livestock, and these he was obliged to purchase on credit.
Two kinds of loans were available. The wealthy planters engaged in
lending money on fairly long terms, while the merchants of the seacoast supplied imported goods on short-term credit. Now, one peculiar

characteristic of the early land system in the colonies was the freedom with which land might be transferred—sold, bequeathed, divided, or taken in payment of every species of debt. Hence the colonial creditors, both merchants and planters, could safely give credit on land security, knowing that the improvements made by the farmer would augment its value and thus provide an increasingly ample guarantee to creditors, should it be necessary for them to foreclose in order to collect existing debts.

In this situation the farmer often found himself at a disadvantage. His debts, which were registered at a fixed sum in pounds, shillings, and pence, had to be paid in farm produce, which was valued at its current market price whenever payments were made. Thus if the price of such produce declined abruptly the farmer might have to deliver all his surplus to his creditor in order to discharge his debts. When this occurred in his dealings with a merchant, the farmer would be obliged to seek a new loan for the purchase of the year's supply of store goods and depend upon the next crop to pay the obligation. This meant that he again had to deliver his surplus produce to his creditor—a circumstance which placed him at a further disadvantage in that he had only one marketing outlet: his creditor was not forced to bid against competitive buyers; hence the complaint of low prices of farm products that were delivered to creditors. And when the farmer became hopelessly involved in debt he might lose his land by foreclosure, thus adding to the holdings of the wealthy class and extending into new areas the trend toward concentrated ownership. In this manner the farmer came to feel that the wealthy merchants and planters were his enemies in a contest for land titles and in a struggle over the prices of farm produce and laws affecting currency and debts.

A second series of social conflicts involved the colonial aristocracy in controversies with groups in England. Just as the colonial merchants became competitors of English merchants, so also the landed aristocracy opposed both the English laws which regulated trade and the claims of the proprietors of Maryland, Pennsylvania, and the Carolinas who held the immediate title to lands desired by the colonial magnates. Since the English merchants and the great proprietors generally had the support of the English government, the colonial aristocracy was impelled to resist imperial control. In the ensuing strife the planters could count upon the aid of the small farmers, who also opposed England's trade regulations, who also disliked to pay quit-rents to the proprietors, and who also desired to acquire proprietary lands. On the other hand, in their conflicts with the small farmers as debtors, the planters and merchants received the support of the English government, always a staunch defender of creditor rights. The strategy of the colonial aristocracy, therefore, was to use the yeoman farmers in opposition to English merchants and proprietors and to depend upon the English government for protection against measures demanded by the yeomen for their relief as a debtor class.

CLEAVAGE IN VIRGINIA

Of all the early conflicts between the small farmers and the upper class the most critical contest occurred in Virginia in 1675–76, by which time the social stratification of the colony had become well marked. The planter class had evolved in response to many circumstances. During the Civil War and the Puritan regime in England many moderately well-to-do partisans of Charles I had migrated to Virginia. Although they were called Cavaliers they were not aristocrats but, rather, substantial members of the English middle class. They invested their money chiefly in tobacco lands and in the fur trade—and at an auspicious time. During the years 1640–60 Virginia enjoyed the benefit of free trade with foreign countries and prospered through relatively high prices of tobacco and furs. Such prosperity prompted the Dutch merchants to extend credit to the planters whereby they might purchase additional lands and servants. Two results followed. The most successful planters enlarged their landholdings in the tidewater area while at the same time a large host of workers completed their terms of servitude and became freedmen. From the profits of tobacco and the fur trade the planters were able to make loans to such freedmen when they acquired small farms on the frontiers.[1]

As a result of the Navigation Acts of 1660 and 1663 and the forcible exclusion of Dutch merchants from the tobacco trade an acute depression fell upon Virginia after 1660, when the planters were required to ship their products directly to England and to depend solely upon English shipping, which was not yet sufficient for their needs. One critic of England's policy wrote: "If the Hollanders must not trade to Virginia how shall the planters dispose of their tobacco? The English will not buy it, for what the Hollander carried thence was a sort of tobacco, not desired by any other people. . . . The tobacco will not vend in England, the Hollanders will not fetch it from England; what must become thereof?" Moreover, the Second Anglo-Dutch War dealt a severe blow to Virginia's trade: in 1667 Dutch warships in Chesapeake Bay captured twenty vessels of the English tobacco fleet. Reduced

---

[1] T. J. Wertenbaker, *Virginia under the Stuarts*, chapters 5–8, is the best discussion of Bacon's Rebellion.

shipping and wartime risks boosted freight rates from the normal figure of £7 a ton of tobacco to charges ranging from £12 to £17 a ton—and this added cost had to be paid indirectly from the planters' profits. As markets contracted, the price of tobacco in the colony fell to a half-penny a pound—a return that did not yield the cost of production to the interior farmers. The secretary of the province in 1667 estimated the yearly income from the crop of the average settler as only fifty shillings—"which, when the taxes . . . shall be deducted, is very little to a poor man who hath perhaps a wife and children to clothe and other necessities to buy." Everywhere the shortage of imported goods was so extreme that observers spoke hyperbolically of "the nakedness of the country."

A brief respite followed the Second Dutch War, only to be succeeded by another spell of hard times during the Third Dutch War of 1672–74. In the winter of 1672–73 an epidemic carried off half the cattle of Virginia—a loss of fifty thousand head before the spring brought relief. Once more the Dutch attacked the English tobacco fleet in the Chesapeake and in 1673 captured nine ships at the mouth of the James River. Vessels coming from England were so few that they brought goods and tools sufficient for only one planter in five; tobacco prices fell to a quarter of what they had been in "normal" times; and the colony seemed filled with "indigent persons who could barely support themselves with their utmost exertions." [2]

This protracted depression further strengthened the wealthy planters at the expense of the poor farmers. As it became necessary to cut the cost of production the planter who had large landholdings and ample credit in England could buy additional servants or slaves, enlarge the scale of his business and reduce the unit cost of production. Menaced by the competition of the larger plantations (which enjoyed another advantage in their superior location for trade), the poor farmer found himself relentlessly squeezed by the necessity of paying fixed debts from sadly depleted income. "The poverty of the country," said Nathaniel Bacon in 1675, "is such that all the power and sway is got into the hands of the rich, who by extortious advantages, having the common people in their debt, have always curbed and oppressed them in all manner of ways."

The desperation of the small farmers led them to demand relief. But the peaceable channels of political action were closed, since the government of Virginia was completely in control of the upper class. The governor, Sir William Berkeley—an inflexible aristocrat, irascible, imperious, and arbitrary—was determined to rule the "rabble" with a

[2] See again P. A. Bruce, *The Virginia Plutarch*, Vol. I, chapters 6–7.

firm hand, convinced that toil, ignorance, and subservience were the proper attributes of the common people. The large planters and merchants, allied with Berkeley, held all the offices in his executive council, which they used to secure personal land grants and to exempt themselves from taxes. Even the House of Burgesses, supposed to represent all the freemen, had become a satellite of the aristocracy. It is probable that between 1661 and 1676 no election of members of the lower house had been held, and it is certain that there was not more than one election, so that the burgesses serving in 1676 were ten or fifteen years removed from a popular mandate. A majority of them had become mere henchmen of the governor, who had secured their compliance by virtue of his power to grant land and to appoint revenue collectors, sheriffs, and officers of the county militia. Accordingly, all agencies of local government, both executive and judicial, were completely dominated by the governor's party. In 1670 the aristocracy enacted a law which denied the ballot to every resident who was not a freeholder.[3]

Similarly the financial system of the colony was honeycombed with favoritism and privilege. Since 1619 the principal revenues for the support of government had been derived from poll taxes levied upon freemen, servants, and slaves. Although the large planters had to pay the taxes for their servants and slaves, the small farmers considered the poll levy unjust and preferred instead a land tax, since the inequalities in land ownership were much more marked than differences in tax payments determined on the poll basis. Moreover, land taxes would have prevented the engrossing of large estates by the planters for speculative purposes and would therefore have opened such holdings to the poorer settlers—a consideration which induced the aristocracy to support the poll tax at all costs. Another grievance of the small farmers grew out of the power of the justices of the peace (representatives of the aristocracy) to impose direct levies without any semblance of the consent of the taxpayers. Moreover, the justices, meeting every second month, composed the county courts, which decided all cases involving less than £10 sterling; hence the poor farmers felt that in disputes with the aristocracy the county courts were merely its champions. Finally, the yeomen charged that the governor's party used public funds to line the pockets of its members and sycophants, so that the colony derived little benefit from taxes levied for fortifications, the construction of buildings at Jamestown, and the encouragement of domestic manufactures.[4]

[3] See again J. Fiske, *Old Virginia and Her Neighbors,* Vol. II, chapters 11–13.
[4] See again Mary Johnston, *Pioneers of the Old South,* chapters 12–13.

When to the other woes of the interior farmers was added the distress of a destructive Indian war their plight became unbearable. In 1675 a raid of the Senecas from the north drove into western Virginia a band of Susquehannocks, who upset the existing balance between settler and Indian on the frontier. Preliminary quarrels and skirmishes in the summer of 1675 finally evoked a general massacre which cost the lives of more settlers than any Indian outbreak of the preceding fifty years. When the farmers appealed to the governor for aid they met a disappointing response. Berkeley and his friends at the time had a virtual monopoly of the western fur trade which they were loath to endanger by harsh measures against the Indians, while their practice of equipping the red men with powder, guns, and shot had been responsible for much of the bloodshed of the frontier war. In January 1676 Berkeley did assemble a military force, only to disband it when he feared that disaffected farmers, once armed, might turn upon the government. Thereafter he favored defensive measures, particularly the building of forts at the falls of the main rivers. This policy did not appease the harassed frontiersmen, who favored vigorous offensive raids into the Indian country and charged that the forts "were a design of the grandees to engross all their [the settlers'] tobacco in their own hands." Meanwhile the governor even refused to issue to frontier officers commissions authorizing them to wage, independently, an offensive war.[5]

Such was the setting when Nathaniel Bacon, a young Englishman who had lived in the colony less than two years, assumed the leadership of the disaffected farmers. As a member of the governor's council Bacon had become contemptuous of Berkeley's defense policy, particularly after the Indians had attacked Bacon's own frontier plantation in Henrico County and killed its overseer. His independent spirit prompted him to organize a force of volunteer frontiersmen and to lead them in vigorous attacks upon the Indians. Berkeley declined to grant him a military commission and proclaimed him a rebel when he refused to disband his men. His followers were described by one of the Virginia aristocrats as "a rabble of the basest sort of people, whose condition was such as by a change could not admit of worse."

Bacon's successful exploits on the frontier made him such a power among the small farmers that Berkeley was obliged to yield concessions, and at last he ordered a new election of burgesses. The free-

---

[5] William E. Dodd has published the first volume of his projected four-volume work, *The Old South*, under the title *Struggles for Democracy* (New York, 1937). This book, written in a liberal spirit and in a leisurely, familiar manner, is the fruit of a long and penetrating inquiry into Southern history.

holders of Bacon's county sent him to Jamestown as their representative. There, however, he failed to obtain his desired commission, nor could he persuade the governor to reverse his frontier policy. Thor-

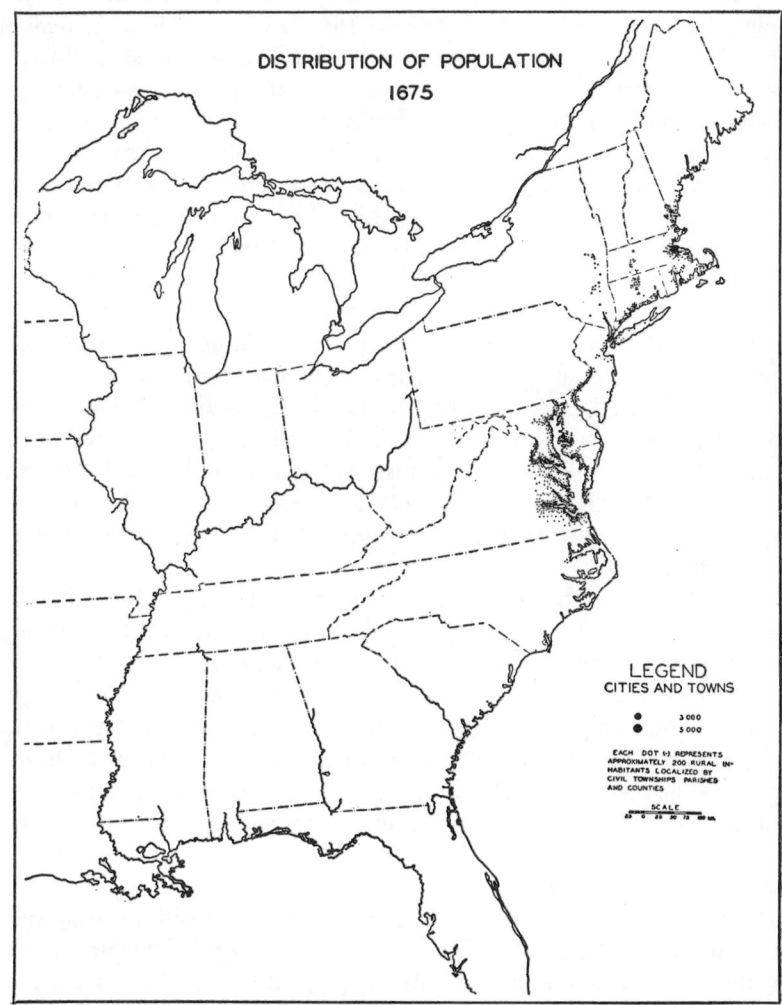

DISTRIBUTION OF POPULATION
1675

LEGEND
CITIES AND TOWNS

oughly exasperated, he finally used force to terrorize the council and to extract a commission from Berkeley. Then, when the insurrectionists had been called away to the frontier by new Indian raids, the governor raised a counter-revolutionary army, whereupon Bacon returned posthaste to Jamestown. Berkeley fled to the eastern shore as Bacon took charge of the government (styling himself "general by the consent of the people") and prepared to resist some royal troops which were presumably on the way to Virginia from England in response to Berkeley's hurried call for aid.[6]

While in control of Jamestown the insurrectionists burned the town, Bacon himself setting fire to the Anglican church. Then in October he died, a victim of fever, and his leaderless following (which now included many runaway servants and slaves) became a disorganized, plundering mob. Berkeley returned from Accomac, rallied the eastern planters, suppressed the revolt, and exacted a terrible vengeance by hanging a score of insurrectionists and decreeing the confiscation of many estates. While this liquidation of the rebels was in progress three commissioners arrived from England with eleven hundred troops. Sent by Charles II to suppress the revolt and to examine into its causes these commissioners were soon at odds with Berkeley, who treated them with the utmost contempt and opposed them in every possible way. Their condemnation of his proceedings finally compelled him to return to England, where he encountered icy reproaches from the Lords of Trade and the displeasure of the king. He died in July 1677, a discredited and broken man. Of his tyranny Charles II is supposed to have said: "That old fool has hanged more men in that naked country than I have for the murder of my father."

Two gains for the yeomanry issued from the rebellion—the dismissal of Berkeley and the negotiation of a treaty with the Indians which restored peace to the frontiers. Otherwise the fundamental institutions of the colony remained intact. There was no change in the personnel and power of the council nor in the privileged status of the aristocracy with respect to landholdings, taxation, credit relations, and local government. The bitter experience of the planters may have antagonized them toward indentured servants and freedmen, may have caused them to depend increasingly upon Negro slaves; at any rate the progress of slavery after 1680 deepened the gulf between rich and poor. Meanwhile the English government did not champion the cause of the "underdog"; instead it insisted that the right to vote be limited to freeholders and attempted, unsuccessfully, to deny to the House of Burgesses the privilege of initiating legislative measures. Nor did England relax the trade and navigation laws which had contributed so materially to the colony's distress.

Continued dissatisfaction and agitation among the small farmers during the 1680's plainly indicated that the causes of popular dis-

[6] *The Story of Bacon's Rebellion*, by Mary N. Stanard (New York, 1907), is a brief account.

content had not been removed. Three unsatisfactory governors served after Berkeley—Sir Henry Chicheley, old, infirm, and "superannuated"; Lord Culpeper, a spoilsman who used his office to enhance his private fortune; and Lord Howard of Effingham, a petty autocrat who mirrored the conceptions of absolute power held by his royal master, James II. The attempt of England to assert her authority over the colony resulted in a government not much more satisfactory than that of Berkeley and his clique. Disaffected groups, however, had been so thoroughly defeated in Bacon's Rebellion that no uprising in Virginia accompanied the Revolution of 1688 in England, although the news of the accession of William and Mary was received with "unfeigned joy and exaltation." [7]

CONFLICTS IN THE PROPRIETARY COLONIES

In seventeenth-century Maryland the upper class consisted of the friends, relatives, and agents of the proprietor, Lord Baltimore, who regarded and administered the colony as his personal estate. As the owner of all ungranted land, as the possessor of several private plantations, and as the receiver of quit-rents paid by all the settlers, the proprietor occupied a commanding position. Upon his relatives and friends he bestowed landed estates, offices, and revenues, thereby dominating the executive, judicial, and military branches of the government. Opposed to the Calvert party were the independent landowners, both large and small, who tended to act in unison against the proprietor. As the owner of ungranted lands desired by the settlers and as the recipient of their quit-rent payments he was more or less their natural enemy. Since they acted through the elected House of Delegates it became imperative for him to hold it in check—a purpose which he accomplished by bribing its members, by limiting each county to two representatives, by vetoing its laws, and by restricting the suffrage (in 1670) to freeholders or owners of personal property worth £40. The staunch Catholicism of the proprietor also set him apart from the majority of his Protestant and Puritan settlers. Among the landowners who did not belong to the proprietary party the cleavage between rich and poor was not so marked as in Virginia—chiefly because of the greater difficulty in securing extensive land grants in Maryland. Not only was the colony much smaller than Virginia; more important was the fact that the land belonged to one man who made grants sparingly, with an eye to his future income, whereas in Virginia the unoccupied land, owned by the king, was

[7] See again Mary Stanard, *Virginia's First Century*, chapters 22–23.

granted by governors who derived no personal advantage by conserving the royal domain but rather profited through generous grants to individuals who could contribute something to the governor's personal fortune. On the whole the royal governors were much more liberal dispensers of the king's acres than were the proprietors in disposing of their lands. Similarly the quit-rents exacted by Lord Baltimore were nominally high: 4*s*. a hundred acres as against 2*s*. in Virginia.[8]

Between 1660 and 1689 five revolts against the proprietor occurred in Maryland. The first (which dominated the colony's history between 1652 and 1657) was engineered by Puritan settlers who had come from Virginia after 1644 to escape religious persecution at the hands of Governor Berkeley. In Maryland, however, these Puritans had little cause of complaint since they enjoyed religious toleration, and since Lord Baltimore submissively acknowledged the Puritan rule of Cromwell in England. But the Puritan colonists, familiar with New England land tenure of fee simple ownership, looked askance upon quit-rents exacted by a proprietary overlord—especially one who was a Roman Catholic. In 1654-55 the Puritans deposed Lord Baltimore's governor, seized control of the colony, defeated a proprietary force sent to subdue them, and erected an independent government. The revolt ended with an agreement in November 1657 which restored Baltimore's authority, guaranteed religious toleration to the Puritans and promised that their land titles would be respected. In the crisis Baltimore had been able to secure the support of the London merchants who desired to terminate all strife in the colonies which was destructive of trade.[9]

A second outbreak in 1660 led by one Josias Fendall, then acting governor for Baltimore, threatened to destroy the proprietary government and to establish a republic to be ruled by the elected house. But when Charles II came to the throne Baltimore recognized him as eagerly as he had submitted to Cromwell and in consequence obtained royal orders which denounced Fendall's revolt and directed the Marylanders to acknowledge the proprietor's rights. Again the revolt collapsed, and during the next fifteen years Lord Baltimore reëstablished a firm grip on his province.

The third revolt, in 1676, which was inspired by Bacon's Rebellion, involved only a handful of malcontents and was speedily suppressed

---

[8] See again C. M. Andrews, *The Colonial Period of American History*, Vol. II, chapters 8–9.

[9] On these conflicts see John H. Latané, *The Early Relations between Maryland and Virginia* (Baltimore, 1895), and B. C. Steiner, *Maryland under the Commonwealth* (Baltimore, 1911).

by an energetic governor who arrested and executed the leaders. Next occurred an outbreak in 1681, engineered by Fendall and another conspirator, John Coode. Once more the proprietary party acted with decision and quelled the revolt by arresting the leaders. Fendall was now fined forty thousand pounds of tobacco and expelled from the province.

Such revolts were significant because they indicated widespread discontent with the proprietary regime. For several reasons the outbreaks had been suppressed with comparative ease: because the proprietor had the backing of the English government, because the division of the colony by Chesapeake Bay into two parts made united action difficult, and because the distress of the farmers was not sufficiently acute to drive them to extremes. The colony had not suffered from an Indian war as had Virginia before Bacon's Rebellion, nor had Lord Baltimore favored the fur traders at the expense of the farmers. Although the quit-rents remained in force, they were payable, after 1671, in tobacco, which was arbitrarily valued for this purpose at 2d. a pound, irrespective of its market price, so that tobacco worth only ½d. a pound would pay a quit-rent of 2d. But in spite of these advantages the Maryland farmers suffered acute distress during the depression of 1664–76, and their poverty made them restless under an overlord who benefited at their expense. Their early revolts demonstrated that they would seize the first opportunity given by events in England to repudiate Lord Baltimore's rule.[10]

Thus when the Marylanders learned of the expulsion of James II from England and when Baltimore (through accidental circumstances) failed to proclaim William III as the new sovereign, they organized a Protestant association with John Coode in command, and in July 1689 seized possession of St. Mary's, the provincial capital. The revolutionary party, now including both the wealthier planters and the small farmers, erected a temporary government in place of the proprietary regime. Then in 1691 England took the colony under her wing and appointed a royal governor. Baltimore retained his position as landlord but not until 1716 did he recover his right to govern the colony, so that Maryland functioned during twenty-five years as a royal province.[11]

The early history of South Carolina also exhibits a bitter conflict between the proprietors and the settlers—a conflict which grew out

[10] Francis E. Sparks, *Causes of the Maryland Revolution of 1689* (Baltimore, 1896), is the most complete account.

[11] B. C. Steiner, "The Protestant Revolution in Maryland," *Report*, American Historical Association, 1898, is excellent.

of the efforts of the former to dominate the government and the economic life of the colony to the detriment of the latter. In 1669 John Locke prepared for the proprietors his famous "Fundamental Constitutions of Carolina," which embodied in particular Lord Ashley's ideas of an aristocratic society. This design for a planned economy proposed to fasten upon the American wilderness a nobility consisting of landgraves and caciques—German and Indian titles respectively, since the charter prohibited the use of English titles in Carolina. The colony was to be divided into counties, each of which was to consist of eight seignories (one for each of the eight proprietors), eight baronies (to be granted to one landgrave and two caciques) and twenty-four colonies to be apportioned among the freemen. Since each seignory, barony, and colony was to contain twelve thousand acres, this scheme meant that two-fifths of the land would belong to the proprietors and the nobles and three-fifths to all the other settlers. Moreover, in the colonies reserved for the freemen, manors of between three thousand and twelve thousand acres might be erected and peopled with leet-men or serfs. Thus the social structure would consist of the proprietary overlords, nobles, owners of large estates, small freeholders, and serfs—a duplication of feudal society of medieval times.

The Fundamental Constitutions further provided for a highly aristocratic government. All executive and judicial power was to be concentrated in the hands of the proprietors and the nobles. Only a landgrave could serve as governor, and although a parliament was to be erected the plan of representation was extremely undemocratic. Each proprietor was entitled to appoint one member and each county was to be represented by its three nobles and four elected delegates, while only owners of five hundred acres or more could qualify as deputies of the freemen.

This elaborate and archaic constitution could not be applied while South Carolina was in its infancy. When the settlers numbered only a few hundred souls it was impossible to create and people counties consisting each of 480,000 acres. Accordingly, the proprietors at first provided for compact settlement in towns. Necessity dictated that the settlers engage in diversified farming and the fur trade, not in the production of staples suited to large estates. The order of nobles could not be created until the land had been surveyed and peopled, although the proprietors did confer the nominal title of landgrave in order to qualify governors. Land grants were also shaped by necessity. The proprietors created a few large holdings and sold or gave away many small tracts, so that in 1685 the majority of farms did not exceed three hundred acres. The widespread distribution of land in turn affected the colony's government, inasmuch as the freeholders dominated the elected assembly and used it as a means of defending their interests against the proprietors.[12]

Early in the 1680's, when the colony was successfully launched and population had increased to about twenty-five hundred, the proprietors at last endeavored to give real force to the Fundamental Constitutions —a move which antagonized the settlers and united the small landowners and the wealthier men in vigorous opposition, since enforcement meant the withdrawal of lands from the reach of the settlers, the imposition of serfdom, and the control of government in the interest of proprietors. The wealthier colonists, who were deeply involved in trade, objected to proprietary restraints. Their chief source of profit, the fur trade, was endangered when the proprietors attempted to monopolize it for their own benefit. Allied to the fur trade was a traffic in Indian slaves who were obtained from the interior—natives enslaved originally by enemy tribes and sold to the white traders. This traffic meant that the South Carolina traders had to ally themselves with one group of warring tribes, thereby tending to embroil the settlers in intertribal strife—a result distasteful to the proprietors who desired peace with the Indians as a condition for the prosperous development of the colony. And when the Charles Town traders evaded the English Navigation Acts (which they did with boldness and ingenuity) they placed the proprietors at a further disadvantage. The English government expected the proprietors to enforce the acts within their province and warned that repeated violations would lead to the annulment of their charter rights—no empty threat in view of the treatment of Massachusetts in 1684. Another issue between proprietors and settlers arose in the 1680's when the proprietors made land grants subject to a quit-rent payable in money. The strife over trade and land induced the settlers to struggle to control the government and to resist the philosophy of the proprietors as expressed in a rebuke to the governor: "Pray, are you to govern the people or the people you?"

The conflict became increasingly sharp until, in 1685, twelve members of the colonial parliament were expelled because they refused to assent to the Fundamental Constitutions. Then occurred a complete break in 1688 when the governor proclaimed martial law and dissolved the parliament. Two years later the settlers launched a counterattack and seized control—only to be dislodged again in 1691. At that time

[12] Edward McCrady's *The History of South Carolina under the Proprietary Government, 1670–1719* (New York, 1897) contains a mass of detailed information, chronologically arranged. See again C. M. Andrews, *The Colonial Period of American History*, Vol. III, chapter 6.

the proprietors appointed Philip Ludwell governor, and although the Fundamental Constitutions were not yet officially abandoned they were now in fact a dead letter. The South Carolinians had successfully resisted the proprietors and their aristocratic program.

In North Carolina the proprietors encountered similar opposition. This region did not seem very attractive to them and had been allowed (before 1673) to go its own way. Settled by poor frontiersmen from Virginia who managed to eke out a niggardly subsistence on isolated farms, the little colony seemed to outsiders the abode of an easygoing, indolent people who regarded self-government as no government and taxes as robbery. Their meager exports consisted of tobacco and furs, and since the settlements had no harbors that could accommodate ocean-going ships, their trade had fallen into the hands of New Englanders who came to the coast in small vessels. Before 1673 the New England traders had been shipping tobacco directly to Europe; hence the North Carolina settlers were indirectly implicated in violations of the enumerated article clause of the Navigation Act of 1660.

Two grievances arose to plague the North Carolinians after 1670. The original settlers had obtained their land titles from Governor Berkeley of Virginia; hence when the Carolina proprietors asserted their claim to the province, there was danger that earlier grants would be annulled. Moreover, the proprietors demanded quit-rents—a real burden to farmers who lived in poverty. Secondly, the Navigation Act of 1673 inflicted a painful blow by levying a duty of 1d. a pound on North Carolina tobacco exported to New England. A part of this tax apparently was shifted by the New England traders to the farmers, and since it equaled the sale price of their tobacco it practically wiped out their profits. The proprietors, however, in order to keep the good will of English colonial officials, insisted upon the enforcement of the hateful tax. A series of riots and outbreaks ensued which culminated in a revolt in 1677–79, when the disgruntled farmers, led by George Durant and John Culpeper, deposed the governor and took possession of the colony. Culpeper was eventually arrested and taken to England for trial, where he was exonerated on the ground that since there was no settled government in North Carolina he had not been guilty of treason. In a later uprising the farmers drove out another governor— Seth Sothell, one of the proprietors. Meanwhile the Fundamental Constitutions had been opposed and frustrated as effectively as in South Carolina. The first phase of the northern colony's tumultuous history ended in 1691 when Philip Ludwell was appointed governor of both the Carolinas and his deputy was placed over the turbulent farmers at Albemarle Sound.

CLASS CONFLICT IN NEW YORK

Between the years 1664 and 1685, when the province of New York was the personal estate of James, Duke of York, there occurred a series of conflicts between proprietor and inhabitants somewhat comparable to those in Maryland and the Carolinas. More fundamental, however, in the early history of New York was a protracted internal strife between aristocratic and democratic forces. The Duke of York did not take a deep personal interest in his province—a fact attested by his gift of New Jersey to Berkeley and Carteret in 1664 and by his failure to insist upon the Connecticut River as the eastern boundary of New York as provided in the duke's grant from Charles II.[13] In the 1680's the Connecticut boundary was fixed at a line running north from a point twenty miles east of the mouth of the Hudson. Hence New York during the duke's rule was a small province—limited to Long Island, Manhattan, other islands along the coast, and a strip of the Hudson valley about fifty miles wide, extending up the river to Albany. The occupation of the Mohawk valley by the Iroquois blocked the extension of settlement into the west.

The economic life of the colonists revolved around four major pursuits. The town of New York domiciled the merchant class engaged in wholesale commerce; at Albany the fur trade was the principal interest; on the mainland and on Long Island small farms produced livestock and grains; and Long Island in addition carried on a whale fishery. Socially the small farmers and fishermen of Long Island and the farmers in the lower Hudson valley, together with the wage-earners, artisans, and small traders of the town of New York, formed a democratic party in opposition to an aristocracy composed of the Albany fur traders, the city merchants, and the owners of large estates. In the early days the lines were not closely drawn between these aristocratic groups. The Albany fur traders and the city merchants both acquired landed estates, while the owners of large landholdings worked by tenants had to engage in trade in order to dispose of the produce in which their tenants paid their rents. The economic pursuits of the province were described in 1684 by the officials of the town of New York: "The manufacture of flour and bread . . . hath been and is the chief support of the trade and traffic to and from this city and the maintenance of its inhabitants in all degrees. . . . All other parts of this province have some particular advantage and way of living, as Long Island by husbandry and whaling; Esopus being the fat of the land by tillage;

<hr>

[13] A. E. McKinley, "The Transition from Dutch to English Rule in New York," *American Historical Review*, VI (July 1901).

Albany by Indian trade and husbandry; this city [has] no other advantage or way of living but by traffic and dependence one on another chiefly upheld by the manufacture of flour and bread."

Prior to 1691 the government of New York was more undemocratic than that of any other of the English colonies. The grant of 1664 from Charles II conferred upon the Duke of York the power to name the governor and council, to impose legislation and taxes, to appoint local officials, and to control the judiciary and militia of the province. He was not obliged to erect a representative legislature, and in the exercise of his almost despotic powers he was subject to only two restraints: his laws must conform to the laws of England and appeals might be made from his provincial courts to the Privy Council. A firm believer in autocratic rule, the duke at first refused to grant the settlers a representative assembly, fearing as he did "the aptness of such bodies to assume to themselves many privileges which prove destructive to or very oft disturb the peace of the government wherein they are allowed." [14]

In view of the concentration of political power in the hands of the proprietor it is not surprising that the aristocratic groups in the colony allied themselves with his appointed agents. In order to derive an income from the province the duke had to rely upon duties levied against its trade, and the collection of such duties was facilitated when commerce was centered in the port of New York. The principal upper-class group, the merchants, desired to monopolize the commerce of the province, so that their interests coincided with the proprietor's desire to have all imports and exports pass through the town which they controlled. The fur traders and the proprietor (who collected a duty on furs exported) united to extend England's sway among the Iroquois and to resist the encroachments of the French *voyageurs* from Canada. And as the owner and grantor of lands, the proprietor was courted by the great men who sought to obtain estates on easy terms. The small farmers and the fishermen, on the other hand, opposed the monopolization of trade by the town merchants and the exaction by the proprietor of duties on trade to which they did not give their consent. Due to the aristocratic temper of the proprietor and the prevailing social standards of the time it was natural for his agents in the province to associate with and heed the advice of the wealthy colonists. The small farmers, finding themselves excluded from a government which increasingly represented the interests of an absentee landlord and a hostile aristocracy, demanded that a representative assembly be erected through which they might defend their own particular interests.

[14] See again J. Fiske, *Dutch and Quaker Colonies*, Vol. II, chapters 10–11, 13.

During the term of Colonel Richard Nicholls, first governor of New York (1664–68), the government of the province assumed the form it retained until 1691. For the benefit of New Englanders who had settled on Long Island and at Westchester on the eastern bank of the lower Hudson, Nicholls prepared a code which he designated as the duke's laws. They guaranteed freedom of worship and existing property rights, provided for a property rather than a religious qualification for voting, and committed the government of the towns to a constable and eight overseers elected by resident freemen. The administration of justice was entrusted to justices of the peace, appointed by the governor, who met yearly as a court of assize where, with the consent of the governor, they might enact laws. Intended primarily for the settlers from New England, the duke's laws in many respects duplicated the codes of New Haven and Massachusetts, although they did not confer the boon of town meetings. A convention of deputies from Westchester and the Long Island towns ratified the laws in 1665, rather unwillingly, but the settlers themselves complained loudly that they were not permitted to assent to taxes, to elect the justices, or to control their local militias. Demanding an elected assembly so that their deputies might "be joined with the governor and council in making the laws," the emigrés from New England waged a continuous fight against the new regime. However, by virtue of the "gentleness, wisdom and intelligence" of Governor Nicholls the province escaped acute strife until 1668, and the duke's laws were extended to the other settlements. A fellow official said of Nicholls's political skill that "he kept persons of different judgments and divers nations in peace when a great part of the world was in wars." [15]

Although the Dutch reconquered New York in 1673 it was restored to England by the Treaty of Westminster, February 19, 1674, and surrendered in the following October to Major Edmund Andros, recently appointed governor by the Duke of York. Imbued with the military spirit, Andros was an honest and able man, a devoted servant of the duke whose interests he placed above those of local groups. Perceiving the weakness of the farmers in the government he recommended that the duke establish an elected assembly, intending possibly to provide a counterweight to the local aristocracy. At any rate Andros incurred the hostility of the merchants, who refused to pay the customs duties from which the duke derived his income from the province, and hence the faithful Andros was summoned to England for an accounting.

[15] See again A. C. Flick (ed.), *History of the State of New York*, Vol. II, chapter 3.

The next governor, Thomas Dongan, who ruled between 1683 and 1688, identified himself chiefly with the upper-class groups in the colony. In 1686 he granted a charter to the city of New York which gave to the merchant class a larger measure of home rule. An earlier charter of 1665, while it granted a monopoly of trade to the freemen of the town, provided that the mayor, aldermen, and sheriff should all be appointed by the governor. Dongan's charter now allowed the freemen of the town to elect the aldermen. Meanwhile the commercial policies in force in the province tended to aggrandize the merchant class. One regulation decreed that all flour exported from the province should be bolted or sifted in the town of New York—a rule which forced the farmers to market their flour through a single channel, gave the merchants control of the flour trade, and brought to their doors the whole provincial supply of wheat and flour, which they could buy after harvest when stocks were large and prices at the lowest level. That the bolting monopoly was used to depress the price of wheat and to uphold the price of flour appears in the establishment, after 1680, of independent mills in the country districts. When such mills threatened the merchants' monopoly Governor Dongan in 1683 instructed the sheriffs to seize all flour bolted and packed outside the town of New York.

Another conflict involved the towns of Southold, Southampton, and Easthampton on eastern Long Island. These settlements fell within the trade area of Boston; hence it was most profitable for them to send thither their grain and whale products to be exchanged for European goods. The New York merchants, desiring to monopolize the Long Island trade, secured an act which levied a duty of 10 per cent *ad valorem* on all European goods imported into Long Island from Boston. When Governor Dongan found that the Long Islanders ignored the act he ordered that all Boston ships should call at the port of New York before they delivered goods to Long Island and return to New York with the outgoing cargoes. To the Long Islanders this policy savored of tyranny. It aimed to force them to depend upon the New York vessels and merchants, thus enabling the latter to dictate prices and freight rates. When prices were higher at Boston than at New York the Long Islanders could not ship directly to their best market, and when the New Yorkers failed to send enough vessels they had no outlet at all for their surplus products.

Governor Dongan also indicated his sympathies by making several large land grants to wealthy men of the province, and in 1686 he favored the fur trading interests by granting Albany a new city charter which conferred upon that town a monopoly of the fur trade.[16]

Due to popular opposition and resistance to his oligarchical regime the Duke of York finally yielded and in 1683 instructed Dongan to call a representative assembly. The Long Island towns since 1665 had been in a state of near rebellion, frequently refusing to pay taxes and issuing protests which were ignored by the magnates in control of the governor's council. Dongan thereupon ordered an election of delegates who met as the first Assembly of New York in October 1683. Its members enjoyed the privileges of free discussion and of considering bills but the measures they approved were subject to vetoes by the governor and the proprietor. This first assembly enacted fifteen laws, the most important being a charter of liberties and privileges which lodged the legislative power with the governor, council, and assembly, extended the ballot to all freeholders and freemen, provided for elections by the "free choice and vote" of the majority, and set up a proportional scheme of representation by counties. Other sections of the charter outlined the principles of land tenure, inheritance, and judicial procedure and guaranteed freedom of worship and trial by jury. Unfortunately for the New York farmers the duke changed his policy after his accession to the throne in 1685 had transformed the province into a royal colony. The acts of the session of 1683 and of two other sessions in 1684 and 1685 were never fully confirmed by James either as proprietor or as king. Instead, new instructions to Dongan in 1685 ordered the abandonment of the representative assembly and once more vested all legislative power in the governor and council—an act in keeping with the autocratic program which the king and the Lords of Trade had in mind for the northern colonies. Then in 1688 New York was annexed to the Dominion of New England and placed under the arbitrary rule of Sir Edmund Andros.

Preoccupied as he was with New England affairs, Andros had to govern New York through a deputy, Captain Francis Nicholson, who, during a brief term until May 1689, continued the policies previously in force, thus allowing the magnates to retain their grip upon the province. Their power was now well-nigh supreme. In 1686 Dongan had given the aristocratic councillors the right to act as justices of the peace in all counties, and as members of the supreme court of the province they were empowered to hear appeals from all subordinate courts. In the towns of New York and Albany the magnates controlled the local governments and dominated the mayor's courts which pronounced

[16] See again C. M. Andrews, *Colonial Self-Government*, chapters 5–6 (New York); chapters 13–14 (Virginia); chapter 15 (Maryland).

final judgment in all cases involving less than £20. So absolute was the sway of the aristocracy in government and so unyielding was its rule that the unprivileged farmers, traders, and workers could not expect concessions through legal channels and accordingly were driven to open revolt.[17]

The news of the flight of James II from England and of the fall of Andros at Boston inspired the discontented groups of New York to revolutionary action. The farmers on Long Island and in Westchester County took up arms and threatened to march on New York City, where they could count upon the support of the unprivileged workers, called mechanics, and many of the small traders and shopkeepers who were restive under the rule of their creditors and competitors. But a march of the farmers became unnecessary when in May 1689 the city "rabble," as the aristocrats styled their opponents, seized the fort at New York. Their aggressive and energetic leader, Jacob Leisler, a German merchant of democratic sympathies who did not belong to the charmed circle of aristocratic families, proved to be more than a match for the indecisive, hot-tempered Nicholson and his council of magnates. On June 24 Nicholson deserted his post and stole away to England, realizing that the revolution in England had erased his authority in the colony. The democratic party then seized control of the customhouse and set up a *de facto* government or council of safety which proclaimed Leisler commander-in-chief. His rule, which endured until March 1691, rested upon the support of the small farmers and the city workers and upon his control of the provincial militia. In April 1690 he summoned a legislature which enacted only two laws, one of which destroyed the trade monopolies of the New York merchants. This significant act declared that "all towns and places shall have equal freedom to bolt and bake and to transport where they please directly to what place or country they think fit, anything their places afford, and that the one place shall have no more privileges than the other."

Leisler's Revolt was primarily an internal class struggle, although the charges which were bandied about at the time tended to confuse the issue. While many of the royal officers under Nicholson were Catholics, the insurrection was not a religious outbreak, since the magnates allied with Nicholson were as staunch in their Protestantism as were the followers of Leisler. The accusations that Nicholson intended to deliver the province to the French also fail to explain the revolt, since Albany, most exposed to French attack, remained hostile to Leisler

---

[17] See again H. L. Osgood, *American Colonies in the Seventeenth Century*, Vol. III, chapters 12, 15 (New York), 16 (Maryland).

until the spring of 1690. The chief magnate at Albany, Robert Livingston, was reinforced by the leading opponent of the insurrectionists, Nicholas Bayard, who escaped from New York City and fled north, where he exerted his influence to keep Albany under the control of the old guard. Only when Indian warfare threatened destruction did the Albany men surrender to Leisler in the spring of 1690 and welcome the protection of his troops.

Not until March 1691 did Colonel Henry Sloughter, first governor appointed by William and Mary, arrive at New York. He was preceded by Major Richard Ingoldsby in command of two companies of British soldiers. Leisler unfortunately disputed Ingoldsby's authority and refused to surrender the fort—an act which his opponents, without just cause, construed as treason. When Sloughter arrived soon afterward, Leisler submitted—only to find that the new governor had permanently allied himself with the aristocratic party. The magnates emerged from their storm cellars, assumed control of the government, and brought ten of the Leisler leaders to trial for treason. Two were acquitted, six were found guilty but pardoned, and Leisler and his son-in-law, Jacob Milborne, were condemned and hanged in May 1691—an act of unwarranted vengeance, since Leisler and Milborne were denied the right of appeal to the king and only casuistry could construe their actions as treason to William III, whose authority, when properly displayed, they had duly recognized. The pressure which the magnates exerted to induce Sloughter to sign the death warrants of the two popular leaders suggests that an appeal to England would have exonerated them. Some tardy justice was done to their memories in 1695 when Parliament reversed the attainder against them and restored their estates to their families.

The outcome of Leisler's Revolt is indicated by a comment of a later governor, Cadwallader Colden, who wrote in 1734 that great changes in society were effected only by the rich and powerful; "any other commotions generally produced only some short lived disorders and confusions." Certainly an era of reaction followed the execution of Leisler. Governor Sloughter died in 1691—a victim of intemperance, his character indicated by the tradition that he signed Leisler's death warrant while intoxicated. Ingoldsby then served as acting governor until he was succeeded by another anti-Leislerian, Colonel Benjamin Fletcher, who abetted the merchant magnates in their adventures in piracy and granted lands with a free hand. In the words of Colden, Fletcher was "a generous man" who "gave away the king's lands by parcels of one hundred thousand acres to a man, and to some particular favorites four or five times that quantity." His government was described by his successor, the Earl of Bellomont, as "corrupted and debauched."[18]

One gain for the democratic forces issued from the confusion of the time. Governor Sloughter was instructed to restore the elected Assembly, and this body held its first meeting in April 1691. Although only about 8 or 10 per cent of the inhabitants were entitled to vote, the elected house afforded the small farmers a means of defending their interests. Thus in 1695 they obtained an act which abolished the flour monopoly of the town of New York and allowed all farmers to engage in bolting, baking, and packing. At this time the Assembly refused to pass any other measures until its free flour act was accepted. The issue arose again in 1700 when the city officials adopted an ordinance placing heavy duties on flour and biscuit imported into the city from the outlying farms. The Assembly then refused to provide for the support of the government until this obnoxious order was repealed. Bellomont wrote that the "city merchants were as obstinate for maintaining their ordinance, so that the money bill was very near miscarrying." Finally, however, he persuaded them to revoke the offending order. Bellomont's successor, Lord Cornbury, in alliance with the merchants, suggested that the city be given as many representatives in the Assembly as all other parts of the province. But this was not done and the city did not recover its monopoly rights.

Leisler's Revolt, as an internal class struggle, was the counterpart of Bacon's Rebellion—not primarily a protest against England's authority as was the Revolution of 1689 in New England, whose leaders represented the upper class. English policy, however, contributed to the causes of the disorders in both Virginia and New York by virtue of the practice of appointing as councillors and advisers of governors the wealthiest men of the colonies. Then when outbreaks against the local aristocracy occurred, England dispatched troops to suppress rebellion and restore the authority of the governor and council. But in the treatment of "rebels" England showed far more leniency in New England than did the colonial magnates in Virginia and New York. Although the aristocratic spirit prevalent in England predisposed the king's advisers to favor the colonial aristocracy, yet when its rule became unduly harsh they insisted upon some concessions to the less influential groups. Bacon's Rebellion gained protection for the frontier settlements of Virginia and Leisler's Revolt brought an elected Assembly to New York.

[18] See again E. Channing, *History of the United States*, Vol. II, chapters 2 (New York), 3 (Virginia), 7 (revolutions, 1689).

Social Conflicts in New Jersey

The struggles of the democracy in New Jersey exhibited the grievances of settlers against proprietors, as in Maryland and Carolina, and the complaints of farmers against merchants, as in New York. It will be remembered that in 1674 Lord John Berkeley sold the western part of New Jersey to Quakers; that in 1676 the colony was divided into two provinces; and that in 1680–82 was sold the Carteret claim to East New Jersey, also to Quakers. The center and capital of East New Jersey was established in 1665 by Philip Carteret, who led an expedition of thirty colonists and founded a settlement at Elizabethtown. During the preceding year many farmers from New England had migrated to East New Jersey and had obtained land grants from Colonel Nicholls, governor of New York. Other emigrants from New England later responded to the generous concessions offered by Carteret, so that by 1675 the New Englanders formed the strongest party in his half of the colony. West New Jersey, which in 1676 had a nucleus of Dutch and Swedish settlers, was peopled afterward principally by the English Quakers, who established their seat of government at Burlington in 1677. Both parts of New Jersey enjoyed elected assemblies.

The principal social conflicts in New Jersey occurred in the eastern province, where the small farmers were squeezed between the proprietors and the merchants of New York. The settlers from New England retained their preference for the land system of the Puritan colonies—grants by the legislature to town proprietors and by them to the individual farmer, so that the latter held his land in fee simple tenure, free from quit-rents or other payments to an overlord. The proprietors of East New Jersey, on the other hand, adopted the method of making grants directly to individuals and of exacting a yearly quit-rent. Those New Englanders who had obtained grants from Governor Nicholls of New York insisted that they were not tenants of the proprietors of New Jersey—a claim that would have made them independent landowners, since the Duke of York had surrendered his rights as overlord of New Jersey. The opposition among the New Englanders to quit-rents became so intense that two of the towns which derived their titles from Nicholls rejected the proprietary authority and established their own governor and assembly—an act of defiance, however, that they were unable to make good. The bitter antagonism between Puritans and Quakers intensified the opposition of the New Englanders to quit-rent payments after East New Jersey passed into the hands of Quaker proprietors in 1682.[19]

[19] H. L. Osgood's *The American Colonies in the Eighteenth Century* (4 vols., New

Commercially, East New Jersey belonged within the trade area of the town of New York, whose merchants were determined to retain their hold upon the trade in this area which they had developed before New Jersey was separated from New York. Both the proprietors of East New Jersey and the resident farmers desired the privilege of free trade with the outside world and accordingly they established a port at Perth Amboy, where trading vessels did not have to pay the heavy import and export duties then in force in New York. This act threatened the New York merchants with the loss of the trade of East New Jersey, since goods sent thither from New York had to pay the New York import duties whereas goods shipped from other places entered Perth Amboy duty free. Moreover, the New York merchants charged that imports could be brought into Perth Amboy and then carried into New York, there to undersell their own wares on which the New York duties had been paid. Similarly, New York produce could be exported via Perth Amboy in order to evade the payment of New York's export duties.

In order to equalize trading conditions the New York merchants insisted that goods entering and leaving East New Jersey should be subject to the duties in force at New York—a demand supported by the Duke of York and later by the king because the free trade of Perth Amboy lessened the proprietary and royal revenues of New York. At first the New Yorkers established an official at Perth Amboy to collect the same duties that were payable in New York and later required that all vessels trading to and from New Jersey should enter the port of New York in order to make the payments there. In this conflict the East New Jersey farmers received the support of the proprietors, who asserted that a free trade was indispensable to the prosperity of their province. New York could not rightfully collect such taxes because the people of New Jersey had never given their consent. And when the New Jersey farmers had to trade exclusively with New York its merchants held a monopoly that enabled them to fix prices as they pleased, free from the competition of other traders.

These contests led eventually to the establishment of a royal government over New Jersey. It had never been clear whether the proprietors of the Jerseys had received the right to govern their territories. The original grant from the Duke of York to Berkeley and Carteret did not openly confer such a right. During the term of Andros as governor of New York he had endeavored to extend the authority of the duke over New Jersey, but the proprietors had resisted and secured an opinion

York, 1924), a work of great scholarship, deals primarily with constitutional controversies. See Vol. I, pp. 382–397.

from an English arbiter which upheld their rights as governors of their provinces. In 1688 the Jerseys were temporarily annexed to the Dominion of New England after the proprietors had consented to surrender their political rights in return for a confirmation of their title to the land. Then, following the overthrow of the Dominion of New England, they resumed their powers of government. During the 1690's, however, East New Jersey was torn by strife over the quit-rents and by the commerical conflict with New York. The proprietors derived no profit from the colony apart from land sales and quit-rents; hence their interest became increasingly that of landlord. Moreover they incurred opposition in England by virtue of their inability to suppress piracy and to enforce the Navigation Acts in New Jersey. Confronted by attacks from the Crown, from their own settlers, and from New York, and realizing that an assertion of their dubious claim to political authority was not worth the cost, they surrendered to the Crown in 1702 the rights of governing their province. The proprietors of West New Jersey did likewise and accordingly New Jersey became a royal province.

The settlement of 1702 allowed the proprietors to retain their rights as landlords and guaranteed to East New Jersey the privilege of free trade through Perth Amboy. England reunited the two little provinces, appointed a royal governor and council and permitted the now consolidated elected assembly to continue. Until 1738 New Jersey was ruled by the governor of New York through a deputy; after 1738 it had its own governor. The commercial policy enforced by England required that the custom duties in force in New York should also be collected in New Jersey.

The internal conflicts of the seventeenth century issued from two main sources—from the antagonism of the workers and small farmers to the merchant-planter upper class, as in New York, Virginia, and New Jersey; and from the animosity of the landowners, both large and small, toward the colonial proprietors, as in Maryland, New Jersey, and the Carolinas. While these conflicts were in progress England had one primary concern—to protect her own stake in the colonies: an interest which made her critical of the proprietary governments, since popular unrest lessened their effectiveness as protectors of that stake. With respect to the internal conflicts in New York and Virginia, England acted to suppress the revolts, to defend her own interests, to restore the colonial aristocracies to power, and to moderate somewhat the harsher features of their rule. Of all the parties involved in these conflicts—the colonial aristocracy, the colonial democracy, the English merchants, the Crown, and the proprietors—the last were in the weakest position, a fact which explains the gradual elimination of the proprietary governments: from New Hampshire in 1679, from New York in 1685–88, from Maine in 1691, from Maryland between 1691 and 1716, from New Jersey in 1702, from the Carolinas in 1719–29, from Georgia in 1751, and from Maryland and Pennsylvania in 1776.

BIBLIOGRAPHICAL NOTE

SECONDARY WORKS: Thomas J. Wertenbaker, *Torchbearer of the Revolution* (Princeton, 1940), a standard account of Bacon's Rebellion, presents the most commonly accepted interpretation. Wilcomb E. Washburn, *The Governor and the Rebel* (Chapel Hill, 1957), a spirited critique of prevailing views of Bacon's Rebellion, deflates Nathaniel Bacon and attempts to exonerate Sir William Berkeley. Jerome R. Reich, *Leisler's Rebellion* (Chicago, 1953), brings out clearly the causes, issues, and results of the conflict. Lawrence H. Leder, *Robert Livingston, 1654–1728, and the Politics of Colonial New York* (Chapel Hill, 1961), a detailed monograph, gives special attention to the conflict between the Leislerian and anti-Leislerian groups.

SOURCES: *The History of Bacon's . . . Rebellion* (Cambridge, 1867), is a contemporary narrative, edited by Charles Deane. See also C. M. Andrews (ed.), *Narratives of the Insurrections*, pp. 3–164, 301–401; and A. B. Hart (ed.), *American History Told by Contemporaries*, I, pp. 242–246, 262–267.

XIV

🌲 England, France,
and Spain

THE success of England in establishing and strengthening her American colonies placed her in a position of potential conflict with any power of Europe bent upon westward expansion, for the fields of colonial exploitation were limited and England's claims to strategic areas denied imperial opportunities to ambitious rivals. Ever since the accession of Henry IV in 1594 France had been growing in stature as a powerful, centralized state. Two crafty and determined prime ministers, the Cardinals Richelieu and Mazarin, had guided the destinies of France between 1624 and 1661, striving relentlessly for an absolute monarchy. By crushing the feudal nobles as a political power, by imposing tax upon tax for the benefit of the king's treasury, by warring against the Protestants as a means of attaining internal religious unity, and by bringing the provinces under the dominance of Paris through royal agents or *intendants* vested with extreme powers in local government—by such methods these two worldly churchmen prepared the way for the triumph of absolutism in the person of the Sun King, Louis XIV.[1]

Animated by a love of power and cherishing illusions of grandeur, this Grand Monarch in 1661 became his own prime minister, taking into his own hands the reins of government, retaining the *intendants* as an agency of local control, reducing his ministers to the status of "yes-men," creating efficient bureaus of central administration, and in general making a reality of the famous phrase attributed to him: "I am the State." As a mirror of his personal splendor and glory he built the gorgeous palace of Versailles, whence emanated the canons of fashion and etiquette that guided aristocratic society throughout Europe. Under his foreign minister, Lionne, he developed the most highly trained and efficient corps of diplomats of the age; his war minister, Louvois, constructed a war machine amply supplied with royal revenues and unrivaled in size and modernization; his finance minister, Colbert, fashioned an integrated system of economics along the lines of mercantilism. All this concentrated force the Sun King aspired to use in

[1] L. B. Packard, *The Age of Louis XIV* (New York, c. 1929), is a readable survey, designed for undergraduates.

355

military conquest for the territorial aggrandizement of his royal house, and circumstances dictated that the arms of France should conquer in the north, toward the Rhine. Such an advance imperiled the Dutch Republic, then screened from French aggression by the Spanish Netherlands (modern Belgium). Meanwhile the colonial ambitions of France menaced England; accordingly after the English and the Dutch had resolved their mutual conflicts in 1674 they united in opposition to the perennial design of Louis XIV for colonial expansion and the conquest of the Spanish Netherlands.[2]

The trend toward absolutism in France prior to 1660 had retarded the growth of industry and trade. The merchant occupied an inferior status in French society, which conferred its honors and prestige upon courtiers, landed nobles, high churchmen, or officials of the king, and betrayed a contemptuous attitude toward men engaged in gainful pursuits. In consequence the wealthy merchants did not train their sons for business and equip them with capital for trade but rather educated them for careers of gentlemen in the service of the court. At the same time the heavy burden of taxes carried by the French people to maintain the monarchy and the army greatly diminished their ability to buy the products of home industry, with the result that —although France had developed certain industries to a high point (cloth, wine, lace, furniture, paper, glass, and thread)—a state of depression and unemployment clouded the early years of the reign of Louis XIV. Foreign commerce was languishing and, excepting her trade with the Levant, France depended upon the shipping of the Dutch, while her imports exceeded her exports, a striking manifestation of the decay of her domestic industries. From this plight Louis XIV and Colbert were determined to extricate the kingdom, and because so much of the national income found its way into the king's treasury it became imperative that the government supply a large part of the capital for economic rehabilitation. The poverty of the mass of the people—in contrast to the great wealth of nobles and courtiers— meant that an adequate domestic market for French products could not be created and consequently Colbert concluded that the way to salvation lay in the development of overseas trade.[3]

As the chief minister of Louis XIV between 1661 and 1683 Colbert adopted and applied the English policy of fostering colonies as pro-

---

[2] A. J. Grant, *The French Monarchy* (2 vols., Cambridge, 1925), is an admirable, brief survey. See Vol. II, chapters 10–15.

[3] An outstanding study of great value is Stewart L. Mims, *Colbert's West India Policy* (New Haven, 1912).

ducing areas rather than the Dutch policy of using overseas possessions primarily as trading posts. He envisaged an integrated empire of four supplementary parts. France, as the center and heart of the system, was to supply manufactured goods, capital, merchants' services, and shipping. Hence he first endeavored to foster home industries and for this purpose a high protective tariff wall was raised in 1665 to exclude competing foreign goods from the French market. In order to procure capital he organized great trading companies in which the king, his officials, and the merchants made large investments. One such firm, the West India Company, formed in 1668, received extensive privileges for trade and colonization in western Africa, North and South America, and the West Indies. The merchants were now elevated in society by favors and honors bestowed upon them at court as the wholehearted patronage of the king was given to their enterprises. Colbert, by insisting that all foreign traders and vessels be excluded from the commerce of the French colonies, reserved it as a monopoly for the native merchant-shipowners. Even the privileges of the West India Company did not exclude private French traders from the colonies, and when the company expired in 1674 all such traders were allowed to share in the national monopoly.[4]

The colonies of France in the West Indies—St. Christopher, Santo Domingo, Martinique, and Guadeloupe—composed the second element in Colbert's imperial scheme. As producers of sugar, tobacco, indigo, cotton, ginger, and dyewoods they fulfilled a threefold function: they supplied articles for consumption in France, thus cutting off payments to foreigners for such commodities of foreign origin; they provided raw materials for French industries; and they afforded articles that might be sold in export trade. The West Indies in turn were to buy French manufactures and employ French capital, shipping, and merchants' services. The denial to the colonies of free trade with foreigners meant that the planters had to pay high prices for their visible and invisible imports from France, and this in turn greatly retarded colonial development. However, Colbert preferred a slow growth in the colonies which would benefit France exclusively to a rapid progress from which foreigners would reap the principal profits.

As the third link in the imperial chain Colbert favored the erection of slave trading stations in Africa where slaves might be purchased with French manufactures and shipped to the planters of the West Indies. Finally, settlements in Canada had their part to play as buyers of

---

[4] See again G. M. Wrong, *The Rise and Fall of New France*, Vol. I, chapters 13–20; Vol. II, chapters 21–23.

French goods and as producers of foodstuffs, work animals, and lumber needed on the West Indian plantations.[5]

How would these colonial possessions benefit France? First, they would stimulate her industries, give employment to her idle workers and take off her surplus manufactures that could not be sold at home. By supplying her with West Indian products the colonies would relieve her from dependence upon foreign states for such commodities, thereby reducing imports for which payment had to be made to foreigners in specie. The earnings of French investors, shippers, and merchants in the form of interest, freights, and profits would give France a favorable balance in colonial trade; similarly, the reëxportation of West Indian staples from France would improve her trading relations with European states. A favorable trade balance in turn would yield an adequate supply of gold and silver, thus providing the sinews of war and a fund of surplus capital that might be devoted to commercial, industrial, and colonial expansion.

Before Colbert's death in 1683 France had driven the Dutch from the trade of the French West Indies, which they had virtually monopolized in 1660. French industries and shipping had been greatly strengthened and extended; the colonies had made substantial if slow progress; and modest success had been attained in the slave trade. At one point, however, Colbert's aims had not been realized: Canada had failed in its role of producer of provisions, lumber, and work animals for the West Indies. New England and New York proved to be better suited to that purpose and consequently they increasingly performed the function originally assigned to Canada. Since Colbert's system aimed to exclude all foreigners from the trade of the colonies, it became imperative that the French West Indies obtain these supplies from French sources. Canada having failed in this connection, the French aspired to acquire New England and New York.[6]

THE ANGLO-FRENCH CONFLICT IN AMERICA

Under the guidance of Colbert France embraced the very policies that had been adopted by England and chose to operate in the same colonial spheres—hence the bitter and prolonged struggle between the two. Besides the ambition of France to acquire England's northern colonies as a feeding ground for the French West Indies she was also determined to monopolize the American fur trade—that source of

---

[5] E. B. Greene, *Provincial America* (New York, 1905), is a notable volume in the *American Nation* series. See chapters 7–10.

[6] Francis Parkman, *The Old Régime in Canada* (Boston, 1880).

fabulous profits which realized so perfectly all the purposes of the mercantilist's creed. By 1660 the Indians of North America had become utterly dependent upon the traffic in furs. Now accustomed to the white man's tools, they were rapidly losing their primitive skill in the art of making and using stone implements. Their dependence on trade increased the importance of trapping and hunting, the source of their purchasing power for European goods; hence their contacts with the white man, instead of leading them to a settled way of life, intensified their roving, predatory characteristics. The fur trade in turn led to a rapid destruction of fur-bearing animals, since peltries and skins had to be obtained in quantities greatly in excess of the Indians' primitive needs. As furs became more scarce and valuable the tribes—now utterly enslaved by the traffic—were forced to struggle against each other for control of the available supply. In the resulting wars European firearms played the decisive role, and the procuring of firearms therefore became a primary concern. In short, the fur trade made the Indians increasingly dependent upon trapping and hunting; the ensuing competition for furs bred intertribal warfare; and such strife in turn intensified the trade which supplied the weapons of war. The Indians had become involved in a vicious circle of trade and strife that carried them toward destruction.[7]

The fur-producing area which the French and English sought to dominate was the vast region adjacent to the Great Lakes. One route which led France westward from Quebec and Montreal followed the St. Lawrence River, Lake Ontario, the Niagara River, and Lake Erie, thus giving access to the upper Ohio valley. Thither went the French *coureurs de bois* in their canoes bound for the hunting lands; along this route the interior tribes brought their furs to Montreal. The great English trading interests at Albany—commanded by the Livingstons and Schuylers—obtained their furs through the Iroquois who dominated the country which links the Hudson River and the Great Lakes. As intermediaries between the English and the inland tribes the Iroquois were natural enemies of the French, since their trade diverted the flow of furs from Montreal to Albany. Repeated hostilities between the Iroquois and the French had not been quieted by a treaty between the two in 1666–67, and after 1680 the strife became more acute as the French began to penetrate into the Illinois country which the Iroquois considered their special domain. In peace the Five Nations could be counted upon to trade with Albany; in war they might cut France's communications with the West at the Niagara River. After 1667 both

---

[7] Harold A. Innes, *The Fur Trade in Canada* (New Haven, 1930), is a detailed, factual treatment. See pp. 1–84.

France and England claimed that the Iroquois were subjects of their respective kings. Not only did England desire to use the Iroquois as suppliers in the fur trade; they also formed a barrier against a French attack on New York via the only likely routes—from the Great Lakes by way of the Mohawk River and from Quebec by way of Lake Champlain and the Hudson.[8]

Representative of the vigor which Colbert infused into colonial affairs was the administration of his governor in Canada between 1672 and 1682—Louis de Buade, Count Frontenac. Instructed by Colbert to develop compact settlements about Quebec in order to foster agriculture, Frontenac instead succumbed to the lure of the great West and became a promoter of interior exploration second only to Champlain. A patron of fur traders rather than of missionaries, Frontenac exalted commercial profit above conversion of the Indians.[9] The French advance westward had halted after Nicolet's memorable expedition to Green Bay in 1634. Now, in 1673, Louis Joliet, a fur trader, and Father Marquette, a Jesuit missionary, resumed the old quest for an inland waterway to the South Sea. Proceeding from Green Bay by the Fox River they crossed the portage to the Wisconsin, whose waters they followed to the Mississippi and then floated down the imperial stream to the mouth of the Arkansas River. Convinced that the Mississippi did not flow into the western ocean they returned to New France, bringing reports of the unrivaled agricultural and timber resources of the great valley.[10] Among those whose imagination was fired by these reports was René Robert Cavelier, Sieur de La Salle—one of the boldest, most resolute figures in the annals of exploration. With the vision of an empire builder La Salle conceived a grand design for the colonization of the interior and the extension of French influence eastward until the English colonies might be conquered and all North America become a province of France. Accordingly, in 1674 he obtained from Louis XIV permission to explore the Mississippi to its mouth—an ambition which he finally accomplished in 1682 after two failures and indescribable hardships which he met with inflexible purpose and heroic courage.[11]

---

[8] Francis Parkman, *Frontenac and New France under Louis XIV* (Boston, 1880).

[9] Charles W. Colby, *The Fighting Governor* (*Chronicles of Canada* series, Toronto, 1915).

[10] Agnes Repplier's *Père Marquette* (Garden City, N. Y., 1929) is brilliantly written. For a more accurate and formal sketch see R. G. Thwaites, *Father Marquette* (New York, 1902). Francis B. Steck, *The Jolliet-Marquette Expedition, 1673* (Washington, 1927), is a detailed, scholarly study, for the special student.

[11] Francis Parkman, *La Salle and the Discovery of the Great West* (2d ed., Boston, 1892), presents La Salle in heroic outlines. The best modern biography of La Salle

The penetration of the French into the Illinois country south of Lake Michigan sharpened their conflict with the Iroquois, who had long regarded this region as their principal source of furs. Thither now

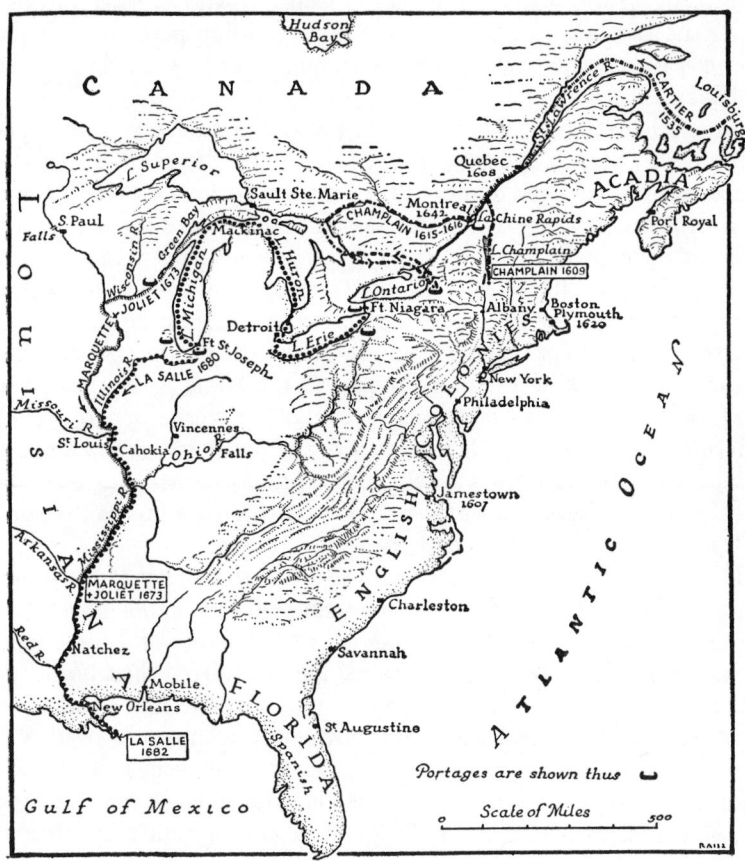

From Wertenbaker and Smith's "The United States of America." © Charles Scribner's Sons.

FRENCH EXPLORATIONS AND SETTLEMENTS

went the *coureur de bois*, the Jesuit missionary, and even the French settler, for the Illinois country—with its rich farming land and its outlet down the Mississippi—promised to realize Colbert's dream of an agricultural colony that would supply the French West Indies with lumber, livestock, and food. The threatened domination of the Illinois country by France aroused the fears of the Albany traders, vigorously

is Frances Gaither, *The Fatal River* (New York, 1931). A popular biography in the romantic vein is Leo F. Jacks, *La Salle* (New York, 1931).

supported after 1683 by Governor Dongan, who aspired to wrest the fur trade from the French. By offering protection to the Iroquois and by sending English traders into the upper Lake country, Dongan incurred the wrath of the authorities in Canada, who accused him of inciting the Iroquois and who in 1687 sent a raiding party into the land of the Senecas, thus foreshadowing an open war between New France and New York.[12]

At another strategic point—the Newfoundland fishery—the impetus given by Colbert to French expansion led to conflict with England. In every respect the Newfoundland fishery conformed to the canons of mercantilism. During the winter season vessels were fitted out in the Atlantic ports of France and in the western ports of England for voyages to Newfoundland. Well stocked with provisions and fishing supplies and manned by French or English seamen, such vessels afforded an export market for capital, labor, and domestic products. The catches of the fishing fleets were carried in part to the home ports, thus curtailing foreign imports of fish, while the remainder were shipped to Portugal, Spain, or Italy—a trade that employed a large volume of shipping, earned freights and profits for the merchants concerned, and gave both states additional exports which contributed toward a favorable balance of trade and the importation of specie.

During the seventeenth century the English fishery at Newfoundland gave rise to a bitter strife between two competing groups—the merchants of the western ports and the merchants of London. The former operated by sending annual fishing fleets from their home ports which returned at the end of the fishing season; the latter endeavored to establish at the island a colony of fishermen who would reside there the year round and exchange their fish for supplies sent from London. Because the West Country merchants had pioneered in developing the industry and because their trade centered in England they generally enjoyed the backing of the English government and held the upper hand in the fishery. However, the London merchants by 1660 had established several fishermen colonists on the southwestern coast of the island and were seriously threatening the vested interest of the West Country ports, although the influence of the latter was still so strong that England did not assist the settlers by providing them with protection or a colonial government.[13]

In 1662 France strengthened her fishery by establishing a fort and

[12] Clarence W. Alvord's *The Illinois Country, 1673–1818* (Springfield, Ill., 1920), is excellent. See chapters 1–6.

[13] Charles B. Judah, *The North American Fisheries and British Policy to 1713* (Urbana, 1933), treats a weighty subject with a light touch. See also R. G. Lounsbury, *The British Fishery at Newfoundland*, chapters 4–7.

settlement at Placentia on the southern coast of Newfoundland, then the principal scene of French activity. Due to a climate more favorable than that of the English settlement, to the subsidizing of the fishermen by the French government, to the stationing of royal troops at the fort, and to protection given by warships, the Placentia colony made material progress as a supply center for the vessels that came from France. The English fishery steadily lost ground to its more efficient rival until by 1689 the French were far in the lead. Meanwhile the English West Country merchants, still bitterly hostile to the English colony, minimized the danger from the French and opposed any measures which would transfer the seat of the fishery from England to the island. In this course they had the support of Charles II and James II, whose pro-French sympathies dictated a policy of inaction. However, the underlying causes of friction remained and were accentuated when William III became king in 1689.

New England also felt the threat implicit in the advance of France. Laying claim to all North America the French had more or less open designs of conquering the Puritan colonies, while the growth of the French fishery at Newfoundland menaced the most important industry of New England. The French settlers of Acadia and the English in Maine struggled for control of the furs, fishery, and timber resources of that region. Here the French, exercising great influence over the Indians (the Abenaki), supplied them with firearms and incited them to resist the encroachments of New England. As long as France retained Acadia and Canada she could use her colonial ports as bases for dispatching vessels to prey upon the commerce and fishery of Massachusetts—perhaps the most menacing threat to New England's security. Should France succeed in conquering New York the Puritan colonies would be isolated and encircled by their foes; hence New England's interest in the defense of Albany equaled that of New York. And when Louis XIV after 1680 enforced a policy of severe persecution of the French Calvinists the determination of the Puritans to resist conquest by their Catholic foes was stirred to a fever heat.[14]

Due to the pro-French policies of Charles II and James II the colonial rivalry in North America was held in abeyance until the English Revolution of 1688. The accession of William III, however, plunged England into a European war that had broken out in 1688. Still intent upon conquering the Spanish Netherlands, Louis XIV had provoked William of Orange to form an alliance with Spain, Austria, and many German states to resist the aggression of France, and the

---

[14] J. T. Adams's vigorously written *Revolutionary New England, 1691–1776* (Boston, 1923) stresses social and economic forces. See chapters 4–5.

primary object of the Dutch Stadtholder in accepting the English crown was to bring England into the war. Thoroughly dissatisfied with the policy of James II which subordinated their commercial ambitions to France the English merchants rallied around William III and accordingly his accession gave the signal for an English offensive against France in those colonial spheres where conflict between the two powers was reaching a critical stage.[15]

King William's War in America was opened with a grand project of Louis XIV for the conquest of New York. In 1689 Count Frontenac was sent back to Canada as governor with instructions to invade New York in conjunction with a naval force that was to sail to Manhattan from France; after the conquest the non-Catholic English settlers in New York were to be expelled. Arriving at Quebec, Frontenac found Canada in a demoralized state due to Iroquois raids, and accordingly he abandoned the design of conquest in favor of counterattacks on the English frontiers. In the winter of 1689–90 he dispatched three expeditions—one of which fell upon a settlement, Salmon Falls, on the Maine-New Hampshire boundary. A second force took possession of the English post, Fort Loyal, where Portland now stands, while the third in February 1690 destroyed the town of Schenectady, thirteen miles west of Albany. In the meantime the English colonists had failed to carry out their plans for a conquest of New France. The collapse of the Dominion of New England destroyed the political unity of the Puritan colonies, while New York was torn by Leisler's Revolt. Frontenac's raids, however, prompted Massachusetts, Plymouth, and Connecticut to send commissioners to New York where, under the leadership of Leisler, plans were made in May 1690 for the conquest of Canada. An expedition of New York and New England troops, supported by a large band of Iroquois, was to advance from Albany by way of Lake Champlain and join at Quebec a naval force to be dispatched by Massachusetts to the St. Lawrence.[16]

In May 1690 the New Englanders won an encouraging victory when a force from Boston commanded by Sir William Phips occupied Port Royal in Acadia and then returned to Boston, amply rewarded with spoils of war. The larger plan of conquest, however, failed. The expedition which set out from Albany—weakened at the start by a disappointing response from the Iroquois—proceeded only to the foot of Lake Champlain and there abandoned the campaign. In the summer of

---

[15] G. N. Clark's *The Dutch Alliance and the War against French Trade* (Manchester, 1923) emphasizes the influence of William III in Anglo-French relations.

[16] See again H. L. Osgood, *American Colonies in the Eighteenth Century*, Vol. I, pp. 42–183, 399–522.

1690 Phips sailed from Boston with two thousand troops and arrived at Quebec, only to procrastinate, to launch a feeble attack, and then to retire when victory was within easy reach. These maneuvers decided the outcome of the war. Neither France nor England contributed much to the American campaigns and the hostile colonies were not yet strong enough for one to overcome the other. The treaty of peace concluded at Ryswick in 1697 provided for a return to the *status quo ante bellum*.[17]

QUEEN ANNE'S WAR

A brief interval of peace after 1697 proved to be merely a prelude to the decisive War of the Spanish Succession, precipitated in 1701 by Louis XIV. In November 1700 the King of Spain, Charles II, died, leaving a will which named as heir to the Spanish throne and its vast possessions the grandson of Louis XIV, Philip of Anjou. Hastily accepting this inheritance for his grandson, Louis established him at Madrid as King Philip V of Spain—a move which meant the domination of the Spanish Netherlands and the Spanish colonies by France. What Louis XIV had failed to accomplish by arms seemed at last within his reach by diplomatic means. William III, still defender of Holland and guardian of England's commercial interests, again assumed command of the anti-French forces and organized another Grand Alliance whose armies took the field in 1702. Refusing to accept Philip V as King of Spain, England recognized the rival claims of an Austrian candidate, the Archduke Charles, and endeavored to place him upon the Spanish throne. Thus during the War of the Spanish Succession (Queen Anne's War in America) Spain was united with France, whereas during King William's War Spain had been a partner in the alliance against Louis XIV. This difference explains a great change that occurred on the colonial stage of the conflict—the extension of the war to the Carolina frontier and to the vast area of the Spanish colonies in America.[18]

Of all the causes of strife between England and France none had greater weight than their rivalry for the trade of the Spanish colonies. The commercial and industrial decline of Spain after 1650 gave to England, France, and Holland a tempting opportunity to divert the major part of the wealth of the Spanish Indies to their respective shores. In every respect the commerce of Spanish America realized the aims of mercantilism. First, it enabled the commercial states to increase their exports of domestic manufactures—either directly to the Spanish

[17] See again J. Winsor, *Cartier to Frontenac*, chapters 9–16.
[18] G. M. Wrong, *The Conquest of New France* (*Chronicles of America*, New Haven, 1918), chapters 1–3.

colonies or to Africa, where they were exchanged for slaves. These in turn were sold to the Spanish planters in the Americas and the West Indies—a trade which netted both silver and gold, thus supplying the European powers with the coveted precious metals. Silver played a vital part in the East India trade: an indispensable export from Europe, it enabled the European traders to purchase those oriental goods which yielded such remarkable profits when reëxported to foreign states and to America. Thus the African, Spanish American, and Far Eastern trades became inseparably united and together they afforded the finest profit opportunities of the age. They employed a vast amount of shipping, enriched the merchants with freights, profits, and interest, provided markets for surplus manufactures and afforded Europe her principal supply of silver—then esteemed more precious than gold. Here certainly was a prize worth fighting for to the end.[19]

England reasserted her ancient interest in this vital trade when Charles II in 1660 incorporated a group of merchants as the Royal African Company and by later charters of 1663 and 1672 gave it the exclusive right to carry slaves from Africa to the English colonies and the exclusive right to hold land in Africa from Morocco to the Cape of Good Hope. The company established forts and trading posts in the Gambia River region and on the Gold Coast, successfully waged war against a rival Dutch company, and profited immensely from the sale of slaves to English planters in the West Indies. Then, after 1680, the company devoted itself primarily to trade with the Spanish colonists. Spain did not engage in the slave traffic but rather sold to assientists or private contractors the exclusive right to supply her colonies with slaves (the assiento). Such contractors customarily purchased Negroes at the West Indies from the great slave trading interests of Europe. Due to war in Africa between France and the Dutch the English company gained a favored position with the assientists, who came to Jamaica to buy Negroes or arranged to have the company deliver slaves to Spanish colonial ports—Cartagena, Havana, and Porto Bello.[20]

The growth of this traffic benefited England in another way: it enabled her merchants to smuggle English merchandise into the Spanish colonies in the slave ships that sailed from Jamaica. Since Spain still required that European goods should go to her colonies by way of

[19] Alfred T. Mahan's *The Influence of Sea Power upon History, 1660–1788* (New York, 1890) discusses international conflicts, considering all important factors and assigning the decisive role to sea power. Mahan wrote so persuasively of this "lesson of history" as to stimulate international competition for naval supremacy. See chapters 1–5.

[20] G. F. Zook, "The Company of Adventurers Trading into Africa, 1660–1672," *Journal of Negro History*, IV (April 1919).

Seville, the English at Jamaica, by shipping directly to the colonists, could undersell the highly taxed goods that arrived over the round-about route from Spain. Two governors of Jamaica in the 1680's, who were virtually agents of the Royal African Company, promoted the traffic so effectively that England secured the lion's share of the assiento business. Again, in 1694, when a Portuguese company obtained the assiento, the English arranged to supply it with slaves at Jamaica. In the meantime the Royal African Company had been neglecting to provide the English planters with slaves—a circumstance which encouraged private traders or interlopers to break in upon its monopoly. So great was the value to England of the traffic with Spanish America—now yielding large quantities of silver annually—and so urgent was the need of supplying the English colonists with slaves that Parliament in 1698 opened the trade to the interlopers on condition that they pay—toward the maintenance of the company's forts—a tax of 10 per cent of the value of the merchandise they imported into Africa.[21]

In 1701 France endeavored to break the grip of England on the Spanish American trade. Since the days of Colbert various French companies had been developing a slave traffic with the French West Indies but as yet France had not profited greatly from the Spanish trade—largely because she was periodically at war with Spain. The tactics of France in the Caribbean had been to plunder Spanish settlements and ships. However, the chief French agent in the West Indies, M. Du Casse, became convinced that France had more to gain from regular commerce with the Spanish colonies than from privateering depredations. Accordingly, he urged that Louis XIV secure the assiento for France. Undoubtedly the latter accepted the Spanish crown for his grandson largely because France might thereby dominate the trade of the Spanish Indies. One of the first acts of Philip V was to confer upon the French Guinea Company a ten-year monopoly of the slave traffic of Spanish America, as well as certain other privileges which promised France a large share of the trade in general merchandise. Perceiving that these concessions would deprive them of all the gains they had made in the Spanish empire the English merchants became vigorous supporters of the war.[22]

"Should the French settle at the disemboguing of the river Mississippi," wrote an English publicist about 1700, "they would not be long before they made themselves masters of that rich province, which would be an addition to their strength very terrible to Europe." The

---

[21] G. Scelle, "The Slave Trade in the Spanish Colonies of America: the Assiento," *American Journal of International Law*, IV.

[22] See again C. P. Nettels, *Money Supply of the American Colonies*, chapter 1.

idea thus expressed by Davenant was not merely a fantasy: as early as 1684 La Salle had given his life in a fruitless, tragic effort to establish a French colony at the mouth of the Mississippi. He had visualized an inland empire that would divert to France the great southern trade in furs and deerskins, then exploited by the merchants of Virginia and South Carolina, and would perhaps enable the French to descend upon the kingdom of New Spain and possess themselves of its silver mines. La Salle's hopes were realized in part when in 1699 one Pierre Le Moyne d'Iberville founded a settlement at Biloxi near the mouth of the Mississippi—a move which forestalled the English, at that very time on the point of sending thither a colonizing expedition. Although the new French province of Louisiana made only slow and painful progress, it served as a base from which French *voyageurs* penetrated into the southwestern area previously dominated by English fur traders. And Louisiana not only threatened the English trade on the southern frontier; it also strengthened the Spaniards in Florida in opposition to their neighbors in South Carolina. The union of France and Spain in Europe thus united their colonies in the remote American wilderness against the common English foe.[23]

The events of King William's War greatly altered the situation on the New York frontier. The raiding parties which Frontenac sent against the Iroquois had wrought widespread destruction and had given them, for the first time, a wholesome respect for France and a lively dread of French arms. Feeling that they had been let down by the English during the war, the Five Nations abandoned the strong pro-English stand they had previously maintained and turned a friendly ear toward Canada, realizing now that war carried a greater threat to their security than did French competition in trade. They divided into pro-French and pro-English factions, received French agents into their villages, began to trade with Montreal, and in 1701 made a peace with Canada that implied a recognition of their subjection to the French king. Thus they adopted what later writers interpreted as a policy of maintaining a balance of power between France and England on the northwestern frontier.

Meanwhile the French were not idle. With the increasing importance of the Mississippi valley, the route to which traversed the Iroquois country, the French perceived the advantage of placating the Five Nations and accordingly sought to secure their good will or at least their neutrality as a condition to the peaceful development of New France. Recognizing the right of the Iroquois to trade with

[23] J. H. Schlarman, *From Quebec to New Orleans* (Belleville, Ill., 1929), is a scholarly study of the French in America. See pp. 15–125.

Albany, although hoping to divert as much of their traffic to Montreal as possible, the French made the peace of 1701, and at the outbreak of Queen Anne's War Louis XIV instructed his officials in Canada not to attack the Iroquois. The latter—determined not to become solely dependent upon the French—agreed that they would remain neutral "on condition that Albany be spared from attack." The new Iroquoian policy of cultivating both sides was extended by an agreement of 1701 in which the Five Nations ceded to the King of England their hunting lands on either side of the Great Lakes.[24]

The lesson of King William's War had not been lost to the Albany traders; they too perceived that France and England were as yet so evenly matched in North America that warfare meant, not a decisive gain for either party, but a virtual destruction of the fur trade—which, during the years 1690–96, had shrunk to trifling proportions. Preferring an understanding with France to the former state of war, fear, and alarms, an important faction of the Albany traders strove to enforce a policy of neutrality and peace. The then governor of New York, Lord Bellomont, favored aggressive measures, chiefly the establishment of English forts and trading posts on the Lakes—a program which would have aroused the French and angered the Iroquois by threatening to deprive them of their status of middlemen between Albany and the West. For these reasons many Albany traders opposed and defeated Bellomont's plans. Meanwhile Albany was developing a traffic with Montreal whereby the French were supplied with cheap English goods for the Indian trade. A delegation of Albany traders visited Montreal in the spring of 1701 and returned with a project for neutrality which they submitted to the council of New York. By virtue of these factors New York and Canada remained at peace during the first half of Queen Anne's War. Between 1702 and 1706 New York spent only trifling sums for frontier defense. On the other hand, New England became at once involved in the renewed hostilities, since the causes of her antagonism toward New France had not been removed; and consequently she had to bear alone the brunt of the early war in the North.[25]

Despite much talk about the conquest of Boston, the French focused their military efforts upon the New England frontier, where their influence among the Indians was paramount—a legacy, in part, of King Philip's War. Raiding parties sent out by the governor of Canada, the

---

[24] Francis Parkman, *A Half-Century of Conflict* (2 vols., Boston, 1892), Vol. I, chapters 1–8.

[25] See again L. P. Kellogg, *The French Regime in Wisconsin and the Northwest*, chapters 9–13.

Marquis de Vaudreuil, harassed exposed settlements from Wells on the Maine coast to Northampton in Massachusetts. Particularly savage was the massacre at Deerfield, where in 1704 the French and Indians launched a surprise attack upon the sleeping villagers, killed fifty-three, and took a hundred and eleven captives, seventeen of whom perished on the subsequent march to Canada. Such raids provoked reproaches in New England against New York, for Albany was prospering by the sale of firearms to the Indians who spread havoc on the eastern frontier. Looking to the conquest of Canada as their only salvation, the New Englanders in 1708 asked Britain to take decisive steps to bring that to pass.[26]

Their chief spokesman was one Samuel Vetch, a Scottish merchant, soldier of fortune, and friend of Joseph Dudley, governor of Massachusetts. Interested in acquiring Canada or Acadia as a region for Scottish colonization, Vetch wrote a tract, *Canada Surveyed,* which convinced the British colonial officials of the necessity of the conquest. Lord Bellomont's earlier policy of aggression had reflected the views of the king's advisers, but England had been unable to act prior to 1708 because of the European war. Successes on the Continent, however, now enabled her to promise aid for a colonial assault upon Canada and accordingly it was arranged that a land expedition should proceed from Albany to the St. Lawrence and that a naval force should sail from Boston to Quebec. The land force was barely under way when news that Britain had not contributed her part to the naval force caused the expedition to disband. New York at this time was participating vigorously in the war, since Britain's offers of aid promised results which the province could not hope to accomplish alone.

After the fiasco of 1709 a congress of colonial governors resolved in favor of the conquest, and Peter Schuyler, now chief director of affairs at Albany, carried their petition to England, taking with him four Iroquois warriors as a means of attracting attention at court.[27] Then, in 1710, a British and colonial force commanded by Francis Nicholson sailed from Boston and conquered Port Royal, Acadia—not a particularly glorious victory, however, since the British outnumbered the Acadians eight to one. Port Royal being the only Acadian settlement of consequence, its seizure meant the conquest of the whole province, and this time Britain did not restore it to France.

[26] Samuel A. Drake, *The Border Wars of New England* (New York, 1897) is a thorough, compact, readable narrative, 1689–1711.

[27] W. T. Morgan, "The Five Nations and Queen Anne," *Mississippi Valley Historical Review,* XIII (Sept. 1926).

The climax or anticlimax of the war came in 1711, when another land force of Iroquois and colonials advanced to Lake Champlain and a grand fleet of seventy-one vessels and twelve thousand men left Boston for Quebec. Commanded by Sir Hovenden Walker, this fleet encountered fog and storms in the St. Lawrence, lost ten ships and nine hundred men, and returned to Boston without striking a blow—an unwarranted retreat, since even after the wreck Walker and his fellow commander, John Hill, an incompetent political appointee, still had enough men for the conquest of all Canada. New York and the Iroquois now sought refuge in their earlier policy of neutrality and the conflict in the North ended in 1713 without other noteworthy events.

In the South the war began in earnest when the Spaniards, early in 1702, launched a land attack from Florida on South Carolina. Warned by friendly Indians (the Creeks), the English managed to raise a defensive force and to drive back the Spaniards and their Indian allies. South Carolina now took the offensive in the autumn of 1702 by dispatching a band of militia and Indians in a small fleet to St. Augustine. Although successful in destroying that ancient Spanish town the English invaders failed to take the fort and were obliged to retreat when two enemy warships appeared. The French and Spaniards retaliated in 1706 by sending a fleet from Havana against Charleston, but the South Carolina farmers rallied to the defense of their port town, routed a part of the enemy force that had landed, and compelled the French commander to beat a hasty retreat. These expeditions demonstrated that the two contestants on the southern frontier were too evenly matched for either to win a campaign for conquest, although the inconclusive engagements indicated that the South Carolinians had a slight advantage over Spaniards and their French and Indian allies.

In the Caribbean, the principal theater of the war in America, the conflict resolved itself into attacks by the European powers upon the commerce and colonies of their foes. The trade between Europe and Spanish America fell largely into the hands of the French—a condition which England met by sending privateers and warships to seize French and Spanish merchantmen, by allowing English traders to carry on an open trade with friendly Spanish colonists, and by conducting a campaign of propaganda among the settlers with the aim of inducing them to reject the authority of Philip V and to recognize the Archduke Charles as King of Spain. While not successful in breaking the power of France and Spain in the Caribbean, England managed to protect her own island colonies, to capture a large number of French and Spanish ships, and to retain and strengthen her grip upon the trade by which her merchants at Jamaica obtained Spanish silver in payment for English goods and slaves—a trade which now supplied England annually with money and bullion worth £200,000.[28]

By the Peace of Utrecht (1713) France ceded to Britain the Hudson Bay region and Acadia, excepting Cape Breton Island, and acknowledged the suzerainty of Britain over the Iroquois. Britain also obtained complete title to Newfoundland and its adjacent islands, although the French received the privilege of drying fish on the western and northern shores between Cape Bonavista and Cape Riche. In return for recognizing Philip V as King of Spain Britain received a thirty-year monopoly of the slave trade of the Spanish Indies. This monopoly conferred the privilege of selling 4,800 slaves a year to the Spanish colonies and of importing directly into Britain (in British vessels) the money, bullion, and produce taken in payment for the slaves. The British assientists were permitted to send once a year a licensed vessel privileged to sell a large cargo of general merchandise to the Spanish colonists at Porto Bello. Britain granted the assiento to the famous South Sea Company, organized in 1711 as a means of establishing Britain in the trade of the Pacific. After 1713 the South Sea Company concentrated upon the trade in general merchandise and used the licensed vessel, permanently stationed off Porto Bello, as a floating warehouse from which British goods were constantly carried to the Spanish colonists. By and large the Peace of Utrecht favored Britain although in two places—Canada and Louisiana—the power of France was not seriously curtailed.

IMPERIAL POLICIES, 1689–1713

As the political victory of the English merchant-capitalists in 1689 led to war against their most potent foreign enemy, France, so also it resulted in the tightening of the imperial system, with the object of restraining their other rivals, the merchants of Scotland and of the colonies. One phase of the colonial policy of William III was a campaign to render the colonial governments more dependent upon England, primarily in order to assure a more stringent enforcement of the Navigation Acts. Thus the Massachusetts charter issued in 1691 provided that the governor of that province be appointed by the king and empowered to reject the nominees to the council who were proposed by a joint assembly of deputies and the existing councillors. Massachusetts, Plymouth, and Maine were now united and since the governor of Massachusetts was also appointed governor of New Hampshire

[28] G. N. Clark, "War Trade and Trade War, 1701–1713," *Economic History Review*, I (Jan. 1928).

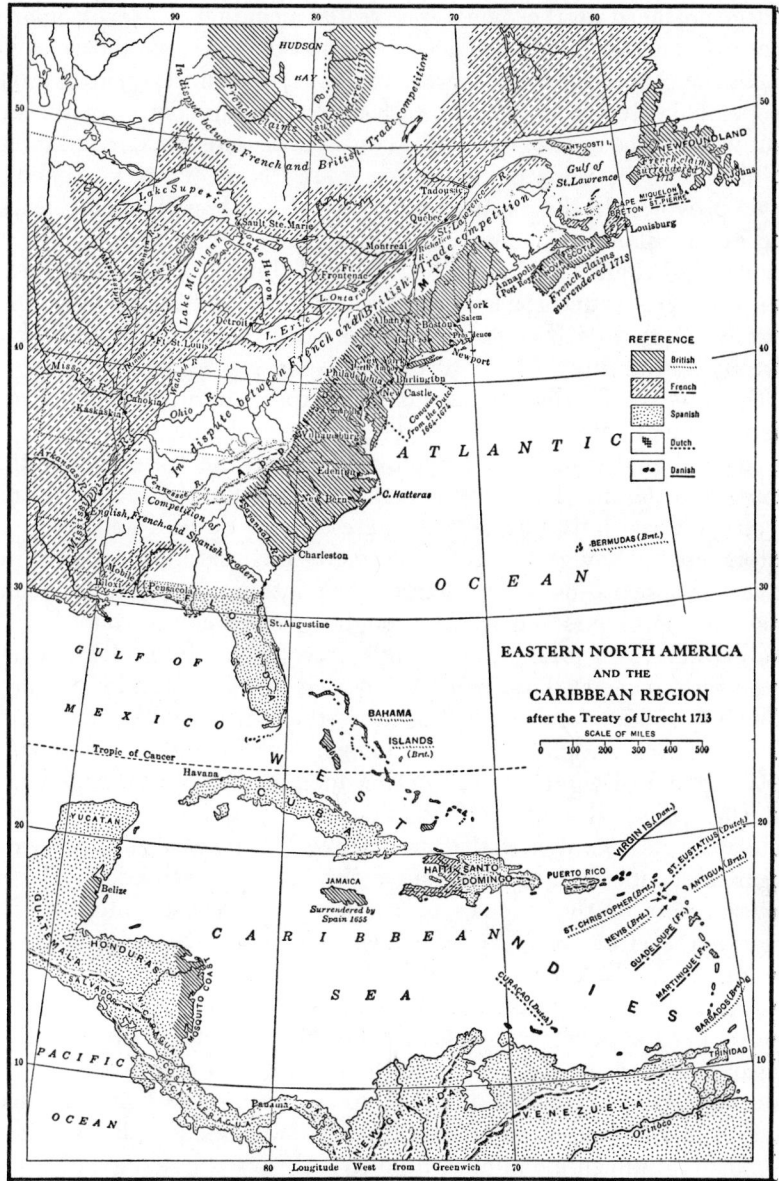

REFERENCE

British
French
Spanish
Dutch
Danish

EASTERN NORTH AMERICA
AND THE
CARIBBEAN REGION
after the Treaty of Utrecht 1713

SCALE OF MILES
0   100   200   300   400   500

From Greene's "The Foundations of American Nationality." © American Book Company.

a large northern royal province was created including all New England except Connecticut and Rhode Island. So also the Crown took into its hands the government of Maryland in 1691, of Pennsylvania in 1693, and of New Jersey in 1702, in each case assuming control of the executive agencies of the province. Penn's political rights were restored to him in 1694, Lord Baltimore's in 1716; New Jersey remained a royal province. In the meantime, English officialdom labored to bring the other colonies (Connecticut, Rhode Island, and the Carolinas) under royal control, and opposed the establishment of new colonies in which governors and councillors were not appointed by the king. Additional rights of self-government were not to be granted, and those already conferred were to be curtailed as soon as possible.[29]

By 1695 the English merchants had become dissatisfied with England's regulation of the colonies. The Lords of Trade, then in charge of colonial affairs, were nobles who represented the aristocracy or the court; and the merchants felt that the colonial administration was indifferent toward the mercantile interests, and careless and inert in enforcing the Navigation Acts. The merchants therefore prepared to have Parliament—now the organ of their interests—assume the management of colonies and trade through a parliamentary council. But William III, ever jealous of his kingly prerogatives, forestalled Parliament's action and at the same time appeased the merchants by creating, May 15, 1696, a new colonial agency—the Lords Commissioners of Trade and Plantations, commonly known as the Board of Trade.

Composed of eight active, working members who represented the merchant class (although high dignitaries of state were nominal members and occasionally attended its meetings) the Board of Trade immediately undertook to subordinate the economic activities and the governments of the colonies to England's mercantile interests. Its creation therefore recognized the power of the merchants in the councils of state. While not empowered to make and enforce decisions it was authorized to investigate all matters pertaining to colonies and trade and to prepare recommendations to Parliament and the executive departments of the Crown. Since the members of the Board served continuously and labored diligently they became the best informed officials in England on colonies and trade and consequently exerted a dominating influence on imperial policy. Always upholding and advocating the principles of mercantilism, the Board made recommendations which were generally given legal force through orders in council or acts of Parliament, and although many such orders were not strictly en-

[29] George H. Guttridge, *The Colonial Policy of William III* (Cambridge, 1922), is a good brief survey.

forced and although many of the policies urged by the Board were not adopted, even so, few actions were undertaken, few measures were approved in the commercial-colonial sphere unless they had first been sanctioned by the Board of Trade.[30]

The English merchants obtained further support in 1696 when Parliament passed a supplementary Navigation Act to strengthen the existing colonial system. In the future all colonial governors (whether elected as in Rhode Island or appointed by proprietors as in Carolina) were to serve only when approved by the king and were required to take an oath to enforce the Navigation Acts under pain of dismissal if they did not. Merchants who reëxported from a colonial port any of the enumerated articles which had been brought from another colony were now required to give bond to assure that such articles would not be carried to foreign ports. Should such bonds prove to be forged or fraudulent a fine of £500 awaited the offender. English customs agents in the colonies received the rights of search possessed by similar officials in England and owners of ocean-going and coastwise vessels engaged in colonial trade were required to register them at London.

The Navigation Act of 1696 did not extend the basic principles of the colonial system; it merely provided for a more efficient administration of existing laws. Of similar effect was the establishment of admiralty courts for the trial and punishment of violators of the acts. Prior to 1697 persons accused of such violations were generally tried in the regular courts of the colonies—a practice upon which English official-dom looked with disfavor: first, because the judges were colonists who tended to deal leniently with colonial merchants; secondly, because such courts granted jury trials, with the result that juries were partial to their accused neighbors. It is not surprising therefore that the colonial courts rarely gave judgments in favor of the English merchants at the expense of colonial merchants or that English agents like Edward Randolph found the judicial cards in the colonies stacked against England.[31]

In 1697 the Privy Council authorized the colonial governors to erect vice-admiralty courts and to appoint the necessary judges, advocates, registrars, and marshals. Eventually, twelve such courts were established in the colonies—all subject to a ruling of the king's Attorney-General in 1702 which forbade them to allow the accused a trial by jury. Presumably these measures should have given England complete

---

[30] One of the best studies of British policy and administration is W. T. Root, *The Relations of Pennsylvania with the British Government* (New York, 1912).

[31] Helen J. Crump, *Colonial Admiralty Jurisdiction* (London, 1931), is the best study (technical).

judicial power over violators of the Navigation Acts, but one question remained: how far did the jurisdiction of the admiralty courts extend? The English navy was too small to make numerous captures on the high seas of vessels engaged in illegal trade; consequently English agents commonly made such seizures in colonial ports and waters. The colonial courts claimed jurisdiction in the ensuing cases and fought stubbornly to remove them from the admiralty courts. To this end the colonial courts reversed decisions rendered by the admiralty judges and freed from prison the traders whom the latter had sentenced. This intensely bitter struggle for control of the means of enforcing the Navigation Acts continued until the Revolutionary War.

By 1690 illegal trade had assumed the virulent form of piracy. Since the time of Drake and the Elizabethan sea dogs pirates had been wont to prey upon the commerce of rival nations in distant waters, even in time of peace. When open war broke out such marauders were commissioned as privateers in the king's service, but after the end of formal hostilities they were prone to resume their old piratical ways.[32] A revival of English privateering and piracy swept over the Caribbean region after Cromwell's expedition against the Spanish Indies in 1654–55. Jamaica now became the center of operations and the treasure of the Spanish colonies the principal source of ill-gotten wealth. Since gold and silver could be disposed of at any place (and no questions asked) the pirates were always on the lookout for ships bearing treasure. Although the English government prior to 1665 had done little to suppress piracy in the Caribbean a new trend of policy appeared afterward as the result of two treaties with Spain in 1667 and 1670 which recognized England's claims to the colonies she actually possessed in the West Indies. Then occurred the growth of the legal slave trade between Jamaica and the Spanish colonies—a traffic which promised greater profits to English merchants than the old game of piracy. Because the outlaws preyed upon friendly Spanish vessels trading with Jamaica, and therefore retarded the growth of peaceful commerce, England undertook to suppress piracy in the Caribbean. Warships were provided to convoy vessels in the Jamaica trade, privateers were ordered not to molest friendly Spaniards, and pirates were offered pardons on condition that they surrender and forsake their evil ways. Due to these measures English piracy and privateering in the Caribbean declined rapidly after 1680.[33]

[32] Violet Barbour, "Privateers and Pirates of the West Indies," *American Historical Review*, XVI (April 1911).

[33] C. H. Haring, *The Buccaneers in the West Indies* (New York, 1910), is an authentic, well-written narrative.

But it soon broke out in a new quarter—in the Red Sea and Indian Ocean, where the pirates now fell upon English vessels carrying silver to the Orient or returning with valuable cargoes of East Indian goods. Many merchants of Massachusetts, New York, South Carolina, and Pennsylvania became involved in this traffic. Some of them actually financed the pirates and shared the plunder; some supplied them with provisions in return for money and East Indian goods; while others carried on a regular trade with Madagascar, which was the base of the pirates' operations for the Red Sea. Colonial officials—particularly Governor Benjamin Fletcher and Councillor Nicholas Bayard of New York and Governor William Markham of Pennsylvania—were accused of selling protection to pirates who sought refuge in American ports, while shopkeepers and the people generally were receptive to the ill-gotten wealth which was liberally spent in shops and taverns or used to refit marauding vessels for new exploits. Such gains of the colonists, however, were destructive of the coveted India trade and consequently England extended her campaign against piracy to the Red Sea.

The foremost enemy of the pirates in North America was the Earl of Bellomont, governor of New England and New York between 1697 and 1701, one of the most energetic, efficient, and industrious of England's colonial administrators—a governor who attempted to subordinate all groups in the colonies to England's mercantile interests. Bringing emphatic instructions for the suppression of piracy and illegal trade, Bellomont made New York the principal target of his attack. He endeavored to prevent pirate ships from landing, instituted searches for money and goods already brought in, insisted that departing vessels should give bond as an assurance against piracy, and removed from the council five of its members who were charged with illegal trade. So effective were his efforts that his enemies complained he had kept £100,000 out of the province in less than a year.[34]

Before leaving England Bellomont joined with other great men to finance an expedition for the suppression of piracy in the Red Sea—a venture that was expected to yield profits through the recovery of spoil. In command was one Captain William Kidd, who proceeded from New York to Madagascar, only to find that the pirates there had made themselves scarce. Apparently Kidd's crew grew restive when no pirates' plunder came their way and thereupon took to piracy on their own account. Whether they forced Kidd into submission or whether he joined willingly remains a mystery. At any rate they captured some

[34] John Masefield, *On the Spanish Main* (New York, 1906), relates pirate exploits with the art of a great writer. See chapters 8–15.

vessels in the India trade and eventually put into port at Boston, where Kidd was arrested on Bellomont's order and later sent to England for trial. Convicted of both murder and piracy Captain Kidd paid for his conduct on the gallows—an execution that may be regarded as the climax of England's war against piracy.

In 1700 Parliament provided legal machinery for the trial of pirates in the colonies by authorizing the king to erect special courts consisting of governors, councillors, admiralty judges, captains of naval vessels, and customs agents. Although distinct from the admiralty courts these special tribunals functioned in the same manner—without jury trial— and were empowered to sentence convicted pirates to death. After the outbreak of Queen Anne's War the pirates once more found a legal course open to them as privateers; their enlistment under one of the flags of the belligerent powers transformed them into allies or enemies at war, and measures taken by England against enemy privateers, together with the campaign against ordinary pirates, removed the old evil from the mainland colonies.[35]

In extenuation of piracy William Penn once said that all the money which they brought into Pennsylvania was remitted to England in the course of trade—a reference to the difficulty with which the northern colonies had long grappled in seeking to find means of payment for their imports of English goods. Without doubt the money derived from piracy had afforded the colonies a large fund of returns during the years 1680–1700; hence its suppression promised to curtail colonial buying power and thus to diminish the market value to England of New England, Pennsylvania, and New York. Due to the population growth of the northern colonies they had been rapidly extending their purchases of English goods and were becoming more and more valuable as markets—thus realizing one objective of English mercantilism. And yet the native products of the northern colonies could not, for the most part, be sold in England, with the result that the colonists had been forced to engage in various pursuits like piracy and illegal trade in order to obtain the necessary means of payment.

In the fields of general commerce the northern merchants had developed their trades with Newfoundland, southern Europe, the Wine Islands, and the West Indies in order to obtain remittances for English imports—coin, bills of exchange, and foreign commodities that could be traded in England for English goods. In many respects, however,

---

[35] C. N. Dalton seeks to rehabilitate Kidd in *The Real Captain Kidd* (New York, 1911). Harold T. Wilkins, *Captain Kidd* (London, 1935), is mainly a selection of source quotations.

these trades were detrimental to England. They built up a class of colonial merchants who competed effectively with the merchants of England for the freights and profits of American commerce and gave to the colonists a variety of trading contacts which enabled them easily to violate the Navigation Acts. To Portugal New Hampshire sold ship timber needed by the royal navy; to Newfoundland the Boston merchants sold rum which induced drunkenness among the resident fishermen and weakened the English fishery there; from the Dutch in the West Indies the Northerners bought European goods which were smuggled into the English colonies; and at Newfoundland colonial ship captains enticed sailors away from English vessels, thus building up the colonial merchant marine at the expense of English shipping.[36]

The suppression of piracy and the closer regulation of colonial trade promised to benefit English merchants but in the process the colonists might lose a large part of their remittances to England and that in turn would curtail their value as markets. Moreover, the colonial demand for manufactures was so great that if the colonists could not buy them in England they would be forced to produce them at home. The progress of manufacturing industries in the northern colonies would inevitably yield a surplus of articles above the needs of local consumption with the result that the Northerners, sooner or later, would export that surplus to the tobacco colonies and the West Indies. England therefore would lose not only the markets of the northern colonies but also those of the plantation area. Such a loss would mean that colonial merchants would gain control of the marketing of southern produce, since they would receive it in exchange for colonial manufactures. Hence the progress of manufacturing industry in the northern colonies threatened to break the grip of English merchant capitalism on Americant trade.

In 1699 the manufacture of woolens, still the mainstay of English industry and object of the tender solicitude of the government, was in a declining state, because—as Parliament asserted—"great quantities of . . . manufactures . . . have of late been made and are daily increasing in the kingdom of Ireland and in the English plantations in America which will inevitably sink the value of the lands and tend to the ruin of the trade and woolen manufactures of this realm." Undoubtedly the cloth industry had made great progress in New England and Long Island, where the people were fabricating their own woolen goods and rapidly improving the quality of their products. In order to

[36] C. P. Nettels, "The Menace of Colonial Manufacturing," *New England Quarterly*, IV (April 1931).

check this trend Parliament inserted a clause in the Woolen Act of 1699 which prohibited the exportation of wool or woolen cloth of American production from any colony, thus permitting household manufacturing but thwarting the growth of the woolen industry on a commercial scale.[37]

England's campaign against piracy and illegal trade, by diminishing colonial remittances for English goods, tended to foster colonial manufactures. These in turn were proscribed by the Woolen Act of 1699. Yet the crucial problem of the trade of the northern colonies remained unsolved, since they could not long be restrained both from obtaining buying power in England and from manufacturing for themselves; something had to be done to supply them with the means of paying for English goods. In this connection the Board of Trade—which strongly advocated the enforcement of the Navigation Acts and the suppression of colonial manufactures—undertook to develop in the northern area staple commodities, similar to tobacco and sugar, which could be exchanged in England for manufactured wares.

The timber resources of New England and New York, the needs of English shipping for naval stores, and the fact that England had been buying such stores from northern Europe, paying for them presumably with specie rather than with her manufactures, formed the basis of the plan proposed by the Board of Trade to solve the problem of colonial returns. After an extended survey made by the Board of the productive capacity of the New England forests, Parliament in 1705 passed an act to encourage the naval stores industry in the northern colonies. Three things about this act deserve notice. First, it granted substantial bounties for pitch, resin, tar, turpentine, ship timber, masts, and hemp which were produced in the colonies and imported into England. Secondly, it placed these products on the enumerated article list, thereby assuring that they would be sold exclusively in England as a means of paying for English exports to the northern colonies. Thirdly, the act provided that pine trees in the forests of New England, New Jersey, and New York should be reserved for the production of naval stores—not used for ordinary lumber. Behind this act lay the assumption that the northern colonies would produce all the stores required by English shipping, yield a surplus which could be reëxported to Europe, provide the colonies with purchasing power for English goods, divert them from competing manufacturing industries, and center their trade in Eng-

---

[37] Robert G. Albion's *Forests and Sea Power* (Cambridge, 1926), an admirable study, discusses the English background of the colonial naval stores industry. See chapters 3–6.

land, thereby lessening their dependence on piracy, illegal trade, and other branches of commerce which had proved detrimental to the English merchants.[38]

Immediately after the passage of the act of 1705 the Board of Trade sent one John Bridger to New England to instruct the inhabitants in the art of producing naval stores and to preserve the most suitable trees in the northern woods from destruction by the colonial lumbermen. Primarily an agent of the English merchants trading to the colonies, Bridger labored with all diligence at his task, only to encounter heated opposition from the lumbermen of New Hampshire, who, he said, threatened to shoot him "if they ketch me in the woods." As long as New Englanders served as colonial officials, he concluded, "the king must not expect any justice as to the woods, for all the people on the frontiers depend on the woods for their livelihood and say the king has no woods . . . and [that] they will cut what and where they please."

Another effort made by England in behalf of colonial naval stores centered in New York, whither the Board of Trade in 1710 sent a company of three thousand refugees from Germany to establish the industry. Parliament voted £10,000 for their support, and they were placed in charge of Governor Robert Hunter. For two years after their arrival he supported the project against numerous odds and then was forced to admit defeat and abandon the cause, just as the first products were nearing completion. Neither New York nor New England, therefore, developed naval stores as staple returns to England; instead the industry took root in the pine forests of the Carolinas where conditions of production were more favorable than in the North. The merchants of New England, however, were able to export the Carolina products by way of Boston to England, thus obtaining the bounty and adding to their purchasing power for English goods. This outcome increased the external commercial activity of New England instead of diminishing it, as the authors of the naval stores program had intended.[39]

Fundamentally the new industry did not take root in New England because it was antagonistic to the major interests already developed there—lumbering, manufacturing, and external commerce. The leading merchants of New England contributed little to this policy which was designed to center their trade in England and to render them

[38] Eleanor Lord, *Industrial Experiments in the British Colonies of North America* (Baltimore, 1898), emphasizes the Baltic trade in English policy.

[39] See again E. B. Greene, *Provincial America,* chapters 1–5 (British policy, 1690–1713).

tributary to their English rivals. During the last years of Queen Anne's War the problem of returns was solved when England transmitted large sums of money to New England and New York for the prosecution of the war—money that was immediately utilized to pay for English goods imported into the colonies. After 1713 the northern colonies found another means of obtaining purchasing power in England—trade with the foreign colonies in the West Indies. This trade, however, soon menaced the English sugar planters in the Caribbean and provoked a deadly conflict between them and the northern merchants which finally terminated in the Revolutionary War.

BIBLIOGRAPHICAL NOTE

SECONDARY WORKS: John B. Wolfe, *The Emergence of the Great Powers* (New York, 1951), describes realistically the European backgrounds of the Anglo-French conflict. Two intensive studies of the economy of France and its commercial policies are Charles W. Cole, *Colbert and a Century of French Mercantilism* (2 vols., New York, 1939), and Charles W. Cole, *French Mercantilism, 1683–1700* (New York, 1943). Nellis M. Crouse, *French Pioneers in the West Indies, 1624–1664* (New York, 1940), and Nellis M. Crouse, *The French Struggle for the West Indies, 1665–1713* (New York, 1943), are useful studies of the West Indian matrix of international strife. W. J. Eccles, *Frontenac the Courtier Governor* (Toronto, 1959), emphasizes the defects of Frontenac as an administrator. Jean Delanglez, *Life and Voyages of Louis Jolliet* (Chicago, 1948), is the most authoritative biography.

Jean O. McLachlan, *Trade and Peace with Old Spain* (New York, 1940), is a valuable study of Anglo-Spanish relations, 1667–1750. K. G. Davies, *The Royal African Company* (New York, 1957), is an intensive study of the English slave traffic of the years 1672–1713. Cyrus H. Karraker, *Piracy was a Business* (Rindge, N. H., 1953), supersedes other studies of its subject. G. M. Waller, *Samuel Vetch* (Chapel Hill, 1960), illumines Britain's plans for the conquest of New France. Ruth Bourne, *Queen Anne's Navy in the West Indies* (New Haven, 1939), is a useful monograph.

SOURCES: On the French in the interior see Louise P. Kellogg (ed.), *Early Narratives of the Northwest* (New York, 1917). Isaac J. Cox (ed.), *The Journeys of René Robert Cavelier Sieur de La Salle* (2 vols., New York, 1905), is an attractive collection. J. F. Jameson (ed.), *Privateering and Piracy in the Colonial Period* (New York, 1923), will appeal to the advanced student. For source materials on Captain Kidd see Graham Brooks (ed.), *The Tryale of Capt. William Kidd* (Edinburgh, 1930). *The Walker Expedition to Quebec, 1711* (London, 1953), reproduces the journal of Sir Hovenden Walker (ed. Gerald S. Graham).

XV

 Immigration and Expansion

PRIOR to the year 1680 the American colonies had in the main realized the early ambition of Sir Walter Raleigh to create little Englands beyond the sea, for nine-tenths of the colonists were of English stock. Only the Dutch and Swedish colonists in the middle region broke the racial unity of the settlements, since the white inhabitants of New England and the southern colonies were almost exclusively of English descent. After 1680, however, England ceased to be the chief source of emigration to the colonies, being superseded in that role by six other regions—France, Germany, Ireland, Scotland, Switzerland, and Africa, which sent out hordes of emigrants who began the historic American process of racial amalgamation. In respect to America the eighteenth century was preëminently the century of the foreigner: in 1760 the foreign-born represented a third of the colonial population whereas in 1912 they accounted for only a sixth of the people of the United States.[1] Crèvecoeur, writing at the time of the Revolutionary War, described the fusion in the colonies of the diverse European national groups which was producing the American type, citing the case of a grandson of an Englishman who had married a Dutch woman and whose five sons had married wives of different nationalities. The formation of the American people from several European stocks introduced a new principle in nation-building: the voluntary union of many national groups hitherto hostile to one another in Europe—a fusion achieved through self-selection or intermarriage among free settlers, not, as previously in history, through conquest and the subjugation of the conquered by the conquerors. Of all the factors at work in eighteenth-century America none had greater influence than the immigration of the foreigners, for this made possible that vigorous expansion which is the dominant note of the age. The population of the colonies, which in 1690 amounted to about a quarter of a million, was to double every twenty-five years (thanks partly to the foreigners) until in 1775 it numbered more than two and a half million souls.[2]

[1] See four important articles by Max Farrand, "Immigration in the Light of History," *New Republic*, IX (Dec. 2, 9, 16, 23, 1916).

[2] E. B. Greene and Virginia D. Harrington have prepared statistical estimates of colonial population in *American Population before the Federal Census of 1790* (New York, 1932). Valuable as a reference work.

383

The Causes and Process of Immigration

The social and economic system of Europe, which increasingly concentrated control over the means of production in the hands of a relatively few landowners and merchants, condemned large masses of the peasants and workers to such a low level of subsistence that serious disturbances in the economic order spread havoc and starvation. The mercantile theory that commerce was one nation's loss and another's gain bred destructive wars and repressive legislation, while European states still resorted to religious persecution as a means of bolstering up the ruling classes. To the poor peasants and workers of Europe, immersed in poverty, war, and religious persecution, the English colonies beckoned with an irresistible appeal. There at least one might enjoy peace and security, freedom of Protestant worship, and the economic opportunities of cheap land and high wages: there perhaps one might pass beyond the grasp of the tax-collector and the sound of marching armies.[3]

So great was the emigration from Germany to America that it has been likened to the Germanic migrations at the dawn of the Middle Ages. From the Rhine country—the Palatinate, Wurtenberg, and Baden—thousands of peasants fled from wars that had intermittently devastated their fertile land. First the Thirty Years' War; then the campaigns of Louis XIV against the Dutch; then the War of the League of Augsburg, and finally the War of the Spanish Succession: what horror, suffering, famine, and pestilence they spread throughout southern Germany. Fighting for their independence in alliance with the enemies of Louis XIV, the German princes periodically felt the scourge of armies which he sent into their lands to destroy the crops that otherwise would have fed the anti-French forces. The War of the League of Augsburg witnessed the burning of the cities of Heidelberg, Mannheim, Speyer, and Worms, and when in 1707 Louis XIV again dispatched an army into the Palatinate on a food-destroying mission, that unhappy country seemed indeed a land of doom. This last invasion gave the final impetus to the modern German *völkerwanderung* which transplanted thousands of peasants to the New World.

To wartime distress were added other causes of discontent. In the Palatinate the peasants who had become radical Protestants or Pietists (Mennonites, Moravians, Socinians, Schwenkfelders, Dunkers, Amish, Quakers) were ruled by Catholic princes bent upon enforcing religious uniformity. The confiscation of property, the seizure of churches and

---

[3] Albert B. Faust, *The German Element in the United States* (2 vols., Boston, 1909; New York, 1927), is preëminent in its field. See Vol. I, chapters 1–10.

the expulsion of the most refractory Protestants—such were the measures employed to subdue and impoverish the peasants. Moreover, the German princes, enamored of the court of Louis XIV and striving to imitate its splendors, drew from the substance of the peasantry the means to sustain their vicarious glory.[4]

The impoverishment of the German peasants meant that the great majority of them could not pay the costs of emigration to America. However, merchants and ship captains able to advance the necessary money employed agents called "newlanders" who visited the peasants and persuaded them to leave the fatherland. Posing as American settlers temporarily sojourning in Germany, wearing flashy clothes and displaying watches and jewelry, the newlanders told wondrous tales of the riches of the colonies. "They would convince one that there are in America, none but Elysian fields abounding in products which require no labor; that the mountains are full of gold and silver, and that the wells and springs gush forth milk and honey; that he who goes there as a servant becomes a lord; as a maid, a gracious lady; as a peasant, a nobleman. . . . Law and authority, they say, is created by the people and abrogated at their will." When the newlander had persuaded a group of peasants to migrate he took them down the Rhine to Amsterdam or Rotterdam, where they were packed in vessels bound for America. In return for their passage they agreed to allow the ship captain to sell their labor in the colonies for a term of years. This traffic in human hopes netted a large profit to the newlanders and their employers.[5]

Quite different were the forces which drove emigrants from France to English America. In order to consolidate his kingly power Louis XIV in 1685 revoked the Edict of Nantes, which had given the Huguenots something of the status of a state within the state. New royal decrees now forbade Protestants to leave the country, to worship in churches, or to hold services in private homes. Having successfully withstood earlier persecution the Huguenots were too strong and loyal to their faith to be subdued by mild measures, and Louis XIV did not shrink from crushing all who would not enter the Catholic fold. Royal troops, employed to break up Huguenot conventicles, perpetrated several massacres; soldiers were quartered in Huguenot homes and given every license; the faithful who tried to escape were thrust into underground prisons or consigned as slaves to the galleys; and other

---

[4] A good introductory study is Lucy F. Bittinger, *The Germans in Colonial Times* (Philadelphia, 1901).

[5] Frank R. Diffenderffer, *The German Immigration into Pennsylvania* (Lancaster, 1900), is a factual, topical treatment.

dissenters were sold as servants to Catholic planters in the French West Indies. Whippings, denial of burials, indignities inflicted upon bodies of the dead—such were added horrors of the persecution, the spirit of which was expressed by the Secretary of War in an official order: "If it happen again to be possible to fall upon such [Huguenot] gatherings, let orders be given to the dragoons to kill the greatest part of the Protestants that can be overtaken, without sparing the women, to the end that this may intimidate them and prevent others from falling into a similar fault." Confronted now by the absolute power of the state and unable to offer armed resistance, the Huguenots had to choose between submission and flight.[6]

On one occasion the French government withdrew its decree against the emigration of Huguenots, only to be greeted by such an outrush of the oppressed that the ban was immediately restored. Even so, a large number of the Huguenots managed to escape—by avowing Catholicism at the frontier, by bribing or evading guards, or by using false passports. Forced to depend upon such methods of stealth the Huguenots could not make preparations in France for a direct voyage to America; instead they were obliged to convert their property into money or foreign credits and then to steal away to near-by states, Holland, Germany, Denmark, or England. For this reason an emigration traffic could not be carried on within France by newlanders; moreover, the expense and difficulty of escape limited the body of emigrants to a group of relatively well-to-do exiles who could finance their removal to America.[7]

Comparable to the Germans in influence and numbers were the Scotch-Irish emigrants driven from Northern Ireland after 1700 by poverty induced by oppressive measures of the English government. Here was a people already accustomed to the status of colonists under the English crown. One phase of colonizing activity of the seventeenth century had been the establishment in 1607–09 of the Plantation of Ulster in Northern Ireland. At the time of the accession of James I the Irish Catholics, long restive under English rule, had launched an armed revolt against the new sovereign. This uprising, like its many predecessors, was suppressed by the English overlords, and this time the king determined to subdue Northern Ireland by establishing garrisons and Protestant settlers among the disaffected Irish. Lands of the

<hr/>

[6] A strongly pro-Huguenot view is presented in Henry M. Baird, *The Huguenots and the Revocation of the Edict of Nantes* (2 vols., New York, 1895).

[7] Charles W. Baird, *History of the Huguenot Emigration to America* (2 vols., New York, c. 1885), emphasizes Huguenot leaders and families. See Vol. II.

"rebels" were widely confiscated in the northern counties (Donegal, Londonderry, Tyrone, Fermanagh, Armagh, and Cavan) and entrusted to companies and "undertakers" on the condition that they be peopled with non-Catholic farmers. The promoters then brought in thrifty, hard-working Scottish tenants, whose industry soon converted Ulster from the most backward to the most prosperous part of Ireland. Presbyterianism now replaced Catholicism as the dominant religion of Ulster, while the Plantation created a new "racial" group, the so-called Scotch-Irish, although the phrase "the Scots settled in Ireland" gives a more accurate description.[8]

Unfortunately for the Scotch-Irish they became too efficient competitors of English landlords and manufacturers. First they developed such a thriving livestock industry that Irish cattle became famous for their excellence. But since the best export markets were in England and Scotland, the Scotch-Irish farmers soon ran afoul of the powerful landed interests in those countries. At the behest of the English landlords, Parliament between 1665 and 1680 prohibited the importation into England of Irish cattle, sheep, swine, beef, pork, bacon, mutton, butter, and cheese, while similar acts of the Scottish Parliament excluded such products from the Scottish markets. As these measures threatened to ruin their cattle industry the Scotch-Irish, with commendable enterprise and adaptability, shifted their production to wool growing and the manufacture of cloth. Now they were able to export light and non-perishable products to all countries, with the result that they encroached upon England's markets and menaced her woolen industry. Parliament struck again through the Woolen Act of 1699 which prohibited the exportation of raw wool and woolen cloth from Ireland to any country. Ruin now visited the farmers and artisans of Ulster, whose doleful plight was described in the 1720's by Dean Swift in his *Irish Tracts*. "Whoever travels through this country," he wrote, "and observes . . . the faces and habits and dwellings of the natives, would hardly think himself in a land where either law, religion or common humanity was professed." "The old and sick" are "every day dying and rotting by cold and famine and filth and vermin. The younger laborers cannot get work, and consequently pine away for want of nourishment to a degree that if at any time they are accidentally hired at common labor, they have not the strength to perform it." [9]

[8] William E. H. Lecky, *A History of England in the Eighteenth Century* (8 vols., 1878–1890), describes vividly the condition of Ireland and Scotland. See Vol. II, chapters 5–7.

[9] Henry J. Ford, *The Scotch-Irish in America* (Princeton, c. 1915), is an outstanding study of an immigrant group.

The loss of foreign markets might not have been disastrous had the Scotch-Irish farmers been allowed to retain all the produce of their farms, but that was impossible when they had to pay rent to absentee landlords. Shortly after 1685 many thousand families had migrated from Scotland to Ireland and had taken up land on long-term leases. When these leases expired in 1717, the landlords demanded double or treble rents for the future and evicted the Scot-Irish who would not pay, replacing them with Irish tenants whose standard of living was incredibly low. Meanwhile the Scotch-Irish had been denied any influence in government, for an act of the English Parliament in 1704 excluded Presbyterians from civil and military offices. Thus like the Germans the Scotch-Irish had to choose between poverty, hunger, and legal discrimination or escape to the New World.

The precursors of the great Scotch-Irish exodus migrated to New England in 1714. Belfast, the commercial center of Ulster and the chief port of embarkation, sent fifty-five shiploads of immigrants to America during the following six years. Due to the poverty of the Scotch-Irish the great majority of the emigrants came as indentured servants, aglow with hopes inspired by newlanders who plied their artful traffic from Belfast. In many instances congregations migrated *en masse* under the leadership of pastors who had made advance investigations and arrangements whereby the emigrants placed themselves under colonial employers in one locality and were thus able to maintain their group solidarity and Old World culture and religion.

Southern Ireland also sent forth a considerable stream of emigrants, among whom were doubtless a large number of Roman Catholics. Some were probably driven from Ireland by the exactions of landlords; others sought to escape the impoverishment that afflicted the artisan and laboring classes at home; still others responded to the lure of commercial opportunity in the colonies. Such emigrants appear to have migrated as individuals or in small groups, and to have settled in all the thirteen colonies—especially in Maryland and in Pennsylvania. Because they generally did not preserve their national identity, either through churches or by other means, they have been very hard to trace. As Roman Catholics they found sentiment in most of the colonies extremely hostile toward their faith. For the most part they seem to have been compelled to conform to Protestant ways, with the result that they were absorbed into their adopted communities. Among noteworthy men of Irish descent at the time of the Revolution were two American generals, John Sullivan and Richard Montgomery, the well-known naval officer, John Barry, two state governors, George Clinton of New York and Thomas Burke of North Carolina, and many other political leaders, including George Bryan of Pennsylvania and Charles Carroll of Maryland.[10]

Another body of emigrants came directly from Scotland—victims of a social revolution within their homeland which occurred after 1745. Previously the Scots of the Highlands had lived in clans which kept alive the spirit of independence so characteristic of that wild and picturesque country. Under the clan system the people owned their land in common and while they gave services and payments to their chieftains they regarded the latter only as leaders to whom they accorded voluntary allegiance. In 1745 the Highlanders participated in an uprising which aimed to place the Young Pretender, Bonnie Prince Charley (Charles Edward Stuart), upon the throne from which his grandfather, James II, had been driven in 1688. After decisively defeating the Highlanders at the battle of Culloden Moor in 1746 the English prepared to erase from Scotland that spirit of devotion to the ancient Scottish royal house which had periodically threatened the security of the Hanoverian dynasty, established in Britain as a result of the Revolution of 1688. Accordingly Parliament enacted a series of laws which forbade the clansmen to wear their peculiar national dress, deprived the chiefs of their hereditary jurisdiction, abolished the communal ownership of the soil, and parceled the land anew among renegade chieftains and commissioners representing the Crown. Then there followed a revolution in the mode of production as small farmers were evicted and their holdings united to form large sheep pastures. The exaction of rents was particularly hateful to the clansmen, reducing them as it did from the status of proud freemen to that of semi-servile tenants. Moreover, the chiefs were forced to disband their armed retainers, thus swelling the ranks of the landless unemployed. The earlier migrations from Scotland to Ulster had attested the fact that Scotland was a poor farming country, and now when eviction, tenantry, and dependence were added to the lot of the Highlanders their condition became indescribably miserable. George Buchanan, the foremost Scottish writer of the time, has left descriptions of terrible want and suffering which eloquently explain the emigration of the Highlanders to America.[11]

The fifth country that contributed to the peopling of the colonies was Switzerland, where in the eighteenth century unemployment was

[10] Michael J. O'Brien, in *A Hidden Phase of American History* . . . (New York, 1920), argues that the Irish composed 35.8 per cent of the American soldiers in the Revolution—a somewhat exaggerated claim refuted by J. F. Jameson in the *American Historical Review*, XXVI (July 1921), 797–799.

[11] J. P. MacLean, *An Historical Account of the Settlements of Scotch Highlanders in America* (Cleveland, 1900), is useful to the special student.

a common specter and poverty and pauperism the lot of a people oppressed by a landowning nobility composed of a few patrician families.
The poor and unprivileged, utterly without opportunity to improve
their living conditions or social status, were harassed by laws such as
that prohibiting artisans from carrying wares under the arcades of
Bern, "so that the patricians might walk through them in comfort," and
another which closed the vegetable market to the common people until
after the nobles had had opportunity to buy all the choice produce. In
1740 there were 69,000 Swiss mercenaries serving for low pay in the
armies of Europe—convincing proof of the lack of economic opportunity at home. Since such mercenaries were recruited by Swiss noblemen,
the poverty of the people became a source of profit to their masters.
Of the Swiss emigrants to America we learn that one Hans Märchen
had "one wife, four children and otherwise nothing," and that Martin
Gass had "one wife, eight children and nothing more." [12]

Early in the eighteenth century the governments of the Swiss cantons
encouraged the emigration of paupers, religious radicals, and com-
munists in an effort to be rid of such undesirables. But when emigration
became general and menaced the business of supplying mercenary
soldiers the official attitude changed. Decrees were issued which prohibited the sale of property by prospective emigrants and which defined
emigration as an act of desertion punishable by loss of property, citizenship, and inheritance rights. Moreover, the governments examined
mail from America in order both to suppress letters which presented
an attractive picture of conditions there and to distribute accounts which
described the hardships and disappointments of a settler's life. Other
acts made it an offense for any person to persuade or assist another to
migrate, so that the newlanders had to operate in secret and to use
many subterfuges to escape detection by watchful officials. Even then
they were often arrested, imprisoned, and in extreme cases executed.
As a result of these measures the Swiss emigrants had to steal out of
the country to Holland or France for embarkation to America.[13]

No form of profit-making enterprise—not even the slave trade or
slavery itself—exhibited the horrors which accompanied the immigrant
traffic in indentured servants. From the time the vessels sailed from
Rotterdam, Amsterdam, Belfast, etc., until they arrived in the colonies
the passengers endured a fate worse than that of most prisoners on
land. With between three hundred and six hundred immigrants packed
into the vessels each person was allotted quarters six feet by two feet

[12] A. B. Faust, "Swiss Emigration to the American Colonies in the Eighteenth Century," American Historical Review, XXII (Oct. 1916).
[13] See again J. T. Adams, Provincial Society, chapter 7.

between decks—forced to lie flat for days when the ship pitched about in terrifying storms. "Imagine the vile atmosphere in an unventilated space containing hundreds of people many ill with all manner of contagious diseases, living and dead side by side, without medical attendance, moaning and shrieking, praying and crying, and perhaps crazed by hunger and thirst" (Jernegan).

During the dreary voyage lasting from four weeks to four months or longer, scurvy, smallpox, and other afflictions took a toll of between a third and a half of the passengers; children under seven rarely survived: one passenger reported that on a single voyage thirty-two little children perished. In extremities food was doled out at the rate of three ounces daily—dirty, spoiled biscuit, repulsive with worms, and even rats and mice were eaten.[14]

What little property the servant immigrant possessed was frequently either lost, destroyed, or stolen en route. His contract with the ship captain contained loopholes which allowed the latter to extend the term of service in order to pay extra charges occasioned by a protracted voyage. Similarly, a husband or a wife might be sold for a longer term as a means of paying the passage of the mate who had died at sea. Should the immigrants refuse to consent to such modified terms they might be kept prisoners on shipboard after the arrival in port—a form of exquisite torture to sea-weary travelers who longed to leave the hateful vessel as soon as possible. When the servants were auctioned on the ship children were frequently separated from parents; husbands and wives were sold to different masters; and the old and sick, instead of being succored at once, were kept longest on board as buyers chose the most vigorous of the workers. Among the purchasers was a class of "soul drivers" who took their human merchandise for sale to employers in the towns and at the country fairs.[15]

THE INFLUENCE OF IMMIGRATION

The coming of the foreigners made possible in large measure the growth of settlement and the vigorous expansion of productive forces which characterized the colonies during the eighteenth century. By providing an enlarged labor force immigration supported the development of enterprises conducted on an increasingly large scale: farming, the fishery, shipbuilding, shipping, plantation production, and the fur trade; and by virtue of the employment of such labor the colonial

[14] See again K. F. Geiser, *Redemptioners and Indentured Servants in Pennsylvania,* chapter 1.
[15] See again C. A. Herrick, *White Servitude in Pennsylvania.*

merchants and planters were able to increase their capital accumulations and thereby to strengthen their position in colonial society. Thus the rise of Philadelphia between 1700 and 1770 from a minor status among colonial towns to the rank of the largest and most prosperous commercial center in North America is traceable to the growth of adjacent settlements which afforded wonderful profit opportunities to the city merchants. The main stream of immigration flowed into Philadelphia and from there fed the settlements of interior Pennsylvania and the piedmont and mountainous regions of Maryland, Virginia, and Carolina—a population trend which raised Pennsylvania and the back country of the South to a position of influence equal to that previously held by New England and the southern tidewater area. The reasons why the immigrants settled in this area are obviously of primary importance.[16]

Due to a variety of causes New England did not attract the foreigners. The poor farming land of the region, the occupation of the most accessible areas during the seventeenth century, the presence of hostile Indians on the frontiers, the need of outlets for the growth of native population, and the unfriendly attitude of the Puritans toward foreigners—all these had a deterring influence upon immigration. Moreover, lands were granted in the New England towns by the town itself, with the result that (in view of the small size of the original townships) the inhabitants struggled to obtain any ungranted lands for themselves. Indentured servants were not promised farms at the end of their service, and care was taken to prevent undesirable settlers from obtaining land in the Puritan towns. The early experience of the Scotch-Irish in New England after 1715 illustrates many of these factors. Drawn thither by the bond of common Calvinistic religion the Scotch-Irish immediately found themselves discriminated against wherever they settled. They were not permitted to establish their own Presbyterian churches; instead they were required to attend the existing Puritan churches and contribute toward their support. When they learned of more favorable conditions in Pennsylvania many of them repaired thither and drew after them the great body of their kinsmen who later migrated from Ulster. Some of the Scotch-Irish pioneers in New England moved northward to the frontiers where they were welcomed and tolerated for their unexcelled prowess as Indian fighters. Illustrative of this group was John Stark, a settler on the New Hampshire frontier and a leader in the French and Indian War. New England as a whole, however, remained overwhelmingly English in its

[16] See again H. L. Osgood, *American Colonies in the Eighteenth Century*, Vol. II, pp. 483–525 (important).

racial composition: only 5 per cent of its population in 1775 was of non-English descent.[17]

For somewhat different reasons New York did not draw a large body of immigrants. There the preëmption of vast estates by the local magnates, the system of tenantry in vogue, the presence of the Iroquois in the Mohawk valley, and the barriers of the Catskills and the Adirondacks made settlement unattractive. Moreover, the unhappy experience of the Palatine Germans who arrived in New York in 1710 advertised the drawbacks of the province. Sent over by the English government to produce naval stores, the Palatines endured a terrible voyage during which a fourth of their number died. Their children were apprenticed in other colonies, the land which was promised to them in return for seven years of labor devoted to naval stores production proved to be pine barrens unsuited to farming, and when they became rebellious they were worked in gangs under military discipline. Finally in 1712 Governor Hunter's funds for the project ran out and it was abandoned. Thereupon the Palatines moved to the Schoharie valley only to find soon afterward that the land upon which they settled had been granted by Hunter to seven Albany partners who demanded rents. Hopeful of securing aid from England the harassed Palatines sent thither three agents who were clapped into a debtors' prison when they finally arrived after many misfortunes. The upshot of the episode was that some of the Palatines remained on the Schoharie as tenants, some removed to other parts of New York, and the remainder, at the invitation of Governor Keith, migrated to Pennsylvania, where at last they received friendly treatment. Their sufferings in New York were vividly reported to their countrymen abroad and thereafter the Germans shunned that province and regarded Pennsylvania as the promised land.[18]

Apart from a sizable migration of the Swiss and French to South Carolina, the southern colonies as a whole did not serve as ports of entry for many of the newcomers from Europe. In Virginia and Maryland the available lands of the tidewater area had been occupied by 1700 and the planters there were depending chiefly upon the slave trade for their labor supply. North Carolina lacked ports suitable for ocean vessels, while direct immigration into both Carolinas was retarded by the pine barrens—a strip of land about a hundred miles wide,

[17] C. K. Shipton, "Immigration to New England, 1680–1740," *Journal of Political Economy*, XLIV (April 1936).

[18] Sanford H. Cobb, *The Story of the Palatines* (New York, 1897), a readable, unpretentious narrative, has now been superseded by Walter A. Knittle, *Early Eighteenth Century Palatine Emigration* (Philadelphia, 1937), the most thorough study of one phase of colonial immigration.

lying between tidewater and the piedmont, where the soil was too light for cultivation in the days before fertilizers came into use. Immense landholdings—like that of Lord Granville, which included the north-

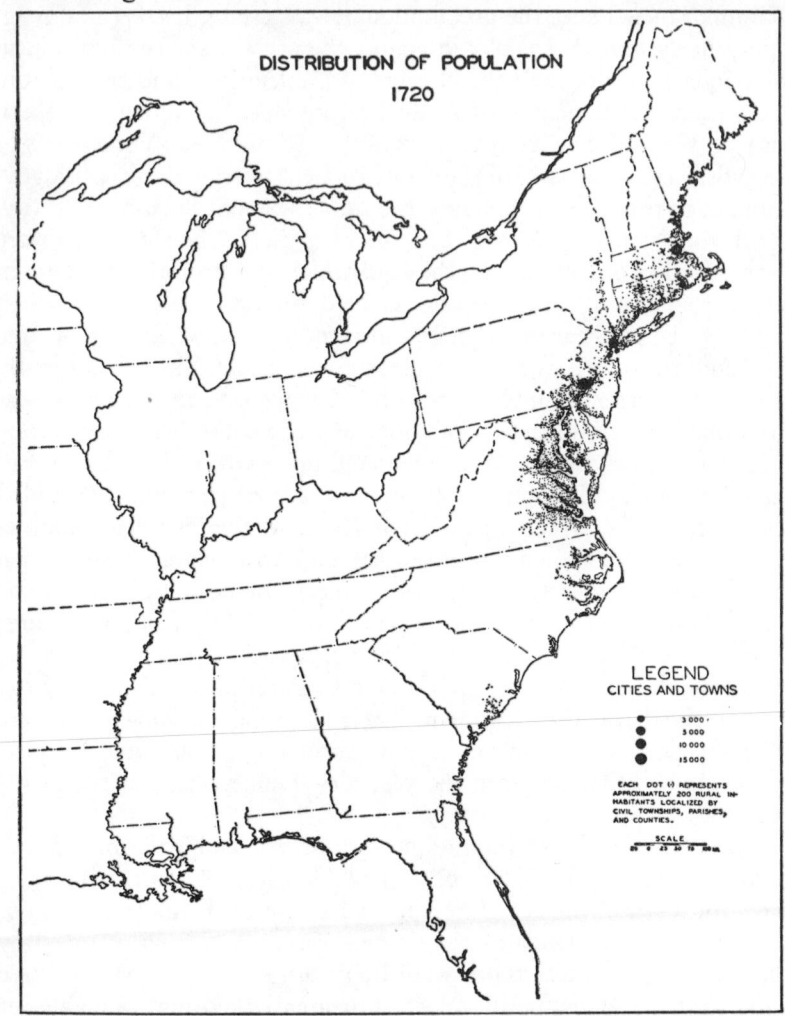

DISTRIBUTION OF POPULATION
1720

LEGEND
CITIES AND TOWNS

● 3 000 ·
● 5 000
● 10 000
● 15 000

EACH DOT (·) REPRESENTS
APPROXIMATELY 200 RURAL IN-
HABITANTS LOCALIZED BY
CIVIL TOWNSHIPS, PARISHES,
AND COUNTIES.

SCALE

ern third of North Carolina—also made the southern area unattractive to settlers. Among the Germans North Carolina received a bad reputation by virtue of the sufferings of a group of Palatine fugitives who had migrated thither in 1710. A Swiss nobleman, Baron de Graffenried, together with other associates, purchased a large tract of land from the Carolina proprietors and arranged for the transportation of six hundred and fifty Germans and a hundred Swiss—only half of whom survived the voyage. Their experiences upon arrival at the Neuse River included acute suffering from disease and hunger before they established their settlement, New Bern, and then within two years they were attacked

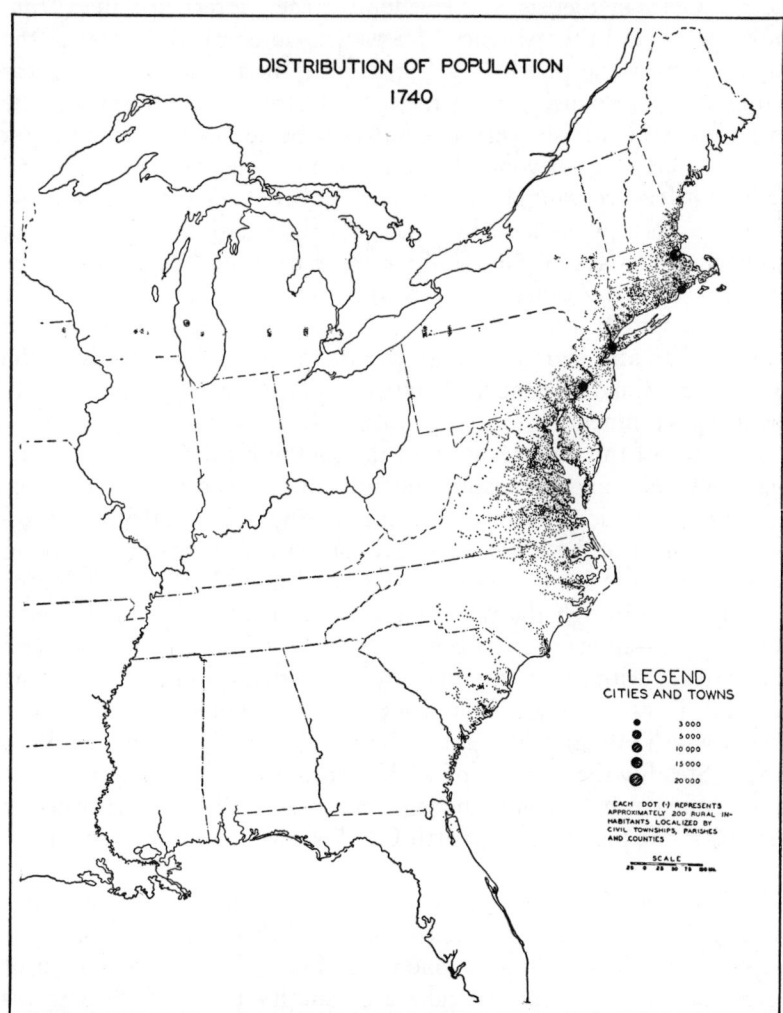

DISTRIBUTION OF POPULATION
1740

LEGEND
CITIES AND TOWNS

•   3 000
•   5 000
◉   10 000
●   15 000
◉   20 000

EACH DOT (•) REPRESENTS
APPROXIMATELY 200 RURAL IN-
HABITANTS LOCALIZED BY
CIVIL TOWNSHIPS, PARISHES
AND COUNTIES

SCALE

by Indians and forced to disperse throughout the southern part of the province. This tragic outcome, coinciding with the sufferings of the Palatines in New York, helped to divert the later German migration to Pennsylvania.[19]

[19] C. M. Andrews, "Immigration and Population of the South to 1783," in *The South in the Making of the Nation*, Vol. V.

The excellent port of Philadelphia, the large area of fertile farm lands in the Delaware, Schuylkill, and Susquehanna valleys, the absence of a tax-supported state church, the affinity between the Quakers and the German Pietists, the freedom of the western frontiers from Indian wars, and the existence of a well-to-do employing class in the eastern part of the province—all these factors account for the great immigration to Pennsylvania after 1710. In the westward advance the aggressive Scotch-Irish were generally to be found on the remotest frontiers, one stage beyond the peace-loving Germans. Scarcely had the Scotch-Irish servant become a freeman before he plunged into the wilderness, occupying land by squatter's right and asserting that "it was against the laws of God and nature that so much land should be idle while so many Christians wanted it to work on and to raise their bread." In spite of the fact that the Penns were selling western lands at only 2s. an acre in 1719 and at 3s. in 1732 nearly two-thirds of the land occupied at this time was settled without grants from the proprietary government.[20]

By virtue of the low elevation of the southern ridge of the Appalachian mountains and the water gaps therein, it was relatively easy for the immigrant pioneers to gain access to the great valley of Pennsylvania. Thence, the course of migration moved southward, carrying settlers after 1726 into western Maryland and the great valley of Virginia and through the water gaps of the Blue Ridge to the piedmont region—an area described as a "rare combination of woodland and pasture, with clear running streams and mild climate." In the Shenandoah valley, Virginia land speculators had obtained large tracts of land which in the 1720's and '30's they offered for sale at a shilling an acre. Steadily the pressure of settlement continued until by 1750 the frontiersmen were passing through the water gaps in southwestern Virginia to the piedmont of North Carolina. Moving in this stream of pioneers were the ancestors of Abraham Lincoln, Jefferson Davis, and John C. Calhoun. The society which took form in the mountain valleys and in the piedmont, based upon small diversified farms, was a projection southward of the economy of Pennsylvania rather than of the plantation system of the tidewater South—a fact which explains the protracted social conflicts between east and west in the southern colonies.[21]

In the economic sphere the eighteenth century immigration tended

---

[20] S. G. Fisher's *The Making of Pennsylvania* (Philadelphia, 1906) describes the colony's racial elements.

[21] A readable, compact, popular account is Oscar Kuhns, *The German and Swiss Settlements of Colonial Pennsylvania* (New York, 1901).

to weaken the survivals of feudalism in America and to strengthen the position of the colonial merchant capitalists. The Germans, the Swiss, the Scotch-Irish, and the Scots had all been sorely oppressed by Euro-

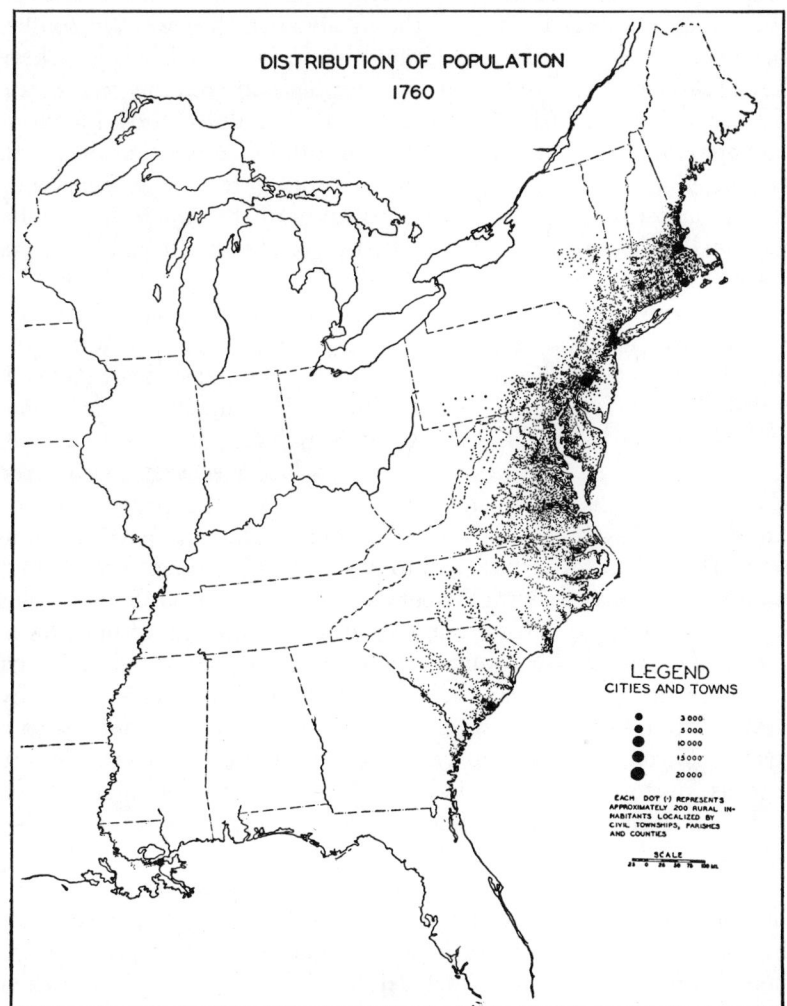

DISTRIBUTION OF POPULATION
1760

LEGEND
CITIES AND TOWNS

● 3 000
● 5 000
● 10 000
● 15 000
● 20 000

EACH DOT (·) REPRESENTS
APPROXIMATELY 200 RURAL IN-
HABITANTS LOCALIZED BY
CIVIL TOWNSHIPS, PARISHES
AND COUNTIES

SCALE

pean landlords and the state churches, military establishments, and burdensome taxes associated therewith. Quite naturally these immigrant groups brought to the colonies a deep-seated hatred of the institutions which had exploited them—an antagonism which inspired them to fight against such semi-feudal survivals in America as huge speculative estates, quit-rents, and tax-supported religions. By 1775 the Scotch-

Irish and Germans formed a powerful group in four colonies still dominated largely by landlords. In Pennsylvania, where they composed two-thirds of the population, they struggled against the Penn family for the control of the proprietary lands; in North Carolina, where they numbered a half of the inhabitants, they were in conflict with the land claims of Lord Granville; in western Virginia, where they composed a third of the settlers, they encountered the great estate of Lord Fairfax; in Maryland, where they accounted for a fourth of the population, they ran afoul of Lord Baltimore's rights as overlord. By occupying lands without title and by refusing to pay quit-rents they steadily undermined existing landlordism until the American Revolution finally destroyed the Penn, Baltimore, Granville, and Fairfax estates.

The French Huguenots, on the other hand, took up residence principally in the plantation area and in the commercial towns. A well-to-do middle-class group to begin with, they soon produced some of the leading commercial families of colonial times—the Faneuils of New England, the Bayards and De Lanceys of New York, and the Laurenses and Manigaults of South Carolina.[22] In a larger sense, however, the whole eighteenth-century immigration fostered the growth of the commercial class. The poor servant immigrants, once they had completed their terms of service, had to begin an independent life without capital assets. Obviously their labor as servants had produced a surplus to the employing capitalist groups; otherwise the system of indentured servitude would have been unprofitable. Such surplus was used in part to finance the freed servant at the expiration of his term—either by means of long-term loans which enabled him to acquire and equip a farm or through short-term credits extended by merchants for the purchase of store goods. The indebted farmers were thereupon obliged to deliver their produce to their creditors immediately after harvest, with the result that the price of farm produce fell to low levels when deliveries were made. On the other hand the prices paid by the farmers for store goods and credit remained practically constant; consequently the merchant creditors were able to extract handsome profits from their dealings with their farmer debtors. This, in fact, was the chief source of the capital accumulations of the merchant class.

The growth of the body of small farmers strengthened the democratic movement in the colonies, since when the freed servant acquired land he became entitled to vote for representatives in his colonial assembly. Against absentee landlords he fought for title to land; against

[22] Arthur H. Hirsh's *The Huguenots of South Carolina* (Durham, N. C., 1928) is one of the best studies of immigration.

his merchant creditors he struggled for relief from debt. In this manner the progress of settlement intensified the conflict between the democratic and aristocratic forces in colonial society.

The growth of population in the middle colonies and the back country of the South also sharpened the antagonism between the colonial merchants and their English rivals. The surplus products of these settlements—grains and livestock—required market outlets which the colonial merchants sought increasingly in the French West Indies. This trade, however, tended to undermine the British sugar plantations and thus to imperil the shipping interests and investments of the British merchants in the Caribbean. The latter could protect themselves only by injuring the trade of the northern merchants and that in turn menaced the economy of the middle region which was expanding so rapidly under the impact of immigration. The policies which England eventually adopted to protect her stake in the West Indies bore a strong resemblance to the measures by which Parliament had destroyed the cattle and woolen industries in Ireland after 1665. When the revolutionary crisis occurred in the colonies the Scotch-Irish rose almost as a man in opposition to Parliament's authority, their attitude eloquently expressed by their foremost orator, Patrick Henry.[23]

A third major conflict of the eighteenth century—that between England and France—was also accentuated as the immigrants rapidly extended England's settled area toward the western outposts of the French.

Although immigration tended to diversify social life in the colonies it did not materially modify the basic political institutions which the English settlers had established during the seventeenth century. In most colonies the foreigners at any given time were a minority; hence in their external relations they had little choice except to conform to the customs of the country. Political thought in the colonies remained essentially English; the immigrants were compelled to become an English-speaking people; and political leadership resided chiefly in the English group—a fact attested by the names of Franklin, Washington, Jefferson, Adams, Madison, Marshall, and Lee.[24]

Similarly, by virtue of naturalization, the foreigners became English subjects. Ordinarily in eighteenth-century Europe emigration meant loss of civil rights such as the privileges of voting, holding office, acquiring land, and inheriting property. The colonies, however, in order to attract settlers, liberally bestowed upon foreigners the benefits of

---

[23] Maude Glasgow, *The Scotch-Irish in Northern Ireland and in the American Colonies* (New York, 1936).

[24] See again E. B. Greene, *Provincial America*, chapter 14.

citizenship and even extended unusual privileges: Virginia and Maryland, for instance, gave to foreigners a five-year exemption from suits for the recovery of debts contracted before emigration. Prior to 1740 the rights of colonial citizenship were conferred by act of an individual colony, with the result that a naturalized immigrant, as a citizen of Massachusetts or Virginia, lost his civil rights if he moved to another colony. Parliament in 1740 enacted that a foreigner who became a citizen of one colony automatically became a citizen in all the English colonies. First he must have resided in one colony for seven years, have taken the oath of supremacy, and have received the sacrament according to the rites of the Anglican Church. Such religious tests, however, were modified to permit the naturalization of Jews and Quakers. After these conditions had been met the foreigner was entitled to civil rights in all the colonies, although he could neither become a privy councillor of the king, serve as a member of Parliament, or hold offices under the Crown in Great Britain and Ireland. The parliamentary statute of 1740, slightly modified, endured throughout the remainder of the colonial period and later formed the pattern of the first naturalization law of the United States.[25]

In the sphere of private family life and religion the immigrants were able to retain their Old World traditions and thus to contribute to the diversity of colonial society. Since most of the non-English groups were Protestant in faith they strengthened the Protestant character of the existing settlements, while the Scots and Scotch-Irish, as sturdy Calvinists, reinforced the Puritanism of New England. Sectarianism received a fresh impetus by virtue of the numerous sects among the Germans, the tendency of the French Huguenots to become Anglicans, and the growth of the Baptist and Methodist churches on the frontiers. The non-Anglican immigrants who settled in the back country of the southern colonies became bitter opponents of the Anglican church which they were called upon to support by taxes, and by resisting its dominance they helped to effect the separation of church and state in the plantation colonies.

English Migration and the Genesis of Georgia

The triumph of the English middle class in the Revolution of 1688, which installed the Whig party in power, altered the course of English emigration to America. As representatives of the commercial and manu-

[25] A brief introduction is Emberson E. Proper, *Colonial Immigration Laws* (New York, 1900). See also A. H. Carpenter, "Naturalization in England and the American Colonies," *American Historical Review*, IX (Jan. 1904).

facturing groups the Whigs rejected the earlier policies of the Crown and the landed aristocracy which had oppressed the religious dissenters of the middle class. The Toleration Act of 1689, by granting freedom of public worship to Protestants who believed in the divinity of Christ, terminated the persecution which had previously driven Quakers and other dissenters to the colonies. Thereafter political and religious oppression ceased to operate in England as a cause of emigration.[26]

Deeply interested in the development of the colonies the Whigs endeavored to people them with foreign Protestants, in view of the decline of emigration from England. Thus a Whig Parliament financed the transportation of Palatines to New York in 1710, and in the 1720's Whig colonial officials worked out a scheme for the systematic colonization of South Carolina by foreign Protestants. Townships of twenty thousand acres were laid out along the main rivers east of the fall line and divided into farms of fifty acres. Because of an unfavorable climate and the poor soil of the pine barren region this project failed: only one settlement of German redemptioners, at Orangeburg on the North Edisto River, survived. Nevertheless, the Whig policy of encouraging Protestant exiles to settle in America made possible the great eighteenth-century immigration and is therefore a memorable feature of English colonization, sharply differentiated from the French and Spanish practice of excluding all but Catholic subjects from New France and New Spain.

The rising middle-class groups in England profited immensely by colonial immigration, for it converted aliens into buyers of English manufactures and producers of surplus produce from which English merchants made their profits. The increase of colonial population provided a major stimulus to the growth of English commerce: thus in 1662–69 the American and West Indian colonies supported about a tenth of England's external trade; in 1770 about a third. Between 1700 and 1770 England's commerce with America and the West Indies increased about fourfold, whereas her total trade, foreign and colonial, increased only twofold.

This commercial expansion in large measure sustained the English Industrial Revolution of the eighteenth century. The American demand for manufactures kept the workshops of England busy and provided employment for her artisans and sailors. No longer did England seem overpopulated; in fact the relative shortage of workers now inspired inventors to develop labor-saving machines and to unleash new sources of industrial power. In response to this trend English officials increasingly discouraged the emigration of efficient workers and sea-

---

[26] See again E. Channing, *History of the United States*, Vol. II, chapter 14.

men and encouraged the emigration of certain "undesirables"—criminals, paupers, and debtors.[27]

In pursuance of these aims several measures were taken. For one thing the government maintained agents at port towns to scrutinize the contracts of servants embarking to the colonies, seeking by this means to stop the business of kidnaping able-bodied workers and of spiriting them to America. In 1765 Parliament forbade the emigration of skilled industrial operatives—a measure which also intended to prevent the dissemination of England's industrial secrets abroad. In like manner the Board of Trade tried to check the desertion of seamen and fishermen from English vessels at Newfoundland and their subsequent employment in New England, where—lured by higher wages and better working conditions—they strengthened the colonial fisheries and merchant marine to the detriment of their English competitors. As early as 1691 it was reported that in this way England was losing more than a hundred seamen and fishermen annually. Prior to 1729 England did not establish a settled government at Newfoundland; instead the commodores in command of the annual fishing fleets from England were empowered to regulate the fishery. They were instructed by the Crown to curtail the exodus to New England, and toward this end they required that masters of vessels from Boston give bond not to take English seamen to the mainland colonies. For many years after 1715 the Board of Trade urged that the settlers at Newfoundland be removed in order to destroy their trade with New England which occasioned the drain of seamen, and when in 1729 England established a civil government in the island one of its objectives was to suppress this long-standing "abuse."

On the other hand England continued to use the colonies as a dumping ground for her criminal population. Parliamentary statutes of 1662 and 1717 authorized judges to sentence convicts to servitude in America: for seven-year terms in case of lesser crimes and for fourteen-year terms in case of offenses punishable by death. Primarily a means of decreasing prison costs in England and of converting convicts into productive workers, this policy was rationalized as a method of enabling them to start life anew, free from the stigma of a criminal past. All told, about fifty thousand convicts were shipped to America—to nine colonies at least: in Maryland, which alone received twenty thousand, they formed the mass of indentured servants during the eighteenth

[27] Notable among recent works is Lawrence H. Gipson's *The British Empire before the American Revolution* (3 vols., Caldwell, Idaho, 1936)—a work planned to give a bird's-eye view of the whole empire about 1750. Volume I describes British and Irish backgrounds.

century. Particularly unsavory was the trade in convict servants carried on by contractors with the English government. Undoubtedly the presence of the convict element depressed the condition of all the indentured servants and aggravated the harsh and oppressive features of the entire immigrant traffic. To the colonists the whole business seemed outrageous. Franklin objected that "these thieves and villains introduced among us spoil the morals of the youth and the neighborhoods that entertain them." It would be as reasonable, he said, for America to send its rattlesnakes to England as for the English to send their jailbirds to America. "Their emptying their jails into our settlements is an insult and a contempt, the cruelest that ever one people offered to another." From 1670 onward the southern and middle colonies passed laws to exclude these undesirables: acts which placed prohibitive duties on imported convicts or which required ship captains to give bond for the good behavior of such immigrants. All such acts, however, were declared null and void by the English government, with the result that the English policy of convict dumping became a serious cause of estrangement between the colonies and the mother country.[28]

Writing in 1729 an English mercantilist, Joshua Gee, suggested that criminals and the unemployed be transported to the frontiers of the southern colonies, "by which means those vast tracts of land now waste will be planted, and secured from the danger we apprehend of the French over-running them." For thirty years after 1700 the unoccupied region between South Carolina, Florida, and Louisiana had evoked proposals in England for the establishment of a buffer colony against the French and Spaniards. Here was a land, presumably, which—in conformity with the mercantilist creed—might produce such commodities as silk, wine, rice, dyes, naval stores, and even gold. More immediately, the control of this region (present-day Georgia and Alabama) meant the control of the lucrative fur trade of the southwest. Before 1729 the English title to the area was vested in the Carolina proprietors, but they had neglected both to colonize and to defend it. The South Carolina Assembly, responding to the interests of the local fur traders, had been more active and after 1715 had established forts on the Savannah and Altamaha Rivers. Only a little aid had come from Britain so that the South Carolinians had had to stagger alone under this burden of frontier defense.

Among the members of Parliament after 1722 was James Edward Oglethorpe, "a young gentleman of very public spirit"—once an English officer in the war with Spain and now a vigorous defender of Eng-

[28] James D. Butler, "British Convicts Shipped to American Colonies," *American Historical Review*, II (Oct. 1896).

land's interests against the Spaniards in America. A man of liberal and humane sympathies, he served as chairman of a parliamentary prison board which exposed the degrading conditions of prison life and the brutal treatment of the inmates, many of whom were decent people, victims of debt, injustice, and poverty. Oglethorpe's interest in these outcasts reflects a humanitarian spirit that was growing among the Anglican clergy and a few enlightened members of the upper class. To such men it appeared that imprisoned debtors might be rescued from the horrors of English jails and be sent to establish the much-needed buffer colony north of Florida. Accordingly in 1732 they obtained from George II a charter which authorized them to colonize the land extending between the Savannah and Altamaha Rivers, from the Atlantic Coast to the South Sea.[29]

The charter of Georgia differed sharply from all other grants to English colonial promoters. It placed control over the province in a board of trustees empowered to raise money, grant lands, enact laws, and levy taxes. The trustees could not derive any personal profit from the enterprise; their actions were subject to close supervision by the king; and their powers were to endure but twenty-one years, after which Georgia was to become a royal province. In addition the charter provided for a common council of trustees, resident in England, authorized to appoint the governor, judges, and other officers of the colony. In a larger sense the enterprise was not strictly philanthropic because it aimed to reduce the cost of maintaining the poor in England, to protect the profitable South Carolina plantations against Spanish incursions, and to strengthen England's grip on the southern fur trade. Earlier experience with profit-making corporations as colonizing agencies had proved, as in the case of Virginia, that such ventures were not profitable; hence the ordinary corporate form of colonization could not be employed. Similarly, English merchants and officials were now unalterably opposed to the creation of new proprietary colonies which transferred too much power to proprietors and local interests and thereby tended to weaken that imperial control which was deemed necessary to assure to England the profits of colonial development. Since neither the corporate nor proprietary type of colony could be established, the charter of Georgia created a new method of control—the trust—which guaranteed that the powers of colonial government and

---

[29] The best recent biographies are Leslie F. Church, *Oglethorpe: A Study in Philanthropy in England and America* (London, 1932), and Amos A. Ettinger, *James Edward Oglethorpe, Imperial Idealist* (New York, 1936). For an older narrative see Henry Bruce, *Life of General Oglethorpe* (New York, c. 1890).

the ownership of ungranted lands should revert to the Crown as soon as the colony had become firmly established on a profitable basis.

Given the principal object of the colony—to raise a bulwark against the Spaniards—the trustees decided that Negroes, both slave and free, should be excluded, lest they join the enemy in time of war. The ban on slavery in turn outlawed large plantations in accordance with the aim of trustees to foster an economy of small farms in order to create the most numerous body of soldier-settlers—a policy which determined the course of Georgia's history before 1750.

The money spent in founding the colony came from two principal sources. First, the trustees solicited contributions from philanthropic persons and in this manner obtained about £20,000; secondly, Parliament made yearly grants ranging from £8,000 to £26,000—the larger part of which was devoted to defense. Most of these funds were spent by the trustees in England and transmitted to Georgia in the form of provisions and equipment, although the governor in the colony was permitted to draw bills on the trust for the purchase of supplies from English merchants. Indicative of the work of the trust were the separate funds into which the money was divided—a fund for establishing the colony, one for religion, one for agriculture, one for schools, and one for the transportation of Swiss and German settlers. Besides money grants the trustees also received other gifts for the settlers—principally Bibles, catechisms, prayer books, and furniture. Financial transactions were handled in London through the Bank of England.[30]

Shortly before the colony was founded Parliament passed an act which released a large number of prisoners from jail but such was the stigma of their past that Oglethorpe soon found that these "miserable wretches" were "starving for want of employment." To such unfortunates the trustees appealed in a well-conducted advertising campaign which portrayed the attractions of a free and independent status in a new country. Before accepting applicants as settlers the trustees required that their good character be certified by their parish officials; by this means it was hoped to exclude criminals, idlers, and drunkards, and because the colonists were prospective soldiers against Catholic Spain, no papists were accepted. Otherwise, the trustees guaranteed religious freedom to Protestants, foreign as well as English, and offered to each settler a farm of fifty acres, while the charter conferred the liberties and privilege of English subjects. Particular efforts were made to secure ambitious, industrious young men and heads of large families, and when they enlisted they were given instructions in farming and

[30] See again V. W. Crane, *The Southern Frontier*, chapter 13.

trained in the art of war by sergeants of the royal guard. The trust provided free transportation to the colony, supplied each settler with adequate food, clothing, tools, and utensils and provided for community production during the first year until individual self-supporting farms could be established by each family.

Other victims of misfortune and oppression—particularly persecuted Protestants of Germany and Switzerland—were welcomed to Georgia by the trustees. Such composed a band of Lutheran exiles driven from their homeland by their Catholic ruler, the Archbishop of Salzburg. First they found refuge in England, where in 1733 the trustees agreed to transport them to the colony and to equip them as ordinary settlers. Led by a nobleman, the Baron von Reck, they arrived in Georgia in 1734, there to establish a settlement, Ebenezer, on a small tributary of the Savannah River. Other Germans, however, especially the peace-loving Pietists, did not respond to the appeal of a military outpost, and although a few Moravians came in 1735 their aversion to war soon led them to move to Pennsylvania.[31]

Not all the settlers brought to Georgia were sent by the trustees: the latter made arrangements which allowed men of means to secure tracts up to five hundred acres, provided they transport ten servants to the colony; after four years of labor each servant was entitled to a twenty-acre farm. Since the cost of transporting and maintaining a servant was relatively high (£20) the trustees allowed such masters to borrow the money from the trust on condition that it be repaid within three years. And if the master had not peopled his five hundred-acre tract after ten years it should revert to the trust.

With Oglethorpe in command the first band of colonists—thirty-five families or 130 settlers—embarked from England in September 1732. Well supplied with provisions (they stopped at Madeira and took on board five tuns of wine—an indication of unusual affluence) their good ship *Ann* carried them without mishap to Charleston, where, as prospective defenders of the southern frontier, they received a most cordial welcome. When they later reached the Savannah River Oglethorpe made good use of his military knowledge by selecting an easily defended site on a high bluff. Since the trustees had not sought profit from the expedition they had provided for the emigrants so amply that only two of them died during the voyage. Soon the colonists were constructing their first town, Savannah—erecting a palisade, clearing land, and building log houses; working in gangs under Oglethorpe's martial

[31] The best short work is James R. McCain, *Georgia as a Proprietary Province* (Boston, c. 1917); the best state history is E. Merton Coulter, *A Short History of Georgia* (Chapel Hill, 1933). See chapters 1–8.

PLAN OF SAVANNAH, GEORGIA, 1734

This shows the land already cleared and laid out, with public mill, guesthouse, public oven, well, public store, fort, parsonage, palisades, and houses beginning to be built.

discipline and supported by provisions supplied by the trust, all with the understanding that at the end of the year they were to receive land and livestock and to work for themselves thereafter.

Early life in Georgia exhibits an illustration of a planned economy under a paternalistic government in which the workers had no part. In order to keep settlement compact, grants of land in excess of five hundred acres were outlawed, settlers were not allowed to sell, rent, mortgage, or lease their small farms (their fifty acres included a town lot sixty by ninety feet), nor could such farms be divided by inheritance; the whole passed to the eldest son. Freed servants who could not immediately become independent farmers were allowed to work at wages fixed by the trust—8d. a day for men and 6d. a day for women. By virtue of the scarcity of labor and small landholdings, grain and cattle farming became the first mainstay of the colony. The trust did not conduct the trade in farm products (this was opened to private merchants) although it did establish and operate the necessary saw- and gristmills. By October 1741 the workers sent by the trust had been allotted 41,600 acres of land, and importers of about 560 servants had received 28,185 acres. Between 1733 and 1740 the trust transported 915 English settlers and 606 foreign Protestants.[32]

Endeavoring to introduce staple commodities that might be exchanged in England for manufactured goods the trustees encouraged the production of wine, silk, and naval stores. They sent over a skilled botanist to instruct the inhabitants in the art of silk culture, required that two mulberry trees be planted on each acre of land allotted, and gave bounties to the producers of raw silk. So also the trustees collected the English bounty on naval stores exported from the colony and remitted the money to the producers in Georgia. In order to preserve friendly relations with the Indians (which Oglethorpe had taken pains to establish at the start), fur traders were strictly regulated by the trustees, who prohibited the importation of rum, fixed the prices of trading goods and furs, required that the traders renew their licenses every year, and designated the areas and trails that could be used. Lest the settlers be drawn away into the forest traffic the trustees forbade any trader to employ servants; each trader had to operate single-handed, under penalty of a fine of £8. One purpose governed all these economic regulations: the settlements should be kept compact and enterprise should remain on a small scale; by this means the colony would consist of a concentrated force of self-sustaining farmer-soldiers.[33]

[32] See again H. L. Osgood, *American Colonies in the Eighteenth Century*, Vol. III, pp. 34–74.
[33] See again E. B. Greene, *Provincial America*, chapter 15.

Like earlier attempts to shape colonial development from England the plans of the Georgia trustees retarded the growth of the province and provoked intense opposition among the settlers. Fundamentally the difficulty arose from the land and labor policy of the trust. The poorer elements became dissatisfied—the servants because they received only a mere twenty acres, and younger sons of proprietors because they could not share in the inheritance of their fathers' lands. The small farmers considered their fifty-acre farms inadequate; moreover, since the landowners could not alienate their land they could not use it as a credit base and consequently could not borrow needed capital. The prospect of a yearly quit-rent of 2s. for each fifty acres was equally displeasing. To the fur traders the ban on rum and servants seemed an unnecessary means of curtailing profits. The larger enterprisers could not obtain all the land or laborers they wanted: in order to acquire the maximum five-hundred-acre tracts they were obliged to import ten servants at a cost of £200. They could not purchase Negroes, and white servants were not attracted to a colony where their freedom dues amounted to only twenty acres of land. Both the large and small proprietors were excluded from the government which seemed to them a despotism of absentee trustees who imposed unpopular policies through the agency of the governor, a military dictator. Owing to the cost of acquiring land and servants the experiments in wine and silk production failed, while the richest lands of Georgia, admirably suited to rice cultivation, could not be exploited because the hot climate and malaria-carrying insects precluded the utilization of white labor. Only by importing slaves could large enterprisers hope to compete with the rice plantations of South Carolina.

About 1737 discontent with the regime of the trustees became acute. The poor settlers left the colony in large numbers, thus diminishing the inadequate labor force. The landed proprietors now complained so loudly of their lot that the trust sent an investigator to the colony. Nothing less than the abandonment of the principal policies of the trust would satisfy the malcontents: they demanded the privilege of importing Negroes, a reduction of the quit-rents, complete freedom in disposing of their farms, the right to elect local officers, and the opportunity of acquiring more land. Although the trustees stoutly opposed these demands they were forced to make concessions gradually until by 1750 their whole regime had been overthrown. The land grant to a freed servant was increased in 1742 to fifty acres; the farmers were conceded the right to sell and otherwise dispose of their lands; the law of inheritance was changed so as to give all sons and daughters equal shares; the maximum limit for plantations was raised from five hundred to two thousand acres; the importation of rum was permitted (in response to a vote of the House of Commons) and in 1749 the introduction of Negro slaves was authorized. These changes enabled large enterprisers, many of whom soon came in from South Carolina, to acquire and consolidate small holdings that had been prepared for cultivation, to obtain an adequate dependent labor force, and thus to perpetuate the large plantation in the economy of Georgia. In the meantime but little progress had been made toward self-government; in 1751 the trustees granted an assembly—not, however, a law-making body but merely an agency through which the property owners could voice their demands and discontents. For the trustees the end was now in sight. Dismayed by the trend of affairs in the colony and the failure of their principal plans they relinquished their rights to the king in 1751. Georgia took its place in the ranks of the royal colonies, ruled thereafter by an elected assembly and by a governor and council appointed by the king, while the growth of a class of large landowners rapidly brought the colony within the circle of the plantation aristocracy of the South.[34]

The economic trend in early Georgia has a significance broader than that of purely local interest. The trustees had deliberately tried to develop an economy of small farms, to prevent the monopolization of land, and to provide an economic basis of independence for a body of once impoverished people. The outcome demonstrated the impracticability of the program; the underlying conditions in America fostered the growth of large enterprise and the concentration of property ownership in a relatively few hands. In this respect Georgia epitomizes the tendency in all colonies toward economic inequality—toward the progress of capitalistic economy.

[34] See again L. H. Gipson, *The British Empire before the American Revolution*, Vol. II, chapter 6.

BIBLIOGRAPHICAL NOTE

SECONDARY WORKS: Stella H. Sutherland, *Population Distribution in Colonial America* (New York, 1936), a standard work, estimates the extent of the population of the colonies and describes its distribution. Marcus L. Hansen, *The Atlantic Migration, 1607–1860* (Cambridge, 1940), a leading authority on the peopling of the United States, includes a survey of the colonial era.

Dieter Cunz, *The Maryland Germans* (Princeton, 1948), a scholarly work, contains a section on the colonial period. Paul A. W. Wallace, *The Muhlenbergs of Pennsylvania* (Philadelphia, 1950), is an interesting, reliable account of members of an outstanding German Lutheran family. Otto Zoff, *The Huguenots* (New York, 1942), is a readable, popular history of French Protestantism. Wayland F. Dunaway, *The Scotch-Irish in Pennsylvania* (Chapel Hill, 1944), gives a good account of the author's chosen people. Ian C. Graham, *Colonists from Scotland*

(Ithaca, 1956), and Duane Meyer, *The Highland Scots of North Carolina* (Chapel Hill, 1961), are careful studies of the Scottish backgrounds of emigration and of the settlements and influence of Scots in the colonies. Abram V. Goodman, *American Overture: Jewish Rights in Colonial Times* (Philadelphia, 1947), studies the Jewish element in the colonies—a group that did not include, at any one time, more than one thousand members. Hyman B. Grinstein, *The Rise of the Jewish Community in New York, 1654–1860* (Philadelphia, 1945), a penetrating analysis, contrasts the life of Jews in New York with their Old World experience. Jacob R. Marcus, *Early American Jewry* (Philadelphia, 1951), is a detailed study pertaining to New York, New England, and Canada, 1649–1794, based on letters, many previously unpublished.

The growth of settlement in back country areas into which many immigrants penetrated is traced in John A. Caruso, *The Appalachian Frontier* (Indianapolis, 1959); Freeman H. Hart, *The Valley of Virginia in the American Revolution, 1763–1789* (Chapel Hill, 1942); and Robert L. Meriwether, *The Expansion of South Carolina, 1729–1765* (Kingsport, 1940).

James E. Caldwell, *The Early Settlement of Georgia* (Athens, 1948), gives a satisfactory account of its subject.

SPECIAL STUDIES FOR ADVANCED STUDENTS: For the student making special studies the following are useful as reference works: G. D. Bernheim, *History of the German Settlements in . . . North and South Carolina* (Philadelphia, 1872); C. K. Bolton, *Scotch Irish Pioneers* (Boston, 1910); Lucian J. Fosdick, *French Blood in America* (New York, c. 1906); Charles A. Hanna, *The Scotch-Irish* (2 vols., New York, 1902); Herrmann Schuricht, *History of the German Element in Virginia* (Baltimore, 1898); John W. Wayland, *The German Element in the Shenandoah Valley* (Charlottesville, Va., 1907).

SOURCES: V. H. Todd has edited *Christoph von Graffenried's Account of the Founding of New Bern* (Raleigh, 1920). On Georgia see W. MacDonald (ed.), *Documentary Source Book of American History*, no. 27 (Georgia charter); *A True and Historical Narrative of the Colony of Georgia by Pat. Tailfer and Others* (ed. Clarence L. Ver Steeg, Athens, 1960); and E. Merton Coulter (ed.), *The Journal of William Stephens, 1741–1745* (2 vols., Athens, 1958–59). The trials of German immigrants are forcefully described in Gottlieb Mittelberger, *Journey to Pennsylvania* (ed. Oscar Handlin and John Clive, Cambridge, 1960).

XVI

The Growth of
American Capitalism

In an address in 1932 former President Coolidge expressed his opinion that the unemployed would be put to work again when somebody could make money by hiring them—a statement which expresses the essence of the American capitalist society as it has developed from early beginnings in colonial times. During the eighteenth century, particularly, the history of the colonies was notable for the growth of capitalist enterprise. The central features of early American capitalism were the ownership of the means of production and transportation (land, tools, shops, buildings, machines, warehouses, ships, etc.) by private individuals—merchants, master artisans, landowning farmers, and planters—and the existence of a class of dependent laborers—wage-earners, slaves, servants, and tenant farmers—who did not share in the ownership of the means of production. Capitalist enterprise functioned through the employment of the dependent workers by the owners of land and capital goods who claimed in consequence a part of the commodities produced by joint use of capital and labor. In the simplest form of capitalist economy, the share of the owners consisted of farm produce and manufactured articles. With the growth of enterprise, the owners obtained more of such "consumers' goods" than they themselves could consume, with the result that they desired to convert their surpluses into capital goods of some durable form.[1]

A first step necessary in the process of converting surplus consumers' goods into capital was to sell them for hard money or its equivalent—a fact which explains the great value attributed to coin and bullion, since they were a non-perishable form of wealth, inexpensively stored and transported, and in such universal demand that they might at any time be converted into any other kind of property. More particularly the owners of money could use it to pay the wages of workers engaged in producing machines, buildings, ships, etc. In reality this practice meant the conversion of the surplus farm and manufactured products received by the capitalists into the labor of those who pro-

---

[1] Special attention is called to a very important chapter (22 on mercantilism) by J. F. Rees in *The Cambridge History of the British Empire*, Vol. I.

duced capital goods. Such capital goods belonged of course to the capitalists and, when used in new production, augmented their stock of income-producing property. Capital, therefore, displayed a tendency to multiply and to enlarge the income of its owners, while the earnings of the dependent workers did not increase proportionately.

Three principal types of colonial enterprise may be differentiated, although the lines dividing them were by no means hard and fast.

In the first category we find the southern planters, whose labor force was composed of servants and slaves, whose gains consisted, in the first instance, of surplus tobacco, rice, and indigo or their equivalents in other products, and whose investments were made in additional slaves, implements of production, buildings, and lands. Comparable to the southern planters were the landed magnates of New York; only the employment by the latter of tenants instead of slaves and the collection of interest and rents in grain and livestock instead of plantation produce differentiated such magnates from the planters. In the same category belonged the large independent farmers in the northern colonies who employed several servants. Obviously the farmer would not have employed servants if their labor, when applied to his capital, had not yielded a return above the cost of purchasing and maintaining them.[2]

Quite distinct from the rural capitalists was the merchant capitalist of the towns. As a shipowner he employed wage-earning sailors and received his return on his invested capital in the form of freight payments; in the fur traffic he invested in trading goods and trading posts, hired traders to whom he paid wages, and profited so greatly by reason of a dominant position that he may be regarded as the employer of the Indians, whose return for their labor probably did not exceed that obtained by Negro slaves. The key to the position of the merchant capitalist, however, is to be found in his relations with the small farmers within his trading area. Here was a class sprung from poor immigrants, freed servants, younger sons without property, and once independent proprietors who had been dispossessed and obliged to start anew. Although it was relatively easy for the poor farmer to secure a small piece of land, yet he could not cultivate it without capital, and that, ordinarily, he did not possess. The town merchants, however, from their surplus earnings, were ready to extend credit, either long-term loans which enabled the farmer to provide himself with land, tools, buildings, and livestock, or short-term credit for the purchase of store goods such as cloth, notions, and utensils. In thus supplying the farmer the merchant became entitled to several re-

[2] See again J. T. Adams, *Revolutionary New England,* chapters 7–8, 10.

turns; freights on goods imported in his vessels, warehouse charges, insurance premiums, profits or commissions on goods sold, and interest on loans. These payments had to be made by the debtor farmers in the form of produce; hence they were required to deliver their surplus to the merchant or his country agents in order to discharge past debts and to obtain fresh credit for the purchase of the next year's supply of store goods.[3]

Once a farmer had become a debtor he discovered that the odds were heavily against him. His class consisted of unorganized producers who could not exert any influence over the prices of the goods they bought and sold. Each year after harvest they had great supplies of produce which temporarily flooded the market and sent prices to their lowest level during the year. At such times the merchants made their purchases or received the produce of their debtors, thereby obtaining at low cost a maximum share of the farmer's output. On the other hand the prices paid by the farmers were not subject to seasonal fluctuations. Interest charges of course did not vary at all; transportation costs remained practically stationary and even the prices of store goods were fairly constant. By selling high and buying low the merchant acquired a considerable share of the farmers' surplus which he was able to sell at a handsome profit, thereby gaining new funds for investment.[4]

Similarly the cyclical movement of prices worked against the debtor farmer. When depressions came the price of his produce dropped drastically and yet the credit charges against him did not change and the prices of transportation and store goods did not fall in proportion. At such times all his surplus was needed to pay his debts and often it did not suffice for that, so he was compelled to go deeper into debt. When his credit had been exhausted and his surplus would not pay existing debts his merchant creditor commonly foreclosed and took possession of his farm—an action whereby the creditor acquired the permanent improvements which the farmer had added to the land. In this manner the holdings of the merchant were enlarged and the trend toward the concentration of capital was intensified.

The acquisition of a large part of the agricultural surplus by the merchants had another important effect; it slowly developed a class of propertyless workers forced off the farms because the meager profits of farming would not sustain all the sons and daughters of the

[3] C. P. Gould, "The Economic Causes of the Rise of Baltimore," in *Essays in Colonial History Presented to C. M. Andrews.*

[4] Leila Sellers, *Charleston Business on the Eve of the American Revolution* (Chapel Hill, 1934), is a careful study of the economy of the Lower South.

family on the land or enable its head to give tł 'm the training and capital necessary for an independent status. Many of these surplus workers found employment as wage-earners in industry but most of them took up land of their own. The latter—as propertyless farmers —were obliged to borrow capital, thus gradually extending the scale of business carried on by the merchants and providing new employment for their accumulated capital. The small profits of agriculture meant further that the debtor farmers did not receive an income sufficient to justify intensive improvements on their land; instead they were compelled to "mine" the soil of its resources and its fertility, with the result that agriculture in the older areas was soon menaced by the competition of newly opened and more fertile lands—a pressure which enlarged the ranks of pioneers who migrated to the West.

In the third category of capitalist enterprise were included the various industries which employed wage-earners: such were the fishery, lumbering, flour milling, iron manufacturing, shipbuilding, the production of naval stores, hat making, sugar refining, and the manufacture of rum.[5] In all these industries the manufacturing capitalists steadily increased their stocks of invested capital and the number of employed hands. Their profits in the first instance assumed the form of a share of the commodities produced by the labor of their workers —a surplus that was in part converted into money and then invested in additional capital goods.

Colonial capitalism had many distinguishing characteristics. As a common rule the owners of capital goods controlled and managed the enterprises in which they were concerned, since large-scale corporations had not yet come into vogue. The class of such owners was relatively large, considering all the planters, independent farmers, master artisans, merchants, and small traders. Yet there were marked differences among the capitalists and the trend toward the concentration of capital set the most affluent apart in a superior category. The mass of the people, as servants, tenants, wage-earners, debtor farmers, or slaves, remained in a dependent condition. There was not as yet a visible specialization of capitalist function: the town merchant invested in ships, lands, buildings, industries, insurance, and mortgages, and the large planter was also often a trader, land speculator, manufacturer, and money-lender. On the whole the merchants occupied the strongest position. Manufacturing employers were cramped by high wages of workmen while the planters suffered both from England's restrictions upon their trade and from the relative inefficiency of slave

---

[5] Virginia D. Harrington, *The New York Merchant on the Eve of the Revolution* (New York, 1935), is a detailed study of the mechanisms of northern business.

labor. Inasmuch as the merchants made their profits from their dealings with the farmers and because nine-tenths of the people were engaged in agriculture the economy of the colonies offered well-nigh
unlimited opportunities to the merchant class.[6]

PLANTATION ECONOMY

The trend toward the concentration of capital operated with full
force in the southern colonies where the soil and climate afforded
staples in great demand in Europe. With the fall in the price of tobacco in Virginia and Maryland after 1660 the larger enterprisers
with capital extended their plantations and labor force, thereby cutting costs and driving small producers to the wall, so that by 1700
the plantation dominated the economy of the tidewater area. Two
new crops, rice and indigo, supported large-scale capitalist farming in
South Carolina and Georgia during the eighteenth century.

In 1694–96, when rice was first successfully cultivated in South
Carolina, the demand for the product in Europe and the resulting
high prices yielded the planter a return of 40 per cent on his labor
and investment. The crop required a considerable capital outlay in
that the cultivated fields had to be flooded two or three times during
the growing season: this was accomplished by damming a river and
erecting a reservoir above the fields, which were enclosed by a levee;
water was then admitted through an upper gate in the levee, and
when the fields had been sufficiently flooded it was drained off through
a lower gate. Another method employed after 1758 which utilized
the tides brought into cultivation the rich swampy lands along the
principal rivers. The rising tide forced the river water onto the rice
fields through the levee gates; drainage was possible whenever the
tide was out. This method, however, proved to be expensive: floods
occasionally broke the levees or they were undermined by alligators
or muskrats, thus effecting drainage at the wrong time, while hurricanes occasionally drove salt water onto the fields, thereby making
them sour and unproductive until after they had been bleached for
several years. After the introduction of Negro slavery in Georgia
(1750) rice plantations developed rapidly, largely under the auspices
of South Carolina planters.[7]

Because of the tedious labor required (hoeing, harvesting by sickle,

---

[6] Gertrude S. Kimball, *Providence in Colonial Times* (Boston, 1912), a broad study,
discusses business interests in chapter 7.

[7] A. S. Salley, *The Introduction of Rice Culture into South Carolina* (Columbia,
S. C., 1919).

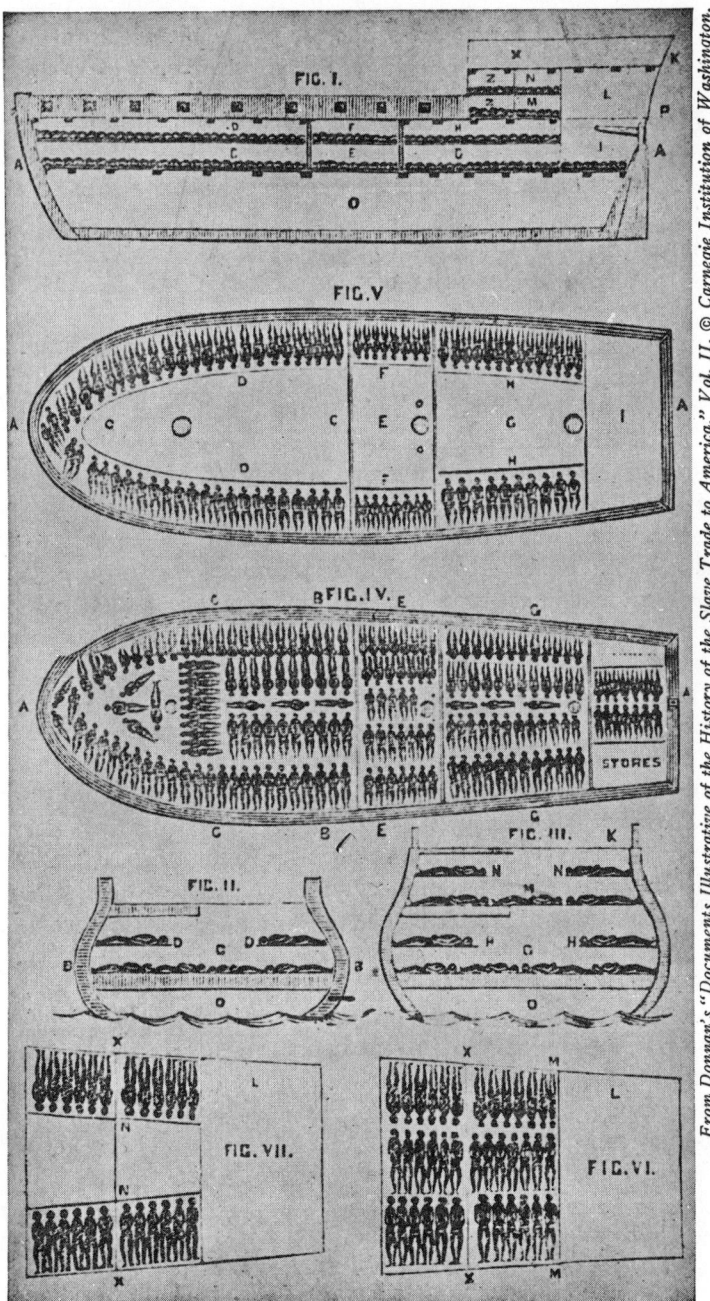

PLAN OF THE *BROOKES*, A SLAVE TRADING VESSEL OF THE EIGHTEENTH CENTURY

threshing by hand flail, and winnowing, sifting, and polishing the grains) and by virtue of the malarial condition of the swamp lands, slave labor was particularly necessary in the rice fields, since long residence in the jungles of Africa had made the Negro immune to malaria, while the white worker was highly susceptible to the disease. As a heavy, low-priced product (2*d*. or 3*d*. a pound in America) rice could be cultivated only along the rivers which afforded cheap transportation to Savannah or Charleston, whence vessels carried it to England and Europe. It was placed on the enumerated article list in 1705, with the result that the cost of shipment through England deprived the colonies of one of their markets, Portugal, and Parliament was forced to yield concessions in 1730, 1735, and 1737 by allowing rice exported from South Carolina, Georgia, and North Carolina to be shipped directly to points in Europe south of Cape Finisterre. Exports from Charleston (in barrels) increased from 3,000 in 1713 to 100,000 in 1724 and 125,000 in 1775. The growth of the plantation in South Carolina is indicated by the fact that after 1708 the Negro and white populations increased at the ratio of three to two.

Indigo supplemented rice in South Carolina after 1742. This product was introduced from the West Indies by Miss Eliza Lucas and cultivated under her supervision on an estate of her father, then governor of Antigua.[8] When it was found that South Carolina could not subsidize the new industry, Parliament in 1748 provided for a continuing bounty to producers of 6*d*. a pound. Due to the decline of indigo production in the West Indies there was a brisk demand for the Carolina product: its price in England ranged from 3*s*. to 6*s*. a pound, netting profits of 33 to 50 per cent to the planters and enabling them to bring the uplands of the interior under cultivation. The dyestuff was a bluish substance extracted from the indigo leaf by fermentation and pressed and cut into cubes—a process so disagreeable, even repulsive, that only slave labor could yield such handsome profits.

Although in its early stages the large plantation was efficient enough to crowd out the small producers yet in the long run it tended to become unprofitable—a trend clearly discernible in the tobacco area. During the eighteenth century the price of tobacco did not rise, whereas the costs of production advanced considerably. True, there was an enlarged production of tobacco; England's yearly imports from America consisted of 28,000,000 pounds in 1700–10 while in 1771–75 England and Scotland together received annually 102,000,000 pounds. Accompanying this growth in production was a large increase

[8] The standard biography is Harriott H. Ravenel, *Eliza Pinckney* (New York, 1902).

in the slave trade: in Virginia, Negroes composed 43 per cent of the population in 1756 as against 24 per cent in 1724; in North Carolina 26 per cent in 1767 as against 22 per cent in 1754; and 29 per cent in Maryland in 1755 as against 18 per cent in 1712. Yet despite such increases in production and in the labor force there are many evidences to show that tobacco growing became less and less profitable due to two primary causes: soil exhaustion and the mounting burden of fixed charges and debt. Both of these causes are traceable to the methods of trade upon which the planters had to depend.[9]

In 1764 a merchant wrote that "the African trade in Virginia must soon be at an end, for the people will not soon pay for the slaves they have already bought." With the progress of rice and indigo in the lower South the demand for slaves boosted their price, and in consequence the tobacco planters were obliged to pay a larger share of their profits to slave traders. Whereas the price of slaves in 1650 had been about £20 a head, it had risen to £25 in 1700, to £30 in 1741, to £40–£60 in 1750 and to £50–£80 in the 1770's. Since slave importations averaged about 3,500 in the years 1715–70, it is apparent that in the eighteenth century the planters had to pay, due to higher prices alone, from £20,000 to £100,000 or more a year.

The slave trade was but one part of a commercial system that frequently did not function for the planters' benefit. It will be recalled that the Navigation Acts required that tobacco should be exported to Europe, its chief market, by way of Britain; that imports to the colonies should pass through Britain; and that only British ships should be employed in the trade. These acts obliged the planters to deal with British merchants, who employed three methods in their colonial business. The wealthy tidewater planters commonly consigned their tobacco to merchants in England who sold it for them and remitted the proceeds to the colonies. Supplementing this method was the factorage system, whereby the merchant hired an agent in the colony to collect tobacco from the smaller planters and to deliver the goods sent from England in return. Then, with the growth of small farms in the interior, the merchants established stores which supplied the farmers with English goods on credit and collected tobacco in payment. With respect to the fundamental relations between farmer and merchant these three methods tended toward a common result.[10]

---

[9] See again L. C. Gray, *History of Agriculture in the Southern United States*, Vol. I. chapters 5, 12–13, 18–20.

[10] Charles C. Crittenden has written a scholarly history of *The Commerce of North Carolina, 1763–1789* (New Haven, 1936). See chapters 1–8.

As it has been previously explained, a planter who consigned his tobacco to England assumed the chief risks of the trade, whereas the merchant occupied a protected position. From the proceeds of a consignment which the latter sold several charges had to be deducted before the planter received anything. Such were the English import duties (6½d. a pound), the freights and insurance on the shipment to England, and the merchant's commission (2½ per cent of the gross proceeds), unloading, trucking, and warehouse fees, a charge for giving bond for the payment of import duties, and an assessment for maintaining a parliamentary lobby of the merchants; moreover the planter had to bear the loss arising from waste and shrinkage. All these charges were of a fixed character and the customs and earnings of the merchants constituted a first claim against the proceeds. In time of war the merchants insured their freight earnings, thus doubling freight rates and greatly increasing the sum deducted from the proceeds before the planters received a penny.[11]

If trade conditions were good and tobacco prices were high the planters secured a substantial profit but when depressions occurred the price of tobacco often fell so low that all the proceeds were consumed by the English charges, and if those charges exceeded the proceeds the planter became indebted to the merchant for the deficit. Several severe and protracted depressions (1703–13, 1720–34, and 1756–65) plunged the planters so deeply in debt that they were never able to extricate themselves. As debtors they were obliged to consign their future crops to their creditor merchants—an arrangement which gave birth to the tradition in Virginia that a delegation of the merchants "would meet annually and settle the price of tobacco for the year, . . . and at the same time have a similar understanding as to the profits of their merchandise, which was often 100 per cent of the prime cost."[12]

The planters also complained that the goods shipped to America by the merchants were of poor quality, that they were carelessly packed and damaged en route, and that orders were improperly or only partially filled. The debts contracted for slaves and merchandise during depressions took a heavy toll of the planters' surplus in better times. Writing in the 1730's Sir Robert Walpole said that the planters were reduced almost "to a state of despair by the many frauds that have been committed in that trade, by the heavy duties which the

[11] E. Donnan, "Micajah Perry," *Journal of Economic and Business History*, IV (Nov. 1931).

[12] For a good account of Virginia's trade see Leonidas Dodson, *Alexander Spotswood* (Philadelphia, 1932), chapter 4. T. J. Wertenbaker's *Norfolk* (Durham, N. C., 1931) is one of the best histories of a colonial town. See chapter 2 (trade).

importers of tobacco are obliged to pay . . . , and by the ill usage they have met with from their factors and correspondents here in England, who from being their servants are now become their lords and masters."

Because of the slender profits of agriculture the planters could not invest in improving and conserving their land, with the result that soil exhaustion rapidly undermined the older plantation areas. The high cost of slaves and their character as workers also impaired plantation economy which, by failing to utilize fertilizers, crop rotation, and deep-soil plowing, rapidly reduced the yield per acre: in Maryland it had fallen, by the end of the eighteenth century, from four thousand to two thousand pounds of tobacco. Although in Virginia in 1700 "soil wastage was everywhere evident and barren fields that would not grow crops profitably," yet the burden of fixed charges—slaves and debts—remained unchanged, thus cutting the planters' profits to the bone.[13]

In hope of extricating themselves from their plight the planters advocated many abortive remedies. After 1700 they secured colonial laws which levied high import duties on slaves, with the object of protecting the older plantations adequately supplied with labor against their rising competitors. Such a duty of £5 was levied by Virginia in 1710. The English government, ever desirous both to extend tobacco production and to promote the slave traffic, consistently opposed all colonial acts designed to curtail the importation of Negroes. Thus the Virginia act of 1710 was disallowed by the Privy Council and in 1731 the Crown ordered colonial governors not to sign any bills which levied duties upon imported slaves.

Of similar intent was another scheme: that of curtailing tobacco production by legal means. When tobacco prices fell to ruinous levels during depressions the assemblies of Virginia and Maryland passed laws which limited the number of plants that could be grown on each plantation and provided for the destruction of all inferior tobacco. Such acts, however, could not be enforced because they penalized the planter who complied and benefited the "chiseler"; moreover, it was impossible to induce all producing areas to coöperate; curtailment in one place led to expansion elsewhere so that the supply and price of tobacco were not materially altered. Crop restriction was also opposed by the small planters who paid officers' fees, taxes, and quit-rents in tobacco at a fixed number of pounds: hence they refused to curtail

[13] An especially important study is Avery O. Craven, *Soil Exhaustion as a Factor in the Agricultural History of Virginia and Maryland, 1606–1860* (Urbana, c. 1926). See chapters 1–2.

the quantity of tobacco money which they minted on their farms. In Maryland (1727–30) the small farmers refused to consent to restrictive schemes unless the quantity of tobacco which they were obliged to pay to the proprietor was correspondingly reduced. Lord Baltimore vetoed the latter proposal, realizing that a mere reduction of the amount of tobacco grown in the colony would not necessarily raise the price; he might merely receive a smaller quantity of tobacco which, when sold in England, would yield less money than a larger quantity. Virginia could not act without the coöperation of Maryland and therefore the whole plan fell through.[14]

Next the colonists appealed to England for relief when in 1732 they presented a petition, *The Case of the Planters of Tobacco in Virginia,* which requested that the heavy fixed charges collected in London be reduced. The import duties should be cut from 6½d. to 4d. a pound, the government should provide warehouses where tobacco could be stored without bond until the duties had been paid, and no duty should be collected on tobacco reëxported. Sir Robert Walpole, then chief minister of England, favored reduction or abolition of the import duties in order to prevent smuggling—a practice, incidentally, which lowered the price of tobacco and cut down the planters' proceeds from shipments which paid the duties. Walpole's scheme failed, due to political opposition and to the antagonism of the tobacco merchants, and the old abuses of the trade continued.[15]

The planters also endeavored to reduce their debts by legal action. In 1708 Maryland enacted a law that debtors without property might declare bankruptcy and escape punishment for debt. This act was disallowed by the Privy Council when English merchants objected that it permitted a planter to assign his lands and slaves to friends or relatives and by feigning bankruptcy to defraud his creditors. A comparable act of Virginia in 1749 allowed the planters to pay debts with depreciated Virginia currency: a debt of £100 in English money might be paid with £125 in Virginia money, even though the latter was not actually worth the former. The English government responded in 1754 by instructing the governor not to sign bills which allowed the planters to pay debts in Virginia currency at a fixed evaluation in English money. All colonial acts which scaled down debts were disallowed by the Privy Council; after 1710 the royal governors were instructed to see that courts were held fre-

---

[14] P. H. Giddens, "Trade and Industry in Colonial Maryland, 1753–1769," *Journal of Economic and Business History,* IV (May 1932).

[15] St. George L. Sioussat, "Virginia and the English Commercial System, 1730–1733," *Report,* American Historical Association, 1905, Vol. I.

quently so that English creditors might conveniently collect their "just dues," and in 1732 Parliament made the lands and slaves of the planters liable for debts.

The reforms sought by the planters—crop restriction, changes in the marketing system, lower import duties, reduction of debts and curtailment of the slave trade—were opposed by English interests which had the support of the imperial government; consequently the planters were obliged to look elsewhere for enduring relief. The most successful planters, who had made profits during good times, found two ways out of the distress of their class. First, they developed a real-estate business in the newer parts of their colonies, acquiring huge tracts of land which they leased to tenants or sold to small farmers.[16] When Robert Carter died in 1752 he possessed 300,000 acres of land, an area too vast to be cultivated by even his large force of a thousand slaves. William Byrd II held eighty thousand acres in 1744; Charles Carroll in Maryland between 1740 and 1765 acquired improved tracts ranging from five to ten thousand acres; Daniel Dulany, also in Maryland, obtained large holdings in Frederick County; in the years 1714–22 Governor Spotswood built up a vast estate in Spotsylvania County, Virginia. The profitableness of such acquisitions is indicated by the fact that land values in Maryland rose threefold between 1730 and 1760.

In the first stage of land speculation the planter ordinarily did not sell his tracts but rather imported tenants (Germans, Scotch-Irish, and settlers from the northern colonies) whom he supplied with tools, seed, and livestock, receiving rent in tobacco, grain, and other produce —an income which obliged him to assume the role of merchant. The rents received by Daniel Dulany in 1764 included fifty thousand pounds of tobacco. In leasing land the speculator often hoped merely to develop it and to pay expenses until a rise in values permitted sales at a profit.

The more efficient planters also found a way out of their difficulties by operating additional plantations on newer, more fertile soil and by diversifying production, so that southern economy became increasingly self-sufficing. The industrial development of the plantation exhibits three general stages. First, the individual estate produced a variety of things for its own use: cattle, sheep, hogs, horses, wheat, corn, rye, cotton and woolen clothing and coarse shoes for the slaves, certain farm implements and utensils, cooperage stock, bricks, soap, candles, salt, beer, and wine. The workers employed were indentured

[16] Halsted L. Ritter's *Washington as a Business Man* (New York, 1931) is an introductory study.

servants or slaves trained as carpenters, coopers, weavers, brick makers, brewers, sawyers, blacksmiths, etc. In the second stage of development the plantation sold a surplus of such products in its neighborhood: to smaller farmers and freed servants and to shipowners who purchased cereals and meats. Then came the final stage when a regular export trade was conducted. Staves, hoops, and headings were exported to the West Indies; thither also went flour, bacon, pork, and livestock; in 1755 Virginia's exports included 200,000 bushels of corn and 40,000 bushels of wheat.[17]

Despite this trend toward diversification the industrial opportunities of the plantation area were limited. The employment of slaves as artisans operated to prevent free craftsmen from migrating to the South, since the social status of their trades was degraded by slavery. Moreover, slave labor—deprived of incentive—was generally inefficient, while the purchase of slaves required a long-term investment that was avoided in the North by the employment of free wage-earners. When slaves were hired by their owners to employers the wage rate was necessarily high because it had to provide not only for the maintenance of the worker but also for a payment to the owner which would cover the principal and interest on his investment. As an industrial force slave labor also lacked the mobility and adaptability attainable when an employer might bargain with a laborer who was free to go where he pleased and who could be discharged at will. Only the scarcity of free wage-earners in the South (a scarcity induced largely by slavery itself) made it profitable for employers to utilize slave artisans as a labor force.[18]

The Progress of Industry

During the eighteenth century the economy of the middle colonies and New England was shaped largely by their commerce with Britain. They continued to purchase great quantities of manufactured and other European goods from England: by 1770 their imports amounted to £1,410,000 a year. Yet the northern colonies had not succeeded in developing domestic staples like tobacco which could be sent to England in payment for their large volume of imports: only a few native products—fur, ship timber, whale products, and lumber —were available as direct returns. Thus in 1770 the visible exports from the northern colonies had a value of only £178,000 and the

[17] See again M. W. Jernegan, *Laboring and Dependent Classes in Colonial America*, pp. 3–23.

[18] See again U. B. Phillips, *American Negro Slavery*, chapter 5.

nominal balance of trade against them amounted to £1,232,000. It is true that the unfavorable trade balance was not so great as these figures indicate because they do not include one very important export from the northern colonies—the ships which were built there and sold to English merchants. Even so, however, the value of imports greatly exceeded the value of the exports sent directly from the northern colonies to England.

Their lack of staples marketable in England had two profound effects on the northern colonies. First, it compelled them to engage in diversified production in order to satisfy as many of their wants as possible. Their agriculture afforded wheat, Indian corn, oats, rye, barley, cattle, sheep, swine, horses, mules, vegetables, fruits, and dairy products, while their domestic industries supplied them with coarse woolen and linen cloth, shoes, furniture, implements, household utensils, candles, soap, paper, glass, hats, sugar, beer, fish, flour, lumber, rum, cooperage stock, ships, saddles, earthenware, ironware, and woodenware. Secondly, the Northerners were obliged to engage in a complex trade in order to dispose of their surplus products in such a way as to provide them with purchasing power in England. The markets available for this surplus included the southern colonies, the West Indies, Africa, the Wine Islands, southern Europe, Newfoundland, Canada, Nova Scotia, and the interior fur trading areas; in each case the exports from the northern mainland were exchanged for commodities that could be used as remittances to England: coined money, bullion, sugar, indigo, dyewoods, ginger, cottonwool, rice, tobacco, naval stores, furs, wine, and bills of exchange. By virtue of these external trades the merchants of the northern colonies not only acquired the means of completing their payments for imports from England but also obtained excess profits from their marketing, shipping and credit services which explain the accumulation of capital in the northern commercial towns.[19]

Northern agriculture did not change materially after 1700 except for the rapid expansion of the settled area: the products raised and the methods of farming were the same as those previously described. In industry, however, the eighteenth century witnessed considerable progress in the form of diversification, specialization, and improved techniques. Household manufacturing, it is true, remained the backbone of industrial production, although it advanced to a more ma-

---

[19] Robert E. Peabody, *Merchant Venturers of Old Salem* (Boston, 1912), tells the story of Richard Derby, merchant. See chapter 1. See also E. Edelman, "Thomas Hancock, Colonial Merchant," *Journal of Economic and Business History*, I (Nov. 1928).

ture stage. In the frontier regions the family carried on a primitive form of production simply to supply itself with such articles as furniture, leather goods, utensils, soap, candles, fuel, and food products. A slightly more advanced community employed the services of traveling artisans who worked on materials supplied by the farmer:

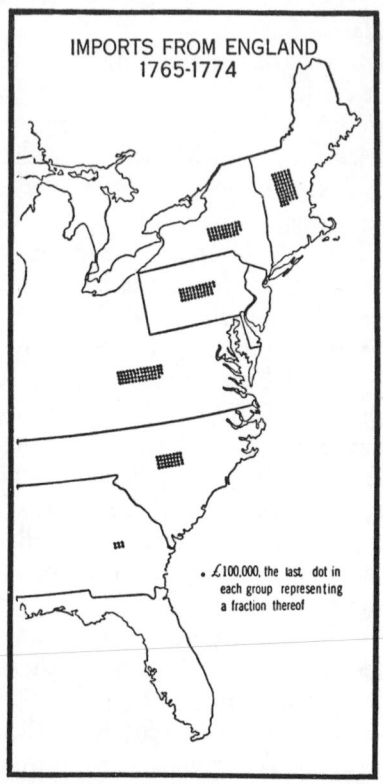

From Charles O. Paullin's "Atlas of the
Historical Geography of the United States."
© Carnegie Institution of Washington. Reprinted by courtesy of the American Geographical Society of New York.

among such artisans were masons, weavers, carpenters, and candle-makers. A third stage occurred when the family produced a surplus of manufactures which were at first exchanged in the neighborhood for other local products. Then, as an area became well settled, with improved transportation facilities, the farmers produced for general sale, more or less as employees of merchant manufacturers. Thus in the seaboard areas the latter supplied the farmers with flax, wool, and cotton which their families spun and wove into cloth—a form of capitalist production, since the merchants owned the raw materials and paid the farmer-workers a wage. This advanced stage of household manufacturing attained in the northern colonies by 1775 resembled the domestic system in vogue in England at the close of the six-

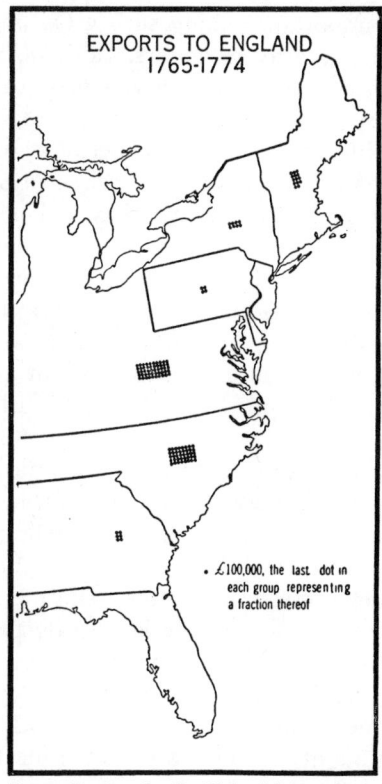

From Charles O. Paullin's "Atlas of the Historical Geography of the United States." © Carnegie Institution of Washington. Reprinted by courtesy of the American Geographical Society of New York.

teenth century, when her merchant capitalists became interested in colonization as a means of extending their markets.[20]

A similar evolution brought the small settled artisan within the circle of capitalist production. In the simplest form of handicraft industry, common to new settlements, a craftsman worked in his own

[20] L. H. Gipson's *The British Empire before the American Revolution* is especially good on economic themes. See Vol. II, chapter 3 (tobacco), pp. 165–185 (South Carolina), chapters 7–9 (sugar islands), chapter 10 (Africa); Vol. III, chapters 8 (iron), 10 (fishery), 11 (British colonial system).

shop, using his own tools with which he fabricated raw materials brought to him by the farmers of the neighborhood. This stage of production for local custom on advance orders was soon followed by a second stage in which the artisan purchased raw materials and manufactured goods for general sale which he displayed at his shop or sold to peddlers. Most important among such artisans were blacksmiths, hatmakers, shoemakers, weavers, tailors, saddlers, and wheelwrights. In colonial times the work of such artisans was not fully specialized: a shoemaker was also a tanner and a currier, a weaver a cloth dresser and a dyer, and a blacksmith a tool maker. Although employers of journeymen or servants and owners of their own tools, these settled craftsmen were not capitalists because they did not employ enough hands to receive substantial profits, so that their income was derived chiefly from their labor, not from their investments. The capital possessed by such artisans was not large: a blacksmith worked at a "bloomery" or small forge, operated by a power-driven bellows, where he manufactured wrought-iron goods; an estate of a leading Boston weaver in 1696 included four looms, a fulling mill, and two dye furnaces.

Ordinarily the small workshop of the artisan did not expand into a large industrial plant, largely because the owner did not possess capital sufficient to sustain production for distant markets which required payments for material and wages before the finished goods could be sold. As the chief possessors of capital the merchants played the principal part in the organization of large-scale production. At first they contracted with the artisans for the wares they produced—a practice virtually equivalent to the employment of the latter as wage-earners. Thus the merchant who received livestock from the farmers hired butchers to slaughter it and to pack the meat products for the market. Inasmuch as the merchants were the owners of the raw material and had control over the marketing processes, they were able to reap the profits arising from the spread between production costs and the sale price of manufactured wares.[21]

For those industries which had advanced beyond the handicraft to the mill stage and which required expensive plants and machinery, the artisans could not provide the necessary capital: that had to be obtained from merchants, large landowners and European investors. In order to establish mills, ironworks, distilleries, breweries, furnaces, etc., the promoters organized partnerships or companies. This method allowed a successful artisan to contribute a share of the capital and to

<hr/>

[21] See again J. R. Commons, *History of Labor in the United States*, Vol. I.

assume control of production, while the merchant investors took charge of financial and marketing operations.

What were the capital requirements of colonial industry? A sawmill, with water wheel and dam, which cut a thousand feet of boards daily, cost between $500 and $1,000. By 1765 flour mills (with a producing capacity of between a hundred and two hundred bushels a day) included besides the mill proper a storehouse or grain elevator, screens for cleaning wheat, a bolting house, ovens, and a cooper's shop "Most of the merchant mills in the central colonies were covered by substantial structures, usually of stone, two or three stories high. . . . The wheels were protected from ice and weather by being enclosed in the building itself." Ironworks consisted of blast furnaces for smelting the ore, refining forges at which a tilt hammer operated by water power fashioned bar iron, and slitting mills and plating mills equipped with rollers and cutters which worked the iron bars into rods, flat iron, and sheeting. Two iron establishments in the late colonial period—the Principio works in Maryland and the Peter Hasenclever works in New Jersey—represented an investment of $250,000 each: the latter consisted of six blast furnaces, seven forges, a stamping mill, three sawmills, and a gristmill. At New York in 1767 one company operated a linen factory which contained fourteen looms. The famous Stiegel glass plant at Mannheim, Pennsylvania, was so large that it was related "that a coach and four could turn around within the brick dome of its melting-house." In the Carolina naval stores industry tar kilns were constructed which had a capacity of 960 barrels; as early as 1664 a tile kiln in New York cost $25,000. The equipment of a brewery (a malt cellar, storehouse, and horses for operating the malt mill) required an outlay of between $1,000 and $3,000, while the equipment of a Trenton, New Jersey, tannery in 1778 included sixty-four vats, two water pools, a bark house, a currying shop and skin dresser's shop, and facilities for making leather breeches.[22]

Judged by modern industrial plants these colonial enterprises seem small enough, yet when it is considered that a colonial artisan, in a lifetime of labor, ordinarily did not accumulate more than $500, it is apparent that the capital outlays were considerable for the time. Whence came such capital? Foreign investors contributed a part: the Principio ironworks was an English concern, while German capital founded the Stiegel glass plant and the Hasenclever ironworks. Otherwise the capital was advanced by colonial enterprisers whose

[22] See again V. S. Clark, *History of Manufactures in the United States, 1607–1860,* chapters 1–9.

initial profits were derived from investments in land and commerce. A schedule of prices drawn up in Maryland in 1775 indicates the profits of trade: a merchant should not sell imported goods whole-sale for more than 112.5 per cent above their prime cost, nor at cash retail prices in excess of 130 per cent, while retail credit prices should not exceed 150 per cent. Land rents in New England in 1720–30 yielded a return of between 6 and 8 per cent. Such gains explain the growth of mercantile fortunes in the North. When Thomas Amory, Boston merchant, died in 1728 his estate exceeded $100,000; in 1737 Peter Faneuil owned English securities worth at least $75,000. Such foreign investments by a Boston merchant prince show that colonial fortunes were accumulating at a faster rate than the opportunities for traditional colonial investments in land and shipping—a trend that continued unabated between 1725 and 1775, and that explains in part the flow of colonial capital into industrial enterprises. Merchants of Philadelphia found an outlet for their surpluses in the iron industry, not only in works located in Pennsylvania but also in Virginia and Carolina. So common were investments in flour that many mills were known as merchant's mills. The employment of butchers, meat pack-ers, cloth workers, and shipwrights by the merchants who provided the raw materials afforded additional capital outlets. At Newport a leading Jewish merchant, Aaron Lopez, turned to the manufacture of spermaceti candles. Rope walks, rum distilleries, the fur trade, and the fishery also gave employment to the excess accumulations of the merchant class. Benjamin Franklin invested in paper mills and print-ing establishments: in 1733, he wrote, "I sent one of my journeymen to Charleston, . . . where a printer was wanting. I furnished him with a press and letters, on an agreement of partnership, by which I was to receive one-third of the profits of the business, paying one-third of the expense." [23]

Large-scale production afforded a high rate of profit by virtue of operating economies and a more effective control over markets and prices. The pioneer glass manufacturer of New Jersey accumulated an estate of approximately $150,000; similarly the Stiegel glass works for a time earned $13,000 a year. In 1705 the income of a Pennsylvania sawmill was £400, only a third of which was necessary to pay maintenance and labor costs. Of the flour industry V. S. Clark says that the miller "usually remained a local magnate, whose home assumed with increasing affluence something like manorial dignity." A Philadelphia cloth manufacturing society earned profits of 41 per

[23] Joseph S. Davis, *Essays in the Earlier History of American Corporations* (2 vols., Cambridge, 1917), gives the best discussion of the corporation in the eighteenth century.

cent during the first two years of operations (1775–76). Wherever possible industrial promoters endeavored to establish monopolies. The merchants and flour millers purchased or received grain when prices were low, attempted to obtain all local supplies, held flour from the market at dull seasons, and sold when prices were high. In the 1760's the spermaceti candlemakers formed an association in order to fix the prices of candles and raw materials (which they purchased through a single agent) and to prevent the "setting up of any new spermaceti works." Conditions of employment also favored the owners of industries: Clark states that "many colonial iron-masters ruled with almost feudal sway over a neighborhood settlement of their laborers and country people." When a sawmill was erected it frequently became the nucleus of a settlement where the owners established a store and a gristmill to serve at first the lumbermen-employees and later the farming community which developed on the cleared land. After 1720 industrial promoters in Boston, Philadelphia, and New York organized societies for the employment of the poor: workhouses were erected and skilled artisans were engaged to instruct children in the production of yarn, thread, cordage, bagging, and cloth. The products belonged to the promoters: "the idea was well fixed in the popular mind that the employment of children in such arts served the general welfare and that the profit of their labor, even when unremunerated, properly belonged to the person who undertook the burden of their instruction."

THE PROBLEM OF SURPLUS CAPITAL

It is notable that the colonial enterprises which assumed large proportions—the fishery, lumbering, flour milling, shipbuilding, etc.—afforded surpluses in excess of colonial needs and that other industries such as the textile, iron, and leather manufactures did not produce enough goods to meet the colonial demand.[24] Why, then, did some industries expand beyond the requirements of American consumption while others lagged behind? Primarily because the "surplus" industries yielded commodities which in the course of external trade were exchanged for English manufactures of the type not produced in sufficient abundance in the colonies. This industrial evolution was not wholly the outgrowth of natural conditions: it was shaped in large measure by English colonial policy, which dictated that the colonies should buy English manufactures, paying for them with staple commodities that could not be produced conveniently and

---

[24] On the whaling industry the best recent account is Elmo P. Hohman, *The American Whaleman* (New York, 1928), chapter 2.

cheaply in England; therefore the colonies should not develop industries in competition with those of the mother country. However, there was a class of products which England did not desire either to obtain from or sell to the colonies: such were fish, meats, cereals, flour, lumber, bread, and rum: consequently she placed no restraints upon the production or sale of such articles in America. On the other hand she restrained the colonial production of leather goods, woolens, hats, and ironware—all major products of her own export industry. This twofold policy of encouraging some colonial enterprises and of restraining others explains why the favored ones produced in excess of colonial needs while the progress of the others was arrested; also why the surpluses of the favored industries had to be exchanged for English manufactures of the sort which the colonies were not encouraged to produce.[25]

By a long train of measures England sought to retard the growth of colonial industries. The Woolen Act of 1699 prohibited the exportation of American wool, woolen yarn, and woolen cloth from any colony—a restriction which denied to colonial producers an extensive market needed to support large-scale enterprise. When Pennsylvania passed an act to encourage shoemaking the Board of Trade in 1706 recommended that it be disallowed on the ground that "it cannot be expected that encouragement should be given by law to the making any manufactures made in England . . . , it being against the advantage of England." About the same time the Board rejected a suggestion for producing sailcloth at New York because it would "be more advantageous to England that all hemp and flax of the growth of the plantations should be imported hither, in order to the manufacturing of it here." Whenever a colonial assembly levied duties on English goods imported with the object of giving tariff protection to colonial industries such acts were speedily disallowed by the Privy Council. Similarly the colonial governors were instructed by the Crown not to sign any bills which discriminated against English manufactures in the colonies or which aimed to foster competing industries there. Of this latter policy the authority on the subject, E. B. Russell, states: "Largely as a result of the government's determined attitude in the matter, comparatively few laws for this purpose were enacted in the plantations." Comparable to the Woolen Act was the Hat Act of 1732, which prohibited the exportation of American-made hats from the colony in which they were produced and which restricted

---

[25] C. M. Andrews, *The Colonial Background of the American Revolution* (New Haven, 1924), in chapter 2 discusses economic aspects of British policy in terms of political factors.

each hatmaker to two apprentices—another safeguard against large-scale production in the colonies.[26]

As early as 1710 the iron manufacturers of England complained of growing competition from the colonial iron industry. The latter developed rapidly from that date until by 1750 numerous furnaces, forges, and mills were operating in New England, the middle colonies, Virginia, and Maryland. When the first large shipments of colonial bar iron entered England in 1735 the product proved to be of such excellent quality that English ironmakers became involved in an acrimonious controversy over the fate of the colonial industry. One group—the ironmasters, who smelted native ores into pig iron—insisted that colonial pig iron be excluded from England by high import duties and went farther to urge that the whole colonial iron industry be suppressed. Allied with this group were the owners of English mines and forests (charcoal then being used in smelting ores). On the other side were the iron manufacturers who desired an abundant supply of cheap pig and bar iron which they might fashion into nails, tools, and other iron wares. The iron manufacturers therefore sought to encourage the production of pig and bar iron in the colonies by admitting it into England duty free, but at the same time they demanded that the colonists should not be allowed to work their crude iron into finished products. Allied with the iron manufacturers were the merchant shipowners who foresaw many weighty cargoes for their vessels in the transportation of crude iron from America to England and of iron manufactures from England to the colonies. The woolen industry sided with the iron manufacturers on the assumption that colonial exports of crude iron would provide the colonists with buying power for English cloth, thus retarding the growth of the woolen manufactures in America.[27]

After a long struggle between the ironmasters and the iron manufacturers the latter triumphed when Parliament in 1750 passed the famous Iron Act, which removed all duties on colonial pig iron imported into England and on colonial bar iron shipped to London. Nor were the colonies to develop iron manufactures; after June 24, 1750, the erection of three types of ironworks was prohibited; slitting mills which cut iron for nails, plating forges which made sheet iron, and steel furnaces which produced blister steel for tools. Such works

---

[26] Sir William J. Ashley defends British colonial policy in his *Surveys, Historic and Economic* (London, 1900). See essays on commercial legislation and American smuggling.

[27] Arthur C. Bining's *British Regulation of the Colonial Iron Industry* (Philadelphia, 1933) is a splendid study.

already established were not to be destroyed; only new ones were proscribed.

The purpose of the English measures against colonial manufactures—to outlaw enterprises which could profit by the economies of large-scale production—was generally realized. Extensive plants could not be concealed from the king's officials, and colonial investors (a cautious class) would not put their money into forbidden enterprises that might be suppressed overnight with the penalty of a fine. The English acts therefore diverted colonial capital from advanced manufactures and intensified the problem which had long confronted the northern colonies—that of finding adequate means of paying for imported goods.[28]

It will be recalled that the bounties on colonial naval stores granted by Parliament in 1705 were intended to provide the northern colonies with exports to England. The industry, however, took root in Carolina, fostered by the generous premiums paid to importers of colonial supplies: £4 a ton for pitch and tar; £3 a ton for resin and turpentine; £6 a ton for hemp; and £1 a ton for masts, yards, and bowsprits. Under the impetus of the bounties, pitch and tar shipped from the Carolinas, 1705–18, amounted to 134,000 barrels a year; from New England, 86,000 barrels. The exports from New England were not produced there but came originally from Carolina; however, the effect of this trade was to provide New England with additional returns. During four years, 1725–29, when the bounties were discontinued, the colonial trade fell off so abruptly that Parliament restored certain of the bounties in 1729 at a reduced rate: £2 4s. a ton for tar and £1 a ton for pitch. The yearly exports for the period 1763–75 were approximately twice as large as those for the years 1730–50; the bounties paid by England were as follows: from 1730 to 1750, about £17,000 a year; from 1750–63, about £24,000; and from 1763–75 about £34,000. Yet despite the substantial growth of naval stores exports they failed to provide the northern colonies with adequate exports to England: when the industry was at its height in 1770 the year's unfavorable trade balance against those colonies amounted to £1,230,000.[29]

Ships built in America and sold to English merchants supplied additional purchasing power for English imports—a value not accounted for in the estimates of colonial exports, since such vessels were not entered in the English custom records from which such estimates have been compiled. The colonial shipbuilding industry made steady progress throughout the eighteenth century—a trend explained

---

[28] See again E. Lipson, *Economic History of England*, Vol. III, chapter 4.

by the fact that American vessels could be constructed at costs 20 to 50 per cent below those prevailing in England. So severe was the competition of the colonial industry that in 1724 the shipbuilders of the Thames district in England, complaining that it was ruining their business, petitioned the government for protection. But despite the emigration of skilled shipwrights to America England did not interfere with the colonial industry: her merchants needed cheap vessels and the colonists obtained purchasing power for English manufactures by providing them. By 1775 30 per cent of the vessels in England's merchant marine were of American construction and 75 per cent of the commerce of the colonies was served by colonial ships. New England remained the center of the industry: in 1772 she produced 68 per cent of all colonial-built vessels as against 10 per cent constructed in Pennsylvania, 8 per cent in New York, and 14 per cent in the southern colonies. Important as such vessels were as an invisible export to England, even so they made but a slight impression on the unfavorable balance of trade: in 1763–66, when that balance against the northern colonies stood at £1,000,000 a year, the value of vessels annually built for sale in New England, Pennsylvania, and New York was only £80,000.

Despite the encouragement given by England to colonial shipbuilding and naval stores, the staple exports of the northern colonies consisted of commodities that could not be marketed in England. Of the value of the exports of New England, 1763–66, the fishery contributed 52 per cent, lumbering 14 per cent, and agriculture 7 per cent; for New York the figures were: farm products 80 per cent and lumber 10 per cent; for Pennsylvania, farm products 80 per cent and lumber 5 per cent. Such commodities, by and large, had to be sold in intermediate markets in order to supply the Northerners with buying power for English goods.

One trade in which the northern colonists did not participate during the seventeenth century—the slave traffic—afforded after 1715 a new outlet for colonial products and additional employment for colonial ships.[30] Newport, Boston, New York, and other towns sent forth vessels laden with rum to purchase slaves in Africa, then to make the famous middle passage to the West Indies and there to dispose of their cargoes, chiefly for commodities marketable in England, and partly for molasses to be returned to the northern colonies as raw

[29] J. Williams, "English Mercantilism and Carolina Naval Stores, 1705–1776," *Journal of Southern History*, I (May 1935).

[30] A brief sketch of the slave trade appears in W. E. B. DuBois, *The Suppression of the African Slave-Trade* . . . (New York, 1896), chapters 1–4.

material for more rum. So important was this heady beverage in the trade that rum distilleries sprang up rapidly in New England (there were sixty-three of them in Massachusetts in 1750 and about thirty in Rhode Island). By 1771 the colonial slave traders employed between sixty and seventy vessels, each capable of transporting sixty-five Negroes—an investment equal to about a fourth of England's stake in the traffic. When a slaver sailed for Africa from a colonial port its value (including cargo and supplies) was about £1,000; after sixty-five Negroes had been transported the owners derived a profit of 33 per cent over and above all costs of the voyage and a depreciation allowance of a third of the value of the vessel. Such handsome profits explain the readiness of colonial merchants to engage in the traffic: of Peter Faneuil of Boston the New England historian, W. B. Weeden, asks: "Did Peter slap his fair round belly and chuckle when he named the snow *Jolly Bachelor?* or was it the sad irony of fate that his craft deliberately designed to be packed with human pains and echo with human groans should in its very name bear the fantastic image of the luxury-loving chief owner? If these be the sources of profit and property, where is the liberty of Faneuil Hall, where the charity of good Peter's alms?" [31]

The growth of the slave traffic intensified the dependence of the northern colonies upon their commerce with the Caribbean region as the principal outlet for their surplus capital and products. Prior to 1700, the northern colonies had traded chiefly with the British West Indies; afterward, however, the British islands did not afford adequate markets for northern produce: population and production increased much more rapidly on the mainland than in the islands—and at a time when English policy induced the Northerners to produce an export surplus of fish, lumber, provisions, and work animals. An additional market therefore became necessary, and this the northerners found in the French West Indies—Guadeloupe, Martinique, and Santo Domingo, also producers of sugar, molasses, and rum.[32]

The trade which ensued greatly benefited the northern colonies but its effect upon the British sugar islands was not so happy. As a more efficient producing area the French colonies were able to undersell the British islands and thus to curtail the profits of the British planters. Established nearly a half century after the British plantations, the French sugar industry had the advantage of newer, more

[31] David D. Wallace, *The Life of Henry Laurens* (New York, 1915), devotes chapter 6 to the slave trade. See also E. Donnan, "The Slave Trade into South Carolina before the Revolution," *American Historical Review*, XXXIII (July 1928).

[32] H. C. Bell, "The West India Trade before the American Revolution," *American Historical Review*, XXII (Jan. 1917).

fertile soils and the benefit of the efficiency and enterprise of energetic planters unburdened by heavy fixed charges and wasteful methods. The British plantations, on the other hand, had been sadly reduced by a long process of exploiting the land for the sake of immediate gain. It was the ambition of the British planter to live luxuriously in England—a practice which diverted the earnings of his class from plantation improvements to extravagant living, while such absenteeism necessitated the employment of overseers who commonly "mined" the soil for the sake of quick profits. In the French islands the plantations were generally smaller and operated by their owners, who reinvested their surplus in plantation improvements, took pains to conserve the soil, and managed their estates with that care, prudence, and economy for which French farmers are famous.[33]

Because the French plantations had to be developed under the shadow of the established English sugar industry the French government encouraged them with privileges which the British planters did not enjoy. Whereas the latter had to ship their sugar first to British ports their French competitors were allowed to export directly to their best European markets without the added charges of visiting a French port. In order to meet the costs of local government the British planters were obliged to pay heavy duties on their sugar exports; France on the other hand supported her colonial governments from national revenues, with the result that the island duties on French sugar exported were only a fourth of those collected by England. By virtue of these many advantages the French islands could sell sugar and its products from 25 to 30 per cent cheaper than Barbados and the Leeward Islands; they could also pay higher prices for northern products which were seeking wider markets. France could not supply her sugar islands with the necessary provisions, nor could her fur trading settlements in North America do so. Neither did France desire to buy West Indian molasses and rum: the French people did not like the taste of molasses, and rum was discriminated against in order to protect the French producers of wine and brandy. For these reasons France allowed her sugar colonies to obtain provisions, lumber, and work animals from the northern colonies in exchange for molasses and rum, and English colonial vessels were permitted to carry on the trade.[34]

As early as 1710 the planters of the British islands demanded pro-

[33] Two significant articles are C. M. Andrews, "Anglo-French Colonial Rivalry: the Western Phase," *American Historical Review*, XX (April, July 1915).

[34] Frank W. Pitman, *The Development of the British West Indies, 1700–1763* (New Haven, 1917), is the best analysis of West Indian economy.

tection against their French competitors. When England and France were locked in a fateful struggle was it not intolerable that the sugar colonies of England should be undermined by a trade through which her own colonies provisioned the French plantations, thereby enlarging the supply of sugar and depressing its price? Did not the northern colonial merchants sell their products in the British West Indies and obtain money there which was used to buy sugar and molasses from the French planters? And did not the Northerners relabel French sugar as British sugar and then ship it to England, thus depriving the British planters of the home market especially reserved for them? What a nefarious traffic was this which strengthened France's hold upon the sugar trade at the expense of England! Not only were the British planters concerned; the British merchants had a vast stake in the islands—a huge investment built up through loans to the debtor planters, a profitable commission business in London, and a fleet of vessels which carried products to and from the West Indies. If the British sugar industry fell it would drag down with it one of the most prosperous branches of England's overseas trade.[35]

In a campaign of self-protection the whole West Indian interest, planters and merchants, brought pressure upon the English government through a powerful parliamentary lobby, and after a long agitation secured the Molasses Act of 1733. Designed to impoverish the French West Indies, this statute imposed extremely high duties on foreign sugar, molasses, and rum imported into the English colonies (the molasses duty was 6d. a gallon.) The spokesmen of the northern colonies protested bitterly: the act, by lowering the prices of the northern staples and raising the price of sugar, molasses, and rum, would curtail the profit of colonial trade or destroy it altogether. Molasses and rum were ingredients in the slave trade, the fur trade, the Newfoundland trade, and the fishery: if the northern colonies could not obtain cheap rum they would lose those all important sources of profit and employment. And for what? Merely to protect the indolent, inefficient planters of the British West Indies! [36]

Obviously the Molasses Act involved the British empire in a serious contradiction. The northern colonists, not permitted to manufacture in competition with English industry, were encouraged to produce a

---

[35] Lowell J. Ragatz, *The Fall of the Planter Class in the British Caribbean, 1763–1833* (New York, c. 1928)—an outstanding book—devotes chapters 1–3 to West Indian society, agriculture, and trade.

[36] On the political influence of the West Indies see Lillian M. Penson, *The Colonial Agents of the British West Indies* (London, 1924.) For a briefer statement see L. M. Penson, "The London West India Interest in the Eighteenth Century," *English Historical Review*, XXXV (July 1921).

surplus of fish, lumber, provisions, and rum—products which had to be sold in outside markets in order to procure purchasing power for English goods. Yet the Molasses Act would have destroyed one of the necessary markets for that surplus. Two parts of the British empire were out of balance: the sugar islands were not keeping pace with the northern colonies, and when the issue became acute England prepared to sacrifice the northern farmers, fishermen, lumbermen, and merchants to the sugar planters and the English merchant-investors concerned in the West Indies. The Northerners presumably were neither to manufacture for themselves nor to sell their crude products where they could obtain purchasing power for English manufactures. How then could colonial investors find new outlets for their surplus capital?

The critical issue thus raised was evaded for twenty-five years by smuggling on a grand scale. The Northerners regarded the Molasses Act as grossly unjust, ignored it completely, and continued the foreign West Indian trade with unabated vigor.[37] Colonial labor and capital therefore continued to flow into shipbuilding, shipping, lumbering, agriculture, the fishery, distilleries, and all the trades dependent upon rum. Instead of resolutely enforcing the act the English government in 1739 offered a concession to the planters by permitting the exportation of sugar directly from the West Indies to points in Europe south of Cape Finisterre. But this availed little, because the best sugar markets were in northern Europe. Meanwhile, as the French plantations and the northern colonies continued to prosper in their unlawful partnership, the British planters repeatedly demanded the suppression of the trade which sustained their rivals. And when they forced the issue after 1758 they helped to precipitate the Revolutionary War.

[37] William S. McClellan, *Smuggling in the American Colonies* . . . (New York, 1912), is a good, compact discussion.

BIBLIOGRAPHICAL NOTE

SECONDARY WORKS: Klaus E. Knorr, *British Colonial Theories, 1570–1850* (Toronto, 1944), summarizes the ideas and attitudes underlying British colonial policies. Philip W. Buck, *The Politics of Mercantilism* (New York, 1942), sees in mercantilism a policy by which national states, seeking the national well-being, moved toward managed economies.

Richard Pares, *Merchants and Planters* (Cambridge, Eng., 1960), consists of four outstanding essays on the economics of the tobacco colonies and the West Indies. Arthur P. Middleton, *Tobacco Coast* (Newport News, 1953), is a first-rate study of the maritime trade and shipping of the Chesapeake Bay area. Louis Morton, *Robert Carter of Naomi Hall* (Princeton, 1941), affords an intimate view of economic life in the tobacco country, as seen on the domains of a leading planter. Jacob M. Price, *The Tobacco Adventure in Russia* (Philadelphia, 1961), describes English efforts to market colonial tobacco in Europe, 1672–1722.

The best studies of colonial merchants are James B. Hedges, *The Browns of Providence Plantations: Colonial Years* (Cambridge, 1952)—an outstanding work; Frederick B. Tolles, *Meeting House and Counting House* (Chapel Hill, 1948)— an attractive group portrait of Philadelphia Quakers; W. E. Baxter, *The House of Hancock* (Cambridge, 1945)—a well-informed analysis of business in Boston; Byron Fairchild, *Messrs. William Pepperrell: of Piscataqua* (Ithaca, 1954)—a scholarly monograph; and Glenn Weaver, *Jonathan Trumbull* (Hartford, 1956) —a realistic description of the actualities of colonial trade. Margaret E. Martin, *Merchants and Trade of the Connecticut River Valley, 1750–1820* (Northampton, 1938, 1939), is one of the best studies of the commerce of an important area. Bernard Bailyn and Lotte Bailyn, *Massachusetts Shipping, 1697–1714* (Cambridge, 1959), provides a modern computation of official data pertaining to shipbuilding, shipping, and shipowning. Richard Pares, *Yankees and Creoles* (Cambridge, 1956), is the best survey of the West Indian trade.

Arthur C. Bining, *Pennsylvania Iron Manufacture in the Eighteenth Century* (Harrisburg, 1938), is a leading study of a colonial industry. Carl Bridenbaugh, *The Colonial Craftsman* (New York, 1950), is an interesting introduction to the skilled trades, as carried on mainly in the principal towns.

SOURCES: Guy S. Callender's *Selections from the Economic History of the United States* (New York), is highly valuable. See chapters 1–3 and note particularly the discriminating introductory essays. The anonymous *American Husbandry* (2 vols., London, 1775; ed. H. J. Carman, New York, 1939), gives an inside view of colonial agricultural techniques. The first two volumes of *A Documentary History of American Industrial Society* (10 vols., Cleveland, 1910–11), edited by U. B. Phillips under the title *Plantation and Frontier, 1649–1863*, contain much material on the eighteenth-century plantation. Elizabeth Donnan (ed.), *Documents Illustrative of the History of the Slave Trade* (4 vols., Washington, 1930–1935), is a collection of great importance. Two well-known statements of mercantilism are Joshua Gee, *The Trade and Navigation of Britain Considered* (London, 1767), and William Wood, *A Survey of Trade* (London, 1718). N. S. B. Gras and Henrietta Larson, *Casebook in American Business History* (New York, 1939), contains valuable material on early American trade. Ruth S. Gottesman, *The Arts and Crafts of New York* (2 vols., New York, 1938, 1954), is a first-hand record, drawn from newspaper advertisements of skilled workers, 1726–1799.

XVII

 Colonial Society

From Europe, and particularly from England, came the cultural traits which contained the germs of American society. The transplanted customs and ideals which survived in America were those best suited to the new environment; and they in turn were modified by it. Occupations, primitive contacts with nature, and the economic organization of society: such influences shaped the mold and spirit of colonial life. If there was diversity of manners and customs traceable to racial, religious, geographical, and class differences, so also—and more important—there were fundamental similarities arising from psychological and physiological traits common to all people, from the common inheritance of Christian morality, and from an economic organization that cut across racial, religious, and geographical lines.[1]

The Colonial Family

The most important element in colonial society, the family, gave a dominant tone of domesticity to the age. It was the unit of production and business enterprise, the means of perpetuating the race, and the chief agency of human association. Often containing as many as twenty or thirty people (counting servants and odd relatives), the family was a large unit primarily because of the numerous children that swarmed about the home. Families of ten or twelve children were considered common; those of twenty or twenty-five were not regarded as phenomenal. Patrick Henry was one of nineteen; John Marshall the first of fifteen. Not all the children survived; in Pennsylvania it was estimated that four in ten died before the age of sixteen. A New England versifier paid tribute to Mrs. Sara Thayer, who died in 1751:

> Also she was a fruitful vine,
> The truth I may relate

[1] Charles A. and Mary R. Beard's *The Rise of American Civilization* (2 vols., New York, 1930) is a stimulating synthesis. See Vol. I, chapter 4.

Fourteen was of her body born
And lived to man's estate.

From these did spring a numerous race,
    One hundred thirty-two;
Sixty and six each sex alike
    As I declare to you.

And one thing more remarkable,
    Which I shall here record:
She'd fourteen children with her
    At the table of the Lord.

An observer of North Carolina in 1760 wrote: "the necessaries of life are so cheap and so easily acquired, and the propagation being unrestricted, that the increase of people there is inconceivable, even to themselves." Oglethorpe advertised in 1732 that a husband, wife, and child over seven could earn six times as much in Georgia as in England. At any rate, economic productivity explains the rapid growth of population and the custom of early marriage. Girls in all the colonies were commonly married when sixteen or eighteen (occasionally when only thirteen or fourteen); young men became husbands more often "under twenty years than above." Such early marriages enabled parents, while still young and adaptable, to become adjusted to each other and to the wear and tear of little children. Nor did youth have to contend with the psychological strain of abstinence when the urge of sex was strong.[2]

As the custodian of property the family played an important economic role. Marriage portions, dowries, marriage settlements, and inheritance figured prominently in family affairs in all the colonies. Due to the property aspects of marriage the early Protestant reformers considered marriage primarily as a civil contract and authorized that the wedding ceremony be performed by civil magistrates. Such was the practice in the middle and New England colonies during the seventeenth century; not until 1692 was marriage by clergymen legalized in Massachusetts. In the eighteenth century, when religious ceremonies became common, the minister acted as an agent of the state. The Anglican Church in the South affirmed the principle of marriage by the clergy, but due to the union of church and state, the clergyman acted as a representative of the civil government as well as of the church. In all the colonies the disposition of

[2] Arthur W. Calhoun, *A Social History of the American Family* (3 vols., Cleveland, 1917–1919), though not a definitive work, contains much interesting information, with intelligent comments. See Vol. I.

property by marriage settlement or inheritance was regulated by civil law; fundamentally marriage was a civil rather than a religious institution.[3]

Since marriage involved a transfer of property, either immediate or in the future, the consent of parents—as the owners of the property concerned—was necessary to a match. Thus custom in all the colonies required that a young man secure the permission of his father and of the father of the young lady of his choice before he began his suit—a custom reinforced by laws which voided marriages entered into without parental consent. Such parental authority, however, was not unlimited: in New England the civil authorities might overrule parental objections made on capricious or unjustifiable grounds. In order to assure parental consent all the colonies condemned secret marriages and required that advance notice be given and that a wedding ceremony be performed. Families of the lower middle class gave notice by having banns thrice published in church; the wealthier folk obtained marriage licenses from governors or ministers, paying fees which the poor could not afford. In Pennsylvania the issuance of a minister's license required two men of good repute to certify that the bridegroom was free to marry; they in turn became liable for damages if he could not legally perform his part of the contract. The rustic wedding in Pennsylvania, which took place in church or in the bride's house, was followed by many a bucolic joke and an all-night celebration given over to feasting and dancing. "Whoever stole off to get some sleep was hunted up, dragged out on the floor, and the fiddler ordered to play, 'Hang on till tomorrow morning.' "[4]

Among upper-class groups there prevailed an acute awareness of the property status of wooer and wooed. An important New Englander wrote of his daughter: "she may stay here long 'ere she meet with a better [match] unless I had more money for her than I can now spare." Certainly few of the upper class "married beneath them"; practical considerations kept a tight rein on romantic fancies. "Where passion and affection sway, that man is deprived of sense and understanding." A suitor of Nancy Shippen, belle of Philadelphia in 1781, lamented that a girl "who has all the advantages of a good education must be married in a hurry and given up to a man she dislikes." Due to the class limitations of courtship the wealthy families became closely related by intermarriage. In 1767 the relatives of Abram De

---

[3] C. L. Powell, "Marriage in Early New England," *New England Quarterly*, I (July 1928).

[4] C. M. Andrews, *Colonial Folkways* (*Chronicles of America*, New Haven, 1919), chapters 1–5, 8.

Peyster of New York included Van Cortlandts, Beekmans, Livingstons, De Lanceys, Philipses, Schuylers, Stuyvesants, Jays, Roosevelts. So also the first families of Virginia—the Carters, Balls, Fitzhughs, Lees, Washingtons, Stuarts, Ludwells, and Corbins—were bound together by ties of marriage. Since the number of prospective husbands among the upper class was limited, the young ladies did their utmost to make themselves attractive in order to charm as many eligible young men as possible and thus to have a wide range of choice. Washington's condemnation of loveless marriages indicates that the romantic ideal survived despite pecuniary handicaps.

Among artisans and small farmers parents considered, not so much the property assets of a prospective mate (although that was not to be scorned), as his or her industry and efficiency as a provider or housewife. Franklin [5] voiced the contempt of this class for mercenary marriages in a "jingle" written in 1721:

> A swarm of sparks, young, gay, and bold
> Loved Sylvia long, but she was cold, . . .
> At last came Dulman, he was old,
> Nay he was ugly, but had gold.
> He came and saw and took the hold,
> While t'other beaux their loss consoled.
> Some say, she's wed; I say she's sold.

Theoretically the husband was lord and master of the family, but numerous references to housewives in *Poor Richard's Almanac* suggest that not all women were meek and submissive. Unquestionably the personal status of women was rapidly improved in colonial America—a fact explained by their high economic value and by their relative scarcity. As cook, seamstress, nurse, laundress, baker, teacher, cloth maker, and supervisor of household production the colonial woman was indispensable in rural economy, her value being attested by the high price of women indentured servants. One writer estimated that a wife and child earned as much as a man. "A good husband," said a commentator on New Hampshire, "with his wife to attend the cattle and make butter and cheese will be profitable, for maids they are soon gone in this country." Throughout colonial times immigration brought to America more men than women; consequently wives were at a premium. So scarce were women in Virginia in 1619 that the Virginia company sent over a shipload of marriageable girls who were disposed of to the planters at the rate of 120 pounds of tobacco each. Oglethorpe wrote of a settlement in Georgia:

[5] Carl Van Doren, *Benjamin Franklin* (New York, 1938), gives the best view of Franklin's career as a whole.

"there is now in this place . . . above 700 men more than there are women. Most of these would marry if they could get wives." In view of the prevailing scarcity, every woman was supposed to marry: an act of Maryland provided a woman must forfeit land inherited if she did not marry within seven years. And a woman who could not "get a husband" was deemed deficient indeed; hence the odium and even disgrace attached to spinsterhood. Similarly, widows and widowers re-married quickly; one man in Pennsylvania proposed to a young lady the day his wife died and remarried within a week. Third and even fourth marriages of bereaved husbands and wives were common in all the colonies.[6]

> Luke, on his dying bed, embraced his wife
> And begged one favor: swear my dearest life,
> Swear if you love me, never more to wed. . . .
> Anne dropped a tear. You know my dear, says she,
> Your least desires have still been laws to me;
> But from this oath, I beg you'd me excuse
> For I'm already promised to J[ohn] H[ughes].

Although colonial women did not attain equality with men, it is certain that they gained a better status than they had enjoyed in Europe. Employments out of doors conferred personal freedom upon girls of the farm; the ideal of maidenly seclusion could not be ad-hered to. A. W. Calhoun, social historian of the American family, states: "If a young man took it into his head that his betrothed should not be free and gay in her social intercourse, he would run the risk of being discarded, incur the reputation of jealousy, and find it very difficult to get married." In the southern and middle colonies the scarcity of women enabled "maid servants of good honest stock" to "choose their husbands out of the better sort of people." A jealous servant in Maryland disparaged a successful rival:

> What if as planter's wife you go
> Nature designed you for the hoe.

Wertenbaker believes that the handicap of poor, degraded men in finding wives acted as a selective factor to improve the race. Mittel-berger, observing eighteenth-century Pennsylvania, was struck by the fact that a wife could not be compelled to do anything against her will, that her husband could not box her ears, and that he might be punished at law for maltreating her. The New England colonies also provided penalties for the ill usage of wives: Plymouth enacted "that

[6] Alice M. Earle, *Colonial Dames and Goodwives* (Boston, 1895), is an entertaining account.

every married woman shall be free from bodily correction or stripes by her husband." [7]

The economic status of women is evident in laws governing property. Widows received either a third or a half of the estate of husbands who died without making wills—a rule which acknowledged the claim of the wife to property produced by joint effort. Connecticut, a colony conservative in family matters, reversed in 1723 its rule which gave husbands complete control over real estate inherited by their wives: a new law prescribed that such property was not to be alienated without the wife's consent. As early as 1675 a marriage contract in Virginia gave the wife full power over the property bestowed upon her by her father. In the middle and southern colonies widows whose husbands had died intestate became administrators of the family estate. The experience of women with the practical affairs of shop or household and their training in industry, economy, and thrift qualified them to serve as managers of the family business or estate: many widows carried on as shopkeepers, merchants, shipowners, innkeepers, farm and plantation operators, printers, editors, and workers in the household crafts. Such careers employed women in all the colonies. Widows without independent estates commonly remarried or lived with relatives; there were few opportunities available to women as wage-earners. [8]

Despite the improved status of women in the colonies, their station in life was determined primarily by the position of their husbands or fathers. Thus women of the poorest families, compelled to work in the fields, stood at the bottom of the social scale. Such was the lot of the many women pioneers, and, according to William Byrd, of the wives of the small farmers in North Carolina. Crèvecoeur states that German farm women "often share . . . the most severe toils of the field." An observer of early Virginia said of women servants: "Yet some wenches that are nasty, beastly, and not fit to be so employed [in household work] are put into the ground." The words "dirty" and "soiled" indicate the opprobrium associated with work in the fields. One of the surest signs of the social advancement of a family was the exemption of its womenfolk from such toil. In middle-class circles the wife, as mistress of the other dependents of the family (the children and servants), confined her activities to work within the household. Such being women's approved function, there was in all the

---

[7] Carl Holliday, *Woman's Life in Colonial Days* (Boston, 1922), a sentimental eulogy, contains many good quotations.

[8] Elisabeth A. Dexter's *Colonial Women of Affairs* (Boston, 1924) is a "study of women in business and the professions in America before 1776."

colonies before 1740 a strong opposition to literary education for girls; they should rather be trained in the household crafts and the practical arts of family management. An ideal housewife was described by John Dunton, a visitor to New England in 1686: "Her pride was to be neat and cleanly, and her thrift not to be prodigal, which made her seldom a non-resident of her household."

The women of the upper class occupied themselves chiefly with planning the work of the home and with supervising the domestic servants, although they also performed lighter duties such as baking, nursing, and sewing. Upper-class girls, exempt from common toil and not yet prepared for the responsibilities of management, were disciplined by training in fancy needlework, drawing, music, refined manners, and care of the person. All such attainments, being decorative rather than utilitarian, indicated that the aristocratic lady, exempt from menial work, belonged to a family of superior status.[9] The intellectual training given to upper-class girls was superficial; at the end of the colonial period James Franklin said that southern ladies "seldom read or endeavor to improve their minds"—a remark that bears out the earlier comments of William Byrd: "We supped at nine and then prattled with the ladies." "Our conversation with the ladies was like whip-syllabub, very pretty but nothing in it." Dr. Shippen's ideal for his daughter was to make her "one of the finest women in Philadelphia."

Occupying a dependent position in society, the colonial women were particularly prone to improve their status by emulating the upper class. Of a visit to his overseer a planter wrote in 1772: "I was sorry to see his wife act the part of a fine lady in all her wearing apparel, with at least two maids besides her own girl to get dinner and wait upon her; but this I do suppose she did to show respect. . . ." An English traveler in the Revolutionary period noted a zest for fashion among American women, both rural and urban, and was impressed by the fact that an innkeeper's daughter "went regularly three times a week seven miles to attend the lessons of one de Grace, a French dancing master, who was making a fortune in the country."

The place of children in colonial society was determined largely by the value of their labor on the farm and in the shop.[10] Boys sowed seed, weeded fields, combed wool, shelled corn, sawed and chopped wood, fed the pigs, watered horses, picked berries, gathered vegetables, made brooms, and ran errands; the girls helped in all the tasks

---

[9] Mary S. Benson, *Women in Eighteenth-Century America* (New York, 1935) is an interesting, informative, scholarly study.

[10] See again Alice M. Earle, *Child Life in Colonial Days.*

about the house. The Reverend Francis Higginson wrote of New England in 1629, "Little children here by setting of corn may earn much more than their own maintenance"—a condition that continued throughout colonial times, as indicated by the traffic in child indentured servants and by the custom of binding poor children to enterprisers who employed them at a profit in workshops. Describing the German settlers in 1789 an observer said: "Upon the birth of a son, they exult in the gift of a plowman or waggoner; and upon the birth of a daughter they rejoice in the addition of another spinster or milkmaid to the family." The high death rate among colonial children meant that the weak and sickly perished; those who survived were generally able to perform the required labor. In 1737 a Dr. Brickell noted that the children of North Carolina were "seldom or never troubled with rickets, and many other distempers that the Europeans are afflicted with, and you seldom see any of them deformed in body."

The customs governing the inheritance of property reflected the diversity of colonial society.[11] The small farmers and artisans believed that each child should receive an equal share of the family estate—a principle which recognized that the labor of the child conferred a claim to the accumulated property. Moreover, equal inheritance was an incentive to labor during childhood. The merchant families also divided estates among the children: dowries, settlements, and inheritances induced intermarriage within this class, thereby multiplying business contacts, reducing competition, and bringing to one family the assistance, in time of need, of other mercantile houses. On the other hand, the wealthy landed families, whose eminence rested upon a large ancestral estate, favored both the principle of primogeniture, which preserved the estate intact in the possession of the eldest son, and the law of entail, which vested the title to a property in a future heir, thus preventing its sale or alienation by the family. Primogeniture and entail did not become prominent in America until large estates developed which were cultivated by tenants, servants, or slaves; on such estates the children of the owner did not work; consequently they had no claim to the family property, nor was an assured inheritance needed as a spur to child labor within the family. Primogeniture, however, was unpopular in the colonies because social development had not gone far enough to provide the younger sons with honorable, well-paid positions in an army, navy, church, or civil service, in business, or in the legal and learned professions. Hence

[11] Richard B. Morris, *Studies in the History of American Law* (New York, 1930), is a significant though technical treatment. See chapters 1–3.

among the colonial aristocracy it was customary to provide subsidiary plantations for the younger sons—a practice which gave the landed interest a strong bent toward expansion.[12]

The law of inheritance governing the estates of landowners who died without making wills illustrates the foregoing observations. Massachusetts in 1641 provided for equal inheritance, except that the eldest son was granted a double portion; Connecticut in 1699 enacted that all children should share equally in the family estate. The Georgia trustees were forced to abandon primogeniture and to allow all sons and daughters to share alike. The Dutch brought from Holland to New Netherland the custom of equal inheritance. In the eighteenth century several colonies (Virginia, Maryland, Pennsylvania, the Carolinas, New York, and Massachusetts) permitted landowners to will estates by the rule of primogeniture; similarly, lands could be entailed by will in all the southern colonies and in Pennsylvania and New York.[13]

THE OUTLOOK ON LIFE

Of the influences that shaped the colonial way of life none had greater force than the determination of the people not to relapse into savagery but to maintain a European standard of living. That ideal necessitated unremitting labor which contact with a primitive environment rendered doubly onerous. Moreover, social betterment depended upon thrift and saving, since the standard of living could be raised only by means of the accumulation of capital so necessary to improved efficiency of production. To the mass of farmers and workers life meant incessant toil; similarly, members of the upper class, possessed of relatively small fortunes, could achieve superiority in society only by that vigilant attention to the details of business through which the accumulation of capital was effected. The hard conditions of life fostered a stern moral code, the essence of which was the condemnation of everything deemed to have a weakening, injurious effect upon oneself and one's neighbors. Health, strength, stamina, endurance, and vitality: such were the desiderata of colonial morality. "If thou would'st live long," said Poor Richard, "live well; for folly and wickedness shorten life." [14]

High among the approved virtues ranked the habit of industry.

[12] R. B. Morris, "Primogeniture and Entailed Estates in America," *Columbia Law Review*, XXVII.

[13] C. M. Andrews, *The Connecticut Intestacy Law* (New Haven, 1933—Connecticut Tercentenary Commission, no. 2).

[14] See again E. Eggleston, *The Transit of Civilization*, chapter 4.

Crèvecoeur noted with approval "that restless industry which is the principal characteristic of these colonies"; an act of Massachusetts condemned "divers loose, vain and corrupt persons . . . [who] insinuate into the fellowship of the young people . . . , drawing them both by night and day from their callings, studies and honest occupations." Of sleep Poor Richard said:

> Nature needs but five,
> Custom gives us seven,
> Laziness takes nine,
> And wickedness eleven.

Since waste destroyed the fruits of industry, thrift and saving were properly in order. Among Poor Richard's maxims the exhortations to economy are numerous: "All things are cheap to the saving, dear to the wasteful"; "Silks and satins put out the kitchen fire"; "Too much plenty makes mouth dainty"; "Spare and have is better than spend and crave"; "A fat kitchen makes a lean will"; "Many dishes, many diseases." So also Franklin commended the utility of honesty, observing that "there being in the world a number of rich merchants, nobility, states and princes who have need of honest instruments for the management of their affairs . . . no qualities . . ." are "so likely to make a poor man's fortune as those of probity and integrity." [15]

The code of sexual morality also condemned all practices considered injurious to the individual and the race. A. W. Calhoun states that the "Puritan emphasis on sexual restraint was of a piece with the general gospel of frugality so appropriate among a class of people trying to accumulate capital in an age of deficit." The New England colonies imposed various restrictions on unmarried men with the object of protecting community morality by keeping bachelors under surveillance or by forcing them to marry or to depart. Womanly modesty everywhere held a high place among the virtues: Dr. Brickell observed of North Carolina: "the women are very shy in their discourses, till they become acquainted": a traveler wrote in 1745 of American girls: "their dress is neat and clean, and not much bordering on the ridiculous humor of the mother country, where the daughters seemed dressed up for a market." In rural communities, where women were somewhat unprotected in their associations, the canon of modesty was particularly imperative. Southern society fostered among men of the upper and middle classes an attitude akin to chivalry, in

---

[15] The most important literary work of the colonial period is *The Autobiography of Benjamin Franklin* (ed. Max Farrand, Berkeley, 1949).

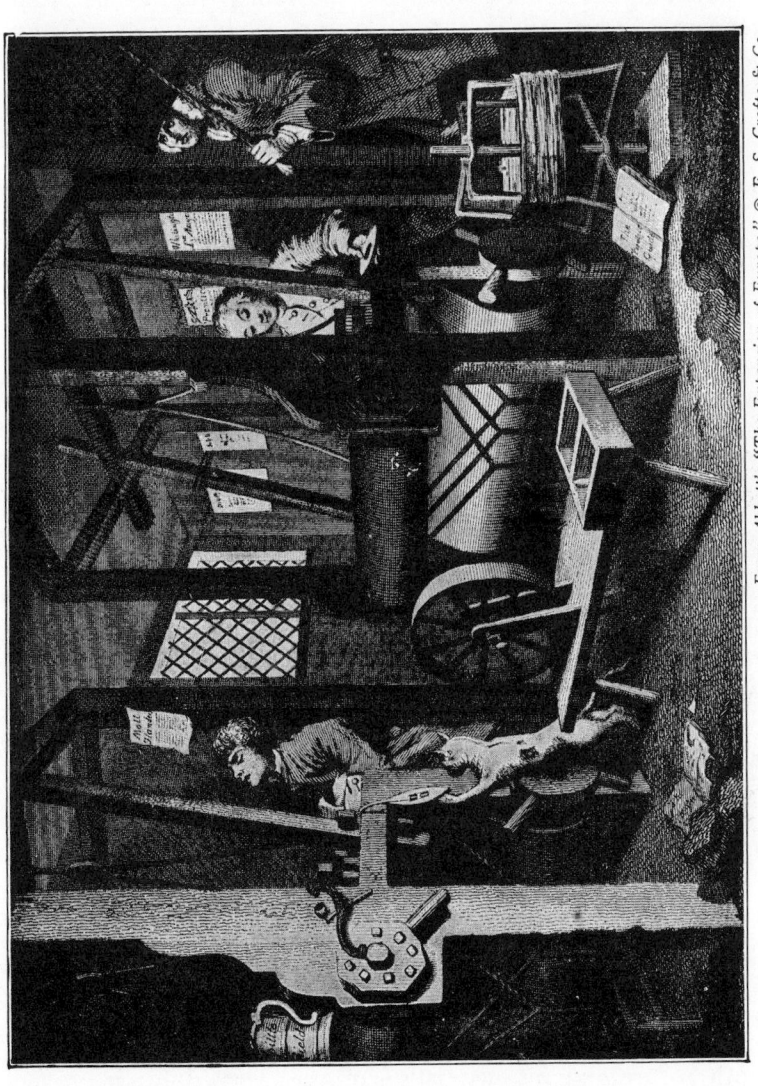

From *Abbott's "The Expansion of Europe."* © *F. S. Crofts & Co.*

THE INDUSTRIOUS AND THE LAZY APPRENTICE

One of the series of drawings entitled *Industry and Idleness*, executed
by William Hogarth in 1747.

view of the necessity of protecting the ladies of the plantation in the presence of servants and slaves.[16]

The training of youth reveals the prevailing moral tone. John Adams wrote to his wife in 1774: ". . . make your children *hardy*, *active*, and *industrious*; for strength, activity and industry will be their only resource and dependence." Little children were not sheltered from the rigors of nature: "Josiah Quincy at three years was taken from his warm bed, winter and summer, carried to the cellar kitchen, and dipped three times in water just from the pump." Winter life in icy rooms had a toughening effect. Numerous children in crowded quarters, busy parents, and the natural distaste of youth for steady work made obedience a cardinal virtue. Teach your child to obey, said Poor Richard, and you may teach him anything. Cotton Mather made his children sensible that " 'tis a folly for them to pretend unto any wit or will of their own . . . my word must be their law." Slaveowners demanded filial obedience on the assumption that "he that cannot obey cannot command." A colonial book of etiquette instructed children thus: "Never sit down at the table till asked. . . . Ask for nothing; tarry till it be offered thee. . . . Sing not, hum not, wriggle not. Spit nowhere in the room but in the corner. When any speak to thee, stand up." [17]

Religious teaching enforced the parental discipline—particularly through the fear of damnation: violators of the fifth commandment would certainly go to the wrong place. Children were told what to do, not coaxed or argued with, and the rod reinforced religious instruction. "Love well, whip well." A whip used in rural Pennsylvania consisted of a piece of leather about six inches in diameter, fastened to a pliable handle. Among educated people in New England, stern parental discipline induced intellectual precocity; some children were taught reading at three and Latin at six! In accordance with Calvin's teachings the Puritan colonies provided severe punishments for children who should curse or smite their parents or be guilty of "stubborn or rebellious carriage."

Two conceptions of life contended for mastery in colonial times. One, a materialistic outlook, assumed that life evolved in response to external forces of environment and social organization; man's struggle with nature and his material necessities shaped his ideas and habits; so also man, through the conquest of nature, might lighten

---

[16] See again T. J. Wertenbaker, *The First Americans*, chapter 8.

[17] T. H. Johnson, "Jonathan Edwards and the 'Young Folks' Bible" (*New England Quarterly*, V, Jan. 1932), discusses attitudes toward sex education of youth.

his burdens on earth. The second—a religious or spiritual conception —affirmed that life moved in response to a divine will; God, an ideal being governing an ideal universe, had foreordained man's destiny; hardship and misfortune chastened man and attuned him to the divine purpose; morality was not a reflection of man's experience but an unchanging decree of God: "the moral law is written on the tablets of eternity." Divine revelation and inspiration were the light of the world. Man could not change his fate through the conquest of nature or the reorganization of society; he must conform to the divine will as recorded in the Scriptures. Nor was man a mere physical mechanism, a product of material forces, but a creature made in the image of God, possessing an immortal soul and destined for eternal life.

In a society as diverse as that of the colonies religion was compounded of numerous ideas.[18] Many forces of nature, not understood by the unlearned, were attributed to a supernatural power. A hard life, in which pain, sickness, hardship, accidents, loss, and death were frequent and beyond control, was more easily borne when such afflictions were regarded as the will of God, who would one day reward the sufferer. A New Englander wrote of his wife: "She would sometimes say to me that bearing, tending and burying children was hard work, and that she had done a great deal of it for one of her age . . . yet would say it was the work she was made for and what God in his providence had called her to, and she could freely do it all for Him." The belief in heaven and hell gave an intensely personal quality to religion; so also attitudes of fear and reverence instilled in youth persisted, often in the recesses of the mind, throughout life. Moreover, some religious sects taught the submission of dependents to their superiors, who were invariably identified with an important church. On the other hand, the New Testament, condemning as it did the rich and exalting the poor and downtrodden, contained the seeds of social revolution; equality before God might also mean equality on earth.[19] To the sensitive, the beauty and order of nature and the feeling that life was essentially good were proof of the existence of a benevolent God. Some embraced mysticism, seeking by prayer and meditation to become suffused with a sense of peace and oneness with God; others inclined toward deism, a creed which denied revelation and the divine

[18] For a view of the influence of American environment see Peter G. Mode, *The Frontier Spirit in Christianity* (New York, 1923).

[19] Thomas C. Hall, *The Religious Background of American Culture* (Boston, 1930), finds the clue to colonial religion in the dissenting tradition of pre-Reformation times.

inspiration of the Scriptures, but accepted the view of a benevolent God, whom man should worship by doing good to one's fellow men.[20]

Despite the religious inheritance of the colonists, their preoccupation with practical concerns, their day-long labor in field and shop, and the necessity of subduing nature in order to mitigate the rigors of life: all these influences strengthened the materialistic conception of life.[21] New Englanders gained a reputation as shrewd traders and investors; travelers in the middle colonies noted that the religious impulse there was at a low ebb (Christian sects tended "to wear themselves out"; "religious indifference becomes prevalent"). Jernegan says that the "main energies and thoughts" of most of the southern planters "were centered on material gains." Of the American farmer Crèvecoeur wrote: "He conceives no other idea of a clergyman than that of a hired man; if he does his work well, he will pay him the stipulated sum; if not he will dismiss him and do without his sermons, and let his church be shut up for years. But notwithstanding this coarse idea, you will find his house and farm to be the neatest in all the country; and you will judge by his wagon and fat horses, that he thinks more of the affairs of this world than of those of the next." In keeping with this materialistic outlook was an engrossing interest in all things useful. Even Cotton Mather aspired to "enkindle" in his children "a mighty desire of being useful in the world." "Sometimes," wrote Crèvecoeur, "I delight in inventing and executing machines, which simplify my wife's labor. I have been tolerably successful that way." Franklin, the most significant American of the eighteenth century and a utilitarian *par excellence,* directed his scientific thought to the improvement of material conditions; he once apologized for making a mathematical study which had no utility.[22]

As in other societies, the colonists faced the problem of harmonizing the need of individual achievement and self-expression with the necessity of coöperation, association, and the social control of property. Individualism, a vital force generated by private ownership of the means of production and by the resulting scheme of individual enterprise in farming, trade, and industry, was intensified by the desire to acquire more capital, and diffused throughout the population by reason of the widespread ownership of land, which conferred upon a

[20] Herbert M. Morais, *Deism in Eighteenth Century America* (New York, 1934), is the best study of this aspect of religious thought.

[21] I. Woodbridge Riley, *American Philosophy: The Early Schools* (New York, 1907), an important pioneer work, discusses idealism, materialism, Puritanism, realism, and deism.

[22] Paul L. Ford, *The Many-Sided Franklin* (New York, 1899), is an analysis of Franklin's thought and personality rather than a narrative of his career.

multitude of small producers the boon of independence and self-directed activity. Crèvecoeur put it thus: "Here the rewards of his [the farmer's] industry follow with equal steps the progress of his labor; his labor is founded on the basis of nature, self-interest, can it want a stronger allurement. . . . As farmers they will be careful and anxious to get as much as they can, because what they get is their .own." Some manifestations of the prevailing individualism were the authority of parents and masters over children, servants and slaves; the ideal of individual improvement, morally and intellectually (note Franklin's efforts toward self-education and moral perfection); and the emphasis placed by religion on the salvation of individual souls. Individualism was naturally strongest among big property owners who had the greatest opportunity to exercise their managing talents and to direct the labor of others; on the other hand, there was no scope for initiative among slaves and but little among servants and wage-earners, since such workers carried out the commands of their masters.[23]

Necessity forced the small farmers to coöperate with one another; unable to command dependents, they were obliged to exchange services among themselves. Pioneers occasionally migrated in companies for the sake of protection, association, and mutual assistance in opening roads and fording streams. House-raisings, huskings, quilting parties, road and bridge building, funerals, the erection of schools and churches—all called forth the coöperative labor of the settlers. In early New England the ideal of community life was particularly strong. On the voyage of 1630 John Winthrop told his fellow emigrants that "they must be knit together in this enterprise as one man, they must rejoice and mourn together, labor and suffer together, 'always having before our eyes our commission and community in the work'" (P. G. Miller). In another vein Poor Richard said: "He that drinks his cider alone, let him catch his horse alone."

The amusements of the common folk reflect the coöperative spirit. Boys indulged in various sports: racing, coasting on sleds, street games, hunting, fishing, trapping. Samuel Sewall condemned April Fools' Day jokes, first practiced in Boston in 1708: "What an abuse of precious time; what a profanation!" Many rural pastimes combined pleasure and utility: such were the "drive" (to clear the neighboring woods of wolves and bears), the house raising, the log rolling, and the deer hunt. At the country fairs, held in Pennsylvania twice a year,

[23] One of the most influential interpretations of American society is F. J. Turner's "The Significance of the Frontier in American History," reprinted in *The Frontier in American History*, chapter 1.

spring and autumn, the rural folk transacted business, consorted with friends and relatives and enjoyed many a rustic diversion. At the side show one saw the polar bear, the camel, the tightrope walker, the juggler, the puppet show, and the musical clock. Foot races, wrestling matches and target shooting contests engaged the young men of prowess; the chief attractions for all were quarter-mile horse races.[24] Apart from the Sabbath, holy days were not observed; the economic creed of Protestantism condemned such "waste" of time in an age of scarcity. Except among the Germans even Christmas was just another day. Thanksgiving in New England, not only a religious observance but also a week-long harvest festival celebrated by feasting, afforded relaxation after the toil of summer. Church services, Thursday lectures, town meetings, and training days also brought the New Englanders together; in the South the ever-popular folk dances (jigs, square dances, the Virginia reel) bore witness to a vigorous community spirit.

The regulation of private property by law imposed another restraint upon individualism.[25] "Particular estates," wrote John Winthrop, "cannot subsist in the ruin of the public." All the colonies resorted to social control, particularly in time of calamity or depression. Laws governing interest rates, forbidding the exportation of needed products, regulating coinage, weights, and measures, offering bounties and other public aid to encourage new industries (mining, cloth making, iron manufacturing), prohibiting monopolies (except of limited duration, for the introduction of new enterprises), providing for the inspection of commodities, and authorizing deferred payment of debts due—all such acts swell the bulk of colonial statute books. In early Massachusetts, efforts to regulate wages failed because workmen "would either remove to other places where they might have more, or else being able to live by planting and other employments of their own, they would not be hired at all." Although many regulatory acts served the interests of particular groups, even so they asserted in theory the right of public control of property.

Nor was the head of the family a law unto his individualistic self. Pennsylvania in 1683 decreed that persons in charge of young children who failed to instruct them in reading and writing should pay a fine of £5 for each child. The New England colonies adopted similar

[24] John A. Krout, *Annals of American Sport* (*Pageant of America*, XV, New Haven, 1929), chapter 1.
[25] Lewis J. Carey, *Franklin's Economic Views* (Garden City, N. Y., 1928), is a satisfactory recent discussion. See also W. A. Wetzel, *Benjamin Franklin as an Economist* (Baltimore, 1895).

acts, enforced by county courts, sheriffs, and grand juries; parents who defied the law were fined or otherwise punished. Massachusetts in 1668 provided that men delinquent in the care of their families should be classed as idle persons and "subject to the house of correction." Due to the prevailing sense of social responsibility and of human solidarity, such acts were necessary because a family head who ignored his duties thereby imposed a burden upon the community.[26]

Life in the colonial towns also exhibited a lively spirit of coöperation. Five urban centers may be classed as major commercial towns: Boston, Philadelphia, Newport, New York, and Charleston. In 1774 Charleston was the only "city" in the South; Philadelphia, with a population of nearly 40,000, had gained first rank in the colonies; New York (25,000 to 30,000) was on the upgrade; Boston, with 20,000, was stationary or declining; Newport, with 12,000, was feeling the competition of Providence. Other port towns of local commercial importance, with populations of less than 12,000, were Salem, New Haven, Providence, Perth Amboy, Newcastle, Baltimore, Richmond, Wilmington (North Carolina), and Savannah. There were also small country towns tributary to the commercial centers—the many villages of New England, Albany, Burlington, Princeton, Trenton, Germantown, Chester, Lancaster, Norfolk, etc. Annapolis, Maryland, and Williamsburg, Virginia, deserve notice as political and social capitals rather than as commercial centers.

The major commercial cities and many of the minor towns operated markets, daily, weekly, or semi-weekly, to which the farmers of the vicinity brought produce for sale to traders and to the townspeople. The rules for the Boston market provided in 1696 that produce must be offered to the householders before traders could buy. New York had six markets in 1774; that of Philadelphia, then described as the best regulated in North America, was "raised upon pillars and covered over for a quarter of a mile in length." Market days broke the monotony of the farmer's life with a taste of town associations and a sojourn at the tavern at the end of the day's bargaining.

The common problems of the towns called forth common efforts. In early times police protection was a community responsibility shared by all able-bodied men. The smaller New England towns utilized trainbands in which all males over sixteen were liable for guard duty at night. In Philadelphia, prior to 1751, all householders were required to serve in the night watch. It became the practice for wealthy men to pay the

[26] Henry B. Parkes, "New England in the Seventeen-Thirties," *New England Quarterly*, III (July 1930).

constable 6s. a year for exemption from duty. Two defects in this custom, pointed out by Franklin,[27] had appeared by the 1740's: the wealthier inhabitants paid no more for protection of their property than the less wealthy, and the constables often employed shiftless, incompetent substitutes. In 1751 a regular, paid watch was established, the cost being assessed against the inhabitants according to property holdings. "In 1772 the watch was instructed to patrol the streets from 10 P. M. to 4 A. M. and call out the time of night and the state of the weather."

By 1775 the leading towns had made some progress toward the paving of streets. An observer said of Philadelphia in 1774: "The streets are all straight, and well paved, about thirty-six . . . feet wide, with foot paths on every side, raised a little above the carriage way, and laid with bricks for the conveniency of the foot passengers." New York's streets (built of "large pebble stones" and made to slope toward a gutter in the middle of the street) were described in 1774 as "ill paved, irregular and too narrow," although they impressed John Adams as "vastly more regular and elegant than those of Boston."

Franklin was an American pioneer in devising city fire protection. At Philadelphia he organized a company of thirty volunteers who equipped themselves with leather buckets and bags and baskets (for removing articles from burning houses), whereupon other companies were soon formed "till they became so numerous as to include most of the inhabitants who were men of property." Later, the companies raised money for the purchase of engines, hooks, and ladders. New York in 1772 had eleven fire companies and engines, with a force of 163 men organized under a fire chief. Every householder had to pay a shilling a year for each chimney of his dwelling, the money being used to have the chimneys swept once a week. "And when a fire happens, a premium is always allowed to the captain and his men who can first make their engines play upon the fire." By 1775 the fire menace in New York and Philadelphia was well under control.[28]

Little progress was registered in other municipal activities. Philadelphia installed street lamps in 1751; New York in 1775 was the only town which regularly cleaned its streets. Elsewhere, trash and ashes were dumped in vacant lots; hogs roamed about in search of garbage; at Charleston, buzzards were welcomed and protected as

[27] Verner W. Crane, *Benjamin Franklin and a Rising People* (Boston, 1954), is a superior study, by a leading authority. I. Bernard Cohen, *Benjamin Franklin* (Indianapolis, 1953), emphasizes Franklin's experimental methods.

[28] Carl Bridenbaugh, *Cities in the Wilderness* (2d ed., New York, 1955), is the best study of early colonial towns.

scavengers. For water supply, reliance was placed upon "pumps sunk at convenient distances in the streets." No house had a bathroom or running water. The impurities of water from wells or streams help explain the vogue of taverns and homemade drinks. New York was erecting a central pumping system, with a reservoir and conduits, when the Revolution cut short the work.

The American town-dweller's relish for clubs, fraternal orders, and other societies appeared in colonial times, a strong urge of that sort manifesting itself after 1710. A Masonic lodge existed in Philadelphia in 1715; by 1770 the order—which included Franklin and Washington among its members—was well represented in the principal seacoast towns. Other clubs, formed along national, professional, or craft lines and avowing the pursuit of knowledge as their aim, brought gregarious spirits together once a week for an evening's comradeship in taverns or private homes. Most of such clubs seem to have forsaken their high aims and to have yielded to the delights of conviviality and good fellowship.

> Boy, bring a bowl of china here,
> Fill it with water cool and clear:
> Decanter and Jamaica right,
> And spoon of silver, clear and bright
> Sugar twice fin'd, in pieces cut,
> Knife, sieve and glass, in order put,
> Bring forth the fragrant fruit and then
> We're happy till the clock strikes ten.

Despite numerous economic or class conflicts, colonial society was held together by strong integrating forces.[29] Religious toleration, made possible largely by the scarcity of labor and vast open lands, diminished Old World tensions among Christian sects. Wealthy groups practiced in business the virtues of industry and thrift which were taught to the lower orders; there were no idle rich, and no gulf between upper-class social theory and practice. Widespread ownership of land—the squatter ideal—diffused the spirit of acquisitive individualism throughout the population. It was easy to convince oneself that personal success and the pursuit of self-interest best served society as a whole: did not the frontier welcome the dispossessed; was not the lot of the common man better in America than in Europe: was not failure due to the defects of the man who fell by the wayside? The standards of the upper class penetrated to the lower classes,

---

[29] A. M. Schlesinger's *New Viewpoints in American History* (New York, 1922) discusses some of the major problems of American society. See chapters 1–7.

binding all with the cement of emulation. "How many poor men, common men, and mechanics," queried a Philadelphia "democrat" at election time in 1776, "have been made happy within this fortnight by a shake of the hand, a pleasing smile, and a little familiar chat with gentlemen who have not for these seven years past condescended to look at them."

The colonial outlook may be described as an expression of a middle-class psychology which exalted industry and thrift and which exposed both a core of utilitarianism overlaid with religious tradition and a spirit of individualism, tempered by coöperation and association. It was an outlook which took economic inequality for granted: how, indeed, might the small property owner become a large owner if the latter were legislated out of existence? [30]

The literature of the eighteenth century, largely a product of the upper middle class, expressed the prevailing sense of social integration. Serenity, zest for life and faith in progress were its distinguishing traits. John Adams wrote in 1765: "I always consider the settlement of America with reverence and wonder, as the opening of a grand scheme and design in Providence for the illumination and the emancipation of the slavish part of mankind all over the earth." Confidence, optimism and a sense of an historic mission were the fruits of such an attitude. "Americans," wrote Crèvecoeur, "are the western pilgrims, who are carrying along with them the great mass of arts, sciences, vigor and industry which began long since in the east; they will finish the great circle." The processes of social growth and construction turned men's thoughts from the past to the future; said a traveler in 1794: "Every first settler in a new country labors less for the present than for the future; less for himself than for posterity; and it is this honorable consciousness that invigorates his toil, cheers his solitude, and alleviates his privations." Colonial society, moreover, called into play the energies of youth: ability, prowess and initiative were not sacrificed to mediocrity and inertia entrenched in aged authority. Washington at twenty-two and George Rogers Clark at twenty-five commanded in the West; Patrick Henry argued the "parson's cause" at twenty-seven; Franklin composed a philosophical work at eighteen; Jefferson wrote the Declaration of Independence at thirty-three; Hamilton became Secretary of the Treasury at thirty-two.[31]

[30] See again V. L. Parrington, *The Colonial Mind*, Book II, chapter 1.
[31] For suggestive essays on American society see Albert F. Pollard's *Factors in American History* (New York, 1925).

Social Problems

The felicity portrayed by promoters of settlement and by writers of the upper middle class is only a part of the picture of colonial life. Many families lived so close to poverty that misfortune reduced them to destitution. Hence arose the problem of caring for the impotent poor—the aged, the blind, the sick, the lame, and the insane. Moreover, there was a class of able-bodied poor: idlers, misfits, tramps, troublemakers, and criminals. The presence of such undesirables is accounted for in part by the English practice, authorized by Parliament in 1662 and 1717, of shipping rogues, vagabonds, and beggars to the colonies. Many of these immigrants had acquired a distaste for work which did not forsake them in the New World.

The principles of poor relief introduced into America were those with which the colonists had been familiar in England. After the dissolution of the English monasteries the burden of caring for the poor was assumed by the state, the work being assigned to the localities and the funds obtained through taxes levied on the property owners. All these features characterized the poor relief systems devised in the colonies. The assemblies acknowledged the public duty of caring for the poor and made the taxpayers of each locality responsible. Plymouth adopted such an act in 1642, Virginia in 1646, Connecticut in 1673, Massachusetts in 1692. In New England, where the town was the unit of administration, the town meeting provided specific regulations which were executed by the selectmen, tithingmen, or overseers of the poor; in the southern colonies the parish was the administrative unit, governed by the vestry—a group of twelve men, chosen after 1676 by the freeholders, and empowered to assess and collect parish taxes, to care for the poor, and to preserve religion and morality. Two of the vestrymen served as church wardens—the "executive arm" of the vestry in discharging its duties.

In New England the simplest mode of poor relief was for each family to care for a destitute person during part of the year. Thus Hadley, Massachusetts, voted in 1687 that a widow should be sent "round the town" to live two weeks with each family "able to receive her." Some of the poor, not wholly incapacitated, were given money from the town treasury and allowed to live alone. The most common practice followed by the smaller towns before the Revolution was the "putting out" system. The selectmen paid a householder who agreed to provide food and shelter for a destitute person; the town generally supplied clothing and medical care. Doctors who served the poor received payment from the town. In the larger settlements almshouses soon appeared; Boston had one in 1660. Prior to 1712 it housed criminals as well as the "honest poor," so great was the stigma attached to poverty. After 1712 efforts were made to realize the "primitive and pious design" of the almshouse, i. e., "the relief of the necessitous, that they might lead a quiet, peaceable and godly life there." [32]

Convinced that all able-bodied poor could find work, the New Englanders wasted little sympathy upon vagabonds and sturdy beggars. Such idlers were either bound out as indentured servants, whipped out of town, or clapped into jail. As the number of the able-bodied poor increased, the costs of confining them in prison (or the house of correction) led to the construction of workhouses. Massachusetts in 1699 provided for the erection of such institutions and authorized the confinement of idlers, tramps, "common pipers, fiddlers, runaways, stubborn servants or children, common drunkards, common night-walkers, pilferers, wanton and lascivious persons, . . . common railers or brawlers such as neglect their callings. . . ." The town provided materials and tools with which the inmates were required to earn their living. Connecticut erected a colony workhouse in 1727; the Boston workhouse began to function in 1729. Whipping supplied discipline and the incentive to work.

A specialization of function was evident in the system of poor relief at the end of the colonial period.[33] The almshouse cared for the "honest poor," the workhouse employed idlers and minor offenders, the prison housed criminals, and the hospital domiciled the sick. Insane asylums had not yet appeared. The care given to the insane poor is suggested in a vote of Braintree in 1689: the town agreed to pay for the erection of a house seven feet long and five feet wide where a man might "secure his sister and good wife Witty, being distracted. . . ."

The prudential New Englanders used prevention as well as relief in dealing with the poor. A master of a vessel who imported immigrants into Massachusetts had to give bond that they would not become a public charge; thus it was hoped "to prevent the importation of poor, vicious and infirm persons." Should an inhabitant bring servants into a town, he must agree to maintain them if they became "diseased, lame or impotent." Again: a householder who received

---

[32] See again M. W. Jernegan, *Laboring and Dependent Classes in Colonial America*, pp. 175–209.

[33] This illustrates one principle of American social development presented in D. R. Fox's charming essays, *Ideas in Motion* (New York, 1935).

outsiders must give notice of their presence; if they seemed likely to become a public burden, they were "warned out" of the town and deported if they would not go willingly. Since each town had to care for its own poor, destitute strangers were speedily returned to their home localities.

Poor relief in the southern colonies may be illustrated by the practices of Virginia, where drifters, runaway servants, and delinquent family heads raised problems akin to those of the northern colonies. The vestries in Virginia disposed of the able-bodied poor, destitute orphans, and the illegitimate children of indentured servants by binding them to masters as apprentices or servants. Almhouses, hospitals, and workhouses do not appear in the parish records; the impotent poor were placed in private homes, the parish supplying clothing and paying the householder the costs of maintenance. Outlays for poor relief, as in New England, varied from 9 per cent to 33 per cent of all expenditures for local purposes. These early forms of relief are the antecedents of modern orphan asylums, poorhouses, public hospitals, widows' pensions, free medical service, and insurance against accidents, unemployment, sickness, and old age.

Criminal tendencies in the colonial population also bear witness to social maladjustments. From England the early settlers brought those conceptions of wrongdoing and those forms of punishment which gave a rough uniformity to the legal practices of all the colonies. Certain crimes were commonly regarded as serious enough to incur the penalty of death. Such were murder, treason, piracy, and acts of sexual perversion. The codes of New England in 1664 also imposed the death penalty for denying the true God, for invading a town, for giving false evidence with the intent of taking a person's life, and—in the case of children over sixteen—for the unprovoked cursing or smiting of parents. Pennsylvania in 1718 prescribed the death penalty for arson, infanticide, burglary, murder, and the malicious mutilation of a person. After the colonies issued paper money they soon added counterfeiting to the list of capital crimes.

Other serious offenses were punished by imprisonment, branding, whipping, compulsory labor, or heavy fines.[34] In this category were theft, burglary, highway robbery, sexual immorality, forgery, serious profanity, and habitual drunkenness. In seventeenth-century New England, women guilty of repeated moral lapses were whipped or occasionally forced to wear the scarlet letter; after 1720, whipping was resorted to only for serious offenders. The law of Pennsylvania

[34] Alice M. Earle, *Curious Punishments of Bygone Days* (New York, 1907)—a readable sketch.

provided, after 1720, that a person thrice guilty of adultery should receive twenty-one lashes, serve seven years in prison, and be branded on the forehead with the letter A; thieves and housebreakers might be branded with the letter T; a fourth offense of serious profanity incurred a fine of £5 and two months of labor, while the culprit became liable to twenty-one stripes every three months for seven years. Five crimes were punishable by branding in Pennsylvania in 1767.

Minor offenses, such as occasional drunkenness and Sabbathbreaking (including unnecessary labor and travel) drew fines and short prison sentences. In colonies with established churches, attendance at divine service was required by law, but only persistent violators were fined; in most places the churches were not large enough to accommodate the whole community at one time.[35] The New England colonies fined persons guilty of owning or playing cards and of disporting themselves at such time-consuming games as shuffleboard, ninepins, and billiards. The Puritans also outlawed lotteries and games of chance. As late as 1717 two dancing masters were ordered not to practice their art in Boston; however, the ban did not extend to folk dances. Among the minor iniquities condemned by the Pennsylvania code of 1682 were stage plays, masques, bullbaiting, and cockfighting.

The New England Puritans, never idealistic regarding human nature, adopted at the start a strict legal code and proceeded to enforce it. The Massachusetts court of assistants considered 286 cases between 1636 and 1644. On the whole the criminal record of colonial New England makes a good showing. After 1692 the death penalty was inflicted for only two crimes—piracy and murder; the white inhabitants of Connecticut, between 1663 and 1775, were involved in but twelve murders, only five of which were premeditated. Sexual irregularities exceeded all other classes of offenses three to one; the number of illegitimate births doubled, trebled, and even quadrupled in the various towns between 1730 and 1770. Other frequently committed offenses included drunkenness, Sabbathbreaking, non-attendance at church, and breach of the peace. A marked increase of heavy drinking occurred in eastern Massachusetts after 1700 and extended to the western counties and to Connecticut after 1725. The number of tavern licenses in many New England towns doubled or trebled between 1700 and 1730 and increased sixfold or eightfold between 1700 and 1770.[36]

---

[35] Alice M. Earle, *The Sabbath in Puritan New England* (New York, 1902), is light reading.

[36] H. B. Parkes, "Morals and Law Enforcement in Colonial New England," *New England Quarterly*, V (July 1932).

In accordance with William Penn's humanitarianism, Pennsylvania in 1682 adopted an extremely mild criminal code which inflicted the death penalty for only one crime—murder. Such liberalism, together with lax enforcement of the law, did not suffice for the province: in 1697 Penn referred to scandalous things done in Philadelphia, "openly committed in defiance of law and virtue: facts so foul, I am forbid by common modesty to relate them." The attractions of Pennsylvania for runaway servants, convicts, and other outcasts account in part for the conditions described by Penn. Beginning in 1701 the criminal law was made progressively severe: branding, whipping, and mutilation were frequently resorted to against stubborn criminals and the number of crimes punishable by death was increased to sixteen by 1767. Between 1683 and 1715 only three serious criminal cases came before the Pennsylvania council; the court records of the years 1715–45 indicate that twenty-three persons were sentenced to death; in the period 1745–75 such sentences numbered at least 112. As a board of review and pardons the council often changed the penalty from death to banishment from the colony. Of the 112 offenders just mentioned only sixty-one were executed.[37]

In all the colonies indentured servants frequently ran afoul of the law. Since they received but a bare subsistence they were tempted to steal; ordinarily not permitted to marry, they were driven to sexual irregularities. The latter problem was particularly acute in the southern colonies, where a number of servants and slaves lived together in comparative isolation. If a servant woman became the mother of an illegitimate child, her efficiency as a worker was temporarily lessened; moreover, the master had to care for the child, and since such children were born free, the master could not command their future labor, as he could in the case of slaves. In grappling with this problem, the southern colonies first enacted that a servant mother should compensate her master with additional service. But this law did not check the evil: it "put a premium on immorality and there seem to have been masters base enough to profit by it." The servant codes respecting illegitimate children were modified after 1660 so as to incorporate the following principles. If the master were not responsible, he was entitled to additional service; if he were responsible, his servant was to be sold by the parish and the sale money used for the support of the child; if the father were known, he was held liable for such support. In any case the mother was fined or flogged.

The early court records suggest that crime and moral lapses were

[37] L. H. Gipson, *Crime and Its Punishment in Provincial Pennsylvania* (Lehigh University, Bethlehem, Pa., 1935).

most common among the lower classes. But such an inference should be guarded against because the upper classes were frequently able to keep their offenses out of the courts. Servants, tenants, and wage-earners had little recourse against their masters; the slaves had none. The offenses of dependents were punished severely; those of the masters often received no legal notice. Similarly, a person of means might make a financial settlement out of court, whereas the poor had to be punished through the legal agencies that authorized whipping, branding, and prison sentences.

Negro slavery constituted another exception to the happy conditions portrayed by writers of the middle class.[38] Estimates of the total slave population after 1700 are unreliable, due to inadequate statistics for the tobacco colonies. In South Carolina the number of slaves increased from 32,000 in 1724 to 90,000 in 1765—representing about 69 per cent of all inhabitants in each year. Connecticut had 6,500 slaves in 1775 as against thirty in 1720; Massachusetts had more than 5,000 in 1775 as against 550 in 1708; Rhode Island's total rose from 3,077 in 1749 to 3,668 in 1774. By 1750 the Negroes in Pennsylvania numbered about 11,000; in New York, after the mid-century, slaves accounted for a seventh of the population.

Slavery came into being in the colonies by virtue of force and custom, without the sanction of positive law; originally the line between slave and indentured servant was indistinct. Not until about 1660 did Virginia recognize slavery by law; after that year each colony enacted a slave code, patterned after the laws of the West Indies, where legal regulations were first adopted. Such codes presumed that every Negro was a slave; emancipation by individual masters was so rare that free Negroes formed an extremely small group. As misfits sharing the stigma attached to their race which exposed them to abuse and exploitation, they held an unprotected, degraded place in society.[39]

Four purposes may be discerned in the colonial slave codes. First, the law safeguarded the master's property right in the slave. Children of a slave woman became the property of her owner. If any freeman injured, stole, or killed a slave, the offender was required to satisfy the owner with double or treble damages. The slave could not leave his master's premises without a permit or unless accompanied by a white person. Fugitives could be arrested by anyone who

[38] Two surveys by a Negro historian are Benjamin Brawley, *A Social History of the American Negro* (New York, 1921), chapters 1–4; and *A Short History of the American Negro* (New York, 1919), chapters 1–4.

[39] John H. Russell, *The Free Negro in Virginia, 1619–1865* (Baltimore, 1913).

encountered them, whereupon they were to be advertised and returned to their owners. Both in Africa and on some plantations slaves
were branded as a means of identification.

Secondly, the slave codes aimed to protect the personal property
of the master. A slave guilty of theft might be punished by death
or by severe whipping; similarly, trading with slaves was made unlawful on the assumption that a slave would sell only his master's property. Owners were commanded to search the slave quarters for stolen
goods.

Thirdly, other acts placed the slave in utter subordination to the
master as a means of enforcing work and discipline. The owner committed no offense if he killed or maimed a slave; he could punish at
his discretion; he might work the slave fourteen or fifteen hours a
day; if a slave struck a white person he might be imprisoned or
severely whipped. The slave could not sue or testify in court or
otherwise secure legal redress of grievances. The law also forbade the
sale of liquor to slaves without the master's consent.

A fourth object of the slave codes was to prevent insurrections.
Thus the laws decreed that three or more slaves were not to assemble
unless with the owner's permission, ordered that slaves should not be
kept on plantations unless white persons were in residence, required
that slaves remain indoors at night after curfew, commanded owners
to search the slave huts for weapons, and forbade the slaves to beat
drums or blow horns.[40]

The punishments prescribed for the misdeeds of slaves resembled
those for other crimes, with whipping the most common penalty.
Court records do not disclose the extent of slave offenses, since masters ordinarily inflicted punishments without trial; the slave could not
pay fines, and prison sentences were rare, due to the cost of maintenance and the loss of the slave's labor. The most dangerous, intractable slaves, guilty of arson, murder, or insurrection, were hanged,
broken at the wheel, burned at the stake, or deported. Thus Massachusetts in 1681 ordered one slave burned and another hanged—both
convicted of arson.

Although the treatment of slaves varied with the temperament of
the master, it is certain that most of them endured a hard lot. They
enjoyed no protection against a vicious owner; even the considerate
master insisted upon full subservience. John Taylor of Caroline,

---

[40] J. C. Ballagh, *A History of Slavery in Virginia* (Baltimore, 1902), is an outstanding study of the legal aspects of slavery. See also the introductions to material on
the various colonies in Helen T. Catterall (ed.), *Judicial Cases Concerning American
Slavery and the Negro* (4 vols., Washington, 1926–36).

urging liberal treatment in 1809, said that "a stern authority, strict discipline and complete subordination must be combined . . . to gain any success at all."

Numerous insurrections bear witness to maladjustments among the slaves.[41] Revolts in Virginia occurred or were plotted in 1663, 1687, and 1709—none, however, of serious proportions. Despite the fact that conspirators in South Carolina in 1720 were punished by hanging, burning at the stake, or deportation, an important insurrection broke out there in 1739. A score of slaves armed themselves by robbing a store and set out for Florida, gathering recruits and murdering whites as they advanced. A white force, assembled when the alarm was sounded, finally attacked the fugitives and captured all but ten. This plot cost the lives of twenty-one whites and forty-four Negroes. In New Jersey a slave accused of plotting an insurrection in 1734 met death on the gallows. A band of slaves in New York (1712) set fire to a house at night and killed citizens as they rushed to the scene. After the revolt had been suppressed by soldiers, twenty-one participants were executed, one being sentenced "to be burned with a slow fire, that he may continue in torment for eight or ten hours." Again, at New York in 1741, charges that a gang of slaves had set fire to several houses and had perpetrated several robberies led the supreme court to ferret out the culprits, who were also suspected of plotting an insurrection. Four white persons implicated were hanged, twenty-nine Negroes were hanged or burned at the stake, and eighty Negroes were deported. Only when forced confessions implicated people of "known credit, fortune and reputation" did the hysteria subside.

In Pennsylvania—where slave insurrections did not threaten—were uttered the first emphatic protests against slavery. In 1688 four men in the Mennonite settlement at Germantown took a public stand against bringing "men hither to rob or sell them against their will." During the next seventy years opposition to slavery found expression among individual Quakers until in 1758 the yearly meeting registered a formal protest.[42] Foremost among the Quaker opponents was John Woolman (1720–72), originally a New Jersey tailor, whose religious mysticism and humane spirit moved him to devote his life to crusades in behalf of peace, the poor, the Indians, and the slaves. After a visit to Virginia in 1746 to observe slavery he wrote: "I saw in these southern provinces so many vices and corruptions increased by this trade and way of life, that it appeared to me as a dark gloominess

---

[41] See again U. B. Phillips, *American Negro Slavery.*

[42] On this theme see Stephen B. Weeks, *Southern Quakers and Slavery* (Baltimore, 1896), chapter 9.

hanging over the land." He condemned slavery in his famous *Journal* (1774) and in an essay, *Some Considerations on the Keeping of Negroes* (1754). Partly in response to his labors, the Philadelphia yearly meeting of the Quakers in 1776 disowned members who refused to free their slaves. Among the New England Puritans early protests against slavery had been voiced by John Eliot and Samuel Sewall. By 1775 men of strongly democratic tendencies in the middle colonies and New England (artisans and small farmers) regarded slavery with disfavor. Emancipation came in these states between 1775 and 1800, while the Northwest Ordinance of 1787 forbade the extension of slavery into the territory north of the Ohio River.

BIBLIOGRAPHICAL NOTE

SECONDARY WORKS: Carl Bridenbaugh, *Cities in Revolt* (New York, 1955), emphasizes the unifying and stimulating force of leading towns. F. B. Tolles, *James Logan and the Culture of Provincial America* (Boston, 1957), is an attractive biography. I. Bernard Cohen, *Franklin and Newton* (Philadelphia, 1956), treats Franklin as an experimental scientist.

Edmund S. Morgan, *The Puritan Family* (Boston, 1944), is an interesting study, of first-rate importance. Edmund S. Morgan, *Virginians at Home* (Williamsburg, 1952), is a worthy addition to the author's study of family life. Julia C. Spruill, *Women's Life and Work in the Southern Colonies* (Chapel Hill, 1938), is a valuable contribution. John Duffy, *Epidemics in Colonial America* (Baton Rouge, 1953), is the best work on its subject.

Emil Oberholzer, Jr., *Delinquent Saints* (New York, 1956), gives a good account of discipline in Congregational churches. Ola E. Winslow, *Meetinghouse Hill* (New York, 1952), revives many disputes of New England towns. J. F. Kelly, *Early Connecticut Meetinghouses* (2 vols., New York, 1948), is a definitive work.

In *The Colonial American in Britain* (Madison, 1956), William L. Sachse relates visits of colonists abroad and reveals a growing sense of Americanism.

SOURCES: Readable travel accounts are Andrew Burnaby, *Travels through the Middle Settlements of North America* [1759–60] (Ithaca, 1960); Peter Kalm, *Travels into North America* (2 vols., London, 1772); and N. D. Mereness (ed.), *Travels in the American Colonies* (New York, 1916; reprinted, New York, 1961). The American Bookshelf editions (ed. Mark Van Doren) contain *Samuel Sewall's Diary* [1675–1724] (1927), and William Byrd's *A Journey to the Land of Eden and Other Papers* (1928).

XVIII

Culture and Religon

THE COLONIAL CHURCHES

THE most prominent feature of religion in the English colonies was the dominance of Protestantism; in every colony the Roman Catholics formed only a small minority. A few dwelt in Virginia, New York, and New Jersey; where they were most numerous—in Maryland and Pennsylvania—they numbered between but four and seven thousand in 1756. Always exposed to the animosity inherited by Protestants from Old World religious strife, the colonial Catholics were further weakened by the Anglo-French wars—by the identification of their faith with the cause of the principal enemy of the English settlers.[1]

The Protestant Reformation, which popularized the idea that man might commune with God without the medium of a priest, emphasized in thought and religion those forces of individualism which early capitalism fostered in the economic sphere. Rejecting the authority of any single ecclesiastical hierarchy, the Protestants divided into numerous sects: many interpreters meant many interpretations. Moreover, the Protestant sects gave expressions to social distinctions—to the interests and outlooks of the various classes. Class differences fostered diversity in religion, while changes within the class structure affected established sects.

Three tendencies are evident in early American Protestantism. Some churches, like the Anglican, expressed the aristocratic spirit of an upper class in control. They vested authority in the clergy and the most wealthy parishioners, favored formal services, frowned upon religious emotionalism, and tended to emphasize external observances rather than the inner spiritual life of the individual. Another upperclass tendency was the effort to establish a church by law and to force it upon all the people, irrespective of individual belief.[2]

A second Protestant trend, which may be described as democratic

---

[1] The best introduction, popular, scholarly and attractive, is William W. Sweet, *The Story of Religions in America* (New York, 1931).

[2] Luther A. Weigle, *American Idealism* (*Pageant of America*, X, New Haven, 1928), chapters 2–4.

or popular, is manifest in such churches as the Baptist, the Methodist (after 1750), and the German Pietist sects like the Moravians and the Mennonites. These churches, dominated by middle-class groups, emphasized the right of individual judgment (soul liberty) as against ecclesiastical authority, favored informal services, stressed an inner spiritual life as against mere outward conformity, and lodged control in the body of believers rather than in a priestly caste or an oligarchy of wealthy laymen. Believing firmly in freedom of conscience, these popular churches resisted all efforts to impose by law a religion not wanted by the people themselves.

A third group of churches included the Quaker, the Presbyterian, the Dutch Reformed, the Lutheran, the German Reformed, and the Congregational. In the eighteenth century they exhibited an inner conflict between aristocratic and democratic tendencies. Originally composed of middle-class groups, these churches became divided in America partly because some of the members rose into the upper class, whereas the majority remained in their former circumstances. The upper-class groups generally stood for the aristocratic principles just mentioned; the lower middle-class elements adhered to the democratic ideas of the popular churches.

Throughout colonial times the Baptist Church retained its democratic character. Its creed affirmed that each man might commune directly with God and thus know religious truth at first hand; hence it rejected the office of priest and the authority of ecclesiastical officials. Only true believers should belong to the church—that is, those who had been converted or awakened by God to a spiritual life. Baptism should follow conversion, and because conversion visited only the mature, infant baptism was held to be ineffectual. Some Baptists accepted the doctrine of predestination; others believed that salvation might be attained through faith and good works. Religion being a relationship between God and each individual, the state should not interfere in matters of conscience. After 1650 the American Baptists regarded immersion as the correct mode of baptism. In keeping with their democratic beliefs they adopted the congregational form of church organization, vesting all power in the church members. After 1707 the Baptist congregations of the middle colonies coöperated through an association which held its meetings in Philadelphia.[3]

The expulsion of Roger Williams from Massachusetts (he may be regarded as the first outstanding American Baptist) illustrates the position of this radical sect in early times. The Baptists were objec-

---

[3] Albert H. Newman, *A History of the Baptist Churches* . . . (New York, 1904), is the most satisfactory treatment.

tionable to established churches because they opposed the union of church and state and because their doctrine of baptism seemed dangerous to those Protestants who believed that each child should be brought under the discipline of the church through the agency of infant baptism. In 1644 Massachusetts ordered the expulsion of Baptists; six years later two Baptists from Rhode Island were fined and expelled from the Bay colony, while another, Obadiah Holmes, who refused to pay a fine, was given thirty lashes. Due to such persecution the Baptists became strongest in those colonies which rejected state coercion in religion—Plymouth, Rhode Island, New Jersey, Pennsylvania, and Delaware. In the eighteenth century they were generally tolerated, though frequently in conflict with Puritans and Anglicans over the question of paying taxes for the support of an established church.

Many of the German and Swiss settlers in the colonies belonged to churches which espoused democratic ideals. Such churches were offshoots of German Pietism—a movement of the seventeenth century in protest against formalism that had crept into the two principal churches, the Lutheran and the German Reformed. The early Pietists organized private societies devoted to Bible study and prayer and designed to promote personal holiness. The chief sects which emerged —the Mennonites, the Moravians, and the Dunkers—resembled the English Quakers and Baptists. Drawing their strength from the German peasantry, these radical groups emphasized the worth of the common man, affirmed that salvation might be achieved through personal piety, rejected external authority in religion, believed in direct communion between God and man, resisted social inequality, and some were even inclined toward an agrarian type of communism. They seemed a threat to privileged classes, since they opposed tax-supported churches, military service, the use of force, slavery, severe punishments, and oaths of allegiance to the *status quo*. They settled where peace and toleration prevailed, principally in Pennsylvania.[4]

By 1640 the Congregational churches of Massachusetts had fallen under the control of conservative groups, although democratic tendencies survived among the people. The men who shaped the early religious policy had belonged to the upper middle class in England; in the colony they composed the local upper class. Consequently, they established a conservative church which was ruled by the clergy and an oligarchy of influential laymen. Only members of an approved congregation could vote or hold office in the general government; all

[4] Lucy F. Bittinger, *German Religious Life in Colonial Times* (Philadelphia, 1907), is a readable survey of the external aspects of pietism.

inhabitants must attend the Puritan services; all must contribute toward the support of the church, either voluntarily or through public taxes.[5] Moreover, the creed of Puritanism gave great influence to the clergy. Man, who was born and lived in sin, could not effect the salvation of his soul; that was a gift of God to the elect. And God would indicate those of his creatures to whom he had granted salvation. The sign of election was a spiritual awakening or conversion which inspired one to forsake sinful ways and to live a godly life. Only after such a conversion might one be admitted to membership in the church and become a partaker of communion. In this process the clergy had a threefold role. They were God's instrument to awaken the soul—to prepare sinful man for his conversion or calling; they then examined the convert to determine whether he had received a true calling and was entitled to church membership, and they strengthened the members in their determination to live in the manner which God required of the elect. The use of political authority to assure religious uniformity and the influence of the clergy were essentially conservative features of Puritanism; democratic features were the selection of the minister by the congregation, the congregational plan of church organization, and the mystical ideal of conversion which meant that salvation required an inner experience of the individual—not mere conformity to an established system.[6]

In the seventeenth century the conservative principle triumphed in the official policy of the Massachusetts church. This outcome is explained in part by the expulsion of the radicals—Roger Williams, Anne Hutchinson, and other mystics who exalted the spiritual experience of the individual as against the authority of the clergy and the state. Then came the persecution of the Quakers. About 1656 Quaker missionaries entered Massachusetts, preaching their doctrine of the inner light (direct inspiration) which was so obnoxious to orthodox leaders because it avowed that the people did not need a trained ministry for spiritual guidance. Quaker doctrines also irked the governing class because they diffused among humble folk a sense of their importance by virtue of their presumed kinship with God. Accordingly, the General Court ordered that Quakers be banished on pain of death if they returned—a law which resulted in the execution in 1659–60 of four intractable missionaries who refused to stay in exile. The early purges in Massachusetts placed in control of the churches men

[5] Perry G. Miller, *Orthodoxy in Massachusetts, 1630–1650* (Cambridge, 1933), supersedes all other studies of the origins and nature of Congregationalism in the Bay Colony.

[6] Herbert W. Schneider's *The Puritan Mind* (New York, c. 1930) presents in modern form a concise analysis of New England Puritanism.

who looked askance at a personal, emotional type of religion in which the persecuted mystics had indulged. Meanwhile, the increasing wealth of the upper class strengthened the trend toward formalism in the Puritan church.[7]

In 1662 this trend received further recognition when the clergy of Massachusetts and Connecticut adopted the "halfway covenant." The issue then considered was the admission of the children of the church founders as church members. Many of the second generation did not experience a conversion; were they to be excluded from membership, thus losing the privilege of having their own children baptized? The clergy decided to admit all children of members to a sort of half membership, reserving full membership (i. e., the privilege of communion) to those who have been converted. Afterward, the clergy tended to emphasize observance of the church discipline and an outward moral life as tests of election. This outcome was conservative in that inheritance and family connections were favored at the expense of the spiritual life of the individual. Conservative people disapproved of excessive religious fervor: it might find expression in an uncouth manner and it might evoke the sort of radicalism that unsettled the status quo by questioning the moral foundations of property and government.[8]

After 1684 the interference of the English government in the affairs of Massachusetts threatened to undermine the Puritan church, since England insisted upon equal privileges for Anglicans and the toleration of dissenters. Hence the new royal charter of 1691 outlawed religious tests for voting and promised liberty of conscience to all Christians except papists. But Puritanism was not crushed. The new property qualifications for voting left the Puritans in control of elective offices, since they were the largest body of property owners. In 1692 the General Court again enacted that all taxpayers must contribute toward the support of the Congregational churches. In the years 1690–1720 the chief spokesmen of orthodoxy were Increase Mather and his son, Cotton Mather—both men of essentially conservative views. Somewhat prone to morbid introspection and ambitious to be the prophet of his age, Cotton Mather was doomed to disappointment. Mistrustful of the common man, too self-centered to be a popular leader, and yet too much given to middle-class religious fervor to appeal to conservative laymen who were growing

[7] Perry G. Miller, "The Marrow of Puritan Divinity," *Publications*, Colonial Society of Massachusetts, XXXII, 247–300.

[8] Perry G. Miller, "The Half-way Covenant," *New England Quarterly*, VI (Dec. 1933).

complacent in the accumulation of wealth, he failed to satisfy either the democratic or the aristocratic parties. Now that Britain appointed the governor of Massachusetts, the clergy no longer exerted their former influence in the executive councils, and Cotton Mather's ambitions to be a power behind the throne were likewise frustrated. His abilities and temperament did not fit him for the leadership to which he aspired, although he taxed his strength to exhaustion, wrote voluminously and became the most widely read author in the colonies.[9]

In order to strengthen the power of the clergy Cotton Mather and other orthodox ministers proposed in 1705 a church organization along Presbyterian lines. The churches of each county were to form an association and to set up a council composed of the ministers and important laymen. Each county council in turn was to send delegates to a general colonial conference, which was to examine and license candidates for the ministry, to ordain, install and dismiss ministers, and to hear appeals from the congregations and the county councils. Designed to impose a uniform doctrine and discipline on all the people, this new plan (called the Consociation) aimed to strengthen the clergy, who were to control the general council; the rule of the many in the various congregations was to give way to the rule of a few at the top. Connecticut adopted the scheme in 1708 (the Saybrook Platform) by authorizing each church to join an association, whereupon the congregations so affiliated became the established churches of the colony. In Massachusetts two factors thwarted the plan. The British government opposed it, fearing to enlarge the power of anti-British, anti-Anglican ministers in a colony none too loyal to the Crown. And the local democratic elements protested. In 1717 appeared the *Vindication of the Government of the Churches of New England,* written by the minister of Ipswich, the Reverend John Wise—a vigorous democrat whose father had been an indentured servant. Wise argued that church government by the congregation was the true principle of New England Puritanism, declaring that "an aristocracy is a dangerous constitution in the church of Christ" and that the "end of all good government is to cultivate humanity and promote the happiness of all." [10]

With the failure of the Consociation movement in Massachusetts the conservative Puritans utilized the General Court to control the congregations. This the General Court did by authorizing the establish-

[9] Ralph and Louise Boas, *Cotton Mather, Keeper of the Puritan Conscience* (New York, 1928), is excellent. Among earlier studies Barrett Wendell, *Cotton Mather* (New York, 1891), is especially recommended.

[10] Williston Walker, *A History of the Congregational Churches* . . . (New York, 1904), is a brief, factual survey.

ment of new churches, by removing objectionable ministers, by settling contests among rival candidates for a pastorate, and by enforcing laws for the public support of all churches. Such legislation perpetuated the old conflict between dissenters and the orthodox church. By absorbing Plymouth Colony in 1691 Massachusetts assumed jurisdiction over numerous Quakers and Baptists settled there. Both sects protested vigorously against paying taxes to support Puritan ministers, the less numerous Baptists accepting the leadership of the more influential Quakers. When such protests to the Massachusetts authorities proved fruitless, the Quakers appealed to the British government through English Quakers who were influential in the Whig party, then in power in England. Such political pressure induced Massachusetts in 1731 and 1734 to exempt the Quakers and Baptists from paying taxes for the support of the Puritan ministers.[11]

The Presbyterian Church gained a foothold in the colonies largely through the work of Francis Makemie, a missionary who, arriving in 1683, traveled through the settlements from New York to South Carolina. The first American presbytery, established in 1708, bore witness to his labors. Since the American congregations were independent of the Presbyterian Church in Scotland and Ulster they were obliged to provide their own ministers—a task to which they proved unequal after the Scotch-Irish immigrants began to arrive in large numbers in 1714. Accordingly, frontier communities commonly lacked a settled ministry and were prone to neglect religion. Presbyterianism was conservative in that its church organization vested large authority in the presbytery or district council of elders and ministers; moreover, it rejected the doctrines of the inner light and salvation through personal effort, adhering instead to the idea of predestination which affirmed the unworthiness of ordinary men in the sight of God. On the other hand the mass of the Scotch-Irish settlers, in their demands for land and political rights, exhibited a strongly democratic spirit. The Presbyterians were most numerous in Pennsylvania and in the western parts of Virginia, Maryland, South Carolina, and North Carolina.[12]

Similar to the Presbyterian Church in organization, creed and internal divisions were two other Calvinist churches—the Dutch Reformed and the German Reformed. The latter had thirty churches

---

[11] *Church and State in Massachusetts, 1691–1740,* by Susan M. Reed (Urbana, 1914), emphasizes the relation of the dissenters to the orthodox church. This story is continued in Jacob E. Meyer, *Church and State in Massachusetts, from 1740 to 1833* (Cleveland, 1930)—a detailed monograph.

[12] For the special student Charles A. Briggs, *American Presbyterianism* (New York, 1885), is the best work.

in Pennsylvania in 1750. The Dutch Reformed Church had been the official church of New Netherland until disestablished by the English after they took over the province in 1664. Ruled by the aristocratic families of New York and northern New Jersey, the Dutch Reformed churches remained under the jurisdiction of the mother church in Holland, where ministers were ordained before they were sent to the colonies.[13] The Lutheran Church, first introduced by the Swedes on the Delaware, grew very slowly until the great influx of the Germans after 1730. By 1750 the Lutherans were supporting forty churches in Pennsylvania. Although the Lutheran Church was a state church in Germany and in the Scandinavian kingdoms, the American Lutherans, as a minority without much political influence, objected to being taxed for the support of any non-Lutheran church and thus strengthened the movement for religious liberty in the colonies.

In the eighteenth century the American Quakers did not display the fervor that had characterized them before 1700. After England granted toleration in 1689 the colonies ceased to attract dissenters animated by religious zeal. In Rhode Island, New Jersey, and Pennsylvania, where the Quakers were most numerous, they were not driven to extremes by persecution. Meanwhile, many Quakers had grown wealthy; moreover, children commonly did not feel the ardor of their once persecuted parents. In eastern Pennsylvania many Quaker merchant families became quite conservative, inclining toward a comfortable way of living, to decorous manners, and to formality in religious worship. Sharing political power through their control of the assembly (to 1757) they betrayed a complacency that generally comes to those long in office. The more conservative Quakers owned slaves, consented to increasingly harsh punishments for criminals, and forsook the early ideal of non-resistance, although they continued to adhere to the forms of their religion and to oppose persecution and appropriations for the defense of the frontiers.[14]

In Massachusetts, Virginia, North Carolina, and Maryland, where the Quakers belonged to the small farmer-artisan class, contests with state churches weeded out the indifferent and kept alive religious zeal. Among such Quakers opposition to oaths, tithes, military service, social inequality, and slavery remained active. The democratic organization of the church enabled the various elements to work together

[13] E. T. Corwin, *A History of the Reformed Church, Dutch* (New York, 1905), is a convenient manual.

[14] Rufus M. Jones, *The Quakers in the American Colonies* (London, 1911), ranks high among religious histories. See also his *The Later Periods of Quakerism* (2 vols., London, 1921), Vol. I.

with reasonable harmony. Each congregation governed itself through its weekly and monthly meetings; hence the majority controlled. The quarterly meeting—a gathering of the people themselves, not an assembly of church officers—provided social life and religious fellowship. And the yearly meetings (the New England Quakers met at Newport; those of the middle colonies and the South at Burlington or Philadelphia) did not attempt to dictate to each congregation. These meetings heard reports of persecutions, provided relief for Friends in distress, and sustained missionary work. Quakerism thus afforded religious freedom to the individual; congregations of radical tendencies were not severely repressed by conservative elements; instead the latter coöperated to protect all Quakers from persecution and to support missionaries who labored among the Indians and the slaves.

By a series of laws, 1619–64, Virginia established the Anglican as the official church of the colony. Maryland followed in 1692, New York in 1693, North Carolina in 1701 and 1715, South Carolina in 1704 and 1706, and Georgia in 1758. But the strength of Anglicanism in these colonies varied greatly. The Church was established in only four counties in New York; in 1775 its communicants numbered only one in fifteen of the population of the province. North Carolina then had only six Anglican churches; Georgia in 1769 had only two. The influence of the Anglicans was declining in Virginia before the Revolution; in Maryland they were a small minority; the condition of the Church was most flourishing in South Carolina.

After 1685 the Anglican churches in America were under the jurisdiction of the Bishop of London. Unable to visit the colonial parishes, he sent thither his personal representatives (called commissaries) who inquired into conditions, advised the clergy, and undertook to improve the morale of communities and to promote religious education by building up schools and parochial libraries. Although the commissaries did not possess the bishop's power to confirm church members or to ordain ministers, in exceptional cases they could discipline and even suspend unworthy rectors. The best-known commissaries were Thomas Bray (Maryland), noted for his work in establishing numerous parish libraries, and James Blair (Virginia), instrumental in securing a royal charter for the Anglican College of William and Mary (1693).[15] By virtue of the colonial charters many royal governors claimed the power of selecting the clergy—a claim successfully disputed by the church members. Except in Maryland, where the governor or proprietor exercised the appointing power, selections were made commonly by the vestry—a board of twelve men who repre-

---

[15] Daniel E. Motley, *Life of Commissary James Blair* (Baltimore, 1901)—a brief sketch.

sented the most wealthy parishioners. Since the vestry also controlled the finances of the parish church it became the center of gravity. Home rule by the vestry, the isolation of churches, and the weakness of external authority gave American Anglicanism an independence somewhat suggestive of Congregationalism.[16]

The Anglican clergyman usually received the use of a house and a glebe or farm, together with a salary from parish taxes plus wedding and funeral fees. In New York, although other means were tried, salaries were provided through voluntary contributions; in South Carolina dissenters were taxed, not directly, but through custom duties. In fifty years the people of North Carolina paid taxes sufficient only to support two ministers for one year! Except in South Carolina the Anglican clergy did not exhibit much religious zeal. Security of tenure, lax discipline, and small incomes all contributed toward a complacency to be expected of a church sustained by law rather than by the fervor of its members. All the Anglican clergy had to be ordained by the Bishop of London—a rule which hindered the recruiting of Americans; hence a large majority were Englishmen. Frequently those who came to the colonies were the unaspiring who had been unable to obtain better places at home. Nor was the spiritual ardor of the Church of England particularly high. In Virginia and Maryland the clergy brought discredit upon the Church by their fondness for horse racing, fox hunting, and other worldly pleasures. The urge to uplift was weak, since the clergy ministered chiefly to people already at the top of the social scale.

Nor was it deemed desirable to agitate members of the lower classes, particularly the slaves. Six colonies between 1664 and 1706 enacted laws declaring that the conversion of slaves did not make them freemen. The planters were lukewarm or hostile to religious instruction for Negroes, partly because Christianity and membership in the owners' church might inculcate ideas of equality and independence, partly because attendance at remote services interfered with work on the plantations. A Presbyterian minister in 1756 deplored "the almost universal neglect of many thousand of poor slaves . . . who generally continue heathens in a Christian country." "It is too manifest to be denied," wrote a Quaker missionary in 1765, "that the life of religion is almost lost where slaves are very numerous; and it is impossible it should be otherwise, the practice being as contrary to the spirit of Christianity as light is to darkness." [17]

[16] Arthur L. Cross, *The Anglican Episcopate and the American Colonies* (New York, 1902), traces the relations between the colonies and the Church of England.

[17] M. W. Jernegan, "Slavery and Conversion in the American Colonies," *American Historical Review*, XXI (April 1916).

One remedy proposed for the weakness of the Anglican Church in America was to establish a resident bishop vested with the power to confirm members and to ordain and discipline ministers. Prelates and colonial officials in England pressed this plan in the years 1710–13, when the Tories (strict Anglicans) were in control. The strengthening of the Anglican Church in the colonies might bind them more closely to Britain by fostering attitudes of obedience to the Crown, since the Anglicans at home stood for the submission of the people to the royal power. However, the Whigs regained control in 1714 and the scheme was dropped. Then the Whig policy of encouraging foreign Protestants to settle in the colonies further lessened the influence of Anglicanism. Nor did the Whigs care to antagonize the colonists by taxing them for the support of an Anglican bishop at a time when their assistance was needed against the French. Non-Anglicans in America opposed the plan; so also did most of the Anglicans, who were satisfied to have their local churches governed by the leading families of their neighborhoods.

In 1701 William III chartered the Society for Propagating the Gospel in Foreign Parts (the S.P.G.)—a small organization dominated by prelates of the Anglican Church. Its purpose was to support missionaries in the colonies for the conversion of Indians, slaves, and non-Anglicans among the white settlers. Accordingly, the S.P.G. centered its efforts upon those regions without an established Anglican Church—particularly upon the middle colonies and Rhode Island. But the society accomplished little. It lacked popular support, as indicated by its small yearly income (£1,000 to £1,500—obtained chiefly from high churchmen), and for this reason it could sustain only a few missionaries. Due to the dearth of enthusiasm among Anglicans for missionary hardships, the agents assigned to the Indians soon left the frontiers and sought a more pleasant life in the settlements. The failure of a missionary sent among the Iroquois in 1704 frustrated plans to use the S.P.G. as a means of combating the political influence of the French Jesuits on the northern frontiers. By virtue of the opposition of the planters to the conversion of slaves little could be accomplished in that direction. The mass of the colonists were either confirmed in a particular faith or indifferent toward religion. Despite the efforts of the S.P.G. Anglicanism steadily lost ground as a popular religion in eighteenth-century America.[18]

[18] E. B. Greene, "The Anglican Outlook on the American Colonies," *American Historical Review*, XX (Oct. 1914).

The Great Awakening

In the 1730's occurred a stirring revival, the Great Awakening—the first spontaneous outburst of popular feeling in American history. Cutting across racial and denominational lines, it affected the mass of the small farmers and artisans, bearing witness to their class solidarity and to their antagonism toward aristocratic influences. Opposed by the Anglican clergy and welcomed by the Baptists, the Great Awakening split the Presbyterian, Congregational, and Dutch Reformed churches into conservative and popular factions. This American movement was only one aspect of a worldwide protest against the complacency, formalism, authoritarianism, and lack of emotional fervor that had come to characterize most of the Protestant churches. From German Pietism a wave of religious zeal swept over Europe after 1700; in England John and Charles Wesley launched the Methodist movement in an effort to infuse new life into complacent Anglicanism.[19] In America the lack of churches in many settlements had caused a neglect of religion which was favorable to an emotional reaction when once the people living in comparative isolation were subjected to the spell of eloquent evangelists.

The Great Awakening exhibited many democratic features, the most important being the conception of salvation popularized by Jonathan Edwards, graduate of Yale College and Congregational minister at Northampton, Massachusetts. Edwards adhered to the Calvinistic view that man was steeped in sin and that a spiritual awakening was God's sign to those whom he had predestined to salvation. By portraying vividly the torments of hell, Edwards aroused in his hearers a dread of sin and a longing for purification that blossomed in a joyful sense of God's presence in the soul. Not wealth or social status but one's individual experience was the condition of salvation. Now it so happened that such a conversion was most likely to visit humble, uneducated people; its effect therefore was to diffuse among the common folk the belief that they were the chosen of the Lord—and thus to intensify their dissatisfaction with an inferior place in society.[20]

The Great Awakening also enabled the common man to participate in the church services, even though such activity took the form of wailing, shouting, rolling on the ground, praying, singing, and leaping in

[19] James Laver, *Wesley* (New York, 1933), is an admirable brief summary.
[20] The best study of Edwards's ideas is Arthur C. McGiffert, *Jonathan Edwards* (New York, 1932); the most readable biography is H. B. Parkes, *Jonathan Edwards* (New York, 1930); the best older study is Alexander U. G. Allen, *Jonathan Edwards* (Boston, 1889).

ecstasy. No longer was religion a monopoly of a few educated, conservative clergymen. The evangelist who aroused the people addressed them in the language they knew. He spoke to the heart rather
than to the intellect; he held services in fields and groves where all
might attend. Rank, formality, and exclusiveness had no place among
a company of worshippers equal in the sight of God.

The Great Awakening popularized the idea that the truth was to
be found by each person in the Bible—not in man-made laws, sermons,
or creeds. Authorities who violated the divine law did not merit respect; institutions contrary to the Scriptures were deemed invalid:
here were the seeds of revolution. Every congregation should govern
itself, since each member had received in full the divine benediction.
And because any person might be revealed as one of God's elect, all
(including Indians and slaves) were entitled to dignified and humane
treatment.[21]

One precursor of the revivalists was Theodore Frelinghuysen, a
Dutch Reformed minister educated in Germany, where he had fallen
under the influence of Pietism. Taking a pastorate in the Raritan valley he traveled in the 1720's a circuit of four churches, championing
a strict morality and the doctrine of spiritual rebirth. Opposed by the
conventional ministers of the Dutch Reformed Church, he coöperated
with Presbyterian revivalists. A pioneer evangelist among the Presbyterians was William Tennent, who arrived in Philadelphia from
Ireland about 1717 and soon undertook to supply ministers for the
Scotch-Irish settlers near the frontiers. To carry out this purpose he
established a log college (1736) at his farm between Philadelphia and
New York, where he trained zealous young preachers and inspired
them with the new evangelism. His son Gilbert, who became a co-
worker with Frelinghuysen, carried forward at New Brunswick the
work in northern New Jersey.[22] In 1740 Gilbert visited Boston,
where his preaching moved a conservative minister to describe him as
"impudent and saucy" and to lament that in the "dreadfullest winter
I ever saw, people wallowed in the snow night and day for the benefit
of his beastly braying." Even before this the younger Tennent had
become the most powerful revivalist in the middle colonies. Meanwhile, in the Connecticut valley Jonathan Edwards, dismayed by the
moral laxity of the age, was calling sinners to repentance and a righteous life, combining in his utterances the qualities of poet, mystic, and

---

[21] See again H. L. Osgood, *American Colonies in the Eighteenth Century*, Vol. III,
pp. 407–450.

[22] Charles H. Maxson, *The Great Awakening in the Middle Colonies* (Chicago,
1920), is a concise, informative study.

stern Calvinist. Although he remained at Northampton, his influence extended so widely through his sermons and writings that he re-awakened all New England to the dangers of hell-fire and sin.[23]

English Methodism contributed to the American revival the greatest evangelist of the age. In 1739 George Whitefield arrived at Philadelphia, whence he visited New York, Charleston, Savannah, and New England. At Northampton he was cordially received by Jonathan Edwards and in Pennsylvania by the Tennents. Already known as the foremost preacher of Britain, Whitefield attracted immense and eager audiences wherever he spoke. Not intellectual in his discourses, he spoke on the simple themes of sin, repentance, and regeneration, swaying thousands of humble folk by his superlative oratory. A tireless worker, he did more than anyone else to spread the spirit of revivalism and to keep it alive.[24]

The most important result of the Great Awakening was the division of the churches into parties which corresponded roughly to existing social classes. The Presbyterians in 1741 divided into the "old lights" and the "new lights"; the Congregationalists into orthodox and separatist. Not until 1758 was the breach closed in the Presbyterian Church. Of the Congregationalist separatists, some eventually returned to the old churches, some formed independent congregations, and many joined the Baptists—the sect which benefited chiefly by the revival in New England. The revivalists insisted that salvation and church membership depended upon conversion; they received as ministers untrained laymen who had been particularly moved by the divine spirit; they supported itinerant preachers and desired to receive them into the existing churches; they favored soul-stirring sermons and emotional demonstrations by the laity. The anti-revivalists (most of the educated ministers, the well-to-do parishioners, and the professors at Yale and Harvard colleges) stressed the fine points of theology and adherence to creeds and church discipline, favored dignified, decorous, unemotional services, recognized only ordained ministers, and protested vehemently against receiving itinerant preachers and their "rabble" followers into the churches.

Other effects of the revival may be noted briefly. It intensified the religious criticism of slavery, gave a short-lived impetus to missionary work among the Indians, and strengthened the humanitarian spirit, as evinced by Whitefield's work in founding an orphans' asylum in

[23] M. H. Mitchell, The Great Awakening (New Haven, 1934—Connecticut Tercentenary Commission, no. 26).

[24] The most recent biography is Albert D. Belden, George Whitefield, the Awakener (Nashville, c. 1930); the most complete is Luke Tyerman, The Life of the Rev. George Whitefield (2 vols., New York, 1876–77).

Georgia. Four new colleges grew out of the movement: Princeton (Presbyterian), Brown (Baptist), Rutgers (Dutch Reformed), and Dartmouth (Congregationalist). The opposition among dissenters to established churches received a fresh stimulus, while defiance of authorized institutions prepared men's minds for the next act of resistance—the American Revolution.[25]

THE EDUCATION OF YOUTH

In colonial times the pursuit of knowledge exhibited two phases. The organized schools trained the youth in the body of existing knowledge; outside the schools, learned and ingenious men speculated anew about nature and the destiny of man. However, both the formal instruction of the schoolroom and the creative intellectual life outside were affected by similar influences, five of which should be understood.[26]

First, the colonists started with the cultural heritage of Europe. They brought with them the European conceptions of the natural world—a strange mixture of folklore, superstition, and scientific truth—and thereafter they were continually affected by cultural currents emanating from the Old World. To New England alone before 1650 came about a hundred and thirty men (most of them ministers) who had been educated in the universities of Europe and Britain. A few colonists maintained close connections with the centers of thought overseas, importing books and scientific apparatus and reporting to European correspondents their observations of natural phenomena in America. The Royal Society of London, incorporated in 1662 and devoted to scientific inquiry, numbered among its correspondents such men as John Winthrop, Jr., and Cotton Mather in New England, William Byrd and John Mitchell of Virginia, and Benjamin Franklin and David Rittenhouse of Pennsylvania. Harvard College, founded at Cambridge (then Newtown) Massachusetts, in 1636, was originally conceived of as a refuge for English Puritans in exile, as a center to which the English Puritans might send their sons, and as a means of preserving the Puritan flame which Charles I sought to extinguish in the English universities. Supported in part by benefactions from English sources, drawing its teachers from England, and shaped by the course of English politics, Harvard retained its inter-

---

[25] F. I. Carpenter, "The Radicalism of Jonathan Edwards," *New England Quarterly*, IV (Oct. 1931). Wesley M. Gewehr's *The Great Awakening in Virginia, 1740–1790*, an excellent study, emphasizes the social aspects of the revival.

[26] Intellectual trends are ably summarized in I. Woodbridge Riley, *American Thought* (New York, 1923).

national character until the Puritans, seizing power in England, no longer needed their "university in exile" after 1650.[27] In Virginia, the College of William and Mary was established in 1693 in order to train the southern youth in the ideals of the Church of England.

Foremost among the cultural influences inherited from Europe was the religious impulse. The medieval union of education and religion had not been dissolved when the colonies were founded. To the colonial clergy more than to any other group belonged the task of preserving and fostering learning in the New World. Most Protestant sects held that an educated ministry was necessary that the Scriptures might be fully understood by men competent to read the original records in Hebrew and Greek; moreover, it was appropriate that the clergy investigate the mysteries of nature and thus be qualified to explain the ways of God to man. Religion also had its part in the education of youth. The Calvinists believed that all should be taught to read in order that they might know the sources of divine truth; children should be reared in the true faith; and the virtues of obedience, industry, and honesty should be inculcated through religious schools. The major sects, both Protestant and Catholic, accepted private property as a sacred institution; two of the Ten Commandments enjoin respect for property rights.[28]

Long before 1600 European thought had manifested a practical, utilitarian bent, as scientific inquiry sought to master the forces of nature in order to lighten men's burdens on earth. To enlarge production and to increase the physical comforts of life: such was the underlying aim, which also dominated the training of the youth of the lower and middle classes, whose education as apprentices taught the skills of craft and trade. To the colonial farm boy or girl incessant contacts with tools, materials, plants, animals, and the soil—a continual preoccupation with the processes of production—gave an education that was extremely practical and concrete.

The environment of the New World strengthened the practical, secular, utilitarian influence in thought at the expense of theology. Concern with the physical aspects of society was imperative since the colonists had to provide in a short time a material equipment (houses, buildings, fences, clearings, roads) which Europe had been generations in acquiring. Moreover, the strange aspects of life in America intensified the curiosity of men about the natural world: the

---

[27] S. E. Morison, *The Founding of Harvard College* (Cambridge, 1935), combines broad knowledge, keen scholarship, and literary charm.

[28] Harvey G. Townsend, *Philosophical Ideas in the United States* (New York, 1934), finds in idealism the key to American philosophy.

contrast between the familiar and the strange is always a potent stimulus to inquiry. There were new plants, soils, minerals, climates, animals, and trees to be observed and utilized—new routes of travel, new seas, ocean currents, lakes, rivers, and harbors to be mastered; even the heavens wore a strange aspect. Animals and plants brought from Europe developed surprising characteristics. Probably every colonist encountered some manifestation of nature that seemed to him strikingly novel—hurricanes, comets, electrical storms, eclipses, heavy snows, clouds of insects or birds, intense heat, bitter cold. Many an intelligent man employed his idle hours in the study of the new nature—the ways of the bee, the migration of birds, the strange face of the seasons, the movements of the stars, the habits of the beasts of the forest. The strongest voice the colonist heard was the voice of nature, and for many years it spoke in unfamiliar accents. It is not surprising, then, that the first American scientists occupied themselves with descriptive botany, zoölogy, geography, and astronomy and with native curiosities among natural phenomena.[29]

Colonial education reflected the class standards of Europe, where the higher learning was closely identified with the higher classes. Exempt from physical toil, the children of the well-to-do needed an intellectual discipline to provide that regularity, application, and restraint, without which leisure and wealth are likely to lead to deterioration. Difficult subjects like Latin, Greek, and mathematics had a high disciplinary value and hence were especially esteemed by the upper-class groups. Higher education also furnished the fortunate with intellectual adornments which set them off from the poor; correct literary usage, an approved accent, the use of Latin or Greek phrases, a knowledge of ancient literature—all served to distinguish the gentleman from peasants and workers. Assuming that superior intellect was the basis of their supremacy, the upper classes emphasized the training of the mind and pursued those studies, like the law and the military arts, which reinforced the economic and military bases of political power. Cultural activities also gratified one's curiosity and esthetic sense and provided an agreeable employment for the leisure hours of the upper-class gentleman.[30]

Since members of the lower classes were disciplined by poverty and toil, and because they enjoyed but little leisure, the studies deemed appropriate for them were of a useful rather than a decorative char-

[29] Edwin E. Slosson, *The American Spirit in Education* (*Chronicles of America*, New Haven, 1921), chapters 1–5.

[30] Merle Curti, *The Social Ideas of American Educators* (New York, 1935), is an excellent study. See chapter 1.

acter. Book learning consisted only of reading, writing, and arithmetic; in addition the poor should acquire physical strength and the skills of artisan or laborer. To masters and employers it seemed equally desirable that the lower classes be trained in the habits of obedience, industry, and honesty.

The most significant influence on education was exerted by the colonial middle class. A desire to emulate the upper class induced the middle class to pursue some studies of a decorative, disciplinary, and esthetic nature; and yet, because the middle class was not exempt from work, it was forced to concern itself largely with the gainful arts and professions—with business, the law, medicine, agricultural improvements, and the skilled trades. Middle-class education therefore combined the useful and the ornamental: as Franklin put it, the preferred studies were the *most* useful and the *most* decorative. "Write with the learned, pronounce with the vulgar," advised Poor Richard. From the middle class came the demand for extending educational opportunities among the people, and because the lower class followed the lead of the middle class, popular education in the colonies aimed to prepare the individual for a useful, gainful life and to confer upon him some of the cultural advantages previously associated with the upper class.

The most distinctive feature of American educational history is the growth of the system of public schools. To New England goes much of the credit for this evolution—a fact explained by many circumstances. The New England colonies, products of an intellectual movement in England, were founded in order to preserve a cultural ideal. Accordingly the Puritan leaders imposed religious unity and erected compact settlements in order to achieve coöperation and cultural solidarity. Since education was permeated with the religious spirit, the New Englanders (except in Rhode Island) could act together in education as a single public body and bring to bear upon the school the concentrated resources of the community.[31] In the middle colonies, religious differences made it impossible for the people to develop one system of public education; religious diversity bred educational diversity. In the southern colonies, the strong economic impetus to emigration resulted in a similar religious diversity; and, moreover, settlements were so dispersed that the localities lacked the concentration of people and resources necessary for the effective support of schools. The advantage of New England's unity becomes apparent when the religious aspect of early education is considered.

[31] Thomas G. Wright, *Literary Culture in Early New England* (New Haven, 1920), is a group of incisive, penetrating essays (for the advanced student).

When the colonies were established there were few state-supported public schools in Europe; most instruction, directly or indirectly, was under the influence of the various churches. Accordingly, the first schools erected in America were established and supported by religious groups. Elementary schools taught reading, writing, church doctrine, and rules of conduct; ministers often served as teachers; and the subject matter of instruction was drawn largely from the Bible. Early textbooks, like the hornbook and *The New England Primer,* abound with religious allusions.

> Young Obadias
> David, Josias
> All were pious.

A colony like Massachusetts or Connecticut, where the people adhered to one creed, could develop a unified public, state-supported religion, whereas other colonies that contained many sects could not act together through the state. In Pennsylvania and New Jersey the Quaker objection to the union of church and state imposed a special obstacle to religious instruction through public (political) agencies.

One other factor influenced education in New England.[32] In most towns the class distinctions were not so marked as to induce the upper-class groups to provide separate schools for their children. In the South, however, with its sharply drawn class lines, the wealthy planters did not want their children to associate with the poor; hence all the youth could not readily be brought together in a single school. Virginia acted upon the assumption that education was a private, not a public, responsibility. The wealthy planters who had to pay for the schooling of their sons in private schools did not care to support public schools for the poor, and since servants, workers, poor farmers, and slaves did not control the colonial governments, they could not provide a system of public schools for themselves.

Between 1635 and 1645 the principal towns of New England, excepting in mainland Rhode Island, made provision for the public support of a local schoolmaster. Massachusetts, caught in an economic depression in 1642, endeavored to foster home industry by requiring that parents and masters teach their children and apprentices to read and to master a trade; if a parent failed, the child might be apprenticed to a master who would give the proper instruction. Then in 1647 Massachu-

---

[32] S. E. Morison's *The Puritan Pronaos* (New York, 1936) embodies the latest researches into the intellectual life of seventeenth-century New England. Especially recommended.

setts ordered that each town of fifty families provide a schoolmaster to teach the children to read and write. This extremely important act permitted the town to pay the schoolmaster through either a tax levy or tuition fees collected from the parents. Unfortunately, many of the poorer towns preferred to pay a fine of £5 rather than support a schoolmaster; hence the act did not have the colony-wide effect which its authors intended. The act was copied by Connecticut and in part by New Hampshire and Plymouth Colony. Rhode Island, as a colony, made no move to establish schools because public religious instruction seemed to savor of that coercion in matters of conscience to which Roger Williams and his followers objected.[33]

When the Dutch controlled New Netherland they established a group of public schools which by 1664 had been extended to nearly all the towns in the colony. But inasmuch as these schools were under the control of the Dutch Reformed Church, the English, while not forcing Anglican instruction upon the Dutch, did not care to entrust all elementary education to the Dutch Church, and consequently did not provide for the public support of schools after 1664. In Maryland an opposite set of factors thwarted the development of a public school system which English officials sought to build up after 1696. In this case failure was due largely to the effort to foster Anglican schools in a colony composed mainly of Catholics and dissenters. Pennsylvania, New Jersey, North Carolina, and Virginia did not establish many elementary public schools; in South Carolina an act of 1712 authorized optional grants for the support of teachers in the parishes.

Outside New England, the lack of public instruction compelled reliance upon private schools, of which there were two principal types —those maintained by religious bodies and those supported by well-to-do families. By 1800 the Quakers had established between sixty or seventy schools; in New York the Society for Propagating the Gospel gave Anglican instruction, especially to the poor. Other sects active in supporting schools were the Dutch Reformed Church and the Presbyterian Church. In the plantation area the planters joined together to hire a schoolmaster and to provide a schoolhouse. Some southern schools received endowments from philanthropic men which provided a little free schooling for poor children. In the religious schools the poor were given free instruction; only parents who could afford to pay were charged tuition fees. Outside rural New England

[33] See again M. W. Jernegan's definitive studies of early education in *Laboring and Dependent Classes in Colonial America*, pp. 59–171.

free education lost caste by virtue of its identification with poverty. Most private schools in the plantation South, when conducted by the local minister, inculcated the beliefs of the Anglican Church.[34]

In considering the meager facilities of colonial schools it should be remembered that the home, the farm, and the shop had a high educational value. There the child learned how to avoid injury, how to do the practical things that sustain life, how to get along with associates; from his elders he learned a thousand lessons taught by the experience of the race. In the elementary schools there was no marked class influence on the subjects taught; nor did the American environment alter the course of instruction. Reading, writing, arithmetic, and rules of conduct were the foundations of all education, both vocational and cultural, serviceable alike in America and in Europe, to rich and poor, to children destined to be farmers, artisans, or gentlemen of leisure. The most important trend in elementary education appeared in New England after 1690—the result of demands that facilities be extended so as to serve all the people. As the settled areas of the towns increased, families remote from the local school petitioned that the town be divided into districts and that their tax money be used to support a new school near at hand. The creation of such district schools kept education close to the people, although the instruction was often of poor quality and the school term only a month.

In the field of secondary education, American experience led to a sharp break with the past.[35] At the start the colonists attempted to duplicate the Latin grammar schools of England, which provided a thorough training in Latin for young gentlemen and students for the ministry. In 1647 Massachusetts enacted that each town of a hundred families maintain such a grammar school. However, the Latin curriculum proved unsuited to the needs of the colonists; and not every town cared to support a school for a few prospective ministers. Accordingly, the Latin grammar school was supplanted after 1750 by the academy—a private school which retained Latin and Greek as the backbone of the curriculum but also emphasized English composition and literature, mathematics, modern languages, and philosophy (including natural science). The academy, well suited to American needs, took root in all the colonies. It retained the instruction necessary for clergymen; it emphasized the disciplinary and decorative studies

[34] Two outstanding texts are Ellwood P. Cubberley, *Public Education in the United States* (Boston, 1934), and Edwin G. Dexter, *A History of Education in the United States* (New York, 1922).
[35] Elmer E. Brown, *The Making of Our Middle Schools* (New York, 1921), is the standard work.

suitable to young gentlemen; and it imparted some knowledge useful in business and the professions.[36]

As the number of wealthy families increased after 1700 a host of private schools appeared, established by enterprising schoolmasters who offered polite instruction to ladies and gentlemen, either in small refined classes or in the home. Such schools taught higher mathematics, geography, Latin, Greek, letter-writing, French, philosophy, and civil government, while special studies of practical value included mechanics, optics, drawing, gauging, astronomy, navigation, fortification, and gunnery. Shorthand was recommended to gentlemen for "dispatch in what they would write for their own memory, and [for] concealing what they would not have lie open to every eye." Fencing and swordsmanship were presented as honorable attainments of young gentlemen, while the youth of both sexes were urged to achieve refinement through dancing (minuets and cotillions), instrumental music (the flute, violin, spinet, and harpsichord), psalmody, French (increasingly popular after 1763), and horsemanship ("an art justly admired and courted as a part of polite education"). We learn that one object of education was to enable youth to enter "the stage of life with advantage and to make an amiable figure in the world." One music master taught by the methods of "the organist of his majesty's chapel," and shorthand was reputable because "many of the nobility, gentry, ministry, etc. [of England] have taken pains to learn it." There were also private schools giving instruction in reading, writing, and arithmetic to children of the well-to-do, thus exempting them from attending the public schools. Another type of private school, designed for aspiring tradesmen, taught the three R's, spelling, and merchants' accounts.[37]

Excepting a little public or private assistance given to poor candidates for the ministry, the colonial college served the youth of the upper and upper middle classes. This explains in part why higher instruction resisted change more effectively than the utilitarian branches of education. One mark of such conservatism was the continued dominance of the religious influence on the curriculum. Of the nine colleges established in colonial times, three were founded by the Congregationalists: Harvard (1636), Yale (1701), and Dartmouth (1769); two by the Anglicans: William and Mary (1693) and King's College, now Columbia (1754); one by the Presbyterians—the Col-

---

[36] C. K. Shipton, "Secondary Education in the Puritan Colonies," *New England Quarterly*, VII (Dec. 1934).

[37] For other books on education see J. T. Adams, *Provincial Society*, pp. 341–342.

lege of New Jersey, now Princeton (1747); one by the Dutch Reformed Church—Queen's College, now Rutgers (1766); and one by the Baptists—Rhode Island College, now Brown (1764). The only institution not under sectarian auspices was the "Academy," established at Philadelphia in 1749.

Higher education is best illustrated by the history of Harvard, the most important of the colonial colleges. Its purpose was to train ministers, to educate young gentlemen, to sustain the Puritan faith and to preserve learning, good manners, and Christian morality in the wilderness. To this end students and teachers lived in the same building, under a fixed discipline, studying, dining, and worshipping together. All the decencies and comforts of life which the times afforded were deemed necessary for the gentleman scholars.[38]

The college students received preparatory training from the Latin grammar schools or through private instruction from ministers. The main entrance requirement was the ability to speak, write, and translate Latin, since the college textbooks were written and classroom instruction given in that tongue. The early curriculum consisted of logic, rhetoric, Greek, Hebrew, ethics, and metaphysics. After his freshman year the student became a sophomore, one who was doing his "sophomes" or exercises in logical disputation. Then he became a junior sophister (one sufficiently adept in logic to take part in public disputations); then a senior sophister. Each tutor taught all subjects; there were no "courses," credits, or written examinations; promotion came upon the tutor's certification of the capacity and application of the student. At the end of the four-year term the seniors had to take open examinations ("sitting solstices"), when they might be examined in every subject of the curriculum "by all comers." At commencement (which centered in the conferring of the B.A. degree) the great men of the colony assembled early in July to listen to orations, to hear the students debate propositions printed on a thesis sheet, and to partake of a great feast. To Cambridge thronged a multitude of country folk, pleasure seekers, sharpers, and riffraff who gave to the occasion something of the character of a modern football game, Fourth-of-July celebration, and county fair.

The student for the ministry commonly remained in residence three years after commencement, reading in theology and philosophy "on his own," whereupon he received the M.A. degree and assumed a place of great prestige in his community. Undergraduates were sub-

[38] S. E. Morison's *Harvard College in the Seventeenth Century* (2 vols., Cambridge, 1936) is the definitive work. For a delightful summary of Professor Morison's researches see chapters 1–6 of his *Three Centuries of Harvard* (Cambridge, 1937).

ject to a strict routine of study, prayers, lectures, and recitations which, together with four meal hours and two periods for relaxation, occupied the day from five in the morning till nine at night. Freshmen lived in abject subjection to all superiors, both upper students and faculty. The natural exuberance of youth often broke out in nocturnal excursions and practical jokes, which were generally tolerated on the theory that "a wild colt often makes a good horse." The flogging of culprits, practiced before 1700, gave way to ear-boxing; that in turn passed out about 1765. Since all students were ranked and given privileges according to the social position of their families, an effective punishment was to lower an offender's college status. In 1772 the college adopted an alphabetical classification; social ratings were then causing too much jealousy and envy among the elite of the province.

Despite the innate conservatism of higher education, it too responded to the trend away from theology toward secular interests.[39] In the late 1690's Harvard's hospitality toward general literature and philosophy as against Puritan dogma moved many strict Puritans to support a new, orthodox college in Connecticut, founded by Harvard graduates in 1701 and named in 1718 at the suggestion of Cotton Mather, leader of the Puritan old guard, in honor of Elihu Yale, a rich merchant benefactor. In the eighteenth century the college curriculum placed increasing emphasis upon mathematics, science, literature, and French. A similar non-sectarian influence appeared in the founding of the Medical College of Philadelphia (1765), soon followed by the establishment of a medical department at King's College in 1767. Benjamin Franklin in 1749 published a plan for higher education, proposing a non-sectarian institution devoted to useful and ornamental studies, of which he deemed the most essential to be English, mathematics, astronomy, geography, history, politics, logic, and morality; the languages, ancient and modern, should be required only when needed in professional training. The general student might choose languages as electives, but not to the neglect of "English, arithmetic, and the other studies absolutely necessary." Franklin's ideas bore some fruit when the Philadelphia Academy was chartered in 1754 as a non-sectarian institution, although the prestige of Latin won it a larger place than Franklin had intended.[40] The launching of the College of Rhode Island (Brown) further weakened the theologi-

[39] J. J. Walsh, "Scholasticism in the Colonial Colleges," *New England Quarterly,* V (July 1932).
[40] Thomas Woody (ed.), *Educational Views of Benjamin Franklin* (New York, 1931).

cal influence in education. Although a Baptist school, its charter granted equal opportunities to the youth of all denominations, guaranteed liberty of conscience, permitted the recruiting of teachers and officers (except the president) from all Protestant elements, banned sectarianism from the general curriculum, and decreed that "the public teaching shall in general respect the sciences."

THE NATURAL WORLD

The colonial period registered notable progress in scientific inquiry. The early settlers came steeped in fears and superstitions drawn from the ancient stock of mythology and folklore. Primitive man had interpreted the natural world in terms of his own welfare: whatever inflicted injury, pain, or illness he deemed evil; whatever induced health, contentment, strength, and prosperity he deemed good. The Christian concept of a single, just God raised the problem of evil; how could the manifold torments and misfortunes that afflicted mankind be reconciled with a God who was both good and all-powerful? The most popular solution of this problem was the conception of Satan—the master evil spirit who had led a host of angels in a revolt against God's rule in heaven, had been hurled with his cohorts into hell, and had thereafter devoted himself to wreaking vengeance upon God by corrupting His creature, man. Another idea affirmed that God kept evil spirits in chains, occasionally lengthening the chain so that the evil ones might torment those deserving divine punishment. Thus there were evil spirits to torment the wicked, and emissaries of Satan who sought to injure the chosen of God.[41]

The concrete evidences of the activity of evil spirits included accidents that befell man, misfortunes, human suffering, and aberrations of nature. To Cotton Mather thunderbolts that struck churches seemed necessarily the work of Satan; superstitious mariners readily attributed stormy weather to evil spirits. Unfortunately, the manifestations of evil extended beyond natural occurrences that all could witness; apparitions, dreams, and delusions of deranged minds were believed to reveal authentic evidences of the powers of darkness—a fact which gave a wider scope to Satan's genius than would have been the case had all his "actions" been subject to tests applied by sane observers. The Devil also operated by taking possession of people (witches), through whom he inflicted torments upon those faithful to the Lord.

Between 1647 and 1662 fourteen people were hanged as witches in

[41] See again Edward Eggleston, *The Transit of Civilization.*

Connecticut and Massachusetts. Then the interest abated until about 1681, when the ministers of Massachusetts revived it. The colony had suffered many afflictions and people were drifting away from the old faith; clearly Satan was at work in the land. In 1684 Increase Mather published *An Essay for the Recording of Illustrious Providences,* wherein he recited various instances of witchcraft—a work prepared at the suggestion of the Puritan divines. Cotton Mather further stimulated interest by studying a "bewitched" child at Boston and by charging in a book, *Memorable Providences* (1689), that the denial of witchcraft was "a dangerous stroke" to "settle men in atheism." Obviously, the belief in evil spirits exalted the power of the ministers, since the people must rely upon the church to protect them against Satan. In March 1691 began the witchcraft delusion at Salem, instigated by some young girls who probably had been unstrung by weird stories they had heard from West Indian slaves. The girls, giving signs of mental derangement, accused neighbors right and left of bewitching them. A wave of hysteria engulfed the village; when it subsided in 1692 twenty persons had been hanged for witchcraft and fifty-five others had confessed their "guilt." Eventually the hysterical accusers (who had at first named as witches only old, poor, unattractive women) began to implicate important people, whereupon the governor and the special trial court of seven judges stopped proceedings, emptied the jails and pardoned those who had confessed. The belief in witchcraft prevailed in the other colonies, but only in New England did executions occur—a fact which suggests the exceptional influence of the Puritan clergy.[42]

Witchcraft was only one superstition entertained by the colonists. Among prevalent notions were the ideas that the earth was the center of the universe, that different stars exerted influence over particular persons, plants, and animals, that comets were signs of impending calamity, that earthquakes were caused by winds imprisoned within the earth, that insects were generated by decaying matter, and that migratory birds wintered on the moon or in the bottoms of rivers. Hogs should be slaughtered during the waxing of the moon or they would shrink and be poor; brushwood should be cut during the waning of the moon so that it would not grow again. "The moon in the wane, gather fruit for to last." Snakes hypnotized animals; water could be detected by moving a forked willow branch over the earth (if water were present, the stick would bend downward). Unlucky days, signs, and charms had a great vogue. A bird's entering a room,

[42] George L. Kittredge's erudite *Witchcraft in Old and New England* (Cambridge, 1929) places the Salem episode in its general historical setting.

a dog's barking all night were portents of approaching death; a cock's crowing at ten o'clock at night foretold a morning rain; horseshoes and brooms placed at doors would keep out witches.

The study of science did not dispel all such popular notions, but during colonial times the groundwork was prepared for the rapid progress to come. When the colonies were founded most scientific inquiry was motivated by religious objectives—to understand God's mysteries and to demonstrate the reality of the world of spirits. The method employed was medieval scholasticism—the process of thought that applies evidence and inductive logic to religious principles, with the purpose of coming at new conclusions consistent with Scriptural premises. Increase and Cotton Mather collected accounts of natural curiosities and monstrosities in order to reinforce their views of Satan's influence and of God's providence.

At the close of the colonial period science was freeing itself from the restrictions of religion. American conditions favored a science that was practical—that would serve the profit motive in industry, shipping, and agriculture; hence the emphasis placed upon plant study, astronomy, surveying, mapmaking, mathematics, chemistry, physics, and medicine. In a sense the process of settlement was a continuation of the great achievements of geographical discovery: new observations of nature, new adjustments to the hard material facts of life had to be made on an ever-extending scale. Hence the American experience proved especially receptive to the inductive, experimental study of nature developed by Copernicus, Galileo, Bacon, Newton, Kepler, and Boyle. By testing and measuring with instruments of precision one drew conclusions from the evidences of the senses, not from past revelations of God to man, and such conclusions might or might not harmonize with prevailing religious conceptions.[43]

The line between revealed religion and experimental science cannot be drawn too sharply, however, because some ministers conducted experiments, used the observational method, kept accurate records of findings, exploded superstitions, and accepted new ideas. Increase and Cotton Mather championed inoculation for smallpox when colonial doctors opposed the innovation.[44]

The leading man of science in the seventeenth century was Governor John Winthrop, Jr., of Connecticut (1606–1676). Convinced that manufactured goods were the basis of a mature civilization and

---

[43] Holland Thompson, *The Age of Invention* (*Chronicles of America*, New Haven, 1921), chapter 1.

[44] Henry R. Viets, *A Brief History of Medicine in Massachusetts* (Boston, 1930), is admirable.

acutely aware of New England's difficulty of buying them from England, Winthrop concluded that New England's salvation lay in the development of home industries and mining. His interest in chemistry, astronomy, and mining were largely those of an industrial promoter. As an astronomer he predicted the discovery of a fifth satellite to Jupiter, although unable to prove his theory due to inadequate instruments. The foremost colonial botanist, John Bartram, a Quaker farmer of Pennsylvania (1699–1777), was drawn to plant study by his love of nature. Not content merely to classify plants, he established a botanic garden near Philadelphia, where he conducted experiments in hybridization and grew many exotic plants sent by friends in Europe. His religious ideas were probably responsible for his expulsion from the Quaker society into which he was born. He traveled the frontiers extensively in search of new seeds, bulbs, and roots for his garden. As a lover of nature he worked chiefly alone, for he found that most Americans had little interest in pure science and that they were prone to exploit rather than to worship nature. Among other contributions he explained the formation of limestones and marbles along lines which geologists now accept.

The first creative scientist in academic circles was John Winthrop, professor of mathematics and natural philosophy at Harvard between 1738 and 1779. As the son of a Boston merchant, Professor Winthrop was in touch with that element among the colonial capitalists which was turning from Puritan dogma to science, and his appointment was viewed with misgivings by the theologians. He established the first laboratory of experimental physics in an American college, using the best available scientific apparatus to demonstrate the laws of heat, light, and mechanics, and in 1751 he introduced the study of calculus at Harvard. He made observations of sunspots, studied electricity, and proved that earthquakes are the result of natural forces, not of divine anger. In 1761 he led an official expedition to Newfoundland to observe the transit of Venus over the sun. His scientific contributions were printed in the *Transactions of the Royal Society*—the main channel of publication for the papers of colonial scientists.[45]

An outstanding thinker like Benjamin Franklin was also a symbol of a broad movement in which a host of lesser figures were taking part. Franklin's early life as a printer—his practice of applying handwork to ideas—explains in large measure the practical cast of his thought. No activity satisfied him so much as scientific inquiry—a mistress who did not have to be flattered and cajoled as did the human

---

[45] T. Hornberger, *Science and the New World* (San Marino, Calif., 1937), is an excellent brief résumé.

beings through whom he sought to accomplish his useful aims. His experiments that proved the identity of lightning and electricity established his international renown as a scientist. The invention of the Franklin stove (which sent the heat into the room instead of up the chimney), of the lightning rod, and of a clock having only three wheels and two pinions, all testify to the practical nature of his work and to the simplicity and economy of his devices. One of his most interesting studies demonstrated that northeast storms on the Atlantic move against the wind. In keeping with his honesty, clarity of thought, and desire to serve his fellow men he dispelled obscurity and mystery from the subjects of which he wrote.[46]

When the colonial period ended the practice of medicine had made but slight progress. The first colonists commonly regarded disease as the work of supernatural agencies. Plagues and severe distempers were caused by evil spirits; common ailments and disturbances were God's means of punishing or purifying the soul. Many people therefore resorted to the ministrations of the clergy as an antidote to illness and pain. Home remedies, the chief reliance of the household, were efficacious largely because, by lessening the patient's fears, they aided natural processes of recuperation. John Winthrop, Jr., advised this cure for ague: "Pare the patient's nails when the fever is coming on; and put the parings into a little bag of fine linen . . . ; and tie that about a live eel's neck, in a tub of water. The eel will die and the patient will recover." Particularly defective were the care given women at childbirth and the treatment of children's diseases; hence the high death rate among young women and infants. Once a person had survived childhood illnesses and had reached the age of twenty he had become so hardened that he could look forward to a ripe old age.[47]

Many doctors came to the colonies in the seventeenth century, some trained in medical centers of Europe and Britain. The physicians of the second generation were educated in the colonies as apprentices or students of individual practitioners—a training inferior to that of Europe—with the result that medical competence declined noticeably after 1670. The failure of the colonies to impose standards and supervision upon the profession opened the door to a variety of quacks, who flourished by virtue of the dread of pain which makes the ignorant so susceptible to easy cures. Even the most competent physicians had

---

[46] See the sketches of early scientists in the *Dictionary of American Biography*, particularly Carl Becker's essay on Franklin.

[47] E. Eggleston, "Some Curious Colonial Remedies," *American Historical Review*, V (Jan. 1900).

little to offer: bleeding was the sovereign remedy, even though the patient might actually need a blood transfusion. Many doctors believed in witchcraft, explaining their failures by the intervention of evil spirits. After 1700 medical students from the colonies sought education in Paris, London, and Edinburgh, thereby raising the level of technical competence, and in the 1760's two medical schools were founded in Philadelphia and New York. Although the colonists showed a common-sense appreciation of the effects of unhealthful sites and of contact with diseased persons, they had no knowledge of bacteria, antiseptics, or most antitoxins. Internal surgery had to wait upon anesthetics, not discovered until after colonial times. The state of colonial medicine is illustrated by the views of Dr. Benjamin Rush (1745–1813), professor at the Philadelphia Medical College, and probably the foremost physician of his day. Believing that all diseases arose from the excessive excitability of the blood vessels, he advocated bleeding as the universal cure. Although he freed himself from denominationalism, his early religious background often cropped out in his use of theological arguments to support his medical theories.[48] Since the Bible affirmed that man was made in the image of God, many pious people believed that to experiment on the human body or to modify natural processes was darkly iniquitous.

THE COMMUNICATION OF IDEAS

In the seventeenth century the ground was being prepared for the growth of an American culture through the adaptation of the English cultural heritage to the frontier environment. However, most colonists then lived in comparative isolation, and it was not until after 1700 that new facilities of communication sprang up to foster and give expression to a slowly emerging culture.[49] In the process of Americanization the colonial towns played the decisive role of radiating centers of trade and thought. The merchants of each town strove to improve their land and sea transportation facilities in order to dominate as wide a market as possible. This urge led to the building and improving of roads, over which flowed an increasing stream of traffic.

Prior to 1700 most travelers journeyed by sea. Roads were little

[48] Nathan G. Goodman, *Benjamin Rush* . . . (Philadelphia, 1934) gives in full the story of a varied public career. James T. Flexner, *Doctors on Horseback* (New York, 1937), though dealing mostly with the postcolonial period, describes earlier conditions.

[49] An admirable introduction to this theme is Michael Kraus, *Intercolonial Aspects of Culture on the Eve of the Revolution* (New York, 1928).

more than paths marked on trees through the forest, compelling the overland traveler to go by horseback or on foot. In 1704 Madam Knight took five days to reach New Haven from Boston, travel at night being exceedingly difficult. However, by 1770 roads had assumed a more modern aspect. A main highway, in fairly good condition—particularly in summer—ran from Boston via Providence, New York, Philadelphia, and Jamestown to Charleston, while first-class roads extended thirty or forty miles inland from the principal port towns. At mid-century the first traveler's guidebook had been published (1732); milestones marked the main roads; and rivers were being crossed by ferries, toll bridges, and an occasional free or public bridge. In 1754 a certain James Wells opened a regular semi-weekly stage and boat line between New York and Philadelphia (extended to Annapolis in 1757); a second line between New York and Philadelphia began to operate in 1760; a third advertised a four-day journey from New York to Boston in 1775. Over the improved dirt roads freight wagons passed to and fro; wealthy folk were jostled onward in their private carriages; the common people rode horseback; the poorest straggled along on foot.[50]

Along the highways life came to a rude but lusty focus at the welcome inns. There the weary traveler found shelter for himself and his horse; there his travel-sharpened appetite made endurable the coarse food and strong drink; there on cold days he warmed himself before the open fire. There, too, he might find fellow travelers with news of distant parts or native inhabitants to regale him with the lore of the district. High and low mingled together with a democratic, inquisitive familiarity. The guests often slept four in a room, men and women together, chance companions of the road. In the South the scarcity of inns obliged the traveler to seek the freely given hospitality of private homes. Coffeehouses, fashioned on the London model, appeared about 1700 in the larger port towns, to become centers of news, business dealings, and good fellowship. At the ordinary tavern one might meet many an eccentric fellow, drawn thither by the lure of the bottle, by lively arguments over politics and religion, and by the opportunities for gambling afforded by the bowling alley and the billiard table.[51]

One figure who paused at the country inn—the post rider—played an important if humble part in binding the colonies together. In the

[50] *A History of Travel in America,* by Seymour Dunbar (4 vols., Indianapolis, c. 1915), is a useful, interesting, well-illustrated compilation. See Vol. I, chapters 1–9.
[51] Alice M. Earle, *Stage Coach and Tavern Days* (New York, 1900); Edward Field, *The Colonial Tavern* (Providence, 1897); Elsie Lathrop, *Early American Inns and Taverns* (New York, 1926).

early days letters were carried by travelers or entrusted to sea captains; official papers were sent by special messengers or borne from town to town by local officials. Legally, the regulation of mails was a function of the colonial governments, which gradually established colony-wide postal services—Massachusetts in 1677, Pennsylvania in 1683. The assemblies fixed the postal rates and designated the places (taverns as a rule) where letters should be posted and delivered. In 1691, when the English government desired a greater wartime efficiency of communication with the colonies, William III granted to Thomas Neale a twenty-year monopoly of the postal business in Massachusetts, Pennsylvania, and New York. Neale chose Andrew Hamilton as his deputy—an efficient lawyer who organized a regular service between Portsmouth, New Hampshire, and Philadelphia, even though postal rates were still fixed by the individual colonies. Neale, finding his monopoly unprofitable, surrendered it in 1707, whereupon Parliament in 1710 ordered that the postal service be placed under the English post office. Not until 1732 did Virginia come into the general American system.[52]

The imperial postal administration was notable for Franklin's term as deputy-postmaster (1753–75), when he instigated three important reforms. He strove to increase the speed, aiming to cut the Boston to Philadelphia run from three weeks to six days, introducing shorter routes, road markings, and day and night riding. He advocated lower postal rates, and when he secured reductions in 1765 the volume of business and postal revenues increased as he had anticipated. He also urged that regular charges be assessed ·against newspapers in the mails. Previously, publishers had paid the riders a bonus; and moreover, since publishers were often postmasters they were able to exclude the papers of their rivals from the mails. Franklin's objections to such irregularities bore fruit in 1758 when the British government ordered that all newspapers be admitted to the mails at prescribed rates. At the onset of the Revolution the patriots immediately seized control of the postal service, so essential had it become to American unity.[53]

The principal agency for the expression of an American point of view was the provincial press. As early as 1638 a printing press was brought to Cambridge, Massachusetts, there to be operated in connection with Harvard College, feeding New England with Puritan

[52] William Smith, *The History of the Post Office in British North America, 1639–1870* (Cambridge, 1920), devotes chapters 1–4 to the thirteen colonies. See also W. Smith, "The Colonial Post Office," *American Historical Review*, XXI (Jan. 1916).

[53] Wesley E. Rich, *The History of the United States Post Office to the Year 1829* (Cambridge, 1924), contains three precise, complete chapters on the colonial service.

tracts, catechisms, sermons, statutes, broadsides, poems, and copies of English books. By 1715 eight presses existed in the colonies: six in New England, one in New York, and one in Philadelphia. Boston's priority as a publishing center explains the appearance there in 1704 of the first American newspaper, *The Boston News-Letter*. Between 1713 and 1745 twenty-two new papers were launched, seven in New England, ten in Pennsylvania (including three published in German), and five in the South. Excepting Delaware and New Jersey, every colony had at least one newspaper by 1765.

The Boston News-Letter, a weekly, appeared as a "tiny four-page, two-column folder," offering a meager fare of local items (such as shipping notices) and of European news. In 1719 Andrew Bradford printed at Philadelphia *The American Weekly Mercury*—soon to be followed at Boston by James Franklin's *New England Courant* (1721), now noted for its publication of the youthful Benjamin Franklin's attacks on Puritan orthodoxy shortly before he migrated to Philadelphia, where in 1729 he bought *The Pennsylvania Gazette*. At this time editors were hearing the call of culture; poems, essays, and reprints of English articles now kept company in the papers with news items, local and foreign. Advertisements, informative if often flowery, revealed that advertisers had not yet learned how to capitalize fear, sex, and snobbishness. After 1750 the press devoted more and more space to politics and to sensational happenings such as crimes and accidents; letters from eminent men, signed with classical *noms de plume*, presented their thoughts on the issues of the day; in 1754 appeared the first American cartoon—Franklin's picture of a snake (symbol of the colonies) divided into eight parts, with the caption, "Unite or Die." In the South, papers like *The Virginia Gazette* and *The South Carolina Gazette* (in the latter Franklin had an interest) equaled the northern papers in range and quality.[54]

Although these early papers had each but a small subscription list, they were handed about from reader to reader until worn out, and moreover they were exchanged freely among the various editors, so that an outstanding article was likely to be reprinted throughout the colonies. Native writers now found a vent for their thoughts—a condition indispensable to the growth of American culture. Without the provincial press one can scarcely envisage the unified action of the

[54] Brief surveys of the colonial press appear in Willard G. Bleyer, *Main Currents in the History of American Journalism* (Boston, c. 1927), chapters 1–3; James M. Lee, *History of American Journalism* (Boston, 1917), chapters 1–6; and George H. Payne, *History of Journalism in the United States* (New York, 1920), chapters 1–8.

Revolutionary era—that upsurge of American sentiment which bore out the early fears of Governor Berkeley that learning fostered "disobedience and heresy" and that printing divulged "libels against the government."

Before the colonial press could play its part in the Revolution it had to be freed from the shackles of British control. Where there were vested interests menaced by new ideas, the privileged classes strove to silence the dissenting voice. Thus, in the early eighteenth century, royal governors and clergymen of influence (especially in Massachusetts) kept a tight rein on journalistic utterance, by direct or indirect means.[55] In 1733 Peter Zenger, a German printer at New York, published in *The New York Weekly Journal* a series of articles written by Lewis Morris (formerly chief justice of the province) which attacked the royal governor, William Cosby. When Zenger was arrested on the charge of false and scandalous libel, the Morris faction employed as his counsel the eighty-year-old Nestor of the American bar, Andrew Hamilton of Philadelphia. In a masterly plea Hamilton proved that the statements printed by Zenger were true and persuaded the jury to find him innocent. Previously juries had decided only whether the accused had published the statements complained of, whereupon the judges decided whether they were libelous or not. Hamilton's success in inducing the jury to decide that the articles were not libelous went far to deprive the judges (Cosby's friends, in this case) of that all-important power and thus set an important precedent for the freedom of the press. Channing states that by reason of the Zenger victory the American newspapers "kept alive and directed the forces of liberty and finally brought about the inevitable separation from the mother country sooner than it would otherwise have occurred."

Newspapers reached readers of all classes; the almanac was addressed primarily to the farmer. *Poor Richard's* was but the leader of a numerous company. After 1750 the almanac became a small magazine which kept the enterprising farmer informed about scientific discoveries (particularly in agriculture and astronomy), told him the year's tale of the moon, stars, and seasons, instructed him through maps, bits of worldly wisdom, and notices of important events, entertained him with jokes and stories, and enriched his culture with portraits, poems, and essays. Circulating by the thousands, read and reread from cover to cover, the almanacs expressed the practical,

[55] Clyde A. Duniway, *The Development of Freedom of the Press in Massachusetts* (New York, 1906), is a pioneer study in censorship.

homespun quality of life on the farm and the rural zest for self-improvement.[56]

In the path of the newspaper and the almanac followed the literary magazine. In 1741 Franklin launched *The General Magazine,* the first or second to be published, significant because it was addressed to "all the British plantations in North America" and because it reprinted American articles and reviewed American publications (the birth of book reviewing in the colonies). In his prospectus Franklin promised to print important political documents, news briefs, "select pieces of poetry," and "essays, controversial, humorous, philosophical, religious, moral or political." With the object of printing things of enduring value, in order—as Washington later put it—"to preserve the liberty, stimulate the industry and meliorate the morals of an enlightened and free people," the numerous magazines which appeared after 1741 (usually published by a printer-editor and priced at about a shilling a copy) were addressed to the elite and supported by only five hundred to fifteen hundred subscribers. This fact explains why most such magazines expired after a year or two, although *The Massachusetts Magazine* and *The New York Magazine* each lasted eight years. Discussions of economic issues (especially the currency) and of education, religion, temperance, prison reform, and slavery animated many an essay written in the strain of the Addison-Steele *Spectator Papers,* while uncertain native bards contributed verses in the manner of Milton, Pope, or Dryden.[57]

The scarcity of books in colonial times gave unusual importance to libraries, private, semi-public, and public. In the South the Society for Propagating the Gospel did useful work in providing parochial libraries, Thomas Bray managing to establish one in nearly every parish in Maryland after he became commissary in 1696. South Carolina founded a general library in 1700, requiring by law that it be open to the public. In 1731 Franklin induced some of his tradesman and artisan friends to pool their slender resources and to buy books for their common use—a practice soon copied by other communities. The largest private collections, like those of Cotton Mather and William Byrd II, contained as many as four thousand volumes. Each college steadily added to its store of treasures; well-to-do students built up personal libraries; and privately owned books circulated almost as freely as the gossip of the neighborhood. To such institutions as the

---

[56] G. L. Kittredge, *The Old Farmer and His Almanac* (Boston, 1904), is interesting reading.

[57] The best general introduction is F. L. Mott, *A History of American Magazines, 1741–1850* (New York, 1930); the most detailed analysis is Lyon N. Richardson, *A History of Early American Magazines, 1741–1789* (New York, 1931).

Newport, New York, and Charleston libraries (all active after 1754) Franklin attributed in part that "enlightened sentiment" so essential to the defense of American liberties.

Indicative of the forces of unity was the genesis of the first important intercolonial society of learned men. As early as 1727 Franklin had taken part in organizing the Junto Club at Philadelphia—a society of young artisans who composed, read, and discussed papers on philosophical and practical themes—and so successfully that Franklin called the club "the best school of philosophy, morality and politics that then existed in the province." With the model of European learned societies before him, Franklin and other "virtuosi or ingenious men residing in the several colonies" organized in 1744 an American academy, which in 1769 was reorganized as the American Philosophical Society. Although destined for a later career of distinction, the Society was significant before 1775, not because of its scientific accomplishments, but as a symbol of the increasing integration of American life.

Meanwhile the common people were slowly fashioning an American language. "Colleges and books," says Emerson, "only copy the language which the field and work-yard make." First of all the Indians enlarged the common speech. One might visit the *wigwam*, there to see the *medicine man*, the *sachem*, the *squaw*, and the *papoose*, to smoke the *pipe of peace*, with the *tomahawk* lying idle, to trade *wampum* and *firewater* for the skins of *raccoon*, *moose*, and *opossum*, and to eat *squash*, *hominy*, *hickory* nuts, *pawpaws*, and *succotash*. The *paleface* might attend a *powwow* just before the *big chief*, covered with *war paint*, took to the *warpath*. Or perhaps in *Indian summer* one might receive *moccasins* from an *Indian giver*. In the settlements of the Dutch the *Yankee* visitor might take a *sleigh* ride to the home of a *boss* or *patroon*, where one dared not *snoop*, and where one might eat *cookies* or *waffles* and hear tales of *spooks* or *Santa Claus*. The French *voyageurs* crossed *portages* and *prairies*, encountering *gophers* and *braves* that were not *bogus*, hiding their treasures in a *cache*, far away from a *bureau*.[58]

From the English vocabulary the colonists coined many Americanisms, either by forming new terms from familiar words or by giving an old word a new meaning. One might set out from a *back-street* or a *back-lane* in a town, round a *bluff* or *cliff*, traverse *barrens*, *bottoms*, and a *hollow*, ascend the *foothills*, pass through a *water gap*, cross a *watershed* and reach a *clearing* in the *back country*, surrounded by *underbrush* where a *log house* near a *salt lick* domiciled a *squatter* adept

[58] An important work of scholarship and literary charm is H. L. Mencken, *The American Language* (4th ed., New York, 1936). See chapters 1–3.

at *logrolling,* who had a *corncrib* and a *hog wallow* frequented by *razor-backs.* Inside the cabin one might be served *hoecake, sweet potatoes, eggplant, roasting ears, mush, apple butter, clingstone* peaches, *johnny-cake,* and *popcorn.* Outside one encountered the *garter snake,* the *bull-frog,* the *ground hog,* the *copperhead, bluegrass,* the *lightning bug,* the *June bug,* the *muskrat.* In summer the *back settler* feared the *prickly heat;* in winter he made a *beeline* from *bobsled* or *snowplow* to a fire of *pine knots* and *backlog.* The established settler might have a *frame house* covered with *shingles,* employ a *hired girl, advocate* or *oppose* a cause, *dicker* or *negotiate* with a *mossback, deed* his land at a *land office* or *camp meeting,* watch his wife make a *crazy quilt,* or see his son *shin up* a *pitch pine.* If a *hired man* should *fly off the handle* or *go on the warpath* and be unable *to whitewash* himself or *to face the music,* he might be told *not to darken one's door again* and be compelled *to take to the woods.*[59]

The Refinement of Taste

In his *Conduct of Life* Emerson observes that genius creates manners and artistic forms, that the upper class adopts and utilizes them, and that the common people follow the example of the upper class. He also remarks that men of genius arise largely from the middle class. In the colonial period, when the American middle class produced few artistic geniuses, the American upper class looked to European genius and to English upper-class standards for guidance in the art of living. Consequently, with respect to manners and elegant pursuits, early American culture was derivative, imitative, provincial.[60]

Inasmuch as imaginative power and technical perfection are the secrets of great achievements in the arts, the lack of such genius in the colonies explains their cultural shortcomings. The activities of the educated colonists, centering in business, public affairs, and religion, assumed a practical or a theological cast. When the first cares of life are over, wrote Franklin, we shall begin to think of the embellishments. The colonies produced no masters of the most creative arts—no outstanding poets, dramatists, sculptors, or composers. In literature, practical concerns largely absorbed the energies of the most original minds: witness the excellent discussions of the public issues of the day. Historical writing (not the most original art form) appealed to many learned gentlemen and divines who became competent practitioners. The colonies had no native theater or virtuosi of the concert stage;

[59] Richard H. Thornton, *An American Glossary* (2 vols., Philadelphia, 1912), is the great pioneer collection of Americanisms.
[60] See again J. T. Adams, *Provincial Society,* chapters 3, 5, 6, 10–11.

their painters for the most part were copyists rather than creators; their architecture (excepting that of the farmhouse, designed for the new environment) followed English models; their higher craftsmen —furniture makers, glaziers, etc.,—drew inspiration from Europe; their fashions in dress and refined conduct came from over sea.

Colonial painters produced three principal types of pictures—portraits, landscapes, and historical scenes. The religious impulse in art was weak, due partly to the Calvinistic belief that things divine should be apprehended by the mind, not pictured to the senses. Since most patrons of art were upper-class families, the chief demand was for portraits that would preserve family traditions, celebrate the virtues of the subject portrayed, and clothe the aristocratic figure in graceful forms.[61]

All the leading colonial painters arose from the middle class—sons of artisans, preachers, shopkeepers. The first artists of note came to America from Europe: such were Gustavus Hesselius (1682–1755), who emigrated from Sweden to Delaware in 1711, and John Smibert of Edinburgh (1688–1751), who settled at Boston in 1730. Soon, however, American-born artists appeared, young artisans often self-taught, able to eke out a bare living with paintbrush if they traveled in search of patrons. In 1760 Benjamin West of Pennsylvania (1728–1820) arrived in Italy to initiate foreign study by aspiring American artists—an example followed by Charles W. Peale of Maryland (1741–1827) at London and by Gilbert Stuart of Rhode Island (1755–1828), also at London. Three Americans—Stuart, West, and John Singleton Copley of Boston (1738–1815)—remained long in London, where cultural atmosphere and artists' fees were more appealing than in America. West eventually became court painter to George III, executing many historical scenes in a stilted, classical style now out of date. Copley and Stuart achieved high distinction as portrait painters; the work of other colonial artists, though precise, faithful, and pleasing, was generally formal, conventional, and uninspired.[62]

The origins of the American theater appear in amateur performances given privately in the southern colonies. The first records of professional companies relate to Charleston (1703) and New York (1704). Early plays were presented in taverns, warehouses, and court-

---

[61] Samuel Isham, *The History of American Painting* (New York, 1936), is the standard authority. See chapters 1–2.

[62] Frank J. Mather *et al*, *The Spirit of American Art* (*Pageant of America*, XII, New Haven, 1927), chapter 1. See also William Dunlap's *The History of the Arts of Design in the United States* (1834), an important pioneer work, which has been corrected in a new edition by F. W. Bayley and C. E. Goodspeed (3 vols., Boston, 1918). See Vol. I.

rooms, but in the 1730's makeshift theaters were being erected, rude, unadorned, barnlike. In 1750 Mr. and Mrs. Lewis Hallam of London arrived in America with a competent English company—to remain for twenty years, playing not only at New York, Philadelphia, Annapolis, and Williamsburg, but also at such places as Hobb's Hole and Port Tobacco. Their career was notable for a season at New York (1753–54), when they gave twenty-one performances of standard English plays. In 1766 the first permanent theater, the Southwark, was built in Philadelphia; in 1767 the first play written by an American, Thomas Godfrey's *The Prince of Parthia*, was offered to the Philadelphia public. The early dramas were either ephemeral pieces which sounded loudly the note of love, or the classical English plays of Congreve, Steele, Addison, and Shakespeare (including *The Tempest, King Lear, Hamlet*, and *Romeo and Juliet*). After 1750 the colonial aristocrats frequented the theater quite regularly, its class character being indicated by a resolve of the Continental Congress in 1774 "to discourage . . . shows, plays and other expensive diversions." Although the Puritan conception of the theater as a "house of Satan" kept it out of colonial New England, the Quaker opposition to plays had subsided sufficiently to permit the Hallams to perform in Philadelphia in 1754.[63]

Concerts and noteworthy musicians were non-existent before 1715. Apparently the first recitals and concerts given in Boston, New York, and Charleston came in the 1730's: by 1750 they had become a regular feature of life in the larger towns. Thereafter interest was sustained by select organizations such as the Orpheus Club of Philadelphia (founded in 1759) and the celebrated St. Cecilia Society of Charleston, organized in 1762. Francis Hopkinson's "My Days Have Been So Wondrous Free," written in 1759, was probably the first musical composition of a native American. Since the colonists had not attained individual excellence in music, the soloist was overshadowed by group performances, choral or orchestral. The principal instruments then employed were the violin, viola, bass viol, 'cello, flute, French horn, harpsichord, spinet, organ, guitar, and pianoforte. Such group performances must have been of very uneven quality, although the trend was probably toward greater precision.[64]

[63] Three excellent histories of the early stage are: Arthur H. Quinn, *A History of the American Drama . . . to the Civil War* (New York, 1923), chapter 1; George C. D. Odell, *Annals of the New York Stage* (8 vols., New York, 1927–36), Vol. I, Book I; and Arthur Hornblow, *A History of the Theatre in America* (2 vols., Philadelphia, 1919), Vol. I, chapters 1–6.

[64] John T. Howard, *Our American Music* (New York, 1931), is the most valuable

Puritanism limited musical expression in seventeenth-century New England to psalm singing, unaccompanied by organ or other instruments. The effect of many untrained voices seems to have been pretty bad, even though the various psalms were sung to about only a half-dozen tunes. To one sensitive hearer it seemed that the congregation was singing five hundred different tunes at once; another remarked, "We used frequently to have some people sing a note or two, after the rest had done." Many efforts after 1700 to achieve vocal harmony gave psalmody a more sedate character. In the 1740's the hymns of Isaac Watts became immensely popular with people responsive to the Great Awakening, although the psalms—now accompanied by bass viol or flute—remained triumphant in the more formal churches. Outside of religious circles, ballads and other secular music had won good repute by 1750; then the Revolution gave birth to a host of marching songs (e. g., "Yankee Doodle") and new ballads celebrating the deeds of military heroes.[65] At Bethlehem, Pennsylvania, founded in 1741, the Moravians established a musical center which soon became famous for its performances of German religious music, particularly the works of Johann Sebastian Bach.

Although the mode of living of the poorer farmers (as described in chapter XII) did not change materially during the eighteenth century, that of the upper class was almost completely transformed. In architecture the most striking feature was the construction of the new mansions of the aristocracy. After 1720 English books on architecture, and after 1740 English plans of houses, were followed, often literally, by colonial builders. That many colonists used wood when brick and stone were in vogue in England did not alter the style of construction. Despite numerous variations in the designs of the houses, three principal types were evident. The rich merchants of New England and of the middle colonies built town dwellings and country or summer houses (the latter often fifteen miles or so from their places of business)—houses commonly rectangular, three stories high, with dormer windows lighting the third-floor rooms, with chimneys at each end, and with either a pitched roof or a roof slanting on all sides from a railed platform on top. In the plantation area a common type of house exhibited a square central section (the family's living quarters); on each side, separate or joined to the main dwelling, were wings contain-

work on the early history of music. O. G. Sonneck, *Early Concert-Life in America, 1731–1800* (Leipzig, 1907), is a careful and detailed, if not very readable, account.

[65] J. H. Kouwenhoven, "Singing in New England," *New England Quarterly*, VI (Sept. 1933).

ing kitchen, pantry, office, and carriage house. At Charleston, South Carolina, many planters had town houses, built adjacent to one another, with principal rooms above the ground floor, a balcony at the front or street, and at the rear a veranda overlooking a private garden.[66]

Most of the later colonial mansions adhered to the Georgian style of architecture that reigned in England after 1720. Designed to be as durable as possible, the mansion expressed the desire of the owner to give permanence to his superior social status and to perpetuate it in his descendants, thus indicating a society of fixed class lines. Naturally the mansion also satisfied the esthetic sense and the demands of health (high sites) and of comfort (summer retreats). Moreover, an expensive dwelling proclaimed the owner's wealth to the world; its size (guest chambers and servants' rooms) and its decorative (non-utilitarian) features signified his mastery of the services of other people. Externally, the lines and proportions gave an impression of solidity and stateliness; inside, high ceilings, spacious rooms, and numerous windows denoted that the owner did not live a cramped existence. The interior effect was one of elegance rather than of easy comfort—an effect attained by means of graceful stairways, polished floors, delicately carved doors, doorways, and mantelpieces, by colored tapestries or figured paper hung on the walls, and by paneling and woodwork painted in light colors or treated so as to bring out the texture of fine woods. Outside one would find flower beds, shrubs, groves, lawns, walks or drives lined with trees, fish ponds, and perhaps a bowling green or a "Roman" temple.[67]

Had one been able to step from a room in the house of a well-to-do colonist in 1670 into a room of a mansion of 1770, the difference would have been startling. In place of the straight, somber, heavy pieces of the early period, one would have found light, polished, and gracefully curved furniture. To a large extent the use of mahogany after 1725 explains the change, for here was a strong, lustrous wood capable of producing objects both sturdy and graceful. Other woods commonly used included oak, pine, maple, and cypress. By 1775 colonial cabinet-makers had attained a high degree of skill, although they copied English models, particularly the work of Chippendale, whose influence prevailed between 1760 and 1775.

[66] The most outstanding work is Fiske Kimball, *Domestic Architecture of the American Colonies and of the Early Republic* (New York, 1927).

[67] Thomas E. Tallmadge, *The Story of Architecture in America* (New York, c. 1927), gives a brief résumé of the colonial period in chapter 2. Harold D. Eberlein,

In the colonial mansion of 1770 one would have observed elegant furnishings in the parlor or drawing room. The easy wing chair, the Windsor chair, introduced from England and popular after 1725, numerous straight-back chairs with rush, leather, or upholstered seats, tall, graceful candle stands, the circular tea table, a settee or sofa that did not invite lounging—all these bespoke a rather stiff refinement. As a rule there were small rugs on the floor, "Turkey carpets" used as table covers, portraits, engravings, and prints on the walls, a mirror over the fireplace, and embroidered or painted fire screens that were fastened to slender posts and might be raised or lowered. A common type of desk, reaching nearly to the ceiling, consisted of a bookcase, the desk proper (with a slanting lid that opened outward to rest on pulls), and a chest of drawers. Only a few hall or "grandfather" clocks were made before 1800 but a mantel clock or a wall clock served as well. Near the colored tiles of the fireplace stood the coal tongs and the warming pan, which, with the andirons, might be of polished brass.[68]

The dining room contained a mahogany table with straight-back chairs to match—accommodations sufficient, perhaps, for twenty guests. A built-in corner cupboard displayed the family chinaware (of oriental designs, in subdued colors) and held the silverware and linen. Forks were then a mark of gentility; ivory-handled knives were fashionable; and silverware served many a purpose, as described earlier by William Fitzhugh: it "gives myself the present use and credit, is a sure friend at a dead lift or is a portion for a child at my decease." Silver serving dishes and candlesticks, glass bowls and goblets, and linen tablecloths and napkins gave a tone of authentic elegance—an effect enhanced by graceful side tables of the "piecrust," "dish-top," or "drop-leaf" design.

At night one retired to a well-appointed chamber where stood the high, massive, carved four-poster, covered perhaps with a hand-woven bedspread of intricate pattern, and enclosed by a canopy and curtains of damask, chintz, or silk. Gauze protected the sleeper from the ravenous mosquito. Other furnishings included linen sheets, hair or feather mattresses, feather pillows, and woolen blankets. In early times personal articles were stored in boxes, later in chests, and finally in highboys. The highboy, distinctively American, was a chest of drawers graced usually with delicately carved shell ornaments and brass handles, and raised two or three feet above the floor by a frame of four or

---

The Architecture of Colonial America (Boston, 1927), is a popular, well-illustrated outline.

[68] L. V. Lockwood, *Colonial Furniture* (2 vols., New York, 1913), is the foremost treatment.

six legs. For a dressing table one used a lowboy—a single drawer, resting on a frame and furnished with a mirror and a dressing box. Objects of art such as one found in the rooms below might also decorate the bedrooms.[69]

Polite society required elegant attire. The ladies and gentlemen of town and tidewater evinced a deep interest in fashion, adopting the upper-class modes of London almost as soon as they appeared there. Many a London tailor or dressmaker was kept busy filling orders placed by the colonial elite through their English correspondents. "Whatever goods you may send me," wrote Washington to his London agent, "let them be fashionable." Colonial dress reached its peak of elegance, richness, and profusion in the years 1740–75, when delicate decoration, flowered and checked patterns, and varied colors (scarlet, blue, maroon, rose, gold, silver, and claret) held sway.

For the most select occasions the gentlemen of that day wore a suit of velvet or satin (breeches and a long decorated coat reaching to the knee), a satin or velvet waistcoat of a different color, silk stockings, and low shoes of black kid. Lace ruffles at the neck and sleeves, coat buttons covered with cloth to match the suit, silver shoe buckles set with sparkling stones: all such finery, together with powdered wig and ornamented sword, denoted in the wearer, not effeminacy, but mastery, showing that he did not engage in physical toil and was thus able to satisfy his common wants through the labor of others.[70]

The colonial lady's apparel in 1760 included petticoats, richly embroidered and brocaded gowns of silk or satin billowing from a tight waist, silk stockings, shoes covered with silk or satin, hoods of velvet or silk, lace caps with ribbons, kid or silk gloves, and jeweled ornaments for the hair, neck, ears, and hands—costumes that reflected dignity, poise, and self-restraint, even though now they might appear none too comfortable. It was fashionable for the upper-class lady to keep her skin "delicately white, smooth and soft," for then everyone would know that all her time was given to refined pursuits. The children of the upper class were dressed in clothes patterned after those of the adults—a means of training the young aristocrat in those rigid manners and disciplines deemed necessary by people of wealth and leisure in order both to avoid individual deterioration and to overawe social inferiors. For out-of-doors wear, for traveling, and for indoor occupations the ladies and gentlemen had outfits less costly than those

[69] Marion Harland (Mary V. H. Terhune), *Some Colonial Homesteads* (New York, 1897), describes many well known upper-class dwellings.

[70] Elisabeth McClellan, *Historic Dress in America, 1607–1800* (Philadelphia, 1904), is the best study of early costume.

for social functions, yet even so such common apparel also served the purpose of establishing one's social superiority by a conspicuous display of wealth.

Perhaps all the diversions of the upper class did not signify an increased refinement of taste, but at least they denoted the enjoyment of means and leisure. The colonial aristocrat was much given to entertaining: one might expect to find guests at his table at any of the four meals of the day. The formal dinner had a great vogue. At the close of a sumptuous repast the gentlemen remained in the dining room, there to imbibe many a glass of wine (Madeira was the aristocratic drink) and to converse at ease over their pipes of tobacco, neither cigars nor cigarettes having yet come into use. The ladies, having retired to the drawing room, entertained themselves until the gentlemen rejoined them for a game of whist or a round of dancing to the strains of a stringed orchestra engaged for the occasion. When gentlemen enjoyed only their own company they resorted freely to the card table or the billiard cue, playing commonly for sizable stakes. One observer at Wilmington noted that "an intolerable itch for gambling prevailed in all companies." The IOU and the cardsharper were not unknown, and more than one scion of the aristocracy dissipated his patrimony at the gambling table.[71]

For diversion out of doors the colonial gentlemen turned to fishing, hunting, fencing, horse racing, and an occasional game of cricket. In 1674 a tailor was fined in Virginia for participating in a horse race—a sport then deemed suitable only for gentlemen. Southern fox hunters imported foxes from England; the devotees of the race track imported blooded stallions and mares, making a business of breeding, trading, and racing thoroughbreds. In the summer young gentlemen of the North might go boating to some near-by cove, there to partake of a picnic dinner, and return at night in jovial spirits. So also it was proper to drive in one's carriage to some picturesque spot, refreshing oneself at a fashionable tea house along the way. The evening promenade graced the social life of the larger towns. At New York sleighing became very popular in the winter. Late in the day a party of twenty or thirty would set out, four to a sleigh, drive to an inn, and enjoy a festive supper.

From such pastimes sprang many select societies. Jockey clubs became prominent in the southern and middle colonies—clubs of sportsmen who arranged rather elaborate programs, particularly on Long Island, in New Jersey and in the South, where three- or four-year-olds and fillies (pacers and runners, for trotters had not yet been intro-

[71] See again C. M. Andrews, *Colonial Folkways*, chapters 3–7, 9.

duced) ran on race tracks or on the greensward for money prizes or trophies. The dancing club or "assembly" sponsored parties at which the stately minuet was performed, as well as informal jigs, reels, marches, hornpipes, and country dances. There were also hunting clubs (e. g., the Gloucester Hunt of Philadelphia), fishing clubs, and miscellaneous societies, like the Friday Night Club at Newport, evidently a company of epicures. After 1750 many aristocrats from Carolina and Pennsylvania summered at Newport, where the climate suggested that of Italy. There a succession of diversions occupied the visitors, who sought to regain health or to escape the heat of regions farther south.[72]

The young ladies, excluded from most of the daytime pursuits of the gentlemen, devoted some of their leisure hours to study, learning to write gracious "epistles," to read "with elegance and propriety," and to speak with correct diction. Other polite pursuits included painting on glass, working with wax, drawing with pencil, and painting with water colors. Fancy needlework of a dozen intricate varieties produced decorative objects which signified that the aristocratic lady was exempt from ordinary tasks—the mark of superior affluence. One teacher advertised that French, "when taught agreeable to its native purity and elegance," was "acquired with becoming ease and gracefulness, as renders it truly ornamental." French dancing masters, Parisian milliners, and French hairdressers (adept at making "hair cushions for ladies") were generously patronized after 1760. At sixteen the young lady's polite education was sufficiently advanced to warrant her formal introduction to the "world of fashion."

[72] Carl Bridenbaugh, "Colonial Newport as a Summer Resort," *Rhode Island Historical Society Collections*, XXVI (Jan. 1931).

BIBLIOGRAPHICAL NOTE

SECONDARY WORKS: F. J. Klingberg, *Anglican Humanitarianism in Colonial New York* (Philadelphia, 1940), emphasizes missionary work among Negroes and Indians. H. P. Thompson, *Thomas Bray* (London, 1954), is a useful study of Anglican promotive work. Nelson R. Burr, *The Anglican Church in New Jersey* (Philadelphia, 1954), is both scholarly and readable. Two valuable studies are Guy S. Klett, *Presbyterians in Colonial Pennsylvania* (Philadelphia, 1937), and L. J. Trinterud, *The Formation of an American Tradition* (Philadelphia, 1949), a reappraisal of early Presbyterianism, emphasizing the Great Awakening. Celestine J. Nuesse, *The Social Thought of American Catholics* (Westminster, Md., 1945), reveals that Catholics, while holding to their faith, conformed to the practical world. Reba C. Strickland, *Religion and the State in Georgia* . . . (New York, 1939), is a detailed monograph.

E. S. Gaustad, *The Great Awakening in New England* (New York, 1957), is an important contribution to the history of evangelism. For a general survey of the Great Awakening, see C. C. Goen, *Revivalism and Separatism in New England*

(New Haven, 1962). Stuart C. Henry, *George Whitefield* (New York, 1957), presents an accurate, vivid portrait of the great revivalist. Ola E. Winslow, *Jonathan Edwards* (New York, 1941), is excellent.

M. L. Starkey, *The Devil in Massachusetts* (New York, 1949), a readable narrative, vitalizes the actors in the witchcraft delusion. Brooke Hindle, *The Pursuit of Science in Revolutionary America* (Chapel Hill, 1956), a careful study, surveys strivings and achievements in the natural sciences. Theodore Hornberger, *Scientific Thought in the American Colleges* (Austin, 1945), is a competent sketch. Edward Ford, *David Rittenhouse* (Philadelphia, 1946), is an admirable brief biography of a leading American scientist. R. H. Shryock, *Medicine and Society in America, 1660–1860* (New York, 1960), is a good introductory account; in *Cotton Mather* (Baltimore, 1954), O. T. Beall, Jr., and R. H. Shryock present Mather as "the first significant figure in American medicine."

Nelson R. Burr, *Education in New Jersey* (Princeton, 1942), gives special weight to religious influences.

G. P. Winship, *The Cambridge Press, 1638–1692* (Philadelphia, 1945), is a meticulous study of early printing. Sidney Kobre provides a useful introduction to the colonial press in *The Development of the Colonial Newspaper* (Pittsburgh, 1944). Anna J. De Armond, *Andrew Bradford, Colonial Journalist* (Newark, Del., 1949), discusses fully one Philadelphia newspaper. *The Trial of Peter Zenger* (ed. Vincent Buranelli, New York, 1957), introduces records of the trial with a pro-Zenger essay.

T. J. Wertenbaker, *The Golden Age of Colonial Culture* (New York, 1942), gives animated portrayals of life in six towns. Virgil Barker, *American Painting* (New York, 1950), ranks as one of the foremost discussions of its subject. J. T. Flexner, *American Old Masters* (New York, 1939), presents attractive sketches of four leading painters. Biographies of individual artists are: C. C. Sellers, *Charles Wilson Peale* (2 vols., Philadelphia, 1947); H. W. Foote, *John Smibert* (Cambridge, 1950); and Grose Evans, *Benjamin West . . .* (Carbondale, Ill., 1959). Carl Bridenbaugh, *Peter Harrison* (Chapel Hill, 1949), introduces the first American architect.

In the field of letters, Barrett Wendell, *A History of American Literature* (New York, 1900), explains colonial writings in terms of English tradition. Charles Angoff's incisive *A Literary History of the American People* (2 vols., New York, 1931), belittles the literature of the colonial era in a manner reminiscent of H. L. Mencken. V. F. Calverton, *The Liberation of American Literature* (New York, 1932), interprets literary expression in terms of economic influences. Two well-known surveys by able scholars are Bliss Perry, *The American Spirit in Literature* (New Haven, 1918), and S. T. Williams, *The American Spirit in Letters* (New Haven, 1926). For other works on American literature, see the note at the end of chapter I.

XIX

 The Struggle for
Land and Currency

The social upheavals of the seventeenth century had not resolved the underlying conflicts of interest which separated various groups within the colonies. After 1700 the growth of commerce and of plantation economy had greatly increased the wealth and power of the colonial aristocracy, while at the same time the extended immigration from abroad enlarged the class of farmers and workers who formed the backbone of the democratic party. The conflict between aristocratic and democratic forces therefore continued with unabated vigor, revolving around the issues of land, currency, and the control of the colonial governments.[1] In South Carolina, prior to 1720, the two parties faced a common enemy in the absentee proprietors who ruled those colonies in the narrow spirit of self-interest, thereby imposing restraints which retarded the advancement of all groups. The latter united in revolutionary action to overthrow the proprietary government in 1719, but once the common enemy had been defeated the latent antagonisms between the aristocratic and democratic parties transformed the struggle into an internal conflict.

The Overthrow of the Carolina Proprietors

Five different parties were concerned in the South Carolina revolution of 1719. Far removed from the province, the proprietary board after 1700 was composed in the main of indifferent and inferior men who cared little about the welfare of the inhabitants, regarding them merely as a source of income. To sell land at a high price and to exact quit-rents indefinitely; to take as much as possible from the province and to give as little in return: such was the ambition of the absentee proprietors; such were their policies which provoked the popular revolt.

With the progress of rice cultivation after 1695 the large planters acquired a predominating influence within the province. Plantation economy forced a rapid growth of the settled area until by 1720 it ex-

---

[1] W. E. Dodd, "The Emergence of the First Social Order in the United States," *American Historical Review*, XL (Jan. 1935).

tended a hundred and fifty miles along the coast. But as plantations moved southward they encroached upon the lands claimed by the Spaniards at St. Augustine and their Indian allies. In this situation the rice planters were at a grave disadvantage: their Negro slaves might turn against them when the Spaniards and the Indians attacked, while their servants and slaves who escaped found refuge and protection at St. Augustine. What the planters desired most was an aggressive policy of defense, including the establishment of frontier settlements of Protestant farmers who would shield the planters from the double menace of slave insurrection and Indian attack. When the proprietors failed to provide for such defenses, the planters were not merely antagonized; they felt it necessary to control the colonial government in order to act for themselves.

In this contest the planters were supported by the small farmers, who were equally eager for assistance from the proprietors and desirous also of obtaining lands which the proprietors granted with a niggardly hand. Yet when Indian war came, the farmers—receiving no aid from the proprietors—were obliged to finance the war themselves and at the same time to pay tribute in the form of quit-rents. Somewhat similar was the plight of the Charleston merchants who engaged in the western fur trade. Confronted now by the competition of the French in Louisiana, the English fur traders felt the need of a strong government to support them in the wilderness. However, the proprietors, indifferent as usual, refused to contribute funds for frontier troops and forts or for presents and diplomatic missions to the Indian tribes.[2]

The fifth party involved was the British government. It was imperative, first of all, that the southern frontier be adequately defended against the French and Spaniards. Not only would a conquest of South Carolina deprive Britain of the western fur traffic and the growing rice trade; it would also bring the French and Spaniards so close to Virginia as to imperil the more important tobacco trade. Moreover, the Acts of Trade and Navigation must be enforced, and piracy—which had taken a new lease of life in the Carolinas—must be suppressed. So inefficient had the proprietors proved in protecting England's commercial interests in the southern region that the Board of Trade had recommended repeatedly since 1700 that the Crown assume control of the government of the two colonies. In view of these interests it is understandable how the planters, small farmers, and fur traders of South Carolina combined with the British government to accomplish the overthrow of the proprietary regime.

[2] See again H. L. Osgood, *American Colonies in the Eighteenth Century*, Vol. II, pp. 347–384.

The power exercised by the proprietors before 1719 also explains the cause of the revolt. At Charleston there existed a party of officials appointed by the proprietors—the governor, the councillors, the secretary, the chief justice, the marshals, the receiver-general, and the surveyor-general—who held the reins of government and ruled in the proprietary interest. Of the councillors the inhabitants complained that they were wholly subservient to the proprietors "and think themselves obliged to carry everything they can in favor of the lords proprietors' intentions and advantage." The elected assembly of the province was a veritable shadow, restricted by the proprietors on three sides—by the negative vote of the council, by the veto of the governor, and by the veto of the proprietors in London. The inhabitants insisted that when the governor signed an act it should stand as if approved by the proprietors; an additional proprietary veto tended "to the great confusion of their administration, contrary to any power given them by the charter."

Even the elected house (or Commons House of Assembly) was not immune from the proprietary influence. Prior to 1716 the election of deputies had been held in Charleston, but with the establishment of remote plantations the assembly in 1716 enacted that elections be held in the respective precincts, "apportioning members according to the largeness of each parish." This act the proprietors rejected and substituted a new electoral scheme whereby the freemen were summoned to two bodies, there to vote "by subscribing their names to lists of representatives to the major part of whom the freemen are generally strangers," thus "giving room for faction, corruption, and tumultuous meetings, and to the great expence of time, travel and money to the freemen."

The judicial system of South Carolina seemed to the inhabitants equally autocratic. The proprietors had not established county courts for the administration of local justice; instead they made Charleston the sole judicial center, presided over by their chief justice—a virtual dictator who performed the functions of the county courts and of the courts of king's bench, exchequer, and common pleas and from whose decisions there was no appeal except to himself. He named attorneys, took fees at his discretion, forced the inhabitants from remote parts to attend courts at Charleston, and delayed suits "in order to multiply his perquisites"; he held himself beyond the control of the assembly, asserting that he was accountable only to the proprietors, and when the inhabitants appealed to them for relief their appeals were ignored.[3]

---

[3] Edward McCrady, *History of South Carolina under the Proprietary Government*, chapters 14–31.

And how had the proprietors used their extensive powers for the benefit of the colony? They had not erected a single mission, church, school, or college: the youth of the country "by imbibing irreligion for want of due education" were in danger of becoming "as barbarous as the native savages." The proprietors had not done anything in recent times to people the colony or "so much as contribute one penny toward the raising of forts and fortifications." Nor had they conferred titles of nobility upon colonists who merited them but instead had offered them for sale—"a procedure so mean" that decent men would not accept the honor.

An early conflict over religion taught the colonists that they had a better friend in the English government than in the proprietors. Freedom of worship having been extended by an act of 1696 to all Christians except Roman Catholics, the assembly, probably packed by the governor, Sir Nathaniel Johnson, a resolute Anglican, enacted in 1704 two laws which established the Anglican Church, taxed even the dissenters for its support, and required members of the elected house to take an oath to conform to the Anglican faith. The dissenters thus excluded sent an agent to England, where they enlisted the aid of the Bishop of London, of whose diocese South Carolina was a part—a later act of the colony having deprived him of some of his ecclesiastical power in the province. Believing that the Church Acts would retard the growth of the colony and its commerce with England, the Board of Trade espoused the cause of the dissenters, whereupon the proprietors yielded and agreed to the repeal of the offensive acts, although they had refused concessions until this official pressure was brought to bear. A new act now established the Anglican Church, provided for its support by all taxpayers, and allowed the laymen of each parish to select the minister, vestrymen, and churchwardens. The dissenters had won a major victory in the removal of the religious test for officeholding, and a precedent for resisting the proprietary power had been established.

While this controversy was in progress the colony was called upon to defend itself during Queen Anne's War; then in 1715 a destructive Indian War ravaged the frontier and penetrated to the heart of the colony. A southern tribe, the Yamassees, incited by the Spaniards at St. Augustine, launched a surprise attack upon the border settlements, massacred two hundred whites, and forced the other farmers to flee into Charleston. Under the leadership of Governor Craven, and with the aid of troops from North Carolina and Virginia, the South Carolinians drove the Yamassees back. Meanwhile appeals to the proprietors brought no aid except one hundred and fifty small arms; later the colonists complained that during the two and a half years of "that unhappy time" the proprietors "took no more notice of us than if they had abandoned the province," acting apparently on the assumption that "if the inhabitants were destroyed the country might be settled by a better people." Forced to shoulder the financial burden of the war without assistance from the proprietors the colony became so deeply involved in debt that its credit by 1719 was exhausted.[4]

Depredations of pirates were also attributed to proprietary neglect. In 1718 a notorious pirate, one Teach or Blackbeard, seized several ships trading to the province and took as prisoners several important South Carolinians; thence he proceeded to North Carolina and there committed further acts of piracy, "with the governor's connivance." And instead of punishing such crimes the proprietors "according to their wonted supineness and negligence took no notice of the same."

On the western frontier other distressing events occurred: in May 1715 the French prevailed upon the Alabama Indians to murder the South Carolina traders within their midst, and following this the French erected a fort, New Toulouse, at Mobile. Next they occupied the Spanish fort at Pensacola, thus surrounding South Carolina on the south and west, strengthening their influence among the Indians and giving force to the charge that they intended to seize the English colony. Again the South Carolinians besought the proprietors for protection; again without avail.

The struggle for land ultimately precipitated the revolt. After the Yamassees had been driven out of their country the assembly enacted that their lands should be settled by British Protestants and thereupon five hundred immigrants were encouraged to come to the province. The proprietors, however, reserved the whole Yamassee tract for themselves, and reversing the land policy of the local government, refused to confirm the titles of the newcomers or to refund their purchase money. The latter, "by sickness contracted by their often removings and spending all their substance they brought to begin their settlements," were reduced to such "want and poverty that they are daily . . . perishing and those that have anything left [are] removing off the province to the great weakening of the same."

Before 1718 the proprietors had allowed the governor and council to dispose of land, only to find that exorbitant grants were made—and in such an underhand manner that the records of titles and quit-rents soon fell into a state of utter confusion. Accordingly, in September 1718 the proprietors decreed that no additional lands be surveyed or granted "to any person whatsoever without our consent and approbation be

[4] See again V. W. Crane, *The Southern Frontier*, chapter 7.

first obtained." Once more the interests of the planters were to give way to those of the proprietors.

In 1719, when a Spanish invasion threatened and Governor Robert Johnson called out the militia, the colonists used the occasion to march upon Charleston and to seize control. A newly elected assembly transformed itself into a revolutionary convention, took charge of the province in the name of the king, and sent an agent, Colonel John Barnwell, to England. The cordial reception which he received gave color to the charge that the revolt had been instigated by British officials. The Crown now assumed the powers of governing South Carolina and dispatched Sir Francis Nicholson thither as the first royal governor. The rights of the proprietors to seven-eighths of the land were finally purchased for the Crown in 1728–29 at a price of £22,500. One proprietor, Lord Carteret (later Lord Granville), refused to sell and retained his claim to the soil. The dominating parties in the revolution were the large rice planters and the English merchants, both of whom regarded the proprietors as an obstacle to the progress of the colony.[5]

THE STRUGGLE FOR LAND

North Carolina, having failed to participate in the revolt of 1719, remained under the proprietary government until 1728, when it too joined the ranks of the royal colonies by reason of the surrender of the proprietary rights. The Crown in 1729 became the owner of ungranted lands; it now appointed the governor, councillors, and other executive and judicial officers of the northern province. Primarily interested in the growth of settlement as a means both of increasing the colony's trade with England and of extending the naval stores industry, British officials pursued a liberal policy in disposing of ungranted lands. To speculative promoters huge tracts were sold at less than a penny an acre on condition that the grantee establish one settler to each two hundred acres received; if lands were not thus settled within a given time they were to revert to the Crown. Likewise the British government liberally bestowed small tracts upon bona fide settlers and readily confirmed the claims of squatters after they had established farms. One object of this lenient policy was to extend the chain of English settlements westward and thus to hold the interior against the French. In order to obtain money for the governor's salary and for other costs of administration the Crown insisted that all lands which it granted pay

[5] See again Justin Winsor (ed.), *Narrative and Critical History of America*, Vol. V, pp. 316–327.

a yearly quit-rent—a measure which gave the governor a special interest in the collection of such revenues.

Second in influence to the Crown were certain large landowners who acquired immense holdings in North Carolina. In 1744 the Privy Council ordered that Lord Granville's proprietary estate should consist of a tract extending from sea to sea between the Virginia border and the line of 35° 34': within this area he was entitled to receive the quit-rents.[6] After the other proprietors had surrendered their land claims in 1728–29 the British government granted large tracts to certain London merchants, the foremost of whom was Henry McCulloch: he and his partners received nearly a million and a half acres during the early 1730's. Their plans included the utilization of the pine barren land for the production of naval stores and the selling or renting of the better farm lands to settlers whom they transported to the colony. Land speculation thus offered a field of investment for the surplus capital of the English merchants and at the same time promised an expansion of trade. In 1739 McCulloch was appointed supervisor of the royal revenues and land grants in North Carolina; later, in 1752, his influence was strong enough to secure the appointment of one Arthur Dobbs, an Irish gentleman, as governor. Also a large-scale land speculator, Dobbs, in the 1730's had secured three hundred thousand acres in the southern part of the province, where he had established seven hundred colonists.[7]

Another group of speculators had been active after 1729—wealthy residents of the colony who had obtained land by means of "blank patents" which were issued and signed by the governor in advance of surveys, thus conferring a general claim to unspecified areas. By this method the Moore and Moseley families and other rich speculators obtained title to a half million acres and by 1750 all the good farming lands except in the back country near the mountains had been patented.

From the neighboring colonies a large stream of small farmer pioneers poured into North Carolina during the eighteenth century and occupied the lands of the piedmont region. Too poor to buy land outright or to go to the seat of government on the coast in order to get titles from the governor and council, such settlers as squatters came into conflict with the claims of the large speculators. They expressed their aspirations in the elected house of the legislature, and since the large

[6] Beverley W. Bond's *The Quit-Rent System in the American Colonies* (New Haven, 1919), a book of fundamental importance, is technical and detailed; the general student should read an article: B. W. Bond, "The Quit-Rent System in the American Colonies," *American Historical Review*, XVII (April 1912).

[7] See again H. L. Osgood, *American Colonies in the Eighteenth Century*, Vol. IV, chapters 5, 9, 11.

landowners controlled the council the conflicts between Assembly and council generally revolved around the issue of land. Nor did the small farmers care to pay quit-rents to either Lord Granville or the king.[8]

During the term of Governor Gabriel Johnston (1734–52) the quit-rents were responsible for the most heated conflict within the colony. Johnston insisted that the rents be paid promptly at a few designated places, that arrears be collected, and that payments be made in full at the rate of 4s. sterling per hundred acres. The Assembly on the other hand demanded that the rents be collected at the individual farms, that arrears be overlooked, that payments be made in produce instead of money, and that when such produce was tendered it should be given a higher monetary value than its mere market price. Unable to get his bills passed the governor dissolved several assemblies and when the two parties agreed upon compromise measures they were disallowed in England. The upshot of the controversy was the complete disorganization of the quit-rent system. Collections virtually ceased, the receiver-general grew indolent and indifferent, the rent rolls were kept in a slipshod fashion, and the deficit became so great that the governor's salary was not paid for thirteen years after 1740. As the menace from France on the western frontiers was increasing at this time Britain did not harass the small farmers of the interior; they were even favored as against the large landowners of the seaboard area, and in consequence the conflict between the frontiersmen and the eastern speculators over land patents and other related issues outranked the contest with Britain over the quit-rents.

The land question also played a decisive role in the rather complicated politics of Pennsylvania.[9] In a general way the province after 1720 was divided into two antagonistic sections. In the eastern counties of Bucks, Chester, and Philadelphia lived the wealthy merchants and farmers who composed a conservative party which controlled the elected assembly. In this alliance the Quakers furnished the political leadership, while the Germans, a group inexperienced in government, provided support at the polls. Sharing similar religious beliefs and united by opposition to the proprietary land system, the eastern Quakers and German Pietists strove to make the assembly superior to the governor representing the Penn family, while at the same time they used their legislative power to withhold protection desired by the set-

[8] See again L. H. Gipson's *British Empire before the American Revolution*, Vol. II, pp. 143–163.

[9] See two works by W. R. Shepherd: *History of Proprietary Government in Pennsylvania* (New York, 1896) and "The Land System of Pennsylvania," *Report*, American Historical Association, 1895.

tlers on the western frontiers—a stand dictated by the Quakers' aversion to war and by their dislike of paying taxes for the benefit of other people.[10]

On the frontiers the Scotch-Irish rapidly became the dominant group. Encouraged at first to come into the province by the Penns in order to buy land and to build up a party against the anti-proprietary Quakers, the Scotch-Irish increased so prodigiously that by 1750 they constituted a third of the population. But as settlers they disappointed the Penns; although they pretended they would buy land "not one in twenty" had "anything to buy with." As early as 1726 it was estimated that there were fifty thousand Scotch-Irish squatters on the frontiers; in 1730 Penn's agent, James Logan, wrote: "I must own, from my experience in the land office, that the settlement of five families from Ireland gives me more trouble than fifty of any other people." Moreover, these "poor but presumptuous people" refused to pay quit-rents to the proprietary family. Equally spirited was their opposition to the eastern Quakers who refused to grant public money for frontier defense; in addition many of the eastern conservatives were speculators who, demanding more for their lands than did the proprietors, viewed the squatters with unbounded contempt. The poorer German settlers on the frontier, finding themselves at odds with their wealthier countrymen of the eastern counties, accepted the political leadership of the aggressive Scotch-Irish. The interior fur trade contributed another cause of antagonism between east and west as the Germans at Lancaster broke in upon the monopoly of trade in the Susquehanna region previously held by Philadelphia merchants. And with the founding of Baltimore in 1729 the Scotch-Irish and German pioneers were able to export their surplus produce by way of the Susquehanna River, thereby lessening their dependence upon Philadelphia and accentuating the cleavage between the sections within the province. Eastern Germans and Quakers against western Germans and Scotch-Irish, and both parties against the proprietor: such was the alignment of political forces until the close of the French and Indian War.[11]

Prior to 1757 the Quakers retained control of the province but their unwillingness to provide for frontier defense finally induced Britain to threaten to enact a parliamentary statute to exclude them from the assembly. They parried this threat in 1757 when several of them withdrew and allowed a non-Quaker majority to assume control. The critical issue at this time was: should the assembly tax the ungranted lands

---

[10] See again H. L. Osgood, *American Colonies in the Eighteenth Century*, Vol. IV, chapter 6.

[11] See again E. Channing, *History of the United States*, Vol. II, chapter 9.

of the Penns? To raise money for defense and to force a more rapid disposal of the proprietary lands (a proposal agreeable to both speculators and small farmers)—such were the purposes of the assembly in contending that the Penns should "give a part to save the whole and not only save it but render it of double or treble value." The assembly also desired to appoint the assessors of lands, to tax the proprietor's income from quit-rents, and to allow the settlers to pay the rents in depreciated currency. To all these measures the Penns objected strenuously: they would consent to the taxation of their lands which netted an income, but, in the words of W. T. Root, "to impose a tax on the vast areas of unlocated and unsurveyed lands appeared to them subversive of the principles of right." [12]

Over these issues raged one of the sharpest legislative battles of colonial times. After being thwarted by the governor in the sessions of 1755–58 the representatives carried the day in 1759 when they induced him to violate his instructions and sign a bill which taxed the ungranted proprietary lands and allowed the assembly to name the assessors. Governor Denny received a legislative gift of £1,000 and a promise that the province would compensate him if his assent should cost him the £5,000 bond he had given to enforce the proprietors' instructions. In spite of the refusal of the assembly to make any appropriations for the war unless he agreed to the tax; in spite of the fact that pressure had been brought to bear upon him by General Amherst, Denny was dismissed by the Penns, who likewise called upon the Crown to disallow the law. In 1760 agents of the province in England agreed to a compromise which excluded the ungranted, unsurveyed land from taxation, provided that surveyed but unimproved lands be taxed at the same rate at which similar lands owned by private persons were taxed, gave the Penns a voice in the selection of accessors, and required that quit-rents be paid according to contracts. However, the assembly refused to ratify this agreement or to repeal the tax of 1759. Then when Indian war again ravaged the frontiers in 1763 the assembly declined to grant defense money except upon its early conditions. Once more a deadlock ensued as the governor vetoed the land tax; no defense funds were voted and the frontier was left to shift for itself. Organizing themselves as the "Paxton Boys," the frontiersmen took up arms, killed some Indians, and then descended upon Philadelphia, demanding relief. This turn of events enabled the governor to extract defense money from the assembly without consenting to the debated tax. So indignant now were the representatives that they sent Benjamin Franklin to

[12] See again W. T. Root, *Relations of Pennsylvania with the British Government*, chapter 7.

England with a petition praying that the Crown assume the powers of the proprietor on the assumption that it was necessary "to fly from petty tyrants to the throne." [13]

Inasmuch as the eastern counties controlled the assembly during this conflict its history demonstrates that the wealthier, conservative groups were the chief opponents of the proprietary land system. Many of the easterners favored the proprietary land tax merely as a means of shifting the defense burden to the proprietors from themselves. Land speculators on the other hand had a twofold motive. They desired to make it unprofitable for the Penns to withhold vast tracts from the speculative buyers, and they hoped to force the Penns to charge higher prices for lands they sold to settlers in competition with private speculative offerings. With regard to the frontier settlers, their main interest for the time was in adequate defense.

The farmers of New Jersey outdid even their Pennsylvania neighbors in opposing an unpopular land system. When in 1702 the numerous and weakly organized proprietors of New Jersey surrendered to the Crown their rights to govern the province they retained possession of the soil, and the English government thereafter attempted to enforce their claims as landlords by decreeing that only they could extinguish Indian titles and that all the settlers should pay to them the required quit-rents. Essentially land speculators, the proprietors parceled the province among themselves, each laying claim to large tracts and carrying on an individual land office business. Politically they were united; they controlled the governor's council and the courts and used their power to enforce their rights as overlords. Before 1747 they enjoyed the backing of the British government, made effective through its agent, the royal governor.[14]

The settlers who occupied the hilly parts of New Jersey west of Newark (for the most part they were of Dutch, English, and Scottish stock) took up unsurveyed land, justifying themselves with the frontier philosophy that the land belonged to him who would use it. They ignored the proprietors by buying their titles from the Indians, by refusing to pay quit-rents, and by cutting timber on lands which the proprietors reserved for themselves. In this conflict the frontiersmen could count upon assistance from the established, more prosperous farmers in Elizabethtown and Monmouth County—settlers who also resisted the proprietary claims, contending that since they had origi-

[13] An exceptionally good study is Charles H. Lincoln, *The Revolutionary Movement in Pennsylvania* (Philadelphia, 1901), chapters 1–4.

[14] See again H. L. Osgood, *American Colonies in the Eighteenth Century*, Vol. IV, chapter 5.

nally derived their titles from the Duke of York they were exempt from quit-rent payments to the New Jersey overlords. And because the farmers dominated the assembly and the militia the proprietors could not depend upon them for protection of their interests; accordingly they were forced to rely upon the council and the courts. The struggle over land therefore assumed a legal character as the proprietors sought by court actions to evict trespassers and the latter directed their attack upon lawyers, judges, and jails.[15]

In 1745 a certain Samuel Baldwin was arrested for cutting trees on a proprietary tract. His neighbors rallied to his defense and forcibly removed him from jail, whereupon some of the rioters were arrested. They too were soon freed by mob violence, the frontier settlers now being well organized under their chosen leaders. The governor who had to deal with these riots was Jonathan Belcher—previously a vigorous opponent of the rural democracy of Massachusetts. Although Belcher "was surpassed by none in his love for the rich and powerful" (Osgood), at the same time as a New Englander he had little sympathy for quit-rents. Accordingly he did nothing to suppress the unrest or to punish the rioters. Nor did the assembly act, except to offer pardons. Inasmuch as legal actions against the farmers invariably evoked new riots, the proprietors finally appealed to England for protection. The Board of Trade favored the use of British troops to quell the revolt but the Privy Council decided to send a commission of inquiry and to arrange for a legal settlement of the proprietors' claims. However, before such steps could be taken the French and Indian War compelled the proprietors to abate their zeal against the farmers in order to enlist their support for the war, while the rioters found a new outlet for their fighting energies. Meanwhile the rioters for nearly a decade had successfully sustained one of the most important of the colonial rebellions against a narrow, semi-feudal land system.

Even New England with its freedom from proprietary overlords and quit-rents did not escape the prevalent controversy over land.[16] During the seventeenth century the Puritan land system had been reasonably conducive to social integration. The title to the lands of Massachusetts, Connecticut, and Rhode Island was vested by the charters in the colonial legislatures and they in turn made initial township grants to small bodies of settlers called town proprietors. Usually the Indians' claim to the land was first extinguished—not by individuals but by the authority of the colonial governments. In disposing of lands

[15] See again L. H. Gipson's *British Empire before the American Revolution,* Vol. III, chapter 6.
[16] See again J. T. Adams, *Revolutionary New England,* chapters 6–8, 10.

the legislatures did not require a money payment but they did impose conditions in order to provide for group settlement conducive to defense, coöperation in economic pursuits, and a common social and religious life. The townships (usually eight or ten square miles) were laid out by the colony, while the town proprietors were required to keep the bounds well marked.[17]

At the outset the proprietors composed the main body of working settlers; hence the township was originally a democratic institution. When the proprietors met together they formed the town meeting, and there they decided upon the utilization and disposition of the land. Each proprietor received a home lot (from two to five acres) located near the village common where the church, school, minister's residence, and town market were placed. Surrounding the common lay the planting and mowing fields; these were divided into small plots which were distributed among the proprietors by lot. The ungranted land belonged to the proprietors in common: pasturage, timber lands affording wood and stone, undivided arable and mowing fields, and waste and swamp lands. In order to build up the community the proprietors attracted outsiders by granting them small plots and by permitting them to attend and participate in the town meetings. Thus there occurred a division between the proprietors and non-proprietors or newcomers, but as long as the former constituted the majority the cleavage was not important. The proprietors continued to exercise alone the right of granting land, but they permitted the newcomers to vote for the selectmen who managed the town's public affairs. Moreover, in the early days the proprietors apportioned lands on a fairly equal basis: although the wealthiest settlers received more land than their poorer neighbors the former got disproportionately small shares—an arrangement necessary to prevent dissatisfaction in the initial period of extreme hardship and privation.[18]

The gradual influx of newcomers sharpened the competition for the ungranted lands as they became increasingly valuable. Then there appeared a pronounced antagonism between the original proprietors or their heirs and the non-proprietors. In the later apportionments of the commons the proprietary party insisted that it alone had the right to give title to land, whereas the non-proprietors urged that the whole body of inhabitants possessed that power. And in granting individual lands the proprietors now tended to assign tracts on the basis of indi-

[17] Lois K. Matthews [Rosenberry], *The Expansion of New England* (Boston, 1909), has a good factual discussion in chapter 4.
[18] Roy H. Akagi's *The Town Proprietors of the New England Colonies* (Philadelphia, 1924) is a monograph of unusual merit and importance.

vidual wealth. Thus the town of Lancaster resolved in 1653 "that in the second division and so through all other divisions of land the matter shall be drawn as near to equality of men's estates as we are able to do": to him that hath shall be given. Similarly the town proprietors began to deny to non-proprietors the privilege of using the commons for grazing purposes or as sources of timber and stone. And bit by bit the wealthier townsmen purchased the small plots of their poorer neighbors so that by 1715 the process of accumulation was propelling the landless outward toward the frontiers. At the same time it supplied the proprietary class with surplus funds which they could use for speculating in wilderness lands.

The growth of a class of propertyless farmers in conjunction with the rise of a class of wealthy men who had surplus capital but who did not desire to leave their established homes—this twofold evolution forced a change in the New England method of creating new towns. After 1725 Massachusetts, Connecticut, and New Hampshire, instead of granting townships to *bona fide* settlers, sold them to speculative promoters. Thus Connecticut in 1737 sold six townships at public auction, each purchaser being allowed to buy one of about fifty proprietary rights in a township at a minimum cost of between £30 and £60. Massachusetts went farther in 1762 when she disposed of ten large tracts at prices ranging from £380 to £3,200, and allowed a single purchaser to acquire an entire township. Because the colonial governments had an interest in settling the frontiers for protection against the French and Indians the speculative purchasers were required to establish a certain number of families within a given time (forty within four years, for instance) and to provide them with a minister, church, and school.[19]

After such purchases had been made (usually on the partial payment installment plan), the speculators operated land offices in eastern towns like Boston, whence they sent their agents on sales missions, not only throughout New England, but to the other colonies and to England as well. Many of their customers were non-pioneering investors who bought titles with the hope of a profitable resale. Among the most noted of the speculators were Josiah Willard of Massachusetts and James Fitch and Roger Wolcott of Connecticut. It soon appeared that grants had been made far in excess of the potentialities of settlement; consequently the speculators were unable to fulfill the prescribed conditions respecting the establishment of families on their lands: however, the colonial governments commonly granted generous extensions. Two principal results issued from the new land system. The early New

[19] Lois K. M. Rosenberry, *Migrations from Connecticut prior to 1800* (New Haven, 1934—Connecticut Tercentenary Commission, no. 28).

England ideal of community solidarity and the use of land grants to promote compact settlement gave way to unregulated competition for individual holdings, while on the frontiers isolated farms replaced the integrated towns common to the seventeenth century. Secondly, the frontier farmers viewed the speculators as their natural enemies who withheld land from cultivation, waged war against squatters, forced the price of land upward, controlled town governments as absentee voters, and failed to contribute toward the defense and welfare of the new communities. The most important legacy of speculation was this sharpened antagonism between seaboard wealth and frontier poverty.[20]

CURRENCY CONFLICTS

Equal in importance with the colonial struggles over land titles was a series of dramatic conflicts over currency—contests to determine the prices which the farmers should receive for their produce. Such prices in turn determined whether debtors should remain in a dependent state and perhaps eventually lose their improved lands through foreclosure or whether they should achieve financial independence and security. The peculiar weakness of the farmers arose from the fact that the prices of their produce fluctuated widely whereas their debts remained fixed; hence when prices went down all their surplus might be required to satisfy their creditors. The farmers therefore desired to keep prices at high levels and they concluded that the best means of doing this was to obtain a large supply of money. For opposite reasons the creditors favored a "sound" or contracted currency.

The monetary expedients adopted by the colonies prior to 1700 had not solved the basic problem of currency supply; the unfavorable balance of trade continually drained them of the gold and silver coin and bullion which they obtained from Europe and the West Indies.[21] The resulting lack of a metallic money compelled them to issue paper currency—a natural culmination of financial practices long in vogue. Since the beginnings of settlement the colonists had used personal promissory notes as a medium of exchange—notes that circulated from hand to hand upon endorsement until they fell due and were paid by the issuer. Similarly at an early date the colonial treasurers issued such notes promising to pay to the holder a certain sum when taxes voted by the assembly had been collected: by this means the colony could obtain funds, say in January, when tax money would not be available

[20] On New England speculation and strife over land rights see C. K. Shipton, *Sibley's Harvard Graduates* (Boston, 1945), Vol. VII, pp. 209, 252, 333, 505, 521, 608.
[21] See again C. P. Nettels, *The Money Supply of the American Colonies*, chapter 10.

until December. The next development occurred in Massachusetts in 1690 when the legislature itself issued the promissory notes in anticipation of tax collections. Such notes or bills were now printed in a form similar to modern paper money and they circulated in the same manner, without individual endorsement. During the years 1700–15 New York, New Jersey, all the other New England colonies, and the two Carolinas printed such bills of credit, while Pennsylvania followed in 1723, Maryland in 1733, Virginia in 1755, and Georgia in 1760. In most colonies the bills were issued originally to raise money for war expenditures and ordinarily they circulated only a year or so until the colony retired them by buying them from their owners with the tax money that had been collected. Although not generally made legal tender they were supposed to represent a certain amount of silver: 8s. in bills for one ounce of silver was the most common rating. Issued in relatively small amounts before 1710, this paper currency did not depreciate materially even though never actually redeemable in silver on demand.[22]

Bills of credit proved to be such a satisfactory currency substitute that the colonists desired to use them in time of peace. However, the termination of Queen Anne's War meant that the bills outstanding would be withdrawn within a short time and that new issues would not be needed for public expenditures; hence a new method of putting bills into circulation and a form of security other than taxes had to be devised. By this time also the farmers began to realize that a large volume of bills of credit would raise prices and lessen their debt burdens. These facts explain the growing popularity of "land banks." It was now proposed that the colonial governments issue a large sum in bills (say £50,000) and lend them to the farmers on the security of their land, up to half of its assessed value. The farmer should then retire the loan in twenty yearly installments and also pay an interest charge to the colony of 5 per cent on the principal due—an income which might enable the colony to dispense with taxes. In short, the colony should use its property assets as a credit base, issue notes thereon, lend to farmers needing money, and use the interest received to support the colonial governments.

A little experience with land banks made the colonial merchants suspicious of them. When land was the security behind the bills there was practically no limit to the amounts that could be issued and therefore no effective barrier against depreciation. In addition the land banks modified the credit relations between farmer and merchant. A farmer

---

[22] Kathryn L. Behrens, *Paper Money in Maryland, 1727–1789* (Baltimore, 1923), is a satisfactory technical study.

who could borrow from a land bank might obtain enough money to pay his debts and thus gain greater freedom in buying supplies and selling his crops; as a debtor he could deal only with his merchant-creditor. Contrariwise, when ordinary bills of credit based on taxes were issued, the merchants usually obtained the money in the first instance (by selling supplies to the colony); then they could lend it to the farmers. Should the farmers first secure the credit their bargaining power with the merchants would be greatly improved; similarly if the merchants obtained the bills in the first instance they could lend on terms profitable to themselves. And another thing: the common legal rate of interest for land bank bills was only 5 per cent whereas the farmers had to pay a much higher charge for credit obtained from the merchants. Finally, if the farmer could not repay his loan from the colony he could expect more lenient treatment than from a private creditor.[23]

In order to make bills of credit completely effective the debtors endeavored to force creditors to accept them as legal tender, and accordingly many acts were passed to that effect. But since the legal tender principle menaced British creditors they appealed to the Crown for protection as early as 1706, whereupon an imperial currency policy was formulated. The royal governors were permanently instructed not to sign acts which declared bills of credit legal tender or which provided for the issuance of bills unless they were accompanied by acts levying taxes for redeeming them within a restricted period. Nor were the governors to sign any extraordinary measures affecting British trade unless they contained clauses suspending their enforcement until the king's consent had been given. And when paper currency laws were enacted contrary to these instructions they were commonly disallowed by the Privy Council. On the currency issue, therefore, colonial creditors could depend upon Britain to protect them against colonial debtors.

Paper money first became a subject of controversy in South Carolina. The expenses of wars waged by the province against the Spaniards and the Indians between 1703 and 1715 were met largely by bills of credit backed by taxes. But such taxes were not collected in amounts sufficient to retire the bills at the times designated and accordingly they were retained in circulation. Moreover, a land bank authorized in 1712 added £32,000 of bills to the colony's stock of currency and by 1715 the total volume outstanding was about £74,000. Later issues caused depreciation: an ounce of silver was worth 8s. in bills in 1710 as against

[23] See again C. J. Bullock, *Essays in the Monetary History of the United States,* Part I, chapter 4; Part II, chapters 1–2; Part III, chapters 1–2.

27s. in 1720 and 36s. in 1730. Inasmuch as the South Carolina bills were made legal tender they had a pronounced effect upon the relations between creditors and debtors.[24]

The merchants of Charleston and the wealthier rice planters formed a creditor party which controlled the governor's council—their instrument for resisting further currency issues. Against them were arrayed the less affluent planters and the small farmers—a debtor party determined to use its control of the Commons House of Assembly (the lower house) to evade tax payments for the redemption of outstanding bills and even to force new issues upon the colony. The antagonism between the creditor council and the debtor assembly became so intense in the late 1720's that a complete legislative deadlock ensued. When the council rejected new currency issues demanded by the assembly the latter refused to assent to bills of any other character, whereupon the colony approached the brink of anarchy as existing laws of a temporary nature expired without substitute legislation being passed. Finally in August 1731 a compromise provided that no new issues should be made —on condition that the existing quantity of bills remain in circulation, £7 in paper being rated as worth £1 sterling. Thereafter the creditors, the council, and the royal governor held the debtors in check, partly by the exercise of their legislative vetoes and partly by controlling the membership of the lower house in such a manner as to deprive the frontier debtor districts of the full representation to which they were entitled.

The most acrimonious conflict over the currency broke out in Massachusetts in the late 1730's.[25] The province had issued large quantities of paper money after 1713, and because the bills of other New England colonies also gravitated to Boston, the currency became superabundant and rapid depreciation ensued: in 1730 bills supposed to equal an ounce of silver were worth only two-fifths of an ounce. When Governor Belcher in 1733 assented to acts which emitted £106,000 in additional bills the British government instructed him not to consent to future issues in excess of £30,000 a year and to see to it that all outstanding bills were not reissued or allowed to circulate after the date originally set for cancellation. These orders meant that by 1742 most of the paper would be withdrawn, with disastrous effects upon prices and debts. Determined not to permit such a currency contraction the debtor farm-

---

[24] W. Roy Smith's *South Carolina as a Royal Province* (New York, 1903), an important study devoted principally to land and financial questions, is best suited to the advanced student.

[25] The foremost work on eighteenth-century finance is Andrew M. Davis's *Currency and Banking in the Province of Massachusetts-Bay* (2 vols., New York, 1900, 1901). It is too technical for the general reader.

ers devised a means of issuing bills which would not be subject to the governor's veto.

This was the famous land bank of 1740 which proposed to print £150,000 in bills to be lent to farmers on land mortgages at 3 per cent interest, with provision for repaying the principal in twenty equal yearly installments. Beginning operations in September 1740 the bank issued £49,250 in bills to about a thousand subscribers—bills without legal authorization which had to depend upon popular support for their effectiveness. That, however, seemed assured, since the mass of the farmers were heavily in debt to the merchants, whom they denounced as "griping and merciless usurers" bent upon building up "vast estates" and making themselves "lords of manors." "Hundreds of thousands are due to them." Without such currency relief the yeomen would surely sink to the status of laborers or tenants and the marchants would "swallow up" thousands of families.[26]

Styling the land bankers as the "needy, idle and extravagant," and charging that the "rabble" would transform "this province noted for trade" into "a habitation of rude rustics," the leading merchants combined, refused to accept any of the newly issued bills and launched a bank of their own for emitting bills to be redeemed in silver after fifteen years. In Governor Belcher they had a determined ally who said of the debtor farmers that they "are grown so brassy and hardy as to be now combining in a body to raise a rebellion." In fact the farmers did organize a march upon Boston in 1741, where they dominated the elections and chose a new set of councillors hostile to the merchants. Belcher, however, dissolved the House of Representatives (which was overwhelmingly pro-land bank), jailed the ringleaders, removed justices of the peace and officers of the militia who were sympathetic to the popular cause, refused to allow attorneys to plead before the council unless they were on the right side, and rejected the new councillors who had been nominated by the general assembly in 1741.

In danger of being engulfed by the popular tide the merchants appealed to Britain for protection and obtained immediate aid when Parliament in 1741 extended to the colonies a statute called the Bubble Act, which outlawed joint-stock companies operating without special authority from Parliament. Although enacted in 1720 this statute had been construed afterward as not applying to the colonies; now, however, it was not only made to apply but also broadened so as to include land banks. With one stroke Parliament made all the transactions of

[26] J. C. Miller, "Religion, Finance, and Democracy in Massachusetts," *New England Quarterly*, VI (March 1933).

the Massachusetts land bank illegal and forced it to wind up its affairs.[27]

The participants in the bank were at once exposed to ruin. As an illegal institution it could not enforce the contracts it had made or recover loans it had extended to its members. Yet each individual subscribed was held individually responsible for all the debts of the bank (or compelled to make good all the bills it had issued). Now it so happened that many of the subscribers were insolvent; hence the solvent participants had to redeem all outstanding bills. So bitter had the conflict grown that the merchants who had been forced to accept the bills were determined to make the subscribers pay to the last farthing. The upshot was a series of lawsuits which harassed the land bankers for nearly twenty years and which ruined many. Foremost among these was one of the bank directors, Samuel Adams, father of the Revolutionary leader. In 1757 two notices appeared simultaneously in the Boston press. One announced a public auction sale of the estate of Samuel Adams, the elder; the other was a notice from the son warning that the sale was illegal and that he would prosecute anyone who trespassed on his father's estate. The embittering of the relations between local creditors and debtors and a legacy of rural antagonism to Parliament's authority—such were the offspring of the Massachusetts land bank episode.

After 1740 Rhode Island became the principal scene of strife between debtors and creditors. There the small farmers who dominated the elected assembly for many years had the wealthy merchants of Newport at their mercy, since the farmers elected the governor as well as the deputies and moreover the governor did not possess the veto power, nor were Rhode Island's acts subject to the royal disallowance. The democratic spirit for which the colony had always been noted expressed itself largely in the paper money crusade; in fact democracy and inflation were kindred spirits in colonial times: let the people have money as well as votes.

So firm was this faith among the Rhode Islanders that between 1710 and 1750 they created nine land banks, the total currency issues of which amounted to £465,000. As a rule the farmers did not bother to pay their loans obtained from land banks; instead, when the payments were well in arrears, they would create another bank and borrow its bills in order to pay their old debts. New banks were also created to supply additional bills for the farmers to borrow. Meanwhile the

[27] See again W. B. Weeden, *Economic and Social History of New England*, Vol. II, pp. 473-491.

colony continued to issue tax-supported bills for public purposes and then failed to pay the taxes when due. In 1740 the paper in circulation amounted to £340,000 and when by 1750 the total had reached £525,-000, depreciation had gone so far that bills supposedly worth an ounce of silver were actually worth only about an eighth of an ounce. Although Rhode Island did not make its bills legal tender yet so strong was the pressure of popular sentiment and so prone were rural judges to require creditors to accept them that in effect they circulated as lawful currency.

About 1730 the Newport merchants began to oppose additional issues, arguing that the farmers were deliberately striving to multiply the bills in order to wipe out private debts, that new loans would be obtained by debtors whose land was already mortgaged to the limit, that the interest rates which the farmers were supposed to pay were unreasonably low, and that the time allowed for the payment of such loans was too long. To these arguments the debtors replied that the merchants, by charging exorbitant prices for their goods, had obtained most of the old bills and had sent them to Boston in the course of trade. In 1730–31, when Governor Jenks attempted to veto a new land bank act the assembly successfully maintained that he did not possess the veto power, and when the merchants appealed to Britain for protection the Crown refused to act because Rhode Island's bills were not legal tender. Encouraged by such success the land bankers set up four new banks between 1733 and 1744 and in so doing nearly drove the merchants to distraction. After they had failed to exclude the debtors from the assembly by raising the property qualifications for voting (meanwhile the depreciation of the currency had greatly extended the franchise by increasing the nominal value of all property) and when in 1750 the debtors were on the point of creating a new bank, the merchants made a last desperate appeal to Britain. Ruin, they said, would visit them if the Assembly continued its reckless conduct.

The British government at last decided to take a hand. Due largely to the exigencies of King George's War the Crown had permitted the New England colonies to issue large quantities of paper but the resulting depreciation had wrought havoc with property rights and trade. Now when the war was over it was deemed necessary to stabilize New England's currency; hence in 1751 Parliament passed the Currency Act in response to the pleas of the Rhode Island and other merchants. This statute prohibited the New England colonies from erecting new land banks and from making bills of credit legal tender; it also required that outstanding bills be retired at the time appointed in the act of issue. In the future only bills backed by taxes could be issued: those emitted for ordinary purposes of government should be retired within two years and those issued for military emergencies should not run for more than five years. Inasmuch as this act sounded the death knell of New England land banks it intensified the opposition of rural debtors to Parliament's authority.

TIDEWATER VERSUS FRONTIER

After 1720 the social cleavage in Virginia, Maryland, North Carolina, and South Carolina assumed a sectional as well as a class character, due to the rough division of those colonies into two antagonistic areas—the seaboard or tidewater and the piedmont or back country.[28] Separated from the interior by the line of the falls of the southern rivers, the seaboard area was distinguished by its large plantations, its highly stratified society, and the supremacy of its slaveholding aristocracy which ruled through the established governments. As a frontier region of small farms varying from fifty to two hundred acres, the back country had not yet become socially stratified; rather it expressed the informal and democratic spirit of laboring farmers among whom slavery was insignificant. And since they were cut off from direct access to the ocean they were forced to rely upon diversified farming and household manufacturing, their chief exports consisting of cattle driven overland to port towns like Baltimore and Richmond—a trade which enabled them to buy essential manufactures such as firearms, ammunition, notions, and ironware.

A host of interests divided these interior farmers from the tidewater aristocracy. As a debtor group they clamored for cheap paper money with which to pay their debts to eastern merchants and planter capitalists—a demand which explains the opposition of the aristocracy to currency inflation. Sorely in need of roads and bridges which they were too poor to construct by themselves, the frontiersmen called upon the colonial governments for assistance, only to find that the aristocracy refused to tax itself for such improvements. A similar opposition met their demands for frontier defense against the Indians, and as squatters they ran afoul of the land claims of the seaboard speculators. They strongly favored the system of small farms and the division of property equally among all children, whereas the tidewater planters preferred the law of primogeniture which awarded the whole ancestral estate to the eldest son. Recognizing that slavery was the basis of the power of their planter enemies the frontiersmen readily criticized that institution

[28] See again F. J. Turner, *The Frontier in American History*, chapters 2–3 (important).

and thereby not only provoked the planters to justify slavery as inherently right but also to deride the small farmers as shiftless and inefficient. And over taxation raged many a fierce battle as the back country, objecting to poll taxes, either insisted upon shifting the burden to the vast landholdings of the planter class or demanded heavier levies upon slaves. As Baptists, Quakers, Methodists, or simply as people indifferent to religion, the frontiersmen also objected strenuously to the parish taxes required by law for the support of the Anglican Church.[29]

In view of such fundamental differences of interest and outlook the control over government was a primary concern to both parties. Not only was the aristocracy determined to retain its mastery over the governor's council; it also sought to curb the influence of the back country in the elected assembly. The tidewater originally obtained control of the lower houses because it was the area first settled; then when the back country was peopled it had to appeal to the tidewater for representation. The South Carolina planters retained power by granting six or eight representatives to each of the coast counties and by allowing only one or two to the western counties. In Virginia the aristocracy erected more counties in the east than in the west and gave each two representatives, even though the tidewater counties were far less populous than those of the piedmont. In 1710 Governor Spotswood remarked that some of the western counties in Virginia were ninety miles in length and inhabited by three times as many people as some of the eastern counties, while in 1780 Jefferson wrote that "19,000 men below the falls give the law to more than 30,000 living in other parts of the state." So also in South Carolina: as late as 1790 the back country complained that the governing class included only a fifth of the white people. The blame for unequal representation may be laid in part to the British government, which feared the leveling tendencies of the interior and reserved to the royal governors the power of apportioning seats in the assembly—a power they used to perpetuate the existing inequalities.[30]

To the tidewater aristocracy it seemed equally imperative that local governments in the back country should be in "proper" hands—that justices of the peace should render correct decisions and that sheriffs

[29] Henry R. McIlwaine, *The Struggle of Protestant Dissenters for Religious Toleration in Virginia* (Baltimore, 1894), treats this theme briefly. See also Stephen B. Weeks, *Church and State in North Carolina* (Baltimore, 1892, 1893).

[30] Charles H. Ambler's excellent *Sectionalism in Virginia* . . . (Chicago, 1910) sketches the colonial conflict in chapter 1. See also William A. Schaper, "Sectionalism in South Carolina," *Report*, American Historical Association, 1900, Vol. I, a standard work.

should duly execute the judgments of the courts. Since such officers were appointed by the governors and councils the interests of the aristocracy were not seriously neglected. Moreover, the excessive size

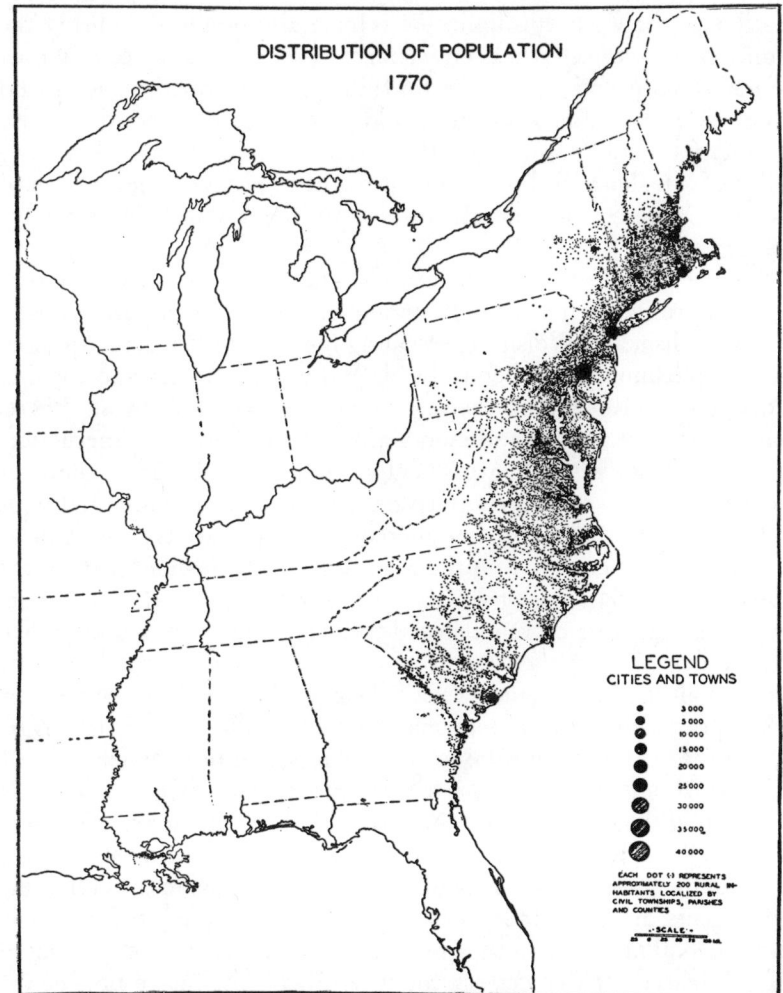

DISTRIBUTION OF POPULATION
1770

LEGEND
CITIES AND TOWNS

of the interior counties worked a hardship upon poor farmers who had to choose between a journey of thirty or forty miles to the county courts or adverse judgments for failure to attend. Nor did the large counties provide adequate police protection to the farmers against cattle thieves and other lawless elements. Above all, the highest provincial courts of appeal were located on the seacoast and were presided over by the very aristocrats who were the oppressors of the interior farmers.[31]

In resisting such conditions the back country at first petitioned for equal representation in the assembly, to be achieved through reducing the size of the western counties—a reform also designed to bring the county courts closer to the frontier farms and to make the county governments more efficient agencies for the suppression of crime. Fees paid to courts, lawyers, and officers should be drastically reduced; so also the sheriffs should not be permitted to steal the tax money which they collected. In short local government ought to promote the welfare of the back country, not merely protect the interests of the seaboard aristocracy.

The most bitter conflict between tidewater and frontier occurred in North Carolina. After 1763 a stream of settlers—Germans, Scotch-Irish, English, and Welsh, representing most Protestant sects—poured into the piedmont from Pennsylvania and western Virginia, occupying the area from Raleigh on the east to Morganton on the west. There, eking out a bare existence, they ran afoul of the great land speculators of the seaboard, whose engrossment of the best lands forced the poor pioneers either to cultivate unfertile tracts or to pay a substantial price to the magnates. The poll tax, moreover, bore relatively much more heavily on the poor than on the rich. A trade depression gripped the colony after 1763; money was scarce or non-existent in the back country, since the paper currency issued to finance the French and Indian War was rapidly withdrawn from circulation. This meant that the farmers must make payments with their produce, and due to the low prices prevailing many a poor man found that all his surplus was required for land payments, taxes, officers' fees, and private debts.

Meanwhile, the aristocracy of merchants and large landowners, dominating the governor and the council, held complete control of the executive and judicial branches of the colonial government. Closely allied to the eastern aristocracy was a rising upper class in the back country—agents of the former, such as surveyors, lawyers, and debt collectors; local merchants and land speculators; and, most conspicuous of all, the officials of the western counties. First came the justices of the peace, appointed by the governor and council, usually the wealthiest men of the back country, who composed the county court, which decided most cases at law, levied parish and county taxes, and was in fact almost the only unit of local government. Next in influence was the county sheriff, appointed by the governor from a panel of three nomi-

[31] St. George L. Sioussat, *Economics and Politics in Maryland, 1720–1750* (Baltimore, 1903), has a brief discussion of social conflicts.

nees prepared by the county justices, and usually assisted by a host of deputies in collecting taxes and executing the orders of the county court. The official party also included a number of clerks, registers, and lawyers who lived by the fees they collected for registering deeds, witnessing papers, and tying and untying the official redtape.

Supported by the governor and council, and free from local restraints, the western officials acted about as they pleased in upholding the *status quo*. It is evident that they interpreted the colony's fee laws to allow the taking of three or four fees when the farmers thought they were entitled to only one, and that the sheriffs kept their tax accounts secret and pocketed part of the tax money collected. When the poor farmers could not pay their debts or the high fees and taxes, the county courts ordered the sale of their property; and in the face of a depressed price level the local upper-class elements were able to buy or acquire such foreclosed property for a trifle and thus improve their style of living.

In 1765 a preliminary outbreak occurred against one George Selwyn, a large land operator, and his surveyor, John Frohock, who attempted to evict settlers in Mecklenburg County who refused to pay the high prices Selwyn asked for land. Three years later the farmers of Orange County formed an association, the Regulators, pledging to pay only legal taxes and legal fees and to act together under majority rule.[32] The local upper-class party, charging that the Regulators were taking the law into their own hands by usurping the functions of the officials and thus seeking to overthrow the government, immediately gained the backing of Governor Tryon and the provincial council. Thus fortified, the officials sought to suppress the uprising by jailing a few leaders, whereupon the Regulators stormed the jails, released their friends and began to threaten their enemies with violence. Governor Tryon, while promising to investigate grievances and to punish lawbreaking officials, betrayed much antagonism toward the Regulators and their methods. Seeking to overawe them he led an armed expedition into their country in 1768, but by avoiding fighting and punishments he quieted them for a time with more promises of reform.

An election in 1769 gave the Regulators control of the provincial assembly. But popular hopes for legal reforms ended abruptly in November when Governor Tryon dissolved the house for its opposition to British policies—an action which served notice that the Regulators could not depend upon the assembly to defend them against Tryon and the council. Meanwhile, the elements in power refused to

[32] The best account is J. S. Bassett, "The Regulators of North Carolina," *Report*, American Historical Association, 1894.

yield. To the Regulators the trials of accused officials appeared a farce: juries were packed; the justices declared their friends and allies innocent, or if technically guilty, fined them a penny; orders for the sale of debtors' property continued apace. Convinced that the courts and officers were adamant, the Regulators resorted to more direct action. They raided jails to free their imprisoned leaders; they assembled at the county courts and intimidated the justices; they whipped their enemies, drove them away, and burned their houses and stables.

In response to such activities Governor Tryon raised a small army which consisted of the eastern aristocrats, the officials, and soldiers recruited through bounties. On May 16, 1771, this force fell upon a large body of poorly armed and unsuspecting Regulators at the Alamance River, routing them after a battle of two hours. Seven Regulator leaders were summarily executed. Tryon's course received the hearty approval of the British government, which however recommended amnesty for the surviving leaders. The movement collapsed completely, since the Regulators had not sought an overthrow of government and were unwilling to fight on. Hundreds of them migrated to Tennessee; the others submitted. When the American Revolution broke out the remaining Regulators still regarded the eastern aristocrats as their chief enemies, and because the latter joined the Revolutionary party, many of the Regulators adhered to the British cause.

BIBLIOGRAPHICAL NOTE

SECONDARY WORKS: L. W. Labaree, *Conservatism in Early American History* (New York, 1948), effectively portrays the colonial aristocracy. Richard A. Lester, *Monetary Experiments* (Princeton, 1939), demonstrates that the middle colonies managed paper currencies successfully. Thomas Hutchinson, *The History of . . . Massachusetts-Bay* (ed. L. S. Mayo, 3 vols., Cambridge, 1936), is an important source for the land bank war. George A. Billias, *The Massachusetts Land Bankers of 1740* (Orono, 1959), interprets the land bank as an agency of speculative business. Kenneth Scott, *Counterfeiting in Colonial America* (New York, 1957), is an adequate treatment. Aaron M. Sakolski, *Land Tenure and Land Taxation in America* (New York, 1957), is an indictment of land speculation, by a leading authority on the subject. Irving Mark, *Agrarian Conflicts in Colonial New York, 1711–1775* (New York, 1940), is a careful study.

SOURCES: The Publications of the Prince Society contain Andrew M. Davis's edition of *Colonial Currency Reprints, 1682–1751* (4 vols., Boston, 1910–11)— the best collection of sources on paper money. For a more convenient selection see A. M. Davis (ed.), *Tracts relating to the Currency of Massachusetts Bay, 1682–1720* (Boston, 1902). F. J. Klingberg (ed.), *Carolina Chronicle* (Berkeley, 1946), portrays trying times in South Carolina, 1708–1716, as described by an Anglican churchman.

XX

Self-Government and
Imperial Control

From the preceding chapters it is evident that the growing economic value of the colonies to Britain and their habit of acting contrary to her interests constantly magnified the problem of imperial control. The ensuing conflicts raised the central issue of government and statecraft—the problem of authority. Were the colonies helpless dependencies of Britain or were they virtually independent countries? And if dependencies, where did the power of governing them rest? Where did sovereignty reside in the British state?

The Power of Parliament

The political struggles in seventeenth-century England between king and Parliament were decided for the future by the Revolution of 1688, which demolished the doctrine of the divine right of kings and demonstrated conclusively that in a profound conflict the forces identified with Parliament were far more powerful than the Crown. After that momentous victory Parliament slowly and gradually, yet remorselessly and irresistibly, extended its power in all directions. The Bill of Rights of 1689 denied to the king for all time the privilege of dispensing with laws or of suspending their enforcement, and it also prohibited the maintenance of a standing army without Parliament's consent. By the Toleration Act of 1689 the religious liberties of the English Protestants were safeguarded against royal encroachments, while a Mutiny Act, also of 1689, necessitated that the king call Parliament into session every year. Through statutes of 1692, 1694, and 1696 Parliament assumed control of national finances by authorizing public loans, by chartering the Bank of England, and by regulating the coinage—acts previously within the sphere of the king's prerogative. The Triennial Act of 1694 and the Septennial Act of 1716 deprived the sovereign of the right to dispense with parliamentary elections, the first act requiring that they be held at least once in three years, the second specifying seven years. Particularly significant was the Act of Settlement of 1701 by which Parliament decreed that the British crown should be worn only by Protestants and designated that after the death of Anne (soon to succeed William III) it should pass to the Electress Sophia of Hanover, a granddaughter of James I. For the future the sovereign must be a member of the Church of England; he or she could not marry a Roman Catholic or involve England in war in behalf of foreign possessions without Parliament's consent. Judges were no longer removable at the sole command of the king. Finally in 1720 Parliament assumed the once royal prerogative of chartering joint-stock • companies.[1]

The character of the sovereigns who ruled between 1702 and 1760 contributed largely to the growth of Parliament's power. Queen Anne (1702–14) was a meek, passive woman of mediocre talents; wholly incompetent to deal with great issues of state, she was dominated by friends and ministers who represented the powerful parties of the day. Then followed the reign of George I (1714–27), a king imported from Hanover, whose ignorance of the English language caused him to ignore the meetings of his ministers, leaving to them the business of government while he occupied himself with unimportant foreign affairs. His successor, George II (1727–60), also born in Hanover, was a timid, pedantic man whose indifference to England and whose interest in Hanover prompted him to give Parliament a free rein. Thus it happened that during these reigns the gains of the Revolution of 1688 assumed the form of parliamentary supremacy over the sovereign.[2]

Since it was undesirable to resort to revolution in order to control the monarchy the task of Parliament after 1688 was to devise some machinery by which it might dictate the course of policy from day to day. One step toward this end was taken during the reign of Queen Anne when Parliament practically deprived the sovereign of the veto power. Earlier, in 1694, William III had begun the practice of mollifying Parliament by choosing ministers who represented the majority of its members—a custom which rapidly developed into the principle of ministerial responsibility or the right of the majority party in the House of Commons to designate and remove the king's advisers, thereby enabling Parliament to dominate the executive branches of the government. Later, after Robert Walpole became the chief financial minister in 1721, he so distinguished himself from his colleagues as to set a precedent for the office of Prime Minister and he also established the idea of cabinet solidarity—the principle that officials who opposed

---

[1] See again G. B. Adams, *Constitutional History of England*, chapters 15–16.
[2] An engaging study of British politics, 1710–35, is Frederick S. Oliver, *The Endless Adventure* (2 vols., London, 1931). Charles Grant Robertson, *England under the Hanoverians* (New York, 1911), is an attractive survey.

the policy of the majority of the ministers should resign. It is true that Parliament's power was often only nominal—that influential ministers like Walpole kept control by bribing members and by manipulating elections and that in consequence a small circle of men dictated to Parliament rather than submitted to its freely formed judgments. Yet this technique of manipulation acknowledged the theoretical supremacy of Parliament as expressed by Blackstone in the 1750's: "So long therefore as the English constitution lasts we may venture to affirm that the power of Parliament is absolute and without control." [3]

Ordinarily the members of Parliament did not originate or frame legislation pertaining to the colonies; most commonly English merchants or other special groups appealed first to colonial officials for a certain action, whereupon the latter would draft a bill for Parliament's consideration. Because the Whig party (representing the merchant class) held power during most of the time between 1689 and 1760 the laws then enacted were designed as a rule to promote the interests of that class. Thus one series of acts aimed to protect the investments of the merchants in the colonies: the Coin Act of 1708, the statute of 1731 which made the lands and slaves of planters liable for debt, the extension to the colonies of the Bubble Act in 1741, and the Currency Act of 1751. A second group of laws were intended to increase colonial exports both in order to provide raw materials for English industry and to supply the colonies with purchasing power for English goods. In this category belong the naval stores Bounty Acts (1705, 1729), the acts placing rice (1705) and copper ore, beaver skins, and other furs (1722) on the enumerated article list, a White Pine Act of 1711 which reserved for the use of the royal navy certain trees on ungranted lands in New England, New York, and New Jersey, and the indigo bounty act of 1746. Other statutes provided for the protection, regulation, or promotion of colonial trade: the Navigation Act of 1696, a statute canceling the monopoly of the Royal African Company (1698) and another dissolving the company (1750), the act for the suppression of colonial piracy (1700), a law of 1708 designed to promote England's trade with Spanish America, the Molasses Act of 1733, and the acts of 1730, 1735, 1737, and 1739 permitting the plantation colonies to ship sugar and rice to points in Europe south of Cape Finisterre. Similarly the Woolen Act (1699), the Hat Act (1732), and the Iron Act (1750) sought to curtail manufacturing in the colonies. Of more particular interest was a statute of 1699 which regulated the English fishery at Newfound-

[3] Edward Jenks, *Parliamentary England* (New York, 1903), is a good, brief, readable introduction to the development of the cabinet.

land. Two facts emerge from this legislation: the extension of Parliament's activity and its preoccupation with issues of industry and trade.[4]

The need for parliamentary legislation touching the colonies came to light in 1705 when they were freely violating the queen's proclamation of 1704 which regulated the value of foreign coin. The Attorney-General of England then pointed out that the proclamation could not be enforced because it carried no penalties; in addition he insisted that the sovereign, single-handed, could not create new offenses for which punishments could be inflicted. This meant that the sovereign, acting alone, could not exert any real power in the sphere of policy—that Parliament must act in order to authorize those penalties necessary for the enforcement of new decrees. Accordingly, in 1708 Parliament passed the coin act which gave legal force to the queen's proclamation of 1704. Since this action was taken at the time when Parliament deprived the sovereign of the veto power it helped to establish the principle of parliamentary supremacy over the colonies; the sovereign could not act without Parliament's approval whereas Parliament could in effect act without the sovereign's. Two other cases reveal the altered status of Parliament and the king. Prior to 1700 Parliament had had no part in either the founding of colonies or the revocation of charters. Now, however, in 1729 it authorized the transfer to the Crown of the rights of the Carolina proprietors and in the 1730's it appropriated large sums of money toward the establishment of Georgia.

Because most parliamentary statutes were designed for Britain they could not be applied to the colonies, where local conditions required special legislation. Hence there existed a distinction between the realm (England, Wales, and after 1707 Scotland) and the dominions (Ireland and the colonies). A statute of the realm did not apply to the colonies unless it was expressly stated in the law that it should so apply, unless it was extended to the dominions by special parliamentary action, as in the case of the Bubble Act, or unless it was adopted by one of the colonial legislatures. Inasmuch as both Parliament and the colonial assemblies exercised the lawmaking power, a rather indefinite distinction between internal and external legislation was allowed to develop. Parliament generally confined itself to the regulation of the external affairs of the colonies (trade, currency, etc.) and permitted the colonial assemblies to legislate for domestic concerns. At best, however, such a distinction was a bit nebulous, since laws regulating trade and debts had important bearings upon local groups while most domestic issues like Indian relations, religion, and the administration of justice might

[4] Mary T. Blauvelt, *The Development of Cabinet Government in England* (New York, 1902), is a concise, lucid outline for the general reader.

readily affect groups outside the colony. Yet the acts passed by Parliament before 1763 were so generally confined to external affairs as to confirm the view of the colonists that domestic legislation was reserved exclusively to the colonial assemblies. On the other hand Parliament assumed that it had full power over both the external and the domestic concerns of the colonies—that it might legislate on any subject and that its statutes would always take precedence over acts of colonial legislatures. From these conflicting conceptions arose a serious misunderstanding between England and the colonies over the limits of Parliament's authority.[5]

THE AGENCIES OF COLONIAL ADMINISTRATION

Throughout the eighteenth century the executive administration of the colonies was performed in the name of the sovereign—a practice which kept alive the fiction of the royal prerogative which the Revolution of 1688 and the subsequent growth of Parliament had in reality dispelled. To enforce British statutes in the colonies, to apply general principles to special situations, and to provide a corps of officials who could safeguard Britain's interests in America: such was the task of British colonial administration. Due to its preoccupation with the legislative needs of Britain proper and to the difficulty of legislating in detail for subjects three thousand miles away, Parliament could only lay down general rules of policy and then permit executive officers to make detailed applications in day-to-day administration. Nor did Parliament create a special executive machinery for governing the colonies; instead the regular executive agencies of Britain assumed that task. The colonies were esteemed by England primarily for their trade; and because such trade was inseparably tied up with all British commerce it seemed desirable to govern them through the same agencies which regulated British affairs. Moreover, since colonies were valuable to England chiefly as sources of revenue it was imperative that they be supervised at a minimum cost; hence the utilization of the established executive departments for colonial administration.[6]

To American students the problem of imperial government becomes intelligible when one understands its similarity to the problem of federalism in the history of the United States. How might a central government regulate the concerns common to all the colonies or states;

[5] Charles H. McIlwain, *The High Court of Parliament* (New Haven, 1934), is an acute study of parliamentary supremacy.

[6] For an excellent résumé of imperial relations see C. M. Andrews, *The Colonial Background of the American Revolution*, chapter 1.

how might disputes among the members of the empire or the federal union be resolved? In the colonial-imperial phase the central government of England conducted all diplomatic negotiations with foreign states, declared and waged war, made treaties of peace, supervised commerce, collected custom duties and quit-rents, regulated currency, managed and disposed of the royal lands, provided naval protection, maintained an army and a postal service, heard appeals from colonial courts, and reviewed legislation enacted by the colonial assemblies. Thus Parliament and the Crown exercised those general powers over the colonies which are now exercised by the President, the Congress, and the federal judiciary over the states.

Among the most important British officials who had a hand in managing the colonies was the Secretary of State for the Southern Department. As the director of Britain's diplomatic relations with France and southern Europe he issued declarations of war, raised armies, conducted military campaigns, and negotiated treaties of peace. Because the numerous wars with France and Spain always involved the colonies he played an important part in colonial administration, acting through the royal governors who were chosen by him (except during the years 1752–61) and were therefore primarily his representatives, responsible to him for colonial defense and military operations. He countersigned their commissions and instructions, transmitted special orders to them, and required that they inform him of events in their colonies. Only once, however, did a secretary infuse vigor into the conduct of colonial affairs: that occurred during the years 1757–61 when William Pitt prosecuted the successful campaigns of the French and Indian War. Otherwise the office failed to provide effective imperial control, for three reasons. First, the ordinary tenure of a secretary was too brief: thirteen ministers served between 1696 and 1724 and nine between 1748 and 1768, so that the incumbent usually did not hold office long enough to become familiar with the remote colonies. Secondly, the minister who enjoyed the longest term (the Duke of Newcastle, 1724–48) had little interest in colonial matters. Finally, the diplomatic and military duties of the office were so onerous as to preclude serious consideration of the details of colonial administration.[7]

The overseas trade of the colonies, coupled with the fact that war and defense against France and Spain called principally for maritime operations, explains the role of the British navy in American waters. After 1708 the management of the navy was entrusted to the

[7] See again L. H. Gipson's *British Empire before the American Revolution*, Vol. I, chapters 1–3, 5.

Admiralty, a board of high officials who formed general policies and executed them through subordinate bureaus such as the Navy Board, the Transport Board, the Victualling Office, and the Navy Pay Office. Acting in close touch with the Secretary of State, the Admiralty and its various offices directed the movements of the navy, appointed naval officers and employees, provided guard-ships for the protection of the coasts of the colonies, supplied convoys and licenses to merchantmen in time of war, issued letters of marque and reprisal to privateers, and issued commissions to vice-admiralty officials in America. To the Admiralty also fell the tasks of suppressing piracy, of inspecting colonial naval stores and paying the bounties due, of enforcing the Acts of Trade and Navigation, and of providing transports and convoys for expeditions against the colonies of France and Spain.

Far less important than the Admiralty was the War Office headed by the Secretary at War, whose duties were of a routine nature—since plans of campaign were mapped out by the Secretary of State and the commander-in-chief of the army. The recruiting, inspection, quartering, and payment of the troops constituted the chief duties of the Secretary at War. Thus two of his subordinate officers were the Paymaster of the Forces and the Paymaster of Guards and Garrisons, while independent of the War Office was the Ordnance Board in charge of artillery, engineers, and fortifications. In the thirteen colonies the principal task of the War Office before 1756—to look after four companies of British troops stationed at New York—was performed in a scandalously inefficient manner. The French and Indian War however imposed the great burden of organizing and equipping the British forces in America, whereupon the War Office developed into a department of major importance.[8]

The financial operations of the British government exhibit the reality of Parliament's power after 1688. The Treasury department, descended from the medieval Exchequer, was managed by a board of high officials consisting of the First Lord of the Treasury (usually the Prime Minister), the Chancellor of the Exchequer (the financial leader of the House of Commons) and three Junior Treasury Lords. They supervised the collection of all revenues and the payment of all moneys appropriated by Parliament, making such disbursements through treasury warrants countersigned by the Board. Since Parliament could not foresee every trifling expenditure that might become necessary it was obliged to give the Treasury Board a large measure of discretion in

[8] See again *The Cambridge History of the British Empire*, Vol. I, chapters 14, 21 (important).

meeting irregular claims arising from emergencies. This power, coupled with the authority to withhold payments in cases involving error or peculation, enabled the Treasury officials to exert a decisive influence in colonial administration, for such irregularities and emergencies arose most frequently in the far-away colonies and moreover the outcome of important colonial policies often depended upon the granting or with-holding of funds. Most of the money appropriated by Parliament was released by the Treasury to designated spending departments but even so the Treasury Board acted as a sort of court of appeal in cases of an extraordinary nature.[9]

An influential board under the Treasury—the Commissioners of the Customs—supervised the collection of import and export duties and helped to enforce the Navigation Acts. These commissioners also advised other departments on all phases of commercial policy and drafted special instructions to the royal governors to guide their actions with reference to trade and revenue. In the colonies the Customs Board was responsible for the collection of the Virginia tax of 2s. on each hogshead of tobacco exported, the plantation duties on enumerated articles shipped to other colonies (act of 1673), and the duties levied by the Molasses Act of 1733. The act of 1673, which provided for erecting customhouses in the colonies, required the Customs Board to maintain the necessary collectors and searchers. The colonies were then (1683) grouped into districts in charge of a Surveyor of the Customs; after 1720 there were two such surveyors, one presiding over the West Indies and the mainland south of Delaware Bay, the other over the remaining colonies and Newfoundland. A second group of officers—naval clerks—entered and cleared vessels in colonial ports, examined ships' papers, and kept records of the cargoes, voyages, tonnage, owner-ship, etc., of vessels engaged in colonial trade.[10]

The Crown also claimed a host of other revenues in the colonies: quit-rents, forfeitures, escheats, fines for violation of the Navigation and other acts, license fees, and a share of prize goods and money and of property recovered from wrecks. The duty of collecting this money was assigned, after 1679, to the Surveyor and Auditor-General of the king's revenue in America—an officer under the Treasury Board whose deputies in the colonies collected and remitted the funds and forwarded accounts for his scrutiny. First to hold this office was William Blath-

---

[9] See again W. T. Root, *Relations of Pennsylvania with the British Government*, chapters 1–6, 11.

[10] Bernard Holland, *Imperium et Libertas* (London, 1901), interprets the imperial relationship as a constitutional problem. See chapter 1.

wayt, probably the most influential figure in colonial administration during the years 1679–1706.

Another important body of officials under the Treasury Board—the Commissioners of the Mint—not only managed England's coinage system but also gave advice pertaining to colonial currency policy. The most famous of these commissioners, Sir Isaac Newton, outlined the monetary principles which England applied to the colonies after 1700.

Separate from the executive boards such as those for the Treasury and the Admiralty were the Attorney-General and the Solicitor-General who assisted in drafting charters, parliamentary statutes, and royal decrees and gave opinions to guide officials on the legal side of colonial relations. They also served as representatives of the Crown in preparing and prosecuting cases in the English courts.

When it is recalled that the first five cabinet positions created in the United States government after 1788 were those of the Attorney-General and the Secretaries of State, War, the Treasury, and the Navy, the bearing of imperial administration on American federalism becomes self-evident. And there is another parallel: in colonial times the English Privy Council exercised a function similar to that later assumed by the Supreme Court of the United States.[11]

Before the Puritan Revolution of the 1640's the Privy Council had been a powerful body of the king's chief ministers who acted as a unit in framing and executing official policies. After 1700, however, the influence of the Council declined, partly because the great executive commissions like the Admiralty assumed their special tasks of administration and partly because a new council of ministers—the cabinet—took form as a means of rendering the chief officials responsible to Parliament rather than to the king. The Privy Council therefore became increasingly an honorary body which either ratified ministerial acts in the king's name or supervised minor interests that did not fall within the jurisdiction of the main executive departments. With reference to the colonies the Council received petitions and complaints, disallowed colonial laws, heard appeals from colonial courts, appointed the royal governors and councillors, put the seal of approval to the commissions and instructions of the governors, and settled disputes among royal agents in the colonial service. It issued orders-in-council or royal decrees which, having the force of law, elaborated parliamentary statutes or applied to the colonies established English legal principles in cases where Parliament had not provided specific legislation.

The Privy Council did its work as a committee of the whole, assum-

[11] See again E. B. Greene, *Provincial America*, chapters 11–13.

ing special names for particular business. Thus it acted as a committee for plantation affairs when it disallowed or approved colonial laws and as a separate committee for hearing appeals from the colonial courts. When it received a petition or complaint it called upon the appropriate executive department for a recommendation, which as a rule it ratified offhand, although in rare instances such "representations" were ignored. Generally speaking it was merely a registering, not a deliberative, body.[12]

Apart from special agents in America who served under the executive departments—collectors of customs, naval clerks, commanders of naval vessels, etc.—the Crown made its will effective through a group of officials whom it placed over each royal colony. Such were the governor, the councillors, the secretary, the attorney-general, the receiver-general, the surveyor-general, and the justices of the supreme court. The appointment of these officials gave England great control over the executive and judicial branches of the colonial governments—a fact that explains in part why Virginia was made a royal province in 1624, New Hampshire in 1679, New York in 1685, Massachusetts in 1691, New Jersey in 1702, the Carolinas in 1719–29, and Georgia in 1751. Only Pennsylvania-Delaware and Maryland survived as proprietary governments in which a proprietor exercised the appointive powers, but inasmuch as the proprietors were bound to enforce parliamentary statutes and were restrained from approving any colonial acts contrary to English law, their governments functioned very much like those of royal provinces. Connecticut and Rhode Island retained their early privilege of electing their governors and lesser officials and hence exercised more autonomy than any of the other thirteen colonies.[13]

Each royal governor received both a commission approved by the Privy Council which vested in him the general powers of his office and a long set of instructions which recited in minute detail what acts he should perform or shun. Though legally such instructions were "private orders of the king," they "were in fact a composite draft, showing the handiwork of nearly every prominent official who had to do with the colonies" (Andrews). As the guardian of all English interests in his colony the royal governor also received numerous letters, special instructions, and orders from the various executive departments. Generally the temper of such executive control was ultra-conservative. British officials high and low frowned upon innovations, adhered to the

[12] The detailed, scholarly work of Edward Raymond Turner, *The Privy Council of England in the Seventeenth and Eighteenth Centuries* (Baltimore, 1927, 1928), is best suited to the advanced student.

[13] C. M. Andrews, *Connecticut and the British Government* (New Haven, 1933—Connecticut Tercentenary Commission, no. 1.).

same policies decade after decade, and viewed the colonies as tributary to all groups in England which had an economic stake in America.

THE COLONIAL ADMINISTRATION AT WORK

Because the principal executive departments acted more or less in isolation and because they regarded the colonies as a side issue, some machinery was necessary to keep the latter under constant surveillance and to draw together the many threads of imperial administration. After 1696 this task fell to the Board of Trade—a commission of eight active and eight honorary members charged with the duty of making the colonies profitable to England and of assuring that their trade show a balance in her favor. As ardent mercantilists the eight active members (representatives of the English merchants) performed the actual work of the Board, often meeting as frequently as four times a week. They drafted the commissions and instructions of the royal governors, examined applicants for posts in the colonial service and recommended appointments, heard complaints from the colonies, conducted investigations, gave information and advice to the executive departments, to Parliament, and to the Privy Council, and drafted decrees, letters, and statutes. After considering colonial laws they recommended to the Privy Council that such acts be approved or disallowed; they corresponded regularly with the colonial governors, receiving official reports and transmitting special instructions; and they kept a library of newspapers, statutes, customs records, maps, documents, legislative proceedings, and treaties—the most extensive collection of material pertaining to the colonies.[14]

The personnel of the Board (a secretary, a dozen or more clerks, and after 1718 a special legal adviser) acted in a systematic manner. As a rule matters were placed before the Board by English merchants, by executive departments, by colonial governors, by Parliament, or by petitioners in the colonies. Thereupon the Board assembled pertinent information from interviews with interested parties, from colonial officials and from other government offices; then after securing legal counsel it framed a representation which urged that either Parliament, the Privy Council, or one of the executive departments take a recommended action. If the proper authority complied the Board informed the colony of the decision and endeavored to put it into effect. Quite obviously the Board did not have the power of decision; it was merely an investigating and advisory body. But inasmuch as of all agencies in

[14] Oliver M. Dickerson, *American Colonial Government, 1696–1765* (Cleveland, 1912), is the standard work on the Board of Trade.

England it possessed the most knowledge of the colonies its recommendations were generally approved—except when they called for sizable outlays of money.[15]

The history of the Board of Trade exhibits four well-marked phases. Between 1696 and 1725 it met regularly, considered a vast amount of business, and labored diligently to make the colonies subordinate to England, particularly by placing them under royal governors. During the next period, 1725–48, the Board became a prey of politics; indifferent members were appointed who were interested chiefly in their salaries (£1,000 a year); hence indolence and inefficiency were the rule. A revival occurred in 1748 when the Earl of Halifax assumed the presidency and endeavored to elevate the Board to the rank of an effective, independent department of state. However, after his retirement in 1761 a relapse ensued and the Board grew increasingly feeble until it expired in 1784.

The power of the Privy Council and the Board of Trade to approve or disallow colonial laws was gradually extended until after 1730 it applied to all the colonies except Connecticut and Rhode Island. A colonial act might be disallowed on the ground that it was contrary to a parliamentary statute, to the common law, to a colonial charter, or to a governor's instructions. A careful examination of the act in question usually preceded the exercise of the royal disallowance and even then the latter was used sparingly: of 8,563 colonial laws only 469 are recorded as disallowed. The scaling down of debts, the inflating of colonial currency, discrimination against English trade and shipping, the fostering of colonial manufactures, the injuring of other colonies, the usurpation of the powers of the royal governors, and encroachments upon the rights of minority groups—such were the measures denied to the colonial legislatures by the royal disallowance.[16]

The complexity of English administration and the lack of integration among the executive departments aggravated the inherently difficult task of governing settlements three thousand miles away. Despite the numerous activities of the Board of Trade it never became a fully effective colonial office, primarily because it lacked the authority to decide and to enforce. "The Lords of Trade," said Governor Belcher of Massachusetts, "are not very mighty lords; nor are they able to administer life or death," while Governor Pownall remarked that "even the

[15] Mary P. Clarke, "The Board of Trade at Work," *American Historical Review*, XVII (Oct. 1911).

[16] An excellent survey is Elmer B. Russell, *The Review of American Colonial Legislation by the King in Council* (New York, 1915). The best brief discussion is C. M. Andrews, "The Royal Disallowance," *Proceedings*, American Antiquarian Society, N. S. XXIV (Oct. 1914).

meanest . . . officers in the plantations looking up solely to the *giving power*, will scarce correspond with the *directing;* nay, may perhaps make court to the one by passing over the other." Similarly, the division of authority among several agencies often resulted in confusion: as the Earl of Shelburne put it in 1763: "it frequently happened that contradictory orders were given by different officers on the same points, and more frequently in affairs of difficulty and delicacy no orders were given at all, the responsibility of both officers being set aside by each having it in his power to throw the blame on the other." As early as 1721 the Board of Trade complained that too many agencies had to do with the colonies, "from whence it happens that no one office is thoroughly informed of all matters relating to the plantations, and sometimes orders are obtained, by surprise, disadvantageous to your Majesty's service."

Another weakness marred the Board of Trade: of all its members none had ever resided in the colonies; accordingly they did not share the American outlook or possess first-hand knowledge of conditions in the colonies. In 1701 William Penn suggested that former governors be appointed to the Board, arguing that they would "supply the rest with that knowledge their experience has given them, that they who have never been in those parts of the world, cannot, though otherwise oracles, comparably understand." The Board, it is true, endeavored to overcome its lack of American experience by consulting persons who had lived in the colonies or who were authorized to present the colonial point of view.[17] To this end most of the colonies maintained agents in London to look after their interests at Whitehall. Such a colonial agent, somewhat comparable to a lobbyist, was appointed, paid, and instructed by the assembly to answer complaints, to protest against unwanted measures and in general to make known colonial desires. "In and out of the colonial offices he passed, encountering the armies of clerks, minor officials, and members of committees, attending hearings in the hope of furthering the interests of the colonies, keeping a watchful eye on bills and debates in Parliament, writing voluminous letters to his lawyers, and to his American correspondents."[18] Although the Board of Trade almost invariably consulted these colonial agents when framing a policy, even so the bulk of its information came from British merchants and royal officials; consequently the Board generally saw things through British eyes and acted without sufficient regard for

[17] James J. Burns, *The Colonial Agents of New England* (Washington, 1935); E. P. Tanner, "Colonial Agencies in England during the Eighteenth Century," *Political Science Quarterly*, XVI (March 1901).

[18] M. Appleton, "Richard Partridge: Colonial Agent," *New England Quarterly*, V (April 1932).

colonial interests. Many agents like Jeremiah Dummer (Massachusetts), Richard Partridge (Rhode Island), and Benjamin Franklin exerted much influence, yet at best they could only protest and retard action; in matters of primary importance interested groups in England usually had their way.[19]

Not all the policies recommended by the Board of Trade were officially adopted. Occasionally it ran against vested interests, as in its campaign to vacate the colonial charters it encountered the opposition not only of proprietary families like the Penns and the Calverts but also of the great English chartered companies which feared that the attack upon the colonial charters might also spread to them. Again, many of the plans urged by the Board (particularly with reference to colonial defense), called for large expenditures which neither Parliament nor the Treasury would authorize. In such cases the Board might appeal to the colonial assemblies for funds, but the latter felt perfectly free to ignore such requests. In fact, the unwillingness of Britain to spend money on the colonies was the primary cause of inefficient administration.

In 1721 the Board of Trade presented a plan for more effective imperial control. It proposed that all the colonies be converted into royal provinces to be ruled by a single governor-general who would be represented in each colony by a deputy-governor. The governor-general should be subordinate to the Board of Trade, which in turn should be converted into a first-class executive department with full powers of decision and action. However, it was not until Halifax became president of the Board that any reforms were made. Then in 1752 it received the right to appoint the colonial governors and to receive all their ordinary correspondence. But the Board lost the appointing power in 1761 and control over colonial correspondence in 1766.[20]

A final gesture toward effective administration was made in 1768 when the Crown created the office of Secretary of State for the Colonies. Probably designed as an independent department coördinate with the other great executive branches, this office failed to bear its intended fruit, for three reasons. First, the colonies had been so long habituated to lax administrative methods that they could not now be subjected to rigorous control. Second, the colonial secretaries were chosen for political reasons, not because they were especially qualified. Finally, the powers of the new secretary were not sharply defined, nor was his

[19] B. W. Bond, "The Colonial Agent as a Popular Representative," *Political Science Quarterly*, XXXV (Sept. 1920).

[20] A. H. Basye, *The Lords Commissioners of Trade and Plantations* (New Haven, 1925), is the best survey of the later history of the Board of Trade (1748–1782).

relationship to other officials made sufficiently clear, with the result that even during the Revolutionary crisis the colonial administration faltered as ministers debated whether the Colonial Secretary was merely the head of the Board of Trade or whether he had full jurisdiction over the colonies as an official coördinate with the other secretaries of state.[21]

Conditions in the colonial civil service also contributed to the ineffectiveness of imperial control. All sorts of considerations dictated colonial appointments: bribery, party politics, friendship, family relationship—nearly anything except merit. No civil service tests existed; training for colonial administration was unknown. Appointments that paid past personal or party debts implied that appointees need not slave at their work, else where was the reward? Hence it was deemed proper for an officeholder to draw his salary and enjoy life in England while a deputy performed his duties in America. And since such deputies received but a pittance from their principals they were forced to accept bribes in order to piece out a living. Of bribery in the customs service Governor Bernard of Massachusetts observed in 1764 that "if conniving at foreign sugars and molasses and Portugal wines and fruits be reckoned corruption, there never was, I believe, an uncorrupt customs house officer in America until within twelve months." Inadequate compensation made it difficult to obtain competent men to occupy subordinate posts; some deputies could not prepare an intelligible report. Far removed from effective supervision many an agent found it easier to live well by complying with colonial wishes than to undergo poverty for the sake of duty. And why not, when bribery, corruption, and favoritism were the accepted means by which the Whig statesmen manipulated Parliament itself? Even well-paid and conscientious colonial officials were often rendered ineffectual—thwarted by colonial opposition. Such resistance encountered by colonial governors and judges sheds additional light upon the weakness of imperial administration.[22]

Royal Governors versus Colonial Assemblies

Fundamentally the antagonism between the colonists and royal officials in America arose from differences of economic interest—because the merchants and other groups in England, through Parliament and the Crown, strove to direct colonial development and to utilize colonial resources for their own profit, whereas the colonists stubbornly resisted such exploitation. And since each side had to rely upon government

---

[21] A. H. Basye, "The Secretary of State for the Colonies, 1768–1782," *American Historical Review*, XXVIII (Oct. 1922).

[22] See again J. T. Adams, *Revolutionary New England*, chapters 1–2.

in America to promote its interests, the struggle for control increased with the growing productivity of the colonies. Who should own land? In whose interest should commerce and industry be regulated? By whom should taxes be paid? Who should provide for defense? And who should have the final word about currency and debts? English groups depended upon the royal governors and other officials; the colonists resisted through their elected assemblies. The ensuing contest seemed on the surface to range the assemblies against the king, but back of the king stood Parliament and behind it the English merchants, while behind the assemblies stood the colonial farmers, planters, and merchants.

In a rough way the three branches of colonial government resembled those of England: the royal governor occupied the place of the king, the governor's council that of the House of Lords, and the elected assembly that of the House of Commons. As in English politics the House of Commons became the center of gravity, so also the colonial assemblies strove for supremacy over the royal governors. England, on the other hand, sought to maintain her executive power over the colonies unimpaired and therefore insisted that the governor exercise those powers of which the king, as ruler of England proper, had been deprived. However, colonial leaders, familiar with the fight made by Parliament against the king, claimed its victories for their own assemblies. Thus an English official, Robert Quary, observed in 1703 that the Virginia legislature insisted that it was "entitled to all the rights and privileges of an English Parliament." Obviously, if the colonists made good this claim their assemblies would come to dominate the royal governors in the same manner that Parliament had triumped over the king.[23]

By 1700 the colonial assembly had won two privileges of the utmost importance: the right to assent to laws and taxes and the right to initiate legislation; hence it could make its demands known and refuse to grant money for the support of government unless they were met. Moreover, the colonists had learned what the English House of Commons had discovered long before: that the executive might nullify parliamentary privileges by manipulating the legislature and that many other liberties were necessary in order to ward off such executive encroachments. First, the members of the legislature must enjoy freedom of debate, the privilege of electing their speaker, and the right to frame their course of action. Secondly, the executive must not determine the membership

[23] Frederic A. Ogg, *Builders of the Republic* (*Pageant of America*, VIII, New Haven, 1927), chapter 1.

of the elected house. In case of disputes arising from elections the members themselves should decide which contestant had the better title; otherwise the executive might manipulate elections in such a way as to pack the house with his own partisans. Nor should any officeholder appointed by the king occupy a seat in the House of Commons. So also elections should be held at prescribed intervals, lest the king keep in office indefinitely a set of members friendly to himself. Thirdly, the sessions of the legislature should be held independently of the sovereign's will. The members should assemble frequently and their meetings should not be adjourned, prorogued, or dissolved except with their consent. Finally, in cases of acute conflict between the legislature and the executive, the latter should give way. Such were the powers and rights which the English House of Commons had won from the sovereign by 1710 and to which the colonial assemblies laid claim during the eighteenth century.[24]

That the assemblies enjoyed a few parliamentary privileges England conceded without protest. Thus when contests over seats arose from elections the assemblies were allowed to decide the issue. Occasionally royal governors attempted to usurp this power, but the assemblies stood firm and successfully asserted their rights. One such contest drew from the Board of Trade an instruction to Lord Cornbury, governor of New Jersey, that he would "do well to leave the determination about elections of representatives to that house, and not to intermeddle therein." Similarly, England did not deprive the assemblies of the privilege of free discussion or the right to choose their own mode of procedure. And as a rule the assemblies met frequently (at least once a year, with a few exceptions); in fact the Massachusetts charter of 1691 definitely provided for annual elections and sessions at fixed dates. The possession of such privileges gave color to the colonial contention that the assembly was in effect a miniature House of Commons. That, however, English officials would not admit; they insisted instead that the colonial governments resembled municipal corporations and that the legal position of the assembly was akin to a municipal council, entirely subordinate to the powers of Parliament.[25]

Accordingly Britain denied to the assemblies certain rights which Parliament exercised openly after 1688. Inspired by the English Triennial Act of 1694 the assemblies periodically passed laws which required

[24] Mary P. Clarke, "Parliamentary Privilege in the American Colonies," in *Essays in Colonial History Presented to C. M. Andrews.*

[25] Attention is again called to H. L. Osgood, *The American Colonies in the Eighteenth Century;* each of its four volumes contains lengthy discussions of imperial administration and local politics.

that new elections be held every two, three, or five years. This issue arose in New York, the Carolinas, New Hampshire, and Virginia when the long continuance in office of representatives friendly to the governor made the assemblies unresponsive to colonial needs; as the New York assemblymen put it in 1737: "in some counties even their very representatives have become their greatest grievance." The British government, however, insisted that the power of calling new elections belonged to the royal governors; consequently they were instructed to veto all triennial acts, and whenever such measures were approved by governors they were disallowed by the Privy Council. Governor Montgomerie of New Jersey explained the secret of Britain's attitude when he said that his predecessors "could not have carried on the public business so quietly and successfully as they did, if they had been obliged to call a new assembly every three years."

The colonists also endeavored to put into effect a clause in the English Act of Settlement of 1701 which excluded officeholders appointed by the king from membership in the House of Commons. In 1713 Governor Spotswood of Virginia demonstrated the need for such legislation when he secured the passage of an act which created forty new offices, each with a large yearly stipend, explaining that he would distribute them among the burgesses and thereby control their votes. Since similar practices prevailed in Massachusetts, South Carolina, Maryland, and New York the assemblies of those colonies enacted laws at various times providing that appointees of the governor should not hold seats in the elected house. Opposing such measures as an infringement upon the governor's appointing power, Britain even went so far in 1770 as to disallow a New York act which excluded royal judges from the assembly.[26]

Most conflicts between governor and assembly involved privileges which Parliament exercised in fact although actions were performed in the name of the king. For instance: the early power of the king to reject speakers elected by the House of Commons became after 1688 a matter of mere form as the king automatically ratified the action of the house. In the colonies the royal governors endeavored to make this power really effective by rejecting as well as approving the speakers chosen by the assembly, whereas the colonists insisted that the governor, like the king, should simply register approval. The governors' instructions generally conferred the power both to reject and to approve. A contest on this issue went against the assembly in New Hampshire, and when the Massachusetts House of Representatives successfully defied

[26] See again W. Roy Smith, *South Carolina as a Royal Province* (section 2, on government).

two governors a clause was inserted in a supplementary charter of 1725 which definitely vested the governor with the power in question.

Before 1688 the king created new electoral districts in England and determined the number of representatives for each; after 1688, however, this power was never exercised and eventually it was assumed by Parliament itself. So also the colonial assemblies claimed the right to erect new electoral districts and to apportion seats; contrariwise, English officials asserted that the governor's right to issue writs to the sheriffs calling for new elections conferred the power to determine representation—to which the colonists objected that such power enabled the governor to give undue weight to districts favorable to the Crown. When the North Carolina Assembly forced a governor to yield on this issue its law governing representation was disallowed; in New Hampshire the assembly was defeated by the governor. In 1767 the Crown instructed all the royal governors not to sign "any law . . . by which the number of the assembly shall be enlarged or diminished." [27]

In the political struggles of seventeenth-century England the king had possessed great influence over Parliament by virtue of his control over its meetings. His power of prorogation enabled him to end a session; his power of dissolution allowed him to terminate the life of a particular Parliament, whereupon a new election had to be held. Although these powers continued to be exercised after 1688 in the king's name, in fact the decisions were made by Parliament itself. As the representative of the king in the colonies the royal governor was authorized by his commission to prorogue and dissolve the assembly. The power of prorogation (the governor could prorogue to any time or place) was used to bring refractory delegates to terms or to delay action when passions ran high. On the other hand the governor exercised the right of dissolution when, utterly at odds with an assembly, he hoped to secure a more tractable house through another election. However, as the antagonisms between England and the colonies deepened before 1775 dissolution lost its effectiveness because a new assembly was generally as hostile as the old. The frequent use of the power of dissolution after 1763 indicated a revolutionary crisis, just as the dissolution of Parliament by Charles I in 1629 and by Charles II in 1681 foreshadowed the English Revolutions of 1642 and 1688.

As a part of the colonial legislature the governor possessed the right to propose legislation desired by groups in England. But since his recommendations, when contrary to colonial interests, were generally ineffective, he was obliged to exert his legislative influence through the

[27] E. B. Greene, *The Provincial Governor* . . . (Cambridge, 1898), is a standard study of the constitutional relations between England and the colonies.

veto power, with which he was vested by the king's commission "to the end that nothing may be passed or done . . . to the prejudice of us, our heirs and successors." Unlike the modern American veto, that of the royal governor was final: a bill could not be passed over his negative by a special vote of the legislature. His instructions told him what sort of bills to oppose; in general they were the kind to which the royal disallowance was applied. If, contrary to his instructions, he failed to veto an important bill his disobedience might cost him his office or work a forefeiture of his bond. A compromise between the veto and the royal disallowance was the suspending clause which provided that a doubtful act should not go into effect until the king's approval had been given. Just as Parliament deprived the sovereign of the veto power in 1707 so also the colonial assemblies resorted to many ingenious devices in order to nullify the power of the royal governors.[28]

Of the privileges enjoyed by Parliament after 1688 three—free discussion, the determination of contests for seats, and control over procedure—were accorded to the colonial assemblies. Two powers which Parliament made effective by statute—the regulation of elections and the exclusion of royal appointees from the elected house—were denied to the colonies, while five other functions which the king did not in fact perform in England after 1707—the rejection of the speaker, prorogation, dissolution, the creation of new electoral areas, and the veto—remained a part of the royal prerogative in America. But even so the governors' power over the colonial assemblies was not absolute because they possessed the same weapon that Parliament had used to wrest concessions from the king—the right to levy taxes and to grant supplies.

The instructions of the royal governor stated the salary to which he was entitled and enjoined him from receiving other emoluments from the colony. However, except in the case of Georgia (where the Crown paid the salaries of executive officials), the governor had to depend upon colonial revenues for his means of support. And only in two colonies did there exist a permanent fund for this purpose: in Virginia, the revenues from the 2s. tax per hogshead on tobacco exported; in North Carolina, the uncertain quit-rents. The governors of New York, New Jersey, Massachusetts, South Carolina, and New Hampshire, on the other hand, had to rely for their income upon temporary grants from the assembly—a dependence which enabled the assembly to coerce the governor by withholding his salary until he had assented to measures which it desired. By this method the governor could be forced to

[28] Leonard W. Labaree, *Royal Government in America* (New Haven, 1930), is an outstanding study of British colonial policy as revealed in the workings of imperial administration.

violate instructions that directed him to veto designated bills. And in order to keep the governor permanently in a state of subordination these five assemblies habitually limited the salary grants to a single year. Of the representatives of New York it was remarked in 1741 "that if a governor will not blindly consent to their bills, however unreasonable or contrary to instructions, they will starve him into compliance." [29]

Endeavoring to break this financial power of the assembly the Crown as early as 1703 instructed the governors to secure permanent appropriations for the salaries of all executive officials. But since the assemblies understood the issue perfectly they steadfastly refused to comply. After a long contest in New York, 1710–15, Governor Hunter surrendered and accepted the principle of the annual grant. A similar controversy occurred in Massachusetts during the term of Governor Burnet (1728–29), whose predecessors had labored in vain to place the salary on a permanent basis. Citing the practice of Parliament in granting the king a fixed income for the duration of his reign, Burnet insisted that the governor should enjoy a similar privilege; otherwise he would be a mere creature of the assembly. The latter rejected the analogy: unlike the king, the royal governor was generally a stranger serving a brief term who had little personal interest in the province; only his financial dependence on the assembly gave assurance of his good conduct. Since Burnet would not accept a grant for a single year he had to finance himself during his short stay in office. His successor, Jonathan Belcher (1730–41), yielded to the assembly. Even the Board of Trade later admitted the hopelessness of its case when in 1755 it ordered the governor of New York to accept temporary grants without further protest.

Not content with reducing upon the governors' legislative power, the assemblies, like the House of Commons, used their control over the purse to usurp many executive functions, insisting that certain conditions be met before appropriation bills were sanctioned. Thus the assemblies extended their sway over financial matters by stating in detail how money was to be spent, by appointing provincial treasurers (except in New Hampshire, New Jersey, and Georgia), by naming collectors of the revenues levied by the colonies (as distinct from Crown revenues), and by setting up committees to supervise the spending of money appropriated.[30] Similarly the assemblies usurped much

[29] See again E. Channing, *History of the United States*, Vol. II, pp. 282–366.

[30] For a detailed study of party organization and legislative committees see Ralph V. Harlow, *The History of Legislative Methods in the Period before 1825* (New Haven, 1917), chapters 1–3.

of the governor's power over Indian affairs by appointing their own agents to transact such business. In the military sphere the governor's power as commander of the colony's armed forces was controlled in various ways: appropriation acts dictated when and where troops were to be used; legislative committees took charge of the management of military operations; and the assemblies determined appointments by withholding officers' pay. All these powers of the legislature issued from the primary power of taxation as asserted by the Massachusetts assembly in 1692: "no aid, tax . . . or imposition whatsoever" shall be "levied on any of their majesties' subjects or estates, but by the act and consent of the governor, council and representatives of the people assembled in general court."

To the colonists the outcome was pleasant indeed; the people's money, declared a Pennsylvania publication of 1759, "is never so well disposed of as in the . . . purchase of good laws." When colonial autonomy was at stake it mattered little that the assembly's power over the purse resulted in coercion and even bribery and that it placed the governors in an intolerable situation by making them responsible to two hostile parties—to British officials who issued their instructions and to colonial legislators who appropriated money. If the governor was a corruptionist like Fletcher or Cornbury he could get a good price for violating the king's orders; if, like Burnet, he was uncompromisingly faithful to the king he usually ran afoul of the assembly and accomplished little. Even the most effective administrators (from Britain's point of view)—honest, tactful, and able men like Hunter, Spotswood, and Shirley had to make many concessions contrary to their instructions.[31] All which explains the steady growth of the assembly's powers —a trend particularly marked during the years of war, 1744–63. Of Massachusetts the Board of Trade observed in 1757: "Almost every act of executive and legislative power, whether it be political, judicial or military, is ordered and directed by votes and resolves of the general court, in most cases originating in the house of representatives." The Privy Council complained in 1745 that the assembly of New York had assumed control of practically the entire executive branch of the government; of South Carolina Governor Glen remarked in 1748 that "the people have the whole of the administration in their hands"; while Governor Lewis Morris said of New Jersey that there was a strong "inclination . . . in the meanest of the people (who are the

---

[31] Outstanding studies of colonial governors are Alice M. Keyes, *Cadwalader Colden* (New York, 1906); George A. Wood, *William Shirley* (New York, 1920); Leonidas Dodson, *Alexander Spotswood;* Everett Kimball, *Public Life of Joseph Dudley.*

majority and whose votes make the assembly) to have the sole direction of all the affairs of the government."

The extension of the influence of the assemblies over the royal governors magnified the importance of the courts as the last line of defense for Britain's interests in America. Not only did the trial and punishment of violators of British laws determine the effectiveness of colonial administration; all rules for individual cases could not be prescribed in detail by a general statute; hence many decisions had to be left to the discretion of judges. But the manner in which judges decided doubtful points of law and evidence determined whether British policies were to be actually enforced or ignored. For these reasons both Britain and the colonists desired to dominate the courts.[32]

The English theory of law, derived from the Middle Ages, defined the king as the fountain of justice. Accordingly, he appointed the judges, established courts, and prosecuted criminals on the assumption that crime was a breach of "the king's peace" and an affront to his dignity. English history, however, had demonstrated before 1688 that judges are human beings, swayed by their associates and superiors and that the king's power of appointment often placed justices in office who merely registered his desires. Accordingly, Parliament in 1701 endeavored to make the judges independent by depriving the king of his power to remove them at will so that he might pack the courts with his satellites.

The earlier principle of the king's control of justice was extended to the colonies before the Revolution of 1688. The royal governors, as agents of the king, were commissioned to erect courts and to appoint the judges—both the local justices of the peace (who were also judges of the county courts) and the justices of the superior courts of appeal. Moreover, the governor and council served as the highest appellate court within a colony—not in criminal cases but in civil suits involving sums in excess of £50, £100, or £300. Final appeals in both civil and criminal cases could be made to the Privy Council. Acting under orders from the governor, the attorney-general of a royal colony prosecuted cases for the king in the higher courts.[33]

Four major issues arose in the contest between the assemblies and Britain over the control of colonial justice. One question was: should the governor or the legislature erect the necessary courts? During the

---

[32] George A. Washburne's *Imperial Control of the Administration of Justice in the Thirteen American Colonies, 1684–1776* (New York, 1923) is the most complete study of this theme.

[33] A. M. Schlesinger, "Colonial Appeals to the Privy Council," *Political Science Quarterly*, XXVIII (June and Sept. 1913).

early colonial period the assemblies had exercised this power and thereafter they insisted that the governor could not act alone. Although a
few special courts were created by executive order, the assemblies
generally made good their contention; hence the main judicial structure of the colonies rested upon laws to which they had given their consent.

A second controversy involved the jurisdiction of the courts. The
colonists generally desired to make the county courts supreme, partly
because the judges were neighbors of suitors and therefore inclined to
favor them in contests with outsiders, partly because local justice saved
the expense of travel to courts far away. For opposite reasons British
merchants and landlords desired to enlarge the powers of the central or
superior courts—to grant to them original jurisdiction in order to save
the cost of attending numerous county courts and to widen their appellate jurisdiction as a means of protection against decisions influenced
by local pressures. In this controversy the British government favored
the central courts and therefore consistently disallowed colonial acts
which extended the jurisdiction of the county courts.[34]

The appointment and removal of judges occasioned the third—and
most active—conflict. The tendency of British policy was to give the
governor the power to dismiss judges at will, thus enabling him to appoint new men who were properly respectful of British interests.
Claiming the same power that Parliament had exercised in 1701—that
of protecting judges against summary dismissal at the mere pleasure of
the executive—the assemblies of New York, Pennsylvania, and North
Carolina passed bills between 1759 and 1761 which provided that
judges should hold office during good behavior. Such measures, however, were either vetoed by the governor or disallowed; and in 1761
general instructions sent to all the governors ordered that they veto any
acts which regulated judicial tenure and that, when appointing new
judges, they reserve the executive's right to dismiss them at his pleasure.

Even then, however, the assembly was not helpless: if a governor
removed colonially minded judges and appointed unpopular successors
it might withhold their salaries, force them to resign, and compel him
to respect its desires. Once again the assemblies claimed a power exercised by Parliament after 1688; once more the Board of Trade objected, arguing that to grant permanent tenure to judges would "lessen
that just dependence which the colonies ought to have upon the government of the mother country."

During the colonial period only a few cases were appealed from

[34] O. P. Chitwood, *Justice in Colonial Virginia* (Baltimore, 1905), is a lucid
analysis, for the advanced student.

American courts to the Privy Council; hence that phase of judicial control did not seriously antagonize the colonists. The rules governing such appeals had a restraining effect: in case an appellant failed to secure a reversal of a colonial decision he was obliged to bear the expense of the appeal and to pay any damages incurred by the appellee. The cost of transporting witnesses to England, the delays involved, and the uncertainty of the outcome deterred such appeals except when a litigant had a strong sense of the justice of his cause.[35]

In the administration of the colonies prior to 1763 British officials adopted two contradictory policies: they conceded to the assembly the right to vote taxes and to make appropriations but they also denied that it possessed the status and the other privileges of the English House of Commons. The colonies, however, tended to duplicate English experience in that the elected house used its control over the purse in order to establish its supremacy over the executive; hence it became evident that its financial power conflicted with the theory that it was an inferior body. Two alternatives therefore confronted British officials: they might limit the financial independence of the assembly, or they might acknowledge that as the master of the governor it was in effect supreme. When, after 1763, they chose the first alternative they forced the political issue of the Revolutionary War.

[35] H. D. Hazeltine, "Appeals from Colonial Courts to the King in Council," *Report*, American Historical Association, 1894.

BIBLIOGRAPHICAL NOTE

SECONDARY WORKS: Basil Williams, *Carteret and Newcastle* (Cambridge, Eng., 1943), contrasts the characters and careers of two British leaders. Dora M. Clark, *The Rise of the British Treasury* (New Haven, 1960), a study of first-rate importance, traces the growing power of the Treasury in colonial affairs and shows its potent influence on the decisions that led to the Revolution. Margaret M. Spector, *The American Department of the British Government* (New York, 1940), is the standard work on the functioning of the office of Secretary of State for the Colonies. Joseph Henry Smith, *Appeals to the Privy Council from the American Plantations* (New York, 1950), is an intensive, thorough, definitive treatise. Ella Lonn, *The Colonial Agents of the Southern Colonies* (Chapel Hill, 1945), and Edward P. Lilly, *The Colonial Agents of New York and New Jersey* (Washington, 1936), are scholarly monographs. Two careful biographical studies by John A. Schutz, *Thomas Pownall* (Glendale, Calif., 1951), and *William Shirley* (Chapel Hill, 1961), throw much light on British colonial administration. W. W. Abbot, *The Royal Governors of Georgia, 1754–1775* (Chapel Hill, 1959), illustrates imperial rule as it operated through an executive department.

Chilton Williamson, *American Suffrage from Property to Democracy* (Princeton, 1960), an important study, summarizes qualifications for voting in the late colonial era. Mary P. Clarke, *Parliamentary Privilege in the American Colonies*

(New Haven, 1943), an excellent monograph, describes the efforts of the assemblies to gain and retain rights and privileges.

Robert E. Brown, *Middle-Class Democracy and the Revolution in Massachusetts, 1691–1780* (Ithaca, 1955), an outstanding book, demonstrates the strength of democracy in the Bay colony. Charles S. Grant, *Democracy in the Connecticut Frontier Town of Kent* (New York, 1961), reveals a transition from pioneer democracy to social differentiation. Donald L. Kemmerer, *Path to Freedom* (Princeton, 1940), is the leading study of political trends in New Jersey as a royal province. Richard P. McCormick, *The History of Voting in New Jersey* [1664–1911] (New Brunswick, 1953), shows the workings of a modified democracy during the colonial age. Theodore Thayer, *Pennsylvania Politics and the Growth of Democracy, 1740–1776* (Harrisburg, 1954), is a competent study of political issues and conflicts. Roy N. Lokken, *David Lloyd, Colonial Lawmaker* (Seattle, 1959), portrays a Pennsylvania defender of local interests and legislative power. *Gentlemen Freeholders* by Charles S. Sydnor (Chapel Hill, 1952), is an essay on the arts of practical politics in Virginia.

STUDIES USEFUL TO THE SPECIAL STUDENT: Among detailed, technical studies the following are useful to the special student: Arthur G. Dorland, "The Royal Disallowance in Massachusetts" (Kingston, Ontario, 1917); Edgar J. Fisher, *New Jersey as a Royal Province, 1738–1776* (New York, 1911); Percy S. Flippin, *The Financial Administration of . . . Virginia* (Baltimore, 1915); William H. Fry, *New Hampshire as a Royal Province* (New York, 1908); Charles L. Raper, *North Carolina, A Study in English Colonial Government* (New York, 1904); Charles W. Spencer, *Phases of Royal Government in New York, 1691–1719* (Columbus, 1905); Henry R. Spencer, *Constitutional Conflict in Provincial Massachusetts* (Columbus, 1905); David D. Wallace, *Constitutional History of South Carolina from 1725 to 1775* (Abbeville, S.C., 1899).

SOURCES: Orders in council on important issues are contained in *Acts of the Privy Council of England, Colonial Series* (ed. W. L. Grant and James Munro, 6 vols., Hereford, 1908–12). The orders are arranged chronologically, for the period 1613–1783. A most important collection. Another highly important collection is Leo F. Stock's edition of the *Proceedings and Debates of the British Parliaments respecting North America* (3 vols., Washington, 1924–30). *Royal Instructions to British Colonial Governors* (ed. by L. W. Labaree, 2 vols., New York) is also of primary value. A political classic, Jeremiah Dummer's *A Defense of the New England Charters* [1721] is reprinted in Vol. I of J. Almon, *A Collection of the Most Interesting Tracts . . . on the . . . American Colonies . . .* (2 vols., London, 1766). Thomas Pownall, *The Administration of the Colonies* (4th ed., London, 1769), discusses constitutional problems of empire in a spirit friendly to the colonies, from the point of view of a colonial governor. Two works which give insight into the problems of a colonial governor are: C. H. Lincoln (ed.), *Correspondence of William Shirley* (2 vols., New York, 1912), and Gertrude S. Kimball (ed.), *The Correspondence of the Colonial Governors of Rhode Island* (2 vols., New York, 1902–03).

XXI

Britain Conquers
New France

THE rivalry between Britain and France for supremacy in North America which continued with full force after 1713 determined the later course of colonial development. While war was in progress Britain had to grant concessions to the colonies as the price of their necessary coöperation; hence she failed to enforce many of the oppressive features of her colonial system. But once she had expelled France from North America she attempted a vigorous enforcement of her imperial policies. Victory, however, came too late; the colonists had become so accustomed to acting as they pleased that they could not then be effectively repressed. In short, the French conflict fostered an American spirit of independence; British success inspired efforts to curb the colonies; and that in turn drove them to revolt.

PEACE AS A PRELUDE TO WAR

After the Peace of Utrecht one sentiment dominated the principal powers of Europe: let there be peace; let the nations recover from the exhaustion of war and seek in industry and commerce the strength to sustain them when the conflict should be renewed. Bitter dynastic hatreds and economic rivalries remained; innumerable points of friction kept Europe in a threatening state of "universal combustion." In the shifting diplomatic alignments of the time three constant factors were at work: the enmity between France and Britain, the intense antagonism between Britain and Spain, and the accord between Spain and France. Once the Hanoverian dynasty had been established in Britain (1714) the Whig statesmen desired at all costs to avoid a general war lest it give the signal for an internal revolution which would put a Catholic Stuart upon the throne—not an imaginary menace, since two uprisings did occur and until 1748 France championed the Stuart cause. To consolidate the gains of Queen Anne's War (which had added £300,000 to Britain's favorable trade balance), to restore commerce with France, always one of Britain's best customers, and to strengthen her grip on colonial trade: such motives lay behind the British desire for peace. "Trade," said Robert Walpole, "is the main riches of the nation and enhances the value of our lands." Dominant in English politics between 1721 and 1739, Walpole labored to keep France and Spain apart, refused to force a war with France, and played one power against another in his effort to prevent a European combination aimed at Britain. Material well-being for the nation was the end which he pursued with easygoing, unruffled assurance, with unwearied patience, and with a cynical disregard for abstractions and ideals. "We have one minister," wrote a contemporary, "that does everything with the same ease and tranquillity as if he were doing nothing." [1]

France too desired nothing so much as an interval of peace. Confronted by Austria on the Continent and by Britain on the seas and ruled now by a boy king (Louis XV was only five when he succeeded his grandfather in 1715) the French willingly joined the concert of Europe to maintain the balance of power and embraced the British policy of peaceful penetration in the colonial sphere. During the regency of Philip, Duke of Orleans (1715–23), who valued peace abroad and pleasure at home, France combined in 1717 with Britain and Holland to form the Triple Alliance which became the Quadruple Alliance when Austria entered in 1718 and the Quintuple Alliance when Spain joined in 1720. By such coöperation the powers maintained the peace of Europe until 1733. [2]

In the meantime America had lost none of its attraction as a source of riches to European investors and speculators; both Britain and France indulged in frenzied financial schemes inspired by the American dream. France had its Mississippi Company, fathered by John Law in 1717, given at first a monopoly of the trade of Louisiana and the beaver trade of Canada and then allowed to absorb other companies until it virtually monopolized the commerce of France. Acting in harmony with Law's companion national bank (which issued France's paper currency), the Mississippi Company took charge of the mint and the collection of the nation's taxes. Britain had its South Sea Company, now holding the assiento and, as rumor affirmed, about to fall heir to the silver mines of Peru. In 1720 Parliament gave this company official sanction by authorizing it to manage the national debt. Both companies promised such fabulous dividends to stockholders that a speculative craze drove the price of shares to ten times their par values; then in 1721 both bubbles burst; stock prices declined to almost nothing and thousands of investors were

---

[1] George R. Sterling Taylor's *Robert Walpole and His Age* (London, 1931) is a well-rounded, readable survey of society and politics.
[2] See again *The Cambridge History of the British Empire*, Vol. I, chapters 11, 15–18.

ruined. In England the crash resulted in placing Walpole in power while Law was forced to leave France. Both episodes demonstrated that schemes of colonial exploitation were now uppermost in the public mind.

The long interval of peace after 1713 did nothing to remove the causes of strife between France and Britain; in fact each nation seized the opportunity to extend its power in America, thereby intensifying instead of allaying the underlying antagonisms.[3] During the 1720's and 1730's the Board of Trade repeatedly recognized the menace of French competition and urged aggressive measures to combat the French influence in Newfoundland and Nova Scotia and on the New York and Carolina frontiers. But since a strong forward policy meant war with France the more drastic recommendations of the Board were ignored by Walpole and his fellow ministers. And because both France and Britain avoided war in order to gain greater strength, peace merely postponed the time of reckoning. The English accused the French of "pushing into an universal commerce as the way of coming at their darling scheme of universal dominion"; in 1740 the Duke of Newcastle declared: "From what I can see France will sooner or later dominate Europe, and perhaps America also."

After 1713 France compensated herself for the loss of Nova Scotia and Newfoundland by erecting Fort Louisbourg on Cape Breton Island. Spending money lavishly upon this stronghold she rapidly made it the most powerful fortress in America. Favored by an Atlantic harbor open during the winter it became the focus of vigorous activities, naval, commercial, and diplomatic, by which France strove to safeguard Canada and to exert a preponderating influence in Nova Scotia, upper New England, and the northern fishery. Moreover, in time of war French privateers from Louisbourg could prey upon the fishing boats and trading vessels of New England, thereby undermining the prosperity of Massachusetts.[4]

Determined to achieve the mastery of the northern fishery the French removed their settlers from Placentia to Cape Breton Island and continued to pursue the codfish so aggressively that their loss of Newfoundland had little effect. Meanwhile, the British fishery at Newfoundland had declined, weakened and disorganized by Queen Anne's War and torn by the rivalries between the resident settlers and the fishermen of western England who desired to conduct the fishery from English ports. In 1718 the Board of Trade estimated

[3] See again G. M. Wrong, *The Rise and Fall of New France*, Vol. II, chapters 24-27.
[4] William Wood, *The Great Fortress* (*Chronicles of Canada* series, Toronto, 1915).

that England's annual income from the Newfoundland fishery had diminished by £314,000 since 1644—a loss attributed to the inefficiency of the fishermen settled on the island; consequently the Board recommended that they be removed to Nova Scotia and that the fishery be carried on exclusively from England. However, the profits of the London merchants who supported the settlers told in the long run and the latter were not removed; instead they became so important that Britain finally accepted the settlement as inevitable and sanctioned it in 1729 by establishing a civil government at the island. Newfoundland proper was not a subject of dispute between Britain and France, but the fishery was; and because by 1740 it yielded Britain between £225,000 and £300,000 annually it was a prize well worth holding against the French.

A more pressing dispute between the two powers involved Nova Scotia, a province which Britain esteemed, not for its fur trade, now shrunk to trifling proportions, but for its forests capable of producing the best of masts and other naval stores and for its fishery, the finest in America. After 1710 Britain allowed the French settlers either to leave or to remain; having neither purchasers for their lands nor vessels in which to leave the Acadians had to stay. The British occupied Annapolis and established there a governor and four companies of fifty soldiers; otherwise the inhabitants of Nova Scotia were French (between 2,500 and 12,000), concentrated in three settlements: one in the south near Annapolis and two in the north near the Basin of Minas and Chignecto Bay. Failing to erect other forts or to bring in non-French settlers, the British allowed the Acadians to retain their property, to adhere to their Roman Catholic faith, and to trade with Cape Breton, Quebec, and France. Nor did Britain exact quit-rents or levy taxes.[5]

France in the meantime, still hoping to control the region, exerted her influence from Louisbourg, whose officials encouraged the Acadians to remain and to adhere to the French interest. The boundary of the province provoked controversy as France contended that she had ceded only the peninsula south of the Bay of Fundy, while the British claimed all the peninsula north to Cape Breton and all the mainland north of the St. Croix River. From the resident Indians (the Micmac and Malecite tribes, closely allied with the Abenakis of Maine—a tribe bitterly hostile to New England) France could count upon unwavering support. The political mentors of the submissive, inarticulate Acadians were Jesuit priests who acted in con-

[5] J. B. Brebner, *New England's Outpost* (New York, 1927), treats the English rule of the Acadians as a political problem.

cert with French officials at Louisbourg to incite the Indians and the settlers against the British with the object of preventing their fishing off the coast. So also the Jesuits instructed the Acadians not to take an oath of loyalty demanded by Britain which would have pledged them to bear arms against their countrymen in Canada. So firm was the resistance on this score that when an oath was finally taken by the Acadians in 1730 it was so ambiguous as to be wholly ineffectual.

The weakness of Britain's rule in Nova Scotia prompted the Board of Trade to call repeatedly for drastic measures. It recommended that the Acadians be removed from the province and replaced by Protestant settlers, that new forts be erected, that four regiments and a warship be added to British defenses, and that a tract of 200,-000 acres of timber land be reserved for the royal navy. But because of the expense involved and the desire of the Whig ministers for peace with France the proposals of the Board were long ignored.[6]

By 1715 land speculation and settlement on the New England frontier had replaced the earlier interest in the fur trade. As the New Englanders advanced up the Kennebec and Penobscot Rivers they encroached upon the hunting lands of the Abenakis, thereby threatening them with extinction. The governor of Canada, promising ammunition and supplies to the Indians if they would drive the English from the eastern frontier, influenced them through Jesuit priests, particularly Père Râle, in charge of a mission at Norridgewock on the Kennebec. In New England Indian missionary work had practically ceased; moreover, the haughty, superior attitude which the New Englanders displayed at the council fire enraged their forest neighbors. In June 1722 the Abenakis, incited by the French, attacked the English settlements on the Kennebec; in July Governor Shute of Massachusetts declared war. Only New Hampshire and Massachusetts participated in the expeditions which proceeded up the Penobscot and Kennebec Rivers, destroyed the Jesuit missions there, killed Père Râle, and drove the Indians inland more than a hundred miles from the coasts of New Hampshire and Maine. So weakened were the Abenakis by Râle's war that eastern New England thereafter was exempt from attack, and settlement moved rapidly toward the interior.[7]

To the west of New England the Anglo-French conflict revolved around the fur trade. After 1713 the French resumed their advance in the Great Lakes country, reoccupying strategic sites previously abandoned and constructing new forts and trading posts. Two routes

[6] See again F. Parkman, *Half-Century of Conflict*, chapters 9–24.

[7] See again J. T. Adams, *Revolutionary New England*, chapters 11–13.

led from Montreal, the metropolis of the fur trade, to the great West. One traversed the Ottawa River and Georgian Bay to the northern end of Lake Huron; there it divided, one branch leading to Sault Ste. Marie and Lake Superior, the other to Michilimackinac and Lake Michigan. On northern Lake Superior the French established a fort, Kaministiquia, which commanded the country adjacent to the northern shore; to the southwest, in Chequagemon Bay, they erected Fort La Pointe which gave access to the upper waters of the Mississippi and also served the traders who frequented the lands of the Chippewa south of Lake Superior. From Michilimackinac the French *voyageurs* entered Green Bay (at the foot of which stood Fort La Baye); thence the route followed the Fox and Wisconsin Rivers to Fort Marin at the junction of the Wisconsin and the Mississippi. Here again the route divided: on the upper waters of the Mississippi were several small forts, while south of Fort Marin the traders paddled down the Mississippi to Fort de Chartres near the French settlements of Cahokia and Kaskaskia in the Illinois country. From Michilimackinac the *voyageurs* also traversed Lake Michigan to its southeastern end, where Fort St. Joseph on the St. Joseph River dominated the surrounding region, and to the southwestern end, where a fort on the Chicago River was the key to the Illinois River route to the Mississippi.[8]

The second and more important route led from Montreal by way of the St. Lawrence and Lake Ontario to the western end of Lake Erie. There the settlement at Detroit commanded the lands of the Ottawa between Lakes Erie and Huron and gave the French control of the southern entrance to Lake Huron as well as a second approach to Lakes Superior and Michigan. The Maumee River, flowing into the western end of Lake Erie, opened the way to the Ohio valley where the French had Fort Miami on the Maumee and forts Quiatanon and Vincennes on the Wabash. It was this lower lakes route which became the scene of Anglo-French rivalry for the interior trade.

The organization of the French fur trade exhibited the common features of early merchant capitalism. Wealthy merchants of Montreal imported from France the trading goods required and sold them on credit to interior traders called *bourgeois* who in turn employed *voyageurs* or *engagés*—men versed in woodcraft and adept in navigating canoes and bargaining with the Indians. The *bourgeois* usually had their *engagés* in debt; moreover they supplied the Indian

[8] See again L. P. Kellogg, *The French Regime in Wisconsin*, chapters 14–20.

on credit, taking in payment the furs with which they in turn paid their debts to their Montreal creditors. In order to reduce the frauds incident to the trade the French government required that the *bourgeois* buy licenses (and at a high price) and submit to the regulations imposed by the commander of the fort in their sphere of operations. Usually a favored company held the exclusive right of buying all furs exported from Canada—a privilege which enabled the company to keep prices at low figures. This monopoly, plus the licensing system, meant that the interior traders could not pay high prices to the Indians, thereby creating an opportunity for English interlopers to cut in by overbidding the French concessionaires.[9]

After 1713 the New York fur trade divided into three branches. The Iroquois continued to bring furs to Albany, encouraged to do so by acts of the New York Assembly, 1714–17; and yet this source of supply steadily decreased until by 1725 only 17 per cent of the furs reaching Albany were brought thither by the Indians. The aggressive advance of the French in the Ohio and Mississippi valleys convinced the more enterprising Albany traders that they too must go directly to the west. By 1716 they were journeying to Lake Ontario in quest of furs; during the 1720's Governor Burnet of New York advocated direct penetration and sent out trading parties each year; in 1725–27 the New Yorkers constructed a post and fort, Oswego, at the mouth of the Onondaga River on Lake Ontario. Fearing that this direct trade would alienate the Iroquois, many of the Albany men opposed it at the start, but it proved such an effective answer to French expansion that by 1725 68 per cent of the furs arriving at Albany were brought in by the western traders. The French met the English advance by erecting a post and fort at Niagara (1716, 1726) to protect their stake in the Ontario region.

Recognizing the fur trade as a grand prize of North America the Board of Trade in 1721 urged that Britain adopt aggressive measures to detach the interior Indians from their alliance with France.[10] British traders should be encouraged to take Indian wives and to live among the tribes; Anglican missions should be established as a counterweight to the Jesuits, who were now regarded as political agents of France; forts should be erected on Lakes Erie and Ontario; the good will of the Indians should be secured by presents and treaties of alliance; the fur trade should be so regulated as to eliminate

[9] See again H. A. Innis, *The Fur Trade in Canada*, pp. 84–192.
[10] See again H. L. Osgood, *American Colonies in the Eighteenth Century*, Vol. III, pp. 363–404, 491–539; Vol. IV, chapters 14–17.

those incessant frauds which angered the Indians; and monopolies should be avoided in order to enable British traders to overbid the French. These elaborate plans, however, were not adopted by the Crown (the expense was too great); hence the only concrete evidence of British advance between 1713 and 1740 was Fort Oswego.

Albany also obtained interior furs through a trade with Montreal made possible by the cheapness of English dry goods—particularly strouds, "a coarse woolen blanketing." Fifteen per cent of the furs entering Albany in 1725 were sent from Montreal in payment for such English merchandise. Although this traffic seemed an easy way of tapping the profits of the French fur trade it was strongly opposed by Governor Burnet and the Albany expansionists on the ground that it did not challenge the French influence among the Indians and that at any time it might be destroyed by France. The New York Assembly therefore passed laws (1720–27) to prohibit the sale of English goods to Canada; however, New York importers and London merchants who supplied the Canadians with traders' goods protested to the Privy Council and in 1729 secured the disallowance of the restraining acts. Nor did the French government suppress this traffic with the ancient enemy.[11]

Although both France and Britain claimed supremacy in the Great Lakes country and demanded that the other withdraw; although the competition of the interior traders of the two nations was sharpened year by year; and although the Board of Trade recommended strong measures against France, nevertheless the rival claims were not pressed to the point of war, largely because the home governments favored peace and economy. Meanwhile the Iroquois were losing their earlier status of middlemen for the English; now, about 1740, many Albany magnates were buying lands from the Six Nations and promoting settlement in the eastern part of the Mohawk valley. Numerous frauds in such land deals estranged the Iroquois from the British cause: in 1744 Governor Colden of New York lamented that the "Indians . . . will on no occasion trust an Albany man."

The progress of the French colony, Louisiana, shaped the relations between Britain and France on the southern frontier.[12] So great were the capital outlays needed for the development of the Mississippi valley that the French government had to offer generous

[11] Peter Wraxall's *An Abridgement of the Indian Affairs . . . transacted in the Colony of New York* [1678–1751] (ed. C. H. McIlwain, Cambridge, 1915), contains an excellent introduction on the northern fur trade.

[12] For a good introductory survey, brief, accurate, well-written, see Albert Phelps, *Louisiana* (Boston, 1905), chapters 1–4.

privileges and monopolies to enterprisers in the new colony. Thus between 1712 and 1715 Louisiana was held as the private domain of one Antoine Crozat; in 1717 John Law's Mississippi Company received the province along with the right to govern it and a monopoly of its trade. Because an underlying object was to supply France with rice, tobacco, silk, and indigo, large estates were granted to promoters who hoped at first to people them with emigrants from Switzerland, the Palatinate, and the Low Countries. But this scheme failed: John Law himself was able to send only two hundred and fifty Palatines to his estate on the Arkansas River instead of the nine thousand he intended to transport thither. Hence the promoters had to rely principally on slave labor; in 1745 Negroes accounted for 36 per cent of the population. Rice became the principal product of the province; tobacco and indigo cultivation made moderate progress; experiments with silk and cotton failed. Four centers of settlement existed in 1745: at New Orleans (founded in 1718), at Natchez, at Natchitoches on the Red River, and in the Illinois country. The latter, an offshoot of Canada but annexed to Louisiana in 1717, produced wheat, Indian corn, and livestock. In 1731 the Mississippi company surrendered its political rights to the king and thereafter Louisiana, like Canada, was governed as a royal province.[13]

Wedged in between Louisiana and the English colonies were four important Indian tribes: the Chickasaws and Choctaws, adjacent to Louisiana, and the Cherokees and Creeks, on the Carolina-Georgia frontier. The French controlled the Choctaws and the English the Cherokees; both wooed the other tribes, the English more successfully. Two policies of the French favored the English. First, the Mississippi Company used its monopoly of the fur trade to exploit the Indians by exacting exorbitant prices for traders' goods, thus driving the red men into the arms of the South Carolina traders. In 1731 Charleston exported 250,000 deerskins. Secondly, the agricultural program of Louisiana called for the removal of the Indians from desirable planting lands. Fearing such deportation the Natchez tribe in 1729 massacred two hundred and fifty French settlers, thereby inaugurating the Natchez wars which until 1750 imposed a severe drain upon the infant colony: in 1745 it could boast of only 3,200 white settlers and 2,000 Negro slaves.[14]

[13] N. M. M. Surrey, *The Commerce of Louisiana during the French Regime* (New York, 1916), is a comprehensive, technical study, for the special student.

[14] Justin Winsor's *The Mississippi Basin* (Boston, 1895) treats the Anglo-French conflict with emphasis upon Louisiana. Very useful.

Britain's greatest defensive effort between 1713 and 1740—the establishment of Georgia—indicated that war with Spain (which would involve the southern colonies) was more imminent than war with France. Britain claimed the land south to a line midway between the thirtieth and thirty-first parallels; the Spaniards in Florida denied that Britain was entitled to Georgia and demanded that she evacuate all posts south of St. Helena Sound, near Beaufort, South Carolina. Charging that the Spaniards assaulted British vessels along the coast, that they incited the slaves of South Carolina to revolt (a dangerous uprising occurred there in 1739), that at St. Augustine they harbored runaway Negroes and servants, and that they induced the Indians to attack Georgia, Britain made vigorous preparations for war. In 1738 Oglethorpe returned to America from England, bringing a newly formed regiment and a commission as commander of the forces of Georgia and South Carolina. After stationing most of the regiment on the Altamaha River, Oglethorpe visited Charleston whence he journeyed westward to secure the alliance of the Creeks in the impending struggle.[15]

The strife on the Florida frontier was primarily a by-product of a commercial conflict between Britain and Spain which culminated in war in 1739. The trade concessions which Britain had forced from Spain in Spanish America had only whetted the appetite of British merchants for a larger share of the silver of Mexico and Peru. It will be recalled that in 1713 the South Sea Company had obtained a thirty-year monopoly of the slave trade with the Spanish colonies and the right to send each year one vessel of five hundred tons (one thousand tons, after 1716) with a cargo of general merchandise for sale at Porto Bello. The company might employ British ships in the slave trade and transport silver and other Spanish products directly from Spanish America to Britain, and in British ships. Otherwise all British vessels and traders were excluded from the Spanish colonies and all legal commerce had to be carried on by way of Spain. These concessions did not appease Britain because they left intact the main features of Spanish policy which closed the Spanish Indies to British merchants; Spain in turn was irked because the concessions, wrung from her by force, threatened to wreck her whole colonial system.

After 1713 the South Sea Company concentrated on the general trade in merchandise rather than on the traffic in slaves, stationing its "annual ship" off the coast of Porto Bello where it was frequently restocked with manufactured goods brought by trading sloops under

---

[15] See again V. W. Crane, *The Southern Frontier*, chapters 8–13.

the cover of night.[16] The value of a single cargo sent out in 1717 was £256,800. Moreover, when the company dispatched vessels with slaves to the Spanish colonies it sent along forbidden merchandise which was received on the sly and sold by its agents in such towns as Havana, Vera Cruz, Porto Bello, Cartagena, and Buenos Aires. Private British merchants at Jamaica joined in this illegal trade so that after 1713 British shipping "abounded in Spanish waters." Spanish officials used two methods to drive out the British smugglers: they arrested and imprisoned British traders in Spanish towns and confiscated their goods; and they stationed guard-ships in the Caribbean which seized British vessels laden with such products as dyewoods, indigo, and silver. Since these commodities were also obtained from the British islands many innocent British vessels were taken by the *guarda-costas*, to the intense exasperation of British merchants who raised the issue of the freedom of the seas. As the House of Commons put it in 1738: "It was the undoubted right of British subjects to sail their ships in any part of the seas of America." Although the British retaliated by seizing Spanish vessels, the Spaniards were the more active: in 1738 Britain's losses from such depredations exceeded Spain's by £95,000.

The interest in the Spanish American trade was shared by all British merchants because it afforded a large part of the nation's bullion supply. And because a bullion shortage in the 1730's was deemed the principal cause of currency troubles and a stagnation of British trade, the mercantile interests demanded strong measures against Spain, for which they prepared public sentiment by circulating tales of atrocities inflicted upon British traders by the Spaniards. A certain Captain Jenkins, who claimed that Spanish officials had cut off one of his ears, stirred up a wave of hysteria by exhibiting his affliction and relating the cruelties he had suffered. Walpole wanted peace, but his plan of pacification was defeated by the South Sea Company and the merchants. Rumors that France had joined the Spaniards in an alliance whereby France would receive commercial privileges in Spanish America and help Spain expel the British traders—such reports intensified the excitement in England. In May 1739 Spain suspended the English held assiento; in October the British merchants, Parliament, and the Whig ministers forced Walpole to consent to war.[17]

[16] Richard Pares, *War and Trade in the West Indies* (New York, 1936), is excellent on the Anglo-Spanish conflict.

[17] V. L. Brown, "The South Sea Company and Contraband Trade," *American Historical Review*, XXXI (Oct. 1925); E. Donnan, "The Early Days of the South Sea Company," *Journal of Economic and Business History*, II (May 1930)—technical.

THE CONFLICT RESUMED

Once more aiming at the conquest of the Spanish Indies Britain captured Porto Bello in November 1739 and then sent an expedition of eight thousand men against Cartagena. But when disease took a toll of half the British force this grand design collapsed in May 1741. Another expedition under Admiral Anson rounded Cape Horn to the Pacific and repeated Drake's exploit of plunder but did not conquer Spain's western settlements. By 1742 Britain's failure in the Spanish Indies was overshadowed by a general European war which had broken out in November 1740. The Austrian Emperor, Charles VI, had died in October, leaving the vast Hapsburg possessions to his daughter, Maria Theresa. In May a new sovereign, Frederick II, had ascended the throne of Prussia; in November he despoiled the inheritance of Maria Theresa by invading the Austrian province of Silesia. Since Austria had long been Britain's counterweight to French influence on the Continent, France took the side of Prussia. In 1742–43 British diplomacy secured support for Austria from Holland, Russia, and Saxony; in 1743 France openly allied herself with Spain, still at war with Britain; and in 1744 Britain declared war against France.[18]

Only one event, the British conquest of Louisbourg, gives significance to the War of the Austrian Succession in America—an achievement provoked by French efforts to seize Annapolis in Nova Scotia and by the desire of the merchants of Massachusetts to protect their trade and fishery against the onslaughts of the French. Prodded by the merchants, Massachusetts voted £50,000 for the expedition and obtained cannon from New York, provisions from New Jersey and Pennsylvania, troops from the other New England colonies, and three naval vessels from Britain. The chief promoter of the project, Governor William Shirley of Massachusetts (one of the better royal governors), feared the menace of Louisbourg to New England; the leader of the colonial forces, William Pepperrell of Kittery Point, Maine, one of the richest men in the colonies, had large investments in northern lands and in the fishery; the British commander, Sir Peter Warren, allied by marriage to the New York De Lanceys, had landholdings in the Mohawk valley. The religious enthusiasm engendered by the Great Awakening found vent in this crusade against the Catholic foe: Pepperrell was a pillar of the Congregational Church; and the war preparations were blessed by

[18] The seventh volume of the *Cambridge Modern History* devotes chapters 3 and 4 to the Anglo-French conflict.

the New England clergy with sermons and prayers. On March 24, 1745, the expedition of four thousand men and nearly a hundred vessels sailed from Boston; on June 15 Louisbourg surrendered after a forty-nine-day siege during which nine thousand cannon balls were poured into the town. Great rejoicing in Britain and New England greeted the news of success; Pepperrell was made a baronet, the first American-born colonist to be so favored.[19]

Shirley now raised a force for the conquest of Quebec, but naval aid promised by Britain did not materialize; instead the Crown in 1747 ordered the disbanding of the troops. France made two imposing but abortive efforts to recover Louisbourg in 1746–47. Much to the disgust of the New Englanders Britain restored the prize to France in 1748 in order to regain for the British East India Company the post of Madras in India which the French had taken during the war. But Britain did send large sums of money to the New England colonies to enable them to redeem the now sadly depreciated paper currency which they had issued to finance the expedition. By the Treaty of Aix la Chapelle (1748) all conquered territories were returned to their former possessors and the points of conflict remained as in 1740.

The center of strife now shifted to the area of present-day Ohio, western Pennsylvania, and West Virginia—a region of crucial importance, the key to the control of the interior.[20] The shortest route from Canada to Louisiana traversed the Ohio country via the Maumee, Great Miami, and Wabash Rivers; hence the French believed that the security of their whole American empire depended upon their possession of this pivotal territory. In like manner the mastery of the interior, by 1748, had become indispensable to the British, in view of the peculiar economy of their seaboard colonies. Not only was settlement rapidly pressing westward in Pennsylvania and Virginia; the capitalists of those colonies needed new fields for the investment of their surplus capital, due to the contraction of opportunities for investment in commerce, the relative unprofitableness of tobacco cultivation, and the refusal of Britain to permit the colonies to develop manufacturing industries. The needed outlets for excess capital had been found by Pennsylvania merchants and Virginia planters in speculation in western lands; in 1768 an observer said of Philadelphia that "It is almost a proverb in this neighborhood that 'Every great fortune made here within these fifty years has been

[19] George A. Wood, *William Shirley*, an excellent study, devotes chapters 9–19 to war problems.
[20] See again C. W. Alvord, *The Illinois Country*, chapters 7–11.

by land.' " In the process of land speculation and the financing of
indigent settlers colonial promoters hoped to utilize the Ohio valley
fur trade: not only would it provide profits to meet the costs of erecting forts to hold the interior against the French; it would also afford
those contacts with the Indians necessary for acquiring title to their
lands.[21]

Pennsylvania traders had penetrated beyond the mountains in the
1720's; Virginians followed in the 1730's. New York's preoccupation with her Oswego trade and South Carolina's preoccupation with
the far southern trade left the Ohio region open to the Pennsylvanians and Virginians, between whom a heated contest for supremacy ensued. Pennsylvania had a shorter route to the Ohio but the
provincial assembly, dominated by the Quakers who always strove
to avoid Indian wars incident to the fur trade and settlement, did
not give adequate backing to the Pennsylvania expansionists. In Virginia, on the other hand, land speculation had become such a primary
concern that the colonial government pursued a more vigorous forward policy. At a conference held at Lancaster, Pennsylvania, in
1744 the Iroquois ceded to Virginia all their lands within that province (lands which they claimed as overlords of weaker tribes, particularly the Delaware and Shawnee). Then, in order to overcome
Pennsylvania's advantages in the West, a group of Virginia gentlemen organized the Ohio Company; among them were such representatives of the planter aristocracy as Thomas Lee, Thomas Nelson,
George Fairfax, Lawrence and Augustine Washington and, later,
George Mason and Governor Robert Dinwiddie. That one of the
original promoters was John Hanbury, a London merchant, indicates that English capitalists were also looking to the Ohio valley as
a field of investment. Because settlement was the principal object of
the company it obtained from the king in 1749 a grant of 200,000
acres on both sides of the Ohio between the Monongahela and Great
Kanawha Rivers, together with a promise of 300,000 acres more if a
hundred families were settled upon the first tract within seven years.
Immediately thereafter the company imported a large stock of
goods for the Indian trade and dispatched to the West one Christopher Gist, who traversed large parts of present-day Ohio, Kentucky,
and West Virginia as well as western Maryland and southwestern
Pennsylvania in his search for lands best suited to settlement. The
company also erected a trading house on the Potomac opposite the
mouth of Will's Creek (now the site of Cumberland, Maryland) and

---

[21] Louis K. Koontz, *The Virginia Frontier* (Baltimore, 1925), emphasizes the role
of Washington.

in 1752 it negotiated an Indian treaty which authorized the construction of a fort at the forks of the Ohio.[22]

For more than a decade the British traders had been strengthening their influence among the Ohio valley Indians by virtue of their ability to overbid the French in the fur trade. In 1741 France adopted a new commercial policy: all traders' licenses were revoked and thereafter the interior posts were leased by the government to individuals on a monopoly basis. The merchant princes of Montreal purchased such leases, but at rates so high as to oblige them to charge extortionate prices for the goods which they supplied to the natives. Exempt from such payments, and exposed to more vigorous competition, the British traders offered better bargains. When the disaffection of the Indians had become critical the governors of Canada prepared to protect the monopolists by force. First, in 1749, an expedition under Céloron de Blainville was sent from Canada to assert France's claim to the upper Ohio. Taking the route of Lake Erie, the Allegheny, the Ohio, the Great Miami, and the Maumee, Blainville's party deposited at the mouth of each important river a lead plate inscribed with the French claim. Next, in 1752, the French destroyed an English fort, Pickawillany, in what is now Miami County, Ohio; then in 1753 a newly arrived governor of Canada, the marquis Duquesne de Menneville, dispatched a second expedition which erected Fort Presque Isle on Lake Erie and Fort le Boeuf on French Creek and took possession of Venango, a British trading post, at the junction of French Creek and the Allegheny River.[23]

When the news of this advance reached Governor Dinwiddie he sent young George Washington to demand that the French withdraw (1753). Washington as yet did not belong to the inner circle of the Virginia aristocracy but he was already one of its most trustworthy agents. He journeyed as far as Fort le Boeuf only to have the French ignore his demands. Dinwiddie immediately retaliated by sending Captain William Trent with a small force to erect a fort at the forks of the Ohio. No sooner was the work under way than a stronger French force expelled the Virginians and thereupon erected Fort Duquesne. Dinwiddie, having raised a small body of troops, again dispatched Washington with orders to drive out the French. Near a place called Great Meadows in the Alleghenies Washington encountered and defeated a French force; then he retreated to

---

[22] In Charles H. Ambler's *George Washington and the West* (Chapel Hill, 1936) there is a careful narrative of the beginnings of the French and Indian War. See chapters 1–7.

[23] G. A. Wood, "Céloron de Blainville and French Expansion in the Ohio Valley," *Mississippi Valley Historical Review*, IX (March 1923).

Great Meadows and hurriedly erected Fort Necessity, which the French attacked and captured in July 1754. Virginia and Canada were now at war.[24]

The replacement of New York by Virginia as the challenger of French supremacy requires an explanation. After 1713 the western problem occasioned a factional strife in New York over two alternatives of policy. One course of action, which may be styled the anti-French program, entailed large expenditures for frontier defense and unceasing efforts to retain the Iroquois as allies in war. The second or neutrality policy, which aimed to preserve peace with Canada, involved the neglect of frontier defenses and an indifferent attitude toward the Iroquois. Advocates of neutrality were the New York and Albany merchants, headed by James De Lancey, who carried on the trade with Montreal. In alliance with them were land speculators, particularly the Livingstons, active in the Mohawk valley: their method of buying land from the Iroquois and of occupying more than they bought made it difficult to propitiate the Six Nations as the anti-French policy demanded. The neutrality party could count upon the political support of the residents of other parts of the province who, having no interest in the frontier, wished merely to avoid expenditures for defense and war.

The anti-French policy derived its impetus from the British government's insistence that New York play a leading role in winning America from France; hence the royal governors, especially William Burnet and George Clinton, were its principal sponsors. The traders who operated at Oswego also inclined toward the anti-French camp; because they traversed the Iroquois country they desired to conciliate the Iroquois in all ways consistent with their trade. The most effective advocate of this policy, William Johnson, an Irishman, had settled on the Mohawk valley frontier, where he engaged in the fur trade and by reason of his fair dealings won the unlimited confidence of the Six Nations, even being "adopted" by the Mohawk tribe. His residence, Mount Johnson, became the center of his rather dubious diplomacy, which consisted largely of warning the Iroquois that France was seeking their destruction.[25]

During King George's War the neutrality party had frustrated Governor Clinton's plans for war against the French; and although Clinton made Johnson the Indian agent of the province, the opposi-

---

[24] See again E. Channing, *History of the United States*, Vol. II, chapters 18–19.

[25] The best biography is Arthur Pound, *Johnson of the Mohawks* (New York, 1930). A briefer, popular narrative is Flora W. Seymour, *Lords of the Valley* (New York, 1930).

tion was so strong in the Assembly that he could accomplish little
and was obliged to finance the Oswego garrison and Indian negotiations from his own pocket: when he was forced to resign in 1750
the province owed him £7,000 for his outlays. At several abortive
conferences held between 1745 and 1753 the Iroquois eloquently

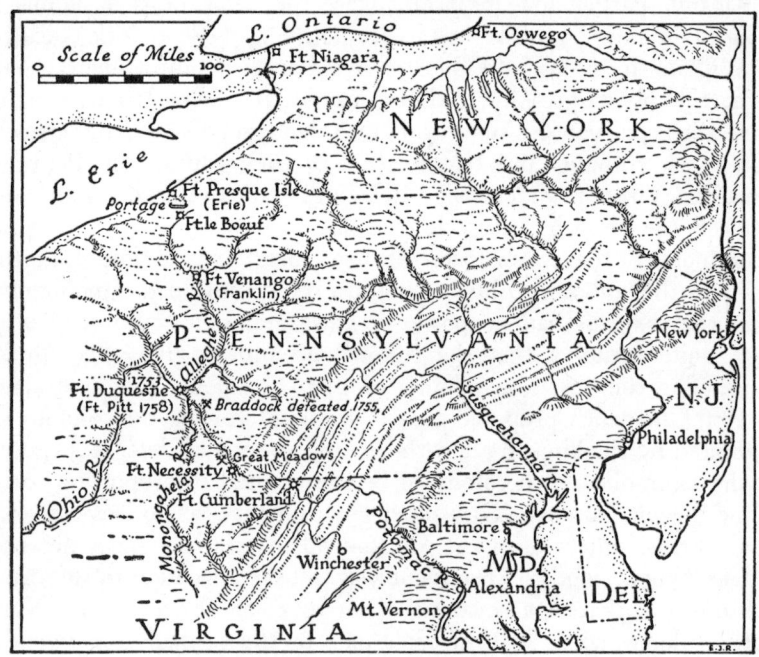

From Adams and Vannest's "The Record of America." © *Charles Scribner's Sons.*

WHERE THE FRENCH AND INDIAN WAR BEGAN

voiced their wrongs: their lands were being filched by speculators
and the great English father did nothing to protect them from the
French. Meanwhile the traders from Virginia and Pennsylvania did
not pursue a policy of neutrality; by inciting the Indians against the
French they inspired the latter to send out the Blainville expedition
and to erect the Lake Erie-Ohio River forts. This show of strength
so impressed the Indians that most of them now sided with France.
In the impending war the Iroquois were certain to be involved, and
yet New York had done nothing for their protection. Their disgust
with Britain's indecision had created a crisis on the New York frontier by the end of 1753.[26]

[26] A. H. Buffinton, "The Policy of Albany and English Westward Expansion,"
Mississippi Valley Historical Review, VIII (March 1922).

To meet this situation the Board of Trade issued a call for a general colonial congress designed to induce the Indians south of the Great Lakes to cease intertribal warfare and to join Britain against France. Hence in June 1754 representatives of New York, Pennsylvania, Maryland, and the New England colonies met the Iroquois at Albany. Particularly important were the delegations of Pennsylvania (Benjamin Franklin was its leader) and of New York (headed by William Johnson and Governor De Lancey). Unfortunately Virginia, the pivotal colony, did not participate. The Iroquois again aired their grievances, such as British land frauds, the defenseless New York frontier, and the invasion of their country by Pennsylvania and Virginia traders. The delegates framed a report which denounced the French, acknowledged the grievances of the Iroquois, recommended the construction of new forts, and advised that the limits of the seaboard colonies should extend only to the mountains. Since the congress had no power to raise money it could only urge (and quite futilely) that the colonial assemblies give effect to its plans. The congress also adopted a plan of colonial union drafted by Franklin which proposed that a president for all the colonies be appointed by the king to act with a grand council of delegates chosen by the assemblies, each colony to be represented in proportion to its financial contributions. This super-government was to have charge of all British interests in the West—Indian treaties, trade, defense, and settlement; and the president was to bear a relation to the council similar to that of a royal governor to a colonial assembly. None of the colonies accepted Franklin's plan or the general recommendations of the congress: none wished to surrender to an outside body both the power of taxation and control over the development of the West. More particularly, the Albany plan would have thwarted the Ohio Company, now dominant in the government of Virginia.

Upon learning of Washington's defeat at Fort Necessity British officials ceased considering their own plans of colonial union and dispatched a force of two regiments to Virginia under the command of Edward Braddock, an aged general, brave and headstrong—a firm disciplinarian who had learned on the battlefields of Europe what he considered the entire art of warfare.[27] Through the influence of John Hanbury and the Ohio Company, Braddock's force landed in Virginia instead of Pennsylvania, thereby necessitating an unduly long march through the wilderness to Fort Duquesne, the first objective of the expedition. Exposure, sickness, and the strain

[27] T. W. Riker, "The Politics behind Braddock's Expedition," *American Historical Review*, XIII (Oct. 1907).

of building wilderness roads for army supply had exhausted Braddock's men by the time they arrived within seven miles of Fort Duquesne, where on July 9, 1755, a force of nine hundred French and Indians sheltered by trees inflicted a decisive defeat in a day's fighting. Braddock perished and the British survivors fled until they reached Fort Cumberland in Maryland. All supplies were lost so that the whole campaign had to be abandoned. The Indians, having now chosen France as the stronger party, ravaged the frontiers of Virginia and Pennsylvania far and wide. "The undeclared war of 1755 had not gone well for Britain."

The continued opposition of the French settlers in Nova Scotia to Britain's authority evoked drastic measures against them in the autumn of 1755. After restoring Louisbourg to France, Britain had strengthened her hold upon the province by establishing in 1749 twenty-five hundred settlers at Halifax—a force which had increased to four thousand by 1752. The French residents (now numbering about nine thousand) occupied a strategic position, since Nova Scotia lay athwart the British route to Louisbourg and Canada, both of which Britain was at last determined to conquer. Hence a part of the campaign of 1755 had been the seizure of a French fort, Beauséjour, at the northern part of the Bay of Fundy. Having succeeded there in June, Britain gained undisputed control of Nova Scotia which she perpetuated in the autumn by deporting more than six thousand Acadians to her colonies south of New Hampshire. Although this action was taken when France and Britain were still nominally at peace, its extreme harshness signified that North America was no longer large enough to accommodate two such bitterly hostile powers.[28]

Colonial rivalry was the underlying cause of the Seven Years' (or French and Indian) War, officially declared in May 1756. That it grew into a general European conflict is explained in the main by the hatred of Austria for Prussia, a legacy of Prussia's seizure of Silesia during the preceding war. When Austrian diplomats after 1748 effected a combination against Prussia, the latter countered with an alliance with Britain—a bargain which assured Prussia of financial backing and gave Britain a powerful ally against France. No longer seeking territorial dominance in Europe but rather striving for supremacy in America, France joined hands with Austria, the power which had long opposed her designs of European conquest. Thus in the spring of 1756 was consummated the Diplomatic Revo-

---

[28] Arthur G. Doughty, *The Acadian Exiles* (*Chronicles of Canada* series, Toronto, 1916).

lution by which those ancient enemies, the French Bourbons and the Austrian Hapsburgs, united in opposition to Prussia and Britain.

In America the plans of campaign revolved around Fort Duquesne and Quebec, or the control of the Ohio valley and Canada.[29] Britain's determination to conquer the latter brought into prominence three approaches to the north: the sea route to the St. Lawrence, guarded for France by Louisbourg; the path of the Richelieu River and Lake Champlain, where France had forts at Ticonderoga and Crown Point; and the Great Lakes-St. Lawrence route, which the French commanded through Forts Niagara and Frontenac on the southwestern and northeastern sides of Lake Ontario. Until 1758 the fortunes of war frowned upon the British; the French destroyed Fort Oswego in 1756, repulsed a large expedition sent against Louisbourg in July 1757, captured Fort William Henry on Lake George in the following August, and maintained their prestige among the upper Ohio valley Indians, particularly the Delaware and Shawnee, whose raids upon the Virginia-Pennsylvania frontier drove the British settlers to or beyond the Allegheny Mountains.[30]

These reverses brought into power the resolute and energetic William Pitt, who, as Secretary of State for the Southern Department, 1757–61, directed Britain's successful campaigns for the conquest of Canada. Exhibiting unlimited self-confidence ("I believe," he said, "that I can save this nation and that no one else can"), he purged the army of the corrupt spoils system, chose the ablest commanders he could find, and inspired the nation with his own zeal for empire. Convinced that "when trade is at stake you must defend it or perish," he concentrated upon America as the decisive theater of the war, at the same time subsidizing Prussia in order to keep France occupied in Europe.[31] Success greeted his first efforts in 1758 when British forces, by conquering Louisbourg, Fort Duquesne (renamed Fort Pitt), and Fort Frontenac, opened the way to Canada. The campaign of 1759 involved a threefold attack: one expedition was to take Fort Niagara and sever Canada from the West; a second, under General Jeffrey Amherst,[32] was to proceed northward by way

[29] The most elaborate study of military operations is *A History of the British Army* (13 vols., London, 1899–1930) by the Hon. Sir John W. Fortescue. Volume II covers the years 1713–63.

[30] Julian S. Corbett, *England in the Seven Years War* (2 vols., London, 1907), is a standard, intensive study of naval and military strategy, politics, and warfare.

[31] For the general reader the best biography is Basil Williams, *The Life of William Pitt* (2 vols., London, 1914).

[32] Two satisfactory biographies stress the military aspect: Laurence S. Mayo, *Jeffrey Amherst* (New York, 1916), and John C. Long, *Lord Jeffrey Amherst* (New York, 1933).

of Lake Champlain; and the third, a combined land and sea force under General James Wolfe, was to advance upon Quebec from the East. The first expedition took possession of Niagara but could not advance down the St. Lawrence; Amherst seized Ticonderoga and Crown Point but had to halt for the winter on Lake Champlain; hence Wolfe's force was compelled to act alone. Tense was the situation during the winter following Wolfe's success in September as both the conquered and the conquerors, cooped up in Quebec, awaited reinforcements from Europe. But in 1759 Britain had shattered the French navy, and the fleet which arrived in May 1760 confirmed the victory of Wolfe. Montreal fell in September and all Canada lay prostrate before Britain's arms.[33]

Britain's relation to war underwent a decisive change as the result of the accession of George III in 1760. Both education and inclination prompted this ambitious, headstrong king to assert his right to rule in fact as well as in name. And since he had been born and bred in England and "gloried in the name of Briton"; because his conventional moral virtues commended him to the powerful English middle class; and because the Hanoverian dynasty was now safely established upon the throne and reinforced by forty-five years of kingship, George III found circumstances favorable to his design of breaking the power of the great Whig families which had ruled continuously since 1715. Pitt was now the chief symbol of Whig influence, and because his power stemmed from the war, George III was determined to restore peace as the means both of ousting Pitt and of gaining the sovereign power. The Achilles' heel of Pitt's policy was the expensive and unpopular practice of subsidizing Prussia; in opposition to this policy George III built up a peace party which forced the great war minister to resign. Meanwhile, France and Spain in 1761 had entered into treaties which renewed the Bourbon family compact: one agreement provided that if France and Britain were at war in May 1762, Spain would aid France. Urging an attack upon Spain but thwarted by George III, Pitt resigned in October 1761 rather than remain in office without power. Nevertheless Britain was forced to declare war against Spain in January 1762 and to prolong the conflict another year—during which she conquered the French

[33] On this famous engagement see Parkman's masterly narrative, *Montcalm and Wolfe* (2 vols., Boston, 1884); Frederick E. Whitton, *Wolfe and North America* (Boston, 1929), an attractive, reliable account of military campaigns; and William Wood, *The Fight for Canada* (London, 1904), a well-informed description of the conquest which glorifies Pitt and Wolfe. Biographies are: Arthur G. Bradley, *Wolfe* (London, 1895)—a brief sketch; and William T. Waugh, *James Wolfe* (Montreal, 1928), which incorporates the latest information.

sugar island, Martinique (she had already taken Guadeloupe in 1759), and occupied Havana and Manila, thereby gaining control of Cuba and the Philippine Islands.[34]

During the negotiations for peace Britain held Canada, Guadeloupe, and Martinique, but because France would rather continue the war than surrender all three colonies, and because George III insisted upon peace, the question arose: should Britain retain Canada or the two sugar islands? Over this issue raged a spirited public debate. Those who urged the retention of Guadeloupe and Martinique argued that their trade was much greater than Canada's: in 1761 the exports of Guadeloupe to Britain exceeded those of Canada more than fortyfold. Similarly, the two islands would increase the markets of Britain's northern mainland colonies, encourage them to continue to produce provisions, lumber, etc., supply them with buying power for British goods, and divert them from manufacturing in competition with British industries. Should France be expelled from Canada, the mainland colonies—no longer in need of Britain's protection—would break away from the mother country. Island colonies were generally secure dependencies because they could never successfully defy a naval power like Britain. And if France lost Guadeloupe and Martinique her naval strength in the Caribbean would be annihilated.

The advocates of Canada urged that its retention would give Britain control of the North American fur trade and greatly enlarge the market for British manufactures, since the northern colonies adjacent to Canada were now surpassing the British West Indies as purchasers of European goods. If Canada and the Ohio valley were restored to France, the English colonies, hemmed in at the mountains, would have to turn to manufactures in order to support their expanding populations. Moreover, the mainland settlements now needed protection from French onslaughts as the condition of their prosperous development. Nor was a revolt of the thirteen colonies likely; local rivalries and jealousies would keep them apart, and Britain could always subdue them by virtue of her mastery of the sea. Finally, the vast extent of Canada would add immeasurably to Britain's prestige in the eyes of the world.[35]

The decision to retain Canada was shaped by three influences. First, British planters and investors in the old British sugar islands did not wish to admit Guadeloupe and Martinique into the empire,

[34] Lewis B. Namier, *England in the Age of the American Revolution* (London, 1930), treats English society and politics, 1760–63.

[35] W. L. Grant, "Canada versus Guadeloupe," *American Historical Review*, XVII (July 1912).

fearing that they would flood the British sugar markets and ruin the British plantations. Secondly, British merchants regarded the fur trade of Canada as a prize of the first magnitude. And thirdly, the mainland colonies, having spent so much blood and treasure in winning Canada, could not be condemned indefinitely to the horrors of war by returning their conquests to the enemy. The conflict in America had reached the point where it could be resolved only by the expulsion of the French.

The Treaty of Paris of 1763 awarded Canada to Britain, as well as the territory west to the Mississippi. Spain ceded Florida to Britain as the price for the restoration of Cuba and the Philippines, while France compensated Spain for the loss of Florida by giving her that part of Louisiana west of the Mississippi and a small strip of land east of the mouth of the river. Britain and Spain were now the premier colonial powers of the world.[36]

THE DECENTRALIZED EMPIRE

The imperial crisis which precipitated the American Revolution issued directly from the French and Indian War. Having expelled France from North America, Britain no longer needed to make political concessions to the colonies in order to secure their assistance against the French; hence she was free to enforce those parts of her colonial system which had previously been neglected. Secondly, the conquest of Canada and the Ohio valley imposed upon Britain the task of governing the whole interior; and in shaping a western policy she antagonized powerful interests in the colonies which were bent upon exploiting the newly won territories. Finally, the war exposed many deep-seated conflicts between Britain and the colonies and demonstrated that the latter were prone to ignore British interests and to evade imperial restrictions. Animosity and mistrust were the results.[37]

One of the most bitter conflicts between the colonies and the mother country arose from the wartime commerce which the former carried on with Canada and the French West Indies—a trade that in British eyes wore the treasonable aspect of giving aid to the enemy. Not only were French military and naval forces furnished with indispensable provisions; equally important, such colonial exports to the enemy made it difficult for British forces to obtain necessary supplies except

[36] W. R. Shepherd, "The Cession of Louisiana to Spain," *Political Science Quarterly*, XIX (Sept. 1904).

[37] Eugene I. McCormac, *Colonial Opposition to Imperial Authority during the French and Indian War* (Berkeley, 1911), is an excellent brief analysis.

at high prices. A similar trade with the French West Indies during King George's War had been blamed by a British admiral for the failure at that time of Britain's naval operations in the Caribbean. Moreover, it was charged that the northern colonies, by trading with the French sugar islands, forced down the price of sugar, molasses, and rum, thereby rendering unprofitable the British plantations in the West Indies. The French sugar obtained by the northern traders was disguised as British sugar and sent to Britain where it deprived the British planters of the home market especially reserved for them.[38]

When at the outbreak of war Britain prohibited all commerce between her subjects and the French, the mainland colonies engaged in an indirect trade whereby they used the Spanish and Dutch islands as depots for the goods which they sold to or received from Guadeloupe, Martinique, and Santo Domingo. In this case neutral vessels made the direct exchanges with the French. In order to stamp out such traffic Parliament in 1757 prohibited the exportation of all provisions (excepting fish, roots, and rice) from a British colony to any place except Britain, Ireland, or other British colonies. With the same object an English admiralty court promulgated the Rule of 1756, which declared that neutrals could not carry on in time of war a trade which was legally closed to them in time of peace. France, of course, regularly excluded the Dutch and Spaniards from the peacetime trade with her colonies; however, due to Britain's naval superiority, she opened her ports to neutrals as a means of continuing her commerce when at war. The Rule of 1756 said in effect that Britain could regulate the trade of other nations with France.[39]

The merchants of the thirteen colonies exhibited much ingenuity and boldness in evading Britain's anti-French statutes and decrees. For one thing, the merchants obtained licenses from colonial governors which authorized their vessels to proceed under a "flag of truce" to the French islands in order to effect an exchange of prisoners of war. Thus colonial ships could transport cargoes of provisions under the shelter of such licenses, which were issued so profusely (especially by the governors of Rhode Island and Pennsylvania) that a more or less open traffic in them developed, as they multiplied and fell in price. Other colonial vessels, having cleared for British ports, traded with the French colonies and then visited British

---

[38] G. L. Beer, *British Colonial Policy, 1754–1765* (New York, 1907), is of primary importance. See chapters 1–9.

[39] Kate Hotblack, *Chatham's Colonial Policy* (London, 1917), is an able, intensive study of the years 1739–65.

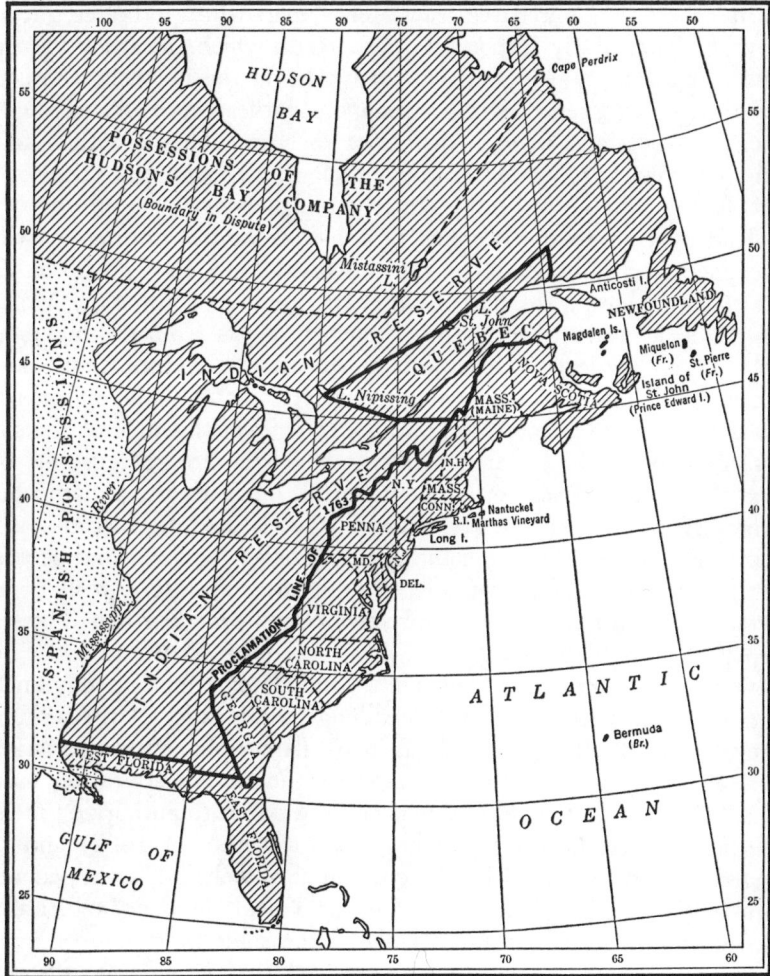

Based on Charles O. Paullin's "Atlas of the Historical Geography of the United States."
© Carnegie Institution of Washington. Reprinted by courtesy of the American Geographical
Society of New York.

British and Spanish possessions after the Treaty of Paris, 1763, and
the organization of British territory under the Royal Proclamation of
October 7, 1763. Besides authorizing the "Proclamation Line," the
Proclamation of 1763 created the three British provinces of Quebec,
East Florida, and West Florida.

ports, where they purchased fraudulent papers which indicated a legal voyage. Particularly important was a trade which the colonists conducted with a Spanish port, Monte Cristi, on the northern shore of Haiti, close to French Santo Domingo. Thither the French brought their produce, and in such quantities that in 1760 more than four hundred vessels unloaded cargoes of sugar, although the little town had had no commercial importance before the war.

Endeavoring to enforce her prohibitions against commerce with the enemy, Britain made use of the royal navy to capture vessels which were abusing the flag of truce, attempted to enforce the Molasses Act as a means of excluding French products from the mainland colonies, and ordered her subjects not to trade at Monte Cristi. Such measures angered the colonial merchants, whose antagonism was sharpened by the introduction into the colonies at this time of writs of assistance or general search warrants which authorized customs officials to enter houses and ships, to break down doors, and to open containers in their search for smuggled goods. Because special search warrants required that the name of the informer be given and because local sentiment made life unpleasant for such informers, writs of assistance proved to be far more effective. They were first issued by the superior court of Massachusetts in 1755; when they had to be renewed in 1760 the Bay merchants banded together and employed James Otis as their attorney to challenge the legality of the writs in court. Described by John Adams as a "flame of fire" who attacked with "a torrent of impetuous eloquence the terrible menacing monster," Otis denied that Parliament had the power to authorize the use of the writs (their legality rested upon a statute of 1662) and asserted instead that British subjects, colonists included, possessed certain fundamental rights which even Parliament could not take away. In this case writs of assistance violated the subjects' right to be free from unreasonable searches and seizures. The superior court affirmed the legality of the writs, but in the meantime Otis had crystallized public indignation against them and had inaugurated the constitutional debate of the Revolutionary era by denying that Parliament possessed unlimited power over the colonies.[40]

The methods used by Britain to finance the war in America also provoked friction within the empire. Because the British colonists on the mainland outnumbered the French settlers by about fourteen to one, Britain possessed a tremendous military advantage over France, provided of course that her colonists could be welded into an effec-

[40] E. Hickman, "Colonial Writs of Assistance." *New England Quarterly*, V (Jan. 1932).

tive army. Having decided to employ colonial troops (as in previous wars), British ministers were confronted by two questions: what should be the relation between the colonial troops and British regulars in America and how could the colonists be made to share the expenses of the war? The first question was answered by subordinating colonial forces to British commanders, thus providing for centralized military operations as directed by the ministry in Britain. Although this method produced many rivalries and antagonisms between colonial officers and British commanders it did not produce nearly so much enmity as that evoked by the means of financing the colonial forces. Due to the cost of the war on the Continent Britain felt unable to pay all the expenses of the colonial campaigns. Between 1748 and 1754 British officials had proposed that Parliament tax the colonies for imperial defense; however, since the colonists were strongly opposed to such levies, this plan had to be abandoned in order to secure colonial coöperation during the critical years of war. In consequence, Britain resorted to the "requisition system"—a scheme whereby each colonial assembly was called upon to furnish a prescribed quota of men and money as its contribution to the war.

As developed by Pitt the requisition system obliged the assembly to vote the money for recruiting, clothing, and paying the wages of the colonial troops; Britain in turn supplied the necessary provisions, tents, arms, and ammunition. Moreover, in order to encourage the assemblies to provide their quotas, Parliament reimbursed the colonies for part of their outlays of the previous year. All told the colonies in this manner received from Britain about two-fifths of the money they spent for recruiting, clothing, and paying their own troops. To British officials this plan seemed fair and generous, especially when the benefits to America from the war were taken into account; hence they expected an equally generous response from the colonies and were sorely exasperated when it was not forthcoming.[41]

Of the colonial attitude the British commander-in-chief in America, Lord Loudoun, said in 1757: "it is the constant study of every province here to throw every expense on the Crown and bear no part of the expense of this war themselves." Three sources of colonial opposition may be distinguished. Some colonies (New Hampshire, Georgia, North Carolina) considered themselves so poor that they could not afford to meet the British requisitions. In New Jersey and Pennsylvania, where the Quakers were powerful, their aversion to war expressed itself in resistance to military appropriations. Generally, the

---

[41] Hubert Hall, "Chatham's Colonial Policy," *American Historical Review*, V (July 1900).

residents of the seaboard area who were not concerned in the fur trade or in western land speculation had little interest in the frontier and were unwilling to be taxed for its defense—an attitude particularly strong in Rhode Island, Delaware, and New Jersey, since those colonies did not possess claims to the territory around which the conflict revolved. Each colony, fearful that it might contribute more than its share, delayed action in order to see what its neighbors would do; the failure of one then provided an excuse for the remissness of the others. Moreover, the assemblies refused to fill their quotas unless they believed that the money would be spent for their particular advantage. Thus British plans for the conquest of Louisiana in 1762 had to be abandoned because the colonies failed to provide their quotas, so indifferent were they to that faraway country. Only Massachusetts, Connecticut, and New York responded effectively throughout the war: the general failure of the requisition system is apparent from the fact that those three colonies contributed seven-tenths of all the troops raised in America.[42]

Even when the assemblies complied with Britain's requests the delay involved often hampered military operations. "The sloth of the colonies," wrote General Amherst, "in raising their troops and sending them to their rendezvous makes it impracticable for me to move the troops on so soon as I could have wished." Nor did the quality of the colonial soldiers satisfy British officers: as General Forbes put it in 1758, the forces from Pennsylvania and Virginia, excepting a few of their principal officers, were "an extreme bad collection of innkeepers, horse jockeys and Indian traders . . . a gathering from the scum of the worst people . . . who have wrought themselves up into a panic at the very name of Indians." Most grievous of all the features of the requisition system was the use made of it by the colonial assemblies to wrest political concessions from the royal governors and the proprietors as the price of military grants—a practice that in British eyes seemed as reprehensible as trade with the enemy.[43]

Contests over the currency illustrate the wartime tactics of the assemblies. Unwilling to tax themselves to meet the immediate costs of the war the colonists again issued paper money in large amounts and the resulting depreciation increased the old tension between debtors and creditors. Virginia now became the principal scene of conflict; there the struggle over currency and debts bore witness to the im-

---

[42] See again W. T. Root, *Relations of Pennsylvania with the British Government,* chapter 10.

[43] Stanley M. Pargellis, *Lord Loudoun in America* (New Haven, 1933), is an able study of problems facing the British army in America, 1756–58.

pending bankruptcy of the tobacco planters, caught as they were in the grip of British merchant capitalism. In 1748 Virginia enacted a law which provided that debts might be paid in Virginia currency (foreign coin or tobacco) at the rate of £125 Virginia money for each £100 sterling due. When the British merchants complained that £100 sterling was worth £140 in Virginia currency the province in 1755 passed a new act which authorized judges to decide the sterling value of the Virginia currency that was tendered in payment of debts. This act evoked two objections from the merchants: first, the judges might overvalue Virginia currency, thereby defrauding British creditors; secondly, Virginia's currency was steadily depreciating, so that a remittance of £100 might lose ten or fifteen per cent of its value between the time a court acted and the time the creditor received the money. The currency issue was intensified at this time (1755) when Virginia issued its first paper currency and made it legal tender in payment of debt. Depreciation followed: in 1757 it took £135 in Virginia paper currency to buy £100 sterling; in 1759 the ratio was 140:100; in 1762 it stood at 165:100. Yet despite the demands of British creditors that they should not be compelled to accept such depreciated paper at more than its sterling value, the assembly refused to provide money for the war except in the form of legal tender paper currency. On the other hand, after the conquest of Canada had satisfied Virginia's military ambitions, the assembly refused to grant money for the war on the ground that such grants would increase the supply of paper currency. Britain thus had either to accept new currency issues or to forego colonial military aid. The exigencies of the war forced her to accept legal tender paper—a concession that embittered British creditors and impelled them to insist upon an anti-paper currency policy as soon as peace deprived the assemblies of their powers of coercion.[44]

The money question became a crucial issue in Virginia in connection with the famous "parson's cause." Prior to 1755 the Anglican clergy of the province had received their salaries in tobacco, each stipend consisting of 17,280 pounds. When poor crops afflicted the colony in 1755 and 1758 the price of tobacco rose to the unusual figure of 5½d. a pound—an increase occasioned in part by the depreciation of Virginia's currency. Had the clergy been paid their salaries in tobacco, the 17,280 pounds to which each was entitled would have amounted to £400. However, the assembly in 1758 passed an act which provided that salaries, dues, and fees might be paid in money

[44] *Virginia and the French and Indian War*, by Hayes Baker-Crothers (Chicago, 1928), stresses imperial defense as a political issue.

at the rate of 2*d.* for each pound of tobacco due, an arrangement that reduced the salaries of the clergy to £144 each. The clergy objected strenuously, arguing that they had been paid in tobacco when its price was low; now when the price was high they ought to receive a compensating benefit. They were joined in their opposition to the "twopenny act" by the British merchants; consequently word arrived in Virginia in 1760 that the act had been disallowed. The clergy, having generally received £144 in money rather than £400 in tobacco, were now entitled to sue for the balance due to them under the former law. Among the suits that followed one gained especial prominence.[45] The Reverend James Maury of Fredericksville sued the vestrymen of his parish; the latter employed Patrick Henry as their attorney. Since the legal technicalities favored the minister, Henry directed his attack against the royal disallowance, asserting that Britain and the colonies were bound together in a mutual compact which neither party could violate without dissolving it. The disallowance of the "twopenny act" was such a manifest piece of tyranny that the colonists must defend their rights. In response to Henry's oratory the court awarded the minister damages of one penny—a thinly disguised defiance of Britain's authority over the colony.

Thus during the French and Indian War two notable attacks upon British merchant capitalism gave evidence of a critical situation within the empire. Speaking for the merchants of New England James Otis repudiated the supreme authority of Parliament which underlay the British acts restraining the commercial opportunities of the northern colonies; speaking for the Virginia planters Patrick Henry voiced their dissatisfaction with the Privy Council, that final guardian of British investments in America.[46] Restraints upon trade which menaced the profits of the colonial merchants; debts which consumed the profits of the southern planters: those two features of British mercantilism had at last evoked an opposition so determined as to indicate the approach of a revolutionary crisis.

[45] A. P. Scott, "The Constitutional Aspect of the 'Parson's Cause,' " *Political Science Quarterly,* XXXI (Dec. 1916).

[46] A standard biography is M. C. Tyler, *Patrick Henry* (Boston, 1887). For a popular account see George Morgan, *The True Patrick Henry* (Philadelphia, 1907).

BIBLIOGRAPHICAL NOTE

SECONDARY WORKS: Walter L. Dorn, *Competition for Empire, 1740–1763* (New York, 1940), describes the situation in Europe as it entered into the Anglo-French conflict. Lawrence H. Gipson, *Zones of International Friction* (Volume V of *The British Empire before the American Revolution,* New York, 1942), surveys the principal areas involved in imperial rivalries, 1748–1754.

John T. Lanning, *The Diplomatic History of Georgia* (Chapel Hill, 1936), amplifies the record of the War of Jenkins' Ear.

Nellis M. Crouse, *La Vérendrye* (Ithaca, 1956), is an attractive narrative of exploration and the fur trade in the trans-Mississippi Northwest during the 1730's. Paul A. W. Wallace, *Conrad Weiser* (Philadelphia, 1945), an outstanding study of the Indian relations of the middle colonies, 1730–1760, is supplemented by Arthur D. Gaeff, *Conrad Weiser* (Fogelsville, Pa., 1945)—a sympathetic biography of the friend of the Indians and apostle of peace. Nicholas B. Wainwright, *George Croghan* (Chapel Hill, 1959), is a first-rate study of trade, land speculation, and Indian affairs in the frontier advance of the middle colonies. Anthony F. C. Wallace, *King of the Delawares* (Philadelphia, 1949), is a moving narrative recording the tragic fate of an Indian leader in the New Jersey-Pennsylvania area.

Specialized treatments which give full accounts of Washington's early activities on the frontier are Charles H. Ambler, *Washington and the West* (Chapel Hill, 1936), thorough and detailed; and Hugh Cleland, *George Washington in the Ohio Valley* (Pittsburgh, 1955), which also provides the documentary record. The best biography of Washington of moderate length is Nathaniel W. Stephenson and Waldo H. Dunn, *George Washington* (2 vols., New York, 1940)—a laudatory work.

Louis K. Koontz, *Robert Dinwiddie* (Glendale, Calif., 1941), views the Anglo-French conflict from the standpoint of the Virginia governor. Kenneth P. Bailey, *The Ohio Company of Virginia* (Glendale, Calif., 1939), elucidates the role of the Company in the Anglo-French conflict. Robert C. Newbold, *The Albany Congress and Plan of Union* (New York, 1955), gives a convenient, well-grounded summary of the Congress and its work. Lee McCardell, *Ill-Starred General* (Pittsburgh, 1958), a biography of Edward Braddock, contains a lively narrative of his disastrous defeat. Wilbur R. Jacobs, *Diplomacy and Indian Gifts* (Stanford, 1960), is an interesting treatment of a neglected phase of the Anglo-French conflict, 1748–1763. A good study of the West Indian theater of the war is Marshall Smelser, *The Campaign for the Sugar Islands, 1759* (Chapel Hill, 1955). Zenab E. Rashed, *The Peace of Paris, 1763* (Liverpool, 1951), provides a careful discussion of war aims, diplomatic maneuvers, and the terms of the Treaty of Paris.

SOURCES: For the Albany plan of union, see A. H. Smyth (ed.), *The Writings of Benjamin Franklin* (10 vols., New York, 1905–07), III, pp. 197–226. Gertrude S. Kimball (ed.), *Correspondence of William Pitt* (2 vols., New York, 1906), pertains to the years 1757–61. S. M. Pargellis has edited an important set of documents, *Military Affairs in North America, 1748–1765* (New York, 1936). Isabel M. Calder (ed.), *Colonial Captivities, Marches, and Journeys* (New York, 1935), throws interesting sidelights on the Anglo-French conflict. See also *The Journal of Jeffrey Amherst* (ed. J. C. Webster, Toronto, 1931). *Illinois on the Eve of the Seven Years' War, 1747–1755* (ed. T. C. Pease and E. Jenison, Springfield, 1940), is a collection emphasizing the Anglo-French rivalry in the fur trade. Wilbur R. Jacobs (ed.), *Indians of the Southern Colonial Frontier* (Columbia, S. C., 1954), makes available a report of 1755 by Edmund Atkin concerning the management of Western and Indian affairs in the South. Lois Mulkearn (ed.), *George Mercer Papers Relating to the Ohio Company of Virginia* (Pittsburgh, 1954), is a valuable collection.

XXII

 The Revolutionary Crisis

HAVING expelled the French from North America in 1763, Britain proceeded to consolidate her new territories and to strengthen her colonial system, long weakened by concessions to the colonies in return for their assistance against the French. The measures adopted after the war exposed a crisis in British mercantilism, indicated alike by antagonisms among commercial groups within Britain and by irreconcilable conflicts between British merchants on one side and colonial merchants and planters on the other. Because the colonies had copied the English methods of business enterprise they tended rapidly to duplicate the merchant capitalism of the mother country—with the result that mercantilistic tendencies took shape in America and clashed violently with British mercantilism. Both Britain and the colonies operated through expanding economies, the essential features of which were the accumulation of surplus capital by merchants and planters and the investment of such surpluses in a manner that opened new areas for exploitation and created new employments for the poor, the unemployed, and the dispossessed. Two fundamental conditions had to be met if eighteenth-century mercantilism was to function successfully: first, both British and colonial capitalists must protect those enterprises in which they had previously invested; second, both groups needed new fields of exploitation in which they could utilize their newly acquired profits.[1]

The central fact governing such investments in America was Britain's policy of prohibiting the development of colonial manufactures that would compete with the products of her own industry. Necessarily this policy greatly limited the opportunities for investment in the colonies, since it confined colonial and British enterprisers to non-manufacturing pursuits. Prior to 1760 there had been three general outlets in North America for the surplus capital of British and colonial investors. First, the tobacco, rice, and indigo plantations had attracted British investments in the form of merchants' loans to planters and had also absorbed colonial capital through the purchase of lands

[1] A brilliant, original interpretation is L. M. Hacker, "The First American Revolution," *Columbia University Quarterly*, XXVII (Sept. 1935).

and slaves. Secondly, the northern economy, revolving around the fishery, lumbering, grain and cattle farming, shipbuilding, and the manufacture of rum, flour, bread, cooperage stock, and crude iron had employed the vessels and other capital of the northern merchants and had enabled them to accumulate new capital to invest in lands, warehouses, trading goods, ships, mills, mortgages, and short-term loans. Thirdly, the fur trade and investments in western lands afforded outlets when plantation economy and northern enterprises were insufficient to absorb the surplus of new capital.[2]

By 1750–60 several tendencies had become apparent in colonial economy. Tobacco production, due to soil exhaustion, the burden of debt, heavy fixed labor costs, and the restraints of the British Acts of Trade, had reached the limits of expansion; in the late 1750's the demands for currency inflation in Virginia as a means of reducing the debt burden and the complaints of the planters against the British colonial system revealed that opportunities for investment of British and colonial capital in tobacco production had ceased to be attractive. After 1763 George Washington, one of the most efficient of the Virginia planters and one of the most unsparing critics of British merchant capitalism, shifted his principal economic activities from tobacco to wheat, flour, plantation manufactures, and investments in western lands. Similarly, by 1760 the commerce of the northern colonies and the economy on which it rested had reached a point where its expansion, depending upon the foreign sugar colonies, threatened Britain's investments in her own sugar islands. Clearly the commercial opportunities within the empire were not sufficient to support both the British merchants and their vigorous colonial rivals. With respect to the fur trade and western land speculation, British and colonial interests had acted in concert prior to 1760, a fact explained by the presence of the common enemy, France. Once the French had been removed, the vast interior awaited exploitation. But since both British and colonial capital could not find adequate outlets in plantation production, in colonial manufacturing, and in imperial commerce, a crucial question arose: should colonial investors or British investors reap the profits of the available enterprises, including the fur trade and the development of the West?[3]

[2] A. M. Schlesinger, "The American Revolution Reconsidered," *Political Science Quarterly*, XXXIV (March 1919).

[3] The passages from W. E. H. Lecky's *History of England* bearing on the Revolution have been edited by J. A. Woodburn as *The American Revolution* (New York, 1929).

The Western Problem

By 1730 most of the vast unoccupied land west of Pennsylvania, Maryland, and the southern colonies had come under the direct control of the British government. The land policy which Britain then pursued reflected the purposes of British merchant capitalism. The Crown did not seek to obtain a revenue for itself through land sales and quit-rents; instead the object was to increase British trade. This was to be accomplished by opening the land to *bona fide* settlers who would enlarge the supply of colonial commodities from which British merchants made their profits. Accordingly, British policy provided for free grants of small farms to actual settlers, and large tracts were given to speculative promoters like the Ohio Company on condition that they establish a prescribed number of families on their land. Otherwise the Crown objected to large grants to speculators who intended merely to acquire great holdings without contributing anything to the peopling of unoccupied areas. Little effort was made to collect the quit-rents nor were other conditions imposed upon land grants which would have stunted the growth of settlement. If, in the northern colonies, the use of certain lands was restricted for the production of naval stores, the object was to provide those colonies with commodities to support their commerce with Britain. And ever since 1700 the Crown had manifested an inflexible opposition to the creation of new proprietary colonies—partly because the proprietary land system generally retarded settlement and therefore curtailed the profits which British merchants made by trading in colonial produce. The proprietary system was allowed to continue in Pennsylvania partly because, in that exceptional instance, the liberal land policy of the Penns led to rapid settlement and increased production and trade with Britain.[4]

Prior to 1763 the necessity of opposing France and Spain in North America had reinforced Britain's policy of extending settlement as rapidly as possible, since the English colonist was a soldier as well as a farmer. Thus Britain's efforts to occupy Georgia and Nova Scotia reflect the Spanish-French menace; so also the Crown was careful to respect the land rights of Indians like the Iroquois whose assistance Britain needed against the French. Later, land policy became an instrument by which the British strengthened their hold in the upper Ohio valley. In 1754 Governor Dinwiddie of Virginia offered land bounties in that region to colonial soldiers and in the same year the

---

[4] C. W. Alvord's *The Mississippi Valley in British Politics* (2 vols., Cleveland, 1916) is one of the most outstanding studies of the colonial period. Very important.

Crown instructed Dinwiddie to grant tracts west of the Alleghenies up to a thousand acres; by 1757 two million acres had been so granted.[5]

After 1760 several factors gave a new slant to Britain's attitude toward the West. First, now that France and Spain had been expelled from the territory east of the Mississippi, Britain no longer needed to encourage settlement as a defense measure. Secondly, the region into which colonial pioneers were now penetrating lay west of the mountains. Would settlements there serve British commerce; were not the Westerners going beyond the reach of British merchants? Thirdly, migration to the West constituted a threat to the established seaboard area. British merchants now had a substantial investment in the tobacco plantations; if the people moved West, would not the tobacco industry be ruined and the debts which the planters owed to British merchants be shuffled off? Fourthly, investors in England were affected by a new speculative craze; one colonist, George Croghan, when visiting England, found his associates there "land crazy." [6] If money was to be made from Britain's newly won territories, certainly British investors should have a substantial share. Moreover, the North American fur trade was now in Britain's possession, and the British merchants who proposed to exploit it looked askance at settlers who would drive the Indians away and destroy the fur-bearing animals. Finally, a new British land policy might be made to protect Britain's established commerce. The French and Indian War had shown that the Acts of Trade and Navigation were but poorly enforced—largely because colonial officials were paid from legislative appropriations and consequently were not dependent upon the Crown. But if the king's lands in America might be made to yield more revenue through sales and quit-rents a fund could be obtained which would make colonial officials independent of legislative support and therefore attentive to the commands of their new paymaster, the British Crown.

Such being the factors involved, it was natural that British land policy should now aim to protect the North American fur trade and to regulate the settlement of the West in such a manner that British investors would have an opportunity to make profits, that existing British investments in the seaboard area would not be wiped out by sudden population shifts, and that the Crown would obtain a revenue

[5] Justin Winsor's *The Westward Movement* (Boston, 1897), a detailed factual survey of events, 1763–98, is valuable as a reference work.

[6] Albert T. Volwiler, *George Croghan and the Westward Movement, 1741–1782* (Cleveland, 1926), is a detailed study of one of the central figures in western trade, Indian affairs, and land speculation.

for the support of colonial officials, thereby enabling them to function more effectively in Britain's interest. Each of these objectives entailed a much more cautious disposal of unused lands than that characteristic of the period of the Anglo-French conflict when the settlers were occupying a region easily accessible to British traders. A more cautious land policy in turn required that the western lands be severed from the thirteen colonies and incorporated into new provinces, the governments of which would be thoroughly subservient to British interests. Hence British colonial officials (Lord Halifax in 1757 and the Earl of Shelburne in 1767) proposed that new royal colonies be erected in the West.[7]

To many colonial capitalists no enterprise seemed more attractive than investments in western lands. The region which now beckoned to the colonial promoters was that of present-day West Virginia, southern Ohio, and Kentucky. Not only were important merchants like Thomas and Samuel Wharton of Pennsylvania interested; so also were leading planter families of Virginia such as the Washingtons and the Lees. The Ohio valley, an excellent wheat country, appealed to the more enterprising planters who were shifting production from tobacco to wheat. Washington now expressed his desire to "increase our export of wheat, gently lead our people off from tobacco, as well as render a vast extent of back country useful to trade."[8] Colonial speculators organized numerous companies, seeking to obtain title to far-reaching areas upon part of which they might establish settlers whose labor would enhance the value of the land which the company retained for future sale. By this means, also, the promoters hoped to obtain choice tracts as their personal estates. In the meantime a company might engage in the fur trade until settlement matured; thus the company might increase its capital and also establish contacts with the Indians preparatory to removing them from its grant. Foremost among such speculative ventures were the Loyal Company, a company of New Yorkers for establishing a colony of New Wales, the Company of Military Adventurers, the Illinois Company, the Wabash Company, the Mississippi Company, and the Susquehannah Company.[9] The proposed land acquisitions of these corporations varied from 200,000 to 12,000,000 acres; the great West inspired great visions.

[7] Clarence E. Carter, *Great Britain and the Illinois Country, 1763–1774* (Washington, 1910), is a thorough, detailed critique for the advanced student.

[8] Paul L. Haworth, *George Washington: Farmer* (Indianapolis, 1915), has been republished (1925) as *George Washington: Country Gentleman.*

[9] J. P. Boyd, "Connecticut's Experiment in Expansion: the Susquehannah Company," *Journal of Economic and Business History,* IV (Nov. 1931).

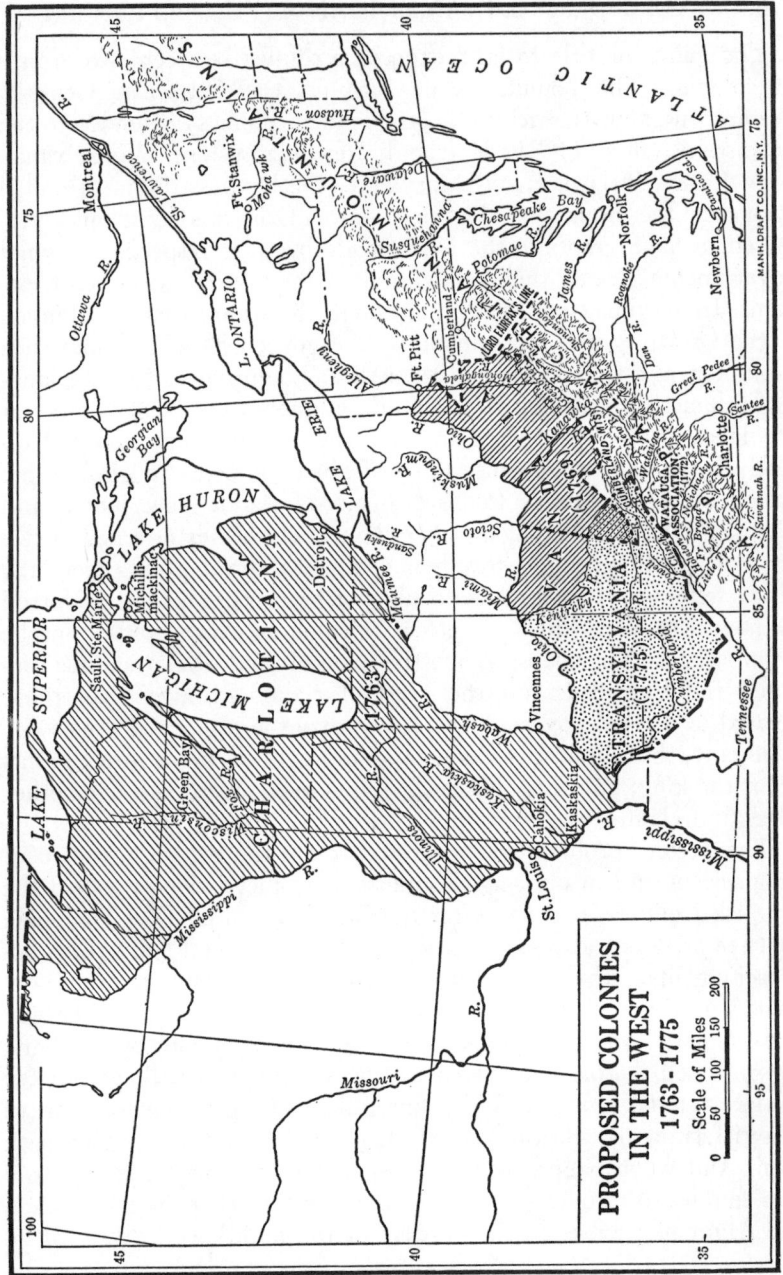

PROPOSED COLONIES IN THE WEST: 1763–1775

The quest for title to land exposed a conflict between two groups of colonies. The boundaries of Virginia, the Carolinas, Georgia, Connecticut, and Massachusetts (the landed colonies) extended to the Mississippi; those of Rhode Island, New Hampshire, Pennsylvania, New Jersey, Delaware, and Maryland (the landless colonies) ended at or near the mountains. The promoters of the landed colonies preferred to have grants in the West made by their respective colonial governments because their influence at home assured preferred treatment. In Virginia, for instance, although the western lands belonged to the Crown, grants were made by the governor—with whom such promoters as a rule had friendly contacts. The promoters of the landless colonies, fearful that they would be ignored by the governors of the landed colonies, desired to have the western lands granted directly by the Crown.[10] Since only Virginia claimed the whole Ohio valley the promoters of Pennsylvania, Maryland, New Jersey, and New York were united against her claims, which they attacked in two ways. First, they sought for their companies direct grants from the king; secondly, if such grants could not be procured, they preferred to have the West divided into new colonies which would not be dominated by Virginians. When the issue of land titles was thus confused the Virginians felt the need of claims stronger than those created by a royal governor and hence they too organized (the Ohio Company, the Mississippi Company) and petitioned for direct grants from the king, knowing that such grants took precedence over other titles and claims.[11]

The western problem was projected before the British government by a serious Indian uprising, Pontiac's conspiracy, which ravaged the English frontiers in 1763. After the British captured Fort Duquesne in 1758 settlers had pressed forward into the upper Ohio valley, encroaching upon the land of the Indians and threatening their destruction. Tribes that had been wooed by the British during the war were angered after the peace when the Crown, in a fit of economy, discontinued the presents which had won their good will. British fur traders (at the time practically unregulated by government) spread dissatisfaction by cheating the Indians and debauching them with rum. And when French agents whispered that a large French army was coming to recover the Ohio valley for the red man and France, the Algonquin tribes on the borders of the middle colonies went on

---

[10] A brief sketch of western trade and land interests appears in Max Savelle's *George Morgan, Colony Builder* (New York, 1932).

[11] C. W. Alvord, "Virginia and the West," *Mississippi Valley Historical Review,* III (June 1916).

the warpath and drove the English settlers from all the frontier posts except Fort Pitt and Detroit. Due to a conference between British agents and the southern Indians in 1763 the latter were pacified and did not enter the conspiracy. Before the revolt was suppressed by British regulars and colonial troops late in 1763 it had convinced British statesmen that a new policy was needed for regulating the fur trade, the settlement, and the defense of the West.[12]

In October the British government issued the Proclamation of 1763 —a highly important state paper drafted by the Earl of Shelburne when president of the Board of Trade. It provided that for the time being colonial settlement was not to extend westward beyond a line running through the sources of the rivers flowing into the Atlantic. Colonial governors were not to authorize surveys or issue patents for any land west of this line—nor for any other land to which the Indian title had not been extinguished. Drafted in order to pacify the Indians, the Proclamation of 1763 was regarded by Shelburne as a temporary measure that would give Britain time in which to form a permanent western policy. Its immediate effects were to remove the western lands from the control of the colonial governors and to compel colonial land speculators to appeal directly to the king for desired grants.

In 1767 Shelburne, now Secretary of State for the Southern Department, proposed that the western country be opened to settlement and that three new colonies be established: at Detroit, on the Ohio, and in the Illinois country.[13] A change in the ministry which occurred soon afterward transferred colonial administration to the Earl of Hillsborough, who occupied in 1768 the newly created post of Secretary of State for the Colonies. Hillsborough rejected Shelburne's proposals of 1767 and advised instead that new colonies should not be erected and that the flow of settlement westward should be carefully regulated, arguing that the interior would drain population from the seaboard and that new settlements should be placed under the military rule of the British commanders of the western posts as a means of avoiding colonial insubordination. In conformity with Hillsborough's program, Britain in 1768 adopted the idea of an Indian boundary line to be located periodically with the consent of the Indians concerned. For the future the title to Indian lands should be purchased by the imperial government; settlement should proceed under the

[12] Francis Parkman's *The Conspiracy of Pontiac* is a fascinating narrative.

[13] The standard biography is Lord Fitzmaurice, *Life of William Earl of Shelburne* (2 vols., 2d ed., London, 1912). See also R. A. Humphreys, "Lord Shelburne and British Colonial Policy, 1766–1768," *English Historical Review*, L (April 1935).

supervision of British agents; the boundary should be moved westward gradually; and white settlers were not to cross the existing
line.[14] By 1770 the line had been located as follows: "Beginning at
Lake Ontario, it bent westward so that it opened up for settlement
the upper waters of the Ohio as far as the mouth of the Great
Kanawha; thence it turned south and east, closing for settlement the
back country of the southern colonies" (Alvord).

Hillsborough's policy and the boundary line of 1768 thus dealt a
hard blow to Virginia's efforts to dominate the West. Only a small
area was now opened to settlement, which was to proceed directly
under the Crown, thus making it possible for the speculators of the
middle colonies to secure land at Virginia's expense. Foremost among
such speculators were Samuel Wharton and William Trent, Pennsylvania merchants and spokesmen in the late 1760's for a group of
"suffering" fur traders who had lost much property during Pontiac's
conspiracy. Since 1763 the suffering traders had been asking Britain
for a large piece of land in the West. Failing in that quarter they had
attended a conference at Fort Stanwix in 1768 where they persuaded
the Six Nations to cede to them a large tract in what is now West
Virginia. And when this area was opened to settlement by the boundary line of 1768 the suffering traders applied to the Crown for a
confirmation of the cession, proposing that it form the basis of a new
colony, Vandalia. Many men of influence in England were induced
to back the Vandalia project and Benjamin Franklin acted as agent
for the promoters at court. Lord Hillsborough opposed the scheme,
but his successor in the colonial office, Lord Dartmouth (1772), approved. However, the forces behind Hillsborough, acting through
the Board of Trade, effectively thwarted the Vandalians at Whitehall,
so that in 1774 the project was still hanging fire.[15]

The year 1774 brought a major development in Britain's western
land policy—the Quebec Act. With the object of reserving the lands
north of the Ohio and west of Pennsylvania as an Indian country and
fur trading area, this act annexed this territory to the province of
Quebec and thereby removed it from the influence of the settlers and
speculators of Virginia and the middle colonies. Virginia's position
was now desperate. Excluded from the country north of the Ohio by
the Quebec Act and on the point of being excluded from West Virginia and Kentucky by the Vandalia project and the Indian boundary

[14] M. Farrand, "The Indian Boundary Line," *American Historical Review*, X (July,
1905). The best recent study is Thomas P. Abernethy, *Western Lands and the American Revolution* (New York, 1937)—important.

[15] Louis P. Kellogg's *The British Regime in Wisconsin and the Northwest* (Madison,
Wis., 1935) is an able survey. See chapters 1–8.

line, the Virginians were forced to act aggressively in defense of their western claims.[16]

Fortunately for the Virginians their governor, Lord Dunmore, stood behind the speculators and pioneers. Himself a speculator who hoped to make his fortune from western lands, Lord Dunmore had ignored Britain's policies by making grants in the Vandalia tract and in the country west of the boundary line. The Virginians were now ready to occupy Kentucky, Daniel Boone having led the way in 1769. Realizing in 1774 that, in the face of the Vandalia project, Virginia needed to defend her claims in the West, Lord Dunmore instigated a war against the Shawnee in the neighborhood of Wheeling, defeated them and wrung from them the right of Virginia pioneers to hunt in Kentucky. In Dunmore's War the Shawnee were isolated; their overlords, the Six Nations, had already granted to Britain the lands occupied by the Shawnee south of the Ohio and west to the Tennessee River (Treaty of Fort Stanwix, 1768). The Iroquois, by sacrificing the Shawnee and their lands, evidently hoped to divert the whites to the country south of the Ohio and thus to preserve intact their own territory in the Mohawk valley.[17]

The landed interest in the colonies received another shock from Britain when the Crown in 1774 promulgated new regulations for the disposal of ungranted lands in Virginia, New York, North Carolina, South Carolina, New Hampshire, Georgia, Florida, and throughout the West. Previously, fertile lands had been occupied by colonists in irregular parcels, thus leaving uneven tracts in between, which the farmers adjacent often appropriated without ceremony. The usual quit-rent of 2s. a hundred acres had not been excessive and great quantities of land had been given away by the Crown. Now the king ordered that for the future all grants must be surveyed in regular lots (minimum, one hundred acres; maximum, a thousand); the quit-rents exacted for such lands should amount to 4s. 2d. a hundred acres (twice the rate prevailing in Virginia); governors were not to make further gifts of land; and all tracts should be sold at auction to the "best bidder" at a price not less than 6d. an acre. Thomas Jefferson objected to these new regulations on the ground that "the ac-

[16] Alfred L. Burt, *The Old Province of Quebec* (Minneapolis, 1933), is a thorough study of the period 1760–91, emphasizing economic influences. R. Coupland's *The Quebec Act* (Oxford, 1925) is a study in British efforts to conciliate the French Canadians.

[17] On settlement west of the southern colonies see Archibald Henderson, *The Conquest of the Old Southwest* (New York, 1920)—well written, in a romantic strain; and Constance L. Skinner, *Pioneers of the Old Southwest* (*Chronicles of America*, New Haven, 1919).

quisition of lands being rendered difficult, the population of our country is likely to be checked"—an indictment which he included in the Declaration of Independence.

British land policy as finally formulated in 1774 declared a virtual embargo on colonial expansion in the West. It closed to speculators and settlers the territories north of the Ohio and south of Virginia, it opened only a small tract in western Virginia, it subjected all ungranted lands in the East to rigorous and hampering conditions of purchase, and it deprived the landed colonies of their claims to the interior. Even the Vandalia speculators had not gained approval for their project, and despite the powerful forces making for westward expansion in Virginia that colony was denied independent access to the West.[18] The restrictive policy applied to the thirteen colonies did not mean, however, that British investors and speculators were being ignored. After 1763 the Crown conferred numerous large tracts upon merchants, army officers, and wealthy landowners (all residents of Britain), such tracts being located in Canada, Nova Scotia, Florida, and Prince Edward Island—regions accessible to British trade and not likely to produce commodities that would compete with the products of industries in which British investors had a large stake. By opening these areas Britain created speculative opportunities for her own investors while opposing the schemes of colonial promoters to develop the trans-Allegheny West.

Britain's regulation of the fur trade north of the Ohio River exhibited the same tendencies which made her land policy odious to the thirteen colonies. The furs of this region were regarded in England as its most valuable form of wealth—a resource that Britain must monopolize in order to provide new outlets for the capital of her merchants and in order also to render the Indians dependent upon herself as the means of controlling their movements in peace and war.[19] More particularly, the British must prevent the French traders who remained in the Northwest from diverting the fur trade down the Mississippi to Spanish New Orleans. After the conquest of Canada British merchants replaced the French capitalists at Montreal; then Pontiac's conspiracy gave the British Canadians a further advantage by disrupting the fur trade of Pennsylvania and New York. Although the traffic was less important to the middle colonies than land specula-

[18] Justin Winsor, "Virginia and the Quebec Bill," *American Historical Review*, I (April 1896).
[19] Wayne E. Stevens, *The Northwest Fur Trade* (Urbana, 1928), is an excellent analysis of the economics of the fur trade and of the political influence of the British fur traders. See also W. E. Stevens, "The Organization of the British Fur Trade, 1760–1800," *Mississippi Valley Historical Review*, III (Sept. 1916).

MAGNA *Britannia: her Colonies* REDUCED

BRITAIN WEAKENED BY OPPRESSIVE MEASURES AGAINST HER COLONIES (1768)

tion it remained a worth-while source of profit: in 1767 the Philadelphia firm of Baynton, Wharton, and Morgan employed three hundred boatmen in the trade with the Illinois country. Each colony
with western aspirations desired to dominate the trade and the Indians—a purpose which provoked colonial opposition to imperial regulations in the interest of British merchants at Montreal.

After a decade of experimentation with such regulations Britain in
the Quebec Act of 1774 proclaimed a new policy for the area north
of the Ohio. Its object was to divert the movement of furs from New
York and Pennsylvania to Montreal; hence all traders were to be
regulated by the governor of the province of Quebec. Thus were the
merchants of the thirteen colonies to be excluded from the northern
fur trade, precisely in the manner that colonial promoters were to be
denied the profits arising from speculation in western lands.[20]

ANGLO-COLONIAL COMMERCIAL RIVALRY

A third phase of the western problem, frontier defense, touched
upon two related issues—taxation and the regulation of commerce.
Pontiac's conspiracy had demonstrated to British officials the urgent
need of protecting the frontiers, and since the colonies could not be
counted upon to support a large army or to act together in harmony,
the British ministry, headed by George Grenville, decided in 1763
to station an imperial force of ten thousand men in North America.
But Britain was not in the mood to pay in full the estimated expense
of £350,000 a year; she had now accumulated a debt of £130,000,000
which cost the nation £4,500,000 yearly in interest; and she staggered
under oppressive taxes, those on land amounting to four shillings in
the pound. Arguing that the colonists should bear part of the charge
for their own defense, Grenville induced Parliament to enact two
momentous statutes. The first—the Sugar Act of 1764—imposed
many new taxes on colonial trade and reduced the molasses duty of
the act of 1733 from 6d. to 3d. a pound, making provision at the
same time for efficient collection of the new tax, whereas the former
duty had yielded next to nothing. The Stamp Act of 1765 required
the colonists to pay stamp duties on legal and commercial documents
(to the dismay of merchants and lawyers), on newspapers, almanacs,
and pamphlets (to the distress of newspaper publishers), and on
playing cards and dice. From all these taxes the Crown hoped to de-

[20] Victor Coffin's *The Province of Quebec and the Early American Revolution*
(Madison, Wis., 1896), a technical study of Britain's problems in governing Canada
after 1760, emphasizes the importance of the fur trade.

rive a revenue of about £100,000 to defray nearly a third of the cost of frontier defense.[21]

The Sugar Act and the Stamp Act at once focused the attention of the colonists upon their long-standing commercial conflicts with Britain. The colonies now supplied British capitalists with income from three principal sources: the general commerce and shipping of the empire, investments in the British sugar islands, and manufacturing industries in England sustained by colonial markets. But because the colonial merchants had to resort to similar enterprises they constantly menaced their British rivals—partly by obtaining a large share of the profits of imperial commerce and partly by trading with the foreign sugar colonies, thus undermining British investments in the British islands. Britain's interests therefore dictated that the colonies should be regulated in such a manner as to protect her West Indian investments, to strengthen her manufacturing industries, and to safeguard the profits of her merchants in colonial trade. These objectives were to be realized in two ways: by imposing new restrictions upon colonial commerce and by enforcing more rigidly the existing Acts of Trade. The importance of such a policy is indicated by a report of the Duke of Newcastle in 1766 that the trade of Britain was declining in every part of the world except America.[22]

Of the new measures adopted after 1760 one group of acts aimed to extend further aid to British manufacturers. Bounties were now offered to stimulate production in the colonies of hemp and flax, raw materials needed by British cloth-workers and rope-makers. The Sugar Act added to the enumerated article list a new group of products desired by British manufacturers—whale fins, hides, skins, raw silk, potashes, pearl ashes, coffee, pimiento, and cocoanuts. The Sugar Act also tightened the hold of British manufacturers on the colonial market: first, by removing most of the drawbacks previously allowed on European goods passing through England to the colonies, thereby increasing their prices so that they could be undersold by British products; secondly, by placing new duties on other competing goods such as oriental silks and calicoes, foreign linens, and French lawns. Finally, an act of 1774 carried forward the prohibitions on colonial manufactures by prohibiting the exportation from Britain to the colonies of tools used in linen, cotton, silk, and woolen manufactures.

[21] C. E. Carter, "The Significance of the Military Office in America, 1763–1775," *American Historical Review*, XXVIII (April 1923).

[22] An intensive, highly important study is Arthur M. Schlesinger, *The Colonial Merchants and the American Revolution* (New York, 1918). Very valuable.

These measures also promised to aid British merchants in that they tended to center colonial trade in England and therefore assured that the freights, commissions, profits, and interest charges involved would go to British firms. Similarly, acts of 1766–67 required that non-enumerated articles bound for parts of Europe north of Cape Finisterre should first pass through a British port. A major clause of the Sugar Act was designed to protect British merchants in the colonial wine trade. Prior to 1763 the colonial merchants had imported great quantities of wine from Madeira, the Canaries, and the Azores. Now, however, all such wines imported from the Wine Islands were to pay in the colonies a duty of £7 a tun, whereas wine imported from Britain was to pay only 10s. a tun. Were such duties efficiently collected, wines exported by British merchants from London to the colonies might compete with wine brought from the Wine Islands by colonial merchants.[23]

Both the Sugar Act and the Stamp Act contained a further threat to colonial business. This was the rule that the taxes collected in America were to be remitted to the British exchequer and disbursed by order of Parliament. Once more the old problem of returns raised its head. The colonial merchants argued that such remittances would deprive them of specie or its equivalent in buying power for English goods and thus make it impossible for them to pay for needed imports, since their "returns" to England had never been adequate, even when they had not had to make remittances of tax money to the Crown. It is true that the tax money was to return to the colonies for the army, but it would come back in the form of English goods which would be exchanged for colonial products and colonial currency needed by the army. If the Crown should contract with British merchants to supply the army, they would obtain the money in England, invest it in English goods, and thereby strengthen their hold upon colonial trade. In other words Britain might deprive the colonial merchants of their means of buying English goods, transfer such buying power to English merchants, and drive the colonial merchants from their customary trade.

In 1773 the British government made its most open move to favor British merchants when Parliament in effect gave the East India Company a monopoly of the colonial trade in tea. A discussion of this measure appears in chapter XXIII.[24]

Five clauses in the Sugar Act extended protection to British in-

[23] See again G. L. Beer, *British Colonial Policy, 1754–1765*, chapters 10–14.
[24] M. Farrand, "The Taxation of Tea," *American Historical Review*, III (Jan. 1898).

vestors in the British West Indies. The English colonists were prohibited from importing rum from a foreign sugar colony; they must now pay an added duty of £1 2s. a hundredweight on all white sugar which they bought from the foreign islands; a new duty of 6d. a pound was placed upon foreign indigo which they purchased; foreign coffee was subject to a duty of £2 19s. 9d. a hundredweight; and foreign molasses to a duty of 3d. a gallon. All these taxes were designed to raise the colonial price of foreign West Indian products in order that the British planters might obtain higher prices for their products.

Hand in hand with these duties and trade restrictions came a series of measures for the strict enforcement of all British regulations, old and new. The Grenville ministry, 1763–65, ordered that absentee officials should take themselves to the colonies and perform their duties in person rather than through low-paid and inefficient deputies; it authorized anew the use of writs of assistance; and it put British naval vessels in American waters to the task of enforcing the Acts of Trade. Parliament in 1764 decreed that customs officials who made seizures and arrests with good cause could not be sued for damages by colonists who were not proved guilty as charged; the burden of proof as to whether duties had been paid or whether goods were of foreign origin was placed upon the accused; and an act of 1764 authorized the erection of a general vice-admiralty court for all the colonies, with the provision that penalties arising from violation of the acts of trade might be recovered in any colonial admiralty or vice-admiralty court, thus removing trials from the neighborhood of the defendant. Next came the Townshend Acts of 1767, strengthening the admiralty courts and reorganizing the American customs service, whereupon the king immediately appointed an American Board of Commissioners of the Customs whose authority extended over all British North America. With energies concentrated upon a single task and with virtually complete powers, this board set about vigorously to enforce the British Acts of Trade.[25]

Before 1763 British customs and trade laws had not seriously injured the colonial merchant class, such acts having not been rigidly enforced—and that because Britain was unwilling to pay for enforcement and shrank from raising the necessary funds by taxing the colonies. But the time had now come to be done with such weakness; hence the decision of 1763 to maintain an army in America and to tax the colonists for its support. (Incidentally the army might be used to enforce the Acts of Trade.) Although Parliament in 1766 re-

[25] See again E. Channing, *History of the United States*, Vol. III, chapters 1–4.

pealed the Stamp Act and lowered the molasses duty of the Sugar Act from 3*d*. to 1*d*., the principle of taxing the colonies for the army remained, since the other duties of the Sugar Act were not removed. Then in 1767 Parliament extended the principle by levying new taxes (the Townshend duties) to be paid in the colonies on imported tea, paper, glass, painter's colors, and lead. The money thus raised was to go to the support, not only of the army, but also to pay expenses of colonial government and the administration of justice; thus might Britain enjoy a revenue independently of the colonial assemblies and free its American agents of their dependence upon the colonists for their pay.[26] The land ordinance of 1774 promised more revenue for this purpose. And when the colonial merchants warred against the Sugar Act, the Townshend duties, and the British customs agents, the Crown in 1768 transferred the army from the West to the East and prepared to crush opposition with military force.

The efficiency of the new enforcement policy contrasted sharply with the lax conditions prevailing before. Between 1767 and 1770 the number of British customs agents in Philadelphia was trebled and new revenue cutters were added to the coast patrol. Channing estimates that in seven years, 1768–74, the colonists paid £200,000 in taxes to the British customs service; British levies collected in America rose from less than £2,000 a year before 1763 to £30,000 a year after 1767. And all this for the purpose of making colonial trade profitable to British merchants at the expense of their American competitors who paid the taxes.

The relation between taxation and enforcement appeared also in the Quartering Act of 1765, which required the colonists to supply additional funds for the support of the imperial army. For that part of the forces stationed within any colony its assembly was to provide barracks, "certain necessary utensils," salt, vinegar, rum or beer, and part of the money to pay the costs of transportation. Since New York was the gateway to the interior the Quartering Act imposed upon that province a disproportionately large share of this extra expense, much to the annoyance of the New Yorkers, who contended that they should not be so penalized simply because the army crossed their territory en route to the West. After 1767 the same problem confronted Massachusetts when royal troops were moved to Boston.[27]

Meanwhile, Britain had adopted a new Currency Act of 1764 in

---

[26] C. M. Andrews, "The American Revolution: an Interpretation," *American Historical Review*, XXI (Jan. 1926).

[27] George E. Howard's *The Preliminaries of the Revolution, 1763–1775* (New York, 1905) is one of the less distinguished volumes of the *American Nation* series.

order to protect the investments of her merchants in the colonies. During the French and Indian War Virginia had issued £250,000 in bills of credit which were declared legal tender in payment of private debts, old and new. As the value of such bills in terms of English money declined, British merchants complained that they diminished debts due in sterling money "of certain and fixed value" by permitting payments to be made in a currency "of a local, uncertain value." Not even the bills of the Bank of England or exchequer notes issued by the British government were legal tender. In 1764 the Board of Trade condemned colonial paper currency as a device whereby colonial debtors could defraud their creditors, and Parliament thereupon forbade the issuance of legal tender bills and ordered that all such bills emitted during the war should be retired at the time appointed by the act of issue. Should any governor sign an act for legal tender currency he should pay a fine of £1,000, lose his post, and be forever barred from offices of trust. The Currency Act of 1764 extended to all the colonies the provisions of the Currency Act of 1751, which the Board of Trade deemed to have had a salutary effect in New England.

THE PLIGHT OF THE COLONIES

Had all the acts on the British statute books after 1763 been rigidly enforced their cumulative force would undoubtedly have crushed the colonies. Let us consider first the region north of Maryland, where the producers of fish, lumber, and farm commodities were steadily enlarging their output and therefore in need of expanding markets, and where the merchants required an extended field of investment for their surplus capital. Prior to 1763 the foreign West Indies and the Wine Islands had afforded two such necessary markets and outlets. The Sugar Act, however, burdened the trade with both regions and tended to raise the prices of the products involved—particularly of rum and molasses, ingredients in nearly every important branch of colonial commerce. Restraints upon trade made shipowning unprofitable and not only depressed the colonial shipbuilding industry but also induced shrewd merchants to sell vessels previously acquired. More particularly the Sugar Act made it difficult for the Northerners to obtain their customary means of buying in England, while the payment of tax money to Britain promised to deprive them of a large part of such remittances as remained.[28] Since colonial com-

[28] F. B. Wiener, "The Rhode Island Merchants and the Sugar Act," *New England Quarterly*, III (July 1930). See also B. M. Bigelow, "Aaron Lopez, Merchant of Newport," *New England Quarterly*, IV (Oct. 1931).

merce revolved around the import trade from Britain, anything which reduced the buying power of the colonial merchants for British goods threatened to dislocate all their other trades. When in 1773 Britain endeavored to give the British East India Company a monopoly of the colonial tea trade the denial of profits to colonial merchants was beyond question. The general effect of Britain's measures, if enforced, would have been to raise the price of all imported goods (the Townshend duties taxed imports even from Britain) and to reduce the prices of colonial exports; losses sustained by colonial producers and merchants through being compelled to buy dear and sell cheap were to provide the gains of British merchants and the tax revenues of the Crown. And if foreign commerce became inadequate and unprofitable, what could the northern colonies do? They were not allowed to develop manufacturing industries and they were to be excluded from the fur trade and the development of the West. In place of the growth long characteristic of the colonies, British policy now threatened repression, contraction, and decay.[29]

Nor did the prospects of the tobacco colonies appear in a happier light. As the profits of the tobacco industry vanished the energetic planters had turned to the production of new commodities—fish, grain, and livestock; they had tried to check the importation of slaves; they had fostered home manufacture of textiles and leather goods; and they had invested in western lands. Yet each of these activities inspired hostile orders from Britain. The slave trade was to remain open and unhampered; home manufactures were not to expand; the markets for southern grain and livestock in the foreign islands were to be curtailed; and the West was to be closed to Virginia speculators. The planters should continue to produce tobacco, even though forced to use inefficient slave labor on exhausted lands, to stagger under an oppressive burden of debt, and to market their crops through creditor-merchants who took the cream of the profits. British policy decreed that the tobacco planters remained wedded to a declining productive system, faced with the certain prospect of economic bondage.[30]

By 1763 the contradictions in mercantilism had become self-evident. If the colonies were to buy more in goods and services from Britain than they sold to her, the deficit could be cared for in only a

[29] C. M. Andrews, *The Boston Merchants and the Non-Importation Movement* (Cambridge, 1917), is an excellent résumé.

[30] See chapter 1 of an admirable study by Isaac S. Harrell, *Loyalism in Virginia* (Philadelphia, 1926).

few ways. Gold and silver might have been used to settle the adverse balance, but the supply in the colonies was not adequate. The other alternative was to sell goods to the colonies on credit. But this solution had its dangers: first because the interest charges ensuing increased the demands on the colonies and enhanced their unfavorable balance of trade; secondly, because the increasing debt burden required an expanding economy if it were to be carried successfully by the debtors. But the investments of British creditors created an interest in established enterprises that might be destroyed by the development of new and competing enterprises. And if new enterprises were retarded, if expansion were stopped, the burden of fixed debts which pressed upon old enterprises would become unbearable, since the debts themselves had been created on the assumption that an expanded production would provide for future payment. Clearly, by 1763 the colonies had to expand in order to prosper, and yet Britain sought to restrain their manufactures, their foreign trade, and their westward settlements, seeking thereby to protect her own commerce, industry, and investments in the tobacco-sugar areas, and to reserve the West as a field for British enterprise. Such enterprises as Britain proposed to leave free to the colonists would have yielded little beyond a subsistence living and the means of paying their sterling debts. Mercantilist tendencies had previously created critical situations but the colonists had escaped because British acts had not been enforced. Now, however, when Britain taxed the colonists for an army and prepared to use it to keep them in an economic strait jacket, a reckoning was at hand.[31]

In a conflict so profound as the American Revolution the interests of all classes were vitally affected by the issues at stake. In some way or other every man's fortune felt the impact of British policies, and for the most part the effect was injurious. A common foe across the sea drew the colonists together, and yet within colonial society were cleavages as deep as those which separated the colonies from the mother country—class divisions that common opposition to British policies could not efface. In the words of Carl Becker, the American Revolution "was the result of two general movements; the contest for home-rule and independence, and the democratization of American politics and society." In order to account for this dualism two questions must be considered: what factors worked to unite the colo-

[31] H. E. Egerton, *The Causes and Character of the American Revolution* (Oxford, 1923), attributes American resistance to the English settler's opposition to an inferior status within the empire.

nial classes against British rule, and what counter-forces arrayed class against class?

A large section of the upper class in America objected strenuously to the lot assigned to them by Britain after 1763. Many southern planters, thoroughly aroused against Britain's dominance of their trade, complained that the British merchants paid unduly low prices for their crops and sent them inferior European goods, poorly packed and shipped and priced excessively high. In the face of such conditions the debt burden had become insupportable: as Jefferson put it, "these debts had become hereditary from father to son, for many generations, so that the planters were a species of property annexed to certain mercantile houses in London." Accepting Jefferson's estimate that the debts of Virginia amounted to £2,000,000 sterling, it is safe to assume that a yearly interest charge of 6 per cent or £120,000 was enough to absorb the income of the planters after all other fixed costs had been deducted. "With their plantations, slaves, and sometimes their furniture and ungrown crops mortgaged beyond their actual value, it seemed in 1775 that nothing less than virtual repudiation could save them" (Carman). The planters, however, were not repudiationists; their status as property owners inculcated a strong sense of the sanctity of private contracts. But when Britain increased the difficulty of debt payment there was no alternative except to resist. The attempted closing of the West to planters' investments threatened to cut off a principal source of income by which they previously had carried their debt burdens, while the new British taxes increased the price of imported goods without adding a penny to their income. The Crown's refusal to permit restrictions on the slave trade also antagonized those planters who were overstocked with now unprofitable workers. For these various reasons the planters raised a voice of protest against Britain's rule. Among them were George Washington, Thomas Jefferson, Benjamin Harrison, Richard Blair, Edmund Pendleton, Richard Henry Lee, Francis Lightfoot Lee, George Mason, Edmund Randolph, Peyton Randolph, James Madison, and Thomas Nelson of Virginia, Charles Carroll and Thomas Johnson of Maryland, and Edmund Rutledge, John Rutledge, Arthur Middleton, Rawlins Lowndes, and Charles C. Pinckney of South Carolina. Among such planters two groups may be distinguished. One, represented by Thomas Jefferson, consisted of agriculturists whose investments and activities were centered upon their plantations and who relished the life of a country gentleman; the second, represented by George Washington, was composed of planters who were also businessmen—merchants, moneylenders, investors in western lands, and promoters of industrial enterprises.[32]

From a large body of colonial merchants came an equally spirited resistance. Their grievances against Britain included the restraints upon their commerce, their exclusion from the northern fur trade and western land speculation, the prohibitions against colonial manufactures, the added burden of taxes, the new measures to enforce the British colonial system and the tendency of these measures to reduce their profits and increase the difficulty of paying debts due to England. (Such debts of Pennsylvania in 1765 amounted to £300,000.) In short, British measures imperiled the existing investments of the colonial merchants and closed new outlets for their surplus capital. The chief merchant opponents of British measures were John Hancock, James Bowdoin, and Elbridge Gerry of Massachusetts, John Langdon of New Hampshire, Jonathan Trumbull and Roger Sherman of Connecticut, Stephen Hopkins, William Ellery, Samuel Ward, and Moses Brown of Rhode Island, Alexander MacDougall, Isaac Sears, and John Lamb of New York, Isaac Pemberton, Thomas Mifflin, Robert Morris, Samuel Wharton, Thomas Wharton, and George Clymer of Pennsylvania, and Henry Laurens, Gabriel Manigault, and Christopher Gadsden of South Carolina. Somewhat akin to the merchants were the New York aristocrats, with their threefold interests in land, commerce, and the fur trade, whose opposition to Britain was voiced by Philip Livingston, Stephen Van Rensselaer, Philip Schuyler, Gouverneur Morris, Robert Livingston, and Lewis Morris.

Many members of the professional class, who were affiliated with the aristocracy by ties of marriage and business or property ownership, directed the campaign against Britain on the legal and intellectual plane. Among them were John Witherspoon, president of Princeton college, George Wythe, professor of law at the College of William and Mary, Dr. Benjamin Rush of Pennsylvania, and an able group of lawyers which included or was to include John Adams and James Otis of Massachusetts, John Jay and Alexander Hamilton of New York, and James Wilson, John Dickinson, and James Smith of Pennsylvania.[33]

---

[32] Burton J. Hendrick, *The Lees of Virginia* (Boston, 1935), a vigorous, fascinating study of a family, is highly recommended to the general reader. Edward S. Delaplaine, *The Life of Thomas Johnson* (New York, 1927), is too detailed for the general reader, considering the importance of the subject.

[33] Gilbert Chinard's *Honest John Adams* (Boston, 1933) is a good modern study, though not equal to the same author's biography of Jefferson. For older standard

The small farmers who composed the backbone of the colonial democracy also had their reasons for resisting Britain's encroachments. All restraints on colonial trade which curtailed markets meant lower prices for the farmers' surpluses, just as British taxes increased the cost of their purchases, while British currency policy now made it impossible for debtors to obtain cheap currency in the form of land bank loans. The Currency Act of 1764 required that the colonists tax themselves to redeem immediately the bills of credit issued during the war—debts which in 1763 amounted to £750,000. Once currency contraction had taken place private debts incurred when money was plentiful and cheap became more burdensome, since payments had to be made in a scarce and dear currency. Franklin in 1766 informed British officials that the restraints on paper money were one of the principal causes of colonial disaffection. If a debtor farmer lost his land through foreclosure, the difficulty of obtaining a new farm was now enhanced, thanks to Britain's new western program and the land ordinance of 1774; hence the land policy of the Crown benefited speculative holders of large estates in the East at the expense of the small farmers and their large and none too affluent families. In the southern colonies the unpopular quit-rents and taxes for the support of the Anglican Church were associated with the oppressions of the British government. The colonial yeomen now controlled the elected house of the legislature in New Jersey, North Carolina, and the New England colonies, while in the South Carolina, Pennsylvania, and Virginia assemblies, although under-represented, they were able to assert their demands.[34] Their leading spokesmen were Samuel Adams of Massachusetts, Patrick Henry and Thomas Jefferson of Virginia, and George Clinton of New York.

Even the unprivileged workers in the towns and the tenants on large estates felt the heavy hand of Britain's rule. The gulf between the small landowning farmers and unprivileged tenants, and workers, skilled, semi-skilled, and unskilled, was not wide. All performed rough and heavy labor, all felt oppressed by the upper class, whether they were debtors, employees, servants, or tenants, and all were imbued with the democratic ideal of the dignity of man. Parrington in his *Colonial Mind* relates an incident showing the antagonism between the working farmers and the aristocratic governor of Massachusetts, Joseph Dudley. "One December day in 1705, as he was

biographies consult John Quincy Adams and Charles Francis Adams, *The Life of John Adams* (2 vols., Philadelphia, 1874), and John T. Morse, *John Adams* (Boston, 1887).

[34] E. Francis Brown's *Joseph Hawley* (New York, 1931) is an admirable study of a Massachusetts radical.

driving along a country road with high snowdrifts on each side, he met with two loads of wood. The chariot coming to a stop, Dudley thrust his head out of the window and bade the carters turn aside and make way for him: but they were inclined to argue the matter in view of the drifts. Words were multiplied, and one of the carters cried . . . 'I am as good flesh and blood as you . . . you may go out of the way.' In a rage the governor drew his sword and struck at the fellow, who snatched the sword away and broke it. . . . He arrested both carters and threw them into jail. . . . They were of good yeoman families, yet the matter hung on for nearly a year before they were discharged from their bonds." [35]

When yeomen could experience such treatment from a royal governor, it is evident that unprivileged workers and tenants were even more at the mercy of their masters. Not that the latter were the British government, but the king's officials in America were the symbol of prerogative, power, and privilege, and in conflicts between workers and masters Britain generally used its power to maintain the authority of the owning class. Hence the unprivileged workers, oppressed by a sense of political and social discrimination, degraded by an economic status derived from and maintained by Britain, and aflame with anti-British feeling, were prepared to remonstrate against any British measures which intensified their unhappy lot.[36]

The British acts of 1763–65 fell upon the colonies when in the midst of an economic depression. Wartime prosperity had been sustained by British military expenditures in America, by privateering, and by the inflation of colonial currency. When all these artificial factors were removed after 1762, trade dwindled, prices declined, and unemployment gripped the towns. The new British taxes and trade restrictions levied a toll upon a shrunken colonial trade that could only mean further impoverishment to the working class, dependent as it was upon the industries that served external commerce. More particularly the artisans resented both the British restrictions upon colonial manufactures and Britain's currency policy which denied to the colonies a money and credit structure necessary to sustain industrial activity. In denouncing Britain's restraints upon colonial manufactures and paper money Benjamin Franklin voiced the protests of the artisan class, of which he himself was the greatest product. A writer in a Boston paper of April 29, 1765, lamented that a "colonist

---

[35] Quoted from the 1929 edition, p. 126, by permission of the publishers, Harcourt, Brace and Co., New York.

[36] A pioneer work analyzing class relationships is Carl Becker's penetrating study, *The History of Political Parties in the Province of New York, 1760–1776* (Madison, Wis., 1909).

cannot make a button, a horseshoe, nor a hobnail, but some sooty ironmonger or respectable button-maker of Britain shall bawl and squall that his honor's worship is most egregiously maltreated, injured, cheated, and robbed by the rascally American republicans." Nor could the colonial workers look with favor upon Britain's new land policy which retarded the movement of surplus farmers and workers into unoccupied areas. As Franklin wrote in 1751: "It is the multitude of poor without land in a country, . . . who must work for others at low wages or starve. . . ." All the British measures adopted after 1760 tended toward a common result: to curtail those industries dependent upon the foreign commerce of the colonies, to deny to the American workers employment in new industries, and to increase the host of landless workers competing for employment in a restricted economy. It is not surprising, then, that such men as Isaac Sears and John Lamb of New York and Paul Revere of Boston could lead the workers in opposition to British rule—and in alliance with outraged farmers of the middle class.[37]

Although the farmers and workers and the colonial upper class had many common grievances against Britain, in other respects the two groups were antagonistic. With respect to paper money the colonial merchants and the more prosperous planters looked with disfavor upon the demands of the colonial debtors, while colonial landlords and speculators were frequently at war with tenant farmers and squatters. Moreover, the employers and owners of large property dreaded the specter of mob rule, fearing that if the lower classes gained control of the colonial governments they would become imbued with a spirit of insubordination, repudiate debts, and seize and redistribute large estates. The merchants, moreover, had long enjoyed certain benefits within the British empire—the protection of the British navy, access to all the markets of the empire, the right to employ their vessels in imperial trade, British support of the slave traffic, and the backing of British diplomacy in disputes with foreign states. Such advantages were not to be surrendered lightly—especially when the destruction of Britain's authority would expose the upper class to mob rule and deprive the colonial merchants of Britain's protection against currency inflation and the repudiation of debts.[38]

In such circumstances the colonial aristocracy found itself in a difficult position. A few merchants like John Hancock perceived that

[37] See again C. A. and M. R. Beard, *Rise of American Civilization*, Vol. I, chapter 5.
[38] See three stimulating, well-written essays, *The Spirit of '76*, by Carl Becker, J. M. Clark, and W. E. Dodd (Washington, 1927).

there was an irreconcilable conflict between British profits and colonial profits, and accordingly waged a persistent war against British rule. However, the majority of the disaffected merchants and planters desired to retain the advantages of the empire and at the same time to free themselves from its shackles of restraint. When it became apparent after 1774 that such advantages could be had only at the cost of British taxes and trade restrictions, a large number of the merchants and planters decided that the restraints outweighed the advantages. Interested primarily in the growth of their influence and fortunes through continued colonial expansion, such members of the upper class were forced to recognize that American development had to be freed from the blight of British mercantilism.

But not all members of the colonial upper class joined the revolutionary movement; others remained firm in their attachment to Britain. At the head of the loyalist party stood the royal governors, the most prominent of whom was Thomas Hutchinson of Massachusetts.[39] As the son of a New England merchant prince Hutchinson inherited an ample fortune which enabled him to devote himself to politics, serving as a multiple officeholder under the Crown before he became royal governor in 1770. Upon his friends, relatives, and dependents he conferred minor royal offices, thus creating a pro-British party animated alike by his own reverence for large property, aristocracy, and British institutions and by his hostility to the political demands of the lower classes. Perceiving the exposed position of the colonial aristocracy, he concluded that it could best be protected from the "mob" by British force. "I wish the good of the country," he wrote, "when I wish to see some further restraint of liberty rather than the connection with the parent state should be broken; for I am sure such a breach must prove the ruin of the colony." When it is recalled that after 1768 the colonists paid £30,000 a year in British taxes for the support of the royal officials in America it is evident that there was a breach between the payers and receivers that was not easily closed.

In Pennsylvania and Maryland the position of the proprietary governors and their officers, emissaries, and employees was analogous to the status of the British officials in the royal colonies. Both the Penn and the Calvert families enjoyed the full support of the British government; the attack in England on the proprietary governments had long since subsided. An estimate that the lands in possession of

39 James K. Hosmer defends the loyalist view in his *Life of Thomas Hutchinson* (Boston, 1896).

the Penn family were now worth £1,000,000 suggests a reason why the Penns should desire to maintain the connection with Britain, whence their title to this princely estate was derived. Nor were the quit-rents and other revenues of the proprietors an income to be willingly surrendered. A recent study by C. A. Barker shows that in 1766 the income of Lord Baltimore from Maryland amounted to £12,500, and that £12,000 went to a hundred and fifty officials of the colony whom he appointed. Since the exports of Maryland were then valued as between £175,000 and £225,000 a year, the proprietary system meant a drain of between 12 and 14 per cent of the purchasing power of the Maryland farmers. "And as more than half of all the income controlled by the proprietary element was concentrated in the hands of the lord proprietor and half a dozen high officials, the preponderance of privilege is evident." [40]

Moreover, the land policy of the Crown as formulated in 1774 was highly beneficial to Baltimore and the Penns. Neither had claims to the land severed from the old colonies by Britain, while the Crown's restrictions on settlement in the Ohio valley and the new conditions imposed upon the sale of unoccupied royal lands would have forced upward the price of ungranted lands still in possession of the Penn and Calvert families. A like good fortune would have visited the holders of large tracts in the area east of Quebec and the Indian boundary line. Among the great speculative holders whose lands would have risen in value through Britain's policy of restricting the area open to settlement were some of the most prominent loyalists. Sir William Pepperrell had an estate stretching for thirty miles along the coast of Maine; Sir John Johnson (son of Sir William Johnson, who died in 1774) had title to fifty thousand acres in the Mohawk valley; [41] the Philipse family in New York possessed lands to the extent of three hundred square miles; Sir James Wright claimed an estate in Georgia later valued at $160,000; and there were besides these the vast domains of Lord Fairfax (over five million acres) and of Lord Granville, one-third of North Carolina. British land policy also promised to benefit the substantial, employing, non-debtor farmers of the seacoast area: first by minimizing the competition of newer lands of the interior; secondly by increasing the force of landless workers who could be hired at low wages. And when

---

[40] C. A. Barker, "Property Rights in the Provincial System of Maryland," *Journal of Southern History*, II (Feb., May 1936).

[41] M. G. Walker, "Sir John Johnson, Loyalist," *Mississippi Valley Historical Review*, III (Dec. 1916).

the British army created a cash market for the farm products of the seacoast area, another potent factor influenced the attitude of this class.

An important section of the merchant class likewise remained loyal to Britain. There were those of ultra-aristocratic temper who feared the mob spirit and the debtor's cry for cheap money more than they feared British restrictions. Particularly was this true of those merchants who were contractors with the Crown for supplying the British army in America, those whose established trading contacts were within the empire, those who were factors of British mercantile firms, and those who did business for British merchants on a commission basis. The merchants of New York usually did not trade with Britain in an independent capacity but rather bought and sold for British correspondents. Other New Yorkers were deeply involved in trade with Montreal. The loyalist group among the New York merchants was particularly strong, represented by members of such families as De Lancey, Bayard, Van Cortlandt, Smith, Cruger, and Walton.

In the professional classes the most prominent loyalists were lawyers and Anglican clergymen. In Massachusetts the wealthy and aristocratic Daniel Leonard, a defender of the British constitution and the class system which supported it, manifested dismay at the democratic trend in America. "It would . . . be the highest degree of impudence and disloyalty," he wrote, "to imagine that the king, at the head of his Parliament, could have any but the most pure and perfect intentions of justice, goodness and truth, that human nature is capable of." The richest man in Pennsylvania, Joseph Galloway, another loyalist attorney (who derived a large income from the legal business of the proprietary land system), led the seaboard aristocracy in opposition to the Philadelphia mechanics and the back-country farmers. The outstanding loyalist of Connecticut, Jared Ingersoll, was also a lawyer.[42] As to the Anglican clergy: not only were many of them Anglo-Americans, trained in loyalty to the king and imbued with respect for authority; in the southern colonies they were menaced by the anti-British democracy, which aimed to abolish the taxes which supported the Anglican Church. In the 1760's the income of the Anglican clergy in Maryland amounted to £8,000 a year. The most outspoken Loyalist among the Virginia clergy, Jonathan Boucher, declared that existing social and political institutions were divinely ordained and lamented that "the laboring classes, instead of

[42] L. H. Gipson, *Jared Ingersoll* (New Haven, 1920), an excellent biography, gives a full account of pre-Revolutionary events in Connecticut.

regarding the rich as their guardians, patrons and benefactors, now look upon them as so many overgrown colossuses whom it is no demerit in them to wrong." [43]

Although the small farmers as a whole did not entertain loyalist sympathies, there was an important exception. In the Carolinas the yeomen and squatters of the back country were first of all enemies of the planter-merchant aristocracy, and since the aristocracy was predominantly anti-British, many of the frontiersmen looked upon Britain —the enemy of their enemies—as a friend. Moreover, the back country of South Carolina was not yet sufficiently settled to make British land policy a serious menace to land-hungry farmers. Finally, the naval stores industry—an important source of income to Carolinians who occupied the sandy, pine-bearing lands beyond the plantation area—was threatened by a rupture with Britain which promised to cut off the British bounties that sustained production in the Carolinas.[44]

From the standpoint of economic issues a broad line may be drawn to separate the colonists who remained loyal to Britain from those who became hostile. Those whose business, investments, and income were menaced by Britain's measures pertaining to land, currency, taxation, trade, and manufacturing enlisted in the opposition, while those whose property would have been protected or enhanced in value by British measures enlisted in the loyalist ranks. And since Britain's policies, in their total effect, meant restriction and contracting opportunity, they antagonized those colonists who were concerned primarily with American expansion; on the other hand, those who stood to gain generally had vested interests that would have been served by a rigid maintenance of the *status quo*. This division meant that the more enterprising and aggressive men joined the struggle against Britain, whereas the most satisfied, conservative and inert remained loyal to the Crown—a fact which explains why the colonial upper class contributed so many more vigorous leaders to the Revolution than to the British cause. And because the mass of the colonists aspired to a better life that could be attained only through an expanding economy, Britain's policies of contraction and repression endangered a much larger part of the democracy than they benefited. Thus British measures, when imposed upon the economy and social structure of the colonies, evoked widespread unrest and inspired a group of able men from the

[43] *Reminiscences of an American Loyalist, 1738–1789: being the Autobiography of the Reverend Jonathan Boucher* (ed. Jonathan Bouchier, Boston, 1925).

[44] *Essays in Honor of William E. Dodd* (ed. Avery Craven, Chicago, 1935) contains a significant study by Philip Davidson, "The Southern Backcountry on the Eve of the Revolution."

upper class to lead the popular resistance to a menace that Franklin once described as "grievous tyranny and oppression." [45]

[45] Carl Becker's *The Eve of the Revolution* (New Haven, 1918) is an outstanding volume in the *Chronicles of America* series.

BIBLIOGRAPHICAL NOTE

SECONDARY WORKS: E. B. Greene, *The Revolutionary Generation* (New York, 1943), contains accurate sketches of many aspects of American society. Bernhard Knollenberg, *Origin of the American Revolution, 1759–1766* (New York, 1960), shows that British decisions which led to the Revolution were made before 1767. John C. Miller, *Origins of the American Revolution* (Boston, 1943), is a vigorous, well-written résumé of the years 1763–76.

Murray G. Lawson, *Fur: A Study in English Mercantilism, 1770–1775* (Toronto, 1943), treats the English hat industry in relation to the fur trade.

Standard monographs on British activities in the South are John R. Alden, *John Stuart and the Southern Colonial Frontier* (Ann Arbor, 1944); Charles L. Mowat, *East Florida as a British Province, 1763–1784* (Berkeley, 1943); and Cecil Johnson, *British West Florida, 1763–1783* (New Haven, 1943).

Other useful studies of Western themes are George E. Lewis, *The Indiana Company, 1763–1798* (Glendale, Calif., 1941), a careful, detailed account; Howard H. Peckham, *Pontiac and the Indian Uprising* (Princeton, 1947), an excellent biography, adding information which was not available to Parkman; John R. Alden, *General Gage in America* (Baton Rouge, 1948), a study of the British commander, 1762–76; and Jack M. Sosin, *Whitehall and the Wilderness* (Lincoln, 1961), which gives data on the British army in America.

Carl Ubbelohde, *The Vice-Admiralty Courts and the American Revolution* (Chapel Hill, 1960), is the foremost study of its subject. O. M: Dickerson, *The Navigation Acts and the American Revolution* (Philadelphia, 1951), throws some light on the enforcement of British laws.

Important studies of the resistance to Britain within individual colonies are: Oscar Zeichner, *Connecticut's Years of Controversy* (Chapel Hill, 1949); David S. Lovejoy, *Rhode Island Politics and the American Revolution, 1760–1776* (Providence, 1958), largely a study of factional party strife; Charles A. Barker, *The Background of the Revolution in Maryland* (New Haven, 1940), which portrays clearly the political and economic state of the colony, 1725–1775; Kenneth Coleman, *The American Revolution in Georgia* (Athens, 1958), which treats the colony as an American community, influenced by outside pressures; and Richard Walsh, *Charleston's Sons of Liberty* (Columbia, 1959), an admirable study which describes the support of the Revolution by artisans and explains the reasons for their stand.

SOURCES: S. E. Morison, *Sources . . . illustrating the American Revolution, 1764–1788* (Oxford, 1929), is a valuable collection, made with discrimination. See pp. 1–148. Three volumes of documents on the British in the Illinois country have been edited by C. W. Alvord and C. E. Carter, all published at Springfield, Ill. They are: *The Critical Period, 1763–1765* (1915); *The New Regime, 1765–1767* (1916); and *Trade and Politics, 1767–1769* (1921). *The Grenville Papers* (ed. William J. Smith, 4 vols., London, 1852–53) include George Grenville's correspondence and his "diary of memorable transactions" during his administration (Vols. II, III).

XXIII

The Imperial Conflict

THE COLONIES OPPOSE THE STAMP ACT AND THE TOWNSHEND ACTS

SPEAKING in the House of Lords in 1766 on the repeal of the Stamp Act the Duke of Grafton said: "If . . . America is not sufficiently taxed, there are other means by which they may be taxed—don't tax them universally. By that means you join them when you should keep them asunder." This advice was amply justified by the storm of opposition which had greeted the Stamp Act in the colonies. Each of the other British measures of 1763–65—the Sugar Act, the Currency Act, the Quartering Act, the Proclamation of 1763 and the new enforcement decrees—affected directly only particular classes and sections. The Stamp Act, however, struck a blow at many groups; hence it became the focus of discontent, a symbol of the iniquities of the British government. More particularly it antagonized four influential and vocal parties: the lawyers, the printer-editors, the merchants, and the planters, constituting as it did a direct levy on the income of all. Seldom in American history have the newspapers been so united behind a single cause as in 1765–66. To most men of the upper class and to the democracy alike the Stamp Act meant a challenge to political liberty. Should Britain collect taxes directly from the colonies, it would be only a matter of time until all the colonial governments might be supported by parliamentary levies. Then the assemblies would lose the power of coercing royal officials and thus of undoing British policies; then Britain might control the economy and the resources of the colonies in a manner most beneficial to British merchants and investors; then all the threatened oppressions of British mercantilism which the colonies had previously evaded by ignoring parliamentary statutes and by bending royal officials to their will would become effective. Unless the colonists were to be squeezed as in a vise they must retain that power over taxes and expenditures which was the means of enforcing economic policy.[1]

---

[1] S. G. Fisher's *The True History of the American Revolution* (Philadelphia, 1902) and *The Struggle for American Independence* (2 vols., Philadelphia, 1908) portray

How was the well-nigh universal opposition to the Stamp Act to be made effective? Those members of the upper class most friendly to Britain—men like Joseph Galloway—favored dignified petitions and remonstrances. The more disaffected planters and merchants were willing to use stronger measures. In the northern colonies some lawyers and merchants refused to use the stamps; the courts were closed; business requiring stamps was not transacted. In the South the planters gave a forecast of the later doctrine of nullification by ignoring the law and doing business without the stamps. In the commercial towns, merchants promised not to import British goods (the non-importation agreements), and artisans and farmers pledged themselves to foster the production and use of American articles. New York led in this movement; Philadelphia and Boston followed; by the summer of 1765 colonial orders for British goods were cut by £600,000. The merchants complained that the Sugar Act deprived them of their means of getting hard money; the Currency Act forbade new issues of legal tender paper money; trade was stagnant; where then could the towns obtain more money, without which the Stamp Act would ruin their already prostrate commerce? On the other hand, critics of the non-importation agreements asserted that the merchants used them to unload on the colonists their accumulated stocks, charging "high prices for old, moth-eaten goods which couldn't have been sold but for the patriotic fervor." [2]

The most radical merchants and the artisans and laborers in the towns were not content with mere petitions and non-resistance. Instigated by radical leaders and by the most anti-British merchants, the farmers and workers formed loose societies, called Sons of Liberty, whereby they gave vent to both their hatred of the British ruling class and their opposition to the new British measures, to which they attributed the unemployment and impoverishment of the postwar depression. Two demonstrations occurred in Boston in the summer of 1765. First a band of townspeople hanged in effigy the stamp distributor and then burned the image on the wreckage of a demolished stamp office; twelve days later another throng swooped down upon the homes of a customs officer and of Lieutenant-Governor Hutchinson and seized and burned records, particularly those pertaining to violation of the Acts of Trade. The "real authority of the government is at an end; some of the principal ringleaders in the late riots walk the streets with impunity; no officers dare attack them; no

the Revolution as conflict with many ugly features, not as a polite disagreement among gentlemen.

[2] See again *The Cambridge History of the British Empire*, Vol. I, chapters 22-23.

attorney-general prosecute them, and no judges sit upon them"—thus Hutchinson described the unruly spirit of the Boston people. Similar occurrences took place in North Carolina, Charleston, Newport, and New York.[3]

The small farmers and planters expressed their dissatisfaction chiefly through the elected assembly. Those of Virginia first sounded the "alarm bell to the disaffected" in May 1765 when the House of Burgesses adopted a series of resolves which declared that the colonists were entitled to the rights and liberties of English subjects and therefore should not be taxed except through their own representatives. Patrick Henry, mindful of his victory in the parsons' cause over the Anglican clergy and British currency policy, spoke so ardently that the speaker warned him against treason. In Massachusetts, the House of Representatives—spurred on by James Otis, then the legal spokesman of the merchants in arms against the Sugar Act—issued a circular letter to all the colonies urging them to send delegates to a conference at New York. Nine colonies complied, and in October twenty-nine representatives assembled in the city hall at New York, there to adopt a declaration of rights and grievances, and to petition king and Parliament for a repeal of the Stamp Act on the ground that the colonists, as British subjects, could be taxed only by their representatives in their own assemblies.

The most telling weapons used by the colonists were the non-importation agreements, which struck the British merchants at a time when trade was bad. The latter clamored for repeal of the Stamp Act, asserting that one hundred thousand workmen were unemployed in Britain because of the breach in American trade. But how could Parliament back down without losing face? Many members of the House of Lords feared the "mob" spirit in the colonies and insisted that Britain must crush it at all costs. The colonists were not really opposing the Stamp Act; their object, said Lord Sandwich, was to determine "whether by resistance they can get themselves loose from other acts more disagreeable and detrimental to them." But if the Stamp Act were not repealed what would be the consequence to Britain? The Duke of Grafton gave the answer: "An increase of poor rates. A diminution of the revenues of excise. A loss of the great debt from America to England." [4]

The British merchants triumphed in 1766 when Parliament repealed the Stamp Act, and—in order to assert Britain's supremacy—

[3] See again J. T. Adams, *Revolutionary New England*, chapters 14–18.
[4] W. T. Laprade, "The Stamp Act in British Politics," *American Historical Review*, XXXV (July 1930).

passed the Declaratory Act which affirmed that Parliament possessed the power to enact laws to bind the colonies in all cases whatsoever. As a concession to British manufacturers and merchants concerned in the trade of the northern colonies, Parliament also modified the Sugar Act. The molasses duty was lowered from 3*d.* a gallon to 1*d.* a gallon and now made to apply to molasses from the British islands as well as from foreign sources. Since the northern colonies had complained that the Sugar Act made it difficult for them to buy British goods, the lowering of the molasses duty meant a slight sacrifice of the British West Indian interest to that of the British merchants and manufacturers who supplied the markets of New England and the middle colonies. Meanwhile, the principle of raising a revenue in the colonies by parliamentary taxes was stoutly reaffirmed.[5]

Throughout the colonies the news of the repeal of the Stamp Act evoked spirited rejoicing. In the excitement the Declaratory Act was ignored; the colonial remonstrants felt that by their opposition they had forced Parliament to retreat. The grievance that had united the colonies vanished; there remained only the acts which had previously not been rigidly enforced or which were of local or restricted application. The merchants gave up the non-importation agreements; the Sons of Liberty subsided; trade resumed its course; and peace seemed at hand. But it was only a respite—for in 1767 came another series of measures which stirred anew all the elements of discord.

The debates in Parliament on the Stamp Act had disclosed a widely held opinion that the colonies were determined to shake off the Acts of Trade and Navigation. In repealing the Stamp Act the British ruling class—the wealthy landowners and merchants—had had no intention of encouraging the unruly temper of the colonists; rather there was manifested a stiff determination to assert Britain's unqualified right to rule. The opportunity came in 1767, when the Chancellor of the Exchequer, Charles Townshend—a veritable embodiment of the hard attitude of the ruling class toward the colonies—was called upon to draft the fiscal measures of the government. Intent upon reducing British taxes by making more efficient the collection of duties levied on American trade, Parliament in 1767, by substantial majorities, passed a group of acts which Townshend had prepared. One authorized the superior courts of the colonies to issue writs of assistance, thus giving specific legal authority to those general search warrants so hateful to colonial merchants. A second created the American Customs Board, previously described in chapter XXII. These two measures

[5] H. L. Osgood, "The American Revolution," *Political Science Quarterly*, XIII (March 1898).

were an effective answer to those colonial merchants who continued to protest against British commercial restrictions after the Stamp Act had been repealed.[6]

During the Stamp Act controversy a Maryland attorney, Daniel Dulany, an ultra-conservative, had written an essay in which he had drawn a nice distinction between internal taxes (stamp taxes, land taxes, poll taxes) and external taxes, or duties on imports and exports. Dulany had also intimated that although it was improper for Parliament to lay internal taxes upon the colonies, external taxes had been in force for more than a century and therefore Parliament had the right to levy them. This distinction gained great popularity among men of the colonial upper class who desired to preserve the imperial connection and at the same time to ward off further parliamentary encroachments. To Townshend such a distinction was nonsense, but if the colonists were foolish enough to prefer external to internal taxes, very well, let them have the external kind. Accordingly, the Townshend Acts levied duties on paper, glass, lead, painters' colors, and tea exported from Britain to the colonies. Designed to raise £40,000 for the support of colonial governors, judges, customs officers, and the British army in America, these duties were to be collected in colonial ports—an arrangement designed to prevent the smuggling of such commodities from foreign countries which would certainly have resulted had the duties been collected in Britain.

Another one of the Townshend Acts singled out the Assembly of New York for special punitive treatment, that province having been previously selected by General Gage as the headquarters of British troops in the colonies. When the Assembly refused to provide all the army supplies called for by the Quartering Act of 1765, great was the indignation in Britain. Accordingly, Parliament in 1767 ordered the legislative "privileges" of the Assembly suspended until compliance was duly made. This action informed the colonies that their assemblies were simply creatures of Britain which Parliament might change or destroy at will. Granted this assumption, the right of the colonists to tax and govern themselves became a repudiated fiction.[7]

The hostility bestowed upon these new measures rivaled that which had greeted the Stamp Act. Leading Bostonians complained that the

---

[6] The works of Claude H. Van Tyne, which emphasize political and intellectual factors and lean toward the British-loyalist point of view, include *The American Revolution* (New York, 1905)—see chapters 1–4; *The Causes of the War of Independence* (Boston, 1922); and *The War of Independence* (Boston, 1929)—see chapters 10–12, 15–17.

[7] The political ideas of the period are admirably stated in Charles E. Merriam's *A History of American Political Theories* (New York, 1928), chapters 1–2.

new revenue officers had come "to plunder our trade and drain the country of its money"; in Charleston a conservative merchant, Henry Laurens, compared such officers to the "miscreants who were driven out of the temple by Jesus with a scourge of small cords." From the quiet of his country estate a Pennsylvania conservative, John Dickinson, issued a series of *Letters from a Farmer in Pennsylvania*, which carried the taxation argument of the colonial upper class a step farther. Perceiving in the Townshend duties a means of wresting from the assemblies their real power by depriving them of their control of the purse, Dickinson abandoned the early distinction between internal and external taxes and introduced a new criterion. What was the *purpose* of a British levy? Was it to regulate trade? If so, the colonists could accept it. But the Townshend duties were levied on British exports to America; such duties could not benefit any commercial group within the empire; hence they were not intended to regulate trade but merely to raise a revenue. If the colonial assemblies were to retain a semblance of power they could not concede that Parliament had the right to levy even an external tax merely for revenue. In addition, Dickinson pointed out that the Stamp Act aimed to raise money for the defense of only the thirteen colonies, whereas the Townshend duties embraced Florida and Canada, so that the old colonies were "to be drained of the rewards of their labor, to cherish the scorching sands of Florida and the icy rocks of Canada and Nova Scotia, which never will return to us one farthing that we send to them." [8]

The colonial merchants again resorted to the non-importation agreements as the most effectual means of compelling Britain to repeal the Townshend Acts. Boston led the way in March 1768; New York followed in April; and the Philadelphia merchants, under pressure from the city populace and the other towns, reluctantly joined in March 1769. The import trade of Boston was cut in half, while Philadelphia's purchases from Britain dropped from £441,000 in 1768 to £134,800 in 1770. When the Virginia Assembly was dissolved by the governor the burgesses met privately in May 1769 and agreed not to import the dutied articles, British luxuries, or slaves. In Charleston the merchants were forced to fall in line by coercion from the city workers led by the anti-British merchant, Christopher Gadsden. Throughout the plantation area non-importation agreements could not be strictly enforced because the trade with Britain was not centered in a few ports. Meanwhile, individual citizens banded into

[8] The best biography is Charles J. Stillé, *The Life and Times of John Dickinson* (Philadelphia, 1891).

associations, pledging themselves to boycott British wares and to purchase American-made goods. The whole movement revealed that,
when the conditions of their foreign trade became unfavorable, the
colonies were compelled to divert their surplus labor and capital to
manufacturing pursuits. Many colonial leaders, among them Washington and Franklin, saw in non-importation a means of fostering
American manufactures as an escape from the thraldom of British
mercantilism.[9]

Once again the mechanics of the towns, in alliance with the most
anti-British merchants, resorted to direct action. In Philadelphia, fifty
pipes of Madeira wine were seized from the king's officers who had
sequestered them as smuggled goods; in Newport some of the townspeople burned a British revenue ship which had taken two vessels
charged with illegal trade; in Boston, Providence, and New York
the wrath of the populace, expressed in personal assaults and coats of
tar and feathers, visited British customs agents and informers who
exposed illegal traders. Such acts brought to Boston harbor in 1768
the *Romney*, a British man-of-war. Then, in June 1768, arrived
John Hancock's sloop, *Liberty*, bearing a cargo which included Madeira wine. The British customs searcher who went aboard was imprisoned in the cabin, there to hear "a hoisting out of goods"; soon
afterward the customs officials ordered the seizure of the *Liberty* by
the *Romney*. That done, the townsmen attacked the customs officers
and their houses, forcing them to flee to Castle William for safety.
Immediately they called upon the British ministry for military protection, and in October 1768 two regiments of British regulars en-
camped in Boston. The Townshend Acts and the Sugar Act, with its
tax of £7 a tun on wine imported by the colonies from Madeira, had
created a situation akin to war.[10]

The issue, however, was not forced at the time because in 1770
Parliament repealed all the Townshend duties except the threepence
tax on tea. A new Prime Minister, Lord North, servant of the British
ruling class and of George III, effected the repeal because he and his
colleagues believed it unwise for Britain to tax her own goods sold
abroad—not because the non-importation agreements had driven the
British merchants to demand the removal of the duties. The British
merchants were now prospering by a trade revival sustained by war
in Europe and by good harvests in England; their commerce with
the tobacco and sugar colonies was not seriously curtailed; and the

[9] See again A. M. Schlesinger, *The Colonial Merchants and the American Revolution*.
[10] John Fiske, *The American Revolution* (2 vols., Boston, 1891), finds in the political ambitions of George III the cause of the Revolution.

non-importation agreements of the northern towns did not become fully effective until 1769—and even then there was much evasion. Moreover, it appeared now that the disaffected colonial merchants, farmers, planters, and artisans were bent upon overthrowing the whole British colonial system; where would such treason end if Britain again supinely gave way? At the suggestion of George III Parliament readily retained the tea duty in order to assert Britain's right to tax the colonies. The partial repeal of the Townshend duties seemed to moderate men in America a concession that justified peace. Boston merchants strove to preserve the non-importation agreements until the tea tax and all the duties of the Sugar Act had been repealed, but the other commercial towns resumed trade and Boston had to follow, lest her near-by rivals engross her former commerce.

Despite the confusion of British politics after 1763, a consistent, unyielding attitude toward the colonies was exhibited: they must be kept in economic subordination to those powerful interests which profited from colonial commerce and investments oversea.[11] It mattered little whether the king's influence were strong or weak, or whether one or another faction of the Whig party held office: British merchants and landowners successfully asserted their purpose of extending and perfecting the colonial system which served their interests so well. The apparent concessions offered to the colonies were also made for the benefit of groups in Britain. Neither Parliament nor the king had demonstrated any intention of abandoning mercantilism in order that colonial economy might expand and function in the interest of a large majority of the colonial farmers, artisans, and merchants.

THE RISE OF COLONIAL DEMOCRACY

During the first period of opposition to British measures (1763–66) there had been substantial agreement among the different classes in the colonies. The Stamp Act had menaced both the conservative merchants whose business was carried on within the British empire (the fair traders) and the anti-British merchants who dealt with foreign countries or colonies (the smugglers or free traders). In the towns the unskilled workers and artisans—the oppressed, the unemployed, and the employees of the free traders—were ripe for action that would assert their political importance and at the same time give vent to their hatred of the British ruling class and its agents in America, to whose measures was attributed the depression of 1763–65.

[11] Lewis B. Namier, *The Structure of Politics at the Accession of George III* (London, 1929), is an intensive analysis of the composition of Parliament.

Deeming it desirable that the colonies present a mass opposition to the Stamp Act, even men of conservative temper, although condemning violence, gave approval to popular demonstrations. Thus in New York many merchants acted with the mechanics as Sons of Liberty; in Boston the popular agitation was directed by such moderates as John Adams and James Otis. Since the principal targets of the populace in 1765 were the stamp distributors, the colonists of the upper class did not at once feel endangered by the outbursts of popular feeling. However, the Stamp Act demonstrations let loose forces not easily controlled. For the first time the mechanics, hitherto denied any influence in politics, became aware of their latent power.[12] When resisting British measures the spokesmen of the colonial upper class had been compelled to speak for all the colonists; they could not with propriety assert the right of a small minority to be free from parliamentary restraints; hence they had spoken in terms of the rights and liberties of every man, of every British subject. Such appeals made the unprivileged workers politically conscious. If Parliament did not have the right to tax the colonists without their consent, then why should workers in America be denied the vote and thus be taxed by the assemblies without *their* consent? As John Adams put it: the Stamp Act controversy filled the minds of the people with sentiments of liberty—liberty that could mean freedom from the oppressions of the colonial aristocracy as well as freedom from British rule.

In the agitation against the Townshend Acts, the demonstrations of the city workers assumed a new character. Those merchants who traded chiefly with Britain did not object to the Townshend measures which aimed to suppress illegal trade with foreign ports; in fact the suppression of colonial smuggling promised to benefit such fair traders. The free traders, however, were violently opposed to the Townshend Acts; hence there occurred a sharp division within the merchant class. In New York, for instance, the unwillingness of the pro-British merchants to oppose the Townshend acts delayed the adoption of a non-importation agreement but this was finally agreed to as a protest against other British measures, particularly the Currency Act of 1764. Even then many merchants proceeded to evade the non-importation agreement, whereupon the free traders again turned to direct action and stirred the mechanics to assaults upon their pro-British rivals. Such attacks raised fears among men of wealth that unbridled mechanics might launch a social revolution that would transfer property and political power to the lower middle classes. Thus frightened for

[12] See again Carl Becker, *History of Political Parties in the Province of New York*.

the security of their own goods and persons many conservative men looked to British officials and troops for protection.[13]

After 1768, when the British troops arrived in Boston to defend the king's officials and the pro-British merchants, the leaders of the mechanics adopted new tactics. In 1770 John Adams wrote that endeavors "had been systematically pursued for many months, by certain busy characters, to excite quarrels, rencounters, and combats, single or compound, between the inhabitants of the lower class and the soldiers, and at all risks to enkindle an immortal hatred between them." Such efforts bore fruit on the evening of March 5, 1770, in the form of the Boston Massacre. A group of boys and young men threw snowballs at a sentry stationed before the customs office in front of the State House; a band of soldiers rushed to his aid; a crowd which quickly assembled assaulted two of the troopers; musket shots answered the attack; five of the townspeople were killed and several others wounded, among them apprentices, shipwrights, a mulatto laborer, a sailor, a ropemaker, and a tailor.[14]

> Unhappy Boston! See thy sons deplore
>   Thy hallow'd walks besmeared with guiltless gore.
> While faithless P[resto]n and his savage bands
> With murd'rous rancour stretch their bloody hands
> Like fierce barbarians grinning o'er their prey,
> Approve the carnage and enjoy the day.

Acting-Governor Hutchinson, under pressure from the popular elements, removed the troops—previously quartered in the town proper —to Castle William in the harbor. In the ensuing trial of the soldiers accused of firing into the crowd, two privates were convicted of manslaughter and the charge against the officer in command of the guard was dismissed. The removal of the troops quieted the nerves of the Boston people, while in all the towns the news of the partial repeal of the Townshend duties, the rescinding of the non-importation agreements, and the revival of prosperity occasioned a lull in the storm of opposition (1771–73).

During this "interval of calm" one man—Samuel Adams of Massachusetts, the first organizer of American democracy as a political force—did more than anyone else to keep alive the flame of colonial discontent. His hostility to the wealthy merchants of Boston and to the British government probably arose from their part in destroying

---

[13] A. P. Peabody, "Boston Mobs before the Revolution," *Atlantic Monthly*, LXII.

[14] R. S. Longley, "Mob Activities in Revolutionary Massachusetts," *New England Quarterly*, VI (March 1933).

the Massachusetts land bank of 1740, which had all but ruined the fortunes of his father. After graduating from Harvard College, he had forsaken the practice of law and devoted himself to politics, living an abstemious life animated by hatred of aristocracy and faith in the common man. To the management of the colony's affairs he proposed to bring the spirit of the New England town meeting. On two counts he opposed British rule: first, because he regarded Britain as the sponsor of the colonial aristocracy; secondly, because he believed that the British colonial system exploited the colonists for the benefit of the British upper class.[15]

In politics Adams's major achievement was the welding of the small farmers and the town workers into a democratic party. His experience with the land bank made him as one with the hard-pressed farmers who demanded currency relief; as an associate in Boston of tradesmen and mechanics he won their confidence and support. His first task was to free these plain people from their awe of their social and political superiors—to arouse among them a sense of their own importance. This he accomplished largely by attacking the royal officials and judges, and by tearing away the veil of secrecy from government so as to expose the aristocrats as actuated by selfish motives, thereby divesting them of noble traits and reducing them to the level of ordinary men. For this his enemies labeled him a character assassin.[16]

His second task was to arouse the people to action. That meant banding them together in order that the weakness of individuals might be transfused into collective strength. In newspapers he published many articles, written under different names and in various literary styles so as to suggest that a host of colleagues labored at his side. He used a Boston political society, the Caucus Club, as a training school for political leaders; in the town meeting and in the provincial assembly he instigated resolutions and speeches which appealed to democratic impulses and emphasized the oppressions of British rule. Then in 1772 he induced the Boston town meeting to select a committee of correspondence to state the rights and grievances of the colonists, to communicate with other towns in the province, and to request them to draft replies. Gradually the towns fell in line, appointing their own committees, until by 1773 the democracy of Massachusetts was prepared for quick, united action under his com-

---

[15]An excellent, scholarly study by John C. Miller, *Sam Adams* (Boston, 1936), is an intensive analysis of early propagandist activities.

[16] R. V. Harlow, *Samuel Adams* (New York, 1923), is a stimulating study in psychology.

mand. Daniel Leonard, the loyalist attorney, described the committees of correspondence "as the foulest, subtlest, and most venomous serpent ever issued from the egg of sedition." [17]

In 1773 Britain played directly into the hands of Samuel Adams and his co-workers when Parliament adopted new regulations for the American tea trade of the East India Company. Mismanagement and corruption had brought the company to the brink of ruin: in the early 1770's its stock dropped to 60, its debts exceeded £1,000,000 and it had on hand 17,000,000 pounds of unsold tea. Due to the Townshend tea tax of 3d. a pound, the colonists had boycotted British tea and such a flourishing illegal trade had developed that after 1770 about nine-tenths of the tea consumed in America was of foreign origin and imported duty free. The loss of the colonial tea trade was one cause of the distress of the East India Company; hence Parliament proposed to restore the company's fortunes, in part, by granting it an effective monopoly of the American market. After May 10, 1773, the company (which had previously been compelled by law to sell its tea at auction to merchants in London) was privileged to reëxport tea to America without paying the existing duty collected on imports of tea into England. Only the threepence tax was to burden the company's tea sold to the colonies; thus the tax to be paid by the American consumer was to amount to considerably less than the tax assessed against the English consumer.

Instead of selling the tea to American merchants in London, the East India Company decided to dispose of it through pro-British merchant correspondents in the colonies. Even Governor Hutchinson admitted that the company could sell the tea through its factors "at a much lower price than it could be afforded by particular merchants who purchased it in England"; thus American fair traders who imported tea from England were in danger of losing their business to the company. The free traders, who already had on hand large stocks of Dutch tea, were also due to be undersold, and perhaps ruined. The opponents of the new policy argued that if Parliament, by adjusting duties, could give the East India Company a monopoly of the tea trade, it might grant similar monopolies to other British firms until colonial merchants were driven from American commerce. The opponents of the company also charged that Britain was offering a bribe of cheap tea to induce the colonists to pay the threepence Townshend tax—tempting them "to barter liberty for luxury." [18]

[17] The best of the older biographies is J. K. Hosmer, *Samuel Adams* (Boston, 1885).
[18] A. M. Schlesinger, "The Uprising against the East India Company," *Political Science Quarterly*, XXXII (March 1917).

Once more the disaffected merchants, the city mechanics and the small farmers presented a united front against a common foe. In New York and Philadelphia great popular demonstrations forced the commanders of the East India Company's tea ships to return to England with their cargoes; in Charleston the tea was locked up in a government warehouse, there to remain for three years; at Boston on December 16, 1773, occurred the most decisive action of the pre-revolutionary era when a band of men, disguised as Indians and unidentified to this day, dumped the tea of three vessels into the harbor. This "most magnificent movement of all" followed a series of negotiations between the popular leaders and the royal officials; when the latter refused to send back the tea, Samuel Adams climaxed a demonstration with the cryptic remark: "This meeting can do nothing more to save the country," whereupon the self-invited guests rushed to the Boston Tea Party.

A fateful crisis now confronted Britain. The East India Company had carried out a parliamentary statute; if the destruction of the tea (property worth £15,000) went unheeded, Parliament would admit to the world that its authority over the colonies had vanished. Official opinion in Britain almost unanimously condemned the Boston Tea Party as an act of vandalism and insurrection and gave wholehearted support to the measures by which the North ministry proposed to bring the insurgent colonists to their senses.[19]

The first of these measures, the Boston Port Bill, effective June 1, 1774, removed the British customhouse from Boston and closed the port to all shipping until the town had compensated the East India Company for its tea. An Administration of Justice Act provided that British agents charged with offenses committed when suppressing riots in Massachusetts or when enforcing British laws might be tried in another colony or in Britain. The Massachusetts Government Act gave to the governor the power to appoint the provincial councillors (previously elected by the General Assembly), forbade the holding of town meetings without the governor's consent, and provided that juries should be selected by the sheriffs (appointees of the governor) instead of by the town meetings. In order that the British troops in Boston might be domiciled where they would be needed, a Quartering Act provided that they might be stationed in the town proper; if the barracks there were inadequate, they might be quartered in taverns, alehouses, and unoccupied buildings. These four acts against Massachusetts were accompanied by the Quebec Act (not designed as a punitive measure), which extended the boundaries of Quebec to

[19] See again E. Channing, *History of the United States,* Vol. III, chapters 5–7.

VIRTUAL REPRESENTATION. 1775.

April 8 1775   Price 6ᵈ

1.... One String Jack ... Deliver your Property.
2.... Begar Tax ... so on France? Accomplice
3.... Let Drum... ... ...
4.... I Gov...you thus meins money for my use

5.... I will not be Robbed
6.... I shall be wounded with you
7.... I am Blind
8.... My French Romin Cabolick Town of Quebeck
9.... The English Protestant Town of Boston

The Rt. Revᵈ
for Order.

Courtesy of the Massachusetts Historical Society.

A SATIRICAL VIEW OF COLONIAL ASSENT TO TAXES LEVIED BY PARLIAMENT

the Ohio and the Mississippi and among other things granted religious freedom to French Catholics residing in the province.[20]

In one way or another these five acts of 1774 denied all the rights and privileges which the colonists had been demanding since 1763. The Boston Tea Party having been nominally a revolt against the tax on tea, the punitive measures affirmed the power of Parliament to tax the colonies for the support of government in America. In the Boston Port Bill, Parliament asserted unlimited power, not only to regulate commerce, but also to destroy commerce in order to punish all the inhabitants, guilty and innocent alike, of a town wholly dependent upon trade. And what of colonial rights of self-government? The town meeting was made subservient to a royal governor; a colonial charter was altered by Parliament overnight, without allowing the colony concerned to present its case; and an ominous shadow fell over the elected assemblies, since the Quebec Act did not grant a representative legislature to that province. So also the judicial system was to function to England's advantage: royal officials were to choose juries for local trials, while the king's agents in America were to be given immunity from local sentiment through the removal of trials to friendly British courts. At one stroke the Quebec Act swept away the western land claims of Massachusetts and Connecticut and curtailed the area claimed by Virginia. The menace of military rule became more formidable as Britain adhered to the principle of parliamentary taxation for the support of a colonial army and insisted that royal troops be domiciled where they were needed to suppress disorders. More menacing still was the appointment of General Gage, the commander of the king's forces in America, as governor of Massachusetts early in 1774. These measures could mean but one thing to the colonies: the destruction of privileges long enjoyed and the establishment of an arbitrary government upheld by military force.[21]

All the economic and political causes of colonial discontent were heightened by utterances of the clergymen who ministered to the Congregational churches in New England and to the Presbyterian churches of the Scotch-Irish settlers on the frontiers. The Quebec Act, by protecting the property of the Roman Catholics in Quebec, by granting them freedom of worship, and by virtually excluding Protestant settlers from the province, promised to create a bulwark against the extension of the Protestant religions in America. And

[20] G. M. Wrong, *Canada and the American Revolution* (New York, 1935), is a good modern account. See chapters 1–13.

[21] Sir George O. Trevelyan, *The American Revolution* (4 vols., New York, 1899–1907) excoriates the Tory ministers for disrupting the British empire by unjustly goading the colonists to an unwilling revolt.

while Catholicism was to wax strong on the borders of the northern colonies, the various popular churches within those colonies were seemingly to be sacrificed to the Church of England. Since 1748, proposals had been made in Britain for an imperial establishment in the colo-

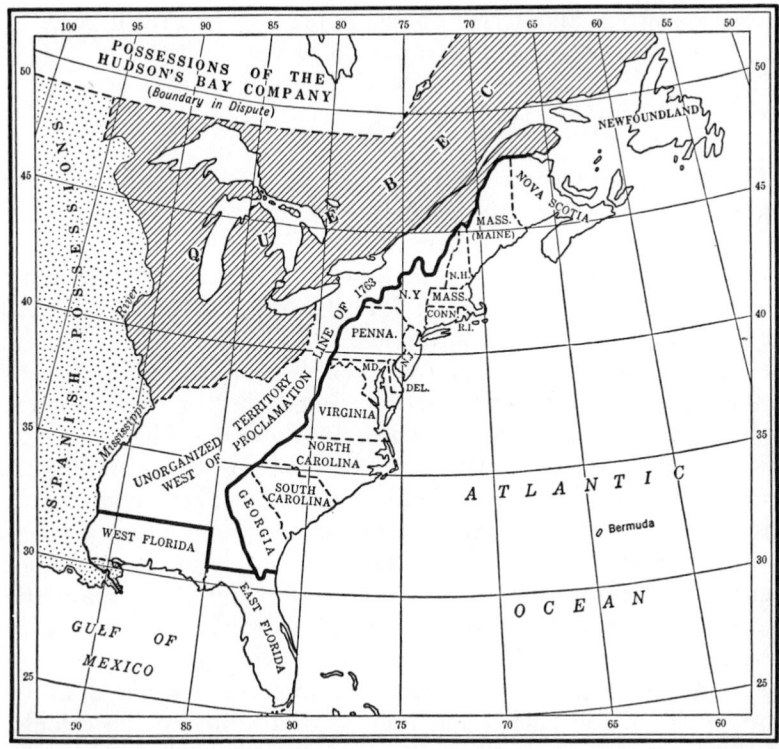

Based on Charles O. Paullin's "Atlas of the Historical Geography of the United States." © Carnegie Institution of Washington. Reprinted by courtesy of the American Geographical Society of New York.

THE CLOSING OF THE NORTHWEST TO THE THIRTEEN COLONIES BY THE QUEBEC ACT OF JUNE 22, 1774

nies of the Anglican Church, to be presided over by an American bishop and supported by parliamentary taxes levied on all the people. Much significance was attached to such proposals when the colonists learned that five Anglican bishops had voted against the repeal of the Stamp Act. Ministers of the Congregational and Presbyterian churches, always prone to discuss political subjects, aroused their parishioners against the Anglican danger. The repeal of the Stamp Act inspired the Reverend Charles Chauncey to preach on the text: "As cold waters to a thirsty soul, so is good news from a far country"; the Boston Massacre elicited from the Reverend John Lathrop a sermon on the theme: "Innocent blood crying to God from the streets of Boston." Such sermons were printed in pamphlet form and widely distributed and read. They revived among radical Protestants the memories of the oppressions of Charles I and Laud and gave religious sanction and fervor to the opposition to British rule: the American cause enjoyed the benediction of the Lord.[22]

THE MOVEMENT FOR INDEPENDENCE

Of the colonial response in 1774 in defense of Massachusetts, Professor Channing wrote: "Never before in American history, and possibly never before in any history had the waves of sympathetic enthusiasm mounted so high as those which now rolled from South to North and from North to South." The Coercive Acts had placed all the colonies in a position comparable to that occupied by Britain after the Boston Tea Party: either the colonists must surrender abjectly, admitting that they possessed no inherent rights, or they must take an unequivocal stand in self-defense, since it was evident that what Britain did to Massachusetts might be done to all. From Virginia, Philadelphia, Charleston, and Connecticut supplies were sent to Boston; the Virginia burgesses, when the legislature was dissolved by the governor for anti-British expressions, met privately and voiced their sympathy for Boston; everywhere town meetings, committees of correspondence, elected assemblies, and colonial leaders denounced the Coercive Acts—in speeches, resolutions, and pamphlets; while the mechanics of the towns again staged demonstrations and dealt violently with British agents and their partisans among the colonists. At the suggestion of the Virginia burgesses, all the thirteen colonies except Georgia sent delegates to a Continental Congress, which assembled in Carpenters' Hall, Philadelphia, on September 5, 1774. Fifty-five members appeared, some chosen legally by the assemblies, some by extra-legal bodies, and others by the assemblies acting in defiance of royal governors. Although united in opposition to the Coercive Acts, the members divided roughly into two parties: moderates and radicals. Among the moderates were Joseph Galloway and John Dickinson of Pennsylvania, John Rutledge and Henry Middleton of South Carolina, and John Jay of New York; among the radi-

[22] Alice M. Baldwin, *The New England Clergy and the American Revolution* (Durham, N. C., 1928), is a superior study. See also C. H. Van Tyne, "The Influence of the Clergy . . . on the American Revolution," *American Historical Review*, XIX (Oct. 1913).

cals: Samuel Adams and John Adams of Massachusetts, Richard Henry Lee and Patrick Henry of Virginia, Roger Sherman of Connecticut, Charles Thomson of Pennsylvania, Christopher Gadsden of South Carolina, and Stephen Hopkins of Rhode Island. Two questions divided the parties: What was the extent of Britain's authority over the colonies? And what measures should they adopt in reply to the Coercive Acts? [23]

The moderate party was composed of men of conservative temper who wished to retain the benefits of the British empire and the protection afforded by British rule against the democratic movement in America. They desired also to preserve the old colonial rights of self-government now threatened by British encroachments. In order to accomplish this double purpose, they had evolved a political theory designed to harmonize British and colonial interests. Many of their leading thinkers were lawyers educated in the English Inns of Court (or law schools), where they had been indoctrinated with English constitutional history and the English common law, the principles of which they now asserted. First, they contended that the colonists were entitled to certain constitutional rights of Englishmen which were embodied in Magna Carta, the Petition of Right of 1628, and the Bill of Rights of 1689—rights which transcended the power of government; neither king nor Parliament could usurp them without violating the British constitution. They were guaranteed to the colonies by the colonial charters in the same manner that royal patents, deeds, and warrants conferred individual title to private property. Foremost among such rights was that expressed in the maxim: "a citizen's property may not be taken from him without his consent." Now the colonists, not being represented in Parliament, did not assent to parliamentary taxes; therefore they could be taxed only by their own assemblies. The moderate leaders, however, recognized that Parliament possessed the power to regulate imperial trade; hence a distinction was drawn between right to tax and the power of general legislation. But what if Parliament should encroach upon the civil rights of the colonists? Fearing that forceful resistance to British rule might lead to a democratic upheaval in America, the moderates regarded petitions and remonstrances as the proper means of securing relief.[24]

The radical party consisted of men who disliked British regulations

[23] Allan Nevins, *The American States during and after the Revolution* (New York, 1924), contains a mass of accurate information, admirably classified. On Revolutionary opinion and organization see pp. 1–116.

[24] Charles F. Mullett, *Fundamental Law and the American Revolution* (New York, 1933), is a study in constitutional doctrines.

more than they valued the benefits of empire and more than they feared the dangers of popular rule. The events of the period 1763–74 had demonstrated to such men many weaknesses in the philosophy of the moderates. For one thing, too much reliance could not be placed upon the colonial charters; that of Pennsylvania specifically recognized the right of Parliament to tax the province; in addition Britain claimed the right to modify or to nullify the charters for reasons of which she was the sole judge. As to taxation: British apologists claimed that the colonies were *virtually* represented in Parliament and that the great mass of the English people had no more voice in its deliberations than did the colonists. Clearly a stronger argument than the rights of Englishmen was needed in order to ward off parliamentary taxes. Moreover, there was no valid distinction between taxation and legislation when laws regulating trade also levied taxes. Finally, the tea episode and the Boston Port Bill had demonstrated that the power of Parliament to regulate trade might be more oppressive than the power of taxation.[25]

The radicals did not give up the claim to the civil rights of British subjects; rather they reinforced that claim with the doctrine of the "natural rights of man." There were two principal sources of this doctrine: Calvinist writers of the seventeenth century and a treatise, *Of Civil Government*, written by John Locke to justify the English Revolution of 1688. Locke's argument was as follows: Men originally dwelt in a state of nature, enjoying by virtue of natural law the rights of life, liberty, and property. Civil government had been created by a contract between the people and a ruler in order to preserve these natural rights; therefore if the ruler should deny them to the people, it was their duty to depose him and choose a successor. In this doctrine political sovereignty and property rights were derived, not from the English constitution, but from the people themselves, acting in conformity with the laws of God and nature. The natural rights theory appealed particularly to those colonists who had occupied land without title from the king and who argued that nature intended that land should belong to those who use it.[26]

The radicals in 1774 were not united: a few like Samuel Adams probably desired complete separation from Britain, but the majority desired to remain within the empire—if they could remain on their own terms. To whom then did the colonists owe allegiance? Benjamin Franklin in 1766 suggested the answer which the radicals had

[25] See again V. L. Parrington, *The Colonial Mind*, Book II, Part II.
[26] H. D. Foster, "International Calvinism through Locke and the Revolution of 1688," *American Historical Review*, XXXII (April 1927).

accepted by 1774: that the colonies were not subject to Parliament but only to the king.[27] This theory (which appealed to men who believed that as a result of the British Acts of Trade "the American goose was reserved for British plucking") implied that the colonies were in fact independent states, inasmuch as the king (after the English Revolution of 1688 had established the principle of limited monarchy) could not rule except in coöperation with Parliament; acting alone he could not regulate colonial commerce, currency, and manufactures, or tax, coerce, and punish as the means of enforcement. Thus had Parliament's authority been eliminated, the king, singlehanded, would have been helpless, and all the oppressions of mercantilism which stemmed from parliamentary statutes would have vanished. But if Parliament should insist upon its authority over the colonists and enforce laws which deprived them of their natural rights, then they must resist—by economic pressure, and if need be by force. Such were the views in 1774 of Richard Henry Lee, Roger Sherman, Stephen Hopkins, Christopher Gadsden, John and Samuel Adams, Benjamin Franklin, Thomas Jefferson, George Washington, and Patrick Henry.[28]

Although the most advanced radicals like Samuel Adams had feared the Continental Congress as a potential agency of conciliation, the events of September and October, along with the spirit of indignation which animated the mass of the people, rapidly weakened the moderates and enabled the radicals to have their way. On October 14 they triumphed when the Congress adopted a Declaration of Rights which embodied their constitutional theories. Asserting that the colonists were entitled by the law of nature, the British constitution, and the colonial charters to the rights of life, liberty, and property, this Declaration affirmed that the colonies were not (and could not be) represented in Parliament and that their local assemblies alone possessed the powers of taxation and legislation. However, the colonists would *voluntarily* accept acts of Parliament regulating external trade provided that such acts did not embody any "idea of taxation, external or internal." In line with this position the Congress would not accept the British acts passed since 1763. The Congress also drafted petitions to the king, to the several colonies, to the province of Quebec, and to the people of Britain—petitions in which colonial rights and grievances were vigorously asserted. The Declaration of

[27] V. W. Crane's *Benjamin Franklin* (Baltimore, 1936) is primarily a study of Franklin's political thought. Malcolm R. Eiselen, *Franklin's Political Theories* (Garden City, N. Y., 1928), is a good brief statement.

[28] Randolph G. Adams, *The Political Ideas of the American Revolution* (Durham, N. C., 1922) is an admirable, well-written study.

Rights, by rejecting the authority of Parliament, placed the Congress in a state of virtual rebellion.[29]

But the Congress did not stop with mere resolutions; on October 20 it adopted the momentous Continental Association, by which the members pledged that, unless Britain surrendered, they would not import certain British goods after December 1, 1774, that they would not consume any tea after March 1, 1775, and that they would not export to Britain after September 10, 1775. Article Eleven of the Association provided that the voters of each city, town, or county should select a committee, "whose business it shall be to observe the conduct of all persons touching the association; and when it shall be made to appear to the satisfaction of a majority of any such committee, that any person . . . has violated the association, that such majority do forthwith cause the truth of the case to be published in the *Gazette,* to the end that all such foes to the rights of British America may be publicly known, and universally contemned as enemies of American liberty; and henceforth we respectively will break off all dealings with him or her." Two other articles authorized the local committees to inspect customs entries and "to seize all goods imported contrary to the Association." [30]

Immediately the radicals throughout the colonies, in town meetings, general conventions, and county gatherings, adopted agreements in support of the Association and set up the designated committees. Next the committee members, by house-to-house canvass, called upon the people to join the Association; then followed the publication of the names of non-signers and the use of coercion. The boycott again became effective; outspoken opponents were tarred and feathered; goods seized from persons who violated the Association were burned; in Virginia and the Carolinas the courts were closed when British merchants sued the planters for debt; criticism and force were applied to those who indulged in luxuries, finery, and expensive amusements (all dependent upon trade with Britain); and in the commercial towns the rigid enforcement of the non-importation agreement brought British commerce to a standstill, the imports from Britain to New York falling from £437,000 in 1774 to £1,228 in 1775. Everywhere it was the fashion to use American-made articles as home industries grew by leaps and bounds.

The Continental Association ranks in importance with the Boston

---

[29] C. H. McIlwain's *The American Revolution* (New York, 1923) defends the constitutional theories of the colonial radicals in the light of English precedent.

[30] P. L. Ford, "The Association of the First Congress," *Political Science Quarterly,* VI (Dec. 1891).

Tea Party and the Coercive Acts because it obliged all persons to take an open stand on the issue of resistance. The Congress in effect renounced the authority of Parliament and assumed the power of a sovereign government when it adopted a general policy and created the machinery to enforce it throughout all the colonies. The other non-importation agreements had been local, private, voluntary; the Association was general, public, compulsory. Many of the moderates, continuing to recognize the authority of Parliament and to adhere to their faith in petitions, denounced the action of the Congress as usurpation. Other moderates and the radicals now accepted the Congress as a *de facto* government and joined in acts of coercion in order to destroy the power of Parliament over the colonies. Thus the two parties of the years 1775–76—loyalists and patriots—superseded the loose political groupings of former days.[31]

In eastern Massachusetts the presence of British troops in Boston drove the local committees to accumulate materials of war. So pronounced was the popular hostility to Britain in this quarter during the winter of 1774–75 that General Gage made no attempt to carry out instructions from Britain that he arrest Samuel Adams and John Hancock and ship them to England to stand trial for their lives. Later in the winter, when Gage dispatched small bands of officers to locate the military supplies of the patriots, the opposition they encountered was overwhelming. On April 18, 1775, Gage, ready at last to strike, sent from Boston about a thousand British regulars to take Adams and Hancock at Lexington and to seize the military stores of the patriots at Concord. Adams's chief partner in revolution, Joseph Warren, touched off the signals to arouse the countryside and dispatched William Dawes and later Paul Revere to warn Hancock and Adams. When the British troops reached Lexington they encountered fifty armed colonists. Shots rang out; several of the colonists were killed; and the British pushed on to Concord, where they destroyed a few war materials which the patriots had not removed. On the return march the British met a continuing fire from the now embattled farmers who lined the roadside. Near Lexington a force of fifteen hundred troops joined the harassed soldiers, only to serve as targets on the way to Boston. So widespread was the response of the countryside in this first battle of the Revolution that the British force of twenty-five hundred men suffered losses nearly three times those sustained by the colonists.

The news of Lexington and Concord struck the other colonies like

[31] W. C. Abbott's *New York in the American Revolution* (New York, 1929) is reliable and readable. See chapters 1–7.

an electric shock. The activities of the patriots immediately assumed a military character as the organs of resistance they had already created were devoted to defense.[32] To Washington the choice now lay between slavery and war. Fortunately for the patriots, their revolutionary organization could readily be converted into a war machine. Reaching into most communities were the committees of correspondence, set up in 1773–74, and the committees created to enforce the Continental Association of October 1774. Upon the foundation of the committees of correspondence all the royal and proprietary colonies except Georgia, Pennsylvania, and New York had, by the close of 1774, erected provincial congresses. Patterned after the colonial assemblies, these congresses were formed when royal and proprietary governors dissolved the legal assemblies or refused to call them into session. Determined not to submit to the shelving of representative government, the anti-British leaders of the assemblies of New Hampshire, Massachusetts, North Carolina, Virginia, and Delaware made provision for the elected delegates to meet independently in provincial congresses. In Maryland, South Carolina, and New Jersey the calls for elections were issued by popular meetings in Baltimore, Charleston, and Newark. Not openly revolutionary bodies, the congresses at first confined their activity to protests against the Coercive Acts, to the election of delegates to the First Continental Congress, and to the enforcement of the Continental Association. In Massachusetts, however, the provincial congress, presided over by John Hancock, established a council of safety which made the military preparations that culminated in the engagements at Lexington and Concord.[33]

When the news of the war reached New York and Georgia, the townspeople seized control of the ports of New York and Savannah, whereupon the patriot leaders called upon the electoral districts to send delegates to provincial congresses, which met respectively in May and July 1775. Elsewhere the war gave the signal for the provincial congresses to take over the legislative and financial functions of government. Next they seized the executive powers as the royal and proprietary governors were driven from office. By the end of 1775 all such governors except those of Pennsylvania, New Jersey, and Maryland had been expelled; by July 1776 they too were gone. In Rhode Island and Connecticut, where there were no royal gov-

[32] H. J. Eckenrode, *The Revolution in Virginia* (Boston, 1916), is excellent on political events and conflicts. See chapters 1–5.

[33] Harry A. Cushing, *History of the Transition from Provincial to Commonwealth Government in Massachusetts* (New York, 1896), is a detailed study of the State's politics to 1780, from a legal point of view.

ernors, the patriots converted their established institutions of government into revolutionary agencies. Since the principal task of the provincial congresses after May 1775 was to wage war against Britain they had then become distinctly revolutionary bodies.[34]

At the apex of the revolutionary structure stood the Continental Congress. In January 1775 Britain had ordered the colonial governors to prevent the election of delegates to a second congress; hence they could not be chosen by old legal methods. But the patriot leaders ignored Britain's orders and arranged to have the provincial congresses elect the new delegates. Accordingly, the Second Continental Congress, merely by assembling at Philadelphia in May in defiance of Britain, took another step toward revolution. There was now no evading the issue of war: Lexington and Concord had been fought and the patriot soldiers of Massachusetts were encircling the British troops in Boston. The Second Continental Congress therefore had either to plunge into the war or yield to Britain completely by disowning all Americans who had taken up arms. There was little hesitation. After declaring war in May the Congress in June organized an army into which it incorporated the forces besieging Boston and over which it placed Washington as commander-in-chief. It also adopted a declaration which stated the causes and necessity for taking up arms in defense of American liberty and property, promising that the colonies would disarm "when hostilities shall cease on the part of the aggressors, and all danger of their being renewed shall be removed, and not before."

The patriot party composed of the disaffected merchants, most southern planters, city tradesmen, artisans, and laborers, and the mass of the small farmers and frontiersmen had now completed a revolutionary organization. It may be likened to a pyramid—if one may compare the dynamic with the static. At the base stood the town, parish, and county committees of correspondence; the middle layer consisted of the provincial congresses and their committees or councils of safety; the Continental Congress and its army crowned the structure. As between patriots and loyalists, it may be stated with assurance that, despite the absence of statistics on the subject, an overwhelming majority of the colonists were hostile to British policy in 1775. The number of loyalists was so small that in most places (except in the presence of British troops) they were ruthlessly kept down by mass

[34] Two able studies of revolutionary action in Virginia are James M. Leake, *The Virginia Committee System and the American Revolution* (Baltimore, 1917)—thorough, detailed, best suited to advanced students—and Charles R. Lingley, *The Transition in Virginia from Colony to Commonwealth* (New York, 1910)—a lucid, concise monograph.

pressure. Early in 1775, however, patriot sentiment was not united: only a small minority of the leaders then favored immediate separation from Britain; a large majority still hoped that Britain would yield. In July 1775, the conciliationists in the Congress, led by John Dickinson and supported by the conservatives of the town of Philadelphia, secured the adoption of a last humble appeal to the king (the Olive Branch Petition).[35] Such moderate men sought a settlement that would protect colonial interests; they expected Parliament to repeal the Coercive Acts, to withdraw the troops, and to renounce its claim to unqualified supremacy over the colonies. In the meantime, since the conciliationists were unwilling to surrender abjectly to Britain, they were impelled upon a course of resistance that steadily widened the breach. The futility of their hopes was speedily to be demonstrated by the conduct of the British ruling class.

THE DECLARATION OF INDEPENDENCE

In November 1774 George III declared to Lord North that the New England colonies were "in a state of rebellion" and that "blows must decide whether they are to be subject to this country or independent." Even before 1774 Britain had shown little disposition to humor the colonies; of all the British measures after 1763 only two or three could be construed as concessions. And, in the opinion of British officials, such concessions had merely inflated the colonists with self-importance; not the slightest hint of weakness on the part of Britain could now be permitted. Even the small, uninfluential minority in Britain on whose behalf Edmund Burke addressed his eloquent appeal for conciliation accepted the theory of parliamentary supremacy over the colonies, while the majority was determined not only to assert the theory in words but also to put it into operation.[36] "A minister who had announced as part of his policy, in 1775, the giving up of the idea of parliamentary supremacy could not have held office for a day; a king who had proposed such a thing would have lost his throne" (Channing). In February 1775 the Earl of Chatham (William Pitt) presented to the House of Lords a plan which proposed that an American congress be invited to recognize Parliament's supremacy and to grant a perpetual revenue for the disposal of Parliament, whereupon Parliament would refrain from taxing the colonies. On the first reading of the bill it was rejected. About the same

[35] See again C. H. Lincoln, *The Revolutionary Movement in Pennsylvania*.
[36] An excellent brief biography is John Morley, *Burke* (London, 1879). For a more extended, recent treatment see Robert H. Murray, *Edmund Burke* (Oxford, 1931).

time the House of Commons adopted Lord North's conciliation plan which affirmed Britain's supremacy and promised that if the colonial assemblies would make suitable grants of money each year to Britain, Parliament would not exercise its taxing powers except in acts regulating trade. As this plan made no concession to the colonists on any vital point, it was rejected by every colony, and by the Continental Congress. The latter, in a report of July 31, 1775, stated that the colonies could not safely make gifts without strings attached, lest the money be "wasted among the venal and corrupt for the purpose of undermining the civil rights of the givers" or "diverted to the support of standing armies."

Two measures adopted by Britain in 1775 closed the door to conciliation. In August, George III refused to receive the Olive Branch Petition (on the ground that it was drafted by an illegal, disloyal body) and on August 23 he issued a proclamation stigmatizing the Americans as rebels and ordering that all persons refrain from giving them assistance. Parliament completed the work of repression by an act of December 22, 1775, which prohibited all trade with the thirteen colonies—an act embodying the view of Lord North that because "the Americans had refused to trade with Great Britain, it was but just that they be not suffered to trade with any other nation." [37]

Having accepted the theory that the colonies were bound to Britain, not through Parliament but through the king, the patriot leaders who now perceived that independence was inevitable were forced to direct their attack upon the person of George III. If Parliament actually possessed no authority over the colonies, then independence must be justified by the misdeeds of the king; if he had not acted unjustly, they could not properly renounce his authority. There was little difficulty, however, in preparing a case against George III, especially after he had refused to receive the Olive Branch Petition and had stigmatized the colonists as rebels. Moreover, all British officials in America were nominally agents of the king; consequently any offenses they committed might plausibly be blamed upon him. Late in October 1775 word reached the Continental Congress that a British naval force had burned the town of Falmouth, Maine. In January 1776 the Virginia patriots burned the town of Norfolk, lest it fall prey to Lord Dunmore, who—driven from Williamsburg to a warship—had used naval vessels to ravage the country along the Virginia rivers.

[37] Dora Mae Clark, *British Opinion and the American Revolution* (New Haven, 1930) is a thorough, informative monograph. Fred J. Hinkhouse, *The Preliminaries of the American Revolution as Seen in the English Press, 1763–1775* (New York, 1926), is useful for the special student.

Such actions the patriot leaders were now ready to attribute to a tyrannical king, thereby appealing to the latent democratic sentiments of the mass of the colonists. Among the underprivileged classes smoldered a hatred of aristocracy and royalty that might be quickly fanned into a consuming blaze.

In the winter of 1775–76 one man in particular sensed the public attitude and the need of the hour. This was Thomas Paine, a restless English adventurer in radicalism and idealism, who had come to America with credentials from Franklin in 1774. In January 1776 he published a fifty-page pamphlet, *Common Sense*,[38] written in a rough, vigorous, flamboyant style that drove home with fierce blows the necessity of independence. Ridiculing the idea of hereditary monarchy, he proclaimed that one honest man was worth more to society "than all the crowned ruffians that ever lived." The British ruling class, with the king at the head, lived by exploiting the common people, not only of the colonies, but of Britain as well. It was contrary to nature, he said, that a whole continent should be tributary to an island. In America the goddess of liberty, hunted from other lands, might find a secure abode. The time for separation had come; it was folly for the colonists to avow loyalty while in arms against the king; gather at once, he urged, the ripe fruit of independence, for "now your *rotting time comes on.*" [39]

Thousands of copies of *Common Sense* sent throughout the colonies crystallized the conviction then forming in men's minds. New England, at war, needed only allies in order to embrace independence. As early as May 31, 1774, a band of North Carolina frontiersmen gathered at Charlotte, Mecklenburg County, there to resolve that all military and civil commissions "heretofore granted by the Crown, to be exercised in these colonies, are null and void, and the constitution of each particular colony wholly suspended." [40] Then, on February 27, 1776, the North Carolina patriots defeated at Moore's Creek a force of sixteen hundred loyalists, taking nine hundred prisoners, whereupon ten thousand patriots assembled to repel a threatened British invasion. Fired with the war spirit the North Carolina provincial congress on April 12th instructed its delegates in the Con-

[38] Reprinted in Arthur W. Peach (ed.), *Selections from the Writings of Thomas Paine* (New York, c. 1928).

[39] The best of the older biographies, Moncure D. Conway's *The Life of Thomas Paine* (2 vols., New York, 1892), is sympathetic toward Paine. Mary A. Best, *Thomas Paine* (New York, 1927), is a lively, popular biography, written from a liberal point of view. In its defense of Paine it "out-Conways Conway."

[40] This resolution is not to be confused with the so-called Mecklenburg Declaration. For the latter, see A. S. Salley, Jr., "The Mecklenburg Declaration," *American Historical Review*, XIII (Oct. 1907).

tinental Congress to vote for independence. The opposition to Britain having risen to the boiling point in Virginia by virtue of Lord Dunmore's warlike measures, the patriots there on May 15 directed their delegates in the Continental Congress to introduce a motion for separation. During these weeks the Congress itself had moved forward by ordering that the loyalists be disarmed (March 14), by authorizing that privateers be equipped to prey upon British vessels (March 23), by opening American ports to foreign ships (early April), and by advising all the colonies to reject Britain's authority and to erect new governments based upon the people's will (May 10, 15).

On June 7 Richard Henry Lee introduced in the Congress a three-fold resolution declaring in favor of independence, foreign alliances, and American federation. The conciliationists headed by John Dickinson postponed a vote, but a committee composed of Jefferson, Franklin, Roger Sherman, R. R. Livingston, and John Adams was named to draft a declaration of independence. On July 1 Lee's resolution was approved by the delegates of nine colonies; on the next day South Carolina, Delaware, and Pennsylvania voiced their assent. Jefferson's declaration was then debated and, slightly modified, was adopted on July 4. New York—the only colony that had not acted—joined its sister states when its provincial congress ratified the Declaration, July 9. Not until August 2 and afterward was it signed by the members of the Continental Congress. One last impetus for separation was the news received at Philadelphia in June that Britain had hired twenty thousand German mercenaries for the American war.[41]

Into the Declaration of Independence Jefferson incorporated the political theories of the most democratic wing of the patriot party. He did not mention Parliament, but allusions to its "pretended legislation" and "unwarranted jurisdiction" implied that the colonists had been bound to Britain solely through the king. They had received their inalienable rights of "life, liberty and the pursuit of happiness" —not from the British monarch—but from "the laws of nature and of nature's God." Their ancestors, presumably, had entered into a contract with the king for the establishment of a just government deriving its powers from the consent of the governed and reserving to the people the right to change that government, should it become destructive of those natural rights it was instituted to preserve. By "a long train of abuses and usurpations" the king had evinced a desire

[41] Herbert Friedenwald, *The Declaration of Independence* . . . (New York, 1904), traces the growth of sentiment in favor of separation and analyzes the Declaration.

to reduce the colonists "under an absolute despotism"; it therefore became their right and duty "to throw off such government, and to provide new guards for their future security." Jefferson next presented a long list of American grievances—which were all attributed to the tyranny of George III. The Declaration then closed with the affirmation "that these United Colonies are, and of right ought to be, free and independent states; that they are absolved from all allegiance to the British Crown, and that all political connection between them and the State of Britain is and ought to be totally dissolved; and that as free and independent states, they have full power to wage war, conclude peace, contract alliances, establish commerce and to do all the acts and things which independent states may of right do." [42]

The Declaration served a purpose beyond that of a public notice of separation; its ideas inspired mass fervor for the American cause. First, by asserting the rights and worth of man ("all men are created equal") it instilled among ordinary folk a sense of their own importance that helped to sustain them at war, inspiring them to struggle for personal freedom, self-government, and a dignified place in society. Secondly, by simplifying the issues of the conflict, the Declaration made it a personal contest—not a protest against lifeless statutes and an abstract Parliament but a struggle against an enemy of flesh and blood—and one who embodied the odious features of European despotism which so many colonists had fled from Europe to escape. Few people in 1776 could have mastered all the issues of the Revolution, but even the simplest mind could grasp the idea of a despotic king. By giving to the common man a personal cause and a personal enemy, the ideas of the Declaration brought the Revolution within the range of popular aspiration and strengthened it with the force of popular emotion.[43]

[42] Carl Becker's *The Declaration of Independence* (New York, 1922) is a fascinating essay—the best of its kind.
[43] John H. Hazelton, *The Declaration of Independence* (New York, 1906), is a detailed critique, for the special student.

BIBLIOGRAPHICAL NOTE

SECONDARY WORKS: Two outstanding studies of British politics are D. A. Winstanley, *Personal and Party Government* (Cambridge, Eng., 1910), and D. A. Winstanley, *Lord Chatham and the Whig Opposition* (Cambridge, Eng., 1912). C. R. Ritcheson, *British Politics and the American Revolution* (Norman, 1954), shows the influence of American issues on party strife and imperial policy. S. Maccoby, *English Radicalism, 1762-1785* (London, 1955), is a thorough account of the opposition to the British governing class. R. W. Postgate, *That Devil Wilkes* (New York, 1929), is the best biography of its colorful subject. E. S. Morgan and H. M. Morgan, *The Stamp Act Crisis* (Chapel Hill, 1953), is mainly a description of the resistance to the Stamp Act. A. C. Land, *The Dulanys of Maryland* (Baltimore, 1955), gives a satisfactory treatment of a leading critic of the Stamp Act. A. M. Schlesinger, *Prelude to Independence* (New York, 1958), describes in detail the role of the press in the resistance to Britain. C. P. Nettels, *George Washington and American Independence* (Boston, 1951), reveals the leadership of Washington in the movement for independence.

Important biographies of leaders of the Revolution are: E. Wilder Spaulding, *His Excellency George Clinton* (New York, 1938); R. D. Meade, *Patrick Henry* (Philadelphia, 1957); Marie Kimball, *Jefferson: the Road to Glory* (New York, 1943); Dumas Malone, *Jefferson the Virginian* (Boston, 1948); and Charles Page Smith, *James Wilson* (Chapel Hill, 1956). Other notable biographies are: Ellen Hart Smith, *Charles Carroll* (Cambridge, 1942); G. C. Groce, Jr., *William Samuel Johnston* (New York, 1937); L. S. Mayo, *John Langdon* (Concord, N. H., 1937); R. A. Rutland, *George Mason* (Williamsburg, 1961); Richard Barry, *Mr. Rutledge of South Carolina* (New York, 1942); R. S. Boardman, *Roger Sherman* (Philadelphia, 1938); and John Cary, *Joseph Warren* (Urbana, 1961).

SOURCES: *The Debate on the American Revolution* (ed. Max Beloff, New York, 1949), is a well-chosen selection of writings of leading men, British and American. E. S. Morgan has edited a collection of sources on the Stamp Act episode, *Prologue to Revolution* (Chapel Hill, 1959). V. W. Crane, *Benjamin Franklin's Letters to the Press, 1758–1775* (Chapel Hill, 1950), presents many of the arguments of the debate on imperial issues. Ross S. J. Hoffman, *Edmund Burke, New York Agent, with His Letters to the New York Assembly . . .* (Philadelphia, 1956), shows the limitations of Burke as a friend of the colonies. Robert L. Schuyler, *Josiah Tucker* (New York, 1931), reprints writings of a liberal English publicist on Anglo-American themes. Harry H. Clark, *Thomas Paine: Representative Selections* (New York, 1944), is prefaced by an excellent statement of Paine's ideas. J. P. Boyd, *The Declaration of Independence* (Washington, 1943), prints facsimiles of differing versions of the document, thereby tracing its evolution. Clarence E. Carter (ed.), *The Correspondence of General Thomas Gage* (2 vols., New Haven, 1931, 1933), is a collection of major importance. Sir John Fortescue has edited the very important *Correspondence of George the Third* (6 vols., London, 1927–28). *The Barrington-Bernard Correspondence* (ed. E. Channing and A. C. Coolidge, Cambridge, 1912), contains Boston-London letters on the imperial problem, 1760–70. *Letters and Diary of John Rowe, Boston Merchant* (ed. A. R. Cunningham, Boston, 1903), gives a running account of events, 1759–79. Edmund Burke's *Letters and Speeches on American Affairs* and John Locke's *Of Civil Government* are available in Everyman's Library editions.

PAPERS OF AMERICAN LEADERS: Important collections of personal material are: R. G. Adams (ed.), *Selected Political Writings of James Wilson* (New York, 1930); J. G. Ballagh (ed.), *Letters of Richard Henry Lee* (2 vols., New York, 1911); H. A. Cushing (ed.), *The Writings of Samuel Adams* (4 vols., New York, 1904–08); C. F. Mullett (ed.), *Some Political Writings of James Otis* (Columbia, Mo., 1929); and J. C. Fitzpatrick (ed.), *The Writings of George Washington* (39 vols., Washington, 1931–44). New editions of the writings of the following men are in the process of publication: John Adams (ed. L. H. Butterfield); Benjamin Franklin (ed. L. W. Labaree); Alexander Hamilton (ed. H. C. Syrett); and Thomas Jefferson (ed. J. P. Boyd).

XXIV

The Revolution Within

DURING the contest for independence the American opponents of Britain divided into two opposing camps: those who pressed for immediate separation and those who wished to postpone the fateful decision. Inasmuch as independence was almost certain to lead to social upheaval in America, many men of conservative temperament feared to release the powerful forces making for internal change. On the other hand those who desired a reconstruction of American society realized that they must first erase the authority of Britain which maintained existing class relationships and the political power of the colonial aristocracy. A cleavage on such a profound issue could not be obliterated by the Declaration of Independence; it persisted afterward, dividing the patriot ranks into contending groups.[1]

For want of a better term one of these groups may be styled the democratic or popular party, keeping in mind that there was then no organization bearing that name. Among the people of this party were the mass of the small farmers and frontiersmen, represented by such leaders as Israel Putnam of Connecticut, John Stark of New Hampshire, Ethan Allen of Vermont, Thomas Person of North Carolina, and Francis Marion and Thomas Sumter of South Carolina. Associated with them were the artisans and laborers of the towns (directed by that resolute democrat, Samuel Adams) and one section of the merchant class—free traders sympathetic toward the popular cause: Hancock and Gerry in Massachusetts, Gadsden in South Carolina, Sears and Lamb in New York, and Stephen Hopkins in Rhode Island. The southern planter class also contributed a few able leaders to the democratic party, notably Jefferson, George Mason, and, before 1777, Patrick Henry and Richard Henry Lee. Particularly important were the lawyers: Luther Martin of Maryland, Joseph Reed and George Bryan of Pennsylvania, William Henry Drayton of South Carolina, Thomas Burke of North Carolina, and John Morin Scott and George Clinton of New York. Towering above all other

[1] For an able analysis of this cleavage see C. E. Merriam, *A History of American Political Theories*, chapter 3.

leaders of the democracy were Jefferson,[2] Samuel Adams, and Benjamin Franklin.

The conception of democracy in 1776 included many principles. First of all, man was a dignified being, capable of governing himself in a rational, orderly manner. Realizing that governments in the past had usually been employed for the oppression of the common people, the democracy viewed all government with suspicion, endorsing the view of Tom Paine that "Government, like dress, is the badge of lost innocence." The powers of government should therefore be reduced to a minimum; each man should govern himself, and such social restraints as were necessary should be imposed by the community in which one lived. The farther governmental agencies were removed from the people the less power they should possess; hence a state government should be more important than a federal or national government. In accordance with Franklin's view that property is the basis of virtue ("An empty bag cannot stand upright"), the democrats believed that each individual should be a property owner, preferably of land, thereby assuring him an independent means of livelihood.[3]

In order to check the tendency inherent in government toward tyranny and oppression, two safeguards were necessary. First, the powers of government should be narrowly restricted. All power resided in the people; they must reserve to themselves the rewards of their labor (low taxes) and their rights of life and liberty, permitting government to exercise only such powers as would serve their interests. In their sovereign capacity the people should form constitutions both to confer upon government the powers it might exercise and to reserve to the people their fundamental rights. Secondly, the limited powers of government ought to be exercised by the people themselves through equal representation in the legislature, a liberal suffrage, and the right of the common man to hold office.[4]

Such political conceptions gave great importance to land as the source of wealth and power. The divine order in nature had decreed that the land should be used by man and that it should belong to those who would cultivate it. "All the property," wrote Franklin, "that is necessary to a man, for the conservation of the individual and the propagation of the species, is his natural right, which none can

[2] For the general student the best biography is Gilbert Chinard, *Thomas Jefferson* (Boston, 1929).

[3] Francis W. Hirst, *Life and Letters of Thomas Jefferson* (New York, 1926), is excellent.

[4] Albert J. Nock's *Jefferson* (New York, c. 1926) is an interpretation by a brilliant essayist.

justly deprive him of: but all property superfluous to such purposes is the property of the public, who by their laws have created it, and who may therefore by other laws dispose of it, whenever the welfare of the public shall demand such disposition." In keeping with such ideas the democracy rejected the king's claim to unoccupied lands, opposed the proprietary overlords, and favored the division of great estates into small holdings. But ownership alone was not enough: the husbandman should enjoy also the fruits of his labor, and that might be effected by means of an adequate currency which would keep up the price of the products which he offered for sale. An ample cash income in turn meant that he might pay his debts and avoid losing his land by foreclosure.[5]

In opposition to the democracy of small property owners and expectant property owners stood a conservative party composed of men of large capital which they combined with the labor of dependent workers in such a manner as to obtain abundant incomes for themselves. To this party belonged many of the wealthiest landowners: Benjamin Harrison, Richard Bland, Edmund Pendleton, Thomas Nelson, Edmund Randolph, and George Washington of Virginia, Charles Pinckney, Charles Coatsworth Pinckney, Edward Rutledge, John Rutledge, Henry Middleton, Arthur Middleton, and Rawlins Lowndes of South Carolina, Charles Carroll and Thomas Johnson of Maryland, Samuel Johnston and Richard Henderson of North Carolina, and Robert R. Livingston, Gouverneur Morris, Lewis Morris, James Duane, and Philip Schuyler of New York. The merchant class also contained many conservatives—James Bowdoin of Massachusetts, Roger Sherman and Jonathan Trumbull of Connecticut, the four Brown brothers of Rhode Island (Nicholas, John, Joseph, and Moses), Henry Laurens and Gabriel Manigault of South Carolina, Joseph Hewes of North Carolina, and George Clymer, Thomas Mifflin, Thomas and Samuel Wharton, Robert Morris, and Edward Biddle of Pennsylvania. Outstanding lawyers of the conservative group were Alexander Hamilton and John Jay of New York, James Iredell of North Carolina, and John Dickinson, James Wilson, and George Ross of Pennsylvania.[6]

The conservative philosophy of society assumed that the common people were ignorant, slothful, and incompetent; as individuals, weak; in the mass, rapacious and violent. The natural order of things

[5] A substantial though brief biography is David S. Muzzey, *Thomas Jefferson* (New York, 1918). Of the older biographies, Henry S. Randall's *The Life of Thomas Jefferson* (3 vols., New York, 1858) is the most valuable.

[6] An admirable study of a conservative leader is Frank Monaghan, *John Jay* (New York, 1935).

had decreed that a few able, well-bred, well-educated men should be the custodians of wealth and the repositories of virtue, charged with the duty of preserving order, decorum, and culture in society. To this select few the mass of the people (slaves, tenants, employees, servants, and debtors) should be subservient. At all times the "greed" of the masses should be curbed, lest it lead to attacks upon the persons and property of the upper class. "The mob," wrote Gouverneur Morris in 1774, "begins to think and reason. Poor reptiles! it is with them a vernal morning; they are struggling to cast off their winter's slough, they bask in the sunshine, and ere noon they will bite."

The most conservative men of the upper class believed that popular uprisings should be guarded against with every precaution. Education of the poor should inculcate habits of industry and attitudes of obedience, an established church should teach respect for authority and property, and government should uphold the existing order by protecting the interests of men of wealth. Since in each state the poor outnumbered the rich it was unwise to rely wholly upon state government; a strong central government, equipped with an army, should be empowered to curb the democracy in its efforts to effect a redistribution of wealth, should such a thing be attempted either by state laws or by the use of force. All offices of government should be controlled by the aristocracy; hence the need of high property qualifications for voting and officeholding. Constitutional restraints on majority rule in elected legislatures should give protection against popular laws which threatened to injure the upper class, and taxes for the support of armed forces and state churches should be collected equally from all the people, not from the wealthy in accordance with their ability to pay. For the benefit of creditors a sound or limited currency should be maintained and managed by them in such a manner as to circumvent the scaling down of debts. For similar reasons the courts should not be unduly sympathetic toward debtors, servants, employees, tenants, or anyone disposed to challenge the supremacy of the upper class.[7]

State Government and Federal Union

On the issue of British rule the democratic elements, unanimous in opposition to king and Parliament, provided the driving force which culminated in independence. On the other hand, the conservatives (who had largely directed the campaign against Britain on legal grounds) were divided. One group, which included Washington,

[7] See again V. L. Parrington, *The Colonial Mind*, Book III.

Carroll, John Adams, Sherman, Trumbull, Thomas Johnson, John Witherspoon, and John Hewes realized that the dangers of British policy exceeded the menace of convulsions within the colonies and acted with the democracy for separation. Excepting pro-British merchants, most of the conservatives of New England, North Carolina, Virginia, Maryland, New Jersey, and South Carolina who joined the revolutionary movement had decided in favor of independence by July 1776. Another group, however, particularly strong in Pennsylvania and New York and represented by James Wilson, Dickinson, Jay, Robert Morris, James Duane, and R. R. Livingston—and in South Carolina by Laurens, Manigault, and John Rutledge—worked to delay independence, fearing that internal upheavals might follow the destruction of British rule. But once the decision for independence had been reached, such conciliationists felt it necessary to take part in the revolutionary movement in order to direct it into what they deemed the proper channels.[8]

Independence erased the authority of the king on which the colonial governments had previously rested, thereby forcing the Americans to establish new state governments on another foundation. And because the Revolution was in part a protest against monarchy and aristocracy, it followed that the will of the people should be declared the source of all political power. The first thing the people had to do was to transform their revolutionary organizations into permanent governments—a task accomplished by means of written constitutions. Even before July 4, 1776, four of the colonies—New Hampshire, South Carolina, Virginia, and New Jersey—had adopted such constitutions. In the autumn and winter of 1776 Delaware, Pennsylvania, Maryland, and North Carolina acted; Georgia and New York followed in 1777; South Carolina formed a new constitution in 1778; and Massachusetts joined the procession in 1780. Rhode Island and Connecticut retained their colonial charters, which they modified by deleting all references to the king. In ten states (Pennsylvania, New York, Virginia, New Hampshire, South Carolina, North Carolina, Delaware, Georgia, New Jersey, and Maryland) the provincial congresses drafted the constitutions, and since the congresses served at the same time as legislative bodies, there was little distinction between the constitution and ordinary law. Not until Massachusetts acted in 1779–80 was a special convention elected which confined itself solely to the task of framing a constitution; and not until then was a constitution submitted to a popular referendum.

[8] See again Allan Nevins, *The American States during and after the Revolution*, pp. 117–630 on political issues and paper money.

In most states the problem of erecting a new government evoked a bitter struggle between the democratic and conservative forces. One section of the democracy stood for three main principles: a liberal franchise, equal representation of all districts in proportion to population, and the supremacy of the popular house of the legislature over the upper house, the executive, and the judiciary. Such was the program of radical democratic leaders like Franklin, Tom Paine, and Samuel Adams. More moderate democratic leaders, including Jefferson, Mason,[9] and R. H. Lee, mistrustful of all government and fearing that an elected lower house might become as tyrannical as an oligarchy of aristocrats, favored a government of limited powers in which the executive, judicial, and legislative branches would keep each other in check. The ultra-conservatives desired to withhold the right to vote from the poor, to give wealthy districts an influence greater than their population alone would warrant, and to provide a strong upper house and an independent executive and judiciary, all three to serve as brakes on the lower house. Radical democrats thus favored popular rule, moderate democrats wanted as little government as possible, and conservatives believed with John Jay that "those who own the country ought to govern it." The radical democrats were small farmers, small tradesmen, artisans, and mechanics; the conservatives were generally the largest property owners; while the moderate democrats were men of liberal sympathies and substantial property, often at odds with the largest property owners and yet not disposed to countenance mob rule or unrestrained attacks upon property rights. In four states (Pennsylvania, North Carolina, Delaware, and Georgia) the new constitutions were essentially democratic, whereas in Virginia, South Carolina, New York, Massachusetts, New Jersey, Maryland, and New Hampshire the conservative influence predominated. The form of government in both Rhode Island and Connecticut after 1776 was democratic, but in Connecticut men of conservative temperament were in control, while in Rhode Island the democratic forces were particularly strong.[10]

Pennsylvania attained the closest approach to pure democracy in its constitution of 1776, adopted by a convention in which delegates from the democratic interior counties outnumbered the representatives of the conservative East by two to one. Its authors (among them Benjamin Franklin) provided for a one-house legislature whose mem-

---

[9] The best work, Kate M. Rowland, *The Life of George Mason* (2 vols., New York, 1892), consists chiefly of Mason's writings.

[10] See again C. H. Van Tyne, *The War of Independence,* chapters 2, 9–12, and *The American Revolution,* chapters 9, 11, 14.

bers were elected annually by all the taxpayers of their districts. An executive council of thirteen, chosen every three years by the voters, and a president without power took the place of the old proprietary governor and council. Neither the president nor the executive council could veto acts of the legislature or otherwise hamper it. Of the state judiciary a critic of the constitution complained that it was wholly dependent upon the legislators, "who may remove any judge from his office *without trial*, for anything they please to call 'misbehavior.'" So bitter was the opposition of the eastern conservatives like Dickinson and Robert Morris that they organized an anticonstitutionalist party and directed their delegates in the assembly to obstruct the new government in every way. Although the eastern conservatives controlled only a third of the legislature their power was strong enough to bring about a deadlock and a disruption of the new government (December 1776). Only when the Continental Congress threatened to take over the state government did the eastern conservatives agree to coöperate. A new election was held in February 1777 and on March 4 the constitution at last began to function as its authors intended.[11]

The democrats of North Carolina in October 1776 held an election of members to a new provincial congress which was authorized to draft the state constitution. Four seats in five were captured by men of advanced democratic views. A leading conservative, Samuel Johnston (who was burned in effigy after his election defeat), lamented that everyone "who has the least pretensions to be a gentleman is borne down *per ignobile vulgus*—a set of men without reading, experience, or principles to govern them." By the new constitution of December 8 every adult freeman of the state received the right to vote for assemblymen, while the latter were required to possess one hundred acres of land. Any resident who owned fifty acres of land enjoyed the right to vote for state senators, each of whom had to possess an estate of three hundred acres. Although the constitution provided for a governor (elected by the legislature) his powers were only nominal: he could not veto its acts or make important appointments, and his term lasted but one year. One ultra-conservative, William Hooper, contemptuously remarked that the only power given to the governor was the right "to sign a receipt for his salary."[12]

[11] Burton A. Konkle, *George Bryan and the Constitution of Pennsylvania, 1731–1791* (Philadelphia, 1922), a vigorously written biography, surveys Pennsylvania politics through the career of a leading radical. See also P. L. Ford, "The Adoption of the Pennsylvania Constitution of 1776," *Political Science Quarterly*, X (Sept. 1895).

[12] A good brief political account is Enoch W. Sikes, *The Transition of North Carolina from Colony to Commonwealth* (Baltimore, 1898).

The first outstanding example of a conservative constitution was the work of a South Carolina provincial congress in which the seaboard had 144 representatives as against forty for the democratic back country, even though the interior section then contained three-fourths of the white population. The first constitution, probably drafted by the ultra-conservative John Rutledge, remained in force from March 1776 until March 1778, when it was superseded by another, also essentially conservative. The distinguishing features of the second constitution were the senate and the scheme of representation for the lower house. If a senator resided in the district he represented he must own property worth £2,000; if he represented a district of which he was not a resident he must be worth £7,000. Only a man with an estate of £10,000 could serve as governor. Although the legislature possessed much power, it was not a democratic body in that the wealthy eastern aristocracy dominated both the senate and the lower house. In the latter, the lowlands were entitled to 144 seats; the populous upcountry to only fifty-eight. Moreover, the wealthy, aristocratic senate was a check on the lower house, and only residents who owned fifty acres of land received the right to vote. Allan Nevins states that the new government was distinctly "for the rich, well-born lowlanders, who had made it for themselves, and meant to keep it their own."

The provincial congress which in June 1776 adopted the first constitution of Virginia was composed of two delegates from each county and therefore reflected the interests of the small wealthy counties of the seaboard as against those of the larger and more populous counties of the interior. Both the conservatives and the liberal democrats took part in the proceedings: Edmund Randolph, for instance, as president of the congress and George Mason as the chief author of the constitution. Although the legislature was made superior to the governor (whose powers were only nominal), although both the lower house and the senate were elected by all residents who possessed fifty acres, and although the two houses chose the governor, even so the constitution did not establish a popular government. Each county continued to be represented by two delegates, with the result that a small eastern county with a few hundred voters ranked as equal to a large western county containing several thousand. Moreover, the seaboard area obtained a disproportionately large influence in the senate, a fourth of whose twelve members were chosen once a year for four-year terms; and, besides, the senate enjoyed nearly coördinate powers with the lower house. Thus despite the centering of power in the legislature, the tidewater aristocracy remained in control by virtue of the checks on the elected house and the unequal mode of representation; self-government in Virginia continued to mean the rule of the upper class.[13]

Drafted by a trio of conservatives—Jay, R. R. Livingston, and Gouverneur Morris—the New York constitution of 1777 provided for a democratic lower house of seventy members elected by the freemen of the towns and by freeholders worth £20. However, four curbs on the elected house restrained the democracy. The governor, chosen for a three-year term by a restricted electorate, commanded the armed forces and received the power to prorogue the legislature. (All previous state constitutions had provided that the legislature should elect a weak executive—a reaction against the influence exercised by the royal and proprietary governors of colonial times.) The New York senate, which shared coördinate powers with the lower house, was certain to be dominated by wealthy men, a fourth of whom were elected each year for four-year terms by voters who possessed freeholds (clear of debt) worth at least £100 each. A council of appointment consisting of the governor and four senators exercised the appointing power, while a council of revision (the governor, the chancellor, and three supreme court judges) could veto acts of the legislature—and only by a two-thirds vote of each house could such a veto be overridden. In 1790 only one adult male in ten in New York City could vote for governor. The power and nature of the senate gave assurance that it would be the center of gravity in a government dominated by wealthy landowners.[14]

In Massachusetts the conservatives also won a decisive victory. The constitution of 1780 provided for a governor elected by property owners and entrusted with the veto and appointive powers, including the right to appoint judges who were to hold office during good behavior. Although each town was privileged to have a representative in the lower house, no salaries were provided for members, and many poor communities could not afford to send delegates. The senate—an effective check on the lower house—represented the wealthy men of the state. Property qualifications were: for a voter, £60; for a representative, a freehold of £100 or other property worth £200; for a senator, a freehold of £300 or other property worth £600; and for the governor, a freehold of £1,000. Taxation for the support of the Congregational churches remained intact. S. E. Morison has de-

---

[13] See again I. S. Harrell, *Loyalism in Virginia*, chapters 2–4, and C. H. Ambler, *Sectionalism in Virginia*, chapter 2.

[14] E. W. Spaulding's *New York in the Critical Period* is an admirable study of the social and economic results of the Revolution.

scribed the constitution of 1780 as "a lawyers' and merchants' constitution, directed toward something like quarterdeck efficiency in government and the protection of property against democratic pirates." [15]

While constitution-making was in progress in the states, the Continental Congress was wrestling with the problem of a federal union. Two circumstances forced the Americans to devise a scheme of confederation. First, they had to coöperate in prosecuting the war—on the assumption that they must hang together or they would hang separately. Secondly, the common problems of the states necessitated a permanent machinery for joint action; the American economy of industry, trade, and credit relations cut across state boundaries and involved perpetual contacts with foreign countries, while numerous rival land claims of the states required some agency for the arbitration of disputes. Prior to 1776 Britain had provided the general government to supervise foreign and intercolonial affairs. Now, however, that government had been renounced and a new one had to be erected. The task presented the same difficulty of adjusting local and external interests which had precipitated the Revolution. On the issue of a central authority the Americans divided into two parties which corresponded roughly to the democratic and conservative groups which were contending for mastery within the states.[16]

One of these parties preferred to make the states the center of a federal system, around which a weak general government should revolve as a satellite. Among the small farmers and the southern planters the sentiment in favor of state sovereignty was particularly strong. Remembering that the British government had used its authority to support the British merchants and landlords in their conflicts with American farmers, the agrarian leaders did not intend to create new institutions vested with the old powers of king and Parliament. The program of the democratic-agrarian forces therefore included the following points. A general government should not possess the power of taxation; all levies on the people should be voted by their state legislatures. So also the states must retain control over military forces, lest these be utilized against the people as the British army had been used. Nor should the general government be granted the exclusive power to regulate trade and enact navigation laws; by such measures the commercial class might oppress the farmers. There

---

[15] J. T. Adams's *New England in the Republic* (Boston, 1926) concludes his three-volume history of New England. See chapters 2–4.

[16] C. H. Van Tyne, "Sovereignty in the American Revolution," *American Historical Review*, XII (April 1907).

should be no federal judiciary empowered to set aside the decisions of state courts, nor should state laws be nullified by an external agency in the manner that the British Privy Council had disallowed colonial acts. In the sphere of domestic legislation the states should be sovereign, vested with the power of coining money, issuing bills of credit, and regulating credit relations and property rights. In those states which had western land claims (Georgia, the Carolinas, Virginia, and Connecticut) the state rights sentiment was reinforced by the desire of settlers and land speculators to vest the title to the western lands in the respective state governments which they controlled.[17]

Against the state rights party were arrayed the advocates of a strong central government—merchants, investors, and men of large wealth whose property interests extended over many states. In their opinion the central government should be sovereign over the states in certain fields. It should regulate trade, establish a uniform currency, enact navigation laws, and conduct diplomatic negotiations with foreign nations. Moreover, it should possess an army and a navy and be able to use them to suppress domestic insurrections which might imperil existing property rights. The laws of a general congress regulating currency and debts should take precedence over acts of the states, and a central judiciary should be empowered to reverse the judgments of state courts detrimental to non-resident creditors. No state should exclude the merchants of other states from its trade, and owners of large tracts of land should be protected against settlers who might swarm in from other states and help themselves to farms. In those states without western land claims (especially in Maryland, Pennsylvania, and New Jersey) land speculators preferred that a general government own the western territory in order that the citizens of all states might stand on an equal footing before the grantor of the land. And should the general government take possession of the western lands it would need vigorous powers in order to defend and administer them properly.[18]

In June 1776 the Continental Congress appointed a committee to draft a plan of union. Men of conservative views dominated this committee, whose guiding spirit was John Dickinson. On July 12 he presented a plan of union which proposed to establish a fairly strong central government. The state rights leaders attacked the Dickinson draft

[17] Merrill Jensen, *The Articles of Confederation* (Madison, 1940), offers an original and stimulating interpretation.

[18] Edmund C. Burnett, *The Continental Congress* (New York, 1941), is an elaborate compilation, useful as a reference work.

and because they dominated the Congress they succeeded in modifying it to suit their views. The Articles of Confederation emerged from the debate, ratified by the Congress on November 15, 1777.

Designed to create a "perpetual union," the Articles granted to the general government only limited powers to be exercised by a Congress in which each state was given one vote. No provision was made for an independent executive department or for a permanent federal judiciary, and no agency was created to review or disallow state laws. The Congress could exercise only such powers as were specifically granted to it by the articles; all power not mentioned was reserved to the states. Only by a unanimous vote of all states could the articles be amended. The Congress could not levy taxes; it could only make requisitions upon the states, trusting that they would raise the money. Such quotas were to be apportioned among the states in proportion to the value of lands and buildings legally in private hands. The Congress might enter into commercial treaties and regulate Indian affairs, yet if its acts in those fields conflicted with certain state laws, the latter were to be supreme. Of the powers granted to the Congress, the most important could be exercised only with the assent of the delegations of nine states—that is to say, the power to engage in war, to coin, borrow or appropriate money, to issue bills of credit, and to decide the number of vessels to be acquired for the navy and the number of land and sea forces to be raised. The states retained the concurrent right to issue bills of credit and to coin money, and the sole right to enact laws governing contracts and debts. Moreover, the states could exercise many of the powers granted to the Congress, if they were exercised with its consent: the right to make treaties, to send and receive diplomatic agents, to maintain navies and armies, to engage in war, and to fit out vessels against pirates. In ordinary times the principal military forces should consist of state militias. If a state did not respect its obligations under the Articles there was no legal means of compelling it to conform.

As an embodiment of the revolutionary opposition to the authority of the British Parliament, the Articles of Confederation reserved to the states most of the powers which Parliament had previously claimed. And the powers granted to the Congress were so hedged about that they could not be used by minority groups in control of the general government to the detriment of the people of the states.[19]

The Articles of Confederation were not ratified by all the states—and hence did not become operative—until March 1, 1781. This delay

[19] E. S. Corwin, "The Progress of Constitutional Theory . . ." [1776–87], *American Historical Review*, XXX (April 1925).

was occasioned by a spirited debate in the Congress over the ownership of the western lands. Those promoters of western settlement
who had been seeking land grants from the king prior to 1776 now
became supplicants before the Congress, contending that it superseded the Crown as the proprietor of the West. Two companies of
speculators dominated the scene: the Indiana Company, sponsors of
the Vandalia project; and the Illinois-Wabash Company, a combination formed in 1779. Both companies were vehicles for the promoters of the middle states. Samuel Wharton, George Morgan, and
Benjamin Franklin were leaders in the Indiana Company, which
sought a large tract in present-day West Virginia; Robert Morris,
James Wilson, and George Ross of Pennsylvania and Charles Carroll, Thomas Johnson, and Samuel Chase of Maryland led the
Illinois-Wabash Company, which proposed to operate in the region
north of the Ohio River. Both companies needed confirmation of
their claims, and despairing of obtaining such confirmations from
Virginia, they insisted that Virginia cede her western lands to the
Congress—from which body they hoped to receive favored treatment.
In June and July 1776 Virginia in effect rejected the claims of the
companies and announced that all the lands within her charter limits
should be disposed of through her state government.[20]

Since the Articles of Confederation as finally drafted proposed to
leave the western lands in possession of the states with charter claims,
the landed interest of the middle states worked to prevent ratification
of the Articles. Maryland thereupon refused to ratify until Virginia
ceded her claims. As an inducement to Virginia, New York on February 19, 1780, abandoned its shadowy title to lands west of the present
boundary of the state. The political leaders of New York agreed to
give up the state's claim (derived from Britain's recognition of New
York as the protector of the Iroquois) because the lands reserved to
the state in 1780 offered ample scope for its land speculators. Then
when Virginia was threatened by British troops and hoped to invigorate the defense measures of the Congress, her legislature on
January 2, 1781, ceded to the United States most of the land north of
the Ohio River, with the condition—sponsored by George Mason—
that all existing grants from the Indians to private interests be nullified. Although the Virginia cession cut the ground from under the land
promoters of the middle states, it induced Maryland to ratify the
Articles of Confederation, March 1, 1781. The land companies then
tried to persuade the Congress to reject the Virginia cession, but their

---

[20] M. M. Jensen, "The Cession of the Old Northwest," *Mississippi Valley Historical
Review*, XXII (June 1936).

efforts proved fruitless; the Congress accepted it on March 1, 1784.[21]

Inasmuch as the Articles of Confederation did not become effective until 1781, the Congress acted until then as a *de facto* government, without the benefit of a written constitution. The foundations of its authority were twofold: the necessity of waging war and the powers with which its members were vested by the people of the several states. Thus between 1776 and 1781 the union was a confederation of the people of the thirteen states united, forced to coöperate by the menace of a common enemy.

THE COSTS OF WAR

To provide the sinews of war was the most urgent task confronting the Congress and the states. That part of the military burden assumed by the Congress in June 1775 included the raising, paying, equipping, and provisioning of a continental army, the appointment of the commander-in-chief and other high officers, the directing of the campaigns of the war, and the apportionment of the expenses of the army among the states on the basis of population (the requisition or quota system). But how was the Congress to raise money in advance of the payment of the state quotas? It could not levy taxes; it could not at first commandeer property (lest it turn the people against the American cause); and it could not obtain adequate funds on loan from men of wealth. Many of the richest men, as loyalists, were unwilling to lend money to the Congress, and their property could be confiscated only by the states. Due to a trade depression in 1775–76, occasioned by Britain's war on American commerce, wealthy patriots were unable to convert commodities into cash, while cautious capitalists feared to lend to the United States when the outcome of the war was in doubt. Should Britain win, all such loans would be repudiated. For similar reasons foreign investors and foreign governments held back; moreover, open support to the Americans might involve a foreign state in war with Britain. The United States had no common currency, either paper or metallic; there were no banks which could extend credit to the government; and the supply of foreign coins and state paper money, thanks to Britain's imperial currency policy, was woefully inadequate for financing an extended war.

In these circumstances the Congress had to issue bills of credit or promissory notes, printed in the form of general currency so that they would circulate without individual endorsements. Such bills had proved serviceable during the earlier wars; and moreover they ap-

[21] Herbert B. Adams, *Maryland's Influence upon Land Cessions to the United States* (Baltimore, 1885).

peased the debtor wing of the revolutionary party which had long clamored for a cheap and abundant currency. They were not redeemable in specie from day to day, but the Congress called upon the states to provide money from taxes for the redemption of the bills at designated times.[22]

All in all the Congress emitted in bills of credit, between June 22, 1775, and November 29, 1779, a sum of $191,500,000. This huge issue was made necessary by the failure of the states to collect the tax money which was supposed to take the bills out of circulation. When such tax money was not paid to the Congress by the states, the old bills remained in use, while money for fresh outlays had to be provided by printing new bills. Prior to September 3, 1779, when the Congress had issued nearly $160,000,000 in bills, the states had provided only about $3,000,000 in tax money for their redemption. Moreover, the states issued notes and bills of their own—$250,000,-000 in all. Since the state and the Congress bills circulated side by side they constituted a uniform currency; each affected the value of the other. The tremendous expansion of the paper currency was not accompanied by an equivalent increase in the supply of silver and commodities; hence the value of the paper currency steadily depreciated. On January 14, 1779, the ratio of silver dollars to paper dollars was $1:8$; on May 5 it stood at $1:24$; on November 17 at $1:38\frac{1}{2}$.

The superabundance of the Continental bills, their depreciation, and the ability of the Congress after 1779 to borrow money from private sources led to a decision to retire the bills from circulation. Accordingly, the Congress enacted, March 18, 1780, that the states should collect taxes and use the money to redeem the bills at the rate of one silver dollar to forty paper dollars. If a taxpayer were assessed a tax of one dollar (silver) he could pay forty dollars in Continental bills, whereupon they would be sent to the Congress and destroyed. After the redemption period had expired, any bills outstanding were to have no further value. Eventually about $120,000,-000 of the Continental bills were retired in this manner; $71,000,000 remained in circulation. After 1781 remaining bills depreciated to the vanishing point, giving rise to the phrase, "not worth a Continental." Speculators bought them for a song, hoping that in the future the Congress might redeem them at part of their face value.[23]

[22] R. V. Harlow, "Aspects of Revolutionary Finance, 1775–1783," *American Historical Review*, XXXV (Oct. 1929).

[23] An older pioneer work, not too technical or detailed, is Albert S. Bolles, *The Financial History of the United States from 1774 to 1789* (2d ed., New York, 1884).

The paper currency issued by the states consisted of both ordinary bills of credit and interest-bearing treasury notes. All told they amounted to about $250,000,000. The only security behind most of this paper was the promise of the state legislatures to levy taxes for redemption. However, such taxes were not collected (often they were not even assessed), and accordingly the state bills traveled the road of depreciation hand in hand with the Continental bills. After 1780 they were drawn in as tax money at various rates of depreciation: in Georgia and Virginia at $1,000 paper to $1.00 silver, in North Carolina at 800 to 1; in New York at 128 to 1; in Maryland at 40 to 1. Through this mode of redemption the indebtedness of the states represented by the bills of credit was effaced by the end of the war, depreciation having served as a tax upon most of the people through whose hands the bills had passed.[24]

Who benefited by the depreciation of the paper currency? Certainly not the mass of the people—not even the debtor class. In order to maintain the face value of both the state and Continental bills of credit in terms of silver dollars the state legislatures in the years 1775–77 enacted that they pass as legal tender in payment of existing debts. Some states went so far as to provide that the tender of bills to a creditor automatically canceled the obligation. Creditors, however, were not wholly unprotected. In the first place, depreciation caused a rapid rise in the price of commodities; in many cases so much of a debtor's increased income in paper money was required for the purchase of new supplies that he had nothing left for debt payments. Secondly, creditors took advantage of the natural disposition of debtors to defer payment and thus extended loans until collections might be made in a better currency. In other cases poorly paid military service forced men to borrow money to operate their farms while they were away in the army. If a debtor did succeed in clearing himself of debt, the rise in the prices of what he bought often forced him to borrow again. When depreciation became acute the creditors secured laws in 1780–82 which provided that past debts be paid in paper currency of a value in silver equivalent to that which the debtor had received. Thus if a debtor had borrowed in 1776 $100 in paper which was then worth $100 in silver, and if he repaid the debt in 1781 when $100 in paper was worth but one dollar in silver, he must pay $10,000 in the depreciated paper. Finally, by 1781 all the states but South Carolina had repealed their legal tender laws, and South Carolina made it unanimous in 1782.[25]

[24] A. Bezanson, Prices . . . During the . . . Revolution [Penn] (Philadelphia, 1951).
[25] The most detailed of the older accounts is W. G. Sumner, The Financier and

Similarly, the day-to-day operation of the paper currency did not benefit the mass of the farmers, workers, and consumers; instead, those who profited were men skilled in money transactions who devoted all their time to the study of prices and currency values. Merchants who anticipated depreciation raised the prices of the goods they sold; and such prices undoubtedly rose faster than wages and the prices of farm products. Soldiers who received fixed pay in a depreciating currency were particularly hard hit. A conference of New Englanders at Providence in December 1776 warned that "the avaricious conduct of many persons, by daily adding to the price of every necessary and convenient article of life . . . , will be attended by the most fatal and pernicious consequences, as it . . . disheartens and disaffects the soldiers . . . and distresses the poorer part of the community." "The rapid and exorbitant rise upon the necessaries . . . of life," declared the Connecticut legislature in 1776, "is chiefly occasioned by monopolizers, the great pest of society." In order to combat such wartime profiteering the states prepared schedules of prices at which sellers were supposed to part with their goods. But price-fixing failed; either sellers would hoard their commodities if the legal prices were too low or they would evade the law. No government could supervise millions of transactions involving the prices of all commodities. Those persons who did abide by the law merely penalized themselves while "chiselers" grew rich. A conference on price-fixing to which all states but Virginia and New York sent delegates in 1780 finally admitted the hopelessness of the policy and abandoned it as a lost cause.

The ever-prevalent complaints of profiteering and allusions to "sharpers, monopolizers and extortioners" indicate that many traders made a good thing out of the war. Realizing that the currency bubble would one day burst, the shrewdest investors converted their paper profits into some durable form—into land, commodities, mortgage loans, capital goods, and the securities of the state and federal governments, thereby acquiring claims to future incomes to be realized in a better currency. At the end of the war, the investments of the creditor class (as expressed in dollars) greatly exceeded their prewar investments, and the burden of debt, both public and private, was correspondingly increased.[26]

the Finances of the American Revolution (2 vols., New York, 1891). For a condensed version see W. G. Sumner, Robert Morris (1892).

[26] W. B. Norton, "Paper Money in Massachusetts during the Revolution," New England Quarterly, VII (March 1934).

The conversion of depreciated paper into income-producing property is illustrated by the long-term loans floated during the war by the Congress and the states. As early as October 1776 the Congress authorized the sale of long-term securities (similar to government bonds), but until September 1777 purchasers did not respond readily, in part because the Congress could not guarantee the payment of interest and principal. However, after 1777 the United States could borrow from France ($6,353,000, specie value, was obtained between 1777 and 1784) and this money the Congress used to pay the interest on its long-term securities. At the same time occurred the depreciation of the Continental bills of credit. Because these bills could be exchanged for United States securities which now yielded interest in sound money, the demand for the latter became so great that the Congress was able, after September 1777, to dispose of securities amounting to $63,000,000, although the paper it received had a specie value of only $7,684,000. Part of this debt was repaid in 1783–89 from proceeds from the sale of the public lands. In 1790 the total domestic indebtedness of the United States was estimated by Alexander Hamilton as $40,000,000 ($27,000,000 principal and $13,000,-000 unpaid interest). At that time unpaid long-term debts incurred by the states exceeded $18,000,000. Since the United States in 1790 provided for the repayment of both the state and federal debts in specie, those investors who had bought government securities in 1777–81 and who retained them until 1790 succeeded in converting depreciated currency into a durable value.

THE REVOLUTION AND THE LAND

Of all the results of the Revolution none exceeded in importance the transformation of the system of land ownership. The landed aristocracy of colonial times, imported from England with feudal trimmings, went down before the onrush of democracy—a change effected by the confiscation of estates, some of which were characterized by feudal survivals, and by the sweeping away of quit-rents, entails, primogeniture, and the colonial establishments of the Anglican Church. Even slavery felt the impact of the rights of man.[27]

The mainspring of this revolution was the seizure by the states of the ungranted lands in possession of the king. New Hampshire, New York, Virginia, the Carolinas, and Georgia took possession of the

---

[27] Benjamin Quarles, *The Negro in the American Revolution* (Chapel Hill, 1961), shows the effect of slavery and portrays the fortunes of Negroes during the war.

royal acres within their borders, thus freeing themselves from the British land ordinance of 1774 and democratizing the power of land disposal by vesting it in the state legislatures. By obtaining title to the territory north to the Great Lakes and west to the Mississippi, the United States swept away the obstacles to settlement imposed by the Quebec Act and the Indian boundary line, opening the West to farmers and land speculators—at first the area of Kentucky-Tennessee; then the region north of the Ohio and the Southwest.[28]

Proprietary estates also fell into the hands of the states. Pennsylvania took over the ungranted lands of the Penn family—a domain valued at £1,000,000, for the loss of which the state granted the Penns £130,000 "in remembrance of the enterprising spirit of the founder and of the expectations and dependence of his descendants." When Maryland confiscated the lands of its proprietor in 1780, the compensation it provided was so inadequate (£10,000) that the British government paid him an additional £90,000. The only surviving proprietorship in the Carolinas (Lord Granville's estate, a third of North Carolina) also passed into the hands of the state government. Virginia took possession of Lord Fairfax's domain of more than five million acres between the Rappahannock and the Potomac Rivers (the Northern Neck).[29] Originally granted in 1649 by Charles II to Lord Culpeper and a group of his associates as a retreat for English Cavaliers, this estate had been acquired *in toto* by Culpeper's son, from whom it descended to Lord Fairfax. After obtaining a confirmation of his title from the Crown in 1745, Fairfax had surveyors run the "Fairfax line" which connected the head springs of the Rappahannock with the northern branch of the Potomac (1746). The next year Fairfax removed to Virginia and thereafter enjoyed the distinction of being the only British peer among the permanent residents of the colonies. He lived in rustic simplicity at "Greenway Court" (near the site of present-day Winchester, Virginia), occupying himself with his interests as a landed magnate. Despite unproved charges that he was a loyalist during the war he was not molested. The confiscation of his estate (after his death in 1781) was the result, not of his loyalism, but of the revolutionary opposition to feudal survivals.

As the war in America progressed the hatreds of patriots and loyalists for each other deepened, fed by patriot attacks on the civil rights and persons of the loyalists and by their counterattacks upon

---

[28] For western land projects see George H. Alden's *New Governments West of the Alleghanies before 1780* (Madison, Wis., 1897). Consult also F. J. Turner, "Western State Making in the Revolutionary Era," *American Historical Review*, I (Oct. 1895).

[29] J. F. Jameson's *The American Revolution Considered as a Social Movement* (Princeton, 1926) is the best general discussion of themes treated in this chapter.

the patriots.[30] By 1778 the intensity of civil strife had driven the patriots to wholesale confiscation of loyalist property. Moderate loyalists who strove to maintain a neutral stand were harassed on all occasions—by fines for evading militia duty, for harboring members of their families active in the British cause, and for every minor misdeed of which they were accused. New York and South Carolina held them financially responsible for robberies committed in their neighborhoods; they were forced to pay double or treble taxes; they were compelled to receive rents and to sell goods priced in depreciated currency and then to meet their obligations with specie. They lost all offices they had held; professional practice was denied to them; they were boycotted, robbed, and cheated. If they resisted such treatment they exposed themselves to the charge of treason and the confiscation of their property—a punishment ordinarily reserved for those loyalists who joined the king's forces or openly gave them assistance. By such measures moderate loyalists were stripped of their personal property and often driven to overt resistance.[31]

On November 27, 1777, the Congress recommended that the states seize and sell the property of all men who adhered to the king and invest the proceeds in Continental loan certificates. By October 1781 every state except South Carolina had followed this advice, and South Carolina fell into line early in 1782. New Hampshire confiscated the estates of twenty-nine persons; Pennsylvania prepared a "black list" naming 490 loyalists, most of whom had left the state after the withdrawal of the British army from Philadelphia; New York seized the lands of fifty-five loyalists, including those of James De Lancey, Roger Morris, John T. Kemp, and Beverly Robinson. The South Carolina act of 1782 confiscated the property of and banished all men who had openly supported the British or who had proved themselves "inveterate enemies of the state"; those who had accepted the king's protection or had supplied his forces with money were fined 12 per cent of their property. Among the large landed estates lost by the loyalists were those of John Wentworth in New Hampshire, Sir William Pepperrell in Maine, Sir John Johnson in New York, and Sir James Wright in Georgia. At the end of the war five thousand loyal-

---

[30] The best introductory sketch is C. H. Van Tyne, *The Loyalists in the American Revolution* (New York, 1902). See also M. C. Tyler, "The Party of Loyalists in the American Revolution," *American Historical Review*, I (Oct. 1895).

[31] Other works on the loyalists are: A. C. Flick, *Loyalism in New York during the American Revolution* (New York, 1901); J. H. Stark, *The Loyalists of Massachusetts* (Boston, 1907); W. H. Siebert, *The Loyalists of Pennsylvania* (Columbus, 1920); E. Peck, *The Loyalists of Connecticut* (New Haven, 1934); H. B. Hancock, *The Delaware Loyalists* (Wilmington, 1940); and R. O. DeMond, *The Loyalists of North Carolina* (Durham, 1940).

ists asked the British government to compensate them for their lost property, which they valued at £10,000,000. After paring such claims to the minimum Britain awarded them £3,292,000. These losses signify that a large amount of loyalist property passed into the hands of the patriots during the war.[32]

As soon as the war broke out, patriot landowners in the royal and proprietary colonies ceased to pay the quit-rents, which amounted in all to $100,000 a year. Then after appropriating the royal and proprietary lands the state governments abolished the quit-rents altogether; the democratic state now took the place of king and proprietors, substituting for the quit-rents a public tax for the benefit, not of absentee landlords, but of the taxpayers themselves.

In keeping with the attack on semi-feudal survivals was the removal of the two bulwarks of the native landed aristocracy—entails and primogeniture. Jefferson led the assault on both. In 1776 he drafted the Virginia law which permitted landholders to convey entailed property in fee simple—an act which removed entails from nearly three-fourths of the settled lands of the state.[33] South Carolina had already legislated against entails by 1775, Pennsylvania and Georgia acted in 1776 and 1777; North Carolina, Maryland, and New York in 1784 and 1786. Of the southern states only Georgia rejected primogeniture during the Revolution (1777), but Virginia, North Carolina, South Carolina, and Maryland, as well as New York and Massachusetts, fell in line during the years 1784–90. After 1800 the rule prevailed in all states but two that real estate and personal property should be shared equally by all children. North Carolina withheld land from daughters if there were surviving sons; New Jersey allowed only half portions to daughters. Inasmuch as both entails and primogeniture had confined the ownership of large estates in the tidewater area to a few families, they had preserved the rule of the southern aristocracy in the colonial governments. With the division of land equally among direct heirs the economic basis of a landed aristocracy was shattered, as estates had to be sold or divided in order to provide the inheritances of all the children. In the 1830's de Tocqueville explained the democratic trend in the United States partly by the practice of equal inheritance. Only large landed estates which could not be alienated, he believed, could provide the permanence of property necessary for a continuing aristocracy; fortunes dependent

[32] William S. Wallace, *The United Empire Loyalists* (*Chronicles of Canada* series, Toronto, 1914).

[33] See again H. J. Eckenrode, *The Revolution in Virginia*, chapters 6–12.

upon the vicissitudes of trade were too mutable to sustain aristocratic families generation after generation.

The disestablishment of the Anglican Church required the repeal of laws which levied taxes for the support of its ministers and which ordered that all inhabitants attend its services. Because the Anglican Church was a symbol of British authority and because a large percentage of Anglicans and the Anglican clergy were loyalists, the opponents of the establishment, strong in the back country, opened their attack at the outbreak of the Revolution. In their state constitutions of 1776 Maryland and North Carolina stripped the Church of its legal privileges, North Carolina declaring that "there shall be no establishment of any one religious church or denomination in preference to any other." After contests described by Jefferson as the severest "in which I have ever been engaged," the Virginia legislature in 1776 repealed most of the old ecclesiastical laws and exempted non-Anglicans from paying church taxes; in 1779 Anglicans also were relieved. The state constitutions of New York (1777), Georgia (1777), and South Carolina (1778) granted religious freedom and equal privileges to Christians of all sects. Inasmuch as many southern Anglicans like Washington were patriot leaders, the religious contest did not partake of the intensity of the strife between patriots and loyalists, and the outcome was a compromise rather than the destruction of the Anglican Church. The non-Anglican patriots gained religious equality

¶ *A Prayer for the King's Majesty.*

O Lord, our heavenly Father, ~~high and mighty, King of kings, Lord of lords, the only Ruler of princes,~~ who doft from thy throne behold all the dwellers upon earth; Moft heartily we befeech thee, with thy favour to behold ~~our moft gracious Sovereign Lord King George; and fo replenifh him~~ with the grace of thy Holy Spirit, that ~~he~~ may alway incline to thy will, and walk in thy way: Endue ~~him~~ plenteoufly with heavenly gifts; grant ~~him~~ in health and wealth long to live; ftrengthen ~~him~~ that ~~he~~ may vanquifh and overcome all ~~his~~ enemies; and finally after this life, ~~he~~ may attain everlafting joy and felicity, through Jefus Chrift our Lord. *Amen.*

¶ *A Prayer for the Royal Family.*

AN ANGLICAN PRAYER FOR THE KING, AS MODIFIED FOR USE IN THE UNITED STATES

while the Anglicans retained their Church, with its property intact.[34]

Not content with destroying semi-feudal and aristocratic survivals in the existing states the democratic leaders took precautions against their extension into the West. The most crucial action along this line was taken with reference to the settlement of Kentucky in 1775–76. In the early 1770's a group of North Carolina merchants and landowners launched a project to establish a great proprietary province beyond the mountains. Foremost among them was Richard Henderson, a conservative judge of Granville County, whose class affiliations are indicated by his marriage to the daughter of an English peer. As a foe of the North Carolina Regulators, Henderson was the victim of an attack which reduced his home, stables, and crops to ashes. His interest in the West moved him to employ as his personal scout the intrepid Daniel Boone, who in 1769–71 explored the wild lands of Virginia, Tennessee, and Kentucky with an eye to settlement prospects. Then with a group of wealthy North Carolinians, all enemies of the Regulators, Henderson formed the Transylvania Company, January 6, 1775. In March the company negotiated a treaty with the Cherokees, holders of the only surviving Indian title to the region, purchasing for £10,000 in goods and money some twenty million acres comprising parts of present-day Virginia and Tennessee and most of Kentucky (Treaty of Sycamore Shoals). Under Henderson's leadership a band of three hundred frontiersmen built a settlement, Boonesborough, where the promoters erected a proprietorship of the Maryland type, reserving quit-rents, retaining title to the land and subjecting an elected assembly to a proprietary veto, for they "clearly realized that if they resigned that power, the delegates . . . would have it in their power to annul the claims and rights of the proprietors" (A. Henderson).[35]

Having acted in defiance of British western land policy, the Transylvania Company evoked the wrath of Lord Dunmore in Virginia, while its members were denounced by Governor Martin of North Carolina as an infamous band of "land pirates." When the Revolutionary War was in progress, the Transylvanians turned to the Continental Congress for a confirmation of their claims, sending an agent

---

[34] Edward F. Humphrey's *Nationalism and Religion in America, 1774–1789* (Boston, 1924), a monograph for the advanced student, discusses church and state in Part III. See again H. J. Eckenrode, *Church and State in Virginia*, chapters 4–8.

[35] See two articles by A. Henderson: "The Creative Forces in Westward Expansion: Henderson and Boone," *American Historical Review*, XX (Oct. 1914) and "Richard Henderson and the Occupation of Kentucky," *Mississippi Valley Historical Review*, I (Dec. 1914).

in September 1775 to represent them before that body. But the appeal fell on deaf ears; Samuel Adams and Jefferson objected to the proprietary government and quit-rents, Jefferson advising the use of Virginia's charter rights to prevent the establishment of "any arbitrary or oppressive government" in the West. Unsuccessful before the Congress, the Transylvania Company next turned to Virginia, only to have the latter confiscate its lands and to organize Kentucky as a county of Virginia in October 1776. However, the company, in view of its purchase of the Cherokee title, received from Virginia in 1778 a grant of 200,000 acres located between the Green and the Ohio Rivers, south of the present site of Evansville, Indiana.[36]

Virginia's action, along with its success in undermining the claims of the Indiana Company and the Illinois-Wabash Company, sealed the doom of great proprietorships which combined the title to land and the powers of government in a few hands. Instead, the colonization of the West was to proceed through individual land grants to promoters and settlers, to be regulated by governments set up at first by the states with western land claims and later by the United States, and to culminate finally in new commonwealths of the democratic type.

The confiscation of the lands of king, proprietors, and loyalists put the state governments into the real estate business on a large scale. Maryland derived £450,000 from the sale of the lands it confiscated; New York obtained $3,085,000. The disposal of such lands did not establish economic equality among the people because those in the best position to buy were those who already possessed wealth. The state legislatures, however, asserted in theory the principle of equal distribution: in New York, where the sale of tracts in excess of five hundred acres was discouraged, two large estates were divided into 525 farms; North Carolina sold land at 50s. a hundred acres; all the southern states and New York gave land bounties to soldiers; and squatters were given preëmption rights. But despite such liberality, shrewd operators were able to amass huge speculative holdings. In New York, small holdings were acquired through dummy purchases, subsequently to be consolidated into large properties.[37] In New Jersey Governor Livingston charged that state commissioners who sold confiscated property used the proceeds to buy land for themselves and later settled their accounts with the state in depreciated currency

---

[36] For an antidote to A. Henderson's eulogistic treatment of Richard Henderson see William S. Lester, *The Transylvania Colony* (Spencer, Ind., 1935), a careful study.

[37] A scholarly, technical work by Thomas C. Cochran, *New York in the Confederation* (Philadelphia, 1932), treats finance and land.

which they procured for a trifle. Since Virginia was the grantor of land *par excellence* the fruits of redistribution are best observed in her experience.

Virginia's practice was to sell vacant lands as a means of paying state debts incurred during the war. Acts of 1779 authorized the sale of hundred-acre tracts at the rate of £40 each and provided that the holders of state certificates of indebtedness might exchange them for land. In 1776 the state promised bounties of a hundred acres to Virginians who enlisted in the Continental army; in 1779 the grants were enlarged and offered to those who served under George Rogers Clark and to commissioned and non-commissioned officers. Upon settlers who had, before 1778, occupied land without title, acts of 1777 and 1779 conferred preëmption rights to four hundred acres per family on condition that the settlers remain on the land one year and raise a crop of corn. In 1781 squatters were allowed to purchase hundred-acre tracts for 20*s*. each and were given two and a half years in which to pay.

Bending these laws to their purposes, promoters obtained great tracts in the West. They purchased at a discount the bounty warrants of soldiers unable or unwilling to migrate; they sent out servants to secure preëmption rights; and they converted state certificates of indebtedness (which represented the values of depreciated currency) into claims upon the land. Estates as large as 140,000 acres came into being. Likewise grants made before the war survived; in 1783 Washington's holdings beyond the mountains amounted to 58,000 acres. Richard Henderson and his partners received 200,000 acres in Kentucky from Virginia and 200,000 acres in Tennessee from North Carolina. By reason of large speculative acquisitions settlers found it difficult to obtain titles (the price of private lands in Kentucky was double the state sale price) and bitter antagonisms ensued, giving birth to reports in 1779 that pioneers were fleeing from speculators to lands held by Spain. Of the abuses of land speculation James Madison wrote, September 8, 1783: "Why did not the assembly stop the sale of land warrants? They bring no profit to the public treasury, are a source of constant speculation on the ignorant, and will finally arm numbers of citizens of other states and even foreigners with claims . . . against the faith of Virginia. Immense quantities have from time to time been vended in this place [Philadelphia] at immense profit. . . . The credulity here being exhausted I am told the land jobbers are going on with their commodity to Boston and other places." [38]

---

[38] C. H. Laub, "Revolutionary Virginia and the Crown Lands," *William and Mary Quarterly*, 2d Series, XI (Oct. 1931)—technical.

The revolution within the states did not resolve the underlying conflicts between the democratic forces and the upper class, despite their coöperation against the common foe. Several factors account for that coöperation during the war. First, both groups accepted the institution of private property, and since many small property owners hoped to become large owners, no general attack was made upon concentrated wealth *per se*. Again: the ideal of a government of limited powers which appealed to the democracy could also serve the aristocracy; constitutional guarantees of civil rights protected men of fortune as well as ordinary citizens, while the check and balance system safeguarded minorities against majority encroachments. Finally, an economy of small, privately owned farms forced the mass of the farmers (deficient as they were in capital) to depend upon merchants for credit and markets, thus enabling the merchants to accumulate substantial profits. For these reasons the democracy and the upper class could act together, each making gains that perpetuated its influence.[39]

In the sphere of government the democratic forces won some notable victories. The two requirements of political democracy were that the majority should rule within a state and that such a majority should not be curbed by an external government. Through the Articles of Confederation the democratic leaders triumphed by creating a weak central government that could not be used by the conservative elements to stifle the democratic forces when in control of a state. The new state constitutions gave the right to vote for members of the lower house of the legislature to practically all landholders and to small property owners in the towns. The upper house was somewhat democratized in that the senate, elected by property owners, replaced the old royal and proprietary councils, while in most states weak executives, chosen by state legislatures or by a popular electorate, superseded the royal and proprietary governors, who—in theory at least—had possessed extensive powers. In Georgia and Pennsylvania there was no senate to curb the house of representatives.[40] The states which most nearly attained the democratic ideal were New Jersey, Rhode Island, Pennsylvania, and Georgia.

In the economic and social sphere the gains of the democracy consisted principally in the destruction of feudal and aristocratic survivals: the quit-rents, primogeniture, entails, and the establishments of the

---

[39] An admirable study of the social aspects of the Revolution is Richard F. Upton's *Revolutionary New Hampshire* (Hanover, 1936).

[40] W. R. Smith, "Sectionalism in Pennsylvania during the Revolution," *Political Science Quarterly*, XXIV (June 1909).

Anglican Church. Nor were such vestiges of the past to extend into new settlements. And through military bounties and the sale of con-fiscated lands at low prices, landowning among the mass of the peo-ple was greatly increased.

Most of the gains of the democracy were made at the expense of British interests and the loyalists rather than at the expense of the conservatives who supported the Revolutionary cause. The latter held their own. First, the large landholdings of patriot leaders remained intact, thus preserving the plantation system and slavery and the tenant-occupied estates of the Van Rensselaer, Livingston, and Schuy-ler families in New York. Large landowners like James Duane, Charles Carroll, Thomas Johnson, Samuel Johnston, and Willie Jones of North Carolina retained their vast possessions. The conserva-tive influence manifested itself in the state governments in two ways: in New York, Massachusetts, and Maryland the democracy was checked by the senate and the governor or by other executive de-vices which protected the larger property owners; in South Carolina and Virginia the back country was not given full representation in the lower house. At the end of the war the conservatives, though op-posed by democratic forces, predominated in New Hampshire, Mas-sachusetts, Connecticut,[41] New York, Maryland, Virginia, and South Carolina.

On the economic front the merchant class benefited through con-tracts for supplying the army, through wartime privateering, and through the paper profits from currency inflation which were invested partly in government loans later paid in more substantial values. Similarly, the confiscation of royal, proprietary, and loyalist property allowed investors to convert depreciated currency or its equivalent in state securities into warrants for land—a process which favored men of the greatest wealth. By 1791 twenty-one men had acquired claims to 5,432,200 acres in western New York. New commercial fortunes arose upon the ruined businesses of loyalist merchants, while the southern planters freed themselves from the debts they owed to Brit-ish firms.

At two points, however, the conservative groups in 1783 were ex-posed to attack. In states where the democracy held control, the legis-latures might at any moment enact laws detrimental to merchants, creditors, employers, and large landowners. Secondly, the federal government lacked the power to protect. It could not curb the state legislatures when they overissued legal tender paper money or passed

---

[41] Richard J. Purcell, *Connecticut in Transition, 1775–1818* (Washington, 1918), is an able analysis of social, economic, and political changes in the state.

laws enabling debtors to evade their obligations. So also the state courts, not subordinate to a federal judiciary, did not offer security to creditors in states where leveling tendencies prevailed. The Congress lacked the power to collect money for the payment of interest and principal on the national debt—a power necessary in order to give value to the securities which wealthy investors had purchased. Likewise, the Congress could not protect American commerce with foreign countries; and as long as the states retained the right to enact tariff laws the Congress could not guarantee that free flow of commodities across state boundaries which was so essential to the merchant class. Finally, should armed revolts against the upper class occur within the states the general government could not assure protection to those attacked. These defects of the Articles of Confederation became evident to the conservative leaders during the years 1783–86. The result was the formation in 1787 of the Federal Constitution, which provided new safeguards against ultra-democratic tendencies within the states.

BIBLIOGRAPHICAL NOTE

Margaret B. Macmillan, *The War Governors in the American Revolution* (New York, 1943), provides a good introduction to state politics. E. P. Douglass, *Rebels and Democrats* (Chapel Hill, 1955), dwells upon conflicts between friends of majority rule and defenders of the plan of checks and balances. Outstanding studies of economic aspects of the war are: E. James Ferguson, *The Power of the Purse* (Chapel Hill, 1961); Clarence L. Ver Steeg, *Robert Morris* (Philadelphia, 1954); and Robert A. East, *Business Enterprise in the American Revolutionary Era* (New York, 1938). See also C. P. Nettels, *The Emergence of a National Economy* (New York, 1962). Scholarly works on states and state leaders are: Robert J. Taylor, *Western Massachusetts in the Revolution* (Providence, 1954); Lee N. Newcomer, *The Embattled Farmers* (New York, 1953); Herbert S. Allan, *John Hancock* (New York, 1948); J. Paul Selsam, *The Pennsylvania Constitution of 1776* (Philadelphia, 1936); Robert L. Brunhouse, *The Counter-Revolution in Pennsylvania, 1776–1790* (Harrisburg, 1942); Kenneth R. Rossman, *Thomas Mifflin and the Politics of the American Revolution* (Chapel Hill, 1952); John A. Munroe, *Federalist Delaware, 1775–1815* (New Brunswick, 1954); Janet B. Johnson, *Robert Alexander, Maryland Loyalist* (New York, 1942); Marie Kimball, *Jefferson: War and Peace* (New York, 1947); David J. Mays, *Edmund Pendleton* (2 vols., Cambridge, 1952); and George Dangerfield, *Chancellor Robert R. Livingston of New York* (New York, 1960). Robert J. Taylor (ed.), *Massachusetts, Colony to Commonwealth* (Chapel Hill, 1961), reproduces important documents relative to constitution-making, 1775–1780.

XXV

 War and Diplomacy

Six and a half years elapsed between the opening of the Revolutionary War and the surrender of Cornwallis at Yorktown, October 19, 1781. The conflict lasted so long because the British and American antagonists each possessed peculiar advantages which made impossible a speedy triumph by either side.[1]

Factors in the War

Let us consider first the influences which favored Britain, the foremost of which was her superior commercial and financial strength. By 1775 Britain had achieved supremacy in world commerce and a large favorable trade balance which represented a part of the profits of her merchants and manufacturers. In time of peace such surplus profits were commonly invested in overseas enterprises and in domestic industry. When war came it was the practice of the British capitalists to lend their surpluses to the government—a process which gave the government command of commodities, cash, and credit in foreign lands. Such public loans benefited the merchants in two ways: first, they received interest from the government; secondly, contracts for supplying the armed forces afforded new sources of profit. The leading merchants, said Edmund Burke in 1775, "are kept full fed with contracts and remittances and jobs of all descriptions and are indefatigable in their endeavors to keep the others quiet. . . . They all, or the greatest number of them, begin to sniff the cadaverous *haut goût* of lucrative war."

Britain's financial strength exhibited itself at first in the superiority of its army. In 1775 the British forces in the thirteen colonies numbered about nine thousand men. Some strategists in Britain proposed to subdue the colonies by naval blockades, but since an army was already on the ground and under attack the North ministry decided that it could not be withdrawn without loss of prestige, and hence Britain was committed to a war on land. General Gage's estimate that twenty thousand men were required to subdue New England

---

[1] See again C. H. Van Tyne, *The War of Independence,* chapters 3–14, 18–23.

necessitated an expansion of the British army, which in 1775 contained only thirty thousand men in far-flung garrisons throughout the empire. Because the iron discipline and the low pay of the army did not appeal to the English people (who disliked militarism to begin with) the enlistment of volunteers failed to provide a desired force of twenty thousand new men; and even the impressment of vagabonds and convicts did not suffice. Accordingly the government sought mercenaries abroad. After a plan to secure Russian troops fell through, Britain contracted in 1775 with the rulers of small German states (Hesse-Cassel, Brunswick, Waldeck, and Ansbach) for eighteen thousand men. By its contract with the Duke of Brunswick, Britain agreed to pay him £7 4s. 4½d. for each soldier he supplied, an equal sum for each of his subjects killed in the war, half this sum for each man wounded, and a yearly subsidy of £11,517 during the war, plus £23,034 a year for two years after the war. The total number of mercenaries obtained before 1781 was about twenty thousand.[2]

Other British forces consisted of American loyalists and the Indians. On several occasions British campaign plans anticipated that uprisings of loyalists would strengthen the king's army—a hope rarely realized. The loyalist forces reached their peak in December 1780 when about eight thousand were attached to the British army at New York. A few loyalist units such as Ferguson's American Riflemen, Lincoln's Queen's Rangers, Tarleton's Legion, and Butler's Tory Rangers did effective work. For two reasons the northern Indians sided with Britain. First, the British monopolized the northern fur trade upon which the Indians were utterly dependent; secondly, the Americans now threatened the Indians' hunting lands, whereas Britain was endeavoring to preserve them against the inroads of settlement.

The discipline, organization and equipment of the British army gave it the initial advantage. The German mercenaries were seasoned soldiers, accustomed to obey orders and not subject to panic when under fire. However, they were poorly paid, indifferent, and unwilling to "fight their hearts out" for a cause. Since the loyalists in most places were a minority their adherence to a British army of occupation raised a serious problem: when the army moved, they could not be left to the vengeance of their neighbors, yet their removal greatly hampered the progress of the troops. Again, since there were more non-combatants than fighters among the loyalists they often impaired the offensive strength of the army by compelling it to defend civilians. As to the Indians: although they were used to harry the frontiers,

[2] See again E. Channing, *History of the United States*, Vol. III, pp. 210-408.

their outrages served chiefly to embitter the Americans. Moreover, the Indians could be counted upon to take to the woods when the war went against the British.

While Britain could rely chiefly upon trained veterans enlisted for the duration of the war, the Americans had to depend upon an improvised army of uncertain composition. The ordinary farmer, who had to keep his farm going, could not remain for long away from home; this meant short-term enlistments, a large turnover in army personnel, and the frequent replacement of seasoned soldiers with raw recruits. Such changes weakened the army because the American volunteer was inexperienced in the art of fighting an organized force in open warfare. The first exposure to gunfire is certain to be a terrible experience to the novice; a series of engagements is usually necessary to harden the soldier against the ever-present danger of panic. Established armies cope with fright by means of the sternest discipline. But such an advantage was denied to the Americans because in 1775 they were intensely individualistic; not accustomed to obeying orders, they regarded their officers as equals whose commands need not be heeded if one's life were at stake.[3] Nor did the American army at the outset possess seasoned officers. Washington, who towered above the others, had earned his reputation in frontier Indian fighting and had not devoted himself to military affairs for a decade. When he took command at Cambridge in 1775 he found such a motley array of citizens that he suggested the uniform of the hunting shirt to give some semblance of order. Of Israel Putnam, the fifth ranking general in June 1775, Beard states that he "insisted on riding at the head of his men at Boston in his shirt sleeves with an old hat on his head as if he were still in the cornfield."

To sustain the war fever at a pitch conducive to recruiting proved to be a task of the first magnitude, especially when the people were not directly menaced by British invasion. Relying chiefly upon volunteers, the states were compelled to offer material inducements: of patriotism Washington said that "a great and lasting war can never be supported on this principle alone. It must be aided by a prospect of interest and some reward." Cash bounties to recruits were increased as the paper money in which they were paid depreciated; slaves who enlisted received their freedom; deserters from the British army were taken into the American ranks. In New England the towns were required to raise quotas of soldiers; when volunteers did not respond, the draft and the hiring of substitutes were resorted to. Two men in

[3] C. K. Bolton, *The Private Soldier under Washington* (New York, 1902), is a brief, careful, realistic study of army conditions.

Connecticut could escape service if they kept one soldier in the field—
a practice which brought many free Negroes into the army. In 1781
Virginia gave three hundred acres of land and a prime Negro slave
or £60 in specie to volunteers. But despite such practices heroic efforts
were needed to keep a Continental army of five thousand men intact. Numerous desertions enhanced the difficulty.[4]

Britain's attack on the import trade of the states curtailed their
normal supply of manufactured goods at a time when American industries were not geared to high-speed production. Throughout the
war there was an acute stortage of clothing, blankets, tents, shoes,
muskets, cannon, powder, and shot. The American stock of gunpowder in April 1775 consisted of the stores seized from government
garrisons; by December the supply was exhausted and for two months
Washington's army besieging Boston had practically no powder at
all.[5] There was no Red Cross, Y.M.C.A., or adequate hospital service
for the relief of the distressed; hence the prevalence of such conditions as those described by General Wayne: "No medicine or regimen
suitable for the sick, no beds of straw to lie on, no covering to keep
them warm other than their own wretched clothing." "Our hospital,
or rather our house of carnage, beggars all description and shocks all
humanity to visit." In 1776 Washington told of the difficulty of operating an army "without any money in our treasury, powder in our
magazines, arms in our stores . . . and by and by, when we shall
be called upon to take the field, shall not have a tent to lie in." General Schuyler testified in 1777 that "our army . . . is weak in numbers, dispirited, naked, in a manner, destitute of provisions, without
camp equipage, with little ammunition, and not a single piece of
cannon." Such conditions persisted until the end of the war.[6]

Britain's naval supremacy gave superior mobility to her army, enabling it before 1778 to move up and down the coast and to occupy
almost at will any American seaport. Philadelphia was easily taken,
though evacuated; at the end of the war the British occupied New
York, Charleston, Wilmington, and Savannah. Between 1776 and
1778 British vessels seized nine hundred American ships and practically ruined New England's fishery. But even the British navy

[4] Louis C. Hatch, *The Administration of the American Army* (New York, 1904),
emphasizes state jealousies as a cause of the ineffective, decentralized conduct of the war.
"The people were often indifferent, the officers captious and quarrelsome, and Congress
inefficient and negligent" (p. 196).

[5] O. W. Stephenson, "The Supply of Gunpowder in 1776," *American Historical
Review*, XXX (Jan. 1925).

[6] John C. Fitzpatrick, *The Spirit of the Revolution* (Boston, 1924), treats neglected
phases of war administration.

could not enforce an effective blockade of the entire coast; armed merchantmen slipped in and out of the ports, maintaining a hazardous trade with Europe and the West Indies which kept the American cause on its feet.[7]

Against the advantages of Britain the Americans possessed one supreme asset—a blended influence of geography, economic organization, and the character of the people. In 1775 there were about 250,000 men of military age in the American population of nearly three million souls. The mass of the people were tough-fibered and inured to hardship and privation. Overwhelmingly anti-British in sentiment, they were determined when fighting for the security of their homes, even if unwilling to enlist for remote campaigns. Adept in the use of firearms, they were masters of guerilla warfare, accustomed to the climate, and familiar with the country they were defending. Courage and hardihood counted for more in the long run than discipline and obedience. Of his men at Valley Forge Washington wrote: "Naked and starving as they are we cannot enough admire the patience and fidelity of the soldiery." Nor should the sacrifices and achievements of the American women be ignored. They plied their spinning wheels and knitting needles, nursed the stricken, tended the farms, worked in the fields, and carried on occupations while their menfolk were away at war. The economic organization of thousands of settlements extending more than a thousand miles along the coast and over three hundred miles into the interior was so decentralized that British control of a single seaport or a river did not give command of a large territory; most communities might eke out an existence in virtual isolation. To hold an area the British were obliged to occupy it with troops; their influence did not then extend beyond their lines, which were constantly exposed to attack; and when they moved they left behind, not a conquered territory, but a defiant people in arms.[8]

Had the British army been able to strike any community at a moment's notice, a permanent conquest might have been effected. But transportation conditions made that impossible; forest trails, roads that at times resembled mudholes, creeks and rivers without bridges, the lack of supply centers and a woeful shortage of wagons, horses, and oxen made troop movements cumbersome in the extreme. The heavier equipment of the British army delayed its advances and en-

[7] C. O. Paullin, *The Navy in the American Revolution* (Cleveland, 1906), a specialized study of naval policy and administration, concludes that the lack of seamen was the chief weakness of the American navy.

[8] Edward E. Curtis, *The Organization of the British Army in America* (New Haven, 1927), describes many of the difficulties encountered by the British.

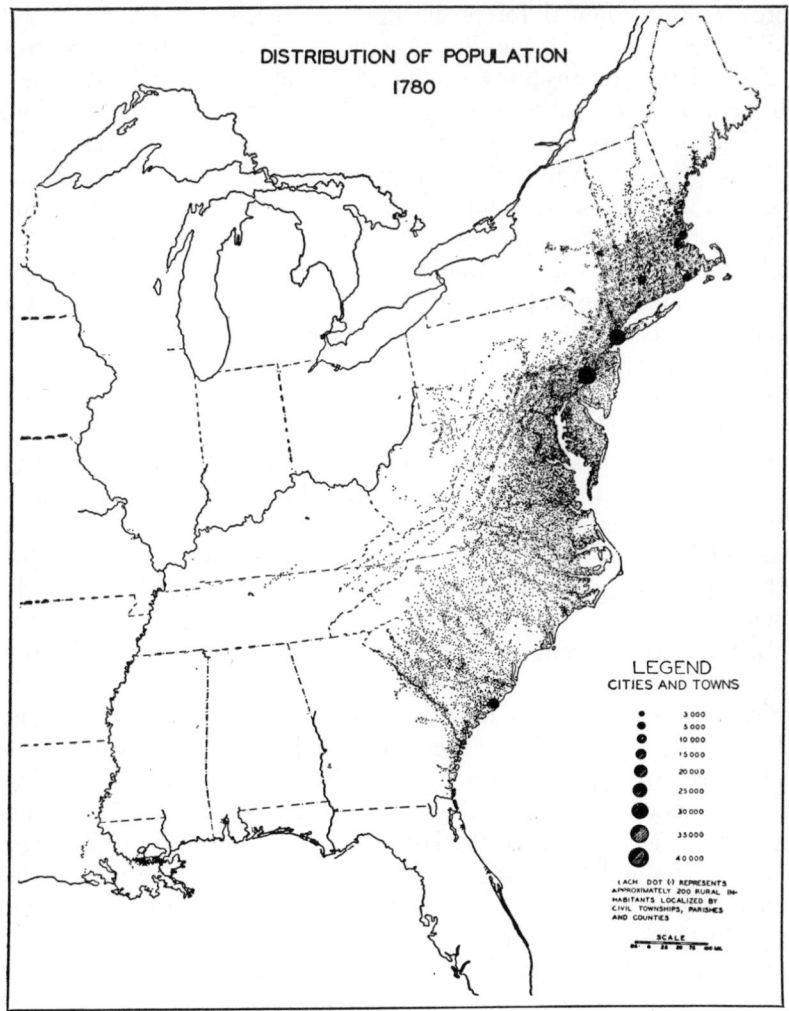

DISTRIBUTION OF POPULATION
1780

LEGEND
CITIES AND TOWNS

abled the American forces, lightly burdened, to elude their pursuers. All the greater were the difficulties of transport when horses, wagons, provisions, gunpowder, and artillery had to be sent from Britain. The uncertainties of transportation made it well-nigh impossible for the British to calculate the time element in campaigns. Since the British ministry directed the war from Westminster, weeks and months elapsed before orders reached officers in America; serious mistakes could not be rectified within a year. The handicaps which now confronted Britain demonstrated how important had been the aid of the once despised colonial forces during the French and Indian War.[9]

The remoteness of the British army from its center of control magnified the responsibility of the officers in command in America. Unfortunately for Britain her generals did not rise to the occasion. Sir William Howe, commander-in-chief from 1775 to February 1778 did not press the war with vigor. Some of his critics attributed his laxity to dissipation and love of luxury; others believed him too friendly to the Americans. Since he had opposed the Coercive Acts and had declared that he would not serve against the colonies, his appointment to the chief command is something of a mystery. As a believer in conciliation he may have reasoned that a savage, destructive war would so antagonize the Americans that they would never afterward feel that sense of loyalty necessary to bind to Britain settlements so dispersed and so remote. At any rate military experts agree that on several occasions Howe let slip the opportunity to deal the American army a crushing blow.[10] His successor, Sir Henry Clinton—who replaced Howe in February 1778—was a mediocre man, while Lord Cornwallis, in command of the southern campaigns, 1780–81, "distinguished" himself chiefly by his surrender at Yorktown.

Britain's naval strength enabled her only to impair—not to destroy —American commerce. The states commissioned a host of privateers which by February 1778 had captured six hundred British vessels. "The damage we have done their West India trade," wrote Franklin in February 1777, "has been estimated by the merchants of London at £1,800,000 sterling, which has raised insurance to 28 per cent, higher than at any time in the last war with France and Spain." The sale of prizes and their cargoes in American ports helped sustain the import trade: one prize sold in Georgia netted £21,138 sterling. Prior to 1780 the southern states, free from invasion, continued normal production, and American blockade runners and European vessels, as neutrals, carried tobacco to northern Europe and rice to the Mediterranean regions. Some of the British West Indian merchants, needing American provisions, connived in illegal trade with the states, while the foreign islands—Dutch St. Eustatius, Danish St. Thomas, and

[9] Francis V. Greene's *The Revolutionary War* . . . (New York, 1911), a concise, well-told story of the military events, emphasizes the elements of strength in the American cause.

[10] Troyer S. Anderson, *The Command of the Howe Brothers during the American Revolution* (New York, 1936), an elaborate critique for the advanced student, criticizes the theory of Howe's Whiggish sympathies for the colonists and explains his failure by the material obstacles encountered in America and by lack of support at home.

French Martinique—served as depots for goods en route to and from Europe.[11] Prior to the autumn of 1777 nearly 80 per cent of the American supply of gunpowder was imported—chiefly from France via the West Indies. The gains of American merchants engaged in privateering are suggested by Franklin's remark in 1779: "The extravagant luxury of our country in the midst of all its distress is to me amazing."

The profits of privateering diverted capital from manufacturing industry and thus retarded its progress during the war, despite the stimuli of the needs of the army, the removal of British restraints on American industry, and the dearth of European goods in the states. Shipbuilders, no longer able to sell to British merchants, went in for the construction of "sharp-prowed, speedy vessels" to serve as privateers. Under the impetus of state bounties, the production of gunpowder yielded about 10 per cent of the quantity used by the American army before the autumn of 1777: 115,000 pounds from domestic saltpetre and 698,245 from imported saltpetre. Powder made at Weymouth, Massachusetts, had the force to drive leaden balls two inches into an oak tree at a distance of eight rods. Philadelphia produced brass and iron cannon, and an arsenal at Springfield, Massachusetts, supplied the army in part with artillery and rifles. The shortage of salt (a necessity previously imported) led the New Englanders to evaporate salt water in shallow pans; the supply thus obtained however was small, as indicated by the price of salt—18¢ a bushel in 1774; $6.00 a bushel in 1781. In 1775 Philadelphia investors organized a company "for promoting American manufactures" which concentrated upon the production of linen, woolen, and cotton cloth; however, homespun continued to be the mainstay of domestic textile production. The shortage and dearness of labor, together with the enemy's menace to mills and factories, deterred cautious capitalists from investing in such enterprises. Thus the Congress had to establish the government munition works at Springfield in 1778. Since most of New England escaped the ravages of war and because its fishery was all but ruined, conditions for manufacturing industries were the most favorable there. Hence the establishment of gun factories or powder mills at Sutton, Andover, Stoughton, Bradford, Waterbury, and North Providence. Due to wartime destruction of old property and of articles currently produced, workshops and mills could not meet the demand for new capital and consumers' goods: in 1781 the states

[11] J. F. Jameson, "St. Eustatius in the American Revolution," *American Historical Review*, VIII (July 1903).

—with respect to their supply of manufactured products—resembled a dry sponge.[12]

The critical events of 1763–75 had brought to the front a group of leaders in each colony, made them known to each other, steeled them in opposition to Britain, and tested their abilities. For one such leader who, like Benedict Arnold, broke under the strain of war, there were a score who stood firm. A country that could produce a general like Washington, a diplomat like Franklin, political leaders like John Adams, Jefferson, and Samuel Adams, and a group of energetic war governors such as Hancock, Trumbull, William Livingston, Thomas Johnson, George Clinton, and Patrick Henry was certainly not deficient in resolute men. Above them all towered the statuesque figure of Washington, determined, patient, persevering, and practical, a man who made concrete knowledge the basis of thinking and who translated thought into action—a completely integrated, fearless personality. His greatest asset was his ability to rise above discouragement and to gain strength by conquering adversity. "Defeat," he said, "is only a reason for exertion. We shall do better next time." [13]

In an accounting of the factors which aided the American cause the assistance received from foreign sources must be given much weight. That will become evident as we review the events of the war.

THE FIRST PHASE OF THE WAR, 1775–77

When the British fell back from Concord to Boston on April 19, 1775, the farmer militiamen of New England immediately besieged the city. By June the British army numbered ten thousand men and Gage had been joined by Generals Howe, Clinton, and Burgoyne. Occupying a narrow peninsula, the British forces were in effect cooped up on an island, since the besieging Americans held the approaches to the mainland. Boston had little strategic value but both contestants sought an early victory for the sake of prestige. On the night of June 16–17 the Americans occupied the heights of Charlestown north of Boston proper, across the Charles River. Realizing that from such

[12] See again V. S. Clark, *History of Manufactures in the United States to 1860,* chapter 10.

[13] Rupert Hughes, *George Washington* (3 vols., New York, 1926–30), the most extensive and the most readable modern biography, traces Washington's career to 1781. Of many older biographies the best for the general reader is P. L. Ford, *The True George Washington* (Philadelphia, 1896—republished in 1924 as *George Washington*). This is a character study, not a military history. John C. Fitzpatrick's *George Washington Himself* (Indianapolis, 1933) supplements the orthodox biographies with much out-of-the-way information.

positions (Bunker Hill, Breed's Hill) the Americans could bombard the British forces in the town and harbor, the British generals immediately ordered an attack. After twice repulsing British charges the Americans had to retreat from Breed's hill when their ammunition gave out, but only after they had inflicted losses three times those sustained by themselves.[14] The continued siege of Boston, which lasted until March 1776, imposed severe hardship and suffering on the townspeople during the winter, since the American army was able to cut off most supplies from the outside. Meanwhile, the Americans had so strengthened their position that a British victory could have been won only at a cost far in excess of any possible advantage. Accordingly, on March 17, 1776, the British evacuated Boston and moved to Halifax, Nova Scotia, accompanied by nine hundred civilian loyalists.

British strategists continued to regard New England as the center of American resistance but, despairing of subduing that stubborn region by direct conquest, they turned to the plan of dominating New York, thereby severing New England from outside reinforcements and supplies. This project entailed the occupation of Manhattan Island, whence an expedition might ascend the Hudson to join a companion force from Canada. Having obtained reinforcements in Nova Scotia, Howe took possession of Staten Island in July 1776. Washington, in anticipation of Howe's plans, shifted his army from Boston and occupied Brooklyn Heights which commanded the town of New York, then confined to the southern tip of Manhattan Island. But Howe quickly crossed to Long Island, defeated an American army in front of Brooklyn Heights and compelled Washington to take refuge on Manhattan Island, north of Harlem.[15] In September Howe occupied the town of New York. In order to gain mastery of the Hudson valley he was soon compelled to attack three American strongholds: Fort Washington at the northern end of Manhattan Island, Fort Lee across the Hudson in New Jersey, and the territory about White Plains, a few miles east of the Hudson. A narrow British victory at White Plains, October 28, placed Howe in a position to menace either New England or the middle states. Accordingly, Washington divided his army, placing one force in New Jersey between the Hudson and the Hackensack Rivers (to guard Philadelphia) and leaving another force under Charles Lee in the vicinity of White

---

[14] Allen French's *The First Year of the American Revolution* (Boston, 1934) is a detailed history of the military events of 1775.

[15] Charles F. Adams, *Studies Military and Diplomatic* (New York, 1911), contains four essays which portray Washington as an inferior general saved by Howe's incompetence.

Plains. The British then seized Fort Lee and advanced upon Washington's army in New Jersey, compelling him to call upon Lee for aid. But Lee, ever jealous of Washington, delayed until too late and was finally captured by the British. Greatly outnumbered, Washington's army had to flee, passing through Newark to the Delaware River, which they crossed near Trenton just before Howe's army occupied that town on December 8. When Lee surrendered on December 13 the American cause seemed lost.[16]

By seizing all boats along the Delaware, Washington checked the pursuit of the British at that river. Desirous of a victory to restore the sagging morale of his troops Washington executed the desperate stroke of crossing the Delaware on Christmas night—a surprise movement which enabled his men to defeat the British at Trenton and to take as prisoners over a thousand Hessians (December 26). This victory revived the spirits of the American army and rekindled hope throughout the states. After defeating the British at Princeton, January 3, 1777, Washington went into winter quarters at Morristown, New Jersey, while Howe's retirement to Burlington left most of New Jersey free from British control.[17]

As in the French and Indian War, so also in the Revolution Canada played a decisive role. The Americans desired to acquire the province in order to gain a fourteenth state and to prevent British attacks from the north. Early in 1775 Massachusetts and Connecticut sent expeditions which united (under the command of Ethan Allen) and took Forts Ticonderoga and Crown Point (May 10, 12), valuable for their stores of war supplies and for their strategic location on the route to Canada. This success opened the path for a Continental force under Richard Montgomery which traversed Lake Champlain and entered Montreal, November 12, 1775. About the same time Benedict Arnold led an expedition through the Maine wilderness, via the Kennebec and Chaudière Rivers, arriving before Quebec on November 13 with less than half of his original force of eleven hundred men. Arnold's attack on Quebec having failed, he waited until Montgomery joined him for a combined assault, which the British repulsed on December 31. Arnold, taking command by virtue, of Montgomery's death, continued the siege until desertions, sickness (smallpox), and the arrival of a British fleet compelled him to evacuate Canada (June 1776). Sir Guy Carleton, governor-general of Quebec

---

[16] The military campaigns are given exhaustive treatment in Vol. III of the Hon. Sir John W. Fortescue's *A History of the British Army.*

[17] Louis M. Sears, *George Washington* (New York, c. 1932), is a factual, conventional treatment, heavily weighted on the military side.

"The Yankie Doodle's Intrenchments near Boston, 1776."
"Publish'd as the Act Directs"

and commander of Britain's northern army, pursued Arnold to Lake Champlain. By skillfully contesting Carleton's advance, Arnold held the British from Crown Point till October 14, thus keeping them from the Hudson and saving Washington's army from a northern attack when it was being hard pressed from the south by Howe.[18]

Britain's war strategy in 1777 called for an invasion of the Hudson valley. General John Burgoyne was to lead an army from Canada via Lake Champlain to Albany; a second force under Lieutenant-Colonel Barry St. Leger was to proceed to Albany by way of Lake Ontario and the Mohawk River; and an army from New York was to ascend the Hudson for a junction with Burgoyne. Such maneuvers would either divide the thirteen states at the Hudson (which the Americans still commanded above the northern boundary of New Jersey) or, by engaging American forces in the north, prevent their giving aid to Washington's army against Howe farther south. But there was one flaw in British plans. Burgoyne was not responsible to Howe at New York; instead he was under the orders of the British Colonial Secretary at Westminster, Lord George Germain, an incompetent man, poorly informed of American conditions. In the meantime Howe had decided to move his main army against Philadelphia, hoping that Washington would defend the city and thus expose himself to a pitched battle that would annihilate his army and end the war. Accordingly, Howe notified the army in Canada that he could not give it aid beyond his "endeavor to have a corps on the lower part of Hudson's River sufficient to open the communications by shipping through the Highlands . . . which corps may afterward act in favor of the northern army." Howe's Philadelphia plans received the approval of Germain, who expressed the hope that Howe might return from the Quaker city in time to coöperate on the Hudson. Burgoyne in turn interpreted his orders to mean that he must advance down the Hudson at all costs.[19]

On July 23, 1777, Howe embarked for Philadelphia with sixteen thousand men; on August 25 he arrived at the Head of Elk in Chesapeake Bay. The protracted voyage had enabled Washington to place his forces between the Chesapeake and Philadelphia at Chad's Ford, where the road from the Head of Elk met Brandywine Creek. In the ensuing battle of Brandywine (September 11), Washington was again able to extricate his inferior army intact, but not to turn back the

[18.]Justin H. Smith, *Our Struggle for the Fourteenth Colony* (New York, 1907), is a definitive treatment of the role of Canada. See also William Wood, *The Father of British Canada* (*Chronicles of Canada* series, Toronto, 1916).

[19] G. H. Guttridge, "Lord George Germain in Office," *American Historical Review*, XXXIII (Oct. 1927).

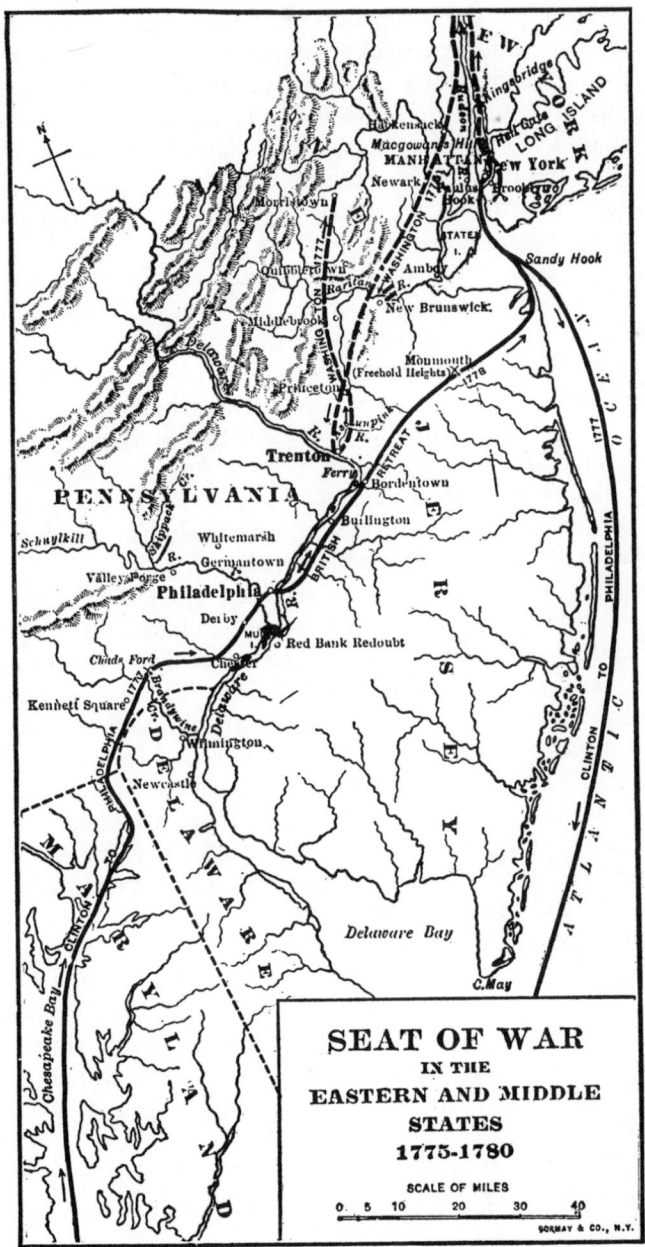

SEAT OF WAR
IN THE
EASTERN AND MIDDLE
STATES
1775-1780

SCALE OF MILES

0 5 10 20 30 40

GORMAY & CO., N.Y.

From "Atlas of American History." © *Harper & Brothers.*

British, who began the occupation of Philadelphia on September 25. Howe then needed three weeks in order to gain control of the Delaware River. Washington's attack at Germantown was repulsed on October 4, whereupon he retired for the winter to Valley Forge on the Schuylkill, a few miles above Philadelphia—a position which restricted the area from which Howe could obtain supplies.

Having set forth from Canada on June 20, 1777, Burgoyne had little trouble taking Ticonderoga (July 6), after which he advanced to Skenesborough, only twenty miles from the Hudson. But to traverse that distance, through a wilderness whose difficulties General Schuyler increased with every sort of impediment, required three weeks before the British gained Fort Edward on the Hudson (July 30). By this time transportation troubles and the inadequacy of army supplies had become so painfully evident that Burgoyne sent a force of Germans under Colonel Baum to seize American stores of provisions at Bennington (now Vermont). The resolute Indian-fighter, John Stark, rallied the frontiersmen, who dealt the British a decisive defeat that cost them eight hundred men.

Elsewhere the fortunes of war frowned upon Burgoyne. Colonel St. Leger, having collected a force of six hundred European troopers and a band of Indians and loyalists, advanced from Oswego to Fort Stanwix, to which he immediately laid siege. The German settlers of the Mohawk valley came to its relief and fought off the invaders in a savage engagement at Oriskany near the fort. Meanwhile, Benedict Arnold [20] had been sent up the Mohawk with a small force. When about twenty miles from the fort he dispatched a messenger with the false report that Burgoyne had surrendered. The Indians mutinied and plundered their British companions, whereupon St. Leger retreated posthaste to Oswego and returned to Canada.

When Howe departed for Philadelphia he left Sir Henry Clinton in command at New York. The cautious Clinton awaited for reinforcements before he moved up the Hudson; not until October 5 did he take the American forts, Clinton and Montgomery, which guarded the river between the Highlands, and by the time British ships had reached Esopus, sixty miles below Albany, Burgoyne's position had become hopeless.

After Burgoyne arrived at Fort Edward (July 30) he was compelled to wait for supplies until the middle of September before he

[20] The affair of Benedict Arnold is effectively narrated in Carl Van Doren, *Secret History of the American Revolution* (New York, 1941); J. T. Flexner, *The Traitor and the Spy* (New York, 1953); W. M. Wallace, *Traitorous Hero* (New York, 1954); C. C. Sellers, *Benedict Arnold* (New York, 1930); and M. Decker, *Benedict Arnold* (New York, 1961).

could proceed down the Hudson. Meanwhile the fight at Bennington had given the signal for the farmers of New England to join the American army in Burgoyne's path. They responded with such alacrity that the British force was soon outnumbered four to one. The Americans, commanded by General Horatio Gates, occupied Bemis Heights about twenty-five miles below Fort Edward—a site which enabled them to dominate the road along the west bank of the Hudson. Two attacks by Burgoyne having been repulsed (September 19, October 7), the British fell back to Saratoga, where—surrounded by the Americans—they surrendered, October 14. A convention of October 17 permitted Burgoyne's exhausted men (now numbering only 4,880) to go to Boston for embarkation to England on condition that they would not again participate in the American war.[21]

THE UNITED STATES SECURE FOREIGN AID

Saratoga ranks as one of the decisive events of the Revolution because it induced France to join the United States in an alliance which contributed greatly to the final victory. Although the peace of 1763 had effected a redistribution of colonial possessions it had not removed the old antagonisms which divided Britain, France, and Spain.[22] After 1762, European capital and labor previously devoted to war sought the channels of trade and oversea investments, thereby prolonging the contest for colonial supremacy. Inasmuch as the three powers adhered to the rule of excluding all foreigners from access to the markets, raw materials, and profit opportunities of their empires, the aggrandizement of one promised to weaken the others, and because imperialism was animated by economic expansion, each state felt it necessary to enlarge its possessions; hence a permanent pacification was impossible. Deprived of Canada and Louisiana, France now concentrated upon her sugar islands, Santo Domingo, Martinique, and Guadeloupe, bringing them to such a high peak of development that she threatened to engross the sugar trade. An estimate of 1766 indicated that France's West Indian commerce exceeded Britain's by 50 per cent and that of the Dutch by 300 per cent. The Duc de Choiseul, France's foreign minister until 1770, proposed to build a new French empire (*La France Equinoxile*) in the region of the Gulf of Mexico and the West Indies, intending, in part, to expel Britain from the trade of

---

[21] Jane Clark, "Responsibility for the Failure of the Burgoyne Campaign," *American Historical Review*, XXXV (April 1930).

[22] James B. Perkins, *France in the American Revolution* (Boston, 1911), thorough, readable, and scholarly, explains American success in terms of French aid.

Spanish America and to divert it to France. Spain, now holding three-fourths of the habitable parts of the Americas and the richest and largest of the West Indian islands, possessed an empire that surpassed her power of control. The British continued to carry on illegal trade with Spanish colonial ports, much to the dismay of the Spanish king, Charles III, the key of whose policy was the preservation of the territory of his empire plus the exclusion of foreigners from its trade and whose animating spirit was hatred of Britain. He denied to the British the right even to navigate the Pacific Ocean, to which the Earl of Chatham replied that "England would sooner consent to give up the Tower of London than to abandon that right." Bitterly resenting Britain's previous conquests of Gibraltar, Minorca, and Florida, the Spaniards, like the French, awaited an opportunity for revenge.[23]

A series of disputes pertaining to the Mediterranean, India, Africa, America, and the West Indies kept the antagonists at swords' points after 1763, Britain and Spain even venturing to the brink of war in 1770. Satisfied with the spoils of 1763, Britain desired peace; France's depleted finances restrained her ambitions; Spain was in a state of chronic unpreparedness. However, some coöperation between the two Bourbon states was maintained as Spain granted commercial privileges to France in Spanish America and France sent engineers to Spanish dockyards to bolster up the Spanish navy.[24]

In her search for new allies France turned her gaze toward Britain's disaffected colonists, to whom after 1762 she dispatched secret agents instructed to fan the flames of discontent, to express the friendly attitude of France, and to get information about the resources, topography, and defenses of the colonies. Realizing that Britain's strength arose from her commerce, to which North America contributed so handsomely, the French saw in a war of revenge the means of gaining that commerce for themselves, thereby weakening their rival and reëstablishing their sorely damaged prestige.

When the American crisis was reached in 1775, both in England and in the colonies the likelihood of French intervention was discussed. The Earl of Chatham likened France to a "vulture hovering over the British empire, and hungrily watching the prey that she is only waiting for the right moment to pounce upon." American sentiment was at first unprepared for a French alliance, due to the hatreds

---

[23] See again *The Cambridge History of the British Empire*, Vol. I, pp. 685–783.

[24] E. S. Corwin, *French Policy and the American Alliance of 1778* (Princeton, 1916), interprets French and Spanish objectives in terms of self-interest and hostility toward Britain.

engendered by the colonial wars, to the dominant Catholicism of France, and to her despotic government. However, the need of foreign military supplies and of the aid of a strong naval power soon overcame such repugnance, which had already been lessened by trade with the French West Indies and by commerce with France at the time of the non-importation agreements. In November 1775 the Congress appointed a secret committee to correspond "with the friends of America"; in the ensuing winter the committee received hopeful assurances of assistance from a French agent, one Bonvouloir; on March 2, 1776, the Congress sent Silas Deane to buy supplies in Paris.[25] One argument in favor of the Declaration of Independence was the necessity of cutting loose from Britain before America could expect substantial foreign aid. In September the Congress decided to appeal to France for a formal recognition of independence and for a treaty of commerce, whereupon Franklin and Jefferson were named to act with Deane in Paris. Jefferson did not serve, his place being taken by Arthur Lee, a young Virginian then in London. The bait offered to France was the commerce of the United States and American aid for a French conquest of the British sugar islands.[26]

Several influences active before 1778 impelled the French king, Louis XVI, to withhold open assistance. His finance minister, Turgot, warned that a war with Britain would bankrupt France; moreover, he discounted the benefits of American commerce, believing that it would continue to center in Britain, regardless of the outcome of the war. On two occasions news of an American defeat cooled the ardor of the French—in October 1776 and a year later when Howe occupied Philadelphia. And yet another thing deterred Louis XVI: France might set a bad example to subject peoples at home and abroad by encouraging the American rebels. Eager "to wound and yet afraid to strike," France proclaimed her neutrality and granted secret aid.

Other forces worked for an open alliance. The foreign minister of Louis XVI, the Comte de Vergennes, an inflexible enemy of Britain, labored incessantly to convince the court that the American war offered France an ideal opportunity to restore her own fortunes by striking down Britain. "She is an enemy," he wrote, "at once grasping, ambitious, unjust, and perfidious. The invariable and most cherished purpose in her politics has been, if not the destruction of France, at

[25] George L. Clark's brief study, *Silas Deane* (New York, 1913), deals principally with the French episode.
[26] C. H. Van Tyne, "French Aid before the Alliance of 1778," *American Historical Review*, XXXI (Oct. 1925).

least her overthrow, her humiliation and her ruin." France must aid the Americans, argued Vergennes, lest Britain make peace and conciliate them by seizing the French sugar islands and by opening them to American trade; or, if the colonies should win their independence, Britain would seek compensation by seizing the French islands. Of similar views was an influential courtier, merchant capitalist, and versatile man of letters and fashion, Caron de Beaumarchais, whose enthusiasm for the Americans and liberty was exceeded only by his detestation of Britain and his patriotic fervor. With every sort of argument he urged, even commanded, the king: *"We must aid the Americans."* [27]

When Deane arrived in Paris he had no official status, since France had not recognized the United States as an independent country; hence he had to approach the court in devious ways. The British, following his every move through a highly efficient secret service, asked that he be expelled from Paris—a request which Vergennes flatly refused.[28] The British found themselves in a dilemma: they did not care to press France to the point of war and they wanted to discourage the Americans by minimizing the possibility of French participation; hence they could not make of French assistance a public issue or a *casus belli*. To Beaumarchais the French government granted a million livres wherewith he operated a commercial house, Hortalez and Company, which supplied the Americans with the sinews of war. By October 1776 Deane had procured clothing for twenty thousand men, muskets for thirty thousand, and large quantities of gunpowder. "Nor was this all. Restrictions upon trade were relaxed in favor of American vessels; American privateers were harbored and fitted out, and their prizes sold in French ports; the construction of ships of war was carried on under the superintendence of French naval officers" (Headlam). With the connivance of the government, many French volunteers sailed for America—idle army officers, bankrupt adventurers, soldiers of fortune, and enthusiastic friends of liberty—seeking new careers, new opportunities to smite Britain, new excitements. Most prominent of such volunteers was the Marquis de Lafayette, a young army officer who longed to exalt France, to abase England, and to demonstrate his military talents. He joined Washington's army as a general, serving without pay and giving such a good account of himself that he won the respect of the great American whom he re-

[27] C. H. Van Tyne, "Influences which determined the French Government to make the Treaty with America, 1778," *American Historical Review*, XXI (Oct. 1915).

[28] S. F. Bemis, "British Secret Service and the French-American Alliance," *American Historical Review*, XXIX (April 1924).

garded with a measure of hero-worship.[29] The chief contribution of France before 1778 was the supplying of munitions, without which the American army would have been quite helpless.

On December 18, 1776, Benjamin Franklin arrived in Paris. Quickly realizing that he could not induce the French to join the United States in open alliance until American arms had demonstrated the likelihood of success, he undertook to make himself agreeable to the king, whose caution was now the chief obstacle to French participation. When Franklin perceived that the French people expected him to embody the homespun virtues of "natural" men dwelling in a rustic, Arcadian society, he affected the simplest garb, manners, and style of living and made his plainness conspicuous in a world of finery and luxury. As a democrat, once an artisan, he delighted the urban masses; as the author of Poor Richard's maxims of prudence, thrift, and industry he was adored by the Parisian middle class; as a philosopher and scientist of European reputation he appealed to nobles and intellectuals—followers of Voltaire or Rousseau—who were then riding the crest of the "enlightenment." By flattery, patience, and good will he became the idol of Paris and the symbol of an oppressed people struggling heroically against the ancient enemy of France.[30]

The victory at Saratoga gave Franklin and Deane a trump card. Britain immediately made overtures for peace. Vergennes now pressed with all his might for an alliance, arguing that if France did not enter the war, the Americans would come to terms with Britain and join her in a war for the conquest of the French West Indies. Better, then, to fight Britain with America as an ally than as an enemy. Besides, American success now seemed assured. On February 6, 1778, France and the United States signed two treaties—one of commerce and one of alliance. By the latter France recognized the independence of the United States and promised military coöperation until independence became an established fact. France consented to recognize American conquests of British territory on the continent of America in return for American recognition of French conquests of British islands near the Gulf of Mexico. Each party agreed not to make peace without the approval of the other.[31]

Hoping to add Spain's navy to the forces opposed to Britain, Ver-

[29] Louis R. Gottschalk in *Lafayette Comes to America* (Chicago, 1935) and *Lafayette Joins the American Army* (Chicago, 1937) demonstrates that Lafayette became a champion of political liberty after his contacts with America.

[30] Bernard Faÿ, *The Revolutionary Spirit in France and America* (New York, c. 1927), treats cultural relationships, 1770–83, in chapters 1–3.

[31] E. S. Corwin, "The French Objective in the American Revolution," *American Historical Review*, XXI (Oct. 1915).

gennes redoubled his efforts to unite France and Spain in an anti-British alliance. The Spaniards craved the recovery of Gibraltar, Minorca, and Florida, but they shrank from giving aid to the Americans. They detested the spirit of democracy and republicanism prevalent in the United States and feared that one successful revolt of colonial subjects might provoke rebellion in their own colonies. Besides, the Spaniards looked askance at a powerful American state which was likely to expand westward and encroach upon their territory in Louisiana and Mexico. Accordingly, they informed Vergennes that they must acquire the lands of the Mississippi valley east to the mountains and possess the exclusive right of navigating the Mississippi River. Vergennes desired to placate Spain; he too did not wish to see the United States become a New World colossus; consequently he was willing to concede to Spain the territory west of the mountains and the sole right of navigating the Mississippi. Before entering the war the Spanish king, Charles III, assumed in 1778 the role of mediator between France and Britain, requesting that each power inform Madrid of its conditions for a peace. Britain replied that she could not desist from war until France ceased to aid the Americans; France replied that she could not forsake her treaty engagements. Finally, Charles III became convinced that Britain was acting in bad faith by deliberately delaying peace negotiations while plundering Spanish vessels and colonial territory. In a fit of rage he denounced Britain and signed a treaty of alliance with France, April 12, 1779.[32] By going to war against Britain Spain hoped to recover Gibraltar, Minorca, and Florida. France agreed not to make peace until Spain had regained Gibraltar, and since French approval was now necessary to an Anglo-American peace, France seemingly bound the United States, without its consent, to the Spanish conquest of Gibraltar. This move on the part of Spain, along with her well-known antagonism toward the Americans, made the Spanish-French alliance highly unpopular in the United States.

When the fortunes of the Americans were at a low ebb in February 1781 the Congress instructed John Jay to negotiate a treaty of alliance with Spain, authorizing him to give up the American right of navigating the Mississippi below the thirty-first parallel. Later the Congress was willing even to relinquish the territory west of the mountains. But the war ended soon afterward and Jay did not even

[32] For details of negotiations see French E. Chadwick, *The Relations of the United States with Spain: Diplomacy* (New York, 1909)—a work that overemphasizes racial factors in diplomacy.

disclose his instructions. Spain acted to the end solely in defense of her own interests, not as a champion of the United States.[33]

France's entrance into the war intensified the difficulties of neutral nations engaged in peaceful trade. Vessels sailing to British ports were subject to capture by the French; those bound to France and the United States were liable to seizure by the British. But since Britain was the superior naval power she had the chief advantage. International law in 1779 recognized the right of a belligerent to stop neutral vessels, to search them, and to seize goods belonging to subjects of the enemy. However, a new principle then gaining popularity asserted that goods on neutral vessels should be regarded as neutral and thus not liable to seizure—a doctrine which appealed to states deficient in naval power. As mistress of the seas, Britain adhered to the old rule which permitted the seizure of enemy goods from neutral ships.

Among the European powers, Prussia and the Netherlands were disposed to join France in protests against Britain's war on neutral trade. Frederick the Great, King of Prussia, had become an ardent foe of the British, believing that they had betrayed him, their one-time ally, when dividing the spoils of the Seven Years' War. Like the Spaniards, King Frederick had no love for the Americans, but he was willing to give them indirect aid in order to humiliate Britain. He encouraged France to enter the war by promising that Prussia would not help Britain, and he used his great influence with Russia to induce Catherine the Great to organize a league of neutral states for the protection of neutral commerce. Formed in 1780, the League of Armed Neutrality eventually embraced Russia, Prussia, Denmark, Sweden, the Netherlands, and the German empire. It asserted the principle that neutral ships carried only neutral goods.

Of the members of the new League the Dutch, as the chief shippers of Europe, were the greatest menace to Britain.[34] They took over most of France's foreign commerce; they traded with the United States through their island, St. Eustatius; and they allowed American privateers to operate from Dutch ports. When the Dutch joined the League, December 10, 1780, and thus gained the backing of the other neutral powers, Britain sought a pretext for declaring war, thus depriving the Dutch of their status as neutral shippers. But Britain did not wish to antagonize the other League members, particularly Russia; hence she could not press the issue of neutral rights. How-

---

[33] See again Frank Monaghan's scholarly and entertaining *John Jay*, chapters 7–11.
[34] Friedrich Edler, *The Dutch Republic and the American Revolution* (Baltimore, 1911), is a standard work.

ever, she had obtained information that the Dutch had been negotiating a treaty with the United States since August 1778. When the Dutch government refused to punish the official who had signed the draft of the proposed treaty, Britain declared war on the Netherlands, December 20, 1780.

Of the financial assistance granted directly to the United States by the enemies of Britain, only that from France ($6,352,000 received on loan between 1777 and 1784) contributed materially to American success. Spain in 1781–82 advanced $174,000, while Dutch bankers did not venture loans ($1,304,000 in 1782–83) until the war had been won.

THE WAR CONCLUDED

The participation of France and Spain gave the United States the benefit of sorely needed naval power, since in 1779 the combined French and Spanish navies included more than a hundred and twenty ships. In July 1780 Washington wrote that "a decisive naval superiority is the basis upon which every hope of success must ultimately depend." The menace of the French and Spanish fleets deprived Britain of her former ability to move troops at will in America. Britain now had to dissipate her energies in order to guard her own shores against invasion (one such attempt being made by the French and Spaniards in July 1779) and to protect her colonial outposts in the Mediterranean, India, Africa, and Florida. Both France and Spain directed their main attack on the British West Indies, thereby forcing Britain to divert thither a large part of her fleet in order to protect her heavy investments in the islands. American privateers now became more efficient in their raids on British shipping and the British coast by virtue of their free access to French ports. The United States had no navy in the modern sense—only a few vessels; hence American naval engagements did not involve the maneuvering of fleets but rather isolated attacks of a few ships on British merchantmen and their naval convoys.[35] The most sensational combat was fought September 23, 1779, between the American ship *Bonhomme Richard*, commanded by John Paul Jones, and the British frigate *Serapis*, then guarding a Baltic merchant fleet off Scarborough Head. Jones's old, weather-beaten ship overcame the new, well-conditioned *Serapis*, and the Americans then sailed to a Dutch port with their prizes. The refusal· of the Dutch to surrender Jones to the British led the latter to renounce all Anglo-Dutch treaties—an important step toward the

[35] A. T. Mahan, *Major Operations of the Navies in the War of Independence* (Boston, 1913), discounts American naval achievements as minor operations.

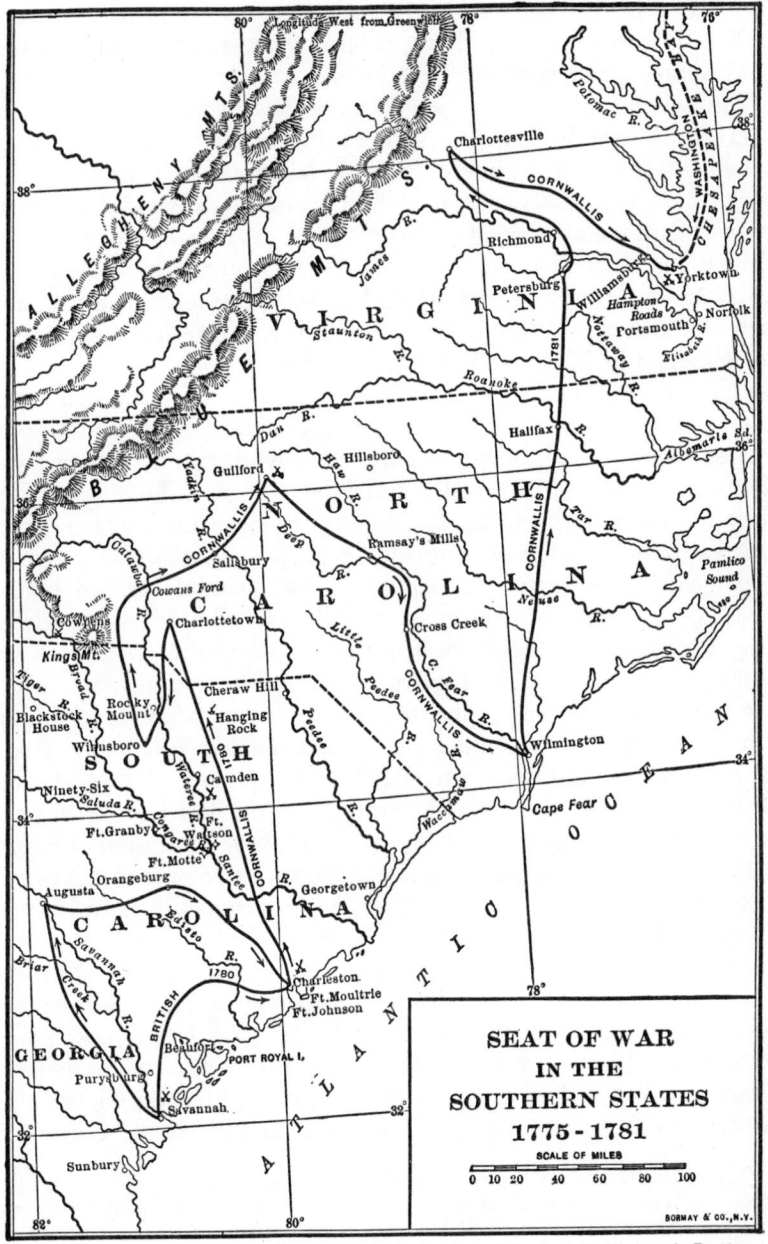

SEAT OF WAR
IN THE
SOUTHERN STATES
1775 - 1781

SCALE OF MILES

0 10 20   40   60   80   100

BORMAY & CO., N.Y.

From "Atlas of American History." © Harper & Brothers.

Anglo-Dutch War declared in the following year. The damage done to British war transport and supply service was the chief contribution of American privateers and frigates.[36]

The military events of 1778 in America revolved around the naval operations of the French. On April 5 a French fleet of twelve vessels, commanded by the Comte d'Estaing, sailed from Toulon and arrived, July 8, at Delaware Bay, shortly after the British had evacuated Philadelphia. Fearing a French naval attack on New York, the British had decided to station there the army that had occupied the Quaker city—a move which would also release troops for the protection of the British West Indies. Sir William Howe having departed for England in May, the British evacuation of Philadelphia was conducted by Clinton. A section of Washington's army, poorly commanded by General Charles Lee, met Clinton at Monmouth Court House, New Jersey, June 28, in an indecisive battle, after which the British escaped at night and reached New York. The French fleet followed the British thither, but finding the British too strong for an attack, proceeded to New England. A projected assault on Newport (occupied by the British in December 1776) was abandoned by the French, whereupon in November 1778 they sailed to the West Indies. The absence of the French fleet in the Caribbean then permitted the British to undertake the conquest of the southern states.[37]

Since the failure of a British attack on Charleston in 1776, the southern seaboard had escaped the ravages of the war. Hoping that a British army would be greeted by a great uprising of loyalists, the British in 1778 decided to occupy Georgia as the base for a northward advance. On December 29, 1778, the British took possession of Savannah, but combined French and American forces recovered the city in October 1779. Soon afterward, while the French navy was in Europe, Clinton moved seven thousand troops from New York to Charleston and forced the surrender of a small American army under General Lincoln (May 1780). The British thereupon overran Georgia and South Carolina. Compelled to go north to protect New York against Washington's army (again occupying the Hudson above Manhattan Island), Clinton left Cornwallis in command in the South. An American army under General Gates was sent to oppose Cornwallis

---

[36] *John Paul Jones*, by Phillips Russell (New York, 1927), a lively journalistic account, gives an accurate impression of a "man of action." Mrs. Reginald De Koven's *The Life and Letters of John Paul Jones* (2 vols., New York, 1913) is thorough and scholarly though burdened with details and biased in favor of Jones.

[37] Gardner W. Allen, *A Naval History of the American Revolution* (2 vols., Boston, 1913), treats intensively the engagements in American waters, relating the navy to other phases of the war.

as he advanced to invade North Carolina. The two forces met at Camden, August 16, 1780, where Gates's North Carolina and Virginia militiamen fled the scene and about a thousand of his regulars were killed or captured—a defeat that ended Gates's career as an American commander. However, a regiment of loyalists led by Patrick Ferguson, which had left Cornwallis's army to recruit in the upcountry, was defeated decisively by the Carolina farmers, who stormed the British position at King's Mountain, October 7, 1780, and took or killed about a thousand of the enemy—an engagement significant because it showed that Britain could not count upon the aid of the back country in the conquest of the Carolinas.

General Nathanael Greene, succeeding to the American southern command, reached Charlotte, North Carolina, early in December 1780. Anticipating a British invasion of that state he divided his army into two parts to straddle the British line of advance. The western force, under General Daniel Morgan, won a victory over Tarleton's Tory Legion at Cowpens in the southwestern part of North Carolina (January 17, 1781). Greene and Cornwallis met at Guilford Court House, May 15, 1781, and fought an indecisive battle which obliged Greene to retreat and caused Cornwallis to retire to Wilmington, North Carolina. Greene then moved into South Carolina, where—aided by the upcountry farmers under Sumter, Pickens and Marion—he forced the British to withdraw to Charleston (1781).[38]

The campaign of 1780 suggested to the British that they must occupy Virginia in order to hold the lower South, since Virginia had poured militiamen into North Carolina. Accordingly, in April 1781 Cornwallis marched north from Wilmington to Virginia where he joined other British forces sent from New York by Clinton late in 1780 to ravage the tidewater area. Lafayette, now in command of a small American army in Virginia, succeeded in eluding Cornwallis, while always keeping within striking range. Cornwallis's peregrinations in Virginia finally brought him to the York River, where he took up a position at Yorktown in August 1781.[39]

Two things were necessary for an American victory over Cornwallis—naval control of the Chesapeake and a land attack by a strong army. In December 1780 the Comte de Grasse sailed "with a great armament" from Brest to Martinique, where he joined another French squadron. He then took his whole fleet to the Chesapeake in

[38] For the general student: Francis V. Greene, *General Greene* (New York, 1893); for the special student, George W. Greene, *The Life of Nathanael Greene* (3 vols., New York, 1871).

[39] G. M. Wrong, *Washington and His Comrades in Arms* (*Chronicles of America*, New Haven, 1921).

the summer of 1781, concealing his plans so well that the British admiral in the Caribbean, Sir George Rodney, dispatched only a small fleet in a blind pursuit. Thus De Grasse gained the Chesapeake without opposition.

In the winter of 1779–80, Lafayette had returned to France, there to persuade Louis XVI to send a large army to America. Five thousand strong, a French force under the Comte de Rochambeau arrived, July 10, 1780, at Newport, recently evacuated by the British in order to prosecute the southern campaign. Rochambeau remained idle a year at Newport, but his presence there greatly strengthened Washington's position on the lower Hudson. Sir Henry Clinton at New York was convinced in the summer of 1781 that the American and French armies and navy were preparing an attack on that city; consequently he not only failed to reinforce Cornwallis but even asked the latter to send troops to New York. Instead of attacking Clinton, Washington and Rochambeau slipped away, united at the Head of Elk, ferried down the Chesapeake, and joined Lafayette in a siege of Yorktown. Most of these maneuvers were accomplished while Clinton was preparing for an attack on New York. Meanwhile, a British fleet had met De Grasse's ships at the Chesapeake, September 5 in what proved to be a decisive engagement because the British retired to New York, leaving De Grasse in command of the bay and thus cutting off Cornwallis's communications by sea. When the British at New York learned of Cornwallis's plight they made frantic efforts to get an expedition ready for his relief, outnumbered as he now was by three to one. But the expedition from New York could not reach the Chesapeake until Cornwallis had given up his army of seven thousand men on October 19. As R. G. Adams puts it, Britain for once "failed to muddle through." [40]

Long before the victory at Yorktown, the American frontiersmen beyond the mountains had defeated the British in the contest for control of the Northwest. The Ohio valley was a prize of the first magnitude—an empire in itself, as well as a line of defense of the middle and southern states against inland attacks by the British and their Indian allies. The British, operating from Detroit, incited the Ohio valley tribes to drive out the American settlers in order to preserve the West for the hunt and the British fur trade. A few settlements in the Illinois country—Cahokia, Kaskaskia, and Vincennes—contained small bands of French woodsmen—a people peaceably inclined, yet antagonistic toward Britain and ready to aid the Americans after the

[40] R. G. Adams, "A View of the Surrender of Cornwallis at Yorktown," *American Historical Review*, XXXVII (Oct. 1931).

American-French alliance of 1778. Across the Ohio, the Kentucky country had become, after 1770, a magnet that was drawing pioneers westward from Virginia and North Carolina.

When the Revolution broke out, the pro-British Indians immediately attacked the Kentucky settlements and by the end of 1776 had driven the pioneers to seek protection at three fortified points: Boonesborough, Harrodsburg, and Logan's Fort. Such was the setting for the exploits of a stalwart young Virginian—George Rogers Clark—a pioneer farmer, surveyor, Indian-fighter, and representative of Virginia land promoters who were struggling with Richard Henderson and his North Carolina partners for the mastery of Kentucky. After urging Patrick Henry, governor of Virginia, to provide for the defense of the frontier, Clark was commissioned a major and authorized to organize the Kentucky militia and to undertake the conquest of the Illinois country. Gathering a band of 175 men he occupied Kaskaskia, July 4, 1778, and later secured possession of Cahokia and Vincennes. His plan to seize Detroit was frustrated when Lieutenant-Governor Henry Hamilton (the British "hair-buying general") raised a war party of Michigan and Wisconsin Indians and captured Vincennes in the autumn of 1778. When Clark learned of this counterstroke he took his small force on a harrowing two hundred and thirty mile march in the dead of winter—one of the epics of American heroism— and reconquered Vincennes, February 25, 1779. Thereafter he led the frontiersmen successfully in border warfare, protecting the Kentucky settlements, keeping the British at bay at Detroit, retaining the Illinois country posts, and guarding the southern states against a British attack from the interior. Due largely to his exertions the Americans, in effect, occupied the Northwest at the end of the war.[41]

British Politics and the Peace

The Revolution differed in one significant respect from the other imperial conflicts in which Britain had participated. In the earlier struggles against Spain, Holland, and France, England had been able to secure allies to aid in defeating a commercial and colonial rival. But in 1775–83 the United States (led by men of English descent) used the old English tactics of forming a coalition against the enemy. The earlier triumphs of Britain now recoiled upon her as her former antagonists, Spain, Holland, and France, joined forces against her,

---

[41] The most authoritative biography is James A. James, *The Life of George Rogers Clark* (Chicago, 1928). Others are Temple Bodley, *George Rogers Clark* (Boston, 1926), and Frederick Palmer, *Clark of the Ohio* (New York, 1929).

while Prussia, her strongest ally in 1756–61, was also hostile. Britain, the architect of coalitions *par excellence*, was for once bereft of allies.

The political situation within Britain also affected the course of the war. The country remained divided into two general classes: those who ruled through the court and Parliament—the nobles, the squires, the merchants, the prelates of the Anglican Church, and the lawyers —and those who were governed without their consent—the wage-earners, tenants, servants, and small tradesmen. But the ruling classes, acting through the dominant political parties, Whig and Tory, were not united in their attitude toward America. After 1775 the Tory party, led by George III and his personal Prime Minister, Lord North, controlled the government until 1782, representing the most powerful section of the upper class composed of the landed interest, the Anglican Church, and the most conservative merchants.[42] In British politics the Tories insisted upon the right of the rich to rule the poor with a free hand; they regarded the British constitution as the world's best; in foreign affairs they considered Britain invincible. They viewed the mass of the colonists as belonging in the same category with the dependent, unprivileged classes in England. "Sir," said the foremost Tory man of letters, Dr. Samuel Johnson, "they [the colonists] are a race of convicts, and ought to be content with anything we may allow them short of hanging." Should the colonists succeed in their nefarious revolt, their triumph might stir the English masses to demand greater political power and more of the good things of life. Moreover, the Tories, adhering firmly to mercantilism, intended to keep the colonists in the strait jacket of the old colonial system in order to extract maximum profits for the British ruling class. Hence the Tories asserted the supremacy of king and Parliament over America—that is, the right of British merchants and investors to regulate colonial trade, manufactures, currency, and settlement in their own interests. Until 1780 the Tories commanded 260 of the 350 seats in Parliament.[43]

Although George III labored to restore the influence of the monarchy, the methods and policies which he pursued satisfied the more conservative members of the middle class who had once opposed the power of the king. George III acted through Parliament; he did not attempt to dissolve it or to dispense with its statutes; instead he endeavored to control it by giving bribes, offices, titles, and privileges to its members. He defended the Anglican Church, upheld the prin-

[42] There is no outstanding biography of Lord North. Reginald Lucas's *Lord North* (2 vols., London, 1913) may be used by the special student.
[43] See again G. O. Trevelyan, *The American Revolution.*

ciples of mercantilism, and treated the empire as sacred and inde-structible. Hence he did not encounter the fierce opposition which had greeted the anti-parliamentary, pro-French, pro-Catholic, and anti-mercantile policies of James II; in addition, George III's ideal of popular submission to king and Parliament satisfied the desire of the ruling class to keep the colonists and the English masses in their place. Lord North personally disliked the American war and favored con-ciliatory measures, but to please the king he stayed on as Prime Minis-ter, against his better judgment. George III even threatened to ab-dicate in 1778 unless Lord North saved him from the humiliation of a Whig ministry headed by the man he disliked above all others, the Earl of Chatham.[44]

The Whig party, which held only about a fourth of the seats in Parliament, was divided into factions. The smaller of these, led by the Marquess of Rockingham, proposed to give the colonies their in-dependence. This sound, enlightened position was fortified by two considerations. First, the American war would inevitably draw in France and Spain; Britain then would be unable to subdue the colo-nists. Secondly, the old colonial system had outlived its usefulness. In 1776 Adam Smith published his attack on mercantilism in *The Wealth of Nations,* arguing that a country would benefit most if it al-lowed capital and labor to flow, under the spur of competition, into the most profitable enterprises. Were the Acts of Trade and Naviga-tion repealed Britain would continue to enjoy the trade of America which was economically most advantageous; only unproductive and inefficient industries and trades needed the protection of law. Why, then, said the Rockingham Whigs, should Britain waste her resources upon a war for the maintenance of an unprofitable colonial system—a war, moreover, that she could never win?

The main body of the Whigs, followers of Chatham and Shel-burne, holding to the theory of parliamentary supremacy, resented the personal government of George III. They adhered to mer-cantilism, refused to recognize the independence of the colonies, and proposed to govern America by conciliation, compromise, and conces-sions. They would repeal the acts that had precipitated the revolt and restore the relations existing between the colonies and Britain before 1760. However, the majority of the British ruling class failed to grant concessions until the Americans had taken a firm stand in favor of independence. Since the Chatham Whigs emphatically refused to concede independence, they were forced to endure a war which rapidly

---

[44] Mary A. Marks, *England and America, 1763 to 1783* (2 vols., New York, 1907), is a detailed, readable narrative, useful on military operations and British politics.

intensified the antagonisms they hoped to allay, and which eventually placed France in arms against Britain. And because opposition to the French had long been a chief stock in trade of the Chathamites, the participation of France made them even more bellicose than George III.[45]

Little can be said of the attitude of the common people of Britain toward the war, inasmuch as they were not represented in Parliament or heeded by the press. The best index of their sentiments— their refusal to enlist in the army—indicates that they were either indifferent or hostile to the purposes of the ruling class.

As early as November 20, 1775, Parliament authorized negotiations looking toward peace—a commission entrusted to Sir William Howe. Meeting Franklin, John Adams, and Edward Rutledge— special representatives of the Congress—in September 1776 at Staten Island, Howe proposed the redress of American grievances, pardons for the insurgents and the renunciation of the Declaration of Independence, whereupon the American delegation broke up the rather amiable conference by taking a firm stand in favor of separation. In May 1777 Chatham moved in Parliament to end the war on the basis of British concessions but his resolution was defeated, November 20. Then, in order to circumvent the French alliance, Parliament early in 1778 passed two conciliation bills introduced by Lord North. One renounced the right of taxing the colonies except in the regulation of trade; the other authorized the appointment of peace commissioners empowered to arrange an armistice. The tea duty of 1767 was at last repealed. Three British commissioners arrived at Philadelphia in June 1778, just as the British army was evacuating the city. Their proposals to the Congress assumed the restoration of the colonial status, to which that body replied that it could not "consider propositions so derogatory to the honor of an independent nation." Again the negotiations broke down because Britain would not recognize independence and the Americans would not remain colonists.[46]

The disaster at Yorktown placed Britain in a critical position. The war had dragged on six and a half years and yet the prospect of success seemed as remote as ever. With France, Spain, and Holland now arrayed against her, Britain was forced to protect her empire in Africa, India, Ireland, the Mediterranean, and the West Indies—a crushing

---

[45] The best account of all diplomatic aspects is Samuel F. Bemis, *The Diplomacy of the American Revolution* (New York, 1935).

[46] For a condensed version of S. F. Bemis's work see his important *A Diplomatic History of the United States* (New York, 1936), chapters 2–5.

From Muzzey's "The United States of America." © Ginn and Company.

THE UNITED STATES BY THE TREATY OF 1783

burden to assume after the long, expensive war in America. The cost of the war (£12,000,000 a year) had been met largely by government borrowings, with the result that British credit in 1782 showed signs of exhaustion. Due to the interruption of peacetime industry and trade, British investors had placed their surplus funds with the government—a form of investment now ceasing to be attractive as government securities fell in value. Moreover, there was danger that previous investments in war loans might be lost if the national debt grew beyond the government's capacity to pay it from future taxes. As the war continued to take a heavy toll of British trade, the investing or ruling classes realized that peace was necessary, both to safeguard investments in government securities by terminating war expenditures, thus protecting the government's credit, and to restore normal commerce as an outlet for new investments. Accordingly, the House of Commons, February 27, 1782, voted to end the war. On March 20 Lord North resigned, whereupon Lord Rockingham took over the premiership and the task of concluding peace on the basis of American independence. Rockingham died soon afterward and Shelburne became Prime Minister, July 1.[47]

Peace negotiations began in earnest in April 1782 and continued until November 30, when Franklin, Jay, Henry Laurens, and John Adams—named as special negotiators by the Congress—signed a preliminary treaty with the British representative, Richard Oswald. During the negotiations the United States had demanded the territory north to the Great Lakes, west to the Mississippi, and south to Florida, together with the right to navigate the Mississippi. The Americans also wished to continue their fishery adjacent to British territory north of Maine, and they refused to promise to compensate the loyalists for their property confiscated during the war. Spain—conducting independent negotiations with Britain—sought Florida and the land south of the Ohio River and west from the mountains to the Mississippi, hoping thus to gain complete control of the great river and of the Gulf of Mexico. France insisted upon the recognition of the independence of the United States, but otherwise seemed to support Spain's claims to the transmontane West and the navigation of the Mississippi. The British declined to make reparation for American property losses occasioned by the war, insisted that American debts due to British creditors before 1775 be paid, asked com-

---

[47] Andrew C. McLaughlin, *The Confederation and the Constitution* (New York, 1905), one of the outstanding volumes of the *American Nation* series, devotes chapters 1 and 2 to the peace.

pensation for the loyalists, and refused to give up Canada. Otherwise, the British were inclined to favor the United States at the expense of France and Spain.[48]

While the negotiations were in progress, Jay became convinced that France and Spain were acting in concert to deprive the United States of the territory west of the mountains. He persuaded Franklin to make a separate treaty with Britain—a course which violated the instructions of the Congress that negotiations were to proceed with "the knowledge and concurrence" of France, but which did not violate the American-French Treaty of Alliance, since the preliminary treaty was to be approved by France before it became effective. Spain and France concluded their tentative agreement with Britain in January 1783, and on September 3 the preliminary treaties were signed as final and definitive.

Spain recovered Minorca and Florida (but not Gibraltar), while France received only a few minor concessions. The American treaty acknowledged the independence, freedom, and sovereignty of the thirteen United States. Article Four provided that it "is agreed that creditors on either side shall meet with no lawful impediments to the recovery of the full value in sterling money of all *bona fide* debts heretofore contracted." The Congress was to recommend to the states that they restore the confiscated property of the loyalists, while the people of the United States received the privilege of fishing off Newfoundland and of drying their fish in unsettled parts of Nova Scotia and Labrador. To the United States went the much coveted territory west to the Mississippi. At the northeast the American boundary was to follow the St. Croix River to its source and then proceed due north to the highlands dividing the rivers flowing into the Atlantic from those flowing into the St. Lawrence. Along the highlands the line was to run to the northwesternmost head of the Connecticut River; then down that river to the forty-fifth parallel and along that parallel to the St. Lawrence River; thence through the middle of the St. Lawrence and the Great Lakes to western Lake Superior and through the northwestern point of the Lake of the Woods to the Mississippi. The boundary then followed the Mississippi southward to the thirty-first parallel, along which it proceeded eastward to the Chattahoochee River and down that river to its junction with the Flint River; then straight to the head of the St. Mary's River, and along the St. Mary's to the Atlantic Ocean.

[48] E. Wead, "British Public Opinion of the Peace with America in 1782," *American Historical Review*, XXXIV (April 1929).

And thus in 1783 the United States joined the society of nations. Born of revolution, combining in its complex make-up the conflicting principles of aristocracy and democracy, scorned by the polite of Europe and confronted by a hostile world, this lusty youth now embraced its destiny of building a continental republic through the conquest of nature, for the satisfactions of the many and the aggrandizement of the few.

BIBLIOGRAPHICAL NOTE

The best military history of the Revolution is Christopher Ward, *The War of the Revolution* (2 vols., New York, 1952); the best shorter account is Willard M. Wallace, *Appeal to Arms* (New York, 1951). Good brief surveys of military operations appear in John R. Alden, *The American Revolution* (New York, 1954), and John R. Alden, *The South in the Revolution* (Baton Rouge, 1957). More comprehensive is John C. Miller, *Triumph of Freedom* (Boston, 1948). Leonard Lundin, *Cockpit of the Revolution* (Princeton, 1940), is an admirable study, with emphasis on military affairs. Christopher Ward, *The Delaware Continentals* (Wilmington, 1941), skillfully reports much of the military history of the war.

Good accounts of specific episodes are Arthur H. Bill, *Valley Forge* (New York, 1952); Carl Van Doren, *Mutiny in January* (New York, 1943); and John D. Barnhart, *Henry Hamilton and George Rogers Clark in the American Revolution* (Crawfordsville, Ind., 1951).

Douglas S. Freeman, John A. Carroll, and Mary W. Ashworth, *George Washington* (7 vols., New York, 1948–57), is a monumental work. Volume V ends with an admirable portrait of Washington. Thomas G. Frothingham, *Washington: Commander in Chief* (Boston, 1930), is an attractive summary. Bernhard Knollenberg, *Washington and the Revolution* (New York, 1940), doubts the existence of the Conway Cabal. Other notable studies of military figures are: S. W. Patterson, *Horatio Gates* (New York, 1941); Theodore Thayer, *Nathanael Greene* (New York, 1960); Broadus Mitchell, *Alexander Hamilton, Youth to Maturity* (New York, 1957); North Callahan, *Henry Knox* (New York, 1958); John R. Alden, *General Charles Lee* (Baton Rouge, 1951); Don Higginbotham, *Daniel Morgan* (Chapel Hill, 1961); and C. P. Whittemore, . . . *John Sullivan* (New York, 1961).

Weldon A. Brown, *Empire or Independence* (University, La., 1941), explains the failure to attain a negotiated peace. Gerald Stourzh, *Benjamin Franklin and American Foreign Policy* (Chicago, 1954), gives a realistic account of Franklin's ideas. Helen Augur, *The Secret War of Independence* (New York, 1956), and Amandus Johnson, *Swedish Contributions to American Freedom* (Philadelphia, 1953), deal with international aspects of the Revolution.

Naval warfare is reviewed in William B. Clark, *George Washington's Navy* (Baton Rouge, 1960); William J. Morgan, *Captains to the Northward* (Barre, 1959); S. E. Morison, *John Paul Jones* (Boston, 1959); Lincoln Lorenz, *John Paul Jones* (Annapolis, 1943); and Charles L. Lewis, *Admiral De Grasse and the American Revolution* (Annapolis, 1945).

Index

Julios
FS
1967.

E 188   E 195
A572   P4

E 123
R42

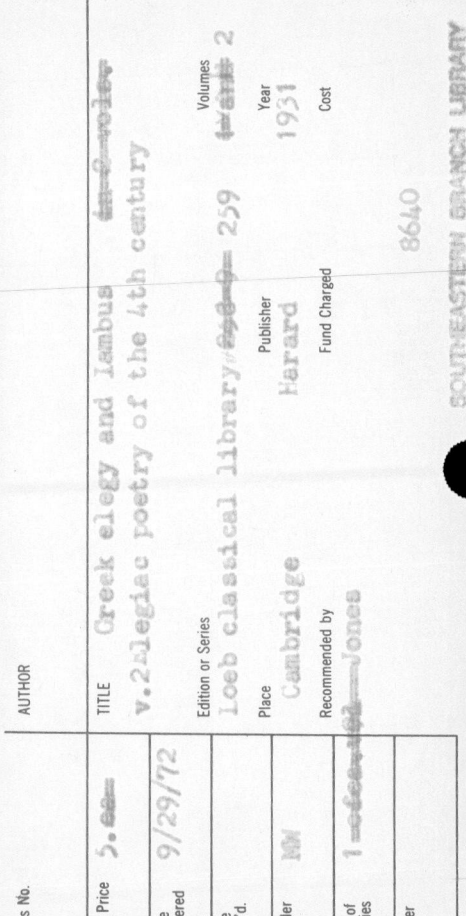

Class No.	5.00	AUTHOR

TITLE Greek elegy and Iambus ~~in 2 vols~~ v.2 elegiac poetry of the 4th century

List Price	5.00
Date Ordered	9/29/72

Edition or Series
loeb classical library/~~p's D~~ 259   Volumes ~~trans~~ 2

Date Rec'd.		Place	Publisher	Year
Dealer	NW	Cambridge	Harard	1931

Recommended by
1 ~~professiol~~—Jones

No. of Copies	1	Fund Charged	Cost
Order No.		8640	

L.C. or Wilson Card

THE
BOWKER
ANNUAL

39th Edition • 1994

THE BOWKER ANNUAL

Library and Book Trade Almanac™

Editor • Catherine Barr

Consultant • Mary Jo Lynch

R.R. Bowker®
A Reed Reference Publishing Company
New Providence, New Jersey

Published by R. R. Bowker,
a Reed Reference Publishing Company
Copyright © 1994 by Reed Elsevier Inc.
All rights reserved
Printed and bound in the United States of America
Bowker is a registered trademark of Reed Publishing (USA) Inc.
The Bowker Annual Library and Book Trade Almanac is a trademark of Reed
Properties Inc., used under license.

International Standard Book Number 0-8352-3481-9
International Standard Serial Number 0068-0540
Library of Congress Catalog Card Number 55-12434

Contents

Part 1
Reports from the Field

National Association Reports

International Reports

Part 2
Legislation, Funding, and Grants

Legislation

Funding Programs and Grant-Making Agencies

Part 3
Library/Information Science
Education, Placement, and Salaries

Part 4
Research and Statistics

Library Research and Statistics

Book Trade Research and Statistics

Part 5
Reference Information

Part 6
Directory of Organizations

Preface

This thirty-ninth edition of *The Bowker Annual* once again incorporates both practical information and thoughtful analysis in the areas most important to librarians, publishers, and others in the information world.

Peter Young and Jane Williams have contributed a special report on Libraries and the National Information Infrastructure, examining the influence of network communications technology on all aspects of libraries and reviewing the prospects for national information policies that balance public and private interests. JoAn Segal's special report gives an overview of Library Cooperation and Networking and covers key issues of the last two years: diversification, duplication, planning, Internet challenges, and more. Legislative efforts in these areas are covered in these two articles as well as in Part 2 of the *Annual*.

The Special Reports section in Part 1 also includes an article by Shirley Ainsworth on the diverse electronic formats (online databases, CD-ROMs, Internet resources) available in Mexico—from the standpoints of both ease of access and database quality; an overview of the International Role of the U.S. Librarian by Hannelore Rader; an account of 17 foreign library professionals' visit to the United States as part of the American Libraries Project; and an assessment of the achievements of the Book Industry Systems Advisory Committee (BISAC) on the occasion of its twentieth birthday, by Tom Clarkson and Sandy Paul.

The International Reports section brings you details of IFLA activities and the Frankfurt Book Fair, as well as an article on library developments in Canada in 1993.

The *SLJ, LJ,* and *PW* news reports and the sixteen reports from federal agencies and libraries and from national associations round out Part 1 of the *Annual*. In addition to a report on activities of the Library of Congress itself, we have added an article on the Center for the Book and its various projects around the country to promote literacy and motivate reading.

Parts 3 and 4 of the *Annual* bring you the usual professional information for librarians (employment, education, and scholarship sources, salary survey, award recipients), the statistics you need to put together budget requests, reports on book pricing and sales, library construction, and where to find book reviews. Don't forget that Part 2 also gives information on where library dollars are being allocated, particularly those under the control of the Department of Education, and that Part 4 starts off with a report by Mary Jo Lynch on the research on libraries and librarianship that took place in 1993. This year we have also added a table giving state rankings of selected public library data so that you can see quickly where your state stands in five key areas.

Part 5 is a ready-reference tool listing toll-free numbers, information on ISBNs and ISSNs, and the best books, bestsellers, and literary prizes of the year. Part 6 is a Directory of Organizations—library and book trade, domestic and foreign—with contact names, phone and FAX numbers, E-mail addresses, and many other useful details.

In addition to all this you'll find at the back of the book a list of National Information Standards Organization (NISO) standards, a calendar of domestic and international events, a list of the authors and contributors to this edition, a list of acronyms, and two indexes giving access to the *Annual's* resources by organization and by subject.

Thanks are owed to Mary Jo Lynch, consultant editor, to Judith Balsamo, assistant editor of the *Annual,* and to all those who contributed reports and replied to questionnaires.

Catherine Barr
Editor

Part 1
Reports from the Field

News of the Year

LJ News Report: Pockets of Prosperity Amid Tight Public Library Budgets

Evan St. Lifer

Senior Editor, News, *Library Journal*

Michael Rogers

Assistant News Editor, *Library Journal*

The results are in on *LJ*'s Fourth Annual Budget Report—its most extensive to date—and the message that emerges for our nation's public libraries is clear: As we move into a new era of fiscal retrenchment and more moderate growth, only those libraries that become an integral part of their communities' long-term mission will thrive.

Undoubtedly, external circumstances—eroding tax bases, continued economic slumps, a reprioritizing of funds away from libraries—have altered public libraries' budgetary landscape. However, for every unfortunate shortfall, we were encouraged to hear about an example of enterprise or support. As California libraries were enduring their worst cuts since the arrival of Proposition 13 in 1978, New York City libraries were receiving six-day-a-week service for the first time in almost 50 years; as Baltimore County was closing eight branches in an effort to downsize, Baltimore's Enoch Pratt library was preparing to reopen two branches with its $1.8 million budget increase; as California's Merced County library system with its 18 branches was scheduled to close, the Friends of the Folsom branch of the Sacramento County PL revived it and helped form a partnership to run it independently; while Colorado libraries are mulling over how to deal with the budgetary restrictions imposed by the statewide TABOR Amendment, Illinois PLs are eagerly awaiting the proceeds of a recently passed bill that will provide them with $18.9 million.

Although the 1990 and 1991 fiscal years of Draconian budgets cuts are behind us—California notwithstanding—the big, budgetary home run is now a rarity. Many libraries—although still groping and thrashing for a secure financial toehold—would be surprised to learn they are in the embryonic stages of a fiscal turnaround, as evidenced by *LJ*'s latest statistics.

LJ sent out questionnaires in October 1993 to 1,629 libraries; 527 libraries responded, giving *LJ* its largest survey and highest response rate (32 percent)

Note: Reprinted from *Library Journal*, January 1994.

since it debuted the survey results in 1991. *LJ* divided responding libraries into three groups: the smaller libraries—those that serve a population of fewer than 50,000; the medium-sized libraries—those that serve between 50,000 and 99,999; and the larger libraries—those that serve 100,000 or more. The names were selected from R. R. Bowker's American Library Directory database and the study was conducted by Cahners Research.

The smaller libraries showed some encouraging signs, averaging a 7 percent jump in their materials funding, 5 percent increases in salaries, and an overall 7 percent increase in total budgets. Medium-sized libraries were up 5 percent across the board—in materials, salaries, and total budget appropriations. The larger libraries were not as fortunate but held their own—up less than 1 percent in materials, up 1 percent in salaries, and up 2.5 percent in total budgets.

Having leafed through every one of the 527 survey responses, including every piece of anecdotal information provided, the editors at *LJ* learned that our Fourth Annual Budget Report is about more than weighing libraries' gains and pains. When asking library officials about their library's future prospects, *LJ* found that perspective was everything. Many librarians with similar financial situations reacted diametrically. What was considered "bleak" for one librarian was labeled "encouraging" by another. Some libraries that traditionally have enjoyed strong support expressed their concern over the possibility of their future funding sources being imperiled, while other libraries with per capitas a fraction of the size were buoyed by the future rather than threatened by it.

Another survey finding only confirmed what we at *LJ* have come to know for some time: That libraries propagate the loudest sentiment, the most aggressive public relations campaign in times of crisis when their collective backs are against the wall or after heavy-handed cuts have been administered. What this Budget Report reveals convincingly is that the country's libraries are illustrative examples of innovative grants, private sector partnerships, and aggressive fundraising campaigns. We ask public libraries to spread the word on their achievements: we need to hear the success stories as loudly and clearly as the warning bells.

New England

Connecticut

Connecticut libraries report small increases, led by a 5 percent surge by Hamden Library. Fairfield PL, with its gaudy $46 per capita funding, is rebounding from an unkind FY 1991/92. The library's funding authority has committed to restoring the 20 percent in materials budget monies that it took away two years ago. While Milford PL finds itself having to deal with a city-imposed freeze on its operating budget, a librarian at the Danbury PL (1 percent increase) said, "unless funds become available . . . enabling librarians to keep pace, we will soon be obsolete in the eyes of the community and funding authorities." Still, another library in the Danbury system, Long Ridge, was able to garner a 9 percent increase.

Maine

Maine's Portland PL saw its budget increase by 3 percent, as did Old Orchard Beach's. One librarian from Old Orchard Beach reported on a statewide move—justified by budget cuts—to replace professionals with paraprofessionals, technicians, and volunteers. "As a 20-year professional, I do not feel hopeful for the future of public libraries," she said. However, Wilton Free PL has an entirely different outlook, having received a 10 percent budget increase. Wilton has incorporated a number of cost-saving measures including recycling books, as well as book and magazine adoptions. "We will do fine," said a librarian at Wilton. "Library funding will bounce back. We must be aggressive in our public relations and let our needs be known."

Massachusetts

Massachusetts is holding the line on state funding to public libraries this year, making an already tight fiscal situation even tighter. Many libraries have made it clear that unless the state's economy picks up, their collective futures will remain cloudy. The Boston PL saw its budget increase by $426,000 or 2 percent. The Needham Free PL, which saw its budget evaporate by 4.5 percent in the last five years, barely had a budget increase—2 percent—for FY 1994. The libraries in Wilmington and Grafton both had small budget increases of 1 percent and 2 percent, respectively. "If funding sources for libraries in Massachusetts continues as is," said a librarian from East Longmeadow PL, "libraries in wealthier communities will continue to keep pace or even improve in some cases while libraries in poorer municipalities continue to deteriorate . . ." If one library is the state's model of prosperity, it's the Newton Free Library. With a per capita of $29, Newton has seen its budget jump by 50 percent since 1988. The library also opened a 90,000 square foot building in 1991. Chelmsford PL, which has absorbed some big cuts in recent years, said it is "recovering," having garnered a 9 percent increase. Chelmsford tried to get a $98,000 bond issue on the ballot to fund additional hours, staff, and materials. However, local voters rejected the measure.

New Hampshire

New Hampshire is no different than its New England neighbors, having been hit hard by the economy. Thus New Hampshire libraries, including the Concord PL, have crept along at a snail's pace. Concord's budget has increased by about 1 percent in the last five years, despite per capita funding of $29.90. For libraries in Londonderry and Deerfield, 1994 represents a pivotal year: Deerfield PL is asking the town for an appropriation to help it purchase books, audiocassettes, videos, and large print books. Londonderry is presenting a $1.3 million bond issue to its local pols in March to expand its facility.

Rhode Island

If the staffs at fellow Rhode Island libraries find themselves a tad envious of the South Kingstown PL in Peace Dale, they have good reason: The librarian there describes the fiscal situation as "excellent and not likely to change." The town staunchly supports library services, as evidenced by its funding of a building program that provided for the renovation of the central library and its two branches in the last six years. Elsewhere, Providence, East Providence, and Warwick PLs are holding their own with increases of 7 percent, 5 percent, and 8 percent, respectively.

Vermont

Vermont's Springfield PL exhibited a 5 percent budget gain, in line with its 25 percent increase since 1988. Springfield and other Vermont areas have been struggling with job losses and shrinking property taxes, slowing their libraries' improvement. The State Library, which runs five regional libraries, is still attempting to rebound from $400,000 worth of cuts since FY 1990, which resulted in the loss of 20 percent of the staff.

Mid-Atlantic

New Jersey

New York's cross-river counterparts polled by *LJ* are holding their own—for the most part. New Jersey libraries in Pompton Plains, Bloomingdale, and Irvington have experienced budget increases of 10 percent, 6 percent, and 16 percent, respectively. Trenton PL and the library systems in Sussex, Gloucester, and Mercer counties also had moderate increases. Libraries having a more difficult time include the Free PL of Woodbridge—which saw its hours cut by 18 percent—Ocean County Library, South Orange PL—which received virtually the same budget as last year—and Clifton PL, foundering with a 6 percent drop in its FY 1994 budget.

New York

Library patrons in the New York metropolitan area are riding the crest of a wave of good fortune: They currently have five-day-a-week service and in June will receive six-day-a-week service for the first time since 1947. However, the financial health of the state's other public libraries is not as clear-cut. Libraries in Greater Poughkeepsie, Liverpool, Binghamton, Mount Vernon, and Dover Plains are using the adjectives "bleak, very poor, awful, flat, and frozen" to describe their fiscal predicaments. Libraries also attribute their struggles to plant closings and declining property taxes. A Broome County PL official (Binghamton) describes the library's plight: "The library board has set standards of operations for staffing, materials budgets, and hours and has actually merged two branch sites, due to insufficient funding, to keep both going at minimal levels. Meanwhile, city and county officials have committed themselves to a new central library building project. It's like being in a Kafka novel." Still, New York City libraries are not alone in their prosperity: institutions in Rochester, Mamaroneck, and Middletown have enjoyed some across-the-board growth in materials, salaries, and total budgets. Long Island libraries in Westhampton and Baldwin continue to garner strong support, although Baldwin is concerned that a Long

Island tax revolt would hurt its funding. The Buffalo & Erie County Library District expects to "no more than hold our own" in 1994 and 1995, while Cherry Valley Memorial Library will remain "status quo."

Pennsylvania

Pennsylvania is grappling with a proposal to revise its state aid formula to provide for stronger incentives to encourage local funding. At press time, Pennsylvania had at least ten different municipalities voting on library bond issues. *LJ* did learn that voters approved a statewide $2.5 million bond issue that should give libraries a needed lift. The Free Library of Philadelphia doesn't expect any local increases but is looking to revenue generated through private funds from a new initiative to be implemented by the library's Foundation Directors and Board of Trustees. Philadelphia's AIDS Library was buoyed by a 17 percent increase in its budget, while Pittsburgh saw two of its libraries—Penn Hills and Northland—garner 10 percent and 7 percent increases, respectively. Erie County Library System absorbed a 9 percent blow to its FY 1993 budget over FY 1992, and public library budgets in Monessen, Annville, Bradford County, and Bessemer also have dipped. Libraries in State College, Williamsport, and Abington made moderate fiscal gains.

South Atlantic

Delaware

Responding Delaware libraries are more encouraged then they've been in recent years, with the possibility of new branches through additional capital funding in county and state budgets. PLs in Wilmington and Newark underwent budget increases of roughly 3 percent.

Florida

Just three of 22 Florida libraries report falling budgets, while two of the state's largest library systems—Miami-Dade and Broward County—had their budgets upped by 10 percent and 8 percent, respectively. The two libraries, which combine to serve a population of almost three million, are upbeat about their funding prospects for the not-too-distant future. Broward County's Financial Assessment Taskforce has found "little evidence" that its libraries would face cutbacks in the next couple of years, while Miami-Dade is based in a stable, dedicated taxing district. A growing local economy has helped lift Stuart's Martin County Library System to a 22 percent budget increase. Other big gainers: Sewanee River Regional Library in Live Oak, 16 percent this year, 55 percent since 1988; Bay County PL Association in Panama City, 14 percent this year, 71 percent since 1988; and Hernando County Library System in Brooksville, 13 percent this year, 101 percent since 1988. Poor local economies have hurt many libraries, however, including Hudson's Pasco County Library (26 percent drop) and the West Palm Beach PL (14 percent drop).

Georgia

Georgia libraries are hopeful that their fiscal predicaments are beginning to change for the better. Jonesboro's Clayton County Library System, Madison's Uncle Remus Regional Library System, and Valdosta's Lownds County PL have exhibited gains of 8 percent, 9 percent, and 8 percent. Two libraries that continue to make big gains are the Sequoyah Regional Library, with a 7 percent gain this year after a five-year gain of 70 percent, and the Lake Lanier Regional Library, which had a budget increase of 11 percent after being paced by a five-year jump of 120 percent. A librarian at the DeKalb County PL in Decatur (up 2 percent) said the institution's biggest challenge is "maintaining the library's forward momentum in the face of enormous technological change and uncertain resources."

Maryland

The sluggishness of Maryland's economy, combined with rapidly rising Medicaid and prison costs, has contributed to a large deficit at the state level, according to Charles W. Robinson, director of the Baltimore County Public Library (BCPL). The lag in state funds to the county level has hurt Baltimore County, which saw its budget drop by about 4 percent for FY 1993/94. Budgetary distress forced Baltimore County to close eight branches in 1993. Despite the budget hits, BCPL will be the recipient of a $1 million county bond initiative in FY 1994/95. "The library has great support from the county government, library trustees, and staff," said Robinson. "But money is tight for all public services." Baltimore's Enoch Pratt library was more fortunate, garnering a 10 percent increase from the City Council. The additional $1.8 million will be used to buy books, reopen and fill positions in two branches that had been closed, and provide for a small salary increase for library staffers. PLs in Westminster and Elkton had increases of 12 percent and 8 percent, while the Wicomico library (5 percent increase) said its future is "brightening." Having endured a 36 percent budget drop since 1988, the Western Maryland PLs in Hagerstown were less sanguine, saying they see "little improvement in the near future."

North Carolina

Of the 18 North Carolina libraries responding, all except one (Greensboro PL, 1 percent drop) exhibited very moderate increases, ranging from 3 percent to 5 percent. Libraries used the adjectives "tentative and tight" to characterize their situations. While Probeson (up 5 percent) and Lincoln (up 3 percent) counties are struggling with unsympathetic politicians and high unemployment, High Point PL (8 percent increase) is "encouraged by the level of support for public library service" in its community. Although Charlotte-Mecklenburg County predicts a "very tight" fiscal future, it garnered a 10 percent increase for FY 1993/94 and has sought $9 million for new branches after recently opening three. North West Hanover County PL in Wilmington is considering increasing fees to help cover its shortfall in staffing funds.

"More budget reductions, further erosion of service," said a librarian from Virginia's Richmond PL. "No more cuts are possible without closing branches in

FY 1995," said a staff member at Loudoun County PL in Leesburg. Other quotes include "severely stressed," from Portsmouth PL (up 5 percent) and "apprehensive," from Suffolk PL System (up 2 percent). A more positive outlook abounds from Roanoke County PL (up 2 percent), "Growth in local revenues appears to be slowly improving"; and from Prince William PL System (up a substantial 18 percent), which reports that "although the county continues to experience the effects of the recession . . . the library has experienced a high level of support, thus prospects are generally positive." Prince William, which experienced an 18 percent jump for FY 1993/94, will open a new facility this year. In tallying information from 19 responding Virginia libraries, *LJ* found six—or just about one out of three—with decreasing budgets for FY 1993/94. Libraries on the downside cite their local economies, decreasing tax bases, and a reprioritizing of funds away from libraries.

West Virginia

West Virginia libraries will get a small boost from a statewide reevaluation of property. Parkersburg Wood, Charleston's Kanawha and Cabell county libraries experienced increases of 4 percent, 9 percent, and 3 percent, respectively.

East North Central

Illinois

For most Illinois public libraries, the best news of 1993 came when State Librarian and Secretary of State George Ryan submitted a plan to the state's General Assembly that will generate $33 million in motor vehicle fees, $18.9 million of which will be dedicated to public libraries. Revenues of the Live & Learn program will increase state aid to libraries by 60 percent. The $18.9 million will be divided among restoration and automation ($8 million); construction grants ($4.9 million); per capita grants ($3.5 million); school library grants ($1 million); family literacy and services for the blind and physically handicapped ($800,000); and research and reference center aid ($700,000). Fifteen of 17 responding libraries registered increases, led by the Northern Illinois Library System, based in Rockford, with a 27 percent surge. Budget increases were also had at PLs in Rolling Meadows (14 percent), Saint Charles (11 percent), Springfield (9 percent), and Decatur (6 percent). Schaumberg Township District Library said its outlook is "good" and its next few years "fine," despite a FY 1993/94 budget drop of about 6 percent.

Indiana

Indiana libraries find themselves in a position that their counterparts nationwide only dream about: They are independent taxing authorities, with a much-desired fiscal autonomy. Still, some Indiana libraries are finding themselves in dire straits because their jurisdictions have decided to freeze their respective tax rates. Allen County is in a "positive" situation, its 1994 budget having increased by 5 percent. Kokomo Howard County PL's budget is also up 5 percent, describing its prospects for the future as "darn good." Two of 12 Indiana libraries report budget decreases, one of which, the Rushville PL, had a 14 percent decrease after "windfall" years in 1992 and 1993 that allowed it to replace old books, make long-needed building improvements, raise salaries, and buy equipment. The other institution, Earl Park PL, dropped by 6 percent.

Michigan

Eight of 25 Michigan libraries report a drop in their FY 1993/94 budget appropriations. Gordon Conable, director of the Monroe County Library System, has voiced his concern about future restrictions posed by property tax reform in Michigan. "Those libraries run by school districts have lost their ability to collect operating levies," he said. "Other public libraries will see new hurdles to overcome in maintaining millages." However, Conable said legislative remedies are being discussed. The Detroit PL, which serves a population of more than one million, saw its budget drop by a hair—less than 1 percent. Other libraries on the budgetary bubble are Sterling Heights PL (up 1 percent); Port Huron's Blue Water Library Federation (down 1 percent) and St. Clair County Library System (down 2 percent); Clinton Township's Macomb County Library (up 1 percent); Albion's Woodlands Library Cooperative (up 1 percent); Sturgis PL (up 2 percent); Veterans Memorial Library in Mount Pleasant (down 2 percent); East Lansing PL (down 2 percent); and Rochester Hills PL (down 2 percent). PLs that have seen a more pronounced jump—between 10 percent and 12 percent—include Escanaba PL, Ann Arbor PL, Monroe County Library System, Ypsilanti District Library, and Grosse Point PL. One of Michigan's big budget winners for FY 1993/94 is Battle Creek's Willard Library, with a 29 percent increase.

Ohio

If there's a darling of *LJ*'s annual budget report, Ohio is it: of 31 responding libraries, not one suffered a decline, and most jumped by at least 5 percent. The magic number for Ohio libraries has been 6.3, as in receiving 6.3 percent of the state's income tax revenues. However, state legislators reduced the 6.3 percent rate to 5.7 percent for FY 1992/93. The 5.7 percent rate is slated to remain at least until FY 1995. Ohio libraries are hoping to return the allocation to 6.3 percent in 1995. The state's larger libraries demonstrated modest gains: Dayton Montgomery County, 10 percent; Youngstown & Mahoning County, 5 percent; Toledo Lucas County, 5 percent; Parma's Cuyahoga County PL, 5 percent; and Columbus's Metropolitan, 2 percent.

Wisconsin

With the exception of Sheboygan's Mead PL, all of Wisconsin's dozen library respondents come out on top in FY 1993/94. Nonetheless, Sheboygan characterized its economy as "stable," while West Allis PL (up 2 percent) referred to itself as "very fortunate." The Milwaukee PL posted a 6 percent gain; Green Bay's Brown County, 7 percent. Ten libraries in St. Croix County are wrangling over county allocations as the area's growth continues to outpace the library services it can provide. "Everybody loves libraries until it comes to funding them," said one librarian from Woodville Community Library.

East South Central

Tennessee

Virtually every one of the 14 Tennessee public libraries polled by *LJ* recorded budget increases, led by Clarksville Montgomery County Library with a whopping 24 percent increase. Other increases by public libraries in Athens, Cookeville, Johnson City, Columbia, Greenville, Maryville, Sparta, Chattanooga Hamilton County, and Elizabethton Center County ranged from 4 percent to 13 percent. Knoxville saw its most recent library budget increase by more than 6 percent; Memphis PL officials report a budget increase for the coming year, albeit a slight one—less than 1 percent.

Alabama

Responding libraries from Alabama are reporting budget growth, but some are garnering them through grants and special fundraising rather than through typical allocations. Huntsville Madison PL and Decatur's Wheeler Basin Regional Library, both with 5 percent increases, are among the group. The Baldwin County Library System in Robertsdale represents a bright spot in the state: After five years of neglect, the library, with the help of a new director, obtained a 22 percent increase for FY 1993/94. Further, voters were to have decided on a millage that would mean an additional $855,000 for the area's public, college, and school libraries. Gadsden (up 5 percent) and Selma Dallas County (which recently passed a $1.2 million bond for expansion and renovation) PLs are also faring well, enjoying solid support from their communities. Two of the state's larger libraries, Tuscaloosa and Mobile, experienced moderate budgetary boosts of 5 percent and 2 percent, respectively. The Mobile PL, however, has seen itself sink on the city's budgetary priority list, behind the police, the courts, and jails.

Mississippi

There is evidence that Mississippi's record on statewide library support, long regarded among the country's worst, may be improving. Almost all reporting libraries had budget increases, led by the DeSoto County Library (14 percent), which describes its fiscal situation as "brighter than at any time during the past ten years." Although still way under the national per capita average of roughly $18, some of the state's libraries have seen subtle per capita increases. Institutions in Greenville, Brookhaven, Hattiesburg, and DeSoto County all have per capitas between $7 and $9. Other less fortunate Mississippi libraries have remained at between $4 and $5, including PLs in West Point, Laurel, and Quitman. "If it weren't for the increases in state aid, we would have no raises at all," said one librarian. "We are getting less than one mill from each county. They figure we have books on the shelves, why do we have to keep buying more?"

Kentucky

Kentucky libraries, with the exception of those in Owensboro, report conservative increases. The Owensboro-Daviess County PL took an 11 percent hit, losing almost one quarter of its materials budget for FY 1993/94.

West North Central

Iowa

The *LJ* survey points to a flat year for Iowa libraries: five of the 11 institutions responding report that their budgets stayed even or decreased. A statewide tax freeze and a downturn in the state's farming industry are at the root of the malaise. Three of the state's largest public libraries—Cedar Rapids, Sioux City, and Iowa City—had respective increases of 3 percent, 4 percent, and 5 percent.

Kansas

"The future looks good!" exclaimed a librarian from Kansas's Oswego PL. Despite taking an 11 percent cut in FY 1993/94, Oswego staffers are buoyed by two community grants totaling $239,000. Having the economy of Johnson County "moving along nicely," as one librarian described it, has helped the library garner a "nice" 18 percent increase for FY 1993/94. Being the library in the state's fastest growing city hasn't hurt the Olathe Public Library: The library's circulation jumped 11 percent, its budget, 15 percent. Since 1988, Olathe's library budget has increased by 100 percent. But Kansas public libraries are lagging in certain parts of the state, including Iola and Shawnee Mission. Both institutions cite a potential reduction in state aid as the primary factor for their sluggish fiscal situations.

Minnesota

If the Minneapolis Public Library is any indication, libraries in Minnesota are holding their own on budgets. Minneapolis, with its 8 percent gain, is joined by libraries in Cambridge (10 percent), Ramsey County (12 percent), and Pine River (16 percent). Pine River benefited from state funding, which made up more than 25 percent of the regional library's total budget. Libraries in Eagan, Northfield, Rochester, and Duluth say they are attracting strong support and that the "future looks bright." Anoka County Library, based in Blaine, saw its budget fall by slightly less than 1 percent.

Missouri

Special districts have meant good things for those Missouri libraries that have them, especially for St. Charles City County Library District in Saint Peters, which has seen its budget jump 59 percent in the last five years, with a 5 percent increase for FY 1993/94. The Mid-Continent PL's budget has undergone similar growth, garnering a 59 percent increase in the last five years, 3 percent for the coming fiscal year. Other hotbeds of budget growth: Ozark Regional in Ironton (11 percent) and Jefferson County in High Ridge. Meanwhile, Kansas City PL's per capita funding topped the $40 mark in FY 1993/94. Despite a fairly stable funding situation in the present, many Missouri libraries expressed concern over how an "eroding tax base" would affect their future funding lot.

Nebraska

Nebraska's Blue Hill and Gordon PLs have seen increases of 8 percent and 11 percent, while Ponca PL has remained even on the fiscal scoreboard, after exhibiting 23 percent budget growth in the last five years.

North Dakota

The North Dakota libraries responding to *LJ*'s poll have budgets that neither improved nor deteriorated significantly: The McKenzie PL in Watford City saw its budget remain the same, while the PL system in Grand Forks traded a 4 percent increase in its materials budget for a 3 percent decrease in salaries.

South Dakota

Although a move is afoot throughout South Dakota to limit property taxes, it hasn't happened yet. Healthy increases were the norm for public libraries in Rapid City (10 percent), Spearfish (11 percent), and Brookings (9 percent).

West South Central

Arkansas

Heady times are ahead for Arkansas libraries, with the recent passage of a constitutional amendment raising the cap on local funding. For the first time, libraries statewide will be allowed to introduce bond issues for capital improvements. The new measure also raises the cap on local funding for public libraries from one to five mills. "There is still a long, hard struggle to go," said Harrison's North Arkansas Regional Library, referring to Arkansas past history of poor library support. "But at least now we are able to ask for more." Little Rock's Central Arkansas Library System is optimistic that the new measure will enable it to "nearly double its operating budget by 1995." The North Little Rock PL echoes its neighbor's outlook, calling its situation "outstanding." The measure will allow the library to double its budget in 1994 and incorporate automation and other services.

Louisiana

New Orleans's continuing financial woes have slowed its library's budget growth (less than 1 percent), while outside the city, two Louisiana public libraries— Ascension Parish (Donaldsville) and Ouachita Parish (Monroe)—had 10 percent and 11 percent budget gains. Iberia Parish's PL, maintaining a relatively static budget for almost five years, is biding its time until 1996, when it can request a tax increase. This past year, Iberia Parish PL had to cut its materials budget by almost 5 percent. The state's best outlook may belong to Calcasieu Parish PL in Lake Charles, which is in the process of building a new main library. Calcasieu Parish library officials have reason to be optimistic: three out of four voters approved a 100 percent increase in its library budget in 1990. Many of the parish's library branches have been expanded and/or renovated, and all 13 branches are going online.

Oklahoma

Library officials across Oklahoma are counting on a new mandate allowing for single county special library districts to help alleviate the long-simmering problem of unequal funding/unequal service. The state's multicounty special districts have suffered because of the inability of all the counties in each district to pass bond issues. Despite the special district controversy, Norman's Pioneer Library System received a boost of 24 percent in its budget for FY 1993/94. The Oklahoma City Public Library is enjoying prosperous times: Its residents recently passed a mill levy that will add up to 14 percent to its budget. Muskogee's Eastern Oklahoma District Library System was not as fortunate, taking a 6 percent hit for FY 1993/94.

Texas

Only two of Texas's 26 responding libraries report decreases in budget appropriations. Two county libraries—in Waco and Conroe—led the way with increases of 24 percent and 20 percent, respectively. Three of the state's largest libraries— Houston (4 percent), Dallas (1 percent), and Fort Worth (4 percent)—made minor gains, while public libraries in Lubbock and Arlington improved by 7 percent and 8 percent, respectively. The Fort Bend County Libraries in Richmond describe themselves as part of a "fast-growing county," whose budget has surged by more than 60 percent in the last five years. "We at the library must work proactively to remain as highly regarded as in the past," said a librarian there. "We are also planning and defining the role of our library system . . . in view of the national information highway and new, emerging technologies."

Mountain States

Arizona

Arizona had five libraries reporting double-digit increases: Peoria PL at 19 percent, Chandler PL at 16 percent, Mesa and Page PLs each at 14 percent, and Glendale PL at 10 percent. Phoenix's Maricopa County Library District, preoccupied by the controversy surrounding the departure of Library Director Kamala Stillwell, took a 6 percent hit. Apache County Library in Saint Johns reports that it has succeeded in meeting its funding needs, despite a slight increase of only 2 percent for FY 1993/94; the PL system in Flagstaff has maintained a stable level of funding (6 percent).

Colorado

When the TABOR (Taxpayer's Bill of Rights) Amendment passed in 1992, it profoundly affected Colorado libraries' future prospects for ameliorating their fiscal situations. The law requires voter approval for the incursion of any new debt or attempted raising of mill levies by a public library. Lakewood's Jefferson County PL budget sank 16 percent after a five-year growth spurt exceeding 50 percent. Boulder PL (5 percent increase) reports that it doesn't anticipate any great financial peaks or valleys, while libraries in Westminster and Pueblo claim modest gains of 7 percent and 8 percent.

Idaho

Librarians across Idaho are holding their collective breaths over a 1 percent property tax limitation, due on the ballot in this year's general election, which would severely hobble their operations. Boise PL (3 percent increase for FY 1993/94) officials have said they would lose 40 percent—50 percent in revenues. Libraries in Soda Springs and Pinehurst—both of which serve populations of about 3,000—had budget increases of 3 percent and 5 percent.

Montana

While Montana's West Yellowstone PL (19 percent increase) proclaims that "Southwest Montana is booming!" and "County property values are sky-high," three other Montana public libraries find themselves in the doldrums. Missoula PL, which has managed just a 2 percent increase in the last five years and was hit with a 7 percent loss this year, said it has only half the staff it needs to serve its community. "We'll be fortunate to stay open," said a librarian there. The public library in Helena also came up empty in FY 1993/94, showing a 6 percent loss. Flathead County Library in Kalispell shows more positive signs, with a 13 percent increase.

Nevada

Two of Nevada's largest public libraries sustained healthy increases: The Las Vegas-Clark County Library District had a 9 percent jump to go along with a 93 percent increase since 1988. The library is in the midst of a facilities development program that will build or expand nine branches. Reno's Washoe County Public Library (10 percent), which has sought additional tax monies, is awaiting a decision from county officials on whether it can put the issue before voters this year.

New Mexico

New Mexico's Roswell and Hobbs public libraries are holding their own; both institutions have histories of consistent support. The State Library, which provides library service to New Mexico's rural areas, had an 8 percent increase.

Utah

Every one of Utah's libraries responding to *LJ*'s survey report at least a 5 percent gain, with the highest budget increase registered by Ogden's Weber County Library at 23 percent. Weber County Library has everything going its way: a new branch on the way this year, more than 50 percent growth in the last five years and a healthy per capita of more than $18. No mere happenstance, Weber County's success can be traced to its commissioners, who in a recent unanimous decision hiked the library property tax rate by more than 40 percent. Salt Lake City public libraries are the beneficiaries of a surging local economy and strong local support. Librarian Dennis Day of the Salt Lake City PL (9 percent increase), which has a per capita of $38.16, cites a "strong level of public services as a core value of the library board/staff" and an "effective community relations program" as two primary reasons for the library's success. Salt Lake County Library System's Eileen Longsworth said with revenues from real estate and construction increasing, "everything is booming." Salt Lake City Public Library's hefty 18 percent budget increase for FY 1994 includes funds for the construction of another library. High growth continues to spur needed library budget increases in Provo (7 percent), Farmington's Davis County (7 percent projected), and St. George's Washington County (8 percent).

Wyoming

Natrona County PL in Casper, Wyoming reports that zero growth in property values has created a stagnant fiscal situation there. The library, facing increased competition for funds from a penal facility in the area, has seen its budget decrease by 30 percent since 1988, topped off by a negligible increase in FY 1993/94 of 1 percent. Friends groups are playing a larger role, helping to raise library funds not only in Natrona County but in neighboring Teton, Johnson, and Sheridan counties.

Pacific States

Alaska

Libraries in Alaska find themselves searching for a reliable revenue source as monies from oil decline. The Anchorage Public Library, which has seen its 1993 circulation edge up by 1 percent to 1,334,893, had a 1 percent drop in its FY 1993/94 budget, in line with its five-year growth of less than 2 percent.

California

The grim news reported by California libraries only confirms a statewide economic library crisis, exacerbated by the state's calamitous reallocation of local property tax revenue from libraries and other local services to fund school districts. Thirty-four of the 45 public libraries responding—or roughly three out of four—experienced cuts in their budgets ranging from less than 1 percent to 41 percent. A quick snapshot of the carnage: Alameda County Library, down 41 percent; County of Los Angeles Public Library, down 36 percent; National City Public Library, down 28 percent; Palos Verde Valley District Library, down 22 percent; Ventura County Public Library, down 21 percent; Monterey County Free Libraries, down 19 percent; Modesto's Stanislaus County Free Library, down 22 percent; San Jose's Santa Clara County Free Library, down 21 percent, and the list goes on. "As long as the governor and legislature bleed the counties dry by shifting property tax monies away from the counties and special districts to the schools, libraries will barely continue to cling to life," said a librarian from Oroville's Butte County Library. "[It's] poor commentary on the priorities of our elected officials."

Merced County suffered the worst fate: its county supervisors voted to permanently close the main library and 18 branches after a .5 percent sales tax issue was rejected by 66 votes. The library employed 83 people.

California's libraries, desperate for some alternative, are hoping that revenue from a proposed sales tax will help them restore chunks of their budgets. Despite all the doom and gloom, the reopening of the Los Angeles Public Library, the increasing growth of Cerritos Public Library (62 percent in five years), and an encouraging budget victory by Pasadena Public Library are bright spots.

Oregon

There's nothing like a statewide fiscal crisis to put things in perspective for California's neighbors to the north: All of Oregon's nine responding libraries report increases, led by Hillsboro and Beaverton City PLs at 17 percent each; libraries in Stayton and Albany weighed in with 9 percent increases. Oregon's property tax cap has yet to pose a problem, according to the responding libraries. Buoyed by a recently passed $31 million bond issue, Portland's Multnomah County Library heads into 1994 with a 7 percent budget increase. Jackson County Library System, which prides itself on being "one of the best-funded libraries in the state," received an 11 percent boost.

Washington

Several of Washington's largest libraries enjoy strong per capita support, including Seattle ($41.45), King County ($35.23), Spokane ($33.59), and Tacoma ($42.12). With the exception of Tacoma, which saw its budget edge up by barely 1 percent, King County's budget jumped by 8 percent—65 percent over five years—and Spokane's budget increased by 6 percent, a whopping 502 percent over five years. The key to Spokane's success has been a $28 million bond fund that provides "alternative creative funding" to pay for staff, materials, and automation in addition to capital improvements. Still smarting from a loss of 20 FTE positions between 1991 and 1992, Seattle PL is finally on the mend: Staffers there are anticipating a restoration of branch hours and the enhancement of several programs after a budget gain of 11 percent. In an effort to improve its lot, Tacoma PL officials detailed plans to collaborate with community organizations to foster "added political support and power."

SLJ News Report:
A Second Look at the Top Stories of 1993

Michael Sadowski

News and Features Editor, *School Library Journal*

Randy Meyer

Assistant News and Features Editor, *School Library Journal*

Bill Clinton stepped in, and Chris Whittle stepped back. The government got tough on television violence, and the networks got defensive. California libraries, already reeling from budget cuts, took another hit. And more schools discovered an exciting new alternative to outmoded energy sources—Library Power.

These are a few of the stories readers followed in the pages of *School Library Journal (SLJ)* over the course of the year. In keeping with annual tradition, there follows an end-of-the-year recap of major news from 1993, along with updates and glimpses of things to come in 1994.

"Good Morning, America"

With a little help from poet Maya Angelou, Bill Clinton said "good morning" to the nation on January 20 as he became the 42nd president of the United States. Indeed, many librarians and educators had great expectations for the dawning of a new day in Washington.

When the Clinton administration unveiled its first budget proposal, however, some of this optimism turned to disappointment. Reminding the nation of the need for painful sacrifices to reduce the federal deficit, Clinton's initial budget was sobering. For one thing, it called for an education hike less than that proposed by President Bush the previous year. Educators feared that many federally funded programs would be unable to keep pace with inflation and that some might have to be cut altogether.

For libraries, the prospects were worse. Clinton called for an overall reduction in federal aid of nearly $14 million and the elimination of several budget lines, including library construction and renovation, foreign-language materials, and library literacy programs.

Over the course of the year, however, the system of checks and balances ran its inevitable course. The House and Senate rejected most of the proposed library program eliminations and called for an increase of nearly 6 percent in overall federal funding for library programs. On the education front, Congress ended up being even less generous than the president, proposing a total education budget $2 billion lower than Clinton's. On October 18, the president approved Congress's changes on both library and education funding and signed them into law.

But there were also two pieces of good news for educators in October. Concerned that some of their programs might be trimmed in Vice President Al

Note: Adapted from *School Library Journal,* December 1993.

Gore's "Reinventing Government" streamlining plan, educators were relieved to find out that education would not be on the rescission list after all. And the "Goals 2000: Educate America Act," a $420 million reform bill introduced by Education Secretary Richard W. Riley, passed the House of Representatives by nearly a three-to-one margin. This revamping of the Bush administration's "America 2000" proposal calls for U.S. students to meet a list of six education goals by the year 2000, national standards in various subject areas, and a more active role for the federal government in education reform.

In addition, school librarians will see many positive changes if the Elementary and Secondary School Library Media Act passes. This legislation would establish federal support for school library media services and restore earmarked funds for the purchase of school library materials.

Midwest Dries Out

As record floods devastated much of the Midwest over the summer, leaving 50 dead and 70,000 homeless, most public libraries survived with relatively little damage. This was due in part to stipulations in the Library Services and Construction Act (LSCA) that prohibit the use of LSCA funds on libraries built in flood plains.

Most libraries suffered only small setbacks that forced them to close for several days—minor book damage, power outages, flooded basements—but a handful of libraries fared worse. The Pattonsburg branch of the Davies County (Mo.) Library lost virtually all of its collection after a levee broke nearby.

School buildings also fared well considering the severity of the flooding. Most schools were able to reopen in the fall, but the flood left in its wake a host of problems: damage to buses, supplies, and equipment; the displacement of students to temporary residences; and the anticipated loss of property tax revenue due to destroyed homes, farms, and businesses.

The total cost of the damage caused by the flood is still unknown, but assistance has come from many sources. President Clinton signed a $4.8 billion flood relief bill in August, including $100 million earmarked for education programs. The National Endowment for the Humanities has set aside $1 million for book preservation grants, and several vendors to the school and library community—including Reed Reference Publishing and PBS Video—have offered to replace flood-damaged materials free of charge.

Tough Talk on Violence

A Harris poll released in August presented some startling statistics about the prevalence of violence in the lives of American children. For example, roughly one in 10 children surveyed (ages 10–19) said they had been shot at in the past year, and about the same number said they had fired a gun at someone else.

Psychologists have long cited violence in television and movies as a factor in violent behavior among children. Youth librarians and others concerned about this issue (and the questions about censorship it raises) watched with interest as Congress met with the heads of the four major TV networks. To ward off congressional action, the network executives presented their solution: parental advisories before programs deemed (by the networks) to have "violent content."

This solution seemed to appease Congress for the time being and to assuage the fears of those concerned about the abridgement of First Amendment rights. But in October, after deaths that allegedly were linked to the feature film "The Program" and the animated MTV series "Beavis and Butt-head," Attorney General Janet Reno told the TV network executives point-blank to stem violence in their programming or face regulation.

"If voluntary steps are not taken and deadlines established [for cleaning up violence in television], government should respond, and respond immediately," Reno said in a Senate Commerce Committee hearing. The committee was considering three bills to curb television violence, all of which were decried by top network executives as government censorship: banning violent programming during hours when children make up a substantial part of the audience; rating television programs according to their violent content; and federally mandated warnings before shows considered violent.

California Budget Woes

Libraries all over the United States have been feeling the pain of budget cuts in recent years, but 1993 was an especially painful year for California's county libraries.

First, Governor Pete Wilson announced plans to dismantle the Special District Augmentation Fund, a measure passed in the late 1970s to keep county agencies such as libraries from feeling the full brunt of tax-cutting Proposition 13. The elimination of the fund essentially shifted $2.6 billion in property tax revenue from libraries to school districts.

In response, the California Library Association authored a benefit assessment bill as a strategy to recover some of the lost funds. (Benefit assessments are basically supplemental taxes on property used to fund services that result in increased property value.) As the library community had hoped, both the State Senate and Assembly passed the legislation—but hopes were dashed when the governor vetoed the bill in October.

County library systems must now come up with alternative strategies on their own. The County of Los Angeles Public Library system, one of the nation's largest, planned to close half of its libraries and drastically reduce services in the remaining half when the funding shift was first announced. It gained a reprieve with a $3.5 million "special assistance fund," but this fund was only intended to support the system with reduced hours until the benefit assessment bill, which the governor vetoed, could take effect.

"Now we are in a holding pattern," said Youth Services Coordinator Penny Markey. "We're hoping the county will provide the funds to keep us going until June, but that may not happen."

A June 1993 statement from the library said: "It is ironic that county public libraries, an integral part of the state's educational system, will close because their budgets have been shifted to fund public schools. Many schools have already been forced to close their libraries, and students have depended on public libraries for completion of their school assignments. Now with public libraries closing, where will there be support for children doing their homework?"

Where Have All the Library Schools Gone?

California's graduate library schools didn't fare much better than its county libraries in 1993. Two of the West Coast's most prestigious programs in library and information science, those at the University of California's Berkeley and Los Angeles campuses, faced closure because of severe university–wide cutbacks.

In February, UC–Berkeley's Academic Planning Board recommended that admissions to the 75-year-old library school be suspended pending a review to define the field of information science and "an administrative and programmatic structure suitable for establishment at Berkeley." The review process is still under way and the admissions freeze stands. Library school Dean Nancy Van House said it is unlikely that the school will accept students for fall 1994 admission.

In June the administration of UC–Los Angeles announced that its library school would be "disestablished." But good news came in July when Executive Vice Chancellor Andrea Rich authorized admission of an MLS class under the rubric of the Graduate School of Education, which appears to be the library school's new permanent home.

Only two other graduate schools of library science now remain on the West Coast: San Jose State University and the University of Washington.

More Media Centers Running on Library Power

More good news was heard throughout the year from the National Library Power Program. Funded by the DeWitt Wallace–Reader's Digest Fund and administered by the American Association of School Librarians (AASL), the project is designed to revamp America's school libraries through the establishment of model programs at selected sites.

In September the fund awarded Library Power implementation grants to local education funds in five additional cities: Chattanooga, Tenn.; Miami, Fla.; Lincoln, Neb.; Cleveland, Ohio; and Denver, Colo. Eight cities already have Library Power projects under way.

In Paterson, N.J., now in its second year as a Library Power city, the local education fund announced plans for a fund–raising campaign to double the library materials budgets at the city's three public high schools. Last year the city went from zero to 15 full-time, certified school library media specialists in its elementary schools.

The fund awards Library Power grants not directly to schools but to local education funds, which in turn work within their communities to optimize the use of grants in public schools. In 1993 local education funds reported the following Library Power expansions:

- Providence, R.I.: four more schools designated for the program, for a total of 14

- New York City: five new school libraries opened
- Baton Rouge, La.: 23 elementary schools added, for a total of 53 participating schools
- Tucson, Ariz.: Double the number of schools participating (from eight to 16)

The DeWitt Wallace–Reader's Digest Fund is committed to establishing up to 25 Library Power districts by 1995 with a total investment of up to $45 million.

Reform Plans Whittled Down

Much to the relief of his opponents, Christopher Whittle suffered major setbacks this year in his plans to reform American education from the private sector.

Time Warner, an important investor in Whittle's Edison Project to establish a system of technology-rich, for-profit schools, backed out. Whittle also failed to attract some of the new investors he had hoped for. As a result, the project was scaled down from one that would build 1,000 schools from the ground up to one that would renovate 100 existing schools in a pilot program.

Whittle Communications officials remain upbeat, but Whittle's other major education venture, Channel One, also faced difficulties this year. The *Wall Street Journal* has speculated that the network, which requires participating schools to show daily commercial news programs in exchange for free video equipment, may be having financial difficulties. And Channel One, already illegal in New York, may be banned in California if a current bill is passed by state legislators and signed by the governor.

Many professional organizations such as the American Federation of Teachers and the National Council of Teachers of English have issued statements against in-school advertising. Now they have a new ally—the students themselves. Unplug, a national coalition of grass-roots, student-run groups, sprang up this year with the goal of ridding all types of commercial messages in schools.

The Year Ahead

Many of these stories will continue to develop in 1994. Library Power will keep fueling change in school library media centers around the country. Christopher Whittle, a dogged entrepreneur, will keep trying to bring his unique brand of education into the marketplace. And lobbyists will be hard at work to get the School Library Media Act, the Goals 2000 legislation, and a host of other items to the top of the national education agenda.

But there will also be new challenges and unforeseen opportunities. Major changes in school financing law could result as more state courts consider measures to ensure equity. The House of Representatives will be up for re-election next year, a vote many believe will be a national referendum on Clinton's administration. And AASL will attempt to "Shape the Vision" for the future of school library media services at its seventh National Conference, to be held in November in Indianapolis.

PW News Reports, 1993

Signposts to the Future

John F. Baker
Editorial Director, *Publishers Weekly*

In the Chinese sense, these are the most interesting times book publishers and booksellers have ever lived through. It's always tempting to call each new year pivotal, but we do see signs that some of the decisions made by book people in 1994 will determine the future of the industry.

Many of the current signs are contrary: the hottest bestsellers can reach previously undreamed–of sales levels, so that these days first printings of half a million copies are by no means uncommon; but the readership for many previously solid book categories—perhaps even general fiction itself—seems to be actually shrinking.

New and bigger bookstores proliferate in the chains, so that a wider choice of books is placed before a constantly growing number of people; but the vast sums spent on expansion have not yet begun to register as improved bookstore profits, and meanwhile worthy independent stores continue to struggle mightily with the discount competition, and occasionally to fall off the map.

The Latest Merger Mania

Publishers have continued to merge into ever larger conglomerate groupings—and then, just when growth mania seemed to be ebbing, Paramount buys Macmillan and will also join either Viacom or QVC, and Morrow seems likely to become part of Putnam. Yet publisher profit margins, except in such predictable areas as el–hi and college texts and some parts of professional publishing, continue to dwindle year by year.

Book retailing, even in a lingering recession, continues to pace much of the merchandise market, and book publishing to increase its overall gross sales by an average 6 to 7 percent a year. But most houses are trimming their staff and lists, focusing their promotional efforts more sharply.

New Concepts of Publishing

The economic uncertainties are matched—perhaps even in part inspired by—the extraordinary fluidity that has infiltrated the very concept of publishing. When the technology already exists that can create a book, one copy at a time, while the customer who has custom-ordered it waits at a "bookstore" (see "Books While U Wait," below); when scholarly journals can be passed to their subscribers by way of computer networks; when college coursepacks can be created by on-campus businesses licensed by the publisher; when scholarly publishers start to join with their local university libraries and computer operations to create academic "pub-

Note: These three articles are adapted from *Publishers Weekly,* January 3, 1994.

lications"; and when even fiction (let alone reference) begins to appear online and in multimedia interactive formats, a sort of instant book into movie—then conventional publishers have many hard choices to make.

The Gold of "Content"

They sit atop golden mountains of "content"—the prize for which so many new and strange media alliances are being forged (see "New Alliances for New Media," below). But how best to mine that gold? The recent PaineWebber media presentations, and the innumerable "electronic conferences" that dot our calendars, show that publishers are all seeking the best way to make the most of this brave new world. Some, like Time Warner, are digitizing all the way; others, like Bantam Doubleday Dell and Penguin, are taking a much more cautious approach. But all now realize that the electronic revolution will certainly proceed, with or without them. And even the thorny issue of where and how the new multimedia products will be sold is being taken in hand by determined entrepreneurs.

These are some of the issues we examine in more detail below.

Books While U Wait

Paul Hilts
Technology Editor, *Publishers Weekly*

John Mutter
Executive Editor, Bookselling, *Publishers Weekly*

Sally Taylor
Far East Correspondent, *Publishers Weekly*

Here's one scenario for a bookstore of the not-so-distant future: In a small space, proprietors stock one copy of each book they can supply for the customer; some stores forgo sample copies altogether and have only a catalog. When a customer wants a book, the bookseller asks the customer's preferences: What typeface and size, what color and grade of paper, plain or fancy binding? Once these and other matters are decided, the bookseller presses a few buttons on the in-store printer. Within minutes, the book, whose digitally encoded text is transferred via modem from the publisher or is stored in the machine having been scanned earlier, is printed out and bound in the store. The finished book can look as handsome as anything currently available through traditional book manufacturing and distribution—and this includes books with color pictures and illustrations.

Seem far-fetched? A look at on-demand printing, which swept college campuses in 1993, proves that the technology is nearly in place. As this movement continues in 1994, it raises some interesting questions for trade publishers, wholesalers, general booksellers, and even writers.

Coursepacks—customized textbooks that are electronically assembled and printed at or near the campus—are now the fastest-growing area in the college store world, according to *Campus Marketplace,* the National Association of College Stores' weekly newsletter. NACS's most recent sales data for the industry show that sales in October 1993 of "custom-published/locally produced materials" rose 148.1 percent over October 1992, the tenth month in a row that total sales dollars in this category had risen.

Many campus stores and nearby copying shops are doing coursepacks: Stanford and Southern Cal are among the largest campus custom publishing operations. One example of what a store can do with the new technology is offered by the Cornell Campus Store at Cornell University, where sales of coursepacks grew 30 percent during the fall semester (3.5 million impressions in course packets from 80,000 different originals). Cornell is one of the few stores doing coursepacks electronically. It is also doing them completely legally.

Cornell uses a Documents on Demand system manufactured by Xerox and prints on a Xerox DocuTech Network Publisher Model 90. The material is scanned and stored electronically. The system has been in use since fall 1992. "About three-quarters of the material is data used in previous semesters," explains Rod Perkins, Cornell's digital-imaging specialist. "Each semester it is fine-tuned, and the reprints can save time in copyright clearance and electronic scanning. As professors become more aware of our service, more are using it."

Cornell's coursepacks generally include articles from newspapers and periodicals, sections of books, and papers by faculty members. Heavy paper stock is used for covers and most of the jobs are three-hole-punched and shrink-wrapped, although 40 percent are perfect-bound and 1 percent are plastic spiral-bound. In the bookstore, coursepacks are shelved with other titles required for a particular course. The Cornell Business School is the single-largest customer.

The store has been able to reduce waste to 7 percent. In cases where the store has printed too few copies, reprints can be made easily and quickly, drawing on the data stored in the system's optical disc "jukebox."

The Cornell Campus Store charges 5 cents a page for production services and a binding fee. Even though copyright fees can raise the cost of coursepacks to the range of conventional textbooks, they are preferred by professors, according to Jim Lawrence, manager of electronic publishing.

Cornell is aboveboard about copyrights, says Lawrence. "All the material is analyzed for copyright needs and the data is entered into the system's management computer, which automatically generates letters for copyright approvals." The store uses the Copyright Clearance Center as much as possible. (CCC charges 0.75 cents per page.) Otherwise, the store goes directly to publishers for copyright clearances, and the store usually pays whatever the publisher asks. However, "if the publisher wants 15 cents a page," Lawrence says, "the professor will usually opt to put the book on reserve at the library."

Broadening Markets

The market for instant books is now broadening to scholarly publishers. John Paeglow and two partners formed Integrated Book Technology (IBT) three years ago to fulfill a new need for electronic printing.

"Publishers were constantly requesting lower quantities (for reprints)," Paeglow says. "At these low quantities, it wouldn't pay to set up a conventional binding line. The only machine we found to be satisfactory for the quality we wanted was a Xerox DocuTech. Then Jim Ryan, one of my partners, came up with a binding solution incorporating library repair techniques. We've tested the binding and found it is stronger than Smyth-sewn."

Some of the most highly respected scholarly publishers—including Cambridge University Press, John Wiley, and Marcel-Dekker—are now using IBT for reprints and very-short-run originals.

Richard Hollick, Cambridge University Press production director, says, "We'll reprint 30 copies of a book, just to have stock on hand. The unit cost is higher than printing 1,000 copies conventionally, but by reducing the minimum run we can keep books in print indefinitely. In 1991, for example, we had orders for 24,000 units we could not fill because the books were out of print.

"While we have only done about 50 titles so far with IBT, the potential of never having a book out of print and never having overstock would make a tremendous impact on our total economic picture," Hollick says.

Bill Clockel at John Wiley & Sons reports a 50 percent increase in these short-run high-quality reprints since last year. The company is now doing 15 titles a month.

"One of the big applications of this will be global utilization," says Clockel. "Instead of sending books to Asia and Europe, we'll be able to send files. The DocuTech is good at reproducing exactly the same image every time from a file." IBT's Paeglow is also beginning to work with Xerox to develop other production sites around the country.

Brave New Bookstore

This leads us back to the scenario of the on-demand general trade bookstore. While the technology will soon be available, tradition and customers' love of the ambiance of bookstores could inhibit the growth of such modernistic retailing.

Imagine what would happen if all bookstores converted to on-demand, in-store printing. Printing plants wouldn't be necessary. Wholesalers would have no books to stock and distribute. Publishers' warehouses would not be needed. Reps might still call on stores, but not so much to sell to stores as to help stores sell. Publishers would still edit and market titles, but they might lose the tight control they now have over what the book looks like and how it reaches the ultimate customer.

Among the many advantages of this brave new book world: a sale would be a sale—returns would no longer exist; publishers wouldn't need to tie up money in inventory; paper would not be wasted; freight costs would vanish; a book would never have to go out of print or out of stock. In addition, the new technology could be a boon for independents. With on-demand printing, they could claim to offer as many titles as chain superstores currently offer today. A shop the size of the smallest of today's bookstores could "stock" a million titles.

Some high hurdles stand in the way of these new bookstores: redefining the relationships among the various elements in the bookselling chain of publisher, printer, distributor, and bookseller; attitudes of the bookseller toward being involved with printing; and consumers' feelings about the bookstore and their demand for "instant books." The music industry is dealing with these issues, too, and its experience might be instructive for booksellers.

Much like on-demand printing, on-demand "pressing" of music CDs has already been proposed. Earlier this year IBM and Blockbuster Entertainment announced two joint ventures to make and dispense music CDs on demand, both in Blockbuster stores and in other retail outlets. (Making the CD would take about six minutes, IBM and Blockbuster estimate.)

The joint ventures were received coolly by music publishers, according to an article in December's *Musician* magazine, more because they challenged a well-defined business structure from which the publishers and distributors profited than because of significant fears about the new technology. The publishers say that this new system could make their current manufacturing and distribution capabilities redundant—perhaps useless. They don't object to the idea of better access to obscure titles; they just want to be the ones controlling the dollars.

One crucial issue concerning the acceptance of the custom CDs as well as custom books is who decides what goes into the custom product, and who will profit. Even though IBM and Blockbuster announced that they intend the system to copy whole CDs intact, the music publishers are wary of technology that would allow songs to be mixed and matched from various albums. McGraw-Hill's Primis electronic custom publishing system was similarly hobbled by other publishers that wanted to keep control over their copyrights and would not release materials to be included in a McGraw-Hill product, even though they knew they would be paid proper royalties, not only on hot items but also on items that never sold well before.

This limited availability of titles might also hobble consumers' acceptance of custom electronic products. In the late 1980s they showed little enthusiasm for an experiment by which they could create audiotapes in booths supplied by Personics Corp. in some Tower Records shops. The company offered a limited selection because of difficulties getting copyrights from publishers, and customers seemed to prefer to buy the prepackaged tapes.

Crossing Over

Of course, even assuming there is a wholesale changeover among retailers to on-demand printing, there are many areas where the new technology wouldn't completely wash away the old forms. Certainly on-demand printing would make sense for many backlist and midlist titles, for which demand is steady but without a concentrated rush at any given time. For blockbuster titles, however, huge demand concentrated within a relatively short period would make printing in-store less attractive, mainly because of the amount of time required.

An alternate view is that the crossover from collegiate bookstores to trade stores might first come in mass market paperbacks. There has been a shift in attitude in recent years among bookstore clients, from being "book readers" to being "book consumers." The distinction is that consumers buy more, but want to do so at the lowest possible price, regardless of quality of production or point of purchase—from book clubs, chain stores, or drugstores.

If the largest single piece of a book's cost is distribution, then eliminating the cost of warehousing and distribution by truck and rail will lead to greater profits for the publisher, and lower cost to the buyer—which might be just the market impetus necessary to force the issue.

Wholesalers on the Hot Seat

Overall, the effect of new technology would be to rationalize the business, increase competition, improve service, and allow for more flexible marketing decisions. But revolutionary change doesn't come easily. Of all segments of the book industry, traditional printing and distribution companies are the most aware of the new technology and have the most to lose.

Wholesalers are expanding their traditional bounds: nearly every wholesaler is now a marketer as well, offering a slew of buying programs, catalogs, recommendations, and more to booksellers. Ingram Book Co., for example, is putting more emphasis on its Publisher Resources Inc. subsidiary, which acts as a distributor in the Publishers Group West mode.

Wholesalers who want to fill their traditional role could specialize, cultivating nonbookstore outlets such as cooking stores, gift shops, and other places outside the traditional trade sales channels (the costs of a printer wouldn't be justified for a few shelves of garden books at the garden center, for example). Wholesalers could print books themselves, too. Mail-order books, particularly from book clubs, by definition, would require some use of traditional printing.

Even the world's largest printer is adapting. R. R. Donnelley has a *Books on Demand* software program that operates much like Cornell's coursepack program. Donnelley also has taken other measures, including the purchase of printer Haddon Craftsman, in large part because Haddon adds a computerized fulfillment system that can provide a range of services, from taking orders to shipping books directly to bookstores.

Last year saw the first real impact of on-demand delivery in collegiate coursepacks. Because the campus bookstore and the university press have interlocking spheres of influence, look for the further entrenchment of coursepacks, but also the expansion of demand into scholarly publishing, and perhaps even into some trade shops that serve local campus needs.

The wave of the future is hitting shore already, and the biggest push may come from end-users. When readers understand what it means to be able to get any title in a matter of minutes at their local "bookstore," those in the industry who are prepared will fare the best.

New Alliances for New Media

Jim Milliot

Business and Finance Editor, *Publishers Weekly*

Evolution, not revolution, should be the hallmark of the book business in 1994, as trends that began developing in 1993 continue. And if these trends accelerate, the convergence of the industry—both its publishing and retail sides—with other segments of the media industry could advance significantly.

In many ways 1993 can be characterized as the year of alliances in the book business, both in traditional and nontraditional ways. As is traditional, certain book publishers were acquired by others; most notable were the purchase of Macmillan by Paramount and of Price Stern Sloan by Putnam Berkley. But there were less traditional alliances formed as well that may presage the direction of the book business. Random House engaged in two electronic publishing joint ventures—one with Broderbund to form Living Books and the other through Fodor's and Worldview Systems to create electronic Fodor's guides. Another unique partnership resulted from Bertelsmann's decision to back financially the new media unit at Bantam Doubleday Dell competitor Putnam Berkley. The potential benefits of combining print and electronic media were also a factor in the Tribune Company's purchase of a traditional book publisher, Contemporary, as well as a leader in multimedia publishing and distribution, Compton's NewMedia.

The year of alliances, however, was illustrated most dramatically, if still inconclusively, by the battle for Paramount. Both Viacom and QVC saw Paramount, with its array of copyrighted properties, as a linchpin in their respective plans to prepare for the multimedia future. A similar need to own more intellectual properties is what is driving Putnam to become even bigger in the book business, by following up the purchase of Price Stern Sloan, potentially, with that of Morrow and Avon. Putnam is just one aspect of the "software side" of parent company's Matsushita empire, which includes Universal Pictures and MCA Records. When Matsushita acquired MCA its aim was to ensure that it would always have access to the content that was played on its machines (such as VCRs). The development of multimedia, with its dependency on content, will further encourage Matsushita to look for ways to join its various copyright properties together.

Importance of Size Re-emerges

While the potential of multimedia is a powerful—if somewhat risky—incentive for publishers and their parent companies to expand their copyright holdings, mergers and acquisitions of various parts of the book and media industry are likely to increase for some old-fashioned reasons: Money is available at low rates and companies are again viewing size as a crucial factor in survival. In the trade book industry in particular, if Putnam does indeed buy the Hearst book properties of Morrow and Avon, the ranks of the largest trade houses will be changed significantly. The new round of mergers and acquisitions has created seven giant trade houses with revenues of over $250 million while thinning the ranks of the moderate to large publishers (those with sales between $100 million and $250 million) to two—St. Martin's and Houghton Mifflin. St. Martin's is making its own effort to expand, although without an acquisition it will be hard-pressed to keep pace with its larger competitors.

The question is whether there are any existing companies that are ready to move into the second tier of moderate to large publishers. Candidates include a crop of independents such as Workman, Andrews & McMeel, Norton, and Zebra. But the more likely scenario is that the next company to grow its book revenues significantly will be run by a major conglomerate. Turner is one possibility, but the company appears more intent on building its movie and television businesses than its print holdings. Microsoft has been an aggressive player in acquiring electronic rights and owns a stake in Dorling Kindersley, but to date has shown no serious interest in broadening its book group beyond the publication of computer books. This leaves Disney. Disney has the resources and the apparent motivation to increase the size of its book group. In conjunction with Harcourt General, Disney was involved in trying to buy Macmillan and took a look at Morrow and Avon. Its motivation for getting involved in books is the same as that of other media conglomerates—it has the ability to leverage content through a variety of distribution formats that, in addition to books, include movies, television programs, and theme parks. Unlike some of its competitors, such as Time Warner, which is interested in building both the superhighway and providing content for it, Disney's strategy is to add to its ownership of content, theorizing that the owners of the superhighway will come to it.

Terra Incognita for Booksellers

On the retail side of the industry, alliances and expansion are also in vogue, but here the participants are navigating uncharted territories. To help combat superstores, two sets of independents broke new ground by establishing buying consortiums during 1993. In July, 21 of the largest independent booksellers formed the Independent Booksellers Consortium in an effort to receive the best terms possible from publishers. Later in the year the book franchise company Little Professor announced that it was establishing the Alliance of Independent Booksellers in an effort to receive higher discounts. If these efforts prove at all successful, it is certain more alliance-building among independents will take place.

The move by independents to form alliances among themselves comes in the face of the unprecedented competition from superstores. The ability of superstores to generate sales was proven in 1993, although what has not been clearly demonstrated is whether superstores will turn significant profits, how profitable superstores can be, and how much they increase the size of the overall book market. Among the chains that operate a large number of superstores—Barnes & Noble, Borders, Crown, Books-A-Million—the growth in sales at the giant outlets is impressive. At Barnes & Noble, Books-A-Million and Crown, superstores are commanding an increasingly larger share of total sales, with superstore sales generating about 48 percent of Barnes & Noble's third-quarter sales and 40 percent at Crown. Both chains expect superstores to account for over 50 percent of sales in 1994. In addition, the superstore-only chain, Borders, had the largest growth of any of the major chains in 1993, with sales up almost 80 percent for the first nine months of the year.

The rapid growth in sales, however, has not meant growth in profits. On the contrary, the costs of opening new superstores have cut into margins at Crown, while Barnes & Noble and Borders operated at a loss through the first nine months of the year, as did Encore Books, which is establishing its own superstore presence. While start-up costs were expected, investors will want to see signs that the superstore strategy can bring profits as well as sales.

The debate over whether superstores expand the market or cannibalize it is being fought only with anecdotal information. On the negative side of the ledger are the flat results from Waldenbooks and Barnes & Noble's mall stores. In addition, scattered reports of independents closing up shop continue to come in, and the explanation for going out of business is usually the same: a weak economy and the competition of superstores. And while the Commerce Department reports that nine-month bookstore sales were up 6 percent through September, that increase is actually behind the 16 percent growth the six major chains posted in their first nine months of the year. The figure was made all the more impressive at the chains since it did not include January 1993, a very strong month for booksellers, topping out at over $1 billion in sales. On the positive side, there are few signs that independents will be closing en masse, and many of the formerly healthy, well-established independents are reportedly still doing well.

Chicago as Microcosm

The city of Chicago was a microcosm of the nationwide bookstore battle, and by the end of the year a decisive blow was struck there: the sale of Kroch's & Brentano's.

It became clear very early in 1993 that there was no way the Chicago market was going to be able to absorb the huge growth in bookstore space that took place when virtually every major superstore chain opened outlets in the area. Before too long, Kroch's & Brentano's, complacent after dominating the market yet without the technical and financial resources of its competitors, was forced into a major downsizing that led to its eventual sale. The lessons are clear. Bookselling continues to be an extremely competitive business, where survival depends on the booksellers' market acumen. And even that may not be enough for independent booksellers who are unlucky enough to be confronted by multiple superstore openings in their area.

The acquisition of Kroch's by Businessship International, however, may also be a precursor to the new challenges confronting all book retailers. Businessship plans to use Kroch's as a base for expanding—perhaps into multimedia. And the signs are clear that independents and chains will have to compete not only among themselves but also with other merchants selling a variety of entertainment and education products.

Musicland is aggressively opening Media Play and On Cue stores, outlets that carry books as well as music and other electronic goods. Learningsmith is steadily increasing its presence and, in the view of some analysts, has such a strong business strategy that it will be a candidate for going public by 1995. And while giant Blockbuster remains on the sidelines in the book business, it is testing the multimedia waters. If multimedia proves successful, the sale of complementary book items at Blockbuster would not be a surprise.

Booksellers are already responding to challenges from other retailers. Borders offers a large selection of music in many of its outlets. And late last year multimedia publishers teamed up with Apple to test the sale of their titles in a variety of bookstores including Barnes & Noble, Tower Books, and The Tattered Cover. The book retail industry appears headed toward a future where stores will become information centers, supplying customers with an array of entertainment and education products in a variety of formats.

Moving Forward

Executives in both the publishing and retailing segments of the industry will be devoting more of their time and effort to determining what the new media mean for their respective industries. While few expect 1994 to be a breakthrough year for multimedia, publishers and booksellers will be looking to see how far the new media combinations have advanced. An early indicator is favorable: computer hardware sales were reportedly brisk during Christmas. An increase in installed machines is crucial if the multimedia market is to become a mass market, something many of the largest publishers are waiting to see before making commitments.

Another object of study for executives will be the profitability of companies in the multimedia market. Some bellwether efforts to follow are Living Books, Putnam NewMedia and Compton's. Compton's indicates some of the promise and, at the moment, frustrations of the multimedia market. Sales of the company, which is regarded as one of the major players in the multimedia field, are a rather modest $28 million.

This may or may not be a watershed year for the book industry's relationships with other media industries, but it is not unreasonable to assume that the foundation for a new publishing business will be laid.

Special Reports

Libraries and the National Information Infrastructure

Peter R. Young

Executive Director

Jane Williams

Research Associate

U.S. National Commission on Libraries and Information Science
1110 Vermont Ave. N.W., Suite 820, Washington, DC 20005
202-606-9200

> Turning and turning in the widening gyre
> The falcon cannot hear the falconer;
> Things fall apart; the centre cannot hold;
> Mere anarchy is loosed upon the world,
> The blood-dimmed tide is loosed, and everywhere
> The ceremony of innocence is drowned;
> The best lack all conviction, while the worst
> Are full of passionate intensity. . . .
>
> And what rough beast, its hour come round at last,
> Slouches towards Bethlehem to be born?
>
> —William Butler Yeats, "The Second Coming"[1]

Like the image in Yeats's poem "The Second Coming," many in the library and information fields sense that they are "turning and turning in the widening gyre" of the electronic frontier. Increasingly soft distinctions among library services, interactive multimedia communications, and information networks raise concerns about future library roles. Some express fear that "the centre cannot hold" and that library roles will diminish in a flood of new commercial information services. Others see interactive multimedia and network technologies providing the potential for transforming libraries and social interrelationships in general. Forecasting the impact of revolutionary change on the library of the future from today's perspective, however, is as difficult as defining Yeats's image of a

Note: The authors' views and opinions in this report do not necessarily represent official policies or positions of the U.S. National Commission on Libraries and Information Science or the U.S. government.

"rough beast, its hour come round at last" that is slouching toward the twenty-first century to be born.

Aside from any reaction from the library community to announcements about the "information superhighway," the general public is increasingly conditioned to anticipate a radical transformation in computer-mediated communications and network services. Will this transformation produce a "mere anarchy" of new interactive multimedia services that are like a "blood-dimmed tide"? Do libraries really "lack all conviction" in the face of the "passionate intensity" of commercial competition for interactive service markets?

Will policymakers address the role of the library, even as they focus legislative and regulatory attention on removing the barriers for telephone companies, cable television broadcasters, and telecommunications firms to compete against one another in the rapidly expanding field of information networks? Will new interactive media service offerings result in the decline of libraries in a future where we amuse ourselves to death with "infotainment" ("Things fall apart; the centre cannot hold")? Or will libraries play an integral role in the emerging information and communications infrastructure, allowing for the continued free public expression of ideas that is essential to the maintenance of our democratic community? These issues and questions are increasingly of concern to those in the library community. These same topics are the basis for this special report.

The report examines the influence of network communications technology within a rapidly progressing movement to construct, organize, and evolve a national information infrastructure. The report attempts to project the impact of networking technology and changing telecommunications policy on the functions, services, and missions of libraries. It also reviews the prospects for national information policies that balance public with private interests through proposed changes in federal regulatory functions and statutory authority relating to universal communications services and affordable access to information.

The article examines prospects for libraries within the emerging national information infrastructure by identifying various issues arising from a consideration of the opportunities and challenges associated with the development of a national "information superhighway." Opportunities and threats for libraries are explored and possible strategies for relating libraries to the information infrastructure are identified. Information policy issues are reviewed that may influence the nature, extent, and involvement of libraries in the formation of global digital information network services and in the emergence of commercial markets for network services, including services based on networked interactive multimedia technologies. Finally, the concept of the networked interactive multimedia digital library is explored within the context of civic networks for possible future development and evolution.

Information Network Infrastructure Development

Like reports in previous editions of the *Bowker Annual*, this article addresses trends and developments affecting library and information services resulting from the convergence of computing and network communication technologies.

Previous reports addressing issues related to this topic include Clifford A. Lynch's 1991 "Visions of Electronic Libraries"[2] and Charles R. McClure et al.'s 1993 "Toward a Virtual Library: Internet and the National Research and Education Network."[3] The current report builds on themes and observations included in these earlier special reports. Unlike these earlier reports, which explore the vision of electronic and virtual libraries as an extension of traditional library functions and services, this report focuses on libraries within a developing infrastructure that functions as "a seamless web of communications networks, computers, databases, and consumer electronics that will put vast amounts of information at users' fingertips."[4] Whether we understand it or not, the public's perceptions of the "information superhighway" will have a fundamental impact on their relationships with and expectations for libraries.

Visions of electronic or virtual libraries do not necessarily depend upon the concept of an information infrastructure within the social context of a public communications architecture. The metaphor of Internet as an electronic highway is useful for differentiating this distinction. Internet has been compared to "a blisteringly fast, multilane roadway where the vehicles are traveling in at least three dimensions at once, the directional signage changes all the time, and there are no rest stops."[5]

An "information infrastructure" implies a conceptual analogy that incorporates all facets and aspects of transportation systems and the structures supporting these systems, regardless of the specific mode of transportation. Thus the information infrastructure analogy cannot be confined to the national interstate highway system. The U.S. Office of Technology Assessment (OTA) is explicit in defining the "communications infrastructure" as "the underlying structure of technical facilities and institutional arrangements that supports communication via telecommunication, broadcasting, film, audio, and video recording, cable, print, and mail."[6] Similarly, the Clinton administration assigns an expansive meaning to the phrase "information infrastructure" in characterizing it to include

> A wide range and ever-expanding range of equipment including cameras, scanners, keyboards, telephones, fax machines, computers, switches, compact disks, video and audio tape, cable, wire, satellites, optical fiber transmission lines, microwave nets, switches, televisions, monitors, printers, and much more.[7]

A national information infrastructure is seen to integrate and interconnect physical components to provide an advanced technological foundation for living in the Information Age and to make these technological advances useful to the public, libraries, business, and other nongovernmental entities. The value of this information infrastructure to users thus depends on the quality of the information, the applications and access software, the network standards and transmission codes, and those who create the information and construct the facilities, applications, and services. We are moving away from the information highway toward a wider concentration on communications infrastructure. Similarly, in the terms of the "information superhighway" analogy, our attention is shifting from the lanes of the roadbed to the impact of networking technologies on social interaction within the global community.

Background on Internet, NREN, and NII

Over the past several years, network telecommunications links between information resources and users have generated excitement and concern within the library community. This interest builds on the increasingly important influence of digital computing and network communication on library functions over several decades. These traditional library functions relate to the acquisition, organization, access, delivery, retrieval, presentation, and preservation of information resources. Such technological influences are justified by the library investment in automating internal systems and processes. The library community's interest in Internet capabilities and potential has centered primarily on the use of computer networks to improve the sharing of resources, access to information, and the dissemination of documents. These functions extend and build upon traditional services offered by libraries to patrons and to other institutions.

More recently, the commercial media and telecommunications industries have shown increasing interest in the development of services supported by a national "information superhighway." These services combine the interactive switching functionality of telephone service with the multimedia bandwidth capabilities of cable television. The potential formation of global information service markets motivates commercial interests to explore service development using electronic transcontinental information thoroughfares.

The explosive growth of Internet use, estimated to be increasing at the rate of 20 percent per month, is attracting the attention of commercial interests based on the logarithmic growth of Internet's 6,000 domestic regional, state, and local networks in the United States connected to more than 2 million host systems worldwide. This growth is maintained by Internet's interconnection of over 12,000 networks worldwide, providing global network interconnections to an estimated 17 million users. Development of Internet navigational tools and software agents responds to a growing demand from network users. Such services include the World Wide Web (WWW) hypertext-based search system for linking related documents and servers; gopher access by menu-based search facilities; Internet file transfer protocol (ftp) allowing access, retrieval, and movement for remote archives of text files, software, graphics, and other types of documents and files; as well as Wide Area Information Server (WAIS), Archie, Veronica, and Rosebud services.

It is becoming commonplace to read newspaper stories and articles in mass market journals about revolutionary commercial alliances that promise a futuristic array of information and entertainment services available in the home. These articles reflect widespread public interest in interactive multimedia services that combine the capabilities of the telephone with cable video services and high-performance computers. The continued rapid development in Internet use, increased network service functionality, and announcements about major federal investment to develop the "information superhighway" seem to have all but eclipsed the concept and intent of the National Research and Education Network (NREN), which was originally conceived as a federal initiative to extend U.S. technology leadership in computer communications through a program of research and development designed to advance the leading edge of networking technology and services. NREN was not originally conceived as a general-purpose communications network. However, the emerging concept of a national information infrastructure constitutes a different transitional stage of technology moving toward a fundamental transformation in those communications, commercial entertainment, and information transfer functions that are inherent to human interactions and interrelationships.

There is a growing realization that the original interests represented by federal investment in technology research and development for interconnecting computer networks are shifting toward an emphasis on commercial investment and innovation. The information infrastructure involves not just technology; it also incorporates the human skills and the content resources required to establish, organize, and sustain communication functions throughout society. Individual and institutional communication functions constitute an essential component of social interaction and form the core of community. The communications infrastructure consists of that human and capital investment that is involved with the technical, economic, and cultural basis of organized society.

The technology perspective associated with the information infrastructure concentrates attention on the nature of the conduit that functions as the roadbed for the "information superhighway." The telephone and cable companies propose to build the on and off ramps, as well as the toll booths, on the new highways using existing copper wire, fiber optic cable, and coaxial cable, or some combination of these technologies, perhaps also incorporating microwave transmission and satellite communications technologies. The economic perspective on the information infrastructure concentrates attention on the nature of industrial and commercial interests forming new alliances that will use the conduit of the "information superhighways" to deliver content, programming, and services to customers and institutions. The cultural perspective concentrates attention on the values and expectations that are reflected by the policies and political agendas related to the formation of the "information superhighway."

Recent popularization of the "information superhighway" reflects growing public response to the commercial interest in developing new markets for network infrastructure-based services. The topic is attracting the attention of editorial writers, conference speakers, and others in the library and information services community and beyond. The digital interstate "high-speed" superhighway and the interactive multimedia marketplace are the subject of recent feature stories in *Time*,[8] *Scientific American*,[9] and *Newsweek*.[10] These articles promise that major cable operators and telephone companies will soon bring a "communicopia" of information services to the neighborhoods of America. They also include warnings about new corporate partnerships made in preparation for range wars over control of the new information pipelines. Observations about the potential of new information technologies for fundamentally altering creativity itself by forging virtual communities are also included in these popular articles, with predictions that the "information superhighway" will redefine the normal sense of community, the pace of intellectual life, and the very nature of knowledge itself.

The various institutional, state, commercial, and federal roles and agendas associated with information and communications are undergoing a fundamental shift in relation to the development of digital high-capacity, high-speed communications networks. Reviews of major recent legislative, regulatory, and administration proposals and policies relating to the building and organizing of a national information superhighway reveal an economic and competitive justification for encouraging commercial investment in developing services based on a digital services network infrastructure. The principles and policies supporting development of digital information communication services and network infrastructure policies have a direct relationship to the roles that libraries will assume within the emerging information infrastructure.

Never has there been a more exciting, confusing, troublesome, or potentially more transformational development involving the future of the library than the recent convergence of computing and telecommunications technologies. The transformational nature of this convergence affects all aspects of the information creation-dissemination-consumption process, from authoring to retrieving. The institutional consequences of this transformation are causing deep soul-searching and examination by librarians and other information professionals, as public policy and private industry representatives move rapidly forward to implement change.

The movement toward a national information and communication infrastructure based on digital technologies is closely related to the enactment of PL 102-194, the High-Performance Computing (HPC) Act of 1991, and specifically, provisions in Title I of that act calling for the development of a national research and education network (NREN). These developments involve policy decisions that bridge both telecommunications and information policy concerns. The HPC program evolved out of the recognition in the early 1980s that advanced computer and telecommunications technologies could provide huge benefits throughout the research community and the entire U.S. economy. NREN is planned to extend U.S. technology leadership in computer communications by a program of research and development that advances the leading edge of networking technology and services. NREN will widen the research and education community's access to high-performance computing and research centers and to electronic information resources and libraries.

Federal, Public, and Private Roles in NII

According to a recent *New York Times* article, a record number of corporate mergers occurred in 1993. In fact, the Securities Data Company[11] reported that the total value of corporate mergers in the third quarter of 1993 was $86.77 billion, almost triple that of the third quarter of 1992. The number of billion-dollar megamergers in this year's third quarter was the second-highest on record, with 12 deals valued at a total of $54.5 billion, up more than sevenfold from a year earlier. Not only are there more deals, the deals are bigger. Not surprisingly, telecommunications and the motion picture industry were dominant themes. The largest deal of the quarter was the American Telephone and Telegraph Company's acquisition of McCaw Cellular Communications Inc. for $17.6 billion. If the players are able to complete their current series of mergers in time, the fourth quarter of 1993 will reflect even bigger billion-dollar deals with the announcement of a $33 billion merger between Raymond W. Smith's Bell Atlantic and John C. Malone's TeleCommunication Inc.[12] The situation remains unresolved.

These frantic billion-dollar deals reflect strategic corporate realignments motivated by a vision of global media market dominance. These empires are based on vertically integrating and segmenting the emerging interactive multimedia services commercial marketplace. Corporate investments, competition, alliances, and partnerships are forming through the convergence of telephones, computers, and television for applications such as video-conferencing and home shopping services. This new virtual services marketplace is estimated to be worth hundreds of billions of dollars a year.

Besides the Bell Atlantic–TCI deal, some of the recent high-profile activity includes the following:

- High-stakes bidding by Viacom (a cable television programming and media company) with help from Blockbuster Entertainment Corp. (the video rental store chain) and Nynex (the regional Bell operating company that owns New York Telephone and New England Telephone) against QVC Network (which operates a home shopping service) partnered with TeleCommunication Inc. (the largest cable television company in the United States), in an effort to purchase Paramount Communications Inc. (an entertainment empire that includes professional sports teams, book publishing houses, and the last major independent movie studio in America)

- The partnership of Continental Cablevision Inc. (the nation's third-largest cable television company) with Performance Systems International Inc. (the nation's largest provider of commercial access to Internet) to offer an interactive data service linking 2.9 million customers to Internet

- US West's investment of $2.5 billion in Time Warner (owner of Home Box Office with 7 million cable subscribers), which means that the regional Bell operating company will develop advanced technology for consumer video services

- Spiegel Inc. (the catalog company with large-scale order fulfillment and distribution operations) teaming up with Time Warner (operating cable systems in 36 states serving 7.1 million customers) to create two home shopping interactive cable channels for "video shopping mail" services that will allow "Catalog Channel" customers to call up any "virtual store" on a television screen, view merchandise from all angles, and place orders interactively[13]

- The plan by Comcast Corporation (the nation's third-largest cable provider and fifth-largest independent cellular phone company) to link wireless communications services to its cable networks[14]

- Rupert Murdoch's acquisition of Delphi Internet Services[15] to provide a global gateway to Internet services, together with his acquisition of Star TV, a satellite broadcasting system based in Hong Kong that reaches 38 countries, which provide Murdoch's News Corp. with capability to extend satellite programming to two-thirds of the planet's population[16]

The list of commercial alliances, cross-industry mergers, and global rivalries is almost endless. Hardly any commercial high-stakes player doubts the rapid emergence of the global marketplace combining elements of the entertainment, media, cable TV, telecommunications, and digital network system industries. The competitive action between the cable operators and the telephone companies is not confined to corporate board rooms, however. The presence of government regulation is an important factor in these developing megamarkets.

An indication of the sensitivity of the communications industry toward government involvement can be seen from comments made at a Washington summit meeting held October 20, 1993, involving Bell Atlantic, AT&T, MCI Communications, and Apple Computer.[17] The message to Washington from this industry gathering was that government should not get in the way. "It's impossible for regulators to move as quickly and effectively as the private sector," said John Sculley. The former chairman of Apple Computer added: "Government needs to give the private sector a green light to go ahead with investment and innovation."

As increasingly sensitive and complex battles are waged in the federal regulatory and statutory arenas, the issue of public interest becomes more apparent. A *New York Times* article about the antitrust implications of the Bell Atlantic–TeleCommunication Inc. proposed merger mentions these concerns.

> Out of the spotlight, some industry executives said today that the trend toward cable-telephone alliances could lead to a world in which a few big conglomerates restrained competition, behaving like geopolitical superpowers that avoid direct confrontation through a policy akin to the "mutual assured destruction" philosophy that at times underpinned the cold war buildup by the United States and the Soviet Union but also helped keep each power too frightened to attack the other.[18]

At present, to the outsider, the results of these commercial activities are unclear. What is clear, however, is that serious consequences could result from these mergers for those dependent upon the library and information services community.

Libraries and NII

At the Spring 1993 Coalition for Networked Information (CNI) conference in San Francisco, Doug van Houweling, vice provost for information technology at the University of Michigan, questioned whether future federal involvement in networking would "follow the vision or follow the bottom line." He asked who will guard the public interest in an increasingly business-oriented network environment. This concern is not unfounded. It is based on the historic development of Internet through federal funding and involvement. Before we explore the nature of civic or community networking, a bit of background history of network development would be helpful.

Craig A. Summerhill's article on the "Impact of Technology on Resource Sharing" is an excellent summary of this history:

> The term "Internet" with a capital "I" refers specifically to the DARPA Internet. The National Science Foundation (NSF) established six national supercomputing centers in 1984. In order to provide researchers with better access to these resources, NSF initiated a program to link

these computing centers via a network called NSFNet. Since Open Systems Interconnection standard (OSI) was not widely available, NSF adopted the TCP/IP protocol suite for use on NSFNet. NSFNet was built upon a three-tiered network topology: (1) a national backbone consisting of switching hubs in NSF supercomputing sites, (2) regional (mid-level) networks linking municipalities and organizations in like geographic regions of the country to the NSFNet backbone sites, and (3) local area networks linking individual organizations (universities, colleges, military sites, businesses) to the national network via the mid-level regionals.[19]

Following passage of the High-Performance Computing Act of 1991 (PL 102-194) in December 1991, the National Research and Education Network (NREN) authorized federal funding for research and development in advanced computing and networking applications. The Interagency Interim NREN (IIN-REN) is a term that is increasingly used to refer to the existing Internet. This IIN-REN is a hierarchy of networks ranging from high-speed, cross-country networks, to regional and mid-level networks, to state and campus network systems. The major federal components of IINREN are the national research agency networks: NSF's NSFNet, the Department of Energy's Energy Sciences Network (ESNet), and the National Aeronautics and Space Administration's NASA Science Internet (NSI). These agencies' networks constitute national network backbones that are planned to collaborate in attaining NREN's gigabit speeds.[20]

Released on September 15, 1993, by the Information Infrastructure Task Force, the document titled *The National Information Infrastructure: Agenda for Action* sets forth the Clinton administration's agenda for developing an advanced National Information Infrastructure that "can help unleash an information revolution that will change forever the way people live, work, and interact with each other."

Clearly, the developmental history of ARPANET, Internet, NREN, and now NII involves federal funding, regulation, standards, research and development, as well as private-sector investment incentives for advanced telecommunications and computing innovation. Throughout the uneven development of the existing network information infrastructure, the federal role has provided an essential focus through which commercial investments have produced the technology and standards required for development and deployment of a national system. This federal role is crucial for the future, but it is far from clear just how it will evolve and develop.

Chuck McClure, in a recent talk on network literacy, expressed this concern:

Until the Clinton administration, the federal policy framework for creating the Internet/NREN has emphasized the development of new networking technologies and creating a "level playing field" for the private sector to develop the network. Inadequate policy exists supporting public sector uses of the Internet/NREN. The library and education community had minimal input and impact on developing the NREN plan. The policy framework has promoted the use of the Internet/NREN among researchers and scientists working primarily on "grand challenges" rather than developing it as a "public right" to which all citizens are entitled.[21]

This same concern was expressed in an interview with Paul Evan Peters, executive director of the Coalition for Networked Information, appearing in *Library Administration and Management*:

... it is not clear that libraries are being heard or that our interests are even on the table as national network programs are being developed. As federal funding for libraries is threatened, we must ask ourselves whether we can effectively reorient LSCA and HEA titles to the national network priority and maintain and expand national interest in library development. . . . I also worry that the essential role of individual state and local governments and of individual institutions and organizations in building the "local roads" and "on-and-off-ramps" of the national information "superhighway" will not get the attention it requires as many of us focus our efforts even more than has been the case on the national level.[22]

Further in this interview, Peters talks about the implications of a shift in development responsibilities from NSF to the Commerce Department:

The current Internet is anchored in the United States by the NSFNet, which employs special electronics to enhance the performance of an underlying infrastructure that most folks in the networking trade refer to as "plain old telephone service (POTS)."

The near-future Internet will be anchored in the United States by the NREN program, which will also use special electronics to enhance the performance of POTS. The next-future Internet will likely be anchored in the United States by a marketplace in which numerous for-profit and not-for-profit network providers will use special electronics to enhance the performance of the NII. This conception calls upon the NII to replace POTS, to enable performance and benefits typical of the Internet to be delivered to a population much wider than that which will ever, for a number of reasons, be served by the Internet per se.[23]

The Vision of Civic Networking

Clearly, the networking issues of concern to the library and information services community correspond with those of the communities working toward a public or noncommercial use of the "information superhighway." The Center for Civic Networking defines its concerns as follows:

Grassroots initiatives using information infrastructure to provide civic and community services are influencing new State policies which can in turn shape Federal communication policy for the 21st century. With accelerating social mobility, political representatives serving millions rather than thousands, long commutes to jobs not connected to local communities and increased cultural diversity, traditional community forums for public deliberation have eroded. Civic networking can revitalize them. A definition of civic networking encompasses:

- The transformational power of information infrastructure to create opportunities, new public works and new public spaces for the 21st century
- The "loadbearing" power of information infrastructure to support and even revitalize civic institutions and Local economies in sustainable ways that replace layers of bureaucratic hierarchy and deplete fewer natural resources
- The public's power to use information infrastructure to recapture the nearly lost art of democratic decision-making and community building—the essential discourse and debate around important issues that informs before the vote, where the public shares views, and learns tolerance
- A new interdisciplinary ethic among information architects, community activities, organizers and planners, public policy analysts, facilitators and engineers who, with the public, can reforge the democratic partnership between citizens and the government they own[24]

Civic networks involve community use of computers and telecommunications to provide services that promote access to members of the community. This definition does not address the provision of private commercial network services to users or customers for a fee. Use of the community network infrastructure is not dependent upon technical expertise, profession, official status, or age. The common denominator in civic networking is the common interest of those in the community for using the capabilities of the network infrastructure for community-based activities.

Steve Cisler of Apple Computers describes civic networking activities as follows:

> The information contained in such [community] networks as well as the relationships that form between the participants make up what I call an electronic greenbelt to reinforce and add value to the community. These communities do include a variety of other interest groups whose needs and interests transcend the geographic boundaries of the town, region, or state. The decisions these communities have made are similar, in some ways, to what happened with the spread of electrical networks a century ago.[25]

Cisler continues with a comparison of community computer networks with the spread of electrical networks. Between 1890 and 1920 a discussion took place about the role of electricity, its benefits, how distribution should be accomplished, what standards should govern its use, and whether the electrical generation plants should be public or private. Equity of access to electrical power is comparable to concerns for equity in access to network capabilities, according to this comparison. Cisler continues:

> . . . the electrical infrastructure developed along two basic models: a power grid confined to a geographical area controlled by a local government or a system developed by private corporations whose operations usually crossed city and state boundaries. The latter entities were usually larger than the former. The consolidation of small private utilities produced an enormous production and distribution grid which was efficient but served the populace unequally. These systems produced more electricity than any other in the world, but there was little rural service, special considerations for large customers, and the public utilities commissions were influenced by the power of the holding companies and the publicity campaigns that they were able to mount. This difference between the electrified urban landscape and the under-served rural area contrasted with Europe and New Zealand where there was almost universal service. In America, the electrical networks were a business, whereas in Scandinavia they were also seen as an instrument of social policy. In Europe, for example, electric streetcars were viewed as an essential service and were operated at a loss. In America they were treated as a business.[26]

The role of the government in electrifying America a century ago provides an example of the "datafication" that can transform America through universal availability of community network capability in preparation for the 21st century.

Review of 1993 Legislation and Outlook for 1994

Major legislation on high-performance computing, NREN, and the National Information Infrastructure (NII) was not enacted in the first session of the 103rd Congress. Various bills regarding telecommunications were introduced and the administration was expected to have its versions introduced shortly after the second session convened on January 25, 1994. A predecessor of those bills may be the National Communications Infrastructure bill, H.R. 3635, introduced by Representative Edward Markey (D-Mass.) November 22. A summary of 1993 legislation follows.

S. 4—National Competitiveness Act of 1993

This bill authorizes funds to promote U.S. industrial competitiveness and economic growth by strengthening and expanding the civilian technology programs of the Department of Commerce. Title VI of the bill deals with applications for the proposed National Research and Education Network and is the same as H.R. 1757. The bill was dubbed "NREN II." The full Senate did not act on S. 4.

H.R. 1757—High-Performance Computing and High Speed Networking Applications Act of 1993/National Information Infrastructure Act of 1993

Introduced April 21, 1993, by Representative Rick Boucher (D-Va.) and referred to Committee on Science, Space, and Technology, this bill amends the High Performance Computing Act of 1991, which provided for NREN. The House passed the bill July 26. The bill gives NREN three parts: networking research and development, experimental test-bed networks, and network access support for education, especially K–12, health care, libraries, and government. A National Science Foundation (NSF) program would foster local networks to connect colleges, schools, libraries, museums, and state and local governments to each other and to Internet.

S. 1086—Telecommunications Infrastructure Act of 1993

Introduced June 9 by Senator John Danforth (R-Mo.) and referred to Committee on Commerce, Science, and Transportation, the bill would permit regional Bell operating companies (RBOCs) to provide electronic publishing services through separate subsidies and to own and operate cable TV systems under certain conditions. Hearings were conducted July 14 and September 8. H.R. 1504 is the companion bill.

H.R. 1504—Communications Competitiveness and Infrastructure Modernization Act of 1993

Introduced March 29, 1993, by Representative Boucher and referred to Committee on Energy and Commerce, this is a bill "to encourage the modernization of the Nation's telecommunications infrastructure, to promote competition in the cable television industry and to permit telephone companies to provide video programming." S. 1086 is the companion bill.

H.R. 2639—Telecommunications and Information Infrastructure and Public Broadcasting Facilities Assistance Act of 1993

This bill aims to help spur development of "model communications projects in health-care facilities, rural areas, schools, libraries and museums." The measure would authorize more than $150 million in fiscal 1995 and again in fiscal 1996 for federal grants to communities or organizations that develop innovative uses for a nationwide network of computer "information superhighways." The House approved an amended bill November 8.

H.R. 3635—National Communications Infrastructure

Introduced November 22, 1993, by Representative Edward Markey (D-Mass.) and referred to Committee on Energy and Commerce, the bill would "encourage deployment of advanced communications services through competition." Markey chairs the committee's Subcommittee on Telecommunications and Finance.

S. 626—Electronic Library Act of 1993

Introduced March 22, 1993, by Senator Joseph Kerrey (D-Neb.) and referred to Committee on Commerce, Science, and Transportation, this would establish a system of state-based electronic libraries. There was no action on the bill.

S. 1782—Electronic Freedom of Information Improvement Act of 1993

Introduced November 23 by Senator Patrick Leahy (D-Vt.) and Senator Hank Brown (R-Colo.), this bill was first introduced in 1991. Mr. Leahy's remark included the following:

> New FOIA guidelines are needed to address new issues arising with the increased use of computers. While FOIA covers all Government information in any format, this bill redefines agency records to make that clear, requires an assessment of agency computer capability, and requires agencies to provide requested formats when possible.
> Making Government information readily available electronically on people's computers can help to revitalize citizens' interest in learning what their Government is doing and better their understanding of the reasons underlying Government actions.[27]

Public Law 103-40—Government Printing Office (GPO) Electronic Information Enhancement Act

Signed June 8, this new law requires GPO to maintain a directory of federal electronic information and an electronic storage facility and to provide the *Congressional Record and Federal Register* online. GPO has begun work on all three parts of the act and aims to have its prototype locator in operation by the middle of 1994.

Major Recent Publications Related to NII

As noted above, much was written, said, and discussed in 1993 regarding the new information environment. The stance of the Clinton-Gore administration was confirmed in several publications that set the tone for most of the year's discussions:

- President William J. Clinton, *A Vision of Change for America*, Washington, D.C., February 17, 1993. This report accompanied the president's address to Congress and describes the economic plan the president proposed. The report outlines technology investments in the president's stimulus package, including information highway demonstrations linking libraries, health-care facilities, governments, and other information producers.

- President William J. Clinton and Vice President Albert Gore, Jr., *Technology for America's Economic Growth, A New Direction to Build Economic Strength*, Washington, D.C., February 22, 1993. Viewed by some as the beginnings of industrial policy for this administration, this paper defines movement in a new direction that includes "forging a closer working partnership among industry, federal and state governments, workers, and universities" and "redirecting the focus of our national efforts toward technologies crucial to today's businesses and a growing economy, such as information and communication, flexible manufacturing, and environmental technologies."

- Vice President Al Gore, *From Red Tape to Results: Creating a Government that Works Better & Costs Less,* Washington, D.C., September 7, 1993. This report made 1993 the year in which "NPR" in Washington came to mean the "National Performance Review," the mammoth effort led by the vice president to examine, redefine, and refine the goals and operations of the federal government. "Reinvention" joined the governmental lexicon as well, as agencies began solving the problems pointed out in *From Red Tape to Results* and producing the savings called for. Part of the chapter "Cutting Back to Basics" deals with electronic government: "We will reengineer the work of government agencies in two ways. First, we will expand the use of new technologies . . . Second, we will speed up the adoption of new ways to improve federal operations . . ."

- Information Infrastructure Task Force, *The National Information Infrastructure: Agenda for Action,* Washington, D.C., September 15, 1993. Describing NII as "a seamless web of communications networks, computers, databases, and consumer electronics that will put vast amounts of information at users' fingertips," this report outlines nine of the administration's principles and objectives in implementing NII. Government is seen as enhancing private efforts and assuring the growth of a system available to everyone at reasonable cost.

Two pertinent publications from the legislative branch are the following:

- Library of Congress, *Delivering Electronic Information in a Knowledge-Based Democracy; Summary of Conference Proceedings 14 July 1993.* This conference explored the public policy framework and agenda, topics for which include updating the regulatory structure, ensuring equitable access, protecting intellectual property, enhancing security and privacy, and supporting the creation of digital libraries. Vice President Gore and Librarian of Congress James E. Billington led conference sessions, and Gore termed libraries the "safety net" in an electronic, networked environment.

- Office of Technology Assessment, *Making Government Work: Electronic Delivery of Federal Services,* Washington, D.C., September 1993. OTA's study warns that transition to electronic government will not automatically improve the government's delivery of services to people or save money.

Examples from 1993's multitude of nongovernmental publications related to NII are:

- Center for Civic Networking, *A National Strategy for Civic Networking: A Vision for Change*, Charlestown, Mass.: The Center, October 1993.
- Commission on Preservation and Access, *The Evolving National Information Network: Background and Challenges*, Washington, D.C.: The Commission, July 1993.
- Computer Professionals for Social Responsibility, *Serving the Community: A Public Interest Vision of the National Information Infrastructure*, Washington, D.C.: CPSR, October 1993.
- National Academy of Public Administration, *The Information Government: National Agenda for Improving Government through Information Technology*. Recommendations from a forum, April 23-24, 1993. Washington, D.C.: The Academy, 1993.

Future Challenges and Opportunities

Inclusion of references to library involvement in the emerging national information infrastructure by President Clinton and Vice President Gore is important to placing the future library challenges and opportunities into perspective. The president's January 25, 1994, State of the Union message included the statement that " . . . we must also work with the private sector to connect every classroom, every clinic, every library, every hospital in America into a national information superhighway by the year 2000."

Prior to the president's speech, the vice president's January 11, 1994, address at UCLA outlined plans for regulatory reform that will allow telecommunications companies to enter new business ventures. Vice President Gore's talk also outlined a series of legislative initiatives aimed at promoting the construction of an advanced nationwide network that can link classrooms, electronic libraries, rural doctors, and ordinary people in their own homes. Mr. Gore "challenged" telephone and cable companies to link all classrooms, libraries, and health clinics to an interactive video and data network by the year 2000.[28]

Clearly, the Clinton administration is promoting more competition, greater network access, and more coherent technical standards to facilitate network interconnections. At the same time, however, policy proposals are needed to balance the public interest in universal access with the economic incentives that are required to increase competition and innovation in new media services markets. Just what reforms and policies are appropriate to allow libraries to provide affordable, open, and flexible public access network channels for their communities is not yet clear. What is clear, however, is that the pace of change is increasing as the commercial and governmental sectors forge the basis for the new information/communications infrastructure. The library community must not only be able to articulate its vision of libraries in this infrastructure; we must have specific proposals and policies that address the governmental and commercial actions required for libraries to continue to serve as vital information and communication institutions for their communities and for the emerging global information infrastructure of the 21st century.

Notes

1. William Butler Yeats, *Selected Poems and Two Plays of William Butler Yeats* (New York: Collier Books, 1966), p. 91.

2. Clifford A. Lynch, "Visions of Electronic Libraries," *The Bowker Annual Library and Book Trade Almanac* (New Providence, N.J.: Bowker, 1991), pp. 75–82.

3. Charles R. McClure et al., "Toward a Virtual Library: Internet and the National Research and Education Network," *The Bowker Annual Library and Book Trade Almanac* (New Providence, N.J.: Bowker, 1993), pp. 24–45.

4. Information Infrastructure Task Force, *The National Information Infrastructure: Agenda for Action* (Washington, D.C., 1993).

5. Jean Armour Polly and Steve Cisler, "Connecting to the Global Internet," *Library Journal* 119 (January 1994): 38.

6. *Critical Connections: Communication for the Future* (OTA-CIT-407) (Washington, D.C.: U.S. Government Printing Office, 1990).

7. Information Infrastructure Task Force, *The National Information Infrastructure: Agenda for Action* (Washington, D.C., 1993).

8. "Electronic Superhighway: A New World of Video Entertainment and Interactive Services Is Coming to Your Home—Sooner Than You Think," *Time* (April 12, 1993): 50–58.

9. Gary Stix, "Domesticating Cyberspace," *Scientific American* (August 1993): 100–110.

10. "Eyes on the Future: And Big Money on the Table. The Race Is On to Find the Bonanza Vein Hidden in Interactive Technology," *Newsweek* (May 31, 1993): 39–47.

11. "Record Number of Mergers," *New York Times* (October 4, 1993): D9.

12. "The Makings of a Multimedia Marriage: How Two CEO's with a Shared Vision Pushed Bell Atlantic and TCI into a $26 Billion Merger," *Washington Post* (October 17, 1993): H1.

13. "Home Shopping Plans for Spiegel-Time Warner," *New York Times* (September 28, 1993): D5.

14. "Head Start on Data Superhighway," *New York Times* (September 8, 1993): D1.

15. "A New Information Mass Market," *New York Times* (September 3, 1993): C1.

16. "Rupert Murdoch: Global Gatekeeper: Tycoon Makes Series of Deals in Effort to Expand Reach with New Technologies," *Washington Post* (October 2, 1993): C1.

17. "Sudden Synergy Among Communications Rivals: Enthusiasm for Alliances at a Conference," *New York Times* (October 21, 1993): D1.

18. "Record Number of Mergers," *New York Times.* op. cit.

19. Craig A. Summerhill, "Impact of Technology on Resource Sharing," *Resource Sharing & Information Networks* 8, no. 1, 1992, p. 106.

20. Donald A. B. Lindberg, Congressional Testimony at a Hearing March 25, 1993, on National Technology Policy: Information Infrastructure ("Information Superhighways" and High Performance Computing) before the House Subcommittee on Technology, Environment, and Aviation of the Committee on Science, Space, and Technology.

21. Charles R. McClure, "Network Literacy: A Role for Libraries?" (paper presented at VTLS Inc., Third Annual Library Directors' Conference, Charlotte, N.C., October 10, 1993).

22. "The Emerging National Information Infrastructure: An Interview with Paul Evan Peters and Jim Neal," *Library Administration and Management* 7, no. 4 (Fall 1993): 201–204.

23. Ibid.

24. The Center for Civic Networking, *A National Strategy for Civic Networking: A Vision of Change* (Washington, D.C.: October 1993): ii–iii.

25. Steve Cisler, *Community Computer Networks: Building Electronic Greenbelts* (Cupertino, Calif.: Apple Library, 1993).

26. Ibid.

27. *Congressional Record* (November 23, 1993): S. 17056.

28. Edmund L. Andrews, "New Tack on Technology: U.S. Tries Coaxing Not Crash Program, for the Advanced Information Network," *New York Times* (January 12, 1994): 1.

Library Cooperation and Networking

JoAn Segal

Vintage Ventures, Boulder, Colorado

History

Beginnings

Cooperation among American libraries had begun by 1853, when Charles Coffin Jewett, then librarian of the newly established Smithsonian Institution, proposed a national cataloging program. Though the plan failed, it suggested shared cataloging and national distribution of cataloging copy later implemented.[1]

The American Library Association published its *Catalog Rules: Author and Title Entries* in 1908. These eventually developed into the *Anglo-American Cataloging Rules (AACR)* in 1967, following international efforts at standardization. The Cataloguing Secretariat of the International Federation of Library Associations and Institutions (IFLA) developed the International Standard Bibliographic Description (ISBD), particularly well suited to the use of computers, which soon came into widespread usage.[2] The development in 1966 of the MARC (Machine-Readable Cataloging) record by Henriette Avram and others at the Library of Congress was "an essential prerequisite"[3] for resource sharing, providing both a format and a communication protocol for bibliographic records. At the end of 1978 the second edition of the *AACR (AACR2)* appeared and has effectively served as a truly international standard for cataloging

Librarians forged the first interlibrary loan code in 1917; the Union List of Serials was first published in 1927; and the Union List of Newspapers began in 1936. The Library of Congress issued the *National Union Catalog* from the 1940s through the completion of the Mansell compilation in the early 1980s.

Since 1950, the practice of interlibrary borrowing and lending has moved from an infrequently invoked privilege to a regularly expected part of the user's rights to service. In the 1970s, the Association of Research Libraries (ARL) undertook research on academic interlibrary loans.[4] The major issues that emerged continue to plague research and other libraries. These include: purchasing and copyright problems, bibliographic access, and the establishment of interlibrary loan protocols.

Regional Union Catalogs were started in the 1930s and 1940s to maintain bibliographic records for libraries in their respective regions and to serve as interlibrary loan clearinghouses. Beginning in the 1960s, groups of libraries banded together regionally to harness the power of the MARC record and communications protocols. Eventually, the old regional union catalogs yielded to the superior power of the computer.

Processing centers were used by relatively small groups of libraries as early as the 1950s, but they failed because of problems in cost accounting. Sharing of the cataloging task took a more serious turn in the mid-1960s when automation and the development of the MARC record and the ISBD gave rise to the bibliographic utilities.

National Networks

OCLC

Under the auspices of the Ohio College Association in 1965 the academic libraries in Ohio hired Fred Kilgour and Ralph Parker to investigate the possibility of harnessing the power of the new MARC record and communications protocols to deliver catalog cards produced through automation. Kilgour and Parker proposed the Ohio College Library Center (OCLC) to serve this purpose. In 1967 Kilgour became its first president. The system went online in 1971 in Ohio and quickly grew to a de facto national network that necessitated a revision (1978) in the governance structure.

In addition to becoming a national shared-cataloging system, OCLC branched out into other areas of librarianship. One of the most successful was the Interlibrary Loan (ILL) Subsystem, which came online in the spring of 1979, allowing libraries to locate and request materials easily and to track requests.

RLG

The Research Libraries Group (RLG) was organized in 1974 to identify collection strengths and minimize duplication among three major research libraries: New York Public, Yale, and Columbia. In 1979 these were joined by Stanford University, whose automated library system, BALLOTS, was modified to become the Research Libraries Information Network (RLIN). Within the next three years, virtually all the large research libraries began to use RLIN for shared cataloging. Other RLG cooperative projects have included preservation and conservation of materials, acquisitions, and interlibrary loan systems. Although a serious competition for members characterized the relationship between the new RLIN and OCLC, negotiations have resulted in RLG members tapeloading records into the OCLC database and other cooperative projects between the two utilities. An attempt at closer collaboration failed in 1991, leaving librarianship in the United States with divided loyalties and without a single national bibliographic database.

WLN

The Washington State Library established the Washington Library Network (WLN) in the early 1970s. Noted for its quality control mechanisms (every record being reviewed before being entered into the database), the system served the northwestern United States, encompassing Washington, Oregon, Idaho, and Montana. In 1990 WLN separated from the State Library, changed its name to the Western Library Network (WLN) and continues operation largely in the Northwest, but with scattered membership throughout the United States and abroad.

Regional OCLC Networks

After OCLC went online in Ohio in 1971 it entered into agreements with several of the regional networks. These arrangements ranged from plans to replicate OCLC regionally to contracts to market the OCLC system in a particular region. Today, there are 19 OCLC networks in the United States and Canada. The relationship between the Regional OCLC Networks and OCLC itself has weathered many crises, but these organizations clearly serve OCLC and their members effectively.

State Networks

The concept that the state is the optimum level for networking among libraries is a time-honored one. Interlibrary loan networks and protocols focused on the state level for decades, coming into question only with the advent of computerized systems, which made it as easy to locate and borrow materials from across the nation as from across the state. OCLC itself was founded as a statewide system, but grew to national size because of the demand of libraries in other parts of the country for the services it was able to provide. The larger and more successful state networks also expanded beyond their borders. The Washington (later Western) Library Network (WLN) has long served libraries in a multistate region, as well as customers abroad. CLASS began as the California Library Authority for Systems and Services, but changed its name in 1983 to Cooperative Library Authority for Systems and Services, acknowledging that its members and services extended well beyond the California borders.

In the 1970s many states began to build databases—often using libraries' OCLC records—to produce union catalogs, at first in microform, and later on CD-ROM. Developments in library networking at the state level have included the establishment of interlibrary loan networks and resource sharing and many states are working toward a goal of an inclusive database accessible either free or at low cost by all citizens of the state wherever they are, with prompt document delivery. This ideal has not yet been fully implemented in any state, although most state libraries are supporting statewide databases and ILL systems.

Other Ties

Interlibrary cooperation also occurs at other levels. Some of the strongest interlibrary ties are among libraries in metropolitan areas, such as the Greater Cincinnati Library Cooperative (GCLC), Metronet in Minneapolis, or Metro in

New York City. CARL, originally the Colorado Alliance for Research Libraries, which included the major university libraries in the state plus the Denver Public Library, became successful as libraries outside its membership used its computerized system. It has spun off CARL Systems Inc., a for-profit subsidiary, and has added libraries, including the University of Wyoming, to the original members. CARL is not the only library cooperative that has grown because of local success; in relation to library networking and cooperation, these developments have had a mixed effect. A cooperative that has created a superior computerized system may have its cooperative aspects threatened by the commercial success of its system, which then becomes a product.

Philosophy of Library Networking and Cooperation

Basic Beliefs

Library cooperation and networking are founded on the belief that the good of all transcends that of each individual entity; that librarianship can move ahead more effectively if all cooperate than if each goes it alone.

In his May 1992 editorial in the *Journal of Academic Librarianship,* Dick Dougherty asked: "Is library cooperation a success story? Or is it a noble gesture that constantly falls short of the mark?" He later concluded that "interlibrary lending has been and remains partly an altruistic activity: . . . the large, well-endowed institutions helping those less fortunate. This is a worthy activity, and I'm sure elements of this philosophy will survive, but . . . resource sharing and interlibrary lending must be placed on a more business-like basis."[5]

Writing about OhioLINK,[6] David Kohl stressed that cooperation is not a "marginal nicety," but a "central necessity for a viable cooperative activity." He characterized cooperative activities as a kind of stewardship for the larger library community. A commitment to quality and to the development and implementation of standards means that each library is part of a total system of libraries. He argued the necessity for "separating one's ego from the seduction of autonomy and attaching it instead to service," thus giving up the illusion of autonomy for a real increase in the power to accomplish the library's mission.[7]

Multitype Participation

Another belief is that cooperation should extend to a variety of types of libraries. Sharyn Ladner studied resource sharing in sci-tech and business libraries and found that most participated in networks.[8] Van Orden and Wilkes identified a significant number of school library media centers in regional networks.[9]

Resource Sharing as Money Saving

Some early supporters of networking and cooperation held that resource sharing would save money. Richard De Gennaro, then at the New York Public Library, and now at Harvard, wrote in 1977:

> The importance of resource sharing mechanisms . . . is not so much that they will save us
> funds we can relocate to other purposes, but that they will permit us to continue to have access

to a large universe of materials we can no longer afford, spending our diminishing funds on the materials we need and use most. In sum, effective resource sharing will help ease the pain that will accompany the scaling-down of commitments and expectations we face in the years ahead.[10]

Over the years, cooperation and resource sharing have not resulted in enhancing library coffers nor even in allowing for major shifts in expense from one cost center to another. As Mary Jackson has pointed out, the fact that libraries may not charge for interlibrary loans does not mean there is no cost associated with them.[11] Yet some administrators believe cooperation can be justified only if it reduces costs.

Cooperative Collection Development

The Research Libraries Group (RLG) has always proposed cooperation in collection development as one of its desired activities. In a 1986 research project supported by Conoco, RLG examined the possibilities for resource sharing among its members. The results indicated cost savings and potential shareability of materials, but subsequent practice has shown that selectors still rely much more heavily on institutional self-interest than on an idealistic notion of national interaccessibility.[12]

Definitions

By "library networks," we may mean cooperatives at various levels, as described above, up to and including the large bibliographic utilities, such as OCLC and RLIN, or the communications systems linking computers in libraries with users or other libraries.

As Keys points out, "OCLC networks are not properly networks at all, at least in any sense that computer people and communications engineers would recognize. . . . They are really resource-sharing cooperatives that deliver some of their services to libraries over networks."[13] For a few of these organizations, the advent of Internet marks the first time they have truly created a network for the delivery of services.

Interlibrary Loan and Resource Sharing

In her "Library to Library" articles in the *Wilson Library Bulletin,* Mary Jackson has consistently emphasized the issue of ownership as related to access and the impact of alternative document delivery sources, such as commercial suppliers, fee-based services, and full-text databases available on line, on traditional interlibrary loan.[14] Mary and Shirley Baker prepared a white paper on interlibrary loan and resource sharing in which they posited an ideal interlibrary loan system. They suggested three major developments that would enhance interlibrary loan: improving the ILL systems of OCLC, RLIN, and WLN; establishing linkages between these major national systems and local systems, and developing an interlibrary loan management system to track and organize current and completed ILL transactions. They set possible time frames and costs for such developments and suggested potential agents for carrying them out.[15]

1992–1993 Developments

National Networks

OCLC

As characterized by John Berry, "OCLC is . . . an information research center; an innovative marketing agency; a major information and database holder, supplier, distributor, and creator; a national network; and a huge membership organization."[16] In its Strategic Plan, distributed in spring 1992, President K. Wayne Smith described a bold strategy:

> OCLC will maintain its position as a world-class database of bibliographic information through a steady stream of enhancements in cataloging and resource sharing. We will move beyond bibliography to become a world-class provider of reference services, including full-text information. And, we will become fully integrated into the digital, broadband, global community that is emerging. We fully intend to move with all deliberate speed toward the ultimate goal of providing information to people in the form required, when and where needed, and at an affordable price.[17]

At the OCLC President's Luncheon during the American Library Association's 1992 Annual Conference, Smith declared that OCLC had three major priorities for 1992: establishing the "new network," starting up the new online system, and starting a new core business: Reference Services.[18]

The new telecommunications network is an Open Systems Interface X.25 packet-switched system whose redundancy reduces the risk of outages, whose fiber optic nature represents the most modern medium of transmission,[19] and whose future growth is secured through modular design and standardized interfaces.[20] However, OCLC's August 1992 paper on Internet and NREN anticipated that "over time, a transition from the OCLC network to Internet and NREN is likely" and that "OCLC is not committed to maintaining a proprietary network that is not in the membership's best interests."[21] In his interview with John Berry, Smith explained that OCLC will amortize the cost of the sorely needed new network before Internet or NREN can replace it.[22]

The new online system includes a new computer system architecture, enhanced capabilities, and a vision of how information will be used in the future.[23] For library professionals, it provides easier editing, enhanced searching, and greater effectiveness and efficiency.

Reference Services include EPIC, the online reference system for library professionals; FirstSearch: EPIC for *patrons*; ArticleFirst and ContentsFirst, databases of article citations and tables of contents for some 11,500 serials, and Electronic publishing, including the *Online Journal of Current Clinical Trials* and the *Online Journal of Knowledge Synthesis for Nursing*.

During 1990–1995, according to the plan, "OCLC will return to basics, will totally retool its factory, will consolidate its market for traditional products and services, will lay the foundation for a new core business in reference services, will pursue more rapid international growth, will refocus its product line, and will develop the necessary alliances for a steady stream of new reference products and services."[24]

Having accomplished the first three priorities, Smith declared in the middle of 1993 that the next three would be expansion of the reference services and international programs and enhancement of PRISM.[25] Activities abroad are already extensive. A special report in the *OCLC Newsletter* detailed an extremely energetic program in Europe, the Middle East, and Africa.[26]

Business and Growth. The number of participating libraries (17,205 as of October 1993), of general members (6,507 in June 1993), of books cataloged (38.2 million online and tapeloaded), of records in the Online Union Catalog (27 million), of holdings locations (493 million), of online serials union lists (129 lists including 12,338 libraries), and of Group Access arrangements for small libraries (50 groups including 5,402 libraries) demonstrates impressive growth. Financially, OCLC had assets of $175 million, and corporate equity of $68.6 million in July 1993.[27] Financial developments include an in-depth study of pricing strategy, and a 9 percent decrease in telecommunications charges.[28]

But OCLC still nurtures its core business, the maintenance and improvement of its Online Union Catalog (OLUC) through its Conversion and Contract Cataloging operations, database quality and enrichment, and internal operation improvement.

Conversion and Contract Cataloging includes current cataloging for libraries at OCLC's central offices in Dublin, Ohio. Major recent customers include Wayne State University[29] and the Library of Congress (for its Hungarian and Romanian materials),[30] but most users of the service are small libraries with insufficient work to justify the hiring of a full-time cataloger. Retrospective conversion (Retrocon) activities have been used recently by Harvard University,[31] six French academic libraries,[32] and the Royal Gardens at Kew.[33] Some 80 million records have been entered into the OLUC through its cataloging projects.[34]

Recent database quality and enrichment efforts have included a massive subject headings improvement project[35] and the development of computer algorithms to detect and delete duplicate records or upgrade incomplete records.[36] OCLC believes efforts to improve the quality of the database are better carried out at the national, rather than the local or regional levels.[37]

Enhancements to the current systems included improved authority-file searching,[38] recent computer room automation such as the robotization of tape storage through the addition of an Automated Cartridge System and "nearline" storage,[39] and the introduction of more powerful workstations.[40]

Research. Targeted areas are Internet, cataloging productivity tools, graphical browsing interfaces, information retrieval, and interface design.[41] A major interlibrary loan study is currently under way[42] and a study of information available on Internet was recently completed.[43]

New Products and Services. OCLC initiated three telecommunications linking projects: the Telecommunications Linking Program (TLP), a hardware-based alternative for libraries with their own networks; Gateway software, which can be added to TLP to allow the library to gain access to OCLC services using terminals or workstations that formerly could not be linked to the OCLC system; and Internet, used by OCLC for several of its reference services and electronic journals.

Governance. The cumbersome nature of OCLC's extensive governance and advisory structure was described by President K. Wayne Smith: "Due process sometimes outlasts the window of opportunity."[44] Major players are: the 16-member board of trustees, nine of whom are librarians; the Users Council, a representative body consisting of delegates from networks and service centers, which elects six members to the board of trustees; and the OCLC Executive Committee, consisting of the top staff officers. Key issues examined by the Users Council over the past two years included governance, networking, future uses of the Online Union Catalog, and a revision of the *Code of Responsible Use.*[45] A variety of advisory groups also bring the opinions of users to OCLC.

RLG and RLIN

Early in 1992 *The Chronicle of Higher Education* featured RLG and its president, James Michalko, noting the organization's redirection from a society of research libraries to one that supports collective efforts to solve the problems facing researchers. This means, according to Michalko, "creat(ing) a whole different set of alliances . . . bring(ing) . . . other constituencies into the mix."[46] This shift also means less emphasis on cataloging and more on other services, a streamlining of governance, and growth in membership.

In its ambitious published plan, *RLG in Perspective: Focusing Collaboration in the 1990s,*[47] RLG invited nonprofit organizations with an educational, scientific, or cultural mission to join it in support of cooperative solutions for scholarship. Plans call for adding new data to existing RLIN files, especially archival and manuscript, visual material, and computer files. Also to be added are new files for materials not available in other databases. Plans to add reference files and to enhance collection access and document delivery were also set forth. Although some similar products and services are available through OCLC and commercial vendors, the emphasis is on materials and services valuable for scholars and not otherwise accessible.

Membership. The effort to move beyond university research libraries yielded returns promptly. In 1992 membership grew from 112 to 121.[48] Among these members was the British Library, the first overseas library in the group, and it was announced that London would become the hub of the RLIN telecommunications system abroad.[49] In early 1993 RLG announced that the Library of Congress had become its 126th member.[50]

Finance. In its publication *RLG in Perspective,*[51] RLG released extensive financial information. RLIN is the main revenue source (70 percent to 80 percent), of which 14 percent to 17 percent comes from membership dues and fees for collaborative activities and 8 percent to 9 percent from grants and contracts. From 1986 to 1991 RLG received more than $8.6 million in grants and contracts. (In 1992 the National Endowment for the Humanities (NEH) awarded it $906,224 for a preservation microfilming project,[52] and the Hewlett Foundation provided an enabling fund of $750,000 to RLG to "improve access to information that supports research and learning.")[53] Revenues in 1991 were $17.6 million, of which $1.6 million was in grants, and expenses totaled $16.5 million.

Additions and Enhancements. In accordance with its announced plans, RLG added to and enhanced the RLIN database. Additions included:

• Arabic-script capability (RLIN is now the only online network that can support the entire JACKPHY[54] menu of languages using non-Roman scripts)[55]

- Access to UMI/Data Courier databases[56]
- The Rigler and Deutsch Record Index, a union catalog of pre-LP discs held by six research libraries
- The art catalogs of the University of California Santa Barbara Arts Library[57]
- Databases of INION, the Russian Academy of Sciences' Institute of Scientific Information in the Social Sciences, with over 1.2 million records[58]
- An inventory of some 1,450 Vatican Archival files[59]

A special project added 7,000 records to the RLIN file of archives and manuscripts.[60]

Research. A major study of the costs of interlibrary loans in research libraries was launched by RLG and the Association of Research Libraries (ARL). With partial support from the Council on Library Resources (CLR), the study was to present cost data in aggregate form for libraries to use as comparative information. Results, released late in 1993, showed a significant increase in interlibrary loan activities as libraries move to an access or demand model for providing information to users. One goal of the research was to help libraries better assess the economics of their own borrowing and lending practices, to evaluate alternative methods of providing these services, and to study the impact of local serials cancellations.[61]

Products and services. RLG announced the availability of Ariel, a software package that enables fast, reliable, high-quality transmission of documents and images over Internet. The system works independently of RLIN and operates on a standalone PC-to-PC system.[62] Faster, more reliable, and less expensive to use than FAX machines, the software compresses images, corrects data transmission errors, and uses Internet, which is a free telecommunications mode for most non-profit organizations.[63]

After being previewed at Rutgers and Brigham Young universities,[64] CitaDel, RLG's new citation and document-delivery service, was released late in 1992.[65] Delivery of materials is available via mail, express courier, FAX, or Internet (Ariel).[66] RLG introduced a videodisc system, AVIADOR, in the summer of 1993.[67]

RLG also announced that it had developed a Z39.50 server for searching its RLIN and CitaDel databases over Internet. This will make it easier for users of a given library's online system to search the many library catalogs available through Internet without having to learn the specific systems used by each.[68]

Publications. In addition to *RLG in Perspective,* RLG published *Preferred Futures for Libraries,* which grew out of six workshops on academic libraries and information resources sponsored by the Andrew W. Mellon Foundation. Although there was consensus on the concept of universal access to multiple information sources from a single workstation, there was no agreement on how to achieve the objective or who should take the leadership in its development.[69] The

RLG Preservation Microfilming Handbook superseded the 1986 version. It contains detailed information on all aspects of the process.[70] *Discovering RLIN,* a description of the database and its contents, was greeted enthusiastically because of its broad approach to human thought and knowledge as expressed in such a database.[71]

WLN

The Western Library Network (WLN) might be considered a regional network, in that the major geographical location of its members is the Pacific Northwest. But, unlike the Regional OCLC networks, it is a true network, creating a cataloging database and making access to it available over its own telecommunications system. Although smaller than either RLIN or OCLC, it is also a supplier of many other products and services, is noted for the quality of its database, and has broad national and international connections.

In his 1992–1993 summary Miller recapped WLN developments, including:

- Full-service Internet access, including entry to the WLN database through WLN Easy Access and dial-up and leased line access to Internet via an 800 number or a local call
- Access to online reference databases and full-text files via the WLN Easy Access system
- The WLN MARC Record Service (MARS), an authority control and database preparation service
- New graphical user interfaces allowing access to LaserCat, WLN's CD-ROM database of more than 4 million MARC records, and to LaserPac, local catalogs on CD-ROM or hard disk using LaserCat software via a Windows and Macintosh interface
- The creation of multimedia databases and retrieval systems, such as one prepared for the Washington Department of Wildlife
- The enhancement of WLN collection assessment services, including development of the WLN/RLG Conspectus Software

Network governance has been modified with the formation of a WLN Multi-State Users Group to reflect the relatively new (1990) status of WLN as an independent nonprofit corporation, rather than a subdivision of the Washington State Library.[72] Growth of this magnitude will prove a challenge for WLN, which will need to identify and measure new markets for its products (including end users, in addition to librarians) and find a niche in an information world enticed by the lure of local systems, rather than centralized creation and storage of records. The problem of pricing for services of high quality—in a market where customers often select on the basis of price only—is particularly pressing for WLN.[73]

Regional Networks

Regional networks have added new products and services to their repertoire and have invested heavily in alliances and sharing relationships with one another. While competition among the regionals is still a reality, with some networks providing certain services to libraries in other networks' "territories," the emphasis has been on collaboration between and among them. A cooperative understanding among AMIGOS, BCR, NELINET, and SOLINET to explore the possibilities of sharing network services was announced early in 1993.[74] In fact, these networks have shared budget and administrative information and even some training staff.[75]

In mid-1993, 17 of the regional OCLC networks formed the Alliance of Library Service Networks to provide services to the libraries they represent. As partners, they will strive to strengthen their ability to provide services and support to their members, contribute to the development and evolution of the national information infrastructure, sustain and enhance their partnership with OCLC and other suppliers, collaborate in negotiating collectively with vendors, and develop and carry out joint programs.[76]

Another forum for these networks is the Regional OCLC Network Directors Advisory Committee (RONDAC), an OCLC-sponsored arena for discussion of OCLC-related issues. At its meeting in August 1993 the group confirmed the value of the strong OCLC/network partnership in meeting the current and future needs of libraries. Some of the new programs into which the networks are entering include: teleconferencing and videotape for disseminating information and training users; Internet access and training; cooperative purchasing/discount programs; continuing education other than OCLC; consulting services; hardware and software sales and training; and preservation services.[77]

AMIGOS

After feasibility studies and board discussion, a pilot project resulted in the fall 1992 broadcast of a satellite teleconference on OCLC/PRISM ILL, distribution of video recordings of the teleconference, and production of a workbook providing instruction about the use of OCLC PASSPORT software version 2.0. Participants rated these alternative methods as effective, although most indicated a preference for instructor-led training. AMIGOS plans to add alternative methods to its other training options, especially when member travel time and costs and timely distribution of information are significant concerns.[78]

The AMIGOS Preservation Service (APS) presents seminars and workshops on preservation-related topics, provides site surveys and preservation management consultation for libraries and archives, and focuses on staff and patron education about preservation. A $498,247 grant from the National Endowment for the Humanities (NEH) will allow the program to continue and expand in 1993–1995.[79]

The new AMIGOS Internet Service became available in November. It features 800-number access to full Internet services, with technical support available 24 hours a day, seven days a week.[80]

AMIGOS Consulting Services (ACS) got off to a good start in 1993 by playing an active role in a Total Quality Management (TQM) program at Texas A&M University.[81] ACS also produced a self-instructional manual on cataloging and classification for small libraries for the New Mexico State Library, and was selected to conduct the planning phase of Tex-Share, a program of resource sharing for Texas academic libraries.[82]

BCR

There was a constant increase in the amount and type of training offered, not only for OCLC systems, but for a variety of other topics.[83] In November 1992 the network moved into a building it purchased outright.[84] Members may now gain access to *The Third Indicator,* its bimonthly publication on OCLC-related topics, via Internet.[85]

CAPCON

Like most other networks, CAPCON has responded to the new technology by offering training and access to Internet.[86] The network also undertook contract cataloging for several of its libraries.[87] Its continuing education program included management and other library topics.[88]

ILLINET and MLNC

Two midwestern networks, ILLINET and the Missouri Library Network Corporation (MLNC), have established the first OCLC no-charge Group Access Capability (GAC) group. Libraries Very Interested in Sharing (LVIS) includes Illinois and Missouri libraries that have contributed holdings to OCLC and have agreed to no-charge loans of monographs and no-charge photocopies for up to 30 pages per bibliographic citation among group members.[89] ILLINET continues to rely heavily on volunteers to train on OCLC and other topics.[90]

MLC

The Michigan Library Consortium (MLC) became a MichNet Affiliate and is now offering dial access passwords to Internet.[91] The tenth edition of the MLC Union List of Serials became available.[92]

MINITEX

MINITEX was founded in December 1968. Its central activity has always been document delivery, with technical services seen as a means to that end. By the close of its twenty-fifth year, the network reached an annual volume of over 300,000 document delivery requests.[93] An ARIEL workstation was installed in the MINITEX Office and is being used to transmit document delivery requests.[94]

NEBASE

NEBASE, a State-Library-based consortium of Nebraska Libraries, also experimented with teleconferencing by broadcasting its fall 1992 Update meeting to eight downlink sites.[95] The NEBASE Offices moved with the Nebraska Library Commission into new offices July 1, 1993.

NELINET

DIAL, a menu-driven gateway to Internet resources for NELINET libraries, began operation in November 1992.[96] The membership reached 515 by June 1993, an increase of over 14 percent in one year.[97] However, early 1992 saw the network go through some belt-tightening, which included one-day-per-month furloughs for all staff and freezing of 1.8 positions.[98] Broadening access and reducing costs for those least able to afford services, NELINET established a new participation category, Affiliate Members, to give small libraries access to NELINET training and group purchases at member rates;[99] it also invites unemployed librarians to take NELINET workshops at half the regular price.[100] An interesting addition to the NELINET Interlibrary Loan Code requires that "signers agree to maintain a level of lending activity on OCLC that is equal to at least 10 percent of their borrowing activity" and "to respond positively to at least 20 percent of pending requests on OCLC."[101] This makes it clear that libraries that intend to use the OCLC ILL Subsystem only to borrow may encounter lending charges from signers.

OHIONET

In early 1992 OHIONET was in the middle of the board's strategic planning process. The plan was completed at the board's March meeting. The mission statement, strategic direction, and strategic elements were published in summary form in the network's newsletter in April 1992 and discussed at the Membership Meeting in May 1992.[102] Partly as a follow-up to the strategic plan, the network did extensive surveys in several areas to develop a marketing plan.[103, 104]

PALINET

PALINET offered continuing education units for its workshops.[105] In October 1992 PALINET joined in an informal agreement with CAPCON to make certain services offered by each network available to all member libraries at member rates. While there are mutual exchanges of services, an important aspect of the agreement is that PALINET members may reach Internet via CAPCON Connect.[106] In mid-1993 PALINET announced a list-serv, Pal-First, for PALINET Internet users.[107]

SOLINET

SOLINET's training and workshop program also broadened in subject matter and in format, with videoconferencing added to other media.[108] By early 1993 SOLINET's workshop program was established as an independent department, Continuing Education & Training.[109] For the second time, NEH awarded a large ($2.4 million) grant for cooperative preservation microfilming to SOLINET, supporting a three-year project with the Association of Southeastern Research Libraries (ASERL).[110] The network announced in the fall of 1992 that it would be offering access to Internet for its members.[111] The Internet SOLutions Access Program was announced in 1993; it is a full-service gateway to Internet resources for SOLINET members that lack other Internet access or those who wish to consolidate these information activities under their network contract.[112]

SOLINET celebrated its twentieth anniversary in 1993 with a membership of more than 700 members[113] and an ambitious plan to establish a "regional information network." This concept responds to the board's vision statement, which begins "SOLINET will establish itself as a major force in the information infrastructure of the Southeast."[114, 115] The board and Executive Director Frank Grisham met with members of the Southeastern University Research Association (SURA) to develop plans for a joint seminar and explore other cooperative activities.[116, 117]

Utlas

Utlas International Canada, whose rope-skipping back and forth across the fine line dividing the private and public sector has been at the least interesting, became a regional network for OCLC in Canada. The company was purchased by ISM Information Services Management Corp., Canada's largest information systems management firm.[118]

WILS

The most exciting special contribution of WILS (Wisconsin InterLibrary Services) is its New Technologies Information Service program, which publishes the monthly *New Tech News (NTN)* (also available online).[119] The program's purpose is to help all librarians, including those in small and medium-sized libraries, to keep abreast of relevant technological developments. WILS has installed a gopher server, offered access to Internet,[120] and begun an E-mail list for Wisconsin librarians.[121] Interesting *NTN* articles address not only library automation issues, but computer-related philosophical, ethical, and political issues, tutorials about various microcomputer topics, and news and gossip about the latest technology. Celebrating its twentieth anniversary in 1992, WILS examined questions of its future and the nature of the evolving national network.[122]

State Networks

A recent survey of state libraries indicated that 11 states have fully developed networks providing some or all of the following: an online public access catalog, book and article delivery systems, Internet (and future NREN) support, E-mail, common hardware and software, and coordinated governance. Another eight states are progressing toward such a level of service. A major stumbling block for all is financing;[123] federal funds have been used by a number of states. Louisiana State University won a recent competition for $2.48 million in Higher Education Act (HEA) funds for statewide networking.[124]

A number of statewide initiatives (mostly academic) were reported in the literature. The implementation of OhioLINK has included patron-initiated checkout, a 48-hour book delivery system among the libraries, active exploration of FAX technology for journal article delivery, provision of full-text commercial databases, and Internet access. In fact, the (now 18) academic institutions involved constitute a "virtual" library with 24-hour access. The Innovative Interfaces Inc. installation includes common basic hardware and software for each institution, with local sites adding modules if desired. The Ohio Board of Regents has provided some $20 million in hardware and about $2 million annually in operating costs. David Kohl cited several major "issues/lessons" from the experience. Among these is a strong support for cooperation as the libraries move to being "mutual branch libraries." He noted that OhioLINK is being held up as a model for cooperation in other areas of higher education in Ohio, and mentioned the value of a large group in increasing clout with vendors.[125]

Florida's Library Information Network for Community Colleges (LINCC) now connects 18 community colleges with nine state universities via the Florida Information Resources Network (FIRN). Students will have access to the combined holdings of all 37 institutions for E-mail, interlibrary loan, and some online reference services.[126] The University of Oregon and four regional college libraries have connected to offer their combined resources to users.[127] New Mexico's ZiaNet now links the Albuquerque Public Library, the University of New Mexico, and New Mexico State University, Las Cruces. The link allows the libraries' users to search the holdings of the other libraries, patch into OCLC and CARL, and have access to Internet.[128] Maryland's Seymour Plan is designed to interconnect all types of libraries by 1999.[129] The New York State Library prepared a plan for network services in the last decade of the twentieth century.[130]

Key Issues in Networking, 1992–1993

Perceptions of Networks

At a time when the national "utilities" like OCLC and RLG are finding success in broadening their base of products and enhancing their core businesses, regional networks continue to seek appropriate niches for their services. Clarifying what is done best at the regional, rather than the national or state or local level, has always been a key question for these groups, which continue to serve their customers/members well, but seem particularly vulnerable to market vagaries. They provide valuable services the utilities could not afford to offer and are "closer to home" psychologically, but they are sometimes seen by librarians as unnecessary middlemen or as undifferentiated from vendors in the private sector. From the point of view of the utilities, they may be perceived as annoying but necessary.

Network directors must balance pricing decisions against the provision of quality services, avoid offending those providing services at national, state, and local levels, and serve as spokespersons and advocates for libraries in their regions. These directors are concerned about libraries failing (or waiting) to load cataloging records produced through local systems into the national databases; they worry about the profusion of products on the market and their ability to provide accurate information to their members; they observe conflicts between library directors and their staff members concerning the trade-off between "professional values" and "productivity." They experience a lack of interest on the part of members, once fiercely involved in network affairs but now taking for granted smooth network operation, perhaps because of preoccupation with financial and other exigencies at home. After years of "representing" their members in national forums, at OCLC, and to the vendor community, they find their organizations increasingly perceived as "just another kind of vendor," rather than an extension of the library via a cooperative effort.

Directors of many large libraries are not always comfortable in the regional networks. Some handle this discomfort by expecting network boards to accede to demands for special perks or reduced prices; others simply withdraw, leaving the regional network weakened without the major library players in the region to work together (or at least side by side) with the rest of the region's librarians. The plethora of networks—state nets, private nets, cooperative groups of all kinds, Internet and NREN, and the groups surrounding them—blurs the lines of discernment. Which is a membership group with responsibilities to the members? Which a discussion forum? Which a supplier of products and services only?

Which just an electronic medium for the transmission of messages? The expansion of the regional networks to include ever-smaller libraries has brought new technological possibilities to these institutions and expanded the types of libraries cooperating,[131] but has also obscured the view of regional networks as major players in the larger library scene, confusing both the small and large library world about the role of the network. Is it the Walmart of the library world, where any library can buy needed products and services at a discount? If so, what loyalty can one expect from a member who finds it possible to buy one product somewhere else at a cheaper price? What responsibility do librarians have to support their regional networks as advocates for their needs in national forums if they have this perception? Several networks are discovering that the "network loyalty" of their members is weaker than at an earlier time in their history. They sometimes find themselves torn between a traditional commitment to inter-network cooperation and the ongoing competition that continues to characterize these organizations.

National Information Infrastructure

Perhaps the single most significant and still growing factor in library (and other) networking today is the emerging National Information Infrastructure. What role should library networks play in providing training, access, and even creating menus, gophers, and other improvements that help users to "navigate" Internet more successfully? Again, turf issues interfere with the provision of service: who should "own" a piece of Internet? Academic institutions? State libraries? State telecommunications departments? Is this an area for inter-network cooperation? How many networks should get into the same "business"? How can a regional network ensure that libraries can have access without coming into conflict with someone at another level of librarianship or government? What is the role of library cooperation and networking in mitigating the impact of Internet on information access and use; in helping people deal with the mass of information now becoming available over Internet; in dealing with questions of information overload and of bibliographical control; and in facilitating the fundamental change in the ways in which individuals get their information now and in the near future.

[A special report on public policy and the national information infrastructure precedes this article—*Ed.*]

Local Systems

As more sophisticated systems support cataloging at the local library, some old problems resurface, the most serious being duplication of effort by library staff cataloging the same materials in different libraries and failing (or seriously delaying) to load records into a national database for the use of others. How can utilities and networks—through pricing strategies, education, and other means—encourage libraries to load catalog records into OCLC (or RLIN or WLN)?

Centralized Cataloging

The suggestion that all cataloging be done centrally, rather than locally, has begun to take root. OCLC and WLN and several of the regional OCLC networks offer cataloging services: not just retrospective conversion, but actual cataloging of previously uncataloged materials. Wayne State University elected to have OCLC serve as its catalogers; it expects to save up to $250,000 a year through this change.[132] The other side of this coin is the fear on the part of library staff that library jobs are being "outsourced" and that quality will inevitably be sacrificed.

Diversification

For regional networks, the emphasis is on diversification, offering a broader mix of OCLC and non-OCLC products; non-cataloging products and services, such as database access and training; microcomputer group purchasing contracts, training, and trouble-shooting; and evaluation of microcomputer products for libraries. Almost all the networks provide some form of consulting services, either informally or formally. Regional networks are trying to become decreasingly dependent on OCLC, fearing that over-reliance on one large vendor is too risky.

Duplication

Still at issue is the lack of a single unified national bibliographic database. Although RLIN and OCLC came close to an agreement in 1991, negotiations fell through, leaving many libraries to catalog on RLIN and then tapeload into OCLC—almost always at a later date. Overlap in the OCLC, RLIN, and WLN databases is great; the major objection to consolidation is the search for perfection in cataloging.

Planning

National, regional, and state networks have placed a strong emphasis on planning in the past two years. An awareness of the major transformations in the environment, together with the speed of change, has stimulated consideration of possible information futures. An interesting task would be a consolidation of some of these planning processes in which a projection of the information world of the future might emerge from the insights gained in the various planning processes.

Internetwork Cooperation

Cooperation among the regional OCLC networks seems to have reached new dimensions with the network directors taking collaborative steps outside the OCLC umbrella, such as representation in the National Information Infrastructure arena.

Aging

As a phenomenon of the later twentieth century, library networking is "new." Or is it? With OCLC passing its twenty-fifth anniversary, RLIN its fifteenth, and several of the regionals celebrating 20 and 25 years, the aging of the networks may be an issue to be reckoned with. Perhaps some new phenomenon needs to be invented to deal with the next phase in the information revolution.

Development of a National Information Infrastructure

NREN: National Research and Education Network

The High-Performance Computing Act of 1991 established the NREN concept together with other aspects of high-speed computing; the legislation was "to provide for a coordinated Federal Program to ensure continued U.S. leadership in high-performance computing"[133] and to "provide for the linkage of research institutions and educational institutions, government and industry in every state."[134]

NREN was not to be one network, but a web of cooperating networks, formal and informal standards bodies, and high-speed transmission facilities. Many policy issues were raised by the act. Some of these were identified during a policy workshop held in September 1992:[135] funding, future operation and evolution, economic and technological aspects of linking with commercial information services, copyright issues, and security and privacy issues. In addition, concerns have been expressed about the need for the national network to be available to all, regardless of ability to pay; about balancing the rights to the network of various constituencies (private enterprise, educational institutions at all levels,[136] and public sector enterprises); and about "last-mile" deployment, that is, bringing fiber optic cable into every home and business.[137]

Developments

The Information Infrastructure and Technology Act of 1993, enacted by Congress on July 26, 1993, represents a second phase of the High Performance Computing Program. In his talks about the program, Vice President Al Gore emphasized a commitment to extending the concept of "universal access," long a tenet of telephone communication, to the networked environment. To do this with the cooperation of the private sector, he proposed changes in the regulatory environment and suggested that all carriers contribute to the cost of "basic" service.[138]

Internet: Its Use and Role in Library Cooperation and Networking

Internet is an "international network of networks in which a common set of protocols allows networks to exchange information."[139] In practical terms, it is a system for information sharing with global dimensions. Among the services available on Internet are:

- E-mail
- Bulletin boards
- Electronic publications
- Access to library catalogs (OPACs) and databases
- The capability to download texts and software

Internet offers librarians access to a wide array of information and reference sources, including major library catalogs, full text of documents and books, commercial services, economic indicators, and international events.

"Everybody wants to get into the (Internet) act";[140] and everybody wants to provide the help people need to do so. A bevy of regional OCLC networks offer training, a smaller but significant number provide access, a few have special lists, and two provide gophers—software assistance for "navigating" Internet. Local system vendors and other companies also offer access. Regional and state telecommunications networks present seminars,[141] associations feature articles about Internet in their newsletters and journals and include courses about it in their continuing education offerings; and OCLC released a major position paper about its future relationship with Internet and NREN.[142]

Librarians are users of Internet, but they may well be an avant-garde; if they are to play a role in anticipating what other end users will want and need as Internet grows, they need to begin thinking about those users. What does the average non-technically-astute individual want and need from Internet and its limitless resources? "They want to know what information resources are available, want to be able to access them and print them, and they want to be able to do this" easily. They want assistance in obtaining the actual information they need in the format they can use. These users may need training; perhaps librarians can provide it. But there may be many other services librarians can provide to help users get what they want and need from Internet.[143]

Coalition for Networked Information

The Coalition for Networked Information (CNI), which was formed in 1990 by the Association of Research Libraries (ARL); CAUSE, the association for academic administrative computing; and EDUCOM, the association for academic computing, held several interesting meetings during 1992 and 1993. The meetings examined opportunities to learn about finding information on Internet,[144] identified action items for attendees to take home with them,[145] and featured access to government information.[146]

National Information Infrastructure

On September 15, 1993, the Clinton administration issued its agenda for action on the National Information Infrastructure (NII), "a seamless web of communications networks, computers, databases, and consumer electronics that will put vast amounts of information at users' fingertips," and will help "unleash an information revolution that will change forever the way people live, work, and interact with each other."[147] As described, NII is not limited to NREN or other networked information ventures, but is comprehensive, including Internet, telecommunications technology, "plain old telephone service" (POTS), and cable and television delivery systems.

Also in September, a small group of library representatives met to discuss what role libraries would play in NII. The National Information Infrastructure Policy Forum, representing 15 library organizations and funded by the American Library Association (ALA), the Council on Library Resources, and the National Science Foundation, provided a forum where leaders could hear the latest developments and begin discussion of common principles.

According to Maurice Mitchell and Laverna Saunders, the term National Information Infrastructure will probably replace NREN as a broader concept and better way of discussing all the issues.[148] They see several important implications for libraries in these developments: the possibility of a virtual library and the ability to expand Internet-based services and build clients' use of them.

Future of Library and Information Networks

Continuities

The need for links with others to share work and information will militate for the continuation of library networks structured much as they are today, probably for at least another decade or two. Librarians will continue to join networks that are effective in helping them use technology to share this work and make these links. Network boards and administrators will continue to modify structures, rethink pricing schemes, and conceive of new ways to be useful to their member-constituents.

Developments

In search of these new modes of usefulness, networks will turn to services and products that are increasingly market-driven. The customer service philosophy will grow in importance, first as a necessity for survival and success, but also as a model for network members. For the regional OCLC networks, the trend toward decreasing dependence on OCLC will spread; they will remain independent but mutually interdependent.

The multistate regional networks and single-state networks that are not state-library-related must come to terms with state networks that are effective competitors, often undergirded by statewide telecommunications networks and supported by state subsidies. Network managers and state librarians will need to determine cooperatively what services each can best provide to ensure optimum service to libraries.

Networks will need to be even more involved in work on the many standards that will enable the development of the National Information Infrastructure. Networks can play a significant role in educating their members, coalescing agreement, and seeing that the new standards are implemented.

Possible Discontinuities

Although jeopardized by institutions that will not accept others' work and by failure to load locally produced records into a national database such as OCLC's, the idea of shared cataloging is widely accepted. Even the Library of Congress is now using OCLC records for copy cataloging.[149] The next stage in streamlining the cataloging process is already beginning. To reduce the workload on our technical services departments, release librarians for more public service tasks, and yet ensure the quality of catalog records so they are acceptable even to the most demanding catalogers, a high-quality centralized cataloging facility, operating to standards set by the library community, is very likely to emerge over the next decade.

As we face the increased use of electronic media and networked information, which many fear will erode the traditional "library," library networks must define their role in helping librarians deal with these media and must also recognize that networked information and services also alter the market for networks themselves. Many networks are heavily involved in helping their members get access to Internet and learn how to "navigate" on it. But in the future not all network users will be librarians. Who will provide direct services to homes and offices—an entirely new market/constituency? OCLC has already announced it considers this market a target. Networks may not want to compete with libraries in this area, but they may have an important role in helping libraries to provide such services if they decide to do so, or in supplementing and complementing library services.

Vision

Librarians and their networks need to take still another step in rethinking the world of library cooperation and networking in light of the development of networked information resources, the physical networks themselves, and the mechanics needed to ensure[150] that all citizens can get the information they need when they need it and in a form they can use.

Ronald Larsen suggested that "as library networks and services evolve . . . so does the need to have them interoperate."[151] This means building online databases and using protocols like the ANSI Z39.50 standard to make it easier for patrons to use them. It also means having reference staff who know how to find and use networked information resources and how to use the network to collaborate and help others do so.

Marshall Keys drew a compelling analogy between library networks and cable television providers,[152] asserting that networks should take a cue from these providers:

> To ensure their futures . . . the multipurpose regional networks will have to become gateways and systems integrators for a variety of services. They will . . . help . . . (their members) make choices among options and . . . provid(e) . . . training and administrative and technical support for the broad range of services their members want.[153]

Conclusion

The rapid development of NII demands modification of traditional librarianship and hence of interlibrary cooperation. Librarians can enhance the information-finding capabilities of their users, enable them to find information resources never before available to them, link them physically to these resources, and teach them how best to use them.

Notes

1. Russell Shank, "Charles Coffin Jewett," *ALA World Encyclopedia of Library and Information Services* (Chicago: American Library Association, 1980), pp. 283–285.

2. Doralyn J. Hickey, "Cataloging," *ALA World Encyclopedia of Library and Information Services* (Chicago: American Library Association, 1980), pp. 121–124.

3. Alice Wilcox, "Resource Sharing," *ALA World Encyclopedia of Library and Information Services* (Chicago: American Library Association, 1980), pp. 479–482.

4. Ibid. p. 480.

5. Richard M. Dougherty, "Editorial: Making Resource Sharing Really Work," *Journal of Academic Librarianship* (May 1992): 75.

6. David Kohl, "OhioLINK: Plugging into Progress," *Library Journal* 118, no. 6 (October 1, 1993): 42–44, 46.

7. Ibid. p. 44.

8. Sharyn J. Ladner, "Resource Sharing in Sci-Tech and Business Libraries: Formal Networking Practices," *Special Libraries* (Spring 1992): 96–111.

9. Phyllis J. Van Orden and Adeline W. Wilkes, "School Library Media Centers and Networks," *Library Resources and Technical Services* 37, no. 1 (January 1993): 7–17.

10. Richard De Gennaro, "Copyright, Resource Sharing, and Hard Times: A View from the Field," *American Libraries* 8, no. 8 (September 1977): 430–435.

11. Mary E. Jackson, "Fitting the Bill" (Library to Library column), *Wilson Library Bulletin* 66, no. 10 (June 1992): 95–97.

12. Richard Hacken, "The RLG Conoco Study and Its Aftermath: Is Resource Sharing in Limbo?" *Journal of Academic Librarianship* 18, no. 1 (March 1992): 17–23.

13. Marshall Keys, "On the Future of the OCLC Regional Networks," *Library Administration and Management* 6, no. 1 (Winter 1992): 10.

14. Mary E. Jackson, "Library to Library," appears monthly in *Wilson Library Bulletin*.

15. Mary E. Jackson, "Maximizing Interlibrary Loans" (Library to Library column), *Wilson Library Bulletin* 67, no. 8 (April 1993): 86–87.

16. John Berry, "K. Wayne's World: OCLC Confronts the Future," *Library Journal* (May 15, 1993): 28–31.

17. K. Wayne Smith, "Letter from the President," *Journey to the 21st Century, A Summary of OCLC's Strategic Plan*. Dublin, Ohio: OCLC, 1991, p. 1.

18. "OCLC to Focus on Core Businesses in Next Two Years, Says Smith," *Advanced Technology/Libraries* (August 1992): 5–6.

19. "Technological Platform," *OCLC Annual Report* 1992/1993, pp. 16–17.

20. Larry Learn and George I. Carpenter, "Planning for Network Disaster: Telecommunications Diversity in the New OCLC Network," *Library Hi Tech* 9, no. 4 (1991): 63–73.

21. *OCLC's Linking Strategy: Internet and NREN*. Dublin, Ohio: OCLC, 1992.

22. John Berry, "K. Wayne's World," op. cit. p. 30.

23. *Journey to the 21st Century: A Summary of OCLC's Strategic Plan* (Dublin, Ohio: OCLC, 1992), p. 13.

24. *Journey to the 21st Century*, op. cit. p. 13.

25. K. Wayne Smith, "Making Progress on Our Three New Priorities," *OCLC Newsletter* no. 205 (September/October 1993): 3.

26. David Buckle, "OCLC Europe, an Overview," *OCLC Newsletter* no. 201 (January/February 1993): 14–24.

27. Figures from *OCLC Annual Report* 1992/1993 pp. 5–7 and *OCLC Newsletter* no. 205 (September/October 1993): 7.

28. "OCLC Reduces Telecommunications Charges by $3 Million," *OCLC Newsletter* no. 201 (January/February 1993): 4.

29. "OCLC Saves Univ. $200,000," *Library Journal* 118, no. 19 (November 15, 1993): 26.

30. *OCLC Annual Report* 1992/1993, p. 19.

31. "Harvard Recon Project," *Wilson Library Bulletin* (November 1992): 12.

32. "French Libraries Sign 600,000-record Retrospective Conversion Contract with OCLC," *WILS Memo* no. 130 (February 7, 1992): 5.

33. "OCLC to Convert 120,000 Records for Royal Botanic Gardens, Kew," *OCLC Newsletter* no. 199 (September/October 1992): 29–30.

34. "Conversion and Contract Cataloging Services," *OCLC Newsletter* no. 205 (September/October 1993): 9–19.

35. "OCLC Subject Headings Improvement Project," *Information Retrieval and Library Automation* (July 1992): 6.

36. Karen Calhoun, Nancy Campbell, and Donna Gehring, "How OCLC and Member Libraries Are Improving the Online Union Catalog," *OCLC Newsletter* no. 204 (July/August 1993): 16–20.

37. Karen Calhoun, "Database Quality: Its Cost, Focus, and Future," *OCLC Newsletter* no. 204 (July/August 1993): 15.

38. "OCLC Enhances Authority File Searching," *Library Hi Tech News* no. 96 (October 1992): 17–18.

39. "Robots Move into OCLC Computer Room," *OCLC Newsletter* no. 204 (July/August 1993): 7.

40. Bill Carney, "OCLC Offers More Powerful Workstations," *OCLC Newsletter* no. 201 (January/February 1993): 28–29.

41. *Annual Review of OCLC Research 1992* (Dublin, Ohio: OCLC, 1993).

42. Erik Jul and Chandra Prabha, "Office of Research Project Will Determine Costs, Workflows, and Usage Data on ILL and Document Delivery," *OCLC Newsletter* no. 199 (September/October 1992): 12–15.

43. Erik Jul, "Internet Research Report Available," *OCLC Newsletter* no. 201, (January/February 1993): 13.

44. John Berry, "K. Wayne's World," op. cit. p. 28.

45. "OCLC Code of Responsible Use to Be Reviewed," *Illinois OCLC Users' Group Newsletter* no. 66 (December 1993): 1.

46. David L. Wilson, "Research Libraries Group Seeks New Focus and New Members," *The Chronicle of Higher Education* (January 22, 1992): A21–22.

47. *RLG in Perspective: Focusing Collaboration in the 1990s* (Mountain View, Calif.: Research Libraries Group, 1991).

48. "RLG Gains Twelve New Members," *Advanced Technology/Libraries* 21, no. 10 (October 1992): 6.

49. "Research Libraries Group Welcomes First Overseas Member, Opens New Chapter of International Collaboration," *Library Hi Tech News* no. 92 (May 1992): 19.

50. "LC Joins RLG," *Library Journal* 118, no. 4 (March 1, 1993): 13.

51. Op. cit.

52. "$906,224 NEH Grant to RLG for Preservation Microfilming," *Library Hotline,* March 30, 1992, p. 3.

53. "Research Libraries Group Awarded $750,000 from Hewlett Foundation to Support New Directions," *Library Hi Tech News* no. 90 (March 1992): 10.

54. Defined by the Library of Congress as Japanese, Arabic, Chinese, Korean, Persian, Hebraic, and Yiddish.

55. "RLIN Adds Arabic-script Capability," *Advanced Technology/Libraries* 20, no. 11 (November 1991): 5–6.

56. "Access to UMI/Data Courier Databases on RLIN," *Information Today* 9, no. 2 (February 1992): 3.

57. "RLIN Adds RDI, UCSB Art Catalogs," *Advanced Technology/Libraries* (September 1992): 1, 11.

58. "RLG to Offer Russian Databases," *Wilson Library Bulletin* 66, no. 2 (October 1992): 17.

59. "Vatican Archives on RLIN," *Library Journal* 118, no. 16 (October 1, 1993): 28.

60. "RLG Project Adds 7,000 Records to RLIN AMC File," *Advanced Technology/Libraries* 22, no. 5 (May 1993): 10.

61. "RLG and ARL to Study Interlibrary Loan Costs," *Information Today* (May 1992): 68.

62. "RLG Announces Ariel Document Transmission System," *Advanced Technology/Libraries* 20, no. 12 (December 1991): 3.

63. *ARIEL: The Document Transmission System for the Internet,* product description from RLG.

64. "Rutgers and BYU to Showcase RLG's CitaDel Service," *Information Today* 9, no. 6 (June 1992): 11–12.

65. "RLG Offers 30 Day Trial of CitaDel Service," *Advanced Technology/Libraries* 21, no. 11 (November 1992): 3.

66. "RLG Announces CitaDel Service," *Advanced Technology/Libraries* 21, no. 5 (May 1992): 1, 10.

67. "RLG Introduces AVIADOR," *Advanced Technology/Libraries* 22, no. 6 (June 1993): 3.

68. "Dateline: Mountain View, CA; RLG Develops Z39.50 Server for Internet Use," *Information Today* 9, no. 10 (November 1992): 1.

69. "RLG Reports on the Future of Libraries," *Information Retrieval and Library Automation* 27, no. 10 (March 1992): 6.

70. "RLG Publishes Handbook for Preservation Microfilming," *C&RL News* (June 1992): 407.

71. Nancy Melin Nelson, "Library Technology," *Information Today* 9, no. 6 (June 1992): 49.

72. Ron Miller, "1993: A Year of Tremendous Productivity," *WLN Participant* 12, no. 6 (November/December 1993): 2–4.

73. Ron Miller, personal communication, January 1994.

74. "Networks to Share Networks," *American Libraries* 24, no. 4 (April 1993): 346.

75. David Brunell, personal communication, January 1994.

76. "Network Vendors Unite for Library Services," *Library Journal* 118, no. 16 (October 1, 1993): 26.

77. Leslie E. Vasquez, "RONDAC Meets in Massachusetts," *OCLC Newsletter* no. 205 (September/October 1993): 6–7.

78. "AMIGOS' Alternative Training Methods Assessment Culminates with Survey," *¿Qué Pasa?,* 14, no. 2 (April 1993): 5.

79. "Grant Facilitates Expansion of AMIGOS Preservation Service," *¿Qué Pasa?* 14, no. 2 (April 1993): 3.

80. "Introducing . . . Internet," *¿Qué Pasa?* 14, no. 4 (October 1993): 1.

81. "Consulting Services Kicks Off TQM at Texas A&M," *¿Qué Pasa?* 14, no. 3 (July 1993): 3.

82. "AMIGOS Consulting Team Starts Work on Tex-Share Planning Project," *¿Qué Pasa?* 14, no. 4 (October 1993): 1.

83. "FY 1991–92: Gradual Recovery from the Recession," *Action for Libraries* 19, no. 1 (January 1993): 2.

84. "New Home for BCR," *Technicalities* 12, no. 10 (October 1992): 3.

85. "Third Indicator to Be Available Through Internet," *Action for Libraries* 18, no. 3 (March 1993): 6.

86. "CAPCON to Offer Dial-in Internet Access," *Information Today* 9, no. 6 (June 1992): 3.

87. "CAPCON Initiates Contract Cataloging Service," *CAPCON Newsletter* (Winter 1992): 1.

88. CAPCON Continuing Education Series, Spring 1993.

89. Suzanne Schriar, *LVIS Is Alive in Illinois and Missouri* (unattributed publication, probably issued by ILLINET/OCLC, Springfield, Illinois, 1993).

90. "Thank You, Trainers!" *Illinois OCLC Users' Group Newsletter* no. 65 (August 1993): 2.

91. "MLC Offers Affordable Access to the INTERNET," *Automation Highlights* (August 31, 1993): 7–8.

92. "OCLC Corner: MLC Union List of Serials," *Automation Highlights,* August 31, 1993, p. 9.

93. Bill DeJohn, "On My Mind," *MINITEX Messenger* 11, no. 3 (September 29, 1993): 4–5.

94. "MINITEX Transmits via ARIEL," *MINITEX Messenger* 10, no. 1 (August 21, 1992): 4–5.

95. "NEON User Libraries' Program Beamed," *NEBASE News* 5, no. 1 (Fall 1992): 1.

96. "Internet Access through NELINET DIAL," *The NELINET Liaison* 14, no. 11 (November 1992): 1–2.

97. Marshall Keys, "NELINET Tops 500 Members," *The NELINET Liaison* 15, no. 9 (September 1993): 1, 5.

98. "The Balance Sheet," *The NELINET Liaison* 14, no. 2 (February 1992): 1–7.

99. "Affiliates: NELINET's Newest Participants," *The NELINET Liaison* 14, no. 4 (April 1992): 1, 5.

100. "NELINET to Help Unemployed Librarians Maintain/Upgrade Skills," *The NELINET Liaison* 14, no. 4 (April 1992): 1, 4.

101. "NELINET ILL Code Revision," *The NELINET Liaison* 14, no. 6 (June 1992): 1–2.

102. "Strategic Plan Complete," *OHIONETwork* 14, no. 4 (April 1992): 1.

103. "The Surveys are Coming!," *OHIONETwork* 15, no. 1 (January 1993): 1.

104. "OHIONET's Three-Year Marketing Plan," *OHIONETwork* 15, no. 4 (April 1993): 1.

105. "PALINET Workshops Now Offer CEUs," *PALINET News* no. 80 (January 1992): 1.

106. "CAPCON Connect Offers Internet Access," *PALINET News* no. 87 (September/October 1992): 3.

107. "Introducing the Pal-First Internet List," *PALINET News* no. 92 (August 1993): 1.

108. Amy Bernath, "Workshop Program Breaks Records, Expands Topics and Technologies," *Solinews* 18, no. 3 (Winter 1992): 1–2.

109. Amy Bernath, "New Continuing Education & Training Department to Expand Offerings," *Solinews* 20, no. 2 (March/April 1993): 1.

110. Sandra Nyberg, "SOLINET Receives Second NEH Grant for Cooperative Preservation Microfilming," *Solinews* 19, no. 1 (Summer 1992): 1–2.

111. Liz Hornsby, "SOLINET Now on Internet; Internet Access Option for Members Slated for Spring," *Solinews* 19, no. 1 (sic) (Fall 1992): 1–2.

112. Dawn Lamade, "Internet SOLutions Access Program Launched," *Solinews* 20, no. 1 (January/February 1993): 4–5.

113. Martha Richardson, "SOLINET Celebrates 20th Anniversary," *Solinews* 20, no. 1 (January/February 1993): 1.

114. Frank Grisham, "The Link: Regional Information Network," *Solinews* 20, no. 1 (January/February 1993): 3–4.

115. Paula T. Kaufman, "Message from the Board Chair: Strategic Vision," *Solinews* 20, no. 1 (January/February 1993): 3.

116. Paula T. Kaufman, "Message from the Board Chair: Of SURA and SOLINET," *Solinews* 20, no. 2 (March/April 1993): 3.

117. Frank Grisham, "The Link: SOLINET/SURA Update," *Solinews* 20, no. 5 (September/October 1993): 3.

118. "Utlas Purchased by ISM," *American Libraries* 24, no. 2 (February 1993): 119.

119. Tom Zillner, "Prototype Online Version of *New Tech News* Debuts," *New Tech News* (February 1992): 1.

120. "WILS Announces Internet Access for Members," *New Tech News* (September 1992): 1.

121. *WILS Annual Report* 1992–1993.

122. "Come Join Us in Celebrating 20 Years of WILS!" *Access* (March 1992): 2.

123. Michael Rogers, "Nets Around the Nation," *Library Journal* 118, no. 6 (October 1, 1993): 46, 45. (This article is extremely valuable for its analysis of the survey in chart and map format.)

124. Personal correspondence from U.S. Department of Education, Office of Library Programs.

125. David Kohl, op. cit. *Library Journal* (October 1, 1993): 46.

126. "Florida Libraries Launch Information Network," *Library Journal* 118, no. 11 (June 15, 1993): 22.

127. "Oregon and New Mexico Offer Statewide Networks," *Library Journal* 118, no. 19 (November 15, 1993): 26.

128. Ibid.

129. *The Seymour Plan: Electronically Connecting Maryland's Libraries* (Baltimore: Maryland State Department of Education, 1992).

130. *New York State Library Network Services Planning Task Force Report: Defining the Services, Roles and Relationships of the State Library as Information Provider, Broker, Publisher, Switch and Catalyst in a Networked Environment* (Albany: New York State Library, 1992).

131. Phyllis J. Van Orden and Adeline W. Wilkes, "School Library Media Centers and Networks," *Library Resources and Technical Services* 37, no. 1 (January 1993): 7–17.

132. "OCLC Saves Univ. $200,000," op. cit. *Library Journal* (November 15, 1993).

133. Public Law 102-194.

134. Ibid., Sec. 102(a).

135. *Proceedings of the NREN Workshop, Monterey, California, September 16–18, 1992.* Sponsored by Computing Research Association, EDUCOM, IEEE U.S. Activities Board, 1992.

136. John Clement, "Where We Are in Networking for K–12 Education: A First Annual Review," *EDUCOM Review* (September/October 1992): 20–23.

137. Rick Boucher, "The Challenge of Transition," *EDUCOM Review* (September/October 1992): 30–35.

138. "The Clinton Administration Wants to Make Sure That Every Citizen Has Access to the Proposed National Data Highway at a Reasonable Price," *The Chronicle of Higher Education* 40, no. 18 (January 5, 1994): A21.

139. *Proceedings of the NREN Workshop, Monterey, California, September 16–18, 1992.* Sponsored by Computing Research Association, EDUCOM, IEEE U.S. Activities Board, 1992.

140. A famous Jimmy Durante line.

141. *The Merit Networking Seminars* brochure (Ann Arbor, Michigan: Merit Network, 1992).

142. *OCLC's Linking Strategy: Internet and NREN* (Dublin, Ohio: OCLC, 1992).

143. Ibid. p. 54.

144. Paul Evan Peters, "Network Navigating and Navigators," *EDUCOM Review* (July/August 1992): 40–42.

145. Noreen Alldredge and Thomas G. Kirk, "Transformational Potential of Networked Information," *C&RL News* 54, no. 1 (January 1993): 18.

146. "Coalition for Networked Information," *NELINET Liaison* 15, no. 5 (May 1993): 1, 5.

147. "Librarians Seek Lane on National Information Highway," *Library Journal* 118, no. 7 (October 15, 1993): 12–13.

148. Maurice Mitchell and Laverna Saunders, "The National Information Infrastructure: Implications for Libraries," *Computers in Libraries* 13, no. 10 (November/December 1993): 53–56.

149. "Cataloging Directorate Hosts Copy Cataloging Seminar," *Library of Congress Information Bulletin* (July 1992).

150. Readers will recognize a paraphrase of Ranganathan's Rules.

151. Ronald L. Larsen, "The Library as a Network-Based Information Server," *EDUCOM Review* (Fall/Winter 1991): 42.

152. Marshall Keys, "On the Future of the OCLC Regional Networks," *Library Administration & Management* 6, no. 1 (Winter 1992): 10–14.

153. Ibid. p. 12.

Mexican Information Resources in Electronic Format

Shirley Ainsworth

El Colegio de México, Mexico, D.F.*

The world's economies are becoming increasingly interlinked and the role of information is assuming a greater importance. The expanding use of electronic communication brings to the foreground the issue of information flow, hitherto predominantly from north to south. The ability to access information resources from other countries, reflecting differing perspectives, may lead to a more profound understanding of questions of common interest.

A concrete example of the trend toward world globalization is the North American Free Trade Agreement (NAFTA), which promotes greater economic cooperation among Canada, Mexico, and the United States. This has stimulated much interest in Mexican information. But while Mexico is one of the foremost producers of databases in Latin America, it is difficult to find out what is available and how to access it, and these potentially useful resources are little exploited by librarians outside the country.

This report attempts to trace the development within Mexico of the diverse electronic formats—online databases, CD-ROMs, and Internet resources—covering such issues as access and database quality. Some of the major products currently available are reviewed, with emphasis on how these can be accessed. Addresses are included in the appendix to this report, along with a list of acronyms.

*On sabbatical leave as an ALA Library Fellow at the Mortenson Center for International Library Programs, University of Illinois at Urbana-Champaign.

Thanks to Micaela Chávez Villa for her help in verifying addresses for the appendix.

Origins and Development of Online Databases

In contrast to the United States and Western Europe, where commercial database vendors have dominated the online industry, in Mexico (as indeed in all of Latin America) most of the major bibliographic and other databases have been created by government or academic institutions, which have not been able to market them well. Much Mexican research, particularly in the scientific field, is published outside the country in foreign journals, a situation stimulated by academic promotion policies. The bibliographical control of this information is covered by the major indexing and abstracting services. For research published in Mexico—much of which in the social sciences and humanities is of a high quality—bibliographical control is still rather patchy and in many cases not very up to date. These databases, however, do contain much information not available elsewhere.

Access to online databases began in 1976, when the Servicio de Consulta a Bancos de Información (SECOBI), part of CONACYT, the Mexican equivalent of the United States's National Science Foundation, began to offer access to international systems such as DIALOG, BRS, ORBIT, QUESTEL, and ESA-IRS for Mexican searchers, centralizing contracts and billing in the national currency. SECOBI once played an important part in stimulating the creation of Mexican databases (several of which are loaded on the CONACYT computers) but has lost this role because of changing priorities within CONACYT.

The other important online database provider is the Centro de Informacíon Científica y Humanística (CICH), of the Universidad Nacional Autónoma de México (UNAM). Since 1978, CICH has produced not only online databases, but also print versions of indexes generated from these. The online databases mostly use MINISIS software, which along with Micro CDS/ISIS (Microisis) has been widely promoted in developing countries by UNESCO (the United Nations Educational, Scientific, and Cultural Organization). These databases must, of course, be searched in Spanish.

Online Access

One of the fundamental problems with using Mexican databases has been that of access. A recent enquiry to LALA-L,[1] the Latin Americanist librarians' listserv, confirmed that these online databases are not being utilized. Until fairly recently, access to online databases was via TELEPAC, the Mexican public data transmission network, under the jurisdiction of the Department of Telecommunications of the Secretaría de Comunicaciones y Transportes (SCT). Connections exist between TELEPAC and TYMNET, TELENET, and SPRINTNET in the United States, TRANSPAC in France, IPSS in the United Kingdom, ITALPAC in Italy, and so forth, so in theory there should be no problem in gaining access to Mexican online information. But TELEPAC use is heavy, making initial connection difficult, and it operates at a slow 1,200 bps asynchronous transmission. It is also prone to line noise, a condition exacerbated in bad weather. These factors have greatly hampered Mexican online development. Since the 1989 privatization of the Mexican telephone company, upon which TELEPAC depends, there has been extensive modernization of parts of the system, increasing the data transmission rate. However, this has not yet been carried over into online access.

The TELEPAC connection to the SECOBI databases had not been functioning for many months in early 1994 and SECOBI has been unable to give a date for the renewal of remote online access. At present it offers several direct dial-up access ports in Mexico City. A contract may be established with SECOBI (see Appendix) to enable access to its databases.

The CICH databases at UNAM, which were previously available through the SECOBI connection, are now available via Internet. These databases are being reloaded onto new equipment that will provide more remote access ports and faster response times. A contract can be established with CICH, which will provide access instructions.

CD-ROM Products

Because of the precarious state of online connections in Mexico, there has been a significant trend in the last few years toward CD-ROM production. The Centro Nacional Editor de Discos Compactos was established in 1983 at the University of Colima and has enjoyed much government support. The center to date has published 36 CD-ROMs—mostly, though not exclusively, of Mexican databases—with plans for a further 11 in the short term. It has made a concerted effort to offer little-known databases, compiling several CD-ROMs containing numerous smaller databases that would otherwise have remained totally inaccessible. One CD-ROM offers more than 50 multidisciplinary Latin American databases, but unfortunately each database must be searched separately. Colima has been exploiting the Micro CDS/ISIS software, which, while it has the benefit of being familiar to database users in developing countries, can be slow in data retrieval. Colima has published many other CD-ROMs on behalf of database producers, making available its equipment and expertise.

UNAM has also ventured into CD-ROM production after using a commercial producer for several years. UNAM uses a software called cd-unam, based on Rommaker with local modifications. It has produced some five CD-ROMs in the last year and more are planned. CICH will be the new production center for UNAM CD-ROMs.

CD-ROM production in Mexico is not the preserve of academic institutions, however, nor do the CD-ROMs produced contain exclusively bibliographical information. A noticeable trend in the last two years has been the inclusion of many more full-text databases and the entry of commercial enterprises into the market. These have tended to concentrate on the production of business directories and the full text of newspapers. The publication by INEGI, the national statistical agency, of the excellent CODICE90, covering the 1990 General Population and Housing Census, perhaps marks the beginning of statistical CD-ROM databases. INEGI also offers statistical information on diskettes.

For high-volume end-user usage, CD-ROMs are obviously a better option than remote online access because a subscription allows unlimited searching. But the trend toward CD-ROM production limits the casual user, who with online access offered through a system pays only for the amount of connect time. Some of these CD-ROMs are quite costly, and only larger or more specialized libraries may have sufficient funds, and the need, to purchase them.

Given that CD-ROM databases are inherently out of date compared to online services, more attention must be paid to the regular updating of the CD-ROMs.

Internet

Internet, which allows computers all over the world to connect with each other, offers both a way to solve problems of access to databases and a wealth of information available from them. One of Internet's greatest strengths is the ease with which information providers of all types and sizes can make files available on the network, which has obvious benefits for the small database producer.

Within Mexico there have been several proposals to form a national network, linking the universities via Internet. One proposal has been led by CONACYT, another by the Secretaría de Educación Pública (SEP), and a third, MEXnet, by the Instituto Tecnológico y de Estudios Superiores de Monterrey. The MEXnet directory currently includes some 33 participating institutions, although not all of these are yet connected.[2]

Some of the more interesting resources currently available via Internet include online catalogs—an excellent source of bibliographical information, current national newspaper texts and summaries, and statistical databases, as well as access to online databases. These are described in some detail below. Internet resources are growing constantly; a good way of exploring what is available is via the Mexican gopher servers. At present there are at least 12, mostly created during the past year.[3]

Databases Within Mexico

Database Quality

Electronic format in itself does not offer any guarantee of quality. While there are several outstanding products available in Mexico at present, it must be said that many suffer, to differing degrees, from a lack of quality control in indexing, coverage, timeliness, and continuity. It should be noted that indexing and abstracting are not part of the library school curriculum nor indeed of any other (witness the lack of back-of-the-book indexing in many Latin American books), which—together with a lack of Spanish-language thesauruses—contributes to descriptor control problems. Most databases do not, in fact, include abstracts. Frequent personnel changes, along with the desire to leave one's mark, have led to the creation of many new projects that are not continued, and to a duplication of resources. As a result, there has been a proliferation of smaller decentralized databases. In many cases there are few alternatives, and each must be judged on its merit.

With that caveat, descriptions follow of some of the major electronic resources currently available in Mexico.[4]

Newspapers

It has traditionally been very difficult to use Mexican newspapers. On the one hand, libraries have had difficulty in maintaining subscriptions to more than a select few because of cost and storage factors, and on the other there has been a lack of adequate indexing. One of the more recent indexes was

Cronologías e indicadores nacionales e internacionales (nos. 1–62, 1984–1989, published in Mexico by Servicios Informativos Procesados, 1985–1989). A monthly, this has now ceased publication. It provided a summary with sources of news drawn from ten Mexican national newspapers and two weekly magazines.

At present there are several alternatives:

CD-Press (CD-ROM) includes the full text of selected articles from some 20 Mexican national and regional newspapers, concentrating on Mexican issues. June 1991–date. Quarterly updates after 1993. Summaries available for 1987–1991. Software: romware from Nimbus Information Systems. [Difusión Científica][5]

El Financiero (CD-ROM). Full text of the newspaper, including statistical tables. 1993–date. Updated quarterly. Software: romware. [Difusión Científica]

SINF (CD-ROM) contains 107,000 references and abstracts from six Mexican dailies, covering January 1990–June 1992. Produced by the Dirección General de Información, UNAM. [CETEI]

NOTIMEX (CD-ROM, online). Complete text in Spanish of news stories transmitted over Notimex, the Mexican news service. January 1992–date. Semiannual updates include about 40,000 news stories. [NISC] Available online through Nexis.

INFOSEL (online), a commercial service, one of several of its type, offers online access to summaries of Mexican newspaper articles, but without reference to the original source. A document delivery service is available. [INFOSEL] PRODATO offers a similar service. [PRODATO]

Online newspapers available via UNAM. [Internet] These include the current daily headline stories of the major national newspapers and a weekly summary of major events.
Access procedure: ftp condor.dgsca.unam.mx
login: anonymous
password: (your E-mail address)
cd pub/Periodicos/Nacionales
ls (to list the files)
binary
get (the current daily headline story)
or for the weekly summary

cd pub/Periodicos/sint.seman
It is also possible to retrieve the following newspapers as compressed (zipped) files: *El Economista, El Nacional, La Jornada,* and *Uno+Uno,* by anonymous ftp to the condor as above, then
cd pub/imagen/noticia/periodicos
ls (to list the files)
binary
get (the required file)
Part of the text of *El Nacional* is also available via a menu. Here the text is arranged in fortnightly date ranges and is keyword searchable. Display is in pico, the text editor of the mail program pine.
Access procedure: telnet condor.dgsca.unam.mx
login: info
option 8 Sistemas de información
option 3 El Nacional

Business Mexico (online, print). Published by the American Chamber of Commerce in Mexico, contains the full text of the journal *Business Mexico,* a monthly dedicated to the promotion of trade and investment between the United States and Mexico. March 1989–date. Available online through Nexis.

Statistics

There are comparatively few databases available to the public concerning Mexican statistics. The more important issuing agencies are the Instituto Nacional de Estadística, Geografía e Informática (INEGI), which has a very large publishing program, the Banco de México, and the Secretaría de Comercio y Fomento Industrial (SECOFI).

CODICE90 (CD-ROM) contains the complete results of the 1990 General Census of Population and Housing, including the census cartography, detailing individual street blocks. It includes more than 26,000 variables not only at national, state, and municipal level, but also utilizes a smaller unit, known as AGEB—area geoestadística básica. Links can be made between geographical and statistical information, and data can be manipulated via the CD-ROM software, or downloaded into either spreadsheets or geographical information systems. This is an excellent product. Published in 1992. [INEGI] The 1990 Census results, together with the census cartography, are also available in a series of diskettes. [INEGI]

Sistema Automatizado de Información Censal (SAIC). *Resultados de los Censos Economicos 1986 y 1989* (diskette) contains the definitive results from the 1986 Economic Censuses, and the preliminary results from 1989, along with comparative data from these two. The 33 packets cover both national and state levels. Published 1991. [INEGI]

Bases de Datos de Series de Tiempo (CD-ROM) contains time series statistics from the System of National Accounts, along with data from surveys organized by INEGI. Geared toward historical, structural, and short-term analysis of the Mexican economy. The software permits manipulation of the data. Published in 1992. [INEGI]

SIE-BANXICO (online-SECOBI) is the database of the Banco de México. It contains around 35,000 statistical series covering the last 20 years in the following sectors: balance of payments and foreign trade, industrial activity, money and banking, price trends, and public sector finances. The database offers programs to perform mathematical operations, but it may be easier to download the information into a spreadsheet. It is a little unwieldy to use, but contains much valuable information. Temporarily inaccessible; there may be renewed online access during 1994.

SICM (Internet, diskette), the Sistema de Información Comercial de México is produced by SECOFI, covering foreign trade information classified according to the Harmonized System, and includes trade statistics by volume and value, 1988–date. Updated monthly.
>   Access procedure: ftp condor.dgsca.unam.mx
>   login: anonymous
>   password: (your E-mail address)
>   cd pub/docs/sicm
>   binary
>   get sicm.zip

It is also available from BANCOMEXT covering 1990–date, with quarterly updates.

Disco de Información Oportuna (DIO) (diskette) contains statistics relating to economic activity, employment, prices, public finances, money and banking, foreign trade, and so forth. Published in 1990 with LOTUS software. [INEGI]

Disco de Información Oportuna Regional (DIOR) (diskette) covers similar statistics at a state level. Published in 1991. [INEGI]

Standards and Patents

BANAPA (online-SECOBI, CD-ROM) is the Mexican patents database, containing more than 72,000 records since 1972. Abstracts are available 1980–date. Produced by SECOFI. Accessibility: local dial-up, probable renewed remote access during 1994. The CD-ROM version contains 50,000 records, covering 1980–1992. [Difusión Científica]

NORM (online-SECOBI, CD-ROM), the standards database, provides citations to documents containing official Mexican standards. Includes 33 specific industries and hundreds of products. Produced by SECOFI. Accessibility: local dial-up, probable renewed remote access during 1994. CD-ROM version published as *Normas Oficiales Mexicanas*, 1994. [Difusión Científica]

Legal Sources

There are a number of resources in this area.

UNAM-JURE (online-SECOBI) contains citations, summaries, and the full text of legal documents appearing in the official dailies of the Mexican federal and state governments. Coverage 1918–1940, 1976–date. Updates: bimonthly. Produced by the Instituto de Investigaciones Jurídicas of UNAM. Accessibility: local dial-up, probable renewed remote access during 1994.

DIALEX (CD-ROM) contains more than 360,000 judicial expositions published in the *Diario Oficial de la Federación*, 1917–1990. Compiled from the summaries appearing in the *Diario Oficial*. An updated edition covering 1917–1992 is planned for 1994. Produced by the Archivo General de la Nación. [Colima]

DATALEX. *Indice de disposiciones de caracter general publicadas en el Diario Oficial de la Federación* . . . Mexico: DATALEX, 1982–date, monthly updates (print), is an outstanding print index. Legal reforms approved during this period cause extensive links to be made to the original legislation, along with any intervening reforms, even though these may lie outside the time coverage of the index. It has a controlled vocabulary and extensive cross references that help in keeping track of the many terminological variations. A help phone line is available, as well as a document delivery service. Updates: monthly [DATALEX]

Legislación Federal Mexicana (CD-ROM) contains the full text of 222 Mexican laws in force, including reforms until July 1992. Compiled from the *Diario Oficial*. Also contains a directory of the Cámara de Diputados. Produced by the Cámara de Diputados. [Colima]

Poder Judicial de la Federación. Jurisprudencia y Tesis Aisladas, 1917–1992. IUS II (CD-ROM) contains the full text of the decisions and working documents of the Mexican Supreme Court on five CD-ROMs, as well as that of 24 Mexican laws currently in force. CD-ROMs also available singly. Produced by the Suprema Corte de Justicia de la Nación. [Colima]

Directories

There are two useful directories for Latin American databases.

Barbarena Blásquez, Elsa, et al., *Directorio de bases de datos de América Latina y el Caribe: DIBALC.* Mexico: Universidad Nacional Autónoma de México, Facultad de Filosofía y Letras, 1992. 144 p. Contains some 659 listings of databases produced in Latin America.

LAIB, Latin American Information Base (Internet, diskette) lists more than 800 databases, CD-ROMs, and networks, produced in Latin America and elsewhere. This is an electronic directory, currently mounted on the Latin American gopher at the University of Texas. Available as a DOS database in Clipper, or in Windows, in English, Spanish, and Portuguese. Produced by Kinloch C. Walpole, Jr. Regular updating.

Access procedure: ftp lanic.utexas.edu
Name: anonymous
Password: (your E-mail address)
cd pub/lanic/laib
binary
get LAIB.ZIP
get AREADME.DOC
get PKUNZIP.EXE
Also available on diskette from Kinloch C. Walpole, Jr. [LAIB]

Other directories include:

Kompass Mexico (CD-ROM, print), the Mexican version of the Kompass international business directories. Includes some 20,000 Mexican companies at a basic directory level. Published 1993 by INFOTEC. Software: romware. [Difusión Científica]

IBCON (CD-ROM, diskette, print), a directory publisher in Mexico City, published ten of its most popular print directories on a CD-ROM in 1992. This includes directories of information centers and libraries, government functionaries, and large exporters and importers, and permits the printing of mailing labels. The directories are also available singly as diskettes (without search software) and or in print versions. [IBCON]

Industridata (CD-ROM, diskette, print), includes 3,187 large and medium-sized businesses from the whole of Mexico, corresponding to the print directories of the same name, published by Mercamerica S.A. CD-ROM [Difusión Científica], diskette [IBCON]

Bibliographic Databases

The majority of Mexican databases are bibliographic; included here is a selection of the more useful.

CLASE (online-CICH, CD-ROM, print), produced by CICH, UNAM, indexes Latin American journals in the social sciences and humanities. Until 1982 the print version also carried a citation index (similar to the ISI Citation Indexes). Online coverage: 1979–1993, 98,000 references. Updating: quarterly, latest update 1993(I) [via Internet]

Periodica (online-CICH, CD-ROM, print) indexes Latin American journals in science and technology, and has a keyword index in English. Online its title is PERIODIC. Online coverage: 1979–1993, 95,000 references. Updating: quarterly, latest update, 1993(I) [via Internet]

BIBLAT (online-CICH, CD-ROM, print) covers multidisciplinary research published outside the region by Latin American authors, and by foreign authors about Latin America. Online coverage: 1979–1991, 78,000 references. Latest update: 1991 [via Internet]

Mexinv (online-CICH, CD-ROM) records specifically Mexican research in all fields, and is a subset of CLASE, Periodica, and BIBLAT. Online coverage: 1978–1989, 44,000 references. Latest update: 1991(II) [via Internet]

The CICH databases were available until January 1988 as BIBLAT on the Questel system in France. Alternative electronic access has been via a CD-ROM:

Bibliografia Latinoamericana (CD-ROM), includes more than 200,000 records and 6 databases, 5 from CICH (CLASE, Periodica, BIBLAT, MEXINV, and DESA, a small database on disasters consisting of some 500 references, which is no longer carried online) and 1 from the Centro Universitario de Investigaciones Bibliotecológicas of UNAM (INFOBILA, covering library and information science in Latin America, which is only accessible on-site at the present). 2nd ed. produced by Multiconsult in 1990 using Microbiblos Laser software. [Multiconsult] CICH is to publish an updated version of the CD-ROM in 1994, using cd-unam software. [CETEI]

TESIUNAM (CD-ROM) includes some 180,000 references to theses, from *licenciatura* (undergraduate) to doctorate, granted by UNAM and other major Mexican universities. Coverage: 1914–1992. Produced by the Dirección General de Bibliotecas of UNAM, 1993. Software: cd-unam. [CETEI]

SERIUNAM (CD-ROM) is a union list of periodicals held not only in the UNAM libraries but also in 62 other academic libraries in Mexico. Includes 31,000 journal titles. Produced by the Dirección General de Bibliotecas of UNAM, 1993. Software: cd-unam. [CETEI]

This updates, but does not completely replace, the

Catálogo colectivo de publicaciones seriadas existentes en unidades de información de la República Mexicana, CCPS. Mexico: CONACYT, 1988 (CD-ROM, microfiche). The CD-ROM version is included on one of the first University of Colima CD-ROMs, *Bancos Bibliográficos Mexicanos I,* published in 1989. Until recently it was also available as an online database through SECOBI.

A third partial union list of serials is much smaller, including titles held in five of the nine Mexican libraries participating in the AMIGOS cooperative interlibrary loan project. It is available as part of the online library catalog at the University of the Americas, Puebla.

Access via Internet:
telnet bibes.pue.udlap.mx
login: library
option 4 Catalogo de revistas Grupo Amigos Mexico

ARIES (CD-ROM) contains descriptions of 14,000 research projects conducted by 6,000 academics at all the major Mexican universities, and the San Carlos University of Guatemala. Published in 1993 by the Dirección General de Intercambio Académico of the UNAM. This was previously available as an online database with CICH, but at the moment online access is on-site. [CETEI]

CIBIMEX (CD-ROM), a bibliography of Mexican publications, contains 102,500 titles of books published between 1970 and 1992. Compiled from diverse sources, including automated Mexican library catalogs. Produced by the Centro de Información Bibliográfica Mexicana, 1992. [Colima]

ISBN México (CD-ROM), 2nd ed. 1990, includes 32,000 records of books published in Mexico, 1985–1990. Produced by Multiconsult. [Multiconsult]

ARGENA (CD-ROM) is an interesting product from the Archivo General de la Nación. It contains a description of the 322 document groups held in the Archivo, and lists the contents of 22 of these, along with bibliographical references, illustrations, and so forth. Produced in 1993. [Colima]

Mexican Library Online Catalogs

Comparatively few Mexican libraries have online catalogs, and fewer are available via Internet. Unfortunately among the unavailable is that of the Biblioteca Nacional, the National Library, whose only off-site access remains an author catalog:

Catálogo Oficial, Biblioteca Nacional de México, 39 reels of 16 mm. microfilm. Mexico: UNAM, Instituto de Investigaciones Bibliográficas, 1982.

Similarly, the Biblioteca Nacional de Antropología e Historia is still served by a dictionary catalog:

Catálogo de la Biblioteca Nacional de Antropología e Historia, 10 vols. Boston, Mass.: G. K. Hall, 1972. Also available on microfilm.

Online Catalogs Available on Internet

Perhaps the most important online catalog currently available on Internet is that of the UNAM library system, including its more than 160 libraries.

Access procedure:
telnet condor.dgsca.unam.mx (132.248.10.3)
login: info (Or, "library" bypasses the submenus)
option 9, Consulta a bibliotecas,
option 1, Dirección General de Bibliotecas
login: dgb

Via this interface, access is by keyword, without Boolean operators. The display format is short and provides locations in individual libraries.
A more standard interface to the catalog, allowing structured searching and Boolean operators, is also available via Internet. Apart from LIBRUNAM, the part corresponding to books, TESIUNAM and SERIUNAM are also available on this interface, but only the parts corresponding to the UNAM holdings.

Access procedure:
telnet 132.248.67.1
enter terminal type and memory required: vt100 150k
login: anonymous
password: guest

The Dirección General de Bibliotecas of UNAM plans to publish in August of 1994 a new edition of LIBRUNAM on CD-ROM, using its cd-unam software [CETEI]. A previous edition, updated until June 1990, included 400,000 titles, along with locations. This was produced by Multiconsult, using Microbiblos Laser software.

Other library catalogs available include:

The Instituto Tecnológico y de Estudios Superiores de Monterrey (ITESM)
Access procedure:
telnet academ02.mty.itesm.mx (131.178.4.15)
login: mtycat
Choose Información Bibliográfica from menu

ITESM—Chihuahua Campus
Access procedure:
available through gopher
other gopher servers
North America
Mexico
ITESM-Chihuahua
Biblioteca del Campus
Searching is by keyword

Universidad de Guadalajara
Access procedure:
telnet udgserv.cencar.udg.mx (148.202.3.2)
login: tequila
password: informa
Also via Hytelnet, and gopher
other gopher servers
North America
Mexico
Universidad de Guadalajara
menu item 12, Sistema de información tequila

University of the Americas, Puebla
Access procedure:
telnet bibes.pue.udlap.mx (140.148.5.4)
login: library
vt100 emulation only
Includes some 95,000 items, books, and journal titles. Uses Sidney's Library Software. Note: exit via telnet escape sequence ^], not "salida" from the menu. Slow. Also via Hytelnet.

Universidad de Monterrey
  Access procedure:
  telnet umhp01.mty.udem.mx (148.238.1.9)
  login: library
Uses Dynix software

Note: The addresses given here may differ somewhat from those provided in gopher and Hytelnet, which are not always up to date. Bear in mind that Internet resources change frequently.

CD-COLMEX (CD-ROM) lists some 300,000 titles from the library of the Colegio de México, specialized in social sciences and the humanities. Published 1994, using cd-unam software. Internet access was planned for 1994. [COLMEX]

Universidad Autónoma Metropolitana (CD-ROM) lists the library holdings of the three campuses. Published in 1991, with an update planned for 1994. Not yet accessible on Internet from outside Mexico City. [Colima]

Access to the Documents

The full-text information resources clearly represent no further problem, but how is one to get access to the documents included in the bibliographical databases? A little must be said about the interlibrary loan (ILL) system in Mexico. There is no centralized ILL system, and indeed no national union catalog. (Serials fare rather better.) Many libraries are not yet automated, and the mail system is woefully inadequate. Traditionally an ILL agreement must be made library to library, which makes for a great number of agreements!

A significant beginning has been made with the creation of AMIGOS, a grouping of nine academic libraries in the Mexico City area with some 23 libraries in the southwestern part of the United States, for the purpose of cooperative loans. The program is coordinated by Robert Seal of the University of Texas at El Paso, and has already begun to make a real difference to the Mexican libraries involved. However, neither the UNAM libraries nor the Biblioteca Nacional are a part of this project, and clearly much remains to be done.

There are, however, several options for librarians and information specialists outside Mexico to gain access to the documents themselves:

INFOTEC, a document center specializing in services to industry, offers document delivery of material not only from its own collections, which include standards, patents, and statistical information, but also from libraries in the Mexico City area. Another of their services is database searching.

CICH, already mentioned several times, offers photocopies of material held in the UNAM libraries. The material included in its databases is all located within UNAM. CICH will also search its databases for the casual user who balks at the thought of accessing them directly.

SECOBI also offers database searching, and a document delivery service.

It might also be useful to contact the Biblioteca Nacional for the loan of Mexican books, the Hemeroteca Nacional for journals, or major academic libraries such as that of El Colegio de México.

Notes

1. Lala-l@uga.bitnet
2. The file MEXnet_directorio.rtf is available by anonymous ftp to telecom.mty.itesm.mx in the directory pub/incoming/contactos.
3. Some of these are available via gopher/other gopher servers/North America/Mexico.
4. The information contained in the following sections is correct as of January 1994.
5. The producers/distributors are included in the appendix.

Appendix

Useful Addresses

Online Searches

Centro de Informacíon Científica y Humanística (CICH)
Universidad Nacional Autónoma de México
Enrique Barreto
Secretario Técnico Administrativo
Apdo. 70-392
C.P. 04510 México, D.F.
Tel. (525) 622-3967
FAX (525) 616-2557
E-mail enrique@selene.cichcu.unam.mx
For a search carried out by CICH staff, contact Georgina Ortega at the same address;
Tel. (525) 622-3955, 622-3956;
E-mail gortega@selene.cichcu.unam.mx.

Servicio de Consulta a Bancos de Información (SECOBI)
Ing. Lourdes Villagran
Coordinadora Ejecutiva de SECOBI
Patricio Sanz 1317, p.b.
Col. del Valle,
C.P. 03100 México D.F.
Tel. (525) 559-2005
FAX (525) 327-7476

CD-ROM and Diskette Producers/ Distributors in Mexico

These are included for reference purposes. There are many distributors in the United States, which I have not attempted to include.

Banco Nacional de Comercio Exterior (BANCOMEXT)
Lic. Paula Rusinsky
Subgerente de Recursos Informativos
Periférico Sur 4333
Col. Jardines en la Montaña
C.P. 14210 México D.F.
Tel. (525) 227-9000
FAX (525) 227-9070

Centro de Tecnología Electrónica e Informática (CETEI)
Lic. Amparo Castillo
Camino Real a Xochimilco 60
Tepepan
C.P. 16020 México D.F.
Tel. (525) 675-3001, 675-4514
FAX (525) 675-4484

Colima
Profa. Blanca Alvarez
Centro Nacional Editor de Discos Compactos
Universidad de Colima
Avenida Universidad 333
C.P. 28000 Colima
México
Tel. (331) 49621, 43004, 43381
FAX (331) 43006

El Colegio de México (COLMEX)
Biblioteca Daniel Cosío Villegas
Camino al Ajusco 20
Col. Pedregal de Sta. Teresa
C.P. 01000 México, D.F.
Tel. (525) 645-5083
FAX (525) 645-4584

DATALEX Información Legislativa
  Mexicana S.A. de C.V.
Carlos Gordillo, Gerente
Canoa 571-702
Tizapán
C.P. 01090 México, D.F.
Tel. (525) 616-0847, 616-1686
FAX (525) 550-2314

Difusión Científica CD-ROM
Lic. Norma Montesdeoca León
Directora General
Glorieta Clavería 123
Col. Clavería
C.P. 02080 México D.F.
Tel. (525) 341-3767, 341-3707
FAX (525) 341-3647, 341-7651

IBCON S.A.
Gutenberg 224
Col. Anzures
C.P. 11590 México D.F.
Tel./FAX (525) 255-4577, 255-5087, 255-5183, 255-5117

**Instituto Nacional de Estadística, Geografía e
  Informática (INEGI)**
Patriotismo 711, 7o.piso
Col. San Juan Mixcoac
C.P. 03920 México D.F.
Tel. (525) 598-8935, 563-9935
FAX (525) 598-8941

**Información Selectiva S.A. de C.V.
  (INFOSEL)**
Washington 629 Ote.
Monterrey, Nuevo León
C.P. 64000, México
Tel. (583) 45 51 00 Ext. 3084
FAX (583) 40 05 60

Latin American Information Base (LAIB)
Kinloch C. Walpole, Jr.
Box 13856
Gainesville, Florida 32604
Tel. (904) 371-0458
FAX (904) 371-4495
compuserve 76200.3533@compuserve.com

Multiconsult S.C
Insurgentes Sur 949, piso 9
Col. Napoles
C.P. 03810 México D.F.
Tel. (525) 536-8672
FAX (525) 687-7482

**National Information Services Corporation
  (NISC)**
Suite 6, Wyman Towers
3100 Saint Paul St.
Baltimore, Md. 21218
Tel. (410) 243-0797
Fax (410) 243-0982

PRODATO
Prosperidad 31A
Col. Escandón
C.P. 11800 México, D.F.
Tel. (525) 277-4060
FAX (525) 277-4791

Major Interlibrary Loan Sites

Biblioteca Nacional de México
Instituto de Investigaciones Bibliográficas
Universidad Nacional Autónoma de México
Centro Cultural
Ciudad Universitaria
Apdo. Postal 29-124
Deleg. Coyoacan
C.P. 04510 México D.F.
Tel. (525) 622-6801
FAX (525) 665-0951

Hemeroteca Nacional (for journals)
Above Address
Tel. (525) 622-6820, 622-6800
FAX (525) 665-0951

El Colegio de México
Biblioteca Daniel Cosío Villegas
Camino al Ajusco 20
Col. Pedregal de Sta. Teresa
C.P. 01000 México D.F.
Tel. (525) 645-5083
FAX (525) 645-4584

INFOTEC
Mtra. Guadalupe Carrión
Directora de Recursos Informativos
Av. San Fernando 37
Col. Torriello Guerra
Deleg. Tlalpan México, D.F.
Tel. (525) 606-0011, 606-1620
FAX (525) 606-0386
dialmail 15782

Acronyms

ARGENA	Archivo General de la Nación
ARIES	Acervo de Recursos de Instituciones de Educación Superior
BANAPA	Banco Nacional de Patentes
BANCOMEXT	Banco Nacional de Comercio Exterior
BIBLAT	Bibliografía Latinoamericana
CIBIMEX	Centro de Información Bibliográfica Mexicana
CICH	Centro de Información Científica y Humanística
CLASE	Citas Latinoamericanas en Ciencias Sociales y Humanidades
CODICE90	Consulta Dinámica Censal
CONACYT	Consejo Nacional de Ciencia y Tecnología
DIALEX	Legislación al Día
INEGI	Instituto Nacional de Estadística, Geografía e Informática
INFOSEL	Información Selectiva
LAIB	Latin American Information Base
SCT	Secretaría de Comunicaciones y Transportes
SECOBI	Servicio de Consulta a Bancos de Información
SECOFI	Secretaría de Comercio y Fomento Industrial
SEP	Secretaría de Educación Pública
SICM	Sistema de Información Comercial de México
SIE-BANXICO	Sistema de Información Económica del Banco de México
UNAM	Universidad Nacional Autónoma de México

References

Colson, Harold, and Peter Stern. "Databases." *In Latin America and the Caribbean: A Critical Guide to Research Sources*, edited by Paula H. Covington. (Bibliographies and Indexes in Latin American and Caribbean Studies, 2) pp. 139–153. New York: Greenwood Press, 1992.

Levison, Andrew, and Heberto Reynel Iglesias. "The Online Industry in Mexico." *Online* 17 (May 1993): 116–119.

Marcaccio, Kathleen Young, ed. *Gale Directory of Databases*. 2 vols. Detroit, Mich.: Gale Research Corp., 1993.

Rosenberg, Victor, and Gretchen Whitney, eds. *The Transfer of Scholarly, Scientific and Technical Information between North and South America: Proceedings of a Conference*. Metuchen, N.J.: Scarecrow, 1986.

United Nations Centre on Transnational Corporations. *Transborder Data Flows and Mexico: A Technical Paper*. New York: United Nations, 1991.

The International Role of U.S. Librarians

Hannelore B. Rader

Director of the Main Library
Cleveland State University

As ambassadors of culture, information, and ideas, U.S. librarians have for generations helped remove boundaries separating cultures and peoples. They have fought courageously to provide access to books and information for the broad spectrum of the United States' populace and to oppose censorship and other restrictions on libraries as centers for learning. They have instituted a wide array of user services to help create a literate citizenry for a democratic society; they have collaborated to set standards for library collections, cataloging, processing, and services; and they have successfully built impressive automated library and information systems while integrating the latest technology and electronic inventions into their user services. U.S. librarians also have much to offer the world in creating, operating, and maintaining libraries and user services, and have been actively involved in numerous international activities since the late 1800s. In the last decade of the twentieth century it will be even more important for American librarians in increasing numbers to continue to involve themselves in international activities.

ALA's International Activities

U.S. librarians have shown an active interest in international cooperation since the first conference of the American Library Association (ALA) in 1876, in which librarians from other countries participated. In 1900 a committee on international cooperation was founded and international cooperation became a regular activity of ALA. In 1927 ALA was instrumental in founding the International Federation of Library Associations and Institutions (IFLA). In 1920 and 1941, respectively, ALA opened the American Library in Paris and the Biblioteca Benjamin Franklin in Mexico City. As early as 1929 international exchanges took place and overseas librarians began to arrive in the United States to study in library schools.

During the 1940s ALA took an active role in library and cultural activities around the world. U.S. librarians became advocates for books and libraries everywhere and future leaders from other countries were introduced to librarianship through visits, practice, and education. In 1942 ALA instituted the Board of International Relations and established an International Relations Office; in 1949 the International Relations Round Table (IRRT) came into being. Many of these international endeavors were supported by special grants and ceased to exist as soon as funding was terminated. The International Relations Office closed in 1947 for lack of funding. The level of international activities within ALA has fluctuated since the 1950s with rising and falling funding support and membership interest.

Exchange Programs

During the 1980s a resurgence of interest in international relations was evident. The establishment of the Library/Book Fellows Program in 1986, under the able leadership of Robert Doyle at ALA and with support from the United States Information Agency (USIA), provided a strong impetus to U.S. librarians to become more involved internationally through service as information ambassadors around the world. To date, groups of 15 to 17 American librarians have served as Library/Book Fellows in six countries. ALA and USIA initiatives call for an expansion of this program as well as an additional program to bring groups of librarians from other countries to the United States to work with American librarians in order to gain new library expertise.

U.S. librarians have also been involved in a variety of international exchange programs. Some of these exchanges have been with public, school, and special librarians; most have been among academic librarians. These exchanges have been arranged by individual libraries, or through associations, groups, and agencies. Within ALA, more than 20 committees and subcommittees concern themselves with international relations. A joint subcommittee created in 1986, the IRC/IRRT (International Relations Committee/International Relations Round Table) Subcommittee on International Exchanges, has prepared guidelines and lists of funding sources and groups sponsoring exchanges, and is a major source of information on international library exchanges. The Special Libraries Association, the Music Library Association, and the American Association of Law Libraries also have international relations committees and foster international librarian exchanges.

[For an account of the 1993 visit to the United States by 17 library professionals from 15 countries, see the article "The American Libraries Project" in this section.—*Ed.*]

Globalization of Information

There are many reasons for the increased interest and need to become more globally involved, especially for those working in information-related jobs and education. Thanks to the globalization of telecommunications and electronic information networks such as Internet, people everywhere, particularly educators and information specialists, can communicate instantly, share information, and hold discussions at a moment's notice. It is commonplace nowadays to communicate on a daily basis with colleagues around the world on Internet. Librarians are major participants in these networks and information sharing groups.

Business Information

Business is likewise becoming globalized. Companies are expanding internationally at a rapid rate; few wholly American businesses will be left by the end of this century. Today one out of six U.S. jobs bears directly on some aspect of international trade and one of three farm acres is used to produce food for export. Tourism has also increased greatly with more U.S. citizens traveling abroad and more visitors from other countries coming to the United States. Information needed in the internationalization of American business must be provided quickly and competently. Librarians in special libraries are particularly aware of this and have quickly become acclimated to their new environment. The Special Libraries Association has for several years sponsored an International Special Librarians Day in April and organized an annual international special library conference with a variety of business and information needs themes.

Higher Education

Higher education is also becoming more international, as evidenced by the tremendous growth in the number of foreign students attending U.S. universities and colleges. In 1992–1993, 419,585 foreign students were enrolled in U.S. universities, 48 percent of them from East Asia and the Pacific. Almost half were graduate students pursuing studies in the sciences, engineering, and business. At the same time, there has been a dramatic increase in the number of foreign instructors in U.S. universities in the last decade, again particularly in these fields. Additionally, the higher education curriculum itself has become more internationalized. Non-Western and multicultural studies and courses have been created, and business, law, engineering, medicine, and education curricula have been reviewed and made more international. In 1988 the American Association of State Colleges and Universities reissued its statement on "The International Responsibility of Higher Education," stressing the importance of international education in preparing students to address global issues.

Given this internationalization, librarians in institutions of higher education must refine the role of the library. This can be accomplished by creating access to global information and by establishing instructional programs for foreign students, to help them acquire information retrieval and assessment skills. Librarians can offer special orientation and information skills programs to ease students into the American system of library and information access and use. Many U.S. students also spend a year studying abroad and need preparation in how to use libraries in other countries.

New Technology

The emerging information highway will eventually change the nature of scholarly communication, which still employs print publishing as its major vehicle. Librarians must work with scholars to build worldwide information and communications systems using evolving electronic technology. This will mean that librarians must be knowledgeable both about new electronic information communication systems and about the activities of librarians and scholars in other countries.

Conclusion

Librarians have much to contribute to the newly evolving information society, whether in business, education, or society. While U.S. librarians can assume a leadership role by sharing their experiences with librarians in other countries through exchanges, workshops, institutes, and electronic communication, they must also realize that they have much to learn about information and library work from other cultures and from librarians in other countries who have developed innovative systems of their own and who have different and unique approaches to information access and sharing.

References

American Association of State Colleges and Universities. *The International Responsibilities of Higher Education.* Washington, D.C.: AASCU 1975/1988.

Barry, Barbara. "International Exchanges and Curricular Change," *Phi Kappa Phi Journal* 68 (Fall 1988): 31–34.

Doyle, Robert. *Activities, Observations, Strategies and Plans of Action.* Chicago: American Library Association and International Relations Committee, 1989.

Duffy, Joseph. "Opinions/Essays: Foreign Student; US Surplus with Asia." *Christian Science Monitor* 85 (November 19, 1993): 23.

The American Libraries Project

Pamela Barton
Project Director
International Education and Exchange Programs
Academy for Educational Development
1255 23rd St. N.W., Washington, DC 20037
202-862-1900

Since 1982 the United States Information Agency (USIA) has sponsored an annual project that brings library professionals from around the world to the United States for a four-week examination of U.S. libraries, library and information science education, and librarianship. The project provides opportunities for approximately 15 participants each year to become familiar with the dominant characteristics of American libraries, and exposes them to current techniques and approaches to library management in the United States. Through site visits—to libraries ranging from the Library of Congress to the Champlain Valley Union High School library in Vermont—and discussions with scholars, government officials, librarians, and volunteers, these visiting librarians see the diversity that exists in American libraries. Attendance at the annual conference of the American Library Association has provided further contacts and insight into current issues and trends for the visitors.

The program is a collaborative effort by the federal government, nonprofit organizations, and volunteers across the United States.

This report focuses on the American Libraries project that took place June 13 through July 8, 1993.

Project Goals

The goals of the project, as specified by USIA, are:

- To provide firsthand information on a wide variety of American libraries in diverse geographic and social settings
- To promote a better understanding of the role of American libraries in U.S. society and the involvement of libraries in educational, informational, cultural, and recreational activities
- To address mutual concerns in librarianship and to foster institutional linkages between foreign and American libraries

Program Sponsor

The program sponsor, USIA, is part of the executive branch of the U.S. government. It administers the international educational exchange program widely known as the Fulbright Program. This was established in 1946, under legislation introduced by Senator J. William Fulbright of Arkansas, to stimulate and facilitate mutual understanding among nations through governmental and private educational and cultural activities. Several types of exchange activities are sponsored under this legislation, allowing students, teachers, scholars, and professionals from the United States to study, teach, lecture, and conduct research in other countries, and creating similar opportunities for foreign nationals traveling to the United States. [For further information on USIA, see the article in the Federal Agency and Federal Library Reports section—*Ed.*]

The American Libraries project is a major activity of the Fulbright Program's International Visitor Program, which works to strengthen and improve communication through the sponsorship of direct contacts. It provides the opportunity for visitors from other nations to study and observe the United States through experiences close to their own professional and personal interests, and for Americans, in turn, to learn about the intellectual and cultural diversity of other societies.

Program Administrator

The Academy for Educational Development (AED), a private, nonprofit organization, was contracted to design and implement the 1993 program. USIA determines the overall goals and themes of the project, and AED develops the itinerary, determines issues to be pursued, identifies resources, and arranges events, often in cooperation with local sponsors. The local sponsors may be either interested library professionals or members of a network of local Councils for International Visitors that exists in communities across the country.

Since 1979 AED has designed and conducted more than 250 projects for USIA, involving some 2,500 visiting professionals. Project topics have included print and broadcast journalism, radio and television broadcasting, communications and development, American theater, American film, higher education, work and education, and drug abuse prevention.

Community Support

The National Council for International Visitors (NCIV) is an association of community groups, most volunteer, in 102 cities and towns across the United States, that provide specialized services to international visitors and foreign scholars. In cooperation with AED, NCIV community affiliates arrange local professional and cultural exchange programs for international visitors and groups sponsored by USIA and the U.S. Agency for International Development.

Local Councils for International Visitors in Cincinnati, Tulsa, Austin, and Chicago participated in the 1993 American Libraries project.

Escort Officers

The group was accompanied throughout the monthlong program by three escort officers contracted by USIA through the U.S. Department of State. The escort officers have extensive experience in cross-cultural communication, and in assisting professionals from other countries to understand and explore U.S. society and culture. One, a librarian, has accompanied the libraries group annually for eight years. The escorts ensured that the logistical and professional content of the project flowed smoothly throughout the month and acted as liaisons between AED and program coordinators in individual cities.

Program Participants

Seventeen library professionals from 15 countries participated in the 1993 American Libraries project. They were chosen by USIA from nominations submitted by officers of the U.S. Information Service (USIS, as USIA is known overseas) in U.S. Embassies around the world. USIS officers nominate established or potential leaders who hold positions of importance, and who can produce a multiplier effect by sharing information with colleagues and others in their countries. USIS also attempts to choose people with little or no professional experience in the United States.

Among the visitors were the assistant chief of the Supreme Court of Justice Library in Buenos Aires, Argentina; the head of the Readers' Service Department at Moricz Zsigmond Library in Nyiregyhaza, Hungary; and the head of the Central Library at Sebelas Maret University in Solo, Central Java, Indonesia.

Other countries represented were the Bahamas, Costa Rica, the Czech Republic, Grenada, India, Jamaica, Mexico, Nigeria, Pakistan, Russia, Saudi Arabia, and Zimbabwe.

Despite the participants' varied backgrounds, they shared many common concerns. In written questionnaires, they listed the following themes and subjects as most relevant to their work:

- Automated library systems and networking
- Preservation, conservation, and storage

- Services for rural communities
- Fund raising and public relations
- Library science education
- Access to information
- The future of libraries
- Reference work
- Services offered by public libraries
- Online services
- Academic and law libraries
- Use of volunteers
- Library management
- The Library of Congress

Itinerary

The 1993 project commenced in Washington, D.C., with an orientation to U.S. libraries, an explanation of federal library policy, an introduction to library education, and visits to the Library of Congress and other important libraries in the Washington area. Next, participants traveled to Burlington, Vermont, where they explored a state library system that uses computer technology to link rural, regional, and university libraries. The group then traveled to New York for a program that focused on library resources in the city: the New York Public Library, the Schomberg Center for Research in Black Culture, and the library at the Metropolitan Museum of Art. Next, participants went to New Orleans, Louisiana, to attend the annual conference of the American Library Association.

The group then divided into three teams according to professional specialization. Participants involved in the management of special libraries visited Cincinnati, Ohio, where they sampled some of the more than 200 special libraries in the area. In Tulsa, Oklahoma, participants who worked in public libraries had the staff and facilities of one of the finest public library systems in the country at their disposal. Participants interested in library science education and university libraries visited Austin, Texas, where they examined the School of Library and Information Science at the University of Texas. The group reassembled in Chicago where the final module featured the advanced technology developed by the Northwestern University Library, the Harold Washington Library Center, and the Center for Research Libraries, as well as a project synthesis and evaluation.

The itinerary was based on the strength and diversity of library resources in each location, on the success of past visits to a certain area, and on the enthusiasm of local Councils for International Visitors to host this group of librarians. An effort was made to include large cities and small towns in geographically and culturally diverse regions of the United States. This itinerary afforded participants opportunities to examine a variety of types of libraries: federal, university, college, public, special, research, and museum. The group also examined related associations, academic programs, and advisory committees.

Washington

The project's opening week in Washington, D.C., (June 14–20) was designed to provide participants with a foundation of common knowledge about libraries in the United States. It also enabled them to explore the abundance of library resources in the Washington metropolitan area. To provide a context for understanding the role of libraries in this country, a professor of government at Georgetown University presented an overview of the U.S. government, and an official from the U.S. Department of Education explained the education system.

Peter Young, executive director of the National Commission on Libraries and Information Science, spoke to the group on national information policy and the role of the federal government in libraries. This initiated a monthlong debate among group members and the American library professionals they met about the transition from print- or text-based information to an interactive, multimedia environment.

Evan Farber, college librarian of Earlham College in Richmond, Indiana, presented an introduction to libraries and librarianship in the United States, including types, history, governance, federal involvement, funding, management, current issues, education, and future trends. Frank Burke, professor of library and information studies at the University of Maryland, College Park, discussed the history of libraries in the United States and provided an overview of library science education, including where and how the subject is taught and current issues in the field.

The group toured the Library of Congress and received a presentation by the chief of the National Reference Service on its history, mandate, holdings, and organization. Later in the week they had full and small-group discussions with representatives of Collections Services, the Congressional Research Service, the Preservation Office, Humanities/Social Sciences, and various area studies divisions.

Members of the group also visited the Folger Shakespeare Library, the Smithsonian Institution Libraries, the Supreme Court Library, and the National Agricultural Library.

The Washington program included an introduction to USIA's network of libraries around the world and training programs available to foreign librarians, a tour of the city's attractions, and a performance by the National Symphony Orchestra.

Vermont

From June 20 to 23, the group was in Vermont. The state has proven to be an excellent choice for groups of visiting international librarians, many of whom recognize the problems posed by its rurality, its scant library resources, and its lack of trained librarians.

Vermont has no county or middle-level governmental structure, and therefore has only small town libraries and a state library department to provide the mostly rural population with library service. More than 90 percent of the 210 existing public libraries are in towns with populations of less than 1,500; one-third of these libraries have no telephone, and 90 percent of the librarians have no formal library training.

The Vermont Department of Libraries, with the support of several foundations, has designed and developed the Vermont Automated Library System (VALS) to ensure that rural Vermonters have the same access as urban residents. This system brings together the major public and private academic and state library resources and makes them available upon request to rural libraries and individuals, without limitation. Individual libraries can access all information and books available within the network, using only a personal computer and a telephone line (computer training of librarians and citizens has been a major component of this project).

The participants received in-depth exposure to VALS in a two-day program hosted by the state Department of Libraries. State Librarian and Commissioner of Libraries Patricia Klinck gave an overview of the history and operation of VALS, explaining how the state library department forged a coalition among many institutions.

Participants then divided into teams to visit public, academic, school, and regional libraries. One team visited the Champlain Valley Union High School, a public library in the town of Bristol, and the Middlebury College library. Another visited the University of Vermont library, a public library in Essex, and the Northwest Regional library. These site visits enabled participants to talk with volunteers and staff about the transition to a computerized system, how such a system has affected access to information, and questions of local control of rural libraries versus participation in a statewide network.

On the second day of the program, participants visited the State Library in Montpelier, where Klinck discussed the technology used by VALS and how the computer hardware and software were chosen.

New York

From June 23 to 25, the group visited New York, where calls included the New York Public Library and the Metropolitan Museum of Art. Participants from the Bahamas, Jamaica, and Nigeria met with Howard Dodson, the director of the Schomberg Center for Research in Black Culture, a visit the three mentioned as a highlight of the monthlong program.

ALA Conference

From June 25 to 30, the group attended the 1993 American Library Association Annual Conference in New Orleans, Louisiana. Many made important contacts with vendors of automated systems and other library supply companies.

City Visits

After the ALA conference, the group divided into three parts according to professional interests: special libraries were the subject in Cincinnati, public libraries in Tulsa, and university libraries and library science education in Austin.

The program in Austin featured the Graduate School of Library and Information Science at the University of Texas. Participants met with the dean to discuss the school's curriculum and admissions process; with the coordinator of the conservation program; and with the associate dean, a professor in archival enterprise. The team also visited the Perry-Casteneda Library, the Harry Ransom Humanities Research Center, and the Lyndon Baines Johnson Library and Museum.

In Tulsa, the program focused on the role of public libraries in a community. The group visited several branches of the Tulsa City-County Library and talked with librarians and administrators about public library management, funding, personnel issues, reader services, collections, technology, volunteer programs, and programs for children.

In Cincinnati, the theme was special libraries. (The Cincinnati area has one of the fastest-growing chapters of the Special Libraries Association in the country.) Participants met with the head librarian of Lloyd Library, the world's largest private repository of material on pharmacy, botany, and chemistry; the library director of the Hebrew Union College, a rabbinical seminary; the director of the Cincinnati Historical Society Library; and the head librarian at the University of Cincinnati College of Law Library.

The last visit by the full group was to Chicago, where the themes were research libraries, academic libraries, and library management, automation, and technology.

The July 3–9 program highlighted the library at Northwestern University. At the Harold Washington Public Library they learned about programs for children, services for the disabled, and a literacy initiative; and the head librarian at the Museum of Natural History described ways in which the library serves scientists. The group also visited the Center for Research Libraries.

Participants' Comments

At the conclusion of the project, participants discussed three topics: the most surprising aspects of libraries in the United States, the most disappointing aspects, and the most useful aspects in terms of their own situations.

The most surprising aspects included:

- The level of networking among American libraries
- The importance of public relations and advertising
- The common use of laser discs as a storage medium, and their low cost and durability
- The wide range of activities that take place in public libraries
- The use of volunteers in public libraries
- The fact that the Vermont library system works via telephone lines, using technology available in most of the world
- The organization of the ALA conference and the high quality of its content
- The participation of the private sector in libraries
- The organization, NOTIS system, and hospitality of the Northwestern University Library

- The delicate and time-consuming nature of a conservator's job
- The dedication and professionalism of American librarians in serving the needs of their users

Participants were most disappointed by:

- A perceived lack of accessibility of the many holdings of the Library of Congress for the general public
- The observation that some rare books are not properly preserved
- The closing of a number of important and prestigious library schools
- The fact that many university libraries receive only a small percentage of a university's overall budget

Among the most useful practices and programs observed were:

- The use of consultants when purchasing new technology
- Simple preservation techniques, such as wrapping books in polyester while they are waiting to be repaired
- Comment boards and suggestion boxes in public libraries
- The computer-controlled compact shelving and book transportation systems used in the New York Public Library
- The practical uses of various networks and databases
- "Friends of the Library" programs

A number of the visitors developed plans to implement new programs upon their return home. Galina Kislovskaya from the All-Russian State Library of Foreign Literature planned to set up a division for fund raising and hoped to organize a national committee on preservation issues. Agnes Varga, the head of the Readers' Service Department at a public library in Hungary, said there was no OCLC-type service in Hungary and was pondering how she might organize one. Ruth John, the director of libraries in Grenada, wanted to initiate a summer reading program for children, an idea she picked up in Tulsa. The parliamentary library in India is moving to a new building, and Ravinder Chadha, its deputy director, identified the shelving system to be used for infrequently requested books. Victoria James, the assistant director of library and archives in Nigeria, planned to write a proposal for the automation of ten museum libraries. The Costa Rican-American Cultural Center is developing a network among four university libraries in Costa Rica and reference librarian Priscilla Hidalgo felt better prepared to implement this plan following her time in the United States. Bushra Riaz of the Lahore University of Management's library hoped to write articles about the Vermont Automated Library System and make a presentation on it to a library association in Pakistan.

All of the international librarians agreed that the project renewed their enthusiasm and commitment to their library endeavors, and hoped to invigorate their colleagues by sharing their experiences.

BISAC at 20

Tom Clarkson
Barnes & Noble

Sandy Paul
Book Industry Study Group

BISAC, the Book Industry Systems Advisory Committee, was founded 20 years ago in response to opportunities afforded by then-new business technologies. The intervening years have seen ongoing technological changes and successful adaptations to them, and the mission of BISAC remains what it was at the beginning: establishing technical standards to facilitate intercommunication and enhance efficiency throughout publishing, wholesaling, librarianship, and bookselling, as well as promoting the implementation and use of those standards.

The use of the International Standard Book Number (ISBN), electronic ordering and invoicing, electronic dissemination of title information, marking books to permit scanning at point of sale, and development of the Standard Address Number (SAN) are some of the more visible elements of bookselling that BISAC has advocated and shepherded into reality.

Today, BISAC remains at the forefront of technical and procedural innovation. Current efforts include

- Setting the stage for a change to national from industry-specific standards for electronic communication within the book industry
- Promoting this change
- Encouraging the use of electronic packing lists and carton receiving
- Exploring functions such as payment advice and returns processing through electronic communication

Would some or all of this have happened without BISAC? Probably. But how long the processes might have taken and how satisfactory they might have been is anyone's guess.

The bottom line is that BISAC does exist and its accomplishments continue to facilitate bookselling.

BISAC's Origins

BISAC began as two separate committees: the ISBN Publicity Committee and the ISBN Data Transmission Committee. Both resulted from invitations sent out by Bud Baker, then president of Baker & Taylor Company, in September 1974. The two committees functioned as separate, cooperating entities until 1977, when they combined to form BISAC.

ISBN Advocacy

Although the publicizing and promotion of the ISBN was a prime objective of BISAC's founding, the number itself was not developed by BISAC. The origins of the ISBN are in the Standard Book Numbering System adopted in the United Kingdom during the late 1960s. [For more information on ISBNs, see the article "How to Obtain an ISBN" in Part 3—*Ed.*]

The concept of using standard book numbers, issued by a standards agency and compatible across the industry, was revolutionary in 1974, and BISAC had its work laid out for it in the initial years.

The need to explain the ISBN and the benefits of its use led to the publication of "How to Improve your Book Ordering and Distribution." This booklet has served, in several revisions, to guide the industry in the use of the ISBN, subsequent BISAC standards, and other BISAC-supported standards and activities.

Use of the ISBN has saved bookselling millions of dollars while dramatically enhancing the availability of books to readers and book buyers.

Electronic Ordering and Other Transactions

Frustrated implementors of today's technology sometimes complain that the book industry is behind the times in terms of electronic intercommunication. Ironically, this impression is at least partly a result of the success of work done in the late 1970s.

One of the motivations for the founding of BISAC was the desire to transmit purchase orders electronically. To address this interest, BISAC developed first a Purchase Order format, and then Invoice and Purchase Order Acknowledgment formats. A logical extension of these efforts was the Title Status format, used to send both initial title information and changes.

The original intent was to exchange business data on magnetic tape until the systems of sender and receiver were running smoothly, then to switch to transmission via telephone lines. However, the economics of telecommunications during the 1970s and 1980s and the nature of the information being sent was such that the exchange of tapes was found to be more appropriate and more cost-effective in most cases than direct transmission.

Several changes have now occurred that make the exchange of data on magnetic tape increasingly obsolete, although even today there are instances where a case can be made for sending purchase orders via tape.

SAN—The Standard Address Number

The utility and increasing success of the ISBN led logically to a proposal for a similar number, the Standard Address Number (SAN), that could be used to identify universally the organizations trading within the book industry.

Prior to the SAN, each vendor had to "look up" the number that identified each customer before an order could be processed or an inquiry handled. In addition, electronic communication was all but impossible without a standard identification system.

BISAC worked in cooperation with the National Information Standards Organization (NISO) and the American National Standards Institute (ANSI) to develop the ANSI/NISO Standard Address Number standard in 1980 and has continued to publicize it and advocate its use. In 1990, BISAC representatives worked with NISO on the revision of that standard to include the numbering of book manufacturers.

The SAN has not enjoyed adoption on the scale of the ISBN, although as electronic communication becomes more widespread this is changing. More and more vendors are announcing that the SAN will be their customer identification number.

OCR Numbers

In the late 1970s the benefits of being able to scan products electronically at various stages of the distribution process, up to and including the point of sale, were becoming obvious, and interest arose in marking books so that they could be scanned. BISAC worked with retailers in the United States and the United Kingdom to review the various methods of marking products and chose an approach called Optical Character Recognition, Version A, or OCR-A. In this marking method, the characters appear similar to the numbers encoded on checks, but they are in fact a different technology.

OCR-A was chosen because it represents the ISBN well and is easily read by humans. At the time of its selection, it was the marking of choice for several major retail organizations. In accordance with the BISAC recommendation, many publishers marked their books with OCR-A, and scanning systems that used this approach performed with varying success. Other factors began to arise, however, that led to a re-examination of the approach, and BISAC formed the Machine Readable Coding Subcommittee in September 1983.

Bookland EAN and the Bar Code

As retailing gained experience with scanning, bar codes gained standing as the coding technology of choice. The Universal Product Code (UPC) and its associated bar code had been developed by the supermarket industry in the early 1970s.

The UPC was not chosen to convey the ISBN because of a limit on the product numbers available within the UPC. In addition, the UPC could not represent the "X" check digit that appears in some ISBNs.

These obstacles to using the UPC were removed by the development of the EAN, first known as the European Article Number and later renamed the International Article Number. The EAN is an extension of the U.S./Canadian UPC; it both encompasses the existing UPC assignments and provides for nine times as many other product numbers around the world.

The EAN was made to incorporate the ISBN by assigning all the existing and possible future book numbers to the fictitious country of Bookland. The result is a number and an associated bar code known as Bookland EAN. This numbering and bar code brings books into a truly global system that can include all products intended for retail trade worldwide.

Recognizing the superiority of the Bookland EAN approach, BISAC in November 1985 adopted the newer method of coding in place of OCR-A. In view of the increasing mix of book and nonbook information products, the decision to move to bar coding has proved to be correct.

Publisher/Manufacturer Intercommunication Standards

As publishers began to realize benefits from electronic communication with their customers, it became obvious that benefits could also be obtained by implementing similar systems for standardizing communication with book manufacturers. At the request of several publisher members, the Publisher/Manufacturer Subcommittee was formed in September 1990. This subcommittee has developed formats for transmitting job specifications, planning schedules, production status, and invoices. To support these formats, standard cost codes and a data dictionary were also developed.

Reproduction Permissions for Custom Publishing

A development seen by many as having great significance for the future of information dissemination is the custom publishing of textbooks. More and more professors are tailoring textbooks to the needs of their courses, using material either from databases maintained by publishers or from works already published.

So that copyrights can be protected and proper royalties paid while facilitating the assembly of custom-published textbooks, BISAC has worked in conjunction with the National Association of College Stores (NACS), the American Association of Publishers (AAP), and the Copyright Clearance Center (CCC) to develop standards for electronic reprint requests and permissions.

The initial standards were adopted in April 1993, but were placed on hold at the end of that year as NACS agreed to work more closely with CCC in processing faculty course pack requests.

ASC X12 and Electronic Data Interchange (EDI)

BISAC's direction in electronic data communication took a significant turn in May 1990 when several major booksellers and distributors said they planned to move to a newer method of communication already adopted by other industries, replacing the original BISAC formats and the tape exchanges of data.

This new method is known as Electronic Data Interchange (EDI) and the formats in which the data is sent are referred to as ASC X12 or simply X12, after the Accredited Standards Committee of the American National Standards Institute (ANSI) that develops them.

A major motivation for the change is the widespread implementation of ASC X12 throughout most other industries. Using X12 allows organizations to exchange data across industry lines in the same nationally agreed forms, rather than using different forms for each industry. Specifically, publishers are able to use the same technology to communicate with traditional booksellers, department stores, mass merchandisers, and specialty chains.

The national implementation of ASC X12 has enabled the establishment of an infrastructure (Value Added Networks or VANs) that eliminates the scheduling headaches that made direct transmission between publishers and booksellers cumbersome. In addition, the ASC X12 approach is more efficient technically than the older methods on which BISAC work in the 1970s was based.

For these reasons, BISAC agreed to adopt the relevant portions of ASC X12 for book industry use. To date, subsets of the ASC X12 standards have been prepared for purchase orders, invoices, purchase order acknowledgments, title status information, and advance ship notices (electronic packing lists).

In many ways, ASC X12 simply represents a better way to perform standard functions. In other areas, however, BISAC is establishing subsets of the ASC X12 standards that will usher in entirely new ways of doing business.

One area new to the book industry is the electronic transmission of financial information, starting with electronic payment advice intended to eliminate the manual advice attached (sometimes in pages and pages) to most checks and to eliminate the manual cash application process.

Another new function involves the Advance Ship Notice (ASN). This function is an electronic packing list that includes a unique reference number for each carton shipped by a publisher or distributor. Nicknamed the "license plate number," it is encoded in a bar code printed on the shipping label.

When books are shipped to a customer, the ASN will be transmitted to the customer's computer. Upon receipt, the customer can scan the bar code and immediately know what is contained in the carton. This technique should translate directly into books being shelved more quickly, and thus available more quickly to readers and buyers.

Challenges

Foremost among today's challenges is accelerating the implementation of Electronic Data Interchange (EDI) using ASC X12. Despite the dedicated efforts of several pioneering organizations, adoption of EDI using ASC X12 has not been as rapid as its benefits would appear to justify. In the spring of 1994, only 50 to 75 organizations were using ASC X12 in some manner, but BISAC has designated 1994 as the "Year of Implementation" for EDI using ASC X12 and activity is picking up. About 200 organizations are actively working to begin using X12.

The practice of EDI is continuing to evolve nationally and internationally; BISAC is participating in this evolution to ensure that book industry needs are addressed, and that the book industry stays abreast of the developments.

Refining and promoting the standards for title status data transmission is another area of opportunity. There is need for a truly industrywide, readily accessible title database (or databases). Several efforts have shown that such databases can provide benefits, but much remains to be done.

Although the use of Bookland EAN bar coding has proved to be valuable across the book industry, there are unresolved bar coding issues that must be addressed before all systems will function smoothly. There are conflicting needs that require different bar codes on mass market paperbacks for different markets and there is the question of appropriate bar coding for such items as maps that are sold in stores other than bookstores.

The world of EDI is moving at a rapid pace. ASC has agreed to synchronize its U.S. standards with the international EDI standard, EDIFACT, in 1997. Work is already under way in Europe to use BISAC formats as the basis for EDIFACT standards for the book industry. Work is also under way in the national and international arena to allow "interactive" EDI (where responses are received in the same session a query is posted) and for "open" EDI, where business relationships take precedence over data transmission.

Thus while BISAC at 20 can look back at a record of significant leadership and accomplishment, the job is by no means finished; assuming continuing technological innovations, we can expect that it will never be. Nor is there much doubt that in 2004 a 30-year review will find both additional accomplishments and challenges yet to be addressed.

Federal Agency
and Federal Library Reports

National Commission on Libraries
and Information Science

1110 Vermont Ave. N.W., Suite 820, Washington, DC 20005-3522
202-606-9200, FAX 202-606-9203
Internet: py_nclis@inet.ed.gov; jw_nclis@inet.ed.gov

Jane Williams
Research Associate

The National Commission on Libraries and Information Science (NCLIS) enjoyed an eventful year in 1993, administratively and programmatically. The new administration's priorities and initiatives included two major concerns already reflected in NCLIS programming: education and the information infrastructure. In addition to public forums and other activities, NCLIS arranged for sample surveys of school library media centers and public libraries to provide data on which to base policy advice in the education and information infrastructure programs.

Budget and Staffing

As required by the General Services Administration, the NCLIS staff moved the commission office in April 1993. The staff further developed its local area network of computers and applications, modernized telephone and mail operations and, courtesy of the U.S. Department of Education, was connected to Internet. NCLIS staff size remained at five full-time permanent employees, aided by the contractual staff operating the Library Statistics Program and part-time consultants. Peter R. Young continued as the executive director of NCLIS.

Congress appropriated $889,000 for FY 1993 for NCLIS, a 7 percent increase over the previous year's appropriation of $831,000. Funds covered operations and programs and enabled NCLIS to conduct meetings and hold open forums in cities across the United States. For example, the commissioners were able to see four major urban public libraries in Boston, Chicago, Philadelphia, and Washington, D.C., and to feed those firsthand experiences into their programs on education and the information infrastructure.

Commission Members

NCLIS Chairperson J. Michael Farrell and Commissioners Jerald Newman and Julia Wu ended their carry-over years on the commission in July 1993 (their initial terms ended July 1992 but they were eligible to serve an extra 12 months). James Lyons, Jr., resigned from the commission in April 1993 and Commissioners Wanda Forbes, Ben-chieh Liu, and Charles Reid began carry-over years in July 1993. Elinor Swaim, vice chairperson, presided over NCLIS affairs after July 19, 1993, when Mr. Farrell's final year ended. Other continuing members of the commission are Shirley Adamovich, Daniel Casey, Carol DiPrete, Norman Kelinson, Kay Riddle, and Barbara Taylor. Winston Tabb represents the Librarian of Congress, a permanent NCLIS member.

On November 16 the President appointed Jeanne Hurley Simon of Illinois to the commission for a term ending July 19, 1997, replacing Mr. Farrell. The Senate confirmed her nomination on November 20 and she was appointed chairperson the same month. The Senate also received the following nominations: Martha Gould of Nevada, replacing Julia Wu; Frank Lucchino of Pennsylvania, replacing Charles Reid; Bobby Roberts of Arkansas, replacing Wanda Forbes; and Gary Sudduth of Minnesota, replacing Jerald Newman.

Support for Legislative and Executive Branches

Throughout the year the NCLIS commissioners and staff maintained contact with various officials and their staffs in the Congress and the administration on matters affecting library and information services nationally. With a new administration, there were many opportunities to acquaint or reacquaint officials with the status and needs of library and information services and with NCLIS's roles in determining and assessing the status and needs. NCLIS undertook program activities summarized below to give it the basis for advising the administration and the Congress.

The recommendations from the July 1991 White House Conference on Library and Information Services, planned and carried out under the commission's auspices, were another source of advice for the federal government. NCLIS commissioned two analyses of the recommendations from a public policy perspective to help NCLIS, the administration, and the Congress assess the pertinence of the conference recommendations for federal initiatives and legislation, such as the 1994/1995 reauthorization of the Library Services and Construction Act.

Library and Information Services in a Networked Environment

Following up on its July 1992 open forum and November 1992 report on library and information services' roles in the National Research and Education Network, in mid-1993 the commission named Syracuse University Professor Charles McClure as NCLIS Distinguished Researcher to examine the impacts of networking on libraries and information services. The scope of Dr. McClure's work for the commission was later extended to include a survey and analysis of public libraries and Internet. Wisconsin Professor Douglas Zweizig and Dr. McClure, principal investigators for the project, planned a quick-response sample survey for January 1994. Dr. McClure will analyze survey findings on the extent of public library involvement with Internet to identify potential federal policies on the public library role in developing a national networked information infrastructure. NCLIS, Dr. McClure, and Dr. Zweizig were to report initial findings in March 1994 at the Public Library Association conference. NCLIS will publish the findings for general distribution as well.

In 1993 NCLIS also reviewed and responded to legislation, to the administration's initiatives, and to reports and other documents pertinent to libraries in a networked environment. NCLIS also participated in meetings such as those of the Digital Resources for Education and Training Work Group, coordinated by the Office of Science and Technology Policy. These and related activities were part of follow-up to a priority recommendation from the 1991 White House Conference on Library and Information Services on sharing information via a network "superhighway."

Libraries and Education

Much commission activity focused on another priority recommendation from the 1991 White House Conference, the Omnibus Children and Youth Literacy Initiative. From late 1992 through mid-1993 NCLIS arranged several meetings with representatives from the American Library Association and the Chief Officers of State Library Agencies to share information and plans for children's and youth services in libraries. While the meetings proceeded in 1993, so did action on pertinent legislation such as the Elementary and Secondary School Library Media Act, Goals 2000 bills on educational reform, and reauthorization of the Elementary and Secondary Education Act.

NCLIS also conducted three open forums to hear views of interested parties across the country on the status, needs, and visions for services to children and youth in school library media centers and public libraries. Also aired were the possible federal roles and responsibilities in providing those services. The 1993 forums were held in May at the Boston Public Library, in September at the California State Library in Sacramento, and in December in Des Moines, coordinated by the Iowa State Library. The commission is publishing the proceedings of the forums, which also serve as the basis for NCLIS to advise Congress and the administration in formulating policy related to children and youth.

Another component of the commission's program on libraries and education was a cooperative project with the American Library Association's Office for Research and Statistics and the American Association of School Librarians to gather statistics from a sample of school library media centers. The most recent statistics were collected by the National Center for Education Statistics in 1985. Results of the next national survey are not expected until late 1995. The June–December 1993 NCLIS/ALA project is to provide current information for activities related to the legislation cited above.

Library Statistics

In addition to the special statistical projects mentioned above, the commission continued its collaboration with the National Center for Education Statistics (NCES), which is part of the U.S. Department of Education, on a comprehensive and consistent national Library Statistics Program (LSP). The original component of the LSP is the Federal-State Cooperative System for public library data (FSCS). In March 1993 NCES electronically released the 1991 public library data for the 50 states and the District of Columbia. Public library data from U.S. territories will be added to the state statistics, beginning with the cycle for collecting 1992 data. [See also the following NCES report—*Ed.*]

The Library Statistics Program coordinated drafting of a survey instrument for the state library agencies, with the survey to take place in the 1993/1994 fiscal year. In September NCLIS and NCES hosted a Library Statistics Forum to assess present and next-decade changes in library and information services and the implications of these changes for the collection, analysis, and use of data relating to national library and information services.

The American Library Association in 1993 honored John Lorenz, LSP coordinator, with its annual Joseph W. Lippincott Award, presented for distinguished professional service in librarianship.

International Activities

J. Michael Farrell, NCLIS chairperson, and Commissioner Riddle attended the ninth session of the UNESCO Intergovernmental Council for the General Information Programme (PGI) in Paris in November 1992. The PGI conference's programs address information activities in member states and plan UNESCO's information program. Mr. Farrell attended the National Summit on Information Policy in Ottawa in December 1992 as an invited observer. He and NCLIS Executive Director Peter Young presented papers at the April 1993 International Conference on National Libraries: Toward the Twenty-first Century, in Taipei, Taiwan.

Commissioners Swaim, DiPrete, and Tabb attended the conference of the International Federation of Library Associations and Institutions (IFLA) in Barcelona in August 1993. Ms. Swaim also attended the IFLA preconference seminar for school librarians from developing countries. The seminar was partially supported with State Department funds administered by the commission. NCLIS coordinated the distribution of $175,000 to seven organizations in 1993, from the State Department's allocation for International Convention and Scientific Organization Contributions.

Awards

NCLIS began an awards program in 1987 to recognize outstanding initiatives by individuals other than librarians and by nonlibrary organizations to improve and promote library and information services. Recipients of 1993 awards were:

- Chrysler Learning Corporation, for a free educational video and booklet,

"Learn at Every Turn," and grants of $1,000 each to 50 elementary and middle school libraries

- Ruth J. Colvin, founder and first president of Literacy Volunteers of America
- Della Jackson, founder of a library for African Americans in a community in western North Carolina
- KENS-TV, for support of San Antonio Public Library's fund-raising telethon
- Mott's USA, provider of up to $500,000 to public libraries for books and other educational materials
- Jerry Neuman, creator, producer, and host of "Check It Out: The Radio Library Program," a daily two-minute public radio program
- The Screen Actors Guild Foundation, for Book PALS, Performing Artists for Literacy in Schools

Publications

Report to the Office of Science and Technology Policy on Library and Information Services' Roles in the National Research and Education Network. November 1992. Available from NCLIS.

Information 2000: Final Report of the White House Conference on Library and Information Services. November 1992. GPO, Stock No. 040-000-0580-3.

Pathways to Excellence: A Report on Improving Library and Information Services to Native American Peoples. January 1993. GPO, Stock No. 040-000-0587-1.

Annual Report of the U.S. National Commission on Libraries and Information Science, 1991-1992. January 1993. Available from NCLIS.

Open Forum on Children and Youth Services: Redefining the Federal Role for Libraries. Report on May 1993 forum in Boston. July 1993. Available from NCLIS.

Briefing and Open Forum on Children and Youth Services: Redefining the Federal Role for Libraries. Report on September 1993 forum in Sacramento. December 1993. Available from NCLIS.

Briefing and Open Forum on Children and Youth Services: Redefining the Federal Role for Libraries. Report on December 1993 forum in Des Moines. February 1994. Available from NCLIS.

Conclusion

Continuation of programs in education and the information infrastructure, involvement with legislative matters such as the reauthorization of the Library Services and Construction Act, preparing for the commission's twenty-fifth year in 1995, orientation and planning with new and veteran commissions, and working with a budget of $904,000 are among the challenges and assets facing NCLIS in 1994.

National Technical Information Service

Technology Administration
U.S. Department of Commerce, Springfield, VA 22161
703-487-4650

Kitt Rodkey
Writing Coordinator

The National Technical Information Service (NTIS) is a self-supporting federal agency within the Department of Commerce that makes available to the public the results of research and development and other information produced by and for the U.S. government. It also disseminates similar information from foreign governments and from domestic and foreign nongovernmental sources.

Products include technical reports, periodicals, databases, software, and online services. A characteristic of the information available from NTIS is that it has not been published commercially and is not generally available from any other source.

The NTIS collection exceeds 2 million works, most of which are in its electronic database. The collection covers technology, scientific and technical information, current events, business and management studies, translations of foreign reports, foreign and domestic trade, general statistics, environment and energy, health and the social sciences, and hundreds of other areas.

NTIS is self-supporting because all costs associated with collecting, abstracting, indexing, archiving, reproducing, and disseminating the information it supplies are paid for by sales of its products and services.

Its direct ancestor was the Publications Board, established by President Harry S. Truman in 1945 to evaluate and disseminate technical material seized from enemy nations at the end of World War II. The agency went through several name changes and expansion of its mission before being renamed the National Technical Information Service in 1970.

All NTIS materials are permanently available. When government agencies and their contractors submit reports and other items to NTIS, they are entered into the NTIS computerized bibliographic database and remain available to the public. The database can be accessed through a number of commercial online vendors, which are listed in the free *NTIS 1994 Catalog of Products and Services*. To obtain a catalog, call 703-487-4650 and ask for PR-827.

NTIS also provides technology transfer services such as patent licensing, business partnerships, and technology descriptions. The FEDRIP (Federal Research in Progress) database includes advance information on some 150,000 research projects currently under way. Its *Published Searches*™ bibliographies provide the most recent data on specific topics from an individual database source. The updated *Directory of Federal Laboratory and Technological Resources* summarizes 1,900 unique resources organized within 70 subject areas.

FedWorld

FedWorld™ is NTIS's electronic marketplace of U.S. and foreign government information. It connects the public to more than 130 U.S. government computer systems that contain databases, programs, and press releases. It also provides the latest information about NTIS products and services that can be searched and downloaded.

The number of FedWorld users has grown to more than 35,000, spurred in part by the availability of widely promoted White House files. Some of the more popular items on FedWorld in 1993 were:

- White House press releases
- North American Free Trade Agreement (NAFTA) updates
- National Performance Review report and updates
- Health care reports
- The National Information Infrastructure (NII) Agenda for Action
- NTIS product information

Access is free of charge. To connect, call 703-321-8020. For more information on FedWorld, call 703-487-4608. FedWorld is also available via Internet.

Acquisition Authority

American Technology Preeminence Act

Until recently, NTIS relied upon voluntary transfers by federal agencies to ensure the comprehensiveness of its collection of federal scientific and technical literature. The American Technology Preeminence Act (ATPA) of 1991 requires all federal agencies to submit public scientific, technical, and engineering information (STEI) for dissemination, making the comprehensiveness of the NTIS collection the responsibility of each federal agency that performs or finances the development of such information. During 1993 NTIS developed procedures to implement the requirements of ATPA. Briefly, the procedures require each agency to provide NTIS with a copy of all unclassified final STEI products within 15 days of the date they are made publicly available. The requirement applies to agency-produced STEI as well as contractor- and grantee-produced STEI.

Domestic Acquisitions

In 1993 the White House made the first in a series of widely publicized publications available through NTIS: the President's Health Security Plan, the report of the National Performance Review (*Creating a Government That Works Better and Costs Less*), and *National Information Infrastructure: Agenda for Action.*

NTIS acquired additional publications of major national importance, including:

- Environmental, safety, and health information from the Environmental Protection Agency, the Food and Drug Administration, and the Occupational Safety and Health Administration

- Business and trade information from the Commerce Department's International Trade Administration and General Counsel's Office

Sources of Information

U.S. Government

More than 200 U.S. government agencies contribute to the NTIS collection, among them the National Aeronautics and Space Administration (NASA), the Environmental Protection Agency (EPA), the National Institute of Standards and Technology, the National Institutes of Health, and the Departments of Agriculture, Commerce, Defense, Energy, Health and Human Services, Interior, and Transportation. NTIS adds more than 70,000 new titles each year to its collection of more than 2 million.

NTIS has established important marketing partnerships with federal agencies in growing areas such as international trade, health care and medicine, and the environment. Superfund documents distribution is centralized by EPA through NTIS; examples of major titles are *Access EPA* and the *EPA Publications Bibliography, Quarterly Abstract Bulletin.* The Food and Drug Administration (FDA) has placed numerous information products with NTIS for sale; an example is the 1994 Food Code. A FedWorld subsystem contains the Department of Labor Davis–Bacon Wage Determination database. For the past seven years NTIS has assisted the National Library of Medicine (NLM) by providing production and distribution for its Grateful Med software program.

Worldwide

NTIS is the leading U.S. government agency in international technical and business information exchange. It actively acquires and distributes information produced by a large number of foreign government departments and other overseas organizations. About a third of the NTIS collection is acquired from international sources, including Japan, Western Europe, the nations of the former Soviet Union, and other Eastern European countries.

Joint Ventures

The National Technical Information Act of 1988 authorized NTIS to work with private industry to build strategic alliances. This is to be done through contracts or cooperative agreements with the private sector, individuals, firms, or other organizations. As a result of the legislation, NTIS established its Joint Ventures Program, which allows it to enter into joint ventures with businesses to create new information products from U.S. government-produced data and software. In addition, NTIS is looking for partnerships to open new channels of sales and distribution for U.S. government information products. For more information about joint ventures with NTIS, call 703-487-4674.

A recent joint venture resulted in the creation of the *Published Search Master Catalog 1993*. The NTIS joint venture partner in this case is NERAC Inc. of Tolland, Connecticut. Another example is the *Environmental Monitoring Methods Index (EMMI)*, a joint venture with Viar & Company, Alexandria, Virginia.

Global Information

More than 30 percent of NTIS's total product offerings came from 77 foreign countries and international organizations in 1993. Topics included technology transfer, tariffs, export markets, and international economics and politics. Emerging export markets in this hemisphere, the Pacific Rim, and in Russia and Eastern Europe motivated the enhancement of existing programs and the development of new ones in these markets.

NTIS is negotiating agreements to improve the coverage of reports from major industrialized countries, as well as from newly industrialized countries producing advanced technologies. NTIS is working with existing sources to focus its acquisition efforts on topics of major interest to NTIS customers. In December NTIS cosponsored an International Conference on Gray Literature in Amsterdam along with European and Japanese counterpart organizations. (Gray literature is literature, in this case technical literature that is published by or for the U.S. government, that is not available to the public.)

New International Products

NTIS has responded to the rapid changes in the world trading environment by targeting regions with exceptional promise. Information dissemination specialties cover three regions and more will be added. A bibliography of more than 2,000 export-related reports was prepared by the International Trade Administration of the U.S. Department of Commerce and released via NTIS.

Market intelligence on Central and Eastern Europe is available as part of a partnership with the Department of Commerce's Eastern Europe Business Information Center. To obtain a free catalog of legal texts concerning this area, call 703-487-4650 and ask for PR-883. Russia is covered by PR-910.

An existing program focusing on Japan was augmented in 1993 with four publications on the computer software market in that country. The Japanese Information Center of Science and Technology (JICST) reports on selected high technology areas. An online information system to Japanese research and development is available through NTIS. During 1993 NTIS cosponsored a conference on access to Japanese technical information with JICST.

The enlarged collection on Latin America, Mexico, and the Caribbean reflects the region's rise in commercial and political significance. A variety of information products have been made available on the North American Free Trade Agreement (NAFTA).

Competitive Intelligence Tracking Tools

The Foreign Broadcast Information Service (FBIS) *Daily Reports* contain news accounts, commentaries, and government statements. The material is gathered from foreign broadcasts, press agency transmissions, newspapers, and periodicals released within the previous 48 to 72 hours. Published Monday through Friday, *Daily Reports* include political, military, economic, environmental, and sociological news, as well as scientific and technical data and reports. Areas covered include Eastern Europe, China, East Asia, Central Eurasia (including Russia and the independent states), Western Europe, and sub-Saharan Africa.

A new subscription, *Science and Technology Perspectives*, is issued monthly. It reports on current, leading-edge scientific, technological, and industrial developments throughout the world. *Science and Technology Perspectives* covers eight high-tech fields in the context of government policy, technological advancement, marketing strategies, and technology transfer issues.

The Joint Publications Research Service *Reports* provide translations of articles and reports from publications around the world. The reports are available by specific country or region and by topics within regions. The translated articles cover the political, economic, and military aspects of each particular country, region, or topic. They contain information that is less time-sensitive than the FBIS *Daily Reports*.

Dispatch is a weekly bulletin published by the Department of State. It provides a diverse compilation of major speeches, congressional testimony, policy statements, fact sheets, and other foreign policy information. Contents include profiles of countries currently in the news, lists of ambassadorial appointments, treaty actions, and updates on current events worldwide and on public- and private-sector assistance to Eastern and Central Europe.

For more information, call the NTIS Subscription Branch at 703-487-4630.

Customized Information

Prepackaged database searches on over 2,000 topics of wide interest may be ordered from NTIS. These are listed in the *Published Searches Master Catalog 1993*, which is available free of charge; ask for PR-186. Direct online access to the NTIS Bibliographic Database may be arranged through eight commercial services, which are listed in PR-827.

The *Government Reports Announcements and Index* journal lists summaries of U.S. government research reports on a biweekly basis. It is indexed by keyword, personal and corporate author, government/contract grant number, and report number. For more information, ask for PR-195.

NTIS Alerts

More than 1,300 new titles are added to the NTIS collection every week. *NTIS Alerts* were developed to help customers tap into this information by providing summaries of reports and studies. Two formats are available. The *Custom Alert* provides twice-monthly summaries of technical reports in any combination of more than 200 subjects tailored to the needs of individual users. The *Pre-*

packaged Alert, also issued twice a month, contains summaries of new technical reports within certain subject areas. For a free catalog, call 703-487-4650, and ask for PR-797.

Selected Research in Microfiche

The Selected Research in Microfiche (SRIM) service automatically provides full-text microfiche copies of reports in the customer's field of interest. The cost is $1.45 for each report in microfiche. There are 350 existing subject areas to choose from, and categories also can be custom-designed for the individual user. SRIM is particularly valuable for corporate and special libraries that need new information as soon as possible or a complete collection on a particular topic. Call 703-487-4630 to start a subscription or to get the free brochure PR-271.

Continuous Acquisition and Life-Cycle Support

The CALS/CE (Continuous Acquisition and Life-Style Support/Concurrent Engineering) Information Center is operated in cooperation with the Department of Defense. CALS, originally conceived by the Department of Defense and private industry as a strategy to streamline acquisition of weapon systems, has become a major government initiative to speed the transition from a paper-intensive environment to a highly automated and integrated operation.

With CALS becoming an international movement, the center expects to join with interested organizations in Europe, Canada, and Australia to expand access to the CALS Electronic Bulletin Board as a component of FedWorld, with worldwide access via Internet.

For more information about the CALS/CE Information Center, call 703-487-4819.

Total Quality Management

The NTIS modernization program encompasses "total quality management" concepts and techniques. NTIS is a "reinvention laboratory," part of a government-wide program of improving services to the public. New equipment has increased customer awareness of and access to NTIS information. Customers benefit from a variety of ordering and delivery means: via modem, Internet, FAX, telephone, and mail. The expanded use of all-electronic printing technology will further enhance the quality of documents available from NTIS.

National Archives and Records Administration

8601 Adelphi Rd., College Park, MD 20740-6001
301-713-6730

David R. Kepley
Chief, Program Analysis Branch
Office of Management and Administration

The National Archives and Records Administration (NARA) is the agency of the federal government responsible for identifying, preserving, and making available to the public and to the federal government all forms of government records not restricted by law that have been determined to have sufficient historical, informational, or evidential value to warrant continued preservation. All federal agencies are obliged by law to cooperate with NARA and to transfer all historically valuable federal records more than 30 years old to NARA if the records are not needed for continuing business of the agency. In 1993, NARA served nearly 300,000 walk-in researchers nationwide and NARA units in the Washington, D.C., area responded by letter to more than 206,000 telephone and written requests.

Archives II

NARA's new facility, located on 33 acres in College Park, Maryland, opened in 1993. Staff began moving to the new building in late October, and the first records began their journey in November with the move of the Nixon Presidential Materials Project from NARA's Pickett Street facility in Alexandria, Virginia, to Archives II. Archives II has a storage capacity of approximately 2 million square feet, spread over 520 miles of shelving space in 21 stack areas. To maximize storage capacity for archival records at Archives II, NARA has equipped all record stacks with electric high-density mobile shelving. Typically, stacks will have fixed perimeter shelving and map cases around the walls to store oversized materials or indexes.

The research complex at Archives II is located on five floors and has separate research rooms for cartographic and architectural records; motion pictures, sound, and video records; microfilm; still pictures; and electronic records.

Archives II is also equipped with nine sophisticated preservation and conservation laboratories, state-of-the-art office space, an auditorium and multipurpose lecture rooms, a day-care center, and a cafeteria.

The Move

Textual holdings in the National Archives Building in Washington, D.C., and the Washington National Records Center in Suitland, Maryland, will be moved to Archives II by record groups within subject-matter clusters. The move of records is scheduled to be completed in 1996. In all, 1,292,000 cubic feet of records will be transferred and rearranged.

Table 1 / Records Being Moved to Archives II

Record Type	Volume (in cubic feet)
Textual	631,534
Cartographic and architectural	45,000
Motion picture, sound, and video	38,000
Still pictures	15,000
Electronic records (tapes and textual documentation)	35,000

Table 2 / Dates for Moving Textual Records, by Cluster

Cluster	Timeframe
Agriculture	Jan.–Oct. 1994
Air Force	July–Sept. 1995
Commerce	Feb.–Oct. 1994
Defense	Oct. 1995–March 1996
Education	June–Sept. 1995
Energy	July–Sept. 1994
Executive Office of the President and presidential agencies	April–June 1995
General government	Oct. 1994–April 1995
Health	April–July 1995
Housing	Sept.–Oct. 1995
Interior	Jan.–Sept. 1994
Justice	Nov. 1994–May 1995
Labor	Sept. 1994–April 1995
Modern Army	April 1995–March 1996
Science	Dec. 1994–April 1995
State/foreign relations	Sept. 1994–April 1995
Transportation	Jan.–July 1994
Treasury	April–Dec. 1995

Table 3 / Dates for Moving Nontextual Records

Records	Timeframe
Cartographic	Dec. 1993–Jan. 1994
Electronic	March 1994
Motion picture, video	Jan.–Feb. 1994
Still photography	Feb.–March 1994

Some NARA services were temporarily discontinued as nontextual records were relocated in late 1993 and early 1994.

Each cluster of textual records should be closed to the public for only a few weeks while the records are being transported. NARA is planning special reference services for researchers during the move.

National Archives Building

Despite the move of the administrative offices and much of NARA's holdings, the National Archives Building on Pennsylvania Avenue in Washington, D.C., will remain the centerpiece of the National Archives. The rotunda on the Constitution Avenue side of the building will continue to house the Declaration of Independence, the Constitution, and the Bill of Rights, and NARA will still create exhibits and programs at the National Archives Building. Materials relating to genealogy and legislative, State Department, Bureau of Indian Affairs, Navy, and pre–World War II Army records will remain downtown. After the move of records to Archives II is complete, all permanent records still held at the Washington National Records Center in Suitland will be transferred to the National Archives Building in Washington. All of the records in the National Archives Building will then be integrated and relocated to bring related records together. In all, 495,430 cubic feet of textual records will remain in or be relocated to the National Archives Building.

Master Location Register

In tandem with this move, NARA is creating a master location register so that archivists will be able to pinpoint the location of records both at Archives II and at the National Archives Building in Washington.

Electronic Access

NARA's Center for Electronic Records is offering electronic access to its Title List, a preliminary and partial listing of data files in the National Archives and selected other materials, through the Internet computer network. The center's materials may be accessed on Internet (cu.nih.gov) by using file transfer protocol (ftp) software.

The Motion Picture, Sound, and Video Branch and the Still Picture Branch have begun to make information about NARA's audiovisual holdings available online. Currently, the online information includes:

- READ.ME, describing the contents of other online files
- NA-GIL33.TXT, Motion Pictures and Sound and Video Recordings in the National Archives
- NA-GIL34.TXT, National Archives Gift Collection Acquisition Policy: Motion Pictures and Sound and Video Recordings
- NA-GIL35.TXT, National Archives Gifts Acquisitions Policy: Still Pictures

- NA-GIL38.TXT, Information for Prospective Researchers about the Still Pictures Branch of the National Archives
- WW2-PIX.TXT, Select Audiovisual Records: Pictures of World War II

ICASS

Archives II is supported by a new computer system, the Integrated Communications and Administrative Support System (ICASS), which, aside from its main administrative support functions, will allow access to electronic databases of information on the archival holdings of NARA. ICASS will provide support for up to 50 dial-in public users, who will be able to access such reference databases as the Archival Information System (AIS; scheduled to be implemented in 1994) and communicate with staff members via E-mail. The ICASS system will also be accessible through Internet.

John F. Kennedy Assassination Materials Collection

On August 23, 1993, NARA opened the records pertaining to President Kennedy's assassination. Material from the following agencies was made available for research:

- Warren Commission records previously opened and a small amount of newly released material
- House Select Committee on Assassinations (approximately 600 boxes)
- Central Intelligence Agency previously opened and newly released materials, the majority of which are redacted copies
- Kennedy, Ford, and Johnson Presidential Libraries previously opened and a small amount of newly released materials, including records from the Rockefeller Commission
- Records of other agencies

The John F. Kennedy Records Collection Act, signed into law on October 26, 1992, mandates that all assassination-related material be housed in a single collection in the National Archives. On December 28, 1992, NARA established the John F. Kennedy Assassination Records Collection. Initially, the collection consisted of open assassination-related material that was already in NARA's custody. The collection continues to grow as agencies complete their reviews and transfer their open records to NARA. The collection may not be complete for several years.

In addition to establishing the physical collection, the John F. Kennedy Assassination Records Collection Act mandated the creation of an electronic index to those documents not open and available to the National Archives when the declassification was signed into law. Each agency with custody of assassination-related materials entered information about its own records into the system. Eventually, all the electronic entries will be transferred to the National Archives.

It will be possible to search the system in a variety of ways, including by subject, date, and originating agency.

Records in the JFK Collection began moving to Archives II in the latter half of March 1994.

Department of Housing and Urban Development Photo Collection

NARA recently approved the transfer of 750,000 photographs from the Department of Housing and Urban Development headquarters to the National Archives. The photographs, slides, and accompanying indexes collected from 1935 to 1990 represent one of the most comprehensive and significant visual collections of the federal government's housing programs from the late Depression era to the present. It includes thousands of images of mobile home "trailer parks" located nationwide (1945–1965), slides and prints of structures that were demolished to make space for agency housing projects, and prints of the interiors of American kitchens (1937–1965). These records provide valuable visual documentation to support research in a broad range of architectural, sociological, and demographic studies.

George Bush Presidential Materials Project

In 1978, presidential records, formerly considered the private property of the president who created them, were declared government property and subject to NARA's archival authority. With the election of President Clinton, NARA began the process of gathering the records of the Bush administration for inclusion in a future presidential library. NARA personnel oversaw the removal, transfer, and storage of the records of the administration to College Station, Texas, the site of the future George Bush Presidential Library. As with all other presidential libraries, the facility will be constructed with private funds. Construction of the library is being directed by the Bush Foundation at Texas A&M University. After construction, the operation and funding of the library will be assumed by NARA. The library is scheduled to open to the public in 1996.

Electronic Access to Hoover Library Collections

As of April 30, 1993, access to the archival and manuscript holdings of the Hoover Library in West Branch, Iowa, is available online through the Research Libraries Information Network (RLIN). The Hoover Library is the first presidential library to have all of its collections included in the massive RLIN database. The downloading of the Hoover Library data has resulted in improved access around the world to the library's 150 collections.

New Philadelphia Federal Records Center

On July 20, 1993, the General Services Administration (GSA) awarded the contract to construct a 300,000-square-foot replacement facility for the 64-year-old building now occupied by the Philadelphia Federal Records Center. The new records center, with a capacity of 1.6 million cubic feet, will be located in northeast Philadelphia. It is targeted for completion 15 months from the date of award of the contract. It is hoped that dedication of this facility will take place before October 1, 1994.

New Pittsfield Federal Records Center and Regional Archives

On May 21, 1993, GSA announced that the Berkshire Land Development Corporation will construct the Silvio O. Conte Federal Record Center and Regional Archives in Pittsfield, Massachusetts. The facility will contain 125,740 square feet of warehouse and related space and 7,700 square feet of office and public space. The center will house long-term records currently located in other Federal Records Centers. The regional archive will house and make available to the public a collection of NARA microfilm publications (federal census and selected other records) of interest to genealogists.

Dedication of this 650,000-cubic-foot facility is expected to occur in the spring of 1994.

Administration

NARA received $165,454,000 in appropriations for FY 1993, of which $5,000,000 is allocated for the National Historic Publications and Records Commission. NARA has a full-time staff of 1,123 in the Washington, D.C., area and 3,472 full-time employees nationwide.

United States Information Agency Library and Book Programs

Library Programs Division
301 Fourth St. S.W., Washington, DC 20547
202-619-4915

The United States Information Agency (USIA), an independent organization within the executive branch, is responsible for the U.S. government's overseas information, educational exchange, and cultural programs. The work of the agency is carried out by a staff of foreign service officers assigned to U.S. missions abroad and by a professional staff of career civil servants in Washington, D.C. Known abroad as the USIS (United States Information Service), the agency has more than 200 posts in 146 countries that are grouped in five geographic areas: Africa; Europe; East Asia and the Pacific; the American Republics; and North Africa, the Near East, and South Asia. Posts in these areas report to area offices in Washington, D.C.

The agency's Bureau of Educational and Cultural Affairs, whose mandate is contained in the United States Information and Educational Exchange Act of 1961 (commonly referred to as the Fulbright-Hays Act), supports exchange-of-persons programs and various other activities and programs to increase mutual understanding between the people of the United States and other countries.

[A report on the 1993 American Libraries project, which brought 17 library professionals from 15 countries to visit their counterparts in the United States, appears in the Special Reports section of Part 1-*Ed.*]

Office of Cultural Centers and Resources

Within the Bureau of Educational and Cultural Affairs, the Office of Cultural Centers and Resources is responsible for USIA's book and library programs. Two of its divisions, Library Programs and Book Programs, are directly concerned with the use of American books and electronic media abroad. Through an international network of libraries and through the translation, promotion, and exhibition of American books, the Office of Cultural Centers and Resources provides foreign audiences with authoritative information about U.S. government policies as well as a greater understanding of American society and culture, past and present.

Library Programs

History of USIS Library Programs

Today's worldwide system of USIS libraries evolved from a matrix of programs. First, in Latin America, came libraries associated with President Franklin Roosevelt's "Good Neighbor" program. In 1941 the coordinator of inter-American affairs, Nelson Rockefeller, contracted with the American Library Association (ALA) to establish and operate a library in Mexico City, the now-famous Biblioteca Benjamin Franklin. Under similar contracts, ALA opened and operated on behalf of the U.S. government two other libraries in Latin America: in Managua, Nicaragua (1942), and Montevideo, Uruguay (1943). These libraries came under Department of State supervision in 1947 and 1948, respectively.

Beginning in 1942, the Office of War Information (OWI) began to establish reference libraries as part of its overseas information program. These were separate and distinct from U.S. Embassy reference libraries at the outset. Later, parts of many embassy collections were turned over to USIS libraries. The American Library in London started operations in December 1942 and officially opened in April 1943. The London library was the first overseas library directly under U.S. government control. Between 1942 and 1945 OWI established libraries in 40 more locations throughout the world. On January 1, 1945, OWI was abolished and the Department of State assumed responsibility for overseas libraries.

Shortly after World War II the U.S. Military Government began opening Information Center (Amerika Häuser) libraries and reading rooms in Germany, throughout the American Zone and in the major cities of the British and French zones. In 1949 responsibility for these installations was transferred from the

Army to the Department of State. In 1955 four Amerika Häuser were converted to binational operations, with the German government assuming financial responsibility for housing and local maintenance and the United States supplying an American director and program materials. Also in 1945 Information Center libraries were started under the auspices of the United States Forces in Austria, the Supreme Commander for the Allied Powers in Japan, and the United States Armed Forces in Korea. The State Department assumed responsibility for these centers when civilian control was restored in each country. Nine centers came under the department's auspices in January 1949, and ten centers in Austria were added in 1950. In April 1952, with the ratification of the peace treaty in Japan, 23 information centers in that country and Korea were transferred to the State Department. On August 1, 1953, the United States Information Agency was established, and responsibility for overseas libraries and reading rooms was transferred to the new agency.

Present Status of Library Programs

More than 5 million patrons visited the more than 160 USIS libraries that were in operation worldwide during 1993.

USIS library services and holdings vary significantly from country to country, depending on the objectives of the USIS post (the public affairs office of the U.S. Embassy), the information needs of audiences served, and the communications environment in the host country. All USIS libraries, however, perform two mutually supportive functions: providing the latest and most accurate information about U.S. government policies and serving as continuing sources of informed commentary on the origin, growth, and development of American social, political, economic, and cultural life.

As greater emphasis is placed on outreach and reference/research services for foreign opinion leaders, USIS librarians function increasingly as subject specialists with direct access to the wealth of information sources in the United States. In recent years more than 100 USIS libraries in Europe, Latin America, Asia, Africa, and the Near East have begun accessing online databases (principally DIALOG, NEXIS, LEGI-SLATE, and the in-house public affairs database PDQ), using international value-added networks for this purpose, as well as dedicated lines provided by the Department of State.

At the same time, USIS libraries are giving increased attention in their circulating collections to long-term objectives, including improved understanding of American intellectual and cultural history, American economic and social institutions, and American political traditions. With collections ranging in size from several hundred to more than 30,000 volumes, USIS libraries seek to provide a balanced cross section of outstanding American contributions in the social sciences and humanities, often in cities where such access is extremely limited or virtually nonexistent.

USIA also provides substantial support for more than 50 libraries located in binational centers in about 20 countries. These USIS-supported libraries, as distinct from USIS libraries, operate primarily under the direction of an indigenous organization rather than a USIS post. USIS support usually consists of donations of materials and services or a grant of funds for rent, materials, and staff. The ongoing nature of USIS support distinguishes such libraries from other indigenous libraries to which USIS may donate collections on an occasional one-time basis.

Library Administration

With a staff of 50 in Washington, D.C., the Library Programs Division provides library services and support for USIA staff in Washington and at USIS posts and offices abroad. The Library Programs Division operates one of the federal government's most dynamic special libraries, each year fielding about 18,000 requests for information, half from USIA Washington staff and half from overseas posts. The headquarters library maintains 50,000 books, 800 journals, and 1,000 online text sources, allowing staff to respond to a wide range of complex bibliographic and information queries. The headquarters library is increasingly involved in training overseas USIS librarians, either through internships of one to two months or during visits of a week or less.

Public Diplomacy Query Database

In addition to its more traditional services, the Library Programs Division indexes most program and foreign policy materials acquired by USIA for overseas distribution and makes them available through a family of databases called Public Diplomacy Query (PDQ). The index and full texts of most of the indexed documents are available online to USIS posts and Washington program offices on a USIA computer using Battelle Lab's BASIS information storage and retrieval software. PDQ databases are also produced in CD-ROM format.

Library Fellows Programs

In 1987 the Library Programs Division, in cooperation with the American Library Association, inaugurated an annual Library Fellows program, which enables U.S. librarians with special expertise to serve in institutions abroad for periods ranging from three months to a year. The general objectives of the program are to improve host country or regional access to important information from and about the United States and to establish wherever possible ongoing linkages between American library professionals and institutions and their overseas counterparts in the interest of improving mutual understanding.

Under the terms of the program, which is administered by the American Library Association through a grant from USIA, prospective host institutions abroad are invited to submit proposals through local USIS posts. Project proposals are evaluated and ranked by a committee convened by the Library Programs Division in Washington, after which the American Library Association announces the positions available and oversees the recruitment and selection of candidates.

Typical Library Fellow projects include planning automation of library functions in a national library, developing an American studies collection in an academic library, designing programs for teaching library skills to children and young adults through public library systems, establishing the organizational framework for a national law library, centralizing cataloging and technical services in an academic library, conducting an assessment of public library networking requirements, or managing a retrospective bibliographic conversion project.

In 1993 the Fellows program was expanded to a two-way exchange, with librarians from foreign institutions coming to libraries in the United States for periods of several months to carry out prearranged programs designed to broaden their professional skills and strengthen their role as participants in the steadily growing worldwide movement toward free access to information.

For more information on USIA library programs, write to the Office of Public Liaison, USIA, Washington, DC 20547.

Book Programs

The USIA Book Programs Division supports the publication of American books abroad in English and in translation, as well as the export of American books that contribute to a better understanding of the United States. The division works with foreign publishers to produce more than half a million copies annually of full-length U.S. trade books, textbooks, condensations, and serializations in English and in foreign languages. Titles are chosen to reflect a broad range of American thought on subjects of importance to long-term U.S. interests.

The Book Programs Division also conducts programs to promote the sale and distribution of American books overseas in close cooperation with the book export efforts of the American publishing industry. Circulating book exhibits provide opportunities to acquaint foreign publishers, booksellers, and readers with American books. Up to a half-dozen major exhibits in multiple sets are produced each year for circulation worldwide. The exhibits travel to as many as 150 USIS posts overseas, where they are displayed at book fairs, scholarly and professional meetings, and other cultural events. The books are eventually donated to foreign institutions.

American publishers often donate books with small sales to nonprofit organizations. Many of these books have great value overseas, particularly in developing countries where commercial distribution of American books is difficult or impossible. USIA works with private-sector organizations to get hundreds of thousands of these books into the hands of both individual and institutional recipients who can benefit from them.

USIA has a special interest in encouraging respect for international copyright conventions by all nations. The Book Programs Division works closely on this issue with other government and private entities interested in promoting awareness of the importance of this issue. Foreign publishers from developing market areas are introduced to U.S. copyright norms and the U.S. freedom-to-publish tradition through short-term professional publishing workshops and courses.

American publishers should direct inquiries about export problems, rights, book exhibits, and participation in other USIA book activities to the Book Programs Division, Bureau of Educational and Cultural Affairs, USIA, Washington, DC 20547. Non-U.S. publishers should turn for assistance to the Cultural Affairs Office of the U.S. Embassy in their country or directly to the Book Programs Division in Washington, D.C.

National Center for Education Statistics
Library Statistics Program

U.S. Department of Education, Office of Educational Research and Improvement
555 New Jersey Ave. N.W., Washington, DC 20208-5652

Adrienne Chute
Library Statistics Program

The NCES mandate to collect library statistics is included in the Hawkins-Stafford Elementary and Secondary School Improvement Amendments of 1988 (PL 100-297). NCES regularly collects and disseminates statistical information on public, academic, and elementary and secondary school libraries. These data provide the only current, comprehensive, national data on the status of libraries. They are used by federal, state, and local officials, professional associations, and local practitioners for planning, evaluation, and making policy. These data are also available to researchers and educators to analyze the state of the art of librarianship and to improve its practice.

Public Libraries

Descriptive statistics for about 9,000 public libraries are collected and disseminated annually through a voluntary census, the Federal-State Cooperative System for public library data (FSCS). In 1993 FSCS completed its fifth data collection.

FSCS is an example of the synergy that can result from combining federal/state cooperation with state-of-the-art technology. FSCS was the first national NCES data collection in which the respondents supplied the data electronically. It was also edited and tabulated completely in machine-readable form. The software—the most recent version is called DECPLUS—is cost-effective and has improved data quality.

During 1993 the 50 states and the District of Columbia participated in the collection of 1992 data. The respondents were about 9,000 public libraries in the 50 states and the District of Columbia, identified by state library agencies. In general, both unit response and response to specific items are very high and item response rates have increased annually. Efforts to improve FSCS data quality are ongoing. Over the past year the clarity of FSCS definitions, software manual, and tables has been significantly improved.

At the state level, FSCS is administered by state data coordinators, appointed by each state's chief officer of the state library agency. FSCS is a working network. An annual training conference is provided for the state data coordinators and a steering committee that represents them is active in the development of the FSCS data collection program and its software. Technical assistance to states is provided by phone and in person by state data coordinators and by NCES staff and contractors. NCES also works cooperatively with the National Commission on Libraries and Information Science (NCLIS), the Chief Officers of State

Note: Jeffrey Williams, Library Statistics Program, contributed to this article.

Library Agencies (COSLA), the American Library Association (ALA), and the U.S. Department of Education's Library Programs Office.

Data files on diskette that contain 1992 data on about 9,000 responding libraries are expected to be available in 1994. These 1992 data will also be aggregated to state and national levels in an E.D. TABS, an NCES publication designed to present major findings with minimal statistical analyses. FSCS collects data on staffing; service outlets; operating income and expenditures; size of collection; service measures such as reference transactions, interlibrary loans, circulation, public service hours, and attendance; and services to children. The 1993 FSCS data will be collected in July 1994, with release of these data scheduled for spring 1995.

Additional information on FSCS may be obtained from Adrienne Chute (202-219-1772), Postsecondary Education Statistics Division, National Center for Education Statistics, Room 311A, 555 New Jersey Ave. N.W., Washington, DC 20208-5652.

The following are highlights from *E.D. TABS Public Libraries in the United States: 1991,* released in April 1993.

- 9,050 public libraries were reported in the 50 states and the District of Columbia in 1991 (Table 1).
- Over 69 percent of the population of legally served areas in the United States is served by 959 (nearly 11 percent) public libraries and their outlets. Each of these public libraries has a legal service area population of 50,000 or more (Tables 1A and 1B).
- 1,416 public libraries (about 16 percent) reported one or more branch libraries, with a total of 6,542 branches. The total number of library buildings reported (central libraries and branches) was 15,482. Ten percent of reporting public libraries had one or more bookmobiles. The total number of bookmobiles reported was 1,125 (Table 2).
- Public libraries reported a total of 108,187 paid full-time-equivalent (FTE) staff (Table 3).
- Public libraries reported that 76.8 percent of total operating income came from local sources, 13.1 percent from the state, 1.2 percent from federal sources, and 9.0 percent from other sources (Table 5).
- Total operating expenditures for public libraries were about $4.3 billion in 1991. Of this, nearly 64 percent was for paid FTE staff and over 15 percent for the library collection (Table 7). The United States' total per capita operating expenditure for library legal service area population was $17.80. The highest per capita was $35.62 and the lowest was $6.75 (Table 15).
- Forty-four percent of public libraries reported operating expenditures of less than $50,000 in 1991. Nearly 37 percent expended between $50,000 and $399,999, and just over 19 percent exceeded $400,000 (Table 9).
- Nationwide, public libraries reported nearly 629 million book and serial volumes in their collections or 2.6 volumes per capita of legal service area population. The volumes per capita ranged from 4.9 to 1.4 (Table 12).

- Nationwide, public libraries reported collections of over 20 million audio materials, about 615,000 films, and over 5.5 million video materials (Table 12A).
- Total nationwide circulation of library materials was over 1.4 billion or 6.1 per capita of legal service area population. Highest statewide circulation per capita was 10.6 and lowest was 3.1 (Table 16).
- Nationwide, over 6 million library materials were loaned by public libraries to other libraries (Table 16).

The numbers and percentages in the highlights above are based entirely on reporting public libraries. There was no imputation for public libraries that did not respond or for items left blank. The percent of public libraries not responding to a given item varies across states, ranging from zero to 100 percent. The reader should take this into account in making inferences or forming conclusions. The impact of nonresponse, especially on totals, can be significant.

Per capita figures in these highlights are based not on the total population of the nation or state but on their population of legal service areas. Population of legal service area means the population of those areas in the state or nation where library service is available. It does not include the population of unserved areas.

Academic Libraries

NCES surveyed academic libraries on a three-year cycle between 1966 and 1988. Since 1988, the Academic Libraries Survey (ALS) has been a component of the Integrated Postsecondary Education Data System (IPEDS) and is on a two-year cycle. ALS provides data on about 3,500 academic libraries. In aggregate, these data provide an overview of the status of academic libraries nationally and statewide.

The survey collects data on the libraries in the entire universe of accredited higher education institutions and on the libraries in nonaccredited institutions with a program of four years or more. ALS produces descriptive statistics on academic libraries in postsecondary institutions in the 50 states, the District of Columbia, and the outlying areas.

NCES has developed IDEALS, a software package for states to use in submitting ALS data to NCES. Its model was DECTOP, the predecessor of DEC-PLUS, the software developed for the collection of public library data in the FSCS program. IDEALS was used by 45 states in the collection of 1992 data.

ALS, using FSCS as a model, has established a steering committee, composed of representatives of the academic library community. Its mission is to improve data quality and the timeliness of data collection, processing, and release. This network of academic library professionals works closely with state IPEDS coordinators (representatives from each state who work with NCES to coordinate the collection of IPEDS data from postsecondary institutions in each of their states). NCES also works cooperatively with ALA, NCLIS, the Association of Research Libraries, the Association of College and Research Libraries, and numerous academic libraries in the collection of ALS. ALS collects data on total operating expenditures, full-time-equivalent library staff, service outlets, total volumes held at the end of the fiscal year, circulation, interlibrary loans, public service hours, gate count, reference transactions per typical week, and online services. The most recent Academic Libraries Survey was conducted in fall 1992, with release of these 1992 data scheduled for spring 1994.

The following are highlights from *E.D. TABS Academic Libraries: 1990,* released in December 1992.

- In 1990, total operating expenditures for libraries at the 3,274 institutions of higher education totaled $3.3 billion.
- The three largest individual expenditure items were salaries and wages, $1.7 billion (52.0 percent); current serial subscription expenditures, $549 million (16.8 percent); and print material expenditures, $402 million (12.3 percent).
- The libraries of the 488 doctoral-granting institutions (14.9 percent of the total institutions) accounted for $1.9 billion, or 58 percent of the total operating expenditure dollars at all college and university libraries.
- The number of volumes held at all academic libraries at the end of fiscal year 1990 totaled about 717 million.
- Libraries at institutions granting doctoral degrees held about 437 million volumes, or 61 percent of the total volumes held.
- The total number of full-time-equivalent (FTE) staff members in college and university libraries equaled about 100,000 including about 26,000 librarians and other professional staff, 42,000 other paid staff, 30,000 student assistants, and 1,400 staff who contributed their services.
- Libraries at institutions granting doctoral degrees accounted for 52,000, or half of all, FTE staff at all academic libraries.
- Academic libraries had 199 million circulation transactions; 80.4 percent from general collections, and 19.6 percent from reserve collections.
- Libraries at institutions granting doctoral degrees accounted for more than half of this total circulation with 105 million circulation transactions.

Additional information on academic library statistics may be obtained from Jeffrey Williams, Postsecondary Education Statistics Division, National Center for Education Statistics, 320A, 555 New Jersey Ave. N.W., Washington, DC 20208-5652 (202-219-1362).

School Library Media Centers

The last national survey exclusively on school library media centers was conducted in school year 1985–1986.

In 1991, a small amount of data on school libraries was collected as embedded items from a sample of public and private elementary and secondary schools as part of the NCES 1990–1991 Schools and Staffing Survey (SASS). Data collected included number of students served; number of professional staff and aides; number of full-time-equivalent librarians/media specialists; number of vacant positions, positions abolished, and approved positions; and amount of librarian input in establishing curriculum. NCES expects to release a short report on these data in 1994.

In addition, in 1991, as a separate part of the same SASS, NCES field-tested two new more comprehensive questionnaires for school libraries. One questionnaire covered the school library media center and the other the school library media specialist. A statistics committee has been established by the American Association of School Librarians to work with the federal government on the statistical needs and concerns of the school library media center community. The committee evaluated the results of the field test and helped to revise collection procedures and both the school library media center questionnaire and the school library media specialist questionnaire for the full-scale survey. NCES, with the assistance of the U.S. Bureau of the Census, will conduct this survey as part of the 1994 SASS. Release of these data is scheduled for 1995. The school library media specialist questionnaire will provide a nationwide profile of the school library media specialist workforce. The school library media center questionnaire will provide a national picture of school library collections, expenditures, technology, and services. This effort will be used to assess the status of school library media centers nationwide and to assess the federal role in their support.

Additional information on school library media center statistics may be obtained from Jeffrey Williams, Postsecondary Education Statistics Division, National Center for Education Statistics, 320A, 555 New Jersey Ave. N.W., Washington, DC 20208-5652 (202-219-1362).

Plans for the Library Statistics Program

NCES plans to continue collecting public library data through FSCS. NCES has annually funded technical assistance to states for library data collection.

Several topical surveys are also under way. In 1993, under the sponsorship of Library Programs, NCES conducted a fast response survey on public library services to children and young adults. The results are expected to be available in 1994. NCES pretested a survey on federal libraries in 1993 and plans data collection for late 1994, with data release in 1995. NCES plans to pretest a survey on state library agencies in 1994 and plans data collection for late 1994 or 1995. The state library survey is a cooperative effort between NCES and COSLA and the federal library survey is a cooperative effort between NCES and the staff of the Federal Library and Information Center Committee (Library of Congress).

NCES has also developed the first comprehensive, public library universe file. This automated file, to be updated annually, is part of DECPLUS. It includes identifying information on all known public libraries (including outlets), all state libraries, and some library systems and cooperatives. Beginning in 1994 this resource will be available for drawing samples for special surveys on such topics as literacy, access for the disabled, library construction, and the like.

NCES has also fostered the use and analysis of FSCS data. A Data Use Subcommittee of the FSCS Steering Committee has been addressing the dissemination, use, and analysis of FSCS data. Data dissemination has also been broadened with electronic release of the data and the E.D. TABS. In 1993 NCES sponsored an invitational forum on policy analysis using library data from all types of libraries. Another expanded invitational forum is planned for 1994. FSCS is also exploring the potential of software, including mapping software, to make customized analysis of public library data available to data users.

The collection of academic library data through IPEDS will also be continued. NCES plans to improve the quality of the data by promoting the use of IDEALS software for data collection. New data elements focusing on electronic access and other new technologies may be added to the survey. The ALS reports will contain more detailed analyses of the data.

NCES will continue school library data collection through SASS.

Publications

Public Libraries in Forty-Four States and the District of Columbia: 1988; An NCES Working Paper (November 1989). o.p.

E.D. TABS: Academic Libraries: 1988 (September 1990). o.p.

E.D. TABS: Public Libraries in Fifty States and the District of Columbia: 1989 (April 1991). o.p.

E.D. TABS: Public Libraries in the U.S.: 1990 (June 1992). o.p.

E.D. TABS: Academic Libraries: 1990 (December 1992). For sale through the Government Printing Office, No. 065-000-00549-2. $4.25.

E.D. TABS: Public Libraries in the United States: 1991 (April 1993). For sale through GPO, No. 065-000-00561-1. $7.50.

More recent publications may be available through the Superintendent of Documents (GPO). Write to: New Orders, Box 371954, Pittsburgh, PA 15250-7954. Tel. 202-783-3238 (Washington, D.C.), FAX (202) 512-2250.

Data Files Released on Diskette

Public Libraries in Forty-Four States and the District of Columbia: 1988 (March 1990).

Public Libraries in Fifty States and the District of Columbia: 1989 (May 1990).

Academic Libraries: 1988 (October 1990).

Public Libraries Data, 1990 (July 1992).

Academic Libraries: 1990 (February 1993).

The NCES data files above are generally available on computer diskette through the U.S. Department of Education, Office of Educational Research and Improvement, Data Systems Branch, 555 New Jersey Ave. N.W., Washington, DC 20208-5725.

Electronic Releases of Publications and Data Files

OERI Toll-Free Electronic Bulletin Board System (EBBS)

E.D. TABS: Public Libraries: 1990 (March 1992)

E.D. TABS: Public Libraries in the United States: 1991 (March 1993)

For more information, call 202-219-1547.

U.S. Department of Education (NCES) Gopher

E.D. TABS: Public Libraries in the United States: 1991 (March 1993). The file name is: Public Libraries in the U.S.: (All Files) (Zip) <PcBin>

Public Libraries Data 1991 (November 1993). The file name is: Public Libraries 1991 Data <PcBin>

The gopher address is: gopher. ed. gov port 10,000.

Library of Congress

Washington, DC 20540
202-707-5000

The *Library of Congress Strategic Plan (1993–2000),* states:

"The Library of Congress's mission is to sustain, to celebrate, and to preserve for future generations a universal collection of knowledge and creativity. It seeks to serve and inspire a free people by:

- Making the Library's resources available and useful to the Congress of the United States in ever more efficient ways;
- Assembling, organizing, and making its universal collection of human knowledge and expression increasingly accessible and useful to the American people and their libraries; and
- Encouraging and celebrating free intellectual creativity by all people in all subjects."

During 1992 and 1993 the Library of Congress expanded its collections to more than 100 million items; announced a number of important acquisitions, including the Leonard Bernstein Archive; made its bibliographic databases available worldwide; successfully pursued its arrearage reduction goals; sought innovation in facing budgetary restraints; implemented new security measures; presented four new major exhibitions; called for support of public libraries; and pursued goals for public-private partnerships on behalf of the intellectual life of the nation.

Milestones

Celebrating the Collections: Thomas Jefferson

The library celebrated the 250th anniversary of the birth of Thomas Jefferson April 13, 1993, by announcing its 100-millionth acquisition: a collection of 745

American watercolor paintings, pencil drawings, and prints by John Rubens Smith, an influential nineteenth-century drawing master. The number of items in the Library of Congress collections had risen to 101,395,257 by the end of fiscal 1992. The James Madison Council, the library's private-sector advisory body, provided funds for purchase of the Smith Collection, and John Kluge, chairman of the council, joined Librarian of Congress James H. Billington in presenting the collection to Representative Vic Fazio (D-Calif.), chairman of the House Subcommittee on Legislative Branch Appropriations, who accepted on behalf of the nation.

The library also marked the Jefferson anniversary by publishing *Jefferson's Legacy: A Brief History of the Library of Congress,* which summarizes the library's history from its founding in 1800 through 1992, and by cooperating in the publication of a new edition of Jefferson's *Manual of Parliamentary Practice* (Applewood Books) and *Jefferson the Man: In His Own Words* (Fulcrum Publishing). The library cosponsored, with the Thomas Jefferson Memorial Foundation, the national lecture series "Thomas Jefferson at 250: The Legacy of an American Genius," which continued for most of 1993. In May 1993, in cooperation with the Institute of Early American History and Culture, the library presented the three-day seminar "Thomas Jefferson and the Education of a Citizen in the American Republic." Funding for the seminar was provided by the Madison Council.

In another Madison Council-related development, the Edward Lowe Foundation provided the library with a $1 million gift to establish a Business Research Fund to support creation and distribution throughout the United States of a variety of business information tools and services to assist the nation's entrepreneurs and small businesses. Edward Lowe, president of the foundation, is a member of the Madison Council.

Foundation gifts also enabled the library to continue its educational programs for librarians from Central and Eastern Europe. A grant of $75,000 from the Margaret Thatcher Foundation was used for a summer 1993 program for ten Russian librarians to train at the Library of Congress and at selected local libraries. The Soros Foundation, beginning in 1992, also has provided funding for three-month fellowships for librarians from Central and Eastern Europe and the former Soviet Union.

Library of the Future

The Library of Congress took a major step toward becoming the electronic library of the future on April 30, 1993, when it made its bibliographic databases available worldwide to users of Internet, a nonprofit collection of computer networks linking an estimated 20 million computer users in more than 100 countries. Initially, access was provided to 26 million Library of Congress records in 35 files. In October, the library announced the availability of a new online information system, LC Marvel (Library of Congress Machine-Assisted Realization of the Virtual Electronic Library), available to Internet users as well as to readers and staff for searches at the library and to congressional offices. The LC Marvel Main Menu offers the following selections:

1 About LC Marvel
2 Library of Congress: Facilities, Activities, and Services
3 Research and Reference
4 Library of Congress Online Systems
5 The U.S. Congress
6 Federal Government Information
7 Services to Libraries and Publishers
8 Copyright
9 Employee Information
10 The Global Electronic Library (by Subject)
11 Internet Resources
12 What's New on LC Marvel

The library in 1992 established the Library of Congress News Service, an online source of information about the library available to anyone with access to a computer and a modem. This service offers news stories about the library and its activities; information on exhibitions, hours, and services; and information of special interest to librarians.

Public Libraries' Importance

The new electronic age makes the nation's 15,000 public libraries more rather than less important to the progress of the United States in the twenty-first century, according to Librarian of Congress James H. Billington. Testifying before Congress on April 21, 1993, Billington warned that cutbacks in local funding of public libraries mean that Americans are "in serious danger of eroding a unique legacy laboriously created by our forebears," even as public demands for modern library services increase and two-thirds of all Americans use a library in the course of a year. Electronic online information "will vastly supplement, not destroy, the book," he said.

As the President and Congress look to the electronic future and the country's needs, they should pay special attention to public libraries, Billington said. Linked by new technology to one another, to university libraries, and to the Library of Congress, these local libraries, "unpublicized yet deeply cherished and heavily used in thousands of communities," can play a vital role in the coming Age of Information, he stated.

Reducing the Backlog of Unprocessed Materials

Library staff working to reduce the arrearages of unprocessed materials in the library's collections met their targets for 1992 and 1993, reducing the backlog by millions of items each year, for a 30.8 percent drop in the backlog since 1989, when goals were set for Phase I of the arrearage reduction project.

Library staff reported a reduction of 12,225,366 items as FY 1993 ended September 30. The backlog was reduced by 4,750,243 items in 1992 and by 6,119,409 in 1993. As 1993 ended, the arrearage total stood at 27,456,787.

Phase II of the project is expected to reduce the 1989 arrearage total by 80 percent by the year 2000.

Collection Security

Intensified security became a major priority after discovery of thefts and mutilations of materials in the library's general and special collections. In 1992 and 1993 protective procedures were significantly tightened. In 1992 the book stacks were closed first to the public and subsequently to all staff except those with work-related reasons for access. The delivery of materials through the book conveyor system was limited and the movement of materials within the buildings was curtailed. Electronic surveillance gates, with alarms triggered by security devices embedded in library materials, were placed at every library exit.

In 1993 electronic surveillance equipment was installed in the Newspaper and Current Periodicals Reading Room, the Manuscript Reading Room, and the Law Library. Phase I of a new security measure began December 13, 1993, when an electronic locking system went into use on the doors to the south stacks in the Thomas Jefferson Building. These stacks, housing materials from the general collections, now are accessible only by use of magnetic cards. There are plans to install the magnetic locks on all doors to stack areas in the Jefferson and Adams buildings. The Madison Building, which was completed in 1980, was designed with stack security in mind.

Budget Tightening

The library's budgets for fiscal 1992, 1993, and 1994 reflected Congress's efforts to reduce spending and the national deficit. As appropriations declined in real dollars, the library had to determine how best to maintain its level of service.

Although Congress approved annual increases for 1992 and 1993, the total for each year was substantially less than requested. The budget for 1994 is $2.5 million less than the total for 1993.

	Request	Appropriation
FY 1992	$359,962,000	$322,228,000
FY 1993	$357,500,000	$334,316,000
FY 1994	$364,400,000	$331,864,000

Increased costs in almost every area, including mandated pay raises, caused the library to look at every possible means of reducing expenditures during 1992 and 1993, while continuing to fulfill its mission. In January 1993, Tuesday and Friday evening hours were eliminated in the six general reading rooms and in the Law Library. Sunday hours were eliminated in the same reading rooms from Memorial Day through Labor Day. The Manuscript Reading Room began closing on Saturdays. Hours of service were being reevaluated as 1993 ended. The National Translations Center was closed and interlibrary loans to foreign libraries were suspended because under present law the library cannot collect postage costs from borrowers. A limited hiring freeze on new appointments was announced May 21, 1992. As FY 1993 ended the size of the library's staff was 5,033, compared with 5,050 at the end of FY 1992.

In the last three months of 1993 the library offered retirement incentives to 250 employees. Positions will be abolished as retirements take place.

In another economy measure, the Special Projects and the Science and Technology Information service units were abolished in May 1993. In an organizational change earlier in the year, the Office of the Associate Librarian for Management and the Center for Innovative Management were eliminated.

National Film Preservation Board

The life of the National Film Preservation Board, authorized by Congress in 1988 to advise the Librarian of Congress on selections for the National Film Registry, was extended for four years in legislation passed by Congress and signed by President Bush on June 26, 1992. The Librarian selected 25 films in 1992 and 25 more in 1993 for addition to the National Film Registry. This brings to 125 the number of films selected for the registry and for preservation by the library because they are culturally, historically, or aesthetically significant.

The National Film Preservation Act of 1992 also authorized the board to conduct a one-year study for Congress on the status of film preservation as a preliminary to the establishment of a comprehensive national film preservation program by the library in conjunction with film archivists and owners of film copyrights. After a year of study, the board reported to Congress on June 25, 1993, that there is a dire need for a comprehensive national program to preserve films now threatened with deterioration. The board immediately began work on such a plan, with assistance from staff of the library's Motion Picture, Broadcasting, and Recorded Sound Division. Its four-volume report, *Film Preservation 1993: A Study of the Current State of American Film Preservation*, was published by the Government Printing Office.

Major Exhibitions

Columbus Quincentenary

The library's celebration of the Christopher Columbus quincentenary in 1992 marked the high point of this multiyear effort. The exhibition "1492: An Ongoing Voyage" and its accompanying catalog were well received by the press, scholars, and the general public. The exhibition provided historical context to the raging debate surrounding the commemoration of the explorer's voyage. Drawing largely from the library's collections, the bilingual exhibition included maps and globes, documents, codices, and navigational tools.

Another quincentenary project—the exhibition "Old Ties, New Attachments: Italian-American Folklife in the West," based on field work done by the American Folklife Center—opened in California at the University of Santa Clara. This survey of Italian-American contributions to the culture of the American West also documents the transformation of Italians in the West into Italian-Americans. The exhibition, accompanied by a publication of the same title, opened at the Library of Congress in October 1993 to run through March 27, 1994.

Russian Archives

A month-long exhibition in June 1992 of 300 previously secret documents from the Communist archives of the former Soviet Union evoked major interest in these materials spanning the creation, rise, and dissolution of the modern Soviet state, from the October Revolution of 1917 to the attempted coup against Mikhail Gorbachev in August 1991.

Vatican Treasures

Two hundred of the Vatican Library's most precious books, manuscripts, and maps were brought for display in the library's first major exhibition of 1993: "Rome Reborn: The Vatican Library and Renaissance Culture." Many of the items had never been on public display anywhere in the world. The exhibition attracted record numbers of visitors to the library's Jefferson Building, where the Great Hall, closed for renovation since 1990, reopened to the public for the four months the Vatican treasures were on display. After the exhibition ended on April 30, the Great Hall was again closed to the public so that renovation could continue, with completion expected in late summer 1994.

Dead Sea Scrolls

"Scrolls from the Dead Sea," running from April 29 through August 1, 1993, in the library's Madison Building, also attracted record crowds. The exhibition featured 12 fragmentary scrolls, only one of which had been brought to the United States before, and 88 related archeological artifacts excavated at Qumran, the ancient site whose inhabitants may have produced the scrolls. This exhibition went on display later in 1993 in the New York Public Library.

Other Developments

National Demonstration Laboratory

The relocation of the National Demonstration Laboratory for Interactive Technology (NDL) from the Smithsonian Institution to the library's Madison Building was recognized at a ribbon-cutting ceremony on March 26, 1992. Funded entirely by private contributions and supported primarily by the Atrium Group—a consortium of private companies that donate funds, software, or equipment—NDL is a showcase of new technology for Library of Congress and congressional staff, educators, and those who make public policy. The facility offers such demonstrations as a "virtual reality" system that places a participant on camera within an interactive video environment and a voice-activated "video patient" that teaches diagnostic techniques to medical students.

Congressional Research Service

The Congressional Research Service (CRS), which provides research, analysis, and information services to Congress, in 1993 received and responded to requests from every member of the Senate and House of Representatives and every congressional committee.

CRS encountered a number of challenges and opportunities at the convening of the 103rd Congress in January 1993. The record number of new members (129), extensive turnover in committee leadership, and potential for legislative reorganization all contributed to changes in congressional needs and interests served by CRS. The service planned well in advance to help ease this transition by effectively introducing new members and their office staffs to the wide range of products, services, and subject expertise it offers and by establishing CRS contacts and information resources for these new members to use.

As part of its objective of providing timely, comprehensive products and services to Congress and keeping abreast of major issues of concern to Congress, CRS developed interdisciplinary teams to address some of the complex issues of greatest congressional interest in FY 1993. Two examples of such issues are the North American Free Trade Agreement (NAFTA) and health care reform.

CRS responded to more than 600,000 requests from congressional offices and committees during 1993 and to a similar number in 1992.

In 1992 CRS specialists and other library staff completed their second year of efforts on behalf of Congress to foster the development of emerging democratic parliaments in Eastern Europe. Among CRS contributions were a three-day conference in Sofia, Bulgaria, at which CRS conducted its first member training program outside the United States, for the newly elected Bulgarian Parliament, and six parliamentary institutes held in Washington, D.C., to train some 100 parliamentary and library staff from seven Eastern and Central European nations.

Copyright

The Copyright Office took a major step toward the twenty-first century in 1992 when it contracted for the development of an optical storage system that will eliminate repetitive manual tasks, such as hand-stamping of applications, and permit retrieval of information in a matter of seconds. Security of applications will be increased, as paper copies will not need to be handled after information is put into the system. Originals can be stored off site, freeing library space for other uses.

A new regulation permits group registration of daily newspapers for a single $40 fee, provided the deposit is a month's issues on microfilm, resulting in a savings to the library in costs of purchasing newspapers on microfilm.

The Recording Industry Association of America honored the Copyright Office on March 10, 1992, with its Cultural Award, recognizing its years of service in behalf of the U.S. recording industry both domestically and internationally. The award honored the Copyright Office for effective administration of U.S. copyright law since 1897, for serving as an international advocate of copyright, and for nurturing the creative process by providing protection for intellectual property.

CD-ROM Regulations

The library is expected to benefit from two new procedures on copyright deposits adopted in 1992. New regulations require deposit of material in CD-ROM format for which copyright is claimed, along with operating software and manuals. The deposit requirements are in direct support of the Machine-Readable Collections Reading Room. The first CD-ROM publications deposited under the new procedure were received by the library September 29, 1993. The first deposit marked the conclusion of a year and a half of negotiations among the Library of Congress, the Information Industry Association, the National Federation of Abstracting and Information Services, and the Association of American Publishers. These negotiations set ground rules for the use of CD-ROM materials by the public using the library and aimed to induce prompt voluntary deposit of such materials at the library.

Law Library

At the invitation of retired Supreme Court Associate Justice William Brennan, a group of eminent attorneys, legal publishers, and other interested persons met in March 1992 to revive the Friends of the Law Library of Congress, an organization founded in the 1930s. The group has constituted a board of directors (of which the Law Librarian is an ex officio member), elected its first officers, and sought and received its status as a nonprofit, tax-exempt organization. By the end of 1993 the Friends had 200 corporate and individual members. The group's fund-raising activities concentrate on special projects not covered by appropriated funds, such as supporting exchange programs for legal scholars.

Americans with Disabilities Act

Library staff worked to conform with the 1992 Americans with Disabilities Act, which will have a profound impact on the staff as well as on readers and tourists covered by this legislation. One of the first implementations was to make an on-call interpreter available for hearing-impaired staff and visitors.

During the library's observance of Disability Awareness Month in October 1993, Librarian Billington described actions by the library to make the collections more accessible to both readers and staff with disabilities.

In the Main Reading Room, the Kurzweil Personal Reader synthesizes type and reads the words aloud, enabling the visually impaired researcher to use the library's printed books and periodicals. The Computer Catalog Center has a large-screen terminal with a variable-font printer as well as two stations designed for wheelchair access. Two librarians, one of whom has taken classes in American Sign Language, are assigned to help persons with disabilities. Closed-circuit magnification systems are available in each of the library's three main buildings. The library's orientation film is open-captioned for the hearing-impaired; elevators are equipped to serve those in wheelchairs and instructions for use are in braille; and elsewhere, special phones and sign language interpreters assist hearing-impaired staffers.

Acquisitions

Important acquisitions during 1992 and 1993 include

- The personal and professional archives of conductor and composer Leonard Bernstein

- The papers of Associate Supreme Court Justice Thurgood Marshall
- A collection representing the life work of composer Irving Berlin
- More than 20,000 documents relating to prisoners of war and missing-in-action servicemen in Southeast Asia received from the Department of Defense, for which the Federal Research Division has created a computerized index
- A collection of research documents on the Vespucci family of Florence presented by distinguished Colombian historian German Arciniegas
- Papers, manuscripts, recordings, photographs, and other materials purchased from the widow of jazz musician and composer Charles Mingus
- The 10,000-item Gwen Verdon/Bob Fosse Collection, donated to the library by Miss Verdon
- The Altshuler collection of approximately 500,000 phonodiscs (78 r.p.m.) and books, magazines, and files related to recorded popular American music, especially jazz
- Marcus Welser's *Bayerische Geschicht,* a work actually written by Elector Maximilian of Bavaria, which documents Bavarian history up to the seventeenth century
- Joducus Hondius's *Vera Totius Expeditionis Nauticae . . .* ("an accurate description of the voyage round the world of Sir Francis Drake who set out from England with five well-equipped ships the 13th December 1577"), a rare map dated 1595
- *The English Poetry Full-Text Database,* published by Chadwyck-Healey
- The Global Jewish Database, a CD-ROM with the full Hebrew text of the Bible, the Jerusalem and Babylonian Talmuds, and a collection of more than 200 books of rabbinic responses
- *Yijo sillok,* the annals of the Yi dynasty (1392–1819) in 400 volumes, a valuable original source on Korean history published in Pyongyang in the North Korean vernacular and available in the West for the first time
- *Dabistan,* a very rare edition of the only complete translation of a major work in Persian on comparative religions
- A series of letters (133 items) from Russian-born novelist Vladimir Nabokov and his wife, Vera, to fellow émigré Gleb Struve
- A manuscript journal of voyages by two U.S. whaling ships, the *Margaret* (1840) and the *York* (1841–1843)
- Nineteen Soviet feature films made during the Stalinist era
- A collection of Charlotte Brooks's negatives, contact sheets, and color transparencies from *Look* magazine
- A collection of illustrations published between 1926 and 1931 in *The Forum,* an influential public opinion magazine

- George Gershwin material from the archives of the Theatre Guild relating to the original and subsequent productions of *Porgy and Bess*
- The first cookbook to be published west of the Rocky Mountains

Public Programs

Joseph Brodsky, Poet Laureate Consultant in Poetry at the Library of Congress, presided over poetry programs in early 1992 and was succeeded for the 1992–1993 literary season by Mona Van Duyn. Rita Dove made her first appearance as poet laureate on October 7, 1993, and promised an ambitious year of programs, including an evening of poetry and jazz. The 1992 Rebekah Johnson Bobbitt National Prize for Poetry, given and named in memory of the sister of President Lyndon Johnson, was shared by poets Louise Glück and Mark Strand. It was presented at the library on October 29, 1992.

Although the library's Coolidge Auditorium in the Jefferson Building remained closed for renovation, the Music Division was able to present its 1992 and 1993 seasons of chamber concerts in the National Academy of Sciences Auditorium. The American Folklife Center's summer outdoor concerts were presented each year on the Neptune Plaza at the entrance to the Jefferson Building.

Barbara Bush was honorary chair for the Center for the Book's 1992 reading promotion, "Explore New Worlds—Read!" In 1992, with support from a grant of more than $500,000 from the Lila Wallace–Reader's Digest Fund, the center launched a three-year "Literary Heritage of the States" education program to look at maps depicting places and people who are part of the U.S. literary landscape. Early efforts produced an exhibition, "Language of the Land," on display at the library from August 5, 1993, through January 17, 1994, with plans for it to travel to more than 20 states.

"Books Change Lives" was selected as the center's theme for 1993 and 1994. During 1993, the number of state Centers for the Book, organized with assistance from the Library of Congress, grew to 29. As a Center for the Book project, the library published a new edition of *The Community of the Book: A Directory of Organizations and Programs* (1993), a guide to national organizations that promote books and reading, administer literary projects, and encourage the study of books and print culture.

[For more information on The Center for the Book, see the following article—*Ed.*]

Center for the Book

John Y. Cole
Director, The Center for the Book
Library of Congress

The Library-Head Start Partnership and the Literary Heritage of the States project are the major 1993–1994 projects of the Center for the Book, one of the Library of Congress's most dynamic and visible educational outreach programs. Since 1977 the center has used the library's prestige and resources to stimulate public interest in books, reading, and libraries and to encourage the study of books and the printed word. Today its reading promotion network includes 29 state affiliates and 128 national civic and educational organizations.

The Center for the Book is a successful public-private partnership; the Library of Congress supports its four full-time positions, but its projects and publications are funded through contributions from individuals, corporations, and foundations.

Background

A half-day symposium on "Reading Promotion around the World" at the 1993 Frankfurt Book Fair was one indication of increasing interest worldwide in book and reading promotion. Two trends help to explain this intensified effort: increased awareness of the severe consequences of illiteracy and failure to read, both for individuals and for society; and a growing conviction that individuals and organizations outside the book and educational worlds must become involved if progress is to be made. The technological revolution since the 1970s, with the emergence of television and the computer as major communications and social forces, has added urgency to the task.

The Center for the Book, part of the renewed effort in the United States to promote literacy and motivate reading, was created by Public Law 95-129, approved October 13, 1977. The legislation was introduced at the behest of Librarian of Congress Daniel J. Boorstin, who felt that a new national office at the Library of Congress for promoting books and reading was a logical way for the institution to play a more prominent role in the nation's educational and cultural life. Through the new law, Congress affirmed its belief in "the importance of the printed word and the book" and recognized the need for the continued study of the written record as "central to our understanding of ourselves and our world." When he approved the legislation, President Jimmy Carter emphasized his personal commitment "to scholarly research and the development of public interest in books and reading."

The Center for the Book's initial planning meetings and programs were supported by contributions from McGraw-Hill and Mrs. Charles W. Engelhard. More than a dozen people who had been closely associated with the National Book Committee (1954–1974), the U.S. Government Advisory Committee on Book and Library Programs (1962–1977), and Franklin Book Programs Inc. (1952–1979), became valuable members of the center's national advisory board.

Many of them returned for a March 1994 Center for the Book program on the "Origins of the American Community of the Book."

Themes

Since 1987 the center has introduced reading promotion themes as a way of stimulating interest and support for projects that benefit all age groups. Used by the affiliated state centers, national organizational partners, and others, the themes remind Americans of the joys of reading and the importance of books in today's world.

In 1989 First Lady Barbara Bush was the honorary chairperson of "1989—The Year of the Young Reader," a campaign to stimulate the love of reading among young people. Her support continued in 1991's effort, "The Year of the Lifetime Reader," which concentrated on family literacy, and in the 1992 campaign, "Explore New Worlds—READ!," which focused on reading as a way of learning about the world, emphasizing geography and the literature of travel and exploration. "Books Change Lives" was the theme for 1993–1994, and "Shape Your Future—READ!" will be featured in 1995–1996. In recent years Pizza Hut Inc. has supported the publication of theme brochures and the American Library Association has produced posters, T-shirts, and other promotional materials.

One of the most successful "Books Change Lives" projects in 1993 was a writing contest for students sponsored by the center and Weekly Reader Corporation's *Read* magazine. More than 9,000 students in grades 6 through 12 wrote letters to authors, living or dead, describing how that author somehow changed the student's outlook on life. Twelve national finalists and ten state finalists (selected by state centers for the book) were chosen. The grand prize winner, Aslum Adad, age 17, of Rolling Meadows, Ill., wrote author Alex Haley about the influence of Haley's *The Autobiography of Malcolm X.*

State Centers

When James H. Billington became Librarian of Congress in 1987, there were ten affiliated state centers. The number increased dramatically in subsequent years, and with the addition of Idaho, Louisiana, and Vermont early in 1994, it reached 29.

Each state center works with the Library of Congress to promote books, reading, and libraries as well as the state's own literary and intellectual heritage. Each center develops and funds its own operations and projects, using Library of Congress promotion themes and occasionally hosting traveling exhibits from the library. When its application is approved, a state center is granted affiliate status for three years. Renewals are for three-year periods.

In 1993–1994, 16 state centers received grants from the Lila Wallace-Reader's Digest Fund to host the Library of Congress traveling exhibition, "Language of the Land: Journeys into Literary America," and to develop programming in connection with the exhibition. Another exhibition, "Bonfire of Liberties: Censorship of the Humanities," was seen in five states and a third, the photo exhibit "A Nation of Readers," was seen in Alaska, Arizona, and Connecticut on the final leg of a six-year journey.

Also in 1993–1994, 11 state centers received "Writing Life" grants from the National Book Foundation. Supported by the Lila Wallace-Reader's Digest Fund, the grants enabled the centers to host authors who were National Book Award winners or finalists. For example, novelist Norman Rush presented programs in Seattle on April 24–25, 1993, under the auspices of the Washington Center for the Book.

On April 18, 1994, representatives from the state centers participated in an idea-sharing session at the Library of Congress, held in conjunction with the library's National Library Week reception, sponsored by the Center for the Book. Projects discussed included "Connecticut Voices," the Connecticut Center for the Book's series of author programs on Connecticut Public Radio; televised author interview programs developed and sponsored by the Arizona and the Florida centers; Colorado's enormously successful Rocky Mountain Book Festival, held October 1–2, 1993; Missouri's Author Recognition Day, which brought more than 200 Missouri authors to a program in the State Capitol and a reception hosted in the Governor's Mansion by Jean Carnahan, the state's First Lady; the 1994 state book award events sponsored by Minnesota and Oklahoma; Nebraska's third annual literature festival; California's photography exhibition, "California Reads!," offered for loan to California libraries; Iowa's daylong, statewide reading marathon; Michigan's children's book fair; the Oregon Intellectual Freedom Clearinghouse, a new project of the Oregon Center for the Book; and Alaska's "Buckets of Books" book collection project for child care organizations. These and many other state center projects were described in an article in the December 1993 issue of *Wilson Library Bulletin*.

Reading Promotion Partners

The center's organizational partnership program now includes 128 governmental, civic, and educational groups. Private and governmental organizations become reading promotion partners of the Library of Congress by agreeing to participate in each year's reading promotion campaign. They develop their own projects, publicize the national theme and the work of the Center for the Book, and sometimes make an in-kind or financial contribution to support the campaign.

The most recent additions to the partnership program are the American Association of Community Colleges, the Auxiliary of the National Rural Letter Carriers Association, and the National Science Teachers Association. Other partners are major professional literacy and library organizations, labor unions, two national newspaper associations, major service organizations (including Kiwanis, the Lions Clubs, and the General Federation of Women's Clubs) as well as those that speak for senior citizens, the scientific community, lawyers, and those engaged in the education of prison inmates. Nine of the 128 partners are U.S. government agencies: the Departments of Agriculture (4H Youth Programs), Defense (Dependents' School System), Education, Energy, Health and Human Services (Head Start Bureau), Justice (Federal Bureau of Prisons) and Labor; the U.S. Information Agency; and the U.S. National Commission on Libraries and Information Science. Also participating are major African-American, Hispanic, and Native American organizations and associations grouping—among others—

the governors and lieutenant-governors of the 50 states, cartoonists, rural electric cooperatives, and U.S. swimmers.

On January 19, 1994, organizational partners gathered at the Library of Congress to share ideas about using the "Books Change Lives" theme. Examples of projects developed by partners and discussed at the meeting included: the restocking of a flood-devastated library in Kansas by American Mensa Ltd., with all the books supplied carrying an American Mensa/"Books Change Lives" bookplate; a student essay contest in Dallas/Fort Worth sponsored by the North Texas Association of the Phi Beta Kappa Society, with a $1,000 scholarship as the prize; and the issuance by the U.S. Postal Service of a "Books Change Lives" poster announcing four new 29-cent stamps that depict favorite childhood books.

Projects

The Library-Head Start partnership project, funded with a transfer of funds from the U.S. Department of Health and Human Services to the Center for the Book, entered its second phase in 1993–1994 with regional workshops sponsored by the California Center for the Book (December 10–11, 1993); the Virginia Center for the Book (March 18–19, 1994); and the Kansas Center for the Book (May 13–14, 1994).

The Library-Head Start project, carried out in collaboration with the Association for Library Service to Children (ALSC), a division of the American Library Association, is designed to demonstrate in communities nationwide how libraries that serve children and Head Start programs can work together in family literacy projects. The project began with the production and distribution of a 40-minute video that describes how to form a library-Head Start partnership. The video and an accompanying guide were discussed by librarians and Head Start teachers in three regional workshops.

The Literary Heritage of the States project, funded with a grant of $503,329 to the Center for the Book from the Lila Wallace-Reader's Digest Fund, began in August 1993 with the opening at the Library of Congress of the traveling exhibition "Language of the Land: Journeys into Literary America." Featuring literary maps and photographs from the library's collections, the exhibit's four regional sections (Northeast, South, Midwest, West) feature the voices of writers deeply rooted in a particular place, e.g. James Fenimore Cooper celebrates the undefiled New York State wilderness, Richard Wright conveys Chicago's urban tumult, Willa Cather portrays a sweltering Nebraska cornfield, and N. Scott Momaday depicts a lonely Oklahoma mountain sacred to his Kiowa ancestors.

A collaborative effort of the Center for the Book and the library's Geography and Map Division and Interpretive Programs Office, the exhibit will be seen around the country through 1995 at 16 state centers and other sites. It began its national tour on October 1, 1993, in Denver at the Rocky Mountain Book Festival under the sponsorship of the Colorado Center for the Book.

The Center for the Book's best-known media project is the Library of Congress/CBS Television "Read More About It" book project. Since 1979, more than 350 CBS television programs have included a thirty-second message in which a performer mentions books suggested by the Center for the Book and sends viewers to their local libraries and bookstores to "Read More About It." Millions of viewers see the messages each time they appear on major CBS telecasts including the Super Bowl, the World Series, and the Olympic Games.

Events

Sponsorship of significant events and meetings at the Library of Congress is an important way the Center for the Book informs others about its projects and goals. Recent examples include a Halloween Mystery Celebration, which included a program on "The Art of Writing Mysteries" featuring writers Tony Hillerman, Mary Higgins Clark, and Elizabeth Peters; "USIA Libraries Abroad," a conference sponsored with the U.S. Information Agency; "Publishing and Book Culture in Russia and the New States: Challenges for the West," a conference sponsored with Pubwatch and the Kennan Institute for Advanced Studies; "Thomas Jefferson and the Education of an American Citizen," a symposium sponsored with the Library of Congress's Rare Book and Special Collections Division and the Institute of Early American History and Culture in Williamsburg, Va; and, with the Public Broadcasting Service, a celebration of the tenth anniversary of the PBS series "Reading Rainbow" that featured readings from favorite children's books by many celebrities, including Associate Supreme Court Justice Ruth Bader Ginsburg, U.S. Senators Carol Moseley-Braun and Paul Simon, Attorney General Janet Reno, and television correspondents Cokie Roberts and Robert MacNeil.

Publications

In recognition of its "services in advancing understanding of the history of printing and its allied arts," in January 1994 the Center for the Book received the American Printing History Association's annual institutional award. The center's active publishing program was specifically cited. Since 1978, the Center for the Book has sponsored the publication of more than 25 books and 50 pamphlets. Recent publications include *The Community of the Book: A Directory of Organizations and Programs* (1993), compiled by Maurvene D. Williams; *A Description of Descriptive Bibliography* (1992), by G. Thomas Tanselle; *Developing Lifetime Readers: A Report on the 1991 "Year of the Lifetime Reader" Promotion of the Library of Congress* (1993), compiled by Michael Thompson; *Earth, Stars, and Writers* (1993), lectures by National Book Award winners Philip Levine, Orlando Patterson, and Norman Rush, published in cooperation with the National Book Foundation; *Jefferson's Legacy: A Brief History of the Library of Congress* (1993), by John Y. Cole; and *Publishing and Readership in Revolutionary France* (1993), edited by Carol Armbruster, a volume based on a symposium sponsored by the Center for the Book and the library's European Division.

The Library of Congress is an international resource of unparalleled dimensions, collecting research materials from all parts of the world and in more than 450 languages. The Center for the Book, through its projects and publications, shares the worldwide concerns of its parent institution. Publications reflecting

Acquire the information resources you need—with a little friendly help.

Now any group or individual can purchase a tax-deductible Reed Reference Publishing Friends of the Library Bond with a face value of $100, $250, $500, $750, or $1,000—at a 20% discount—and donate it to your library. Your library receives full face value on a first-time purchase of any Reed Reference Publishing product—books, CD-ROMs, microfiche, as well as tape leasing services.

Let local support groups know their contributions can go further with the 20% discount offered by this program. *Sign up by calling 1-800-521-8110. Dial "1" for Customer Service and ask for the Library Bonds Department. You can also fax your request to (908) 665-6688.*

BCR1

☐ **YES!** Our sponsor(s) is interested in purchasing Reed Reference Publishing Friends of the Library Bonds in the following denominations:

QTY		TOTAL
____ $100 Bond at $80 each		_____
____ $250 Bond at $200 each		_____
____ $500 Bond at $400 each		_____
____ $750 Bond at $600 each		_____
____ $1,000 Bond at $800 each		_____
	Total $	_____

Library:

Name _____

Library _____

Address _____

City/State/Zip _____

Sponsor:

Name _____

Organization _____

Address _____

City/State/Zip _____

Daytime Phone (_____)_____

PAYMENT:

☐ Check or money order enclosed for $_____
(Please make checks payable to Reed Reference Publishing.)

Charge my: ☐ VISA ☐ MC ☐ AMEX

Card # _____ Exp._____

Signature _____
(Please enclose all credit card orders in an envelope.)

An Exciting Way to Help You Save Money— Reed Reference Publishing's Friends of the Library Bonds

"I think that the Friends of the Library Bonds Program is an excellent idea. This is just the kind of opportunity that allows Friends groups to respond to library needs in an appropriate and cost-effective manner."

—Sandy Cody, Program Coordinator, Friends of the Libraries, The Ohio State University

Alert *all* your friends and supporters to **Reed Reference Publishing's Friends of the Library Bonds** Program! Just call us and we'll send you a brief press release to place in your local newspapers, library newsletter, or other local publications.

this interest include *U.S. Books Abroad: Neglected Ambassadors* (1984), by Curtis G. Benjamin; *Multiple Meanings: The Written Word in Japan* (1987), edited by J. Thomas Rimer, a publication based on a major exhibition and two symposia; *International Library Horizons* (1989), by Robert Vosper; and, most recently, *Donated Book Programs: A Dialogue of Partners Handbook* (1993).

The Role of the Center for the Book

The high visibility and national partnership approach of the Center for the Book complement the plans of Librarian of Congress James H. Billington for the future development of the Library of Congress. With congressional approval, Billington has encouraged the Library of Congress to undertake a new educational role, sharing its resources and influence with the rest of the country in new and imaginative ways. The Center for the Book has become a small pilot project in the library's effort to link itself more creatively and effectively to the nation's intellectual, educational, and cultural life. It is pointing the way to what might be possible through closer alliances among the Library of Congress, other organizations, and the private sector.

The Center for the Book's role as a public advocate on behalf of books, reading, and libraries also focuses attention on the essential link between books, reading, and democracy. In a speech entitled "Books and the World," published by the Center for the Book in 1988, librarian Billington vividly described this relationship and its importance:

> It is important to stress the central moral importance of the enterprise of reading itself for our kind of society. (It) arises first of all from the simple fact that our type of democracy has depended on knowledge and grown through books. By their very nature, books foster freedom with dignity. Books do not coerce, they convince. . . Historically books have been the companions of a responsible democratic citizenry. They provide keys to the dynamism of our past and perhaps to our national competitiveness in the future. Books link the record of yesterday with the possibilities of tomorrow.

Federal Library and Information Center Committee

Library of Congress, Washington, DC 20540
202-707-4800

Joseph W. Price
Acting Director

Looking to the future during fiscal 1993, the Federal Library and Information Center Committee (FLICC) streamlined its organizational structure, promoted forward-looking initiatives in automation and networking on behalf of the nation's federal libraries and information centers, and sponsored programs that helped define the emerging role of federal librarians and improve the management of federal libraries. FLICC's network arm, FEDLINK, sharply improved its fiscal operations while offering expanded and enhanced FEDLINK training programs both locally and regionally. In FY 1993 the FEDLINK procurement program provided discounts and contract cost avoidance benefits that saved the federal government more than $12 million.

Organizational strides and administrative changes marked FY 1993. FLICC worked with Library of Congress (LC) units on a draft reorganization plan submitted in July and continued to work on the plan through the end of 1993. In August, Mary Berghaus Levering, FLICC executive director since 1989, was detailed to operate the Copyright Office at LC and participate in work advising Congress on the need for copyright legislation. Joseph Price, chief of LC's Science and Technology division, was named acting FLICC director and Joseph Banks, FEDLINK business manager, acting FEDLINK director, working with Milton MeGee, FEDLINK Network Operations (FNO) coordinator, and Lee Power, FLICC chief program analyst, in a consultative approach to ongoing management of the organization.

The FLICC Personnel Working Group played a major role in advising and assisting the Office of Personnel Management (OPM) in developing OPM's draft classification standards for the GS-1410 Librarian Series, GS-1411 Library Technician Series, and GS-1412 Technical Information Specialist Series. The FLICC Statistics Working Group, in concert with the National Center for Education Statistics (NCES), continued to develop the nationwide survey of federal libraries and information centers to update 1978 statistics. The FLICC Policy Working Group responded to release of the Office of Management and Budget's (OMB's) "Federal Information Resources Management (Circular A-130), Revision," by preparing a summary analysis for federal librarians. The FLICC Binding Working Group continued to provide input to the new Government Printing Office (GPO) federal binding contract, which it helped shape, and to acquaint federal libraries with contract provisions and binding personnel.

FLICC also promoted the evolving role of federal librarians in meeting government's changing information needs and the administration's desire to "reinvent government." Key FLICC events spotlighted the challenges facing the federal library and information center community: the 1993 Annual FLICC Forum on Federal Information Policies, "Government's Role in the Electronic

Information Era: User Needs and Government's Response," and a special forum devoted to "Federal Librarians in the 21st Century: Changing Roles in the Electronic Age."

Membership Meetings

At the first FLICC quarterly membership meeting, held on December 10, 1992, members were briefed on GPO's Library Programs Service and Office of Electronic Information Dissemination Services by Judith Russell of GPO. The second quarterly meeting, held on February 22, 1993, featured a preview of the 103rd Congress agenda by Harold Relyea of the LC Congressional Research Service. At the June 3 meeting, Sara C. Jones of the Joint Committee on Printing reviewed the GPO Electronic Information Access Enhancement Act of 1993 (S. 564) and Roxanne Williams of the Agriculture Department discussed the Draft Policy Framework for Public Access to Government Information. During the September 23 meeting, the following public access topics were presented: "Inventory Locator," by Timothy Gauslin, U.S. Geological Survey; "OMB Circular A-130 Implementation," by Peter Weiss, OMB; and "The Z39.50 Standard for Information Retrieval," by Ray Denenberg, LC. Members also received updates on OPM's Librarian Classification Standards by Jean Stewart, OPM, and activities of the White House Conference on Library and Information Services Task Force (WHCLIST) by Doria Grimes, National Oceanic and Atmospheric Administration, federal library delegate, and Davis McCarn, user representative for federal librarians.

Working Groups

Binding Working Group

The FLICC Binding Working Group worked closely with the new GPO contract binder, selected in August 1992, to ensure satisfactory service to federal libraries. At the behest of the group, GPO's Term Contracts Division and Quality Assurance Division directed the binder to take corrective action when problems arose. The group also succeeded in getting GPO to modify the binding contract so that volumes needing corrections could be returned directly to the binder and developed the GPO form "Notice of Quality Defects in Library Binding" to support this arrangement.

Education Working Group

The FLICC Education Working Group planned and organized programs on the use of Internet, strategic planning, space planning, user satisfaction, imaging technologies, issues and advances related to the binding of books, and total quality management. The popular "Orientation to LC Collections and Services for Federal Libraries" series was continued in FY 1993, as was the highly successful "Great Escapes" series of "brown-bag" orientations hosted at various federal libraries in the District of Columbia metro area.

Federal Depository Libraries Working Group

The FLICC Federal Depository Library Working Group was established in the spring of 1993 in response to funding problems and proposed cuts in the GPO Federal Depository Library Program (FDLP). During May the members toured GPO's distribution and cataloging facility and discussed the future of federal libraries in the FDLP with GPO officials. The group also alerted federal libraries to restructuring and financial concerns of GPO.

Federal Law Librarians

FLICC continued the dialogue on redescribing and clarifying the relationship between FLICC and the Federal Law Librarians.

Finance Working Group

The FLICC Finance Working Group held numerous sessions to develop the FY 1994 FLICC budget and reported to members that increasing program costs and lower service dollar projections for FY 1994 necessitated an increase in FEDLINK fees and a major effort to secure network customers. Members approved changes in the FEDLINK fee structure that increased the transfer pay fee from 6.75 percent to 8 percent and established a two-level direct-pay structure providing that members with orders up to $25,000 pay a flat fee of $850 per service account and members with orders over $25,000 pay an additional 0.5 percent of service dollars over $25,000.

Membership and Governance Working Group

The FLICC Membership and Governance Working Group remained on standby to advise FLICC on the selection and eligibility of FLICC members and interpretation of the FLICC bylaws.

Nominating Working Group

The FLICC Nominating Working Group oversaw FLICC's annual three-phase election process under the FLICC bylaws.

Personnel Working Group

The FLICC Personnel Working Group continued to coordinate with FLICC members, OPM, and interested library professionals and associations to achieve revised classification standards for the GS-1410 (Librarian), GS-1411 (Library Technician), and GS-1412 (Technical Information Specialist) series. OPM's release of classification standards for the 1411 series in August incorporated several changes in response to FLICC's suggestions, but at the end of FY 1993 all OPM classification projects were placed on hold indefinitely.

Policy Working Group

The Policy Working Group prepared a comparison of the revised OMB Circular A-130 with comments that FLICC had made previously to OMB on the proposed

A-130 draft, and established a tracking system to monitor several bills significant to FLICC.

Preservation Working Group

The Preservation Working Group forcefully articulated the status and importance of preservation in federal libraries and archives, supported continuing education initiatives to assist federal libraries and information centers in meeting challenges associated with effective preservation programs, developed a checklist of preservation procedures for libraries, and sponsored a presentation in September at the Smithsonian Institution on preservation programs in Kiev, St. Petersburg, and Budapest depositories.

Reference/Public Services Working Group

Reconstituted in FY 1993 to reflect an expanding mission in circulation, interlibrary loan (ILL), and new technology, the FLICC Reference/Public Services Working Group presented a demonstration of Housing and Urban Development's Conquest retrieval program in August, suggested alterations to existing Interlibrary Loan Request Form LC SF-162 to reflect current technology and provide increased information for both borrowing and lending libraries, and focused on the need for developing a federal employee "pathfinder" to communicate different agency rules governing facility and library access.

Statistics Working Group

Organized in FY 1991 to update 1978 federal library statistics prepared by FLICC (then known as the Federal Library Committee), the FLICC Statistics Working Group mailed a survey pretest in September to nearly 300 federal library and information centers, developed a definition of "information centers" to be fine-tuned in the pretest, and minimized the potential that survey data could be used to support the privatization of federal libraries.

Publications and Education

The FLICC Publications and Education office (FPE) continued to provide communications and education outreach to the federal library and information center community by issuing FLICC and FEDLINK publications and administrative reports, organizing educational events and technical programs, coordinating more than 50 meetings of the FLICC working groups, and providing logistical, program development, and organizational support for quarterly meetings of FLICC's membership and bimonthly meetings of the FLICC Executive Board.

FPE produced *FEDLINK Technical Notes* monthly from October 1992 through April 1993 and bimonthly for the remainder of the fiscal year, issued the FLICC Education and FEDLINK Training Calendar during the interim months, and published the quarterly *FLICC Newsletter.* FPE's annual publications included the *1993 Directory of FLICC Members and Working Groups,* the *FY 1993 FEDLINK Services Directory,* and the *FY 1994 FEDLINK Registration Package.* FPE compressed the publication cycle of the summaries and papers of two annual

FLICC Forums to assure more timely release, producing the 1992 Forum summary and papers in January 1993, followed nine months later by the 1993 Forum summary and papers. FPE produced FY 1993 FLICC management reports including FLICC monthly, quarterly, and annual reports, as well as minutes for FLICC Quarterly Membership Meetings and bimonthly Executive Board meetings.

In conjunction with the FLICC Education Working Group, FLICC offered 12 all-day educational programs in FY 1993 geared to helping federal libraries and information centers manage change. The programs focused on the impact of developing information technologies and services on the library world and the role of federal librarians, as well as the challenge of managing federal libraries in such an environment.

FEDLINK (Federal Library and Information Network)

In FY 1993, 892 federal agencies received cost-effective access to an array of automated information retrieval services for online research, cataloging, and interlibrary loan through FEDLINK. Member federal agencies also procured publications, serials, and books through FEDLINK via LC/FEDLINK contracts with major vendors.

The FEDLINK Advisory Council (FAC) established a FAC Marketing Task Force to advise and assist FEDLINK with marketing efforts designed to reach a broader segment of the federal community in an effort to increase FEDLINK's customer base. FEDLINK's Internet Planning Group (IPG) continued to explore FEDLINK's role in introducing and informing federal libraries about Internet.

FEDLINK Network Operations

During FY 1993 FEDLINK Network Operations (FNO) functioned as the regional library network for 825 Online Computer Library Center (OCLC) member federal libraries. FNO conducted 125 training events in the Washington, D.C., area and nationally and provided daily technical and program support to all federal libraries and information centers. FNO staff prepared solicitations and other required contract documents for LC Contracts and Logistics (C&L) Services in support of the FEDLINK procurement program for information products and services, served on Technical Evaluation Review Panels (TERPs) to evaluate vendors' responses, and served as Contract Officer Technical Representatives (COTRs) for the awarded FEDLINK contracts.

OCLC Network Activity

During the first quarter of FY 1993 FEDLINK network librarians implemented the OCLC PRISM ILL migration plan begun in 1992. This national training program prepared more than 500 OCLC Interlibrary Loan system users for transition to the new PRISM ILL environment in December 1992. In the second quarter OCLC continued expansion of its Reference Services products, EPIC and Firstsearch, which generated member interest and an increased demand for user support. As an increasing number of members developed local systems, FNO provided expert support in local database creation through OCLC MARC tapes and other MARC services. FNO prepared the membership for cancellation of the FEDLINK network archival tape known as the FLC tape effective July 1, 1993. In the third quarter, when OCLC announced keyword access to the Online Union Catalog, FEDLINK recognized the need to promote strategic and cost-effective searching in a more complex searching environment and offered four new searching courses: PRISM Searching Overview, Advanced PRISM Searching, PRISM Searching for Cataloging, and PRISM Searching for Interlibrary Lending.

FEDLINK Training

FEDLINK staff conducted 108 OCLC classes and 17 Internet classes. Nearly one half of FEDLINK's 1,502 FY 1993 students received training outside the District of Columbia metro area. FEDLINK conducted regional and on-site training in Alaska, Arizona, Arkansas, California, Colorado, Louisiana, Maryland, New Mexico, Ohio, Texas, Virginia, and Washington, and national OCLC training programs for the Army Corps of Engineers in Alabama and for the Air Force in Louisiana. FEDLINK's OCLC Training Agreements with five OCLC Regional Support Networks provided additional training options to FEDLINK members.

FEDLINK OCLC Member Activity

FEDLINK OCLC members during the reporting period July 1992–June 1993 showed slightly less OCLC online activity than in the same period in 1992, although usage was slightly higher than the comparable 1991 period. Total interlibrary lending requests and referrals dropped from 312,195 to 303,362, a decrease of 2.8 percent. Total union list holdings displays rose from 26,778 in 1992 to 43,800 in 1993, a 63.6 percent increase, while other On Line Union Catalog (OLUC) holdings displays decreased from 586,236 in 1992 to 560,079 in 1993. Activity on the OCLC Online Cataloging system decreased from 1992, but approximated prior years' usage. One indicator was that total master records created by FEDLINK libraries in 1993 dropped 14.77 percent from 77,833 in 1992 to 66,335 in 1993, a decrease from the previous year, but only slightly lower than 1991, when FEDLINK members created 66,925 OLUC records. Activity on OCLC Reference Products continued upward with total EPIC OLUC per record displays (including both online and offline charges) increased to 101,705 in 1993, a 6.9 percent rise over 1992 activity.

Library Automation Resource Service

Through LARS (the Library Automation Resource Service), FNO offered expert counsel to federal libraries in the application of automation and telecommunications in their library environment. LARS continued to focus on introducing Internet to federal librarians through briefings held at the Defense Technical Information Center Annual Users Group Meeting, Alaska Resources Library, U.S. Circuit Court, Department of Labor Library, National Aeronautics and Space Administration, and Denver Federal Service Center. FNO continued to respond to inquiries, conduct Internet demonstrations, create documents, and implement a collection of downloadable files for federal libraries on the LC Sequent computer.

When LC unveiled Marvel (Machine-Assisted Realization of the Virtual Electronic Library) to the Internet world in July, FEDLINK launched an Internet training program comprising Internet Demonstrations, half-day Internet Overviews, and two-day Internet Workshops.

[For more information on LC's Marvel, see the preceding article on the Library of Congress, under the heading "Library of the Future"—*Ed.*]

Development of the FEDLINK ALIX electronic bulletin board continued. Access to, and visibility of, ALIX increased when the NTIS FedWorld bulletin board gateway added ALIX to its more than 100 bulletin boards. Internet access to FedWorld made ALIX available worldwide.

LARS also initiated the use of the OCLC PASSPORT Software by the Patent and Trademark Depository Library Program for access to FTS 2000 E-mail.

FEDLINK Procurement Program

FEDLINK analyzed the discounts offered through LC/FEDLINK basic ordering agreements (BOAs) and typical contracting costs for information procurements to assess the cost effectiveness of the FEDLINK procurement vehicle. A brief review of FY 1992 invoices suggested that BOA discounts, which ranged from 0 percent to 57 percent off commercial rates, saved members at least $2.5 million in service dollars. Analysis of comparable contracting costs for establishing 84 BOAs and providing competition for 403 individual orders over $25,000 suggested that centralizing contracting activity at FEDLINK saved the government approximately $9,740,000 in cost avoidance (estimating $20,000 per contracting action). Thus, through discounts and contracting cost avoidance alone—not considering FEDLINK's invoice processing, education, and other services—the FEDLINK program saved $12,240,000, an amount triple the program's annual operating budget.

SYMIN System Activities

The FEDLINK fiscal accounting system, SYMIN, continued productive operations throughout the year. The database management system was upgraded to Paradox 4.0 from Paradox 3.5 to allow a smoother transaction flow on the network and enable the systems staff to develop further improvements to the system.

FEDLINK Fiscal Operations

FEDLINK Fiscal Operations (FFO) establishes federal agencies' membership in FEDLINK, determines FEDLINK service fees for members, prepares member interagency agreements (IAGs) and IAG amendments and FEDLINK vendor delivery orders, and administers FEDLINK member accounts, including processing all FEDLINK vendor invoices and generating individual FEDLINK member account statements.

FY 1993 was the most successful year of operating performance in the history of the FEDLINK program. No temporary obligation was necessary for FY 1993 because of the complete reconciliation of the FY 1993 transfer-pay service dollar obligation. In other significant accomplishments, FFO developed and

Figure 1

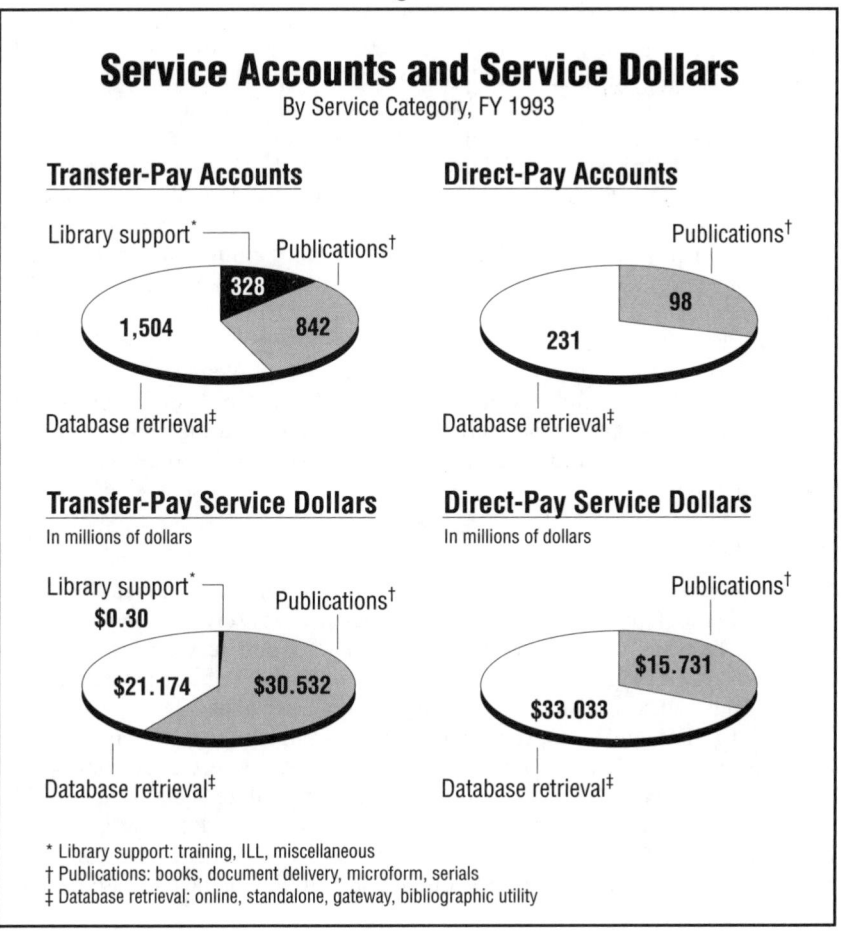

Service Accounts and Service Dollars
By Service Category, FY 1993

Transfer-Pay Accounts

Library support* — Publications[†]

328

1,504 842

Database retrieval[‡]

Direct-Pay Accounts

Publications[†]

98

231

Database retrieval[‡]

Transfer-Pay Service Dollars
In millions of dollars

Library support* — Publications[†]
$0.30

$21.174 $30.532

Database retrieval[‡]

Direct-Pay Service Dollars
In millions of dollars

Publications[†]

$15.731

$33.033

Database retrieval[‡]

* Library support: training, ILL, miscellaneous
† Publications: books, document delivery, microform, serials
‡ Database retrieval: online, standalone, gateway, bibliographic utility

implemented guidelines to successfully control and monitor the delivery order process; decreased the amount of interest net of discounts remitted to FEDLINK vendors for late payment by more than $37,000, from the FY 1992 total of $38,360 to approximately $1,200 in FY 1993; reconciled FEDLINK accounts from FY 1986 through FY 1989; completed the block move of multiyear funds, processing more than 800 delivery orders representing $1.5 million; ensured that administrative expenditure obligations did not exceed program fee projections; successfully performed Financial Management Systems (FMS) reviews; and continued to inform the FEDLINK member/vendor community through information alerts, meetings, vendor fairs, and newsletters.

Summary Statistics

FFO processed FY 1993 registrations from federal libraries, information centers, and other federal offices resulting in 892 signed FY 1993 IAGs compared to

1,127 basic IAGs processed in FY 1992. In addition, FFO processed 3,487 IAG Amendments (1,535 FY 1993 and 1,952 prior year adjustments) for agencies adding, adjusting, or terminating service funding. These IAGs and IAG Amendments represented 4,256 individual service requests to begin, renew, convert, or cancel service from 84 FY 1993 FEDLINK vendors. The service requests were executed by delivery orders generated by FFO and issued to vendors by Contracts and Logistics (C&L) Services. Delivery orders represented $48,412,900 in FY 1993 and prior year transfer-pay service dollars. For FY 1993 alone, FEDLINK processed approximately $52 million in service dollars for 2,810 transfer-pay accounts and approximately $48.7 million in service dollars for 329 direct-pay users. FY 1993 activity represented a total of 3,003 FEDLINK agency accounts.

On behalf of transfer-pay users, FFO processed for payment 50,078 invoices during FY 1993 for both current and prior year orders. Vendor payments from agencies' FY 1993 transfer-pay accounts totaled $25,206,631. FFO continued to maintain open accounts for three prior years for members using book and serials services, paying publications services invoices based on the order date of the invoiced items.

Vendor Statistics

Vendor services are classified as database retrieval services (online, CD-ROM, gateway, bibliographic utility), publications acquisitions services (books, serials, document delivery, and microform), and library support services (training and ILL fee payment). Figure 1 shows the relative volume of transfer-pay and direct-pay accounts and service dollars according to service category.

FEDLINK handles approximately twice as many transfer-pay database accounts as publications accounts, but total publications service dollars exceed database dollars. Serials services alone represent $23 million, compared with $21 million for databases overall. The average transfer-pay database account is approximately $14,100; the average publications account is $36,300. Direct-pay database users represent $33 million of the $48.8 million in the database retrieval category.

National Agricultural Library

U.S. Department of Agriculture, NAL Bldg., Beltsville, MD 20705
Internet: agref@nalusda.gov

Brian Norris
Public Affairs Officer

The Library of Congress, the National Library of Medicine, and the National Agricultural Library (NAL) are the three national libraries of the United States. NAL also serves as the departmental library for the U.S. Department of Agriculture (USDA), serving thousands of USDA employees worldwide.

Established in 1862, NAL is now the largest agricultural library in the world, with more than 2.2 million volumes. The library has an annual budget of about $18 million and a staff of 225. In addition to serving scientists, researchers, farmers, universities, businesses and the general public in the United States, in recent years NAL has begun serving an ever-increasing international clientele.

Merger with New Research Agency

NAL is to be merged into a new Agricultural Research and Education Service under a USDA reorganization proposed by Secretary Mike Espy on September 7, 1993. Under the plan, NAL will join the Agricultural Research Service (ARS), the Extension Service (ES), and the Cooperative State Research Service (CSRS) in the new agency.

NAL Plays Key Role in E. Coli Response

To assist government officials in dealing with the outbreak of food-poisoning in the western United States attributed to E. coli bacteria, NAL made a crash effort to identify information on the bacteria from the NAL collection and those of other major research libraries. In a matter of hours after the first outbreak, a bibliography of E. coli literature plus copies of 65 articles on the bacteria were produced and provided to USDA officials. NAL also made the materials available nationwide, free of charge.

Jefferson Letters Found

Letters written by or to Thomas Jefferson, dealing with various agricultural matters, were found among old files in the NAL collection in August 1993. The 11 letters date from April 24, 1786, to October 20, 1819, and include requests to Jefferson for appointments to federal agricultural offices, letters from Jefferson transferring "millet seed" and "succory seed" to acquaintances in the United States, and a letter to Jefferson from "Lord Sheffield" of the Board of Agriculture in London, England, commenting on Jefferson's invention of a "mould board" for use in farming.

NAL Aids European Agricultural Libraries

NAL has agreed to cooperate more closely in exchanging agricultural information with counterparts in several Central European countries. The countries are Albania, the Czech Republic, Estonia, Hungary, Latvia, Lithuania, Poland, Romania, the Slovak Republic, and Slovenia. An agreement was signed at the second U.S./Central European Agricultural Library Roundtable in Budapest in October 1992. It calls for continued and improved exchange of agricultural information, personnel exchanges, cooperation in developing electronic information systems and products, and efforts to improve document delivery. The agreement was the result of proposals made at the first U.S./Central European Roundtable, held at NAL in November 1991.

AGRICOLA Marks a Milestone

NAL added the 3-millionth record to its AGRICOLA bibliographic database in the summer of 1993, marking a major milestone. AGRICOLA is the backbone of the NAL collection, allowing NAL users speedy retrieval of needed materials from among the millions of items in the collection.

Electronic Information Study Funded

NAL received FY 1993 funds to initiate a study on developing structures for managing electronic information. NAL will evaluate a number of electronic information provisional models, focusing primarily on USDA materials. In the first phase, NAL will evaluate its internal policies and procedures to determine changes needed to acquire, store, and access electronic materials. Next, NAL will work with USDA to facilitate electronic dissemination of the department's materials. Finally, NAL will study how Internet can be used to disseminate agricultural information.

Plant Genome Activities Grow

NAL's Plant Genome Database and Information Center (PGDIC), established in 1991, convened a database workshop to discuss the nature, goals, and direction for the public access database. Participants included database experts from the University of California, Los Alamos National Laboratory, the National Science Foundation, and USDA's Germplasm Resources Information Network. A model database will soon be available and a general database will be available for public access within three years. In support of USDA's Plant Genome Research Program, NAL continued to add plant genetics literature, accumulating in the AGRICOLA database more than 15,000 citations related to molecular genetics.

Strategic Planning

NAL has launched strategic planning to help guide library operations into the next century. Under the technical guidance of the Office of Management Studies, Association of Research Libraries, a half-day orientation meeting was held for all NAL staff, followed by a three-day retreat during which about 35 NAL staff members were introduced to the planning process.

In April 1993 the NAL Planning Study Group, a steering committee, was named. The NAL staff was encouraged to join work groups dealing with "vision," "history," "internal situation," "external situation," and "communications." About half of NAL's staff, representing all branches and levels of management, volunteered for the work groups.

NAL Accepts Reference Requests on Internet

People all over the world now have computer access to NAL reference services through the Internet telecommunications system. On May 1, 1993, NAL's Reference Section began accepting requests for reference services via Internet. NAL's Internet address is agref@nalusda.gov.

NAL's Reference Section provides both reference and information assistance. The NAL Internet mailbox is screened for reference requests daily and an NAL reference librarian is assigned to respond to them. In most cases, requests for bibliographic information are searched on NAL's bibliographic database, AGRICOLA.

NAL may require a fee for "comprehensive searches." Fees are assessed only upon prior agreement with the user and are only charged for work requiring more than one hour.

Food Labeling Education Database

A database of food labeling education activities throughout the United States is now available at NAL's Labeling Education Information Center. The database includes projects and research and educational materials (brochures, videotapes, etc.) that have been produced to inform the public about new food labeling laws.

This program, part of NAL's Food and Nutrition Information Center, is a cooperative effort between NAL, the Food Safety Inspection Service of USDA, and the U.S. Food and Drug Administration.

Food Irradiation Evaluation Study Funded

NAL received funds in 1993 to begin study on providing international access to food irradiation materials. NAL will convert an NAL-produced food irradiation CD-ROM to another software package, improving its usability, and will employ a food irradiation expert to select documents for electronic storage. Germany and France are interested in providing documents and databases to NAL. It is expected that NAL will become the international center for food irradiation information.

NAL Participates in National Cataloging Program

NAL has been selected to participate in the National Coordinated Cataloging Program (NCCP). This is a cooperative cataloging program of the Library of Congress (LC) in which selected libraries produce full, high-quality cataloging for the LC database and bibliographic utility (OCLC). NAL began full participation in 1993.

In addition, NAL continues to be an active participant with LC in the National Coordinated Cataloging Operations (NACO), the Cooperative Online Serials Program (CONSER), and the Cooperative Subject Cataloging Program (CSCP).

Document Delivery Improvements

The coordinator of the NAL Regional Document Delivery System (RDDS) and eight regional RDDS coordinators are working to improve and streamline services provided by the NAL RDDS. Following up on two planning meetings in 1992, another was held at Cornell University May 6–7, 1993, at which a "nearly final" version of the RDDS Guidelines was produced. Major initiatives resulting from the meetings include providing systemwide standards in procedures and policies via RDDS Guidelines (expected to be completed and distributed in the summer of 1994) and producing both a systemwide RDDS manual and a brochure. Another goal is increasing communication among NAL and participating land-grant universities through annual coordinator meetings, periodic regional meetings, and use of the RDDS-L Internet listserv.

Text Digitizing Program Advances

NAL's ongoing National Agricultural Text Digitizing Program (NATDP) continued to move ahead in FY 1993. The project began in 1987 with NAL and over 40 land-grant university libraries developing and evaluating the use of CD-ROM technology in improving access to agricultural literature. During the pilot study, NAL evaluated the usefulness of optical scanning and optical character recognition in the library environment, and the land-grant universities evaluated four CD-ROM databases and several retrieval software products. An evaluation study final report was completed and published, officially ending the NATDP pilot study.

NATDP became a fully operational "program" in January 1992. Since then, NAL has developed CD-ROMs containing the *Agronomy Journal* of 1907–1924, selected papers of George Washington Carver, and extensive information on aquaculture. Currently in production is a disc on food irradiation.

NAL Links with Food Service Institute

Authorized under the Child Nutrition and Women, Infant and Children (WIC) Reauthorization Act of 1989, the National Food Service Management Institute (NFSMI) entered into a trust fund cooperative agreement with NAL to link the resources of NAL's Food and Nutrition Information Center (FNIC) with NFSMI at the University of Mississippi. An NFSMI nutritionist is now located at FNIC offices in NAL and reference calls to the institute's toll-free telephone number are switched directly to FNIC. NAL provides document delivery services to NFSMI clientele.

Health Bulletin Board Use Encouraged

NAL's Rural Information Center Health Service (RICHS), the U.S. Department of Health and Human Services, and the North Central Wisconsin State Office of Rural Health collaborated in an effort to encourage State Offices of Rural Health (SORH) to use the networking capabilities of NAL's computer bulletin board

ALF. RICHS staff have trained SORH staff in the use of ALF and encourage state use through a "health question of the week."

Climate Change Packet Updated

An information packet on global climate change was made available to the general public free of charge in February 1993. It is an update of a packet NAL originally developed in August 1991. Described are the concerns surrounding, and potential effects of, global climate change. Included are reprints of articles both supporting and rejecting these concerns. The packet contains bibliographies of other readings on climate change, lists of books and journal articles, a directory of global climate-change organizations, and guides to additional information sources.

Animal Welfare Workshops

In 1993 NAL's Animal Welfare Information Center (AWIC) held three workshops on meeting the information requirements of the Animal Welfare Act. The workshops, targeted at members of the biomedical research community, provided an overview of the reporting requirements of the act with regard to animals used in research. The workshops also discussed the concept of alternatives, and where to find information on alternatives. Details on accessing the information electronically were included.

Thesaurus Project Moves Ahead

NAL continued to be a key player in the international effort to produce a Unified Agricultural Thesaurus (UAT), a project to improve worldwide access to agricultural information through an improved thesaurus system. NAL, CAB International (CABI), and the Food and Agricultural Organization (FAO) of the United Nations are working to develop versions of both AGROVOC, the thesaurus used by FAO for the AGRIS database, and the CAB Thesaurus, used by CABI for CAB Abstracts and by NAL for AGRICOLA. NAL and FAO have signed a letter of agreement to complete the classification of AGROVOC, work representing the first step in unifying the thesauri.

Another effort focuses on development of management software to support the thesaurus project, in conjunction with the Canadian International Development Research Centre.

Agriculture Network Active

Since September 1992 NAL's Alternative Farming Systems Information Center (AFSIC) has been the site of the central coordinating office for the Sustainable Agriculture Network (SAN). Called SANlink, the office links the widely dispersed personnel and activities of SAN and helps in coordinating sustainable agriculture projects. The office also provides staff support to the Sustainable

Agriculture Research and Education (SARE) program, a USDA competitive-grants project authorized by the 1990 farm bill. SAN comprises people from universities, government, businesses, and non-profit organizations who produce information on "ecologically based, knowledge-intensive" farming.

Home Landscaping Aid Developed

In cooperation with the University of Florida Institute for Food and Agricultural Sciences (IFAS) and the Michigan State University Cooperative Extension Service, NAL developed an interactive multimedia CD-ROM on home landscaping. The disc contains information on do-it-yourself landscaping, including 24 designs to cover various yard sizes and characteristics.

Called "Plant It!-CD," the disc provides information on plants that grow best in various U.S. climate zones. Nearly 1,000 plants are covered.

Image Transfer Project Under Way

NAL, the University of Pittsburgh School of Library and Information Sciences, and Michigan State Cooperative Extension Service are examining the use of images in information retrieval. A test database of 2,000 digitized slides of rare botanical prints, plus common plant pests and diseases, will be accessed online through a server at Pittsburgh, as well as through CD-ROM distribution.

The first client-server mode will run under Windows (with later clients to be developed by the University of Pittsburgh), allowing interactive access through Internet. A user can search the image database and retrieve desired digitized photographs in a variety of formats and resolutions.

The evaluation will examine the operation of image transfer in a networked environment, will determine the preferred formats and resolutions, and will compare online access with individual workstation access through CD-ROM.

Computer-Assisted Indexing Software Evaluated

NAL evaluated a computer-assisted indexing system that could potentially produce more indexing records for the AGRICOLA database while maintaining current quality standards. The PC-based system under evaluation was created by DataCentralen, Denmark, and is named LINXS, for library indexing system. LINXS was designed to assist the human indexer by examining text and suggesting descriptors from the CAB Thesaurus and alphanumeric codes from the AGRICOLA Subject Category Codes, two of the most important components of the AGRICOLA record. A report will be issued.

Publication Aids U.S. Industry

NAL's Technology Transfer Information Center worked with the Federal Laboratory Consortium to produce the 220-page publication "Tapping Federal Technology: Inventions, Expertise, and Facilities." The publication has more than 150 entries for federal government information intermediaries—information, analysis, and software centers; clearinghouses; electronic bulletin boards; databases; and catalogs—to assist U.S. industry in locating technology that will help it compete in the world marketplace.

Youth Development Information

NAL's Youth Development Information Center (YDIC) worked with USDA's Extension Service and the 4-H Program to identify and make available, in digital format, information on youth development for extension agents. YDIC also worked with the National Collaboration for Youth and the National Society for Fund Raising Executives on projects to improve computer networking for the youth development and resource development communities. Cooperative agreements will allow for more youth development information to be made available and will improve the quality of that information.

Water Quality Information Tap Opens

In 1993 the amount of water quality information provided over the Water Information Network (WIN) of NAL's electronic bulletin board ALF increased dramatically. WIN is managed by NAL's Water Quality Information Center. The center added approximately 20 new documents to WIN including water quality hotlines; a calendar of upcoming regional, national, and international water quality meetings; and bibliographies covering agriculture's impact on water quality.

Commodity Trading Program

NAL help in gathering information on commodity futures trading was requested by USDA's Extension Service (ES) and the Commodity Futures Trading Commission (CFTC). Under the "Commodity Futures Trading, Agricultural Option Pilot Program," ES and CFTC are working to introduce farmers to commodity options as a way to generate income. ES and CFTC asked NAL's Agricultural Trade and Marketing Information Center to expand its scope to include multimedia materials on risk management, futures and options markets, legislation and regulations, commodity trading, and related fields.

National Library of Medicine

8600 Rockville Pike, Bethesda, MD 20894
301-496-6308
Internet: publicinfo@occshost.nlm.nih.gov

Robert Mehnert
Public Information Officer

The National Library of Medicine (NLM) took a significant step in opening up its collections to the world in 1993 when it introduced "NLM Locator." This online catalog system makes the library's entire catalog listing of book, serial, and audiovisual holdings available over Internet. The library levies no charge for access to Locator.

Internet Offerings

Users of Internet can now search the same databases that are available at the public terminals at NLM. NLM Locator allows searching of CATLINE®, with its 700,000 cataloging records for books; AVLINE®, which contains 25,000 records for videorecordings and other audiovisual materials; and SERLINE®, containing records for 80,000 serial titles, more than 20,000 of them active publications. To access NLM Locator, set terminal emulator to VT100, telnet to locator.nlm.nih. gov, and enter locator at the log-in prompt.

Concurrent with the creation of Locator, the library also made available the full text of a number of its publications via Internet. These include the monthly *AIDS Bibliography,* the series known as *Current Bibliographies in Medicine,* and fact sheets describing NLM's many programs and services. As with Locator, there is no charge for access. To retrieve NLM publications, Internet users should ftp to nlmpubs.nlm.nih.gov and log in as nlmpubs.

MEDLINE Use Grows

The library's major bibliographic database, MEDLINE®, contains 7.6 million references to journal articles published between 1966 and the present. An abstract in English is included with most MEDLINE records and may be printed at the user's option. MEDLINE is available via NLM's online MEDLARS® network, on CD-ROMs produced by private companies, through commercial database vendors, and through some 20 institutional partners in other countries.

The number of online users of NLM's own network has risen to about 78,000. Users not only have 24-hour access to MEDLINE, but to some 50 other NLM databases covering AIDS, cancer, toxicology, environmental health, bioethics, health planning and administration, and other specialized topics. The user base increased in 1993 when Internet access to NLM's computers made MEDLINE searching available to scientists at the National Institutes of Health.

The primary mode of access for individuals to the databases on NLM's computers is Grateful Med®. This is a microcomputer software program for IBM-compatible and Macintosh personal computers. An update for the Macintosh Grateful Med was released in 1993 with no cost to registered users. More than 60,000 copies of the software have been distributed by the National Technical Information Service. The charge for online access was reduced on January 1, 1993, and the average cost of a MEDLINE search via Grateful Med is now less than $1.25. An experimental arrangement in 1992 allowing members of the American College of Physicians access to MEDLINE at a flat rate was successful and was renewed in 1993; a similar arrangement with the American College of Cardiology went into effect.

Networking

Although many individuals have direct access to MEDLINE and the other NLM databases, a substantial portion of the total usage consists of database searching by members of the National Network of Libraries of Medicine (NN/LM) for patrons of those 4,000 institutions. NLM's mandate to create and support the national network is grounded in the Medical Library Assistance Act of 1965. It is clear now, as it was to Dr. Michael DeBakey and the other framers of that legislation, that networking of information resources is key to their being used efficiently and effectively to promote health. NLM supports through contracts the operation of eight Regional Medical Libraries, which in turn support the hospital and other health science libraries in their geographic areas.

NLM's network of international MEDLARS Centers was expanded in 1993 with the addition of Israel. The Berman National Medical Library at Hebrew University–Hadassah Medical School is the first center to rely on Internet for online access to NLM using Grateful Med.

Publications

NLM's primary bibliographic publication is the *Index Medicus®*, a monthly listing of articles from some 3,000 journals published worldwide. With the references from some 600 additional journals, primarily in dentistry and nursing, indexed citations for the *Index Medicus* serve also as the foundation for MEDLINE. NLM ceased as of December 1993 publication of the *NLM Current Catalog* and the *NLM Audiovisuals Catalog*. In the face of easy and inexpensive access to the online databases CATLINE and AVLINE, subscriptions had fallen below a level to warrant continued publication.

A new edition of the *Collection Development Manual of the National Library of Medicine* was published in 1993. It reflects a comprehensive review and revision of selection criteria for the NLM collections, with emphasis on reducing the overlap among the three U.S. national libraries by focusing NLM's collecting more sharply on biomedical subjects.

Health Services Research Information

An area of increasing concern to the library is the application of research results to improve patient care and to contain health care costs. This information is of vital importance to physicians, administrators, policymakers, and payers. Researchers also need effective access to information to help design and conduct new studies.

A big step toward fulfilling these needs was the addition of $8 million to the library's fiscal 1994 budget to create at NLM a new National Information Center on Health Services Research and Health Care Technology. The goals of the new center are to make the results of health services research, including technology assessments and practice guidelines, readily available to health care practitioners, administrators, policymakers, and the information professionals who serve these groups. The center will also serve health services researchers and will contribute to the information infrastructure needed to foster patient record systems. The new legislative mandate and increased budget will allow NLM to develop quickly an online bibliographic database for health services research, a health services research-in-progress database, and a full-text retrieval system for clinical practice guidelines.

Table 1 / Selected NLM Statistics*

Library Operation	Volume
Collection (book and nonbook)	4,970,000
Serial titles received	22,400
Articles indexed for MEDLINE	376,000
Circulation requests filled	401,000
For interlibrary loan	220,000
For on-site users	181,000
Computerized searches (all databases)	5,964,000

*For the year ending September 30, 1993.

High Performance Computing and Communications

The multiagency High Performance Computing and Communications (HPCC) initiative has become a keystone of the American science and technology enterprise. The National Library of Medicine continues to provide the physical facilities for the HPCC Coordination Office, and the NLM director serves in a concurrent position as head of the office. The library supports several HPCC-related projects, including those concerned with connecting health professionals to computerized information resources, medical imaging, biotechnology, and information retrieval tools.

Computer Connections

Among the thousands of research and education institutions in the United States that connect to federally supported computer networks, medical institutions are only sparsely represented. To help correct this, NLM has created (in collaboration with the National Science Foundation) a Medical Connections Program to provide "jump-start" grants to medical centers wishing to connect to the National Research and Education Network (NREN). Another aspect of "connections" is

NLM's Integrated Advanced Information Management Systems (IAIMS) program. Rather than attempting to connect an institution to the "outside world," these are grants to build institution-wide computer networks that link and relate library systems with a variety of individual and institutional databases and information files for patient care, research, education, and administration.

Digital Imaging

The goal of several NLM projects is to develop ways to transfer medical images of such a high quality that they can be used remotely for diagnosis or treatment. Perhaps the most exciting NLM undertaking in digital imaging is the Visible Human project. This is an attempt to build a digital image library representing x-y-z numerical coordinates of submillimeter slices of the male and female human body. The first phase of the program—to acquire image data from photographic, computed tomography and magnetic resonance imaging—is now under way and the data are expected to be available in 1994 as a set of digital images that NLM will make available over NREN. Once retrieved, the 3-D anatomic coordinates will form the basis of "living images" rendered by computer graphics. These can be rotated, viewed from any angle, and reversibly "dissected." The Visible Human project promises to provide an unprecedented image resource for the education of health professionals, and will foster the development of computer graphics tools that will support computer-aided surgical planning and patient education.

Biotechnology

The National Center for Biotechnology Information (NCBI), a part of NLM, is creating automated systems for storing and analyzing knowledge about molecular biology, biochemistry, and genetics. In October 1992 responsibility for the GenBank DNA Sequence Database was transferred from another NIH component to NCBI. NCBI scientists created GenBank's literature component, exchanged sequence data with the other sequence database centers in Europe and Japan, and now distribute this information internationally. It is estimated that some 3 million searches are being done each year on NCBI's databases—both online and on compact disc. NCBI scientists also perform research into advanced methods of computer-based information processing for analyzing the structure and function of biologically important molecules and compounds. Sequence comparison and predicting three-dimensional macromolecular structure, for example, are extremely computer intensive and the target of HPCC application programs supported by the library, both intramurally and extramurally.

Information Retrieval Tools

The goal of the Unified Medical Language System is to give practitioners and researchers easy access to machine-readable information from diverse sources, including the scientific literature, patient records, factual databanks, and knowledge-based expert systems. The approach is to develop "knowledge sources" that can compensate for differences in the way concepts are expressed, identify relevant information sources, and negotiate the telecommunications and search procedures necessary to retrieve information from the sources.

Much work on UMLS has been accomplished over the last several years by NLM and its collaborators, and a variety of products—Metathesaurus, Semantic Network, and Information Sources Map—are now in the hands of systems builders around the country. A fourth experimental UMLS Knowledge Sources disk was sent without charge to system developers in 1993. The new edition substantially enhanced the Metathesaurus, which now contains 152,000 concepts and 279,000 terms, including synonyms and lexical variants, from 15 vocabularies.

The library is expanding its extramural support of medically related High Performance Computing and Communications programs. In April 1993 NLM solicited applications for support from academic and research centers with experience in the medical applications of advanced computing and digital communications. More than 130 applications were received for developing testbed networks for linking hospitals, doctors' offices, medical libraries, and universities; software for visualizing human anatomy and analyzing images; real-time treatment of patients at remote sites; and database technology, including the development of computerized patient records. In October 1993 the library announced a $4.15 million award to a consortium of West Virginia agencies for a statewide project titled "Collaborative Technology for Real-Time Treatment of Patients." The library hopes to be able to fund more such projects in 1994.

Outreach

The NLM outreach program is a cooperative effort with the 4,000 member institutions of the National Network of Libraries of Medicine. NLM has undertaken more than 200 outreach projects involving 400 institutions since the publication of a 1989 Board of Regents report on the need for such a program. The concern of the panelists was that the library's various information services, including MEDLINE and the other online databases, were not as widely known and used as they should be.

The projects include extensive efforts to train physicians and other health professionals to use Grateful Med. This is being done by staff of the Regional Medical Libraries and through awards to small and medium-sized libraries to improve local resources and access to online information. There is a special emphasis on libraries in rural and inner-city areas and those that serve minority populations.

A number of larger outreach programs are being undertaken directly by NLM. These include projects in the Lower Mississippi Delta (a 214-county, 7-state region characterized as the most impoverished area of the nation); an Information Access Project at Meharry Medical College (Nashville) to train more than 300 faculty, residents, students, and practicing health professionals to use Grateful Med and MEDLINE; and a project to strengthen the capacity of 20 historically black colleges and universities to train health professionals in the use of NLM's toxicological, environmental, occupational, and hazardous waste databases.

Administration

For the year ending September 30, 1993, NLM had an appropriated budget of $103,613,000 and a full-time staff of 596.

Educational Resources Information Center

ERIC Processing and Reference Facility
1301 Piccard Drive, Suite 300, Rockville, MD 20850-4305
301-258-5500, 800-799-3742, FAX 301-948-3695
Internet: ericfac@inet.ed.gov

Ted Brandhorst
Director

Database Size and Growth

The ERIC database consists of two files: *Resources in Education (RIE)* and *Current Index to Journals in Education (CIJE)*. The ED records announced in *RIE* represent documents; they are approximately 1,800 characters long on average. The EJ records announced in *CIJE* represent journal articles; they are approximately 650 characters long on average. Overall, the ERIC database through 1993 contains 353,419 records for documents and 468,113 records for journal articles, for a grand total of 821,532 bibliographic records. Approximately 13,000 document records and 18,000 article records are added annually, for a total of 31,000 records per year. Overall, the ERIC database through 1993 is approximately 943 million bytes in size and growing at a rate of around 35 million bytes per year.

	No. of Records		
File	1966–1992	1993	Total
Resources in Education (1966–) ED Records	341,419	12,000	353,419
Current Index to Journals in Education (1969–) EJ Records	449,542	18,571	468,113
	790,961	30,571	821,532

ERIC Clearinghouse Competition

The contracts for all 16 ERIC clearinghouses were competed during the first six months of 1993. After the dust had settled, two clearinghouses had relocated and seven had changed their names:

Old Name	New Name	New Location
Counseling and Guidance	Counseling and Student Services	Univ. of North Carolina, Greensboro
Reading and Communication Skills	Reading, English, and Communication	
Handicapped and Gifted Children	Disabilities and Gifted Education	
Information Resources	Information and Technology	
Junior Colleges	Community Colleges	
Teacher Education	Teaching and Teacher Education	
Tests, Measurement, and Evaluation	Assessment and Evaluation	Catholic Univ. of America

Adjunct Clearinghouses

Adjunct clearinghouses are organizations that, at no cost to ERIC, assist ERIC in covering a specialized segment of the literature of education. Two new adjunct clearinghouses were established in 1993, as follows:

Adjunct ERIC Clearinghouse on Clinical Schools
American Association of Colleges for Teacher Education (AACTE)
One Dupont Circle N.W., Suite 610
Washington, DC 20036-1186
202-293-2450, FAX 202-457-8095, Internet: iabdalha@inet.ed.gov
Note: Adjunct to ERIC Clearinghouse on Teaching and Teacher Education (SP)

Adjunct Test Collection Clearinghouse
Educational Testing Service (ETS)
ETS Test Collection
Rosedale and Carter Roads, Princeton, NJ 08541
609-734-5737, FAX 609-683-7186, Internet: mhalpern@rosedale.org
Note: Adjunct to ERIC Clearinghouse on Assessment and Evaluation

800 Numbers/Internet Addresses

All ERIC components have acquired (or are in the process of acquiring) national toll-free 800 numbers as well as Internet addresses and connectivity. These two developments should result in a marked increase systemwide in question-answering and other reference activity.

ERIC Component	800 Number	Internet Address
ERIC Program Office		
Office of Educational Research and Improvement (OERI)	—	eric@inet.ed.gov
ACCESS ERIC	800-538-3742	acceric@inet.ed.gov
ERIC Document Reproduction Service (EDRS)	800-443-3742	edrs@gwuvm.gwu.edu
ERIC Processing and Reference Facility	800-799-3742	ericfac@inet.ed.gov
Oryx Press (*CIJE* Publisher)	800-279-6799	arhjb@asuvm.inre.asu.edu
ERIC Clearinghouse on/for:		
Adult, Career, and Vocational Education	800-848-4815	ericacve@magnus.acs.ohio-state.edu
Assessment and Evaluation	—	eric_ae@cua.edu
Community Colleges	800-832-8256	eeh3rie@mvs.oac.ucla.edu
Counseling and Student Services	800-414-9769	ericcass.uncg.ed
Disabilities and Gifted Education	800-328-0272	ericec@inet.ed.gov
Educational Management	800-438-8841	ppiele@oregon.uoregon.edu
Elementary and Early Childhood Education	800-583-4135	ericeece@ux1.cso.uiuc.edu
Higher Education	—	eriche@inet.ed.gov
Information and Technology	800-464-9107	eric@ericir.syr.edu

Languages and Linguistics	800-276-9834	jeannie@cal.org
Reading, English, and Communication	800-759-4723	ericcs@ucs.indiana.edu
Rural Education and Small Schools	800-624-9120	u56d9@wvnvm.wvnet.edu
Science, Mathematics, and Environmental Education	—	ericse@osu.edu
Social Studies/Social Science Education	800-266-3815	ericso@ucs.indiana.edu
Teaching and Teacher Education	—	jbeck@inet.ed.gov
Urban Education	800-601-4868	cue-eric@columbia.edu

Adjunct ERIC Clearinghouses on:

Chapter 1 (Compensatory Education)	800-456-2380	
Clinical Schools	—	iabdalha@inet.ed.gov
Consumer Education	—	cse_bonner@emunix.emich.edu
ESL Literacy Education	—	
Test Collection	—	mhalpern@rosedale.org
United States-Japan Studies	—	risinger@ucs.indiana.edu

ACCESS ERIC

In 1993 ACCESS ERIC, the ERIC System's outreach component, fielded more than 1,200 information requests per month, most of them through the toll-free line, 1-800-LET-ERIC. ACCESS ERIC also continued to work with the increasing number of computer networks, such as America Online, America Tomorrow, CompuServe, and GTE Educational Network Services, to provide ERIC information to the burgeoning number of users of these systems.

To aid librarians and other ERIC providers, ACCESS ERIC began in 1993 an extensive revision of the systemwide brochure, *All About ERIC*. The totally new *All About ERIC*, which will include reproducible worksheets and reference sections, was to be available by spring 1994. Other publication highlights of 1993 included the release of *Striving for Excellence: The National Education Goals, Vol. II*, a compilation of clearinghouse-produced ERIC Digests particularly relevant to the national education goals, and the production of both print and computer disk versions of the comprehensive *ERIC Directory of Education-Related Information Centers*.

To broaden awareness and use of the ERIC System, ACCESS ERIC, working with the ERIC Public Information Task Force, developed and disseminated 500 press kits to education, library, and general media members. In the fall of 1993 ACCESS ERIC, in conjunction with the ERIC Document Reproduction Service (EDRS), launched a promotional campaign to inform librarians and other information providers about the latest ERIC developments. The campaign was kicked off with an ad in the journal *American Libraries* and "Know It All" kits for all those responding to the ad.

ERIC Document Reproduction Service

The ERIC Document Reproduction Service (EDRS) is the document delivery arm of ERIC and handles all subscriptions for ERIC microfiche and on-demand requests for reproduced paper copy or microfiche. During 1993 the volume of

Standing Order Customers (SOCs) subscribing to the total ERIC microfiche collection (about 12,750 titles, or 17,000 fiche cards, for approximately $2,000 annually) rose above the 900 level for the first time after several years in the 800 range. SOCs include over 100 overseas addresses.

EDRS prices were increased effective January 1, 1994:

Product	Price*
Microfiche (price per card)**	
Monthly subscription	$0.120 (diazo)
(approximate annual cost: $2,000)	$0.249 (silver)
Back collections (1966–previous month)	$0.146
Clearinghouse collections	$0.280
On-demand documents	
Per title (up to 5 fiche = 480 pages)	$1.23
Each additional fiche (96 pages)	$0.25
Reproduced paper copies	
First 1–25 pages	$3.53
Each 25-page increment (or part thereof)	$3.53
1993 Cumulative indexes on microfiche	
Subject, author, title, institution, descriptor,	
and identifier indexes	$75.00

*Prices do not include shipping. Prices are valid for calendar 1994.
**Diazo, unless otherwise specified.

ERIC Usage Fees

In April 1993 the director of ERIC announced that the tentative plan to charge online and CD-ROM vendors a 10 percent usage fee for use of the ERIC database in electronic form was being withdrawn indefinitely due to objections from the Information Industry Association and the American Library Association. The objective had been to use the income from usage fees for needed system improvements.

ERIC on CD-ROM

Four vendors now offer the ERIC database on CD-ROM:

Company	Telephone Number
SilverPlatter	617-769-2599
DIALOG Information Services	415-858-2700
EBSCO	508-535-8500
National Information Services Co.	410-243-0797

ERIC Digests

ERIC Digests (two-page concentrated treatments of key education topics, with suggestions for further reading) continue to be the most popular form of ERIC publication. The clearinghouses each produce approximately 10 digests per year, for a systemwide total of around 150 annually. Through March 1993 ERIC had produced a total of 1,504 digests, of which 1,339 have been entered into the ERIC database (the remaining 165 are considered out-of-date or obsolete).

Of the 1,339 in the database, 1,062 have had their full text added to their basic bibliographic record and can be read or downloaded in full text via both the online and CD-ROM systems that carry the ERIC database. The full text of these 1,062 ERIC Digests has also been made available from several locations via Internet.

A January 1994 update to the digest full-text file added approximately 150 new ERIC Digests and for the first time began to add digest-like publications from non-ERIC sources.

A printed bibliography describing all ERIC Digests through March 1993 can be obtained from the ERIC Facility.

ERIC Ready References

ERIC Ready References are brief handouts (usually one page, front and back) on database-related topics repeatedly of interest to users, such as ERIC component names, addresses, and telephone numbers; document types in the database; microfiche and document prices by size of document; accession number ranges by year; digest titles; and so forth. New ERIC Ready References are created regularly in response to user suggestions. During 1993 the following new titles were generated:

Ready Reference		Date Published
17A&B	Journals currently covered by *CIJE* A (arranged by title) B (arranged by clearinghouse)	July 1993
18	Field labels/tags in use by online and CD-ROM system Vendors for the ERIC database	July 1993
19	ERIC-at-a-Glance: ERIC system components graphically displayed	August 1993

All ERIC Ready References can be obtained free of charge from the ERIC Facility.

Publications about ERIC

In January 1993 ERIC published *The Educational Resources Information Center (ERIC): An Annotated Bibliography of Documents and Journal Articles about ERIC (Covering the Period 1960-1993)* (ED-355 974). This comprehensive compilation contains a total of 689 citations (574 to items in the database; 115 to items not in the database). It supersedes all previous bibliographies on this topic. It can be obtained free from the ERIC Facility.

The *ERIC Annual Report* gives the most comprehensive summary of ERIC's last full year of operations. It is available free of charge from ACCESS ERIC (800-LET-ERIC) and is also entered into the database as soon as it is available.

Books in ERIC

In 1993 a policy decision was reached that ERIC should begin to cover education-related books, including the output of major commercial publishers. This literature had previously not been covered because it was copyrighted and could not be microfiched by ERIC and because it was already under good bibliographic control by conventional library mechanisms. During 1993, as a result of this new policy, a total of nearly 500 books were cataloged into the ERIC database. It is anticipated that as many as 1,000 books will be accessioned in 1994. The publisher's address or other source of availability, and price, is always included in the ERIC resume. Such items can be identified in searching by the Publication Type code 010 (representing "Books").

ERIC Videotape

The ERIC Clearinghouse on Information and Technology (IR) has produced a new videotape, *ERIC: In Action,* that offers libraries and educators an effective way to introduce ERIC to their users. The 15-minute videotape is organized under four major topics: basic structure, major benefits, key index features, and options for locating materials. Librarians training new ERIC users and library or education professors introducing students to ERIC as an education resource are invited to try it. The cost is $17 (including postage). Call 1-800-LET-ERIC for more information.

International ERIC

In October 1993 DIALOG Information Services announced a new CD-ROM product called International ERIC, containing separate databases for the *Australian Education Index (AEI), British Education Index (BEI),* and *Canadian Education Index (CEI).* This product captures the educational literature from the major non-U.S. English-speaking countries and is the first tangible product of the informal InterEd cooperation that has been going on between ERIC, AEI, BEI, and CEI for the last few years. It is available from DIALOG for an annual subscription price of $1,295 (U.S.), $900 (non-U.S.).

Internet Activities

During 1993 ERIC's Internet activities increased dramatically. By the beginning of the year, all components (and most individual staff) had acquired Internet addresses and stable connectivity. Internet-based E-mail has in many cases replaced correspondence and telephone calls for internal communications. Internet-based file transfer is now the basis for the transmission of bibliographic data from the dispersed ERIC Clearinghouses to the ERIC Facility (for editorial and database-building purposes). ERIC's sponsoring agency, the Office of Educational Research and Improvement (OERI), acquired an Internet node (INet) and rapidly became a so-called gopher site. As a result, numerous ERIC publications and files are being loaded on INet and made available to the world at large via Internet.

AskERIC

AskERIC, a project of the ERIC Clearinghouse on Information and Technology, provides question-answering, help, and referral to K–12 educators through Internet. AskERIC now receives an average of 250 electronic mail inquiries weekly. AskERIC draws on the total resources of the ERIC system to generate and send Internet responses to all inquiries within 48 hours.

In addition, AskERIC has established a growing file of full-text resources on their ftp/gopher site. This full-text databank, referred to as the AskERIC Electronic Library, includes hundreds of lesson plans, news and information about ERIC and AskERIC, ERIC Digests in full text, completed searches on current topics, resource guides, popular questions and answers, and the archives of some education-related listservs. This resource now receives electronic visits at the phenomenal rate of 15,000 a week. In 1994 the AskERIC Electronic Library is being expanded to include the full text of many publications of the ERIC Clearinghouses and other components. Eventually, contributors of documents to ERIC will be asked to provide both printed and electronic versions (if available), with electronic versions being considered as candidates for the full-text Electronic Library. AskERIC can be reached by telephone at 315-443-9114 or Internet: askeric@ericir.syr.edu.

National Association Reports

American Library Association

50 E. Huron St., Chicago, IL 60611
312-944-6780, 800-545-2433

Hardy R. Franklin
President

Founded in 1876, the American Library Association (ALA) is the world's oldest and largest national library association, with 55,836 members representing all types of librarians and libraries—academic, school, and public, as well as special libraries serving business, government, hospitals, and other institutions. Members also include trustees and other library supporters.

The association encompasses 11 membership divisions focused on various types of libraries and library services. ALA maintains headquarters in Chicago, a Washington, D.C., office, and an editorial office for *Choice,* a review journal for academic libraries, in Middletown, Connecticut.

Priority areas of concern are access to information, legislation and funding, intellectual freedom, public awareness, personnel resources, and library services, development, and technology.

Conference Highlights

ALA holds two major membership meetings each year. The 112th ALA Annual Conference, held June 24 to July 1, 1993, in New Orleans, attracted 17,165 members, exhibitors, and guests. The theme, selected by 1992–1993 ALA President Marilyn L. Miller, was "Empowering People through Libraries." The keynote speaker was former President Jimmy Carter.

In his address at the conference's Opening General Session, Carter recalled the libraries of his childhood and touched on Miller's theme of empowerment, saying that libraries are essential to help prevent "the discrimination of the rich against the poor." Carter also noted the futility of talking about education reform and student achievement while at the same time curtailing library services. "We cannot ask our children to read and take away their books," Carter said. "We cannot call for improving education and close our libraries."

In his inaugural speech, 1993–1994 ALA President Hardy R. Franklin introduced his theme, "Customer Service: The Heart of a Library." Franklin said: "During my term as president, we will focus on improving service to the library user, expanding services to those underserved, and offering services to those whom we have been unable to serve."

ALA planned to broadcast a videoseminar titled "Achieving Breakthrough Service in Libraries" on May 12, 1994.

More than 9,600 people attended the 1993 ALA Midwinter Meeting in Denver, January 22–28. The meeting was marked by protests against Amendment 2, a constitutional change approved by Colorado voters that revoked anti-discrimination protection for homosexuals. The ALA Executive Board voted not to hold future meetings in Denver unless the legislation was overturned.

Upcoming conferences include the 1994 ALA Annual Conference, to be held June 23–30 in Miami Beach, and the 1995 Midwinter Meeting, scheduled for January 20–26.

Issues

Threatened library school closings, continued funding problems, and ALA's "foreign policy" were among the issues addressed by the association during 1993.

At the 1993 Annual Conference, the ALA Council passed resolutions objecting to proposed closings of graduate programs in library and information science at the University of California's Berkeley and Los Angeles campuses. Library school admissions at UC–Berkeley were frozen while a panel conducted a review of the library school. In June UCLA administrators announced that the campus's School of Library and Information Science would be "disestablished." It was later announced that MLS candidates would continue to be admitted and classes administered through the UCLA Graduate School of Education.

The budget woes that plagued libraries during the recent recession did not go away during 1993. Major cutbacks were reported in such cities as Baltimore and New Orleans, and California's county libraries lost $2.6 billion in a statewide funding shift. ALA continued to combat the problem of library budget cuts through public awareness activities.

A 1992 ALA Council resolution condemning the government of Israel for alleged censorship activities sparked controversy throughout 1993. After much debate about the resolution—and the appropriateness of ALA's involvement in what many consider to be "foreign policy" issues—Council voted at the 1993 ALA Annual Conference to revoke the resolution.

Washington Report

ALA's 19th annual Legislative Day in Washington April 20 gave library supporters from all 50 states an opportunity to meet with legislators—many of them newly elected—on a number of key issues affecting library service.

The ALA Washington Office called the Clinton administration's first budget "good news/bad news" for libraries. Although funds for improving public library services were to be increased by 14 percent, several programs were set for elimination, and total federal support to libraries was to be cut by 11 percent in fiscal 1994. The House and Senate rejected most of the cuts after vigorous protests by

ALA and others. The final budget, signed by the President, called for a 6 percent increase in funding although talk of rescission continued at the end of the year.

Several pieces of legislation that would have tremendous impact on library services moved forward in 1993 with leadership from ALA. These included the Elementary and Secondary School Library Media Act (S. 266 and H.R. 1151), which would establish federal support (both administrative and financial) specifically for school library media programs; and the National Information Infrastructure (NII) Act of 1993 (H.R. 1757), which would support national networking applications in education, health care, libraries, and government information.

In September 1993 ALA joined with 14 other organizations to establish a national Telecommunications Policy Roundtable, concerned with safeguarding public access to the national information highway endorsed by the Clinton administration. Chief among ALA's concerns is that libraries be a key access point to this vast electronic information network.

ALA applauded President Clinton for signing into law the Government Printing Office (GPO) Electronic Access Act, which provides for direct public access to various government databases, including the Congressional Quarterly, through an online system to be established at GPO. The system will be available without charge to depository libraries.

Intellectual Freedom

For the 12th year, ALA commemorated the defense of intellectual freedom with "Banned Books Week—Celebrating the Freedom to Read" (September 25–October 2). Cosponsors are the American Booksellers Association, the American Society of Journalists and Authors, the Association of American Publishers, and the National Association of College Stores.

The ALA Office for Intellectual Freedom (OIF) received reports on more than 600 censorship attempts in 1992–1993 (many more went unreported). Popular targets included children's self-esteem guides, Madonna's *Sex,* and books with gay characters and/or themes, especially the children's picture books *Heather Has Two Mommies* by Leslea Newman and *Daddy's Roommate* by Michael Willhoite.

OIF also reported increased involvement by national organizations in local censorship attempts, and the Freedom to Read Foundation told the ALA Council that attempts by conservative religious groups to gain footholds in local government could lead to an increase in censorship cases.

Children's Book and Media Awards

Cynthia Rylant, author of *Missing May,* received the 1993 Newbery Medal for the most distinguished contribution to American literature for children in 1992. Emily Arnold McCully won the 1993 Caldecott Medal, awarded for the most distinguished American picture book for children, for her illustrations in *Mirette on the High Wire.* The awards are presented by the Association for Library Service to Children (ALSC), a division of ALA.

Patricia C. McKissack received the 1993 Coretta Scott King Author Award, presented for an outstanding book by an African-American author, for *The Dark Thirty: Southern Tales of the Supernatural,* published in 1993. Kathleen Atkins Wilson received the 1993 King Illustrator Award for her first book, *The Origin of Life on Earth: An African Creation Myth.*

The third annual Andrew Carnegie Medal for Excellence in Children's Video was awarded to John Kelly and Gary Soto for *The Pool Party.* The Mildred L. Batchelder Award, awarded for outstanding translation of a children's book, was not presented in 1993.

M. E. Kerr received the 1993 Margaret A. Edwards Award for outstanding contribution to literature for young adults. The award is sponsored by *School Library Journal* and administered by the Young Adult Library Services Association, a division of ALA.

Public Awareness

The National Library Week theme, "Libraries Change Lives," was the focus for the third year of ALA's "Rally for America's Libraries," a campaign to raise public awareness about the need to support libraries. Members of the public were invited to "Write for America's Libraries" and share stories of how a library had made a difference in their lives. More than 10,000 letters and 46,000 statements of support were received. Almost half a million people have registered their support for libraries since the rally was launched in 1991. Those expressing their support in 1993 included such well-known library users as President Clinton, *60 Minutes* correspondent Ed Bradley, Nobel Prize winner Linus Pauling, pop singer Gloria Estefan, and actress Katharine Hepburn.

The letters and testimonials received in ALA's "Write for America's Libraries" campaign reached millions via coverage in local and national media. An unprecedented number of editorials endorsing funding for libraries appeared in major newspapers, including *USA Today,* the *Christian Science Monitor, Boston Globe, Atlanta Constitution,* and *San Francisco Examiner.* Nationally syndicated columnist Bob Greene wrote three columns in support of increased funding for libraries, using letters received in ALA's campaign. In October, ABC TV's *American Agenda* carried a special report on the funding difficulties experienced by many libraries.

"Libraries Change Lives" is also the title of an exhibition, produced by ALA with support from the Microsoft Corporation, that will travel to more than 60 libraries over the next three years. The ten-panel exhibit features testimonials from notable library users collected during the campaign.

Introduced in 1984, ALA's celebrity "Read" posters have become one of the association's most popular public awareness tools. Those lending their support in 1993 included Olympic gold medalist Kristi Yamaguchi and actors Sean Connery, Graham Greene, and Roseanne Arnold.

"Together is better . . . Let's Read" was the title of the first national reading incentive program sponsored by ALA in cooperation with McDonald's Family Restaurants. A free kit of promotional materials was sent to all 16,000 public libraries in the United States.

Other public awareness activities included the annual observances of Library Card Sign-Up Month in September and the Night of a Thousand Stars/Great American Read-Aloud, which continued to spark activities at libraries nationwide. "Libraries Change Lives" was once again the theme for National Library Week in 1994 (April 17–23).

Special Projects

Family literacy continued to be a major focus for ALA special projects, with three organizations supporting separate programs in cooperation with the association.

Eleven additional libraries received grants of up to $10,000 to participate in the Bell Atlantic/ALA Family Literacy Project. Begun in 1989, the program provides financial and training assistance to projects throughout the Mid-Atlantic region. It is scheduled to continue at least through January 1995.

Cargill, the Minneapolis-based corporation, also continued its partnership with ALA to promote family literacy with an additional $50,000 grant. The project links Cargill offices and employees around the United States with organizations in their local communities to work on a variety of family literacy projects, from tutoring to fund raising.

The Viburnum/ALA Rural Family Literacy Project, established in 1992, also grew through additional funding in 1993. Funded by the Viburnum Foundation Inc., a private nonprofit foundation based in Rochester, N.Y., the project gave $3,000 grants to six rural libraries in Louisiana to support family literacy programs intended to break the intergenerational cycle of illiteracy.

The National Library Power Program, funded by the DeWitt Wallace–Reader's Digest Fund and administered by the American Association of School Librarians (AASL), a division of ALA, continued to fuel change in school libraries in 1993. Thirteen communities have received Library Power funding to improve public school libraries, and the fund is committed to establishing up to 25 Library Power sites by 1995 with a total investment of up to $45 million.

Other ALA special projects:

- The "Writers Live at the Library" pilot project, funded with a $521,841 grant from the Lila Wallace–Reader's Digest Fund, brought such writers as Gwendolyn Brooks and Walter Mosley to 19 public libraries in Michigan, Illinois, and Wisconsin.

- The Library–Head Start Partnership Project, a cooperative effort between ALA's Association for Library Service to Children (ALSC), the Library of Congress Center for the Book, and the Head Start Bureau, aimed to show how libraries and Head Start educators can work together to promote literacy and learning.

- In its sixth year, the Library/Book Fellows program, supported by the United States Information Agency, placed 15 U.S. librarians in library assignments in countries including Namibia, Scotland, South Korea, Greece, and Nicaragua.

Officers and Staff

Hardy R. Franklin, director of the District of Columbia Public Library, assumed the presidency of ALA at the end of the 1993 Annual Conference in New Orleans. Arthur Curley, director of Boston Public Library, was elected vice-president/president-elect for 1994–1995.

ALA Executive Director Peggy Sullivan announced that she would not remain in the job beyond 1994, and a search committee was formed to find the next executive director. Interviewing for the position was scheduled to begin in early 1994.

ALA Deputy Executive Director Roger H. Parent resigned to become executive director of the American Association of Law Libraries.

New ALA staff include Patricia Martin, director of development, and Karen Whittlesey, deputy executive director of the Association for Library Collections and Technical Services (ALCTS). Cathleen Bourdon, former deputy executive director of the Association of College and Research Libraries (ACRL), was named executive director of ALA's Reference and Adult Services Division (RASD) and Association of Specialized and Cooperative Library Agencies (ASCLA). Rob Carlson returned to ALA as deputy executive director of the Library and Information Technology Association (LITA).

Publishing Highlights

The ALA President's Special Committee on Project Century 21, appointed by 1992–1993 ALA President Marilyn L. Miller, published *Project Century 21: A Research and Action Program for Meeting the Information Needs of Society— Background Papers,* an examination of society's needs for information into the 21st century and the human resources that will be needed to meet them.

Notable items published by ALA Books in 1993 included Hazel Rochman's *Against Borders: Promoting Books for a Multicultural World,* which was endorsed by Archbishop Desmond Tutu as a "useful and fascinating tool to understanding"; Joseph Lazarro's *Adaptive Technologies*; and Henry Reichman's *Censorship and Selection: Issues and Answers for Schools,* a joint publication with the American Association of School Administrators.

Special Libraries Association

1700 18th St. N.W., Washington, DC 20009-2508
202-234-4700, FAX 202-265-9317

Lauren M. Emmolo
Manager, Communications

Headquartered in Washington, D.C., the Special Libraries Association (SLA) is an international organization serving more than 14,000 special librarians and information managers, brokers, and consultants. As the second-largest library and information-related association in North America, SLA provides a variety of programs and services in the areas of professional development, public relations, research, specialized publications, government relations, and career and employment services.

More than 50 percent of the association's members are employed by corporations, with the remainder at government agencies, museums, associations, universities, hospitals, and other organizations with specialized information needs.

At year-end 1993, SLA had 56 regional chapters in the United States, Canada, the Caribbean, the Pacific, Europe, and the Middle East; 28 subject-area divisions; seven special-interest caucuses; and 43 student groups. New units include the Legal Division, Baseball Caucus, and three student groups—Kent State University, University of Maryland, and Université de Montréal.

Association activities are developed with specific direction toward achieving SLA's strategic goals, which are to advance the leadership role of its members in putting knowledge to work for the benefit of decision makers in their organizations and the general public and to shape the destiny of the information society.

Professional Development

SLA's continuing education courses provide information professionals with opportunities for intensive, hands-on learning experiences. The professional development programs integrate technology and management techniques that meet the varied needs of SLA members. For example, the Middle Management Institute benefits those without formal management education. The Executive Management Program addresses such themes as "Advanced Topics in Managerial Decision Making" and "Principles of Accounting and Financial Management."

The 1993 Winter Education Conference was the first to focus on a single theme, "Total Quality: A Vision for the Future." The conference, designed exclusively for information professionals, offered workshops, focus groups, and a keynote address on "learning organizations."

In recognition of the continuous advancements in computer and telecommunications technology that have revolutionized the library profession, SLA's 1994 Winter Education Conference, InfoTech '94, also focused on a single topic—information technology. It featured a series of courses and seminars on recent technological developments and ramifications, such as use of Internet, implementing CD-ROM networking, exploring the ethical implications in information technology, and harnessing interactive computer-based multimedia. InfoTech '94, held in Dallas January 23–25, also offered one-stop shopping of tabletop and permanent Infomart exhibits.

SLA's State-of-the-Art Institute, "Latin America: The Emerging Information Power," held in November 1993, was timely—the meeting took place within a week of the decisive vote in the U.S. Congress endorsing the North American Free Trade Agreement (NAFTA). Held in Washington, D.C., the institute attracted a record number of information, business, and government professionals from the United States and abroad, giving them the opportunity to discuss the impact of the economic and political developments in Latin America and the access and exchange of business, scientific, technical, and legal information.

The theme of SLA's 84th Annual Conference, held June 5–10, 1993, in Cincinnati, Ohio, was "Looking to the Year 2000: Information Professionals Chart the Course." The conference, which provides members and other information professionals with the opportunity to gain knowledge from industry experts, share experiences with their peers, and make valuable career contacts, featured several hundred workshops, field trips, and continuing education courses to provide information and ideas that could be implemented in attendees' libraries. Hot topics were Internet, copyright law, and CD-ROM networking. Despite the lingering effects of the recession, the conference attracted 5,166 attendees.

The theme of SLA's 85th Annual Conference, to be held June 11–16, 1994, in Atlanta, is "Information Vision." To help information professionals cultivate an "information vision," conference programming will stress such concepts as recognizing the need to be innovative, learning to anticipate critical changes in the workplace, and developing new measures to achieve excellence.

Recognizing the need to make learning more convenient and cost-effective, SLA co-sponsors programs with its chapters and other library associations. SLA's self-study program, established in 1988, responds to the education needs of members who cannot attend continuing education courses on-site or who wish to learn at their own pace. In 1993 SLA published *The ABC's of Cataloging,* a primer on the "how-to's" of setting up a catalog for a specialized collection. The self-study program now totals eight courses on such topics as business writing, time management, database design, and public speaking.

Commitment to Research

In 1989 the SLA Board of Directors approved a Research Agenda, focusing on what special librarians need to know in order to improve the performance of libraries, information centers, and information professionals. The agenda comprises five broad categories: Futures, Current/User Issues, Measures of Productivity and Value, Client/User Satisfaction Measures, and Staffing.

In 1993 SLA awarded its Research Grant to Marilyn D. White, associate professor at the College of Library and Information Services, University of Maryland, for a project titled "Measuring Customer Satisfaction and Quality of Service in Special Libraries."

The 1992 Research Grant recipients, José-Marie Griffiths and Donald King, reported their research results at the 1993 Annual Conference. They conducted an analysis of more than 10,000 statistical survey responses, providing detailed evidence of the usefulness, value, and worth of organizations' libraries. Griffiths and King found that in-house libraries save organizations as much as three times the cost of their operation by reducing the time that professionals would otherwise have to spend to acquire needed information. The results of their study were published by SLA in *Special Libraries: Increasing the Information Edge.*

The results of the 1991 Research Grant recipient's work were published in 1993. In her study, titled *The Impact of the Special Library on Corporate Decision Making,* Joanne Marshall found that library and information services significantly facilitate individual and organizational performance. Eighty-four of the 299 managers and executives surveyed at five financial institutions in Toronto responded that information provided by special librarians contributed to better-informed decision making.

In addition, SLA sponsored a research project on the emerging job opportunities for librarians and information professionals. The results were published in the fourth in a series of SLA Occasional Papers, *Extending the Librarian's Domain: A Survey of Emerging Occupational Opportunities for Librarians and Information Professionals,* by Forest Woody Horton, Jr.

Creating Information Pathways

SLA's Nonserial Publications Program provides information professionals with useful literature on a variety of critical topics, such as salaries, careers, value, research, Internet, and a broad range of management issues.

Among the books published by SLA in 1993 were *The Internet and Special Libraries: Use Training, and the Future,* by Hope Tillman and Sharyn Ladner; *Opening New Doors: Alternative Careers for Librarians,* by Ellis Mount; and *Valuing Special Libraries and Information Centers,* an information kit. In addition, SLA provided information professionals with a unique collection of handbooks, brochures, and posters.

The association's monthly newsletter, *SpeciaList,* published numerous feature articles about new trends and developments in the information profession, such as multimedia, accessing European Community information, Internet, AIDS information, outreach to Eastern and Central Europe, and the emergence of Latin America as an information power. Many of these articles were written by SLA members. In addition, the newsletter served as a conduit to SLA programs and services, informing members of professional opportunities and background on association-related issues.

Special Libraries, the association's quarterly journal, offers guest-edited issues on special topics. The summer 1993 issue was guest-edited by Guy St. Clair, an SLA past president, and addressed benchmarking, total quality management, and the learning organization. The fall 1993 special issue was titled "Standing in the Future." Guest-edited by Jane I. Dysart and Stephen Abram, the issue covered the virtual library, a prospective outlook of the information profession in 2005, and ideas and opportunities on the future of librarianship. Other issues of *Special Libraries* addressed a variety of topics, such as developing an in-house database from online sources, atmospheric sciences information resources, similarities between legal and scientific literature, and state library online search services.

Supporting Professional Achievement

Each year SLA honors members of the information community for outstanding contributions to the association or profession and to encourage future efforts. The association's extensive awards and honors program helps members gain recognition from their peers in the information industry and from their colleagues in their own organizations.

The association also realizes the need to recruit and assist top college students in entering the profession. In 1993 SLA awarded four scholarships totaling $24,000 to students pursuing degrees in library and information science.

Enhancing the Profession's Image

The primary goal of the SLA Public Relations Program is to increase awareness and appreciation of the important role that special librarians play in their organizations and society. Along with research, public relations remains a priority of the association.

International Special Librarians Day was created as a way to gain recognition for the contributions of the profession in the international sharing of information. The theme for International Special Librarians Day, April 22, 1993, was "Global Understanding through Information."

To recognize outstanding public relations efforts made by members during International Special Librarians Day and National Library Week, the SLA Public Relations Committee presents an annual award. In addition, public relations awards are presented to members for significant contributions to the public relations goals of their chapter, division, or employer, and to a journalist for writing an interesting and informative feature about the profession.

SLA co-sponsored the second in a series of video training programs with Mead Data Central. This new program, The Information Partnership: Recognizing a VIP, provides insights on the contributions that information centers make to their organizations.

SLA hosted a special reception as a pre-Annual Conference celebration for Cincinnati business and civic leaders to meet with VIPs of the information profession. This provided members of the profession with an opportunity to describe how information professionals can cooperate to put knowledge to work for their organizations and communities. Procter & Gamble President John E. Pepper was honored at the reception in recognition of his commitment to the twin goals of information literacy and lifelong learning.

Serving as the Profession's Government Relations Advocate

Government relations staff work closely with SLA members to influence the formulation, change, and dissemination of national and international information policies. Staff work with legislative and regulatory leaders to see that access to government information remains open for all users.

Members of SLA's Copyright Committee work in concert with government relations staff to monitor activities on myriad issues relating to copyright. This past year, the committee members were busy keeping track of the fallout from the *American Geophysical Union* v. *Texaco* case, which ruled that companies in the for-profit sector that make copies of copyrighted scientific and technical journals violate fair use under the 1976 Copyright Act. This decision goes against SLA's position on copyright, which is "that libraries in the public and private sectors (should) receive equitable treatment." SLA did not agree with the decision handed down in this court case and supported the Texaco position. The association, in conjunction with the Association of Research Libraries, the American Association of Law Libraries, and the Medical Library Association, prepared an *amicus curiae* (friend of the court) brief on behalf of the Texaco position. The appeal was heard in May 1993, but a decision had not been handed down by the court at the time this report was written.

In addition, SLA voiced opposition to the severe federal funding cuts for certain classes of postal rates. Such cuts will have a severe budgetary impact on nonprofit associations such as SLA that disseminate a wide array of materials to its members.

SLA also prepared a paper for the Clinton–Gore transition team and other administration officials, titled "Revitalizing America: Information Strategies for the 1990s." The paper calls for the establishment of a National Academy of Information, as well as a number of other options to coordinate the policies that govern information in the United States. This paper includes other recommendations that will be of value to the administration as it examines ways to create a U.S. national information infrastructure

Library Legislative Day continues to be a focal point for the government relations program. Held annually during National Library Week, the day's activities include briefings by congressional staff, meetings with representatives and senators and a congressional reception on Capitol Hill. Library Legislative Day is an opportunity for members of the profession to come to Washington, D.C., to contact their federal elected officials and express their opinions on issues of concern to the special library community. Since 1988 SLA has been an official sponsor of the day, which is also cosponsored by the American Library Association and the District of Columbia Library Association.

Players in the Information Age

SLA's primary goal is to advance the leadership role of information professionals by providing a variety of services to enhance their professional skills and advancing the interests of the special libraries community. The association aims to show policymakers and decision makers in the business community that special librarians are key players in the Information Age.

Association of Research Libraries

21 Dupont Circle N.W., Washington, DC 20036
202-296-2296, FAX 202-872-0884
Internet: arlhq@cni.org

Duane E. Webster

Executive Director

The Association of Research Libraries (ARL) represents the 120 principal research libraries that serve major research institutions in the United States and Canada. ARL's mission is to identify and influence forces affecting the future of research libraries in the process of scholarly communication. ARL articulates the concerns of research libraries and their institutions and promotes equitable access to recorded knowledge in support of teaching, research, and scholarship through coalitions for action, information policy development, and innovation in research library programs.

ARL fulfills its mission through the work of its programs and services, which include Statistics, Communications and Scholarly Relations, Management Services, Federal Relations and Information Policy, Collection Services, Access and Technology, Scientific and Academic Publishing, and Research and Development.

Statistics

ARL's Statistics Program collects and distributes quantifiable information describing the characteristics and operations of member libraries and conducts research on new measures and interpretive approaches. In 1993 the program focused on improving methods of collecting, verifying, and analyzing member library data. In addition, the association began collecting more detailed data on nonprint collections. Kendon Stubbs, Associate University Librarian at the University of Virginia and consultant to the program, prepared a study of the library expenditures and university E&G (education and general) expenditures data ARL has collected since 1980. His findings were presented in the January 1994 issue of the ARL newsletter.

The ARL Statistics Program produces two major publications annually, the *ARL Annual Salary Survey* and *ARL Statistics*. The 1992 salary survey presents trends in professional positions and salaries for fiscal 1993, with special sections on minority librarians, Canadian librarians, and librarians in ARL university law and medical libraries. In 1992 the average salary for all ARL university librarians was $42,144 ($44,464 for men and $40,809 for women). For minority librarians, the average salary was $39,737. The 1992–1993 *ARL Statistics* presents data on ARL member libraries in the areas of collections, staffing, expenditures, and interlibrary loan (ILL). These data are also available in machine-readable form.

Communications and Scholarly Relations

The ARL Communications Program has as its goal the education of academic communities regarding research library issues as well as influencing policy and decision makers within higher education and other fields related to research and scholarship. Through the ARL newsletter and press releases, members of the library, higher education, and scholarly communication communities are apprised of current developments of importance to research libraries and are informed of ARL positions on issues that affect the research library community.

In 1993 the ARL newsletter, *ARL: A Bimonthly Newsletter of Research Library Issues and Actions,* addressed such issues as the cost of interlibrary loan, NREN (the National Research and Education Network) and the information infrastructure, foreign publishing trends, copyright and fair-use rights, and public interest values in telecommunications policy. The newsletter also contained regular reports about the association's project on diversity and minority recruitment.

The Leadership Role in Library Fund Raising, Minutes of the 120th Membership Meeting (May 1992) and *Charting the Future: Research Libraries Prepare for the 21st Century, Minutes of the 121st Membership Meeting* (October 1992) were published and distributed in July and September 1993, respectively.

In the area of scholarly relations, ARL continues to build strategic allegiances with other national organizations including extensive participation in activities of the National Humanities Alliance, the Association of American Universities, and the American Council of Learned Societies.

Collaborative efforts with the Association of American Universities (AAU) resulted in the 1992 adoption of a joint ARL-AAU action agenda. As a result, with support from the Andrew W. Mellon Foundation, the AAU Research Libraries Project was established with three task forces: intellectual property rights in the electronic environment; a national strategy for managing scientific and technological information; and acquisition and distribution of foreign languages and area studies materials. Each task force seeks to develop strategies with dual purposes: first, to exploit the full potential of communications and computing technologies for innovative applications in research and teaching, and second, to seek investments and/or changes that will demonstrate long-term cost advantages for universities. Throughout 1993 some three dozen individuals from the academic community—librarians, faculty, technologists, and academic administrators—served as members of the three project task forces. Discussions were hosted at the AAU and ARL membership meetings during the fall; the project was scheduled to conclude in April 1994. A report on the preliminary findings of the task forces was published in *ARL* No. 170, September 1993, pp. 1–3.

In December 1992 ARL published *University Libraries and Scholarly Communication,* a study undertaken by the Andrew W. Mellon Foundation. The report is an analysis of the operations and economics of research libraries with special attention to the impact of new information technologies. The study is distinctive in taking a long view of the library landscape and provides a basis for evaluating new directions in a thoughtful way. During the year, over 5,000 copies of the study were distributed and ARL undertook to broaden the visibility of the report by encouraging discussions among members of the higher education and scholarly communications communities. In addition, the report was made available in electronic form for Internet retrieval from three sites: the University of Virginia Libraries, the American Mathematical Society, and the Coalition for Networked Information. ARL was also instrumental in development of a HEIRAlliance report that summarizes the Mellon study (see under the heading Access and Technology below for details on HEIRAlliance).

Office of Management Services

The ARL Office of Management Service (OMS) functions as a bridge between the business world and the world of academic and research libraries. Constantly seeking concepts and techniques with the potential to contribute to the effective management of libraries, OMS is dedicated to staying abreast of current management theory and practice. OMS provides consulting, training, and information services on the management of human and material resources in libraries.

The OMS Training and Staff Development Program offers institutes and workshops designed to strengthen the organizational, analytical, creative, and interpersonal skills of library staff. It seeks to promote personal responsibility for improvements in library services and programs and for effective individual performance. The institutes, designed to strengthen leadership skills and professional performance, are conducted by OMS staff with the assistance of librarians who have completed training and consultation skills programs with OMS. In 1993 over 750 library staff attended OMS training institutes and workshops.

The OMS Information Services Program gathers, analyzes, and distributes information on contemporary library management techniques, conducts surveys and analytical reviews, and answers inquiries on library issues and trends. The overall goals of the program are: to identify expertise and encourage its exchange; to promote experimentation and innovation; to improve performance; and to facilitate the introduction of change. These goals are accomplished through an active publication and information service program whose principal components are the Systems and Procedures Exchange Center (SPEC), the OMS Occasional Paper Series, the Quick-SPEC survey service, and the new OMS Conference Program.

OMS publications in 1993 included SPEC Kits on providing public services to remote users, library development and fund-raising practices, cooperative strategies for foreign acquisitions, quality improvement programs, and benefits for professional staff.

The OMS Consulting Service Program is designed to facilitate change in libraries. The most recent focus has been on assisting libraries in the transition from an archival role to an information gateway. OMS provides a wide range of consulting services, incorporating new research on service delivery, marketing, and organizational effectiveness. Using an assisted self-study approach, the Consulting Service Program helps libraries investigate current practices and future trends, and develop workable plans for collection management, technical and public services, leadership development, organizational screening, and organizational review and design.

The newest OMS service is the Diversity Program. Begun in 1990 as a research and development project, this program seeks to respond to rapidly changing demographics by encouraging an awareness of human differences that leads to a value of and respect for these differences. It assists libraries in the development of workplace environments that welcome, develop, foster, and support diversity. Presentations, consultation, and training are all offered as part of this program. A special effort has been made to use a partnership approach to work with other organizations within the field of librarianship and higher education to support the goals of this program.

Federal Relations and Information Policy

The ARL Federal Relations and Information Policy program actively tracks and seeks to influence a number of federal programs and issues of concern to research libraries, among them information policy, networking and telecommunications, privacy, preservation, and higher education, with an emphasis on issues relating to networking, intellectual property, and dissemination of government information.

Networking and telecommunications policies have been at the forefront of congressional and executive branch activities in the past year. ARL, with others in the library and higher education communities, supported the House-passed follow-on legislation to the High-Performance Computing Act of 1991 (HPCA)— the National Information Infrastructure Act of 1993 (H.R. 1757). The bill amends HPCA and calls for the establishment of an interagency program to implement the broad-based view of NREN via applications in four key areas: government information dissemination, libraries, health care, and education. Several other bills relating to telecommunications policy from a regulated perspective have been introduced and will be the focus of ARL activity in 1994.

ARL, with more than 70 other nonprofit organizations, established the Telecommunications Policy Roundtable in an effort to ensure a public voice in the emerging national information infrastructure. The group was launched to encourage the nonprofit community to participate more fully in the many critical information infrastructure debates under way. The roundtable developed a set of principles "to guide policy making in order to ensure that future generations inherit an information infrastructure that enhances the quality of life for everyone."

ARL was active on a number of copyright and intellectual property issues. With other members of the scholarly, library, and research communities, ARL filed an *amicus* brief re *American Geophysical Union* v. *Texaco*. Second, ARL joined with seven other associations in the library and scholarly communities and expressed concerns about possible changes to copyright policy as proposed in the Copyright Reform Act of 1993. Third, with 12 library, scholarly, and research associations, ARL presented testimony before the Clinton administration's Working Group on Intellectual Property, Information Infrastructure Task Force.

Finally, during the past year there has been a great deal of activity on government information dissemination issues. ARL supported passage of the Government Printing Office (GPO) Electronic Access Act, which moves GPO forward in the delivery of online federal information. ARL and others in the library community have encouraged the rethinking of current programs, and two recent reports, by the Dupont Circle Group and the Chicago Conference on the Future of Federal Government Information, identified possible new directions for access to and dissemination of government information.

Collection Services

The Collection Services Program addresses the broad issues facing research libraries in the areas of collection management and preservation. The association's collection development efforts promote needed government and foundation support for collections of national importance in the United States and Canada and work to improve the structures and processes needed for effective cooperative collection development programs, including the North American Collections Inventory Project (NCIP).

In 1991 ARL launched the Foreign Acquisitions Project, funded by the Andrew W. Mellon Foundation. A central focus is the consideration of service models for the collection and distribution of foreign materials. A corollary effort is the exploration of the implications of electronic information resources and the consideration of innovative approaches and structures aimed at facilitating electronic resource sharing. The key 1994 strategy is the development of demonstration projects that would show how different world areas can be incorporated into an overall program of distributed access to and delivery of foreign acquisitions.

Collection management consulting through the Collection Analysis Program and training programs is also provided by ARL staff.

ARL's preservation efforts include advocacy for strengthening and encouraging broad-based participation in national preservation efforts in the United States and Canada; support for development of preservation programs within member libraries through the Preservation Planning Program; support for effective bibliographic control of the preservation-related process; encouragement for development of preservation information resources; and monitoring technological developments that may have an impact on preservation goals.

A current focus is development of an ARL action plan for preservation. The plan will build on the discussions at the May 1992 Chicago Preservation Planning Conference as well as the recommendations resulting from the 1993 evaluation of the impact of the National Endowment for the Humanities (NEH) preservation programs on ARL libraries. A corollary effort is consideration of issues in the utilization of digital technology for preserving retrospective scholarly resources.

Access and Technology

The Access and Technology Program of ARL addresses issues related to scholarly information resources such as bibliographic control, technology, and public services. Four ARL groups contribute to this program and include the Committee on Access to Information Resources, the Working Group on

Scientific and Technical Information, and the ARL representatives to the Steering Committee of the Coalition for Networked Information.

The fourth group is the ARL Advisory Committee on the ARL-RLG Interlibrary Loan Cost Study, which oversaw a major investigation of the interlibrary loan process. The study was undertaken in collaboration with the Research Libraries Group (RLG) and with the support of Council on Library Resources (CLR). In June ARL published the *ARL/RLG Interlibrary Loan Cost Study*. The report details the finding that, on average, an ILL transaction costs $30 ($19 to initiate a request to borrow an item, and $11 to lend an item to another library) and that 77 percent of this cost is for library staff.

The year also saw wide circulation of a "white paper" titled *Maximizing Access, Minimizing Costs,* that was prepared for ARL by Shirley K. Baker, Washington University at Saint Louis, and Mary E. Jackson, University of Pennsylvania. The paper critiqued the current ILL system, made a series of recommendations for association activity, and led to the development of the ARL North American Interlibrary Loan and Document Delivery (NAILDD) Project. The project's purpose is to promote developments that will improve delivery of materials to users, including materials from remote sites. Those developments will enable the user to choose sources for requesting materials, streamline the request process, and facilitate delivery of material; from the library's perspective, the project seeks to ensure user access to research resources, minimize paperwork required to track ILL and document delivery requests, streamline the financial tracking associated with such requests, and minimize staff involvement, thus reducing unit costs.

The access and technology capability also encompasses the relationship established among ARL, CAUSE, and EDUCOM—the Higher Education Information Resources (HEIR) Alliance, which prepared and distributed two briefing papers in the series *What Presidents Need to Know*. HEIRAlliance Executive Strategies Report No. 2 was *What Presidents Need to Know . . . about the Future of University Libraries: Technology and Scholarly Communication* (June 1993) and Report No. 3 was *What Presidents Need to Know . . . about the Impact of Networking on Campus* (October 1993). The series of reports is available through the CAUSE office in Boulder, Colorado.

Office of Scientific and Academic Publishing

The objective of the Office of Scientific and Academic Publishing (OSAP) is to maintain and improve scholars' access to information. OSAP undertakes activities to understand and influence the forces affecting the production, dissemination, and use of scholarly and scientific information. The office seeks to promote innovative, creative, and alternative ways of sharing scholarly findings, particularly through championing newly evolving electronic techniques for recording and disseminating academic and research scholarship. The office also maintains a continuing educational outreach to the scholarly community in order to encourage a shared "information conscience" among all participants in the scholarly publishing chain: academics, librarians, and information producers. The capability is advanced and OSAP receives guidance through the work of the ARL

Committee on Scholarly Communication. As part of its interest in the newly emerging Internet scholarly communications movement, the office produced the third edition of the *Directory of Electronic Journals, Newsletters, and Academic Discussion Lists*, increased by some 30 percent in both its coverage and level of sophistication.

In August, an Internet list, moderated by Ann Okerson, the OSAP director, was started to provide a place for creators of new electronic journals to report their plans and announcements to the subscriber list. On average, about two new start-ups have been reported each week. NewJour-L supports the directory project; its Internet address is: NewJour-L@e-math.ams.org. The Association of American University Presses and ARL held their third joint Symposium on Electronic Publishing in November. The proceedings of the second joint AAUP/ARL Symposium on Electronic Publishing were published in March.

An electronic version of the Andrew W. Mellon Foundation's study *University Libraries and Scholarly Communication* was produced during the spring. It was mounted for ftp and gopher retrieval with the University of Virginia libraries as a principal Internet site. In its first full month (July), it was the single most highly retrieved set of files at the university. A hyperlinked version for World Wide Web was prepared. It is available from the same site.

The ARL Firm Subscription Prices Working Group (chaired by Don Koepp, Director of Libraries, Princeton University) continues to work toward getting firm and timely prices from journal publishers. ARL's group letter was circulated widely throughout the vendor and publisher communities and directors of Irish and British libraries prepared and signed similar letters. ARL was assisted by the Scientific, Technical and Medical Publishers (STM) Library Relations Committee and by the subscription vendor community in its efforts.

Office of Research and Development

The Office of Research and Development (ORD) consolidates the administration of grants and grant-supported projects administered by ARL. The major goal within ORD is to promote the ARL research agenda by identifying and developing projects in support of the research library community's mission. ORD also works to develop funding support for those projects. Another part of this capability is the ARL Visiting Program Officer project. This project provides ARL staff and staff from member libraries the opportunity to collaborate on programs of interest to the association. There were four Visiting Program Officers in 1993, contributing to the Latin American Studies Assessment Project, the Foreign Acquisitions Project, the North American Interlibrary Loan and Document Delivery Project, and a visiting officer who contributed to ARL's development of positions and strategies on government information policy issues.

Among the funded projects in 1993:

- The National Endowment for the Humanities (NEH) awarded ARL a grant to support the enhancement and revision of the Preservation Planning Program resources. Under this grant, ARL completed updating the

Preservation Planning Program Manual and Resources Notebook and developed a series of seven resource guides.

- ARL, in conjunction with the Library of Congress, administered an NEH-funded project to convert into machine-readable records approximately 529,000 monographic reports that represent the records for microform masters held by libraries, archives, publishers, and other producers. NEH will also support another ARL project to convert serials records in the National Register of Microform Masters (NRMM), this activity in conjunction with Harvard University Library, the Library of Congress, and the New York Public Library.
- Under the Scholarship, Research Libraries and Foreign Publishing in the 1990s Project, and with the support of the Andrew W. Mellon Foundation, ARL is developing projects to provide a clearer understanding of the forces influencing the ability of North American research libraries to build collections of foreign materials.
- The Japan-U.S. Friendship Commission awarded ARL a grant to develop pilot projects to help Japanese studies librarians to test various approaches to information access. This is a joint project with the National Coordinating Committee for Japanese Library Resources (NCC).
- ARL was also awarded a grant from the H. W. Wilson Foundation for the North American Interlibrary Loan and Document Delivery (NAILDD) Project.

Association Governance and Membership Activities

The 1993 spring ARL Membership Meeting was held in Honolulu in May. The theme, "Gateway to the Pacific Rim: Information Resources for the 21st Century," highlighted the key issues of East–West scholarship and research libraries' response. Panels examined efforts by the academic library community to respond to scholars needs for enhanced access to resources, and trends in publishing, collecting, and foundation support to enhance access to Pacific Rim information resources. The program was hosted by the University of Hawaii Libraries.

The fall ARL Membership Meeting was held in Arlington, Virginia, October 21-22. The theme was "The Emerging Information Infrastructure: Players, Issues, Technology, and Strategies." The program highlighted the convergence of the telecommunications and entertainment industries and the profound impact that this phenomenon will have on the characteristics and the very nature of emerging information infrastructures. Discussions centered on two themes: the need to understand the substantial investment that is required to build the global information infrastructure and how libraries and other educational organizations must join forces to promote a public interest dimension.

At the conclusion of the ARL business meeting in October, ARL President Susan Nutter of North Carolina State University handed over the presidency to John Black, University of Guelph. During the business meeting, three directors were elected to serve three-year terms on the ARL board: Kent Hendrickson, University of Nebraska; Gloria Werner, UCLA; and James Williams, University of Colorado. Two directors whose board terms ended at this meeting, Joan Chambers, Colorado State University, and Emily Mobley, Purdue University, were acknowledged.

Membership approved a dues increase to establish an ongoing ARL program to support efforts to recruit minorities to careers in research libraries.

ARL presented Congressman Vic Fazio (D-Calif.) with an award honoring his contributions to and continued support of research libraries and higher education. Rep. Fazio has consistently recognized and garnered support for library programs and public access issues including the introduction of electronic products and services to the Depository Library Program, support for the Library of Congress and Government Printing Office budgets, and the promotion of the use of permanent paper for publications of long-term value. This was only the third time in the history of the association that such an award was given.

Two new committees—the Working Group on Copyright and the Advisory Committee for the Minority Recruitment Program—were established in 1993. Standing committees in 1993 included Information Policies, Access to Information Resources, Research Collections, Preservation of Research Library Materials, Management of Research Library Resources, and Scholarly Communication. Advisory committees and project groups include the Advisory Committee on ARL Statistics, Advisory Committee on the Office of Management Services, and the Working Group on Scientific and Technical Information.

Coalition for Networked Information

The Coalition for Networked Information (CNI) was founded in March 1990 to help realize the promise of advanced networks and high-performance computing for information access and delivery. The coalition was established by three associations: ARL, CAUSE, and EDUCOM. ARL promotes equitable access and effective use of recorded knowledge supporting teaching, research, and scholarship. CAUSE and EDUCOM are dedicated to introducing, using, and managing information technology and related resources in research in general and higher education. CNI promotes the creation of and access to information resources in networked environments in order to enrich scholarship and enhance intellectual productivity.

A task force of institutions and organizations able and willing to contribute resources and attention to the mission of the coalition was created in 1990 and continues to grow. This task force now provides a common vehicle by which over 190 institutions and organizations pursue a shared vision of information management and how it must change in the 1990s to meet the social, educational, and economic opportunities and challenges of the 21st century. Members of the task force include higher education institutions; publishers; network service providers; computer hardware, software and systems companies; library networks and organizations; and public and state libraries.

Association of American Publishers

220 E. 23 St., New York, NY 10010
212-689-8920

1718 Connecticut Ave. N.W., Washington, DC 20009
202-232-3335

Judith Platt
Director of Communications

The Association of American Publishers (AAP), with more than 200 members located in every region of the United States, is the principal trade association of the book publishing industry.

AAP members publish hardcover and paperback books in every field, including general fiction and nonfiction; poetry; children's books; textbooks; Bibles and other religious books; reference works; scientific, medical, technical, professional, and scholarly books and journals; and classroom instructional and testing materials. Members of the association also produce computer software and electronic products and services, including online databases, CD-ROM, and CD-I.

The association's highest priorities are

- Expanding domestic and foreign markets for American books, journals, and electronic publishing products
- Promoting the status of publishing in the United States and abroad
- Defending freedom of expression, at home and abroad
- Keeping AAP member publishers informed on legislative, regulatory, and policy issues that affect the industry, and serving as the industry's voice on these issues
- Protecting the rights of creators through ongoing efforts in defense of copyright
- Offering practical educational programs to assist members in selected areas

The association is structured to serve both the general and specific interests of its members.

AAP's core programs, carried out under the guidance of standing committees, deal with concerns that affect all publishers, such as copyright, postal rates and regulations, First Amendment concerns, international freedom to publish, tax and trade policy, education and library funding, and new technology.

The association's six divisions—General Publishing, Paperback Publishing, School, Higher Education, Professional and Scholarly Publishing, and International—deal with specific market areas. Each division operates under the guidance of its own executive body, within policy guidelines set by AAP's 18-member board of directors. Members of the board are elected to four-year terms, under a chairperson who serves for two years. Charles R. Ellis, president and CEO of John Wiley & Sons, served as chairperson from 1992 until 1994;

Jack Hoeft (Bantam Doubleday Dell president and CEO) took over on April 1, 1994. Ambassador Nicholas A. Veliotes is president of the association.

AAP maintains two offices, in New York and Washington, D.C., with a total of approximately 40 professional and support staff members.

Highlights of 1993

- Book sales in 1992 showed a modest 4.4 percent gain over 1991, totaling $16.8 billion.
- AAP joined Reading Is Fundamental in a new literacy effort.
- A massive raid on book pirates in Indonesia marked a high point in AAP's intensified overseas copyright enforcement campaign.
- The International Division spearheaded AAP's successful campaign on English-language open-market rights in Western Europe.
- Following discussions with an AAP delegation in London and New York, the British Library announced its decision to pay U.S. publisher-set prices for copyrighted material used in document delivery services to U.S. customers.
- The Paperback Publishing Division sponsored the first industrywide symposium on publishing and the environment.
- The School Division continued its successful efforts to retain categorical funding for instructional materials in California, Texas, and Florida.
- AAP joined PEN and others in an initiative to keep public attention focused on the plight of author Salman Rushdie, helping to establish a U.S. committee for Rushdie's defense and securing a meeting for Rushdie with President Clinton.
- James Lichtenberg joined the AAP staff as vice president, Higher Education Division.
- Carol Risher was named AAP vice president for Copyright and New Technology.
- AAP held its 23rd annual meeting in Washington, D.C., with United Nations Secretary-General Boutros Boutros-Ghali and Supreme Court Justice Antonin Scalia among the featured speakers.
- The International Freedom to Publish Committee sponsored a human rights fact-finding mission to Egypt.
- The Higher Education Division launched an ambitious "Invest in Your Future" marketing campaign.
- AAP extended its program for publishers on the West Coast, sponsoring a Rights and Permissions seminar and a Professional and Scholarly Publishing Division (PSP) marketing workshop in San Francisco.
- AAP joined in sponsoring a memorial tribute to Jeremiah Kaplan, marking the passing of a great publisher.
- Among those honored in 1993: Donald Eklund received the School

Division's Mary McNulty Award; Jason Epstein was named recipient of the Curtis Benjamin Award; Jack Thornton received the Higher Education Division's Leisy Award; and the Professional and Scholarly Publishing Division's R. R. Hawkins Award went to the University of Chicago Press.

Divisions

General Publishing Division

The General Publishing Division (GPD) represents publishers of fiction, nonfiction, poetry, children's literature, reference and religious books. Its programs strive to broaden the audience for books and are often carried out in conjunction with other AAP divisions. GPD maintains close ties with the bookselling and library communities, wholesalers, and authors groups, through a number of joint liaison committees. It provides major support for literacy programs, for the National Book Awards, and for the reading promotion efforts of the Center for the Book in the Library of Congress. William Shinker (HarperCollins) chaired the committee during 1993.

The division's concern for literacy continued in 1993 as GPD explored, with the Barbara Bush Foundation for Family Literacy, ways to promote literacy effectively. The division is formulating plans for a forum on literacy issues.

Marking the 1993 celebration of National Book Week, GPD joined with PEN American Center in sponsoring "My Life in Books/Books in My Life," a symposium featuring a dozen industry professionals—authors, literary agents, publishers, editors and designers—discussing their careers.

GPD and the Paperback Publishing Division provided funding for a second study of consumer book-buying behavior, released by the Book Industry Study Group in March. The study revealed an encouraging 7 percent increase in book purchasing over the previous year.

The AAP Reading Initiative, a project of GPD's Children's Publishing Committee, works to promote the use of children's literature in school classrooms. In 1991 the Reading Initiative, in collaboration with the Virginia State Reading Association, launched the Teachers as Readers (TAR) Project—a pilot program of educator reading groups designed to engage teachers, school administrators, and others in the world of contemporary children's trade books. By the end of 1993, Teachers as Readers groups had been set up in 41 states, the District of Columbia, and Guam, and the project had won endorsements from eight major organizations, including the International Reading Association, the National Council of Teachers of English, and the American Library Association. New York has two dozen active, registered TAR groups, Texas 18, and California 8. Current efforts focus on launching the program in the nation's nursery schools, including Head Start and independent chains, and in Chapter One-financed public programs.

GPD continued to sponsor its popular educational programs, the Publishers Forum Luncheons. In February the division inaugurated a new series of symposia, the Direct Marketing Roundtables.

Higher Education Division

The Higher Education Division (HED) is concerned with all aspects of marketing, production, and distribution of textbooks and related multimedia materials for postsecondary education. The division works to enhance the perceived value of instructional materials from college publishers and to protect and expand intellectual property rights within the college marketplace. The division serves as a link between publishers, college bookstores, faculty, and students, working in close cooperation with the National Association of College Stores. Michael Needham (McGraw-Hill) chaired the division in 1993.

Following an extensive search, James Lichtenberg was named AAP vice president, Higher Education Division. A communications expert specializing in the field of higher education, Lichtenberg served for five years as a special consultant to AAP on higher education affairs. He took over his new post on March 8, 1993.

Concern over significant shifts in student buying behavior in the past several years prompted HED to refocus its marketing efforts. "Marketing to Students" was the central theme of the division's 11th annual meeting, held in Boston in May.

Following a successful pilot program carried out in collaboration with bookstores on nine campuses, the division's Marketing Services Committee launched a nationwide marketing campaign—"Invest in Your Future"—to encourage students to buy, use, and retain textbooks.

Seeking to redefine the division's mission and goals in light of profound changes in the academic environment, 14 members of the HED Executive Council met in Boston in June for a strategic planning session. Three goals emerged from that session: 1) enhancing the perceived value of instructional materials; 2) protecting and expanding intellectual property rights; and 3) developing contemporary standards for granting and obtaining rights in all media. Two new divisional entities have been given specific responsibilities in implementing these goals: a new Faculty Relations Committee was formed to work directly with professors and faculty associations, and a new Permissions Standard Committee has been charged with exploring and developing ways of handling the permissions process with a special focus on materials in nontraditional format. (In addition, the HED Marketing Services Committee has developed its own strategic plan to improve the "perceived value" of college publishers' materials.)

Encouraging tests in the field prompted HED member publishers to begin including prepaid return Tyvek mailers with complimentary copies of textbooks sent to faculty members for review. Use of the mailers—which was expanded with AAP support—was shown to substantially increase the percentage of unwanted books returned to their publishers and to result in return of books in usable condition so that they can be recycled to other faculty members.

HED continued to sponsor its popular AAP/WEST seminars for publishers on the West Coast. Seminars in 1993 covered changes in higher education curricula and new opportunities in educational publishing.

Jack Thornton, retired president of Wadsworth Inc., was named to receive the division's James F. Leisy Award for distinguished contributions to college publishing.

For the 17th year, the division sponsored Pubcenter at the annual meeting and Campus Market Expo (CAMEX) of the National Association of College Stores, held in Denver in 1993.

International Division

The International Division's membership reflects the range of the general AAP membership in terms of size and market. Alun Davies (Bantam Doubleday Dell) chairs the committee.

The division is concerned with marketing American books and related products overseas through direct sales, copublishing ventures, sales of English-language and translation rights, and the promotion of English as a second language. The International Division (ID) sponsors educational programs to help publishers strengthen their international capability and assists U.S. publishers in participating at international book fairs. The division serves as liaison with various agencies involved in promoting American books overseas, including the State and Commerce Departments, the United States Information Agency (USIA), and the World Bank.

Through its International Copyright Protection Committee, the division seeks to secure overseas markets by promoting effective international protection for U.S. copyrights.

Inside Export, the division newsletter, reports on specific trade opportunities for American publishers. The newsletter is available on a subscription basis to publishers who are not International Division members.

The division traditionally sponsors a major seminar for publishers attending the American Booksellers Association convention. The 1993 program was a ground-breaking symposium on "The New Spanish-Language Market in the United States—Publishing and Distribution."

The division hosted meetings between U.S. and foreign publishers, including delegations from China and Eastern European publishers visiting the United States under USIA sponsorship.

For the first time, the division sponsored an internship program, which brought nine publishers from Eastern Europe to the Frankfurt Book Fair and gave them an opportunity to work at the stands of division members. The program was viewed as a success both by the interns and their sponsoring U.S. publishers and plans call for an expanded program for 15 interns next year.

The division again sponsored an international rights directors meeting at Frankfurt. This year the focus was on rights and licensing in electronic publishing.

The division published *Supplement 1* to its *Handbook of International Rights.* The new supplement, which can be purchased alone or in combination with the *Handbook,* deals with the 1991 amendment to the Australian copyright law. The division's Executive Council approved funding for a guide to U.S. publishing for foreign publishers. A project of the division's Rights and Co-Publishing Committee, the guide will provide practical assistance to international rights buyers and sellers, especially those in Eastern Europe and other developing markets.

ID member publishers worked with the AAP Washington staff in an unsuccessful effort to head off a move to close all Stars and Stripes military bookstores
overseas and turn their operations over to the military post exchanges.

At the division's request, AAP copyright counsel undertook a study of the
legal situation in the European Community with respect to exclusive rights contracts. The study was initiated to dispel the confusion over British publishers'
contention that a contract establishing exclusive rights for the United Kingdom
and open-market English-language rights for other EC states violated EC
antitrust law. The conclusion of AAP counsel's study is that such contracts do
not violate EC law. This subject and AAP's position were featured in meetings at
the 1993 Frankfurt Fair.

Anti-Piracy: The International Copyright Protection Committee

The committee operates under the administrative umbrella of the International
Division and its activities are coordinated with AAP's domestic copyright program. The committee works with other U.S. copyright industries in the
International Intellectual Property Alliance to focus U.S. government attention
on efforts to protect American copyrights overseas and eliminate market access
barriers for U.S. copyrighted works. The International Copyright Protection
Committee coordinates AAP's overseas copyright enforcement campaign, which
is now operating in Indonesia, Japan, South Korea, Malaysia, Puerto Rico,
Singapore, and Taiwan.

AAP participated in the alliance filing to the U.S. Trade Representative targeting countries whose failure to protect American copyrights warrants special
attention under the "Special 301" provisions of the Omnibus Trade and
Competitiveness Act of 1988. [For further information on this subject, see the
report "Legislation and Regulations Affecting Publishing in 1993" in Part 2—
Ed.]

In the spring of 1993 confusion over implementation of Taiwan's new parallel import law created a real problem for American publishers, whose book shipments were held up by Taiwan Customs. Responding to requests from AAP and
other alliance members, U.S. government officials reviewed the problem with
officials from Taiwan and secured an agreement under which book shipments
from AAP member publishers will be given immediate clearance to a list of
AAP-authorized importers.

AAP's vigorous anti-piracy enforcement campaign continued to gather
momentum. On March 8, in two separate raids on book pirates in Seoul, South
Korea, more than 2,000 pirated copies of AAP members' titles were seized.
Settlements reached in April required the pirates to pay substantial fines and
issue public apologies in the major Korean-language newspapers.

A significant blow in the anti-piracy war was struck in Indonesia in
November with action initiated by AAP and the Business Software Alliance (representing major U.S. software publishers), which resulted in coordinated raids
against three printers and two publishers. More than 17,000 pirated computer
manuals and books, along with pirated software, were seized. The raids were the
first of their kind in Indonesia and yielded, in addition to the pirated material,

names and addresses of retail syndicates and major customers in North America, Europe, Asia, and the Middle East, which may lead to further prosecutions.

A hard-won copyright victory was achieved with passage and signing of a new Russian copyright law, which took effect August 3. AAP and other members of the alliance played a significant role in the process of bringing Russia into the international copyright community. Enforcement is a priority for 1994.

AAP prepared a detailed report on the status of copyright reform and anti-piracy activities in 62 countries. The report outlines the considerable progress made over the past year as a result of AAP's overseas enforcement efforts and the activities of the alliance—a year in which more than 20 former pirate countries enacted new Berne-compatible copyright laws. An additional 26 countries prepared draft copyright laws on which AAP (through the alliance) provided comments.

Paperback Publishing Division

Concentrating on issues of special concern to mass market paperback publishers, the Paperback Publishing Division (PPD) works to expand the market for paperback books. Laurence Kirshbaum (Warner Books) chaired the division during 1993.

The division sponsors a Book Preview program at the annual meeting and cover design exhibit of the National Association of College Stores. In 1993 for the first time the Book Preview Program, highlighting forthcoming mass market paperback titles, was presented in video form. The Educational Marketing Committee also prepared an informal guide to help first-time attendees at various conventions make the most of their visits to publishers' exhibits.

PPD members have been wrestling for several years with the problem of uniform bar code placement for mass market paperback books. Standard practice for other segments of the publishing industry is to print the Bookland EAN code on the back cover. Bookland EAN is item-specific, containing information such as title and ISBN, and is the code preferred by bookstores. Supermarkets, drug stores, and other retail outlets where mass market paperback books are sold prefer the Universal Product Code (UPC) on the back of these books. The PPD Head of House Council, following a meeting in November, affirmed the continued utility of carrying the UPC on the back cover and keeping the Bookland EAN code on the inside front cover.

A PPD-sponsored symposium, "Book Publishing and the Environment," marked the industry's first comprehensive effort to address environmental concerns. Divided between legislative and technical issues, the seminar provided a framework for understanding recycling issues from a variety of perspectives. Paper recycling standards, debinding, the impact of books on the solid waste stream, and environmental concerns in the printing process, including the contentious question of chlorine bleaching, were some of the issues addressed at the September symposium.

The Rack Clearance Center, now entering its 16th year of operation, serves as liaison between participating publishers and wholesalers, auditing reimbursement claims for mass market paperback book racks installed in retail locations. The center currently processes claims for 28 publishers/imprints.

Professional and Scholarly Publishing Division

The Professional and Scholarly Publishing (PSP) Division is concerned with the publication of technical, scientific, medical, and scholarly materials. Division members produce books, journals, computer software, databases, and CD-ROM and CD-I products. Professional societies and university presses play an important role in the division. Linda Scovill (Scovill/Patterson Primary Eyecare Communications) is division chairperson.

The division publishes a quarterly newsletter, *PSP Bulletin.*

The division's 1993 meeting in Washington was the first PSP annual meeting to feature an exhibit of scientific and educational new technology services in addition to the program sessions. Fifteen exhibitors participated. More than 40 speakers at a dozen plenary and concurrent sessions offered PSP publishers programs on a range of subjects, from document delivery to the National Research and Education Network (NREN) and networked information, sales opportunities in Asia, and the significance of international reproduction rights organizations. Outstanding PSP publications were honored at the annual awards banquet; the R. R. Hawkins Award went to the University of Chicago Press for *The History of Cartography, Volume 2, Book I: Cartography in the Traditional Islamic and South Asian Societies.*

In response to concerns raised by the PSP Task Force on Cross Border Document Delivery over the failure of the British Library Document Supply Center (BLDSC) to comply with U.S. copyright law in providing document delivery services to customers in the United States, a delegation headed by AAP Chairperson Charles Ellis went to London in June to meet with representatives of the British Library board and the BLDSC. The discussions continued in New York the following month. Late in the summer, the British Library announced its intention to pay fees set by individual publishers for copies of U.S.-copyrighted material delivered to customers in the United States.

The division offered a number of educational programs throughout the year, including seminars on direct marketing, and opportunities for journal sales beyond subscriptions.

In conjunction with the American Booksellers Association, PSP undertook a comprehensive study to reexamine the Levin Echo Effect—the correlation between publishers' direct mail promotions and sale of the same titles through scientific and technical bookstores. The division also began a new library survey to examine the impact of electronic information on collection development and access in the humanities and social sciences.

Recipients of the PSP minority student scholarships at the New York University Summer Publishing Institute and the Radcliffe Summer Publishing Program were chosen. The scholarships were established as part of a divisional program to encourage minorities in publishing.

PSP offered an educational program on the West Coast for the first time. The division's popular "Basics of Marketing Professional/Educational Publications" was presented November 5 in conjunction with the San Francisco Bay Area Book Festival. The enthusiastic response will encourage the division to plan more seminars for the West Coast.

The PSP Journals Committee's electronic publishing case studies seminar drew an unprecedented attendance of more than 180 registrants, eager to hear reports on new electronic publishing projects. TULIP, a two-and-a-half-year-old project exploring the use of Internet and campus networks to distribute journals, and Red Sage, an electronic journal delivery project, were discussed at the September seminar, along with McGraw-Hill's PRIMIS customized book operation, the Institute of Electrical and Electronics Engineers (IEEE) journal conversion project, and Faxon's tables-of-contents database.

School Division

The School Division is concerned with publishing for the elementary and secondary school (K–12) market. The division works to enhance the role of instructional materials in the education process, to secure increased funding for these materials, and to simplify the procedures under which educational materials are "adopted" by various states. The School Division serves as a bridge between the publishing industry and the educational community. It works in the cause of education at the state and local level, and maintains an effective lobbying network in key adoption states. The evolving funding crisis has focused attention on how the division can best serve AAP's educational publishing constituency in increasingly difficult times. Alfred McDougal (McDougal Littell & Company) served as chairperson during 1993.

The division opened the year with its annual meeting in Boston, taking a close look at the role of the publisher in a changing educational environment. Retired School Division Vice President Donald Eklund was presented with the Mary McNulty Award.

With *Electronic Learning* magazine, the School Division sponsored a conference on "Multiple Media: The New Curriculum" in Chicago in February. The enthusiastic response from the conference's 200 participants has prompted the division to plan a similar conference for 1994.

In collaboration with Recording for the Blind and the American Printing House for the Blind, the division sponsored a workshop, "Serving the Print-Disabled Student." The conference looked at how the braille laws in various states, along with the new Americans with Disabilities Act, are changing the traditional production and adoption processes for K–12 publishers.

The division worked closely with the AAP Washington staff on a host of federal legislative initiatives of concern to educational publishers. [See the article "Legislation and Regulations Affecting Publishing in 1993" in Part 2—*Ed.*]

Some of the division's most important work is carried on at the state level to provide legislators with a better understanding of the importance of instructional materials and the need to preserve the integrity of the funding for these materials. The division's work in three key states—Florida, California, and Texas—produced significant results in 1993.

The Florida legislature voted late in the year to maintain categorical funding for instructional materials, despite efforts by the State Commissioner of Education to "block grant" instructional materials funding into a broader program that might have allowed these funds to be used for any educational purpose.

The Florida legislature also increased instructional materials funding by more than $12.4 million over the previous year, to $80.5 million.

California's fiscal crisis continues to be of primary concern. The work of the division's legislative advocate in California was crucial in maintaining categorical funding for instructional materials, although all categories were reduced to some degree. The division is working on a long-term strategy to impress upon California legislators the importance of instructional materials in providing all children in the state with equal access to educational opportunities.

The Texas legislative budget office approved allocation of a two-year fund totaling $272 million, with approximately $190 million of that allotted for basal reading. AAP School Division publishers were also invited to meet with Texas state education officials to discuss the current restructuring of the Texas Education Agency and to offer recommendations for streamlining the process of evaluating and selecting instructional materials.

The division, along with the National Association of State Textbook Administrators and the Book Manufacturers Institute, compose the Advisory Commission on Textbook Specifications (ACTS). In 1993 the commission issued newly revised *Manufacturing Standards & Specifications for Textbooks,* setting acceptable manufacturing standards for school textbooks. Adoption states and many large school districts use these standards as baseline specifications to ensure quality and durability of print materials used in schools.

The division established two new committees in 1993:

- The Committee for Serving Disabled Students will seek ways to facilitate timely, efficient and cost-effective production of accessible educational materials for disabled students. One of the committee's functions will be to establish clear guidelines regarding ownership and underlying rights for electronic files and final product produced from files.

- As the only School Division committee not focused on a state or a single issue, the Professional Development Committee can direct its activities as needed in the school text publishing community. The committee will play an important role in the developing relationship between the Human Rights Division of the National Education Association (NEA) and the AAP School Division.

Core Committees

Copyright Committee

The Copyright Committee coordinates AAP efforts to protect and strengthen the proprietary rights of authors and publishers and to enhance public awareness of the importance of copyright. Edward Stanford (Paramount Publishing) chairs the committee.

Year's end brought a significant copyright victory for AAP and the three publishers that sued Michigan Document Services in February 1992 for copyright infringement. A federal magistrate in Michigan issued an opinion on December 17 that the production of "coursepacks" for sale to college students, without the permission of the publishers whose copyrighted works are photocopied for inclusion in the coursepacks, is an infringement of copyright. The Michigan ruling, in keeping with the 1989 *Basic Books, Inc.* v. *Kinko's Graphics Corporation* decision, refutes the defendant's claim of "fair use."

Much of the Copyright Committee's energy in 1993 was devoted to legislative issues, analyzing proposals before Congress with specific reference to their copyright implications, and advising the AAP board and membership on appropriate industry responses. Among these legislative issues were the proposed Copyright Reform Act repealing sections 411(a) and 412 of the Copyright Act; legislation authorizing fee-based services and products from the Library of Congress; bills expanding the National Research and Education Network (NREN) and efforts to further the National Information Infrastructure (NII), and proposals to extend the term of copyright. [For more information, see "Legislation and Regulations Affecting Publishing in 1993" in Part 2—*Ed.*]

The Copyright Committee, working with AAP's New Technology Committee, guided the association's participation in 18 months of negotiation between the private sector and the Library of Congress, leading to the development of new voluntary model agreements under which the Library of Congress may permit patrons to use and copy from CD-ROM products obtained as part of the copyright registration and deposit system.

The committee and AAP copyright counsel provided guidance for the discussions held with representatives of the British Library concerning document delivery services (see under Professional and Scholarly Publishing Division above).

The committee's Rights and Permissions Advisory Committee (RPAC) established an RPAC/WEST group to serve members on the West Coast, and held its first workshop in September in San Francisco. The seminar looked at the role of permissions professionals in the context of the new information technologies. RPAC also sponsored a workshop in New York in April on the impact of the new Copyright Renewal Act on rights and permissions.

Freedom to Read Committee

The Freedom to Read Committee coordinates AAP's efforts to promote and protect First Amendment rights and intellectual freedom. Its activities include intervention in court cases, lobbying efforts at the national and state level, educational programs, and publications. The Freedom to Read Committee works closely with allied organizations, such as the American Library Association's Intellectual Freedom Committee and the American Booksellers Foundation for Intellectual Freedom, and coordinates AAP participation as a member of the Media Coalition, a group of trade associations formed to defend First Amendment rights. Jane Isay (Grosset Books/G.P. Putnam's Sons) was 1993 committee chair, succeeding Betty Prashker of Crown Publishing.

The committee produced a new publication, perhaps the first of its kind targeted specifically to American book publishers, providing a broad overview of First Amendment issues that have a direct bearing on day-to-day publishing operations. The publication, *Book Publishing and the First Amendment (The State of Free Expression for Book Publishers, Present and Future)*, draws heavily on the expertise of members of the Freedom to Read Committee. It is a series of essays covering such topics as libel law, privacy, sexually explicit materials, the copyright law's fair-use provisions, and censorship in public schools and libraries. The 70-page book is available for purchase.

The Freedom to Read Committee again joined with ALA's Intellectual Freedom Committee to sponsor a First Amendment program at the ALA annual conference in New Orleans. The program—"Hearing Children's Voices, Respecting Children's Choices"—featured two award-winning African-American authors, Virginia Hamilton and Walter Dean Myers. The AAP/ALA program also included a screening of *Damned in the USA,* a controversial British documentary about pressure groups and censorship.

Freedom to Read Committee representatives were part of a small delegation who met with the Justice Department's director of public affairs in October to discuss a variety of First Amendment concerns.

AAP again participated in the observance of "Banned Books Week— Celebrating the Freedom to Read," an annual event jointly sponsored by AAP, ALA, the American Booksellers Foundation for Free Expression, the National Association of College Stores, and others.

AAP wrote to Congress endorsing the nomination of Jane Alexander as chair of the National Endowment for the Arts, stressing the importance of Ms. Alexander's "strong commitment to non-partisan, non-politicized support for the arts."

Early in December, AAP and the ALA-affiliated Freedom to Read Foundation were among those who successfully petitioned the U.S. Court of Appeals for the District of Columbia to release the report of the independent prosecutor in the Iran-contra case.

During 1993 the committee was involved in a number of court cases with First Amendment implications:

- With other members of the Media Coalition, AAP filed an *amicus* (friend of the court) brief in the 11th Circuit in *Pompano Book and Video* v. *Satz,* supporting the owners of three Florida adult bookstores in their claims of illegal harassment by local prosecutors. The brief argues that ultimately it is mainstream publishers and booksellers who are the victims of "government-orchestrated efforts to suppress protected expression."

- Following the Justice Department's decision to appeal the ruling of a Los Angeles federal judge striking down the "general standards of decency" language for NEA (National Endowment for the Arts) grants, AAP signed on to an *amicus* brief originated by People for the American Way, asserting that the "decency" clause cannot be applied without violating First Amendment principles.

- In an obscenity case involving the operator of a chain of adult book and video stores, the U.S. Supreme Court handed down a 5–4 ruling rejecting the argument that application of the forfeiture provisions of federal anti-racketeering (RICO) laws in pornography cases violates the First Amendment. The defendant in the case, Ferris J. Alexander, had been found guilty of violating anti-obscenity laws by selling four magazines and three videotapes, the total value of which was less than $200. In addition to his $200,000 fine and six-year prison sentence, his $25 million business was confiscated and its inventory subsequently burned. AAP, ALA, and the ALA-affiliated Freedom to Read Foundation had filed an *amicus* brief contending that application of the RICO forfeiture provisions in such cases is a serious violation of free speech guarantees. Justice Anthony Kennedy wrote a strong dissent challenging the majority's "grave repudiation of First Amendment principles."

- AAP joined the Magazine Publishers of America in an *amicus* brief defending the right of Standard and Poor's to the qualified privilege from subpoena accorded journalists and challenging the contention of a New York bankruptcy court that Standard and Poor's is not engaged in journalistic activity.

- In September the Ninth Circuit Court of Appeals in San Francisco overturned the contempt citation of an Arizona author who refused to give up confidential materials amassed in researching a book. With the support of the Freedom to Read Committee, AAP counsel represented the author, Ronald Watkins, *pro bono*. In its ruling, the appellate court not only recognized a qualified shield for journalists subpoenaed in civil cases, but affirmed that the privilege applies to all investigative journalists, whether their work is published in books, newspapers, magazines, or via electronic media.

- In a case similar to *Watkins,* AAP, joined by New Orleans librarians, filed an *amicus* brief in the Fifth Circuit protesting the order of a district court judge that author Joseph Bosco turn over notes and tapes used in the writing of *Blood Will Tell* (Morrow), a nonfiction account of a murder. The AAP brief argues that both the U.S. and Louisiana State constitutions "demand vigilant protection of the journalistic process in order to protect the free flow of information to the public."

- In December the Justice Department agreed to drop further prosecution of a North Carolina distributor of "adult" materials in the face of pending civil litigation in which the distributor, PHE Inc., challenged the practice of instituting successive multiple obscenity prosecutions of the same defendant in different jurisdictions. PHE maintained that the prosecutions were intended to stop distribution of all sexually explicit materials, even those protected by the First Amendment. AAP and other members of the Media Coalition had filed an *amicus* brief opposing the Justice Department's tactics and a federal appellate court held in June 1992 that the Justice Department acted improperly. The practice of multi-district obscenity prosecutions is currently under review by the Justice Department.

- AAP and other members of the Media Coalition were plaintiffs in a suit filed three years ago challenging the provisions of a Tennessee law restricting the display and sale to minors of harmful materials, including those containing "excess violence." In December, the Tennessee Supreme Court ruled that the restriction on "excess violence" was unconstitutionally vague.

International Freedom to Publish Committee

AAP's International Freedom to Publish (IFTP) Committee is the only group formed by a major publishers organization for the specific purpose of defending and promoting freedom of written communication worldwide. The committee monitors human rights issues and provides moral support and practical assistance to publishers and authors outside the United States who are denied basic freedoms. The committee carries on its work in close cooperation with other human rights groups, including Human Rights Watch and PEN International. Wendy Wolf (HarperCollins) is committee chairperson.

The committee and the Fund for Free Expression joined in sponsoring a mission to Egypt to look into human rights abuses, with specific reference to authors and publishers. Wendy Wolf, with Gara LaMarche, executive director of the Fund for Free Expression, and Mary Lynne Werlwas, an FFE fellow, spent two weeks in Egypt in early spring examining issues related to freedom of expression. In trying to cover as broad a spectrum as possible, the mission met with some 70 individuals including writers (among them Nobel laureate Naguib Mahfouz); publishers from a range of traditional, feminist, leftist, and Islamic houses; journalists; members of the professional community; government officials; and human rights activists. The mission's report will provide background and guidance for future IFTP activity.

Responding to the plight of reform-minded legal scholars in China who are being denied access to libraries and institutional support because of their political beliefs, the committee solicited and received from AAP members a number of books on constitutional law and democratic rights theory. The donated books, including works by Ronald Dworkin, Anthony Lewis, Laurence Tribe, and Archibald Cox, were sent to the Chinese scholars to facilitate their research and writing on legal issues.

Approaching the fifth anniversary of the death sentence against author Salman Rushdie, PEN American Center and AAP, along with a number of other organizations, joined in establishing a U.S. Committee for the Defense of Salman Rushdie. The committee's objective is to "reawaken public concern" about the danger to Rushdie and others connected with publication of *The Satanic Verses.* Barely two months after the committee's establishment, Rushdie was received at the White House, meeting briefly with President Clinton and for a longer period with Secretary of State Warren Christopher and National Security Adviser Anthony Lake.

The committee voiced concern to the Justice and State Departments over denial of a visa to Irish author Gerry Adams. Adams is president of Sinn Fein, the political arm of the Irish Republican Army, and the author of two recently published books, one of which deals with his years in a British prison. His planned visit to the United States had included a 10-city book promotion tour.

The committee continued to voice protests on behalf of writers, journalists, and publishers who have been denied basic freedom of expression. In 1993 letters were sent to the Turkish government protesting severe restrictions on freedom of the press and the murder and mistreatment of journalists and authors, especially those with pro-Kurdish sympathies; to Egyptian President Hosni Mubarak on behalf of writer Alaa Hamed; to officials of the Norwegian government regarding the shooting of William Nygaard, publisher of the Norwegian edition of *The Satanic Verses;* and to Fidel Castro regarding the arrest and detention of Cuban writer Norberto Fuentes.

The committee makes small grants to assist publishers overseas. In 1993 such grants went to the Romanian publishing house Humanitas, and to *Srpski Glasnik,* a Serbian newspaper in Croatia.

Committee plans for 1994 include missions to China and Cuba.

Committee for Managing Diversity

The Committee for Managing Diversity develops programs to foster understanding of the growing diversity in our nation's population and to aid publishers in successfully managing that diversity. Dundee Holt (McGraw-Hill) chaired the committee during 1993.

To offer AAP member publishers meaningful assistance in identifying and establishing long-term, sustainable publishing industry diversity programs, the committee in 1993 prepared a new mission statement.

A dozen AAP member publishers bolstered the committee's support for the Howard University Press Book Publishing Institute by donating scholarships for the 1993 course.

The committee serves as liaison between the nonprofit Greater New York Hospital Foundation's "Walks of Life" program and the AAP membership. The program, which is designed to introduce young people to the workplace, operates at nine New York City schools and includes corporate mentoring, career days, and other in-school volunteer options.

The committee has also established connections with Black Women in Publishing, a professional development group, to provide information on a new scholarship program offering summer corporate internships to New York City public high school juniors and seniors.

New Technology Committee

The New Technology Committee serves as a resource for the membership on new technologies for print and electronic publishing products. Paul Constantine (John Wiley & Sons) chairs the committee.

The committee holds open meetings at which publishers have an opportunity to hear about new technological developments. Among the presentations made to the committee in 1993 were programs on ADOBE's new Acrobat technology, Kaleida's Scriptex language (which permits products to run on both MAC and DOS platforms), Electric Book Company's proposed new hand-held device, and "ebooks," a service for distributing page-by-page replicas of print books over Internet.

As a result of efforts by the New Technology Committee, working with AAP's Copyright Committee, the private sector and the Library of Congress were able to develop voluntary model agreements governing the use of CD-ROM products obtained by the Library of Congress through the copyright registration and deposit system. The first three CD-ROM publications deposited for copyright and public use under the new model agreements were presented to the Library of Congress (LC) in a formal ceremony on September 29. Four documents have been endorsed that it is hoped will encourage voluntary deposit of CD-ROMs. Two of the documents, authorizing either network or stand-alone access, are for use by publishers. The third is an agreement to be signed by LC patrons when downloading or copying material from a CD-ROM; the fourth document is a general statement of LC policy on CD-ROM use.

The committee has oversight responsibility for the *AAP Standard for Electronic Manuscript Preparation and Markup* and the Electronic Publishing Special Interest Group (EPSIG), which governs its development and use. Beginning with AAP's important first steps in the mid-1980s in developing an SGML (Standard General Markup Language) standard for use by book publishers, the *AAP Standard* has evolved into a new International Standard—ISO 12083:1993—that reaches far beyond the initial efforts. A new collaboration between AAP, the Graphic Communications Association Research Institute, and the consulting firm of McAfee & McAdam, has redefined EPSIG, which will function as a self-contained membership organization.

Postal Committee

The AAP Postal Committee coordinates AAP activity in the area of postal rates and regulations. It monitors developments at the U.S. Postal Service and the independent Postal Rate Commission and intervenes on the industry's behalf in formal proceedings before the commission. The committee also directs AAP lobbying activities on postal issues. Stephen Bair (Time Life Books) continued to serve as chairperson during 1993.

The revenue-forgone subsidy, which has supported overhead costs associated with mailings by nonprofit groups since the early 1970s, was virtually eliminated by Congress this year. The costs of supporting the congressionally mandated preferred postal rate structure will now be divided between nonprofit and commercial mailers. The first step of a six-year phase-in of higher rates for nonprofit mailers went into effect in November.

Congressional action also changed the rules regarding use of the Library Rate. Although publishers will still be able to use the Library Rate to ship books purchased by libraries, schools, and colleges, this rate will no longer be available for mailing complimentary review copies of textbooks.

Postmaster General Marvin Runyon has stated that he intends to hold off any general postal rate increases until 1995 and has denied rumors that the next rate increase would average 20 percent, indicating that he hopes to hold increases to the rate of inflation.

Administrative Committees

Three administrative committees direct and coordinate AAP member services:

Compensation Survey Committee

This committee coordinates and supervises preparation of the *AAP Survey of Compensation and Personnel Practices in the Publishing Industry*. Published every two years (a *Survey* was published in 1993), the report is designed to provide members of the association with current and accurate information on prevailing compensation levels for representative management and professional positions in the industry. The survey is prepared by Organization Resources Counselors Inc., a compensation firm with extensive experience in the book publishing industry. Christine Names (Random House) chaired the 1993 committee.

Lawyer's Committee

The Lawyer's Committee is composed of both in-house and outside counsel of AAP member companies. It meets quarterly to discuss such areas as libel and invasion of privacy, First Amendment, antitrust, product liability, and insurance coverage. Ellis Levine (Random House) is committee chairperson.

Statistics Committee

The Statistics Committee oversees the preparation of monthly and annual statistics reports published by AAP. The committee coordinates the efforts of the various divisional statistics committees as they update and modify data for their various market segments. The AAP industry report includes information on sales, operating costs, inventory turnover, and accounts receivable aging. The Statistical Service Center, an independent consulting firm, collects and analyzes data under procedures guaranteed to protect confidentiality. William Grace (D. C. Heath) chaired the committee in 1993.

Pubnet

The year 1993 brought continued growth for Pubnet, AAP's electronic database interchange service for book ordering. More than 2,400 bookstores and some 70 publishers are now on the system. Steven Vana-Paxhia (Houghton Mifflin) continued to chair the Pubnet Executive Committee.

Originally established to serve the college publishing community, Pubnet has successfully expanded in recent years to trade, mass market, and university press publishing. Key trade book wholesalers and vendors for the academic library market are Pubnet customers.

The number of orders processed on the network grew by almost 29 percent from 416,000 in 1992 to more than 535,000 in 1993.

Following successful field tests, Pubnet*Express, a new service for Pubnet users that offers instant order acknowledgement and provides immediate shipping status, was launched in May with the shipment of new Pubnet*Express software to the more than 2,000 bookstores on the system.

Pubnet hosted a number of sessions at the American Booksellers Association convention in Miami, including a panel discussion on Pubnet as a competitive solution for booksellers and a luncheon for Pubnet bookseller users.

During 1993 a new version of the Pubnet Permissions software was developed and made available. Pubnet Permissions, AAP's electronic mail system designed for copyright permissions requests, became compatible with Internet in 1993. Through the use of a gateway between General Electric's Electronic Mail Service and Internet, any person with an Internet account can send permissions requests over Pubnet Permissions. Opening of the gateway will further simplify the permissions request process, especially for college faculty and students.

Over the past year, Pubnet has been working with General Electric Information Services and HarperCollins to develop a prototype online information service for booksellers and publishers. This is the first attempt to broaden Pubnet's focus from a distribution service to include an online marketing service for publishers.

In the spring of 1994 Pubnet was to undergo a fundamental change, moving to the recently approved BISAC file formats known as ASC X12. The move is designed to increase the efficiency of electronic trading by putting the industry on a single format.

Washington Office

The AAP Washington office is the industry's front line on matters pertaining to federal legislation and government policy. The Washington staff keeps the membership informed about developments on Capitol Hill and in the agencies of the Executive Branch. The Washington office serves as the industry's voice, communicating publishers' views and concerns to members of Congress, government officials, and the media.

A number of AAP member houses maintain a corporate presence in Washington, either through their own offices or representation by Washington legal counsel. This "AAP Washington Representatives Group," which meets at the AAP Washington office to share information and coordinate legislative strategy, is a valuable resource for the association.

AAP maintains a modest Political Action Committee, allowing industry members to take an active part in the political process by supporting Senate and House candidates who share the industry's concerns on such issues as First Amendment rights, education and library funding, and copyright protection.

Literacy

A major focus of the association's work is to encourage reading and literacy in the United States. The association participated in the first International Publishers Association Reading Seminar, held in Frankfurt October 5, reporting on publisher-supported reading promotion efforts in the United States.

AAP is a member of the national network of "Reading Promotion Partners" supporting the work of the Center for the Book in the Library of Congress. The Association also provides funding for the annual observance of National Book Week in January, which serves to focus national attention on reading and books through the staging of book-related events.

A new literacy initiative undertaken in 1993 joins AAP with Reading Is Fundamental (RIF). With AAP support, RIF began a program in Maryland that takes advantage of a statewide requirement that all high school students earn community service credits in order to graduate. The AAP/RIF project, "Teens as Literacy Leaders," enables students to earn this credit by serving as reading tutors and mentors to younger children. The hope is that, in addition to offering practical tutoring, the high school students can serve as reading role models for the younger children.

Communications and Public Affairs

The primary objective of the communications program is the creation and dissemination of a coherent body of informational materials to provide an accurate picture of the association and its activities, as well as the concerns of its members that have industrywide implications.

The public affairs program disseminates information to the trade press and other media and to the general public about the association, presenting the views of the publishing industry on salient issues.

Both programs work to focus attention on the ways in which the association serves its members and advances the cause of publishing in the United States.

The association's newsletter, the AAP *Monthly Report,* provides information on AAP initiatives, core committee and divisional activities, legislative and regulatory developments, activity in the courts, and international developments of interest to the AAP membership.

American Booksellers Association

828 South Broadway, Tarrytown, NY 10591
914-591-2665

Carol Miles
Director of Research

Early in 1993 the American Booksellers Association (ABA) Board of Directors, under the leadership of President Chuck Robinson of Village Books in Bellingham, Washington, approved a new strategic plan to guide ABA into the twenty-first century. Based on more than a year's worth of meetings, focus groups, telephone surveys, and other activities designed to obtain and integrate member input, the plan outlines ABA's mission and key challenges for the future and offers proposals and strategies to achieve them. The four major themes of the strategic plan are: 1) to create and provide access to information, knowledge, and tools to support business success for member booksellers; 2) to promote efficient operation and standardization within the industry; 3) to fight encroachments against free expression and to build the widest possible market for books; and 4) to ensure a fair and nondiscriminatory trade environment.

Consistent with ongoing member concern about the impact of unconventional aggressive competition for market share, the board acted early in the year to establish a special task force to work with ABA legal counsel and staff to implement those portions of the strategic plan that deal with ensuring a fair and nondiscriminatory trade environment.

Overall, meanwhile, amid signs of a slowly improving economy, retail sales for bookstores continued to increase over the previous year, albeit at a somewhat slower rate than during 1992. Preliminary estimates for 1993—based on figures reported monthly by the Current Retail Trade branch of the Bureau of the Census (U.S. Department of Commerce) and compiled by the ABA Research Department for publication in *Newswire,* ABA's weekly newsletter—indicate that bookstore sales increased an estimated 5.9 percent over 1992, up from an estimated $8.8 billion to approximately $9.3 billion.

Membership

Concurrently, ABA membership figures continued to grow, the total climbing to 8,309 in fiscal 1992–1993. Confidence in the future of retail bookstores was evidenced by the record 1,205 members in the Provisional category of membership held by prospective booksellers—the first time in ABA history that the 1,000-member barrier had been broken. Total bookstore membership reached 4,271, more than 720 bookstores having joined the association in the 1992–1993 fiscal year.

During 1993 the association established a Scientific/Technical specialty membership segment for sellers of books in these categories as well as for others interested in the field. This segment joined the previously established Travel, Science Fiction, Gay/Lesbian, and African-American segments. Specialty segment members receive a quarterly newsletter, assistance in organizing meetings, and a directory of their members.

A Disaster Response Team was formed to engage in outreach to member bookstores that have sustained physical damage due to natural disasters such as floods, earthquakes, and hurricanes. The team is composed of bookstore members who serve on ABA's Association & Membership Development Committee. They offer replacement copies of essential ABA operational tools such as the *Returns Handbook* to stores whose copies have been damaged or lost. Publishers are also notified and asked to extend every courtesy to stores that have been damaged.

1993 Convention and Trade Exhibit

"Bringing the World to Readers" was the theme of ABA's annual Convention and Trade Exhibit, held in Miami Beach, Florida, May 29 through June 1, 1993. Called the largest convention of the year in Dade County by the *Miami Herald,* the event was attended by more than 24,000 booksellers, trade visitors, exhibitors, and members of the press.

More than 7,000 attendees took part in the convention's popular educational component. Organized by ABA's Department of Professional Development and Education, the educational smorgasbord featured 52 panels, roundtables, and presentations. Highlights included sessions on electronic books, competition and the future, foreign-language books, using and understanding financial documents, selling bargain books, visual merchandising, and First Amendment censorship issues.

An educational resource center was a new addition at the 1993 convention. Samples of all the educational materials provided by ABA to its members were on display, and training videos were available for review. In addition, members of the Education Committee were on hand at all times to answer questions and to explain the wide range of services and opportunities available to members.

Adult and children's book authors were in attendance in profusion. In addition to autographing their latest books, they were featured speakers at four book and author breakfasts, two reading rooms, and a mystery salon. Speakers included Jean Craighead George, Maya Angelou, Walter Mosley, Betty Friedan, Oprah Winfrey, Frank Conroy, Patricia Cornwell, William Styron, former British Prime Minister Margaret Thatcher, and Dave Barry.

Outstanding achievements in the book community were honored at a wide variety of convention events. Prominent among them were the American Booksellers Book of the Year (ABBY) presentations honoring the books that booksellers most enjoyed handselling over the previous year. In Miami Beach ABA presented its first-ever ABBY award for children's books to *Old Turtle,* written by Douglas Wood, with watercolors by Cheng-Khee Chee, and published by Pfeifer-Hamilton. The third annual ABBY award in the adult trade category went to Robert James Waller for *The Bridges of Madison County*, published by Warner Books. The four ABBY honor books for 1993 (in alphabetical order) were: *Animal Dreams* by Barbara Kingsolver; *A River Runs Through It & Other Stories* by Norman Maclean; *A Thousand Acres* by Jane Smiley; and *Women Who Run with the Wolves* by Clarissa Pinkola Estes.

The Miami gathering was the last to be totally managed in-house by ABA staff. ABA entered into an agreement early in 1993 with Reed Exhibition Companies, a division of Reed Publishing (USA) Inc., to form a joint venture company that will own and operate the annual ABA Trade Show. Booksellers Show Associates (BSA), the new joint venture company in which ABA holds majority interest, has assumed responsibility for the 1994 Trade Exhibit, which is being managed by Reed's Association Exposition Services of Stamford, Connecticut. The convention portion, however, including the annual membership meeting, educational seminars, hospitality suites, book and author breakfasts, and other events, continues to be handled directly by ABA.

American Booksellers Foundation for Free Expression

In its fourth year of operation the American Booksellers Foundation for Free Expression (ABFFE) continued its vigorous efforts to oppose censorship and to support free expression. A highlight was ABFFE sponsorship of a Socratic dialogue, "The Fine Line," at the 1993 ABA convention. The program featured such notables as Robert Bork, Catharine MacKinnon, Maya Angelou, Terry Anderson, Erica Jong, Michael Medved, John Frohnmayer, Judy Blume, Nicholas Veliotes, Clarissa Pinkola Estes, and others in a frank exchange on First Amendment and free expression issues. The program was moderated by Harvard University Law School's Arthur Miller. A videotape version of the program was also created for use in bookstores, schools, and libraries to help frame discussions on First Amendment issues.

In another major initiative during 1993, ABFFE helped organize the Rushdie Defense Committee USA and ran a full-page advertisement in the *New York Times Book Review* section urging President Clinton to join the effort to pressure the Iranians to end the death threat against Salman Rushdie for the "crime" of writing a book. In addition, thousands of bookstore patrons signed a petition circulated by ABFFE urging the president to meet with Mr. Rushdie. Such a meeting did, in fact, take place at the White House in late November.

ABFFE became a member of the National Coalition against Censorship during 1993 and once again sponsored, together with the American Library Association (ALA), the annual observance of Banned Books Week. The 1993 material featured completely redesigned posters and kits that were adaptable for use by a wide range of bookstores, resulting in the participation of more than 1,000 establishments.

Finally, ABFFE has continued to monitor efforts to interfere with the availability of First Amendment-protected material, a project on which the Media Coalition and FEN (Free Expression Network) and ABA's members and staff have worked cooperatively. In light of the growing debate over violence in the media, the ABFFE board of directors adopted a resolution "to oppose acts of censorship by government in establishing content-based restrictions on access to otherwise protected material."

Education and Professional Development

In addition to the extensive educational component at the ABA convention, the Education Department conducted six booksellers schools in 1993 with a combined attendance of approximately 400 students. Three of the schools were for prospective booksellers, one was a professional school for experienced booksellers, and one was for booksellers specializing in children's books. ABA, jointly with the National Association of College Stores (NACS), also sponsored a general trade booksellers school. Minority grants were once again awarded, in 1993 to ten booksellers, to facilitate their attendance at a booksellers school. Grants covered the full cost of tuition, lodging, meals, and materials for the school selected.

ABA and the Soros Open Society Foundation again jointly sponsored a booksellers school in Eastern Europe. The 1993 school, held in Cluj Napoca, Romania, was taught by three booksellers and one publisher and attracted 105 students from Russia, Moldova, and Romania.

As part of the Education Department's ongoing effort to raise the professional competency of ABA's Booksellers School faculty, a Train-the-Trainer school was offered immediately preceding the Miami convention to enhance the teaching skills of the 12 participants. Attendance at a Train-the-Trainer program is now a requirement for anyone aspiring to become a faculty member for one of ABA's schools or seminars.

The ABA Video Lending Library continued to be popular and a frequently used member resource. Several new videos covering such subjects as customer service, hiring procedures, and effective telephone marketing were added to the video library, bringing the total now available to 19.

Publications

The ABA Publications Department continued to expand its efforts to provide retail booksellers with a wide range of informational and practical books and periodicals. For example, *The American Booksellers Association 1992–1993 Membership Directory* debuted and was offered as a new member benefit. The directory contains a listing of all ABA main bookstore members, categorized by state, as well as a complete guide to ABA volunteers and staff, activities, and services. The 1993–1994 edition of the ever-popular *ABA Book Buyer's Handbook* is more extensive than ever before, containing over 2,000 publisher listings, together with distribution and ISBN indexes and updated information on sources of supply for many products. Further, a project was begun in 1993, in cooperation with the Publisher Relations Committee and the Research Department, that is intended to culminate in production of a supplement to the *Handbook,* which will incorporate more detailed terms and conditions for the major publishers. The supplement will further increase the utility of this volume and its companion *ABA Book Buyer's Returns Handbook.*

Booksellers Publishing Inc. (BPI), the book publishing subsidiary of ABA, continued to expand its list of professional titles for people in the book community. In addition to the titles offered under the Booksellers House imprint (*Parnassus on Wheels* and *The Haunted Bookshop* by Christopher Morley, *Fifty Years in My Bookstore* by Harry W. Schwartz, *Sunwise Turn* by Madge Jenison, and *Operating a Bookstore* by Eliot Leonard), BPI published a new edition of *ABACUS Expanded,* a financial survey of member bookstores compiled by the ABA Research Department. The 1993 edition, based on 1991 operations, contains data collected by Industry Insights Inc. from 199 ABA-member independent booksellers doing business in 232 locations. Balance sheet data and a series of operating ratios are included for the first time in the current edition of the book. Also in 1993 BPI began distribution of *Independent Bookstore Planning & Design,* a new book by renowned bookstore designers Ken White and Frank White. This book, which contains 200 photos and illustrations, is an important resource on planning, building, and remodeling all types of bookstores.

The Publications Department also inaugurated a new quarterly newsletter for members interested in scientific & technical bookselling. The new quarterly joins those previously launched in African-American, science fiction, gay/lesbian, and travel bookselling, respectively. In addition, the Publications Department continued to publish ABFFE's quarterly newsletter, *Free Expression,* and the association's weekly newsletter, *ABA Newswire.*

Throughout the year, the staff of *American Bookseller* magazine worked to fashion editorial content that would help readers both to improve their business practice and to understand better the retailing trends that are shaping the business environment they will face in the years ahead. In each regular issue—as well as in a thirteenth issue, the *Bookstore Source Guide*—the magazine's features covered everything from the "Bookselling Wars" of Chicago and the book industry's "Coming to Terms with Multiculturalism" to candid, in-depth interviews with such figures as Warner Books President Laurence Kirshbaum and Waldenbooks President Charles Cumello. In addition, articles by such leading figures as Jay Conrad Levinson and Don Peppers (Tom Peters's choice for business book author of the year) gave booksellers cutting-edge strategies for successfully competing in the 1990s.

Ever mindful of the expanding role of new media and evolving technology in bookselling, *American Bookseller* established a feature department on new media during 1993; launched "Info Exchange," a free service to help readers considering the purchase of a computerized inventory system; increased coverage of the rapidly changing world of computer publishing; and even began communicating with booksellers and others in the industry via Internet, thereby bringing the magazine even closer to an increasingly diverse readership. *American Bookseller* also debuted a redesign for its expanded editorial departments in 1993. This, together with its focus on special issues such as children's books and small press publishing, continued to bring books and booksellers together. Finally, a special insert featuring a generous excerpt from the ABACUS report was once again mailed to subscribers with the magazine, as was a stand-alone ABA merchandising calendar.

Research

In its continuing effort to provide knowledge that helps booksellers do their jobs better, the Research Department made available to all ABACUS participants— for the first time in 1993—a "Company Performance Report." This document consisted of a computerized printout of the participant's own financial ratios shown alongside the appropriate "industry comparatives." Further, for a nominal fee, participants could request a "report card," which provided a written evaluation of each key ratio, including a description of what the ratio means, its possible uses, and what other areas or ratios affect a given variable.

Other research results published by the department included findings from a reader survey concerning bookseller reactions to promotional materials distributed by publishers and other vendors and, for the second consecutive year, those of a reader survey of booksellers covering various aspects of bookstore magazine sales. Current bookselling statistics, such as retail sales for bookstores, continued to be published regularly in *Newswire,* and the results of pre- and post-holiday consumer surveys on books as gifts conducted by the Wirthlin Group and the Gallup Organization, respectively, were once again released to the press and subsequently reported by a wide variety of trade and consumer media, including *Newswire.*

Two other consumer research studies were undertaken during 1993, both as joint endeavors with other industry groups. For the second consecutive year ABA joined with the Association of American Publishers (AAP) and the Book Industry Study Group (BISG) in the publication of the *1991–1992 Consumer Research Study on Book Purchasing.* The study contained, among other things, information on the demographics of book buyers and types of books purchased. In the other cooperative venture, new in 1993, AAP's Professional and Scholarly Books Division and ABA formed a Direct Marketing Study Group that undertook a joint study. Conducted by the Wirthlin Group, the study will survey end consumers of professional and scholarly books and incorporate data from interviews with booksellers and publishers of the genre. The ultimate goal of the Direct

Marketing Study Group is to increase sales of professional and scholarly books in trade bookstores, to the mutual benefit of booksellers and publishers alike.

Two information modules developed by the Research Department in 1992, "Opening a Bookstore" and "Children's Bookselling," were introduced early in 1993. Also in 1993, two additional modules were developed. Entitled "Audio, Video, and Multimedia Books" and "Statistical Overview of Retail Bookselling," respectively, the new modules will be available in 1994, together with updated versions of the earlier modules. All of the modules were developed based on analyses of records of the large number of requests for technical, reference, and general bookselling information directed to the department.

In addition to carrying out various research projects and studies for internal use by ABA departments and committees in making management decisions concerning development and monitoring of new products and services, the Research Department continued to handle the myriad tasks required to operate and maintain ABA's extensive bookselling and publishing library. The department's staff also further expanded the computerized indexes of both *American Bookseller* and *Newswire* during 1993, and plans were made to increase the amount of both domestic and international reference material available through the library's CD-ROM equipment.

Other Activities

ABA's new Government Affairs Department, created in 1992, was active throughout 1993 in monitoring the potential effect of the various health care reform proposals on the operation of retail bookstores. Proposals requiring employer payment of a fixed percentage of health insurance premiums received particularly close scrutiny. In addition, the Government Affairs Department provided material to bookstores on compliance with the new Family and Medical Leave Act of 1993 and the Americans with Disabilities Act. Efforts to insure bookstore eligibility for government loan programs are also under way. Underscoring its involvement in these and other issues, ABA has become an active participant in the government affairs activities of the National Retail Federation.

Booksellers Order Service (BOS), an ABA subsidiary, continued to offer many diverse products to bookstores through its group buying program. New products introduced during calendar year 1993 include Kermit T-shirts for adults and children, courtesy of Jim Henson Productions; a new "alligator" children's gift-wrapping paper designed by renowned children's illustrator Thacher Hurd; and a new heavyweight totebag optionally bearing the imprint of a bookstore's name and logo. Other items that BOS continues to stock include 3M security strips for booksellers using that system, gift certificates, gift-wrapping paper with a book design, and photodegradable plastic and paper bags imprinted with BOS's definition of a book on one side and of a bookstore on the other. Also available are cotton totebags, recycled paper shopping bags, and T-shirts, each with optional imprinted store name and logo.

ABA, as part of its ongoing program of generic advertising to promote awareness of books and bookstores, continued its sponsorship of "The American Reader," a weekly radio show highlighting books and authors. Hosted by Milton

Rosenberg, the show is carried by more than 150 stations across the country. ABA also began partial underwriting of two additional programs in 1993. One of these, "Tell Me a Story," is a new radio show in which celebrated writers read short stories. The inaugural program on October 5, 1993, featured a recording of the late Raymond Carver reading "What We Talk About When We Talk About Love" and began a 26-week series of shows that is being broadcast on the NPR satellite. Among the authors scheduled for the initial year were Alice Walker, V. S. Pritchett, Amy Tan, and Paul Bowles. The second new recipient of an ABA grant was "First Edition," a half-hour television newsmagazine devoted to books and authors. The show, which will use the funding to produce five new episodes and re-edit a previously produced pilot episode first shown at the Miami Beach convention, aims to air on public television starting in the spring of 1994.

The ABA Publisher Relations Committee continued its work as a conduit through which information can travel between booksellers and their vendors. To this end, the committee conducted 40 meetings with 32 publishers in 1993, presenting them with a range of board-approved issues of mutual interest to member booksellers and their suppliers. These same issues were also presented, in the form of an educational seminar, at the annual meeting of the Association of University Presses and at the Publishing University sponsored by the Publishers Marketing Association. The Publisher Relations Committee also conducted a pilot test of a new Publisher Intern Program, scheduled to debut in 1994, in which publishing industry employees will each spend two and a half days working in a bookstore. Other 1993 activities include the production and distribution of three educational brochures to the publishing community, as well as distribution, in cooperation with the Industry Standardization Committee, of standards approved by the Book Industry Systems Advisory Committee (BISAC) for title abbreviations and "hard copy" invoice.

The Industry Standardization Committee's work plan for 1993, based on the standardization component of ABA's strategic plan, had a two-pronged focus in its continuing quest to identify and resolve ways in which lack of standardization in the book industry is harmful to booksellers and vendors alike. First, the committee continued to work closely with BISAC in proposing, developing, approving, updating, and reacting to standards for paperwork and the exchange of information; BISAC, the organization with paramount responsibility for setting standards for the book industry, was chaired during 1992–1993 by the ABA Liaison to BISAC, also a member of the Industry Standardization Committee. In addition to the aforementioned "hard copy" credit memo standard and Book Industry Standard for Title Abbreviations (including subject/category codes), the committee sent board-approved "hard copy" standards for statement/remittance advice and for an eye-readable indicator of "strippability" (to be placed adjacent to the bar code on mass market paperbacks) to BISAC in 1993. Second, the committee continued its work in encouraging voluntary adoption of BISAC standards by booksellers and publishers alike, to their mutual benefit. To further this aim, the Industry Standardization Committee published an article on standardization in *American Bookseller,* worked closely with the Publisher Relations Committee in distribution of BISAC-approved standards (see above), and undertook a joint

Standard Address Number (SAN) promotion at the 1993 Convention and Trade Exhibit with BISAC and the R. R. Bowker Company, the SAN administrator. [For more information on BISAC, see the article in the Special Reports section of Part 1—*Ed.*]

Finally, the last week of 1993 saw ABA's move to its permanent national headquarters in Tarrytown, N.Y. In addition to ample office space for its expanding activities, the association's new headquarters will contain state-of-the-art facilities for its extensive bookselling and publishing library, as well as for booksellers schools and meetings.

International Reports

International Federation of Library Associations and Institutions

Nancy D. Anderson

Mathematics Librarian and Associate Professor of Library Administration
University of Illinois at Urbana–Champaign

Founded in 1927, the International Federation of Library Associations and Institutions (IFLA) has moved from a primarily European-focused organization to one that is truly international. Its membership is made up of 135 associations, 891 institutions, 180 personal affiliates, and 15 bodies with consultative status in 135 countries. Membership and financial matters were the most pressing concerns for IFLA in 1993. The annual conference, in Barcelona, was attended by a record number of delegates.

Organization

IFLA consists of 32 sections (standing committees) and 14 roundtables that funnel information to eight divisions. Section and roundtable members are elected by association and institutional members, and every two years—in odd-numbered years—section members elect section officers who, in turn, elect division officers. Division chairpersons form the Professional Board, which oversees the program activities of the organization. The Executive Board, which is responsible for general policy, management, finance, and external communications, is also elected every two years.

Underlying the activities of the sections are IFLA's five core programs: Universal Availability of Publications (UAP); Universal Bibliographic Control International MARC (UBCIM); Universal Dataflow and Telecommunications (UDT); Preservation and Conservation (PAC); and Advancement of Librarianship in the Third World (ALP).

To inform divisions, sections, and roundtables of one another's activities, IFLA prepares a Medium-Term Program (MTP) every six years. Once a year the standing committees of the sections, the roundtable executive committees, and the coordinating boards of the divisions are asked to update their work plans and approve them at the IFLA annual conference. This information is then compiled, published, and distributed to IFLA officers and other interested individuals. In this way, all IFLA professional groups are kept up-to-date on one another's work and can note opportunities for cooperative action.

Annual Conference

The annual IFLA conference is the highlight of the association's activities. The 1993 conference (the 59th) was held in Barcelona August 22–28 with the theme "The Universal Library: Libraries as Centers for the Global Availability of Information." This was the organization's largest conference ever, with 3,049 delegates from more than 90 countries attending. The strong showing was due in part to the fact that this was an IFLA election year and therefore a meeting of the association's voting body, the IFLA Council, was scheduled. Barcelona also was seen as an attractive venue; the political uncertainties of Moscow and the high cost of travel to New Delhi had kept many from attending the previous two conferences.

The Barcelona organizing committee, especially Ester Omella and Mercè Figuerola, presented a well-managed conference. There were 93 open program sessions, 17 workshops, and five satellite meetings. A total of 209 papers were presented, with nearly 300 translations. (A complete listing of the papers is available from IFLA headquarters, and copies of the papers are available from the regional clearinghouses.)

At the opening session of the conference, IFLA President Robert Wedgeworth introduced three honorary IFLA presidents: Herman Liebaers, Else Granheim, and Hans-Peter Geh.

Poster sessions (visual rather than oral presentations) by 28 presenters were favorably received, and the Professional Board inaugurated a new program session, the Guest Lecture Series. One session that attracted considerable interest was on Internet. Visits to libraries were scheduled daily and receptions were held each evening (always with lots to eat and drink and sometimes with fireworks or a laser light show). The only negative incidents were a temporary cancellation of programs after a violent thunderstorm knocked out power to much of Catalonia and the level of street crime in Barcelona. Extra security measures were instituted by the City of Barcelona, but only after IFLA Secretary General Leo Voogt broke his wrist and heel in an accident as he chased a purse snatcher.

Marcelle Beaudiquez, IFLA treasurer, told Council that IFLA's financial situation had worsened since 1991, becoming "worrying and requiring appropriate measures." This was due to several factors, among them geopolitical upheavals resulting in loss of dues from national associations in Eastern Europe and the relative stagnation of growth in institutional membership. Council approved a moratorium on dues-in-arrears action and heard plans to undertake a membership campaign. David Clements, Professional Board chairperson, reported on how the board was tackling its enhanced role in coordinating the work of all professional units, including the core programs. Gboyega Banjo, chairperson of the IFLA Fact-Finding Mission to South Africa, spoke on the recommendations of the mission; copies of the report were mailed to the membership after the conference and members were asked to comment. Russell Bowden, acting chairperson of the Publications Committee, reported on the committee's thorough review of what, why, and for whom IFLA publishes. He then asked IFLA members to write IFLA headquarters to express their views on whether the *IFLA Annual* should be discontinued and its contents included in *IFLA Journal.*

Nancy John, chairperson of the Copyright Committee, reported that it had identified three areas where decisions were needed to help define long-term strategy on issues of intellectual property. The Executive Board appointed a permanent copyright adviser, Sandy Norman, in response to the committee's recommendations.

The Executive and Professional boards are also studying the possibility of holding biennial rather than annual conferences and planned to prepare a position paper on that issue for discussion at the 1994 conference in Havana.

Two roundtables were approved by the Professional Board: the Roundtable on User Education and the Roundtable on Women's Issues in Librarianship. New officers of the Professional Board were announced, and outgoing officers were thanked. Council approved a proposal to make Marcelle Beaudiquez, IFLA treasurer, an honorary fellow of IFLA.

Resolutions

Each IFLA conference produces a number of resolutions arising from conference or preconference activities. A general resolution on the destruction of libraries in Croatia and Bosnia-Hercegovina was accepted by Council and forwarded to UNESCO, which has taken some action. A resolution containing nearly 30 recommendations from the IFLA pre-session seminar on school librarianship as well as other resolutions coming from IFLA's professional groups were forwarded to the Professional Board for action. The Copyright Committee resolved to recognize the work of Ross Shimmon on its behalf. A resolution by the Section on Acquisition and Exchange condemned the growing tendency by governments at various levels to impose taxes on library materials, recommending that all library materials be free from taxation. The Section on Library Services to Multicultural Populations urged IFLA to request UNESCO to facilitate and support preservation of the oral tradition of African mother-tongue languages, as part of UNESCO's Memory of the World Project. The same section, along with the Section on Information Technology and the Section on Cataloging, resolved to strengthen IFLA's role in international standards. The Roundtable on Audiovisual Media urged the Council of Europe to include all AV formats in its "Draft Convention to Protect the European AV Heritage." Finally, the Section of Libraries for the Blind asked IFLA's acceptance of and requested its support for the statement on Access for Information for All.

1994 Conference

IFLA's sections and roundtables are planning a full program for the 1994 annual conference in Havana, set for August 21–27. The theme is "Libraries and Social Development." Despite Cuba's economic difficulties, it appears that resources are being allocated to the tourist and convention industry. IFLA headquarters reports that the convention center will offer the best facilities of any IFLA conference yet and that lodging will be good, with reasonable prices. An up-to-date list of the airlines flying to Cuba has been delivered to Cuban embassies around the world to make travel arrangements easier for IFLA delegates. Visas can be obtained from Cuban consulates, in person and on the spot or by mail with very little delay. Although U.S. Department of the Treasury regulations at present forbid the spending of money for tourist, business, and recreational trips to Cuba, many U.S. delegates are determined to attend the conference because they believe these regulations amount to censorship. Some may qualify for one of the exemptions to the regulations. The organizing committee planned to post more information and a registration form on Internet. Registration payment should be made directly to IFLA Headquarters. A one-day tourist excursion follows the conference and is included in the registration fee.

Other Activities

The Professional Board held a retreat, "IFLA Trends," in The Hague April 3–4, 1993. The topic of the retreat was "Developing a Strategic View of IFLA's Program Objectives." Duane Webster, executive director of the Association of Research Libraries (ARL), served as facilitator to the group, composed of Professional Board members, core program directors, and senior IFLA staff. They examined a variety of issues affecting the future development of IFLA, focusing on the role of the Professional Board in determining program priorities and strategies. A brief report of this retreat appears in *IFLA Journal* 19 (1993), pp. 421–422. Building on the results achieved in 1993, IFLA scheduled a follow-up session, "Trends 2," for April 1994 to develop an action plan and timetable.

IFLA's groups held a lively series of meetings during 1993. The IFLA UAP program cosponsored a Workshop on Universal Availability of Publications in Arab-Speaking Countries in Cairo January 12–14, and the following month the thirteenth annual meeting of the Roundtable on Audiovisual Media met in The Hague, bringing together the five nongovernmental organizations involved in audiovisual archiving with UNESCO. The Section of Libraries for the Blind sponsored a training seminar on library services for the blind and visually handicapped in developing countries in Havana during February. The IFLA Division of Bibliographic Control, with the assistance of the IFLA Section for Latin America and the Caribbean, sponsored the first seminar on universal bibliographic control in Rio de Janeiro March 23–26. The third Interlending and Document Supply International Conference was held in Budapest from March 29 to April 1, cosponsored by the IFLA UAP program. IFLA's core programs for ALP and PAC organized the first Pan-African Conference on the Preservation and Conservation of Library and Archives Material in Nairobi June 20–25. Also in June, the IFLA UBCIM program sponsored the first workshop on UNIMARC with CDS/ISIS, with demonstrations of the UNIBASE project.

Awards and Grants

IFLA awarded a number of special grants during the year:

- The Gustav Hoffmann Study Grant, the successor award to its Martinus Nijhoff Study Grant, was offered by K. G. Saur. It allows a librarian in a country in which librarianship is a newly developing profession to study an issue in one or more countries of Western Europe. This year's grant went to Samuel Oke Ogunniyi of Nigeria, to study the use of computers in libraries for acquisition, storing, and dissemination of information.

- The IFLA Jury for the Guust van Wesemael Literacy Prize awarded the 1992 prize to the Public Library Service of Namibia to purchase books for public libraries. This prize commemorates the late IFLA Coordinator of Professional Activities and Deputy Secretary General.
- The Hans-Peter Geh Study Grant, enabling a librarian from the former Soviet Union to attend a conference in Germany or elsewhere, was awarded to Mariko Karo of Estonia, who attended the Barcelona annual conference and presented a paper at the meeting of the Section on Acquisition and Exchange.
- The Dr. Shawky Salem Grant was awarded to Atlaf Alzawawi of Kuwait, who will study advanced cataloging, and to Maud Stephan Hacham of Lebanon, who will study information technology and advanced services.

Recent Publications

Each year, IFLA sections and core programs offer a growing number of useful professional publications. The following were published in 1993:

- *Advanced Reading in Multicultural Countries,* compiled by Krista Talvi and ed. by Kalju Tammaru under the auspices of the Roundtable on Research in Reading. Tallinn, Estonia: National Library of Estonia.
- *Availability of Western Periodical Literature in Polish Libraries,* by Barbara Stefaniak. Boston Spa, Wetherby, UK: IFLA Office for UAP. ISBN 0-7123-2097-0.
- *Continuing Professional Education and IFLA: Past, Present, and a Vision for the Future: Papers from the IFLA CPERT Second World Conference on Continuing Professional Education for the Library and Information Science Professions,* ed. by Blanche Woolls under the auspices of the Roundtable. Munich: K. G. Saur (IFLA Publications, No. 66/67). ISBN 3-598-21794-3.
- *Documentation of Nordic Art—Design, Bibliographies, Databases/ Documentation de l'Art des Pays Nordiques—Design, Bibliographies, Bases de Données: Proceedings for the Art Libraries Satellite Meeting, Stockholm, August 16–19, 1990,* ed. by Charlotte Hanner under the auspices of the Section of Art Libraries. Munich: K. G. Saur (IFLA Publications, No. 65). ISBN 3-598-21793-5.
- *Electronic Data Interchange: An Overview of EDI Standards for Libraries.* Ottawa, Canada: IFLA UDT Office (UDT Series in Data Communication Technologies and Standards for Libraries, No. 4).
- *Guidelines for Legislative Libraries,* compiled by Dermot Englefield under the auspices of the Section of Parliamentary Libraries. Munich: K. G. Saur (IFLA Publications, No. 64). ISBN 3-598-21792-7.

- *Guidelines for Subject Authority and Reference Entries*, prepared by the Working Group on Guidelines for Subject Authority Files of the Section on Classification and Indexing. Munich: K. G. Saur (UBCIM Publications, New Series, No. 12). ISBN 3-598-11180-8.
- *IFLA Communications 1992: A Bibliography of IFLA Conference Papers.* The Hague: IFLA (Professional Reports, No. 36). ISBN 90-70916-44-4.
- *Interlibrary Loan of Alternative Format Materials: A Balanced Sourcebook*, ed. by Bruce E. Massis and Winnie Vitzansky under the auspices of the Section of Libraries for the Blind. Binghamton, N.Y.: Haworth Press (Journal of Interlibrary Loan & Information Supply, Vol. 3, No. 1/2). ISBN 1-56024-394-5.
- *International Cooperation in the Field of Authority Data: An Analytical Study with Recommendations*, English translation by Ruth Webb of the study by Françoise Bourdon. Munich: K. G. Saur (UBCIM Publications, New Series, No. 11). ISBN 3-598-11169-X.
- *OSI for Libraries: From Standards to Services*, ed. by Fay Turner, Paula Tallim, and J. C. Zeeman. Ottawa, Canada: IFLA UDT Office (UDT Series on Data Communication Technologies and Standards for Libraries, No. 3). ISBN 0-9694214-4-3.
- *Packet Radio: Applications for Libraries in Developing Countries.* Ottawa, Canada: IFLA UDT Office (UDT Series on Data Communication Technologies and Standards for Libraries, No. 5).
- *Pautas para Servicios Bibliotecarios para Prisoneros*, ed. by Frances E. Kaiser under the auspices of the Section of Libraries Serving Disadvantaged Persons. Spanish translation of *Guidelines for Library Services to Prisoners*. The Hague: IFLA (Professional Reports, No. 37). ISBN 90-70916-46-0.
- *World Directory of Map Collections*, compiled by the Section of Geography and Map Libraries and ed. by Lorraine Dubreuil. 3rd ed. The Hague: IFLA (IFLA Publications, No. 63). ISBN 3-598-21791-9.
- *World Directory of Parliamentary Libraries of Federated States and Autonomous Territories*, compiled by Section of Parliamentary Libraries and ed. by Ernst Kohl. 1st ed., 2 vol. Bonn: Deutscher Bundestag. ISBN 3-89372-011-1.

Frankfurt Book Fair, 1993: Electronics Arrive But Books Survive

Herbert R. Lottman
International Correspondent, *Publishers Weekly*

John F. Baker
Editorial Director, *Publishers Weekly*

At breakfast on opening morning, a packager demonstrated his product for a table companion on a hand-held reader—an indication of what was in store for visitors to the 45th postwar Frankfurt Book Fair last October.

The fair was preparing its (and everybody's) future, opening the door wide to new media in every shape and form, offering considerable how-to in a daily round of lectures and panels. Some 170 exhibitors from 14 countries were in the new electronic publishing hall. Would fusion between those dissimilar elements—books and bytes—take place?

Once again the traditional print pavilions were thronged (more than 180 would-be exhibitors, mostly German, never got a stand at all). At final count there were 6,167 individual exhibits, up from 1992's 6,096. The U.S. contingent—notoriously one of the complainingest, including more "never again-ers" than are found elsewhere—grew by nearly 7 percent (with 45 more exhibitors; 724 in all). Britain rose by 23 stands (to 859), while French, Italian, and Spanish participation showed significant declines, reflecting the economic realities of "Latin" Europe.

The context, once again, was all-but-universal recession, with near-zero growth in industrial countries one had learned to count on. But in some countries—Japan, for one—glum economic statistics hadn't yet affected the book business, certainly not the translation rights market. Internationally known German imprints were prospering. "There's no crisis here!" Suhrkamp Verlag's Siegfried Unseld insisted. But Germany's trade is still a cottage industry; the fear is that problems will come when the country's unique network of solidly implanted independent booksellers is dismantled by that universal epidemic, soaring downtown rentals.

Visitors from the far side of the Atlantic weren't necessarily affected by the down side, since they were more likely to be meeting the most dynamic of their foreign counterparts, those least affected by business cycles (although Milan agent Susanna Zevi was able to say she was getting better money than ever from Italian publishers, despite economic conditions there—with blind offers of a kind she hadn't had at last year's fair). And a number of publishers got a shot in the arm from Toni Morrison's Nobel Prize, announced smack in the middle of fair week.

Note: Adapted from *Publishers Weekly,* November 1, 1993.

The Electronics Invasion

The posters had warned everybody what to expect this year, and no matter that the electronics hall (Hall 1.1) was a 10-minute walk from the main action in Hall 4. All of the 15,000 square feet available for electronics was booked, and more space is planned on the floor below for the 1994 fair ("There is no way to bring electronics closer—or inside the book fair proper," fair director Peter Weidhaas told *PW*).

Some 550 visitors signed up for seminars and working breakfasts connected to the show. Indeed, one of the surprises was the assiduity with which leading book traders attended two- to three-hour meetings describing their digital future, deserting the booths and aisles of the book fair to do so; and more than 300 fair-goers jammed into the Tuesday pre-fair international rights meeting, devoted this year to problems related to electronic publishing.

Well-attended breakfast presentations included a first demonstration of Philips's striking digital video (the company's John Hawkins said that funding was being sought for a major educational CD-I publishing program in Europe); Elsevier showed its innovative Interactive Anatomy for doctors; and Franklin Electronics described sales of 12 million of its hand-held electronic books, now being distributed through 30,000 stores in the United States and currently in 10 percent of schools in the United Kingdom. Sony spoke of its new Electronic Book Authoring System, a $7,500 tool package that enables publishers to create their own CDs, and said it now has 300 titles worldwide in 17 countries and eight languages for its own platform. A company called Eurotronics described an exclusive Xerox-based technology for compressing information that lowers costs (it already has licenses with Berlitz, Larousse, and Michelin, among others), and Langenscheidt described its work with Sony to expand the German market by use of a CD-ROM translating device that enables the company's dictionaries to be run on various platforms.

One wondered whether two separate fairs were being staged simultaneously this year, one in Hall 1.1. "We spend our lives going to the electronics shows," remarked Mark Pattis of the NTC Publishing Group. "At least they're on our turf this time." NTC had decided to exhibit both in its traditional location in the American section of international Hall 4 and in Hall 1.1. (On the fair's opening day, Pattis finalized an agreement that gives NTC exclusive rights to BBC language-teaching methods—including audiovisual materials—for the U.S. market.) Springer-Verlag was another house with a foot in each world.

At times, however, it did seem as if traditional publishers were shying away from confrontation. Some were placing intermediaries to stand between them and the hardware manufacturers. Penguin's Peter Mayer predicted that electronics specialists will become more like publishers, publishers more like technologists. ("We'll always need editors. The hardware people can't replace them.")

Speaking not as the leading European bibliographical and directory publisher he is but as chairman of the publishers group of the Börsenverein, Munich's Klaus G. Saur called the new media ideal for reference works, insisting that "the function of the publisher does not consist of trading in paper."

A number of electronics activists, such as Voyager, preferred to perform in the bookish atmosphere of the traditional fair pavilions. Random House showed electronic publishing alongside print-and-paper. Dorling Kindersley presented its products, notably a much-admired Microsoft collaboration called Musical Instruments, in both Halls 4 and 1. And in a corner of the U.S.A. Book-Expo sector, downstairs in Hall 4, bookman and attorney Martin Levin introduced trade associates to the miracles of ADAM, a medical image and voice program that also permits manual-quality printouts.

Multimedia wizard Byron Preiss, who has a number of new products up his sleeve (including a Dell book on massage, a "Fashion Field Guide," and a reference series with Ballantine), found the German technology "way ahead of the pack" in visuals, but lamented Philips's determination to stick with its own base, commenting: "If they made it generally available they could own the market."

And Back in Books . . .

It should have been no surprise that the fair seemed quiet for many of the major book traders. "There isn't a lot of energy here, something you feel from the first day," reported New York scout Mary Anne Thompson. "I didn't find out about a single book I hadn't known about before." She was quite familiar with the fair's "hot" book, Knopf's pseudonymous *The Girls,* as well as much-touted thrillers from agents Ed Victor and Fred Hill. London agent Deborah Owen also thought it was a quiet fair, offering as evidence the fact that people came to her begging for new talent. In the perspective of Doubleday's Carol Lazare, this year's Frankfurt was "a kinder, gentler fair." Then what to make of that steamroller Tom Mori and his large team of Japanese assistants and their partners from nearly everywhere else in Asia? For the first time in his career, Mori had placed U.S. titles in the No. 1 spot in all categories of the Japanese bestseller lists—yes, even *The Bridges of Madison County,* in a million-copy sale.

Although English-language product continued to drive the fair, the action seemed to have shifted from the American booths on the ground floor to the British sector a flight above. Agent Fred Hill believed that was because more and more conglomerates chose to exhibit their U.S. imprints with the British.

Commented Milan's Susanna Zevi, "They say it's a quiet fair, but I find it very active." Reported New York's Lynn Franklin, "You have to get to the Agents Center at 8:30 in the morning to get a seat." By fair's end, New York agent Roslyn Targ had signed up eight languages for Henry Roth's gargantuan *Mercy of a Rude Stream* (St. Martin's). New York scout Chandler Crawford of Sanford Greenburger found the level of bidding at this Frankfurt more than satisfactory. At Henry Holt, Bruno Quinson, Wendy Sherman, and Janette Carrier were close to signing up several key countries for Shimon Peres's *The New Middle East* (with Germany, Spain, and France already on board).

Among other American visitors, how busy things seemed sometimes appeared to be a matter of temperament. While Simon & Schuster's Marcella Berger found it "quiet but businesslike—a very serious fair this time," Warner's Larry Kirshbaum, who had skipped the last two Frankfurts, was ebullient. "It seems tremendously successful and energetic," he enthused. "I sense a real quickening of the economic pulse. American sales have been strong lately, and for once we seem to be exporting some of our success. I have a real feeling that

Americans are right on the publishing pulse. Our novelists work in translation better than ever."

St. Martin's Sally Richardson also found interest in American fiction stronger than ever: "People are taking manuscripts back to their rooms and reading them, and that's a big change from recent years." At Hyperion, Bob Miller, who has doubled his list since last year, was busier than usual, and reported strong interest—with preemptive offers from several countries—on a book by a noted medical school professor whose specialty is interviewing murderers right after their crimes. Another very special interest was represented by Jack Jensen of Chronicle Books, who had finally sold foreign rights in all three of the phenomenally successful Griffin and Sabine epistolary books, "though there are some formidable translation problems."

The troubled world economy was good for some publishers. Sally Wechsler, representing Drake Beam Morin, a major international employment and career counseling firm that has recently launched its own book operation, said world interest in these books, many aimed at people about to lose their jobs, had grown greatly. "Several countries, including Japan and some of the Scandinavian countries, are now facing this problem for the first time, and most business publishers don't do such books," she said. Leslie Smith of San Diego's Pfeiffer & Co., publishers of management training books, agreed: "People want to learn to work more efficiently, especially the East Europeans and the Russians."

Dutch Treat

For the first time, a publishing country offering itself as the fair's focal theme made an attempt to link this largely cultural manifestation to the no-nonsense business side of the fair. The spotlight had been turned on Flanders and the Netherlands, and in addition to the usual round of cultural events on and off the fairgrounds there were trade-related aspects to the focus. Just inside the entrance to the Dutch sector of Hall 4, literary imprint J. M. Meulenhoff of Amsterdam displayed posters calling attention to its young Dutch authors, while a nearby information booth staffed by Dutch publishers guided visitors to their particular interests. Meulenhoff's Maarten Asscher said the choice of this region as focal theme began showing effects as early as two years ago, when German publishers started fishing for Dutch authors they could publish in time for the fair.

Frankfurt management, with the help of publisher donors, had again invited leading publishers from Russia and Eastern Europe to the fair (some received air tickets, some hotels only, some free stands). A few had driven all the way—including the Romanian contingent, which arrived in a book-filled minibus. The pavilion devoted to Eastern Europe included a large auditorium for daily panel discussions. The U.S. technical assistance group Pubwatch, with the British Council, sponsored a fairgrounds forum on Western support of the book trades of Russia and Eastern Europe.

One of the most exciting things happening in Eastern European publishing—privatization—could be seen up close at an off-fair gathering of Western investors in PWN, Poland's leading scientific publisher. The firm was born in the heyday of Stalinism, and the Solidarity government had placed it in the hands of

Grzegorz Boguta (who had masterminded underground imprint Nowa and gone to prison for it). "The most exciting experience of my life!" declared Polish-American businessman Richard Knauff, chairman of PWN's supervisory board, whose mission is to transform the Polish house into a "world-class publisher."

As always, the International Group of Scientific, Technical, and Medical Publishers (STM) held its annual assembly at a downtown hotel on the morning preceding the fair (see report below). The International Publishers Association staged an impressive round of meetings. The Motovun Group of publishers and packagers—which no longer meets in its Istrian hilltop town because of the war raging in the former Yugoslavia—held its regular Sunday morning breakfast. At another hotel breakfast, Jerusalem Book Fair alumni editorial fellows were joined by some of their seniors (including Peter Mayer of Penguin, Bruno Quinson of Holt, Monika Schoeller of Fischer, Michael Naumann of Rowohlt, and Lothar Menne of Hoffmann & Campe) for a moment of nostalgia.

As always, the fair day was lengthened—sometimes until midnight—by the parties; each fairgoer had a list of "musts." The Bertelsmann receptions are usually among them, along with the Saturday night Heyne bash. This year Americans were invited back to the traditional Reader's Digest party. One of the biggest one-shot events was the self-celebration of his 25th Frankfurt by Bonnier publisher Karl Otto Bonnier.

It wasn't the happiest of fairs; the next one (October 5–10, 1994) may be more joyous; the focal theme will be Brazil.

STM Tackles the Publisher's Right

Herbert R. Lottman
International Correspondent, *Publishers Weekly*

If the world were as it should be, the general assembly of the International Group of Scientific, Technical, and Medical Publishers (STM) would be *the* event of the Frankfurt Book Fair, representing as it does the top half of the industry—heads of houses whose aggregate balance sheets would blow away all but the giants of general trade. At this year's gathering, the 25th, the mood seemed buoyant.

There are now 117 member companies, and "I'm personally convinced that our role is growing every year," declared STM's chairman, Frans van Eysinga, until now head of the Wolters Kluwer Academic group, henceforth director of Wolters Kluwer U.S. He remains chairman of STM from his New York base, while STM moves its offices from a cramped canal house in Amsterdam to more ample quarters in Amersfoort.

Committee Work

Much of STM's year-round work takes place in committees. In the copyright committee, now chaired by Lynette Owen of Britain's Longman Group, members

Note: Adapted from *Publishers Weekly,* November 8, 1993.

hammer out policy with respect to cooperation with their countries' rights reproduction organizations, and other problems inherent in moving into electronic
publishing. The committee was instrumental in preparing "The Publisher in the
Electronic Age," a position paper drafted by general counsel Charles Clark for
the International Publishers Copyright Council (IPCC).

The marketing committee, in the charge of Malik Lechelt of Germany's
Georg Thieme Verlag, stages training seminars in the United States and Europe.
An innovations committee, headed by Herman Frank of Elsevier Sequoia, runs an
annual seminar in London (this year's topic is networking). Chaired by Herman
Pabbruwe of Kluwer Academic Publishers, the library relations committee bird-
dogs potential conflicts with librarians over new publishing technologies, pricing, and standardization. STM's only committee organized on regional lines, the
Iberoamericano chapter chaired by Claudio Rothmuller of Brazil's Campus,
mounts panels and marketing seminars both in Spain and in Latin America, often
linked with regional book fairs.

A major event this year, the STM conference for heads of houses and policymakers called STM 2000, is to include discussion of updating the group's objectives in the light of new technologies.

Legal Implications of Creative Role

Meanwhile at Frankfurt, the general assembly was providing food for thought
through a panel on the legal implications of the creative role of the publisher, a
session presided over by Sara Finnegan of Williams & Wilkins (formerly STM's
chairperson). "It is not at all simple anymore," she warned in her opening
remarks; publishers can no longer take their rights for granted, and often they
don't even know which rights they control. She urged a close reading of Charles
Clark's IPCC position paper; indeed, the next speaker was Clark himself, who
addressed the "publisher's right," promising that much energy over the next two
years would be devoted to defining it. Clark quoted the Dutch Copyright Society,
which uses the term "electronic fixation" to define digital publishing, and insisted that the publisher holds the exclusive right to authorize what the society calls
"electronic disclosure." The fear, added Clark, is that some "author-biased" governments might ignore the publisher's right.

Jon Baumgarten of Proskauer, Rose, Goetz & Mendelsohn, former general
counsel of the U.S. Copyright Office, was introduced to the panel as the man
who fought through the Texaco case. He made it clear that the American publishing community in general, American STM publishers in particular, back the
international STM position. He did worry that talk of neighboring rights could be
"troublesome," in that it implied something other than copyright was being discussed. Karel Leeflang of Elsevier Science Publishers thought that any new protection should not be limited to digital products. He recommended "strategic
alliances" with authors and end users—customers, distributors—"because in this
new environment there's a lot to learn and we'll learn faster together."

The final speaker was Charles Ellis, CEO of John Wiley and chairperson of
the Association of American Publishers; he was there to announce that U.S. publishers have not been "on the outside, sniping," although he admitted that

American reticence was one reason it had taken so long to attain today's level of cooperation. Speaking as a "multinational" publisher, Ellis said that preference had always been given to enforcement of existing national copyright laws without fundamental modifications because "we didn't see the need for them." In the past the notion of neighboring rights had worked against the copyright owner; indeed, in both the film and recording industries it had been used to withhold compensation to U.S. copyright holders in world markets, and there was concern that defining such a right might lead to a more cumbersome system, when all parties now call for greater simplicity.

Defining Publisher's Right

There had been fear, said Ellis, that a "publisher's right" could conceivably limit the ability of copyright holders to protect their rights and recover compensation for use of their works until the United States adopted an equivalent neighboring right, "a step that could well be considered wholly unnecessary or politically unattainable." But the new approach to legal protection of the creative role of the publisher, as outlined by Charles Clark and Jon Baumgarten, offers a happier alternative. "It is focused on protection in the context of electronic uses, and pledges that whether a new provision is adopted as part of the national copyright laws or as a new neighboring right, it will still be extended to all the signatories of Berne, not just to those who have an equivalent form of protection." The recommendation had been formulated in an IPCC resolution recently adopted by the World Intellectual Property Organization (WIPO) board of governors as part of its biennial program for 1994–1995; Ellis urged all STM members to support IPCC's position.

Canadian Library Trends in 1993

Michael Williamson
Head, Library Development Centre
National Library of Canada

Bonnie Oakes
Liaison Officer (Student)
Library Development Centre
National Library of Canada

Canadian libraries have again faced a number of challenges over the past year. Although the very serious recession showed some signs of relenting, there was no wholesale recovery that could alleviate the economic stress on Canadian society in general. The library community therefore faced familiar trends—shrinking budgets, demands from users for a wide range of both new and traditional services, user fees, a renewed emphasis on resource sharing, a notable increase in censorship, and the pervasive and powerful influence of technologies that saw increased use of Internet and networked information in general, the burgeoning of community-based networks, and related information policy issues at all levels of government and in the private sector. Canada held a federal election in 1993, and a new Liberal majority government took office; from the onset, this new government made it clear that it was committed to establishing a Canadian information infrastructure that would not only relate to the National Information Infrastructure (NII) in the United States, but would clearly address Canadian concerns from a public policy perspective and from an economic perspective. The new government made it clear that it was supporting the CANARIE initiative (Canadian Network for the Advancement of Research, Industry, and Education), introduced by the previous government. This network will upgrade the current CA*net backbone network and will be crucial to the success of the information superhighway in Canada.

Canadian librarians have therefore been organizing—as their counterparts in the United States have done through the American Library Association (ALA) and other associations—in order to ensure that their voices are heard and reflected in the development of related public policy.

Regional Trends

Two unifying factors that cut across practically all sectors of Canadian society were the need to cut public deficits at all levels of government and the need for jobs—unemployment continued to top 11 percent nationally. Canada is a federation of regions that are quite distinct, particularly economically. Only the British Columbia economy continued to grow and prosper, although by year's end there were signs that the manufacturing sector in Eastern Canada was showing sparks of life. The potential impact of the North American Free Trade Agreement (NAFTA) remains to be seen.

The information, media, and technology economy continued to grow, however. Governments wanted to make a commitment to rapid growth of the information infrastructure without over-regulating or erecting unnecessary barriers. The province of New Brunswick appointed a cabinet minister responsible for the development of the superhighway. Other provinces such as British Columbia—the most "connected" province in the country—had a number of initiatives that supported the growth of the information infrastructure. A number of other provinces followed suit in varying degrees.

Parallel to these developments were the concerns of public policy groups, including librarians. Librarians in all regions expressed concern over equitable and affordable access, copyright, regulation, standards, privacy, gender issues, verification of networked information, and future roles and responsibilities. The Community Networks, or Freenets (of which seven are operational at the present time and up to 50 are under development), also organized and held the first International Community Networks Conference at Carleton University in Ottawa in August. Over 200 people attended. "Freeneters" were active in expressing their public policy views from a grassroots democracy perspective.

Resource Sharing

Due to economic uncertainty, there has been tremendous growth and interest in resource sharing. Interlibrary loan (ILL) traffic has increased dramatically world-wide, and numerous national, regional, and local projects are under way across Canada. In British Columbia, the Greater Vancouver Library Federation has become "InterLINK." The new organization comprises 12 autonomous public libraries in the Lower Mainland and allows residents access to the full range of services and materials available in the participating branch libraries. In the Yukon, a new association called the Information Providers is under development. The group plans to promote professional development and resource sharing in order to be less dependent on libraries outside the Yukon. Pilot projects include a Union List of Serials and a Union List of Professional Literature. Electronic interlibrary loan and document delivery are creating new opportunities. The problems of searching multiple databases are being resolved as the American National Standards Institute (ANSI) Z39.50 protocol standard is implemented. The National Library of Canada has taken a leadership role by incorporating a new ILL system using the interface AMICUS Z39.50/SR searching module. This allows both librarians and users to verify citations and locate needed materials more easily. Efficiency will be the key to successful service, as librarians must compete with commercial document providers.

Major Technology Projects

A number of projects are under way that could have a significant impact on the future of librarianship in Canada. Aside from the CANARIE initiative mentioned above, there are a number of multimedia network projects that range from "virtual library" scenarios to small networks that carry a variety of graphic, textual, and sound information between such institutions as hospitals and universities. These networks, most of which are in pilot project mode, will eventually connect with the superhighway and provide wide access for users. Many libraries are experimenting with everything from basic innovation in library automation to multimedia projects. Interactive CD-ROM is very popular and users have made clear that they require access to Internet at their local library or via their local library. Certainly the growth of Freenets has accelerated end-user demands for access to the wider spectrum of networked information. Libraries made success-ful inroads into gopher, Mosaic, WWW, and other locator tools. The National Library of Canada has produced a number of related guides, such as "Dial-up Internet Access Providers in Canada," to help libraries to connect to Internet. Some particularly noteworthy initiatives are outlined below:

- The National Library of Canada's AMICUS database. Throughout the development of AMICUS, National Library user representatives have been on the project team to ensure the applications reflect the needs of external clients. The system supports library operations in ILL, cataloguing, reference, and collection development. The system was programmed during the summer of 1993, and will be operational after an extensive period of system testing and user training in 1994. AMICUS will permit users to access through a "graphical user interface" viewing data through multiple windows on a single screen.

- In the United States, the National Research and Education Network (NREN) plans to upgrade and expand the existing network infrastructure by 1996. CANARIE (the Canadian Network for the Advancement of Research, Industry, and Education) is Canada's corresponding initiative. Information is becoming more communal, and this project creates an intermediary with the ability to connect users to knowledge, striving to expand Canada's telecommunications infrastructure. CANARIE's information highway will be capable of carrying voice, text, data, graphics, and video services to and from all Canadians. An integrated information highway will ensure that Canada remains competitive globally, and provides ready access to the best resources in Canada and in other countries. Government and industry are working together to finance, build, operate, and maintain the project.

- Freenet developments. The National Capital Freenet was very active in 1993 and organized the first International Community Networks Conference. The Toronto Freenet will be operational in early 1994, and other cities and towns in Ontario are planning Freenets. British Columbia is especially involved in Freenet development. The Victoria Freenet is operating, and others are planned in Trail, Vancouver, Prince George, the Sparwood-Fernie area, and the Squamish-Whistler-Pemberton area.

- Schoolnet. Schoolnet is an ambitious initiative of Industry and Science Canada (a large federal government department). The goal of Schoolnet is to have all 17,000 schools in Canada online and connected by 1997. Library information is heavily represented in Schoolnet.

Planning Information Policy

In response to new technology and more limited funding, libraries have been assessing their long-term plans for public service. A steady decline in funding has been coupled with an increased demand for a higher level of service. The new chief executive officer of the Toronto Public Library, Gabriele Lundeen, has assumed a leadership role in this area. Streamlining operations and moving toward the electronic publication are two mainstays of a plan formed on the basis of meetings with all concerned parties at one of the country's largest public libraries. Pilot projects in 1993 included an automated phone renewal system, and the 3M Self Checkout system at one branch. Planning for a project based on a full-text database of magazines is under way.

Reports on the National Summit on Information Policy have been published. The goal of the summit—which brought together government, the private sector, writers, publishers, and associations—was to define the effects of a national information policy on the technological changes taking place in Canadian society. Four themes were discussed, arising from briefs submitted prior to the summit: "Achieving Equitable Access," "Developing the Human Potential," "Strengthening the Infrastructure," and "Maximizing the Economic Benefits." Five main points emerged:

- Support for privacy principles
- Creation of new education and training requirements
- The need to offer new technologies and market them successfully
- The need for a National Policy Board to coordinate policies and government agencies
- The need for new vision and strong leadership from government

Librarians at the conference urged government to fund and mandate libraries as focal points for public access to electronic highways. Some library delegates felt the agenda focused on information as a commodity, rather than as the foundation of democracy.

Representatives from British Columbia, the Maritime provinces, and the Northwest Territories were more critical of the format than those from central Canada. Librarians from these areas felt that there was a lack of public interest, awareness and understanding of the modern library community. However, the summit was a discussion forum and did not issue a final resolution. Participants will take the recommendations and set their own agendas for action.

Censorship

Censorship has continued to increase in Canada. Trustees of the public library in Thunder Bay, Ontario, were so concerned about censorship activities in their community that they decided to produce a video about censorship and distribute it widely. Anti-censorship groups and several Canadian booksellers were angered when Canada Customs officials detained several hundred books and magazines. (Officials are able to detain material indefinitely, and the review process can take up to two years.) The action seemed to target small publishers and minority viewpoints. In response, the Book and Periodical Council, the Canadian Booksellers Association, and Censorstop organized a letter campaign aimed at Revenue Minister Otto Jelinek. The Forum on Censorship and Intellectual Freedom is a new electronic discussion group serving as a national registry of censorship challenges in Canada. It is an open forum for faculty, librarians, teachers, and interested international subscribers.

Services for Persons with Disabilities

As a participant in the National Strategy for the Integration of Persons with Disabilities, the National Library administers two initiatives. The first is under development and involves a program to encourage alternate format publishing. No information is available yet on the number of Canadians who are print-impaired, but initial consultations have been held with publishers, librarians, and vendors. The Adaptive Technology for Libraries Program continues and 21 libraries across the country will receive 1993–1994 grants. More than $150,000 will be given for the purchase of equipment that will provide direct access to special format materials. Recipients include: the University of Manitoba Libraries, Winnipeg; the Library Resource Centre, Seneca College of Applied Arts and Technology, North York; Bibliothèque municipale de Saint-Laurent, Saint-Laurent; and the Halifax City Regional Library, Halifax.

Construction Projects

The past year has seen very few new construction projects. There is a new public library building in Reston, Manitoba. In Toronto, an extension was approved for the Metropolitan Toronto Reference Library. British Columbia has several projects planned: a new building is under construction in Port Moody, and a new Humanities and Social Sciences Library is scheduled at the University of British Columbia. Work continues on the new central public library for Vancouver. Plans currently include a day-care centre, natural light for all staff work areas, and a roof garden. The major sources of funding will be city borrowing, the municipal Property Endowment Fund, sale of the existing site, a contribution from the federal and provincial governments, and a corporate and public fundraising campaign. The design is flexible in nature, and anticipates a period of rapid change. This community project has generated tremendous support and enthusiasm.

Library Education and Employment Trends

Library schools have been under pressure from university administrations to be more competitive, more broadly based in terms of training and skill enhancements, and more contemporary. The influx of other disciplines and the trends toward career marketability and interdisciplinary studies have converged to bring about changes in degree names, curricula, and school affiliations. Special-interest groups are also bringing changes at several library and information faculties. At the University of Western Ontario, women's studies are having a significant impact on the curriculum. The University of Toronto is considering a name change to Master of Information Studies and schools are integrating computer applications into traditional core classes in hopes of reflecting the job market more effectively. The program at Dalhousie University in Nova Scotia is facing closure or amalgamation with other programs such as Business Administration. School alumni and current students started a letter campaign to the university administration, the premier, and members of the provincial legislature. It appears that this campaign was successful.

The past year offered limited opportunities for new graduates. There was a significant loss of entry-level positions. The number of graduates finding full-time permanent library positions was down, and the number finding any type of library employment also fell. Graduates found themselves in contract positions and in non-traditional related employment such as small software companies and information management companies. There was also a trend towards graduates leaving Canada and finding library work in the United States.

Part 2
Legislation, Funding, and Grants

Legislation

Legislation and Regulations Affecting Libraries in 1993

Carol C. Henderson

Director, Washington Office, American Library Association

In its first year in office, the Clinton administration proposed an ambitious technology plan and National Information Infrastructure (NII) agenda, and created an extraordinary climate for change, increasing its chances for succeeding in much of this agenda. The new administration recognized the societal impact of its proposed "information superhighway," but was sketchy on actions required to ensure that it serves a societal good.

While the administration highlighted the role of libraries in its NII documents, it also delivered a serious threat to several federal library programs, including the funds libraries are using to make their resources available electronically. Once again it was up to Congress, after a roller-coaster series of ups and downs, to restore library program funds to approximately previous levels.

The administration's agenda included the improvement of access to government information. The Government Printing Office (GPO) Electronic Access Act was signed into law in June. An earlier Senate version had been sponsored by then-Senator Al Gore. However, in September, the report of the vice president's National Performance Review was at odds with the GPO Electronic Access Act, recommending a shift of printing authority to individual federal agencies with no provision for free distribution of government information to the public.

Other pieces of the administration's agenda were partway through the legislative process at year's end. These included bills for networking technology applications in education, health care, libraries, and government information dissemination; and for pilot projects to assist community institutions such as libraries to connect to networks and improve service delivery.

Funding

President Clinton submitted his first budget request on April 8, and it was a disappointment for those who welcomed his campaign statement about supporting Department of Education library programs. While the fiscal 1994 budget proposed increasing the Library Services and Construction Act (LSCA) Title I public library services by 14 percent, and level-funding LSCA III interlibrary cooperation and resource sharing, it would have eliminated three other currently funded LSCA titles, as well as all Higher Education Act (HEA) library programs.

By the time library supporters arrived on Capitol Hill on April 20 for the annual Library Legislative Day during National Library Week, Representative Dale Kildee (D-Mich.) was leading a campaign to restore funding for the library programs proposed for elimination in the administration's budget. Kildee sponsored a joint letter requesting funding for all library programs at current-year levels. By early May, 84 members of the House had signed on to the Kildee letter to the chairman of the House Appropriations Subcommittee on Labor, Health and Human Services, and Education.

Less than a month later, the House Appropriations Committee, searching for funds to pay for the administration-proposed summer jobs stimulus package, approved a supplemental appropriations bill that removed all FY 1993 funds for a number of education programs, including two HEA library programs and LSCA VI library literacy projects. All three programs were only weeks away from sending out awards. (The committee had asked the administration to propose specific program cuts to fund the stimulus package. When the administration declined, the committee focused on cuts the administration had proposed in the FY 1994 budget.) The House passed this measure, but the Senate version funded the president's summer jobs program by using $500 million appropriated for a program that was never authorized. House-Senate conferees followed the Senate lead and included no cuts in education and library programs.

While this threat to FY 1993 funding was being averted, the appropriations committees were acting on FY 1994 library funding. The House-passed version of H.R. 2518 contained current-level funding for all LSCA and HEA library programs, except that no funds were included for LSCA V, Foreign-Language Materials Acquisition. On September 29 the Senate passed H.R. 2518 with only one library program change—an increase of $2.4 million in LSCA II, Public Library Construction. House-Senate conferees split the difference, leaving LSCA II with $17,792,000, a 7.3 percent increase over FY 1993, and LSCA V with no funds. Table 1 lists final amounts for library and related programs.

Further threats to library funding were emerging, however. A major priority of the administration, and of a majority of the newly elected legislators, was to address the deficit. In addition to a jobs stimulus package, the administration proposed a deficit reduction bill that would reduce program expenditures, cut entitlements, and increase some taxes. The deficit reduction package was hotly debated and squeaked through Congress with the slimmest of margins just before the August recess.

In order to obtain passage, the president made promises to a number of legislators to allow further cuts to be voted on in the fall. These promises set the stage for an amendment offered by Representatives Tim Penny (D-Minn.) and John Kasich (R-Ohio) that included such draconian cuts in discretionary programs that it forged one of the most unusual lobbying alliances of the year to defeat it.

By the end of September it was clear that all HEA library programs as well as LSCA II and VI were targeted for rescission by the vice president's National Performance Review report. Education and library programs were singled out for $3.7 billion worth of cuts or redirection. With much work by the Committee for Education Funding, a major coalition of education groups in which the American

Table 1 / **Appropriations for Federal Library and Related Programs, FY 1994**
(figures in thousands)

Library Programs	FY 1993 Appropriation	FY 1994 Authorization	FY 1994 Clinton Request	FY 1994 Appropriation
El/Sec Education Act I, Chap. 2 (incl. school libraries)	$458,413	needs new auth	$435,461	$394,696
GPO Superintendent of Documents	29,082	necessary sums	33,707	29,082
Higher Education Act				
Title II-A: College Library Technology and Cooperation	3,873	such sums	0	3,873
Title II-B: Library Education	4,960	such sums	0	4,960
Title II-B: Research and Demonstration	2,802	such sums	0	2,802
Title II-C: Improving Access to Research Library Resources	5,808	such sums	0	5,808
Title VI: Section 607 Foreign Journals	982	such sums	0	0
Library of Congress	334,316[1]	2 USC 131	364,352[2]	331,864[1]
Library Services and Construction Act	128,626	such sums	114,749	128,866
Title I: Public Library Services	83,227	such sums	95,000	83,227
II: Public Library Construction	16,584	such sums	0	17,972
III: Interlibrary Cooperation	19,749	such sums	19,749	19,749
IV: Indian Library Services[3]	—	—	—	—
V: Foreign Language Materials	968	such sums	0	0
VI: Library Literacy Programs	8,098	such sums	0	8,098
National Agricultural Library	17,715	7 USC 3125a	17,915	18,155
National Commission on Libraries and Information Science	889	such sums	904	904
National Library of Medicine and MLAA	116,743	42 USC 275	116,679	119,981

[1]Includes authority to obligate $24.2 million in receipts.
[2]Includes authority to obligate $24.4 million in receipts.
[3]Funded at 2% of appropriations for LSCA I, II, and III.

Table 1 / Appropriations for Federal Library and Related Programs, FY 1994 (cont.)
(figures in thousands)

Library Programs	FY 1993 Appropriation	FY 1994 Authorization	FY 1994 Clinton Request	FY 1994 Appropriation
Library-Related Programs				
Adult Education and Literacy	$304,718	such sums	$315,707	$304,908
Bilingual, Immigrant, Refugee Education	225,745	needs new auth	232,251	240,155
ESEA Chapter I (Disadvantaged Children)	6,698,601	needs new auth	7,099,770	6,914,112
Education of Handicapped Children (state grants)	2,718,175	formula based	2,877,494	2,858,973
Educational Partnerships	4,136	needs new auth	2,120	0
Educational Research	73,984	needs new auth	90,750	78,000
Eisenhower Math and Science Education	246,016	such sums	252,658	250,998
Even Start	89,123	such sums	110,000	91,373
HEA Title III: Developing Institutions	203,332	such sums	208,823	212,870
HEA Title IV-C: College Work-study	616,508	such sums	526,941	616,508
HEA Title VI: International Education	49,283	such sums	48,301	52,283
Inexpensive Book Distribution (RIF)	10,029	needs new auth	10,029	10,300
National Archives and Records Administration	160,045	necessary sums	189,182	190,232
National Center for Education Statistics	77,850	such sums	125,000	77,850
National Endowment for the Arts	174,460	needs new auth	174,593	170,228
National Endowment for the Humanities	177,413	needs new auth	177,491	177,491
National Historical Publications and Records Commission	5,000	needs new auth	4,000	5,250
Postal Revenue Forgone	121,912	39 USC 2401	91,434	91,434
Postsecondary Education Improvement Fund	15,872	such sums	17,872	17,372
Star Schools (ESEA IX)	22,777	needs new auth	27,000	25,944
Women's Educational Equity	1,984	such sums	1,984	1,984

Library Association (ALA) participates, the administration was persuaded to remove all education and library cuts from its proposed deficit reduction legislation (H.R. 3400, the Government Reform and Savings Act of 1993).

However, this "reinventing government" report served as a primer for budget cutters on both sides of the Hill. The Penny–Kasich proposal referred to above included rescission of all FY 1994 funds for LSCA II, and would eliminate the title altogether from the statute. Belatedly, the administration and congressional leaders realized the depth of support for Penny–Kasich and the deep cuts it would impose on discretionary programs over five years.

Thus was born a loose coalition of all those parties who would suffer the most under Penny–Kasich—education, senior citizens, the Department of Defense and defense contractors, housing advocates, and every other part of government affected by the proposed cuts, including the administration. In the days before adjournment, the administration hastily crafted a substitute that was incorporated in a revised version of H.R. 3400. The House-passed H.R. 3400 included a reduction of $8,500,000 in Department of Education salaries and expenses, and a cut of $900,000 from the Library of Congress (LC). The measure also incorporated proposed changes to the Depository Library Program and GPO. The Senate did not act on the bill before the end of the session.

Copyright and Intellectual Property Issues

Copyright Reform Act

ALA and seven other library and scholarly organizations submitted a statement for House judiciary subcommittee hearings in March on H.R. 897, the Copyright Reform Act. Title I of the bill would remove two of the three incentives for registration of claims and deposit of copyrighted works, would move the Register of Copyrights from appointment by the Librarian of Congress to appointment by the president, and remove from the Librarian of Congress any authority over Copyright Office regulations and staff. The ALA statement noted that the bill had the potential to disrupt longstanding and productive partnerships, and should not be acted upon without a thorough investigation of its impact and its costs.

In response to the legislation, the Librarian of Congress in May appointed a 20-member advisory group to look at possible improvements to the copyright registration and deposit process. This Advisory Committee on Copyright Registration and Deposit (ACCORD) is cochaired by Barbara Ringer, now acting Register of Copyrights, and Robert Wedgeworth, now university librarian at the University of Illinois, Urbana–Champaign. They submitted their report on the first phase of their work to the Librarian of Congress on September 15.

The comparable Senate subcommittee held a hearing on S. 373, the Senate version of the Copyright Reform Act, on October 19. Robert Oakley, representing the American Association of Law Libraries (AALL), testified on behalf of AALL, ALA, the Association of Research Libraries (ARL), the National Humanities Alliance, and the Special Libraries Association (SLA). Oakley said the legislation puts the unrivaled collections of LC at risk by removing significant incentives for voluntary registrations and deposit. Oakley, a member of ACCORD, noted that the panel was divided on the question of repealing sections

411(a) and 412 of the Copyright Act. He indicated many ACCORD members thought its recommendations were useful in and of themselves, but weaker than the inducements to registration and deposit in the current system. The House passed a revised version of H.R. 897 in November; the Senate had not acted on S. 373 at the end of the session.

Intellectual Property and NII Hearing

More than 25 witnesses with a variety of personal and organizational points of view testified at the November 18 public hearing on intellectual property issues involved in the National Information Infrastructure initiative. The hearing was held by the Working Group on Intellectual Property of the Information Policy Committee of the administration's Information Infrastructure Task Force. Bruce Lehman, assistant secretary of commerce and commissioner of patents and trademarks, and chair of the working group, presided at the all-day event.

Robert Oakley testified on behalf of AALL, ALA, the Association of Academic Health Science Library Directors, the Association of American Universities, ARL, CAUSE, the Coalition for Networked Information, EDUCOM, the Medical Library Association (MLA), the National Association of State Universities and Land-Grant Colleges, the National Coordinating Committee for the Promotion of History, and SLA. Oakley commented on the specific questions asked by the working group, and stated the need to reaffirm that the rights granted to educators and to libraries and their users apply in the electronic environment as they have in the paper environment. John Masten, executive vice president of the New York Public Library, also testified, emphasizing democratic access to information.

Software Lending by Libraries

The Copyright Office was preparing a required report for Congress at year's end on the extent to which the Computer Software Rental Amendments Act of 1990 had achieved its intended purpose with respect to lending by nonprofit libraries. The act permits nonprofit libraries to lend computer programs for nonprofit purposes, provided that each copy lent by the library bears a warning of copyright in accordance with regulations prescribed by the Register of Copyrights. In July the Copyright Office sought public comment; library groups were among those responding.

Government Information

GPO Access Act

On June 8 President Clinton signed into law S. 564, the Government Printing Office (GPO) Electronic Access Act, making it PL 103-40 and assuring that GPO's role in distributing information electronically will increase. A statement released by the president said that "this important step forward in the electronic dissemination of federal information will provide valuable insights into the most effective means of disseminating all public government information."

The law establishes a means of enhancing electronic public access to a wide range of federal electronic information. Under the GPO Access legislation, the Superintendent of Documents is required to

- Provide a system of online access to the *Congressional Record,* the *Federal Register,* and other appropriate publications
- Maintain an electronic directory of federal electronic information
- Operate an electronic storage facility for federal electronic information

The GPO Access System will be available without charge to depository libraries; other users will be charged approximately the incremental cost of dissemination.

The legislation that became the GPO Access Act built on the consensus developed when the House passed a similar bill in the fall of 1992. That bill was a refinement of the original GPO WINDO/Gateway bills introduced in the 102nd Congress, and strongly supported by ALA, the Taxpayers Assets Project, and other organizations, most of them members of the ALA-initiated Coalition on Government Information.

OMB Circular A-130

Office of Management and Budget (OMB) Circular A-130, "Management of Federal Information Resources," was issued on June 25. The revised circular incorporated new policies for managing government information that encourage agencies to use electronic technologies to improve public access. Sally Katzen, administrator of OMB's Office of Information and Regulatory Affairs, said that the revision "will help bring the federal government information into the information age. This is a major step toward realizing the vision of a government that uses technology better to communicate with the American people."

Of particular note was OMB's change in the restrictive interpretation of the definition of "government publication" in its April 1992 draft circular, to which the library community had strenuously objected. In the newly issued circular, agencies are to establish procedures to ensure compliance with the law requiring that government publications be made available to depository libraries through GPO. OMB now said agencies shall "provide electronic information dissemination products to the Government Printing Office for distribution to depository libraries."

Further, OMB recognized that "Depository libraries are major partners with the Federal Government in the dissemination of information and contribute significantly to the diversity of information sources available to the public. They provide a mechanism for wide distribution of government information that guarantees basic availability to the public. Executive branch agencies support the depository library program both as a matter of law and on its merits as a means of informing the public about the government."

National Performance Review

Trying to implement some of the National Performance Review (NPR) recommendations, the administration in late October sent Congress H.R. 3400, the Government Reform and Savings Act. Among other things, Title XIV of H.R.

3400 would have dismantled GPO and made each agency procure its own printing and be responsible for dissemination to depository libraries.

When the House passed H.R. 3400 on November 22, it approved an entirely different version of Title XIV. In a move that would restructure the Depository Library Program administered by GPO, the House bill transferred to the Library of Congress the position and all functions of the Superintendent of Documents. The Senate Committee on Rules and Administration planned hearings on the bill and related NPR issues in February 1994.

Libraries Subject of Hearing

On April 21 the Joint Committee on the Library held a hearing on the Library of Congress and its link to the nation's state and local libraries. Scheduled for the day following Library Legislative Day, the event attracted a full room to hear 14 witnesses testify, including the Librarian of Congress, the librarian *in* Congress (Representative Major Owens, D-N.Y.), ALA President Marilyn Miller, and librarians from urban and rural public and state libraries. The hearing represented a unique grassroots snapshot of the inventiveness, the partnerships, and the technological innovation librarians are using to meet the challenges and opportunities they face.

Library of Congress

Budget

The Library of Congress (LC) FY 1994 budget request of $364,352,000, although a 9 percent increase, was a bare-bones budget. The House-passed level was 1 percent below FY 1993 funding; the Senate provided $642,595 more than the House. Conferees agreed on FY 1994 funding of $331,864,000, less than the FY 1993 amount of $334,316,000, necessitating severe cuts in personnel and service levels. LC also faces the possibility of further cuts to FY 1994 appropriations in deficit reduction measures to come up in the Senate during the second session.

Fund Act

A revised version of legislation authorizing LC to charge fees for certain services was introduced as S. 345, the Library of Congress Fund Act of 1993, on February 4 by Senator Claiborne Pell (D-R.I.). The legislative counsel for the Senate Rules and Administration Committee made a number of changes to LC's November 1992 draft, most of which were technical. The most significant substantive change removed earlier copyright language to which library associations had objected. On May 20 the Senate committee approved the bill with technical corrections, but no substantive changes. None of the wording changes recommended jointly by ALA, AALL, and ARL were incorporated by the Senate committee, although report language addressed some of these points.

Senator Dennis DeConcini (D-Ariz.), a member of the committee and chairman of the Judiciary Subcommittee on Patents, Copyrights, and Trademarks, announced his intention to offer amendments dealing with copyright when the bill reached the Senate floor. The amendments, proposed by the information and publishing industries, included some language opposed by ALA, AALL, and ARL. Numerous meetings took place among interested parties and LC and congressional staff, but no further action had taken place at year's end.

National Information Infrastructure

Administration's NII Initiative

The new administration on February 22 announced a technology initiative, "Technology for America's Economic Growth: A New Direction to Build Economic Strength," followed by a September 15 document, "The National Information Infrastructure: Agenda for Action." Strengths of the proposals included recognition of NII's transforming potential for social purposes, of the need for assistance for school and library applications, of the potential for enhancing access to government information, of the need for an expanded definition of universal service, and of the need for representation from public interest groups on the proposed Advisory Council on NII.

The administration successfully called attention to a crucial policy area, emphasized that the stakes for a democratic society are high, and created a climate for change. The highlighting of libraries and information access in these documents was due in part to intensive work by ALA, other library groups, and public sector and public interest organizations, but many details are still lacking, and some questions cannot yet be answered.

The White House formed a federal Information Infrastructure Task Force (IITF) chaired by Secretary of Commerce Ronald Brown under the aegis of the White House Office of Science and Technology Policy and the National Economic Council. IITF includes policy committees on telecommunications, applications, and information policy. Each committee has working groups that have been exploring specific issues.

President Clinton issued Executive Order 12864 on September 15 to establish the U.S. Advisory Council on the National Information Infrastructure, a group of nonfederal members to be appointed by the secretary of commerce. Several library and related organizations submitted nominations, but at year's end appointments had not been made.

Telecommunications Policy

One of the most ambitious goals of the administration was to accomplish a major rewrite of the Communications Act of 1934. Vice President Gore outlined the principles underlying this policy initiative in a December 21 speech:

- Encourage private investment
- Promote and protect competition
- Provide open access to the network
- Avoid creating a society of information haves and have-nots
- Encourage flexibility

Meanwhile, several bills were pending in Congress to rewrite the regulatory landscape of telecommunications policy; the administration indicated it would build on these.

Library and Public Sector Efforts

Representatives from 15 national library and information associations met in Washington, D.C., September 8–10 to discuss critical national policy issues dealing with NII. The group reached consensus on several key areas of principles that must be used to guide NII development—First Amendment, privacy, intellectual property, ubiquity, equitable access, and interoperability. At year's end, the principles, together with the full proceedings of the policy forum, were being distributed for appropriate action by participating organizations, including ALA.

The policy forum was chaired by Elaine Albright, chair of the ALA Legislation Committee's Ad Hoc Subcommittee on Telecommunications, and grew out of subcommittee work. Sponsored by ALA's Library and Information Technology Association, it was supported through major funding from ALA, the Council on Library Resources, and the National Science Foundation, as well as through contributions from participating organizations.

Several library groups joined more than 60 organizations in announcing a new coalition and unveiling a blueprint for America's twenty-first century information infrastructure. The Telecommunications Policy Roundtable called on Americans to make their voices heard on vital issues of communications policy. The group issued seven public interest principles in the areas of universal access, freedom to communicate, vital civic sector, diverse and competitive marketplace, equitable workplace, privacy protection, and democratic policy making.

Elaine Albright spoke at the coalition's October 26 press conference in Washington, D.C., announcing the principles. Albright noted that several library groups—ALA, AALL, ARL, the Coalition for Networked Information, Libraries for the Future, MLA, and SLA—had all endorsed the principles. Albright also said that these public interest principles were consistent with the outcome of the library associations' policy forum held in September.

Networking Applications Bills

H.R. 1757 and S. 4

The House in July passed H.R. 1757, the National Information Infrastructure Act, authorizing computer networking applications in education, health care, libraries, and government information. Similar Senate provisions (Title VI of S. 4, the National Competitiveness Act) are pending, but did not make it to the Senate floor before adjournment. The library community supported such measures, which originated in legislation introduced in the previous Congress by then-Senator Gore and known as "Gore II" because the applications were a follow-up to the Gore-sponsored High-Performance Computing Act that established the National Research and Education Network (NREN).

The House Science Subcommittee held a series of hearings both before and after the introduction of H.R. 1757. On February 2, Sara Parker, the Pennsylvania commissioner of libraries, represented ALA. She strongly supported passage of an NREN applications bill, and made several recommendations to strengthen it, including addition of a new component to provide applications for government information, including connections to depository libraries. Other witnesses, including Representative Owens and John Masten of the New York Public Library, supported library applications at later hearings, on May 6.

Both H.R. 1757 and S. 4 defined NREN as a program with several components. In addition to application areas, the bills included an expanded connections program at the National Science Foundation to include connections for libraries, schools, and state and local governments; and research and training programs, including training for librarians and for librarians to instruct the public.

S. 4 included a component called electronic libraries in the states, clearly taken from S. 626, the Electronic Library Act, introduced by Senator Robert Kerrey (D-Neb.). However, S. 4 included troublesome language promoted by large regional telecommunications companies that would hamper state library agencies and state and regional library and education networks wishing to act on behalf of libraries and schools in meeting the goals of the legislation.

A number of constituencies expressed strong support for the House-passed H.R. 1757 and recommended that some of its provisions be substituted for certain language in S. 4. Senate action was delayed due to a variety of factors, including differences of opinion between the administration and some congressional and other interested parties about how much direction should be given to federal agencies in the application areas. A version cleared for Senate floor action but never acted upon was a compromise that was neither as bare-bones as the administration preferred nor as detailed as H.R. 1757.

NTIA Pilot Projects

The House in November passed another piece of the administration's agenda, a bill (H.R. 2639) to authorize the National Telecommunications and Information Administration (NTIA) in the Department of Commerce to award matching grants to assist community institutions such as schools, libraries, museums, state and local governments, and health and social service agencies to connect to networks, access electronic information, and improve service delivery. Although the Senate had not yet acted, the NTIA pilot projects received $26 million in a separate FY 1994 funding measure.

Permanence and Recycled Paper

President Clinton's Executive Order 12873 of October 20 requires the use of recycled paper within the federal government, but makes no mention of permanence considerations, or of the 1990 law (PL 191-423) that established a national policy to promote the use of permanent alkaline paper. In June, ALA, together with several other library, archival, and scholarly organizations, sent a letter to the White House that recommended that the executive order accommodate needs for alkaline permanent paper so that costs for preserving the federal record would be minimized.

Preferred Postal Rates

Major statutory changes were made to preferred postal rates in 1993, although two kinds of mail were not affected by the changes—free mail for the blind and overseas voting by U.S. citizens. For other nonprofit rates that have been partially supported by congressional appropriations, the administration requested no funds.

Congress responded by enacting a major postal rate restructuring that eliminated the authority for revenue-forgone funding but retained some preferential treatment for nonprofit mailers. These rates increase modestly over a six-year phase-in period, but are still considered "preferred," because they have been assigned overhead costs equal to half of the corresponding commercial rate overhead.

New rates took effect November 21. Third-class letter-size piece rates increased by two-tenths of a cent. Restrictions on the kinds of mail sent at the special bulk third-class rates will also be imposed. The fourth-class library rate increased by 1 cent for the first pound. The average 3.5-pound library rate package went up from $1.37 to $1.38.

Also effective November 21, publishers are allowed to mail books and other eligible materials at the library rate only if they are mailed in response to a purchase order from a qualifying institution or organization. The preferred postal rate restructuring passed originally by both House and Senate would have eliminated all publisher use of the fourth-class library rate. The champions in restoring library-rate eligibility for items ordered by libraries and educational institutions were Senators Thad Cochran (R-Miss.), Ted Stevens (R-Alaska), and Christopher Bond (R-Mo.), who discussed such an amendment on the Senate floor in August. The final version of the postal funding bill (H.R. 2403) incorporated this change as part of the postal rate restructuring (now PL 103-123).

School Library Media Act

First introduced in October 1992, the Elementary and Secondary School Library Media Act was reintroduced by Senator Paul Simon (D-Ill.) in January and by Representative Jack Reed (D-R.I.) in February. By the end of the year, 59 representatives and 10 senators had cosponsored S. 266 and H.R. 1151.

The major thrust of the legislation is to provide targeted support for school library media resources—support that has been lacking for more than a dozen years under the current Elementary and Secondary Education Act (ESEA) Chapter 2 block grant program. The identical House and Senate bills would authorize a unit in the Department of Education to administer the program, a major grant program in which each state's allocation would be passed on to local education agencies for purchase of school library resources in all formats, and competitive grant programs for school library media specialists and teachers to design collaborative curriculum projects, and to expand use of computers and computer networks in the curriculum.

The key features of the bills were developed by ALA to help implement the School Library Services portion of the Omnibus Children and Youth Literacy

Table 2 / Status of Legislation of Interest to Librarians

(103rd Congress, 1st Session, Convened: January 5, 1993, Adjourned: November 26, 1993)

Legislation	House					Senate					Final Action		
	Introduced	Hearings	Reported by Subcommittee	Committee Report No.— H. Rept. 103-	Floor Action	Introduced	Hearings	Reported by Subcommittee	Committee Report No.— S. Rept. 103-	Floor Action	Conference Report— H. Rept. 103-	Final Passage	Public Law— PL 103-
Arts and Humanities reauthorization	H.R. 2351	•		186	•	S. 1218	•	•	182	•		•	
Communications and Antitrust Reform	H.R. 3626												
Communications, Competitiveness, Infrastructure	H.R. 1504												
Congressional Budget Resolution	H.Con.Res. 64	•		31	•	S.Con.Res. 18							
Copyright Reform Act	H.R. 897	• •		388	•	S. 373			19	•	48		
DOE National Competitiveness Technology	H.R. 2875					S. 473							
El/Sec School Library Media Act	H.R. 1151					S. 266			69	•			
Electronic Library Act						S. 626							
Emergency Book Fund Act	H.R. 2256												
ESEA reauth. (Improve America's Schools Act)	H.R. 3130	•			•	S. 1513	•						
Family and Medical Leave Act	H.R. 1	• •		8	•	S. 5	•		3	•	none	•	3
Goals 2000: Educate America	H.R. 1804	• •		168	•	S. 1150	•		85	•	none	•	
GPO Electronic Access	H.R. 1328	• •		108	•	S. 564	•	•	27	•			40
HBCU Restoration of Historic Buildings	H.R. 2921			398	•								
Improvement of Information Access Act	H.R. 629	•			•		•						
LC American Folklife Center	H.R. 2074	•		•	•	S. 685	•	•	47	•		•	101
LC Fund Act						S. 345			50				
Lobbying Disclosure Act	H.R. 823	•				S. 570			37	•			
Local Exchange Infrastructure	H.R. 1312	•											
Natl. Communications, Competitiveness, and II Act	H.R. 3636	•											
National Community Service	H.R. 2010	• •		155	•	S. 919	• •	•	70	•	219	•	82
National Competitiveness Act	H.R. 820	• •		77	•	S. 4	•	•	113	•			
Networking Applications bills	H.R. 1757	• •		173	•	S. 4	•	•	113	•			
NHPRC reauthorization	H.R. 2139	•		215		S. 314		•	145				

Table 2 / Status of Legislation of Interest to Librarians (cont.)

(103rd Congress, 1st Session, Convened: January 5, 1993, Adjourned: November 26, 1993)

Legislation	House Introduced	House Hearings	House Reported by Subcommittee	House Committee Report No.—H. Rept. 103-	House Floor Action	Senate Introduced	Senate Hearings	Senate Reported by Subcommittee	Senate Committee Report No.—S. Rept. 103-	Senate Floor Action	Conference Report—H. Rept. 103-	Final Passage	Public Law—PL 103-
NIH reauthorization (NLM/MLAA)	H.R. 4	•	•	28	•	S. 1	•	•	2	•	100	•	43
NTIA Pilot Projects	H.R. 2639	•	•	325	•								
OERI reauthorization	H.R. 856	•	•	209	•	S. 286	•	•	183				
Omnibus Budget Reconciliation	H.R. 2264			111	•	S. 1134		•	•	•	213	•	66
Paperwork Reduction Act	H.R. 2995					S. 560, 681							
Privacy Protection Act						S. 1735							
Technology for Education Act	H.R. 2728	•				S. 1040	•						
Telecommunications Infrastructure Act						S. 1086	•						
Appropriations													
Emergency supplemental, FY 1993	H.R. 1335	•	•	30	•	H.R. 1335	•	•	none	•	none	•	24
Second supplemental, FY 1993	H.R. 2244	•	•	105	•	H.R. 2244	•	•			none		
Supplemental, FY 1993	H.R. 2118	•	•	91	•	H.R. 2118	•	•	54	•	165	•	50
Agriculture, FY 1994	H.R. 2493	•	•	153	•	H.R. 2493	•	•	102	•	212	•	111
Commerce, State, FY 1994	H.R. 2519	•	•	157	•	H.R. 2519	•	•	105	•	293	•	121
Interior, FY 1994	H.R. 2520	•	•	158	•	H.R. 2520	•	•	114	•	299	•	138
Labor-HHS-Education, FY 1994	H.R. 2518	•	•	156	•	H.R. 2518	•	•	143	•	275	•	112
Legislative branch, FY 1994	H.R. 2348	•	•	117	•		•	•	103	•	210	•	69
Treasury, Postal, FY 1994	H.R. 2403	•	•	127	•	H.R. 2403	•	•	106	•	256	•	123

For free copies of bills, reports, and laws, write: House Document Rm., B-18 Annex No. 2, Washington, DC 20515; Senate Document Rm., B-04 Hart, Washington, DC 20510.

Initiative, which was the top priority of the 1991 White House Conference on Library and Information Services. The intention is that the bills could serve as appropriate amendments to the pending reauthorization of ESEA.

The administration's 452-page proposal (Improving America's Schools Act) to amend and extend ESEA was introduced in the fall as H.R. 3130 and S. 1513. The proposal would eliminate the current Chapter 2 block grant program, and does not propose any school library program elsewhere in the legislation.

Valerie Wilford, executive director of the Illinois Valley Library System, testified on behalf of ALA's American Association of School Librarians on a related bill before the Senate Labor and Human Resources Committee on July 21. S. 1040, the Technology for Education Act, included the technology grant portions of S. 266. Wilford stressed that while technology will be an important part in the achievement of the national education goals, strong school library media collections and programs are also needed.

Table 2 indicates the status of legislation of interest to librarians.

Legislation and Regulations Affecting Publishing in 1993

Judith Platt

Director of Communications, Association of American Publishers

Copyright

Copyright Reform Act of 1993

Senators Dennis DeConcini (D-Ariz.) and Orrin Hatch (R-Utah) and Representative William Hughes (D-N.J.) introduced legislation (S. 373 and H.R. 897) that would, among other things, repeal Section 411 (a) of the Copyright Act so that copyright registration would no longer be a requirement for instituting suit, and repeal Section 412 of the Copyright Act, which requires timely registration as a condition for the award of statutory damages and attorney's fees.

Because copyright registration is voluntary under U.S. copyright law, the Copyright Act contains incentives to encourage copyright owners to register their works. Registration and its accompanying deposit requirement are essential to the integrity of the Library of Congress's vast collections, to the public record of registrations maintained by the Copyright Office, and to the scholars, researchers, and members of Congress who use these collected works and registration records.

At Senate hearings on October 19, the Association of American University Presses (AAUP) and the Association of American Publishers (AAP) offered testimony to the effect that repeal of Section 412 would "upset the careful and critical balance . . . among the interests of authors and publishers of pre-existing works and those who would transform, build upon and make reasonable use of those works." In addition, repeal would "put at risk both the Library of Congress' vast collections . . . and the Copyright Office's invaluable public record." AAP is working with a broad coalition of historians, authors, and others who share these concerns, to mitigate the impact of the proposed changes.

Fair Use and Video Monitoring Services

In January Senator Hatch reintroduced legislation to amend the copyright law to designate "news reporting monitoring" as a "fair use exception to the exclusive right of a copyright owner," making the fair-use defense available to for-profit video monitoring services and insulating them from copyright infringement liability when they clip and sell copies of cable and broadcast programming.

The bill (S. 23) is particularly troubling because news reporting monitoring is a for-profit business that uses the works of copyright owners without compensating them. The legislation could undermine a key premise of the fair-use doctrine: the presumption that a commercial use of copyrighted material is not fair use under our copyright law.

No hearings have been held on S. 23, and no companion bill has been introduced in the House.

Postal Funding

Revenue-Forgone Subsidy

The revenue-forgone subsidy, which has supported overhead costs associated with mailings by nonprofit groups since the early 1970s, was virtually eliminated by Congress in 1993 (with the exception of mailings for the blind and for overseas voters). The costs of supporting the congressionally mandated preferred postal rate structure will now be divided between nonprofit and commercial mailers. The first step of a six-year phase-in of higher rates for nonprofit mailers went into effect in November.

Congressional action also changed the rules regarding the use of the Library Rate. Although publishers will still be able to use the Library Rate to ship books purchased by libraries, schools, and colleges, it will no longer be available for mailing complimentary review copies of textbooks.

Education

FY 1994 Appropriations

The fiscal 1994 Department of Education appropriations bill, which President Clinton signed in October, allocates $30.1 billion for Education Department programs, a decrease of $200 million from the 1993 level. Of particular concern to publishers is the $64 million cut in funding for the Chapter 2 block grant program, which supports a variety of important activities including "the acquisition of instructional and educational materials such as library books, reference materials, computer hardware and software, multimedia equipment and other instruction enhancing materials."

AAP joined with 12 other organizations in an unsuccessful attempt to restore Chapter 2 funding to the 1993 level. Despite its lack of success, the effort was significant in bringing together an alliance that may prove effective in other legislative battles.

Elementary and Secondary Education Act (ESEA) Reauthorization

Legislation (H.R. 6) providing a six-year extension for programs carried out under the ESEA of 1965 was introduced early in the session. Following a number of hearings, the original bill was replaced by the administration's own version, the Improving America's Schools Act (H.R. 3130, S. 1513).

The legislation would require states to adopt academic and testing standards for Chapter 1 schools (Chapter 1 provides supplemental services to disadvantaged students and is the largest federal program for elementary and secondary education), and to expand existing technology programs. Also of significance for educational publishers, the legislation would merge the existing Chapter 2 block grant program with the Dwight D. Eisenhower Mathematics and Science state grant program. The new program would focus solely on helping teachers upgrade their knowledge and skills, and this "professional development" stricture could mean a significant loss of funding currently available for the purchase of instructional materials.

AAP sent a package of suggested amendments, including express statutory recognition of instructional materials and specific definitions of equipment and technology, to Capitol Hill. Efforts to amend the legislation along these lines will continue in the second session of the 103rd Congress.

Goals 2000

The House passed its version (H.R. 1804) of the administration's education reform bill—Goals 2000: The Educate America Act—on October 13. The Senate version (S. 1150) was reported out of the Senate Labor and Human Resources Committee and at year's end was awaiting action by the full Senate. Of particular interest to educational publishers are proposed new "opportunity to learn" standards that could result in a significant increase in the demand for high quality, up-to-date instructional materials.

Office of Educational Research and Improvement

In August the House passed H.R. 856, legislation authorizing a four-year renewal and expansion of the Office of Educational Research and Improvement (OERI). A similar Senate bill (S. 286) was reported out of committee in November and at year's end was awaiting action by the full Senate. Among other provisions, the legislation would establish a National Education Library within OERI as the central location within the federal government for information about education. Included in the activities envisioned for this National Education Library are search and retrieval of electronic databases, document delivery by mail and FAX, interlibrary loan, resource-sharing networks, and development of directories and indices for textbooks and other specialized collections held by education libraries throughout the United States. Of particular concern to AAP is the absence of language specifically recognizing the need to safeguard copyright in connection with the National Education Library's activities.

Government Competition with the Private Sector

Library of Congress Fund Act

The Library of Congress Fund Act of 1993 (S. 345) was introduced in February by Senator Claiborne Pell (D-R.I.) at the request of Librarian of Congress James Billington. Like predecessor legislation in the 102nd Congress, the bill would enable the Library of Congress to engage in a wide range of "fee-for-service" activities, including document delivery, customized research reports, database products and services, and translation services. At the request of Congress, AAP continues to participate in negotiations with the Library of Congress, the library community, and the Information Industry Association (IIA) in an attempt to address serious concerns raised by the bill. Among these concerns:

- Some of these activities would put the Library of Congress in direct competition with the private sector without regard to the availability of such products or services in the marketplace
- The legislation fails to adequately address the question of protecting copyrighted works utilized or compensating the owners of these works
- The legislation does not expressly proscribe the Library of Congress, a government entity, from asserting proprietary claims for its newly created information products

The legislation was reported out of the Senate Rules Committee in May, but no further action was taken in the first session of Congress. The AAP/IIA/library community talks with the Library of Congress are slated to continue.

Intellectual Freedom

Free Trade in Ideas

Congressman Howard Berman (D-Calif.) reintroduced his "Free Trade in Ideas" bill (H.R. 1579), which is identical to his bill in the 102nd Congress. The legislation would 1) lift existing restrictions prohibiting U.S. citizens from traveling at their own expense to countries such as Cuba; 2) clarify the "Berman Amendment" to the 1988 Omnibus Trade Act, which prohibits the Executive Branch from regulating the import and export of books, publications, films, and other informational materials; 3) prohibit restrictions on academic, cultural, and scientific exchanges; and 4) insure that import and export of informational materials could not be restricted as a result of U.S. adherence to United Nations embargoes.

AAP testified in favor of the original bill in the 102nd Congress. In addition, AAP President Nicholas Veliotes raised the question of including books under United Nations embargoes with U.N. Secretary-General Boutros Boutros-Ghali during an AAP-sponsored dinner at the State Department, and followed up this discussion with a letter to the secretary-general asking the United Nations to modify its rules to ensure that books and educational materials are excluded from embargoes.

Supporters of the "Free Trade in Ideas" legislation failed in their attempt to incorporate the bill into H.R. 2333, the International Relations Act of 1993, which was considered and passed by the House in June. Similar efforts will be made in connection with the Senate Foreign Relations Committee's consideration of H.R. 2333 during the second session.

Recycling

While no major recycling legislation was introduced in the first session of the 103rd Congress, the administration fulfilled its promise to issue an executive order establishing recycling guidelines for federally procured materials, including printing and writing paper. The executive order was issued on October 20, and while it addresses only federal procurement of printing and writing paper (an estimated 2 percent to 3 percent of the total market), attention is now focused on the paper industry to see how the order will affect the availability of recycled paper that meets or exceeds the new federal requirements. In the months leading up to issuance of the executive order, AAP communicated with the White House on two separate occasions, urging openness in the drafting process and a realistic approach to setting standards. The executive order does not establish any chlorine reduction or chlorine elimination goals, but pressure on the paper industry to reduce its use of chlorine is expected to continue.

The Information Superhighway

National Information Infrastructure

Creation of a National Information Infrastructure (NII) continues to be a top Clinton administration priority. On September 15 the administration released its *NII: Agenda for Action,* establishing an NII Task Force composed of several committees, including one on Information Policy.

One of this committee's three working groups, the Working Group on Intellectual Property, held a hearing on November 18 to discuss the protection of copyright and other intellectual property rights in an electronic world. Two AAP members and a member of the American Association of University Presses (AAUP) testified at the hearing. In a written statement and comments filed subsequently, AAP told the Working Group that 1) the basic principles of existing copyright law appear to be adequate to protect AAP members' copyrighted materials in a networked environment; 2) there does not at present appear to be a need to change the fair-use provisions of the copyright law; and 3) supplementary provisions may be needed in other laws (and possibly in the Copyright Act itself) to ensure adequate implementation of the copyright law in a digital environment.

AAP also noted that there are a number of non-copyright issues in connection with NII that must be carefully considered, including the role of the First Amendment in a networked environment, the question of how both providers and users of information will gain access to the information superhighway, and the availability of the network to minorities and rural communities.

NREN Legislation

During the first session of the 103rd Congress, proposals were introduced in both houses of Congress to address various aspects of the emerging National Information Infrastructure. Two bills are of particular interest to AAP: H.R. 1757 (introduced by Representative Rick Boucher, D-Va.), the National Information Infrastructure Act, and Title VI of S. 4 (introduced by Senator Ernest Hollings, Democrat of South Carolina), the National Competitiveness Act. Both deal with the development of new technologies to improve the performance of high-speed computer networks. (One section of the House bill, for example, calls for the development of high-speed, highly accurate technology to convert information from print to electronic format for "digital libraries.")

AAP succeeded in having important copyright language included in the House bill, and on July 26 the House passed H.R. 1757 with all of the AAP-endorsed copyright language included.

The association has worked closely with the Senate Commerce Committee staff to ensure that significant copyright language is included in several sections of Title VI of S. 4. The full Senate was expected to vote on S. 4 early in 1994, at which time the most recent draft of the bill, containing all of the language AAP successfully lobbied for, was expected to be offered as a substitute bill.

Trade Policy

NAFTA

In a close and highly publicized vote, Congress passed the North American Free Trade Agreement (NAFTA) implementing legislation in November. The publishing industry, and other copyright industries, strongly supported NAFTA because the treaty incorporates the strongest intellectual property protection language thus far achieved by U.S. negotiators, including a broad "national treatment" provision that will prevent discrimination against U.S. copyrighted material. As it did in the Canadian Free Trade Agreement, Canada again took a "cultural industries" exclusion, which in NAFTA includes intellectual property protection. However, the United States retains its ability to retaliate under Section 301 of the Trade Act. The U.S. copyright industries have also urged that the administration closely monitor Mexico's copyright protection enforcement in light of that country's past ineffectiveness in stemming widespread piracy.

GATT

After seven years of negotiation, the Uruguay Round of trade talks under the General Agreement on Tariffs and Trade (GATT, soon to become the World Trade Organization) was successfully concluded on December 15 with the signing of a new GATT accord that for the first time covers intellectual property protection issues. Of particular importance to American publishers are the TRIPS (Trade Related Intellectual Property Rights) agreement and the dispute settlement/enforcement provisions of the pact. At year's end, the publishing industry was still analyzing the final text to determine its impact on the industry. On the plus side, the new GATT accord establishes a high level of protection for U.S.

copyrights as the international norm, binding at least the 111 current members of GATT. A GATT member country's failure to live up to this standard will call the dispute settlement mechanism into play, subjecting that country to possible cross-sectoral retaliation. This leverage will greatly assist in forcing countries to amend their laws and improve enforcement. A possible downside of the agreement is that the long transition periods given developing countries to improve their laws (five years from July 1, 1995, for less developed countries, 10 years for "least developed" countries) might affect the ability of the United States to call into play the "Special 301" provisions of the Omnibus Trade and Competitiveness Act of 1988. However, the bilateral negotiation process, which has proven effective in the past in obtaining overseas protection for U.S. copyrights, will continue to play an important role.

"Special 301" Provisions of the U.S. Trade Act

Under the "Special 301" provisions of the Omnibus Trade and Competitiveness Act of 1988, the U.S. Trade Representative (USTR) is required to identify countries where abuses of U.S. intellectual property rights are particularly egregious, and to set in motion an accelerated process for correcting these abuses. AAP, through the International Intellectual Property Alliance, provides data on copyright piracy and market access barriers for U.S.-copyrighted works to aid USTR in identifying problem areas. In February 1993 the alliance named a total of 28 countries whose failure to protect American copyrights warranted their designation as 1993 "Priority Foreign Countries," "Priority Watch List," or "Watch List" countries. According to the alliance report, trade losses from copyright piracy in those countries exceeded $4.6 billion in 1992. At a Senate hearing in April 1993, the alliance reasserted the copyright industries' support for "Special 301" as a weapon in the fight against copyright piracy. That same month, a delegation of copyright industry representatives that included Deborah Wiley (John Wiley & Sons), a member of the AAP International Copyright Protection Committee, called on U.S. Trade Representative Mickey Kantor to press the case against copyright piracy. On April 30 Ambassador Kantor announced the "Special 301" designations for 1993, sending a welcome signal that the Clinton administration intends to take a tough stand on piracy.

GSP

AAP and its copyright industry allies in the International Intellectual Property Alliance supported efforts in Congress to extend the Generalized System of Preferences (GSP) trade program until September 30, 1994, and to make the 14 independent states of the former Soviet Union eligible for duty-free access to U.S. markets under the GSP program. By conditioning preferential trade benefits on a requirement that these countries provide high levels of protection and enforcement of U.S. intellectual property rights, the GSP program is seen by the U.S. copyright industries as an effective means of encouraging countries to improve their protection for U.S. copyrights and to open their markets to U.S.-copyrighted works. AAP, presenting testimony on behalf of the Coalition for GSP Renewal, made these points to Congress at House hearings in April. Congress approved the GSP extension as part of the budget reconciliation bill.

Subsequently, AAP (working through the alliance) petitioned the government to deny GSP benefits to six countries whose protection was particularly lax. The petitions were accepted and the government is now engaged in negotiations to effect needed changes.

Other Legislative Issues

Stars and Stripes Bookstores

As part of the 1994 Defense Department reauthorization bill, Congress included a provision to close all Stars and Stripes military bookstores outside the United States and to turn their operations over to the military post exchanges. A similar proposal was put forward several years ago but not implemented following a study mandated by Congress.

Despite an AAP letter to the House and Senate Armed Services Committee expressing concern that books would not fare as well in a general retail operation and that, consequently, U.S. service personnel would lose the benefit of a wide range of books, Congress approved closing the Stars and Stripes bookstores and turning their operations over to the PXs by April 1994.

Funding Programs and Grant-Making Agencies

National Endowment for the Humanities

Old Post Office, 1100 Pennsylvania Ave. N.W., Washington, DC 20506
202-606-8438

Thomas C. Phelps
Humanities Project in Libraries and Archives

The National Endowment for the Humanities (NEH) is an independent grant-making agency of the federal government created by Congress in 1965. It supports research, education, and public understanding of the humanities through grants to individuals, organizations, and institutions. NEH grant-making operations are conducted through six major divisions: Public Programs, Preservation and Access, Research Programs, Education Programs, Fellowships and Seminars, and State Programs. In addition, aid is available to libraries through the Office of Challenge Grants.

Division of Public Programs

This division endeavors to fulfill NEH's mandate to foster public appreciation and understanding of the humanities. It includes programs that assist institutions and organizations such as public, college and university, and special libraries, and library associations, in developing projects for presentation to the general public. The division is composed of four programs: Museums and Historical Organizations, Media, Public Humanities Projects, and Libraries and Archives. The single program within the division that supports libraries directly is Humanities Projects in Libraries and Archives, although other programs offer indirect support. Humanities Projects in Libraries and Archives encourages all types of libraries to plan and present humanities programs in many different formats. Cooperative projects among public, academic, and special libraries, and among libraries, museums, historical societies, and other cultural institutions are also encouraged. Programs may take place at locations other than libraries; however, the primary objective of using library collections and resources to enhance public understanding and appreciation of the humanities must be evident in the design of projects.

Among the many possible ways applicants to the program might fulfill the endowment's mandate to foster public understanding and appreciation of the humanities are the following: investigate the history of systems of thought; explore language as a reflection of culture; examine American diversity and what it means to be an American; pose a philosophical debate concerning fundamental human rights; trace the development of the origins of social, political, or religious systems; or examine central themes such as love, war, family, or work through literature. A variety of methods and formats may be employed for the exploration of topics within the disciplines of the humanities. Some formats that have proven useful include reading and discussion groups; lecture series; conferences; film series accompanied by discussion and supplementary readings; exhibition of library material or small exhibitions subordinate to other program formats; and such written material as anthologies devoted to specific themes, essays illuminating specific topics, annotated bibliographies, or reading lists.

Applicants for support of such projects are urged to consider carefully the most appropriate means of implementing their programs in libraries and archives and to discuss them with NEH staff. Projects should involve librarians and the active collaboration of scholars from the appropriate disciplines of the humanities during both the planning and presentation of the programs. Programs should create an opportunity for thoughtful examination of scholarship or a dialogue between the scholarly community and the public based on the existing collection of humanities resources held in libraries and archives. Programs should include the active use of such collections and fulfill those parts of any library's mission having to do with the education of constituent users.

Humanities Projects in Libraries and Archives also encourages libraries to design out-of-school projects for young people. By involving youth in projects, libraries can help them to acquire and apply new knowledge and skills in the disciplines of the humanities. Projects for this age group are intended to encourage a lifelong interest in the humanities by introducing young people to the range of resources and activities in the humanities available to them through collections found in libraries and archives.

The following are examples of such projects:

• To bring humanities projects to those who live in the rural isolation of Montana, an award of $177,799 was made to the Flathead County Library System for a series of 12 interactive book discussion programs on radio through which a diverse and geographically scattered audience could interact with scholars via toll-free telephone lines to discuss the myths and realities of life in the West as portrayed by Montana writers. Questions are raised by listeners regarding early and modern settlers in the West, notions of Western identity, and the disparities and conflicts between native tribalism and non-native individualism. All of these questions emanate from the project's theme: the myths and realities of living in the "last best place," a theme based on an anthology of critical essays on Montana literature by William Bevis, *Ten Tough Trips: Montana Writers and the West.* Other books, available from local public or academic libraries, read and discussed over the air include A. B. Guthrie's *The Big Sky*, James Welch's *Fools Crow*, Norman MacLean's *A River Runs Through It*, and Ivan Doig's *This House of Sky*.

- An award of $195,000 was made to the Southwest Texas State University Library in San Marcos, Texas, for an exhibition of library material resources entitled "No Traveller Remains Untouched: Journeys of Transformation." Books, manuscripts, letters, documents, and maps were presented in the original stationary exhibition. These items, along with written texts, were also formatted into a traveling poster exhibition that— together with an interpretive catalogue, lectures, guides, bibliographies, and resource booklets—illustrate the cultural evolution of the Southwest as seen through the glass of seven paradigmatic journeys that influenced regional history.

- Justice, love, loyalty, religious faith, honor, and the conflict of public and private selves are among the topics that exhibition visitors will be prompted to consider by a traveling panel exhibition about the evolution of the Arthurian legend in literature, history, and the arts. In collaboration with the Newberry Library and the New York Public Library, the American Library Association received an award of $385,000 in outright support and $75,000 in matching funds to support a traveling exhibition and a reading and discussion theme unit, curriculum guides, and interpretive catalogue on "The Many Realms of King Arthur." A 15-minute videotape will greet exhibition visitors at 68 libraries (including libraries in Alaska, Hawaii, and Puerto Rico) in order to refresh their memory of the basic Arthurian story (using Sir Thomas Mallory's version). After seeing the exhibition, visitors are encouraged to participate in reading and discussion programs at site libraries where versions of the Arthur stories by Mallory, Alfred Lord Tennyson, and T. H. White, as well as more modern versions such as Marion Zimmer Bradley's *The Mists of Avalon*, and Walker Percy's *Lancelot*, are to be discussed with local scholars.

- Reading, listening, and discussion programs featuring the works of major contemporary American poets, taped interviews with them, and scholar-led discussions at 30 library sites throughout the nation were supported by an award of $314,666 made to the Modern Poetry Association for a series entitled "Poets in Person—Reading, Hearing, and Talking about Contemporary Poetry in America's Libraries." The association collaborated with the American Library Association in selecting site libraries, training librarians and scholars, and publicizing the programs.

Awards were also made in 1993 to libraries in Florida, Hawaii, and states in the Midwest for flood and hurricane relief. Most of these awards were under $25,000 and were made to support the restoration or replacement of damaged or destroyed items in library or archival collections.

Division of Preservation and Access

This division's grants are made to institutions for projects that will preserve and increase the availability of resources important for research, education, and public programming in the humanities. Resources may include books, journals, newspapers, manuscripts and other archival materials, maps, photographs, film, sound recordings, and objects of material culture held by libraries, archives, museums, historical organizations, and other repositories.

The division accepts applications that address problems of preservation and access from a variety of perspectives. Support may be sought for microfilming projects conducted by individual libraries and archives or by institutions acting as a consortium; the conservation treatment of endangered materials, where conversion to a more stable medium is not appropriate; projects to preserve material-culture collections; projects that will provide intellectual access to textual and nontextual collections; education and training projects on a regional or national level; the work of regional preservation services; the preparation of statewide preservation plans; research and demonstration projects to improve procedures and technology; and projects involving issues of national significance to the library and archives field. Proposals may combine preservation and access activities.

Through awards from this division, NEH established the National Heritage Preservation Program to support efforts to stabilize material-culture collections important to the humanities through the appropriate housing and storage of objects, improved climate control, and the installation of security, lighting, and fire prevention systems. Grants are also available to establish regional or national training programs for the care and conservation of material-culture collections, as well as for projects that will document collections significant to the humanities.

Support for access projects can involve the arrangement and description of archival and manuscript collections; archival surveys; the cataloging of graphic, film, sound, or artifact collections; the bibliographic control of printed works; the microfilming of collections in non-U.S. repositories; the preparation of oral histories; and the exploration of issues that have a national impact on the library and archival fields.

These are some examples:

- The Association of Research Libraries received an award of $884,520 to convert into machine-readable form 50,000 manual records for Roman-alphabet monographs from the master file of the *National Register of Microform Masters,* which ceased publication in 1983.
- The preservation microfilming of 15,000 monographs in theology, histories of U.S. religious denominations, and the history of religions was accomplished through a grant of $600,000 to the American Theological Library Association.
- The Frick Art Reference Library received $112,500 to duplicate the A. C. Cooper Nitrate Negatives Collection. With the grant, 6,340 unstable nitrate negatives were duplicated and 1,615 glass plate negatives were cleaned and rehoused. All of the photographs were taken by A. C. Cooper between 1920 and 1932, covering works of art auctioned by Christie's and other London auction houses.

- The library at the University of North Carolina at Chapel Hill was awarded $220,000 to preserve endangered sound recordings that document the oral traditions of the American South.
- With a grant of $393,962, the University of Texas at Austin Library will preserve via microfilm as many as 4,000 volumes pertaining to Brazilian literature and materials relating to Caribbean, South American, and Central American history, geography, and biography.
- To support the preservation of deteriorating newsreels in the Hearst-Metrotone Newsreel collection that document political events worldwide during the 1930s, the University of California/Los Angeles Library was granted $255,000.
- The African-American Manuscript Access Project at the Virginia Historical Society was awarded a grant of $37,880 to support the enhancement of catalogue entries and other finding aids to collections documenting over three centuries of African-American history in Virginia.

Division of Research Programs

The division provides support for the preparation for publication of editions, translations, and other important works in the humanities; the preparation of reference materials; the conduct of large or complex interpretive studies; research conferences; and research opportunities offered through independent research centers (many of which are libraries) and scholarly organizations. The Editions, Translations, and Reference Materials programs within the division are of particular interest to libraries and librarians.

The Editions Program supports various stages in the preparation of authoritative and annotated editions of works and documents valuable to both scholars and general readers and generally accessible through libraries. The Translation Program supports individual or collaborative projects to translate into English works that provide insight into the history, literature, philosophy, and artistic achievements of other cultures. The Reference Materials Program supports the preparation of works that will enhance the availability of information and research materials such as dictionaries, atlases, encyclopedias, concordances, reference grammars, databases, text bases, and other projects that will provide essential scholarly tools for libraries.

These are examples:

- The preparation of a catalogue of 300 medieval and Renaissance manuscripts in the Plimpton Collection was supported by a grant of $89,760 to the Columbia University Library.
- With a grant of $28,160, Stanford University planned and presented a conference to enhance access to Russian archives through the Research Libraries Information Network.
- An online bibliography of published works for theater research, a comprehensive database of references to current theater-related periodicals and books published around the world, was supported with a grant of $140,000 to the City University of New York/Brooklyn College Library.

- The University of California at Riverside Library was awarded $600,000 to support the continued preparation of the *Eighteenth-Century Short-Title Catalogue,* which records all publications produced in Britain and its dependencies during the years 1701–1800.

Division of Education Programs

Libraries may receive Division of Education Programs grants directly or as part of a college or university effort to strengthen teaching in the humanities. Direct grants to libraries usually support humanities institutes at which elementary and secondary school teachers or college and university faculty use the library's resources as part of a program of study directed by recognized scholars.

Division of Fellowships and Seminars

This division's seminar programs enable individuals to pursue their work and to exchange ideas in the collegial atmosphere of a community of scholars. None of the awards from this division's fellowships programs are given to institutions or organizations such as libraries, but librarians are eligible for fellowship awards. Awards are sometimes made to faculty and institutions to conduct seminar programs. Sometimes libraries such as the Newberry or the Folger gain such awards.

Office of Challenge Grants

Libraries are eligible for support within the Challenge Grant Program. By inviting libraries to appeal to a broader funding public, challenge grants assist them to increase long-term financial stability and capital support and thereby improve the quality of humanities activities and collections. To receive each federal dollar, a challenge grant recipient must raise $3 to $4 from nonfederal funding sources. Both federal and nonfederal funds may be used to support the costs of renovation and construction and the purchase of equipment and the acquisition of collections. Funds may also be invested in interest-bearing accounts to ensure annual revenues to support educational programs in the humanities in perpetuity. Awards in this category are limited to two per institution; second awards require the 4:1 match.

The following are examples:

- The Wittenberg University Library in Springfield, Ohio, received a $200,000 challenge grant to support collection development and cataloguing to establish an endowment for humanities acquisitions in the university library.
- The New Orleans Public Library received a $200,000 challenge grant to support the endowment of acquisitions in Louisiana history, culture, and literature, ethnic history and culture, and literary criticism, as well as to support public programs such as exhibits and reading and discussion programs.

- An endowment for five research fellowships, two internships in archival conservation and management, and staff positions was supported by a $1 million challenge grant to the New York State Archives.
- The Corpus Christi Public Library received a $75,000 challenge grant to support an endowment for the acquisition of humanities materials.

Division of State Programs

The endowment annually makes grants to state humanities councils in the 50 states, the District of Columbia, Puerto Rico, the U.S. Virgin Islands, Guam, and the Northern Marianas. The state councils, in turn, award grants to institutions and organizations within each state or territory according to guidelines and application deadlines determined by each council. Most grants are for projects that promote or foster public understanding and appreciation of the humanities, and many awards are made to libraries for such projects. Guidelines and application deadlines may be obtained by contacting the state or territorial council directly.

Office of Publications and Public Affairs

For publications or information about any of the endowment divisions, offices, or programs, contact the Public Information Office at 1100 Pennsylvania Ave. N.W., Room 407, Washington, DC 20506 (telephone 202-606-8438).

State Humanities Councils

Alabama Humanities Foundation
Robert Stewart, Exec. Dir.
2217 Tenth Ct. S.
Birmingham, AL 35205
205-930-0540

Alaska Humanities Forum
Stephen Lindbeck, Exec. Dir.
430 W. Seventh Ave., Suite 1
Anchorage, AK 99501
907-272-5341

Arizona Humanities Council
Dan Shilling, Exec. Dir.
Ellis-Shackelford House
1242 N. Central Ave.
Phoenix, AZ 85004
602-257-0335

Arkansas Humanities Council
Robert E. Bailey, Exec. Dir.
10816 Executive Center Dr., Suite 310
Little Rock, AR 72211
501-221-0091

California Council for the Humanities
James Quay, Exec. Dir.
312 Sutter St., Suite 601
San Francisco, CA 94108
415-391-1474

Colorado Endowment for the Humanities
James Pierce, Exec. Dir.
1623 Blake St., Suite 200
Denver, CO 80202
303-573-7733

Connecticut Humanities Council
Bruce Fraser, Exec. Dir.
41 Lawn Ave., Wesleyan Sta.
Middletown, CT 06457
203-347-6888

Delaware Humanities Forum
Henry Hirschbiel, Exec. Dir.
1812 Newport Gap Pike
Wilmington, DE 19808-6179
302-633-2400

D.C. Community Humanities Council
Francine Cary, Exec. Dir.
1331 H St. N.W., Suite 902
Washington, DC 20005
202-347-1732

Florida Humanities Council
Ann Henderson, Exec. Dir.
1514 1/2 E. Eighth Ave.
Tampa, FL 33605-3708
813-272-3473

Georgia Humanities Council
Ronald E. Benson, Pres.
50 Hurt Plaza S.E., Suite 440
Atlanta, GA 30303-2936
404-523-6220

Hawaii Committee for the Humanities
Annette M. Lew, Exec. Dir.
First Hawaiian Bank Bldg.
3599 Wai'alae Ave., Rm. 23
Honolulu, HI 96816
808-732-5402

Idaho Humanities Council
Thomas H. McClanahan, Pres.
217 W. State St.
Boise, ID 83702
208-345-5346

Illinois Humanities Council
Kristina Valaitis, Exec. Dir.
618 S. Michigan Ave., 7th fl.
Chicago, IL 60605
312-939-5212

Indiana Humanities Council
Kenneth L. Gladish, Pres.
1500 N. Delaware St.
Indianapolis, IN 46202
317-638-1500

Iowa Humanities Board
Rick Knupfer, Exec. Dir.
Oakdale Campus
Univ. of Iowa
Iowa City, IA 52242
319-335-4153

Kansas Humanities Council
Marion Cott, Exec. Dir.
112 W. Sixth St., Suite 210
Topeka, KS 66603
913-357-0359

Kentucky Humanities Council
Virginia Smith, Exec. Dir.
417 Clifton Ave.
Univ. of Kentucky
Lexington, KY 40508-3406
606-257-5932

Louisiana Endowment for the Humanities
Michael Sartisky, Pres.
The Ten-O-One Bldg.
1001 Howard Ave., Suite 3110
New Orleans, LA 70113
504-523-4352

Maine Humanities Council
Dorothy Schwartz, Exec. Dir.
Box 7202
Portland, ME 04112
207-773-5051

Maryland Humanities Council
Barbara Wells Sarudy, Exec. Dir.
601 N. Howard St.
Baltimore, MD 21201-4585
410-625-4830

Massachusetts Foundation for the Humanities
David Tebaldi, Exec. Dir.
One Woodbridge St.
South Hadley, MA 01075
413-536-1385

Michigan Humanities Council
Ronald Means, Exec. Dir.
119 Pere Marquette Dr., Suite 3B
Lansing, MI 48912-1231
517-372-7770

Minnesota Humanities Commission
Cheryl Dickson, Pres.
26 E. Exchange St.
Saint Paul, MN 55101
612-224-5739

Mississippi Humanities Council
Cora Norman, Exec. Dir.
3825 Ridgewood Rd., Rm. 311
Jackson, MS 39211-6453
601-982-6752

Missouri Humanities Council
Christine Reilly, Exec. Dir.
911 Washington Ave., Suite 215
Saint Louis, MO 63101-1208
314-621-7705

Montana Committee for the Humanities
Gerald Fetz, Acting Exec. Dir.
Box 8036, Hellgate Sta.
Missoula, MT 59807
406-243-6022

Nebraska Humanities Council
Jane Renner Hood, Exec. Dir.
Lincoln Center Bldg., Suite 225
215 Centennial Mall S.
Lincoln, NE 68508
402-474-2131

Nevada Humanities Committee
Judith K. Winzeler, Exec. Dir.
1034 N. Sierra St.
Reno, NV 89503
702-784-6587

New Hampshire Humanities Council
Charles G. Bickford, Exec. Dir.
19 Pillsbury St.
Box 2228
Concord, NH 03302-2228
603-224-4071

New Jersey Committee for the Humanities
Cynthia M. Koch, Exec. Dir.
390 George St., Suite 602
New Brunswick, NJ 08901-2019
908-932-7726

New Mexico Endowment for the Humanities
John Lucas, Exec. Dir.
209 Onate Hall
Cnr. Campus and Girard N.E.
Albuquerque, NM 87131
505-277-3705

New York Council for the Humanities
Jay Kaplan, Exec. Dir.
198 Broadway, 10th fl.
New York, NY 10038
212-233-1131

North Carolina Humanities Council
Alice Barkley, Exec. Dir.
425 Spring Garden St.
Greensboro, NC 27401
919-334-5325

North Dakota Humanities Council
Everett Albers, Exec. Dir.
Box 2191
Bismarck, ND 58502
701-255-3360

Ohio Humanities Council
Eleanor Kingsbury, Exec. Dir.
695 Bryden Rd
Box 06354
Columbus, OH 43206-0354
614-461-7802

Oklahoma Foundation for the Humanities
Anita May, Exec. Dir.
Festival Plaza
428 W. California, Suite 270
Oklahoma City, OK 73102
405-235-0280

Oregon Council for the Humanities
Richard Lewis, Exec. Dir.
812 S.W. Washington St., Suite 225
Portland, OR 97205
503-241-0543

Pennsylvania Humanities Council
Harry Ausprich, Exec. Dir.
320 Walnut St., Suite 305
Philadelphia, PA 19106
215-925-1005

Rhode Island Committee for the Humanities
Thomas H. Roberts, Exec. Dir.
60 Ship St.
Providence, RI 02903
401-273-2250

South Carolina Humanities Council
Randy L. Akers, Exec. Dir.
1610 Oak St.
Columbia, SC 29204
803-771-8864

South Dakota Humanities Council
John Whalen, Exec. Dir.
Box 7050, Univ. Sta.
Brookings, SD 57007
605-688-6113

Tennessee Humanities Council
Robert Cheatham, Exec. Dir.
1003 18th Ave. S.
Nashville, TN 37212
615-320-7001

Texas Committee for the Humanities
James Veninga, Exec. Dir.
3809 S. Second St.
Austin, TX 78704
512-440-1991

Utah Humanities Council
Delmont Oswald, Exec. Dir.
350 S. 400 E., Suite 110
Salt Lake City, UT 84111-2946
801-359-9670

Vermont Council on the Humanities
Victor R. Swenson, Exec. Dir.
Box 58
Hyde Park, VT 05655
802-888-3183

Virginia Foundation for the Humanities and
   Public Policy
Robert C. Vaughan, Pres.
145 Ednam Dr.
Charlottesville, VA 22903
804-924-3296

Washington Commission for the Humanities
Hidde Van Duym, Exec. Dir.
615 Second Ave., Suite 300
Seattle, WA 98104
206-682-1770

West Virginia Humanities Council
Charles Daugherty, Exec. Dir.
723 Kanawha Blvd., Suite 800
Charleston, WV 25301
304-346-8500

Wisconsin Humanities Council
Max Harris, Exec. Dir.
716 Langdon St.

Madison, WI 53706
608-262-0706

Wyoming Council for the Humanities
Robert Young, Exec. Dir.
Box 3643, Univ. Sta.
Laramie, WY 82071-3643
307-766-6496

Guam Humanities Council
Jillette Leon-Guerreo, Exec. Dir.
123 Archbishop Flores St., Suite C
Agana, GU 96910
671-472-4507

Commonwealth of the Northern Mariana
   Islands Council for the Humanities
William Barrineau, Exec. Dir.
Caller Box AAA 3394
Saipan, MP 96950
670-235-4785

Fundación Puertorriqueña de las
   Humanidades
Juan M. Gonzalez Lamela, Exec. Dir.
Box S-4307
Old San Juan, PR 00904
809-721-2087

Virgin Islands Humanities Council
Magda Smith, Exec. Dir.
Box 1829
Saint Thomas, VI 00803
809-776-4044

Council on Library Resources, 1993

1400 16th St. N.W., Suite 510, Washington, DC 20036
202-483-7474

Ellen B. Timmer
Publications Consultant

The Council on Library Resources (CLR) is an exempt operating foundation established in 1956 to "aid in the solution of library problems; to conduct research in, develop, and demonstrate new techniques and methods; and to disseminate through any means the results thereof." The council awards grants and contracts to institutions and individuals, with the objective of helping to find solutions to the generic problems of libraries and information services. In addition, as an operating foundation, the council directs its own projects. It often performs a catalytic role by bringing individuals and organizations together to define problems and help determine priorities for action in the council's areas of interest. Areas currently receiving most attention include human resources, the economics of information services, infrastructure, and access and processing.

Support is not provided for construction or renovation, collection acquisitions, routine operating costs, activities judged to be of limited influence, or work that essentially repeats previous research. CLR does not fund indirect costs or, with rare exceptions, equipment purchases.

The board of directors consists of individuals from libraries, academic institutions, the business community, and the professions. Council officers are Maximilian W. Kempner, chairperson; Charles D. Churchwell, vice chairperson; W. David Penniman, president; and Mary Agnes Thompson, secretary and treasurer. During the fiscal year ending June 30, 1993, the council received support for its activities from the J. Paul Getty Trust, the William and Flora Hewlett Foundation, the W. K. Kellogg Foundation, and the Andrew W. Mellon Foundation.

Highlights of FY 1993

During the year, CLR took a close look at the environment in which it and the libraries it serves must operate, and kept an eye on several trends that could affect its work. These trends and the need for libraries to be able to respond to them in new ways were underscored as the council held focus group sessions for research librarians and urban public librarians. The session participants identified the role of the library, financing and accountability, technology, and adaptation to change as major areas of concern. All of these issues fit into CLR's current program areas and must be addressed in order for the council to work toward its overall goals: to help libraries embrace a forward-looking mission and vision and to help foundations see a close relationship between their objectives and the objectives of the libraries of the future. The following four sections describe CLR's current program areas and discuss some of the grants awarded or active in FY 1993.

Human Resources

The council's human resources program is intended to develop leaders on a continuing basis who can build and manage the information support systems needed by society and to assist current leaders in developing the skills needed to transform their institutions in response to changing societal needs. This program area emphasizes leadership and management development, recruitment, education, and research.

CLR's longstanding Academic Library Management Intern Program concluded after providing 55 librarians with the chance to observe the day-to-day management of a large academic library during a one-year internship. The last class of interns included Heather Gordon, who interned with Jerry D. Campbell, University Librarian at Duke University, and Judy McQueen, who interned with Richard De Gennaro, Roy E. Larsen Librarian at Harvard College.

While the program was highly successful, evaluation has suggested that there may not be the same need for this kind of program as there was at its inception in 1974, and that different kinds of programs could serve more people at a lower cost. One example of these newer programs is the College Library Director Mentor Program, which was funded by the council in 1992 for a two-year period to enhance the leadership capabilities of newly appointed college library directors. The program was developed by the College Libraries Section of the Association of College and Research Libraries and was coordinated by Larry Hardesty of Eckerd College. New directors participating in the program are matched with experienced college library directors, who act as their mentors or peer consultants. Fourteen first-year directors participated in the program during the 1992–1993 academic year. Initial reactions have been positive from the new directors and their mentors, as well as from academic deans.

CLR made a grant in 1993 to the Graduate School of Library and Information Studies at Queens College/City University of New York (CUNY) to conduct a series of four workshops centered around multiculturalism and diversity in the workplace. The workshops will contribute to new strategies for redesigning the school's curriculum in order to provide improved services to a multicultural library audience.

Economic Data

In order to assure that the resources invested in libraries and related information services are allocated effectively to maximize the benefits to society, CLR has been addressing projects that focus attention on the costs and benefits of specific library services. The results from such projects should lead to a more systematic decision-making process regarding allocation of funding and cost sharing. The economics studies completed or initiated in 1993 tended to focus on microeconomic issues, addressing such topics as serial pricing, journal use, interlibrary loan (ILL), and public library financing. In addition, CLR continued to encourage the application to library services of continuous quality techniques, and supported the development of functional tools for libraries to use to determine their own costs and benefits.

CLR provided partial support for a project to examine the costs to research libraries of ILL services. Data was collected from 76 libraries on the typical costs of ILL transactions, based on a survey instrument developed by the Research Libraries Group (RLG) and distributed by the Association of Research Libraries (ARL).

CLR is also providing support for an ARL Visiting Program Officer working to improve ILL and document delivery services. The results of the ARL/RLG interlibrary loan study point to a need for an ideal ILL system as proposed in a white paper prepared for the ARL Committee on Access to Information Resources. The program officer will follow up on the recommendations in the white paper and will work with libraries and ILL/document delivery system designers to move toward a more comprehensive and integrated system for interlibrary loan and document delivery.

CLR funded a proposal from Rutgers University to develop tools to assess the costs, and classify and measure the benefits of diverse library functions. The project's objectives are to adapt functional cost analysis to all types of library functions and services, to develop a system to classify libraries' beneficial impacts, and to develop a system for measuring those benefits. The project investigators will develop techniques and a methodology that will be assembled into a manual, which will subsequently enable other libraries to use the measurements that are defined from the project or to define their own, as appropriate.

Infrastructure

Infrastructure is an umbrella term for the systems, services, and facilities that help libraries and other information services operate more efficiently and effectively. Elements covered under this term include buildings, communications networks, bibliographic utilities, software and hardware vendor communities, and publishers. The goal of CLR's infrastructure program is to establish continuing communication and cooperation among the various information systems and services that support libraries and to ensure that economic, sociopolitical, technical, and legal changes do not inhibit library functions or access to information by individuals and groups.

The main emphasis of CLR's infrastructure program continues to be in the area of engineering information. A June 1992 conference partially sponsored by the council resulted in an integrated action plan to improve access to engineering information in libraries and specialized information services in the United States. The council's report of the conference proceedings, *Exploration of a National Engineering Information Service*, was published in December 1992. This effort has since become known as the National Engineering Information Initiative (NEII). CLR has taken responsibility for maintaining the progress of NEII toward the realization of a national engineering information network. The NEII work is proceeding in accordance with the integrated action plan developed at the June 1992 conference, and includes:

- Forming a panel that will provide direction and oversight for the development of the network
- Obtaining funding to carry out the NEII action plan
- Establishing a listserv to enable interested parties to share ideas and information about NEII via computer
- Conducting focus group sessions with engineers in government, academia, and industry

Another ongoing activity in this area is the special grant program, Setting Library Policies and Priorities in Research Universities, which provided four $100,000 grants to universities or consortia to study management and services issues in research libraries and to develop strategic plans for dealing with those issues. All four projects are nearing completion, but the process of planning will continue in all of the institutions involved. Grant recipients report that major benefits from this program have been the establishment of a process for planning, the engagement of university faculty and administrators in that process, a new look at how the institution can respond to the changing environment, and the development of tools to support data-driven decision making.

Project participants at Columbia University have completed data collection and analysis for a study and survey of library use and users in three science departments. The costs of interlibrary borrowing and document delivery were compared with the cost of ownership; factors such as the value of browsing were also considered. The Columbia study team visited libraries at six other institutions to identify different models for information delivery that could be incorporated into Columbia's existing electronic infrastructure.

At Harvard University, the strategic planning grant coincided with a period of significant change in the Harvard College Library. In addressing the need to respond to new developments in technology, economics, scholarship, and teaching within a research institution, Harvard found that a key to success was an initial emphasis on vision and a continuing focus on organizational development. Harvard's vision statement presents a future scenario based not on the current organization but on the role and function of the Harvard College Library ten years hence. Harvard project participants scheduled invitational symposia in late 1993 to address the changing role of the library in learning, teaching, and research.

Building on a strong foundation of interinstitutional collaboration, the State University of New York (SUNY) University Center libraries have been developing multilevel committee structures for planning and policy setting related to cooperative collection development and resource sharing among four institutions within the statewide system. The libraries conducted a journal overlap study, a current journal titles use study, an interlibrary loan survey, and a faculty electronic access survey, all of which not only gathered data on which to base decisions but helped to increase communication, raise awareness, and enlist the cooperation of the communities served by the four libraries.

Duke University, the University of North Carolina at Chapel Hill, and North Carolina State University have also been conducting user surveys and studies to gather data on their collective collection strengths. A large-scale survey of all faculty and a large sample of the graduate students in science and engineering departments of the three universities was conducted in 1992. The data complements findings from Columbia and SUNY regarding the use of materials and library services. After careful analysis of the data, the research team is exploring some key policy questions with focus groups on each campus.

CLR awarded a grant to Rice University with the aim of investigating how librarians can work with computer scientists and university faculty to demonstrate a virtual library concept. The grant provides partial support for a project to develop materials for an undergraduate course within the university's electronic studio project. The project will incorporate a distributed multimedia hypertext system, the Virtual Notebook System. Materials collected by librarians, faculty, and students in fully developed electronic studios will include notes, assignments, documents, images, video, and sound. The project investigators will assess the roles and responsibilities of the librarians, faculty members, and computer scientists, as well as the management and utilization of technologies.

CLR partially supported a conference organized by the Getty Art History Information Program and the American Council of Learned Societies to address the implications of electronic information for scholarship in the humanities. The participants developed recommendations that included the initiation of a national collaborative effort for the humanities, promotion of the creation of a national "digital" library, development of model collaborative projects, support for training, promotion of an understanding of the role that information technology can play in research and teaching, and establishment of descriptive standards for primary materials.

Over the next three years, high-speed data connections and Internet access will be brought to homes, schools, libraries, and businesses in the community of Blacksburg, Virginia. This effort, the Blacksburg Electronic Village Project, is serving as a prototype for bringing interactive library resources to people in the community. The council funded an initial evaluation that will gauge the impact of new electronic information services on libraries and individuals; determine which information services have the greatest value to users; assess the user interface and other technical aspects of the information services; and refine evaluation methods and techniques in order to make improvements before a subsequent full-scale evaluation of the project.

Access and Processing

In recent years, changes in information availability, means of delivery, and costs of processing have challenged the traditional processing and access activities of libraries. The purpose of the council's efforts in this area is to create ongoing mechanisms that encourage improvement in the internal processes performed by libraries so that access to information is enhanced and the resources invested in libraries are used more efficiently and effectively. Put simply, CLR seeks to help libraries provide information to their users in an efficient and usable form.

In the area of bibliographic control, CLR supported a survey by SKP Associates that assessed the value of the Cataloging in Publication (CIP) program, which provides prepublication cataloging records for the books most likely to be acquired by libraries. The council was instrumental in the establishment of the CIP program at the Library of Congress in 1971 and supported a similar study conducted after the program's first ten years of operation. Results from the 1993 study indicated that the scope and quality of the data are above average and that savings in cataloging costs for libraries are significant. The program clearly continues to be a valuable service.

In another cataloging-related effort, the council supported a planning meeting of the Cooperative Cataloging Council, which was established to develop a strategic plan for cooperative cataloging among the nation's libraries. The effort came out of a joint meeting of representatives of the National Coordinated Cataloging Program and the CONSER (Cooperative Online Serials) Program who saw the need for a model program that would take the best from existing programs and set the stage for a more cost-effective, participatory process. The group prepared a mission statement, established goals, and formed several task forces to address specific issues.

Preservation is another element of this program area. In conjunction with an effort of the United States Agricultural Information Network, the council provided partial support for an Advisory Panel on Preservation to consider how best to preserve agricultural science literature, including primary unpublished resources and the most important pre-1950 published literature. Land-grant institutions, the

National Agricultural Library, and other libraries, societies, and archives with important historical collections will participate in the program.

An ongoing project researching how to develop an online catalog search system that incorporates aids for clustering and organizing useful retrieval sets is being conducted in the Computer Science Department of Indiana University of Pennsylvania, with funding from CLR. The system takes advantage of the data included in a bibliographic record, tables of contents, and expert system technology to improve subject access for catalog retrieval.

The concept of the digital library or electronic information center is being considered actively by many organizations. In order to provide the necessary background information for developing plans related to the electronic library, CLR has contracted with the University of Michigan's School of Information and Library Studies to conduct an analytical review of the literature on the future library.

Further information about other new and ongoing grants can be found in CLR's *37th Annual Report* for FY 1993.

Grants and Contracts Over $5,000, FY 1993

Association of Research Libraries, Washington, D.C.
ARL visiting program officer to improve interlibrary
loan and document delivery services — $10,700

Indiana University of Pennsylvania, Indiana, Pa.
Hypermedia for improved subject access — $6,600
Vocabulary control tools for online searching — $14,852

Kansas State University, Manhattan, Kans.
National preservation plan for the historical literature
of agriculture — $7,000

Queens College, Flushing, N.Y.
Seminar series on mapping curricular revision — $6,600

Rice University, Houston, Texas
The Rice humanities electronic studio — $65,000

Rutgers University, New Brunswick, N.J.
Study of the costs and beneficial impacts of library functions — $97,612

University of Michigan, Ann Arbor, Mich.
The library of the future: an analytical report and bibliography — $7,000

Virginia Polytechnic Institute and State University, Blacksburg, Va.
Blacksburg Electronic Village project — $9,665

U.S. Department of Education Library Programs, 1993

555 New Jersey Ave. N.W., Washington, DC 20208-5571
202-219-2293, FAX 202-219-1725

Ray M. Fry

Director, Library Programs
Office of Educational Research and Improvement
U.S. Department of Education

The U.S. Department of Education's Office of Library Programs contributes to the improvement of the nation's libraries and library education by administering the 11 programs under the Library Services and Construction Act (LSCA) and the Higher Education Act, Title II (HEA II). The programs

- Promote resource sharing and cooperation among all types of libraries by facilitating development and access to information that permit individuals to find and use books and other materials from libraries across the country
- Assist state library agencies in improving local library services for all citizens, with a focus on underserved populations such as the handicapped and disadvantaged
- Support local and state efforts to construct new public library facilities and upgrade existing ones
- Improve library services to native populations—Indian tribes, Alaskan native villages, and Hawaiian natives—through basic and special projects
- Support the acquisition of foreign-language materials in state and local public libraries
- Support adult literacy programs conducted by state library agencies and local public libraries
- Strengthen major research libraries, including those of postsecondary institutions, by helping them improve access to important collections, preserve deteriorating materials, and acquire unique, distinctive, and specialized materials
- Advance the education of librarians through fellowships and training institutes
- Encourage colleges and universities to promote and develop exemplary uses of technology for resource sharing and networking
- Fund research and demonstration projects on library and information science issues

Note: The following Library Programs' staff assisted in writing and/or compiling data for this article: Nancy Cavanaugh, Christina Dunn, Beth Fine, Clarence Fogelstrom, Donald Fork, Jane Heiser, Barbara Humes, Neal Kaske, Dorothy Kittel, Robert Klassen, Carol Cameron Lyons, Linda Miles, Evaline Neff, Jan Owens, Kathy Perkinson, Trish Skaptason, and Louise Sutherland.

In addition to administering LSCA and HEA II, Library Programs provides leadership to the library community by

- Planning for library development
- Implementing federal policies and programs
- Providing guidance and technical assistance to grant recipients
- Promoting the evaluation of library programs
- Recognizing exemplary library programs
- Conducting research to address national issues
- Interpreting federally funded library activities for library and nonlibrary audiences
- Integrating the contributions of libraries into the framework of the National Education Goals

In FY 1993, the Office of Library Programs undertook two special projects: a survey of public library services to children and young adults, a cooperative effort with the U.S. Department of Education's National Center for Education Statistics; and Evaluating Federally Funded Library Programs, a contract with the University of Wisconsin–Madison to train state library personnel in planning and evaluation. (This contract is further described under HEA II-B, Research and Demonstration Program.)

Higher Education Act (HEA, PL 99-498)

Title II of the Higher Education Act has been the backbone of federal financial assistance to college and university libraries for more than two decades. With the continuing expansion of information resources and the increasing demands on higher education libraries, Title II has been an important factor in helping these libraries to preserve, acquire, and share resources; to train and retrain personnel; and to use new technologies to improve services. In 1986 HEA Title II was reauthorized and some parts rewritten to accommodate further change, including establishment of the College Library Technology and Cooperation Grants program (HEA, Title II-D; now HEA II-A). In 1987 these amendments were implemented fully through revisions in the regulations and development of new regulations for the II-D program. Changes in HEA Title II under the 1992 reauthorization reflect a new emphasis on the electronic networked environment. Changes include:

- Under Library Education, Research, and Development (HEA II-B), "Library Career Training" became "Library Education and Human Resource Development," with a focus on meeting critical needs, such as minority recruitment. Determining critical needs in library education and research priorities requires the Secretary to consult with library and information science professional bodies.

- "Strengthening Research Library Resources" (HEA II-C) was changed to "Improving Access to Research Library Resources." The new title reflects the new emphasis on access.
- Part D under HEA Title II, College Library Technology and Cooperation Grants program, became Part A.
- "Strengthening Library and Information Science Programs and Libraries in Historically Black Colleges and Universities and Other Minority-Serving Institutions" (HEA II-D) was added as a new part. However, no funds were appropriated for its administration.

The 1992 amendments were implemented in FY 1993 through revisions in the regulations.

College Library Technology and Cooperation Grants Program (HEA, Title II-A)

The College Library Technology and Cooperation Grants Program, HEA Title II-A (formerly HEA Title II-D), was added to the Higher Education Act when the law was reauthorized in 1986. The program awards grants to institutions of higher education for technological equipment to enhance resource-sharing activities among colleges and universities. In FY 1993, the sixth year of program funding, $3,872,768 was appropriated for Title II-A.

In addition to encouraging resource-sharing projects among libraries of institutions of higher education, this program promotes innovative research and demonstration projects that meet special needs in utilizing technology to enhance library services. Grants are awarded in four categories:

- Networking grants to plan, develop, acquire, maintain, or upgrade technological equipment necessary to organize, access, or utilize material in electronic formats and to participate in electronic networks for sharing of library resources
- Combination grants to establish and strengthen joint-use library facilities, resources, or equipment for the accessing and sharing of library and information resources
- Services to Institutions grants to establish, develop, or expand programs or projects that improve information services provided to institutions of higher education
- Research and Demonstration grants to conduct research or demonstration projects that improve information services to meet specialized national or regional needs in using technology to enhance library and information services such as through the National Research and Education Network (NREN)

In FY 1993, the College Library Technology and Cooperation Grants Program awarded grants (33 new, 4 continuation) totaling $3,872,768 to institutions in 22 states, Puerto Rico, and the District of Columbia. Of the total amount, $3,437,780 supported 33 new grants and $434,988, 4 continuation grants. Of the

Table 1 / Applications Received and FY 1993 Awards by Category, College Library Technology and Cooperation Grants Program

	Networking	Combination	Services to Institutions	Research and Demonstration
Number of awards	19	5	2	7
Total dollars awarded	$845,792	$829,406	$231,027	$1,531,555
Average award	$44,516	$165,881	$115,514	$218,794
Applications received	123	52	22	60
Total dollars requested	$6,343,373	$12,361,948	$4,240,527	$12,725,183
Average request	$51,572	$237,730	$192,751	$212,086

four continuation awards, two were Research and Demonstration projects, one was a Services to Institutions project, and one was a Networking project.

Awards promote networking and resource-sharing activities and were made primarily to academic libraries, although state and public libraries and other non-profit organizations are eligible.

A total of 257 applications, requesting $35,671,031, were received for the FY 1993 competition. Table 1 reports the number of new awards made and applications received for each of the four grant categories.

The projects funded in FY 1993 demonstrate the broad range of resource sharing through technology. The following represent each category of grants:

Networking. Tougaloo College (Tougaloo, Mississippi) will implement a program of resource sharing with other libraries through membership in the Southeastern Library Network (SOLINET), a regional affiliate of the Online Computer Library Center Inc. (OCLC). This networking project will make possible online searching of very large bibliographic databases to which Tougaloo College will add its records, including a unique archival collection of manuscripts and documents relating to the Mississippi Civil Rights Movement.

Combination. The Michigan Research Libraries Triangle (MRLT), a consortium of the University of Michigan (Ann Arbor), Michigan State University (East Lansing), and Wayne State University (Detroit) libraries, will electronically link their online catalogs. This effort will make it possible for students and faculty members at any one of these universities to search the holdings of the other two as well as their own. A function also will be added to their online systems enabling the patrons of these libraries to initiate borrowing (interlibrary loans) among these institutions.

Services to Institutions. South Central Research Library Council (Ithaca, New York) will be working through New York's nine Reference and Research Library Resources Systems to provide on-site advice, guidance, education, and technical support to librarians of 111 New York academic libraries that will enable them either to establish Internet connections or to increase and enhance staff knowledge and skills in using Internet. (Internet is part of the developing national—and international—information infrastructure.)

Research and Demonstration. Librarians at the University of Tennessee (Knoxville) will be developing and testing an electronic scholar's workstation that will enable scholars to move seamlessly among the works they are creating, online library catalogs, citation databases, electronic journals and reference resources, and links to information experts. The scholar's workstation of the future—"an electronic version of a branch library"—will be installed and field-tested at four different locations on the campus in Knoxville.

Table 2 lists projects funded under each category.

Library Education and Human Resource Development Program (HEA, Title II-B)

The Library Education and Human Resource Development Program (Title II-B of the Higher Education Act) authorizes a program of federal financial assistance to institutions of higher education and other library organizations and agencies to assist in training persons in library and information science and to establish, develop, and expand programs of library and information science. Grants are made for fellowships and traineeships at the master's, post-master's, and doctoral levels. Grants may also be used to assist in covering the costs of institutes, or courses, to upgrade the competencies of persons serving in all types of libraries, information centers, or instructional materials centers offering library and information services, and of those serving as educators.

In FY 1993 Congress appropriated $4,960,000 for the HEA II-B, Library Education and Human Resource Development Program. One hundred and fifteen fellowship awards were made to 47 institutions to support 298 fellowships (122 doctoral, 17 post-master's, and 159 master's). The total of all grants was $3,870,400. Stipends were $5,400 for master's, and $7,400 for post-master's and doctoral candidates. Institutions received an amount equal to the stipend to cover the cost of training.

Areas of study reflect the Secretary's priorities:

- Master's-level studies fall mainly into four areas: children's and young adult services; science reference; school library media; and cataloging.
- Training and retraining at the post-master's level will focus on library services to youth science reference; and library management.
- Funded doctoral fellowships will prepare candidates to teach in some area of study in librarianship or to engage in library planning, evaluation, and research.

Table 3 shows the Library Education and Human Resource Development fellowship grants awarded in FY 1993.

Between 1966 and 1993 institutions of higher education were awarded a total of 4,802 awards—1,361 doctoral, 282 post-master's, 3,311 master's, 16 bachelor's, and 53 associate's fellowships; and 77 traineeships. Table 4 reviews the fellowship program's history.

In FY 1993 the Library Education and Human Resource Development Program made awards totaling $1,089,600 to support institutes or training workshops primarily for school and public librarians. Seventeen institute grants were awarded to institutions of higher education and library organizations. These grants, training approximately 1,700 participants, ranged from $13,965 to $122,456.

(text continues on p. 296)

Table 2 / College Library Technology and Cooperation Grants Program
Projects Funded under HEA Title II-A, Summary Listing for FY 1993

	City	State	Funds Granted
Networking			
Southern Arkansas University[1]	Magnolia	AR	$49,145
Wartburg College[1]	Waverly	IA	50,000
Highland Community College	Freeport	IL	42,725
Illinois Valley Community College[1]	Oglesby	IL	47,394
North Park College and Theological Seminary	Chicago	IL	48,510
Shawnee Community College[1]	Ullin	IL	49,982
Spertus College of Judaica	Chicago	IL	49,690
Bangor Theological Seminary	Bangor	ME	36,600
College of the Atlantic[1]	Bar Harbor	ME	49,955
Crowder College[1]	Neosho	MO	40,008
Delta State University[1]	Cleveland	MS	47,365
Tougaloo College[1]	Tougaloo	MS	41,839
Mount Olive College[1]	Mount Olive	NC	32,576
New Hampshire Technical College[1]	Stratham	NH	33,494
Cleveland State University	Cleveland	OH	49,200
Saint Francis College[1]	Loretto	PA	50,000
Universidad Adventista de las Antillas[1]	Mayaguez	PR	49,964
Tri-County Technical College[1]	Pendleton	SC	49,900
Presentation College[1]	Aberdeen	SD	27,445
(mean award size $44,516)		Subtotal	$845,792
Combination			
Alabama Commission on Higher Education	Montgomery	AL	$225,000
University of Michigan[2]	Ann Arbor	MI	237,000
Penn Valley Community College[2]	Kansas City	MO	55,800
State University of New York at Cortland	Cortland	NY	77,006
York Technical College[2]	Rock Hill	SC	234,600
(mean award size $165,881)		Subtotal	$829,406
Services to Institutions			
Washington Research Library Consortium	Lanham	MD	$71,777
South Central Research Library Council	Ithaca	NY	159,250
(mean award size $115,514)		Subtotal	$231,027
Research and Demonstration			
University of California at Berkeley School of Library and Information Studies[2]	Berkeley	CA	$ 117,770
University of California at Berkeley Library	Berkeley	CA	228,183
Georgetown University Medical Center[2]	Washington	DC	91,640
University of Illinois[2]	Champaign	IL	641,866
University of Michigan, Ann Arbor[2]	Ann Arbor	MI	115,551
Oregon State University[2]	Corvallis	OR	214,247
University of Tennessee, Knoxville[2]	Knoxville	TN	122,298
(mean award size $218,794)		Subtotal	$1,531,555
Noncompeting Continuations			
Arizona State University[2]	Tempe	AZ	$95,081
Center for Research Libraries	Chicago	IL	133,315
University of Minnesota–Twin Cities	Minneapolis	MN	95,885
Rutgers, State University of New Jersey	New Brunswick	NJ	110,707
(mean award size $108,747)		Subtotal	$434,988
		Total	$3,872,768

[1] Developing institutions
[2] Eligible for noncompeting continuation awards in fiscal year 1994

Table 3 / HEA Title II-B, Library Education
FY 1993 Fellowship Grantees

Grantee	Number and Level	Amount	Area of Study
Catholic University	3 master's	$32,400	Young adult services
Clarion University	1 master's	10,800	Rural public libraries, school library media
Clark Atlanta University	1 master's	10,800	Children and young adult services, school library media
CUNY, Queens College	1 master's	10,800	Children and young adult services, school library media, science reference
Drexel University	8 doctoral	118,400	Library education and research
Emporia State University	1 master's	10,800	Children and young adult services, school library media, science reference, cataloging
Florida State University	8 doctoral	126,400	Children and young adult services
Indiana University	2 doctoral	29,600	Library education and research
	3 post-master's	47,400	School library media, children and young adult services
	3 master's	32,400	Science reference
	1 master's	12,800	Youth services, school library media
Kent State University	3 master's	34,400	Children and young adult services
Long Island University, C.W. Post Campus	1 master's	10,800	School, public, academic, and special libraries
	3 master's	33,400	Public library services, young adult services
	1 master's	10,800	Science reference
Louisiana State University	4 post-master's	59,200	Science reference, youth services
	3 master's	32,400	Library education, automation of library services
	5 master's	58,000	Science reference
	1 master's	10,800	Cataloging
	1 master's	10,800	School library media, services for children, young adults, and disabled persons
North Carolina Central University	1 master's	10,800	Science reference
Ohio University	1 master's	10,800	School library media
Rosary College	5 master's	54,000	Science reference
	3 master's	32,400	School library media
Rutgers University	7 doctoral	107,600	Library education
	1 master's	10,800	School library media, children and young adult services
Sam Houston State University	1 master's	10,800	School library media
San Jose State University	1 master's	10,800	Children and young adult services in public libraries
Simmons College	1 master's	10,800	Children and young adult services, school library media
St. John's University	1 master's	10,800	School library media, public library services
SUNY at Albany	3 doctoral	44,400	Library education and research
	5 master's	54,000	Cataloging and preservation
	1 master's	10,800	Science reference
	1 master's	10,800	School library media
SUNY at Buffalo	1 master's	10,800	Science reference, school library media

Table 3 / HEA Title II-B, Library Education
FY 1993 Fellowship Grantees *(cont.)*

Grantee	Number and Level	Amount	Area of Study
Syracuse University	1 master's	11,800	Youth services
Texas Woman's University	6 doctoral	88,800	Library education
	3 master's	32,400	School library media
	1 master's	10,800	Cataloging
	3 master's	32,400	Young adult services in public libraries
	3 master's	37,400	Children's services with emphasis on early childhood
University of Alabama	2 doctoral	29,600	Library and information science education
	2 doctoral	31,600	Library education and research in youth services
	1 master's	10,800	School library media
	3 master's	32,400	Cataloging, information technology management
University of Arizona	4 doctoral	62,200	Library education and research
	5 master's	57,000	Science reference
University of California, Berkeley	4 doctoral	60,200	Library education
	5 doctoral	74,000	Research in new technologies
	2 doctoral	30,600	Management, planning and evaluation
	1 master's	10,800	Organization of information
	1 master's	10,800	Technical services using information technologies
	1 master's	11,800	Children and young adult services, school library media
University of California, Los Angeles	7 doctoral	106,600	Library education, planning, evaluation, and research
	3 master's	32,400	School library media, children and young adult services
University of Central Arkansas	4 master's	54,200	School library media
University of Houston, Clear Lake	3 master's	32,400	School library media
University of Illinois	4 doctoral	59,200	Library education, children and young adult services, school library media
	3 master's	32,400	Youth services, science reference, cataloging
University of Iowa	1 master's	10,800	Children and young adult services
University of Kentucky	1 master's	10,800	School library media
	1 master's	10,800	Science reference
University of Maryland	1 master's	10,800	School library media, children and young adult services, science reference
University of Michigan	2 doctoral	31,600	Library education and research
	3 master's	33,400	Science reference
University of Missouri	4 master's	43,200	Science reference
	3 master's	32,400	School library media, public library services
	1 master's	10,800	Science reference (health)
	1 master's	12,800	School library media
	1 master's	10,800	Children's services, school library media
	1 master's	12,800	Cataloging

**Table 3 / HEA Title II-B, Library Education
FY 1993 Fellowship Grantees** *(cont.)*

Grantee	Number and Level	Amount	Area of Study
University of North Carolina, Chapel Hill	7 doctoral	105,600	Library education and research
	3 master's	32,400	Cataloging
	1 master's	10,800	Systems management in technical services
	1 master's	10,800	Children and young adult services in public libraries
	1 master's	10,800	Information systems analysis and design
University of North Carolina, Greensboro	1 master's	10,800	Public and academic library services
University of North Texas	5 doctoral	77,000	Library education
	5 doctoral	79,000	Library and information science education
	6 doctoral	90,800	Science reference
	4 doctoral	59,200	Library education
	1 master's	10,800	School, public, academic, and special libraries
	1 master's	10,800	Cataloging, library education with emphasis on managing with new technologies
	1 master's	10,800	Science reference
	1 master's	10,800	Library education, automation of library services
University of Oklahoma	3 master's	32,400	Science reference
	3 master's	32,400	Young adult services
	1 master's	12,800	School library media
	1 master's	10,800	Cataloging
University of Pittsburgh	8 doctoral	119,400	Library education and research
	6 doctoral	92,800	Library education and research, information management
	6 post-master's	88,800	Library management
	5 master's	54,000	Children and young adult services, school library media
	3 master's	32,400	Science reference
	1 master's	10,800	Services for elderly, illiterate, and disadvantaged
University of South Carolina	4 post-master's	59,200	Children and young adult services, school library media
	1 master's	13,800	Children and young adult services, school library media
University of Southern Mississippi	1 master's	13,800	Children and young adult services
University of Tennessee	3 master's	32,400	Children's services
	3 master's	32,400	School library media
	1 master's	10,800	Science reference
University of Texas	4 doctoral	59,200	Library education, planning, and evaluation
	3 master's	32,400	Children and young adult services
	1 master's	10,800	Preservation and program management
	1 master's	10,800	Public library services
	1 master's	10,800	Services for "at-risk" youth in school and public libraries

Table 3 / HEA Title II-B, Library Education
FY 1993 Fellowship Grantees *(cont.)*

Grantee	Number and Level	Amount	Area of Study
University of Wisconsin, Madison	6 doctoral	88,800	Library education, planning, evaluation, and research
	3 doctoral	44,400	Library education, financial management
	2 doctoral	29,600	Information science, planning, evaluation and research
	1 master's	10,800	School library media, children and young adult services
University of Wisconsin, Milwaukee	3 master's	35,400	Children and young adult services
	1 master's	10,800	Science reference
Wayne State University	3 master's	36,400	School library media
	1 master's	11,800	Science reference
	1 master's	11,800	Technical services
Subtotal	159 master's		
	17 post-master's		
	122 doctoral		
Total	298 fellowships	$3,870,400	

The institutes represent a variety of subject matter and approaches. However, all address at least one of the Secretary's priorities:

- Areas of library specialization where there are currently shortages, such as school media, children's services, young adult services, science reference, and cataloging
- Serving the information needs of people who are elderly, illiterate, disadvantaged, or residents of rural America

Because libraries are in a unique position to aid community efforts in support of the National Education Goals, the Secretary invited applicants to tie their proposals to the goals. Many of the institutes also reflect this commitment particularly in the areas of

- Preparing children to learn in school
- Helping students to achieve in mathematics and science and other challenging subjects
- Improving the public library as a center for lifelong learning for adults

Since the utilization of information technologies will play a key role in how well libraries will serve Americans' information needs, many of the institutes place heavy emphasis on training and retraining in information technology and management to improve services, especially in K–12 programs. Table 5 shows institute grants awarded in FY 1993.

Table 4 / HEA, Title II-B, Library Education
Fellowship/Trainee Program, Academic Years 1966–1993

Academic Year	Insti- tutions	Fellowship/Traineeship					Total	FY
		Doctoral	Post- Master's	Master's	Bachelor's	Associate's		
1966/67	24	52	25	62	—	—	139	1966
1967/68	38	116	58	327	—	—	501	1967
1968/69	51	168	47	494	—	—	709	1968
1969/70	56	193	30	379	—	—	602	1969
1970/71	48	171	15	200	20*	—	406	1970
1971/72	20	116	6	—	20*	—	142	1971
1972/73	15	39	3	20*	—	—	62	1972
1973/74	34	21	4	145+14*	—	20	204	1973
1974/75	50	21	3	168+3*	—	5	200	1974
1975/76	22	27	6	94	—	—	127	1975
1976/77	12	5	3	43	—	—	51	1976
1977/78	37	18	3	134	—	5	160	1977
1978/79	33	25	9	139	10	5	188	1978
1979/80	36	19	4	134	2	3	162	1979
1980/81	32	17	5	72	—	7	101	1980
1981/82	34	13	2	59	—	5	79	1981
1982/83	33	13	2	56	—	3	74	1982
1983/84	33	8	7	56	4	—	75	1983
1984/85	41	5	4	67	—	—	76	1984
1985/86	38	11	4	57	—	—	72	1985
1986/87	39	14	3	51	—	—	68	1986
1987/88	29	10	5	45	—	—	60	1987
1988/89	20	9	0	14	—	—	23	1988
1989/90	20	10	0	12	—	—	22	1989
1990/91	21	10	2	21	—	—	33	1990
1991/92	27	24	3	23	—	—	50	1991
1992/93	38	104	12	300	—	—	416	1992
1993/94	47	122	17	159	—	—	298	1993
Totals		1,361	282	3,311+37*	16+40*	53	5,100	

* Indicates traineeships

Library Research and Demonstration Program (HEA, Title II-B)

The Library Research and Demonstration Program (Title II-B of the Higher Education Act) authorizes grants and contracts for research and demonstration projects related to the improvement of libraries, training in librarianship, and the dissemination of information derived from these projects. Table 6 presents a chronological funding history of the program.

Title II, Part B, of the Higher Education Act was amended by the Higher Education Amendments of 1986. In 1987, by statutory mandate, "information technology" was deleted from the list of authorized research and demonstration subjects. This amendment precludes research on or about information technology but allows use of technology to accomplish the goals of a research or demonstration project.

Table 5 / HEA, Title II-B, Library Education and Human Resource Development
FY 1993 Institute Awards

Grantee	Award Amount	Project Title
Auburn University	$48,377	Telecommunications and electronic information retrieval institute
University of California, Los Angeles	43,452	Information Tools for Young Scientists: An Intensive Institute for Children's Librarians
American Association for the Advancement of Science	107,816	Science Library Institute
American Library Association	95,131	Library Media Specialists, Teachers and Administrators Collaborate to Help Middle School Students Learn Science and Math
University of Iowa	122,456	Geographic Information Systems (GIS) Literacy Institute
Baltimore County Public Library	47,415	Reaching Out to Information Schools, Networks: School and Public Telecommunications Institute
Massachusetts Board of Library Commissioners	60,960	Massachusetts Science Reference Institute
University of Michigan	51,775	Use of Telecommunications in K-12 Education
Wayne County (MI) Regional Educational Service Agency	94,465	Project Gateway: An Institute to Provide School Media Specialists Training and Long-Term Support in Information Technology
Rutgers University	26,691	Towards a Nation of Readers: Community Partnerships for Fostering the Reading Habit in Childhood and Early Adolescence
Southern Westchester Board of Cooperative Educational	77,667	Retraining for School Library Media Specialists in New Information Services Technologies
University of North Carolina, Greensboro	50,945	Ready to Learn: Kids Need Libraries
Case Western Reserve	40,500	Training the Librarian of the Future
Kent State University	63,001	Information Technology and Instruction: An Institute for the 21st Century
Sam Houston State University	13,965	Infusing Curricula with a Global Perspective
University of Texas	83,227	Achieving Readiness for School
University of Wisconsin	61,757	Internetworking Rural Libraries Institute

In FY 1993 Congress appropriated $2,802,400 for the HEA II-B, Research and Demonstration Program. Funds supported one grant and one contract:

- From the 21 applicants requesting more than $43.9 million under the Library Research and Demonstration Program—Statewide Multitype Library Network and Database competition, a grant of $2,480,000 was awarded to Louisiana State University and Agricultural and Mechanical College (LSU) to expand electronic library networking statewide. LSU proposed to expand the existing Louisiana Academic Libraries Network at LSU into a statewide library network via the state's fiberoptic telecommunications network. The expanded network will connect academic libraries throughout the state and extend access to all 64 parish libraries and some larger K–12 schools.

Table 6 / HEA Title II-B, Library Research and Demonstration Program, 1967–1993

Fiscal Year	Appropriation	Grants and Contracts Obligations	Number of Grants and Contracts
1967	$3,550,000	$3,381,052	38
1968	3,550,000	2,020,942	21
1969	3,000,000	2,986,264	39
1970	2,171,000	2,160,622	30
1971	2,171,000	2,170,274	18
1972	2,750,000	2,748,953	31
1973	1,785,000	1,784,741	24
1974	1,425,000	1,418,433	20
1975	1,000,000	999,338	19
1976	1,000,000	999,918	19
1977	1,000,000	995,193	18
1978	1,000,000	998,904	17
1979	1,000,000	980,563	12
1980	1,000,000 *	319,046	4
1981	1,000,000 *	239,954	12 (2 contracts, 10 commissioned papers)
1982	1,000,000 *	243,438	1 contract
1983	1,000,000 *	237,643	4 contracts
1984	1,000,000 *	250,764	3 contracts
1985	1,000,000 *	360,000	3 contracts
1986	1,000,000 *	378,000	3 contracts
1987	1,000,000 *	336,522	5 (3 grants, 2 contracts)
1988	718,000 *	306,303	5 grants
1989	709,000 *	297,325	5 grants
1990	855,000 *	285,000	5 grants
1991	976,000	320,753	4 grants 2 commissioned papers 1 contract
1992	325,000	324,894	2 contracts
1993	2,802,400	2,802,400	1 grant 1 contract

* Includes the II-B training appropriation

- The contract with the University of Wisconsin–Madison ($322,400) begun in FY 1992 to provide training for state library agency personnel in planning and evaluating federally funded library programs was continued. Training is designed to strengthen state library agencies' capabilities in evaluating projects, demonstrating greater accountability for federal funds, and identifying and disseminating information about effective programs. The contractor presented two workshops and developed two manuals, introducing participants to the TELL IT Evaluation Process.

Improving Access to Research Library Resources Program (HEA, Title II-C)

Title II-C of the Higher Education Act, Improving Access to Research Library Resources Program (formerly Strengthening Research Library Resources Program), promotes quality research and education throughout the United States by awarding funds to research libraries to make accessible collections that are rare, exclusively held, and of interest to a national research audience. This is achieved by making the content and location of the materials known through machine-readable catalog records contributed to national databases; and by making handling and perusal of the materials possible through conservation of the physical items and preservation of their intellectual content. The program also funds the acquisition of rare and unique research materials to fill gaps and strengthen existing collections.

In authorizing the Improving Access to Research Library Resources Program, Congress recognized that expansion of educational and research programs, together with the rapid increase in the production of recorded knowledge, places unprecedented demands on major research libraries by requiring programs and services beyond their financial capability. Authorized funding activities include:

- Creating and making available machine-readable catalog records via nationwide databases
- Acquiring specialized rare material to enhance or complete a library collection that may be a focus for national or international research
- Preserving collections of unique materials for scholarly use via microfilming, encapsulation, deacidification, and other chemical and manual processes
- Developing improved methods and procedures to provide bibliographic access, enhance collections, and meet preservation needs
- Demonstrating the cost benefits and advantages of cooperative cataloging ventures among major research libraries

Major research libraries are defined as public or private nonprofit institutions that contribute significantly to higher education and research, with unique collections containing material that is not widely available but is in substantial demand by researchers and scholars not connected with the institution and of national or international significance for research.

An amendment regarding eligibility (as a major research library) was added in 1986 with the reauthorization of the Higher Education Act. It permits institutions that do not qualify as a major research library under the criteria listed in the program regulations to provide information or documentation to demonstrate the national or international significance for scholarly research of the collection described in the grant application. This amendment allows the applicant's project to be evaluated if the collection is of national or international significance.

During the 16 years of program operation, $93,169,348 has been awarded to acquire rare and unique materials; to augment special collections in demand by researchers and scholars; to preserve fragile and deteriorating materials not generally available elsewhere; and to provide access to research collections by converting bibliographic information into machine-readable form and entering the records into national databases. Overall, 1,440 applications have been received and 549 funded.

In FY 1993, 96 applications requesting more than $13.5 million were received. With an allotment of $5,808,160, 35 new and 11 continuation grants were awarded, supporting projects at 39 institutions. Bibliographic control again emerged as the major activity in FY 1993, accounting for 87 percent of the funds. Preservation was second, accounting for 11 percent, and collection development accounted for 2 percent.

Following are examples of FY 1993 funded projects:

- Holdings of the Electronic Text Service of the Columbia University Libraries will provide machine-readable records for 50 electronic text sets. The cataloging will provide analytics for the sets, which will be available through OCLC's Major Microforms Program. The Electronic Text Service was the first facility in an American library devoted to collecting and providing access to authoritative editing of electronic primary-source texts and research in the humanities. The records will be available in RLIN and OCLC.
- Iowa State University will preserve and provide access to the films in the American Archives of the Factual Film, which include business, industrial, educational, technical, documentary, and other types of non-theatrical films. Records will be added to OCLC and to the National Moving Image Database (NAMID).
- Ohio State University will make available the papers of Admiral Richard E. Byrd, polar explorer and pioneer aviator and navigator, by arranging, describing, and cataloging them. Records will be entered into OCLC and fragile items will be reformatted for preservation purposes.
- At the University of Nevada's Getchell Library (Reno) records for 10,000 monographs in the Basque Studies Collection will be created, upgraded, edited, and holding library information added to records in OCLC. The Basque Studies Collection consists of materials by or about Basque people worldwide, published in Basque country and of general research concern to Basques.

Table 7 analyzes FY 1993 grant awards by major activity and Table 8 summarizes Improving Access Research Library Resources Program grant activities since FY 1978.

Library Services and Construction Act

Library Services for Indian Tribes and Hawaiian Natives Program (LSCA, Title IV)

LSCA Title IV discretionary grants awarded in FY 1993 will improve public library services to 209 Indian Tribes and 170,000 Hawaiian Natives. Funds are being used in 28 states to support a variety of activities, including salaries and

Table 7 / HEA, Title II-C, Improving Access to Research Library Resources Program Analysis of FY 1993 Grants, by Major Program Activity

Institute	Total	Bibliographic Control	Preservation	Collection Development
		Program Activity		
American Museum of Natural History	$139,662	$139,662	$—	$—
Balch Institute for Ethic Studies	62,988	62,988	—	—
Brooklyn Historical Society	63,000	47,250	15,750	—
Brown University	77,018	77,018	—	—
Carnegie Museum of Natural History	124,000	62,000	62,000	—
Center for Research Libraries	194,000	194,000	—	—
Chicago Historical Society	117,000	80,871	36,129	—
Columbia University	88,000	54,784	33,216	—
Columbia University	58,000	58,000	—	—
Cornell University	127,685	66,931	60,754	—
Duke University	41,000	41,000	—	—
Duke University	150,331	150,331	—	—
Folger Shakespeare Library	90,191	42,350	47,841	—
Harvard University	170,739	170,739	—	—
Harvard University	358,000	358,000	—	—
Harvard University	165,000	165,000	—	—
Iowa State University	45,000	43,759	1,241	—
Library Company of Philadelphia	104,388	92,388	12,000	—
New York Public Library	65,000	53,597	11,403	—
Ohio State University	62,144	58,371	3,773	—
Ohio State University	60,500	60,500	—	—
Ohio University	180,101	180,101	—	—
Princeton University	99,068	99,068	—	—
Rutgers University	90,000	52,434	37,566	—
Stanford University, Hoover Institution	475,000	475,000	—	—
State Historical Society of Wisconsin	60,000	60,000	—	—
SUNY at Binghamton	132,500	32,500	100,000	—
University of California, Berkeley	221,000	69,000	152,000	—
University of California, Los Angeles	141,000	141,000	—	—
University of California, Riverside	250,000	250,000	—	—
University of Chicago	85,000	68,914	16,086	—
University of Florida	107,402	107,402	—	—
University of Kansas	135,000	96,287	38,713	—
University of Maine	160,000	55,925	104,075	—
University of Michigan	81,580	81,580	—	—
University of Minnesota	90,516	90,516	—	—
University of Minnesota	86,196	86,196	—	—
University of Missouri	97,000	91,050	5,950	—
University of Nevada, Reno	199,997	199,997	—	—
University of North Carolina	161,000	160,570	430	—
University of Oklahoma	110,829	110,829	—	—
University of Oklahoma	85,000	85,000	—	—
University of South Carolina	65,825	65,825	—	—
University of Texas	72,000	55,361	16,639	—
Wayne State University	90,000	90,000	—	—
Yale University	168,500	168,500	—	—
Total	$5,808,160	$5,052,594	$639,491	$116,075

Table 8 / HEA, Title II-C, Strengthening Research Library Resources Program,
Summary of Funding, by Major Activity, FYs 1978–1993

Fiscal Year	Total Funding	Bibliographic Control	Percent of Funding	Preservation	Percent of Funding	Collection Development	Percent of Funding
1978	$4,999,996	$2,864,339	57	$1,340,554	27	795,103	16
1979	6,000,000	3,978,366	66	1,393,201	23	628,433	11
1980	5,992,268	4,345,765	73	805,383	13	841,120	14
1981	6,000,000	4,249,840	71	1,298,542	22	451,618	7
1982	5,760,000	4,042,549	70	1,521,258	27	196,193	3
1983	6,000,000	4,738,575	79	909,612	15	351,813	6
1984	6,000,000	4,526,772	76	1,044,973	17	428,255	7
1985	6,000,000	4,236,695	70	1,729,997	29	33,308	*
1986	5,742,000	4,429,374	77	1,122,409	20	190,217	3
1987	6,000,000	4,732,543	79	1,202,696	20	64,761	1
1988	5,744,000	4,804,408	84	850,570	15	89,022	1
1989	5,675,000	4,674,002	82	591,729	11	409,269	7
1990	5,738,000	5,141,888	90	510,255	9	85,857	1
1991	5,854,924	4,447,920	76	851,780	15	555,224	9
1992	5,855,000	4,720,805	81	766,648	13	367,547	6
1993	5,808,160	5,052,594	87	639,491	11	116,075	2
Total	$93,169,348	$70,986,435	76	$16,579,098	18	$5,603,815	6

*Less than 1 percent

training of library staff, purchase of library materials, and the renovation or construction of library facilities.

Since FY 1985, 2 percent of the appropriations for LSCA Titles I, II, and III has been set aside as the available funding for LSCA Title IV (1.5 percent for Indian Tribes and 0.5 percent for Hawaiian Natives). Only federally recognized Indian Tribes and Alaska Native Villages and organizations serving Hawaiian Natives that are recognized by the governor of Hawaii are eligible to participate in the program. For the past nine years, Alu Like Inc. has been the only organization recognized to apply for the Hawaiian Native set-aside.

Two types of grants are awarded—Basic Grants and Special Projects Grants. The Basic Grant is noncompetitive, and if an Indian Tribe or Alaska Native Village is eligible and pursues authorized activities, funding is guaranteed. In FY 1993 the established Basic Grant for Indian Tribes was $4,290. Alu Like Inc. applied for the entire Hawaiian Native set-aside of $597,799 under the Basic Grant program.

These funds continue to be used to support projects emphasizing outreach, collection development, and training of Hawaiian Natives for librarianship.

Indian Tribes are using the majority of this year's Basic Grant funds to support library personnel and purchase library materials. The Squaxin Island Tribe in Shelton, Washington, will use its $4,290 basic grant to pay partial wages of the librarian. The grant will also purchase library materials that encourage tribal members in Adult Basic Education classes to read; support the activities of the Child Development Center; and attract members of neighboring communities to view displays and use available materials. In Miami, Florida, the Miccosukee Tribe will use its basic grant to purchase selected reference materials, books, and

Table 9 / Library Services & Construction Act, Title IV, Library Services for Indian Tribes & Hawaiian Natives Program, Basic Grant Awards, FY 1993

State	Number of Awards	Amount
Alabama	1	$4,290
Alaska	35	205,920
Arizona	9	38,610
California	37	171,600
Connecticut	1	4,290
Florida	2	8,580
Hawaii	1	597,799
Iowa	1	4,290
Kansas	1	4,290
Louisiana	1	4,290
Massachusetts	1	4,290
Michigan	7	30,030
Minnesota	3	12,870
Mississippi	1	4,290
Missouri	1	4,290
Montana	6	25,740
Nebraska	2	8,580
Nevada	6	25,740
New Mexico	13	55,770
New York	3	12,870
North Carolina	1	4,290
North Dakota	3	12,870
Oklahoma	19	85,800
Oregon	7	30,030
South Dakota	3	12,870
Utah	1	4,290
Washington	19	85,800
Wisconsin	7	30,030
Total	192*	$1,494,409

* Five awards serve more than one Indian Tribe. A total of 209 Tribes and one Hawaiian Native Organization received Basic Grants.

periodicals to satisfy the user population. Reference materials on Native American rights, children's books and videos, periodicals, adult books, Native American research materials, and newspapers will be added to the existing collection. The Pedro Bay Village in Alaska will use more than half of the grant to purchase educational videos, books, and magazines to attract tribal members to the library. Grant funds will also pay for needed shelving to display the library materials.

The Native Hawaiian Library Project is using its $597,799 Basic Grant to support several different projects that target Hawaiian Natives. These projects include a library resource van that travels by boat to four islands to circulate books, artifacts, brochures, and videotapes; books-by-mail and outreach for the elderly in remote areas; Parent Workshops to encourage parents to read to their children; Homework Centers to improve students' study habits; collection of literacy materials and literacy referral service for patrons; public service announcements, posters, and bookmarks to inform the Hawaiian Native community of the importance of lifelong learning and the public library; and one fellowship for a Hawaiian Native to pursue a graduate degree in library science.

Forty percent of the eligible Indian Tribes and Alaska Native Villages applied for and received Basic Grants. Approximately $900,000 was awarded under the Basic Grant program (see Table 9 for Basic Grant awards); the remaining $896,709 was used for Special Projects grants.

Although the Special Projects program supports the same types of activities as the Basic Grant program, the two programs are very different in the amount of support and the required effort for funding. All Special Projects proposals are reviewed for quality of project, scored, and then ranked on a competitive basis.

Each grantee is required to have a librarian, provide a long-range program of three to five years, and contribute a minimum of 20 percent of the total project costs. Twelve Indian Tribes successfully competed for Special Projects funds, with grants ranging from more than $23,000 to the San Juan Southern Paiute Tribe in Arizona, for the training of library personnel who will help expand community services, to $168,137 to the Pueblo of Laguna in New Mexico for the construction of a new 2,800-square-foot library facility.

With its first Special Projects grant of $154,800, the Coquille Tribe in Oregon will build a 3,000-square-foot library. The library will be one part of a multi-use building that includes an Assisted Living Facility and a Cultural Center/Museum. Tribal members, researchers, and the general public will have access to lending collections and special collections of cultural and historical materials.

In contrast, the Three Affiliated Tribes of North Dakota, with its ninth Special Projects grant of $75,134 will pay salaries of the library technical assistant, the library programmer, and the children's programmer. The staff addresses the specialized needs of youth and seniors.

Library holdings will increase by 2,000 volumes when the Lac Courte Oreilles Tribe in Wisconsin uses its Special Projects grant of $55,179. The tribe will also hire and train a full-time Native American library aide. As a result, the library will increase hours of service and provide more outreach services.

Table 10 is a listing of the grants made under the Special Projects program in FY 1993, including a breakdown of the federal funds awarded and the nonfederal funds contributed.

Foreign-Language Materials Acquisition Program (LSCA, Title V)

The Foreign-Language Materials Acquisition Program, Title V of LSCA, supports the efforts of state and local public libraries to develop foreign-language materials collections that serve the needs of their communities.

Although the program was established in 1984, Congress did not appropriate funds ($976,000) until FY 1991. Funding for FY 1993, the third year of the program, was $968,192. During that year 104 applications were received from 29 states, requesting more than $3.5 million. In July 1993 DOE awarded grants to one state library and 29 to public libraries, supporting projects in 13 states. By law, 30 percent of the funds available were designated for grants between $35,000 and $125,000 (large grants). The remaining grants could not exceed

Table 10 / Library Services and Construction Act, Title IV, Library Services for Indian Tribes & Hawaiian Natives Program, Special Projects Awards, FY 1993

State/Tribe	Nonfederal Funds	Federal Funds
Arizona		
San Juan Southern Paiute Tribe, Tuba City	$6,233	$23,069
Minnesota		
Red Lake Band of Chippewa Indians, Red Lake	16,288	28,461
Montana		
Confederated Salish & Kootenai Tribes, Pablo	8,375	23,616
New Mexico		
Pueblo of Laguna, Laguna	52,600	168,137
Pueblo of Santa Clara, Espanola	19,720	55,235
Pueblo of Zuni, Zuni	29,498	68,308
North Dakota		
Three Affiliated Tribes, Newtown	45,722	75,134
Oklahoma		
Cherokee Nation of Oklahoma, Tahlequah	65,818	132,297
Oregon		
Coquille Indian Tribe, Coos Bay	106,910	154,800
Washington		
Confederated Tribes and Bands of the Yakima Indian Nation, Toppenish	76,014	46,200
Nisqually Indian Tribe, Olympia	29,590	66,273
Wisconsin		
Lac Courte Oreilles Tribal Governing Board, Haywood	27,584	55,179

$35,000. Three large grants were awarded, the remaining were small grants. Since FY 1991 nearly $3 million have been awarded, funding 90 projects in 20 states.

The FY 1993 applications were reviewed by 57 peer reviewers. The peer review panels were composed of public, state, academic, and school librarians. The applications included requests for a variety of Asian, American Indian, Polish, Russian, and Romance languages; over 50 percent of the applications focused on Spanish-language projects.

The Title V grant funds are for the purchase of foreign-language books, magazines, newspapers, audio and videocassettes, and computer software. The materials assist libraries to improve, expand, or initiate library services to patrons who require materials in a language other than English. The materials support the National Education Goals by supporting educational and instructional library programs, such as homework help centers, and adult education programs and literacy efforts. The materials support preschool story hour programs, helping parents read to their children in their native language. Magazines and newspapers provide access to current information to seniors, adults, young adults, and children. Libraries across the nation report dramatic changes in populations served and significant increases in the request for materials in a variety of formats and languages. Information from the 1990 census confirms the demographic changes that libraries report. Large numbers of recent immigrants, speaking dozens of languages, require materials for education, information, recreation, and life-coping skills. Libraries also indicate that funding limitations and budget cutbacks directly affect their ability to provide new or expanded services to both children and adults.

The projects funded will enable 30 libraries—large urban, suburban, and rural—to improve direct services to their communities. Table 11 lists the grants made under the Foreign-Language Materials Acquisition Program in FY 1993, giving the name of the library, its location, funding level, and the language(s) to be collected. Projects funded under the program include (1) supporting adult literacy classes, particularly health issues, and basic job skills; (2) expanding collections to enhance curriculum materials for both elementary and junior high school libraries; (3) initiating materials for Head Start and other preschool programs; (4) assisting a cooperative regional initiative for improving library services by acquiring an array of materials for adults and children; (5) developing a core reference collection of materials to be shared throughout the state through a statewide interlibrary loan network; and (6) supporting the development of educational and cultural collections that reflect the heritage of library patrons.

Congress did not include funding for this discretionary library program in FY 1994, reporting that funding for foreign-language library materials was the responsibility of individual libraries. Consequently, on December 16, 1993, a notice was published in *Federal Register* 58 (FR No. 240, 65703) announcing the withdrawal of a previous notice inviting applications for new awards for FY 1994. DOE will not make new awards in FY 1994.

Library Literacy Program (LSCA Title VI)

Title VI of the Library Services and Construction Act authorizes a discretionary grant program to support adult literacy programs in state and local public libraries. The program received an appropriation of $8,097,696 for FY 1993.

Under the Library Literacy Program, state and local public libraries may apply directly to the U.S. Department of Education for grants of up to $35,000. State libraries may use grants to coordinate and plan library literacy programs and to train librarians and volunteers to carry out such programs. Local public libraries may use grants to promote use of voluntary services of individuals, agencies, and organizations in literacy programs and to acquire library materials, use library facilities, and train volunteers for the programs.

In FY 1993 LSCA Title VI awarded 248 grants totaling over $8 million to 236 local public libraries and 12 state libraries. The grants were reviewed by a panel of 74 literacy experts representing local and state libraries, literacy councils, state departments of education, institutions of higher education, and private or other literacy efforts. Grants ranged in size from $7,000 to the maximum amount of $35,000. The average amount was $32,767. Grantees planned and

**Table 11 / Projects Funded under LSCA Title V,
Foreign-Language Materials Acquisition Program, FY 1993**

Library	City/State		Funding	Language
Nogales-Santa Cruz County Public Library	Nogales	AZ	$29,559	Spanish, Korean
Alhambra Public Library	Alhambra	CA	$8,338	Vietnamese
Corona Public Library	Corona	CA	$35,000	Spanish
Daly City Public Library	Daly City	CA	$25,000	Spanish
Livermore Public Library	Livermore	CA	$11,735	Spanish
Merced County Library	Merced	CA	$35,000	Spanish
Napa City-County Library	Napa	CA	$35,000	Spanish
Sacramento Public Library	Sacramento	CA	$35,000	Russian
San Diego Public Library	San Diego	CA	$96,819	Spanish, Asian
San Francisco Public Library	San Francisco	CA	$35,000	Spanish, Chinese
Stockton-San Joaquin County	Stockton	CA	$35,000	Spanish, Vietnamese
Watsonville Public Library	Watsonville	CA	$10,000	Spanish
Southern Peaks Public Library	Alamosa	CO	$9,687	Spanish
Athens Regional Library	Athens	GA	$22,520	Spanish, Chinese
Gail Borden Public Library	Elgin	IL	$21,176	Spanish, Asian
Urbana Free Library	Urbana	IL	$15,000	Multi
Waukegan Public Library	Waukegan	IL	$27,000	Spanish
Lake County Public Library	Merrillville	IN	$13,002	Spanish
Nevada State Library and Archives	Carson City	NV	$35,000	Spanish
Monmouth County Library	Manalapan	NJ	$35,000	Chinese
Newark Public Library	Newark	NJ	$35,000	Multi
Albuquerque/Bernalillo County Public Library	Albuquerque	NM	$35,000	Spanish
New York Public Library	New York	NY	$96,819	Multi
Westchester Library System	Elmsford	NY	$34,966	Spanish
Free Library of Philadelphia	Philadelphia	PA	$19,502	Multi
Corpus Christi Public Library	Corpus Christi	TX	$15,000	Spanish
Harris County Public Library	Houston	TX	$31,750	Spanish
San Antonio Public Library	San Antonio	TX	$96,819	Spanish
Tyler Public Library	Tyler	TX	$18,500	Spanish
Fairfax County Public Library	Fairfax	VA	$15,000	Spanish

coordinated literacy activities with literacy councils, schools, private agencies, and other literacy providers in the state or community. They were also encouraged to coordinate literacy activities with recipients of grants under Title I of the Library Services and Construction Act.

The Library Literacy Program supported coordinating and planning library literacy programs, training volunteers as tutors, recruiting adult literacy students to participate, and purchasing books, videocassette, and other teaching materials.

Examples of library literacy activities in FY 1993 include (1) establishing penpal connections between adult literacy students in different programs to encourage writing and self-expression; (2) introducing senior citizen learners and tutors to computerized literacy instruction; (3) teaching adult basic education students how to use the library; and (4) providing library literacy collections for inmates in a statewide prison system. Specific projects funded in FY 1993 follow.

The South San Francisco Library in California received $35,000 to field-test training and instructional methods at three sites, in Indiana, Michigan, and Pennsylvania. The method uses multisensory lessons that are adapted to the individual learner's ability and learning style. The project will focus on national dissemination and testing of the training activities and teaching materials and on developing additional materials, including a tutor training guide and parent teaching activity cards.

The Logan Library in Utah, which has a nationally recognized adult literacy project, received $28,500 to support a full-time coordinator for the program. This allows the library to continue its excellent cooperative arrangements with schools and other agencies in the community. Cooperative activities include in-service training to employees and department heads of a retirement home that also offers pay incentives to their employees who become literacy students; providing literacy and ESL instruction for parents of children in the local Head Start program; training practicum students from the Department of Social Work in working with adult literacy students; and training students of the state university to work as literacy volunteers, for which they will receive university credit. The library also coordinates its services with those of the local adult basic education programs and the local applied technology center, offering basic literacy or English-as-a-second-language (ESL) instruction to those students who need one-to-one tutoring before they can participate in a classroom setting.

The Broward County Library in Florida received $33,775 to continue to expand the extensive student empowerment component of its adult literacy program. It offers student support groups, has a field trip club, and has set up a student speakers bureau to recruit other students and to increase awareness of the problem of illiteracy in the community. A student advisory committee provides guidance and recommendations on the management and services offered by the literacy program. In 1994 the library will work with an aerospace company in the area to set up a career and training center. One branch library has been designated an adult literacy library.

The Menlo Park Library in California received $27,725 to expand its computer-assisted instruction to include CD-ROM capability, with linkage by modem to other literacy programs in the area. A committee of volunteers will be established to provide guidance on the use of technology in the program. An annotated bibliography will be developed.

See Table 12 for a complete list of FY 1993 grantees under the Library Literacy Program.

Table 12 / Library Literacy Program Grants, FY 1993

Alabama
Anniston and Calhoun County Library
Anniston
Bonnie Seymour, 205-548-2686
Award amount: $22,665

Pickens County Cooperative Library
Carrollton
Lori Ward Smith, 205-367-2142
Award amount: $32,000

Alaska
Fairbanks North Star Borough Public Library
Fairbanks
Greg Hill, 907-459-1020
Award amount: $34,991

Arizona
Apache Junction Public Library
Apache Junction
Spencer Paden, 602-982-6342
Award amount: $34,850

Camp Verde Public Library
Camp Verde
Phyllis Hazekamp, 602-567-6631
Award amount: $33,690

Chandler Public Library
Chandler
Karen Drake, 602-786-2312
Award amount: $24,860

Gila County Library District
Miami
Lynn Carey, 602-425-0229
Award amount: $21,224

Yuma County Library District
Yuma
Anna L. Martin, 602-782-1871
Award amount: $34,881

Arkansas
Arkansas State Library
Little Rock
John A. Murphey, Jr., 501-682-1526
Award amount: $35,000

Hot Springs County Library
Malvern
Jane Goodwin, 501-332-4039
Award amount: $25,000

California
Alameda County Library ESOL (English for
Speakers of Other Languages) Tutoring
Fremont
Sherry Drobner, 510-745-1484
Award amount: $34,984

Alameda County Library Small Group Tutor-
ing
Fremont
Sherry Drobner, 510-745-1484
Award amount: $34,986

Alameda County Library Tutoring in Jails
Fremont
Sherry Drobner, 510-745-1484
Award amount: $34,388

Auburn-Placer County Library
Auburn
Delana Rudd, 916-889-4114
Award amount: $34,950

Chula Vista Public Library
Chula Vista
Meg Schofield, 619-425-4784
Award amount: $34,845

Colton Public Library
Colton
Mary Ann Ponder, 909-370-5170
Award amount: $24,851

Coyote Valley Tribal Community Library
Redwood Valley
Judy Fisch, 707-485-8723
Award amount: $35,000

El Dorado County Library
Placerville
Marilyn Crouch, 916-621-5546
Award amount: $21,700

Huntington Beach Library
Adult Literacy Services
Huntington Beach
Linda Light, 714-375-5102
Award amount: $35,000

Huntington Beach Library
Family Literacy Project
Huntington Beach
Ronald Hayden, 714-960-8836
Award amount: $34,832

Lake County Library
Lakeport
Dallas Cook, 707-263-7633
Award amount: $35,000

Livermore Public Library
Livermore
Susan Gallinger
510-373-5509
Award amount: $34,628

Marin County Free Library
San Rafael
Barbara Hughes, 415-499-6051
Award amount: $35,000

Mariposa Free County Library
Mariposa
Lynda Campbell, 209-966-5905
Award amount: $34,527

Menlo Park Public Library
  ESL Tutoring
Menlo Park
Judith Wilczak, 415-321-8818
Award amount: $34,900

Menlo Park Public Library
  Literacy Computer Lab
Menlo Park
Judith Wilczak, 415-321-8818
Award amount: $27,725

Monterey County Free Libraries
Salinas
Karen J. Albertus, 408-899-0417
Award amount: $33,453

Napa City-County Library
Napa
Frances Williams Houser, 707-253-4283
Award amount: $33,938

National City Public Library
National City
Russell Hamm, 619-474-2129
Award amount: $30,343

Oakland Public Library
  Student Oral History
Oakland
Leslie McGinnis, 510-238-3432
Award amount: $34,500

Oakland Public Library
  Student Retention and Support

Oakland
Leslie McGinnis, 510-238-3432
Award amount: $28,500

Orange County Public Library
Santa Ana
Scott Cheney, 714-566-3070
Award amount: $34,860

Redwood City Public Library
Redwood City
David Miller, 415-780-7077
Award amount: $35,000

Rincon Public Library
  Rincon, San Luiseno Band of Mission
  Indians
Valley Center
James J. Fletcher, 619-749-1051
Award amount: $27,516

Salinas Public Library
Salinas
Julia Orozco, 408-758-7314
Award amount: $32,005

San Bernardino City Library
San Bernardino
S'Ann Freeman, 909-381-6530
Award amount: $22,340

San Bernardino County Library
San Bernardino
Patricia Laudisio, 909-387-5728
Award amount: $34,922

San Francisco Public Library
  Project Read Outreach
San Francisco
Ana Linder, 415-557-4388
Award amount: $34,965

San Francisco Public Library
  Support Services for Adult Readers
San Francisco
Ana Linder, 415-557-4388
Award amount: $34,997

San Francisco Public Library
  Support Services for Volunteer Tutors
San Francisco
Ana Linder, 415-557-4388
Award amount: $28,455

San Jose Public Library
San Jose

Ruth Kohan, 408-277-3230
Award amount: $34,816

San Rafael Public Library with Marin County
Free Library
San Rafael
Barbara Barwood, 415-485-3318
Award amount: $35,000

Santa Clara County Library with four other
libraries
Milpitas
Taylor Willingham, 408-262-1349
Award amount: $170,593

South San Francisco Public Library
Computer Assisted Instruction
South San Francisco
Leslie Shelton, 415-877-5329
Award amount: $32,500

South San Francisco Public Library
Tutoring Training Model
South San Francisco
Leslie Shelton, 415-877-5329
Award amount: $35,000

Tuolumne County Library with Amador
County Public Library
Sonora
Leon Casas, 209-533-5663
Award amount: $70,000

Ventura County Library Service Agency
Project JOBS
Ventura
Pat Flanigan, 805-652-6294
Award amount: $34,989

Ventura County Library Service Agency
Project Special Help
Ventura
Pat Flanigan, 805-652-6294
Award amount: $35,000

Ventura County Library Service Agency
Project Success
Ventura
Pat Flanigan, 805-652-6294
Award amount: $20,284

Willows Public Library
Willows
Susan M. Rawlins, 916-934-5156
Award amount: $26,162

Colorado
Canon City Public Library
Canon City
Gary Shook, 719-269-9021
Award amount: $24,067

Colorado Department of Education
State Library
Denver
Mary Willoughby, 303-866-6743
Award amount: $35,000

Delta County Public Library
Delta
Ethel Jackson, 303-874-9630
Award amount: $24,900

Durango Public Library
Durango
Daniel Brassell, 303-247-2492
Award amount: $34,998

Eagle Valley Library District
Eagle
Robyn Bryant, 303-328-6273
Award amount: $34,950

Fort Collins Public Library
Adult Literacy Services
Fort Collins
Jane B. Davis, 303-221-6742
Award amount: $32,167

Fort Collins Public Library
Coordination of Literacy Services
Fort Collins
Jane B. Davis, 303-221-6742
Award amount: $35,000

Garfield County Public Library
New Castle
Linda Halloran, 303-984-3121
Award amount: $35,000

Heginbotham Library
Holyoke
Rose Kreher, 303-854-2597
Award amount: $35,000

Loveland Public Library
Loveland
Marcia Lewis, 303-962-2404
Award amount: $31,822

Mesa County Public Library District
Grand Junction

Caryl Duke, 303-245-5522
Award amount: $35,000

Pikes Peak Library
Colorado Springs
Jean Maio, 719-531-6333
Award amount: $34,425

Security Public Library
Security
Beverly McFarland, 719-392-4443
Award amount: $22,000

Upper San Juan Library District
Pagosa Springs
Gloria G. Macht, 303-264-2835
Award amount: $31,606

Connecticut
Bugbee Memorial Library
Danielson
Marie C. Chartier, 203-774-9429
Award amount: $35,000

Connecticut State Library
Hartford
Patricia Owens, 203-566-2712
Award amount: $35,000

Meriden Public Library
Meriden
Bruce MacCabe, 203-235-1714
Award amount: $34,200

Stratford Library Association
Stratford
Barbara Moren, 203-385-4164
Award amount: $34,376

Willimantic Public Library
Willimantic
Theodore Perch, 203-423-6182
Award amount: $35,000

Delaware
Corbit-Calloway Memorial Library
Odessa
Susan Menei, 302-378-8838
Award amount: $12,448

Kent County Department of Library Services
Dover
Martha Hadaway, 302-736-2265
Award amount: $34,500

Sussex County Department of Libraries
Georgetown

Christel Shumate, 302-855-7890
Award amount: $35,000

Wilmington Institute Library
Wilmington
Carmen Knox, 302-658-5624
Award amount: $35,000

Florida
Broward County Library
Fort Lauderdale
Janet Hansen, 305-765-4271
Award amount: $33,775

Columbia County Public Library
Lake City
Mary Browder, 904-758-2101
Award amount: $25,539

Gadsden County Public Library
Quincy
Jane Mock, 904-627-7106
Award amount: $34,945

St. John's County Public Library
St. Augustine
Michael R. Rouse, 904-823-2651
Award amount: $35,000

Tampa/Hillsborough County Public Library
Tampa
Marcee Challener, 813-273-3659
Award amount: $33,437

Wilderness Coast Public Libraries with two
   other libraries
Crawfordville
Cheryl Turner, 904-926-4571
Award amount: $105,000

Georgia
Brooks County Public Library
Quitman
Liza Newman, 912-263-4412
Award amount: $34,970

Cobb County Public Library
Marietta
J. Nicholas Fogarty, 404-528-2324
Award amount: $15,000

Conyers-Rockdale Library System
Conyers
Deborah Manger, 404-388-5041
Award amount: $15,980

DeKalb County Public Library
Decatur
Sherry De Enfants, 404-370-8450
Award amount: $34,632

Lake Blackshear Regional Library
Americus
Frances Seaver, 912-924-8091
Award amount: $33,200

Ocumulgee Regional Library
Eastman
Dottie Welch, 912-374-4711
Award amount: $35,000

Peach Public Libraries
Fort Valley
Gilda Stanberry-Cotney, 912-825-8540
Award amount: $34,922

Sara Hightower Regional Library
Rome
Carrol Maloof, 706-236-4617
Award amount: $34,992

Southwest Georgia Regional Library
Bainbridge
Susan Whittle, 912-248-2665
Award amount: $34,500

Hawaii
Hawaii State Public Library System
    Hilo Public Library
Hilo
Maile Williams, 808-933-4650
Award amount: $29,840

Idaho
Bear Lake County Free Library District
Montpelier
Vivienne Dimick, 208-847-1664
Award amount: $32,040

Clearwater Memorial Public Library
Clearwater
Jill Lynch, 208-476-3411
Award amount: $27,042

East Bonner County Library
Sandpoint
James Murray, 208-263-6930
Award amount: $32,375

Illinois
Chicago Public Library
    ABLA Homes Literacy Center

Chicago
Elio DeArrudah, 312-747-4162
Award amount: $29,000

Chicago Public Library
    Independence/Albany Branch
Chicago
Margaret Dunne, 312-744-0900
Award amount: $15,500

Chicago Public Library
    Rogers Park Branch
Chicago
Jacqueline Hui, 312-744-0156
Award amount: $31,900

Eisenhower Public Library
Harwood Heights
Ronald Stoch, 708-867-7828
Award amount: $35,000

Rockford Public Library
Rockford
Marcia Cook, 815-965-6731
Award amount: $26,535

St. Charles Public Library
St. Charles
Peg Coker, 708-584-2811
Award amount: $19,853

Indiana
Anderson City, Anderson, Stony Creek and
    Union Townships' Public Library
Anderson
Donna Cumberland, 317-641-2462
Award amount: $35,000

Hammond Public Library
Hammond
Arthur Meyers, 219-931-5100
Award amount: $32,460

Indiana State Library
Indianapolis
Sherrill Franklin, 317-232-3719
Award amount: $35,000

Indianapolis-Marion County Public Library
Indianapolis
Sarah Jane Batt, 317-269-1745
Award amount: $35,000

Johnson County Public Library
Franklin
Rose Marie Stiffler, 317-738-2833

Award amount: $26,006

Knox County Public Library
Vincennes
Emily Bunyan, 812-886-4380
Award amount: $29,335

Lake County Public Library
Merrillville
Sharon Ball, 219-769-3541
Award amount: $35,000

Lowell Public Library
Lowell
Virginia Maravilla, 219-696-7704
Award amount: $34,939

Vigo County Public Library
Terre Haute
Katherine Hackleman, 812-232-1113
Award amount: $15,738

Wayne Township Public Library
Richmond
Carol Smyth, 317-966-8291
Award amount: $35,000

Kansas
Johnson County Library
Shawnee Mission
Mona Carmack, 913-967-8600
Award amount: $32,800

Kansas City, Kansas Public Library
Kansas City
Carolyn Nicholson, 913-596-5800
Award amount: $17,650

Kentucky
Bullitt County Public Library District
Sheperdsville
Randall Matlow, 502-543-7675
Award amount: $24,167

Hopkinsville-Christian County Public
    Library
Hopkinsville
Robert Satterwhite, 502-887-4624
Award amount: $18,000

Laurel County Public Library
London
Lori Schecter, 606-864-5759
Award amount: $35,000

Lexington Public Library
Lexington

Virginia McHenry-Hepner, 606-231-5519
Award amount: $29,364

Louisiana
Claiborne Parish Public Library
Homer
Pam Suggs, 318-927-3845
Award amount: $35,000

Evangeline Parish Library
Ville Platte
Janice A. Smith, 318-363-1369
Award amount: $35,000

Ouachita Parish Public Library
Monroe
Ben Brady, 318-387-1950
Award amount: $35,000

Shreve Memorial Library
Shreveport
Sharyn M. Gilsoul, 318-226-5864
Award amount: $29,421

Maine
Maine State Library
Augusta
Julia Walkling, 207-725-6353
Award amount: $34,997

Sanford Library Association
Sanford
Kenneth Scott, 207-324-4714
Award amount: $35,000

Maryland
Anne Arundel County Public Library
Annapolis
Betty Morganstern, 410-222-7371
Award amount: $20,758

Enoch Pratt Free Library
Baltimore
Rhea Lawson, 410-396-0970
Award amount: $33,000

Ruth Enlow Library
Oakland
Barbara Pentz, 301-334-8606
Award amount: $33,979

Wicomico County Free Library
Salisbury
Linda Perry, 410-749-3612
Award amount: $15,390

Massachusetts
Cary Memorial Library
Lexington
Donna Salacuse, 617-862-3706
Award amount: $34,939

Chicopee Public Library
Chicopee
Michael Barron, 413-594-6679
Award amount: $34,750

Fall River Public Library
Fall River
Regina Slezak, 508-324-2700
Award amount: $32,950

Fitchburg Public Library
Fitchburg
Elizabeth Watson, 508-345-9639
Award amount: $33,190

Haverhill Public Library
Haverhill
Virginia Behan, 508-373-1588
Award amount: $29,330

Holyoke Public Library
Holyoke
Mary Kates, 413-534-2211
Award amount: $35,000

Hudson Public Library with Marlborough
   Public Library
Hudson
Patricia Desmond, 508-568-9644
Award amount: $29,060

Lee Library Association with Pittsfield Pub-
   lic Library
Lee
Georgia Massucco, 413-243-0385
Award amount: $63,164

Massachusetts Board of Library Commis-
   sioners
   ESL Curriculum Model
Boston
Shelly Quezada, 617-267-9400
Award amount: $32,387

Massachusetts Board of Library Commis-
   sioners
   Family Literacy for Inmates
Boston
Shelly Quezada, 617-267-9400
Award amount: $29,790

Morrill Memorial Library
Norwood
Bettina Blood, 617-769-0200
Award amount: $34,750

Plymouth Public Library
Plymouth
Mary Anne Odell, 508-830-4260
Award amount: $34,011

Springfield Library and Museums Associa-
   tion
Springfield
Janet Kelly, 413-788-8806
Award amount: $35,000

Vineyard Haven Public Library with two
   other libraries
Vineyard Haven
Marjorie Convery, 508-696-4211
Award amount: $12,891

Watertown Free Public Library
Watertown
Susan Viskin, 617-924-8797
Award amount: $ 35,000

Michigan
Adrian Public Library
Adrian
Jule Fosbinder, 517-265-7525
Award amount: $35,000

Dearborn Department of Libraries
Dearborn
R. Patrick Coady, 313-943-2037
Award amount: $34,996

Grand Rapids Public Library
Grand Rapids
Robert Raz, 616-456-3623
Award amount: $34,928

Greenville Public Library
Greenville
Virginia Schantz, 616-754-6359
Award amount: $30,716

Jackson District Library
Jackson
Joy Rosynek, 517-788-4317
Award amount: $31,658

Jordan Valley District Library
East Jordan
Dawn Pringle, 616-536-7131

Award amount: $22,495

Kalamazoo Public Library
Kalamazoo
Mary Doud, 616-342-9837
Award amount: $35,000

Lansing Public Library
Lansing
Edward Spink, 517-374-4600
Award amount: $35,000

Library Cooperative of Macomb
Mt. Clemens
Marsha DeVergilio, 313-286-2750
Award amount: $34,928

Mitchell Public Library
Hillsdale
Diana Pierson, 517-437-2581
Award amount: $29,527

Ypsilanti District Library
Ypsilanti
Donna DeButts, 313-482-0565
Award amount: $34,989

Mississippi
Bolivar County Library
Cleveland
Ronnie W. Wise, 601-843-2774
Award amount: $35,000

Elizabeth Public Library
Grenada
Hardy McElwain, 601-226-2072
Award amount: $35,000

Madison County-Canton Public Libraries
Canton
Beverly Herring, 601-859-3202
Award amount: $35,000

Mid-Mississippi Regional Library
Kosciusko
Richard O. Greene, 601-289-5151
Award amount: $31,500

Sunflower County Library
Indianola
Teresa K. Raymond, 601-887-2641
Award amount: $35,000

Missouri
Dunklin County Library
Kennett
Benny Freeman, 314-888-3561

Award amount: $32,885

Montana
Big Horn County Public Library
Hardin
Helen Turney, 406-665-1808
Award amount: $33,495

Bitterroot Public Library
Hamilton
Nansu Haynes, 406-363-1670
Award amount: $31,326

Butte-Silver Bow Public Library
Butte
Karen Shipley, 406-723-7905
Award amount: $29,277

Glendive Public Library
Glendive
Gail Nagle, 406-365-3633
Award amount: $22,307

Lewistown City Library
Lewistown
Sharon Stead, 406-538-7849
Award amount: $34,861

Rocky Boy Community Public Library
Box Elder
Peggy Nagel, 406-395-4313
Award amount: $34,547

Nevada
Las Vegas-Clark County Library District
Las Vegas
Caron Schwahn, 702-382-3493
Award amount: $34,336

Nevada State Library and Archives
Carson City
Emmy Bell, 702-687-8340
Award amount: $26,000

New Hampshire
Carpenter Memorial Library
Pittsfield
Leslie Vogt, 603-435-8406
Award amount: $28,507

Concord Public Library
Concord
Nancy Morse, 603-224-2775
Award amount: $34,572

Exeter Public Library
Exeter

Ellen Hardsog, 603-772-3101
Award amount: $29,317

Fuller Public Library
Hillsboro
Tamara McClure, 603-464-3595
Award amount: $34,112

Richards Free Library
Newport
Andrea Thorpe, 603-868-3430
Award amount: $34,984

New Jersey
Camden County Library
Voorhees
Sivya Romisher, 609-772-1636
Award amount: $61,845

Irvington Public Library
Irvington
Lorelei McConnell, 201-372-6400
Award amount: $26,360

Jersey City Public Library
Jersey City
Annie Kessler, 201-547-4518
Award amount: $35,000

Newark Public Library
Newark
Linda Duesinger, 201-623-4001
Award amount: $35,000

Old Bridge Public Library with 23 other
    libraries
Old Bridge
Elissa Director, 908-679-1004
Award amount: $90,029

Paterson Free Public Library
Paterson
Kwaku Ameabeng, 201-357-3001
Award amount: $28,000

Westwood Free Public Library
Westwood
Leonard LoPinto, 201-664-0583
Award amount: $30,000

New Mexico
Harwood Public Library
Taos
Tracy McCallum, 505-758-3063
Award amount: $34,623

New Mexico State Library
Santa Fe
Scott Sheldon, 505-827-3809
Award amount: $35,000

Socorro Public Library
Socorro
Lucie Olson, 505-835-1114
Award amount: $15,431

New York
Amsterdam Free Library
Amsterdam
Franklin Wendell, 518-842-2553
Award amount: $27,861

Brentwood Public Library
Brentwood
Doris Lewis Sargent, 516-273-7883
Award amount: $34,500

Brooklyn Public Library
Brooklyn
Susan O'Connor, 718-780-7819
Award amount: $35,000

Huntington Memorial Library
Oneonta
Marie Bruni, 607-432-1980
Award amount: $26,540

Mastics-Moriches-Shirley Community
    Library
Shirley
Denise Boinay, 516-399-1511
Award amount: $34,271

Nassau Library System
Uniondale
Dorothy Puryear, 516-292-8920
Award amount: $35,000

New York Public Library
    Centers for Reading and Writing
New York
Diane Rosenthal, 212-932-7893
Award amount: $35,000

Southern Adirondack Library System
Saratoga Springs
Elaine Baker, 518-584-7300
Award amount: $32,600

Westchester Library System
Elmsford
Diane Courtney, 914-592-8214

Award amount: $35,000

Wyandanch Public Library
Wyandanch
Rita Liversedge, 516-643-4848
Award amount: $35,000

North Carolina
Ashe County Public Library
West Jefferson
Cheryl Earnhardt, 919-246-2041
Award amount: $35,000

Gaston County Public Library
Gastonia
Lucinda W. Moose, 704-868-2167
Award amount: $22,575

North Dakota
Fort Berthold Reservation Library
New Town
Quincee Baker, 701-627-4738
Award amount: $35,000

North Dakota State Library
Bismarck
Nancy Maxwell, 701-224-3681
Award amount: $35,000

Ohio
Clark County Public Library
Springfield
Robert Saunter, 513-323-9751
Award amount: $28,650

Columbus Metropolitan Library
Columbus
Rubye Kyles, 614-645-2800
Award amount: $34,670

Oklahoma
Anadarko Community Library
Anadarko
Joan Hines, 405-247-3087
Award amount: $24,996

Bosewell Public Library
Bosewell
Virginia Watson, 405-566-2320
Award amount: $30,000

Lawton Public Library
Lawton
Marion F. Donaldson, 405-581-3450
Award amount: $28,200

Oklahoma Department of Libraries
Oklahoma City
Leslie Gelders, 405-521-2502
Award amount: $33,160

Southern Prairie Library System
Altus
Katherine Hale, 405-477-2890
Award amount: $34,941

Tulsa City-County Library
Tulsa
Lynn Yasser, 918-596-7958
Award amount: $35,000

Oregon
Eugene Public Library
Eugene
Sandra Carrick, 503-687-5450
Award amount: $35,000

Oregon State Library
Salem
Mary Ginnane, 503-378-2112
Award amount: $34,992

Pennsylvania
Bayard Taylor Memorial Library
Kenneth Square
Alice Peters, 215-444-2988
Award amount: $22,896

Bucks County Free Library
Doylestown
Susan Rork, 215-348-0332
Award amount: $15,500

Crawford County Federated Library System
Meadville
Mary Lindquist, 814-337-7323
Award amount: $33,200

Free Library of Philadelphia
Philadelphia
Nancy Laskowski, 215-686-5346
Award amount: $35,000

J. Lewis Crozer Library
Chester
A. Karen Dalie, 215-494-4179
Award amount: $33,000

Juniata County Library
Mifflintown
Thomas Hipple, 717-436-6378
Award amount: $7,000

Rhode Island
Coventry Public Library
Coventry
Deborach Barchi, 401-822-9100
Award amount: $20,395

East Providence Public Library
East Providence
Eileen Socha, 401-434-2719
Award amount: $29,375

Providence Public Library
  Family Literacy
Providence
Roseanne Trissler, 401-455-8041
Award amount: $34,991

Providence Public Library
  Family Writing Centers
Providence
Roseanne Trissler, 401-455-8041
Award amount: $34,983

Rhode Island Department of State Library
  Services
Providence
Ann Piascik, 401-277-2726
Award amount: $34,383

Woonsocket Harris Public Library
Woonsocket
Kathy Ellen Bullard, 401-769-9044
Award amount: $18,890

South Carolina
Chester County Library
Chester
Ann Ramsey, 803-377-8145
Award amount: $16,000

Texas
Andrews County Library
Andrews
Kay Robins, 915-524-1432
Award amount: $34,000

Commerce Public Library
Commerce
Candance Mathews, 903-886-6858
Award amount: $35,000

Corpus Christi Public Libraries
Corpus Christi
Dorothy Castanon, 512-854-2357
Award amount: $35,000

Delta County Public Library
Cooper
Cindy Switzer, 903-395-4575
Award amount: $35,000

Fort Bend County Libraries
Richmond
Linda Behling, 713-341-2640
Award amount: $33,815

Fort Worth Public Library
Fort Worth
Connie Barnes, 817-624-7350
Award amount: $22,891

Franklin County Public Library
Mt. Vernon
Jean Shelby, 903-537-4916
Award amount: $35,000

Harris County Public Library
Houston
Rhoda L. Goldberg, 713-749-9011
Award amount: $31,642

Houston Public Library
Houston
Barbara J. Price, 713-869-1307
Award amount: $32,319

Lubbock City-County Library
Lubbock
Jeffrey Rippel, 806-767-2822
Award amount: $33,515

San Antonio Public Library
  Bazan Branch
San Antonio
Mary L. Cantu, 210-223-5687
Award amount: $35,000

San Antonio Public Library
  Collins Gardens Branch
San Antonio
Mary L. Cantu, 210-223-5687
Award amount: $35,000

Smithville Public Library
Smithville
Karen Bell, 512-237-2707
Award amount: $34,670

Sterling Municipal Library
Baytown
Denise Fischer, 713-427-7331
Award amount: $35,000

Unger Memorial Library
Plainview
Minnie Ruth Rigler, 806-296-1147
Award amount: $23,837

Utah
Logan Library
Logan
Ronald Jenkins, 801-750-9870
Award amount: $28,500

Payson City Library
Payson
Connie Carrasco, 801-465-5225
Award amount: $35,000

Price City Library
Price
Paula Lewis, 801-637-4747
Award amount: $19,350

Provo City Library
Provo
Norma Henrie, 801-379-6667
Award amount: $31,018

San Juan County Library
Monticello
Joyce Martin, 801-537-2967
Award amount: $34,119

Ute Indian Tribal Library
Fort Duchesne
Everet Cesspooch, 901-722-3941
Award amount: $34,159

Virginia
Botetourt County Library
Roanoke
Stephen Vest, 703-977-3433
Award amount: $15,785

Jefferson-Madison Regional Library
Charlottesville
Karen Morris, 804-971-7151
Award amount: $32,807

Smyth-Bland Regional Library
Marion
Judith A. Taminger, 703-783-7950
Award amount: $35,000

Southside Regional Library
Boydton
E. Frances Trimmer, 804-676-2006
Award amount: $22,195

Washington
Lummi Reservation Library System
Bellingham
Pam Hillaire, 206-676-2772
Award amount: $34,999

Nisqually Indian Tribe Community Library
Olympia
Maria Fletter, 206-456-5221
Award amount: $35,000

West Virginia
Cabell County Public Library
Huntington
Judy Rule, 304-523-9451
Award amount: $35,000

Hamlin-Lincoln County Public Library System
Hamlin
Margaret Smith, 304-824-5481
Award amount: $29,123

Martinsburg-Berkeley County Public Library
Martinsburg
Margaret Batten, 304-267-8933
Award amount: $35,000

Monroe County Library with Peterson Public Library
Union
Judith Azulay, 304-772-3038
Award amount: $70,000

Wyoming
Converse County Public Library
Douglas
Sandra Johnson, 307-358-3644
Award amount: $24,065

Total number of awards: 248
Total award amount: $8,126,196

Table 13 / Funding for LSCA Titles I, II, and III, FY 1994

State	Title I	Title II	Title III
Alabama	$1,333,329	$293,824	$315,082
Alaska	360,831	127,506	79,037
Arizona	1,250,222	279,611	294,910
Arkansas	857,370	212,425	199,557
California	8,658,923	1,546,664	2,093,151
Colorado	1,150,998	262,642	270,826
Connecticut	1,099,131	253,771	258,237
Delaware	388,875	132,302	85,844
District of Columbia	361,309	127,587	79,153
Florida	3,896,223	732,136	937,148
Georgia	2,050,190	416,424	489,079
Hawaii	517,787	154,349	117,133
Idaho	492,475	150,020	110,990
Illinois	3,387,461	645,127	813,661
Indiana	1,751,590	365,356	416,602
Iowa	970,738	231,813	227,074
Kansas	891,299	218,228	207,792
Kentucky	1,228,964	275,976	289,750
Louisiana	1,374,887	300,932	325,169
Maine	538,553	157,900	122,174
Maryland	1,545,139	330,049	366,492
Massachusetts	1,843,829	381,131	438,991
Michigan	2,786,064	542,275	667,690
Minnesota	1,427,732	309,970	337,995
Mississippi	916,436	222,526	213,893
Missouri	1,623,018	343,368	385,395
Montana	425,731	136,605	94,789
Nebraska	640,009	175,251	146,799
Nevada	563,764	162,212	128,293
New Hampshire	504,410	152,061	113,886
New Jersey	2,334,558	465,057	558,100
New Mexico	633,327	174,108	145,177
New York	5,165,544	949,218	1,245,238
North Carolina	2,075,210	420,703	495,151
North Dakota	374,272	129,804	82,299
Ohio	3,218,992	616,315	772,770
Oklahoma	1,080,289	250,549	253,664
Oregon	1,015,924	239,541	238,041
Pennsylvania	3,491,111	662,853	838,819
Rhode Island	475,436	147,106	106,854
South Carolina	1,187,447	268,875	279,673
South Dakota	394,887	133,330	87,303
Tennessee	1,576,803	335,464	374,178
Texas	5,038,451	927,483	1,214,390
Utah	696,876	184,977	160,602
Vermont	356,145	126,704	77,900
Virginia	1,947,627	398,883	464,184
Washington	1,607,426	340,701	381,611
West Virginia	696,623	184,934	160,540

Table 13 / Funding for LSCA Titles I, II, and III, FY 1994 *(cont.)*

State	Title I	Title II	Title III
Wisconsin	1,572,037	334,649	373,022
Wyoming	327,757	121,850	71,010
American Samoa	52,818	22,192	13,111
Guam	76,490	26,241	18,857
Northern Marianas	51,879	22,031	12,883
Puerto Rico	1,165,198	265,070	274,273
Virgin Islands	67,900	24,772	16,772
Palau	44,144	20,709	11,006
Total	$81,562,460	$17,436,160	$19,354,020

LSCA State-Administered Programs

More than 80 percent of the Office of Library Programs' funding is allocated under the LSCA state-administered programs (Titles I, II, and III). Awards are made to the state library administrative agencies to:

- Upgrade local public library services
- Improve public library services to targeted populations
- Strengthen state library administrative agencies to improve statewide public library services
- Meet designated public library institutional needs, such as for major urban libraries
- Assist public libraries in the construction, acquisition, remodeling, and alteration of existing buildings and support technology enhancements
- Establish, develop, and expand local, state, regional, and interstate cooperative library networks
- Promote library resource-sharing activities among public, academic, school, and special libraries
- Develop the technological capacity of libraries for resource sharing
- Promote preservation of fragile library materials

In FY 1994 the funds appropriated for these programs totaled $118,352,640. Table 13 gives a state-by-state breakdown of the FY 1994 funding for LSCA, Titles I, II, and III.

Public Library Services (LSCA Title I)

The state library agencies made Title I subgrants in 18 legislated service categories, ranging from library-based literacy efforts to strengthening the regional library resources of metropolitan public libraries. The most recent state reports (1992) reflect the following ranking of these 18 funding categories:

1 Areas with inadequate library services

2 Strengthening state library administrative agencies to meet the library and information needs of the state

3 Areas without library services

4 Disadvantaged

5 Strengthening the national or regional resources of major urban public libraries

6 Blind and physically handicapped

7 State institutional library services

8 Literacy programs

9 LSCA administration at the state level

10 Strengthening the regional library resources of metropolitan public libraries

11 Community information referral centers

12 Limited English-speaking proficiency

13 Elderly

14 Drug abuse prevention

15 Other handicapped

16 Child-care-center library programs

17 Intergenerational library programs

18 Model literacy centers

To provide a more focused perspective on Title I Public Library Services projects, state library reports for FY 1991, 1992, and when available, for FY 1993 were reviewed to identify innovative activities and trends in selected LSCA program areas. These analyses follow.

Library Services to Special Populations: Literacy

Since 1988 there has been a steady decline in the amount of LSCA Title I funds used to support library literacy programs. In FY 1991 public libraries reported expenditures of approximately $2.6 million for literacy activities, and in FY 1992, $2.4 million. In these same years, states reported expenditures of approximately $5.5 million (FY 1991) and $4.8 million (FY 1992) in state and local dollars for literacy activities. In addition, in FY 1991 and 1992 Ohio and the District of Columbia supported Model Literacy Centers using $20,936 in federal and $7,000 in state funds.

There are several factors that make it difficult to give a complete picture of expenditures or to determine whether the overall level of support for literacy programs is actually increasing or declining. In many states, literacy activities are reported under broad categories: Services to the Disadvantaged or Inadequately Served. In other instances, libraries choose to focus on Literacy Services to the Limited English-speaking and report under that LSCA category. States reported more than $1.4 million in LSCA funds was spent in FY 1991 and $1.1 million in FY 1992. Tables 14 through 17 show the state-by-state breakouts.

Table 14 / LSCA Title I Expenditures for Literacy, FY 1991

	Federal	State	Local	Total
Alabama	$7,523	$0	$970	$8,493
Alaska	0	0	0	0
Arizona	0	0	0	0
Arkansas	7,420	0	0	7,420
California	164,103	0	0	164,103
Colorado	84,568	0	0	84,568
Connecticut	25,000	0	0	25,000
Delaware	8,961	0	0	8,961
District of Columbia	88,418	16,300	0	104,718
Florida	117,945	0	47,368	165,313
Georgia	15,309	0	5,241	20,550
Hawaii	7,845	0	0	7,845
Idaho	28,742	0	0	28,742
Illinois	83,690	5,216,166	0	5,299,856
Indiana	0	0	0	0
Iowa	0	0	0	0
Kansas	42,668	0	0	42,668
Kentucky	31,050	0	0	31,050
Louisiana	18,496	10,695	0	29,191
Maine	0	0	0	0
Maryland	25,568	0	0	25,568
Massachusetts	53,352	0	0	53,352
Michigan	58,857	0	0	58,857
Minnesota	0	0	0	0
Mississippi	0	0	0	0
Missouri	56,741	0	0	56,741
Montana	0	0	0	0
Nebraska	4,496	0	0	4,496
Nevada	0	0	0	0
New Hampshire	0	0	0	0
New Jersey	0	0	0	0
New Mexico	0	0	0	0
New York	252,787	0	0	252,787
North Carolina	0	0	0	0
North Dakota	0	0	0	0
Ohio	57,411	9,506	97,761	164,678
Oklahoma	45,541	0	0	45,541
Oregon	0	0	0	0
Pennsylvania	0	0	0	0
Rhode Island	0	26,082	0	26,082
South Carolina	50,570	8,844	35,758	95,172
South Dakota	1,704	3,199	0	4,903
Tennessee	108,508	0	0	108,508
Texas	469,995	0	0	469,995
Utah	41,796	0	0	41,796
Vermont	0	0	0	0
Virginia	405,635	0	0	405,635
Washington	40,576	0	0	40,576
West Virginia	0	0	0	0
Wisconsin	76,219	0	0	76,219
Wyoming	0	0	0	0
Guam	0	0	0	0
Puerto Rico	0	0	0	0
Virgin Islands	0	0	0	0
Total	$2,481,494	$5,290,792	$187,098	$7,959,384

Table 15 / LSCA Title I Expenditures for Literacy, FY 1992

	Federal	State	Local	Total
Alabama	$1,477	$0	$3,007	$4,484
Alaska	0	0	0	0
Arizona	0	0	0	0
Arkansas	10,000	0	0	10,000
California	216,297	0	0	216,297
Colorado	41,579	0	0	41,5790
Connecticut	25,000	0	0	25,0000
Delaware	2,498	9,068	2,779	14,345
District of Columbia	112,852	92,365	0	205,217
Florida	142,100	0	47,386	189,486
Georgia	0	0	0	0
Hawaii	0	0	0	0
Idaho	26,024	0	0	26,024
Illinois	317,996	4,636,511	0	4,954,507
Indiana	29,433	0	0	29,433
Iowa	5,000	0	0	5,000
Kansas	44,257	0	0	44,257
Kentucky	26,156	0	0	26,156
Louisiana	24,384	6,225	0	30,609
Maine	0	0	0	0
Maryland	41,800	0	0	41,800
Massachusetts	109,815	0	0	109,815
Michigan	102,372	0	0	102,372
Minnesota	0	0	0	0
Mississippi	0	0	0	0
Missouri	36,032	0	0	36,032
Montana	0	0	0	0
Nebraska	3,691	0	0	3,691
Nevada	0	0	0	0
New Hampshire	0	0	0	0
New Jersey	200,000	0	0	200,000
New Mexico	0	0	0	0
New York	255,428	0	0	255,428
North Carolina	0	0	0	0
North Dakota	0	0	0	0
Ohio	68,235	36	50,561	118,832
Oklahoma	52,835	0	0	52,835
Oregon	0	0	0	0
Pennsylvania	23,770	0	0	23,770
Rhode Island	1,582	19,685	0	21,267
South Carolina	45,135	803	34,836	80,774
South Dakota	87	3,903	0	3,990
Tennessee	128,042	0	0	128,042
Texas	341,117	0	0	341,117
Utah	30,000	0	0	30,000
Vermont	0	0	0	0
Virginia	42,854	0	0	42,854
Washington	16,194	0	0	16,194
West Virginia	0	0	0	0
Wisconsin	69,797	0	0	69,797
Wyoming	0	0	0	0
Guam	0	0	0	0
Puerto Rico	0	0	0	0
Virgin Islands	0	0	0	0
Total	$2,593,839	$4,768,596	$138,569	$7,501,004

Table 16 / LSCA Title I Expenditures for the Limited English-Speaking, FY 1991

	Federal	State	Local	Total
Alabama	$0	$0	$0	$0
Alaska	0	0	0	0
Arizona	0	0	0	0
Arkansas	5,015	0	0	5,015
California	153,283	0	0	153,283
Colorado	130,045	0	0	130,045
Connecticut	0	0	0	0
Delaware	8,450	0	0	8,450
District of Columbia	16,500	2,000	0	18,500
Florida	0	0	0	0
Georgia	0	0	0	0
Hawaii	0	0	0	0
Idaho	0	0	0	0
Illinois	310,644	0	0	310,644
Indiana	0	0	0	0
Iowa	850	0	0	850
Kansas	0	0	0	0
Kentucky	0	0	0	0
Louisiana	15,936	8,912	0	24,848
Maine	0	0	0	0
Maryland	104,525	0	0	104,525
Massachusetts	18,450	0	0	18,450
Michigan	16,726	0	0	16,726
Minnesota	0	0	0	0
Mississippi	0	0	0	0
Missouri	0	0	0	0
Montana	0	0	0	0
Nebraska	0	0	0	0
Nevada	17,000	0	0	17,000
New Hampshire	0	0	0	0
New Jersey	62,500	0	0	62,500
New Mexico	0	0	0	0
New York	110,291	0	0	110,291
North Carolina	130,420	0	24,713	155,133
North Dakota	0	0	0	0
Ohio	5,718	4,753	2,159	12,630
Oklahoma	0	0	0	0
Oregon	43,291	0	0	43,291
Pennsylvania	0	0	0	0
Rhode Island	3,974	3,981	0	7,955
South Carolina	0	0	0	0
South Dakota	0	0	0	0
Tennessee	0	0	0	0
Texas	204,525	0	0	204,525
Utah	4,333	7,844	0	12,177
Vermont	0	0	0	0
Virginia	0	0	0	0
Washington	0	0	0	0
West Virginia	0	0	0	0
Wisconsin	6,206	0	0	6,206
Wyoming	0	0	0	0
Guam	2,500	2,000	0	4,500
Puerto Rico	0	0	0	0
Virgin Islands	0	0	0	0
Total	$1,371,182	$29,490	$26,872	$1,427,544

Table 17 / LSCA Title I Expenditures for the Limited English-Speaking, FY 1992

	Federal	State	Local	Total
Alabama	$0	$0	$0	$0
Alaska	0	0	0	0
Arizona	0	0	0	0
Arkansas	0	0	0	0
California	263,780	0	0	0
Colorado	0	0	0	0
Connecticut	0	0	0	0
Delaware	2,500	0	2,000	4,500
Dist. of Columbia	18,510	23,703	0	42,213
Florida	0	0	0	0
Georgia	6,500	0	0	6,500
Hawaii	0	0	0	0
Idaho	0	0	0	0
Illinois	39,591	0	0	39,591
Indiana	0	0	0	0
Iowa	364	0	0	364
Kansas	0	0	0	0
Kentucky	0	0	0	0
Louisiana	20,320	5,187	0	25,507
Maine	0	0	0	0
Maryland	52,263	0	0	52,263
Massachusetts	46,756	0	0	46,756
Michigan	42,568	0	0	42,568
Minnesota	0	0	0	0
Mississippi	0	0	0	0
Missouri	16,395	0	0	16,395
Montana	0	0	0	0
Nebraska	0	0	0	0
Nevada	5,000	0	0	5,000
New Hampshire	0	0	0	0
New Jersey	222,500	0	0	222,500
New Mexico	0	0	0	0
New York	128,614	0	0	128,614
North Carolina	0	0	0	0
North Dakota	0	0	0	0
Ohio	25,208	18	8,794	34,020
Oklahoma	0	0	0	0
Oregon	13,031	0	0	13,031
Pennsylvania	30,000	0	0	30,000
Rhode Island	0	0	0	0
South Carolina	0	0	0	0
South Dakota	0	0	0	0
Tennessee	0	0	0	0
Texas	135,897	0	0	135,897
Utah	0	0	0	0
Vermont	0	0	0	0
Virginia	0	0	0	0
Washington	0	0	0	0
West Virginia	0	0	0	0
Wisconsin	6,500	0	0	6,500
Wyoming	0	0	0	0
Guam	2,000	2,000	0	4,000
Puerto Rico	0	0	0	0
Virgin Islands	0	0	0	0
Total	$1,078,297	$30,908	$10,794	$1,119,999

Further, family literacy programs often appear under the LSCA categories for intergenerational literacy, child care and services to the elderly. There are numerous descriptions of new library buildings and renovations built with LSCA Title II funds that include space for literacy activities, such as tutoring, tutor training, computer-assisted instruction, and other support activities. Also, the figures reported here do not include the $8 million available during this period under LSCA Title VI. The $3 million increase in LSCA Title VI in 1991 may account for some of the decrease in expenditures in LSCA Title I.

The percentage of LSCA funds used by states for literacy activities varies widely. The national average was 3.14 percent of Title I funds in FY 1991 and 2.97 percent in FY 1992. However, several states committed substantially more than the average:

FY 1991		FY 1992	
State	Percentage	State	Percentage
CO	7	DC	31.81
DC	24	IL	9.67
ID	7	NJ	7.33
TN	7	TN	7.97
UT	6	TX	6.82
VA	26		

Average expenditures of Title I funds under the Limited English-speaking category were 1.84 percent in FY 1991 and 1.70 percent in FY 1992. Those states reporting expenditures above the average were:

FY 1991		FY 1992	
State	Percentage	State	Percentage
CO	10	CA	3.56
DC	4	DC	5.22
IL	10	MD	3.47
MD	7	NJ	8.15
NC	12		
OR	5		
TX	4		

The District of Columbia was the leader in the expenditure of Title I funds in the three targeted areas of Literacy, Limited English-speaking, and Model Literacy Centers. The district used 28 percent of its allotment in FY 1991 and 41.8 percent in FY 1992 on these activities.

With literacy activities becoming a more integrated part of mainstream public library services, the use of LSCA Title I funds has shifted from the establishment of local literacy programs to an increased emphasis on coalition building and coordination at the local level, as well as coordinated statewide services such as training, collection building, literacy hotlines for tutor recruitment and student placement, and consultation at the state level. Several of the areas being addressed are illustrated in the following highlights.

Recruitment of minority participants is an ongoing problem in many areas of the country. The Fort Collins (CO) Public Library used a Title I subgrant to increase the number of minority tutors in its literacy programs. The 18 community organizations participating in the effort trained and matched with students 34 minority tutors. In addition, two in-service training sessions were held for all tutors to enhance their awareness of multicultural issues related to tutoring. A multicultural literacy festival promoted library literacy activities.

The San Diego (CA) Public Library (like many of the 81-member programs of the California Literacy Campaign) found that only a small percent of tutors (13 percent) participating in READ San Diego, represented minority groups. As a result of this finding, the library developed a pilot project to design messages specifically targeted to ethnic communities. Phase I involved research, concept testing, identification of appropriate media, development of print and TV ads, and audience testing. Issues related to teaching, education, and volunteerism were explored with the help of seven area literacy providers. Focus groups facilitated the process. General Colin Powell contributed time to the first public service announcements, which went to eight television and 13 radio stations in the area. In Phase II of the project, the library tested the results and disseminated the public service spots to the other 81 libraries in the California Literacy Campaign. Success indicators include a 27 percent increase in inquiries from potential ethnic tutors and a 44 percent increase in minority tutor/student matches.

Many new readers who are academically ready to go on to adult basic education (ABE), GED preparation, or job skills training are reluctant to leave one-to-one tutoring situations. To ease this transition the Adult Learning Center at the Queens Borough (NY) Public Library developed the "Extension Class" program. Classes were conducted on a semester basis, and consisted of two three-hour sessions twice a week. At the time of enrollment each of the 84 students completed an intake questionnaire and participated in an individual conference to discuss his/her educational goals and plans. Reading level was monitored by use of the TABE test at the beginning, mid-point, and end of the semester. Median reading level gain was 1.7. Two teachers and two paraprofessionals kept student interest by regularly alternating between whole group instruction and small group work that allowed for peer interaction. Students had the opportunity to apply skills learned in class through participation in the Extension Class Writing Group, which produces a magazine of student work. The writing group uses the computers in the Adult Learning Center to write, revise, and edit their work. The program has a high motivation factor as shown by the high retention rate. Over 70 percent of those involved went on to ABE classes.

Hoping to break the cyclical pattern of illiteracy the Spring Green (MO) County Library joined forces with the Friends of the Library and the Parents as Teachers program to initiate family literacy programs that targeted 400 inner city families with infants and toddlers to teach them the importance of reading aloud to their children and to make families aware of the public library's role in literacy and children's library services. Members of Parents as Teachers distributed "Wee Read" packets during regularly scheduled home visits and demonstrated how to read aloud to children. Information about the library's Literacy Outreach program was also distributed. The Mobile Learning Center staff and the literacy coordinator were part of the in-library education program that consisted of read-aloud sessions, storytelling, and tours of the library. Incentives to visit the library were provided through coupons redeemable for free books and T-shirts imprinted with the "Wee Read" logo and the legend "Read Me a Story," which were given away at a "Wee Read Fair." The library had hoped to issue 50 new library cards to families who had not used the library. At the end of the project year 43 new cards had been issued and the library was pleased to discover that 45 percent of the families already had library cards. A key element in the success of the program was the continuous followup provided by Parents as Teachers workers. The Friends of the Library provided funding for a second year of the program in which 300 more families will be targeted.

To promote family literacy, the Allegan (MI) Public Library developed a more direct relationship with the existing literacy network and the Head Start program. Head Start workers introduced the program to 194 families during home visits and parent activities at the Head Start Center. Parents in need of literacy skills were matched with tutors. The library purchased picture books for the six Head Start classrooms and paperbacks and read-along audio cassettes that parents could use with their children in the classroom and at home. Each month, tutors helped the parents learn to read a new book. Head Start teachers also made extensive use of the materials. While the number of parents participating in the program was lower than expected, the library still feels that this program was a success. Parents were exposed to opportunities that helped them to improve their literacy skills and, in turn, helped their children. Head Start received a grant to continue the program for a second year. A local church agreed to provide space and transportation and two community organizations agreed to provide funds to purchase additional books.

State libraries used LSCA funds for a variety of activities during this period of funding. The California State Library joined with the State Board of Education to take advantage of an opportunity to survey adult literacy needs in the state as part of the National Adult Literacy Survey (NALS) conducted by the U.S. Department of Education NCES and the Educational Testing Service. In 1991 the District of Columbia published the second edition of *Adult Basic Education/English as a Second Language Collection: An Annotated List of Titles,* which was distributed free to adult literacy providers in the district and at cost to libraries throughout the United States. The Texas State Library conducted *A Summative Evaluation of the Public Library Services to Disadvantaged Populations Grant Project: 1988–1992* to determine how well public libraries were meeting the needs of those with less than a 12th-grade education, limited English speakers, the unemployed, the poor, and the elderly. Finally, the Missouri State Library funded the writing and publication of *Libraries and Literacy: A Program Planning Manual for Missouri Libraries* as part of its ongoing effort to promote literacy activities in state libraries.

Library Services to Special Populations: The Blind and Physically Handicapped

Nearly all states and most outlying areas provide services on a statewide, or territorial, basis through a regional library for the blind and physically handicapped.

This program serves as a service and distribution center for audio-recorded materials and playback equipment available from the National Library Service (NLS) of the Library of Congress. In addition to these statewide programs, many states use LSCA funds to reach persons whose disabilities prevent them from coming to a library, by funding projects at the local level.

The types of services offered on a statewide basis are based primarily on books and magazines recorded on disc, cassette, and magnetic tape, along with appropriate playback equipment, and materials in braille. Projects at the area and community levels focus on outreach activities such as visits to shut-ins, programs for the deaf and hearing-impaired, and radio reading services.

Major trends noted include the automation of records concerning users, materials, equipment, and circulation, enabling the libraries to serve increasing numbers of users with the same or fewer staff; specialized toys designed for handicapped children; greater use of assistive devices such as print-to-voice; print-to-braille; text on computer screen to either large print, voice, or braille for the visually impaired; telecommunications devices for the deaf (TDDs); and closed captioned video/television programs for the hearing-impaired; radio reading programs for the blind and physically handicapped, and special services for the orthopedically impaired.

The amount of federal, state and local funds expended for services to the blind and physically handicapped in FY 1991 was $26.6 million. Of this amount, $5.7 million came from federal funds. Table 18 shows the state-by-state breakout.

A sampling of LSCA-funded projects for the handicapped illustrates some of the types of services provided:

Brevard County (FL) Library System. Assistive Reading Devices Collection. These devices enable persons with limited vision to read print on their own. They range from handheld illuminated magnifiers to talking calculators. Hanging bags and racks were used to shelve and circulate the items, which were also listed in the online catalog. The 42 items were arranged into sets for circulation from each of the system libraries in addition to one set for reference. Rechargeable batteries were used for all of the devices as a long-term cost-effective measure. A collection of assistive device catalogs was assembled and made available to the public. As a result of the publicity announcing the initiation of this service, the circulation of the Subregional Library for the Blind and Physically Handicapped registered a 270 percent increase in circulation over the previous year.

Memphis/Shelby County (TN) Public Library and Information Center. In 1991 the former WTTL radio station became WYPL, and accomplished a decade long goal by becoming an open-air channel, FM 89.3. The channel's programs are now available to the print-impaired citizens of Shelby County without the need for special radio receivers. WYPL reaches listeners in a 50-mile radius, including up to 420,000 blind and visually impaired persons. One of the unique programs produced is "Hands on Cooking" where two hosts, one sighted and one blind, cook during the program. There is a half hour of children's stories each weeknight. Adolescent listeners may tune into "Young Adult Books" and "Seventeen and Sassy." "WYPL Reports" is a community affairs program, and "Mid-day" broadcasts a weekday local news and information program. More than 100 volunteers read the books and magazines used in the broadcasts.

Table 18 / LSCA Title I Expenditures for the Blind and Physically Handicapped,
FY 1991

	Federal	State	Local	Total	Population Served
Alabama	$31,281	$325,869	$0	$357,150	5,019
Alaska	0	71,963	0	71,963	618
Arizona	0	430,714	0	430,714	11,072
Arkansas	117,401	50,958	0	168,359	4,435
California	0	1,881,252	0	1,881,252	32,500
Colorado	105,544	208,707	0	314,251	9,587
Connecticut	302,831	0	0	302,831	8,500
Delaware	43,847	73,488	0	117,335	1,200
District of Columbia	17,516	113,847	0	131,363	9,000
Florida	188,324	606,295	55,456	850,075	58,675
Georgia	120,423	937,007	2,620	1,060,050	17,320
Hawaii	0	336,598	0	336,598	1,870
Idaho	0	182,716	0	182,716	2,449
Illinois	157,905	2,177,134	0	2,335,039	33,500
Indiana	358,073	193,965	0	552,038	12,864
Iowa	33,911	18,089	0	52,000	10,124
Kansas	122,500	314,400	0	436,900	14,247
Kentucky	90,100	200,000	0	290,100	5,059
Louisiana	163,954	192,628	0	356,582	5,502
Maine	250,608	16,392	0	267,000	3,700
Maryland	98,975	431,025	0	530,000	15,000
Massachusetts	35,782	126,473	0	162,255	33,654
Michigan	465,485	480,702	0	946,187	16,273
Minnesota	12,633	294,642	0	307,275	6,294
Mississippi	22,197	185,891	0	208,088	4,803
Missouri	88,309	244,620	0	332,929	12,000
Montana	110,017	38,017	0	148,034	2,472
Nebraska	73,062	381,583	0	454,645	4,789
Nevada	60,477	29,875	0	90,352	1,500
New Hampshire	63,099	115,058	0	178,157	2,500
New Jersey	476,014	36,934	0	512,948	12,000
New Mexico	0	141,129	0	141,129	2,047
New York	431,664	1,062,347	0	1,494,011	42,791
North Carolina	195,779	710,346	0	906,125	8,524
North Dakota	115,237	0	0	115,237	1,674
Ohio	254,530	1,371,938	0	1,626,468	27,000
Oklahoma	25,179	0	0	25,179	12,000
Oregon	10,388	236,041	0	246,429	6,680
Pennsylvania	105,000	1,793,200	0	1,898,200	66,000
Rhode Island	129,590	182,521	0	312,111	14,068
South Carolina	86,303	592,288	0	678,591	7,518
South Dakota	194,786	42,883	0	237,669	2,911
Tennessee	134,000	619,875	0	753,875	9,638
Texas	0	1,149,660	0	1,149,660	24,516
Utah	109,100	190,283	0	299,383	6,760
Vermont	31,868	15,143	0	47,011	1,377
Virginia	87,213	143,361	0	230,574	21,858
Washington	73,170	1,083,613	0	1,156,783	8,447
West Virginia	51,760	160,212	0	211,972	5,602
Wisconsin	0	482,271	0	482,271	10,577
Wyoming	0	55,383	0	55,383	2,500
Guam	3,750	23,617	0	27,367	400
Puerto Rico	35,586	42,798	0	78,384	1,343
Virgin Islands	14,456	48,709	0	63,165	500
Total	$5,699,627	$20,844,460	$58,076	$26,602,163	643,257

The Vision Center, which opened in July, gives library users the opportunity to use existing technology to access the library's print materials. This is accomplished through six workstations: a Kurzweil computer, two magnification stations, a braille computer, a large-print/physically disabled workstation, and the Media/Training Center, which helps to accommodate various sight-related needs.

Utah State Library. Service to Persons Who Are Orthopedically Impaired. The library works closely with organizations and agencies that serve the orthopedically impaired and includes orthopedically impaired patrons on its Consumer Advisory Council. As a result there was a period of considerable growth in circulation (26 percent in books, 52 percent in magazines) and a 12 percent increase in the number of patrons served. The professional staff held four training workshops for nursing home employees—specialized training that continues to be part of the curriculum at the Salt Lake Community College. The library also trains its own staff in meeting the needs of orthopedically impaired patrons.

Vermont State Library. Planning for Accessibility—a publication designed to get librarians and trustees started in addressing physical access to libraries. This publication of the Vermont Board of Libraries Access Task Force includes excerpts from the Americans With Disabilities Act that are of concern to public libraries as well as other laws and regulations related to the disabled. It covers such topics as low-cost alterations and requirements for parking, walks, ramps, entrances, and doors. It lists libraries that exhibit examples of the requirements being discussed and includes a selected annotated bibliography.

Library Services to Special Population: The Institutionalized

Library Services to the Institutionalized is one of the mandated areas for states receiving grants under LSCA. In previous years, each state was required to spend as much, or more, for library services under this program as they had in the second preceding year. For the first time, in FY 1991, states were allowed to ratably reduce their expenditures to correspond with reductions in populations served. The state reports indicate that $2.4 million was spent in FY 1991 and $4.1 million in FY 1992. When pooled with state and local funds $21.9 million was used to support such efforts in FY 1991 and $30 million in FY 1992. (Tables 19 and 20 show the state-by-state breakout.)

Since reasons for institutionalization vary, each institutional library focuses on the special needs of its clientele through specially tailored programs and collections. This report highlights projects funded during FY 1990 and 1991.

Alabama. The Alabama Department of Corrections used LSCA funds to open three new libraries in correctional institutions. This brings the total of such libraries to eight, with ten correctional institutions needing library service.

Arizona. Of the estimated 14,000 inmates in the Arizona State Prison System, about 30 percent are of Spanish origin. Funds were used to purchase Spanish-language materials for nine institutions.

Connecticut. The state library gave workshops for the librarians in institutional libraries, which included "Space Planning for Small Libraries," and an open forum was held to discuss issues and the grant program.

Delaware. An extended Books-by-Mail program provided library services to the institutionalized.

Table 19 / LSCA Titie I Expenditures for the Institutionalized, FY 1991

	Federal	State	Local	Total	Population Served
Alabama	$30,483	$121,740	$3,785	$156,008	13,837
Alaska	0	80,297	0	80,297	3,372
Arizona	6,169	206,336	0	212,505	32,000
Arkansas	78,492	13,663	0	92,155	53,000
California	20,520	2,995,618	0	3,016,138	0
Colorado	81,436	240,478	0	321,914	9,067
Connecticut	31,412	4,657	200,497	236,566	18,404
Delaware	10,980	4,657	0	15,637	3,704
District of Columbia	1,170	24,450	0	25,620	7,500
Florida	224,912	419,963	0	644,875	4,833,560
Georgia	53,046	9,638	15,316	78,000	3,800
Hawaii	4,160	269,170	0	273,330	0
Idaho	1,618	15,000	0	16,618	2,200
Illinois	0	2,231,590	0	2,231,590	0
Indiana	105,317	369,408	0	474,725	18,128
Iowa	44,551	0	0	44,551	0
Kansas	121,607	1,429	0	123,036	10,551
Kentucky	39,500	50,000	0	89,500	11,400
Louisiana	80,053	62,274	0	142,327	34,080
Maine	0	218,500	0	218,500	0
Maryland	10,050	24,000	0	34,050	10,483
Massachusetts	27,267	296,609	0	323,876	17,475
Michigan	95,016	0	0	95,016	5,429
Minnesota	19,259	301,542	0	320,801	5,000
Mississippi	102,201	63,237	0	165,438	29,621
Missouri	75,446	300,495	0	375,941	5,499
Montana	46,251	60,670	0	106,921	2,345
Nebraska	26,779	380,557	0	407,336	0
Nevada	25,000	69,390	0	94,390	4,740
New Hampshire	28,066	170,191	0	198,257	2,100
New Jersey	84,253	304,544	0	388,797	0
New Mexico	3,800	48,917	0	52,717	4,264
New York	121,086	2,280,406	0	2,401,492	560
North Carolina	45,000	181,979	0	226,979	25,000
North Dakota	33,985	80,740	0	114,725	1,025
Ohio	116,083	443,505	0	559,588	2,071,154
Oklahoma	125,447	223,246	0	348,693	11,000
Oregon	0	434,763	0	434,763	0
Pennsylvania	9,000	1,712,649	0	1,721,649	49,556
Rhode Island	5,185	191,502	0	196,687	0
South Carolina	64,738	535,262	0	600,000	19,703
South Dakota	59,225	172,801	0	232,026	2,510
Tennessee	50,000	25,000	0	75,000	12,660
Texas	63,403	357,838	0	421,241	57,931
Utah	29,219	156,353	0	185,572	5,036
Vermont	8,840	93,879	0	102,719	1,453
Virginia	0	260,000	0	260,000	20,428
Washington	15,263	1,387,574	0	1,402,837	0
West Virginia	49,543	148,908	0	198,451	0
Wisconsin	75,939	1,045,774	0	1,121,713	50,918
Wyoming	21,318	69,462	0	90,780	1,850
Guam	9,000	2,250	0	11,250	0
Puerto Rico	69,186	63,469	0	132,655	12,112
Virgin Islands	8,540	48,985	0	57,525	0
Total	$2,458,814	$19,275,365	$219,598	$21,953,777	7,484,455

Table 20 / LSCA Title I Expenditures for the Institutionalized, FY 1992

	Federal	State	Local	Total	Population Served
Alabama	$61,017	$225,538	$0	$286,555	22,250
Alaska	0	82,359	0	82,359	3,562
Arizona	42,000	216,922	0	258,922	35,000
Arkansas	78,119	16,547	0	94,666	53,000
California	0	3,641,515	0	3,641,515	146,102
Colorado	82,473	223,801	0	306,274	9,067
Connecticut	14,855	0	205,487	220,342	7,350
Delaware	10,635	10,807	12,774	34,216	10,628
District of Columbia	0	26,760	0	26,760	7,500
Florida	290,884	323,112	29,793	643,789	863,822
Georgia	47,372	12,440	3,181	62,993	6,681,235
Hawaii	5,936	262,434	0	268,370	3,000
Idaho	0	16,200	0	16,200	0
Illinois	0	2,531,559	0	2,531,559	0
Indiana	112,633	341,961	0	454,594	18,128
Iowa	50,000	363,217	0	413,217	0
Kansas	59,184	1,429	0	60,613	2,461,000
Kentucky	89,499	59,650	0	149,149	0
Louisiana	95,580	23,619	0	119,199	34,080
Maine	7,662	215,180	0	222,842	2,000
Maryland	176,108	231,910	0	408,018	42,942
Massachusetts	60,845	294,886	0	355,731	16,488
Michigan	109,116	0	0	109,116	15,000
Minnesota	43,259	915,385	0	958,644	8,447
Mississippi	25,001	87,602	0	112,603	18,414
Missouri	51,278	320,442	0	371,720	0
Montana	45,928	43,857	0	89,785	2,400
Nebraska	24,991	389,394	0	414,385	4,442
Nevada	35,000	67,062	0	102,062	9,014
New Hampshire	27,616	189,750	0	217,366	2,021
New Jersey	94,478	339,779	0	434,257	0
New Mexico	38,000	49,768	0	87,768	4,375
New York	1,344,180	6,467,739	0	7,811,919	17,773,173
North Carolina	46,401	192,948	0	239,349	10,412
North Dakota	36,620	81,550	0	118,170	1,025
Ohio	116,810	460,161	0	576,971	52,016
Oklahoma	99,778	301,722	0	401,500	0
Oregon	0	450,229	0	450,229	11,080
Pennsylvania	78,164	1,527,357	0	1,605,521	82,270
Rhode Island	36,822	226,700	0	263,522	43,000
South Carolina	76,426	523,574	0	600,000	4,000
South Dakota	54,254	186,245	0	240,499	0
Tennessee	50,000	25,000	0	75,000	22,300
Texas	64,636	360,182	0	424,818	57,931
Utah	30,000	87,753	0	117,753	5,125
Vermont	28,561	74,829	0	103,390	1,453
Virginia	0	260,000	0	260,000	20,428
Washington	74,769	1,424,211	0	1,498,980	0
West Virginia	5,440	188,303	0	193,743	4,415
Wisconsin	78,013	1,065,119	0	1,143,132	61,738
Wyoming	14,806	83,234	0	98,040	2,344
Guam	9,000	56,259	0	65,259	9,000
Puerto Rico	72,213	85,770	0	157,983	11,156
Virgin Islands	8,545	50,500	0	59,045	1,800
Total	$4,104,907	$25,704,270	$251,235	$30,060,412	28,655,933

Georgia. The Georgia Mental Health Institute, Regional Hospital for Northeast Georgia purchased materials on health issues related to the causes for hospitalization for use by the patients and their families.

Idaho. In support of the *Teens for the Restoration of the Earth's Environment* (TREE) group, the Idaho State School for the Deaf and Blind purchased high-interest, low-reading level reference materials, books by Idaho authors, and materials on recycling and ecology.

Kentucky. After the 1991 Kentucky Institutional Librarians Conference identified the lack of reference materials as the major shortcoming of state-supported institutional libraries, a major push to purchase reference materials for ten of these institutions was undertaken.

Maryland. Three correctional education libraries introduced the multimedia "Success in the Workplace" program. This is a self-directed computerized modular course.

Massachusetts. The Paul A. Denver State School, serving 391 mentally retarded clients of whom 35 percent are also elderly, funds a program especially for this over-50-year-old group. The program is designed to help them preserve their functional abilities.

Michigan. The Kinross Correctional Facility Library serves a population of 1,200, of whom 60 percent are functionally illiterate. Federal funds were used to train 30 men to serve as tutors at the facility and to publish a directory, *Resource for Prison Literacy Projects.*

Montana. Flathead County Library provided a rotating collection, including large-type books, periodicals and newspapers to the Montana Veterans' Home.

New Jersey. Funds were used to establish libraries in restricted hospital wards such as the AIDS units.

New York. Young male inmates at three New York State correctional facilities were offered programs on parenting issues that covered infant and child development, family law, the father's role in the family, and dysfunctional families.

Ohio. The Ohio Department of Rehabilitation & Corrections involved inmates in book discussions to increase their awareness of literature and available library resources.

Pennsylvania. The library at the State Correctional Unit at Waynesburg developed a Spanish-language collection to provide reference, drug/alcohol therapy and self-help books for its female Hispanic population.

Rhode Island. Five institutional libraries participate in the statewide library network and receive materials through the delivery system, while four libraries have been loaned CD-ROM equipment with copies of the statewide database (QUAHOG).

Washington. The institutional librarians determined roles for their libraries using the Planning and Role-Setting Process developed by the Public Library Association. The two primary roles selected were to serve as a reference library and a popular materials library. One secondary role was selected: education support center.

Wisconsin. A grant to the Winding Rivers Library System provided service to inmates in county jails through rotating collections of paperback books, Spanish-language materials, and a basic reference collection.

Virgin Islands. Institutional libraries requested materials to upgrade their collections to support literacy activities and legal reference services.

Library Services to Special Populations: The Elderly

There are now on file more than twenty years (1971–1992) of state reports on the Library Services to the Elderly category. The FY 1991 reports indicate that $1.5 million of LSCA funds supported such efforts, while FY 1992 reports show $1.7 million. When combined with state and local funds, the total reached almost $1.8 million in FY 1991 and $2.1 million in FY 1992. (See Tables 21 and 22 for state breakouts.)

In the first few years of LSCA funding, almost all projects were for delivery of books to the homebound or were special programs at the library. The energy crisis caused a revamping of programs dependent on either cars or bookmobiles. During that period, Books-by-Mail took the place of on-site delivery. Since energy costs are now down and postal rates and personnel costs are up, many of the Books-by-Mail projects rely on delivery by volunteers. Analysis of the projects conducted in FY 1992 (the latest reports available) listed only five projects that included mail delivery. Forty projects funded delivery of programs and materials to homes, nursing homes, senior centers, and other such sites. All but one of these projects included rotating and/or deposit collections. The Washoe County (NV) Library project located a collection of large-print and other books of interest to the elderly in the county senior center. This project has proven so successful that the library will continue to support the program after the federal funds lapse; plans are under way to move it from an extension branch to a full branch with its own budget.

Projects that funded rotating collections, as well as collections housed in the library, centered on large-print books (82 projects). Audiovisual materials purchased (69 projects) included talking books and adapted games. Also noted was the purchase of materials of special interest to the elderly (21 projects for special reference materials, craft and travel books, etc.). The Newton County (GA) Library found that the addition of new large-print books and books on cassette increased circulation considerably—circulation of audio books was up 55 percent and large-print was up 33 percent. When the Mississippi Library Commission (MLC) added new large-print books to its collection, these materials represented 30.5 percent of MLC's total circulation in 1992.

Materials added to collections included multisensory kits to aid in life review and stimulation of the senses (14 projects). Several projects, like the one at the White Pine (MI) Library Cooperative, checked kits out to local libraries for extended periods before they rotated to another library for use. The White Pine Library Cooperative used the kits in over 30 locations in an 11-county area. Visual aids were mentioned in 13 projects, with most citing the Americans with Disabilities Act as an impetus to develop such collections. The Laurens County (SC) Library provided a low-vision center, allowing the visually impaired to try the various aids prior to purchase.

A large number of projects in FY 1992 supported special programming (41). These included book talks, use of BiFolkal kits, read-aloud sessions, and travel and other films. Location appears to have much to do with the type of program-

Table 21 / LSCA Title I Expenditures for the Elderly, FY 1991

	Federal	State	Local	Total	Population Served
Alabama	$29,900	$0	$13,981	$43,881	15,115
Alaska	0	0	0	0	0
Arizona	10,025	0	0	10,025	109,722
Arkansas	9,000	0	0	9,000	23,452
California	401,600	0	0	401,600	141,500
Colorado	30,825	0	0	30,825	515
Connecticut	0	0	0	0	0
Delaware	5,569	4,040	0	9,609	5,500
District of Columbia	72,000	73,530	0	145,530	76,000
Florida	74,280	0	43,966	118,246	188,334
Georgia	10,000	2,000	2,120	14,120	138,590
Hawaii	0	0	0	0	0
Idaho	0	0	0	0	0
Illinois	0	0	0	0	0
Indiana	20,399	0	0	20,399	21,000
Iowa	3,876	0	0	3,876	10,482
Kansas	39,625	0	0	39,625	54,576
Kentucky	73,728	0	0	73,728	290,269
Louisiana	11,747	6,684	0	18,431	468,991
Maine	0	42,158	0	42,158	500
Maryland	11,297	0	0	11,297	6,173
Massachusetts	0	0	0	0	0
Michigan	9,510	0	0	9,510	2,549
Minnesota	5,146	0	0	5,146	21,716
Mississippi	0	0	0	0	0
Missouri	48,681	0	0	48,681	200
Montana	0	0	0	0	0
Nebraska	1,501	0	0	1,501	205,684
Nevada	5,800	0	0	5,800	12,500
New Hampshire	3,177	1,000	0	4,177	165,000
New Jersey	0	0	0	0	0
New Mexico	0	0	0	0	0
New York	153,970	0	0	153,970	58,874
North Carolina	0	0	0	0	0
North Dakota	0	0	0	0	0
Ohio	20,527	8,605	0	29,132	20,672
Oklahoma	48,430	0	0	48,430	0
Oregon	906	0	0	906	20,000
Pennsylvania	34,470	0	0	34,470	21,000
Rhode Island	0	0	0	0	0
South Carolina	23,950	0	19,450	43,400	10,000
South Dakota	12,942	14,434	0	27,376	123,063
Tennessee	51,167	0	0	51,167	841,907
Texas	152,506	0	0	152,506	130,285
Utah	0	0	0	0	0
Vermont	0	0	0	0	0
Virginia	20,128	0	0	20,128	3,030
Washington	20,993	0	0	20,993	665
West Virginia	0	0	0	0	0
Wisconsin	107,847	0	0	107,847	104,655
Wyoming	0	0	0	0	0
Guam	2,000	2,000	0	4,000	0
Puerto Rico	0	11,525	0	11,525	4,135
Virgin Islands	0	0	0	0	0
Total	$1,527,522	$165,976	$79,517	$1,773,015	3,296,654

Table 22 / LSCA Title I Expenditures for the Elderly, FY 1992

	Federal	State	Local	Total	Population Served
Alabama	$0	$0	$0	$0	0
Alaska	0	0	0	0	0
Arizona	3,500	0	0	3,500	550
Arkansas	0	0	0	0	0
California	0	0	0	0	0
Colorado	28,175	0	0	28,175	833
Connecticut	0	0	0	0	0
Delaware	10,690	0	12,774	23,464	5,628
District of Columbia	3,005	103,921	0	106,926	76,000
Florida	151,814	0	111,343	263,157	60,083
Georgia	16,000	2,000	2,290	20,290	97,991
Hawaii	0	0	0	0	0
Idaho	697	0	0	697	447
Illinois	31,234	0	0	31,234	60,000
Indiana	5,826	0	0	5,826	100
Iowa	9,313	0	0	9,313	500
Kansas	30,000	0	0	30,000	7,776
Kentucky	62,830	0	0	62,830	347,002
Louisiana	15,240	3,891	0	19,131	468,991
Maine	124	41,624	0	41,748	500
Maryland	32,050	0	0	32,050	3,675
Massachusetts	20,800	0	0	20,800	3,030
Michigan	76,284	0	0	76,284	1,505,154
Minnesota	5,185	0	0	5,185	22,000
Mississippi	2	94	0	96	15,132
Missouri	47,360	0	0	47,360	200,000
Montana	0	0	0	0	0
Nebraska	1,845	0	0	1,845	205,684
Nevada	25,000	0	0	25,000	266,800
New Hampshire	1,423	1,500	0	2,923	168,522
New Jersey	20,000	0	0	20,000	250
New Mexico	0	0	0	0	0
New York	103,970	0	0	103,970	10,752
North Carolina	21,602	0	0	21,602	not available
North Dakota	0	0	0	0	0
Ohio	16,969	1,120	21,000	39,089	21,859
Oklahoma	49,365	0	0	49,365	1,641
Oregon	12,116	0	0	12,116	1,600
Pennsylvania	409,209	0	0	409,209	71,710
Rhode Island	11,098	24,449	0	35,547	239,750
South Carolina	29,824	37,839	24,483	92,146	19,409
South Dakota	7,445	6,223	13,668	27,336	not available
Tennessee	58,650	0	0	58,650	131,548
Texas	264,840	0	0	264,840	187,295
Utah	0	0	0	0	0
Vermont	0	0	0	0	0
Virginia	0	0	0	0	0
Washington	0	0	0	0	0
West Virginia	0	0	0	0	0
Wisconsin	111,452	0	0	111,452	122,983
Wyoming	0	0	0	0	0
Guam	2,000	2,000	0	4,000	not available
Puerto Rico	0	11,525	0	11,525	1,307
Virgin Islands	0	0	0	0	0
Total	$1,696,937	$236,186	$185,558	$2,118,681	4,326,502

ming that is successful, with crafts and travel sessions more popular in rural areas, crime prevention and social services in urban areas, and book talks and other cultural activities popular in all areas. The Words and Memories project at the Brooklyn (NY) Public Library presented 178 programs at 23 sites, using multimedia materials, read-aloud, storytelling, poems, and songs to stimulate reading and share memories. Another excellent project is the Nassau (NY) Library System's Lively Minds, a lifelong learning program that used library resources for mental stimulation, enjoyment, and empowerment to prove that neither age nor physical infirmity can limit the power of the mind.

The major change in intergenerational projects is one of emphasis. As mentioned in earlier reports, these projects tended to have youth reading to or delivering books to the homebound or those in nursing homes. Current projects (16) aim for the elderly to aid children who need to develop better reading skills or who need after-school help with homework. The project in Fort Scott, Kansas, taught the seniors about the number of children reading below grade level and why they have such poor reading skills. An outstanding project in Broward County, Florida, is Prime Time, which matches the elderly and children attending federally supported day-care centers. This project produced a video that captures the joy of seniors and children interacting. (The video is available for the cost of reproduction.) Even when reading assistance is being provided by senior citizens, projects like Read to Me in New Bedford, Massachusetts, found that the critical element for success is often the work done by the librarian overseeing the volunteers. The organizational skills and the enthusiasm of the project leader can be a critical factor.

The number of projects on genealogy and community history (5) is down from previous reports. However, the project at the Westchester (NY) Library System is notable. Approximately 35 persons attended four sessions to study a variety of memoirs by Americans and to hear a talk by a senior who had written his memoirs for his grandchildren; six sessions on how to write memoirs; and finally a computer instruction course on word-processing skills. A second project, at the Harvin Clarendon County (SC) Library, used video equipment to record the oral history of the senior citizens of the community and to capture the historical sites in the county to show to the immobile elderly.

Six projects noted that Information and Referral serves as an integral part of the project. The Bethel Park (PA) Public Library project developed a Senior Information Area in the library for use by the elderly, nursing home activity directors, and families of those in nursing homes or with Alzheimer's disease.

More and more libraries realize that they need to promote their programs. Forty-two projects noted the various ways they promoted their services to the elderly. Interagency cooperation was mentioned in 20 project reports and training of librarians and volunteers in 19 projects. The OWLS project offered by the Mohawk Valley (NY) Library Association received the Bessie Boehm Moore award. This project included three continuing education workshops on improving services to the elderly for the librarians in four counties. A statewide training institute was presented by Pennsylvania's state library agency as the kickoff for a funding push in this area of service. It was patterned after an earlier program in New Jersey. Catalogs and bibliographies were produced in large-print in ten projects; production was made possible by computerization and other new technologies (noted in five projects).

There are still areas in which projects serving the elderly fall short. The use of advisory groups (usually seniors) was noted only twice and manuals were produced in only five projects. However, many more projects noted their inability to produce written materials. Manuals and resource guides tend to take a back seat to other programming activities. The potential of such manuals as the Read Aloud Handbook produced by the Brown County (WI) Library and Library Service to Florida's Elders by the Florida Division of Library and Information Services to be reproduced and disseminated is great.

Library Services to Targeted Institutions: Major Urban Public Libraries

The Library Services and Construction Act (LSCA) requires that when the total appropriation for LSCA Title I exceeds $60 million, each state must reserve a percentage of such funds under the Major Urban Resource Libraries (MURL) Program for urban libraries whose collections and services reach beyond their local jurisdiction. In FY 1991, there were 167 cities (excluding the District of Columbia) that received LSCA Title I funds under the program.

LSCA defines a major urban resource library as "any public library located in a city having a population of 100,000 or more individuals, as determined by the Secretary." However, before a library serving a city of 100,000 or more can receive funds to serve as a MURL, it must design a program to provide services to individual users and to other libraries beyond its local jurisdiction. For example, in Kentucky the criteria established for a grant under the MURL program had to meet all of the following standards:

- A MURL shall have a collection at least 50 percent larger than the next smaller public library collection.
- A MURL collection shall be maintained by annual additions and replacements averaging 1/7 volume per capita per year over the previous five years.
- A MURL shall make its collection accessible through interlibrary loan and participation in the Kentucky Library Network.
- A MURL shall possess five special resource collections of major significance to the Regional Area.
- A MURL shall employ one professional staff person per 100,000 population served, based on its MURL population.
- A MURL shall communicate its programs and services to all Kentucky public libraries at least once per quarter.

The Kentucky FY 1991 annual report identifies the Lexington Public Library and the Louisville Free Public Library as meeting or exceeding all standards; both libraries therefore qualified as a MURL in FY 1991.

The Lexington Public Library ($12,728) grant assisted the library in enhancing the existing special resource business collection for individual users and other libraries in the regional area, made accessible through telephone reference service and or in-house use, free of charge.

The primary tool purchased was a microform copy of the *Business Collection,* which included text of approximately 450 business periodicals. (This collection is accessed through Infotrac, which is an automated index already owned by the library.) Ten other major reference tools were also purchased, including *Dun's Business Identification Service, Diamond's Japan Business Directory, Standard Trade Index of Japan, and Pratt's Guide to Venture Capital Sources.*

The library promoted the collection through a community newsletter and talks with community groups. It also sponsored a workshop, "The Basic Business Collection For the 90s—A Workshop for Librarians," which informed librarians in the regional area about basic business resources and CD-ROM and online data bases for business reference work.

The project objectives were met by the purchase of materials and promotional efforts of the library. This project took on new importance in FY 1991 as networking efforts in the state progressed. Because the library's holdings are in the OCLC data base, and that data base is now accessible to all member libraries in the state's library network, the potential for resource sharing has been greatly enhanced.

The library has promoted use of the collection with individuals and other libraries for the past three years. While usage has been difficult to track (because individuals help themselves once they are taught to use the systems), a test count (taken between April 15 and 28, 1991) of the number of microfilm cartridges used from the business collection revealed that 448 were used, which extrapolated to 11,648 uses in the year.

The Louisville Free Public Library (LFPL) grant ($32,000) enhanced the "Patent and Trademark Depository Library," which consists of copies of utility and design patents on microfilm, hard copy of various finding guides, indexes and directories, and CASSIS, a CD-ROM data base used to search for specific patents and trademarks by subject.

In March 1988 the library was designated as a patent depository library by the U.S. Patent and Trademark Office. This designation entitled the library to a variety of support services from the Washington, D.C., office, as well as certain materials, such as updates on CD-ROM. In return, the library was obligated to purchase 20 years of backfiles of patents to be housed and used on site. Grant funds have been used to make backfile and necessary equipment purchases over the last four years.

The library mounted a strong publicity effort within the regional area and throughout the state to create awareness and encourage use of the collection. Project staff sponsored several training workshops for librarians and potential users (attorneys, inventors, scientists and students). The FY 1991 workshop was in conjunction with the Government Documents Roundtable, a branch of the Kentucky Library Association. The session resulted in the production of a booklet that identified patent and trademark holdings in 21 libraries, as well as basic reference search aids and a procedure for patent searching. The Louisville Free Public Library compiled and published the booklet with non-matching local funds.

The library sponsored a Science Fair Readiness Workshop on November 4, 1990. This event encouraged and assisted students to use the patent library in preparing science fair entries. The Library also participated in the Young Inventors and Creators Contest sponsored by the Foundation for a Creative America in cooperation with the U.S. Patent Office and the U.S. Copyright Office. LFPL was one of only 16 of the over 60 libraries in the patent depository program to participate.

Library staff participated in several other events, making presentations and disseminating material on the collection. These opportunities included a "patents basics" seminar hosted by the University of Louisville's Center of Entrepreneurship and Technology and Small Business Development Center, and the Louisville Bar Association, as well as the inaugural meeting of the Bluegrass Inventors Guild.

Articles and announcements appeared in a number of library newsletters and other periodicals, as well as in a newly designed brochure on the collection which is distributed by the Chamber of Commerce and Service Corps of Retired Executives (SCORE). Announcements also ran on the Library's public access electronic bulletin board and on SCIBOARD, operated by the University of Louisville.

The objectives of the grant were achieved. The collection, known as the Patent Library, was enhanced by the addition of utility patent backfiles from 1963–1958 and design patents from 1969–1968. The addition of these backfiles fulfilled the library's obligation concerning ownership of 20 years of backfiles in order to be a patent depository library of the U.S. Patent Office in Washington. The library owns 30 years of backfiles and will continue to receive all new patents from the Patent Office at a nominal cost. As a depository, they will receive other patent depository reference materials.

The library estimated that more than 500 people used the collection during FY 1991. Another significant usage figure was reflected by the number of copies made on the patent microfilm printer. In FY 1990 a total of 5,268 copies were made; in FY 1991 the total was 6,513, a 19.1 percent increase. Although actual counts were not kept, copies were faxed to patrons beyond the immediate regional area. As the Kentucky Library Network establishes access to LFPL's holdings through the OCLC interlibrary loan system, it is anticipated that usage will continue to increase across the state.

Other libraries have been encouraged to use the service, as LFPL staff made numerous presentations and conducted training for librarians around the state. One such effort resulted in production of a booklet that identifies patent holdings in other libraries. This document is used to help patrons throughout the state locate the nearest geographic location of resources, which may lead the patrons to LFPL as a final step in locating needed material.

As the LFPL mission statement indicates, the library is the "primary access point for information, materials and services to support educational, economic, and recreational development of this community. As such, the library will be a part of local government's efforts to promote economic development . . . and enhance the quality of life for all citizens." A public library resource of this importance and accessibility will have a long-term impact on not only local development, but on the state as well. Coupled with the resource-sharing capabilities now in place among 250 Kentucky libraries, Kentuckians can now move into new markets and realize potential for growth as entrepreneurs.

Section 103 after clause (7) and Section 102(c)(3) of LSCA provides that the state may not reduce the amount it reserves to a MURL below the amount that it reserved to the MURL in the preceding fiscal year. Two additional conditions in Section 102(c)(3) of the act, became effective in FY 1991 that the amount reserved to each MURL may be ratably reduced to the extent that the total Federal allocations to the state are reduced, or the 1990 census shows the population of the city served by such library has decreased. These two conditions were not applicable in FY 1991 because the total federal allocations to the states were not reduced, and the 1990 census of cities with populations of 100,000 or more had not been released by the Bureau of Census.

The following shows the amount expended for MURLs from FY 1979 through FY 1992 and the amount obligated in FY 1993:

FY 1979	FY 1980	FY 1981	FY 1982
$1,666,225	$1,722,990	$1,776,609	$-0-*
FY 1983	FY 1984	FY 1985	FY 1986
$-0-*	$2,142,102	$4,256,151	$4,231,144
FY 1987	FY 1988	FY 1989	FY 1990
$4,921,172	$4,857,391	$5,086,800	$5,393,628
FY 1991	FY 1992	FY 1993	Total
$5,460,369	$5,802,397	$6,233,717	$53,550,695

*In FY 1982 and FY 1983, the Title I appropriation was $60,000,000. States therefore did not reserve funds for MURLs.

The following examples are from the state FY 1991 annual reports and are representative of how MURL funds were used in FY 1991.

Louisiana. Three major public libraries—Shreve Memorial Library (Caddo Parish), the East Baton Rouge Parish Library, and the New Orleans Public Library—received funds for resource development. Each played a central and crucial role in its region because of the general and special collections that may be used by persons outside their normal service area. The sophisticated interlibrary loan network, Lasernet, made available the resources of these libraries to citizens throughout the state.

Shreve Memorial Library, known for its service to business, historians, and those seeking government publications, received $34,174 for expansion and improvement of these and other areas of the collections. Figures show that 14,000 titles were added to the collection from the previous year.

East Baton Rouge Parish Library has one of the most comprehensive genealogy collections in the nation. Its busy main library and branches circulate over 2,000,000 items annually. One of the reasons for its popularity is the free availability of these materials and services to those who reside outside the service area itself—an unusual cooperative arrangement across complex political subdivisions. The $58,569 distributed as MURL funds developed an important major collection that is shared widely with residents throughout the state.

The state's largest urban area is New Orleans, with a population just under 500,000. The New Orleans Public Library is known for its service to adult new readers, for its programs in the humanities, and for music, business, science, census and marketing information. MURL funds totaling $91,492 were made available to ensure the growth and updating of the collections, which are widely used by citizens throughout the state through interlibrary loan or personal visits.

Missouri. The St. Louis Public Library ($36,046) acquired a broader selection of quality materials relating to the fine, performing, practical and recreational arts for the public libraries of the state to access on behalf of their patrons. Circulation and interlibrary loan (ILL) figures were monitored and as of August 1991 a total of 146 ILLs had been filled in the subject areas covered by this grant. Local circulation for the Fine Arts Department more than doubled that of the previous year.

New York. The Brooklyn Public Library ($194,701) purchased about 9,500 volumes and 254 audiovisual items with MURL funds in FY 1991. Most of these materials updated and filled gaps in the reference collections. For example, funds allowed the Art and Music Division to buy many of the expensive items in their reference collection. Many other divisions of the central library benefitted from these funds as well. Duplicate copies of less expensive circulating materials were also purchased. The increase in circulation and in reference use are largely attributed to the increased numbers of materials available to the users.

Buffalo ($35,026) and Erie County Public Library used MURL funds to strengthen heavily used special collections. Funds were used to purchase 1,638 volumes and 39 tapes to supplement the collections in seven areas, including computer science, small business/export-import, substance abuse, literature, Middle East/Holocaust, and environment.

The New York Public Library ($258,467) allocated its funds to specialized units of two of its central libraries. Selections were based on prioritized requests submitted to the associate director by the librarians responsible for collections management in these units. Funds helped support the continuation of heavily used CD-ROM subscriptions and the development of the film/video collection by allowing the library to purchase 644 audiovisual items and 985 periodical subscriptions on CD.

Syracuse ($22,259) and the Onondaga County Public Library's grant focussed on upgrading print holdings in five major areas: standards and codes, materials and metallurgy, construction and remodeling, interior design, and adult curricula. The library purchased 409 print items and the Health Index in CD-ROM format. Staff felt that the addition of these materials greatly increased patrons' success in finding what they needed in these areas.

Queens Borough Public Library ($163,639) purchased 5,113 books and 1,197 audiovisual items. Both print materials and audiotapes were purchased for the foreign language collection—a heavily-used and important collection in this borough. A little under 10 percent of the MURL grant was used for preservation and duplication of photographs of local history in the library's Long Island collection, making the collection more accessible to users and copies available for out-of-building use.

Ten divisions of the Rochester Public Library ($28,338) shared MURL funds, purchasing 520 volumes, 726 audiovisual items and 207 microfilm items. The subject areas included art, business, children's services, science and technology, education, and local history. Microforms were used to fill gaps in the collection and replace hardcopy and save space.

In Yonkers ($24,605) the MURL funds were used to purchase specialized reference sources not readily available in other public libraries. Obtaining these reference tools has enabled the library to locate and provide information in the rapidly growing high technology area.

Texas. In FY 1991, 18 public libraries met the state's criteria and participated in the Major Urban Resource Libraries (MURL) grant program. MURL libraries received grants totaling $587,601 to purchase library materials, equipment and services that would improve their ability to serve, without charge, persons residing outside their tax-supporting political subdivisions. The evaluation reports received from subgrantees at the end of the project year indicate that a total of 23,244 library materials were purchased with MURL grant funds to better serve non-residents.

The grant program requires each MURL library to set one or more service objectives to non-residents during the grant year. The following table summarizes the free services received by non-residents. Since it is not always possible to identify every non-resident patron using the library, the actual number served is probably higher than the figures show.

Service Objective	Libraries Setting Objective	Non-Residents Served
Non-residents making on-site use of collections and services	15	2,054,180
Non-residents using reference services	11	1,945,404
Circulation to non-residents	8	421,203

A breakdown of the MURLs expenditures by state for FY 1991, 1992, and funds that were reserved for FY 1993 is in Table 23.

Library Services to Targeted Institutions: Metropolitan Libraries

Under LSCA, states may provide funds to cities to strengthen metropolitan public libraries that serve as national or regional resource centers. This provision has allowed states to determine which metropolitan public libraries have the capacity to serve as library resource centers without the requirement that the city have a population over 100,000.

The amount spent from FY 1984 through FY 1992 and the amount that was obligated in FY 1993 are shown here:

FY 1984	FY 1985	FY 1986	FY 1987
$2,726,236	$3,571,713	$3,514,961	$2,959,216

FY 1988	FY 1989	FY 1990	FY 1991
$2,972,531	$2,892,955	$2,623,184	$2,613,508

FY 1992	FY 1993	Total
$2,306,264	$2,532,502	$28,713,070

Table 23 / Major Urban Resource Libraries (MURLs) Expenditures
for FYs 1991, 1992, and Funds Reserved for FY 1993

State	FY 1991	FY 1992	FY 1993
Alabama	$59,870	$40,130	$200,000
Alaska	18,274	18,462	19,888
Arizona	76,652	177,291	120,226
Arkansas	18,820	20,000	20,000
California	914,166	1,036,092	1,121,426
Colorado	195,682	195,682	185,365
Connecticut	54,305	55,235	55,235
Delaware	0	0	0
District of Columbia	0	0	0
Florida	149,373	202,373	202,380
Georgia	70,613	73,680	29,329
Hawaii	39,723	38,878	39,724
Idaho	18,190	18,190	31,850
Illinois	268,815	284,996	284,945
Indiana	113,015	110,719	110,719
Iowa	27,605	27,615	27,615
Kansas	60,592	60,761	60,761
Kentucky	45,688	45,688	44,728
Louisiana	184,262	184,262	184,262
Maine	0	0	0
Maryland	62,619	67,099	67,099
Massachusetts	78,789	87,864	87,864
Michigan	163,032	172,649	172,656
Minnesota	53,777	56,195	54,492
Mississippi	16,652	17,578	17,192
Missouri	90,645	96,664	97,422
Montana	0	0	0
Nebraska	45,150	47,908	46,420
Nevada	28,307	31,564	34,769
New Hampshire	0	0	0
New Jersey	68,265	68,006	68,006
New Mexico	33,842	0	67,684
New York	727,035	739,725	739,725
North Carolina	83,580	89,300	93,890
North Dakota	0	0	0
Ohio	233,983	233,167	234,072
Oklahoma	65,696	60,270	71,397
Oregon	47,349	9,912	114,813
Pennsylvania	302,809	302,809	302,809
Rhode Island	13,038	13,826	27,685
South Carolina	0	0	0
South Dakota	0	0	8,817
Tennessee	132,000	132,000	132,000
Texas	587,601	628,752	628,773
Utah	25,000	25,000	25,000
Vermont	0	0	0
Virginia	117,397	135,603	135,603
Washington	75,622	0	132,339
West Virginia	0	0	0
Wisconsin	82,536	98,590	23,810
Wyoming	0	0	0
American Samoa	0	0	0
Guam	0	0	0
Northern Marianas	0	0	0
Palau	0	0	0
Puerto Rico	0	97,862	110,927
Virgin Islands	0	0	0
Total	$5,450,369	$5,802,397	$6,233,717

The following projects from the FY 1991 annual reports are representative of activities carried out under this provision:

California. The State of California Answering Network (SCAN) at the Los Angeles Public Library ($645,662). SCAN is a regional reference center and backup resource for referral of questions from the California Library Services Act system reference centers, which help local public libraries handle questions beyond their capacity. SCAN has been funded with LSCA Title I funds for over 15 years although the state has attempted to move SCAN to a state-funded program that would build and expand upon the LSCA program.

Examples of projects funded at SCAN are:

- Salaries of reference staff and operating expenses to provide answers to questions referred from other libraries, including materials augmentation to build area resource strengths
- Consultant studies and similar planning activities
- Demonstration projects in cooperative library systems and in libraries of various types to gather data and field test various methods of reference services enhancement or provision
- Intensive study and evaluation to ascertain the most suitable patterns in this changing area of service

During FY 1991 SCAN was located in the temporary Central Library as the main Los Angeles Public Library was under reconstruction. Through the cooperation of the University of California Los Angeles (UCLA), SCAN continued to have an office in the University Research Library, staffed at least three days a week. SCANLOG, the database program to record and compile statistics, continued to be refined, with new log-in and log-out procedures proving helpful. Three issues of the SCAN/INFO newsletter were published with a 1,375-copy distribution. SCAN conducted 590 computer searches and answered 3,180 questions.

Michigan. Ann Arbor Public Library ($12,467). The library acquired a CD-ROM Wilsonline periodical index search station, a complete set of Gale's *Twentieth Century Literacy Criticism,* woodwind and brass sheet music, educational and cultural videos, and large-print books for adults and youth.

The Wilsonline CD-ROM has become so popular that the library will probably begin having a time limit for terminal use by patrons. The literary criticism materials are heavily used by students from high schools, community colleges and major universities in the area and the sheet music for woodwinds and brass meets an important need for the hundreds of instrumentalists in the community. The educational and cultural video collection is heavily used by those for whom the printed word may be a difficult cultural option as well as those who are more educationally sophisticated. The large-print books are heavily used by both adults and youth with visual and physical handicaps.

Minnesota. Metropolitan Library Service agency (MELSA) ($350,278). The goal of this project was to reimburse the major municipal information centers of the Minneapolis Public Library and the St. Paul Public Library for providing reference service and materials to patrons who live outside of their city boundaries. These two major cities circulated 339,985 items and answered 189,390 reference questions for the residents of the seven-county area.

A second grant assisted the public libraries in the Twin City metropolitan area in making effective use of technology to improve library and information service through the use of CD-ROM workstations and CD software. The grant enabled the purchase of 16 CD ROM workstations with supporting maintenance. Preliminary evidence shows that there was an estimated $18,000 savings by using the CD-ROM products instead of online services.

Tennessee. ($215,090). There are four metropolitan libraries in Tennessee: Chattanooga-Hamilton County Bicentennial Library, Chattanooga; Knox County Public Library, Knoxville; Memphis-Shelby County Public Library and Information Center; and the Public Library of Nashville and Davidson County.

These libraries, designated as single-county metropolitan library regions, are a part of the Tennessee Regional Library System. Each is administered by a library board composed of representatives of all types of library users throughout the metropolitan county. These library boards enter into a contractual relationship with the state that allows them to receive and expend state and federal funds as a supplement to locally authorized funds.

The four libraries completed long-range plans in FY 1991. In accordance with these plans, they provided materials and services to all residents of their metropolitan areas. They also provided resources to public libraries statewide, through the Area Resource Centers (ARCs) housed at each metropolitan library. The ARCs provided reference and interlibrary loan service to designated multi-county regional library systems. The Memphis ARC served 20 county libraries in the Forked Deer, Reelfoot and Shiloh regions. The Nashville ARC served 26 counties in the Blue Grass, Highland Rim and Warioto regions. The Chattanooga ARC served 26 counties in the Caney Fork, Fort Loudoun, and Upper Cumberland regions. The Knoxville ARC served 19 counties in the Clinch-Powell, Nolichucky, and Watauga regions.

The ARCs are not designed to supplant the services of the local public libraries, but rather to ensure that all library users have access to all of Tennessee's public library resources. Monies provided in this project enhanced the ability of the metropolitan libraries to provide all types of materials to meet the needs of metropolitan residents and residents of the counties within each ARC service area. All four metropolitan libraries used the money provided through this project to purchase library materials which were made available through the ARC system to public library users throughout Tennessee.

Table 24 presents a breakdown of the expenditures for Metropolitan Public Libraries serving as national or regional resource centers for FY 1991 and FY 1992, and funds that were obligated in FY 1993.

Public Library Construction (LSCA Title II)

During FY 1991 the states obligated more than $18.2 million in federal funds for public library construction projects. Funding included more than $9.8 million from the FY 1991 appropriation of $18,883,640 and $8.2 million carried over from previous years' allotments. This left $8.9 million from the FY 1991 allotment and over $4.4 million of carryover funds available to use for approved projects in FY 1992.

During the same year, FY 1991, 36 states completed 127 public library construction projects involving LSCA Title II funds. (Table 25 lists the completed

Table 24 / Metropolitan Public Libraries Serving as National or Regional Resource Centers, Expenditures for FYs 1991, 1992, and Funds Obligated in FY 1993

State	FY 1991	FY 1992	FY 1993
Alabama	$0	$7,950	$0
Alaska	0	0	0
Arizona	0	0	0
Arkansas	0	0	0
California	645,662	722,200	804,176
Colorado	0	0	0
Connecticut	0	0	0
Delaware	0	0	0
District of Columbia	111,495	123,126	80,000
Florida	228,409	302,500	302,500
Georgia	20,000	0	0
Hawaii	0	0	0
Idaho	0	0	0
Illinois	0	0	0
Indiana	0	0	0
Iowa	0	0	0
Kansas	16,592	16,592	16,592
Kentucky	0	0	0
Louisiana	0	0	0
Maine	0	0	0
Maryland	0	0	0
Massachusetts	0	0	0
Michigan	97,088	160,762	175,000
Minnesota	350,278	301,672	589,842
Mississippi	0	0	0
Missouri	0	0	0
Montana	0	0	0
Nebraska	0	0	0
Nevada	161,327	34,000	0
New Hampshire	0	0	0
New Jersey	573,633	74,007	0
New Mexico	0	0	0
New York	0	0	0
North Carolina	193,934	348,365	346,302
North Dakota	0	0	0
Ohio	0	0	0
Oklahoma	0	0	0
Oregon	0	0	0
Pennsylvania	0	0	0
Rhode Island	0	0	0
South Carolina	0	0	0
South Dakota	0	0	0
Tennessee	215,090	215,090	215,090
Texas	0	0	0
Utah	0	0	0
Vermont	0	0	0
Virginia	0	0	0
Washington	0	0	0
West Virginia	0	0	0
Wisconsin	0	0	0
Wyoming	0	0	0
American Samoa	0	0	0
Guam	0	0	0
Northern Marianas	0	0	0
Palau	0	0	0
Puerto Rico	0	0	3,000
Virgin Islands	0	0	0
Total	$2,613,508	$2,306,264	$2,532,502

Table 25 / LSCA Title II Construction Projects Completed in FY 1991

	Project	Federal	State	Local	Total
Alabama	Wetumpka P.L.	$36,950	$0	$39,233	$76,183
Arizona	Safford	250,000	0	413,637	663,637
Arkansas	Crowley Ridge	57,046	0	68,620	125,666
Colorado	Eagle Cnty P.L.	15,000	0	74,001	89,001
	Garfield Cnty P.L.	75,000	0	89,500	164,500
	Adams Cnty P.L.	34,613	0	45,150	79,763
	Pitkin Cnty P.L.	75,000	0	2,030,903	2,105,903
	Library of the BPH	138,140	750,000	0	888,140
	Ignacio P.L.	40,000	0	72,000	112,000
	Dacono P.L.	5,500	0	6,500	12,000
	Garfield Cnty P.L.	9,000	0	11,000	20,000
	Custer Cnty P.L.	34,040	0	39,960	74,000
	Basalt P.L.	6,038	0	7,142	13,180
	Adams Cnty P.L.(b)	7,820	0	9,180	17,000
Connecticut	Brookfield Library	6,012	4,008	4,590	14,610
	Booth/Dimock Mem.	100,000	350,000	1,290,000	1,740,000
	Harwinton P.L.	25,902	287,976	622,469	936,347
	Sherman Library	88,297	120,624	214,000	422,921
Florida	Lakewood Park Br.	200,000	0	797,451	997,451
	Pompano Beach City	155,000	0	181,800	336,800
	Volusia Cnty Lib. Ctr	200,000	0	540,000	740,000
Idaho	Twin Falls P.L.	245,909	0	2,308,413	2,554,322
Illinois	Fairview Hghts P.L.	200,000	0	1,081,309	1,281,309
	North Chicago P.L.	200,000	0	1,364,089	1,564,089
	Chester P.L.	200,000	0	651,630	851,630
	Flagg Township Lib.	200,000	0	1,600,000	1,800,000
	Prospect Hghts P.L.	250,000	0	2,336,000	2,586,000
	Poplar Creek	115,685	109,315	625,000	850,000
	Nippersink P.L.	250,000	0	547,080	797,080
Indiana	Kolomo-Howard Cnty	200,000	0	572,000	772,000
	Delphi P.L.	271,116	0	558,619	829,735
Iowa	Belle Plaine	140,704	0	259,296	400,000
	Cresco	150,000	0	386,000	536,000
Kentucky	Madison Cnty Pub. Lib.	350,072	0	487,179	837,251
Louisiana	St. Martin Parish	100,000	0	100,000	200,000
Maine	Buck Memorial Library	93,160	0	95,790	188,950
	Ellsworth City P.L.	75,000	0	150,000	225,000
	Pendleton P.L.	2,300	0	2,300	4,600
	Witherle	17,562	0	17,562	35,124
	Salmon	5,220	0	6,000	11,220
	Bass Harbor	41,606	0	54,000	95,606
Maryland	Baltimore Cnty Pub. Lib.	92,970	0	135,000	227,970
Massachusetts	Fall River P.L.	75,000	0	225,000	300,000
	Westwood	24,996	35,000	86,504	146,500
Minnesota	Galaxie	200,000	0	2,827,510	3,027,510
Mississippi	Ricks Memorial Library	65,000	0	65,000	130,000
	Elise Jurgens Memorial	200,000	0	253,628	453,628
Missouri	Albany P.L.	26,500	0	34,718	61,218
	Cameron P.L.	69,443	0	75,543	144,986

Table 25 / LSCA Title II Construction Projects Completed in FY 1991 *(cont.)*

	Project	Federal	State	Local	Total
	Festus P.L.	52,647	0	56,587	109,234
	Grundy Cnty (Jewett)	185,000	0	217,966	402,966
	Maryville P.L.	10,000	0	16,610	26,610
	Palmyra Bicent Lib.	14,597	0	22,658	37,255
	St. Charles	241,875	0	261,901	503,776
	St. Louis P.L.	250,000	0	250,000	500,000
	Scenic Reg. Lib.	298,378	0	484,712	783,090
Montana	Daniels	5,000	0	5,800	10,800
	Meagher	58,000	0	62,000	120,000
New Hampshire	Acworth Silsby Lib.	21,000	0	21,000	42,000
	Colebrook P.L.	10,000	0	10,000	20,000
	Derry P.L.	43,000	0	150,000	193,000
	New castle P.L.	37,500	0	37,500	75,000
	Ossipee P.L.	20,000	0	20,000	40,000
	Wilmont P.L.	35,433	0	35,433	70,866
	NH State Library	27,583	28,315	0	55,898
New Jersey	Hamilton Township P.L.	73,046	0	292,187	365,233
	Long Branch P.L.	12,690	0	19,046	31,736
	Norwood P.L.	81,000	0	300,000	381,000
New York	Darwin R. Baker Lib.	7,464	0	13,863	21,327
	Bay Shore-Bghtwaters	24,728	0	1,111,185	1,135,913
	Brooklyn P.L. (a)	200,467	0	1,826,749	2,027,216
	Brooklyn P.L. (b)	157,505	0	726,211	883,716
	Floyd Mem. Lib.	7,000	0	15,219	22,219
	Hamburg P.L.	5,273	0	17,872	23,145
	Hicksville P.L.	9,852	0	166,948	176,800
	Lewiston P.L.	251,096	100,000	1,216,728	1,567,824
	NY P.L.	121,541	0	1,678,227	1,799,768
	Newark P.L.	38,119	0	936,881	975,000
	North Bellmore P.L.	39,096	0	1,250,110	1,289,206
	Oswego City Library	10,649	0	24,009	34,658
	Utica P.L. (A)	94,150	0	350,713	444,863
	Utica P.L. (B)	58,512	0	154,620	213,132
North Carolina	Cleveland Cnty Mem.	80,000	62,500	1,412,268	1,554,768
	Canton P.L.	120,032	125,000	786,959	1,031,991
	Pender Cnty Lib.	250,102	0	749,644	999,746
	Phillip Leff Mem.	80,000	37,000	130,208	247,208
North Dakota	Bottineau Cnty Lib.	112,000	0	112,000	224,000
	Harvey P.L.	124,500	0	192,228	316,728
	Grand Forks P.L.	30,660	0	61,320	91,980
Ohio	Streetsboro Br. Lib.	197,228	0	224,322	421,550
	Seastern OH Reg. Lib.	155,400	219,600	0	375,000
	New Bremen Br. Lib.	177,102	0	203,359	380,461
	Carnegie P.L.	102,996	0	231,489	334,485
Oklahoma	Anadarko	125,000	10,000	393,874	528,874
	Ethel Briggs Mem. Lib.	53,277	0	53,277	106,554
Oregon	Siuslaw P.L.	135,641	0	1,342,687	1,478,328
Pennsylvania	Cranberry P.L.	200,000	0	263,831	463,831
	Allentown P.L.	400,000	0	400,000	800,000

Table 25 / LSCA Title II Construction Projects Completed in FY 1991 *(cont.)*

	Project	Federal	State	Local	Total
	Berks Cnty P.L. Sys.	220,000	0	225,895	445,895
South Dakota	Baltic Br. Minnehaha	1,020	0	1,020	2,040
Tennessee	Chattanooga/Hamilton	100,000	35,784	346,586	482,370
	Franklin County Library	100,000	35,784	99,652	235,436
	Lake City Public Library	100,000	35,784	95,527	231,311
	W.G. Rhea Public Library	100,000	35,784	137,480	273,264
	Westmoreland Public Lib.	54,526	35,784	18,742	109,052
Texas	Boerne P.L.	100,000	0	864,751	964,751
	Harris Cnty P.L. (a)	100,000	0	243,756	343,756
	Calhoun Cnty P.L.	200,000	0	708,180	908,180
	Kaufman Cnty Lib.	200,000	0	380,338	580,338
	Keller P.L.	100,000	0	775,000	875,000
	Hudspeth Cnty	100,000	0	145,490	245,490
	Goliad Cnty Lib.	100,000	0	233,941	333,941
	Allen Memorial P.L.	100,000	0	176,100	276,100
	Sachse P.L.	100,000	0	251,057	351,057
	Welhausen	100,000	0	291,054	391,054
	Harris Cnty P.L. (b)	38,248	0	578,870	617,118
Utah	American Fork P.L.	47,481	0	47,625	95,106
Vermont	Brandon Free P.L.	5,500	0	6,160	11,660
	Rutland Free Library	100,000	0	1,096,028	1,196,028
Washington	Everett Pub. Lib.	72,873	0	1,372,194	1,445,067
	Shelton Pub. Lib.	285,000	0	661,328	946,328
	Blaine Pub. Lib.	151,388	0	285,936	437,324
Wisconsin	Milwaukee Pub. Lib.	125,000	0	1,711,396	1,836,396
	New Berlin Pub. Lib.	125,000	0	450,000	575,000
	Matheson Mem. Lib.	125,000	0	314,377	439,377
	Lodi Women's Club	125,000	0	497,770	622,770
	Lakes Cnty P.L.	37,411	0	89,224	126,635
Wyoming	Carbon Cnty Library	3,440	0	6,296	9,736
Total		$13,484,627	$2,454,042	$54,034,286	$69,972,955

projects.) This represents nine fewer completed projects than in FY 1990. The combined federal, state, and local expenditures for those projects totaled $69 million with 19 percent coming from Title II funds.

When compared with expenditures for FY 1990, there was an increase of 22 percent in the amount of LSCA funds that were used to support these projects. This same period saw a decrease of 23 percent in state matching funds and an increase of 7 percent in matching local funds.

These combined state and local matching funds totaled more than $56 million or 80 percent of the total costs for all completed public library construction projects in FY 1991. Of this amount, local contributions made up the largest percentage (77 percent).

Interlibrary Cooperation and Resource Sharing (LSCA Title III)

Federal funds under Title III have been used effectively by the state library administrative agencies to

- Promote institutional cooperation so that it is now a common feature of everyday library and information service delivery patterns
- Create and upgrade statewide databases of bibliographic holdings using the standardized MARC format
- Provide access to the cost-sharing benefits of OCLC directly or through other regional bibliographic services networks
- Train library staff in all aspects of networking activities involving library automation, use of machine-readable databases, and other technological skills
- Support improvements in storing and disseminating bibliographic data, delivering library materials, and transmitting documents and information

The FY 1992 annual reports indicate continued tie-ins with specialized and national database networks and services, such as those of the Library of Congress, National Library of Medicine, National Agricultural Library, and National Science Foundation, for access to specialized information resources as well as bibliographic data. Frequently members of the specialized networks are also members of the statewide multitype network, thus providing access to these materials to users of any libraries on the statewide network.

With the appearance on the national scene of the National Information Infrastructure and Internet, some state library administrative agencies are using LSCA Title III funds to explore and/or experiment with methods of enabling the library networks in their states to participate in and take advantage of these opportunities.

Listed below are some of the Title III activities reported by the states:

Alaska. All libraries in Alaska depend on the WLN network for cataloging, interlibrary loan (ILL) service, and collection development purposes. During FY 1990 WLN made a transition from the Washington State Library to a private non-profit corporation. In order to ensure that programs needed by Alaska's libraries would be developed to meet their demands, the Alaska State Library provided special one-time funding. The $200,000 grant came from a combination of LSCA Title I ($64,526), LSCA Title III ($42,253), and state ($93,221) funds. The larger public libraries use WLN for cataloging and the public library community is the major user of WLN (primarily through the ALNCAT) for ILL purposes.

Arkansas. Network planning continued to have a broadened scope. The tele-facsimile network now has 71 administrative units with 127 telefacsimile sites. School libraries have joined the network to expand the resource-sharing ties established through Resource Arkansas as well as to increase the number of public, academic, and school libraries working together.

Georgia. Georgia Library Information Network (GLIN) has for 21 years served public, academic, and special libraries with information and materials. A manual system is being phased out and replaced by the Georgia Online Database (GOLD). This enables members to do their own online searching and electronically initiate their own electronic requests. By July 1, 1993, all GLIN libraries will be using GOLD.

Idaho. On November 19, 1992, the state library sponsored a teleconference on Networking for Resource Sharing at eight downlink sites around the state. The presenter was Bernard G. Sloan, director of the Illinois Library Computer Systems and author of *Linked Systems for Resource Sharing.*

Kansas. Eight Kansas junior/senior high school libraries received a grant of $1,000 each to teach online searching skills to students. Using a computer in the school library, students were able to connect with Dialog Information Services. Students learned to search databases on such subjects as drama, engineering, chemistry, social studies, and agriculture. Students were given access to topics and information previously not available to them—student debaters especially found it useful. Student dread of speech assignments, written reports, and research papers has greatly diminished.

Colorado. LSCA Title III funds play an important part in the implementation of the Access Colorado Library and Information Network. This network was created by the Colorado legislature to provide free access to the information resources of the libraries in the state, as well as to computerized databases. A telecommunications network has been established that links libraries and other databases. Toll-free dial access for all residents is provided so that they can access the network from home, school, library, or business using microcomputers and modems. The first phase of Access Colorado contains databases from CARL, MARMOT, Pikes Peak Library District, Boulder Public Library, University of Colorado, Colorado College, and University of Southern Colorado. Dial access is available in 11 locations. Those parts of the state not covered can use toll-free 800 numbers.

Connecticut. To ensure that all Connecticut citizens have equal access to information through interlibrary loan cooperation, resource sharing, and networking, the state library has established the Connecticut Library and Information Network (CONLINET), to become fully operational by the year 2000 and be accessible through Internet. Current activities include a competitive grant program among all types of libraries to fund projects implementing CONLINET and the hiring of a "network planner" to complete design and implementation plans for the new network, including cost estimates and technical specifications.

Illinois. ILLINET ONLINE is the statewide network and database involving 800 libraries of all types. ILLINET is accessible to local libraries seven days a week through regional library systems and is connected to OCLC. Serials of Illinois Online (SILO) lists more than 500,000 journals in over 1,200 libraries.

Maine. To increase access to library services the state library is expanding and enhancing MaineCat, which is Maine's union catalog on CD-ROM. MaineCat is being meshed with the University of Maine URSUS (University Resources Serving Users Statewide) system, which includes the seven state campus libraries and three large private college libraries. The inclusion in this online automated library system enables the state library to access Internet for all Maine libraries wishing to participate.

Nebraska. Operation of NEBASE, the state network, is supported largely through state funds with supplemental funding for some services provided through LSCA Title III for the OCLC activity of the state library agency. The network is critical to Nebraska which has many rural communities. NEON, the statewide database, provides access to information for 13.1 percent of the 139 public, school, special, and academic libraries in the state.

New York. The state library uses the funds to augment the state interlibrary loan and database services network and staff other network development and services. Title III support is meshed with state funding. The major goal is to enable all libraries to become "Electronic Doorways" through which any New Yorker can have access to the information resources of the state.

Oregon. The state is trying to increase its technological capacity for interlibrary cooperation and resource sharing through four projects using LSCA Title I funds for the public library participation and Title III funds for the other types of libraries. The Southeast Oregon Library Network (SOLN) is designed to serve 26,000 people residing in Malheur County, an area larger than Delaware, Connecticut, and Rhode Island combined. The shared integrated network to be completed in two phases will improve access to materials held in 15 or more libraries in the region, through the development of an automated database of 150,000 records and online cataloging, circulation, and acquisition control. Each citizen will have the ability to locate and obtain immediately any of the items held throughout the region, and would be tied to other regional network nodes and to the state library. Components will include an online catalog with dial access, computerized database searching, E-mail, local courier service, and a regional borrower's card.

Washington. Support is being provided for the development and testing of a model statewide referral network. Preliminary activities will include the enhancement and expansion of existing databases by conversion to an electronic mode; upgrade of existing holdings in the Pacific Northwest Union List of Serials (PULSe); and a coordinated strategy to access Internet for all public and academic libraries.

Part 3
Library/Information Science Education, Placement, and Salaries

Guide to Employment Sources in the Library and Information Professions

Margaret Myers

Director, Office for Library Personnel Resources
American Library Association

This guide updates the listing in the 1993 *Bowker Annual* with information on new services and changes in contacts and groups previously listed. The sources given primarily assist professionals in obtaining positions, although a few assist paraprofessionals, who tend, however, to be recruited through local sources.

General Sources of Library and Information Jobs

Library Literature

Many national, regional, and state library journals and newsletters carry classified ads of library job vacancies and positions wanted. Association members can sometimes list a position-wanted ad free in association publications. *American Libraries, Chronicle of Higher Education, College & Research Libraries News, Library Journal,* and *Library Hotline* regularly carry listings of available positions. State and regional library association newsletters, state library journals, foreign library periodicals, and other types of periodicals that carry such ads are listed in later sections of this guide.

Newspapers

In addition to the regular classifieds, the *New York Times* Sunday Week in Review includes a special section of jobs for librarians. Local newspapers—particularly the larger city Sunday editions, such as the *Washington Post, Los Angeles Times,* and *Chicago Tribune*—often carry listings for both professional and paraprofessional positions in libraries.

Internet

A number of openings are beginning to appear as announcements on the library-related electronic listservs on Internet, although these are interspersed with other news items. This may be a growing trend in the future.

Note: The author wishes to thank Maxine Moore, OLPR administrative assistant, for her help in gathering and compiling updated information.

Library Joblines

Library joblines, or job hotlines, provide recorded telephone messages of job openings in a specific geographic area. Most tapes are changed once a week, although a listing may sometimes be carried for several weeks. The information is fairly brief and the cost of calling is borne by the individual job seeker, but a jobline provides a quick and up-to-date listing of vacancies that is not usually possible with printed listings or journal ads.

Most joblines only carry listings for their state or region, although some occasionally accept out-of-state positions if there is room on the tape. A few list technician and other paraprofessional positions, but the majority include only professional jobs. Callers sometimes find that the jobline doesn't answer; this usually means that the tape is being changed or that there are no new jobs for that period. The classified section of *American Libraries* carries jobline numbers periodically as space permits.

The following joblines are in operation:

Jobline Sponsor	Job Seekers (To Hear Job Listings)	Employers (To Place Job Listings)
American Association of Law Libraries	312-939-7877	53 W. Jackson Blvd., Suite 940, Chicago, IL 60604. FAX 312-431-1097
Arizona Department of Library, Archives and Public Records (Arizona libraries only)	602-275-2325	Research Div., Rm. 300, 1700 W. Washington, Phoenix, AZ 85007. FAX 602-255-4312
British Columbia Library Association (B.C. listings only)	604-430-6411	Jobline, 110-6545 Bonsor Ave., Burnaby, BC V51 1H3, Canada
California Library Association (identical listings)	916-443-1222 (north) 818-797-4602 (south)	717 K St., Suite 300, Sacramento, CA 95814-3477. 916-447-8541
California Media and Library Educators Association	415-697-8832	1499 Old Bayshore Hwy., Suite 142, Burlingame, CA 94010. 415-692-2350
Colorado State Library[1] (includes paraprofessionals)	303-866-6741	Jobline, 201 E. Colfax, 3rd fl., Denver, CO 80203-1704. 303-866-6732, FAX 303-866-6940; also via Libnet
Connecticut Library Association (24 hours)	203-645-8090	Box 1046, Norwich, CT 06360
Delaware Division of Libraries (Del., N.J., and Pa. listings)	800-282-8696 (in-state) 302-739-4748 (out-of-state)	43 S. Dupont Hwy., Dover, DE 19901

Jobline Sponsor	Job Seekers (To Hear Job Listings)	Employers (To Place Job Listings)
Drexel University College of Information Studies	215-895-1672	College of Information Studies, Philadelphia, PA 19104. 215-895-2478
State Library of Florida	904-488-5232 (in-state)	R. A. Gray Bldg., Tallahassee, FL 32399-0251. 904-487-2651
Library Jobline of Illinois[2]	312-828-0930 (professional) 312-828-9198 (support staff)	Illinois Library Assn., 33 W. Grand, Suite 301, Chicago, IL 60610. 312-644-1896; $40/2 weeks
Indiana Statewide Library Jobline	317-926-6561	Central Indiana ALSA, 1100 W. 42 St., Indianapolis, IN 46208
State Library of Iowa (professional jobs in Iowa; only during regular business hours)	515-281-6788	East 12 & Grand, Des Moines, IA 50319
Kansas State Library Jobline (also includes paraprofessional and out-of-state)	913-296-3296	c/o Jana Renfro, 3rd fl., State Capitol, Topeka, KS 66612
Kentucky Job Hotline (24 hours)	502-564-3008	Dept. for Libs. and Archives, Box 537, Frankfort, KY 40602. 502-875-7000
Maryland Library Association (24 hours)	410-685-5760	115 W. Franklin St., Baltimore, MD 21201. 410-727-7422 (Mon.–Fri., 9:30 A.M.–2:30 P.M.)
Medical Library Association Jobline (24 hours)	312-553-4636	N. Michigan Ave., Suite 300, Chicago, IL 60602. 312-419-9094
Metropolitan Washington Council of Governments Library Council (D.C.)	202-962-3712	1875 I St. N.W., Suite 200, Washington, DC 20006. 202-223-6800, Ext. 458
Michigan Library Association	517-694-7440	1000 Long Blvd., Suite 1, Lansing, MI 48911. 517-694-6615 ($20/week)
Missouri Library Association Jobline	314-442-6590	1306 Business 63 S., Suite B, Columbia, MO 65201-8404. 314-449-4627
Mountain Plains Library Association[3]	605-677-5757	c/o I. D. Weeks Library, University of South Dakota, Vermillion, SD 57069. 605-677-6082, FAX 605-677-5488
Nebraska Job Hotline (in-state and other openings during regular business hours)	402-471-2045 800-307-2665 (in-state)	Nebraska Library Commission, 1200 N St. 120, Lincoln, NE 68508-2023
New England Library Jobline (New England jobs only)	617-738-3148	GSLIS, Simmons College, 300 The Fenway, Boston, MA 02115
New Jersey Library Association	609-695-2121	Box 1534, Trenton, NJ 08607; non-members $25/4 weeks

Jobline Sponsor	Job Seekers (To Hear Job Listings)	Employers (To Place Job Listings)
New York Library Association	518-432-6952 800-232-6952 (in-state)	252 Hudson Ave., Albany, NY 12210-1802. 518-432-6952 (members $15/3 months, non-members $25/3 months)
North Carolina State Library (professional jobs in N.C. only)	919-733-6410	Division of State Library, 109 E. Jones St., Raleigh, NC 27601-2807. 919-733-2570
Oklahoma Department of Libraries Jobline (5:00 P.M.–8:00 A.M., Monday–Friday and all weekend)	405-521-4202	200 N.E. 18 St., Oklahoma City, OK 73105. 405-521-2502
Oregon Library Association (Northwest listings only)	503-585-2232	Oregon State Library, State Library Bldg., Salem, OR 97310. 503-378-4243
Pacific Northwest Library Association[4]	206-543-2890	c/o Graduate School of Library and Information Science, University of Washington, FM-30, Seattle, WA 988195. 206-543-1794
Pennsylvania Jobline[5]	717-234-4646	Pennsylvania Library Assn., 1919 N. Front St., Harrisburg, PA 17102. 717-233-3113 (weekly fee for non-members)
Pratt Institute SLIS Job Hotline	718-636-3742	SLIS Dept., Brooklyn, NY 11205.
Special Libraries Association	202-234-3632	1700 18th St. N.W., Washington, DC 20009. 202-234-4700
Special Libraries Association, New York Chapter	212-740-2007	David Jank, FIND/SVP, 625 Ave. of the Americas, New York, NY 10011. FAX 212-645-7681
Special Libraries Association, San Andreas-San Francisco Bay Chapter	415-856-2140	415-858-4070; FAX 415-858-4043
Special Libraries Association, Southern California Chapter	818-795-2145	818-302-8966; FAX 818-302-8015
Texas Library Association Job Hotline (24 hours; Texas listings only)	512-328-0651	3355 Bee Cave Rd., Suite 401, Austin, TX 78746. 512-328-1518
Texas State Library Jobline (Texas listings only)	512-463-5470	Library Development, Box 12927, Austin, TX 78711. 512-463-5447
University of South Carolina College of Library and Information Science (no geographic restrictions)	803-777-8443	University of South Carolina, Columbia, SC 29208. 803-777-3858
Virginia Library Association Jobline (Virginia libraries only)	703-519-8027	669 S. Washington St., Alexandria, VA 22314

Jobline Sponsor	Job Seekers (To Hear Job Listings)	Employers (To Place Job Listings)
University of Western Ontario School of Library and Information Science	519-661-3543	London, Ontario N6G 1H1, Canada. 519-661-2111 Ext. 8494

1. Weekly printed listing sent on receipt of stamps and mailing labels.
2. Cosponsored by the Special Libraries Association Illinois Chapter and the Illinois Library Association.
3. 800-356-7820 available from all MPLA states, 10:00 P.M.–8:00 A.M., Sunday–Thursday; 5:00 P.M. Friday–5:00 P.M. Sunday (includes listings for the states of Arizona, Colorado, Kansas, Montana, Nebraska, Nevada, Oklahoma, North and South Dakota, Utah, and Wyoming, also paid listings from out-of-region institutions—$10/week).
4. Alaska, Alberta, British Columbia, Idaho, Montana, Oregon, and Washington; includes both professional and paraprofessional jobs.
5. Sponsored by the Pennsylvania Library Association; also accepts paraprofessional out-of-state listings.

Specialized Library Associations and Groups

The National Registry for Librarians, formerly housed in the Illinois State Job Service at 40 W. Adams St., Chicago, IL 60603, is no longer in operation. Referral service is still available through state and local job service offices, but no independent registry will be maintained for librarians.

Advanced Information Management

444 Castro St., Suite 320, Mountain View, CA 94041 (415-965-7799). This placement agency, with offices in Southern California (900 Wilshire Blvd., Suite 1424, Los Angeles, CA 90017; 213-243-9236) as well as in the San Francisco Bay area, specializes in library and information personnel. It offers professional librarians and paraprofessionals work on a temporary, permanent, or contract basis in special, public, and academic libraries. It also places consultants on special projects in libraries or as managers of library development projects. There is no fee for applicants.

American Association of Law Libraries Career Hotline

53 W. Jackson Blvd., Suite 940, Chicago, IL 60604 (312-939-4764). The hotline (312-939-7877) is a 24-hour-a-day recording updated each Friday at noon and available as an index in geographic order of positions currently available in full text in the AALL Job Data Base. AALL members receive the complete Job Data Base free on request. Others must send a written request with $5 to AALL, Dept. 77-6021. To list a position, contact AALL, Placement Assistant, FAX 312-431-1097.

American Libraries "Career LEADS"

c/o *American Libraries,* 50 E. Huron St., Chicago, IL 60611. Classified job listings are published in each monthly issue of *American Libraries.* Some 100 job openings are grouped by type, and "Late Job Notices" are added near press time. Subsections are Positions Wanted, Professional Exchange, Requests for Proposals, Librarians' Classified, joblines, and regional salary scales. "ConsultantBase" (see below) appears four times a year.

American Libraries "Career LEADS EXPRESS"

c/o Georgia Okotete, 50 E. Huron St., Chicago, IL 60611. Advance galleys (3–4 weeks) of classified job listings with approximately 100 "Positions Open" to be published in the next issue of *American Libraries* are sent about the 17th of each month. Galleys do not include editorial corrections and late changes, but they do include some "Late Job Notices." For each month, send a $1 check made out to AL EXPRESS and a self-addressed, standard business-size envelope (4 x 9) with 52 cents postage.

American Libraries ConsultantBase (CBase)

This *AL* service helps match professionals offering library/information expertise with institutions. Published quarterly, CBase appears in the "Career LEADS" section of *AL*'s January, April, June, and October issues. Rates: $4.50/line (classified); $45/inch (display). Inquiries should be made to Jon Kartman, LEADS Editor, *American Libraries,* 50 E. Huron St., Chicago, IL 60611 (312-280-4211).

American Library Association, ASCLA/SLAS State Library Consultants to Institutional Libraries Discussion Group

This group compiles a list of job openings in institutional libraries throughout the United States and its territories. Send self-addressed, stamped envelope(s) to Institutional Library Jobline, c/o Gloria Spooner, State Library of Louisiana, Box 131, Baton Rouge, LA 70821-0131. Send job listings to the same address, or call 504-342-4931 or FAX 504-342-3547. Listings appear for one month unless re-submitted.

American Library Association, Association of College and Research Libraries

50 E. Huron St., Chicago, IL 60611-2795 (312-280-2513). Classified advertising appears each month in *College & Research Libraries News.* Ads are also posted to C&RL NewsNet, an abridged electronic edition of *C&RL News* accessible on Internet through the gopher server at the University of Illinois at Chicago. You can connect your favorite gopher client directly to host gopher.uic.edu 70. Select "The Library" from the menu and "C&RL NewsNet" from the next menu.

American Library Association, Office for Library Personnel Resources

50 E. Huron St., Chicago, IL 60611 (312-280-4277). A placement service is provided at each annual conference (June or July) and midwinter meeting (January or February). Request job seeker or employer registration forms before the conference. Those unable to attend a conference can register with the service and have job or applicant listings sent directly to them from the conference site for a fee. Handouts on interviewing, preparing a résumé, and other job-seeking information are available from the ALA Office for Library Personnel Resources.

ALA divisions also usually have a placement service at national conferences. See *American Libraries* "Datebook" for dates of upcoming divisional conferences (not held every year).

American Society for Information Science

8720 Georgia Ave., No. 501, Silver Spring, MD 20910-3602 (301-495-0900). ASIS operates an active placement service at annual meetings (usually October). Locales change. All conference attendees (both ASIS members and nonmembers), as well as ASIS members who cannot attend the conference, are eligible to use the service to list or find jobs. The service accepts listings from employers who cannot attend the conference, arranges interviews, and sponsors special seminars. Throughout the year, job openings are listed in *ASIS JOBLINE,* a monthly publication sent to all members and available to nonmembers on request.

Art Libraries Society/North America (ARLIS/NA)

c/o Executive Director, 3900 E. Timrod St., Tucson, AZ 85711 (602-881-8479, FAX 602-322-6778). *ARLIS/NA UPDATE* (6 issues a year) lists jobs for art librarians and slide curators, and the society maintains a job registry at its headquarters. Any employer may list a job with the registry, but only members may request job information.

Asian/Pacific American Libraries Newsletter

c/o Anna Wang, Ohio State University, 124 Main Library, 1858 Neil Ave. Mall, Columbus, OH 43210-1286 (614-292-6151). This quarterly newsletter includes some job ads. It is free to members of the association.

Association for Educational Communications and Technology

Placement and Referral Service, 1025 Vermont Ave., Suite 820, Washington, DC 20005 (202-347-7834, FAX 202-347-7839). A referral service is available free to AECT members. The placement center at the annual conference is free to all conference registrants. Members also receive a free monthly newsletter of job vacancies.

Association for Library and Information Science Education

4101 Lake Boone Trail, Raleigh, NC 27606 (919-787-5181). ALISE provides a placement service for library education faculty and administrative positions at its annual conference in January or February.

C. Berger and Company

327 E. Gundersen Dr., Carol Stream, IL 60188 (708-653-1115 or 800-382-4222). CBC conducts nationwide executive searches to fill permanent management, supervisory, and director positions in libraries, information centers, and related firms. It also supplies special, academic, and public libraries in Illinois, Wisconsin, Indiana, Pennsylvania, and Texas with temporary professional personnel and clerks to work under contract or for short- or long-term assignments. In addition, CBC offers library and records management consultant services and provides staff to manage projects for clients.

Black Caucus Newsletter

c/o George C. Grant, Ed., Rollins College, Campus Box 2654, Winter Park, FL 32789 (407-646-2676, FAX 407-646-1515). Published bimonthly by Four-G Publishers, this newsletter lists paid advertisements for job vacancies and complementary brief summaries of others, as well as news reports, biographies, essays, and book reviews of interest to members. Free to members; $8.50/year to others.

Canadian Association of Special Libraries and Information Services/Ottawa Chapter Job Bank

c/o CASLIS Job Bank Coordinator, 266 Sherwood Dr., Ottawa, ON K1Y 3W4, Canada. Job seekers should send a résumé; employers who want to list a job should call 613-728-9982.

Canadian Library Association

200 Elgin St., Suite 602, Ottawa, ON K2P 1L5, Canada (613-232-9625). This national association operates a Jobmart at its annual conference in June and publishes classified job ads in *Feliciter* (10 issues/year).

Catholic Library Association

9009 Carter St., Allen Park, MI 48101. Personal and institutional members can advertise for jobs or list job openings (up to 35 words) free in *Catholic Library World* (4/year). Others should contact the advertising coordinator for rates.

Chinese-American Librarians Association Newsletter

c/o Meng-Xiong Liu, Clark Library, San Jose State University, One Washington Sq., San Jose, CA 95119-0028 (408-924-2817, FAX 408-924-2701). The association newsletter issued in February, June, and October includes job listings. Free to members.

Council on Library/Media Technicians, Inc.

c/o Ruth A. Tolbert, Membership Chairperson, Central Indiana ALSA, 1100 W. 42 St., No. 305, Indianapolis, IN 46208. *COLT Newsletter* appears bimonthly in *Library Mosaics*. Personal dues: $25; students: $20; institutions, U.S.: $40, foreign: $55.

Gossage Regan Associates

25 W. 43 St., New York, NY 10036 (212-869-3348, FAX 212-997-1127). Gossage Regan Associates is a full-service library personnel and consulting firm that places librarians and information managers in permanent positions nationwide. The emphasis, however, is on the New York metropolitan area, where the agency is the leading provider of temporary professional support personnel to libraries. Other services include executive search for library directors, division heads, and information vice presidents and managers, and information management consultation.

Indiana Jobline, Central Indiana Area Library Services Authority

1100 W. 42 St., Suite 305, Indianapolis, IN 46208 (317-926-6561). Libraries may access this computer-based listing of job openings in all types of libraries in Indiana through telex or other electronic communication system by calling 317-924-9584. A printed listing is available on request.

Labat-Anderson, Inc.

2200 Clarendon Blvd., Suite 900, Arlington, VA 22201 (703-525-9400). Labat-Anderson supports various federal agencies in 27 states, with most positions located in the Washington, D.C., area. Résumés with cover letters are accepted from librarians with an ALA-accredited MLS and from records managers for part-time and full-time employment.

The Library Co-Op, Inc.

3840 Park Ave., Suite 107, Edison, NJ 08820 (908-906-1777, 800-654-6275). This employment agency supplies permanent and temporary personnel and consultants to work in a variety of information settings, from library moving to database management, catalog maintenance, reference, retrospective conversion, and more. The agency recently formed a new division, ABCD Filing Services, and hired two specialists in space planning.

Library Management Systems

4730 Woodman Ave., Suite 330, Sherman Oaks, CA 91423 (818-789-3141, 714-251-1020, 310-277-9012, 619-456-4083). Established in 1983 to provide contract library services and personnel to public and special libraries and businesses, Library Management Systems organizes and manages small- to medium-sized special libraries and designs and implements major projects such as retrospective data conversions, automation studies, reference services, and records management. LMS has 75 librarians and library assistants on call for long- and short-term projects and provides permanent placement at all levels.

Library Mosaics

Box 5171, Culver City, CA 90231 (310-410-1573). This bimonthly magazine accepts job listings for library/media technicians but does not handle correspondence relating to advertised jobs.

Medical Library Association

6 N. Michigan Ave., Suite 300, Chicago, IL 60602-4805 (312-419-9094). *MLA News* (10 issues/year, June/July and November/December combined issues) lists positions wanted and available in its "Employment Opportunities" column. The position-available rate is $13.50/line for nonmembers and for advertisements received through an employment or advertising agency or other third party. Up to 10 lines are free for MLA members; each additional line is $12. Both members and nonmembers may rerun ads once in the next consecutive issue for $25. Positions-available advertisements must list a salary range. Positions-wanted rates are $8.50/line for nonmembers; 20 free lines for members and $7.50 for

each additional line. Advance mailing of "Employment Opportunities" is available for six months for a prepaid fee: MLA members, $15; nonmembers, $25. MLA also offers a placement service and job market sessions at its annual conference each spring. Job advertisements received for publication in *MLA News* are posted to the MLANET Jobline the week of receipt. The jobline can be accessed 9:00 A.M. to 5:00 P.M. Central Time by calling 312-419-9094, Ext. 343; for 24-hour access, call 312-553-4636. In the MLA jobline, positions are categorized by type, salary range, and regional area.

Pro Libra Associates Inc.

6 Inwood Place, Maplewood, NJ 07040 (201-762-0070, 800-262-0070). A multi-service agency, Pro Libra specializes in consulting, personnel, and project support for libraries and information centers.

REFORMA, National Association to Promote Library Service to the Spanish-Speaking

Employers wishing to send direct mailings to the REFORMA membership (600+) may obtain mailing labels arranged by zip code for $100 per set. For those who want to mail job fliers to REFORMA Executive Board members, a set of mailing labels is available for $5. Contact Al Milo, 714-738-6383. Job ads are also published quarterly in the REFORMA Newsletter. For rate information, contact Ed Erazo, 505-646-6930.

School Library Career Awareness Network (SCAN)

School of Information Studies, Syracuse, NY 13244 (315-443-2740). In coordination with the New York Library Association, School Library Media Section, Syracuse University operates a clearinghouse for recruitment and placement of school library media specialists in New York State. *SCANsheet* is mailed biweekly from April to September and monthly from October to March to members of the NYLA School Library Media Section for a $10 fee ($15 for nonmembers). *SCANfolio* gives school administrators information from the database directory of participating library media specialists seeking positions. *SCANline* is a 24-hour hotline. Employers are not charged to list jobs; a *SCANfolio* search costs $25. Payment of $10/year ($15 for nonmembers) entitles registrants to all SCAN services.

Society of American Archivists

600 S. Federal, Suite 504, Chicago, IL 60605 (312-922-0140). The bimonthly *Archival Outlook* (sent only to members) contains features about the archival profession and other timely topics, such as courses in archival administration, meetings, and professional opportunities (job listings). The "SAA Employment Bulletin" is a bimonthly listing of job opportunities available to members by subscription for $24/year and to nonmembers for $10/issue. Prepayment is required.

Special Libraries Association

1700 18th St. N.W., Washington, DC 20009-2508 (202-234-4700). SLA operates a telephone jobline called SpeciaLine, 202-234-3632, available 24 hours a day, seven days a week. Most SLA chapters have employment chairpersons who provide referral services for employers and job seekers. Several SLA chapters have joblines. The association's monthly newsletter, *The SpeciaList,* carries classified advertising, and SLA offers an employment clearinghouse at the annual conference in June. SLA also provides a discount to members using the résumé evaluation service offered through Advanced Information Management.

State Library Agencies

Some state library agencies issue lists of job openings within their area. These include Colorado (weekly, sent on receipt of SASE or stamps and mailing labels; also available via E-mail, Libnet); Indiana (monthly on request); Iowa (*Joblist,* monthly on request); Massachusetts (*Massachusetts Position Vacancies,* monthly, sent to all state public libraries and to interested individuals on a one-time basis); Mississippi (*Job Vacancy List,* monthly); and Ohio (*Library Opportunities in Ohio,* sent monthly to accredited library education programs and to interested individuals on request).

The Georgia, Nebraska, North Carolina, and South Carolina state libraries have an electronic bulletin board service that lists job openings in each state. Nebraska can be accessed via Nebraska Online (402-471-4020, 800-307-2665 in Nebraska). North Carolina can be accessed nationally by Internet. South Carolina can be accessed in-state by users of the South Carolina Library Network.

On occasion, state library newsletters or journals list vacancies. These include Alabama (*Cottonboll,* quarterly); Alaska (*Sourdough,* bimonthly); Arizona (*Libraries News Week*); Indiana (*Focus on Indiana Libraries,* 11/year); Iowa (*Joblist*); Kansas (*Kansas Libraries,* bimonthly); Louisiana (*Library Communique,* monthly); Missouri (*Show-Me Libraries,* quarterly); Nebraska (*Overtones,* quarterly); New Hampshire (*Granite State Libraries,* bimonthly); New Mexico (*Hitchhiker,* weekly); North Carolina (*NEWS FLASH,* monthly, public libraries only); Utah (*Directions for Utah Libraries,* monthly); and Wyoming (*Outrider,* monthly).

Many state library agencies do not have formal placement services but refer applicants informally when they know of vacancies. The following states primarily make referrals to public libraries: Alabama, Alaska, Arizona, Arkansas, California, Georgia, Louisiana, Pennsylvania, South Carolina (institutional also), Tennessee, Utah, Vermont, and Virginia. Those that refer applicants to all types of libraries are Alaska, Delaware, Florida, Idaho, Illinois, Kansas, Kentucky, Maine, Maryland, Mississippi, Montana, Nebraska, Nevada (largely public and academic), New Hampshire (public, school, and academic), New Mexico, North Carolina, North Dakota, Ohio, Pennsylvania, Rhode Island, South Dakota, West Virginia (on Pennsylvania Jobline, public, academic, and special), and Wyoming.

The following state libraries post job notices for all types of libraries on a bulletin board: California, Connecticut, Florida, Georgia, Illinois, Indiana, Iowa, Kentucky, Michigan, Montana, Nevada, New Jersey, New York, North Carolina, Ohio, Oklahoma, Pennsylvania, South Carolina, South Dakota, Utah, and Washington. [For the addresses of state agencies, see Part 6—*Ed.*]

State and Regional Library Associations

State and regional library associations often make referrals, run ads in association newsletters, or operate a placement service at annual conferences. Some also sponsor joblines. The following associations refer applicants when they know of jobs: Arkansas, Delaware, Hawaii, Louisiana, Michigan, Nevada, Pennsylvania, South Dakota, Tennessee, and Wisconsin.

Although listings are infrequent, the following association newsletters and journals do announce job vacancies: Alabama (*Alabama Librarian,* 7/year); Alaska (*Newspoke,* bimonthly); Arizona (*Newsletter,* 10/year); Arkansas (*Arkansas Libraries,* 6/year); Connecticut (*Connecticut Libraries,* 11/year); Delaware (*Delaware Library Association Bulletin,* 3/year); District of Columbia (*Intercom,* 11/year); Florida (*Florida Libraries,* 10/year); Indiana (*Focus on Indiana Libraries,* 11/year); Iowa (*Catalyst,* 6/year); Kansas (*KLA Newsletter,* 6/year); Minnesota (*MLA Newsletter,* 10/year); Missouri (bimonthly); Mountain Plains (*MPLA Newsletter,* bimonthly, lists vacancies and positions wanted for individuals and institutions); Nebraska (*NLAQ*); Nevada (*Highroller,* 4/year); New Hampshire (*NHLA Newsletter,* 6/year); New Jersey (*NJLA Newsletter,* 10/year); New Mexico (shares notices via State Library's *Hitchhiker,* weekly); New York (*NYLA Bulletin,* 10/year; free for institutional members; $25/week, $40/2 weeks for others); Ohio (*ACCESS,* monthly); Oklahoma (*Oklahoma Librarian,* 6/year); Rhode Island (*RILA Bulletin,* 6/year); South Carolina (*News and Views*); South Dakota (*Book Marks,* bimonthly); Tennessee (*TLA Newsletter*); Vermont (*VLA News,* 10/year); Virginia (*Virginia Librarian,* quarterly), and West Virginia (*West Virginia Libraries,* 6/year).

At their annual conference, the following associations have some type of placement service, although it may only consist of bulletin board postings: Alabama, California, Connecticut, Georgia, Idaho, Illinois, Indiana, Kansas, Louisiana, Maryland, Massachusetts, Mountain Plains, New England, New Jersey, New York, North Carolina (biennial), Oregon, Pacific Northwest, Pennsylvania, South Dakota, Southeastern, Tennessee, Texas, Vermont, and Wyoming.

The following associations have no placement service at this time: Kentucky, Middle Atlantic Regional Library Federation, Midwest Federation, Minnesota, Mississippi, Montana, Nebraska, Nevada, New Mexico, North Dakota, Ohio, Utah, West Virginia, and Wisconsin. [State and regional association addresses are listed in Part 6—*Ed.*]

Library and Information Science Programs

Library and information science programs offer some type of service for current students as well as alumni. Most schools provide job-hunting and résumé-writing seminars. Many invite outside speakers who represent different types of library or recent graduates who relate career experiences. Faculty members or a designated placement officer offer individual advisory services or résumé critiques.

Of the ALA-accredited programs, the following handle placement activities through the library school: Alabama, Albany, Alberta, British Columbia, Buffalo (compiles annual graduate biographical listings), Dalhousie, Drexel, Hawaii, Illinois, Kent State, Louisiana, McGill, Michigan, Missouri, Pittsburgh (Department of Library Science only), Pratt, Puerto Rico, Queens, Rhode Island, Rosary, Rutgers, Saint John's, South Carolina, Syracuse, Tennessee, Texas–Austin, Toronto, UCLA (compiles graduate profile booklets), Western Ontario, Wisconsin–Madison, and Wisconsin–Milwaukee.

Although the central university placement center handles placement activities for California–Berkeley and Emporia, in most cases faculty in the library school still counsel job seekers informally.

Some schools handle placement services in a cooperative manner; in most cases, the university placement center sends out credentials and the library school posts or compiles the job listings. Such schools include Alabama, Albany, Arizona, Buffalo, Catholic, Clarion, Florida State, Illinois, Indiana, Iowa, Kent State, Kentucky, Long Island, Maryland, Montreal, North Carolina–Chapel Hill, North Carolina–Greensboro, North Carolina Central, North Texas, Northern Illinois, Oklahoma, Pittsburgh, Queens, Saint John's, San Jose, Simmons, Southern Connecticut, Southern Mississippi, Syracuse, Tennessee, Texas Woman's, Washington, Wayne State, and Wisconsin–Milwaukee.

Schools may distribute placement credentials free, charge a general registration fee, or request a fee for each file or set of credentials sent out.

Schools that post job notices for review but do not issue printed lists include Alabama, Alberta, Arizona, British Columbia, Buffalo, Catholic, Clark–Atlanta, Dalhousie, Drexel, Florida State, Hawaii, Kent State, Kentucky, Louisiana, Maryland, McGill, Montreal, North Carolina–Chapel Hill, North Carolina–Greensboro, North Carolina Central, Oklahoma, Puerto Rico, Queens, Rutgers, Saint John's, San Jose, Simmons, South Carolina, Southern Mississippi, Syracuse (general postings), Tennessee, Texas Woman's, Toronto, UCLA, Washington, Wayne State, Western Ontario, and Wisconsin–Madison.

In addition to posting job vacancies, some schools offer printed listings, joblines, or database services:

- Albany (free to School of Information Science and Policy students and for one year following graduation; $10/year for others)
- British Columbia (uses British Columbia Library Association Jobline, 604-430-6411)
- California–Berkeley (weekly out-of-state job list and jobline free to students and graduates for six months after graduation; $55 annual fee for University of California alumni; call 510-642-3283)
- Clarion (free with SASE to alumni)
- Drexel (job hotline listing local jobs only, changed each Monday, 215-895-1672)
- Emporia (weekly bulletin of school, university, and public jobs; separate bulletin for special libraries positions; $15.71/6 months for Emporia graduates; $30 plus tax/6 months for others)
- Florida State
- Hawaii

- Illinois (8 issues by mail for $4 and 8 No. 10 SASEs to alumni, $8 and 8 SASEs to nonalumni; also free online placement JOBSearch database on campus and via dial access through Internet)
- Indiana (free for one year following graduation; alumni and others may send SASEs)
- Iowa ($15/year for registered students and alumni)
- Michigan (free for one year following graduation; all other graduates, $15/year for 24 issues; $20 for others)
- Missouri (Library Vacancy Roster, monthly printout, $1/issue, with minimum of 6 issues, to anyone)
- North Texas ($5/6 months, students and alumni)
- Oklahoma
- Pittsburgh (free online placement to alumni)
- Pratt (free to students and alumni for full-time or part-time professional positions only)
- Rhode Island (monthly, $5/year)
- Rosary (*Placement News* every 2 weeks, free for 6 months following graduation, $15/year for students and alumni, $25 to others; *Placement News* is also on Lincolnet and can be accessed by telephone)
- Simmons operates the New England Jobline, which announces professional vacancies in New England, 617-521-2815
- South Florida (in cooperation with ALIS; $10/year)
- Southern Connecticut (printed listing twice a month, free in office, mailed to students and alumni free)
- Syracuse (lists selected jobs online through electronic mail to students; School Media–New York State Listings, $10 for NYLA members, $15 for nonmembers)
- Texas–Austin (bimonthly *Placement Bulletin* free to students and alumni for one year following graduation, $15/6 months and $26/year thereafter; Austin/Central Texas Area Job-Hunters' List—full job descriptions are sent as often as notices are received—$14/6 months, $24/year)
- Washington operates the Pacific Northwest Library Association jobline, which announces professional vacancies, 206-543-2890
- Wisconsin–Madison (now sends listings from Wisconsin and Minnesota to Illinois for its JOBSearch and placement bulletin)
- Wisconsin–Milwaukee sends selected jobs online through electronic mail to students
- Western Ontario operates the SLIS (School of Library and Information Science) Jobline, which announces openings for professionals, 519-661-3543; to list positions, 519-661-2111, Ext. 8495

Employers often list jobs only with schools in their geographic area; some library schools give nonalumni information in person regarding specific locales, but are not staffed to handle mail requests. Schools that allow librarians in the area to view listings are Alabama, Albany, Alberta, Arizona, British Columbia, Buffalo, California–Berkeley, Catholic, Clarion, Clark–Atlanta, Dalhousie, Drexel, Emporia, Florida State, Hawaii, Illinois, Indiana, Iowa, Kent State, Kentucky, Louisiana, Maryland, McGill, Michigan, Missouri, Montreal, North Carolina–Chapel Hill, North Carolina–Greensboro, North Carolina Central, North Texas, Oklahoma, Pittsburgh, Pratt, Puerto Rico, Queens, Rhode Island, Rosary, Rutgers, Saint John's, San Jose, Simmons, South Carolina, South Florida, Southern Connecticut, Southern Mississippi, Syracuse, Tennessee, Texas–Austin, Texas Woman's, Toronto, UCLA, Washington, Wayne State, Western Ontario, Wisconsin–Madison, and Wisconsin–Milwaukee. [For a list of accredited library schools, see later in Part 3. For information on the placement services of other library education programs, contact the school directly.]

Federal Library Jobs

To be considered for employment in many federal libraries, an applicant must establish civil service eligibility and be placed on the Office of Personnel Management (OPM) register in the appropriate geographic area. As of November 1987, OPM terminated its nationwide register and each office in the OPM network became responsible for hiring librarians in its area.

Eligibility can be established by meeting education and/or experience requirements and submitting appropriate forms to OPM during designated "open" periods. Interested applicants should contact their local Federal Job Information/Testing Center (FJI/TC) periodically to find out when the next open period will be and to obtain the proper forms. FJI/TCs are listed under "U.S. Government" in metropolitan telephone directories. Current library job openings in the Washington, D.C., area are listed on a recorded phone message with other federal jobs (202-606-2700; press 1, 2, 406). You may obtain additional information on jobs nationwide by visiting the FJI/TC in your area and using its touch screen computer.

Applications are evaluated by the grade(s) for which applicants are qualified. Information on beginning salary levels can be obtained from FJI/TC. To qualify for librarian positions, applicants must possess a master's degree in library science, a fifth-year bachelor's degree in library science, or 30 semester hours of graduate study in library science. (Candidates who have a combination of education and/or experience may qualify to take the written subject-matter test, which is administered in the Washington, D.C., metropolitan area. To be considered for librarian positions and testing outside the D.C. metropolitan area, contact the nearest FJI/TC.)

The OPM office that maintains the register refers candidates but does not hire and therefore is unaware of a vacancy until an agency requests candidates to fill it. Applications are evaluated according to the agency's requirements. OPM refers only the most qualified candidates.

In addition to filing the appropriate forms, applicants can contact federal agencies directly. More than half the vacancies occur in the Washington, D.C., area. Most positions are in three agencies: the Army, Navy, and Veterans Administration.

The Department of Veterans Affairs (VA) employs more than 350 professional librarians at 176 health care facilities throughout the United States and Puerto Rico. Although most VA positions require training in medical librarianship, many entry-level GS-9 positions require no previous experience; each GS-11/13 position requires specific experience. The VA has examining authority for library positions throughout the agency. This register is open continuously. To receive information and application forms, contact the VA Special Examining Unit, Box 24269, Richmond, VA 23224. For a copy of the current job vacancy list, call 202-233-2820 Monday–Friday, 8:00 A.M.–4:30 P.M. (Eastern Time).

Some "excepted" agencies are not required to hire through usual OPM channels. Although these agencies may require the standard forms, they maintain their own employee selection policies and procedures. Agencies with positions outside the competitive civil service include the Board of Governors of the Federal Reserve System, Central Intelligence Agency, Defense Intelligence Agency, Department of Medicine and Surgery, Federal Bureau of Investigation, Foreign Service of the United States, General Accounting Office, Library of Congress, National Science Foundation, National Security Agency, Tennessee Valley Authority, U.S. Nuclear Regulatory Commission, U.S. Postal Service, judicial branch of the government, legislative branch of the government, U.S. Mission to the United Nations, World Bank, International Finance Corporation, International Monetary Fund, Organization of American States, Pan American Health Organization, and United Nations Secretariat.

The Library of Congress (LC), the world's largest and most comprehensive library, administers its own merit selection system. Job classifications, pay, and benefits are the same as in other federal agencies, and job qualifications generally correspond to those required of the U.S. Office of Personnel Management. LC does not use registers but announces vacancies as they become available. A separate application must be submitted for each position. Announcements for most professional positions stating required qualifications and ranking criteria are widely distributed and remain posted for a minimum of 30 days. The Library of Congress Human Resources Operations Office is located in the James Madison Memorial Bldg., 101 Independence Ave. S.E., Washington, DC 20540 (202-707-5620).

Additional Sources: General and Specialized Jobs

Affirmative Action Register

8356 Olive Blvd., Saint Louis, MO 63132. The goal of the register is to "provide female, minority, handicapped, and veteran candidates with an opportunity to learn of professional and managerial positions throughout the nation and to assist employers in implementing their Equal Opportunity Employment programs." The monthly bulletin is distributed free to leading businesses, industrial and academic institutions, and more than 4,000 agencies that recruit qualified minorities and women, as well as to all known professional organizations for women, minorities, and the handicapped; placement offices; newspapers; magazines; rehabilitation facilities; and more than 8,000 federal, state, and local governmental employment units. The bulletin's total readership is more than 3.5 million (audited). Individual mail subscriptions are available for $15 a year (free to libraries on request). Almost every issue has library job listings.

Chronicle of Higher Education

1255 23rd St. N.W., Suite 700, Washington, DC 20037 (202-466-1055, FAX 202-296-2691). Forty-eight issues a year with breaks in August and December. This publication lists a variety of library positions each week, including administrative and faculty jobs.

National Faculty Exchange

4656 W. Jefferson, Suite 140, Fort Wayne, IN 46804. This program brokers the exchange of faculty and staff at U.S. institutions. Librarians interested in participating should ascertain whether their academic institution is a member.

Additional Sources: School Libraries

School librarians often find that the channels for locating positions in education, such as contacting county or city school superintendent offices, are of more value than the usual library channels. Primary sources include university placement offices, which carry listings for a variety of school system jobs, and local information networks of teachers and library media specialists. A list of teachers' agencies may be obtained from the National Association of Teachers' Agencies, Sandra R. Alexander, CPC, Treas., c/o G. A. Agency, 104 S. Central Ave., Valley Stream, NY 11580-5442 (516-568-8871).

Overseas

Opportunities for employment in foreign countries are limited, and interested candidates should investigate the immigration policies of individual countries. Employment for Americans is virtually limited to U.S. government libraries, libraries of U.S. firms doing worldwide business, and American schools abroad. Library journals from other countries sometimes list job vacancies. Some individuals have obtained jobs by contacting foreign publishers or vendors directly. Non–U.S. government jobs usually call for foreign-language fluency. "Job-Hunting in the UK" by Diane Brooks, *Canadian Library Journal*, 45:374–378 (December 1988), offers advice for those interested in the United Kingdom. *Career Opportunities for Bilinguals and Multilinguals: A Directory of Resources in Education, Employment and Business* by Vladimir F. Wertsman (Scarecrow Press, 1991, ISBN 0-8108-2439-6, $35) includes contact names for foreign employment and business resources. "International Jobs" by Wertsman (*RQ*, Fall 1992, pp. 14–19) provides a listing of library resources for finding jobs abroad.

Council for International Exchange of Scholars (CIES)

3007 Tilden St. N.W., Suite 5M, Washington, DC 20008-3097 (202-686-7877). CIES administers U.S. government Fulbright awards for those wishing to lecture at universities or do advanced research abroad; usually 10 to 15 awards are made to specialists in library science each year. In addition, many countries offer research or lecture awards for which specialists in library and information science may apply. Open to U.S. citizens with university or college teaching experience. Opportunities exist for professional librarians as well. Applications and information may be obtained, beginning each year in March, directly from CIES.

Department of Defense, Dependents Schools

2461 Eisenhower Ave., Alexandria, VA 22331-1100. With overall management and operational responsibilities for the education of dependent children of active-duty U.S. military personnel and DOD civilians stationed in foreign areas, this agency is responsible for teacher recruitment. Write for the complete application brochure. The latest edition of Overseas Opportunities for Educators provides information on employment opportunities in about 225 schools worldwide operated for the children of U.S. military and civilian personnel stationed overseas.

International Association of School Librarianship

Box 1486, Kalamazoo, MI 49005. Informal contacts can be established through this group.

International Schools Services

Box 5910, Princeton, NJ 08543 (609-452-0990). This private, not-for-profit organization, founded in 1955, serves U.S. schools, other than Department of Defense schools, overseas. These include international elementary and secondary schools that enroll children of businessmen and -women and diplomats living abroad. ISS services to overseas schools include recruitment and recommendation of personnel, curricular and administrative guidance, purchasing, and facility planning. ISS also publishes a comprehensive directory of overseas schools and a bimonthly newsletter, *NewsLinks*, for those interested in the intercultural educational community. Write for information regarding these and other services.

Library Fellows Program

c/o Robert P. Doyle, American Library Association, 50 E. Huron St., Chicago, IL 60611 (312-280-3200). ALA administers a grant from the U.S. Information Agency for a program that places American library and book service professionals in institutions overseas for several months to one year. Assignments vary depending on the projects requested by host countries. Candidates should have foreign-language skills, technical expertise, and international interests or expertise. Positions are announced in January, interviews are held in April, and fellows start assignments in mid-September. A similar program places midlevel librarians from other countries in U.S. libraries for three to ten months. Non-U.S. librarians interested in participating should contact the public affairs or cultural affairs officer at the U.S. Embassy in their country.

Peace Corps

1990 K St. N.W., 9th fl., Washington, DC 20526. The Peace Corps needs several professionals with experience in medicine, agriculture, automated systems, cataloging, and technical services. Write for a brochure and application form.

U.S. Information Agency (USIA)

Special Services Branch, USIA, 301 Fourth St. S.W., Washington, DC 20547. USIA, known overseas as the U.S. Information Service (USIS), seeks librarians with an MLS and at least four years' experience for regional library officer positions. Candidates must have a master's degree in librarianship from an ALA-accredited graduate library program, proven administrative ability, and the skills to coordinate the overseas USIS library program with other USIS information functions in various cities worldwide. Practical experience in at least one of the major functional areas of adult library services is required. Other relevant experience could include cooperative library program development, community outreach, public affairs, project management, and personnel training. USIA maintains about 160 libraries in nearly 90 countries, with 1 million books and about 400 local library staff. Libraries provide reference service and publications about the United States for foreign audiences. U.S. citizenship is required. Benefits include overseas allowances and differentials where applicable, vacation, term life insurance, and medical and retirement programs. To apply, send the standard U.S. government application (SF171).

Overseas Exchange Programs

Most exchanges are handled by direct negotiation between interested parties. A few libraries have established exchange programs for their own staff. To facilitate exchange arrangements, the *IFLA Journal* (issued February, May, August, and November) lists individuals wishing to exchange their position for one outside their country. Listings must include the following information: full name, address, present position, qualifications (with year obtained), language abilities, and preferred country, city, library, and type of position. Send to International Federation of Library Associations and Institutions Secretariat, Box 95312, 2509 CH The Hague, Netherlands.

The ALA International Relations Committee/International Relations Round Table (IRC/IRPT) Joint Committee on International Exchange is developing a database of U.S. and international libraries and librarians interested in international study or exchanges. The committee welcomes requests for information and for inclusion in the database by all countries, although initially the focus will be on Eastern and Central Europe, the former Soviet Union, and Asia. The committee can be contacted by writing to Lucinda Covert-Vail, Bobst Library, B Level, Rm. 13-43, New York University, 70 Washington Sq., New York, NY 10012.

The two-page "Checklist for Preparing for an International Exchange," prepared by the ALA International Relations Committee/International Relations Round Table (IRC/IRRT), is available from the ALA Office for Library Personnel Resources (OLPR) or the ALA International Relations Committee. Also available from OLPR is a short bibliography on international exchanges. Under the auspices of the IRC/IRRT Joint Committee on International Exchange of Librarians and Information Professionals, Linda E. Williamson wrote *Going International: Librarians' Preparation Guide for a Work Experience/Job Exchange Abroad* (1988, 74 pp., ISBN 0-8389-7268-3, $15 from ALA Order Services, 50 E. Huron St., Chicago, IL 60611).

LIBEX Bureau for International Staff Exchange

c/o A. J. Clark, Information and Library Studies Library, University of Wales, Aberystwyth (formerly College of Librarianship Wales Library), Llanbadarn Fawr, Aberystwyth, Dyfed SY23 3AS, Wales (Tel. 0970-622417, Telecom Gold/LA-NET 79:2039, FAX 0970-622190, JANET E-mail ILSLIB@UK.AC. ABER). LIBEX assists in two-way exchanges for British librarians wishing to work abroad and for librarians from the United States, Canada, the European Community, the Commonwealth, and many other countries who wish to work in Britain.

Using Information Skills in Nonlibrary Settings

Information professionals have shown a great deal of interest in "alternative careers" and in using information skills in a variety of settings. These jobs are not usually found through regular library placement channels, although many library schools are trying to generate such listings for students and alumni. Listings for jobs that require information management skills may not specifically call for librarians, so job seekers may need to use ingenuity to find them. Some librarians offer their services on a free-lance basis to businesses, alternative schools, community agencies, legislators, and the like; these opportunities are usually not advertised but are found through contacts developed over time. A number of businesses that broker information have developed from individual free-lance experiences. Small companies or other organizations often need a one-time service for organizing files or collections, bibliographic research for special projects, indexing or abstracting, compiling directories, or consulting work. Bibliographic networks and online database companies are using librarians as information managers, trainers, researchers, systems and database analysts, and online services managers. Jobs are sometimes advertised in library network newsletters or data-processing journals. Librarians can be found working in law firms as litigation case supervisors (organizing and analyzing records for legal cases); in publishing companies as sales representatives, marketing directors, editors, and computer services experts; in community agencies as adult education coordinators, volunteer administrators, and grant writers. The three-page handout "Alternative Career Directions for Librarians," available from OLPR/ALA (50 E. Huron St., Chicago, IL 60611), provides a list of job titles.

The classifieds in *Publishers Weekly* and *National Business Employment Weekly* may lead to information-related positions. One might also consider reading the Sunday classified sections in metropolitan newspapers to locate job descriptions under a variety of job titles calling for information skills.

The *Burwell Directory of Information Brokers* is an annual publication that lists information brokers, free-lance librarians, independent information specialists, and institutions that provide services for a fee. Individuals do not need to pay to be listed; the 1994 directory is available for $79.50 plus $5.50 postage and handling (foreign postage, $25.50) from Burwell Enterprises, 3724 FM 1960 West, Suite 214, Houston, TX 77068 (713-537-9051, FAX 713-537-8332). It is supplemented by the bimonthly *Information Broker* ($40; foreign postage, $15), which includes articles by, for, and about individuals and companies in the fee-based information field, book reviews, a calendar of events, and issue-oriented articles.

The Independent Librarians Exchange Round Table is a unit within the American Library Association that serves as a networking source for owners of information businesses, consultants, and those who work for a company that provides support services to libraries or other information services outside traditional library settings. The membership fee is $8, in addition to ALA dues, and includes the newsletter *ILERT Alert*. A directory of members is available free to ILERT members, for $5 to other ALA members, and for $10 to nonmembers. At the 1993 ALA annual conference, ILERT sponsored a program, "Jobs for Indexers," which is available on cassette No. ALA332 for $24 from Teach'em Inc., 160 E. Illinois St., Chicago, IL 60611 (800-224-3775).

The Association of Independent Information Professionals, not affiliated with ALA, was formed in 1987 for individuals who own and operate for-profit information companies. Contact Marilyn Levine, 2266 N. Prospect, Suite 314, Milwaukee, WI 53202.

A growing number of publications describe opportunities for librarians in the broader information arena. "Information Entrepreneurship: Sources for Reference Librarians" by Donna Gilton, *RQ,* Spring 1992, pp. 346–355; "Information Brokering: The State of Art" by Alice Sizer Warner, *Wilson Library Bulletin,* April 1989, pp. 55–57, and "The Information Broker: A Modern Profile" by Mick O'Leary, *Online,* November 1987, pp. 24–30, provide an overview of information brokerage. *The Information Broker's Handbook* by Sue Rugge and Alfred Glossbrenner (Blue Ridge Summit, PA: Windcrest/McGraw-Hill, 1992, 379 pp., ISBN 0-8306-3798-2, $29.95) covers the market for information, getting started, pricing and billing, and more. *Mind Your Own Business: A Guide for the Information Entrepreneur* by Alice Sizer Warner (New York: Neal-Schuman, 1987, 165 pp., ISBN 1-55570-014-4, $24.95) describes planning for and managing an information business, including marketing, sales, and record keeping. *Opening New Doors: Alternative Careers for Librarians,* edited by Ellis Mount (Washington, D.C.: Special Libraries Association, 1993) provides profiles of librarians who are working outside libraries.

New Options for Librarians: Finding a Job in a Related Field, edited by Betty-Carol Sellen and Dimity S. Berkner (New York: Neal-Schuman, 1984, 300 pp., ISBN 0-918212-73-1, $27.95), covers how to prepare for and initiate a job search and examines career possibilities in publishing, public relations, abstracting and indexing, association work, contract service companies, information management, and more. Also included is a survey of librarians working in related fields and an annotated bibliography. The survey results are summarized in "Librarians in Alternative Work Places," *Library Journal* 110 (February 15, 1985): 108–110.

Guide to Careers in Abstracting and Indexing by Wendy Wicks and Ann Marie Cunningham (Philadelphia: NFAIS, 1992, 126 pp.) is available for $25 from the National Federation of Abstracting and Information Services, 1429 Walnut St., Philadelphia, PA 19102 (215-563-2406). The American Society of Indexers, Box 386, Port Aransas, TX 78373 (512-749-4052), has a number of publications that would be useful for individuals who are interested in indexing careers. Send for membership and publication information.

Careers in Information, edited by Jane F. Spivack (Boston: G. K. Hall, 1982, ISBN 0-914236-83-0, $27.50), includes chapters on the work of information specialists, entrepreneurship in the information industry, and information professionals in the federal government, as well as guidance on finding a job and information on placements and salaries for the broader information field as well as librarianship. "Atypical Careers and Innovative Services in Library and Information Science," edited by Walter C. Allen and Lawrence W. S. Auld, composes the entire issue of *Library Trends* 32 (Winter 1984): pp. 251–358. It focuses on new directions with potential employment opportunities for librarians and some of the implications for the changing role of the information professional.

Infomediary, an international, professional quarterly journal, edited by an international board of experts and published since 1985, focuses on information brokerage, consulting, and the entrepreneurial aspects of the library and information field. Since 1989 (vol. 3), the journal has been published by IOS Press, Van Diemenstr. 94, 1013 CN Amsterdam, Netherlands. The subscription price for 1993 (vol. 6) is $175. A personal subscription costs $60.

Although out of print, some earlier publications are still useful sources: *What Else You Can Do with a Library Degree,* edited by Betty-Carol Sellen (New York: Neal-Schuman and Gaylord Brothers, 1979); *The Information Brokers: How to Start and Operate Your Own Fee-Based Service* by Kelly Warnken (New York: Bowker, 1981); and *Careers in Other Fields for Librarians . . . Successful Strategies for Finding the Job* by Rhoda Garoogian and Andrew Garoogian (Chicago: ALA, 1985). Chapters in the latter book include bridging traditional and nontraditional employment; opportunities in business, government, education, and entrepreneurship; and employment techniques (where to look for jobs, résumés and letters, and interviewing). Of particular interest is the chapter describing the process of translating traditional library tasks and skills into new types of job responsibility. Scattered throughout are sample job descriptions in other fields that incorporate information functions.

Temporary/Part-Time Positions

Working as a substitute librarian or in temporary positions may be an alternative career path or interim step while looking for a regular job. This type of work can provide valuable contacts and experience. Organizations that hire library workers for part-time or temporary jobs include Pro Libra Associates, Inc., 6 Inwood Place, Maplewood, NJ 07040 (201-762-0070); C. Berger and Co., 327 E. Gundersen Dr., Carol Stream, IL 60188 (708-653-1115, 800-382-4222), in the Chicago area; Gossage Regan Associates, Inc., 25 W. 43 St., New York, NY 10036 (212-869-3348); The Library Co-Op, Inc., 3840 Park Ave., Suite 107, Edison, NJ 08820 (908-906-1777, 800-654-6275); Library Management Systems, 4730 Woodman Ave., Suite 330, Sherman Oaks, CA 91423 (818-789-3141); and Advanced Information Management, 444 Castro St., Suite 320, Mountain View, CA 94041 (415-965-7799) or 3020 Old Ranch Pkwy., 3rd fl., Seal Beach, CA 90740-2751 (310-799-5538).

Part-time jobs are not always advertised, and they are often found by canvassing local libraries and leaving applications.

Job Hunting in General

Wherever information needs to be organized and presented to patrons in an effective, efficient, and service-oriented fashion, professional librarians can apply their skills. However, one must be prepared to invest considerable time, energy, imagination, and money to create or obtain a satisfying position in a conventional library or other type of information service. Usually, one job-hunting method or source is not enough.

"How to Find a Job Online" by Ann J. Van Camp, *Online* 12 (July 1988): 26–34, offers guidance on databases that might lead to library or information-related positions.

Public and school library certification requirements often vary from state to state; contact the state library agency for such information. Certification requirements are summarized in *Certification of Public Librarians in the United States* (4th ed., 1991), available from the ALA Office for Library Personnel Resources. A summary of school library/media certification requirements by state is included in *Requirements for Certification of Teachers, Counselors, Librarians and Administrators for Elementary and Secondary Schools,* published annually by the University of Chicago Press. "School Library Media Certification Requirements: 1992 Update" by Patsy H. Perritt also provides this information. [See 1993 edition of *The Bowker Annual—Ed.*] For information on a specific state, contact the state supervisors of school library media services. [For a list of the state supervisors, see Part 6—*Ed.*]

Civil service requirements—be they on the local, county, or state level—can add another layer of procedures to the job search. Some civil service jurisdictions require written and/or oral examinations; others assign a ranking based on a review of credentials. Jobs are usually filled from a list of qualified candidates. As the exams are held only at certain times and a variety of jobs can be filled from a single list of applicants (e.g., all Librarian I positions, regardless of type of function), candidates should be certain that the library of interest falls under civil service regulations.

For a position in a specific specialty or geographic area, remember those reference skills to ferret information from directories and other tools regarding local industries, schools, subject collections, and the like. Directories such as the *American Library Directory, Subject Collections, Directory of Special Libraries and Information Centers,* and *Directory of Federal Libraries,* as well as state directories and directories for other special subject areas, can provide a wealth of information for job seekers. "The Job Hunter's Search for Company Information" by Robert Favini (*RQ,* Winter 1991, pp. 155–161) lists general reference business sources that might also be useful for librarians seeking employment in corporations. Some students have pooled resources to hire a clipping service for a specific period to get classified ads for a particular geographic area.

For information on other job-hunting and personnel matters, request a checklist of materials from the ALA Office for Library Personnel Resources, 50 E. Huron St., Chicago, IL 60611.

Placements and Salaries, 1992:
Salaries Rise as Programs Decline

Fay Zipkowitz

Associate Professor, Graduate School of Library and Information Studies
University of Rhode Island, Kingston

The annual *Library Journal* Placements and Salaries survey allows us to monitor trends and to assess supply and demand for new graduates in librarianship. Of the 51 accredited library schools in the United States, 41 responded in some fashion to *LJ's* 42nd annual survey. Columbia University is notably absent from this year's report because its library school has closed. Brigham Young University's library school has also closed and is reporting on the last graduates in the pipeline. Northern Illinois University is allowing students already enrolled to complete their course work but is accepting no new students

In the 1950s when this annual survey began, there were 33 accredited library schools in the United States (and only 3 in all of Canada). In the late 1970s, the number of accredited U.S. schools peaked at 61, with a sharp decline in programs during the next decade. The recent spate of closings, as well as those institutions on the verge of disbanding their library schools, confirms that we are in the midst of another decline. Still, as with the earlier decline, the closings have not necessarily had much relationship to enrollments and application rates, or regard for the geographical location of alternative programs.

There are now large areas of the country with no accredited library school and in some cases very few unaccredited programs. The geographical distribution of accredited programs affects recruitment of newcomers to the profession as well as placement of newly graduated professionals. Some students may elect to enroll in library programs because of their proximity. Other qualified potential applicants may shun the field because there is no program accessible to them without major relocation. Of the former group, many are tied to their location after graduation, sometimes creating a local surplus of qualified librarians and conceivably depressing local salary levels. (There is anecdotal evidence of this phenomenon in Boston, Ann Arbor, and the San Francisco Bay area.)

Further attrition of library schools is bound to have an effect on recruitment and placement; distance education may address some of these needs, but at the present time there are distressing gaps in program opportunities.

Minority Placements

This report reflects responses from 41 institutions concerning salaries and placement trends as experienced by their 1992 graduates. One institution provided

Note: Adapted from *Library Journal,* October 15, 1993.
The author thanks Eric Barden, Rebecca Armitage, and Julie Handren, graduate students, for their help with this project.

Table 1 / Status of 1992 U.S. Graduates, Spring 1993*

	Graduates	Not in Lib. Positions			Employment Not Known			Perm. Prof. Placements			Temp. Prof. Placements			Nonprof. Lib. Placements			Total in Lib. Positions		
	Total	Women	Men	Total	Women	Men	Total	Women	Men	Total	Women	Men	Total	Women	Men	Total	Women	Men	Total
Northeast	1,213	19	9	28	43	12	55	407	83	490	17	2	19	30	4	34	454	89	543
Southeast	564	10	9	19	32	7	39	213	41	254	6	0	6	4	2	6	223	43	266
Midwest	1,268	14	1	15	126	27	153	366	95	461	9	2	11	35	11	46	410	108	518
Southwest	178	5	2	7	43	4	47	87	13	100	5	0	5	2	0	2	94	13	107
West	402	9	3	12	18	8	26	145	38	183	16	5	21	4	4	8	165	47	212
All schools	3,625	57	24	81	262	58	320	1,218	270	1,488	53	9	62	75	21	96	1,346	300	1,646

*For an explanation of why totals don't necessarily add up, see section titled "Minority Placements."

Table 2 / Placements and Full-Time Salaries of 1992 U.S. Graduates: Summary by Region

	Total Placements*	Placements			Low Salary		High Salary		Average Salary			Median Salary		
		Women	Men	Total	Women	Men	Women	Men	Women	Men	Total	Women	Men	Total
Northeast	718	368	78	446	$11,200	$18,000	$90,000	$60,000	$28,080	$28,620	$28,175	$26,900	$26,950	$26,900
Southeast	342	206	39	245	11,000	17,400	61,300	40,000	25,048	24,615	24,979	24,000	24,000	24,000
Midwest	688	350	97	447	12,000	16,000	58,000	42,700	25,175	25,855	25,322	24,800	25,000	25,000
Southwest	154	86	13	99	12,245	23,000	43,800	31,000	26,047	27,222	26,201	32,000	27,680	25,500
West	265	135	34	169	14,151	13,603	43,000	47,000	28,959	28,286	28,959	35,500	27,000	33,000
All schools	2,167	1,145	261	1,406	$11,000	$13,603	$90,000	$60,000	$26,618	$26,881	$26,666	$25,700	$26,000	$25,968

*Includes placements undifferentiated by sex.

summary information but no data for individual placements. Of the remaining 40 programs, the completeness and accuracy of individual data vary between and within the institutional reports.

For example, gender and type of placement might be supplied, but no salary figure reported; or, salary, gender, and type of library might be reported but not location and type of position. In addition, there are some graduates for whom no information is available because the school was unable to report specific information, or only able to report for some, but not all, of its graduates who were placed.

For the first time, this year's survey included a category for minority status and most respondents supplied that information. Thus, we were able to report some comparison between general and minority salary levels for new graduates. This data category also allowed us to examine minority placements within the context of geographical distribution of new graduates in general.

Once again I want to express my appreciation for the time, effort, and thought that went into gathering and reporting data in the survey responses.

The 1992 Data

In 1992 the average beginning salary of full-time, permanent, professional placements was $26,666 (see Table 2), representing a 6.5 percent increase over the revised 1991 salary of $25,583. The median salary increased 3.9 percent, from $25,000 in 1991 to $25,968 in 1992. The average salary for 123 full-time professional minority placements was $27,539. (As noted above, this was the first time minority identification had been reported, so no comparison with previous years was possible. These data are reported in Table 7.) The median men's salary for 1992 placements was $300 higher than the women's salary, and the average for men was $263 higher than the average for women. See Table 2 for more detail.

In response to questions about numbers of position listings received by library schools, 11 schools stated that their listings were up compared with 1991. Estimates of the increases range from 2 percent to 100 percent. Four schools indicated no appreciable change in 1992 postings, while 13 schools reported a decrease in openings listed. The magnitude of decreased listings ranges from 1 percent to about 40 percent.

Thirty-six institutions responded to the question asking for a comparison of 1993 placements at the time they submitted their report with placements at the same time one year before. Nine schools reported increased placements, 18 schools indicated no change from 1992, and 9 schools registered a downturn in placements.

A question about the comparison of starting salaries in 1992 with 1991 was answered by 33 schools. Sixteen reported that salaries increased in 1992, 12 indicated no discernible change, and 5 asserted there was a decline in 1992 salaries.

(text continues on p. 391)

Table 3 / Placements by Type of Library of 1992 U.S. Graduates by School

School	Public			Elementary & Secondary			College & University			Special			Other			Total		
	Women	Men	Total	Women	Men	Total	Women	Men	Total	Women	Men	Total	Women	Men	Total	Women	Men	Total
Alabama	14	2	16	15	0	15	17	2	19	3	1	4	1	2	3	50	7	57
Brigham Young	4	2	6	2	0	2	2	2	4	1	2	3	0	1	1	9	7	16
Calif., Berkeley	7	2	9	1	0	1	12	5	17	14	1	15	6	3	9	40	11	51
Calif., Los Angeles	16	0	16	2	0	2	17	0	17	20	0	20	3	0	3	58	0	58
Catholic	2	1	3	6	0	6	3	0	3	4	2	6	2	1	3	17	4	21
Clarion	9	0	9	3	2	5	6	3	9	3	0	3	1	0	1	22	5	27
Drexel	11	3	14	8	0	8	7	0	7	20	3	23	8	6	14	54	12	66
Florida State	12	3	15	3	1	4	6	3	9	2	0	2	0	0	0	23	7	30
Hawaii	9	3	12	14	0	14	6	9	15	7	0	7	2	2	4	38	14	52
Indiana	30	4	34	9	1	10	16	12	28	14	2	16	0	0	0	69	19	88
Iowa	8	2	10	5	1	6	6	4	10	5	2	7	0	0	0	24	9	33
Kent State	19	6	25	8	5	13	7	4	11	7	2	9	3	1	4	44	18	62
Long Island	9	4	13	6	0	6	1	0	1	6	0	6	0	0	0	22	4	26
Louisiana State	7	2	9	10	0	10	9	0	9	6	1	7	2	1	3	34	4	38
Michigan	23	7	30	17	0	17	12	4	16	7	2	9	7	0	7	66	13	79
Missouri	11	5	16	5	0	5	11	2	13	9	2	11	1	0	1	37	9	46
N.C., Central	17	1	18	13	1	14	4	2	6	3	0	3	1	3	4	28	7	35
N.C., Chapel Hill	4	2	6	2	0	2	11	3	14	8	1	9	2	2	4	27	8	35
N.C., Greensboro	4	2	6	18	1	19	7	0	7	1	0	1	0	0	0	30	3	33
Northern Illinois	12	5	17	7	0	7	7	2	9	2	1	3	2	0	2	30	8	38
Pittsburgh	13	4	17	5	1	6	14	8	22	12	2	14	5	4	9	49	19	68
Pratt	6	5	11	1	1	2	2	0	2	5	5	10	1	1	2	15	12	27

Table 3 / Placements by Type of Library of 1992 U.S. Graduates by School (cont.)

School	Public			Elementary & Secondary			College & University			Special			Other			Total		
	Women	Men	Total	Women	Men	Total	Women	Men	Total	Women	Men	Total	Women	Men	Total	Women	Men	Total
Queens	10	4	14	10	0	10	0	4	4	5	3	8	1	0	1	26	11	37
Rhode Island	13	0	13	12	0	12	2	0	2	2	1	3	0	0	0	29	1	30
Rosary	29	7	36	19	1	20	14	4	18	10	7	17	0	0	0	72	19	91
Rutgers	31	5	36	14	0	14	17	2	19	19	3	22	5	1	6	86	11	97
St. John's	7	0	7	4	0	4	1	2	3	2	0	2	0	0	0	14	2	16
Simmons	19	6	25	6	0	6	24	10	34	28	4	32	6	1	7	83	21	104
South Carolina	12	1	13	18	1	19	6	2	8	1	0	1	3	2	5	40	6	46
Southern Connecticut	12	1	13	5	0	5	3	0	3	5	0	5	1	0	1	26	1	27
Southern Mississippi	8	0	8	7	2	9	3	1	4	2	1	3	1	0	1	21	4	25
SUNY Buffalo	19	2	21	18	3	21	13	1	14	5	0	5	4	3	7	59	9	68
Syracuse	0	0	0	9	0	9	8	2	10	2	1	3	2	0	2	21	3	24
Tennessee	1	1	2	6	0	6	1	0	1	4	0	4	1	0	1	13	1	14
Texas, Austin	18	2	20	18	1	19	9	7	16	19	2	21	7	2	9	71	14	85
Texas Woman's	5	0	5	16	0	16	6	0	6	5	0	5	1	0	1	33	0	33
Washington	16	6	22	2	1	3	18	0	18	15	2	17	0	0	0	51	9	60
Wayne State	25	7	32	12	1	13	15	2	17	13	1	14	3	0	3	68	11	79
Wisconsin, Madison	10	0	10	8	0	8	8	0	8	5	0	5	3	0	3	34	0	34
Wisconsin, Milwaukee	10	7	17	12	0	12	5	5	10	9	7	16	1	2	3	37	21	58
Total	482	114	596	356	24	380	336	107	443	310	61	371	86	38	124	1,570	344	1,914

Table 4 / Placements and Full-Time Salaries of 1992 U.S. Graduates by School

School	Total Placements	Placements			Low Salary		High Salary		Average Salary			Median Salary		
		Women	Men	Total	Women	Men	Women	Men	Women	Men	Total	Women	Men	Total
Alabama	57	26	6	32	$20,780	$21,000	$32,000	$35,000	$25,388	$24,833	$25,284	$25,000	$23,250	$25,000
Brigham Young	16	8	7	15	21,500	23,000	38,000	47,000	25,786	29,586	27,559	24,872	27,100	26,000
Calif., Berkeley	51	31	8	39	15,540	22,500	43,000	37,000	31,710	28,481	31,047	31,596	27,250	31,000
Calif., Los Angeles	58	28	0	28	21,000	—	41,000	—	30,432	—	30,432	29,250	—	29,250
Catholic	21	13	3	16	15,000	30,000	43,000	60,000	27,197	41,000	29,785	27,000	33,000	27,716
Clarion	27	21	4	25	12,000	20,000	43,000	26,500	22,635	23,710	22,807	24,000	24,170	24,000
Drexel	66	36	7	43	17,800	21,000	52,000	24,000	28,499	28,271	28,462	26,500	30,000	27,000
Florida State	30	21	6	27	20,000	21,730	36,500	32,200	24,586	25,468	24,782	23,662	24,500	24,000
Hawaii	52	30	10	40	14,150	19,220	41,000	42,400	29,850	31,190	30,185	28,972	30,486	28,972
Indiana	88	61	18	79	14,700	20,000	39,000	41,500	23,985	26,765	24,619	23,000	25,300	24,000
Iowa	33	16	6	22	20,966	20,800	44,500	34,000	25,474	25,967	25,608	23,375	24,500	24,000
Kent State	62	37	14	51	17,000	20,000	36,000	42,700	24,771	29,514	26,073	23,500	27,000	25,000
Louisiana State	38	22	5	27	11,000	20,500	43,500	40,000	24,319	28,056	25,011	24,000	24,500	24,000
Michigan	79	58	11	69	18,000	23,370	58,000	33,500	27,608	27,082	27,524	26,000	26,000	26,000
Missouri	46	18	8	26	14,000	20,000	40,000	27,000	25,272	24,281	24,967	24,000	24,250	24,000
N.C., Central	35	25	6	31	18,800	17,400	38,000	29,300	25,978	23,317	25,463	24,000	24,250	24,000
N.C., Chapel Hill	35	23	5	28	24,000	22,000	40,000	33,696	27,044	26,539	26,954	26,000	25,000	25,558
N.C., Greensboro	33	25	2	27	18,000	21,300	30,000	26,000	24,159	23,650	24,121	23,500	23,650	23,500
Northern Illinois	38	21	8	29	16,000	16,000	43,000	34,000	25,652	24,117	25,229	25,000	24,500	25,000
Pittsburgh	68	1	2	3	24,000	18,000	24,000	30,000	24,000	24,000	24,000	24,000	24,000	24,000
Pratt	27	12	11	23	22,100	19,500	37,000	40,000	28,667	29,018	28,835	27,500	28,000	28,000

Table 4 / Placements and Full-Time Salaries of 1992 U.S. Graduates by School (cont.)

School	Total Placements	Placements Women	Men	Total	Low Salary Women	Men	High Salary Women	Men	Average Salary Women	Men	Total	Median Salary Women	Men	Total
Queens	37	19	7	26	26,000	22,000	52,000	28,630	33,391	26,484	31,532	30,000	26,280	28,315
Rhode Island	30	22	0	22	11,200	—	40,000	—	24,527	—	24,527	23,500	—	23,500
Rosary	91	37	8	45	18,000	24,620	37,000	28,500	25,248	27,265	25,606	25,000	28,000	25,000
Rutgers	97	64	9	73	18,000	20,000	90,000	45,000	30,592	29,798	30,493	27,957	26,000	27,573
St. John's	16	11	2	13	15,000	34,000	35,868	38,000	27,768	36,000	29,034	26,290	36,000	28,000
Simmons	104	57	13	70	17,000	19,074	42,500	42,000	27,335	26,422	27,165	27,000	24,000	27,000
South Carolina	46	35	5	40	18,000	18,000	36,000	28,000	25,506	23,000	25,192	24,500	23,000	24,246
Southern Connecticut	27	19	0	19	13,520	—	56,000	—	31,211	—	31,211	30,000	—	30,000
Southern Mississippi	25	13	2	15	18,000	20,000	28,000	23,000	21,308	21,500	21,333	21,000	21,500	21,000
SUNY Buffalo	68	33	6	39	15,500	21,840	50,000	31,000	25,054	27,400	25,415	24,900	27,850	26,000
Tennessee	14	12	1	13	18,500	19,000	61,300	19,000	27,950	19,000	27,262	24,500	19,000	24,000
Texas, Austin	85	55	13	68	17,400	23,000	43,800	31,000	25,497	27,222	25,827	24,300	27,680	25,000
Texas Woman's	33	29	0	29	18,000	—	42,500	—	27,359	—	27,359	26,500	—	26,500
Washington	60	33	5	38	15,803	23,500	39,500	30,450	26,340	26,655	26,381	26,280	26,000	26,238
Wayne State	79	37	4	41	17,900	17,000	53,000	26,281	25,917	23,390	25,671	26,000	25,140	26,000
Wisconsin, Madison	34	24	0	24	14,000	—	40,000	—	26,358	—	26,358	25,859	—	25,859
Wisconsin, Milwaukee	58	14	11	25	22,000	19,240	43,500	34,000	27,903	24,613	26,455	26,000	25,000	25,000

Table 5 / Average Salary Index
Starting Library Positions, 1985–1992*

	Library Schools	Average Beginning Salary	Dollar Increase in Average Salary	Beginning Index	BLS-CPI
1985	58	$19,753	$962	111.6	109.3
1986	54	20,874	1,121	118.0	110.5
1987	55	22,247	1,373	125.7	115.4
1988	51	23,491	1,244	132.8	120.5
1989	43	24,581	1,090	138.9	124.0
1990	38	25,306	725	143.0	130.7
1991	46	25,583	277	144.6	136.2
1992	41	26,666	1,083	150.7	140.5

*Bureau of Labor Statistics Consumer Price Index based on 1982–1984 = 100. Average beginning salary for 1982–1984 figured at $17,693.

Placement Success and Failure

Comparing the placements of 1992 graduates with 1991 graduates, 5 schools said they had experienced more difficulty in 1992 than in 1991, 23 said the placement was about the same, and 10 said they had experienced less difficulty in 1992 than with 1991 graduates.

For the placement of 1993 graduates, 11 respondents indicated they expect more difficulty in placements than in 1992, 23 expect the placements will be about the same, and 4 expect less difficulty.

The survey asked for specialties or concentrations that were required for posted positions that graduates did not have, or positions for which there may be increasing demand and a short supply. The responses focused on chemistry, engineering, sciences, math, foreign languages, music, cataloging, medicine, computer science, and information systems. One school stated, however, "[W]e have more difficulty placing graduates because they will not relocate than because they are not fully qualified for positions." Another reported that they "had qualified candidates but many don't want to catalog." Others noted the need for children's librarians, archivists, and people with knowledge of very technical library systems. Several schools indicated that many positions listings they receive are for experienced librarians; they are seeing fewer entry-level positions.

Overall, salaries and placements have not changed dramatically over the past few years. Many variables that make up the profile of the MLS graduate affect starting salaries—continued employment, part-time study, return to a senior-level position, other graduate degrees already held, collective bargaining contracts, to name just a few. The picture that emerges is not exactly bleak, but we still feel the unease of the economy, the shortage of new and replacement jobs, and the diminution of opportunity to study for the MLS.

Table 6 / Special Placements, 1992

	Women	Men	Total
Government jurisdictions (U.S.)			
National libraries	4	1	5
State and provincial libraries	0	1	1
Armed Services libraries (domestic)	1	0	1
Overseas agencies (incl. Armed Services libraries abroad)	1	0	1
Other government agencies (except USVA hospitals)	8	6	14
Library science			
Advanced study	3	3	6
Other			
Architecture	2	0	2
Art and museums	12	0	12
Audiovisual and media centers	191	15	206
Bibliographic instruction	12	2	14
Book trade (wholesale and retail)	7	0	7
Business (finance, industrial, corporate)	16	9	25
Children's services (other than public or school libraries)	1	0	1
Communications industry (advertising, newspaper, etc.)	10	1	11
Correctional institutions	1	1	2
Database publishing and services	3	1	4
Freelance	5	1	6
Government documents	7	2	9
Historical societies, agencies, archives	7	0	7
Hospitals (incl. USVA hospitals)	2	2	4
Indexing and abstracting	8	2	10
Information services (nonlibrary)	39	6	45
Law	46	5	51
Library services to the handicapped	0	1	1
Medicine (incl. nursing schools)	25	13	38
Networks, consortia, and utilities	2	0	2
Outreach activities and services	4	0	4
Pharmaceutical	6	0	6
Rare books, manuscripts, archives	24	8	32
Records management	8	1	9
Religion (seminaries, theological schools)	3	1	4
Research and development	2	0	2
Science and technology	9	6	15
Social sciences	3	0	3
Spanish-speaking centers	1	1	2
Systems analysis, automation	15	8	23
Theater, motion pictures, dance, music	6	0	6
Youth services (public libraries)	94	11	105
Youth services (school)	28	1	29
Youth/young adult (other)	22	7	29
Total special placements	638	116	754

Table 7 / Salaries of Minority Placements by Type of Library

	Number	Percent of Total	Low Salary	Average Salary	High Salary
Academic	46	37.4	$13,680	$27,825	$42,400
Public	34	27.6	15,540	24,657	32,292
School	23	18.7	19,000	30,336	49,387
Special	16	13.0	14,560	29,406	40,000
Other	4	3.3	19,800	25,200	35,000
Total	123	100	$13,680	$27,539	$49,387

Table 8 / Comparison of Salaries by Type of Library, 1992

	Total Placements	Placements			Low Salary		High Salary		Average Salary			Median Salary		
		Women	Men	Total	Women	Men	Women	Men	Women	Men	Total	Women	Men	Total
Public libraries														
Northeast	196	49	12	61	$15,500	$19,074	$31,990	$30,500	$24,445	$25,070	$24,568	$24,550	$26,000	$24,900
Southeast	83	17	5	22	20,000	20,500	29,500	26,000	24,041	22,760	23,750	24,492	23,000	23,924
Midwest	227	29	13	42	20,000	16,000	30,000	34,000	23,536	24,346	23,787	24,000	25,000	24,000
Southwest	25	20	2	22	19,300	23,000	29,600	27,680	23,581	25,340	23,741	23,830	25,340	23,830
West	65	21	6	27	22,048	23,500	35,500	47,000	27,034	29,879	27,666	26,280	27,163	26,280
All schools	596	136	38	174	15,500	16,000	35,500	47,000	24,474	25,292	24,652	24,496	25,000	24,500
School libraries														
Northeast	114	48	2	50	11,200	29,857	52,000	31,000	30,315	30,429	30,320	28,000	30,429	28,250
Southeast	98	37	1	38	18,000	24,000	36,000	24,000	26,085	24,240	26,030	24,800	24,000	24,740
Midwest	111	19	0	19	18,900	—	53,000	—	29,771	—	29,771	26,700	—	26,700
Southwest	35	27	1	28	17,400	31,000	42,500	31,000	26,529	31,000	26,689	26,000	31,000	26,300
West	22	5	0	5	20,000	—	38,000	—	26,747	—	26,747	26,743	—	24,743
All schools	380	136	4	140	11,200	24,000	53,000	31,000	28,205	28,964	28,227	26,850	30,429	26,904
College/university libraries														
Northeast	133	30	8	38	20,000	22,500	39,000	42,000	27,573	28,613	27,791	27,000	27,500	27,000
Southeast	77	15	1	16	11,000	18,000	27,500	18,000	22,698	18,000	22,404	24,000	18,000	23,500
Midwest	140	16	7	23	16,000	19,240	44,500	28,000	26,486	23,534	25,588	25,000	24,000	24,960
Southwest	22	10	6	16	18,000	24,000	41,890	30,000	28,559	27,167	28,037	27,666	27,000	27,166
West	71	24	5	29	15,803	22,500	35,500	27,000	27,410	24,300	26,874	28,416	24,000	27,000
All schools	443	95	27	122	11,000	18,000	44,500	42,000	26,683	25,783	26,484	26,000	25,000	26,000
Special libraries														
Northeast	142	38	7	45	17,000	21,000	43,000	34,000	27,911	27,597	27,919	27,000	28,000	27,000
Southeast	34	4	1	5	18,500	40,000	43,500	40,000	27,125	40,000	29,700	23,250	40,000	24,000
Midwest	107	16	9	25	22,000	17,000	32,250	34,000	26,659	25,756	26,334	26,750	25,000	26,500
Southwest	26	18	2	20	20,000	23,000	35,000	28,200	26,882	25,600	26,753	27,635	25,600	27,435
West	62	30	2	32	20,000	25,000	41,000	29,000	31,214	27,000	30,095	31,250	27,000	31,000
All schools	371	106	21	127	17,000	17,000	43,500	40,000	28,452	27,271	28,257	27,605	26,500	27,500
Other libraries														
Northeast	53	9	4	13	21,000	23,400	52,000	31,400	31,444	26,925	30,054	30,000	26,450	29,000
Southeast	21	3	3	6	23,000	22,000	29,000	32,280	25,493	27,427	26,460	24,480	28,000	26,240
Midwest	23	2	0	2	17,900	—	22,000	—	19,950	—	19,950	19,950	—	19,950
Southwest	10	5	2	7	19,800	28,000	43,800	30,000	27,820	29,000	28,157	25,000	29,000	25,000
West	17	4	3	7	20,779	28,000	38,000	37,000	31,570	31,667	31,611	33,750	30,000	32,500
All schools	124	23	12	35	17,900	22,000	52,000	37,000	28,903	28,582	28,793	27,000	28,000	28,000

Accredited Master's Programs in Library and Information Studies

This list of graduate programs accredited by the American Library Association was issued in fall 1993. The list of accredited programs is updated semiannually in the spring and fall and is available from the ALA Committee on Accreditation. A list of more than 200 institutions offering both accredited and nonaccredited programs in librarianship appears in the forty-sixth edition of the *American Library Directory* (R. R. Bowker, 1993).

Northeast: Conn., D.C., Md., Mass., N.J., N.Y., Pa., R.I.

Catholic University of America, School of Lib. and Info. Science, Washington, DC 20064. Jean L. Preer, Acting Dean. 202-319-5085.

Clarion University of Pennsylvania, College of Communication, Computer Info. Science, and Lib. Science, Clarion, PA 16214. Rita Rice Flaningam, Dean. 814-226-2328.

Drexel University, College of Info. Studies, Philadelphia, PA 19104. Richard H. Lytle, Dean. 215-895-2474.

Long Island University, Palmer School of Lib. and Info. Science, Brookville, NY 11548. Anne Woodsworth, Dean. 516-299-2856.

Pratt Institute, School of Info. and Lib. Science, Brooklyn, NY 11205. S. M. Matta, Dean. 718-636-3702.

Queens College, City University of New York, Grad. School of Lib. and Info. Studies, 254 Rosenthal Lib., Flushing, NY 11367. Marianne Cooper, Dir. 718-997-3790.

Rutgers University, School of Communication, Info., and Lib. Studies, 4 Huntington St., New Brunswick, NJ 08903. Betty J. Turock, Chair and Program Dir. 908-932-7917.

Saint John's University, Div. of Lib. and Info. Science, Jamaica, NY 11439. James A. Benson, Dir. 718-990-6200.

Simmons College, Grad. School of Lib. and Info. Science, Boston, MA 02115-5898. Robert D. Stueart, Dean. 617-738-2225.

Southern Connecticut State University, School of Lib. Science and Instructional Technology, New Haven, CT 06515. Edward C. Harris, Dean. 203-397-4532.

State University of New York at Albany, School of Info. Science and Policy, Albany, NY 12222. 518-442-5115.

State University of New York at Buffalo, School of Info. and Lib. Studies, Buffalo, NY 14260. George S. Bobinski, Dean. 716-645-2412.

Syracuse University, School of Info. Studies, 4-206 Center for Science and Technology, Syracuse, NY 13244-4100. Donald A. Marchand, Dean. 315-443-2911.

University of Maryland, College of Lib. and Info. Services, College Park, MD 20742. Ann E. Prentice, Dean. 301-405-2033.

University of Pittsburgh, School of Lib. and Info. Science, Pittsburgh, PA 15260. Toni Carbo Bearman, Dean. 412-624-5230.

University of Rhode Island, Grad. School of Lib. and Info. Studies, Rodman Hall, Kingston, RI 02881-0815. Elizabeth Futas, Dir. 401-792-2947.

Southeast: Ala., Fla., Ga., Ky., La., Miss., N.C., S.C., Tenn., P.R.

Clark Atlanta University, School of Lib. and Info. Studies, Atlanta, GA 30314. Charles D. Churchwell, Dean. 404-880-8697.

Florida State University, School of Lib. and Info. Studies, R106, Tallahassee, FL 32306-2048. F. William Summers, Dean. 904-644-5775.

Louisiana State University, School of Lib. and Info. Science, Baton Rouge, LA 70803. Bert R. Boyce, Dean. 504-388-3158.

North Carolina Central University, School of Lib. and Info. Sciences, Durham, NC 27707. Benjamin F. Speller, Jr., Dean. 919-560-6485.

University of Alabama, School of Lib. and Info. Studies, Tuscaloosa, AL 35487-0252. Philip M. Turner, Dean. 205-348-4610.

University of Kentucky, School of Lib. and Info. Science, Lexington, KY 40506-0039. Thomas J. Waldhart, Dir. 606-257-8876.

University of North Carolina, School of Info. and Lib. Science, Chapel Hill, NC 27599-3360. Barbara B. Moran, Dean. 919-962-8366.

University of North Carolina at Greensboro, Dept. of Lib. and Info. Studies, Greensboro, NC 27412. Marilyn L. Miller, Chair. 919-334-5100.

University of Puerto Rico, Escuela Graduada de Bibliotecologia y Ciencia de la Información, San Juan, PR 00931. Annie F. Thompson, Dir. 809-763-6199.

University of South Carolina, College of Lib. and Info. Science, Columbia, SC 29208. Fred W. Roper, Dean. 803-777-3858.

University of South Florida, Div. of Lib. and Info. Science, Tampa, FL 33620-7800. Kathleen de la Peña McCook, Dir. 813-974-3520.

University of Southern Mississippi, School of Lib. and Info. Science, Hattiesburg, MS 39406. Joy Greiner, Dir. 601-266-4228.

University of Tennessee, Knoxville, Grad. School of Lib. and Info. Science, Knoxville, TN 37996-4330. José-Marie Griffiths, Dir. 615-974-2148.

Midwest: Ill., Ind., Iowa, Kan., Mich., Mo., Ohio, Wis.

Emporia State University, School of Lib. and Info. Management, Emporia, KS 66801. Martha L. Hale, Dean. 316-341-5203.

Indiana University, School of Lib. and Info. Science, Bloomington, IN 47405. Blaise Cronin, Dean. 812-855-2848.

Kent State University, School of Lib. and Info. Science, Kent, OH 44242. Rosemary R. DuMont, Dean. 216-672-2782.

Northern Illinois University, Dept. of Lib. and Info. Studies, DeKalb, IL 60115. Cosette N. Kies, Chair. 815-753-1733.

Rosary College, Grad. School of Lib. and Info. Science, River Forest, IL 60305. Michael E. D. Koenig, Dean. 708-524-6844.

University of Illinois, Grad. School of Lib. and Info. Science, 1407 W. Gregory, 410 DKH, Urbana, IL 61801-3680. Leigh Estabrook, Dean. 217-333-3281.

University of Iowa, School of Lib. and Info. Science, Iowa City, IA 52242-1420. Carl F. Orgren, Dir. 319-335-5707.

University of Michigan, School of Info. and Lib. Studies, Ann Arbor, MI 48109-1092. Daniel E. Atkins, Dean. 313-764-9376.

University of Missouri, School of Lib. and Info. Science, Columbia, MO 65211. Mary F. Lenox, Dean. 314-882-4546.

University of Wisconsin–Madison, School of Lib. and Info. Studies, Madison, WI 53706. Jane B. Robbins, Dir. 608-263-2900.

University of Wisconsin–Milwaukee, School of Lib. and Info. Science, Milwaukee, WI 53201. Mohammed M. Aman, Dean. 414-229-4707.

Wayne State University, Lib. and Info. Science Program, Detroit, MI 48202. Joseph J. Mika, Dir. 313-577-1825.

Southwest: Ariz., Okla., Tex.

Texas Woman's University, School of Lib. and Info. Studies, Denton, TX 76204-0905. Keith Swigger, Dean. 817-898-2602.

University of Arizona, School of Lib. Science, Tucson, AZ 85719. Charlie D. Hurt, Dir. 602-621-3565.

University of North Texas, School of Lib. and Info. Sciences, Denton, TX 76203. Raymond F. von Dran, Dean. 817-565-2445.

University of Oklahoma, School of Lib. and Info. Studies, Norman, OK 73019. June Lester, Dir. 405-325-3921.

University of Texas at Austin, Grad. School of Lib. and Info. Science, Austin, TX 78712-1276. Brooke E. Sheldon, Dean. 512-471-3821.

West: Calif., Hawaii, Wash.

San Jose State University, School of Lib. and Info. Science, San Jose, CA 95192-0029. Stuart A. Sutton, Dir. 408-924-2492.

University of California at Berkeley, School of Lib. and Info. Studies, Berkeley, CA 94720. Nancy Van House, Acting Dean. 510-642-9980.

University of California at Los Angeles, Grad. School of Lib. and Info. Science, Los Angeles, CA 90024-1520. Beverly P. Lynch, Dean. 310-825-8799.

University of Hawaii, School of Lib. and Info. Studies, Honolulu, HI 96822. Miles M. Jackson, Dean. 808-956-7321.

University of Washington, Grad. School of Lib. and Info. Science, Seattle, WA 98195. Phyllis Van Orden, Dir. 206-543-1794.

Canada

Dalhousie University, School of Lib. and Info. Studies, Halifax, NS B3H 4H8. Mary Dykstra, Dir. 902-494-3656.

McGill University, Grad. School of Lib. and Info. Studies, Montreal, PQ H3A 1Y1. J. Andrew Large, Dir. 514-398-4204.

Université de Montréal, Ecole de Bibliotheconomie et des Sciences de l'Information, Montreal, PQ H3C 3J7. Marcel Lajeunesse, Dir. 514-343-6044.

University of Alberta, School of Lib. and Info. Studies, Edmonton, Sheila Bertram, Dir. 403-492-4578.

University of British Columbia, School of Lib., Archival, and Info. Studies, Vancouver, BC V6T 1Z1. Ken Haycock, Dir. 604-822-2404.

University of Toronto, Faculty of Lib. and Info. Science, Toronto, ON M5S 1A1. Adele M. Fasick, Dean. 416-978-3234.

University of Western Ontario, School of Lib. and Info. Science, London, ON N6G 1H1. Jean Tague-Sutcliffe, Dean. 519-661-3542.

Library Scholarship Sources

For a more complete list of scholarships, fellowships, and assistantships offered for library study, see *Financial Assistance for Library and Information Studies,* published annually by the American Library Association.

American Association of Law Libraries. (1) A varying number of scholarships of a minimum of $1,000 for graduates of an accredited law school who are degree candidates in an accredited library school; (2) a varying number of scholarships of varying amounts for library school graduates working on a law degree, nonlaw graduates enrolled in an accredited library school, and law librarians taking a course related to law librarianship; (3) a stipend of $3,500 for an experienced minority librarian working toward an advanced degree to further a law library career. For information, write to: Scholarship Committee, AALL, 53 W. Jackson Blvd., Suite 940, Chicago, IL 60604.

American Library Association. (1) The David

H. Clift Scholarships of $3,000 for a varying number of U.S. or Canadian citizens who have been admitted to accredited library schools. For information, write to: Staff Liaison, Clift Scholarship Jury, ALA, 50 E. Huron St., Chicago, IL 60611; (2) the Tom C. Drewes Scholarships of $3,000 for a varying number of support staff currently working in libraries. For information, write to Staff Liaison, Drewes Scholarship Jury, ALA, 50 E. Huron St., Chicago, IL 60611; (3) the Louise Giles Minority Scholarship of $3,000 for a varying number of minority students who are U.S. or Canadian citizens and have been admitted to accredited library schools. For information, write to: Staff Liaison, Giles Minority Scholarship Jury, ALA, 50 E.

Huron St., Chicago, IL 60611; (4) the Miriam L. Hornback Scholarship of $3,000 for a varying number of ALA support staff or support staff currently working in a library. For information, write to: Staff Liaison, Hornback Scholarship Jury, ALA, 50 E. Huron St., Chicago, IL 60611.

ALA/American Association of School Librarians. The AASL School Librarians Workshop Scholarship of $2,500 for a candidate admitted to a full-time ALA-accredited MLS or school library media program. For information, write to: AASL/ALA, 50 E. Huron St., Chicago, IL 60611.

ALA/Association for Library Service to Children. (1) The Bound to Stay Bound Books Scholarship of $2,500 for two students who are U.S. or Canadian citizens and who have been admitted to an ALA-accredited program who will work with children in a library for one year after graduation; (2) the Frederic G. Melcher Scholarship of $5,000 each for two U.S. or Canadian citizens admitted to an accredited library school who plan to work with children in school or public libraries for two years after graduation. For information, write to: Exec. Dir., ALSC, ALA, 50 E. Huron St., Chicago, IL 60611.

ALA/Association of College and Research Libraries and the Institute for Scientific Information. (1) The ACRL Doctoral Dissertation Fellowship of $1,000 for a student who has completed all coursework in the area of academic librarianship; (2) the Samuel Lazerow Fellowship of $1,000 for research in acquisitions or technical services in an academic or research library; (3) the ACRL and Martinus Nijhoff International West European Specialist Study Grant pays travel expenses, room, and board for a ten-day trip to the Netherlands and two other European countries for an ALA member. Selection based on proposal outlining purpose of trip. For information, write to: Althea Jenkins, ACRL/ALA, 50 E. Huron St., Chicago, IL 60611.

ALA/International Relations Committee. The Bogle International Library Travel Fund grant of $500 for a varying number of ALA members to attend a first international conference. For information, write to: Robert P. Doyle, ALA, 50 E. Huron St., Chicago, IL 60611.

ALA/Library and Information Technology Association. Two LITA Scholarships in Library and Information Technology of $2,500 each for students (one of whom is a minority student) who have been admitted to an ALA-accredited program in library automation and information science. For information, write to: LITA/ALA, 50 E. Huron St., Chicago, IL 60611.

ALA/New Members Round Table. NRMT/EBSCO Scholarship of $1,000 for a U.S. or Canadian citizen and member of the ALA New Members Round Table. Based on financial need and professional goals. For information, write to: Paula Hering, Warren County Community College Lib., Rte. 57 W., Box 55A, Washington, NJ 07882.

ALA/Public Library Association. The New Leaders Travel Grant Study Award of up to $1,500 for a varying number of PLA members with five years' or less experience. For information, write to: PLA/ALA, 50 E. Huron St., Chicago, IL 60611.

American-Scandinavian Foundation. Fellowships and grants for 25 to 30 students, in amounts from $2,500 to $15,000, for advanced study in Denmark, Finland, Iceland, Norway, or Sweden. For information, write to: Exchange Div., American-Scandinavian Foundation, 725 Park Ave., New York, NY 10021.

Association for Library and Information Science Education. (1) A varying number of research grants of up to $2,500 for members of ALISE; and (2) the Jane Anne Hannigan Research Award of $500 for an untenured faculty member or doctoral student. For information, write to: Exec. Dir., ALISE, 4101 Lake Boone Trail, Raleigh, NC 27607.

Association of Jewish Libraries. The May K. Simon Memorial Scholarship Fund offers a varying number of scholarships of at least $500 each for MLS students who plan to work as Judaica librarians. For information, write to: Sharona R. Wachs, AJL, 1000 Washington Ave., Albany, NY 12203.

Association of Seventh-Day Adventist Librarians. The D. Glenn Hilts Scholarship of $1,000 to a member of the Seventh-Day Adventist Church in a graduate library program. For information, contact: Ms. Foutz, Assn. of Seventh-Day Adventist Libns., 3800 S. 48 St., Lincoln, NE 68506.

Beta Phi Mu. (1) The Sarah Rebecca Reed Scholarship of $1,500 for a person accepted in an ALA-accredited library program; (2) the Frank B. Sessa Scholarship of $750 for a Beta Phi Mu member for continuing education; (3) the Harold Lancour Scholarship of $1,000 for study in a foreign country related to the applicant's work or schooling. For information, write to: Exec. Secy., Beta Phi Mu, School of Lib. and Info. Science, Univ. of Pittsburgh, Pittsburgh, PA 15260.

Canadian Association of Law Libraries. The Diana M. Priestly Scholarship of $2,000 for a student with previous law experience or for entry to an approved Canadian law school or accredited Canadian library school. For information, contact: Suzan Hebditch, Chair, Scholarship Committee, Canada Department of Justice, 928 Royal Trust Tower, Edmonton, AB T5J 2Z2.

Canadian Library Association. The Howard V. Phalin–World Book Graduate Scholarship in Library Science of $2,500, the CLA Dafoe Scholarship of $1,750, and the H. W. Wilson Foundation Scholarship of $2,000 are each given to a Canadian citizen or landed immigrant to attend an accredited Canadian library school; the Phalin scholarship can also be used for an accredited U.S. school. For information, write to: CLA Membership Services Department, Scholarships and Awards Committee, CLA, 200 Elgin St., Suite 602, Ottawa, ON K2P 1L5, Canada.

Catholic Library Association. The World Book, Inc., Grant of $1,500 divided among no more than four recipients for workshops, institutes, etc. Open to CLA members only. For information, write to: Jean R. Bostley, SSJ Scholarship Committee, St. Joseph Central High School Lib., 22 Maplewood Ave., Pittsfield, MA 01201.

Chinese-American Librarians Association. The Sheila Suen Lai Scholarship of $500 for a Chinese descendant who has been

accepted in an ALA-accredited program. For information, write to: Ling H. Jeng, 3773 Belleau Wood Dr., Lexington, KY 40517-1804.

Church and Synagogue Library Association. The Muriel Fuller Memorial Scholarship of $131.54 for a correspondence course offered by the Univ. of Utah Continuing Education Div. Open to CSLA members only. For information, write to: CSLA, Box 19357, Portland, OR 97280-0357.

Massachusetts Black Librarians' Network Scholarship of at least $500 for a minority student entering an accredited master's program in library science with no more than 12 semester hours toward a degree. For information, write to: Pearl Mosley, Chair, MBLN, 27 Beech Glen St., Roxbury, MA 02119.

Medical Library Association. (1) A scholarship of $2,000 for a person entering an ALA-accredited library program, with at least one half of the program yet to be completed; (2) a scholarship of $2,000 for a minority student for graduate study; (3) a varying number of Research, Development and Demonstration Project grants of $100–$500 for U.S. or Canadian citizens who are ALA members; (4) continuing education awards of $100–$500 for U.S. or Canadian citizens who are ALA members; (5) the Cunningham Memorial International Fellowship of $3,000 plus travel expenses for a foreign student for postgraduate study in the United States; (6) the MLA Doctoral Fellowship of $1,000 for postgraduate work in medical librarianship or information science. For information, write to: Professional Service Area, MLA, Suite 300, 6 N. Michigan Ave., Chicago, IL 60602.

Mountain Plains Library Association. (1) A varying number of grants of up to $600 each; and (2) a varying number of grants of up to $150 each for MPLA members with at least two years of membership for continuing education. For information, write to: Joseph R. Edelen Jr., MPLA Exec. Secy., Univ. of South Dakota, I. D. Weeks Lib., Vermillion, SD 57069.

REFORMA, the National Association to Promote Library Services to the Spanish-Speaking. A varying number of scholarships of $1,000 each to attend an ALA-accredited program. For information, write to: Orlando Archibeque, Auraria Lib., Univ. of Colorado, Lawrence at 11 St., Campus Box 101, Denver, CO 80204.

Society of American Archivists. The Colonial Dames Awards, two grants of $1,200 each for specific types of repositories and collections. For information, write to: SAA, 600 S. Federal, Suite 504, Chicago, IL 60605.

Southern Regional Education Board. (1) A varying number of grants of varying amounts to cover in-state tuition for residents of Arkansas, Georgia, Kentucky, Louisiana, Maryland, Mississippi, Oklahoma, South Carolina, Tennessee, Texas, Virginia, and West Virginia, for graduate or postgraduate study in an accredited library school. For information, write to: SREB, 592 Tenth St. N.W., Atlanta, GA 30318-5790.

Special Libraries Association. (1) Two $6,000 scholarships for students interested in special libraries; (2) the Plenum Scholarship of $1,000 and (3) the ISI Scholarship of $1,000, also for students interested in special library work; (4) the Affirmative Action Scholarships of $6,000 each for two minority students interested in special library work. For information, write to: Laura Devlin, Manager of Membership Development, SLA, 1700 18th St. N.W., Washington, DC 20009; (5) two Pharmaceutical Division Stipend Awards of $750 and $250 for students with an undergraduate degree in chemistry, life science, or pharmacy entering or enrolled in an ALA-accredited program. For information, write to: Susan E. Katz, Awards Chair, Knoll Pharmaceuticals Science Information Center, 30 N. Jefferson St., Whippany, NJ 07981.

Library Scholarship and Award Recipients, 1993

Library awards are listed by organization. An index listing awards alphabetically by title follows this section.

American Association of Law Libraries (AALL)

AALL Scholarships. *Offered by:* AALL; Matthew Bender & Company; Columbia University Law School Library; Information America; Mead Data Central; Thomson Professional Publishing; and/or West Publishing Company. *Winners:* (Type I: Library Degree for Law School Graduates) Melinda Elder, Annette Klingman, Sandra Lamar, Margaret Martinke, Mary Mulligan, Diane Murley, Billie Olson, Lisa Peters, Susan Sokoll, Cheryl Stephen, Veyis Sucsuz, Melanie Williamson, Elizabeth Woodruff; (Type II: Law Degree for Library School Graduates) Kevin Gray, Barbara Morgan; (Type III: Library Degree for Non–Law School Graduates) Linda Baltrush, Michael Brantley, Sandra Deane, Tracy Fritz, Mark Heutmaker,

Robert King, Holly Mohler, Laura Weidig; (Type IV: Meira Pimsleur Scholarship) Melinda Elder; (Type V: George A. Strait Minority Stipend) Evelyn Marie Campbell, Iris Lee, Charlcie Pettway, Alicia Randolph, Dan Wong.

Joseph L. Andrews Bibliographical Award. For significant contribution to legal bibliographical literature. *Winner:* Jürgen Christoph Gödan for *International Legal Bibliographies: A Worldwide Guide and Critique,* trans. by John F. Pickron (Transnational Publishers, 1992).

Marian Gould Gallagher Distinguished Service Award. To recognize extended and sustained service to law librarianship, for exemplary service to the association, or for contributions to the professional literature.

Winners: Jane L. Hammond, Blanka Kudej.

Law Library Journal Article of the Year Award. *Winner:* Katherine Topulos, for "A Common Lawyer's Bookshelf Recreated: An Annotated Bibliography of a Collection of Sixteenth Century English Law Books," *Law Library Journal* 641 (Fall 1992).

Law Library Publication Award. To recognize achievements in in-house, user-oriented library materials that are outstanding in quality and significance. *Winners:* (Print) Georgetown University Law Center Library for Law; Massachusetts Trial Court Law Libraries; (Nonprint) Not awarded in 1993.

American Library Association (ALA)

ALA/Meckler Library of the Future Award ($2,500). For a library, consortium, group of librarians, or support organization for information technology in a library setting. *Donor:* Meckler Corporation. *Winner:* Albert R. Mann Library, Cornell Univ.

Hugh C. Atkinson Memorial Award ($2,000). For outstanding achievement (including risk taking) by academic librarians that has contributed significantly to improvements in library automation, management, and/or development or research. *Offered by:* ACRL, ALCTS, LAMA, and LITA divisions. *Winner:* Richard De Gennaro.

Carroll Preston Baber Research Grant ($7,500). For innovative research that could lead to an improvement in library services to any specified group(s) of people. *Donor:* Eric R. Baber. *Winner:* Debra Wilcox Johnson.

Beta Phi Mu Award ($500). For distinguished service in library education. *Donor:* Beta Phi Mu International Library Science Honorary Awards Committee. *Winner:* Kathryn Luther Henderson.

David H. Clift Scholarship ($3,000). To a worthy U.S. or Canadian citizen to begin an MLS degree in an ALA-accredited program. *Donor:* Scholarship endowment

interest. *Winners:* Marylou Hale, Karyn F. Everham.

Melvil Dewey Medal. To an individual or group for recent creative professional achievement in library management, training, cataloging and classification, and the tools and techniques of librarianship. *Donor:* OCLC/Forest Press Inc. Not awarded in 1993.

EBSCO ALA Conference Sponsorships. To allow librarians to attend ALA's Midwinter Meetings and Annual Conferences. *Donor:* EBSCO. *Winners:* Faith Brautigan, Mary Hedrick, Eva D. Poole, Burley J. Scales, Ann Sparanese.

Equality Award ($500). To an individual or group for an outstanding contribution that promotes equality of women and men in the library profession. *Donor:* Scarecrow Press. *Winner:* Patricia Glass Schuman.

Loleta D. Fyan Award ($10,000). For projects in public library development. *Winner:* Franklin Lakes (NJ) Free Public Library.

Gale Research Company Financial Development Award ($2,500). To a library organization for a financial development project to secure new funding resources for a public or academic library. *Donor:* Gale Research Company. *Winner:* Mazomanie (WI) Free Library.

Grolier Foundation Award ($1,000). For stimulation and guidance of reading by children and young people. *Donor:* Grolier Foundation. *Winner:* Michael L. Printz.

G. K. Hall Award for Library Literature ($500). For outstanding contribution to library literature issued during the three years preceding presentation. *Donor:* G. K. Hall & Company. *Winner:* James Rettig for *Distinguished Classics of Reference Publishing* (Oryx Press).

Honorary ALA Membership. *Winner:* Robert Vosper.

Tony Leisner Scholarship ($3,000). For a library support staff person to enter a master's library program. *Winner:* Patricia Anne Scott.

Joseph W. Lippincott Award ($1,000). To a librarian for distinguished service to the profession. *Donor:* Joseph W. Lippincott, Jr. *Winner:* John G. Lorenz.

Bessie Boehm Moore Award ($1,000). Presented to a public library that has developed an outstanding and creative program for public library services to the aging. *Donor:* Bessie Boehm Moore. *Winner:* Salem (OR) Public Library.

Herbert W. Putnam Honor Award ($500). To an American librarian of outstanding ability for travel, writing, or other use to improve service to the library profession or society. No award until 1996.

H. W. Wilson Library Periodical Award ($1,000). To a library, library group, or association for a periodical making a contribution to librarianship. *Donor:* H. W. Wilson Company. *Winner:* Pacific Northwest Library Association for *PNLA Quarterly,* ed. by Katherine Eaton.

H. W. Wilson Library Staff Development Grant ($2,500). To a library organization for a program to further its goals and objectives. *Donor:* H. W. Wilson Company. *Winner:* DeKalb County (GA) Public Library.

World Book–ALA Goal Awards ($8,000). To ALA units for the advancement of public, academic, or school library service and librarianship through support of programs that implement the goals and priorities of ALA. *Donor:* World Book Inc. *Winner:* ALA's Young Adult Library Services Association (YALSA) for their project "Serving the Underserved: Customer Services for Young Adults."

American Association of School Librarians (AASL)

AASL ABC/Clio Leadership Grant (up to $1,750). For planning and implementing leadership programs at state, regional, or local levels to be given to school library associations that are affiliates of AASL. *Donor:* ABC/Clio. *Winner:* Massachusetts School Library Media Association.

AASL Information Plus Continuing Education Scholarship ($500). To a school library media specialist, supervisor, or educator to attend an ALA or AASL continuing education event. *Donor:* Information Plus. Not awarded in 1993.

AASL Intellectual Freedom Award ($2,000 to recipient, $1,000 to media center of recipient's choice). For a school library media specialist who has upheld principles of intellectual freedom. *Donor:* Social Issues Resources Series Inc. (SIRS). *Winner:* Jean Kern.

AASL School Librarians Workshop Scholarship ($2,500). To a full-time student preparing to become a school library media specialist at the preschool, elementary, or secondary level. *Donor:* Library Learning Resources Company. *Winner:* Julia Moysich.

Distinguished School Administrators Award, AASL/SIRS ($2,000). For expanding the role of the library in elementary and/or secondary school education. *Donor:* Social Issues Resources Series Inc. (SIRS). *Winner:* Susan Robinson.

Distinguished Service Award, AASL/Baker & Taylor ($3,000). For outstanding contributions to librarianship and school library development. *Donor:* Baker & Taylor Books. *Winner:* Marilyn Miller.

"Emergency Librarian" Publication Award ($500). For an outstanding publication in school librarianship to be given to a school library association affiliated to AASL. *Donor: Emergency Librarian. Winner: Ohio Media Spectrum.*

Frances Henne Award ($1,250). To a school library media specialist with five or fewer years in the profession to attend an AASL regional conference or ALA Annual Conference for the first time. *Donor:* R. R. Bowker Company. *Winner:* Susan Elizabeth Bucko.

Microcomputer in the Media Center Award ($1,000 to the specialist and $500 to the library). To library media specialists for innovative approaches to microcomputer applications in the school library media center. *Donor:* Follett Software Company. *Winner:* Pamela Hill.

National School Library Media Program of the Year Award (up to $3,000). To school districts and a single school, for excellence and innovation in outstanding library media programs. *Donor:* Encyclopaedia Britannica Educational Corporation. *Winners:* (Single School District) Not awarded in 1993; (Small School District) Indian

Prairie #204, Naperville, IL; (Large School District) Blue Valley #229, Overland Park, KS.

American Library Trustee Association (ALTA)

ALTA/Gale Outstanding Trustee Conference Grant Award ($750). *Donor:* Gale Research Company. *Winners:* Elaine M. Melisi, Patricia S. Baur.

ALTA Major Benefactors Honor Award. To individual(s), families, or corporate bodies who have made major benefactions to public libraries. *Winners:* Charles and Philip Bosserman.

Literacy Award. To a library trustee or an individual who in a volunteer capacity has made a significant contribution to addressing the illiteracy problem in the United States. Not awarded in 1993.

Trustee Citations. To recognize public library trustees for individual service to library development on the local, state, regional, or national level. *Winners:* Charlotte M. Forgeron and J. A. (Jake) Killian.

Armed Forces Libraries Round Table

Armed Forces Library Achievement Citation. For contributions toward development of interest in libraries and reading in armed forces library service and organizations. Candidates must be members of the Armed Forces Libraries Round Table. *Winner:* Marlow Peters.

Armed Forces Library Certificate of Merit. To librarians or "friends" who are members of AFLRT who provide an exemplary program to an Armed Forces library. *Winner:* Edwin Williams.

Armed Forces Library Newsbank Scholarship Award ($1,000 to the school of the recipient's choice). To members of the Armed Forces Libraries Round Table who have given exemplary service in the area of library support for off-duty education programs in the armed forces. *Donor:* Newsbank Inc. *Winner:* Marion Fontish.

Association for Library Collections and Technical Services (ALCTS)

Hugh C. Atkinson Memorial Award. *See under* American Library Association.

Best of "LRTS" Award. To the author(s) of the best paper published each year in the division's official journal. *Winner:* Ross Atkinson for "The Acquisitions Librarian as Change Agent in the Transition to the Electronic Library," *Library Resources and Technical Services* 36, no. 1 (January 1992): 7–20.

Margaret Mann Citation. To a cataloger or classifier for achievement in the areas of cataloging or classification. *Winner:* Janet Swan Hill.

Esther J. Piercy Award ($1,500). To a librarian with fewer than ten years' experience for contributions and leadership in the field of library collections and technical services. *Donor:* Yankee Book Peddler. *Winner:* Barbara A. Winters.

Resources Section

Blackwell/North America Scholarship Award. To the author(s) of an outstanding monograph, published article, or original paper on acquisitions, collection development, or areas of resources development in libraries ($2,000 to library school of winner's choice). *Donor:* Blackwell/North America. *Winner:* Ann L. Okerson for "With Feathers: Effects of Copyright and Ownership on Scholarly Publishing" in *College and Research Libraries,* 52, no. 5 (September 1991): 425–438.

Serials Section

Bowker/Ulrich's Serials Librarianship Award ($1,500). For contribution to serials librarianship in areas of professional association, participation, library education, serials literature, research, or development of tools leading to better understanding. *Donor:* R. R. Bowker Company/Ulrich's. *Winner:* Ann L. Okerson.

First Step Award, Serials Section/Wiley Professional Development Grant ($1,500). For librarians new to the serials field to attend

ALA's Annual Conference. *Donor:* John Wiley & Sons. *Winner:* Christa Easton.

Association for Library Service to Children (ALSC)

ALSC/Book Wholesalers Summer Reading Program Grant ($3,000). To an ALSC member for implementation of an outstanding public library summer reading program for children. *Donor:* Book Wholesalers Inc. *Winner:* Hurst Public Library.

ALSC/Econo-Clad Literature Program Award ($1,000). To an ALSC member who has developed and implemented an outstanding library program for children involving reading and the use of literature, to attend an ALA conference. *Donor:* Econo-Clad Books. *Winner:* Margaret Serpico, J. F. Kennedy Library.

May Hill Arbuthnot Lecturer for 1993. *Winner:* Virginia Hamilton.

Bound to Stay Bound Books Scholarship ($5,000). Two awards for study in the field of library service to children toward the MLS or beyond in an ALA-accredited program. *Donor:* Bound to Stay Bound Books. *Winners:* Melissa Zymboly Depper, Janice Marilyn Wall.

Distinguished Service to ALSC Award ($1,000). To recognize significant contributions to, and an impact on, library services to children and/or ALSC. *Winner:* Augusta Baker.

Frederic G. Melcher Scholarship ($5,000). To students entering the field of library service to children for graduate work in an ALA-accredited program. *Winners:* Jon Michael Theisen, Marla Joy Ehlers.

Putnam and Grosset Book Group Awards ($600). To children's librarians in school or public libraries with ten or fewer years of experience to attend ALA Annual Conference for the first time. Must be a member of ALSC. *Donor:* Putnam and Grosset Book Group. *Winners:* Mary Ann Bursk, Kay A. Elliasen, Katherine K. Matsil, Kirsten Jeanne Parrish.

Association of College and Research Libraries (ACRL)

ACRL Academic or Research Librarian of the Year Award ($3,000). For outstanding contribution to academic and research librarianship and library development. *Donor:* Baker & Taylor. *Winner:* William A. Moffett.

ACRL Doctoral Dissertation Fellowship ($1,000). To a doctoral student in the field of academic librarianship whose research indicates originality, creativity, and interest in scholarship. *Winner:* Weijing Yuan.

Hugh C. Atkinson Memorial Award. *See under* American Library Association.

EBSCO Community College Learning Resources Achievement Awards ($500). Two awards to individuals, groups, or institutions to recognize significant achievement in the areas of programs and leadership. *Donor:* EBSCO Subscription Services. *Winners:* Lois Mariott, Gloria Terwilliger.

Samuel Lazerow Fellowship for Research in Acquisitions or Technical Services ($1,000). To foster advances in acquisitions or technical services by providing librarians a fellowship for travel or writing in those fields. *Sponsor:* Institute for Scientific Information (ISI). Not awarded in 1993.

Katharine Kyes Leab and Daniel J. Leab *American Book Prices Current* Exhibition Catalogue Awards. For the three best catalogs published by American or Canadian institutions in conjunction with exhibitions of books and/or manuscripts. *Winners:* (First Division) "Encountering the New World 1493–1800," John Carter Brown Library; (Second Division) "Evolution of the Heart," Thomas Fisher Rare Book Library, University of Toronto; (Third Division) "Ties That Bind: Communities in American History," National Archives.

Martinus Nijhoff International West European Specialist Study Grant. Supports research pertaining to West European studies, librarianship, or the book trade. Focus on acquisitions, organization, or use of library materials. *Sponsor:* Martinus Nijhoff International. Not awarded in 1993.

Oberly Award for Bibliography in the Agricultural Sciences. For the best English-language bibliography in the field of agriculture or a related science in the preceding two-year period. *Donor:* Eunice R. Oberly Fund. *Winner:* Albert H. Joy.

K. G. Saur Award for Best *College and Research Libraries* Article ($500 to each author). To author(s) to recognize the most outstanding article published in *College and Research Libraries* during the preceding year. *Donor:* K. G. Saur. *Winners:* Peter Hernon and Cheryl Metoyer-Duran; Charles B. Lowry.

Bibliographic Instruction Section (BIS)

Bibliographic Instruction Publication of the Year Award. *Winners:* Terrence F. Mech, Donald W. Farmer.

Miriam Dudley Bibliographic Instruction Librarian Award ($1,000). For contribution to the advancement of bibliographic instruction in a college or research institution. *Donor:* Mountainside Publishing. *Winner:* Hannelore Rader.

Association of Specialized and Cooperative Library Agencies (ASCLA)

ASCLA Exceptional Service Award. To recognize effective programming, pioneering activity, or significant research in service to special populations. *Winner:* Rhea Joyce Rubin.

ASCLA Leadership Achievement Award. To recognize leadership and achievement in the areas of consulting, multitype library cooperation, and state library development. *Winner:* Keith Michael Fiels.

ASCLA/National Organization on Disability Award. To institutions or organizations that have made the library's total service more accessible through changing physical and/or additional barriers. *Donor:* National Organization on Disability, funded by J. C. Penney. *Winner:* Pioneer Library System, Newark, N.Y.

ASCLA Professional Achievement Award. For professional achievement within the areas of consulting, networking, statewide services and programs. *Winner:* Laurence A. Miller.

ASCLA Service Award. For outstanding service and leadership to the division. *Winner:* Lorraine E. Summers.

Section on Library Service to the Blind and Physically Handicapped

Francis Joseph Campbell Citation. For contribution of recognized importance to library service for the blind and physically handicapped. *Winner:* Mary A. Roatch.

Federal Librarians Round Table (FLRT)

Federal Librarians Achievement Award. For leadership or achievement in the promotion of library and information science in the federal community. Not awarded in 1993.

Government Documents Round Table (GODORT)

James Bennett Childs Award. To a librarian or other individual for distinguished lifetime contributions to documents librarianship. Not awarded in 1993.

CIS/GODORT/ALA Documents to the People Award ($2,000). To an individual, library, organization, or noncommercial group that most effectively encourages or enhances the use of government documents in library services. *Donor:* Congressional Information Service Inc. (CIS). *Winner:* Susan Tulis.

Readex/GODORT/ALA Catharine J. Reynolds Award ($2,000). Grants to documents librarians for travel and/or study in the field of documents librarianship or area of study benefiting performance as documents librarians. *Donor:* Readex Corporation. *Winner:* Kate Lee.

Intellectual Freedom Round Table (IFRT)

John Phillip Immroth Memorial Award for Intellectual Freedom ($500). For notable contribution to intellectual freedom fueled by personal courage. *Winner:* William A. Moffett.

Eli M. Oboler Memorial Award ($1,500). Biennially, to an author of a published work in English, or in English translation dealing with issues, events, questions, or controversies in the area of intellectual freedom. *Donor:* HBW Associates. Not awarded in 1993.

State Program Award ($1,000). To a state library association intellectual freedom committee, state library media association intellectual freedom committee, or state intellectual freedom coalition, for the most successful and creative project during the calendar year. *Donor:* Social Issues Resources Series Inc. (SIRS). *Winner:* Oregon Library Association Intellectual Freedom Committee.

International Relations Committee

Bogle International Library Travel Fund ($500). To ALA member(s) to attend first international conference. *Donor:* Bogle Memorial Fund. *Winner:* Ann Joyner.

John Ames Humphry/OCLC/Forest Press Award ($1,000). To an individual for significant contributions to international librarianship. *Donors:* OCLC/Forest Press. Not awarded in 1993.

Library Administration and Management Association (LAMA)

Hugh C. Atkinson Memorial Award. *See under* American Library Association.

John Cotton Dana Library Public Relations Awards. To libraries or library organizations of all types for public relations programs or special projects ended during the preceding year. *Donor:* H. W. Wilson Company. *Winners:* (Annual Coordinated Public Relations Program) Indiana Library Federation, Nappanee (IN) Public Library; (Public Library Category) Birmingham (AL) Public Library, Brooklyn (NY) Public Library, Columbus (OH) Metropolitan Library, County of Los Angeles Public Library, San Juan Capistrano (CA) Regional Library of the Orange County Public Library System, Orange (CA) Pub-

lic Library, Patchogue-Medford (NY) Library, Worthington (OH) Public Library; (School Library Category) School District of Lancaster (PA); (College and University Category) Indiana University Libraries; (State Library Category) Kentucky Department for Libraries and Archives; (Library Association Category) Palm Beach County Library Association; (Library Consortia Category) Allen Parish Libraries, NOLA Regional Library System; (Recognition of Achievement) Dale B. Canelas, Donald G. Kelsey (Appreciation), Franklyn F. Bright, Lynn Scott Cochrane (Special Thanks).

AIA/ALA–LAMA Library Buildings Award Program. For excellence in architectural design and planning. *Donors:* American Institute of Architects (AIA) and LAMA. *Winners:* Krochina Architects, Anchorage, Alaska, for Hope (AK) Library; CBT/Childs Bertman Tseckares Inc., Boston, Massachusetts, for Parlin Memorial Library, Everett, Massachusetts; David W. Osler Associates, Ann Arbor, Michigan, for Howell (MI) Carnegie District Library; Schwartz/Silver Architects, Boston, Massachusetts, for Library of Art, Architecture and Planning, Massachusetts Institute of Technology; Koetter, Kim & Associates Inc., Boston, Massachusetts, for Harvey Firestone Library, Princeton, N.J.; Esherick, Homsey, Dodge and Davis, San Francisco, California, for Science Library, University of California at Santa Cruz; Shepley Bulfinch Richardson and Abbott, Boston, Massachusetts, for Library and Science Complex, Albuquerque (NM) Academy; Hodgetts and Fung Design Associates, Santa Monica, California, for Powell Library Staging Facility, University of California, Los Angeles.

Library and Information Technology Association (LITA)

Hugh C. Atkinson Memorial Award. *See under* American Library Association.

LITA/CLSI Scholarship in Library and Information Technology ($2,500). *Winner:* Mary Farris.

LITA/Gaylord Award for Achievement in Library and Information Technology ($1,000). For achievement in library and information technology. *Donor:* Gaylord Bros. Inc. *Winner:* Steve Cisler.

LITA/*Library Hi Tech* Award ($1,000). To an individual or institution for a work that shows outstanding communication for continuing education in library and information technology. *Donor:* Pierian Press. *Winner:* Charles W. Bailey.

LITA/OCLC Minority Scholarship in Library and Information Technology ($2,500). To encourage a qualified member of a principal minority group, with a strong commitment to the use of automation in libraries, to enter library automation. *Donor:* OCLC. *Winner:* Shirley Ann Fonseca.

Library History Round Table (LHRT)

Phyllis Dain Library History Dissertation Award ($500). To the author of a dissertation treating the history of books, libraries, librarianship, or information science. Given every two years. *Winner:* Plummer Alston Jones, Jr., for *American Public Library Service to the Immigrant Community, 1876–1948.*

Justin Winsor Prize Essay ($500). To an author of an outstanding essay embodying original historical research on a significant subject of library history. Not awarded in 1993.

Library Research Round Table (LRRT)

Jesse H. Shera Award for Research ($500). For an outstanding and original paper reporting the results of research related to libraries. Not awarded in 1993.

Map and Geography Round Table

MAGERT Honors Award. *Winner:* Helen-Jane Armstrong.

National Library Week Committee

Grolier National Library Week Grant ($2,000). To libraries or library associations of all types for a public awareness campaign in connection with National Library Week in the year the grant is awarded. *Donor:* Grolier Educational Corporation. *Winner:* Grosse Pointe (MI) Public Library.

New Members Round Table (NMRT)

NMRT EBSCO Scholarship ($1,000). To a U.S. or Canadian citizen to begin an MLS degree in an ALA-accredited program. Candidates must be members of NMRT. *Donor:* EBSCO Subscription Services. *Winner:* Pamela Witte.

Shirley Olofson Memorial Award. For individuals to attend their second ALA Annual Conference. *Winner:* Jeannie A. Dilger.

3M/NMRT Professional Development Grant. To NMRT members to encourage professional development and participation in national ALA and NMRT activities. *Donor:* 3M. *Winners:* Ann Patricia Snoeyenbos, Darlene Ada Mahone, Stephanie Lorayne Sterling.

Office for Library Personnel Resources

Louise Giles Minority Scholarship ($3,000). To a worthy U.S. or Canadian minority citizen to begin an MLS degree in an ALA-accredited program. *Donor:* Scholarship endowment interest. *Winners:* Roberta E. Kemp, Fran Martinez-Scott.

Public Library Association (PLA)

Excellence in Small and/or Rural Public Service Award. *Winner:* Kingman (KS) Carnegie Library.

International Study Grant. *Winner:* Linda Payne-Button.

Library Video Award ($1,000). To a public library demonstrating excellence and innovation in library programming with video and the ability to market and promote the use of these services to library users. *Donor:* Baker & Taylor Video. *Winner:* Hempstead (NY) Public Library.

Allie Beth Martin Award ($3,000). Honors a librarian who, in a public library setting, has demonstrated extraordinary range and depth of knowledge about books or other library materials and has distinguished ability to share that knowledge. *Donor:*

Baker & Taylor Books. *Winner:* Kay K. Martin.

Leonard Wertheimer Multilingual Public Library Service Award ($1,000). To a person, group, or organization for work that enhances and promotes multilingual public library services. *Sponsor:* NTC Publishing Group. Not awarded in 1993.

Adult Lifelong Learning Section

Advancement of Literacy Award. Honors a publisher, bookseller, hardware and/or software dealer, foundation, or similar group that has made a significant contribution to the advancement of adult literacy. *Donor: Library Journal. Winner:* Friends of Literacy through Libraries.

Publishing Committee

Carnegie Reading List Awards (amount varies). To ALA units for preparation and publication of reading lists, indexes, and other bibliographical and library aids useful in U.S. circulating libraries. *Donor:* Andrew Carnegie Fund. *Winners:* American Library Trustee Association (ALTA), $3,550 for "Reading List for Public Library Board Orientation"; Association for Library Service to Children (ALSC), $4,135 for "Book Some Time Together: Books for Intergenerational Reading."

Whitney-Carnegie Awards ($5,000 maximum). For the preparation of bibliographic aids for research, with scholarly intent and general applicability. *Donor:* James Lyman Whitney and Andrew Carnegie Funds. *Winners:* Ana Maria Cobos and Analya Sater for *Latin American Studies: A Core List;* Association for Library Service to Children for *Multicultural Reading List* and *Coping through Books.*

Reference and Adult Services Division (RASD)

Dartmouth Medal. For creating current reference works of outstanding quality and significance. *Donor:* Dartmouth College, Hanover, NH. *Winners: Encyclopedia of Sociology* (Macmillan); (honorable mention) *The Oxford Companion to the English Language* (Oxford Univ. Pr.).

Denali Press Award ($500). For creating reference works of outstanding quality and significance that provide information specifically about ethnic and minority groups in the United States. *Donor:* Denali Press. *Winner:* Lyn Miller-Lachmann for *Our Family, Our Friends, Our World: An Annotated Guide to Significant Multicultural Books for Children and Teenagers* (R. R. Bowker).

Facts on File Grant ($2,000). To a library for imaginative programming that would make current affairs more meaningful to an adult audience. *Donor:* Facts on File Inc. *Winner:* Los Angeles (CA) Public Library.

Margaret E. Monroe Library Adult Services Award. To a librarian for impact on library service to adults. *Winner:* Kathleen Weibel.

Isadore Gilbert Mudge Citation ($1,500). For distinguished contribution to reference librarianship. *Winner:* Andrew M. Hansen.

Reference Service Press Award ($1,000). To the author of the most outstanding article published in *RQ* during the preceding two volume years. *Donor:* Reference Service Press Inc. *Winner:* Lydia Olszak for "Mistakes and Failures at the Reference Desk," *RQ* 31 (Fall 1991): 39–41.

John Sessions Memorial Award. To a library or library system in recognition of work with the labor community. *Donor:* AFL/CIO. *Winner:* Texas Labor Archives, University of Texas at Arlington.

Louis Shores-Oryx Press Award ($1,000). To an individual, team, or organization to recognize excellence in reviewing of books and other materials for libraries. *Donor:* Oryx Press. *Winner:* William Katz.

Business Reference and Services Section (BRASS)

Gale Research Award for Excellence in Business Librarianship/BRASS ($1,000). To an individual for distinguished activities in the field of business librarianship. *Donor:* Gale Research Inc. *Winner:* Lorna Daniells.

Gale Research Award for Excellence in Reference and Adult Services ($1,000). To a library or library system for developing an imaginative and unique library resource to meet patrons' reference needs. *Donor:* Gale Research Inc. *Winner:* Kalamazoo (MI) Public Library.

Social Responsibilities Round Table (SRRT)

SIRS/Peace Award ($500). To honor a library or librarian who has contributed to advancement of knowledge related to issues of international peace. *Donor:* Social Issues Resources Series Inc. (SIRS). *Winner:* The Lion and the Lamb Peace Arts Center of Bluffton, Ohio.

SRRT/Gay and Lesbian Task Force, Gay and Lesbian Book Awards. *Winners: Ceremonies: Prose and Poetry* by Essex Hemphill; *Making History: The Struggle for Gay and Lesbian Equal Rights, 1945–1990* by Eric Marcus.

Young Adult Library Services Association (YALSA)

Baker & Taylor Conference Grants ($750). To young adult librarians in public or school libraries to attend an ALA Annual Conference for the first time. Candidates must be members of YALSA and have one to ten years of library experience. *Donor:* Baker & Taylor Books. *Winners:* Cheryl K. Ward, Janet Ake.

Margaret A. Edwards Award ($1,000). To an author whose book or books have provided young adults with a window through which they can view their world and which will help them to grow and to understand themselves and their role in society. *Donor: School Library Journal. Winner:* M. E. Kerr.

Frances Henne/YALSA/*Voice of Youth Advocates (VOYA)* Research Grant. Not awarded in 1993.

YALSA/Econo-Clad Literature Program Award ($1,000). To a YALSA member for development and implementation of an outstanding program for children involving reading and the use of literature. *Donor:* Econo-Clad Books. *Winner:* Margaret Serpico.

American Society for Information Science (ASIS)

ASIS Award of Merit. For an outstanding contribution to the field of information science. *Winner:* Robert Hayes.

ASIS Best Information Science Book. *Winner:* Samuel Neill.

ASIS Best Information Science Teacher Award ($500). *Winner:* Carol Tenopir.

ASIS Doctoral Forum Award. *Winners:* Dee A. Michel, Margaret Wilkinson, Carol Barry.

ASIS Research Award. For an outstanding research contribution in the field of information science that consists of a systematic program of research in a single study. *Winner:* Howard White.

ASIS Special Award. For contributions outside the everyday activities of information professionals. *Winners:* Robert Kahn, Vinton Cerf.

Cretsos Leadership Award. *Winner:* Amanda Spink.

Watson Davis Award. For a significant long-term contribution to ASIS. *Winner:* Debora Shaw.

ISI Information Science Doctoral Dissertation Scholarship. *Donor:* Institute for Scientific Information (ISI). *Winner:* Sam Gyun Oh.

JASIS Paper Award. For the outstanding paper published in the *Journal of the American Society for Information Science (JASIS). Winner:* Ray Larson.

Art Libraries Society of North America (ARLIS/NA)

Chadwyck-Healey Professional Development Award ($500). To encourage contribution to the society by participating as a moderator, panelist, or presenter of a paper at the ARLIS/NA annual conference. *Winner:* Judy Dyki.

Jim and Anna Emmett Travel Award ($600). To assist information professionals who are physically challenged to participate in the ARLIS/NA annual conference. *Winner:* Karen Genet.

G. K. Hall Conference Attendance Award ($400). To encourage attendance at the annual conference by ARLIS/NA committee members, chapter officers, and moderators. *Winner:* Jeanne Brown.

Howard Karno Travel Award ($500). To provide financial assistance to a professional art librarian from Mexico or Latin America to attend the ARLIS/NA annual conference. *Cosponsor:* Howard Karno Books. *Winner:* Martha Urrunaga.

Léonce Laget Travel Award ($1,000). To provide financial assistance for an art information professional from outside North America to attend the ARLIS/NA annual conference. *Cosponsor:* Librairie Léonce Laget. *Winner:* Gerard Regimbeau.

Fraiser McConnell Travel Award ($500). For members of an ethnic or cultural group under-represented within ARLIS/NA. *Winner:* Mary Hernandez.

David Mirvish Books/Books on Art Travel Award ($500). To encourage art librarianship in Canada. *Winner:* Francoise Roux.

Norman Ross Travel Award. To encourage professional development through attendance at the ARLIS/NA annual conference. *Winner:* Tracey Lemon.

Association for Library and Information Science Education (ALISE)

ALISE Award for Professional Contribution to Library and Information Science Education. *Winner:* Thomas J. Galvin.

ALISE Doctoral Students Dissertation Awards ($400). To promote the exchange of research ideas between doctoral students and established researchers. *Winner:* Kathleen Eisenbeis.

ALISE Research Award ($2,500). For a project that reflects ALISE goals and objectives. *Winner:* Linda C. Smith.

ALISE Research Paper Competition ($500). For a research paper concerning any aspect of librarianship or information studies by a member of ALISE. *Winner:* Wayne Weigand.

ALISE Service Award. For outstanding contributions to the association. *Winner:* John N. Berry III.

Jane Anne Hannigan Research Award ($500). *Winner:* Joy McGregor.

Association of Jewish Libraries (AJL)

May K. Simon Scholarship ($500). For a student who intends to become a Judaica librarian. *Winners:* Katrina Kolt, Sharon Rotter.

Association of Records Managers and Administrators (ARMA)

ARMA International Scholarships ($750). To students pursuing an associate's degree, diploma program, or certification in information and records management at the professional/managerial level. *Winners:* Angela Foster, Jeanne Fugate, Tammy Michalak, Robert Tamela.

Beta Phi Mu

Beta Phi Mu Award. *See under* American Library Association.

Harold Lancour Scholarship for Foreign Study ($1,000). For graduate study in a foreign country related to the applicant's work or schooling. No award in 1993.

Sarah Rebecca Reed Scholarship ($1,500). For study at an ALA-accredited library school. *Winner:* Lisa Willette Janicke.

Frank B. Sessa Scholarship for Continuing Professional Education ($750). For continuing education for a Beta Phi Mu member. *Winners:* Trudi E. Jacobson, Dianne S. Stalker.

Canadian Association of College and University Libraries (CACUL)

CACUL Distinguished Academic Librarian

Award. *Winner:* Sandra Black, Mohawk College.

CACUL Innovation Achievement Award ($1,500). No award in 1993.

CACUL Micromedia Award of Merit ($500). *Winner:* Judith Stonehewer.

Canadian Association of Public Libraries (CAPL)

CAPL Outstanding Public Library Service Award. *Winner:* Marianne Hall.

CAPL Public Relations Award. *Donor:* Faxon Canada. *Winner:* Hinton (AB) Public Library.

Canadian Association of Special Libraries and Information Services (CASLIS)

CASLIS Special Librarian of the Year Award. *Winner:* Jane Beaumont.

Canadian Library Association (CLA)

CLA Meckler Award for Innovations in Technology. *Donor:* Meckler Corporation. *Winner:* North York (ON) Public Library.

CLA Outstanding Service to Librarianship Award. *Donor:* R. R. Bowker. *Winner:* Gerald Brown.

CLA Research and Development Grants ($500 each). *Winners:* Rae Hazelwood, Beth Tompkins.

Canadian Library Journal Student Article Contest. *Winner:* MacGregor Patterson.

NFB/CLA Award for Outstanding Film or Video Librarian. *Donor:* National Film Board of Canada. *Winner:* Cynthia Bartholomew.

Canadian Library Trustees Association (CLTA)

CLTA Achievement in Literacy Award. For an innovative literacy program by a public library board. *Donor:* ABC Canada. *Winner:* London (ON) Public Library.

CLTA Merit Award for Distinguished Service as a Public Library Trustee. For outstanding leadership in the advancement of public library trusteeship and public library service in Canada. *Winner:* Margaret Andrewes.

Canadian School Library Association (CSLA)

Canadian School Executive Distinguished Service Award for School Administrators. No award in 1993.

Canebsco School Library Media Periodical Award. *Winner: The Bookmark,* the professional journal of the Columbia Teacher-Librarians Association.

Grolier Award for Research in School Librarianship in Canada ($1,000). For theoretical or applied research that advances the field of school librarianship. *Winner:* Joy McGregor.

National Book Service Teacher Librarian of the Year. *Winner:* Reesa Cohen.

Margaret B. Scott Award of Merit ($400). For the development of school libraries in Canada. *Cosponsor:* Ontario Library Association. No award in 1993.

Carnegie Corporation of New York

Andrew Carnegie Medal for Excellence in Children's Video. To U.S. producer of the most distinguished video for children in the previous year. *Donor:* Carnegie Corp. of New York. *Winner:* Gary Soto for *A Summer Life* (Fast Forward).

Chinese-American Librarians Association (CALA)

CALA Distinguished Service Award. *Winners:* Amy D. Seetoo, Irene Yeh.

CALA President's Award. *Winner:* Chuan-Hua Lowe.

Sheila Suen Lai Scholarship ($500). To a student of Chinese nationality or descent pursuing full-time graduate studies for a master's degree in an ALA-accredited library school. *Winners:* Ying Wang, Bin Gong.

Church and Synagogue Library Association (CSLA)

CSLA Award for Outstanding Congregational Librarian. For distinguished service to the congregation and/or community through devotion to the congregational library. *Winner:* Maria Bellevance.

CSLA Award for Outstanding Congregational Library. For responding in creative and innovative ways to the library's mission of reaching and serving the congregation and/or the wider community. *Winner:* Jane Burghduff, Clear Lake United Methodist Church.

CSLA Award for Outstanding Contribution to Congregational Libraries. For providing inspiration, guidance, leadership, or resources to enrich the field of church or synagogue librarianship. *Winner:* Marjorie Cook.

Helen Keating Ott Award for Outstanding Contribution to Children's Literature. *Winner:* Tomie dePaola.

Pat Tabler Memorial Scholarship Award. *Winner:* Juanita Garner-Wahe.

Council on Library Resources (CLR)

Grants. For a partial list of the recipients of CLR grants for the 1992–1993 academic year, see the report from the Council on Library Resources in Part 2.

Gale Research Company

ALTA/Gale Outstanding Trustee Conference Grant Award. *See under* American Library Association, American Library Trustee Association.

Gale/*Library Journal* Library of the Year Award ($5,000). *Winner:* Austin (TX) Public Library.

Gale Research Award for Excellence in Business Librarianship; and Gale Research Company Award for Excellence in Refer-

ence and Adult Services. *See under* American Library Association, Reference and Adult Services Division, Business Reference and Services Section.

Gale Research Financial Development Award. *See under* American Library Association.

Medical Library Association (MLA)

Estelle Brodman Award for the Academic Medical Librarian of the Year. To honor significant achievement, potential for leadership, and continuing excellence at mid-career in the area of academic health sciences librarianship. *Winner:* Julia Sollenberger.

Cunningham Memorial International Fellowship ($3,500). A six-month grant and travel expenses in the United States and Canada for a foreign librarian. *Winner:* Gu Xiaohong.

Louise Darling Medal. For distinguished achievement in collection development in the health sciences. *Winner:* Anne M. Pascarelli.

Janet Doe Lectureship ($250). *Winner:* Alison Bunting.

Ida and George Eliot Prize ($200). For an essay published in any journal in the preceding calendar year that has been judged most effective in furthering medical librarianship. *Donor:* Login Brothers Books. *Winner:* Joanne G. Marshall.

Murray Gottlieb Prize ($100). For the best unpublished essay submitted by a medical librarian on the history of some aspect of health sciences or a detailed description of a library exhibit. *Donor:* Ralph and Jo Grimes. *Winner:* Glenda Wiese.

Joseph Leiter NLM/MLA Lectureship. *Winner:* Suzanne Stensaas.

MLA Award for Distinguished Public Service. No award in 1993.

MLA Award for Excellence and Achievement in Hospital Librarianship. To a member of the MLA who has made significant contributions to the profession in the area of overall distinction or leadership in hospital librarianship. *Winner:* Bernie Todd Smith.

MLA Continuing Education Award. *Winners:* Sarah Knox Morley, Melanie J. Tennyson.

MLA Doctoral Fellowship ($1,000). *Donor:* Institute for Scientific Information (ISI). *Winner:* Valerie Florance.

MLA President's Award. For exceptional contributions to medical librarianship. No award in 1993.

MLA Research, Development, and Demonstration Projects Grants. *Winners:* Jennifer Bayne, Joan Leishman.

MLA Scholarship ($2,000). For graduate study in medical librarianship at an ALA-accredited library school. *Winner:* Alicia Rehn Busch.

MLA Scholarship for Minority Students ($2,000). *Winner:* Velora Avis Jernigan.

John P. McGovern Award Lectureship ($500). *Winner:* Patricia Aburdene.

Marcia C. Noyes Award. For an outstanding contribution to medical librarianship. The award is the highest professional distinction of MLA. *Winner:* Nina W. Matheson.

Rittenhouse Award ($500). For the best unpublished paper on medical librarianship submitted by a student enrolled in, or having been enrolled in, a course for credit in an ALA-accredited library school, or a trainee in an internship program in medical librarianship. *Donor:* Rittenhouse Medical Bookstore. *Winner:* Marsha Greer.

Frank Bradway Rogers Information Advancement Award ($500). For an outstanding contribution to knowledge of health science information delivery. *Donor:* Institute for Scientific Information (ISI). *Winner:* Jay Daly.

K. G. Saur (Munich, Germany)

Award for Best *College and Research Libraries* Article. *See under* American Library Association, Association of College and Research Libraries.

Hans-Peter Geh Grant. To enable a librarian from the former Soviet Union to attend a conference in Germany or elsewhere. *Winner:* Mariko Karo (Estonia).

Gustav Hoffmann Study Grant. To allow a librarian in a country where librarianship is a newly developing profession to study an issue in one or more countries of Western Europe. *Winner:* Samuel Oke Ogunniyi (Nigeria).

Society of American Archivists (SAA)

C. F. W. Coker Prize for Finding Aids. *Winners:* Diane Vogt-O'Connor for the *Guide to Photographic Collections at the Smithsonian Institution.*

Colonial Dames Scholarships. To archivists who have been in the field less than two years and who are working with holdings predating 1825, for a portion of the tuition, travel, and housing expenses at the Modern Archives Institute, Washington, D.C. No award in 1993.

Fellows' Posner Prize. For the best article in the *American Archivist* journal. *Winners:* (for 1991) Frederick J. Stielow for "Archival Theory Redux and Redeemed," *American Archivist* 54, no. 1, 14–26; (for 1992) Avra S. Michelson and Jeff Rothenberg for "Scholarly Communication and Information Technology: Exploring the Impact of Changes in the Research Process on Archives," *American Archivist* 55, no. 2, 236–315.

Philip M. Hamer–Elizabeth Hamer Kegan Award. To an individual and/or institution that has increased public awareness of a specific body of documents. *Winner:* Carl Albert Congressional Research Center for "The Congress, the Constitution and Oklahoma: A Series of Traveling Exhibits."

Oliver Wendell Holmes Award. To allow overseas archivists, already in the United States or Canada for training, to augment their visit by traveling to the SAA annual meeting. No award in 1993.

J. Franklin Jameson Award. For archival advocacy. *Winners:* Thomas D. Clark, Louise McBee, John Marshall.

Sister M. Claude Lane Award. For a significant contribution to the field of religious archives. *Winner:* Peter J. Wosh.

Waldo Gifford Leland Prize. For writing of superior excellence and usefulness in the field of archival history, theory, or practice. *Winner:* Helen W. Samuels for *Varsity Letters: Documenting Modern Colleges and Universities* (Scarecrow).

Theodore Calvin Pease Award. For superior writing achievement by a student of archival administration. *Donor:* Marguerite Pease. No award in 1993.

SAA Distinguished Service Award. No award in 1993.

SAA Fellows. No award in 1993.

Special Libraries Association (SLA)

John Cotton Dana Award. For exceptional support and encouragement of special librarianship. *Winner:* Roger K. Haley.

ISI Scholarship ($1,000). For beginning doctoral candidates in library/information science. *Donor:* Institute for Scientific Information (ISI). Not awarded in 1993.

Plenum Scholarship ($1,000). For graduate study leading to a doctorate in library and information science. Not awarded in 1993.

SLA Affirmative Action Scholarship ($6,000). *Winner:* Aravinda Pillalamarri.

SLA Fellows. *Winners:* Toni Carbo Bearman, Mary E. Dickerson, Muriel Regan, Marilyn McAnally Stark.

SLA Meckler Award for Innovations in Technology. *Winner:* Karen Bleakley.

SLA President's Award. *Winner:* John Ganly.

SLA Professional Award. *Winner:* William Andrew Moffett.

SLA Public Relations Award ($1,000). For an outstanding article on special librarianship. *Winner:* Diana Westbrook.

SLA Research Grant. *Winner:* Marilyn D. White.

SLA Scholarships ($6,000). For students with financial need who show potential for special librarianship. *Winners:* John Alita, Tina Chrismore, Michele Tennant.

SLA Special Recognition for Excellence in Public Relations During National Library Week/International Special Librarians Day. *Winner:* corporate information services staff, RMT Inc.

SLA H. W. Wilson Award. For the most outstanding article in the past year's *Special Libraries. Donor:* H. W. Wilson Company. *Winner:* Sharyn Ladner.

Alphabetical List of Award Names

Individual award names are followed by a colon and the name of the awarding body; e.g., the Bound to Stay Bound Books Scholarship is given by ALA/Association for Library Service to Children. Consult the preceding list of "Library Scholarship and Award Recipients, 1993," which is alphabetically arranged by organization, to locate recipients and further information. Awards named for individuals are listed by surname.

AALL Scholarships: American Association of Law Libraries

AASL/ABC/Clio Leadership Grant: ALA/American Association of School Librarians

AASL Information Plus Continuing Education Scholarship: ALA/American Association of School Librarians

AASL Intellectual Freedom Award: ALA/American Association of School Librarians

School Librarians Workshop Scholarship: ALA/American Association of School Librarians

ACRL Academic or Research Librarian of the Year Award: ALA/Association of College and Research Libraries

ACRL Doctoral Dissertation Fellowship: ALA/Association of College and Research Libraries

AIA/ALA–LAMA Library Buildings Award Program: ALA/Library Administration and Management Association

ALA/Meckler Library of the Future Award: ALA

ALISE Award for Professional Contribution to Library and Information Science Education: Association for Library and Information Science Education

ALISE Doctoral Students Dissertation Awards: Association for Library and Information Science Education

ALISE Research Award: Association for Library and Information Science Education

ALISE Research Paper Competition: Association for Library and Information Science Education

ALISE Service Award: Association for Library and Information Science Education

ALSC/Book Wholesalers Summer Reading Program Grant: ALA/Association for Library Service to Children

ALSC/Econo-Clad Literature Program Award: ALA/Association for Library Service to Children

ALTA/Gale Outstanding Trustee Conference Grant Award: ALA/American Library Trustee Association

ALTA Major Benefactors Honor Awards: ALA/American Library Trustee Association

ARMA International Scholarships: Association of Records Managers and Administrators

ASCLA Exceptional Service Award: ALA/Association of Specialized and Cooperative Library Agencies

ASCLA Leadership Achievement Award: ALA/Association of Specialized and Cooperative Library Agencies

ASCLA/National Organization on Disability Award: ALA/Association of Specialized and Cooperative Library Agencies

ASCLA Professional Achievement Award: ALA/Association of Specialized and Cooperative Library Agencies

ASCLA Service Award: ALA/Association of Specialized and Cooperative Library Agencies

ASIS Award of Merit: American Society for Information Science

ASIS Best Information Science Book: American Society for Information Science

ASIS Best Information Science Teacher Award: American Society for Information Science

ASIS Doctoral Forum Award: American Society for Information Science

ASIS Research Award: American Society for Information Science

ASIS Special Award: American Society for Information Science

Advancement of Literacy Award: ALA/Public Library Association, Adult Lifelong Learning Section

Joseph L. Andrews Bibliographical Award: American Association of Law Libraries

May Hill Arbuthnot Lecturer: ALA/Association for Library Service to Children

Armed Forces Library Achievement Citation: ALA/Armed Forces Libraries Round Table

Armed Forces Library Certificate of Merit: ALA/Armed Forces Libraries Round Table

Armed Forces Library Newsbank Scholarship Award: ALA/Armed Forces Libraries Round Table

Hugh C. Atkinson Memorial Award: ALA

Carroll Preston Baber Research Grant: ALA

Baker & Taylor Conference Grants: ALA/Young Adult Library Services Association

Best of "LRTS" Award: ALA/Association for Library Collections and Technical Services

Beta Phi Mu Award: ALA

Bibliographic Instruction Publication of the Year Award: ALA/Association of College and Research Libraries, Bibliographic Instruction Section

Blackwell/North America Scholarship Award: ALA/Association for Library Collections and Technical Services, Resources Section

Bogle International Library Travel Fund: ALA/International Relations Committee

Bound to Stay Bound Books Scholarship: ALA/Association for Library Service to Children

Bowker/Ulrich's Serials Librarianship Award: ALA/Association for Library Collections and Technical Services, Serials Section

Estelle Brodman Award for the Academic Medical Librarian of the Year: Medical Library Association

CACUL Distinguished Academic Librarian Award: Canadian Association of College and University Libraries

CACUL Innovation Achievement Award: Canadian Association of College and University Libraries

CACUL Micromedia Award of Merit: Canadian Association of College and University Libraries

CALA Distinguished Service Award: Chinese-American Librarians Association

CALA President's Award: Chinese-American Librarians Association

CAPL Outstanding Public Library Service Award: Canadian Association of Public Libraries

CAPL Public Relations Award: Canadian Association of Public Libraries

CASLIS Special Librarian of the Year Award: Canadian Association of Special Libraries and Information Services

CIS/GODORT/ALA Documents to the People Award: ALA/Government Documents Round Table

CLA Meckler Award for Innovations in Technology: Canadian Library Association

CLA Outstanding Service to Librarianship Award: Canadian Library Association

CLA Research and Development Grants: Canadian Library Association

CLTA Achievement in Literacy Award: Canadian Library Trustees Association

CLTA Merit Award for Distinguished Service as a Public Library Trustee: Canadian Library Trustees Association

CSLA Award for Outstanding Congregational Librarian: Church and Synagogue Library Association

CSLA Award for Outstanding Congregational Library: Church and Synagogue Library Association

CSLA Award for Outstanding Contribution to Congregational Libraries: Church and Synagogue Library Association

Francis Joseph Campbell Citation: ALA/Association of Specialized and Cooperative Library Agencies, Section on Library Service to the Blind and Physically Handicapped

Canadian Library Journal Student Article Contest: Canadian Library Association

Canadian School Executive Distinguished Service Award for School Administrators: Canadian School Library Association

Canebsco School Library Media Periodical Award: Canadian School Library Association

Andrew Carnegie Medal for Excellence in Children's Video: Carnegie Corporation of New York

Carnegie Reading List Awards: ALA/Publishing Committee

Chadwyck-Healey Professional Development Award: Art Libraries Society of North America

James Bennett Childs Award: ALA/Government Documents Round Table

C. F. W. Coker Prize for Finding Aids: Society of American Archivists

David H. Clift Scholarship: ALA

Colonial Dames Scholarships: Society of American Archivists

Cretsos Leadership Award: American Society for Information Science

Cunningham Memorial International Fellowship: Medical Library Association

Phyllis Dain Library History Dissertation Award: ALA/Library History Round Table

John Cotton Dana Award: Special Libraries Association

John Cotton Dana Library Public Relations Award: ALA/Library Administration and Management Association

Louise Darling Medal: Medical Library Association

Dartmouth Medal: ALA/Reference and Adult Services Division

Watson Davis Award: American Society for Information Science

Denali Press Award: ALA/Reference and Adult Services Division

Melvil Dewey Medal: ALA/Reference and Adult Services Division

Distinguished School Administrators Award, AASL/SIRS: ALA/American Association of School Librarians

Distinguished Service Award: AASL/Baker & Taylor: ALA/American Association of School Librarians

Distinguished Service to ALSC Award: ALA/Association for Library Service to Children

Janet Doe Lectureship: Medical Library Association

Vincent H. Duckles Award: Music Library Association

Miriam Dudley Bibliographic Instruction Librarian of the Year Award: ALA/Association of College and Research Libraries, Bibliographic Instruction Section

EBSCO ALA Conference Sponsorships: ALA

EBSCO Community College Learning Resources Achievement Awards: ALA/Association of College and Research Libraries

Margaret A. Edwards Award: ALA/Young Adult Library Services Association

Ida and George Eliot Prize: Medical Library Association

Emergency Librarian Publication Award: ALA/American Association of School Librarians

Jim and Anna Emmett Travel Award: Art Libraries Society of North America

Equality Award: ALA

Excellence in Small and/or Rural Public Service Award: ALA/Public Library Association

Facts on File Grant: ALA/Reference and Adult Services Division

Federal Librarians Achievement Award: ALA/Federal Librarians Round Table

Fellows' Posner Prize: Society of American Archivists

First Step Award, Serial Sections/Wiley Professional Development Grant: ALA/Association for Library Collections and Technical Services, Serials Section

Loleta D. Fyan Award: ALA

Gale/*Library Journal* Library of the Year Award: Gale Research Company

Gale Research Award for Excellence in Business Librarianship/BRASS: ALA/Reference and Adult Services Division, Business Reference and Services Section

Gale Research Award for Excellence in Reference and Adult Services: ALA/Reference and Adult Services Division, Business Reference and Services Section

Gale Research Company Financial Development Award: ALA

Marian Gould Gallagher Distinguished Service Award: American Association of Law Libraries

Hans-Peter Geh Grant: K. G. Saur

Louise Giles Minority Scholarship: ALA/Office for Library Personnel Resources

Murray Gottlieb Prize: Medical Library Association

Grolier Award for Research in School Librarianship in Canada: Canadian School Library Association

Grolier Foundation Award: ALA

Grolier National Library Week Grant: ALA/National Library Week Committee

G. K. Hall Award for Library Literature: ALA

G. K. Hall Conference Attendance Award: Art Libraries Society of North America

Philip M. Hamer–Elizabeth Hamer Kegan Award: Society of American Archivists

Jane Anne Hannigan Research Award: Association for Library and Information Science Education

Frances Henne Award: ALA/American Association of School Librarians

Frances Henne/YALSA/*Voice of Youth Advocates (VOYA)* Research Grant: ALA/Young Adult Library Services Association

Gustav Hoffmann Study Grant: K. G. Saur

Oliver Wendell Holmes Award: Society of American Archivists

Honorary ALA Membership: ALA

John Ames Humphry/OCLC/Forest Press Award: ALA/International Relations Committee

International Study Grant: ALA/Public Library Association

ISI Information Science Doctoral Dissertation Scholarship: American Society for Information Science

ISI Scholarship: Special Libraries Association

John Phillip Immroth Memorial Award for Intellectual Freedom: ALA/Intellectual Freedom Round Table

International Special Librarians Day. *See* Special Recognition for Excellence in Public Relations During National Library Week

JASIS Paper Award: American Society for Information Science

J. Franklin Jameson Award: Society of American Archivists

Howard Karno Travel Award: Art Libraries Society of North America

LITA/CLSI Scholarship in Library and Information Technology: ALA/Library and Information Technology Association

LITA/Gaylord Award for Achievement in Library and Information Technology: ALA/Library and Information Technology Association

LITA/*Library Hi Tech* Award: ALA/Library and Information Technology Association

LITA/OCLC Minority Scholarship in Library and Information Technology: ALA/Library and Information Technology Association

Léonce Laget Travel Award: Art Libraries Society of North America

Sheila Suen Lai Scholarship: Chinese-American Librarians Association

Harold Lancour Scholarship for Foreign Study: Beta Phi Mu

Sister M. Claude Lane Award: Society of American Archivists

Law Library Journal Article of the Year Award: American Association of Law Libraries

Law Library Publication Award: American Association of Law Libraries

Samuel Lazerow Fellowship: ALA/Association of College and Research Libraries

Katharine Kyes Leab and Daniel J. Leab *American Book Prices Current* Awards: ALA/Association of College and Research Libraries

Tony Leisner Scholarship: ALA

Joseph Leiter NLM/MLA Lectureship: Medical Library Association

Waldo Gifford Leland Prize: Society of American Archivists

Library Video Award: ALA/Public Library Association

Joseph W. Lippincott Award: ALA

Literacy Award: ALA/American Library Trustee Association

MAGERT Honors Award: ALA/Map and Geography Round Table

MLA Award for Distinguished Public Service: Medical Library Association

MLA Award for Excellence and Achievement in Hospital Librarianship: Medical Library Association

MLA Continuing Education Award: Medical Library Association

MLA Doctoral Fellowship: Medical Library Association

MLA President's Award: Medical Library Association

MLA Research, Development, and Demonstration Projects Grants: Medical Library Association

MLA Scholarship: Medical Library Association

MLA Scholarship for Minority Students: Medical Library Association

Fraiser McConnell Travel Award: Art Libraries Society of North America

John P. McGovern Award Lectureship: Medical Library Association

Margaret Mann Citation: ALA/Association for Library Collections and Technical Services

Allie Beth Martin Award: ALA/Public Library Association

Frederic G. Melcher Scholarship: ALA/Association for Library Service to Children

Microcomputer in the Media Center Award: ALA/American Association of School Librarians

David Mirvish Books/Books on Art Travel Award: Art Libraries Society of North America

Margaret E. Monroe Library Adult Services Award: ALA/Reference and Adult Services Division

Bessie Boehm Moore Award: ALA

Isadore Gilbert Mudge Citation: ALA/Reference and Adult Services Division

NFB/CLA Award for Outstanding Film or Video Librarian: Canadian Library Association

NMRT EBSCO Scholarship: ALA/New Members Round Table

National Book Service Teacher Librarian of the Year: Canadian School Library Association

National School Library Media Program of the Year Award: ALA/American Association of School Librarians

Martinus Nijhoff International West European Specialist Study Grant: ALA/ Association of College and Research Libraries

Marcia C. Noyes Award: Medical Library Association

Oberly Award for Bibliography in the Agricultural Sciences: ALA/Association of College and Research Libraries

Eli M. Oboler Memorial Award: ALA/Intellectual Freedom Round Table

Shirley Olofson Memorial Award: ALA/New Members Round Table

Eva Judd O'Meara Award: Music Library Association

Helen Keating Ott Award for Outstanding Contribution to Children's Literature: Church and Synagogue Library Association

Theodore Calvin Pease Award: Society of American Archivists

Esther J. Piercy Award: ALA/Association for Library Collections and Technical Services

Plenum Scholarship: Special Libraries Association

Putnam and Grosset Book Group Awards: ALA/Association for Library Service to Children

Herbert W. Putnam Honor Award: ALA

Readex/GODORT/ALA Catharine J. Reynolds Award: ALA/Government Documents Round Table

Sarah Rebecca Reed Scholarship: Beta Phi Mu

Reference Service Press Award: ALA/Reference and Adult Services Division

Rittenhouse Award: Medical Library Association

Frank Bradway Rogers Information Advancement Award: Medical Library Association

Norman Ross Travel Award: Art Libraries Society of North America

SAA Distinguished Service Award: Society of American Archivists

SAA Fellows: Society of American Archivists

SIRS/Peace Award: ALA/Social Responsibilities Round Table

SRRT/Gay and Lesbian Task Force, Gay and Lesbian Book Awards: ALA/Social Responsibilities Round Table

SLA Affirmative Action Scholarship: Special Libraries Association

SLA Fellows: Special Libraries Association

SLA Hall of Fame Award: Special Libraries Association

SLA Honorary Member: Special Libraries Association

SLA Meckler Award for Innovations in Technology: Special Libraries Association

SLA Member Recognition for Excellence in Public Relations: Special Libraries Association

SLA President's Award: Special Libraries Association

SLA Professional Award: Special Libraries Association

SLA Public Relations Award: Special Libraries Association

SLA Research Grant: Special Libraries Association

SLA Scholarships: Special Libraries Association

SLA Special Recognition for Excellence in Public Relations During National Library Week/International Special Librarians Day: Special Libraries Association

SLA H. W. Wilson Award: Special Libraries Association

K. G. Saur Award for Best *College and Research Libraries* Article: ALA/Association of College and Research Libraries

Margaret B. Scott Award of Merit: Canadian School Library Association

Frank B. Sessa Scholarship for Continuing Professional Education: Beta Phi Mu

John Sessions Memorial Award: ALA/Reference and Adult Services Division

Jesse H. Shera Award for Research: ALA/Library Research Round Table

Louis Shores-Oryx Press Award: ALA/Reference and Adult Services Division

May K. Simon Scholarship: Association of Jewish Libraries

State Program Award: ALA/Intellectual Freedom Round Table

Pat Tabler Memorial Scholarship Award: Church and Synagogue Library Association

3M/NMRT Professional Development Grant: ALA/New Members Round Table

Trustee Citations: ALA/American Library Trustee Association

Leonard Wertheimer Multilingual Public Library Service Award: ALA/Public Library Association

Whitney-Carnegie Awards: ALA/Publishing Committee

H. W. Wilson Library Periodical Award: ALA

H. W. Wilson Library Staff Development Grant: ALA

Justin Winsor Prize Essay: ALA/Library History Round Table

World Book–ALA Goal Awards: ALA

YALSA/Econo-Clad Literature Program Award: ALA/Young Adult Library Services Association

Part 4
Research and Statistics

Library Research and Statistics

Research on Libraries and Librarianship in 1993

Mary Jo Lynch

Director, Office for Research and Statistics, American Library Association

The most significant research development of 1993 relates not to the traditional libraries of yesterday and today but to the digital libraries of tomorrow. In the July/August issue of *Educom Review,* John R. Garrett of the Corporation for National Research Initiatives described the research need to "meet the grand challenges that face us in building a national, networked, distributed, on-line system of linked digital libraries." Several months later *High Performance Computing and Communications Week* (October 28, 1993) carried an announcement that "Three government agencies have set aside several million dollars to accelerate the development of digital libraries. The National Science Foundation (NSF), the Advanced Research Projects Agency (ARPA) and the National Aeronautics and Space Administration (NASA) together could award as much as $25 million over the next four years for . . . electronic library research."

The program announcement for this "Digital Library Initiative" asks for research proposals in any or all of the following areas:

- Systems for capturing data of all forms (text, sound, image)
- Organizing electronic information in a variety of formats
- Advanced software for searching, filtering, and summarizing large volumes of data, imagery, and all kinds of information
- Visualization and other interactive technologies for quickly browsing large volumes of imagery
- Networking protocols and standards needed to insure the ability of the digital network to accommodate the high volume, bandwidth and switching requirements of a digital library
- Simplifying the utilization of networked databases distributed around the nation and around the world
- Social and economic issues (such as intellectual property rights and charging mechanisms)

Each proposal must show 25 percent cost sharing and each must involve active participation of a partner from each of the following:

- Client groups (such as specific research communities)
- Commercial enterprises (such as publishers)
- Archival establishments (such as libraries)
- Researchers (such as supercomputer centers)

Several libraries and schools of library and information science/studies are known to be involved in proposals submitted in response to this initiative. Proposals were due in early February 1994 and results are to be announced in June or July 1994.

The excitement generated by this initiative is evident in an Internet message sent to individuals and groups in mid-February announcing a "Symposium on Theory and Practice of Digital Libraries" and calling for papers on any topics related to design, implementation, and use. The symposium "Digital Libraries 94" will be held June 19–21, 1994, in College Station, Texas, chaired by Richard Furuta and John Leggett of the Hypermedia Research Laboratory at Texas A&M University. In a message describing the upcoming event, Furuta noted that

> An unprecedented opportunity exists for forming a community of scholars to study the theory and practice of digital libraries. The catalyst has been the Digital Library Initiative, jointly sponsored by the National Science Foundation, ARPA, and NASA. In preparing responses to the call for proposals, hundreds of researchers have spent uncounted thousands of hours evaluating and re-evaluating the characteristics of a digital library. Innovative, exciting alliances have been formed, bringing together distributed teams drawn from independent research laboratories, client organizations, and industrial entities. In the past few months we have seen what is certainly the greatest collective application of thought to date on issues of digital libraries.

The symposium is an opportunity to share insights and "take steps toward building a wide-ranging, open, research community that reflects the diversity of knowledge needed to address the problems of digital libraries." Proceedings will be published.

Academic Libraries

Libraries serving large research universities have been very active in exploring possibilities of computer and communications technologies. That reality, as well as the increasing financial constraints faced by university research libraries, has been of concern recently to the Andrew W. Mellon Foundation, which has always believed that libraries are central to scholarly communication. In 1989 the foundation began a study of the economics of research libraries and their response to the rapidly developing electronic technologies. The project involved several collaborators and was done "to inform [Mellon's] subsequent activities, including grantmaking." The report of this work, *University Libraries and Scholarly Communication,* was published for the Mellon Foundation by the Association of Research Libraries (ARL) in November 1992.

Original data collection was not part of this project. Instead, the collaborators analyzed existing data, primarily statistics collected annually by ARL. Results are presented in Part 1 of the report, "Historical Trends: Collections,

Expenditures, Publications," which features numerous figures and tables showing long-term trends in those three areas. Part 2 of the report is largely text and covers "Information Needs and New Technologies." Central to these chapters is the idea that "electronic technologies may permit different assumptions and practices to characterize scholarly communication in the future" as compared to the past. For example, "the ability to share materials readily in electronic form alleviates the need for each institution to attempt to build a comprehensive collection." Part 2 raises many fundamental issues in chapters on "Information as a Commodity," "Bibliographic Information in Electronic Form," "Electronic Publishing," "Resource Sharing: Collection Development and Document Delivery," "Economic and Legal Issues," and "Networks and the National Telecommunications Infrastructure."

The report was published not because these important issues were settled but because the foundation believed the work would be useful to a wider audience. Also, Mellon will continue to work in this arena. In his foreword to the report, foundation President William G. Bowen announced:

> This Foundation intends to continue to pursue aggressively a number of the issues raised in the report but not resolved. Specifically, we are examining the possibility of evaluating systematically some of the "natural experiments" in new modes of electronic publication and dissemination now going on, and we might simultaneously encourage the development of some carefully structured experiments designed to address some of the open questions of quality, means of access to materials, convenience, and costs.

Research done along those lines and research sponsored by the NSF-ARPA-NASA initiative described earlier will certainly transform libraries as we have known them.

Interlibrary Loan

Resource sharing among academic research libraries was one of the major issues addressed by the Mellon report. In June 1993 ARL published a slim volume devoted entirely to one aspect of the topic—interlibrary loan (ILL). Marilyn M. Roche of the Research Libraries Group (RLG) is the author of *ARL/RLG Interlibrary Loan Cost Study: A Joint Effort by the Association of Research Libraries and the Research Libraries Group.*

This 64-page report contains findings on the present costs of interlibrary lending and borrowing in North American research libraries. Seventy-six U.S. and Canadian research libraries collected ILL cost data for 1991, which was then verified, analyzed, and distilled into the published study. As explained in its introduction, the purpose of the study was twofold:

- To produce substantive Benchmark Data on costs of interlibrary lending and borrowing, which are key components of resource sharing programs
- To provide a Management Tool that would enable participating libraries to make preliminary cost comparisons between ILL and alternative methods of obtaining materials for patrons

Participants in the study completed an extensive questionnaire covering costs of staff, network and communications, delivery, photocopying, supplies, equipment and software, rental and maintenance, and direct and indirect borrowing charges, as well as income recovered.

Each participant received a customized ILL cost analysis report illustrating its costs for lending and borrowing along with summary statistics of aggregated unit costs for all participants. The published report presents aggregate data only, primarily through a series of clear and attractive scatter diagrams and bar charts. Several key findings of the report were summarized in ARL's press release as follows:

- The major cost of ILL operations is for staff; less than one-fourth of the total goes to all other elements—communications, photocopying, supplies, equipment, materials delivery, and so on.
- More than half of all filled ILL transactions are done through photocopies rather than transmitting the original item.
- The average cost for a completed ILL transaction (incurred by both the lender and the borrower) is close to $30—nearly $19 for the requester and $11 for the lender.

This report is part of a series of initiatives by ARL and the Council on Library Resources (CLR) to help librarians cope with increasing costs, volume, and complexity of ILL activity. ARL will publish in 1994 *System Design for Interlibrary Loan and Document Delivery: A Description of Priority Needs*. This volume, developed by Visiting Program Officer Mary Jackson of the University of Pennsylvania, will describe ARL's North American Interlibrary Loan and Document Delivery Project (NAILDD)—an attempt to reconceptualize interlibrary loan, including the use of computer and communications technology to make the process less labor-intensive. The publication will give background and context for the technical developments ARL would like to influence and includes background papers and working documents of NAILDD's Developers/Implementors Group.

School Libraries

The research reported in *Seeking Meaning: A Process Approach to Library and Information Services* (Ablex, 1993) will be of interest to both academic and school librarians. In it, author Carol Collier Kuhlthau describes the "process approach" to information seeking that she developed through a series of projects beginning with her dissertation at Rutgers University. Once a high school librarian, Kuhlthau was puzzled by the negative feelings expressed by students using the library for "research" papers and wondered: "Why was there hesitation to get started, confusion about the task, lack of confidence in ability, and low motivation and interest?"

Using theoretical constructs from thinkers such as John Dewey, George Kelly, Jerome Brunner, and Robert Taylor, Kuhlthau planned and conducted a series of five studies of information seeking from the user's perspective. The studies used both quantitative techniques and a variety of qualitative techniques including journals, search logs, short written statements, case studies, conceptual maps, teachers' assessment, and a perceptions questionnaire. Kuhlthau's first study was in a high school; she later tested her results in academic libraries and public libraries. She concludes her work with thoughtful chapters on the "Uncertainty Principle," "Roles of Mediators in the Process of Information Seeking," "Intervention into the Process of Information Seeking," and a final chapter redefining the mission of the librarian in a technological age.

Kuhlthau's doctoral dissertation was the beginning of a research career with impressive results, but this happens too rarely in our field. Many dissertations stand alone and results are never used by practitioners. To remedy the problem, Ken Haycock produced *Research about Teaching and Learning through the School's Library Resource Center* (Rochland Press, 1992). Haycock, director of the School of Library, Archival, and Information Studies at the University of British Columbia, took as his model a book called *What Works,* published several years ago by the U.S. Department of Education to inform educators about doctoral research with practical implications for classroom teachers. Part I of Haycock's book lists 30 "research findings," comments briefly on the implications of each, and cites several dissertations that support the finding. Part II is an annotated bibliography of almost 600 North American dissertations and Part III consists of indexes—author, geographic area, title.

The bibliography is comprehensive, not critical, but there is definite focus: the selection of dissertations is aimed toward developing an organized body of knowledge about factors affecting effectiveness—generalizations, principles, theories—that will guide professional practice in schools and school districts. Haycock's introduction notes that although almost 600 dissertations are listed as relevant to the chosen topic, fewer than 200 were included in references to the findings. Those 200 were chosen carefully according to criteria explained in the introduction. The author makes no claim that the findings represent ultimate truth, but concludes that "in this field, to wait for absolute certainty is to wait forever."

Stephen Krashen, author of *The Power of Reading: Insights from the Research* (Libraries Unlimited, 1993), is much surer of the one research finding he describes—that voluntary free reading is the single best way to improve both reading and writing skills.

Krashen's book was the centerpiece for Treasure Mountain IV, a one-day "research retreat" for researchers in the school library community held at Tulane University before the 1993 American Library Association (ALA) annual conference in New Orleans. The retreat was named Treasure Mountain in reference to the first such retreat held in 1989 before the Salt Lake City conference of the American Association of School Librarians (AASL). As before, David Loertscher of Libraries Unlimited was the main organizer.

As keynote speaker, Krashen described numerous studies—some good, some not so good—that, collectively, present a solid case for his thesis

... that if children or less literate adults start reading for pleasure ... good things will happen. Their reading comprehension will improve, and they will find difficult, academic-style texts more comprehensible. Their writing style will improve, and they will be better able to write prose in a style that is acceptable to schools, business, and the scientific community. Their vocabulary will improve and will improve at a better rate than if they took one of the well-advertised vocabulary building courses. Also, their spelling and control of grammar will improve.

The rest of the day was devoted to presentation of related studies—some by Krashen's doctoral students—and discussion of plans for a national reading promotion campaign sparked by AASL President Blanche Woolls.

Public Libraries

The literature of public librarianship is filled with references to the belief that public libraries are educational institutions. Results of a Gallup poll released at the 1993 ALA annual conference confirm that the American people share that belief. The survey was supported by a 1992 grant from the U.S. Department of Education under the Library Research and Demonstration Program (Title IIB of the Higher Education Act). The grant was made to George D'Elia of the Information and Decision Sciences Department at the Carlson School of Management of the University of Minnesota. D'Elia was advised by a panel of librarians and collaborated with the University of Minnesota Center for Survey Research and the Gallup Organization. The final report of this project, *The Roles of the Public Library in Society,* was published in the fall of 1993 by the Urban Libraries Council (ULC).

A national sample of the general public and a national sample of community opinion leaders were asked to evaluate the importance to their communities of ten different roles of the public library. These roles included the public library serving as

- Community activities center
- Center for information about the community
- Educational support center for students of all ages
- Learning center for adult independent learners
- Recreational reading center of popular materials and bestsellers
- Discovery and learning center for preschool children
- General information center for community residents
- Information center for community business
- Research center for scholars and researchers
- Comfortable, quiet place where residents can go to read, to think, or to work

The respondents evaluated each role in terms of its importance to their community using the response categories "not important," "slightly important," "moderately important," or "very important." Figures in the executive summary of the report show that more than 80 percent of the general public rated the following roles as "very important:"

- Educational support center for students of all ages (88 percent)
- Learning center for adult independent learners (85 percent)
- Discovery and learning center for preschool children (83 percent)

All other roles were rated "very important" by from 41 percent to 68 percent of the general public. More than 78 percent of the opinion leaders rated the same top three goals as "very important" and from 38 percent to 65 percent rated the other goals as "very important."

In addition to questions about public library roles, the questionnaire asked about financial support for public libraries. The respondents were informed that communities in this country spend from as little as $4 per capita to as much as $100 per capita, with the national median at $16 per capita. Respondents were asked to choose from a possible range of values from zero dollars per capita to more than $100 per capita in increments of $20. The average per capita expenditure that respondents thought the community should spend annually on the public library was $39.86 for African Americans, $33.73 for Caucasian Americans, $39.22 for Hispanic Americans, and $41 for the community opinion leaders. All these responses suggested that levels of library support are well above the national median (for 1990) of $16.

Data was gathered through two national telephone surveys—a national probability sample of 1,001 adults aged 18 or older and a survey of 300 community opinion leaders (defined as "individuals who, because of the positions they hold in the community, have an influence on the shaping of public opinion," such as newspaper editors). The basic survey of the general public was supplemented by two additional national probability samples—401 African Americans and 399 Hispanic Americans (the budget did not allow for samples of smaller minority groups).

The full report contains details on methodology and procedure as well as 123 tables and accompanying text. Most of the tables show differences in evaluation of importance of libraries' roles by different segments (i.e., demographic characteristics) of the three samples—Caucasian Americans, African Americans, and Hispanic Americans—and by both public library users and nonusers in each group. For each of the three racial/ethnic groups, data is given for each of 22 demographic characteristics (such as marital status and total annual household income) and four categories of library use (personal visit, phone call). The executive summary of the report suggests how public librarians can use this data:

> These demographic comparisons of the data can be used to generate a tentative set of roles for a library or even for branches within a library system. For example, a library could begin by identifying the significant service populations of its community based on race, gender, age, education level, size of household, or any of the other demographic characteristics reported in these surveys. For each of these significant service populations (for example, African-American households with preschoolers), the library could then identify the roles that are reported in these surveys to be most important to the respondents who represent the service population. . . . The library could then draw the reasonable inference that the service populations in its community would most likely share the same opinions about the importance of the roles as the respondents in the survey who represented those service populations. A library could then develop a tentative set of roles for its community that could be tested by a small

community survey, or by interviews with representatives of its various service populations, or by town meetings, or by any other method appropriate to local conditions or resources.

Additional commentary on the importance, meaning, and use of these results is provided by researcher George D'Elia and Urban Libraries Council (ULC) President Joey Rodger in the January/February 1994 issue of *Public Libraries*.

Private-Sector Funding

Although D'Elia's research may indicate that the American people are willing to financially support public libraries at a much higher level, the reality is that many public libraries are finding it increasingly difficult to provide the programs people expect with funds currently available from public sources. As a result, many are turning to the private sector, often establishing local public library foundations to receive and dispense private funds. This solution is not without problems, however, and ULC received a $37,950 grant from the H. W. Wilson Foundation in 1993 to study the issues involved.

Principal investigator for the study is Thomas Jeavons, director of the Center on Philanthropy and Nonprofit Leadership at Grand Valley State University, Grand Rapids, Michigan. Issues to be examined include:

- What happens to the commitment of local government to provide support for public library services when major private fund raising is done
- Why the independent sector should give money to historically tax-supported institutions such as the public library
- If tax-supported institutions begin to seek major funding from the independent sector, with whom they are competing
- Whether public library boards and directors risk skewing the priorities of the public library in order to attract or retain private funds

The study was to be completed early in 1994.

Data on Literacy

In fulfilling their educational roles, many public libraries have become involved in various activities that promote literacy. The recent report on *Adult Literacy in America* therefore should be of great interest to the library community. The work reported was requested by Congress in 1988 because of a growing concern that a large proportion of the U.S. population lacks literacy skills adequate to keep the United States competitive in the global society. Congress knew something had to be done but lacked information about the extent and nature of the problem. To gather such data, the National Center for Education Statistics (NCES) sponsored the National Adult Literacy Survey through a contract to Educational Testing Service and a subcontract to Westat. The report presents an overview of the results; six other reports will present more details or specific issues (among them "literacy among older adults" and "literacy and cultural diversity").

Adult Literacy in America is based on household interviews with nearly 27,000 adults aged 16 and older. This number includes 1,100 inmates of federal and state prisons and 11 sample supplements within participating states. In addition to completing literacy tasks, participants answered questions about such matters as their demographic characteristics, educational backgrounds, reading practices, and labor-market experiences. The "literacy tasks" were designed so that each participant could be ranked at level 1 (low), 2, 3, 4, or 5 (high) for each of three different skills:

- Prose literacy—locating, understanding, and using information from texts that include editorials, news stories, instruction manuals, and fiction
- Document literacy—locating, integrating, and using information contained in schedules, lists, order forms, indexes, maps, graphical displays, and tables
- Quantitative literacy—locating quantities embedded in prose or documents, inferring the appropriate arithmetic needed to obtain the needed results, and applying the proper operations to the numbers

The report presents results for each level of each skill by 10 demographic characteristics (such as age and level of education). It also shows literacy skills by social and economic characteristics such as voting behavior, economic status, and employment status. The executive summary of the report notes that

> While the literacy levels on each scale can be used to explore the range of literacy demands, these data do not reveal the types of literacy demands that are associated with particular contexts in this pluralistic society. That is, they do not enable us to say what specific level of prose, document, or quantitative skill is required to obtain, hold, or advance in a particular occupation, to manage a household, or to obtain legal or community services, for example. Nevertheless, the relationships among performance on the three scales and various social or economic indicators can provide valuable insights, and that is the goal of this report.

Internet Use

Today's public libraries serve an important social role by providing literacy services. Vice President Al Gore has suggested that in the future they will probably serve a quite different social role by serving as a "safety net" for access to Internet. Late in 1993 the National Commission on Libraries and Information Service (NCLIS) announced plans to investigate the readiness of public libraries to fill this role by supporting a survey of public library involvement with Internet. Findings will be analyzed to identify potential federal policies relating to the public library role in developing a networked information infrastructure for the nation.

Charles R. McClure, professor at the School of Information Studies at Syracuse University, and Douglas L. Zweizig, professor at the School of Library and Information Studies at the University of Wisconsin–Madison, are co-principal investigators for this study. Questionnaires were mailed to a national sample in January 1994 and a preliminary report was to be presented at the Public Library Association (PLA) National Conference in Atlanta in March. The four-page questionnaire was designed to provide information about such topics as the following:

- Degree to which public libraries have operational connections to Internet
- Type of provider the library uses to obtain connectivity
- Number and type of people in the library who have Internet addresses
- Internet services and resources that are used by the librarians and their assessment of these services and resources
- Library programs or services that have been developed incorporating use of Internet
- Barriers or problems related to using Internet
- Estimated expenditures and costs for connecting to and using Internet
- Special arrangements by which libraries are connected to Internet, such as state network users, federal grant recipients, subsidized Internet access rates, and so on
- Libraries that are not connected but are planning for Internet access in the near future

Special Libraries

An innovative exploratory study of Internet use was published by the Special Libraries Association (SLA) in April 1993. In the introduction to *The Internet and Special Librarians,* Sharyn J. Ladner and Hope N. Tillman explain that

> We wrote this book because we think the Internet and what it represents has the potential to make or break the profession of special librarianship. We believe that the impact of networked information on twenty-first century life and industry will be as great as that of the steam engine which ushered in the Industrial Revolution in the late eighteenth century.

Ladner and Tillman are extremely optimistic about the potential of networked information to transform special librarianship and about the potential of librarians to play key roles in the development and use of networked information.

This study used Internet to identify participants, to administer the survey, and to release results before formal publication. Its purpose was not to determine extent of use by special librarians but to find out how and for what purpose a self-selected group of people who consider themselves special librarians use Internet. Fifty-four individuals participated in the study. Based on their responses the authors were able to

- Describe how special librarians who have access to Internet (or BITNET) use these networks and how they pay for access
- Determine what advantages or opportunities these networks have for special librarians
- Identify barriers to access or other disadvantages for special librarians
- Identify training needs and protocols for special librarians

In addition to these results, the report includes speculation about the future (that Internet use is essential to the viability of the special library, for example) and numerous appendices to help a beginner get started.

Value of Libraries

SLA also published *Special Libraries: Increasing the Information Edge* by José-Marie Griffiths and Donald W. King. This report, SLA Research Series No. 9, is the result of a 1992 SLA research grant that enabled the authors to compile and analyze results of a series of their studies beginning with a project performed in 1981–1982 for the U.S. Department of Energy, Office of Scientific and Technical Information (OSTA):

> The purpose of the book is to summarize and present accumulated evidence of the usefulness, value, and impact of information, and of the contribution that organization libraries make to the benefits gained from its use. This evidence is derived from 27 independent studies performed with 16 companies, 7 government agencies, and including 4 national surveys of professionals (collectively more than 10,000 statistical survey responses from scientists, engineers, lawyers, and management, administration, marketing, and other professionals).
>
> We show that professionals who use information extensively and effectively are more successful than those who do not. Increased productivity and improved quality are among the benefits gained. Furthermore, substantially greater benefits are achieved from information provided through organization libraries. This relative advantage or gain achieved through effective use of information and libraries is what we refer to as the "information edge."

Librarians in all types of libraries are increasingly concerned about demonstrating the value of libraries and librarians to the people they serve. This concern has been most acute in the special library community, and the topic has a prominent place on SLA's research agenda. The Griffiths–King report is an impressive contribution to the literature on this important topic and is an essential base for any additional work. The ten chapters present detailed information and succinct analysis accompanied by 64 tables and 94 figures.

Awards That Support Research

ALISE

The first library and information science research awards of the year were presented in January at the annual meeting of the Association for Library and Information Science Education (ALISE), which preceded the 1993 ALA midwinter meeting in Denver. Darlene Weingand and Rebecca Watson-Boone (Wisconsin–Madison), winners of the ALISE Research Grant for 1992, described results of their project entitled "Dimensions of Effectiveness of Schools of Library and Information Studies." Adapting the research model of the Public Library Effectiveness Study (1989) by Thomas Childers and Nancy Van House, the investigators surveyed a sample of each of four constituencies of a universe of ALA-accredited library and information science (LIS) schools. When asked to identify indicators that are most useful in evaluating the effectiveness of a LIS school, all four constituent groups (Committee on Accreditation, senior university administrators, employers, and alumni) place accreditation status, faculty awareness of new developments in the field, the reputation of the school, and how employers view the school's graduates among their "top ten" indicators. They also focus on the goals and objectives of the school, the reputation of the faculty, and the direction the school provides to professional practice. Beyond these, each constituent group prefers a slightly different set of indicators. Detailed results will be published in a series of articles, the first to appear in the *Journal of Library and Information Science Education* in the spring of 1995.

The 1993 ALISE Research Grant was awarded to Linda C. Smith (Illinois) for a project entitled "Interdisciplinarity in Schools of Library and Information Science." Smith will gather baseline data to characterize the nature and extent of interdisciplinarity in U.S. schools by means of two questionnaires: one sent to all full-time faculty in schools with ALA-accredited master's programs and a second sent to deans and directors of those schools. The questionnaires will gather a considerable amount of descriptive data and will also invite comments through open-ended questions.

The 1992 Jane Anne Hannigan Research Award winner, Christine Jenkins (Wisconsin–Madison), presented results of her study of "Youth Service Librarians, the American Library Association and Intellectual Freedom for Young People, 1940–1973." The 1993 Hannigan Research Award winner, Joy McGregor (Florida State), described her plans for a study of "Cognitive Processes and the Use of Information: A Qualitative Study of Higher-Order Thinking Skills used in the Research Process by Gifted Students."

Library Acquisition: Practice and Theory (LAPT)

In the spring, *Library Acquisition: Practice and Theory (LAPT)* announced the recipients of its 1993 Research Award: Samuel Demas, Anne S. Caputo, and William J. Kara. Demas is head of collection development and preservation at Cornell University's Albert R. Mann Library in Ithaca, New York. Caputo is manager, academic programs, at Dialog Information Services. Kara is acquisitions librarian at Cornell's Albert R. Mann Library.

Their proposal, "Viability of the Vendor Model of Information Delivery through a Library Gateway," describes a study that

> . . . aims to determine the viability of the "vendor model" of information delivery through a library gateway. By offering a campus community unrestricted access to an unprecedented scope of electronic information, libraries and vendors will learn for the first time: which files are used, how much they are used, by whom they are used (e.g., faculty, staff, students), and at what times of the day and night. This data is essential for database vendors trying to structure fixed fee pricing schedules, and for libraries in selecting files, choosing access mechanisms, and planning information delivery systems.

AASL

At the 1993 annual conference of ALA in New Orleans, winners of three American Association of School Librarians (AASL) research grants were announced. Judy M. Pitts of Tallahassee, Florida, and the team of Julie I. Tallman and Jean Donham van Deusen of Iowa City, Iowa, are the first recipients of AASL/Highsmith Research Grants. The grants, up to $2,500 for each project, are sponsored by the Highsmith Co. Inc. of Fort Atkinson, Wisconsin, to enable school library media specialists, library educators, library information science or education professors to conduct innovative research aimed at measuring and evaluating the impact of school library media programs on learning and education.

Pitts, who is currently completing her doctorate in the School of Library and Information Studies at Florida State University, will receive $2,098.90 for a project titled "Intuitive Understandings and Mental Models of Information: A Qualitative Study of Factors Associated with the Information Seeking and Use Behavior of Adolescents." She will explore how students learn by attempting to discover the effect of prior knowledge on decision-making processes related to information seeking and use. The results will be designed to aid educators in developing teaching strategies to improve information-seeking and information-use behaviors in students.

Tallman and van Deusen will receive $2,500 for a project titled "Scheduling Impact on Curriculum Involvement and Information Skills Instruction: Should We Switch to Flexible Scheduling?" The project will investigate flexible scheduling in terms of curriculum involvement of the library media program, integration of library skills into the content areas, and accessibility to students to determine the effect of those factors on student learning. Tallman is an assistant professor in the School of Library and Information Science at the University of Iowa. Van Deusen is the districtwide library media and technology coordinator for the Iowa City Community School District.

Other ALA Units

The Association of College and Research Libraries (ACRL) announced the winner of ACRL's Doctoral Dissertation Fellowship at its President's Program on June 28. Weijing Yuan, library technician and teaching assistant at the University of Toronto, received the award for her dissertation "Long-Term Monitoring of End-User Searching Behavior in Adapting to an Information Retrieval System."

The winner of ALA's Carrol Preston Baber research award was announced at the ALA Membership Meeting. Debra Wilcox Johnson, assistant professor in the School of Library and Information Studies at the University of Wisconsin–Madison, will develop and test performance measures for family literacy programs in public libraries. The work to be supported by the Baber grant builds on Johnson's 1992 national survey of public library family literacy programs, which found that evaluation was the weakest component. Johnson will identify and evaluate existing measurement techniques, develop new measures, if needed, and explore ways to use technology in the measurement effort. One result will be a manual of measurement techniques for public libraries with family literacy programs.

Two ALA grants that support research were not made in 1993 because of a lack of suitable proposals: ACRL's $1,000 Samuel Lazerow Fellowship for Research in Acquisition or Technical Service and the $500 Frances Henne Young Adult Library Services (YALSA)/VOYA (Voices of Youth Advocates) Research Grant.

Medical Library Association (MLA)

At its 1993 annual meeting in Chicago, the Medical Library Association (MLA) presented its 1993 Research, Development, and Demonstration Project Grant to

Joan Leishman, executive director, Health Sciences Information Consortium, Toronto, Ontario, and Jennifer Bayne, director, Fudger Health Sciences Library, Toronto Hospital. The two librarians will apply the grant to "A Study to Measure the Impact of a Problem-Based Learning Curriculum on the Teaching Hospital Library of the University of Toronto."

MLA also announced the awarding of its doctoral fellowship to Valerie Florance, of the Edward G. Miner Library at the University of Rochester School of Medicine and Dentistry in Rochester, New York. Florance is a doctoral candidate at the University of Maryland–College Park and is working on a dissertation entitled "A Clinical Extract of Biomedical Literature for Patient-Care Problem Solving."

SLA

The $15,000 Research Grant offered by the Special Libraries Association (SLA) was awarded this year to a team headed by Marilyn D. White of the University of Maryland College of Library and Information Services (CLIS) for a project entitled "Measuring Customer Satisfaction and Quality of Service in Special Libraries." Others working on this project are Eileen Abels of CLIS and Danuta Nitecki of the University Library.

The project will assess customer satisfaction in an information service context with several objectives: identifying existing models in business that may be applicable, comparing values and perceptions of service quality held by information center users and providers, and developing a data-gathering instrument that can be used to derive customer satisfaction measures about the delivery of information services.

Awards that Recognize Research

ALISE

The first awards for research well done were also made at the January 1993 conference of the Association for Library and Information Science Education (ALISE) in Denver. The $400 ALISE Doctoral Dissertation Award for 1993 went to Kathleen Eisenbeis (Texas–Austin) for "Privatizing Space-Derived Data: A Case Study of the Effects of the Land Remote-Sensing Commercialization Act of 1984 on the Academic Geography Community." A book based on this dissertation is to be published by Scarecrow in 1994.

The 1993 ALISE Research Paper Award ($500) was won by Wayne Weigand who presented a paper entitled "Catalog of 'A.L.A.' Library (1893): Origins of a Genre." The paper will be included in *For the Good of the Order: Essays in Honor of Edward G. Holley,* a festschrift to be published in 1994 by JAI Press.

ALA

ALA usually announces winners of two awards for research papers at its annual conference—the Library Research Round Table (LRRT) Jesse H. Shera Award for Research and the Library History Round Table (LHRT) Justin Winsor Prize.

Neither award was given for 1993. LHRT was able to find a winner for its new Phyllis Dain Library History Dissertation Award—Plummer Alston Jones, Jr., head librarian/director of learning resources, Iris Holt McEwen Library/LaRose Resources Center at Elon College in North Carolina. Jones received the award for his dissertation "American Public Library Service to the Immigrant Community, 1876–1948; A Bibliographical History of the Movement and its Leaders: Jane Maud Campbell (1869–1947), John Foster Carr (1869–1939), Eleanor (Edwards) Ledbetter (1870–1954), and Edna Phillips (1890–1954)."

ASIS

In October, at its 56th annual meeting, the American Society for Information Science (ASIS) announced awards to several researchers. Its general award, the Award of Merit, was given to Robert M. Hayes, retired dean of the Graduate School of Library and Information Science at the University of California at Los Angeles. Hayes, who served as 1963 president of the American Documentation Institute (the forerunner of ASIS), is a highly respected educator and researcher and widely published author whose efforts in the field of information science have affected the academic and professional careers of thousands of scientists and practitioners.

The ASIS Research Award, which honors a systematic program of research in a single area at a level beyond the single study and recognizes outstanding research contributions in the field of information science, was presented to Howard White, professor at Drexel University. White has been active in diverse areas of information science, through his own research and through that of his students, and is an articulate spokesman for the quantitative point of view in information science. The Research Award recognizes his substantial body of research representing the evolution of information science in the last two decades.

The Best JASIS Paper Award went to Ray R. Larson of the School of Library and Information Studies at the University of California, Berkeley, for a paper in the January 1992 issue of the *Journal of the American Society for Information Science* entitled "Evaluation of Advanced Retrieval Techniques in an Experimental Online Catalog." The abstract to that lengthy article reads as follows:

Research on the use and users of online catalogs conducted in the early 1980s found that subject searches were the most common form of online catalog search. At the same time, many of the problems experienced by online catalog users have been traced to difficulties with the subject access mechanisms of the online catalog. Numerous proposals have been made for methods intended to improve subject access to online catalog records. These commonly involve enhancing the catalog's bibliographic records with additional terms, or incorporating subject authority files or additional thesauri in the database. Another stream of research has concentrated on applying retrieval techniques derived from information retrieval (IR) research to replace the Boolean search methods of conventional online catalog systems. This study describes the results of retrieval tests using a variety of these search methods in the CHESIRE experimental online catalog system.

Three doctoral students were winners of the ASIS Doctoral Forum Award presented for outstanding doctoral research done in the information field. The winners are:

- Margaret Wilkinson, University of Western Ontario, for "Impact of the Ontario Freedom of Information and Protection of Privacy Act of 1987 upon Affected Organizations"
- Carol Barry, Louisiana State University, for "User Defined Relevance Criteria: An Exploratory Study"
- Dee Andy Michel, University of California at Los Angeles, for "A File Structure Model of Library Search Behavior"

OCLC

This annual article usually includes a good bit of detail about research at OCLC based on what appears in the yearly *Annual Review of OCLC Research.* Since that publication was not available yet for 1992–1993 when this article was written, the full story cannot be told. News reports of three Library and Information Science Research Grants to library school faculty have appeared, however, and are summarized below:

- Carolyn Frost, associate dean, School of Information and Library Studies, University of Michigan, will study gopher users' information searching behavior, identifying patterns and problems in the searching behavior and recommending changes for improvement. Her study is entitled "An Empirical Test of Gopher Searching Using Three Organization Schemes."
- Richard Smiraglia, associate professor, Palmer School of Library and Information Science, Long Island University, will further the bibliographic control of works by verifying the extent of derivative bibliographic relationships in the OCLC Online Union Catalog and by testing a conceptual model for a database of bibliographic works. His study is entitled "Toward the Bibliographic Control of Works: Derivative Bibliographic Relationships in the Online Union Catalog."
- James Sweetland, associate professor, and Judith Senkevitch, assistant professor, School of Library and Information Science, University of Wisconsin, Madison, will question whether there is a core of widely held adult fiction in the OCLC database that can be used as a list of classics. "Evaluating Public Library Fiction Collections: Is There a Core List of Classics?" will study the feasibility for OCLC to consider using the core list concept to develop a machine-readable product to assist public libraries in evaluating their fiction collections.

One reason for the delay in publishing the *Annual Review* was the transfer of Martin Dillon from director of the Office of Research to director of Library Resources Management at OCLC. Tom Hickey and Ed O'Neill will be co-directors of the Office of Research.

CLR and DOE Library Programs

Articles that appear elsewhere in this edition of the *Bowker Annual* on the Council on Library Resources (CLR) and the U.S. Department of Education (DOE) Library Programs include information about sponsored research as well as other programs funded by these agencies. Of particular interest in the CLR article is the $97,612 grant to Rutgers University to develop tools that measure the costs and benefits of university library functions. Paul B. Kantor and Tefko Seracevic are principal investigators on this project.

As was noted last year, Library Programs no longer calls for field-initiated proposals to be funded by Title II-B of the Higher Education Act. Instead, funds available under this title are going to the School of Library and Information Studies at the University of Wisconsin–Madison for a program to train personnel in state library agencies to plan and conduct evaluations of library programs. As part of that effort, however, one field-initiated project was funded in 1993. ALA's Young Adult Library Services Association (YALSA) received funds to develop a manual of output measures for public library services to young adults similar to the general manual developed by the Public Library Association (PLA)—*Output Measures for Public Libraries*—and the companion volume developed by PLA and the Association for Library Services to Children (ALSC).

Title II-A of the Higher Education Act, also administered by Library Programs, authorizes four different types of grants under the College Library Technology and Cooperation Grants Program. Of the 33 new grants funded by this program in 1993, seven were classified as research and development.

Library Associations

AALL

The American Association of Law Librarians (AALL) has been planning a more active role in the research arena for several years. In the spring of 1993 the AALL board accepted the research agenda prepared by a special committee. The agenda lists researchable questions under five broad headings. Examples of the questions are:

- How can librarians determine whether a researcher has successfully used an end-user access tool, gotten the correct answer to a reference question, or found the information that he or she was looking for?
- What is the appropriate role for law librarians in the provision of pro bono (free) services to indigent and pro se patrons (those representing themselves)?
- How is the public affected by the growing reliance on electronic sources for legal research and restrictions on access to electronic tools?

The full agenda was published in the October 1993 issue of the *AALL Newsletter*.

ALA

The 1993 annual conference of ALA in New Orleans featured a preconference on "Research in Cataloging and Classification: Ways and Means" sponsored by the Research Committee of the Cataloging and Classification Section of the Association for Library Collection and Technical Services (ALCTS). Elaine Svenonius of UCLA was the keynote speaker. Other presenters included Ruth Carter (University of Pittsburgh) on getting published, Richard Smiraglia (Long Island University) on research methods, and Carol Mandel (Columbia University) on developing research questions.

At the first breakout session, small groups discussed general development of a research project. Later breakout sessions focused on research projects in one of four areas: classification, descriptive cataloging, authority control, or subject cataloging. A brief report on the preconference was prepared by Catherine S. Herlihy for the *ALCTS Newsletter* (Volume 4, No. 6/7, 1993). *Cataloging and Classification Quarterly,* Volume 19, No. 1 will publish a bibliography prepared for the preconference by Martha O'Hara Conway and the paper by Ruth Carter on how to get research results published.

Among the several meetings focusing on research at the 1993 conference, one deserves special mention. The Library Research Round Table (LRRT) sponsored a presentation by Janice Radway, author of *Reading the Romance,* who described her current research on the Book-of-the-Month-Club. Radway focused on the early judges of the club and their attitudes toward book selection and evaluation. Placing her remarks within the context of qualitative methodology, she talked about the possibilities and difficulties of combining archival and ethnographic research while exploring difficulties in trying to address the complexities of reading and the ways books are actually used.

In November, ALA's Reference and Adult Services Division (RASD) published proceedings of a preconference on "Research in Reference Effectiveness" held at the 1992 annual conference in San Francisco. Published as RASD Occasional Paper No. 16, the publication was edited by Marjorie E. Murfin and Jo Bell Whitlatch. Eight papers are included from one or more of the following authors: Sharon Bostick, Danuta Nitecki, W. Michael Havener, Anna M. Donnelly, Karen Williams, Janet J. Fore, John M. Budd, Helen R. Tibbo, John V. Richardson, Matthew Schall, Nancy F. Stimson, Kathleen Gunning, and Kimberly Spyers-Duran.

Two chapter titles indicate the content of this volume:

- "The Development and Validation of the Library Anxiety Scale" by Sharon L. Bostick
- "User Criteria for Evaluating the Effectiveness of the Online Catalog" by Danuta Nitecki

Another ALA division formed a research committee in 1993. At the midwinter meeting in Denver, the LITA (Library Information Technology Association) Task Force on Library Research recommended to the LITA board the establishment of a LITA research committee. The board accepted the suggestion and charged the new committee as follows:

To promote the development and diffusion of research skills in the LITA membership; encourage the conduct of research about, and application of research results to, information technology issues of concern to the profession; support the dissemination of information technology research; and influence the quality and direction of information technology research. To foster communication and research relationships with other units of the American Library Association, vendors of information technology products and services, graduate schools of library and information science, and other organizations involved in information technology research, both nationally and internationally. To work with other units of the Association to develop and define statistical measures related to the availability, cost, use, and effectiveness of electronic information resources and systems in libraries.

It is fortunate that this committee is in place, given the NSF/ARPA/NASA initiative described at the beginning of this article.

Number of Libraries in the United States and Canada

Statistics are from the forty-sixth edition of the *American Library Directory 1993-94 (ALD)* (R. R. Bowker, 1993). Data are exclusive of elementary and secondary school libraries.

Libraries in the United States

Public Libraries	15,312*
Public libraries, excluding branches	9,097†
Main public libraries that have branches	1,299
Public library branches	6,215
Academic Libraries	4,619*
Junior college libraries	1,255
Departmental	88
Medical	7
Religious	3
University and college	3,364
Departmental	1,455
Law	179
Medical	212
Religious	104
Armed Forces Libraries	463*
Air Force	130

Note: Numbers followed by an asterisk are added to find "Total libraries counted" for each of the three geographic areas (United States, U.S.-administered regions, and Canada). The sum of the three totals is the "Grand total of libraries listed" in *ALD*. For details on the count of libraries, see the preface to the forty-sixth edition of *ALD—Ed.*

Medical	17
Army	182
Law	1
Medical	36
Navy	151
Law	1
Medical	19
Government Libraries	1,871*
Law	424
Medical	229
Special Libraries (excluding public, academic, armed forces, and government)	10,149*
Law	1,140
Medical	1,925
Religious	1,011
Total Special Libraries (including public, academic, armed forces, and government)	11,257
Total law	1,745
Total medical	2,445
Total religious	1,118
Total Libraries Counted(*)	32,414

Libraries in Regions Administered by the United States

Public Libraries	27*
Public libraries, excluding branches	12†
Main public libraries that have branches	3
Public library branches	15
Academic Libraries	51*
Junior college libraries	7
University and college	44
Departmental	21
Law	2
Medical	1
Armed Forces Libraries	3*
Air Force	1
Army	1
Navy	1
Government Libraries	9*
Law	1
Medical	2

Special Libraries (excluding public, academic, armed forces, and government)	17*
Law	4
Medical	5
Religious	1

Total Special Libraries (including public, academic, armed forces, and government)	21
Total law	7
Total medical	8
Total religious	1

Total Libraries Counted (*)	107

Libraries in Canada

Public Libraries	1,755*
Public libraries, excluding branches	751†
Main public libraries that have branches	139
Public library branches	1,004

Academic Libraries	522*
Junior college libraries	146
Departmental	45
Medical	1
Religious	3
University and college	376
Departmental	183
Law	20
Medical	21
Religious	21

Government Libraries	387*
Law	20
Medical	6

Special Libraries (excluding public, academic, armed forces, and government)	1,260*
Law	106
Medical	248
Religious	77

Total Special Libraries (including public, academic, and government)	1,365
Total law	146
Total medical	276
Total religious	101

Total Libraries Counted (*)	3,924

Summary

Total U.S. Libraries	32,414
Total Libraries Administered by the United States	107
Total Canadian Libraries	3,924
Grand Total of Libraries Listed	36,445

†Federal, state, and other statistical sources use this figure (libraries *excluding* branches) as the total for public libraries.

Library Acquisition Expenditures, 1992–1993: U.S. Public, Academic, Special, and Government Libraries

For more than two decades, the R. R. Bowker Company has compiled statistics on public and academic library acquisition expenditures (Tables 1 and 2) from information reported in the *American Library Directory (ALD)*. Since 1987, statistics also have been compiled for special and government libraries (Tables 3 and 4). The information in these tables is taken from the forty-sixth edition of the directory (1993) and in most cases reflects expenditures for the 1992–1993 period. The total number of U.S. libraries listed in the forty-sixth edition of *ALD* is 32,414, including 15,312 public libraries, 4,619 academic libraries, 10,149 special libraries, and 1,871 government libraries.

Understanding the Tables

Number of libraries includes only those U.S. libraries in *ALD* that reported annual acquisition expenditures (5,894 public libraries, 2,867 academic libraries, 2,231 special libraries, 535 government libraries). Libraries that reported annual income but not expenditures are not included in the count. Academic libraries include university, college, and junior college libraries. Special academic libraries, such as law and medical libraries, that reported acquisition expenditures separately from the institution's main library are counted as special libraries.

The amount in the *total acquisition expenditures* column for a given state is generally greater than the sum of the categories of expenditures. This is because the total acquisition expenditures amount also includes the expenditures of libraries that did not itemize by category.

Figures in *categories of expenditure* columns represent only those libraries that itemized expenditures. Libraries that reported a total acquisition expenditure amount but did not itemize are only represented in the total acquisition expenditures column.

Unspecified includes monies reported as not specifically for books, periodicals, audiovisual materials and equipment, microform, preservation, other print materials, manuscripts and archives, machine-readable materials, or database fees. This column also includes monies reported for categories in combination— for example, audiovisual *and* microform. When libraries report only total acquisition expenditures without itemizing by category, the total amount is not reflected as unspecified.

Table 1 / Public Library Acquisition Expenditures

State	Number of Libraries	Total Acquisition Expenditures	Books	Other Print Materials	Periodicals	Manuscripts & Archives	AV Materials	AV Equipment	Microform	Machine-Readable Materials	Preservation	Database Fees	Unspecified
Alabama	84	5,724,140	2,881,454	310,778	400,591	—	359,923	18,276	366,308	41,706	16,051	64,555	233,369
Alaska	23	2,060,289	821,350	63,437	111,481	—	161,951	20,957	27,020	7,758	9,776	170,382	2,457
Arizona	58	10,351,512	6,620,987	28,685	1,135,708	—	387,065	27,520	274,806	216,561	125,681	82,548	6,578
Arkansas	32	2,374,709	1,355,078	1,941	176,977	6,500	32,486	13,462	45,706	5,850	13,478	41,945	16,711
California	176	104,482,788	45,864,752	392,203	26,421,543	30,354	5,488,272	121,272	3,645,574	365,606	510,355	1,096,259	2,887,651
Colorado	93	10,892,128	6,083,297	4,772	1,089,095	10,970	459,099	9,373	206,272	61,799	29,838	284,935	153,458
Connecticut	137	12,716,337	6,558,151	54,348	1,216,462	350	735,332	83,750	199,740	96,936	50,253	415,500	84,491
Delaware	22	2,128,472	698,541	1,000	107,587	—	55,713	24,528	17,021	20,048	—	31,218	—
District of Columbia	3	36,181,700	30,000	—	5,000	—	5,000	—	—	—	15,000	—	5,000
Florida	111	36,054,484	15,849,312	84,861	2,189,213	—	1,081,091	117,604	484,336	162,294	135,183	348,320	222,270
Georgia	49	11,142,145	5,286,409	60,132	443,906	—	579,012	36,066	200,470	27,748	9,125	8,080	15,996
Hawaii	3	3,197,279	2,387,676	110	787,594	—	21,899	—	—	—	—	—	—
Idaho	64	2,880,554	2,102,919	3,385	180,775	—	105,672	7,650	7,975	11,426	24,467	71,730	8,592
Illinois	403	46,200,415	23,934,724	653,348	3,286,685	2,500	2,826,427	226,022	770,135	269,721	105,459	701,968	516,122
Indiana	168	22,548,058	12,648,204	48,158	1,894,744	3,000	1,894,507	180,716	222,265	312,160	124,382	210,667	766,993
Iowa	298	7,775,475	5,054,132	39,297	710,312	148	448,436	49,448	70,802	101,464	39,240	59,992	49,829
Kansas	198	8,995,092	5,980,505	65,200	813,063	—	423,141	14,683	44,066	76,479	27,146	149,098	313,185
Kentucky	85	5,583,783	2,444,218	10,967	247,471	60	245,972	45,524	67,397	19,124	15,717	31,649	111,628
Louisiana	55	10,658,075	5,201,210	5,000	966,688	—	299,062	51,183	122,174	12,999	48,744	54,277	774,853
Maine	115	2,216,757	1,302,042	2,168	227,964	3,017	92,907	11,700	28,827	5,410	18,987	33,377	11,296
Maryland	29	93,756,616	12,438,507	25,001	727,805	50,838	77,053,684	3,274	38,374	176,534	3,383	170,161	147,840
Massachusetts	273	22,479,500	14,677,700	35,020	1,767,330	5,500	962,947	59,091	224,165	225,572	37,395	159,978	477,648
Michigan	258	29,476,989	11,581,988	236,302	1,925,370	5,764	2,364,730	53,482	339,594	89,884	37,950	236,568	456,279
Minnesota	106	14,631,115	8,632,498	153,680	1,049,608	—	969,695	25,282	85,107	224,903	44,278	653,549	19,663
Mississippi	42	3,409,109	1,890,379	9,702	287,391	2,963	157,340	7,930	33,667	22,823	14,477	6,090	17,390

State												
Missouri	88	12,208,241	6,337,709	4,880	1,033,267	219	784,229	25,907	351,508	103,117	91,361	79,603	758,152
Montana	52	1,709,834	620,679	2,374	134,077	—	40,923	10,119	5,388	10,469	5,138	78,419	204,704
Nebraska	112	3,321,699	1,834,417	8,094	349,007	—	95,063	12,931	41,479	12,170	19,147	48,981	104,652
Nevada	18	4,159,618	1,863,298	2,050	369,999	—	16,019	5,585	49,772	500	3,075	4,600	5,500
New Hampshire	136	5,610,730	1,552,200	8,290	179,730	621	86,327	8,564	44,364	6,956	12,143	8,130	13,014
New Jersey	250	31,118,328	17,317,613	104,595	2,969,783	1,316	1,571,506	224,337	483,150	451,729	111,236	380,344	570,990
New Mexico	36	3,425,859	2,099,670	5,500	353,437	550	43,300	65,085	21,750	14,360	24,070	5,514	138,350
New York	485	89,891,330	55,231,429	939,810	7,188,012	43,300	4,274,669	234,540	1,105,178	259,662	228,226	363,679	2,758,603
North Carolina	102	15,982,585	11,206,940	108,378	1,605,596	2,209	1,064,205	276,819	205,829	154,472	107,321	59,177	203,635
North Dakota	31	1,176,088	577,879	20,150	133,594	—	48,515	2,000	16,383	6,802	4,893	3,025	4,503
Ohio	217	59,692,151	32,330,733	870,310	6,632,344	7,532	5,956,544	114,060	1,598,279	520,716	985,668	705,637	417,923
Oklahoma	61	5,816,308	3,130,104	15,847	778,167	—	364,263	14,872	72,213	77,935	33,639	196,227	249,159
Oregon	86	7,305,123	4,551,903	19,261	926,758	—	604,865	6,400	8,609	40,234	51,766	62,274	29,530
Pennsylvania	338	26,170,384	14,573,118	128,705	2,661,970	4,402	1,420,231	84,389	1,273,493	146,091	183,798	340,459	1,243,700
Rhode Island	35	2,280,029	1,453,453	—	216,008	1,592	128,925	5,030	43,050	60,850	33,897	64,482	3,027
South Carolina	39	10,879,143	5,090,164	6,457	675,289	3,100	348,012	26,361	71,763	119,713	47,595	35,400	2,715,751
South Dakota	43	2,161,188	1,025,117	8,649	191,344	—	163,413	21,250	27,536	7,965	1,861	336,840	27,486
Tennessee	80	9,630,623	5,503,054	34,570	952,899	—	669,781	15,544	180,606	27,313	74,689	138,733	1,618,399
Texas	287	27,395,076	16,263,300	109,733	3,757,710	1,652	1,639,598	79,845	343,283	226,763	176,359	279,161	677,301
Utah	30	4,390,972	3,280,901	52,319	410,537	—	425,420	42,876	21,950	310	26,034	38,791	14,000
Vermont	97	1,886,207	1,012,078	3,506	144,038	—	57,973	200	63,430	179	6,614	2,059	6,281
Virginia	78	22,689,071	12,035,310	261,501	2,200,913	48,983	853,765	42,776	389,231	223,207	95,122	106,239	690,527
Washington	60	18,477,424	11,807,892	43,232	2,352,231	100	1,261,946	12,898	366,994	50,751	53,277	233,999	66,146
West Virginia	62	3,019,199	1,039,109	2,050	179,946	5,238	94,377	7,123	6,871	5,445	6,460	18,033	82,528
Wisconsin	253	14,787,083	8,612,313	72,585	1,745,384	145	1,190,680	59,437	139,316	76,412	45,810	284,307	742,507
Wyoming	22	1,483,849	706,000	21,969	125,750	500	60,056	25,090	39,140	3,745	13,230	71,090	14,557
Pacific Islands	1	180,000	—	2,500	—	—	—	—	—	—	—	—	—
Puerto Rico	4	2,070,578	591,560	4,000	1,405,765	—	—	—	—	200	53,024	8,029	8,000
Virgin Islands	—	—	—	—	—	—	—	—	—	—	—	—	—
Total U.S.	5,988	896,836,241	423,973,976	5,150,810	87,843,918	243,423	120,497,753	2,589,496	14,484,976	5,172,581	3,933,262	9,168,914	20,529,874
Estimated % of Acquisition Expenditures			61.13	0.74	12.67	0.04	17.37	0.37	2.09	0.75	0.57	1.32	2.96

Table 2 / Academic Library Acquisition Expenditures

State	Number of Libraries	Total Acquisition Expenditures	Books	Other Print Materials	Periodicals	Manuscripts & Archives	AV Materials	AV Equipment	Microform	Machine-Readable Materials	Preservation	Database Fees	Unspecified
Alabama	48	17,002,952	5,465,508	202,437	8,793,704	6,429	166,696	100,933	351,089	62,821	561,532	119,233	293,779
Alaska	7	2,515,737	513,246	4,190	653,314	1,500	6,586	2,000	80,152	52,537	56,843	47,100	29,444
Arizona	26	21,629,857	2,378,385	18,000	2,148,053	—	197,759	76,836	173,978	169,445	51,693	104,370	648,957
Arkansas	29	8,613,393	2,570,943	20,545	4,050,942	63,396	103,540	45,099	253,380	206,508	177,608	232,272	123,052
California	215	118,646,571	29,439,476	2,717,332	45,077,812	33,708	1,554,312	1,922,113	2,397,155	1,057,931	4,143,202	1,159,763	5,762,116
Colorado	43	20,910,014	5,630,175	73,701	6,464,915	5,330	265,253	99,473	551,524	323,826	331,848	239,418	111,735
Connecticut	67	34,268,247	11,158,488	989,315	14,822,271	2,114,300	183,384	122,120	1,805,767	269,054	1,165,797	104,927	487,099
Delaware	7	5,301,800	2,593,744	29,000	2,352,380	45	13,532	21,800	16,578	32,100	10,700	38,778	71,630
District of Columbia	28	21,368,784	4,495,553	168,879	7,143,719	500	93,356	14,721	253,883	54,810	319,954	140,651	38,681
Florida	85	39,599,694	9,388,476	358,726	15,906,828	6,966	807,218	459,546	1,454,084	865,978	829,235	514,874	535,392
Georgia	67	27,413,340	7,795,186	486,817	13,390,818	27,000	285,459	178,816	1,520,838	474,320	229,014	739,045	679,068
Hawaii	13	5,843,667	1,706,749	600	2,895,340	—	65,737	19,000	48,609	17,930	254,489	12,580	163,825
Idaho	11	5,273,145	1,200,308	49,400	2,663,762	500	25,620	15,618	73,510	17,094	130,524	43,252	395,747
Illinois	117	58,953,296	16,813,581	404,869	21,938,418	12,262	819,127	559,972	1,058,534	735,958	997,162	787,012	837,250
Indiana	62	26,994,825	7,841,296	564,732	13,636,730	258,144	321,617	307,551	210,212	244,436	915,085	470,753	142,244
Iowa	47	16,182,244	3,280,446	13,764	4,533,624	1,200	200,948	111,817	86,380	108,821	118,388	89,884	159,171
Kansas	46	9,903,128	1,942,262	42,860	2,840,730	42,500	117,934	111,074	105,615	129,648	123,777	70,256	75,433
Kentucky	51	16,563,862	3,427,099	728,102	5,877,469	2,500	177,874	41,346	396,673	168,074	379,701	232,504	84,789
Louisiana	33	18,602,915	5,235,898	112,491	7,404,771	10,939	109,356	328,452	301,620	412,984	482,005	219,382	—
Maine	24	6,280,596	2,180,165	179,480	2,818,817	9,000	73,668	51,627	148,893	52,783	146,525	130,521	80,864
Maryland	49	23,857,972	7,006,714	52,900	10,105,517	500	237,701	178,243	288,738	248,943	340,546	220,219	3,199,146
Massachusetts	111	66,940,267	18,394,843	922,943	19,645,788	8,023	583,047	324,823	870,524	740,683	2,286,870	1,420,056	4,646,177
Michigan	100	47,449,822	12,132,700	387,798	19,681,969	16,057	466,419	297,416	633,004	391,856	984,119	607,177	1,081,905
Minnesota	56	22,888,029	8,019,545	469,579	8,825,194	2,855	347,418	259,805	164,908	183,381	1,123,034	180,588	683,873
Mississippi	34	9,835,671	1,470,763	6,950	4,056,205	500	210,851	184,605	185,915	133,872	125,270	32,331	64,495

Missouri	76	27,934,358	79,898	13,300,668	14,734	410,810	322,808	688,749	393,954	395,555	333,031	1,018,697
Montana	13	3,301,922	3,310	2,010,215	2,000	38,410	8,850	23,723	41,132	33,370	37,922	62,000
Nebraska	29	9,553,797	123,228	2,610,078	—	131,357	113,838	235,471	62,786	97,459	94,561	49,621
Nevada	7	5,072,508	165	2,058,573	—	122,231	183,717	320,398	134,126	177,032	20,031	95,772
New Hampshire	21	3,713,397	6,700	1,854,861	—	43,085	24,720	112,925	58,520	27,662	28,598	31,342
New Jersey	61	25,930,790	927,671	10,484,089	167,687	214,061	77,453	632,534	346,682	486,815	246,260	379,893
New Mexico	23	7,114,537	469,411	3,579,210	4,292	125,758	65,263	160,260	94,188	208,839	51,212	14,565
New York	227	115,250,232	2,202,320	43,623,011	17,263	1,059,401	507,983	2,195,032	1,214,086	2,337,000	1,319,109	4,456,601
North Carolina	104	38,133,541	66,220	18,494,271	8,101	755,391	586,412	896,291	711,323	886,706	543,580	500,832
North Dakota	15	5,288,837	19,200	1,512,992	—	64,020	35,797	61,533	13,361	28,543	66,612	33,920
Ohio	137	59,422,964	169,274	28,415,768	6,821	655,551	203,965	587,531	354,981	1,363,186	535,330	1,712,891
Oklahoma	40	12,182,198	73,123	5,993,540	800	155,520	116,786	296,094	147,350	221,700	127,401	109,047
Oregon	41	12,581,596	59,902	6,521,402	3,000	223,416	84,182	319,491	232,960	206,252	228,252	214,364
Pennsylvania	169	72,885,944	513,175	21,900,234	22,380	746,153	335,569	875,562	693,917	1,666,834	933,155	1,000,865
Rhode Island	11	9,817,649	—	3,951,789	625	40,664	62,461	102,742	67,743	285,211	166,338	2,397,978
South Carolina	54	13,751,804	390,092	6,627,442	1,781	209,542	56,089	342,226	182,014	437,417	226,683	113,239
South Dakota	17	3,839,664	—	1,936,239	500	39,716	64,590	25,192	23,583	92,888	104,884	56,698
Tennessee	63	23,791,504	738,842	12,522,196	50,820	274,154	171,564	302,400	221,384	388,969	343,950	1,239,950
Texas	155	70,333,104	621,721	28,999,738	79,745	1,445,112	722,497	2,025,182	1,075,996	1,453,525	1,250,100	1,011,309
Utah	11	8,204,740	27,573	3,543,979	14,611	70,928	41,296	44,532	172,365	230,176	64,560	6,313
Vermont	21	6,172,463	5,590	2,051,877	43,555	89,762	37,792	226,219	95,038	140,112	200,376	873,425
Virginia	73	37,429,715	577,700	18,483,831	2,100	541,480	368,907	879,529	593,435	620,653	465,766	1,050,201
Washington	45	22,573,521	169,432	12,260,050	25,978	359,793	474,832	366,764	277,884	171,786	229,596	129,125
West Virginia	26	6,724,439	36,180	1,043,110	102,396	56,421	116,374	147,215	68,653	25,310	138,371	702,655
Wisconsin	69	27,004,926	45,466	7,168,762	14,415	585,454	235,997	523,327	403,702	271,387	327,722	727,911
Wyoming	7	3,590,393	—	2,073,406	—	79,580	—	6,396	34,548	96,380	29,587	318,720
Pacific Islands	4	472,725	400	136,322	—	33,000	1,850	800	5,000	—	5,000	—
Puerto Rico	33	4,707,478	3,902	2,204,256	500	208,850	65,791	38,204	6,200	47,112	150,750	47,198
Virgin Islands	2	418,455	—	134,000	—	8,500	—	19,304	4,037	6,093	10,100	—
Total U.S.	579	70,895,447	2,229,122	19,237,644	40,670	1,184,205	223,960	801,732	820,053	2,338,937	4,856,247	1,305,170
Estimated % of Acquisition Expenditures		36.28	4.30	37.10	0.08	2.28	0.43	1.55	1.58	4.51	9.37	2.52

Table 3 / Special Library Acquisition Expenditures

| | | | | | | | Categories of Expenditure | | | | | | |
State	Number of Libraries	Total Acquisition Expenditures	Books	Other Print Materials	Periodicals	Manuscripts & Archives	AV Materials	AV Equipment	Microform	Machine-Readable Materials	Preservation	Database Fees	Unspecified
Alabama	9	632,550	139,450	1,000	252,000	1,000	1,000	—	17,000	33,000	7,000	34,100	104,000
Alaska	7	83,950	22,200	3,000	15,550	800	—	1,700	—	14,500	4,200	17,000	—
Arizona	29	1,146,449	194,262	13,000	273,142	1,100	7,020	1,000	20,732	14,041	10,500	288,093	166,877
Arkansas	3	54,572	13,760	250	30,012	150	10,200	—	200	—	—	—	—
California	217	15,084,189	2,870,258	127,322	3,051,213	77,920	277,038	53,451	151,378	455,749	189,989	2,361,885	157,101
Colorado	43	2,733,899	356,944	16,000	1,015,000	26,000	74,830	51,980	115,811	71,050	29,278	272,507	128,870
Connecticut	51	3,434,214	581,385	126,311	586,495	16,260	39,765	14,900	17,515	24,850	147,192	143,153	40,247
Delaware	10	1,490,719	258,304	—	148,921	4,263	5,428	5,309	7,435	—	32,399	76,260	568,000
District of Columbia	68	5,378,892	1,350,533	148,850	1,936,024	8,800	6,550	12,700	43,689	30,209	38,693	325,387	37,050
Florida	59	2,851,519	783,122	63,440	848,834	5,200	42,378	16,953	31,378	48,939	29,013	437,569	37,085
Georgia	31	1,361,070	209,319	1,300	250,631	1,000	33,064	10,200	7,220	11,814	27,321	64,235	3,219
Hawaii	10	692,682	137,146	200	360,716	—	4,137	100	—	6,200	1,281	36,450	—
Idaho	8	213,429	54,000	—	71,000	—	1,000	—	—	10,800	—	8,200	—
Illinois	133	10,603,377	2,101,622	154,351	2,801,254	70,875	129,862	56,775	341,108	172,055	238,060	387,729	84,793
Indiana	49	1,656,028	284,522	117,700	541,417	2,002	27,426	30,078	38,620	104,745	8,225	221,022	64,738
Iowa	35	981,670	278,968	28,639	308,900	500	19,128	41,218	550	11,000	11,743	58,972	5,745
Kansas	22	355,558	77,860	7,209	85,002	—	6,162	7,575	19,300	5,578	4,223	12,421	775
Kentucky	18	613,059	97,041	500	101,909	39,413	7,850	7,000	39,413	7,500	7,048	11,145	—
Louisiana	13	415,459	81,091	2,925	223,746	12,425	8,951	2,653	3,900	5,400	8,477	30,610	3,851
Maine	25	646,274	76,331	1,600	324,209	2,115	19,824	2,787	250	1,000	11,959	43,084	4,565
Maryland	62	2,604,807	536,031	72,245	965,047	2,550	49,281	35,682	80,555	40,157	41,400	469,171	708
Massachusetts	113	9,486,702	3,479,952	58,930	2,191,065	21,173	85,912	18,499	34,595	179,693	110,230	873,596	44,283
Michigan	66	4,913,650	1,366,182	55,846	1,478,650	3,100	75,318	34,640	53,126	126,027	38,573	332,151	49,585
Minnesota	47	3,031,592	1,237,112	179,562	386,098	22,373	18,461	28,331	111,202	48,662	50,456	191,910	26,375
Mississippi	5	59,875	5,900	1,025	45,116	—	800	100	2,225	—	1,634	—	—

State												
Missouri	49	5,171,876	701,607	75,512	1,991,974	8,315	38,020	8,639	6,100	19,780	205,197	551,500	128,452
Montana	12	143,817	38,279	1,730	51,040	1,050	14,450	—	12,197	—	5,183	9,738	—
Nebraska	15	203,535	41,679	500	26,193	2,000	2,420	735	35,102	300	1,250	2,445	3,127
Nevada	7	627,539	28,214	—	49,766	3,000	5,400	12,000	8,023	10,200	4,200	3,525	501,971
New Hampshire	13	936,131	231,095	8,500	369,505	4,800	1,000	631	1,100	40,680	23,300	37,600	500
New Jersey	70	6,360,539	1,748,533	55,225	2,058,932	1,500	44,577	26,753	74,390	79,928	17,575	421,540	49,110
New Mexico	23	1,961,425	578,663	2,700	1,313,089	400	11,394	2,400	1,450	3,742	9,250	18,000	19,737
New York	217	25,666,890	4,187,709	902,956	3,451,162	45,750	106,392	2,049,687	177,200	189,150	368,004	4,089,410	258,260
North Carolina	38	1,751,806	504,580	4,450	586,092	57	23,735	45,500	101,077	7,580	3,600	59,458	51,500
North Dakota	8	220,659	51,853	1,427	90,295	—	5,430	7,900	—	20,833	28,267	10,970	1,802
Ohio	112	8,039,962	1,891,030	327,460	1,879,660	2,097	113,287	24,473	89,347	39,572	119,485	484,461	116,321
Oklahoma	18	507,768	231,360	2,249	207,193	—	3,150	4,000	25,000	7,600	1,000	15,775	2,420
Oregon	25	620,949	125,028	6,075	213,341	—	3,482	3,300	125	2,684	11,919	65,050	5,000
Pennsylvania	152	7,947,152	1,119,466	388,065	2,222,888	66,926	58,991	46,962	132,811	497,995	194,229	358,884	169,155
Rhode Island	14	120,438	21,961	75	38,684	1,400	1,348	1,500	1,100	5,692	6,747	7,128	349
South Carolina	15	391,645	66,236	1,695	80,985	3,500	12,299	13,727	20,900	—	11,714	20,544	9,770
South Dakota	6	140,297	45,131	95	51,405	—	6,244	129	—	—	—	15,066	337
Tennessee	31	1,980,162	508,491	32,314	836,759	1,000	57,313	30,783	27,968	73,097	31,645	44,843	5,435
Texas	83	6,472,625	1,543,651	156,331	1,870,192	23,250	70,883	28,313	73,717	136,283	105,623	320,529	65,467
Utah	7	483,020	87,105	26,550	69,015	15,000	—	—	178,400	—	5,000	2,770	24,000
Vermont	15	121,787	52,470	419	17,715	1,845	850	200	—	65	6,729	1,560	6,823
Virginia	74	5,589,597	670,596	67,975	910,685	46,263	42,678	66,530	180,511	150,500	60,094	579,929	63,722
Washington	32	2,056,033	294,459	5,314	820,013	17,161	33,510	107,000	32,000	181,700	9,661	66,200	4,611
West Virginia	9	339,409	34,810	500	244,598	—	7,000	1,900	1,700	3,000	945	8,900	12,075
Wisconsin	56	1,608,202	547,117	49,315	493,328	8,866	23,387	27,449	13,619	19,261	22,728	118,162	68,034
Wyoming	8	42,850	3,100	1,150	2,200	—	300	—	200	—	100	600	200
Pacific Islands	1	118,367	112,932	—	2,424	—	—	—	2,965	—	—	46	—
Puerto Rico	3	605,118	121,437	—	9,890	—	9,492	—	3,000	—	2,239	—	—
Virgin Islands	—	—	—	—	—	—	—	—	—	—	—	—	—
Total U.S.	2,944	1,300,354,595	334,872,560	16,341,405	520,345,300	3,208,258	16,286,870	10,922,189	25,890,189	14,886,741	28,725,704	16,235,783	38,751,004
Estimated % of Acquisition Expenditures		32.62		1.59	50.69	.31	1.59	1.06	2.52	1.45	2.80	1.58	3.78

Table 4 / Government Library Acquisition Expenditures

State	Number of Libraries	Total Acquisition Expenditures	Books	Other Print Materials	Periodicals	Manuscripts & Archives	AV Materials	AV Equipment	Microform	Machine-Readable Materials	Preservation	Database Fees	Unspecified
Alabama	5	237,442	88,172	1,277	16,856	—	3,000	—	3,000	2,150	3,720	5,670	5,645
Alaska	7	192,724	30,200	500	120,343	—	—	2,000	17,843	7,500	—	11,200	3,138
Arizona	12	951,570	79,800	4,000	50,800	1,000	3,800	100	5,500	—	3,500	40,000	—
Arkansas	2	182,589	37,159	4,807	103,696	—	17,523	—	335	—	—	14,633	—
California	60	8,916,462	1,841,146	667,784	2,647,219	—	180,141	19,358	95,754	17,450	80,514	295,394	141,700
Colorado	22	1,084,893	263,092	5,782	526,889	550	20,412	14,191	24,223	12,000	1,300	130,648	16,536
Connecticut	5	93,145	5,756	200	55,056	—	—	4,000	—	—	1,700	11,000	1,278
Delaware	2	104,598	85,388	1,000	7,000	—	1,000	2,000	7,310	—	900	—	—
District of Columbia	28	6,375,138	1,683,700	89,200	1,828,700	200	31,100	20,800	85,000	121,988	24,750	1,636,000	208,300
Florida	35	3,212,760	618,112	13,946	1,605,551	2,000	58,405	5,562	14,196	15,210	15,909	127,789	12,464
Georgia	3	142,370	63,100	5,800	61,200	—	4,200	—	20	—	2,000	3,500	6,750
Hawaii	3	777,088	165,790	480,120	19,200	—	—	—	56,000	—	—	1,000	49,778
Idaho	2	32,070	6,700	—	17,600	—	470	—	300	—	—	4,000	3,000
Illinois	13	4,182,947	864,964	—	469,931	—	7,300	3,000	49,958	700	86,500	16,000	—
Indiana	8	449,870	82,402	—	28,807	—	4,911	1,260	4,697	—	4,044	1,698	1,650
Iowa	7	148,747	33,225	1,654	87,800	20	1,900	—	3,000	—	—	6,200	5,000
Kansas	5	530,991	180,014	165,456	147,760	—	3,400	—	100	—	5,432	23,729	5,000
Kentucky	5	1,118,112	524,307	15,000	65,263	—	220,979	—	1,000	—	2,500	258,463	9,200
Louisiana	5	220,890	10,450	786	59,600	—	954	—	2,000	26,000	—	2,800	7,300
Maine	5	331,961	19,771	—	204,801	—	4,143	20,000	3,908	20,000	1,140	38,987	19,111
Maryland	13	10,592,299	1,231,677	32,000	3,673,750	6,500	201,000	6,500	10,000	32,000	1,856,150	499,536	142,805
Massachusetts	20	1,649,939	1,116,054	—	224,436	1,000	8,434	6,000	14,882	51,120	3,200	33,037	30,000
Michigan	15	877,488	174,321	14,483	204,995	—	10,827	1,100	17,434	8,015	2,535	22,629	834
Minnesota	8	617,709	81,300	210,650	182,459	3,000	8,700	13,400	11,000	8,000	1,500	75,600	9,675
Mississippi	5	346,918	14,794	—	34,052	—	4,495	—	—	—	494	4,924	—

State	No.											
Missouri	7	420,953	22,400	11,400	67,600	—	6,400	27,950	750	1,800	24,840	—	—
Montana	5	455,773	13,980	—	172,240	—	1,650	—	4,550	9,200	7,860	1,710	2,430
Nebraska	5	212,039	19,262	—	46,957	—	52,570	8,000	—	50	—	45,133	4,000
Nevada	6	848,384	413,365	—	66,648	—	7,900	5,100	7,842	300	3,610	76,619	1,000
New Hampshire	2	57,500	2,000	5,000	18,000	—	1,000	—	31,500	—	—	—	—
New Jersey	10	376,451	157,212	—	69,227	3,000	5,000	3,000	2,000	200	1,500	14,000	12,512
New Mexico	6	553,827	108,283	158,242	71,402	—	1,000	—	1,000	7,000	8,000	40,000	—
New York	50	4,232,373	1,549,912	71,133	392,226	—	19,796	8,000	86,562	58,978	18,693	50,375	19,102
North Carolina	10	1,354,535	487,596	3,050	577,852	—	4,963	—	13,109	3,526	16,525	202,000	3,889
North Dakota	3	85,480	28,471	—	47,004	—	785	—	2,295	360	165	5,700	700
Ohio	17	1,230,090	317,360	15,150	526,680	—	16,600	—	3,350	4,600	2,700	17,691	28,855
Oklahoma	9	516,204	123,901	27	55,098	—	10,768	1,009	—	70	6,748	9,634	2,271
Oregon	5	449,939	129,200	—	186,500	—	—	—	500	1,300	500	129,939	—
Pennsylvania	25	1,771,743	662,626	33,175	103,769	—	24,938	4,458	14,500	—	26,980	8,000	42,497
Rhode Island	3	426,245	34,344	—	53,749	—	10,040	—	6,195	12,917	4,000	26,000	—
South Carolina	5	166,293	51,600	—	20,600	—	22,500	5,600	—	—	—	63,355	—
South Dakota	6	77,336	23,435	—	35,625	—	5,217	4,002	2,000	559	800	800	4,698
Tennessee	8	255,862	78,846	500	135,195	500	9,000	10,300	—	2,200	5,421	7,700	3,000
Texas	11	139,178	52,180	3,050	45,332	3,050	3,770	3,144	7,524	9,000	9,000	7,672	605
Utah	6	298,928	38,969	—	104,500	600	28,084	—	61,880	10,760	9,200	25,295	5,513
Vermont	4	101,818	22,850	1,700	1,300	1,200	—	—	3,000	—	5,000	200	—
Virginia	20	5,059,946	3,382,507	5,500	747,561	—	21,210	1,626	64,848	257,000	13,681	418,363	350
Washington	13	1,692,464	172,484	500	266,102	10,000	16,320	—	5,000	2,000	24,126	16,330	35,443
West Virginia	5	827,474	401,876	10,400	106,237	600	75,500	—	30,100	10,000	10,000	31,500	6,861
Wisconsin	15	615,163	370,763	3,050	137,666	3,050	4,500	—	16,467	4,000	500	34,237	5,180
Wyoming	6	259,749	171,392	1,000	56,000	1,000	8,500	10,000	7,400	500	5,057	—	—
Pacific Islands	—	—	—	—	—	—	—	—	—	—	—	—	—
Puerto Rico	3	868,500	233,990	105,300	486,110	—	2,000	500	9,000	—	7,100	20,000	4,500
Virgin Islands	—	—	—	—	—	—	—	—	—	—	—	—	—
Total U.S.	2,252	151,461,183	32,368,887	3,300,737	38,657,574	573,199	1,665,417	2,945,342	2,342,204	2,912,611	2,308,778	14,067,483	3,117,245
Estimated % of Acquisition Expenditures			31.05	3.17	37.08	0.55	1.60	2.83	2.25	2.79	2.21	13.49	2.99

Library Price Indexes for Colleges and Schools

Kent Halstead

Research Associates of Washington, 2605 Klingle Rd. N.W., Washington, DC 20008

A rise in prices with the gradual loss of the dollar's buying power has been a continuing phenomenon in the U.S. economy. Libraries have been especially affected by the higher prices of books and periodicals. Price indexes are useful in documenting the impact of inflation. A measure of composite yearly price changes in the items libraries purchase can be projected to determine the additional funding required to maintain buying power. Price indexes can also be used to ascertain if spending has kept pace with inflation. A decline in constant dollars per user means a loss in real investment.

A price index compares the aggregate price level of a fixed market basket of goods and services in a given year with the price in the base year. To measure price change accurately, the *quality* and *quantity* of the items purchased must remain constant as defined in the base year. Weights attached to the importance of each item in the budget are changed infrequently—only when the relative *amount* of the various items purchased clearly shifts or when new items are introduced.

The indexes in Tables 1 through 6 are calculated with FY 1983 as the base year. This means that current prices are expressed as a percentage of prices for 1983. (Prices for library materials are generally quoted for the calendar year. They are reported here for the corresponding *fiscal year*—for example, calendar year 1985 prices are reported for FY 1985–1986.) An index of 110 means that prices have increased 10 percent since the base year. The indexes may be converted to any desired base period by dividing each index number by the value of the index for the selected base year.

Two composite library price indexes and their subcomponents are reported here for 1976–1991. For higher education, the academic library price index (LPI) reports relative price levels affecting the *total operating budget* of college and university libraries. For elementary-secondary schools, price levels for *new acquisitions* are reported. Subsequent data are currently available from Research Associates of Washington.

Academic Library Price Index

The Academic Library Current Operations and Acquisitions Price Index (LPI), together with its various subcomponents, is reported in Tables 2 through 5. The LPI reflects the relative year-to-year price level of the goods and services purchased by college and university libraries for their current operations. Table 1 shows the composition of the library budget for pricing purposes and the 1982–1983 estimated national weighting structure. The priced components are organized in three major categories—personnel compensation; acquisitions; and contracted services, supplies, and materials. Because the size, responsibilities, and collections of academic libraries vary widely within the higher education community, individual libraries may want to compile the price index for their

Table 1 / Budget Composition of College and University Library Operations by Object
Category, FY 1983 Estimate

Category	Percent	Distribution
Personnel Compensation		
1.0 Salaries and wages		50.0
1.1 Administrators	15.0	
1.2 Librarians	30.0	
1.3 Other professionals	5.0	
1.4 Nonprofessional staff	40.0	
1.5 Students	10.0	
	100.0	
2.0 Fringe benefits		10.0
Acquisitions		
3.0 Books and periodicals		26.0
3.1a U.S. college books	20.0	
3.1b North American academic books	20.0	
3.2 Foreign books	10.0	
3.3 U.S. periodicals for academic libraries	40.0	
3.4 Foreign periodicals	10.0	
	100.0	
4.0 Other materials		2.0
4.1 Microfilm	60.0	
4.2 16-mm film	5.0	
4.3 Videocassettes	15.0	
4.4 Filmstrip	10.0	
4.5 Prerecorded cassette tape	10.0	
	100.0	
Contract Services, Supplies, Equipment		
5.0 Binding		1.2
6.0 Contract services		5.4
7.0 Supplies and materials		3.0
8.0 Equipment		2.4
		100.0

Source: Derived from the National Center for Education Statistics, U.S. Department of Education, library
budget data for 1985 and earlier years.

own operations, using the price series in Tables 2 through 5 weighted by the composition of their local library budget. The tailoring procedure using a computer disk is outlined in *Inflation Measures for Schools & Colleges: 1993 Update.*[1]

The LPI reports inflation affecting a fixed market basket of goods and services and hence measures only the added funding necessary to buy the equivalent of last year's purchases. But library operations are seldom "business as usual." The collection acquisitions component in particular requires special attention.

The acquisition budget should consist of three parts, each of which must be separately defended:

(text continues on p. 465)

Table 2 / Academic Library Price Indexes for Major Components, FYs 1976–1991*

1983=100 Fiscal Year	Personnel Compensation		Acquisitions			Contracted Services, Supplies, and Materials			Library Price Index† LPI
	Salaries and Wages (L1.0)	Fringe Benefits (L2.0)	Books and Periodicals (L3.0)	Other Acquisitions (L4.0)	Binding (L5.0)	Contract Services (L6.0)	Supplies and Materials (L7.0)	Equipment (L8.0)	
1976	61.0	47.8	52.7	69.0	60.7	60.0	64.6	61.7	57.8
1977	64.2	52.8	57.8	70.9	64.7	63.5	67.8	64.8	61.6
1978	67.9	58.4	63.4	78.4	69.4	67.0	70.7	69.3	66.1
1979	73.1	64.5	70.9	79.5	75.2	71.0	75.2	74.7	71.8
1980	79.5	72.6	79.2	85.0	83.3	76.5	85.0	81.6	78.9
1981	86.5	81.8	89.7	83.7	89.7	85.3	92.9	89.6	87.0
1982	94.1	91.5	95.1	102.5	97.9	94.8	99.8	96.4	94.6
1983	100.0	100.0	100.0	100.0	100.0	100.0	100.0	100.0	100.0
1984	105.0	108.3	103.8	103.6	105.2	104.7	105.9	102.2	104.9
1985	110.4	117.7	108.7	104.8	106.8	109.2	112.1	104.8	110.4
1986	115.3	127.7	117.7	110.5	107.9	114.3	112.5	106.9	116.6
1987	119.5	137.4	131.7	101.2	111.6	117.8	118.8	108.8	123.6
1988	123.7	147.2	141.4	97.4	116.1	122.1	125.3	110.9	129.7
1989	130.3	158.8	153.1	99.8	124.0	129.0	137.9	115.8	138.2
1990	136.6	171.4	167.8	98.5	125.1	134.2	138.4	120.8	146.8
1991*	142.7	184.5	183.6	107.3	126.8	140.2	138.6	123.4	155.9

*Data for 1992 and 1993 are available from Research Associates of Washington.

†1983 weights: LPI=50.0% salaries and wages + 10% fringe benefits + 26.0% books and periodicals + 2.0% other materials + 1.2% binding + 5.4% contracted services + 3.0% supplies and materials + 2.4% equipment.

Sources: Personnel compensation, see Table 3; acquisitions, see Tables 4 and 5; binding, Bureau of Labor Statistics (BLS), earnings in the printing and publishing industry; contract services, Inflation Measures for Schools & Colleges: 1992 Update (Research Associates of Washington); supplies and equipment, Producer Price Index components, BLS.

Table 3 / Academic Library Price Indexes for Personnel Compensation, FYs 1976–1991

1983=100 Fiscal Year	Salaries and Wages						Fringe Benefits (L2.0)
	Administrators (L1.1)	Librarians (L1.2)	Other Professionals (L1.3)	Non-Professionals (L1.4)	Students (L1.5)	Total* (L1.0)	
1976	62.7	62.7	63.9	59.0	60.0	61.0	47.8
1977	65.1	65.1	66.9	62.9	64.4	64.2	52.8
1978	67.6	67.6	70.4	67.7	69.2	67.9	58.4
1979	73.0	73.0	74.5	72.7	74.7	73.1	64.5
1980	78.6	78.6	79.8	79.6	82.2	79.5	72.6
1981	85.4	85.4	86.7	87.0	89.4	86.5	81.8
1982	93.7	93.7	93.9	94.3	95.5	94.1	91.5
1983	100.0	100.0	100.0	100.0	100.0	100.0	100.0
1984	104.9	104.9	104.7	105.6	103.6	105.0	108.3
1985	111.3	111.3	111.6	109.9	107.4	110.4	117.7
1986	117.6	116.8	118.4	114.2	110.3	115.3	127.7
1987	124.2	120.2	125.4	118.3	112.1	119.5	137.4
1988	127.6	123.1	131.6	123.5	116.5	123.7	147.1
1989	138.2	130.6	139.2	128.7	119.9	130.3	158.8
1990	146.0	136.8	147.7	134.5	124.5	136.6	171.4
1991	154.6	143.0	155.7	139.7	129.8	142.7	184.5

*1983 weights: total salaries = 15% administrators + 30% librarians + 5% other professionals + 40% nonprofessionals + 10% students.

Sources: College and University Personnel Association, American Association of University Professors, and U.S. Bureau of Labor Statistics.

Table 4 / Academic Library Price Indexes for Books and Periodicals, FYs 1976–1991

| 1983=100 Fiscal Year | Hardcover Books | | | | | | Periodicals | | | Books and Periodicals |
| | U.S. College Books | | North American Academic Books | | Library of Congress Foreign Books | | U.S. Academic | | Foreign (7 countries) | |
	Price	Index (L3.1a)	Price	Index (L3.1b)	Price	Index (L3.2)	Price	Index (L3.3)	Index (L3.4)	Index* (L3.0)
1976	$13.20	52.8	$14.00	47.2	$7.91	65.4	$38.94	49.9	62.0	52.7
1977	14.80	59.2	15.50	52.3	8.89	73.5	41.85	53.6	67.0	57.8
1978	16.50	66.0	17.60	59.4	9.41	77.8	45.14	57.8	74.0	63.4
1979	18.02	72.1	19.60	66.1	11.52	95.3	50.11	64.2	80.0	70.9
1980	19.70	78.8	21.98	74.2	13.05	107.9	57.23	73.3	84.5	79.2
1981	21.50	86.0	25.00	84.4	13.84	114.5	67.81	86.9	93.8	89.7
1982	23.10	92.4	27.87	94.1	11.91	98.5	73.89	94.7	100.8	95.1
1983	25.00	100.0	29.63	100.0	12.09	100.0	78.04	100.0	100.0	100.0
1984	27.00	108.0	30.34	102.4	11.78	97.4	82.47	105.7	97.0	103.8
1985	29.00	116.0	31.77	107.2	11.66	96.4	86.10	110.3	102.9	108.7
1986	31.00	124.0	33.60	113.4	13.52	111.8	92.32	118.3	116.9	117.7
1987	33.40	133.6	36.93	124.6	15.94	131.8	104.69	134.1	132.1	131.7
1988	35.07	140.3	39.14	132.1	14.59	120.7	117.75	150.9	144.6	141.4
1989	38.14	152.6	41.21	139.1	17.97	148.6	125.87	161.3	153.4	153.1
1990	40.52	162.1	44.19	149.1	20.15	166.7	139.75	179.1	172.7	167.8
1991	42.01	168.0	46.53	157.0	22.84	188.9	158.53	203.1	184.5	183.6

Note: Prices of library materials are generally quoted for the calendar year, but they are reported here for the corresponding *fiscal year,* e.g., calendar year 1985 prices are reported for FY 1985–1986.

*1983 weights: books and periodicals = 20% U.S. college books + 20% North American academic books + 10% foreign books + 40% U.S. periodicals for academic libraries + 10% foreign periodicals.

Sources: U.S. College Books compiled by Kathrine Soupiset, Trinity University. North American Academic Books compiled by Stephen Bosch, University of Arizona. Foreign book prices compiled by Linda Pletzke, U.S. Library of Congress. U.S. Periodicals for Academic Libraries average subscription price, the Faxon Institute. Foreign periodical price indexes compiled from the Faxon Institute price data for Canada, France, Germany, Italy, Japan, the Netherlands, and the United Kingdom.

Table 5 / Academic Library Price Index for Other Acquisitions Components, FYs 1976–1991

1983=100 Fiscal Year	Microfilm Price	Index (L4.1)	16-mm Film Price	Index (L4.2)	Videocassettes Price	Index (L4.3)	Filmstrip Price	Index (L4.4)	Prerecorded Cassette Tape Price	Index (L4.5)	Machine-Readable CD-ROM Price	Index (L4.6)	Other Acquisitions Index* (L4.0)
1976	$0.1190	54.5	$12.85	85.6	$ —	—	$73.91	90.6	$10.32	96.1	$ —	—	69.0
1977	0.1335	61.1	12.93	86.1	—	—	58.41	71.6	12.08	112.5	—	—	70.9
1978	0.1475	67.5	13.95	92.9	—	—	76.26	93.4	10.63	99.0	—	—	78.4
1979	0.1612	73.8	12.56	83.7	—	—	62.31	76.3	12.47	116.1	—	—	79.5
1980	0.1750	80.1	13.62	90.7	—	—	65.97	80.8	12.58	117.1	—	—	85.0
1981	0.1890	86.5	12.03	80.1	7.58	72.4	67.39	82.6	9.34	87.0	—	—	83.7
1982	0.2021	92.5	16.09	107.2	14.87	142.0	71.12	87.1	12.48	116.2	—	—	102.5
1983	0.2184	100.0	15.01	100.0	10.47	100.0	81.62	100.0	10.74	100.0	—	—	100.0
1984	0.2274	104.1	15.47	103.1	11.04	105.4	79.57	97.5	11.23	104.6	—	—	103.6
1985	0.2450	112.2	16.93	112.8	8.44	80.6	85.76	105.1	9.99	93.0	—	—	104.8
1986	0.2612	119.6	16.50	109.9	10.24	97.8	83.50	102.3	8.99	83.7	—	—	110.5
1987	0.2350	107.6	16.85	112.3	7.44	71.1	85.33	104.5	10.61	98.8	—	—	101.2
1988	0.2198	100.6	17.00	113.3	6.79	64.9	112.15	137.4	8.50	79.1	—	—	97.4
1989	0.2352	107.7	18.96	126.3	7.21	68.9	74.45	91.2	10.12	94.2	1,533	99.8	99.8
1990	0.2244	102.7	20.63	137.4	5.67	54.2	89.14	109.2	10.58	98.5	1,740	113.3	98.5
1991	0.2507	114.8	18.40	122.6	5.60	53.5	121.76	149.2	10.47	97.5	1,710	111.3	107.3

*1983 weights: other acquisition materials = 50% microfilm + 5% 16-mm film + 15% videocassettes + 10% filmstrip + 10% prerecorded cassette tape + 10% CD-ROM disks.

Sources: Microfilm compiled by Imre Jarmy, U.S. Library of Congress. 16-mm film, videocassettes, filmstrip, and prerecorded cassette tape compiled by David Walch, California Polytechnic State University; CD-ROM disks by Pamela R. Mason, National Agricultural Library.

Table 6 / School Library Acquisitions Price Indexes, FYs 1976–1991

1983=100 Fiscal Year	Hardcover Books					Mass Market Paperback Books					
	Elementary*		Secondary		Total Index‡	Elementary		Secondary		Total Index§
	Average Price	Index	Average Price	Index		Average Price	Index	Average Price	Index	
1976	$5.82	65.6	$16.19	52.9	59.0	$1.07	53.0	$1.46	49.5	51.2
1977	5.87	66.2	17.20	56.2	61.0	1.22	60.4	1.60	54.2	57.3
1978	6.64	74.9	18.03	58.9	66.6	1.41	69.8	1.71	58.0	63.9
1979	6.59	74.3	20.10	65.7	69.8	1.47	72.8	1.91	64.7	68.8
1980	7.13	80.4	22.80	74.5	77.3	1.48	73.3	2.06	69.8	71.6
1981	8.21	92.6	23.57	77.1	84.5	1.65	81.7	2.50	84.7	83.2
1982	8.29	93.5	25.48	83.3	88.2	1.79	88.6	2.65	89.8	89.2
1983	8.87	100.0	30.59	100.0	100.0	2.02	100.0	2.95	100.0	100.0
1984	9.70	109.4	31.19	102.0	105.5	2.24	110.9	3.13	106.1	108.5
1985	10.11	114.0	29.82	97.5	105.4	2.28	112.9	3.38	114.6	113.7
1986	9.95	111.5	31.46	102.8	107.0	2.71	132.2	3.62	121.7	127.0
1987	10.64	118.5	32.43	105.9	112.0	2.71	134.2	3.86	131.2	132.7
1988	11.48	127.8	36.28	118.5	123.0	2.80	138.6	4.00	135.9	137.3
1989	11.79	131.3	39.00	127.4	129.3	3.18	157.4	4.55	154.6	156.0
1990	13.01	144.9	40.61	132.7	138.5	3.19	157.9	4.32	146.8	152.4
1991†	13.07	145.6	42.12	137.6	141.4	3.56	176.2	4.57	155.3	165.8

*Juvenile books (age 8 or younger), fiction.

†Data for 1992 and 1993 are available from Research Associates of Washington.

‡Hardcover books total = 47.9% elementary + 52.1% secondary.

§Mass market paperback books total = 50.2% elementary + 49.8% secondary.

Note: Prices for library materials are generally quoted for the calendar year. They are reported here for the corresponding *fiscal year*, e.g., calendar year 1985 prices are reported for FY 1985–1986.

Table 6 / School Library Acquisitions Price Indexes, FYs 1976–1991 (cont.)

1983=100 Fiscal Year	U.S. Periodicals					Microfilm		Audiovisual Materials						
	Elementary		Secondary		Total Index‖			16-mm Film		Videocassette		Filmstrip		
	Average Price	Index	Average Price	Index		Average Price	Index	Average Price	Index	Average Price	Index	Average Price	Index
1976	$4.69	47.4	$14.36	60.0	54.0	$0.1190	54.5	$12.85	85.6	$—	—	$73.91	90.6
1977	5.32	53.7	15.24	63.7	58.9	0.1335	61.1	12.93	86.1	—	—	58.41	71.6
1978	5.82	58.8	16.19	67.7	63.4	0.1475	67.5	13.95	92.9	—	—	76.26	93.4
1979	6.34	64.0	17.26	72.1	68.3	0.1612	73.8	12.56	83.7	—	—	62.31	76.3
1980	6.70	67.7	18.28	76.4	72.2	0.1750	80.1	13.62	90.7	—	—	65.97	80.8
1981	7.85	79.3	19.87	83.0	81.2	0.1890	86.5	12.03	80.1	7.58	72.4	67.39	82.6
1982	8.56	86.5	21.83	91.2	88.9	0.2021	92.5	16.09	107.2	14.87	142.0	71.12	87.1
1983	9.90	100.0	23.93	100.0	100.0	0.2184	100.0	15.01	100.0	10.47	100.0	81.62	100.0
1984	11.49	116.1	26.43	110.4	113.1	0.2274	104.1	15.47	103.1	11.04	105.4	79.57	97.5
1985	12.21	123.3	27.90	116.6	119.8	0.2450	112.2	16.93	112.8	8.44	80.6	85.76	105.1
1986	13.31	134.4	26.41	110.4	121.9	0.2612	119.6	16.50	109.9	10.24	97.8	83.50	102.3
1987	13.76	139.0	26.95	112.6	125.3	0.2350	125.9	16.85	112.3	7.44	71.1	85.33	104.5
1988	15.19	153.4	27.79	116.1	134.0	0.2198	117.8	17.00	113.3	6.79	64.9	112.15	137.4
1989	16.39	165.6	28.29	118.2	140.9	0.2352	126.0	18.96	126.3	7.21	68.9	74.45	91.2
1990	16.95	171.2	29.69	124.1	146.7	0.2244	120.2	20.63	137.4	5.67	54.2	89.14	109.2
1991	17.51	176.9	31.24	130.5	152.7	0.2507	134.3	18.40	122.6	5.60	53.5	121.76	149.2

‖ U.S. periodicals total = 47.9% elementary + 52.1% secondary.

Table 6 / School Library Acquisitions Price Indexes, FYs 1976–1991 (cont.)

1983=100 Fiscal Year	Audiovisual Materials (cont.)						Free Textbooks to Students					
	Prerecorded Cassette Tape		Multimedia Kits		Audiovisual Total Index**	Library Materials Index†† (7.1)	Hardbound		Paperbound		Total Index‡‡ (7.2)	Library Materials and Textbooks Index§§ (7.0)
	Average Price	Index	Average Price	Index			Average Price	Index	Average Price	Index		
1976	$10.32	96.1	$140.25	n/a	89.5	64.5	$4.10	57.7	$2.08	58.4	57.8	60.6
1977	12.08	112.5	93.63	n/a	76.1	63.8	4.67	65.7	2.27	63.8	65.3	64.7
1978	10.63	99.0	93.65	n/a	93.0	71.7	5.23	73.6	2.40	67.4	72.4	72.1
1979	12.57	117.0	117.38	n/a	79.9	71.8	5.78	81.3	2.70	75.8	80.2	76.7
1980	12.58	117.1	85.70	n/a	84.3	78.1	6.12	86.1	2.87	80.6	85.0	82.1
1981	9.34	87.0	92.71	n/a	81.9	83.6	6.42	90.3	3.05	85.7	89.4	86.9
1982	12.48	116.2	46.99	n/a	95.4	89.9	6.64	93.4	3.23	90.7	92.9	91.6
1983	10.74	100.0	57.52	n/a	100.0	100.0	7.11	100.0	3.56	100.0	100.0	100.0
1984	11.23	104.6	Discontinued		99.2	105.1	7.80	109.7	3.75	105.3	108.9	107.3
1985	9.99	93.0			103.3	107.1	8.40	118.1	4.05	113.8	117.3	113.0
1986	8.99	83.7			101.7	108.6	9.12	128.1	4.98	139.9	130.4	121.2
1987	10.61	98.8			102.5	112.6	9.71	136.4	5.73	161.0	141.2	129.1
1988	8.50	79.1			125.0	125.1	11.82	156.1	5.62 ‖ ‖	175.0	159.8	145.2
1989	10.12	94.2			94.0	124.0	12.63	166.9	6.10	190.0	171.4	151.4
1990	10.58	98.5			107.7	133.0	15.41	203.6	7.15	222.4	207.3	175.9
1991	10.47	97.5			135.1	142.1	17.64	233.1	7.89	245.4	235.5	196.1

**Total audiovisual = 12.3% 16-mm film + 7.9% videocassettes + 73.5% filmstrips + 6.3% prerecorded tapes.

††Library materials index = 61.2% hardcover books + 3.6% paperback books + 11.7% periodicals + 2.3% microfilm + 21.2% audiovisual.

‡‡Textbook index = 80.5% hardbound + 19.5% paperbound.

§§Library material and textbook index = 42.2% library materials + 57.8% textbooks.

‖ ‖Price source changed in FY 1988 and linked to previous series.

Sources: The following prices are published in Part 4 of the *Bowker Annual:* hardcover and paperback books; U.S. periodicals; 16-mm film, videocassettes, filmstrip, and prerecorded cassette tape; free textbooks, compiled from prices reported by the Association of American Publishers.

1 The basic acquisition budget is the amount required to maintain and update the collection; that is, sufficient funds to purchase annually the number of volumes that equals 5 percent of the collection (discounting older materials). The L3.0 and L4.0 components of the LPI preserve the purchasing power of this basic acquisition budget.

2 Additional acquisition funding is the amount required annually to *extend* the collection in breadth and/or depth to satisfy changes in curriculum and other educational programs, changes in institutional level, or in faculty needs. The LPI does not account for this funding.

3 Additional acquisition funding is the amount required annually to *upgrade* the overall rating of the collection by extending the quantity and price range of new acquisitions. This quality change is not accounted for by the LPI. In the event that additional funding becomes a permanent part of the basic funding requirement, the purchasing power of the enlarged basic acquisition budget may be maintained by using the L3.0 and L4.0 price series as deflators.

L1.0 Salaries and Wages

For pricing purposes, library personnel are organized in five divisions. *Administrators (L1.1)* consists of the chief, deputy, associate, and assistant chief librarian—that is, staff members having administrative responsibilities for management of the library. L1.1 is based on the head librarian salary series reported by the College and University Personnel Association (CUPA). *Librarians (L1.2)* are all other professional library staff. Since 1984–1985, the L1.2 price series is based on the average median salary for circulation, acquisition, technical service, and public service librarians reported by CUPA. *Other professionals (L1.3)* includes personnel who are not librarians in positions normally requiring at least a bachelor's degree, including curators, archivists, computer specialists, budget officers, information and system specialists, subject bibliographers, and media specialists. The Higher Education Price Index (HEPI) faculty salary price series is used as a proxy. *Nonprofessional staff (L1.4)* includes technical assistants, secretaries, clerical, shipping, and storage personnel specifically assigned to the library and covered by the library budget, but excludes general custodial and maintenance workers and student employees. As the category is dominated by office workers, its wages are based on the HEPI clerical workers price series reported by the BLS (Bureau of Labor Statistics) Employment Cost Index. *Students (L1.5)* are usually employed part time for nearly minimum hourly wages. In some instances, wages are set by work-study program requirements of the institution's student financial aid office. The proxy price series used for student wages is the Employment Cost Index series for nonfarm laborers reported by the Bureau of Labor Statistics.

L2.0 Fringe Benefits

The price of fringe benefits is based on the HEPI fringe benefit price series for all college and university personnel.

L3.0 Books and Periodicals Acquisitions

The price of U.S. book acquisitions for smaller college libraries (L3.1a) is based on the U.S. college books price series, which is derived from the prices of approximately 6,000 titles reviewed in *Choice* during the calendar year. The prices of books acquired by larger university libraries (L3.1b) are based on the North American academic books price series, which is derived from data on approximately 85,000 titles in approval plans. (In this national LPI the college and university price series have equal weight; however, in tailoring the LPI to its own needs, a library should use the more suitable series.) The price of *foreign books (L3.2)* is based on Library of Congress data on appropriated funds for foreign books and titles purchased.[2] The price of *U.S. periodicals (L3.3)* is based on the U.S. periodicals for academic libraries price series compiled by the Faxon Institute. *Foreign periodicals (L3.4)* prices are based on a fixed weighted index of unit prices for seven major countries from data provided by the Faxon Institute.[3]

L4.0 Other Materials

The five other materials—microfilm, 16-mm film, videocassettes, filmstrip, and prerecorded cassette tape—are representative of all collected library material other than books and periodicals. The largest estimated weight is assigned to microform used in the collection of government documents, newspapers, and preservation works. (Only the microfilm price is given; no price series for microfiche is available.) For the price sources, see Table 5.

L5.0 Binding

Binding is increasingly being contracted out at all but the largest libraries. As no wage series focuses exclusively on binding, L5.0 is based on the average weekly earnings of production or nonsupervisory workers in the printing and publishing industry (BLS, Employment and Earnings series).

L6.0 Contract Services

Services contracted by libraries include communications, postal service, data processing, and printing and duplication. The L6.0 price is based on the HEPI contracted services subcomponent. (In this instance the data processing component generally represents the library's payment for use of a central campus computer service.) Libraries may also contract out such specialized activities as ongoing public access cataloging (OPAC), which are not given separate prices in the L6.0 component.

L7.0 Supplies and Materials

Prices of office supplies, which constitute the bulk of library supplies and materials, are based on the BLS Producer Price Indexes.

L8.0 Equipment

Equipment is limited to small, easily movable, relatively inexpensive and short-lived items, such as hand calculators, projectors, fans, cameras, tape recorders, and small televisions, which are not regarded as depreciable capital equipment. Prices are based on the HEPI equipment price series.

School Library Acquisitions Price Index

The School Library Acquisitions Price Index measures year-to-year price changes for a typical fixed market basket of books, periodicals, and other materials purchased by elementary-secondary school libraries. Table 6 shows the index and its subcomponents as well as prices paid by schools for students' textbooks. See the footnotes to Table 6 for a brief description of the various price series and sources.

Notes

1. *Inflation Measures for Schools & Colleges: 1993 Update* (Research Associates of Washington, Washington, D.C., 1993) includes overall inflation measures for the higher education and school communities for 1976 through 1993.
2. The Library of Congress acquires much standard foreign material through exchange programs. Purchased foreign materials include exceptional monographs that would not normally be acquired by academic libraries.
3. Canada, Germany, France, Italy, Japan, the Netherlands, and the United Kingdom.

Expenditures for Resources in School Library Media Centers, FY 1991–1992

Marilyn L. Miller and Marilyn Shontz

This is the sixth in a series of *School Library Journal* reports summarizing specific developments in public and private school library media programs in the United States. The purpose of this series, begun in 1983, has been to provide readers of *SLJ* with an up-to-date account of national trends in expenditures for program development dependent on funding. It also provides a longitudinal review of trends in expenditures and program development. This report covers the school year 1991–1992. Previous reports were published in the October 1983, May 1985, June/July 1987, June 1989, and August 1991 issues of *SLJ*.

All of the articles have focused attention on the status of school library resources, expenditures for those collections, media center staffing, and instructional involvement. In addition, we have reported on the steady escalation in library media center use of microcomputers for management and program development and the emergence of communications technology in library media centers (LMCs).

Each *SLJ* report outlining expenditures for resources has provided additional, current data on one or more aspects of library media programs. The 1993 report broadens reporting on the use of microcomputers and other technologies and provides brief information on the use of the whole language strategy for teaching reading and its impact on the library media program.

All references to LMCs and staff in this report refer *only* to those schools that subscribe to *SLJ*. This year, all tables reflect data from both public and private schools. We are reporting no separate data for private schools, since responses were received from only 75 schools, reflecting 8 percent of the total survey response. The data are presented in a total of 19 charts and tables, offering readers several ways to compare their own LMC expenditures, services, and programs with a national norm.

This series of surveys has filled a need for up-to-date information about school library media program development. Since the publication in 1960 of *Standards for School Library Programs* (American Association of School Librarians/ALA), the landmark national standards that introduced the concept of the library as a program of multimedia services, only four comprehensive national surveys have been conducted by the federal government on the status of school library media programs. The most recent was published in 1986 by the U.S. Department of Education [National Center for Education Statistics. Statistics of Public and Private School Library Media Centers, 1985–1986 (with historical comparisons from 1958–1985). U.S. Department of Education, 1987].

Note: Reprinted from *School Library Journal,* October 1993. Marilyn L. Miller is professor and chair, Department of Library and Information Studies, School of Education, University of North Carolina at Greensboro, and immediate past president of the American Library Association. Marilyn Shontz is assistant professor, Department of Library and Information Studies, School of Education, UNC at Greensboro.

Major Findings

Two major findings, both with strong implications for the school library profession, emerged from this study. First, our commitment to the teaching and motivating of reading is crashing headlong into our fascination with technology. The nation is concerned about the fact that children are either learning to read and then not reading or they are not learning to read at all. Government officials and many organized groups talk about national goals for education, many of which depend on reading if they are to be met. School officials tout new reading programs, avow their concern with reading goals, and cut LMC book budgets or leave them at 1960 levels to purchase microcomputers, software, CD-ROMs, and videodiscs.

Access to books is being seriously curtailed by the rapidly deteriorating state of school library collections and community unwillingness to fund them. Or, is it lack of school leadership in informing communities of the sad state of school library media programs? Added to this is the current plight of public libraries. Failing public libraries are becoming the rule in community after community with closed branches, reduced hours, lower expenditures for resources, and increased demand for service and materials from children who cannot find the resources where and when they need them at school.

In many schools, funds are being diverted from print resources to computer software, CD-ROM, videotapes, and videodiscs. The funds being diverted or added, however, are not enough in many cases to develop a fully electronic library so that all can completely access the resources at the point of need. In other schools, LMCs are being developed as full-fledged modern information centers: a basic print collection and electronic access are being developed side-by-side, and young people have access to a rich environment of needed information.

This leads to the second major finding. For some time now, prognosticators have been worrying about the emergence of the information haves and have-nots. This series of studies has been describing the decline of school library collections for a decade. The most recent survey provides proof that we definitely have some learners who are information haves and others who are information have-nots.

The data reveal the emergence of electronic, or high-tech, library media centers. These centers, in technologically "smart" schools, are being developed with the requisite additional funds or, as noted above, at the expense of book collections. The high price of books, the popularity of video recordings for instructional purposes, inflation, the rapidity with which books go out of date, the addition of the costs of machines, and the software to use those machines are combining to make many of our school library media centers obsolete.

The problems associated with the clash between books and technology are further compounded by the increasing pressures on library media specialists. Library media specialists are struggling to keep up with constant changes in "the latest style" of managing schools. Yesterday we were concerned about teaching critical thinking skills; today we call the process "outcomes based education." Library media specialists are struggling to become teaching partners with teachers who don't want them. They are struggling to help reeducate teachers who are either out-of-date themselves or are entering teaching jobs ill-prepared by their teacher education programs to meet the demands of a society being reshaped by the parameters of "information literacy."

The North Carolina Public Schools Forum announced on July 12, 1993, that 80 percent of classroom teachers do not have basic computer skills. At the same time, media positions are being cut, support staff positions are being abolished, and media specialists' responsibilities are being broadened.

Methodology

In mid-September 1992, a questionnaire was mailed to 1,560 school library media centers in the 50 states. These were chosen by systematic random sampling from the *SLJ* school-based subscription list. (Questionnaires were mailed only to subscribers who indicated either the name of a school or some form of the title "school library media specialist" in the address.) Two subsequent mailings were sent to nonrespondents. By December 15, 918 responses had been received. The usable response rate was 57.8 percent, two and one-half percentage points higher than that of the last report.

Each response was checked for accuracy, then coded and entered into the computer. Data analysis was done using the Statistical Package for the Social Sciences (SPSS). Measures of central tendency (means and medians) were produced for all of the budget items listed on the survey. Chi Square and ANOVA tests were used in statistical analysis of data presented in Tables 18 and 19. (For purposes of this study, both means and medians are reported, wherever appropriate, to give a more accurate description of the data. The means provide comparability with earlier studies that have used this measure; the medians indicate accurately the expenditures reported by most LMCs.)

Although the mean (or average) is the descriptive statistic most commonly used in studies of this type, analysis of the data showed that much of it was positively skewed because a few respondents reported spending extremely large amounts for various kinds of library materials. With data distribution like this, the few large scores make the mean a less desirable measure of central tendency because those scores cause the mean to be unrealistically large.

In instances where the data were skewed, simply to report the mean would be misleading. For example, one respondent reported spending $10,000 for computer software, while another reported spending $3. This is a range of $9,997, resulting in a mean for all respondents of $1,055 but a more realistic median of $500. (The median represents the "middle" number if all responses were ordered from lowest to highest.)

As in previous surveys, each school library media specialist was asked to report the specific amounts expended for a variety of materials, including audiovisual rental fees and leasing costs, and microcomputer equipment purchases and maintenance costs. Respondents also were asked to note the size of the book collection and to estimate the extent to which it is out of date; to describe the LMC staff; and to report whether a system media coordinator was employed by the district.

Other questions, also asked in previous surveys, included those on the availability of online bibliographic and technical services and the availability and use of microcomputers, both by students and by library media specialists. In this survey, we continued the questions introduced in the previous survey about the use of resource-sharing networks. We also expanded the number of questions about other technologies and requested specific expenditures for CD-ROM and information about the use of videodisc technology.

The new survey also provides data on factors that affect the selection of resources for the LMC program and the availability of whole language reading instruction. It explores the relationship of the library media specialist to the whole language program and the impact of the program on the library media collection and its use.

There is no foolproof method for ascertaining all of the possible funding sources for the LMC program in a relatively short questionnaire. To our knowledge, no other national survey has attempted to report all major sources of funding. Table 4 presents mean and median expenditures for all resources in 1991–1992 from all traditional funding sources. It is acknowledged that this accounting does not consider district or regional funds or services that might be provided to the LMC.

In the latest survey, we continued to request information on expenditures from local, federal, and gift monies, including those from fundraisers, an ever more common occurrence in schools. "Local" is defined as money allocated by local school boards, states, and/or counties that fund all or part of local school expenses and are administered through the local education agency. Slightly over one-half of the LMCs received some type of gift funds. Although 82 percent of those receiving gift funds purchased books, the largest expenditures from this category were for microcomputer and audiovisual resources/equipment.

More than one-third of the respondents received federal funding. Federal funding is still available for some schools from the Education Consolidation and Improvement Act of 1981, commonly known as block grants. Some 113 respondents reported spending an average of $4,127 in federal funds on microcomputer resources, while 241 reported spending an average of $2,016 on books and 142 spent $2,100 on audiovisual resources. (Not shown on the table: The majority of the schools receiving federal funds were elementary, reporting a median expenditure of $2,000 and a mean expenditure of $5,181.)

Tables 5–8 summarize public and private school expenditures of funds reported categorically from local sources in fiscal year (FY) 1991–1992 and provide comparisons with the five previous studies. Table 5 reports mean and median amounts spent per school from local funds on books, AV, microforms, periodicals, software, and CD-ROM products. Table 6 shows a comparison of the median expenditures from all six *SLJ* reports. Table 7 summarizes per-pupil expenditures of local funds for resources in the same categories.

Table 8 shows modest increases in median pupil expenditures from local sources in FY 1991–1992 for all resources except AV materials. The 40 cents per pupil increase for books actually reflects a decline in allocations, since the inflation rate was 4.2 percent in 1990 and 3 percent in 1991. The average price for a hardcover children's book was $16.64 in 1992; the average price for an adult nonfiction book was $45.85. The average elementary media specialist could therefore purchase only about one-third of a book per child.

In all of these tables, the funds reported for AV materials include expenditures for new materials, videos, rentals, and leasing. From observation and conversations with many library media specialists, we assume the largest share of expenditures for audiovisual resources is used to purchase recorded videotapes. Amounts expended for microcomputer resources include software, online fees, and technical processing charges. The amount reported for periodicals includes money spent for magazines, journals, and newspapers for both student and professional use. The amount expended for books includes titles designated for the reference collection and all preprocessing costs.

Tables 5 and 7 introduce a new reporting category for CD-ROM. Figures for total median expenditures of $762 per school and $1.00 a pupil in 203 schools expand the description of all major resources in the developing electronic school library media centers.

In spite of the increasing availability of microcomputers being used for management in LMCs, many library media specialists have yet to establish an accounting method for their expenditures that permits them to retrieve specific amounts spent by category of resource. (Those respondents did estimate by category, which is helpful.) Other respondents just provided lump sums for materials such as print items, audiovisual and computer software, and services.

Respondents

Respondents were asked to describe themselves in terms of: gender; certification; educational background; employment status; years of experience both in education and in librarianship; and salary. Table 14 presents a summary of some of these data.

Tables 1–3 describe demographic characteristics of the respondents. Thirty-one percent of the total respondents to this survey were from high schools, up from 24 percent in the previous study. The percentage from elementary schools dropped to 40 percent from 45 percent. There was little change in junior high/middle school and "other" representation.

Regional reporting changes included a drop in the percentage of respondents from the Northeast and gains for those in the West and North Central regions. The percentage of respondents from the South remained steady at 39 percent.

Collections and Expenditures

Data about collections and expenditures are organized in Tables 9–13. Data on size of collections and expenditures reported categorically from local funds and organized by school level, region, and enrollment category are shown in Tables 9–11. In order to display the total amounts reported, whether categorically or in a lump sum, from all sources—local, federal, and gifts and fundraising—Total Materials Expenditures (TME) are reported at the bottom of each table for purposes of comparison. TME reflects *all* expenditures for resources, including audiovisual equipment, computer hardware, on-line services, rentals, leasing, supplies, and maintenance, but excluding salaries.

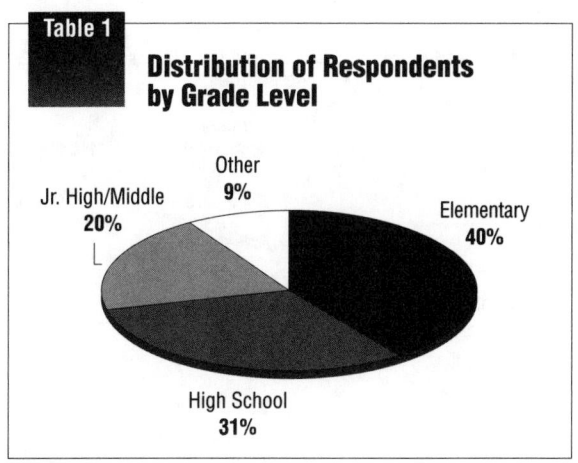

Table 1

Distribution of Respondents by Grade Level

Other
9%

Jr. High/Middle
20%

Elementary
40%

High School
31%

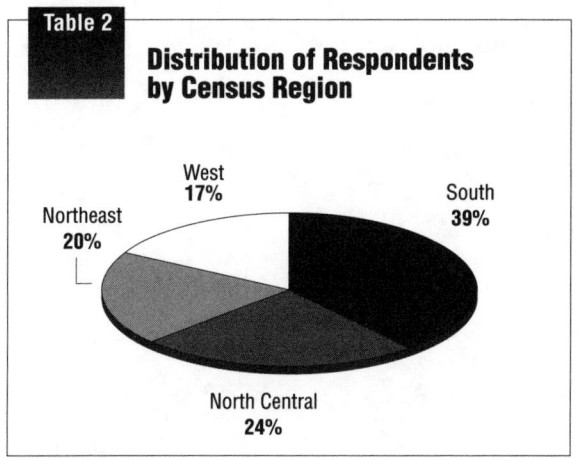

Table 2

Distribution of Respondents by Census Region

West
17%

Northeast
20%

South
39%

North Central
24%

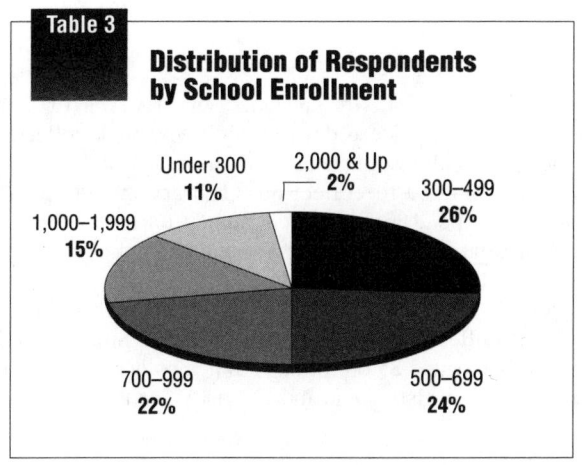

Table 3

Distribution of Respondents by School Enrollment

Under 300
11%

2,000 & Up
2%

300–499
26%

1,000–1,999
15%

700–999
22%

500–699
24%

Table 4 / Mean and Median Expenditures for All Resources, 1991–1992
(all funding sources)

	Number Responding	Mean	Median
Local			
Books	783	$4,949	$3,632
Periodicals	784	1,291	988
Microforms	136	1,199	800
AV resources/equipment	681	3,088	1,850
Microcomputer resources/equipment	458	3,259	1,063
Total All Local	831	$11,815	$7,425
Federal			
Books	241	$2,016	$1,500
Periodicals	25	1,691	843
Microforms	15	1,049	1,000
AV resources/equipment	142	2,100	966
Microcomputer resources/equipment	113	4,127	1,895
Total All Federal	324	$4,133	$2,140
Gift Funds			
Books	381	$1,108	$500
Periodicals	71	211	100
Microforms	7	564	500
AV resources/equipment	144	1,229	600
Microcomputer resources/equipment	127	2,086	1,000
Total All Gift	460	$1,928	$852
Total All Funds			
Books	810	$5,866	$4,602
Periodicals	808	1,324	1,000
Microforms	151	1,200	850
AV resources/equipment	716	3,548	2,200
Microcomputer resources/equipment	539	4,093	1,800
Total Materials Expenditures	847	$14,171	$9,609

Regardless of how the data are presented, the news on LMC book collections in the United States is indeed devastating. LMC book collections are stagnant. Only in the very smallest of schools with under 250 students enrolled is one book per child being added to collections. Library media specialists in the Northeast continue to spend more of their money on books, but each year the amount lessens in relationship to expenditures for audiovisual and computer resources—including CD-ROM.

Southern schools continue to have the smallest book collections and the largest audiovisual collections. Table 10 reveals that Southern schools spend $5.07 per pupil for books and $5.60 for all resources other than books. Schools in the North Central region also spend more money for all resources other than

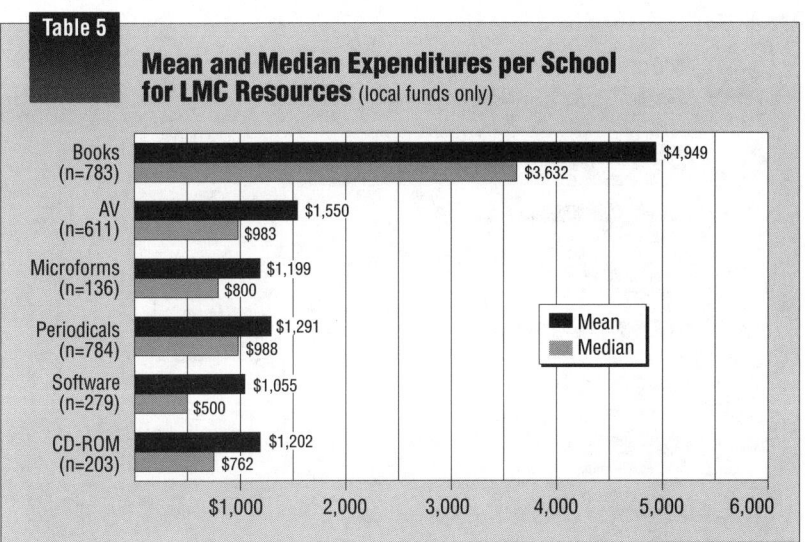

Table 5

Mean and Median Expenditures per School for LMC Resources (local funds only)

Books (n=783): Mean $4,949; Median $3,632
AV (n=611): Mean $1,550; Median $983
Microforms (n=136): Mean $1,199; Median $800
Periodicals (n=784): Mean $1,291; Median $988
Software (n=279): Mean $1,055; Median $500
CD-ROM (n=203): Mean $1,202; Median $762

■ Mean
▨ Median

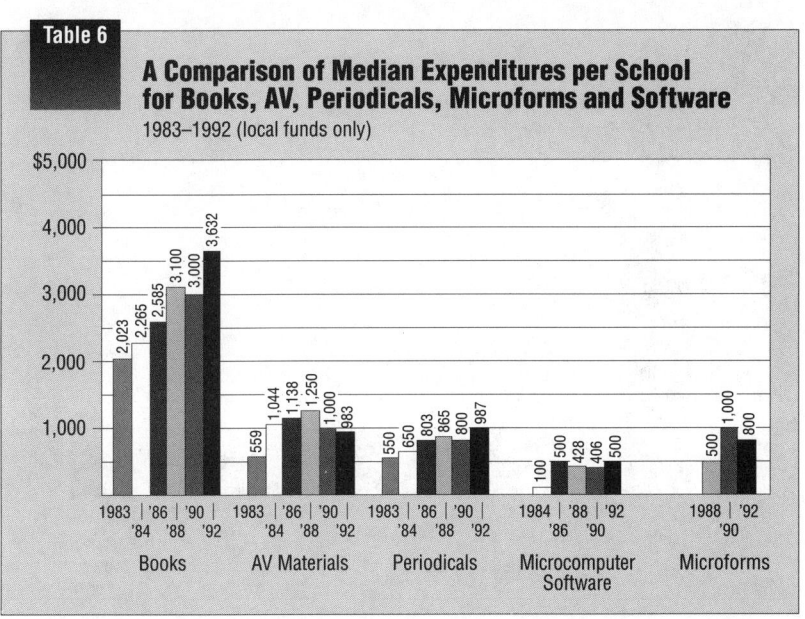

Table 6

A Comparison of Median Expenditures per School for Books, AV, Periodicals, Microforms and Software
1983–1992 (local funds only)

Books: 1983 2,023; '84 2,265; '86 2,585; '88 3,100; '90 3,000; '92 3,632
AV Materials: 1983 559; '86 1,044; '88 1,138; '90 1,250; '92 1,000; 983
Periodicals: 1983 550; '84 650; '86 803; '88 865; '90 800; '92 987
Microcomputer Software: 1984 100; '86 500; '88 428; '90 406; '92 500
Microforms: 1988 500; '90 1,000; '92 800

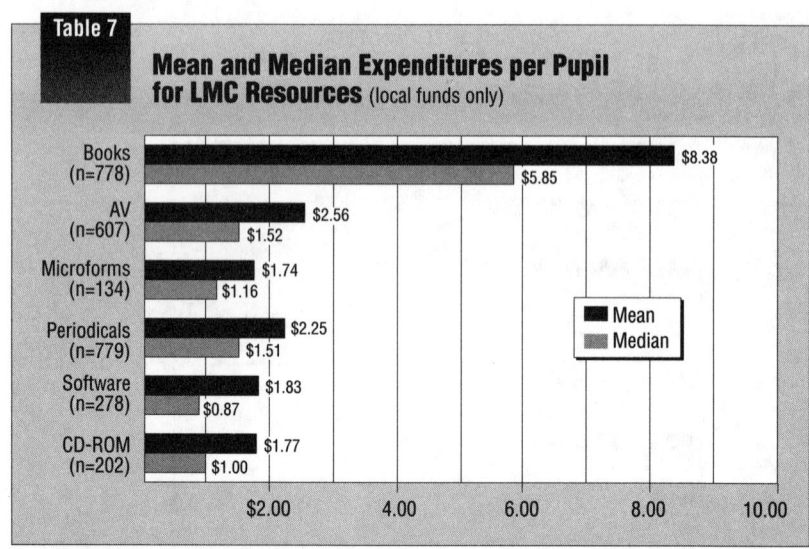

Table 7

Mean and Median Expenditures per Pupil for LMC Resources (local funds only)

Books (n=778): Mean $8.38, Median $5.85
AV (n=607): Mean $2.56, Median $1.52
Microforms (n=134): Mean $1.74, Median $1.16
Periodicals (n=779): Mean $2.25, Median $1.51
Software (n=278): Mean $1.83, Median $0.87
CD-ROM (n=202): Mean $1.77, Median $1.00

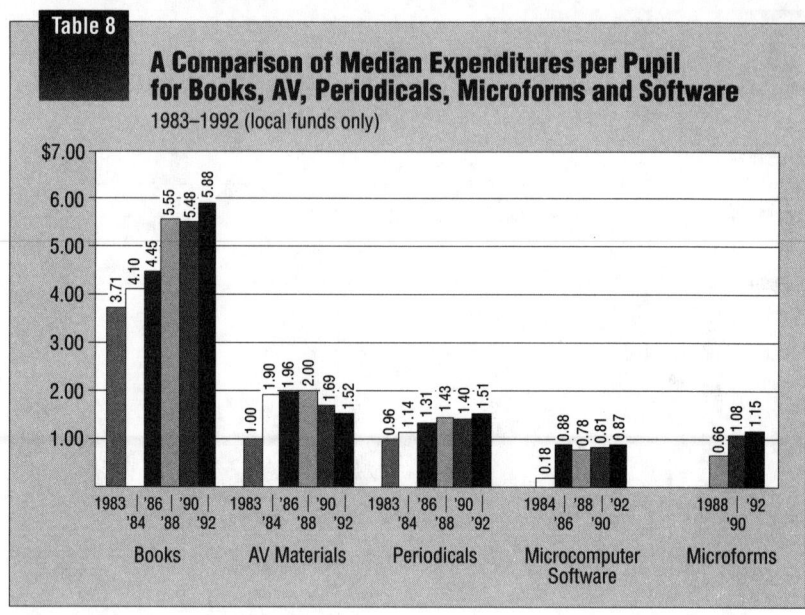

Table 8

A Comparison of Median Expenditures per Pupil for Books, AV, Periodicals, Microforms and Software
1983–1992 (local funds only)

Books: 3.71, 4.10, 4.45, 5.55, 5.48, 5.88
AV Materials: 1.00, 1.90, 1.96, 2.00, 1.69, 1.52
Periodicals: 0.96, 1.14, 1.31, 1.43, 1.40, 1.51
Microcomputer Software: 0.18, 0.88, 0.78, 0.81, 0.87
Microforms: 0.66, 1.08, 1.15

Table 9 / LMC Collection Size and Local Expenditures by School Level

	Elementary n=361		Jr. High/Middle n=177		Senior High n=281		Other n=79	
	median	mean	median	mean	median	mean	median	mean
Size of Book Collection	8,697	8,694	10,000	10,529	12,000	13,151	9,481	10,387
Volumes Added, 1991–92	363	501	320	527	300	420	350	435
Number of Books per Pupil	15	18	15	17	15	18	19	22
Volumes Discarded, 1991–92	125	293	160	357	105	315	100	253
Size of AV Collection	595	1,000	473	1,158	500	1,467	378	639
Number of AV Items Added, 1991–92	25	44	20	48	25	53	17	40
Number of AV Items per Pupil	1	2	1	2	1	2	1	2
AV Items Discarded, 1991–92	5	28	3	62	4	71	0	17
Size of Microcomputer Software Collection	71	139	34	152	15	65	3	73
Microcomputer Software Added, 1991–92	5	19	4	21	2	10	0	11
Microcomputer Software per Pupil	0	0	0	0	0	0	0	0
Microcomputer Software Discarded, 1991–92	0	4	0	3	0	2	0	1
Expenditures								
Books	$3,253.00	$4,278.00	$4,000.00	$4,827.00	$4,337.00	$6,068.00	$3,400.00	$4,271.00
Books per Pupil	$5.73	$8.51	$6.05	$7.57	$5.75	$8.88	$7.42	$8.08
Periodicals	529.00	623.00	1,100.00	1,220.00	1,726.00	2,185.00	950.00	1,348.00
Periodicals per Pupil	0.98	1.33	1.66	2.05	2.35	3.46	2.17	2.80
Microforms	350.00	781.00	1,200.00	1,244.00	883.00	1,280.00	675.00	723.00
Microforms per Pupil	0.47	1.17	1.32	2.11	1.17	1.78	1.07	1.13
Audiovisual Materials	769.00	1,351.00	1,400.00	2,013.00	1,000.00	1,583.00	500.00	1,343.00
Audiovisual Materials per Pupil	1.48	2.57	2.03	2.98	1.29	2.37	1.20	2.23
Microcomputer Software	500.00	965.00	500.00	1,047.00	390.00	1,126.00	823.00	1,319.00
Microcomputer Software per Pupil	0.94	1.95	0.90	1.43	0.68	1.89	1.34	2.10
CD-ROM Products	500.00	670.00	750.00	872.00	800.00	1,620.00	790.00	1,099.00
CD-ROM Products per Pupil	0.83	1.40	1.05	1.28	1.06	2.13	1.64	1.90
*Total Materials Expenditures (TME)	$8,000.00	$11,591.00	$10,445.00	$12,122.00	$12,295.00	$19,650.00	$7,457.00	$10,851.00
TME per Pupil	$14.08	$22.09	$14.64	$18.78	$16.86	$27.75	$17.28	$20.61

*See narrative for explanation of TME

Table 10 / LMC Collection Size and Local Expenditures by Region

	Northeast n=182		South n=344		North Central n=213		West n=154	
	median	mean	median	mean	median	mean	median	mean
Size of Book Collection	10,000	12,031	8,831	9,494	9,744	10,490	10,412	12,035
Volumes Added, 1991–92	320	399	364	547	300	385	385	500
Number of Books per Pupil	19	21	14	15	18	21	15	18
Volumes Discarded, 1991–92	98	246	150	353	110	321	140	273
Size of AV Collection	500	1,062	700	1,185	445	946	350	1,392
Number of AV Items Added, 1991–92	15	25	35	57	20	54	20	44
Number of AV Items per Pupil	1	2	1	2	1	2	1	2
AV Items Discarded, 1991–92	1	84	5	36	2	36	2	48
Size of Microcomputer Software Collection	25	87	40	128	50	135	15	77
Microcomputer Software Added, 1991–92	2	11	3	19	5	18	3	12
Microcomputer Software per Pupil	0	0	0	0	0	0	0	0
Microcomputer Software Discarded, 1991–92	0	2	0	4	0	3	0	2
Expenditures								
Books	$4,200.00	$5,626.00	$3,500.00	$4,851.00	$3,630.00	$4,731.00	$3,390.00	$4,705.00
Books per Pupil	$7.80	$9.31	$5.07	$7.45	$6.83	$9.96	$5.46	$7.20
Periodicals	1,081.00	1,399.00	750.00	1,012.00	1,265.00	1,569.00	1,000.00	1,363.00
Periodicals per Pupil	1.90	2.45	1.20	1.69	2.14	2.95	1.28	2.25
Microforms	788.00	1,207.00	888.00	1,236.00	900.00	1,128.00	833.00	1,224.00
Microforms per Pupil	1.25	2.35	1.13	1.57	1.11	1.54	1.09	1.53
Audiovisual Materials	1,000.00	1,822.00	892.00	1,456.00	1,000.00	1,575.00	880.00	1,411.00
Audiovisual Materials per Pupil	1.46	3.20	1.40	2.19	1.93	2.81	1.17	2.30
Microcomputer Software	500.00	1,268.00	307.00	1,004.00	500.00	937.00	500.00	1,105.00
Microcomputer Software per Pupil	1.20	2.06	0.61	1.63	0.93	1.86	0.80	2.00
CD-ROM Products	800.00	1,188.00	744.00	1,149.00	600.00	1,052.00	800.00	1,467.00
CD-ROM Products per Pupil	0.90	2.28	0.90	1.54	1.03	1.60	1.61	1.86
*Total Materials Expenditures (TME)	$9,350.00	$12,866.00	$9,947.00	$14,058.00	$9,600.00	$16,782.00	$9,801.00	$12,507.00
TME per Pupil	$16.78	$21.84	$14.79	$23.17	$18.36	$26.75	$12.31	$19.25

*See narrative for explanation of TME

Table 11 / LMC Collection Size and Local Expenditures by Enrollment Category

	Under 300 Students n=97		300–499 Students n=234		500–699 Students n=218		700–999 Students n=191		1000–1999 Students n=137		2000 and up n=19	
	median	mean	median	mean	median	mean	median	mean	median	mean	median	mean
Size of Book Collection	5,488	6,430	8,000	8,514	9,540	9,990	10,650	11,672	14,450	15,655	20,000	19,931
Volumes Added, 1991–92	200	284	300	419	350	507	432	582	400	493	400	478
Number of Books per Pupil	27	33	20	21	16	17	13	14	11	11	8	8
Volumes Discarded, 1991–92	80	176	100	288	116	284	150	331	200	411	200	310
Size of AV Collection	265	583	450	703	500	1,465	675	1,313	800	1,463	1,000	1,577
Number of AV Items Added, 1991–92	15	34	20	35	25	49	25	48	35	72	70	65
Number of AV Items per Pupil	1	3	1	2	1	2	1	2	1	1	0	1
AV Items Discarded, 1991–92	8	22	3	38	5	36	5	72	5	64	5	66
Size of Microcomputer Software Collection	0	78	35	99	50	132	25	135	21	104	25	66
Microcomputer Software Added, 1991–92	0	13	5	12	5	20	2	18	3	14	2	4
Microcomputer Software per Pupil	0	0	0	0	0	0	0	0	0	0	0	0
Microcomputer Software Discarded, 1991–92	0	2	0	2	0	6	0	2	0	2	0	1
Expenditures												
Books	$2,025	$2,961	$2,950	$3,450	$3,382	$4,807	$4,500	$5,885	$5,300	$6,837	$11,000	$10,557
Books per Pupil	$9.40	$17.07	$6.94	$8.63	$5.67	$8.07	$5.49	$7.30	$4.23	$5.16	$3.92	$4.18
Periodicals	854	1,052	700	984	850	1,038	1,077	1,347	1,600	2,121	1,900	2,180
Periodicals per Pupil	3.89	5.43	1.65	2.49	1.45	1.76	1.30	1.64	1.28	1.58	0.79	0.86
Microforms	516	880	1,020	1,150	775	1,129	600	1,087	962	1,325	1,500	2,220
Microforms per Pupil	4.06	3.93	2.63	2.90	1.34	1.94	0.73	1.33	0.84	1.01	0.49	0.92
Audiovisual Materials	506	920	768	1,156	1,000	1,756	1,000	1,519	1,506	2,045	3,000	2,955
Audiovisual Materials per Pupil	2.43	4.27	1.91	2.87	1.54	2.98	1.27	1.86	1.10	1.59	0.94	1.23
Microcomputer Software	323	681	410	920	725	1,056	300	1,058	345	1,465	1,018	971
Microcomputer Software per Pupil	1.91	3.01	1.04	2.50	1.30	1.79	0.40	1.29	0.24	1.04	0.31	0.33
CD-ROM Products	793	725	962	739	645	915	500	996	1,000	2,100	800	1,521
CD-ROM Products per Pupil	3.16	3.82	1.65	2.43	1.09	1.56	0.66	1.24	0.90	1.63	0.40	0.62
*Total Material Expenditures (TME)	$5,198	$8,415	$7,332	$8,986	$9,507	$13,319	$11,600	$15,316	$14,509	$25,633	$15,869	$19,234
TME per Pupil	$23.60	$43.15	$18.31	$22.61	$15.68	$22.67	$13.82	$19.04	$11.56	$18.43	$6.94	$8.06

*See narrative for explanation of TME

Table 12 / Total Budget, Book Budget, AV Budget, Microcomputer Resources Budget, and Book Collection Size by Middle/Junior High School Enrollment
(local funds only)

	Under 300 Students (n=9)	300–499 Students (n=38)	500–699 Students (n=45)	700–999 Students (n=56)	1000–Over Students (n=27)
Expenditures					
Total Budget (median)					
per school	$2,300.00	$6,570.00	$7,950.00	$8,852.00	$13,375.00
per student	$10.71	$17.81	$11.94	$10.20	$10.40
Total Budget Range					
per school	580–14,007.00	480–21,300.00	2,795–32,900.00	600–38,700.00	255–45,850.00
per student	2.17–60.90	1.50–60.86	4.99–59.82	.62–45.53	.24–42.69
Book Budget (median)					
per school	1,350.00	3,050.00	3,968.00	4,750.00	5,000.00
per student	7.62	8.74	6.55	5.27	4.86
Book Budget Range					
per school	500–8,500.00	80–8,500.00	1,000–12,095.00	607–30,500.00	1,500–13,665.00
per student	2.40–36.96	.25–22.97	1.69–18.61	.74–41.94	1.11–11.39
AV Resources Budget (median)					
per school	430.00	1,787.00	2,067.00	2,509.00	3,900.00
per student	1.48	2.75	3.29	3.05	3.04
AV Resources Budget Range					
per school	120–1,502.00	131–8,000.00	120–16,100.00	24–16,000.00	1,800–27,650.00
per student	0.60–6.53	0.32–16.50	0.23–29.27	0.03–19.05	1.13–25.75
Computer Resources Budget (median)					
per school	350.00	1,300.00	1,200.00	982.00	2,235.00
per student	2.42	2.61	2.09	1.06	1.79
Computer Resources Budget Range					
per school	300–4,000.00	100–11,000.00	52–13,600.00	76–7,751.00	100–40,000.00
per student	1.20–13.79	0.31–31.88	0.08–23.27	0.08–8.09	0.06–22.22
Collections					
Size of Book Collection (median)	7,250.00	7,800.00	10,000.00	11,050.00	13,500.00
Range of Book Collection (median)	4,000–16,370.00	1,900–19,456.00	990–19,000.00	3,000–28,000.00	8,000–23,000.00

Table 13 / Out-of-Date Collection Category and Region

Percent of Collection Out-of-Date:	Northeast n=170		South n=331		North Central n=209		West n=149	
	<45%	>45%	<45%	>45%	<45%	>45%	<45%	>45%
Size of Book Collection	12,123	10,811	9,500	8,899	10,793	8,692	12,250	11,176
Volumes Added, 1991–92	407	325	565	387	411	267	551	246
Number of Books per Pupil	21	15	15	15	21	21	18	16
Volumes Discarded, 1991–92	253	211	334	471	332	268	276	260
% with Selection Policy	78%	54%	80%	85%	84%	78%	83%	73%
% with Advisory Committee	11%	12%	45%	43%	15%	3%	15%	18%
% with Added Funds for Micro Software	28%	5%	30%	25%	29%	14%	26%	22%
% with Added Funds for Online	11%	4%	7%	6%	8%	6%	12%	4%
% with Added Funds for CD-ROM	30%	18%	23%	25%	28%	19%	28%	13%
% with Added Funds for Interactive Video	8%	2%	11%	14%	13%	8%	11%	0%
% with Added Funds for Interlibrary Loan	12%	2%	8%	17%	19%	4%	21%	0%
% Member of Network	66%	76%	43%	35%	60%	62%	48%	42%
% with Online Catalog	21%	16%	25%	10%	25%	16%	36%	33%
% with Computerized Circulation	41%	30%	55%	25%	44%	27%	63%	54%
% with Telephone	69%	69%	73%	50%	76%	68%	86%	67%
% Using Whole Language	60%	30%	53%	37%	45%	45%	52%	50%
Expenditures								
Books: Local Funds	$5,574.00	$3,451.00	$5,122.00	$2,636.00	$5,208.00	$2,618.00	$5,086.00	$2,910.00
Books: Federal Funds	1,699.00	3,942.00	2,259.00	1,665.00	2,030.00	1,463.00	1,766.00	1,676.00
Books: Gift Funds	1,170.00	1,269.00	1,195.00	1,378.00	1,091.00	887.00	790.00	712.00
Books: Total All Funds	6,479.00	4,371.00	6,449.00	3,658.00	5,867.00	3,293.00	5,746.00	3,482.00
Total Book Funds per Pupil	$10.03	$4.61	$7.84	$4.27	$10.84	$6.27	$7.86	$4.19
*Total Materials Expenditures (TME)	$13,335.00	$8,501.00	$14,775.00	$8,300.00	$18,585.00	$8,876.00	$13,559.00	$7,794.00
TME per Pupil	$23.58	$11.09	$24.44	$13.20	$28.18	$20.95	$20.95	$11.93

*See narrative for explanation of TME

books. Library media specialists in that region are spending more money now for CD-ROM than they are for microcomputer software.

CD-ROM expenditures are extraordinary. Table 11, which organizes the data by enrollment category, shows that small schools are spending one-third as much for CD-ROMs as they are for books and more on CDs than either audiovisual materials or computer software. And, the electronic schools of all sizes are spending a significant part of their financial resources for CD-ROM access.

In the 1989 report, we presented a table of total expenditures and collection sizes for high school respondents; in the 1991 report, we displayed the same data for elementary schools. In this current report, Table 12 presents total local expenditures and holdings of middle/junior high schools by size of school enrollment. As was true in the other reports, the data presented this way, with budget ranges per school and per student, highlight the inequities of resources in middle/junior high schools of all sizes. The data for schools with enrollments of 700–999 and over 1,000 are particularly dramatic. Except for the smallest of schools, the question is: How are students presented with adequate reading materials, much less other types of instructional materials?

Expenditures for LMC resources are affected by a variety of factors. To determine if those factors varied among schools, the respondents were asked to rank nine factors that influenced their expenditures for resources. The nine factors were: budget cuts; curriculum needs and relevance; favorable reviews; need for new or replacement technology; needs of exceptional students; possibility of censorship; predetermined budget allocations; replacement of lost or worn-out materials; and, results of previewing or examination.

The three factors ranked most important with all respondents replying were: 1) curriculum needs and relevance (43 percent); 2) budget allocations (20.5 percent); 3) budget cuts (18 percent). The three factors influencing selection that were ranked lowest in importance were: results of previewing or examination of resources; needs of exceptional students; and, possibility of censorship.

Table 13 displays data that describe the percentage of the book collection that is out of date by collection category and region of the nation. Library media specialists were asked to provide their self-assessment of the "up-to-dateness" of their book collections. The data show—quite dramatically—the library media specialists' estimates of the deteriorating quality of books available to students in many of the nation's LMCs.

Schools with the lowest per-pupil expenditures also have the highest percentage of out-of-date books. Schools in the Northeast have tried to keep current information available for students and teachers. They have used more of their federal and gift monies for books than the other regions, and a higher percentage of them belong to networks.

The use of the whole language method of teaching reading is widespread in the latest survey's schools, but a third and more of the schools (one-half in the West) have collections that are more than 45 percent out of date. Schools in the Northeast, North Central, and West regions that use advisory committees have collections that are more up-to-date. Having a selection policy, however, does not insure that necessary weeding will be done.

A surprising finding is the number of library media specialists using computerized circulation that still report a quarter or more of their collections as out-of-

Table 14 / School Library Media Specialist Experience, Salary, and Supporting Staff

	Elementary		Middle/Jr. High		Senior High		Other	
	median	mean	median	mean	median	mean	median	mean
No. Media Specialists in School	1.00	0.92	1.00	1.04	1.00	1.22	1.00	1.06
Years Experience in K–12 Schools	17	17	21	20	20	20	17	17
Years Experience Library/Media	12	12	15	14	15	15	10	12
Salary of Head Media Specialist	$32,000	$33,378	$35,000	$36,724	$35,350	$34,916	$27,093	$25,711
Student Assistants	0.00	4.07	4.00	7.40	4.00	6.02	0.00	2.52
Support Staff/ Paid Clerks	0.50	0.61	0.50	0.65	1.00	0.88	0.50	0.49
Adult Volunteers	2.00	3.99	0.00	1.82	0.00	0.68	0.00	4.12

date. More than one-half of the schools in the West with an average collection size of 11,000 and automated circulation reported that their collections are more than 45 percent out of date. The schools that appear to have the most up-to-date collections are those that receive extra funding for online access, interactive video resources, and interlibrary loan resources.

Human Resources

According to our survey, verbal reports of staffing cutbacks are well-founded. Table 14 shows that the average number of media specialists working in elementary and high schools has decreased; the number of paid support staff in elementary schools has been cut by one-half; and the number of adult volunteers has doubled.

Salary increases have continued in spite of the poor economy. Increases over the last survey range from $2,000 for elementary and "other" library media specialists to $3,000 for middle/junior high professionals and $4,000 for library media specialists in high schools. Respondents to this survey reported nearly the same number of years' experience in the LMC as did those responding to the previous survey. Current respondents report a median of 12 years' experience in elementary school library media centers, 14 in middle/junior high LMCs, and 14 in high school LMCs. Once again, the means and medians are nearly identical, reflecting the status quo of the ages of personnel being recruited and retained in the LMC.

Technology in the LMC

Although book collections are static and deteriorating, Tables 15 and 16 reveal that technology is faring much better in LMCs. Over two-thirds of the LMCs in

Table 15 / LMCs and Technology

	Number Responding	Percent
Additional Funds Provided for:		
Microcomputer Software	231	25.6
Online Bibliographic Services	71	7.9
CD-ROM	218	24.2
Interactive Video	89	9.9
Technical Processing Services	80	8.9
LMC Uses Cable TV Transmissions	593	65.8
LMC Uses Videodisc Technology	311	34.5
LMC Has Online Computer Catalog On-Site	219	24.3
LMC Plans to Develop Online Computer Catalog	297	33.0
LMC Has Computerized Circulation System On-Site	426	47.3
LMC Plans to Develop Computerized Circulation	214	23.8
Student Access to Electronic Database Searching:		
On-Site Online Access to Databases	190	21.1
Off-Site Online Access to Databases	68	7.5
On-Site CD-ROM	377	41.8
Off-Site CD-ROM	32	3.6
LMC Has Access to Fax Machine:		
Yes, in LMC	68	7.5
Yes, in School	225	25.0
Yes, Elsewhere	135	15.0
No Access	457	50.7
LMC Member of a Network	467	53.0
LMC Has Telephone	638	72.7

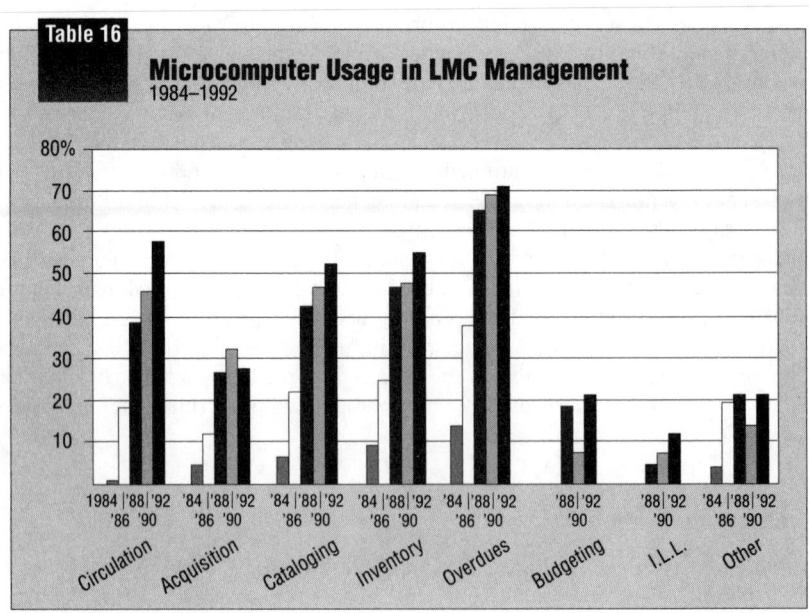

Table 16

Microcomputer Usage in LMC Management
1984–1992

the survey now have telephones, and 53 percent belong to a formal or informal network. The next-most pervasive technology in the LMC for information delivery is cable TV, but funding for nearly all electronic resources has increased over the past two years. Forty-two percent of the schools have CD-ROMs available for students; on-site online access to databases has nearly doubled; and access to fax machines in the LMC or elsewhere in the school is increasing steadily.

Additional funds continue to be provided for microcomputer software as well as online bibliographic and technical processing services. More than one-third of the schools are using videodisc technology, and 10 percent of the library media specialists received additional funds to help develop interactive video resources. Twenty-four percent received extra funds to purchase CD-ROMs. LMCs with online public access catalogs (OPACs) have tripled, but the number making plans to develop an online catalog has dropped from 40 percent in the last survey to 33 percent now, implying that many respondents still do not see online cataloging as a possibility in the near future. Nearly one-half of the respondents now have computerized circulation systems, and 24 percent are planning to develop them.

Library media specialists continue to extend their use of microcomputers for most management tasks. As displayed in Table 16, the largest increases in automated tasks were in the management of budgeting, representing an increase of 14 percentage points, and the management of circulation, representing an increase of 12 percentage points over the previous study. Discouragingly, the production of overdues remains at the top of the list of automated functions, with 71 percent of the respondents reporting this use of microcomputers.

Planning with Teachers

As reported in Table 17, more than 92 percent of the library media specialists reported planning weekly, either formally or informally, with teachers for the integration of resources and services into the curriculum. Formal planning is defined as planned meetings scheduled in advance of a specific instructional unit, while informal planning is defined as spur-of-the-moment planning with no advance notice. This is a significant increase over the 71 percent who reported in the previous survey that they participated in cooperative planning with teachers.

The current data show, however, that less *time* is spent in regular, formal planning in all schools except in the middle/junior high. And, although in the current survey a few more library media specialists reported informal planning

Table 17 / LMS/Teacher Instructional Planning by Grade Levels

	Mean No. Hours Formal Instructional Planning	Mean No. Hours Informal Instructional Planning
Elementary	0.86 (n=331)	2.04 (n=336)
Jr. High/Middle	1.80 (n=170)	3.08 (n=169)
High School	1.23 (n=263)	2.68 (n=267)
Other	0.63 (n=67)	2.10 (n=69)
Total	1.15 (n=834)	2.45 (n=844)

Table 18 / Comparison of Schools with and without District Level Media Coordinators: Collection, Expenditures, and Planning Time

	With Full-Time n=270		With Part-Time n=128		Without n=482	
	median	mean	median	mean	median	mean
*Enrollment	680	814	577	700	550	643
Total Materials Expenditure (TME)	$9,869	$16,891	$10,328	$14,021	$9,413	$12,542
Total Materials Expenditure (TME) per Pupil	$12.45	$21.35	$16.54	$23.06	$16.15	$23.82
Size of Book Collection	10,000	11,200	10,000	10,393	9,772	10,403
Number of Books per Pupil	13.88	16.80	14.95	17.34	17.11	19.27
Volumes Added, 1991–92	371	521	330	478	314	446
*Volumes Discarded, 1991–92	150	393	158	322	100	257
Size of AV Collection	711	1,114	500	1,141	500	1,196
Number of AV Items per Pupil	0.97	1.61	0.90	2.12	0.89	2.03
*Number of AV Items Added, 1991–92	31	60	25	43	20	41
Number of AV Items Discarded, 1991–92	6	73	10	52	1	34
*Size of Software Collection	50	157	46	102	20	91
Microcomputer Software per Pupil	0.08	0.26	0.06	0.20	0.03	0.18
Microcomputer Software Added, 1991–92	5	18	5	23	2	13
Microcomputer Software Discarded, 1991–92	0	3	0	3	0	2
Microcomputer Software Local Funds per Pupil	$0.76	$1.65	$0.94	$2.12	$0.83	$1.77
CD-ROM Local Funds per Pupil	$0.76	$1.36	$1.31	$2.15	$0.94	$1.77
*Library Media Specialist Salary	$36,000	$36,174	$34,192	$35,016	$31,247	$32,640
*Clerical Assistance	1.00	0.76	1.00	0.76	0.50	0.64
Adult Volunteers	1.00	2.46	0.00	2.02	0.00	2.59
*Weekly Time of Formal Planning with Teachers (hrs.)	1.00	1.40	1.00	1.24	0.00	0.99
Weekly Time of Informal Planning with Teachers (hrs.)	2.00	2.66	2.00	2.41	2.00	2.35

*Statistically significant relationship (p=.05 or above)

Table 19 / Comparison of Schools with and without District Level
Media Coordinators: Administration and Services

	Percent with Full-Time District Coordinator n=270	Percent with Part-Time District Coordinator n=128	Percent without District Coordinator n=482
*Use of Library Media Advisory Committee	35	33	17
*Availability of Selection Policy	86	86	75
*Planning with Teachers for Integrated Instruction	74	78	62
Added Funds for Microcomputer Software	27	27	28
Added Funds for Online Searching	7	8	9
Added Funds for Technical Processing	9	12	9
Added Funds for CD-ROM	23	26	27
Added Funds for Interactive Video	14	7	10
LMC Member of Network	55	54	51
Added Funds for Interlibrary Loan	10	13	15
*Telephone in LMC	80	77	68
*LMC Uses Cable TV	72	73	63
*LMC Uses Videodiscs	45	38	30
Online Computer Catalog On-Site	27	29	22
Plans to Develop Online Computer Catalog	61	62	53
Computerized Circulation System On-Site	52	52	45
Plans to Develop Computerized Circulation System	63	63	52
Online Access to Databases On-Site	23	24	21
CD-ROM Access On-Site	47	53	40
Access to Fax Machine	40	56	50
Whole Language Used for Reading Instruction	55	48	48
Materials Budget More Than 1990–91	46	47	46
Author Visit to School	29	26	29

*Statistically significant relationship (p=.05 or above)

than reported using this strategy previously, the amount of time spent planning informally also has decreased except in the high schools. The decline in staffing may be the critical factor in this change.

The whole language approach as the primary way of teaching reading skills and motivating reading has been receiving a great deal of attention. Respondents to the recent survey were asked to comment on the use of the whole language method in their schools, to identify their role in the program, and to report the effects of the method on the library media collection and its use.

While the use of the whole language method is concentrated in elementary schools, 49 percent of the respondents from all levels of schools reported that the whole language method was in use in their buildings. Nearly all of those reporting were full-time library media specialists. The method is most common in the schools reporting from the South; it is least common in the schools reporting from the West. Ten percent reported that they had helped plan and implement whole language in their schools, while 21 percent reported that they had been consulted in the development. Nine percent reported no involvement.

The other 60 percent provided many examples of the ways they had been involved. Library media specialists in 27 percent of the schools using the whole language method reported greater demands on the entire collection than with other strategies; nine percent reported a greater demand for fiction, including picture books and easy books; three percent noted no change because teachers use classroom collections.

District Coordination

Tables 18 and 19 reveal a slight decline in the number of schools with district media coordinators. Forty-four percent reported in the current survey that they had access to district assistance, while 47 percent had reported affirmatively in the previous survey. The data further reveal an increase in part-time coordinators and a decrease in full-time coordinators. This survey continues to reveal several factors related to the availability of district coordinators that are statistically significant—at the .05 level or above.

From Table 18 these factors include the size of school, number of volumes discarded, number of AV items added, size of the microcomputer software collection, expenditures of local funds for CD-ROM products, library media specialist salary, availability of clerical assistance, and the strategy of weekly formal planning time with teachers. On Table 19, the significant statistical factors include the use of a library media advisory committee, availability of a materials selection policy, planning with teachers for integrated instruction, and the availability of a telephone, cable television, and videodiscs in the LMC.

Need for More Data

Compounding the outrage of the deterioration of LMC collections and programs is the fact that we do not have enough precise data to support these claims. This study provides many indicators. These indicators should be backed up with state-collected data, data from regional accrediting associations, and national data collected by the National Center for Education Statistics to provide the information needed by the states, the U.S. Department of Education, and Congress.

There seems to be one avenue left to us, and that is for state associations to become militant on the issue of sinking school library media centers. We are talking about rural children, inner city children, the children of migrant workers, the children of immigrant families. We are talking about the voters, the workers, and the parents of tomorrow. Local control, local autonomy, local decision-making means local exposure of conditions that are crippling and will continue to cripple the learning possibilities for our children. Local leadership has to be developed, organized, motivated, and led by state associations. These may be our last hope.

State Rankings of Selected Public Library Data, 1991

The rankings were compiled by the National Data Resource Center of the National Center for Education Statistics (NCES) using data submitted in July 1992 to NCES through the Federal State Cooperative System for public library data (FSCS). A full report was published as *Public Libraries in the U.S.: 1991;* data are also available on diskette (for details see the NCES article in Part 1).

The District of Columbia contributes to FSCS as do the 50 states and is therefore shown in the rankings. The reader is cautioned, however, that this library is probably more appropriately compared to libraries serving large urban areas rather than to states.

	Circulation Transactions per capita*	Reference Transactions per 1,000 pop.	Book and Serial Vols. per capita	Staff (FTE) per capita†	Operating Expenditures per capita	Local Income per capita
Alabama	47	45	47	48	41	40
Alaska	30	35	21	24	3	2
Arizona	24	14	44	34	24	19
Arkansas	46	50	39	51	51	48
California	38	7	43	38	20	17
Colorado	17	17	25	15	14	10
Connecticut	15	13	7	9	6	5
Delaware	44	44	48	50	45	45
D.C.	49	3	23	2	1	1
Florida	39	4	50	37	30	25
Georgia	45	39	41	43	40	41
Hawaii	31	12	33	14	15	51
Idaho	14	26	17	26	33	33
Illinois	20	11	19	7	10	4
Indiana	5	18	15	4	9	9
Iowa	9	33	10	21	31	27
Kansas	7	5	6	1	21	12
Kentucky	36	49	42	42	46	43
Louisiana	40	34	36	28	37	31
Maine	16	28	1	18	28	32
Maryland	2	1	24	10	7	11
Massachusetts	22	20	2	12	12	13
Michigan	37	21	30	32	26	29
Minnesota	4	8	26	19	13	14
Mississippi	51	48	40	47	49	47
Missouri	21	37	12	27	27	22
Montana	32	43	22	35	47	37
Nebraska	13	25	9	20	29	24
Nevada	34	24	46	33	23	18
New Hampshire	18	29	5	16	22	21
New Jersey	33	22	14	6	5	3
New Mexico	28	46	29	29	32	30
New York	23	2	13	8	2	7
North Carolina	35	38	45	40	39	35
North Dakota	25	30	18	39	42	44
Ohio	1	6	16	3	4	49
Oklahoma	29	27	37	36	38	34
Oregon	6	23	31	25	19	15
Pennsylvania	42	31	38	41	36	39
Rhode Island	26	51	11	11	18	23
South Carolina	48	47	49	45	43	42
South Dakota	12	41	8	23	34	28
Tennessee	50	36	51	49	50	46
Texas	43	19	35	46	44	36
Utah	11	16	27	30	25	26
Vermont	27	42	3	31	35	38
Virginia	19	10	32	22	17	20
Washington	3	9	28	13	8	6
West Virginia	41	32	34	44	48	50
Wisconsin	10	15	20	17	16	16
Wyoming	8	40	4	5	11	8

Source: National Center for Education Statistics, July 1993.
* Per capita calculations are based on libraries that reported the specific item and a nonzero value for population of legal service areas.
† FTE = full-time-equivalent.

Library Buildings 1993:
Construction Hits the Ceiling

Bette-Lee Fox

Managing Editor, *Library Journal*

Corinne O. Nelson

Editorial Assistant, *Library Journal*

It would appear that library construction has finally been slowed by public reluctance to increase taxes and public spending. The number of completed public library projects in fiscal 1993 (July 1, 1992, through June 30, 1993) is the lowest in the last seven years and the second-lowest in the last nine years. Nevertheless, the amount of spending—the second-highest ever—remains high as construction costs hold steady. The 113 new buildings and 105 addition and renovation projects cost more than $428 million (Tables 1–3).

In the December 1992 issue, *LJ* expressed the hope that a new administration in Washington would bring an end to the downslide of America's libraries. We haven't given up hope since then, but there is little to report that would indicate significant change. On the local level, the tax revolt continues to be the culprit behind the slowdown in construction projects. The numerous offspring of Proposition 13 (California's 1979 measure reducing property taxes) have made new libraries a luxury most communities would prefer to do without. The monies previously allocated from referenda finally have been spent.

Academic projects seem unfazed by economics or politics (Tables 4–7). Fifty-one completed academic projects are reported for fiscal 1993 compared with 49 in FY 1992, the most expensive being the new Indiana University–Purdue University at Indianapolis (IUPUI) library, which cost $32 million.

The most expensive public project is the new facility at Bellevue, Wash., at $25.8 million. Funding for all public projects is, as always, predominantly from the local sector.

There are still hundreds of library buildings in progress (though the fewest in six years—614 public and 114 academic), and we'll report on those that are completed in the 1994 Architectural Issue. To receive a list of these "Still to Come" projects, write to Library Journal, In Progress, 249 W. 17 St., New York, NY 10011; 212-463-6819; FAX 212-463-6734.

Note: Adapted from the December 1993 issue of *Library Journal*, which also lists architects' addresses.

Table 1 / New Public Library Buildings, 1993

Community	Pop. in M	Code	Project Cost	Const. Cost	Gross Sq.Ft.	Sq.Ft. Cost	Equip. Cost	Site Cost	Other Costs	Volumes	Reader Seats	Federal Funds	State Funds	Local Funds	Gift Funds	Architect
Alabama																
Birmingham	20	B	$1,000,000	$651,000	8,140	$79.97	$157,000	$59,000	$133,000	45,000	78	0	0	$1,000,000	0	Davis Speake
Elba	5	M	348,371	281,698	5,200	54.17	26,489	17,000	23,184	113,000	n/a	$245,000	$187,000	18,000	$17,000	Barganier Davis Sims
Greenville	22	M	890,586	715,926	13,777	51.97	80,809	40,338	53,513	65,000	n/a	192,788	0	503,436	194,362	McKee & Assocs.
Prichard	40	M	945,741	783,689	11,413	68.67	0	89,876	72,176	n/a	n/a	851,167	94,574	0	0	Glazner Assocs.
Arkansas																
Perryville	8	B	573,500	459,647	5,000	91.93	27,368	46,809	39,676	20,000	21	70,000	0	238,500	265,000	Polk, Stanley…
California																
Benicia	28	M	5,985,174	4,603,857	31,700	145.23	718,161	Owned	663,156	100,000	200	0	4,735,362	1,249,812	0	Frants Albert
San Diego	22	B	4,575,000	1,800,000	13,200	136.37	250,000	975,000	1,550,000	45,000	129	0	0	4,575,000	0	Rusty Coombs
San Diego	50	B	5,265,000	2,400,000	20,650	116.23	450,000	500,000	1,915,000	60,000	148	0	0	5,265,000	0	Gene Cipparone
San Diego	18	B	6,520,000	2,900,000	21,700	133.64	430,000	2,050,000	1,140,000	60,000	157	0	0	4,470,000	2,050,000	Richard Bundy
Vacaville	81	B	5,982,664	2,927,286	25,186	116.23	525,000	462,000	2,068,378	150,000	200	0	0	5,962,664	20,000	Spencer Assocs.
Westlake Village	8	B	n/a	n/a	6,000	n/a	n/a	Leased	n/a	22,500	54	0	0	n/a	50,000	Wally Gordon
Florida																
Bronson	2	B	106,748	94,740	2,500	37.90	6,908	Owned	5,100	5,000	50	0	0	0	106,748	Darrell Fleeger
Gainesville	37	B	2,593,107	1,661,023	24,174	68.71	139,090	295,571	497,423	100,000	105	0	250,000	2,343,107	0	Hunter-McKellips
Gainesville	36	B	2,376,394	1,583,662	24,174	65.51	138,365	127,531	526,836	100,000	105	0	0	2,376,394	0	Hunter-McKellips
Odessa	26	B	1,167,000	850,000	10,500	80.95	100,000	Owned	217,000	40,000	72	0	0	67,000	1,100,000	Charles Batech
Ponte Vedra Beach	22	B	1,121,799	717,345	12,251	58.55	107,280	185,700	111,474	44,000	62	0	0	1,121,799	0	Pappas Associates
Port St. Lucie	50	B	1,940,140	1,380,369	20,000	69.02	100,200	Owned	459,571	50,000	68	0	792,892	1,147,248	0	James H. Howell
W. Palm Beach	62	B	2,824,123	1,669,931	17,000	98.23	284,876	721,321	147,995	70,000	110	0	0	2,824,123	0	Gee & Jenson
Georgia																
Atlanta	20	B	1,110,077	877,762	10,500	83.60	116,010	13,676	102,629	40,000	50	0	0	1,110,077	0	R.L. Brown
Atlanta	15	B	892,024	578,336	6,500	88.97	92,980	118,184	102,524	30,000	40	0	0	892,024	0	Harris & Partners
Atlanta	40	B	1,596,419	1,191,060	17,000	70.06	225,323	Owned	180,036	75,000	80	0	0	1,596,419	0	Carl Trimble
Atlanta	20	B	894,816	630,474	7,500	84.06	97,553	55,439	111,350	35,000	40	0	0	894,816	0	Harris & Partners

Symbol Code: B—Branch Library; BS—Branch & System Headquarters; M—Main Library; MS—Main & System Headquarters; S—System Headquarters; n/a—not available

Table 1 / New Public Library Buildings, 1993 *(cont.)*

Community	Pop. in M	Code	Project Cost	Const. Cost	Gross Sq.Ft.	Sq.Ft. Cost	Equip. Cost	Site Cost	Other Costs	Volumes	Reader Seats	Federal Funds	State Funds	Local Funds	Gift Funds	Architect
Chickamauga	9	B	508,473	385,172	5,200	74.07	92,259	Owned	31,042	25,000	40	0	450,000	0	58,473	Bruce Jennings
Columbus	49	B	1,915,244	1,387,700	19,450	71.34	447,240	Owned	80,304	125,000	158	0	1,212,858	702,386	0	Brittain, Thompson
Columbus	22	B	932,415	651,345	9,400	69.29	252,951	Owned	28,119	55,000	74	0	787,142	145,273	0	J.R.A. Architects
Doraville	5	B	128,739	0	200	643.70	0	Owned	0	5,000	0	0	0	128,739	0	none
Homer	7	B	433,811	301,404	4,120	73.16	73,257	Owned	59,150	15,000	40	0	390,417	43,394	0	Bramlett Assocs.
Jackson	16	M	1,170,000	770,570	11,730	65.69	195,000	Owned	204,430	50,000	66	0	878,886	200,000	91,114	Spangler & Manley
Jefferson	8	B	499,898	345,103	4,800	71.90	89,700	Owned	65,095	20,000	52	0	449,904	8,000	41,994	Bramlett & Assocs.
Maysville	7	B	493,707	334,745	4,120	81.25	70,087	Owned	88,875	15,000	40	0	390,417	101,790	1,500	Bramlett & Assocs.
Pearson	3	B	324,468	212,249	2,800	75.80	68,135	2,099	41,985	6,770	18	0	278,586	45,882	0	James W. Buckley
Thomasville	40	M	3,401,961	2,000,000	23,000	86.96	700,000	512,000	189,961	100,000	250	0	1,999,961	890,000	512,000	Jinright, Ryan, Lynn
Wadley	3	B	296,004	218,031	2,750	79.28	48,227	Owned	29,746	8,500	59	0	255,414	40,590	0	Brittain, Thompson
Willacoochee	3	B	288,239	182,937	2,500	73.18	72,143	2,533	30,626	6,770	18	0	257,252	30,987	0	James W. Buckley
Wrens	3	B	543,179	388,339	5,220	74.39	84,848	Owned	69,992	15,800	113	0	470,744	72,435	0	Brittain, Thompson
Idaho																
Athol	1	B	256,416	220,160	2,200	100.07	28,758	Owned	7,498	11,000	17	0	0	256,416	0	Gordon Longwell
Rathdrum	7	B	482,945	355,779	3,805	93.50	60,607	39,672	26,887	20,000	28	238,668	0	244,277	0	Gordon Longwell
Spirit Lake	2	B	256,731	220,476	2,200	100.21	28,758	Owned	7,497	11,000	17	0	0	256,731	0	Gordon Longwell
Illinois																
Chicago	55	B	2,548,480	1,742,434	13,572	128.38	265,955	Owned	540,091	70,000	84	0	1,442,000	1,106,480	0	Dubin, Dubin...
Chicago	64	B	3,563,078	2,217,079	13,274	167.02	279,206	267,000	799,793	58,000	90	0	3,420,300	142,778	0	Kendall J. Fleming
Naperville	40	B	4,469,304	2,604,376	32,000	81.38	291,895	201,587	1,371,446	160,000	90	0	0	4,469,304	0	LZT/Filling
Indiana																
Clarksville	54	B	1,542,018	1,154,600	10,800	106.91	183,055	100,000	104,363	40,000	66	100,995	0	1,441,023	0	Robert Kissinger
Fishers	29	BS	4,618,132	3,353,551	35,621	94.15	289,222	250,000	725,359	51,051	132	0	0	4,368,132	250,000	Everett I. Brown
Rensselaer	10	MS	2,064,805	1,572,905	17,000	92.52	164,069	170,000	157,831	53,000	98	0	0	2,062,582	2,223	Donald K. Rothenberger
Kentucky																
Lexington	55	B	2,379,725	1,513,508	15,000	100.90	217,985	462,133	186,099	70,000	84	0	333,875	2,030,990	14,860	Omni Architects

Symbol Code: B—Branch Library; BS—Branch & System Headquarters; M—Main Library; MS—Main & System Headquarters; S—System Headquarters; n/a—not available

City		Symbol														Architect
Mayfield	33	M	1,400,846	966,842	17,636	54.82	136,622	57,475	239,907	100,000	102	0	350,000	1,050,846	0	Kenar Architectural
Louisiana																
Baton Rouge	50	B	4,966,559	3,634,716	37,607	96.65	557,259	454,476	320,108	160,000	300	0	0	4,966,559	0	Richard Brown
Cecilia	8	B	299,979	227,770	3,590	63.44	46,493	Owned	25,716	20,000	30	0	0	299,979	0	Glen Angelle
Lacombe	10	B	440,000	0	1,600	0	n/a	56,000	0	11,000	0	0	0	440,000	0	Modular Structures
Maryland																
Baltimore	80	MS	7,500,000	5,375,000	47,000	114.36	287,854	1,000,000	837,146	300,000	38	0	6,490,000	0	1,010,000	Ayers/Saint/Gross
Mount Airy	14	B	2,572,287	1,936,136	16,431	117.85	236,604	153,202	246,345	54,000	80	59,400	178,200	2,215,887	118,800	Cho, Wilks & Benn
Massachusetts																
West Tisbury	2	M	686,190	377,956	4,900	77.13	62,161	166,000	80,073	18,500	43	57,500	0	347,763	280,927	Benjamin Moore
Michigan																
Rochester	77	M	13,115,051	7,536,017	70,000	107.65	819,360	3,000,000	1,759,674	257,000	450	200,000	0	10,315,051	2,600,000	TMP Assocs.
Minnesota																
Benson	6	M	576,000	431,000	6,154	70.04	45,000	70,000	30,000	30,000	45	183,480	0	340,000	52,520	Johnson, Sheldon...
Maplewood	31	B	3,006,451	2,561,451	34,000	75.34	210,000	Owned	235,000	190,000	161	0	0	3,006,451	0	Buetow & Assocs.
Saint Paul	40	B	2,710,300	2,049,137	14,500	141.32	161,340	279,707	220,116	60,000	92	0	0	2,710,300	0	Jeffrey A. Scherer
Springfield	5	M	1,025,465	757,823	8,470	89.47	83,447	100,787	83,408	2,500	50	0	0	49,500	975,965	Group II Architects
West Saint Paul	52	B	5,626,847	3,813,546	28,500	133.80	346,857	1,004,315	462,129	100,000	64	0	0	5,626,847	0	Leonard Parker Assocs.
Missouri																
Blue Springs	20	B	790,515	608,307	15,204	40.01	105,200	53,102	23,906	105,000	96	0	0	790,515	0	Tognascioli/Gross...
Lee's Summit	23	B	1,037,072	639,194	15,204	42.04	112,002	261,443	24,433	105,000	96	0	0	1,037,072	0	Tognascioli/Gross...
Parkville	25	B	922,132	629,303	17,664	35.63	90,232	176,447	26,150	120,000	108	0	0	922,132	0	Tognascioli/Gross...
Nevada																
Las Vegas	50	B	6,341,940	4,487,610	38,900	115.36	400,890	1,000,000	453,440	160,000	200	0	0	6,341,940	0	Welles-Pugsley
New Hampshire																
Springfield	1	M	132,500	120,000	2,736	43.86	2,500	Owned	10,000	18,000	22	40,000	0	21,000	71,500	Brian Rodonets
New Jersey																
Barnegat	13	B	1,787,213	1,392,149	11,236	123.90	165,972	Owned	229,092	25,000	45	0	0	1,787,213	0	James W. Hyres
Forked River	22	B	1,741,092	1,384,723	9,942	139.28	161,409	Owned	194,960	30,000	66	0	0	1,741,092	0	James W. Hyres
Westmont	53	B	3,242,627	2,577,716	14,500	177.77	303,136	Owned	361,775	52,000	91	0	0	2,492,627	750,000	Harry DiFazio

Symbol Code: B—Branch Library; BS—Branch & System Headquarters; M—Main Library; MS—Main & System Headquarters; S—System Headquarters; n/a—not available

Table 1 / New Public Library Buildings, 1993 *(cont.)*

Community	Pop. in M	Code	Project Cost	Const. Cost	Gross Sq.Ft.	Sq.Ft. Cost	Equip. Cost	Site Cost	Other Costs	Volumes	Reader Seats	Federal Funds	State Funds	Local Funds	Gift Funds	Architect
New York																
New York	50	B	16,833,614	15,737,614	15,000	1,049.17	296,000	Leased	800,000	45,558	88	0	0	4,200,000	12,633,614	Davis, Brody
Walworth	7	M	417,926	227,356	3,260	69.74	37,570	153,000	n/a	14,000	24	0	37,570	380,356	0	Al Pardi
North Carolina																
Charlotte	40	B	2,417,702	1,513,152	15,000	100.88	220,000	500,000	184,550	80,000	72	0	0	1,827,702	590,000	Gantt Huberman
Durham	25	B	1,236,700	695,082	10,500	66.20	70,427	219,735	251,456	50,000	64	0	50,000	1,186,700	0	Nicholson Assocs.
Wilmington	25	B	818,150	558,584	6,897	80.99	104,231	70,000	85,335	40,000	46	231,238	50,000	535,912	1,000	John Sawyer
Ohio																
Bedford	34	B	1,896,305	1,479,205	14,480	102.16	364,100	Leased	53,000	60,000	90	0	0	1,896,305	0	Design Group
Kirtland	7	M	1,873,674	1,356,814	13,700	99.04	205,672	104,745	206,443	120,000	85	0	0	601,154	1,272,520	Collins, Rimer...
McArthur	11	M	1,061,649	806,940	10,556	76.44	127,584	Owned	127,125	40,000	37	335,891	0	725,758	0	Beck & Tabeling
South Point	16	B	832,885	582,000	7,495	77.65	155,885	68,000	27,000	16,500	47	0	0	832,885	0	Robert L. Dalton
Pennsylvania																
Lower Burrell	36	B	803,479	573,665	5,500	104.30	60,700	69,000	100,114	30,000	50	233,170	7,000	50,000	513,309	Lorenzi, Dodds...
Saxton	5	M	222,816	203,426	3,312	61.42	7,990	2,000	9,400	20,000	18	212,826	0	0	9,990	Joseph A. Oricko
South Carolina																
Blythewood	20	B	448,791	255,749	4,000	63.93	58,400	108,683	25,959	25,000	29	0	0	448,791	0	Don Golightly
Columbia	35	B	878,466	544,904	10,000	54.49	92,901	190,738	49,923	50,000	45	0	0	878,466	0	Curt Davis
Columbia	286	MS	19,293,429	12,133,888	242,000	50.14	1,632,389	2,839,617	2,687,535	750,000	745	0	0	18,915,708	377,721	Stevens & Wilkinson
Columbia	30	B	1,032,124	542,442	10,000	54.24	98,561	333,988	57,133	50,000	45	0	0	727,624	304,500	Curt Davis
Columbia	15	B	420,133	255,377	4,000	63.83	56,539	80,420	27,797	25,000	29	0	0	420,133	0	Don Golightly
Tennessee																
Antioch	107	B	1,218,455	898,264	12,114	74.15	143,417	28,000	148,774	51,422	81	100,000	35,784	1,054,671	28,000	Hart-Freeland-Roberts
Greenfield	5	M	149,258	120,205	2,400	50.09	14,341	7,500	7,212	3,200	19	73,445	0	75,813	0	Thomas, Ross...
Ooltewah	36	B	719,931	581,030	8,000	72.63	89,508	Owned	49,393	40,000	53	0	0	719,931	0	Frank McDonald
Texas																
Buda	3	M	262,267	221,267	5,200	42.55	27,000	Owned	14,000	24,000	30	0	100,000	0	162,267	Robert Hill Jr.

Symbol Code: B—Branch Library; BS—Branch & System Headquarters; M—Main Library; MS—Main & System Headquarters; S—System Headquarters; n/a—not available

City		Code													Architect
Buffalo	2	M	42,200	35,000	1,620	21.60	200	7,000	0	8,000	14	0	42,000	200	Mike Campbell
Canton	38	M	516,725	394,245	10,000	39.43	95,000	Owned	27,480	70,000	50	0	262,260	254,465	Joseph F. Gordon
DeSoto	34	M	2,743,276	1,727,868	30,000	57.60	156,997	704,000	154,411	100,000	110	0	2,743,276	0	H H Architects
Hamilton	8	M	252,369	181,356	5,000	36.27	15,315	27,200	28,498	10,000	50	0	0	0	James W. Coats
Harlingen	65	M	4,064,471	3,630,853	45,000	80.69	329,200	Owned	404,418	160,000	238	300,000	4,064,471	0	Hideil Architects
Pasadena	30	B	1,572,808	823,891	10,300	79.98	203,069	420,826	125,022	40,000	60	82,186	1,490,622	0	Dansby & Miller
Saginaw	9	M	435,000	271,800	5,767	47.13	44,600	73,000	45,600	45,000	40	0	435,000	0	Rady & Assocs.
San Antonio	38	B	1,565,951	1,081,920	12,000	90.16	142,779	232,550	108,702	80,000	60	0	1,565,951	0	O'Neill, Conrad...
Sugar Land	35	B	2,785,587	1,560,744	19,400	80.45	385,992	241,652	597,199	80,000	142	0	2,785,587	0	Brooks Assn.
Tatum	4	B	213,598	180,048	3,206	56.16	7,459	10,990	15,101	13,000	26	0	14,630	198,968	Phillip D. Thacker
Utah															
Murray	33	M	1,281,676	846,881	19,500	43.43	255,995	39,000	139,800	100,000	191	0	1,281,676	0	Pasker Gould Ames
Virginia															
Chesapeake	24	B	2,248,608	1,611,380	17,640	91.35	351,567	Owned	285,661	90,000	115	0	2,248,608	0	Walter Wildman
Chester	9	B	714,300	425,000	4,000	106.25	30,000	137,600	121,700	22,500	36	0	714,300	0	Williams Tazewell
Franklin	12	B	1,122,805	765,418	10,600	72.21	130,632	108,800	117,955	38,000	52	100,000	121,000	901,805	Greaves, Finch
Glen Allen	12	B	2,375,000	1,576,970	18,900	83.43	338,860	241,800	217,370	82,500	88	0	2,375,000	0	Motley & Assocs.
Stafford	42	B	3,000,000	2,157,262	23,000	93.79	290,000	Owned	552,738	100,000	117	0	2,915,000	85,000	Lukmire Partnership
Washington															
Bellevue	250	B	25,813,000	19,570,000	138,000	141.81	1,900,000	3,080,000	1,263,000	300,000	408	0	25,813,000	0	Zimmer, Gunsul, Frasca
Covington	50	B	3,924,680	2,300,000	15,250	150.82	330,000	824,680	470,000	70,000	104	0	3,924,680	0	Eskilsson Architecture
Graham	20	B	1,364,245	939,150	7,152	131.31	133,137	157,395	134,563	32,000	49	0	1,364,245	0	Erickson-McGovern
Sno-Isle	n/a	M	1,263,554	1,025,356	11,200	91.54	148,700	Owned	89,498	n/a	n/a	0	1,263,554	0	Cheney/Page
Summit	21	B	1,673,616	992,993	7,424	133.75	115,856	443,018	121,749	32,000	49	0	1,673,616	0	Lewis Architects
University Place	21	B	2,534,138	1,491,946	12,000	124.33	205,735	661,519	174,938	60,000	82	0	2,534,138	0	Cardwell/Thomas
Woodinville	50	B	3,463,000	2,000,000	15,000	133.33	380,000	413,000	670,000	65,000	94	0	3,463,000	0	Buffalo Design
West Virginia															
Summersville	9	M	626,116	504,770	6,858	73.60	53,859	35,477	32,010	34,000	46	200,000	426,116	0	Jeff Goff
Wisconsin															
Kenosha	83	B	2,595,000	2,089,783	24,600	84.95	209,000	85,000	211,217	90,000	100	125,000	2,470,000	0	Durrant Group
Shell Lake	3	M	293,934	209,803	3,765	55.72	22,727	35,845	25,559	16,000	18	88,180	87,909	117,845	not reported
Stevens Point	62	M	4,400,000	3,900,000	45,000	86.67	100,000	Owned	400,000	250,000	200	0	3,860,000	540,000	Jay Carow

Symbol Code: B—Branch Library; BS—Branch & System Headquarters; M—Main Library; MS—Main & System Headquarters; S—System Headquarters; n/a—not available

Table 2 / Public Library Buildings: Additions and Renovations, 1993

Community	Pop. in M	Code	Project Cost	Const. Cost	Gross Sq.Ft.	Sq.Ft. Cost	Equip. Cost	Site Cost	Other Costs	Volumes	Reader Seats	Federal Funds	State Funds	Local Funds	Gift Funds	Architect
Alabama																
Mobile	379	S	$686,504	$510,153	6,200	$82.28	$40,113	$100,000	$36,238	0	0	$125,000	$109,720	$356,336	$95,448	Timothy J. Spafford...
Valley	40	M	23,406	21,898	1,694	12.93	1,508	Owned	0	2,000	n/a	0	0	8,406	15,000	John Woodham...
Alaska																
Wrangell	3	M	669,515	579,793	5,900	98.27	20,589	Owned	69,133	30,000	35	240,424	350,000	66,591	12,500	Minch Ritter Voelckers
Arizona																
Glendale	70	B	250,000	250,000	15,000	16.68	0	Owned	0	100,000	60	0	0	250,000	0	none
Arkansas																
Mena	17	B	147,870	132,600	3,041	43.60	5,995	Owned	9,275	5,000	36	60,000	0	10,000	77,870	Doug Arnold
California																
Burbank	150	MS	570,000	508,000	30,100	16.88	7,500	Owned	54,500	252,000	75	0	0	570,000	0	Charles Walton Assocs.
Corona	90	MS	10,840,180	9,200,000	87,239	105.51	963,849	Owned	672,000	200,000	305	0	0	10,840,180	0	Charles Walton Assocs.
El Segundo	15	M	4,065,000	3,234,000	28,460	113.63	507,000	Owned	324,000	130,000	150	159,000	0	3,906,000	0	Charles Walton Assocs.
Los Altos	38	B	3,500,000	2,800,000	28,000	100.00	4,000,000	Owned	200,000	180,000	n/a	0	0	3,400,000	100,000	Rich Kasten
Norco	25	B	85,000	70,000	9,000	7.78	15,000	Leased	0	44,000	32	0	0	85,000	0	none
Oakland	22	B	64,500	20,000	3,000	6.67	30,000	Leased	14,500	15,600	41	0	0	64,500	0	George Matsumoto
San Francisco	44	B	1,056,112	717,972	8,576	83.71	47,777	Owned	290,363	48,000	93	0	0	1,056,112	0	Norm Karasick
Santa Ana	308	MS	2,282,784	1,749,897	41,300	42.37	479,725	Owned	53,162	411,000	168	1,219,769	219,886	781,128	0	Allen & Gardner
Colorado																
Boulder	112	MS	14,971,987	8,809,000	92,164	95.58	1,180,820	1,907,800	3,074,367	500,000	210	42,600	0	14,800,000	129,387	Midyette, Seieroe...
Denver	n/a	B	790,916	606,392	11,444	52.98	45,649	Owned	138,875	45,000	76	0	0	790,916	0	Bennett, Wagner...
Denver	n/a	B	802,016	616,833	11,560	53.36	45,229	Owned	139,954	60,000	60	0	0	802,016	0	Bennett, Wagner...
Denver	n/a	B	612,910	436,504	10,388	42.02	50,085	Owned	126,321	35,000	74	0	0	612,910	0	Murata Outland...
Denver	n/a	B	566,854	417,518	3,968	105.22	0	Owned	149,336	10,000	15	0	0	566,854	0	Pouw & Assocs.
Denver	n/a	B	1,630,442	1,252,905	17,808	70.36	71,595	Owned	305,942	68,000	77	0	0	1,560,442	70,000	Michael Brendle
Denver	n/a	B	1,127,240	901,465	12,965	69.53	25,906	Owned	199,869	53,000	45	0	0	1,127,240	0	Oz Architecture
Fowler	2	M	41,289	32,749	800	40.93	5,743	Owned	2,797	9,000	15	18,817	0	0	22,472	Robert L. Shrum
Longmont	50	M	6,273,085	4,995,921	75,946	65.78	445,931	Owned	831,233	n/a	n/a	0	0	6,273,085	0	RNL Design

Symbol Code: B—Branch Library; BS—Branch & System Headquarters; M—Main Library; MS—Main & System Headquarters; S—System Headquarters; n/a—not available

Connecticut																
Ellington	10	M	3,500,000	2,705,000	25,745	105.07	250,000	225,000	320,000	60,000	120	100,000	350,000	3,025,000	25,000	Moser Pilon Nelson
New Milford	24	M	96,830	37,828	1,330	28.44	44,004	Owned	14,998	n/a	n/a	0	32,276	64,554	0	Joanne Devry...
Norwich	39	M	166,695	110,105	983	112.07	38,000	Owned	18,590	90,000	86	57,431	46,700	51,564	11,000	F. Biebesheimer...
Florida																
Deerfield Beach	46	B	2,318,001	2,090,025	15,120	138.00	100,000	Owned	127,976	55,000	110	0	250,000	2,028,001	40,000	Gee & Genson
Lake Park	7	M	146,556	108,300	1,700	63.71	22,778	Owned	15,478	8,000	18	73,278	0	73,278	0	Palm Beach...
Naples	31	B	394,700	303,700	7,000	43.39	54,000	Owned	37,000	40,000	60	0	0	370,000	24,000	Gee & Jensen
Orange Park	81	B	2,116,088	1,557,791	28,000	55.64	334,417	Owned	223,880	120,000	232	0	0	2,116,088	0	Stephen Lazar
Georgia																
Carrollton	250	MS	1,094,886	799,630	27,866	28.70	209,051	Owned	86,205	181,465	130	250,000	672,875	172,011	0	Southern Eng.
Ochlocknee	800	B	52,500	38,000	1,100	34.55	12,000	Owned	2,500	4,500	20	0	0	52,500	0	Jinright, Ryan...
Pavo	800	B	59,500	37,000	1,500	24.67	20,000	Owned	2,500	5,000	20	0	0	59,500	0	Jinright, Ryan...
Idaho																
Boise	47	M	164,251	124,988	4,600	27.17	27,500	Owned	11,763	30,000	44	0	0	156,251	8,000	Dennis Fitzgerald
Hayden	25	BS	1,213,284	892,175	13,484	66.16	171,705	75,632	73,772	50,000	85	0	0	1,207,784	5,500	Gordon Longwell
Illinois																
Bloomingdale	17	M	372,689	184,471	14,998	12.30	101,997	Owned	86,221	72,500	103	28,000	0	334,689	10,000	Dahlquist...
Chicago	55	B	4,557,346	3,171,414	30,001	105.71	506,030	Owned	879,902	45,000	108	0	3,269,346	1,288,000	0	Kendall Fleming
Clinton	10	M	3,964,857	3,353,884	2,900	115.65	310,973	Owned	300,000	90,000	178	0	0	3,964,857	25,000	Frye Gilvan...
Morris	15	M	1,130,000	930,000	14,200	65.50	42,500	Owned	127,500	70,000	115	0	0	1,130,000	0	Wendt...
Northbrook	32	M	1,620,000	1,179,000	36,389	32.40	250,000	Owned	191,000	203,000	251	0	0	1,620,000	0	Otis Associates
Pekin	32	M	18,625	15,525	555	28.00	0	Owned	3,100	80,000	140	9,312	0	9,313	0	Jost Becker Jost
Shorewood	13	M	302,972	260,743	6,454	40.40	23,177	Owned	19,052	40,000	86	75,000	0	227,972	0	Ross DeYoung
Skokie	59	M	2,146,993	1,617,096	100,000	16.17	228,255	Owned	301,642	400,000	365	0	0	2,146,993	0	Johnson...
Stickney	6	M	999,174	878,008	7,305	120.19	0	Owned	121,167	n/a	75	0	226,000	773,174	0	John Frega
Indiana																
DeMotte	10	B	1,868,793	1,537,643	17,300	88.88	162,819	10,500	157,831	52,000	105	0	0	1,867,393	1,400	Rothenberger
Seymour	31	M	2,926,452	2,072,349	24,000	86.35	565,103	Owned	289,000	120,000	158	0	0	2,866,452	60,000	Koster...
South Bend	167	MS	8,735,421	6,075,194	114,002	53.29	1,375,227	Owned	1,285,000	550,000	400	0	0	8,735,421	0	Woollen...
Iowa																
Audubon	8	M	382,154	339,227	4,261	79.62	14,927	Owned	28,000	45,000	40	89,000	0	17,576	275,578	Brooks...

Symbol Code: B—Branch Library; BS—Branch & System Headquarters; M—Main Library; MS—Main & System Headquarters; S—System Headquarters; n/a—not available

Table 2 / Public Library Buildings: Additions and Renovations, 1993 (cont.)

Community	Pop. in M	Code	Project Cost	Const. Cost	Gross Sq.Ft.	Sq.Ft. Cost	Equip. Cost	Site Cost	Other Costs	Volumes	Reader Seats	Federal Funds	State Funds	Local Funds	Gift Funds	Architect
Boone	17	M	2,639,210	1,992,835	33,600	59.31	436,882	Owned	209,493	100,000	120	0	0	2,637,210	2,000	Haila Eng.
Clinton	30	M	18,003	16,149	n/a	n/a	0	Owned	1,854	n/a	n/a	n/a	0	18,003	0	Phil Feddersen
Kansas																
Moundridge	2	M	89,544	79,560	2,566	31.00	1,918	Owned	8,066	20,000	16	29,100	0	60,444	0	Alan Parker
Norton	48	M	979,061	792,862	19,004	41.72	127,000	Owned	59,199	100,000	65	0	0	779,061	200,000	Jack Gillam
Kentucky																
Covington	140	M	65,000	n/a	n/a	n/a	n/a	Owned	n/a	n/a	n/a	0	0	65,000	0	Robert Ehinet
Greenup	37	M	159,377	123,794	1,794	69.00	24,595	400.00	10,588	40,000	30	0	81,949	77,428	0	John Meyers
Paducah	70	M	885,929	632,319	25,293	25.00	185,879	Owned	67,731	100,000	110	0	0	885,929	0	Peck...
Maryland																
Laurel	70	B	1,310,000	1,060,000	21,040	50.38	160,000	Owned	90,000	150,000	65	0	0	1,292,930	17,070	Navy Marshall
Massachusetts																
Orleans	6	M	1,147,247	891,743	15,975	55.82	92,295	Owned	163,209	40,000	84	0	467,937	181,310	498,000	Gaffney Arch.
Plympton	2	M	418,238	349,139	4,310	81.00	0	Owned	69,099	22,958	42	100,000	193,910	58,870	65,449	Roscrea Arch.
Rockland	15	M	1,359,057	1,067,415	9,401	113.54	156,752	Owned	134,890	50,000	100	0	534,057	755,000	70,000	Paul Blanchard
Michigan																
Holly	17	M	109,090	87,380	1,500	58.25	12,110	Owned	9,600	20,000	32	0	0	109,090	0	Tom Yaste
Wyandotte	31	M	459,499	325,448	6,905	47.13	39,051	25,000	70,000	63,000	62	0	0	459,499	0	Ed Laupmanis
Mississippi																
Waynesboro	5	B	198,371	142,765	2,413	59.16	41,760	Owned	13,846	30,000	50	25,000	125,335	73,036	0	Eng. Assocs.
New Hampshire																
Brookline	3	M	296,055	194,147	5,070	54.17	37,730	53,960	10,218	25,000	47			233,325	37,730	PMR
New Jersey																
Mount Holly	312	MS	2,418,930	2,025,476	13,968	145.00	146,690	Owned	246,764	500,000	263	0	0	2,418,930	0	Garrison Arch.
West Milford	25	M	43,432	28,026	5,379	5.21	8,276	Owned	7,130	22,500	38	0	0	43,432	0	Galliher & Baier

Symbol Code: B—Branch Library; BS—Branch & System Headquarters; M—Main Library; MS—Main & System Headquarters; S—System Headquarters; n/a—not available

New York

Location		Sym														
New York City	42	M	219,950	196,900	2,625	75.00	3,800	Owned	19,250	150,000	191	39,184	180,766	0	0	Alan Ballou
New York	49	B	182,058	155,000	1,300	119.23	0	Owned	27,058	n/a	n/a	0	182,058	0	0	WBTL...
Staten Island	8	B	1,087,000	1,007,000	6,645	151.54	80,000	Owned	0	25,024	36	0	1,087,000	0	0	Ellis...

North Carolina

Location		Sym														
Greensboro	30	B	153,975	128,850	6,088	21.16	17,650	Owned	7,475	20,000	34	0	153,975	0	0	D. de Bettencourt
Mocksville	28	M	885,802	731,802	15,800	46.32	51,000	5,000	98,000	60,000	102	180,000	300,000	50,000	355,802	Paul Briggs

Ohio

Location		Sym														
Bexley	989	M	4,486,013	3,367,719	44,432	75.79	678,680	Owned	439,614	250,000	230	0	4,486,013	0	0	Robert Loversidge
Canal Fulton	12	M	632,535	546,246	7,003	78.00	42,159	Owned	44,130	50,000	39	0	630,035	0	2,500	GLC Architects
Cincinnati	14	B	2,796,800	2,147,843	15,424	139.25	206,099	150,000	292,858	100,000	89	2,559,588	237,212	0	0	J. Richard Savage
Columbus	18	B	610,000	405,000	8,560	47.31	126,676	14,000	64,324	25,000	50	0	610,000	0	0	Curt Moody
Columbus	33	B	810,000	561,000	7,580	74.01	150,076	Owned	98,924	52,000	43	0	810,000	0	0	Curt Moody
Crestline	9	M	713,454	609,387	9,600	63.48	23,167	21,000	59,900	60,000	62	0	300,000	0	413,454	Marr Knapp
Elyria	70	M	296,967	224,489	16,500	13.61	56,901	Owned	15,577	200,000	131	0	296,967	0	0	Dan Weaver
Medina	30	MS	1,217,529	709,868	24,035	29.53	71,420	340,089	96,152	150,000	273	0	1,217,529	0	0	David Holzheimer

Oklahoma

Location		Sym														
Chandler	4	M	142,500	53,895	2,500	21.56	12,992	69,000	6,613	15,000	18	67,500	50,000	0	25,000	Don Beck
Jenks	8	B	308,625	250,697	2,170	115.53	26,366	Owned	31,562	30,000	42	50,000	308,625	0	0	Olsen-Coffey

Oregon

Location		Sym														
Lincoln City	12	M	1,211,278	648,500	19,774	32.80	130,083	375,000	57,695	32,000	119	112,466	1,098,812	0	0	Lee Ruff...
Toledo	6	M	257,139	251,898	3,000	83.97	2,039	Owned	3,202	35,000	n/a	126,610	0	0	130,979	Wattex Gordon

Pennsylvania

Location		Sym														
Abington	60	M	164,143	99,453	3,850	25.83	31,494	Owned	33,196	140,000	179	0	0	10,000	154,143	Paul Remus
Glenside	35	S	37,333	24,450	1,776	13.77	11,773	Owned	1,110	0	0	0	12,333	25,000	12,333	E.A. Panassow
New Florence	6	M	27,901	7,287	702	10.38	20,614	Leased	0	20,000	15	0	5,395	0	22,507	not reported
Pittsburgh	19	B	604,769	331,762	4,000	82.94	104,776	108,391	59,840	18,000	39	0	454,769	150,000	0	John Krusienski

South Carolina

Location		Sym														
Beaufort	105	MS	2,850,000	2,400,000	33,783	71.04	300,000	Owned	150,000	180,000	250	0	2,850,000	0	0	Hayes, Seay
Columbia	45	B	1,221,705	500,464	13,000	38.49	107,622	558,187	558,187	60,000	50	0	1,221,705	0	0	Don Golightly
Spartanburg	33	B	36,400	0	6,000	0	36,400	Leased	0	50,000	155	0	36,400	0	0	none
West Columbia	60	B	1,508,304	596,555	20,512	29.08	184,757	685,000	41,992	60,000	39	100,000	1,386,304	0	22,000	W. Daniel Shelley

Symbol Code: B—Branch Library; BS—Branch & System Headquarters; M—Main Library; MS—Main & System Headquarters; S—System Headquarters; n/a—not available

Table 2 / Public Library Buildings: Additions and Renovations, 1993 (cont.)

Community	Pop. in M	Code	Project Cost	Const. Cost	Gross Sq.Ft.	Sq.Ft. Cost	Equip. Cost	Site Cost	Other Costs	Volumes	Reader Seats	Federal Funds	State Funds	Local Funds	Gift Funds	Architect
York	20	B	96,876	41,929	4,000	10.48	35,971	Owned	18,976	25,000	18	10,000	0	56,540	30,336	F. Earle Gaulden
Tennessee																
Covington	38	M	99,934	78,154	1,442	54.20	11,610	Owned	10,170	40,000	25	43,966	0	51,551	4,417	Hall & Waller
Elizabethton	52	M	1,071,855	819,041	13,507	60.64	99,772	76,006	77,036	45,000	86	100,000	35,784	436,071	500,000	Reedy & Sykes
Texas																
Deer Park	28	M	662,500	622,500	12,500	49.80	0	Owned	40,000	52,000	74	0	0	662,500	0	Dansby & Miller
Montgomery	15	B	239,612	68,445	6,000	10.07	50,872	120,095	200	30,000	33	100,000	0	119,612	20,000	Sid Shackelford
Utah																
Park City	6	M	1,337,441	988,566	21,730	45.49	300,000	Owned	48,875	80,000	114	0	0	1,337,441	0	Wallace N. Cooper
Virginia																
Arlington	171	MS	13,429,000	10,648,000	132,847	80.37	1,544,000	Owned	1,237,000	350,000	350	0	0	13,429,000	0	Lukmire Partnership
Chesapeake	171	MS	5,464,703	3,962,237	67,839	58.41	948,042	Owned	554,424	290,000	342	0	0	5,464,703	0	Edward G. Lazaron
Chesterfield	224	MS	2,852,000	2,424,000	48,000	50.50	35,700	Owned	392,300	185,000	111	0	0	2,852,000	0	Design Collab.
Purcellville	25	B	2,981,489	1,743,728	17,172	101.54	406,173	62,771	309,082	74,500	57	0	0	2,951,795	29,694	Einhorn, Yaffee...
Richmond	32	B	1,840,700	1,344,800	15,000	89.65	140,000	61,100	294,800	90,000	98	0	1,080,700	0	760,000	Design Collab.
Washington																
Burien	46	B	2,727,983	2,050,097	20,448	100.26	353,202	Owned	324,684	130,000	n/a	0	0	2,727,983	0	Olson Sundberg
West Virginia																
Harman	2	M	30,656	27,087	768	35.27	3,569	Owned	0	1,500	12	15,300	0	15,356	0	none
Morgantown	76	MS	1,019,784	920,085	24,000	38.34	79,412	Owned	20,287	150,000	100	0	0	1,019,784	0	Jerry Goff
Wisconsin																
Deforest	11	M	9,113	0	9,000	0	8,000	Leased	1,113	50,000	25	0	0	9,113	0	none
Horicon	4	M	497,480	430,480	8,640	49.82	38,000	Owned	29,000	24,000	46	0	0	477,480	20,000	Bray & Assoc.

Symbol Code: B—Branch Library; BS—Branch & System Headquarters; M—Main Library; MS—Main & System Headquarters; S—System Headquarters; n/a—not available

Table 3 / Public Library Buildings: Six-Year Cost Summary, 1988–1993

	Fiscal 1988	Fiscal 1989	Fiscal 1990	Fiscal 1991	Fiscal 1992	Fiscal 1993
No. of new buildings	101	111	127	120	118	113
No. of ARRs*	142	124	123	108	115	105
Sq. ft. new buildings	1,449,397	1,760,743	1,592,389	1,520,121	1,935,111	1,896,197
Sq. ft. ARRs	1,280,321	1,612,495	1,707,313	1,689,484	1,819,787	1,878,628
New buildings						
Construction cost	$100,984,847	$160,937,343	$128,175,181	$121,884,749	$188,143,273	$183,978,065
Equipment cost	20,489,527	19,450,410	16,922,110	18,603,687	27,234,207	22,651,001
Site cost	10,403,705	14,191,713	13,147,809	14,504,740	21,011,768	28,353,201
Other costs	12,349,755	16,693,362	13,357,985	18,521,472	31,315,471	32,275,926
Total—project cost	144,237,174	211,716,128	176,628,983	176,127,088	267,704,719	267,770,932
ARRs—project cost	104,179,480	135,015,044	113,769,695	141,262,919	205,103,863	160,825,726
New and ARR project cost	$248,416,654	$346,731,172	$290,398,678	$317,390,007	$472,808,582	$428,596,658
Fund sources						
Federal, new buildings	$7,352,110	$8,140,109	$10,593,149	$8,139,146	$9,851,065	$4,320,934
Federal, ARRs	7,321,967	8,264,044	6,984,747	6,533,719	7,413,576	3,646,307
Federal, total	$14,674,077	$16,404,153	$17,577,896	$14,672,865	$17,264,641	$7,967,241
State, new buildings	$13,849,248	$48,714,905	$29,450,257	$14,349,412	$10,753,499	$26,376,138
State, ARRs	6,922,165	6,997,782	7,315,892	11,439,866	43,002,552	10,841,063
State, total	$20,771,413	$55,712,687	$36,766,149	$25,789,278	$53,756,051	$37,217,201
Local, new buildings	$112,230,599	$137,650,121	$124,136,070	$138,176,957	$230,815,119	$208,363,930
Local, ARRs	79,197,138	108,753,024	84,323,211	111,788,933	139,135,045	141,961,411
Local, total	$191,427,737	$246,403,145	$208,459,281	$249,965,890	$369,950,164	$350,325,341
Gift, new buildings	$11,084,832	$17,428,326	$13,094,262	$15,810,151	$16,487,880	$28,878,559
Gift, ARRs	10,805,194	11,219,980	15,928,366	11,561,261	15,849,230	4,389,236
Gift, total	$21,890,026	$28,648,306	$29,022,628	$27,371,412	$32,337,110	$33,267,795
Total funds used	$248,763,253	$347,168,291	$291,825,954	$317,799,445	$473,307,966	$428,777,578

*Additions, remodelings, and renovations.

Table 4 / New Academic Library Buildings, 1993

Institution	Project Cost	Gross Sq.Ft.	Sq.Ft. Cost	Construction Cost	Equipment Cost	Book Capacity	Seating Capacity	Architect
Indiana Univ.– Purdue Univ. Indianapolis (IUPUI) Education Lib.,	$32,000,000	285,000	$95.17	$27,124,144	$2,000,000	1,000,000	1,740	Barnes/Lee
Indiana Univ., Bloomington	22,000,000	21,285	98.74	2,101,681	n/a	100,000	310	CRSS Architects
Gonzaga Univ., Spokane, Wash.	20,000,000	137,000	124.08	17,000,000	3,000,000	500,000	1,000	Tan, Boyle, Heyamoto
Music Lib. Middlebury College, Vt.	16,000,000	98,900	n/a	n/a	n/a	n/a	51	Hardy, Holzman, Pfeiffer
California State Univ., San Marcos	15,343,000	35,000	102.29	3,580,033	724,538	101,000	291	CRSS, Inc.
Biomedical Information Communications Center, Oregon Health Sciences Univ., Portland	14,500,000	75,692	157.36	11,911,103	830,271	60,000	160	G.H.A. Architects
Univ. of Scranton, Pa.	13,300,000	80,000	130.00	10,400,000	2,900,000	330,000	896	Leung, Hemmler & Camayd
Science and Engineering Lib., Ohio State Univ., Columbus	12,500,000	96,987	104.75	10,160,000	2,340,000	450,000	725	John Burgee Assocs.
Philadelphia College of Textiles & Science	10,750,000	54,000	146.48	7,910,000	645,000	120,000	450	Shepley Bulfinch...
U.S. Marine Corps Univ. Research Lib.	n/a	100,000	101.00	10,100,000	n/a	340,000	830	Shepley Bulfinch...
Valencia Community College —East Campus, Orlando, Fla.	9,300,000	100,573	n/a	n/a	860,000	95,000	494	Hunton Brady Pryor Maso
Drake Univ. Law School, Des Moines, Iowa	8,500,000	71,110	98.40	6,997,066	420,000	296,454	701	Leonard Parker Assocs.
Norwich Univ., Northfield, Vt.	8,100,000	58,000	94.82	5,500,000	800,000	300,000	434	Perry Dean Rogers
Center for Law and Management Lib., Wake Forest Univ., Winston-Salem, N.C.	7,420,000	51,000	109.80	5,600,000	1,200,000	235,000	610	Cesar Pelli & Assocs.
Xavier Univ. of Louisiana, New Orleans	7,000,000	88,000	68.18	6,000,000	1,000,000	300,000	740	Blitch Assocs./Billes-Manning
Davis & Elkins College, Elkins, W.Va.	6,934,499	45,000	143.53	6,459,232	475,267	187,000	215	Architects Collaborative
Immaculata College, Pa.	6,818,950	52,500	119.47	6,272,320	438,275	240,000	300	Breslin-Ridyard-Fadero
Albany State College, Ga.	6,000,000	73,197	62.54	4,577,700	421,500	200,000	905	Allain & Assocs.
Georgian Court College, Lakewood, N.J.	5,910,000	48,000	86.25	4,140,000	660,000	150,000	350	Geddes Brecher Qualls...
Univ. of California at Los Angeles	2,800,000	36,000	77.78	2,800,000	0	200,000	400	Hodgett's & Fung
Univ. of Texas at Austin	1,993,000	31,165	46.17	1,439,000	554,000	1,600,000	0	Arch & Eng. Svcs., UT-Austin

Table 5 / Academic Library Buildings: Additions and Renovations, 1993

Institution	Status	Project Cost	Gross Sq.Ft.	Sq.Ft. Cost	Construction Cost	Equipment Cost	Book Capacity	Seating Capacity	Architect
Univ. of California San Diego	Total	$36,448,000	369,556	$77.39	$28,600,000	$1,262,000	1,473,345	2,283	Gunnar Birkerts;
	New	28,125,000	195,000	111.80	21,800,000	946,000	723,345	1,039	Buss, Silvers, Hughes
	Renovated	8,323,000	174,056	39.07	6,800,000	316,000	750,000	1,244	
Univ. of Maryland, College Park	Total	32,400,000	230,000	119.13	27,400,000	5,000,000	2,080,000	2,069	MFE, Inc.
	New	16,200,000	100,000	137.00	13,700,000	2,500,000	1,040,000	1,365	
	Renovated	16,200,000	100,000	105.38	13,700,000	2,500,000	1,040,000	704	
Willamette College of Law, Salem, Ore.	Total	8,167,439	93,680	75.67	7,089,000	404,000	160,000	490	Soderstrom Architects
	New	n/a	46,550	n/a	n/a	n/a	n/a	n/a	
	Renovated	n/a	47,130	n/a	n/a	n/a	n/a	n/a	
Univ. of Guam, Mangilao	Total	7,902,880	54,201	134.74	7,302,880	600,000	130,000	400	J.B. Jones
	New	4,270,988	26,201	163.00	4,270,988	n/a	110,000	300	
	Renovated	3,031,892	28,000	108.28	3,031,892	n/a	20,000	100	
Univ. of New Mexico, Albuquerque	Total	7,000,000	126,500	45.06	5,700,000	428,000	657,000	350	Van H. Gilbert
	New	4,130,000	38,000	89.47	3,400,000	330,000	360,000	50	
	Renovated	2,870,000	88,500	25.99	2,300,000	98,000	297,000	300	
St. Michael's College, Colchester, Vt.	Total	6,000,000	68,500	71.04	4,866,400	325,000	256,000	438	Steve Foote
	New	n/a	28,600	n/a	n/a	n/a	n/a	n/a	
	Renovated	n/a	39,900	n/a	n/a	n/a	n/a	n/a	
Earlham College, Richmond, Ind.	Total	4,993,350	60,954	54.33	3,311,700	822,600	338,000	420	Jack Hodell
	New	3,041,000	18,054	109.82	1,982,700	358,200	125,000	120	
	Renovated	1,952,350	41,900	31.72	1,329,000	464,000	213,000	300	

Table 5 / Academic Library Buildings: Additions and Renovations, 1993 *(cont.)*

Institution	Status	Project Cost	Gross Sq.Ft.	Sq.Ft. Cost	Construction Cost	Equipment Cost	Book Capacity	Seating Capacity	Architect
Olivet College, Mich.	Total	4,978,334	36,000	n/a	n/a	432,174	140,000	300	WBTL Architects
	New	3,318,906	24,000	n/a	n/a	288,117	90,000	200	
	Renovated	1,659,428	12,000	n/a	n/a	144,057	50,000	100	
Whitworth College,	Total	4,698,500	53,420	70.32	3,756,500	596,000	267,000	553	Northwest Architectural
Spokane, Wash.	New	2,944,150	26,160	88.31	2,310,250	421,100	n/a	n/a	
	Renovated	1,754,350	27,260	53.05	1,446,250	174,900	n/a	n/a	
Atlanta Univ. Center	Total	4,000,000	185,000	18.38	3,400,000	600,000	1,000,000	1,500	J.W. Robinson
	New	n/a	25,000	n/a	n/a	n/a	n/a	n/a	
	Renovated	n/a	160,000	n/a	n/a	n/a	n/a	n/a	
Pennsylvania State Univ.,	Total	2,656,369	37,500	60.81	2,380,559	300,810	98,696	299	Geddes, Brecher,
Hershey	New	2,415,007	12,500	167.68	2,096,000	269,007	n/a	n/a	Qualls…
	Renovated	241,362	25,000	7.38	284,559	31,803	n/a	n/a	
Univ. of Wyoming	Total	2,022,935	21,380	68.48	1,464,065	208,168	n/a	n/a	Gorder/South Group
College of Law,	New	n/a	17,642	n/a	n/a	n/a	93,492	129	
Laramie	Renovated	n/a	3,378	n/a	n/a	n/a	n/a	n/a	
Thompson-Pell Research	Total	750,000	7,800	89.74	700,000	50,000	20,000	30	Pamela W. Hawkes
Center, Fort Ticonderoga,	New	47,700	500	90.00	45,000	0	0	0	
Ticonderoga, N.Y.	Renovated	702,100	7,300	89.73	655,000	50,000	20,000	30	
Grand View College,	Total	637,900	25,000	20.92	522,900	115,000	130,000	380	Brooks, Borg & Skiles
Des Moines	New	n/a	5,000	n/a	n/a	n/a	30,000	40	
	Renovated	n/a	10,000	n/a	n/a	100,000	340	25	

Table 6 / Academic Library Buildings: Additions Only, 1993

Institution	Project Cost	Gross Area	Sq.Ft. Cost	Construction Cost	Equipment Cost	Book Capacity	Seating Capacity	Architect
Carl A. Kroch Lib., Cornell Univ., Ithaca, N.Y.	$25,000,000	97,000	$206.18	$20,000,000	$500,000	1,300,000	180	Shepley Bulfinch...
Knight Lib., Univ. of Oregon, Eugene	16,812,785	132,000	98.90	13,054,817	512,667	n/a	n/a	TBG Architects
Naval Postgraduate School, Monterey, Calif.	7,160,000	45,000	96.89	4,360,000	2,800,000	800,000	350	Ishimaru Design Group
Henderson State Univ. Arkadelphia, Ark.	2,000,000	22,000	84.55	1,860,000	140,000	75,000	122	Sims, Grisham, Blair

Table 7 / Academic Library Buildings: Renovations Only, 1993

Institution	Project Cost	Gross Area	Sq.Ft. Cost	Construction Cost	Equipment Cost	Book Capacity	Seating Capacity	Architect
Chemistry Lib.,Indiana Univ., Bloomington	$19,123,000	8,400	$17.84	$149,856	n/a	60,000	55	Boyd, Sobieray
Univ. of Calif., Davis	10,555,000	204,750	47.76	9,780,500	774,500	802,815	2,173	Simon, Martin-Vegue...
Mount Mercy College, Cedar Rapids, Iowa	6,200,000	65,000	87.70	5,700,000	500,000	150,000	500	Durrant Architects
Williams College, Williamstown, Mass.	3,275,000	100,506	24.47	2,460,000	815,000	590,000	835	Weese Langley Weese
Princeton Univ., Princeton, N.J.	n/a	12,000	129.17	1,550,000	0	665,000	0	Kehrt Shatken Sharon
Ohio State Univ. Columbus,	922,292	52,624	17.53	922,292	0	125,000	1,055	Feinknopf Macioce Schappa
Music/Dance Lib., Ohio State Univ., Columbus	460,268	21,774	18.15	395,268	65,000	175,000	131	Feinknopf Macioce Schappa
Science-Math Center Lib., Knox College, Galesburg, Ill.	185,000	9,918	18.65	185,000	0	70,000	87	Metzger Johnson
Reed College, Portland, Ore.	170,000	1,050	113.33	119,000	18,500	19,000	16	Zimmer Gunsul Frasca
George Washington Univ., Washington, D.C.	140,903	1,114	41.75	46,508	94,395	0	36	John Cox
Warner Pacific College, Portland, Ore.	100,000	11,296	2.73	30,889	69,111	50,000	95	Robert L. Hicks
Northwestern School of Law, Lewis & Clark College, Portland, Ore.	22,000	1,000	22.00	22,000	0	0	0	none

Book Trade Research and Statistics

Prices of U.S. and Foreign Published Materials

Adrian W. Alexander

Chair, ALA ALCTS Library Materials Price Index Committee

For a number of years now, price increases for library materials have borne little relation to those of most consumer goods and services in the United States; 1993 was no exception in one sense. As the chart below illustrates, the average cost of several categories of materials tracked by the Library Materials Price Index Committee (LMPIC) did decline in 1993; the Consumer Price Index (CPI) dropped significantly as well. This means that most library materials increased in price in 1993 at a rate three to four times that of the CPI. The major change for 1993, however, is the fact that the increase in cost of U.S. periodicals was closer to that of other types of materials than in recent years.

		Percent Change	
Index	1991	1992	1993
Consumer price index	3.1	2.9	1.3
Periodicals	11.7	12.2	5.5
Serial services	9.3	8.0	4.8
Hardcover books	4.9	2.0	-4.0*
Academic books	5.3	6.4	3.3
College books	6.0	6.6	3.0
Mass market paperbacks	11.2	2.8	9.2*
Trade paperbacks	5.4	2.2	2.3*

preliminary

U.S. Published Materials

Tables 1 through 8 report average prices and price indexes for library materials published in the United States. Categories include periodicals (Table 1), serial services (Table 2), hardcover books (Table 3), North American academic books (Table 4), college books (Table 5), mass market paperback books (Table 6), trade paperback books (Table 7), and nonprint media (Table 8).

(text continues on p. 521)

Table 1 / U.S. Periodicals: Average Prices and Price Indexes, 1992–1994

(Index Base: 1977 = 100)

Subject Area	1977 Average Price	1992 Average Price	1992 Index	1993 Average Price	1993 Index	1994 Average Price	1994 Index
U.S. periodicals excluding Russian translations*	$24.59	$117.11	476.3	$123.55	502.4	$135.37	550.5
U.S. periodicals including Russian translations	33.42	155.93	466.6	165.25	494.5	179.53	537.2
Agriculture	11.58	49.48	427.3	53.17	459.2	57.06	492.7
Business and economics	18.62	78.09	419.4	81.33	436.8	88.10	473.1
Chemistry and physics	93.76	549.50	586.1	605.46	645.8	678.03	723.2
Children's periodicals	5.82	19.48	334.7	19.83	340.7	20.43	351.1
Education	17.54	67.42	384.4	70.48	401.8	74.76	426.2
Engineering	35.77	192.77	538.9	180.00	503.2	195.62	546.9
Fine and applied arts	13.72	41.15	299.9	42.08	306.7	44.92	327.4
General interest periodicals	16.19	34.56	213.5	35.73	220.7	37.39	230.9
History	12.64	43.27	342.3	42.46	335.9	44.99	355.9
Home economics	18.73	75.13	401.1	77.33	412.9	82.23	439.0
Industrial arts	14.37	69.47	483.4	74.66	519.6	78.78	548.2

Journalism and communications	16.97	68.68	404.7	75.89	447.2	80.14	472.3
Labor and industrial relations	11.24	66.69	593.3	72.95	649.0	78.42	697.7
Law	17.36	60.53	348.7	73.44	423.0	76.06	438.2
Library and information sciences	16.97	59.42	350.2	60.81	358.3	63.04	371.5
Literature and language	11.82	35.77	302.6	37.46	316.9	39.72	336.0
Mathematics, botany, geology, general science	47.13	235.26	499.2	240.92	511.2	271.68	576.4
Medicine	51.31	276.01	537.9	288.38	562.0	321.39	626.4
Philosophy and religion	10.89	35.96	330.3	37.84	347.5	40.25	369.6
Physical education and recreation	10.00	35.81	358.1	37.74	377.4	39.47	394.7
Political science	14.83	56.93	383.9	65.57	442.1	70.50	475.4
Psychology	31.74	145.22	457.5	156.74	493.8	171.80	541.3
Russian translations	175.41	842.42	480.3	906.26	516.7	964.13	549.6
Sociology and anthropology	19.68	91.19	463.4	97.04	493.1	106.28	540.1
Zoology	33.69	197.89	587.4	219.58	651.8	243.38	722.4
Total number of periodicals						
Excluding Russian translations	3,218	3,731	3,731	3,731	3,731	3,731	3,731
Including Russian translations	3,418	3,942	3,942	3,941	3,941	3,941	3,941

Compiled by Adrian W. Alexander and Kathryn Hammell Carpenter. For further comments see *American Libraries*, May 1993 and May 1994 issues. The price index is based on subscription price information supplied, compiled, and analyzed by the Faxon Company, and follows guidelines, definitions, and criteria established by the American National Standards Institute in *American National Standard for Library and Information Services and Related Publishing Practices—Library Materials—Criteria for Price Indexes* (ANSI Z39.20—1983).

* The category Russian Translations was added in 1986.

Table 2 / U.S. Serial Services: Average Prices and Price Indexes, 1990–1993
(Index Base: 1977 = 100)

Subject Area	1977 Average Price	1990 Average Price	1990 Index	1991 Average Price	1991 Percent Increase	1991 Index	1992 Average Price	1992 Percent Increase	1992 Index	1993 Average Price	1993 Percent Increase	1993 Index
U.S. serial services*	$142.27	$377.24	265.2	$412.38	9.3	289.9	$445.37	8.0	313.0	$466.57	4.8	327.9
Business	216.28	523.79	242.2	584.93	11.7	270.5	625.67	7.0	289.3	641.28	2.5	296.5
General and humanities	90.44	274.39	303.4	292.23	6.5	323.1	317.15	8.5	350.7	336.71	6.2	372.3
Law	126.74	390.98	308.5	424.68	8.6	335.1	467.27	10.0	368.7	490.44	5.0	387.0
Science and technology	141.16	443.36	314.1	483.90	9.1	342.8	529.35	9.4	375.0	560.45	5.9	397.0
Social sciences+	145.50	370.40	254.6	398.76	7.7	274.1	420.24	5.4	288.8	448.88	6.8	308.5
U.S. documents	62.88	101.45	161.3	107.74	6.2	171.3	112.18	4.1	178.4	117.93	5.1	187.5
Wilson Index	87.51	237.99	272.0	262.97	10.5	300.5	281.73	7.1	321.9	301.17	6.9	344.2
Total number of services	1,432	1,308		1,307			1,294			1,294		

1992 compiled by Andrew Shroyer, New York University, and Laura Nanna, University of California, Santa Barbara, and 1993 compiled by Mark Sandler, University of Michigan, from data supplied by the Faxon Company, publishers' price lists, and library acquisition records. For further comments, see *Library Journal*, April 15, 1992, "Serial Services 1992" by Andrew Shroyer and Laura Nanna, and *American Libraries*, May 1993, "Serial Services 1993" by Mark Sandler. 1994 data not available at press time.

* The definition of a serial service has been taken from *American National Standard for Library and Information Services and Related Publishing Practice—Library Materials—Criteria for Price Indexes* (ANSI Z39.20—1983).

+ Excludes "Wilson Index"; excludes Russian Translations as of 1988.

Table 3 / U.S. Hardcover Books: Average Prices and Price Indexes, 1991–1993
(Index Base: 1977 = 100)

Subject Area	1977 Average Price	1990 Volumes	1990 Average Price	1990 Index	1991 Volumes	1991 Average Price	1991 Index	1992 Volumes	1992 Average Price	1992 Index	1993 (Preliminary) Volumes	1993 (Preliminary) Average Price	1993 (Preliminary) Index
Agriculture	$16.24	359	$54.24	334.0	371	$57.73	355.5	359	$53.76	331.0	268	$57.15	351.9
Art	21.24	759	42.18	198.6	717	44.99	211.8	815	44.59	209.9	671	46.29	217.9
Biography	15.34	1,337	29.58	192.8	1,416	27.52	179.4	1,359	30.41	198.2	1,174	30.38	198.0
Business	18.00	748	45.48	252.7	790	43.38	241.0	832	43.91	243.9	708	42.34	235.2
Education	12.95	562	38.72	299.0	556	41.26	318.6	653	48.77	376.6	548	42.02	324.5
Fiction	10.09	1,962	19.83	196.5	2,062	21.30	211.1	2,052	20.39	202.1	1,956	20.35	201.7
General works	30.99	1,035	54.77	176.7	1,071	51.74	167.0	1,160	56.29	181.6	801	53.58	172.9
History	17.12	1,450	36.43	212.8	1,442	39.87	232.9	1,533	39.19	228.9	1,293	40.69	237.7
Home economics	11.16	357	23.80	213.3	341	24.24	217.2	369	24.88	222.9	358	20.70	185.5
Juvenile	6.65	3,675	13.01	195.6	3,705	16.64	250.2	3,646	14.46	217.4	3,410	14.30	215.0
Language	14.96	312	42.98	287.3	240	51.72	345.7	362	49.68	332.1	291	60.87	406.9
Law	25.04	596	60.78	242.7	753	64.90	259.2	766	76.21	304.4	592	70.70	282.3
Literature	15.78	1,312	35.80	226.9	1,265	36.76	233.0	1,409	39.23	248.6	1,146	38.58	244.5
Medicine	24.00	2,215	72.24	301.0	2,078	71.44	297.7	2,277	75.22	313.4	1,794	75.17	313.2
Music	20.13	184	41.86	207.9	173	41.04	203.9	207	47.37	235.3	180	41.65	206.9
Philosophy and psychology	14.43	963	40.58	281.2	945	42.74	296.2	1,032	46.85	324.7	886	44.91	311.2
Poetry and drama	13.63	486	32.19	236.2	511	33.29	244.2	462	36.76	269.7	453	38.11	279.6
Religion	12.26	977	31.31	255.4	958	32.33	263.7	1,110	35.31	288.0	1,100	32.22	262.8
Science	24.88	2,028	74.39	299.0	1,818	80.14	322.1	1,955	81.95	329.4	1,472	79.39	319.1
Sociology and economics	29.88	4,504	42.10	140.9	4,306	48.43	162.1	4,861	45.53	152.4	3,990	46.46	155.5
Sports and recreation	12.28	403	30.52	248.5	440	30.68	249.8	465	34.62	281.9	410	33.42	272.1
Technology	23.61	1,521	76.80	325.3	1,620	76.40	323.6	1,621	82.18	348.1	1,096	78.40	332.1
Travel	18.44	181	30.41	164.9	156	32.43	175.9	182	33.28	180.5	142	28.51	154.6
Total	$19.22	27,926	$42.12	219.1	27,734	$44.17	229.8	29,487	$45.05	234.4	24,739	$43.26	225.1

Compiled by Adrian W. Alexander, Faxon Company, from data supplied by the R. R. Bowker Company. Price indexes on Tables 3 and 7 are based on books recorded in the R. R. Bowker Company's *Weekly Record* (cumulated in *American Book Publishing Record*). The 1992 preliminary figures include items listed during 1992 with an imprint date of 1992. Final data for previous years include items listed between January and June of that year and June of the following year with an imprint date of the specified year.

Table 4 / North American Academic Books: Average Prices and Price Indexes, 1990–1991 to 1992–1993, Figure 1
(Index Base: 1979–1980 = 100)

Subject Area	LC Class	1979–1980 No. of Titles	1979–1980 Average Price	1990–1991 No. of Titles	1990–1991 Average Price	1990–1991 Index	1991–1992 No. of Titles	1991–1992 Average Price	1991–1992 Percent Increase	1991–1992 Index	1992–1993 No. of Titles	1992–1993 Average Price	1992–1993 Percent Increase	1992–1993 Index
Agriculture	S	1,275	$22.80	1,640	$56.09	246.0	1,437	$60.65	8.1	266.0	1,415	$63.94	5.4	280.4
Anthropology	GN	688	18.23	914	37.45	205.4	974	37.72	0.7	206.9	1,194	38.46	2.0	211.0
Botany	QK	428	30.06	411	81.45	271.0	369	91.44	12.3	304.2	384	97.39	6.5	324.0
Business and economics	H	6,980	18.92	10,778	42.90	226.7	10,735	45.46	6.0	240.3	10,944	49.52	8.9	262.0
Chemistry	QD	950	43.44	1,035	104.50	240.6	1,121	102.56	-1.9	236.1	968	110.16	7.4	253.6
Education	L	2,682	14.37	3,197	34.39	239.3	3,329	36.14	5.1	251.5	3,354	36.75	1.7	255.8
Engineering and technology	T	5,277	28.83	7,979	67.55	234.3	7,961	72.10	6.8	250.1	8,310	74.32	3.1	257.8
Fiction, children's literature	PZ	572	11.47	1,791	20.07	175.0	1,776	20.31	1.2	177.1	1,994	20.29	-0.1	176.9
Fine and applied arts	M,N	4,846	21.82	5,238	43.81	200.8	4,967	45.48	3.8	208.4	4,927	48.03	5.6	220.1
General works	A	322	22.71	345	73.14	322.1	343	73.26	0.2	322.6	382	86.01	17.4	378.7
Geography	G	554	23.22	665	54.54	234.9	666	56.88	4.3	245.0	725	58.78	3.3	253.1
Geology	QE	475	31.59	507	70.69	223.8	473	73.43	3.9	232.5	483	77.66	5.8	245.8
History	C,D,E,F	5,713	18.95	8,571	36.25	191.3	8,746	38.45	6.1	202.9	8,772	37.11	-3.5	195.8
Home economics	TX	492	16.71	656	30.06	179.9	478	32.41	7.8	194.0	467	36.13	11.5	216.2
Industrial arts	TT	111	16.14	232	23.98	148.6	128	32.11	33.9	198.9	107	34.20	6.5	211.9
Law	K	1,122	19.82	1,804	49.56	250.1	2,046	55.70	12.4	281.0	1,887	60.69	9.0	306.2

Subject	Class												
Library and information science	Z	774	21.82	1,734	49.70	227.8	1,646	52.42	5.5	240.2	1,470	55.18	5.3	252.9
Literature and language	P	8,823	15.43	15,091	31.39	203.4	15,463	34.02	8.4	220.5	15,424	34.74	2.1	225.1
Mathematics and computer science	QA	2,281	24.62	5,427	49.33	200.4	5,719	52.85	7.1	214.7	6,082	54.58	3.3	221.7
Medicine	R	6,636	26.02	9,472	65.29	250.9	9,608	68.61	5.1	263.7	9,727	71.97	4.9	276.6
Military and naval science	U,V	599	18.14	1,144	37.19	205.0	1,013	40.05	7.7	220.8	907	46.58	16.3	256.8
Philosophy and religion	B	3,319	15.63	6,042	35.71	228.5	6,353	36.89	3.3	236.0	6,715	37.65	2.1	240.9
Physical education, recreation	GV	1,391	12.43	1,034	23.22	186.8	780	26.31	13.3	211.7	797	28.41	8.0	228.6
Physics and astronomy	QB	1,114	35.63	2,313	71.74	201.3	2,569	77.98	8.7	218.9	2,354	82.33	5.6	231.1
Political science	J	2,861	17.25	3,703	39.92	231.5	4,032	42.87	7.4	248.5	4,083	43.73	2.0	253.5
Psychology	BF	1,752	18.84	1,746	39.14	207.7	1,564	42.76	9.3	227.0	1,671	44.88	5.0	238.2
Science (general)	Q	313	22.85	636	47.78	209.1	619	57.91	21.2	253.5	652	55.92	-3.5	244.7
Sociology	HM	4,851	16.87	5,356	36.10	214.0	5,531	38.14	5.7	226.1	5,919	38.98	2.2	231.1
Zoology	QH,QL,QP,QR	2,982	32.70	3,773	79.91	244.4	3,676	82.18	2.8	251.3	3,386	82.62	0.5	252.7
Totals, averages for all subjects		70,183	$21.98	103,234	$46.53	211.7	104,122	$49.53	6.5	225.3	105,500	$51.15	3.3	232.7
Canadian history		348	$9.17	332	$24.57	267.9	303	$24.93	1.5	271.9	402	$25.15	0.9	274.3
Canadian literature		540	$5.37	795	$13.69	254.9	831	$14.17	3.5	263.9	933	$14.25	0.5	265.3

Compiled by Stephen Bosch, University of Arizona, from data collected from approval plan statistics supplied by Baker & Taylor, Coutts Library Services, and Blackwell/North America. Baker & Taylor and Blackwell/North America used a fiscal year from July 1 to June 30. Coutts Library Services used a fiscal year from June 1 to May 31 from 1979–1980 to 1982–1983; in 1983–1984 Coutts changed its fiscal year to February 1 to January 31. This table covers titles published or distributed in the United States and Canada. Baker & Taylor data include continuations (series, serials, and sets) and paperbacks of 48 pages or less. "General Supplementary" and "Extracurricular" (non-academic) categories are included by Baker & Taylor in 1979–1980 but excluded beginning with 1980–1981.

Table 4 / North American Academic Books: Average Prices and Price Indexes, 1990–1992, Figure 2
(Index Base: 1989 = 100)

| Subject Area | LC Class | 1989 | | Electronic Version 1990 | | | Electronic Version 1991 | | | Electronic Version 1992 | | | % Change |
		No. of Titles	Average Price	No. of Titles	Average Price	Index	No. of Titles	Average Price	Index	No. of Titles	Average Price	Index	1991–1992 Price
Agriculture	S	897	$45.13	935	$48.80	108.1	781	$56.97	126.2	870	$52.63	116.6	-7.6
Anthropology	GN	406	32.81	396	33.56	102.3	400	35.34	107.7	487	35.07	106.9	-0.8
Botany	QK	251	69.02	200	78.85	114.2	199	85.12	123.3	188	91.03	131.9	6.9
Business and economics	H	5,979	41.67	5,568	39.10	93.8	5,908	41.39	99.3	5,489	45.21	108.5	9.2
Chemistry	QD	577	110.61	575	102.50	92.7	544	110.63	100.0	520	127.47	115.2	15.2
Education	L	1,685	29.61	1,531	32.53	109.9	1,692	35.55	120.1	1,802	36.10	121.9	1.5
Engineering and technology	T	4,569	64.94	4,092	65.28	100.5	4,563	70.67	108.8	4,615	75.70	116.6	7.1
Fine and applied arts	M,N	3,040	40.72	2,847	41.07	100.9	2,826	43.11	105.9	2,765	41.83	102.7	-3.0
General works	A	333	134.65	96	33.21	24.7	129	41.42	30.8	119	38.09	28.3	-8.0
Geography	G	396	47.34	364	46.58	98.4	384	50.44	106.6	458	54.40	114.9	7.9
Geology	QE	303	63.49	234	68.85	108.4	209	71.51	112.6	202	76.40	120.3	6.8
History	C,D,E,F	5,549	31.34	5,757	33.98	108.4	5,545	37.04	118.2	5,638	32.29	103.0	-12.8
Home economics	TX	535	27.10	603	27.74	102.4	510	28.64	105.7	556	27.66	102.1	-3.4

Subject	Class												
Industrial arts	TT	175	23.89	283	21.78	91.2	159	30.25	126.6	172	24.26	101.5	-19.8
Law	K	1,252	51.10	1,093	48.19	94.3	1,414	54.62	106.9	1,406	59.67	116.8	9.2
Library and information science	Z	857	44.51	934	43.96	98.8	659	41.35	92.9	934	44.46	99.9	7.5
Literature and language	P	10,812	24.99	11,141	25.60	102.4	10,804	30.02	120.1	10,469	27.62	110.5	-8.0
Mathematics and computer science	QA	2,707	44.68	2,868	46.72	104.6	2,629	50.47	113.0	3,124	52.33	117.1	3.7
Medicine	R	5,028	58.38	5,272	61.85	105.9	5,244	63.58	108.9	5,109	65.99	113.0	3.8
Military and naval science	U,V	715	33.57	596	34.15	101.7	507	39.03	116.3	399	40.49	120.6	3.7
Philosophy and religion	B	3,518	29.06	3,626	30.93	106.4	3,672	25.15	86.6	3,534	22.77	78.4	-9.5
Physical education, recreation	GV	814	20.38	883	19.67	96.5	644	35.14	172.4	726	33.69	165.3	-4.1
Physics and astronomy	QB	1,219	64.59	1,267	66.39	102.8	1,285	82.90	128.3	1,222	83.78	129.7	1.1
Political science	J	1,650	36.76	1,294	38.00	103.4	1,378	49.25	134.0	1,479	42.11	114.5	-14.5
Psychology	BF	890	31.97	936	33.61	105.1	932	36.61	114.5	896	38.52	120.5	5.2
Science (general)	Q	433	56.10	405	49.28	87.8	362	59.40	105.9	382	74.19	132.2	24.9
Sociology	HM	2,742	29.36	2,878	33.33	113.5	2,906	36.07	122.9	3,085	34.64	118.0	-4.0
Zoology	QH,QL,QP,QR	1,967	71.28	2,202	71.98	101.0	1,985	79.20	111.1	1,789	78.76	110.5	-0.6
Totals, averages for all subjects		59,299	$41.69	58,876	$41.91	100.5	58,270	$45.84	109.9	58,435	$45.91	110.1	0.2

Compiled from electronic data provided by Baker & Taylor, Coutts Library Services, Blackwell/North America, and Yankee Book Peddler. See narrative for more details.

Table 5 / U.S. College Books: Average Prices and Price Indexes, 1978, 1991, 1992, 1993
(Index Base for all years: 1978 = 100. 1992 also indexed to 1991; 1993 also indexed to 1992)

Subject Area	1978 Number of Titles	1978 Average Price per Title	1991 Number of Titles	1991 Average Price per Title	1991 Prices Indexed to 1978	1992 Number of Titles	1992 Average Price per Title	1992 Prices Indexed to 1978	1992 Prices Indexed to 1991	1993 Number of Titles	1993 Average Price per Title	1993 Prices Indexed to 1978	1993 Prices Indexed to 1992
General	47	$15.25	13	$42.85	281.0	12	$69.77	457.5	162.8	16	$54.45	357.0	78.0
Humanities	92	$16.14	18	$43.30	268.3	20	$35.48	219.8	81.9	15	$40.41	250.4	113.9
Art and architecture	315	26.60	296	55.62	209.1	325	57.88	217.6	104.1	297	57.76	217.1	99.8
Photography[1]	—	—	15	47.85	—	16	53.18	—	111.2	16	48.92	—	92.0
Communication	71	14.03	42	36.82	262.4	45	38.68	275.7	105.1	59	42.67	304.1	110.3
Language and literature	97	13.38	84	36.71	274.4	141	24.17	180.6	65.8	53	36.94	276.1	152.8
English and American	834	12.42	565	31.22	251.4	489	39.75	320.0	127.3	573	36.30	292.3	91.3
Germanic	51	12.35	37	28.79	233.1	55	32.92	266.6	114.3	49	34.25	277.3	104.0
Romance	101	12.27	114	30.11	245.4	100	42.39	345.5	140.8	91	34.82	283.8	82.1
Slavic	46	13.22	27	26.50	200.5	44	33.77	255.4	127.4	34	36.83	278.6	109.1
Other	67	13.03	68	35.62	273.3	82	35.68	273.8	100.2	58	40.70	312.4	114.1
Performing arts	16	15.07	20	33.49	222.2	9	54.19	359.6	161.8	20	35.22	233.7	65.0
Dance	21	12.95	14	52.20	403.1	13	22.40	173.0	42.9	13	38.67	298.6	172.6
Film	80	15.70	66	39.11	249.1	70	38.89	247.7	99.4	87	39.68	252.7	102.0
Music	138	15.10	144	42.92	284.3	140	48.09	318.5	112.0	176	43.06	285.2	89.5
Theater	34	13.84	40	44.44	321.1	38	43.15	311.8	97.1	56	39.97	288.8	92.6
Philosophy	197	14.21	253	41.30	290.7	233	44.58	313.7	107.9	236	42.62	299.9	95.6
Religion	300	11.98	126	34.68	289.5	177	37.66	314.4	108.6	141	36.74	306.7	97.6
Total humanities[2]	2,500	$14.86	1,929	$38.69	260.3	1,997	$42.24	284.3	109.2	1,974	$41.54	279.5	98.3
Science and technology	102	$21.31	97	$39.46	185.2	93	$44.29	207.8	112.2	89	$44.94	210.9	101.5
History of science/technology	85	17.37	73	38.19	219.9	81	44.62	256.9	116.8	46	37.62	216.6	84.3
Astronautics/astronomy	22	23.78	37	39.41	165.7	43	47.91	201.5	121.6	51	51.36	216.0	107.2
Biology	231	23.67	70	68.97	291.4	138	53.66	226.7	77.8	122	53.50	226.0	99.7
Botany[1]	—	—	54	54.74	—	86	67.83	—	123.9	83	53.32	—	78.6
Zoology[1]	—	—	43	51.25	—	66	53.52	—	104.4	70	46.48	—	86.8
Chemistry	95	28.59	44	76.24	266.7	58	66.05	231.0	86.6	75	86.55	302.7	131.0
Earth science	84	29.99	58	64.02	213.5	65	63.09	210.4	98.6	49	71.57	238.6	113.4
Engineering	241	25.75	85	66.86	259.7	114	76.43	296.8	114.3	125	68.27	265.1	89.3
Health sciences	92	14.88	111	44.93	302.0	111	41.29	277.5	91.9	158	41.72	280.4	101.0

Information/computer science	53	20.37	74	44.73	219.6	83	42.57	209.0	95.2	60	46.54	228.5	109.3
Mathematics	70	22.54	62	50.48	224.0	82	47.88	212.4	94.8	74	49.17	218.1	102.7
Physics	47	28.77	38	52.04	180.9	53	58.40	203.0	112.2	57	56.11	195.0	96.1
Sports and physical education	73	10.32	24	34.87	337.9	21	39.55	383.2	113.4	30	38.29	371.0	96.8
Total sciences	1,195	$22.77	870	$51.79	227.4	1,094	$54.09	237.5	104.4	1,089	$53.68	235.7	99.2
Social/behavioral sciences	156	$16.37	55	$34.58	211.3	31	$36.66	223.9	106.0	49	$43.46	265.5	118.5
Anthropology	102	16.97	143	39.56	233.1	195	46.30	272.8	117.0	152	42.38	249.7	91.5
Business, management, labor	136	14.36	127	39.84	277.5	135	40.49	282.0	101.6	153	41.63	289.9	102.8
Economics	242	17.65	321	44.32	251.1	348	46.30	262.3	104.5	295	46.09	261.1	99.5
Education	129	12.48	163	40.38	323.6	92	40.66	325.8	100.7	113	47.18	378.0	116.0
History/geography/area studies													
Africa	116	16.26	59	43.08	264.9	50	46.77	287.6	108.6	39	38.38	236.0	82.1
Asia and Oceania	38	16.34	35	36.18	221.4	43	43.31	265.1	119.7	28	48.73	298.2	112.5
Europe	78	19.03	58	39.50	207.5	87	42.83	225.1	108.4	55	47.09	247.5	109.9
Latin America and Caribbean	308	16.52	355	44.59	269.9	354	50.42	305.2	113.1	336	47.95	290.3	95.1
Middle East and North Africa	47	15.82	42	53.42	337.7	54	40.50	256.0	75.8	47	42.88	271.0	105.9
North America	40	16.80	37	47.62	283.5	49	46.37	276.0	97.4	63	47.90	285.1	103.3
Political science	275	16.08	350	33.98	211.3	380	33.01	205.3	97.1	400	36.37	226.2	110.2
Comparative politics[3]	281	14.74	19	38.51	261.3	12	55.80	378.6	144.9	30	40.21	272.8	72.1
International relations[3]	—	—	227	40.75	—	162	41.82	—	102.6	171	44.48	—	106.4
Political theory[3]	—	—	160	40.32	—	162	41.21	—	102.2	122	44.97	—	109.1
U.S. politics[3]	—	—	62	37.12	—	106	41.70	—	112.3	69	41.95	—	100.6
Psychology	142	15.39	178	36.47	237.0	146	41.02	266.5	112.5	153	44.56	289.5	108.6
Sociology	280	14.69	210	37.07	252.3	200	39.77	270.7	107.3	213	42.09	286.5	105.8
Total social/behavioral sciences[2]	2,437	$15.98	2,785	$39.81	249.2	2,801	$42.07	263.3	105.7	2,660	$43.14	270.0	102.5
Total (excluding reference)[2]	6,179	$16.83	5,597	$41.29	245.4	5,904	$44.41	263.9	107.5	5,739	$44.62	265.1	100.5
Reference	453	$34.15	660	$72.20	211.4	655	$75.13	220.0	104.1	720	$83.15	243.5	110.7
Grand total[2]	6,632	$18.02	6,257	$44.55	247.2	6,559	$47.48	263.5	106.6	6,459	$48.92	271.3	103.0

Compiled by Donna Alsbury, Florida Center for Library Automation, from book reviews appearing in Choice during the calendar year indicated. The cooperation of the Choice editorial staff is gratefully acknowledged. Additional information about this data appears in the April issue of Choice.
1 Began appearing as a separate section in September 1983.
2 1978 totals include Linguistics (incorporated into Language and Literature in December 1985) and Classical Language and Literature and Ancient History (incorporated into Classical Studies in 1985).
3 Began appearing as a separate section in March 1988.

Table 6 / U.S. Mass Market Paperback Books: Average Prices and Price Indexes, 1990–1993
(Index Base: 1981 = 100)

Subject Area	1981 Average Price	1981 Total Volumes	1990 Average Price	1990 Index	1991 Total Volumes	1991 Average Price	1991 Index	1992 (Final) Total Volumes	1992 (Final) Average Price	1992 (Final) Index	1993 (Preliminary) Total Volumes	1993 (Preliminary) Average Price	1993 (Preliminary) Index
Agriculture	$2.54	1	$3.95	155.5	5	$5.00	196.9	14	$7.40	291.3	22	$6.23	245.3
Art	5.49	11	13.40	244.1	7	10.13	184.5	3	10.33	188.2	5	19.79	360.5
Biography	3.82	58	7.24	189.5	76	6.18	161.8	92	6.18	161.8	68	6.55	171.5
Business	4.63	16	7.86	169.8	13	8.36	180.6	21	8.30	179.3	21	10.41	224.8
Education	3.96	15	8.08	204.0	5	5.98	151.0	15	9.96	251.5	31	11.31	285.6
Fiction	2.47	2,855	4.06	164.4	2,265	4.49	181.8	2,587	4.63	187.4	2,046	4.78	193.5
General works	3.63	44	6.87	189.3	52	7.48	206.1	65	7.25	199.7	42	8.70	239.7
History	3.53	28	6.25	177.1	28	8.37	237.1	43	7.14	202.3	14	8.60	243.6
Home economics	4.35	44	6.75	155.2	60	7.97	183.2	69	7.41	170.3	56	6.67	153.3
Juvenile	1.79	433	3.56	198.9	448	3.38	188.8	489	3.61	201.7	381	3.68	205.6
Language	3.42	17	5.36	156.7	9	7.26	212.3	11	6.26	183.0	10	7.64	223.4
Law	3.09	3	6.62	214.2	4	9.85	318.8	1	4.99	161.5	0	0.00	161.5
Literature	3.42	28	6.45	188.6	24	5.89	172.2	29	7.16	209.4	18	6.77	198.0
Medicine	3.66	31	8.24	225.1	32	5.88	160.7	21	9.02	246.4	12	9.81	268.0
Music*	5.68	7	14.66	258.1	1	2.75	48.4	1	2.75	48.4	1	11.00	193.7
Philosophy and psychology	2.84	121	6.82	240.1	67	7.78	273.9	89	6.71	236.3	83	6.31	222.2
Poetry and drama	3.22	4	6.09	189.1	12	6.55	203.4	12	6.24	193.8	7	7.27	225.8
Religion	2.70	13	6.96	257.8	11	7.79	288.5	9	7.88	291.9	3	9.97	369.3
Science	4.45	9	9.17	206.1	15	8.27	185.8	9	8.16	183.4	8	7.87	176.9
Sociology and economics	3.43	50	6.89	200.9	42	7.56	220.4	59	6.48	188.9	43	8.09	235.9
Sports and recreation	3.05	136	5.29	173.4	139	7.50	245.9	142	6.84	224.3	92	7.17	235.1
Technology	4.20	14	24.16	575.2	29	25.58	609.0	40	31.18	742.4	62	30.83	734.0
Travel	3.23	29	11.23	347.7	26	10.95	339.0	5	9.10	281.7	7	10.56	326.9
Total	$2.65	3,967	$4.57	172.5	3,370	$5.08	191.7	3,826	$5.22	197.0	3,032	$5.70	215.1

Compiled by Adrian W. Alexander, Faxon Company, from data supplied by the R. R. Bowker Company. Average prices of mass market paperbacks are based on listings of mass market titles in *Paperbound Books in Print*.

* 1982 is used as the index base for Music.

Table 7 / U.S. Trade (Higher Priced) Paperbook Books: Average Prices and Price Indexes, 1990–1993
(Index Base: 1977 = 100)

Subject Area	1977 Average Price	1990 No. of Books	1990 Average Price	1990 Index	1991 No. of Books	1991 Average Price	1991 Index	1992 (Final) No. of Books	1992 (Final) Average Price	1992 (Final) Index	1993 (Preliminary) No. of Books	1993 (Preliminary) Average Price	1993 (Preliminary) Index
Agriculture	$5.01	142	$16.42	327.7	129	$14.90	297.4	179	$16.73	333.9	138	$19.35	386.2
Art	6.27	462	17.90	285.5	509	19.11	304.8	549	19.52	311.3	400	19.90	317.4
Biography	4.91	520	13.05	265.8	536	13.38	272.5	516	13.59	276.8	469	14.89	303.3
Business	7.09	398	19.61	276.6	477	21.20	299.0	484	22.94	323.6	380	21.71	306.2
Education	5.72	436	19.20	335.7	453	23.30	407.3	480	23.25	406.5	411	22.39	391.4
Fiction	4.20	885	11.32	269.5	1,027	12.17	289.3	928	13.68	325.7	723	13.59	323.6
General works	6.18	629	29.67	480.1	650	34.74	562.1	868	29.20	472.5	535	31.29	506.3
History	5.81	701	17.39	299.3	717	16.99	292.4	724	17.42	299.8	581	18.42	317.0
Home economics	4.77	351	12.97	271.9	371	12.89	270.2	374	14.29	299.6	290	13.68	286.8
Juvenile	2.68	938	6.79	253.4	810	7.60	283.6	869	7.49	279.5	945	7.88	294.0
Language	7.79	292	16.67	214.0	250	16.83	216.0	230	17.61	226.1	212	20.98	269.3
Law	10.66	269	25.15	235.9	331	24.62	231.0	277	25.17	236.1	232	26.36	247.3
Literature	5.18	671	15.54	300.0	654	15.31	295.6	727	17.04	329.0	632	17.35	334.9
Medicine	7.63	696	22.82	299.1	702	24.20	317.2	855	26.16	342.9	699	28.30	370.9
Music	6.36	92	19.17	301.4	115	17.03	267.8	121	20.56	323.3	117	20.50	322.3
Philosophy and psychology	5.57	563	15.29	274.5	657	16.54	296.9	637	17.24	309.5	546	18.07	324.4
Poetry and drama	4.71	368	12.43	263.9	338	11.88	252.2	395	13.06	277.3	346	12.65	268.6
Religion	3.68	1,248	12.12	329.3	1,334	12.50	339.7	1,371	13.08	355.4	1,092	13.60	369.6
Science	8.81	621	28.01	317.9	567	28.31	321.3	640	27.98	317.6	478	31.55	358.1
Sociology and economics	6.03	2,333	19.60	325.0	2,294	19.68	326.4	2,354	19.72	327.0	2,066	21.21	351.7
Sports and recreation	4.87	422	13.67	280.7	449	15.03	308.6	490	15.64	321.1	388	15.40	316.2
Technology	7.97	509	30.06	377.2	586	33.39	418.9	589	28.75	360.7	400	29.12	365.4
Travel	5.21	280	13.32	255.7	301	14.06	269.9	276	14.75	283.1	176	15.84	304.0
Total	$5.93	13,286	$17.45	294.3	14,257	$18.40	310.3	14,933	$18.81	317.2	12,256	$19.24	324.5

Compiled by Adrian W. Alexander, Faxon Company, from data supplied by the R. R. Bowker Company. Price indexes on Tables 3 and 7 are based on books recorded in the R. R. Bowker Company's *Weekly Record* (cumulated in *American Book Publishing Record*). The 1992 preliminary figures include items listed during 1992 with an imprint date of 1992. Final data for previous years include items listed between January of that year and June of the following year with an imprint date of the specified year.

Table 8 / U.S. Nonprint Media: Average Prices and Price Indexes, 1989–1993
(Index Base: 1980 = 100)

Category	1980 Average Price	1989 Average Price	1989 Index	1990 Average Price	1990 Index	1991 Average Price	1991 Index	1992 Average Price	1992 Index	1993* Average Price	1993* Index	1993+ Average Price	1993+ Index
16mm films													
Rental cost per minute	$1.41	$2.87	203.5	$2.02	143.3	$2.46	174.5	$1.95	138.3	$2.68	190.1	$1.97	139.7
Purchase cost per minute	12.03	20.63	171.5	18.40	153.0	20.08	166.9	20.85	173.3	22.14	184.0	16.23	134.9
Cost of film	279.09	421.00	150.8	517.72	185.5	525.50	188.3	412.83	147.9	381.25	131.1	391.79	140.4
Length per film (min.)	23.2	20.4	—	28.1	—	26.2	—	19.8	—	17.2	—	24.1	—
Videocassettes													
Purchase cost per minute	7.58	5.67	74.8	5.60	73.9	4.81	63.5	3.23	42.6	2.35	31.0	2.38	31.4
Cost of video	271.93	169.21	62.2	215.34	79.2	199.67	73.4	112.92	41.5	94.59	34.8	93.22	34.3
Length per video (min.)	—	29.9	—	35.9	—	41.5	—	35.0	—	40.3	—	38.2	—
Filmstrips													
Cost of filmstrip	21.74	33.14	152.4	37.38	171.9	36.90	169.7	34.63	159.3	35.10	161.5	31.54	145.1
Cost of filmstrip set	67.39	89.14	132.3	121.76	180.7	97.90	145.3	81.73	121.3	75.11	111.5	81.06	120.3
Number of filmstrips per set	3.1	2.7	—	3.3	—	2.7	—	2.4	—	2.1	—	2.6	—
Number of frames per filmstrip	67.9	55.9	—	46.5	—	56.6	—	49.4	—	58.7	—	64.4	—
Sound recordings													
Average cost per cassette	9.34	10.58	113.3	10.47	112.1	12.18	130.4	11.73	125.6	8.11	86.8	8.20	87.8
Cost per compact disc	—	—	—	—	—	—	—	—	—	14.78	—	13.36	—

Compiled by Dana L. Alessi, Baker & Taylor, from selected issues of Booklist, Library Journal, School Library Journal, and Wilson Library Bulletin.

* Old methodology.
+ New methodology.

Periodical and Serial Prices

The Library Materials Price Index Committee and the Faxon Company jointly produce the U.S. periodical price index. Subscription prices shown are publishers' list prices, and do not include publishers' discounts or vendor service charges. This year's index includes data for 1992, 1993, and 1994. An expanded report, including subject breakdowns, LC class comparisons, and rankings by rate of increase and average price, was published annually in the April 15 issue of *Library Journal* through 1992 and is now published in the May issue of *American Libraries*.

After a second consecutive double-digit increase in 1992 of 12.2 percent, the average U.S. periodical price increase (Table 1), excluding Russian translations, had dropped in 1993 to only 5.5 percent. In 1994, however, the average price rose once again, at a rate of 9.6 percent, to $135.37, a level more typical of the five-year period from 1986 to 1990. Chemistry and physics titles continue to be much more expensive than all other subject categories surveyed, except for Russian translations, with an average price in 1994 of $678.03 (12 percent higher than in 1993). Mathematics, however, posted the highest rate of increase, with 12.8 percent, followed by chemistry and physics, medicine (11.4 percent), and zoology (10.8 percent).

Price data for U.S. serial services (Table 2) for 1994 was not available at press time. Next year's survey will include average prices and price indexes for 1992, 1993, 1994, and 1995.

Book Prices

The 1993 average price of U.S. hardcover books, based on preliminary data, was $43.26 (Table 3), 4 percent less than the figure for 1992. This category has previously been characterized by low increases (less than 5 percent per annum over the previous four years). This index is compiled from information published in R. R. Bowker's *Weekly Record.*

Table 4 shows average prices and price indexes for North American academic books. LMPIC has been studying the feasibility of changing the way this table has been compiled. This table, therefore, includes both an "old" and a "new" version of this data. Figure 1 is the standard approach that has been used since the mid-1980s and is produced from data collected from approval plan cost/coverage statistics supplied by Baker & Taylor, Coutts Library Services, and Blackwell North America. Its coverage is based on titles treated by these vendors during their respective fiscal years for the period shown. Figure 2 is based on electronic data provided by these three vendors, plus Yankee Book Peddler, and covers titles with an imprint date of 1989, 1990, 1991, or 1992 that were treated by one or more of these vendors' approval programs.

The database does not duplicate information on titles treated by more than one vendor, as did the old approach, and provides a more comprehensive representation of the academic book market for a given imprint year. Periods of coverage in the two versions are almost identical. Figure 1, for example, reports data only through June 30, 1993, but all of the participating vendors treated a large number of 1992 imprints during the first six months of 1993. LMPIC recommends that the new version of the index be adopted and the old version discontinued. We welcome reaction from our constituents.

Figure 1 of Table 4 shows an average price in 1992–1993 of $51.15, for an increase of 3.3 percent over the prior year. Figure 2, however, shows an average price of $45.91 for 1992–1993, for an increase over 1991–1992 of only 0.2 percent.

U.S. college book prices (Table 5) averaged $48.92 in 1993, only 3 percent higher than in 1992. Humanities titles, as a group, actually decreased in price in 1993, from $42.24 to $41.54, as did science titles, which dropped in average price from $54.09 to $53.68. Reference titles, which increased in price by 10.7 percent, accounted mainly for the fact that there was any increase at all; without reference books included, the sample rose in average price by only 21 cents, from $44.41 to $44.62. Data for this index is compiled from *Choice* book reviews, and expanded data appears in the April 1994 issue of *Choice*.

U.S. mass market paperback books (Table 6) and U.S. trade paperbacks (Table 7) varied somewhat in 1993, based on preliminary data from R. R. Bowker. In 1992, both categories posted increases in average price of between 2 percent and 3 percent. In 1993, however, trade paperbacks increased by about the same rate (2.3 percent) as in the prior year (from $18.81 to $19.24), but mass market paperbacks behaved in a fashion more similar to 1991 (11.2 percent increase), by jumping 9.2 percent, from $5.22 to $5.70.

Prices of Other Media

The U.S. nonprint media index (Table 8) is somewhat different for 1993. Compiler Dana Alessi has developed a new methodology, using a Lotus spreadsheet, which ensures that each title is counted only once. In the old methodology, there was not always consistency among the review sources with respect to price or length, so some titles could be counted more than once. Data for 1993 was compiled using both methodologies and both are presented in Table 8 this year. Also, the number of sources used to compile the index was expanded to include *Library Journal* and *Wilson Library Bulletin* as well as the previous sources, *School Library Journal* and *Booklist*. Finally, compact discs have been added to the sound recordings category for 1993.

The number of 16mm films produced continues to decline sharply as videocassettes dominate as a viewing medium. The average cost of videocassettes continued to drop in 1993, from $3.23 per minute to $2.38 per minute. This is due in part to the increasing number of titles reviewed that are intended for home viewing as well as library usage. Audio cassettes also continue to decline in cost, down significantly in 1993 to $8.20 from $11.73 in 1992. According to Dana Alessi, much of this can be attributed to the increasing number of audiobooks being reviewed.

The CD-ROM price inventory (Table 9) covers the period 1991–1993, and contains some significant changes over last year's inventory:

1 The former distinction between CD-ROM products as "monographs" or "serials" has been dropped. The ease of updating CD-ROM products has made the distinction less meaningful.

2 Data for the 1993 inventory were gathered primarily from the *Faxon Guide to CD-ROM 1993*, supplemented by *CD-ROMs in Print 1993*, and publisher

catalogs. CD-ROM products were included that meet the ANSI Standard Z39.20-1983 for Price Indexes.

3 In the LC subject classification arrangement, class H was separated into two sections: Business (HB-HJ) and Social Sciences (H, HM-HV). Class J (Political Science) and K (Law) were combined to include CD-ROM products for government data in one class.

As in prior years, all prices listed are single-user (non-networked) prices, at the "highest level of service," meaning the most frequent interval plus all available archival discs. CD-ROM production continues to increase, from 808 titles listed in 1992 to 949 in 1993. However, while the average price increased in 1992 by 12 percent, 1993 saw a more moderate change, from $1,750 to $1,846, an increase of only 5 percent.

Foreign Prices

Indexes are included for British academic books (Table 10), German academic books (Table 11), German academic periodicals (Table 12), and Latin American books (Table 13).

British Prices

Prices for British academic books are compiled from information supplied by B. H. Blackwell. The average price in 1993 was £35.39, which reflects an increase of 2.5 percent over the 1992 average price of £34.51. The increase for 1993 was only one-third that posted in 1992 (7.5 percent). Indeed, compiler Curt Holleman notes that both inflation (2.5 percent) and the increase in output of British books (1.1 percent) were comparatively small in 1993. The significant decrease in the value of the pound against the U.S. dollar in late 1992 more than offset the modest increases caused by inflation and title output, so that the real cost for U.S. libraries fell approximately 11.8 percent in 1993.

German Prices

German academic book prices (Table 11) rose by 6.8 percent in 1993, from DM58.20 to DM62.18, after only a 1.2 percent increase in 1992. Data for this table is provided by Otto Harrassowitz Inc., based on books supplied to its North American approval plan customers. This year, compiler John Haar determined that the data include titles published in Austria and Switzerland, as well as Germany. If only titles published in Germany are considered, the rate of increase is 6.6 percent, so the net impact of the inclusion of Austrian and Swiss titles was negligible. A more significant factor in the higher increase for 1993 was the discontinuation of discounts previously offered by associations and other non-trade German publishers. Beginning with 1994 data, we will recompute the German book price index to include only titles published in Germany.

(text continues on p. 530)

Table 9 / CD-ROM Price Inventory 1991–1993: Average Costs by Subject Classification

Classification	LC Class	Number of Titles			Average Price per Title			Percent Change	
		1991	1992	1993	1991	1992	1993	1991–1992	1992–1993
General works	A	65	104	127	$1,684	$1,697	$1,468	1	-13
Philosophy, psychology, religion	B	10	17	20	1,223	1,063	1,224	-13	15
History: general & Old World	D	3	5	6	325	722	888	122	23
History: America	E-F	11	16	16	146	595	568	308	-5
Geography, anthropology, recreation	G	24	30	35	1,909	1,643	1,507	-14	-8
Social sciences	H	66	72	75	2,342	1,866	2,022	-20	8
Business	HB-HJ	24	50	73	4,085	3,825	4,208	-6	10
Political science, law	J-K	10	28	35	2,331	1,796	1,776	-23	-1
Education	L	15	21	24	948	1,086	1,008	15	-7
Music	M	9	11	12	227	400	831	76	108
Fine arts	N	29	31	33	520	1,175	1,122	126	-5
Language and literature	P	25	40	46	380	2,926	2,907	670	-1
Science	Q	107	138	142	1,267	1,395	1,516	10	9
Medicine	R	67	93	123	1,500	1,386	1,485	-8	7
Agriculture	S	21	22	31	1,126	2,464	3,063	119	24
Technology	T	23	38	55	2,289	2,822	2,351	23	-17
Military science	U-V	3	22	24	716	789	948	10	20
Bibliography, library science	Z	50	70	72	1,530	1,432	1,424	-6	-1
Totals		562	808	949	$1,562	$1,750	$1,846	12	5

Compiled by Martha Kellogg and Theodore Kellogg, University of Rhode Island. Prices were obtained primarily from *Faxon Guide to CD-ROM 1993*, augmented by publishers' catalogs, and *CD-ROMs in Print 1993, An International Guide to CD-ROM, CDi, CDTV, & Electronic Book Products* (Meckler), compiled by Norman Desmarais. Note that the average prices used here are for the current subscription or current edition, received at the "highest level of service," i.e., (if a serial) at the most frequent level of service, and including all archival discs.

Table 10 / British Academic Books: Average Prices and Price Indexes, 1991–1993

(Index Base: 1985 = 100)

Subject Area	1985		1991			1992			1993		
	No. of Titles	Average Price	No. of Titles	Average Price	Index	No. of Titles	Average Price	Index	No. of Titles	Average Price	Index
General works	29	£30.54	44	£38.12	124.8	43	£47.79	156.5	30	£71.86	235.3
Fine arts	329	21.70	436	32.00	147.5	400	32.00	147.5	411	34.28	158.0
Architecture	97	20.68	119	30.35	146.8	141	31.34	151.5	185	31.60	152.8
Music	136	17.01	166	25.84	151.9	146	33.73	198.3	127	29.89	175.7
Performing arts except music	110	13.30	92	25.06	188.4	138	22.60	169.9	164	24.93	187.4
Archaeology	146	18.80	151	28.75	152.9	143	30.01	159.6	141	32.55	173.1
Geography	60	22.74	72	30.91	135.9	64	37.62	165.4	62	32.69	143.8
History	1,123	16.92	1,321	26.85	158.7	1,381	28.65	169.3	1,282	30.42	179.8
Philosophy	127	18.41	180	33.06	179.6	154	42.84	232.7	182	37.12	201.6
Religion	328	10.40	368	19.72	189.6	291	22.24	213.8	408	21.43	206.1
Language	135	19.37	144	30.44	157.2	112	32.22	166.3	150	39.24	202.6
Miscellaneous humanities	59	21.71	62	34.57	159.2	54	30.00	138.2	59	25.37	116.9
Literary texts (excluding fiction)	570	9.31	461	12.96	139.2	501	14.09	151.3	431	18.91	203.1
Literary criticism	438	14.82	494	28.58	192.8	590	29.13	196.6	532	29.99	202.4
Law	188	24.64	239	41.68	169.2	236	52.77	214.2	285	47.96	194.6
Library science and book trade	78	18.69	102	27.61	147.7	85	33.40	178.7	80	42.42	227.0
Mass communications	38	14.20	82	29.71	209.2	106	25.70	181.0	107	24.12	169.9
Anthropology and ethnology	42	20.71	66	31.45	151.9	84	33.03	159.5	70	37.15	179.4
Sociology	136	15.24	156	35.71	234.3	190	35.55	233.3	180	34.93	229.2
Psychology	107	19.25	126	34.88	181.2	114	33.92	176.2	145	35.73	185.6

Table 10 / British Academic Books: Average Prices and Price Indexes, 1991–1993 *(cont.)*
(Index Base: 1985 = 100)

Subject Area	1985		1991			1992			1993		
	No. of Titles	Average Price	No. of Titles	Average Price	Index	No. of Titles	Average Price	Index	No. of Titles	Average Price	Index
Economics	334	20.48	520	41.29	201.6	511	44.23	216.0	548	47.46	231.7
Political science, international relations	314	15.54	440	31.08	200.0	432	33.21	213.7	414	33.95	218.5
Miscellaneous social sciences	20	26.84	10	36.61	136.4	22	32.64	121.6	23	38.63	143.9
Military science	83	17.69	72	24.72	139.7	55	24.48	138.4	54	27.09	153.1
Sports and recreation	44	11.23	69	16.79	149.5	61	18.99	169.1	56	17.32	154.2
Social service	56	12.17	47	23.28	191.3	89	23.56	193.6	81	25.31	208.0
Education	295	12.22	300	25.38	207.7	302	24.95	204.2	328	25.17	206.0
Management and business administration	427	19.55	416	35.48	181.5	462	38.27	195.8	483	41.15	210.5
Miscellaneous applied social sciences	13	9.58	14	40.90	426.9	21	23.72	247.6	14	28.95	302.2
Criminology	45	11.45	68	23.16	202.3	66	25.88	226.0	54	24.64	215.2
Applied interdisciplinary social sciences	254	14.17	370	25.44	179.5	385	31.21	220.3	421	29.85	210.7
General science	43	13.73	45	35.13	255.9	33	34.18	248.9	31	37.10	270.2
Botany	55	30.54	51	42.24	138.3	52	38.77	126.9	49	41.25	135.1
Zoology	85	25.67	110	37.39	145.7	89	36.10	140.6	80	38.95	151.7
Human biology	35	28.91	25	42.62	147.4	17	40.38	139.1	42	45.07	155.9
Biochemistry	26	33.57	28	43.64	130.0	36	44.65	133.0	24	49.99	148.9
Miscellaneous biological sciences	152	26.64	164	36.51	137.0	158	42.64	160.1	150	36.31	136.3
Chemistry	109	48.84	98	77.00	157.7	108	67.34	137.9	91	72.40	148.2
Earth sciences	87	28.94	102	54.73	189.1	102	52.05	179.9	89	52.03	179.8
Astronomy	43	20.36	35	32.36	158.9	35	38.90	191.1	44	37.13	182.4

Physics	76	26.58	94	45.72	172.0	103	52.72	198.3	100	50.19	188.8
Mathematics	123	20.20	139	30.71	152.0	143	33.82	167.4	131	34.27	169.7
Computer sciences	150	20.14	259	31.25	155.2	248	32.73	162.5	259	29.85	148.2
Interdisciplinary technical fields	38	26.14	66	35.26	134.9	82	40.50	154.9	65	43.15	165.1
Civil engineering	134	28.68	167	51.99	181.3	153	59.51	207.5	151	61.38	214.0
Mechanical engineering	27	31.73	45	47.12	148.5	42	62.74	197.7	47	60.66	191.2
Electrical and electronic engineering	100	33.12	115	49.34	149.0	107	46.10	139.2	108	46.57	140.6
Materials science	54	37.93	103	71.86	189.5	105	79.82	210.4	93	81.76	215.6
Chemical engineering	24	40.48	46	53.66	132.6	31	62.73	155.0	46	64.55	159.5
Miscellaneous technology	217	36.33	222	51.54	141.9	268	54.87	151.0	247	60.09	165.4
Food and domestic science	38	23.75	54	44.61	187.8	54	57.06	240.3	42	58.12	244.7
Non-clinical medicine	97	18.19	99	31.46	173.0	125	29.93	164.5	144	29.79	163.8
General medicine	73	21.03	59	38.44	182.8	69	45.60	216.8	65	42.29	201.1
Internal medicine	163	27.30	168	40.18	147.2	182	50.99	186.8	186	48.24	176.7
Psychiatry and mental disorders	71	17.97	113	30.47	169.6	107	27.88	155.1	103	28.37	157.9
Surgery	50	29.37	39	50.14	170.7	54	59.96	204.2	53	62.88	214.1
Miscellaneous medicine	292	22.08	287	37.73	170.9	290	40.37	182.8	319	39.16	177.4
Dentistry	20	19.39	23	36.41	136.2	28	33.57	173.1	25	36.26	187.0
Nursing	71	8.00	48	13.53	169.1	56	14.90	186.3	56	15.71	196.4
Agriculture and forestry	78	23.69	82	37.85	159.8	95	39.68	167.5	95	40.61	171.4
Animal husbandry and veterinary medicine	34	20.92	47	34.30	164.0	48	32.32	154.5	53	41.90	200.3
Natural resources and conservation	58	22.88	54	31.20	136.4	58	43.32	189.3	50	39.38	172.1
Total, all books*	9,049	£19.07	10,561	£32.06	168.1	10,805	£34.51	181.0	10,925	£35.39	185.6

Compiled by Curt Holleman, Southern Methodist University, from data supplied by Chris Tyzack of B. H. Blackwell and John Sumsion of Loughborough University of Technology. The committee uses 1985 as the base year because that is the first year that the BHB database was used as the source of prices.

* Includes other small categories not listed in this table.

Table 11 / German Academic Books: Average Prices and Price Indexes, 1991–1993
(Index Base: 1989 = 100)

Subject Area	LC Class	1989 No. of Titles	1989 Average Price	1991 No. of Titles	1991 Average Price	1991 Percent Increase	1991 Index	1992 No. of Titles	1992 Average Price	1992 Percent Increase	1992 Index	1993 No. of Titles	1993 Average Price	1993 Percent Increase	1993 Index
Agriculture	S	240	DM50.06	192	DM62.46	34.6	124.8	248	DM57.99	-7.2	115.8	358	DM57.64	-0.6	115.1
Anthropology	GN	86	83.17	48	76.98	12.8	92.6	78	79.83	3.7	96.0	84	80.29	0.6	96.5
Botany	QK	70	88.44	76	98.59	7.2	111.5	80	97.91	-0.7	110.7	96	94.75	-3.2	107.1
Business and economics	H-HJ	1,152	51.21	1,443	56.98	6.4	111.3	1,551	60.22	5.7	117.6	1,518	61.53	2.2	120.2
Chemistry	QD	65	100.61	80	95.39	2.0	94.8	101	97.72	2.5	97.1	90	110.12	12.7	109.5
Education	L	243	45.10	273	39.39	-1.6	87.4	372	41.14	4.4	91.2	351	45.90	11.6	101.8
Engineering and technology	T	593	84.44	505	89.28	17.1	105.7	561	84.64	-5.2	100.2	581	102.84	21.5	121.8
Fine and applied arts	M-N	2,131	52.35	1,762	56.24	-1.4	107.4	2,268	60.81	8.1	116.2	2,512	64.80	6.5	123.8
General works	A	45	47.68	47	47.21	-15.6	99.0	67	50.14	6.2	105.2	50	165.09	229.3	346.2
Geography	G	332	51.29	212	58.55	6.2	114.2	207	55.43	-5.3	108.1	188	61.38	10.7	119.7
Geology	QE	41	75.91	41	110.41	32.8	145.4	52	110.94	0.5	146.1	70	92.19	-16.9	121.4
History	C,D,E,F	1,281	53.29	1,583	47.13	-8.3	88.4	2,316	50.09	6.3	94.0	2,347	54.78	9.4	102.8
Law	K	613	83.11	1,091	67.85	-6.6	81.6	1,347	70.69	4.2	85.1	568	81.73	15.6	98.3
Library and information science	Z	137	77.88	151	94.77	44.9	121.7	173	76.46	-19.3	98.2	157	87.39	14.3	112.2
Literature and language	P	3,535	47.45	2,878	46.83	3.1	98.7	4,355	46.91	0.2	98.9	4,631	51.28	9.3	108.1
Mathematics and computer science	QA	212	79.92	300	76.21	-3.8	95.4	239	86.00	12.8	107.6	346	94.75	10.2	118.6
Medicine	R	1,289	72.47	1,431	73.64	13.6	101.6	1,743	71.74	-2.6	99.0	1,427	75.68	5.5	104.4
Military and naval science	U-V	99	50.50	69	48.99	-0.8	97.0	68	78.63	60.5	155.7	64	68.99	-12.3	136.6
Natural history	QH	91	89.25	132	77.09	5.4	86.4	96	77.74	0.8	87.1	105	72.75	-6.4	81.5
Philosophy and religion	B	1,109	59.27	1,097	53.67	-14.5	90.6	1,628	58.31	8.6	98.4	2,022	57.55	-1.3	97.1
Physical education and recreation	GV	104	36.56	79	35.95	10.5	98.3	83	43.56	21.2	119.1	85	39.49	-9.3	108.0
Physics and astronomy	QB-QC	148	81.45	177	85.37	9.5	104.8	160	87.02	1.9	106.8	191	102.03	17.2	125.3
Physiology	QM-QR	144	99.59	140	102.52	-6.2	102.9	146	98.94	-3.5	99.3	125	133.71	35.1	134.3
Political science	J	622	40.87	487	44.71	-4.0	109.4	515	49.99	11.8	122.3	530	45.76	-8.5	112.0
Psychology	BF	135	54.13	193	46.17	6.3	85.3	227	51.13	10.7	94.5	181	56.29	10.1	104.0
Science (general)	Q	86	56.47	114	59.16	10.5	104.8	125	65.37	10.5	115.8	171	81.85	25.2	145.0
Sociology	HM-HX	838	39.50	959	38.86	-2.4	98.4	1,200	41.09	5.7	104.0	1,131	45.80	11.5	116.0
Zoology	QL	52	124.77	48	99.24	33.1	79.5	35	127.65	28.6	102.3	101	86.03	-32.6	69.0
Total		15,493	DM56.80	15,608	DM57.49	2.8	101.2	20,041	DM58.20	1.2	102.5	20,080	DM62.18	6.8	109.5

Compiled by John Haar, Vanderbilt University, from approval plan data supplied by Otto Harrassowitz. Data represent a selection of materials relevant to research and documentation published in Germany, Austria, and Switzerland (see text for more information regarding the nature of the data). Unclassified material as well as titles in home economics and industrial arts have been excluded. The index is not adjusted for high-priced titles.

Table 12 / German Academic Periodicals: Average Prices and Price Indexes, 1992–1994
(Index Base: 1990 = 100)

Subject Area	LC Class	1990 Average Price	1992 No. of Titles	1992 Average Price	1992 Percent Increase	1992 Index	1993 No. of Titles	1993 Average Price	1993 Percent Increase	1993 Index	1994 No. of Titles	1994 Average Price	1994 Percent Increase	1994 Index
Agriculture	S	DM235.11	176	DM259.15	5.8	110.2	167	DM269.87	4.1	114.8	174	DM272.07	0.8	115.7
Anthropology	GN	112.88	10	124.60	14.3	110.4	7	162.97	30.8	144.4	7	166.90	2.4	147.9
Botany	QK	498.79	22	544.40	6.2	109.1	18	609.33	11.9	122.2	18	642.80	5.5	128.9
Business and economics	H-HJ	153.48	262	170.99	4.6	111.4	273	195.27	14.2	127.2	226	211.69	8.4	137.9
Chemistry	QD	553.06	65	699.70	10.1	126.5	47	696.32	-0.5	125.9	49	776.90	11.6	140.5
Education	L	70.86	60	71.30	0.3	100.6	62	74.69	4.8	105.4	63	78.50	5.1	110.8
Engineering and technology	T-TS	239.40	369	279.76	15.0	116.9	304	342.11	22.3	142.9	397	280.97	-17.9	117.4
Fine and applied arts	M-N	84.15	257	92.10	6.5	109.4	159	97.04	5.4	115.3	168	101.39	4.5	120.5
General works	A	349.37	84	349.26	-5.1	100.0	89	348.32	-0.3	99.7	102	375.46	7.8	107.5
Geography	G	90.42	17	115.10	24.4	127.3	16	114.27	-0.7	126.4	16	133.10	16.5	147.2
Geology	QE	261.30	41	300.70	12.9	115.1	40	323.34	7.5	123.4	40	346.80	7.3	132.7
History	C,D,E,F	66.09	136	80.62	24.5	122.0	136	81.54	1.1	123.4	137	79.59	-2.4	120.4
Law	K	193.88	134	240.50	16.5	124.0	142	250.69	4.2	129.3	146	263.60	5.1	136.0
Library and information science	Z	317.50	57	336.10	27.3	105.9	58	373.04	11.0	117.5	59	404.70	8.5	127.5
Literature and language	P	102.69	169	122.13	15.4	118.9	168	119.74	-2.0	116.6	172	121.74	1.7	118.6
Mathematics and computer science	QA	1,064.62	36	1,165.50	6.1	109.5	36	1,138.83	-2.3	107.0	38	1,193.50	4.8	112.1
Medicine	R	320.62	534	350.29	6.9	109.3	533	368.19	5.1	114.8	561	388.78	5.6	121.3
Military and naval science	U-V	86.38	21	90.06	8.2	104.3	23	100.51	11.6	116.4	23	103.69	3.2	120.0
Natural history	QH	728.36	59	828.50	10.7	113.7	51	921.68	11.2	126.5	53	984.40	6.8	135.2
Philosophy and religion	B	65.00	176	74.56	11.8	114.7	185	89.32	19.8	137.4	193	94.64	6.0	145.6
Physical education and recreation	GV	81.96	51	78.60	-3.6	95.9	52	92.38	17.5	112.7	52	97.40	5.4	118.8
Physics and astronomy	QB-QC	684.40	61	865.02	6.5	126.4	53	945.91	9.4	138.2	55	969.83	2.5	141.7
Physiology	QM-QR	962.83	10	1,140.17	9.5	118.4	8	1,378.18	20.9	143.1	8	1,450.48	5.2	150.6
Political science	J	80.67	142	87.60	3.8	108.6	140	87.46	-0.2	108.4	142	89.10	1.9	110.4
Psychology	BF	94.10	37	102.40	8.8	108.8	41	104.39	1.9	110.9	41	112.00	7.3	119.0
Science (general)	Q	310.54	33	341.30	-3.4	109.9	33	396.33	16.1	127.6	35	415.30	4.8	133.7
Sociology	HM-HX	109.61	59	121.69	8.4	111.0	60	120.87	-0.7	110.3	60	124.31	2.8	113.4
Zoology	QL	161.02	33	214.70	22.0	133.3	32	211.86	-1.3	131.6	33	223.60	5.5	138.9
Total		DM228.40	3,011	DM265.88	10.9	116.4	2,933	DM277.58	4.4	121.5	3,068	DM287.14	3.4	125.7

*Compiled by Steven E. Thompson, Brown University, from data supplied by Otto Harrassowitz. The data represent periodical and newspaper titles published in Germany. Price information for 1994 is preliminary; price data is 87% complete.

Table 13 / Number of Copies and Average Cost of Latin American Books Purchased by Seven Selected U.S. Libraries in FYs 1992 and 1993

	Number of Books		Average Cost*		Percent Change in Cost
	1992	1993	1992	1993	
Argentina	5,688	4,838	$16.87	$18.02	6.82
Bolivia	1,790	1,919	10.24	11.07	8.11
Brazil	7,634	11,518	15.55	9.11	-41.41
Chile	1,802	1,724	17.08	18.04	5.62
Colombia	2,868	3,423	13.93	15.05	8.04
Costa Rica	909	784	14.56	19.81	36.06
Cuba	298	391	14.99	17.71	18.15
Dominican Republic	440	255	17.58	24.60	39.93
Ecuador	1,835	2,347	9.79	10.52	7.46
El Salvador	285	338	11.95	10.27	-14.06
Guatemala	491	400	14.68	14.86	1.23
Guyana	8	7	6.25	32.48	419.68
Haiti	55	27	19.11	29.17	52.64
Honduras	217	263	8.47	11.93	40.85
Jamaica	74	67	17.64	20.21	14.57
Mexico	7,738	6,311	22.02	30.15	36.92
Nicaragua	209	319	17.79	18.18	2.19
Panama	181	290	14.11	16.23	15.02
Paraguay	801	467	11.97	13.00	8.60
Peru	2,651	1,525	15.57	20.23	29.93
Puerto Rico	355	180	22.59	28.20	24.83
Suriname	18	2	31.17	8.65	-72.25
Trinidad	123	27	17.54	26.12	48.92
Uruguay	1,511	1,416	19.22	23.18	20.60
Venezuela	2,211	1,999	11.86	11.52	-2.87
Other Caribbean	530	1,174	14.64	20.00	36.61
Total	40,722	42,011	$16.29	$16.36	0.43

Compiled by David Block, Seminar on the Acquisition of Latin American Library Materials (SALALM) Acquisition Committee, from reports on the number and cost of current monographs purchased by the libraries of Cornell University, Library of Congress, New York Public Library, University of Arizona, University of Illinois, University of Texas, and University of Wisconsin.

* Some figures include binding costs.

German periodical prices (Table 12) rose in 1994 at an even more moderate rate than German book prices, from an average price in 1992 of DM277.58 to DM287.14, or 3.4 percent. The 1993 inflation rate is one point lower than the 1992 rate of 4.4 percent. Since this index first appeared only last year, its base year (1990) is much more recent. The largest increase in 1994 for a single subject category was in geography, at 16.5 percent, followed by chemistry at 11.6 percent. These were the only categories with increases of 10 percent or higher, while the average price for engineering and technology actually dropped by 17.9 percent.

Latin American Prices

Data reported for books published in over 25 Latin American countries (Table 13) are compiled from acquisitions records of seven large research libraries. They are not, therefore, a true price index based on the total publishing output of these nations. Prices may also be affected by the state of the book trade in each country, the lack of meaningful list prices for many countries, varying rates of inflation, currency revaluations, changes in the scope of dealer coverage, and other inconsistencies in reporting practice.

Compiler David Block reports that the data for 1993 are skewed by a statistical anomaly resulting from a change in acquisitions patterns at one of the libraries surveyed. In 1992–1993 the Library of Congress received 7,357 monographic items, as compared to 2,250 and 1,395 items reported in 1992 and 1991. This huge increase, along with a very low reported unit cost (about $2.70 per title) achieved by the LC Field Office staff (particularly for Brazilian titles) is a major reason why the average cost for Latin American titles remained almost constant between 1992 and 1993. David Block notes that if LC's Brazilian titles were extracted from the survey, the overall average price for 1993 would have been $18.75, for an increase over 1992 of 15.1 percent.

U.S. Purchasing Power Abroad

In 1993 the U.S. dollar continued to gain strength against most key foreign currencies related to publishing. Unlike in 1992, there were almost no midyear fluctuations in exchange rates. The only exceptions were the Japanese yen, which gained strength against the dollar, and the British pound, which strengthened slightly at midyear but finished 1993 weaker than at the end of 1992. The following chart reports rates in currency per U.S. dollar based on quotations in the *Wall Street Journal*. Readers interested in quotations for earlier years may examine earlier volumes of the *Bowker Annual*.

	12/31/91	1/31/92	6/30/92	12/31/92	6/30/93	12/31/93
Canada	1.1555	1.1750	1.1955	1.2695	1.2820	1.3296
France	5.1800	5.5025	5.1035	5.5045	5.6835	5.8930
U.K.	0.5349	0.5615	0.5247	0.6614	0.6607	0.6774
Germany	1.5150	1.6150	1.5177	1.6160	1.6877	1.7353
Japan	124.80	125.70	125.45	124.60	106.32	111.83
Netherlands	1.7070	1.8175	1.7105	1.8156	1.8928	1.9385

Using the Price Indexes

Librarians are encouraged to monitor both trends in the publishing industry and changes in economic conditions when preparing budget projections. The ALA ALCTS Library Materials Price Index Committee endeavors to make information on publishing trends readily available by sponsoring the annual compilation and publication of the price data contained in Tables 1–13. The indexes cover newly published library materials and document prices and rates of price changes at the national level. They are useful benchmarks against which local costs may be compared, but because they reflect retail prices in the aggregate, they are not a substitute for cost data that reflect the collecting patterns of individual libraries.

In part, differences arise because the national indexes exclude discounts, service charges, shipping and handling fees, or other costs that libraries may bear. Discrepancies may also be related to subject focus, mix of current and retrospective materials, and the portion of total library acquisitions comprising foreign imprints. Such variables can affect the average price paid by a particular library, although the library's rate of price increase may not significantly differ from national price indexes. The Library Materials Price Index Committee is interested in pursuing studies correlating a particular library's costs with national prices and would appreciate being informed of any planned or ongoing studies. The committee welcomes interested parties to its meetings at the ALA annual and midwinter conferences.

Current members of the Library Materials Price Index Committee are Adrian Alexander (chair), Dana Alessi, Donna Alsbury, Richard Brumley, Marifran Bustion, Virginia Gilbert, Cynthia Hepfer, John Lazar (intern), Genevieve Owens, Mark Sandler, Andrew Shroyer, and Wilba Swearingen. Consultants and other advisers who contributed to the preparation of indexes are David Block, Stephen Bosch, Kathryn Hammell Carpenter, John Haar, Curt Holleman, Martha Kellogg, Frederick Lynden, Kathryn Soupiset, Sharon Sullivan, and Steven Thompson.

Book Title Output and Average Prices: 1993 Preliminary Figures

Gary Ink

Research Librarian, *Publishers Weekly*

American book title output, which recorded a total of 49,276 titles in 1992, continued its upward recovery from the low point reached in 1990 (Tables 1–3). However, there may be early indications that this trend will not continue when final 1993 figures are in. Preliminary 1993 data compiled for *Publishers Weekly* by R. R. Bowker show a total decline of 2,311 titles from the preliminary 1992 total indicated in March 1993.

American book title output reached a peak in 1987, with the grand total of 56,027; three successive years of falling figures bottomed out in 1990, when total output stood at only 46,743. In 1991 title output rebounded to 48,146, with 1992 output continuing the upward movement. The preliminary data received for 1993 seem to indicate that the total will be less than 49,000 when all figures are tabulated.

Note: Adapted from *Publishers Weekly,* March 7, 1994.

Declines by Category

By category (Table 1), there continue to be significant declines: sociology is down by 1,024 titles from the levels of 1992; fiction, which increased slightly between 1991 and 1992, shows a decline of 849 titles from the 1992 final total; and the growth in the children's category (Juveniles) continues to show a flattening trend. When final figures are available, it is unlikely that any category will show substantial gains over 1992's figures.

Mass market output by category (Table 3) shows what may be the beginning of an upward trend for mass market publishing. The preliminary total of 3,032 titles represents an increase of 424 titles over the preliminary total recorded in March 1993. The precipitous decline in fiction, which began between the years 1990 and 1991, has been reversed. Preliminary figures for 1993 indicate that the upward trend in fiction will likely continue. In the nonfiction categories, it is interesting to note that significant gains have been recorded in agriculture, education, and technology. The nonfiction categories in which preliminary figures indicate marked declines are history and poetry.

Prices Rise Moderately

Average prices rose moderately in 1992. Figures shown here are derived from two R. R. Bowker databases—*American Book Publishing Record* for hardcovers and trade paperbacks and *Paperbound Books in Print* for mass market paperbacks (Tables A–C).

While final price averages will vary somewhat from these preliminary ones, the latter do suggest some trends. Hardcover fiction averages continue to remain below the $20 price point; prices in this area have gone up only 43 cents in the last three years. Mass market fiction averages show only a small increase—15 cents—over 1992. Trade paperback fiction, which took a significant jump between 1991 and 1992, shows a decline of 9 cents in the preliminary figures for 1993. Overall, however, trade paperback averages show a preliminary increase of 43 cents.

Preliminary 1993 figures indicate that hardcover books on all subjects priced under $81 (Table A-1) have decreased by $1.10, which includes a 36-cent decline in fiction, to $19.35.

Each of the 23 standard subject groups used here represents one or more specific Dewey Decimal Classification numbers, as follows:

Agriculture, 630–639, 712–719; Art, 700–711, 720–779; Biography, 920–929; Business, 650–659; Education, 370–379; Fiction; General Works, 000–099; History, 900–909, 930–999; Home Economics, 640–649; Juveniles; Language, 400–499; Law, 340–349; Literature, 800–810, 813–820, 823–899; Medicine, 610–619; Music, 780–789; Philosophy, Psychology, 100–199; Poetry, Drama, 811, 812, 821, 822; Religion, 200–299; Science, 500–599; Sociology, Economics, 300–339, 350–369, 380–399; Sports, Recreation, 790–799; Technology, 600–609, 620–629, 660–699; Travel, 910–919.

Table 1 / American Book Title Production, 1991–1993

Category	1991 All Hard and Paper	1992 Final Hard and Trade Paper — Books	Editions	Totals	1992 All Hard and Paper	1993 Preliminary Hard and Trade Paper — Books	Editions	Totals	1993 All Hard and Paper*
Agriculture	523	465	86	551	565	339	82	421	443
Art	1,283	1,227	162	1,389	1,392	976	143	1,119	1,124
Biography	2,120	1,671	244	1,915	2,007	1,561	172	1,733	1,801
Business	1,421	1,025	321	1,346	1,367	918	247	1,165	1,186
Education	1,129	1,015	154	1,169	1,184	901	133	1,034	1,065
Fiction	5,424	2,922	181	3,103	5,690	2,708	87	2,795	4,841
General works	1,886	1,776	312	2,088	2,153	1,240	200	1,440	1,482
History	2,331	1,924	355	2,279	2,322	1,674	272	1,946	1,960
Home economics	789	637	120	757	826	582	93	675	731
Juveniles	5,111	4,379	276	4,655	5,144	4,485	196	4,681	5,062
Language	566	481	125	606	617	432	106	538	548
Law	1,177	729	333	1,062	1,063	660	244	904	904
Literature	2,087	1,918	280	2,198	2,227	1,673	176	1,849	1,867
Medicine	3,027	2,499	714	3,213	3,234	2,014	625	2,639	2,651
Music	300	289	56	345	346	258	56	314	315
Philosophy, psychology	1,766	1,444	273	1,717	1,806	1,315	191	1,506	1,589
Poetry, drama	890	841	46	887	899	792	40	832	839
Religion	2,389	2,167	364	2,531	2,540	1,950	321	2,271	2,274
Science	2,710	2,182	538	2,720	2,729	1,741	404	2,145	2,153
Sociology, economics	7,241	6,427	946	7,373	7,432	5,525	840	6,365	6,408
Sports, recreation	1,063	850	121	971	1,113	718	104	822	914
Technology	2,421	1,692	420	2,112	2,152	1,273	385	1,658	1,720
Travel	492	352	111	463	468	229	104	333	340
Total	48,146	38,912	6,538	45,450	49,276	33,964	5,221	39,185	42,217

* Includes mass market paperbacks (see Table 3).

Note: Figures for mass market paperbound book production are based on entries in R. R. Bowker's *Paperbound Books in Print*. Other figures are from the *Weekly Record (American Book Publishing Record)* database. Figures under "Books" and "Editions" designate new books and new editions.

Table 2 / Paperbacks (Excluding Mass Market), 1991–1993

Category	1991 Totals	1992 Final			1993 Preliminary		
		New Books	New Editions	Totals	New Books	New Editions	Totals
Fiction	526	382	113	495	300	98	398
Nonfiction	14,661	12,195	2,772	14,967	10,337	2,157	12,494
Total	15,187	12,577	2,885	15,462	10,637	2,255	12,892

Table 3 / Mass Market Paperbacks, 1990–1993

Category	1990 Final	1991 Final	1992 Final	1993 Preliminary
Agriculture	1	5	14	22
Art	12	7	3	5
Biography	58	76	92	68
Business	16	13	21	21
Education	15	5	15	31
Fiction	2,855	2,266	2,587	2,046
General works	44	52	65	42
History	28	28	43	14
Home economics	44	60	69	56
Juveniles	433	449	489	381
Language	17	9	11	10
Law	3	4	1	0
Literature	28	24	29	18
Medicine	31	32	21	12
Music	7	1	1	1
Philosophy, psychology	121	67	89	83
Poetry, drama	4	12	12	7
Religion	13	11	9	3
Science	9	15	9	8
Sociology, economics	50	42	59	43
Sports, recreation	136	139	142	92
Technology	14	29	40	62
Travel	29	29	5	7
Total	3,968	3,375	3,826	3,032

Table 4 / Imported Titles, 1991–1993
(Hard and Trade Paper Only)

Category	1991 Totals	1992 Final Books	1992 Final Editions	1992 Final Totals	1993 Preliminary Books	1993 Preliminary Editions	1993 Preliminary Totals
Agriculture	81	80	13	93	43	22	65
Art	101	146	10	156	90	9	99
Biography	124	110	14	124	80	5	85
Business	140	116	10	126	158	22	180
Education	176	222	10	232	192	15	207
Fiction	250	207	39	246	73	3	76
General works	252	281	32	313	208	19	227
History	314	308	40	348	242	25	267
Home economics	23	23	2	25	3	2	5
Juveniles	69	48	2	50	31	1	32
Language	171	151	13	164	117	10	127
Law	171	151	46	197	130	37	167
Literature	196	256	18	274	188	15	203
Medicine	447	452	62	514	319	64	383
Music	71	62	7	69	47	1	48
Philosophy, psychology	256	264	27	291	262	29	291
Poetry, drama	115	123	13	136	85	4	89
Religion	129	145	20	165	127	18	145
Science	795	719	121	840	531	91	622
Sociology, economics	1,278	1,425	96	1,521	1,162	113	1,275
Sports, recreation	93	99	13	112	83	7	90
Technology	558	404	54	458	278	59	337
Travel	57	40	12	52	19	2	21
Total	5,867	5,832	674	6,506	4,468	573	5,041

Table 5 / Translations into English, 1988–1993
(Hard and Trade Paper Only)

	1988 Final	1989 Final	1990 Final	1991 Final	1992 Final	1993 Prelim.
Arabic	27	45	26	24	26	23
Chinese	34	26	45	35	49	40
Danish	23	49	24	20	25	12
Dutch	49	33	40	30	30	29
Finnish	3	3	10	1	42	4
French	570	442	389	365	383	288
German	501	453	252	402	337	306
Hebrew	45	56	35	45	47	36
Italian	129	142	79	87	91	77
Japanese	95	84	82	83	70	53
Latin	43	38	51	49	10	49
Norwegian	12	12	7	8	62	2
Russian	256	251	185	168	146	115
Spanish	162	121	120	125	122	125
Swedish	47	36	30	25	25	20
Yiddish	14	12	5	13	4	2
Total	2,010	1,803	1,380	1,480	1,469	1,181

Note: "Total" covers only the languages listed here.

Table A / Hardcover Average Per-Volume Prices, 1990–1993

Category	1990 Prices	1991 Prices	1992 Final Vols.	1992 Final $ Total	1992 Final Prices	1993 Preliminary Vols.	1993 Preliminary $ Total	1993 Preliminary Prices
Agriculture	$54.24	$57.73	359	$19,300.99	$53.76	268	$15,316.76	$57.15
Art	42.18	44.99	815	36,339.49	44.59	671	31,062.03	46.29
Biography	29.58	27.52	1,359	41,325.89	30.41	1,174	35,660.69	30.38
Business	45.48	43.38	832	36,533.25	43.91	708	29,977.67	42.34
Education	38.72	41.26	653	31,848.10	48.77	548	23,025.38	42.02
Fiction	19.83	21.30	2,052	41,849.26	20.39	1,956	39,798.85	20.35
General works	54.77	51.74	1,160	65,297.65	56.29	801	42,918.90	53.58
History	36.43	39.87	1,533	60,073.99	39.19	1,293	52,606.14	40.69
Home economics	23.80	24.23	369	9,179.47	24.88	358	7,408.70	20.70
Juveniles	13.01	16.64	3,646	52,717.35	14.46	3,410	48,776.65	14.30
Language	42.98	51.71	362	17,984.20	49.68	291	17,711.63	60.87
Law	60.78	64.89	766	58,375.15	76.21	592	41,856.11	70.70
Literature	35.80	36.76	1,409	55,274.85	39.23	1,146	44,209.49	38.58
Medicine	72.24	71.44	2,277	171,284.29	75.22	1,794	134,861.37	75.17
Music	41.86	41.04	207	9,804.60	47.37	180	7,496.07	41.65
Philosophy, psychology	40.58	42.74	1,032	48,346.29	46.85	886	39,787.45	44.91
Poetry, drama	32.19	33.29	462	16,982.20	36.76	453	17,263.51	38.11
Religion	31.31	32.33	1,110	39,192.80	35.31	1,100	35,445.83	32.22
Science	74.39	80.14	1,955	160,208.75	81.95	1,472	116,864.64	79.39
Sociology, economics	42.10	48.43	4,861	221,318.81	45.53	3,990	185,386.66	46.46
Sports, recreation	30.52	30.68	465	16,096.10	34.62	410	13,702.21	33.42
Technology	76.80	76.40	1,621	133,207.23	82.18	1,096	85,929.73	78.40
Travel	30.41	32.43	182	6,057.55	33.28	142	4,048.25	28.51
Total	$42.12	$44.17	29,487	$1,348,598.10	$45.05	24,739	1,071,114.72	$43.26

Table A-1 / Hardcover Average Per-Volume Prices—Less Than $81, 1990–1993

Category	1990 Prices	1991 Prices	1992 Final Vols.	1992 Final $ Total	1992 Final Prices	1993 Preliminary Vols.	1993 Preliminary $ Total	1993 Preliminary Prices
Agriculture	$33.90	$31.92	293	$10,293	$35.13	214	$7,996.06	$37.36
Art	37.31	37.92	741	27,221	36.74	618	23,604.59	38.20
Biography	25.47	25.23	1,320	35,453	26.86	1,141	31,520.89	27.63
Business	36.43	38.01	792	31,349	39.58	665	24,846.02	37.36
Education	36.35	36.51	616	24,429	39.66	514	19,914.58	38.74
Fiction	19.27	19.55	2,038	40,172	19.71	1,940	37,547.45	19.35
General works	40.60	39.76	996	42,721	42.89	706	30,699.50	43.48
History	33.77	35.31	1,469	52,785	35.93	1,252	46,919.29	37.48
Home economics	22.44	23.89	366	8,495	23.21	357	7,318.75	20.50
Juveniles	12.88	13.37	3,640	50,424	13.85	3,404	47,719.75	14.02
Language	34.74	40.32	311	12,022	38.66	254	8,671.62	34.14
Law	40.42	41.31	524	22,672	43.27	423	18,582.51	43.93
Literature	33.50	33.64	1,368	48,176	35.22	1,124	39,428.74	35.08
Medicine	41.53	40.19	1,460	61,075	41.83	1,133	46,483.63	41.03
Music	38.20	38.17	195	7,762	39.81	168	6,172.22	36.74
Philosophy, psychology	35.76	36.75	962	37,519	39.00	829	31,366.85	37.84
Poetry, drama	29.93	31.32	443	14,231	32.12	439	13,361.56	30.44
Religion	29.30	29.70	1,060	32,880	31.02	1,057	30,606.03	28.96
Science	45.45	45.77	1,278	60,073	47.01	969	44,460.55	45.88
Sociology, economics	37.78	39.19	4,580	184,598	40.31	3,757	153,887.10	40.96
Sports, recreation	30.00	29.42	458	15,213	33.22	403	12,765.71	31.68
Technology	45.73	46.38	1,092	53,325	48.83	727	33,935.12	46.68
Travel	29.12	29.00	176	5,416	30.77	138	3,572.25	25.89
Total	$31.60	$31.95	26,178	$878,304	$33.55	22,232	$721,380.77	$32.45

Table B / Mass Market Paperbacks Average Per-Volume Prices, 1991–1993

	1991 Prices	1992 Final Vols.	1992 Final $ Total	1992 Final Prices	1993 Preliminary Vols.	1993 Preliminary $ Total	1993 Preliminary Prices
Agriculture	$5.00	14	$103.57	$7.40	22	$137.00	$6.23
Art	10.13	3	30.99	10.33	5	98.94	19.79
Biography	6.18	92	568.57	6.18	68	445.28	6.55
Business	8.36	21	174.21	8.30	21	218.55	10.41
Education	5.98	15	143.36	9.96	31	350.68	11.31
Fiction	4.49	2,587	11,972.60	4.63	2,046	9,786.41	4.78
General works	7.48	65	471.06	7.25	42	365.55	8.70
History	8.37	43	307.16	7.14	14	120.38	8.60
Home economics	7.97	69	511.46	7.41	56	373.90	6.67
Juveniles	3.38	489	1,766.79	3.61	381	1,401.59	3.68
Language	7.26	11	68.90	6.26	10	76.36	7.64
Law	9.85	1	4.99	4.99	0	0	0
Literature	5.89	29	207.78	7.16	18	121.92	6.77
Medicine	5.88	21	189.43	9.02	12	117.76	9.81
Music	2.75	1	2.75	2.75	1	11.00	11.00
Philosophy, psychology	7.78	89	597.24	6.71	83	523.95	6.31
Poetry, drama	6.55	12	74.89	6.24	7	50.90	7.27
Religion	7.79	9	70.96	7.88	3	29.90	9.97
Science	8.27	9	73.48	8.16	8	62.94	7.87
Sociology, economics	7.56	59	382.53	6.48	43	347.64	8.09
Sports, recreation	7.50	142	971.26	6.84	92	659.58	7.17
Technology	25.58	40	1,247.12	31.18	62	1,911.41	30.83
Travel	10.95	5	45.48	9.10	7	73.93	10.56
Total	$5.08	3,826	$19,986.58	$5.22	3,032	$17,285.57	$5.70

Table C / Trade Paperbacks Average Per-Volume Prices, 1990–1993

Category	1990 Prices	1991 Prices	1992 Final Vols.	1992 Final $ Total	1992 Final Prices	1993 Preliminary Vols.	1993 Preliminary $ Total	1993 Preliminary Prices
Agriculture	$16.42	$14.90	179	$2,994.34	$16.73	138	$2,669.88	$19.35
Art	17.90	19.11	549	10,715.55	19.52	400	7,958.40	19.90
Biography	13.05	13.38	516	7,011.67	13.59	469	6,984.60	14.89
Business	19.61	21.20	484	11,104.80	22.94	380	8,249.87	21.71
Education	19.20	23.30	480	11,159.05	23.25	411	9,201.89	22.39
Fiction	11.32	12.17	928	12,692.18	13.68	723	9,827.17	13.59
General works	29.67	34.74	868	25,347.77	29.20	535	16,742.35	31.29
History	17.39	16.99	724	12,613.96	17.42	581	10,699.93	18.42
Home economics	12.97	12.89	374	5,346.13	14.29	290	3,966.99	13.68
Juveniles	6.78	7.60	869	6,508.49	7.49	945	7,444.43	7.88
Language	16.67	16.83	230	4,051.00	17.61	212	4,447.80	20.98
Law	25.15	24.62	277	6,971.50	25.17	232	6,115.33	26.36
Literature	15.54	15.31	727	12,391.18	17.04	632	10,965.29	17.35
Medicine	22.82	24.20	855	22,364.88	26.16	699	19,784.80	28.30
Music	19.17	17.03	121	2,488.10	20.56	117	2,397.95	20.50
Philosophy, psychology	15.29	16.54	637	10,981.43	17.24	546	9,865.69	18.07
Poetry, drama	12.43	11.88	395	5,159.16	13.06	346	4,375.25	12.65
Religion	12.12	12.50	1,371	17,936.85	13.08	1,092	14,851.13	13.60
Science	28.01	28.31	640	17,910.15	27.98	478	15,079.78	31.55
Sociology, economics	19.60	19.68	2,354	46,425.55	19.72	2,066	43,810.06	21.21
Sports, recreation	13.67	15.03	490	7,662.07	15.64	388	5,975.53	15.40
Technology	30.06	33.39	589	16,936.47	28.75	400	11,649.81	29.12
Travel	13.32	14.06	276	4,071.75	14.75	176	2,787.90	15.84
Total	$17.45	$18.40	14,933	$280,837.00	$18.81	12,256	$235,851.83	$19.24

Book Sales Statistics, 1993: AAP Preliminary Estimates

Association of American Publishers

The industry estimates shown in the following table are based on the U.S. Census of Manufactures. This census is conducted every fifth year—the most recent being the 1987 census.

Between censuses, the Association of American Publishers (AAP) estimates are "pushed forward" by the percentage changes that are reported to the AAP statistics program, and by other industry data that are available. Some AAP data are collected in a monthly statistics program, and it is largely this material that is shown in this preliminary estimate table. More detailed data are available from, and additional publishers report to, the AAP annual statistics program, and this additional data will be incorporated into Table S1 which will be published in the (forthcoming) AAP 1993 Industry Statistics.

Table 1 / Estimated Book Publishing Industry Sales 1982, 1987, 1991–1993
(Millions of Dollars)

	1982 $	1987 $	1991 $	1992 $	1992 % Change from 1991	1993 $	1993 % Change from 1992	Compound Growth Rate (%) 1982–1993	1987–1993	1991–1993
Trade (total)	1,513.0	2,712.8	4,252.6	4,661.6	9.6	4,997.4	7.2	11.5	10.7	8.4
Adult hardbound	770.8	1,350.6	1,958.3	2,222.5	13.5	2,552.8	14.9	11.5	11.2	14.2
Adult paperbound	458.2	727.1	1,130.5	1,261.7	11.6	1,283.7	1.7	9.8	9.9	6.6
Juvenile hardbound	206.9	478.5	859.0	850.8	-1.0	783.1	-8.0	12.9	8.6	-4.5
Juvenile paperbound	77.1	156.6	304.8	326.6	7.2	377.8	15.7	15.5	15.8	11.3
Religious (total)	425.5	638.8	854.7	907.1	6.1	955.5	5.3	7.6	6.9	5.7
Bibles, testaments, hymnals, etc.	149.1	177.6	250.8	260.1	3.7	267.3	2.8	5.5	7.1	3.2
Other religious	276.4	461.2	603.9	647.0	7.1	688.2	6.4	8.7	6.9	6.8
Professional (total)	1,536.4	2,207.3	2,860.7	3,106.7	8.6	3,402.7	9.5	7.5	7.5	9.1
Business	224.2	388.8	488.8	490.3	0.3	—				
Law	560.9	780.0	1,011.9	1,128.1	11.5	—				
Medical	287.2	406.5	580.5	622.7	7.3	—				
Technical, scientific, other prof'l	464.1	632.0	779.5	865.6	11.0	—				
Book clubs	522.9	678.7	749.8	742.3	-1.0	787.9	6.1	3.8	2.5	2.5
Mail order publications	568.6	657.6	733.6	630.2	-14.1	582.3	-7.6	0.2	-2.0	-10.9
Mass market paperback, rack-sized	703.4	913.7	1,243.9	1,263.8	1.6	1,341.5	6.1	6.0	6.6	3.9
University presses	125.4	170.9	265.5	280.1	5.5	292.9	4.6	8.0	9.4	5.0
Elementary and secondary text	1,108.2	1,695.6	2,054.2	2,080.9	1.3	2,307.2	10.9	6.9	5.3	6.0
College text	1,206.1	1,549.5	2,001.3	2,084.1	4.1	2,144.3	2.9	5.4	5.6	3.5
Standardized tests	70.4	104.0	133.5	140.4	5.2	146.8	4.6	6.9	5.9	4.9
Subscription reference	306.9	437.6	552.4	572.3	3.6	602.0	5.2	6.3	5.5	4.4
AV and other media (total)	148.0	213.0	216.4	198.4	-8.3	—				
El-hi	130.1	174.7	164.3	154.7	-5.2	—				
College	7.9	15.1	21.9	14.4	-34.2	—				
Other	10.0	23.2	30.2	29.3	-3.0	—				
Other sales	162.1	210.8	224.7	250.6	11.5	—				
Total	8,396.9	12,190.3	16,143.3	16,918.5	4.8	18,039.8	6.6	7.2	6.8	5.7

Source: Association of American Publishers.

Preliminary data from the 1992 U.S. Census of Manufactures should be available in summer 1994, and data back to 1987 will then be adjusted accordingly. These estimates should also be available for the AAP 1993 Industry Statistics.

Readers comparing the estimated data with census reports should recall that the U.S. Census of Manufactures does not include data on most university presses nor on other institutionally sponsored and not-for-profit publishing activities, nor (under SIC 2731: Book Publishing) for the audiovisual and other media materials that are included in this table. On the other hand, AAP estimates have traditionally excluded Sunday school materials and certain pamphlets that are incorporated in the census data.

It should be noted that the Other Sales category includes only incidental book sales, such as music, sheet sales (both domestic and export, except those to prebinders), and miscellaneous merchandise sales.

Estimates include domestic sales and export sales of U.S. product and do not cover indigenous activities of publishers' foreign subsidiaries.

Non-rack-size Mass Market Publishing is included in Trade—Paperbound. Prior to the 1988 AAP Annual Statistics, this was treated as Adult Trade Paperbound. It is recognized that part of this is Juvenile (1987 estimate: 20 percent), and adjustments have been made in this respect. AAP also notes that this area includes sales through traditional "mass market paperback channels" by publishers not generally recognized as being "mass market paperback."

U.S. Book Exports and Imports, 1991–1992

Unesco World Book Output and Translations

Chandler B. Grannis
Contributing Editor, *Publishers Weekly*

U.S. book exports of over $1.63 billion and imports of almost $990 million were reported for 1992 by the Bureau of the Census, Department of Commerce (Tables 1 and 2). The figures are deceptive because, as in previous years, export shipments valued under $2,500 are not counted, nor are import shipments valued below $1,250.

In any case, the figures actually reported are sufficient to indicate year-to-year trends. Exports in 1992 increased 9.2 percent over 1991 and imports increased almost 12.8 percent (Tables 1 and 2). The ratio of exports to imports was about 62-38—midway between the 1990 and 1991 ratios (Table 3). The imports include shipments of books manufactured abroad for U.S. publishers.

The figures serve also to indicate the year-to-year trends in trade with specific countries. Among the larger customers for U.S. book exports, percentage changes in the reported dollar values in 1992 included United Kingdom, +9.8;

Note: Adapted from *Publishers Weekly,* November 22, 1993.

Canada, +9.1; Australia, +3.4; Japan, +4.6; West Germany, +5; Mexico, +41.2; Netherlands, -11.9; Singapore, +1. Among countries from which the United States imported books, percentage changes included United Kingdom, +10.1; Hong Kong, +19.8; Japan, +3.3; Singapore, +16.1; Canada, +49.3; Italy, -23.3; West Germany, +3.8 (Tables 5 and 6).

Unreported Shipments

It is in calculating the proportion of publishers' sales attributable specifically to exports that the unreported shipments are significant. The reported exports in 1992 accounted for at least 9.9 percent of the $16.8 billion total sales of U.S. publishers (Table 4), to judge by comparing the Commerce data with the annual total sales estimates of the Association of American Publishers (AAP).

But if the small shipments could be recorded, and thus included in the Census totals, the export share of the U.S. book industry would prove to be even more important. William S. Lofquist, printing and publishing industry specialist at the Department of Commerce, who prepares the data from Census information, suggested that the actual export totals are "not less than"—and probably more than—5 percent above those reported; and that the import totals may be at least 2 percent above the totals given.

Therefore, the actual 1992 U.S. export total may be considered not less than $1.71 billion, or 10.2 percent of the publishers' total sales. And the import total is probably over $1 billion. Moreover, the adjustments are probably very conservative.

International Title Output

International book title output figures, among many other cultural statistics, are compiled by the United Nations Educational, Scientific and Cultural Organization (Unesco) and printed in the annual *Unesco Statistical Yearbook*. Extracts from the current edition have been selected and augmented by *PW* and are presented here in Tables A, B, and C.

Translations published in major book producing countries are shown in Table A. In place of Unesco's figures for the United States, we show figures prepared each year for *PW* by R. R. Bowker. These figures, while larger than those of Unesco, are still incomplete.

Table B offers a partial picture of the relative positions of the languages from which reported translations are made.

Table C presents title output of principal publishing countries, taken from the *Unesco Yearbook*. Unesco does not include totals from the United States, United Kingdom and Canada. *PW* therefore for several years has obtained these figures directly—from Bowker data prepared for *PW*; from *The Bookseller* of London; and from the Book Publishing Survey manager at Statistics Canada, Ottawa. Figures have not been obtained for three additional countries—Japan, Australia, and Argentina—not counted by Unesco.

One reason why some figures are not given by Unesco is that the United States and several other sources do not use the same subject or topical category

Table 1 / U.S. Book Exports, 1991–1992
(Shipments Valued at $2,500 or More)
(Dollars and Units in Thousands)

	1992 $	% Chg. 1991–1992	1992 Units	% Chg. 1991–1992
Dictionaries	$9,841.0	+9.9	2,021.2	+18.4
Encyclopedias	60,708.0	+6.2	10,396.6	+2.6
Textbooks	276,345.0	+14.1	38,796.7	+6.8
Bibles & other religious books	54,474.0	-10.1	42,682.2	+2.6
Technical, scientific, & professional books	499,097.0	+7.0	77,266.3	+7.5
Art & pictorial books	22,370.0	+18.8	11,037.5	+10.3
Hardbound books not elsewhere indicated	126,396.0	+15.4	37,593.7	+4.6
Rack-size paperbound	165,913.0	+17.4	99,909.0	+13.4
Books over 48 pp. not elsewhere indicated*	371,176.0	+4.8	467,244.8	+5.4
Children's picture, coloring, drawing	27,626.0	+44.4	49,603.5	+44.0
Music books	18,109.0	+10.6	2,860.4	+17.7
Atlases	3,941.0	+31.2	463.9	-2.3
Totals	$1,635,995.0	+9.2	839,875.8	+8.2

*Plus covers; includes paperbacks not counted elsewhere.

Table 2 / U.S. Book Imports, 1991–1992
(Shipments Valued at $1,250 or More)
(Dollars and Units in Thousands)

	1992 $	% Chg. 1991–1992	1992 Units	% Chg. 1991–1992
Dictionaries, thesauruses	$7,554.0	+21.0	2,131.9	+33.6
Encyclopedias (incl. installments)	5,957.0	-21.1	846.3	-21.2
Textbooks	110,994.0	+37.6	23,095.6	+44.1
Bibles & other religious books	42,429.0	+30.0	37,206.1	-7.5
Technical, scientific, & professional	132,328.0	+4.7	26,063.7	+8.8
Art, pictorial: under $5 each	15,661.0	-5.4	20,470.7	-34.1
$5 and up each	27,879.0	+13.9	1,992.3	-13.0
Hardbound books not elsewhere indicated	330,270.0	+1.8	108,484.7	+13.6
Rack-size paperbound	69,084.0	+27.9	62,327.8	+49.5
Books 48+ pp. or more not elsewhere indicated	145,725.0	+9.4	69,053.6	-2.3
Children's picture, coloring, drawing	95,185.0	+45.4	105,354.3	+36.7
Music not elsewhere indicated	3,051.0	+11.2	980.5	+35.1
Atlases	3,690.0	+10.7	828.1	+8.5
Totals	$989,807.0	+12.8	458,835.5	+14.0

Table 3 / Book Export-Import Ratios, 1975–1992
(in Millions of Dollars)

	Exports	Imports	Approx. Ratio
1992	$1,636.0	$989.8	62–38
1991	1,497.8	877.8	63–37
1990	1,428.0	902.2	61–39
1985	591.2	564.3	51–49
1980	518.9	511.6	50.1–49.9
1975	269.3	147.6	60–40

Table 4 / U.S. Book Exports Compared to Total U.S. Book Sales, 1975–1992
(in Millions of Dollars)

	Exports	Total Sales*	Exports as % of Total Sales
1992	$1,635.9	$16,845.6	9.9
1991	1,497.8	16,144.9	9.3
1990	1,428.0	15,365.1	9.4
1985	591.2	10,156.0	5.8
1980	518.9	6,411.0	8.1
1975	269.3	3,789.3	7.1

*Totals from Association of American Publishers.

counts as those used by Unesco; the conversion of figures from one database to another, involving different definitions, presents obvious difficulties. Data collection is also complicated by the many contemporary shifts in national boundaries and authorities and by uncertainties in the importance given to cultural statistics.

Translations

Titles in translation worldwide continued to trend upward, in the period for which figures are available—1984–1986. From 52,405 in 1984 the figure hit 63,293 in 1986. Spain led the way with 9,649 titles in translation. The U.S. figures rose to 1,762, from 1,439 in 1984.

The most popular language for translating into remains English. The 1986 figures (the latest available) show 29,294 titles translated into English worldwide; Russian came in second, with about 6,600.

Table 5 / U.S. Book Imports from Principal Countries, 1991–1992
(Shipments Valued at $1,250 or More)
(Ranked by 1992 Dollar Amounts, in Thousands)

	1992 $	1991 $	1992 Units	1991 Units
United Kingdom	205,962	187,008	51,442.9	47,463.8
Hong Kong	187,354	156,345	85,932.6	69,089.4
Japan	91,551	88,636	25,790.5	25,106.5
Singapore	88,725	76,428	47,568.3	37,742.4
Canada	86,385	57,664	84,615.8	61,772.5
Italy	63,535	82,683	54,754.7	77,001.5
Germany, West	49,594	47,792	6,530.2	7,334.4
Spain	30,822	29,688	9,696.6	10,320.4
Mexico	24,278	16,586	14,381.2	5,757.9
Colombia	19,554	14,164	13,829.5	11,524.2
France	18,322	12,546	6,260.8	4,191.8
Korea, South	16,262	13,609	9,386.0	6,217.4
Netherlands	16,043	14,960	2,371.5	2,484.6
Taiwan	12,037	8,381	6,927.5	5,687.0
Belgium	11,143	9,821	4,950.9	4,936.3
China	10,932	5,213	12,346.1	6,869.3
Switzerland	7,634	7,534	806.5	978.9
Israel	7,277	6,675	1,699.3	1,630.1
Australia	6,401	5,578	1,799.4	1,945.7
Ireland	5,978	3,928	824.7	403.4
Sweden	5,013	5,364	2,375.1	1,283.3
Thailand	4,300	1,627	4,440.8	1,379.5
Denmark	3,289	5,495	894.2	990.3
Bermuda	1,653	324	769.5	129.6
India	1,552	822	1,182.7	363.8
Czechoslovakia	1,444	676	495.1	269.5
Austria	1,358	1,884	331.0	683.3
Saudi Arabia	1,224	399	166.4	31.1
New Zealand	953	739	1,281.1	745.8
Portugal	750	1,297	235.6	488.7
Malaysia	609	1,537	291.2	1,119.2
Norway	592	1,973	68.5	147.2
Venezuela	461	832	664.1	1,214.7
Yugoslavia	277	4,378	63.4	1,983.1
World Totals	$989,807	$877,757	458,835.1	402,622.1

Table 6 / U.S. Book Exports to Principal Countries, 1991–1992
(Shipments Valued at $2,500 or more)
(Ranked by 1992 Dollar Amounts, in Thousands)

	1992 $	1991 $	1992 Units	1991 Units
Canada	702,174	643,911	429,130.6	390,885.5
United Kingdom	228,475	208,091	96,594.6	92,500.4
Australia	121,993	118,043	54,161.1	55,075.7
Japan	89,605	85,638	33,691.3	38,717.8
Germany, West	50,980	48,550	20,351.6	17,872.8
Mexico	50,968	36,109	23,516.7	12,553.2
Netherlands	33,169	37,642	9,544.5	13,844.8
Singapore	32,848	32,605	17,179.4	19,468.4
France	23,264	23,030	8,502.4	7,773.6
South Africa	20,662	13,572	12,085.8	10,906.3
Taiwan	19,501	18,029	8,685.2	6,605.5
Hong Kong	18,231	14,495	10,666.5	9,547.3
Philippines	16,054	10,863	8.924.8	6,770.5
India	14,656	9,821	5,288.6	3,462.0
Spain	14,538	14,985	4,599.0	4,557.1
Switzerland	13,693	11,235	3,965.8	4,125.9
Ireland	12,714	7,692	2,174.7	2,292.7
Korea, South	12,690	12,313	5,955.5	5,650.0
Italy	11,894	10,426	4,485.0	3,563.6
Argentina	10,706	7,637	9,742.8	5,626.9
Brazil	10,063	13,414	3,890.7	4,701.8
Saudi Arabia	8,602	4,675	3,895.8	2,294.2
New Zealand	7,598	7,711	3,362.1	3,956.1
Belgium	6,115	5,655	1,778.5	2,076.0
Malaysia	5,751	4,981	1,928.9	1,807.5
Venezuela	5,474	5,170	5,840.4	5,404.3
Israel	4,886	4,161	2,752.0	2,160.9
Sweden	4,823	5,655	1,569.1	2,036.1
Thailand	4,496	3,318	1,288.7	1,076.1
Greece	4,304	1,247	683.5	564.0
China	3,808	2,671	3,251.8	883.4
Colombia	3,664	2,116	2,185.5	1,226.3
Chile	3,541	2,955	2,174.3	1,900.0
United Arab Emirates	3,412	2,030	973.4	418.1
Denmark	3,181	5,150	977.8	1,885.7
Norway	2,983	2,186	1,611.0	1,135.0
Nigeria	2,729	5,020	2,627.3	2,864.2
Austria	1,923	3,297	1,105.1	912.0
Finland	1,240	4,149	480.5	1,276.3
World Totals	$1,635,995	$1,497,767	839,875.8	776,454.3

Table A / Translation Publishing by Principal Countries, 1984–1986

	1984	1985	1986
Brazil	1,331	3,570	2,291
Czechoslovakia	1,272	1,319	1,395
Denmark	1,659	1,610	1,771
Finland	1,421	1,487	1,111
France	3,821	4,679	1,710
Germany, East	674	746	797
Germany, West	6,868	5,559	8,139
Hungary	1,238	1,202	1,144
Italy	—	—	961
Japan	2,698	2,892	2,875
Mexico	—	—	2,087
Netherlands	—	4,286	3,945
Norway	1,251	448	400
Portugal	738	729	872
Spain	7,741	7,944	9,649
Sweden	1,916	1,900	2,043
Switzerland	1,084	998	888
Turkey	1,152	987	701
USSR	7,758	8,039	8,202
United Kingdom	1,153	1,121	914
United States	1,439	1,389	1,762
Yugoslavia	1,280	1,590	1,440
All Reporting Countries	52,405	57,374	63,293

Table B / Books in Translation, 1984–1986
(From Selected Languages)

	1984	1985	1986
English	22,724	26,690	29,294
French	5,422	6,327	6,502
German	4,311	4,847	5,079
Russian	6,230	6,337	6,620
Italian	1,544	1,581	1,754
Scandinavian*	2,192	1,675	1,718
Spanish	839	828	864
Classical Greek, Latin	1,035	896	995
Hungarian	679	563	619
Arabic	536	233	445
Japanese	204	254	232
Chinese	163	161	156
Others	7,470	7,545	9,015
World Totals	52,405	57,374	63,293

*Swedish, Danish, Norwegian, Icelandic

Table C / World Book Title Output, 1988–1990: Principal Publishing Countries

	1988	1989	1990
Africa			
Egypt	1,451	—	—
Nigeria	1,424	1,466	—
South Africa	4,480	6,696	4,950
North America			
Canada	7,550	8,249	8,126
Cuba	2,069	2,199	—
Mexico	4,826	3,490	—
United States	52,069	53,446	48,146
South America			
Chile	1,840	2,350	—
Colombia	—	1,486	—
Asia			
Bangladesh	1,209	—	2,795
China	—	74,973	73,923
India	14,408	11,851	13,837
Indonesia	1,687	1,396	1,518
Iran	3,401	6,289	—
Korea, South	42,842	39,267	39,330
Malaysia	—	3,348	4,578
Philippines	1,072	—	1,112
Sri Lanka	2,175	2,188	2,455
Thailand	—	11,217	7,783
Turkey	—	—	6,291
Europe			
Austria	8,360	9,462	10,305
Belgium	8,289	6,822	—
Bulgaria	4,379	4,543	3,412
Czechoslovakia	9,558	9,294	8,585
Denmark	10,584	10,762	11,082
Finland	10,386	10,097	10,153
France	39,026	40,115	41,720
Germany, East	6,526	6,018	—
Germany, West	68,611	65,980	61,015
Greece	—	—	3,255
Hungary	8,621	8,631	8,322
Iceland	1,244	1,250	1,515
Italy	19,620	22,647	25,068
Netherlands	13,845	15,392	13,691
Norway	4,894	5,331	3,712
Poland	10,728	10,286	10,242
Portugal	—	6,527	—
Romania	—	3,867	2,178
Spain	35,426	38,353	36,239
Sweden	11,794	11,197	12,034
Switzerland	12,698	13,270	13,839
United Kingdom	62,069	61,195	63,980
Yugoslavia	12,100	11,339	9,797
USSR			
USSR	—	76,711	—
Byelorussia	2,962	—	2,823
Ukraine	8,311	—	7,046

Source: *Unesco Statistical Yearbook, 1992*, except U.S. figures derived by *Publishers Weekly* from R. R. Bowker Data Services; U.K. figures from *The Bookseller*, London; Canadian figures from *Statistics Canada* (Michel Frève, Book Publishing Survey manager), Ottawa. U.S. figures do not include publications of state and local governments, some institutions, company reports, proceedings, lab manuals, yearbooks, U.S. Government Printing Office output, and university theses. However, the books of university presses, religious organizations, and other nonprofit publishers are included.

Number of Book Outlets in the United States and Canada

The *American Book Trade Directory* has been published by R. R. Bowker since 1915. Revised annually, it features lists of booksellers, wholesalers, periodicals, reference tools, and other information about the U.S. and Canadian book markets. The data shown in Table 1 are from the 1993–1994 edition of the directory.

The 30,271 stores of various types shown are located throughout the United States, Canada, and regions administered by the United States. "General" bookstores stock trade books and children's books in a general variety of subjects. "College" stores carry college-level textbooks. "Educational" outlets handle school textbooks up to and including the high school level. "Mail order" outlets

Table 1 / Bookstores in the United States and Canada, 1993

Category	United States	Canada
Antiquarian general	1,060	74
Antiquarian mail order	548	18
Antiquarian specialized	256	9
Art supply store	81	1
College general	3,274	171
College specialized	157	11
Computer software	230	0
Department store	2,612	92
Drugstore	23	9
Educational*	236	58
Exporter-importer	14	1
Federal sites†	310	1
Foreign language*	133	28
General	7,257	1,087
Gift shop	292	27
Juvenile*	496	50
Law*	40	3
Mail order general	439	18
Mail order specialized	172	6
Medical*	38	1
Museum store and art gallery	574	28
Newsdealer	175	8
Office supply	75	16
Other§	3,232	302
Paperback‡	571	30
Religious*	3,869	249
Remainders	29	6
Science-technology*	36	4
Stationer	74	30
Used*	1,506	124
Total	27,809	2,462

* Includes mail order shops for this topic, which are not counted elsewhere in this survey.

† National historic sites, national monuments, and national parks.

‡ Includes mail order. Excludes used paperback bookstores, stationers, drugstores, or wholesalers handling paperbacks.

§ Stores specializing in subjects or services other than those covered in this survey.

sell general trade books by mail and are not book clubs; all others operating by mail are classified according to the kinds of books carried. "Antiquarian" dealers sell old and rare books. Stores handling secondhand books are classified as "used." "Paperback" stores have more than 80 percent of their stock in paperbound books. Stores with paperback departments are listed under the appropriate major classification ("general," "department store," "stationer," etc.). Bookstores with at least 50 percent of their stock on a particular subject are classified by subject.

Book Review Media Statistics

Compiled by the staff of *The Bowker Annual*.

Number of Books Reviewed by Major Book-Reviewing Publications, 1992–1993

	Adult		Juvenile		Young Adult		Total	
	1992	1993	1992	1993	1992	1993	1992	1993
Booklist[1]	3,612	3,690	2,647	2,696	891	—	7,150	6,386
Bulletin of the Center for Children's Books	—	—	772	729	—	—	772	729
Chicago Sun Times[2]	800	500	100	100	—	100	900	700
Chicago Tribune	1,100	730	150	55	—	—	1,250	785
Choice[3]	6,633	6,520	—	—	—	—	6,633	6,520
Horn Book Magazine	20	—	400	500	75	—	495	500
Horn Book Guide[4]	—	—	3,200	3,750	600	—	3,800	3,750
Kirkus Services[5]	4,209	5,000	—	—	—	—	4,209	5,000
Library Journal[6]	5,203	5,500	—	—	—	—	5,203	5,500
Los Angeles Times	1,700	1,750	150	100	—	—	1,850	1,850
New York Review of Books	448	400	—	—	—	—	448	400
New York Times Sunday Book Review[7]	2,000	2,000	300	300	—	—	2,300	2,300
Publishers Weekly[8]	6,122	4,860	1,300	1,513	—	—	7,422	6,373
School Library Journal[9]	—	—	3,120	3,256	360	366	3,480	3,622
Washington Post Book World[10]	1,874	1,764	107	91	—	35	1,981	1,890
West Coast Review of Books (Rapport)	920	592	—	1	—	—	920	593

[1] All figures are for a 12-month period from September 1 to August 31; 1993 figures are for September 1, 1992–August 31, 1993 (vol. 89). Totals do not include the 458 reference and subscription books reviewed and the reviews of special bibliographies—6,250 in 1992–1993. In addition, *Booklist* publishes reviews of nonprint materials—1,193 audiovisual titles (vol. 89). The number of books reviewed for juveniles and young adults is combined.

[2] Includes books mentioned in columns.

[3] All figures are for a 12-month period beginning September and ending July/August; 1993 figures are for September 1992–July/August 1993. Total for 1992 includes 79 nonprint materials.

[4] 1993 juvenile figures include young adult titles.

[5] Adult figures include both adult and juvenile books.

[6] *LJ* reviewed 114 magazines and 1,068 nonprint materials in 1992, and 121 magazines and 1,066 nonprint materials in 1993. There were 126 books reviewed in the round-ups and 503 reviewed in "Prepub Alert" in 1992, and 103 books reviewed in the round-ups and 609 reviewed in the "Prepub Alert" in 1993.

[7] Juvenile figures include books reviewed in the "Bookshelf" column.

[8] Includes reviews of paperback originals and reprints.

[9] *SLJ*'s 1993 figures include 94 reference books and 91 books in Spanish.

[10] The 1992 total includes 68 recorded books.

Part 5
Reference Information

Ready Reference

Publishers' Toll-Free Telephone Numbers

Publishers' toll-free numbers continue to play an important role in ordering, verification, and customer service. This year's list comes from *Literary Market Place* (R. R. Bowker) and includes distributors and regional toll-free numbers, where applicable. The list is not comprehensive and toll-free numbers are subject to change. Readers may want to call for toll-free directory assistance (800-555-1212).

Publisher/Distributor	Toll-Free No.
A-R Editions Inc, Madison, WI.	800-736-0070
Abacus, Grand Rapids, MI.	800-227-7210
Abbeville Publishing Group, New York, NY.	800-227-7210
Abbot, Foster & Hauserman Co, Spokane, WA.	800-562-0025
ABC-CLIO, Santa Barbara, CA.	800-422-2546
Aberdeen Group, Addison, IL.	800-323-3550
Abingdon Press, Nashville, TN.	800-251-3320
Harry N Abrams Inc, New York, NY.	800-345-1359
ACA Books, New York, NY.	800-321-4510
Academic Press Inc, San Diego, CA.	(cust serv) 800-321-5068
Academic Therapy Publications, Novato, CA.	800-422-7249
Academy Chicago Publishers, Chicago, IL.	800-248-READ
The Academy of Producer Insurance Studies Inc, Austin, TX.	800-526-2777
Accelerated Development Inc, Muncie, IN.	800-222-1166
Acropolis Books Ltd, Reston, VA.	800-451-7771
ACS Publications Inc, San Diego, CA.	800-888-9983
ACTA Publications, Chicago, IL.	800-397-2282
Active Parenting Publishers, Marietta, GA.	800-825-0060
ACU Press, Abilene, TX.	800-444-4228
Bob Adams Inc, Holbrook, MA.	800-872-5627
ADAPT Publishing Co Inc, Austin, TX.	800-333-8429
Addison-Wesley Publishing Co Inc, Reading, MA.	800-447-2226
Adventure Publications, Cambridge, MN.	800-678-7006
Aegean Park Press, Laguna Hills, CA.	800-736-3587
The AEI Press, Washington, DC.	800-223-2336
Aequus Institute Publications, Hendersonville, TN.	800-441-1963
Aerofax Inc, Arlington, TX.	800-733-2329

Publisher/Distributor	Toll-Free No.

AGES (Ancestral Genealogical Endexing Schedules),
Salt Lake City, UT. — 800-733-0844
Agora Inc, Baltimore, MD. — 800-433-1528
Ahsahta Press, Boise, ID. — 800-992-TEXT
Airmont Publishing Co Inc, New York, NY. — 800-223-5251
Alaska Northwest Books, Seattle, WA. — 800-331-3510
Alba House, Staten Island, NY. — 800-343-ALBA
The Alban Institute Inc, Washington, DC. — (book orders) 800-457-2674
Alfred Publishing Co Inc, Van Nuys, CA. — 800-292-6122
Allworth Communications Inc, New York, NY. — 800-247-6553
Allyn & Bacon, Needham Heights, MA. — 800-223-1360
Alpine Publications Inc, Loveland, CO. — 800-777-7257
Altweger & Mandel Publishing Co, West Bloomfield, MI. — 800-472-3485
AMACOM Books, New York, NY. — (orders) 800-538-4761
Frank Amato Publications, Portland, OR. — 800-541-9498
Amboy Associates, San Diego, CA. — 800-448-4023
America West Pubs, Tehachapi, CA. — 800-729-4131
American Academy of Orthopaedic Surgeons, Rosemont, IL. — 800-626-6726
American Academy of Pediatrics, Elk Grove Village, IL. — 800-433-9016
American & World Geographic Publishing, Helena, MT. — 800-654-1105
American Association for Vocational Instructional Materials,
Athens, GA. — 800-228-4689
American Association of Cereal Chemists, St Paul, MN. — 800-328-7560
American Association of Engineering Societies,
Washington, DC. — 800-658-8897
American Bible Society, New York, NY. — 800-543-8000
American Brain Tumor Association, Chicago, IL. — 800-886-2282
American Camping Association, Martinsville, IN. — 800-428-CAMP
American Chemical Society, Washington, DC. — 800-227-5558
American College of Physician Executives, Tampa, FL. — 800-562-8088
American Correctional Association, Laurel, MD. — 800-825-2665
American Counseling Association,
Alexandria, VA. — 800-545-2223; 800-347-6647
American Diabetes Association, Alexandria, VA. — 800-232-3472
American Education Publishing Co, Columbus, OH. — 800-542-7833
American Foundation for the Blind, New York, NY. — 800-232-5463
American Guidance Service Inc, Circle Pines, MN. — 800-328-2560
American Health Publishing Co, Dallas, TX. — 800-736-7323
American Hospital Publishing Inc, Chicago, IL. — 800-621-6902
The American Institute of
Architects Press, Washington, DC. — (orders) 800-457-3239
American Institute of Physics Inc, New York, NY. — 800-AIP-PHYS
American Law Institute, Philadelphia, PA. — 800-CLE-NEWS
American Law Institute-American Bar Association
Committee on Continuing Professional Education. — 800-CLE-NEWS
American Library Association (ALA), Chicago, IL. — 800-545-2433

Publisher/Distributor	Toll-Free No.
American Map Corp, Maspeth, NY.	800-432-MAPS
American Mathematical Society, Providence, RI.	800-321-4267
American Nurses Association, Washington, DC.	800-637-0323
American Phytopathological Society, St Paul, MN.	800-328-7560
American Printing House for the Blind Inc, Louisville, KY.	800-223-1839
American Psychiatric Press Inc, Washington, DC.	800-368-5777
American Society for Nondestructive Testing, Columbus, OH.	800-222-2768
American Society of Civil Engineers, New York, NY.	800-548-2723, (NY) 800-628-0041
American Society of Mechanical Engineers (ASME), New York, NY.	800-843-2763
American Standard Text Corporation, New York, NY.	800-533-4027
American Technical Publishers Inc, Homewood, IL.	800-323-3471
Ameritype & Art Inc, Cleveland, OH.	800-544-5314
The Analytic Press, Hillsdale, NJ.	(orders only) 800-926-6579
Ancestry Inc, Salt Lake City, UT.	800-531-1790
Anderson Publishing Co, Cincinnati, OH.	800-543-0883; 800-582-7295
Andrews & McMeel, Kansas City, MO.	800-826-4216
Annabooks, San Diego, CA.	800-462-1042
Annual Reviews Inc, Palo Alto, CA.	800-523-8635
AOCS Press, Champaign, IL.	800-336-AOCS
Aperture, New York, NY.	800-929-2323
Appleton & Lange, East Norwalk, CT.	800-423-1359
Aqua Quest Publications Inc, Locust Valley, NY.	800-933-8989
Archer Fields Press, New York, NY.	800-338-2665
The Archives Press, Los Altos, CA.	800-338-4454
Ardis Publishers, Ann Arbor, MI.	(orders) 800-877-7133
ARE Press, Virginia Beach, VA.	800-723-1112
Ariel Press, Alpharetta, GA.	800-336-7769
Jason Aronson Inc, Northvale, NJ.	800-782-0015
Arrow Mapp Inc, Taunton, MA.	800-343-7500
Artabras Inc, New York, NY.	800-227-7210
Arte Publico Press, Houston, TX.	800-633-ARTE
Artech House Inc, Norwood, MA.	800-225-9977
ASCP Press, Chicago, IL.	800-621-4142
Ashgate Publishing Co, Brookfield, VT.	800-535-9544
Aslan Publishing, Lower Lake, CA.	800-275-2606
Aspen Books, Murray, UT.	800-748-4850
Aspen Publishers Inc, Gaithersburg, MD.	(orders) 800-638-8437
Association for the Advancement of Medical Instrumentation, Arlington, VA.	800-332-2264
Asylum Arts Publishing, Santa Maria, CA.	(orders only) 800-253-3605
ATLA Press, Washington, DC.	800-424-2727
Augsburg Fortress Publishers, Minneapolis, MN.	800-328-4648
August House Publishers Inc, Little Rock, AR.	800-284-8784
Avalon Books, New York, NY.	800-223-5251

Publisher/Distributor	Toll-Free No.
Ave Maria Press, Notre Dame, IN.	800-282-1865
Avery Publishing Group Inc, Wayne, NJ.	800-548-5757
Aviation Book Co, Santa Clarita, CA.	800-423-2708
Avon Books, New York, NY.	800-238-0658
B & B Publishing Inc, Fontana, WI.	800-325-6125
Back to the Bible, Lincoln, NE.	800-759-2425
Baha'i Publishing Trust, Wilmette, IL.	800-999-9019
Baker Book House, Grand Rapids, MI.	800-877-2665
Balcony Publishing, Austin, TX.	800-777-7949
Ballantine/Del Rey/Fawcett/Ivy Books, New York, NY.	800-638-6460
Bancroft-Sage Publishing, Marco, FL.	800-942-1745
Banks-Baldwin Law Publishing Co, Cleveland, OH.	(AZ, IN, OH, PA) 800-362-4500; (KY) 800-221-2630
Bantam Books, New York, NY.	800-223-6834
Bantam Doubleday Dell Books for Young Readers, New York, NY.	800-223-6834
Bantam Doubleday Dell Publishing Group Inc, New York, NY.	800-223-6834
Baptist Spanish Publishing House, El Paso, TX.	800-755-5958
Barbour & Co Inc, Uhrichsville, NJ.	(orders) 800-852-8010
Barclay Press, Newberg, OR.	800-962-4014
Barnes & Noble Books (Imports & Reprints), Lanham, MD.	800-462-6420
Barron's Educational Series Inc, Hauppauge, NY.	800-645-3476
Battele Press, Columbus, OH.	800-451-3543
Baywood Publishing Co Inc, Amityville, NY.	800-638-7819
Beacham Publishing Inc, Washington, DC.	800-466-9644
Beacon Hill Press of Kansas City, Kansas City, MO.	800-877-0700
Bear & Co Inc, Santa Fe, NM.	800-932-3277
Beautiful America Publishing Co, Wilsonville, OR.	800-874-1233
Peter Bedrick Books Inc, New York, NY.	800-788-3123
Beginning Press, Seattle, WA.	800-831-4088
Behrman House Inc, West Orange, NJ.	800-221-2755
Frederick C Bell Publisher Inc, Savannah, GA.	800-829-8406
Bellerophon Books, Santa Barbara, CA.	800-253-9943
Matthew Bender & Co Inc, New York, NY.	(outside NY) 800-223-1940; 800-422-2022
The Benjamin-Cummings Publishing Co, Redwood City CA.	800-950-2665
John Benjamins North America Inc, Philadelphia, PA.	800-562-5666
Benroc Press Ltd, Rochester, NY.	800-724-4691
Robert Bentley Inc, Cambridge, MA.	800-423-2595
Benziger Publishing Co, Mission Hills, CA.	800-423-9534
Berkley Publishing Group, New York, NY.	800-223-0510
Berkshire House Publishers, Stockbridge, MA.	800-321-8526
Berlitz Publishing Co Inc, New York, NY.	800-628-4808
Best Publishing Co, Flagstaff, AZ.	800-468-1055
Bethany House Publishers, Minneapolis, MN.	800-328-6109

Publisher/Distributor	Toll-Free No.
Bethel Publishing Co, Elkhart, IN.	800-348-7657
Betz Publishing Co Inc, Rockville, MD.	800-634-4365
Beverage Marketing Corp, Mungo Junction, OH.	800-332-6222
Beyond Words Publishing Inc, Hillsboro, OR.	800-284-9673
Bhaktivedanta Book Publishing Inc, Los Angeles, CA.	800-559-4455
Birkhauser Boston, Cambridge, MA.	800-777-4643
George T Bisel Co, Philadelphia, PA.	800-247-3526
Walter J Black Inc, Port Washington, NY.	800-4-MURDER
Blackbirch Press Inc, Woodbridge, CT.	800-831-9183
John F Blair, Publisher, Winston-Salem, NC.	800-222-9796
Blue Dolphin Publishing Inc, Nevada City, CA.	800-643-0765
Blue Moon Books Inc, New York, NY.	800-535-0007
Blue Mountain Press Inc, Boulder, CO.	800-525-0642
Blue Note Publications, Cape Canaveral, FL.	800-624-0401
Blue Poppy Enterprises Press, Boulder, CO.	800-487-9296
BNA Books, Washington, DC.	800-372-1033
Bob Jones University Press, Greenville, SC.	800-845-5731
Bonus Books Inc, Chicago, IL.	800-225-3775
Book-Lab, New York, NY.	800-654-4081
Book Lures Inc, O'Fallon, MO.	800-444-9450
Book Publishing Co, Summertown, TN.	800-695-2241
Book Sales Inc, Secaucus, NJ.	800-526-7257
R R Bowker, New Providence, NJ.	(sales) 800-521-8100
Boyd & Fraser Publishing Co, Danvers, MA.	800-225-3782
Boynton/Cook Publishers Inc, Portsmouth NH.	(orders) 800-541-2086
William K Bradford Publishing Co Inc, Acton, MA.	800-421-2009
Branden Publishing Co Inc, Boston, MA.	800-537-7335
BRAT Inc, Santa Fe, NM.	800-359-2728
Breakthrough Publications, Ossining, NY.	800-824-5000
Brethren Press, Elgin, IL.	800-323-8039
Brick House Publishing Co, New Boston, NH.	(orders only) 800-446-8642
Bridge Publications Inc, Los Angeles, CA.	800-722-1733; (CA) 800-843-7389
E J Brill USA Inc, Kinderhook, NY.	800-962-4406
Bristol Publishing Enterprises Inc, San Leandro, CA.	800-346-4889
Broadman Press, Nashville, TN.	800-251-3225
Broadway Press, Shelter Island, NY.	800-869-6372
Paul H Brookes Publishing Co, Baltimore, MD.	800-638-3775
The Brookings Institution, Washington, DC.	800-275-1447
Brookline Books Inc, Cambridge, MA.	800-666-2665
Brooks/Cole Publishing Co, Pacific Grove, CA.	800-354-9706
Wm C Brown Group, Dubuque, IA.	800-338-5578
Brunner/Mazel Inc, New York, NY.	800-825-3089
Bull Publishing Co, Palo Alto, CA.	800-676-2855
Burning Gate Press, Mission Hills, CA.	800-258-9919
Business & Legal Reports Inc, Madison, CT.	800-727-5257
Business News Publishing Co, Troy, MI.	800-837-1037

Publisher/Distributor	Toll-Free No.
Business One Irwin, Homewood, IL.	800-634-3961
Business Research Services Inc, Washington, DC.	800-845-8420
Butterworth-Heinemann, Stoneham, MA.	(orders) 800-366-2665;
	(cust serv) 800-544-1013
Butterworth Legal Publishers, Salem, NH.	800-548-4001
C & T Publishing, Martinez, CA.	800-284-1114
Caddylak Systems Inc, Brentwood, NY.	800-523-8060
Calgre Press, Antioch, CA.	800-397-8423
California College Publishing, National City, CA.	800-221-7374
Cambridge Career Products, Charleston, WV.	800-468-4227
Cambridge University Press, New York, NY.	800-221-4512
Camden House Publishing, Charlotte, VT.	800-344-3350
Camelot Books, New York, NY.	800-238-0658
Cameron & CO, San Francisco, CA.	800-779-5582
Care Communications Inc, Chicago, IL.	800-458-3544
The Career Press Inc, Hawthorne, NJ.	800-CAREER-1
Career Publishing Inc, Orange, CA.	800-854-4041
William Carey Library, Pasadena, CA.	800-777-6371
Carlson Publishing Inc, Brooklyn, NY.	800-336-7460
Carolrhoda Books Inc, Minneapolis, MN.	800-328-4929
Carroll & Graf Publishers Inc, New York, NY.	800-365-3453
Castle Books Inc, Secaucus, NJ.	(orders) 800-526-7257
CAT Publishing, Redding, CA.	800-767-0511
The Caxton Partners Ltd, Caldwell, ID.	800-657-6465
CEF Press, Warrenton, MO.	800-748-7710
Celestial Arts, Berkeley, CA.	800-841-BOOK
Center for Career Development Inc, Cincinnati, OH.	800-992-ICAN
Center for Research & Development in Law-Related Education, Winston-Salem, NC.	800-437-1054
Chadwyck-Healey Inc, Alexandria, VA.	800-752-0515
Chalice Press, St Louis, MO.	800-366-3383
Charlesbridge Publishing, Watertown, MA.	800-225-3214
Chariot Family Publishing, Elgin, IL.	800-323-7543
Chartwell Books Inc, Secaucus, NJ.	(orders) 800-526-7257
Chelsea Green Publishing Co, Post Mills, VT.	800-639-4099
Chess Combination Inc, Bridgeport, CT.	800-354-4083
Chicago Review Press Inc, Chicago, IL.	800-888-4741
Childrens Press, Chicago, IL.	800-621-1115
Child's Play, New York, NY.	800-472-0999
Chilton Book Co, Radnor, PA.	800-695-1214
Chilton Publications, Wilmette, IL.	(orders only) 800-397-8109
Chivers North America Inc, Hampton, NH.	800-621-0812
Chrestendom Press, Front Royal, VA.	800-877-5456
Christian Brothers Publications, Romeoville, IL.	800-433-7593
Christian Classics, Inc, Westminster, MD.	800-888-3065
Christian Schools International, Grand Rapids, MI.	800-635-8288

Publisher/Distributor	Toll-Free No.
The Christian Science Publishing Society, Boston, MA.	800-288-7090
Chronicle Books, San Francisco, CA.	(orders) 800-722-6657;
	(order in CA) 800-445-7577
Chronicle Guidance Publications Inc, Moravia, NY.	800-622-7284
Chronimed Publishing, Minnetonka, MN.	800-444-5951
Churchill Livingstone Inc, New York, NY.	(IL only) 800-553-5426
The Citizens Call Publishers, Phillipsburg, MT.	800-875-HEAL
CKE Publications, Olympia, WA.	800-428-7402
Clarity Press, Atlanta, GA.	(orders only) 800-247-6553
Clark City Press, Livingston, MT.	800-835-0814
Cleaning Consultant Services Inc, Seattle, WA.	800-622-4221
Clear Light Publishers, Santa Fe, NM.	800-253-2747
Cliffs Notes Inc, Lincoln, NE.	800-228-4078
Clinical Psychology Publishing Co Inc, Brandon, VT.	800-433-8234
Clymer Publications, Overland Park, KS.	800-654-6776
CNW Publishing, North Sandwich, NH.	800-351-9278
Cold Spring Harbor Laboratory Press, Cold Spring Harbor, NY.	800-843-4388
Cole Group Inc, Santa Rosa, CA.	800-959-2717
Collector Books, Paducah, KY.	800-626-5420
College Press Publishing Co, Joplin, MO.	800-289-3300
Colonial Press, Bessemer, AL.	(orders) 800-280-6941
The Color Resource, San Francisco, CA.	800-827-3311
Colorado School of Mines Press, Golden, CO.	800-446-9488
Columba Publishing Co, Akron, OH.	800-999-7491
Columbia Publishing Co Inc, Baltimore, MD.	800-544-0042
Comex Systems Inc, Mendham, NJ.	800-543-6959
Commerce Clearing House Inc, Chicago, IL.	800-248-3248
Communication Publications & Resources, Blackwood, NJ.	800-888-2086
Community Intervention Inc, Minneapolis, MN.	800-328-0417
Compact Books, Hollywood, FL.	800-771-FELL
CompCare Publishers, Minneapolis, MN.	(outside MN) 800-328-3330
Compton's Learning Company, Chicago, IL.	800-382-3228
Computer Publishing Enterprises, San Diego, CA.	800-544-5541
Conari Press, Emeryville, CA.	800-685-9595
Concept Management, Mesa, AZ.	800-258-0877
Concordia Publishing House, St Louis, MO.	800-325-3040
The Conference Board Inc, New York, NY.	800-872-6273
Congressional Information Service, Bethesda, MD.	800-638-8380
Congressional Quarterly Books, Washington, DC.	800-638-1710
Consulting Psychologists Press Inc, Palo Alto, CA.	800-624-1765
The Continuum Publishing Corp, New York, NY.	800-937-5557
Cool Hand Communications Inc, Boca Raton, FL.	800-428-0578
Copley Publishing Group, Acton, MA.	800-562-2147
Cornell Maritime Press Inc, Centreville, MD.	800-638-7641
Cornell University Press, Ithaca, NY.	(outside NY State) 800-666-2211
CorpTech, Woburn, MA.	800-333-8036

Publisher/Distributor	Toll-Free No.
Cortina Learning International Inc, Westport, CT.	800-245-2145
Council Oak Publishing Co Inc, Tulsa, OK.	800-247-8850
Country Roads Press, Castine, ME.	800-729-9179
The Countryman Press Inc, Woodstock, VT.	800-245-4151
Countrysport Press, Traverse City, MI.	800-367-4114
Course Technology Inc, Cambridge, MA.	800-648-7450
Covenant Publications, Chicago, IL.	800-621-1290
Covered Bridge Press, North Attleboro, MA.	800-752-3769
Cowley Publications, Boston, MA.	800-225-1534
Crabtree Publishing Co, New York, NY.	800-387-7650
Craftsman Book Co, Carlsbad, CA.	800-829-8123
CRC Publications, Grand Rapids, MI.	800-333-8300
Creative Arts Book Co, Berkeley, CA.	800-848-7789
Creative Education Inc, Mankato, MN.	800-445-6209
Creative Homeowner Press, Upper Saddle River, NJ.	800-631-7795
Creative Learning Consultants Inc, Beavercreek, OH.	800-729-5137
Creative Publishing Co, College Station, TX.	800-245-5841
Creative Teaching Press Inc, Cypress, CA.	800-444-4287
Crisp Publications Inc, Menlo Park, CA.	800-442-7477
Croner Publications Inc, Jericho, NY.	800-441-4033
The Crossing Press, Freedom, CA.	800-777-1048
The Crossroad Publishing Co Inc, New York, NY.	800-937-5557
Crossway Books, Wheaton, IL.	800-323-3890
Crystal Clarity Publishers, Nevada City, CA.	800-424-1055
Crystal Productions, Glenview, IL.	800-255-8629
Da Capo Press Inc, New York, NY.	800-221-9369
Dake Bible Sales, Lawrenceville, GA.	800-241-1239
Dance Horizons, Pennington, NJ.	800-220-7149
John Daniel & Co, Publishers, Santa Barbara, CA.	800-662-8351
The Dartnell Books, Chicago, IL.	800-621-5463
DATA Business Publishing, Englewood, CO.	800-447-4666
Data Research Inc, Eagan, MN.	800-365-4900
Database Publishing Co, Newport Beach, CA.	800-888-8434
F A Davis Co, Philadelphia, PA.	800-523-4049
Davis Publications Inc, Worcester, MA.	800-533-2847
DAW Books Inc, New York, NY.	800-526-0275
The Dawn Horse Press, Clearlake, CA.	800-524-4941
Dawn Publications, Nevada City, CA.	800-545-7475
Dawbert Press, Duxbury, MA.	800-93-DAWBERT
DBI Books, Inc, Northbrook, IL.	800-767-6310
Cy De Cosse Inc, Minnetonka, MN.	800-328-0590
De Vorss & Co Inc, Marina Del Rey, CA.	(CA) 800-331-4719; (outside CA) 800-843-5143
Deaconess Press, Minneapolis, MN.	800-544-8207
Ivan R Dee Inc, Chicago, IL.	(orders) 800-634-0226
Marcel Dekker Inc, New York, NY.	(outside NY) 800-228-1160

Publisher/Distributor	Toll-Free No.
Dell Publishing, New York, NY.	800-223-6834
Delmar Publishers Inc, Albany, NY.	(NY) 800-347-7707
Delta Books, New York, NY.	(outside NY State only) 800-223-6834
Demos Publications, New York, NY.	800-532-8663
T S Denison & Co Inc, Minneapolis, MN.	800-328-3831
Derrydale Press Inc, Lyon, MS.	800-443-6753
Deseret Book Co, Salt Lake City, UT.	800-453-3876
Destiny Image, Shippensburg, PA.	800-722-6774
Devyn Press, Louisville, KY.	800-274-2221
DGC Associates Inc, Cedarhurst, NY.	800-442-2342
Dharma Publishing, Berkeley, CA.	800-873-4276
Dictation Disc Co, New York, NY.	800-528-3897
Digital Press, Maynard, MA.	800-223-1360
Dimensions for Living, Nashville, TN.	800-281-3320
Discovery Enterprises Ltd, Lowell, MA.	800-729-1720
Discovery House Publishers, Grand Rapids, MI.	800-653-8333
Distinctive Publishing Corp, Plantation, FL.	800-683-3722
Diversity Press, Idabel, OK.	800-642-0779
DLM, Chicago, IL.	800-767-8420
FW Dodge Residential Statistical Services, Lexington, MA.	800-541-9913
DOK Publishers Inc, Cheektowaga, NY.	800-458-7900
Dominie Press Inc, San Diego, CA.	800-232-4570
Don Bosco Multimedia, New Rochelle, NY.	800-342-5850
The Donning Co/Publishers, Virginia Beach, VA.	800-296-8572
Doral Publishing, Wilsonville, OR.	800-876-8093
Dorset House Publishing Co Inc, New York, NY.	800-DHBOOKS
Doubleday, New York, NY.	800-223-6834
Douglas Charles Press, North Attleboro, MA.	800-752-3769
Dover Publications Inc, Mineola, NY.	(orders) 800-223-3130
Down East Books, Camden, ME.	800-432-1670
The Dramatic Publishing Co, Woodstock, IL.	800-448-7469
Duke Communications Intenational, Loveland, CO.	800-621-1544
Duquesne University Press, Pittsburgh, PA.	800-666-2211
Durkin Hayes Publishing, Niagara Falls, NY.	800-962-5200
Dustbooks, Paradise, CA.	800-477-6110
Eagle's View Publishing, Liberty, UT.	(orders) 800-547-3364
East Coast Publishing, Poughkeepsie, NY.	800-327-4212
Eastland Press, Seattle, CA.	800-453-3278
Eclipse Books, Forestville, CA.	800-468-6828
ECS Learning Systems Inc, San Antonio, TX.	800-68-TEACH
EDC Publishing, Tulsa, OK.	800-475-4522
Ediciones del Norte, Hanover, NH.	800-782-5422
Edition Q Inc, Carol Stream, IL.	800-621-0387
Editorial Caribe, Miami, FL.	800-633-6248
Editorial Unilit, Miami, FL.	800-767-7726
EDL, Columbia, SC.	800-227-1606

Publisher/Distributor	Toll-Free No.
Education Systems, Sandy, UT.	800-288-3987
Educational Assessment Publishing Co, San Diego, CA.	800-888-5111
Educational Impressions, Hawthorne, NJ.	800-451-7450
Educational Insights Inc, Dominguez Hills, CA.	800-933-3277
Educational Ministries Inc, Prescott, AZ.	800-221-0910
Educational Technology Publications, Englewood Cliffs, NJ.	800-952-BOOK
Educators Publishing Service Inc, Cambridge, MA.	800-225-5750
Wm B Eerdmans Publishing Co, Grand Rapids, MI.	800-253-7521
Elysium Growth Press, Los Angeles, CA.	800-350-2020
Embassy Marine Publishing & Foremost Books, Old Saybrook, CT.	800-999-1075
EMC Corp, St Paul, MN.	800-328-1452
Encyclopedia Britannica Educational Corp, Chicago, IL.	800-554-9862
Encyclopedia Britannica Inc, Chicago, IL.	800-323-1229
Engineering Information Inc, Hoboken, NJ.	800-221-1044
EPM Publications Inc, McLean, VA.	800-289-2339
ERIC Clearinghouse on Reading and Communication Skills, Bloomington, IN.	800-759-4723
Lawrence Erlbaum Associates Inc, Hillsdale, NJ. (for orders only)	800-9-BOOKS-9
Essential Medical Information Systems Inc, Durant, OR.	800-225-0694
ETR Associates, Santa Cruz, CA.	800-321-4407
Evangelical Literature League, Jeniston, MI.	800-426-8255
Evanston Publishing Inc, Evanston, IL.	800-594-5190
Event Horizon Press, Desert Hot Springs, CA.	800-528-1747
Everton Publishers, Logan, UT.	800-443-6325
Everyday Learning Corp, Evanston, IL.	800-382-7670
Exley Giftbooks, Mount Kisco, NY.	800-423-9539
Faber & Faber Inc, Winchester, MA. (outside NY)	800-666-2211;
	(inside NY) 607-666-2211
Facts & Comparisons Inc, St Louis, MO.	800-223-0554
Facts on File Inc, New York, NY.	800-322-8755
Fairchild Books & Visuals, New York, NY.	800-247-6622
Falcon Press Publishing Co Inc, Helena, MT.	800-582-2665
W D Farmer Residence Designer Inc, Atlanta, GA.	800-225-7526;
	(GA) 800-221-7526
Farrar, Straus & Giroux Inc, New York, NY. (orders, cust serv)	800-631-8571
FASA Corp, Chicago, IL.	800-424-FASA
Father & Son Publishing, Tallahassee, FL.	800-741-2712
R H Faulkner Books Inc, Marion, IN.	800-352-5725
Faxon Co, Ann Arbor, MI.	800-999-3594
Fearon Teacher Aids, Carthage, IL.	800-242-7272
Philip Feldheim Inc, Spring Valley, NY.	800-237-7149
Fell Publishers, Hollywood, FL.	800-771-FELL
The Fisherman Library, Point Pleasant, NJ.	800-553-4745
Five Corners Publications Ltd, Plymouth, VT.	800-972-3868

Publisher/Distributor	Toll-Free No.
Fliptrack One On One, Computer Training, Addison, IL.	800-242-8668
Fisher Books, Tucson, AZ.	800-255-1514
J Flores Publications, Miami, FL.	800-472-2388
Flower Valley Press, Rockville, MD.	800-753-5197
Focus Information Group Inc, Newburyport, MA.	(orders) 800-848-7236
Focus on the Family Publishing, Colorado Springs, CO.	800-232-6459
Fodor's Travel Publications Inc, New York, NY.	800-733-3000
Foghorn Press, San Francisco, CA.	(CA) 800-842-7477
Fondo de Cultura Economica USA Inc, San Diego, CA.	800-532-3872
Food First Books, San Francisco, CA.	800-888-3314
Fordham University Press, Bronx, NY.	800-666-2211
Foreign Policy Associates, New York, NY.	(orders only) 800-477-5836
Forest House Publishing Co Inc, Lake Forest, IL.	800-394-READ
Forward Movement Publications, Cincinnati, OH.	800-543-1813
The Foundation Center, New York, NY.	800-424-9836
Franciscan University Press, Steubenville, OH.	800-783-6357
Franklin Watts Inc, Chicago, IL.	800-621-1115
The Free Press, New York, NY.	(cust serv) 800-257-5755;
	(orders) 800-323-7445
Free Spirit Publishing Inc, Minneapolis, MN.	800-735-7323
Friends United Press, Richmond, IN.	800-537-8838
Front Row Experience, Byron, CA.	(voice and fax) 800-524-9091
Fulcrum Publishing Inc, Golden, CO.	800-992-2908
Futura Publishing Co Inc, Mount Kisco, NY.	800-877-8761
P Gaines Co, Oak Park, IL.	800-578-3853
Gale Research Inc, Detroit, MI.	(cust serv) 800-877-GALE;
	(edit) 800-347-GALE
Gallaudet University Press, Washington, DC.	800-451-1073
Gareth Stevens Inc, Milwaukee, WI.	800-341-3569
Garrett Educational Corp, Ada, OK.	800-654-9366
Garrett Publishing Inc, Deerfield Beach, FL.	800-638-7571
Wm W Gaunt & Sons Inc, Holmes Beach, FL.	800-942-8683
GemStone Press, Woodstock, VT.	800-962-4544
Genealogical Publishing Co Inc, Baltimore, MD.	800-296-6687
General Publishing Group Inc, Santa Monica, CA.	800-745-9000
Geological Society of America (GSA), Boulder, CO.	800-GSA-1988
Gessler Publishing Co Inc, New York, NY.	800-456-5825
The C R Gibson Co, Norwalk, CT.	800-243-6004
Gleim Publications Inc, Gainesville, FL.	800-87- GLEIM
Glen Abbey Books Inc, Seattle, WA.	(cust serv) 800-782-2239
Glencoe, Westerville, OH.	800-848-1567
Peter Glenn Publications Ltd, New York, NY.	800-223-1254
Global Professional Publications, Engelwood, CO.	800-854-7179
Global Travel Publishers, Pompano Beach, FL.	800-882-9453
The Gold Book Co, Atlanta, GA.	800-842-6848
Golden Educational Center, Redding, CA.	800-800-1791

Publisher/Distributor	Toll-Free No.
Golf Gifts Inc, Lombard, IL.	800-552-4430
Good Books, Intercourse, PA.	(PA) 800-762-7171
Goodheart-Willcox Co, South Holland, IL.	800-323-0440
Gordon & Breach, Science Publishers Inc, New York, NY.	800-545-8398
Christopher Gordon Publishers Inc, Norwood, MA.	800-934-TEACH
Gospel Publishing House, Springfield, MO.	800-641-4310
Gould Publications, Binghamton, NY.	800-847-6502
Government Research Service, Topeka, KS.	800-346-6898
Grapevine Publications Inc, Corvallis, OR.	800-338-4331
Graphic Arts Center Publishing Co, Portland, OR.	800-452-3032
Graphic Learning, Waterbury, CT.	800-874-0029
Grayson Bernard Publishers, Bloomington, IN.	800-925-7853
Great Quotations Inc, Glendale Heights, IL.	800-354-4889
Green Hill Publishers Inc, Ottawa, IL.	800-426-1357
Green Valley Area Education Agency Fourteen, Creston, IA.	800-362-1864
Warren H Green Inc, St Louis, MO.	800-537-0655
Greenhaven Press Inc, San Diego, CA.	800-231-5163
Greenwillow Hooks, New York, NY.	800-631-1199
Greenwood Publishing Group Inc, Westport, CT.	(orders) 800-225-5800
Grey House Publishing Inc, Lakeville, CT.	800-562-2139
Grolier Educational Corp, Danbury, CT.	800-243-7256
Grove/Atlantic, New York, NY.	800-521-0178
Grove's Dictionaries of Music Inc, New York, NY.	800-221-2123
Gryphon Editions Inc, New York, NY.	800-633-8911
Gryphon House Inc, Mount Rainier, MD.	800-638-0928
The Guilford Press, New York, NY.	(orders) 800-365-7006
Gulf Publishing Co, Book Division, Houston, TX.	(TX) 800-392-4390; (all other except AK & HI) 800-231-6275
Hagstrom Map Co Inc, Maspeth, NY.	800-432-MAPS
Alexander Hamilton Institute, Maywood, NJ.	800-879-2441
Hammond Inc, Maplewood, NJ.	800-526-4953
Hampton-Brown Co Inc, Carmel, CA.	800-933-3510
Hampton Roads Publishing Co Inc, Norfolk, VA.	800-766-8009
Hanley & Belfus Inc, Philadelphia, PA.	800-962-1892
Harbinger House, Tucson, AZ.	800-759-9945
Harcourt Brace Jovanovich Inc, Orlando, FL.	(cust serv) 800-225-5425
HB Trade Division, San Diego, CA.	800-543-1918
Harcourt Brace College Publishers, Fort Worth, TX.	(cust serv) 800-782-4479
HB School Department	(cust serv) 800-225-5425
Harcourt Brace Professional Publishing, San Diego, CA.	800-543-1918
HarperCollins Publishers, New York, NY.	800-242-7737; (PA) 800-982-4377
The Harrington Park Press, Binghamton, NY.	800-342-9678; 800-3-Haworth
Harris Media/Newspower, Northfield, MA.	800-346-8330
Harris Publishing Co, Twinsburg, OH.	800-888-5900

Publisher/Distributor	Toll-Free No.
Harrison House Publishers, Tulsa, OK.	800-888-4126
Harvard Business School Press, Boston, MA.	800-545-7685
Harvard University Press, Cambridge, MA.	800-448-2242
Harvest House Publishers Inc, Eugene, OR.	800-547-8979
The Haworth Press Inc, Binghamton, NY.	800-342-9678
Hawthorne Educational Services, Columbia, MO.	800-542-1673
Hay House Inc, Carson, CA.	(orders) 800-654-5126
Haynes Publications Inc, Newbury Park, CA.	800-442-9637
Hazelden Publishing Group, Center City, MN.	800-328-9000
HBJ College Publishers, Fort Worth, TX.	800-782-4479
HBJ Professional Publishing, San Diego, CA.	800-543-1918
HBJ Trade, San Diego, CA.	800-543-1918
Health Communications Inc, Deerfield Beach, FL.	(cust serv) 800-851-9100
Health for Life, Los Angeles, CA.	800-874-5339
Health Leadership Associates Inc, Potomac, MD.	800-435-4775
Health Press, Santa Fe, NM.	800-643-BOOK
Health Science, Santa Barbara, CA.	800-446-1990
Healthcare Management Group McGraw-Hill, New York, NY.	800-544-8168
Heartland Samplers Inc, Minneapolis, MN.	800-999-2233
D C Heath & Co, Lexington, MA.	800-235-3565
William S Hein & Co Inc, Buffalo, NY.	800-828-7571
Heinemann Educational Books Inc, Portsmouth, NH.	800-541-2086
Heinle & Heinle Publishers, Boston, MA.	800-237-0053
Hemisphere Publishing Corp, Bristol, PA.	800-821-8312
Hendrickson Publishers Inc, Peabody, MA.	800-358-3111
Virgil W Hensley Inc, Tulsa, OK.	800-288-8520
Herald House, Independence, MO.	800-767-8181
Herald Press, Scottdale, PA.	800-245-7894
Heritage Books Inc, Bowie, MD.	800-398-7709
Hi-Time Publishing Corp, Milwaukee, WI.	800-558-2292
Highsmith Press, Fort Atkinson, WI.	800-558-2110
Hill & Wang, New York, NY.	(orders, cust serv) 800-631-8571
Lawrence Hill Books, Brooklyn, NY.	(order only) 800-888-4741
Hillcrest Press Inc, Santa Ana, CA.	800-248-8057
Hillsdale College Press, Hillsdale, MI.	800-437-2268
Himalayan Publishers, Honesdale, PA.	800-444-5772
Hive Publishing Co, Easton, PA.	800-355-HIVE
Peg Hoenack's MusicWorks, Bethesda, MD.	800-466-8668
Hogrefe & Huber Publishers, Kirkland, WA.	800-228-3749
Holman Bible Publishers, Nashville, TN.	800-251-3225; (TN) 800-342-0021
Henry Holt & Co Inc, New York, NY.	800-488-5233
Holt, Rinehart and Winston Inc, Orlando, FL.	(cust serv) 800-782-4479
Holt, Rinehart and Winston School Division, Austin, TX.	(cust serv) 800-782-4479
Home Builder Press, Washington, DC.	800-223-2665
Home Planners Inc, Tucson, AZ.	800-521-6797

Publisher/Distributor	Toll-Free No.
Homestyles Publishing & Marketing Inc, Minneapolis, MN.	800-547-5570
Hope Publishing Co, Carol Stream, IL.	800-323-1049
Hope Publishing House, Pasadena, CA.	(orders only) 800-326-2671
Horizon House Publishers, Camp Hill, PA.	800-233-4443
Horizon Publishers & Distributors Inc, Bountiful, UT.	800-453-0812
Houghton Mifflin Co, Boston, MA.	(trade books) 800-225-3362;
	(textbooks) 800-257-9107;
	(college texts) 800-225-1464
Howard University Press, Washington, DC.	800-441-1303
Howell Press Inc, Charlottesville, VA.	800-868-4512
Human Kinetics Publishers Inc, Champaign, IL.	800-747-4457
Human Resources Development Press, Amherst, MA.	800-822-2801
Humanics Ltd, Atlanta, GA.	800-874-8844
Huntington House Publishers, Lafayette, LA.	800-749-4009
Hyperion, New York, NY.	(orders) 800-343-9204
I Do Publishing, Boulder, CO.	800-888-0385
IAP Inc, Casper, WY.	800-443-9250
IBC USA (Publications) Inc, Ashland, MA.	800-343-5413
ICP, Indianapolis, IN.	800-428-6179
ICS Books Inc, Merrillville, IN.	800-541-7323
ICS Press, San Francisco, CA.	800-326-0263
Ideals Publishing Corp, Nashville, TN.	800-558-4383
IDG Books Worldwide Inc, San Mateo, CA.	800-762-2974
IEEE Computer Society Press, Los Alamitos, CA.	800-272-6657
IFSTA/Fire Protection Publications, Stillwater, OK.	800-654-4055
Igaku-Shoin Medical Publishers Inc, New York, NY.	800-765-0800
Ignatius Press, San Francisco, CA. (orders, catechisms only)	800-322-1531
Illuminated Way Publishing Inc, Golden Valley, MN.	800-457-9063
Imaginart Press, Bisbee, AZ.	800-828-1376
Imagine Inc, Pittsburg, PA.	800-926-6653
Incentive Publications Inc, Nashville, TN.	800-421-2830
Index Publishing Group, San Diego, CA.	800-334-8152
Indiana University Press, Bloomington, IN.	(orders only) 800-842-6796
Infobooks, Santa Monica, CA.	800-669-0409
Information Guides, Hermosa Beach, CA.	800-347-3257
Information Resources Press, Arlington, VA.	800-451-7363
Inner Traditions International Ltd, Rochester, VT.	800-448-2665;
	(VT call collect) 802-878-0315
Institute for Language Study, Westport, CT.	800-245-2145
Institute for Palestine Studies, Washington, DC.	800-874-3614
Interarts Ltd, Cambridge, MA.	800-626-4655
Interchange Inc, St Louis Park, MN.	800-669-6208
The International Center for Creative Thinking, Mamaroneck, NY.	800-328-4465
International Information Associates Inc, Morrisville, CA.	800-645-6973
International Library-Book Publishers Inc, Gaithersburg, MD.	800-359-3349
International Linguistics Corp, Kansas City, MO.	800-237-1830

Publisher/Distributor	Toll-Free No.
International Wealth Success, Merrick, NY.	800-323-0548
Interstate Publishers Inc, Danville, IL.	800-843-4774
Interurban Press, Glendale, CA.	800-899-8722
InterVarsity Press, Downers Grove, IL.	800-843-7225
Iowa State University Press, Ames, IA.	(orders only) 800-862-6657
Richard D Irwin Inc, Homewood, IL.	(Continental US) 800-634-3961
Ishiyaku EuroAmerica Inc, St Louis, MO.	800-633-1921
Island Press, Washington, DC.	800-828-1302
Ivory Tower Publishing Co Inc, Watertown, MA.	800-322-5016
J-Mart Press, Virginia Beach, VA.	800-487-4060
Jalmar Press, Rolling Hills Estates, CA.	800-662-9662
Jameson Books Inc, Ottawa, IL.	800-426-1357
Jamestown Publishers, Providence, RI.	800-USA-READ
Jane's Information Group, Alexandria, CA.	800-243-3852
Janson Publications Inc, Dedham, MA.	800-322-MATH
January Productions, Hawthorne, NJ.	800-451-7450
Jewish Lights Publishing, Woodstock, VT.	800-962-4544
Jewish Publication Society, Philadelphia, PA.	800-234-3151
Jist Works Inc, Indianapolis, IN.	800-648-JIST; (trade) 800-JIST-USA
Johnson Institute, Minneapolis, MN.	800-231-5165; (MN) 247-0484; (Canada) 800-447-6660
Jones & Bartlett Publishers Inc, Boston, MA,	800-832-0034
Joy Publishing, San Juan Capistrano, CA.	800-783-6265
JSA Publications Inc, Farmington Falls, MI.	800-345-0096
Judson Press, Valley Forge, PA.	800-331-1053
Justice Systems Press, Port Angeles, WA.	800-553-1903
Kalmbach Publishing Co, Waukesha, WI.	800-558-1544
Kar-Ben Copies Inc, Rockville, MD.	800-4-KARBEN
Kaye Wood Publishing, West Branch, MI.	800-248-KAYE
KC Publications, Las Vegas, NV.	800-626-9673
Keate Publishing Inc, New Canaan, CT.	800-858-7014
Kendall/Hunt Publishing Co, Dubuque, IA.	(orders only) 800-228-0810
Kennedy Publications, Fitzwilliam, NH.	800-531-0007
Kent State University Press, Kent, OH.	(orders) 800-247-6553
Key Curriculum Press, Berkeley, CA.	800-338-7638
Kingfisher Books, New York, NY.	800-497-1657
Kirkbride Bible Co Inc, Indianapolis, IN.	800-428-4385
Neil A Kjos Music Co, San Diego, CA.	800-854-1592
The S Klein Library on Computer Graphics, Norwell, MA.	800-874-9980
Alfred A Knopf Inc, New York, NY.	800-638-6460
Knopf Publishing Group, New York, NY.	800-638-6460
Knowledge Ideas & Trends Inc, Manchester, CT.	800-826-0529
Knowledge Industry Publications Inc, White Plains, NY.	800-800-5474
Kodansha America Inc, New York, NY.	(except NJ) 800-631-8571
Kola Publishing, New York, NY.	800-435-2433
Kraus International Publications, Millwood, NY.	800-223-8323

Publisher/Distributor	Toll-Free No.
Kraus Reprint, Millwood, NY.	800-223-8323
Kraus Sikes Inc, Madison, WI.	800-969-1556
Kregel Publications, Grand Rapids, MI.	(orders only) 800-733-2607
Kumarian Press Inc, West Hartford, CT.	(orders only) 800-289-2664
Ladybird Books Inc, Auburn, ME.	800-523-9247
Laffing Cow Press, Saratoga, NY.	800-722-6932
Lakewood Publications, Minneapolis, MN.	800-328-4329
G Landes Co, Austin, TX.	800-346-5994
Langenscheidt Publishers Inc, Maspeth, NY.	800-432-MAPS
Langmarc Publishing, San Antonio, TX.	800-864-1648
Laser Institute of America, Orlando, FL.	800-34-LASER
Lawyers Co-Operative Publishing Co, Rochester, NY.	800-527-0430
Lea & Febiger, Malvern, PA.	800-882-8LEA
Leading Edge Reports, Cleveland, OH.	800-866-4648
Learning Links Inc, New Hyde Park, NY.	800-724-2616
Learning Publications Inc, Holmes Beach, FL.	(orders) 800-222-1525
Learning Resources Network (LERN), Manhattan, KS.	800-678-5376
The Learning Works Inc, Santa Barbara, CA.	800-235-5767
Lectorum Publications Inc, New York, NY.	800-345-5946
Legacy Publishing Group, Clinton, MA.	800-322-3866
J Hardy Legwin, Newton Centre, MA.	800-334-7510
Lerner Publications Co, Minneapolis, MN.	800-328-4929
Lewis & Roth Publishers, Littleton, CO.	800-477-3239
Lexington Books, New York, NY.	(cust serv) 800-257-5755; (orders) 800-323-7445
Liberty Fund Inc, Indianapolis, IN.	800-955-8335
Libraries Unlimited Inc, Englewood, CO.	800-237-6124
Life Action Press, Los Angeles, CA.	800-367-2246
Liguori Publications, Liguori, MO.	800-325-9521
Lincoln Institute of Land Policy, Cambridge, MA.	800-848-7236
LinguiSystems Inc, East Moline, IL.	800-PRO-IDEA
Linton Day Publishing Co, Stone Mountain, GA.	800-927-0409
Lion Publishing Corp, Batavia, IL.	800-447-5466
J B Lippincott Co, Philadelphia, PA.	(MA) 800-638-3030; (PA) 800-242-7737
Little, Brown & Co Inc, Boston, MA.	800-343-9204
Littlefield, Adams Quality Paperbacks, Lanham, MD.	800-462-6420
The Liturgical Press, Collegeville, MN.	800-858-5450
Liturgy Training Publications, Chicago, IL.	800-933-1800
Llewellyn Publications, St Paul, MN.	800-843-6666
Lloyds of London Press Inc, New York, NY.	800-955-6937
Loizeaux Brothers Inc, Neptune, NJ.	800-526-2796
Lone Eagle Publishing Co, Los Angeles, CA.	800-345-6257
Lonely Planet Publications, Oakland, CA.	(orders) 800-275-8555
Longman Publishing Group, White Plains, NY.	(orders only) 800-447-2226
Longriver Books/Truck Press, East Haven, CT.	800-243-0138

Publisher/Distributor	Toll-Free No.
Longstreet Press, Marietta, GA.	800-927-1488
Lothrop, Lee & Shepard Books, New York, NY.	800-843-9389
Lotus Light Publications, Twin Lakes, WI.	(orders only) 800-824-6396
Loyola University Press, Chicago, IL.	800-621-1008
Lucent Books Inc, San Diego, CA.	800-231-5163
LuraMedia Inc, San Diego, CA.	800-367-5872
M & H Publishing Co Inc, LaGrange, TX.	800-521-9950
McClanahan Publishing House Inc, Kuttawa, KY.	800-544-6959
McCutchan Publishing Corp, Berkeley, CA.	800-227-1540
Madison Books, Lanham, MD.	800-462-6420
Mage Publishers Inc, Washington, DC.	800-962-0922
Magna Publications Inc, Madison, WI.	800-433-0499
MARC Publications, Monrovia, CA.	(US only) 800-777-7752
Marinelli Publishing, Lowell, MI.	800-NEED-A-PI
Mariposa Publishing Co, St Paul, MN.	800-735-3001
Market Data Retrieval Inc, Shelton, CT.	800-333-8802
Marketcom Inc, Fenton, MO.	800-325-3884
Marlor Press Inc, St Paul, MN.	800-669-4908
MasterMedia, Kansas City, MO.	800-821-3303
Marsilio Publishers Corp, New York, NY.	800-992-9685
Master Books, El Cajon, CA.	800-999-3777
MasterMedia Ltd, New York, NY.	800-334-8232
Masters Press Inc, Indianapolis, IN.	800-722-2677
The Mathematical Association of America, Washington, DC.	800-331-1622
Maupin House, Gainsville, FL.	800-524-0634
Maverick Publications Inc, Bend, OR.	800-800-4831
Mayfair Games Inc, Niles, IL.	800-432-4376
Mayfield Publishing Co, Mountain View, CA.	800-433-1279
Meadowbrook Press Inc, Deephaven, MN.	800-338-2232
R S Means Co Inc, Kingston, MA,	800-448-8182
Meckler Publishing, Westport, CT.	800-635-5537
Media & Methods, Philadelphia, PA.	800-523-4540
Media Publishing, Kansas City, MO.	800-347-2665
Medical Device Register, Montvale, NJ.	800-222-3045
Medbooks, Houston, TX.	800-443-7397
Medical Physics Publishing Corp, Madison, WI.	800-442-5778
The Russel Meerdink Co Ltd, Menasha, WI.	800-635-6499
Melius Publishing Inc, Pierre, SD.	800-882-5171
Menasha Ridge Press, Birmingham, AL.	800-247-9437
Mercer Inc, New York, NY.	800-348-7583
Mercer University Press, Macon, GA.	800-637-2378; 800-342-0841
Mercury House Inc, San Francisco, CA.	800-998-9129
Meriwether Publishing Ltd/Contemporary Drama Service, Colorado Springs, CO.	800-93PLAYS
Merriam-Webster Inc, Springfield, MA.	800-828-1880

Publisher/Distributor	Toll-Free No.
Merryant Publishers, Vashon, WA.	800-228-8958
Mesorah Publications, Brooklyn, NY.	800-637-6724
Metal Bulletin Inc, New York, NY.	800-METAL-25
Metamorphous Press Inc, Portland, OR.	800-937-7771
Michelin Travel Publications, Greenville, SC.	800-423-0485; 800-223-0987
The Michie Co, Charlottesville, VA.	800-446-3410
Microsoft Press, Redmond, WA.	800-MSPRESS
Midwest Plan Service, Ames, IA.	800-562-3618
Milady Publishing Co, Albany, NY.	800-836-5239
The Millbrook Press Inc, Brookfield, CT.	800-462-4703
Miller Freeman Inc, San Francisco, CA.	(orders only) 800-848-5594
Milliken Publishing Co, St Louis, MO.	800-325-4136
Mills & Sanderson Publishers, Bedford, MA.	800-441-6224
The Minerals, Metals & Materials Society (TMS), Warrendale, PA.	800-759-4867
Minnesota Historical Society Press, St Paul, MN.	800-647-7827
MIS: Press, Inc, New York, NY.	800-488-5233
The MIT Press, Cambridge, MA.	(orders only) 800-356-0343
Mitchell McGraw-Hill, Watsonville, CA.	800-435-2665
MMB Music Inc, St Louis, MO.	800-543-3771
Mockingbird Books, Marietta, GA.	800-497-6663
Monday Morning Books Inc, Palo Alto, CA.	800-435-7234
Moody Press, Chicago, IL.	800-678-8812
Moon Publications Inc, Chico, CA.	800-345-5473
More Than a Card Inc, New Orleans, LA.	800-635-9672
Thomas More Press, Chicago, IL.	800-835-8965
Morehouse Publishing Co, Harrisburg, PA.	800-877-0012
Morgan-Rand Inc, Philadelphia, PA.	800-441-3839
Morrow Junior Books, New York, NY.	800-843-9389
William Morrow & Co Inc, New York, NY.	800-843-9389
Mosaic Press Miniature Books, Cincinnati, OH.	800-932-4044
Mosby-Year Book Inc., St Louis, MO.	800-325-4177
Motorbooks International Publishers & Wholesalers Inc, Osceola, WI.	800-826-6600; 800-458-0454
Mountain Meadow Press, Wrangell, AK.	800-368-8277
Mountain n' Air Books, Tujunga, CA.	800-446-9696
Mountain Press Publishing Co, Missoula, MT.	800-234-5308
Mountaineers Books, Seattle, WA.	800-553-4453
Mulberry Books, New York, NY.	800-843-9389
John Muir Publications Inc, Santa Fe, NM.	800-888-7504
Multnomah Press, Portland, OR.	800-929-0910
Munchkin Publications Etcetera, Lynbrook, NY.	(orders) 800-247-6553
Municipal Analysis Services Inc, Austin, TX.	800-488-3932
Mike Murach & Associates Inc, Fresno, CA.	800-221-5528
MUSA Video Publishing, Dallas, TX.	800-421-5355

Publisher/Distributor	Toll-Free No.
Music Sales Corp, New York, NY.	800-431-7187
The Naiad Press Inc, Tallahassee, FL.	(order desk only) 800-533-1973
National Academy Press, Washington, DC.	(orders only) 800-624-6242
National Association of Broadcasters Washington, DC.	800-368-5644
National Association of Secondary School Principals, Reston, VA.	800-235-7746
National Association of Social Workers (NASW), Silver Spring, MD.	800-638-8799
National Council of Teachers of English, Urbana, IL.	800-369-6283
National Council on Radiation Protection & Measurements, Bethesda, MD.	800-229-2652
National Geographic Society, Washington, DC.	800-638-4077
National Information Center for Educational Media Albuquerque, NM.	800-468-3453
National Institute for Trial Advocacy, Notre Dame, IN.	800-225-6482
National Learning Corp, Syossett, NY.	800-645-6337
National Practice Institute, Minneapolis, MN.	800-328-4444
National Press Books Inc, Bethesda, MD.	800-275-8888
National Publishing Co, Philadelphia, PA.	(orders only) 800-873-8384
National Textbook Co (NTC), Lincolnwood, IL.	(orders only) 800-323-4900
Naturegraph Publishers Inc, Happy Camp, CA.	800-775-5352
Naval Institute Press, Annapolis, MD.	800-233-8764
NavPress Publishing Group, Colorado Springs, CO.	800-366-7788
Nelson Publications, Port Chester, NY.	800-333-6357
Thomas Nelson Inc, Nashville, TN.	800-251-4000
New Amsterdam Books, Franklin, NY.	800-944-4040
New City Press, New Rochelle, NY.	(orders only) 800-462-5980
New Creation Publishing Group, LaQuinta, CA.	800-875-HEAL
New Dimensions in Education Inc, Waterbury, CT.	800-227-9120
New Directions Publishing Corp, New York, NY.	(PA) 800-233-4830
New Harbinger Publications Inc, Oakland, CA.	(orders only) 800-748-6273
New Horizon Press, Far Hills, NJ.	800-533-7978
New Leaf Press Inc, Green Forest, AR.	800-643-9535
New Readers Press, Syracuse, NY.	(orders only) 800-448-8878
New Society Publishers, Philadelphia, PA.	800-333-9093
New World Library, San Rafael, CA.	(retail orders) 800-227-3900; (CA) 800-632-2122
New York Academy of Sciences, New York, NY.	800-THE-NYAS
New York Zoetrope, New York, NY.	800-CHAPLIN
Newcastle Publishing Co Inc, North Hollywood, CA.	800-932-4809
Nippan Publications, Carson, CA.	800-562-1410
The Noble Press Inc, Chicago, IL.	800-486-7737
Nolo Press, Berkeley, CA.	800-992-6656
Norman Publishing, San Francisco, CA.	800-544-9359
North River Press Inc, Croton-on-Hudson, NY.	800-486-2665
North-South Books Inc, New York, NY.	800-282-8257
Northland Publishing Co, Flagstaff, AZ.	800-346-3257

Publisher/Distributor	Toll-Free No.
Northwest Publishing Inc, Salt Lake City, UT.	800-398-2102
Northwind Press, Sandpoint, ID.	800-235-7756
NorthWord Press Inc, Minocqua, WI.	(order line only) 800-336-6398
Jeffrey Norton Publishers Inc, Guilford, CT.	800-243-1234
W W Norton & Co Inc, New York, NY.	(orders cust serv) 800-233-4830
Nucleus Publications, Willow Springs, MO.	800-762-6595
Nutrinfo Corp, Norwood, MA.	800-676-6686
Nystrom, Chicago, IL.	800-621-8086
The Oasis Press, Grants Pass, OR.	800-228-2275
Offender Preparation Education Network Inc (OPEN), Dallas, TX.	800-966-1966
Official Airline Guide Inc, Oak Brook, IL.	800-323-3537
Ohara Publications Inc, Santa Valencia, CA.	800-423-2874
Ohio University Press, Athens, OH.	800-621-2736
Oliver-Nelson Books, Nashville, TN.	800-251-4000
Oliver Wight Ltd Publications Inc, Essex Junction, VT.	800-343-0625
Online Press Inc, Bellevue, WA.	800-854-3344
Omnigraphics Inc, Detroit, MI.	800-234-1340
Open Court Publishing Co, Peru, IL.	800-435-6850; (IL) 800-892-6831
Optical Society of America, Washington, DC.	800-584-0416
Orbis Books, Maryknoll, NY.	(orders) 800-258-5838
Orchard Books, New York, NY.	800-433-3411
Orchard House Inc, Concord, MA.	800-423-1303
O'Reilly Associates Inc, Sebastopol, CA.	800-998-9938
Organization for Economic Cooperation & Development OECD Publications & Information Center, Washington, DC.	800-456-6323
Orion Research Corp, Scottsdale, AZ.	800-844-0759
ORS Publishing, Tallahassee, FL.	800-462-8913
The Oryx Press, Phoenix, AZ.	800-279-6799
Osborne/McGraw-Hill, Berkeley, CA.	800-227-0900
Our Sunday Visitor Publishing, Huntington, IN.	(orders) 800-348-2440
The Overmountain Press, Johnson City, TN.	800-992-2691
Richard C Owen Publishers Inc, Katonah, NY.	800-336-5588
Oxbridge Communications Inc, New York, NY.	800-955-0231
Oxford University Press Inc, New York, NY.	(cust serv) 800-451-7556
Oxmoor House Inc, Birmingham, AL.	800-366-4712
Pacific Press Publishing Association, Boise, ID.	8000-447-7377
Pagananiana Publications, Neptune, NJ.	800-631-2188
Paladin Press, Boulder, CO.	800-392-2400
Palindrome Press, Washington, DC.	800-843-5990
Panel Publishers Inc, New York, NY.	800-638-8437
Panoptic Enterprises, Woodbridge, VA.	800-594-4766
Pantheon Books/Schocken Books, New York, NY.	800-638-6460
Papier-Mache Press, Watsonville, CA.	800-776-1956
PAR Publishers, Homewood, IL.	800-634-3961
PAR Publishing Co, Santa Barbara, CA.	800-PARAPUB
Paraclete Press, Orleans, MA.	800-451-5006

Publisher/Distributor	Toll-Free No.
Paragon House, New York, NY.	800-PARAGON
Paramount Publishing, New York, NY.	(cust serv) 800-223-2348;
	800-223-2336
Parenting Press Inc, Seattle, WA.	800-99-BOOKS
Parker & Son Publications Inc, Carlsbad, CA.	800-452-9873
Parkside Publishing Corp, Park Ridge, IL.	(US & Canada) 800-221-6364
Passport Books, Lincolnwood, IL.	(orders only) 800-323-4900
Pathway Book Service, Gilsum, NH.	800-345-6665
Pathway Press, Cleveland, TN.	800-553-8506
Patrick's Press, Columbus, GA.	800-654-1052
PBC International Inc, Glen Cove, NY.	800-527-2826
Peachpit Press Inc, Berkeley, CA.	800-283-9444
Peachtree Publishers Ltd, Atlanta, GA.	800-241-0113
Pelican Publishing Co Inc, Gretna, LA.	800-843-1724
The Pennsylvania State University Press, University Park, PA.	800-326-9180
PennWell Publishing Co Inc, Tulsa, OK.	800-752-9764
Per Annum Inc, New York, NY.	800-548-1108
The Perfection Learning Corp, Des Moines, IA.	800-762-2999
Performance Dimensions Publishing, Powers Lake, WI.	800-877-7413
Peter Pauper Press Inc, White Plains, NY.	800-833-2311
Peterson's Guides Inc, Princeton, NJ.	800-338-3282
Pfeifer-Hamilton Publishers, Duluth, MN.	800-247-6789
Phanes Press Inc, Grand Rapids, MI.	800-678-0392
Phi Delta Kappa Educational Foundation, Bloomington, IN.	800-766-1156
Philosophy Documentation Center, Bowling Green, OH.	800-444-2419
Pictorial Histories Publishing Co Inc, Missoula, MT.	800-638-6873
The Pierian Press, Ann Arbor, MI.	800-678-2435
The Pilgrim Press/United Church Press, Cleveland, OH.	800-537-3394
The Pilgrim's Path, Ojai, CA.	800-284-5864 ext "H"
PJS Publications Inc, Peoria, IL.	800-521-2885
Planning Communications, River Forest, IL.	800-829-5220
Pleasant Co Publications Inc, Middleton, WI.	800-233-0264
Plenum Publishing Corp, New York, NY.	800-221-9369
PMA Publishing Corp, Costa Mesa, CA.	800-654-4425
PMD Publishers Group Inc, Winter Park, FL.	800-438-5911
Pocahontas Press Inc, Blacksburg, VA.	800-446-0467
Pomegranate Artbooks Inc, Rohnert Park, CA.	800-227-1428
Popular Culture Ink, Ann Arbor, MI.	800-678-8828
Clarkson Potter Publishers, New York, NY.	800-526-4264
Powerhouse Publishing, Fawnskin, CA.	800-366-3119
Praeger Publishers, Westport, CT.	800-225-5800
Prairie House Inc, Fargo, ND.	800-866-Book
Prakken Publications Inc, Ann Arbor, MI.	(orders only) 800-530-9673
Precept Press, Chicago, IL.	800-225-3775
Prentice Hall Canada, Scarborough, ON.	800-567-3800
Presbyterian & Reformed Publishing Co, Phillipsburg, NJ.	800-631-0094

Publisher/Distributor	Toll-Free No.
Preservation Press, Washington, DC.	800-766-6847
Presidio Press, Novato, CA.	800-966-5179
Price Stern Sloan Inc, Los Angeles, CA.	800-421-0892
Princeton Architectural Press, New York, NY.	800-458-1131
Princeton Book Co Publishers, Pennington, NJ.	800-326-7149
Princeton University Press, Princeton, NJ.	800-777-4726
The Printers Shopper, Chula Vista, CA.	800-854-2911
Pro Lingua Associates, Brattleboro, VT.	800-366-4775
Probus Publishing Co, Chicago, IL.	800-PROBUS-1
Productivity Press Inc, Cambridge, MA. (cust serv only)	800-394-6868
Professional Development Institute, Huntington Beach, CA.	800-833 7979
Professional Publications Inc, Belmont, CA.	800-426-1178
Professional Resource Exchange Inc, Sarasota, FL.	800-443-3364
Programs for Education, Rosemont, NJ.	800-627-5867
Prometheus Books, Buffalo, NY.	800-421-0351
ProStar Publications Ltd, Los Angeles, CA.	800-292-6657
Pruett Publishing Co, Boulder, CO.	800-247-8224
Psychological Assessment Resources Inc (PAR), Lutz, FL.	800-331-8378
The Psychological Corporation, San Antonio, TX. (cust serv)	800-228-0752
Public Utilities Reports Inc, Arlington, VA.	800-368-5001
Purdue University Press, West Lafayette, IN.	800-933-9637
Purple Mountain Press Ltd, Fleischmanns, NY.	800-325-2665
The Putnum Berkley Group Inc, New York, NY.	800-631-8571
The Putnam & Grosset Book & Activity Group, New York, NY.	800-691-8571
PWS-Kent Publishing Co, Boston, MA.	800-343-2204
QED Publishing Group, Wellesley, MA.	800-343-4848
Quail Ridge Press, Brandon, MS.	800-343-1583
Quality Medical Publishing Inc, St Louis, MO.	800-423-6865
Quality Press, Milwaukee, WI.	800-248-1946
Quality Resources, White Plains, NY.	800-247-8519
Questar Publishers Inc, Sisters, OR.	800-933-0910
Quintessence Publishing Co Inc, Carol Stream, IL.	800-621-0387
Rainbow Books, Highland City, FL. (book orders)	800-356-9315
Raintree/Steck-Vaughn Publishers, Milwaukee, WI.	800-558-7264
RAM Research Corp, Frederick, MD.	800-874-8999
Rand McNally & Co, Skokie, IL.	800-333-0136
Random House Inc, New York, NY.	800-726-0600
Random House Trade Sales and Marketing	800-726-0600
Knopf Publishing Group, New York, NY.	800-638-6460
Ransom Hill Press, Ramona, CA.	800-423-0620
Rapha Publishing, Houston, TX.	800-383-4673
Reader's Digest Association, Pleasantville, NY.	800-431-1726
Recovery Publications, San Diego, CA.	800-873-8384
Recruiting & Search Report, Panama City Beach, FL.	800-634-4548
Red Crane Books, Santa Fe, NM.	800-992-3392
Redleaf Press, St Paul, MN.	800-423-8309

Publisher/Distributor	Toll-Free No.
Thomas Reed Publications Inc, Boston, MA.	800-995-4995
The Reference Press Inc, Austin, TX.	800-486-8666
Regal Books, Ventura, CA.	800-235-3415
Regnery Gateway Inc, Washington, DC.	800-462-6420
Regular Baptist Press, Schaumburg, IL.	800-727-4440
Rei America Inc, Miami, FL.	800-726-5337
REPAIRMASTER, West Jordan, UT.	800-347-5163
Research Publications Inc, Woodbridge, CT.	800-444-0799
Resource Media, Philadelphia, PA.	800-441-3839
Resurrection Press Ltd, Williston Park, NY.	800-892-6657
Retail Reporting Corp, New York, NY.	800-251-4545
Retail Strategies & Publishing Inc, Overland Park, KS.	800-733-6160
Fleming H Revell Co, Grand Rapids, MI.	800-877-2665
Review & Herald Publishing Association, Hagerstown, MD.	800-234-7630
Rip Off Press Inc, Auburn, CA.	800-468-2669
The Riverside Publishing Co, Chicago, IL.	800-323-9540
Rizzoli International Publications Inc, New York, NY.	800-462-2387
Roberts Rinehart Publishers, Niwot, CO.	800-352-1985
Rockwell Publishing, Redmond, WA.	800-221-9347
Rodale Press Inc, Emmaus, PA.	800-441-7761
Roper Press Inc, Dallas, TX.	800-284-0158
The Rosen Publishing Group Inc, New York, NY.	800-237-9932
Ross Books, Berkeley, CA.	800-367-0930
Norman Ross Publishing Inc, New York, NY.	800-648-8850
Roth Publishing Inc, Great Neck, NY.	800-899-ROTH
Fred B Rothman & Co, Littleton, CO.	800-457-1986
Roundtable Publishing Inc, Malibu, CA.	800-222-5322
Rowman & Littlefield Publishers Inc, Lanham, MD.	800-462-6420
Rudra Press, Portland, OR.	800-876-7798
Running Press Book Publishers, Philadelphia, PA.	(orders) 800-345-5359
Russell Sage Foundation, New York, NY.	800-666-2211
Rutgers University Press, New Brunswick, NJ.	(orders only) 800-446-9323
Rutledge Hill Press, Nashville, TN.	800-234-4234
William H Sadlier Inc, New York, NY.	800-221-5175
Sagamore Publishing Inc, Champaign, IL.	(orders) 800-327-5557
St Anthony Messenger Press, Cincinnati, OH.	800-488-0488
St Anthony Publishing Inc, Alexandria, VA.	800-632-0123
St James Press, Detroit, MI.	800-345-0392
St Martin's Press Inc, New York, NY.	800-221-7945
Saint Mary's Press, Winona, MN.	800-533-8095
St Nectarios Press, Seattle, WA.	800-643-4233
St Paul Books & Media, Boston, MA.	800-876-4463
Salem Press Inc, Englewood Cliffs, NJ.	800-221-1592
Santillana Publishing Co Inc, Compton, CA.	800-245-8584
Sasquatch Books, Seattle, WA.	800-775-0817
W B Saunders Company, Philadelphia, PA.	(cust serv) 800-545-2522

Publisher/Distributor	Toll-Free No.
K G Saur, New Providence, NJ.	(orders only) 800-521-8110
Scarborough House, Lanham, MD.	800-462-6420
Scarecrow Press Inc, Metuchen, NJ.	800-537-7107
Sceptor Publishers, Princeton, NJ.	800-322-8773
Schaffer Frank Publications Inc, Torrance, CA.	800-421-5565
Scholarly Publications, Houston, TX.	800-275-7825
Scholarly Resources Inc, Wilmington, DE.	800-772-8937
Scholars Press, Atlanta, GA.	(cust serv) 800-437-6692
Scholastic Inc, New York, NY.	800-392-2179
Scholastic Professional Books, New York, NY.	800-325-6149
School Zone Publishing Co, Grand Haven, MI.	800-253-0564
Arthur Schwartz & Co Inc, Woodstock, NY.	800-669-9080
Science & Behavior Books, Palo Alto, CA.	800-547-9982
Scientific American Medicine, New York, NY.	800-545-0554
The Scientific Press Inc, San Francisco, CA.	800-451-5409
Scott & Daughters Publishing Inc, Los Angeles, CA.	800-547-2688
Scott, Foresman & Co, Glenview, IL.	(orders only) 800-782-2665
Scott Publications, Livonia, MI.	800-458-8237
Scott Publishing Co, Sidney, OH.	800-572-6885; (OH) 800-327-1259
Scripture Press Publications Inc, Wheaton, IL.	800-323-9409
The Seedsowers, Beaumont, TX.	800-228-2665
Self-Counsel Press Inc, Bellingham, WA.	800-663-3007
Servant Publications, Ann Arbor, MI.	(US orders) 800-458-8505; (MI orders) 800-533-8505
Seven Locks Press Inc, Arlington, VA.	800-354-5348
Dale Seymour Publications Inc, Palo Alto, CA.	800-872-1100
M E Sharpe Inc, Armonk, NY.	800-541-6563
Harold Shaw Publishers, Wheaton, IL.	800-SHAW-PUB
Sheed & Ward, Kansas City, MO.	(cust serv) 800-333-7373; 800-444-8910
Sheep Meadow Press, Bronx, NY.	800-972-4491
Sheridan Worldwide Inc, Scottsdale, AZ.	800-548-7841
Signature Books Inc, Salt Lake City, UT.	800-356-5687
Singular Publishing Group Inc, San Diego, CA,	800-521-8545
Skidmore-Roth Publishing, El Paso, TX.	800-825-3150
Skillpath Publications Inc, Mission, KS.	800-873-7545
SkippingStone Press Inc, Denver, CO.	800-333-6073
Sky Publishing Corp, Cambridge, MA.	800-253-0245
Slack Incorporated, Thorofare, NJ.	800-257-8290
Slawson Communications Inc, Carlsbad, CA.	800-SLAWSON
Smith & Kraus Inc Publishers, Newbury, VT.	800-862-5423
Lee Smith Publishers & Printers, North Nashville, TN.	800-274-6774
Smithmark Publishers Inc, New York, NY.	800-645-9990
Smithsonian Institution Press, Washington, DC.	800-678-2675
Snow Lion Publications Inc, Ithaca, NY.	800-950-0313
Society for Industrial & Applied Mathematics, Philadelphia, PA.	800-447-SIAM
Society of Manufacturing Engineers, Dearborn, MI.	800-733-4SME

Publisher/Distributor	Toll-Free No.
Sophia Institute Press, Manchester, NH.	800-888-9344
Soundprints Corp, Norwalk, CT.	800-228-7839
Source Books, Trabuco Canyon, CA.	800-695-4237
South Carolina Bar, Columbia, SC.	(SC only) 800-768-7787
South-Western Publishing Co, Cincinnati, OH.	800-543-0487
Southern Institute Press, Indian Rocks Beach, FL.	800-633-4891
Southpark Publishing Group Inc, Dallas, TX.	800-669-5657
Specialty Press, Stillwater, MN.	800-888-9653
Sphinx Publishing, Clearwater, FL.	800-226-5291
Spirit Dance Publishing, Sorrento, FL.	800-223-5333
Spoken Arts Inc, St Petersburg, FL.	800-726-4090
Springer-Verlag New York Inc, New York, NY.	800-SPRINGER
Springhouse Corp, Springhouse, PA.	800-346-7844
SPSS Inc, Chicago, IL.	800-543-9263
SRA School Group, Chicago, IL.	(school) 800-843-8855; (ISED orders) 800-772-1277
ST Publications Book Division, Cincinnati, OH.	800-925-1110
Stackpole Books, Harrisburg, PA.	800-732-3669
Standard Publishing Co, Cincinnati, OH.	800-543-1301
Standard Publishing Corp, Boston, MA.	800-682-5759
Star Books Inc, Wilson, NC.	800-476-1591
Starwood Publishing Inc, Washington, DC.	800-525-3444
State University of New York Press, Albany, NY.	800-666-2211
Statesman Examiner Inc, Colville, WA.	800-488-5676
Steck-Vaughn Co, Austin, TX.	800-531-5015
Sterling Publishing Co Inc, New York, NY.	800-367-9692
Stewart, Tabori & Chang, Publishers, New York, NY.	800-722-7202
Stillpoint Publishing International Inc, Walpole, NH.	800-847-4014
Stockton Press, New York, NY.	800-221-2123
Stoeger Publishing Co, South Hackensack, NJ.	800-631-0722
Storey/Garden Way Publishing, Pownal, VT.	800-359-7436
Strang Communications Co/Creation House, Altamonte Springs, FL.	800-451-4598
Studio Press, Soulsbyville, CA.	800-445-7160
Success Advertising & Publishing, Palm Beach Gardens, FL.	800-330-4643
Sulzburger & Graham Publishing Co Ltd, New York, NY.	800-366-7086
Summers Press Inc, Bedford, TX.	800-743-6491
Summit University Press, Livingston, MT.	800-323-5228
SunCity Publishing, Tri-Cities, WA.	800-831-5208
Sundance Publishers, Littleton, MA.	800-343-8204
Sunset Books, Menlo Park, CA.	800-227-7346
Sunstone Publications, Cooperstown, NY.	800-327-0306
Surrey Books Inc, Chicago, IL.	800-326-4430
Swan, Raven & Co, Newburg, OR.	800-488-4849
Swedenborg Foundation Inc, West Chester, PA.	(cust serv) 800-355-3222
SYBEX Inc, Alameda, CA.	800-227-2346

Publisher/Distributor	Toll-Free No.
Syracuse University Press, Syracuse, NY.	800-365-8929
Tabor Publishing, Allen, TX.	800-527-4747
Tambourine Books, New York, NY.	800-843-9389
Tapestry Press Ltd, Acton, MA.	800-535-2007
The Taunton Press Inc, Newtown, CT.	800-283-7252; (orders) 800-888-8286
Taylor & Francis Publishers Inc, Bristol, PA.	800-821-8312
Taylor Publishing Co, Dallas, TX.	(voice & fax) 800-677-2800
TEACH Services, Brushton, NY.	800-367-1844
Teacher Ideas Press, Englewood, CO.	800-237-6124
Teachers Friend Publications Inc, Riverside, CA.	800-343-9680
Technical Association of the Pulp & Paper Industry (TAPPI), Atlanta, GA.	800-332-8686
Technical Insights Inc, Fort Lee, NJ.	800-245-6217
Technomic Publishing Co Inc, Lancaster, PA.	800-233-9936
Techware Corp, Altamonte Springs, FL.	800-34-REACH
Telecom Library Inc, New York, NY.	800-542-7279
Temple University Press, Philadelphia, PA.	800-447-1656
Templegate Publishers, Springfield, IL.	800-367-4844
Ten Speed Press, Berkeley, CA.	800-841-BOOK
Tesla Book Co, Chula Vista, CA.	800-398-2056
Texas A & M University Press, College Station, TX.	(orders) 800-826-8911
Texas Instruments Inc Data Book Marketing, Dallas, TX.	800-336-5236
Texas Tech University Press, Lubbock, TX.	800-832-4042
Texas Western Press, El Paso, TX.	800-488-3789
TFH Publications Inc, Neptune, NJ.	800-631-2188
Thames & Hudson Inc, New York, NY.	800-233-4830
That Patchwork Place Inc, Bothell, WA.	800-426-3126
Theosophical Publishing House, Wheaton, IL.	800-669-9425
Thieme Medical Publishers Inc, New York, NY.	800-782-3488
Thinking Publications, Eau Claire, WI.	800-225-4769
Charles C Thomas, Publisher, Springfield, IL.	800-258-8980
Thomas Geale Publications Inc, Montara, CA.	800-554-5457
Thomasson-Grant Publishers, Charlottesville, VA.	800-999-1780
Thomson Financial Publishing, Skokie, IL.	800-444-0064
Tidewater Publishers, Centreville, MD.	800-638-7641
Time Being Books-Poetry in Sight & Sound, St Louis, MO.	800-331-6605
Time Life Inc, Alexandria, VA.	800-621-7026
Times Books, New York, NY.	800-733-3000
Todd Publications, West Nyack, NY.	800-747-1056
TODTRI Productions Ltd, New York, NY.	800-241-4477
Tor Books, New York, NY.	(cust serv) 800-221-7945
Torah Aura Productions, Los Angeles, CA.	800-238-6724
Tower Publishing Co, Portland, ME.	800-287-7323
Traders Press Inc, Greenville, SC.	800-927-8222
Tradery House, Memphis, TN.	800-727-1034

Publisher/Distributor	Toll-Free No.
Trails Illustrated, Evergreen, CO.	800-962-1643
Trakker Maps Inc, Miami, FL.	800-432-1730
Treasure Chest Publications Inc, Tucson, AZ.	800-969-9558
Tree by the River Publishing, Carson City, NV.	800-487-6610
Tree of Life Publications, Joshua Tree, CA.	(orders only) 800-247-6553
Treehaus Communications Inc, Loveland, OH.	(orders) 800-638-4287
Tribune Publishing, Orlando, FL.	800-788-1213
Trinity Press Intenational, Valley Forge, PA.	800-421-8874
TriQuarterly Books, Evanston, IL.	(orders only) 800-621-2736
Troll Associates, Mahwah, NJ.	800-526-5289
Tself/Editorial CLIE, Fort Lauderdale, FL.	800-327-7933
TSR Inc, Lake Geneva, WI.	800-DRAGONS
Charles E Tuttle Co Inc, Rutland, VT.	800-526-2778
21st Century Education Inc, Kingston, NY.	800-866-5559
Twenty-Third Publications Inc, Mystic, CT.	800-321-0411
Tyndale House Publishers Inc, Wheaton, IL.	800-323-9400
Type & Temperment Inc, Gladwyne, PA.	800-IHS-TYPE
ULI-The Urban Land Institute, Washington, DC.	800-462-1254
UMI Publications Inc, Charlotte, NC.	800-462-5831
Unarius Academy of Science Publications, El Cajon, CA.	800-842-2725
Unique Publications, Burbank, CA.	800-332-3330
The United Methodist Publishing House, Nashville, TN.	800-251-3320
United Nations, New York, NY.	800-253-9646
United States Institute of Peace, Washington, DC.	800-537-9359
United States Pharmacopeial Convention Inc, Rockville, MD.	800-227-8772
United States Tennis Association, White Plains, NY.	800-223-0456
Universal Unity, Fremont, CA.	800-995-1938
University Microfilms International (UMI), Ann Arbor, MI.	800-521-0600; (Canada) 800-343-5299
The University of Arizona Press, Tucson, AZ.	(orders) 800-426-3797
The University of Arkansas Press, Fayetteville, AR.	800-525-1823
University of California Press, Berkeley, CA.	800-822-6657
University of Chicago Press, Chicago, IL.	(orders) 800-621-2736
University of Denver Center for Teaching International Relations Publications, Denver, CO.	800-967-2847
University of Illinois Press, Champaign, IL.	(orders) 800-545-4703
University of Iowa Press, Iowa City, IA.	(orders only) 800-235-2665
The University of Michigan Press, Ann Arbor, MI.	800-876-1922
University of Minnesota Press, Minneapolis, MN.	800-388-3863
University of Missouri Press, Columbia, MO.	800-828-1894
University of Nebraska at Omaha Center for Public Affairs Research, Omaha, NE.	800-227-4533
University of Nebraska Press, Lincoln, NE.	(orders) 800-755-1105
The University of North Carolina Press, Chapel Hill, NC.	(orders only) 800-848-6224

Publisher/Distributor	Toll-Free No.
University of Oklahoma Press, Norman, OK.	(orders) 800-627-7377
University of Pennsylvania Press, Philadelphia, PA.	(orders & cust serv only) 800-445-9880
University of Pittsburgh Press, Pittsburgh, PA.	800-666-2211
University of South Carolina Press, Columbia, SC.	800-763-0089
University of Tennessee Press, Knoxville, TN.	(warehouse, Continental US except IL) 800-621-2736
University of Utah Press, Salt Lake City, UT.	800-444-8638 ext 6771
University of Washington Press, Seattle, WA.	800-441-4115
University Press of America Inc, Lanham, MD.	800-462-6420
University Press of Florida, Gainesville, FL.	800-226-3822
The University Press of Kentucky, Lexington, KY.	800-666-2211
University Press of Mississippi, Jackson, MS.	800-737-7788
University Press of New England, Hanover, NH.	800-421-1561
University Publications of America, Bethesda, MD.	800-692-6300
University Publishing Group, Frederick, MD.	800-654-8188
Upstart Publishing Co Inc, Dover, NH.	800-235-8866
Upward Way Inc, Pleasant View, TN.	800-367-2665
The Urban Institute Press, Washington, DC.	800-462-6420
US Catholic Conference, Washington, DC.	800-235-8722
US Games Systems Inc, Stamford, CT.	800-544-2637; 800-54GAMES
Useable Portable Publications Inc, Winchester, MA.	800-648-3166
Van Patten Publishing, Portland, OR.	800-345-0096
Vanderbilt University Press, Nashville, TN.	(orders only) 800-937-5557
VCH Publishers Inc, New York, NY.	800-422-8824
Ventana Press, Chapel Hill, NC.	800-743-5369
Venture Press, Plantation, FL.	800-373-5957
VGM Career Horizons, Lincolnwood, IL.	(orders only) 800-323-4900
Victor Books, Wheaton, IL.	800-323-9409
Visible Ink Press, Detroit, MI.	800-776-6256
Vision Books International, Santa Rosa, CA.	800-377-3431
Visual Education Association, Springfield, OH.	(USA) 800-243-7070
Vitesse Press, Brattleboro, VT.	800-848-3747
Voyageur Press, Stillwater, MN.	800-888-9653
Wadsworth Publishing Co.	800-354-9706
Waite Group Press, Corte Madera, CA.	800-368-9369
J Weston Walch Publisher, Portland, ME.	800-341-6094
Walker & Co, New York, NY.	800-AT-WALKER
Walker Western Research Co, San Mateo, CA.	800-258-5737
Wallace Homestead Book Co, Radnor, PA.	800-695-1214
Warren Gorham Lamont, New York, NY.	800-922-0066
Warren Publishing House Inc, Everett, WA.	800-334-4769
Washington State University Press, Pullman, WA.	800-354-7360
Waterfront Books, Burlington, VT.	(orders) 800-639-6063
Watson-Guptill Publications, New York, NY.	800-451-1741
Franklin Watts Inc, Chicago, IL.	800-672-6672

Publisher/Distributor	Toll-Free No.
Weatherhill Inc, New York, NY.	800-788-7323
Webster International Inc, Brentwood, TN.	800-727-6833
Samuel Weiser Inc, York Beach, ME.	800-423-7087
Weka Publishing, Greenwich, CT.	800-222-9352
Wellspring, York, PA.	800-533-3561
Wesleyan University Press, Middletown, CT.	800-421-1561
West Publishing Co, St Paul, MN.	(orders only) 800-328-9352
Westchester Publishing, Los Altos, CA.	800-950-4095
Westcliffe Publishers Inc, Englewood, CO.	800-523-3692
Western Psychological Services, Los Angeles, CA.	(US & Canada) 800-648-8857
Western Publishing Co Inc, Racine, WI.	(ordering & shipping information) 800-558-5972
The Westminster Press/John Knox Press, Louisville, KY.	800-395-7234
Westport Publishers Inc, Kansas City, MO.	800-347-BOOK
WH&O International, Wellesley, MA.	800-553-6678
Whitaker House, Springdale, PA.	800-444-4484
White Cliffs Media Co, Crown Point, IN.	800-359-3210
Whitehorse Press, Boston, MA.	800-531-1133
Albert Whitman & Co, Morton Grove, IL.	800-255-7675
Whole Person Associates Inc, Duluth, MN.	800-247-6789
Wide World of Maps Inc, Phoenix, AZ.	800-279-7654
Wilderness Press, Berkeley, CA.	800-443-7227
John Wiley & Sons Inc, New York, NY.	(order only) 800-CALL WILEY
Williams & Wilkins, Baltimore, MD.	800-638-0672
Williamson Publishing Co, Charlotte, VT.	800-234-8791
The H W Wilson Co, Bronx, NY.	800-367-6770
Windward Publishing Inc, Miami, FL.	(FL) 800-330-6232
The Wine Appreciation Guild Ltd, San Francisco, CA.	800-242-9462
Winston-Derek Publishers Inc, Nashville, TN.	800-826-1888
Wisdom Publications, Boston, MA.	800-272-4050
Wolfe Publishing Co, Prescott, AZ.	800-899-7810
Woodbine House, Rockville, MD.	800-843-7323
Woodbridge Press Publishing Co, Santa Barbara, CA.	800-237-6053
Woodland Books, Provo, UT.	800-777-2665
Word Inc, Irving, TX.	800-933-9673
Wordware Publishing Inc, Plano, TX.	800-229-4949
Workman Publishing Co, New York, NY.	800-722-7202
World Bible Publishers Inc, Iowa Falls, IA.	800-247-5111
World Book Inc, Chicago, IL.	(cust serv) 800-621-8202
World Book Direct Marketing, Evanston, IL.	800-937-7720
World Book Educational Products, Elk Grove Village, IL.	800-433-6580
World Book Publishing, Chicago, IL.	800-255-1750
World Eagle Inc, Wellesley, MA.	800-634-3805
World Information Technologies Inc, Northport, NY.	800-WORLD-INFO

Publisher/Distributor	Toll-Free No.
World Resources Institute, Washington, DC.	800-822-0504
World Scientific Publishing Co Inc, River Edge, NJ.	800-227-7562
Worth Publishers Inc, New York, NY.	800-321-9299; 800-223-1715
The Wright Group, Bothell, WA.	800-523-2371 (training dept); 800-345-6073
Write Source Educational Publishing House, Burlington, WI.	800-445-8613
Writer's Digest Books, Cincinnati, OH.	800-289-0963
Wyrick & Co, Charleston, SC.	800-227-5898
YMAA Publication Center, Jamaica Plain, MA.	800-669-8892
Young Discovery Library, Ossining, NY.	800-343-7854
Zaner-Bloser Inc, Columbus, OH.	800-421-3018
Zebra Books, New York, NY.	800-221-2647
Zebrowski Historical Services & Publishing Co, Bloomburg, NY.	800-753-3727
Ziff-Davis Press, Emeryville, CA.	800-688-0448
Zondervan Publishing House, Grand Rapids, MI.	(cust serv) 800-727-1309

How to Obtain an ISBN

Emery Koltay
Director
United States ISBN Agency

The International Standard Book Numbering (ISBN) system was introduced into the United Kingdom by J. Whitaker & Sons Ltd., in 1967 and into the United States in 1968 by the R. R. Bowker Company. The Technical Committee on Documentation of the International Organization for Standardization (ISO TC 46) defines the scope of the standard as follows:

> . . . the purpose of this standard is to coordinate and standardize the use of identifying numbers so that each ISBN is unique to a title, edition of a book, or monographic publication published, or produced, by a specific publisher, or producer. Also, the standard specifies the construction of the ISBN and the location of the printing on the publication.
>
> Books and other monographic publications may include printed books and pamphlets (in various bindings), mixed media publications, other similar media including educational films/videos and transparencies, books on cassettes, microcomputer software, electronic publications, microform publications, braille publications and maps. Serial publications and music sound recordings are specifically excluded, as they are covered by other identification systems. [ISO Standard 2108]

The ISBN is used by publishers, distributors, wholesalers, bookstores, and libraries, among others, in 83 countries to expedite such operations as order fulfillment, electronic point-of-sale checkout, inventory control, returns processing, circulation/location control, file maintenance and update, library union lists, and royalty payments.

Construction of an ISBN

An ISBN consists of 10 digits separated into the following parts:

1 Group identifier: national, geographic, language, or other convenient group
2 Publisher or producer identifier
3 Title identifier
4 Check digit

When an ISBN is written or printed, it should be preceded by the letters *ISBN,* and each part should be separated by a space or hyphen. In the United States, the hyphen is used for separation, as in the following example: ISBN 1-879500-01-9. In this example, 1 is the group identifier, 879500 is the publisher identifier, 01 is the title identifier, and 9 is the check digit. The group of English-speaking countries, which includes the United States, Australia, Canada, New Zealand, and the United Kingdom, uses the group identifiers 0 and 1.

The ISBN Organization

The administration of the ISBN system is carried out at three levels—through the International ISBN Agency in Berlin, Germany; the national agencies; and the publishing houses themselves. Responsible for assigning country prefixes and for coordinating the worldwide implementation of the system, the International ISBN Agency in Berlin has an advisory panel that represents the International Organization for Standardization (ISO), publishers, and libraries. The International ISBN Agency publishes the *ISBN System User's Manual*—the basic guide for all national agencies—and the *Publishers International ISBN Directory,* which is distributed in the United States by R. R. Bowker. As the publisher of *Books in Print,* with its extensive and varied database of publishers' addresses, R. R. Bowker was the obvious place to initiate the ISBN system and from which to provide the service to the U.S. publishing industry. To date, the U.S. ISBN Agency has entered more than 73,000 publishers into the system.

ISBN Assignment Procedure

Assignment of ISBNs is a shared endeavor between the U.S. ISBN Agency and the publisher. The publisher is provided with an application form, an Advance Book Information (ABI) form, and an instruction sheet. After an application is received and verified by the agency, an ISBN publisher prefix is assigned, along with a computer-generated block of ISBNs. The publisher then has the responsibility to assign an ISBN to each title, to keep an accurate record of the numbers assigned by entering each title in the ISBN Log Book, and to report each title to the *Books in Print* database. One of the responsibilities of the ISBN Agency is to validate assigned ISBNs and to retain a record of all ISBNs in circulation.

ISBN implementation is very much market-driven. Wholesalers and distributors, such as Baker & Taylor, Brodart, and Ingram, as well as such large retail chains as Waldenbooks and B. Dalton recognize and enforce the ISBN system by requiring all new publishers to register with the ISBN Agency before accepting their books for sale. Also, the ISBN is a mandatory bibliographic element in the International Standard Bibliographical Description (ISBD). The Library of Congress Cataloging in Publication (CIP) Division directs publishers to the agency to obtain their ISBN prefixes.

Location and Display of the ISBN

On books, pamphlets, and other printed material, the ISBN shall be on the verso of the title leaf or, if this is not possible, at the foot of the title leaf itself. It should also appear at the foot of the outside back cover if practicable and at the foot of the back of the jacket if the book has one (the lower right-hand corner is recommended). If neither of these alternatives is possible, then the number shall be printed in some other prominent position on the outside. The ISBN shall also appear on any accompanying promotional materials following the provisions for location according to the format of the material.

On other monographic publications, the ISBN shall appear on the title or credit frames and any labels permanently affixed to the publication. If the publication is issued in a container that is an integral part of the publication, the ISBN shall be displayed on the label. If it is not possible to place the ISBN on the item or its label, then the number should be displayed on the bottom or the back of the container, box, sleeve, or frame. It should also appear on any accompanying material, including each component of a multitype publication.

Printing of ISBN in Machine-Readable Coding

In the last few years, much work has been done on machine-readable representations of the ISBN, and now all books should carry ISBNs in bar code. The rapid worldwide extension of bar code scanning has brought into prominence the 1980 agreement between the International Article Numbering, formerly the European Article Numbering (EAN), Association and the International ISBN Agency that allows the ISBN to be translated into an EAN bar code.

All EAN bar codes start with a national identifier (00–09 representing the United States), *except* those on books and periodicals. The agreement replaces the usual national identifier with a special "Bookland" identifier represented by the digits 978 for books (see Figure 1) and 977 for periodicals. The 978 Bookland/EAN prefix is followed by the first nine digits of the ISBN. The check digit of the ISBN is dropped and replaced by a check digit calculated according to the EAN rules.

Figure 1 / Printing the ISBN in Bookland/EAN Symbology

ISBN 1 - 879500 - 01 - 9

9 781879 500013

The following is an example of the conversion of the ISBN to ISBN Bookland/EAN:

ISBN	1-879500-01-9
ISBN without check digit	1-879500-01
Adding EAN flag	978187950001
EAN with EAN check digit	9781879500013

Five-Digit Add-On Code

In the United States, a five-digit add-on code is used for additional information. In the publishing industry, this code can be used for price information or some other specific coding. The lead digit of the five-digit add-on has been designated a currency identifier, when the add-on is used for price. Number 5 is the code for the U.S. dollar; 6 denotes the Canadian dollar; 1 the British pound; 3 the Australian dollar; and 4 the New Zealand dollar. Publishers that do not want to indicate price in the add-on should print the code 90000 (see Figure 2).

Figure 2 / Printing the ISBN Bookland/EAN Number in Bar Code
with the Five-Digit Add-On Code

ISBN 0-9628556-4-2

50995>

9 780962 855641

978 = ISBN Bookland/EAN prefix
5 + Code for U.S. $
0995 = $9.95

ISBN 1 - 879500 - 01 - 9

90000

9 781879 500013

90000 means no information
in the add-on code

Reporting the Title and the ISBN

After the publisher reports a title to the ISBN Agency, the number is validated and the title is listed in the many R. R. Bowker hard-copy and electronic publications, including *Books in Print, Forthcoming Books, Paperbound Books in Print, Books in Print Supplement, Books Out of Print, Books in Print Online, Books in Print Plus-CD ROM, Children's Books in Print, Subject Guide to Children's Books in Print, On Cassette: A Comprehensive Bibliography of Spoken Word Audiocassettes, Variety's Complete Home Video Directory, Software Encyclopedia, Software for Schools,* and other specialized publications.

For an ISBN application form and additional information, write to United States ISBN Agency, R. R. Bowker Company, 121 Chanlon Rd., New Providence, NJ 07974, or call 908-665-6770.

How to Obtain an ISSN

National Serials Data Program
Library of Congress

Two decades ago, the rapid increase in the production and dissemination of information and an intensified desire to exchange information about serials in computerized form among different systems and organizations made it increasingly clear that a means to identify serial publications at an international level was needed. The International Standard Serial Number (ISSN) was developed and has become the internationally accepted code for identifying serial publications. The number itself has no significance other than as a brief, unique, and unambiguous identifier. It is an international standard, ISO 3297, as well as a U.S. standard, ANSI/NISO Z39.9. The ISSN consists of eight digits in arabic numerals 0 to 9, except for the last, or check, digit, which can be an X. The numbers appear as two groups of four digits separated by a hyphen and preceded by the letters ISSN—for example, ISSN 1234-5679.

The ISSN is not self-assigned by publishers. Administration of the ISSN is coordinated through the ISSN Network, an intergovernmental organization within the UNESCO/UNISIST program. The network consists of national and regional centers, coordinated by the ISSN International Centre. Centers have the responsibility to register serials published in their respective countries.

Because serials are generally known and cited by title, assignment of the ISSN is inseparably linked to the key title, a standardized form of the title derived from information in the serial issue. Only one ISSN can be assigned to a title; if the title changes, a new ISSN must be assigned. Centers responsible for assigning ISSNs also construct the key title and create an associated bibliographic record.

The ISSN International Centre handles ISSN assignments for international organizations and for countries that do not have a national center. It also maintains and distributes the collective ISSN database that contains bibliographic records corresponding to each ISSN assignment as reported by the rest of the network. The database contains more than 600,000 ISSNs.

In the United States, the National Serials Data Program at the Library of Congress is responsible for assigning and maintaining the ISSN for all U.S. serial titles. Publishers wishing to have an ISSN assigned can either request an application form from or send a current issue of the publication to the program and ask for an assignment. Assignment of the ISSN is free, and there is no charge for its use.

The ISSN is used all over the world by serial publishers to distinguish similar titles from each other. It is used by subscription services and libraries to manage files for orders, claims, and back issues. It is used in automated check-in systems by libraries that wish to process receipts more quickly. Copyright centers use the ISSN as a means to collect and disseminate royalties. It is also used as an identification code by postal services and legal deposit services. The ISSN is included as a verification element in interlibrary lending activities and for union catalogs as a collocating device. In recent years, the ISSN has been incorporated into bar codes for optical recognition of serial publications and into the standards for the identification of issues and articles in serial publications.

For further information about the ISSN or the ISSN network, U.S. libraries and publishers should contact the National Serials Data Program, Library of Congress, Washington, DC 20540-4160 (202-707-6452; FAX 202-707-6333). Non-U.S. parties should contact the ISSN International Centre, 20 rue Bachaumont, 75002 Paris, France. Telephone: (1) 42-36-73-81.

Distinguished Books

Best Books of 1993

This is the forty-seventh year in which the Notable Books Council of the Reference and Adult Services Division of the American Library Association has issued its list of "Notable Books" for adults.

Fiction

Coyle, Beverly. *In Troubled Waters*. Houghton. $19.45.

Eugenides, Jeffrey. *Virgin Suicides*. Farrar. $18.

Gaines, Ernest. *A Lesson Before Dying*. Knopf. $21.

Jones, Thom. *The Pugilist at Rest and Other Stories*. Little, Brown. $18.95.

Klima, Ivan. *Judge on Trial*. Knopf. $25.

McCracken, Elizabeth. *Here's Your Hat, What's Your Hurry?* Random. $20.

Malouf, David. *Remembering Babylon*. Pantheon. $20.

Nordan, Lewis. *Wolf Whistle*. Algonquin. $16.95.

Proulx, E. Annie. *The Shipping News*. Macmillan. $20.

Russo, Richard. *Nobody's Fool*. Random. $23.

Watson, Larry. *Montana 1948*. Milkweed. $18.95.

Poetry

Fiser, Karen. *Words Like Fate and Pain*. Zoland. $9.95.

Van Duyn, Mona. *If It Be Not I*. Knopf. $25.

Nonfiction

Arenas, Reinaldo. *Before Night Falls*. Viking. $23.

Chernow, Ron. *The Warburgs*. Random. $30.

Delany, Sarah and A. Elizabeth. *Having Our Say: The Delany Sisters' First 100 Years*. Kodansha. $20.

Drakulic, Slavenka. *Balkan Express*. Norton. $19.95.

Kaplan, Robert D. *Balkan Ghosts*. St. Martin's. $22.95.

Kaysen, Susanna. *Girl, Interrupted*. Turtle Bay. $17.

Kelly, Michael. *Martyr's Day*. Random. $23.

Kennedy, Paul. *Preparing for the Twenty-First Century*. Random. $14.

Mills, Kay. *This Little Light of Mine*. Dutton. $24.

Prejean, Helen, C.S.J. *Dead Man Walking*. Random. $21.

Remnick, David. *Lenin's Tomb*. Random. $25.

Schaller, George B. *The Last Panda*. Univ. of Chicago Press. $24.95.

Vidal, Gore. *United States: Essays, 1952–1992*. Random. $37.50.

Best Young Adult Books of 1993

In January each year a committee of the Young Adult Library Services Association of the American Library Association (ALA) compiles a list of best books published for young adults in the last 16 months, selected for their proven or potential appeal to the personal reading taste of the young adult. *School Library Journal (SLJ)* also provides a list of best books for young adults. Books on the 1993 list, which was published in the December 1993 issue of the journal, all meet one or a combination of criteria including topical appeal to young adults and outstanding literary quality. The following list combines the titles selected for both lists. The notation "ALA" or *"SLJ"* following the price indicates the source of each selection.

Alcock, Vivien. *Singer to the Sea God.* Delacorte. $15. ALA.

Anderson, Rachel. *The Bus People.* Holt. $13.95. ALA.

Ashe, Arthur. *Days of Grace.* Random. $24. ALA.

Atkin, S. Beth. *Voices from the Fields: Children of Migrant Farmworkers Tell Their Stories.* Little, Brown. $16.95. ALA.

Bedford, Simi. *Yoruba Girl Dancing.* Viking. $19. *SLJ.*

Berg, Elizabeth. *Durable Goods.* Random. $17. ALA, *SLJ.*

Block, Francesca Lia. *Missing Angel Juan.* Harper. $14. ALA.

Blume, Judy. *Here's to You, Rachel Robinson.* Orchard. $14.95. ALA.

Brandenburg, Jim. *To the Top of the World: Adventures with Arctic Wolves.* Photos by the author. Walker. $16.95. ALA.

Bruchac, Joseph. *Dawn Land.* Fulcrum. $19.95. ALA.

Cohen, David. *America: Then and Now.* Harper. $40. *SLJ.*

Conly, Jane Leslie. *Crazy Lady!* Harper. $13. ALA.

Cooney, Caroline B. *Whatever Happened to Janie?* Delacorte. $15.95. ALA.

Crutcher, Chris. *Staying Fat for Sarah Byrnes.* Greenwillow. $14. ALA.

Delany, Sarah, and A. Elizabeth. *Having Our Say: The Delany Sisters' First 100 Years.* Kodansha. $20. ALA.

deLint, Charles. *Dreams Underfoot.* Tor. $22.95. *SLJ.*

Deuker, Carl. *Heart of a Champion.* Little, Brown. $15.95. ALA.

Dickinson, Peter. *A Bone from a Dry Sea.* Delacorte. $16. ALA.

Drucker, Olga Levy. *Kindertransport.* Holt. $14.95. ALA.

Esquivel, Laura. Tr. from Spanish by Carol and Thomas Christensen. *Like Water for Chocolate.* Doubleday. $18.95. ALA.

Faragher, John Mark. *Daniel Boone: The Life and Legend of an American Pioneer.* Holt. $27.50. *SLJ.*

Feelings, Tom. *Soul Looks Back in Wonder.* Illus. by the author. Dial. $15.99. ALA.

Fleischman, Paul. *Bull Run.* Harper. $14. ALA.

Freedman, Russell. *Eleanor Roosevelt: A Life of Discovery.* Houghton. $17.95. ALA.

Gaines, Ernest J. *A Lesson Before Dying.* Knopf. $21. ALA, *SLJ.*

Garland, Sherry. *Shadow of the Dragon.* Harcourt. $10.95. ALA.

Gee, Michael. *The Champion.* Simon & Schuster. $14. ALA.

Gibbons, Kaye. *Charms for the Easy Life.* Putnam. $19.95. ALA, *SLJ.*

Grant, Cynthia. *Shadow Man.* Macmillan. $13.95. ALA.

———. *Uncle Vampire.* Macmillan. $13.95. ALA.

Guiley, Rosemary Ellen. *The Encyclopedia of Ghosts and Spirits.* Facts on File. $40. *SLJ.*

Hahn, Mary Downing. *The Wind Blows Backward.* Houghton. $13.95. ALA.

Haynes, David. *Right by My Side: A Novella.* New Rivers. $9.95. ALA.

Hobbs, Will. *Beardance.* Macmillan. $14.95. ALA.

Hodge, Merle. *For the Life of Laetitia.* Farrar. $15. ALA.

Huong, Duong Thu. *Paradise of the Blind.* Tr. from Vietnamese by Phan Huy Duong and Nina McPherson. Morrow. $20. *SLJ.*

Isaacson, Philip M. *A Short Walk Around the Pyramids and Through the World of Art.* Knopf. $20. ALA.

Janeczko, Paul B. *Stardust Otel.* Orchard. $14.95. ALA.

Janeczko, Paul B., ed. *Looking for Your Name: A Collection of Contemporary Poems.* Orchard. $14.95. ALA.

Johnson, Angela. *Toning the Sweep: A Novel.* Orchard. $13.95. ALA.

Jones, Edward P. *Lost in the City.* Photos by Amos Chan. Morrow. $19. *SLJ.*

Jordan, Sherryl. *Winter of Fire.* Scholastic. $13.95. ALA.

Katcher, Philip. *The Civil War Source Book.* Facts on File. $35. *SLJ.*

Kaysen, Susanna. *Girl, Interrupted.* Random. $17. ALA.

Kingsolver, Barbara. *Pigs in Heaven.* Harper. $22. *SLJ.*

Le Mieux, A. C. *The TV Guidance Counselor.* Morrow. $13. ALA.

Levine, Ellen. *Freedom's Children.* Putnam. $15.95. ALA.

Littlefield, Bill. *Champions: Stories of Ten Remarkable Athletes.* Little, Brown. $21.95. ALA.

Lowry, Lois. *The Giver.* Houghton. $13.45. ALA.

Lynch, Chris. *Shadow Boxer.* Harper. $14. ALA.

McKinley, Robin. *Deerskin.* Ace. $17.95. ALA, *SLJ.*

MacLachlan, Patricia. *Baby.* Delacorte. $13.95. ALA.

Macy, Sue. *A Whole New Ball Game: The Story of the All-American Girls Professional Baseball League.* Holt. $14.95. ALA.

Mazer, Harry. *Who Is Eddie Leonard?* Delacorte. $14.95. ALA.

Mazer, Norma Fox. *Out of Control.* Morrow. $14. ALA.

Merrick, Monte. *Shelter: A Novel.* Hyperion. $19.95. ALA.

Meyer, Carolyn. *White Lilacs.* Harcourt. $10.95. ALA.

Mori, Kyoko. *Shizuko's Daughter.* Holt. $15.95. ALA.

Myers, Walter Dean. *Malcolm X: By Any Means Necessary.* Scholastic. $13.95. ALA.

Napoli, Donna Jo. *The Magic Circle.* Dutton. $14.99. ALA.

Olmert, Michael. *Smithsonian Book of Books.* Smithsonian. $45. *SLJ.*

Paulsen, Gary. *Harris and Me: A Summer Remembered.* Harcourt. $13.95. ALA.

———. *Nightjohn.* Delacorte. $14. ALA.

Philbrick, Rodman. *Freak the Mighty.* Scholastic. $13.95. ALA.

Qualey, Marsha. *Revolutions of the Heart.* Houghton. $13.45. ALA.

Rendell, Ruth. *The Crocodile Bird.* Random. $20. ALA.

Reynolds, Marilyn. *Detour for Emmy.* Morning Glory. $15.95. ALA.

Rinaldi, Ann. *In My Father's House.* Scholastic. $13.95. ALA.

Roberson, Jennifer. *Lady of the Forest: A Novel of Sherwood.* Kensington. $22. ALA.

Rochman, Hazel, and Darlene Z. McCampbell, compilers. *Who Do You Think You Are? Stories of Friends and Enemies.* Little, Brown. $15.95. ALA, *SLJ.*

Ruby, Lois. *Miriam's Well.* Scholastic. $13.95. ALA.

Sleator, William. *Oddballs.* Dutton. $14.99. ALA.

Smith, Wayne. *Thor.* St. Martin's. $24.95. ALA.

Staples, Suzanne Fisher. *Haveli.* Knopf. $18. ALA.

Sutcliff, Rosemary. *Black Ships Before Troy: The Story of the Iliad.* Illus. by Alan Lee. Delacorte. $19.95. ALA.

Sweeney, Joyce. *The Tiger Orchard.* Delacorte. $15. ALA.

Tamar, Erika. *Fair Game.* Harcourt. $3.95. ALA.

Taylor, Theodore. *Timothy of the Cay.* Harcourt. $13.95. ALA.

Temple, Frances. *Grab Hands and Run.* Orchard. $14.95. ALA.

Van der Rol, Ruud, and Rian Verhoeven. *Anne Frank: Beyond the Diary—A Photographic Remembrance.* Viking. $17. ALA.

Vick, Helen Hughes. *Walker of Time.* Harbinger. $9.95. ALA.

Volavkova, Hanna, ed. *I Never Saw Another Butterfly . . . Children's Drawings and Poems from Terezin Concentration Camp, 1942–1944.* Schocken. $25. ALA.

Walker, Kate. *Peter.* Houghton. $13.95. ALA.

Watson, Larry. *Montana 1948.* Milkweed. $18.95. ALA.

Weaver, Will. *Striking Out.* Harper. $15. ALA.

The Wild West. Warner. $49.95. *SLJ.*

Wittinger, Ellen. *Lombardo's Law.* Houghton. $13.95. ALA.

Wolff, Virginia Euwer. *Make Lemonade.* Holt. $15.95. ALA.

Yep, Laurence, ed. *American Dragons: Twenty-Five Asian American Voices.* Harper. $15. ALA.

Yolen, Jane. *Briar Rose.* Tor. $17.95. *SLJ.*

Best Children's Books of 1993

A list of notable children's books is selected each year by the Notable Children's Books Committee of the Association for Library Service to Children of the American Library Association (ALA). The committee is aided by suggestions from school and public children's librarians throughout the United States. The book review editors of *School Library Journal (SLJ)* also compile a list each year, with full notations, of best books for children. The following list is a combination of ALA's 1994 choices and *SLJ*'s "Best Books of 1993," published in the December 1993 issue of *SLJ*. The source of each selection is indicated by the notation "ALA" or "*SLJ*" following each entry. [See "Literary Prizes, 1993" later in Part 5 for Newbery, Caldecott, and other award winners—*Ed.*]

Appelbaum, Diana. *Giants in the Land.* Illus. by Michael McCurdy. Houghton. $14.95. ALA, *SLJ.*

Armstrong, Jennifer. *Chin Yu Min and the Ginger Cat.* Illus. by Mary GrandPre. Crown. $15. ALA.

Asbjørnsen, Peter Christen. *Three Billy Goats Gruff.* Retold and illus. by Glen Rounds. Holiday. $14.95. *SLJ.*

Bartone, Elisa. *Peppe the Lamplighter.* Illus. by Ted Lewin. Lothrop. $14. ALA.

Bash, Barbara. *Shadows of Night: The Hidden World of the Little Brown Bat.* Illus. by the author. Sierra Club. $16.95. *SLJ.*

Bawden, Nina. *The Real Plato Jones.* Houghton. $13.95. *SLJ.*

Beake, Lesley. *Song of Be.* Holt. $14.95. ALA.

Bial, Raymond. *Amish Home.* Illus. by the author. Houghton. $14.45. ALA.

Bible. *The Story of the Creation: Words from Genesis.* Illus. by Jane Ray. Dutton. $16. *SLJ.*

Block, Francesca Lia. *Missing Angel Juan.* Harper. $14. *SLJ.*

Brandenburg, Jim. *To the Top of the World: Adventures with Arctic Wolves.* Photos by the author. Walker. $16.95. *SLJ.*

Carey, Valerie Scho. *Tsugele's Broom.* Illus. by Dirk Zimmer. Harper. $15. ALA.

Carrick, Carol. *Whaling Days.* Illus. by David Frampton. Houghton. $15.45. ALA.

Cerullo, Mary M. *Sharks: Challengers of the Deep.* Photos by Jeffrey Cobblehill. $15. *SLJ.*

Coerr, Eleanor. *Sadako.* Illus. by Ed Young. $16.95. ALA.

Cohn, Amy L., compiler. *From Sea to Shining Sea: A Treasury of American Folklore and Folk Songs.* Scholastic. $29.95. ALA, *SLJ.*

Coman, Caroline. *Tell Me Everything.* Farrar. $15. ALA, *SLJ.*

Conly, Jane Leslie. *Crazy Lady!* Harper. $13. ALA.

Cooper, Susan. *The Boggart.* Macmillan. $14.95. ALA, *SLJ.*

Cross, Gillian. *The Great American Elephant Chase.* Holiday. $14.95. *SLJ.*

Crutcher, Chris. *Staying Fat for Sarah Byrnes.* Greenwillow. $14. *SLJ.*

Cutler, Jane. *Darcy and Gran Don't Like Babies.* Illus. by Susannah Ryan. Scholastic. *$14.95. SLJ.*

Demarest, Chris L. *Lindbergh.* Illus. by the author. Crown. $15. *SLJ.*

Dickinson, Peter. *A Bone from a Dry Sea.* Delacorte. $16. ALA, *SLJ.*

Fleischman, Paul. *Bull Run.* Harper. $14. ALA, *SLJ.*

Fleming, Denise. *In the Small, Small Pond.* Illus. by the author. Holt. $15.95. ALA, *SLJ.*

Fox, Paula. *Western Wind.* Orchard. $14.95. *SLJ.*

Freedman, Russell. *Eleanor Roosevelt: A Life of Discovery.* Houghton. $17.95. ALA, *SLJ.*

Garland, Sherry. *Lotus Seed.* Illus. by Tatsura Kiuchi. Harcourt. $14.95. ALA.

Giblin, James Cross. *Be Seated: A Book about Chairs.* Harper. $15. ALA.

Gowell, Elizabeth Tayntor. *Sea Jellies: Rainbows in the Sea.* Watts. $15.90. *SLJ.*

Green, Kate. *Number of Animals.* Illus. by Christopher Wormell. Creative Ed. $19.95. ALA.

Greenberg, Jan, and Jordan Greenberg. *The Sculptor's Eye: Looking at Contemporary American Art.* Delacorte. $19.95. ALA.

Griffin, Peni R. *The Switching Well.* Macmillan. $15.95. *SLJ.*

Griffith, Helen V. *Grandaddy and Janetta.* Illus. by James Stevenson. Greenwillow. $14. ALA.

Hamilton, Virginia. *Many Thousand Gone: African Americans from Slavery to Freedom.* Illus. by Leo and Diane Dillon. Knopf. $16. ALA.

———. *Plain City.* Scholastic. $13.95. ALA, *SLJ.*

Henkes, Kevin. *Owen.* Illus. by the author. Greenwillow. $14. ALA, *SLJ.*

Hesse, Karen. *Lester's Dog.* Illus. by Nancy Carpenter. Crown. $13. *SLJ.*

Heymans, Annemie, and Margriet Heymans. *The Princess in the Kitchen Garden.* Illus. by the authors. Farrar. $16. ALA.

Hoose, Phillip. *It's Our World, Too! Stories of Young People Who Are Making a Difference.* Little, Brown. $19.95. ALA.

Isaacson, Philip M. *A Short Walk Around the Pyramids and Through the World of Art.* Knopf. $20. ALA, *SLJ.*

Johnson, Angela. *Julius.* Illus. by Dav Pilkey. Orchard. $14.95. ALA, *SLJ.*

———. *Toning the Sweep: A Novel.* Orchard. $13.95. ALA, *SLJ.*

Johnson, Paul Brett. *The Cow Who Wouldn't Come Down.* Illus. by the author. Orchard. $14.95. *SLJ.*

Johnston, Julie. *Hero of Lesser Causes.* Little, Brown. $14.95. ALA, *SLJ.*

Joyce, William. *Santa Calls.* Illus. by the author. Harper. $18. ALA, *SLJ.*

Kindl, Patrice. *Owl in Love.* Houghton. $13.95. ALA.

King-Smith, Dick. *The Cuckoo Child.* Illus. by Leslie W. Bowman. Hyperion. $13.95. *SLJ.*

Klause, Annette Curtis. *Alien Secrets.* Delacorte. $14.95. ALA, *SLJ.*

Konigsburg, E. L. *T-Backs, T-Shirts, Coat, and Suit.* Macmillan. $13.95. *SLJ.*

Kraus, Scott, and Kenneth Mallory. *The Search for the Right Whale: How Scientists Rediscovered the Most Endangered Whale in the Sea.* Crown. $14. *SLJ.*

Krull, Kathleen. *Lives of the Musicians: Good Times, Bad Times (And What the Neighbors Thought).* Illus. by Kathryn Hewitt. Harcourt. $18.95. ALA, *SLJ.*

Lavies, Bianca. *Compost Critters.* Photos by the author. Dutton. $14.99. *SLJ.*

———. *A Gathering of Garter Snakes.* Photos by the author. Dutton. $14.99. ALA.

Lawrence, Jacob. *The Great Migration: An American Story.* Illus. by the author. Harper. $22.50. ALA.

Levine, Ellen, ed. *Freedom's Children: Young Civil Rights Activists Tell Their Own Stories.* Putnam. $15.95. *SLJ.*

Lewin, Ted. *I Was a Teenage Professional Wrestler.* Illus. by the author. Orchard. $16.95. ALA, *SLJ.*

Lisle, Janet. *Forest.* Orchard. $15.95. *SLJ.*

Llorente, Pilar Molina. *The Apprentice.* Illus. by Juan Ramon Alonso. Farrar. $13. ALA.

Lowry, Lois. *The Giver.* Houghton. $13.95. ALA, *SLJ.*

Lynch, Chris. *Shadow Boxer.* Harper. $14. *SLJ.*

Lyons, Mary. *Starting Home: The Story of Horace Pippin, Painter.* Macmillan. $15.95. ALA.

McDermott, Gerald. *Raven: A Trickster Tale from the Pacific Northwest.* Illus. by the author. Harcourt. $14.95. ALA.

MacLachlan, Patricia. *Baby.* Delacorte. $13.95. ALA.

McPhail, David. *Pigs Aplenty, Pigs Galore.* Illus. by the author. Dutton. $13.99. ALA.

Macy, Sue. *A Whole New Ball Game: The Story of the All-American Girls Professional Baseball League.* Holt. $14.95. *SLJ.*

Mahy, Margaret. *The Good Fortunes Gang.* Illus. by Marian Young. Delacorte. $13.95. *SLJ.*

Martin, James. *Hiding Out: Camouflage in the Wild.* Illus. by Art Wolfe. Crown. $13. ALA.

Mazer, Anne. *The Oxboy.* Knopf. $13. ALA.

Mitchell, Margaree King. *Uncle Jed's Barbershop.* Illus. by James Ransome. Simon & Schuster. $15. ALA.

Murphy, Jim. *Across America on an Emigrant Train.* Houghton. $16.95. *SLJ.*

Myers, Walter Dean. *Brown Angels: An Album of Pictures and Verses.* Harper. $16. ALA.

Patron, Susan. *Maybe Yes, Maybe No, Maybe Maybe.* Illus. by Dorothy Donahue. Orchard. $14.95. ALA, *SLJ.*

Paulsen, Gary. *Nightjohn.* Delacorte. $14. ALA.

Peck, Richard. *Bel-Air Bambi and the Mall Rats.* Delacorte. $14.95. *SLJ.*

Pomerantz, Charlotte. *Outside Dog.* Illus. by Jennifer Plecas. Harper. $14. ALA.

Qualey, Marsha. *Revolutions of the Heart.* Houghton. $13.95. *SLJ.*

Raschka, Chris. *Yo! Yes?* Illus. by the author. Orchard. $14.95. ALA.

Reid, Barbara. *Two by Two.* Illus. by the author. Scholastic. $14.95. ALA.

Rochman, Hazel, and Darlene Z. McCampbell, compilers. *Who Do You Think You Are? Stories of Friends and Enemies.* Little, Brown. $15.95. *SLJ.*

Ross, Ramon Royal. *Harper and Moon.* Macmillan. $14.95. ALA, *SLJ.*

Sandburg, Carl. *More Rootabagas.* Illus. by Paul O. Zelinsky. Knopf. $18. ALA, *SLJ.*

Sattler, Helen Roney. *The Earliest Americans.* Illus. by Jean Day Zallinger. Houghton. $16.95. *SLJ.*

Say, Allen. *Grandfather's Journey.* Houghton. $15.95. ALA, *SLJ.*

Scieszka, Jon. *Your Mother Was a Neanderthal.* Illus. by Lane Smith. Viking. $11.99. *SLJ.*

Scott, Ann Herbert. *Cowboy Country.* Illus. by Ted Lewin. Houghton. $14.95. *SLJ.*

Seidler, Tor. *Wainscott Weasel.* Illus. by Fred Marcellino. Harper. $20. ALA.

Sendak, Maurice. *We Are All in the Dumps with Jack and Guy.* Illus. by the author. Harper. $20. ALA.

Seymour, Tres. *Hunting the White Cow.* Illus. by Wendy Anderson Halperin. Orchard. $15.95. ALA, *SLJ.*

Shannon, George. *Climbing Kansas Mountains.* Illus. by Thomas B. Allen. Macmillan. $15.95. *SLJ.*

Sills, Leslie. *Visions: Stories about Women Artists.* Whitman. $18.95. ALA.

Sis, Peter. *Komodo!* Illus. by the author. Greenwillow. $15. *SLJ.*

———. *A Small Tall Tale from the Far Far North.* Illus. by the author. Knopf. $15. ALA.

Stevens, Janet, reteller. *Coyote Steals the Blanket: A Ute Tale.* Illus. by the reteller. Holiday. $15.95. *SLJ.*

Temple, Frances. *Grab Hands and Run.* Orchard. $14.95. *SLJ.*

Trivizas, Eugene. *The Three Little Wolves and the Big Bad Pig.* Illus. by Helen Oxenbury. Macmillan. $15.95. ALA, *SLJ.*

Van Allsburg, Chris. *The Sweetest Fig.* Illus. by the author. Houghton. $17.95. ALA, *SLJ.*

Van der Rol, Ruud, and Rian Verhoeven. *Anne Frank: Beyond the Diary—A Photographic Remembrance.* Viking. $17. ALA.

Walker, Kate. *Peter.* Houghton. $13.95. ALA.

Walsh, Ellen Stoll. *Hop Jump.* Illus. by the author. Harcourt. $13.95. ALA.

Walsh, Jill Paton. *Matthew and the Sea Singer.* Illus. by Alan Marks. Farrar. $13. ALA.

Wells, Rosemary. *Max and Ruby's First Greek Myth: Pandora's Box.* Illus. by the author. Dial. $11.99. *SLJ.*

Westray, Kathleen. *Color Sampler.* Illus. by the author. Ticknor & Fields. $14.95. ALA.

Williams, Vera B. *Scooter.* Illus. by the author. Greenwillow. $15. ALA.

Wolff, Ashley. *Stella and Roy.* Illus. by the author. Dutton. $12.99. *SLJ.*

Wolff, Virginia Euwer. *Make Lemonade.* Holt. $15.95. ALA, *SLJ.*

Yep, Laurence. *Dragon's Gate.* Harper. $15. ALA.

Young, Ronder Thomas. *Learning by Heart.* Houghton. $13.95. ALA.

Bestsellers of 1993: The Sky's the Limit

Daisy Maryles

Executive Editor, *Publishers Weekly*

One of the big stories of 1993 was the expansion of superstores. *Publishers Weekly* noted that the nation's largest chains had reported sales increases of about 17 percent for the first six months, and bookstore sales in general topped $1 billion in both January and August. And while figures for the last quarter are not yet available, one can guess that they will reach an all-time high, given that 15 of the top fiction and nonfiction titles for last year garnered their astoundingly high sales in the last quarter.

Thus far in the 1990s, all of our year-end bestseller analyses have reported new sales heights. That trend continues. In 1993 just about all previous sales records were broken—sometimes by impressive margins. And since the economic news is still discouraging, and consolidations and cutbacks continue, the impressive gains enjoyed by the bestsellers can be credited to the massive amounts of retail space made available by the superstore expansion. To hit big, a title had to succeed at the national chains and discount stores.

Setting Some New Records

Nine books topped the 1 million mark in 1993, one more than the 1992 record. Three books went over 2 million, another first. And one of these (yes, *The Bridges of Madison County*) is the fastest-selling novel in publishing history, with more than 4.3 million copies sold within the year. Consider that only 10 years ago, in 1983, the top 10 bestsellers of the year *combined* did not total 4.3 million.

The number of fiction and nonfiction titles with reported sales of 100,000 copies or more (not counting religion bestsellers) also set an all-time high: 157 books—11 more than in 1992. Fiction generated most of that growth, with 85

Note: Adapted from *Publishers Weekly,* March 7, 1994.

novels passing the 100,000 sales mark. Last year the record was 75 novels. The 1993 count for nonfiction was a tad better than 1992—72 vs. 71, but it did not beat 1989's all-time high of 78.

Perhaps more significant than the sheer number of six-figure-sales titles is the huge increase in units at almost every sales level. Last year, 48 books—25 fiction and 23 nonfiction—sold more than 300,000 copies, easily beating the 1992 record of 39 titles. In 1993, 81 books sold more than 200,000 copies, outpacing 1992's 62.

In fiction, six novels reported end-of-year sales topping 1 million, nine more went over 500,000 and five others passed the 400,000 point. That was more than enough to surpass the 1992 total of 13. For 1993's nonfiction, three titles sold more than a million copies, and a fourth was just shy of that amount at year's end. Seven more passed 500,000 and another seven went over 400,000 (18 in total). Previously 1992 had held these records, also with a total of 13.

Net vs. Gross Sales

All our calculations here are based on shipped and billed figures supplied by publishers for new books issued in 1993 and 1992 (a few older titles that had made the 1993 weekly charts are also included). These figures reflect only 1993 U.S. trade sales—that is, sales to bookstores, wholesalers, and libraries. Publishers were asked not to include book club, overseas, and direct-mail sales. Also, while they were instructed to take into account returns through the end of January 1994, in many instances the 1993 sales reports include books that may still be returned.

Many more books than usual at the 100,000+ level did not appear on *PW*'s weekly bestseller lists last year, and there were even more titles that enjoyed only brief appearances. Yet the sales figures are at an all-time high, and some of the shorter stays on the weekly lists are due to bestseller competition that was keener than ever.

The big question is what the returns will be on these crucial titles, for it will be some time until the final net is figured for many of them. For all the books on the top-15 list, bestselling runs were always in the double digits. But the average weekly rates of sale for the superstars were outstanding. Rush Limbaugh's *See, I Told You So* was on the list for 13 weeks, seven in the No. 1 slot during the frenzied holiday season; reported sales were more than 2.5 million copies. It took about 52 weeks to move 2.6 million copies of his first book, *The Way Things Ought to Be*. It took about 48 weeks to move 1.3 million copies of *The Pelican Brief* in 1992; it took two weeks less for *The Client* to sell more than twice that amount in 1993.

Around the Blockbusters

It's almost a publishing truism to note that nearly all of the top 15 novelists are veterans. It's no surprise to see Grisham, Clancy, King, Steel, Rice, Turow, Ludlum, Clark, Follett, Koontz, and Clavell. In fact, except for Clavell, all of these authors made at least one appearance on these top-15 lists within the last three years.

There are some newcomers. The author who dominated the 1993 fiction charts was Robert James Waller, and he set what may be an unbeatable record with his first novel, *The Bridges of Madison County*. Waller's second novel, *Slow Waltz at Cedar Bend*, enjoyed sales of more than 1.9 million in 1993, ahead of most of the bestselling veterans.

There are a few other newcomers to the fiction top 15. Laura Esquivel's debut novel, *Like Water for Chocolate*, was still among the top five on *PW*'s weekly lists in March 1994, after 47 weeks. Its first printing was 30,000. Nick Bantock is another new name on our end-of-the-year charts (though he established a record of his own when all three Griffin and Sabine volumes appeared on our bestseller list simultaneously). The combined sales for all three—*Griffin & Sabine, Sabine's Notebook,* and *The Golden Mean*—totaled almost 1.9 million copies by the end of 1993.

In nonfiction, too, the name of the game is generally the author's name. Media personalities—Limbaugh, Howard Stern, and Jerry Seinfeld—dominate the top three spots. Bestselling authors Maya Angelou and M. Scott Peck secure the last two spots on the list. Susan Powter's ubiquitous "infomercial" certainly helped *Stop the Insanity* achieve mega-sales. Deepak Chopra, a leading writer on mind/body issues, was one of the many authors last year propelled onto the list by a successful *Oprah* appearance. Harvey Penick has two golf titles in the top 15, one a return from last year; his 1993 sales secure his spot (for the time being) as the bestselling hardcover sportswriter. Wall Street guru Peter Lynch returns with another bestselling financial advice tome: *Beating the Street*. His earlier *One Up on Wall Street* sold more than 600,000 in hardcover and paperback.

Two newcomers to the year-end nonfiction bestseller lists seem to have captured the current zeitgeist. Clarissa Pinkola Estes's exploration of the female unconsciousness in *Women Who Run with the Wolves* touched a nerve, as did John Gray's contribution to better communications between the sexes in *Men Are from Mars, Women Are from Venus*. It didn't hurt that both are accomplished and riveting speakers who did extremely well on the publicity circuit. A more curious entry in the top 15 group is anthropologist/novelist Elizabeth Marshall Thomas's *The Hidden Life of Dogs*. The high point of her media blitz was a *Newsweek* cover.

Certainly the most curious mega-seller in recent years is Betty Eadie's *Embraced by the Light* (which heads our year-end religion bestsellers). Eadie's debut, the chronicle of a near-death experience, was Gold Leaf's first publication, and it began as a regional bestseller.

Fiction Top 15

1. *The Bridges of Madison County* by Robert James Waller. Warner (4/92); 4,362,352

2. *The Client* by John Grisham. Doubleday (3/93); 2,927,376

3. *Slow Waltz at Cedar Bend* by Robert James Waller. Warner (11/93); 1,978,342

4. *Without Remorse* by Tom Clancy. Putnam (8/11/93); 1,814,173
5. *Nightmares and Dreamscapes* by Stephen King. Viking (10/93); 1,328,927
6. *Vanished* by Danielle Steel. Delacorte (8/93); 1,121,716
7. *Lasher* by Anne Rice. Knopf (10/3/93); 736,010
8. *Pleading Guilty* by Scott Turow. Farrar (6/93); 710,152
*9. *Like Water for Chocolate* by Laura Esquivel. Doubleday (10/92); **675,000
*10. *The Scorpio Illusion* by Robert Ludlum. Bantam (6/93); **600,000
11. *The Golden Mean* by Nick Bantock. Chronicle (9/6/93); 590,044
12. *I'll Be Seeing You* by Mary Higgins Clark. Simon & Schuster (5/5/93); 564,218
13. *A Dangerous Fortune* by Ken Follett. Delacorte (11/93); 529,460
14. *Mr. Murder* by Dean Koontz. Putnam (10/27/93); 529,430
15. *Gai-Jin* by James Clavell. Delacorte (6/83); 528,334

Nonfiction

1. *See, I Told You So* by Rush Limbaugh. Pocket (11/93); 2,587,600
2. *Private Parts* by Howard Stern. Simon & Schuster (10/15/93); 1,228,298
3. *Seinlanguage* by Jerry Seinfeld. Bantam (9/93); 1,106,000
4. *Embraced by the Light* by Betty J. Eadie with Curtis Taylor. Gold Leaf Press (12/92); 956,122
5. *Ageless Body, Timeless Mind* by Deepak Chopra. Crown. (7/93); 802,417
6. *Stop the Insanity* by Susan Powter. Simon & Schuster (10/13/93); 688,816
7. *Women Who Run with the Wolves* by Clarissa Pinkola Estes. Ballantine (5/92); 652,423 in 1993
8. *Men Are from Mars, Women Are from Venus* by John Gray. Harper (6/92); 582,624
9. *The Hidden Life of Dogs* by Elizabeth Marshall Thomas. Houghton (8/3/93); 548,177
10. *And If You Play Golf, You're My Friend* by Harvey Penick with Bud Shrake. Simon & Schuster (10/93); 509,219
11. *The Way Things Ought to Be* by Rush Limbaugh. Pocket (10/92); 2.6 million since publication
12. *Beating the Street* by Peter Lynch with John Rothchild. Simon & Schuster (3/10/93); 496,899

Note: Rankings are determined by sales figures provided by publishers; the numbers generally reflect reports of copies "shipped and billed" in calendar year 1993 and take into account some early returns through the end of January 1993. Publishers do not yet know what their total returns will be so none of these figures should be regarded as final net sales.

* Sales figures were submitted to *PW* in confidence, for use in placing the title on the list.

** Numbers shown are rounded down to the nearest 25,000 to indicate relationship to sales figures that are printed.

13. *Harvey Penick's Little Red Book* by Harvey Penick with Bud Shrake. Simon & Schuster (5/15/92); 496,436 in 1993

14. *Wouldn't Take Nothing for My Journey Now* by Maya Angelou. Random (3/93); 455,876

15. *Further Along the Road Less Traveled* by M. Scott Peck, M.D. Simon & Schuster (10/15/93); 435,674

The Fiction Runners-Up

This was the first time in bestseller history that novels with sales of 400,000 or more did not make the year-end top 15; there were five such in 1993. Most of the runners-up spent between two and three months on *PW*'s weekly charts, though a few fell off so quickly that the "shipped and billed" figure seems likely to drop. *Homeland* had a one-week run, *Star Wars #4: The Truce at Bakura* was on for three weeks, and *November of the Heart* was on for five weeks. These ranked sixteenth through thirtieth:

16. *The Hope* by Herman Wouk (Little, Brown, 474,000)

17. *Streets of Laredo* by Larry McMurtry (Simon & Schuster)

18. *Griffin & Sabine* by Nick Bantock (Chronicle Books, 1993 sales were 436,764; since fall 1991 publication, total sales 756,000+)

19. *Star Wars #4: The Truce at Bakura* by Kathy Tyers (Bantam)

20. *Sacred Clowns* by Tony Hillerman (Harper, 403,229)

21. *Star Wars #3: The Last Command* by Timothy Zahn (Bantam)

22. *The Night Manager* by John le Carré (Knopf, 344,258)

23. *Homeland* by John Jakes (Doubleday)

24. *Decider* by Dick Francis (Putnam, 308,883)

25. *November of the Heart* by LaVyrle Spencer (Putnam, 302,817)

26. *Honor Among Thieves* by Jeffrey Archer (Harper, 298,964)

27. *A Case of Need* by Michael Crichton (Dutton, 292,322)

28. *Cruel & Unusual* by Patricia Cornwell (Macmillan, 280,317)

29. *"J" Is for Judgment* by Sue Grafton (Holt, 279,181)

30. *Talismans of Shannara* by Terry Brooks (Ballantine, 267,671)

Higher Numbers, Lower Ranks

The big news back in 1992 was that there were six novels with reported sales of 200,000+ copies that did not make it to the list of top 30. That was a record then, but not such a big deal after viewing the 1993 group; an astounding 14 novels over the 200,000 mark didn't even make the list of fiction runners-up.

In some cases, these books performed very well on the weekly lists. *Pigs in Heaven* was on *PW*'s chart for 19 weeks and was among the top 15 fiction bestsellers at a number of the stores polled for our lists. *Sabine's Notebook* was on for 14 weeks, after an 11-week 1992 showing. *A Season in Purgatory* enjoyed an

11-week run on our weekly charts; *Close Combat* was on the lists for eight weeks, *American Star* and *Angel* had seven weeks apiece, and *Fire in Heaven*, five. Both *Pot of Gold* and *The Death and Life of Superman* placed on the weekly charts for four weeks; *Thunderpoint* was on for three.

Books that did not appear even once on our charts include *Where There's Smoke, Finnegan's Week,* and *A Time to Kill.* Because the latter—Grisham's debut—was a hardcover reissue of a 1993 mass market bestseller, many booksellers perhaps didn't bother to count it among their top-selling frontlist. But for most of the books that had a brief or no presence on the weekly national charts, these impressive "shipped and billed" sales figures may come back to haunt publishers' ledgers.

The 14 books with sales of more than 200,000 are: *Sabine's Notebook* by Nick Bantock (Chronicle, 254,755 in 1993; 537,716 since fall 1992 publication); *American Star* by Jackie Collins (Simon & Schuster); *A Season in Purgatory* by Dominick Dunne (Crown, 243,810); *Where There's Smoke* by Sandra Brown (Warner, 243,500); *A Time to Kill* by John Grisham (Doubleday); *Pot of Gold* by Judith Michael (Poseidon); *Finnegan's Week* by Joseph Wambaugh (Morrow, 224,979); *Fires of Heaven* by Robert Jordan (Tor, 222,199); *The Death and Life of Superman* by Roger Stern (Bantam); *Pigs in Heaven* by Barbara Kingsolver (Harper, 213,976); *Angel* by Barbara Taylor Bradford (Random, 212,999); *Close Combat* by W. E. B. Griffin (Putnam, 207,982); and *Thunderpoint* by Jack Higgins (Putnam, 204,315).

More No-Shows for High Numbers

A record number of 16 novels with sales of 150,000+ didn't make 1993's top 30 list, breaking the record of 11 set in 1992. Once again the performance of these books on *PW's* weekly charts varied greatly. *Degree of Guilt* had an impressive 15-week run, followed by *After All These Years,* with 10 weeks. Books that had a run of four or more weeks included *Hill Towns, Devil's Waltz, Perfect, The Robber Bride, Shining Ones,* and *Forward the Foundation.* Books by Susan Hill, Dale Brown, Diane Duane, and John Saul did not appear at all.

The 16 titles are: Judith McNaught's *Perfect* (Pocket); Susan Hill's *Mrs. DeWinter* (Morrow); Susan Isaacs's *After All These Years* (Harper); Dale Brown's *Chains of Command* (Putnam); Phillip Margolin's *Gone, but Not Forgotten* (Doubleday); Diane Duane's *Dark Mirror* (Pocket); Lawrence Sanders's *McNally's Risk* (Putnam); Garrison Keillor's *Book of Guys* (Viking); Richard North Patterson's *Degree of Guilt* (Knopf); David Eddings's *The Shining Ones* (Ballantine); Margaret Atwood's *The Robber Bride* (Doubleday); John Saul's *Guardian* (Fawcett); Anne Rivers Siddons's *Hill Towns* (Harper); Jonathan Kellerman's *Devil's Waltz* (Bantam), and Isaac Asimov's *Forward the Foundation* (Doubleday).

The 1993 total for 125,000+ is 12 books, down from the all-time high of 15 such performers in 1992. Last year there were nine additional fiction titles that racked up sales of 100,000 or more; in 1992, that figure was 13.

In the 125,000+ group, half of the titles were on the 1993 weekly charts for more than one month, with *Einstein's Dreams* spending an impressive 19 weeks.

Much of this longevity was due to the book's impressive performance at the independents. *Saving Grace* and *Whispers* had brief stays of two weeks and one week, respectively. Meanwhile Stephen Coonts, Eugenia Price, Sandra Brown, and Nick Bantock never cracked the national weekly charts last year.

The dozen 1993 titles with sales over 125,000 are: *Red Horseman* by Stephen Coonts (Pocket); *Along Came a Spider* by James Patterson (Little, Brown); *Einstein's Dreams* by Alan Lightman (Pantheon); *Where Shadows Go* by Eugenia Price (Doubleday); *Saving Grace* by Julie Garwood (Pocket); *Winter Prey* by John Sandford (Putnam); *Strip Tease* by Carl Hiaasen (Knopf); *Whispers* by Belva Plain (Delacorte); *Paper Doll* by Robert B. Parker (Putnam); *Adam's Fall* by Sandra Brown (Bantam); *Hotel Pastis* by Peter Mayle (Knopf); and *The Egyptian Jukebox* by Nick Bantock (Viking).

In the group of 14 more novels with sales over 100,000, only four made it to *PW*'s weekly charts: *Prime Witness* by Steve Martini and Lilian Jackson Braun's *The Cat Who Went into the Closet* (both Putnam); *Smilla's Sense of Snow* by Peter Hoeg (Farrar); and Amanda Quick's *Deception* (Bantam).

The other 10 have yet to make an appearance. They are: *Creatures of the Kingdom* by James A. Michener (Random), *Texas Sunrise* by Fern Michaels (Ballantine), *The Black Opal* by Victoria Holt (Doubleday), *Fortune's Favorites* by Colleen McCullough (Morrow), *The Chronicles of Pern: First Fall* by Anne McCaffrey (Ballantine), *The Wyndham Legacy* by Catherine Coulter (Putnam), *Star Flight* by Phyllis Whitney (Crown), *Assumed Identity* by David Morrell (Warner); *Interest of Justice* by Nancy Taylor Rosenberg (Dutton); and *Cauldron* by Larry Bond (Warner).

Nonfiction Runners-Up

Many of the titles in the second tier of top sellers had long tenures on the weekly charts, often more than four months. These included *Eat More, Weigh Less,* Dean Ornish's tome for good health; *Reengineering the Corporation* (27 weeks in 1993 alone); *Healing & the Mind* (23 weeks, twice at No. 1); *A Woman's Worth* (19 weeks, four times in the lead); and *Listening to Prozac* (18 weeks, and also a *Newsweek* cover story). All were also ranked frequently by the chains and independents among their top 25.

Two books, by Charles Givens and Jeff Smith, never secured a footing on the 1993 weekly charts, although the latter came very close many times.

16. *Maybe (Maybe Not)* by Robert Fulghum (Villard, 428,806)

17. *Eat More, Weigh Less* by Dean Ornish, M.D. (Harper, 427,881)

18. *A Marriage Made in Heaven . . . or Too Tired for an Affair* by Erma Bombeck (Harper, 420,975)

19. *Reengineering the Corporation* by Michael Hammer & James Champy (Harper, 375,499).

20. *Healing and the Mind* by Bill Moyers (Doubleday, 362,768)

21. *Love Can Build a Bridge* by Naomi Judd with Bud Schaetzle (Random, 345,770)

22. *Star Trek Memories* by William Shatner with Chris Kreski (Harper, 335,004)
23. *A Woman's Worth* by Marianne Williamson (Random, 314,401)
24. *The Downing Street Years* by Margaret Thatcher (Harper, 287,521)
25. *The Winner Within* by Pat Riley (Putnam, 272,738)
26. *Superself: Doubling Your Personal Effectiveness* by Charles J. Givens (Simon & Schuster)
27. *The Frugal Gourmet Cooks Italian* by Jeff Smith (Morrow, 267,680)
28. *The Book of Virtues,* ed. by William J. Bennett (Simon & Schuster, 258,153 last year, but considering how well it's doing so far in 1994, that figure will likely mushroom)
29. *Listening to Prozac* by Peter Kramer (Viking, 236,534)
30. *How to Satisfy a Woman Every Time . . .* by Naura Hayden (Bibli O'Phile, 222,013 in 1983, in addition to about 1 million copies sold in 1992)

More Nonfiction Hits

Eighteen books with sales over 150,000 copies are not among the top 30 for 1993; seven of these sold more than 200,000. That's a drastic increase over 1992, when only five titles boasted 150,000+ sales, and a 200,000-copy seller earned the No. 26 spot.

The longest-running bestseller in this group was *Care of the Soul* by Thomas Moore. According to Harper, total hardcover sales for the book since its May 1992 publication are close to 280,000 copies. The books by Arthur Ashe and David Halberstam enjoyed the No. 1 spot for two weeks apiece.

Eight books did not achieve a rank on *PW*'s weekly charts. Four of these are cookbooks—a category that is often is not counted by booksellers when calculating frontlist bestsellers.

Titles with sales of 150,000+ are: *The Best Cat Ever* by Cleveland Amory (Little, Brown); *Days of Grace* by Arthur Ashe (Knopf); *Secrets of a Sparrow* by Diana Ross (Random); *The Fifties* by David Halberstam (Random); *Better Homes and Gardens New Dieter's Cookbook* (Meredith); *Having Our Say* by Sarah and A. Elizabeth Delany (Kodansha); *Richard Simmons' Never Give Up* by Richard Simmons (Warner); *Food: Your Miracle Medicine* by Jean Carper (Harper); *Fountain of Age* by Betty Friedan (Simon & Schuster); *More Memories* by Ralph Emery (Putnam); *Care of the Soul* by Thomas Moore (Harper); *Den of Lions: Memoirs of Seven Years* by Terry Anderson (Crown); *Chef Paul Prudhomme's Fork in the Road* by Paul Prudhomme (Morrow); *Black Holes & Baby Universes* by Stephen Hawking (Bantam); *I Took a Lickin' and Kept on Tickin'* by Lewis Grizzard (Random); *Complete Book of Baking* by Pillsbury (Viking); *Fannie Flagg's Original Whistle Stop Cafe Cookbook* by Fannie Flagg (Fawcett); and *The Real Anita Hill* by David Brock (Free Press).

Twelve titles had sales between 125,000 and 149,000 in 1993, three less than 1992's tally. Six of these didn't make the weekly charts, including books by Oliver North, Dennis Byrd, and Alex Haley.

The 1993 125,000+ group: *Mama Makes Up Her Mind* by Bailey White (Addison Wesley); *One More Mission* by Oliver North (Harper); *A World Waiting to Be Born* by M. Scott Peck (Bantam); *Rise & Walk: The Trial & Triumph of Dennis Byrd* by Dennis Byrd (Harper); *Grow Rich Slowly* by Don Underwood & Paul Brown (Viking); *Alex Haley's Queen* by Alex Haley & David Stevens (Morrow); *Case Closed* by Gerald Posner (Random); *Official & Confidential* by Anthony Summers (Putnam); *The Stanley Complete Step-by-Step Book of Home Repair and Improvement* by James A. Hufnagel (Simon & Schuster); *The Last Brother* by Joe McGinniss (Simon & Schuster); *Weight Watchers' Favorite Homestyle Recipes* (Dutton); and *Cooking with Regis and Kathie Lee* by Regis Philbin and Kathie Lee Gifford (Hyperion).

There were 12 nonfiction titles with reported sales of 100,000 or more in 1993, nine less than in 1992. Only four achieved the weekly charts: *Outsmarting the Female Fat Cell* by Debra Waterhouse (Hyperion); *The Angel Book: A Handbook for Aspiring Angels* by Karen Goldman (Simon & Schuster); *Secret Ceremonies* by Deborah Laake (Morrow); and *A History of God* by Karen Armstrong (Knopf).

The other 100,000+ nonfiction: *Nothin' but Good Times Ahead* by Molly Ivins (Random); *Power Thoughts* by Robert Schuller (Harper); *New Times in the Old South* by Marilyn Schwartz (Crown); *Bread Machine Baking: Perfect Every Time* by Lora Brody & Millie Apter (Morrow); *The Whole Ten Yards* by Frank Gifford (Random); *Thinking Out Loud* by Anna Quindlen (Random); *Sharkproof* by Harvey Mackay (Harper); and *President Kennedy* by Richard Reeves (Simon & Schuster).

Children's Books: Hollywood and Horror

Diane Roback
Children's Book Editor, *Publishers Weekly*

With slashers stalking shopping malls and mummies lurking in graveyards, the horror genre hit its stride in 1993—to the obvious delight of young fans and savvy publishers, but to the dismay of many parents and educators. Hollywood provided the inspiration for some of the biggest picture book titles—even the latest Waldo adventure. But even though Jurassic Park brought T. rex back to life for some gigantic sales, it was another dinosaur—a grinning purple fellow named Barney—that topped the charts.

For this roundup, publishers supplied sales figures for frontlist hardcovers that sold more than 75,000 copies in 1993; and frontlist paperbacks, backlist hardcovers, and backlist paperbacks that sold more than 100,000 copies. We asked publishers to supply trade sales figures only, reflecting returns as of February 1. Since figures do not include total returns, they consequently do not necessarily represent net sales. Some books appear without sales figures; these were submitted to *Publishers Weekly* in confidence, for use only in ranking the titles.

Slowing Sales?

Is the children's book industry in a slump, as many have been reporting? The hardcover frontlist figures certainly support this observation. In 1992, 38 new hardcovers sold more than 100,000 copies; in 1993, only 26 titles claimed that distinction. Of the 48 frontlist hardcovers that sold more than 75,000 copies in 1993, 10 are connected to films (seven of which are Disney tie-ins), and another 10 are based on TV shows (seven of which are Barney titles). Other top scorers are new titles by established children's book creators: Maurice Sendak, Jan Brett, William Joyce, Chris Van Allsburg, Alexandra Day.

In other significant showings, the two latest I Spy picture books sold a combined 300,000 copies. Single titles of note are a poetry collection from Jack Prelutsky, *The Dragons Are Singing Tonight;* a folklore anthology, *From Sea to Shining Sea,* which sold 90,600 copies with a $29.95 list price; a first picture book from greeting-card artist Mary Engelbreit, *The Snow Queen;* and, novels being a rarity on this list, Lynne Reid Banks's *The Mystery of the Cupboard.*

A Horror-ble Year

In paperback frontlist, the dinos of Barney and *Jurassic Park* battle it out for supremacy: four titles from each camp claim spots in the top ten. And horror books follow closely on their heels: books from Christopher Pike (four of his paperbacks sold more than 175,000 copies), R. L. Stine's Fear Street series (with three titles above 150,000 copies and four more above 100,000), and Stine's Goosebumps line, all the rage with middle-graders (three Goosebumps titles sold more than 200,000 copies each, and seven more sold over 150,000 copies).

Also scoring well in paperback frontlist is the now-perennial Baby-sitters Club series (11 titles sold over 150,000 copies; 23 BSC titles sold over 100,000 copies); and the three new American Girls titles from Pleasant Company starring Addy.

If you knock off the scary books, the sitter books and the Barney and Disney titles, what's left (and above 150,000 copies there's very little left indeed) is largely Sweet Valley High, Thomas the Tank Engine, the Berenstain Bears and the sole "literary" title over the 100,000-copy mark, Anne Fine's *Alias Madame Doubtfire,* catapulted to success by the hit Robin Williams film.

Looking Back on Backlist

Although backlist is still the heart of the children's book business, this year's numbers reflect a noticeable fall-off in the category. In 1993, only 47 backlist hardcovers sold over 100,000 copies, compared to 73 titles in 1992. That peripatetic Waldo traveled below the 100,000 mark (in 1992 three Waldo titles sold more than 200,000 copies each); Random had only 15 titles on the list (13 of which were Dr. Seuss and Beginner Books), compared to 24 titles in 1992; and such success stories as *The Very Hungry Caterpillar, The Wheels on the Bus,* and *Chicka Chicka Boom Boom!* all dropped out of contention.

The paperback backlist list yielded a much more varied set of titles: Disney fare; perennial backlist (and school) staples such as *The Outsiders* and *Roll of Thunder, Hear My Cry*; Berenstain Bears; Sesame Street; Roald Dahl; and Mercer Mayer.

Hardcover Frontlist Bestsellers

200,000+

1. *Barney's Farm Animals.* Kimberly Kearns and Marie O'Brien, illus. by Karen Malzeke-McDonald. Lyons/Barney (1,045,674)
2. *Barney's Favorite Mother Goose Rhymes.* Stephen White, illus. by Mary Grace Eubank. Lyons/Barney (926,150)
3. *Baby Bop's Toys.* Kimberly Kearns and Marie O'Brien. Lyons/Barney (793,902)
4. *Barney's Color Surprise.* Mary Ann Dudko and Margie Larsen. Lyons/Barney (712,175)
5. *Baby Bop's Counting Book.* Mary Ann Dudko and Margie Larsen. Lyons/Barney (604,026)
6. *Where's Waldo? In Hollywood.* Martin Handford. Candlewick (395,421)
7. *Aladdin* (Disney Classic). Penguin (338,671)
8. *Baby Bop Discovers Shapes.* Stephen White, illus. by Larry Daste. Lyons/Barney (290,636)
9. *Poky Puppy's First Christmas.* Justine Korman, illus. by Jean Chandler. Western (250,243)
10. *Beauty and the Beast: Teapot's Tale.* Justine Korman, illus. by Peter Emslie. Western (227,142)

100,000+

11. *Barney Goes to the Zoo.* Linda Cress Dowdy, illus. by Karen Malzeke-McDonald. Lyons/Barney (194,559)
12. *Santa Calls.* William Joyce. Harper (189,079)
13. *Snow White* (Disney Classic). Penguin (187,650)
14. *We Are All in the Dumps with Jack and Guy.* Maurice Sendak. Harper (183,774)
15. *Carl Goes to Daycare.* Alexandra Day. Farrar (175,000)
16. *The Shiny Skates.* Elizabeth Koda-Callan. Workman (168,000)
17. *I Spy Mystery.* Jean Marzollo, photos by Walter Wick. Scholastic (161,800)
18. *Goodnight Opus.* Berkeley Breathed. Little, Brown (145,539)
19. *Christmas Trolls.* Jan Brett. Putnam (142,528)
20. *I Spy Fun House.* Jean Marzollo, photos by Walter Wick. Scholastic (141,000)
21. *The Secret Garden.* Diane Molleson. Scholastic (140,700)

22. *The Baby-sitter's Club Chain Letter.* Ann M. Martin. Scholastic (133,500)
23. *Mary Engelbreit's The Snow Queen.* Hans Christian Andersen, illus. by Mary Engelbreit. Workman (130,000)
24. *Aladdin* (Pop-Up). Illus. by Diana Wakeman. Disney (116,684)
25. *The Dragons Are Singing Tonight.* Jack Prelutsky, illus. by Peter Sis. Greenwillow
26. *Stephen Biesty's Cross-Sections Man-of-War.* Stephen Biesty and Richard Platt. Dorling Kindersley (109,000)

75,000+

27. *The Nightmare Before Christmas.* Tim Burton. Hyperion (98,926)
28. *The Sweetest Fig.* Chris Van Allsburg. Houghton (94,864)
29. *Nutcracker Story Book Set and Advent Calendar.* Mary Packard, illus. by Nan Brooks. Workman (94,000)
30. *Cinderella.* William Wegman. Hyperion (91,123)
31. *From Sea to Shining Sea.* Compiled by Amy L. Cohn. Scholastic (90,600)
32. *Animalia* (new edition). Graeme Base. Abrams (87,000)
33. *Thomas the Tank Engine Storybook.* Rev. W. Awdry, illus. by Owain Bell. Random (86,752)
34. *Carl's Masquerade board book.* Alexandra Day. Farrar (85,000)
35. *The Mystery of the Cupboard.* Lynne Reid Banks. Morrow
36. *Beauty and the Beast.* Leslie McGuire, illus. by Russell Hicks. Western (83,072)
37. *The Cat Next Door.* Elizabeth Koda-Callan. Workman (82,000)
38. *Cinderella.* Francine Hughes, illus. by Russell Hicks. Western (81,846)
39. *George Balanchine's The Nutcracker.* Joel Meyerowitz. Little, Brown (78,302)
40. *Pat the Stimpy.* Putnam (77,556)
41. *The Christmas Star.* Marcus Pfister. North-South (77,387)
42. *Telling Time with Thomas the Tank Engine.* Rev. W. Awdry, illus. by Owain Bell. Random (77,242)
43. *Pat the Puppy.* Edith Kunhardt. Western (76,842)
44. *Little Red Riding Hood.* William Wegman. Hyperion (76,059)
45. *Stellaluna.* Janell Cannon. Harcourt Brace (75,254)
46. *The Little Mermaid.* Mary Fulton, illus. by Russell Hicks. Western (75,068)
47. *Pat the Beastie.* Illus. by Henrik Drescher. Hyperion (75,002)
48. *The Eleventh Hour* (new edition). Graeme Base. Abrams (75,000)

Paperback Frontlist Bestsellers

200,000+

1. *Barney's Hats.* Mary Ann Dudko and Margie Larsen. Lyons/Barney (1,034,031)
2. *Where Are My Shoes?* Mary Ann Dudko and Margie Larsen. Lyons/Barney (644,782)
3. *Jurassic Park: The Movie Storybook.* Adapted by Jane Mason. Putnam (461,460)
4. *Aladdin: The Genie's Tale.* Karen Kreider, illus. by Mark Manderosian. Western (439,184)
5. *Jurassic Park: The Junior Novelization.* Adapted by Gail Herman. Putnam (427,016)
6. *The Dinosaurs of Jurassic Park.* Wendy Larson. Putnam (393,067)
7. *A Tent Too Full.* Stephen White, illus. by Darren McKee and Bill Alger. Lyons/Barney (377,979)
8. *Baby Bop's ABC.* Mark Bernthal, illus. by Larry Daste. Lyons/Barney (352,700)
9. *Jurassic Park: Raptor Attack.* Adapted by Kristin Kiser. Putnam (309,935)
10. *Meet Addy.* Connie Porter, illus. by Melodye Rosales. Pleasant. (246,532)
11. *Road to Nowhere.* Christopher Pike. Pocket
12. *Cinderella.* Nikki Grimes, illus. by Don Williams. Western (231,812)
13. *Snow White.* Teddy Slater. Western (225,865)
14. *Silent Night 2 (Fear Street Super Chiller).* R. L. Stine. Pocket
15. *Jessi and the Jewel Thieves* (Baby-sitters Club Mystery No. 8). Ann M. Martin. Scholastic (211,100)
16. *Let's Get Invisible!* (Goosebumps No. 6). R. L. Stine. Scholastic (208,600)
17. *The Baby-Sitter III.* R. L. Stine. Scholastic (206,200)
18. *Eternal Enemy.* Christopher Pike. Pocket
19. *Night of the Living Dummy* (Goosebumps No. 7). R. L. Stine. Scholastic (204,400)
20. *Welcome to Camp Nightmare* (Goosebumps No. 9). R. L. Stine. Scholastic (203,200)

100,000+

21. *Sea City, Here We Come!* (BSC Super Special No. 10). Ann M. Martin. Scholastic (198,000)
22. *Addy's Surprise.* Connie Porter, illus. by Melodye Rosales. Pleasant Co. (195,194)

23. *Addy Learns a Lesson.* Connie Porter, illus. by Melodye Rosales. Pleasant Co. (194,872)
24. *The Haunted Mask* (Goosebumps No. 11). R. L. Stine. Scholastic (194,800)
25. *Claudia's Friend* (BSC No. 63). Ann M. Martin. Scholastic (194,700)
26. *The Ghost Next Door* (Goosebumps No. 10). R. L. Stine. Scholastic (191,500)
27. *The Tiny Perfect Dinosaur: Presenting Tyrannosaurus Rex.* Dale Russell and John Acorn, illus. by Ely Kish. Andrews and McMeel (191,000)
28. *The Betrayal* (Fear Street Saga No. 1). R. L. Stine. Pocket
29. *Dawn's Family Feud* (BSC No. 64). Ann M. Martin. Scholastic (188,800)
30. *Kristy and the Worst Kid Ever* (BSC No. 62). Ann M. Martin. Scholastic (186,300)
31. *The Berenstain Bears and the Bully.* Stan and Jan Berenstain. Random (185,526)
32. *The Immortal.* Christopher Pike. Pocket
33. *Little House on Rocky Ridge.* Roger Lea MacBride. Harper (184,647)
34. *Jessi and the Awful Secret* (BSC No. 61). Ann M. Martin. Scholastic (182,000)
35. *Halloween Night.* R. L. Stine. Scholastic (180,900)
36. *Stacey's Big Crush* (BSC No. 65). Ann M. Martin. Scholastic (179,900)
37. *The Girl Who Cried Monster* (Goosebumps No. 8). R. L. Stine. Scholastic (179,000)
38. *Dawn's Big Move* (BSC No. 67). Ann M. Martin. Scholastic (175,600)
39. *The Story of the Nutcracker Ballet.* Deborah Hautzig, illus. by Diane Goode. Random (175,332)
40. *The Wicked Heart.* Christopher Pike. Pocket
41. *Dawn and the Disappearing Dogs* (BSC Mystery No. 7). Ann M. Martin. Scholastic (173,900)
42. *The Werewolf of Fever Swamp* (Goosebumps No. 14). R. L. Stine. Scholastic (166,500)
43. *Maid Mary Anne* (BSC No. 66). Ann M. Martin. Scholastic (165,800)
44. *The Secret* (Fear Street Saga No. 2). R. L. Stine. Pocket
45. *Be Careful What You Wish For* (Goosebumps No. 12). R. L. Stine. Scholastic (160,100)
46. *Kristy and the Haunted Mansion* (BSC Mystery No. 9). Ann M. Martin. Scholastic (155,600)
47. *The Curse of the Mummy's Tomb* (Goosebumps No. 5). R. L. Stine. Scholastic (153,900)
48. *Piano Lessons Can Be Murder* (Goosebumps No. 13). R. L. Stine. Scholastic (152,500)
49. *Aliens Ate My Homework.* Bruce Coville, illus. by Katherine Coville. Pocket

50. *Jessi and the Bad Baby-Sitter* (BSC No. 68). Ann M. Martin. Scholastic (147,400)
51. *The Cheater* (Fear Street). R. L. Stine. Pocket
52. *Stacey and the Mystery Money* (BSC Mystery No. 10). Ann M. Martin. Scholastic (146,900)
53. *The Dead Girlfriend.* R. L. Stine. Scholastic (145,900)
54. *Logan Bruno, Boy Baby-Sitter* (BSC Special Request). Ann M. Martin. Scholastic (142,800)
55. *Sunburn* (Fear Street). R. L. Stine. Pocket
56. *Addams Family Values.* Ann Hodgman. Pocket
57. *The Burning* (Fear Street Saga No. 3). R. L. Stine. Pocket
58. *Wave Hello to Thomas.* Rev. W. Awdry, illus. by Owain Bell. Random (136,300)
59. *James in a Mess.* Rev. W. Awdry, illus. by Owain Bell. Random (135,323)
60. *A Night to Remember* (Sweet Valley High Magna Edition). Francine Pascal. Bantam (131,800)
61. *Claudia and the Mystery at the Museum* (BSC Mystery No. 11). Ann M. Martin. Scholastic (131,000)
62. *Get Well Soon, Mallory!* (BSC No. 69). Ann M. Martin. Scholastic (124,400)
63. *Stacey and the Cheerleaders* (BSC No. 70). Ann M. Martin. Scholastic (123,100)
64. *Dawn and the Surfer Ghost* (BSC Mystery No. 12). Ann M. Martin. Scholastic (120,100)
65. *Worf's First Adventure* (Star Trek: The Next Generation: Starfleet Academy No. 1). Peter David, illus. by James Fry. Pocket
66. *The Evil Twin* (SVH No. 100). Francine Pascal. Bantam (117,400)
67. *Alias Madame Doubtfire.* Anne Fine. Bantam (117,300)
68. *Karen's Big Lie* (BSLS No. 38). Ann M. Martin. Scholastic (116,900)
69. *Winnie the Pooh: Merry Christmas Mystery.* Betty Birney, illus. by Nancy Stevenson. Western (116,359)
70. *College Girls* (Sweet Valley University No. 1). Francine Pascal. Bantam (113,900)
71. *Karen's Tuba* (BSLS No. 37). Ann M. Martin. Scholastic (113,600)
72. *Karen's Friend* (BSLS No. 36). Ann M. Martin. Scholastic (113,200)
73. *Aladdin: Monkey Business.* Barbara Bazaldua, illus. by Don Williams. Western (112,586)
74. *The Berenstain Bears and the Nerdy Nephew.* Stan and Jan Berenstain. Random (111,613)
75. *Wonder's Yearling.* Joanna Campbell. Harper (111,599)
76. *The Berenstain Bears and the Drug Free Zone.* Stan and Jan Berenstain. Random (111,049)

77. *Chalk Around the Block.* Sharon McKay and David MacLeod, illus. by Marilyn Mets. Andrews and McMeel (109,000)
78. *The Muppet's Christmas Carol.* Jim Henson. Western (108,722)
79. *The Night Before Christmas.* Illus. by Jean Hirashima. Putnam (108,567)
80. *The Berenstain Bears Gotta Dance.* Stan and Jan Berenstain. Random (107,936)
81. *Loves, Lies, and Jessica Wakefield* (SVU No. 2). Francine Pascal. Bantam (107,800)
82. *The Morning After* (SVH No. 95). Francine Pascal. Bantam (107,600)
83. *Jennifer Murdley's Toad.* Bruce Coville, illus. by Katherine Coville. Pocket
84. *Karen's Wedding* (BSLS No. 39). Ann M. Martin. Scholastic (105,800)
85. *Superman: Doomsday and Beyond.* Louise Simonson. Bantam (105,200)
86. *Karen's Doll Hospital* (BSLS No. 35). Ann M. Martin. Scholastic (105,100)
87. *The Secret Garden.* Jan Carr. Scholastic (102,600)
88. *The Arrest* (SVH No. 96). Francine Pascal. Bantam (101,300)
89. *Broken Hearts* (Fear Street Super Chiller). R. L. Stine. Pocket
90. *Karen's Newspaper* (BSLS No. 40). Ann M. Martin. Scholastic (100,800)

Hardcover Backlist Bestsellers

200,000+

1. *Aladdin.* Karen Kreider, illus. by Darrell Baker. Western, 1992 (1,329,735)
2. *The Poky Little Puppy.* Janette Sebring Lowrey, illus. by Gustaf Tenggren. Western, 1942 (367,684)
3. *Brown Bear, Brown Bear, What Do You See?* Bill Martin Jr., illus. by Eric Carle. Holt, 1992 (364,863)
4. *Green Eggs and Ham.* Dr. Seuss. Random, 1960 (363,672)
5. *The Cat in the Hat.* Dr. Seuss. Random, 1957 (338,680)
6. *Aladdin* (Disney Classic). Penguin, 1992 (338,671)
7. *Oh, the Places You'll Go!* Dr. Seuss. Random, 1990 (290,792)
8. *One Fish, Two Fish, Red Fish, Blue Fish.* Dr. Seuss. Random, 1960 (282,802)
9. *Dr. Seuss's ABC Book.* Dr. Seuss. Random, 1960 (261,896)
10. *Goodnight Moon* board book. Margaret Wise Brown, illus. by Clement Hurd. Harper, 1991 (256,940)
11. *Hop on Pop.* Dr. Seuss. Random, 1963 (245,947)
12. *A Child's Year.* Joan Walsh Anglund. Western, 1992 (242,258)
13. *Snow White.* Lewis Patrick, illus. by Mones. Western, 1992 (241,738)
14. *The Giving Tree.* Shel Silverstein. Harper, 1964 (235,828)
15. *Dumbo.* Rita Balducci, illus. by Phil Ortiz and Diana Wakerman. Western, 1992 (233,104)

16. *Are You My Mother?* P. D. Eastman. Random, 1960 (214,436)
17. *Go, Dog. Go!* P. D. Eastman. Random, 1961 (202,855)
18. *Where the Sidewalk Ends.* Shel Silverstein. Harper, 1974 (201,464)
19. *Pat the Bunny.* Dorothy Kunhardt. Western, 1942 (200,724)

100,000+

20. *The Cat in the Hat Comes Back.* Dr. Seuss. Random, 1958 (176,843)
21. *Beauty and the Beast Word Book.* Barbara Bazaldua, illus. by Darrell Barker. Western, 1992 (175,518)
22. *Stephen Biesty's Incredible Cross-Sections.* Stephen Biesty. Knopf, 1992 (150,286)
23. *The Stinky Cheese Man and Other Stupid Tales.* Jon Scieszka, illus. by Lane Smith. Viking, 1992 (146,391)
24. *Polar Bear, Polar Bear, What Do You Hear?* Bill Martin Jr., illus. by Eric Carle. Holt, 1991 (146,243)
25. *I Can Read with My Eyes Shut!* Dr. Seuss. Random, 1978 (142,484)
26. *Put Me in the Zoo.* Robert Lopshire. Random, 1960 (141,336)
27. *Fox in Socks.* Dr. Seuss. Random, 1965 (136,352)
28. *The Rainbow Fish.* Marcus Pfister. North-South, 1992 (135,761)
29. *Oh, the Thinks You Can Think!* Dr. Seuss. Random, 1975 (133,765)
30. *If You Give a Mouse a Cookie.* Laura Joffe Numeroff, illus. by Felicia Bond. Harper, 1985 (131,613)
31. *The Light in the Attic.* Shel Silverstein. Harper, 1981 (129,690)
32. *The Polar Express.* Chris Van Allsburg. Houghton, 1985 (128,069)
33. *Old Turtle.* Douglas Wood, illus. by Cheng-Khee Chee. Pfeifer-Hamilton, 1991 (123,177)
34. *I Spy Christmas.* Jean Marzollo, photos by Walter Wick. Scholastic, 1992 (117,200)
35. *The Macmillan Dictionary for Children.* Macmillan, 1989 (115,819)
36. *Mirette on the High Wire.* Emily Arnold McCully. Putnam, 1992 (115,702)
37. *The Jolly Christmas Postman.* Janet and Allan Ahlberg. Little, Brown, 1991 (115,352)
38. *Pinocchio.* Diane Muldrow, illus. by Fred Marvin. Western, 1992 (113,346)
39. *Beauty and the Beast.* Teddy Slater, illus. by Ric Gonzalez and Ron Dins. Western, 1991 (112,078)
40. *On the Day You Were Born.* Debra Frasier. Harcourt, 1991 (110,408)
41. *Pinocchio* (Disney Classic). Penguin, 1992 (109,967)
42. *The Runaway Bunny* board book. Margaret Wise Brown. Harper, 1991 (109,464)
43. *The Magic Locket.* Elizabeth Koda-Callan. Workman, 1988 (107,590)
44. *If You Give a Moose a Muffin.* Laura Joffe Numeroff, illus. by Felicia Bond. Harper, 1991 (104,558)

45. *Thomas the Tank Engine and the Hide and Seek Animals.* Rev. W. Awdry, illus. by Owain Bell. Random, 1991 (103,942)
46. *The Mitten.* Jan Brett. Putnam, 1989 (102,268)
47. *The Little Mermaid: Ariel's Secret.* Denise Lewis, illus. by Sue DiCicco. Western, 1991 (100,762)

Paperback Backlist Bestsellers

200,000+

1. *Beauty and the Beast.* Rita Balducci, illus. by John Kurtz and Jose Cardona. Western, 1992 (385,046)
2. *Aladdin.* Ann Braybrooks, illus. by Phil Ortiz and Serge Michaels. Western, 1992 (366,915)
3. *The Bones Book and Skeleton.* Stephen Cumbaa. Workman, 1991 (344,043)
4. *Snow White.* Rita Balducci, illus. by Don Williams. Western, 1992 (336,606)
5. *The Little Mermaid.* Stephanie Calmenson, illus. by Franc Mateu. Western, 1991 (311,938)
6. *The Little Mermaid: Sebastian's Story.* J. Colby, illus. by John Kurtz. Western, 1992 (296,429)
7. *Precious Moments: What a Wonderful World.* Illus. by John Kurtz. Western, 1992 (274,187)
8. *The Outsiders.* S. E. Hinton. Dell, 1968 (247,600)
9. *Roll of Thunder, Hear My Cry.* Mildred Taylor. Puffin, 1991 (239,494)
10. *Charlotte's Web.* E. B. White, illus. by Garth Williams. Harper, 1974 (239,018)
11. *Little House in the Big Woods.* Laura Ingalls Wilder, illus. by Garth Williams. Harper, 1971 (237,228)
12. *Where the Wild Things Are.* Maurice Sendak. Harper, 1988 (236,811)
13. *Bridge to Terabithia.* Katherine Paterson. Harper, 1987 (232,240)
14. *The Indian in the Cupboard.* Lynne Reid Banks. Avon, 1982
15. *Beauty and the Beast.* Michael Teitelbaum, illus. by Serge Michaels. Western, 1991 (221,821)
16. *Little House on the Prairie.* Laura Ingalls Wilder, illus. by Garth Williams. Harper, 1971 (221,439)
17. *Goodnight Moon.* Margaret Wise Brown, illus. by Clement Hurd. Harper, 1977 (217,816)
18. *The Boxcar Children.* Gertrude Chandler Warner. Albert Whitman, 1989 (215,538)
19. *Sarah, Plain and Tall.* Patricia MacLachlan. Harper, 1987 (213,112)
20. *Cinderella.* Walt Disney. Western, 1987 (210,063)
21. *Where the Red Fern Grows.* Wilson Rawls. Bantam, 1984 (209,200)

22. *Alexander and the Terrible, Horrible, No Good, Very Bad Day.* Judith Viorst, illus. by Ray Cruz. Aladdin, 1987 (203,692)

23. *Farm Animals Word Book.* Hans Helweg. Random, 1984 (203,509)

24. *Say Cheese and Die!* (Goosebumps No. 4). R. L. Stine. Scholastic, 1992 (203,200)

25. *Happy Easter, Little Critter.* Mercer Mayer. Western, 1988 (202,918)

26. *The Zoo Book.* Jan Pfloog. Western, 1967 (201,094)

27. *The Lion, the Witch and the Wardrobe.* C. S. Lewis. Aladdin, 1970 (200,879)

150,000+

28. *Welcome to Dead House* (Goosebumps No. 1). R. L. Stine. Scholastic, 1992 (199,000)

29. *The Berenstain Bears and the Messy Room.* Stan and Jan Berenstain. Random, 1983 (198,017)

30. *Sesame Street: Sleep Tight.* Constance Allen, illus. by David Prebenna. Western, 1991 (193,911)

31. *Thomas the Tank Engine and the Freight Train.* Rev. W. Awdry. Random, 1991 (193,623)

32. *Hatchet.* Gary Paulsen. Puffin, 1988 (188,457)

33. *Just Me and My Dad.* Mercer Mayer. Western, 1977 (186,429)

34. *The Berenstain Bears Go to School.* Stan and Jan Berenstain. Random, 1978 (184,395)

35. *The Secret Garden.* Frances Hodgson Burnett, illus. by Tasha Tudor. Harper, 1987 (183,599)

36. *Maniac Magee.* Jerry Spinelli. Harper, 1992 (181,755)

37. *Fantasies (Beverly Hills, 90210).* K. T. Smith. Harper, 1992 (181,304)

38. *Stay Out of the Basement* (Goosebumps No. 2). R. L. Stine. Scholastic, 1992 (175,400)

39. *The Farm Book.* Jan Pfloog. Western, 1964 (174,189)

40. *The Berenstain Bears Forget Their Manners.* Stan and Jan Berenstain. Random, 1985 (173,797)

41. *A Cow on the Line.* Rev. W. Awdry. Random, 1992 (173,222)

42. *Monster* (Goosebumps No. 13). R. L. Stine. Scholastic, 1992 (172,100)

43. *The Mickey Mouse Book.* Walt Disney, illus. by Al White. Western, 1965 (169,939)

44. *Julie of the Wolves.* Jean Craighead George, illus. by John Schoenherr. Harper, 1974 (169,716)

45. *Happy Birthday, Thomas!* Rev. W. Awdry. Random, 1990 (169,609)

46. *Thomas the Tank Engine's Noisy Trip.* Rev. W. Awdry. Random, 1989 (169,187)

47. *The Tiny Perfect Dinosaur: Presenting Leptoceratops.* Dale Russell and John Acorn, illus. by Ely Fish. Andrews and McMeel, 1992 (168,000)

48. *The Berenstain Bears Learn About Strangers.* Stan and Jan Berenstain. Random, 1985 (167,177)
49. *Amelia Bedelia.* Peggy Parish, illus. by Fritz Seibel. Harper, 1992 (165,262)
50. *Merry Christmas, Mom and Dad.* Mercer Mayer. Western, 1982 (164,638)
51. *The Berenstain Bears and the New Baby.* Stan and Jan Berenstain. Random, 1974 (164,401)
52. *Number the Stars.* Lois Lowry. Dell, 1990 (160,400)
53. *James and the Giant Peach.* Roald Dahl. Puffin, 1988 (160,142)
54. *The Mouse and the Motorcycle.* Beverly Cleary. Avon, 1990
55. *Stone Fox.* John Reynolds Gardiner, illus. by Marcia Sewall. Harper, 1983 (159,036)
56. *Dinosaur Days.* Joyce Milton. Random, 1985 (158,734)
57. *Scary Stories 3: More Tales to Chill Your Bones.* Alvin Schwartz, illus. by Stephen Gammell. Harper, 1991 (158,236)
58. *The New Baby.* Mercer Mayer. Western, 1983 (156,724)
59. *Thomas Gets Tricked.* Rev. W. Awdry. Random, 1989 (155,816)
60. *Wrong Number* (Fear Street). R. L. Stine. Pocket, 1990
61. *Island of the Blue Dolphins.* Scott O'Dell. Dell, 1987 (154,100)
62. *The Sign of the Beaver.* Elizabeth Speare. Dell, 1983 (153,100)
63. *The Bug Book and the Bug Bottle.* Hugh Danks. Workman, 1987 (153,053)
64. *Shiloh.* Phyllis Reynolds Naylor. Dell, 1992 (152,200)

125,000+

65. *Beverly Hills, 90210: No Secrets.* Mel Gilden. Harper 1992 (149,183)
66. *The Berenstain Bears Visit the Dentist.* Stan and Jan Berenstain. Random, 1981 (148,654)
67. *Scary Stories to Tell in the Dark.* Alvin Schwartz, illus. by Stephen Gammell. Harper, 1986 (147,802)
68. *The Baby-Sitter.* R. L. Stine. Scholastic, 1989 (146,800)
69. *The Little Engine That Could.* Watty Piper. Putnam, 1978 (146,196)
70. *The Berenstain Bears and Too Much TV.* Stan and Jan Berenstain. Random, 1984 (144,525)
71. *Minnie 'n' Me: The Perfect Bow.* Lynstet Calder, illus. by Sue Shakespeare. Western, 1991 (144,502)
72. *The Puppy Book.* Jan Pfloog. Western, 1968 (141,728)
73. *The Berenstain Bears and the Truth.* Stan and Jan Berenstain. Random, 1983 (141,028)
74. *Baby Kermit's Playtime ABC.* Lily Jones, illus. by David Prebenna. Western, 1992 (140,983)
75. *Big Bird's Book of Big and Little.* Emily Kingsley, illus. by A. Delany. Western, 1977 (140,917)
76. *The Baby-Sitter II.* R. L. Stine. Scholastic, 1991 (140,700)

77. *Ramona Quimby, Age 8.* Beverly Cleary. Avon, 1992

78. *The Ernie and Bert Book.* Norman Stiles, illus. by Joe Mathieu. Western, 1977 (139,872)

79. *Diesel's Devious Deed.* Rev. W. Awdry. Random, 1992 (139,741)

80. *More Scary Stories to Tell in the Dark.* Alvin Schwartz, illus. by Stephen Gammell. Harper, 1986 (139,517)

81. *The Butterfly Book.* Michael Berenstain. Western, 1992 (138,467)

82. *The Return of the Indian.* Lynne Reid Banks. Avon, 1987

83. *A Wrinkle in Time.* Madeleine L'Engle. Dell, 1973 (137,900)

84. *The Berenstain Bears and Too Much Junk Food.* Stan and Jan Berenstain. Random, 1985 (137,841)

85. *My Side of the Mountain.* Jean Craighead George. Puffin, 1991 (136,818)

86. *Trouble for Thomas.* Rev. W. Awdry. Random, 1989 (136,093)

87. *Frosty the Snowman.* Carol North, illus. by Terri Super. Western, 1990 (136,005)

88. *I Was So Mad.* Mercer Mayer. Western, 1985 (134,228)

89. *The Kitten Book.* Jan Pfloog. Western, 1968 (133,017)

90. *The Berenstain Bears Don't Pollute.* Stan and Jan Berenstain. Random, 1991 (132,257)

91. *Rudolph.* Eileen Daly, illus. by Milli Juncar. Western, 1992 (131,844)

92. *Arthur Goes to Camp.* Marc Brown. Little, Brown, 1984 (130,837)

93. *The Berenstain Bears and Trouble with Friends.* Stan and Jan Berenstain. Random, 1987 (130,700)

94. *The Witch of Blackbird Pond.* Elizabeth Speare. Dell, 1972 (130,600)

95. *The Berenstain Bears and Too Much Pressure.* Stan and Jan Berenstain. Random, 1992 (129,714)

96. *The Pigman.* Paul Zindel. Bantam, 1983 (128,700)

97. *The Mother Goose Book.* Illus. by Nina Barbaresi. Western, 1982 (127,884)

98. *The Bravest Dog Ever.* Natalie Standiford. Random, 1989 (127,131)

99. *Surprise Island* (Boxcar Children Mystery No. 2). Gertrude Chandler Warner, illus. by Mary Gehr. Albert Whitman, 1989 (125,708)

100. *The Berenstain Bears and the Trouble with Grownups.* Stan and Jan Berenstain. Random, 1992 (125,491)

101. *The Berenstain Bears Get in a Fight.* Stan and Jan Berenstain. Random, 1982 (125,104)

100,000+

102. *A Very Special Critter.* Mercer Mayer. Western, 1992 (124,847)

103. *The Berenstain Bears Go to the Doctor.* Stan and Jan Berenstain. Random, 1981 (124,684)

104. *The Three Bears.* Yuri Salzman. Western, 1987 (123,781)

105. *The Velveteen Rabbit.* Margery Williams. Putnam, 1987 (123,353)

106. *Sesame Street: Splish-Splashy Day.* Liza Alexander, illus. by Joseph Ewers. Western, 1989 (122,996)

107. *The Bunny Book.* Richard Scarry. Western, 1987 (122,767)

108. *The Berenstain Bears and the Slumber Party.* Stan and Jan Berenstain. Random, 1990 (122,700)

109. *The Secret of the Indian.* Lynne Reid Banks. Avon, 1990

110. *All By Myself.* Mercer Mayer. Western, 1983 (122,287)

111. *Matilda.* Roald Dahl. Puffin, 1990 (121,942)

112. *The Berenstain Bears and the Bad Dream.* Stan and Jan Berenstain. Random, 1988 (121,796)

113. *The Truck Book.* Bill Gere, illus. by Tom LaPadula. Western, 1987 (121,345)

114. *Just Me and My Cousin.* Mercer Mayer. Western, 1992 (120,548)

115. *Tales of a Fourth Grade Nothing.* Judy Blume. Dell, 1976 (120,500)

116. *The Berenstain Bears and No Girls Allowed.* Stan and Jan Berenstain. Random, 1986 (120,355)

117. *Just Grandma and Me.* Mercer Mayer. Western, 1985 (119,453)

118. *Pinocchio.* Walt Disney. Western, 1988 (119,408)

119. *I Just Forgot.* Mercer Mayer. Western, 1988 (117,948)

120. *Cloudy with a Chance of Meatballs.* Judi Barrett, illus. by Ron Barrett. Aladdin, 1982 (117,929)

121. *In the Year of the Boar and Jackie Robinson.* Bette Bao Lord, illus. by Marc Simont. Harper, 1986 (117,735)

122. *Bambi.* Walt Disney. Western, 1987 (117,724)

123. *Bunnicula.* James Howe. Avon, 1980

124. *The Three Little Pigs.* Yuri Salzman. Western, 1988 (116,345)

125. *Chain Letter.* Christopher Pike. Avon, 1986

126. *Knot Now! The Complete Friendship Bracelet Kit.* Margaret Hartelius. Putnam, 1992 (114,857)

127. *The True Confessions of Charlotte Doyle.* Avi. Avon, 1992

128. *When I Get Bigger.* Mercer Mayer. Western, 1983 (114,464)

129. *Corduroy.* Don Freeman. Puffin, 1976 (113,908)

130. *Hopscotch the Tiny Bunny.* Stephanie Calmenson, illus. by Barbara Lanza. Western, 1991 (113,827)

131. *The Friendly Duck.* Gina Ingoglia, illus. by Deborah Bongo. Western, 1989 (112,190)

132. *The Light in the Forest.* Conrad Richter. Dell, 1990 (112,100)

133. *The Fire Engine Book.* Jesse Younger, illus. by Aurelius Battaglia. Western, 1982 (112,006)

134. *Clifford the Big Red Dog.* Norman Bridwell. Scholastic, 1963 (110,000)

135. *Frog and Toad Are Friends.* Arnold Lobel. Harper, 1979 (109,010)

136. *Party Summer* (Fear Street Super Chiller). R. L. Stine. Pocket, 1991 (109,000)

137. *Just Shopping with Mom.* Mercer Mayer. Western, 1989 (108,963)

138. *Clifford the Small Red Puppy.* Norman Bridwell. Scholastic, 1985 (108,900)

139. *Kristy's Great Idea* (BSC No. 1). Ann M. Martin. Scholastic, 1986 (108,800)

140. *The Little Prince.* Antoine de Saint-Exupéry. Harcourt, 1982 (108,718)

141. *The Little Rabbit Who Wanted Red Wings.* Carolyn Bailey. Putnam, 1988 (108,071)

142. *The Easy-to-Read Little Engine That Could.* Watty Piper. Putnam, 1986 (107,176)

143. *Mrs. Frisby and the Rats of NIMH.* Robert C. O'Brien. Aladdin, 1986 (106,659)

144. *Beverly Hills, 90210: Which Way to the Beach?* Mel Gilden. Harper, 1992 (106,038)

145. *The Runaway Bunny.* Margaret Wise Brown, illus. by Clement Hurd. Harper, 1977 (106,034)

146. *Just a Mess.* Mercer Mayer. Western, 1987 (106,008)

147. *Just for You.* Mercer Mayer. Western, 1975 (105,566)

148. *The Magic School Bus Inside the Earth.* Joanna Cole, illus. by Bruce Degen. Scholastic, 1985 (105,500)

149. *Wayside School Is Falling Down.* Louis Sachar. Avon, 1990

150. *Sesame Street: Going Places.* Jessie Smith, illus. by Joseph Ewers. Western, 1987 (104,442)

151. *Caps for Sale.* Esphyr Slobodkina. Harper, 1987 (103,931)

152. *Sideways Stories from Wayside School.* Louis Sachar. Avon, 1985

153. *Ramona the Pest.* Beverly Cleary. Avon, 1992

154. *Charlie and the Chocolate Factory.* Roald Dahl. Puffin, 1988 (102,492)

155. *The Mitten.* Jan Brett. Putnam, 1989 (102,268)

156. *The Yellow House Mystery* (Boxcar Children Mystery No. 3). Gertrude Chandler Warner. Albert Whitman, 1989 (101,858)

157. *The Grouchy Ladybug.* Eric Carle. Harper, 1986 (101,799)

158. *The Magic School Bus Lost in the Solar System.* Joanna Cole, illus. by Bruce Degen. Scholastic, 1992 (101,400)

159. *The Magic School Bus Inside the Human Body.* Joanna Cole, illus. by Bruce Degen. Scholastic, 1990 (100,200)

160. *Socks.* Beverly Cleary. Avon, 1990

161. *Runaway Ralph.* Beverly Cleary. Avon, 1991

162. *Muggie Maggie.* Beverly Cleary. Avon, 1991

163. *Chain Letter 2: The Ancient Evil.* Christopher Pike. Pocket, 1992

164. *Cheerleaders No. 1: The First Evil* (Fear Street). R. L. Stine. Pocket, 1992

Paperback Bestsellers: Banking on Brand Names

Maria Simson

Paperback Editor, *Publishers Weekly*

Saying perennial favorites dominate the lists may be something of an understatement. Stephen King had three books on the mass market list and a combined in-print total of 7,750,000; Michael Crichton's triad had 14,527,000; while John Grisham's *The Firm, The Pelican Brief* (both movie tie-ins), and *A Time to Kill* came in with a whopping 1993 in-print total of 20,342,180 copies.

The biggest in-print total for a single title in past *Publishers Weekly* surveys was 6,938,000 for Scott Turow's *Presumed Innocent* in 1991. But with *The Pelican Brief* boasting an in-print figure of 10,232,480, Grisham has taken the gold by an exceedingly comfortable margin of 3,294,480 copies.

The numbers reflect publishers' claims for copies printed in 1993 of books published in 1992 or 1993, not their sales. Because *PW* has refined the process for determining what makes a mass market bestseller in a particular year, several books published in past years dropped off. Still, the list continued to be heavy with multiple titles by a few authors. In fact, the top 12 slots in 1993 were occupied by only six authors. Other authors with two or more bestsellers were Danielle Steel, Dean Koontz, Johanna Lindsey, Anne Rice, Lawrence Sanders, Sandra Brown, Phyllis Whitney, John Sandford, Anne Rivers Siddons, Catherine Coulter, and Jayne Ann Krentz.

Many of the same names have been around for years, often for over a decade. Danielle Steel, Stephen King, Sidney Sheldon, Johanna Lindsey, Erich Segal, James Herriot, Robert Ludlum, Lawrence Sanders, Robin Cook, Kathleen E. Woodiwiss, and Phyllis Whitney were all ensconced on this year's list—much as they were on *PW*'s 1979 survey, 15 years ago.

Trade Paperbacks

If the art for trade paperbacks looks a little familiar, that's because it is. The cover of Jackson Brown, Jr.'s *Life's Little Instruction Book* has remained a constant for the past two years leading with sales of 1,500,000 in 1991 and 3,390,994 in 1992. This year Brown's *LLIB, Vol. II*, makes its appearance in the second slot with 1,483,573. In number one? Last year's No. 4, *The T-Factor Fat Gram Counter* by Jamie Pope-Cordle and Martin Katahn.

The trade paperback numbers reflect originals, reprints, or dual editions published in 1992 or 1993 for which publishers have billed and shipped at least 55,000 copies to bookstores in 1993; as such, the numbers do not always reflect net sales. As in years past, hope, humor, food, and fat continue to lead the trade paper bestsellers. While some readers looked to advice from Brown, Marianne Williamson, Robert Fulghum, Thomas Moore, Deepak Chopra, M. Scott Peck and *Bart Simpson's Guide to Life,* others were hoping to be amused by comic strips featuring Bill Watterson and Berkeley Breathed, not to mention Gary Larson, Garry Trudeau, and Garfield (trend or conspiracy?).

Note: Titles marked by an asterisk were published in 1992. Sales figures for some books were submitted in confidence, for use only in positioning titles.

Bookbuyers also enlisted a wide assortment of names for help taking off (or putting on) pounds: *T-Factor*'s Pope-Cordle, Weight Watchers, Betty Crocker, Julee Rosso, Molly O'Neill, Regis and Kathie Lee, dear old Dad (*Dad's Own Cookbook*), and TV's Dawn Wells (*Mary Ann's Gilligan's Island Cookbook*). It's worth noting that this last is one of two books based on the 1960s sitcom, along with Russell Johnson's *Here on Gilligan's Isle*.

Although not an election year, 1993 showed if anything an increase in the number of political books over 1992—in part at least because of the paperbacking of cloth originals. Martin Gross boasted two bestsellers (*The Government Racket, A Call for Revolution*) as did Vice President Al Gore (*Earth in the Balance* and *The Gore Report on Reinventing Government*) and debate opponent Ross Perot (*Not for Sale at Any Price* and *Save Your Job, Save Your Country*). Millie Bush dropped off the list, while Michael O'Donoghue's *Socks Goes to Washington* crept in on little cat feet.

One of the most memorable events of Bill Clinton's inauguration was Maya Angelou's reading of her poem *On the Pulse of Morning*, which sold a hefty 361,215 copies. It is part of a slow but marked increase of books by and about African Americans, which goes beyond the perennial Richard Wright titles and a reissue of Carter G. Woodson's 1933 *The Mis-Education of the Negro* to Angelou's *I Shall Not Be Moved*, Toni Morrison's *Jazz*, Michael Jordan's 700,000-copy seller *Rare Air*, Marion Wright Edelman's *Measure of Our Success*, Eric Copage's *Black Pearls: Daily Meditations, Affirmations and Inspirations for African Americans*, and *The Black Family Reunion Cookbook* from the National Council of Negro Women.

Literary titles generally held their own very nicely. In nonfiction, biographical accounts (Truman, Nicholas II, JFK, Richard Feynman) and current events (Andrew Hacker's *Two Nations*, Jonathan Kozol's *Savage Inequalities*, Susan Faludi's *Backlash*) continued to do very well. And in fiction, quite apart from the three movie tie-ins (*Age of Innocence, Remains of the Day*, and *Schindler's List*), there was an impressive array of titles—many by relative newcomers: Cormac McCarthy's *All the Pretty Horses*, Dorothy Allison's *Bastard Out of Carolina*, Nicholson Baker's *Vox*, Annie Dillard's first novel *The Living*, Cristina Garcia's *Dreaming in Cuban*, Susan Sontag's *The Volcano Lover*, Gloria Naylor's *Bailey's Cafe*, Pulitzer Prize-winning Robert Olen Butler's *A Good Scent from a Strange Mountain*, and Jane Smiley, who is represented not only by her NBA-winning *A Thousand Acres* but by three other backlist titles as well.

Trade Paperbacks

500,000+

* *The T-Factor Fat Gram Counter.* Jamie Pope-Cordle and Martin Katahn. Reprint. Norton

Life's Little Instruction Book, Vol. II. H. Jackson Brown, Jr. Original. Rutledge Hill (1,483,573)

The Days Are Just Packed. Bill Watterson. Original. Andrews and McMeel (1,122,000)

The Age of Innocence. Edith Wharton. Movie tie-in. Collier (932,833)

The Far Side Gallery 4. Gary Larson. Original. Andrews and McMeel (830,000)

Rare Air: Michael on Michael. Michael Jordan. Dual. Collins San Francisco (700,000)

The Chickens Are Restless. Gary Larson. Original. Andrews and McMeel (642,000)

Schindler's List. Thomas Keneally. Movie tie-in. Touchstone

* *Live and Learn and Pass It On.* H. Jackson Brown, Jr. Original. Rutledge Hill (592,563)

200,000+

Beavis & Butthead: This Book Sucks. Created by Mike Judge. Original. Pocket (415,000)

A Return to Love. Marianne Williamson. Reprint. Harper (400,924)

Submarine. Tom Clancy. Original. Berkley (379,000)

* *A Thousand Acres.* Jane Smiley. Reprint. Fawcett (370,000)

On the Pulse of Morning. Maya Angelou. Original. Random (361,215)

Not For Sale At Any Price. Ross Perot. Original. Hyperion (359,000)

Great Good Food. Julee Rosso. Dual. Crown (349,319)

Teaching Your Children Values. Original. Fireside

Betty Crocker's Cookbook, 7th Edition. Editors of Betty Crocker. Original. Prentice Hall (325,000)

The Remains of the Day. Kazuo Ishiguro. Reissue. Vintage (315,000)

Dianetics. L. Ron Hubbard. Reprint. Bridge (305,095)

Awaken the Giant Within. Anthony Robbins. Reprint. Fireside

Making of Jurassic Park. Don Shay and Jody Duncan. Original. Ballantine (296,000)

Baseball Cards, 13th Edition. Dr. James Beckett. Original. House of Collectibles (280,000)

Bottoms Up. Joyce L. Vedral. Original. Warner (274,322)

The Tightwad Gazette. Amy Dacyczyn. Original. Villard (272,061)

Zapp! The Lightning of Empowerment. William Byham. Reprint. Fawcett (268,000)

500 Beauty Solutions. Beth Barrick-Hickey. Original. Sourcebooks (261,674)

Jazz. Toni Morrison. Reprint. Plume (245,883)

Save Your Job, Save Your Country. Ross Perot and Pat Choate. Original. Hyperion (245,100)

Truman. David McCullough. Reprint. Touchstone

All the Pretty Horses. Cormac McCarthy. Reprint. Vintage (236,000)

The President's Health Security Plan. White House Domestic. Original. Times (224,440)

* *PC/Computing: How Computers Work.* Ron White. Original. Ziff-Davis (220,147)

* *Revolution from Within: A Book of Self-Esteem.* Gloria Steinem. Reprint. Little, Brown (220,000)

* *Politically, Fashionably, and Aerodynamically Incorrect: The Final Outland Collection.* Berkeley Breathed. Original. Little, Brown (206,224)

The Low-Fat Supermarket Shopper's Guide. Jamie Pope-Cordle. Original. Norton

Random Acts of Kindness. Editors of Conari Press. Original. Conari (200,000)

100,000+

Courage to Heal. Ellen Bass. Original. Harper (195,552)

Garfield Takes His Licks. Jim Davis. Original. Ballantine (182,000)

* *If I Had My Life to Live Over I Would Pick More Daisies.* Edited by Sandra Haldeman Martz. Dual. Papier-Mache (179,793)

The One Minute Manager, 10th Anniversary Edition. Kenneth Blanchard and Spencer Johnson. Reprint. Berkley (175,000)

Earth in the Balance. Al Gore. Reprint. Plume (173,605)

* *The Indispensable Calvin and Hobbes.* Bill Watterson. Original. Andrews and McMeel (171,000)

Dr. Dean Ornish's Program for Reversing Heart Disease. Dean Ornish. Reprint. Ballantine (170,000)

776 Stupidest Things Ever Said. Kathryn and Ross Petras. Original. Doubleday

Deeper Thoughts. Jack Handey. Original. Hyperion (160,900)

* *The Whole Internet User's Guide and Catalog.* Ed Krol. Original. O'Reilly and Associates (160,000)

Meditations from the Road. M. Scott Peck. Original. Fireside

The Te of Piglet. Benjamin Hoff. Reprint. Penguin (160,000)

The Entertainment Weekly Seinfeld Companion. Bruce Fretts. Original. Warner (159,214)

Star Trek Chronology. Michael and Denis Okuda. Original. Pocket (158,000)

1001 Ways to Be Romantic. Gregory J. P. Godey. Reprint. Casablanca (157,000

Divorce Busting. Michelle Weiner-Davis. Reprint. Fireside

The Wall Street Journal's Guide to Understanding Money. Wall Street Journal. Original. Fireside

* *Bread Machine Magic.* Linda Rehberg and Lois Conway. Original. St. Martin's (151,084)

The Running Press Cyclopedia: The Portable Visual Encyclopedia. Diagram Group. Original. Running Press (150,000)

Of Mice and Men. John Steinbeck. Reprint. Penguin (150,000)

You Are Not Alone. Julia Thorne. Original. Harper (149,249)

Bastard Out of Carolina. Dorothy Allison. Reprint. Plume (147,461)

* *The Government Racket.* Martin L. Gross. Reprint. Bantam (146,000)

A Call for Revolution. Martin Gross. Original. Ballantine (141,000)

* *Foods That Heal.* Dr. Bernard Jensen. Reprint. Avery (139,000)

Martha Stewart's Christmas. Martha Stewart. Reprint. Clarkson Potter (138,603)

* *Attack of the Deranged Mutant Killer Monster Snow Goons.* Bill Watterson. Original. Andrews and McMeel (137,000)

Reinventing Government. David Osborne and Ted Gaebler. Reprint. Plume (136,369)

Care of the Soul. Thomas Moore. Reprint. Harper (135,242)

Don't Know Much About Geography. Ken Davis. Reprint. Avon (135,000)

Barn Blind. Jane Smiley. Reprint. Ballantine (134,000)

Mostly Harmless. Douglas Adams. Reprint. Fawcett (134,000)

* *Lawyers & Other Reptiles.* Jess M. Brallier. Original. Contemporary (132,485)

* *Deep Thoughts.* Jack Handey. Original. Berkley (131,000)

Measure of Our Success. Marion Wright Edelman. Reprint. Harper (130,640)

Coneheads. Tom Davis and Dan Aykroyd. Original. Hyperion (129,600)

Toujours Provence. Peter Mayle. Reprint. Vintage (129,000)

The Education of Little Tree. Forrest Carter. Reprint. Univ. of New Mexico (127,806)

Simply Light Cooking. Weight Watchers International. Reprint. Plume (122,856)

* *World's Best Card Tricks.* Bob Longe. Original. Sterling (120,000)

Duplicate Keys. Jane Smiley. Reprint. Fawcett (120,000)

Webster's New World Pocket Dictionary, 2nd Edition. Revised. Prentice Hall (120,000)

To Love Again. Bertrice Small. Original. Ballantine (119,000)

* *Don't Squat With Yer Spurs On: A Cowboy's Guide to Life.* Texas Bix Bender. Original. Gibbs Smith (114,945)

Garfield Fat Cat Three Pack. Jim Davis. Original. Ballantine (113,000)

Bankruptcy 1995: The Coming Collapse of America and How to Stop It. Harry E. Figgie, Jr., with Gerald J. Swanson. Reprint. Little, Brown (112,000)

Betty Crocker's Low-Calorie Cooking. Editors of Betty Crocker. Original. Prentice Hall (110,000)

The Legacy. R. A. Salvatore. Reprint. TSR (109,563)

365 Outdoor Activities You Can Do With Your Child. Steve and Ruth Bennett. Original. Bob Adams (108,131)

Bart Simpson's Guide to Life. Matt Groening. Original. Harper (107,268)

Running MS DOS, 6th Edition. Van Wolverton. Reprint. Microsoft (107,016)

The Ditches of Edison County. Ronald Richard Roberts. Original. Plume (105,718)

Top Secret Recipes. Todd Wilbur. Original. Plume (103,735)

Keeping the Love You Find. Harville Hendrix. Original. Pocket (102,000)

* *There Are No Children Here.* Alex Kotlowitz. Reprint. Anchor

The Living Trust. Henry Abts III. Reprint. Contemporary (100,204)

Private Screening. Richard North Patterson. Reprint. Ballantine (100,000)

Acquired Tastes. Peter Mayle. Reprint. Bantam (100,000)

* *Homecoming.* John Bradshaw. Reprint. Bantam (100,000)

* *101 Best Family Card Games.* Alfred Sheinwold. Original. Sterling (100,000)

Health Security. Government Printing Office. Original. Touchstone

75,000+

Black Boy. Richard Wright. Reprint. Harper (99,969)

* *Backlash.* Susan Faludi. Reprint. Anchor

All I Really Needed to Know I Learned in Kindergarten. Robert Fulghum. Reprint. Fawcett (94,000)

Daisy Fay & the Miracle Man. Fanny Flagg. Reprint. Warner (93,650)

A World Lit Only By Fire: The Medieval Mind and the Renaissance Portrait of An Age. William Manchester. Reprint. Little, Brown (92,000)

Lincoln at Gettysburg. Garry Wills. Reprint. Touchstone

Betty Crocker's Mexican Made Easy. Editors of Betty Crocker. Original. Prentice Hall (90,000)

The Pearl. John Steinbeck. Reprint. Penguin (90,000)

Betty Crocker's Quick Dinners in 30 Minutes or Less. Editors of Betty Crocker. Original. Prentice Hall (90,000)

Positive Thinking Everyday. Dr. Norman Vincent Peale. Original. Fireside

* *Cows of Our Planet.* Gary Larson. Original. Andrews and McMeel (90,000)

Your Money or Your Life. Joe Dominquez and Vicki Robin. Reprint. Penguin (90,000)

New Router Handbook. Patrick Spielman. Original. Sterling (88,000)

Unbelievably Good Deals & Great Adventures That You Absolutely Can't Get Unless You're Over 50. Joan Rattner Heilman. Reprint. Contemporary (87,657)

Head to Head. Lester Thurow. Reprint. Warner (87,545)

Native Son. Richard Wright. Reprint. Harper (86,052)

* *The New Joy of Sex.* Alex Comfort. Reissue. Pocket (86,000)

* *How To Study.* Ron Fry. Original. Career Press (86,000)

Realms of Valor. James Lowder. Original. TSR (85,994)

* *Moosewood Revised.* Mollie Katzen. Reprint. Ten Speed (85,852)

Inside Windows NT. Helen Custer. Original. Microsoft (85,413)

Cooking With Regis and Kathie Lee. Regis Philbin and Kathie Lee Gifford with Barbara Albright. Reprint. Hyperion (84,500)

The Seventh Garfield Treasury. Jim Davis. Original. Ballantine (84,000)

Dad's Own Cookbook. Bob Sloan. Dual. Workman (83,368)

The Wall Street Journal Guide to Personal Finance. Wall Street Journal. Original. Fireside

JFK: Reckless Youth. Nigel Hamilton. Reprint. Random (82,791)

More Low-Fat Recipes. Editors of Sunset. Original. Sunset (82,600)

* *The New Houseplant Expert.* D. G. Hessayon. Original. Sterling (82,500)

Dave Barry Does Japan. Dave Barry. Reprint. Fawcett (82,000)

How Software Works. Ron White. Original. Ziff-Davis (80,920)

Chicken Soup for the Soul: 101 Stories To Open the Heart and Rekindle the Spirit. Jack Canfield and Mark Victor Hansen. Original. Health Communications (80,793)

New Our Bodies Ourselves. Boston Women's Health Book Collective. Reprint. Touchstone

Betty Crocker's Holiday Baking. Editors of Betty Crocker. Original. Prentice Hall (80,000)

* *Bringers of the Dawn: Teachings from the Pleiadians.* Barbara Marciniak. Original. Bear (80,000)

The 100 Best Small Towns in America. Norman Crampton. Original. Prentice Hall (80,000)

Give War A Chance. P. J. O'Rourke. Reprint. Vintage (79,000)

A Good Samaritan Strikes Again. Patrick F. McManus. Reprint. Owl/Holt (78,360)

The Living. Annie Dillard. Reprint. Harper (78,241)

Men & Other Reptiles. Original. Contemporary (78,216)

Wreathmaking Basics. Dawn Cusick. Original. Sterling (78,000)

Cooking for Life. Cherie Calbom and Vicki Rae Chelf. Original. Avery (78,000)

Swordsheath Scroll. Dan Parkinson. Original. TSR (77,432)

Never Ask a Man the Size of His Spread: A Cowgirl's Guide to Life. Gladiola Montana. Original. Gibbs Smith (77,119)

Vox. Nicholson Baker. Reprint. Vintage (77,000)

Life Carries On. Editors of Life Magazine. Reprint. Fireside

Cowboys Are My Weakness. Pam Houston. Reprint. Pocket (77,000)

Two Nations. Andrew Hacker. Reprint. Ballantine (77,000)

* *Juicing for Life.* Cherie Calbom and Maureen Keane. Original. Avery (75,000)

Where the Bluebird Sings to the Lemonade Springs. Wallace Stegner. Reprint. Penguin (75,000)

Genius. James Gleick. Reprint. Vintage (75,000)

The Low-Fat Fast Food Guide. Jamie Pope-Cordle and Martin Katahn. Original. Norton

55,000+

* *The Internet Companion: A Beginner's Guide to Global Networking.* Tracey LaQuey Parker and Jeanne C. Ryer. Original. Addison-Wesley (74,006)

The Carbohydrate Addict's Program For Success. Rachael and Richard Heller. Original. Plume (73,968)

Never Confuse A Memo With Reality. Richard Moran. Original. Harper (73,827)

60 Ways to Relieve Stress in 60 Seconds. Manning Rubin. Original. Workman (73,075)

Legacy of the Heart. Wayne Muller. Reprint. Fireside

* *Perennials.* Editors of Sunset. Original. Sunset (73,500)

Covenant of the Forge. Dan Parkinson. Original. TSR (72,955)

We Were Soldiers Once. Harold Moore and Joe Galloway. Reprint. Harper (72,818)

Before the Mask. Michael and Teri Williams. Original. TSR (72,033)

* *50 Fabulous Places to Raise Your Family.* Lee and Saralee Rosenberg. Original. Career Press (72,000)

The Druid Queen. Douglas Niles. Original. TSR (71,913)

The Gore Report. Al Gore. Original. Times (70,934)

* *When Food Is Love.* Geneen Roth. Reprint. Plume (70,560)

Black Pearls. Eric Copage. Original. Quill (70,404)

* *Crockery Cook Book.* Editors of Sunset. Original. Sunset (70,300)

The Joy of Parenthood. Jan Blaustone. Original. Meadowbrook (70,300)

Dreaming in Cuban. Cristina Garcia. Reprint. Ballantine (70,000)

The Price Waterhouse Investor's Tax Adviser. Staff of Price Waterhouse. Revised. Prentice Hall (70,000)

Who Will Tell the People. William Grieder. Reprint. Touchstone

The Black Wing. Mary Kirchoff. Original. TSR (66,902)

Soldiers of Ice. David Cook. Original. TSR (66,058)

At Paradise Gate. Jane Smiley. Reprint. Touchstone

The Mis-Education of the Negro. Carter G. Woodson. Reprint. Africa World Press (66,000)

Emperor of Ansalon. Douglas Niles. Original. TSR (65,527)

Prince of Lies. James Lowder. Original. TSR (65,146)

Pool of Twilight. James M. Ward and Anne K. Brown. Original. TSR (65,070)

Bonsai Basics. Christian Pessey and Remy Samson. Original. Sterling (65,000)

Rolling Stone: The Photographs. Preface by Tom Wolfe, intro. by Jann S. Wenner. Reprint. Fireside

The Black Family Reunion Cookbook. National Council of Negro Women. Reprint. Fireside

Spine-Tingling "True" Ghost Stories. Sheila Barry. Original. Sterling (65,000)

Eleanor Roosevelt, Vol. I. Blanche Wiesen Cook. Reprint. Penguin (65,000)

Hammer and Axe. Dan Parkinson. Original. TSR (64,820)

"And Then Jack Said to Arnie . . . " Don Wade. Reprint. Contemporary (64,617)

The Volcano Lover. Susan Sontag. Reprint. Anchor

The Outcast. Simon Hawke. Original. TSR (64,269)

Star Trek: The Next Generation Companion. Larry Nemecek. Reprint. Pocket (64,000)

Crypt of the Shadowking. Mark Anthony. Original. TSR (63,672)

* *Basic Plumbing.* Editors of Sunset. Reprint. Sunset (63,500)

Postcards From Life's Little Instruction Book. H. Jackson Brown, Jr. Original. Rutledge Hill (63,155)

* *Sharks Don't Get Cancer.* Dr. I. William Lane and Linda Comac. Original. Avery (63,000)

Bury My Heart at Fun-Fun Mountain. Bill Amend. Original. Andrews and McMeel (62,000)

Home Canning. Editors of Sunset. Reprint. Sunset (61,700)

* *Sound Blaster: The Official Book.* Rich Heimlich, David Golden, Ivan Luk, and Peter Ridge. Original. Osborne/McGraw-Hill (61,400)

Written By Herself. Jill Ker Conway. Original. Vintage (61,000)

Tapestry of Dark Souls. Elaine Bergstrom. Original. TSR (60,939)

Dairy Hollow's House Soup & Bread Cookbook. Crescent Dragonwagon. Dual. Workman (60,866)

The Last Tsar. Edvard Radzinsky. Reprint. Anchor

* *Savage Inequalities.* Jonathan Kozol. Reprint. Harper (60,736)

* *Meditations for New Mothers.* Beth Wilson Saavedra. Original. Workman (60,375)

Lincoln on Leadership. Donald Philips. Reprint. Warner (60,101)

13th Gen. Neil Howe and Bill Strauss. Original. Vintage (60,000)

The Creators. Daniel J. Boorstin. Reprint. Vintage (60,000)

Bailey's Cafe. Gloria Naylor. Reprint. Vintage (60,000)

A Good Scent From a Strange Mountain. Robert Olen Butler. Reprint. Penguin (60,000)

The American Heart Association Cookbook, 5th Ed. American Heart Association. Reprint. Times (59,855)

Christmas Day Kitten. James Herriot. Reprint. St. Martin's (59,730)

Mary Ann's Gilligan's Island Cookbook. Dawn Wells, Jim Clark and Ken Beck. Original. Rutledge Hill (59,282)

* *Great Bread Machine Recipes.* Norman A. Garrett. Original. Sterling (59,000)

101 Science Tricks. Roy A. Richards. Original. Sterling (59,000)

The Change. Germaine Greer. Reprint. Fawcett (59,000)

Get Your Act Together. Pam Young and Peggy Jones. Original. Harper (58,958)

Bread Machine Magic: Book of Helpful Hints. Linda Rehberg and Lois Conway. Original. St. Martin's (58,807)

Shampoo Planet. Douglas Coupland. Reprint. Pocket (58,500)

The Popcorn Report. Faith Popcorn. Reprint. Harper (58,417)

How 'Bout Them Cowboys! Frank Coffey, Ernie Wood with Tony Seidl. Original. Taylor (58,093)

High and Mighty. St. Louis Post-Dispatch. Original. Andrews and McMeel (58,000)

Dear Mom. Scott Matthews. Original. Bantam (58,000)

Your Blues Ain't Like Mine. Bebe Moore Campbell. Reprint. Ballantine (57,000)

Socks Goes to Washington: Diary of America's First Cat. Michael O'Donoghue. Original. Thomasson-Grant (57,000)

Ziglar on Selling. Zig Ziglar. Reprint. Ballantine (57,000)

Cerulean Storm. Troy Denning. Original. TSR (56,186)

The Garden Pests & Diseases. Editors of Sunset Original. Sunset (56,100)

The Nitpicker's Guide for Next Generation Trekkers. Phil Ferrand. Original. Dell (56,056)

Say Hello to Cactus Flats. Bill Amend. Original. Andrews and McMeel (56,000)

* *Ideas for Great Window Treatments.* Editors of Sunset. Original. Sunset (56,000)

How Networks Work. Frank Derfler, Jr. and Les Freed. Original. Ziff-Davis (55,705)

* *Wild Swans.* Jung Chang. Reprint. Anchor

The Obsidian Oracle. Troy Denning. Original. TSR (55,040)

Here On Gilligan's Isle. Russell Johnson. Original. Harper (55,038)

Money Doesn't Grow on Trees. Neale Godfrey. Original. Fireside

The Wellness Book. Herbert Benson and Eileen M. Stuart. Reprint. Fireside
Challenging Lateral Thinking Puzzles. Paul Sloane. Original. Sterling (55,000)
Shadows of Forgotten Ancestors. Carl Sagan and Ann Druyan. Reprint. Ballantine (55,000)
Meditations for Cats Who Do Too Much. Michael Cader. Original. Penguin (55,000)
I Shall Not Be Moved. Maya Angelou. Reprint. Bantam (55,000)
Cooking for Good Health. Gloria Rose. Original. Avery (55,000)

Mass Market Paperbacks

3 million +

The Pelican Brief. John Grisham. Reprint. Dell (10,232,480)
* *The Firm.* John Grisham. Reprint. Dell (6,175,800)
* *Jurassic Park.* Michael Crichton. Reprint. Ballantine (6,427,000)
* *A Time to Kill.* John Grisham. Reprint. Dell (3,933,900)
Rising Sun. Michael Crichton. Reprint. Ballantine (5,600,000)
Jewels. Danielle Steel. Reprint. Dell (3,003,580)
Mixed Blessings. Danielle Steel. Reprint. Dell (3,000,020)

2 million +

Gerald's Game. Stephen King. Reprint. Signet/Onyx (2,750,000)
All Around the Town. Mary Higgins Clark. Reprint. Pocket (2,575,000)
Dolores Claiborne. Stephen King. Reprint. Signet/Onyx (2,500,000)
The Waste Lands. Stephen King. Reprint. Signet/Onyx (2,500,000)
Congo. Michael Crichton. Reprint. Ballantine (2,500,000)
Stars Shine Down. Sidney Sheldon. Reprint. Warner (2,479,000)
Darkest Hour. V. C. Andrews. Original. Pocket (2,275,000)
Dragon Tears. Dean Koontz. Reprint. Berkley (2,270,000)

The Way Things Ought to Be. Rush Limbaugh. Reprint. Pocket (2,180,000)
Shadowfires. Dean Koontz. Reprint. Berkley (2,120,000)

1.5 million +

* *Scarlett.* Alexandra Ripley. Reprint. Warner (1,814,385)
The Tale of the Body Thief. Anne Rice. Reprint. Ballantine (1,800,000)
American Star. Jackie Collins. Reprint. Pocket (1,750,000)
Bygones. Lavyrle Spencer. Reprint. Jove (1,726,000)
The Road to Omaha. Robert Ludlum. Reprint. Bantam (1,675,000)
The Magic of You. Johanna Lindsey. Original. Avon (1,625,000)
Keeper of the Heart. Johanna Lindsey. Original. Avon (1,600,000)
Waiting to Exhale. Terry McMillan. Reprint. Pocket (1,562,000)
Scruples Two. Judith Krantz. Reprint. Bantam (1,543,000)
McNally's Secret. Lawrence Sanders. Reprint. Berkley (1,506,000)
The Witching Hour. Anne Rice. Ballantine (1,500,000)
Mitigating Circumstances. Nancy Taylor Rosenberg. Reprint. Signet/Onyx (1,500,000)

1 million+

Along Came A Spider. James Patterson. Reprint. Warner (1,406,292)
Inadmissible Evidence. Philip Friedman. Reprint. Ivy (1,400,000)
Sahara. Clive Cussler. Reprint. Pocket (1,392,000)
Forever In Your Embrace. Kathleen E. Woodiwiss. Original. Avon (1,390,000)
Treasures. Belva Plain. Reprint. Dell (1,365,350)
McNally's Luck. Lawrence Sanders. Reprint. Berkley (1,365,000)
Sweet Liar. Jude Deveraux. Reprint. Pocket (1,350,000)
Fugitive Nights. Joseph Wambaugh. Reprint. Bantam (1,341,000)
The General's Daughter. Nelson DeMille. Reprint. Warner (1,325,200)

French Silk. Sandra Brown. Reprint. Warner (1,321,000)

Blindsight. Robin Cook. Reprint. Berkley (1,318,000)

UH-OH. Robert Fulghum. Reprint. Ivy (1,300,000)

Acts of Faith. Erich Segal. Reprint. Bantam (1,290,000)

All That Remains. Patricia D. Cornwell. Reprint. Avon (1,278,000)

Where Is Joe Merchant? Jimmy Buffett. Reprint. Avon (1,255,000)

Every Living Thing. James Herriot. Reprint. St. Martin's (1,235,000)

Castles. Julie Garwood. Original. Pocket (1,230,000)

* Tangled Vines. Janet Dailey. Reprint. Little, Brown (1,230,000)

I Is for Innocent. Sue Grafton. Reprint. Fawcett (1,200,000)

The Ebony Swan. Phyllis Whitney. Reprint. Fawcett (1,200,000)

* Eyes of Prey. John Sandford. Reprint. Berkley (1,187,000)

Colony. Anne Rivers Siddons. Reprint. Harper (1,182,000)

Silent Prey. John Sandford. Reprint. Berkley (1,159,000)

Devil's Waltz. Jonathan Kellerman. Reprint. Bantam (1,151,000)

Stars. Kathryn Harvey. Reprint. Avon (1,140,000)

Silken Web. Sandra Brown. Reprint. Warner (1,137,700)

* Outer Banks. Anne Rivers Siddons. Reprint. Harper (1,131,000)

The Heiress Bride. Catherine Coulter. Reprint. (1,109,000)

Hidden Talents. Jayne Ann Krentz. Original. Pocket (1,105,000)

Fatherland. Robert Harris. Reprint. Harper (1,101,000)

Red Square. Martin Cruz Smith. Reprint. Ballantine (1,100,000)

Everything She Ever Wanted. Ann Rule. Reprint. Pocket (1,085,000)

It Doesn't Take a Hero. Gen. H. Norman Schwarzkopf with Peter Petre. Reprint. Bantam (1,078,000)

I Can't Believe I Said That. Kathie Lee Gifford. Reprint. Pocket (1,070,000)

Lord of Hawkfell Island. Catherine Coulter. Original. Jove (1,052,000)

Wildest Hearts. Jayne Ann Krentz. Original. Pocket (1,048,000)

The Evening Star. Larry McMurtry. Reprint. Pocket (1,040,000)

Midnight Secrets. Janelle Taylor. Reprint. Kensington (1,035,000)

Oprah! Up Close and Down Home. Nellie Bly. Original. Kensington (1,000,050)

Honest Illusions. Nora Roberts. Reprint. Jove (1,001,000)

Compelling Evidence. Steve Martini. Reprint. Jove (1,001,000)

* Games of the Hangman. Victor O'Reilly. Reprint. Berkley (1,001,000)

* Sky Masters. Dale Brown. Reprint. Berkley (1,001,000)

* For All Their Lives. Fern Michaels. Reprint. Ballantine (1,000,000)

* Woman Without A Past. Phyllis Whitney. Reprint. Fawcett (1,000,000)

* Damage. Josephine Hart. Reprint. Ivy (1,000,000)

Fanta C. Sandra Brown. Reprint. Bantam (1,000,000)

Voice of the Eagle. Linda Lay Shuler. Reprint. Signet/Onyx (1,000,000)

Beyond Eden. Catherine Coulter. Reprint. Signet/Onyx (1,000,000)

Compiled by Ingrid Chevannes & Dermot McEvoy

Almanacs, Atlases, and Annuals

* The World Almanac and Book of Facts 1993. Edited by Mark Hoffman. Annual. World Almanac (2,200,000)

The World Almanac and Book of Facts 1994. Edited by Robert Famighetti. Annual. World Almanac (2,080,000)

J. K. Lasser's Your Income Tax 1994. J. K. Lasser Institute. Annual. Prentice Hall (750,000)

Mobil Travel Guide Series 1993. Prentice Hall Travel Editors. Annual. Prentice Hall (525,000)

Ernst & Young Tax Guide 1993. Ernst & Young. Original. Wiley (500,000)

Gousha's New Deluxe 1994 Road Atlas. H. M. Gousha Editors. Annual. Prentice Hall (450,000)

What Color Is Your Parachute 1993? Richard Bolles. Annual. Ten Speed (316,189)

Ernst & Young Tax-Saving Strategies Guide 1993. Ernst & Young. Original. Wiley (300,000)

Information Please Almanac 1994. Annual. Houghton Mifflin (290,000)

Gousha's Interstate Road Atlas 1994. Editors of H. M. Gousha. Annual. Prentice Hall (265,000)

Information Please Sports Almanac 1994. Annual. Houghton Mifflin (235,108)

The Physicians' Desk Reference Family Guide to Prescription Drugs. PDR Staff. Original. Medical Economics Data (205,000)

Consumer Reports Books Guide to Income Tax 1994. Editors of Consumer Reports. Annual. Consumer Reports (150,000)

Kovel's Antiques and Collectibles Price Guide #25. Ralph and Terry Kovel. Annual. Crown (116,809)

Consumer Reports: Buying Guide 1994. Editors of Consumer Reports. Annual. (110,599)

The 1994 Physicians' Desk Reference. Editors of Physicians' Desk Reference Staff. Annual. Medical Economics Data (110,000)

Sports Illustrated 1994 Sports Almanac. Editors of Sports Illustrated. Original. Little, Brown (106,000)

Places Rated Almanac. David Savageau and Richard Boyer. Revised. Prentice Hall (105,000)

Birnbaum's Walt Disney World, 1994. Edited by Wendy Leskon. Annual. Hyperion (103,900)

Let's Go Europe, 1994. Harvard Student Agencies. Original. St. Martin's (102,362)

* *Birnbaum's Walt Disney World 1993.* Edited by Wendy Leskon. Annual. Hyperion (101,300)

* *The Unofficial Guide to Walt Disney World 1993.* Bob Sehlinger. Annual. Prentice Hall (100,000)

Gousha's Pocket Road Atlas 1993. Editors of H. M. Gousha. Annual. Prentice Hall (95,000)

Information Please Sports Almanac 1993. Original. Houghton Mifflin (93,000)

* *Knock 'em Dead 1993: The Ultimate Job Seeker's Handbook.* Martin Yate. Annual. Bob Adams (85,573)

The Milepost: The Only All-the-North Travel Guide. Annual. Vernon (85,000)

Mobil Road Atlas Trip Planning Guide 1994. Susan Farewell. Annual. Prentice Hall (82,000)

Peterson's Guide to Four Year Colleges, 1994. Original. Peterson's (76,000)

Best American Short Stories 1993. Edited by Louise Erdrich. Dual. Houghton Mifflin (75,200)

The 1994 Black Book Price Guide to United States Coins. Marc Hudgeons. Original. House of Collectibles (66,000)

The Universal Almanac. John W. Wright. Annual. Andrews and McMeel (60,000)

The Princeton Review Word Smart. Adam Robinson and the Staff of the Princeton Review. Reprint. Villard (59,213)

Let's Go USA 1994. Harvard Student Agencies. Original. St. Martin's (55,246)

Roget's International Thesaurus, Fifth Ed. Edited by Dr. Robert L. Chapman. Reprint. Harper (55,170)

Knock 'em Dead 1994: The Ultimate Job Seeker's Handbook. Martin Yate. Annual. Bob Adams (54,954)

The Princeton Review: Cracking the GRE, 1994 Edition. Adam Robinson and John Katzman. Annual. Villard (54,064)

The Essential Guide to Prescription Drugs 1994. James W. Long et al. and James J. Rybacki. Annual. Harper (52,948)

Literary Prizes, 1993

Gary Ink
Research Librarian, *Publishers Weekly*

ABBY Award. *Offered by:* American Booksellers Association. To honor titles that members have most enjoyed hand-selling in the past year. *Winners:* (adult) Robert James Waller for *The Bridges of Madison County* (Warner Books); (children's) Douglas Wood for *Old Turtle,* illustrations by Cheng-Khee Chee (Pfeifer-Hamilton).

Academy of American Poets Fellowship Award. For distinguished poetic achievement. *Winner:* Gerald Stern.

J. R. Ackerly Award (Great Britain). For autobiography. *Offered by:* PEN (UK). *Winner:* Barry Humphries for *More, Please* (Viking).

Jane Addams Children's Book Award. For a book promoting the cause of peace, social justice, and world community. *Offered by:* Women's International League for Peace and Freedom and the Jane Addams Peace Association. *Winner:* Frances Temple for *A Taste of Salt: A Story of Modern Haiti* (Orchard Books).

Jane Addams Picture Book Award. For a book promoting the cause of peace, social justice, and world community. *Offered by:* Women's International League of Peace and Freedom and the Jane Addams Peace Association. *Winner:* Faith Ringgold for *Aunt Harriet's Underground Railroad in the Sky* (Crown).

Ambassador Book Awards. To recognize books that have made an exceptional contribution to the interpretation of life and culture in the United States. *Offered by:* English-Speaking Union. *Winners:* (arts & letters) Joseph Mitchell for *Up in the Old Hotel* (Pantheon); (American Studies) Garry Wills for *Lincoln at Gettysburg* (Simon & Schuster); (biography) Scott Donaldson for *Archibald MacLeish: An American Life* (Houghton Mifflin); (fiction) Robert Stone for *Outerbridge Reach* (Ticknor & Fields).

American Academy of Arts and Letters Awards in Literature. *Offered by:* American Academy of Arts and Letters. *Winners:* Ellen Akins, Richard Bausch, Vance Bourjaily, Deborah Eisenberg, Rolf Fjelde, Tina Howe, Denis Johnson, A. G. Mojtabai.

American Academy of Arts and Letters Gold Medal for Belles Lettres and Criticism. *Offered by:* American Academy of Arts and Letters. *Winner:* Elizabeth Hardwick.

Bancroft Prizes. For books of exceptional merit and distinction in American history, American diplomacy, and the international relations of the United States. *Offered by:* Columbia University. *Winners:* Charles Capper for *Margaret Fuller: An American Romantic Life: The Private Years* (Oxford); Melvyn P. Leffler for *A Preponderance of Power: National Security, the Truman Administration and the Cold War* (Stanford).

James Beard Awards. For cookbooks. *Offered by:* James Beard Foundation. *Winners:* (cookbook of the year) Lynne Rosetto Kasper for *The Splendid Table* (Morrow); (general) Joyce Goldstein for *Back to Square One* (Morrow); (American) Molly O'Neill for *New York Cookbook* (Workman); (food photography) Peter Johnson, photographer, and Gilliam Hewitt, ed., for *France: A Culinary Journey* (Collins); (baking and desserts) Marcel Desaulniers for *Death by Chocolate* (Rizzoli); (entertaining) Rosamond Richardson and Linda Burgess for *Alfresco* (Potter); (fruits, vegetables, and grains) Jeanne Lemlin for *Quick Vegetarian Pleasures* (HarperCollins); (international) Yamuna Devi for *Yamuna's Table* (Dutton); (Italian) Marcella Hazan for *Essentials of Classic Italian Cooking* (Knopf); (light and healthy) Steven Raichlen for *Steve Raichlen's High Flavor, Low-Fat Cooking* (Camden House); (quick and easy) Frances McCullough and Barbara Witt for *Great Food Without Fuss* (Henry Holt); (single subject) Jeanne Lesem for *Preserving Today* (Knopf); (wine and spirits) Hugh Johnson and James Halliday for *The Vintner's Art* (Simon & Schuster);

(writings on food) Amal Naj for *Peppers* (Knopf).

Curtis Benjamin Award for Creative Publishing. *Offered by:* Association of American Publishers. *Winner:* Jason Epstein.

Bennett Award. To honor a writer of significant achievement whose work has not received in the United States the full recognition to which it is entitled. *Offered by: The Hudson Review. Winner:* Charles Tomlinson.

Helen B. Bernstein Award for Excellence in Journalism. *Offered by:* New York Public Library. *Winner:* Samuel G. Freedman for *Upon This Rock* (HarperCollins).

James Tait Black Memorial Prizes (Great Britain). For the best biography and the best novel of the year. *Offered by:* University of Edinburgh. *Winners:* (biography) Charles Nicholl for *The Beckoning: The Murder of Christopher Marlowe* (Cape); (fiction) Rose Tremain for *Sacred Country* (Sinclair-Stevenson).

Bollingen Prize in Poetry. *Offered by:* Yale University. *Winner:* Mark Strand.

Booker of Bookers (Great Britain). To celebrate the silver jubilee of the Booker Prize for Fiction, and to select the best British novel of the past quarter century. *Offered by:* Book Trust. *Winner:* Salman Rushdie for *Midnight's Children* (Cape).

Booker Prize for Fiction (Great Britain). *Offered by:* Book Trust. *Winner:* Roddy Doyle for *Paddy Clarke Ha Ha Ha* (Secker & Warburg).

Michael Braude Award for Light Verse. *Offered by:* American Academy of Arts and Letters. *Winner:* Turner Cassity.

British Literature Prize (Great Britain). To honor sustained achievement by a living writer. *Offered by:* Arts Council. *Winner:* V. S. Naipaul.

British Science Fiction Award. For the best science fiction novel of the year. *Offered by:* British Science Fiction Writers Association. *Winner:* Kim Stanley Robinson for *Red Mars* (HarperCollins).

John Burroughs Medal. For distinguished nature writing. *Offered by:* John Burroughs Association. *Winner:* Vincent G. Dethier for *Crickets and Katydids, Concerts and Solos* (Harvard).

Witter Bynner Foundation Prize for Poetry. *Offered by:* American Academy of Arts and Letters. *Winner:* Patricia Storace.

Caldecott Medal. For the artist of the most distinguished picture book. *Offered by:* R. R. Bowker Company. *Winner:* Emily Arnold McCully for *Mirette on the High Wire* (Putnam).

Italo Calvino Award. *Offered by:* Columbia University Translation Center. *Winner:* Tim Parks for *The Marriage of Cadmus and Harmony,* by Roberto Calasso (Knopf).

John W. Campbell Memorial Award. For outstanding science fiction writing. *Offered by:* Center for the Study of Science Fiction. *Winner:* Charles Sheffield.

Canada–Japan Book Award. For a book about Japan or a book translated from Japanese into English or French. *Offered by:* Canada Council. *Winner:* Barbara Bose for *Tsuda Umeko and Women's Education in Japan* (Yale).

Melville Cane Award. For a critical work on poetry, a poet, or poets. *Offered by:* Poetry Society of America. *Winner:* Jacques Barzun for *An Essay on French Verse* (New Directions).

Carnegie Medal (Great Britain). For the outstanding children's book of the year. *Offered by:* The Library Association. *Winner:* Anne Fine for *Flour Babies* (Hamish Hamilton).

Chicago Sun-Times Books of the Year. *Winners:* (fiction) Leon Forrest for *Divine Days* (Another Chicago Press); (nonfiction) Gary Rivlin for *Fire on the Prairie* (Holt); (best first book) Mitchell Duneier for *Slim's Table* (Univ. of Chicago).

Julia Child Cookbook Awards. For the best cookbooks of the year. *Offered by:* International Association of Culinary Professionals. *Winners:* (best cookbook of year) Lynne Rosetto Kasper for *The Splendid Table* (Morrow); (general) Joyce Goldstein for *Back to Square One* (Morrow); (American) Molly O'Neill for *New York Cookbook* (Workman); (international) Barbara Tropp for *China Moon Cookbook* (Workman); (baking) Ken Haedrich for *Home for the Holidays* (Bantam); (health and diet) Graham Kerr for *Graham Kerr's Minimax Cookbook* (Doubleday); (single subject) Henrietta Green for *A Glorious Feast* (Sedgewood Press); (illustrated/photography) Gilliam Hewitt for *France: A Culinary Journey* (Collins); (literary food writing) John Thorne for *Outlaw Cook* (Farrar, Straus & Giroux); (reference, technical) Elizabeth Lambert Ortiz for *The Encyclopedia of Herbs, Spices and Flavorings* (Dorling Kindersley); (award for a first cookbook) Lynne Rosetto Kasper for *The Splendid Table* (Morrow).

Children's Book Award. Chosen by children. *Winners:* (grand prize) Jacqueline Wilson for *The Suitcase Kid* (Doubleday); (picture book) Berlie Doherty and Keith Bowen for *Snowy* (HarperCollins); (longer novel) Robert Westall for *Gulf* (Methuen).

Gilbert Chinard Prize. For a distinguished scholarly book or manuscript in the history of relations between France and North, Central, and South America published by a Canadian or American author. *Offered by:* Society for French Historical Studies and Institut Français de Washington. *Winner:* Not awarded in 1993.

Cholmondeley Awards (Great Britain). For contributions to poetry. *Offered by:* Society of Authors. *Winners:* Patricia Beer, Mackay Brown, P. J. Kavanagh, Michael Longley.

Christopher Book Awards. For books that affirm the highest values of the human spirit. *Offered by:* The Christophers. *Winners:* (adult) Eric Silver for *The Book of the Just* (Grove); Joseph Iron Eye Dudley for *Chocteau Creek: A Sioux Reminiscence* (Univ. of Nebraska); Robert Ellsberg for *Fritz Eichenberg* (Orbis Books); Marian Wright Edelman for *The Measure of Our Success* (Beacon Press); Judy Barron and Sean Barron for *There's a Boy in Here* (Simon & Schuster); Katie Kelly for *A Year in Saigon* (Simon & Schuster); (children's) Marcus Pfister for *The Rainbow Fish,* tr. by J. Alison James (North–South Books); Paula DePaolo for *Rosie and the Yellow Ribbon,* pictures by Janet Wolf (Little, Brown); Karen Hesse for *Letters From Rifka* (Henry Holt); Mildred Pitts Walter for *Mississippi Challenge* (Bradbury Press).

Arthur C. Clarke Award (Great Britain). For best science fiction novel of the year. *Offered by:* British Science Fiction Association. *Winner:* Marge Piercy for *Body of Glass* (Michael Joseph).

Columbia University Translation Center Awards. *Winners:* Melvin Dixon for *The Collected Poetry of Leopold Sedar Senghor* (Univ. of Virginia); Dorothy Gilbert for *Erec and Enide,* by Chretien de Troyes (Univ. of California); Ron Padgett for *The Complete Poems of Blaise Cendrars* (Univ. of California); Moss Roberts for *Three Kingdoms,* by Luo Guanzhong (Univ. of California).

Commonwealth Club of California Book Awards. For books of exceptional literary merit by authors who are legal residents of California. *Winners: Gold Medals:* (fiction) Irvin Yalom for *When Nietzsche Wept* (Basic Books); (nonfiction) Ramon Eduardo Ruiz for *Triumphs and Tragedy* (Norton). *Silver Medals:* (notable contribution to publishing) Proctor Patterson Jones for *Napoleon: An Intimate Account of the Years of Supremacy, 1800–1814* (Random House); (Californiana) Robert V. Hine for *Josiah Royce: From Grass Valley to Harvard* (Univ. of Oklahoma); (nonfiction) Richard Rodriguez for *Days of Obligation* (Viking); (fiction) Martin Cruz Smith for *Red Square* (Random House); (first novel) Sylvia Lopez-Medina for *Cantora* (Univ. of New Mexico); (juvenile, age 10 and under) Ellen Kindt McKenzie for *A Bowl of Mischief* (Henry Holt); Patricia Polacco for *Chicken Sunday* (Philomel); (juvenile, ages 11–16) Kristiana Gregory for *Earthquake at Dawn* (Harcourt Brace).

Thomas Cook Travel and Guide Book Awards (Great Britain). *Offered by:* Book Trust. *Winners:* (travel) Nik Cohn for *The Heart of the World* (Chatto); (guide book) Paul Gray and Lucy Ridout for *Thailand: The Rough Guide* (Harrap).

Deo Gloria Award (Great Britain). For a work of fiction written from a Christian standpoint. *Offered by:* Deo Gloria Trust. *Winner:* P. D. James for *The Children of Men* (Faber).

Alice Fay Di Castagnola Award. For a work-in-progress to recognize a poet at a crucial stage in his or her work. *Offered by:* Poetry Society of America. *Winner:* Laura Kasischke for *Housekeeping in a Dream* (work-in-progress).

Dr. Seuss Picturebook Award. *Offered by:* Random House. *Winner:* Lisa Horstman for *Fast Friends: A Tail and Tongue Tale* (Knopf).

Margaret A. Edwards Award. For lifetime achievement in writing books for young adults. *See* Library Scholarship and Award Recipients, 1993, in Part 3.

Encore Award (Great Britain). *Offered by:* Society of Authors. *Winner:* Colm Toibin for *The Heather Blazing* (Picador).

Esquire/Volvo/Waterstone's Non-Fiction Award (Great Britain). To give greater prominence to good general nonfiction. *Winner:* Blake Morrison for *And When Did You Last See Your Father?* (Granta).

Geoffrey Faber Memorial Prize (Great Britain). For recognition of a volume of prose fiction or a volume of verse of great literary merit. *Offered by:* Faber & Faber. *Winner:* Will Self for *The Quantity Theory of Insanity* (Bloomsbury).

Norma Faber First Book Award. For a first book of poetry. *Offered by:* Poetry Society of America. *Winner:* Timothy Liu for *Vox Angelica* (Alice James Books).

Faulkner Award for Fiction. To honor the best work of fiction published by an American writer. *Offered by:* PEN American Center. *Winner:* E. Annie Proulx for *Postcards* (Scribner).

E. M. Forster Award in Literature. *Offered by:* American Academy of Arts and Letters. *Winner:* Sean O'Brien.

French–American Translation Prize. *Offered by:* French–American Foundation. *Winner:* Lydia Davis for *The Rules of the Game I: Scratches* by Michael Leiris (Paragon House).

Frost Silver Medal. To a person who has shown lifelong dedication and achievement in poetry. *Offered by:* Poetry Society of America. *Winner:* William Stafford.

Ralph J. Gleason Music Book Awards. To honor outstanding books about music and musicians in all areas of popular music. *Offered by:* Rolling Stone, BMI, and New York University. *Winners:* (first prize) Jon Savage for *England's Dreaming: Anarchy, Sex Pistols and Beyond* (St. Martin's); (second prize) Thomas L. Morgan and William Barlow for *From Cakewalks to Concert Halls* (Elliot & Clark); (third prize) Bill Graham and Robert Greenfield for *Bill Graham Presents* (Doubleday).

Golden Kite Awards. For outstanding children's books. *Offered by:* Society of Children's Book Writers and Illustrators. *Winners:* (fiction) Mary E. Lyons for *Letters from a Slave Girl* (Scribner); (nonfiction) Jim Murphy for *The Long Road to Gettysburg* (Clarion); (illustration) Patricia Polacco for *Chicken Sunday* (Philomel).

Barbara Goldsmith Freedom to Write Awards. To honor writers who have demonstrated great courage in defending freedom of expression. *Offered by:* PEN American Center. *Winners:* Zoran Mutic, Svetlana Slapsak, Nizar Nayyuf.

Kate Greenaway Medal (Great Britain). For children's book illustration. *Offered by:* The Library Association. *Winner:* Anthony Browne for *Zoo* (Julia MacRae).

Eric Gregory Trust Awards (Great Britain). For poets under the age of 30. *Offered by:* Society of Authors. *Winners:* Eleanor Brown, Sean Boustead, Tracey Herd, Joel Lane, Angela McSeveney, Deryn Rees-Jones.

Guardian Children's Fiction Award (Great Britain). To discover fresh new writing and to salute established excellence. *Winners:* William Mayne for *Low Tide* (Cape); Jamila Gavin for *The Wheel of Surya* (Methuen).

Guardian Fiction Prize (Great Britain). For recognition of a novel by a British or Commonwealth writer. *Winner:* Pat Barker for *The Eye in the Door* (Viking).

Guggenheim Fellowships. *Offered by:* Guggenheim Memorial Foundation. *Winners:* (fiction) Blanche McCrary Boyd, Robert Olen Butler, Michael Cunningham, Louis Edwards, Mary Gordon, Allen Kurzweil; (poetry) Nicholas Christopher,

Billy Collins, Cornelius Eady, Lars Gustafsson, Mary Jo Slater, Frederick Siedel.

R. R. Hawkins Award. For the most outstanding professional, reference, or scholarly work of the year. *Offered by:* Association of American Publishers, Professional/Scholarly Publishing Division. *Winner:* J. B. Harley and David Woodward, eds., for *The History of Cartography, Vol. II, Book I* (Univ. of Chicago).

Drue Heinz Literature Prize. To recognize and encourage the writing of short fiction. *Offered by:* Drue Heinz Foundation and Univ. of Pittsburgh Press. *Winner:* Stewart O'Nan for *In a Walled City* (Univ. of Pittsburgh).

Ernest Hemingway Foundation Award. For a work of first fiction by an American. *Offered by:* PEN American Center. *Winner:* Ernest P. Jones for *Lost in the City* (Morrow).

James S. Holmes Award. *Offered by:* Columbia University Translation Center. *Winner:* Stacey Knecht for *Back to the Congo*, by Lieve Joris (Atheneum).

Langston Hughes Award. To individuals who, in the tradition of Langston Hughes, have made a distinguished contribution to arts and letters. *Offered by:* Modern Poetry Association. *Winner:* Chinua Achebe.

International Reading Association Children's Book Awards. *Winners:* (younger reader) *Old Turtle* by Douglas Wood, illustrated by Cheng-Khee Chee (Pfeifer-Hamilton); (older reader) *Letters from Rifka* by Karen Hesse (Holt).

Irish Times International Fiction Prize (Ireland). *Offered by: Irish Times. Winner:* E. Annie Proulx for *The Shipping News* (Fourth Estate).

Irish Times Non-Fiction Prize (Ireland). *Offered by: Irish Times. Winner:* Brian Keenan for *An Evil Cradling* (Hutchinson).

Irish Times Prize for a First Work of Fiction (Ireland). *Winner:* John MacKenna for *The Fallen and Other Stories* (Blackstaff).

Jerusalem Prize (Israel). To a writer whose works best express the theme of freedom of the individual in society. *Offered by:* Jerusalem International Book Fair. *Winner:* Stefan Heym.

Sue Kaufman Prize for First Fiction. *Offered by:* American Academy of Arts and Letters. *Winner:* Francisco Goldman for *The Long Night of White Chickens* (Atlantic Monthly).

Robert F. Kennedy Book Award. To recognize authors whose books faithfully and forcefully reflect Robert Kennedy's concerns: justice and equality for the poor, the minorities, and the young; and the responsible examination of major social issues. *Offered by:* Robert F. Kennedy Memorial. *Winner:* Albert Gore, Jr., for *Earth in the Balance* (Houghton Mifflin).

Coretta Scott King Award. For a work that promotes the cause of peace and brotherhood. *Offered by:* American Library Association Social Responsibilities Roundtable. *Winners:* (author) Patricia McKissack for *The Dark-Thirty* (Knopf); (illustrator) Kathleen Atkins Wilson for *The Origin of Life on Earth*, retold by David Anderson (Sight Productions).

Lamont Poetry Selection. *Offered by:* Academy of American Poets. *Winner:* Rosanna Warren for *Stained Glass* (Norton).

Harold Morton Landon Translation Award. For a book of verse translated into English by a single translator. *Offered by:* Academy of American Poets. *Winner:* Charles Simic for *The Horse Has Six Legs: An Anthology of Serbian Poetry* (Graywolf Press).

Lannan Literary Awards. *Offered by:* Lannan Foundation. *Winners:* (fiction) Paul West; (poetry) Denise Levertov; (nonfiction) Edward Hoagland; (lifetime achievement) William Gaddis.

Lannan Literary Fellowships. *Offered by:* Lannan Foundation. *Winners:* (fiction) Rikki Ducornet, Dennis Johnson, Carole Maso; (poetry) Cyrus Cassells, Benjamin Allen Saenz; (nonfiction) Terry Tempest Williams.

Ruth Lilly Poetry Prize. *Offered by:* American Council for the Arts and Modern Poetry Association. *Winner:* Charles Wright.

Locus Awards. For science fiction writing. *Offered by:* Locus Publications. *Winners:* (best novel) Connie Willis for *Doomsday Book* (Bantam); (best fantasy novel) Tim Powers for *Last Call* (Morrow; (best horror/dark-fantasy novel) Dan Simmons for *Children of the Night* (Putnam); (best first novel) Maureen F. McHugh for *China Mountain Zhang* (Tor Books); (best non-fiction) James Gurney for *Dinotopia* (Turner); (best collection) Robert Silverberg for *The Collected Stories of Robert Silverberg, Vol. 1, Secret Sharers* (Bantam); (best anthology) Gardner Dozois, ed., *The Year's Best Science Fiction: Ninth Annual Collection* (St. Martin's); (best publisher) Tor Books.

Los Angeles Times Book Prizes. To honor literary excellence. *Winners:* (fiction) Barbara Kingsolver for *Pigs in Heaven* (HarperCollins); (poetry) Mark Doty for *My Alexandria* (Univ. of Illinois); (history) Anthony Grafton for *New Worlds, Ancient Texts* (Harvard Univ.); (biography) John Mack Faragher for *Daniel Boone, The Life and Legend of an American Pioneer* (Henry Holt); (science and technology) Daniel McNeill and Paul Freiberger for *Fuzzy Logic* (Simon & Schuster); (current interest) Peter Skerry for *Mexican Americans: The Ambivalent Minority* (Free Press); (Art Seidenbaum Award for First Fiction) Paul Kafka for *Love <Enter>* (Houghton Mifflin); (Robert Kirsch Award) Carolyn See.

McKitterick Prize (Great Britain). For a first novel by a writer over the age of 40. *Offered by:* Society of Authors. *Winner:* Andrew Barrow for *The Tap Dancer* (Duckworth).

McVitie's Prize (Great Britain). For the Scottish writer of the year. *Winner:* John Prebble for *Landscapes and Memories* (HarperCollins).

Lenore Marshall/*The Nation* Poetry Prize. For an outstanding book of poems published in the United States. *Offered by:* *The Nation* and New Hope Foundation. *Winner:* Thom Gunn for *The Man with Night Sweats* (Farrar, Straus & Giroux).

Kurt Maschler Award (Great Britain). For a children's book in which text and illustrations are both excellent and perfectly harmonious. *Offered by:* Book Trust. *Winner:* Karen Wallace and Mike Bostock for *Think of an Eel* (Walker Books).

Somerset Maugham Awards (Great Britain). For young British authors to gain experience in foreign countries. *Offered by:* Society of Authors. *Winners:* Dea Birkett for *Jella* (Gollancz); Duncan McLean for *Out of the Rain* (Bloodaxe).

NCR Book Award (Great Britain). For nonfiction. *Winner:* Peter Hennessy for *Never Again: Britain 1945–1951* (Cape).

National Arts Club Medal of Honor for Literature. *Offered by:* National Arts Club. *Winner:* Aleksandr Solzhenitsyn.

National Book Awards. *Offered by:* National Book Foundation. *Winners:* (fiction) E. Annie Proulx for *The Shipping News* (Scribner); (nonfiction) Gore Vidal for *The United States: Essays 1952–1992* (Random House); (poetry) A. R. Ammons for *Garbage* (Norton).

National Book Critics Circle Awards. *Offered by:* National Book Critics Circle. *Winners:* (fiction) Cormac McCarthy for *All the Pretty Horses* (Knopf); (general nonfiction) Norman Maclean for *Young Men and Fire* (Univ. of Chicago); (biography/autobiography) Carol Brightman for *Writing Dangerously: Mary McCarthy and Her World* (Clarkson Potter); (criticism) Garry Wills for *Lincoln at Gettysburg* (Simon & Schuster); (poetry) Hayden Carruth for *Collected Poems 1946–1991* (Copper Canyon).

National Book Foundation Medal for Distinguished Contribution to American Letters. *Offered by:* National Book Foundation. *Winner:* Clifton Fadiman.

National Jewish Book Awards. *Offered by:* Jewish Book Council. *Winners:* (autobiography/memoir) Norman Manes for *On Clowns* (Grove/Weidenfeld); (children's literature) Karen Hesse for *Letters from Rifka* (Henry Holt); (children's picture book) Michael J. Rosen for *Elijah's Angel* (Harcourt); (contemporary Jewish life) William B. Helmreich for *Against All Odds* (Simon & Schuster); (fiction) A. B. Yehoshua for *Mr. Mani*, tr. by Hillel Halkin (Doubleday); (Holocaust) Christopher R. Browning for *Ordinary Men* (HarperCollins); (Israel) Anita Shapira for *Land and Power*, tr. by William Templer (Oxford); (Jewish folklore and anthropology) Jerome R. Mintz for *Hasidic People* (Harvard); (Jewish history) Naomi W. Cohen for *Jews in Christian America* (Oxford); (Jewish thought) Susan Starr Sared for *Women as Ritual Experts* (Oxford); (scholarship) Ephraim Kanarfogel for *Jewish Education and Society in the High Middle Ages* (Wayne State Univ.); (Sephardic studies) Jane S. Gerber for *The Jews of Spain* (Free Press); (visual arts) Sharon R. Keller, ed., for *The Jews* (Hugh Lauter Levin/Macmillan).

Nebula Award. *Offered by:* Science Fiction Writers of America. *Winners:* (novel) Connie Willis for *Doomsday Book* (Bantam); (novella) James Morrow for *City of Truth* (St. Martin's); (Grand Master) Frederick Pohl.

John Newbery Medal. For the most distinguished contribution to literature for children. *Donor:* ALA Association for Library Service to Children. *Medal contributed by:* Daniel Melcher. *Winner:* Cynthia Rylant for *Missing May* (Orchard Books).

Charles H. and N. Mildred Nilon Excellence in Minority Fiction Award. *Offered by:* Univ. of Colorado/Fiction Collective Two. *Winner:* Omar S. Castaneda for *Remembering to Say "Mouth" or "Face"* (Univ. of Colorado/Fiction Collective Two).

Nobel Prize in Literature. For the total literary output of a distinguished writer. *Offered by:* Swedish Academy. *Winner:* Toni Morrison.

Flannery O'Connor Award for Short Fiction. *Offered by:* Univ. of Georgia Press. *Winners:* Christopher McIlroy for *All My Relations* (Univ. of Georgia); Diane Nelson for *A Brief History of Male Nudes* (Univ. of Georgia).

Scott O'Dell Award for Historical Fiction. *Offered by: Bulletin of the Center for Children's Books,* Univ. of Chicago. *Winner:* Michael Dorris for *Morning Girl* (Hyperion).

PEN/Book-of-the-Month Club Translation Prize. *Offered by:* PEN American Center. *Winner:* Thomas Hoisington for *The Adventures of Mr. Nicholas Wisdom* by Ignacy Krasicki (Northwestern Univ.).

PEN Center USA West Annual Literary Awards. For outstanding literary achievement by writers living west of the Mississippi. *Winners:* (fiction) Rudolfo Anaya for *Albuquerque* (Univ. of New Mexico); (nonfiction) William Kittredge for *Hole in the Sky* (Knopf); (poetry) Thom Gunn for *The Man with Night Sweats* (Farrar, Straus & Giroux); (children's) Randy Powell for *Is Kissing a Girl Who Smokes Like Licking an Ashtray?* (Farrar, Straus & Giroux); (Elinor D. Randall Translation Prize) Wayne Lammers for *Still Life and Other Stories* (Stone Bridge Press).

Fernando Pessoa Award. *Offered by:* Columbia University Translation Center. *Winner:* Lisa Sapinkopf for *Selected Poems of Sophia de Mello Breyner* (Copper Canyon).

Edgar Allan Poe Awards. For outstanding mystery, crime, and suspense writing. *Offered by:* Mystery Writers of America. *Winners:* (novel) Margaret Maron for *Bootlegger's Daughter* (Mysterious Press); (first novel) Michael Connelly for *The Black Echo* (Little, Brown); (original paperback) Dana Stabenow for *A Cold Day for Murder* (Berkley); (fact crime) Harry Farrell for *Swift Justice* (St. Martin's); (critical/biographical) John Loughery for *Alias S.S. Van Dine* (Scribner); (young adult) Chap Reaver for *A Little Bit Dead* (Delacorte); (juvenile) Eve Bunting for *Coffin on a Case* (HarperCollins); (Grand Master) Donald E. Westlake; (Reader of the Year) Bill Clinton.

Poets' Prize. For the best book of verse published by a U.S. poet in the preceding year. *Offered by:* Poets' Prize Foundation. *Winner:* Adrienne Rich for *An Atlas of the Difficult World* (Norton).

Renato Poggioli Translation Award. For an outstanding translation. *Offered by:* PEN American Center. *Winner:* Ann Goldstein for *Journey to the Land of Flies,* by Aldo Buzzi (work-in-progress).

Prix Goncourt (France). For a work of imagination, preferably a novel, exemplifying youth, originality, esprit, and form. *Winner:* Amlin Maalouf for *Le Rocher de Tanios* (Grasset).

Pulitzer Prizes in Letters. To honor distinguished works by American writers, dealing preferably with American themes.

Offered by: Columbia Univ. Graduate School of Journalism. *Winners:* (fiction) Robert Olen Butler for *A Good Scent from a Strange Mountain* (Henry Holt); (history) Gordon S. Wood for *The Radicalism of the American Revolution* (Knopf); (biography) David McCullough for *Truman* (Simon & Schuster); (poetry) Louise Gluck for *The Wild Iris* (Ecco Press); (general nonfiction) Garry Wills for *Lincoln at Gettysburg* (Simon & Schuster).

QPB New Voices Award. For the most distinctive and promising work of fiction offered by the Quality Paperback Book Club. *Winner:* Sandra Cisneros for *Woman Hollering Creek* (Random House).

Rea Award. For an outstanding short story. To honor a living writer who has made a significant contribution to the short story as an art form. *Offered by:* Dungannon Foundation. *Winner:* Grace Paley.

Romance Writers of America RITA Awards. *Winners:* (traditional) Maria Ferrarella for *Father Goose* (Silhouette); (short contemporary) Helen R. Myers for *Navarrone* (Silhouette); (long contemporary) Karen Young for *The Silence of Midnight* (Harlequin); (young adult) Sherry Garland for *Song of the Buffalo Boy* (Harcourt); (single title contemporary) Kathleen Eagle for *This Time Forever* (Avon); (historical series) Cheryl Reavis for *The Prisoner* (Harlequin); (historical single title) Penelope Williamson for *Keeper of the Dream* (Dell); (regency romance) Jo Beverley for *An Unwilling Bride* (Zebra Regency); (romantic suspense/gothic) Nora Roberts for *Divine Evil* (Bantam); (futuristic/fantasy/paranormal) Antoinette Stockenberg for *Emily's Ghost* (Dell); (best first book) Jeane Renick for *Trust Me* (Harper Monogram); (golden choice award) Jill Marie Landis for *Come Spring* (Jove Books).

Rome Fellowship in Literature. *Offered by:* American Academy in Rome. *Sponsored by:* American Academy of Arts and Letters and Philip Morris Companies. *Winner:* Thomas Bolt.

Richard and Hinda Rosenthal Foundation Award. For a work of fiction that is a considerable literary achievement though not necessarily a commercial success. *Offered*

by: American Academy of Arts and Letters. *Winner:* Robert Olen Butler for *A Good Scent from a Strange Mountain* (Henry Holt).

Sagittarius Prize (Great Britain). For a first novel by a writer over the age of 60. *Offered by:* Society of Authors. *Winner:* Brian O'Doherty for *The Strange Case of Mademoiselle P* (Chatto).

Félix-Antoine Savard Award. *Offered by:* Columbia University Translation Center. *Winner:* Daniel Sloate for *Selected Poems* by Marie Uguay (Guernica Press).

Science Book Prize (Great Britain). *Sponsored by:* Rhone-Poulenc. *Winner:* Steven Rose for *The Making of Memory* (Bantam Press).

Shamus Awards. To honor the private eye writer of mystery fiction. *Offered by:* Private Eye Writers of America. *Winners:* (best novel) Harold Adams for *The Man Who Was Taller Than God* (Walker Books); (best first novel) John Straley for *The Woman Who Married a Bear* (Soho); (best paperback original) Marele Day for *The Last Tango of Dolores Delgado* (Allen & Unwin); (lifetime achievement) Marcia Muller.

Smarties Book Prizes (Great Britain). To encourage high standards and to stimulate interest in books for children. *Offered by:* Book Trust. *Winners:* (Grand Prix and ages 6 to 8) Michael Foreman for *War Game* (Pavilion); (under age 5) Rita Philips Mitchell and Carolyn Binch for *Hue Boy* (Gollancz); (ages 9 to 11) Maeve Henry for *Listen to the Dark* (Heinemann).

W. H. Smith Literary Award (Great Britain). For a significant contribution to literature. *Offered by:* W. H. Smith. *Winner:* Michele Roberts for *Daughters of the House* (Virago).

Jean Stein Award for Nonfiction. *Offered by:* American Academy of Arts and Letters. *Winner:* Stanley Crouch.

Bram Stoker Awards. For best horror writing of the year. *Offered by:* Horror Writers of America. *Winners:* (novel) Thomas F. Monteleone for *Blood of the Lamb* (Tor Books); (first novel) Elizabeth Massie for *Sineater* (Pan Books); (collection) Norman Partridge for *Mr. Fox and Other Feral*

Tales (Roadkill Press); (nonfiction) Christopher Golden, ed., for *Cut! Horror Writers on Horror Film* (Berkley); (lifetime achievement) Ray Russell.

Mildred and Harold Straus Living Awards. To enable writers to devote their working time completely to writing. *Offered by:* American Academy of Arts and Letters. *Winners:* John Casey, Joy Williams.

Sunday Express Book of the Year Award (Great Britain). *Offered by: Sunday Express. Winner:* William Boyd for *The Blue Afternoon* (Sinclair-Stevenson).

Sunday Times Young Writer of the Year Award (Great Britain). *Offered by: Sunday Times. Winner:* Simon Armitage for *Xanadu* (Bloodaxe).

Betty Trask Awards (Great Britain). For works of a romantic or traditional nature by writers under the age of 35. *Offered by:* Society of Authors. *Winners:* Mark Blackaby for *You'll Never Be Here Again* (unpublished); Simon Corrigan for *Tommy Was Here* (Deutsch); Joanna Briscoe for *Mothers and Other Lovers* (unpublished); Olivia Fane for *Landing on Clouds* (unpublished).

Kingsley Tufts Poetry Award ($50,000). *Offered by:* Claremont Graduate School. *Winner:* Susan Mitchell for *Rapture* (HarperCollins).

Harold D. Vursell Memorial Award in Literature. *Offered by:* American Academy and of Arts and Letters. *Winner:* T. Coraghessan Boyle.

Lila Wallace–*Reader's Digest* Fund Writer's Awards. *Offered by:* Lila Wallace Foundation. *Winners:* Richard Bausch, Bruce Duffy, Mary Gordon, Jamaica Kincaid, Maxine Hong Kingston, Sharon Olds, Anton Shammas, Ntozake Shange, Tom Sleigh, C. K. Williams, C. D. Wright.

Washington Post/Children's Book Guild Award for Nonfiction. To honor an author or author-illustrator whose total work has contributed significantly to the quality of nonfiction for children. *Winner:* Seymour Simon.

Western States Book Awards. *Offered by:* Western States Arts Federation. *Winners:* (fiction) Carol Orlock for *The Hedge, The Ribbon* (Broken Moon Press); (creative nonfiction) Velma Wallis for *Two Old Women* (Epicenter Press); (poetry) Jane Miller for *August Zero* (Copper Canyon Press).

Whitbread Literary Awards (Great Britain). For literature of merit that is readable on a wide scale. *Offered by:* Booksellers Association of Great Britain. *Winners:* (novel) Joan Brady for *Theory of War* (Deutsch); (first novel) Rachel Cusk for *Saving Agnes* (Macmillan); (biography) Andrew Motion for *Philip Larkin: A Writer's Life* (Faber); (poetry) Carol Ann Duffy for *Mean Time* (Anvil Press); (children's novel) Anne Fine for *Flour Babies* (Hamish Hamilton).

William Allen White Children's Book Award. *Offered by:* Emporia State University. *Winner:* Jerry Spinelli for *Maniac Magee* (Little, Brown).

Whiting Writers Awards. *Offered by:* Mrs. Giles Whiting Foundation. *Winners:* Jeffrey Eugenides, Dagoberto Gilb, Kevin Kling, Mark Levine, Nathaniel Mackey, Dionisio D. Martinez, Sigrid Nunez, Janet Peery, Kathleen Peirce, Lisa Shea.

Walt Whitman Award. For poetry. *Offered by:* Academy of American Poets. *Winner:* Alison Hawthorne for *Science and Other Poems* (Louisiana State Univ.).

Thornton Niven Wilder Awards. *Offered by:* Columbia University Translation Center. *Winner:* (Norwegian) Peter Magnus; (Hungarian) Lazlo Gy Horvath; (Persian) Najaf Daryabandari.

William Carlos Williams Award. For the best book of poetry published by a small, nonprofit, or university press. *Offered by:* Poetry Society of America. *Winner:* Louise Gluck for *The Wild Iris* (Ecco Press).

Robert H. Winner Memorial Award. For a poem or sequence of poems characterized by a delight in language and the possibilities of ordinary life. *Offered by:* Poetry Society of America. *Winner:* Helen Frost.

L. L. Winship Book Award. To an author who has written the best book with a connection to New England. *Offered by: Boston Globe. Winner:* Nicholas Fox Weber for *Patron Saints* (Knopf).

George Wittenborn Memorial Book Awards. *Offered by:* Art Libraries Society of North

America. *Winners:* Nelson–Atkins Museum of Art for *The Century of Tung Ch'i'ch'ang*, Wai-Kam Ho, ed.; American Institute of Architects Press for *Fay Jones: the Architecture of E. Fay Jones, FAIA*, by Robert Adams Ivy; Grupo Azabache for *Pintura y escultura en Nueva Espana (1557–1640)*, by Guillermo Tovar de Teresa; Rizzoli International Publications for *Puerto Rico 1900: Turn-of-the-Century Architecture in the Hispanic Caribbean, 1890–1930*, by Jorge Rigau; Minneapolis Institute of Arts for *Visions of the People: A Pictorial History of the Plains Indian Life*, by Evan M. Maurer.

Paul A. Witty Short Story Award. *Offered by:* International Reading Association. *Winner:* Shizuko Obo for "The Day Mother Sold the Family Swords" (*Cricket* magazine, August 1992).

World Fantasy Convention Awards. For outstanding fantasy writing. *Winners:* (novel) Tim Powers for *Last Call* (Avon Books); (best collection) Jack Cady for *The Sons of Noah* (Broken Moon Press); (best anthology) Dennis Etchison, ed., for *Metahorror* (Dell); (lifetime achievement) Harlan Ellison.

World Science Fiction Convention Hugo Awards. For outstanding science fiction writing. *Winners:* (fiction) Vernor Vinge for *A Fire Upon the Deep* (Tor Books), Connie Willis for *Doomsday Book* (Bantam); (nonfiction) Harry Warner, Jr., for *A Wealth of Fable: An Informal History of Science Fiction Fandom in the 1950's* (SCIFI).

Morton Dauwen Zabel Award in Poetry. *Offered by:* American Academy of Arts and Letters. *Winner:* James Purdy.

Part 6
Directory of Organizations

Directory of Library and Related Organizations

Networks, Consortia, and Other Cooperative Library Organizations

This list is taken from the 1993-1994 edition of *American Library Directory*, (R. R. Bowker),which includes additional information on member libraries and primary functions of each organization.

United States

Alabama

Alabama Health Libraries Association Inc. (ALHeLa), Mobile Infirmary Medical Center, Box 2144, Mobile 36652. SAN 372-8218. Tel. 205-431-3134. FAX 205-431-2529. *Pres.* Joy H. Harriman; *V.P.* Sondra Pfieffer.

Jefferson County Hospital Librarians Association, Medical Lib., AMI, Brookwood Medical Center, 2010 Brookwood Dr., Birmingham 35209. SAN 371-2168. Tel. 205-877-1131. *Coord.* Lucy Moor.

Library Management Network Inc., 915 Monroe St., Box 443, Huntsville 35804. SAN 322-3906. Tel. 205-532-5963. FAX 205-532-5994. *System Coord.* Charlotte Moncrief.

Marine Environmental Sciences Consortium, Dauphin Island Sea Lab, Box 369-370, Dauphin Island 36528. SAN 322-0001. Tel. 205-861-2141. FAX 205-861-4646. *Dir.* George Crozier; *Libn.* Connie Mallon.

Network of Alabama Academic Libraries, c/o Alabama Commission on Higher Education, One Court Sq., Suite 221, Montgomery 36104-3584. SAN 322-4570. FAX 205-240-3349. *Dir.* Sue O. Medina.

Alaska

Alaska Library Network, 3600 Denali, Anchorage 99503. SAN 371-0688. Tel. 907-261-2976. *Coord.* Judy Monroe.

Arizona

Arizona Resources Consortium, c/o Northland Pioneer College, 1200 E. Hermosa Dr., Box 610, Holbrook 86025-0610. SAN 329-5176. Tel. 602-524-6111, Ext. 265. FAX 602-524-2772. *Head Libn.* Ronald J. Kupper; *Co-Dir.* Glen Tiller.

Central Arizona Biomedical Librarians (CABL), c/o Maricopa County Medical Society Lib., 326 E. Coronado, No. 104, Phoenix 85004. SAN 370-7598. Tel. 602-252-3224. FAX 602-251-3224. *Chair* Joe Esposito; *Program Chair, Chair-Elect* Lenore Schnaitman.

Maricopa County Community College District, Lib. Technical Services, 2411 W. 14 St., Tempe 85281-6941. SAN 322-0060. Tel. 602-731-8774. FAX 602-731-8787. *Coord. Acq.* Randi Sher; *Coord. Tech. Services* Kathy A. Lynch; *Dir.* Gilbert Gonzales.

Navajo County Library Consortium, c/o Northland Pioneer College, Box 610, Holbrook 86025. SAN 323-9896. Tel. 602-

524-6111, Ext. 202. FAX 602-524-2772. *Admin.* Ronald J. Kupper.

Arkansas

Arkansas Area Health Education Center Consortium (AHEC), Sparks Regional Medical Center, 1311 S. I St., Box 17006, Fort Smith 72917-7006. SAN 329-3734. Tel. 501-441-5337. FAX 501-441-5339. *Regional Health Science Libn.* Grace Anderson.

Independent College Fund of Arkansas, Twin City Bank Bldg., Suite 610, One Riverfront Place, North Little Rock 72114. SAN 322-0079. Tel. 501-378-0843. *Pres.* E. Kearney Dietz.

Northeast Arkansas Hospital Library Consortium, 223 E. Jackson, Jonesboro 72401. SAN 329-529X. Tel. 501-972-1290. FAX 501-931-0839. *Dir.* Peggy Blair.

South Arkansas Film Coop, Ash and E. Third, Malvern 72104. SAN 321-5938. Tel. 501-332-5442. FAX 501-332-6679. *Coord.* Tammy Lackey; *Project Dir.* Mary Cheatham.

California

Area Wide Library Network (AWLNET), 2420 Mariposa St., Fresno 93721. SAN 322-0087. Tel. 209-488-3229. *Dir. Info. Services* Sharon Vandercook.

Asian Shared Information and Access (ASIA), 2225 W. Commonwealth Ave., Alhambra 91803. SAN 371-5086. Tel. 818-284-7744. FAX 818-284-1475. *Project Dir.* Kate Seifert.

Bay Area Library and Information Network (BAYNET), California Academy of Science, M. W. Malliard Lib., Golden Gate Park, San Francisco 94118. SAN 371-0610. Tel. 415-750-7101. *Pres.* Tom Moritz; *Treas.* Ann Patterson.

Central Association of Libraries (CAL), 605 N. El Dorado, Stockton 95202. SAN 322-0125. Tel. 209-944-8649. FAX 209-944-8292. *Chair.* Susan Walsh.

Consumer Health Information Program & Services (CHIPS), County of Los Angeles Public Lib., 151 E. Carson St., Carson 90745. SAN 372-8110. Tel. 310-830-0909. *Libn.* Ellen Mulkern.

Cooperating Libraries in Claremont (CLIC), c/o Honnold Lib., Claremont Colleges, 800 Dartmouth Ave., Claremont 91711. SAN 322-3949. Tel. 909-621-8045. *Dir.* Bonnie J. Clemens.

Cooperative Library Agency for Systems and Services (CLASS), 1415 Koll Circle, Suite 101, San Jose 95112-4698. SAN 322-0117. Tel. 408-453-0444. FAX 408-453-5379. *Exec. Dir.* Robert A. Drescher; *Chair* Dennis E. Smith.

Dialog Information Services Inc., 3460 Hillview Ave., Palo Alto 94304. SAN 322-0176. Tel. 415-858-3785. FAX 415-858-7069. *Pres.* Patrick Tierney.

Health Information to Community Hospitals (HITCH), c/o Norris Medical Lib., Univ. of Southern California, 2003 Zonal Ave., Los Angeles 90033-4582. SAN 322-4066. Tel. 213-342-1967. FAX 213-221-1235. *Dir.* Nelson J. Gilman; *Coord.* William Clintworth; *Libn.* Louise Adams.

Inland Empire Academic Libraries Cooperative, Univ. of LaVerne, Wilson Lib., 2040 Third St., LaVerne 91750. SAN 322-015X. Tel. 714-593-6251. *Coord.* Marlin Heckman.

Inland Empire Medical Library Cooperative (IEMLC), c/o Kaiser Foundation Hospital, 9961 Sierra Ave., Fontana 92335. SAN 371-8980. Tel. 909-427-5085. FAX 909-427-7356. *Chair* Shirley Younce.

Kaiser Permanente Library System–Southern California Region (KPLS), Health Sciences Lib., 4647 Zion Ave., San Diego 92120. SAN 372-8153. Tel. 619-528-7323.

Learning Resources Cooperative, c/o County Office of Education, 6401 Linda Vista Rd., San Diego 92111. SAN 371-0785. Tel. 619-292-3608. *Dir.* Marvin Barbula.

Los Angeles County Health Sciences Library Consortium, c/o Rancho Los Amigos Medical Center, Health Sciences Lib., 7601 E. Imperial Hwy., Downey 90242. SAN 322-4317. Tel. 310-940-7696. *Coord.* Evelyn Marks.

Medical Library and Information Consortium (MLIC), c/o Planetree at San Jose Medical Center, 98 N. 17 St., San Jose 95112. SAN

371-0513. Tel. 408-998-3212, Ext. 4137. *Chair* Candace Ford.

Metropolitan Cooperative Library System (MCLS), 2235 N. Lake Ave., Suite 106, Altadena 91001. SAN 371-3865. Tel. 818-798-1146. *System Dir.* Linda Katsouleas.

National Network of Libraries of Medicine–Pacific Southwest Region (PSRML), Louise Darling Biomedical Lib., 10833 Leconte Ave., Los Angeles 90024-1798. SAN 372-8234. Tel. 310-825-1200. *Dir.* Alison Bunting.

Northern California and Nevada Medical Library Group, 2140 Shattuck Ave., Box 2105, Berkeley 94704. SAN 329-4617. *Pres.* Peggy Tahir.

Northern California Association of Law Libraries (NOCALL), Univ. of California Law Lib., Davis 95616. SAN 323-5777. Tel. 916-752-3328. FAX 916-752-8768. *Pres.* Judy James.

Northern California Consortium of Psychology Libraries (NCCPL), Pacific Graduate School of Psychology Lib., 935 E. Meadow Dr., Palo Alto 94303. SAN 371-9006. Tel. 415-494-7477, Ext. 11. *Co-Chairs* Christine Dassoff, Peter Hirose.

Northern California Telecommunications Consortium, 2211 Park Towne Circle, No. 4, Sacramento 95825. SAN 329-4412. Tel. 916-483-2496. FAX 916-483-2497. *Exec. Dir.* Michael T. McManus; *Operations Supervisor* Sandra Scott-Smith.

OCLC Pacific Network (PACNET), 9227 Haven Ave., Suite 260, Rancho Cucamonga 91730. SAN 370-0747. Tel. 909-941-4220. FAX 909-948-9803. *Dir.* Bruce Preslan.

Pacific Southwest Regional Medical Library (PSRML), c/o Louise Darling Biomedical Lib., 10833 Le Conte Ave., Los Angeles 90024-1798. SAN 322-0192. Tel. 310-825-1200. FAX 310-825-5389. *Dir.* Alison Bunting.

Peninsula Libraries Automated Network (PLAN), 25 Tower Rd., San Mateo 94402-4000. SAN 371-5035. Tel. 415-571-6798. FAX 415-349-5089. *Project Dir.* Lois Kershner.

Performing Arts Libraries Network of Greater Los Angeles (PALNET), UCLA Arts Lib., Univ. Research Lib., 405 Hil-gard Ave., Los Angeles 90024-1575. SAN 371-3997. Tel. 310-825-3817. *Chair* Brigitte Kueppers.

Research Libraries Group Inc., 1200 Villa St., Mountain View 94041-1100 (see also under National Library and Information Industry Associations). SAN 322-0206. Tel. 415-962-9951. FAX 415-964-0943. *Pres.* James Michalko.

Sacramento Area Health Sciences Librarians, Robert Garlick Lib., Mercy–San Juan Hospital–Carmichael CA, Carmichael 95608. SAN 322-4007. Tel. 916-537-5218. FAX 916-537-5254. *Pres.* Meredith Johanson.

San Bernardino, Inyo, Riverside Counties United Library Services, 312 W. 20 St., Suite D, San Bernardino 92405. SAN 322-0222. Tel. 909-882-7577. FAX 909-882-6871. *Dir.* Vaughn L. Simon.

San Francisco Biomedical Library Group, California College of Pediatric Medicine, 1210 Scotts St., San Francisco 94115. SAN 371-2125. Tel. 415-292-0409. *Coord.* Ron Schultz.

San Francisco Consortium, 513 Parnassus Ave., Box 0400, San Francisco 94143. SAN 322-0249. Tel. 415-476-9155. *Exec. Dir.* Malcolm S. M. Watts.

Santa Clara Valley Medical Center, Milton J. Chatton Medical Lib., 751 S. Bascom Ave., San Jose 95128. SAN 322-0184. Tel. 408-299-5650. FAX 408-299-8859. *Medical Libn.* Shirley Kinoshita.

Santa Clarita Interlibrary Network (SCILNET), 24700 McBean Pkwy., Santa Clarita 91355. SAN 371-8964. Tel. 805-253-7885. *Pres.* Janet Tillman; *Recorder* Leslie Bretall.

Serra Cooperative Library System, 5555 Overland Ave., Bldg. 15, San Diego 92123. SAN 372-8129. Tel. 619-694-3600. *System Coord.* Susan Swisher.

The SMERC Library, 101 Twin Dolphin Dr., Redwood City 94065-1064. SAN 322-0265. Tel. 415-802-5650. *Educational Services Mgr.* Karol Thomas; *Ref. Coord.* Mary Moray.

SOUTHNET, c/o South Bay Cooperative Lib. System, 180 W. San Carlos St., San Jose 95113. SAN 322-4260. Tel. 408-294-2345. FAX 408-295-7388. *Asst. Systems Dir.* Susan Holmer.

State of California Answering Network (SCAN), c/o Los Angeles Public Lib., 630 W. Fifth St., Los Angeles 90071-2097. SAN 322-029X. Tel. 213-612-3216. FAX 213-612-0546. *Dir.* Evelyn Greenwald.

Substance Abuse Librarians and Information Specialists (SALIS), Box 9513, Berkeley 94709-0513. SAN 372-4042. Tel. 510-642-5208. FAX 510-642-7175. *Dir. SALIS Institutional Home* Andrea Mitchell; *Chair* Jill Austin.

Total Interlibrary Exchange (TIE), 5574 Everglades St., Suite A, Ventura 93003. SAN 322-0311. Tel. 805-650-7732. FAX 805-642-9095. *Pres.* John Murray.

Colorado

Arkansas Valley Regional Library Service System (AVRLSS), 635 W. Corona, Suite 113, Pueblo 81004. SAN 371-5094. Tel. 719-542-2156. *Dir.* Donna R. Jones; *Chair* Bev Moore.

Bibliographical Center for Research, Rocky Mountain Region Inc., 14394 E. Evans Ave., Aurora 80014-1478. SAN 322-0338. Tel. 303-751-6277. FAX 303-751-9787. *Exec. Dir.* David H. Brunell.

Central Colorado Library System (CCLS), 4350 Wadsworth Blvd., Suite 340, Wheat Ridge 80033-0200. SAN 371-3970. Tel. 303-422-1150. *Dir.* Gordon C. Barhydt.

Colorado Alliance of Research Libraries (CARL), Bldg. D, 3801 E. Florida Ave., Suite 300, Denver 80210. SAN 322-3760. Tel. 303-758-3030. *Exec. Dir.* Alan Charnes.

Colorado Association of Law Libraries, Box 13363, Denver 80201. SAN 322-4325. Tel. 303-492-2709. FAX 303-492-2707. *Pres.* Bobbie Studwell.

Colorado Council of Medical Librarians (CCML), Webb Memorial Lib., Penrose/St. Francis Healthcare Systems, Box 7021, Colorado Springs 80933. SAN 370-0755. Tel. 719-630-5288. FAX 719-630-5603. *Pres.* Nina Janas.

Colorado Resource Sharing Network, c/o Colorado State Lib., 201 E. Colfax, Denver 80203-1799. SAN 322-3868. Tel. 303-866-6900. FAX 303-830-0793. *Coord.* Susan Fayad.

High Plains Regional Library Service System, 800 Eighth Ave., Suite 341, Greeley 80631. SAN 371-0505. Tel. 303-356-4357. FAX 303-353-4355. *Dir.* Nancy Knepel; *Chair* Verl Manwarren.

Irving Library Network, c/o Jefferson County Public Lib., 10200 W. 20 Ave., Lakewood 80215. SAN 325-321X. Tel. 303-232-7114. *Network Mgr.* Carol Lehman.

Peaks and Valleys Library Consortium, c/o Arkansas Valley Regional Lib. Service System, 635 W. Corona Ave., Suite 113, Pueblo 81004. SAN 328-8684. Tel. 719-542-2156. *Pres.* Dick Maxwell.

Pueblo Library System Software Users' Group, 300 N. Adams, Loveland 80537. SAN 322-4635. Tel. 303-962-2400. FAX 303-962-2905. *Pres.* Ted Schmidt.

Southwest Regional Library Service System (SWRLSS), Drawer B, Durango 81302. SAN 371-0815. Tel. 303-247-4782. FAX 303-247-5087. *Technical Services Resource Sharing Mgr.* Judith M. Griffiths.

Connecticut

Capitol Area Health Consortium, 183 E. Cedar St., Newington 06111. SAN 322-0370. Tel. 203-666-3304, Ext. 302. FAX 203-666-8110. *Dir.* Robert Boardman.

Capitol Region Library Council, 599 Matianuck Ave., Windsor 06095-3567. SAN 322-0389. Tel. 203-549-0404. FAX 203-728-0135. *Exec. Dir.* Dency Sargent.

Connecticut Association of Health Sciences Libraries (CAHSL), Rockville General Hospital, 31 Union St., Rockville 06066. SAN 322-0397. Tel. 203-872-5277. FAX 203-872-5169. *Pres.* Laurie Fornes.

Council of State Library Agencies in the Northeast (COSLINE), Connecticut State Lib., 231 Capitol Ave., Hartford 06106. SAN 322-0451. Tel. 203-566-4301. FAX 203-566-8940. *Pres.* Sara Parker.

CTW Library Consortium, Olin Memorial Lib., Wesleyan Univ., Middletown 06457-6065. SAN 329-4587. Tel. 203-347-9411, Ext. 3143. FAX 203-344-7969. *Dir.* Alan E. Hagyard; *Applications Programmer* Mary Wilson; *Systems Programmer* Bu Yang.

Eastern Connecticut Library Association, 15 Wilson St., Willimantic 06226-1920. SAN 322-0427. Tel. 203-456-4343. FAX 203-423-1839. *Exec. Dir.* Marietta Johnson.

Hartford Consortium for Higher Education, 260 Girard Ave., Hartford 06105. SAN 322-0443. Tel. 203-236-1203. *Dir.* Kimberly Burris.

LEAP (Library Exchange Aids Patrons), 2901 Dixwell Ave., Hamden 06518. SAN 322-4082. Tel. 203-281-7498. FAX 203-288-4052. *Exec. Dir.* Richard Dionne; *Chair* Lois Baldini.

Libraries Online Inc. (LION), 123 Broad St., Middletown 06457. SAN 322-3922. Tel. 203-347-1704. *Pres.* Marie Shaw; *Exec. Dir.* William F. Edge, Jr.

National Network of Libraries of Medicine New England Region 8, NN-LM NE Region 8, Univ. of Connecticut Health Center, 263 Farmington Ave., Farmington 06030-5370. SAN 372-5448. Tel. 203-679-4500. FAX 203-679-1305. *Dir.* Ralph D. Arcari.

Northwestern Connecticut Health Science Libraries, 50 Hospital Hill Rd., Sharon 06069. SAN 329-5257. Tel. 203-364-4095. FAX 203-364-4003. *Libn.* Michael Schott; *Coord.* Jackie Rourke.

Region One Cooperating Library Service Unit Inc., 267 Grand St., Waterbury 06702-1981. SAN 322-046X. Tel. 203-756-6149. FAX 203-757-1117. *Coord.* Tom Lawrence.

Southeastern Connecticut Library Association (SECLA), 1084 Shennecossett Rd., Groton 06340-6097. SAN 322-0478. Tel. 203-445-5577. FAX 203-449-6932. *Dir.* Patricia Holloway.

Southern Connecticut Library Council, 2405 Whitney Ave., Hamden 06518. SAN 322-0486. Tel. 203-288-5757. FAX 203-287-0757. *Dir.* Susan Carlquist Muro.

Southwestern Connecticut Library Council Inc., 925 Broad St., Bridgeport 06604. SAN 322-0494. Tel. 203-367-6439. FAX 203-367-2521. *Admin.* Ann Neary.

Delaware

Central Delaware Library Consortium, Dover Public Lib., 45 S. State St., Dover 19901.

SAN 329-3696. Tel. 302-736-7030. FAX 302-736-0985. *Dir.* Robert S. Wetherall.

Delaware Library Consortium, Delaware Academy of Medicine, 1925 Lovering Ave., Wilmington 19806. SAN 329-3718. Tel. 302-656-6398. FAX 302-656-0470. *Pres.* Gail P. Gill.

Kent Library Network, 412 N. Governor's Ave., Dover 19901. SAN 371-2214. Tel. 302-736-6184. *Pres.* Richard Krueger.

Libraries in the New Castle County System (LINCS), University of Delaware, Newark 19717-5267. SAN 329-4889. Tel. 302-831-2965. *Pres.* Paul Anderson.

Sussex Help Organization for Resources Exchange (SHORE), 109 E. Laurel, Georgetown 19947-1442. SAN 322-4333. Tel. 302-846-9894. *Pres.* Diana McDonnell.

Wilmington Area Biomedical Library Consortium, 1925 Lovering Ave., Wilmington 19806. SAN 322-0508. Tel. 302-656-6398. *Pres.* Gail P. Gill.

District of Columbia

American Association of Zoological Parks and Aquariums–Librarians Special Interest Group (AAZPA–LSIG), National Zoological Park, Washington 20008. SAN 373-0891. Tel. 202-673-4771. *Chair* Kay Kenyon.

CAPCON Library Network, 1320 19th St. N.W., Suite 400, Washington 20036. SAN 321-5954. Tel. 202-331-5771. FAX 202-797-7719. *Exec. Dir.* Dennis Reynolds.

Christian College Coalition, 329 Eighth St. N.E., Washington 20002. SAN 322-0524. Tel. 202-546-8713. FAX 202-546-8913. *Pres.* Myron S. Augsburger.

Cluster of Independent Theological Schools, 391 Michigan Ave. N.E., Washington 20017. SAN 322-0532. Tel. 202-529-5244. *Chair* Richard Murphy.

District of Columbia Health Sciences Information Network (DOCHSIN), Prince Georges Hospital Center Medical Lib., Sheverly, MD 20785. SAN 323-9918. Tel. 301-618-2490. *Pres.* Penny Martin.

Educational Resources Information Center (ERIC), U.S. Dept. of Educ., 555 New Jersey Ave. N.W., Washington 20208-5720.

SAN 322-0567. Tel. 202-219-2289. FAX 202-219-1817. *Dir.* Robert Stonehill.
ERIC Clearinghouses
—ERIC Clearinghouse for Junior Colleges, Math-Sciences Bldg., Rm. 8118, Univ. of California, 405 Hilgard Ave., Los Angeles, CA 90024-1564. SAN 322-0648. Tel. 310-825-3931. FAX 310-206-8095. *Dir.* Art Cohen.
—ERIC Clearinghouse for Science, Mathematics and Environmental Education, Ohio State Univ., 1200 Chambers Rd., Rm. 310, Columbus, OH 43212-1792. SAN 322-0680. Tel. 614-292-6717. FAX 614-292-0263. *Dir.* David Haury.
—ERIC Clearinghouse for Social Studies–Social Science Education, Indiana Univ., Social Studies Development Center, 2805 E. Tenth St., Bloomington, IN 47408-2698. SAN 322-0699. Tel. 812-885-3838. FAX 812-855-7901. *Dir.* John Patrick.
—ERIC Clearinghouse on Adult, Career, and Vocational Education, Center on Education and Training for Employment, 1900 Kenny Rd., Columbus, OH 43210-1090. SAN 322-0575. Tel. 614-292-4353. FAX 614-292-1260. *Dir.* Susan Imel.
—ERIC Clearinghouse on Counseling and Personnel Services, Univ. of Michigan, School of Education, Rm. 2108, 610 E. University St., Ann Arbor, MI 48109-1259. SAN 322-0583. Tel. 313-764-9492. FAX 313-747-2425. *Dir.* Garry Walz.
—ERIC Clearinghouse on Educational Management, Univ. of Oregon, 1787 Agate St., Eugene, OR 97403-5207. SAN 322-0605. Tel. 503-346-5043. FAX 503-346-2334. *Dir.* Phil Piele.
—ERIC Clearinghouse on Elementary and Early Childhood Education, College of Education, Univ. of Illinois, 805 W. Pennsylvania Ave., Urbana, IL 61801-4897. SAN 322-0591. Tel. 217-333-1386. FAX 217-333-3767. *Dir.* Lilian Katz.
—ERIC Clearinghouse on Handicapped and Gifted Children, Council for Exceptional Children, 1920 Association Dr., Reston, VA 22091-1589. SAN 322-0613. Tel. 703-264-9474. FAX 703-264-9494. *Dir.* Fred Weintraub.

—ERIC Clearinghouse on Higher Education, George Washington Univ., One Dupont Circle, Suite 630, Washington, DC 20036-1183. SAN 322-0621. Tel. 202-296-2597. FAX 202-296-8379. *Dir.* Jon Fife.
—ERIC Clearinghouse on Information Resources, Syracuse Univ., Huntington Hall, Rm. 030, Syracuse, NY 13244-2340. SAN 322-063X. Tel. 315-443-3640. FAX 315-443-5448. *Dir.* Michael Eisenberg.
—ERIC Clearinghouse on Languages and Linguistics, Center for Applied Linguistics, 1118 22nd St. N.W., Washington, DC 20037-0037. SAN 322-0656. Tel. 202-429-9292. FAX 202-659-5641. *Dir.* Charles Stansfield.
—ERIC Clearinghouse on Reading and Communication Skills, Indiana Univ., Smith Research Center, Bloomington, IN 47408-2698. SAN 322-0664. Tel. 812-855-5847. FAX 812-855-4220. *Dir.* Carl Smith.
—ERIC Clearinghouse on Rural Education and Small Schools, Appalachia Educational Laboratory, 1031 Quarrier St., Box 1348, Charleston, WV 25325-1348. SAN 322-0672. Tel. 304-347-0400. FAX 304-347-0487. *Dirs.* Todd Strohmenger, Craig Howley.
—ERIC Clearinghouse on Teacher Education, American Association of Colleges for Teacher Education, One Dupont Circle N.W., Suite 610, Washington, DC 20036-1186. SAN 322-0702. Tel. 202-293-2450. FAX 202-457-8095. *Dir.* Mary Dilworth.
—ERIC Clearinghouse on Tests, Measurement and Evaluation, American Institutes for Research, Washington Research Center, 3333 K St. N.W., Washington, DC 20007-3541. SAN 322-0710. Tel. 202-342-5060. FAX 202-342-5033. *Dir.* Lawrence Rudner.
—ERIC Clearinghouse on Urban Education, Teachers College, Columbia Univ., 525 W. 120 St., Box 40, New York, NY 10027-9998. SAN 322-0729. Tel. 212-678-3433. FAX 212-678-4048. *Dir.* Erwin Flaxman.
EDUCOM, c/o 1112 16th St. N.W., Suite 600, Washington 20036. SAN 371-487X. Tel. 202-872-4200. *Pres.* Kenneth King; *Membership Mgr.* John Gehl.

FEDLINK (Federal Library and Information Network), c/o Federal Lib. and Info. Center Committee, Lib. of Congress, Washington 20540-5110. SAN 322-0761. Tel. 202-707-4800. FAX 202-707-4818. *Network Coord.* Milton McGee.

Forest Service Information Network, USDA Forest Service, Rm. 809, RPE, Box 96090, Washington 20090-6090. SAN 322-032X. Tel. 703-235-1042. FAX 703-235-1767. *Mgr.* Seung Ja Sinatra.

NASA Library Network, ARIN (Aerospace Research Information Network), NASA Headquarters, Code JTT, Washington 20546. SAN 322-0788. Tel. 202-358-1388. FAX 202-358-3063. *Program Mgr.* Barbara Everidge; *Project Dir.* Roland Ridgeway.

National Library Service for the Blind and Physically Handicapped, 1291 Taylor St. N.W., Washington 20542. SAN 370-5870. Tel. 202-707-5100. FAX 202-707-0712. *Dir.* Frank Kurt Cylke.

Northeast Medical School Consortium, c/o Dahlgren Memorial Lib.–Georgetown Univ. Medical Center, 3900 Reservoir Rd. N.W., Washington 20007. SAN 371-067X. Tel. 202-687-1176. *Libn.* Naomi C. Broering.

Transportation Research Information Services (TRIS), 2101 Constitution Ave. N.W., TRB, 2133-307, Washington 20418. SAN 370-582X. Tel. 202-334-3250. FAX 202-334-3495. *Mgr.* Jerome T. Maddock.

Veterans Affairs Library Network (VAL-NET), Lib. Div. Programs Office, 810 Vermont Ave. N.W., Washington 20420. SAN 322-0834. Tel. 202-535-7521. FAX 202-535-7539. *Asst. Lib. Programs* Wendy N. Carter.

Washington Theological Consortium, 487 Michigan Ave. N.E., Washington 20017-1585. SAN 322-0842. Tel. 202-832-2675. *Exec. Dir.* David Trickett.

Florida

Central Florida Library Consortium (CFLC), Box 521233, Longwood 32752-1233. SAN 371-9014. Tel. 407-322-3580. FAX 407-322-3727. *Exec. Dir.* John Dooley.

Consortium of South Eastern Law Libraries (COSELL), College of Law Lib., Nova Univ. Law Lib., 3305 College Ave., Fort Lauderdale 33314. SAN 372-8277. Tel. 305-452-6210. *Chair* Carol A. Roehrenbeck; *Pres.* Thomas Steele.

Consortium of Southern Biomedical Libraries (CONBLS), Univ. of Florida Health Science Center Lib., Box 100206, Gainesville 37614. SAN 370-7717. Tel. 904-392-4017. FAX 904-392-6803. *Pres.* Ted F. Sryglen.

Florida Library Information Network, c/o Bureau of Lib. and Network Services, State Lib. of Florida, R. A. Gray Bldg., Tallahassee 32399-0250. SAN 322-0869. Tel. 904-487-2651. FAX 904-488-0978. *Bureau Chief* Linda Tepp Fuchs.

Library Affairs Committee of the Associated Mid-Florida Colleges, c/o Merl Kelce Lib., Univ. of Tampa, Tampa 33606. SAN 322-0877. Tel. 813-253-6231. FAX 813-251-0016. *Dir.* Lydia Acosta.

Miami Health Sciences Library Consortium (MHSLC), c/o Broward General Medical Center, 1600 S. Andrews Ave., Fort Lauderdale 33316. SAN 371-0734. Tel. 305-355-4797. *Chair* Lee A. Whiteside, *Mgr.* Dolores Farooqui.

Palm Beach Health Sciences Library Consortium (PBHSLC), c/o Good Samaritan Medical Center Medical Lib., Box 3166, West Palm Beach 33402. SAN 370-0380. Tel. 407-650-6315. FAX 407-650-6417. *Chair* Linda Kressal.

Panhandle Library Access Network (PLAN), 4 Harrison Ave., Suite 5, Panama City 32401. SAN 370-047X. Tel. 904-763-1950. FAX 904-769-0222. *Dir.* Selma K. Jaskowski.

Southeast Florida Library Information Network Inc. (SEFLIN), 100 S. Andrews Ave., Fort Lauderdale 33301. SAN 370-0666. Tel. 305-357-7318. FAX 305-357-6998. *Exec. Dir.* Elizabeth Curry; *Pres.* Samuel F. Morrison.

Tampa Bay Library Consortium Inc., 10002 Princess Palm Ave., Suite 124, Tampa 33619. SAN 322-371X. Tel. 813-622-8252. FAX 813-628-4425. *Pres.* Ted Haggard; *Exec. Dir.* Barbara J. Stites.

Tampa Bay Medical Library Network (TABAMLN), Box 527, Bay Pines 33504. SAN 322-0885. Tel. 813-953-1730. FAX 813-953-1218 *Pres.* Barbara Hartman.

Georgia

Association of Southeastern Research Libraries, Pullen Lib., Georgia State Univ., 100 Decatur St. S.E., Atlanta 30303-3018. SAN 322-1555. Tel. 404-651-2172. FAX 404-651-2508. *Chair* Ralph E. Russell.

Atlanta Health Science Libraries Consortium, Medical Lib., Eglescon Children's Hospital, 1405 Clifton Ave., Atlanta 30322. SAN 322-0893. Tel. 404-325-6438. FAX 404-325-6437. *Pres.* Mamie Bell.

Central Georgia Associated Libraries, c/o Wesleyan College, Willet Memorial Lib., 4760 Forsyth Rd., Macon 31297. SAN 322-0907. Tel. 912-477-1110, Ext. 200. *Dir.* Mrs. Roberts.

Cooperative College Library Center Inc. (CCLC), Suite 602, 159 Ralph McGill Blvd., Atlanta 30308. SAN 322-0915. Tel. 404-659-6886. FAX 404-577-0131. *Acting Dir.* Dorothy Allen.

Emory Medical Television Network, 1440 Clifton Rd. N.E., Rm. 110, Atlanta 30322. SAN 322-0931. Tel. 404-688-8736. FAX 404-523-4706. *Dir.* Dan Joiner; *Business Mgr. & Producer* Julie S. Budnik.

Georgia Health Sciences Library Association (GHSLA), Medical Lib., Crawford Long Hospital of Emory Univ., 550 Peachtree St. N.E., Atlanta 30365. SAN 372-8307. Tel. 404-686-2678. *Chair* Rosaline K. Lett.

Georgia Interactive Network for Medical Information (GaIN), c/o Medical Lib., School of Medicine, Mercer Univ., 1550 College St., Macon 31207. SAN 370-0577. Tel. 912-752-2515. FAX 912-752-2051. *Dir.* Jocelyn A. Rankin.

Georgia Online Database (GOLD), c/o Div. of Public Lib. Services, 156 Trinity Ave. S.W., Atlanta 30303-3692. SAN 322-094X. Tel. 404-656-2461. FAX 404-656-7297. *Dir.* Joe Forsee; *Coord.* Jo Ellen Ostendorf.

Health Science Libraries of Central Georgia (HSLCG), c/o Medical Lib., Mercer Univ.

School of Medicine, 1550 College St., Macon 31207. SAN 371-5051. Tel. 912-752-2515. FAX 912-752-2051. *In Charge* Jocelyn Rankin.

South Georgia Associated Libraries, 208 Gloucester St., Brunswick 31523-0901. SAN 322-0966. Tel. 912-267-1212. FAX 912-267-9597. *Pres.* Betty Frazier; *Secy.-Treas.* Jim Darby.

Southeast Georgia Health Sciences Libraries (SEGHSL), Memorial Medical Center, Box 23089, Savannah 31413. SAN 373-0867. Tel. 912-350-8619. *Chair* Karen Waters; *Chair-Elect* Susan Barrett.

Southeastern Library Network (SOLINET), 1438 W. Peachtree St. N.W., Suite 200, Atlanta 30309-2955. SAN 322-0974. Tel. 404-892-0943. FAX 404-892-7879. *Exec. Dir.* Frank P. Grisham.

Southwest Georgia Health Sciences Library Consortium (SWGHSLC), Medical Lib., Colquitt Regional Medical Center, Moultrie 31776. SAN 372-8072. Tel. 912-890-3460. *Med. Libn.* Susan Staton.

University Center in Georgia Inc., 50 Hurt Plaza, Suite 465, Atlanta 30303-2923. SAN 322-0990. Tel. 404-651-2668. FAX 404-656-0757. *Exec. Dir.* Charles B. Bedford.

Hawaii

Medical Library Group of Hawaii (MLGH), Tripler Army Medical Center, Honolulu 96859-5000. SAN 371-3946. Tel. 808-433-6391. *Chair* Mabel Trafford; *Chair-Elect* Molly Knippenberg.

Idaho

Boise Valley Health Sciences Library Consortium (BVHSLC), Health Sciences Lib., Saint Alphonsus Regional Medical Center, Boise 83706. SAN 371-0807. Tel. 208-378-2271. FAX 208-378-2702. *Contact* Judy Balcerzak.

Cooperative Information Network (CIN), 8385 N. Government Way, Hayden Lake 83835. SAN 323-7656. Tel. 208-772-7648. FAX 208-772-2498. *Contact* John Hartung.

Eastern Idaho System, 457 Broadway, Idaho Falls 83402. SAN 323-7699. Tel. 208-529-

1450. FAX 208-529-1464. *Contact* Paul Holland.

Health Information Retrieval Center, Saint Luke's Regional Medical Center, 190 E. Bannock St., Boise 83712. SAN 322-1008. Tel. 208-386-2277. FAX 208-384-0254. *Dir.* Pamela Spickelmier.

Idaho Health Information Association (IHIA), c/o Health Sciences Lib., Saint Alphonsus Regional Medical Center, 1055 N. Curtis Rd., Boise 83706. SAN 371-5078. Tel. 208-378-2271. *Pres.* Judy Balcerzak; *Pres.-Elect* Kathy Matlock.

Southeast Idaho Health Information Consortium, Idaho Health Sciences Lib., Idaho State Univ., Box 8089, Pocatello 83209. SAN 322-4341. Tel. 208-236-4686. FAX 208-236-4687. *Dir.* Terry Wiggins.

VALNET, Eighth Ave. and Sixth St., Lewiston 83501. SAN 323-7672. Tel. 208-799-2395. FAX 208-799-2831. *Contact* Ann Harris.

Illinois

American Theological Library Association (ATLA), 820 Church St., Suite 300, Evanston 60201-3707. SAN 371-9022. Tel. 708-869-7788. FAX 708-869-8513.

Areawide Hospital Library Consortium of Southwestern Illinois (AHLC), c/o Memorial Hospital, 4500 Memorial Dr., Belleville 62223. SAN 322-1016. Tel. 618-233-7750, Ext. 5343. FAX 618-233-7750, Ext. 5658. *Coord.* Barbara Grout.

Association of Chicago Theological Schools (ACTS), c/o Catholic Theological Union, 5402 S. Cornell Ave., Chicago 60615. SAN 370-0658. Tel. 312-752-5757. *Pres.* Don Senior.

Capital Area Consortium, Brookins Lib., Sangamon State Univ., Springfield 62794-0251. SAN 322-1024. Tel. 217-786-6601. FAX 217-786-6597. *Coord.* Nancy Stump.

Center for Research Libraries, 6050 S. Kenwood, Chicago 60637-2804. SAN 322-1032. Tel. 312-955-4545. FAX 312-955-4339. *Pres.* Donald B. Simpson.

Chicago and South Consortium, La Grange Memorial Hospital, La Grange 60525. SAN 322-1067. Tel. 708-579-4040. *Coord.* Pat Grundke.

Chicago Library System (CLS), 400 State St., 10th fl., Chicago 60605. SAN 372-8188. Tel. 312-747-4013. *Exec. Dir.* Alice Calabrese.

Consortium of Museum Libraries in the Chicago Area, John G. Shedd Aquarium Lib., 1200 S. Lake Shore Dr., Chicago 60605. SAN 371-392X. Tel. 312-986-2289. *Dir.* Janet E. Powers; *Chair* Janice McNeill.

Council of Directors of State University Librarians of Illinois (CODSULI), Southern Illinois Univ. Lib. at Carbondale, Carbondale 62901. SAN 322-1083. Tel. 618-453-2522. FAX 618-453-3440. *Chair* Carolyn A. Snyder.

East Central Illinois Consortium, Medical Lib., Sarah Bush Lincoln H.C., Box 372, Mattoon 61938. SAN 322-1040. Tel. 217-258-2262. FAX 217-258-2111. *Coord.* Nina Pals.

Fox Valley Health Science Library Consortium, Marianjoy Rehabilitation Hospital, Box 795, Wheaton 60189. SAN 329-3831. Tel. 708-462-4104. FAX 708-260-0143. *Coord.* Nalini Mahajan.

Heart of Illinois Library Consortium, College of Nursing Lib., Saint Francis Medical Center, 211 Greenleaf St., Peoria 61603. SAN 322-1113. Tel. 309-665-2180. FAX 309-829-0707. *Dir.* Joyce Hexdall.

Illinois Department of Mental Health and Developmental Disabilities Library Services Network (LISN), Elgin Mental Health Center, 750 S. State St., Elgin 60120. SAN 322-1121. Tel. 708-742-1040, Ext. 2660. *Chair* Jennifer Ford.

Illinois Health Libraries Consortium, c/o Meat Industry Info. Center, National Livestock and Meat Board, 444 N. Michigan Ave., Chicago 60611. SAN 322-113X. Tel. 312-467-5520, Ext. 272. *Coord.* William D. Siarny, Jr.

Illinois Library and Information Network (ILLINET), c/o Illinois State Lib., 300 S. Second St., Springfield 62701-1796. SAN 322-1148. Tel. 217-782-2994. FAX 217-785-4326. *Dir.* Bridget L. Lamont.

Illinois Library Computer Systems Office (ILCSO), Univ. of Illinois, 205 Johnstowne Centre, 502 E. John St., Champaign 61820. SAN 322-3736. Tel.

217-244-7593. FAX 217-244-7596. *Dir.* Bernard G. Sloan.

Illinois State Curriculum Center–East Central Network (ISCC), Sangamon State Univ., F-2, Springfield 62794-9423. SAN 371-5108. Tel. 217-786-6375. FAX 217-786-6036. *Dir.* Rebecca Douglass; *Libn.* Susie Shackleton.

Illinois Valley Library System (IVLS), 845 Brenkman Dr., Pekin 61554. SAN 371-0637. Tel. 309-353-4110. FAX 309-353-8281. *Exec. Dir.* Valerie J. Wilford.

Judaica Library Network of Metropolitan Chicago (JLNMC), c/o Asher Lib., Spertus College of Judaica, 618 S. Michigan Ave., Chicago 60605. SAN 370-0615. Tel. 312-922-8248. FAX 312-922-6406. *Pres.* Cheryl Banks.

Libras Inc., North Central College, Naperville 60540. SAN 322-1172. Tel. 708-420-3400. *Pres.* Carolyn Sheehy.

Metropolitan Consortium of Chicago, Resurrection Medical Center Lib., 7435 W. Talcott, Chicago 60631. SAN 322-1180. Tel. 312-774-8000, Ext. 5930. FAX 312-792-7900. *Coord.* Laura Wimmer.

National Network of Libraries of Medicine, Greater Midwest Region, c/o Lib. of the Health Sciences, Univ. of Illinois at Chicago, 1750 W. Polk St., Box 7509, Chicago 60680-7509. SAN 322-1202. Tel. 312-996-2464. FAX 312-996-2226. *Acting Dir.* Ann C. Weller.

Northern Illinois Learning Resources Cooperative, 91 Sugar Lane, Suite 4, Box 509, Sugar Grove 60554. SAN 329-5583. Tel. 708-466-4848. FAX 708-466-4895. *Exec. Dir.* Donald E. Drake.

Private Academic Libraries of Illinois (PALI), c/o North Park College Lib., 3225 W. Foster Ave., Chicago 60625. SAN 370-050X. Tel. 312-583-2700, Ext. 4081. FAX 312-463-0570. *Pres.* Dorothy Ellen Gross.

Quad Cities Libraries in Cooperation (QUAD-LINC), 220 W. 23 Ave., Coal Valley 61240. SAN 373-093X. Tel. 309-799-3155. FAX 309-799-7916. *Dir.* Robert McKay.

River Bend Library System (RBLS), Box 125, Coal Valley 61240. SAN 371-0653. Tel. 309-799-3155. FAX 309-799-7916. *Coord.* Mary Root.

Sangamon Valley Academic Library Consortium, Box 19231, Springfield 62794-9231. SAN 322-4406. Tel. 217-782-2658. FAX 217-782-0988. *Chair* Martin Gallas.

Shabbona Consortium, c/o Illinois Valley Community Hospital, 925 West St., Peru 61354. SAN 329-5133. Tel. 815-223-3300, Ext. 494. FAX 815-223-3394. *Dir.* Linda Maciejewski.

Upstate Consortium, Swedish American Hospital, 1400 Charles St., Rockford 61104. SAN 329-3793. Tel. 815-961-2030, Ext. 4556. FAX 815-968-3713. *Coord.* Rachel Garza.

USA Toy Library Association, 2530 Crawford Ave., Suite 111, Evanston 60201. SAN 371-215X. Tel. 708-864-3330. *Exec. Dir.* Judith Q. Iacuzzi.

Indiana

Area Library Services Authority Region 2, 209 Lincolnway E., Mishawaka 46544-2084. SAN 322-1210. Tel. 219-255-5262. FAX 219-255-8489. *Exec. Dir.* Shirleen R. Martens.

Area Library Services Authority Region 3 (TRI-ALSA), 900 Webster St., Box 2270, Fort Wayne 46801-2270. SAN 322-1229. Tel. 219-424-6664. FAX 219-422-9762. *Coord.* Jane Raifsnider; *Reference Center Dir.* Marla Baden.

Central Indiana Area Library Services Authority, 1100 W. 42 St., Suite 305, Indianapolis 46208-3302. SAN 322-1237. Tel. 317-926-6561. FAX 317-923-3658. *Acting Dir.* Pam Holt.

Central Indiana Health Science Libraries Consortium, 1701 N. Senate Blvd., Methodist Hospital Lib., Box 1367, Indianapolis 46206. SAN 322-1245. Tel. 317-929-8021. FAX 317-929-8397. *Coord.* Christine Bockrath.

Collegiate Consortium Western Indiana, c/o Cunningham Memorial Lib., Indiana State Univ., Terre Haute 47809. SAN 329-4439. Tel. 812-237-3700. FAX 812-237-2567. *Dean* Ronald G. Leach.

Eastern Indiana Area Library Services Authority, 111 E. 12 St., Anderson 46016. SAN 322-1253. Tel. 317-641-2471. FAX

317-641-2468, 747-8221. *Admin.* Jan Gillespie.

Evansville Area Library Consortium, 3700 Washington Ave., Evansville 47750. SAN 322-1261. Tel. 812-479-4151. FAX 812-473-7564. *Coord.* E. Jane Saltzman.

Four Rivers Area Library Services Authority, Rm. 5, Old Vanderburgh County Court House, 201 N.W. Fourth St., Evansville 47708-1355. SAN 322-127X. Tel. 812-425-1946. FAX 812-425-1969. *Exec. Dir.* Ida L. McDowell.

Indiana Cooperative Library Services Authority (INCOLSA), 5929 Lakeside Blvd., Indianapolis 46278-1996. SAN 322-1296. Tel. 317-298-6570. FAX 317-328-2380. *Exec. Dir.* Barbara Evans Markuson.
—INCOLSA Processing Center, 5929 Lakeside Blvd., Indianapolis 46278-1996. SAN 322-130X. Tel. 317-298-6570. FAX 317-328-2380.

Indiana State Data Center, Indiana State Lib., 140 N. Senate Ave., Indianapolis 46204-2296. SAN 322-1318. Tel. 317-232-3733. *Coord.* Roberta Eads.

Northeast Indiana Health Science Libraries Consortium (NEIHSL), Caylor-Nickel Clinic, Lutheran Center for Health Services, 3024 Fairfield Ave., Fort Wayne 46807. SAN 373-1383. Tel. 219-458-2277. *Coord.* Lauralee Aven.

Northwest Indiana Area Library Services Authority (NIALSA), 1919 W. 81 Ave., Merrillville 46410. SAN 322-1342. Tel. 219-736-0631. FAX 219-736-0633. *Pres.* Catherine Salyers; *Admin.* Barbara Topp.

Northwest Indiana Health Science Library Consortium, c/o Northwest Center for Medical Education, Indiana Univ. School of Medicine, 3400 Broadway, Gary 46408-1197. SAN 322-1350. Tel. 219-980-6852. FAX 219-980-6566. *Coord.* Rachel Feldman.

Society of Indiana Archivists, c/o Indiana State Archives, 140 N. Senate Ave., Indianapolis 46204. SAN 329-5508. Tel. 317-232-3660. *Pres.* Nancy K. Turner; *Secy.-Treas.* Stephen E. Towne.

Southeastern Indiana Area Library Services Authority (SIALSA), 128 W. Spring St., New Albany 47150-3639. SAN 322-1369. Tel. 812-948-8639. FAX 812-948-0293. *Exec. Dir.* Sue Stultz.

Stone Hills Library Network, 112 N. Walnut, Suite 500, Bloomington 47408. SAN 322-1377. Tel. 812-334-8347. FAX 812-334-8378. *Coord.* Sara G. Laughlin.

Wabash Valley Health Science Library Consortium, Indiana State Univ., Cunningham Lib., Terre Haute 47809. SAN 371-3903. Tel. 812-237-2540. FAX 812-237-2567. *Dir.* Ronald G. Leach; *Coord.* Evelyn J. Birkey.

Wabash Valley Library Network, 629 South St., Lafayette 47901. SAN 322-1385. Tel. 317-429-0250. FAX 317-429-0223. *Admin.* Dennis Lawson; *Reference Libn.* Becky Marthey.

Iowa

Bi-State Academic Libraries (BI-SAL), c/o Marycrest College, Davenport 52804. SAN 322-1393. Tel. 319-326-9254. *Chair* Sister Joan Sheil.

Consortium of College and University Media Centers, Iowa State University, 121 Pearson Hall, Ames 50011. SAN 322-1091. Tel. 515-294-1811. FAX 515-294-8089. *Exec. Dir.* Don A. Rieck.

Dubuque (Iowa) Area Library Information Consortium, 11 Eleventh & Bluff, Dubuque 52001. SAN 322-1407. Tel. 319-589-9620. *Pres.* Sister Jean Murphy.

Iowa Online Users Group, Iowa Dept. of Educ., Grimes State Office Bldg., Des Moines 50319-0146. SAN 322-3728. Tel. 515-281-5286. *Chair* Mary Jo Bruett.

Iowa Private Academic Library Consortium (IPAL), Luther College Lib., Decorah 52101-1060. SAN 329-5311. Tel. 319-387-1190. *Chair* Norma Hervey.

Iowa Resource and Information Sharing (IRIS), State Lib. of Iowa, E. 12 and Grand, Des Moines 50319. SAN 322-1415. Tel. 515-281-4105. FAX 515-281-6191. *Libn.* Sherman B. Smith.

Linn County Library Consortium, 500 Third Ave. S.E., Cedar Rapids 52406. SAN 322-4597. Tel. 319-398-8328. *Pres.* Bridget Janus; *V.P.* Margaret White.

Metro Omaha Health Information Consortium (ICON), Jennie Edmundson Memorial Hospital Lib., 933 E. Pierce, Council Bluffs 51503. SAN 372-8102. Tel. 712-

328-6203. *Pres.* Christine Kirby; *Pres.-Elect* Dorothy Willis.

Polk County Biomedical Consortium, Iowa Hospital Assn. Lib., 100 E. Grand Ave., Des Moines 50309. SAN 322-1431. Tel. 515-288-1955. *Dir.* Roxanne Tovrea.

Quad City Area Biomedical Consortium, Mercy Hospital Medical Lib., W. Central Park, Davenport 52804. SAN 322-435X. Tel. 319-383-1067. *Coord.* Mary Vickrey.

Sioux City Library Cooperative (SCLC), c/o Sioux City Public Lib., 529 Pierce St., Sioux City 51101-1203. SAN 329-4722. Tel. 712-252-5669. *Agent* Janus F. Olsen.

Tri-College Cooperative Effort, Loras College, c/o Wahlert Memorial Lib., 1450 Alta Vista, Dubuque 52004-0178. SAN 322-1466. Tel. 319-588-7125. FAX 319-588-7292. *Dirs.* Paul Roberts, Joel Samuels, Robert Klein.

Kansas

Associated Colleges of Central Kansas, 105 E. Kansas, McPherson 67460. SAN 322-1474. Tel. 316-241-5150. FAX 316-241-5153. *Libn.* Donna Zerger.

Dodge City Library Consortium, 1001 Second Ave., Dodge City 67801. SAN 322-4368. Tel. 316-225-0248. *Chair* Milrea Weber.

Kansas City Regional Council for Higher Education, 8016 State Line Rd., Suite 205, Leawood 66208-3710. SAN 322-211X. Tel. 913-341-4141. FAX 913-341-5768. *Pres.* Frederick Baus.

Kansas Library Network Board, State Capitol, 3rd fl., Topeka 66612-1593. SAN 329-5621. Tel. 913-296-3296. FAX 913-296-6650. *Exec. Dir.* Michael Piper.

Kansas State Audiovisual Center, 223 S. Main, Wichita 67202. SAN 322-1482. Tel. 316-262-0611. FAX 316-262-4540. *Dir.* Sondra B. Koontz.

Kentucky

Bluegrass Medical Librarians (BML), 1740 Nicholasville Rd., Lexington 40503. SAN 371-3881. Tel. 606-275-6297. *Pres.* Luann Matthews; *Secy.-Treas.* Carol Dellapina.

Council of Independent Kentucky Colleges and Universities, Box 668, Danville 40423-0668. SAN 322-1490. Tel. 606-236-3533. FAX 606-236-3534. *Exec. Dir.* John W. Frazer; *Dir. Lib. Consortium* Christy Robinson.

Eastern Kentucky Health Science Information Network (EKHSIN), c/o Camden-Carroll Lib., Morehead State Univ., Morehead 40351. SAN 370-0631. Tel. 606-783-2610. FAX 606-784-3788. *Consortium Coord.* William DeBord.

Kentuckiana Metroversity Inc., 3113 Lexington Rd., Louisville 40206. SAN 322-1504. Tel. 502-897-3374. FAX 502-895-1647. *Exec. Dir.* Thomas Diener.

Kentucky Health Science Libraries Consortium, Methodist Evangelical Hospital, 315 E. Broadway, Louisville 40202. SAN 370-0623. Tel. 502-897-8183. *Pres.* Leslie Pancratz.

Kentucky Library Information Center, c/o Western Kentucky Univ., Helm Lib., Office 101, Bowling Green 42101-3576. SAN 322-1512. Tel. 502-745-6118. FAX 502-745-5943. *Dir.* Michael Binder.

Kentucky Library Network Inc., 300 Coffee Tree Rd., Box 537, Frankfort 40602. SAN 371-2184. Tel. 502-875-7000. FAX 502-564-5773. *Pres.* Brenda Macy.

Northern Kentucky Regional Library Consortia, c/o Northern Kentucky Regional Office, Fifth and Scott St., Covington 41011. SAN 329-5079. Tel. 606-491-7610.

State Assisted Academic Library Council of Kentucky (SAALCK), c/o Blazer Lib., Kentucky State Univ., Frankfort 40601. SAN 371-2222. Tel. 502-227-6852. FAX 502-564-5068. *Chair and Pres.* Karen McDaniel.

Theological Education Association of Mid America (TEAM-A), c/o Southern Baptist Theological Seminary, 2825 Lexington Rd., Louisville 40280-0294. SAN 322-1547. Tel. 502-897-4807. *Dir.* Ronald F. Deering.

Louisiana

Baton Rouge Hospital Library Consortium, Women's Hospital, Airline Way, Baton Rouge 70895. SAN 329-4714. Tel. 504-924-8462. *Dir.* Hilgard Baier.

Lasernet, State Lib. of Louisiana, Box 131, Baton Rouge 70821. SAN 371-6880. Tel. 504-342-4923. FAX 504-342-3547. *Deputy State Libn.* Michael R. McKann.

Louisiana Government Information Network (LaGIN), c/o State Lib. of Louisiana, Box 131, Baton Rouge 70821. SAN 329-5036. Tel. 504-342-4920. FAX 504-342-3547. *Coord., User Services* Blanche Cretini.

New Orleans Educational Telecommunications Consortium, 1215 Prytamia Ave., Suite 205, New Orleans 70130. SAN 329-5214. Tel. 504-523-5737. FAX 504-523-5736. *Chair* Gregory O'Brien; *Exec. Dir.* Robert J. Lucas.

Maine

Health Science Library Information Consortium (HSLIC), Westbrook College, Abplanalp Lib., 716 Stevens Ave., Portland 04103. SAN 322-1601. Tel. 207-797-7261, Ext. 330. *Chair* Elaine Rigby.

Maryland

Cooperating Libraries of Central Maryland (CLCM), 5 Harry S. Truman Pkwy., Annapolis 21601. SAN 322-3914. Tel. 410-222-7288 (voice and FAX). *Exec. Dir.* Cecy Keller.

Criminal Justice Information Exchange Group, c/o National Institute of Justice/NCJRS, 1600 Research Blvd., Rockville 20850. SAN 329-580X. Tel. 301-251-5309. FAX 301-251-5212. *Coord.* Connie Kirkland.

District of Columbia Health Sciences Information Network (DOCHSIN), see under District of Columbia.

ERIC Processing and Reference Facility, 1301 Piccard Dr., Suite 300, Rockville 20850-4305. SAN 322-161X. Tel. 301-258-5500. FAX 301-948-3695. *Dir.* Ted Brandhorst.

Interlibrary Users Association (IUA), c/o Comsat Corp., 22300 ComSat Dr., Clarksburg 20871. SAN 322-1628. Tel. 301-428-4512. FAX 301-428-7747. *Pres.* Merilee Worsey; *V.P.* Charles Gallagher.

Maryland Interlibrary Organization (MILO), c/o Enoch Pratt Free Lib., 400 Cathedral St., Baltimore 21201-4484. SAN 343-8600. Tel. 410-396-5498. FAX 410-396-5837. *Admin.* Mary Anne Denham; *Head* Elizabeth Ruffin.

Metropolitan Area Collection Development Consortium (MCDAC), c/o Arlington County Dept. of Public Libs., 1015 N. Quincy St., Arlington 22201. SAN 323-9748. Tel. 703-358-5981. FAX 703-358-5962. *Chief, Materials Management Div.* Eleanor K. Pourron.

National Clearinghouse for Alcohol and Drug Information (NCADI), Box 2345, Rockville 20847-2345. SAN 371-9162. Tel. 301-468-2600. FAX 301-468-6433. *Project Dir.* David Rowden.

National Library of Medicine, Medical Literature Analysis and Retrieval System (MEDLARS), 8600 Rockville Pike, Bethesda 20894. SAN 322-1652. Tel. 301-496-6193. *Head MEDLARS Management Section* Carolyn Tilley.

—AIDSDRUGS. SAN 323-7427. Tel. 301-496-6193.

—AIDSLINE. SAN 323-7443. Tel. 301-496-6193.

—AIDSTRIALS. SAN 323-746X. Tel. 301-496-6193.

—AVLINE. SAN 326-7180. Tel. 301-496-6193.

—BIOETHICSLINE. SAN 326-7202. Tel. 301-496-6193.

—CANCERLIT. SAN 326-7229. Tel. 301-496-6193.

—CATLINE. SAN 326-7261. Tel. 301-496-6193.

—CCRIS (Chemical Carcinogenesis Information System). SAN 328-8560. Tel. 301-496-6193.

—ChemID. SAN 371-4772. Tel. 301-496-6193.

—CHEMLINE. SAN 322-1679. Tel. 301-496-1131.

—DART (Development and Reproduction Toxicology). SAN 371-4780. Tel. 301-496-6193.

—DBIR (Directory of Biotechnology Information Resources). SAN 323-7486. Tel. 301-496-6193.

—DENTALPROJ. SAN 323-7508. Tel. 301-496-6193.

—DIRLINE. SAN 326-730X. Tel. 301-496-6193.

—DOCUSER. SAN 323-7524. Tel. 301-496-6193.

—EMICBACK (Environmental Mutagen Information BACKfile). SAN 371-4799. Tel. 301-496-6193.

—ETICBACK (Environmental Teratology Information Center BACKfile). SAN 371-4802. Tel. 301-496-6193.

—GENETOX. SAN 371-4756. Tel. 301-496-6193.

—Health Planning and Administration. SAN 326-7326. Tel. 301-496-6193.

—HISTLINE. SAN 326-6796. Tel. 301-496-6193.

—HSDB (Hazardous Substances Data Bank). SAN 326-6818. Tel. 301-496-6193.

—IRIS (Integrated Risk Information System). SAN 371-4764. Tel. 301-496-6193.

—MEDLINE. SAN 322-1695. Tel. 301-496-6193.

—MESH Vocabulary File. SAN 326-6893. Tel. 301-496-6193.

—Name Authority File. SAN 326-6915. Tel. 301-496-6193. *In Charge* Carolyn Tilley.

—PDQ (Physician Data Query). SAN 326-6931. Tel. 301-496-6193.

—POPLINE. SAN 326-6958. Tel. 301-496-6193.

—Registry of Toxic Effects of Chemical Substances (RTECS). SAN 322-1709. Tel. 301-496-6193.

—SDILINE. SAN 326-6974. Tel. 301-496-6193.

—SERLINE. SAN 326-6990. Tel. 301-496-6193.

—TOXLINE. SAN 322-1660. Tel. 301-496-1131.

—TOXLIT. SAN 323-7540. Tel. 301-496-6193.

—TRI (Toxic Chemical Release Inventory). SAN 323-7567. Tel. 301-496-6193.

National Network of Libraries of Medicine, Southeastern-Atlantic, Univ. of Maryland Health Sciences Lib., 111 S. Greene St., Baltimore 21201-1583. SAN 322-1644. Tel. 410-706-2855. FAX 410-706-8403. *Exec. Dir.* Faith A. Meakin.

Washington Research Library Consortium, 901 Commerce Dr., Upper Marlboro 20772. SAN 322-0540. Tel. 301-390-2000. FAX 301-731-1012. *Exec. Dir.* Lizanne Payne.

Massachusetts

Boston Area Music Libraries (BAML), Morse Music Lib., Harvard Univ., 59 Shephard St., Cambridge 02138. SAN 322-4392. Tel. 617-495-8730. FAX 617-496-8760. *Coord.* Martin Schreiner.

Boston Biomedical Library Consortium (BBLC), Saint Elizabeth's Hospital, 736 Cambridge St., Brighton 02135. SAN 322-1725. Tel. 617-789-3000. *Chair* Kathryn Guarcello.

Boston Library Consortium, c/o Boston Public Lib., Rm. 339, 666 Boylston St., Boston 02117. SAN 322-1733. Tel. 617-236-4306. *Exec. Dir.* Hannah M. Stevens.

Boston Theological Institute Library Program, 45 Francis Ave., Cambridge 02138. SAN 322-1741. Tel. 617-495-5780. *Asst. Lib. Coord.* Clifford Putney.

Cape Libraries Automated Materials Sharing (CLAMS), 60 Benjamin Franklin Way, Unit E, Hyannis 02601. SAN 370-579X. Tel. 508-790-4399. *Pres.* Richard J. Connor.

Central Massachusetts Consortium of Health Related Libraries (CMCHRL), c/o Estate Mutual Co., 440 Lincoln St., Worcester 01605. SAN 371-2133. Tel. 508-855-2557. FAX 508-853-6332. *Pres.* Tim Rivard.

Consortium for Information Resources, Emerson Hospital, Nine Acre Corner, Concord 02083. SAN 322-4503. Tel. 508-369-1400. FAX 508-369-7655. *Pres.* Nancy Caloander.

Cooperating Libraries of Greater Springfield (CLGS), Springfield City Lib., 220 State St., Springfield 01103. SAN 322-1768. Tel. 413-739-3871, Ext. 290. *Chair* Ann Keefe.

C W Mars (Central Western Massachusetts Automated Resource Sharing), One Sunset Lane, Paxton 01612-1197. SAN 322-3973. Tel. 508-755-3323. FAX 508-755-3721. *Mgr.* David T. Sheehan; *Supv. User Services* Gale E. Eckerson.

Digital Library Network (DLN), 146 Main St., Maynard 01754. SAN 370-0534. Tel. 508-493-2165. *Mgr.* Jillian Hamer.

Essex County Cooperating Libraries, Abbott Public Lib., 235 Pleasant St., Marblehead 01945. SAN 322-1776. Tel. 508-927-

2300, Ext. 4339. *Pres.* Victor Dyer; *V.P.* Suzanne Nichelson-Wonson.

Fenway Library Consortium, Massachusetts College of Pharmacy, Boston 02115. SAN 327-9766. Tel. 617-732-2800. *Coord.* Anne Pascarelli.

HILC Inc. (Hampshire Interlibrary Center), Box 740, Amherst 01004. SAN 322-1806. Tel. 413-256-8316. *Admin. Asst.* Dora Tudryn; *Business Mgr.* Jean Stabell.

Libraries and Information for Nursing Consortium (LINC), c/o School of Nursing Lib., Saint Elizabeth's Hospital, 159 Washington St., Brighton 02135. SAN 371-0580. Tel. 617-789-2304. *Coord.* Robert L. Loud.

Merrimac Interlibrary Cooperative, Hemingway Lib., Bradford College, 320 S. Main St., Haverhill 01835. SAN 329-4234. Tel. 508-372-7161, Ext. 387. *Chair* Ruth Hooten.

Merrimack Valley Library Consortium, c/o Memorial Hall Lib., Elm Sq., Andover 01810. SAN 322-4384. Tel. 508-475-6960. FAX 508-470-2990. *Chair* Joseph Dionne; *Dir.* Evelyn Kuo.

Minuteman Library Network, 49 Lexington St., Framingham 01701. SAN 322-4252. Tel. 508-879-8575. FAX 508-879-5470. *Exec. Dir.* Joan Kuklinski.

NELINET Inc., Two Newton Executive Park, Newton 02162. SAN 322-1822. Tel. 617-969-0400. FAX 617-332-9634. *Exec. Dir.* Marshall Keys.

New England Law Library Consortium Inc., Harvard Law School Lib., Langdell Hall, Cambridge 02138. SAN 322-4244. Tel. 617-495-9918. FAX 617-495-4449. *Exec. Dir.* Martha Berglund Crane.

North Atlantic Health Science Libraries Inc. (NAHSL), New England College of Optometry, 420 Beacon St., Boston 02115. SAN 371-0599. *Chair* Lynne Silver; *Chair-Elect* Robin Rand.

North of Boston Library Exchange Inc. (NOBLE), 112 Sohier Rd., Suite 117, Beverly 01915. SAN 322-4023. Tel. 508-927-5050. FAX 508-927-7939. *Network Admin.* Ronald A. Gagnon; *Database Mgr.* Elizabeth B. Thomsen.

Northeast Consortium of Colleges and Universities in Massachusetts (NECCUM), c/o

Middlesex Community College, Spring Rd., Bedford 01730. SAN 371-0602. Tel. 617-275-8910. *Coord.* Caryl Dundurf.

Northeastern Consortium for Health Information (NECHI), Anna Jaques Hospital, 25 Highland Ave., Newburyport 01950. SAN 322-1857. Tel. 508-463-1000, Ext. 2480. FAX 508-463-5411. *Pres.* Florence S. Mercer.

Southeastern Automated Libraries Inc. (SEAL), 732 Dartmouth St., South Dartmouth 02748. SAN 371-5000. Tel. 508-996-8700. FAX 508-992-9914. *Network Admin.* Deborah K. Conrad; *Systems Admin.* Barbara Bonville.

Southeastern Massachusetts Consortium of Health Science Libraries (SEMCO), Shattuck Hospital, 170 Morton St., Jamaica Plain 02130. SAN 322-1873. Tel. 617-522-8110, Ext. 0307. *Pres.* Anne Lima.

Southeastern Massachusetts Cooperating Libraries (SMCL), Stonehill College, Cushing-Martin Lib., North Easton 02357-4015. SAN 322-1865. Tel. 508-230-1111. FAX 508-238-9253. *Chair* Edward Hynes.

Wellesley–Lexington Area Cooperative Libraries (WELEXACOL), c/o Solomon R. Baker Lib., Bentley College, 175 Forest St., Waltham 02154-4705. SAN 370-5978. Tel. 617-891-2231. *Pres.* Sherman Hayes; *Treas.* Marion Slack.

West of Boston Network (WEBNET), Horn Lib.-Babson College, Babson Park 02157. SAN 371-5019. Tel. 617-239-4308. FAX 617-239-5226. *Project Coord.* Fae K. Hamilton; *Network Pres.* Elizabeth L. Keenan.

Western Massachusetts Health Information Consortium, Shriners Hospital Medical Lib., 516 Carew St., Springfield 01104. SAN 329-4579. Tel. 413-787-2053. *Chair* Susan LaForte.

Worcester Area Cooperating Libraries, c/o Worcester State College Learning Resources Center, Rm. 221, 486 Chandler St., Worcester 01602-2597. SAN 322-1881. Tel. 508-754-3964, 793-8000, Ext. 8544. FAX 508-793-8083. *Coord.* Gladys Wood.

Michigan

Berrien Library Consortium, Andrews Campus, Berrien Springs 49104. SAN 322-4678. Tel. 616-926-6139. FAX 616-982-3710. *Pres.* Fred Kirby; *Treas.* Marley Soper.

Capital Area Library Network (CALNET), 407 N. Cedar St., Mason 48854. SAN 370-5927. Tel. 517-676-2008. FAX 517-676-9646. *Contact* Kathleen M. Vera; *Chair* David Keddle.

Cloverland Processing Center, c/o Bay de Noc Community College, Learning Resource Center, 2001 N. Lincoln Rd., Escanaba 49829-2511. SAN 322-189X. Tel. 906-786-5802, Ext. 122. FAX 906-786-5802, Ext. 244. *Dean* Christian Holmes.

Detroit Area Consortium of Catholic Colleges, c/o Sacred Heart Seminary, 2701 Chicago Blvd., Detroit 48206. SAN 329-482X. Tel. 313-883-8500. FAX 313-868-6440. *Chair* John Nienstedt.

Detroit Associated Libraries Region of Cooperation (DALROC), Detroit Public Lib., 5201 Woodward Ave., Detroit 48202. SAN 371-0831. Tel. 313-833-4036. FAX 313-832-0877. *Chair* Robert Holley; *Contact* James Lawrence.

Flint Area Health Science Libraries Network, c/o Flint Osteopathic Hospital, Medical Lib., 3921 Beecher Rd., Flint 48532-3699. SAN 329-4757. Tel. 313-762-4587. *Chair* Ria Lukes; *Dir.* Doris Blauet.

Kalamazoo Consortium for Higher Education (KCHE), Kalamazoo College, 1200 Academy St., Kalamazoo 49007. SAN 329-4994. Tel. 616-337-7220. FAX 616-337-7305. *Pres.* Lawrence Bryan; *Coord.* Margie Flynn.

Lakeland Area Library Network (LAKENET), 60 Library Plaza N.E., Grand Rapids 49503. SAN 371-0696. Tel. 616-454-0272. *Coord.* Harriet Field.

Michigan Health Sciences Libraries Association (MHSLA), Providence Hospital, 16001 W. Nine-Mile Rd., Southfield 48037. SAN 323-987X. Tel. 313-424-3294. *Pres.* Carole Gilbert.

Michigan Library Consortium (MLC), Suite 8, 6810 S. Cedar St., Lansing 48911. SAN 322-192X. Tel. 517-694-4242. FAX 517-694-9303. *Exec. Dir.* Kevin C. Flaherty.

Northern Interlibrary System (NILS), 316 E. Chisholm St., Alpena 49707. SAN 329-4773. Tel. 517-356-1622. FAX 517-354-3939. *Dir.* Rebecca E. Cawley.

Sault Area International Library Association, c/o Lake Superior State Univ. Lib., Sault Sainte Marie 49783. SAN 322-1946. Tel. 906-635-2402. FAX 906-635-2193. *Chairs* Ruth Neveu, Brian Ingram.

Smaller Libraries Information Consortium (SLIC), Lawrence Technological Univ., 21000 W. Ten Mile Rd., Southfield 48075. SAN 371-5043. Tel. 313-356-0200, Ext. 3000. *Chair* Gary R. Cocozzoli; *V. Chair* Irvin C. Rabideau.

Southeastern Michigan League of Libraries (SEMLOL), c/o Kresge Lib., Oakland Univ., Rochester 48309. SAN 322-4481. Tel. 313-370-2474. FAX 313-370-2458. *Chair* Indra David.

Southern Michigan Region of Cooperation (SMROC), 415 S. Superior, Suite A, Albion 49224-2315. SAN 371-3857. Tel. 517-629-9469. FAX 517-628-3812. *Fiscal Agent* James C. Seidl.

Southwest Michigan Library Cooperative (SMLC), 200 S. Kalamazoo St., Paw Paw 49079. SAN 371-5027. Tel. 616-657-4698. *Dir.* Auda L. Geppert.

State Council of Michigan Health Science Libraries, 401 W. Greenlawn Ave., Lansing 48910-2819. SAN 329-4633. Tel. 517-334-2270. FAX 517-334-2551. *Pres.* Barbara Kormelink; *Mid-West Rep.* David Keddle.

Upper Peninsula of Michigan Health Science Library Consortium, c/o Marquette General Hospital, 420 W. Magnetic, Marquette 49855. SAN 329-4803. Tel. 906-225-3429. FAX 906-225-3524. *Chair* Kenneth Nelson.

Upper Peninsula Region Library Cooperation Inc., 1615 Presque Isle Ave., Marquette 49855. SAN 329-5540. Tel. 906-228-7697. FAX 906-228-5627. *Pres.* Phyllis Johnson; *Treas.* Suzanne Dees.

Wayne Oakland Library Federation (WOLF), 33030 Van Born Rd., Wayne 48184. SAN 370-596X. Tel. 313-326-8910. FAX 313-326-3035. *Dir.* Harry Courtright.

Minnesota

Arrowhead Health Sciences Library Network, Tilderquist Memorial Medical Lib., 502 E. Second St., Duluth 55805-1982. SAN 322-1954. Tel. 218-720-1362. FAX 218-720-1397. *Coord.* Annelie Sober.

Central Minnesota Libraries Exchange (CMLE), c/o Learning Resources, Rm. 61, Saint Cloud State Univ., Saint Cloud 56301-4498. SAN 322-3779. Tel. 612-255-2950. FAX 612-654-5131. *Dir.* Patricia E. Peterson.

Community Health Science Library, c/o Saint Francis Medical Center, 415 Oak St., Breckenridge 56520. SAN 370-0585. Tel. 218-643-7507. *Dir.* Geralyn Terfehr.

Cooperating Libraries in Consortium (CLIC), 1457 Grand Ave., Suite N, Saint Paul 55105. SAN 322-1970. Tel. 612-699-9300. FAX 612-699-0724. *Consortium Mgr.* David Barton.

METRONET, 226 Metro Sq. Bldg., Seventh and Robert Sts., Saint Paul 55101. SAN 322-1989. Tel. 612-224-4801. FAX 612-224-4827. *Dir.* Mary Treacy Birmingham.

Metropolitan Library Service Agency (MELSA), Griggs-Midway Bldg., 570 Asbury St., Suite 201, Saint Paul 55104-1849. SAN 371-5124. Tel. 612-645-5731. FAX 612-649-3169. *Exec. Dir.* William M. Duncan; *Program Officer* Tzvee Morris.

Minitex Library Information Network, c/o S-33 Wilson Lib., Univ. of Minnesota, 309 19th Ave. S., Minneapolis 55455-0414. SAN 322-1997. Tel. 612-624-4002. FAX 612-624-4508. *Dir.* William DeJohn.

Minnesota Department of Human Services Library Consortium, DHS Lib. and Resource Center, 444 Lafayette, Saint Paul 55155-3826. SAN 371-0750. Tel. 612-297-8708. FAX 612-296-6244. *Dir. and Coord.* Colleen Spadaccini.

Minnesota Theological Library Association, c/o Luther Northwestern Theological Seminary Lib., 2375 Como Ave., Saint Paul 55108. SAN 322-1962. Tel. 612-641-3202. FAX 612-641-3280. *Database Admin.* Tom Walker.

North Country Library Cooperative, Olcott Plaza, Suite 110, 820 Ninth St. N., Vir-

ginia 55792-2298. SAN 322-3795. Tel. 218-741-1907. *Coord.* Sandra L. Romans.

Northern Lights Library Network, Box 845, Alexandria 56308-0845. SAN 322-2004. Tel. 612-762-1032. FAX 612-762-1032. *Dir.* Joan B. Larson.

SMILE (Southcentral Minnesota Inter-Library Exchange), Box 3031, Mankato 56001. SAN 321-3358. Tel. 507-389-5108. FAX 507-389-1772. *Dir.* Lucy Lowry; *Smiline I & R Dir.* Kate Tohal.

Southeast Library System (SELS), 107 W. Frontage Rd., Hwy. 52 N., Rochester 55901. SAN 322-3981. Tel. 507-288-5513. FAX 507-288-8697. *Multitype Libn.* Roger Leachman.

Southwest Area Multi-County Multi-Type Interlibrary Exchange (SAMMIE), Southwest State Univ. Lib., Marshall 56258. SAN 322-2039. Tel. 507-532-9013. FAX 507-532-2039. *Dir.* Mary Ann Hagemeyer.

Twin Cities Biomedical Consortium, c/o Riverside Medical Center, Riverside and 25 Ave. S., Minneapolis 55454. SAN 322-2055. Tel. 612-371-6545. *Chair* Mary Finnegan.

Waseca Interlibrary Resource Exchange (WIRE), Janesville-Waldorf-Pemberton Public Schools, 110 E. Third St., Box 389, Janesville 56048. SAN 370-0593. Tel. 507-234-5181. *Dir.* Pauline Fenelon.

Westlaw, 610 Opperman Dr., Box 64526, Saint Paul 55164-0526. SAN 322-4031. Tel. 612-687-7000. *Mgr.* Thomas McLeod.

Mississippi

Central Mississippi Consortium of Medical Libraries (CMCML), Medical Center, U.S. Dept. of Veterans Affairs, 1500 E. Woodrow Wilson Dr., Jackson 39216. SAN 372-8099. Tel. 601-342-4471, Ext. 1703. *Chair* Rose Anne Tucker.

Central Mississippi Library Council (CMLC), c/o Macklendon Lib., Hinds Community College, Raymond 39154. SAN 372-8250. Tel. 601-857-3378. *Chair* Chris W. Cullnane II.

Gulf Coast Biomedical Library Consortium, c/o Memorial Hospital, Box 1810, Gulf-

port 39502-1810. SAN 322-2063. Tel.
601-865-3159. *Chair* Connie Keel.
Mississippi Biomedical Library Consortium,
c/o U.S. Air Force Medical Center Lib.,
Keesler AFB 39534-5300. SAN 371-
070X. Tel. 601-377-6042. FAX 601-377-
6460. *Pres.* Sherry Nave.

Missouri

Kansas City Library Network Inc., Univ. of
Missouri Dental Lib., 650 E. 25 St.,
Kansas City 64108. SAN 322-2098. Tel.
816-235-2063. *Pres.* Michelle Lahey.
Kansas City Metropolitan Library Network,
15624 E. 24 Hwy., Independence 64050.
SAN 322-2101. Tel. 816-836-5200, Ext.
257. FAX 816-836-5200. *Office Mgr.*
Sharon Jennings.
Missouri Libraries Film Cooperative
(MLFC), 15616 E. Hwy. 24, Independence
64050. SAN 371-4993. Tel. 816-836-
5200. FAX 816-836-5200. *Admin.* Billy F.
Windes; *Pres.* John Mertens.
Missouri Library Network Corporation,
10332 Old Olive St. Rd., Saint Louis
63141. SAN 322-466X. Tel. 314-567-
3799. FAX 314-567-3798. *Dir.* Mary Ann
Mercante.
Municipal Library Cooperative, 140 E. Jef-
ferson, Kirkwood 63122. SAN 322-2152.
Tel. 314-966-5568. *ILL* Barbara Leevy.
PHILSOM-PHILNET-BACS Network, c/o
Washington Univ., Medical Lib. and Bio-
medical Communications Center, 660 S.
Euclid Ave., Saint Louis 63110. SAN 322-
2187. Tel. 314-362-2788. FAX 314-367-
9547. *Dir.* Loretta Stucki.
Saint Louis Regional Library Network, 9425
Big Bend, Saint Louis 63119. SAN 322-
2209. Tel. 314-965-1305. *Admin.* Bernyce
Christiansen.

Montana

Helena Area Health Science Libraries Con-
sortium (HAHSLC), Corette Lib., Carroll
College, Helena 59625. SAN 371-2192.
Tel. 406-447-4341. FAX 406-447-4525.
Chair Lois Fitzpatrick.

Nebraska

Eastern Library System (ELS), 11902 Elm
St., Suite 6A, Omaha 68144. SAN 371-
506X. Tel. 402-330-7884. *Admin.* Kath-
leen Tooker; *Pres.* Michael Poma.
Lincoln Health Sciences Library Group
(LHSLG), Univ. of Nebraska–Lincoln,
Lincoln 68508-0305. SAN 329-5001. Tel.
402-472-2739. *Chair* Richard E. Voeltz.
Meridian Library System, 2022 Ave. A, Suite
14, Kearney 68847. SAN 325-3554. Tel.
308-234-2087. *Pres.* Judy Henning;
Admin. Sharon Osenga.
National Network of Libraries of Medi-
cine–Midcontinental Region (NN-LM-
MR), c/o McGoogan Lib. of Medicine,
Univ. of Nebraska Medical Center, 600 S.
42 St., Omaha 68198-6706. SAN 322-
225X. Tel. 402-559-4326. FAX 402-559-
5498. *Dir.* Nancy N. Woelfl.
NEBASE, c/o Nebraska Lib. Commission,
1200 N St., Suite 120, Lincoln 68508-
2006. SAN 322-2268. Tel. 402-471-2045.
FAX 402-471-2083. *Dir.* Jacqueline
Mundell; *Coord.* Paul Seth Hoffman.
Northeast Library System, 2813 13th St.,
Columbus 68601. SAN 329-5524. Tel.
402-564-1586. *Admin.* Carol Speicher.
Southeast Nebraska Library System, Union
College Lib., 3800 S. 48 St., Lincoln
68506. SAN 322-4732. Tel. 402-486-
2555. FAX 402-486-2678. *Admin.* Kate
Marek.
Western Council of State Libraries Inc.,
Nebraska Lib. Commission, 1200 N. St.,
Suite 120, Lincoln 69508-2006. SAN 322-
2314. Tel. 402-471-4001. *Pres.* Rod Wag-
ner.

Nevada

Information Nevada, Interlibrary Loan Dept.,
Nevada State Lib. and Archives, Capitol
Complex, Carson City 89710-0001. SAN
322-2276. Tel. 702-687-5160. FAX 702-
887-2630. *Contact* Millie L. Syring.
Nevada Cooperative Medical Library, 2040
W. Charleston Blvd., Suite 500, Las Vegas
89102. SAN 321-5962. Tel. 702-383-

2368. FAX 702-383-2369. *Dir. Lib. Services* Aldona Jonynas.

Nevada Medical Library Group (NMLG), c/o West Nevada Community College, Learning Resource Center, 2201 W. Nye Lane, Carson City 89701. SAN 370-0445. Tel. 702-887-3071. *Chair* Valerie Andersen.

New Hampshire

Bearcamp Neighborhood Library Association, Box 209, Madison 03849. SAN 371-8999. Tel. 603-367-8048. *Secy.* Nancy H. Dannies.

Health Science Libraries of New Hampshire and Vermont (HSL-NH-VT), New London Hospital Medical Lib., 270 County Rd., New London 03257. SAN 371-6864. Tel. 603-526-2911. FAX 603-526-2990. *Pres.* Marion L. Allen; *V.P.* Daphne Pringle.

Hillstown Cooperative, 3 Meetinghouse Rd., Bedford 03110. SAN 371-3873. Tel. 603-472-2300. *Chair* Frances M. Wiggin.

Librarians of the Upper Valley Coop (LUV Coop), c/o Cass Memorial Lib., Box 89, Springfield 03284-0089. SAN 371-6856. Tel. 603-763-4381. *Secy.* Celeste Klein.

Merri-Hill-Rock Library Cooperative, Hampstead Public Lib., Box 190, Hampstead 03841. SAN 329-5338. Tel. 603-329-6411. *Chair* Judith L. Crowley.

New Hampshire College and University Council, Libs. Committee, 116 S. River Rd., D4, Bedford 03110. SAN 322-2322. Tel. 603-669-3432. FAX 603-623-8182. *Exec. Dir.* John W. Ryan.

North Country Consortium (NCC), Gale Medical Lib., Littleton Regional Hospital, 107 Cottage St., Littleton 03561. SAN 370-0410. Tel. 603-444-7731, Ext. 164. *Coord.* Linda L. Ford.

Nubanusit Library Cooperative, c/o Peterborough Town Lib., Main St. and Concord, Peterborough 03458. SAN 322-4600. Tel. 603-924-6401. *Contact* Ann Geisel.

Scrooge and Marley Cooperative, 310 Central St., Franklin 03235. SAN 329-515X. Tel. 603-934-2911. *Chair* Randy Brough.

Seacoast Coop Libraries, Weeks Public Lib., Box 430, Greenland 03840. SAN 322-

4619. Tel. 603-436-8548. *Contact* Bonnie Gardner.

New Jersey

AT&T Library Network, 600 Mountain Ave., Rm. 6A-311, Murray Hill 07974. SAN 329-5400. Tel. 908-582-4361. FAX 908-582-3146. *Mgr.* Ronnye Schreiber.

Bergen County Cooperative Library System, 810 Main St., Hackensack 07601. SAN 322-4546. Tel. 201-489-1904. FAX 201-489-4215. *Exec. Dir.* Robert W. White.

Bergen Passaic Health Sciences Library Consortium, c/o Englewood Hospital and Medical Center, 350 Engle St., Englewood 07631. SAN 371-0904. Tel. 201-894-3145. FAX 201-894-9049. *Pres.* Lia Sabbagh.

Central Jersey Health Science Libraries Association, Saint Francis Medical Center Medical Lib., 601 Hamilton Ave., Trenton 08629. SAN 370-0712. Tel. 609-599-5068. FAX 609-599-5773. *Dir.* Donna Barlow; *Technical Info. Specialist* Eileen Monroe.

Central Jersey Regional Library Cooperatives—Region V, 55 Schanck Rd., Suite B-15, Freehold 07728-2942. SAN 370-5102. Tel. 908-409-6484. FAX 908-409-6492. *Exec. Dir.* Dottie Hiebing.

Cosmopolitan Biomedical Library Consortium, c/o Elizabeth General Medical Center, 925 E. Jersey St., Elizabeth 07201. SAN 322-4414. Tel. 908-558-8092. FAX 908-820-8974. *Pres.* Catherine Boss.

County of Essex Cooperating Libraries System (CECLS), Livingston Public Lib., 51 Baker St., Maplewood 07040. SAN 322-4562. Tel. 201-762-1622. *Pres.* Rowland Bennett.

Dow Jones News Retrieval, Box 300, Princeton 08543-0300. SAN 322-404X. Tel. 609-452-1511. FAX 609-520-4775. *Sr. Marketing Coord.* Maggie Landis.

Essex-Hudson Regional Library Cooperative—Region Three, 350 Scotland Rd., Suite 201, Orange 07050. SAN 329-5117. Tel. 201-673-6373. FAX 201-673-6121. *Exec. Dir.* Gladys Odette.

Health Sciences Library Association of New Jersey (HSLANJ), Rutgers University Center for Alcohol Studies, Bush Campus, Piscataway 08855-0969. SAN 370-0488. Tel. 908-932-4442. FAX 908-932-5944. *Pres.* Catherine Weglarz.

LMX Automation Consortium, c/o MCC Lib., 155 Mill Rd., Edison 08818-3050. SAN 329-448X. Tel. 908-548-7113. *Exec. Dir.* James H. Kennedy; *Database Mgr.* Ann MacDonald.

Monmouth-Ocean Biomedical Information Consortium (MOBIC), Community Medical Center, 99 Hwy. 37 W., Toms River 08755. SAN 329-5389. Tel. 908-240-8117. FAX 908-341-8093. *Dir.* Reina Reisler.

Morris Automated Information Network (MAIN), 30 E. Hanover Ave., Whippany 07981. SAN 322-4058. Tel. 201-285-6951. FAX 201-285-6965. *Dir.* Knute Seebohm.

Morris-Union Federation, 214 Main St., Chatham 07928. SAN 310-2629. Tel. 201-635-0603. *Contact* Diane O'Brien.

New Jersey Academic Library Network, c/o Kean College, Nancy Thompson Lib., Union 07083. SAN 329-4927. Tel. 908-527-2017. FAX 908-527-2365. *Chair* Barbara Simpson.

New Jersey Health Sciences Library Network (NJHSN), c/o Health Sciences Lib., Mountainside Hospital, Montclair 07042. SAN 371-4829. Tel. 201-429-6240. FAX 201-680-7850. *Chair* Patricia Regenberg.

Northwest Regional Library Cooperative, 31 Fairmount Ave., Box 486, Chester 07930. SAN 329-4609. Tel. 908-879-2442. FAX 908-879-8812. *Exec. Dir.* Diane M. Solomon; *Project Coord.* Joyce L. Wemer.

Pinelands Consortium for Health Information, c/o Kennedy Memorial Hospital, Washington Township Div. Medical Lib., 435 Huffville-Cross Keys Rds., Turnersville 08012. SAN 370-4874. Tel. 609-582-2675. FAX 609-582-3190. *Coord.* William Dobkowski.

Society for Cooperative Healthcare and Related Education (SCHARE), Union County College, 1033 Springfield Ave., Cranford 07016. SAN 371-0718. Tel. 908-

276-5710. *Coord.* Anne Calhoun; *Chair* Geri Farina.

South Jersey Regional Library Cooperative, Paint Works Corporate Center, 10 Foster Ave., Suite F-3, Gibbsboro 08026. SAN 329-4625. Tel. 609-346-1222. FAX 609-346-2839. *Exec. Dir.* Karen Hyman; *Program Development Coord.* Katherine Schalk-Greene.

Union Middlesex Regional Library Cooperative Inc. (LINX), 44 Stelton Rd., Suite 330, Piscataway 08854. SAN 371-5116. Tel. 908-752-7720. FAX 908-752-7785. *Exec. Dir.* Gail L. Rosenberg; *Program and Services Coord.* Cheryl O'Connor.

New Mexico

New Mexico Consortium of Academic Libraries, Miller Lib., Western New Mexico Univ., Box 680, Silver City 88062. SAN 371-6872. *Pres.* Ben Wakashige; *Pres.-Elect* Harris Richards.

New Mexico Consortium of Biomedical and Hospital Libraries, c/o Lovelace Medical Lib., 5400 Gibson Blvd. S.E., Albuquerque 87108. SAN 322-449X. Tel. 505-262-7158. *Permanent Contact* Sarah Morley.

New York

Academic Libraries of Brooklyn, 175 Willoughby St., Suite 15C, Brooklyn 11201. SAN 322-2411. Tel. 718-260-3626. FAX 718-260-3756. *Pres.* Aline Locascio.

Associated Colleges of the Saint Lawrence Valley, Satterlee Hall, State Univ. of New York, Potsdam 13676-2299. SAN 322-242X. Tel. 315-265-2790. *Exec. Dir.* Susan M. Cypert.

Brooklyn–Queens–Staten Island Health Sciences Librarians (BQSI), 340 Henry St., Brooklyn 11201. SAN 370-0828. Tel. 718-780-1077. *Pres.* George A. Wahlert; *V.P.* Raja Jaytilleke.

Capital District Library Council for Reference and Research Resources, 28 Essex St., Albany 12206. SAN 322-2446. Tel. 518-438-2500. FAX 518-438-2872. *Exec.*

Dir. Charles D. Custer; *Admin. Secy.* Carolyn Houlihan.

Central New York Library Resources Council, 763 Butternut, Syracuse 13208. SAN 322-2454. Tel. 315-478-6080. FAX 315-478-0512. *Exec. Dir.* Keith E. Washburn.

Consortium of Foundation Libraries, c/o International Planned Parenthood Foundation, Western Hemisphere Region, 902 Broadway, New York 10017. SAN 322-2462. Tel. 212-995-8800. Fax 212-995-8853. *Chair* Abigail Hourwich.

Council of Archives and Research Libraries in Jewish Studies (CARLJS), 330 Seventh Ave., 21st fl., New York 10001. SAN 371-053X. Tel. 212-629-0500. FAX 212-629-0508. *Exec. Dir.* Richard Siegel; *Pres.* Sandra Weiner.

Educational Film Library Association, c/o AV Resource Center, Cornell Univ., Business and Technology Park, Ithaca 14850. SAN 371-0874. Tel. 607-255-2090. FAX 607-255-9946. *AV Coord.* Rich Gray; *AV Sales* Liz Powers; *AV Technology* Gerry Kalk.

Health Information Libraries of Westchester (HILOW), c/o New York Medical College, Medical Lib., Basic Sciences Bldg., Valhalla 10595. SAN 371-0823. Tel. 914-993-4204. *Pres.* Chris Hunter.

Library Consortium of Health Institutions in Buffalo, Office of the Consortium, c/o Info. Dissemination Service, Health Sciences Lib., State Univ. of New York, Buffalo 14214. SAN 329-367X. Tel. 716-829-3351. *Dir.* Cindy Bertuca.

Long Island Library Resources Council, Melville Lib. Bldg., Suite E5310, Stony Brook 11794-3399. SAN 322-2489. Tel. 516-632-6650. FAX 516-632-6662. *Dir.* Herbert Biblo.

Manhattan-Bronx Health Sciences Libraries Group, c/o NCI Lib., 41 Madison Ave., New York 10010. SAN 322-4465. Tel. 212-684-0909. FAX 212-213-4694. *Pres.* Judy Lee.

Medical and Scientific Libraries of Long Island (MEDLI), c/o Palmer School of Lib. and Info. Science, C. W. Post Campus, Long Island Univ., Brookville 11548. SAN 322-4309. Tel. 516-299-2866. FAX 516-626-2665. *Pres.* William F. Casey.

Medical Library Center of New York, 5 E. 102 St., New York 10029. SAN 322-3957. Tel. 212-427-1630. FAX 212-860-3496. *Dir.* Lois Weinstein.

Middle Atlantic Region National Network of Libraries of Medicine, New York Academy of Medicine, 2 E. 103 St., New York 10029-5293. SAN 322-2497. Tel. 212-876-8763. FAX 212-534-7042. *Dir.* Arthur Downing.

New York Metropolitan Reference and Research Library Agency (METRO), 57 E. 11 St., New York 10003. SAN 322-2500. Tel. 212-228-2320. FAX 212-228-2598. *Dir.* Joan Neumann; *Coord. of Programs and Services* Alar Kruus.

New York State Interlibrary Loan Network (NYSILL), c/o New York State Lib., Albany 12230. SAN 322-2519. Tel. 518-474-5383. *State Libn.* Joseph F. Shubert; *Dir.* Jerome Yavarkovsky; *Principal Libn.* J. Van der veer Judd.

North Country Reference and Research Resources Council, 7 Commerce Lane, Canton 13617. SAN 322-2527. Tel. 315-386-4569. FAX 315-379-9553. *Exec. Dir.* John J. Hammond.

Research Library Association of South Manhattan, New York Univ. Bobst Lib., 70 Washington Square S., New York 10012. SAN 372-8080. Tel. 212-998-2566. *Coord.* Joan Grant.

Rochester Regional Library Council (RRLC), 302 N. Goodman St., Rochester 14607. SAN 322-2535. Tel. 716-461-5440. FAX 716-461-2721. *Dir.* Janet M. Welch.

South Central Research Library Council, 215 N. Cayuga St., Ithaca 14850. SAN 322-2543. Tel. 607-273-9106. *Exec. Dir.* Janet E. Steiner; *Special Projects Dir.* Jean Currie.

Southeastern New York Library Resources Council, 220 Rte. 299, Box 879, Highland 12528. SAN 322-2551. Tel. 914-691-2734. *Exec. Dir.* Ellen A. Parravano.

State University of New York–OCLC Library Network (SUNY–OCLC), Central Administration, State Univ. of New York, State University Plaza, Albany 12246. SAN 322-256X. Tel. 518-443-5444. FAX 518-432-4346. *Dir.* Glyn T. Evans.

Western New York Library Resources Council, 180 Oak St., Buffalo 14203. SAN 322-2578. Tel. 716-852-3844. FAX 716-852-0276. *Exec. Dir.* Mary W. Ghikas.

North Carolina

Cape Fear Health Sciences Information Consortium, Cape Fear Valley Medical Center, Box 2000, Fayetteville 28302. SAN 322-3930. Tel. 919-323-6601. FAX 919-433-7710. *Chair* Pat Hammond.

Microcomputer Users Group for Librarians in North Carolina, Health Sciences Lib., Univ. of North Carolina, Chapel Hill 27599-7585. SAN 322-4449. Tel. 919-962-0700. FAX 919-966-1537. *Pres.* Julia Shaw-Kolcot.

Mid-Carolina Academic Library Network (MID-CAL), 400 N. ACC Dr., Wilson 27893. SAN 371-3989. Tel. 919-399-6501. *Chair* Marty Smith; *Project Dir.* Ted Waller.

NC Area Health Education Centers, Health Sciences Lib., CB 7585, Univ. of North Carolina, Chapel Hill 27599-7585. SAN 323-9950. Tel. 919-962-0700. FAX 919-966-1537. *Network Coord.* Diana C. McDuffee.

North Carolina Department of Community Colleges, Institutional Services, 200 W. Jones St., Raleigh 27603-1337. SAN 322-2594. Tel. 919-733-7051, Ext. 635. FAX 919-733-0680. *Dir.* Major Boyd.

North Carolina Information Network, 109 E. Jones St., Raleigh 27601-2807. SAN 329-3092. Tel. 919-733-2570. FAX 919-733-8748. *Dir.* Diana Young.

Northwest AHEC Library at Salisbury, c/o Rowan Memorial Hospital, 612 Mocksville Ave., Salisbury 28144. SAN 322-4589. Tel. 704-638-1081. FAX 704-636-5050. *Dir.* Connie Schardt.

Northwest AHEC Library Information Network, Northwest Area Health Education Center, Bowman Gray School of Medicine, Medical Center Blvd., Winston-Salem 27157-1060. SAN 322-4716. Tel. 919-716-9210. *Coord.* Phyllis Gillikin.

Resources for Health Information Consortium (ReHI), Box 14465, Raleigh 27620-

4465. SAN 329-3777. Tel. 919-250-8529. *Dir.* Karen Grandage.

Triangle Research Libraries Network, Wilson Lib., CB 3940, Chapel Hill 27599-3940. SAN 329-5362. Tel. 919-962-8022. FAX 919-962-0484. *Exec. Dir.* David Carlson.

Unifour Consortium of Health Care and Educational Institutions, c/o Northwest AHEC Lib. at Hickory, Catawba Memorial Hospital, 810 Fair Grove Church, Hickory 28602. SAN 322-4708. Tel. 704-326-3662. FAX 704-322-2921. *Dir.* Phyllis Gillikin.

North Dakota

American Indian Higher Education Consortium (AIHEC), c/o UTTC, 3315 University Dr., Bismarck 59501. SAN 329-4056. Tel. 701-255-3285. *Pres.* David Gipp.

Central Dakota Cooperating Libraries (CDCL), 515 N. Fifth St., Bismarck 58501. SAN 373-1391. Tel. 701-222-6410. FAX 701-221-6854. *Chair* Thomas T. Jones; *Secy.-Treas.* Cheryl Bailey.

North Dakota Network for Knowledge, c/o North Dakota State Lib., Liberty Memorial Bldg., Capitol Grounds, 604 E. Blvd. Ave., Bismarck 58505-0800. SAN 322-2616. Tel. 701-224-2492. FAX 701-224-2040. *State Libn.* William Strader.

Tri-College University Libraries Consortium, c/o North Dakota State Univ., 306 Ceres Hall, Fargo 58105. SAN 322-2047. Tel. 701-237-8170. *Coord.* Darrel M. Meinke; *Provost, Tri-College Univ.* William C. Nelson.

Valley Medical Network, 720 N. Fourth St., Fargo 58122. SAN 329-4730. Tel. 701-234-5837. FAX 701-234-5927. *Pres.* Margaret Wagner.

Ohio

Central Ohio Hospital Library Consortium, Medical Lib., Riverside Methodist Hospital, 3535 Olentangy River Rd., Columbus 43214. SAN 371-084X. Tel. 614-566-5230. FAX 614-265-2437. *Archival Records* Jo Yeoh.

Cleveland Area Metropolitan Library System (CAMLS), 20600 Chagrin Blvd., Suite

500, Shaker Heights 44122-5334. SAN 322-2632. Tel. 216-921-3900. FAX 216-921-7220. *Exec. Dir.* Jacqueline Mundell.

Columbus Area Library and Information Council of Ohio (CALICO), c/o Westerville Public Lib., 126 S. State St., Westerville 43081. SAN 371-683X. Tel. 614-882-7277, Ext. 156. *Pres.* Lois Szudy.

Consortium of Popular Culture Collections in the Midwest (CPCCM), c/o Popular Culture Lib., Bowling Green State Univ., Bowling Green 43403-0600. SAN 370-5811. Tel. 419-372-2450. FAX 419-372-7996.

Greater Cincinnati Library Consortium, 3333 Vine St., Suite 605, Cincinnati 45220-2214. SAN 322-2675. Tel. 513-751-4422. FAX 513-751-0463. *Exec. Dir.* Martha J. McDonald.

Miami Valley Libraries (MVL), c/o Tipp City Public Lib., 11 E. Main St., Tipp City 45371. SAN 322-2691. Tel. 513-667-3826. *Pres.* Patricia Liening.

Mideastern Ohio Library Organization (MOLO), 403 N. Mill St., Louisville 44641-1428. SAN 322-2705. Tel. 216-875-4269. FAX 216-875-3404. *Dir.* Dave Simmons.

NEOUCOM Council of Associated Hospital Librarians, Ocasek Regional Medical Info. Center, Box 95, Rootstown 44272-0095. SAN 370-0526. Tel. 216-325-2511, Ext. 542. FAX 216-325-0522. *Chair* Jean Williams Sayre.

NOLA Regional Library System, 4445 Mahoning Ave. N.W., Warren 44483. SAN 322-2713. Tel. 216-847-7744. FAX 216-847-7704. *Dir.* Holly C. Carroll.

North Central Library Cooperative, 27 N. Main St., Mansfield 44902-1703. SAN 322-2683. Tel. 419-526-1337. FAX 419-526-2145. *Dir.* Jennifer J. Davis.

Northeastern Ohio Major Academic and Research Libraries (NEOMARL), c/o Northeastern Ohio Univ. College of Medicine, Box 95, Rootstown 44272-0095. SAN 322-4236. Tel. 216-325-2511, Ext. 542. *Chair* Jean W. Sayre.

Northwest Library District (NORWELD), 251 N. Main St., Bowling Green 43402. SAN 322-273X. Tel. 419-352-2903. FAX 419-354-0405. *Dir.* Allan Gray.

OCLC (Online Computer Library Center) Inc., 6565 Frantz Rd., Dublin 43017-3395. SAN 322-2748. Tel. 614-764-6000. FAX 614-764-6096. *Pres.* K. Wayne Smith.

Ohio Network of American History Research Centers, Ohio Historical Society Archives/Lib., 1982 Velma Ave., Columbus 43211-2497. SAN 323-9624. Tel. 614-297-2510. FAX 614-297-2411. *Archivist* George Parkinson.

Ohio Regional Consortium of Law Libraries (ORCLL), Ohio State Univ. Law Lib., 1659 High St., Columbus 43210-1391. SAN 371-3954. Tel. 614-292-3202. *Pres.* Katherine Carrick; *V.P.* Taylor Fitchett.

Ohio Valley Area Libraries (OVAL), 252 W. 13 St., Wellston 45692-2299. SAN 322-2756. Tel. 614-384-2103. FAX 614-384-2106. *Dir.* Eric S. Anderson.

Ohio-Kentucky Coop Libraries, c/o Cedarville College, Box 647, Cedarville 45314. SAN 325-3570. Tel. 513-766-2211. *Ed.* Janice Bosma.

OHIONET, 1500 W. Lane Ave., Columbus 43221-3975. SAN 322-2764. Tel. 614-486-2966. FAX 614-486-1527. *Exec. Dir.* Michael P. Butler.

Southwest Ohio Regional Library System (SWORL), 505 Kathryn Dr., Wilmington 45177-2274. SAN 322-2780. Tel. 513-382-2503. FAX 513-382-2504. *Dir.* Corinne Johnson.

Southwestern Ohio Council for Higher Education, 2900 Acosta St., Suite 141, Dayton 45420-3467. SAN 322-2659. Tel. 513-297-3150. FAX 513-297-3163. *Dir.* Tamara Yeager; *Chair Lib. Div.* John Montag.

Oklahoma

Greater Oklahoma City Area Health Sciences Library Consortium, Norman Regional Hospital, Health Services Lib., Box 1308, Norman 73071. SAN 329-3858. Tel. 405-360-8385. *Pres.* Michelynn McKnight.

Metropolitan Libraries Network of Central Oklahoma Inc. (MetroNetwork), Box 250, Oklahoma City 73101-0250. SAN 372-8137. Tel. 405-235-0571, Ext. 198. *Chair* Vicki Sullivan.

Mid-America Law School Library Consortium (MALSLC), c/o College of Law Lib.,

Univ. of Tulsa, 3120 E. Fourth Pl., Tulsa 74104-3189. SAN 371-6813. Tel. 918-631-2459. FAX 918-631-3556. *Chair* Richard E. Ducey.

Midwest Curriculum Coordination Center, 1500 W. Seventh Ave., Stillwater 74074-4364. SAN 329-3874. Tel. 405-377-2000. FAX 405-743-5541. *Dir.* Brenda Stacy.

Oklahoma Telecommunications Interlibrary System (OTIS), 200 N.E. 18 St., Oklahoma City 73105-3298. SAN 322-2810. Tel. 405-521-2502. FAX 405-525-7804. *Head* Mary Hardin.

Tulsa Area Library Cooperative, 400 Civic Center, Tulsa 74103. SAN 321-6489. Tel. 918-596-7893. FAX 918-596-7895. *Coord.* Paula Emmons.

Oregon

Association of Visual Science Librarians (AVSL), c/o Good Samaritan Hospital and Medical Center, 1015 N.W. 22 Ave., Portland 97210. SAN 370-0569. Tel. 503-229-7711. *Chair* Madelyn Hall.

Chemeketa Cooperative Regional Library Service, c/o Chemeketa Community College, Box 14007, Salem 97309-7070. SAN 322-2837. Tel. 503-399-5105. FAX 503-399-2514. *Coord.* Linda Cochrane.

Chiropractic Library Consortium (CLIB-CON), Western States Chiropractic College Lib., 2900 N.E. 132 Ave., Portland 97230. SAN 328-8218. Tel. 503-256-3180. FAX 503-256-4021. *Chair* Kay Irving.

Coos Cooperative Library Service District, Extended Service Office, Tioga 107, 1988 Newmark, Coos Bay 97420. SAN 322-4279. Tel. 503-888-7260. FAX 503-888-7285. *Ext. Services Coord.* Mary Jane Fisher.

Library Information Network of Clackamas County, 16201 S.E. McLoughlin Blvd., Oak Grove 97267. SAN 322-2845. Tel. 503-655-8550. FAX 503-655-8555. *Network Admin.* Joanna Rood.

Oregon Health Information Network, Oregon Health Sciences Univ. Lib., Box 573, Portland 97207-0573. SAN 322-4287. Tel. 503-494-3444. FAX 503-494-5241. *Coord.* Steve Teich.

Oregon Health Sciences Libraries Association (OHSLA), c/o Tuality Community Hospital, Box 309, Hillsboro 97123. SAN 371-2176. Tel. 503-681-1121. FAX 503-681-1729. *Chair* Natalie Norcross.

Portland Area Health Sciences Librarians, c/o Oregon Geriatric Educ. Center, Portland State Univ., Box 751, Portland 91207. SAN 371-0912. Tel. 503-725-5149. *Secy.* Jennifer Gregorio.

Southern Oregon Library Federation, c/o Jackson County Public Lib. System, Medford Lib. Branch, 413 W. Main St., Medford 97501. SAN 322-2861. Tel. 503-776-7281. FAX 503-776-7290. *Pres.* Kate McGann.

Washington County Cooperative Library Services, 17880 S.W. Blanton St., Box 5129, Aloha 97006. SAN 322-287X. Tel. 503-642-1544. FAX 503-591-0445. *Mgr.* Peggy Forcier.

Pennsylvania

Associated College Libraries of Central Pennsylvania, c/o Dickinson College, Carlisle 10713. SAN 322-2888. Tel. 717-245-1396. *Chair* John Stachacz.

Basic Health Sciences Library Network, c/o Consortium for Health Information, One Medical Center Blvd., Upland 19013. SAN 371-4888. Tel. 215-447-6163. FAX 215-447-6164. *Pres.* Kathy Kell.

Berks County Library Association (BCLA), Box 1343, R.D. 1, Hamburg 19526. SAN 371-0866. Tel. 215-655-6355. *Pres.* Julie Rinehart.

Berks County Public Library System (BCPLS), Agricultural Center, Box 520, Leesport 19533. SAN 371-8972. Tel. 215-378-5260. FAX 215-378-1525. *Admin.* Julie Rinehart.

Can-Do Consortium, Dauphin County Lib. System, 101 Walnut St., Harrisburg 17101. SAN 372-8196. Tel. 717-234-4961. *Dir.* Richard Bowra; *Dist. Coord.* James Hollinger.

Catholic Library Association, 461 W. Lancaster Ave., Haverford 19041. SAN 329-1030. Tel. 215-649-5251. FAX 215-896-1991. *Pres.* Paul Ostendorf.

Central Pennsylvania Consortium, c/o Franklin and Marshall College, Box 3003, Lancaster 17604-3003. SAN 322-2896. Tel. 717-291-3919. FAX 717-291-3969. *Dir.* Marigrace Bellart.

Confederation of State and State Related Institutions, Somerset State Hospital Staff Lib., Box 631, Somerset 15501. SAN 323-9829. Tel. 814-443-0216. FAX 814-443-0217. *Dir. Lib. Services* Eve Kline.

Consortium for Health Information and Library Services, One Medical Center Blvd., Upland 19013-3995. SAN 322-290X. Tel. 215-447-6163. FAX 215-447-6164. *Exec. Dir.* Kathleen Vick Kell.

Cooperating Hospital Libraries of the Lehigh Valley Area, Saint Joseph Hospital, 12 and Walnut Sts., Reading 19603. SAN 371-0858. Tel. 215-378-2393. FAX 215-378-2390. *Libn.* Kathleen Mazurek.

Delaware Valley Information Consortium, Abington Memorial Hospital, 1200 York Rd., Abington 19001. SAN 329-3912. Tel. 215-576-2096. *Coord.* Marion Chayes.

Eastern Mennonite Associated Libraries and Archives (EMALA), 2215 Millstream Rd., Lancaster 17602. SAN 372-8336. Tel. 717-393-9745. *Chair* Ray K. Hacker.

Erie Area Health Information Library Cooperative (EAHILC), Warren State Hospital, 33 Main St., North Warren 16365-5099. SAN 371-0564. Tel. 814-723-5500, Ext. 223. FAX 814-726-4562. *Chair* Helen Sweitzer.

Film Library Intercollege Cooperative of Pennsylvania (FLIC), c/o Delaware County Community College, Rt. 252, Media Line Rd., Media 19063. SAN 322-2926. Tel. 215-359-5156. *Pres.* Edward Beasley.

Greater Philadelphia Law Library Association (GPLLA), Box 335, Philadelphia 19015. SAN 373-1375. Tel. 215-592-5609. *Pres.* Darlene Moore; *V.P.* Kathleen A. Caron.

Health Information Library Network of Northeastern Pennsylvania, c/o Community Medical Center, Doctor's Lib., 1800 Mulberry St., Scranton 18510. SAN 322-2934. Tel. 717-969-8197. *Chair* Corrine McNabb.

Health Sciences Libraries Consortium, 3600 Market St., Suite 550, Philadelphia 19104.

SAN 323-9780. Tel. 215-222-1532. FAX 215-222-0416. *Exec. Dir.* Joseph C. Scorza.

Interlibrary Delivery Service of Pennsylvania, 471 Park Lane, State College 16803-3208. SAN 322-2942. Tel. 814-238-0254. FAX 814-238-9686. *Admin. Dir.* Janet C. Phillips.

Laurel Highlands Health Sciences Library Consortium, Univ. Lib., Rm. 209, Univ. of Pittsburgh at Johnstown, Johnstown 15904. SAN 322-2950. Tel. 814-269-7280. FAX 814-266-8230. *Dir.* Heather W. Brice.

Lehigh Valley Association of Independent Colleges Inc., Moravian College, 1200 Main St., Bethlehem 18018-6650. SAN 322-2969. Tel. 215-882-5275. FAX 215-882-5515. *Dir.* Galen C. Godbey.

Mid-Atlantic Law Library Cooperative, c/o Allegheny County Law Lib., 921 City/County Bldg., Pittsburgh 15219. SAN 371-0645. Tel. 412-355-5353. FAX 412-355-5889. *Dir.* Joel Fishman; *Coord.* Frank Liu.

NEIU Consortium, 1300 Old Plank Rd., Mayfield 18433. SAN 372-817X. Tel. 717-282-9268. *Dir.* Robert Carpenter; *Program Coord.* Rose Bennett.

Northeastern Pennsylvania Bibliographic Center, c/o Learning Resource Center, Marywood College, Scranton 18509-1598. SAN 322-2993. Tel. 717-348-6211, Ext. 546. FAX 717-348-1817. *Dir.* Catherine H. Schappert.

Northwest Interlibrary Cooperative of Pennsylvania (NICOP), Penn State–Erie, Behrend College Lib., Station Rd., Erie 16563. SAN 370-5862. Tel. 814-898-6106. FAX 814-898-6350. *Chair* Elizabeth Smith.

Oakland Library Consortium (OLC), Carnegie Mellon Univ., Hunt Lib., Rm. 302, Pittsburgh 15213-3890. SAN 370-5803. Tel. 412-268-2890. FAX 412-268-6944. *Exec. Dir.* Sylverna Ford.

PALINET and Union Library Catalogue of Pennsylvania (PALINET), 3401 Market St., Suite 262, Philadelphia 19104. SAN 322-3000. Tel. 215-382-7031. FAX 215-382-0022. *Exec. Dir.* James E. Rush; *Mgr. OCLC Services* Meryl Cinnamon; *Mgr.*

Microcomputer Services Clifford Coughlin; *Mgr. Admin. Services* Donna Wright.

Pennsylvania Citizens for Better Libraries (PCBL), 608 Gladfelte Hall, 502 Ellen Rd., Camp Hill 17011. SAN 372-8285. Tel. 717-737-6451. FAX 717-737-6123. *Pres.* Dennis P. Leeper.

Pennsylvania Community College Library Consortium, c/o Bucks County Community College, Swamp Rd., Newtown 18940. SAN 329-3939. Tel. 215-968-8055. *Pres.* John Bradley.

Pennsylvania Library Association, 1919 N. Front St., Harrisburg 17102. SAN 372-8145. Tel. 717-233-3113. *Exec. Dir.* Margaret S. Bauer; *Pres.* Christine Roysdon.

Philadelphia Area Consortium of Special Collections Libraries (PACSCL), c/o Academy of Natural Sciences, 1900 Benjamin Franklin Pkwy., Philadelphia 19103-1195. SAN 370-7504. Tel. 215-299-1040. FAX 215-299-1028. *Chair Exec. Committee* Carol M. Spawn.

Pittsburgh Council on Higher Education (PCHE), 3814 Forbes Ave., Pittsburgh 15213-3506. SAN 322-3019. Tel. 412-683-7905. FAX 412-648-1492. *Exec. Dir.* Betty K. Hunter.

Pittsburgh-East Hospital Library Cooperative, c/o Saint Francis Medical Center, 400 45th St., Pittsburgh 15201. SAN 322-3027. Tel. 412-622-4110. *Pres.* Pam Sgalio.

Pittsburgh Regional Library Center (PRLC), 103 Yost Blvd., Pittsburgh 15221-4833. SAN 322-3035. Tel. 412-825-0600. FAX 412-825-0762. *Exec. Dir.* Christina Russell.

Somerset–Bedford County Medical Library Consortium, Box 631, Somerset 15501-0631. SAN 322-3043. Tel. 814-445-6501, Ext. 216. FAX 814-443-0217. *Dir.* Eve Kline; *Libn.* Kathy Plaso.

Southeast Pittsburgh Library Consortium (SEPLC), Health Science Lib., South Hills Health System, Box 18119, Pittsburgh 15236. SAN 371-5132. Tel. 412-469-5786. *Chair* Barbara Palso.

Southeastern Pennsylvania Theological Library Association (SEPTLA), c/o Saint Charles Borromeo Seminary, Ryan Lib., 1000 E. Wynnewood Rd., Overbrook 19096-3012. SAN 371-0793. Tel. 215-667-3394, Ext. 280. FAX 215-664-7913. *Pres.* Lorena Boylan.

State System of Higher Education Libraries Council (SSHELCO), c/o Ganser Lib., Millersville Univ., Box 1002, Millersville 17551. SAN 322-2918. Tel. 717-872-3608. FAX 717-872-3854. *Chair* David Zubatsky.

Susquehanna Library Cooperative, c/o Stevenson Lib., Lock Haven Univ., Lock Haven 17745. SAN 322-3051. Tel. 717-893-2309. FAX 717-893-2506. *Pres.* Robert Bravard.

Tri-State College Library Cooperative (TCLC), c/o S. H. Green Lib., West Chester Univ., West Chester 19383. SAN 322-3078. Tel. 215-436-2747. *Pres.* Frank Helms.

Rhode Island

Association of Rhode Island Health Sciences Librarians (ARIHSL), c/o Isaac Ray Medical Lib., Butler Hospital, 345 Blackstone Blvd., Providence 02906. SAN 371-0742. Tel. 401-455-6249. *Pres.* Ruth Ann Gildea.

Consortium of Rhode Island Academic and Research Libraries (CRIARL), Box 40041, Providence 02940-0041. SAN 322-3086. Tel. 401-841-2641. *Pres.* Robert E. Schnare.

Cooperating Libraries Automated Network (CLAN), c/o Warwick Public Lib., 600 Sandy Lane, Warwick 02886. SAN 329-4560. Tel. 401-739-5440. FAX 401-732-2055. *Exec. Dir.* Virginia Taken.

Rhode Island Library Network (RHILINET), 300 Richmond St., Providence 02903-4222. SAN 371-6821. Tel. 401-277-2726. FAX 401-831-1131. *Dir.* Barbara Weaver.

South Carolina

Catawba-Wateree Health Education Consortium, 1020 W. Meeting St., Box 2049, Lancaster 29721. SAN 329-3971. Tel.

803-286-4121. FAX 803-286-4165. *Libn.* Penny Welling.

Charleston Academic Libraries Consortium, College of Charleston, Robert Scott Small Lib., Charleston 29424. SAN 371-0769. Tel. 803-792-5530. *Chair* David Cohen.

Columbia Area Medical Librarians' Association (CAMLA), Professional Lib., Box 202, Columbia 29202. SAN 372-9400. Tel. 803-734-7136. FAX 803-734-7087. *Coord.* Neeta N. Shah.

South Carolina AHEC Consortium (AHEC), 171 Ashley Ave., Charleston 29425. SAN 329-3998. Tel. 803-792-4431. FAX 803-792-4430. *Dir.* Dean Cleghorn.

South Carolina Health Information Network (SCHIN), Medical Univ. of South Carolina Lib., 171 Ashley Ave., Charleston 29425-3001. SAN 370-0542. Tel. 803-792-2374. FAX 803-792-7947.

South Carolina State Library, South Carolina Library Network, 1500 Senate St., Box 11469, Columbia 29211-1469. SAN 322-4198. Tel. 803-734-8666. FAX 803-734-8676. *State Libn.* James B. Johnson, Jr.

Upper Savannah AHEC, Medical Lib., Self Memorial Hospital, 1325 Spring St., Greenwood 29646. SAN 329-4110. Tel. 803-227-4851. FAX 803-227-4838. *Libn.* Thomas Hill.

South Dakota

Colleges of Mid-America Inc. (CMA), c/o Mount Marty College, 1105 W. Eighth St., Yankton 57058. SAN 322-3132. Tel. 605-668-1548. *Dir.* Mary C. Miller.

South Dakota Library Network (SDLN), University Station, Box 9672, Spearfish 57799. SAN 371-2117. Tel. 605-642-6264. *Dir.* Gary Johnson.

Tennessee

Association of Memphis Area Health Science Libraries (AMAHSL), c/o Univ. of Tennessee Health Science Lib., 877 Madison Ave., Memphis 38163. SAN 323-9802. Tel. 901-528-5634. *Pres.* Glenda Mendina; *V.P.* Mary Buckley.

Knoxville Area Health Sciences Library Consortium (KAHSLC), c/o Univ. of Tennessee Medical Center, Preston Medical Lib., 1924 Alcoa Highway, Knoxville 37920. SAN 371-0556. Tel. 615-544-9525. *Libn.* Marjorie A. Caldwell; *Pres.* Shelley Paden.

Mid-Tennessee Health Science Librarians Consortium, c/o Vanderbilt Univ. Medical Center Lib., Nashville 37232-2340. SAN 329-5028. Tel. 615-322-2291. FAX 615-343-6454. *Pres.* Beverly Carlton.

Tennessee Health Science Library Association (THESLA), Vanderbilt Univ. Medical Center Lib., Nashville 37232-2340. SAN 371-0726. Tel. 615-322-2291. FAX 615-343-6454. *Pres.* Evelyn Forbes.

Tri-Cities Area Health Sciences Libraries Consortium, East Tennessee State Univ., James H. Quillen College of Medicine, Medical Lib., Box 70693, Johnson City 37614-0693. SAN 329-4099. Tel. 615-929-6252. FAX 615-461-7025. *Dir.* Janet S. Fisher.

West Tennessee Academic Library Consortium, c/o Jackson State Community College Lib., 2046 N. Parkway, Jackson 38301. SAN 322-3175. Tel. 901-425-2615. FAX 901-425-2647. *Chair* Scott Cohen.

Texas

Abilene Library Consortium, Abilene Christian Univ. Lib. Station, Box 8177, Abilene 79699-8177. SAN 322-4694. Tel. 915-674-2434. FAX 915-674-2202. *System Mgr.* Robert Gillette.

Alliance for Higher Education, 17103 Preston Rd., Suite 250, LB 107, Dallas 75248-1373. SAN 322-3337. Tel. 214-713-8170. FAX 214-713-8209. *Pres.* Allan Watson; *Dir. Lib. Programs and Services* Mary M. Huston.

Amigos Bibliographic Council Inc., 122000 Park Central Dr., Suite 500, Dallas 75251. SAN 322-3191. Tel. 214-851-8000. FAX 214-991-6061. *Exec. Dir.* Bonnie Juergens.

APLIC International Census Network, c/o Population Research Center, 1800 Main Bldg., Univ. of Texas, Austin 78713. SAN 370-0690. Tel. 512-471-5514. FAX 512-471-4886. *Dir.* Gera Draaijer; *Libn.* Diane Fisher.

Council of Research and Academic Libraries (CORAL), Box 290236, San Antonio 78280-1636. SAN 322-3213. Tel. 201-341-1366. *Pres.* Cliff Dawdy.

—Circulation and Interlibrary Loan Group (CIRCILL), c/o San Antonio College, 1001 Howard St., San Antonio 78212. SAN 322-323X. Tel. 210-733-2489. *Chair* John Deosdade.

—Coral Periodicals-Serials Librarians Group (CORPSE), Institute of Texan Cultures, Box 1226, San Antonio 78294. SAN 322-3248. Tel. 210-226-7651. *Chair* Diane Bruce.

—Documents Users Group (DOCS), c/o San Antonio College, 1001 Howard St., San Antonio 78212. SAN 322-3256. Tel. 201-733-2598. *Chair* Christine Petimezas.

—Instructional Media Services Group (IMS), Our Lady of the Lake Univ., 411 S.W. 24 St., San Antonio 78207-4689. SAN 322-3221. Tel. 201-434-6711. *Pres.* Jean Thornblom.

—Special Collections Interest Group (SCIG), Trinity Univ., 715 Stadium Dr., San Antonio 78212. SAN 324-2986. Tel. 201-736-7344. *Pres.* Craig Likness.

—Technical Services Interest Group (TSIG), Southwest Research Institute, 6220 Calebra Rd., San Antonio 78228. SAN 322-3272. Tel. 210-522-2126. *Pres.* Rowland Craig.

Del Norte Biosciences Library Consortium, c/o Reference Dept. Lib., Univ. of Texas at El Paso, El Paso 79968-0582. SAN 322-3302. Tel. 915-747-5643. FAX 915-747-5327. *Pres.* Esperanza A. Moreno.

Harrington Library Consortium, Box 447, Amarillo 79178. SAN 329-546X. Tel. 806-371-5135. FAX 806-371-5370. *Mgr.* Roseann Perez.

Health Library Information Network, c/o Texas College of Osteopathic Medicine, Health Science Lib., 2500 Camp Bowie Blvd., Fort Worth 76107. SAN 322-3299. Tel. 817-735-2588. *Chair* Regina Lee.

Health Oriented Libraries of San Antonio (HOLSA), Briscoe Lib., Univ. of Texas Health Science Center, 7703 Floyd Curl Dr., San Antonio 78284. SAN 373-5907. Tel. 210-567-2425. *Pres.* Linda Siegel.

Houston Area Research Library Consortium (HARLiC), c/o Rice Univ., Fandren Lib., 6100 S. Main St., Houston 77005. SAN 322-3329. Tel. 713-527-4021. *Pres.* Beth Shapiro.

National Network of Libraries of Medicine—South Central Region, c/o HAM-TMC Lib., 1133 M. D. Anderson Blvd., Houston 77030-2809. SAN 322-3353. Tel. 713-790-7053, Ext. 6. FAX 713-790-7030. *Contact* Mary Ryan.

Northeast Texas Library System (NETLS), 625 Austin, Garland 75040-6365. SAN 370-5943. Tel. 214-205-2566. FAX 214-205-2523. *Dir.* Lowell Lindsey; *Coord.* Elizabeth Crabb.

Piasano Consortium, Victoria College, Univ. of Houston at Victoria, 2602 N. Ben Jordan, Victoria 77901-5699. SAN 329-4943. Tel. 512-573-3291, 576-3151. FAX 512-573-4401. *Coord.* Joe F. Dahlstrom.

Regional Information and Communication Exchange, Fondren Lib., Rice Univ., Box 1892, Houston 77251-1892. SAN 322-3345. Tel. 713-528-3553. FAX 713-523-4117. *Dir.* Una Gourlay.

South Central Academic Medical Libraries Consortium (SCAMEL), TCOM Health Sciences Lib., 3500 Camp Bowie Blvd., Fort Worth 76107. SAN 372-8269. Tel. 817-735-2380. *Chair* James Pat Craig; *Chair-Elect* Janet Minnerath.

TAMU Consortium of Medical Libraries, Medical Sciences Lib., Texas A & M University, College Station 77843. SAN 372-9702. Tel. 409-845-7427. FAX 409-845-7493. *Dir.* Dottie Eakin.

Texas Council of State University Librarians, Southwest Texas State Univ., Albert B. Alkek Lib., San Marcos 78666-4604. SAN 322-337X. Tel. 512-245-2133. FAX 512-245-3002. *Chair* Joan Heath.

TEXNET, Box 12927, Austin 78711. SAN 322-3396. Tel. 512-463-5465. FAX 512-463-5436. *Mgr.* Rebecca Linton.

USDA Southwest Regional Document Delivery System, c/o Texas A&M Univ. Lib.,

Interlib. Loan Service, College Station 77843-5000. SAN 322-340X. Tel. 409-845-5641. FAX 409-845-4512. *ILL Head* Susan Raschke.

Utah

Utah College Library Council (UCLC), c/o Brigham Young Univ., 1354 HBLL, Provo 84602. SAN 322-3418. Tel. 801-378-4482. FAX 801-378-6347. *Secy.* Terry Dahlin.

Utah Health Sciences Library Consortium (UHSLC), c/o Saint Benedict Hospital, 5475 S. 500 East, Ogden 84405. SAN 370-5900. Tel. 801-479-2055. *Chair* Sandy Eckersley.

Vermont

Vermont Resource Sharing Network, c/o Vermont Dept. of Libraries, 109 State St., Montpelier 05609-0601. SAN 322-3426. Tel. 802-828-3261. FAX 802-828-2199. *Contact* Marjorie Zunder.

Virginia

American Gas Association–Library Services (AGA-LSC), 1515 Wilson Blvd., Arlington 22209. SAN 371-0890. Tel. 703-841-8400. FAX 703-841-8406. *Dir.* Steven Dorner.

Defense Technical Information Center, Cameron Station, Bldg. 5, Alexandria 22304-6145. SAN 322-3442. Tel. 703-274-3848. FAX 703-274-9274. *Admin.* Kurt N. Molholm.

Infopro Technologies (formerly Maxwell Online Inc.), 8000 Westpark Dr., McLean 22102. SAN 322-2438. Tel. 703-442-0900. FAX 703-893-4632. *Pres.* Andrew Gregory.

Lynchburg Area Library Cooperative, Mary Helen Cochran Lib., Sweet Briar College, Sweet Briar 24595. SAN 322-3450. Tel. 804-381-6139. FAX 804-381-6173. *Pres.* John Jaffe.

Richmond Academic Library Consortium (RALC), VCU Libs., Box 2033, Richmond 23284-2033. SAN 371-3938. Tel. 804-367-1107. *Pres.* Barbara Ford; *V.P.* Theresa Byrd.

Richmond Area Film-Video Cooperative, c/o Virginia Commonwealth Univ., James Branch Cabell Learning Resource Center, Richmond 23284-2033. SAN 322-3469. Tel. 804-367-1088. FAX 804-367-0151. *Dir.* Barbara Ford.

Southside Virginia Library Network (SVLN), Longwood College, 201 High St., Farmville 23909-1897. SAN 372-8242. Tel. 804-395-2433. *Interim Dir.* Rebecca R. Laine.

Southwestern Virginia Health Information Librarians (SWVAHILI), c/o Veterans Administration Medical Center, Salem 24153. SAN 323-9527. Tel. 703-982-2463. *Chair* Jean Kennedy; *Secy.-Treas.* Mary Horner.

Tidewater Health Sciences Libraries (THSL), c/o Eastern Virginia Medical School Lib., Box 1980, Norfolk 23501-1980. SAN 317-3658. Tel. 804-446-5840. *Dir.* Anne Cramer.

U.S. Army Training and Doctrine Command (TRADOC), Lib. and Info. Network (TRALINET) Center, ATBO-N, Bldg. 117, Fort Monroe 23651-5117. SAN 322-418X. Tel. 804-727-4491. FAX 804-727-2750. *Systems Libn.* Edwin Burgess.

Virginia Library and Information Network (VLIN), c/o Virginia State Lib. and Archives, 11 St. at Capitol Sq., Richmond 23219-3491. SAN 373-0921. Tel. 804-786-2320. FAX 804-335-4608. *State Libn.* John C. Tyson; *Dir. Lib. Development & Networking* Anthony Yankus.

Virginia Tidewater Consortium for Higher Education, Health Science Bldg., Rm. 129, 5215 Hampton Blvd., Norfolk 23529-0293. SAN 329-5486. Tel. 804-683-3183. FAX 804-683-4515. *Dir.* Lawrence G. Dotolo.

Washington

Central Washington Hospital Consortium, Box 1887, Wenatchee 98807. SAN 329-3750. Tel. 509-662-1511. *Coord.* Susan Marshall.

Consortium for Automated Library Services, Evergreen State College Lib. L2300, Olympia 98505. SAN 329-4528. Tel. 206-

866-6000, Ext. 6260. FAX 206-866-6790. *Systems Mgr.* Steven A. Metcalf.

Council on Botanical Horticultural Libraries, Lawrence Pierce Lib., Rhododendron Species Federation, 2525 S. 336 St., Box 3798, Federal Way 98063-3798. SAN 371-0521. Tel. 206-927-6960. FAX 206-838-4686. *Chair* Mrs. George Harrison.

Inland Northwest Health Sciences Libraries (INWHSL), 2917 W. Fort Wright Dr., Spokane 99204-5290. SAN 370-5099. Tel. 509-466-3260, Ext. 4488. *Chair* Robert Pringle.

National Network of Libraries of Medicine—Pacific Northwest Region, Univ. of Washington, SB-55, Seattle 98195. SAN 322-3485. Tel. 206-543-8262. FAX 206-543-2469. *Dir.* Sherrilynne S. Fuller.

Seattle Area Hospital Library Consortium, Health Info. Network Services, Everett 98206. SAN 329-3815. Tel. 206-258-7558. FAX 206-258-7266. *Dir.* Rhe Jain; *Pres.* Cheryl Noble.

Spokane Cooperative Library Information System (SCOLIS), E12004 Main, Spokane 99206-5193. SAN 322-3892. Tel. 509-922-1371. FAX 509-926-7139. *Mgr.* Linda Dunham.

WLN, Box 3888, Lacey 98503-0888. SAN 322-3507. Tel. 206-923-4000. FAX 206-923-4009. *Pres.* Ronald F. Miller; *Mgr.* Gwen Culp.

West Virginia

East Central Colleges, c/o Bethany College, Box AJ, Bethany 26032-1434. SAN 322-2667. Tel. 304-829-7812. FAX 304-829-7546. *Exec. Dir.* Dennis Landon.

Huntington Health Science Library Consortium, Marshall Univ. Health Science Libs., Huntington 25755-9210. SAN 322-4295. Tel. 304-696-3170. *Chair* Edward Dzierzak.

Mountain States Consortium, c/o Alderson Broaddus College, Philippi 26416. SAN 329-4765. Tel. 304-457-1700. *Treas.* J. Leonard Lobello.

Southern West Virginia Library Automation Corporation, 221 N. Kanawha St., Box 1876, Beckley 25802. SAN 322-421X.

Tel. 304-255-0511, Ext. 19. FAX 304-255-0516. *Systems Mgr.* Margaret Williamson.

Wisconsin

Council of Wisconsin Libraries Inc. (COWL), 728 State St., Rm. 464, Madison 53706-1494. SAN 322-3523. Tel. 608-263-4962. FAX 608-263-3684. *Dir.* Kathryn Schneider Michaelis.

Fox River Valley Area Library Consortium, c/o Saint Nicholas, 1601 N. Taylor Dr., Sheboygan 53081. SAN 322-3531. Tel. 414-459-4713. FAX 414-452-2499. *Coord.* Jeff Gartman.

Fox Valley Library Council (FVLC), c/o Outagamie/Wayaaca Lib. Council, 225 N. Oneida St., Appleton 54911. SAN 323-9640. Tel. 414-832-6190. *Pres.* Dennis Parks.

Library Council of Metropolitan Milwaukee Inc., 814 W. Wisconsin Ave., Milwaukee 53233. SAN 322-354X. Tel. 414-271-8470. FAX 414-286-2137. *Exec. Dir.* Corliss Rice.

North East Wisconsin Intertype Libraries Inc. (NEWIL), c/o Nicolet Federated Lib. System, 515 Pine St., Green Bay 54301. SAN 322-3574. Tel. 414-448-4412. FAX 414-448-4420. *Coord.* Terrie Howe.

Northwestern Wisconsin Hospital Library Consortium, c/o Health Sciences Lib., Saint Michael's Hospital, 900 Illinois Ave., Stevens Point 54481. SAN 322-3604. Tel. 715-346-5091. FAX 715-341-5077. *Dir.* Jan Kraus.

South Central Wisconsin Health Science Library Cooperative, Watertown Memorial Hospital Research Center, 125 Hospital Dr., Watertown 53094. SAN 322-4686. Tel. 414-262-4278. FAX 414-261-3940. *Coord.* Linda Long.

Southeastern Wisconsin Health Science Library Consortium, c/o VA Medical Center Medical Lib., 5000 W. National Ave., Milwaukee 53295. SAN 322-3582. Tel. 414-384-2000, Ext. 2342. *Contact* Janice Curnes.

Southeastern Wisconsin Information Technology Exchange Inc. (SWITCH), 6801 N. Yates Rd., Milwaukee 53217. SAN 371-

3962. Tel. 414-351-2423. FAX 414-352-6062. *Exec. Dir.* David Weinberg-Kinsey.
Wisconsin Area Research Center Network, ARC Network, 816 State St., Madison 53706. SAN 373-0875. Tel. 608-264-6480. *State Archivist* Peter Gottlieb.
Wisconsin Interlibrary Services (WILS), 728 State St., Rm. 464, Madison 53706-1494. SAN 322-3612. Tel. 608-263-4962, 263-5051. FAX 608-263-3684. *Dir.* Kathryn Schneider Michaelis.
Wisconsin Valley Library Service (WVLS), 400 First St., Wausau 54401. SAN 371-3911. Tel. 715-847-5535. FAX 715-845-4270. *Dir.* Heather Ann Eldred.

Wyoming

Health Sciences Information Network (HSIN), c/o Science and Technology Lib., Univ. of Wyoming, Box 3262, Laramie 82071-3262. SAN 371-4861. Tel. 307-766-4263. FAX 307-766-3611. *Coord.* Janice Gahagan.
Northeastern Wyoming Medical Library Consortium, Campbell County Memorial Hospital, Box 3011, Gillette 82716. SAN 370-484X. Tel. 307-682-8811, Ext. 183. FAX 307-687-5182. *Chair* Dorothy O'Brien.
Wyoming Library Network, c/o Wyoming State Lib., Supreme Court and State Lib. Bldg., Cheyenne 82002. SAN 371-0661. Tel. 307-777-7281. FAX 307-777-6289. *State Libn.* Suzanne LeBarron.

Virgin Islands

VILINET (Virgin Islands Library and Information Network), c/o Division of Libs., Museums and Archives, 23 Dronningens Gade, Saint Thomas 00802. SAN 322-3639. Tel. 809-774-3407 (DLMAS), 774-3725. *Chair* Jeanette Allis Bastian.

Canada

Alberta

Alberta Association of College Librarians (AACL), S. Alberta Institute of Technolo-
gy, 1301 16th Ave. N.W., Calgary T2M 0L4. SAN 370-0763. Tel. 403-284-8408. FAX 403-284-8619. *Chair* Dave Weber.
Alberta Government Libraries Council (AGLC), c/o Alberta Public Service Lib., 10320 146th St., Edmonton T5N 3A2. SAN 370-0372. Tel. 403-451-7178. *Chair* Carol Dawson; *Chair-Elect* Teresa Richey.
Alberta Occupational Health and Safety (AEOH), Alberta Occupational Health Lib. Services, 10709 Jasper Ave., 6th fl., Edmonton T5J 3N3. SAN 370-0801. Tel. 403-427-3530. FAX 403-427-5698. *Public Services Libn.* J. Lavkulich.
Northern Alberta Health Libraries Association (NAHLA), c/o Lib. and Inquiry Services, Alberta Health, 10709 Jasper Ave., Edmonton T5J 3N3. SAN 370-5951. Tel. 403-427-3530. *Pres.* Joanne Lavkulich.

British Columbia

British Columbia College and Institute Library Services, Clearinghouse for the Print Impaired (CILS), Vancouver Community College, Langara Campus Lib., 100 W. 49 Ave., Vancouver V5Y 2Z6. SAN 329-6970. Tel. 604-324-5237. FAX 604-324-5544. *Contact* Phyllis Mason.
British Columbia Post-Secondary Interlibrary Loan Network (NET), Univ. of British Columbia, Box 2139, Vancouver V6B 3T1. SAN 322-4724. Tel. 604-822-4430. FAX 604-822-6465. *Head ILL* Margaret Friesen.
Central Vancouver Librarian Group (CVLG), c/o Lib. Processing Centre–Serials, Univ. of British Columbia, 2206 E. Mall, Vancouver V6T 1Z3. SAN 323-9543. Tel. 604-822-4578. FAX 604-822-3201. *Chair* Kat McGrath.
Media Exchange Cooperative (MEC), Capilano College, 2055 Purcell Way, North Vancouver V7J 3H5. SAN 329-6954. Tel. 604-984-4943. FAX 604-984-1728. *Pres.* Frieda Wiebe.

Manitoba

Manitoba Government Libraries Council (MGLC), 202-880 Portage Ave., Winnepeg R3G 0P1. SAN 371-6848. Tel. 204-945-8002. FAX 204-945-5063. *Chair* Marilyn Brooke.

Manitoba Library Consortium Inc. (MLCI), c/o Aikins, MacAulay and Thorvaldson, Community Exchange Tower, 360 Main St., Winnipeg R3C 4G1. SAN 372-820X. Tel. 304-632-2232. *Chairs* Patricia Bozyk, Kathy Thornborough.

New Brunswick

LINK–Library Information Network, c/o Ward Chipman Lib., Univ. of New Brunswick, Box 5050, Saint John E2L 4L5. SAN 370-0798. Tel. 506-648-5704. FAX 506-648-5701. *Coord.* Susan Collins.

Maritimes Health Libraries Association (MHLA/ABSM), Saint John Regional Hospital Health Sciences Lib., Box 2100, Saint John E2L 4L5. SAN 370-0836. Tel. 506-648-6763. *Pres.* Anne Kilfoil.

Nova Scotia

Council of Metropolitan University Librarians (COMUL), Technical Univ. of Nova Scotia, Box 1000, Halifax B3J 2X4. SAN 370-0704. Tel. 902-420-7700. FAX 902-420-7551. *Chair* M. Riaz Hussain.

Novanet, 1379 Seymour St., Halifax B3H 3J5. SAN 372-4050. Tel. 902-494-1785. FAX 902-494-1536. *System Mgr.* Leslie A. Foster.

Ontario

Bibliocentre, 80 Cowdray Ct., Scarborough M1S 4N1. SAN 322-3663. Tel. 416-754-6600. FAX 416-299-0902. *Dir.* Doug Wentzel.

Canadian Association of Research Libraries (CARLABRC), Univ. of Ottawa, Morisset Hall, Rm. 602, 65 University St., Ottawa K1N 9A5. SAN 323-9721. Tel. 613-564-5864. FAX 613-564-5871. *Exec. Dir.* David L. McCallum.

Canadian Health Libraries Association (CHLA/ABSC), Office of Secretariat, 3332 Yonge St., Box 94038, Toronto M4N 3R1. SAN 370-0720. Tel. 416-485-0377 (Voice & FAX). *Contact* Dorothy Davey; *Pres.* Jennifer Bayne.

Canadian Heritage Information Network (CHIN), 365 Laurier Ave. W., Journal Tower S., 12th fl., Ottawa K1A 0C8. SAN 329-3076. Tel. 613-992-3333, Ext. 186. FAX 613-952-2318. *Dir. Gen.* P. Homulos; *Coord.* Merridy Bradley.

County and Regional Municipal Library (CARML), c/o Lennox and Addington County Lib., 37 Dundas St. W., Napanee K7R 1Z5. SAN 323-9705. Tel. 613-354-2585. FAX 613-354-7527. *Chair* Sam Coghlan; *Secy.* Mary Ann Evans.

Disability Resource Library Network (DRLN), c/o Hugh McMillan Rehab. Center, Health Science Lib., 350 Ramsey Rd., Toronto M4G 1R8. SAN 323-9837. Tel. 416-425-6220, Ext. 517. *Chair* Pui-Ying Wong.

Education Libraries Sharing of Resources—A Network (ELSOR), 45 York Mills Rd., Willowdale M2P 1B6. SAN 370-0399. Tel. 416-397-2523. FAX 416-397-2640. *Chair* Martha E. Murphy.

Hamilton and District Health Library Network, c/o Health Science Lib., McMaster Univ., 1200 Main St. W., Hamilton L8N 3Z5. SAN 370-5846. Tel. 416-525-9140, Ext. 2322. FAX 416-521-0048. *Network Coord.* Linda Panton.

Health Science Information Consortium of Toronto, Univ. of Toronto, 7 King's College Circle, Toronto M5S 1A5. SAN 370-5080. Tel. 416-978-6359. FAX 416-978-7666. *Exec. Dir.* Joan L. Leishman.

Hi-Tech Libraries Network, c/o Cal Corp., 1050 Morrison Dr., Ottawa K2H 8K7. SAN 323-9586. Tel. 613-820-8280. FAX 613-820-8314. *Contact* Sandra Spence.

Kingston Area Health Libraries Association (KAHLA), c/o Saint Lawrence College Learning Resource Center, King and Portsmouth Ave., Kingston K7L 5A6. SAN 370-0674. Tel. 613-544-5400, Ext. 1248. FAX 613-545-3920. *Pres.* Barbara Carr.

Ontario Council of University Libraries (OCUL), Lakehead Univ., Thunder Bay P7B 5E1. SAN 371-9413. Tel. 807-343-8110. *Chair* Fred MacIntosh.

Ontario Hospital Libraries Association, Region 9 (OHLAR9), c/o Rideau Regional

Centre Lib., Box 2000, Smith Falls K7A 4T7. SAN 370-0550. Tel. 613-284-0123, Ext. 225. FAX 613-283-3463. *Chair* Janet Joyce; *Pres.* Pat Kitely.

Ontario Hospital Libraries Association, c/o Victoria Hospital Lib. Services, Box 5375, London N6A 4G5. SAN 370-0739. Tel. 519-685-8500, Ext. 7717. FAX 519-667-6794. *Dir.* Mary Gillet.

Ontario Public Library Information Network, Ministry of Culture & Communications Libs. and Community Info. Branch, 77 Bloor St. W., 3rd fl., Toronto M7A 2R9. SAN 329-5605. Tel. 416-314-7611. FAX 416-314-7635. *Dir.* Barbara Clubb.

Ottawa Hull Health Libraries Association (OHHLA), c/o Canadian Medical Association Lib., 1867 Alta Vista Dr., Ottawa K1G 0G8. SAN 370-0844. Tel. 613-731-9331, Ext. 2144. FAX 613-731-9013. *Pres.* Kathleen Beauboin; *Secy.-Treas.* Judith Bosschart.

QL Systems Limited, One Gore St., Box 2080, Kingston K7L 5J8. SAN 322-368X. Tel. 613-549-4611. FAX 613-548-4260. *Pres.* Hugh Lawford.

—Calgary Branch, 505 Third St. S.W., Suite 1010, Calgary, AB T2P 3E6. SAN 322-3817. Tel. 403-262-6505. *Marketing Mgr.* Anita Manley.

—Halifax Branch, 1819 Granville St., Suite 300, Halifax, NS B3J 1X8. SAN 325-4194. Tel. 902-420-1666. *Mgr.* Ruth Rintoul.

—Ottawa Branch, 901 Saint Andrews Tower, 275 Sparks, Ottawa K1R 7X9. SAN 322-3825. Tel. 613-238-3499. *V.P. Marketing* Adrienne Herron; *Mgr.* Alan Dingle.

—Toronto Branch, 411 Richmond St. E., Suite 101, Toronto M5A 3S5. SAN 322-3833. Tel. 416-862-7656. *Mgr.* Tim Outhit.

—Vancouver Branch, 355 Burrard St., Suite 920, Vancouver, BC V6C 2G8. SAN 322-3841. Tel. 604-684-1462.

Shared Library Services (SLS), South Huron Hospital Shared Lib. Services, 24 Huron St. W., Exeter N0M 1S2. SAN 323-9500. Tel. 519-235-2700, Ext. 49. FAX 519-235-3405. *Dir.* Linda Wilcox.

Sheridan Park Association Library and Information Science Committee (SPA LISC),

2275 Speakman Dr., Mississauga L5K 1B1. SAN 370-0437. Tel. 416-823-6160. *Chair* Laurie Scott; *Mgr.* E. Gordon.

Southern Ontario Library Service–Hamilton (SOLS), 1133 Central Ave., Hamilton L8K 1N7. SAN 371-0629. Tel. 416-544-2780. *Dir.* Gabriele Lundeen.

Toronto Health Libraries Association (THLA), Box 94056, Toronto M4N 3R1. SAN 323-9853. Tel. 416-978-2872. *Pres.* Sylvia Newman.

Toronto School of Theology, c/o Emmanuel College, 75 Queen's Park Crescent E., Toronto M5S 1K7. SAN 322-452X. Tel. 416-585-4551. FAX 416-585-4516. *Secy. Lib. Commission* R. Grant Bracewell.

Wellington Waterloo Dufferin (WWD) Health Library Network, c/o Health Science Lib., Kitchener-Waterloo Hospital, 835 King St. W., Kitchener N2G 1G3. SAN 370-0496. Tel. 519-742-3611, Ext. 2235. *Coord.* Thelma Bisch.

Quebec

Association des Bibliothèques de la Santé Affiliées à l'Université de Montréal (ABSAUM), c/o Health Lib., Univ. of Montreal, Montreal H3C 3J7. SAN 370-5838. Tel. 514-343-6826. FAX 514-343-2550. *Secy.* Bernard Bedard.

Montreal Health Libraries Association (MHLA), 4565 Queen Mary Rd., Montreal H3W 1W5. SAN 323-9608. Tel. 514-340-1424, Ext. 3266. FAX 514-340-2807. *Pres.* Louise Bourbonais.

Montreal Medical Online Users Group (MMOUG), McGill Health Sciences Lib., 3655 Drummond St., Montreal H3G 1Y6. SAN 370-0771. Tel. 514-398-4757. FAX 514-398-3890. *Coord.* Angella Lambrou.

Saskatchewan

Saskatchewan Government Libraries Council (SGLC), c/o Saskatchewan Agriculture and Food Lib., 3085 Albert St., Regina S4S 0B1. SAN 323-956X. Tel. 306-787-5151. FAX 306-787-0216. *Chair* Helene Stewart.

National Library and Information-Industry Associations, United States and Canada

American Association of Law Libraries

Executive Director, Roger Parent
53 W. Jackson Blvd., Chicago, IL 60604
312-939-4764, FAX 312-431-1097
Internet: lawchg@orion.depart.edu

Object

The American Association of Law Libraries (AALL) is established for educational and scientific purposes. It shall be conducted as a nonprofit corporation to promote and enhance the value of law libraries to the public, the legal community, and the world; to foster the profession of law librarianship; to provide leadership in the field of legal information; and to foster a spirit of cooperation among the members of the profession. Established 1906.

Membership

Memb. 4,800. Persons officially connected with a law library or with a law section of a state or general library, separately maintained. Associate membership available for others. Dues (Indiv.) $118; (Inst.) two or fewer professional libns., $236; more than two, $115 times the number of professionals; (Indiv. Assoc.) $118; (Inst. Assoc.) $227 times the number of members; (Retired) $32.50; (Student) $26; (SIS Memb.) $12 each per year. Year. July 1 to June 30.

Officers (July 1993–June 1994)

Pres. Kay M. Todd, Paul Hastings Janofsky and Walker, 133 Peachtree St. N.E., Atlanta, GA 30303. Tel. 404-527-8241, FAX 404-523-1542; *V.P./Pres.-Elect* Carol D. Billings, Law Lib. of Louisiana, 301 Loyola Ave., New Orleans, LA 70112. Tel. 504-568-5706, FAX 504-568-5069; *Past Pres.* Mark E. Estes, Holme Roberts and Owen, 1700 Lincoln St., Suite 4100, Denver, CO 80203. Tel. 303-861-7000, FAX 303-866-0200; *Secy.*

Gayle E. Webb, Riverside County Law Lib., 3989 Lemon St., Riverside, CA 92501. Tel. 909-275-6395, FAX 909-275-6394; *Treas.* Judith Meadows, State Law Lib. of Montana, Justice Bldg., 215 N. Sanders, Helena, MT 59620-3004.

Executive Board (1993–1994)

Margaret Maes Axtmann, Mary Lu Linnane, Robert L. Oakley, Patricia Patterson, Ann Puckett, Thomas H. Reynolds.

Committee Chairpersons

Awards. Donna K. Bauach
Call for Papers. Arturo L. Torrea.
CONELL. Bonnie L. Koneski-White; Jane Halligan.
Constitution and Bylaws. Alva T. Stone.
Copyright. James S. Heller.
Education. James L. Hoover.
Financial Advisory. Anne W. Grande.
Government Relations. Cheryl Rae Nyberg.
Grants. Rhea A.-L. Ballard
Index to Foreign Legal Periodicals. Daniel L. Wade.
Indexing Periodical Literature. William Mills.
Law Library Journal and Newsletter. Myra K. Saunders.
Minorities. Cheryl Smith Cheatham.
National Legal Resources. Bruce M. Kennedy.
Nominations. Barbara Bintliff.
Placement. D. Mahoney.
Preservation. Patricia K. Denham.
Public Relations. Connie Pine.
Publications Policy. Janet Sinder.
Publications Review. Cynthia Larter Cicco.

Recruitment. Pauline Aranas.
Relations with Information Vendors. Richard Vaughan.
Research Agenda. Nancy Carol Carter
Scholarships. Daniel W. Martin.
Statistics. Katherine Belgum.

Special-Interest Section Chairpersons

Academic Law Libraries. Arturo L. Torres.
Automation and Scientific Development. Thomas B. Fleming.
Contemporary Social Problems. Karen J. Edwards.

Council of SIS Chairs. Nancy P. Johnson.
Foreign, Comparative, and International Law. Jonathan Pratter
Government Documents. Veronica Maclay.
Legal History and Rare Books. Daniel L. Wade.
Legal Information Service to the Public. Heather B. Simmons.
Micrographics and Audiovisual. Michael Klepper.
On-Line Bibliographic Services. Phyllis C. Post.
Private Law Libraries. Johanna C. Bizub.
Reader Services. Tim J. Watts.
State, Court, and County Law Libraries. Anita K. Shew.
Technical Services. Hope Breeze.

American Film and Video Association

Film/Video Library, Allegheny Intermediate Unit
17 Terminal Way, Pittsburgh, PA 15219

Object

To promote the production, distribution, and utilization of educational films and videos and other audiovisual materials. Incorporated 1943.

Membership

Memb. 1,500. Dues (Inst.) $210; (Commercial organizations) $315; (Indiv.) $55; (Students and Retirees) $35. Floating membership year.

Officers (1993–1994)

Pres. Kathryn Elder, York Univ. Libs., 125 Scott Lib., 4700 Keele St., North York, ON M3J 1P3, Canada. Tel. 416-736-5508, FAX

416-736-5838; *Past Pres.* Roberto Esteves, San Francisco Public Lib., Civic Center, San Francisco, CA 94102; *Treas.* Kevin Conner, Film/Video Lib., Allegheny Intermediate Unit, 17 Terminal Way, Pittsburgh, PA 15219.

Board of Directors

Officers; Gary Handman, Maria Johns, Paula Murphy.

Publications

AFVA Bulletin (6 per year).
AFVA Evaluations (ann.).
Festival Guide (ann.).
Sightlines (6 per year).

American Library Association

Executive Director, Peggy Sullivan
50 E. Huron St., Chicago, IL 60611
312-944-6780, 800-545-2433

Object

The mission of the American Library Association (ALA) is to provide leadership for the development, promotion, and improvement of library and information services and the profession of librarianship in order to enhance learning and ensure access to information for all. Founded 1876.

Membership

Memb. (Indiv.) 52,925; (Inst.) 2,911; (Total) 55,836. Any person, library, or other organization interested in library service and librarians. Dues (Indiv.) 1st year, $38; renewing memb., $75; (Nonsalaried Libn.) $26; (Trustee and Assoc. Memb.) $34; (Student) $19; (Foreign Indiv.) $45; (Inst.) $70 and up, depending on operating expenses of institution.

Officers (1993–1994)

Pres. Hardy R. Franklin, Dist. of Columbia Public Lib., 901 G St. N.W., Washington, DC 20001; *Pres.-Elect* Arthur Curley, Dir. and Libn., Boston Public Lib., Copley Sq., Boston, MA 02117; *Treas.* Ann K. Symons, Juneau Douglas H.S. Lib., 10014 Crazy Horse Dr., Juneau, AK 99801; *Exec. Dir.* Peggy Sullivan, ALA Headquarters, 50 E. Huron St., Chicago, IL 60611.

Executive Board

Officers; Marilyn L. Miller (*Past Pres.*); Charles E. Beard (term expires 1997); Betty J. Blackman (1995); Nancy M. Bolt (1994); Cesar Caballero (1996); Bruce E. Daniels (1996); Judith A. Sessions (1994); Mary R. Somerville (1997); Betty J. Turock (1995).

Endowment Trustees

Bernard A. Margolis (1995), Eric Moon (1994), Patricia Glass Schuman (1996); *Exec. Board Liaison* Ann K. Symons; *Staff Liaison* Peggy Sullivan.

Divisions

See the separate entries that follow: American Assn. of School Libns.; American Lib. Trustee Assn.; Assn. for Lib. Collections and Technical Services; Assn. for Lib. Service to Children; Assn. of College and Research Libs.; Assn. of Specialized and Cooperative Lib. Agencies; Lib. Admin. and Management Assn.; Lib. and Info. Technology Assn.; Public Lib. Assn.; Reference and Adult Services Div.; Young Adult Lib. Services Assn.

Publications

ALA Handbook of Organization and Membership Directory 1993–1994 (ann.).
American Libraries (11 per year; membs.; organizations $60; foreign $70; single copy $6).
Book Links (6 per year; U.S. $18; foreign $22; single copy $3.50).
Booklist (22 per year; U.S. and possessions $60; foreign $75; single copy $4.50).
Choice (11 per year; U.S. $160; foreign $180; single copy $15).

Round Table Chairpersons

(ALA staff liaison is given in parentheses.)
Armed Forces Libraries. Marsha Drier (Patricia A. Muir).
Continuing Library Education Network and Exchange. Kenna J. Forsyth (Margaret Myers).
Ethnic Materials and Information Exchange. Kay A. Averette (Mattye L. Nelson).

Exhibits. Nancy E. Schwartz (Paul Graller).
Federal Librarians. Dan Orr Clemmer (Patricia A. Muir).
Government Documents. Duncan M. Aldrich (Patricia A. Muir).
Independent Librarians Exchange. Susanne Bjorner (Margaret Myers).
Intellectual Freedom. Pamela Gay Bonnell (Anne Penway).
International Relations. Mohammed Aman (Robert Doyle).
Library History. Mark Tucker (Charles T. Harmon).
Library Instruction. Emily M. Okada (Jeniece Guy).
Library Research. Mary Biggs (Mary Jo Lynch).
Map and Geography. April Carlucci (Judy Hambrick).
New Members. Joanna M. Burkhardt (Judy Hambrick).
Social Responsibilities. Stephen J. Stillwell (Mattye L. Nelson).
Staff Organizations. Leon Bey (Jeniece Guy).
Support Staff Interests. Annamarie Kehnast (Margaret Myers).
Video. Mary A. Keelan (Irene P. Wood).

Committee Chairpersons

Access to Information (Special). Gordon M. Conable (Eileen D. Cooke, Judith F. Krug, Mary Jo Lynch, Mattye L. Nelson).
Accreditation (Standing). Herman L. Totten (Prudence W. Dalrymple).
ALA Self-Study (Special). F. William Summers (Emily Melton).
American Libraries (Advisory). Gail A. Schlachter (Thomas M. Gaughan).
Appointments (Advisory). Arthur Curley (Emily Melton).
Awards. Robert S. Smith (Peggy Barber).
Book Links (Subcommittee). Ginny Moore Kruse (Barbara Elleman).
Chapter Relations (Standing). Florence S. Brown (Gerald G. Hodges).
Committee on Committees (Elected Council Committee). Arthur Curley (Emily Melton).
Conference Program (Standing), Miami (1994). Hardy R. Franklin (Peggy Barber).

Constitution and Bylaws (Standing). Dallas Y. Shaffer (Emily Melton).
Council Orientation (Special). Hannelore Rader (Lois Ann Gregory-Wood).
Customer Service, President's Committee on (Special). Hardy R. Franklin (Peggy Barber, Gerald G. Hodges, Margaret Myers, Carol S. Nielsen).
Customer Service to Youth, President's Committee for (Special). Hardy R. Franklin (Carol S. Nielsen, Bonnie J. Smothers, Linda L. Waddle).
Development (Advisory). J. Dennis Day (Patricia Martin).
Intellectual Freedom (Standing, Council). Candace D. Morgan (Judith F. Krug).
International Relations (Standing, Council). Beverly P. Lynch (Robert P. Doyle).
Legislation (Standing, Council). E. J. Josey (Eileen D. Cooke).
Library Education (Standing, Council). Margaret M. Kimmel (Margaret Myers).
Library Outreach Services, Office for (Standing, Advisory). Virginia H. Mathews (Mattye L. Nelson).
Library Personnel Resources, Office for (Standing, Advisory). Lois Winkel (Margaret Myers).
Membership (Standing). Kay A. Cassell (Gerald G. Hodges).
Minority Concerns and Cultural Diversity (Standing, Council). Fannette H. Thomas (Mattye L. Nelson).
Nominating, 1994 Election (Special). Gloria J. Coles (Emily Melton).
Organization (Standing, Council). Karen A. Whitney (Charles Harmon).
Pay Equity (Standing, Council). Penelope S. Jeffrey (Margaret Myers).
Planning (Standing, Council). Julie A. Cummins (Peggy Sullivan).
Policy Monitoring (Council). Charles A. Bunge (Lois Ann Gregory-Wood).
Professional Ethics (Standing, Council). Jeanne M. Isacco (Judith Krug).
Program Evaluation and Support (Standing, Council). Vivian R. Wynn (Peggy Sullivan).
Project Century 21 (Special Presidential). Jane Robbins (Margaret Myers).
Public Information (Standing, Advisory). Fred E. Goodman (Linda K. Wallace).

Publishing (Standing, Council). Mary K. Biagini (Donald Chatham).

Research and Statistics (Standing). Barbara F. Immroth (Mary Jo Lynch).

Resolutions (Standing, Council). Judith R. Farley (Emily Melton).

Standards (Standing). Keith C. Wright (Mary Jo Lynch).

User Instruction for Information Literacy (Standing). Marsha D. Broadway (To be appointed).

Women in Librarianship, Status of (Standing, Council). Estelle M. Black (Margaret Myers).

Joint Committee Chairpersons

American Association of Law Libraries/American Correctional Association–ASCLA Committee on Institution Libraries (joint). Thea Chesley (ACA); Timothy Brown (ASCLA).

American Federation of Labor/Congress of Industrial Organizations–ALA, Library Service to Labor Groups, RASD. Mary F.

Hicks (ALA); Anthony Sarmiento (AFL/CIO).

Anglo-American Cataloguing Rules Common Revision Fund. Peggy Sullivan (ALA); Karen S. Adams (Canadian Lib. Assn.)

Anglo-American Cataloguing Rules, Joint Steering Committee for Revision of. Janet Swan Hill (ALA).

Association for Educational Communications and Technology–AASL. To be appointed.

Association for Educational Communications and Technology–ACRL. Marilyn McDonald; Gretchen H. Neill.

Association of American Publishers–ALA. Hardy R. Franklin (ALA); To be appointed (AAP).

Association of American Publishers–ALCTS. Sally Somers (ALCTS); Audrey D. Melkin (AAP).

Children's Book Council–ALA. Elizabeth S. Watson (ALA); Jazan Higgins (CBC).

Society of American Archivists–ALA (Joint Committee on Library-Archives Relationships). Karma A. Beal (ALA); Nicholas Burckel (SAA).

American Library Association
American Association of School Librarians

Executive Director, Ann Carlson Weeks
50 E. Huron St., Chicago, IL 60611
312-944-6780, 800-545-2433, FAX 312-664-7459

Object

The American Association of School Librarians (AASL) is interested in the general improvement and extension of library media services for children and young people. AASL has specific responsibility for planning a program of study and service for the improvement and extension of library media services in elementary and secondary schools as a means of strengthening the educational program; evaluation, selection, interpretation, and utilization of media as they are used in the context of the school program; stimulation of continuous study and research in the library field and establishing criteria of eval-

uation; synthesis of the activities of all units of the American Library Association in areas of mutual concern; representation and interpretation of the need for the function of school libraries to other educational and lay groups; stimulation of professional growth, improvement of the status of school librarians, and encouragement of participation by members in appropriate type-of-activity divisions; conducting activities and projects for improvement and extension of service in the school library when such projects are beyond the scope of type-of-activity divisions, after specific approval by the ALA Council. Established in 1951 as a separate division of ALA.

Membership

Memb. 7,700. Open to all libraries, school library media specialists, interested individuals, and business firms with requisite membership in ALA.

Officers (1993–1994)

Pres. Blanche Woolls, 270 Tennyson Ave., Pittsburgh, PA 15213; *V.P./Pres.-Elect* Jacqueline Mancall, Drexel Univ., College of Info. Studies, Philadelphia, PA 19104; *Secy.* Susan D. Ballard, 55 Linda Lane, Manchester, NH 03104; *Treas.* Helen R. Adams, 7743 Hwy. 66, Rosholt, WI 54473; *Past Pres.* Ruth Toor, 61 Greenbriar Dr., Berkeley Heights, NJ 07922.

Board of Directors

Officers; *Regional Dirs.* Frances Bradburn, Marybeth Green, Mary Lou Gregory, Clara G. Hoover, M. Ellen Jay, Marjorie Pappas, Harriet Selverstone; *Affiliate Assembly Delegates* Deborah R. Coleman, Lorrie Monprode-Holt, Frances McDonald; *Section Dirs.* *ELMSS* Michael Eisenberg; *NPSS* Mary (Meb) Norton; *SPVS* Joie Taylor; *Ex officio* Jane C. Terwillegar, Ann Carlson Weeks.

Publications

AASL Presidential Hotline (s. ann.; memb.).
School Library Media Quarterly (q.; memb.; nonmemb. $40). *Ed.* Mary Kay Biagini, SLIS, Univ. of Pittsburgh, 135 N. Bellefield Ave., Pittsburgh, PA 15260.

Committee Chairpersons

Unit I: Organizational Maintenance

Unit Head. Phyllis Heroy.
Budget. Barbara Nemer.
Bylaws and Organizations. Mary Alice Hunt.
Leadership Enhancement. Susan A. Long.
Long-Range Planning. Erlene Killeen.

Membership. Glenda Anderson.
Nominating (1994). Jacqueline G. Morris.

Unit II: Organizational Relationships

Unit Head. To be appointed.
AECT/AASL Joint Committee. To be appointed.
American University Press Services Publication Selection. Raymond Barber.
International Relations. Ruth Cady.
Legislation. Rosemary Chance.
National Council for the Accreditation of Teacher Education. Frank Birmingham.
School Library Statistics Program. Jacqueline Morris.

Unit III: Library Media Personnel Development

Unit Head. Erlene Killeen.
Annual Conference Local Arrangements. Roberta Kaiser.
Annual Conference Program Planning. Doris Epler.
Continuing Education. Elizabeth Polk.
General Conference, Indianapolis. Valerie Wilford.
Professional Development Coordinating. Elizabeth Polk.
Publications Advisory. Lillian Wehmeyer.
Publications Coordinating. Lillian Wehmeyer.
SLMQ Editorial Board. Mary Kay Biagini.

Unit IV: Library Media Program Development

Unit Head. Drucilla Raines.
Count on Reading. Brenda White.
Cultural Diversity. Linda Zoppa.
Intellectual Freedom. Vicki Hardesty.
Literacy. Linda Cornwell.
Research. Ken Haycock.
Resource-Based Teaching. Margaret Tassia.
Students at Risk. Marian Karpisek, Nancy Bluemel.
Technology. Carol Simpson.

Unit V: Public Information

Unit Head. Diane C. Pozar.

Awards. AASL Highsmith Research, A. Jeanie McNamara; ABC/CLIO, Elspeth Goodin; Distinguished School Administrator's Award, AASL/SIRS, Elizabeth Haynes; Distinguished Service Award, AASL/Baker and Taylor, Dawn Heller; Emergency Librarian Periodical Award, Judith Gray; Frances Henne Award, JoAnn V. Rogers; Information Plus Continuing Education Award, vacant; Intellectual Freedom Award, AASL/SIRS, vacant; Microcomputer in the Media Center Award Selection, AASL/Follett, Marybeth Green; National School Library Media Program of the Year Award Selection, AASL/Encyclopaedia Britannica Companies, Pamela Parman; School Librarians Workshop Award, Neata Wiley; National School Library Month, Laura Edwards; Public Awareness, Doris Epler.

Section Chairpersons

Educators of Library Media Specialists (ELMSS). M. Kathryn Holland.
Non-Public Schools (NPSS). Jacquelyn Thomas.
Supervisors (SPVS). Rebecca T. Bingham.

American Library Association
American Library Trustee Association

Executive Director, Susan Roman
50 E. Huron St., Chicago, IL 60611-2795
312-280-2161, 800-545-2433 Ext. 2161, FAX 312-440-9374

Object

The American Library Trustee Association (ALTA) is interested in the development of effective library service for all people in all types of communities and in all types of libraries; it follows that its members are concerned, as policymakers, with organizational patterns of service, with the development of competent personnel, the provision of adequate financing, the passage of suitable legislation, and the encouragement of citizen support for libraries. ALTA recognizes that responsibility for professional action in these fields has been assigned to other divisions of ALA; its specific responsibilities as a division, therefore, are:

1. A continuing and comprehensive educational program to enable library trustees to discharge their grave responsibilities in a manner best fitted to benefit the public and the libraries they represent.

2. Continuous study and review of the activities of library trustees.

3. Cooperation with other units within ALA concerning their activities relating to trustees.

4. Encouraging participation of trustees in other appropriate divisions of ALA.

5. Representation and interpretation of the activities of library trustees in contacts outside the library profession, particularly with national organizations and governmental agencies.

6. Promotion of strong state and regional trustee organizations.

7. Efforts to secure and support adequate library funding.

8. Promulgation and dissemination of recommended library policy.

9. Assuring equal access of information to all segments of the population.

10. Encouraging participation of trustees in trustee/library activities, at local, state, regional and national levels.

Organized 1890. Became an ALA division in 1961.

Membership

Memb. 1,566. Open to all interested persons and organizations. For dues and membership year, see ALA entry.

Officers (1993–1994)

Pres. Ann L. Donoghue; *1st V.P./Pres.-Elect* Sharon A. Saulmon; *2nd V.P.* Judith M. Baker; *Past Pres.* Aileen R. Schrader; *Parliamentarian* Ira B. Harkavy; *Councillor* Terri C. Jacobs.

Board of Directors

Officers; *Council Administrators* Denise E. Botto (1994), Ira B. Harkavy (1994), Helen S. Kohlman (1994), Patricia F. Turner (1994), Leroy D. Williams (1994); *ALTA Newsletter Ed.* Sharon A. Saulmon (1996); *Regional V.P.s* Gloria F. Aguilar (1994), Wayne Coco (1994), Eddie Jackson (1994), Floy Johnson (1994), Esther W. Lopato (1994), Virginia M. McCurdy (1994), Ruth Newell (1994), Barbara S. Prentice (1995), John T. Short (1994), Diane L. Smith (1995), James A. Ulmer III (1995); *PLA Rep.* William T. Balcom (1994); *Ex officio* Susan Roman.

Staff

Exec. Dir. Susan Roman; *Program Officer* Lorelle R. Brown; *Admin. Secy.* Willette Holmes.

Publication

ALTA Newsletter (6 per year; memb.). *Ed.* Sharon A. Saulmon, 12228 High Meadow Ct., Oklahoma City, OK 73170.

Committee Chairpersons

Action Development. Roslyn S. Kurland.
Affiliate Subscription Program (Task Force). Sharon A. Saulmon.
ALTA WILL (Task Force). Jack Cole.
Awards. Paulette H. Holahan.
Budget. Sharon A. Saulmon.
Common Concerns, ALTA/PLA (Interdivisional). William T. Balcom, Ramonda S. Wertz.
Conference Program and Evaluation. Gail Dysleski.
Corporate Funding. Wayne Coco.
Editorial Advisory Board. Sharon A. Saulmon.
Education of Trustees. Nicholas G. Spillios.
Financial Development. Norman Kelinson.
Intellectual Freedom. Lillian Broad, Ezequiel Vargas.
Legislation. Marilyn Borea, Robert D. Terry.
Liability Exemption for Trustees (Ad hoc). Glen R. Dunlap.
Lobbying Seminar (Task Force). To be appointed.
Membership. Alphonse Martin, Jr.
Nominating. Wayne Coco.
Preconference. Shirley A. Barrett, Marie T. Pikul.
President's Program. Catherine S. Wallace.
Publications. Clifford Dittrich.
Resolutions. Charles E. Reid.
Speakers Bureau. Betty Paige Hanchey.
Special Functions. William G. Murphy.
Specialized Outreach Services. Suzine Har-Nicolescu.
Trustee Citations, Jury on. Virginia G. Young.
Trustee Digest Editorial (Task Force). Wayne Coco.
White House Conference Implementation (Subcommittee). Bernard R. Malkmus, Lila Milford.

American Library Association
Association for Library Collections and Technical Services

Executive Director, Karen Muller
50 E. Huron St., Chicago, IL 60611
800-545-2433 Ext. 5031, FAX 312-280-3257
Bitnet: U19466@UICVM; Internet: u19466@uicvm.uic.edu

Object

The Association for Library Collections and Technical Services is responsible for the following activities: acquisition, identification, cataloging, classification, and preservation of library materials; the development and coordination of the country's library resources; and those areas of selection and evaluation involved in the acquisition of library materials and pertinent to the development of library resources. ALCTS has specific responsibility for

1. Continuous study and review of the activities assigned to the division.

2. Conduct of activities and projects within its area of responsibility.

3. Syntheses of activities of all units within ALA that have a bearing on the type of activity represented.

4. Representation and interpretation of its type of activity in contacts outside the profession.

5. Stimulation of the development of librarians engaged in its type of activity, and stimulation of participation by members in appropriate type-of-library divisions.

6. Planning and development of programs of study and research for the type of activity for the total profession.

ALCTS will provide its members, other ALA divisions and members, and the library and information community with leadership and a program for action on the access to, and identification, acquisition, description, organization, preservation, and dissemination of information resources in a dynamic collaborative environment. In addition, ALCTS provides forums for discussion, research, and development, and opportunities for learning in all of these areas. To achieve this mission,

ALCTS has the following organizational goals:

1. To promote the role of the library and information science in an information society.

2. To provide its members with opportunities for information exchange.

3. To promote innovative and effective library education and training, to foster the recruitment of individuals with diverse qualities to library work, and to provide continuing education for librarians and library practitioners.

4. To develop, support, review, and promote standards to meet library and information needs.

5. To provide opportunities for members to participate through research and publications and professional growth.

6. To manage the association effectively and efficiently.

Established 1957; renamed 1988.

Membership

Memb. 5,364. Any member of the American Library Association may elect membership in this division according to the provisions of the bylaws.

Officers (1993–1994)

Pres. Jennifer A. Younger, Univ. Libs., Ohio State Univ., 1858 Neil Ave. Mall, Rm. 106, Columbus, OH 43210-1286; *V.P.* Robert P. Holley, 106 Kresge Lib., Wayne State Univ., Detroit, MI 48202.

Address correspondence to the executive director.

Directors

Officers; *Exec. Dir.* Karen Muller; *Past Pres.* Lizbeth Bishoff; *Dirs.-at-Large* Marjorie E. Bloss (term expires 1995); Katha D. Massey (1994); *ALCTS Councillor* Jean Farrington (1995); *Council of Regional Groups Chair* Laverna Saunders (1994); *Council of Regional Groups V.Chair* Ann Denton (1995); *LC Liaison* Winston Tabb; *LRTS Ed.* Richard P. Smiraglia (1996); *ALCTS Newsletter Ed.* Edward Swanson (1994); *Parliamentarian* Walter M. High (1995); *ALCTS Planning Committee Chair* John P. Webb (1995); *ALCTS Budget and Finance Chair* Shirley Leung (1994).

Publications

ALCTS Network News (irreg.; free). *Ed.* Karen Whittlesey. Available on Bitnet and Internet; subscribe via listserv@uicvm.bitnet.

ALCTS Newsletter (6 per year; memb.; nonmemb. $25). *Ed.* Edward Swanson, Minnesota Historical Society, 345 Kellogg Blvd. W., Saint Paul, MN 55102-1903.

Library Resources & Technical Services (q.; memb.; nonmemb. $45). *Ed.* Richard P. Smiraglia, Palmer School of Lib. and Info. Science, Long Island Univ., Brookville, NY 11548. Tel. 516-299-2866.

Section Chairpersons

Acquisitions. Caroline L. Early.
Cataloging and Classification. Carlen Ruschoff.
Collection Management and Development. Connie McCarthy.
Preservation of Library Materials. Janet Gertz.
Reproduction of Library Materials. Nancy Elkington.
Serials. Miriam Palm.

Committee Chairpersons

Association of American Publishers/ALCTS Joint Committee. Sally W. Somers; Audrey Melkin.

Audiovisual. Eric R. Childress.
Best of *LRTS*. Diane Vizine-Goetz.
Blackwell North America Scholarship Award. Helen I. Reed.
Budget and Finance. Shirley W. Leung.
Catalog Form and Function. Catherine S. Herlihy.
Commercial Technical Services. J. Randolph Call.
Conference Program, Chicago (1995). Robert P. Holley.
Conference Program, Miami (1994). Jennifer A. Younger.
Continuing Education Needs of Paraprofessionals (Task Force). Barry Baker.
Duplicates Exchange Union. David E. Winchester.
Education. John Drew Racine.
Ethics (Task Force). Gay Dannelly.
International Relations. Cecily A. Johns.
Legislation. John R. James.
Library Materials Price Index. Adrian W. Alexander.
LRTS Editor Search (Task Force). William Z. Schenck.
LRTS Editorial Board. Richard P. Smiraglia.
MARBI. Florence J. Wilson.
Membership. Frank A. D'Andraia.
1994 President's Program (Task Force). Sharon Walbridge.
Nominating. Joseph Branin.
Nomination Procedures and Leadership (Task Force). Nancy R. John.
Organization and Bylaws. Liz Bishoff.
Esther J. Piercy Award Jury. Pamela Bluh.
Planning. John P. Webb.
Preservation Microfilming. Margaret M. Byrnes.
Publications. Bill E. Robnett, Jr.
Publisher/Vendor Lib. Relations. Joseph W. Barker.
Research and Statistics. Karen Schmidt.
Scholarly Communication. Paul J. Kobulnicky.
Technical Services Measurements. Kathleen Brown.

Discussion Groups

Automated Acquisitions/In-Process Control Systems. Jeri Van Goethem.

Computer Files. Wilma I. Cromwell.

Creative Ideas in Technical Services. Laurel Jizba, Karen Wilson.

Electronic Publishing. Jean S. Callaghan.

LITA/ALCTS Authority Control in the Online Environment (Interest Group). Karen S. Calhoun.

LITA/ALCTS Innovative Microcomputer Support of Technical Services (Interest Group). Betsy Gamble.

LITA/ALCTS MARC Holdings (Interest Group). Kathryn Loafman.

LITA/ALCTS Retrospective Conversion (Interest Group). Rosario Garza (ALCTS), Birong Ho (LITA).

LITA/ALCTS Serials Automation (Interest Group). Elizabeth Ten Have.

Newspaper. Donnell L. Ruthenberg.

Out of Print. Marilyn Ng.

Pre-Order and Pre-Catalog Searching. Nancy Boggess-Korckach.

Role of the Professional in Academic Research Technical Services Departments. Helen Miller.

Technical Services Administrators of Medium-Sized Research Libraries. Colleen Hyslop.

Technical Services Directors of Large Research Libraries. Harriet Selkowitz.

Technical Services in Public Libraries. Elisabeth A. Konrad.

American Library Association
Association for Library Service to Children

Executive Director, Susan Roman
50 E. Huron St., Chicago, IL 60611
312-280-2163, 800-545-2433

Object

Interested in the improvement and extension of library services to children in all types of libraries. Responsible for the evaluation and selection of book and nonbook materials for, and the improvement of techniques of, library services to children from preschool through the eighth grade or junior high school age, when such materials or techniques are intended for use in more than one type of library. Founded 1901.

Membership

Memb. 3,609. Open to anyone interested in library services to children. For information on dues, see ALA entry.

Officers (1993–1994)

Pres. Ellen M. Stepanian; *Pres.-Elect* Virginia McKee; *Past Pres.* Kathy Ann East.

Address correspondence to the executive director.

Directors

Rita Auerbach, Therese G. Bigelow, Leslie Edmonds, Elizabeth F. Howard, Penny S. Markey, Sara Miller, Virginia A. Walter, Gretchen M. Wronka; *Councillor* Frances V. Sedney; *Staff Liaison* Susan Roman.

Publications

ALSC Newsletter (q.; memb.). *Ed.* Anitra T. Steele.

Journal of Youth Services in Libraries (q.; memb.; nonmemb. $40; foreign $50). *Eds.* Donald J. Kenney, Virginia Polytechnic Institute, Box 90001, Blacksburg, VA 24062-9001; Linda J. Wilson, Dept. of Educational Studies, 206A Russell Hall, Radford Univ., Radford, VA 24142.

Committee Chairpersons

Priority Group I: Child Advocacy

Consultant. Ann Kalkoff, 220 Berkley Place, Apt. 1D, Brooklyn, NY 11217.
Boy Scouts of America (Advisory).
Legislation.
Liaison with Mass Media.
Liaison with National Organizations Serving the Child.

Priority Group II: Evaluation of Media

Consultant. Margaret A. Bush, Grad. School of Lib. and Info. Science, Simmons College, 300 The Fenway, Boston, MA 02115.
Computer Software Evaluation.
Film and Video Evaluation.
Notable Children's Books.
Recording Evaluation.
Selection of Children's Books from Various Cultures.

Priority Group III: Professional Development

Consultant. Patsy Weeks, Box 15, Bangs, TX 76823.
Arbuthnot Honor Lecture.
(Louise Seaman) Bechtel Fellowship.
Distinguished Service Award.
Econo-Clad Literature Program Award.
Education.
Managing Children's Services (Committee and Discussion Group).
Putnam and Grosset Group Awards.
Scholarships: Melcher and Bound to Stay Bound.
Teachers of Children's Literature (Discussion Group).

Priority Group IV: Social Responsibilities

Consultant. Eliza T. Dresang, 440 Virginia Terr., Madison, WI 53705.

Intellectual Freedom.
International Relations.
Library Service to Children with Special Needs.
Preschool Services (Discussion Group).
Preschool Services and Parent Education.
Social Issues (Discussion Group).
Social Issues in Relation to Materials and Services for Children (Committee).

Priority Group V: Planning and Research

Consultant. Jill L. Locke, Dept. of Lib. and Info. Studies, Univ. of North Carolina, 302A Curry Bldg., Greensboro, NC 27412.
Caldecott Medal Calendar.
Collections of Children's Books for Adult Research (Discussion Group).
Grants.
Local Arrangements.
Membership.
National Planning of Special Collections.
National Reading Program.
Nominating.
Oral Record Project Advisory Committee.
Organization and Bylaws.
Planning and Budget.
Preconference Planning.
Publications.
Research and Development.
Storytelling (Discussion Group).

Priority Group VI: Award Committees

Consultant. Ruth I. Gordon, 225 N. Foothill Blvd., Cloverdale, CA 95425-3115.
(Mildred L.) Batchelder Award Selection.
Caldecott Award.
Carnegie Award.
Newbery Award.
Wilder Award.

American Library Association
Association of College and Research Libraries

Executive Director, Althea H. Jenkins
50 E. Huron St., Chicago, IL 60611-2795
312-280-3248, 800-545-2433 Ext. 2516, FAX 312-280-2520
E-mail: U55385@UICVM.UIC.EDU

Object

The mission of the Association of College and Research Libraries (ACRL) is to foster the profession of academic and research librarianship and to enhance the ability of academic and research libraries to serve effectively the library and information needs of current and potential library users. This includes all types of academic libraries— community and junior college, college, and university—as well as comprehensive and specialized research libraries and their professional staffs. Founded 1938.

Membership

Memb. 10,170. For information on dues, see ALA entry.

Officers (1993–1994)

Pres. Thomas Kirk, Libn., Hutchins Lib., Berea College, Berea, KY 40404. Tel. 606-986-9341 Ext. 5266, FAX 606-986-9494; *Pres.-Elect* Susan K. Martin, Univ. Libn., Lauvinger Lib., Georgetown Univ., 37 and O Sts. N.W., Washington, DC 20057-1006. Tel. 202-687-7425, FAX 202-687-7501; *Past Pres.* Jacquelyn A. McCoy, 1590 Linda Vista Ave., Pasadena, CA 91103-1955. Tel. 213-259-2671, FAX 213-341-4991; *Div. Councillor* Rochelle Sager, Dir., Lib. and Media Services, Fashion Institute of Technology Lib., 227 W. 27 St., New York, NY 10001. Tel. 212-760-7884, FAX 212-760-7268; *Budget and Finance Chair* Thomas M. Peischl, Dean of Lib. Services, Memorial Lib., Mankato State Univ., MSU Box 19, Box 8400, Mankato, MN 56002-8400. Tel. 507-389-5953, FAX 507-389-5488; *Exec. Dir. (ex officio)* Althea H. Jenkins, ALA, 50 E. Huron St., Chicago, IL 60611.

Board of Directors

Officers; Karin E. Begg Borei, Frances J. Maloy, Ray E. Metz, Linda L. Phillips, Shelley E. Phipps, Barbara J. Wittkopf; *Planning Committee Chair* Sandra Ready (ex officio).

Publications

ACRL Publications in Librarianship (formerly ACRL Monograph Series) (irreg.). Ed. Jonathan A. Lindsey, Baylor Univ., Waco, TX 76793.

Choice (11 per year; $155; foreign $170). *Choice Reviews-on-Cards* ($235; foreign $255). Ed. Patricia E. Sabosik, 100 Riverview Center, Middletown, CT 06457.

College and Research Libraries (6 per year; memb.; nonmemb. $50). Ed. Gloriana St. Clair, Pennsylvania State Univ., University Park, PA 16802.

College and Research Libraries News (11 per year; memb.; nonmemb.$25). Ed. Mary Ellen Kyger Davis, ACRL, ALA, 50 E. Huron St., Chicago, IL 60611.

Rare Books and Manuscripts Librarianship (2 per year; $35). Ed. Alice D. Schreyer, Univ. of Delaware Lib., Newark, DE 19717-5267.

Committee and Task Force Chairpersons

Academic Library Statistics. Elizabeth Salzer.

Academic or Research Librarian of the Year Award. Wendy Pradt Lougee.

Academic Status. Janice C. Fennell.

Access Policy Guidelines Task Force. Kathleen Gunning.

Appointments (1993) and Nominations (1994) and *College & Research Libraries News*. Pamela Snelson.

Appointments (1994) and Nominations (1995). Suzanne Calpestri.

Association for Educational Communication and Technology. Marilyn M. McDonald, Gretchen Neill.

Audiovisual. Imogene I. Book.

Budget and Finance. Thomas M. Peischl.

Choice Editorial Board. W. Lee Hisle.

Colleagues. William R. Mott.

College & Research Libraries Editorial Board. Gloriana St. Clair.

College & Research Libraries News Editorial Board. Pamela Snelson.

Conference Program Planning, Chicago (1995). Susan K. Martin.

Conference Program Planning, Miami (1994). Thomas Kirk.

Constitution and Bylaws. Richard J. Wood.

Copyright. Sarah E. Cox.

Doctoral Dissertation Award. Lawrence J. McCrank.

Government Relations. Patricia Wand.

Intellectual Freedom Task Force. Judy Gibson Noyes.

International Relations. Maureen D. Pastine.

Samuel Lazerow Award. Julia A. Gammon.

Membership. Mary Ann Griffin.

Membership Communications, Task Force on. Larry R. Oberg.

"MLA Bibliography" Scope and Overlap. Elaine A. Franco.

National Conference Executive Committee. Joanne R. Euster.

New Publications Advisory Board. Paula C. Murphy.

Orientation. Jacquelyn A. McCoy.

Planning. Sandra Ready.

Professional Education. Rochelle Ballard.

Professional Liaison. Barbara J. Ford.

Publications. Karen S. Seibert.

Publications in Librarianship Editorial Board. Stephen E. Wiberley, Jr.

Racial and Ethnic Diversity. Susana A. Hinojosa.

Rare Books and Manuscripts Librarianship Editorial Board. Sidney E. Berger.

Research. Maxine H. Reneker.

K. G. Saur Award. James F. Williams II.

Standards and Accreditation. Carolyn Dusenbury.

Vocational Interest Inventories Task Force. Anne K. Beaubien.

Discussion Group Chairpersons

Academic Librarians' Associations. Roberta J. Kramer.

Australian Studies. Murray S. Martin.

Canadian Studies. Lewis R. Miller.

Electronic Library Development in Academic Libraries. Craig Mulder, Anna M. Wang.

Electronic Text Centers. Marianne I. Gaunt.

English and American Literature. William Baker.

Exhibits and Displays. Michael M. Miller.

Fee-Based Information Service Centers in Academic Libraries. Stephen D. Coffman.

Fundraising and Development. Laura H. Maurer.

Heads of Public/Readers Services. Florence Kell Doksansky.

Home Economics/Human Ecology Librarians. Linda Stein.

Journal Costs in Academic Libraries. James R. Mouw.

Librarians of Library Science Collections. Patricia Stinson Switzer.

Personnel Administrators and Staff Development Officers. Margaret A. Pickering, Teri Switzer.

Philosophical, Religious, and Theological Studies. Kay Tavill.

Popular Culture and Libraries. Douglas B. Highsmith.

Public Relations in Academic Libraries. Karen Hatcher.

Research. Darrell L. Jenkins.

Undergraduate Librarians. J. Louise Malcomb.

Section Chairpersons

Afro-American Studies. William C. Welburn.

Anthropology and Sociology. Kathryn L. Creely.

Arts. Madeleine M. Nichols.

Asian and African. Katharine K. Elsasser.

Bibliographic Instruction. Lori L. Arp.

College Libraries. Barbara J. Brown.

Community and Junior College Libraries. Margaret A. Holleman.

Educational and Behavioral Sciences. Judith Segal.

Extended Campus Library Services. Lynn LaBrake-Harrison.

Law and Political Science. Charles D. Spornick.
Rare Books and Manuscripts. Jackie M. Dooley.
Science and Technology. Janet S. Fore.
Slavic and East European. Leena Siegel-baum.

University Libraries. Noreen S. Alldredge.
Western European Specialists. James H. Spohrer.
Women's Studies. Betty J. Glass.

American Library Association
Association of Specialized and Cooperative Library Agencies

Executive Director, Cathleen Bourdon
50 E. Huron St., Chicago, IL 60611
312-280-4395, 800-545-2433 Ext. 4396, FAX 312-944-8085

Object

To represent state library agencies, specialized library agencies, and multitype library cooperatives. Within the interest of these types of library organizations, the Association of Specialized and Cooperative Library Agencies (ASCLA) has specific responsibility for

1. Development and evaluation of goals and plans for state library agencies, specialized library agencies, and multitype library cooperatives to facilitate the implementation, improvement, and extension of library activities designed to foster improved user services, coordinating such activities with other appropriate ALA units.

2. Representation and interpretation of the role, functions, and services of state library agencies, specialized library agencies, and multitype library cooperatives within and outside the profession, including contact with national organizations and government agencies.

3. Development of policies, studies, and activities in matters affecting state library agencies, specialized library agencies, and multitype library cooperatives relating to (a) state and local library legislation, (b) state grants-in-aid and appropriations, and (c) relationships among state, federal, regional, and local governments, coordinating such activities with other appropriate ALA units.

4. Establishment, evaluation, and promotion of standards and service guidelines relating to the concerns of this association.

5. Identifying the interests and needs of all persons, encouraging the creation of services to meet these needs within the areas of concern of the association, and promoting the use of these services provided by state library agencies, specialized library agencies, and multitype library cooperatives.

6. Stimulating the professional growth and promoting the specialized training and continuing education of library personnel at all levels of concern of this association and encouraging membership participation in appropriate type-of-activity divisions within ALA.

7. Assisting in the coordination of activities of other units within ALA that have a bearing on the concerns of this association.

8. Granting recognition for outstanding library service within the areas of concern of this association.

9. Acting as a clearinghouse for the exchange of information and encouraging the development of materials, publications, and research within the areas of concern of this association.

Membership

Memb. 1,420.

Board of Directors (1993–1994)

Pres. Barbara L. Perkis, Asst. Dir., Illinois Regional Lib. for the Blind and Physically Handicapped, 1055 W. Roosevelt Rd., Chicago, IL 60608. Tel. 312-746-9217, FAX 312-746-9192; *V.P.* Amy Owen, Dir., Utah State Lib. Div., 2150 S. 300 W., Suite 16, Salt Lake City, UT 84115-2579. Tel. 801-466-5888, FAX 801-533-4657; *Past Pres.* Jan Ison, Exec. Dir., Lincoln Trail Libs. System, 1704 W. Interstate Dr., Champaign, IL 61821-1068. Tel. 217-352-0047, FAX 217-352-7153; *Dirs.-at-Large* Laurence A. Miller, Joan Neumann, Diana Ray Tope, Barbara Will; *Div. Councillor* Lorraine S. Summers; *Section Reps.* Thea B. Chesley and Barbara Mates (Libraries Serving Special Populations), Mary Ghikas (Multitype Library Networks and Cooperatives), Bill Crowley (State Library Agencies); *Ex officio* *"Interface" Ed.* Thomas J. Dorst; *Organization and Bylaws Committee Chair* Rod Wagner.

Executive Staff

Exec. Dir. Cathleen Bourdon.

Publications

Interface (q.; memb.; nonmemb. $15). *Ed.* Thomas J. Dorst, Illinois State Lib., 300 S. Second St., Springfield, IL 62701-1796. Tel. 217-782-5012, FAX 217-785-4326.

Committees

American Correctional Association/ASCLA Joint Committee on Institution Libraries. Thea Chesley, Jay Ihrig.
Awards. Bridget Lamont.
Budget and Finance. Jan Ison.
Conference Program Coordination. Brenda Pacey.
Legislation. Barbara Will.
Library Personnel and Education. To be appointed.
Membership Promotion. Carl Beery.
Organization and Bylaws. Rod Wagner.
Planning. Jan Ison.
Publications. Debra Parks.
Research. Jeannette Smithee.
Serials Advisory. Leslie Burger.
Standards Review. Linda Walling; Guidelines for Library Service for People with Developmental Disabilities, Marilyn Irwin, Ruth O'Donnell; Revision of Standards for Library Service to the Blind and Physically Handicapped, Donna Dziedzic.

American Library Association
Library Administration and Management Association

Executive Director, Karen Muller
50 E. Huron St., Chicago, IL 60611
312-280-5031, 800-545-2433 Ext. 5031, FAX 312-280-3257

Object

The Library Administration and Management Association (LAMA) provides an organizational framework for encouraging the study of administrative theory, for improving the practice of administration in libraries, and for identifying and fostering administrative skill. Toward these ends, the division is responsible for all elements of general administration that are common to more than one type of library. These may include organizational structure, financial administration, personnel management and training, buildings and equipment, and public relations. LAMA meets this responsibility in the following ways:

1. Study and review of activities assigned to the division with due regard for changing developments in these activities.

2. Initiating and overseeing activities and projects appropriate to the division, including activities involving bibliogra-

phy compilation, publication, study, and review of professional literature within the scope of the division.

3. Synthesis of those activities of other ALA units that have a bearing upon the responsibilities or work of the division.

4. Representation and interpretation of library administrative activities in contacts outside the library profession.

5. Aiding the professional development of librarians engaged in administration and encouragement of their participation in appropriate type-of-library divisions.

6. Planning and development of those programs of study and research in library administrative problems that are most needed by the profession.

Established 1957.

Membership

Memb. 5,254.

Officers (1993–1994)

Pres. Carol F. L. Liu, Exec. Asst. to Dir., Queens Borough Public Lib., 162-20 Ninth Ave., Apt. 9C, Whitestone, NY 11357. Tel. 718-990-0890, FAX 718-291-8936; *V.P./Pres.-Elect* Donald E. Riggs, Dean, Univ. Lib., Univ. of Michigan, 818 Hatcher Grad. Lib., Ann Arbor, MI 48109-1205. Tel. 313-764-9356, FAX 313-763-5080; *Past Pres.* James G. Neal, Dean, Univ. Libs., Indiana Univ., Lib. C-2, Bloomington, IN 47405. Tel. 812-855-3403, FAX 812-855-2576; *Councillor* Claudya B. Muller, Exec. Dir., Cuyahoga County Public Lib., Administration Bldg., 2111 Snow Rd., Parma, OH 44134-2792. Tel. 216-749-9490, FAX 216-398-1748; *Exec. Dir.* Karen Muller, 50 E. Huron St., Chicago, IL 60611. Tel. 312-280-5031, FAX 312-280-3257.

Address correspondence to the executive director.

Board of Directors

Dirs. Carol L. Anderson, Teresa Edwards, Joline R. Ezzell, Michael S. Freeman, Gerard B. McCabe, John J. McGinnis, Ronald P. Naylor, Joseph A. Starratt, Ann F. Stone; *Dirs.-at-Large* Judith A. Adams, Charles E. Kratz, Jr.; *Ex officio* Charles E. Beard, Deborah Carver, Joyce N. Davis, Joan R. Giesecke, Diane Graves, Susan F. Gregory, Elizabeth C. Habich, Ronald P. Naylor, Gene Rollins, John J. Vasi, Thomas L. Wilding.

Publication

Library Administration and Management (q.; memb.; nonmemb. $50; foreign $60). *Ed.* Diane Graves, 4043 Wolf Rd., Western Springs, IL 60558. Tel. 312-915-6728, FAX 312-915-6637.

Committee Chairpersons

Budget and Finance. Ronald P. Naylor.
Governmental Affairs. Robert A. Daugherty.
Membership. Raul A. Huerta.
Organization. John J. Vasi.
Orientation. Rosemary H. Arneson.
Program. Rod Henshaw.
Publication. Charles B. Lowry.
Recognition of Achievement. William G. Jones.
Small Libraries Public Service. John M. Robson.
Special Conferences and Programs. Kathryn J. Deiss.

Section Chairpersons

Buildings and Equipment. Carol L. Anderson.
Fund Raising and Financial Development. Joline R. Ezzell.
Library Organization and Management. Michael S. Freeman.
Personnel Administration. Ann F. Stone.
Public Relations. John J. McGinnis.
Statistics. Joseph A. Starratt.
Systems and Services. Teresa Edwards.

American Library Association
Library and Information Technology Association

Executive Director, Linda J. Knutson
50 E. Huron St., Chicago, IL 60611
312-280-4270, 800-545-2433

Object

The Library and Information Technology Association (LITA) envisions a world in which the complete spectrum of information technology is available to everyone. People in all their diversity will have access to a wealth of information technology in libraries, at work, and at home. In this world, everybody can realize their full potential with the help of information technology. The very boundaries of human relations will expand beyond the limitations of time and space we experience today. The outer limits are still unknown; what is known is that the exploration will be challenging.

LITA provides its members, other ALA divisions and members, and the library and information science field as a whole with a forum for discussion, an environment for learning, and a program for action on the design, development, and implementation of automated and technological systems in the library and information science field.

LITA is concerned with the planning, development, design, application, and integration of technologies within the library and information environment, with the impact of emerging technologies on library service, and with the effect of automated technologies on people. Its major focus is on the interdisciplinary issues and emerging technologies. LITA disseminates information, provides educational opportunities for learning about information technologies and forums for the discussion of common concerns, monitors new technologies with potential applications in information science, encourages and fosters research, promotes the development of technical standards, and examines the effects of library systems and networks.

Membership

Memb. 5,597.

Officers (1993–1994)

Pres. Tamara J. Miller; *Pres.-Elect* Nancy K. Roderer; *Past Pres.* Walt Crawford.

Directors

Officers; Betty Bengtson (term expires 1996), Michele I. Dalehite (1995), Katharina E. Klemperer (1994), Linda D. Miller (1994), Jean Armour Polly (1995), Nolan F. Pope (1994), Craig A. Summerhill (1996); *Councillor* Carol A. Parkhurst (1997); *Ex officio* David R. McDonald (1994); *Exec. Dir.* Linda J. Knutson.

Publications

Information Technology and Libraries (q.; memb.; nonmemb. $50; single copy $15). *Ed.* Thomas W. Leonhardt, Dir. of Technical Services, Univ. Of Oklahoma Lib., 401 W. Brooks St., Norman, OK 73019-0528. For information or to send manuscripts, contact the editor.

LITA Newsletter (q.; memb.; nonmemb. $25; single copy $8). *Ed.* Walt Crawford, Research Libs. Group, 1200 Villa St., Mountain View, CA 94041-1100.

Committee Chairpersons

Hugh C. Atkinson Memorial Award. Maureen Sullivan.

Budget Review. Walt Crawford.

Bylaws and Organization. David R. McDonald.

Education. William Paul Kane.

Executive. Tamara J. Miller.

Financial. Dan K. Marmion, Jo-Ann Michalak.

Information Technology and Libraries Editorial Board. Thomas J. Leonhardt.

Interest Group Leadership and Continuity (Task Force). Linda Robinson.
International Relations. Charles R. Martell.
Leadership Development. Richard E. Gates.
Legislation and Regulation. Patrick Flannery.
LITA/Gaylord Award. Dan Iddings.
LITA/GEAC-CLSI Scholarship (Subcommittee). Elizabeth L. Lawley.
LITA/*Library Hi Tech* Award. Lynne Lysiak.
LITA Newsletter (Subcommittee). Walt Crawford.
LITA/OCLC Minority Scholarship (Subcommittee). Lucie Chen.
Machine-Readable Form of Bibliographic Information (MARBI), LITA/ALCTS/RASD. Florence J. Wilson.
Membership. Billie Peterson.
Nominating. Carl E. Bengston.
Program Planning. Barbra B. Higginbotham.
Publications. Charles W. Bailey, Jr.
Research. Gary S. Lawrence.
Technical Standards for Library Automation (TESLA). Mark Hinnebusc.
Technology and Access. Mary Alice Ball.

Interest Group Chairpersons

Adaptive Technologies. Christopher G. Lewis.
Artificial Intelligence/Expert Systems. Douglas A. Kranch.
Authority Control in the Online Environment, LITA/ALCTS. Karen S. Calhoun.
Customized Applications for Library Microcomputers. Stephen R. Westman.
Desktop Publishing. Pat Ensor, Xiao-Yan Shen.
Distributed Systems and Networks. Deborah C. Masters.
Electronic Mail/Electronic Bulletin Boards. Ray E. Metz, Maryjane Poulin.
Emerging Technologies. Richard E. Gates.
Geographic Information Systems. Patrick McGlamery, Joan Maier McKean.
Human/Machine Interface. Jennie L. McKee.
Imagineering. Catherine Doyle.
Interest Group Coordinator. Colby Mariva Riggs.
Library Consortia/Automated Systems. Bernard G. Sloan.
MARC Holdings (Interest Group). Kathryn Loafmann.
Microcomputer Support of Technical Services, LITA/ALCTS. Betsy Gamble.
Microcomputer Users. Birong Ho.
Online Catalogs. Jeffrey R. Rehbach.
Optical Information Systems. Pamela R. Mason.
Programmer/Analyst. William W. Jones, Jr.
Retrospective Conversion, LITA/ALCTS. Birong Ho.
Serials Automation, LITA/ALCTS. Elizabeth Ten Have.
Small Integrated Library Systems. Gregory J. Zuck.
Telecommunications. Kathleen A. Wakefield.
Vendor/User. Anita Cook.

American Library Association
Public Library Association

Executive Director, George Needham
50 E. Huron St., Chicago, IL 60611
800-545-2433 Ext. 5025, FAX 312-280-5029

Object

The Public Library Association (PLA) will advance the development and effectiveness of public library service and public librarians. PLA has specific responsibility for

1. Conducting and sponsoring research about how the public library can respond to changing social needs and technical developments.

2. Developing and disseminating materials useful to public libraries in interpreting public library services and needs.

3. Conducting continuing education for public librarians by programming at national and regional conferences, by

publications such as the newsletter, and by other delivery means.

4. Establishing, evaluating, and promoting goals, guidelines, and standards for public libraries.

5. Maintaining liaison with relevant national agencies and organizations engaged in public administration and human services, such as the National Association of Counties, Municipal League, and Commission on Post-Secondary Education.

6. Maintaining liaison with other divisions and units of ALA and other library organizations, such as the Association of American Library Schools and the Urban Libraries Council.

7. Defining the role of the public library in service to a wide range of user and potential user groups.

8. Promoting and interpreting the public library to a changing society through legislative programs and other appropriate means.

9. Identifying legislation to improve and to equalize support of public libraries.

PLA exists to provide a diverse program of communication, publication, advocacy, and continuing education. The program priorities are determined by PLA members and may include some areas or concerns also identified as priorities by ALA. The primary staff program responsibility is to facilitate members' activities and initiatives by providing coordination and support.

The division seeks to

1. Provide leadership for the improvement of public libraries.

2. Provide an effective forum for discussing issues of concern to public librarians.

3. Provide relevant, high-quality continuing education through publications, workshops, and programs.

4. Provide opportunities for developing and enhancing individual professional networks.

5. Develop and disseminate policy statements on matters affecting public libraries.

6. Communicate effectively with the nonlibrary world about matters impacting public library service.

7. Maintain a stable membership and financial base.

PLA's priority concerns are adequate funding for public libraries; improved management of public libraries; recognition of the importance of all library staff in providing quality public service; recruitment, education, training, and compensation of public librarians; effective use of technology; intellectual freedom; improved access to library resources; and effective communication with the nonlibrary world. Organized 1944.

Membership

Memb. 7,000+. Open to all ALA members interested in the improvement and expansion of public library services to all ages in various types of communities.

Officers (1993–1994)

Pres. Pat A. Woodrum, Tulsa City-County Lib., 400 Civic Center, Tulsa, OK 74103; *V.P./Pres.-Elect* Judith A. Drescher, Memphis–Shelby County Public Lib., 1850 Peabody Ave., Memphis, TN 38104; *Past Pres.* Elliot Shelkrot, Free Lib. of Philadelphia, Logan Sq., Philadelphia, PA 19103.

Board of Directors

Dirs.-at-Large Rick Ashton, Ginnie Cooper, Linda P. Elliott, Martin J. Gomez, Donald J. Napoli, Donna Barrett Schremser; *Section Reps.: ALLS Past Pres.* Mary Jo Ryan; *CIS Past Pres.* David L. Searcy; *MLS Pres.* Jean T. Curtis; *MPLSS Pres.* Patricia L. Owens; *PLSS Pres.* Kathleen R. Imhoff; *PPPLS Dir.* Kay K. Runge; *SMLS Rep.* John Allyn Moorman; *ALTA Rep.* Ramonda (Mandy) S. Wertz; *ALA/PLA Councillor* Linda Mielke; *PLA Affiliates Network* Christine L. Hage; *Ex officio: PLA Budget and Finance Rep.* Patrick O'Brien; *PLA Exec. Dir.* George Needham.

Publication

Public Libraries (bi-mo.; memb.; nonmemb. $50; foreign $60; single copy $10). *Feature Ed.* Ellen Altman, 1936 E. Belmont Dr., Tempe, AZ 85284; *Managing Ed.* Sandra Causey Garrison, PLA, 50 E. Huron St., Chicago, IL 60611.

Section Presidents

Adult Lifelong Learning. Kathryn M. Panares.
Community Information. Marlys H. O'Brien.
Marketing of Public Library Services. Patricia L. Owens.
Metropolitan Libraries. Jean T. Curtis.
Public Library Systems. Kathleen R. Imhoff.
Public Policy for Public Libraries. Catherine A. O'Connell.
Small and Medium-Sized Libraries. Jan B. Walsh.

Committee Chairpersons

Audiovisual. Dorothy M. Liegl.
Awards. Michael Madden.
Budget and Finance. Patrick O'Brien.
Business Council. Michael J. Wirt.
Bylaws and Organization. Judith M. Foust.
Cataloging Needs of Public Libraries. Ellen Slotoroff Zyroff.
Children, Service to. Lucinda Frances Ware.
Common Concerns, ALTA/PLA. William T. Balcom.
Conference Program Coordinating (1994). James B. Alsip.
Conference Program Coordinating (1995). Harriet Henderson.
Education of Public Librarians. June Lester.
Intellectual Freedom. Loretta R. O'Brien.
International Relations. Theresa Huang.
Leadership Development (1994). Fran C. Freimarck.
Leadership Development (1995). Donna Mancini.
Legislation. Sarah A. Long.
Liaison with National Organizations. John D. Christenson.

Liaison with Service Clubs. Faye Clow.
Library Video Award. Phyllis Y. Massar.
LSCA Ad Hoc (Special). Sarah A. Long.
Allie Beth Martin Award. Marilyn Prosser.
Membership. Carole Dickerson.
Multilingual Materials and Library Service. John W. Cunningham.
National Achievement Citation. Kay K. Runge.
National Conference (1994). Susan S. Goldberg; National Conference Exhibitors Advisory. Mary L. Shapiro; National Conference Local Arrangements. Ronald A. Dubberly; National Conference Program. Sandra S. Nelson.
National Conference (1996). June M. Garcia; National Conference Exhibitors Advisory. Stephen Kochoff; National Conference Local Arrangements. Ginnie Cooper; National Conference Program. Christine L. Hage.
New Leaders Travel Grant. Louise A. Sevold.
Nominating (1994). Donald J. Sager.
Nominating (1995). Ronald A. Dubberly.
PLA Partners. LaDonna T. Kienitz.
Planning and Evaluation. Karen J. Krueger.
Planning Off-Site Delivery of Library Services (Special). Ernest DiMattia.
Political Effectiveness. Sharon Hammer.
President's Program/Hot Topics (1994). Cathy Audley.
President's Program/Hot Topics (1995). Marilyn Boria.
Public Libraries Advisory Board. Claudia B. Sumler.
Public Library Data Service. Sheldon B. Kaye.
Public Library History. Donald J. Sager.
Public Library Services to the Homeless. Ernestine L. Hawkins.
Publications. Thomas C. Phelps.
Research. Thomas A. Childers.
Retail Outlets in Public Libraries. A. Michael Deller.
Technology in Public Libraries. Susan B. Harrison.
Leonard Wertheimer Multilingual Public Library Service Award. Carmen L. Martinez.

American Library Association
Reference and Adult Services Division

Executive Director, Cathleen Bourdon
50 E. Huron St., Chicago, IL 60611
312-944-6780, 800-545-2433

Object

The Reference and Adult Services Division (RASD) is responsible for stimulating and supporting in every type of library the delivery of reference/information services to all groups, regardless of age, and of general library services and materials to adults. This involves facilitating the development and conduct of direct service to library users, the development of programs and guidelines for service to meet the needs of these users, and assisting libraries in reaching potential users.

The specific responsibilities of RASD are

1. Conduct of activities and projects within the division's areas of responsibility.

2. Encouragement of the development of librarians engaged in these activities, and stimulation of participation by members of appropriate type-of-library divisions.

3. Synthesis of the activities of all units within the American Library Association that have a bearing on the type of activities represented by the division.

4. Representation and interpretation of the division's activities in contacts outside the profession.

5. Planning and development of programs of study and research in these areas for the total profession.

6. Continuous study and review of the division's activities.

Membership

Memb. 5,558. For information on dues, see ALA entry.

Officers (1993–1994)

Pres. Charles Gilreath; *Pres.-Elect* David Kohl; *Secy.* Julia Rholes.

Directors and Other Members

Daniel Barthell, Anita Evans, Linda Friend, Mary Jackson, Mark Leggett, Nancy H. Sherwin; *Councillor* Gail Schlachter; *Past Pres.* James Rettig; *Ed. RASD Update* Jane Kleiner; *Eds. RQ* Connie Van Fleet, Danny Wallace; *Ed. Round-up* John Hepner; *Planning Committee Chair* Elaine Jennerich; *Exec. Dir.* Cathleen Bourdon.

Address correspondence to the executive director.

Publications

RASD Update (memb.; nonmemb. $15). *Ed.* Jane Kleiner, Middleton Lib., Louisiana State Univ., Baton Rouge, LA 70803-7010.

Round-up: Newsletter of the RASD Council of State and Regional Groups (s. ann.) *Ed.* John C. Hepner, Box 507, Denton, TX 76202-0507.

RQ (q.; memb; nonmemb. $42). *Eds.* Connie Van Fleet and Danny Wallace, Louisiana State Univ., 267 Coates, Baton Rouge, LA 70803-7010.

RQ Occasional Papers (irreg.) *Ed.* Nancy Huling, Suzallo Lib. FM-25, Univ. of Washington, Seattle, WA 98195.

Section Chairpersons

Business Reference and Services. Timothy Dixon.
Collection Development and Evaluation. Merle Jacob.
History. Carla Rickerson.
Machine-Assisted Reference. Louis Drummond.
Management and Operation of Public Services. Karen Liston Newsome.
Services to User Populations. Mario Gonzalez.

Committee Chairpersons

Access to Information. Carolyn Radcliff.
AFL/CIO Joint Committee on Library Services to Labor Groups. Mary F. Hicks.
Awards Coordinating. Peter McCallion.
Conference Program. Charles Gilreath.
Conference Program Coordinating. Kelly Janousek.
Dartmouth Medal. Jack Forman.
Denali Press Award. Carolyn Gates.
Executive. Charles Gilreath.
Facts on File Grant. Ree DeDonato.
Finance. James Rettig.
Gale Research Award for Excellence in Reference and Adult Services. Marsha Spyros.
Legislation. James R. Cannon.
Membership. Linda Keir Simons.

Margaret E. Monroe Library Adult Services Award. Patricia M. Hogan.
Isadore Gilbert Mudge/R. R. Bowker Award. Nancy Fisher.
Nominating (1994). Elizabeth F. Stroup.
Organization. Karen J. Chapman.
Planning. Elaine Z. Jennerich.
Publications. Nancy Huling.
Reference Services Press Award. Gary M. Klein.
RQ Editorial Advisory Board. Connie Van Fleet, Danny Wallace.
John Sessions Memorial Award. Barbara Hull.
Louis Shores/Oryx Press Award. Richard Bleiler.
Standards and Guidelines. Larayne Dallas.

American Library Association
Young Adult Library Services Association

Executive Director, Ann Carlson Weeks
50 E. Huron St., Chicago, IL 60611
312-944-6780, 800-545-2433 Ext. 4388, FAX 312-664-7459

Object

To advocate, promote, and strengthen service to young adults as part of the continuum of total library service. The following concerns and activities are interdependent in fulfilling the goal of the Young Adult Library Services Association (YALSA). The association

1. Advocates the young adult's right to free and equal access to materials and services, and assists librarians in handling problems of such access.
2. Evaluates and promotes materials of interest to adolescents through special services, programs, and publications, except for those materials designed specifically for curriculum use.
3. Identifies research needs related to young adult service and communicates those needs to the library academic community in order to activate research projects.
4. Stimulates and promotes the development of librarians and other staff working

with young adults through formal and continuing education.
5. Stimulates and promotes the expansion of young adult service among professional associates and agencies at all levels.
6. Represents the interests of librarians and staff working with young adults to all relevant agencies, government or private, and to industries that serve young adults as clients or consumers.
7. Creates and maintains communication links with other units of ALA whose developments affect service to young adults.

Established 1957.

Membership

Memb. 2,284. Open to anyone interested in library services and materials for young adults. For information on dues, see ALA entry.

Officers (1993–1994)

Pres. Judith Druse, Curriculum/Media Libn., Washburn Univ., 1700 College Ave., Topeka, KS 66621. Tel. 913-231-1010 Ext. 1277, FAX 913-357-1240; *V.P./Pres.-Elect* Jennifer Jung Gallant, 482 Dover Center, Bay Village, OH 44140. Tel. 216-835-6020, FAX 216-835-6115; *Past Pres.* Elizabeth O'Donnell, 39 Lane Rd., Raymond, NH 03077. Tel. 603-624-6550, FAX 603-624-6559; *Councillor* Pamela R. Klipsch, 117 E. Bodley Ave., Kirkwood, MO 63122. Tel. 618-462-0651, FAX 618-462-0665.

Directors

Officers; Betty Carter (term expires 1994), Elizabeth E. Elam (1995), Lesley S. J. Farmer (1996), Patrick Jones (1996), Constance P. Lawson (1994), Amy Oxley (1995); *Ex officio Chair, Budget and Finance* Gayle Keresey; *Ex officio Chair, Long-Range Planning* Pamela G. Spencer; *Ex officio Chair, Organization and Bylaws* Helen Vandersluis; *Exec. Dir.* Ann Carlson Weeks.

Publication

Journal of Youth Services in Libraries (q.; memb.; nonmemb. $40; foreign $50). *Eds.* Donald J. Kenney, Director's Office, Virginia Polytechnic Inst., Box 90001, Blacksburg, VA 24062-9001. Tel. 703-231-5595, FAX 703-231-9263; Linda J. Wilson, Dept. of Educational Studies, Radford Univ., 206A Russell Hall, Radford, VA 24142. Tel. 703-831-5344, FAX 703-831-5302.

Committee Chairpersons

Baker and Taylor Conference Grant. Susan Meck.
Best Books for Young Adults (1994). Joel Shoemaker.
Best Books for Young Adults (1995). Audra L. Caplan.
Budget and Finance. Gayle Keresey.

Computer Applications. Nancy P. Zimmerman.
Division Promotion. Elizabeth M. Reed.
Econo-Clad Program Literature Award. Audra L. Caplan.
Education. Bruce Lee Siebers.
Margaret A. Edwards Award (1994). Judy T. Nelson.
Margaret A. Edwards Award (1995). JoAnn G. Mondowney.
Executive. Judith Druse.
Genre List Coordinator. Michael Cart.
Genre List, Fantasy. Paulette Goodman.
Genre List, Historical Fiction. Carlos Najera.
Genre List, Horror. Jack Forman.
Genre List, Humor. Mary Huebscher.
Genre List, Mystery. Suzanne Manczuk.
Genre List, Romance. To be appointed.
Genre List, Science Fiction. Paul S. Ritz.
Genre List, Sports. Mary Arnold.
Genre Marketing (Task Force). Candace V. Conklin.
Intellectual Freedom. Patricia Muller.
Journal of Youth Services in Libraries, Editorial. Donald J. Kenney, Linda J. Wilson.
Journal of Youth Services in Libraries, Evaluation (ad hoc). Joan L. Atkinson.
Legislation. Jeri Baker.
Local Arrangements (1994). Sharon Bart.
Long-Range Planning. Pamela G. Spencer.
Media Selection and Usage. Connie Adams Bush.
Membership Recruitment. Larry D. Condit.
National Organizations Serving the Young Adult (Liaison). James Rosinia.
Nominating (1994). Chapple Langemack.
Nominating (1995). Mike Printz.
Organization and Bylaws. Helen Vandersluis.
Outreach. James E. Cook.
Outstanding Books for the College Bound, Biographies. Marjorie Lewis.
Outstanding Books for the College Bound, Coordinator. Betty Carter.
Outstanding Books for the College Bound, Fiction. Julie DeMatteis.
Outstanding Books for the College Bound, Fine Arts. To be appointed.
Outstanding Books for the College Bound, Nonfiction. Betty B. Lazarus.
Outstanding Books for the College Bound, Theater. Jo Ann Kingston.
Oversight. Pamela G. Spencer.

Preconference, Miami (1994). Pamela G. Spencer, Mike Printz.
Program Planning. Lily Helwig.
Public Ear: Popular Music and Teenagers (ad hoc). Frances Bradburn.
Publications. Nancy French.
Publishers' Liaison. Barbara Nosanchuk.
Recommended Books for Reluctant Young Adult Readers (1994). Nancy Reich.

Amelia E. Walden Award (ad hoc). Caryn G. Sipos.
White House Conference on Library and Information Services (ad hoc). Virginia Matthews.
Young Adult Literature (Discussion Group). Susan Rosenzweig.
Youth Participation. Barbara L. Blosveren.

American Merchant Marine Library Association

(An affiliate of United Seamen's Service)
Executive Director, Roger T. Korner
One World Trade Center, Suite 2161, New York, NY 10048
212-775-1038

Object

Provides ship and shore library service for American-flag merchant vessels, the Military Sealift Command, the U.S. Coast Guard, and other waterborne operations of the U.S. government. Established 1921.

Officers (1993–1994)

Honorary Chair Adm. Albert J. Harbinger; *Pres.* Talmage E. Simpkins; *Chair, Exec. Committee* Arthur W. Friedberg; *V.P.s* W. J. Amoss, Jr., John M. Bowers, James Capo, Ernest Corrado, C. E. DeFries, H. R. Del Mar, Mario Guidi, John Halas, Lane Kirkland, George E. Murphy, S. Nakanishi, Gregorio Oca, Shannon J. Wall; *Secy.* Lillian Rabins; *Treas.* William G. Croly; *Exec. Dir.* Roger T. Korner.

American Society for Information Science

Executive Director, Richard B. Hill
8720 Georgia Ave., Suite 501, Silver Spring, MD 20910
301-495-0900, FAX 301-495-0810
E-mail: asis@cni.org

Object

The American Society for Information Science (ASIS) provides a forum for the discussion, publication, and critical analysis of work dealing with the design, management, and use of information, information systems, and information technology.

Membership

Memb. (Indiv.) 3,700; (Student) 600; (Inst.) 115. Dues (Indiv.) $95; (Student) $25; (Inst.) $350 and $550.

Officers

Pres. Marjorie M. K. Hlava, Access Innovations, 4314 Mesa Grande S.E., Albuquerque, NM 87196; *Pres.-Elect* James E. Rush, Palinet, 3401 Market St., Suite 262, Philadelphia, PA 19104; *Treas.* Anne M. Buck, New Jersey Inst. of Technology, Univ. Heights, Newark, NJ 07102; *Past Pres.* José-Marie Griffiths, Univ. of Tennessee, 2615 Shoreline Dr., Knoxville, TN 37932.

Address correspondence to the executive director.

Board of Directors

Chapter Assembly Dir. Judith E. Watson; *SIG Cabinet Dir.* Karla Petersen; *Dirs.-at-Large* Joseph A. Busch, Paula L. Galbraith, Elisabeth L. Logan, Clifford Lynch, Nancy K. Roderer, Jane K. Starnes.

Publications

Annual Review of Information Science and Technology. Available from Learned Information, 143 Old Marlton Pike, Medford, NJ 08055.
Bulletin of the American Society for Information Science. Available from ASIS.
Interfaces for Information Retrieval and Online Systems: The State of the Art. Ed. Martin Dillon. Available from Greenwood Press, 88 Post Rd. W., Westport, CT 06881.
Journal of the American Society for Information Science. Available from John Wiley and Sons, 605 Third Ave., New York, NY 10016

Proceedings of the ASIS Annual Meetings. Available from Learned Information, 143 Old Marlton Pike, Medford, NJ 08055.

Committee Chairpersons

Accreditation (Task Force). José-Marie Griffiths.
Awards and Honors. Gregory Newby.
Budget and Finance. Anne Buck.
Career Development. Maurica Fedors.
Conferences and Meetings. Ann Dodson.
Constitution and Bylaws. Norman Horrocks.
Continuing Education. Gloria Caton.
Executive Committee. José-Marie Griffiths.
Information Policy. Sarah Kadec.
Information Science Education. Martha Williams.
Intellectual Property (Task Force). Patrice Lyons.
Membership. Candy Schwartz.
Nominations. José-Marie Griffiths.
Publications. Ben-Ami Lipetz.
Research. Debora Shaw.
Standards. Mark Needleman.

American Theological Library Association

820 Church St., Suite 300, Evanston, IL 60201-5603
708-869-7788, FAX 708-869-8513

Object

To bring its members into close working relationships with each other, to support theological and religious librarianship, to improve theological libraries, and to interpret the role of such libraries in theological education, developing and implementing standards of library service, promoting research and experimental projects, encouraging cooperative programs that make resources more available, publishing and disseminating literature and research tools and aids, cooperating with organizations having similar aims, and otherwise supporting and aiding theological education. Founded 1947.

Membership

Memb. (Inst.) 185; (Indiv.) 500. Membership

is open to persons engaged in professional library or bibliographical work in theological or religious fields and others who are interested in the work of theological librarianship. Dues (Inst.) $75 to $500, based on total library expenditure; (Indiv.) $15 to $100, based on salary scale. Year. Sept. 1–Aug. 31.

Officers (July 1993–June 1994)

Pres. Roger L. Loyd, Duke Divinity School Lib., Duke Univ., Durham, NC 27708-0972. Tel. 919-660-3452, FAX 510-649-1417; *V.P.* Linda Corman, Trinity College Lib., 6 Hoskin Ave., Toronto, ON M5S 1H8, Canada. Tel. 416-978-2653, FAX 416-978-2797; *Secy.* David J. Wartluft, Krauth Memorial Lib., Lutheran Theological Seminary at

Philadelphia, 7301 Germantown Ave., Philadelphia, PA 19119-1794. Tel. 215-248-4616 Ext. 37, FAX 215-248-4577.

Research in Ministry: An Index to Doctor of Ministry Project Reports (ann.).

Board of Directors

Marti Alt, Christopher Brennan, David D. Bundy, Myron B. Chace, Diane Choquette, M. Patrick Graham, Valerie R. Hotchkiss, Mitzi M. Jarrett, Mary Williams; *Exec. Dir.* Albert E. Hurd; *Dir. of Finance* Patricia Adamek; *Dir. of Development* John Bollier; *Rec. Secy.* Joyce L. Farris.

Publications

Index to Book Reviews in Religion (ann.).
Newsletter (q.; memb.; nonmemb. $10). *Eds.* Albert E. Hurd, Gerry Byrne.
Proceedings (ann.; memb.; nonmemb. $20). *Ed.* Dir. of Member Services.
Religion Index One: Periodicals (ann.).
Religion Index Two: Multi-Author Works (ann.).

Committee Chairpersons and Other Officials

Annual Conference. Christine Wenderoth.
Archivist. Boyd Reese.
Automation and Technology. Lewis Day.
Collection Evaluation and Development. Christine Wenderoth.
College and University. Judy Clarence.
Education. René House.
Historical Records. Rosalyn Lewis.
Nominating. Channing Jeschke.
OCLC Theological User Group. Linda Omoh.
Online Reference Resource. Charles Willard.
Oral History. Alice Kendrick.
Public Services. Kirk Moll.
Publication. Rev. George C. Papademetriou.
Rare Books and Special Collections. Paul Schrodt.
Records Manager. Rev. Simeon Daly.
Statistician. Dir. of Member Services.
Technical Services. Chris W. Cullnane.

Archivists and Librarians in the History of the Health Sciences

(formerly the Association of Librarians in the History of the Health Sciences)

President, Edward T. Morman
Johns Hopkins Institute of the History of Medicine,
1900 E. Monument St., Baltimore, MD 21205-2169
410-955-3159, FAX 410-550-6819

Object

This association is established exclusively for educational purposes to serve the professional interests of librarians, archivists, and other specialists actively engaged in the librarianship of the history of the health sciences by promoting the exchange of information and by improving the standards of service.

Membership

Memb. (Voting) 120; (Nonvoting) 60. Voting members shall be limited to persons who have professional responsibilities for library and archives collections and services in the history of the health sciences. Nonvoting membership shall be open to persons interested in the concerns of the association.

Officers (May 1993–May 1994)

Pres. Edward T. Morman, Johns Hopkins Inst. of the History of Medicine, 1900 E. Monument St., Baltimore, MD 21205-2169. Tel. 410-955-3159; *Pres.-Elect* Barbara Irwin, Smith Lib., Univ. of Medicine and Dentistry, 30 12th Ave., Newark, NJ 07103-

2754; *Secy.-Treas.* Susan Rishworth, American College of Obstetrics and Gynecology, 409 12th St. S.W., Washington, DC 20024.; *Eds.* Jodi Koste, Special Collections and Archives, Medical College of Virginia, MCV Box 582, Richmond, VA 23113-0582; and Joan Echtenkamp Klein, Historical Collections, Univ. of Virginia Health Sciences Center, Box 234, Charlottesville, VA 22908.

Steering Committee

Officers; Barbara J. Niss.

Committees

Archives. Jodi Koste, Special Collections and Archives, Medical College of Virginia,

MCV Box 582, Richmond, VA 23113-0582.

Awards. Christopher Hoolihan, Miner Lib., Univ. of Rochester, 601 Elmwood Ave., Rochester, NY 14642.

Nominating. To be appointed.

Program. To be appointed.

Publication

Watermark (q.; memb.; nonmemb. $15). *Eds.* Jodi Koste, Special Collections and Archives, Medical College of Virginia, MCV Box 582, Richmond, VA 23113-0582; and Joan Echtenkamp Klein, Historical Collections, Univ. of Virginia Health Sciences Center, Box 234, Charlottesville, VA 22908.

ARMA International
(Association of Records Managers and Administrators)

Executive Director, James P. Souders
4200 Somerset Dr., Suite 215, Prairie Village, KS 66208
913-341-3808, FAX 913-341-3742

Object

To promote a scientific interest in records and information management; to provide a forum for research and the exchange of ideas and knowledge; to foster professionalism; to develop and promulgate workable standards and practices; and to furnish a source of records and information management guidance through education and publication.

Membership

Membership application is available through ARMA Headquarters. Annual dues are $100 for international affiliation. Chapter dues vary from city to city. Membership categories are chapter member ($100 plus chapter dues), student member ($15), and unaffiliated member.

Officers (1993-1994)

Pres. James Allin Spokes, Records Management, Manitoba Hydro, Box 815, Winnipeg, MB R3C 2P4, Canada. Tel. 204-474-3295, FAX 204-475-9044; *Immediate Past Pres. and Chair of the Board* Pat Dixon, Southland Corp., Box 711, Dallas, TX 75221. Tel. 214-828-5503, FAX 214-841-6672; *Pres.-Elect* Tyrone G. Butler, New York City School Construction Authority, 30-30 Thomson Ave., Long Island City, NY 11101-3045. Tel. 718-472-8824, FAX 718-472-8850; *Secy.-Treas.* Michael P. Flanagan, Union Pacific Railroad Co., 1416 Dodge St., Rm. 830, Omaha, NE 68179. Tel. 402-271-3072, FAX 402-271-5610; *Region V.P.s: Region I* Robert Nawrocki; *Region II* Julie A. Gee; *Region III* J. Michael Pemberton; *Region IV* Karen Shaw; *Region V* Douglas P. Allen; *Region VI* William E. Testerman; *Region VII* Gifford

Salisbury; *Region VIII* Richard Weinholdt; *Region IX* Susan Eichinger; *Region X* Michael S. Cranston; *Region XI* Kenneth Hopkins; *Region XII* Christine M. Ardern.

Publication

Records Management Quarterly. Ed. Ira Penn, Box 4580, Silver Spring, MD 20914.

Committee Chairpersons

Awards. James Allin Spokes, Records Management, Manitoba Hydro, Box 815, Winnipeg, MB R3C 2P4, Canada. Tel. 204-474-3295.

Education Development. Juanita M. Skillman, Corporate Services, American Honda Motor Co., 1919 Torrance Blvd., Torrance, CA 90501-2746. Tel. 310-781-4365, FAX 310-781-4343.

Financial Planning: Management Audit. Michael P. Flanagan, Union Pacific Railroad Co., 1416 Dodge St., Rm. 830, Omaha, NE 68179. Tel. 402-271-3072, FAX 402-271-5610.

IAC Assistants. Timothy W. Hughes, Madison Gas and Electric Co., Box 1231, Madison, WI 53701-1231. Tel. 608-252-4799, FAX 608-252-7098; Wendy L. Sapp, Hercules Inc., 1313 Market St., Wilmington, DE 19894-0001. Tel. 302-594-5396, FAX 302-594-5471.

Industry Action. Joyce W. Ellis, A. H. Robins Co., Box 26609, Richmond, VA 23261-6609. Tel. 804-257-2794, FAX 804-257-2726.

Legislative and Regulatory Affairs: U.S. Frances E. Chartier, Coastal Group, 9 Greenway Plaza, Houston, TX 77046. Tel. 713-877-6384, FAX 713-877-6754.

Legislative and Regulatory Affairs: Canada. Raphaël A. Thierrin, 208, 4515 45th St. S.W., Calgary, AB T3E 6K7, Canada. Tel. 403-686-3310.

Nominating. Pat Dixon, Southland Corp., Box 711, Dallas, TX 75221. Tel. 214-828-5503, FAX 214-841-6672.

Organizational Outreach. Tad C. Howington, County of Tarrant, Dept. of Records and Microfilm, 401 W. Belknap, UO17, Fort Worth, TX 76196-0135. Tel. 817-884-1726, FAX 817-884-3363.

Program (1994). Claire A. Cardina, City of Tampa, Archives and Records Service, 1104 E. Twiggs St., Tampa, FL 33602. Tel. 813-227-7181, FAX 813-223-8076.

Public Relations, Marketing, and Membership. Anne Taylor-Butler, Litigation Support/Records, New York City Dept. of Transportation, 295 Lafayette St., 4th fl., New York, NY 10012. Tel. 212-323-8564, FAX 212-323-8950.

Publications Coordination. Robert E. Miller, Bausch and Lomb Inc., 1400 N. Goodman St., Rochester, NY 14602. Tel. 716-338-6041, FAX 716-338-6653.

Publications Coordination: Publications and Research Development (Subcommittee). Jean K. Brown, Univ. Archives, Univ. of Delaware, 002 Newark Hall, Newark, DE 19716. Tel. 302-831-2750, FAX 302-831-6903.

Publications Coordination: Standards Advisory and Development (Subcommittee). Marti Fischer, Bank of California, 433 California St., 11th fl., San Francisco, CA 94104. Tel. 415-765-3491, FAX 415-765-3121

Publications Coordination: Technology Investigations and Studies (Subcommittee). John T. Phillips, 1803 Nantasket Rd., Knoxville, TN 37922. Tel. 615-574-0328, FAX 615-574-9374.

Art Libraries Society of North America

Executive Director, Lori Bahrman
3900 E. Timrod St., Tucson, AZ 85711
602-881-8479, FAX 602-322-6778

Object

To foster excellence in art librarianship and visual resources curatorship for the advancement of the visual arts. Established 1972.

Membership

Memb. 1,325. Dues (Inst.) $75; (Indiv.) $55; (Business Affiliate) $75; (Student/Retired/Unemployed) $35; (Sustaining) $175; (Sponsor) $500; (Overseas) $75. Year. Jan. 1–Dec. 31. Membership is open and encouraged for all those interested in visual librarianship, whether they be professional librarians, students, library assistants, art book publishers, art book dealers, art historians, archivists, architects, slide and photograph curators, or retired associates in these fields.

Officers (Feb. 1994–Feb. 1995)

Pres. Janis Ekdahl; *V.P./Pres.-Elect* Edward Teague; *Secy.* Sherman Clarke; *Treas.* Edward Goodman; *Exec. Dir.* Lori Bahrman; *Past Pres.* Deirdre C. Stam.

Address correspondence to the executive director.

Executive Board

President, past president, president-elect, secretary, treasurer, and five regional representatives (Northeast, Midwest, South, West, and Canada).

Publications

ARLIS/NA Update (bi-mo.; memb.).

Art Documentation (q.; memb.).
Handbook and List of Members (ann.; memb.).
Occasional Papers (price varies).
Topical Papers (price varies).
Miscellaneous others (request current list from headquarters).

Committees

AAT Advisory.
Cataloging Advisory.
Collection Development.
Conference.
Cultural Diversity.
Development.
International Relations.
Membership.
Gerd Muehsam Award.
Nominating.
Professional Development.
Publications.
Research.
Standards.
Technology.
Travel Award.
George Wittenborn Award.

Chapters

Arizona; Central Plains; DC-Maryland-Virginia; Delaware Valley; Kentucky-Tennessee-West Virginia; Michigan; Midstates; Montreal-Ottawa-Quebec; New England; New Jersey; New York; Northern California; Northwest; Ohio; Ontario; Southeast; Southern California; Texas; Twin Cities; Western New York.

Asian/Pacific American Librarians Association

President, Ravindra N. Sharma
Director, University Libraries, University of Evansville
1800 Lincoln Ave., Evansville, IN 47722
812-479-2485, FAX 812-479-2009

Object

To provide a forum for discussing problems and concerns of Asian/Pacific American librarians; to provide a forum for the exchange of ideas by Asian/Pacific American librarians and other librarians; to support and encourage library services to the Asian/Pacific American communities; to recruit and support Asian/Pacific American librarians in the library/information science professions; to seek funding for scholarships in library/information science schools for Asian/Pacific Americans; and to provide a vehicle whereby Asian/Pacific American librarians can cooperate with other associations and organizations having similar or allied interests. Founded 1980; incorporated 1981; affiliated with ALA 1982.

Membership

Open to all librarians and information specialists of Asian/Pacific descent working in U.S. libraries and information centers and other related organizations and to others who support the goals and purposes of APALA. Asian/Pacific Americans are defined as those who consider themselves Asian/Pacific Americans. They may be Americans of Asian/Pacific descent, Asian/Pacific people with the status of permanent residency, or Asian/Pacific people living in the United States. Dues (Inst.) $25; (Indiv.) $10; (Students/Unemployed Librarians) $5.

Officers (July 1993–June 1994)

Pres. Ravindra N. Sharma, Dir., Univ. Libs., Univ. of Evansville, 1800 Lincoln Ave., Evansville, IN 47722. Tel. 812-479-2485, FAX 812-479-2009; *V.P./Pres.-Elect* Erlinda J. Regner, Chicago Public Lib., 400 N. Franklin St., Chicago, IL 60614. Tel. 312-747-4414; *Secy.* Susan G. Shiroma, New York Univ. Lib., 70 Washington Sq. S., New York, NY 10012. Tel. 212-998-2602; *Treas.* Wilfred W. Fong, Univ. of Wisconsin–Milwaukee, Milwaukee, WI 53211. Tel. 414-229-5421.

Advisory Committee

President, immediate past president, vice president/president-elect, secretary, treasurer, chairpersons of regional chapters, and an elected representative of the standing committees.

Publications

APALA Newsletter. Ed. Wilfred W. Fong, Univ. of Wisconsin–Milwaukee, Milwaukee, WI 53211. Tel. 414-229-5421.

Committee Chairpersons

Awards. Abdul J. Miah.
Constitution and Bylaws. Fazal Kabir.
Finance. Henry C. Chang.
Local Arrangement. Julita Awkard.
Membership. Shushila Shah.
Nominations. Marjorie Li.
Program and Publicity. Abdul Miah, Erlinda J. Regner.
Recruitment and Scholarship. David Liu.

Association for Information and Image Management

Executive Director, Sue Wolk
1100 Wayne Ave., Silver Spring, MD 20910
301-587-8202, FAX 301-587-2711

Object

To increase the effectiveness of public and private organizations by promoting and advancing the development and use of systems, services, and technologies that store, retrieve, and manipulate images of documents.

Officers

Pres. Beverlee Nunnari, Reliance Electric, 24800 Tungsten Rd., Cleveland, OH 44117;
V.P. Paul M. Carman, Eastman Kodak Co., 343 State St., Rochester, NY 14650-0303; *Treas.* David F. Liddell, IBM Corp., 208 Harbor Dr., MD 51, Stamford, CT 06904.

Publications

fyi/im newsletter (24 per year; memb.). *Ed.* Beth Rosenberg.
INFORM (10 per year; memb.). *Ed.* John Harney.

Association for Information Management

Managing Director, David Kahn
6348 Munhall Ct., Box 374, McLean, VA 22101
703-790-0403

Object

To provide leadership in targeting and enhancing the abilities of all managers to ensure the efficient and effective delivery of information in order to further individual and organizational goals. The means to do this are through effective integration and management of technologies, content, and people. Established 1981.

Membership

Memb. (Indiv.) 600. Dues (Indiv.) private $100, public/academician $60; (Foreign) $135. Members include corporate planners, vice presidents of communication and marketing, administration managers, online users, and data processing, telecommunications, library, records management, office automation, and management information systems (MIS) personnel. The primary focus is on the management of these information activities and on making the total information base supportive of management and the decision-making process. The board of directors is made up of leading information professionals in industry, academia, and government.

Board of Directors

Chair Arlen R. Lessin, Chair and Pres., Lessin Technology Group; *V.Chair* Alan S. Linden, Mgr., Dist. Marketing Operations, Wang Laboratories; *Exec. Dir.* Susan Kahn.

Publications

AIM Network (mo.; memb.). Newsletter.
AIM 1990 Membership Profile Survey (memb. $20; nonmemb. $35).

Association for Library and Information Science Education

Executive Director, Penney De Pas
4101 Lake Boone Trail, Suite 201, Raleigh, NC 27607-7507
919-787-5181, FAX 919-787-4916

Object

To promote excellence in research, teaching, and service for library and information science education. Established 1915.

Membership

Memb. 680. Dues (Inst.) for ALA-accredited programs $250; all others $150; (International Affiliate Inst.) $75; (Indiv.) $20 or $40. Year. Sept.–Aug. Any library/information science school with a program accredited by the ALA Committee on Accreditation may become an institutional member. Any school that offers a graduate degree in librarianship or a cognate field but whose program is not accredited by the ALA Committee on Accreditation may become an institutional member at the lower rate. Any school outside the United States and Canada offering a program comparable to that of institutional membership may become an international affiliate institutional member. Any faculty member, administrator, librarian, researcher, or other individual employed full time may become a personal member. Any retired or part-time faculty member, student, or other individual employed less than full time may become a personal member at the lower rate.

Officers (Feb. 1994–Jan. 1995)

Pres. Charles Curran, Univ. of South Carolina, College of Lib. and Info. Science, 113 Davis College, Columbia, SC 29208; *V.P./Pres.-Elect* June Lester, Univ. of Oklahoma; *Past Pres.* Timothy W. Sineath, College of Lib. and Info. Science, Univ. of Kentucky, Lexington, KY 40506; *Secy.-Treas.* Carl Orgren, Univ. of Iowa.

Directors

Officers; Martha Hale (term expires 1997); Margaret Mary Kimmel (1996); Ruth A.

Palmquist (1995); *Ed.* Rosemary R. DuMont; *Exec. Dir.* Penney De Pas; *Parliamentarians* Charles A. Bunge, Norman Horrocks.

Publications

ALISE Library and Information Science Education Statistical Report (ann.; $32; foreign $34).
Journal of Education for Library and Information Science (4 per year; $60; foreign $70).
Membership Directory (ann.; included in *Journal* subscription rate).

Committee Chairpersons

Awards and Honors. Adele Fasick, Univ. of Toronto.
Communications and Public Relations. Judith Weedman, Univ. of California, Berkeley.
Conference Planning. Patricia Feshan, Univ. of South Carolina; Timothy W. Sineath, Univ. of Kentucky.
Editorial Board. Rosemary R. DuMont, Kent State Univ.
Faculty Development. To be announced.
Government Relations. James Baughman, Simmons College.
International Relations. John Agada, Emporia State Univ.
LIS Education Statistical Report Project. Timothy W. Sineath.
Membership. Lynn Connaway, Univ. of Missouri.
Nominating. Terrence Crowley, San Jose State Univ.
Nominations. Charles Curran, Univ. of South Carolina.
Organization and Bylaws. Sidney Pierce, Univ. of Oklahoma.
Recruitment. John B. Hall, Drexel Univ.
Research. Daniel O'Connor, Rutgers Univ.
Resolutions. Amy Warner, Univ. of Michigan.
Tellers. Ellen Crosby, Univ. of South Carolina.

Association of Academic Health Sciences Library Directors

Administrator, Shirley Bishop
2033 Sixth Ave., No. 804, Seattle, WA 98121
206-441-6020, FAX 206-441-8262

Object

To promote—in cooperation with educational institutions, other educational associations, government agencies, and other nonprofit organizations—the common interests of academic health sciences libraries located in the United States and elsewhere, through publications, research, and discussion of problems of mutual interest and concern, and to advance the efficient and effective operation of academic health sciences libraries for the benefit of faculty, students, administrators, and practitioners.

Membership

Dues (Inst.) $500; (Assoc. Inst.) $200. Regular membership is available to nonprofit educational institutions operating a school of health sciences that has full or provisional accreditation by the Association of American Medical Colleges. Regular members shall be represented by the chief administrative officer of the member institution's health sciences library. Associate membership (and nonvoting representation) is available to organizations having an interest in the purposes and activities of the association.

Officers (Nov. 1993–Nov. 1994)

Pres. Lynn Kasher Morgan; *Pres.-Elect* Karen Brewer; *Secy.-Treas.* Frieda Weise; *Past Pres.* Judith Messerle.

Board of Directors

J. Michael Homan, Brett A. Kirkpatrick, Patricia Michelson.

Association of Christian Librarians

Executive Director, Wava Bueschlen
Box 4, Cedarville, OH 45314

Object

To meet the needs of evangelical Christian librarians serving in institutions of higher learning. The association shall promote high standards of professionalism in library work as well as projects that encourage membership participation in serving the academic library community. Established 1956.

Membership

Memb. (Indiv.) 320. Dues (Indiv.) $20–$48, based on salary scale. Year. Jan.–Dec. A full member shall be a Christian librarian subscribing to the purposes of the corporation who is affiliated with an institution of higher learning. Associate members include those who are in agreement with the purposes of the corporation but who are not affiliated with institutions of higher learning or who are nonlibrarians.

Officers (June 1993–June 1994)

Pres. Nancy Olson, Lincoln Christian College, Lincoln, IL 62656; *V.P.* Stanford Terhune, Malone College, 306 37th St. N.W., Canton, OH 44709; *Secy.* Sharon Bull, Point Loma Nazarene College, San Diego, CA 92106; *Treas.* Ferne Weimer, Billy Graham Center, Wheaton, IL 60187; *Public Relations*

Dir. Clyde Root, Bethel College, Mishawaka, IN 46545-5509; *Business Mgr.* Janice Bosma, Cedarville College, Cedarville, OH 45314.

Board of Directors

Sheila Carlblom, Joan Holt, Ronald Jordahl, Lois Lehman, Steven Preston.

Publications

Christian Librarian (q.; memb.; nonmemb. $20). *Ed.* Ronald Jordahl, Prairie Bible Inst., Three Hills, AB T0M 2A0, Canada.
Christian Periodical Index. Ed. Douglas Butler, Asbury College, 202 S. Walnut, Wilmore, KY 40390.

Committee Chairpersons

Archivist. Patricia Ashby, Cedarville College, Cedarville, OH 45314.
Bible College Section. Lynn Anderson, Central Bible College, 1315 E. Wheatridge, Springfield, MO 65803.
Commission for International Library Assistance. William Abernathy, BGC Lib., Wheaton College, Wheaton, IL 60187.
Conference Coordinator. Bea Flinner, Southern Nazarene Univ., 4115 N. College, Bethany, OK 73008.
Liberal Arts Section. Paul Snezek, Wheaton College, Wheaton, IL 60187.
Program, 1994 Conference. Roger Phillips, Taylor Univ., Upland, IN 46989.

Association of Jewish Libraries

c/o National Foundation for Jewish Culture
330 Seventh Ave., 21st fl., New York, NY 10001
212-678-8092

Object

To promote the improvement of library services and professional standards in all Jewish libraries and collections of Judaica; to serve as a center of dissemination of Jewish library information and guidance; to encourage the establishment of Jewish libraries and collections of Judaica; to promote publication of literature that will be of assistance to Jewish librarianship; and to encourage people to enter the field of librarianship. Organized in 1965 from the merger of the Jewish Librarians Association and the Jewish Library Association.

Membership

Memb. 890. Dues (Inst.) $25; (Student/Retired) $18. Year. July 1–June 30.

Officers (June 1992–June 1994)

Pres. Ralph R. Simon, Sindell Lib., Temple EmanuEl, 2200 S. Green Rd., University Heights, OH 44121; *Past Pres.* Linda P. Lerman, Research Libs. Group, 1200 Villa St., Mountain View, CA 94041-1100; *V.P./Pres.-Elect* Zachary Baker, Lib., Yivo Inst. for Jewish Research, 1048 Fifth Ave., New York, NY 10033; *V.P. Memb.* Aviva Astrinsky, Annenberg Research Inst. Lib., 420 Walnut St., Philadelphia, PA 19106. Tel. 215-238-1290 Ext. 104; *Treas.* Toby G. Rossner, Bureau of Jewish Education of Rhode Island, 130 Sessions St., Providence, RI 02906; *Rec. Secy.* Merrily E. Hart, Aaron Gerber Lib., Cleveland College of Jewish Studies, 26500 Shaker Blvd., Beachwood, OH 44122; *Corresponding Secy.* Rita Lifton, Lib., Jewish Theological Seminary of America, 3080 Broadway, New York, NY 10027;

Publications V.P. Esther Nussbaum, Ramaz Upper School Lib., 60 E. 78 St., New York, NY 10021.

Address correspondence to the association.

Publications

AJL Newsletter (q.). *Eds.* Irene S. Levin-Wixman, Judaica Lib., Temple EmanuEl, 190 N. County Rd., Palm Beach, FL 33480; Hazel Karp, Hebrew Academy of Atlanta Lib., 5200 Northland Dr., Atlanta, GA 30342.

Judaica Librarianship (irreg.). *Eds.* Marcia Posner; Bella Hass Weinberg, Yivo Lib., 1048 Fifth Ave., New York, NY 10028.

Miscellaneous (request current list from Esther Nussbaum, Lib., Ramaz Upper School, 60 E. 78 St., New York, NY 10021).

Division Presidents

Research and Special Library. Barry Walfish. Synagogue, School, and Center Libraries. Aileen Grossberg.

Association of Research Libraries

Executive Director, Duane E. Webster
21 Dupont Circle, 8th fl., Washington, DC 20036
202-296-2296

Object

To identify and influence forces affecting the future of research libraries in the process of scholarly communication; to promote equitable access to, and effective use of, recorded knowledge in support of teaching, research, scholarship, and community service. Established 1932 by the chief librarians of 43 research libraries.

Membership

Membership is institutional. Memb. 119. Dues $12,000. Year. Jan.–Dec.

Officers (Oct. 1993–Oct. 1994)

Pres. John Black, Univ. of Guelph Lib.; *Pres.-Elect* Jerry Campbell, Dir., Duke Univ. Libs.; *Past Pres.* Susan K. Nutter, North Carolina State Univ. Libs.

Board of Directors

John Black, Univ. of Guelph; Jerry Campbell, Duke Univ.; Dale B. Canelas, Univ. of Florida; Nancy Cline, Pennsylvania State Univ.; Kent Hendrickson, Univ. of Nebraska; Sul Lee, Univ. of Oklahoma; Susan K. Nutter, North Carolina State Univ.; George W. Shipman, Univ. of Oregon; David H. Stam, Syracuse Univ.; Gloria Werner, UCLA; James Williams, Univ. of Colorado.

Publications

ARL: A Bimonthly Newsletter of Research Libraries Issues and Actions (6 per year; $40)

ARL Annual Salary Survey (ann.; $60).

ARL Minutes (s. ann.; $60).

ARL Statistics (ann.; $60).

Directory of Electronic Journals, Newsletters, and Academic Discussion Lists. Compiled by Michael Strangelove and Diane Kovacs (1992; $20).

Preservation Statistics. Statistics and analysis on personnel, expenditures, and categories of treatments (ann.; $60).

Report of the ARL Serials Prices Project. A compilation of reports examining serials prices problems ($60).

Systems and Procedures Exchange Center (SPEC) Kits (10 issues per year; $235 per year).

Committee Chairpersons

Access. Nancy Eaton, Iowa State.
ARL Statistics. William J. Crowe, Univ. of Kansas Lib.
Information Policies. James Neal, Indiana Univ. Lib.
Management of Research Library Resources. Kent Hendrickson, Univ. of Nebraska Lib.
Nominations. John Black, Univ. of Guelph Lib.
Preservation of Research Library Materials. Robert Street, Stanford Univ. Lib.
Research Collections. Dale B. Canelas, Univ. of Florida Lib.
Scholarly Communications Committee. Millicent D. Abell, Yale Univ. Lib.

Units

Coalition for Networked Information. Formed by ARL, CAUSE, and EDUCOM in March 1990 to explore the promise of high-performance computers and advanced networks for enriching scholarship and enhancing intellectual productivity.
Office of Management Services. Provides consulting, training, and publishing services on the management of human and material resources in libraries.
Office of Research and Development. To pursue the ARL research agenda through the identification and development of projects in support of the research library community's mission.
Office of Scientific and Academic Publishing. Established in 1990 to identify and influence the forces affecting the production, dissemination, and use of scholarly and scientific information.

ARL Membership in 1993

Nonuniversity Libraries

Boston Public Lib., Canada Inst. for Scientific and Technical Info., Center for Research Libs., Linda Hall Lib., Lib. of Congress, National Agricultural Lib., National Lib. of Canada, National Lib. of Medicine, New York Public Lib., New York State Lib., Smithsonian Institution Libs.

University Libraries

Alabama, Alberta, Arizona, Arizona State, Auburn, Boston, Brigham Young, British Columbia, Brown, California (Berkeley), California (Davis), California (Irvine), California (Los Angeles), California (Riverside), California (San Diego), California (Santa Barbara), Case Western Reserve, Chicago, Cincinnati, Colorado, Colorado State, Columbia, Connecticut, Cornell, Dartmouth, Delaware, Duke, Emory, Florida, Florida State, Georgetown, Georgia, Georgia Inst. of Technology, Guelph, Harvard, Hawaii, Houston, Howard, Illinois (Chicago), Illinois (Urbana), Indiana, Iowa, Iowa State, Johns Hopkins, Kansas, Kent State, Kentucky, Laval, Louisiana State, McGill, McMaster, Manitoba, Maryland, Massachusetts, Massachusetts Inst. of Technology, Miami, Michigan, Michigan State, Minnesota, Missouri, Nebraska, New Mexico, New York, North Carolina, North Carolina State, Northwestern, Notre Dame, Ohio State, Oklahoma, Oklahoma State, Oregon, Pennsylvania, Pennsylvania State, Pittsburgh, Princeton, Purdue, Queen's (Kingston, Canada), Rice, Rochester, Rutgers, Saskatchewan, South Carolina, Southern California, Southern Illinois, Stanford, SUNY (Albany), SUNY (Buffalo), SUNY (Stony Brook), Syracuse, Temple, Tennessee, Texas, Texas A & M, Toronto, Tulane, Utah, Vanderbilt, Virginia, Virginia Polytechnic, Washington, Washington State, Waterloo, Wayne State, Western Ontario, Wisconsin, Yale, York.

Association of Visual Science Librarians

Chair, Madelyn Hall, Director of Libraries
Good Samaritan Hospital and Medical Center, 1040 N.W. 22 Ave., Portland, OR 97210
503-229-7678, FAX 503-790-1201

Object

To foster collective and individual acquisition and dissemination of visual science information, to improve services for all persons seeking such information, and to develop standards for libraries to which members are attached. Founded 1968.

Membership

Memb. (U.S.) 55; (Foreign) 13.

Publications

Opening Day Book Collection—Visual Science.
PhD Theses in Physiological Optics (irreg.).
Standards for Visual Science Libraries.
Union List of Vision-Related Serials (irreg.).

Meetings

Annual meeting held in December in connection with the American Academy of Optometry; midyear mini-meeting with the Medical Library Association.

Beta Phi Mu
(International Library and Information Science Honor Society)

Executive Secretary, Blanche Woolls
School of Library and Information Science, University of Pittsburgh, Pittsburgh, PA 15260
412-624-9435, FAX 412-648-7001

Object

To recognize high scholarship in the study of librarianship and to sponsor appropriate professional and scholarly projects. Founded at the University of Illinois in 1948.

Membership

Memb. 24,000. Open to graduates of library school programs accredited by the American Library Association who fulfill the following requirements: complete the course requirements leading to a fifth year or other advanced degree in librarianship with a scholastic average of 3.75 where A equals 4 points (this provision shall also apply to planned programs of advanced study beyond the fifth year that do not culminate in a degree but that require full-time study for one or more academic years); receive a letter of recommendation from their respective library schools attesting to their demonstrated fitness for successful professional careers. Former graduates of accredited library schools are also eligible on the same basis.

Officers

Pres. (1993–1995) Elfreda A. Chatman, School of Lib. and Info. Science, Univ. of North Carolina, Chapel Hill, NC 27599-3360. Tel. 919-962-8366, FAX 919-962-8071; *V.P./Pres.-Elect* Mary Biggs, West Lib., Trenton State College, Hillwood Lakes, CN 4700, Trenton, NJ 08650-4700; *Past Pres.* Norman Horrocks, V.P., Editorial, Scarecrow Press, Box 4167, Metuchen, NJ 08840; *Treas.* Dennis K. Lambert, Head of Collection Management, Falvey Memorial Lib., Villanova Univ., Villanova, PA 19085-1699; *Exec. Secy.* Blanche Woolls, School of

Lib. and Info. Science, Univ. of Pittsburgh, Pittsburgh, PA 15260.

Directors

Barbara J. Barber (term expires 1994), Mary E. Donor (1995), Judith Hopkins (1994), Rhonda Marker (1996), Carol S. Robinson (1995), Zary M. Shafa (1996); *Dirs.-at-Large* W. Michael Havener, Marion T. Reid, Nancy P. Zimmerman.

Publications

Beta Phi Mu Monograph Series. Book-length scholarly works based on original research in subjects of interest to library and information professionals. Available from Greenwood Press, 88 Post Rd. W., Box 5007, Westport, CT 06881-9990.

Chapbook Series. Limited editions on topics of interest to information professionals. Call Beta Phi Mu for availability.

Newsletter. Ed. William Scheeren.

Chapters

Alpha. Univ. of Illinois, Grad. School of Lib. and Info. Science, Urbana, IL 61801; *Beta.* Univ. of Southern California, School of Lib. Science, Univ. Pk., Los Angeles, CA 90007; *Gamma.* Florida State Univ., School of Lib. Science, Tallahassee, FL 32306; *Delta* (Inactive). Loughborough College of Further Education, School of Libnshp., Loughborough, England; *Epsilon.* Univ. of North Carolina, School of Lib. Science, Chapel Hill, NC 27514; *Zeta.* Atlanta Univ., School of Lib. and Info. Studies, Atlanta, GA 30314; *Theta.* Pratt Inst., Grad. School of Lib. and Info. Science, Brooklyn, NY 11205; *Iota.* Catholic Univ. of America, School of Lib. and Info. Science, Washington, DC 20064; Univ. of Maryland, College of Lib. and Info. Services, College Park, MD 20742; *Kappa.* Western Michigan Univ., School of Libnshp., Kalamazoo, MI 49008; *Lambda.* Univ. of Oklahoma, School of Lib. Science, Norman, OK 73019; *Mu.* Univ. of Michigan, School of

Lib. Science, Ann Arbor, MI 48109; *Nu* (Inactive); *Xi.* Univ. of Hawaii, Grad. School of Lib. Studies, Honolulu, HI 96822; *Omicron.* Rutgers Univ., Grad. School of Lib. and Info. Studies, New Brunswick, NJ 08903; *Pi.* Univ. of Pittsburgh, School of Lib. and Info. Science, Pittsburgh, PA 15260; *Rho.* Kent State Univ., School of Lib. Science, Kent, OH 44242; *Sigma.* Drexel Univ., School of Lib. and Info. Science, Philadelphia, PA 19104; *Tau* (Inactive). State Univ. of New York at Geneseo, School of Lib. and Info. Science, Geneseo, NY 14454; *Upsilon.* Univ. of Kentucky, College of Lib. Science, Lexington, KY 40506; *Phi* (Inactive). Univ. of Denver, Grad. School of Libnshp. and Info. Mgt., Denver, CO 80208; *Chi.* Indiana Univ., School of Lib. and Info. Science, Bloomington, IN 47401; *Psi.* Univ. of Missouri at Columbia, School of Lib. and Info. Sciences, Columbia, MO 65211; *Omega* (Inactive). San Jose State Univ., Div. of Lib. Science, San Jose, CA 95192; *Beta Alpha.* Queens College, City College of New York, Grad. School of Lib. and Info. Studies, Flushing, NY 11367; *Beta Beta.* Simmons College, Grad. School of Lib. and Info. Science, Boston, MA 02115; *Beta Delta.* State Univ. of New York at Buffalo, School of Info. and Lib. Studies, Buffalo, NY 14260; *Beta Epsilon.* Emporia State Univ., School of Lib. Science, Emporia, KS 66801; *Beta Zeta.* Louisiana State Univ., Grad. School of Lib. Science, Baton Rouge, LA 70803; *Beta Eta.* Univ. of Texas at Austin, Grad. School of Lib. and Info. Science, Austin, TX 78712; *Beta Theta.* Brigham Young Univ., School of Lib. and Info. Science, Provo, UT 84602; *Beta Iota.* Univ. of Rhode Island, Grad. Lib. School, Kingston, RI 02881; *Beta Kappa.* Univ. of Alabama, Grad. School of Lib. Service, University, AL 35486; *Beta Lambda.* North Texas State Univ., School of Lib. and Info. Science, Denton, TX 76203; Texas Woman's Univ., School of Lib. Science, Denton, TX 76204; *Beta Mu.* Long Island Univ., Palmer Grad. Lib. School, C. W. Post Center, Greenvale, NY 11548; *Beta Nu.* Saint John's Univ., Div. of Lib. and Info. Science, Jamaica, NY 11439; *Beta Xi.* North Carolina Central Univ., School of Lib. Science, Durham, NC 27707; *Beta Omicron.* Univ. of

Tennessee at Knoxville, Grad. School of Lib. and Info. Science, Knoxville, TN 37916; *Beta Pi.* Univ. of Arizona, Grad. Lib. School, Tucson, AZ 85721; *Beta Rho.* Univ. of Wisconsin at Milwaukee, School of Lib. Science, Milwaukee, WI 53201; *Beta Sigma.* Clarion State College, School of Lib. Science, Clarion, PA 16214; *Beta Tau.* Wayne State Univ., Div. of Lib. Science, Detroit, MI 48202; *Beta Upsilon* (Inactive). Alabama A & M Univ., School of Lib. Media, Normal, AL 35762; *Beta Phi.* Univ. of South Florida, Grad. Dept. of Lib., Media, and Info. Studies, Tampa, FL 33620; *Beta Psi.* Univ. of Southern Mississippi, School of Lib. Service, Hattiesburg, MS 39406; *Beta Omega.* Univ. of South Carolina, College of Libnshp., Columbia, SC 29208; *Beta Beta Alpha.* Univ. of California at Los Angeles, Grad. School of Lib. and Info. Science, Los Angeles, CA 90024; *Beta Beta Gamma.* Rosary College, Grad. School of Lib. and Info. Science, River Forest, IL 60305; *Beta Beta Delta.* Univ. of Cologne, Germany; *Beta Beta Epsilon.* Univ. of Wisconsin at Madison, Lib. School, Madison, WI 53706; *Beta Beta Zeta.* Univ. of North Carolina at Greensboro, Dept. of Lib. Science and Educational Technology, Greensboro, NC 27412; *Beta Beta Theta.* Univ. of Iowa, School of Lib. and Info. Science, Iowa City, IA 52242; *Pi Lambda Sigma.* Syracuse Univ., School of Info. Studies, Syracuse, NY 13210.

Bibliographical Society of America

Executive Secretary, Marjory Zaik
Box 397, Grand Central Station, New York, NY 10163
212-647-9171

Object

To promote bibliographical research and to issue bibliographical publications. Organized 1904.

Membership

Memb. 1,300. Dues $30. Year. Jan.–Dec.

Officers (Jan. 1993–Jan. 1995)

Pres. William P. Barlow, Jr.; *V.P.* David Vander Meulen; *Treas.* R. Dyke Benjamin; *Secy.* Marie E. Korey.

Council

Jonathan A. Hill, Katharine Leab, Paul Needham, G. Thomas Tanselle (term expires 1994); Sandra Alston, John Lancaster, Fred Schreiber, Alice Schreyer (1995); James N. Green, Alexandra Mason, Leslie Morris, James E. Walsh (1996).

Publication

Papers (q.; memb.). *Ed.* William S. Peterson, Dept. of English, Univ. of Maryland, College Park, MD 20742.

Committee Chairpersons

Fellowship Program. Richard Landon.
Publications. Katharine Leab.

Canadian Association for Information Science
(Association Canadienne des Sciences de l'Information)

140 Saint George St., Toronto, ON M5S 1A1, Canada
416-978-8876

Object

To bring together individuals and organizations concerned with the production, manipulation, storage, retrieval, and dissemination of information with emphasis on the application of modern technologies in these areas. The Canadian Association for Information Science (CAIS) is dedicated to enhancing the activity of the information transfer process, utilizing the vehicles of research, development, application, and education, and serving as a forum for dialogue and exchange of ideas concerned with the theory and practice of all factors involved in the communication of information.

Membership

Institutions and individuals interested in information science and involved in the gathering, organization, and dissemination of information (computer scientists, documentalists, information scientists, librarians, journalists, sociologists, psychologists, linguists, administrators, etc.) can become members of CAIS. Dues (Inst.) $165; (Personal) $75; (Student) $40.

Board of Directors

Pres. David Lafranchise, External Affairs and International Trade, Lester B. Pearson Bldg., 125 Sussex Dr., Ottawa, ON K1A 0G2. Tel. 613-992-6032; *Past Pres.* Ernst J. Schuegraf, Dept. of Mathematics and Computing Science, Saint Francis Xavier Univ., Antigonish, NS B2G 1C0. Tel. 902-867-2269; *Treas.* Kent Weaver, Univ. of Toronto Lib., 130 Saint George St., Toronto, ON M5S 1A1. Tel. 416-978-7292; *Publications Dir.* Charles Meadow, Faculty of Lib. and Info. Science, Univ. of Toronto, 140 Saint George St., Toronto, ON M5S 1A1. Tel. 416-978-4665; *Journal Ed.* Joan Cherry, Faculty of Lib. and Info. Science, Univ. of Toronto, 140 Saint George St., Toronto, ON M5S 1A1. Tel. 416-978-4663; *Secy.* Mary Nash, Nash Info. Services, 1975 Bel Air Dr., Ottawa, ON K2C 0X1; *Dir.* Margaret E. Gross, Spar Aerospace, 21025 Trans Canada Hwy., Sainte Anne-de-Bellevue, PQ H9X 3R2. Tel. 514-457-2150.

Chapters

CAIS West. Jocelyn Godolphin.
Ottawa. Pat Johnston.
Toronto. Maggie Weaver.

Publication

Canadian Journal of Information and Library Science (q.; $95; outside Canada $110).

Canadian Library Association

Executive Director, Karen Adams
200 Elgin St., Ottawa, ON K2P 1L5, Canada
613-232-9625, FAX 613-563-9895

Object

To provide leadership in the promotion, development, and support of library and information services in Canada for the benefit of association members, the profession, and Canadian society. Offers library school scholarship and book awards; carries on international liaison with other library associations; makes representation to government and official commissions; offers professional development programs; and supports intellectual freedom. Founded in 1946, CLA is a nonprofit voluntary organization governed by an elected executive council.

Membership

Memb. (Indiv.) 4,000; (Inst.) 1,000. Open to individuals, institutions, and groups interested in librarianship and in library and information services. Dues (Indiv.) $55 to $175, depending on salary; (Inst.) from $175 up, graduated on budget basis. Year. Anniversary date renewal.

Officers (1993–1994)

Pres. Françoise Hébert, 7 Thornwood Rd., No. 302, Toronto, ON M4W 2R8. Tel. 416-926-1902; *V.P./Pres.-Elect* Patricia Cavill, 651 Willow Brook Dr. S.E., Calgary, AB T2J 1N6. Tel. 403-278-1630; *Past Pres.* Margaret Andrewes, c/o ISM Lib. Info. Services, 3300 Bloor St. W., West Tower, 16th fl., Etobicoke, ON M8X 2X2. Tel. 416-236-7171 Ext.

353; *Treas.* Deborah deBruijn, Univ. of Calgary Libs., 2500 Univ. Dr. N.W., Calgary, AB T2N 1N4. Tel. 403-220-3461.

Executive Council

Table officers, divisional presidents, and councillors-at-large.

Publications

CM: Canadian Materials for Schools and Libraries (6 per year; $42).
Feliciter (10 per year; newsletter).

Division Representatives

Canadian Association of College and University Libraries. Judith Head, Univ. of Lethbridge, 4401 Univ. Dr., Lethbridge, AB T1K 3M4.
Canadian Association of Public Libraries. Jocelyne LeBel, New Brunswick Lib. Service, Box 6000, Fredericton, NB E3B 5H1.
Canadian Association of Special Libraries and Information Services. Nigel Long, 5310-13531 Deer Run Blvd. S. E., Calgary, AB T2J 6P9.
Canadian Library Trustees Association. Neil Findlay, 18837-99A Ave., Edmonton, AB T5T 3M9.
Canadian School Library Association. Lynne Lighthall, Univ. of British Columbia, 4093 W. 14 Ave., Vancouver, BC V6R 2X3.

Catholic Library Association

Executive Director, Paul J. Ostendorf, Saint Mary's College of Minnesota, Campus Box 26, 700 Terrace Heights, Winona, MN 55987
507-457-6935, FAX 507-459-1565

Object

The promotion and encouragement of Catholic literature and library work through cooperation, publications, education, and information. Founded 1921.

Membership

Memb. 900. Dues $45–$500. Year. July–June.

Officers (1993–1994)

Pres. Paul J. Ostendorf, Saint Mary's College of Minnesota, Campus Box 26, 700 Terrace Heights, Winona, MN 55987-1399. Tel. 507-457-6935; *V.P./Pres.-Elect* Jean R. Bostley, Saint Joseph Central H.S., 22 Maplewood Ave., Pittsfield, MA 01201. Tel. 412-447-9121; *Exec. Dir.* Paul J. Ostendorf.

Address correspondence to the executive director.

Executive Board

Officers; Tina-Karen Forman, UCLA Research Lib., 405 Hilgard Ave., Los Angeles, CA 90024; Nicholas Falco, Queens Borough Public Lib., 1256 Pelham Parkway, Bronx, NY 10461; Mary E. Gallagher, College of Our Lady of the Elms, 291 Springfield St., Chicopee, MA 01013; Kathleen Jastrab Harty, Sacred Heart School of Theology, Box 429, Hales Corners, WI 53130-0429;

Bonaventure Hayes, OFM, Christ the King Seminary, East Aurora, NY 14052-0607; Molly M. Lyons, Saint Patrick's Seminary, 320 Middlefield Ave., Menlo Park, CA 94025; Barbara H. Weathers, Duchesne Academy, 10202 Memorial Dr., Houston, TX 77024.

Publications

Catholic Library World (4 per year; memb.; nonmemb. $60). *Ed.* Allen Gruenke.

Catholic Periodical and Literature Index (q.; $400 for college and university libraries, seminaries, public libraries, and publishers; $200 for school and parish libraries). *Ed.* Dana Cernaianu.

Section Chairpersons

Academic Libraries. Priscilla Berthiaume.
Archives. Mary E. Gallagher.
Children's Libraries. Mary Luke Mulraney.
High School Libraries. Joan B. Richardson.
Parish/Community Libraries. Marcella McGrogan.

Round Table Chairpersons

Bibliographic Instruction. Sister Margaret Ruddy.
Cataloging and Classification. Tina-Karen Forman.

Chief Officers of State Library Agencies

c/o The Council of State Governments
3560 Iron Works Pike, Box 11910, Lexington, KY 40578-1910
606-231-1925, FAX 606-231-1928

Object

To provide a means of cooperative action among its state and territorial members to strengthen the work of the respective state and territorial agencies, and to provide a continuing mechanism for dealing with the problems faced by the heads of these agencies, which are responsible for state and territorial library development.

Membership

The Chief Officers of State Library Agencies (COSLA) is an independent organization of the men and women who head the state and territorial agencies responsible for library development. Its membership consists solely of the top library officers of the 50 states, the District of Columbia, and the territories, variously designated as state librarian, director, commissioner, or executive secretary.

Officers (1992–1994)

Pres. Nancy L. Zussy, State Libn., Washington State Lib., Box 42460, Olympia, WA 98504-2460. Tel. 206-753-2915, FAX 206-586-7575; *V.P./Pres.-Elect* J. Maurice Travillian, Asst. State Superintendent for Libs., Maryland State Dept. of Educ., 200 W. Baltimore St., Baltimore, MD 21201. Tel. 410-333-2113, FAX 410-333-2507; *Secy.* Jane Kolbe, State Libn., South Dakota State Lib., State Lib. Bldg., 800 Governors Dr., Pierre, SD 57501-2294. Tel. 605-773-3131, FAX 605-773-4950; *Treas.* Bridget L. Lamont, Dir., Illinois State Lib., 300 S. Second St., Springfield, IL 62701-1796.

Directors

Officers; *Immediate Past Pres.* Barratt Wilkins; *Dirs.* Amy Owen, John C. Tyson.

Chinese-American Librarians Association

Executive Director, Sheila S. Lai
c/o California State University at Sacramento,
2000 Jed Smith Drive, Sacramento, CA 95819-6039
916-278-6201, FAX 916-363-0868

Object

To enhance communications among Chinese-American librarians as well as between Chinese-American librarians and other librarians; to serve as a forum for discussion of mutual problems and professional concerns among Chinese-American librarians; to promote Sino-American librarianship and library services; and to provide a vehicle whereby Chinese-American librarians may cooperate with other associations and organizations having similar or allied interest.

Membership

Memb. 450. Open to everyone who is interested in the association's goals and activities. Dues (Regular) $15; (Student/Nonsalaried) $7.50; (Inst.) $45; (Permanent) $200.

Officers (July 1993–June 1994)

Pres. Betty L. Tsai; *V.P./Pres.-Elect* Linda Tse; *Exec. Dir.* Sheila S. Lai; *Treas.* Peter Wang.

Publications

Journal of Library and Information Science (2 per year; memb.; nonmemb. $15).
Membership Directory (memb.).
Newsletter (3 per year; memb.; nonmemb. $10).

Committee Chairpersons

Award. Amy D. Seetoo.
Constitution and Bylaws. Eugenia Tang.
Finance. Peter Wang.
Local Arrangements. Nancy Sun Hershoff.
Membership. Corliss Lee, Diana Shih.
Nomination. Carl Chan.
Program Book Editor. Vickie Toy Smith.
Program Planning. Linda Tse.
Public Relations. Angela Yang.
Publications. Wilfred Fong.
Scholarship. Ling-Hwey Jeng.

Task Force (Ad Hoc Committee) Chairpersons

ALA Cultural Diversity Grant Project. Linda Tse.
CALA/APALA Relations. Tze-Chung Li.
Cultural Studies. Marjorie Li.
International Relations. Wei-ling Dai.
Professional Development. Christina Hyun.
Services to Chinese Populations. Linda Tse.

Chapter Presidents

California. Patty Wong.
Greater Mid-Atlantic. Cecilia Chin.
Midwest. Li-Mei Ku.
Northeast. Norma Yueh.
Southwest. Connie Wang.

Journal Officers

Newsletter Eds. Meng-Xiong Liu, Clark Lib., San Jose State Univ., One Washington Sq., San Jose, CA 95192-0028. Tel. 408-924-2817; Emily Fang, c/o 1632 Clement St., San Francisco, CA 94121. Tel. 415-666-0311.

Church and Synagogue Library Association

Box 19357, Portland, OR 97280-0357
503-244-6919

Object

To act as a unifying core for the many existing church and synagogue libraries; to provide the opportunity for a mutual sharing of practices and problems; to inspire and encourage a sense of purpose and mission among church and synagogue librarians; to study and guide the development of church and synagogue librarianship toward recognition as a formal branch of the library profession. Founded 1967.

Membership

Memb. 1,900. Dues (Inst.) $100; (Affiliated) $50; (Church/Synagogue) $30; (Indiv.) $16. Year. July–June.

Officers (July 1993–June 1994)

Pres. William Gentz, 300 E. 34 St., New York, NY 10016; *1st V.P./Pres.-Elect* Russell L. Newburn, 9493 Moulin Ave., Alliance,

OH 44601; *2nd V.P.* Cheri Grout, 132 Foxwood Dr., Brownsburg, IN 46112; *Treas.* J. Robert Waggoner, 413 Robindale Ave., Dearborn, MI 48128; *Past Pres.* Joyce S. Allen, 3815 N. Bolton Ave., Indianapolis, IN 46226.

Executive Board

Officers; committee chairpersons.

Publications

Bibliographies (1–6; price varies).

Church and Synagogue Libraries (bi-mo.; memb.; nonmemb. $18; Canada $21). *Ed.* Lorraine E. Burson.
CSLA Guides (1–16; price varies).

Committee Chairpersons

Awards. Lillian Koppin.
Chapters. Gail Waggoner.
Conference. Mary Beth Conover.
Continuing Education. Naomi Kauffman.
Finance and Fund Raising. Emil Hirsch.
Library Services. Diane van Naerssen.
Nominations and Elections. Eleanor Courtney.
Personnel. Joyce Allen.
Publications. Carol Campbell.

Council of National Library and Information Associations

1700 18th St. N.W., Washington, DC 20009

Object

To provide a central agency for cooperation among library/information associations and other professional organizations of the United States and Canada in promoting matters of common interest.

Membership

Open to national library/information associations and organizations with related interests of the United States and Canada. American Assn. of Law Libs.; American Lib. Assn.; American Society of Indexers; American Theological Lib. Assn.; Art Libs. Society of North America; Assn. of Christian Libns.; Assn. of Jewish Libs.; Catholic Lib. Assn.; Chinese-American Libns. Assn.; Church and Synagogue Lib. Assn.; Council of Planning Libns.; Lib. Binding Inst.; Lutheran Church Lib. Assn.; Medical Lib. Assn.; Music Lib. Assn.; National Libns. Assn.; Society of American Archivists; Special Libs. Assn.; Theatre Lib. Assn.

Officers (July 1993–June 1994)

Chair Madeline Taylor, 36 Park Pl., Brooklyn, NY 11217; *V.Chair/Chair-Elect* Sherry Vellucci, Dept. of Lib. and Info. Science, Saint John's Univ., 8000 Utopia Pkwy., Jamaica, NY 11439; *Past Chair* Kathleen Haefliger, 954 Galen Dr., State College, PA 16803; *Secy./Treas.* Marie F. Melton, RSM, Saint John's Univ. Lib., Rm. 322, 8000 Utopia Pkwy., Jamaica, NY 11439. Tel. 718-990-6735.

Directors

Linda Beck (term expires 1996), Muriel Regan (1994), Norma Yueh (1995).

Council of Planning Librarians

Deborah Thompson-Wise, Editor
552 Hodges Library, University of Tennessee, Knoxville, TN 37996-1000
615-974-0033, FAX 615-974-2708

Object

To provide a special interest group in the field of city and regional planning for libraries and librarians, faculty, professional planners, university, government, and private planning organizations; to provide an opportunity for exchange among those interested in problems of library organization and research and in the dissemination of information about city and regional planning; to sponsor programs of service to the planning profession and librarianship; to advise on library organization for new planning programs; and to aid and support administrators, faculty, and librarians in their efforts to educate the public and their appointed or elected representatives to the necessity for strong library programs in support of planning. Founded 1960.

Membership

Memb. 242. Open to any individual or institution that supports the purpose of the council, upon written application and payment of dues to the treasurer. Dues (Inst.) $45; (Indiv.) $25; (Student) $15. Year. July 1–June 30.

Officers and Board (1993–1994)

Pres. Jane McMaster, Science and Engineering Lib., Ohio State Univ., Columbus, OH 43210. Tel. 614-292-3053; *V.P./Pres.-Elect* Elizabeth Douthitt Byrne, Environmental Design Lib., 210 Wurster Hall, Univ. of California, Berkeley, CA 94720. Tel. 510-643-7323; *Past Pres.* Thelma Helyar, Inst. for Public Policy and Business Research, 607 Blake Hall, Univ. of Kansas, Lawrence, KS 66045-2960; Tel. 913-864-3701; *Treas.* Gretchen Beal, Knoxville–Knox County Metropolitan Planning Commission, 400 Main Ave., Knoxville, TN 37902; *Secy.* Gary Parsons, 373 N.W. 4 Diagonal, No. 204, Boca Raton, FL 33432. Tel. 407-368-9049; *Member-at-Large* Cathy Moulder, McMaster Univ., Hamilton, ON, Canada; *Editor, CPL Newsletter* Lynne De Merritt, Municipal Research and Services Center of Washington, 10517 N.E. 38 Place, Kirkland, WA 98088-7926. Tel. 206-827-4334; *Chair, Editorial Advisory Board* Linda S. Drake, City/Regional Planning Lib., CB#3140, Univ. of North Carolina, Chapel Hill, NC 27599-3140. Tel. 919-962-3983; *Editor, CPL Bibliographies* Deborah Thompson-Wise, 552 Hodges Lib., Univ. of Tennessee, Knoxville 37996-1000.

Publications

Directory of Planning and Urban Affairs Libraries in the United States and Canada ($36).

CPL Bibliographies may be purchased on standing order or by individual issue. Catalog sent upon request. The following is only a partial list of publications:

No. 289. *Tackling Environmental Problems across the Media of Air, Water, and Land.* Feng Liu, 1993 ($18).

No. 290. *Ethics in Planning.* Marta Escuin-Rubio and Jerome Kaufman, 1993 ($20).

No. 291. *Metropolitan Reorganization: A Response to Urban Fragmentation.* Roger K. Hedrick, 1993 ($18).

No. 292. *Bibliography on Growth Management.* Lynne De Merritt, 1993 ($18).

No. 293. *Parking Publications for Planners.* Dennis Jenks, 1993 ($18).

No. 294. *Recent Publications in Planning, Volume 1: Subject Index, Citations 1-1118.* Dennis Jenks, 1993 ($18).

No. 295. *Recent Publications in Planning, Volume 2: Subject Index, Citations 1119-2152.* Dennis Jenks, 1993 ($18).

Council on Library Resources

1400 16th St. N.W., Suite 510, Washington, DC 20036-2217
202-483-7474, FAX 202-483-6410, Internet: clr@cni.org

Object

A private operating foundation, the council seeks to assist in finding solutions to the problems of libraries, particularly academic and research libraries. In pursuit of this aim, the council conducts its own projects, makes grants to and contracts with other organizations and individuals, and calls upon many others for advice and assistance with its work. The council was established in 1956 by the Ford Foundation, and it now receives support from a number of private foundations and other sources. Current program emphases include human resources, access and processing, economics of libraries, and infrastructure.

Membership

The council's membership and board of directors are limited to 25.

Officers

Chair Maximilian Kempner; *V.Chair* Charles Churchwell; *Pres.* W. David Penniman; *Secy.-Treas.* Mary Agnes Thompson.
Address correspondence to headquarters.

Publications

Annual Report.
CLR Reports (newsletter).

Federal Library and Information Center Committee

Executive Director, Mary Berghaus Levering
Library of Congress, Washington, DC 20540-5100
202-707-4800

Object

The committee makes recommendations on federal library and information policies, programs, and procedures to federal agencies and to others concerned with libraries and information centers.

The committee coordinates cooperative activities and services among federal libraries and information centers and serves as a forum to consider issues and policies that affect federal libraries and information centers, needs and priorities in providing information services to the government and to the nation at large, and efficient and cost-effective use of federal library and information resources and services.

Furthermore, the committee promotes improved access to information, continued development and use of the Federal Library and Information Network (FEDLINK), research and development in the application of new technologies to federal libraries and information centers, improvements in the management of federal libraries and information centers, and relevant education opportunities. Founded 1965.

Membership

Libn. of Congress, Dir. of the National Agricultural Lib., Dir. of the National Lib. of Medicine, representatives from each of the other executive departments, and representatives from each of the following agencies: National Aeronautics and Space Admin., National Science Foundation, Smithsonian Institution, U.S. Supreme Court, U.S. Info. Agency, National Archives and Records

Admin., Admin. Offices of the U.S. Courts, Defense Technical Info. Center, Government Printing Office, National Technical Info. Service, and Office of Scientific and Technical Info. (Dept. of Energy), Exec. Office of the President, Dept. of the Army, Dept. of the Navy, Dept. of the Air Force, and chairperson of the FEDLINK Advisory Council. Fifteen additional voting member agencies shall be selected on a rotating basis by the voting members of FEDLINK and nine rotating members through selection by the permanent members of the committee. These rotating members will serve three terms. One representative from each of the following agencies is invited as an observer to committee meetings: General Accounting Office, General Services Admin., Joint Committee on Printing, National Commission on Libs. and Info. Science, Office of Mgt. and Budget, Office of Personnel Mgt., and Lib. of Congress Financial Services Directorate.

Officers

Chair James H. Billington, Libn. of Congress; *Chair Designate* Donald C. Curran, Assoc. Libn. for Constituent Services, Lib. of Congress; *Exec. Dir.* Mary Berghaus Levering, Federal Lib. and Info. Center Committee, Lib. of Congress, Washington, DC 20540-5100.

Address correspondence to the executive director.

Publications

Annual FLICC Forum on Federal Information Policies (summary and papers).
Annual Report.
FEDLINK Technical Notes (mo.).
FLICC Newsletter (q.).

Federal Publishers Committee

Chairperson, John Weiner
Energy Information Administration, EI-23, Mail Sta. BG-057,
1000 Independence Ave. S.W., Washington, DC 20585
202-586-6537, FAX 202-586-0114

Object

To foster and promote effective management of data development and dissemination in the federal government through exchange of information, and to act as a focal point for federal agency publishing.

Membership

Memb. 700. Membership is available to persons involved in publishing and dissemination in federal government departments, agencies, and corporations, as well as independent organizations concerned with federal government publishing and dissemination. Some key federal government organizations represented are the Joint Committee on Printing, Government Printing Office, National Technical Info. Service, National Commission on Libs. and Info. Science, and the Lib. of Congress. Meetings are held monthly during business hours.

Officers

Chair John Weiner; *Secy.* Marilyn Marbrook.

Committee Chairpersons

Programs. Sandra Smith.
Roundtable Activity. June Malina.

Information Industry Association

555 New Jersey Ave. N.W., Suite 800, Washington, DC 20001
202-639-8262, FAX 202-638-4403

Membership

Memb. 500+ companies. Open to companies involved in the creation, distribution, and use of information products, services, and technologies. For details on membership and dues, write to the association headquarters.

Staff

Pres. Kenneth B. Allen; *V.P.* Emily G. Pilk; *V.P. and General Counsel* Steven J. Metalitz; *V.P. Memb.* Judith Angerman; *Dir., Industry Relations* Michael I. Atkin; *Dir., Meetings* Carol Madden; *Dir., Global Issues Council and Optical Publishing Div.* Robert Vitro; *Dir., Small and Emerging Business Council and Voice Info. Services Div.* Terri L. Lageman.

Board of Directors

Chair Hugh Yarrington, Commerce Clearing House Inc.; *Chair-Elect* Andrew Prozes, Southam Info. and Technology Group; *Past Chair* John Hockenberry, Washington Post; *Treas.* Paul Wojcik, Bureau of National Affairs Inc.; *Secy.* W. Leo McBlain, ADP Brokerage Info. Services; *V.Chairs* James E. Coane, Telebase Systems Inc.; Linda J. Laskowski, U S WEST Communications; Paul P. Massa, Congressional Info. Service; *Membs.* Kathleen Bingham, Find/SVP Inc.; Steven Graham, AT&T Microelectronics; Michael Jabara, Jabara and Co.; Natalie S. Lang, Oryx Press; Richard Levine, Dow Jones and Co.; Thomas McClain, Dun and Bradstreet Info. Services; J. Edward McEntire, Info. Handling Services; Thomas J. McLeod, West Publishing; Barbara A. Munder, McGraw-Hill; Joseph Rhyne, Mead Data Central; Peter Simon, Reed Reference Publishing; Patrick J. Tierney, Dialog Info. Services; Lawrence Wills, IBM Corp.

Division Chairpersons

Directory. Russell Perkins, Morgan-Rand Inc.
Electronic Information Services. Huw Morgan, Southam Info. and Technology Group.
Financial Information Services. W. Leo McBlain, ADP Brokerage Info. Services.
Optical Publishing. Paul Earl, Emerging Technology Applications.
Voice Information Services. Thomas Pace, Dow Jones and Co.

Council Chairpersons

Global Issues. Andrew Prozes, Southam Info. and Technology Group.
Public Policy and Government Relations. Cynthia Braddon, McGraw-Hill.
Small and Emerging Business. H. Donald Wilson, Conquest Software.

Publication

Information Sources (annual; memb. $55; nonmemb. $95).

Lutheran Church Library Association

Executive Director, Leanna D. Kloempken
122 W. Franklin Ave., Minneapolis, MN 55404
612-870-3623

Object

To promote the growth of church libraries by publishing a quarterly journal, *Lutheran Libraries;* furnishing booklists; assisting member libraries with technical problems; and providing meetings for mutual encouragement, assistance, and exchange of ideas among members. Founded 1958.

Membership

Memb. 1,800. Dues $25, $37.50, $50, $75, $100, $500, $1,000. Year. Jan.–Jan.

Officers (Jan. 1993–Jan. 1995)

Pres. Robert Kruger, 15180 County Rd. 40, Carver, MN 55315; *V.P.* Charles R. Mann, 21512 Maple Ave., Rogers, MN 55374; *Secy.* Evelyn Pearson, 9550 Collegeview Rd., No. 330, Bloomington, MN 55437; *Treas.* Marilyn Anderson, 5328 51st Ave. N., Minneapolis, MN 55429.

Address correspondence to the executive director.

Directors

Hazel Arndt, Odella Baak, Lucille Christianson, Viola Gering, Ardis Jordahl, Vernita Kennen, Marilyn Miller.

Publication

Lutheran Libraries (q.; memb.; nonmemb. $25).

Board Chairpersons

Advisory. Rev. Rolf Aaseng.
Council of National Library and Information Associations. Wilma W. Jensen.
Finance. L. Edwin Wang.
Library Services. Betty LeDell.
Membership. To be appointed.
Publications. Rod Olson.

Medical Library Association

Executive Director, Carla Funk
6 N. Michigan Ave., Suite 300, Chicago, IL 60602
312-419-9094, FAX 312-419-8950

Object

The major purposes of the Medical Library Association (MLA) are to foster medical and allied scientific libraries, to promote the educational and professional growth of health science librarians, and to exchange medical literature among the members. Through its programs and publications, MLA encourages professional development of its membership, whose foremost concern is dissemination of health sciences information for those in research, education, and patient care. Founded 1898; incorporated 1934.

Membership

Memb. (Inst.) 1,300; (Indiv.) 3,700. Institutional members are medical and allied scientific libraries. Individual members are people who are (or were at the time membership was established) engaged in professional library or bibliographic work in medical and allied scientific libraries or people who are interested in medical or allied scientific libraries. Dues (Student) $25; (Emeritus) $40; (Intro.) $75; (Indiv.) $110; (Sustaining) $345; and (Inst.) $175–$410, based on the number of the library's periodical subscriptions. Members may be affiliated with one or more of MLA's 24 special-interest sections and 14 regional chapters.

Officers

Pres. June H. Fulton, Medical Documentation Service, Inst. for Scientific Info., 3501 Market St., Philadelphia, PA 19104; *Pres. Elect* Fred. W. Roper, *Past Pres.* Jacqueline D. Bastille, Treadwell Lib., Massachusetts General Hospital, Fruit St., Boston, MA 02114.

Directors

Karen Brewer (term expires 1994), Janet S. Fisher (1996), Carole M. Gilbert (1996), Kathryn J. Hoffman (1995), Christiane J. Jones (1996), Wayne J. Peay (1994), Daniel T. Richards (1996), Ada M. Seltzer (1995), M. Sandra Wood (1995).

Publications

Bulletin of the Medical Library Association (q.; $136).
Directory of the Medical Library Association, 1993/94 ($150).
MLA News (10 per year; $48.50).
Miscellaneous (request current list from association headquarters).

Committee Chairpersons

Awards. Nancy W. Clemmons.

Books (Panel). Ruth Holst.
Bulletin Editorial Board. Naomi C. Broering.
Bulletin Evaluation. Alan Carr.
Bylaws. David S. Curry.
Continuing Education. Susan B. Case.
Credentialing. Jo Ann Bell.
Exchange (Advisory Committee). Darel J. Robb.
Governmental Relations. Sara Jean Jackson.
Grants and Scholarship. Jett McCann.
Health Sciences Library Technicians. Diane Robbins Riley.
Hospital Libraries. Bernie Todd Smith.
Joseph Leiter NLM/MLA Lectureship. Lois Ann Colaianni.
Membership. Marion Holena Levine.
National Program (1994). Neil Rambo.
National Program (1995). Linda A. Watson.
News Evaluation. Jeannette C. McCray.
Professional Recognition (Review Panel). Faith A. Meakin.
Publications. Karen M. Bensing.
Publishing and Information Industries Relations. Frances L. Chen.
Status and Economic Interests of Health Sciences Library Personnel. Penny T. Ward.

Ad Hoc Committee Chairpersons

Committee to Establish Cunningham Endowment. Robert G. Cheshier.
Ethics Task Force. Richard A. Lyders.
Executive Committee. June H. Fulton.
Joint MLA/AAHSLD Legislative Task Force. June Glaser.
Nominating Committee. Richard A. Lyders.
Platform for Change Implementation Task Force. Mary M. Horres.
Research Task Force. Prudence W. Dalrymple.
Task Force on MLA/NLM Collaboration. Susan Russell Lessick.

Music Library Association

Box 487, Canton, MA 02021
617-828-8450, FAX 617-828-8915

Object

To promote the establishment, growth, and use of music libraries; to encourage the collection of music and musical literature in libraries; to further studies in musical bibliography; to increase efficiency in music library service and administration; and to promote the profession of music librarianship. Founded 1931.

Membership

Memb. 1,900. Dues (Inst.) $71; (Indiv.) $65; (Student) $35. Year. Sept. 1–Aug. 31.

Officers

Pres. Michael Ochs, 98 Ridge Ave., Newton Centre, MA 02159; *Past Pres.* Don L. Roberts, Music Lib., Northwestern Univ., Evanston, IL 60208-2300; *Rec. Secy.* Nancy Bren Nuzzo, 68 Hillside Dr., Williamsville, NY 14221; *Treas.* Diane Parr Walker, 1437 Rugby Ave., Charlottesville, VA 22901-3848; *Exec. Secy.* Richard Griscom, Anderson Music Lib., Univ. of Louisville, Louisville, KY 40292.

Members-at-Large

Victor Cardell, UCLA; Beth Christensen, Saint Olaf College; Elizabeth Davis, Columbia Univ.; David Hunter, Univ. of Texas at Austin; Paula Matthews, Bates College; Carol Tatian, Brown Univ.

Special Officers

Business Mgr. James S. P. Henderson, Box 487, Canton, MA 02021.
Convention Mgr. Ned Quist, Arthur Friedheim Peabody Conservatory of Music,

One E. Mount Vernon Place, Baltimore, MD 21202.
Placement. Pat Fisken, Paddock Music Lib., Dartmouth College, Hanover, NH 03755.
Publicity. Richard E. Jones, 1904 Sandlewood Dr., Greencastle, IN 46135-9214.

Publications

MLA Index Series (irreg.; price varies).
MLA Newsletter (q.; memb.).
MLA Technical Reports (irreg.; price varies).
Music Cataloging Bulletin (mo.; $25).
Notes (q.; indiv. $60; inst. $65).

Committee Chairpersons

Administration. Charles P. Coldwell, Seattle Public Lib.
Bibliographic Control. Jennifer Bowen, Eastman School of Music.
Development. Geraldine Ostrove, Music Div., Lib. of Congress. Tel. 202-707-5503.
Education. Laura Dankner, Loyola Univ., New Orleans, LA. Tel. 504-865-2367.
Finance. Victor Cardell, UCLA.
Walter Gerboth Award. David C. Hunter, Univ. of Texas at Austin.
Legislation. Mary Davidson, Sibley Music Lib., Rochester, NY. Tel. 716-274-1350.
Nominating. To be appointed.
Preservation. John Shepard, New York Public Lib. Tel. 212-870-1654.
Public Libraries. Carolyn Dow, Lincoln (NE) City Libs.
Publications. Ruth Henderson, City Univ. of New York. Tel. 212-690-4174.
Publications Awards. Pauline S. Bayne, Univ. of Tennessee.
Reference and Public Service. Judy Tsou, Univ. of California, Berkeley. Tel. 415-643-6197.
Resource Sharing and Collection Development. Elizabeth Davis, Columbia Univ.

National Association of Government Archives and Records Administrators

Executive Director, Bruce W. Dearstyne
New York State Archives
10A46 Cultural Education Center, Albany, NY 12230
518-473-8037

Object

Founded in 1984, the association is successor to the National Association of State Archives and Records Administrators, which had been established in 1974. NAGARA is a growing nationwide association of local, state, and federal archivists and records administrators, and others interested in improved care and management of government records. NAGARA promotes public awareness of government records and archives management programs, encourages interchange of information among government archives and records management agencies, develops and implements professional standards of government records and archival administration, and encourages study and research into records management problems and issues.

Membership

State archival and records management agencies are NAGARA's sustaining members, but individual membership is open to local governments, federal agencies, and to any individual or organization interested in improved government records programs.

Officers

Pres. Howard Lowell, Delaware State Archives; V.P. David Hoober, Arizona Dept. of Lib. Archives and Public Records; Secy. Tyrone Butler, New York City Dept. of Records and Info. Services; Treas. James Moore, Western Washington Univ.

Publications

Clearinghouse (q.; memb)
Government Records Issues (series).
Information Clearinghouse Needs of the Archival Profession (report).
Local Government Records.
Preservation Needs in State Archives (report).
Program Reporting Guidelines for Government Records Programs.
Technical Publications (series).

National Federation of Abstracting and Information Services

Executive Diretor, Ann Marie Cunningham
1429 Walnut St., Philadelphia, PA 19102
215-563-2406, FAX 215-563-2848

Object

NFAIS is an international, not-for-profit membership organization comprising leading information producers, distributors, and corporate users of secondary information. Its purpose is to serve the information community through education, research, and publication. Founded 1958.

Membership

Memb. 70+. Full membership (regular and government) is open to organizations that, as a substantial part of their activity, produce secondary information services for external use. Secondary information products are compilations containing printed or electronic summaries of, or references to, multiple sources of publicly available information. For example, organizations that assemble bibliographic citations, abstracts, indexes, and data are all secondary information services.

Associate membership is available to organizations that operate or manage online information services, networks, inhouse information centers, and libraries; conduct research or development work in information science or systems; are otherwise involved in the generation, promotion, or distribution of secondary information products under contract; or publish primary information sources.

Members pay dues annually based on the fiscal year of July 1–June 30. Dues are assessed based on the member's revenue derived from information-related activities.

Officers (1993–1994)

Pres. Kurt Molholm; *Pres.-Elect* Dennis Auld; *Past Pres.* Monica Pronin; *Secy.* Bonnie Maxwell; *Treas.* Jim Ashling.

Directors

Miriam Chall, Gladys Cotter, Taissa Kusma, Delores Meglio, John Regazzi, William Schlegel, Ralph Ubico.

Staff

Exec. Dir. Ann Marie Cunningham; *Publications Coord.* Wendy Wicks; *Promotions Coord.* Shawn Louise Clawson; *Financial Asst.* Wendy Carter; *Admin. Asst.* Katrina LeBlanc.

Publications

Automated Support to Indexing (1992; memb. $80; nonmemb. $100).

CD-ROM for Information Distribution (1992; memb. $80; nonmemb. $100).

Customer Services and User Training (1991; memb. $40; nonmemb. $50).

Developing New Markets for Information Products (1993; memb. $50; nonmemb. $60).

Flexible Workstyles in the Information Industry (1993; memb. $50; nonmemb. $60).

Guide to Careers in Abstracting and Indexing (1992; memb. $20; nonmemb. $25).

NFAIS Newsletter (mo.; North America $110; non-North America, $125).

Recognition Technology in the Information Industry (1992; memb. $80; nonmemb. $100).

Three Views of the Internet (1993; memb. $50; nonmemb. $60).

National Information Standards Organization

Executive Director, Patricia Harris
Box 1056, Bethesda, MD 20827
301-975-2814, FAX 301-869-8071

Object

To develop technical standards used in libraries, publishing, and information services. Experts from the information field volunteer to lend their expertise in the development and writing of NISO standards. The standards are approved by the consensus of NISO's voting membership, which consists of 57 voting members representing libraries, government, associations, and private businesses and organizations. NISO is supported by its membership and corporate grants. Formerly a committee of the American National Standards Institute (ANSI), NISO, formed in 1939, was incorporated in 1983 as a nonprofit educational organization. NISO is accredited by ANSI and serves as the U.S. Technical Advisory Group to ISO/TC 46.

Membership

Memb. 57. Open to any organization, association, government agency, or company—

national in scope—willing to participate in and having substantial concern for the development of NISO standards.

Officers

Chair Michael Mellinger, Data Research Associates, Saint Louis, MO; *Past Chair* James Rush, PALINET, Philadelphia, PA; *V.Chair/Chair-Elect* Michael J. McGill, Univ. of Michigan, Ann Arbor, MI; *Treas.* Heike Kordish, New York Public Lib., NY; *Secy.* Patricia Harris, NISO, Bethesda, MD; Bob Badger, Springer Verlag, New York, NY; Shirley Kistler Baker, Washington Univ., Saint Louis, MO; Joel Baron, Faxon Co., Westwood, MA; Bill Bartenbach, Engi-

neering Info., Hoboken, NJ; Marjorie Hlava, Access Innovations, Albuquerque, NM; John Kolman, NOTIS Systems, Evanston, IL; Rebecca Lenzini, CARL Systems, Denver, CO; Clifford Lynch, Univ. of California, Oakland, CA; Nolan Pope, Univ. of Wisconsin, Madison, WI.

Publications

Information Standards Quarterly (q.; $65; foreign $85). *Ed.* Pat Ensor.

NISO published standards are available from NISO Press, Box 338, Oxon Hill, MD 20750-0338. Tel. 301-567-9522, 800-282-6476, FAX 301-567-9553.

National Librarians Association

Executive Secretary, Peter Dollard
Box 486, Alma, MI 48801
FAX 517-463-8694

Object

To promote librarianship, to develop and increase the usefulness of libraries, to cultivate the science of librarianship, to protect the interest of professionally qualified librarians, and to perform other functions necessary for the betterment of the profession of librarians, rather than as an association of libraries. Established 1975.

Membership

Memb. 200. Dues $20/year; $35/2 years; (Students, Retired, and Unemployed Libns.) $10. Floating membership year. Any person interested in librarianship and libraries who holds a graduate degree in library science may become a member upon election by the executive board and payment of the annual dues. The executive board may authorize exceptions to the degree requirements for applicants who present evidence of outstanding contributions to the profession. Student

membership is available to those graduate students enrolled full time at any ALA-accredited library school.

Officers

Pres. Matthew Kubiak, Bloomington, IL. Tel. 309-828-6091; *V.P./Pres.-Elect* Carol Meyer, Cincinnati, OH. Tel. 513-632-8372; *Secy.-Treas.* Peter Kaatrude, Port Arthur, TX. Tel. 409-983-4921.

Executive Board

Officers; *Past Pres.* Alvin Bailey; *Members-at-Large* Don Barlow, Elizabeth Crabb, Joseph Harzbecker, Don Tipka, Hope Waller.

Publication

National Librarian (q.; $15). *Ed.* Peter Dollard.

REFORMA
(National Association to Promote Library Services to the Spanish Speaking)

President, Camila A. Alire
Auraria Library, Lawrence at 11th, Denver, CO 80204
303-556-3526, FAX 303-556-3528

Object

To support the active recruitment of bilingual and bicultural librarians to meet the needs of the Spanish-speaking community.

Membership

Memb. 559. Any person who is supportive of the goals and objectives of REFORMA.

Officers

Pres. Camila A. Alire, Auraria Lib., Lawrence at 11th, Denver, CO 80204. Tel. 303-556-3526, FAX 303-556-3528; *V.P./Pres.-Elect* Gilda Baeza Ortego, Wildenthal Memorial Lib., Sul Ross Univ., Alpine, TX 79832. Tel. 915-837-8124, FAX 915-837-8400; *Past Pres.* Martin Gomez, Oakland Public Lib., 125 14th St., Oakland, CA 95612. Tel. 510-238-3281, FAX 510-238-2232; *Treas.* Rene Amaya, 1750 Coolidge Ave., Altadena, CA 91001; *Secy.* Ivonne Jimenez, El Paso Public Lib., 501 N. Oregon St., El Paso, TX 79901. Tel. 915-543-5418, FAX 915-543-5410; *Newsletter Ed.* Edward Erazo, New Mexico State Univ., Dept. 3475, Box 30006, Las Cruces, NM 88003-0006. Tel. 505-646-6930, FAX 505-581-4067; *Archivist/Historian* Salvador Guerena, Univ. Lib.-CEMA, Univ. of California, Santa Barbara, CA 93106. Tel. 805-893-8563, FAX 805-893-4676.

Publication

REFORMA Newsletter (q.; memb.). *Ed.* Edward Erazo, New Mexico State Univ., Dept. 3475, Box 30006, Las Cruces, NM 88003-0006. Tel. 505-646-6930, FAX 505-581-4067.

Committees

Book Awards. Sandra Bandarrama.
Children's Services. Oralia Garza de Cortez.
Membership. Al Milo.
Nominations. Ramiro Salazar.
Organizational Development. John Ayala.
Public Relations. Edward Erazo.
Scholarship. Orlando Archibeque.
Ways and Means. Raul Huerta.

Meetings

All meetings take place at the American Library Association's Midwinter meeting and annual conference.

Research Libraries Group Inc.

Director of Corporate Communications, Jennifer Hartzell
1200 Villa St., Mountain View, CA 94041-1100
415-691-2207

Object

The Research Libraries Group (RLG) is a not-for-profit international consortium of over 140 universities, archives, historical societies, museums, and learned societies. Its mission is to improve access to information that supports research and learning. RLG owns and operates RLIN®—the Research Libraries Information Network—to serve the information access and management needs of its members, nonmember institutions, and individuals worldwide.

Membership

Memb. 140+. Membership is open to any nonprofit institution with an educational, cultural, or scientific mission. There are two membership categories: general and special. General members are institutions that serve a clientele of more than 5,000 faculty, academic staff, research staff, professional staff, students, fellows, or members. Special members serve 5,000 or fewer faculty, academic staff, research staff, professional staff, students, fellows, or members.

Directors

Millicent D. Abell, Yale Univ.; Edward W. Barry, Oxford Univ. Press; Edwin C. Bridges, Alabama Dept. of Archives and History; David H. Cohen, Northwestern Univ.; John H. D'Arms, Univ. of Michigan; Joan I. Gotwals, Emory Univ.; Peter S. Homulos, Canadian Heritage Info. Network; Paula T. Kaufman, Univ. of Tennessee; Peter Lyman, Univ. of Southern Calif.; James Michalko, RLG; Charles E. Miller, Florida State Univ.; Paul H. Mosher, Univ. of Pennsylvania;

Roger W. Moss, Athenaeum of Philadelphia; Trudy H. Peterson, National Archives and Records Admin.; David H. Stam, Syracuse Univ.; Winston Tabb, Lib. of Congress.

Staff

Pres. James Michalko; *V.P., Planning and Research Resources* John Haeger; *Dir., Info. Delivery Services* James Campbell; *Dir., Access Services* Wayne Davison; *Dir., Customer and Operations Support* Jack Crantham; *Dir., Corporate Communications* Jennifer Hartzell; *Dir., Member Support and Services* Patricia McClung; *Dir., Development* David Richards; *Dir., Finance and Administration* Molly Singer; *Dir., Lib. and Bibliographic Services* Karen Smith-Yoshimura.

Publications

The Research Libraries Group News (3 per year; newsletter).
Information Needs in the Humanities.
Information Needs in the Sciences.
Information Needs in the Social Sciences.
Photograph Preservation and the Research Library.
RLG in Perspective: Focusing Collaboration in the 1990s.
RLG Preservation Microfilming Handbook.

Society for Scholarly Publishing

Executive Director, Francine Butler
c/o Resource Center for Associations,
10200 W. 44 Ave., Suite 304, Wheat Ridge, CO 80033
303-422-3914

Object

To draw together individuals involved in the process of scholarly publishing. This process requires successful interaction of the many functions performed within the scholarly community. The Society for Scholarly Publishing (SSP) provides the leadership for such interaction by creating opportunities for the exchange of information and opinions among

scholars, editors, publishers, librarians, printers, booksellers, and all others engaged in scholarly publishing.

Membership

Open to all with an interest in scholarly publishing and information dissemination. There are four categories of membership: individual, $50; contributing, $250; sustaining, $500; and sponsoring, $1,500. Year. Jan. 1–Dec. 31.

Executive Committee (July 1992–June 1994)

Pres. Robert Shirrell, Univ. of Chicago Press, 5720 S. Woodlawn Ave., Chicago, IL 60637. Tel. 312-702-8785, FAX 312-702-0694; *V.P.* Christine Lamb, FRS Inc., 238 Main St., Suite 201, Cambridge, MA 02142; *Secy.-Treas.* Michael Leonard, MIT Press, 55 Hayward St., Cambridge, MA 02142.

Directors

Executive Committee; Czeslaw Jan Grycz, Univ. of California, 300 Lakeside Dr., 8th fl., Oakland, CA 94612-3550; Phyllis Hall, IEEE, 345 E. 47 St., New York, NY 10017-2394; Isabella L. Hinds, Copyright Clearance Center, 27 Congress St., Salem, MA 01970; Karen Hunter, Elsevier Science Publishing, 655 Sixth Ave., New York, NY 10010; Stephen Prudhomme, National Research Council–Canada, Sussex Dr., Rm. 1011,

Ottawa, ON K1A 0R6, Canada; Robert H. Marks, Dir., Publications Div., American Chemical Society, 1155 16th St. N.W., Washington, DC 20036; Nina Matheson, Dir., Welsh Lib., Johns Hopkins Univ., 1900 E. Monument St., Baltimore, MD 21205; Cynthia Smith, Aspen Publishers, 200 Orchard Ridge Dr., Gaithersburg, MD 20878; *Exec. Dir.* Francine Butler, 10200 W. 44 Ave., Suite 304, Wheat Ridge, CO 80033; *Assoc. Dir.* Jerry Bowman, 10200 W. 44 Ave., Suite 304, Wheat Ridge, CO 80033.

Committee Chairpersons

Annual Meeting. Nancy Hammerman.
Education. Barbara Meyers.
Executive. Robert Shirrell.
Membership. Mark Meade.
Nominations. Judy Holoviak.

Meetings

An annual meeting is conducted in either May or June. The location changes each year. Additionally, SSP conducts several seminars throughout the year.

Society of American Archivists

Executive Director, Anne P. Diffendal
600 S. Federal St., Suite 504, Chicago, IL 60605
312-922-0140, FAX 312-347-1452

Object

To promote sound principles of archival economy and to facilitate cooperation among archivists and archival agencies. Founded 1936.

Membership

Memb. 4,600. Dues (Indiv.) $55–$155, graduated according to salary; (Assoc.) $55, domestic; (Student) $35, with a two-year maximum on membership; (Inst.) $200; (Sustaining) $400.

Officers (1993–1994)

Pres. Edie Heolin; *V.P.* Maygene Daniels, National Gallery of Art; *Treas.* William Maher, Univ. of Illinois at Champaign.

Council

Karen Benedict, Luciana Duranti, Tim Ericson, Margaret Hedstrom, Tom Hickerson, Mary Janzen, Rand Jimerson, Waverly Lowell, Elizabeth Yakel.

Staff

Exec. Dir. Anne P. Diffendal; *Memb. Asst.* Bernice E. Brack; *System Admin.* Jim Sauder; *Managing Ed.* Teresa Brinati; *Publications Asst.* Troy Sturdivant; *Bookkeeper* Carroll Dendler; *Sr. Archivist* Jane Kenamore; *Meeting Planner* Debra Mills.

Publications

American Archivist (q.; $75; foreign $90). *Ed.* Richard Cox; *Managing Ed.* Teresa Brinati. Books for review and related correspondence should be addressed to the managing editor.

SAA Newsletter (6 per year; memb.). *Ed.* Teresa Brinati.

Special Libraries Association

Executive Director, David R. Bender
1700 18th St. N.W., Washington, DC 20009-2508
202-234-4700, FAX 202-265-9317

Object

To provide an association of individuals and organizations having a professional, scientific, or technical interest in library and information science, especially as these are applied in the recording, retrieval, and dissemination of knowledge and information in areas such as the physical, biological, technical, and social sciences, the humanities, and business; and to promote and improve the communication, dissemination, and use of such information and knowledge for the benefit of libraries or other educational organizations. Organized 1909.

Membership

Memb. 14,000. Dues (Sustaining) $300; (Indiv.) $75; (Student) $15. Year. Jan.–Dec. or July–June.

Officers (July 1993–June 1994)

Pres. Miriam A. Drake, Price Gilbert Memorial Lib., Georgia Inst. of Technology, Atlanta, GA 30332. Tel. 404-894-4510, FAX 404-894-6084; *Pres.-Elect* Didi Pancake, 203 Raymond Ave., Charlottesville, VA 22903-3640. Tel. 804-295-0419, FAX 804-924-4338; *Past Pres.* Catherine Scott, 700 Seventh St. S.W., No. 435, Washington, DC 20024. Tel. 202-357-2139, FAX 202-786-2443; *Treas.* Richard E. Wallace, Technical Info. Center, A. E. Staley Manufacturing Co., 2200 Eldorado St., Decatur, IL 62525-1801. Tel. 217-421-3283, FAX 217-421-2519; *Chapter Cabinet Chair* Janice C. Anderson, Access Info. Assocs., 4710 Bellaire Blvd., Suite 140, Bellaire, TX 77401-4505. Tel. 713-664-4357, FAX 713-664-4825; *Chapter Cabinet Chair-Elect* Bill Fisher, Div. of Lib. and Info. Science, San Jose State Univ., One Washington Sq., San Jose, CA 95192-0029. Tel. 408-924-2494, FAX 408-924-2476; *Div. Cabinet Chair* Jean M. Scanlan, Price Waterhouse Info. Center, 160 Federal St., Boston, MA 02110. Tel. 617-439-7412, FAX 617-439-7453; *Div. Cabinet Chair-Elect* Monica Ertel, Apple Lib. and Info. Services, Apple Computer, 4 Infinite Loop, MS304-2AC, Cupertino, CA 95014. Tel. 408-974-2552, FAX 408-725-8502; *Secy.* Judy Macfarlane, Info. Resources, KPMG Peat Marwick Thorne, 2000 McGill College Ave., No. 1900, Montreal, PQ H3A 3H8, Canada. Tel. 514-840-2254, FAX 514-840-2233.

Directors

Officers; Billie M. Connor (term expires 1995); Betty Eddison (1994); Richard Geiger (1996); Sylvia E. A. Piggott (1994); Ethel Salonen (1996).

Publications

Special Libraries (q.) and *SpeciaList* (mo.). Cannot be ordered separately ($60 for both; foreign $65). *Ed.* Gail Repsher.

Committee Chairpersons

Affirmative Action. Nettie Seaberry.
Association Office Operations. Miriam A. Drake.
Awards and Honors. Guy St. Clair.
Bylaws. M. Kay Mowery.
Cataloging. Lillian R. Mesner.
Committee on Committees. Laura N. Gasaway.
Conference Program, Atlanta (1994). Judith Field.
Conference Program, Montreal (1995). Karen Holloway.

Consultation. Lawrence Himelfarb.
Copyright Implementation. Sarah K. Wiant.
Finance. Richard E. Wallace.
Government Relations. Pamela M. Dragovich.
International Relations. Katherine M. Richards.
Networking. Doris Small Helfer.
Nominating. Helen Manning.
Professional Development. Toby Pearlstein.
Public Relations. Anne K. Abate.
Publications. Susan Fifer-Canby.
Publisher Relations. Annie M. Brewer.
Research. Ann W. Talcott.
SLA Scholarship. Kathleen Eisenbeis.
Special Libraries Education Advisory Board. Marilyn Stark.
Strategic Planning. Billie M. Connor.
Student Relations Officer. Marion Paris.
Technical Standards. Marjorie Hlava.
Tellers. Marcia C. Stone.

Theatre Library Association

Secretary-Treasurer, Richard M. Buck
New York Public Library for the Performing Arts
111 Amsterdam Ave., New York, NY 10023-7498
212-870-1644, 212-870-1670

Object

To further the interests of collecting, preserving, and using theatre, cinema, and performing arts materials in libraries, museums, and private collections. Founded 1937.

Membership

Memb. 500. Dues (Indiv.) $20; (Inst.) $25. Year. Jan. 1–Dec. 31.

Officers (1993–1994)

Pres. (vacant); *V.P.* Bob Taylor, Curator, Billy Rose Theatre Collection, New York Public Lib. for the Performing Arts, 111 Amsterdam Ave., New York, NY 10023-7498; *Secy.-Treas.* Richard M. Buck, Asst. to the Exec. Dir., New York Public Lib. for the

Performing Arts, 111 Amsterdam Ave., New York, NY 10023-7498.

Executive Board

Susan Brady, Lauren Bufferd, Rosemary Cullen, Catherine Johnson, Nena Couch, Geraldine Duclow, Steven Higgins, Paul Newman, Louis A. Rachow, Dorothy Swerdlove, Richard Wall, Walter Zvonchenko; *Ex officio* Madeleine Nichols, Alan J. Pally, Barbara Naomi Cohen-Stratyner, Maryann Chach; *Honorary* Paul Myers; *Historian* Louis A. Rachow.

Publications

Broadside (q.; memb.) . *Ed.* Maryann Chach, Catherine Johnson.
Performing Arts Resources (ann.; memb.). *Ed.* Barbara Naomi Cohen-Stratyner.

Committee Chairpersons

Awards. Steven Vallillo.
Collection Resources. Walter Zvonchenko.
Long-Range Planning. To be appointed.
Membership. Geraldine Duclow.

Nominations. Richard Wall.
Program and Special Events. Richard M. Buck, Bob Taylor.
Publications. Maryann Chach, Catherine Johnson.

Urban Libraries Council

President, Eleanor Jo (Joey) Rodger
1800 Ridge Ave., Suite 208, Evanston, IL 60201
708-866-9999, FAX 708-866-9989

Object

To identify and make known the problems relating to urban libraries serving cities of 50,000 or more individuals, located in a Standard Metropolitan Statistical Area; to provide information on state and federal legislation affecting urban library programs and systems; to facilitate the exchange of ideas and programs of member libraries and other libraries; to develop programs that enable libraries to act as a focus of community development and to supply the informational needs of the new urban populations; to conduct research and educational programs that will benefit urban libraries and to solicit and accept grants, contributions, and donations essential to their implementation.

ULC currently receives all of its funding from membership dues. Future projects will involve the solicitation of grant funding. ULC is a 501(c)(3) not-for-profit corporation based in the state of Illinois.

Membership

Membership is open to public libraries and library systems serving populations of 50,000 or more located in a Standard Metropolitan Statistical Area. Dues are based on the size of the organization's operating budget, according to the following schedule: under $2 million, $700; $2 million to $5 million, $1,000; $5 million to $10 million, $1,250; $10 million to $15 million, $1,500; over $15 million, $2,000. In addition, ULC member libraries may choose Sustaining or Contributing status (Sustaining, $10,000; Contributing, $3,000 to $9,000) for the period 1992–1994. Corporate memberships are also available.

Officers (1993–1994)

Chair James R. Dawe, 750 B St., Suite 2100, San Diego, CA 92101; *V.Chair* Lawrence A. Kane, Jr., Dinsmore and Shohl, 1900 Chemed Center, Cincinnati, OH 45202; *Secy.* Sally Frazier, 7204 Sleepy Hollow Rd., Tulsa, OK 74136; *Treas.* Esther W. Lopato, 1231 E. 21 St., Brooklyn, NY 11210.

Officers and members of the executive board serve two-year terms. New officers are elected and take office at the summer annual meeting of the Council.

Executive Board

Ronald A. Dubberly, Robert B. Croneberger, Paulette H. Holahan, G. Victor Johnson, Samuel F. Morrison, John Alden Philbrick, Michael A. Schott, M. Calvin Shumaker, Patricia F. Turner, Reginald W. Williams.

Staff

Pres. Eleanor Jo Rodger; *V.P., Admin. and Program* Bridget A. Bradley; *Secy.* Fides Julian.

Publications

Balancing the Books: Financing American Public Library Service (1992).

Frequent Fast Facts Surveys: Fees Survey Results (March 1993); Fund Raising and Financial Development Survey Results (November 1993); Staffing Survey Results (June 1993).

Keeping the Books: Public Library Financial Practices (1992).
Large Urban Libraries: Their Roles, Responsibilities and Contributions (1991).
Urban Libraries Exchange (mo.; memb.).

State, Provincial, and Regional Library Associations

The associations in this section are organized under three headings: United States, Canada, and Regional. Both the United States and Canada are represented under Regional associations.

United States

Alabama

Memb. 1,200. Term of Office. Apr. 1994–Apr. 1995. Publication. *The Alabama Librarian* (q.).

Pres. Margaret Blake. Tel. 205-690-8377; *Exec. Dir.* Barbara Black, 400 S. Union St., Suite 255, Montgomery 36104. Tel. 205-262-5210.

Address correspondence to the executive director.

Alaska

Memb. 476. Term of Office. Mar. 1993–Mar. 1994. Publication. *Sourdough* (q.).

Pres. Maurine Canarsky, Wien Lib., 1215 Cowles St., Fairbanks 99701. Tel. 907-459-1020; *V.P.* Rita Dursi Johnson, Egan Lib., 11120 Glacier Hwy., Juneau 99801-8676. Tel. 907-465-6466; *Secy.* Beth Odsen, Anchorage Law Lib., 303 K St., Anchorage 99501. Tel. 907-264-0587; *Treas.* India M. Spartz, Alaska State Lib., Box 110571, Juneau 99811-0571. Tel. 907-465-2910.

Address correspondence to the secretary.

Arizona

Memb. 1,241. Term of Office. Oct. 1993–Oct. 1994. Publication. *ASLA Newsletter* (mo.). Articles for the newsletter should be sent to the attention of the executive secretary.

Pres. Carol Hammond, Fletcher Lib., Arizona State Univ. W., 4701 W. Thunderbird Rd., Box 37100, Phoenix 85069-7100. Tel. 602-543-8504; *Treas.* Bill Pillow, Scottsdale Public Lib., 3839 Civic Center Blvd., Scottsdale 85251. Tel. 602-994-2474; *Exec. Secy.* Jim Johnson, 13832 N. 32 St., Suite D-1, Phoenix 85032. Tel. 602-971-3885.

Address correspondence to the executive secretary.

Arkansas

Memb. 800. Term of Office. Jan.–Dec. 1994. Publication. *Arkansas Libraries* (bi-mo.).

Pres. Alice Coleman, Dir., Texarkana Public Lib., 600 W. Third St., Texarkana 75501. Tel. 903-794-2149, FAX 903-794-2139; *Exec. Dir.* Sherry Walker, Arkansas Lib. Assn., 1100 N. Univ. Ave., Suite 109, Little Rock 72207. Tel. 501-661-1127, FAX 501-663-1218.

Address correspondence to the executive director.

California

Memb. 2,600. Term of Office. Nov. 1993–Nov. 1994. Publication. *California Libraries.*

Pres. Joy Thomas, Lib., California State Univ. at Long Beach; *V.P./Pres.-Elect* Mary Jo Levy, Palo Alto Public Lib.; *Exec. Dir.* Mary Sue Ferrell, California Lib. Assn., 717 K St., Suite 300, Sacramento 95814. Tel. 916-447-8541, FAX 916-447-8394.

Address correspondence to the executive director.

Colorado

Memb. 863. Term of Office. Oct. 1993–Oct. 1994. Publication. *Colorado Libraries* (q.). *Ed.* Nancy Carter, Music Lib., Univ. of Colorado, Campus Box 184, Boulder 80309. *Pres.* Stepheny Liptak, Univ. of Southern Colorado, 2200 Bonforte Blvd., Pueblo 81001; *Treas.* Vicki Nichols, Jefferson County Public Lib., 4305 Brentwood St., Wheat Ridge 80033.

Address correspondence to the association, Box 489, Pinecliffe 80471. Tel. 303-642-0203, FAX 303-642-0201.

Connecticut

Memb. 1,100. Term of Office. July 1993–June 1994. Publication. *Connecticut Libraries* (11 per year). *Ed.* David Kapp, 4 Llynwood Dr., Bolton 06040. Tel. 203-647-0697.

Pres. Sandra Ruoff, Guilford Free Public Lib., 67 Park St., Guilford 06437. Tel. 203-453-6561; *V.P./Pres.-Elect* Janet V. Day, Woodbridge Public Lib., 10 Newton Rd., Woodbridge 06525. Tel. 203-389-3433; *Treas.* Jean Schneider, 20 Lantern Lane, Niantic 06357. Tel. 203-445-5577; *Administrator* Karen Zoller, Connecticut Lib. Assn., Box 1046, Norwich 06360-1046. Tel. 203-885-2758.

Address correspondence to the administrator.

Delaware

Memb. 355. Term of Office. Apr. 1993–Apr. 1994. Publication. *DLA Bulletin* (3 per year). *Pres.* Verlie A. Gaither, Derrickson Memorial Lib., Delaware Technical and Community College, 333 Shipley St., Wilmington 19801-2499. Tel. 302-573-5426, FAX 302-577-2548; *V.P./Pres.-Elect* Jonathan B. Jeffrey, Morris Lib., Univ. of Delaware, Newark 19711-5267. Tel. 302-831-6945, FAX 302-831-1046; *Secy.* Martha Hadaway, Kent County Dept. of Lib. Services, 414 Federal St., Dover 19901. Tel. 302-736-2265, FAX 302-736-2262; *Treas.* Janet D. Shaw,

Newark H.S., E. Delaware Ave., Newark 19711. Tel. 302-454-2254.

Address correspondence to the association, Box 816, Dover 19903-0816.

District of Columbia

Memb. 900. Term of Office. Sept. 1993–Aug. 1994. Publication. *INTERCOM* (mo.).

Pres. Sue Uebelacker, Prince George's County Memorial Lib., Largo-Kettering Branch, 72 Watkins Pk. Plaza, Upper Marlboro, MD 20772. Tel. 301-390-7458; *V.P./Pres.-Elect* Trellis Wright, Lib. of Congress, Special Projects Office, Rm. LM 611, Washington 20540-9100. Tel. 202-707-2422; *Secy.* Rita Thompson-Joyner, DC Public Lib., 901 G St. N.W., Washington 20001. Tel. 202-727-1101; *Treas.* Steve Palincsar, General Accounting Office, 441 G St. N.W., Suite 6430, Washington 20548. Tel. 202-275-3947.

Address correspondence to the president.

Florida

Memb. (Indiv.) 1,378; (In-state Inst.) 83. Term of Office. July 1993–June 1994.

Pres. Susan Anderson, Saint Petersburg Jr. College. Tel. 813-341-3600; V.P./Pres.-Elect Holen Moeller, Leon County Public Lib. Tel. 904-487-2665; Secy. Betty D. Johnson, duPont-Ball Lib., Stetson Univ. Tel. 904-822-7178; Treas. Arthur Viders, 7906 Hopi Place, Tampa 33634-2418. Tel. 813-888-8484; Exec. Secy. Marjorie Stealey, Florida Lib. Assn., 1133 W. Morse Blvd., Suite 201, Winter Park 32789. Tel. 407-647-8839.

Address correspondence to the executive secretary.

Georgia

Memb. 1,055. Term of Office. Oct. 1993–Oct. 1995. Publication. *Georgia Librarian.* *Ed.* Joanne Lincoln, Atlanta Public Schools, 2930 Forrest Hill Dr. S.W., Atlanta 30315. Tel. 404-827-8725.

Pres. Donna D. Mancini, DeKalb County Public Lib., 215 Sycamore St., Decatur 30030. Tel. 404-370-8450; *1st V.P./Pres.-Elect* Sue Hatfield, Dir., Lib. Services, DeKalb College, 555 N. Indian Creek Rd.,

Clarkston 30021. Tel. 404-294-3491; *2nd V.P.* Grace McLeod, DeKalb County Public Lib., 3560 Kensington Rd., Decatur 30032. Tel. 404-508-7190; *Secy.* David Searcy, Community Extension Services, Atlanta Fulton Public Lib., Bldg. B, Suite 105, 3645 Southside Industrial Pkwy., Atlanta 30354. Tel. 404-366-0710; *Treas.* Alan Kaye, Dir., Roddenbery Memorial Lib., 320 N. Board St., Cairo 31728. Tel. 912-377-3632.

Address correspondence to the president.

Hawaii

Memb. 450. Publications. *HLA Newsletter* (q.); *HLA Journal* (ann.); *HLA Membership Directory* (ann.).

Pres. Kenneth R. Herrick, 50-I Malaai Rd., Hilo 96720. Tel. 808-933-3507; *Pres.-Elect/Conference Chair* Jean Ehrhorn, 507 Koko Isle Circle, Honolulu 96825. Tel. 808-956-2472.

Address correspondence to the association, Box 4111, Honolulu 96812-4111.

Idaho

Memb. 500. Term of Office. Oct. 1993–Oct. 1994. Publication. *Idaho Librarian* (q.). *Ed.* Mary Bolin, Univ. of Idaho Lib., Moscow 83844-2363. Tel. 208-885-7737.

Pres. Rand Simmons, Northwest Nazarene College Lib., 623 Holly St., Nampa 83686. Tel. 208-467-8609; *1st V.P./Pres.-Elect* Karen Strege, 633 E. 25 Ave., Spokane, WA 99203; *2nd V.P./Pres.-Elect* Vivian Wells, 3219 E. 3600 N., Kimberly 83341. Tel. 208-733-6551; *Treas.* Tim Brown, Boise State Univ. Lib., 1910 Univ. Dr., Boise 83725. Tel. 208-385-1234; *Secy.* Karen Ganske, Nampa Public Lib., 101 11th Ave. S., Nampa 83651. Tel. 208-465-2263; *Conference Exhibits Coord.* Donna M. Hanson, Idaho Lib. Assn., Box 8533, Moscow 83843. Tel. 208-885-2505.

Address conference exhibits correspondence to the exhibits coordinator. Address all other correspondence to the president.

Illinois

Memb. 4,100. Term of Office. July 1993–June 1994. Publication. *ILA Reporter* (10 per year).

Pres. Jay Wozne, Chicago Lib. System, 400 S. State St., 10th fl., Chicago 60606; *V.P./Pres.-Elect* Lee Logan, Illinois Valley Lib. System, 845 Brenkman Dr., Pekin 61554; *Treas.* Mary Bowman; *Exec. Dir.* vacant.

Address correspondence to the association, 33 W. Grand Ave., Suite 301, Chicago 60610. Tel. 312-644-1896, FAX 312-644-1899.

Indiana

Memb. (Indiv.) 1,000; (Inst.) 200. Term of Office. May 1993–May 1994. Publications. *Focus on Indiana Libraries* (11 per year), *Ed.* Raquel M. Ravinet; *Indiana Libraries* (q.), *Ed.* Steve Schmidt, IUPUI, 815 W. Michigan St., Indianapolis 46219. Tel. 317-274-0470.

Pres. Sandra Sawyer, Fulton County Public Lib., 1099 N. Prairie Wood Dr., Rochester 46975; *Secy.* Connie Patsiner, IVAN, 1100 W. 42 St., Indianapolis 46208; *Treas.* Sally Otte, 5251 N. Delaware, Indianapolis 46220.

Address correspondence to the Indiana Lib. Federation, 6408 Carrollton Ave., Indianapolis 46220. Tel. 317-257-2040, FAX 317-257-1393.

Iowa

Memb. 1,805. Term of Office. Jan.–Dec. 1994. Publication. *The Catalyst* (bi-mo.). *Ed.* Naomi Stovall.

Pres. Ricarda Sauro, Tipton Public Lib., Tipton 52772.

Address correspondence to the association, 823 Insurance Exchange Bldg., 505 Fifth Ave., Des Moines 50309. Tel. 515-243-2172, FAX 515-243-0614.

Kansas

Memb. 1,100. Term of Office. July 1993–June 1994. Publications. *KLA Newsletter* (q.); *KLA Membership Directory* (ann.).

Pres. Kay Bradt, Baker Univ., 606 W. Eighth St., Baldwin City 66006. Tel. 913-594-6451, Ext. 414; *Pres.-Elect* Virginia Prather, Ellinwood School/Community Lib., 210 N. Schiller, Ellinwood 67526-1651; *Exec. Secy.* Leroy Gattin, South Central Kansas Lib. System, 901 N. Main St., Hutchinson 67501. Tel. 316-663-5441, Ext.

110, FAX 316-663-1215; *Secy.* Marianne Eichelberger, Newton Public Lib., 720 N. Oak, Newton 67114. Tel. 316-283-2890, FAX 316-283-2916; *Treas.* Marcella Ratzlaff, Hutchinson Public Lib., 901 N. Main St., Hutchinson 67501. Tel. 316-663-5441.

Address correspondence to the executive secretary.

Kentucky

Memb. 1,900. Term of Office. Oct. 1993–Oct. 1994. Publication. *Kentucky Libraries* (q.).

Pres. Janet Stith; *V.P./Pres.-Elect* June Martin; *Secy.* Elaine Steinberg; *Exec. Secy.* John Underwood, 1501 Twilight Trail, Frankfort 40601. Tel. 502-223-5322.

Address correspondence to the executive secretary.

Louisiana

Memb. (Indiv.) 1,710; (Inst.) 78. Term of Office. July 1993–June 1994. Publication. *LLA Bulletin* (q.). *Ed.* Florence Jumonville, 7911 Birch St., New Orleans 70118. Tel. 504-523-4662.

Pres. Grace G. Moore, 4554 Whitehaven St., Baton Rouge 70808. Tel. 504-342-4929; *1st V.P./Pres.-Elect* Walter W. Wicker, 5027 Stow Creek, Ruston 71270. Tel. 318-257-2577; *Secy.* Mary Norton, 2219 S. Salcedo St., New Orleans 70125. Tel. 504-837-5204; *Parliamentarian* Carol D. Billings, 12 Swallow St., New Orleans 70124. Tel. 504-568-5706.

Address correspondence to the association, Box 3058, Baton Rouge 70821. Tel. 504-342-4928, FAX 504-342-3547.

Maine

Memb. 1,100. Term of Office. (Pres., V.P.) Spring 1992–Spring 1994. Publications. *Mainely Libraries* (4 per year); *Maine Memo* (mo.).

Pres. Barbara Rice, Bangor Public Lib., Bangor 04401; *V.P.* Valerie Osborne, Old Town Public Lib., Old Town 04468; *Secy.* Charles Howell, Millinocket Memorial Lib., Millinocket 04462; *Treas.* Jean Oplinger, Farmington Public Lib., Farmington 04938.

Address correspondence to the association, c/o Maine Municipal Assn., Local Government Center, 37 Community Dr., Augusta 04330. Tel. 207-623-8428, FAX 207-626-5947.

Maryland

Memb. 1,300. Term of Office. July 1993–June 1994. Publication. *The Crab.*

Pres. Shirley Peck, Essex Community College Lib., 7201 Rossville Blvd., Baltimore 21237. Tel. 410-780-6420; *1st V.P./Pres.-Elect* Joyce M. Demmitt, Howard County Lib., 10375 Little Patuxent Pkwy., Columbia 21044. Tel. 410-313-7800; *2nd V.P.* Judith C. Cooper, Prince George's County Memorial Lib. System, 6532 Adelphi Rd., Hyattsville 20783. Tel. 301-699-3500; *Secy.* Carol E. Dausch, Baltimore County Public Lib., 1716 Eastern Ave., Baltimore 21222. Tel. 410-887-7255; *Treas.* Hampton M. Auld.

Address correspondence to the association, 400 Cathedral St., 3rd fl., Baltimore 21201-4401. Tel. 410-727-7422, FAX 410-625-9594.

Massachusetts

Memb. (Indiv.) 950; (Inst.) 100. Term of Office. July 1993–June 1994. Publication. *Bay State Librarian* (10 per year).

Pres. Ellen Rainville, Fletcher Lib., 50 Main St., Westford 01886. Tel. 508-692-5557, FAX 508-692-0287; *V.P.* Ellen Rauch, EMRLS, Boston Public Lib., Copley Sq., Box 286, Boston 02117. Tel. 800-287-4065, FAX 617-267-0364; *Secy.* Brian Donoghue, Massachusetts Board of Lib. Commissioners, 648 Beacon St., Boston 02215. Tel. 800-952-7403, 617-267-9400, FAX 617-421-9833; *Treas.* Dodie Gaudet, WMRLS, 58 Main St., Hatfield 01038. Tel. 800-282-7755, 413-247-9306, FAX 413-247-9740; *Exec. Secy.* Barry Blaisdell, Massachusetts Lib. Assn., Countryside Offices, 707 Turnpike St., North Andover 01845. Tel. 508-686-8543.

Address correspondence to the executive secretary.

Michigan

Memb. (Indiv.) 2,200; (Inst.) 300. Term of Office. June 1993–June 1994. Publication. *Michigan Librarian Newsletter* (10 per year).

Pres. Sandra Yee, Eastern Michigan Univ., Ypsilanti 48197; *Treas.* Marney Cooley, Tecumseh Public Lib., 215 N. Ottawa, Tecumseh 49286; *Exec. Dir.* Marianne Hartzell, Michigan Lib. Assn., 1000 Long Blvd., Suite 1, Lansing 48911. Tel. 517-694-6615.

Address correspondence to the executive director.

Minnesota

Memb. 940. Term of Office. (Pres., Pres.-Elect) Jan.–Dec. 1994; (Treas.) Jan. 1994–Dec. 1995; (Secy.) Jan. 1993–Dec. 1994. Publication. *MLA Newsletter* (10 per year).

Pres. Linda DeBeau-Melting, 499 Wilson Lib., Univ. of Minnesota, Minneapolis 55406; *Pres.-Elect* Judith Gaston, Univ. of Minnesota Film and Video, 1313 Fifth St. S.E., Suite 106, Minneapolis 55455; *ALA Chapter Councillor* Janice Feye-Stukas, Lib. Development and Services, 440 Capitol Sq., 500 Cedar St., Saint Paul 55101; *Secy.* Jeanne Gelinas, 2400 Interlachen Rd., Suite 217, Spring Park 55384; *Treas.* Deborah Struzyk, Minneapolis Public Lib., 300 Nicollet Mall, Minneapolis 55401; *Admin. Secy.* Eileen Moore, Minnesota Lib. Assn., 1315 Lowry Ave. N., Minneapolis 55411-1398. Tel./FAX 612-521-1735.

Address correspondence to the administrative secretary.

Mississippi

Memb. 1,100. Term of Office. Jan.–Dec. 1994. Publication. *Mississippi Libraries* (q.).

Pres. Deb Mitchell; *V.P./Pres.-Elect* Charline Longino; *Treas.* Tom Henderson; *Exec. Secy.* Robin Latham, MLA Office, Box 20448, Jackson 39289-1448. Tel. 601-352-3917.

Address correspondence to the executive secretary.

Missouri

Memb. 1,000. Term of Office. Oct. 1993–Oct. 1994. Publication. *MO INFO* (6 per year). *Ed.* Jean Ann McCartney.

Pres. Julia Schneider, Missouri Western State College, 4525 Downs Dr., Saint Joseph 64507. Tel. 816-271-4369; *V.P./Pres.-Elect* Elizabeth Eckles, Woffner Lib. for the Blind and Physically Handicapped, Box 387, Jefferson City 65102. Tel. 314-751-8720. *Secy.* Karen Hicklin. Tel. 816-646-0547; *Chair, Budget and Finance* Don Gaertner; *Exec. Dir.* Jean Ann McCartney, Missouri Lib. Assn., 1306 Business 63 S., Suite B, Columbia 65201. Tel. 314-449-4627.

Address correspondence to the executive director.

Montana

Memb. 500. Term of Office. July 1993–June 1994. Publication. *Library Focus* (4 per year). *Eds.* Gregg Sapp and Greg Notess, Renne Lib., Montana State Univ., Bozeman 59717-0332. Tel. 406-994-3162.

Pres. Jane Howell, Eastern Montana College, 1500 N. 30 St., Billings 59101-0298. Tel. 406-657-2320, FAX 406-657-2037; *V.P./Pres.-Elect* Susan Nissen, Montana Power Co. Law Lib., 40 E. Broadway, Butte 59701. Tel. 406-496-5000; *Rec. Secy.* David Pauli, Missoula Public Lib., 301 E. Main St., Missoula 59802. Tel. 406-721-2665; *Financial Secy.* Clara Sprague, Box 954, Bozeman 59771-0954. Tel. 406-587-3346.

Address correspondence to the financial secretary.

Nebraska

Memb. 1,000. Term of Office. Oct. 1993–Oct. 1994. Publication. *NLA Quarterly.*

Pres. Carol Connor, Bennett-Martin Lib., 136 S. 14 St., Lincoln 68508; *V.P./Pres.-Elect* Rod Wagner, Nebraska Lib. Commission, Suite 120, 1200 N St., Lincoln 68508-2023; *Secy.* Carol Reed, Kearney Public Lib., 2020 First Ave., Kearney 68847; *Treas.* Tracy Bicknell, 216N Love Lib., Lincoln 68588-0410; *Exec. Dir.* Ken Oyer, 5302 S. 75 St., Ralston 68127-3903. Tel. 402-398-6092, FAX 402-398-6923.

Address correspondence to the executive director.

Nevada

Memb. 400. Term of Office. Jan.–Dec. 1994. Publication. *Highroller* (4 per year). *Pres.* Gary Avent, Elko County Lib., 720 Court St., Elko 89801; *Treas.* Carolyn Rowles-Heiser, Douglas County Lib., Box 337, Minden 89423. Tel. 702-782-9841. Address correspondence to the president.

New Hampshire

Memb. 700. Term of Office. June 1993–May 1994. Publication. *NHLA Newsletter* (bi-mo.). *Pres.* Ann Trementozzi; *Secy.* Carl Heidenblad, Nesmith Lib., 3 N. Lowell Rd., Windham 03087; *Treas.* Pamela Schwotzer, North Hampton Public Lib., Box 628, North Hampton 03862.

Address correspondence to the association, Box 2332, Concord 03302-2332.

New Jersey

Memb. 1,700. Term of Office. May 1993–Apr. 1994. Publications. *New Jersey Libraries* (q.); *New Jersey Libraries Newsletter* (mo.). *Pres.* Norma Blake, Burlington County Lib., Woodlane Rd., Mount Holly 08060. Tel. 609-267-9660; *V.P./Pres.-Elect* Mary Louise Abrams, Paramus Public Lib., E. 116 Century Rd., Paramus 07652. Tel. 201-599-1302; *Treas.* Susan Persak, Chester Lib., 250 W. Main St., Chester 07930; *Exec. Dir.* Patricia Tumulty, New Jersey Lib. Assn., 4 W. Lafayette St., Trenton 08608. Tel. 609-394-8032.

Address correspondence to the executive director, Box 1534, Trenton 08607.

New Mexico

Memb. 550. Term of Office. Mar. 1993–Apr. 1994. Publication. *New Mexico Library Association Newsletter. Ed.* Donnelyn Curtis, Box 3358, Las Cruces 88003.

Pres. Alison Almquist, 12104 Hickory Ct. N.E., Albuquerque 87111; *1st V.P.* Barbara Billey, San Juan College Lib., 4601 College Blvd., Farmington 87401; *Treas.* Virginia Seiser, 919 Silver Ave. S.W., Albuquerque 87102; *ALA Councillor* Susie Sonflieth, 322 Pinos Verdes, Santa Fe 87501.

Address correspondence to the association, Suite 8, El Dorado Sq., 11200 Montgomery N.E., Albuquerque 87111.

New York

Memb. 3,200. Term of Office. Oct. 1993–Nov. 1994. Publication. *NYLA Bulletin* (10 per year). *Ed.* Nancy McRay.

Pres. Sandra Miranda, White Plains Public Lib., 100 Martine Ave., White Plains 10601; *V.P./Pres.-Elect* Rhonna Goodman, New York Academy of Medicine Lib., 2 E. 103 St., New York 10029; *Treas.* Carol Ann Desch, Worthman Lane, Rensselaer 12144; *Exec. Dir.* Susan Lehman Keitel, New York Lib. Assn., 252 Hudson Ave., Albany 12210. Tel. 518-432-6952; *Asst. Dir.* Gail Ghazzawi.

Address correspondence to the executive director.

North Carolina

Memb. 2,500. Term of Office. Oct 1993–Oct. 1995. Publication. *North Carolina Libraries* (q.). *Ed.* Frances Bradburn, Joyner Lib., E. Carolina Univ., Greenville 27858.

Pres. Gwen G. Jackson, S.E. Technical Assistance Center, 2013 Lejeune Blvd., Jacksonville 28546. Tel. 919-577-8920, FAX 919-577-1427; *V.P./Pres.-Elect* David Fergusson, Forsyth County Public Lib., 660 W. Fifth St., Winston-Salem 27101. Tel. 919-727-2556, FAX 919-727-2549; *Secy.* Judy LeCroy, Davidson County Schools, Box 2057, Lexington 27293-2057. Tel. 704-249-8181, FAX 704-249-1062; *Treas.* Wanda Brown Cason, Reynolds Lib., Wake Forest Univ., Box 7777, Reynolda Sta., Winston-Salem 27109-7777. Tel. 919-759-5094, FAX 919-759-9831.

Address correspondence to the secretary.

North Dakota

Memb. (Indiv.) 423; (Inst.) 32. Term of Office. Oct. 1993–Sept. 1994. Publication. *The Good Stuff* (q.). *Ed.* Ellen Kotrba, Fritz Lib., Univ. of North Dakota, Univ. Sta., Grand Forks 58201.

Pres. Sharon Evensen, Hoghaug Lib., Univ. of North Dakota–Lake Region, Devils Lake 58301; *V.P./Pres.-Elect* Kathy Waldera, Bismarck Public Lib., Bismarck 58501; *Secy.* Agnes Jensen, Stutsman County Lib., Jamestown 58401; *Treas.* Neil Price, Dept. of Lib. Science, Univ. of North Dakota, Grand Forks 58202.

Address correspondence to the president.

Ohio

Memb. 2,846. Term of Office. Nov. 1993–Oct. 1994. Publications. *Access* (mo.); *Ohio Libraries* (4 per year).

Pres. Alan Hall, Public Lib. of Steubenville–Jefferson County, 407 S. Fourth St., Steubenville 43952. Tel. 614-282-9782; *V.P./Pres.-Elect* James Bouchard, Lima Public Lib., 650 W. Market St., Lima 45801; *Secy.* Susan Hagloch, Tuscarawas County Public Lib., 121 Fair Ave. N.W., New Philadelphia 44663. Tel. 216-364-4474.

Address correspondence to the association, 35 E. Gay St., Suite 305, Columbus 43215. Tel. 614-221-9057.

Oklahoma

Memb. (Indiv.) 1,050; (Inst.) 60. Term of Office. July 1993–June 1994. Publication. *Oklahoma Librarian* (bi-mo.).

Pres. Jan Keene; *V.P./Pres.-Elect* Robert Swisher; *Secy.* Jonette Ellis; *Treas.* Ken Bierman; *Exec. Dir.* Kay Boies, 300 Hardy Dr., Edmond 73013. Tel./FAX 405-348-0506.

Address correspondence to the executive director.

Oregon

Memb. 1,000. Term of Office. Sept. 1993–Aug. 1994. Publication. *Oregon Library News* (mo.). *Ed.* MLou Williams, Hermiston Public Lib., Hermiston 97838. Tel. 503-567-2882, FAX 503-567-3551.

Pres. Pat Grace, Kerr Lib., Oregon State Univ., Corvallis 97331. Tel. 503-737-7265; *V.P./Pres.-Elect* Anne Billeter, Jackson Co. Lib., Medford 97501. Tel. 503-776-7285; *Secy.* Donetta Sheffold, Kerr Lib., Oregon State Univ., Corvallis 97331. Tel. 503-737-7265; *Treas.* Michael Gaston, Siuslaw Public

Lib., Florence 97439. Tel. 503-997-3132. Address correspondence to the secretary.

Pennsylvania

Memb. 1,750. Term of Office. Jan.–Dec. 1994. Publication. *PLA Bulletin* (mo.).

Pres. Cynthia K. Richey, 439 Austin Ave., Pittsburgh 15243-1959. Tel. 412-531-1912; *V.P.* Kathy K. Kennedy, Monroeville Public Lib., 2615 Mosside Blvd., Monroeville 15146-3381. Tel. 412-372-0500; *Exec. Dir.* Margaret Bauer, CAE, Pennsylvania Lib. Assn., 1919 N. Front St., Harrisburg 17102. Tel. 717-233-3113.

Address correspondence to the executive director.

Rhode Island

Memb. (Indiv.) 451; (Inst.) 37. Term of Office. Nov. 1993–Nov. 1994. Publication. *Rhode Island Library Association Bulletin. Ed.* Mattie Gustafson.

Pres. Florence Doksansky, Brown Univ. Libs., Providence 02903. Tel. 401-253-1040; *V.P./Pres.-Elect* James Giles, Cranston Public Lib., 140 Sockanosset Cross Rd., Cranston 02920. Tel. 401-943-9080; *Secy.* Patience Bliss, Coventry Public Lib., 1672 Flat River Rd., Coventry 02816. Tel. 401-822-9100; *Treas.* Madeleine Telfeyan, Rhode Island Historical Society Lib., 121 Hope St., Providence 02903. Tel. 401-331-8575; *ALA Councillor* Frank Iacono, Dept. of State Lib. Services, 300 Richmond St., Providence 02903. Tel. 401-277-2726; *NELA Councillor* Eileen Socha, Weaver Memorial Lib., 41 Grove Ave., East Providence 02914. Tel. 401-434-2453.

Address correspondence to the secretary.

South Carolina

Memb. 850. Term of Office. Dec. 1993–Feb. 1995.

Pres. Debby Coleman; *V.P./Pres.-Elect* Mary Smalls, South Carolina State Univ., *Exec. Secy.* Drucie Raines, South Carolina Lib. Assn., Box 219, Goose Creek 29445. Tel. 803-764-3668, FAX 803-824-2690.

Address correspondence to the executive secretary.

South Dakota

Memb. (Indiv.) 479; (Inst.) 75. Term of Office. Oct. 1993–Oct. 1994. Publication. *Book Marks* (bi-mo.).

Pres. Glenda Oakley, 1241 Frank S.E., Huron 57350; *V.P./Pres.-Elect* Elvita Landau, Brookings Public Lib., 515 Third St., Brookings 57006; *Secy.* Jackie Traut, Mitchell Public Lib., 221 N. Duff, Mitchell 57301; *Treas.* Margaret Sieg, Hot Springs Public Lib., 145 N. Chicago, Hot Springs 57747; *ALA Councillor* Beth Marie Quanbeck, South Dakota State Lib., 800 Governor's Dr., Pierre 57501-2294; *MPLA Rep.* Jane Larson, Vermillion Public Lib., 18 Church St., Vermillion 57069-3093.

Address correspondence to the association, Box 673, Pierre 57501.

Tennessee

Memb. 1,030. Term of Office. July 1993–July 1994. Publication. *Tennessee Librarian* (q.).

Pres. Carolyn Daniel, Lib., McGavock H.S., Nashville 37214. Tel. 615-758-2635; *V.P./Pres.-Elect* John Evans, Memphis State Univ. Libs., Memphis 38152. Tel. 901-678-4485; *Exec. Secy.* Betty Nance, Box 158417, Nashville 37215-8417. Tel. 615-297-8316, FAX 615-269-1807.

Address correspondence to the executive secretary.

Texas

Memb. 5,600. Term of Office. Apr. 1993–Apr. 1994. Publications. *Texas Library Journal* (q.); *TLAcast* (9 per year).

Pres. E. Dale Cleff, Texas Tech Univ. Lib., Box 40002, Lubbock 79409. Tel. 806-742-2261; *Exec. Dir.* Patricia Smith, TLA Office, 3355 Bee Cave Rd., Suite 401, Austin 78746-6763. Tel. 512-328-1518, FAX 512-328-8852.

Address correspondence to the executive director.

Utah

Memb. 650. Term of Office. May 1993–Feb. 1994. Publication. *UTAH Libraries News* (bi-mo.).

Pres. Marian Karpisek, 1430 Andrew Ave., Salt Lake City 84104. Tel. 801-578-8279; *V.P.* Pete Giacoma, 365 Emery, Salt Lake City 84104. Tel. 801-451-2322; *Secy.* Faye Todd, 2551 Buena Vista Dr., West Jordan 84088. Tel. 801-943-4636; *Treas./Exec. Secy.* Chris Anderson. Tel. 801-581-5266.

Address correspondence to the association, 2150 S. 300 W., Suite 16, Salt Lake City 84115.

Vermont

Memb. 450. Term of Office. May 1993–May 1994. Publication. *VLA News* (10 per year).

Pres. Laurel Stanley, Hall Lib., Lyndon State College, Lyndonville 05851. Tel. 802-626-9371; *V.P./Pres.-Elect* Nancy Wilson, Lawrence Memorial Lib., 40 North St., Bristol 05443. Tel. 802-453-2366; *Secy.* Paula Arnold, Gary Lib., Vermont College, Montpelier 05602. Tel. 802-828-8747; *Treas.* Sandy Duling, Coolidge Lib., Castleton State College, Castleton 05735. Tel. 802-468-5611; *ALA Councillor* Melissa Malcolm, Mount Abraham Union H.S., 7 Airport Dr., Bristol 05443. Tel. 802-453-2333; *NELA Rep.* Russell Moore, Springfield Town Lib., 43 Main St., Springfield 05156. Tel. 802-885-3108.

Address correspondence to the president.

Virginia

Memb. 1,400. Term of Office. Jan.–Dec. 1994. Publications. *Virginia Librarian* (q.), *Eds.* Lucretia McCulley and Daniel Ream, Boatwright Lib., Univ. of Richmond, Richmond 23173; *VLA Newsletter* (10 per year), *Ed.* Sue Trask, College of William and Mary, Williamsburg 23187.

Pres. John Stewart, Virginia Beach Public Lib., 110 Municipal Center, Virginia Beach 23456; *V.P./Pres.-Elect* Linda Farynk, McConnell Lib., Radford Univ., Radford 24141; *2nd V.P.* Suzanne Freeman, Virginia Commonwealth Univ., Box 2033, Richmond 23284; *Secy.* Paulette Thomas, Virginia Historical Society, Box 7311, Richmond 23221; *Treas.* Diana Granger, Fairfax County Public Lib., 13135 Lee-Jackson Hwy., Fairfax 22033; *Exec. Dir.* Deborah Trocchi, Virginia Lib. Assn., 669 S. Washington St., Alexandria 22314. Tel. 703-519-7853, FAX 703-519-7732.

Address correspondence to the executive director.

Washington

Memb. 1,150. Term of Office. Aug. 1993–July 1994. Publications. *Alki* (3 per year); *WLA Link* (5 per year).

Pres. Randall Hensley, OUGL, DF-10, Univ. of Washington, Seattle 98195. Tel. 206-543-1968.

Address correspondence to the association, 1232 143rd Ave. S.E., Bellevue 98007. Tel. 206-747-6917.

West Virginia

Memb. 600. Term of Office. Dec. 1993–Nov. 1994. Publication. *West Virginia Libraries*. Ed. Yvonne Farley, Kanawha County Public Lib. ᴷᵃʳᵉⁿ ᴳᵒᶠᶠ

Pres. J. D. Waggoner, West Virginia Lib. Commission, 1900 Kanawha Blvd. E., Charleston 25305. Tel. 304-558-2531; *V.P./Pres.-Elect* Charles A. Julian, 148 Edgewood St., Apt. C, Wheeling 26003. Tel. 304-242-7377; *2nd V.P.* Jo Ann Calzonetti, Wise Lib., West Virginia Univ., Box 6069, Morgantown 26506-6069. Tel. 304-293-3051; *Treas.* David Childers, West Virginia Lib. Commission, 1900 Kanawha Blvd. E., Charleston 25305. Tel. 304-558-2041; *Secy.* Myra Ziegler, Summers County Public Lib., 201 Temple St., Hinton 25951. Tel. 304-466-4490; *ALA Councillor* Tom Brown, Box 901, Athens 24712. Tel. 304-384-5366.

Address correspondence to the president.

Wisconsin

Memb. 2,000. Term of Office. Jan.–Dec. 1994. Publication. *WLA Newsletter* (6 per year).

Pres. Ethel Himmel, 8015 Portland Ave., Wauwatosa 53213. Tel. 414-453-2126; *V.P./Pres.-Elect* Venora McKinney, 8035 N. Celina, Milwaukee 53224-2903. Tel. 414-286-3025; *Exec. Dir.* Larry J. Martin, 4785 Hayes Rd., Madison 53704-7364. Tel. 608-242-2040, FAX 608-242-2050.

Address correspondence to the executive director.

Wyoming

Memb. (Indiv.) 450; (Inst.) 21; (Subscribers) 24. Term of Office. Oct. 1993–Oct. 1994.

Pres. Laurn Wilhelm, Univ. of Wyoming Libs., Box 3374, Laramie 82071. Tel. 307-766-2527; *V.P./Pres.-Elect* Helen Higby, Sweetwater County Lib., Box 550, Green River 82935. Tel. 307-875-3615; *Exec. Secy.* Laura Grott, Box 1387, Cheyenne 82001. Tel. 307-632-7622, FAX 307-638-3469.

Address correspondence to the executive secretary.

Guam

Memb. 75. Publication. *Guam Library Association News* (mo. during school year).

Pres. Linda Schlekau, Upi Elementary School, Yigo 96930. Tel. 671-653-1371, FAX 671-653-5305; *V.P. Programs and Publicity* Joanne Tarpley, Robert F. Kennedy Memorial Lib., Univ. of Guam, Mangilao 96923. Tel. 671-734-9186; *V.P. Memb.* Nicholas Goetzfridt, Robert F. Kennedy Memorial Lib., Univ. of Guam, Mangilao 96923. Tel. 671-734-9332; *Treas.* Harry Uyehara, College of Ed., Univ. of Guam, Mangilao 96923. Tel. 671-734-9519; *ALA Councillor* Mark Goniwiecha, Robert F. Kennedy Memorial Lib., Univ. of Guam, Mangilao 96923. Tel. 671-734-9332; *Secy.* Hazel Moe, Agueda Johnston Middle School, Ordot. Tel. 671-472-6785.

Address correspondence to the association, Box 22515 GMF, Barrigada 96921.

Puerto Rico

Memb. 250. Publications. *Boletín* (ann.); *Cuadernos Bibliotecológicos* (irreg.); *Informa* (mo.); *Cuadernos Bibliográficos* (irreg.).

Pres. Aura Jiménez de Panepinto.

Address correspondence to the Sociedad de Bibliotecarios de Puerto Rico, Apdo. 22989, UPR Sta., Rio Piedras 00931.

Virgin Islands

Saint Croix Lib. Assn. Memb. 24. Publications. *SCLA Newsletter* (q.); *Studies in Virgin Islands Librarianship* (irreg.).

Pres. Virginia Wilder; *V.P.* Elizabeth Rezende; *Secy.* Gwendolyn Hazard; *Treas.*

WVLA
PO Box 5221
Charleston, WV 25361

Sylvania Golphin; *Exec. Board Members* Wallace Williams, Corinne Broadhurst.

Address correspondence to the president at the association, Box 3017, Christiansted, Saint Croix 00821. Tel. 809-773-4729, FAX 809-778-5724.

Canada

Alberta

Memb. 700. Term of Office. May 1993–Apr. 1994. Publication. *Letter of the L.A.A.* (5 per year).

Pres. Linda C. Cook, Yellowhead Regional Lib., 433 King St., Box 400, Spruce Grove T7X 2Y1. Tel. 403-962-2003, FAX 403-962-2770; *Exec. Dir.* Christine Sheppard, 80 Baker Crescent N.W., Calgary T2L 1R4. Tel. 403-284-5818, FAX 403-282-6646.

Address correspondence to the association, 5512 Fourth St. N.W., Box 64197, Calgary T2K 6J1. Tel. 403-284-5818, FAX 403-282-6646.

British Columbia

Memb. 940. Term of Office. Apr. 1993–May 1994. Publication. *BCLA Reporter. Ed.* Jim Harrington.

Pres. Gordon Ray; *V.P./Pres.-Elect* Leonora Crema.

Address correspondence to the association, 110-6545 Bonsor Ave., Burnaby V5H 1H3. Tel. 604-430-9633, FAX 604-430-8595.

Manitoba

Memb. 440. Term of Office. Spring 1993–Spring 1994. Publication. *Newsline* (mo.).

Pres. Jim Blanchard; *V.P./Pres.-Elect* John Tooth; *Office Mgr.* Jeannette Dankewych.

Address correspondence to the association, 208-100 Arthur St., Winnipeg R3B 1H3. Tel. 204-943-4567.

Ontario

Memb. Over 3,750. Term of Office. Nov. 1993–Nov. 1994. Publications. *Inside OLA* (bi-mo.); *The Teaching Librarian* (q.).

Pres. Janice Hayes, CNIB Lib. for the Blind, Toronto. Tel. 416-480-7545;

V.P./Pres.-Elect Jane Horrocks, Richmond Hill Public Lib. Tel. 905-770-1310; *Treas.* Lenny Goldberg, Vaughan Public Libs. Tel. 905-477-5733.

Address correspondence to the association, 100 Lombard St., Suite 303, Toronto M5C 1M3. Tel. 416-363-3388, FAX 416-941-9581.

Quebec

Memb. (Indiv.) 170; (Inst.) 42; (Commercial) 7. Term of Office. May 1993–May 1994. Publications. *ABQ/QLA Bulletin* (3 per year); *QASL Newsletter* (3 per year).

Pres. Frances Ackerman, Fraser Hickson Lib., 4855 Kensington Ave., Montreal H3X 3S6; *V.P./Pres.-Elect* Maria Varvarikos, Lower Canada College, 4090 Royal Ave., Montreal H4A 2M5; *Exec. Secy.* Marie Eberlin, Quebec Lib. Assn., Box 1095, Pointe Claire H9S 4H9. Tel. 514-630-4875.

Address correspondence to the executive secretary.

Saskatchewan

Memb. 300. Term of Office. July 1993–June 1994. Publication. *Saskatchewan Library Association Forum* (5 per year).

Pres. Bryan Foran, SLA Office, 2431 Eighth Ave., Regina S4R 5J7. Tel. 306-780-9413; *Exec. Dir.* Katherine Fisher, Box 3388, Regina S4P 3H1. Tel. 306-780-9413, FAX 306-757-4422.

Address correspondence to the executive director.

Regional

Atlantic Provinces: N.B., Nfld., N.S., P.E.I.

Memb. (Indiv.) 348; (Inst.) 44. Term of Office. May 1993–May 1994. Publications. *APLA Bulletin* (bi-mo.), *Ed.* Edith Haliburton; *Membership Directory and Handbook* (ann.).

Pres. Marion Pape; *V.P./Pres.-Elect* Charles Cameron; *V.P. Nova Scotia* Laura Jantek; *V.P. Prince Edward Island* Nichola Cleaveland; *V.P. New Brunswick* Jocelyne Thompson; *V.P. Newfoundland* Elinor Benjamin; *V.P. Memb.* Laura Peverill; *Secy.*

Francesco Lai. Tel. 902-893-6669; *Treas.* Caren Mofford.

Address correspondence to Atlantic Provinces Lib. Assn., c/o School of Lib. and Info. Studies, Dalhousie Univ., Halifax, NS B3H 4H8.

Middle Atlantic: Del., D.C., Md., Va., W. Va.

Term of Office. June 1993–July 1994. *Pres.* Kitty Hurrey, Southern Maryland Regional Lib., Box 459, Charlotte Hall, MD 20622. Tel. 301-934-9442; *V.P.* Ernest Kallay, Jr., Lib. Dir., Clarksburg Harrison Public Lib., 404 W. Pike St., Clarksburg, WV 26301. Tel. 304-624-4411; *Treas.* Darrell Lemke, 9207 Chanute Dr., Bethesda, MD 20814.

Address correspondence to the president.

Midwest: Ill., Ind., Minn., Ohio

Term of Office. 1992–1995.
Pres. Patricia Llerandi, Schaumburg Township Lib., 32 W. Library Lane, Schaumburg, IL 60194. Tel. 708-885-3373, Ext. 150; *V.P./Pres.-Elect* Kathy East, Tel. 419-352-5104; *Secys.* Diane Bever, Tel. 317-455-9265, Linda Kolb, Tel. 317-257-2040.

Address correspondence to the president, Midwest Federation of Lib. Assns.

Mountain Plains: Ariz., Colo., Kans., Mont., Neb., Nev., N. Dak., Okla., S. Dak., Utah, Wyo.

Memb. 920. Term of Office. One year. Publications. *MPLA Newsletter* (bi-mo.), *Ed. and Adv. Mgr.* Jim Dertien, Sioux Falls Public Lib., 201 N. Main Ave., Sioux Falls, SD 57102. Tel. 605-339-7115; *Membership Directory* (ann.).

Pres. Ronelle Thompson, Augustana College Lib., Sioux Falls, SD 57197. Tel. 605-336-5447; *V.P./Pres.-Elect* Blaine H. Hall, Brigham Young Univ. Lib., Provo, UT 84602. Tel. 801-378-6117; *Exec. Secy.* Joe Edelen, Weeks Lib., Univ. of South Dakota, Vermillion, SD 57069. Tel. 605-677-6082.

Address correspondence to the executive secretary, Mountain Plains Lib. Assn.

New England: Conn., Maine, Mass., N.H., R.I., Vt.

Memb. (Indiv.) 1,200; (Inst.) 100. Term of Office. One year (Treas., Dirs., two years). Publication. *New England Libraries* (6 per year). *Ed.* Renee Olson, Reading Public Lib., 64 Middlesex Ave., Reading, MA 01867. Tel. 617-944-0840.

Pres. Carol DiPrete, Roger Williams College Lib., Old Ferry Rd., Bristol, RI 02809. Tel. 401-254-3031; *V.P./Pres.-Elect* Krista McLeod, Nevins Memorial Lib., 305 Broad Way, Methuen, MA 01844. Tel. 508-686-4080; *Secy.* Robert Cunningham, NELINET, Inc., Newton, MA 02158. Tel. 617-969-0400; *Treas.* Lucy Gangone, Somers Public Lib., Somers, CT 06071. Tel. 203-763-3501; *Exec. Secy.* Barry Blaisdell, New England Lib. Assn., 707 Turnpike St., North Andover, MA 01845. Tel. 508-685-5966.

Address correspondence to the executive secretary.

Pacific Northwest: Alaska, Idaho, Mont., Oreg., Wash., Alberta, B.C.

Memb. (Active) 725; (Subscribers) 160. Term of Office. Oct. 1993–Sept. 1994. Publication. *PNLA Quarterly. Ed.* Katherine G. Eaton, 1631 E. 24 Ave., Eugene, OR 97403. Tel. 503-344-2027, FAX 503-341-5898.

Pres. Audry Kolb, 2471 N.W. Williams Loop, Redmond, OR 97756. Tel. 503-548-0381; 1st V.P./Pres.-Elect Ann Haley, Walla Walla Public Lib., 238 E. Alder St., Walla Walla, WA 99362-1967. Tel. 509-545-6549, FAX 509-527-3748; 2nd V.P. Terry Heyer, Pocatello Public Lib., 812 E. Clark St., Pocatello, ID 83201-9266. Tel. 208-232-1263, FAX 208-232-9266; Secy. Claire Christiansen, Olympia Timberland Lib., 313 Eighth Ave. S.E., Olympia, WA 98501. Tel. 206-352-0595, FAX 206-586-3207; Treas. Paul E. Jensen, Des Moines Lib., King County Lib. System, 21620 11th Ave. S., Des Moines, WA 98198. Tel. 206-824-6083,

FAX 206-296-5047.

Address correspondence to the president, Pacific Northwest Lib. Assn.

Southeastern: Ala., Ark., Fla., Ga., Ky., La., Miss., N.C., S.C., Tenn., Va., W. Va.

Memb. 1,700. Term of Office. Dec. 1992–Dec. 1994. Publication. The Southeastern Librarian (q.).

Pres. Gail Lazenby, Cobb County Public Lib., 266 Roswell St., Marietta, GA 30060.

Tel. 404-528-2324; V.P./Pres.-Elect Joe Forsee, Dir., Div. of Public Lib. Services, 156 Trinity Ave. S.W., Atlanta, GA 30303-3692; Secy. Ann Hamilton, Henderson Lib., Georgia Southern Univ., Statesboro, GA 30460; Treas. Robert Cannon, Public Lib. of Charlotte and Mecklenburg County, 310 N. Tryon St., Charlotte, NC 28202; Exec. Secy. Claudia Medori, Box 987, Tucker, GA 30085-0987. Tel./FAX 404-939-5080.

Address correspondence to the executive secretary, Southeastern Lib. Assn.

State and Provincial Library Agencies

The state library administrative agency in each of the U.S. states will have the latest information on its state plan for the use of federal funds under the Library Services and Construction Act. The directors and addresses of these state agencies are listed below.

Alabama

Patricia L. Harris, Dir., Alabama Public Lib. Service, 6030 Monticello Dr., Montgomery 36130-2001. Tel. 205-277-7330, FAX 205-272-9419.

Alaska

Karen R. Crane, Dir., Alaska State Libs., Archives, and Museums, Dept. of Educ., Box 110571, Juneau 99811-0571. Tel. 907-465-2910, FAX 907-465-2151.

Arizona

Arlene Bansal, Dir., Dept. of Libs., Archives, and Public Records, State Capitol, 1700 W. Washington, Suite 200, Phoenix 85007-2896. Tel. 602-542-4035, FAX 602-542-4972.

Arkansas

John A. (Pat) Murphey, Jr., State Libn., Arkansas State Lib., One Capitol Mall, Little Rock 72201-1081. Tel. 501-682-1526, FAX 501-682-1529.

California

Gary E. Strong, State Libn., California State Lib., Box 942837, Sacramento 94237-0001. Tel. 916-654-0174, FAX 916-654-0064.

Colorado

Nancy M. Bolt, Asst. Commissioner, State Lib. and Adult Education Office, Colorado Dept. of Educ., 201 E. Colfax Ave., Denver 80203. Tel. 303-866-6732, FAX 303-866-6940.

Connecticut

Richard G. Akeroyd, Jr., State Libn., Connecticut State Lib., 231 Capitol Ave., Hartford 06106. Tel. 203-566-4301, FAX 203-566-8940.

Delaware

Tom W. Sloan, State Libn. and Dir., Div. of Libs., 43 S. DuPont Hwy., Dover 19901. Tel. 302-739-4748, FAX 302-739-6787.

District of Columbia

Hardy R. Franklin, Dir., District of Columbia Public Lib., 901 G St. N.W., Suite 400, Washington 20001. Tel. 202-727-1101, FAX 202-727-1129.

Florida

Barratt Wilkins, State Libn., State Lib. of Florida, R. A. Gray Bldg., Tallahassee 32399-0250. Tel. 904-487-2651, FAX 904-488-2746.

Georgia

Joe B. Forsee, Dir., Div. of Public Lib. Services, 156 Trinity Ave. S.W., Atlanta 30303-3692. Tel. 404-656-2461, FAX 404-651-9447.

Hawaii

Bartholomew A. Kane, State Libn., Hawaii State Public Lib. System, 465 S. King St., Rm. B1, Honolulu 96813. Tel. 808-586-3704, FAX 808-586-3715.

Idaho

Charles A. Bolles, State Libn., Idaho State Lib., 325 W. State St., Boise 83702-6072. Tel. 208-334-5124, FAX 208-334-4016.

Illinois

Bridget L. Lamont, Dir., Illinois State Lib., 300 S. Second St., Springfield 62701-1796. Tel. 217-782-2994, FAX 217-785-4326.

Indiana

C. Ray Ewick, Dir., Indiana State Lib., 140 N. Senate Ave., Indianapolis 46204-2296. Tel. 317-232-3692, FAX 317-232-3728.

Iowa

Sharman B. Smith, State Libn., State Lib. of Iowa, E. 12 and Grand, Des Moines 50319. Tel. 515-281-4105, FAX 515-281-6191.

Kansas

Duane F. Johnson, State Libn., Kansas State Lib., State Capitol, 3rd fl., Topeka 66612-1593. Tel. 913-296-3296, FAX 913-296-6650.

Kentucky

James A. Nelson, State Libn./Commissioner, Kentucky Dept. for Libs. and Archives, 300 Coffee Tree Rd., Box 537, Frankfort 40602-0537. Tel. 502-875-7000, FAX 502-564-5773.

Louisiana

Thomas F. Jaques, State Libn., State Lib. of Louisiana, Box 131, Baton Rouge 70821-0131. Tel. 504-342-4923, FAX 504-342-3547.

Maine

J. Gary Nichols, State Libn., Maine State Lib., State House Sta. 64, Augusta 04333. Tel. 207-622-5600, FAX 207-287-5615.

Maryland

J. Maurice Travillian, Asst. State Superintendent for Libs., Div. of Lib. Development and Services, Maryland State Dept. of Educ., 200 W. Baltimore St., Baltimore 21201-2595. Tel. 410-333-2113, FAX 410-333-2507.

Massachusetts

Keith M. Fiels, Dir., Massachusetts Board of Lib. Commissioners, 648 Beacon St., Boston 02215. Tel. 617-267-9400, FAX 617-421-9833.

Michigan

James W. Fry, State Libn., Lib. of Michigan, 717 Allegan St., Box 30007, Lansing 48909. Tel. 517-373-1580, FAX 517-373-4480.

Minnesota

William G. Asp, Dir., Lib. Development and Services, Minnesota Dept. of Educ., 440 Capitol Sq., 550 Cedar St., Saint Paul 55101. Tel. 612-296-2821, FAX 612-296-5418.

Mississippi

Jame Smith, Acting Dir., Mississippi Lib. Commission, 1221 Ellis Ave., Box 10700, Jackson 39289-0700. Tel. 601-359-1036, FAX 601-354-4181.

Missouri

Monteria Hightower, Assoc. Commissioner for Libs./State Libn., Missouri State Lib., 600 W. Main, Box 387, Jefferson City 65102-0387. Tel. 314-526-4783, FAX 314-751-3612.

Montana

Richard T. Miller, Jr., State Libn., Montana State Lib., 1515 E. Sixth Ave., Box 201800, Helena 59620-1800. Tel. 406-444-3115, FAX 406-444-5612.

Nebraska

Rod Wagner, Dir., Nebraska Lib. Commission, The Atrium, 1200 N St., Suite 120, Lincoln 68508-2006. Tel. 402-471-4001, FAX 402-471-2083.

Nevada

Joan G. Kerschner, State Libn., Nevada State Lib. and Archives, Capitol Complex, Carson City 89710. Tel. 702-687-8315, FAX 702-687-8330.

New Hampshire

Kendall F. Wiggin, State Libn., New Hampshire State Lib., 20 Park St., Concord 03301-6314. Tel. 603-271-2397, FAX 603-271-2205.

New Jersey

Louise Minervino, State Libn., Div. of State Lib., Dept. of Educ., CN520, Trenton 08625-0520. Tel. 609-292-6200, FAX 609-292-2746.

New Mexico

Karen J. Watkins, State Libn., New Mexico State Lib., 325 Don Gaspar St., Santa Fe 87503. Tel. 505-827-3804, FAX 505-827-3888.

New York

Joseph F. Shubert, State Libn./Asst. Commissioner for Libs., New York State Lib., Rm. 10C34, C.E.C., Empire State Plaza, Albany 12230. Tel. 518-474-5930, FAX 518-474-2718.

North Carolina

Sandra M. Cooper, State Libn., Div. of State Lib., Dept. of Cultural Resources, 109 E. Jones St., Raleigh 27601-2807. Tel. 919-733-9923, FAX 919-733-8748.

North Dakota

William R. Strader, State Libn., North Dakota State Lib., Liberty Memorial Bldg., Capital Grounds, 604 East Blvd., Bismarck 58505-0800. Tel. 701-224-2717, FAX 701-224-2040.

Ohio

Richard M. Cheski, State Libn., State Lib. of Ohio, 64 S. Front St., Columbus 43266-0334. Tel. 614-644-6845, FAX 614-466-3584.

Oklahoma

Robert L. Clark, Jr., State Libn., Oklahoma Dept. of Libs., 200 N.E. 18 St., Oklahoma City 73105-3298. Tel. 405-521-2502, FAX 405-525-7804.

Oregon

Jim Scheppke, State Libn., Oregon State Lib., Salem 97310-0640. Tel. 503-378-4367, FAX 503-588-7119.

Pennsylvania

Sara Parker, Commissioner of Libs., Pennsylvania Dept. of Educ., Box 1601, Harrisburg 17105. Tel. 717-787-2646, FAX 717-772-3265.

Rhode Island

Barbara Weaver, Dir., Rhode Island Dept. of State Lib. Services, 300 Richmond St., Providence 02903-4222. Tel. 401-277-2726, FAX 401-831-5140.

South Carolina

James B. Johnson, Jr., Dir., South Carolina State Lib., 1500 Senate St., Box 11496, Columbia 29211. Tel. 803-734-8666, FAX 803-734-8676.

South Dakota

Jane Kolbe, State Libn., South Dakota State Lib., 800 Governors Dr., Pierre 57501-2294. Tel. 605-773-3131, FAX 605-773-4950.

Tennessee

Edwin S. Gleaves, State Libn./Archivist, Tennessee State Lib. and Archives, 403 Seventh Ave. N., Nashville 37243-0312. Tel. 615-741-7996, FAX 615-741-6471.

Texas

William D. Gooch, Dir./Libn., Texas State Lib., Box 12927, Capitol Sta., Austin 78711. Tel. 512-463-5460, FAX 512-463-5436.

Utah

Amy Owen, Dir., Utah State Lib., 2150 S. 300 W., Suite 16, Salt Lake City 84115. Tel. 801-466-5888, FAX 801-533-4657.

Vermont

Patricia E. Klinck, State Libn., Vermont Dept. of Libs., 109 State St., Montpelier 05609-0601. Tel. 802-828-3265, FAX 802-828-2199.

Virginia

John C. Tyson, State Libn., Virginia State Lib. and Archives, 11 St. at Capitol Sq., Richmond 23219-3491. Tel. 804-786-2332, FAX 804-786-5855.

Washington

Nancy L. Zussy, State Libn., Washington State Lib., Box 42460, Olympia 98504-2460. Tel. 206-753-2915, FAX 206-586-7575.

West Virginia

Frederic J. Glazer, Dir., West Virginia Lib. Commission, Science and Cultural Center, Charleston 25305. Tel. 304-558-2041, FAX 304-558-2044.

Wisconsin

William J. Wilson, Asst. Superintendent and Administrator, Div. for Lib. Services, Wisconsin Dept. of Public Instruction, 125 S. Webster St., Box 7841, Madison 53707-7841. Tel. 608-266-2205, FAX 608-267-1052.

Wyoming

Jerry Krois, Acting State Libn., State Lib. Div., Supreme Court and State Lib. Bldg., 2301 Capitol Ave., Cheyenne 82002-0060. Tel. 307-777-7283, FAX 307-777-6289.

American Samoa

Emma F. C. Pen, Program Dir., Office of Lib. Services, Dept. of Educ., Box 1329, Pago Pago 96799. Tel. 011-684-633-1181 or 1182.

Guam

Frank R. San Agustin, Territorial Libn., Nieves M. Flores Memorial Lib., 254 Martyr St., Agana 96910. Tel. 671-477-6417, FAX 671-477-9777.

Marshall Islands

Kinja Andrike, Secy. of Education, Dept. of Educ., Majuro 96960.

Micronesia

Daro Weital, Chief, Div. of Education, Kolonia, Pohnpei 96941.

Northern Mariana Islands

Richard Meldrom, Commonwealth Libn., Joeten-Kiyu Public Lib., Box 1092, Saipan 96950. Tel. 670-235-7550, FAX 670-235-7322.

Palau (Republic of)

William Tabelual, Dir., Bureau of Educ., Koror 96941.

Puerto Rico

Maria de los Angeles Lugo, Dir., Public Lib. Div., Dept. of Educ., Box 759, Hato Rey 00919. Tel. 809-753-9191.

Virgin Islands

Jeannette Bastian, Dir. and Territorial Libn., Div. of Libs., Archives and Museums, 23 Dronningens Gade, Saint Thomas 00802. Tel. 809-774-3407, FAX 809-775-1887.

Alberta

Lucy Pana, Dir., Lib. Services, Alberta Dept. of Community Development, Libs. and Community Development Branch, 16214-114 Ave., Edmonton T5M 2Z5. Tel. 403-427-2556, FAX 403-422-6519.

British Columbia

Barbara Greeniaus, Dir., Lib. Services Branch, Ministry of Municipal Affairs, Recreation, and Housing, 800 Johnson St., Victoria V8V 1X4. Tel. 604-356-1791, FAX 604-387-4048.

Manitoba

Sylvia Nicholson, Dir., Manitoba Culture, Heritage, and Citizenship, Public Lib. Services, Unit 200, 1525 First St., Brandon R7A 7A1. Tel. 204-726-6864, FAX 204-726-6868.

New Brunswick

Jocelyne LeBel, Dir., New Brunswick Lib. Service, Box 6000, Fredericton E3B 5H1. Tel. 506-453-2354, FAX 506-457-4991.

Newfoundland

Pearce J. Penney, Provincial Dir., Public Libs. Service, Arts and Culture Centre, Allandale Rd., Saint John's A1B 3A3. Tel. 709-737-3964, FAX 709-737-3009.

Northwest Territories

Ronald J. Mackenzie, Dir., N.W.T. Public Lib. Services, Government of the Northwest Territories, Box 1100, Hay River X0E 0R0. Tel. 403-874-6531, FAX 403-874-3321.

Nova Scotia

Marion L. Pape, Provincial Libn., Nova Scotia Provincial Lib., 3770 Kempt Rd., Halifax B3K 4X8. Tel. 902-424-2456, FAX 902-424-0633.

Ontario

Barbara Clubb, Dir., Libs. and Community Info. Branch, Ministry of Culture and Communications, 3rd fl., 77 Bloor St. W., Toronto M7A 2R9. Tel. 416-314-7611, FAX 416-314-7635.

Prince Edward Island

Albert MacDonald, Provincial Libn., P.E.I. Provincial Lib., Red Head Rd., Box 7500, Morell C0A 1S0. Tel. 902-961-3200.

Quebec

Michel Bonneau, Dir., Direction du livre, de la lecture, et des bibliothèques publiques, Ministère de la Culture, 225 Grande Allée Est, Bloc A, 3 étage, Quebec G1R 5G5. Tel. 418-644-7206, FAX 418-644-0380.

Saskatchewan

Gloria Materi, Acting Provincial Libn., Saskatchewan Provincial Lib., 1352 Winnipeg St., Regina S4P 3V7. Tel. 306-787-2972, FAX 306-787-8866.

Yukon Territory

Linda R. Johnson, Dir., Dept. of Educ., Libs., and Archives, Box 2703, Whitehorse Y1A 2C6. Tel. 403-667-5309, FAX 403-667-4253.

State School Library Media Associations

Alabama

Children's and School Libns. Div., Alabama Lib. Assn. Memb. 450. Term of Office. Apr. 1993–Apr. 1994. Pub lication. *The Alabama Librarian* (quarterly).
Exec. Dir. Barbara Black, 400 S. Union St., Suite 255, Montgomery 36104.
Address correspondence to the executive director.

Arizona

School Lib. Media Div., Arizona State Lib. Assn. Memb. 500. Term of Office. Dec. 1993–Nov. 1994. Publication. *ASLA Newsletter.*
Pres. Diane Skorupski, Liberty School, 5495 S. Liberty Ave., Tucson 85706. Tel. 602-741-2604; *Pres.-Elect* Mary Morris, Show Low H.S., 11350 N. Central, Show Low 85901. Tel. 602-537-2901.
Address correspondence to the president.

Arkansas

Arkansas Assn. of School Libns. and Media Educators. Term of Office. Jan.–Dec. 1994.
Chair Julie Morgan, 216 Hilltop Dr., Russellville 72801. Tel. 501-968-7364; *Chair-Elect* Linda Taylor, 2906 Pamela Dr., Benton 72015. Tel. 501-778-1667; *Secy.-Treas.* Doris Jones, Caldwell Elementary School, 1800 W. Sevier, Benton 72015. Tel. 501-778-4444.
Address correspondence to the chairperson.

California

California Media and Lib. Educators Assn. Job Hotline. 415-697-8832. Memb. 1,700. Term of Office. June 1993–May 1994. Publication. *CMLEA Journal.* Ed. Barbara Jeffus.
Pres. Robert Skapura, Los Medanos College, 2700 E. Leland Dr., Pittsburg 94565; *Pres.-Elect* John McGinnis, Cerritos Community College, 11110 Alondra Blvd., Norwalk 90650; *Secy.* Judith Toll, San Leandro H.S., 2200 Bancroft Ave., San Leandro 94577; *Treas.* Betty D. Silva, Fairfield H.S., 205 E. Atlantic, Fairfield 94533; *Business Office Secy.* Nancy D. Kohn, CMLEA, 1499 Old Bayshore Hwy., Suite 142, Burlingame 94010. Tel. 415-692-2350.
Address correspondence to the business office secretary.

Colorado

Colorado Educational Media Assn. Memb. 650. Term of Office. Feb. 1994–Feb. 1995.
Pres. Su Eckhardt; *Pres.-Elect* Billie Wolter; *Secy.* Nancy Terman.
Address correspondence to the executive secretary, Box 22814, Wellshire Sta., Denver 80222. Tel. 303-777-9122.

Connecticut

Connecticut Educational Media Assn. Term of Office. May 1993–May 1994. Publications. *CEMA Update Monthly;* CEMA videotape "The School Library Media Specialist—A Continuing Story," available in 1/2" ($35) or 3/4" Umatic ($40); Resource Guide ($13).
Pres. Carolyn Marcato, 155 Catalpa Rd., Wilton 06897. Tel. 203-762-2547; *V.P.* Tally Negroni, 53 Blueberry Hill, Weston 06883. Tel. 203-227-8044; *Secy.* Barbara Rocheleau, 460 Papurah Rd., Fairfield 06430. Tel. 203-259-9869; *Treas.* Michael Quigley, 3 Dittmar Rd., Bethel 06801. Tel. 203-744-3250; *Admin. Secy.* Anne Weimann, 25 Elmwood Ave., Trumbull 06611. Tel. 203-372-2260.
Address correspondence to the administrative secretary.

Delaware

Delaware School Lib. Media Assn. Div. of Delaware Lib. Assn. Memb. 100. Term of Office. Apr. 1993–Apr. 1994. Publications. *DSLMA Newsletter* (irreg.); column in *DLA Bulletin* (3 per year).
Pres. Patricia Woods, Sussex Vo-Tech Center, Box 351, Georgetown 19947. Tel. 302-856-0961; *V.P./Pres.-Elect* Ruth Davis, Delaware City Elementary, Fifth and Bayard St., Delaware City 19706. Tel. 302-834-3180.

Address correspondence to the president.

District of Columbia

District of Columbia Assn. of School Libns. Memb. 93. Term of Office. Aug. 1993–July 1995. Publication. *Newsletter* (4 per year).
Pres. Anita Drayton; *V.P.* Lydia Jenkins; *Rec. Secy.* Olivia Hardison; *Treas.* Mary Minnis; *Financial Secy.* Connie Lawson; *Corres. Secy.* Sharon Sorrels, Banneker H.S., 800 Euclid St. N.W., Washington 20001.

Address correspondence to the association, Box 90488, Washington 20090-0488.

Florida

Florida Assn. for Media in Education. Memb. 1,450. Term of Office. Oct. 1993–Oct. 1994. Publication. *Florida Media Quarterly.* Ed. Pat Conlon, Rte. 4, Box 461, Hawthorne 32640. Tel. 904-620-7587.
Pres. Helen Tallman, 7601 S.W. 94 Ave., Miami 33173. Tel. 305-365-6278; *Pres.-Elect* Linda Schroeder, 4249 N.W. 56 Way, Gainesville 32606. Tel. 904-336-2702; *V.P.* Donna Heald, 1941 N.E. 51 St., Suite 48, Fort Lauderdale 33308. Tel. 305-572-1336, FAX 305-572-1334; *Secy.* Ginger Klega, 7360 Sparkling Lake Rd., Orlando 32819. Tel. 407-656-2424 Ext. 208; *Assn. Exec.* Mary Margaret Rogers, Box 13119, Tallahassee 32317. Tel. 904-893-5396.

Address correspondence to the association executive.

Georgia

School Lib. Media Div., Georgia Lib. Assn. Term of Office. Oct. 1993–Oct. 1995.
Chair Margie McClure, Avondale Elementary School, 10 Lakeshore Dr., Avondale Estates 30002. Tel. 404-284-5324; *Pres.* Donna Mancini, DeKalb County Admin. Bldg., 5th fl., 1300 Commerce Dr., Decatur 30030. Tel. 404-371-3045, FAX 404-371-3057; *Secy.* David Searcy, Atlanta Fulton Public Lib., E. Atlanta Branch, 457 Flat Shoals Ave., Atlanta 30316. Tel. 404-525-8802.

Address correspondence to the association, Box 39, Young Harris 30582. Tel. 706-379-3526, FAX 706-379-4203.

Hawaii

Hawaii Assn. of School Libns. Memb. 299. Term of Office. June 1993–May 1994. Publications. *HASL Newsletter* (1 per semester); *Golden Key Journal* (1 every 5 years).
Pres. Kathleen Cannallo. Tel. 808-536-2756; *1st V.P.* Bev Fujita; *2nd V.P.* Irmalee Choo; *Rec. Secy.* Candace Foster; *Corres. Secy.* Velma Yoshitake; *Treas.* Myles Furubayashi; *Dirs.* Roseyn Devlin, Betsy Young.

Address correspondence to the association, Box 23019, Honolulu 96822.

Idaho

Educational Media Div., Idaho Lib. Assn. Memb. 125. Term of Office. Oct. 1992–Oct. 1994. Publication. Column in *The Idaho Librarian* (q.).
Chair Susan Van Orden, Pocatello H.S., 325 N. Arthur Ave., Pocatello 83204. Tel. 208-233-2056; *Chair-Elect* Larry Gold, School Dist. Office, 3115 Poline Rd., Pocatello 83201. Tel. 208-253-3222; *Secy.* Sue Crofts, 33 Purdue Ave., Pocatello 83204.

Address correspondence to the chairperson.

Illinois

Illinois School Lib. Media Assn. Term of Office. July 1993–June 1994.
Pres. Johanne Grewell, 4118 Westport Ct., Peoria 61615. Tel. 309-685-2567; *Pres.-Elect* Sondra Miller, 29 Providence Lane, Springfield 62707. Tel. 217-546-0907.

Address correspondence to Box 598, Canton 61520. Tel. 309-649-0911, FAX 309-647-0140.

Indiana

Assn. for Indiana Media Educators. Memb. 1,025. Term of Office. May 1993–Apr. 1994. Publications. *AIME News* (mo.); *Indiana Media Journal* (q.).
Pres. Judy Hays, Avon H.S., 13013 W. Rockville Rd., Indianapolis 46234. Tel. 317-272-2586, FAX 317-272-3100; *Pres.-Elect* Bonnie Grimble, Carmel H.S., 520 E. Main St., Carmel 46032. Tel. 317-846-7721, FAX 317-571-4066; *Admin. Asst.* Karen G. Burch, 1908 E. 64 St., South Dr., Indianapolis

46220. Tel. 317-257-8558, FAX 317-259-4191.

Address correspondence to the administrative assistant.

Iowa

Iowa Educational Media Assn. Memb. 600. Term of Office. Apr. 1993–Mar. 1994. Publication. *Iowa Media Message* (5 per year). *Ed.* Margaret White, Grant Wood Area Education Agency, 4401 Sixth St. S.W., Cedar Rapids 52404.

Pres. Thomas Hoffman, Heartland Area Education Agency, 6500 Corporate Dr., Johnston 50131; *Pres.-Elect* Lucille Lettow, 1516 College St., Cedar Falls 50613; *Exec. Secy.* Paula Behrendt, 2306 Sixth, Harlan 51537; *Treas.* Rick Maehl.

Address correspondence to the executive secretary.

Kansas

Kansas Assn. of School Libns. Memb. 700. Term of Office. July 1993–June 1994. Publication. *KASL Newsletter* (s. ann.).

Pres. Shelia Blume, 227 Fifth St., Phillipsburg 67661. Tel. 913-543-5469; *V.P./Pres.-Elect* Roma McConkey, 337 S. Cunningham Rd., Salina 67401; *Treas.* Kathy Schulz, Box 34, Hill City 67642; *Secy.* Kay Weigel, 1915 Montgomery Dr., Manhattan 66502. Tel. 913-539-7976; *Business Mgr.* Kay Mounkes, 2823 Rd. L, Emporia 66801.

Address correspondence to the business manager.

Kentucky

Kentucky School Media Assn. Memb. 628. Term of Office. Oct. 1993–Oct. 1994. Publication. *KSMA Newsletter.*

Pres. Jackie White, Kentucky Dept. of Educ., 500 Mero St., Frankfort 40601; *Pres.-Elect* Donna Hornsby, Beechwood Independent School, Beechwood Rd., Fort Mitchell 41017; *Secy.* Carolyn Hammond, Danville H.S., 203 E. Lexington St., Danville 40422; *Treas.* Margarette Morris, Belfry H.S., Box 457, Belfry 41514. Tel. 606-353-9093.

Address correspondence to the president.

Louisiana

Louisiana Assn. of School Libns. Memb. 580. Term of Office. July 1993–June 1994.

Pres. Mattie Mosley, 2060 Pepper Ridge Dr., Shreveport 71115. Tel. 318-797-5034; *1st V.P.* Mary Ellen Shiflett, 5 Country Club, LaPlace 70068. Tel. 504-758-2116; *2nd V.P.* Claudia J. Fisher, 23990 Reames Rd., Zachary 70791. Tel. 504-654-9201; *Secy.* Grace Guth, 932 Idlewilde Lane, Lake Charles 70605. Tel. 318-433-3497.

Address correspondence to the association, c/o Louisiana Lib. Assn., Box 3058, Baton Rouge 70821.

Maine

Maine Educational Media Assn. Memb. 350. Term of Office. May 1993–May 1995. Publication. *Maine Entry* (with the Maine Lib. Assn.).

Pres. David W. Anderson, Thornton Academy, 438 Main St., Saco 04072. Tel. 207-282-3361; *1st V.P.* Linda Lord, Maine State Lib., State House Sta. 64, Augusta 04333; *2nd V.P.* Susan Allison, Lewiston H.S., 156 E. Ave., Lewiston 04240; *Secy.* Carol King, Wells Jr. H.S., Box 310, Wells 04090; *Treas.* Karen Keller, Winslow Jr. H.S., 10 Danielson St., Winslow 04901.

Address correspondence to the president.

Maryland

Maryland Educational Media Organization. Term of Office. July 1994–June 1995. Publication. *MEMORANDOM.*

Pres. Fred Thomas, 201 Booth St., Elkton 21921; *Treas.* Sylvia Hazzard, 10697 Quarterstaff Rd., Columbia 21044; *Admin. Secy.* Jean Flohr.

Address correspondence to the association, Box 21127, Baltimore 21228.

Massachusetts

Massachusetts School Lib. Media Assn., formerly Massachusetts Assn. for Educational Media. Memb. 500. Term of Office. June 1993–May 1994. Publication. *Media Forum* (q.).

Pres. Rolf Erikson, Minuteman Regional VT, 758 Marrett Rd., Lexington 02173; *Secy.*

Kathy Lowe, Lunenburg H.S., 1079 Massachusetts Ave., Lunenberg 01462; *Treas.* Gail Thomas, Medway High and Middle Schools, 45 Holliston St., Medway 02053; *Admin. Asst.* Sue Rebello, MSLMA, Box 618, Franklin 02038. Tel. 413-283-7119.

Address correspondence to the administrative assistant.

Michigan

Michigan Assn. for Media in Education. Memb. 1,400. Term of Office. Jan.–Dec. 1994. Publications. *Media Spectrum* (4 per year); *MAME Newsletter* (5 per year).

Pres. Victoria DeFields, Bridgman Public School Dist., 9964 Gast Rd., Bridgman 49106. Tel. 616-466-0229; *Pres.-Elect* Sue Schwartz, REMC 13, Ingham ISD, 210 State St., Mason 48854. Tel. 517-676-9726; *V.P. for Special Interest Groups* Terence Madden, Ann Arbor Public Schools, 2555 S. State St., Ann Arbor 48104. Tel. 313-994-2220; *Treas.* LaRene Klink, Genesee School Dist., 7347 N. Genesee Rd., Genesee 48437. Tel. 313-640-3111; *V.P. for Regions* Tricia Lamiman, Reeths-Puffer Schools, 1911 W. Giles Rd., Muskegon 49445. Tel. 616-744-4721; *Secy.* Linda Arbogast, Lewiston Schools, Box 417, Lewiston 49756. Tel. 517-786-2253; *Exec. Dir.* Burton H. Brooks, 6810 S. Cedar St., Suite 8, Lansing 48911. Tel. 517-699-1717, 616-842-9195, FAX 616-842-9195.

Address correspondence to the executive director.

Minnesota

Minnesota Educational Media Organization. Memb. 840. Term of Office. (Pres.) June 1993–June 1994 (other offices 2 years in alternating years). Publications. *Minnesota Media* (3 per year); *ImMEDEAte; MEMOrandum* (mo.). *Ed.* Al Lundquist, 264 Queenan Ave. S., Lakeland 55043. Tel. 612-458-6225.

Pres. Jim Marshall, 205 Birnamwood Dr., Burnsville 55337. Tel. 612-591-4742; *Secy.* Susan Sandell, 6862 Eckles Rd. N.W., Bemidji 56601; *Treas.* Charlie Lindberg.

Mississippi

School Section, Mississippi Lib. Assn. Memb. 1,300. Term of Office. Jan.–Dec. 1994.

Chair Judith Eichman; *Secy.* Florence Box.

Address correspondence to the association, c/o Mississippi Lib. Assn., Box 20448, Jackson 39289-1448.

Missouri

Missouri Assn. of School Libns. Memb. 903. Term of Office. June 1993–May 1994.

Pres. Marilyn Stone, Hickman H.S., Columbia 65202. Tel. 314-886-2541; *Pres.-Elect* Rita Linck, Parkway South H.S., Ballwin 63021. Tel. 314-394-8354, FAX 314-394-8353.

Address correspondence to the association, 5552 S. Kingsway, Saint Louis 63109-3528.

Montana

Montana School Lib. Media Div., Montana Lib. Assn. Memb. 225. Term of Office. Aug. 1993–Apr. 1994. Publication. *Montana Library Focus* (published by Montana Lib. Assn.) (q.).

Pres. Dan Kohnstamm, 573 Somers Ave., Whitefish 59937. Tel. 406-862-8609; *V.P./Pres.-Elect* Polly Taggart, 2515 Silver Blvd., Billings 59102. Tel. 406-652-6692.

Address correspondence to the president.

Nebraska

Nebraska Educational Media. Assn. Memb. 350. Term of Office. July 1993–June 1994. Publication. *NEMA News* (4 per year). *Ed.* c/o Box 286, Henderson 68371.

Pres. Phyllis Brunken, ESU #7, 2657 44th Ave., Columbus 68601. Tel. 402-564-5753, FAX 402-563-1121; *Pres.-Elect* Steve Davis, Kearney Public School, Central Media and Technology, 310 W. 24 St., Kearney 68847. Tel. 308-234-6431, FAX 308-237-5796; *Secy.* Barbara Hansen, Norfolk Jr. H.S., 510 and Pasewalk, Norfolk 68701. Tel. 402-371-7206; *Treas.* Marilyn Scahill, Dodge Elementary School, Grand Island Schools, 641 S. Oak St., Grand Island 68801. Tel. 308-381-5889.

Address correspondence to the president.

Nevada

Nevada School and Children's Lib. Section, Nevada Lib. Assn. Memb. 100. Term of Office. Jan.–Dec. 1994.

Pres. Marsha Haaser, Incline Middle School, Incline Village 89451. Tel. 702-832-4220.

New Hampshire

New Hampshire Educational Media Assn., Box 418, Concord 03302-0418. Memb. 265. Term of Office. June 1993–June 1994. Publications. *Online* (5 per year), *Taproot* (s. ann.).

Pres. Margaret Beale, Hollis Jr. H.S., Hollis 03049. Tel. 603-465-2223; *Pres.-Elect* Deirdre Angwin, McKelvie Middle School, 108 Liberty Hill Rd., Bedford 03110. Tel. 603-472-3729; *V.P.* Kim Carter, Souhegan H.S., Amherst 03031. Tel. 603-673-9940; *Treas.* Jeff Kent, Broken Ground School, Concord 03301. Tel. 603-225-0825; *Rec. Secy.* Joan Abbott, Bicentennial Elementary School, E. Dunstable Rd., Nashua 03062. Tel. 603-594-4383; *Corres. Secy.* Joyce Fisher, Stevens H.S., Broad St., Claremont 03743. Tel. 603-543-4220.

Address correspondence to the president.

New Jersey

Educational Media Assn. of New Jersey. Memb. 1,080. Term of Office. June 1993–May 1994. Publications. *Signal Tab* (mo.); *Emanations* (2 per year).

Pres. Mary Jane Smith, 4 Wilbur Terr., Sayreville 08872; *Pres.-Elect* Pam Chesky, 135 Midwood Way, Colonia 07067; *V.P.* Dagmar Finkle, 81 Lisa Dr., Chatham 07928; *Rec. Secy.* Nina Kemps, 647 Guilford Rd., Cherry Hill 08003; *Corres. Secy.* Judy Dursema, 19 Strong St., Mahwah 07430; *Treas.* Gordon Mann, 902 Roosevelt Blvd., Clayton 08312.

Address correspondence to the president.

New Mexico

School Libs. Children and Young Adult Services Div., New Mexico Lib. Assn. Memb. 240. Term of Office. Apr. 1993–Apr. 1994.

Chair Jerry Klopfer, Paul Horgan Lib., New Mexico Military Academy, 100 W. College, Roswell 88201-5173. Tel. 505-624-8382; *Chair-Elect* Dianah Jentgen.

Address correspondence to the chairperson.

New York

School Lib. Media Section, New York Lib. Assn., 252 Hudson St., Albany 12210. Tel. 518-432-6952, 800-252-6952. Memb. 950. Term of Office. Oct. 1993–Oct. 1994. Publications. *SLMSGram* (q.); participates in *NYLA Bulletin* (mo. except July and Aug.).

Pres. Sara Kelly Johns, Beekmantown Central School, Box 829, Plattsburgh 12901. Tel. 518-563-0041; *V.P., Communications* Donna Chumas, Patchogue Medford H.S., Buffalo Ave., Medford 11763-3703. Tel. 516-447-3143; *V.P., Conferences* Kristine Littrell, Pittsford Mendon H.S., Mendon Rd., Pittsford 14534. Tel. 716-385-4138; *Secy.* Marcia Eggleston, Norwood–Norfolk Central School, Rte. 56, Norwood 13668. Tel. 315-353-6631; *Treas.* Connie Wright, Southwestern Central School, 600 Hunt Rd., Jamestown 14701. Tel. 716-664-6273; *Bureau of School Lib. Media Programs* Robert Barron, State Educ. Dept., Education Bldg. Annex, Rm. 676, Albany 12234. Tel. 518-474-2468; *Div. of Lib. Development* Joseph Mattie, New York State Lib., CED, Rm. 10B41, Albany 12230. Tel. 518-474-7890.

Address correspondence to the president or secretary.

North Carolina

North Carolina Assn. of School Libns. Memb. 1,000. Term of Office. Oct. 1993–Oct. 1995.

Chair Augie Beasley, East Mecklenburg H.S., 6800 Monroe Rd., Charlotte 28212. Tel. 704-343-6430; *Chair-Elect* Karen Perry, High Point Central H.S., 801 Ferndale Dr., High Point 27262. Tel. 919-819-2852.

Address correspondence to the chairperson.

North Dakota

School Lib. and Youth Services Section, North Dakota Lib. Assn. Memb. 108. Term of Office. Sept. 1993–Sept. 1994. Publication. *The Good Stuff.*

Pres. Linda Miller, Wahpeton Middle School, Wahpeton 58075. Tel. 701-642-6687; *Secy.* Sharon Paintner, Carrington H.S., Carrington 58421. Tel. 701-652-3136.

Address correspondence to the president.

Ohio

Ohio Educational Lib. Media Assn. Memb. 1,300. Term of Office. Jan.–Dec. 1994. Publication. *Ohio Media Spectrum.*

Pres. Lynda Sadowski, Mentor Exempted Village Schools, Mentor H.S., 6477 Center St., Mentor 44060; *Exec. Dir.* Ann Hanning, 1631 N.W. Professional Plaza, Columbus 43220. Tel. 614-326-1460, FAX 614-459-2087.

Address correspondence to the executive director.

Oklahoma

Oklahoma Assn. of School Lib. Media Specialists. Memb. 392. Term of Office. July 1993–June 1994. Publication. *Information Powerline.*

Chair Linda Gann, Jenks H.S., 205 E. B St., Jenks 74037. Tel. 918-299-4411, FAX 918-299-9197; *Chair-Elect* Phil Woolverton, McLoud H.S., Box 60, McLoud 74851. Tel. 405-946-3352, FAX 405-964-2801; *Secy.* Linda DeBerry, Idabel H.S., 901 Lincoln Rd., Idabel 74745. Tel. 405-286-7693, FAX 405-286-5585; *Treas.* JoAnne Hope, SDE, 2500 N. Lincoln Blvd. 215, Oklahoma City 73105. Tel. 405-521-2956, FAX 405-521-6205.

Address correspondence to the chairperson.

Oregon

Oregon Educational Media Assn. Memb. 700. Term of Office. Oct. 1993–Sept. 1994. Publication. *INTERCHANGE.*

Pres. Richard Forcier; *Pres.-Elect* Diane Claus-Smith; *Exec. Secy.* Sherry Hevland, 16695 S.W. Rosa Rd., Beaverton 97007. Tel. 503-649-5764.

Address correspondence to the executive secretary.

Pennsylvania

Pennsylvania School Libns. Assn. Term of Office. July 1992–June 1994. Publication. *Learning and Media* (4 per year).

Pres. Sally Myers, 337 Roley St., Belle Vernon 15012.

Address correspondence to the president.

Rhode Island

Rhode Island Educational Media Assn. Memb. 356. Term of Office. June 1993–May 1994. Publication. *RIEMA Newsletter* (5 per year). *Ed.* Bette G. Dion, 8 Evelyn Dr., Bristol 02809. Tel. 401-253-9345.

Pres. Susan Bryan, 26B Tamarac Dr., Greenville 02828. Tel. 401-949-4230; *V.P.* Karen M. Shore, 27 Nancy St., Pawtucket 02860. Tel. 401-722-2108; *Secy.* Janice Carreau, 101 Old North Rd., Mystic, CT 06355. Tel. 203-536-7066; *Treas.* Joseph Light, 34 George St., Westerly 02891. Tel. 401-596-3173; *Memb. Chair* Michael Mello, 486 Water St., Portsmouth 02871. Tel. 401-683-4499, FAX 401-683-5204.

Address correspondence to the association, Box 762, Portsmouth 02871.

South Carolina

South Carolina Assn. of School Libns. Memb. 1,128. Term of Office. June 1993–May 1994. Publication. *Media Center Messenger* (5 per year).

Pres. David Bell, Myrtle Beach H.S., 3300 Central Pkwy., Myrtle Beach 29577. Tel. 803-626-5303; *Pres.-Elect* Elisabeth Hall, Arden Elementary School, 1300 Ashley St., Columbia 29203. Tel. 803-735-3400; *Exec. Secy.* David Cobb, Box 2442, Columbia 29202. Tel. 803-822-5640, FAX 803-822-5665.

Address correspondence to the executive secretary.

South Dakota

South Dakota School Lib. Media Assn., Section of the South Dakota Lib. Assn. and South Dakota Education Assn. Term of Office. Oct. 1993–Oct. 1994.

Pres. Kristen Leite; *Pres.-Elect* Maritta Brown; *Secy.-Treas.* Rosalie Aslesen,

Spearfish H.S., Spearfish 57783. Tel. 605-642-2612.

Address correspondence to the secretary-treasurer.

Tennessee

Tennessee Assn. of School Libns., Tennessee Education Assn. Term of Office. Nov. 1993–July 1995.

Pres. Donna Garrett, 1784 Old Mill Rd., Germantown 38138; V.P. Yuvonne Joslin.

Address correspondence to the president.

Texas

Texas Assn. of School Libns. Memb. 2,905. Term of Office. Apr. 1993–Apr. 1994. Publication. *Media Matters* (3 per year).

Chair Michael Bell, 3009 Hawk Ave., McAllen 78504-5062. Tel. 210-618-8330; *V.Chair* Cyd Sheffy, 2709 Covert Ave., Fort Worth 76133-1807. Tel. 817-370-5870; *Secy.* Nancy J. Newton, 4632 94th St., Lubbock 79424-5016. Tel. 806-766-1666.

Address correspondence to an officer or to the association, 3355 Bee Cave Rd., Suite 401, Austin 78746. Tel. 512-328-1518.

Utah

Utah Educational Lib. Media Assn. Memb. 400. Term of Office. Mar. 1993–Mar. 1994. Publication. *UELMA Newsletter* (5 per year).

Pres. Carolyn Derricott, West Jordan H.S., 8136 S. 2700 W., West Jordan 84088. Tel. 801-565-7576; *2nd V.P.* Richard Siddoway, Davis School Dist., 45 E. State St., Farmington 84025. Tel. 801-451-1135; *Secy.* Dennis Morgan, Riverview Jr. H.S., 751 W. Tripp Lane, Murray 84123. Tel. 801-264-7406; *Treas.* Jan Staheli, Provo School Dist., 931 E. 300 N., Provo 84606. Tel. 801-374-5480; *Exec. Secy.* David Walton, Alpine School Dist., 50 N. Center, American Fork 84003. Tel. 801-756-8470.

Address correspondence to the executive secretary.

Vermont

Vermont Educational Media Assn. Memb. 203. Term of Office. May 1993–May 1994. Publication. *VEMA News* (q.).

Pres. Karen Hennig, Craftsbury Academy, Craftsbury Common 05827. Tel. 802-586-7706; *Pres.-Elect* Mary Prior, Barnet School, W. Barnet Rd., Barnet 05821. Tel. 802-633-4978; *Secy.* Holly Kruse, Cabot School, Cabot 05647. Tel. 802-563-2289; *Treas.* Patricia Nelson, Berlin Elementary School, R.D. 4, Box 2060, Montpelier 05602. Tel. 802-223-2796.

Address correspondence to the president.

Virginia

Virginia Educational Media Assn. Memb. 1,000. Term of Office. Oct. 1993–Oct. 1994. Publications. *Mediagram* (q.); *VEMA Journal* (s. ann.).

Pres. Vickie Pearce, 1077 Lord Dunmore Dr., Virginia Beach 23464. Tel. 804-441-5865; *Pres.-Elect* Verley Dotson, Box 156, Hurley 24620. Tel. 703-566-8334, FAX 703-566-7738; *Secy.* Melinda Younger; *Treas.* Frances Clark.

Address correspondence to the president.

Washington

Washington Lib. Media Assn. Memb. 1,150. Term of Office. Oct. 1993–Oct. 1994. Publication. *The Medium* (3 per year). *Ed.* Sue Weiss, 23708 107th Place W., Edmonds 98020-5238. Tel. 206-546-2715.

Pres. Susan Baker, 304 White Pine Dr., Bremerton 98310; *Pres.-Elect* Eldon Bond, 1135 Wheaton Way, No. A-1, Bremerton 98310; *V.P.* Joanne Sheely, 1312 Dayton Ave. N.E., Renton 98056; *Secy.* Janet Brown, 5702 16th Ave. S.E., Apt. B, Lacey 98503. Tel. 206-459-8594; *Treas.* Barbara Baker, Box 1413, Bothell 98041. Tel. 206-489-6258.

Address correspondence to the president.

West Virginia

West Virginia Educational Media Assn. Memb. 150. Term of Office. Apr. 1993–Apr. 1994. Publication. *WVEMA Newsletter*.

Pres. Lynne Curran, Doddridge County Middle School, West Union 26456. Tel. 304-873-2390; *Pres.-Elect* Janet Underwood, Salem-Teikyo Univ., Salem 26426. Tel. 304-782-5011.

Address correspondence to the president.

Wisconsin

Wisconsin Educational Media Assn. Memb. 870. Term of Office. Mar. 1992–Apr. 1994. Publications. *Dispatch* (6 per year); *Wisconsin Ideas in Media* (ann.). *Pres.* Nels Aakre, N6176 Summerglow Trail, Onalaska 54650. Tel. 608-789-7737; *Pres.-Elect* Terri Iverson, 1835 Ridgeview Acres, Platteville 53818. Tel. 608-822-3276. Address correspondence to the president.

Wyoming

Section of School Library Media Personnel, Wyoming Lib. Assn. Memb. 80. Term of Office. Oct. 1993–Oct. 1994.

Chair E. Douglas Hinkle, Wheatland H.S., 13 and Oak Sts., Wheatland 82201. Tel. 307-322-2075 Ext. 4336, FAX 307-322-2084. Address correspondence to the chairperson.

Puerto Rico

Puerto Rico Assn. of School Libns. (ABE-SPRI). Memb. 498. Publications. *ABE-SPRINF* (4 per year); *BIBESCO* (every 2 years).
Pres. Shirley Kennerly.
Address correspondence to the Asociación de Bibliotecarios Escolares de Puerto Rico, c/o Dept. of Educ., Cesar Gonzalez Ave., Box 1559, Hato Rey 00917. Tel. 809-763-6199.

State Supervisors of School Library Media Services

Alabama

Jane Bandy Smith, Staff Development Specialist, Gordon Persons Bldg., Rm. 3345, 50 N. Ripley St., Montgomery 36130-3901. Tel. 205-242-8082, FAX 205-242-0482.

Alaska

Vacant. 344 W. Third Ave., Suite 125, Anchorage 99501-2337. Tel. 907-269-6568.

Arizona

Irene Munger, Lib. Media Consultant/Literacy Specialist, State Dept. of Educ., 1535 W. Jefferson, Phoenix 85007. Tel. 602-542-3537.

Arkansas

Margaret Crank, Lib. Media Program Specialist, Arkansas Dept. of Educ., Arch Ford Bldg., 4 Capitol Mall, Rm. 107A, Little Rock 72201. Tel. 501-682-4396.

Colorado

Nancy M. Bolt, Asst. Commissioner, Colorado State Lib., 201 E. Colfax Ave., Denver 80203. Tel. 303-866-6900, FAX 303-866-6940.

Lynda Welborn, Sr. Consultant, School Media, Colorado Dept. of Educ., 201 E. Colfax Ave., Denver 80203. Tel. 303-866-6730, FAX 303-866-6940.

Connecticut

Betty B. Goyette, Consultant for Lib. Media Services and Instructional TV, State Dept. of Educ., 165 Capitol Ave., Hartford 06106-1630. Tel. 203-566-6660.

District of Columbia

Marie Harris Aldridge, Supervising Dir., Lib. Services, Dist. of Columbia Public Schools, Wilkinson Admin. Annex, Pomeroy Rd. and Erie St. S.E., Washington 20020. Tel. 202-767-8643, FAX 202-404-1085.

Florida

Sandra W. Ulm, Administrator, School Lib. Media Services, Florida Dept. of Educ., 522 Florida Education Center, 325 W. Gaines St., Tallahassee 32399. Tel. 904-488-8184.

Georgia

Nancy V. Paysinger, Dir., Media Programs, Div. of Curriculum and Instruction, Georgia

Dept. of Educ., Twin Towers E., Suite 2054, Atlanta 30334. Tel. 404-656-2418.

Hawaii

Patsy Izumo, Dir., Special Instructional Programs and Services Branch, State Dept. of Educ., 2530 Tenth Ave., Rm. A20, Honolulu 96816.

Illinois

Mark Wancket, Principal Consultant, and Byron (Bud) Bartlett, Instructional TV Specialist, Instructional Technology Section, Illinois State Board of Educ., 100 N. First St., Springfield 62777. Tel. 217-782-5844, FAX 217-524-6125.

Indiana

Jacqueline G. Morris, Learning Resources, Center for School Improvement and Performance, Indiana Dept. of Educ., 229 State House, Indianapolis 46204. Tel. 317-232-9125.

Iowa

Betty Jo Buckingham, Consultant, Educational Media, State Dept. of Educ., Grimes State Office Bldg., Des Moines 50319-0146. Tel. 515-281-3707.

Kansas

Jacqueline Lakin, Education Program Consultant, Kansas State Board of Educ., 120 S.E. Tenth Ave., Topeka 66612-1182. Tel. 913-296-2144, FAX 913-296-7933.

Kentucky

Jackie White, Info. Resources Consultant, Kentucky Dept. of Educ., 500 Mero St., Frankfort 40601. Tel. 502-564-7168.

Maine

Walter J. Taranko, Coord., Media Services, Maine State Lib., LMA Bldg., State House Sta. 64, Augusta 04333. Tel. 207-287-5620.

Maryland

Gail C. Bailey, Chief, School Lib. Media Services and State Media Services Branch, Div. of Lib. Development and Services, State Dept. of Educ., 200 W. Baltimore St., Baltimore 21201. Tel. 410-333-2125.

Massachusetts

Candace Boyden, Acting Rep., Dept. of Educ., 350 Main St., Malden 02148. Tel. 617-388-3300.

Michigan

Daniel W. Schultz, Asst. Superintendent, Educational Technology and Grants, Michigan Dept. of Educ., Box 30008, Lansing 48909. Tel. 517-373-6331.

Missouri

Carl Sitze, Missouri Dept. of Elementary and Secondary Educ., Box 480, Jefferson City 65102. Tel. 314-751-7754.

Montana

Lorrie Monprode-Holt, Lib. Media Specialist, Office of Public Instruction, 1300 11th Ave., Helena 59601. Tel. 406-444-2979, FAX 406-444-3924.

Nevada

Frank South, Dir., Nevada Dept. of Educ., Capitol Complex, 400 W. King St., Carson City 89710. Tel. 702-687-3136.

New Hampshire

Susan C. Snider, Curriculum Supv., Lib. Media Services, State Dept. of Educ., Div. of Instructional Services, 101 Pleasant St., Concord 03301. Tel. 603-271-3454.

New Jersey

Jean E. Harris, Consultant, State Dept. of Educ., State Lib., 185 W. State St., CN 520, Trenton 08625-0520. Tel. 609-292-6245.

New Mexico

Mary Jane Vinella, Lib./Media Consultant, Dept. of Educ., Education Bldg., Santa Fe 87501-2786. Tel. 505-827-6504.

New York

Robert E. Barron, State Supv., School Lib. Media Programs, State Educ. Dept., Rm. 676 EBA, Albany 12234. Tel. 518-474-2468.

North Carolina

Elsie L. Brumback, Dir., Media and Technology, Dept. of Public Instruction, Raleigh 27601-2825. Tel. 919-715-1530.

North Dakota

Patricia Herbel, Dir., Elementary Education, Dept. of Public Instruction, State Capitol, 600 East Blvd., Bismarck 58505. Tel. 701-224-2295, FAX 701-224-4770.

Ohio

Carl Carter, Lib./Media Consultant, Ohio Dept. of Educ., 65 S. Front St., Rm. 611, Columbus 43266-0308. Tel. 614-466-9272.

Oklahoma

Bettie Estes-Rickner, Dir., and Carol Casey, Coord., Lib. Media Section, State Dept. of Educ., 2500 N. Lincoln Blvd., Oklahoma City 73105-4599. Tel. 405-521-2956.

Oregon

James W. Sanner, Specialist, Instructional Technology, Oregon Dept. of Educ., 255 Capitol St. N.E., Salem 97310. Tel. 503-378-8004.

Pennsylvania

John L. Emerick, Div. of School Lib. Media Services, State Dept. of Educ., 333 Market St., Harrisburg 17126-0333. Tel. 717-787-6704.

Rhode Island

Marie DiBiasio, Dir., Office of Instruction, Rhode Island Dept. of Educ., 22 Hayes St., Providence 02908. Tel. 401-277-2648.

South Carolina

Linda C. Bartone, Education Associate: Library/Media, State Dept. of Educ., 801 Rutledge Bldg., 1429 Senate St., Columbia 29201. Tel. 803-734-8395, FAX 803-734-8624.

South Dakota

Donna Gilliland, School Lib./Media Coord., South Dakota State Lib., 800 Governors Dr., Pierre 57501-2294. Tel. 605-773-3131.

Tennessee

Vacant. State Dept. of Educ., Div. of Curriculum and Instruction, 8th fl., Gateway Plaza, 710 James Robertson Pkwy., Nashville 37243-0379. Tel. 615-532-6300.

Texas

June Kahler, Dir., Lib. Media Program, Texas Education Agency, 1701 N. Congress Ave., Austin 78701-1494. Tel. 512-463-9542.

Utah

Sharyl G. Smith, Instructional Services, State Office of Educ., 250 E. Fifth S., Salt Lake City 84111. Tel. 801-538-7789.

Vermont

Leda Schubert, School Lib./Media Consultant, Vermont Dept. of Educ., Montpelier 05620. Tel. 802-828-3111.

Virginia

Gloria K. Barber, Assoc., Lib./Media, Dept. of Educ., Box 2120, Richmond 23216-2120. Tel. 804-225-2539, FAX 804-786-1703.

Washington

Gayle D. Pauley, Supv., Office of State Superintendent of Public Instruction, Old Capitol Bldg., Box 47200, Olympia 98504. Tel. 206-753-2858.

West Virginia

Brenda Williams, Asst. Dir., Office of Technology, West Virginia Dept. of Educ., Bldg. 6, Rm. 346, 1900 Kanawha Blvd. E., Charleston 25305-0330. Tel. 304-558-7880, FAX 304-558-2584.

Wisconsin

Carolyn Winters Folke, Dir., Bureau for Instructional Media and Technology, State Dept. of Public Instruction, Box 7841, Madison 53707. Tel. 608-266-1965.

Wyoming

Nancy Leinius, Education Programs Specialist, Wyoming Dept. of Educ., Hathaway Bldg., Cheyenne 82002. Tel. 307-777-6226.

American Samoa

Emma Pen, Supv., Office of Lib. Services, Dept. of Educ., Box 1329, Pago Pago 96799. Tel. (011) 684-633-1181.

Marshall Islands

Tamar A. Jordan, Libn., Alele Museum Lib. and National Archives, Box 629, Majuro, Marshall Islands 96960.

Northern Mariana Islands

Robert K. Wright, Dir., Learning Resources, Northern Marianas College, Box 1250, Saipan, MP 96950.

Puerto Rico

Carmen Belén Rivera, Asst. Secy., Education Extension Area, Dept. of Educ., Box 190759, San Juan 00919. Tel. 809-753-9211; Lydia I. Santiago, Dir., Public Lib. Service, Dept. of Educ., Box 190759, San Juan 00919. Tel. 809-754-7227.

Virgin Islands

Fiolina B. Mills, State Dir., State Media Lib. Services, Virgin Islands Dept. of Educ., 44-46 Kongens Gade, Saint Thomas 00801. Tel. 809-776-2573, 809-774-5339.

International Library Associations

Inter-American Association of Agricultural Librarians and Documentalists—AIBDA

c/o IICA-CIDIA, Apdo. 55, 2200 Coronado, Costa Rica
29-0222, FAX 29-4741/29-2659

Object

To serve as liaison among the agricultural librarians and documentalists of the Americas and other parts of the world; to stimulate the exchange of information and experiences through technical publications and meetings; to promote the improvement of library services in the field of agriculture and related sciences; to seek the professional improvement of the agricultural librarians and documentalists of Latin America and the Caribbean.

Officers

Pres. Suzana Sperry; *V.P.* Lidya Revello; *Rec. Secy.* Zayda Caballero; *Treas.* Ana Lorena Yglesias; *Membs. at Large* Vielka Chang, Ofelia Aguilar, Letty Vasconez, Karla Vanessa Bonilla; *Exec. Secy.* Ghislaine Poitevien.

Publications

AIBDA Actualidades (irreg.).
Boletín Especial (irreg.).
Boletín Informativo (3 per year).
Revista AIBDA (2 per year).

International Association of Agricultural Information Specialists

c/o J. van der Burg, Secretary-Treasurer
CIRAD/CIDARC, B.P. 5035, 34032 Montpellier Cedex 1, France
67-61-58-00, FAX 67-61-58-20

Object

The Association shall, internationally and nationally, promote agricultural library science and documentation as well as the professional interest of agricultural librarians and documentalists. Founded 1955.

Malaysia; *Jr. V.P.* W. Laux, Biologische Bundesanstalt, Königin-Luise-Strasse 19, W-1000 Berlin 33, Germany; *Secy.-Treas.* J. van der Burg, CIRAD/CIDARC, B.P. 5035, 34032 Montpellier Cedex 1, France; *Ed.* A. P. Powell, Agriculture Lib., Agriculture Science Center-North, Lexington, KY 40546.

Membership

Memb. 634. Dues (Inst.) $80; (Indiv.) $30.

Officers

Pres. J. H. Howard, National Agricultural Lib., Beltsville, MD 20705; *Sr. V.P.* Syed Salim Agha, Lib. Universiti Pertanian Malaysia, 43400 UPM, Serdang, Selangor,

Executive Committee

C. Boast, USA; E. Herpay, Hungary; J. Kennedy-Olsen, USA; J. R. Metcalfe, UK; T. Niang, Senegal; N. W. Posnett, UK; V. Pozdnyakov, Russia; J. M. Schippers, Netherlands; J. C. Sison, Philippines; W. E. Umbima, Kenya; representatives of national associations of agricultural librarians and documentalists.

Publications

Quarterly Bulletin of the IAALD (memb.).
World Directory of Agricultural Information Resource Centres.

International Association of Law Libraries

c/o Covington & Burling, 1201 Pennsylvania Ave. N.W., Washington, DC 20044-7566
202-662-6152, FAX 202-662-6291

Object

IALL is a worldwide organization of librarians, libraries, and other persons or institutions concerned with the acquisition and use of legal information emanating from sources other than their jurisdictions, and from multinational and international organizations. IALL's basic purpose is to facilitate the work of librarians who must acquire, process, organize, and provide access to foreign legal materials. IALL has no local chapters but maintains liaison with national law library associations in many countries and regions of the world.

Membership

Over 500 members in more than 50 countries on five continents.

Officers (1992–1995)

Pres. Katalin Balazs-Veredy (Hungary); *1st V.P.* Larry Wenger (USA); *2nd V.P.* Jurgen Godan (Germany); *Secy.* Roberta Shaffer (USA); *Treas.* Marie-Louise Bernal (USA).

Board Members (1992–1995)

Bruitt Kjolstad (Switzerland); June Renie (Trinidad); Adolf Sprudzs (USA); Raimund-Ekkhard Walter (Germany); Jacqueline Elliott (Australia); Joachim Schwietzke (Germany); Josep Sort Tico (Spain).

Publications

International Journal of Legal Information (3 per year; US$55 for individuals; $80 for institutions).

Committee Chairpersons

Constitution and Bylaws. Jurgen Godan (Germany).
Nominations. Larry Wenger (USA).

International Association of Metropolitan City Libraries

c/o Charles W. Hunsberger, Secretary-Treasurer
Box 73221, Las Vegas, NV 89170-3221

Object

INTAMEL is a platform for professional communication and information for libraries of cities with 400,000 or more inhabitants.

Membership

More than 100 members in approximately 40 countries.

Officers (1993–1995)

Pres. Edwin S. Holmgren, New York Public

Lib., 455 Fifth Ave., New York, NY 10016; *Secy.-Treas.* Charles W. Hunsberger, Box 73221, Las Vegas, NV 89170-3221.

Publications

Annual International Statistics of City Libraries (INTAMEL).

INTAMEL Newsletter.

Various lecture papers.

International Association of Music Libraries, Archives and Documentation Centres (IAML)

c/o Veslemöy Heintz, Secretary-General
Svenskt Musikhistoriskt Arkiv, Box 16326, S-103 26 Stockholm, Sweden
46-8-666-45-62, FAX 46-8-666-45-65

Object

To promote the activities of music libraries, archives, and documentation centers and to strengthen the cooperation among them; to promote the availability of all publications and documents relating to music and further their bibliographical control; to encourage the development of standards in all areas that concern the association; and to support the protection and preservation of musical documents of the past and the present.

Membership

Memb. 1,900.

Board Members (1992–1995)

Pres. Don L. Roberts, Music Lib., Northwestern Univ., Evanston, IL 60208; *Past Pres.* Catherine Massip, Dir., Département de

la Musique, Bibliothèque Nationale, 58 Rue Richelieu, F-75084 Paris Cedex 02, France; *V.P.s* Blanka Červinková, Mestská Knihovna v Praze, Mariánské Námésti 1, ČR-115 72 Prague, Czech Republic; Hugh Cobbe, Music Libn., British Lib., Great Russell St., London WC1B 3DG, England; Lenore Coral, 1309 E. State St., Ithaca, NY 14850; Wolfgang Krueger, Heumadener Str. 23, O-7302 Ostfildern 4 (Kemnat), Tyskland, Germany; *Secy.-Gen.* Veslemöy Heintz, Svenskt Musikhistoriskt Arkiv, Box 16326, S-103 26 Stockholm, Sweden; *Treas.* Pamela Thompson, Head Libn., Royal College of Music, Prince Consort Rd., London SW7 2BS, England.

Publication

Fontes Artis Musicae (4 per year; memb.). *Ed.* Susan T. Sommer, New York Public Lib. for the Performing Arts, 111 Amsterdam Ave., New York, NY 10023-7498.

Professional Branches

Archives and Music Documentation Centres Branch. Inger Enquist, Svensk Musikhistoriskt Arkiv, Box 16326, S-103 26 Stockholm, Sweden.

Broadcasting and Orchestra Libraries. Helen Faulkner, 26 Vere Rd., Brighton, Sussex BN1 4NR, England.

Libraries in Music Teaching Institutions.

Michèle Lancelin, Bibliothèque du Conservatoire National de Région, 22 Rue de la Belle Feuille, F-92100 Boulogne, France.

Public Libraries. Heikki Poroila, Vantaa City Lib., Box 20, SF-01301 Vantaa, Finland.

Research Libraries. Hugh Cobbe, Music Libn., British Lib., Great Russell St., London WC1B 3DG, England.

International Association of Orientalist Librarians

c/o Kenneth Klein, Secretary-Treasurer
East Asia Library, University of Southern California
University Park, Los Angeles, CA 90089-0182

Object

To promote better communication among Orientalist librarians and libraries, and others in related fields, throughout the world; to provide a forum for the discussion of problems of common interest; to improve international cooperation among institutions holding research resources for Oriental Studies. The term *Orient* specifies the Middle East, East Asia, and the South and Southeast Asia regions.

Founded in 1967 at the 27th International Congress of Orientalists (ICO) in Ann Arbor, Michigan. Affiliated with the International Federation of Library Associations and Institutions (IFLA) and International Congress for Asian and North African Studies (formerly ICO).

Officers

Pres. William S. Wong; *Secy.-Treas.* Kenneth Klein; *Ed.* Raymond D. Lum.

Publication

International Association of Orientalist Librarians Bulletin (s. ann.; memb.).

International Association of School Librarianship

c/o Jean Lowrie, Executive Secretary
Box 19586, Kalamazoo, MI 49019

Object

To encourage the development of school libraries and library programs throughout all countries; to promote the professional preparation of school librarians; to bring about close collaboration among school libraries in all countries, including the loan and exchange of literature; to initiate and coordinate activities, conferences, and other projects in the field of school librarianship. Founded 1971.

Membership

Memb. (Indiv.) 800; (Assn.) 41.

Officers and Executive Board

Pres. Lucille C. Thomas, USA; *V.P.* Sigrun-klara Hannisdöttir, Iceland; *Treas.* Donald Adcock, USA; *Exec. Secy.* Jean Lowrie, USA; *Dirs.* Beatrice Anderson, Jamaica; Gerald Brown, Canada; David Elaturoti, Nigeria; Gloria Hall, Bolivia; Gunilla Janlert, Sweden; Mieko Nagakura, Japan; Fay Nicholson, Australia; Melvin Rainey, Fiji; Felix Tawete, Swaziland.

Publications

Books and Borrowers.
IASL Conference Proceedings (ann.).

IASL Monograph Series.
IASL Newsletter (q.).

U.S. Members

American Assn. of School Libs.; Assn. de Bibliotecarios Escolares de Puerto Rico; Educational Media Assn. of New Jersey; Hawaii School Lib. Assn.; Illinois Assn. for Media in Education; Louisiana Assn. of School Libns.; Maryland Educational Media Organization; Michigan Assn. for Media in Education; Oregon Educational Media Assn.; Virginia Educational Media Assn.; Washington Lib. Media Assn.

International Association of Sound Archives

c/o Sven Allerstrand, Secretary-General
Arkivet för Ljud och Bild
Box 27890, S-115 93 Stockholm, Sweden
FAX 46-8-663-1811

Object

The International Association of Sound Archives (IASA) is a nongovernmental UNESCO-affiliated organization. It was established in 1969 in Amsterdam to allow international cooperation among archives that preserve recorded sound documents. IASA interests lie in a wide variety of recorded sound, including music, and cover problems common to the variety of collections with which the association deals: problems of acquisition, preservation, organization, documentation, copyright, accessibility, distribution, and the technical aspects of recording and playback. The association is actively involved in the preservation, organization, and use of sound recordings, techniques of recording, and methods of reproducing sound in all fields in which the audio medium is used; the exchange of recordings among archives and of related literature and information; and in all subjects relating to the professional work of sound archives and archivists.

Membership

Open to all categories of archives and other institutions that preserve sound recordings, and to organizations and individuals having a serious interest in the purposes or welfare of IASA. The association includes members representing national archives; archives of music, history, literature, drama, and folklife recordings; collections of oral history, natural history, bioacoustic, and medical sounds; recorded linguistic and dialect surveys; and radio and television sound archives.

Officers

Pres. James McCarthy, National Film and Sound Archives, Box 222, Saint Leonards 2065, Australia. FAX 61-2-436-4178; *Past Pres.* Gerald Gibson, M/B/RS Div., Lib. of Congress, Washington, DC 20540. FAX 202-707-3434; *V.P.s* Giorgio Adamo, Discoteca di Stato, Via dei Funari 32, I-00186 Rome, Italy. FAX 6-321-6437; Magdalena Cséve,

Documentation Dept., Hungarian Radio, Bródy Sándor u. 5-7, H-1800 Budapest, Hungary. FAX 36-1-138-7519; Kurt Degeller, Fonoteca Nazionale Svizzera, Via Foce 1, 6905 Lugano 6, Switzerland. FAX 4191-526-169; Treas. Anna Maria Foyer, Arkivet för Ljud och Bild, Box 27890, S-115 93 Stockholm, Sweden. FAX 46-8-663-1811; Ed. Helen Harrison, Media Lib., Open University Lib., Walton Hall, Milton Keynes MK7 6AA, England. FAX 44-908-653744; Secy.-Gen. Sven Allerstrand, Arkivet för Ljud och Bild, Box 27890, S-115 93 Stockholm, Sweden. FAX 46-8-663-1811.

International Association of Technological University Libraries

c/o President, Gerard A. J. S. van Marle
Twente University of Technology Library
Box 217, 7500 AE Enschede, Netherlands

Object

To provide a forum where library directors can meet to exchange views on matters of current significance in the libraries of Universities of Science and Technology. Research projects identified as being of sufficient interest may be followed through by working parties or study groups.

Membership

Ordinary, official observer, sustaining, and nonvoting associate. Membership fee is 160 guilders per year (430 guilders for 3 years, 680 guilders for 5 years). Memb. 198 (in 41 countries).

Officers and Executives

Pres. Gerard A. J. S. van Marle, Twente Univ. of Technology Lib., Box 217, 7500 AE Enschede, Netherlands; Secy. Michael Breaks, Libn., Heriot-Watt Univ., Riccarton, Edinburgh EH14 4AS, Scotland; Treas. Annette Winkel-Schwarz, National Technological Lib. of Denmark, Anker Engellundsvej 1, DK-2800 Lyngby, Denmark; 1st V.P. Nancy Fjällbrant, Sweden; Membs. Tom Cochrane, Australia; Dietmar Brandes, Germany; North American Regional Group Chair Jay K. Lucker, USA; Ed. Nancy Fjällbrant, Sweden.

Publications

IATUL News (irreg.).
IATUL Proceedings (ann.).

International Council on Archives

Charles Kesckeméti, Secretary General
60 Rue des Francs-Bourgeois, F-75003 Paris, France

Object

To establish, maintain, and strengthen relations among archivists of all lands, and among all professional and other agencies or institutions concerned with the custody, organization, or administration of archives, public or private, wherever located. Established 1948.

Membership

Memb. 1,300 (representing 150 countries and territories). Dues (Indiv.) $80 or $120; (Inst.) $120; (Archives Assns.) $120 or $200; (Central Archives Directorates) $250 or $125 minimum, computed on the basis of GNP per capita.

Officers

Secy.-Gen. Charles Kesckeméti.

Publications

Archivum (ann.; memb. or subscription to K. G. Saur Verlag, Ortlerstr. 8, Postfach 70 16 20, W-8000 Munich 70, Germany).

Guide to the Sources of the History of Nations (Latin American Series, 12 vols. pub.; African Series, 14 vols. pub.; Asian Series, 13 vols. pub.).

ICA Bulletin (s. ann.; memb.).

Janus (s. ann.; memb.).

List of other publications available from the secretary general.

International Federation for Information and Documentation (FID)

Executive Director, Ben G. Goedegebuure
Box 90402, 2509 LK The Hague, Netherlands
3140671, FAX 3140667

Object

To promote, through international cooperation, research in and development of information science, information management, and documentation, which includes inter alia the organization, storage, retrieval, repackaging, dissemination, value adding to information, and evaluation of information, however recorded, in the fields of science, technology, industry, social sciences, arts, and humanities.

Program

FID devotes much of its attention to corporate information; industrial, business, and finance information; information policy research; the application of information technology; information service management; the marketing of information systems and services; content analysis, for example, in the design of database systems; linking information and human resources; and the repackaging of information for specific user audiences. The following commissions, committees, and groups have been established to execute FID's program of activities: *Regional Commissions:* Commission for Western, Eastern and Southern Africa (FID/CAF), Commission for Asia and Oceania (FID/CAO), Commission for Latin America (FID/CLA), Commission for the Caribbean and North America (FID/CNA), Commission for Northern Africa and the Near East (FID/NANE), Regional Organization for Europe (FID/ROE); *Committees:* Classification Research, Education and Training, Fundamental Theory of Information, Information for Industry, Information Policies and Programmes, Intellectual Property Issues, Social Sciences Documentation and Information, Universal Decimal Classification; *Special Interest Groups:* Advisory Services for Small and Medium-Sized Enterprises; Archives and Records Management; Banking, Finance, and Insurance Information; Environmental Information; Executive Information Systems; Information for Public Administration; Quality Issues in the Information Sector; Roles, Careers, and Development of the Modern Information Professional; Marketing Systems and Services; Safety Control and Risk Management.

Officers

Pres. Ritva T. Launo, ALKO Ltd., Box 350, SF-00101 Helsinki, Finland; *V.P.s* Margarita Almada de Ascencio, CICH, Universidad Nacional Autonoma, A.P. 70-932, 04510 Mexico D.F., Mexico; Yuzuru Fujiwara, Inst. of Info. Sciences and Electronics, Univ. of Tsukuba, 1-Tennodai, Tsukuba, Ibaraki 305, Japan; Forest W. Horton Jr., Chair USNC-FID, Box 19166, Washington, DC 20036; *Treas.* Roger Bowes, Aslib, Information House, 20-24 Old St., London EC1V 9AP, England; *Councillors* José R. P. Alvarez-Ossorio, Madrid, Spain; Yuri M. Arskij, Moscow, Russia; Christian Galinski, Vienna, Austria; Karl Kalseth, Oslo, Norway; Michel J. Menou, Gentilly, France; Remy Ogwang-Ameny, Kampala, Uganda; Augusta M. Paci, Rome, Italy; Anna Maria Prat Trabal, Santia-go, Chile; Karl A. Stroetmann, Alfter, Germany; Neva Tudor-Silovic, Zagreb, Croatia; T. Viswanathan, New Delhi, India; *Belgian Memb.* L. Van Simaeys, Louvain-la-Neuve, Belgium; *Exec. Dir.* Ben G. Goedegebuure, Box 90402, 2509 LK The Hague, Netherlands; *Pres. FID/CLA* Humberto Arango Sales, Havana, Cuba; *Pres. FID/CNA* Carol Collins, Georgetown, Guyana; *Pres. FID/CAO* Ian Dickson, Burwood, Vic., Australia; *Pres. FID/CAF* Mu'azu H. Wali, Lagos, Nigeria; *Pres. FID/NANE* Shawky Salem, Safat, Kuwait; *Pres. FID/ROE* José R. P. Alvarez-Ossorio, Madrid, Spain.

Address all correspondence to the executive director.

Publications

FID Annual Report (ann.).
FID Directory (bienn.).
FID News Bulletin (mo.) with quarterly inserts *Document Delivery Survey* and *ET Newsletter.*
FID Publications List (irreg.).
International Forum on Information and Documentation (q.).
Newsletter on Education and Training Programmes for Information Personnel (q.).
Proceedings of congresses; Universal Decimal Classification editions; manuals; directories; bibliographies on information science, documentation, mechanization, linguistics, training, and classification.

International Federation of Film Archives (FIAF)

Secretariat, 190 rue Franz Merjay, B-1180 Brussels, Belgium
32-2-343-06-91, FAX 32-2-343-76-22

Object

To facilitate communication and cooperation between its members, and to promote the exchange of films and information; to maintain a code of archive practice calculated to satisfy all national film industries, and to encourage industries to assist in the work of the federation's members; to advise its members on all matters of interest to them, especially the preservation and study of films; to give every possible assistance and encouragement to new film archives and to those interested in creating them. Founded in Paris, 1938. Affiliates: 93 (in 60 countries).

Officers

Pres. Robert Daudelin, Canada; *V.P.s* Hoos Blotkamp, Netherlands; Vladimir Opela, Czech Republic; Ivan Trujillo Bolio, Mexico; *Secy.-Gen.* Eva Orbanz, Germany; *Treas.* Clyde Jeavons, England.

Address correspondence to B. van der Elst, executive secretary, c/o the Secretariat.

Executive Committee

Officers; Hoos Blotkamp, Netherlands; José Manuel Costa, Portugal; Jan-Christopher Horak, USA; Jorge Nieto, Colombia; Vladimir Opela, Czech Republic; José Maria Prado, Spain; Guy-Claude Rochemont, France; Steven Rice, USA; Roger Smither, UK; Ivan Trujillo Bolio, Mexico.

Publications

Annual Bibliography of FIAF Members' Publications.

Bibliography of National Filmographies.

Evaluating Computer Cataloguing Systems, by Roger Smither (a guide for film archivists).

FIAF Bulletin.

FIAF Cataloguing Rules for Film Archives.

Glossary of Filmographic Terms in English, French, German, Spanish, and Russian (a second version in 12 languages).

Handbook for Film Archives (available in English or French).

International Directory to Film & TV Documentation Sources.

International Index to Film Periodicals (cumulative volumes).

International Index to Film Television Periodicals (microfiche service).

International Index to Television Periodicals (cumulative volumes).

Study on the Usage of Computers for Film Cataloguing.

Technical Manual of the FIAF Preservation Commission.

International Federation of Library Associations and Institutions (IFLA)

c/o The Royal Library, Box 95312, 2509 CH The Hague, Netherlands

Object

To promote international understanding, cooperation, discussion, research, and development in all fields of library activity, including bibliography, information services, and the education of library personnel, and to provide a body through which librarianship can be represented in matters of international interest. Founded 1927.

Membership

Memb. (Lib. Assns.) 180; (Inst.) 903; (Aff.) 182; 124 countries.

Officers and Executive Board

Pres. Robert Wedgeworth, Univ. of Illinois, Urbana-Champaign; *V.P.* Russell Bowden, Lib. Assn., London, England; *2nd V.P.* Marta Terry, Biblioteca Nacional, Havana, Cuba; *Treas.* Warren Horton, National Lib. of Australia, Canberra, Australia; *Exec. Board* Ekaterina Genieva, Lib. for Foreign Literature, Moscow, Russia; Robert D. Stueart, GSLIS, Simmons College, Boston, Mass.; Eeva-Maija Tammekann, Lib. of Parliament, Helsinki, Finland; Sun Beixin, China Soc. of Lib. Science, Beijing, China; *Ex officio memb.* Ian M. Johnson, SLIS, Robert Gordon Inst. of Technology, Aberdeen, Scotland; *Secy.-Gen.* Leo Voogt; *Coord. Professional Activities* Winston Roberts; *IFLA Office for Universal Bibliographic Control and International MARC Program Dir.* Kurt Nowak; *Program Officer* Marie-France Plassard, c/o Deutsche Bibliothek, Frankfurt/Main, Germany; *IFLA International Program for UAP Program Dir.* David Bradbury; *Program Officer* Graham Cornish, c/o British Lib. Document Supply Centre, Boston Spa, Wetherby, West York-

shire, England; *IFLA Office for Preservation and Conservation Program Dir.* Jean-Marie Arnoult, c/o Bibliothèque Nationale, Paris; *IFLA Office for University Dataflow and Telecommunications Program Dir.* Leigh Swain; *Program Officer* Paula Tallim, c/o National Lib. of Canada, Ottawa, Canada; *IFLA Office for the Advancement of Librarianship in the Third World Program Dir.* Birgitta Bergdahl, c/o Uppsala Univ. Lib., Uppsala, Sweden; *IFLA Office for International Lending Dir.* David Bradbury.

Publications

IFLA Annual.
IFLA Directory (bienn.).
IFLA Journal (q.).
IFLA Professional Reports.
IFLA Publications Series.
International Cataloguing and Bibliographic Control (q.).
PAC Newsletter.
UAP Newsletter (s. ann.).
UDT Newsletter.

American Membership

American Assn. of Law Libs.; American Lib. Assn.; Art Libs. Society of North America; Assn. for Lib. and Info. Science Education; Assn. for Population Planning/Family Planning Libs.; Assn. of Research Libs.; International Assn. of Law Libs.; International Assn. of Orientalist Libns.; International Assn. of School Libns.; Medical Lib. Assn.; Special Libs. Assn. *Institutional Membs.* There are 143 libraries and related institutions that are institutional members or affiliates of IFLA in the United States (out of a total of 911), and 78 personal affiliates (out of a total of 154).

International Organization for Standardization (ISO)

ISO Central Secretariat
1 rue de Varembé, Case Postale 56, CH-1211 Geneva 20, Switzerland
22-749-01-11, Fax 22-733-34-30

Object

To promote the development of standardization and related activities in the world with a view to facilitating international exchange of goods and services, and to developing cooperation in the sphere of intellectual, scientific, technological, and economic activity.

Officers

Pres. John Hinds; *V.P., Policy* Stewart Horwood, Australia; *V.P., Technical Management* John Kean, Canada; *Secy.-Gen.* Lawrence D. Eicher.

Technical Work

The technical work of ISO is carried out by over 200 technical committees. These include:

ISO/TC 46—Information and documentation (Secretariat, Deutsches Institut für Normung, Burggrafenstr. 6, 10787 Berlin, Germany). Scope: Standardization of practices relating to libraries, documentation and information centers, indexing and abstracting services, archives, information science, and publishing.

ISO/TC 37—Terminology (principles and coordination) (Secretariat, Österreiches Normungsinstitut, Heinestr. 38, Postfach 130, A-1021 Vienna, Austria). Scope: Standardization of methods for creating, compiling, and coordinating terminologies.

ISO/IEC JTC 1 (Joint technical committee for information technology) (Secretariat, American National Standards Institute, 11 W. 42 St., 13th fl., New York, NY 10036). Scope: Standardization in the field of information technology.

Publications

Bulletin (mo.).
Catalogue (ann.).
ISO 9000 News (bi-mo.).
Liaisons.
Member Bodies.
Memento (ann.).

Foreign Library Associations

The following list of regional and national library associations around the world is a selective one. A more complete list of foreign and international library associations can be found in *International Literary Market Place* (R. R. Bowker).

Regional

Africa

Standing Conference of African Lib. Schools, c/o School of Libns., Archivists and Documentalists, Université Cheikh Anta Diop de Dakar, B.P. 3252, Dakar, Senegal. Tel. 25-76-60.

Standing Conference of African Univ. Libs., c/o E. Bejide Bankole, Editor, African Journal of Academic Librarianship, Box 46, Univ. of Lagos, Yaba, Lagos, Nigeria. Tel. 524968.

The Americas

Asociación de Bibliotecas Universitarias, de Investigación e Institucionales del Caribe (ACURIL) (Assn. of Caribbean Univ., Research and Institutional Libs.), Biblioteca Regional del Caribe, Universidad de Puerto Rico, Río Piedras, Puerto Rico 00931. Tel. 809-790-8054. *Exec. Secy.* Oneida R. Ortiz, Apdo. Postal 23317, Estación de la Universidad, San Juan, Puerto Rico 00931, or Calle Humacao 39, Villa Avila, Guaynabo, Puerto Rico 00969.

Seminar on the Acquisition of Latin American Lib. Materials (SALALM), c/o *Exec. Secy.* Sharon Moynahan, General Lib., Univ. of New Mexico, Albuquerque, NM 87131-1466.

Asia

Congress of Southeast Asian Libns. IV (CONSAL IV), c/o Serafin N. Quiason, National Lib. of the Philippines, T. M. Kalaw St., 100 Ermita, Box 2926, Manila, Philippines.

The Commonwealth

Commonwealth Lib. Assn. (COMLA), c/o *Hon. Exec. Secy.* Norma Y. Amenu-Kpodo, Box 144, Mona, Kingston 7, Jamaica.

Standing Conference on Lib. Materials on Africa (SCOLMA), Records Branch, Foreign and Commonwealth Office (LRD), Hanslope Park, Hanslope, Milton Keynes MK19 7BH, England. FAX 0908-511419.

Europe

LIBER—Ligue des Bibliothèques Européennes de Recherche (Assn. of European Research Libs.), c/o H.-A. Koch, Staats- und Universitäsbibliothek, Postfach 330440, W-28334 Bremen, Germany.

Nordisk Videnskabeligt Bibliotekarforbund (Scandinavian Federation of Research Libns.), c/o Tomas Lidman, Stockholm Univ. Lib., S-10691 Stockholm, Sweden.

Pacific Islands

Pacific Islands Assn. of Libs. and Archives, c/o *Exec. Secy.* Arlene Cohen, RFK Lib., Univ. of Guam, UOG Sta., Mangilao, Guam 96923. *Pres.* Dakio Syne.

National

Australia

Australian Lib. and Info. Assn., Box E441, Queen Victoria Terrace, ACT 2600. *Exec. Dir.* Virginia Walsh.

Australian Society of Archivists, Box 83, O'Connor, ACT 2601. FAX 062-5522034. *Pres.* Chris Coggin; *Secy.* Jennifer Davidson.

Austria

Büchereiverband Österreichs (Assn. of Austrian Public Libs. and Libns.), *Chair* Franz Pscher; *Secy.* Heinz Buchmüller, Lange Gasse 37, A-1080 Vienna.

Österreichische Gesellschaft für Dokumentation und Information (Austrian Society for Documentation and Info.), c/o Österreichisches Normungsinstitut, Heinestrasse 38, Postfach 130, A-1021 Vienna.
Vereinigung Österreichischer Bibliothekare (Assn. of Austrian Libns.) c/o Österreichische Nationalbibliothek, Josefsplatz A-1015 Vienna. Secy. Mag Eva Ramminger.

Bangladesh

Lib. Assn. of Bangladesh, c/o Lib. Training Inst., Bangladesh Central Public Lib., Shahbagh, Ramna, Dacca 1000.

Barbados

Lib. Assn. of Barbados, Box 827E, Bridgetown.

Belgium

Archives et Bibliothèques de Belgique/ Archief- en Bibliotheekwezen in België (Archives and Libs. of Belgium), c/o Bibliothèque Royale Albert I, 4 Blvd. de l'Empereur, B-1000 Brussels.
Association Belge de Documentation/Belgische Vereniging voor Documentatie (Belgian Assn. for Documentation), Blvd. L. Schmidt-laan 119, B.3, B-1040 Brussels. *Pres.* J. Louis Janssens.
Association Professionnelle des Bibliothécaires et Documentalistes, B.P. 31, B-1070 Brussels.
Institut d'Enseignement Supérieur Social de la Communauté Française de Belgique, Section Bibliothécaires-Documentalistes-Gradués (State Inst. of Higher Social Education, Libn., and Documentalist Section), Rue de l'Abbaye 26, B-1050 Brussels. *Dir.* Roselyne Simon-Saint-Hubert.
Vereniging van Religieus-Wetenschappelijke Bibliothecarissen (Assn. of Theological Libns.), Minderbroederstr. 5, B-3800 Saint Truiden. *Secy.* K. Van de Casteele, Groenenborgerlaan 149, B-2020 Antwerp.
Vlaamse Vereniging voor Bibliotheek-, Archief-, en Documentatiewezen (Flemish Assn. of Libns., Archivists, and Documentalists), Goudbloemstraat 10-12, B-2060

Antwerp. FAX 3-232-4294. *Pres.* E. Pairon; *Secy.* R. Raeymaekers.

Belize

Belize Lib. Assn., c/o Central Lib., Bliss Inst., Box 287, Belize City.

Bolivia

Asociación Boliviana de Bibliotecarios (Bolivian Lib. Assn.), c/o Biblioteca y Archivo Nacional, Calle Bolivar, Sucre.

Botswana

Botswana Lib. Assn., Box 1310, Gaborone.

Brazil

Associação dos Arquivistas Brasileiros (Assn. of Brazilian Archivists), Praia de Botafoga 186, Sala B-217, CEP 22253 Rio de Janeiro. *Pres.* Jaime Antunes da Silva.
Federação Brasileira de Associações de Bibliotecários (Brazilian Federation of Libn. Assns.), Rua Avanhandava, 40-Conj. 110, 01306 São Paulo. FAX 11-292-2993.

Bulgaria

Sâjuz na Bibliotechnite i Informazionnite Rabotnitzi (Union of Libns. and Info. Officers), 4 Pl. Slaveikov, Rm. 609, P.B. 269, Sofia 1000. *Pres.* Tatyana Yanakieva.

Canada

Bibliographical Society of Canada/La Société Bibliographique du Canada, Box 575, Postal Sta. P, Toronto, ON M5S 2T1. *Secy.* Anne Dondertman.
Canadian Assn. for Info. Science/Association Canadienne de Science de l'Information, Univ. of Toronto, 140 Saint George St., Toronto, ON M5S 1A1. Tel. 416-978-8876, FAX 416-971-1399.
Canadian Council of Lib. Schools/Conseil Canadien des Ecoles de Bibliothéconomie, c/o *Pres.* Adele M. Fasick, Faculty of Lib. and Info. Science, Univ. of Toronto, 140 Saint George St., Toronto, ON M5S 1A1.
Canadian Lib. Assn., c/o *Exec. Dir.* Karen Adams, 200 Elgin St., 6th fl., Ottawa, ON

K2P 1L5. (For detailed information on the Canadian Lib. Assn. and its divisions, see "National Library and Information-Industry Associations, United States and Canada;" for information on the library associations of the provinces of Canada, see "State, Provincial, and Regional Library Associations.")

Chile

Colegio de Bibliotecarios de Chile A.G. (Chilean Lib. Assn.), Diagonal Paraguay 383, Torre II, Departamento 122, Santiago.

Colombia

Asociación Colombiana de Bibliotecarios (ASCOLBI) (Colombian Assn. of Libns.), Calle 10, No. 3-16, Apdo. Aéreo 30883, Bogota.

Costa Rica

Asociación Costarricense de Bibliotecarios (Assn. of Costa Rican Libns.), Apdo. 3308, San Jose. *Secy.-Gen.* Nelly Kopper.

Côte d'Ivoire (Ivory Coast)

Association pour le Développement de la Documentation des Bibliothèques et Archives de la Côte d'Ivoire (Assn. for the Development of Documentation Libs. and Archives), c/o Bibliothèque Nationale, B.P. V180, Abidjan.

Cyprus

Kypriakos Synthesmos Vivliothicarion (Lib. Assn. of Cyprus), Box 039, Nicosia. *Secy.* Paris G. Rossos.

Czech Republic

Svaz Knihovníkůa Informačních Pracovníků Ceské Republiky (Assn. of Lib. and Info. Professionals of the Czech Republic), Klementinum 190, 110 01 Prague 1.
Ústřední Knihovnická Rada ČR (Central Lib. Council of the Czech Republic), Valdštejnské nám. 4, 118 11 Prague 1. *Pres.* Jaroslav Vyčichio.

Denmark

Arkivforeningen (Archives Society), c/o *Exec. Secy.* Steen Ousager, Landsarkivet for Sjaelland, Box 661, Jagtvej 10, DK-2200 Copenhagen N.
Danmarks Biblioteksforening (Danish Lib. Assn.), c/o *Pres.* Søren Møller, Telegrafvej 5, DK-2750 Ballerup.
Danmarks Forskningsbiblioteksforening (Danish Research Lib. Assn.), *Pres.* Lars Bjørnshauge; *V.P.* Niels Mark; *Secy.* Dorthe Skovgaard, Danmarks Tekniske Bibliotek, Anker Engelundsvej 1, DK-2800 Lyngby.
Danmarks Skolebiblioteksforening (Assn. of Danish School Libs.), Vesterbrogade 20, DK-1620 Copenhagen V. *Exec. Secy.* Niels Jacobsen.

Dominican Republic

Asociación Dominicana de Bibliotecarios (Dominican Lib. Assn.), c/o Biblioteca Nacional, Plaza de la Cultura, Cesar Nicolás Penson 91, Santo Domingo. *Pres.* Prospero J. Mella Chavier.

Ecuador

Asociación Ecuatoriana de Bibliotecarios (Ecuadoran Lib. Assn.), c/o *Exec. Secy.* Eulalia Galarza, Casa de la Cultura, Apdo. 67, 794 Avda. 6 de Diciembre, Quito.

El Salvador

Asociación de Bibliotecarios de El Salvador (El Salvador Lib. and Info. Professionals Assn.), c/o Biblioteca Nacional, 8A Avda. Norte y Calle Delgado, San Salvador.

Ethiopia

Ye Ethiopia Betemetshaft ena Information Balemoyawoch Mahber (Ethiopian Lib and Info. Professionals Assn.), Box 30530, Addis Ababa.

Fiji

Fiji Lib. Assn., Govt. Bldgs., Box 2292, Suva. FAX 300830.

Finland

Suomen Kirjastoseura/Finlands Biblioteks-förening (Finnish Lib. Assn.), Museokatu 18-A-5, SF-00100 Helsinki 10. FAX 358-0-441-345. *Secy.-Gen.* Tuula Haavisto.
Tietopalveluseura/Samfundet för Informationstjänst i Finland (Finnish Society for Info. Services), Harakantie 2, SF-02600 Espoo.

France

Association des Archivistes Français (Assn. of French Archivists), *Pres.* Jean-Luc Eichenlaub; *Exec. Secy.* Jean LePottier, 60 Rue des Francs-Bourgeois, F-75141 Paris Cedex 03.
Association des Bibliothécaires Français (Assn. of French Libns.), 7 Rue des Lions-Saint-Paul, F-75004 Paris.
Association Française des Documentalistes et des Bibliothécaires Spécialisés (Assn. of French Info. Scientists and Special Libns.), 25 Rue Claude Tillier, F-75012 Paris.

Germany

Arbeitsgemeinschaft der Kunstbibliotheken (Working Group of Art Libs.), Bibliothek des Deutschen Archäologischen Instituts, Abteilung Rom, Dr. Horst Blanck, Via Sardegna 79, I-00187 Rome. Tel. 488-5617, FAX 488-4973.
Arbeitsgemeinschaft der Spezialbibliotheken (Assn. of Special Libs.), c/o M. Schwarz-er, Kekulé-Bibliothek, Bayer AG, 51373 Leverkusen-Bayerwerk.
Deutsche Gesellschaft für Dokumentation e.V. (German Society for Documentation), Hanauer Landstr. 126-128, 60314 Frank-furt am Main. *Pres.* Arnoud de Kemp.
Deutscher Bibliotheksverband e.V. (German Lib. Assn.), Bundesallee 184/185, 10717 Berlin. *Secy.* Elke Dämpfert.
Verein der Bibliothekare an Öffentlichen Bibliotheken e.V. (Assn. of Libns. at Public Libs.), *Chair* Konrad Umlauf; *Secy.* Katharina Boulanger, Postfach 1324, 72703 Reutlingen.

Verein der Diplom-Bibliothekare an Wis-senschaftlichen Bibliotheken (Assn. of Graduated Libns. at Academic Libs.), c/o *Chair* Marianne Saule, Universitätsbibliothek, 93051 Regensburg.
Verein Deutscher Archivare (Assn. of German Archivists), c/o Generaldirektion der Staatlichen Archive Bayerns, Schönfeldstr. 5, 80539 Munich. FAX 089-28638-615.
Verein Deutscher Bibliothekare e.V. (Assn. of German Libns.), Andreas Anderhub; *Secy.* Monika Hagenmaier-Farnbauer, Universitätsbibliothek Mainz, Saarstr. 21, 55122 Mainz.

Ghana

Ghana Lib. Assn., Box 4105, Accra. *Exec. Secy.* D. B. Addo.

Great Britain

See United Kingdom.

Guatemala

Asociación Bibliotecológica de Guatemala (Lib. Assn. of Guatemala), c/o Dir., Biblioteca Nacional de Guatemala, 5A Avda. 7-26, Zona 1, Guatemala City.

Guyana

Guyana Lib. Assn., c/o *Pres.* Hetty London, 76-77 Main St., Box 10240, Georgetown.

Hong Kong

Hong Kong Lib. Assn., GPO 10095, Hong Kong.

Hungary

Magyar Könyvtárosok Egyesülete (Assn. of Hungarian Libns.), *Pres.* Tibor Horváth; *Secy.* István Papp, Szabó Ervin tér 1, H-1088 Budapest.

Iceland

Bókavaroafélag Islands (Icelandic Lib. Assn.), Box 1497, 121 Reykjavik.

India

Indian Assn. of Special Libs. and Info. Centres, P-291, CIT Scheme 6M, Kankurgachi, Calcutta 700054.

Indian Lib. Assn., Dr. Mukerjee Nagar, A/40-41, Flat 201, Ansal Bldg., Delhi 110009.

Iraq

Iraqi Lib. Assn., c/o National Lib., Bab-el-Muaddum, Baghdad.

Ireland

Cumann Leabharlann Na h-Eireann (Lib. Assn. of Ireland), 53 Upper Mount St., Dublin 2. *Pres.* Deirdre Ellis-King; *Hon. Secy.* B. Teeling.

Israel

Israel Lib. Assn., c/o *Exec. Secy.* Moshe Karov, Box 303, Tel Aviv 61002.

Israel Society of Special Libs. and Info. Centers, Atidim Scientific Pk., 2 Dvora Haneviah St., Tel Aviv 61430.

Italy

Associazione Italiana Biblioteche (Italian Lib. Assn.), c/o *Secy.* L. Bellingeri, C.P. 2461, I-00100 Rome A-D. Tel. and FAX 44-63-532.

Jamaica

Jamaica Lib. Assn., Box 58, Kingston 5.

Japan

Information Science and Technology Assn., Japan (INFOSTA-NIPDOK), *Pres.* Takuya Gondoh; *Dir. and Secy.-Gen.* Yukio Ichikawa, Sasaki Bldg., 5-7 Koisikawa 2-chome, Bunkyo-ku, Tokyo 112.

Nihon Toshokan Kyôkai (Japan Lib. Assn.), c/o *Secy.-Gen.* Reiko Sakagawa, 1-10, 1-chome, Taishido, Setagaya-ku, Tokyo 154.

Senmon Toshokan Kyôgikai (Japan Special Libs. Assn.), National Diet Lib., 10-1 Nagata-cho, 1-chome, Chiyoda-ku, Tokyo 100. FAX 03-3597-9104.

Jordan

Jordan Lib. Assn., Box 6289, Amman.

Korea (Republic of)

Korean Lib. Assn., c/o *Exec. Dir.* Dae Kwon Park, 60-1 Panpo 2 Dong, Seocho-ku, Box 2041, Seoul.

Laos

Association des Bibliothécaires Laotiens (Laos Lib. Assn.), Direction de la Bibliothèque Nationale, Ministry of Education, B.P. 704, Vientiane.

Latvia

Lib. Assn. of Latvia, Latvian State Lib., Kr. Baronaiela 14, 226011 Riga.

Malawi

Malawi Lib. Assn., Box 429, Zomba.

Malaysia

Persatuan Perpustakaan Malaysia (Lib. Assn. of Malaysia), Box 12545, 50782 Kuala Lumpur.

Mauritania

Association Mauritanienne des Bibliothécaires, des Archivistes et des Documentalistes (Mauritanian Assn. of Libns., Archivists, and Documentalists), Bibliothèque Nationale, B.P. 20, Nouakchott.

Mexico

Asociación Mexicana de Bibliotecarios, A.C. (Mexican Assn. of Libns.), Apdo. 27-651, Admin. de Correos 27, 06760 Mexico, D.F.

The Netherlands

Nederlandse Vereniging van Bibliotharissen, Documentalisten en Literatuuronderzoekers (Dutch Lib. Assn.), Verenigingsbureau, Plompetorengracht 11, NL-3512 CA Utrecht.

UKB—Samenwerkingsverband van de Universiteitsbibliotheken, de Koninklijke Bibliotheek en de Bibliotheek van de Koninklijke Nederlandse Akademie van Wetenschappen (Assn. of the Univ. Libs., the Royal Lib., and the Lib. of the Netherlands Academy of Arts and Sciences), c/o *Exec. Secy.* J. H. de Swart, Bibliotheek Vrije Universiteit, De Boelelaan 1103, NL-1081 HV Amsterdam.
Vereniging voor het Theologisch Bibliothecariaat (Assn. of Theological Libns.), c/o *Exec. Secy.* P. J. A. Nissen, Postbus 289, NL-6500 AG Nijmegen.

New Zealand

New Zealand Lib. and Info. Assn., c/o *Gen. Secy.* Lydia Klimovitch, Box 12-212, Wellington. FAX 04-499-1480.

Nicaragua

Biblioteca Universitaria, Universidad Centroamericana, Apdo. 69, Managua. *Dir.* Conny Mendez R.

Nigeria

Nigerian Lib. Assn., c/o Polytechnic Lib., PMB 22, UI P.O., Ibadan.

Norway

Arkivarforeningen (Assn. of Archivists), c/o Riksarkivet, Folke Bernadottes Vei 21, Oslo 8. FAX 02-237489.
Norsk Bibliotekforening (Norwegian Lib. Assn.), c/o *Secy.-Treas.* B. Aaker, Malerhaugveien 20, N-0661 Oslo.
Norsk Fagbibliotekforening (Norwegian Assn. of Special Libs.), Malerhaugveien 20, N-0661 Oslo.

Pakistan

Pakistan Lib. Assn. (FBC), c/o Pakistan Inst. for Development Economy, Univ. Campus, Box 1091, Islamabad.
Society for the Promotion and Improvement of Libs., c/o *Pres.* Hakim Mohammed Said, Al-Majeed, Hamdard Centre, Nazimabad, Karachi 74600.

Panama

Asociación Panameña de Bibliotecarios, c/o Biblioteca Interamericana Simón Bolívar, Estafeta Universitaria, Panama City.

Paraguay

Asociación de Bibliotecarios del Paraguay (Assn. of Paraguayan Libns.), Casilla de Correo 1505, Asuncion.

Peru

Asociación Peruana de Archiveros (Assn. of Peruvian Archivists), Archivo General de la Nación, Calle Manuel Cuadros s/n, Palacio de Justicia, Apdo. 3124, Lima.

Philippines

Assn. of Special Libs. of the Philippines, College of Public Admin. Lib., Univ. of the Philippines, Box 474, Manila D-406.
Philippine Lib. Assn., c/o National Lib. Bldg., Rm. 301, T. M. Kalaw St., Ermita, Manila.

Poland

Stowarzyszenie Bibliotekarzy Polskich (Polish Libns. Assn.), Ul. Konopczyńskiego 5/7, 00-953 Warsaw.

Portugal

Associação Portuguesa de Bibliotecários, Arquivistas e Documentalistas (Portuguese Assn. of Libns., Archivists, and Documentalists), Campo Grande 83, 1751 Lisbon.

Romania

Asociatia Bibliotecarilor din Bibliotecile Publice din România (Assn. of Public Libns. of Romania). *Pres.* Gheorghe-Iosif Bercan; *Secy.* Georgeta Clinca, Strada Ion Ghica 4, 79708 Bucharest.

Senegal

Association Sénégalaise des Bibliothécaires, Archivistes et Documentalistes (ASBAD), c/o EBAD, B.P. 3252, Dakar. *Pres.* Mariétou Diongue Diop; *Secy.-Gen.* Emmanuel Kabou.

Sierra Leone

Sierra Leone Assn. of Archivists, Libns., and Info. Scientists, c/o Sierra Leone Lib. Board, Box 326, Freetown.

Singapore

Lib. Assn. of Singapore, c/o Branch Lib., Bukit Merah Central, Box 0693, Singapore 9115.

Slovak Republic

Spolok Slovenských Knihovníkov (Slovak Libns. Assn.), c/o *Pres.* Dušan Katuščák, Kapitulská 3, 811 01 Bratislava.

Spain

Centro de Información y Documentación Científica, c/o *Secy.* Milagros Villarreal de Benito, Joaquín Costa 22, 28002 Madrid.

Sri Lanka

Sri Lanka Lib. Assn., Professional Center, 275/75 Bauddhaloka Mawatha, Colombo 7. FAX 01-685201.

Sweden

Svenska Arkivsamfundet (Swedish Archival Assn.), c/o Riksarkivet, Box 12541, S-10229 Stockholm. *1st Archivist* Britta Jonell Ericsson. FAX 468-737-6474.
Svenska Bibliotekariesamfundet (Swedish Assn. of Univ. and Research Libs.), c/o Univ. College, Box 874, S-50115 Borås.
Sveriges Allmänna Biblioteksförening (Swedish Lib. Assn.), Box 474, S-10126 Stockholm. FAX 08-723-0038.
Tekniska Litteratursällskapet (Swedish Society for Technical Documentation), Box 5073, S-10242 Stockholm. *Secy.* Katarina Wahl.
Vetenskapliga Bibliotekens Tjänsteman-naförening (Assn. of Research Lib. Employees), c/o *Pres.* Christer Larsson, Royal Library, LiBRiS Dept., Box 5093, S-10241, Stockholm.

Switzerland

Schweizerische Vereinigung für Dokumenta-tion/Association Suisse de Documentation (Swiss Assn. of Documentation), c/o BID PTT, CH-3030 Bern.
Vereinigung Schweizerischer Archivare (Assn. of Swiss Archivists), c/o Hans Ulrich Wipf, Fronwagplatz 24, CH-8200 Schaffhausen.
Vereinigung Schweizerischer Biblio-thekare/Association des Bibliothécaires Suisses/Associazione dei Bibliotecari Svizzeri (Assn. of Swiss Libns.), Effingstr. 35, CH-3008 Bern. FAX 031-264648.

Taiwan

Library Assn. of China, c/o National Central Lib., 20 Chung-shan S. Rd., Taipei. FAX 02-311-0155. *Exec. Dir.* Teresa Wang Chang.

Tanzania

Tanzania Lib. Assn., Box 21659, Dar es Salaam. *Chair* T. E. Mlaki.

Tunisia

Association Tunisienne des Documentalistes, Bibliothécaires et Archivistes (Tunisian Assn. of Documentalists, Libns., and Archivists), B.P. 380, R.P. Tunis.

Turkey

Türk Kütüphaneciler Derneği (Turkish Libns. Assn.), Elgün Sokaği 8/8, 06440 Yenise-hir, Ankara.

Uganda

Uganda Lib. Assn., Box 5894, Kampala.

United Kingdom

ASLIB (The Assn. for Info. Management), Information House, 20-24 Old St., London EC1V 9AP, England. *Chief Exec.* Roger Bowes. Tel. 071-253-4488, FAX 071-430-0514.
Assn. of British Theological and Philosophi-cal Libs., c/o *Hon. Secy.* Alan F. Jesson, Bible Society's Lib., Univ. Lib., West Rd.,

Cambridge CB3 9DR, England. Tel. 0225-333000, FAX 0223-333160.

Bibliographical Society, c/o British Lib., Great Russell St., London WC1B 3DG, England. Tel. 071-323-7567.

British and Irish Assn. of Law Libns., c/o *Hon. Secy.* H. C. Boucher, Info. Mgr., Pinsent & Co., 3 Colmore Circus, Birmingham B4 6BN, England. Tel. 021-200-1050, FAX 021-626-1040

The Lib. Assn., 7 Ridgmount St., London WC1E 7AE, England. *Chief Exec.* Ross Shimmon. Tel. 071-636-7543, FAX 071-436-7218.

Private Libs. Assn., c/o *Hon. Secy.* Frank Broomhead, 16 Brampton Grove, Kenton, Harrow, Middlesex HA3 8LG, England.

School Lib. Assn., Liden Lib., Barrington Close Liden, Swindon, Wiltshire SN3 6HF, England. Tel. 0793-617838. *Exec. Secy.* Valerie Fea.

Scottish Lib. Assn., a branch of The Lib. Assn., Motherwell Business Centre, Coursington Rd., Motherwell ML1 1PW, Scotland. *Dir.* Robert Craig. Tel. 0698-252526, FAX 0698-252057.

Society of Archivists, Information House, 20-24 Old St., London, EC1V 9AP, England. Tel. 071-253-5087/4488 Ext. 65, FAX 071-253-3942. *Exec. Secy.* Patrick Cleary.

Standing Conference of National and Univ. Libs., Secretariat and Registered Office, 102 Euston St., London NW1 2HA, England. Tel. 071-387-0317, FAX 071-383-3197. *Exec. Secy.* G. Pentelow.

Welsh Lib. Assn., a branch of The Lib. Assn., c/o Publications Office, Public Lib., Dew St., Haverford West, Dyfed SA62 1SU, Wales.

Uruguay

Agrupación Bibliotecológica del Uruguay (Lib. Documentation, Numismatics and Archive Science Assn. of Uruguay), Cerro Largo 1666, 11200 Montevideo. *Pres.* Luis Alberto Musso.

Venezuela

Colegio de Bibliotecólogos y Archivólogos de Venezuela (Assn. of Venezuelan Libns. and Archivists), Apdo. 6283, Caracas 1010.

Yugoslavia

Hrvatsko Bibliotekarsko Društvo (Croatian Lib. Assn.), National and Univ. Lib., Marulićev trg 21, 41001 Zagreb, Croatia. Tel. 041-446-322, FAX 426-676. *Pres.* Aleksandra Horvat; *Exec. Secy.* Daniela Živković.

Zambia

Zambia Lib. Assn., Box 32839, Lusaka.

Zimbabwe

Zimbabwe Lib. Assn., Box 3133, Harare.

Directory of Book Trade and Related Organizations

Book Trade Associations, United States and Canada

For more extensive information on the associations listed in this section, see the annual editions of the *Literary Market Place* (R. R. Bowker).

American Booksellers Assn. Inc., 828 S. Broadway, Tarrytown, NY 10591. Tel. 914-591-2665. *Pres.* Chuck Robinson, Village Books, Bellingham, WA 98225; *V.P.* Avin Mark Donnitz, Harry W. Schwartz Bookshops, Milwaukee, WI 53202; *Secy.* Mary Gay Shipley, The Book Rack, Blytheville, AR 72315; *Treas.* Neal Coonerty, Bookshop Santa Cruz, Santa Cruz, Calif.; *Publications Dir.* Dan Cullen.

American Institute of Graphic Arts, 1059 Third Ave., New York, NY 10021. Tel. 212-752-0813. *Pres.* Anthony Russell; *Dir.* Caroline Hightower.

American Medical Publishers Assn. *Pres.* Mary K. Cowell, Raven Press, 1185 Ave. of the Americas, New York, NY 10036. Tel. 212-930-9500; *Secy.-Treas.* Joan Blumberg, W. B. Saunders Co., Curtis Bldg., Philadelphia, PA 19106. Tel. 215-238-7860.

American Printing History Assn., Box 4922, Grand Central Sta., New York, NY 10163. *Pres.* Martin W. Hunter; *V.P. Programs* Anne Anninger; *V.P. Publications* Michael Peich; *V.P. Memb.* James R. Kelly; *Treas.* John Hench; *Ed., Printing History* David Pankow; *Exec. Secy.* Stephen Crook.

American Society of Indexers Inc., Box 386, Port Aransas, TX 78373. Tel. 512-749-4052, FAX 512-749-6334. *Contact Person* Kathy Caldwell; *Pres.* Tom McFadden, Box 23376, Flagstaff, AZ 86002-3376; *V.P.* Carolyn McGovern, 2957 Filbert Dr., Walnut Creek, CA 94598; *Secy.* Barbara

Cohen, 1708 Ridgeland Dr., Champaign, IL 61821; *Treas.* Frances Lennie, Box 18609, Rochester, NY 14618-0609.

American Society of Journalists and Authors, 1501 Broadway, Suite 302, New York, NY 10036. Tel. 212-997-0947, FAX 212-768-7414. *Exec. Dir.* Alexandra Cantor.

American Society of Media Photographers, Suite 502, 14 Washington Rd., Princeton Junction, NJ 08550-1033. Tel. 609-799-8300, FAX 609-799-2233. *Pres.* Matt Herron; *Exec. Dir.* Richard Weisgrau.

American Society of Picture Professionals Inc., c/o *Memb. Chair* Mindy Klarman, Macmillan/McGraw-Hill School Div., 10 Union Sq. E., 5th fl., New York, NY 10003. Tel. 212-702-4705; *National Pres.* Larry Levin, Nation's Business, 1615 H St. N.W., Washington, DC 20062. Tel. 202-463-5447; *National Secy.* Judy Mason, Music St., Box 869, West Tisbury, MA 02575. Tel. 508-696-8716.

American Translators Assn., 1735 Jefferson Davis Hwy., Suite 903, Arlington, VA 22202. Tel. 703-412-1500, FAX 703-412-1501. *Pres.* Edith F. Losa; *Secy.* Anne Cordero; *Treas.* Seth Reames; *Exec. Dir.* John Gillis.

American Wholesale Booksellers Assn., 702 S. Michigan St., South Bend, IN 46601. Tel. 219-232-8500 Ext. 23, FAX 813-626-9782. *Pres.* John Michel, F.E.P. Inc.; *V.P.* George Coe, Brodart Co.; *Treas./Exec. Secy.* Michael Raymond, the distributors.

Antiquarian Booksellers Assn. of America, 50 Rockefeller Plaza, New York, NY 10020. Tel. 212-757-9395, FAX 212-459-0307. *Pres.* Peter Howard; *V.P.* Robert Rulon-Miller, Jr.; *Secy.* Jeffrey Marks; *Treas.* Robert Fleck; *Exec. Dir.* Liane Wood-Thomas. Address correspondence to the executive director.

Assn. of American Publishers, 220 E. 23 St., New York, NY 10010. Tel. 212-689-8920. *Pres.* Nicholas Veliotes; *Exec. V.P.* Thomas McKee; *V.P.s* James Lichtenberg, Roger Rogalin; *Dirs.* Barbara Meredith, Roberta Plutzik, John Zotz; *Washington Office* 1718 Connecticut Ave. N.W., Washington, DC 20009. Tel. 202-232-3335; *V.P.s* Michael Klipper, Carol Risher; *Dirs.* Judith Platt, Diane Rennert, Roger Williams; *Chair* Charles Ellis, John Wiley and Sons; *V.Chair* Jack Hoeft, Bantam Doubleday Dell Publishing Group; *Treas.* Lawrence E. Levinson, Paramount Communications/Paramount Publishing; *Secy.* Alberto Vitale, Random House.

Assn. of American Univ. Presses, 584 Broadway, Suite 410, New York, NY 10012. Tel. 212-941-6610. *Pres.* Colin Day, Univ. of Michigan Press; *Exec. Dir.* Peter Grenquist; *Asst. Exec. Dir.* Hollis Holmes. Address correspondence to the executive director.

Assn. of Authors' Representatives Inc., 10 Astor Place, 3rd fl., New York, NY 10003. Tel. 212-353-3709. *Pres.* Perry Knowlton; *Admin. Secy.* Ginger Knowlton.

Assn. of Book Travelers, Box 1795, New York, NY 10185. Tel. 212-206-7715. *Pres.* Paul Drougas. Address correspondence to the president.

Assn. of Canadian Publishers, 2 Gloucester St., Suite 301, Toronto, ON M4Y 1L5, Canada. Tel. 416-413-4929, FAX 416-413-4920. *Exec. Dir.* Garry Neil. Address correspondence to the executive director.

Assn. of Jewish Book Publishers, 838 Fifth Ave., New York, NY 10021. *Pres.* Rabbi Elliot Stevens. Address correspondence to the president.

Assn. of the Graphic Arts, 330 Seventh Ave., New York, NY 10001. Tel. 212-279-2100. *Pres.* William Dirzulaitis; *Dir. Ed.* Linda Nahum; *Office Mgr.* Susan Turturo.

Book Industry Study Group Inc., 160 Fifth Ave., New York, NY 10010. Tel. 212-929-1393, FAX 212-989-7542. *Chair* Laura Conley; *V.Chair* Paul McLaughlin; *Treas.* Seymour Turk; *Secy.* Robert Bell; *Managing Agent* SKP Assocs. Address correspondence to William Raggio.

Book Manufacturers Institute, 45 William St., Suite 245, Wellesley, MA 02181-4007. Tel. 617-239-0103. *Pres.* Brian Payne, Hamilton Printing Co.; *Exec. V.P.* Stephen Snyder. Address correspondence to the executive vice president.

Book Publicists of Southern California, 6464 Sunset Blvd., 580, Hollywood, CA 90028. Tel. 213-461-3921, FAX 213-461-0917. *Pres.* Irwin Zucker; *V.P.* Sol Marshall; *Secy.* Joe Sorrentino; *Treas.* Nina Mills.

Book Week Headquarters, Children's Book Council Inc., 568 Broadway, New York, NY 10012. Tel. 212-966-1990. *Pres.* Paula Quint; *Asst. V.P.* Maria Juarez; *Chair* Louise Howton, Harcourt Brace, 525 B St., San Diego, CA 92101. Tel. 619-699-6810.

Bookbinders' Guild of New York, c/o *Secy.* Tracy Cabanis, Alfred Knopf, 201 E. 50 St., New York, NY 10022. Tel. 212-572-2004; *Pres.* Paul Stanley, Courier Cos., 60 E. 42 St., Suite 864, New York, NY 10165. Tel. 212-490-8700; *V.P.* Sheila Anderson, W. H. Freeman, 51 Madison Ave., New York, NY 10010. Tel. 212-576-9484; *Treas.* Irwin Wolf, c/o Graphic Design Studio, 108 John St., North Massapequa, NY 11758; *Financial Secy.* Linda Palladino, William Morrow and Co., 1350 Ave. of the Americas, New York, NY 10019. Tel. 212-261-6675.

Bookbuilders of Boston Inc., c/o Tom D'Espinosa, 66 Cummings Pk., Woburn, MA 01801. Tel. 617-933-6878. *Pres.* Martin Rabinowitz.

Bookbuilders West, Box 7046, San Francisco, CA 94120-9727. *Pres.* Barbara Redman, Color Tech Corp., 121 Second St., 2nd fl., San Francisco, CA 94105. Tel. 415-546-4991.

Canadian Book Publishers' Council, 250 Merton St., Suite 203, Toronto, ON M4S 1B1, Canada. Tel. 416-322-7011, FAX 416-322-6999. *Pres.* Gordon S. Bain, Random House of Canada Ltd.; *1st V.P.* Brian

O'Donnell, Irwin Publishing; *Treas.* Andrew Nopper, Distican; *Exec. Dir.* Jacqueline Hushion; *Special Interest Groups* The School Group, The College Group, The Trade Group.

Canadian Booksellers Assn., 301 Donlands Ave., Toronto, ON M4J 3R8, Canada. Tel. 416-467-7883, FAX 416-467-7886. *Dir. Memb. Programs* Lynda Joyet; *Exec. Dir.* Ingrid van Rotterdam.

Catholic Book Publishers Assn. Inc., c/o *Secy.* Charles A. Roth, 333 Glen Head Rd., Old Brookville, NY 11545. Tel. 516-671-9342; *Pres.* Mary Carol Kendzia, Twenty-Third Publications, 185 Willow St., Box 180, Mystic, CT 06355. Tel. 203-536-2611.

Chicago Book Clinic, 111 E. Wacker Dr., Suite 200, Chicago, IL 60601-4298. Tel. 312-946-1700. *Exec. Dir.* Cindy Clark; *Pres.* Robert R. Duncan; *Pres.-Elect* Sue Nisson; *Secy.* Kim Meriwether; *Treas.* Mark Tiberi.

Chicago Publishers Assn., c/o *Pres.* Robert Follett, Follett Corp., 2233 West St., River Grove, IL 60171. Tel. 708-583-2000.

Children's Book Council Inc., 568 Broadway, New York, NY 10012. Tel. 212-966-1990. *Pres.* Paula Quint; *Asst. V.P.* Maria Juarez; *Chair* Elizabeth Gordon, Disney/Hyperion, 114 Fifth Ave., New York, NY 10010. Tel. 212-633-4422.

Christian Booksellers Assn., Box 200, Colorado Springs, CO 80901. Tel. 719-576-7880. *Pres.* William Anderson.

Copyright Society of the U.S.A., 1133 Ave. of the Americas, 33rd fl., New York, NY 10036. Tel. 212-354-6401, FAX 212-354-2847. *Pres.* Roger Zissu; *Administrator* Barbara Pannone.

Education for Mission, Friendship Press, 475 Riverside Dr., New York, NY 10115-0050. Tel. 212-870-2495. *Exec. Dir.* Audrey Miller; *Program Committee Pres.* Sandra Rooney.

Educational Paperback Assn., c/o *Exec. Secy.* Marilyn Able, Box 1399, East Hampton, NY 11937. Tel. 212-879-6850. *Pres.* Sanford Jaffe, The Booksource, Saint Louis, MO 63108. Tel. 800-525-4862.

Evangelical Christian Publishers Assn., 3225 S. Hardy Dr., Suite 101, Tempe, AZ

85282. Tel. 602-966-3998, FAX 602-966-1944. *Exec. Dir.* Doug Ross.

Graphic Artists Guild Inc., 11 W. 20 St., 8th fl., New York, NY 10011-3704. Tel. 212-463-7730. *Natl. Exec. Dir.* Paul Basista; *Pres.* Karen Guancione. Address correspondence to the national executive director.

Great Lakes Booksellers Assn., c/o *Exec. Dir.* Jim Dana, Box 901, 509 Lafayette, Grand Haven, MI 49417. Tel. 616-847-2460, FAX 616-842-0051. *Pres.* Rick Morgenstern, Morgenstern Booksellers, Bloomington, IN 47401; *V.P.* Greg Wybel, Wybel Marketing, 46171 Village Green Dr., Apt. 309, Belleville, MI 48111.

Guild of Book Workers, 201 E. Capitol St. S.E., Washington, DC 20003. Tel. 202-544-4600. *Pres.* Franklin Mowery.

International Assn. of Printing House Craftsmen Inc., 7042 Brooklyn Blvd., Minneapolis, MN 55429-1370. Tel. 612-560-1620. *Pres.* Cheryl Sunness; *Exec. Dir.* Kevin Keane.

International Copyright Information Center, c/o Assn. of American Publishers, 1718 Connecticut Ave. N.W., 7th fl., Washington, DC 20009-1148. Tel. 202-232-3335, FAX 202-745-0694. *Dir.* Carol Risher.

International Standard Book Numbering U.S. Agency, 121 Chanlon Rd., New Providence, NJ 07974. Tel. 908-665-6700, FAX 908-464-3553. *Dir.* Emery Koltay; *Officers* Lynn DeVita, Diana Fumando, Bill McCahery, Don Riseborough, Albert Simmonds, Peter Simon.

Jewish Book Council, 15 E. 26 St., New York, NY 10010. Tel. 212-532-4949, FAX 212-481-4174. *Pres.* Leonard Gold; *Dir.* Paula Gribetz Gottlieb.

Library Binding Institute, 7401 Metro Blvd., Suite 325, Edina, MN 55439. *Exec. Dir.* Sally Grauer.

Magazine and Paperback Marketing Institute, 4000 Coolidge Ave., Baltimore, MD 21229. Tel. 410-525-3355. *Exec. V.P.* Don DeVito.

Metropolitan Lithographers Assn., 950 Third Ave., Suite 1500, New York, NY 10022. Tel. 212-838-8480. *Pres.* Frank Stiuo; *Exec. Dir.* Jane Bernd.

Mid-America Publishers Assn., c/o *Exec. Dir.* Jerry Kromberg, Box 30242, Lincoln,

NE 68503-0242. Tel. 402-466-9665, FAX 402-466-9093. *Pres.* Karen Adler, Two Lane Press, Kansas City, MO 64111. Tel. 816-531-3129, FAX 816-531-6113.

Mid-Atlantic Booksellers Assn., 108 S. 13 St., Philadelphia, PA 19107. Tel. 215-735-9598. *Exec. Dir.* Larry Robin.

Midwest Independent Publishers Assn., 9561 Woodridge Circle, Eden Prairie, MN 55347-2744. Tel. 612-941-5053. *Exec. Secy.* Pat Bell.

Miniature Book Society Inc., c/o *Pres.* Rev. Joseph L. Curran, Box 127, Sudbury, MA 01776. Tel. 617-527-7560; *V.P.* James F. DeLancey, 2212 S. Canterbury Rd., Wilmington, NC 28403; *Secy.* Doris Selmer, 55 E. Arthur Ave., Arcadia, CA 91006; *Treas.* Loretta Gentile, 10 Albert St., Waltham, MA 02154.

Minnesota Book Publishers Roundtable. *Pres.* David Wexler, Chronimed Publishing, 13911 Ridgedale Dr., Minnetonka, MN 55343; *V.P.* Teresa Bonner, Milkweed Editions, 430 First Ave. N., Suite 400, Minneapolis, MN 55401; *Secy.-Treas.* Brad Vogt, Liturgical Press, Collegeville, MN 56321. Tel. 612-363-2538. Address correspondence to the secretary-treasurer.

Mountains and Plains Booksellers Assn., 805 LaPorte Ave., Fort Collins, CO 80521. Tel./FAX 303-484-5856. *Exec. Dir.* Lisa Knudsen; *Pres.* Regina Bullock; *V.P.* Kasha Songer; *Secy.* Gwynne Spencer; *Treas.* Terry Wernick.

National Assn. of College Stores, 500 E. Lorain St., Oberlin, OH 44074-1294. Tel. 216-775-7777, FAX 216-775-4769. *Public Relations Coord.* Jerry L. Buchs; *Pres./Treas.* Pamela A. Mills; *Pres.-Elect/Secy.* Richard McDaniel. Address correspondence to the public relations coordinator.

National Council of the Churches of Christ in the U.S.A. *See* Education for Mission.

New England Booksellers Assn., 45 Newbury St., Boston, MA 02116. Tel. 617-421-9340, FAX 617-421-9341. *Pres.* Carole Horne; *Exec. Dir.* Wayne Drugan.

New Mexico Book League, 8632 Horacio Place N.E., Albuquerque, NM 87111. Tel. 505-299-8940. *Exec. Dir.* Dwight A. Myers; *Pres.* Robert Kadlec; *V.P.* Robert R. White; *Treas.* C. Rittenhouse; *Ed.* Carol Myers.

New York Rights and Permissions Group, c/o *Chair* Jeanne Gough, Gale Research Inc., 835 Penobscot Bldg., Detroit, MI 48226. Tel. 313-961-6813.

Northern California Booksellers Assn. *See* Northern California Independent Booksellers Assn.

Northern California Independent Booksellers Assn., 1144 65th St., Suite B, Emeryville, CA 94608. Tel. 510-601-6922, FAX 510-601-8398. *Exec. Dir.* Ginie Thorp.

Optical Publishing Assn., Box 21268, Columbus, OH 43221. Tel. 614-442-8805, FAX 614-442-8815. *Exec. Dir.* Richard A. Bowers.

Pacific Northwest Booksellers Assn., 1510 Mill St., Eugene, OR 97401-4258. Tel. 503-683-4363. *Pres.* Marilyn Newman; *Exec. Dir.* Thom Chambliss.

Periodical and Book Assn. of America Inc., 120 E. 34 St., Suite 7K, New York, NY 10016. Tel. 212-689-4952, FAX 212-545-8328. *Pres.* Michael McCarthy; *V.P.s* Keith Furman, Mary McEvoy; *Treas.* Edward Handi; *Secy.* Andrea Morris; *Exec. Dir.* Michael Morse; *Legal Counsel* Lee Feltman; *Advisers to the Pres.* Irwin Billman, Norman Jacobs, Adrian Lopez, Robert Woltersdorf.

Periodical Marketers of Canada, c/o *Pres.* Alex Petraitis, Metro Toronto News Co., 120 Sinnot Rd., Scarborough, ON M1L 4N1, Canada. Tel. 416-752-8720, FAX 416-285-2056; *V.P.* John Seebach, Great Pacific News, 2500 Vauxhall Place, Richmond, BC V6V 1Y8, Canada. Tel. 604-278-4841, FAX 604-278-5642; *Secy.-Treas.* Steve Shepherd, Ottawa Valley News Co., Box 157, Arnprior, ON K7S 3H4, Canada. Tel. 613-623-3197. Address correspondence to the association, 2 Berkeley St., Suite 503, Toronto, ON M5A 2W3, Canada. Tel. 416-363-4549, FAX 416-363-6691.

Philadelphia Book Clinic, c/o *Secy.-Treas.* Thomas Colaiezzi, 136 Chester Ave., Yeadon, PA 19050-3831. Tel. 215-259-7022.

Publishers Advertising and Marketing Assn., c/o *Secy.* Cathy Grunewald Collins, Crown Publishing Group, 201 E. 50 St., New

York, NY 10022. Tel. 212-572-2028; *Pres.* Lee Wiggins, Macmillan Publishing Co., 866 Third Ave., New York, NY 10022. Tel. 212-702-6874; *V.P.* Judy Murphy Polvay, The New Yorker, 20 W. 43 St., New York, NY 10036. Tel. 212-840-3800; *Treas.* Stephanie A. Joel, John Wiley and Sons, 605 Third Ave., New York, NY 10158-0012. Tel. 212-850-6365.

Publishers' Publicity Assn., c/o *Pres.* Patricia Eisemann, Macmillan Publishing Co., 866 Third Ave., New York, NY 10022. Tel. 702-6757; *V.P.* Beth Davey, Little, Brown and Co., 1271 Ave. of the Americas, New York, NY 10020. Tel. 212-522-8063; *Secy.* Ben Petrone, Carol Publishing Group, 600 Madison Ave., New York, NY 10022. Tel. 212-418-4090; *Treas.* Lottchen Shivers, Henry Holt and Co., 115 W. 18 St., New York, NY 10011. Tel. 212-886-9269.

Religion Publishing Group, c/o *Secy.* Charles Roth, Roth Advertising Inc., 333 Glen Head Rd., Old Brookville, NY 11545. Tel. 516-671-9292; *Pres.* Hargis Thomas, Oxford Univ. Press, 200 Madison Ave., New York, NY 10016. Tel. 212-679-7300 Ext. 7235.

Research and Engineering Council of the Graphic Arts Industry Inc., Box 639, Chadds Ford, PA 19317. Tel. 215-388-7394. *Pres.* Robert Peters; *Exec. V.P./Secy.* Brian Chapman; *Exec. V.P./Treas.* Bernard Knox; *Managing Dir.* Fred Rogers.

Southern California Booksellers Assn., Box 4176, Culver City, CA 90231-4176. *Pres.* Lise Friedman, Dutton's Brentwood Books, 11975 San Vicente Blvd., Los Angeles, CA 90049. Tel. 310-476-6263, FAX 310-471-0399.

Technical Assn. of the Pulp and Paper Industry, Technology Pk./Atlanta, Box 105113, Atlanta, GA 30348-5113. Tel. 404-446-1400. *Pres.* Ronald Estridge; *V.P.* Jack E. Chinn; *Exec. Dir./Treas.* W. L. Cullison.

West Coast Book People Assn., 27 McNear Dr., San Rafael, CA 94901. *Secy.* Frank Goodall. Tel. 415-459-1227.

Women's National Book Assn., 160 Fifth Ave., New York, NY 10010. Tel. 212-675-7805. *Pres.* Carolyn Wilson, 1115 Grandview Dr., Nashville, TN 37204. Tel. 615-269-1000 Ext. 2441; *V.P.* Sue MacLaurin, 3554 Crownridge Dr., Sherman Oaks, CA 91403. Tel. 818-501-3925; *Secy.* Margaret Auer, Dir. of Libs., Univ. of Detroit, Box 19900, Detroit, MI 48219-3599. Tel. 313-993-1090; *Treas.* Sylvia Cross, 19824 Septo St., Chatsworth, CA 91311. Tel. 818-886-8448; *Chapter Pres.:* *Binghamton* Dorothea Seargent, 277 Nowlan Rd., Binghamton, NY 13904. Tel. 607-724-6253; *Boston* Dorothy S. O'Connor, 192 Howard St., Melrose, MA 02176. Tel. 617-665-5005; *Detroit* Joanne Johnson, Box 46523, Mount Clemens, MI 48046. Tel. 313-469-3548; *Los Angeles* LaVonne Taylor, 15831 Olden St., Suite 71, Sylmar, CA 91342. Tel. 818-367-8085; *Nashville* Lee Fairbend, 210 Britain Ct., Brentwood, TN 37027. Tel. 615-790-0896; *New York* Janet Rosen, 175 W. 12 St., Apt. 2C, New York, NY 10011. Tel. 212-675-7593; *San Francisco* Andrea Brown, Box 808, El Granada, CA 94018.Tel. 415-728-1714; *Washington, DC* Diane Ullius, 5621 Sixth St. S., Arlington, VA 22204. Tel. 703-931-8610.

International and Foreign Book Trade Associations

For Canadian book trade associations, see the preceding section, "Book Trade Associations, United States and Canada." For a more extensive list of book trade organizations outside the United States and Canada, with more detailed information, consult *International Literary Market Place* (R. R. Bowker), which also provides extensive lists of major bookstores and publishers in each country.

International

Afro-Asian Book Council, 4835/24 Ansari Rd., New Delhi 110-002, India. Tel. 11-326-1487, FAX 11-326-7437. *Chair* S. Bissoondoyal; *Secy.-Gen.* Asang Machwe; *Dir. Secretariat* Abul Hasan.

Centre Régional pour la Promotion du Livre en Afrique (Regional Center for Book Promotion in Africa), Box 1646, Yaoundé Cameroon. Tel. 022-4782/2936. *Secy.* William Moutchia.

Centro Regional para el Fomento del Libro en América Latina y el Caribe (CERLALC) (Regional Center for Book Promotion in Latin America and the Caribbean), Calle 70, No. 9-52, Apdo. Aéreo 57348, Bogota 2, Colombia. Tel. 01-249-5141, 01-255-4594, FAX 01-255-4614. *Dir.* Jorge Salazar.

Confederation of Information Communication Industries, 19 Bedford Sq., London WC1B 3HJ, England. Tel. 071-580-6321, FAX 071-636-5375.

Federation of European Publishers, 92 Ave. de Tervuren, B-1040 Brussels, Belgium. Tel. 2-736-36-16, FAX 2-736-19-87. *Pres.* Pere Vicens; *Dir.* Paul Cerf.

Group of Booksellers Associations in the EEC, Blvd. Lambermont, LN-140-B-1, B-1030 Brussels, Belgium. *Pres.* John Hitchin; *Gen. Secy.* Christiane Vuidar.

International Board on Books for Young People (IBBY), Nonnenweg 12, Postfach, CH-4003 Basel, Switzerland. Tel. 061-272-29-17, FAX 061-272-27-57. *Dir.* Leena Maissen.

International Booksellers Federation, Blvd. Lambermont, LN-140-B-1, B-1030 Brussels, Belgium. Tel. and FAX 2-242-0957. *Pres.* John K. Hedgecock; *Gen. Secy.*

Christiane Vuidar.

International League of Antiquarian Booksellers, c/o *Pres.* Anton Gerits, Delilaan 5, NL-1217 HJ Hilversum, The Netherlands. *Secy.* Helen Kahn, Box 323, Victoria Sta., Montreal, PQ H3Z 2V8, Canada.

International Publishers Assn. (Union Internationale des Editeurs), Ave. Miremont 3, CH-1206 Geneva, Switzerland. Tel. 22-346-3018, FAX 22-347-5717. *Secy.-Gen.* J. Alexis Koutchoumow.

International Publishers Copyright Council, 90 Tottenham Court Rd., 5th fl., London W1P 9HE, England. Tel. 071-436-5931, FAX 071-436-3986.

National

Argentina

Cámara Argentina de Publicaciones (Argentine Publications Assn.), Reconquista 1101, 6° piso, 1003 Buenos Aires. *Pres.* Agustin dos Santos.

Cámara Argentina del Libro (Argentine Book Assn.), Avda. Belgrano 1580, 6° piso, 1093 Buenos Aires. Tel. 1-381-8383, FAX 1-381-9253. *Secy.* Norberto J. Pou.

Australia

Australian Book Publishers Assn., 89 Jones St., Suite 60, Ultimo, N.S.W. 2007. *Dir.* Susan Blackwell.

Australian Booksellers Assn., Box 173, North Carlton, Vic. 3054. *Exec. Dir.* Celia Pollock.

National Book Council, Suite 3, 21 Drummond Pl., Carlton, Vic. 3053. FAX 03-663-8658. *Exec. Dir.* Thomas Shapcott.

Austria

Hauptverband des Österreichischen Buchhandels (Austrian Publishers and Booksellers Assn.), Grünangergasse 4, A-1010 Vienna. *Gen. Secy.* Otto Mang.

Österreichischer Buchhändlerverband, Grünangergasse 4, A-1010 Vienna. *Pres.* Michael Kernstock; *Secy.* Otto Mang.

Österreichischer Verlegerverband (Assn. of Austrian Publishers), Grünangergasse 4, A-1010 Vienna. *Gen. Secy.* Otto Mang.

Verband der Antiquare Österreichs (Austrian Antiquarian Booksellers Assn.), Grünangergasse 4, A-1010 Vienna. *Gen. Secy.* Otto Mang.

Belgium

Algemene Vlaamse Boekverkopersbond (Flemish Booksellers Assn.), c/o Vereniging van Uitgevers van Nederlandstalige Boeken, Hof ter Schrieklaan 17, B-2600 Berchem/Antwerp. FAX 3-281-2240.

Association des Editeurs Belges (Belgian Assn. of Publishers of French-Language Books), 140 Blvd. Lambermont, Bte. 1, B-1030 Brussels. *Dir.* Bernard Gérard.

Chambre Professionnelle Belge de la Librairie Ancienne et Moderne/Belgische Beroepskamer van Antiquaren (Belgian Assn. of Antiquarian and Modern Booksellers), Secretariat, 53 Blvd. Saint Michel, B-1040 Brussels. Tel. 2-736-4329.

Vereniging ter Bevordering van het Vlaamse Boekwezen (Assn. for the Promotion of Flemish Books), Frankryklei 93, Bus 3, B-2000 Antwerp. *Secy.* Wim de Mont.

Bolivia

Cámara Boliviana del Libro (Bolivian Booksellers Assn.), Box 682, Edif. Las Palmas, Avda. 20 de Octubre 2005, Planta Baja, La Paz; *Pres.* Rolando S. Condori.

Brazil

Associação Brasileira de Livreiros Antiquarios (Brazilian Assn. of Antiquarian Booksellers), Rua Visconde de Caravelas 17, 22271 Rio de Janeiro. *Pres.* Patrick Levy.

Associação Brasileira do Livro (Brazilian Booksellers Assn.), Av. 13 de Maio 23, 16°, 20031 Rio de Janeiro; *Pres.* Ernesto Zahar.

Câmara Brasileira do Livro (Brazilian Book Chamber), Av. Ipiranga, 1267-10 andar, 01039-907 Sao Paulo, S.P. FAX 11-229-7463. *Gen. Mgr.* Aloysio T. Costa.

Sindicato Nacional dos Editores de Livros (Brazilian Book Publishers Assn.), Av. Río Branco 37, 15 andar, Salas 1503/06 e 1510/12, 20090 Rio de Janeiro. Tel. 21-233-6481, FAX 21-253-8502. *Pres.* Sérgio Machado; *Exec. Secy.* Nilson Lopes.

Chile

Cámara Chilena del Libro (Chilean Book Assn.), Alameda Bernardo O'Higgins 1370, Of. 501, Santiago. Tel. 2-698-9519, 2-672-4088, FAX 2-698-9226. *Pres.* Eduardo Castillo; *Exec. Secy.* Carlos Franz.

China (People's Republic)

Publishers Assn. of China, 85 Dongsi Nandajie, 100703 Beijing.

Colombia

Cámara Colombiana del Libro (Colombian Book Assn.), Carrera 17A, No. 37-27, Apdo. Aéreo 8998, Bogota. Tel. 1-288-6188, FAX 1-287-3320. *Exec. Dir.* Miguel Laverde Espejo; *Chair* Jairo Camacho Cuellar.

Czech Republic

Ministerstvo Kultury České Republiky, Oddělení Knižní Kultury a Tisku (Czech Ministry of Culture, Dept. for Publishing and Book Trade), Valdštejnské nám. 4, 118 11 Prague 1.

Denmark

Danske Antikvarboghandlerforening (Danish Antiquarian Booksellers Assn.), Box 2028, DK-1012 Copenhagen K. *Pres.* Poul Jan Poulsen.

Danske Boghandlerforening (Danish Booksellers Assn.), Boghandlernes Hus, Siljangade 6, DK-2300 Copenhagen S. 3-154-2255, FAX 3-157-2422.

Danske Forlaeggerforening (Danish Publishers Assn.), Købmagergade 11, DK-1150 Copenhagen K. *Dir.* Erik V. Krustrup.

Ecuador

Cámara Ecuatoriana del Libro, Guayaquil 1629, 4° piso, Casilla 17-01-3329, Quito. FAX 2-566340. *Secy.* Luis Mora Ortega.

Egypt

General Egyptian Book Organization, Box 1660, Corniche El-Nile, Boulac, Cairo. FAX 2-754213.

Estonia

Estonian Publishers Assn., Parnu mnt 10, EE-0090 Tallinn. FAX 142-445720. *Dir.* M. Helme.

Finland

Kirja-ja Paperikauppojen Liitto ry (Finnish Booksellers and Stationers Assn.), Eerikinkatu 15-17 D 43-44, SF-00100 Helsinki. Tel. 694-4822, FAX 694-4900. *Managing Dir.* Olli Eräkivi.

Suomen Kustannusyhdistys ry (Finnish Book Publishers' Assn.), Merimiehenkatu 12 A6, SF-00150 Helsinki. *Secy.-Gen.* Veikko Sonninen.

France

Cercle de la Librairie (Circle of Professionals of the Book Trade), 35 Rue Grégoire-de-Tours, F-75006 Paris. Tel. 1-44-41-28-00. *Dir.* Jean-Marie Doublet.

Fédération Française des Syndicats de Libraires (French Booksellers Assn.), 43 Rue de Châteaudun, F-75009 Paris. *Pres.* Patrice Van Moe.

France Edition—Office de Promotion Internationale, 35 Rue Grégoire-de-Tours, F-75006 Paris. Tel. 1-44-41-13-13, FAX 1-46-34-63-83. *Managing Dir.* Patrick C. Dubs; *Secy.-Gen.* Marc Franconie.

Syndicat National de la Librairie Ancienne et Moderne (SLAM), 4 Rue Gît-le-Coeur, F-75006 Paris. Tel. 1-43-29-46-38. *Pres.* Dominique Courvoisier.

Syndicat National de l'Edition (French Publishers Assn.), 35 Rue Grégoire-de-Tours, F-75006 Paris. Tel. 1-43-29-75-75. *Pres.* Serge Eyrolles; *Dir.-Gen.* Gérard Belorgey.

Syndicat National des Importateurs et Exportateurs de Livres (National Assn. of Book Importers and Exporters), 107 Blvd. Saint Germain, F-75006 Paris. *Pres.* André Didier.

Union des Libraires de France, 35 Rue Grégoire-de-Tours, F-75006 Paris. FAX 1-46-33-65-29.

Germany

Börsenverein des Deutschen Buchhandels e.V. (Assn. of German Publishers and Booksellers), Postfach 100442, 60549 Frankfurt-am-Main. FAX 69-130-6201; Gerichtsweg 26, 04103 Leipzig.

Bundesverband der Deutschen Versandbuchhändler e.V. (National Federation of German Mail-Order Booksellers), An der Ringkirche 6, 65197 Wiesbaden. *Dirs.* Stefan Rutkowsky, Kornelia Wahl.

Verband Deutscher Antiquare e.V. (German Antiquarian Booksellers Assn.), Braubachstr. 34, 60311 Frankfurt-am-Main. *Pres.* Christine Grahamer; *V.P.* Edmund Brumme.

Ghana

Ghana Book Publishers Assn., c/o Ghana Universities Press, Box 2419, Accra. *Secy.* W. A. Dekutsey.

Ghana Booksellers Assn., Box 10367, Accra. Tel. 773-002. *Secy.* Fred J. Reimmer.

Great Britain

See United Kingdom

Greece

Panhellenic Federation of Greek Publishers, Arahovis 61, GR-10681 Athens. *Gen. Secy.* D. Pandeleskos.

Syllogos Ekdoton Vivliopolon (Publishers and Booksellers Assn. of Athens), 54 Themistocleous St., GR-10681 Athens. *Pres.* Th. Kastaniotis; *Secy.* M. Bakirtzis.

Hungary

Magyar Könyvkiadók és Könyvterjesztök Egyesülése (Hungarian Publishers' and Booksellers' Assn.), Vörösmarty tér 1X, Postafiók 130, H-1367 Budapest. *Pres.* István Bart; *Secy.-Gen.* Péter Zentai.

Iceland

Félag Íslenskra Bókaútgefenda (Icelandic Publishers' Assn.), Sudurlandsbraut 4A, IS-108 Reykjavik. *Gen. Mgr.* Vilborg Hardardóttir.

India

Federation of Indian Publishers, Federation House, 18/1-C, Institutional Area, JNU Rd., Aruna Asaf Ali Marg, New Delhi 110067. FAX 11-686-4054. *Secy.* Anand Bhushan.

Indonesia

Ikatan Penerbit Indonesia (IKAPI) (Assn. of Indonesian Book Publishers), Jl. Kalipasir 32, Jakarta 10330. FAX 21-314-6050. *Secy. Gen.* Setia Dharma Majid; *Head, Foreign Relations* Aida Joesoef Ahmad.

Ireland

Booksellers Assn. of Great Britain and Ireland, 54 Middle Abbey St., Dublin 1. *Admin.* Penelope Morphew.
CLÉ: The Irish Book Publishers' Assn., The Writers' Centre, 19 Parnell Sq., Dublin 1. Tel. 1-872-9090, FAX 1-872-2035.

Israel

Book and Printing Center of the Israel Export Institute, 29 Hamered St., Box 50084, 68125 Tel Aviv. FAX 3-514-2881. *Dir.* Corine Knafo.
Book Publishers Assn. of Israel, 29 Carlebach St., Box 20123, Tel Aviv. *Chair*

Rachel Edelman; *Managing Dir.* Amnon Ben Shmuel; *International Promotion and Literary Rights Dept. Dir.* Lorna Soifer. Tel. 3-561-4121, FAX 3-561-1996. *Exec. Dir.* Arie Friedler.

Italy

Associazione Italiana Editori (Italian Publishers Assn.), Via delle Erbe 2, I-20121 Milan. *Secy.* Pietro Pizzoni.
Associazione Librai Antiquari d'Italia (Antiquarian Booksellers Assn. of Italy), Via J. Nardi 6, I-50132 Florence. *Pres.* Vittorio Soave.
Associazione Librai Italiani (Italian Booksellers Assn.), Corso Venezia 49, I-20121 Milan.

Jamaica

Booksellers Assn. of Jamaica, c/o Sangster's Book Stores Ltd., 97 Harbour St., Box 366, Kingston.

Japan

Japan Book Importers Assn., Chiyoda Kaikan 21-4, Nihonbashi 1-chome, Chuo-ku, Tokyo 103. *Secy.* Shunji Kanda.
Japan Book Publishers Assn., 6 Fukuromachi, Shinjuku-ku, Tokyo 162. *Pres.* Toshiyuki Hattori; *Exec. Dir.* Toshikazu Gomi.

Kenya

Kenya Publishers Assn., Box 45314, Nairobi. *Secy.* David Mwata.

Korea (Republic of)

Korean Publishers Assn., 105-2 Sagan-dong, Chongno-gu, Seoul 110-190. FAX 2-738-5414. *Pres.* Nark-Joon Kim; *Secy.-Gen.* Jong-Jin Jung.

Latvia

Latvia Publishers Assn., c/o Mars Ozolins, Vega Ltd. Publishers, Lazaretes 3, Riga 1010.

Lithuania

Lithuania Publishers Assn., K. Sirvydo 6, 2600 Vilnius. FAX 122-619696. *Pres.* Vincas Akelis.

Luxembourg

Confédération du Commerce Luxembourgeois, Groupement Libraires-Papetiers (Confederation of Retailers, Group for Stationers and Booksellers), 23 Allée-Scheffer, B.P. 482, L-2014 Luxembourg. Tel. 47-31-25, FAX 22-00-59. *Pres.* Jean-Claude Diderich; *Secy.* Christiane Kuhn.

Malaysia

Malaysian Book Publishers Assn., No. 10, Jalan 217, 46050 Petaling Jaya, Selangor Darul Ehsan. FAX 3-791-0416. *Hon. Secy.* Thomas Soh.

Mexico

Cámara Nacional de la Industria Editorial Mexicana, Holanda No. 13, CP 04120 México 21. FAX 5-604-3147. *Secy.-Gen.* R. Servin.

The Netherlands

Koninklijke Nederlandse Uitgeversbond (Royal Dutch Publishers Assn.), Keizersgracht 391, 1016 EJ Amsterdam. FAX 20-620-3859. *Secy.* R. M. Vrij.

Koninklijke Vereeniging ter Bevordering van de Belangen des Boekhandels (Royal Dutch Book Trade Assn.), Frederiksplein 1, Box 15007, 1001 MA Amsterdam. *Secy.* M. van Vollenhoven-Nagel.

Nederlandsche Vereeniging van Antiquaren (Antiquarian Booksellers Assn. of the Netherlands), Box 664, 1000 AR Amsterdam. *Pres.* F. W. Kuyper; *Secy.* A. Gerits.

Nederlandse Boekverkopersbond (Booksellers Assn. of the Netherlands), Waalsdorperweg 119, Box 90731, 2509 LS The Hague. Tel. 70-324-4395, FAX 70-324-4411. *Pres.* W. Karssen; *Exec. Secy.* A. C. Doeser.

New Zealand

Book Publishers Assn. of New Zealand, Box 386, Auckland 1. FAX 9-309-7798. *Pres.* Tony Harkins; *Exec. Dir.* Dean Reynolds.

Booksellers New Zealand, Book House, 86 Boulcott St., Box 11-377, Wellington. FAX 4-472-8628. *Chief Exec.* Jo Breese.

Nigeria

Nigerian Publishers Assn., 14 Awosika Ave., Off Oshunto Kun Ave., Old Bodija, Box 2541, Ibadan. *Pres.* Victor Nwankwo.

Norway

Bok og Papiransattes Forening (Norwegian Book Trade Employees Assn.), Øvre Vollgate 15, N-0158 Oslo 1.

Den Norske Bokhandlerforening (Norwegian Booksellers Assn.), Øvre Vollgate 15, N-0158 Oslo. *Dir.* Olav Gjerdene.

Norske Forleggerforening (Norwegian Publishers Assn.), Øvre Vollgate 15, N-0158 Oslo 1. Tel. 2-242-1355, FAX 2-233-3830. *Dir.* Paul M. Rothe.

Pakistan

National Book Council of Pakistan, 1st fl., Block 14D, Al-Markaz F-8, Islamabad. *Dir.-Gen.* M. I. Hussain.

Peru

Cámara Peruana del Libro (Peruvian Publishers Assn.), Jirón Washington 1206, Of. 507-508, Apdo. 10253, Lima.

Philippines

Book Development Assn. of the Philippines, 40 Valencia St., New Manila, Quezon City 3008. FAX 2-721-8782.

Philippine Educational Publishers' Assn., 927 Quezon Ave., 1104 Quezon City. *Pres.* J. Ernesto Sibal.

Poland

Polskie Towarzystwo Wydawców Książek (Polish Society of Book Editors), ul.

Mazowiecka 2/4, 00-048 Warsaw. *Pres.* Andrzej Karpowicz.

Stowarzyszenie Ksiegarzy Polskich (Assn. of Polish Booksellers), ul. Mokotowska 4/6, 00-641 Warsaw. *Pres.* Tadeusz Hussak.

Portugal

Associação Portuguesa de Editores e Livreiros (Portuguese Assn. of Publishers and Booksellers), Av. dos Estados Unidos da América 97-6, Esq., 1700 Lisbon.

Romania

Romlibri, Piata Presei Libere 1, R-71341 Bucharest. *Deputy Gen. Dir.* Victor Mircea.

Russia

Publishers Assn., Per Sivtsev Vrazhok 43, 121839 Moscow. FAX 95-241-6353. *Contact* M. Shishigin.

Russian Book Chamber, Kremlevskaya nab 1/9, 121019 Moscow G-19. FAX 95-202-3992. *Dir.-Gen.* J. V. Torsujev.

Singapore

National Book Development Council of Singapore, Bukit Merah Branch Lib., Bukit Merah Central, Box 0693, Singapore 9115. FAX 270-6139.

South Africa

Publishers Assn. of South Africa, Private Bag 91932, Auckland Park 2006. Tel. 11-726-7470, FAX 11-482-3409. *Chair* Mike Peacock; *Admin.* Theresa Edwards.

Spain

Federación de Gremios de Editores de España (Spanish Federation of Publishers Assns.), Juan Ramón Jiménez, 45-9°, Izda. 28036, Madrid. Tel. 1-350-91-05, FAX 1-345-43-51. *Pres.* D. Fermín Vargas; *Secy.-Gen.* Ana Moltó.

Gremi d'Editors de Catalunya (Assn. of Catalonian Publishers), Valencia 279, First

Planta, Barcelona 08009. *Pres.* P. Vicens i Rahola.

Gremi de Llibreters de Barcelona i Catalunya (Assn. of Barcelona and Catalonia Booksellers), C. Mallorca 272-274, 08037 Barcelona.

Sri Lanka

Booksellers Assn. of Sri Lanka, Box 244, Colombo 2. *Secy.* W. L. Mendis.

Sri Lanka Assn. of Publishers, 112 S. Mahinda Mawatha, Colombo 10. *Pres.* Dayawansa Jayakody.

Sudan

Sudanese Publishers Assn., H. Q. Al Ikhwa Bldg., Flat 7, 7th fl., Box 2771, Khartoum.

Suriname

Publishers Assn. Suriname, Domineestr. 26, Box 1841, Paramaribo. FAX 410-563.

Sweden

Svenska Antikvariatföreningen, Box 22549, S-10422 Stockholm. Tel. 8-411-9136, FAX 8-20-9308. *Secy.* Mats Petersson.

Svenska Bokförläggareföreningen (Swedish Publishers Assn.), Drottninggatan 97, S-11360 Stockholm. *Dir.* Kenth Muldin.

Svenska Bokhandlareföreningen (Swedish Booksellers Assn.), Skeppargatan 27, S-11452 Stockholm. *Managing Dir.* Thomas Rönström.

Switzerland

Schweizerischer Buchhändler- und Verleger-Verband (Swiss German-Language Booksellers and Publishers Assn.), Postfach 9045, CH-8050 Zurich. FAX 1-311-3132. *Secy.* Egon Räz.

Società Editori della Svizzera Italiana (Publishers Assn. for the Italian-Speaking Part of Switzerland), C.P. 2600, Viale Portone 4, CH-6501 Bellinzona.

Société des Libraires et Editeurs de la Suisse Romande (Assn. of Swiss French-Language Booksellers and Publishers), 2 Ave.

Agassiz, CH-1001 Lausanne. *Secy.-Gen.* Robert Junod.

Tanzania

Publishers Assn. of Tanzania, Box 1408, Dar es Salaam.

Thailand

Publishers and Booksellers Assn. of Thailand, 323 Mul Soi Thiraphat, Pracha-u-thit Rd., Bangkok 10140. FAX 2-427-1703.

United Kingdom

Assn. of Learned and Professional Society Publishers, 48 Kelsey Lane, Beckenham, Kent BR3 3NE, England. Tel. 81-658-0459, FAX 81-663-3583. *Secy.* B. T. Donovan.

Book Trust, Book House, 45 E. Hill, London SW18 2QZ, England. *Chief Exec.* Beverly Anderson.

Booksellers Assn. of Great Britain and Ireland, Minster House, 272 Vauxhall Bridge Rd., London SW1V 1BA, England. *Chief Exec.* Tim Godfray.

Educational Publishers Council, 19 Bedford Sq., London WC1B 3HJ, England. *Dir.* John R. M. Davies; *Mgr.* Sandra Robertson.

Publishers Assn., 19 Bedford Sq., London WC1B 3HJ, England. Tel. 71-580-6321, FAX 71-636-5375. *Pres.* Nicholas Chapman; *Chief Exec. and Secy.* Clive Bradley; *International Div. Dir.* Ian Taylor; *Educational Publishers Council Dir.* and *Council of Academic and Professional Publishers Dir.* John Davies.

Uruguay

Cámara Uruguaya del Libro (Uruguayan Publishing Council), Juan D. Jackson 1118, CP 11200 Montevideo. FAX 2-241-1860.

Zambia

Booksellers and Publishers Assn. of Zambia, Lotti House, Oldwing, 1st fl., Rm. 6, Cairo Rd., Box 31838, Lusaka. FAX 1-225195. *Exec. Dir.* Basil Mbewe.

Zimbabwe

Zimbabwe Book Publishers Assn., 12 Selous Ave., Harare. FAX 4-729905.

National Information Standards Organization (NISO) Standards

Book Production and Publications

Z39.4-1984*	Basic Criteria for Indexes
Z39.5-1985*	Abbreviation of Titles of Publications
Z39.14-1987*	Writing Abstracts
Z39.21-1988	Book Numbering (ISBN)
Z39.22-1989	Proof Corrections
Z39.41-1990	Printed Information on Spines
Z39.43-1993	Standard Address Number for the Publishing Industry (SAN)
Z39.48-1992	Permanence of Paper for Printed Publications and Documents in Libraries and Archives
Z39.49-1992	Computerized Book Ordering
Z39.59-1987*	Electronic Manuscript Preparation and Markup
Z39.66-1992	Durable Hardcover Binding for Books

Codes and Numbering Systems

Z39.9-1992	International Standard Serial Numbering (ISSN)
Z39.21-1988	Book Numbering (ISBN)
Z39.23-1990	Standard Technical Report Number (STRN), Format, and Creation
Z39.33-1988*	Development of Identification Codes for Use by the Bibliographic Community
Z39.47-1993	Extended Latin Alphabet Coded Character Set for Bibliographic Use
Z39.53-1987	Codes for the Representation of Languages for Information Interchange
Z39.56-1991	Serial Item and Contribution Identifier
Z39.64-1989	East Asian Character Code
ANSI/NISO/ISO 3166	Codes for the Representation of Names of Countries

Indexes, Thesauri, and Directories

Z39.4-1984*	Basic Criteria for Indexes
Z39.19-1993	Guidelines for the Construction, Format, and Management of Monolingual Thesauri

Microforms

Z39.40-1987*	Compiling U.S. Microform Publishing Statistics
Z39.62-1993	Eye Legible Information on Microfilm Leader Send Trailers and on Containers of Processed Microfilm on Open Reels

Acquisitions and Ordering

Z39.49-1992	Computerized Book Ordering
Z39.52-1987*	Standard Order Form for Multiple Titles of Library Materials

Romanization

Z39.11-1972 (R1989)	System for the Romanization of Japanese
Z39.12-1972 (R1984)	System for the Romanization of Arabic

Technical Reports and Papers

Z39.18-1987*	Scientific and Technical Reports—Organization, Preparation, and Production
Z39.23-1990	Standard Technical Report Number (STRN), Format and Creation

Serial Publications

Z39.5-1985*	Abbreviation of Titles of Publications
Z39.9-1992	International Standard Serial Numbering (ISSN)
Z39.44-1986*	Serials Holding Statements
Z39.48-1992	Permanence of Paper for Printed Publications
Z39.56-1991	Serial Item and Contribution Identifiers
Z39.59-1987*	Electronic Manuscript Preparation and Markup

Automation

Z39.2-1994	Information Interchange Format
Z39.44-1986*	Serials Holding Statements
Z39.47-1993	Extended Latin Alphabet Coded Character Set for Bibliographic Use (ANSEL)
Z39.49-1992	Computerized Book Ordering
Z39.50-1992	Information Retrieval Application Service Definition and Protocol Specification for OSI
Z39.57-1989	Holding Statements for Non-Serial Items
Z39.58-1992	Common Command Language for Interactive Information Retrieval
Z39.59-1987*	Electronic Manuscript Preparation and Markup
Z39.63-1989*	Interlibrary Loan Data Elements
Z39.67-1993	Computer Software Description

ANSI/NISO/ISO
3166   Codes for the Representation of Names of Countries
ANSI/NISO/ISO
9660   Volume and File Structure of CD-ROM for Information
Interchange

Standards Committees

SC Q	Periodicals—Format and Arrangement
SC R	Environmental Conditions for Storage of Paper-Based Library and Archival Materials
SC LL	Record Format for Patron Records, Circulation Transaction Format
SC MM	Environmental Conditions for the Exhibition of Library and Archival Materials
SC SS	Information to Be Included in Ads [etc.] for Products Used for the Storage, Binding, or Repair of Library Materials
SC XX	Abbreviations of Captions for Holdings Statements
SC ZZ	Library Binding
SC AC	Guides to Microform Sets
SC AF	Scientific and Technical Reports—Organization, Preparation, and Production
SC OO	Revision of Z39.29-1977 Bibliographic References
SC PP	Revision of Z39.19-1980 Thesaurus Construction
SC UU	Revision of Z39.7-1983 Library Statistics
SC YY	Revision of Z39.4-1989 Basic Criteria for Indexes
SC AE	Format for the Submission of Data for Multimedia CD-ROM Mastering
SC AG	Writing Abstracts

Other Standards in Development

Z39.65-199X	Permanent and Durable Library Catalog Cards
Z39.73-199X	Single-Tier Steel Bracket Library Shelving

*This standard is being reviewed by NISO's Standards Development Committee or is under revision. For further information please contact NISO, Box 1056, Bethesda, MD 20827; Tel. 301-975-2814; FAX 301-869-8071.

Calendar

The list below contains information on association meetings or promotional events that are, for the most part, national or international in scope. State and regional library association meetings are also included. To confirm the starting or ending date of a meeting, which may change after the *Bowker Annual* has gone to press, contact the association directly. Addresses of library and book trade associations are listed in Part 6 of this volume. For information on additional book trade and promotional events, see the *Exhibits Directory*, published annually by the Association of American Publishers; *Chase's Annual Events*, published by Contemporary Books, 180 N. Michigan Ave., Chicago, IL 60601; *Literary Market Place* and *International Literary Market Place*, published by R. R. Bowker; and the "Calendar" section in each issue of *Publishers Weekly* and *Library Journal*.

1994

May

3–6	Midatlantic Regional Library Federation/Maryland Library Association	Baltimore, MD
4–5	Chicago Book Clinic	Chicago, IL
4–8	"Palexpo" International Fair for Books and Press	Geneva, Switzerland
5–6	Wisconsin Library Association	Brookfield, WI
8–12	International Reading Association	Toronto, ON, Canada
9–10	National Online Meeting	New York, NY
9–12	Evangelical Press Association	Saint Paul, MN
10–12	Florida Library Association	Orlando, FL
10–12	London Medical Book Fair	London, England
10–15	Quebec International Book Fair	Quebec, PQ, Canada
12–14	Quebec Library Association	Montreal, PQ, Canada
12–15	Prague International Book Fair/Prague International Library Fair	Prague, Czech Republic
13–19	Medical Library Association	San Antonio, TX
14–17	Periodical Marketers of Canada	Banff, AB, Canada
14–18	Canadian Association of Law Libraries	Montreal, PQ, Canada
17–20	Association of Research Libraries	Austin, TX
18–19	Vermont Educational Media Association	Burlington, VT

May 1994 *(cont.)*

18–23	Warsaw International Book Fair	Warsaw, Poland
19–24	Turin Book Fair	Turin, Italy
22–23	Vermont Library Association .	Burlington, VT
22–24	Maine Educational Media Association/ Maine Library Association	Orono, ME
24–28	German Library Conference	Dortmund, Germany
26–27	Publishers Marketing Association	Los Angeles, CA
26–28	Manitoba Library Association	Winnipeg, MN, Canada
26–29	Atlantic Provinces Library Association	Baddeck, NS, Canada
27–6/2	Seminar on the Acquisition of Latin American Library Materials	Athens, GA
28–31	American Booksellers Association	Los Angeles, CA
31–6/3	"Worlddidac '94" Swiss Industries Fair	Basel, Switzerland
*	"INFOBASE"/International Trade Show for Information	Frankfurt am Main, Germany
*	International Federation of Film Archives	Bologna, Italy

June

2–5	International PEN Regional Conference	Liechtenstein
6–9	Scottish Library Association	Peebles, Scotland
9–10	Rhode Island Library Association	Newport, RI
9–11	Educational Press Association of America	Chicago, IL
9–11	Society for Scholarly Publishing	San Francisco, CA
11–16	Special Libraries Association	Atlanta, GA
12–14	Copyright Society of USA	Bolton Landing, NY
14–16	Library Resources Exhibition	Birmingham, England
14–17	Association of Christian Librarians	Greenville, IL
15–18	American Theological Library Association	Pittsburgh, PA
15–18	Canadian Library Association	Vancouver, BC, Canada
15–18	Scandinavian Federation of Research Librarians	Lillehammer, Norway
18–20	Canadian Booksellers Association	Toronto, ON, Canada
19–22	Association of American University Presses	Washington, DC
19–22	Association of Jewish Libraries	Atlanta, GA
23–26	Australian Book Fair	Sydney, NSW, Australia
23–30	American Library Association/Library Administration and Management Association/Public Library Association	Miami, FL
24	Chief Officers of State Library Agencies	Miami, FL
24–27	Asian Pacific American Librarians Association	Miami Beach, FL

*To Be Determined

June 1994 *(cont.)*

25	Evangelical Christian Publishers Association	Denver, CO
25–30	Christian Booksellers Association	Denver, CO
27	Theatre Library Association	Miami, FL
*	LIBER/Salon Internacional del Libro	Madrid, Spain
*	Bibliographical Society of Canada	Calgary, AB, Canada

July

4–8	International Association of Technological University Librarians	Sheffield, England
6–12	Canadian Booksellers Association	Toronto, ON, Canada
9–14	American Association of Law Libraries	Seattle, WA
17–22	International Association of Music Libraries, Archives and Documentation Centres	Ottawa, ON, Canada
18–25	International Association of School Librarianship	Pittsburgh, PA
21–23	Texas Library Association	Austin, TX
21–25	Hong Kong Book Fair	Hong Kong
24–26	Church and Synagogue Library Association	Raleigh, NC
27–31	International Feminist Book Fair	Melbourne, Australia
*	National Association of Government Archives and Records Administrators	

August

3–7	Zimbabwe International Book Fair	Harare, Zimbabwe
5–7	African American Librarians' National Conference	Milwaukee, WI
6–10	International Association of Printing House Craftsmen	Chicago, IL
11–14	Pacific Northwest Library Association	Eugene, OR
17–28	São Paulo Biennial International Book Show	São Paulo, Brazil
19–20	International Association of Law Libraries	Trinidad
21–27	IFLA Annual Conference	Havana, Cuba
*	Associated Booksellers of South Africa	Durban, South Africa
*	Christian Booksellers Association of Canada	Winnipeg, MB, Canada

September

1–6	Beijing International Book Fair	Beijing, China
2–6	Miniature Book Society	Ottawa, ON, Canada
3–11	Singapore International Festival of Books and Book Fair	Singapore

*To Be Determined

September 1994 *(cont.)*

6–11	Society of American Archivists	Indianapolis, IN
9–11	South–Central Booksellers Association	New Orleans, LA
9–12	British and Irish Association of Law Librarians	Birmingham, England
12–18	4th European Conferences on Archives	Lancashire, England
16–18	Pacific Northwest Booksellers Association	Eugene, OR
17	Antiquarian Book Fair	Sturbridge, MA
21–24	COSMEP: International Association of Independent Publishers	San Francisco, CA
22–23	Publishers Association of the South	Kissimmee/Orlando, FL
22–24	North Dakota Library Association	Bismark, ND
23–25	Mountains and Plains Booksellers Association	Denver, CO
23–25	Northern California Booksellers Association	Oakland, CA
23–25	Southeastern Booksellers Association	Kissimmee, FL
24–30	Distripress	Marrakesh, Morocco
25–26	London Remainder and Promotional Book Fair	London, England
25–28	Pennsylvania Library Association	Harrisburg, PA
26–29	International Association of Law Libraries	The Hague, Netherlands
26–30	New Zealand Library and Information Association/Australian Library and Information Association	Wellington, New Zealand
28–10/1	European Association of Directory Publishers Annual Conference	Algarve, Portugal
28–10/1	Kentucky Library Association	Louisville, KY
28–10/1	South Dakota Library Association	Aberdeen, SD
30–10/2	New England Booksellers Association	Boston, MA
*	Intermedia Europe	Wiesbaden, Germany
*	International Hispanic Book Fair	Miami, FL
*	Mid-America Publishers Association	

October

2–3	Mid-Atlantic Booksellers Association	Atlantic City, NJ
2–4	New England Library Association	Sturbridge, MA
2–9	International Federation for Information and Documentation	Tokyo, Japan
4–6	Ohio Educational Library Media Association	Columbus, OH
5–7	North Carolina Association of School Librarians	Winston–Salem, NC
5–7	Minnesota Library Association	Duluth, MN

*To Be Determined

October 1994 (*cont.*)

5–7	Idaho Library Association	Sun Valley, ID
5–8	Ohio Library Association	Columbus, OH
5–10	Frankfurt Book Fair	Frankfurt, Germany
6–8	Washington Library Media Association	Yakima, WA
7–9	Great Lakes Booksellers Association	Chicago, IL
8–11	Arkansas Association of School Librarians and Media Educators/ Arkansas Library Association	Hot Springs, AR
12–14	Iowa Library Association	Davenport, IA
12–14	Missouri Library Association	Saint Louis, MO
12–15	International Council on Archives	Salonika, Greece
12–16	American Translators Association	Austin, TX
13–15	Georgia Library Association	Augusta, GA
13–15	Oregon Educational Media Association	Seaside, OR
14–16	New England Booksellers Association	Boston, MA
16–18	Chief Officers of State Library Agencies	Oklahoma City, OK
18–21	Association of Research Libraries	Washington, DC
18–21	Michigan Library Association	Grand Rapids, MI
19–23	New York Library Association	Syracuse, NY
19–28	Muscat International Book Fair	Muscat, Oman
20–22	West Virginia Library Association	Wheeling, WV
20–24	International Seminar on Information Technologies and Services	Shanghai, China
20–24	Virginia Educational Media Association	Richmond, VA
23–24	Massachusetts School Library Media Association	Sturbridge, MA
23–25	Magazine Publishers of America	Niguel, CA
25–28	Wisconsin Library Association	Oshkosh, WI
25–29	Southeastern Library Association	Charlotte, NC
26–28	Japanese Library Association	Tattori, Japan
26–28	Nebraska Library Association/ Educational Media Association	Omaha, NE
26–28	Ohio Library Association	Toledo, OH
26–29	Mountain Plains Library Association/ Nevada Library Association	Lake Tahoe, NV
26–29	Virginia Library Association	Williamsburg, VA
28–30	Chicago International Remainder and Overstock Book Exposition	Chicago, IL
29–11/1	Evangelical Christian Publishers Association	San Francisco, CA
*	American Institute of Graphic Artists	New York, NY
*	Children's Book Week	London, England

November

2–4	Florida Association for Media in Education	Fort Lauderdale, FL

*To Be Determined

November 1994 *(cont.)*

3–5	Illinois School Library Media Association	Lincolnshire, IL
5–6	San Francisco Bay Area Book Festival	San Francisco, CA
5–7	Colorado Library Association	Keystone Resort, CO
5–13	Istanbul Book Fair	Istanbul, Turkey
6–9	Book Manufacturers' Institute Inc.	Phoenix, AZ
8–11	Mississippi Library Association	Jackson, MS
9–13	American Association of School Librarians	Indianapolis, IN
12–15	California Library Association	Anaheim, CA
12–15	Periodical Marketers of Canada	Ottawa, ON, Canada
14–20	National Children's Book Week	USA
17–20	Antiquarian Booksellers Association of America Inc.	Boston, MA
17–22	Montreal Book Show/Salon du Livre de Montréal	Montreal, PQ, Canada
20–12/20	Jewish Book Month	USA
23–12/9	Arabic Book Exhibition	Kuwait City, Kuwait
24–12/7	Cairo International Children's Book Fair	Cairo, Egypt
30–12/3	Arizona State Library Association	Phoenix, AZ
*	Pacific Islands Association of Libraries and Archives	Majuro, Marshall Islands
*	PEN International Congress	Prague, Czech Republic

December

3–4	Small Press Book Fair	New York, NY
5–6	Electronic Books Conference	New York, NY
8–12	Association of Visual Science Librarians	San Antonio, TX

1995

January

13–16	Ontario Library Association	Toronto, ON, Canada
25–2/5	Calcutta Book Fair	Calcutta Maidan, India

February

3–9	American Library Association Midwinter Conference	Philadelphia, PA
8–11	Music Library Association	Atlanta, GA
25–3/5	International Book Fair in Mexico	Mexico City, Mexico
*	Colorado Educational Media Association	Colorado Springs, CO

*To Be Determined

March

3–6	International PEN	Perth, WA, Australia
5–7	American Medical Publishers Association	Philadelphia, PA
8–10	Louisiana Library Association	Lafayette, LA
9–12	Luxembourg Book Festival	Luxembourg
12–17	Jerusalem International Book Fair	Jerusalem, Israel
16–18	Association for Indiana Media Educators	Indianapolis, IN
24–25	Hawaii Library Association	Honolulu, HI
29–4/1	Association of College and Research Libraries	Pittsburgh, PA
*	Alaska Library Association	Juneau, AK

April

9–15	National Library Week	USA
10–13	Association for Information & Image Management	San Francisco, CA
20–5/2	International Book Fair	Bogotá, Colombia
22–26	Evangelical Christian Publishers Association	Scottsdale, AZ
22–26	National Association of College Stores	Saint Louis, MO
26–30	Alberta Library Association	Jasper, AB, Canada
26–30	"Palexpo" International Fair for Books and Press	Geneva, Switzerland
28–5/3	Book Manufacturers Institute	Amelia Island, FL
28–5/4	Seminar on the Acquisition of Latin American Library Materials	Athens, GA
30–5/2	Massachusetts Library Association	Sturbridge, MA
30–5/4	International Reading Association	Anaheim, CA
*	Idaho Library Association	

May

5–11	Medical Library Association	Washington, DC
11	Archivists and Librarians in the History of the Health Sciences	Pittsburgh, PA
16–19	Prague International Book Fair & Writers Festival	Prague, Czech Republic
17–22	Warsaw International Book Fair	Warsaw, Poland
*	Atlantic Provinces Library Association	Saint Andrews, NB, Canada
*	Turin National Book Fair	Turin, Italy

June

1–2	Publishers Marking Association	Chicago, IL
3–5	Periodical Marketers of Canada	Winnipeg, MB, Canada

*To Be Determined

June 1995 *(cont.)*

10–15	Special Libraries Association	Montreal, PQ, Canada
13–16	Association of Christian Librarians	Lakeland, FL
15–18	Canadian Library Association	Calgary, AB, Canada
17–20	American Booksellers Association	Chicago, IL
17–20	Association of American University Presses	Nashville, TN
18–23	International Association of Music Libraries, Archives and Documentation Centres	Helsingor, Denmark
22–29	American Library Association Annual Conference	Chicago, IL
*	UK Library Association Biennial Conference	Manchester, England

July

15	Evangelical Christian Publishers Association	Denver, CO
15–20	American Association of Law Libraries	Pittsburgh, PA
15–20	Christian Booksellers Association	Denver, CO
20–24	Hong Kong Book Fair	Wanchai, Hong Kong
*	International Association of School Librarianship	Nigeria

August

2–6	Zimbabwe International Book Fair	Harare, Zimbabwe
18–28	Edinburgh Book Festival	Edinburgh, Scotland
20–26	IFLA Annual Conference	Istanbul, Turkey
29–9/3	Society of American Archivists	Washington, DC
*	Associated Booksellers of South Africa	Johannesburg, South Africa

September

1–4	Miniature Book Society	Los Angeles, CA
15–17	Great Lakes Booksellers Association	Grand Rapids, MI
16	Antiquarian Book Fair	Sturbridge, MA
22–24	Mountains and Plains Booksellers Association	Denver, CO
22–24	Northern California Booksellers Association	Oakland, CA
28–29	Publishers Association of the South	Atlanta, GA
28–10/2	Association of Directory Publishers	San Diego, CA
29–10/2	Colorado Library Association	Snowmass Resort, CO
29–10/3	Pennsylvania Library Association	Pittsburgh, PA
*	International Hispanic Book Fair	California

*To Be Determined

September 1995 *(cont.)*

*	Moscow International Book Fair	Moscow, Russia
*	Worddidac	Mexico

October

1–2	Mid-Atlantic Booksellers Association	Atlantic City, NJ
1–7	Distripress	Istanbul, Turkey
4–7	South Dakota Library Association	Sioux Falls, SD
11–16	Frankfurt Book Fair	Frankfurt, Germany
18–20	Iowa Library Association	Des Moines, IA
18–20	Michigan Library Association	Lansing, MI
18–21	Ohio Educational Library Media Association	Dayton, OH
18–27	Muscat International Book Fair	Muscat, Oman
24–27	Mississippi Library Association	Jackson, MS
29–11/1	Book Manufacturers Institute	Palm Beach, FL
*	Children's Book Week	London, England
*	International Council on Archives	Washington, DC
*	Oregon Educational Media Association	Portland, OR

November

4–5	San Francisco Book Council	San Francisco, CA
4–12	Istanbul Book Fair	Istanbul, Turkey
8–12	American Translators Association	Nashville, TN
11–14	California Library Association	Santa Clara, CA
13–19	National Children's Book Week	USA
16–21	Montreal Book Show	Montreal, PQ, Canada
24–12/7	Cairo International Book Fair	Cairo, Egypt

December

4–5	Electronic Books Conference	New York, NY
27–30	Modern Language Association of America	Chicago, IL

1996

February

14–17	Music Library Association	Seattle, WA
14–18	Association for Educational Communications and Technology/Association for Indiana Media Educators	Indianapolis, IN

April

13–17	National Association of College Stores	San Diego, CA

*To Be Determined

May 1996

9	Archivists and Librarians in the History of the Health Sciences	Buffalo, NY
31–6/6	Medical Library Association	Kansas City, MO

June

6–9	Canadian Library Association	Halifax, NS, Canada
17–20	Association for Information & Image Management	Chicago, IL

July

6–11	American Association of Law Libraries	Indianapolis, IN
*	International Association of School Librarianship	Kingston, Jamaica

August

16–18	Colorado Library Association	Denver, CO
27–9/1	Society of American Archivists	San Diego, CA
*	Colorado Educational Media Association	Denver, CO
*	Alaska Library Association	Fairbanks, AK

September

20–22	Great Lakes Booksellers Association	Toledo, OH
*	International Council on Archives	Beijing, China

October

6–9	Pennsylvania Library Association	Lancaster, PA
8–10	Iowa Library Association	Waterloo, IA
9–12	South Dakota Library Association	Spearfish, SD
14–17	Library and Information Technology Association	Pittsburgh, PA
15–18	Michigan Library Association	Dearborn, MI
22–26	Southeastern Library Association	Lexington, KY
23–25	North Carolina Association of School Librarians	Raleigh, NC
30–11/3	American Translators Association	Colorado Springs, CO

*To Be Determined

Authors and Contributors

Ainsworth, Shirley
Alexander, Adrian W.
Anderson, Nancy D.
Baker, John F.
Barton, Pamela
Brandhorst, Ted
Chute, Adrienne
Clarkson, Tom
Cole, John Y.
Emmolo, Lauren M.
Fox, Bette-Lee
Franklin, Hardy R.
Fry, Ray M.
Grannis, Chandler B.
Halstead, Kent
Henderson, Carol C.
Ink, Gary
Kepley, David R.
Koltay, Emery
Lottman, Herbert R.
Lynch, Mary Jo
Maryles, Daisy
Mehnert, Robert
Meyer, Randy

Miles, Carol
Miller, Marilyn L.
Myers, Margaret
Nelson, Corinne O.
Norris, Brian
Oakes, Bonnie
Paul, Sandy
Phelps, Thomas C.
Platt, Judith
Price, Joseph W.
Rader, Hannelore B.
Rodkey, Kitt
Rogers, Michael
Sadowski, Michael
St. Lifer, Evan
Segal, JoAn
Shontz, Marilyn
Timmer, Ellen B.
Webster, Duane E.
Williams, Jane
Williamson, Michael
Young, Peter R.
Zipkowitz, Fay

Acronyms

A

AALL. American Association of Law Libraries

AAP. Association of American Publishers

AASL. American Association of School Librarians

AAU. Association of American Universities

ABA. American Booksellers Association

ABBY. American Booksellers Book of the Year

ABFFE. American Booksellers Foundation for Free Expression

ACRL. Association of College and Research Libraries

ACTS. Advisory Commission on Textbook Specifications

ADA. Americans with Disabilities Act

AED. Academy for Educational Development

AIBDA. Inter-American Association of Agricultural Librarians and Documentalists

AIM. Association for Information Management

AJL. Association of Jewish Libraries

ALA. American Library Association

ALCTS. Association for Library Collections and Technical Services

ALISE. Association for Library and Information Science Education

ALS. Academic Libraries Survey

ALSC. Association for Library Service to Children

ALTA. American Library Trustee Association

AMMLA. American Merchant Marine Library Association

APALA. Asian/Pacific American Librarians Association

ARGENA. Archivo General de la Nación

ARIES. Acervo de Recursos de Instituciones de Educación Superior

ARL. Association of Research Libraries

ARLIS/NA. Art Libraries Society of North America

ARMA. Association of Records Managers and Administrators, see ARMA International

ASCLA. Association of Specialized and Cooperative Library Agencies

ASIS. American Society for Information Science

ATPA. American Technology Preeminence Act

AWIC. National Agricultural Library, Animal Welfare Information Center

B

BANAPA. Banco Nacional de Patentes

BIBLAT. Bibliografía Latinoamericana

BISAC. Book Industry Systems Advisory Committee

BLDSC. British Library Document Supply Center

BOS. American Booksellers Association, Booksellers Order Service

BPI. Booksellers Publishing, Inc.

BSA. Booksellers Show Associates

C

CACUL. Canadian Association of College and University Libraries

CAIS. Canadian Association for Information Science

CALA. Chinese-American Librarians Association

CALS/CE. Continuous Acquisition and Life-Style Support/Concurrent Engineering

CAPL. Canadian Association of Public Libraries

CASLIS. Canadian Association of Special Libraries and Information Services

CCC. Copyright Clearance Center

CD-ROM. Compact Disc Read-Only Memory

CIBIMEX. Centro de Información Bibliográfica Mexicana

CICH. Centro de Información Científica y Humanística

CLA. Canadian Library Association; Catholic Library Association

CLASE. Citas Latinoamericanas en Ciencias Sociales y Humanidades

CLR. Council on Library Resources

CLTA. Canadian Library Trustees Association

CNI. Coalition for Networked Information

CNLIA. Council of National Library and Information Associations

CODICE90. Consulta Dinámica Censal

COSLA. Chief Officers of State Library Agencies

CPL. Council of Planning Librarians

CRS. Congressional Research Service

CSLA. Canadian School Library Association; Church and Synagogue Library Association

FID. International Federation for Information and Documentation

FLICC. Federal Library and Information Center Committee

FPC. Federal Publishers Committee

FSCS. Federal-State Cooperative System (FSCS) for Public Library Data

G

GATT. General Agreement on Tariffs and Trade

GPO. Government Printing Office

GPO WINDO/Gateway bills. Government Printing Office Wide Information Network Data Online/Gateway to Government bills

GSP. Generalized System of Preferences

H

HEA. Higher Education Act

HPCA. High Performance Computing Act

HUD. Housing and Urban Development, Department of, 124

D

DIALEX. Legislación al Día

DIO. Disco de Información Oportuna

DIOR. Disco de Información Oportuna Regional

E

EAN. European Article Number, renamed International Article Number

EDRS. Educational Resources Information Center, ERIC Document Reproduction Service

ERIC. Educational Resources Information Center

F

FDLP. Government Printing Office, Federal Depository Library Program

FIAF. International Federation of Film Archives

I

IALL. International Association of Law Libraries

IAML. International Association of Music Libraries, Archives and Documentation Centres

IAOL. International Association of Orientalist Librarians

IASA. International Association of Sound Archives

IASL. International Association of School Librarianship

IATUL. International Association of Technological University Libraries

IBT. Integrated Book Technology

ICASS. Integrated Communications and Administrative Support System

IFLA. International Federation of Library Associations and Institutions

IIA. Information Industry Association

IINREN. Interagency Interim NREN

ILL. Interlibrary loan

INTAMEL. International Association of Metropolitan City Libraries

ISBN. International Standard Book Number

ISO. International Organization for Standardization

J

JICST. Japanese Information Center of Science and Technology

L

LAIB. Latin American Information Base

LAMA. Library Administration and Management Association

LINCC. Library Information Network for Community Colleges

LINXS. Library indexing system

LIS. Library/information science

LITA. Library and Information Technology Association

LJ. Library Journal

LSCA. Library Services and Construction Act

LSP. National Center for Education Statistics, Library Statistics Program

M

Marvel. Library of Congress, Machine-Assisted Realization of the Virtual Electronic Library

MLA. Medical Library Association; Music Library Association

MLC. Michigan Library Consortium

MLNC. Missouri Library Network Corporation

MURLs. Major Urban Resource Libraries

N

NAFTA. North American Free Trade Agreement

NAGARA. National Association of Government Archives and Records Administrators

NAL. National Agricultural Library

NARA. National Archives and Records Administration

NATDP. National Agricultural Library, National Agricultural Text Digitizing Project

NCCP. National Coordinated Cataloging Program

NCES. National Center for Education Statistics

NCIV. National Council for International Visitors

NCLIS. National Commission on Libraries and Information Science

NEH. National Endowment for the Humanities

NEII. National Engineering Information Initiative

NFAIS. National Federation of Abstracting and Information Services

NFSMI. National Food Service Management Institute

NII. National information instructure

NISO. National Information Standards Organization

NLA. National Librarians Association; National Library of Australia

NLM. National Library of Medicine

NREN. National Research and Education Network

NSF. National Science Foundation

NTIA. National Telecommunications and Information Administration

NTIS. National Technical Information Service

O

OCLC. Online Computer Library Center

OCR. Optical Character Recognition

OERI. Education, U.S. Department of, Office of Educational Research and Improvement

OLUC. Online Union Catalog

OMB. United States, Management and Budget, Office of

OSAP. Association of Research Libraries, Scientific and Academic Publishing, Office of

OTA. Office of Technology Assessment

P

PDQ. United States Information Agency, library programs, Public Diplomacy Query (PDQ) database

PGDIC. National Agricultural Library, Plant Genome Database and Information Center

PLA. Public Library Association
POTS. Plain old telephone service
PW. Publishers Weekly

R

RASD. American Library Association, Reference and Adult Services Division
RBOCs. Regional Bell Operating Companies
RIF. Reading Is Fundamental
RLG. Research Libraries Group
RONDAC. Regional OCLC Network Directors Advisory Committee
RTSD. American Library Association, Resources and Technical Services Division. *See new name* Association for Library Collections and Technical Services

S

SAA. Society of American Archivists
SAIC. Sistema Automatizado de Información Censal
SAN. Standard Address Number
SECOBI. Servicio de Consulta a Bancos de Información
SICM. Sistema de Información Comercial de México
SLA. Special Libraries Association
SLJ. School Library Journal
SRIM. Selected Research in Microfiche
SSP. Society for Scholarly Publishing
STM. Scientific, Technical, and Medical Publishers

T

TAR. Teachers as Readers

TLA. Theatre Library Association
TLP. Telecommunications Linking Program
TRIPS. Trade Related Intellectual Property Rights

U

ULC. Urban Libraries Council
UMLS. National Library of Medicine, Unified Medical Language System
UNAM. Universidad Nacional Autónoma de México
UPC. Universal Product Code
USIA. United States Information Agency
USIS. United States Information Service, *overseas name for* United States Information Agency
USPS. Postal Service, U.S.

V

VALS. Vermont Automated Library System

W

WHCLIS. White House Conference on Library and Information Services
WILS. Wisconsin InterLibrary Services
WIN. Water Information Network
WLN. Western Library Network

Y

YALSA. Young Adult Library Services Association
YDIC. National Agricultural Library, Youth Development Information Center

Index of Organizations

Please note that this index includes cross-references to the Subject Index. Many additional organizations can be found in Part 6 under the following headings: Networks, Consortia, and Other Cooperative Library Organizations; State, Provincial, and Regional Library Associations; State and Provincial Library Agencies; State School Library Media Associations; State Supervisors of School Library Media Services; Foreign Library Associations; Book Trade Associations, United States and Canada; International and Foreign Book Trade Associations.

A

Academy for Educational Development (AED), 95
Acervo de Recursos de Instituciones de Educación Superior (ARIES), 84–85
Advisory Commission on Textbook Specifications (ACTS), 210
AGRICOLA (AGRICultural OnLine Access), 163
Agricultural Research and Education Service, 161
Alliance of Independent Booksellers, 30
Alliance of Library Service Networks, 59
American Association of Law Libraries (AALL), 674–675
   awards, 399–400
   career hotline, 365
   research and demonstration, 441–443
American Association of School Librarians (AASL), 21, 678–680
   awards, 401–402, 436–437
American Booksellers Association (ABA)
   awards, 221
   Booksellers Order Service (BOS), 225
   convention and trade exhibit, 220–223
   education and professional development, 222
   government affairs, 225
   membership, 220
   publications, 223–224
   publisher relations, 226
   research, 224–225

standardization committee, 226
American Booksellers Foundation for Free Expression (ABFFE), 221–222
American Film and Video Association, 675
American Library Association (ALA), 181–186, 676–678
   awards, 400–408, 438–439
   Banned Books Week, 183
   conference, 54, 442
      highlights, 181–182
   intellectual freedom, 183, 212
   international activities, 91–92
   issues addressed, 182
   personnel, 186
   as placement source, 366
   public awareness, 184–185
   publishing highlights, 186
   Reference and Adult Services Division (RASD), 695–696
      awards, 407–408
      notable books list, 589
      research and demonstration, 442–443
   special projects, 185
   Washington report, 182–183
   See also American Association of School Librarians; American Library Trustee Association; Association of College and Research Libraries; Association for Library Collections and Technical Services; Association for Library Service to Children; Association of Specialized and Cooperative Library Agencies; Library Administration and

Subject Index

Please note that many cross-references refer to entries listed in the Index of Organizations.

A

Academic books, prices and price indexes, 460(table)
British averages, 1991–1993, 525–527(table)
German averages, 1991–1993, 528(table)
North American averages
electronic version, 1990–1992, 514–515(table)
from 1990–91 to 1992–93, 512–513(table)
U.S. college books, averages, 1978, 1991, 1992, 1993, 516–517(table)
See also Association of American Publishers, Professional and Scholarly Publishing Division; Society for Scholarly Publishing
Academic libraries, *see* College and research libraries; Academic Libraries Survey
Academic Libraries Survey (ALS), 132–133
Acquisitions
expenditures, 447–455
academic libraries, 450–451(table)
government libraries, 454–455(table)
public libraries, 448–449(table)
special libraries, 452–453(table)
NISO standards, 796
prices and price indexes
Books and periodicals, 460(table)
for major components, 458(table)
for other components, 461(table)
school libraries, 462–464(table)
See also Association of Research Libraries, collection services program *and* specific types of libraries, i.e., Public libraries
Adams, Gerry, 214

Adults, services for, *see* American Library Association, Reference and Adult Services Division; Literacy programs; Senior citizens, library services for
Advance Ship Notice (ASN), 106
Agencies, library, *see* Library associations and agencies
Agricultural libraries, *see* Inter-American Association of Agricultural Librarians and Documentalists; International Association of Agricultural Librarians and Documentalists; National Agricultural Library
Alabama
LJ report, 11
networks and cooperative library organizations, 641
school library media associations, 752
school library media services, state supervisors, 759
Alaska
LJ report, 16
networks and cooperative library organizations, 641
school library media services, state supervisors, 759
Alexander, Jane, 212
Almanacs, bestselling, 626–627
American Booksellers Book of the Year (ABBY), 221
American Geophysical Union v. Texaco, 191, 195, 240
American Libraries as placement source, 365–366
American Libraries Project, 94–101
administrator, 95
community support, 96
escort officers, 96